Penguin Reference Books
Roget's Thesaurus

D0414464

T.F.K. JOHNSTON

Roget's Thesaurus
of English words and phrases

New edition prepared by
Betty Kirkpatrick MA

Penguin Books

PENGUIN BOOKS

Published by the Penguin Group
27 Wrights Lane, London W8 5TZ, England
Viking Penguin Inc., 40 West 23rd Street, New York, New York 10010, USA
Penguin Books Australia Ltd, Ringwood, Victoria, Australia
Penguin Books Canada Ltd, 2801 John Street, Markham, Ontario, Canada L3R 1B4
Penguin Books (NZ) Ltd, 182–190 Wairau Road, Auckland 10, New Zealand

Penguin Books Ltd, Registered Offices: Harmondsworth, Middlesex, England

First published 1852
This abridged edition first published in Great Britain by Penguin Books 1988. Based
on *Roget's Thesaurus* revised and edited by Betty Kirkpatrick, first published by
Longman Group UK Limited 1987
10 9 8 7 6

This edition copyright © Longman Group UK Limited, 1962, 1982, 1987
All rights reserved

Printed in England by Clays Ltd, St Ives plc
Filmset in Times New Roman
Typesetting by Systemset, Stotfold, Hitchin, Herts

Except in the United States of America, this book is sold subject
to the condition that it shall not, by way of trade or otherwise, be lent,
re-sold, hired out, or otherwise circulated without the
publisher's prior consent in any form of binding or cover other than
that in which it is published and without a similar condition
including this condition being imposed on the subsequent purchaser

Preface
to the first edition, 1852

It is now nearly fifty years since I first projected a system of verbal classification similar to that on which the present Work is founded. Conceiving that such a compilation might help to supply my own deficiencies, I had, in the year 1805, completed a classed catalogue of words on a small scale, but on the same principle, and nearly in the same form, as the Thesaurus now published. I had often during that long interval found this little collection, scanty and imperfect as it was, of much use to me in literary composition, and often contemplated its extension and improvement; but a sense of the magnitude of the task, amidst a multitude of other avocations, deterred me from the attempt. Since my retirement from the duties of Secretary of the Royal Society, however, finding myself possessed of more leisure, and believing that a repertory of which I had myself experienced the advantage might, when amplified, prove useful to others, I resolved to embark in an undertaking which, for the last three or four years, has given me incessant occupation, and has, indeed, imposed upon me an amount of labour very much greater than I had anticipated. Notwithstanding all the pains I have bestowed on its execution, I am fully aware of its numerous deficiencies and imperfections, and of its falling far short of the degree of excellence that might be attained. But, in a work of this nature, where perfection is placed at so great a distance, I have thought it best to limit my ambition to that moderate share of merit which it may claim in its present form; trusting to the indulgence of those for whose benefit it is intended, and to the candour of critics who, while they find it easy to detect faults, can at the same time duly appreciate difficulties.

P.M. Roget
29 April, 1852

Preface to this edition

Since it was first published in 1852 Roget's Thesaurus has sold well over 30 million copies. It has been an indispensable companion to generations of English speakers and writers, and is firmly established as one of the greatest English language reference books in the world. The present edition has been prepared to reflect the major changes in English usage which have emerged during the 1980s.

Roget's Thesaurus is essentially a collection of words and phrases classified according to underlying concepts and meanings. The unique classification invented by Peter Mark Roget has withstood the test of time remarkably well. It has proven infinitely capable of absorbing new concepts and new vocabulary. Improved and expanded in detail by successive editors, it continues to provide an unparalleled key to modern English usage.

Roget's classification system is extensive yet finely focussed and easy to master. It is described fully in the section that follows. There is also an index, which provides an alternative access to the contents.

The unique value of Roget's Thesaurus is to help writers or speakers clarify and shape an idea which they wish to convey, and which is difficult to capture or to express clearly. The Thesaurus thereby helps users to improve their command of English usage, and to develop their ability to communicate precisely and appropriately. The secret to the success of Roget's Thesaurus lies in how it helps people express themselves effectively in writing and speech. This is a creative reference work, unlike simple synonym dictionaries (some of which are misleadingly labelled as thesauri).

This new edition has been made necessary by the unprecedentedly rapid expansion of the English vocabulary in the 1980s, reflecting major scientific, cultural and social changes. Discoveries and inventions in the world of science, medicine and technology have given rise to terms such as *acid rain, AIDS, cellular radio, genetic fingerprinting, nuclear winter, oncogene* and *transputer*. New concepts in politics, finance, industrial relations and sociology include *arbitrageur, creative accounting, insider trading, intrapreneur, junk bond, rate-capping, science park* and *secondary picketing*. New attitudes to life, as well as dramatic changes in life-style, ranging from travel and leisure pursuits to health consciousness and eating habits have given a

wealth of new words including *baby boomer, bag lady, demi-veg, E numbers, Sloane Ranger, streetwise* and *yuppy*.

The language of these and a great many other recent changes has been merged into the ever-changing body of Roget's Thesaurus, making for a uniquely up-to-date version of the great classic.

Betty Kirkpatrick

How to use this book

The Text

The *Thesaurus* is divided into six *Classes*. The first three Classes cover the external world: Class One, *Abstract Relations*, deals with such ideas as number, order and time; Class Two, *Space*, is concerned with movement, shapes and sizes, while Class Three, *Matter*, covers the physical world and humankind's perception of it by means of the five senses. The last three Classes deal with the internal world of human beings: the human mind (Class Four, *Intellect*), the human will (Class Five, *Volition*), and the human heart and soul (Class Six, *Emotion, Religion and Morality*). There is a logical progression from abstract concepts, through the material universe, to mankind itself, culminating in what Roget saw as mankind's highest achievements: morality and religion.

Roget borrowed his scheme from natural history, with its hierarchy of Phyla, Classes, Orders and Families. His system has also been compared to a tree, with ever smaller ramifications diverging from the main branches. This is a workable way of dividing up human experience, as can be seen from the way Roget's system has survived intact through numerous revisions. But life, as Roget himself points out, is not easily compartmentalized. 'Choice', for example, involves both the will (Class Five) and the intellect (Class Four). The language which reflects our experience is equally complex, more like a web than a tree, for it interconnects at all points. Also one word may have many meanings depending on its context. Roget was aware of this problem. His solution was to use copious cross-references to link related groups of words, a method which succeeded in both reflecting the complexity of language and coming to terms with it.

To see at a glance how Roget's system works, look up the *Plan of Classification* on pp. xv—xvi. This shows the Six Classes, further subdivided into *Sections*. Each Section deals with a particular aspect of the Class within which it is found. So under Class One, *Abstract Relations*, we find Sections for *Quantity, Order, Time* and so on. The Sections themselves are further subdivided into *Heads*. Within Class One Section Six, *Time*, for instance, there are 35 Heads dealing with, among others, the ideas of *Present Time, Past Time, Transience,* and *Age*. Each Head is numbered. There are 990 in the present edition, a slight reduction from Roget's original 1,000. It is the Heads which form the basic units of the book, and they follow each other in a logical progression. It is a sign of Roget's skill in compiling the *Thesaurus* that this basic framework has remained virtually intact through edition after edition of the copyright version, of which this is the most recent.

The Heads themselves are divided into paragraphs, grouped together according to their part of speech. Head 852, *Hope*, for example, has three paragraphs of nouns (marked N.), two of adjectives (**Adj.**), two of verbs (**Vb.**), one of adverbs (**Adv.**) and one of interjections (**Int.**). Not all Heads have a full complement of parts of speech, nor are the labels themselves applied too strictly, words and phrases being allocated to the part of speech which most closely describes their function. Each paragraph begins with a word in italics known as the *keyword*. This is both a clue to the kind of words found in that paragraph, and also itself part of the vocabulary. It is *not* a synonym of the words which follow: it was Roget's intention to offer words which express every aspect of an idea, rather than to list the synonyms. It is called the *keyword* because it is both the 'key' to the rest of the paragraph, and the 'open sesame' to the whole book, being used to identify the position of other words in the index and cross-references.

Within the paragraphs, words are grouped between semicolons according to their meaning, context or level of usage (i.e. colloquial, formal, etc.). These groups follow one another in a logical sequence, exploring every aspect of the idea under consideration. By comparing, whether consciously or not, the words and phrases offered, you can now select the most appropriate. It was Roget's expectation that his readers would "recognize" the word they wanted, guided by "an instinctive tact". On this assumption, words having more than one meaning or context are not usually repeated within paragraphs, nor are transitive and intransitive verbs listed separately. Where the right word is not immediately apparent, but an unfamiliar one seems from the context as if it might answer, it is advisable, especially for non-English speakers, to check with a dictionary. Yet more ideas can be obtained by looking up the cross-references. These are found at the end of some groups of words and consist of a Head number and a word in italics. The latter, besides being an item of vocabulary in its own right, is also the *keyword* of a paragraph in the given Head. It is also worth consulting the Heads before and after the one originally looked up. Most Heads are in pairs, representing the positive and negative aspects of an idea, e.g. **852** *Hope*, **853** *Hopelessness*. Sometimes several heads between them cover an idea — 'education' is dealt with in **534** *Teaching*, **535** *Misteaching*, **536** *Learning*, **537** *Teacher*, **538** *Learner* and **539** *School*.

A few conventions should be explained. These have mainly been designed to avoid repetition and save space. Conjugate forms are often indicated by the use of 'etc.' For instance, 'be content, — satisfied etc. adj.' suggests that readers can form further verbs for themselves on the same pattern. In the same way, 'darkness etc. adj.' suggests how more nouns may be formed from the adjectives already given. Where consecutive expressions use the same word, two means are used to avoid repeating it. The phrases may be linked by '*or*', as in 'drop a brick *or* a clanger', 'countryman *or* -woman'. Alternatively, the repeated word is simply indicated by its first letter, followed by a full stop: 'weasel word, loan w., nonce w.,' and so on. Brackets within the text are occasionally used to clarify the context of a word, as in 'dissolve (a marriage)'. 'Tdmk' in brackets following a noun indicates a registered trade mark. An 'e' in brackets added to the end of a word means that it is of French origin and requires a final 'e' if applied to a woman. '**See** . . .' is used to refer the reader to another paragraph within the same Head, where the idea under consideration is dealt with more thoroughly. This often happens where a general paragraph, such as '*killing*'

in Head 362, is followed by more specific paragraphs, in this case '*homicide*' and '*slaughter*'.

The Index

Once familiar with Roget's *Plan of Classification*, readers will be able to find their own way round the book, and this is certainly the most rewarding method of using the *Thesaurus*. However, new readers, and those in a hurry, will probably prefer to use the Index at the back of this book.

The Index is based on a complete computer-listing of all the items in the book. It is intended as a guide to the text rather than as a catalogue of its contents, and the reader should not assume that a word is missing from the book simply because it is not in the Index. Nor is the list of references at each entry intended to be exhaustive. The reader should bear in mind that the Heads offer words to express a given idea or ideas; it really does not matter whether you look up a noun, a verb or an adjective, as once you have found the right Head, all the parts of speech conveying that idea will be available to you.

The Index consists of a list of items, each of which is followed by one or more references to the text. These references consist of: a Head number; a *keyword* in italics, and a part of speech label (n. for nouns, adj. for adjectives, vb. for verbs, adv. for adverbs, and int. for interjections). The *keyword* is given to identify the paragraph which contains the word you have looked up; it also gives an indication of the ideas contained in that paragraph, so it can be used as a clue where a word has several meanings and therefore several references. To use the Index, look up your word, turn to the Head number given in your chosen reference, and under the relevant part of speech you will find a paragraph beginning with the *keyword* given in the Index.

Where several references are given choose the most appropriate *keyword*. For instance, suppose you need another expression for 'feeling happy'. Look up 'happy' in the Index, and you will find a list of references. The *keywords* given include 'apt', 'willing' and 'drunk', which refer to other uses of the word 'happy'. But the *keywords* 'cheerful' and 'happy' are obviously relevant, and looking up **833** *cheerful* and **824** *happy* will offer you an abundance of suitable terms.

Some points to note

1) *Items are listed in alphabetical order*, whether they are words or phrases. For example: "hall, halleluja, halliard, hallmark, hall of residence, halloo, hallow, hallowed, hallowed by custom, Hallowe'en". 'The', 'a', and 'be' are disregarded for this purpose.

2) *References to the same Head* are not usually repeated under different grammatical forms of the same word. For example: "abundance" has references to Heads **32, 171, 632, 625** and **637**, while "abundant" has reference to none of these, but lists **104, 800** and **813**. This means that the adjective is found in three Heads which do not list the noun form: the idea of "abundance", however, is present in all the Heads listed. It is a good idea to check other forms of the word you are looking up, to obtain the fullest list of references to suitable Heads. Forms that do not follow each other immediately are linked by the direction 'See . . .'.

Obvious derivatives of words, such as nouns ending in '-ness', adjectives in '-ing' or '-ed' and adverbs in '-ly', are not usually given an entry of their own unless they have a different meaning from the parent word.

3) *Objects* should be looked up in their simplest form, e.g. "ship" rather than "clipper", "dog" rather than "wolfhound" and "flag" than 'banneret". An object with a compound name, such as "money box" may be dealt with under either or both of its constituent parts.

4) *Phrases* are listed in alphabetical order as noted above. In idioms where the first word is variable, such as "have (*or* know) by heart", the phrase will be indexed under both, or under the next word in the phrase.

5) *General expressions* such as "good example", "bad health", "no meaning" and "not mind" have been retained in the Index as useful guides for the reader.

6) *(s) after a word* indicates that references may apply to either the singular or the plural form.

7) *Alternative spellings* are given after the main form.

PLAN OF CLASSIFICATION

THESAURUS
OF ENGLISH WORDS AND PHRASES

Class one

ABSTRACT RELATIONS

Section one: Existence

1 Existence – N. *existence,* being, entity; aseity, self-existence; monad, a being, an entity, ens, quiddity; Platonic idea; subsistence 360 *life*; eternity 115 *perpetuity*; preexistence 119 *priority*; this life 121 *present time*; prevalence 189 *presence*; realization, evolution 147 *conversion*; creation 164 *production*; potentiality 469 *possibility*; metaphysics; realism, materialism, idealism, existentialism 449 *philosophy*.

reality, realness, actuality; material e. 319 *materiality*; historicity, factuality, factualness 494 *truth*; fact, fact of life, undeniable f., positive f., stubborn f., matter of f., fait accompli 154 *event*; real thing, not a dream, no joke; nitty-gritty, basics, fundamentals, bedrock, nuts and bolts, brass tacks 638 *important matter*.

essence, nature, very n., quiddity, inner being, sum and substance 5 *essential part*; soul, heart, heart of the matter, core, centre 224 *interiority*.

Adj. *existing,* existent; existential; essential 5 *intrinsic*; absolute, given; in existence, under the sun, living 360 *alive*; preexistent 119 *prior*; coexistent 121 *present*; undying, immortal, eternal, enduring 115 *perpetual*; extant, surviving, indestructible 113 *lasting*; rife, prevalent 189 *ubiquitous*; metaphysical.

real, essential, not imagined, actual, positive, factual, well-documented, historical, well-g. 494 *true*; natural, physical, flesh and blood 319 *material*; concrete, solid, tangible 324 *dense*.

Vb. *be,* exist, have being; be the case 494 *be true*; consist in, reside in 5 *be intrinsic*; preexist; coexist, coincide, subsist 121 *be now*; continue 146 *go on*; endure 113 *last*; pass the time, live out one's life, drag out one's l.; be alive, breathe, live, have one's being, draw breath 360 *live*; be found, be met with, lie 186 *be situated*; be here 189 *be present*; prevail, be rife 189 *pervade*; take place, come about, occur 154 *happen*; hold good 494 *be true*;

become, come to be, come into existence, first see the light of day 360 *be born*; spring up 68 *begin*; develop, grow, take shape 316 *evolve*; turn out, change into, metamorphose 147 *be turned to*.

Adv. *actually,* really, essentially, substantially; ipso facto; in essence, to all intents and purposes; in fact, in point of f. 494 *truly*.

2 Nonexistence – N. *nonexistence,* nothingness, nullity; blank, vacuum 190 *emptiness*; nothing, sweet n., nil, cipher, zilch 103 *zero*; a nothing, nonentity 4 *insubstantial thing*; no such thing, no one, nonperson 190 *nobody*; nihilism, negativeness.

extinction, oblivion, nirvana; dying out, obsolescence 51 *decay*; annihilation, nihilism 165 *destruction*; cancellation, erasure, clean slate 550 *obliteration.*

Adj. *nonexistent,* without being; missing, omitted 190 *absent*; negatived, nullified, null and void; cancelled, wiped out.

unreal, without reality, baseless, groundless, unfounded, without foundation; fictitious, fabulous, visionary 513 *imaginary*; intangible 4 *insubstantial*; only supposed.

unborn, uncreated, unmade; unbegotten, unconceived; undiscovered, uninvented, unimagined; as yet unborn, yet to come.

extinct, died out, vanished, lost and gone forever; no more, dead and gone, defunct 361 *dead*; obsolete, dead as the dodo; finished, over and done with 125 *past.*

Vb. *not be,* have no existence *or* life, be null and void; fail to materialize, not come off, abort; be yet unborn.

pass away, cease to exist, become extinct *or* obsolete, die out; be no more 361 *die*; come to nothing, abort 728 *miscarry*; sink into oblivion 506 *be forgotten*; go, vanish, be lost to sight; dematerialize, melt into thin air, go up in a puff of smoke 446 *disappear*; evaporate 338 *vaporize*; dissolve 337 *liquefy.*

nullify, reduce to nothing, annul, annihilate, extinguish; render null and void, suspend 752 *abrogate*; neutralize, negative 533 *negate*; cancel 550 *obliterate*; abolish, wipe out 165 *destroy.*

3 Substantiality – **N.** *substantiality,* essentiality 1 *reality*; substantivity, objectivity; corporeality, visibility, tangibility, palpability, solidity 319 *materiality*; weight 322 *gravity*; pithiness, meatiness; material 319 *matter.*

substance, core, nub, nitty-gritty 5 *essential part*; entity, thing, something, somebody 319 *object*; living matter 360 *life*; concretion 324 *solid body*; pith, marrow, meat 224 *interiority.*

Adj. *substantial,* real, actual, objective, natural, corporeal, phenomenal, physical 319 *material*; concrete, solid, tangible, palpable 324 *dense*; considerable 638 *important*; bulky 195 *large*; heavy 322 *weighty*; pithy, meaty, meaningful, full of substance.

Adv. *substantially,* really 1 *actually*; essentially 5 *intrinsically*; largely, in the main 32 *greatly.*

4 Insubstantiality – **N.** *insubstantiality,* nothingness 2 *nonexistence*; naught, nothing, nothing at all, zilch, not a whit *or* jot, not a scrap 103 *zero*; no one, not a soul 190 *nobody*; incorporeality 320 *immateriality*; lack of substance; meagreness, sparseness 325 *rarity*; superficiality 212 *shallowness*; intangibility, impalpability, invisibility; vacuity, vacancy, void, hollowness 190 *emptiness*; fatuity 497 *absurdity*; hallucination, self-delusion 542 *deception*; dream world, fantasy 513 *ideality*; unreality.

insubstantial thing, token, symbol 547 *indication*; soul 447 *spirit*; abstraction, shadow, ghost, phantom, spectre, vision, dream, mirage, optical illusion 440 *visual fallacy*; air, thin a., mist; bubble, gossamer, snowflake; bauble; vanity, inanity, fatuity, fool's paradise 499 *folly*; flight of fancy, figment of the imagination, pipe dream, castle in the air 513 *fantasy*; all talk, moonshine, cock and bull story; hot air, idle talk, gossip, speculation, rumour 515 *empty talk*; cry of 'wolf' 665 *false alarm*; mockery, pretence 875 *ostentation*; chimera, figment, courtesy title; nine days' wonder, flash in the pan; cipher, figurehead, man of straw 639 *nonentity*; stuffed shirt 873 *vain person*; fictitious person; pseudonym, stage name 562 *no name.*

Adj. *insubstantial,* inessential; nonphysical, nonmaterial 320 *immaterial*; bodiless, incorporeal; aetherial 323 *light*; thin, gossamer 422 *transparent*; pale 426 *colourless*; misty 336 *gaseous*; fragile, delicate, ghostly, spectral 970 *spooky*; vague 419 *dim*, vacuous, vacant,

void 190 *empty*; inane; honorary, nominal, fictitious; emblematic, symbolic, token; without substance, groundless, without foundation, unfounded; visionary, chimerical 513 *imaginary*; senseless 515 *meaningless*; blank, characterless, null; superficial 212 *shallow*.

Vb. *not be,* pass away, nullify.

5 Intrinsicality – N. *intrinsicality,* inherence, immanence; essentialness; inwardness, introversion, autism; subjectiveness, subjectivity; ego 80 *self*; subjectivism.

essential part, sine qua non; prime constituent 1 *essence*; principle, property, attribute 89 *concomitant*; virtue; quintessence, flower, distillation; stuff, quiddity 3 *substance*; incarnation, embodiment; life, lifeblood, heart's blood, sap; jugular vein, artery; heart, heart of the matter, soul, inner man 447 *spirit*; gumption, backbone, marrow, pith, fibre; core, kernel 225 *centre*; nub, nittygritty, nuts and bolts, business end, nucleus 638 *chief thing*.

character, nature, quality; make-up, personality, type, breed 77 *sort*; constitution, characteristics, traits, ethos; cast, colour, complexion; features; diagnosis.

temperament, temper, frame of mind, humour, disposition, mood, spirit 817 *affections*; strain, trait 179 *tendency*; idiosyncrasy, peculiarity 80 *speciality*.

heredity, DNA, chromosome, gene, inherited characteristic; original sin; ancestry 169 *genealogy*; Mendel's law; genetics, genetic counselling, genetic engineering 358 *biology*.

Adj. *intrinsic,* immanent, deep down, deep-seated, deep-set, deep-rooted, ingrained; inherent, integral 58 *component*; inward, internal 224 *interior*; implicit, part and parcel of, built-in 78 *included*; indispensable, unalienable, inseparable 13 *identical*; autistic, subjective, introversive, reflexive, inwardlooking, introspective, introverted; characteristic; indigenous, native; natural,

instinctive, automatic; organic 156 *fundamental*; a priori, original, elemental, cardinal; essential, constitutional.

genetic, inherited, hereditary, familial, atavistic; native, inborn, innate, congenital, inbred.

characteristic, typical, representative, 80 *special*; characterizing, qualitative; indicative, unchanging 153 *established*.

Vb. *be intrinsic,* - immanent etc. adj.; inherit, take after, run in the family; bear the mark of, involve, boil down to 523 *imply*.

6 Extrinsicality – N. *extrinsicality,* objectiveness, objectivity; transcendence 34 *superiority*; otherness, the other, externality, outwardness, outer space 223 *exteriority*; externalization; projection, extrovert; accidence 7 *modality*; accident, contingency 159 *chance*; accessory.

Adj. *extrinsic,* foreign 59 *extraneous*; transcendent 34 *superior*; outward, external, extramural 223 *exterior*; outward-looking, extroverted; environmental, acquired, implanted, inbred, instilled, inculcated; accessory, annexed, appended 38 *additional*; incidental, accidental, contingent, fortuitous 159 *casual*; nonessential, inessential; subsidiary, subordinate 35 *inferior*.

Vb. *be extrinsic,* lie without, be outwith; transcend 34 *be superior*; come from without.

make extrinsic, objectify, realize, project.

7 State: absolute condition – N. *state,* condition; lot, walk of life, station in l., lifestyle; plight 8 *circumstance*; position, place, echelon, category, status, footing, standing, rank; habit, disposition. attitude, frame of mind, vein, temper, disposition, humour, mood 817 *affections*; state of mind, spirits, morale; state of health; kilter, fettle.

modality, mode, manner, way, fashion, trend, style; mould 243 *form*; shape, fabric 331 *structure*; aspect, character, guise 445 *appearance*.

8 Circumstance: relative condition– N. *circumstance,* situation, circumstances, conditions, factors, the times; environment, milieu 230 *surroundings*; context 9 *relation*; status quo, state of affairs, how things stand; régime, set-up 7 *state*; aspect, appearances 445 *appearance*; lie of the land 186 *situation*; footing, standing, status, relative position 73 *serial place*, awkward situation, catch-22 s., plight, pickle, pretty pass, corner, fix, hole, jam, quandary, dilemma 700 *predicament*.

juncture, conjuncture, stage, point 154 *event*; contingency, eventuality; crossroads, turning point, point of no return; moment, hour, right time, opportunity 137 *occasion*; critical moment, crucial m., when the chips are down.

Adj. *circumstantial,* situated; surrounding, environmental, contextual; limiting; modifying 468 *qualifying*; temporary 114 *transient*; variable 152 *changeful*; relative, contingent, incidental; critical, crucial; suitable, seemly 24 *agreeing*; appropriate, convenient 642 *advisable*.

Adv. *thus,* so; like this, in this way. *if,* should it be that; in the event of, in the case of, in case; provided that; given that, supposing, assuming, granting, allowing; if not, unless, except, without.

Section two: Relation

9 Relation – N. *relation,* relatedness, connectedness, rapport, reference, respect, regard; bearing, direction; concern, interest, import 638 *importance*; involvement, implication 5 *intrinsicality*; relationship, homogeneity, affinity; filiation, kinship 11 *consanguinity*; classification; affiliation, alliance 706 *association*; relations, friendly terms, intimacy 880 *friendship*; liaison, connection, merger, take-over, link, tie-up 47 *bond*; something in common, common interest, common denominator; context, milieu, environment 8 *circumstance*.

relativeness, relativity, interconnection, mutual relation 12 *correlation*; correspondence 13 *identity*, 28 *equality*; analogy 18 *similarity*; comparability 462 *comparison*; apposition, approximation 289 *approach*, 200 *nearness*, 202 *contiguity*, 89 *accompaniment*; collaterality 219 *parallelism*, 245 *symmetry*; perspective, proportion, ratio; cause and effect 156 *cause*; dependence 157 *effect*; relative position, status, rank, echelon 27 *degree*; serial order 65 *sequence*.

relevance, logicality, logical argument 475 *reasoning*; thread; due proportion 24 *conformance*; suitability, application, appositeness, pertinence, propriety, comparability 24 *fitness*; case in point, good example, classic e.,

referral, reference, cross-r.; application, allusion, mention; citation, quotation; frame of reference, referent.

Adj. *relative,* not absolute 8 *circumstantial*; relational, respective; referable; related, connected, associated, en rapport, linked, bearing upon, concerning; of import 638 *important*; belonging, appertaining, in common; mutual, reciprocal, corresponding, answering to 12 *correlative*; in the same category 62 *arranged*; consecutive 65 *sequential*; affiliated, filiated, cognate, kindred 11 *akin*; analogous, like 18 *similar*; comparative, comparable 462 *compared*; approximating, approaching 200 *near*; collateral; proportional, proportionate, varying as, in ratio, to scale; in due proportion, commensurate 245 *symmetrical*; in perspective; contextual.

relevant, apposite, pertinent, applicable; to the point, well-directed 475 *rational*; proper, appropriate, suitable, fitting 24 *apt*; alluding, allusive; quotable, worth mentioning.

Vb. *be related,* have a relationship; have reference to, refer to, have to do with; bear upon, have a bearing on, be a factor 178 *influence*; touch, concern, deal with, interest, affect; be a relation 11 *be akin*; belong, pertain, appertain; approximate to 289 *approach*; answer to, correspond, reciprocate 12 *correlate*;

have a connection, tie in with; be proportionate, vary as; be relevant, serve as an example; come to the point, get down to brass tacks, get down to the nitty-gritty.

relate, put in perspective; connect with, gear to, apply, bring to bear upon; link, connect, bracket together, treat as one, tie up with 45 *tie*; put in its context, provide a background, sketch in the b.; compare 18 *liken*; balance 28 *equalize*; establish a connection, draw a parallel; make a reference to, refer to, touch on, allude to, mention, mention in passing, refer to en passant.

Adv. *relatively,* not absolutely, in relation to; to some extent, comparatively; proportionally, in ratio, to scale, in perspective; depending on circumstance.

concerning, touching, regarding; as to, as regards, with regard *or* respect to; relative to, relating to, vis-à-vis, with reference to, about, re, on; in connection with; in relation to; speaking of, apropos, by the way, by the bye, on the subject of; on the point of; in the matter of; whereas; forasmuch, inasmuch; concerning which, whereto; thereto; hereto; whereof, thereof, hereof.

10 Unrelatedness: absence of relation –
N. *unrelatedness,* absoluteness; independence 744 *freedom*; arbitrariness; unilateralism; separateness, isolation 46 *separation*; individuality 80 *speciality*; homelessness, no fixed abode; lack of connection; unclassifiability; randomness 61 *disorder*; inconsequence (see *irrelevance*); dissociation 46 *disunion,* 72 *discontinuity*; wrong association 495 *error*; disproportion, asymmetry 246 *distortion*; incommensurability, disparity 29 *inequality*; diversity, multifariousness 15 *difference,* 17 *nonuniformity,* 82 *multiformity*; incongruence 84 *nonconformity*; irreconcilability 14 *contrariety*; intrusiveness 138 *untimeliness*; no business of, nobody's b.; square peg in a round hole, fish out of water 25 *misfit*; exotic, intruder, cuckoo in the nest 59 *extraneousness.*

irrelevance, irrelevancy; illogicality 477 *sophism*; inapplicability; inconsequence, non sequitur; parenthesis; diversion, red herring, dust in the eyes 282 *deviation*; incidental 154 *event*; nonessential 639 *unimportance.*

Adj. *unrelated,* absolute; independent; owing nothing to 21 *original*; irrespective, regardless, unilateral, arbitrary; unclassified, unidentified; homeless, of no fixed abode; wandering, astray; insular 88 *alone*; uninvolved 860 *indifferent*; floating, detached, unconnected, without context, unallied; parenthetic; episodic, incidental 72 *discontinuous*; separate, individual 80 *special*; without interest, nothing to do with; inessential 6 *extrinsic*; exotic, foreign, alien, strange, extraterrestrial 59 *extraneous*; intrusive; inappropriate, incompatible 25 *disagreeing*; not comparable, incommensurable, disparate 29 *unequal*; disproportionate, out of proportion, asymmetrical 246 *distorted*; discordant 84 *unconformable*; irreconcilable 14 *contrary*; multifarious 82 *multiform.*

irrelevant, illogical; inapposite, inapplicable; impertinent, inept 25 *unapt*; misapplied; misdirected 495 *erroneous*; off-target, off the beam, off-centre, peripheral; wandering 570 *diffuse*; beside the point, beside the mark, neither here nor there; trivial, inessential 639 *unimportant*; inconsequential; incidental 159 *casual*; remote, far-fetched, forced, strained, laboured; academic, immaterial.

Vb. *be unrelated,* have nothing to do w., have no bearing on; owe nothing to; have no right to be there; not be one's business, be nobody's b.; not concern, not touch; be irrelevant, be beside the p., cloud the issue, draw a red herring, throw dust in one's eyes; force, strain, labour; drag in by the heels, drag in screaming; ramble, wander, lose the thread, stray from the point 570 *be diffuse.*

11 Consanguinity: relations of kindred –
N. *consanguinity,* kinship, kindred,

blood 169 *parentage*; affiliation, relationship, affinity, propinquity; blood relationship; ancestry, lineage, descent 169 *genealogy*; connection, alliance, family; ties of family, clanship, tribalism, nationality 371 *nation*; nepotism; atavism 5 *heredity*.

kinsman, kinswoman; kin, kindred, kith and kin, kinsfolk, relations; near relative, next of kin; distant relation, blood r., kissing cousin; one of the family, relation by marriage, in-law, grandparents, father, mother 169 *parentage*; children, offspring, issue, one's flesh and blood 170 *posterity*; twin, identical t., sibling, sister, brother *or* s., blood b. *or* s., half-b. *or* -s., stepbrother *or* -s.; cousin, first c., second c., cousin once removed; uncle, aunt, auntie, great-uncle, great-great-u., great-aunt, great-great-a.; nephew, niece, grand-nephew, grand-niece; clansman, tribesman, compatriot.

family, matriarchy, patriarchy; motherhood, fatherhood, brotherhood, sisterhood; fraternity, sorority; adopted son *or* daughter, foster child, godchild, stepchild, adopted c.; adoptive mother *or* father, biological mother *or* father, natural mother, surrogate m., in-laws; one's people, one's folks; family circle, home c. 882 *fellowship*; the old folks at home, household, hearth and home 192 *home*; nuclear family, extended f.; tribe, clan.

race, stock, breed, strain, line, house, tribe, clan, sept; ethnic group; nation, people.

Adj. *akin,* kindred, twin-born; matrilineal, out of; patrilineal, by; maternal, paternal 169 *parental*; sibling, fraternal, brotherly, sisterly, cousinly; avuncular; related, family, allied; german; near, related 9 *relative*; once removed, twice r.; next-of-kin.

ethnic, racial, tribal, clannish 371 *national*; interbred, inbred 43 *mixed*; Caucasoid, Negroid.

Vb. *be akin,* share the blood of; claim relationship etc. n.; own a connection 9 *be related*; marry into 894 *wed*; father,

sire 167 *generate*; be brother *or* sister to; affiliate, adopt, foster.

12 Correlation: double or reciprocal relation – N. *correlation,* correlativity 9 *relation*; proportion 245 *symmetry*; design, pattern 62 *arrangement*; grid 222 *network*; correspondence 18 *similarity*; opposite number 13 *identity*; mutuality, interrelation, interconnection; interdependence, mutual dependence; interaction, interplay; alternation, turn and turn about, swings and roundabouts, seesaw 317 *oscillation*; reciprocity, reciprocation 151 *interchange*; each, each other, one another; give and take 770 *compromise*; exchange, change, payment in kind 791 *barter*; trade-off, tit for tat 714 *retaliation*.

Adj. *correlative,* reciprocal 9 *relative*; corresponding, opposite, answering to, analogous, parallel 18 *similar*; proportional, proportionate 245 *symmetrical*; complementary, interdependent; interconnecting; mutual, requited; reciprocating; alternating, alternate, seesaw; balancing 28 *equivalent*; interlocking, geared, interacting; patterned, woven; interchangeable, exchangeable; inter -, international; two-way.

Vb. *correlate,* interrelate, interconnect, interlock, interplay, interact; interdepend; vary as, be a function of; correspond, be analogous to, answer to, reflect 18 *resemble*; react 280 *recoil*; alternate 317 *oscillate*; reciprocate 714 *retaliate*; exchange, swap, barter, trade off 791 *trade*; balance 28 *equalize*; set off, act as a foil to 31 *compensate*.

Adv. *correlatively,* proportionately, as... so...; mutually, reciprocally, each to each, each other, one another; interchangeably, in mutual exchange; in kind; alternately, by turns, turn and turn about; vice versa 14 *contrarily*; between, shuttlewise 317 *to and fro*.

13 Identity – N. *identity,* identicalness, sameness; the same, the very same, the very one; genuineness 494 *authenticity*; the real thing, it 21 *no imitation*; the very

words, ditto, tautology, redundancy 106 *repetition*; alter ego, genius, double; identification, coincidence, congruence 24 *agreement*; coalescence, absorption 299 *reception*; convertibility, interchangeability, equivalence 28 *equality*; no difference, indistinguishability; synonymity, synonymy 514 *meaning*; same kind, homogeneity 16 *uniformity*; no change, invariability, constant 153 *fixture*; duplicate 22 *copy*; look-alike, dead ringer, spitting image; fellow, pair, match, twin 18 *analogue*; homonym, homophone, synonym 559 *word*.

Adj. *identical,* same, self, selfsame, of that ilk; one and the same, one and only 88 *one*; coalescent, merging, absorbed; identified with, indistinguishable, lookalike, interchangeable, confusable, unisex, convertible, equivalent 28 *equal*; synonymous, congruent 24 *agreeing*; always the same, invariable, constant, unchanging, unaltered 153 *unchangeable*; monotonous 838 *tedious*; homogeneous, monolithic 16 *uniform*; tautologous, redundant, repetitive, repetitional 106 *repeated*.

Vb. *be identical,* look the same, be as like as two peas in a pod, be look-alikes, be a dead ringer for, be the spitting image of, ditto 106 *repeat*; coincide, coalesce, merge, be one with; be congruent, agree in all respects, be unanimous 24 *accord*; phase 123 *synchronize*.

identify, make as one, unify; treat as the same, not distinguish; equate, tar with the same brush 28 *equalize*; assimilate, match, pair 18 *liken*.

Adv. *identically,* ibidem; ditto; same here.

14 Contrariety – N. *contrariety,* world of d. 15 *difference*; exclusiveness, irreconcilability 10 *unrelatedness*; antipathy, repugnance, hostility 888 *hatred*; adverseness, contrariness, antagonism 704 *opposition*; antidote 182 *counteraction*;

conflict, confrontation, clash 279 *collision*; discord 25 *disagreement*; contradistinction, contrast, relief, light r., variation, undertone, counterpoint 15 *differentiation*; contradiction 533 *negation*; contraindication 467 *counterevidence*; antonym 514 *meaning*; inconsistency 17 *nonuniformity*; paradox, ambivalence 518 *equivocalness*; oppositeness, antithesis, direct opposite, antipodes, poles apart; other extreme, quite the contrary, quite the reverse; other side, opposite s. 240 *contraposition*; reverse, wrong side 238 *rear*; inverse 221 *inversion*; converse, reverse image, mirror i., mirror 417 *reflection*; opposite direction, contraflow; headwind, undertow, countercurrent 182 *counteraction*.

polarity, contraries 704 *opposites*; positive and negative; north and south; east and west; day and night; light and darkness; hot and cold; fire and water; chalk and cheese; black and white; good and evil; yin and yang, male and female.

Adj. *contrary,* nonidentical, as different as chalk from cheese, anything but 15 *different*; contrasting, contrasted, incompatible, clashing, conflicting, discordant 25 *disagreeing*; inconsistent, not uniform 17 *nonuniform*; ambivalent, bittersweet, love-hate, sweet and sour; contradictory, antithetic 533 *negative*; antithetical, antonymous; diametrically opposite, poles apart, antipodean 240 *opposite*; reverse, converse, inverse; antipathetic, hostile; adverse, antagonistic 704 *opposing*; antidotal; counter-, contra-, anti-.

Vb. *be contrary,* have nothing in common, be poles apart 10 *be unrelated*, 15 *differ*; contrast 25 *disagree*; conflict with; run counter to 240 *be opposite*; speak with two voices 518 *be equivocal*; contravene 704 *oppose*, 738 *disobey*; contradict, contraindicate 533 *negate*; cancel out 182 *counteract*; turn the tables 221 *invert*.

Adv. *contrarily,* on the other hand, conversely, contrariwise; vice versa, topsy-turvy, upside down; inversely; on

the contrary; otherwise, the other way round; in contrast, in opposition to.

15 Difference – N. *difference,* unlikeness 19 *dissimilarity*; disparity, odds 29 *inequality*; margin, differential, minus, plus 41 *remainder*; wide margin 199 *distance*; narrow margin 200 *nearness*; heterogeneity, variety, diverseness, diversity 17 *nonuniformity*; divergence, departure from 282 *deviation*; otherness, differentia, distinctness 10 *unrelatedness,* 21 *originality*; discrepancy, incongruity 25 *disagreement*; incompatibility, antipathy 861 *dislike*; disharmony, discord, variance 709 *dissension*; contrast 14 *contrariety*; opposite, antithesis 240 *contraposition*; variation, modification, alteration 143 *change,* 147 *conversion.*

differentiation 463 *discrimination*; contradistinction, distinction, nice d., subtle d.; nuance, nicety 514 *meaning*; conjugation, declension 564 *grammar.*

variant, different thing, another t., something else, something else again; quite another matter, different kettle of fish, a different ball game; another story, horse of another colour, another light on, the other side of the coin; freak, mutation; sport 84 *nonconformist*; new edition 589 *edition.*

Adj. *different,* differing, unlike 19 *dissimilar*; original 126 *new*; various, diverse, diversified, heterogeneous 17 *nonuniform*; multifarious 82 *multiform*; assorted, all manner of 43 *mixed*; distinct, distinguished, differentiated, discriminated 46 *separate*; departing from; odd 84 *unusual*; discordant, clashing, incongruent, incongruous 25 *disagreeing*; disparate 29 *unequal*; contrasting, contrasted, far from it, wide apart, poles apart 14 *contrary*; other, not the same; in a different class 34 *superior,* 35 *inferior*; the same yet not the same, altered 147 *converted.*

distinctive, diagnostic, indicative 5 *characteristic*; differentiating, distinguishing; comparative, superlative.

Vb. *differ,* be different etc. adj.; vary from, diverge f. 282 *deviate*; contrast,

conflict 25 *disagree*; be at variance 709 *quarrel*; change one's tune, modify, vary, make alterations; suffer a sea change 143 *change.*

differentiate, distinguish, single o. 463 *discriminate*; refine, make a distinction; widen the gap 46 *set apart.*

16 Uniformity – N. *uniformity,* uniformness, consistency, constancy, steadiness 153 *stability*; persistence 71 *continuity,* 146 *continuance*; unfailing regularity, conveyor belt 141 *periodicity*; order, regularity, method, centralization 60 *order*; homogeneity 18 *similarity*; monolithic quality; unity, unison, correspondence, accordance 24 *agreement*; evenness, levelness, flushness 258 *smoothness*; roundness 245 *symmetry*; sameness 13 *identity*; monotony; mixture as before, same old story; even pace, rhythm; daily round, routine, treadmill 610 *habit*; monotone; droning, sing-song, monologue; monolith; pattern, mould; type, stereotype 22 *copy*; stamp, set, assortment; suit; standard dress 228 *uniform*; standardization, mass production, automation, computerization 83 *conformity*; cliché 106 *repetition*; regimentation, totalitarianism, closed shop 740 *compulsion.*

uniformist, regimenter; leveller, egalitarian.

Adj. *uniform,* all of a piece, one-piece; same all through, monolithic; of one kind; homogeneous 18 *similar*; same, consistent, constant, steady 153 *fixed*; undeviating, unchanging, invariable 144 *permanent*; equable 823 *inexcitable*; rhythmic 258 *smooth*; undifferentiated, unrelieved 573 *plain*; without contrast, lacking variety, uniformed, characterless, featureless, blank; monotonous, droning, sing-song, monotone; monochrome; repetitive 106 *repeated*; normal 83 *typical*; patterned, standardized, stereotyped, mass-produced, conveyor belt, unisex; sorted, assorted, sized; drilled, aligned, in line; orderly, regular 245 *symmetrical*; straight, even, flush, level, dead l. 216 *flat.*

Vb. *be uniform,* - homogeneous etc. adj.; follow routine 610 *be wont*; sing in unison, chorus 24 *accord*; typify 83 *conform*; toe the line, follow the crowd, fall in, wear uniform.

make uniform, homogenize; characterize, run through 547 *mark*; level, abolish differentials 28 *equalize*; assimilate 18 *liken*; size, grade; drill, align; regiment, institutionalize; standardize, stereotype; mass-produce; put into uniform; regularize 83 *make conform*.

17 Nonuniformity – **N.** *nonuniformity,* variability, patchiness 72 *discontinuity*; unpredictability 152 *changeableness*; inconstancy, inconsistency, capriciousness, whimsy 604 *caprice*; irregularity, haphazardness 61 *disorder*; asymmetry 244 *amorphism*; unevenness 259 *roughness*; heterogeneity 15 *difference*; contrast 14 *contrariety*, 19 *dissimilarity*; divergence 282 *deviation*; diversity, variety 82 *multiformity*; all shapes and sizes, mixed bag, ragbag, lucky dip, hotchpotch, odds and ends 43 *medley*; patchwork, motley, crazy paving, mosaic 437 *variegation*; abnormality, exception, special case, sport, mutation, freak 84 *nonconformity*; odd man out, rogue elephant 59 *extraneousness*; uniqueness.

Adj. *nonuniform,* variable, unpredictable 152 *changeful*; sporadic 142 *fitful*; inconstant, inconsistent 604 *capricious*; temperamental 822 *excitable*; patchy 29 *unequal*; random, haphazard, unsystematic; asymmetrical 244 *amorphous*; untidy, out of order; uneven, bumpy 259 *rough*; erratic, out of step, out of time; contrasted 14 *contrary*; heterogeneous, diverse 15 *different*, 19 *dissimilar*; multifarious, miscellaneous, of all sorts 82 *multiform*; multicoloured, decorated 844 *ornamental*; divergent, diversified; dissenting 25 *disagreeing*; atypical 84 *unconformable*; unusual, unconventional 84 *abnormal*; unique, lone 80 *special*; individual, hand-made; out of uniform, in mufti.

18 Similarity – **N.** *similarity,* resemblance, likeness, similitude; seeming, look 445 *appearance*; fashion, trend, style 243 *form*; point of resemblance 9 *relation*; congruity 24 *agreement*; affinity, kinship 11 *consanguinity*; homogeneity, comparability, analogy, correspondence, parallelism 12 *correlation*; equivalence, parity 28 *equality*; no difference 13 *identity*; family likeness; close resemblance, perfect l.; faithful likeness, photographic l. 551 *representation*; lifelikeness 494 *accuracy*; approximation 200 *nearness*; faint resemblance; suggestion, hint.

assimilation, likening 462 *comparison*; identification 13 *identity*; simulation, camouflage 20 *imitation*; parable, allegory, metaphor; portrayal 590 *description*; portraiture 553 *picture*; alliteration, assonance, rhyme 593 *prosody*; pun, play on words 518 *equivocalness*.

analogue, the like, suchlike, the likes of; type, perfect example, classic e. 83 *example*; correlative 12 *correlation*; simile, parallel, metaphor, allegory, parable; equivalent 150 *substitute*; twin; match, pair, fellow, mate, companion; complement, counterpart, other half, better half 89 *concomitant*; alter ego, genius, doppelgänger; double, dead ringer, lookalike; likeness, reflection, shadow, the picture of 551 *image*; dead spit of, spitting image, living image, chip off the old block; two peas, couple, pair 90 *duality*; two of a kind, birds of a feather; clone 22 *duplicate*.

Adj. *similar,* resembling, like, alike, twin, matching, like as two peas (in a pod), out of the same mould; much of a muchness, 13 *identical*; of a piece 16 *uniform*; analogous; parallel 28 *equivalent*; corresponding, bracketed with; homogeneous, close, approximate 200 *near*; representative; reproducing, reflecting; after, après, in the style of, à la; much the same, something like, such as, quasi.

lifelike, realistic, exact, faithful, typical; just one, true to life, true to type; graphic, vivid.

simulating 20 *imitative*; seeming, deceptive; mock, quasi, pseudo 542 *spurious*; synthetic, artificial, simulated, ersatz 150 *substituted*.

Vb. *resemble,* be similar to, pass for, bear a resemblance; mirror, reflect 20 *imitate*; seem like, sound l., look as if; look like, take after, favour, put one in mind of, have the look of; savour of, smack of; come near to 289 *approach*; match, answer to 24 *accord*; typify 551 *represent*.

liken, approximate 462 *compare*; reduce to 13 *identify*; pair, twin, bracket with 28 *equalize*; allegorize; portray 20 *imitate*.

Adv. *similarly,* as, like, as if, quasi, so to speak, as it were; likewise, so, in the same category, by the same token.

19 Dissimilarity – **N.** *dissimilarity,* incomparability 10 *unrelatedness*; disparity 29 *inequality*; divergence 15 *difference*; variation, variety 17 *nonuniformity,* 82 *multiformity*; contrast 14 *contrariety*; little in common, nothing in c., no common ground, not a pair 25 *disagreement*; novelty, uniqueness 21 *originality*; dissemblance; 527 *disguise*; poor l. 552 *misrepresentation*; foreign body, 59 *extraneousness*; odd man out 25 *misfit*.

Adj. *dissimilar,* unlike, diverse 15 *different*; various 82 *multiform*; disparate 29 *unequal*; unalike, not comparable 10 *unrelated*; unpaired 17 *nonuniform*; unique, peerless, matchless, nonpareil, one and only, original 21 *inimitable*; incongruent 25 *disagreeing*; untypical, atypical, exotic 84 *unconformable*; novel 126 *new*; a far cry from 199 *distant*; not true to life, unrealistic.

Vb. *be unlike,* - dissimilar etc. adj.; bear no resemblance, have nothing in common 15 *differ*.

make unlike, discriminate, distinguish 15 *differentiate*; modify 143 *change*, 147

convert; 246 *distort*; dissemble 542 *deceive*; disguise 525 *conceal*; 541 *fake*.

20 Imitation – **N.** *imitation,* copying etc. vb; sincerest form of flattery; rivalry, emulation 716 *contention*; doing as Rome does 83 *conformity*; want of originality, slavish imitation; imitativeness, parrotry (see *mimicry*); affectedness 850 *affectation*; mimesis 551 *representation*; reflection, mirror, echo, shadow 18 *assimilation*; translation 520 *interpretation*; borrowing, cribbing, plagiarism, piracy 788 *stealing*; forgery, falsification, counterfeit, fake 541 *falsehood*; copying, transcribing, tracing 22 *copy*; duplication 166 *reproduction*, 551 *photography*.

mimicry, mimesis 551 *representation*; onomatopoeia; mime, pantomime, sign language, gesticulation 547 *gesture*; ventriloquism 579 *speech*; portraiture 553 *painting,* 590 *description*; realism 494 *accuracy*; mockery, caricature, parody, spoof, burlesque 851 *satire*; travesty 552 *misrepresentation,* 246 *distortion*; mimicking, apishness, parrotry 106 *repetition,* 850 *affectation*; conjuring, illusionism; simulation, semblance, disguise, cosmetics, make-up, camouflage. mockery.

imitator, copycat, ape, sedulous a.; mockingbird, parrot, myna bird, echo; sheep 83 *conformist*. poseur, mocker, parodist, caricaturist 839 *humorist*, mime, ventriloquist, mimic, impersonator, female i., drag artiste, illusionist 594 *entertainer*; actor, portraitist 556 *artist*; copyist, tracer; translator, paraphraser 520 *interpreter*; simulator, hypocrite 545 *impostor*; borrower, plagiarist, pirate; counterfeiter, forger; duplicator, spirit d., copier, photocopier, Xerox (tdmk), stencil.

Adj. *imitative,* mimetic; emulating; onomatopoeic, echoic; aping, parrotlike; following; echoing; posing 850 *affected*; disguised, camouflaged; mock, mimic; simulating, shamming 541 *hypocritical*; pseudo, quasi, sham, imitation, phony, counterfeit 541 *false*; artificial,

ersatz, synthetic, man-made 150 *substituted*; run-of-the-mill, hackneyed 610 *usual*; unimaginative, derivative, second-hand, handed down 106 *repeated*; paraphrastic, modelled; copied, slavish; caricatured, parodied, travestied, burlesque.

Vb. *imitate,* emulate, ape, parrot, echo, mirror, reflect 18 *resemble*; pretend, masquerade, make-believe, make as if, make like; act, mimic, mime, portray 551 *represent*; parody, take off, spoof, lampoon, caricature, burlesque, travesty 851 *ridicule*; sham, simulate, put on, feign 541 *dissemble*; camouflage 525 *conceal*.

copy, trace; catch; set up 587 *print*; reprint, duplicate, mimeograph, cyclostyle, photocopy, xerox, photostat; copy out, transcribe, type, paraphrase, translate 520 *interpret*; crib, plagiarize, pirate, lift, borrow 788 *steal*; counterfeit, forge 541 *fake*.

do likewise, do as the Romans do, mould oneself on; take a leaf out of another's book; follow suit, tread in the steps of, follow my leader 284 *follow*; echo, ditto, chorus 106 *repeat*; follow precedent, follow another's example, jump on the bandwagon 83 *conform*; emulate.

21 Originality – **N.** *originality,* creativeness, inventiveness 513 *imagination*; all my own work, a poor thing but mine own, 164 *production*; original thought, originality 119 *priority*, 10 *unrelatedness*; uniqueness, the one and only 88 *unity*; new departure 68 *beginning*; something new, novelty, innovation, freshness 126 *newness*; eccentricity, idiosyncrasy, individuality 84 *nonconformity*.

no imitation, genuineness, sincerity 494 *authenticity*; real thing, the real McCoy, the genuine article. 80 *self*; autograph, holograph, manuscript, one's own hand.

Adj. *original,* creative, inventive 513 *imaginative*; underived; archetypal; primordial, primary; first, first-hand, first

in the field, pioneering 119 *prior*; unprecedented, fresh, novel 126 *new*; individual; idiosyncratic 84 *unconformable*.

inimitable, incomparable, out of reach 34 *superior*; not imitated, not emulated, uncopied, atypical 15 *different*; unique, one and only 88 *one*; true 494 *genuine*.

22 Copy – **N.** *copy,* exact c.; clone 166 *reproduction*; replica, facsimile, tracing; fair copy, transcript, transcription; cast, death mask; ectype, stamp, seal, impression, imprint; stereotype, lithograph, print, offprint; 555 *engraving*; photocopy, Xerox (tdmk), photograph 551 *photography*; Photostat (tdmk). microfilm, microfiche 548 *record*; an imitation, dummy, pastiche; fake 542 *sham*; plagiarism, piracy, crib 20 *imitation*; a likeness, semblance 18 *similarity*; portrait, drawing 553 *picture*; icon, image 551 *representation*; model, effigy, statue 554 *sculpture*; reflex, echo, mirror 106 *repetition*, 417 *reflection*; poor likeness, apology for, mockery of 552 *misrepresentation*; caricature, cartoon, travesty, take-off, spoof, lampoon, parody 851 *ridicule*; shadow; outline, sketch, draft; metaphrase, paraphrase 520 *translation*.

duplicate, carbon copy; stencil, master copy; transfer, rubbing; photograph 551 *photography*; reprint, reissue 589 *edition*.

23 Prototype – **N.** *prototype,* archetype; type, norm, everyman 30 *average*; protoplasm 358 *organism*; original, protoplast 68 *origin*; precedent 119 *priority*; guide, rule, maxim 693 *precept*; standard, criterion, touchstone, standard of comparison, yardstick, bench mark, barometer, frame of reference 9 *referral*; ideal 646 *perfection*; keynote, tuning fork, metronome 465 *gauge*; module; specimen, sample 83 *example*; model; exemplar, pattern, template, paradigm; dummy, mock-up; copybook, copy, text, manuscript; blueprint, design, master plan, scheme 623 *plan*; rough plan, outline, draft, sketch.

living model, model, artist's m., poser, sitter, subject; fashion model, mannequin; stroke, pacer, pacemaker; trendsetter; bandleader, conductor.

mould, matrix, mint; stencil, negative; frame 243 *form*; wax figure, lay f., tailor's dummy; last; die, stamp, punch, seal, intaglio 555 *printing.*

Vb. *be an example,* set an e., serve as e., act as a pattern; serve as a model, model, sit for, pose.

24 Agreement – **N.** *agreement,* consent 488 *assent*; accord, accordance, chorus, unison 16 *uniformity*; harmony 410 *melody*; consonance, concordance; concert, understanding, mutual understanding, rapport, entente; concordat, convention, pact 765 *compact*; unity, solidarity, unanimity 488 *consensus*; consortium 706 *cooperation*; union 50 *combination*; peace 710 *concord.*

conformance 83 *conformity*; congruence, coincidence 13 *identity*; consistency, congruity 16 *uniformity*; coherence, consequence, logic, logical conclusion 475 *reasoning*; correspondence, parallelism 18 *similarity.*

fitness, aptness, qualification, capability 694 *aptitude*; suitability, propriety 642 *good policy*; the right man or woman in the right place, the very thing 13 *identity*; relevancy, pertinence, admissibility, appositeness, case in point, good example 9 *relevance*; commensurability, proportion 9 *relation*; timeliness, right moment 137 *occasion*; mot juste.

adaptation, harmonization, synchronization, matching 18 *assimilation*; reconciliation 719 *pacification*; accommodation, negotiation 770 *compromise*; attunement, adjustment 62 *arrangement*; compatibility, fitting, suiting, good fit, perfect f.

Adj. *agreeing,* right, in accord, in accordance with, in keeping with; corresponding, answering; proportional, proportionate, commensurate, according to 12 *correlative*; coinciding, congruent, congruous 28 *equal*; consistent with,

conforming 83 *conformable*; in conformity, in step, in phase, in tune, synchronized 123 *synchronous*; of a piece with, consistent; harmonized 410 *harmonious*; combining, mixing; suiting, matching 18 *similar*; becoming 846 *tasteful*; sympathetic; reconcilable, compatible, coexisting, symbiotic; consentient, agreeable, acquiescent 488 *assenting*; concurrent, agreed, at one, in unison, unanimous; united, concerted; in rapport with, like-minded; in treaty, negotiating 765 *contractual.*

apt, applicable, admissible, germane, appropriate, pertinent, to the point, well-aimed 9 *relevant*; to the purpose, bearing upon; pat, in place, apropos; right, happy, felicitous 575 *elegant*; at home, in one's element; opportune 137 *timely.*

fit, fitting, befitting, seemly, decorous; suited, well-adapted, capable, qualified, groomed for, cut out for 694 *skilful*; suitable, up one's street 642 *advisable*; proper 913 *right.*

adjusted, well-a. 60 *orderly*, 494 *accurate*; synchronized; focused, tuned, fine-t.; strung, pitched, attuned 412 *musical*; trimmed, balanced. 28 *equal*; well-cut, fitting, well-fitting; bespoke, made to measure, tailored, tailor-made.

Vb. *accord,* agree, concur 488 *assent*, 758 *consent*; respond, echo, chorus, chime in, ditto 106 *repeat*; coincide, mesh with, dovetail 45 *join*; fit, fit like a glove, fit like a second skin, fit to a T; tally, correspond, match 18 *resemble*; go with, tone in w., harmonize; come naturally to; take to like a duck to water; fit in, belong, feel at home, be in one's element; answer, do, meet, suit, suit down to the ground 642 *be expedient*; prove timely, fit the occasion; pull t. 706 *cooperate*; be consistent, hang together 475 *be reasonable*; negotiate 766 *make terms*; get on with, be of one mind, be on the same wavelength, hit it off, fraternize 880 *befriend.*

adjust, make adjustments 654 *rectify*; readjust, repair 656 *restore*; fit, suit, adapt, accommodate, conform; attune,

tune, pitch, string 410 *harmonize*; modulate; regulate 60 *order*; graduate, proportion 12 *correlate*; align 62 *arrange*; balance 28 *equalize*; cut, trim 31 *compensate*; tailor, make to measure; focus, synchronize.

25 Disagreement – N. *disagreement,* disaccord; nonagreement, agreement to disagree 489 *dissent*; conflict of opinion, controversy 475 *argument*; confrontation, wrangling, bickering 709 *quarrel*; disunity, faction 709 *dissension*; dissidence 978 *schism*; clash 279 *collision*; challenge, defiance, rupture, breach 718 *war*; variance, divergence, discrepancy 15 *difference*; ambiguity, ambivalence 518 *equivocalness*; inconsistency, credibility gap; variety, inconsistency 17 *nonuniformity*; contradiction, conflict 14 *contrariety*; dissonance, inharmoniousness 411 *discord*; incongruence, incongruity 10 *unrelatedness*; disparity 29 *inequality*; disproportion, asymmetry 246 *distortion*; incompatibility, irreconcilability, hostility 881 *enmity*.

inaptitude, unfitness, incompetence 695 *unskilfulness*; unfittingness, unsuitability, impropriety 643 *inexpedience*, inapplicability, inadmissibility, irrelevancy 10 *irrelevance*; interruption 138 *untimeliness*; maladjustment, incompatibility 84 *nonconformity*.

misfit, maladjustment, bad fit; bad match, mésalliance 894 *marriage*; incongruity, false note, jar 411 *discord*; fish out of water, square peg in a round hole; outsider, alien, foreigner, foreign body 59 *intruder*; dissident 84 *nonconformist*; joker, odd man out, freak, mutation 84 *abnormality*; eccentric, oddity 851 *laughingstock*.

Adj. *disagreeing,* dissenting, not unanimous 489 *dissenting*; in opposition, at odds, at cross purposes, at variance; at one another's throats, at loggerheads, at war 718 *warring*; bickering 709 *quarrelling*; hostile, antagonistic 881 *inimical*; antipathetic; conflicting, contradictory 14 *contrary*; unnatural, against the grain, out of character; incompatible. odd,

alien, foreign 59 *extraneous*; out of proportion, unsymmetrical 246 *distorted*; grating 411 *discordant*; mismatched; ill-matching, badly matched, ill-assorted, incongruous 497 *absurd*.

unapt, unsuited, incompetent 695 *unskilful*; inept, maladjusted 695 *clumsy*; wrong, unfitting, unsuitable, unbecoming, not for one, improper, undue, inappropriate 643 *inexpedient*; impracticable 470 *impossible*; unfit for, ineligible; ill-timed 138 *inopportune*; inapplicable, inadmissible 10 *irrelevant*; out of character, out of keeping; out of one's element, like a fish out of water, like a square peg in a round hole; out of place, out of joint, out of tune, out of time, out of step, out of phase.

Vb. *disagree* 489 *dissent*; differ, dispute 475 *argue*; fall out 709 *quarrel,* clash, confront, collide, contradict 14 *be contrary*; be unapt etc. adj.; diverge 15 *differ*; not play, not play ball 702 *be obstructive*; have nothing to do with 10 *be unrelated*; be incongruous, stick out like a sore thumb, jar.

Section three: Quantity

26 Quantity – N. *quantity,* amount, sum 38 *addition*; total 52 *whole*; extent 465 *measurement*; mass, substance, body, bulk 195 *size*; dimension, dimensions, longitude 203 *length*; width, thickness 205 *breadth*; altitude 209 *height*; deepness 211 *depth*; area, volume, extension 183 *space*; weight 322 *gravity*, 323 *lightness*; force, flow, potential, pressure, tension, stress, strain, torque 160 *energy*; numbers 104 *multitude*; quotient, fraction, multiple.

finite quantity, limited amount; lower limit, upper l., ceiling 236 *limit*; quantum, quota, quorum; measure, dose 465 *measurement*; avoirdupois 322 *weighing*; ration, whack 783 *portion*; spoonful, thimbleful, teaspoonful, dessertspoonful, tablespoonful, cupful; capful, bagful, lot, batch; load, lorryload, containerful 193 *contents*; lock stock and barrel 52

whole; large amount, masses, heaps, mountains 32 *great quantity*; small amount, bit 33 *small quantity*; greater amount, more, most, majority 36 *increase*, smaller amount, less, not so much 37 *decrease*.

Adj. *quantitative*, some, certain, any.

27 Degree: relative quantity – N. *degree*, relative quantity, proportion, ratio, scale 9 *relativeness*, 462 *comparison*; ration, stint 783 *portion*, 53 *part*; amplitude, extent, intensity, frequency, magnitude, size 26 *quantity*; level, pitch, altitude 209 *height*, 211 *depth*; key, register 410 *musical note*; reach, compass, scope 183 *range*; rate, tenor, way, speed 265 *motion*; gradation, graduation, calibration 15 *differentiation*; differential, shade, nuance; grade, remove, stepping-stone; step, rung, tread, stair 308 *ascent*; point, stage, milestone, turning point, crisis 8 *juncture*; mark, peg, notch, score 547 *indicator*; bar, line, interval 410 *notation*; valuation, value 465 *measurement*; ranking, grading 77 *classification*; class, kind 77 *sort*; standard, rank, grade 73 *serial place*; military rank, lieutenancy, captaincy, majority, colonelcy; ecclesiastical rank 985 *church office*; hierarchy 733 *authority*; sphere, station, status, social class, caste, standing, footing 8 *circumstance*; gradualism, gradualness 278 *slowness*.

comparative, relative, proportional, in scale 9 *relative*; within the bounds of; measured by.

Vb. *graduate*, rate, class, rank 73 *grade*; scale, calibrate; compare, measure.

Adv. *by degrees*, gradually, little by little, step by step, drop by drop, bit by bit, inch by inch; by inches, slowly but surely, by slow degrees; to some extent, just a bit; however little, however much.

28 Equality: sameness of quantity or degree – N. *equality*, parity, equal opportunity, coincidence 24 *agreement*; symmetry, balance; evenness. 216 *horizontality*; equability.

equivalence, likeness 18 *similarity*; sameness 13 *identity*, 219 *parallelism*; equation; interchangeability 151 *interchange*; isotropy; synonym; reciprocation, exchange, fair e., trade-off 791 *barter*; par, quits; equivalent, value 809 *price*; six of one and half a dozen of the other, nothing to choose between, nothing in it, level-pegging; even money.

equilibrium, equipoise, equiponderance, balance; even keel, steadiness; balance of nature, balance of power, balance of trade, balance of payments; deadlock, stalemate, logjam 145 *stop*; stable state, homoeostasis; sea legs, seat; fin, aileron, spoiler 153 *stabilizer*; balance.

equalization, equation; balancing 322 *weighing*; coordination, adjustment, levelling up *or* down 656 *restoration*, 31 *compensation*; positive discrimination, affirmative action, equal opportunities legislation, equal division, going halves 92 *bisection*; reciprocity 12 *correlation*; tit for tat 714 *retaliation*, 151 *interchange*; equalizer, counterpoise.

draw, drawn game, no result, drawn battle; level-pegging; tie, dead heat; stalemate, deadlock; neck and neck race, photo finish; love all, deuce.

compeer, peer, equal, match, mate, twin; fellow, brother 18 *analogue*; equivalent, parallel, opposite number, pair, counterpart, shadow.

Adj. *equal*, same 13 *identical*; like 18 *similar*; coordinate, coincident, congruent, homologous 24 *agreeing*; equidistant; isotropic; balanced, in equilibrium; homoeostatic, steady, stable 153 *fixed*; even, level, round, square, flush 258 *smooth*; equilateral, regular 16 *uniform*, 245 *symmetrical*; equable, unvarying; well-matched, drawn, tied; parallel, level-pegging, running level, abreast, neck-and-neck, nip and tuck; bracketed; sharing; equally divided, half-and-half, fifty-fifty; impartial, equitable 913 *just*; on equal terms, on the same footing, on a par, on a level; par, quits, upsides with.

equivalent, comparable, parallel, interchangeable, synonymous, corresponding, reciprocal 12 *correlative*; tantamount, virtually the same, more or less identical, indistinguishable; much the same, all one, as broad as it is long, pot calling the kettle black (**see** *equivalence*) 18 *similar*; worth.

Vb. *be equal,* equal, counterbalance, compensate; come to the same thing, coincide with, agree w. 24 *accord*; be equal to, measure up to; cope with 160 *be able*; make the grade, come up to scratch, pass muster 635 *suffice*; hold one's own, keep up with, keep pace w., be level; parallel; match, twin 18 *resemble*; tie, draw; break even; go halves.

equalize, equate; bracket, match; parallel 462 *compare*; balance, strike a b., poise; trim, dress, square, round off, make flush, level 258 *smooth*, 16 *make uniform*; fit, accommodate, readjust 24 *adjust*; counterpoise, even up; redress the balance, handicap 31 *compensate*; set on an even keel, equilibrate, restore to equilibrium 153 *stabilize*; right oneself, keep one's balance.

29 Inequality: difference of quantity or degree – N. *inequality,* difference of degree 34 *superiority*, 35 *inferiority*; irregularity, patchiness 17 *nonuniformity*; unevenness 259 *roughness*; disproportion, asymmetry 246 *distortion*, 25 *disagreement*; oddness, lopsidedness 220 *obliquity*; disparity 15 *difference*; unlikeness 19 *dissimilarity*; imbalance; dizziness, the staggers; tilting of the scales, preponderance, top-hamper 322 *gravity*; short weight 323 *lightness*; inadequacy 636 *insufficiency*; odds 15 *difference*; counterpoise; partiality, discrimination 481 *bias*.

Adj. *unequal,* disparate, incongruent 15 *different*, 19 *dissimilar*; unique, unequalled; 644 *excellent*; below par 35 *inferior*; disproportionate, asymmetrical 246 *distorted*; irregular, scalene, lopsided 17 *nonuniform*; awry; odd, uneven; variable, patchy 437 *variegated*; deficient, defective, falling short, inadequate 636 *insufficient*; underweight 323 *light*; overweight 322 *weighty*; unbalanced, swaying; untrimmed, unballasted, uncompensated; overloaded, top-heavy, unwieldy 695 *clumsy*; listing, leaning, canting, heeling; off balance, dizzy, giddy, falling; unequitable, partial, 481 *biased*.

Vb. *be unequal,* be mismatched 25 *disagree*; not balance, not equate 15 *differ*; fall short 35 *be inferior*; preponderate, have the advantage, give points to, outclass, outrank 34 *be superior*; outstrip 306 *outdo*; be deficient 636 *not suffice*; overcompensate, overweight, tip the scales 322 *weigh*; be underweight 323 *be light*; unbalance, throw off balance; overbalance, capsize; list, tilt, lean 220 *be oblique*; rock, sway 317 *fluctuate*; vary 143 *change*.

30 Mean – N. *average,* medium, mean, median; middle term 73 *serial place*; balance; happy medium, golden mean 177 *moderation*; standard product 79 *generality*; ruck, ordinary run 732 *averageness*; norm, par; the normal 610 *habit*.

middle point, midpoint, middle distance, half way 70 *middle*; middle years 131 *middle age*; middle class 869 *middle classes*; middle of the road, midway, middle course, middle ground 625 *middle way*; splitting the difference 770 *compromise*; neutrality 606 *no choice*; central position 225 *centre*.

common man 869 *commoner*, everywoman, man *or* woman in the street; joe soap 79 *everyman*; average specimen 732 *averageness*.

Adj. *median,* mean, average 70 *middle*, 225 *central*; lukewarm; intermediate, grey; standard, par, ordinary, commonplace, run-of-the-mill, mediocre 732 *middling*; moderate, middle-of-the-road 625 *neutral*; middle class, middle brow.

Vb. *average out,* average, take the mean; split the difference, go halfway 770 *compromise*; strike a balance 28 *equalize*.

31 Compensation – N. *compensation,* weighting 28 *equalization*; rectification 654 *amendment*; reaction, neutralization, antidote, nullification 182 *counteraction*; commutation 151 *interchange*, 150 *substitution*; redemption, recoupment, recovery; retrieval 771 *acquisition*; indemnification, reparation, damages, redress 787 *restitution*, 656 *restoration*; amends, expiation 941 *atonement*; reimbursement, refund, one's money back; recompense, repayment 962 *reward*, 910 *revenge*, 714 *retaliation*; reciprocity, measure for measure 12 *correlation*.

Adj. *compensatory,* compensating, redeeming, countervailing, balancing 28 *equivalent*; self-correcting, self-cancelling; reimbursing, restitutory; amendatory, expiatory 941 *atoning*; weighed against 462 *compared*.

Vb. *compensate,* offer compensation, make amends, make compensation etc. n.; do penance 941 *atone*; indemnify, restore, pay back 787 *restitute*; make good, make up, make up for; add a makeweight, ballast; pay, repay 714 *retaliate*; bribe, square 962 *reward*; reimburse, pay overtime 804 *pay*; redeem, outweigh; overcompensate, lean over backwards.

recoup, recover 656 *retrieve*; make up leeway, take up the slack; indemnify oneself, take back, get back 786 *take*; make a comeback 656 *be restored*.

32 Greatness – N. *greatness,* largeness, bigness, girth 195 *size*; large scale, generous proportions, ample p., vastness, enormousness, gigantism; muchness, abundance 635 *plenty*; amplitude, ampleness, fullness, maximum 54 *completeness, plenitude*; superabundance, superfluity, embarras de richesses, arm and a leg, more than enough 637 *redundance*;

immoderation 815 *prodigality*; exorbitance, excessiveness, excess 546 *exaggeration*; enormity, immensity, boundlessness 107 *infinity*; numerousness, countlessness 104 *multitude*; dimensions, magnitude 26 *quantity*, 27 *degree*; extension, extent 203 *length*, 205 *breadth*, 209 *height*, 211 *depth*; expanse, area, volume, capacity 183 *space*; spaciousness 183 *room*; might, strength, intensity 160 *power*, 178 *influence*; intensification, magnification, multiplication 197 *expansion*; aggrandizement 36 *increase*; seriousness, significance 638 *importance*; eminence 34 *superiority*; grandeur, grandness 868 *nobility*, 871 *pride*; majesty 733 *authority*; fame, renown 866 *repute, prestige*; noise, din 400 *loudness*.

great quantity, galore 635 *plenty*; crop, profusion, abundance 171 *productiveness*; superfluity, superabundance, torrent 637 *redundance*, 350 *stream*; expanse, lake, sea, ocean, world, universe, sight of, world of; much, lot, whole l., fat l., deal, good d., great d.; not a little, not peanuts, not chickenfeed, not to be sneezed at; too much, more than one bargained for; stock, mint, mine 632 *store*; quantity, peck, bushel, pints, gallons; lump, heap, mass, stack, mountain 74 *accumulation*; load (of), shipload, lorryload, sackload, containerful 193 *contents*; quantities, lots, lashings, oodles, scads, gobs, wads, pots, bags; heaps, loads, masses, stacks; oceans, seas, floods, streams; volumes, reams, sheets, pages and pages, screeds; numbers, quite a f., crowds, masses, millions, hosts, swarms, multitudes 104 *multitude*; all, entirety, corpus, caboodle 52 *whole*.

Adj. *great,* greater, main, most, major 34 *superior*; maximum, greatest 34 *supreme*; grand, big, muckle, mickle 195 *large*; fair-sized, largish, biggish; substantial, considerable, respectable; sizable, king-s., full-s., man-s., life-s.; bulky, massive, heavy 322 *weighty*; prolonged, lengthy 203 *long*; wide, thick 205 *broad*; swollen; ample, generous, voluminous, capacious 183 *spacious*; profound 211

deep; tall, lofty 209 *high*; 162 *strong*; mighty 160 *powerful*, 178 *influential*; intense, violent 174 *vigorous*; noisy 400 *loud*; soaring, climbing; culminating, at the peak, at its height, through the ceiling, at the limit *or* zenith, at the summit 213 *topmost*; plentiful, abundant, overflowing 635 *plentiful*; superabundant 637 *redundant*; many, swarming, teeming, hotching, alive with 104 *multitudinous*; antique, ancient, venerable, immemorial 127 *olden*, 131 *ageing*; imperial, august, of value 644 *valuable*, 868 *noble*; exalted 821 *impressive*; glorious, famed, famous 866 *renowned, worshipful*; grave, solemn, serious 638 *important*; excelling, excellent; 644 *best*.

extensive, wide-ranging, far-flung, far-reaching, widespread, prevalent, epidemic; worldwide, global, universal, cosmic; mass, wholesale, full-scale, all-embracing, across-the-board, comprehensive 78 *inclusive*.

enormous, immense, vast, colossal, giant, gigantic, monumental 195 *huge*; towering, sky-high 209 *high*.

prodigious, marvellous, astounding, amazing, astonishing 864 *wonderful*; fantastic, fabulous, incredible, unbelievable, passing belief; 472 *improbable*, 470 *impossible*; stupendous, tremendous, terrific; dreadful, frightful 854 *frightening*; breathtaking, overwhelming, out of this world 821 *impressive*.

remarkable, signal, noticeable 866 *noteworthy*; outstanding, extraordinary, exceptional, singular, uncommon 84 *unusual*; eminent, distinguished, marked 638 *notable*.

flagrant, blatant, flaring, glaring, stark, staring, staring one in the face; shocking 867 *discreditable*.

unspeakable, unutterable, indescribable, beyond description, indefinable, ineffable; past speaking 517 *inexpressible*.

exorbitant, extortionate, harsh, stringent, severe, Draconian 735 *oppressive*;

excessive, extreme. monstrous, outrageous, swingeing, unconscionable; unbearable 827 *intolerable*; inordinate, unwarranted, preposterous, extravagant, astronomical; beyond the pale, going too far.

consummate 54 *complete*; flawless 646 *perfect*; entire 52 *whole*; thorough, thoroughgoing, utter, total, out and out, dyed in the wool, arch, crass, gross, arrant, rank, regular, downright, desperate, unmitigated.

absolute, essential, positive, unequivocal; stark, pure, sheer, mere 44 *unmixed*; unlimited, unrestricted 107 *infinite*.

Vb. *be great* - large, etc. adj.; loom, loom up; stretch 183 *extend*; rear, tower, soar, mount 308 *ascend*; scale, transcend 34 *be superior*; clear, overtop; exceed, know no bounds, run to extremes, go off the deep end 306 *overstep*; enlarge 36 *augment*; 197 *expand*.

greatly, much, well; very, right, so; very much, mighty, ever so; fully, quite, entirely, utterly, without reservation, 54 *completely*; thoroughly, wholesale; widely, extensively, universally 79 *generally*; largely, mainly, mostly, to a large extent; something, considerably, fairly, pretty, pretty well; a sight, a deal, a great d., ever so much; materially, substantially; increasingly, more than ever, doubly, trebly; specially, particularly; dearly, deeply; vitally; exceptionally; on a large scale, in a big way; vastly, hugely, enormously, gigantically, colossally; heavily, strongly, powerfully, mightily; actively, strenuously, vigorously, heartily, intensely; closely, narrowly, intensively, zealously, fanatically, hotly, bitterly, fiercely; acutely, sharply, shrewdly; exquisitely; enough, more than e., abundantly, profusely, prodigiously; generously, richly, worthily, magnificently, splendidly, nobly; supremely, preeminently, superlatively; rarely, unusually, wonderfully, incomparably, strangely; indefinitely, immeasurably, incalculably, infinitely, unspeakably, ineffably.

17

extremely, ultra, to extremes, to the limit, to the nth degree; no end of, no limit to; beyond measure, beyond all bounds; beyond comparison, beyond compare, incomparably; overly, unduly, improperly, to a fault; out of all proportion; bitterly, harshly, drastically, rigorously, unconscionably, with a vengeance; immoderately, uncontrollably, desperately, madly, frantically, frenziedly, furiously, fanatically, bitterly; exceedingly, excessively, exorbitantly, inordinately, outrageously, prohibitively, preposterously; foully, abominably, grossly, monstrously, horribly; confoundedly, deucedly, devilishly, damnably, hellishly; tremendously, terribly, fearfully, dreadfully, awfully, frightfully, horribly.

remarkably, noticeably, markedly, pointedly; notably, strikingly, conspicuously, signally, emphatically, prominently, glaringly, flagrantly, blatantly, unashamedly; publicly 400 *loudly*; preeminently 34 *eminently*; outstandingly, unco; singularly, peculiarly, curiously, oddly, queerly, strangely, strangely enough, uncommonly, unusually; surprisingly, astonishingly, amazingly, astoundingly, incredibly, magically.

33 Smallness – N. *smallness,* small size, diminutiveness, minuteness 196 *littleness*; brevity 204 *shortness*; leanness, meagreness 206 *thinness*; briefness, momentariness 114 *transience*; paucity 105 *fewness*; rareness, sparseness, sparsity 140 *infrequency*; scarceness, scarcity, inadequacy 636 *insufficiency*, 307 *shortfall*; exiguousness, scantiness; moderateness, moderation; pettiness, insignificance, meanness 639 *unimportance*, 35 *inferiority*; mediocrity 30 *average*, 732 *averageness*; tenuity 4 *insubstantiality*; compression, abbreviation, abridgment 198 *contraction*; diminution 37 *decrease*; miniaturization.

small quantity, fraction, modicum, minimum 26 *finite quantity*; minutiae, trivia; peanuts, chickenfeed 639 *trifle*;

detail, petty detail 80 *particulars*; nutshell 592 *compendium*; drop in the bucket, drop in the ocean; homoeopathic dose, trifling amount infinitesimal a.; thimbleful, spoonful, mouthful, cupful; trickle, dribble, sprinkling, sprinkle, dash, splash, squirt, squeeze; tinge, tincture, trace, smidgen, lick, smell, breath, whisper, suspicion, vestige, soupçon, thought, suggestion, hint, nuance, shade, touch; vein, strain, streak; spark, gleam, flash, flicker, ray; pinch, snatch, handful; snack, sip, bite, scrap, morsel, sop; dole, pittance, iron ration; fragment 53 *piece*; whit, bit, mite, iota, jot, tittle, fig, toss; ounce, gram, pennyweight, scruple, minim 322 *weighing*; inch, micron, millimetre 200 *short distance*; second, moment, nanosecond 116 *instant*.

small thing 196 *miniature*; microcosm; particle, atom; dot, point, pinpoint; dab, spot, fleck, speck, mote; grain, granule, seed, crumb 332 *powder*; drop, droplet; thread, wisp, shred, rag, tatter, fragment 53 *piece*; smithereens, little pieces; flake, snip, snippet, gobbet, small slice, finger; confetti; splinter, chip, clipping, paring, shaving; shiver, sliver, slip; pinprick, prick, nick; hair 208 *filament*. groat, mite, widow's m.; dime, sou; gnat, flea; shrimp, minnow, sprat; manikin, midget 196 *dwarf*.

Adj. *small,* exiguous, not much, moderate, modest, homoeopathic, minimal, infinitesimal; microscopic, tiny, teeny, teeny-weeny, teensy, weeny, wee, minute, diminutive, miniature 196 *little*; smaller 35 *lesser*; least, minimum; small-sized, small-framed, small-built, small-boned, undersized 196 *dwarfish*; slim, slender, lean, meagre, thin, anorexic 206 *narrow*; slight, feeble, puny, frail 163 *weak*; delicate, dainty, fragile 330 *brittle*; flimsy 323 *light*; fine, subtle, quiet, soft, low, faint, hushed 401 *muted*; squat 210 *low*; brief, minute, skimpy, abbreviated 204 *short*; shortened, abridged, cut, concise, compact, thumbnail; scanty, scant, scarce 307 *deficient*; dribbling, trickling

636 *insufficient*; reduced, limited, restricted 747 *restrained*; declining, ebbing, at low ebb, less 37 *decreasing*.

inconsiderable, minor, lightweight, trifling, trivial, petty, paltry, not to be taken seriously, insignificant 639 *unimportant*; not many 105 *few*; imperceptible; marginal, negligible, laughable, remote, slight; superficial, cursory 4 *insubstantial*; so-so 30 *median*; modest, humble, tolerable 732 *middling*; not much of a, no great shakes, second-rate 35 *inferior*.

Vb. *be small*, fit into a nutshell, be put onto a thumbnail; be less 307 *fall short*; get less 37 *decrease*; shrink 198 *become small*.

Adv. *slightly*, exiguously, little; lightly, softly, faintly, feebly; superficially, cursorily, gradually, little by little, imperceptibly, insensibly, invisibly; on a small scale, in a small way, modestly; fairly, moderately, tolerably, quite; comparatively, relatively, rather; indifferently, poorly, badly; hardly, scarcely, barely, only just, just and no more; narrowly, by the skin of one's teeth, by one's fingernails; hardly at all, no more than. at least, at the very least.

partially, to some degree, in some measure, to a certain extent, to some e.; somehow, after a fashion, sort of, in a kind of way, in a manner of speaking; some, somewhat, a little, a bit, just a bit, ever so little; not fully; in part, partly; not perfectly.

almost, all but, within an ace of, within an inch of, on the brink of, on the verge of, within sight of, in a fair way to 200 *near*; close upon, approximately 200 *nearly*; pretty near, just short of, not quite, virtually.

about, somewhere, somewhere about, thereabouts; more or less; near enough; at a guess, say.

in no way, no ways, no wise, by no means, not by any manner of means, in no respect, not at all, not in the least, not a bit, not the least bit, not in the slightest; not a whit, not a jot, not by a long chalk.

34 Superiority – **N.** *superiority*, higher position; loftiness 209 *height*; transcendance 32 *greatness*, 306 *overstepping*; top 213 *summit*; excellence 644 *goodness*; ne plus ultra 646 *perfection*; seniority 64 *precedence*, 119 *priority*; eminence 866 *prestige*; higher rank, higher degree 27 *degree*, 868 *nobility, aristocracy*; paramountcy, supremacy, sovereignty, majesty 733 *authority*; ascendancy, domination, predominance 178 *influence*; leadership 689 *management*; prevalence 29 *inequality*; win, championship 727 *victory*; prominence 638 *importance*; one-upmanship 698 *cunning*, 727 *success*; excess 637 *superfluity*; climax, zenith, culmination 725 *completion*; maximum, top, ceiling, peak, pinnacle, crest, crest of the wave; record, high, new h. 213 *summit*.

advantage, handicap, favour 615 *benefit*; head start, flying s., lead, commanding l., winning position, pole p.; odds, points, vantage, pull, edge; seeded position; command, upper hand, whip h.; one up, something in hand, reserves; trump card, card up one's sleeve; ace up one's sleeve; leverage, clout; vantage ground.

superior, superman *or* woman, wonderwoman 864 *prodigy*; select few 644 *elite*; high-ups, one's betters, top people, best p. 638 *bigwig*; aristocracy 868 *upper class*; overlord, sovereign 741 *master*; commander, chief, guide 690 *leader*; boss, foreman 690 *manager*; primate, president, prime minister, premier, primus inter pares 690 *director*; star, virtuoso 696 *proficient person*; mastermind 500 *sage*; world-beater, record-breaker; chart-topper; prizewinner, champion, record-holder 727 *victor*; prima donna, first lady, head boy *or* girl; big fish in a small pool.

Adj. *superior*, greater 32 *great*; upper, higher, senior, supernormal, above average, in a different class, in a class by himself *or* herself 15 *different*; better, a cut above, head and shoulders above 644 *excellent*; more than a match for; one up, ahead, always one step a., streets a. 64

preceding; record, exceeding, overtopping, vaulting, outclassing; in the lead, on top, winning, victorious 727 *successful*; distinguished 866 *noteworthy*; rare, 84 *unusual*; top-level, high-l., high-powered; 638 *important*; commanding, in authority 733 *ruling*.

supreme, arch-, greatest 32 *great*; highest, above all others, uppermost 213 *topmost*; first, chief, foremost 64 *preceding*; main, principal, leading, overruling, overriding, cardinal, capital 638 *important*; excellent, superlative, super, champion, tip-top, top-notch, first-rate, first-class, A1, 5-star, front-rank, world-beating 644 *best*; facile princeps, top of the class, second to none, none such, nonpareil; dominant, paramount, preeminent, sovereign; incomparable, unrivalled, matchless, peerless, unparalleled, unequalled 21 *inimitable*; unsurpassed, ultimate, the last word in; beyond compare 646 *perfect*; transcendental, out of this world.

Vb. *be superior,* transcend, rise above, surmount, overtop, tower over, overlook, command 209 *be high*; go beyond 306 *overstep*; exceed, out-Herod Herod, take the cake, take the biscuit; carry off the laurels, bear the palm, wear the crown; pass, surpass, beat the record, reach a new high; improve on, better, go one b., cap, trump; excel 644 *be good*; assert one's superiority, be too much for; steal the show, outshine, eclipse, overshadow, throw into the shade; put another's nose out of joint, have the laugh on 851 *ridicule*; best, outrival, outclass, outrank 306 *outdo*; outplay, outpoint, outmanoeuvre, outwit; overtake, leave behind, lap 277 *outstrip*; get the better of, worst, trounce, beat, beat hollow, knock into a cocked hat, beat all comers 727 *defeat*.

predominate, preponderate, tip the scale, turn the s.; change the balance 29 *be unequal*; override, sit on 178 *prevail*; have the advantage, have the whip hand, have the edge on; hold all the cards, hold all the aces; lead, hold the l., be up on, be one up.

culminate, come to a head; cap, cap it all, crown all 213 *crown*; rise to a peak; set a new record, reach new heights, reach a new high 725 *climax*.

Adv. *beyond,* more, over; over the mark, above the m., above par, over the average; above the limit, upwards of, in advance of; over and above; at the top of the scale, on the crest, at its height, at the peak, at the zenith.

eminently, preeminently, outstandingly, surpassingly, prominently, superlatively, supremely; above all, of all things; to crown it all, to cap it all; par excellence; principally, especially, particularly, peculiarly, singularly; a fortiori; far and away, by far 32 *extremely*.

35 Inferiority – N. *inferiority*, minority, littleness 33 *smallness*; subordinacy, subordination, dependence 745 *subjection*; supporting role, second fiddle 639 *unimportance*; lowliness 872 *humility*; second rank, third class, back seat, obscurity; handicap 702 *hindrance*; defect 647 *imperfection*; inadequateness 307 *shortfall*, 636 *insufficiency*; failure 728 *defeat*; second best 645 *badness*, 812 *cheapness*; kitsch 847 *bad taste*; shabbiness 801 *poverty*; decline 655 *deterioration*; low, all-time l., minimum, lowest point, nadir, the bottom, rock b. 214 *base*; depression, trough 210 *lowness*.

inferior, subordinate, subaltern, sub, underling, assistant, sidekick, subsidiary 707 *auxiliary*; agent 755 *deputy*, 150 *substitute*; tool, pawn 628 *instrument*; retainer 742 *dependant*; menial, hireling 742 *servant*; poor relation, small fry 639 *nonentity*; subject, underdog 742 *slave*; backbencher, private, other ranks, lower classes 869 *commonalty*; second, second best, second string, second fiddle, second-rater; also-ran; reject 607 *rejection*; lesser creation, younger, junior, minor.

Adj. *lesser,* less, minor, small-time, one-horse, hick, small-beer 639 *unimportant*; small 33 *inconsiderable*; smaller, diminished 37 *decreasing*; reduced.

inferior, lower, junior; subordinate, subaltern 742 *serving*; dependent, parasitical 745 *subjected, subject*; secondary, tributary, ancillary, subsidiary, auxiliary 703 *aiding,* 639 *unimportant*; second, second-best, second-class, second-rate; third-rate 922 *contemptible*; lowly, below the salt; low-ranking; subnormal, substandard, not up to the mark, not up to scratch; underweight 307 *deficient*; spoilt; defective 647 *imperfect*; failing 636 *insufficient*; shoddy, jerry-built, crummy 645 *bad,* 812 *cheap,* 847 *vulgar*; low 869 *plebeian*; makeshift 670 *unprepared*; temporary, provisional 114 *ephemeral*; feeble 163 *weak*; in a lower class, outclassed, outshone, trounced, beaten 728 *defeated*; unworthy, not fit, not fit to hold a candle to, not in the same league, not a patch on.

Vb. *be inferior,* fall short, come short of, fall below 307 *fall short*; lag, fall behind; want, lack 636 *not suffice*; not make the grade, not come up to scratch, not pass 728 *fail*; bow to 739 *obey*; concede the victory; yield, give in, cede, yield the palm, hand it to, knuckle under 721 *submit*; play second fiddle, play a supporting role 742 *serve*; take a back seat, retire into the shade; sink into obscurity; lose face 867 *lose repute*; get worse 655 *deteriorate*; sink, sink without trace, touch rock bottom, reach one's nadir 309 *descend.*

Adv. *less,* minus, short of; beneath 210 *under*; below average.

36 Increase – N. *increase,* increment, augmentation, waxing, crescendo; progress 285 *progression*; growth, growth area, development a., boom town; buildup, development 164 *production*; extension, protraction; widening; spread, escalation, amplification, inflation, dilation 197 *expansion*; proliferation, swarming 171 *productiveness, abundance*; multiplication; adding 38 *addition*; enlargement, aggrandizement 32 *greatness*; heightening, raising 310 *elevation*; concentration 324 *condensation*; intensification, stepping up, redoubling 91 *duplication,* acceleration, speeding 277 *spurt*; hotting up 381 *heating*; excitation 174 *stimulation*; exacerbation 832 *aggravation*; advancement, boost 654 *improvement*; rise, spiral, upward curve, upward trend, upswing, upturn 308 *ascent*; uprush, upsurge, flood, tide, surge 350 *wave*; progressiveness, cumulativeness, snowball 74 *accumulation.*

increment, augmentation, bulge; accretion, accrual, accession, contribution 38 *addition*; supplement, salary increase, pay rise 40 *extra*; padding, stuffing 303 *insertion*; percentage, commission, expenses, rake-off 771 *earnings.*

Adj. *increasing,* spreading, progressive, escalating; growing, waxing, filling, crescent, on the increase, on the up and up; supplementary 38 *additional*; ever-increasing, snowballing, cumulative 71 *continuous*; intensive; fruitful 171 *prolific*; increased, stretched, enlarged.

Vb. *grow,* increase, gain, develop, escalate; dilate, swell, bulge, wax, fill 197 *expand*; fill out, fatten, thicken;broad; become larger, put on weight 322 *weigh*; sprout, bud, burgeon, flower, blossom 167 *reproduce itself*; breed, spread, swarm, proliferate, mushroom, multiply 104 *be many,* 171 *be fruitful*; grow up 669 *mature*; spring up, shoot up, grow taller, grow by leaps and bounds 209 *be high*; spiral, climb, mount, rise, go through the ceiling, rocket, skyrocket, take off 308 *ascent*; 417 *shine*; gain strength 656 *be restored,* 162 *be strong*; improve 654 *get better*; flourish, thrive, prosper; gain ground, advance, snowball, accumulate 285 *progress*; earn interest 771 *be profitable*; gain in value, appreciate, rise in price 811 *be dear*; boom, break all records, surge, exceed, overflow 637 *superabound,* 32 *be great*; rise to a maximum 34 *culminate.*

augment, increase, bump up, double; redouble; duplicate 106 *repeat*; multiply 166 *reproduce*; propagate, grow, raise, rear 369 *breed stock*; enlarge, magnify, distend, inflate, blow up 197 *expand*;

amplify, develop, build up, fill out, fill in, pad out 54 *make complete*; supplement, enrich; contribute to; accrue 38 *add*; extend, prolong, stretch 203 *lengthen*; broaden, widen, thicken, deepen; heighten, enhance, send up 209 *make higher*; raise, exalt 310 *elevate*; advance, aggrandize 285 *promote*; speed up 277 *accelerate*; intensify, redouble, step up, stimulate, energize 174 *invigorate*; give a boost to, boost 685 *refresh*, 656 *restore*, 162 *strengthen*; glorify 546 *exaggerate*, 482 *overrate*; stoke, add fuel to the flame, exacerbate 832 *aggravate*; maximize.

37 Decrease: no increase – N. *decrease*, lessening, dwindling, falling off, de-escalation; waning, fading; dimming 419 *dimness*; wane 198 *contraction*; shrinking; ebb, reflux, retreat 286 *regression*; ebb tide, neap 210 *lowness*; descending order 71 *series*; subsidence, sinking, decline, declension, downward curve, downward spiral, downward trend, downturn, fall, drop, plunge 309 *descent*, 165 *ruin*; deflation, recession, slump 655 *deterioration*; retrenchment, cutback, cut, cutting back 814 *economy*; loss of value, depreciation 812 *cheapness*; weakening; shortage 636 *scarcity*; diminishing returns, exhaustion 190 *emptiness*; shrinkage, erosion, decay, crumbling 655 *dilapidation*.

diminution, making less; deduction 39 *subtraction*; abatement, reduction, de-escalation, restriction 747 *restraint*; deceleration 278 *slowness*; retrenchment, cut, economization 814 *economy*; cutting back, pruning, paring, shaving, clipping, docking, curtailment, abridgment, abbreviation 204 *shortening*; compression, squeeze 198 *contraction*; abrasion, erosion 333 *friction*; weeding out, elimination 62 *sorting*, 300 *ejection*; mitigation, minimization 177 *moderation*; belittlement, undervaluation 483 *underestimation*, 926 *detraction*; demotion, degradation 872 *humiliation*.

Adj. *decreasing*, dwindling; waning, fading; evaporating; de-escalating; declining, going down, sinking, ebbing; decaying.

Vb. *abate*, diminish, decrease, de-escalate, lessen, take away, detract from, deduct 39 *subtract*; except 57 *exclude*; reduce, scale down, whittle, pare, scrape 206 *make thin*; clip, trim 46 *cut*; shrink, abridge, abbreviate, boil down 204 *shorten*; squeeze, compress, contract 198 *make smaller*; limit, curtail 747 *restrain*; cut down, cut back, retrench 814 *economize*; decelerate 278 *retard*; depress 311 *lower*; minimize, mitigate, extenuate 177 *moderate*; allay, alleviate 831 *relieve*; deflate, puncture; disparage, decry, belittle, depreciate, undervalue 483 *underestimate*, dwarf, overshadow 34 *be superior*; steal one's thunder, put in the shade; degrade, demote 872 *humiliate*; exhaust 300 *empty*; let evaporate, boil away 338 *vaporize*; crumble 332 *pulverize*; rub away, abrade, file 333 *rub*; gnaw, nibble at, eat away 301 *eat*; erode, rust 655 *impair*; strip, peel, denude 229 *uncover*; unman 161 *disable*; dilute 163 *weaken*, thin out, weed o., depopulate 105 *render few*; decimate 165 *destroy*; damp down, crack down on.

decrease, grow less, lessen, de-escalate; abate, slacken, ease, moderate, subside, die down; dwindle, shrink, contract 198 *become small*; wane, waste, decay, wear away, wither away, degenerate 655 *deteriorate*; fade, die away, grow dim 419 *be dim*; retreat, withdraw, ebb 286 *regress*, 290 *recede*; run low, run down, ebb away, drain away, fail 636 *not suffice*; tail off, taper off, peter out; 293 *converge*; subside, sink 313 *plunge*; come down, decline, fall, drop, slump, collapse 309 *descend*; level off, bottom out, lag 278 *decelerate*; melt away 446 *disappear*; evaporate 338 *vaporize*; thin out 105 *be few*, become endangered, become extinct 2 *pass away*; reduce, lose weight, become anorexic 323 *be light*, 946 *starve*; lose one's voice, shut up 578 *be mute*; lose, shed; cast off.

38 Addition – N. *addition,* adding to, annexation, agglutination 45 *union*; superimposing 187 *location*; affixture 65 *sequence*; supplementation, contribution 703 *aid*; superaddition, imposition, load 702 *encumbrance*; accession, accretion, accrual, supervention; interposition, interjection 303 *insertion*, 78 *inclusion*; reinforcement 36 *increase*; increment, supplement, additive, E numbers; add-on; addendum, appendage, tailpiece, appendix 40 *adjunct*; extra time, overtime 113 *protraction*; appurtenance 89 *accompaniment*; summation, adding up, counting up, totalling, total.

Adj. *additional,* additive; added, included etc. vb.; adventitious; supplementary, conjunctive; subsidiary, auxiliary, contributory 703 *aiding*; supernumerary; another, further, more; extra, spare 637 *superfluous*; interjected, interposed 303 *inserted*, prefixed 64 *preceding*.

Vb. *add,* add up, sum, total; carry over 272 *transfer*; add to, annex, append; attach, pin to, clip to, tag on, tack on; hitch to, yoke to, unite to 45 *join, tie*; stick on, glue on; add on, preface, prefix, affix, suffix, infix; introduce; interpose, interject; engraft, let in 303 *insert*; contribute to 36 *augment*; swell, extend, expand 197 *enlarge*; supplement; superadd, superimpose; ornament, embellish 844 *decorate*; mix with 43 *mix*; annex 786 *take*.

accrue, be added 78 *be included*; supervene 295 *arrive*; join 708 *join a party*; combine with 50 *combine*; make one more; reinforce, swell the ranks.

Adv. *in addition,* additionally, more, plus, extra; with interest, with a vengeance, with knobs on; and, too, also, item, furthermore, further; likewise, and also, to boot; else, besides; et cetera; and so on, and so forth, moreover, into the bargain, over and above, including, inclusive of, with, as well as, apart from, not to mention, let alone, not forgetting; together with, along w., coupled w., in conjunction w..

39 Subtraction – N. *subtraction,* deduction, taking away; diminution 37 *decrease*; abstraction, removal, withdrawal; elimination 62 *sorting*; clearance 300 *ejection*; unpacking 188 *displacement*, 304 *extraction*; precipitation, sedimentation, ablation, abrasion, erosion, detrition 333 *friction*; retrenchment, cutting back, curtailment 204 *shortening*; severance, detruncation, amputation, excision 46 *scission*; mutilation 655 *impairment*; expurgation; deletion 550 *obliteration*; minuend 85 *numerical element*; subtrahend.

Vb. *subtract,* take away, deduct, do subtraction; detract from, diminish, decrease 37 *abate*; cut 810 *discount*; take off, knock o., allow; except, take out, leave o. 57 *exclude*; expel 300 *eject*; abstract 786 *take*, 788 *steal*; withdraw, remove; unload 188 *displace*; shift 272 *transfer*; draw off 300 *empty*; abrade, scrape away, file down, erode 333 *rub*; eradicate, uproot, pull up, pull out 304 *extract*; pick, pick out, put on one side 605 *select*; cross out, blot o., delete, censor 550 *obliterate*; expurgate, mutilate 655 *impair*; sever, separate, amputate, excise; shear, shave off, clip 46 *cut*; retrench, cut back, cut down, whittle, lop, prune, pare, decapitate, behead, dock, curtail, abridge, abbreviate 204 *shorten*; geld, castrate, caponize, spay, emasculate 161 *unman*; peel, skin, fleece, strip, divest, denude 229 *uncover*.

40 Adjunct: thing added – N. *adjunct,* addition, additive, something added, add-on, contribution 38 *addition*; addendum, carry-over; supplement, annex; attachment, fixture; inflection, affix, suffix, prefix, adjective, adverb 564 *part of speech*; ticket, tag 547 *label*; appendage, tailpiece, train, following 67 *sequel*; wake 65 *sequence*; appendix, postscript, P.S., P.P.S., envoi, coda, ending 69 *extremity*; codicil, rider 468 *qualification*; marginalia, annotation, footnotes; corollary, complement 725 *completion*; appurtenance, accessory 89 *concomitant*; companion piece, fellow, pair

18 *analogue*; extension, continuation, second part; annexe, wing (of a house), outhouse 164 *edifice*; offshoot 53 *branch*; arm, extremity 53 *limb*; accretion 59 *extraneousness*; increment 36 *increase*; patch, reinforcement 656 *repair*; padding, stuffing 227 *lining*; interpolation 303 *insertion*; interlude, intermezzo 231 *interjacency*; insertion, gusset 228 *garment*; flap, lappet, lapel; ingredient 58 *component*; fringe, 234 *edge*; embroidery 844 *ornamentation*; garnish, seasoning; frills, trimmings; trappings, accoutrements 228 *dressing*.

extra, additive, addendum, increment, something over and above, byproduct; percentage, interest 771 *gain*; bonus, tip, perk, perquisite, graft 962 *reward*; free gift, freebie, giveaway, gratuity, golden handshake, golden hello 781 *gift*; windfall; allowance; oddment, odds and ends; supernumerary; spare parts, spares 633 *provision*; reinforcement 707 *auxiliary*; surplus 637 *superfluity*; extra time, injury time, overtime.

41 Remainder: thing remaining – N. *remainder*, residue; result; balance; surplus; relic, rest, remains, remnant 105 *fewness*; rump, stump, stub, scrag end, fag e., butt e. 69 *extremity*; torso, trunk 53 *piece*; fossil, skeleton, bones 363 *corpse*; husk, shell; wreck, wreckage, debris 165 *ruin*; ashes 332 *powder*; track, spoor, fingerprint 548 *record*, *trace*; afterglow 67 *sequel*; memorabilia 505 *remembrance*; survival 113 *durability*; vestige.

leavings, leftovers; precipitate, deposit, sediment; alluvium, silt 344 *soil*; drift, loess, moraine, detritus 272 *thing transferred*; grounds, lees, dregs; scum, dross, slag, sludge; bilge, scrapings, shavings, filings, sawdust, crumbs 332 *powder*; husks, chaff, stubble; peel, peelings; skin, slough, scurf; combings, trimmings, clippings, remnants, offcuts; scraps, candle-ends, odds and ends, bin-ends, lumber 641 *rubbish*; rejects 779 *derelict*; sweepings, scourings, offscourings; waste, sewage

302 *excrement*; refuse, litter, 649 *dirt*.

Adj. *remaining*, surviving, left, vestigial, resultant; residual; deposited, sedimentary, precipitated; discarded 779 *not retained*; on the shelf 860 *unwanted*; left over, odd; net, surplus; unused; outstanding; spare; superfluous 637 *redundant*; orphaned, widowed.

Vb. *be left*, remain, result, survive.

leave over, leave out 57 *exclude*; leave, discard, abandon 607 *reject*.

42 Decrement: thing deducted – N. *decrement*, deduction, depreciation, cut 37 *diminution*; allowance; remission; clawback, rebate 810 *discount*; refund, shortage, slippage, defect 307 *shortfall*, 636 *insufficiency*; loss, sacrifice, forfeit 963 *penalty*; leak, leakage, escape 298 *outflow*; consumption 634 *waste*; subtrahend, rake-off 786 *taking*; toll 809 *tax*.

43 Mixture – N. *mixture*, mingling, mixing, stirring; blending, harmonization; admixture 38 *addition*; commixture 45 *union*; intermixture, interpolation 231 *interjacency*; interweaving, interlacing 222 *crossing*; amalgamation, integration 50 *combination*; merger 706 *association*; eclecticism; fusion, interfusion, infusion, suffusion, transfusion, instillation, impregnation; adulteration 655 *impairment*; contamination, infection 653 *insalubrity*; infiltration, penetration 297 *ingress*; crossbreeding; interbreeding, miscegenation, intermarriage 894 *marriage*; syngamy, allogamy 167 *propagation*; cross-fertilization, hybridism, hybridization, mongrelism; miscibility, solubility 337 *liquefaction*.

tincture, ingredient 58 *component*; strain, streak, element, vein; sprinkling, infusion; tinge, touch, drop, dash, soupçon 33 *small quantity*; smack, hint, suspicion, flavour 386 *taste*; seasoning; colour, dye 425 *hue*; stain 845 *blemish*.

a mixture, mélange; blend, harmony 710 *concord*; composition 331 *structure*; amalgam, fusion, compound, confection, potpourri, concoction 50 *combination*; pastiche; alloy, bronze, brass, pew-

ter, steel; paste; soup, stew, goulash, ragout, olla podrida, salmagundi 301 *dish*; cocktail, punch, brew; solution, infusion.

medley, variety 17 *nonuniformity,* 82 *multiformity*; motley, mosaic 437 *variegation*; miscellany,miscellanea, mixed bag, job lot, ragbag, lucky dip; gallimaufry, hotchpotch, hodgepodge, mishmash, potpourri; jumble; conglomeration 74 *accumulation*; entanglement, imbroglio 61 *confusion*; phantasmagoria, kaleidoscope; clatter 411 *discord*; motley crew 74 *crowd*; circus 369 *zoo*; variety show 594 *stage show*; all sorts, odds and ends, paraphernalia.

hybrid, cross, cross-breed, mongrel; mule; half-breed, half-caste; mulatto.

Adj. *mixed,* mixed up, stirred; mixed up in, involved in; blended, harmonized; syncretic, eclectic; fused, alloyed 50 *combined*; tempered, qualified, adulterated, sophisticated, watered down 163 *weakened*; merged, amalgamated; composite, half-and-half, fifty-fifty; confused, jumbled; unclassified, out of order; heterogeneous 17 *nonuniform*; kaleidoscopic, phantasmagoric 82 *multiform*; patchy, dappled, motley 437 *variegated*; shot; miscellaneous, random 464 *indiscriminate*; miscible, soluble; pervasive 653 *infectious*; hybrid, mongrel; cross-bred, crossed; half-caste; of mixed blood, multiracial.

Vb. *mix,* mix up, stir, shake; shuffle, scramble 63 *jumble*; knead, mash 332 *pulverize*; brew 56 *compose*; fuse, alloy, merge, amalgamate 45 *join*; blend, harmonize 50 *combine*; mingle, intermingle, intersperse 437 *variegate*; interleave 303 *insert*; intertwine, interweave 222 *weave*; tinge, dye 425 *colour*; imbue, instil, impregnate; sprinkle 341 *moisten*; water down, adulterate 163 *weaken*; temper, doctor, tamper with 143 *modify*; season, spice, fortify, lace, spike; hybridize, mongrelize, cross, cross-fertilize, cross-breed 167 *generate*.

Adv. *among,* amongst, amid, amidst, with; in the midst of; inter alia.

44 Simpleness: freedom from mixture –
N. *simpleness,* homogeneity 16 *uniformity*; purity 648 *cleanness*; oneness 88 *unity*; absoluteness, sheerness; fundamentality 1 *essence*; indivisibility, insolubility; simplicity 516 *intelligibility*, 573 *plainness*, 699 *artlessness*.

Adj. *simple,* homogeneous, monolithic 16 *uniform*; sheer, mere, utter, nothing but; single, unified 88 *one*; elemental, indivisible, entire 52 *whole*; primary, fundamental, nuts and bolts, basic 5 *intrinsic*; elementary, uncomplicated, simplified 516 *intelligible*; direct, unadulterated, unalloyed; unsophisticated; 699 *artless*; sincere; naked.

unmixed, pure and simple, without alloy; clear, pure, undefiled, unpolluted, clarified, purified 648 *clean*; thoroughbred 868 *noble*; free from, excluding; unblemished, untarnished 646 *perfect*; unblended, unalloyed, uncompounded, uncombined; undiluted, unadulterated, neat 162 *strong*; unqualified, unmodified; unfortified; unseasoned.

Vb. *simplify,* render simple 16 *make uniform*; break down, factorize 51 *decompose*; disentangle, unscramble; unite.

45 Union – N. *union,* junction, joining etc. vb.; coming together, meeting, concurrence, conjunction 293 *convergence*; clash 279 *collision*; contact 202 *contiguity*, 378 *touch*; congress, concourse, reunion 74 *assembly*; confluence, rendezvous, meeting-place 76 *focus*; coalescence, fusion, merger 43 *mixture*; unification, synthesis 50 *combination*; cohesion, agglutination 48 *coherence*; concretion, consolidation, solidification, coagulation 324 *condensation*; coalition, alliance, symbiosis 706 *association*; connection, linkage, tieup, hookup, linkup 47 *bond*; syngamy, wedlock 894 *marriage*; interconnection, interlocking 222 *crossing*; communication 305 *passage*; network, intercommunication, intercourse 882 *sociability*; trade, traffic, exchange 151 *interchange*, 791 *trade*; involvement 9 *relation*.

coition, coitus, copulation, sexual intercourse, sex, fucking (vulg.), bonking, intimacy, carnal knowledge; generation 167 *propagation*; pairing, mating, coupling; union 894 *marriage*; consummation; sexual assault 951 *rape.*

joint, joining, juncture; crease 261 *fold*; suture, seam, stitching 47 *bond*; bonding, English bond, Flemish b.; weld; splice; mitre, mitre joint; dovetail, dovetail and mortise joint; ball and socket j.; hasp, latch, sneck, catch 218 *pivot*; hinge-joint; finger, thumb, wrist, ankle, knuckle, knee, hip, elbow; node; junction, meeting-point, intersection, crossroads 222 *crossing*; decussation, figure X 222 *cross.*

Adj. *conjunctive,* adjunctive, connective, copulative, adhesive 48 *cohesive*; coagulating, astringent; coincident; copulatory, coital, venereal, intimate.

firm, close, fast, secure, sound 153 *fixed*; solid, set, solidified 324 *dense*; glued, cemented, stuck 48 *cohesive*; put, pat; planted, rooted, deep-set; ingrown, impacted; close-set, crowded, tight, tight-fitting, wedged, jammed, stuck; inextricable, inseparable, immovable, unshakable; packed, jam-p. 54 *full.*

tied, bound, knotted, roped, lashed, secured, belayed, spliced; stitched, sewn, gathered; attached, fastened, adhering 48 *cohesive*; well-tied, tight; taut, tense, fast, secure; intricate, involved, tangled, inextricable, indissoluble.

Vb. *join,* conjoin, couple, yoke, hyphenate, harness together; pair, match 18 *liken*, 462 *compare*, 894 *marry*; bracket, bracket together 28 *equalize*; put together, throw t., piece t., unite 50 *combine*; gather 74 *bring together*; add to, amass, accumulate 38 *add*, 632 *store*; associate, ally, twin (town); merge 43 *mix*; incorporate, unify; 16 *make uniform*; lump together, roll into one; include, embrace 78 *comprise*; grip, grapple 778 *retain*; hinge, articulate, dovetail, mortise, mitre, rabbet; fit, set, interlock, jam 303 *insert*; weld, solder, fuse, cement, glue; lace, knit, sew, seam,

stitch; pin, buckle; do up, fasten, button up, zip up 264 *close*; lock, latch; darn, patch, mend, heal over 656 *repair.*

connect, attach, annex (see *affix*); staple, clip, pin together; string t., rope t., link t., contact 378 *touch*; make contact, plug in, earth; network, interconnect; link, bridge, span; communicate, intercommunicate; put through to, put in touch; hook up with, link up w.; tie up w. 9 *relate.*

affix, attach, fix, fasten; yoke, leash, harness, saddle, bridle; tie up, moor, anchor; tie to, tether, pin on, hang on, hook on, screw on, nail on; stick on, cement on, sellotape on, gum on; suffix, prefix 38 *add*; splice, engraft, implant 303 *insert*; impact, set, frame 235 *enclose*; drive in, knock in, hammer in 279 *strike*; wedge, jam; screw, nail, rivet, bolt, clamp, clinch.

tie, knot, hitch, lash, belay; knit, sew, seam, stitch, suture; tack, baste; braid, plait, crochet, twine, twist, intertwine, lace, interlace, interweave 222 *weave*; truss, string, rope, strap; do up, lace up, lash up; tether, picket, moor; pinion, manacle, handcuff; hobble, shackle 747 *fetter*; bind, splice, gird, girdle; bandage.

tighten, constrict, compress; fasten, screw up, make firm, make fast, secure; tauten, draw tight, pull t..

unite with, join, meet 293 *converge*; hold t., fit closely, adhere, hang together, hold t., stick t. 48 *cohere*; mesh, interlock, engage, grip, grapple, clinch; embrace, entwine; link up with, hold hands; associate with, partner, mix w. 882 *be sociable*; marry, get hitched 894 *wed*; live with, cohabit; go to bed with, lie with, sleep w., make love, have intercourse, have sex w., fuck (vulg.), bonk, have carnal knowledge; consummate a marriage *or* a union; know, enjoy, possess, have, do; lay, make, bed, tumble; knock off, have it off *or* away with; deflower, rape, ravish, violate, take by force 951 *debauch*; copulate, couple, mate, pair 167 *generate*; mount, tup, cover, serve; cross with, breed w.

46 Disunion – N. *disunion,* disjunction, disconnection, disconnectedness, incoherence, break 72 *discontinuity;* diffusion, dispersal 75 *dispersion;* breakup, disintegration, dissolution, decay 51 *decomposition,* 655 *dilapidation;* absentmindedness 456 *abstractedness;* dissociation, withdrawal, retirement 621 *relinquishment,* 753 *resignation;* moving apart, growing a., widening 294 *divergence,* 282 *deviation;* split, schism (see *separation);* detachment, neutrality 860 *indifference;* isolation, quarantine, segregation 883 *seclusion;* insularity 620 *avoidance;* lack of unity 709 *dissension;* separateness, isolationism, separatism; no connection, no common ground 10 *unrelatedness;* distance apart; dichotomy 15 *difference;* interval, breathing space, space, opening, hole, breach, break, rent, rift, tear, split; fissure, crack, cleft, chasm; cleavage, slit, cut, gash, incision 201 *gap.*

separation, disjoining, severance, parting; uncoupling, breaking up, splitting up 896 *divorce;* untying, undoing, unfastening, unravelling; loosening, freeing 746 *liberation;* setting apart, discrimination, segregation, ghettoization, apartheid 883 *seclusion;* exemption 57 *exclusion;* boycott 620 *avoidance;* expulsion 300 *ejection;* selection 605 *choice;* putting aside 632 *storage;* taking away 39 *subtraction;* expropriation; detaching, withdrawal 188 *displacement,* 272 *transference;* stripping, peeling, plucking 229 *uncovering;* disjointing, dislocation; scattering 75 *dispersion;* dissolution, resolution, disintegration 51 *decomposition;* dissection, analysis, breakdown; disruption, fragmentation 165 *destruction;* splitting, fission, nuclear f. 160 *nucleonics;* breaking, cracking, rupture, fracture 330 *brittleness;* dividing line, caesura; wall, fence, hedge, ha-ha 231 *partition;* curtain 421 *screen;* boundary 236 *limit;* Styx.

scission, section, cleavage, cutting, tearing; division, dichotomy 92 *bisection;* subdivision, segmentation; partition 783 *apportionment;* abscission, cutting off, decapitation, curtailment, retrenchment 204 *shortening,* 37 *diminution;* cutting away, resection, circumcision; cutting open, incision, opening 658 *surgery;* dissection; rending, clawing, laceration, tearing off, nipping, pinching, biting etc. vb.

Adj. *separate,* apart, asunder; adrift, lost; unjoined, unfixed, unfastened; unattached, unannexed, unassociated; distinct, discrete, differentiated, separable, distinguishable 15 *different;* exempt, excepted; hived off, abstracted; unassimilated 44 *unmixed;* alien, foreign 59 *extraneous;* external 6 *extrinsic,* 223 *exterior;* insular, lonely, isolated 88 *alone,* shunned, dropped, avoided, boycotted, sent to Coventry; cast-off; set apart 605 *chosen;* abandoned, left 41 *remaining;* hostile, antipathetic 881 *hostile,* 14 *contrary,* 240 *opposite;* divorced; disjunctive, separative; dichotomous, dividing; selective, diagnostic 15 *distinctive.*

Vb. *separate,* stand apart 620 *avoid;* go away 296 *depart;* go apart, go different ways, radiate 294 *diverge;* go another way 282 *deviate;* part, part company, cut adrift, cut loose, divorce, split up; hive off; get free, get loose 667 *escape;* disengage, cast off, unmoor; leave, quit, fall away 621 *relinquish;* scatter, break up 75 *disperse;* spring apart 280 *recoil;* come apart, fall a., break, come to bits, disintegrate 51 *decompose;* come undone, unravel; fall off 49 *come unstuck;* split, crack 263 *open.*

disunite, dissociate, divorce; split up, break up, part, separate, sunder, sever; uncouple, unhitch, disconnect, unplug; disengage; disjoint, displace, dislocate, wrench; detach, unseat; remove, detract, deduct 39 *subtract,* 272 *transfer;* skin, strip, flay, peel, pluck 229 *uncover;* unfasten, undo, unbutton, unhook, unlace, unzip, unclasp, unlock, unlatch 263 *open;* untie, cut the knot, sever the tie, disentangle; unstitch, unpick; loosen, relax, slacken, unstring 177 *moderate;* unbind, unchain, unfetter, unloose, loose, free, set f., release 746 *liberate;* expel 300

27

eject; dispel, scatter, break up, disband, demobilize 75 *disperse*; disintegrate, break down 51 *decompose*, 332 *pulverize*, 165 *destroy*.

set apart, put aside set a. 632 *store*; mark out, tick off, distinguish 15 *differentiate*, 463 *discriminate*; single out 605 *select*; exempt, leave out 57 *exclude*; boycott, send to Coventry 620 *avoid*; taboo, black, blacklist 757 *prohibit*; insulate, isolate, cut off 235 *enclose*; zone, compartmentalize, screen off, declare a no-go area 232 *circumscribe*; segregate, ghettoize, sequester, quarantine, maroon 883 *seclude*; keep apart, hold a., drive a.; drive a wedge between, estrange, alienate, set against.

sunder (see *disunite*); divide, fragment, fractionate, segment, sectionalize, fractionalize; reduce, factorize, analyse; dissect 51 *decompose*; dichotomize, halve 92 *bisect*; divide up, split, partition, parcel out 783 *apportion*; dismember, quarter, carve (see *cut*); behead, decapitate, curtail, dock, amputate 204 *shorten*; take apart, take to pieces, cannibalize, dismantle, break up, dismount; force open 263 *open*; slit, split; cleave 263 *pierce*. See *break*.

cut, hew, hack, slash, gash 655 *wound*; prick, stab, knife 263 *pierce*; cut through, cleave, saw, chop; cut open, slit 263 *open*; cut into, make an incision, incise 555 *engrave*; cut deep, cut to the bone, carve, slice; cut round, pare, whittle, chisel, chip, trim, bevel; clip; snip; cut short, shave 204 *shorten*; cut down, fell, scythe, mow; cut off, lop, prune, dock, curtail (see *sunder*); cut up, chop up, quarter, dismember; dice, shred, mince, make mincemeat of, pound 332 *pulverize*; bite 301 *chew*; scratch, score, plough 262 *groove*; nick 260 *notch*.

rend, tear (see *sunder*); scratch, claw; gnaw, fret, fray, make ragged; rip, slash, slit (see *cut*); lacerate, dismember; tear limb from limb, tear to pieces, tear to shreds, 165 *destroy*; mince, grind, crunch, scrunch, pound 301 *chew*, 332 *pulverize*; blow to pieces, burst.

break, fracture, rupture, bust; split,

burst; break in pieces, smash, smash to smithereens, shatter, splinter, shiver 165 *demolish*; fragment, crumble, grind 332 *pulverize*; disintegrate, cave in 51 *decompose*; break up, dismantle (see *sunder*); chip, crack, damage 655 *impair*; bend, buckle, warp 246 *distort*; break in two, snap; cleave, force apart 263 *open*.

Adv. *separately,* severally, singly, one by one, bit by bit, piecemeal, in bits, in pieces, in halves, in twain, discontinuously, unconnectedly, disjointedly.

apart, open, asunder, adrift; to pieces, to bits, to smithereens, to shreds; limb from limb.

47 Bond: connecting medium – N. *bond,* connecting medium, vinculum, chain, shackle, fetter, handcuff, tie, band, hoop, yoke; sympathy, empathy, fellow feeling 905 *pity*; nexus, connection, link, liaison 9 *relation*; junction, hinge 45 *joint*; ramification, network 53 *branch*; hyphen, dash, bracket 547 *punctuation*; cement (see *adhesive*); bondstone, binder; tie-beam, stretcher, girder 218 *beam*; strut, stay 218 *prop*; channel, passage, corridor 624 *access*; steppingstone, causeway 624 *bridge*; span, arch; isthmus, neck; col, ridge; stair, steps, stepladder, ladder 308 *ascent*; lifeline; umbilical cord.

cable, line, guy, hawser, painter, moorings; guest-rope, towline, towrope, ripcord, lanyard, communication cord; rope, cord, whipcord, string, tape, twine 208 *fibre*; chain, wire, earth.

ligature, ligament, tendon, muscle; tendril, osier, raffia 208 *fibre*; lashing, binding; string, cord, thread, tape, sticky tape, Sellotape (tdmk), Scotch tape (tdmk), Velcro (tdmk), band, fillet, ribbon, ribband; bandage, tourniquet; drawstring, thong, lace, tag; braid, plait 222 *network*; tie, stock, cravat 228 *neckwear*; knot, hitch, clinch, bend; running k., slip k., granny k., reef k.; half hitch, clove h.; sheepshank; Gordian k.

fastening, fastener, snap f., press-stud, pop-fastener, popper, zip fastener, zip;

drawstring; stitch, basting; button, buttonhole, eyelet, loop, frog; hook and eye; Velcro (tdmk); stud, cufflink; garter, suspender, braces; tiepin, brooch 844 *jewellery*; clip, grip, slide, clasp, curlers; hairpin, hatpin; skewer, spit, pin, drawing p., safety p., toggle p., cotter p., linch p., king p.; peg, dowel, treenail, trenail, nail, brad, tack, tintack 256 *sharp point*; Blutack (tdmk), Sellotape (tdmk), Scotch tape (tdmk); holdfast, staple, clamp, brace, batten, cramp 778 *pincers*; nut, bolt, screw, rivet; buckle, clasp, morse; hasp, hinge 45 *joint*; catch, safety c., spring c.; latch, bolt; lock, lock and key 264 *closure*; combination lock, yale l., mortise l.; padlock, handcuffs, bracelets 748 *fetter*; ring, cleat; hold, bar, post, pile, pale, stake, bollard.

adhesive, glue, fish glue, lime, birdlime, gum, epoxy resin; fixative, hair lacquer, hair spray, brilliantine, grease; solder; paste, size, clay, cement, putty, mortar, stucco, plaster, grout 226 *facing*; wafer, sealing wax; sticker, stamp, adhesive tape, sticky t., Sellotape (tdmk), Scotch tape (tdmk), Blu-tack (tdmk); flypaper 542 *trap*; sticking plaster, Elastoplast (tdmk), Band-Aid (tdmk) 48 *coherence*.

48 Coherence – N. *coherence*, connection, connectedness 71 *continuity*; chain 71 *series*; cohesion, cohesiveness; tenacity 778 *retention*; adherence, adhesion, adhesiveness; stickiness 354 *viscidity*; cementation, cementing, sticking, soldering, agglutination 45 *union*; compaction, conglomeration, consolidation, set 324 *condensation*; inseparability, indivisibility, union 88 *unity*; phalanx, serried ranks, unbroken front, united f.; birds of a feather; monolith, agglomerate, concrete 324 *solid body*.

Adj. *cohesive*, adhesive, adherent; clinging, tenacious; sticky, tacky, gummy, gluey, viscous 354 *viscid*; wellknit, coagulated, concrete, frozen 324 *dense*; shoulder to shoulder, side by side, serried; monolithic 16 *uniform*; united, indivisible, inseparable, inextricable;

close, tight, close-fitting, skintight, figure-hugging, clinging, moulding.

Vb. *cohere*, hang together, grow together 50 *combine*; stick close, hold fast; bunch, close the ranks, rally 74 *congregate*; take hold of 778 *retain*; hug, clasp, embrace, twine round; close with; fit, fit tight, mould the figure; adhere, cling, stick; stick to, cleave to, stick on to, freeze on to; stick like a limpet, cling like a shadow, cling like ivy; cake, coagulate, conglomerate, solidify.

49 Noncoherence – N. *noncoherence*, incoherence 72 *discontinuity*; uncombined state, noncombination, chaos 51 *decomposition*; scattering 75 *dispersion*; separability; looseness, bagginess; loosening, relaxation, freedom 46 *separation*; wateriness 335 *fluidity*; slipperiness 258 *smoothness*; frangibility, friability 330 *brittleness*; nonadhesion, aloofness.

Vb. *come unstuck*, peel off, melt, thaw, run 337 *liquefy*; totter, slip 309 *tumble*; dangle, flap 217 *hang*; rattle, shake, flap.

50 Combination – N. *combination*, composition; coalescence, symphysis 45 *union*; fusion, blending, conflation, synthesis, syncretism 43 *mixture*; amalgamation, merger, assimilation, digestion, absorption 299 *reception*; uniting, unification, integration, centralization 88 *unity*; incorporation, embodiment; synchronization 706 *cooperation*; marriage, union, league, alliance 706 *association*; cabal 623 *plot*; counterpoint 412 *music*; chorus 24 *agreement*; harmony, orchestration 710 *concord*; assembly 74 *assemblage*; synopsis, conspectus, bird's-eye view 592 *compendium*.

compound, alloy, amalgam, blend, composite 43 *a mixture*.

Adj. *combined*, united, unified 88 *one*; integrated, centralized; embodied; inbred, ingrained, absorbed 5 *intrinsic*; fused 43 *mixed*; blended, adapted 24 *adjusted*; connected, linked, networked, conjoint; aggregated; synchronized 123 *synchronous*; in harmony, on the same wavelength, in partnership, in league;

associated 706 *cooperative*; conspiratorial.

Vb. *combine,* put together; make up 56 *compose*; interweave 222 *weave*; harmonize, synchronize 24 *accord*; bind, tie 45 *join*; unite, unify, centralize; incorporate, embody, integrate, absorb, assimilate; merge, amalgamate, pool; blend, fuse 43 *mix*; impregnate, imbue, instil, inoculate; bracket together; lump together 38 *add*; group, rally 74 *bring together*; band together, associate; ally; go into partnership with, join hands, join forces with, team up with 706 *cooperate*; fraternize, make friends 880 *be friendly*; marry 894 *wed*; mate 90 *pair*; conspire 623 *plot*; coalesce, grow together.

51 Decomposition – N. *decomposition* 46 *disunion*; division, partition, 46 *separation*; dissection, dismemberment; anatomization, analysis, breakdown; factorization; syllabification, parsing 564 *grammar*; resolution, electrolysis, hydrolysis, photolysis, catalysis; atomization; dissolving, dissolution 337 *liquefaction*; fission 160 *nucleonics*; hiving off, decentralization, devolution, delegation; regionalism; collapse, breakup, disintegration, entropy 165 *destruction*; chaos 17 *nonuniformity*.

decay 655 *dilapidation*; erosion, wear and tear 37 *diminution*; disintegration 361 *death*; corruption, mouldering, rotting, putridness, putrefaction, adipocere, mortification, necrosis, gangrene, caries 649 *uncleanness*; rot, rust, mould 659 *blight*; carrion 363 *corpse*.

Vb. *decompose,* resolve, reduce, factorize 44 *simplify*; separate, parse, dissect; break down, analyse, take to pieces 46 *sunder*; electrolyse, catalyse; split, fission 46 *disunite*; atomize 165 *demolish*; disband, break up, hive off 75 *disperse*; decentralize 783 *apportion*; unsettle, disturb 63 *derange*; melt 337 *liquefy*; erode 37 *abate*; rot, rust, moulder, decay, consume, waste away, crumble, wear, perish 655 *deteriorate*; corrupt, putrefy, mortify, gangrene 649 *be unclean*; disintegrate, go to pieces 165 *be destroyed*.

52 Whole. Principal part – N. *whole,* wholeness, fullness 54 *completeness*; integration, indivisibility, integrity, oneness 88 *unity*; whole number, integer, entity 88 *unit*; entirety, ensemble, corpus, complex, totality, summation, sum 38 *addition*; holism, universalization, generalization 79 *generality*; comprehensiveness, inclusiveness 78 *inclusion*; collectivity, system, world, globe, cosmos 321 *universe*; microcosm; Lebensraum; bird's-eye v., panorama, overview, conspectus.

all, no exceptions, one and all, everybody, everyone 79 *everyman*; all the world 74 *crowd*; total, aggregate, sum; ensemble, be-all and end-all, lock, stock and barrel; hook, line and sinker; inventory 87 *list*; lot, whole l., the whole caboodle, the whole bang shoot, the works.

chief part, best part, major p., nitty-gritty, nuts and bolts 638 *chief thing*; ninety-nine per cent, bulk, mass; heap 32 *great quantity*; tissue, staple, stuff; body, torso, trunk, bole, stem, stalk; hull, hulk, skeleton; lion's share, biggest slice of the cake; gist, sum and substance, the long and the short of it; almost all, nearly all, everything but the kitchen sink; all but a few, majority.

Adj. *whole,* total, universal; integral, pure 44 *unmixed*; sound 646 *perfect*; gross, full 54 *complete*; integrated 88 *one*; in one piece; fully restored.

intact, untouched, unaffected; unspoiled, virgin 126 *new*; undivided, undiminished, unclipped, uncut; undissolved; unbroken, unimpaired 646 *undamaged*; uncut, unabridged, unedited, uncensored, unexpurgated.

indivisible, 324 *indissoluble*; inseparable, monolithic 16 *uniform*.

comprehensive, omnibus, all-embracing, all-encompassing, across-the-board, full-length 78 *inclusive*; wholesale, sweeping 32 *extensive*; widespread, epidemic 79 *general*; international, world, world-wide, global, cosmic 79 *universal,* 189 *ubiquitous*.

Adv. *on the whole,* by and large, all in all, all things considered, in the long run;

substantially, in essence; virtually, to all intents and purposes, in effect; as good as; mainly, in the main 32 *greatly*; almost, all but 200 *nearly*.

collectively, one and all, all together; comprehensively; in bulk; in the aggregate; en masse, en bloc.

53 Part – N. *part,* portion; proportion, fraction, half, quarter, tithe, percentage; factor, aliquot 85 *number*; surplus 41 *remainder*; quota, contingent; dividend, share 783 *portion*; item, particular, detail 80 *particulars*; clause, sentence, paragraph 563 *phrase*; ingredient, member, constituent, element 58 *component*; schism, faction 708 *party*; heat, leg, lap, round 110 *period*; side 239 *laterality*; group, species (see *subdivision*); detachment; attachment 40 *adjunct*; page, leaf, folio, sheet 589 *book*; excerpt, extract, passage, quotation, quote 605 *choice*; text; segment, sector, section 46 *scission*; arc 248 *curve*; hemisphere 252 *sphere*; instalment, advance, down payment, deposit, earnest 804 *payment*; fragment (see *piece*).

limb, member, organ, appendage; hind limb 267 *leg*; forelimb 271 *wing*; flipper, fin 269 *propeller*; arm, hand 378 *feeler*.

subdivision, segment, sector, section 46 *scission*; division, compartment; group, subgroup, species, subspecies, family 74 *group*; classification 62 *arrangement*; ward, community, parish, department, region 184 *district*; chapter, paragraph, clause, subordinate clause, phrase, verse; part, number, issue, instalment, volume 589 *edition*; canto 593 *poem*.

branch, ramification, offshoot 40 *adjunct*; bough, limb, spur, twig, tendril, leaf, switch, shoot, scion, sucker, slip, sprig, spray 366 *foliage*.

piece, torso, trunk, stump 41 *remainder*; limb, segment, section (see *part*); patch, insertion 40 *adjunct*; length, roll 222 *textile*; strip, swatch; fragment 55 *incompleteness*; bit, scrap, offcut, shred, wisp, rag 33 *small thing*; morsel, bite,

crust, crumb 33 *small quantity*; splinter, skelf, sliver, chip, snippet; cut, wedge, finger, slice, rasher; collop, cutlet, chop, gigot c., steak; hunk, chunk, wad, wodge, portion, slab, lump, mass 195 *bulk*; clod, turf, divot, sod 344 *soil*; shard, flake, scale; dose 783 *portion*; bits and pieces, odds and ends, oddments 43 *medley*; bin ends; clippings, parings, brash, rubble, scree, detritus, moraine, debris 41 *leavings*; parcel, plot, allotment.

Adj. *fragmentary,* broken, crumbly 330 *brittle*; in bits, in pieces, in smithereens; not whole 647 *imperfect*; partial, bitty, scrappy 636 *insufficient*; fractional, aliquot; segmental, sectional, divided; shredded, sliced, minced, ground 33 *small*.

Vb. *part,* divide, partition, segment; compartmentalize 46 *sunder*; share out 783 *apportion*; fragment 46 *disunite*.

54 Completeness – N. *completeness,* entireness, wholeness 52 *whole*; integration 88 *unity*; solidarity 706 *cooperation*; harmony 710 *concord*; self-sufficiency 635 *sufficiency*; entirety, totality 52 *all*; comprehensiveness 79 *generality*; the ideal 646 *perfection*; ne plus ultra, the limit 236 *limit*; peak, culmination, zenith, crown 213 *summit*; finish 69 *end*; last touch, finishing t. 725 *completion*; fulfilment, consummation 69 *finality*.

plenitude, fullness, amplitude, capacity, maximum, one's fill, saturation 635 *sufficiency*; saturation point 863 *satiety*; completion, filling; filling up, brimming, overrunning, swamping, drowning; full house, complement, full c.; requisite number, quorum; full measure, bumper; bellyful, skinful, repletion; full size, full length, full volume.

Adj. *complete,* plenary, full; total; integral 52 *whole*; entire 52 *intact*; full-blown, full-grown, fully-fledged, 669 *matured*; unbroken, undivided 324 *dense*; self-contained, self-sufficient 635 *sufficient*; fully furnished; all-in, comprehensive 78 *inclusive*; exhaustive, detailed 570 *diffuse*; absolute, extreme;

thorough, thoroughgoing, sweeping, wholesale, regular 32 *consummate*; unmitigated, downright, plumb, plain 44 *unmixed*; crowning, culminating, consummating, complementary.

full, replete 635 *filled*; topped up; well-filled, bulging; brimful, brimming; overwhelmed; overflowing, running over, slopping, swamped, drowned; saturated, oozing; bursting at the seams; gorged, fit to burst, full to bursting 863 *sated*; chock-full, chock-a-block, crammed, stuffed, packed, jam-p., packed like sardines; laden, heavy-l., fully charged, all seats taken, standing room only; infested, overrun, crawling with, hotching w., alive w., seething w., jumping w., lousy w., stiff w.; full of, rolling in; soaked in, dripping with.

Vb. *be complete,* be integrated; culminate, come to a head 725 *climax*; come to a close, be all over 69 *end*; be self-sufficient 635 *have enough*; want nothing, lack n. 828 *be content*; become complete, fill out, reach maturity 669 *mature*; be filled.

make complete, complete, complement, integrate 45 *join*; make whole 656 *restore*; build up, construct, make up, piece together 56 *compose*; eke out, supplement; do thoroughly, leave nothing undone, carry out 725 *carry through*; put the finishing touch, put the icing on the cake, round off 69 *terminate*.

fill, fill up, brim, top; saturate 341 *drench*; overfill, swamp, drown, overwhelm; top up, replenish 633 *provide*; satisfy 635 *suffice*, 828 *content*, 863 *sate*; fill to capacity, cram, pack, stuff, line, bulge out, pack in, pile in, squeeze in, ram in, jam in 303 *insert*; load, charge, ram down; freight; fill space, occupy 226 *cover*; reach to, extend to 183 *extend*; spread over, overrun 189 *pervade*; fit tight, be full to overflowing, be chock-a-block 45 *tighten*; fill in, enter 38 *add*.

Adv. *completely,* fully, wholly, totally, entirely, utterly, extremely 32 *greatly*; all told, in all, in toto; on all counts, in all respects, in every way; quite, altogether; outright, downright; thoroughly; to one's

fill, to the top of one's bent, to the utmost, to the end, to the full; out and out, all out, heart and soul; head and shoulders, head over heels; neck and crop; to the brim, up to the hilt, up to the neck, up to the ears, up to the eyes; hook, line and sinker; root and branch; down to the ground; with a vengeance, with knobs on, with all the trimmings, and then some; to the last man, to the last breath; every whit, every inch; at full length, full out, in full; as far as possible; to capacity, not an inch to spare.

throughout, all the way, from first to last, from beginning to end, from end to end, from one end to the other, the length and breadth of, from coast to coast, from sea to sea, from Land's End to John o' Groats 183 *widely*; from north and south and east and west; fore and aft; high and low; from top to bottom; from top to toe, from head to foot, cap-à-pie; to the bitter end, to the end of the road, to the end of the chapter.

55 Incompleteness – N. *incompleteness,* defectiveness; unfinished state 647 *imperfection*; immaturity 670 *undevelopment*; sketch, outline, 623 *plan*; skeleton, torso, trunk 53 *piece*; half measures, a lick and a promise 726 *noncompletion*; perfunctoriness, superficiality. 458 *negligence*; nonfulfilment, deficiency, slippage 307 *shortfall*, 636 *insufficiency*; dissatisfaction 829 *discontent*; impairment 655 *deterioration*; omission, break, gap, lacuna, missing link 72 *discontinuity*, 201 *interval*; part payment 53 *part*.

deficit, screw loose, missing link, omission 647 *defect*; shortfall, slippage; 772 *loss*; default 930 *improbity*; want, lack, need 627 *requirement*.

Adj. *incomplete,* inadequate, defective 307 *deficient*; short, scant, unsatisfactory 636 *insufficient*; like Hamlet without the Prince 641 *useless*; omitting, wanting, lacking, needing, requiring; short of, shy of; halting, mutilated; without, -less, -free; garbled, impaired; cropped, abbreviated, shortened 204 *short*; flawed 647 *imperfect*; partial 53

fragmentary; half-finished, neglected 726 *uncompleted*; not ready 670 *unprepared*; undeveloped, underdeveloped, unripe 670 *immature*; raw, crude, roughhewn 244 *amorphous*; sketchy, scrappy, bitty; thin, poor 4 *insubstantial*; perfunctory, half-hearted, half-done, undone 458 *neglected*; left in the air, left hanging; omitted, missing, lost 190 *absent*; interrupted 72 *discontinuous*.

unfinished, in progress, in hand; in embryo, begun 68 *beginning*; in preparation, on the stocks; on the back-burner.

Vb. *be incomplete,* miss, lack, need 627 *require*, 307 *fall short*; be wanting 190 *be absent*; default, leave undone 458 *neglect*; omit, miss out 57 *exclude*; break off, interrupt 72 *discontinue*; leave in the air, leave dangling, leave hanging 726 *not complete.*

56 Composition – N. *composition,* constitution, setup, make-up; formation, construction, build-up, build 331 *structure*; organization 62 *arrangement*; nature, humour, character, condition 5 *temperament*; embodiment 78 *inclusion*; compound 43 *mixture,* 50 *combination,* 358 *organism*; syntax, sentence 563 *phrase*; artistic composition 412 *music,* 551 *art,* 553 *painting,* 554 *sculpture*; architecture 164 *edifice*; authorship 586 *writing,* 593 *poetry*; dramatic art 594 *drama*; composing, printing, typography 587 *print*; compilation 74 *assemblage*; construction 164 *production*; choreography 594 *ballet*; orchestration, instrumentation, score 412 *musical piece*; work of art, picture, portrait, sculpture, piece of s., model; literary work 589 *book,* 593 *poem,* 591 *dissertation,* 592 *anthology*; play 594 *stage play*; 837 *dance*; pattern, design 12 *correlation.*

Vb. *constitute,* compose, form, make; make up; inhere, belong to, enter into.

contain, subsume, include, consist of 78 *comprise*; hold, have, take in, absorb 299 *admit*; comprehend, embrace, embody 235 *enclose.*

compose, compound 43 *mix,* 50 *combine*; organize, set in order, put in o. 62

arrange; synthesize, put together, make up 45 *join*; compile, assemble 74 *bring together*; compose, set up, computer-set 587 *print*; draft, draw up 586 *write*; orchestrate, score 413 *compose music*; draw 553 *paint*; sculpt, construct, build, make, fabricate 164 *produce*; knit 222 *weave.*

57 Exclusion – N. *exclusion,* preemption; forestalling 702 *hindrance*; exclusiveness, monopoly, closed shop, dog-in-the-manger policy; possessiveness 932 *selfishness*; exception; special case; exemption, dispensation 746 *liberation*; leaving out, including o., omission 607 *rejection*; blackball; no entry, no admission, no-go area, no-man's land, exclusion order; closed door, lockout; picket line; embargo, ban, bar, taboo 757 *prohibition*; ostracism, boycott 620 *avoidance*; segregation, quarantine, caste system, colour bar, apartheid, 883 *seclusion*; intolerance, repression, suppression, discrimination 481 *prejudice*; expulsion, eviction; disbarment, dismissal, suspension, excommunication; deportation, exile, expatriation; removal, elimination, eradication 188 *displacement*; dam, wall, barricade, screen, partition, pale, curtain, Iron C., Bamboo C. 235 *barrier*; great wall of China 713 *defence*; customs' barrier, economic zone, tariff wall 809 *tax*; ghetto.

Adj. *excluding,* exclusive, exemptive; restrictive, clannish, cliquish; preventive, prohibitive; preemptive.

Vb. *be excluded,* not belong, stay outside, not gain admission; suffer exile, go into e., go into voluntary e. 296 *depart*, 190 *be absent.*

exclude, preclude 470 *make impossible*; preempt, forestall 64 *come before*; keep out, warn off 747 *restrain*; blackball, vote against, deny entry, shut out, debar, shut the door on, spurn 607 *reject*; bar, ban, place an embargo on, taboo, black, disallow 757 *prohibit*; ostracize, cold-shoulder, boycott, send to Coventry 620 *avoid*, not include, leave out, include o.; count o.; exempt, dispense, excuse

746 *liberate*; except, make an exception, treat as a special case 19 *make unlike*; omit, miss out, pass over, disregard 458 *neglect*; lay aside, put a., relegate 46 *set apart*; take out, strike o., cross o., cancel 550 *obliterate*; disbar, strike off, remove, disqualify 188 *displace*, 963 *punish*; rule out, draw the line; wall off, fence off, screen off, curtain off, quarantine 232 *circumscribe*, 235 *enclose*; excommunicate, segregate, sequester 883 *seclude*; thrust out, dismiss, sack, declare redundant, deport, extradite, exile, banish, outlaw, expatriate; weed, sift, sieve, sort out; eradicate, uproot 300 *eject*; expurgate, bowdlerize, censor 648 *purify*; deny 760 *refuse*; abandon 779 *not retain*.

Adv. *exclusive of*, excepting, barring, bar, not counting, including out, except, with the exception of, save; short of; let alone, apart from.

58 Component – N. *component*, component part, integral p., element, item; piece, bit, segment; link, stitch; word, letter; constituent, part and parcel 53 *part*; factor, leaven 178 *influence*; additive, appurtenance, feature 40 *adjunct*; one of, member, one of us; staff, workforce, crew, men, company, complement 686 *personnel*; ingredient 193 *contents*, 43 *tincture*; works, inner workings, insides, interior 224 *interiority*; nuts and bolts, machinery 630 *machine*; spare part 40 *extra*; components, set, outfit 88 *unit*.

Adj. *component*, constituent, ingredient; belonging, proper, native, inherent 5 *intrinsic*; built-in; admitted, one of, on the staff.

59 Extraneousness – N. *extraneousness*, foreignness 6 *extrinsicality*, 223 *exteriority*; foreign parts; foreign body, foreign substance, accretion 38 *addition*; alien element, 84 *nonconformity*; exotica.

foreigner, alien, stranger, emmet, outlander; Southerner, Northerner, Easterner, Westerner; Martian, extraterrestrial being, little green men; Celtic fringe; Sassenach, pommie (derog), limey (derog), rooineck (derog); Yank, Yankee, Aussie, Kiwi; wog (derog), wop (derog), dago (derog); gringo (derog), whitey (derog), honkie (derog), paleface; colonial, Creole 191 *settler*; resident alien, expatriate; migrant, migrant worker, guest w., Gastarbeiter, emigrant, émigré, exile; immigrant. refugee. diaspora, ten lost tribes.

intruder, interloper, alien, trespasser, cuckoo in the nest, squatter; uninvited guest, gatecrasher, stowaway; outsider; not one of us, stranger in our midst; arrival, new a., nouveau arrivé, newcomer, new boy, tenderfoot 297 *incomer*; invader 712 *attacker*.

Adj. *extraneous,* ulterior, outside 223 *exterior*, 6 *extrinsic*; ultramundane, extragalactic 199 *distant*; not indigenous, imported; foreign, alien, unearthly; strange, outlandish, barbarian; overseas, transatlantic; continental, extraterrestrial; exotic, unacclimatized; gypsy, nomad, wandering; unassimilated, unintegrated 46 *separate*; immigrant; intrusive, interloping, trespassing, gatecrashing; infringing, invading; exceptional 84 *unusual*; not of this world, unnatural, paranormal, supernatural 983 *magical*; inadmissible.

Section four: Order

60 Order – N. *order*, state of order, orderliness, tidiness, neatness 648 *cleanness*, 258 *smoothness*; quiet 266 *quietude*; harmony 710 *concord*; system, method, methodology, prioritization; fixed order, pattern, rule 81 *regularity*, 16 *uniformity*; custom, routine 610 *habit*; rite 988 *ritual*; discipline 739 *obedience*; due order, hierarchy, gradation, subordination, rank, position 73 *serial place*; unbroken order, even tenor, progression, series 71 *continuity*; logical order, alphabetical o. 65 *sequence*, 12 *correlation*; organization, array 62 *arrangement*, 56 *composition*; a place for everything and e. in its place.

Adj. *orderly*, harmonious, 245 *symmetrical*; well-behaved, decorous 848 *well-bred*; disciplined 739 *obedient*; well-regulated, according to rule 81 *regular*; ordered, classified 62 *arranged*; methodical, systematic; strict 16 *uniform*; steady 610 *habitual*; correct, shipshape, Bristol fashion, trim, neat, tidy, neat and tidy, neat as a pin, out of a bandbox; spick and span, spruce, dapper, well-groomed 648 *clean*; in good trim, well-kept, in apple-pie order, in perfect o., in its proper place 62 *arranged*; direct 249 *straight*; lucid 516 *intelligible*.

Vb. *order*, dispose, prioritize 62 *arrange*; schematize, systematize, organize 62 *regularize*; regulate 24 *adjust*; normalize, standardize 16 *make uniform*; keep order, call to order, police, govern 733 *rule*, 737 *command*.

be in order, be shipshape, harmonize 24 *accord*; range oneself, draw up, line up; fall into place, find one's level; take one's place, station oneself, take up one's position 187 *place oneself*; keep one's place; rally round 74 *congregate*; follow routine 610 *be wont*.

61 Disorder – N. *disorder*, random order, nonclassification; incoordination; muddle, no system; bedlam, chaotic state, chaos, mayhem 734 *anarchy*; irregularity, anomalousness, anomaly 17 *nonuniformity*; disunion, disaccord 25 *disagreement*; disharmony 411 *discord*; disorderliness, unruliness, lack of discipline 738 *disobedience*; outbreak (see *turmoil*); nihilism 738 *sedition*; untidiness, clutter, littering, slovenliness 649 *uncleanness*; neglect 458 *negligence*; discomposure, disarray, dishevelment 63 *derangement*; scattering 75 *dispersion*, 51 *decomposition*; upheaval 149 *revolution*; subversion 221 *overturning*; destruction; welter, jumble, shambles, hugger-mugger, mix-up, medley, embroilment, imbroglio 43 *mixture*; chaos, scramble 74 *crowd*; muddle, litter, clutter, lumber 641 *rubbish*; farrago, mess, mishmash, hash, hotchpotch, ragbag, Babel, bedlam, madhouse (see *turmoil*).

complexity, complication, snarl-up 700 *difficulty*, 702 *hindrance*; implication, involvement, imbroglio, embroilment; intricacy, kink 251 *convolution*; maze, labyrinth, warren; web 222 *network*; coil, tangle, twist, snarl, ravel; knot, Gordian k. 47 *ligature*; puzzle 517 *unintelligibility*; awkward situation, how d'ye do, how-do-you-do, pretty kettle of fish, pickle 700 *predicament*.

turmoil, turbulence, tumult, frenzy, ferment, storm, convulsion 176 *violence*; pandemonium, inferno; hullabaloo, hubbub, racket, row, riot, uproar 400 *loudness*; affray, fracas, dustup, stramash, brawl, mêlée 716 *fight*; hurly-burly, to-do, rumpus, ruction, shemozzle, spot of bother, pother, trouble, disturbance 318 *commotion*; whirlwind, tornado, hurricane 352 *gale*; beargarden, shambles, madhouse, Bedlam; shindig, breach of the peace; roughhouse, rough and tumble, free for all, fisticuffs, all hell broken loose, bull in a china shop; street fighting, gang warfare 709 *quarrel*; fat in the fire, devil to pay, hell to p.

slut, sloven, slag, slattern, draggletail, litterer, litterlout 649 *dirty person*; ragamuffin, tatterdemalion 801 *poor person*.

anarchist, nihilist; lord of misrule, sons of Belial 738 *rioter*.

Adj. *complex*, intricate, involved, elaborate, sophisticated, complicated, over-c., overinvolved 251 *coiled*, problematic 517 *puzzling*; winding, inextricable; entangled, enmeshed, balled up, snarled 702 *hindered*; knotted 45 *tied*.

disorderly, undisciplined, unruly; out of control, out of step, out of line, tumultuous, rumbustious; frantic 503 *frenzied*; orgiastic, Saturnalian, Bacchic, Dionysiac 949 *drunken*; rough, tempestuous, turbulent 176 *violent*, anarchical, nihilistic, lawless 954 *lawbreaking*; wild, harum-scarum, rantipole, tomboyish, boisterous, scatterbrained 456 *lightminded*.

Vb. *be disordered*, fall into disarray, scatter, break up 75 *disperse*; get in a

mess, fall into confusion 49 *come unstuck*; get out of hand, riot, 738 *disobey*; jump the queue 64 *come before*; disorder 63 *derange*.

rampage, go on the r., storm; rush, mob; riot 738 *revolt*; romp 837 *amuse oneself*; play the fool 497 *be absurd*; give a riotous welcome 876 *celebrate*.

62 Arrangement: reduction to order – N.

arrangement, reduction to order; ordering, disposal, disposition, marshalling, arraying, placing 187 *location*; grouping, 74 *assemblage*; division, distribution, allocation, allotment 783 *apportionment*; method, systematization, organization, prioritization, reorganization; restructuring, perestroika; rationalization; streamlining 654 *improvement*; centralization 48 *coherence*; decentralization, hiving off 49 *noncoherence*; administration 689 *management*; planning 623 *contrivance*, 669 *preparation*; taxonomy, categorization, classification 561 *nomenclature*; analysis 51 *decomposition*; codification, consolidation; syntax, conjugation 564 *grammar*; grading, gradation, subordination, graduation, calibration 465 *measurement*, 71 *series*; synchronization 123 *synchronism*; construction 56 *composition*; array, system, form 60 *order*; cosmos 321 *universe*; orchestration, score 412 *music*; layout, pattern; choreography 837 *dance*; collection, assortment 74 *accumulation*; schematism; computer program; register, file 548 *record*; inventory, catalogue, table 87 *list*; code, digest; class, group, sub-g. 77 *classification*.

sorting, grading, seeding; cross-reference 12 *correlation*; file, computer f., folder, filing system, card index, pigeonhole, slot; sieve, strainer 263 *porosity*.

Adj. *arranged*, disposed, marshalled, arrayed etc. vb.; ordered, schematic, tabulated, tabular; methodical, systematic, organizational; precise, definite, cut and dried; classified; straightened out; regulated 81 *regular*; sorted, seeded, graded, streamed, banded.

Vb. *arrange*, set, dispose, set up, set out, lay out; formulate, form, knock into shape, orchestrate, score 56 *compose*; range, rank, align, line up, form up; position 187 *place*; marshal, array; rally 74 *bring together*; put in order; grade, size, group, space; collocate, thread together 45 *connect*; settle, fix, determine, define; allot, allocate, assign, distribute, deal, parcel out 783 *apportion*; rearrange, trim, neaten, tidy, tidy up, arrange for, make arrangements 669 *prepare*, 623 *plan*, 689 *manage*.

regularize, reduce to order, straighten out, put to rights 654 *rectify*, 24 *adjust*; regulate; organize, systematize, prioritize, methodize, schematize; standardize, normalize, centralize 16 *make uniform*.

class, classify, subsume, group; specify 561 *name*; process; analyse, divide; dissect 51 *decompose*; rate, rank, grade, evaluate 480 *estimate*; sort, sift, sieve, seed; tag, label 547 *mark*; file, pigeonhole; index, cross-r.; tabulate, alphabetize; catalogue; register 548 *record*; program.

63 Derangement – N. *derangement*, shuffling 151 *interchange*; translocation, displacement 272 *transference*; obstruction 702 *hindrance*; disarrangement, disorganization, discomposure, dishevelment; dislocation 46 *separation*; disturbance, interruption 138 *untimeliness*; creasing, corrugation 261 *fold*; madness 503 *mental disorder*; upsetting 221 *inversion*; convulsion 176 *violence*, 318 *agitation*; state of disorder 61 *disorder*.

Vb. *derange*, disarrange, disorder, put out of gear, get out of order; disturb, touch 265 *move*; interfere 702 *hinder*; lose 188 *misplace*; disorganize, muddle, confuse, convulse, throw into confusion, make havoc; tamper, spoil, mar, damage, sabotage 655 *impair*; strain, bend, twist 176 *force*; unhinge, dislocate, sprain, rick 188 *displace*; unseat, dislodge, derail, throw off the rails; throw off balance, upset, overturn, capsize 221 *invert*, 149 *revolutionize*; declassify;

shake, jiggle, toss 318 *agitate*; trouble, perturb, unsettle, discompose, disconcert, ruffle, rattle, flurry, fluster 456 *distract*; interrupt 138 *mistime*; misdirect, disorientate, throw one off his bearings 495 *mislead*, 655 *pervert*; unhinge, dement, drive mad 503 *make mad*, 891 *enrage.*

jumble, shuffle, get out of order 151 *interchange*, 272 *transpose*; mix up 43 *mix*; toss, tumble 318 *agitate*; ruffle, dishevel, tousle; rumple, crumple, crease, wrinkle, crush 261 *fold*; untidy, mess, muck up; muddle, mess up, scatter, fling about 75 *disperse.*

bedevil, throw into confusion, make a mess *or* hash of; confound, complicate, perplex, involve, ravel, ball up, foul up, entangle, tangle, embroil; turn topsy-turvy, turn upside down 221 *invert*; send haywire.

64 Precedence – N. *precedence,* antecedence, going before, coming b., queue-jumping 283 *preceding*; front position, prosthesis 237 *front*; higher position, pride of place 34 *superiority*; preference 605 *choice*; preeminence, excellence 638 *importance*; captaincy, leadership, hegemony 733 *authority*; the lead, the pas; leading, guiding, pioneering; precedent 66 *precursor*; past history 125 *past time.*

Adj. *preceding,* foregoing, outgoing; former, ex-, previous 119 *prior*; before-mentioned, above-m.; aforesaid, said; forewarning, premonitory, prodromal; preliminary, prefatory, preparatory.

Vb. *come before,* be first to arrive 283 *precede*; go first, jump the queue; lead, guide, conduct, show the way, point the way 547 *indicate*; be the forerunner of, pioneer, clear the way, blaze the trail 484 *discover*; head, take the lead 237 *be in front*; have precedence, take p. 34 *be superior*; lead the dance, set the fashion, be a trend-setter 178 *influence*; open, lead off, kick off, bully off 68 *begin*; preface; introduce, usher in, herald, ring in 68 *auspicate*; get ahead; antedate 125 *be past.*

put in front, send a reconnaisance party, send ahead, station before 187 *place*; prefix 38 *add*; front, top 237 *be in front*; presuppose 512 *suppose*; preface.

Adv. *before,* in advance; preparatory to, as a prelude to, as a preliminary; earlier 119 *before* (in time); ante, supra, above 237 *in front.*

65 Sequence – N. *sequence,* coming after, descent, line, lineage 120 *posteriority*; going after; inference 475 *reasoning*; suffixion 38 *addition*; succession, successorship, mantle, Elijah's m. 780 *transfer*; rota, Buggin's turn; series 71 *continuity*; successiveness, alternation, serialization; continuation, prolongation 113 *protraction*, 146 *continuance*; pursuance 619 *pursuit*; overtaking 306 *overstepping*, 727 *success*; subordination, second place, proxime accessit 35 *inferiority*; last place 238 *rear*; consequence 67 *sequel.*

Adj. *sequential,* following, succeeding; ensuing; next 200 *near*; posterior, latter, later 120 *subsequent*; another, second 38 *additional*; successive, consecutive 71 *continuous*; alternating 12 *correlative*; alternate, consequent, resulting 157 *caused.*

Vb. *come after,* ensue 284 *follow*; follow close, sit on one's tail, drive bumper to bumper, breathe down one's neck, tread on the heels; succeed, inherit, step into the shoes of, supplant 150 *substitute*; alternate, relieve, take over.

place after, suffix, append.

Adv. *after,* following; afterwards 120 *subsequently*, 238 *rearward*; at the end, as follows, consequentially; in the end 69 *finally*; next, later; infra, below.

66 Precursor – N. *precursor,* predecessor, ancestor, forbear 169 *parentage*; Adam and Eve, early man 371 *humankind*; the ancients 125 *antiquity*; eldest, firstborn; discoverer, inventor 461 *experimenter*; pioneer, pathfinder, explorer 268 *traveller*; guide, pilot 690 *leader*; scout, reconnaissance party; vanguard, avant-garde, innovator, trail-blazer; trend-setter;

forerunner; herald, harbinger, announcer 529 *messenger*; anticipation, foretaste, preview, premonition, 511 *omen*; trailer; prequel; precedent 83 *example*; antecedent, prefix, preposition 40 *adjunct*; eve, vigil, day before 119 *priority.*

prelude, preliminary, preamble, preface, front matter, prologue, foreword; opening, introduction 68 *beginning*; lead, heading, frontispiece 237 *front*; 669 *preparation*; aperitif, appetizer, hors d'oeuvre, starter; overture 412 *musical piece*; presupposition 512 *supposition,* 475 *premise.*

Adj. *precursory,* preliminary, exploratory 669 *preparatory*; introductory, prefatory 68 *beginning*; inaugural; precedent 64 *preceding.*

67 Sequel – N. *sequel,* consequence, result, aftermath, by-product, spin-off 157 *effect*; conclusion 69 *end*; aftereffect; hangover, morning after 949 *crapulence*; aftertaste; afterglow, fallout; afterbirth, placenta 167 *obstetrics*; inheritance, legacy 777 *dower*; surprise 508 *lack of expectation*; afterthought, second thoughts; second try, second bite at the cherry; end matter, epilogue, postscript; envoi, last words; follow-up 725 *completion*; continuation, sequel 589 *book*; tailpiece, colophon, coda 238 *rear*; appendage, appendix, codicil, supplement 40 *adjunct*; suffix, affix, inflection 564 *grammar*; afters, pudding, dessert 301 *dish*; afterlife, 124 *future state*; hereafter.

retinue, following, followers, camp f., groupies 284 *follower*; queue 71 *series*; train, cortège 71 *procession*; tailback, wake 89 *concomitant*; trailer 274 *vehicle.*

successor, descendant, future generations 170 *posterity*; heir 776 *beneficiary*; next man in; replacement, supplanter 150 *substitute*; newcomer, nouveau arrivé 297 *incomer*; satellite, hanger-on 742 *dependant.*

68 Beginning – N. *beginning,* birth, rise (see *origin*); infancy, babyhood 130 *youth*, 126 *newness*; primitiveness 127

oldness; commencement; onset 295 *arrival*; emergence 445 *appearance*; inception, institution, constitution, foundation 156 *causation*; origination, invention 484 *discovery*; creation 164 *production*; innovation 21 *originality*; initiative, introduction 66 *prelude*; alpha, first letter, initial; heading, headline; title page, front matter; van, front, forefront 237 *front*; dawn 128 *morning*; running in, teething troubles, growing pains; first sight, first impression, first lap, first round, first stage; early stages, early days; rudiments, elements, first principles, alphabet, ABC; leading up to 289 *approach*; onset 712 *attack*; starter 538 *beginner*; preliminaries 669 *preparation.*

debut, coming out, presentation, initiation, launching; inauguration, opening, unveiling; first night, premiere, first appearance, first offence; first step, first move; gambit; maiden voyage, maiden speech; baptism of fire.

start, outset; zero hour, D-day; send-off, embarkation, countdown 296 *departure*; rising of the curtain; kick-off; house-warming, honeymoon; flying start.

origin, derivation, conception, genesis, birth, nativity; provenance, ancestry 169 *parentage*; fount, fons et origo; rise 156 *source*; nest, womb; bud, germ, seed; egg, protoplasm 358 *organism*; first beginnings, cradle 192 *home.*

entrance 297 *way in*; inlet 345 *gulf*; mouth, opening 263 *orifice*; threshold 624 *access*; porch 194 *lobby*; gateway 263 *doorway*; border 236 *limit*; suburbs 230 *surroundings*; foothills, outlier; pass, corridor 289 *approach*, 305 *passage.*

Adj. *beginning,* introductory, prefatory 66 *precursory*; inaugural; rudimental 156 *fundamental*; primeval, primordial 127 *primal*; rudimentary, elementary; embryonic, nascent, budding, incipient, in preparation 726 *uncompleted*; early, infant 126 *new.*

first, initial, primary, maiden, starting, natal; pioneering 21 *original*; unprecedented 126 *new*; foremost, front 237

frontal; leading, principal, major, head, chief 34 *supreme*.

Vb. *begin,* commence; open, dawn, spring up; arise, emerge, appear; rise; spring from; sprout, germinate; come into existence, come into the world, see the light of day 360 *be born*; make one's debut, come out; start, enter upon, embark on 296 *start out*; fire away, kick off, strike up; start work, clock in; roll up one's sleeves, limber up 669 *prepare*; run in; begin at the beginning, start from scratch; put one's hand to the plough, put one's shoulder to the wheel, set to, set to work, get cracking, get moving, get weaving; attack, tackle, address oneself; go to it 672 *undertake*.

initiate, found, launch; originate, invent 484 *discover*; usher in, herald, ring in, open the door to, introduce; start, start up, switch on, ring up the curtain; set in motion, get under way; put to work 622 *employ*; handsel, run in; take the initiative, lead, lead off, lead the way, take the lead, pioneer, break new ground 64 *come before*; broach, open, raise the subject; break the ice, kick off, set the ball rolling; throw the first stone, open fire; take the first step, take the plunge; trigger off, spark off, set off.

auspicate, inaugurate, open; establish 156 *cause*; be a founder member, be in on the ground floor, be in with the bricks; baptize, christen, launch 561 *name*; initiate, blood; lay the foundations, cut the first turf 669 *prepare*.

Adv. *initially,* originally, in the beginning; at the very start, from its inception; from the beginning, from the word go; first, firstly, in the first place, primarily, first of all, first and foremost; as a start, for starters, for a kick-off, for a beginning; from scratch.

69 End – N. *end,* close, conclusion, consummation 725 *completion*; payoff, result, end r. 157 *effect*; expiration, lapse; termination, closure, guillotine; finishing stroke, death blow, quietus, coup de grace; knockout, clincher 279 *knock*; denouement; ending, finish, finale, curtain; term, period, stop, halt 145 *cessation*; final stage, latter end 129 *evening*; beginning of the end, last words, swansong, envoi, coda 67 *sequel*; last stage, last round, last lap, home stretch; last over; last breath, last gasp 361 *decease*; terminal illness; final examination, finals 459 *exam*. See *finality*.

extremity, omega; extreme, pole, antipodes; extreme case, ne plus ultra; farthest point, world's end, ultima Thule, where the rainbow ends; fringe, verge, brink 234 *edge*; frontier, boundary 236 *limit*; end of the road, end of the line, terminus, terminal 295 *goal*, 617 *objective*; dregs; foot, toe, bottom, nadir 214 *base*; bottom dollar, last cent, last penny 801 *poverty*; tip, cusp, point 256 *sharp point*; vertex, peak, head, top, zenith 213 *summit*; tail, tail end 67 *sequel*; arm, stump 53 *limb*; shirt-tail, coat-t. 217 *hanging object*; end, butt end, gable e., fag e. 238 *rear*; tag, epilogue, postscript, end matter, appendix 40 *adjunct*; inflection, suffix 564 *grammar*.

finality, bitter end; time, time up, deadline; conclusion 54 *completeness*; breakup, wind-up 145 *cessation*; dissolution 165 *destruction*; doom, destiny 596 *fate*; last trump, crack of doom, Götterdämmerung; Day of Judgment, end of the world 124 *future state*.

Adj. *ending,* final, terminal, last, ultimate, supreme, closing; extreme, polar; definitive, conclusive, crowning. hindmost, rear 238 *back*; caudal.

Vb. *end,* come to an end, expire, run out, become invalid 111 *elapse*; close, finish, conclude, be all over; die out 361 *die*, 2 *pass away*; come to a close, draw to a c., have run its course; stop, clock out, go home 145 *cease*.

terminate, conclude, close, settle; apply the closure, bring to an end, put an end to, put a stop to, put paid to, pull the plug on; discontinue, drop; finish, consummate, see it out 725 *carry through*; ring down the curtain, put up the shutters, shut up shop, wind up, close down,

call it a day; switch off, ring off, hang up, cut off, stop 145 *halt*.

Adv. *finally,* in conclusion; at last, at long last; once for all, for good and all; never again, nevermore. in the end, in the long run, in the final analysis, when all's said and done.

70 Middle – N. *middle,* midst, midpoint; mean 30 *average*; medium; thick, thick of things; heart, heart of the matter, kernel; nave, hub, navel 225 *centre*; nucleus 224 *interiority*; midweek, midwinter, half tide; midstream 625 *middle way*; bisection, midline, equator, the Line 28 *equalization*; midriff, diaphragm 231 *partition*; equidistance, halfway house; mezzo floor.

Adj. *middle,* medial, mean, mezzo, mid 30 *median*; middlemost 225 *central*; intermediate, betwixt and between 231 *interjacent*; equidistant; mediterranean, equatorial.

71 Continuity: uninterrupted sequence – N. *continuity,* continuousness, uninterruptedness, monotony 16 *uniformity*; continuation; successiveness, succession; line, lineage, descent, dynasty; one thing after another, serialization 65 *sequence*; continuum 115 *perpetuity*; assembly line, conveyor belt 146 *continuance*; endless band 315 *rotation*; recurrence, cycle 106 *repetition*, 141 *periodicity*, 139 *frequency*; cumulativeness, snowball 36 *increase*; course, career, flow, steady f., trend 179 *tendency*; progressiveness 285 *progression*; circuit, round 314 *circuition*; daily round, routine, rut, practice, custom 610 *habit*; track, trail, wake 67 *sequel*; chain, food c.; chain reaction. round robin, chain letter; circle 250 *circularity*.

series, gradation 27 *degree*; succession, run; progression; ascending order 36 *increase*; descending order 37 *decrease*; family tree, lineage 169 *genealogy*; chain, line, string, thread; train, parade; unbroken line, line of battle; array 62 *arrangement*; row; range, ridge; colonnade, peristyle, portico; ladder,

steps, stairs, staircase 308 *ascent*; range, tier, storey 207 *layer*; set, suite, suit (of cards); assortment 77 *classification*; spectrum; gamut, scale 410 *musical note*; stepping stones 624 *bridge*; hierarchy, pyramid.

Adj. *continuous,* continued, run-on; consecutive, running, successive 65 *sequential*; serial, serialized; seriate, catenary; progressive; overlapping, unbroken, solid, smooth, uninterrupted, circular; continuing, ongoing; continual, incessant, ceaseless, unremitting, nonstop, constant 115 *perpetual*; cyclical, rhythmic 110 *periodic*; repetitive, recurrent, monotonous 106 *repeated*, 16 *uniform*; linear, lineal, rectilinear 249 *straight*.

continue, run on, prolong, 203 *lengthen*; serialize, arrange in succession, catenate, string 45 *connect*; maintain continuity, keep the kettle boiling 600 *persevere*; keep the succession, provide an heir.

Adv. *continuously,* consecutively etc. adj.; successively, in succession, in turn; one after another; at a stretch, together, running; at one go, without stopping, on the trot; around the clock, night and day 115 *for ever*; progressively; in procession, in file, in single f., in Indian f., in a crocodile, nose to tail.

72 Discontinuity: interrupted sequence – N. *discontinuity,* intermittence; discontinuation 145 *cessation*; interval, hiatus, pause, time lag 145 *lull*; disconnectedness, randomness 61 *disorder*; unevenness 17 *nonuniformity*, 259 *roughness*; dotted line; broken ranks; ladder, run 46 *disunion*; disruption, interruption, intervention; parenthesis 231 *interjection*; caesura, division 46 *separation*, 547 *punctuation*; break, fracture, flaw, fault, split, crack, cut 201 *gap*; lacuna; missing link; broken thread, anacoluthon, non sequitur; alternation 141 *periodicity*; irregularity 142 *fitfulness*.

Adj. *discontinuous,* nonrecurrent; discontinued; interrupted, broken; disconnected; discrete 46 *separate*; few and far

between 140 *infrequent*; irregular, intermittent 142 *fitful*; alternate, alternating, stop-go, on-off 141 *periodical*; spasmodic 17 *nonuniform*; jerky, bumpy, uneven 259 *rough*; incoherent; parenthetic, episodic.

Vb. *be discontinuous,* halt, rest 145 *pause*; alternate.

discontinue, suspend, break off, refrain from, desist; interrupt, intervene, chip in, butt in, break, break in upon 231 *interfere*; interpose, interject, punctuate; disconnect, break the connection, break *or* interrupt one's train of thought, snap the thread 46 *disunite.*

73 Term: serial position – **N.** *serial place,* term, order, remove 27 *degree*; echelon, rank, ranking, grade, gradation; station, place, position, slot; status, standing, footing, social class, caste; point, mark, pitch, level, storey; step, tread, round, rung; stage, milestone, watershed.

Vb. *grade,* rank, rate, place, classify, class; stagger, space out 201 *space.* 27 *graduate.*

74 Assemblage – **N.** *assemblage,* collection 50 *combination,* 62 *arrangement*; collocation; compilation, corpus, anthology 56 *composition*; gathering, harvest 370 *agriculture,* 771 *acquisition*; consolidation, concentration; centering, focusing, zeroing in on; levy, call-up 718 *war measures*; parade 875 *pageant*; march, demonstration, rally; roundup, lineup; herding, shepherding 369 *animal husbandry*; collectivization, collective, 370 *farm*; conspiracy, caucus 708 *party*; collective noun 564 *grammar.*

assembly, getting together, ganging up; forgathering, congregation, concourse, conflux, concurrence 293 *convergence*; gathering, meeting, mass m., protest m., sit-in, meet; coven; conventicle; convention, convocation 985 *synod*; legislature, conclave 692 *council*; eisteddfod, mod, festival 876 *celebration*; reunion, get-together, gathering of the clans, ceilidh 882 *social gathering*; company, at home, party 882 *fellowship*; circle, sewing-bee;

encounter group 658 *therapy*; discussion group, symposium 584 *conference.*

group, constellation, galaxy, cluster 321 *star*; pride (lions), leap (leopards), troop, bevy, swarm, flock, herd; drove, team; pack, kennel; stable, string; nest, eyrie; brood, hatch, litter, kindle (kittens); gaggle, flight, skein, covey, wing (plovers), charm (finches), exaltation (larks); shoal, school; unit, brigade 722 *formation*; batch, lot, clutch; brace, pair, span 90 *duality*; leash, four-in-hand 96 *quaternity*; set, class, genus, species, subs. 77 *sort*; breed, tribe, clan, household 11 *family*; brotherhood, sisterhood, fellowship, guild, union 706 *association*; club 708 *society*; sphere, quarter, circle 524 *informant*; charmed circle, coterie 644 *elite*; social group, the caste system, the classes 868 *nobility,* 869 *commonalty*; in-group, us and them, they 80 *self*; age group, peer g., year g., stream 538 *class*; hand (at cards), set 71 *series.*

band, company, troupe; cast 594 *actor*; brass band, dance b., pop group, rock g. 413 *orchestra*; team, string, fifteen, eleven, eight; knot, bunch; set, coterie, clique, ring; gang, squad, party, work p.; crew, complement, manpower, workforce, staff 686 *personnel*; following 67 *retinue*; squadron, troop, platoon; unit, regiment, corps 722 *formation*; squad, posse; force, body, host 722 *armed force,* 104 *multitude*; (Boy) Scouts, Girl Guides 708 *society*; band of brothers, sisters, merry men 880 *friendship*; committee, commission 754 *consignee*; panel 87 *list.*

crowd, throng 104 *multitude*; huddle, cluster, swarm, colony; knot, bunch; the masses, the hoi polloi, mass, mob, ruck 869 *rabble*; sea of faces, full house 54 *completeness*; congestion, press, squash, squeeze, jam, scrum, rush, crush; rush hour 680 *haste*; flood, spate, deluge, stream, streams of 32 *great quantity*; volley, shower, hail, storm; infestation, invasion 297 *ingress.*

bunch, assortment, lot, mixed l. 43 *medley*; clump, tuft, wisp, handful; pencil (of rays), fan; bag 194 *receptacle*;

hand (tobacco), bundle, packet, wad; batch, pack, package, parcel; portfolio, file, dossier 548 *record*; bale, roll, bolt; load, pack 193 *contents*; fascine, faggot; fascicle; tussock, shock, sheaf, stook, truss, heap; swathe, rick, stack 632 *storage*; thicket, copse 366 *wood*; bouquet, nosegay, posy, spray; skein, hank.

accumulation, agglomeration, conglomeration; massing, amassment; concentration, centralization; pileup 279 *collision*; pile, heap; snowdrift; snowball 36 *increment*; debris, detritus 41 *leavings*; dustheap, midden, dump 641 *rubbish*; cumulus, storm cloud 355 *cloud*; store, storage 633 *provision*, 799 *treasury*; magazine, battery, armoury, quiver 723 *arsenal*; bus garage, car park, parking lot; set, lot 71 *series*; mixed lot, mixed bag 43 *medley*; kit, gear, stock; range, selection, assortment 795 *merchandise*; display 522 *exhibit*; museum 632 *collection*; menagerie, aquarium 369 *zoo*; literary collection 589 *library*; miscellanea, miscellany, compilation 56 *composition*; symposium, festschrift 591 *dissertation*.

Vb. *congregate,* meet, forgather, rendezvous; assemble; associate, come together, get t., join t., flock t., gather, gather round, collect, troop, rally, roll up, swell the ranks; resort to, centre on, focus on, zero in on, make for 293 *converge*; band together, gang up; mass, concentrate; conglomerate, huddle, cluster, bunch, crowd; throng, swarm, seethe, mill around; surge, stream, flood 36 *grow*; swarm in, infest, invade.

bring together, assemble, put together, draw t. 45 *join*; draw 291 *attract*; gather, collect, rally, muster, call up, mobilize; concentrate, consolidate; collocate, lump together, group, brigade, unite; compile 56 *compose*; bring into focus, focus, zero in on, centre; convene, convoke, convocate, summon, hold a meeting; herd, shepherd, get in, whip in, call in, round up, corral 235 *enclose*; mass, aggregate, rake up, dredge up; accumulate, conglomerate, heap, pile, amass; catch, take, rake in, net 771 *acquire*;

scrape together, garner 632 *store*; truss, bundle, parcel, package; bunch, bind 45 *tie*; pack, cram, stuff 54 *fill*; build up, pile up, stack 310 *elevate*.

Adv. *together,* as one, in a oner; collectively, all together, en masse.

75 Nonassembly. Dispersion – N. *dispersion,* scattering, diffraction, breakup 46 *separation*; branching out, fanning o., spread, scatter, radiation 294 *divergence*; sprawl, suburbia; distribution 783 *apportionment*; delegation, decentralization, regionalization; disintegration 51 *decomposition*; evaporation 338 *vaporization,* 337 *liquefaction*; dissipation 634 *waste*; circulation, diffusion; dissemination, broadcasting; spraying, sprinkling; dispersal; disbandment, demobilization.

Vb. *be dispersed,* disperse, scatter, spread, fan out, thin o. 325 *rarefy*; spread like wildfire, be rampant, flood; radiate, branch, branch out 294 *diverge*; break up, break ranks, fall out 46 *separate*; break away 49 *come unstuck*; hive off, go each his *or* her own way 267 *wander*; drift away, drift apart; straggle, trail, fall behind 282 *stray*; spread over, sprawl over, cover, litter 226 *overlie*; explode, blow up, burst, fly apart; evaporate, melt 338 *vaporize,* 337 *liquefy*; disintegrate, dissolve, decay 51 *decompose*.

disperse, scatter, diffract; spread out, splay 294 *diverge*; separate 46 *sunder*; thin out, string o.; disseminate, diffuse, broadcast, sow, strew, spread; dissipate, dispel, disintegrate 51 *decompose*; scatter to the winds 634 *waste*; dispense, deal, deal out, dole out, allot 783 *apportion*; decentralize, regionalize; break up, disband, disembody, demobilize, dismiss, send home 46 *disunite*; draft, draft off, hive off, detach 272 *send*; sprinkle, splash, spray, spatter 341 *moisten*; circulate. rout 727 *defeat*.

76 Focus: place of meeting – N. *focus,* focal point, junction, town centre, city c. 293 *convergence,* 225 *centre*; crossroads; switchboard, exchange, nerve centre;

hub, nub, core, heart, kernel 70 *middle*; civic centre, community c., village hall, village green, town square; campus, quad; market place 796 *market*; stamping ground; club, pub, local 192 *tavern*; headquarters, HQ, depot; rallying point; venue, rendezvous, trysting place 192 *meeting place*; fireside, campfire; cynosure, centre of attraction, honeypot 291 *attraction*; place of pilgrimage, Mecca, Lourdes, Rome, Zion, promised land 295 *goal*, 617 *objective*.

Vb. *focus,* centre on 293 *converge*; centralize, concentrate, focus upon, zero in on; point to.

77 Class – N. classification,

categorization 62 *arrangement*; taxonomy; diagnosis, specification, designation; category, class, bracket; set, subset; head, heading, subhead, section, subsection 53 *subdivision*; division, branch, department, faculty; pocket, pigeonhole, slot 194 *compartment*; tier, rank, caste, status, social class, standing 27 *degree*; province, domain, field, sphere, range; sex, gender; blood group, age g., stream 74 *group*; coterie, clique 74 *band*; persuasion, school of thought, denomination 978 *sect*.

sort, order, type, version, variety, kind, species; manner, genre, style; nature, quality, grade, calibre 5 *character*; mark, brand 547 *label*; ilk, stripe, kidney, feather, colour; stamp, mould, shape, frame, make 243 *form*; assortment, kit, gear, set, suit, lot 71 *series*.

breed, strain, blood, family, kin, tribe, clan, sept, caste, line 11 *race*, 169 *genealogy*; kingdom, phylum, class, order, genus, species, subspecies; genotype, monotype.

78 Inclusion – N. inclusion,

comprising; incorporation, embodiment, assimilation, encapsulation; comprehension, admission, integration 299 *reception*; admissibility, eligibility; membership 775 *participation*; inclusiveness, coverage, full c., blanket c. 79 *generality*; all-

roundness, versatility 694 *skill*; comprehensiveness; set, complete s., complement, package 52 *whole*; package deal 765 *compact*; constitution 56 *composition*; accommodation 183 *room*.

Adj. *inclusive,* including, comprising, counting, containing, having; holding, consisting of; incorporating; fully-furnished, all-inclusive, all-in; overall, all-embracing 52 *comprehensive*; wholesale, blanket, sweeping 32 *extensive*; total, across-the-board, global.

included, admitted, counted; admissible, eligible; integrated; constituent, making up; inherent 58 *component*, 5 *intrinsic*; belonging, pertinent 9 *relative*; classified with, in the same league 18 *similar*; 11 *akin*; entered, noted, recorded, on the list; merged 38 *additional*.

Vb. *be included,* be contained, be comprised, make one of; enlist, enrol oneself, swell the ranks, join 708 *join a party*; come under, go u., fall u.; merge in; appertain to, pertain, refer to 9 *be related*; come in, go in, enter into 297 *enter*; constitute 56 *compose*; overlap, inhere, belong 5 *be intrinsic*.

comprise, include, involve, mean, imply, consist of, hold, have, count, boast 56 *contain*; take, measure 28 *be equal*; receive, take in 299 *admit*; accommodate, find room for; comprehend, encapsulate, cover; embody, incorporate; encompass, embrace, encircle, envelop 235 *enclose*.

Adv. *including,* inclusively; from A to Z; et cetera.

79 Generality – N. generality,

universality; catholicity, catholicism; ecumenicity, ecumenicalism 976 *orthodoxy*; universalism; generalization, universal; macrocosm 321 *universe*; globalization, global view, world-view; panorama, synopsis, conspectus, bird's-eye view 52 *whole*; inclusiveness, dragnet 78 *inclusion*; prevalence, custom 610 *habit*, 848 *fashion*; pervasiveness, ubiquity 189 *presence*; pandemic, epidemic 651 *disease*; imprecision 495 *inexactness*, 464 *indiscrimination*; commonness, ruck,

run of the mill 30 *average*; ordinariness 732 *averageness.*

everyman, everywoman; man *or* woman in the street, Mr *or* Mrs average, man on the Clapham omnibus, joe soap. common type 30 *common man*; everybody, every one, each one, one and all, the long and the short and the tall, all and sundry, every mother's son, every man Jack, all hands 52 *all*; all the world and his wife, Tom, Dick and Harry, Uncle Tom Cobley and all, the masses, the hoi polloi, the rabble, 869 *commonalty*; all sorts, anyone, whosoever, N or M; anything, whatsoever, what have you, what you will 562 *no name.*

Adj. *general,* generic, typical, representative, standard; encyclopaedic, broad-based; collective, all-embracing, blanket, across-the-board 52 *comprehensive*; broad, sweeping, panoramic; prevalent 189 *ubiquitous*; usual, normal, run-of-the-mill, customary 610 *habitual*; vague, loose, indefinite 495 *inexact*; unspecified, impersonal 10 *unrelated*; common, ordinary, average 30 *median*; commonplace 83 *typical*; popular, mass, vulgar 869 *plebeian*; multipurpose.

universal, catholic, ecumenical; national, international, cosmopolitan, global, worldwide, nationwide, widespread 32 *extensive*; pervasive, prevalent, epidemic, pandemic 189 *ubiquitous*; every, each, any, all, all without exception 52 *whole.*

Vb. *generalize,* render general etc. adj.; broaden, widen, universalize, globalize; spread, broadcast, diffuse 75 *disperse.*

Adv. *generally,* without exception, universally etc. adj.; mainly; generally speaking, by and large; loosely, vaguely.

80 Speciality – **N.** *speciality,* personality, uniqueness; singularity 88 *unity*; originality, individuality, particularity; make-up 5 *character*; characteristic, one's middle name; idiosyncrasy, eccentricity, peculiarity, distinctive feature, trademark, mannerism, quirk, foible; trait, mark, feature, attribute; sine qua non 89 *accompaniment*; distinction, differentiae 15 *difference*; idiom; slang, jargon, brogue, patois 560 *dialect*; idiolect 557 *language*; version, lection 15 *variant*; exception, nonce word, special case 84 *nonconformity*; specialty, gift, special study, specialization 694 *skill.*

particulars, details, the nitty gritty, minutiae, items, special points, specification; circumstances; the ins and outs of.

self, ego, id, identity, selfhood, personality 320 *subjectivity*; psyche, soul 447 *spirit*; I, myself, number one, me generation; we, ourselves; yourself, himself, herself, itself, themselves; us, in-group 74 *group*; being 371 *person.*

Adj. *special,* specific, particular; peculiar, singular, unique 88 *one*; individual, idiosyncratic, characteristic, idiomatic, original 21 *inimitable*; personal, private; appropriate 24 *apt*; diagnostic 5 *characteristic*; distinctive, marked, out of the ordinary 84 *unusual.*

definite, definitive, defining; determinate, quantified, specified; distinct, concrete, explicit, clear-cut, cut and dried; certain, exact, precise 494 *accurate*; itemized, detailed.

private, intimate, esoteric, personal, personalized, exclusive; off the record, for one's private ear, confidential, secret 523 *latent.*

Vb. *specify,* enumerate, quantify 86 *number*; particularize, itemize, detail, 87 *list*; cite, reel off, mention, name names 561 *name*; enter into detail, spell out 570 *be diffuse*; define, determine 236 *limit*, 463 *discriminate*; pinpoint, locate 187 *place*; come to the point, explain 520 *interpret*; point out 547 *indicate*; realize, translate into fact, substantiate 156 *cause*; individualize, personalize 15 *differentiate*; specialize.

Adv. *specially,* especially, in particular; personally, for one's own part; specifically, ad hoc, to order.

severally, each, apiece, one by one; respectively, in turn; in detail, bit by bit.

namely, that is to say, videlicet, viz., to wit, i.e..

81 Rule – N. *rule,* norm, formula, canon, code; maxim, principle 693 *precept;* law, law of nature, universal principle; firm principle, hard and fast rule; strict law, law of the Medes and Persians; law of the jungle, sod's law, Murphy's law, Parkinson's law; unwritten rule *or* law, rule of thumb; statute, by-law 953 *law;* regulation, order, party line; guide, precedent, model, pattern 23 *prototype;* form, standard, keynote 83 *example.*

regularity, constancy 16 *uniformity; order;* 60 *order;* normality, normal state; form, routine, drill, practice, custom 610 *habit;* fixed ways, rut, groove; treadmill; methodicalness, method, system 62 *arrangement;* convention 83 *conformity.*

Adj. *regular,* constant, steady 141 *periodical;* even 258 *smooth;* standardized 16 *uniform;* regulated, according to rule, according to the rule-book, methodical, systematic 60 *orderly;* normal, unexceptional 83 *typical;* customary 610 *usual;* conventional 83 *conformable.*

82 Multiformity – N. *multiformity,* multiplicity; heterogeneity, variety, diversity 17 *nonuniformity;* multifariousness, many-sidedness 101 *plurality;* schizophrenia, split personality 503 *personality disorder;* changeability 152 *changeableness,* 437 *variegation;* Proteus, Jekyll and Hyde; kaleidoscope.

Adj. *multiform,* multifarious, polymorphous, polymorphic; multifid; multiple, multiplex, multiplicate, manifold, many-headed, many-sided, many-faceted, hydra-headed, protean, versatile, all-round; variform, heterogeneous, diverse 17 *nonuniform;* motley, mosaic, kaleidoscopic 43 *mixed;* many-coloured 437 *variegated;* divers, sundry; of all sorts and kinds 15 *different;* changeable 152 *changeful;* schizophrenic.

83 Conformity – N. *conformity,* conformation 24 *conformance;* faithfulness 768 *observance;* accommodation, adjustment, reconciliation, conciliation 24 *agreement, adaptation;* malleability 327 *softness;* acquiescence 721 *submission;*

assimilation, acclimatization, naturalization 147 *conversion,* 18 *similarity;* conventionality 848 *etiquette;* traditionalism; orthodoxness 976 *orthodoxy;* formalism, strictness 735 *severity;* convention, form 848 *fashion,* 610 *practice;* emulation 106 *repetition,* 925 *flattery,* 20 *imitation;* ordinariness 79 *generality.*

example, exemplar, type, pattern, model 23 *prototype;* exemplification, stock example, classic e.; case, case in point, instance; illustration, practical demonstration, object lesson; sample, random s., cross-section; representative, specimen, representative selection; trailer, teaser, foretaste 66 *precursor;* precedent.

conformist, conventionalist, traditionalist; company man; formalist, copycat, yes-man 20 *imitator,* 925 *flatterer;* follower, loyalist.

Adj. *conformable,* adaptable, adjustable; malleable, pliant 327 *flexible;* accommodating 24 *agreeing;* conforming, following, faithful, loyal, true-blue 768 *observant;* conventional, traditional 976 *orthodox;* slavish, servile 20 *imitative.*

typical, normal, natural, of daily occurrence, everyday, ordinary, common, common or garden 79 *general;* average 30 *median,* 732 *middling;* true to type; commonplace, prosaic; conventional; habitual 610 *usual;* representative, standard; exemplary.

Vb. *conform,* correspond, conform to 24 *accord;* adapt oneself, accommodate o., adjust o., mould o.; fit in; bend, yield, take the shape of 327 *soften;* fall into line, toe the l., fall in with 721 *submit;* comply with 768 *observe;* fit in with 24 *accord;* stick to the rules, obey regulations, follow precedent 739 *obey;* keep in step, follow the fashion, follow the trend, follow the crowd, do as others do, do as the Romans do; join in the cry, jump on the bandwagon, keep up with the Joneses 848 *be in fashion;* follow suit 20 *imitate, copy;* drift with the tide, swim with the stream 601 *be irresolute;* keep to the beaten track, run on tramlines, run in a groove, stick in a rut 610 *be wont.*

make conform, conform, assimilate, naturalize 18 *liken*; acclimatize 610 *habituate*; systematize 62 *regularize*; normalize, conventionalize, standardize; drill 16 *make uniform*; train, lead 689 *direct*; bend, twist, force 740 *compel*; accommodate, fit, fit in, trim, cut down to size, knock *or* lick into shape 24 *adjust*.

exemplify, illustrate, cite, quote, reel off, instance.

84 Nonconformity – N. *nonconformity,* nonconformance, unconformity, inconsistency 25 *disagreement*, 17 *nonuniformity*; contrast 14 *contrariety*; exceptionality, strangeness 59 *extraneousness*; nonconformism, unorthodoxy 977 *heterodoxy*; disconformity, dissidence 489 *dissent*, 769 *nonobservance*; deviationism 744 *independence*; anomalousness, eccentricity, irregularity 282 *deviation*; unconventionality; freakishness, oddity; rarity 140 *infrequency*; infringement, infraction 954 *illegality*; breach of practice; wonder, miracle 864 *prodigy*; anomaly, exception 57 *exclusion*; exemption, escape clause 919 *nonliability*; special case 80 *speciality*; individuality, trait, idiosyncrasy, quirk, kink, peculiarity, singularity, mannerism; uniqueness 21 *originality*.

abnormality, aberration 282 *deviation*; mutation 15 *variant*; abortion, teratogenesis, monstrosity, monster; sexual abnormality, bisexuality; homosexuality, lesbianism, Sapphism; fetishism, necrophilia, sadism, masochism, sadomasochism; transvestism, gender bending; hermaphroditism 161 *impotence*.

nonconformist, dissident, deviationist, dissenter, maverick 489 *dissentient*, 977 *heretic*, 978 *sectarian*; blackleg, scab 938 *cad*; unconventionalist, Bohemian, hippie, beatnik, dropout; rebel, angry young man, punk, recalcitrant 738 *revolter*; contra; fanatic 504 *crank*; outlaw, criminal 904 *offender*; pariah 883 *outcast*; hermit, loner 883 *solitary*; gypsy, nomad, tramp, bag lady 268 *wanderer*; odd man out, joker; square peg in a round hole, fish out of water 25 *misfit*; deviant, mutant, albino, freak, monster, oddity, original, character, card, caution, odd customer, queer c., oddball, weirdo 504 *crank*; queer fish 851 *laughingstock*; curiosity, rarity; neither fish, flesh, fowl nor good red herring; transsexual, hermaphrodite; homosexual, lesbian, lez *or* les, gay; pansy, fairy, nancy, poof, poofter, homo, fruit, queen, queer; dyke *or* dike; transvestite, drag artist, gender-bender 143 *transformation*; pervert, perv; sadist, masochist, sadomasochist; mongrel, cur 43 *hybrid*.

rara avis, unicorn, phoenix, griffin, roc; sphinx, hippogriff, chimera, centaur, Minotaur; dragon, wyvern, firedrake, cockatrice, basilisk, salamander, hydra; sea serpent, leviathan, kraken, Loch Ness monster; merman, mermaid, siren, Lorelei; gorgon, cyclops 970 *mythical being*; Snark, Jabberwocky, hobbit 513 *fantasy*.

Adj. *unconformable,* unmalleable 326 *rigid*, 602 *obstinate*; recalcitrant 711 *defiant*; eccentric; a law to oneself 744 *independent*; freakish, outlandish; unique 80 *special*; solitary 883 *unsociable*; blacklegging; nonconformist, dissident 489 *dissenting*, 978 *sectarian*; unorthodox, heretical; nonpractising 769 *nonobservant*; unconventional, weird, offbeat, Bohemian, hippie, beatnik, irregular, not done; infringing, lawless, criminal 954 *illegal*; aberrant, off the rails; misplaced, out of one's element, out of place, ectopic, out of order; incongruous, out of step, out of line, out of tune, out of keeping 25 *disagreeing*; alien, exotic, 59 *extraneous*; wandering; ambiguous 518 *equivocal*.

unusual, uncustomary, unwonted 611 *unhabituated*; unfamiliar 491 *unknown*; newfangled 126 *new*; exotic 59 *extraneous*; out of the ordinary, extraordinary, way-out; phenomenal; unparalleled; singular, unique 80 *special*, 140 *infrequent*; rare, choice, recherché 644 *excellent*; strange, bizarre, curious, odd, queer, rum, unco; funny, peculiar, fantastic, grotesque 849 *ridiculous*; noteworthy,

remarkable, surprising, astonishing, miraculous 864 *wonderful*; mysterious, inexplicable, unaccountable 523 *occult*; unimaginable, incredible 470 *impossible*, 472 *improbable*; monstrous, teratoid, teratological; unnatural, preternatural, supernatural; outsize 32 *enormous*; outré.

abnormal, unnatural, supernatural, preternatural (see *unusual*); aberrant, teratological, teratoid, freakish; uncharacteristic, untypical, atypical, unrepresentative, exceptional; anomalous 17 *nonuniform*; kinky, deviant; homosexual, lesbian, lez *or* les, gay, bent, queer; bisexual, AC/DC; epicene, androgynous, gynandrous; mongrel, hybrid 43 *mixed*; irregular; solecistic; nonstandard, substandard, below par, subnormal; supernormal 32 *great*; asymmetrical, deformed, amorphous, shapeless 246 *distorted*.

Vb. *be unconformable,* - unconventional etc. adj.; not fit in, be a fish out of water, be a square peg, be out of one's element; be the exception that proves the rule; infringe custom; break a law, commit a breach of etiquette, break a habit, break with custom; violate a law; drop out, freak o., do one's own thing 744 *be free*; make an exception; leave the beaten track.

Section five: Number

85 Number – N. *number,* real number, imaginary n.; natural n., cardinal n., ordinal n.; round n., complex n.; prime n., odd n., even n., whole n., integer; irrational n., transcendental n.; numeral, cipher, digit, figure, character; numerals, Arabic n., Roman n., algorithm; decimal system, binary s.; quantity, unknown q., unknown, X, symbol, constant; mapping; operator, sign; function, variable, argument; vector, matrix, tensor, quaternion; surd; expression, equation, quadratics; formula, series; set.

numerical element, minuend, subtrahend; multiplicand, multiplier; coefficient, multiple, dividend, divisor, aliquant, aliquot; quotient, factor, submultiple, fraction, proper f., improper f., vulgar f.; mixed number; numerator, denominator; decimal, recurring d., repetend; common factor, common denominator; reciprocal, complement; parameter; power, root, square r., cube r.; exponent, index, logarithm, natural l., mantissa, antilogarithm; modulus, differential, derivative, integral, integrand, determinant, fluxion.

ratio, proportion; progression, arithmetical progression, geometrical p., harmonic p.; trigonometrical ratio, sine, tangent, secant; cosine, cotangent, cosecant; percentage, per cent, percentile.

numerical result, answer, product, equation; sum, total, aggregate 52 *whole*; difference, residual 41 *remainder*; bill, score, tally 38 *addition*.

Adj. *numerical,* numerary, numeral, digital; arithmetical; cardinal, ordinal; round, whole; even, odd; prime; figurate; positive, negative, surd, radical; divisible, aliquot; multiple; reciprocal, complementary; fractional, decimal; incommensurable; commensurable, proportional; exponential, logarithmic, differential, fluxional, integral; algebraic, transcendental; rational, irrational.

86 Numeration – N. *numeration,* numbering, enumeration, census, counting, ciphering, figuring, reckoning, calculating, computing; sum, tally, score; count, countdown; summation, calculation, computation 465 *measurement*; pagination; algorithm, decimal system; accountancy 808 *accounts*; poll, capitation; head-count.

mathematics, pure m., applied m., arithmetic, algebra; quadratic equations; set theory, modern maths; differential calculus, integral c., infinitesimal c., vector c.; fluxions; calculus of variations; topology; geometry, trigonometry; graphs, logarithms; algorithm, systems

analysis (see *data processing*); operational research, critical path analysis, linear programming 623 *policy*; axiomatics 475 *reasoning*.

statistics, figures, tables, averages; mode, mean 30 *average*; significance, deviation, normal d., standard d., standard error; distribution curve, skew; regression; correlation, rank c. test, chi-squared t.; statistical enquiry, market research, poll, Gallup p. (tdmk) 605 *vote*; census, capitation; roll call, muster, muster roll, account 87 *list*; demography, birth rate, death r.; vital statistics; price index, retail p. i., cost of living, cost-of-living index 809 *price*; bar graph, histogram, scatter diagram, pie chart, flow c. 623 *plan*; cartogram 551 *map*.

data processing, electronic d. p., EDP, computing, computation, computer literacy; computer technology, cybernetics; software, program, computer p.; input, output, throughput, feedback; storage, retrieval; batch processing, time-sharing, multiprogramming, downtime; machine code, computer language, hardware (see *counting instrument*); keyboard, keypad, mouse; data, bit, byte; magnetic tape, floppy disk, disk drive; processor, word processor; central processing unit; database, data bank, memory, menu, visual display unit, VDU, visual display terminal, VDT 445 *appearance*; hard copy, printout; viewdata, Prestel (tdmk), Ceefax (tdmk), Oracle (tdmk), teletext 524 *information*.

counting instrument, abacus; ready reckoner, multiplication table; tape measure, yardstick 465 *gauge*; sliding rule, slide r.; Cuisenaire rods, Napier's bones *or* rods; comptometer, adding machine, calculating m., calculator, electronic c., pocket c.; cash register, till, totalizator, tote; computer, digital c., analogue c; mainframe; minicomputer, microcomputer, microprocessor, personal computer, home c., desk-top c., lap-top c..

Adj. *statistical,* expressed in numbers, digital, ciphered, numbered; mathematical, arithmetical, algebraical; geometrical, trigonometrical; in ratio, in proportion, percentile, quartile.

computerized, automatic, robotic, electronic, on-line, off-line; programmable; real-time, random-access, on-screen, user friendly; analogue, digital, binary, alphanumeric.

Vb. *number,* cast, count, reckon, calculate, compute, tell; score, keep the s., notch up; tick off, count down; paginate; enumerate, poll, count heads, count hands; take a poll, take a census; muster, take roll call; take stock, inventory 87 *list*; go over 106 *repeat*; check, audit, balance, keep accounts 808 *account*; aggregate, amount to, add up to, total, tot up to, come to.

computerize, automate; digitize, digitalize; program, process; debug; compute, log on, key in, keyboard, dump, log off 173 *operate*.

87 List – N. *list,* enumeration; inventory, stock list; chart, table, catalogue, listing; portfolio 767 *security*; statement, schedule, manifest, bill of lading; checklist; invoice; score; price list, tariff, bill, account 809 *price*; registry, Domesday Book; file, register 548 *record*; ticket, docket, tag, tally 547 *label*; ledger, books; table of contents, index, card i. 547 *indication*; menu, 86 *data processing*; bill of fare, menu 301 *eating*; playbill, programme, prospectus, synopsis, syllabus 592 *compendium*; roll, electoral r., voting list 605 *electorate*; payroll; Army List, Navy L., active l. 686 *personnel*; census 86 *numeration*; book list, bibliography 589 *reading matter*; rota, roster, panel; waiting list, short l., short leet; dramatis personae; family tree, pedigree 169 *genealogy*; scroll, roll of honour, martyrology, beadroll, diptych; blacklist 928 *accused person*, 924 *censure*; sick list 651 *sick person*; book of days, calendar, engagement book, diary 505 *reminder*; questionnaire; alphabetical list, A-Z, alphabet 60 *order*.

word list, vocabulary, glossary, lexicon, thesaurus 559 *dictionary.*

directory, gazetteer, atlas; almanac, calendar, timetable 117 *chronology*; Bradshaw, ABC 524 *guidebook*; Army List, Navy L., Crockford, Debrett, Burke's Peerage, Who's Who 589 *reference book*; telephone directory, phone book, Yellow Pages.

Vb. *list,* enumerate; itemize, reel off, inventory, catalogue, index, tabulate; file, docket, schedule, enter, book 548 *register*; enlist, matriculate, enrol, empanel, inscribe.

88 Unity – N. *unity,* oneness, absoluteness 44 *simpleness*; integration, wholeness 52 *whole*; uniqueness, individuality 80 *speciality*; monotheism; monism; singleness 895 *celibacy*; isolation, solitude, loneliness 883 *seclusion*; union, undividedness, indivisibility, solidarity 48 *coherence,* 706 *association*; unification 50 *combination.*

unit, integer, one, ace, item, article, piece; individual, atom, monad, entity 371 *person*; single piece, monolith; nonce word; isolated case, only exception; solo, monologue; single person, single, bachelor, bachelor girl 895 *celibate*; single parent 896 *divorce*, hermit, lone wolf, loner 883 *solitary*; set, kit, outfit, package 78 *inclusion.*

Adj. *one,* singular, sole, single, solitary; unique, only, lone, one and only; unrepeated, only-begotten; one-off, custom-built; a, an, a certain 562 *anonymous*; individual 80 *special*; absolute, universal 79 *general*; unitary, unific, univocal, unicameral, unilateral, unicellular; unisex; mono-; monolithic 16 *uniform.*

alone, lonely, homeless, orphaned, deserted, abandoned, forsaken; lonesome, solitary, lone 883 *unsociable*; isolated; insular 199 *distant*; single-handed, on one's own; by oneself, on one's tod; unaccompanied, unescorted, unchaperoned; celibate.

Adv. *singly,* one by one, one at a time; once, once only, once and for all, for the nonce, just this once, never again, only, solely, simply; alone, on one's own, by oneself, per se.

89 Accompaniment – N. *accompaniment,* concomitance 71 *continuity*, 45 *union*, 5 *intrinsicality*; inseparability; society 882 *sociability*; companionship, togetherness 880 *friendship*; partnership, marriage 706 *association*; coexistence 181 *concurrence*; coincidence, contemporaneity, simultaneity 123 *synchronism*; attendance, company; parallel course 219 *parallelism.*

concomitant, attribute, sine qua non 5 *essential part*; complement 54 *completeness*; accessory, appendage, appurtenance, fixture 40 *adjunct*; by-product, corollary; symptom, syndrome 547 *indication*; coincidence 159 *chance*; context, circumstance 7 *state*; background; accompaniment, obbligato; accompanist 413 *musician*; entourage, court 742 *retainer*; attendant, following, suite 67 *retinue*; groupie, camp follower; convoy, escort, guide 690 *leader*; chaperon, bodyguard 660 *protector*, 749 *keeper*; suitor, wooer 887 *lover*; tracker 619 *hunter*; inseparable, shadow, tail 284 *follower*; consort, cohabitee, lover 894 *spouse*; comrade, companion, boon c., best friend 880 *friend*; stable companion, mate, co-worker, partner, associate 707 *colleague*; accomplice 707 *collaborator*; twin, pair, fellow 18 *analogue*; satellite, parasite, hanger-on 742 *dependant.*

Vb. *accompany,* coexist; cohabit, live with, keep company w., consort w., walk out w.; string along with; bear one company, squire, chaperon, protect 660 *safeguard*; convoy, escort, guide, conduct, lead, usher 64 *come before*; track, dog, tail, shadow 619 *pursue*; associate with, partner 706 *cooperate*; gang up with, chum up w. 880 *befriend*; carry with, bring in its train, bring in its wake 156 *cause*; be inseparable, go hand in hand with, follow as night follows day 157 *depend*; belong, go with, go together 9 *be related.*

Adv. *with,* together with, along w., in company w.; in the same boat; hand in

hand, arm in arm, side by side; cheek by jowl.

90 Duality – N. *duality,* dualism; double-sidedness; double life, dual personality, split p., Jekyll and Hyde; positive and negative, yin and yang 14 *polarity*; dyad, two, deuce, duo, twain, couple, Darby and Joan, Jack and Jill, Romeo and Juliet; brace, pair, couple; doublets, twins, Castor and Pollux, Gemini, Siamese twins, identical t., Tweedledum and Tweedledee 18 *analogue*; yoke; couplet; twosome, duel; duet; Janus.

Adj. *dual,* binary, binomial; bilateral, bicameral; twin, biparous; bisexual, double-barrelled, duplex 91 *double*; paired, coupled etc. vb.; two abreast, two by two; in twos, both; in pairs, tête-à-tête, à deux; double-sided, double-edged, bipartisan; amphibious; ambidextrous 91 *double*; bifocal; biform, two-dimensional, two-faced.

Vb. *pair,* couple, match, bracket, yoke; mate, pair off.

91 Duplication – N. *duplication,* doubleness; doubling 261 *fold*; reduplication, encore, repeat, iteration, echo, parrotry 106 *repetition*; renewal 656 *restoration*; copy, carbon c., photocopy, Xerox (tdmk) 22 *duplicate*; living image, look-alike 18 *analogue*.

Adj. *double,* doubled, twice; duplex; biform; twofold, two-sided, two-headed, two-edged; double-faced, two-faced; amphibious, ambidextrous; dual-purpose, two-way; ambiguous 518 *equivocal*; ambivalent; bisexual, AC/DC, hermaphrodite; twin, duplicate; dualistic 90 *dual*.

Vb. *double,* redouble, square; encore, echo, second 106 *repeat*; renew 656 *restore*; duplicate, twin; reduplicate, stencil, xerox, photocopy 20 *copy*.

92 Bisection – N. *bisection,* bipartition, dichotomy; dividing by two, halving etc. vb.; hendiadys; half, moiety, fifty per cent 53 *part*; hemistich; hemisphere 252 *sphere*.

bifurcation, forking, branching, furcation 294 *divergence*; swallowtail, fork, prong 222 *cross*.

dividing line, diameter, diagonal, equator; parting, seam; date line; party wall, garden fence 231 *partition*.

Adj. *bisected,* halved etc. vb.; bifid, bipartite; bicuspid; bifurcated, forked; dichotomous; split, cloven.

Vb. *bisect,* transect; divide, split, cleave 46 *sunder*; cut in two, share, go halves, go fifty-fifty 783 *apportion*; halve, divide by two.

bifurcate, separate, fork; branch off, ramify 294 *diverge*.

93 Triality – N. *triality,* trinity; triplicity 94 *triplication*.

three, triad; Faith, Hope and Charity; threesome, triumvirate, troika; triplet, trio; trimester, triennium; trefoil, shamrock, triangle, trident, tripod, trivet; three-wheeler, tricycle; three-headed monster, Cerberus; triphthong, triptych, trilogy; third power, cube; third person; Third World.

Adj. *three,* triform, trinomial; three in one, tripartite; tricolour; three-dimensional, three-sided, triangular, deltoid, trigonal, trilateral; three-pointed; trifoliate, three-leaved *or* leafed; three-pronged, three-cornered; tricorn, tricuspid; three-monthly, trimestrial, quarterly.

94 Triplication – N. *triplication,* triplicity; trebleness; hat trick; tercentenary.

Adj. *treble,* triple; trine, trinal, ternary; triplex, triplicate, threefold, three-ply; third, tertiary; trihedral; trilateral.

Vb. *treble,* triple, triplicate, cube.

95 Trisection – N. *trisection,* tripartition, trichotomy; third, third part; tierce.

Vb. *trisect,* divide into three parts, divide by three; trifurcate.

96 Quaternity – N. *quaternity,* four, tetrad, tetrarchy; square, tetragon, quadrilateral, quadrangle, quad; tetrahedron; quadrature, quarter; fylfot, swastika 222

cross; tetrapod; tetrameter, quatrain; tetragram; quartet, foursome; four winds, four evangelists; four-in-hand, quadriga; quatrefoil; quadruplet, quad; quadruped, tetrapod; quadrennium; four corners of 52 *whole*.

Adj. *four,* quaternary, quadratic; quadrate, square, quadrilateral, tetrahedral, foursquare; four-footed, quadrupedal; quadrennial.

97 Quadruplication – N. *quadruplication,* quadruplicity; squaring; quatercentenary.

Adj. *fourfold,* quadruple, quadruplicate, quadruplex; squared.

Vb. *quadruple,* quadruplicate, multiply by four; square, quadrate.

98 Quadrisection – N. *quadrisection,* quartering, fourth, fourth part; quarterly; quart, quarter; farthing, quarto.

Vb. *quadrisect,* quarter, divide into four parts, divide by four.

99 Five and over – N. *five,* cinque, quintuplet, quin; quintet; pentagon, pentagram; pentameter; Pentateuch; pentathlon; cinquefoil; quinquereme; five senses, Five Towns, Cinque Ports; five-a-side; a bunch of fives.

over five, six, half-a-dozen, sextet, hexad, sixer; hexagon, hexagram; Hexateuch; hexameter; seven, heptad, week, sabbatical year; septennium; septenary, septet; pleiad; Heptateuch; Seven Deadly Sins, Seven Wonders of the World, Seven Seas; eight, octave, octet, octad; octagon; one over the eight, piece of eight, figure of eight; nine, three times three; nonary; novena; nine Muses, nine days' wonder; ten, tenner, decade; decagon, decahedron, Decalogue; Ten Commandments; eleven, hendecasyllable; twelve, dozen; dodecahedron; twelve apostles, the Twelve, twelve tribes; thirteen, baker's dozen, double figures, teens.

twenty and over, twenty, a score; icosahedron; four and twenty, two dozen; twenty-five, pony; forty, two score; fifty,

half a hundred, jubilee; sixty, three score; sexagenarian; seventy, three score and ten, septuagenarian; eighty, four score, octogenarian; ninety, nonagenarian.

hundred, century, ton, centenary, centennial; hundredweight; centurion; centenarian; centipede; the hundred days; Old Hundredth; hundred per cent; treble figures.

over one hundred, a gross; hundreds and hundreds; thousand, grand; millennium; ten thousand, myriad; hundred thousand, lakh; million; ten million; thousand million, milliard; billion; million million; trillion, quadrillion, centillion, multimillion; zillion.

100 Multisection – N. *multisection,* decimation.

Adj. *multifid,* multipartite; decimal, tenth, tithe; duodecimal, twelfth; sexagesimal, sexagenary; hundredth, centesimal; millesimal.

Vb. *multisect,* decimate, decimalize.

101 Plurality – N. *plurality,* the plural; multiplicity 104 *multitude*; many-sidedness 82 *multiformity*; polygon, polyhedron; polytheism; a number; a few; majority.

Adj. *plural,* composite, multiple; polydactyl, polypod; multiparous; polymorphic, multiform; many-sided; multilateral, multipurpose; in the majority 104 *many*.

102 Fraction: less than one – N. *fraction,* decimal f. 85 *numerical element*; fragment 53 *part*, 783 *portion*; shred 33 *small quantity.*

Adj. *fractional,* partial 53 *fragmentary*, 33 *small.*

103 Zero – N. *zero,* nil, zilch, nothing, simply n., next to nothing, naught, nought, nix; no score, love, duck, blank; cipher; nothingness 2 *nonexistence*, 4 *insubstantiality*; none, nobody, not a soul 190 *absence*; nadir, rock bottom.

Adj. *not one,* not any, zero; infinitely little, null 4 *insubstantial,* 2 *nonexistent.*

104 Multitude – **N.** *multitude,* numerousness, multiplicity; large number, million 99 *over one hundred*; lots, loads, heaps, masses 32 *great quantity*; numbers, scores, myriads, millions, trillions, zillions; a sea of, a mass of, a world of, a sight of; forest, thicket; host, array, fleet, battalions 722 *army*; throng, mob, all the world and his wife 74 *crowd*; tribe, horde.

Adj. *many,* myriad, several, sundry, divers, various, a thousand and one; quite a few, a good f.; considerable, numerous, very many, a good many, ever so m., many more, no end of, umpteen, n; untold, unnumbered, innumerable, uncounted 107 *infinite*; multifarious, manifold 82 *multiform*; ever-recurring 139 *frequent,* 106 *repeated*; much, ample, multiple; profuse, in profusion, abundant, superabundant, generous, lavish, overflowing, galore 635 *plentiful,* 32 *great.*

multitudinous, massed, crowded, thronged 54 *full*; populous, peopled, populated, high-density 324 *dense*; teeming, crawling, humming, lousy with, hotching w., alive w., bristling w. 171 *prolific*; thick, thick on the ground, thick as flies; coming thick and fast 139 *frequent*; incalculable, innumerable, inexhaustible, countless, endless 107 *infinite.*

Vb. *be many,* - various etc. adj.; swarm with, crawl w., hum w., bristle w., teem w., be hotching w., be lousy w., be alive w. 54 *fill*; clutter, crowd, throng, swarm, mass, flock, troop 74 *congregate*; swarm like ants, swarm like locusts, swarm like bees round a honey-pot; flood, overflow, snow under, swamp, overwhelm 637 *superabound*; infest, overrun; swell the ranks 36 *augment*; outnumber, make a majority 32 *be great.*

105 Fewness – **N.** *fewness,* paucity; exiguity, thinness, sparsity, sparseness, rarity 140 *infrequency*; scantiness 636 *scarcity*; a few, a handful; wisps, tuft; poor turnout; small number, trickle, soupçon, smidgen 33 *small quantity*; limited number, no quorum; minority, one or two, not enough to matter, a derisory amount.

Adj. *few,* precious few, scant, scanty, little 636 *scarce*; thin on the ground, sparse, rare, low-density, few and far between 140 *infrequent*; not many, hardly any; to be counted on the fingers of one hand; too few, in a minority, without a quorum.

Vb. *be few,* be few in number, be underpopulated; seldom occur.

render few, reduce, diminish, pare 198 *make smaller*; scale down, slim down, cut back, decimate; eliminate, weed, thin, sort out 300 *eject*; understaff.

Adv. *here and there,* in dribs and drabs, in twos and threes, in a trickle; sparsely, rarely, infrequently.

106 Repetition – **N.** *repetition,* iteration, reiteration; doubling, ditto, reduplication 20 *imitation,* 91 *duplication*; recapitulation; renewal, resumption, reprise 68 *beginning*; saying again, repeating, anaphora 574 *ornament*; tautology, redundancy 570 *diffuseness*; stammering, stuttering 580 *speech defect*; repeat, repeat performance, encore; second helping, seconds; playback, replay, return match, revenge; chorus, refrain 412 *vocal music*; echo, repercussion, reverberation 404 *resonance*; quotation, plagiarism; hardy annual (see *recurrence*); old story, chestnut 838 *tedium*; reprint, reissue 589 *edition*; remake, rehash, recast, revival 656 *restoration.*

recurrence, repetitiveness 139 *frequency*; cycle, round, return, rebirth, renaissance, reincarnation 141 *regular return*; succession, run, series, serial 71 *continuity*; recurring decimal, repetend; throwback, atavism 5 *heredity*; reappearance, comeback, curtain call; rhythm, drumming, hammering 141 *periodicity*; alliteration, assonance, rhyme 18 *assimilation,* 593 *prosody*; 838 *tedium*; same old round, mixture as before, rehash, routine 610 *habit.*

Adj. *repeated,* repetitional; recurrent, recurring, ever-r. 141 *periodical*; haunting 505 *remembered*; tautological, redundant, repetitive, repetitious, harping, iterative; stale, cliché-ridden 572 *feeble*; echoing, rhyming, alliterative, assonant 18 *similar*; monotonous, singsong 16 *uniform*, 838 *tedious*; rhythmical, drumming, hammering; incessant, habitual 139 *frequent*; retold, said before, quoted, cited; above-mentioned, aforesaid 66 *precursory*; plagiarized 20 *imitative*; reheated, rehashed, recycled.

Vb. *repeat,* do again, iterate, cut and come again; duplicate, reduplicate, redouble 91 *double*; multiply 166 *reproduce*; reiterate, say again, recapitulate, go over, ring the changes on; retell, restate, reword, rephrase; trot out; recite, reel off, say over, say after; echo, ditto, parrot, plagiarize 20 *copy*, 925 *flatter*; quote, cite 505 *remember*; go over the same ground, retrace one's footsteps, practise, rehearse; play back, rerun, rewind; recycle, reprocess; begin again, restart, resume 68 *begin*; replay, give an encore; reprint, reissue, republish; rehash, remake, renew, revive 656 *restore*; reheat.

again, afresh, anew, over again, for the second time, once more; ditto; encore; de novo.

107 Infinity – N. *infinity,* infiniteness, boundlessness, limitlessness, illimitability; infinite space, outer s. 183 *space*; eternity 115 *perpetuity*.

Adj. *infinite,* indefinite; immense, measureless; eternal 115 *perpetual*; countless, innumerable, immeasurable, illimitable, interminable; incalculable, unfathomable, incomprehensible, unapproachable, beyond comprehension; inexhaustible, without number, without limit, without end, no end of; without measure, limitless, endless, boundless; untold, unnumbered 104 *many*; unlimited.

Adv. *infinitely,* ad infinitum; indefinitely; immeasurably 32 *greatly*.

Section six: Time

108 Time – N. *time,* tide; tense 564 *grammar*; duration, extent 113 *long duration*; season, term, semester, tenancy, tenure; tour, shift, shot, spell, stint; span, space 110 *period*; a bit, a while; the whole time, the entire period, life, lifetime; eternity 115 *perpetuity*; passage of time, lapse of time, lapse, course 111 *course of time*; years, days; Time, Father Time, Time's scythe, Time's hourglass, sands of time, ravages of t., t. the enemy, t. the healer; fourth dimension; time zone; indefinite time; past time, past tense 125 *past time*, 119 *priority*; prospective time 124 *futurity*; contemporaneity 121 *present time*; recent time 126 *newness*; antiquity, distant time 127 *oldness*.

date, day, age, reign 110 *era*; vintage, year, time of life 117 *chronology*; birthday, Saint's day 141 *anniversary*; day of the week, calends, ides, nones; time of day 117 *clock time*; moment 116 *instant*; target date, zero hour, D-day; term, fixed day, quarter day, payday.

Adj. *continuing,* permanent 115 *perpetual*, in process of, pending; repetitive, recurrent 106 *repeated*; temporal 141 *periodical*.

Vb. *continue,* endure, drag on 113 *last*; roll on, pass 111 *elapse*; live through, sustain; stay, remain, abide, survive 113 *outlast*; wait 136 *be pending*.

pass time, vegetate, breathe, subsist, exist 360 *live*; age; spend time, consume t., use t., employ t. 678 *be busy*; while away time, kill t., summer, winter, weekend; waste time, fritter away t. 679 *be inactive*; mark time.

fix the time, date, put a date to, settle on a date for 117 *time*.

Adv. *while,* whilst, during, pending; day by day 113 *all along*; in the course of, so long as; for the time being, for now, meantime, meanwhile; between whiles, in the meantime, in the interim; from day to day, from hour to hour; hourly 139 *often*; for a time, for a season; till,

until, up to, yet; always, the whole time, all the time 139 *perpetually*; all along 54 *throughout*.

when, what time; one day, once upon a time, one fine morning; in the days of, in the time of, in the year of.

109 Neverness – N. *neverness,* Greek Calends; month of Sundays, blue moon, when pigs fly; jam tomorrow, mañana; dies non; eternity 115 *perpetuity.*

Adv. *never,* not ever, at no time, at no period, on no occasion; not in donkey's years; nevermore, never again; over one's dead body; never before, never in one's born days; without date, sine die.

110 Period – N. *period,* matter of time; season; time of day, morning, evening; time of year, spring, summer, autumn, fall, winter 128 *morning,* 129 *evening*; term; time up, full time 69 *finality*; spell, go, tour, stint, shot, shift, span, stretch, sentence; innings, turn; round, bout, lap; watch; length of time, second, minute, hour; particular time, rush hour; pause, interval; day, weekday, working day; week, working w., five-day w.; fortnight, month, calendar m., lunar m., quarter, trimester; half year, semester; twelve month, year, solar y., sidereal y., light y., leap y.; fiscal y.; quinquennium; decade, Gay Nineties, Hungry Thirties, Swinging Sixties; golden wedding, jubilee 141 *anniversary*; century, millennium.

era, time, period, generation, age, days; epoch; aeon; cycle, Ice Age; Stone A., Iron A., Dark Ages, Middle A. 125 *antiquity*; Renaissance, Age of Enlightenment, A. of Reason, belle époque, fin de siècle; modern times, Computer A., Space A.; Golden A., A. of Aquarius.

Adj. *periodic* 141 *seasonal*; hourly, annual, biennial, quinquennial, centennial; period 127 *olden.*

111 Course: indefinite duration – N. *course of time,* matter of t., process of t., lapse of t., march of t., flight of t.; duration 108 *time*, 146 *continuance.*

Vb. *elapse,* pass, lapse, flow, run, roll, proceed, advance, press on 285 *progress*; wear on, drag on, crawl 278 *move slowly*; flit, fly, fleet, slip, slide, glide 277 *move fast*; run its course; go by, pass by, slip by, fly past.

Adv. *in time,* in due time, in due season; in the course of time, in the process of t., in the fullness of t., with the years.

112 Contingent duration – Adv. *provisionally,* precariously, by favour; at the pleasure of; for the present; so long as it lasts; as *or* so long as.

113 Long duration – N. *long duration,* a long t., unconscionable t.; a month of Sundays, years, donkey's years, years on end, yonks; a lifetime; generations, a century, an age, ages, aeons 115 *perpetuity*; longevity 131 *old age*; corridor of t., antiquity 125 *past time.*

durability, lasting quality, endurance; stamina, staying power 162 *strength*; survival 146 *continuance*; permanence 153 *stability*; long standing, good age, ripe old a. 127 *oldness*; long run, long innings.

protraction, prolongation, extension; dragging out, spinning o., padding o., filibustering, stonewalling 702 *hindrance*, 715 *resistance*; interminability, long haul 136 *delay*, 278 *slowness*; extra time, injury t., overtime.

Adj. *lasting,* abiding; secular, agelong, lifelong, livelong; longtime, longstanding, inveterate, deep-seated, deep-rooted; of long duration, long-term, long-service, marathon 203 *long*; unconscionable; durable, enduring 162 *strong*; long-lived 127 *immemorial*; evergreen, unfading, fresh 126 *new*; eternal, perennial 115 *perpetual*; persistent, chronic 602 *obstinate*; indestructible 162 *unyielding*; constant, stable, permanent 153 *unchangeable.*

Vb. *last,* endure, stand, stay, remain, abide, continue 146 *go on*; defy time, stand the test of time, never end 115 *be eternal*; wear well 162 *be strong*.

outlast, outlive, outwear, outstay, survive; remain 41 *be left*; live to fight another day; have nine lives.

Adv. *for a long time,* long, for long, for ages, for years, since time immemorial, many a long day; for good, for ever, for all time, for better for worse; all one's life, from the cradle to the grave; till blue in the face; till the cows come home.

all along, all day, all day long, the livelong day, as the day is long; all the year round, round the clock; day in day out, year in year out; ever since.

long ago, long since, in the distant past, long long ago, when the world was young; in the past, in ancient days, in bygone times 125 *formerly.*

at last, at long last, in the end, in the long run, after many days, not before time.

114 Transience – N. *transience,* transientness, transitoriness 4 *insubstantiality*; impermanence; evanescence 446 *disappearance*; volatility 338 *vaporization*; fugacity 277 *velocity*; fragility 330 *brittleness*; mortality, perishability 361 *death*; frailty, fragility 163 *weakness*; mutability 152 *changeableness*; capriciousness, fickleness 604 *caprice*; suddenness 116 *instantaneity*; temporariness, interregnum.

brief span, short space of time, a minute or two, short while; briefness, momentariness, brevity 204 *shortness*; mortal span, short life and a merry one; summer lightning, shooting star, meteor, flash in the pan, nine days' wonder; ephemera, bubble, mayfly, snow on a dyke, snows of yesteryear, smoke in the wind; April shower, summer cloud 4 *insubstantial thing*; bird of passage, ship that passes in the night; brief encounter; short run 110 *period*, 277 *spurt*; spasm, moment 116 *instant.*

Adj. *transient,* temporal, impermanent, transitory, fading, passing 4 *insubstantial*; cursory, flying, fleeting, flitting, fugitive 277 *speedy*; volatile, written in water; evanescent; unsettled, restless; flickering, changeable 152 *changeful.*

ephemeral, of a day, short-lived, fleeting, disposable; mortal 361 *dying*; frail, fragile 163 *weak*, 330 *brittle*; impermanent, temporary.

brief, short-term, short-service 204 *short*; summary, short and sweet, to the point 569 *concise*; quick, fleet, brisk 277 *speedy*; sudden, momentary, meteoric, like a flash 116 *instantaneous*; hurried 680 *hasty.*

Vb. *be transient,* - transitory etc. adj.; not stay, not last; flit, fleet, fly, gallop 277 *move fast*; fade, flicker, vanish, evanesce, melt, evaporate 446 *disappear*; fade like a dream, flit like a shadow, pass like a summer cloud, burst like a bubble.

115 Perpetuity: endless duration – N. *perpetuity,* endless time 107 *infinity*; everlastingness; eternity, timelessness; never-endingness, interminability 113 *long duration*; endurance 144 *permanence*, 71 *continuity*; immortality 146 *continuance*; perpetuation, immortalization.

Adj. *perpetual,* perennial, longlasting, enduring, durable 113 *lasting*; agelong 127 *immemorial*; nonstop, constant, continual, ceaseless, incessant; flowing, ever-flowing, uninterrupted 71 *continuous*; dateless, ageless, unageing, unchanging, immutable 144 *permanent*; evergreen, unfading, everlasting; imperishable, undying, deathless, immortal; unending, never-ending, interminable; endless, without end, timeless, eternal.

Vb. *perpetuate,* make permanent, continue, establish; immortalize, eternalize.

be eternal, - perpetual etc. adj.; last for ever, endure for e., live for e.; go on for e., have no end, never cease.

Adv. *for ever,* in perpetuity, on and on; ever and always, for always and always, for aye, evermore, for ever and ever, for ever and a day; time without end, world without e.; for keeps, for good and all, for better for worse; to the end of time, till doomsday, to the crack of doom; to infinity 107 *infinitely.*

116 Instantaneity: point of time – N. *instantaneity,* instantaneousness, immediateness, immediacy; simultaneity 121 *present time*; suddenness, abruptness 508 *lack of expectation*; precise time 135 *punctuality*; momentariness 114 *transience.*

instant, moment, precise m., point, point of time; second, split s., half a s., tick, trice, jiffy, half a j., mo, half a mo; breath; burst, crack; stroke, coup; flash, lightning f.; twinkle, twinkling, the twinkling of an eye; two shakes, two shakes of a lamb's tail; the very moment, the very hour, the stroke of.

Adj. instantaneous, immediate, instant, sudden, abrupt, snap; quick as lightning, with the speed of light, quick as a flash, like a flash 277 *speedy.*

117 Chronometry – N. *chronometry,* chronoscopy, horology; watch-making; calendar-making, timetabling; timing, dating; timekeeping 108 *time.*

clock time, right time, BBC t., astronomer's t., solar t., sidereal t., Greenwich Mean T., G.M.T., British Standard T., British Summer T., B.S.T., local t., Central European T., continental t.; time of day, time of night; bedtime; summer time, double summer t., daylight saving t.

timekeeper, chronometer, timepiece; clock, dial, face; hand, pendulum 317 *oscillation*; electric clock, digital c., quartz c., long-case c., grandfather c., grandmother c., calendar c., carriage c., cuckoo c., alarm c., travelling alarm, travel clock, clock radio, alarum; Big Ben; water-clock; watch, ticker; fobwatch, hunter, repeater; wristwatch, digital watch, analogue w.; sundial; hourglass, sand-glass, egg timer; chronograph, chronoscope; time signal, pip, siren, hooter; gong, bell, five-minute b., time-clock, timer, stopwatch; Tim, speaking clock; parking meter, traffic light 305 *traffic control*; time fuse, time switch, time bomb; metronome.

chronology, dendrochronology; radiocarbon dating; dating; date, age, epoch, style 110 *era*; old style, O.S., new style, N.S.; almanac, calendar, perpetual c., fixed c., Gregorian c., Julian c.; ephemeris, astronomical almanac; chronicle, annals, book of days, diary, journal, logbook 548 *record*; date list, time-chart 87 *list*; tide-table, timetable, schedule 87 *directory.*

chronologist, chronographer, chronologer, calendar-maker, calendarist; chronicler, annalist, diarist 549 *recorder.*

Vb. *time,* clock; timetable, schedule; match times 123 *synchronize*; phase 24 *adjust*; set the alarm 669 *make ready*; calendar, chronologize, chronicle 548 *record*; date, be dated; measure time, mark t., beat t., keep t.; count the minutes, watch the clock; clock in 68 *begin*; clock out 145 *cease.*

Adv. *o'clock,* a.m., p.m.

118 Anachronism – N. *anachronism,* parachronism, wrong date, wrong day, chronological error; mistiming, previousness, prolepsis 135 *anticipation*; disregard of time, unpunctuality 136 *lateness*; neglect of time 506 *oblivion*; wrong moment 138 *untimeliness.*

Adj. anachronistic, misdated; antedated, foredated, previous, before time, too early 135 *early*; parachronistic, postdated 136 *late*; too late, overdue, unpunctual, behind time; out of due time, out of season, out of date, old-fashioned 127 *antiquated.*

119 Priority – N. *priority,* antecedence, previousness, preexistence; primogeniture, birthright; eldest, firstborn, son and heir; flying start 64 *precedence*; leading 283 *preceding*; the past, yesteryear, yesterday 125 *past time*; eve, day before; precedent, antecedent; foretaste, trailer, teaser, preview, prerelease; herald 66 *precursor*; prequel.

Adj. prior, earliest, first, first in the field, precedent 64 *preceding*; previous, earlier, anterior, antecedent; antediluvian, prehistoric; pre-Christian, BC; prewar, preexisting, prenatal, antenatal;

elder, eldest, firstborn; former, ci-devant, onetime, erstwhile, sometime, ex-, retired, emeritus; foregoing, aforementioned, above-mentioned; aforesaid, said; introductory, prefatory, preliminary 66 *precursory*; given, presupposed 512 *supposed*.

Vb. *do before,* presuppose 512 *suppose*; predecease, prefabricate, prearrange, preempt, prejudge, preview; be previous, anticipate, forestall, be beforehand with, jump the gun, jump the queue; steal a march on, have a start on 277 *outstrip*; lead 283 *precede*, 64 *come before*.

Adv. *before,* prior to, beforehand, by; just before, on the eve of; earlier, previously, formerly; ultimo, ult.; afore, ere; aforetime, ere now, before n.; ere then, before t., already, yet; in anticipation; until now, up to now, hitherto, heretofore.

120 Posteriority – **N.** *posteriority,* subsequence; succession 65 *sequence*, days to come, time to come 124 *futurity*; line, lineage, descent, successor, descendant 170 *posterity*; cadet; aftermath 67 *sequel*.

Adj. *subsequent,* posterior, following, ensuing, next, to come, after, later; last in date, junior, cadet, younger, youngest 130 *young*; successive, consecutive, consequent; succeeding, designate, to be 124 *future*; postnatal; posthumous; postwar; after Christ, AD; postprandial 65 *sequential*.

Vb. *ensue,* supervene, follow after 65 *come after*; go after 284 *follow*, 157 *result*; succeed, follow in the footsteps of, step into the shoes of 771 *inherit*.

Adv. *subsequently,* later, in the process of time; after, afterwards; at a later date; next, next time; thereafter, thereupon; since, from that time, from that moment; from the start, from the word 'go'; after a while, after a time; soon after, close upon; next month, proximo.

121 Present time – **N.** *present time,* contemporaneity, contemporaneousness, topicality 126 *modernism*; time being,

the present, present time, present day, present moment; this hour, this moment, this moment in time, this instant 116 *instantaneity*; juncture, opportunity, crisis 137 *occasion*; the nonce; the times, modern t., these days, this day and age; today, twentieth century, nowadays; one's age, present generation, one's contemporaries 123 *contemporary*.

Adj. *present,* actual, instant, current, extant 1 *existing*; of this date, of today's d.; topical, contemporary, contemporaneous; present-day, latter-day, latest, up-to-the-minute, up-to-date, bang up-to-date 126 *modern*.

Adv. *at present,* now, right now, at this time, at this moment, at this moment in time; live; at the present time, contemporaneously, contemporarily; today, nowadays; at this time of day, at this stage, even now; already, but now, just now; this time, on the present occasion; for the time being, for now, for the nonce; on the spot; now or never; now as always.

until now, to this day, to the present day, up to now, to date; through; from the start, from the word 'go' 113 *all along*.

122 Different time – **N.** *different time,* other times 124 *futurity*, 125 *past time*; another time, some other t., not now, not today, any time but this 109 *neverness*; parachronism 118 *anachronism*.

123 Synchronism – **N.** *synchronism,* synchrony; coexistence, coincidence, concurrence, concomitance 89 *accompaniment*; simultaneity, simultaneousness, same time 116 *instantaneity*; contemporaneity, contemporaneousness, same date, same day 121 *present time*; coevality, same age, twin birth 28 *equality*; level-pegging, neck-and-neck, nip and tuck, dead heat 28 *draw*; synchronization, sync, phasing, isochronism.

contemporary, coeval, twin 28 *compeer*; one's contemporaries, one's own generation; age group, peer g., class, year 74 *group*.

Adj. *synchronous,* synchronal; synchronic; contemporary, contemporaneous 121 *present,* 126 *modern*; simultaneous, coinstantaneous, coincident, coexistent, coeternal, conterminous, concomitant 24 *agreeing,* level, neck and neck 28 *equal*; matched in age, coeval, twin; of the same age, of the same year, of the same generation, of the same vintage; synchronized, timed, phased, isochronous, on the beat.

Vb. *synchronize,* sync, concur, coexist 89 *accompany*; encounter, coincide 295 *meet*; keep time 410 *harmonize*; say together, say in unison, chorus; tune, phase 24 *adjust*; be level-pegging, run neck and neck 28 *be equal*; pace, keep in step with; isochronize.

124 Futurity: prospective time – N. *futurity,* future tense; womb of time, time to come, days and years to come; morrow 120 *posteriority*; future, time ahead, prospect, outlook 507 *expectation*; coming events, fate 154 *event,* 155 *destiny*; near future, tomorrow, mañana, the day after tomorrow, next week, next year 121 *present time,* 200 *nearness*; advent 289 *approach*; long run, distant future 199 *distance*; future generations, descendants, heirs, heritage 170 *posterity*; successorship.

future state, what fate holds in store 155 *destiny,* 596 *fate*; latter days; doomsday, crack of doom 69 *finality*; afterlife, life after death, life to come, hereafter, kingdom come 971 *heaven*; damnation 972 *hell*; good time coming, mañana, jam tomorrow, millennium 730 *prosperity*; reincarnation 106 *repetition*.

Adj. *future,* to be, to come; coming 289 *approaching*; nigh, just round the corner, close at hand 200 *near*; on the horizon, in the wind; due, destined, fated, threatening, imminent, overhanging 155 *impending*; in the future, ahead, yet to come, waiting; in embryo, on the stocks 669 *preparatory*; prospective, designate, earmarked 605 *chosen*; promised, looked for, anticipated 507 *expected,*

471 *probable*; predicted, foreseeable; later, ulterior, posterior 120 *subsequent*.

Vb. *be to come,* lie ahead, lie in the future; have in store, be destined, threaten, overhang 155 *impend*; near, draw nigh 289 *approach*; be imminent, be just round the corner, cast its shadow before, stare one in the face.

henceforth, in future, from this time forth, from now on.

125 Past Time: retrospective time – N. *past time* 119 *priority*; retrospection, looking back 505 *remembrance*; past tense, historic t., preterite, perfect, pluperfect 564 *grammar*; the past, recent p., only yesterday 126 *newness*; distant past, history, antiquity; old story, matter of history 127 *oldness*; past times, days of yore, days of old, olden days, good old d., bygone d.; auld lang syne, yesterday, yesteryear, former times.

antiquity, rust of a., eld; creation, when time began, when the world was young, time immemorial; prehistory, protohistory, ancient world, mediaeval times; Stone Age, prehistoric a.; Dark Ages, Middle A. 110 *era*; the ancients, cavemen, Neanderthal man 371 *humankind*; relics, neolith, microlith, 41 *remainder*; 127 *archaism*; ruin, ancient monument, megalith, Stonehenge 548 *monument,* 253 *earthwork*; excavation, dig, archaeology 484 *discovery*; museum 632 *collection*; ancient lineage 169 *genealogy*.

fossil, fossilized remains *or* relics, petrified forest, trilobite, ammonite; trace fossil 548 *record*; coal forest 385 *fuel*; sponge, coral 358 *organism*; Neanderthal man 371 *humankind*; mammoth, dinosaur 365 *animal*.

palaeology, palaeontology, palaeozoology, palaeography; palaeoanthropology 371 *humankind*; archaeology; antiquarianism.

antiquarian, palaeontologist, archaeologist; palaeologist, palaeographer; antiquary 492 *scholar*; historian, prehistorian; medievalist 549 *chronicler*; Egyptologist, classicist 557 *linguist*.

Adj. *past,* in the p., historical; ancient, prehistoric 127 *olden*; early, primitive 127 *primal*; gone, gone for good, bygone, lost, dead and buried 506 *forgotten*; passed away, no more, died out, dead as the Dodo 2 *extinct*, 361 *dead*; passé, has-been, obsolete 674 *disused*, 127 *antiquated*; fossilized 326 *hard*; over, blown o., done, over and done with, behind one; elapsed, lapsed, expired, run out, ended, finished 69 *ending*.

former, late, quondam, sometime, ex- 119 *prior*; retired, emeritus, outgoing.

foregoing, last, latter 64 *preceding*; recent.

retrospective, looking back, backward-looking; reminiscing 505 *remembering*; historical; retroactive, going back; with hindsight, from experience.

Vb. *be past,* have elapsed, have expired; have run its course, have had its day, be burnt out; pass, die, elapse, blow over, be o., be at an end 69 *end*; be a dead letter.

Adv. *formerly,* aforetime, of old, of yore; time was, ago, in olden times; long ago, long since; a long while, a long time ago; once upon a time; years ago, ages a.; lately, some time ago, some time back; yesterday, the day before yesterday; yestreen, yesteryear; last year, last season, last month, last week.

126 Newness – **N.** *newness,* recentness; recent date, recent occurrence, recent past 125 *past time,* 121 *present time*; innovation 560 *neology*, 21 *originality*; novelty, freshness, dewiness 648 *cleanness*; greenness, immaturity, callowness, rawness 130 *youth*; renovation, restoration, renewal, resurrection 656 *revival*; clean slate, new leaf, new broom.

modernism, modernity, modernness, modernization; up-to-dateness, topicality, contemporaneity 121 *present time*; the latest, the latest thing, the in-thing, latest fashion; the last word, dernier cri; new look, contemporary style, trendiness 848 *fashion*.

modernist, neologist, neoteric, futurist; advanced thinker, avant-garde; bright young thing, trendy, yuppy, babyboomer; modern generation, younger g.

Adj. *new,* newish, recent, of recent date, of recent occurrence; upstart, parvenu, nouveau arrivé, nouveau riche, mushroom; novel, inventive, innovative, unprecedented, unheard of 21 *original*; brand-new, spick and span, like new, in mint condition 648 *clean*; green, evergreen, dewy, juicy; fresh, fresh as a daisy, fresh as paint; maiden, virgin, virginal; newborn 130 *young*; raw, unfledged, callow 670 *immature*; just out, just published, hot from the press; new-made, new-laid; straight from the oven, factory-fresh; untouched by human hand; unused, first-hand; untried, untrodden, unbeaten, unexplored 491 *unknown*; untested 461 *experimental.* aspiring 68 *beginning*.

modern, late, latter-day; contemporary, topical 121 *present*; up-to-the-minute, up-to-date, bang up-to-date, with it; à la mode, in the latest fashion, trendy 848 *fashionable*; ultramodern, modernistic, advanced, avant-garde, futuristic, revolutionary; innovating, innovative, neoteric, newfangled, new-fashioned.

Vb. *modernize,* do up, renovate, refurbish; update, bring up to date, give a new lease of life; have the new look, go modern, go contemporary, get with it; move with the times 285 *progress*.

127 Oldness – **N.** *oldness,* primitiveness 68 *beginning*; olden times 110 *era*; age, eld; dust of ages, ruins 125 *antiquity*; maturity, mellowness 129 *autumn*; decline, rust 51 *decay*; senility 131 *old age*.

archaism, antiquities 125 *antiquity*; ancien régime; thing of the past, relic of the p.; listed building, ancient monument; museum piece, antique, heirloom, bygone, Victoriana; dodo, dinosaur 125 *fossil*; golden oldie; old fogy, old fossil, fuddy-duddy. archaist, square, old-timer, has-been, back number.

tradition, lore, folklore, mythology; inveteracy, custom 610 *habit*; common law; word of mouth 579 *speech*.

Adj. *olden,* old, ancient, antique, antiquarian; veteran, vintage; venerable; archaic, ancient; time-worn; prehistoric, mythological; feudal, medieval; historical 125 *past*, 866 *renowned.*

primal, prime, primitive, primeval, primordial, aboriginal 68 *beginning*; fossil, palaeozoic; eolithic, palaeolithic, mesolithic, neolithic; early, antediluvian, before the Flood.

antiquated, of other times, of another age, archaic; old as the hills, old as Methuselah, old as time, age-old 113 *lasting*; old-world, old-time; olde worlde, ye olde; prewar 119 *prior*; anachronistic 125 *retrospective*; fossilized, ossified; behind the times, out of date, out of fashion, dated, antediluvian, before the Flood, out of the ark, horse-and-buggy, silent-screen, black-and-white; conservative, Victorian, old-fashioned, old-school, square, not with it; outworn, outdated, outmoded; passé, démodé, vieux jeu, old hat; gone by 125 *past*; perished 655 *dilapidated*; mouldering; obsolete, obsolescent; superannuated 674 *disused*; old 131 *ageing.*

Vb. *be old,* - antiquated etc. adj.; belong to the past, have had its day, be burnt out 69 *end*; age; decline, fade, wither 655 *deteriorate.*

128 Morning. Spring. Summer – **N.** *morning,* morn, forenoon, a.m.; small hours, wee sma' hours 135 *earliness*; matins; dawn, dawning, cockcrow, dawn chorus 66 *precursor*; sunrise, sun-up, daybreak 417 *light*; peep of day, break of d.; first blush of day; daylight, daytime; full day, full light of day; Aurora, rosy-fingered Dawn; daystar, orb of day 321 *sun.*

noon, high noon, meridian, midday, noonday, noontide; eight bells, twelve o'clock, twelve noon.

spring, springtime, springtide, Eastertide, vernal season, spring s., seed-time, blossom-time, maying; first cuckoo; vernal equinox, first point of Aries.

summer 379 *heat*; summertime, summertide, Whitsuntide; midsummer,

summer solstice, Midsummer's Day, high summer, dog days; haymaking; aestivation; Indian summer.

129 Evening. Autumn. Winter – **N.** *evening,* eventide, even, eve, dewy e.; evensong, vespers, afternoon, p.m.; matinée; afternoon tea, five o'clock; sundowner, soirée; dog-watches; sunset, sundown, setting sun, going down of the sun; evening star, Hesperus, Vesper; dusk, crepuscule, twilight, gloaming 419 *half-light*; candlelight, cockshut, dewfall; moonrise, moonset 321 *moon*; close of day, nightfall, dark, night-time, night-owl 418 *darkness*; bedtime 679 *sleep*; curfew, last post 136 *lateness*, 69 *finality.*

midnight, dead of night, witching time; night-watch, small hours.

autumn, back-end, fall, harvest, harvest-time; harvest moon; Michaelmas; Indian summer.

winter 380 *wintriness*; wintertime, wintertide; yuletide, Christmas; midwinter, winter solstice; hibernation; nuclear winter.

Adj. *wintry,* winter, brumal, brumous, snowbound 380 *cold*; stark, bleak.

130 Youth – **N.** *youth,* freshness 126 *newness*, 174 *vigorousness*; young blood, youthfulness, youngness, juvenility; babyhood, infancy, childhood, childish years, tender age 68 *beginning*; puppyhood; boyhood, girlhood; one's teens, adolescence, pubescence, age of puberty, boyishness, girlishness, awkward age, growing pains; younger generation, rising g. 132 *youngster*; growing boy *or* girl, minor, ward; Peter Pan.

nonage, tender age, immaturity, minority, infancy, pupillage, wardship; cradle, nursery, kindergarten.

salad days, school d., student d., college d., happiest days of one's life; heyday, heyday of the blood, springtime of youth; prime of life, bloom of youth, florescence.

Adj. *young,* youthful, childlike, boyish, girlish; virginal, maidenly, sweet-sixteen; adolescent, pubescent; teenage,

preteen, juvenile; maturing, developing, growing; budding, burgeoning, blooming, flowering; unripe, green, callow, awkward, raw, unfledged 670 *immature*; school-age, under-age, minor, infant, pre-school; younger, minor, junior, cadet; youngest; childish; juvenescent; young at heart, ageless.

131 Age – N. *age,* time of life, years, lifespan 113 *long duration.*

middle age, middle years, middle life; years of discretion 134 *adultness*; maturity, prime of life; a certain age, climacteric, change of life, the change, menopause, male m., mid-life crisis; middleaged spread.

old age, anno domini; pensionable age, retirement age; advanced years, three-score years and ten, allotted span, grey hairs, white hairs 133 *old person*; senescence, declining years, vale of years, evening of one's days, autumn *or* winter of life; infirmity, debility 163 *weakness*; second childhood, dotage, senility, Alzheimer's disease 655 *deterioration*; longevity, ripe old age.

seniority, old man's privilege 64 *precedence*; primogeniture 119 *priority*; higher rank 34 *superiority*; doyen; gerontocracy, elders, presbytery, senate 692 *council.*

gerontology, nostology, geriatrics, care of the aged 658 *therapy*, old people's home, sheltered housing, eventide home.

Adj. *ageing,* aged, old, elderly, matronly; middle-aged, ripe, mature, mellow 669 *matured*; overblown, overripe, run *or* gone to seed; of a certain age, not so young as one was, no chicken; past one's prime, getting on, getting old, going grey, greying; white-haired, grey-h., hoary, hoary-headed, long in the tooth; senescent, waning, declining, moribund 361 *dying*; wrinkled, lined, marked with crow's feet, rheumy-eyed, toothless, shrivelled, wizened, decrepit, rickety; drivelling, doddering, gaga 499 *foolish*; senile, failing; advanced in years, stricken in y., living on borrowed time,

with one foot in the grave; longeval, old as the hills, old as Methuselah; well-preserved 650 *healthy*; venerable, patriarchal; too old, past it; retired 681 *leisurely*; superannuated, passé(e) 127 *antiquated*; gerontologic, geriatric.

older, major; elder, senior 34 *superior*; firstborn, eldest, primogenital 119 *prior*; eldest, maximus.

132 Young person. Young animal. Young plant – N. *child,* children, small fry; babe, baby, bundle of joy; infant, nursling, suckling, weanling, fosterling; bairn, little one, tiny tot, little chap, mite, moppet, toddler; brat, kid, kiddie; papoose, bambino; little darling, little angel, little monkey, little imp; cherub, young innocent; changeling. See *young creature.*

youngster, juvenile, young person, young adult, young hopeful, young'un; young people 130 *youth*; boy, schoolboy, stripling, adolescent; youth, young man, lad, laddie, sonny; urchin, nipper, cub, young shaver, whippersnapper; yob; Ted, mod, rocker, punk, skinhead; girl, young woman; schoolgirl, lass, lassie, missie, wench, maid, maiden, virgin; chit, slip, chick, miss; teenager, teenybopper, weenybopper, groupie; tomboy, hoyden; little minx, baggage; colleen, mademoiselle, damsel, nymph, nymphet. See *young creature.*

young creature, young animal, yearling, lamb, kid, calf, heifer; piglet; fawn, colt, foal, filly; kitten; puppy, pup, whelp, cub; chick, chicken, pullet; duckling, gosling, cygnet 365 *animal, bird*; fledgling, nestling, fry, litter, farrow, clutch, spawn, brood; larva, pupa, nymph; caterpillar, grub; chrysalis, cocoon; tadpole; embryo, foetus 156 *source.*

young plant, seedling, set; sucker, runner, spur, shoot, offshoot, sprout, slip; twig, sprig, scion, sapling 366 *plant.*

133 Old person – N. *old person,* elderly p., retired p., pensioner, old-age p., O.A.P., senior citizen; old dear, old body.

old man, elderly gentleman, patriarch, elder statesman; grandfather, grandad 169 *paternity*; veteran, old soldier, old hand, old stager, old trouper, old-timer 696 *expert*; old'un, old boy, gaffer; old geezer, o. codger, o. buffer, dotard; old fogy.

old woman, elderly lady, dowager; grandmother, grandma, gran, granny; old girl, old trout, old duck, old bag; old dutch 894 *spouse*; no spring chicken, mutton dressed as lamb; gammer, crone, hag.

old couple, Darby and Joan.

134 Adultness – N. *adultness,* adulthood, grown-upness, development; years of discretion, matureness; age of consent, legal age, majority, man's *or* woman's estate; manhood, womanhood, virility, nubility 372 *male*, 373 *female*; key of the door; maturity, prime of life 131 *middle age*.

adult, grown-up, big boy *or* girl; man, gentleman 372 *male*; woman, lady, matron 373 *female*.

Adj. *grown-up,* adult, of age, at the age of consent, old enough to know better; mature, fully-developed, full-grown 669 *matured*; nubile; virile, manly 372 *male*; womanly, matronly 373 *female*; full-blown, full-fledged; in one's prime, adult, X-rated, 18.

135 Earliness – N. *earliness,* early hour, unearthly h.; early stage, primitiveness 68 *beginning*; early riser, early bird; first arrival 66 *precursor*; original settler, earliest inhabitant 191 *native*.

punctuality, timeliness 137 *occasion*; promptitude 678 *activity*; immediacy 116 *instantaneity*.

anticipation, a stitch in time 510 *foresight*, 669 *preparation*; prematurity, precocity; forestalling 64 *precedence*.

Adj. *early,* bright and e., good and e., in the small hours, in the wee sma' hours;

timely, in time, on t., in good t., punctual, prompt; forward, in advance; precocious, ahead of its time 126 *new*; immediate 116 *instantaneous*, 508 *unexpected*; coming shortly, forthcoming, ready 669 *prepared*; imminent, at hand 200 *near*; premature 670 *immature*.

Vb. *be early,* - premature etc. adj.; be betimes, be beforehand etc. adv.; nip in the bud; forestall, preempt 64 *come before*; take the opportunity, take time by the forelock; steal a march on, catch napping 306 *outdo*; engage, book, reserve; secure, order; lose no time 680 *hasten*; jump the gun.

Adv. *betimes,* early, soon; before long; first thing, at the first opportunity; with time to spare; punctually, to the minute, in time, in good time.

beforehand, in advance; precipitately; precociously, prematurely, untimely, too soon.

suddenly, without notice 508 *unexpectedly*; forthwith, right away; at the drop of a hat.

136 Lateness – N. *lateness,* late hour, small hours, wee sma' hours 129 *midnight*; eleventh hour, last minute; backwardness, slow development 670 *non-preparation*, 499 *unintelligence*; tardiness, lagging, dragging one's feet 278 *slowness*; afterthought, delayed reaction; latecomer; late developer 538 *learner*; late riser 278 *slowcoach*; laggard 679 *idler*; Fabius Cunctator.

delay, cunctation, Fabian policy 858 *caution*; delaying tactics, gaining time, stonewalling, filibustering 113 *protraction*, 702 *hindrance*; deceleration 278 *slowness*; holdup 747 *restraint*; postponement, adjournment, cooling-off period; pause, time lag, jet lag 145 *lull*; deferment, moratorium, respite, days of grace; suspension, stay of execution; reprieve 752 *abrogation*; putting off, procrastination, mañana 679 *sluggishness*; dilatoriness, bureaucracy, red tape 678 *overactivity*; shelving, putting on ice, putting on hold, putting on the back-burner, cold storage 679 *inactivity*.

Adj. *late,* late in the day, eleventh-hour, last-minute, deathbed; too late, time up; overdue, delayed, belated, benighted; held up, bogged down 702 *hindered*; behindhand, lagging, behind time, behind schedule; sluggish, tardy; backward 278 *slow*; Fabian 858 *cautious*; unpunctual; procrastinating, dilatory 679 *inactive*; delayed-action; deferred etc. vb.; on ice, on hold, in cold storage, on the back-burner, posthumous 120 *subsequent*.

Vb. *be late,* sit up late, rise late, keep late hours, burn the midnight oil, burn the candle at both ends; lag behind 284 *follow*; drag one's feet, linger, loiter 278 *move slowly*; hang back 679 *be inactive*; miss a chance, miss the boat, oversleep 138 *lose a chance*; be behindhand, have leeway to make up, have a backlog; not move with the times; lose, stop (clock).

wait 507 *await*; bide one's time, hold one's horses, take one's time, wait and see 145 *pause*; sleep on it 677 *not act*; hang fire; hang on, hold on, hold the line; stand about, sit a., hang a.; be kept waiting, wait impatiently, cool one's heels, play the waiting game; count to ten.

put off, defer, postpone, adjourn; hold over; file, pigeonhole; table; shelve, put in cold storage, keep on ice, put on the back-burner; hold in abeyance; procrastinate, protract, delay, retard, set back, hold up, gain time, stonewall, filibuster; temporize, tide over; stall, keep one waiting.

Adv. *late,* after time, behind t.; late in the day, at sunset, at the eleventh hour, at the last minute, last thing; at length, at last, at long l., ultimately; till all hours; too late.

137 Occasion: timeliness – N. *occasion,* happy chance 154 *event*; juncture 181 *concurrence*; timeliness, opportuneness, ripeness; fittingness 24 *fitness*, right time; auspicious hour, right moment, nick of time.

opportunity, favourable opportunity, golden o. 469 *possibility*; one's chance, break, lucky moment, piece of luck 159

chance; opening, look-in, field 744 *scope*; freedom of choice 744 *freedom*; convenience, clear field 159 *fair chance*; stepping-stone 624 *bridge*.

crisis, critical time, key moment; turning point, psychological moment, crucial m., crux, emergency, extremity; eleventh hour, last minute 136 *lateness*; the chips are down.

Adj. *timely,* in time, within the time limit; on time, to the minute, on the dot, punctual 135 *early*; well-timed; just in time, not before time, in the nick of t., at the eleventh hour.

opportune, favourable, providential, heaven-sent, auspicious, propitious; fortunate, lucky, happy 730 *prosperous*; fitting 24 *apt*.

crucial, critical, key, momentous, climactic, pivotal, decisive 638 *important*.

Vb. *profit by,* seize *or* grab the chance, take the opportunity, create an opening; take time by the forelock, carpe diem, strike while the iron is hot, make hay while the sun shines; cash in on, capitalize, exploit, turn to good account 673 *use*.

incidentally, by the way, by the by; en passant, apropos; parenthetically, by way of parenthesis; while speaking of, while on this subject, talking of, that reminds me.

138 Untimeliness – N. *untimeliness,* wrong time, inopportuneness 643 *inexpedience*; mishap, contretemps; evil hour 731 *misfortune*; off day, time of the month; disturbance 72 *discontinuity*; mistiming 118 *anachronism*.

Adj. *ill-timed,* mistimed, ill-judged, ill-advised; out-of-turn, untimely, untoward; malapropos, inconvenient 25 *unapt*, 643 *inexpedient*; unseasonable, unpunctual, not in time 136 *late*; premature, too soon for 135 *early*.

inopportune, untoward, inauspicious, unpropitious, unfavourable, ill-omened, ill-starred, unlucky, unhappy, unfortunate 731 *adverse*.

Vb. *mistime,* time it *or* things badly 481 *misjudge*; disturb, find engaged.

be engaged, be busy, be occupied, be not at home; be otherwise engaged, have a previous engagement, have other fish to fry 678 *be busy.*

lose a chance, miss the bus, miss the boat 728 *fail;* bungle 695 *be unskilful;* lose one's chance, let the opportunity slip 136 *be late;* let slip through one's fingers 458 *neglect;* stand in one's own light, shut the stable door after the horse has bolted 695 *act foolishly.*

139 Frequency – N. *frequency,* rapid succession 71 *continuity;* oftenness, unfailing regularity 141 *periodicity;* redoubling 106 *repetition;* frequenting, haunting, regular visits.

Adj. *frequent,* recurrent 106 *repeated;* common, of common occurrence 104 *many;* thick on the ground 104 *multitudinous;* continual, constant, steady; regular 141 *periodical;* haunting, frequenting, assiduous 610 *habitual.*

Vb. *recur 106 reoccur;* do nothing but; keep, keep on 146 *go on,* frequent, haunt 882 *visit;* pester 827 *trouble.*

Adv. *often,* oft, many a time, time after t., time and time again, times without n.; a thousand t.; frequently, commonly, generally; more often than not; not infrequently, again and again; in quick succession, in rapid succession; thick and fast; regularly, daily, hourly; ad libitum.

perpetually, continually, constantly, incessantly, steadily, without respite 71 *continuously;* at all times, night and day, day and night, day after day, day in, day out, morning, noon and night.

sometimes, occasionally, every so often, once in a while; at times, now and then, now and again, every now and again; from time to time.

140 Infrequency – N. *infrequency,* rarity 105 *fewness;* seldomness, uncommonness; intermittence 72 *discontinuity.*

Adj. *infrequent,* uncommon, sporadic, occasional; intermittent, few and far between 72 *discontinuous;* scarce, rare, scarce *or* rare as hen's teeth 105 *few;* like

gold dust 811 *of price;* almost unheard of, unprecedented 84 *unusual.*

Adv. *seldom,* little, once in a while; rarely, scarcely, hardly, only occasionally; not often, infrequently; scarcely ever, hardly e., once in a blue moon, once in a month of Sundays; few and far between.

141 Periodicity: regularity of recurrence – N. *periodicity,* regularity, rhythm, steadiness, evenness 16 *uniformity;* timing, phasing, serialization 71 *continuity;* alternation, turn and turn about, shot about; reciprocity 12 *correlation;* ebb and flow, alternating current, AC, wave movement 317 *fluctuation;* to-and-fro movement, pendulum m., piston m., shuttle m.; shuttle service; shuttle diplomacy; pulsation, pulse, tick, beat, throb, rhythm, swing 317 *oscillation;* chorus, refrain 106 *recurrence;* drumbeat, tattoo 403 *roll;* tide 350 *wave;* frequency, wave f.; turn, go, round, circuit, lap; shift, relay 110 *period,* cycle.

regular return, rota, cycle, circuit, revolution, life cycle, wheel of life 314 *circuition,* 315 *rotation;* biorhythm; menstrual cycle, menses; yearly cycle, seasons 128 *morning,* 129 *evening;* fixed interval 110 *period;* routine, daily round 60 *order,* 610 *habit.*

anniversary, birthday, saint's day, jubilee, silver j., diamond j., wedding anniversary, silver wedding, ruby w., golden w.; diamond w., centenary, bicentenary; St George's Day, St Andrew's D., St Patrick's D., St David's D., St Valentine's Day 988 *holy day;* Fourth of July, Independence Day, 14 Juillet, Bastille Day 876 *special day.*

Adj. *periodical,* periodic, cyclic, revolving; fluctuating; rhythmical, steady, even, regular, constant, punctual, clocklike, like clockwork 81 *regular;* breathing, pulsating, throbbing, beating; recurrent, intermittent, sporadic, spasmodic, on-again-off-again 106 *repeated;* reciprocal, alternate, alternating 12 *correlative;* serial, successive, serialized 65 *sequential,* 71 *continuous.*

seasonal, anniversary; hourly, daily, nightly, diurnal, quotidian, tertian, biweekly, weekly, hebdomadal, hebdomadary, fortnightly, monthly; menstrual; yearly, annual, biennial, triennial, quadrennial, quinquennial, sextennial, septennial, octennial, decennial; bissextile; centennial, sesquicentennial, bicentennial, tercentennial, quadricentennial, quincentennial, millennial; secular.

Adv. *periodically,* rhythmically etc. adj.; at regular intervals; at fixed periods; punctually etc. adj.; seasonally, hourly, daily, weekly, monthly, yearly; per diem, per annum; at intervals, intermittently, sporadically, spasmodically, fitfully, every now and then, every so often, every once in a while.

142 Fitfulness: irregularity of recurrence
– N. *fitfulness,* irregularity 61 *disorder*; fits and starts 17 *nonuniformity*, 318 *spasm*; remission 114 *transience*, 72 *discontinuity*; unsteadiness, variability 152 *changeableness*, 143 *change*; capriciousness, unpredictability 604 *caprice*; eccentricity; lurching 317 *oscillation*.

Adj. *fitful,* periodic, intermittent, on-off, on-again-off-again, stop-go 72 *discontinuous*; irregular 84 *unconformable*; uneven 29 *unequal*; occasional 140 *infrequent*; unsteady, unstable, fluttering 17 *nonuniform*; inconstant, variable 152 *changeful*; spasmodic, jerky, restless; halting, wavering, flickering, unsystematic; erratic 604 *capricious*; moody.

Section seven: Change

143 Change: difference at different times
– N. *change,* alteration, variation 15 *difference*; mutation, permutation, modulation, inflexion, declension; mutability, variability 152 *changeableness*; modification, adjustment, process, treatment 468 *qualification*; sea change 147 *conversion*; sudden change 149 *revolution*; break, break with the past, innovation, new look 126 *newness*; winds of change; change for the better, reformation 654 *improvement*; change for the worse 655 *deterioration*; change of direction, U-turn, diversion, shift, turn 282 *deviation*, 286 *regression*; relocation, change of position, transition 305 *passage*; translation, transposition 272 *transference*, 151 *interchange*; alternation 141 *periodicity*; overthrow 221 *inversion*; change of mind, c. of heart 603 *change of mind.*

transformation, transfiguration; transmogrification; sea change, metamorphosis, metasomatism; metabolism, anabolism, catabolism; transmutation, transubstantiation 147 *conversion*; transmigration of souls; reincarnation, avatar; version, adaptation, transcription, translation 520 *interpretation*, 521 *misinterpretation.*

Adj. *changeable,* variable, mutable; fickle 604 *capricious*; affected, changed etc. vb.; newfangled 126 *new*; transitional, provisional, alternative, transmutative; chequered, kaleidoscopic 437 *variegated.*

Vb. *change,* be changed, alter 152 *vary*; wax and wane 36 *grow*, 37 *decrease*; change one's clothes; change colour, change countenance 426 *lose colour*; change one's tune 603 *tergiversate*; vacillate, blow hot and cold, chop and change 604 *be capricious*; turn, shift, veer, change course, do a U-turn 282 *deviate*; relocate, seek pastures new, make a transition, pass to 305 *pass*; turn the corner 656 *be restored*; turn over a new leaf, be converted 654 *get better*; submit to change 83 *conform*; move with the times 126 *modernize.*

modify, alter, vary, modulate, diversify 437 *variegate*; superimpose 38 *add*; introduce changes, innovate 126 *modernize*; computerize, automate; turn upside down, subvert 149 *revolutionize*, 221 *invert*; reverse, turn back 148 *revert*; make changes, rearrange, reorder, reset 62 *arrange*; adapt 24 *adjust*; conform 83 *make conform*; recast, remould, reshape 243 *form*; process, treat; revise, edit, correct 654 *rectify*; reform 654 *make better*; revamp, patch, darn 656 *restore*; change for the worse 655 *pervert*; tamper

with, meddle w., spoil 655 *impair*; warp, bend, deform 246 *distort*; dye, discolour 425 *colour*, adulterate, doctor, qualify 43 *mix*, 163 *weaken*; cover, mask, disguise 525 *conceal*; change round, ring the changes 151 *interchange*, 272 *transpose*; effect a change, leaven 156 *cause*; turn the scale 178 *influence*; transform, transfigure, metamorphose, transmute, transubstantiate, 147 *convert*; metabolize, digest.

144 Permanence: absence of change– N. *permanence,* permanency, status quo; invariability, immutability 153 *stability*; persistence 600 *perseverance*; endurance, duration 113 *durability*, 115 *perpetuity*; fixity of purpose, immobility, intransigence 602 *obstinacy*; firmness, bedrock, foundation, solidity 324 *density*; conservation 666 *preservation*, 146 *continuance*; rule 81 *regularity*; fixed law, entrenched clause 153 *fixture*; standing, long s., inveteracy 127 *oldness*; tradition, custom, practice 610 *habit*; fixed attitude, conservatism; routine, rut 60 *order*.

Adj. *permanent,* enduring, durable 113 *lasting*; persisting, continuing, maintained; 115 *perpetual*; inveterate, rocklike, long-standing 127 *immemorial*; perpetuated, standing, well-established, entrenched, in with the bricks, fixed, unchangeable, immutable 153 *established*; well-preserved 666 *preserved*; unchanging, conservative, reactionary, dyed in the wool, true blue, diehard 602 *obstinate*; stationary, static, immobile 266 *quiescent*; always the s. 13 *identical*.

Vb. *stay,* come to stay, be here for good, set in, take root; abide, endure, subsist, outlast 113 *last*; persist, hold, hold good; hold on, hold it, maintain, sustain, keep up, keep on 146 *go on*; rest, remain, tarry, live 192 *dwell*; stand fast, refuse to budge, dig one's toes in, dig one's heels in 600 *persevere*; stand one's ground, keep one's footing 599 *stand firm*; stand still, resist change 266 *be quiescent*; grow moss 127 *be old*; remain the same, not change one's spots.

145 Cessation: change from action to rest – N. *cessation,* ceasing; desistance, discontinuance, discontinuation 72 *discontinuity*; arrest 747 *restraint*; withdrawal 753 *resignation*, 621 *relinquishment*.

stop, halt, dead stop; logjam, impasse, standstill, deadlock, stalemate 28 *draw*; checkmate 728 *defeat*; breakdown 728 *failure*; stoppage; shutdown, closing down, nonresumption 69 *end*; hitch, check 702 *hindrance*; blockage 264 *closure*; interruption 72 *discontinuity*; breaking-off, walkout 709 *dissension*; closure of debate, guillotine 399 *silence*.

strike, stopping work 679 *inactivity*, 715 *resistance*; industrial action, general strike, 'national holiday'; work to rule; stoppage, walkout, sit-in, work-in, sitdown strike, lightning s.; unofficial strike, wildcat s., mutiny 738 *disobedience*; lockout 57 *exclusion*.

lull, interval, pause, remission, letup; break, breather, rest 685 *refreshment*; holiday, day off, time o., leisure time 681 *leisure*; interlude, cooling-off period, breathing space; abeyance, suspension; close season, respite, moratorium, truce, armistice, cease-fire, standstill 136 *delay*.

stopping place, port of call, port, harbour; stop, halt, pull-up, whistle-stop, station; bus stop, request s.; terminus, terminal, air t. 271 *air travel*; dead end, blind alley, cul-de-sac; billet, destination, the grave; 295 *goal*.

Vb. *cease,* stay, desist, refrain, hold, hold one's hand, stay one's h.; stop, halt, pull up, draw up; stand, rest, rest on one's oars, repose on one's laurels 683 *repose*; have done with, see the last of, end, finish 69 *terminate*; interrupt, leave off, knock o.; break o., let up 72 *discontinue*; ring off, hang up 578 *be mute*; withhold one's labour, stop work, down tools, strike, come out, walk out, vote with one's feet 715 *resist*; lock out 57 *exclude*; pipe down 399 *be silent*; come to an end, dry up, peter out, run o., run down 636 *not suffice*; slacken off, fade out, fade away 446 *disappear*; come off, end its run, be taken off; fold up, collapse

728 *fail*; die away, blow over, clear up 125 *be past*; stand down, withdraw, retire 753 *resign*; leave, leave off; give up, give over 621 *relinquish*; shut up, shut down, close; shut up shop, put up the shutters, go out of business, wind up; shut off steam, switch off; cease fire 719 *make peace*; sound the last post, ring down the curtain, call it a day 266 *be quiescent*, 679 *sleep*.

halt, stop, put a stop to; arrest, check, stem 702 *obstruct*; hold up, call off; pull up, cut short, call a halt, interrupt 747 *restrain*; call out, stage a strike; bring to a standstill, cause a logjam, freeze; checkmate, stalemate, thwart 702 *hinder*; check oneself, stop short, stop in one's tracks, stop dead; grind to a halt, seize, seize up, stall, jam, stick, catch; brake, put on the b. 278 *retard*.

pause, halt for a moment, take a breather; hold back, hang fire 278 *move slowly*; stay one's hand, hold one's horses, hesitate 679 *be inactive*; wait awhile, suspend, adjourn, shelve, put on ice, mothball, put on the back-burner 136 *wait*; rest 683 *repose*.

146 Continuance in action – N. *continuance*, continuation 71 *continuity*, 144 *permanence*; flow 179 *tendency*; extension, prolongation 113 *protraction*; maintenance, perpetuation 115 *perpetuity*; sustained action, persistence 600 *perseverance*; progress 285 *progression*; uninterrupted course, break, run, rally 71 *series*; recurrence 106 *repetition*.

Vb. *go on*, keep going, march on, drive on, proceed, advance 285 *progress*; run on, never end 115 *be eternal*; - and - (e.g. rain and rain, pour and pour); roll on, pursue its course, take its c.; endure, stick, hold, abide, rest, remain, linger 144 *stay*; haunt, frequent 139 *recur*; keep at it, persist, carry on, peg away 600 *persevere*; stick it out to the bitter end, sit it out, wait, wait till the end, see the end of, hang on 725 *carry through*; be not out; survive; live out one's time 69 *end*.

sustain, maintain, uphold 218 *support*; follow through 71 *continue*; keep up 666 *preserve*; keep on, harp on 106 *repeat*; keep it up, prolong, protract; 115 *perpetuate*; keep things moving, keep the pot boiling, keep the ball rolling.

147 Conversion: change to something different – N. *conversion*, converting, turning into, making i.; processing 164 *production*; reduction, crystallization; fermentation, leaven; chemistry, alchemy; mutation, transfiguration 143 *transformation*; enchantment 983 *sorcery*; course, lapse, flux 111 *course of time*; development 36 *increase*; evolution 358 *biology*; degeneration 655 *deterioration*; regeneration, reformation 654 *improvement*; rebirth 656 *restoration*; naturalization 78 *inclusion*; denaturalization 916 *loss of right*; brainwashing 178 *influence*; evangelization 534 *teaching*, 612 *inducement*; convertibility 469 *possibility*.

transition, transit 305 *passage*; movement, shift, relocation, translation, transfer 272 *transference*; alteration 143 *change*; life cycle.

Adj. *converted*, turned into, made i. etc. vb.; assimilated, naturalized; reborn, born again; brainwashed; becoming, transitional; evolving, embryonic, developing, growing into; transformed, metamorphosed, transfigured, bewitched, unrecognizable 15 *different*.

Vb. *be turned to*, be converted into, become, get; come to, turn to, ferment, develop into, evolve i., ripen i. 316 *evolve*; fall into, pass i., slide i., shift i. 305 *pass*; melt into, merge i.; settle into, sink i.; mellow 669 *mature*; wax 36 *grow*; degenerate 655 *deteriorate*; take the shape of, assume the character of; be transformed; undergo a personality change, suffer a sea change, turn over a new leaf 143 *change*; metamorphose.

convert, reduce, process, ferment, leaven; make into, reduce to, resolve into, turn i., conjure i., enchant 983 *bewitch*; metamorphose; transmute, alchemize; render, make, mould, shape, hew into shape, knock *or* lick into s. 243

form; brainwash 178 *influence*; proselytize, evangelize 534 *teach*; win over 485 *convince*; regenerate 656 *revive*; paganize 655 *pervert*.

transform, transfigure; landscape 844 *decorate*; camouflage, disguise, paper over the cracks 525 *conceal*; render 520 *translate*; traduce 521 *misinterpret*; reshape, deform 246 *distort*; change the face of, change out of recognition 149 *revolutionize*; metamorphose 143 *modify*; reform, make something of 654 *make better*; remodel, reorganize, restructure, rationalize.

148 Reversion – N. *reversion,* reverting, going back, return, regress, retrogression, retreat, withdrawal, ebb 286 *regression*; tracing back, derivation 156 *source*; return to the past, turning the clock back, harking back 127 *archaism*; atavism, throwback 5 *heredity*; looking back, retrospection 505 *remembrance*; retroaction; reaction 182 *counteraction*, 31 *compensation*; repercussion, boomerang effect, backlash, backfire, ricochet 280 *recoil*; revulsion, disenchantment 830 *regret*; counter-revolution, reversal 149 *revolution*; retraction, backdown 603 *change of mind*; volte face, about-turn, U-t., right-about t. 240 *contraposition*; backsliding, recidivism 657 *relapse*; retroversion; 246 *distortion*; giving back, cession, replacement, reinstatement 787 *restitution*; getting back, recovery, retrieval 771 *acquisition*; taking back; reply, feedback 460 *answer*; retort 479 *confutation*; turn, turning point, watershed, crucial point, turn of the tide, calm before the storm 137 *crisis*; alternation, swing, swings and roundabouts, give-and-take, swing of the pendulum 141 *periodicity*, 106 *recurrence*, 317 *oscillation*; recycling; to-and-fro movement, coming and going, shuttling, commuting; round trip, there and back; return journey, return ticket, day return; back where one started, status quo.

Vb. *revert,* go back, turn b., turn, return, retrace 286 *regress*; reverse, face

about, turn a., do a U-turn 221 *invert*; ebb, retreat, withdraw 290 *recede*; kick back, rebound, backfire, ricochet, boomerang 280 *recoil*; slip back, slide b., backslide 657 *relapse*; back down, retract 603 *recant*; hark back, start again, turn the clock back, go back to the beginning, restore the status quo, revive 656 *restore*; disenchant, open one's eyes, remove the spell 613 *dissuade*.

149 Revolution: sudden or violent change – N. *revolution,* full circle, circuit 315 *rotation*; radical change, organic c.; tabula rasa, clean slate, clean sweep 550 *obliteration*; sudden change, catastrophe, coup d'état 508 *lack of expectation*; landslide; violent change, bouleversement, upset, overthrow 221 *overturning*; convulsion, shake-up, upheaval, reorganization, restructuring, perestroika; eruption, explosion, cataclysm 176 *outbreak*; avalanche, crash, debacle 309 *descent*, rebellion, counter-revolution 148 *reversion*, 738 *revolt*; total change, sea c., metamorphosis, nullification 752 *abrogation, deposal.*

revolutionist, abolitionist, radical, revolutionary, Marxist, Red 738 *revolter*; seditionist 738 *agitator*; anarchist 168 *destroyer*; idealist 654 *reformer*.

Adj. *revolutionary* 126 *new*; innovating, radical, thoroughgoing, out-and-out, root and branch 54 *complete*; cataclysmic, catastrophic, seismic, earth-shaking, world-shaking 176 *violent*; seditious, subversive, Marxist, red 738 *disobedient*; anarchistic 165 *destructive*.

Vb. *revolutionize,* overturn 221 *invert*; switch over 603 *tergiversate*; uproot, eradicate, make a clean sweep 550 *obliterate*, 165 *demolish*; break with the past, remodel, restructure, reorganize, refashion 126 *modernize*; change the face of, metamorphose 147 *transform.*

150 Substitution: change of one thing for another – N. *substitution,* subrogation, surrogation; commutation, exchange,

switch, shuffle 151 *interchange*; supplanting, replacement, transfer 272 *transference*.

substitute, sub, proxy, alternate, agent, representative 755 *deputy*; surrogate; twofer; understudy, stand-in 594 *actor*; ghost, ghost-writer 589 *author*; locum tenens, locum 658 *doctor*; reserve, twelfth man 707 *auxiliary*; supply, replacement; relief 67 *successor*; double, ringer, look-alike, changeling 545 *impostor*; mother figure, father f., foster parent; synonym, doublet 559 *word*; metaphor, symbol 551 *representation*; prosthesis, artificial limb, pacemaker; transplant; alternative, second best, ersatz 35 *inferiority*; whipping boy, scapegoat, sacrifice 981 *oblation*; makeshift, temporary measure, stopgap; sticking plaster, Band-Aid (tdmk) 177 *moderator*; expedient, modus vivendi 770 *compromise*.

Adj. *substituted,* vicarious 931 *disinterested*; interchangeable 28 *equivalent*; dummy, imitation, plastic, mock, ersatz, counterfeit, false 542 *spurious*; makeshift, stopgap, provisional, acting, temporary 114 *ephemeral*.

Vb. *substitute,* change for; exchange, switch 151 *interchange*; take *or* offer in exchange, swap, compound 770 *compromise*; palm off with, fob off w. 542 *deceive*; make do with, put up w., make shift w.; put in the place of, replace with; count as, treat as, regard as; replace, step into the shoes of, succeed 65 *come after*; supersede, supplant, displace, oust 300 *eject*; replace, take the place of, be substitute for, do duty f., count f., stand in f., act f., understudy f. 755 *deputize*; act the part ol, ghost for; hold the fort; shoulder the blame for, accept responsibility for, take the rap f., cover up f.; rob Peter to pay Paul.

Adv. *instead,* in place, in lieu; in favour of; in loco parentis; by proxy; alternatively, as an alternative; in default of, for want of better, faute de mieux.

151 Interchange: double or mutual change – N. *interchange,* interchangeability, reciprocality; swap, exchange, trade-off 791 *barter*; commutation, permutation; transposition, metathesis, mutual transfer; all change; castling (chess), shuffle, shuffling 272 *transference*; reciprocity, mutuality; cross-fire, interplay, two-way traffic, reciprocation 12 *correlation*; quid pro quo; rally (tennis), give and take; retort, repartee 460 *rejoinder*; measure for measure, tit for tat, eye for an eye, tooth for a tooth 714 *retaliation*.

Vb. *interchange,* exchange, counterchange; change money, convert; swap, barter, trade off 791 *trade*; permute, commute, shuttle; change places; switch, shuffle, castle (chess) 272 *transpose*; give and take 770 *compromise*; reciprocate 12 *correlate*; requite, give as good as one gets 714 *retaliate*; bandy words, answer back, return the compliment, rejoin, retort 460 *answer*; take in each other's washing, scratch each other's back 706 *cooperate*.

152 Changeableness – N. *changeableness,* changeability, mutability 143 *change*; changefulness, variability, variety 17 *nonuniformity*, 437 *variegation*; inconsistency, inconstancy, irregularity; instability, imbalance 29 *inequality*; unsteadiness, rockiness; pliancy 327 *softness*; fluidness 335 *fluidity*; lubricity, slipperiness 258 *smoothness*; mobility, restlessness, fidgeting, disquiet 318 *agitation*; fluctuation, alternation 317 *oscillation*; turning, veering, chopping and changing 142 *fitfulness*; impermanence, flash 114 *transience*; vacillation, hesitation, wavering 601 *irresolution*; yea and nay 603 *change of mind*; fickleness, capriciousness 604 *caprice*; flightiness, light-mindedness 456 *inattention*; versatility 694 *aptitude*.

changeable thing, moon, Proteus, chameleon; kaleidoscope; shifting sands; man of straw; wax, clay; mercury, quicksilver 335 *fluid*; wind, weathercock, weathervane; eddy; April showers;

wheel, whirligig; mobile 265 *motion*; fortune, wheel of Fortune; vicissitude, luck 159 *chance*; variable quantity 85 *numerical element*; mobile features 445 *appearance*; grasshopper mind 456 *inattention*; floating voter, don't know 603 *tergiversator*.

Adj. *changeful,* changing, mutable, alterable, phased 143 *changeable*; shifting, vicissitudinous; varying, variant, variable 17 *nonuniform*; kaleidoscopic; protean 82 *multiform*; quick-change, versatile 694 *skilful*; uncertain, unreliable, vacillating, wavering 601 *irresolute*; moody, unpredictable, unaccountable 508 *unexpected*; never the same, everchanging, volatile, mercurial 15 *different*; rootless, of no fixed abode, vagrant, wandering; wayward, fickle, whimsical 604 *capricious*; vibratory, tidal 141 *periodical*; malleable, plastic 327 *soft*; giddy, dizzy, flighty, wanton, irresponsible, frivolous 456 *light-minded*; shifty, inconstant, unfaithful, disloyal, traitorous.

Vb. *vary,* be off with the old and on with the new, show variety 437 *variegate*; ring the changes, go through phases 143 *change*; chop and change, change and change about; dodge, double 620 *avoid*; shuffle, be shifty 518 *be equivocal*; writhe 251 *wriggle*; dart, flit, flitter 265 *be in motion*; leap, dance, flicker, gutter 417 *shine*; twinkle, flash; wave, flutter, flap 217 *hang*; shake, tremble 318 *be agitated*; wobble, stagger, teeter, totter, rock, reel, sway, swing, vibrate 317 *oscillate*; shuttle, alternate, ebb and flow, wax and wane 317 *fluctuate*; veer, tack, yaw 282 *deviate*, 269 *navigate*; puff 352 *blow*; vacillate, waver, shilly-shally, hesitate, float, drift, change one's mind 601 *be irresolute*; hover, blow hot and cold, play fast and loose 603 *tergiversate*; be inconstant 604 *be capricious*.

153 Stability – N. *stability,* immutability; irreversibility, constancy 16 *uniformity*; firmness 144 *permanence*; rest, immobility, immovability 266 *quiescence*; stableness, steadiness, steady state, homoeostasis, balance 28 *equality*;

nerve, iron n., aplomb 599 *resolution*; stiffness, inflexibility 326 *hardness*, 602 *obstinacy*.

fixture, establishment, firm foundation; foundations, cornerstone, rock, bedrock, pillar, tower, pyramid; invariant, constant; fast colour, indelible ink; leopard's spots; law, law of the Medes and Persians, the Twelve Tables, the Ten Commandments, written constitution, droit du seigneur 953 *legality*.

stabilizer, fin, spoiler, keel; counterweight, ballast; buttress 218 *prop*.

Adj. *unchangeable,* inflexible 602 *obstinate*; unwavering, rocklike 599 *resolute*; predictable, reliable 473 *certain*; immutable, unalterable, inconvertible; changeless, unchanging, inalterable, irreversible; unshrinkable, shrinkproof; stereotyped, unvarying, invariable, constant 16 *uniform*; steady, undeviating 81 *regular*; durable, as the hills 113 *lasting*, 144 *permanent*; undying, perennial, evergreen 115 *perpetual*; imperishable, indestructible, inextinguishable 660 *invulnerable*. See *fixed*.

fixed, steadfast, firm, secure, immovable, irremovable; unassailable, unshakable, rocklike, steady as a rock; steady, stable, balanced, homoeostatic; fast, ingrained, indelible; engraved; ineradicable, rooted, deep-r.; deep-seated, entrenched, in with the bricks, foursquare, well-founded, built on a rock; standing, pat; tethered, moored, anchored 45 *tied*; at rest, at anchor; run aground, stuck fast, stranded, grounded, high and dry; pinned down, transfixed; immobile, frozen, rooted to the ground *or* spot, like a statue, still as a stone 266 *still*.

Vb. *stabilize,* root, entrench, found, establish, build on a rock 115 *perpetuate*; erect, set up, set on its feet 218 *support*; float, set afloat; fix, set, stereotype; make valid, validate, confirm, ratify 488 *endorse*; retain, stet; bind, make sure, make fast 45 *tie*; keep steady, hold the road, retain equilibrium, balance 28 *equalize*.

154 Present events – N. *event,* phenomenon; fact, matter of f., actual f. 1 *reality*;

case, circumstance, situation, state of affairs 7 *state*; occurrence, eventuality, incidence, realization, happening, turn of events; incident, episode, adventure 137 *occasion*; milestone, watershed 8 *juncture*; fortune, accident, casualty, contingency 159 *chance*; misadventure, mishap 731 *misfortune*; emergency, pass 137 *crisis*; coincidence 181 *concurrence*; advent 289 *approach*; encounter, meeting; transaction, proceeding, affairs 676 *action*; result, product, consequence, issue, outcome, upshot 157 *effect*; denouement, solution 316 *evolution*; catastrophe 69 *end*.

affairs, matters, doings, transactions 676 *deed*; agenda; involvement, concern, concerns, interests, business i., irons in the fire, axes to grind 622 *business*; world, life, situation 8 *circumstance*; current affairs, affairs in general, state of affairs; course of events 111 *course of time*; chapter of accidents, ups and downs of life, vicissitudes 730 *prosperity*, 731 *adversity*.

Vb. *happen*, become, come into existence 360 *be born*; materialize, appear, be realized, come off 727 *succeed*; take place, occur, come about, come to pass, fulfil expectations; befall, betide 159 *chance*; turn up, pop up, crop up, start up, spring up, arise 295 *arrive*; present itself 189 *be present*; supervene 284 *follow*; issue, transpire, emanate 157 *result*; turn out, fall o., work o., pan o.; be afoot, take its course, advance 285 *progress*; continue 146 *go on*; go off, pass o. 125 *be past*; fall to one's lot, be one's good fortune *or* misfortune; be the case, be so, prove, prove to be; bring about, occasion 156 *cause*.

meet with, incur, encounter 295 *meet*; realize, happen on, chance upon, stumble u., find 484 *discover*; experience, pass through, go t.; have been through 490 *know*, 818 *feel*; have adventures, endure, undergo 825 *suffer*.

Adv. *eventually*, ultimately; in due course, in the course of things, in the natural course of t., in the ordinary course of t.; as times go; as the world goes.

155 Destiny: future events – **N.** *destiny*, what's to come, one's stars 596 *fate*; horoscope, forecast 511 *prediction*; prospect, outlook 507 *expectation*; coming events, future plans 124 *futurity*, 617 *intention*; trouble in store, danger 900 *threat*; proximity 200 *nearness*, 289 *approach*; future existence, hereafter 124 *future state*; next world, Hades, afterworld, world to come, life after death 971 *heaven*; predestination 596 *necessity*, 473 *certainty*.

Adj. *impending*, overhanging, louring, hovering, imminent; preparing, brewing, cooking 669 *preparatory*; destined, predestined, in the stars, in the lap of the gods 596 *fated*; predicted, forthcoming, forecast 511 *predicting*; inescapable, inevitable, going to be, bound to happen 473 *certain*; due, owing 596 *necessary*; in the wind, on the cards 471 *probable*; on the agenda, intended, decided on 608 *predetermined*; in prospect, in view, in the offing, on the horizon, looming on the h., in the distance 443 *visible*; in the future, to come, in the womb of time 124 *future*; at hand, close 200 *near*, 289 *approaching*; instant, immediate, about to be, on the point of 116 *instantaneous*; pregnant with, heavy w. 511 *presageful*; in store, in reserve, ready, kept r., on the stocks 669 *prepared*; in embryo, embryonic 68 *beginning*.

Vb. *impend* 124 *be to come*; hang over, lie o., hover, lour, loom, be on the horizon 900 *threaten*; come on, draw nigh 289 *approach*; front, face, stare one in the f. 237 *be in front*; breathe down one's neck; ripen 669 *mature*.

Section eight: Causation

156 Cause: constant antecedent – N. *causation*, causality, cause and effect, aetiology 158 *attribution*; authorship; origination, creation 21 *originality*; invention 484 *discovery*; inspiration 178 *influence*; evocation, provocation 164 *production*; stimulation, fomentation, encouragement, motivation 612 *motive*; planting, cultivation 370 *agriculture*; abetment 706 *cooperation*.

cause, material c., prime mover, God 965 *the Deity*; creator, maker 164 *producer*; begetter, father 169 *parentage*; author, inventor, originator, founder; agent, leaven; stimulus 174 *stimulant*; contributor, factor, contributory f., moment, determinant; inspirer, mainspring 612 *motivator*; fomenter, aider, abettor; power behind the throne, undercurrents 178 *influence*; planetary influence, astrological i., stars 155 *destiny*; fate 596 *necessity*; force 740 *compulsion*.

source, fountain, fount 68 *origin*; spring, fountainhead, wellspring; mine, quarry 632 *store*; birthplace 192 *home*; genesis, ancestry, lineage, descent 169 *parentage*; parent, ancestor, progenitor; loins 167 *genitalia*; rudiment, element, principle, first p.; nucleus, germ, seed, sperm, spore; egg, foetus, embryo; chrysalis, cocoon 132 *young creature*; bud, stem, stock, rootstock; root, bulb 366 *plant*; radix, radical, etymon, derivation, etymology; foundation, fundamentals, the nitty gritty, bedrock 214 *base*; groundwork, spadework, beginnings 68 *beginning*; nuts and bolts, raw material, ore 631 *materials*.

reason why, reason, cause, the why and wherefore; explanation, key 460 *answer*, 520 *interpretation*; excuse 614 *pretext*; ground, basis, rationale, motive, idea, occasion, raison d'être.

Adj. *fundamental*, primary, elemental, ultimate; foundational, radical, basic 5 *intrinsic*; crucial, central 638 *important*; original, aboriginal 68 *first*; primitive, primordial 127 *primal*.

Vb. *cause*, originate, bring into being, create, make 164 *produce*; beget, be the author of 167 *generate*; invent 484 *discover*; be the reason 158 *account for*; underlie, be *or* lie at the bottom of, be at the root of; sow the seeds of, be answerable, be responsible, have a hand in, be to blame; institute, found, lay the foundations, inaugurate 68 *auspicate*; set up, erect 310 *elevate*; launch, set afloat, set afoot, set going, trigger off, spark off, touch o. 68 *begin*; open, open up, broach 68 *initiate*; seed, sow, plant, water 370 *cultivate*; contrive, effect, effectuate, bring about, bring off, bring to pass 727 *succeed*; procure, provide the means, put up the wherewithal; stage-manage, engineer 623 *plan*; bring on, induce, precipitate 680 *hasten*; bring out, draw o., evoke, elicit 291 *attract*; provoke, arouse, awaken 821 *excite*; stimulate 174 *invigorate*; kindle, inspire, incite, tempt 612 *induce*; occasion 612 *motivate*; have an effect, be a factor, show its result, make or mar 178 *influence*; be the agent, do the deed 676 *do*; determine, decide, give the decision 480 *judge*; decide the result, turn the scale, come down on one side or the other, give the casting vote 178 *prevail*, 34 *predominate*.

157 Effect: constant sequel – N. *effect*, consequence, corollary 65 *sequence*; result; derivation, derivative, precipitate 41 *remainder*; upshot, outcome, issue, denouement 154 *event*; final result, end r., termination 725 *completion*; visible effect, mark, print, impress 548 *trace*; by-product, side-effect, spin-off; aftermath, legacy, backwash, wake, repercussion 67 *sequel*; resultant action, response 460 *answer*; performance 676 *deed*; reaction, backlash, boomerang effect 182 *counteraction*; offspring 170 *posterity*; handiwork 164 *product*; karma 596 *fate*; moral effect 178 *influence*.

growth, development, expansion 36 *increase*; carcinoma 651 *cancer*; bud, blossom, florescence, fruit; ear, spike; produce, crop, harvest; profit 771 *gain*; growth industry.

Adj. *caused,* owing to, due to, attributed to; consequential, resulting from, consequent upon 65 *sequential*; contingent, depending, dependent on 745 *subject*; resultant, derivative, descended; secondary 20 *imitative*; arising, emergent, emanating, developed from, evolved f.; born of, out of, by; ending in, issuing in; effected, done.

Vb. *result,* be the r., come of; follow on, ensue, wait on, accrue 284 *follow*; be owing to, be due to; owe everything to, borrow from 785 *borrow*; have a common origin 9 *be related*; take its source, have its roots in, derive from, descend f., originate f. *or* in, come from *or* out of; issue, proceed, emanate 298 *emerge*; grow from, spring f., arise f., flow f.; develop, unfold 316 *evolve*; bud, sprout, germinate 36 *grow*; show a trace, show an effect, receive an impression, bear the stamp 522 *be plain*; bear the consequences 154 *meet with*, 963 *be punished*; turn out, fall o., pan o., work o., eventuate 154 *happen*; result in 164 *produce*.

depend, hang upon, hinge on, pivot on, turn on, centre on 12 *correlate*, 745 *be subject*.

158 Attribution: assignment of cause – N. *attribution,* reference to, imputation, ascription; theory, hypothesis, assumption, conjecture 512 *supposition*; explanation 520 *interpretation*; aetiology 459 *enquiry*; rationale 156 *reason why*; affiliation 169 *parentage*; derivation, etymology 156 *source*; attribute 89 *concomitant*; credit, credit title, acknowledgment 915 *dueness*.

Vb. *attribute,* ascribe, impute; say of 532 *affirm*; accord, grant, allow 781 *give*; put down to, set down to; assign to, refer to, point to, trace to, connect with, derive from 9 *relate*; lay at the door of, affiliate, father upon; charge with, saddle with *or* on; found upon; make responsible, make a scapegoat, blame for 928 *accuse*; bring home to 478 *demonstrate*; credit, credit with, acknowledge.

account for, explain 520 *interpret*; theorize, hypothesize, assume 512 *suppose*.

Adv. *hence,* thence, therefore; whence, wherefore; for, since, on account of, because, owing to, thanks to, on that account, from this cause, from that cause, ergo, thus, so; that's why.

159 Chance: no assignable cause – N. *chance,* blind c., fortuity, randomness; fortuitousness; unpredictability 474 *uncertainty*; inexplicability 517 *unintelligibility*; lot, fortune, wheel of f., lady luck 596 *fate*; potluck, luck of the draw; good fortune, luck, good l., run of good l. 730 *prosperity*; bad luck, run of bad l. 731 *misfortune*; hazard, accident, misadventure, casualty, coincidence, chapter of accidents 154 *event*; lucky shot, lucky strike, fluke 618 *nondesign*; chance in a million 140 *infrequency*; chance meeting, chance encounter 508 *lack of expectation*; serendipity 484 *discovery*.

equal chance, even c., fifty-fifty 28 *equality*; toss-up, spin of the coin, heads or tails, throw of the dice, turn of the card, spin of the wheel; lucky dip, random sample; lottery, raffle, tombola, sweepstake, premium bond 618 *gambling*.

fair chance, sporting c., fighting c., 469 *possibility*; half a chance, small c. 472 *improbability*; good chance 137 *opportunity*; long odds, odds on, odds 34 *advantage*; safe bet, sure thing, the probabilities 471 *probability*.

Adj. *casual,* fortuitous, serendipitous, chance, haphazard, hit-or-miss, random, stray, out of a hat; adventitious, accidental, unexpected, incidental; coincidental; 10 *unrelated*; chancy, fluky, dicey, incalculable.

Vb. *chance,* turn up, crop up, fall to one's lot, so happen 154 *happen*; chance upon, come u., light u., hit u., stumble u., bump into, run across 154 *meet with*, 484 *discover*; go out on a limb, risk it, try one's luck, chance it, leave it to chance 618 *gamble*.

Adv. *by chance,* by accident; accidentally, fortuitously, serendipitously; perchance, perhaps; according to chance, as it may be.

73

160 Power – N. *power,* potency, mightiness 32 *greatness*; prevalence, predominance 34 *superiority*; omnipotence, almightiness 733 *authority*; control, sway 733 *governance*; moral power, ascendancy 178 *influence*; spiritual power, charisma, mana; witchcraft 983 *sorcery*; staying power, endurance 153 *stability*; driving force 612 *motive*; physical power, might, muscle, brute force *or* strength 162 *strength*; might and main, effort, endeavour 682 *exertion*; force 740 *compulsion*; stress, strain, shear; weight 322 *gravity*; weight of numbers; manpower 686 *personnel*; position of power, position of strength, vantage ground 34 *advantage*.

ability, ableness, capability, potentiality 469 *possibility*; competence, efficiency, efficacy, effectuality 694 *skill*; capacity, faculty, virtue, property 5 *intrinsicality*; qualification 24 *fitness*; attribute 89 *concomitant*; native wit, gift, flair, what it takes 694 *aptitude*; grasp 183 *range*; enablement.

energy, liveliness, vigour, drive, pep, zip, dynamism 174 *vigorousness*; work, kinetic energy, electrical energy, atomic e., nuclear e.; mechanical energy, engine power, horsepower; inertia; resistance 333 *friction*; force, field of f.; force of gravity 322 *gravity*; pressure, head, charge, steam; steam up; tension, high t.; electromotive force; pulling power 288 *traction*; thrust, jet propulsion 287 *propulsion*; momentum, impetus 279 *impulse*; magnetic field 291 *attraction*; 292 *repulsion*; suction 299 *reception*; expulsion 300 *ejection*; unit of work, erg, joule; calorie.

electricity, static e.; lightning; electrodynamics, electrostatics, electromagnetism; induction, inductance, capacitance; resistance, conduction; oscillation, pulsation, frequency; electric charge, pulse, shock; electric current, direct c., alternating c.; circuit, short c., closed c.; electrode, anode, cathode; positive, negative; conductor, semiconductor, nonconductor, insulator; lightning conductor, earth 662 *safeguard*; electrification, live wire 661 *danger*.

electronics, optics; lasers 417 *radiation*; integrated circuit, microprocessor; computer electronics 86 *data processing*; automation 630 *machine*; television, radio 531 *telecommunication*; electrical engineering, electricity supply; power line, lead, flex 47 *cable*; distributor; pylon, grid, national g.; generator, magneto, dynamo; oscillator, alternator; transformer, commutator, power pack; battery, accumulator; cell, photo c., photoelectric c.; valve, tube, transistor; voltage, volt, watt, kilowatt, megawatt; ohm; amperage, ampere, amp.

nucleonics, nuclear physics; fission, fusion, thermonuclear reaction; cyclotron, synchrotron; atomic pile, nuclear reactor, fast breeder r.; fuel rods, coolant; radioactivity, fallout 417 *radiation*; radioactive waste 659 *poison*; nuclear warhead, nuclear missile, atomic bomb 723 *bomb*; nuclear winter.

Adj. *powerful,* potent 162 *strong*; mighty 32 *great*; prevalent, prevailing, predominant 178 *influential*; almighty, omnipotent, irresistible 34 *supreme*; empowered 733 *authoritative*; competent, capable, able, adequate, equal to, up to 635 *sufficient*; with resources 800 *rich*; more than a match for, efficacious, effectual, effective 727 *successful*; operative, workable, having teeth; in force, valid 153 *established*; cogent, compulsive 740 *compelling*.

dynamic, energetic, peppy 174 *vigorous*; supercharged, souped-up; magnetic; propelling; locomotive, kinetic 265 *moving*; powered, engined; mechanized, automated 630 *mechanical*; electric, electrical, electromagnetic, electronic; computerized, atomic, nuclear, thermonuclear; hydroelectric, wave-powered, solar-p., wind-driven, water-d., steam-operated.

Vb. *be able,* - powerful etc. adj.; can, have it in one's power, have it in one; be capable of, have the talent for, have the virtue, have the property; manage 676 *do*; measure up to 635 *suffice*; have power, exercise p., control 733 *dominate*; force 740 *compel*.

161 Impotence – N. *impotence,* lack of power; invalidity, 163 *weakness*; inability, incapacity; incapability, incompetence, inefficiency 728 *failure*, 695 *unskilfulness*; ineptitude, unfitness 25 *inaptitude*; decrepitude 131 *age*; frailness 114 *transience*; invalidation, disqualification 752 *abrogation*; sterility, barrenness 172 *unproductiveness*, *contraception*; disarmament, demilitarization 719 *pacification*; demobilization 75 *dispersion*.

helplessness, defencelessness 661 *vulnerability*; harmlessness 935 *innocence*; powerlessness 745 *subjection*, 747 *restraint*; stamping of feet, gnashing of teeth 891 *anger*; prostration, exhaustion 684 *fatigue*; collapse, breakdown 728 *failure*; unconsciousness, faint, swoon, coma, catatonia; numbness, narcosis 375 *insensibility*; stroke, cerebrovascular accident, CVA, apoplexy, paralysis, hemiplegia, paraplegia 651 *disease*; atrophy 655 *deterioration*; senility, old age 131 *age*; incontinence; dementia, Alzheimer's disease 503 *mental disorder*; imbecility 499 *unintelligence*; pupillage, minority 130 *nonage*; babyhood, infancy 130 *youth*; invalid 651 *sick person*, 163 *weakling*.

Adj. *powerless,* impotent, unable; unauthorized; nominal, figurehead 4 *insubstantial*; invalid, null and void; without a leg to stand on 163 *weak*; inoperative, not working, unemployed, disemployed 677 *nonactive*; suspended, in abeyance, cancelled, withdrawn; abolished, gone by the board; obsolete; mothballed, laid up, out of circulation, kaput; disqualified, deposed; inept 25 *unapt*; unworkable, dud, good for nothing 641 *useless*; inadequate 636 *insufficient*; ineffective,

inefficacious, ineffectual, feeble 728 *unsuccessful*; incapable, incompetent, inefficient 695 *unskilful*; unpowered, unengined.

impotent, powerless, feeble 163 *weak*; emasculated, castrated, gelded, unsexed, unmanned, spayed, sterilized; sexless; sterile, barren, infertile 172 *unproductive*; worn out, exhausted, used up, effete; senile, gaga 131 *ageing*; paralytic, arthritic, stiff 326 *rigid*; unconscious, comatose, drugged, hypnotized, catatonic 375 *insensible*; incapacitated, disabled, paralysed 163 *crippled*; incontinent; all in, dead-beat, clapped out 684 *fatigued*; prostrated 216 *supine*; shellshocked 854 *nervous*; helpless, rudderless; laid on one's back; thwarted, gnashing one's teeth, stamping one's feet 702 *hindered*.

Vb. *disable,* incapacitate 641 *make useless*; disqualify 916 *disentitle*; deprive of power, invalidate 752 *abrogate*; disarm, demilitarize 163 *weaken*; neutralize 182 *counteract*; undermine, sap 255 *make concave*; exhaust, use up, consume 634 *waste*; wind, prostrate, bowl over, knock out 279 *strike*; paralyse 679 *make inactive*; sprain, rick, wrench, twist, dislocate, break, fracture; cripple, lame, maim, hobble, nobble, hamstring 702 *hinder*, 655 *impair*; stifle, smother, throttle, suffocate, strangle 362 *kill*; muzzle, deaden 399 *silence*; spike the guns, draw the teeth, clip the wings, tie one's hands, cramp one's style; sabotage, put a spoke into one's wheel, throw a spanner in the works; deflate, take the wind out of one's sails; put out of action, put out of commission 674 *stop using*.

unman, unnerve, devitalize 163 *weaken*; emasculate, castrate, neuter, spay, geld, unsex.

162 Strength – N. *strength,* might, potency, horsepower, HP 160 *power*; energy 174 *vigorousness*; force 735 *brute force*; resilience; load-bearing capacity, tensile strength; steel 326 *hardness*; heart of oak 329 *toughness*; staying

power, survivability, endurance, grit 600 *stamina*.

vitality, healthiness, fitness 650 *health*; vim, vigour, liveliness 360 *life*; virility 855 *manliness*; guts, nerve, spunk, pluck, backbone 599 *resolution*; aggressiveness 718 *bellicosity*; physique, muscularity, muscle, biceps, sinews, thews and sinews; beefiness, burliness, brawn 195 *size*; grip, iron g., vicelike g. 778 *retention*; Titanic strength, strength of Hercules.

athletics 837 sport, 716 *contest*; athleticism, gymnastics, acrobatics, bodybuilding, pumping iron, feats of strength, callisthenics, aerobics 682 *exercise*; stadium, gymnasium, astrodome 724 *arena*.

athlete, gymnast, tumbler, acrobat, contortionist, trapeze artist, circus rider, bareback r., stunt man, escapologist 594 *entertainer*; marathon runner; Blue, all-rounder 716 *contender*; wrestler 716 *wrestling*; heavyweight 722 *pugilist*; weight-lifter, body-builder, strong man; champion 644 *exceller*; he-man, muscle man 372 *male*; Mr Universe, Tarzan, Hercules; Samson, Goliath, Atlas, Titan 195 *giant*; tower of strength 707 *auxiliary*.

Adj. *strong,* lusty, vigorous, youthful 130 *young*; mighty, potent, armed 160 *powerful*; high-powered, high-tension; all-powerful, omnipotent, overpowering, overwhelming 34 *superior*; incontestable, irresistible, more than a match for, victorious; sovereign, supreme 733 *ruling*; valid, in full force; like a giant refreshed; in high feather, in fine fettle, in tip-top condition, at one's peak, in top form, in good nick, fit as a fiddle, sound as a bell 650 *healthy*; heavy 322 *weighty*; forceful; urgent, compulsive 740 *compelling*; emphatic 532 *assertive*; hard as iron, steely, adamantine 326 *hard*; case-hardened, toughened 329 *tough*; solid, substantial, stable 153 *fixed*; well-built, stout; strong as a horse, strong as a lion, strong as an ox; heady, alcoholic 949

intoxicating; undiluted, neat; strengthened, fortified, double-strength; entrenched, unassailable 660 *invulnerable*; unyielding, staunch 599 *resolute*; stubborn, intransigent 602 *obstinate*; persistent; shatterproof, unbreakable, solid 324 *dense*; impregnable 660 *invulnerable*; indomitable, unconquerable, invincible, unbeatable; unquenchable, unallayed; unflagging, tireless, unexhausted 678 *industrious*; unwithered, indestructible; waterproof, showerproof, weatherproof, rustproof, damp-proof, impermeable, gasproof, leakproof, hermetic; fireproof, bulletproof, bombproof.

stalwart, stout, sturdy, hardy, rugged, robust, doughty 174 *vigorous*; of good physique, able-bodied, muscular, brawny; sinewy, wiry 678 *active*; strapping, well-knit, well set-up, broadshouldered, barrel-chested, thickset, stocky, mesomorphic, burly, beefy, husky, hulking, hefty 195 *large*; gigantic, colossal, titanic, Herculean, Atlantean 195 *huge*.

manly, masculine, macho 372 *male*; amazonian; virile, red-blooded, manful 855 *courageous*; in the prime of manhood 134 *grown-up*.

Vb. *be strong,* - mighty etc. adj.; pack a punch; come in force; overpower, be more than a match for 727 *overmaster*; recover, convalesce, revive 656 *be restored*; blow hard, blow great guns 352 *blow*.

strengthen, confirm, give strength to, lend force to 36 *augment*; underline, stress 532 *emphasize*; reinforce, fortify; prop, sustain 218 *support*; brace, steel, screw up one's courage 855 *give courage*; stiffen, stiffen one's resolve, stiffen one's upper lip, toughen, temper, case-harden 326 *harden*; energize, act like a tonic, put body into, put beef into 174 *invigorate*; beef up, tone up, reinvigorate 685 *refresh*; set one on his legs 656 *cure*; set up, build up 310 *elevate*; power, engine.

163 Weakness – N. *weakness,* lack of strength, feebleness, puniness; vulnerability, helplessness 161 *impotence*;

slightness 323 *lightness*; flimsiness, fragility, frailness 330 *brittleness*; delicacy, tenderness 374 *sensibility*; unsteadiness, shakiness, giddiness, vertigo, disequilibrium 29 *inequality*; feet of clay, instability 152 *changeableness*; ineffectiveness; moral weakness, frailty, infirmity of purpose 601 *irresolution*; debility, infirmity, decrepitude, senility 131 *old age*; delicate health 651 *ill health*; flaccidity, flabbiness 327 *softness*; fleshiness, corpulence 195 *bulk*; loss of strength, enervation, inactivity 679 *sluggishness*; exhaustion, prostration, collapse 684 *fatigue*; decline 655 *deterioration*; weakening, softening, mitigation 177 *moderation*; relaxation 734 *laxity*; loosening 46 *disunion*; adulteration, watering, watering down, dilution 43 *mixture*; debilitation 655 *impairment*; emasculation, evisceration; invalidation 752 *abrogation*; crack, fault 201 *gap*; flaw 845 *blemish*; inadequacy 636 *insufficiency*; weak point, fatal flaw, Achilles' heel 647 *defect*.

weakling, pansy, patsy; lightweight, small fry 639 *nonentity*; softy, sissy, milksop, namby-pamby; old woman, invalid, hypochondriac 651 *sick person*; lame dog, lame duck 731 *unlucky person*; infant, babe-in-arms, kitten 132 *young creature*; baby, big baby, crybaby, chicken 856 *coward*; mummy's boy, mother's darling, teacher's pet 890 *favourite*; doormat, pushover, jellyfish, drip, weed, wimp, nerd, wet.

weak thing, broken reed, thread, rope of sand; sandcastle, house built on sand, house of cards, house of bricks, cobweb 4 *insubstantial thing*; matchstick, eggshell, paper, tissue p.; glass, china 330 *brittleness*; water, dishwater, milk and water.

Adj. *weak,* powerless, 161 *impotent*; unconfirmed 161 *powerless*; unfortified, unstrengthened, vulnerable; harmless 935 *innocent*; namby-pamby, cissy *or* sissy, babyish; effeminate, limp-wristed, womanish 373 *female*; poor, feeble, frail, delicate, slight, puny 33 *small*; lightweight 323 *light*; slightly built, anorexic, skeletal, of poor physique 196

little; thin 206 *lean*; feeble-minded, weak *or* soft in the head, dim-witted, imbecile 499 *foolish*; weak-willed, half-hearted 601 *irresolute*; spineless, weak-kneed, lily-livered, chicken-hearted, yielding 721 *submitting*; pale 426 *colourless*; limp, flaccid, flabby, floppy 327 *soft*; drooping, sagging, giving 217 *hanging*; slack, loose, relaxed 734 *lax*; watery, wishy-washy, milk-and-water, insipid, wersh 387 *tasteless*; low, quiet, faint 401 *muted*; decrepit, old 131 *ageing*; past it, weak as a baby, weak as a kitten; wavering, unreliable 604 *capricious*.

weakened, debilitated, enervated, diminished, deflated 37 *decreasing*; depleted, impoverished, drained, dissipated; effete; sapped, undermined, disarmed, disabled, laid low; exhausted, wearied 684 *fatigued*; strained, overstrained 246 *distorted*; the worse for wear, not what it was, on its last legs, tottering; deactivated, neutralized 175 *inert*; diluted, adulterated, watered, watered down 43 *mixed*. See *crippled*.

weakly, infirm, delicate, sickly 651 *unhealthy*; groggy, rocky; run down, seedy, under the weather, coming apart at the seams, below par, one degree under, poorly; underweight, anorexic, skinny 206 *lean*; listless; faint; sallow, wan, pallid, lacklustre 426 *colourless*.

crippled, disabled, impaired, incapacitated, handicapped 161 *impotent*; halt, lame, game, gammy, limping, hobbling; hamstrung, hobbled; knock-kneed 246 *deformed*; arthritic, rheumatic, gouty; limbless, legless, armless, handless, eyeless 647 *imperfect*.

flimsy, gossamer, wispy, tenuous 4 *insubstantial*; delicate, dainty 331 *textural*; frail, fragile 330 *brittle*; gimcrack, jerry-built, makeshift, shoddy 641 *useless*; rickety, ramshackle, tumbledown, on its last legs, shaky, tottery, teetering, wobbly, wonky, creaky, tumbledown 655 *dilapidated*.

Vb. *be weak,* grow w., grow feeble, weaken; sicken, be in poor health 651 *be ill*; faint, fail, languish, flag 684 *be fatigued*; drop, fall 309 *tumble*; dwindle 37

decrease; decline 655 *deteriorate*; droop, wilt, fade; wear thin, crumble; yield, give way, sag 327 *soften*; split 263 *open*; dodder, totter, teeter, sway, stagger, reel 317 *oscillate*; tremble, shake 318 *be agitated*; halt, limp, go lame 278 *move slowly*; have one foot in the grave, not have long to go, be on the way out 127 *be old*.

weaken, debilitate, enervate; loosen 46 *disunite*; soften up 327 *soften*; strain, sprain 161 *disable*; hurt, injure 655 *wound*; cramp 702 *obstruct*; disarm, take the edge off, cushion 257 *blunt*; impoverish, starve; deprive, rob 786 *take away*; reduce, extenuate, thin, lessen 37 *abate*; dilute, adulterate 43 *mix*; devitalize, eviscerate; deactivate, neutralize 182 *counteract*; decimate 105 *render few*; muffle 401 *mute*; invalidate 752 *abrogate*; sap, deplete, undermine.

164 Production – N. *production,* producing, creation; origination, invention, innovation, original work 21 *originality*, 484 *discovery*; productivity 171 *productiveness*; endeavour 671 *attempt*, 672 *undertaking*; composition, authorship 551 *art*, 553 *painting*, 554 *sculpture*, 586 *writing*; musicianship; performance, output, turnout 676 *action*; execution, accomplishment, achievement; concoction, brewing 669 *preparation*; craftsmanship 243 *formation*; planning, design 623 *plan*; organization 331 *structure*, 62 *arrangement*; engineering, construction; establishment, erection 310 *elevation*; making, fabrication, manufacture, industry, sunrise i. 622 *business*; processing, process 147 *conversion*; production line 71 *continuity*, 630 *machine*; increased output, mass production; productivity deal 706 *cooperation*; development, growth 36 *increase*, 171 *abundance*; factory farming 370 *agriculture*; breeding 369 *animal husbandry*; procreation 167 *propagation*.

product, creature, creation, result 157 *effect*; output; printout; end-product, by-p.; extract, essence; handiwork, artifact; manufacture, article, thing 319 *object*; goods, wares 795 *merchandise*; goods and services, gross national product, GNP; earthenware 381 *pottery*; stoneware, hardware, ironware; fabric, cloth 222 *textile*; production, work, opus, oeuvre, piece 56 *composition*; chef d'oeuvre, magnum opus, crowning achievement 694 *masterpiece*; fruit, flower, blossom, berry; produce, yield, harvest, crop, vintage 157 *growth*; interest, increase, return 771 *gain*; brainwave, brainchild, conception 451 *idea*; fiction 513 *ideality*; offspring, young, egg, spawn, seed 132 *young creature*.

edifice, building, structure, erection, pile, dome, tower, high-rise building, skyscraper 209 *high structure*; pyramid, ancient monument 548 *monument*; church 990 *temple*; mausoleum 364 *tomb*; habitation, mansion, hall 192 *house*; college 539 *school*; fortress 713 *fort*.

producer, creator, maker, Nature; the Creator 965 *the Deity*; originator, inventor, discoverer, mover, prime m., instigator 612 *motivator*; founding father, founder, founder member, establisher 156 *cause*; begetter 169 *parentage*; creative worker, poet, writer 589 *author*; composer 413 *musician*; painter, sculptor 556 *artist*; deviser, designer 623 *planner*; developer, constructor, builder, architect, engineer; manufacturer, industrialist 686 *agent*; executive 676 *doer*; labourer 686 *worker*; artificer, craftsman or - woman 686 *artisan*; grower, planter, cultivator, agriculturalist, gardener 370 *farmer*; stock farmer, stock breeder, sheep farmer, rancher 369 *breeder*; miner, extractor; play-producer 594 *stage manager*; film producer, film director, 445 *cinema*.

Vb. *produce,* create, originate, make; invent 484 *discover*; think up, conceive 513 *imagine*; write, design 56 *compose*; operate 676 *do*; frame, fashion, shape, mould 243 *form*; knit, spin 222 *weave*; sew, run up 45 *tie*; forge, chisel, carve, sculpture, cast; coin 797 *mint*; manufacture, fabricate, prefabricate, process, turn out, mill, machine; mass-produce,

churn out, multiply 166 *reproduce*; construct, build, raise, rear, erect, set up, run up 310 *elevate*; put together, make up, assemble, compose, cobble together 45 *join*; synthesize, blend 50 *combine*; mine, quarry 304 *extract*; establish, found, constitute, institute 68 *initiate*; organize, get up 62 *arrange*; develop, exploit; industrialize, mechanize, automate, computerize; engineer, contrive 623 *plan*; perform, implement, execute, achieve, accomplish 725 *carry out*; bring about, yield results, effect 156 *cause*; unfold, develop 316 *evolve*; breed, hatch, rear 369 *breed stock*; sow, grow, farm 370 *cultivate*; bear young 167 *reproduce itself*; bring up, educate 534 *train*.

165 Destruction – N. *destruction,* undoing 148 *reversion*; blotting out 550 *obliteration*; blowing out, annihilation, nullification 2 *extinction*; abolition, suppression 752 *abrogation*; suffocation, smothering, stifling, silencing 399 *silence*; subversion 221 *overturning*, 149 *revolution*; overthrow 311 *lowering*; felling, levelling, razing, flattening 216 *horizontality*; dissolution 51 *decomposition*; breaking up, tearing down, knocking d., demolition, demolishment 655 *dilapidation*, 46 *disunion*; disruption 46 *separation*; crushing, grinding, pulverization 332 *powderiness*; incineration 381 *burning*; liquidation, elimination, extermination; extirpation, eradication, rooting out, uprooting 300 *ejection*; wiping out, mopping up 725 *completion*; decimation, mass murder, massacre, genocide 362 *slaughter*; hatchet job; destructiveness, vandalism, iconoclasm 176 *violence*; sabotage 702 *hindrance*; fire-raising, arson 381 *incendiarism*.

ruin, downfall, ruination, perdition, one's undoing; crushing blow 731 *adversity*; catastrophe, disaster, act of God 731 *misfortune*; collapse, débâcle, landslide 149 *revolution*; breakdown, meltdown, break-up, crack-up 728 *failure*; crash, smash, smash-up 279 *collision*; wreck, shipwreck, wreckage, wrack, rack and ruin; sinking, loss; Waterloo 728 *defeat*; knockout blow, KO 279 *knock*; beginning of the end, slippery slope, road to ruin 655 *deterioration*; coup de grace 725 *completion*; apocalypse, doom, crack of doom, knell, end 69 *finality*, 961 *condemnation*; ruins 127 *oldness*.

Adj. *destructive,* destroying, internecine, annihilating etc. vb.; root and branch 54 *complete*; consuming, ruinous 634 *wasteful*; sacrificial, costly 811 *dear*; exhausting, crushing; apocalyptic, cataclysmic, overwhelming 176 *violent*; raging 176 *furious*; merciless 906 *pitiless*; mortal, suicidal, cut-throat, life-threatening 362 *deadly*; subversive, subversionary 149 *revolutionary*; incendiary, mischievous, pernicious 645 *harmful*; poisonous 653 *toxic*.

Vb. *destroy,* undo, unmake, dismantle, take apart 148 *revert*; destruct, self-d.; abolish, annihilate, liquidate, exterminate, axe, invalidate 2 *nullify*; devour, consume 634 *waste*; swallow up, engulf 299 *absorb*; swamp, overwhelm, drown 341 *drench*; incinerate, burn up, gut 381 *burn*; wreck, shipwreck, sink (see *suppress*); end, exterminate, put an end to 69 *terminate*; do for, do in, put down, put away, do away with, make away w., get rid of 362 *kill*; poison 362 *murder*; decimate 105 *render few*; exterminate, leave no survivor 362 *slaughter*, 906 *be pitiless*; remove, extirpate, eradicate, deracinate, uproot, root up 300 *eject*; wipe out, expunge, efface, erase, delete, rub out, blot out, strike out, cancel 550 *obliterate*; annul, revoke, tear up 752 *abrogate*; dispel, scatter, dissipate 75 *disperse*; dissolve 337 *liquefy*; evaporate 338 *vaporize*; mutilate, deface 244 *deform*; knock out, flatten out; put the kibosh on, nip in the bud, put the skids under, make short work of, seal the doom of, make mincemeat of, mop up; spifflicate, trounce 726 *defeat*; dish, cook one's goose, sabotage 702 *obstruct*; play hell with, play the deuce with 63 *bedevil*, 634 *waste*; ruin, bring to ruin, be the ruin of, be one's undoing.

demolish, unbuild, dismantle, break down, knock d., pull d., tear d. 46 *disunite*; level, raze, raze to the ground, lay in the dust 216 *flatten*; throw down, steamroller, bulldoze 311 *fell*; blow down, blow away, carry a.; cut down, mow d. 362 *slaughter*; knock over, kick o.; subvert, overthrow, overturn, topple, cause the downfall of, overset, upset 221 *invert*; explode, blast, blow up, blow sky-high; bombard, bomb, blitz, blow to bits 712 *fire at*; wreck, break up, smash up; smash, shatter, shiver, smash to smithereens 46 *break*; pulp, crush, grind 332 *pulverize*; crush to pieces, atomize, grind to bits, make mincemeat of; rend, tear up, rend to pieces, tear to bits, tear to shreds, tear to rags, pull to pieces 46 *sunder*; shake to pieces 318 *agitate*; beat down, batter, ram 279 *strike*; gut, strip bare 229 *uncover*.

suppress, quench, blow out, put o., snuff o. 382 *extinguish*; put the kibosh on, nip in the bud, cut short, cut off, abort 72 *discontinue*; quell, put down, stamp out, trample out, trample under foot, stamp on, sit on, clamp down on 735 *oppress*; squelch, squash 216 *flatten*; quash, revoke 752 *abrogate*; blanket, stifle, smother, suffocate, strangle 161 *disable*; keep down, repress 745 *subjugate*; cover 525 *conceal*; drown, submerge, sink, scuttle, scupper, torpedo, sink without trace 313 *plunge*, 311 *lower*.

consume, devour, eat up, lick up, gobble up; swallow up, engulf, envelop 299 *absorb*; squander 634 *waste*.

be destroyed, go west, go under, be lost 361 *perish*; sink, go down 313 *plunge*; have had it, be all over with, be all up with 69 *end*; cop it, fall, bite the dust 309 *tumble*; founder, go on the rocks, break up, split, go to pieces, crumple up; fall into ruin, go to rack and ruin, crumble 655 *deteriorate*; go to the wall, succumb; go downhill, go to pot, go to the dogs, go to hell, go to blazes.

166 Reproduction – N. *reproduction,* procreation 167 *propagation*; remaking, refashioning, reshaping, remoulding, reconstruction 164 *production*; redoing 106 *repetition*; reduplication, mass production 171 *productiveness*; multiplication, duplication, printing 587 *print*; renovation, renewal 656 *restoration*; regeneration, resuscitation 656 *revival*; resurrection, resurgence; reappearance 106 *recurrence*; atavism 5 *heredity*; reincarnation 124 *future state*; copy 22 *duplicate*; Phoenix.

Vb. *reproduce,* remake, refashion, remould, reconstruct; rebuild; duplicate, clone 20 *copy*, 106 *repeat*; inherit 18 *resemble*, 148 *revert*; renovate, renew 656 *restore*; regenerate, revivify, resuscitate, reanimate 656 *revive*; reappear 106 *reoccur*; resurrect, mass-produce, multiply; breed 167 *reproduce itself,* 104 *be many*.

167 Propagation – N. *propagation* 166 *reproduction*; fertility, fecundity 171 *productiveness*; proliferation, multiplication 36 *increase*; breeding, hatching, incubation 369 *animal husbandry*; eugenics 358 *biology*; sex, facts of life, birds and the bees; copulation 45 *coition*; procreation 156 *source*; parthenogenesis, virgin birth; spontaneous generation; fertilization, pollination, fecundation, impregnation, insemination, artificial i., AID, test-tube baby, fertility drug 171 *fertilizer*; conception, pregnancy, germination, gestation (**see** *obstetrics*); birth, nativity, happy event 68 *origin*; stillbirth, abortion 728 *failure*; birth rate; development 157 *growth*; fruition, flowering 669 *maturation*; puberty 134 *adultness*; parenthood, maternity, paternity 169 *parentage*; procreator, begettor; inseminator, donor; fertilizer, pollinator; propagator, cultivator 370 *gardener*.

obstetrics, midwifery; parturition, birth, childbirth, natural c., childbed, confinement, lying in; epidural 375 *anaesthetic*; labour, labour pains, contractions; delivery, breech d., forceps d.,

Caesarian section, Caesarian; amniotic fluid, waters, bag of w., caul, umbilical cord; placenta, afterbirth; amniocentesis, alpha-fetoprotein test 658 *diagnostic*; gynaecologist, obstetrician, midwife 658 *nurse*; stork, gooseberry bush.

genitalia, loins, womb 156 *source*; genitals, reproductive organs, sex organs; pudenda, private parts, privates; male member, penis, phallus, cock (vulg), prick (vulg); testicles, scrotum, balls (vulg), goolies (vulg); prostate, p. gland; vas deferens; vulva, clitoris, vagina, cunt (vulg), fanny (vulg), pussy (vulg), uterus, cervix, ovary, Fallopian tubes; ovum, egg; semen, seminal fluid; sperm, spermatozoa; seed, pollen.

Adj. *fertilized,* impregnated; pregnant, enceinte, gravid; in an interesting *or* delicate condition; heavy with, big with; expecting, expecting a happy event, expectant, carrying, with child, in the family way; up the spout, up the pole, in the club, having a bun in the oven, fallen, preggers; parturient. obstetric.

Vb. *reproduce itself,* yield, give increase 171 *be fruitful*; hatch, breed, spawn, multiply, teem, 104 *be many*; germinate, sprout, burgeon 36 *grow*; bloom, flower, fruit, bear fruit, fructify 669 *mature*; seed; conceive, get pregnant, fall; carry, bear; be brought to bed of, bring forth, give birth, have a baby; have children, have young; lay (eggs), drop, farrow, lamb, foal, calve, cub, pup, whelp, kitten, litter; have one's birth 360 *be born*.

generate, evolve 164 *produce*; bring into being, bring into the world, give life to, bring into existence, beget, get, engender, spawn, father, sire; copulate 45 *unite with*; impregnate, inseminate, pollinate; procreate, propagate; breed, hatch, incubate, raise, bring up, rear 369 *breed stock*; raise from seed, take cuttings, bud, graft, layer 370 *cultivate*.

168 Destroyer – N. *destroyer,* demolisher, leveller; Luddite, iconoclast, annihilationist, nihilist, anarchist 149 *revolutionist*; wrecker, vandal, arsonist, pyromaniac 381 *incendiarism*; despoiler, ravager, pillager, raider 712 *attacker*, 789 *robber*; saboteur; defacer, eraser, extinguisher 550 *obliteration*; hatchet man, hitman, killer, assassin 362 *murderer*; executioner, hangman; barbarian, Vandal, Hun; time, hand of t., time's scythe 111 *course of time*; angel of death 361 *death*; destructive agency, locust 947 *glutton*; moth, woodworm, dry rot, rust, erosion 51 *decay*; corrosive, acid, mildew, blight, poison 659 *bane*; earthquake, fire, flood; grim-visaged war 718 *war*; instrument of destruction, sword 723 *weapon*; gunpowder, dynamite, blasting powder 723 *explosive*; blockbuster 723 *bomb*; nuclear warhead; juggernaut, bulldozer 216 *flattener*; Four Horsemen of the Apocalypse, Exterminating Angel.

169 Parentage – N. *parentage,* paternity, maternity; parenthood, fatherhood, motherhood; loins, womb 156 *source*; kinship 11 *family*; adoption, fostering, guardianship, surrogateship, surrogacy 660 *protection*; parent, first parents, Adam and Eve 371 *humankind*; single parent 896 *divorce*, godparent, guardian 660 *protection*.

genealogy, family tree, lineage, kin 11 *consanguinity*; pedigree, heredity; line, blood, strain; blue blood 868 *nobility*; stock, stem, tribe, house, clan 11 *race*; descent, extraction, birth, ancestry 68 *origin*.

paternity, fatherhood; father, dad, daddy, pop, papa, pater, governor, the old man; head of the family, paterfamilias; procreator, begetter, author of one's existence; grandfather, grandsire, grandad, grandpa, great-grandfather 133 *old man*; ancestor, progenitor, forefather, forbear, patriarch, predecessor 66 *precursor*; father figure; adoptive father, foster-f., natural f., biological f., stepfather, father-in-law; fatherland.

maternity, motherhood; maternal instinct 887 *love*; expectant mother, mother-to-be 167 *propagation*; mother, unmarried m., dam; mamma, mummy, mum, mater; grandmother, grandma, granny, gran, nan; materfamilias, matron, matriarch; ancestress, progenitrix; grandam 133 *old woman*; mother substitute; foster-mother, stepmother, adoptive mother, natural m., biological m., surrogate m.; mother-in-law; Mother Church, mother country, motherland.

Adj. *parental,* paternal; maternal, matronly; fatherly, fatherlike; motherly, stepmotherly; family, lineal, patrilineal, matrilineal; ancestral; hereditary 5 *genetic*; patriarchal 127 *immemorial*; racial 11 *ethnic*.

170 Posterity – N. *posterity,* progeny, issue, offspring, young, little ones 132 *child*; breed 11 *race*; brood, seed, litter, farrow, spawn 132 *young creature*; children, grandchildren 11 *family*; succession, heirs, inheritance, heritage 120 *posteriority*; rising generation 130 *youth.*

descendant, son, daughter; chip off the old block, infant 132 *child*; scion, shoot, sprout 132 *young plant*; heir, heiress 776 *beneficiary*; love child 954 *bastardy*; branch, ramification, colony; graft, offshoot, offset.

171 Productiveness – N. *productiveness,* productivity, mass production 164 *production*; boom, booming economy 730 *prosperity*; overproductivity, superabundance, glut, butter mountain, wine lake 637 *redundance*; menarche, fecundity, fertility, luxuriance, lushness, exuberance, richness, embarras de richesses 635 *plenty*; baby boom, population explosion; procreation, multiplication 167 *propagation*; fructification 669 *ripening*; fertilization, pollination.

fertilizer, organic f., manure, farmyard m., dung, guano, compost, bonemeal; artificial fertilizer, chemical f.; phosphates, nitrates, potash, lime; top-dressing, mulch 370 *agriculture*; semen, sperm, seed; fertility drug. gonadotrophin 167 *propagation*.

abundance, wealth, riot, profusion, harvest 32 *great quantity*; mother earth; hotbed, nursery, propagator; cornucopia, horn of plenty, land flowing with milk and honey; milch cow; aftermath 67 *sequel*; rabbit warren, ant heap 104 *multitude.*

Adj. *prolific,* fertile, productive, fecund; teeming, spawning; fruitful, fruitbearing, fructiferous; pregnant, heavy with, parturient; exuberant, rife, lush, leafy, verdant, luxuriant, rich, fat 635 *plentiful*; copious, streaming, pouring; paying 640 *profitable*; creative, scribacious.

Vb. *make fruitful,* make productive etc. adj.; fertilize, irrigate, impregnate, inseminate; procreate, propagate 167 *generate.*

be fruitful, - prolific etc. adj.; flourish; burgeon, bloom, blossom; germinate; conceive, bear, give birth, have children 167 *reproduce itself*; teem, proliferate, swarm, multiply, mushroom 104 *be many*; boom; 36 *augment*; populate.

172 Unproductiveness– N. *unproductiveness,* unproductivity, dearth, famine 636 *scarcity*; sterility, barrenness, infertility, infecundity 161 *impotence*; deforestation, erosion; defoliation; scorched earth policy, desertification, desertization; falling birthrate, zero population growth 37 *decrease*; virginity 895 *celibacy*; change of life, the change, menopause; abortion; unprofitableness 772 *loss*; unprofitability, fruitlessness 641 *uselessness*; aridity, aridness, fallowness, stagnation; slump, idleness 679 *inactivity.*

contraception, birth control, planned parenthood, family planning; contraceptive, barrier c.; pill, minipill, coil, loop, diaphragm, Dutch cap, French letter, condom, sheath; spermicide, C-film; rhythm method, Billing's m.; chastity 747 *restraint*; sterilization, vasectomy, hysterectomy.

desert, dryness, aridity, aridness 342 *dryness*; desolation, waste, barren w.,

wastelands, lunar landscape; heath, moor, bush, wild, wilderness; desert sands, sand dunes, Sahara; dustbowl 634 *waste*; desert island; salt flat 347 *marsh*; Artic wastes 380 *ice*.

Adj. *unproductive,* dried up, exhausted, spent; sparse, scarce 636 *insufficient*; waste, desert, desolate; treeless, bleak, gaunt, bare 190 *empty*; poor, stony, shallow, eroded; barren, infertile, sour, sterile; withered, shrivelled, blasted; unprolific, unfruitful, arid, unirrigated 342 *dry*; fallow, stagnating 674 *disused*; unsown, untilled, uncultivated; impotent, sterilized, sterile, on the pill; childless, without issue; celibate; fruitless, unprofitable 641 *profitless*; inoperative, out of action, null and void, of no effect 161 *impotent*; ineffective 728 *unsuccessful*; addled, abortive 670 *unprepared*.

173 Agency – N. *agency,* operation, work, doing 676 *action*; job, position, office 622 *function*; exercise 673 *use*; force, strain, swing 160 *power*; interworking 178 *influence*; procurement 689 *management*; service 628 *instrumentality*; effectiveness, efficiency 156 *causation*; quickening power 174 *stimulation*; support 703 *aid*; co-agency 706 *cooperation*; execution; process.

Adj. *operative,* effectual, efficient, efficacious 727 *successful*; operational, functional; in force, in play, at work; 673 *used*; afoot, up and doing 678 *active*.

Vb. *operate,* be in action, be operative, be in play, play; act, work, go, run 676 *do*; serve, execute, perform 622 *function*; do its job, do its stuff, do one's thing 727 *be successful*; take effect 156 *cause*; have effect 178 *influence*; take action, take industrial a., strike 678 *be active*; crew, man; make operate, bring into play, bring into action, wind up, turn on, plug in, switch on, flick *or* flip the switch, press the button; actuate, power, drive 265 *move*.

174 Vigour: physical energy – N. *vigorousness,* lustiness, energy, vigour, life 678 *activity*; dynamism, pressure, force, impetus 160 *energy*; intensity 162 *strength*; dash, élan, pizzazz, impetuosity 680 *haste*; exertion, effort 682 *labour*; fervour, enthusiasm 571 *vigour*; gusto, relish, zest, zestfulness 824 *joy*; liveliness, spirit, vim, zing, zip, éclat; fire, mettle, pluck, smeddum, blood 855 *courage*; fizz, verve, snap, pep, drive, go, get up and go; enterprise, initiative 672 *undertaking*; vehemence 176 *violence*; aggressiveness, oomph, thrust, push, kick, punch 712 *attack*; grip, bite, teeth, backbone, spunk 599 *resolution*; guts, grit 600 *stamina*; virility 162 *vitality*.

stimulation, activation, turning on, galvanizing, whipping up; intensification, boost, stepping up 36 *increase*; excitement 821 *excitation*; stir, bustle 678 *activity*; perturbation 318 *agitation*; ferment, fermentation.

stimulant, energizer, activator, booster; yeast, leaven, catalyst; stimulus, fillip, shot, shot in the arm; crack of the whip, spur, prick, prod, jolt, goad, lash 612 *incentive*; restorative, tonic, pep pill 658 *tonic*; pick-me-up, aperitif, appetizer 390 *savouriness*; seasoning, spice 389 *sauce*; liquor, alcohol 301 *alcoholic drink*; aphrodisiac, philtre; love potion; pep talk, rousing cheer, egging on 821 *excitant*.

Adj. *vigorous,* energetic 678 *active*; forceful, vehement 176 *violent*; vivid, vibrant 160 *dynamic*; intense, strenuous 678 *industrious*; enterprising, go-getting, go-ahead 285 *progressive*; aggressive, keen, 597 *willing*; potent 160 *powerful*; hearty, virile, full-blooded 162 *strong*; full of beans, peppy, zippy, zingy, zestful, lusty, mettlesome 819 *lively*; blooming, bouncing 650 *healthy*; spry, brisk, nippy, snappy; fizzy, effervescent, heady, racy; tonic, bracing, rousing, invigorating, stimulating 821 *exciting*; thriving, lush 171 *prolific*.

keen, acute, sharp, trenchant 571 *forceful*; mordant, biting, pointed, sarcastic; virulent, corrosive, caustic 388 *pungent*; acrimonious, acrid, acid 393 *sour*.

Vb. *be vigorous,* thrive, be full of zip *or* zing, enjoy life 650 *be healthy*; burst with energy 162 *be strong*; show energy 678 *be active*; be always on the go, be up and doing 682 *exert oneself*; drive; cut right through 176 *force*; get up steam, put on a spurt, get psyched up, pull out all the stops 277 *accelerate*; be thorough, strike home 725 *carry through*; show one's power, make an impression 178 *influence*, 821 *impress*; throw one's weight about 678 *meddle*.

invigorate, energize, activate; galvanize, electrify, intensify, double, redouble; wind up, step up, bump up, hike up, pep up, ginger up, boost, soup up 162 *strengthen*; rouse, kindle, inflame, stimulate, psych up, enliven, quicken 821 *excite*; act like a tonic, hearten, animate, egg on 833 *cheer*; go to one's head, intoxicate 949 *inebriate*; freshen, revive 685 *refresh*; give an edge to 256 *sharpen*.

175 Inertness – N. *inertness,* inertia 677 *inaction*; lifelessness, languor, paralysis, torpor, torpidity 375 *insensibility*; rest, vegetation, stagnation, passivity 266 *quiescence*; dormancy 523 *latency*; apathy, sloth 679 *sluggishness*; immobility, passive resistance 602 *obstinacy*; impassiveness, stolidity 823 *inexcitability*.

Adj. *inert,* passive, dead 677 *nonactive*; lifeless, languid, torpid, numb 375 *insensible*; heavy, lumpish, sluggish 278 *slow*, 679 *inactive*; hibernating 679 *sleepy*; quiet, vegetating, stagnant 266 *quiescent*; fallow 172 *unproductive*; slack; limp, flaccid 163 *weak*; apathetic, neutral 860 *indifferent*, 820 *impassive*; deactivated, suspended, in abeyance; dormant 523 *latent*.

176 Violence – N. *violence,* vehemence, frenzy, fury, ferment, impetuosity 174 *vigorousness*; destructiveness, vandalism 165 *destruction*; boisterousness, turbulence, storminess 318 *commotion*; uproar, riot, row, roughhouse, rumpus, ruckus, brouhaha, stramash, furore 61 *turmoil*; roughness, rough handling 735 *severity*; force, fisticuffs, hammer blows,

strong-arm tactics, terrorism 735 *brute force*; torture 898 *cruel act*; brutality, savagery 898 *inhumanity*; fierceness, ferocity 906 *pitilessness*; rage, hysterics 822 *excitable state*; fit, throes, paroxysm 318 *spasm*; shock, clash 279 *collision*.

outbreak, outburst 318 *agitation*; flood, tidal wave 350 *wave*; cataclysm, convulsion, earthquake, quake, tremor 149 *revolution*; eruption, volcano 383 *furnace*; explosion, blow-up, flare-up, burst, blast 165 *destruction*; bursting open 46 *disunion*; detonation 400 *loudness*; sortie 712 *attack*; gush, torrent 350 *stream*.

storm, turmoil, turbulence, war of the elements; weather, dirty w., rough w., inclement w., inclemency; squall, tempest, typhoon, hurricane, tornado, cyclone 352 *gale*; thunder, thunder and lightning;   rainstorm,   downpour, cloudburst 350 *rain*; hailstorm, snowstorm, blizzard 380 *wintriness*; sandstorm, duststorm, sirocco 352 *gale*; magnetic storm.

violent creature, brute, beast, wild b., savage b.; dragon, tiger, wolf, she w., mad dog; demon, devil, hellhound, Hound of the Baskervilles, hellcat 938 *monster*; savage, barbarian, vandal, iconoclast 168 *destroyer*; he-man, cave m., Neanderthal m. 372 *male*; man of blood, assassin, executioner, Herod 362 *murderer*; homicidal maniac, psychopath 504 *madman*; rough, tough, rowdy, thug, mugger 904 *ruffian*; hooligan, bully, bully boy, bovver b., boot b., terror, holy t. 735 *tyrant*; firebrand, incendiary, pyromaniac 738 *agitator*; revolutionary, militant, nihilist, terrorist 149 *revolutionist*; termagant, Amazon; spitfire, scold 892 *shrew*.

Adj. *violent,* vehement, forcible 162 *strong*; acute 256 *sharp*; unmitigated; excessive, outrageous, extravagant 32 *exorbitant*; rude; extreme, severe, tyrannical, heavy-handed 735 *oppressive*; barbarous, savage, brutal, bloody 898 *cruel*; hot-blooded 892 *irascible*; aggressive, bellicose 718 *warlike*; rampant, charging; struggling, kicking, thrashing about

61 *disorderly*; rough, wild, furious, raging, blustery, tempestuous, stormy 352 *windy*; drenching, torrential 350 *rainy*; uproarious, obstreperous 400 *loud*; rowdy, turbulent, tumultuous, boisterous; incendiary, nihilistic 149 *revolutionary*; intemperate, immoderate, unbridled, unrestrained; ungovernable, unruly, uncontrollable 738 *disobedient*; irrepressible, inextinguishable 174 *vigorous*; ebullient, hot, red-hot, inflamed 381 *heated*; inflammatory, scorching, flaming 379 *fiery*; eruptive, cataclysmic, overwhelming, volcanic, seismic 165 *destructive*; detonating, explosive, bursting; convulsive, spasmodic; full of violence, disturbed, troublous.

furious, fuming, boiling, towering; infuriated, mad, like a mad bull, mad with rage, maddened 891 *angry*; impetuous, rampant, gnashing; roaring, howling; headstrong 680 *hasty*; desperate 857 *rash*; savage, tameless, wild; blustering, threatening 899 *cursing*; vicious, fierce, ferocious 898 *cruel*; blood-thirsty, ravening, rabid, berserk, out of control 362 *murderous*; tigerish; frantic, frenetic, hysterical 503 *frenzied*.

Vb. *force*, use f., smash 46 *break*; tear, rend 46 *sunder*; bruise, crush 332 *pulverize*; blow up 165 *demolish*; strain, wrench, pull, dislocate, fracture, sprain; twist, warp, deform 246 *distort*; force open, prize o., pry o., lever o., jimmy 263 *open*; blow open, burst o.; shock, shake 318 *agitate*; do violence to, mug, beat up, abuse 675 *misuse*; violate, ravish, rape 951 *debauch*; torture 645 *ill-treat*.

177 Moderation – N. *moderation*, nonviolence; mildness, gentleness 736 *leniency*; harmlessness, innocuousness 935 *innocence*; moderateness, reasonableness 502 *sanity*; golden mean 732 *averageness*; temperateness, restraint, self-control 942 *temperance*; soberness 948 *sobriety*, 874 *modesty*; impassivity 823 *inexcitability*; neutrality 625 *middle way*; correction, adjustment, modulation; mitigation 831 *relief*; relaxation,

remission, letup 734 *laxity*; easing, alleviation; détente 719 *pacification*; tranquillization, sedation; quiet, calm, dead c. 266 *quietude*; control, check 747 *restraint*.

moderator, palliative 658 *remedy*; alleviative 658 *balm*; soothing syrup, milk, oil on troubled waters; calmative, sedative, tranquillizer, Valium (tdmk), lullaby; nightcap, bromide, barbiturate, sleeping pill, Mogadon (tdmk); anodyne, opiate, opium, laudanum 375 *anaesthetic*; dummy, pacifier 264 *stopper*; wet blanket, damper, killjoy 613 *dissuasion*; cooler, cold water, cold shower 382 *extinguisher*; clamp, brake 747 *restraint*; neutralizer; anaphrodisiac 658 *antidote*; cushion, shock absorber 327 *softness*; mollifier, peacemaker 720 *mediator*; rein.

Adj. *moderate*, unextreme, nonviolent, reasonable, within reason 913 *just*; innocuous 935 *innocent*, 163 *weak*; measured, restricted, low-key 747 *restrained*; self-controlled, tempered 942 *temperate*, 948 *sober*; cool, calm, composed 823 *inexcitable*; still, quiet, untroubled 266 *tranquil*; peaceable, pacific 717 *peaceful*; leftish, pink, nonextreme, non-reactionary, middle-American, middle-of-the-road 625 *neutral*, 860 *indifferent*.

Vb. *moderate*, mitigate, temper; correct 24 *adjust*; tame, check, curb, control, chasten, govern, limit, keep within limits 747 *restrain*; lessen, diminish, slacken 37 *abate*; palliate, extenuate, qualify 163 *weaken*; take the edge off 257 *blunt*; break the fall, cushion 218 *support*; play down, soft-pedal, tone down, blue-pencil, euphemize 648 *purify*; sober, sober down, dampen, damp, cool, chill, throw cold water on 382 *refrigerate*, 613 *dissuade*; put a damper on, bank down the fires; blanket, muffle, smother, subdue, quell 382 *extinguish*.

assuage, ease, pour balm, mollify 327 *soften*; alleviate, lighten 831 *relieve*; deactivate, neutralize, act as an antidote, take the sting out 182 *counteract*; allay, dull, deaden 375 *render insensible*; soothe, calm, tranquillize, comfort, still,

quiet, hush, lull, rock, cradle, rock to sleep 266 *bring to rest*; disarm, appease, smooth over, bring round, pour oil on troubled waters 719 *pacify*; assuage one's thirst, quench one's t., slake 301 *drink*.

178 Influence – N. *influence*, capability, power, potency 160 *ability*; prevalence, predominance 34 *superiority*; mightiness 32 *greatness*, 638 *importance*; upper hand, whip h., casting vote, final say; vantage ground, footing, hold, grip; leverage, play 744 *scope*; purchase 218 *pivot*; clout, weight, pressure; pull, drag, magnetism 291 *attraction*; counterattraction 292 *repulsion*, 182 *counteraction*; impact 279 *impulse*; climate 8 *circumstance*; occult influence, mana, magic, spell 983 *sorcery*; stars, astrology, horoscope, heavens, destiny 596 *fate*; hypnotism, mesmerism; curse, ruin 659 *bane*; persuasion, insinuation, inspiration 612 *motive*; personality, je ne sais quoi, charisma 866 *prestige*; ascendancy, domination, tyranny 733 *authority*; sway, control, dominance, reign 733 *governance*; sphere of influence, orbit; factor, contributing f., vital role, leading part 156 *cause*; indirect influence, patronage, favour, pull, friend at court, wire-pulling 703 *aid*; strings, lever 630 *tool*; secret influence, hidden hand, hand that rocks the cradle, woman behind the great man, power behind the throne, kingmaker, power broker, Grey Eminence 523 *latency*; lobby, pressure group, vested interest 612 *inducement*; manipulator, mover, manoeuvrer 612 *motivator*; big noise, big shot 638 *bigwig*; superpower; Big Brother, the Establishment 733 *government*.

Adj. *influential*, dominant, predominant, prevalent, prevailing 34 *supreme*; ruling, reigning, commanding, in the driving seat, obeyed; recognized, with authority 733 *authoritative*; rising, ascendant 36 *increasing*; strong, potent, mighty, multinational 32 *great*, 160 *powerful*; leading, guiding, inspiring; active

in, busy, meddling 678 *active*; contributing, effective; weighty, key, momentous, decisive, world-shattering, earth-shaking 638 *important*; telling, moving, attractive; fascinating, charismatic; irresistible, hypnotic, mesmeric 740 *compelling*; persuasive, suggestive, insinuating; addictive; instructive 534 *educational*; pervasive 189 *ubiquitous*.

Vb. *influence*, have i., carry weight, cut ice; be well-connected, know the right people, have friends at court, have friends in high places; have a hold on, have in one's power; have the ear of, be obeyed 737 *command*; dominate, tower over, bestride; lead by the nose, have under one's thumb, wind round one's little finger, wear the trousers 34 *be superior*; exert influence, make one's presence felt, assert oneself; put pressure on, lobby, pull strings 612 *motivate*; make one's voice heard 455 *attract notice*; have a voice, have a say in; affect, be a factor in, turn the scale; bear upon, tell u. 821 *impress*; work on 925 *flatter*; inspire, persuade, carry with one 612 *induce*; force 740 *compel*; brainwash, prejudice 481 *bias*; hypnotize, mesmerize 291 *attract*; put off 292 *repel*; militate against, counterbalance 182 *counteract*; actuate, work 173 *operate*; have a rôle, play a part, play a leading p., guide 689 *direct*; lead the dance, set the fashion, establish a trend, be the model for 23 *be an example*.

prevail, outweigh, override, turn the scale 34 *predominate*; overawe, overcome, subdue, subjugate; hold the whip hand, gain the upper hand, hold all the cards, master 727 *overmaster*; control, rule, monopolise 733 *dominate*; hold 778 *retain*; take root, take hold, settle 144 *stay*; permeate, catch on, spread, rage, be rife, spread like wildfire.

179 Tendency – N. *tendency*, trend, tenor; tempo, rhythm, set, drift 281 *direction*; course, stream, main current, main stream, Zeitgeist, spirit of the times, spirit of the age; climate 178 *influence*; gravitation, affinity 291 *attraction*;

polarity 240 *contraposition*; aptness 24 *fitness*; gift, talent, instinct for 694 *aptitude*; proneness, proclivity, propensity, predisposition, readiness, inclination, penchant, predilection, liking, leaning, bias, prejudice; weakness 180 *liability*; cast, cast of mind, bent, turn, grain; a strain of 43 *tincture*; vein, humour, mood; tone, quality, nature, characteristic 5 *temperament*; special gift, genius, idiosyncrasy 80 *speciality*.

Vb. *tend,* verge, lean, incline; set towards, gravitate t. 289 *approach*; turn 178 *influence*; lead to 156 *conduce*; be calculated to 471 *be likely*.

180 Liability – **N.** *liability,* liableness, weakness 179 *tendency*; exposure 661 *vulnerability*; susceptibility 374 *sensibility*; potentiality 469 *possibility*; likelihood 471 *probability*; obligation, responsibility, accountability, amenability 917 *duty*.

Adj. *liable,* apt to; subject to, given to 745 *subject*; open to, exposed to, in danger of 661 *vulnerable*; dependent on, contingent 157 *caused*; incident to, incidental; possible, within the realms of possibility, on the cards, within the range of 469 *possible*; susceptible 819 *impressible*; answerable, reportable, responsible, accountable 917 *obliged*.

Vb. *be liable,* - subject to etc. adj.; be responsible, the buck stops here, answer for 917 *incur a duty*; incur, lay oneself open to, stand the chance of; run the risk of 661 *be in danger*.

181 Concurrence: combination of causes – **N.** *concurrence,* combined operation, joint effort, collaboration, synergy, synergism 706 *cooperation*; coincidence 24 *conformance*, 83 *conformity*; concord, harmony 24 *agreement*; compliance 758 *consent*; consensus 488 *assent*; acquiescence, nonresistance 721 *submission*; concert, pooling of resources, two heads are better than one, two minds with but a single thought, joint planning, collusion, conspiracy 623 *plot*; league, alliance,

partnership 706 *association*; conjunction, liaison 45 *union*; think tank.

Vb. *concur,* acquiesce 488 *assent*; collude, connive, conspire 623 *plot*; agree, harmonize 24 *accord*; hang together, stick t., pull t. 706 *cooperate*; contribute, help, aid, abet, aid and abet, serve 703 *minister to*; promote, subserve 156 *conduce*; go with, go along w., go hand in hand w., keep pace w., keep abreast of, run parallel to 89 *accompany*; unite, stand together 48 *cohere*.

182 Counteraction – **N.** *counteraction,* polarity 240 *contraposition*; antagonism, antipathy, clash, aggro, conflict, mutual c. 14 *contrariety*, 279 *collision*; reaction, retroaction, repercussion, backfire, backlash, boomerang effect 280 *recoil*; recalcitrance, kicking back 715 *resistance*, 704 *opposition*; inertia, friction, drag, check 702 *hindrance*; interference, counterpressure, repression, suppression 747 *restraint*; intolerance, persecution 735 *severity*; neutralization, deactivation 177 *moderation*; nullification, cancellation 165 *destruction*; crosscurrent, headwind 702 *obstacle*; counterspell, counterirritant, neutralizer 658 *antidote*; counterbalance, counterweight; counterblast, countermove 688 *tactics*; defensive measures, deterrent 713 *defence*; prevention, preventive, preventative; contraception; inhibitor 757 *prohibition*.

Vb. *counteract,* counter, run c., cross, traverse, work against, go a., militate a.; not conduce to 702 *hinder*; react 280 *recoil*; persecute 881 *be inimical*; fight against, resist, withstand, defend oneself 704 *oppose*; antagonize, conflict with 14 *be contrary*; clash 279 *collide*; interfere 678 *meddle*; cancel out, counterpoise, counterbalance; repress 165 *suppress*; undo, cancel 752 *abrogate*; neutralize, act as an antidote, deactivate, demagnetize; cure 658 *remedy*; recover 656 *retrieve*; obviate, be a way round, prevent, inhibit 757 *prohibit*.

Adv. *although,* in spite of, despite, notwithstanding; against, contrary to 704 *in opposition.*

Class two

SPACE

Section one: Space in general

183 Space: indefinite space – N. *space,* expanse, expansion; extension, extent, surface, area; volume, cubic content; continuum, stretch 71 *continuity*; space-time 108 *time*; empty space 190 *emptiness*; abyss 211 *depth*; roominess; infinite s. 107 *infinity*; sky, aerospace, airspace, outer space 321 *heavens*; world, length and breadth of the land; vastness, immensity; terrain, open space, open country; green belt, wide open spaces 348 *plain*; upland, moorland, veld, prairie, steppe 348 *grassland*; outback, hinterland 184 *region*; wild, wilderness, waste 172 *desert.*

measure, proportions, dimension 203 *length,* 205 *breadth,* 209 *height,* 211 *depth*; area, surface a.; square measure, acreage, acres, rods, poles and perches; square inch, square yard, square metre, hectare, hide; volume, cubic content 195 *size.*

range, reach, carry, compass; stretch, grasp, span; radius, latitude, amplitude; sweep, spread, ramification; play, swing, margin 744 *scope*; sphere, field, arena 184 *region*; prospect 438 *view*; perspective, focal distance 199 *distance*; aim; magnifying power.

room, space, accommodation; capacity, stowage, storage space 632 *storage*; seating capacity, seating; standing room; margin, clearance, windage; elbowroom, legroom, room to swing a cat; headroom, headway; leeway, latitude; opening, way 263 *open space*; Lebensraum.

Adj. *spacious* 32 *extensive*; expansive, roomy, commodious; ample, vast, capacious, broad, deep, wide; voluminous, baggy, loose-fitting 195 *large*; broad-based 79 *general*; far-reaching, far-flung,

widespread, wide-ranging, comprehensive, worldwide, global, world 52 *whole*; uncircumscribed, boundless 107 *infinite*; extending, branching.

Vb. *extend,* spread, outspread, spread out, range, cover, encompass; span, straddle, bestride; extend to, reach to 202 *be contiguous*; branch.

Adv. *widely,* extensively, everywhere, with no stone unturned; far and near, far and wide, all over, globally, universally, the whole world over; under the sun, on the face of the earth, in all quarters, from end to end, from pole to pole, from coast to coast, from Land's End to John o' Groats 54 *throughout*; from all the points of the compass, from the furthest corners of the earth; to the four winds, to the uttermost parts of the earth; here, there and everywhere, right and left, high and low.

184 Region: definite space – N. *region,* locality, locale, parts 185 *place*; sphere, orb, hemisphere; zone, section, belt; latitude, parallel, meridian; clime, climate; tract, terrain, country, ground, soil 344 *land*; geographical unit, island, peninsula, continent, landmass; sea 343 *ocean*; Third World 733 *political organization*; compass, circumference, circle, circuit 233 *outline*; boundaries, bounds, shore, confines, marches 236 *limit*; pale, precincts, close, enclave, salient 235 *enclosure*; corridor 624 *access*; area, field, theatre 724 *arena*; economic zone, exclusive area, charmed circle. See *territory.*

territory, sphere, zone; catchment area; beat, pitch, ground; plot, lot, holding, claim 235 *enclosure*; grounds, park 777 *estate*; national boundaries, domain, territorial waters, economic zone; continental shelf, airspace; possession, dependency, protectorate, dominion; colony, settlement; motherland, fatherland, homeland 192 *home*; commonwealth, republic, kingdom, realm, state, empire 733 *political organization*; no-man's-land, Tom Tiddler's ground 774 *nonownership*; no-go area.

district, purlieus, neighbourhood, haunt 187 *locality*; subregion, quarter,

division 53 *subdivision*; state, province, county, shire, bailiwick, riding, lathe, wapentake, hundred, soke, rape, tithing; diocese, bishopric, archbishopric; parish, ward, constituency; borough, community, township, municipality; county, district, metropolitan area; canton, department, arrondissement, commune; hamlet, village, town, market t., county t. 192 *abode*; built-up area 192 *housing*; garden city, new town; suburb, suburbia, dormitory suburb, stockbroker belt; green belt 183 *space*; Home Counties, provinces, back of beyond, the sticks, outback, backwoods, bush, brush, bundu; hinterland, heartland.

city, metropolis, conurbation; Greater London, the Big City, the Big Smoke, the Big Apple; City, Wall Street.

185 Place: limited space – N. *place*, emplacement, site, location, position 186 *situation*; station, substation; quarter, locality 184 *district*; pitch, beat, billet, socket, groove; centre, meeting place, rendez-vous 76 *focus*; birthplace, dwelling place, fireside 192 *home*; address, habitat 187 *locality*, 192 *quarters*; premises, building, mansion 192 *house*; spot, plot; point, dot, pinpoint; niche, nook, corner, cranny, hole, pigeonhole, pocket, slot 194 *compartment*; confines, bounds, baseline, crease (cricket) 236 *limit*; confined place, prison, coffin, grave; precinct, paddock, compound, pen 235 *enclosure*; close, quadrangle, quad, square, town s.; yard, area, backyard, courtyard, court 263 *open space*; farmyard, field 370 *farm*; every nook and cranny.

186 Situation – N. *situation*, position, setting; scene, locale; time and place, when and where; location, address, whereabouts; point, stage, milestone 27 *degree*; site, seat, emplacement, base 185 *place*; habitat, ecosphere, ecosystem, biotype, range 184 *region*; post, station; standpoint, standing, ground, footing 7 *state*; side, aspect, attitude, posture; frontage, orientation 239 *laterality*, 240 *contraposition*; geography, topography,

chorography, cosmography, ecology 321 *earth sciences*; chart 551 *map*.

Vb. *be situated*, be located, be sited, be situate, centre on; be found at, have one's address at, be, lie, stand; be stationed, be posted; live, live at 192 *dwell*; touch.

187 Location – N. *location*, placing, siting, placement, emplacement, collocation, disposition; posting, stationing, relocation; locating, pinpointing; radiolocation, radar; centering, localization 200 *nearness*; settlement, resettlement, lodgment, establishment, fixation, installation; deposition; putting in 303 *insertion*.

locality, quarters, purlieus, environs, environment, surroundings, milieu, neighbourhood, parts, neck of the woods 184 *district*; vicinity; address, postal district, street, place of residence, habitat 192 *abode*; seat, site 185 *place*; meeting place, venue, haunt 76 *focus*.

station, seat, site, emplacement, position 186 *situation*; depot, base, military b., barracks, naval base, air b.; colony, settlement; anchorage, roadstead, mooring 662 *shelter*; cantonment, lines, police l.; camp, encampment, laager, bivouac, campsite, caravan site, temporary abode; hostel 192 *abode*; halting place, lay-by, car park, parking bay, parking lot, parking place 145 *stopping place*.

Vb. *place*, collocate, assign a place 62 *arrange*; situate, position, site, locate, relocate; base, centre, localize; narrow down, pinpoint, pin down; find the place, put one's finger on; place right, aim well, hit, hit the nail on the head, hit the mark 281 *aim*; put, lay, set, seat; station, post, park; install, ensconce, set up, establish, fix 153 *stabilize*; fix in, root, plant, implant, embed, graft, slot in 303 *insert*; bed, bed down, put to bed, tuck in, tuck up, cradle; accommodate, find a place for, find room for, put one up, lodge, house, quarter, billet; quarter upon, billet on; impose; moor, tether, picket, anchor 45 *tie*; dock, berth 266 *bring to rest*; deposit, lay down, put d.,

set d.; stand, put up, erect 310 *elevate*; place with, transfer, bestow, invest 780 *assign*; array, deploy.

place oneself, stand, take one's place, take one's stand, anchor, drop a. 266 *come to rest*; settle, strike root, take r., gain a footing, get a foothold, entrench oneself, dig in 144 *stay*; perch, alight, sit on, sit, squat, park; pitch on, pitch one's tent, encamp, camp, bivouac; stop at, lodge, put up; burrow; ensconce oneself, locate oneself, establish o., find a home, move in, put down roots; settle, colonize, populate, people 192 *dwell*.

188 Displacement – N. *displacement,* dislocation, derailment 63 *derangement*; misplacement, wrong place, ectopia 84 *abnormality*; shift, move 265 *motion*; red shift, Doppler effect; parallax; aberration, perturbation (astronomy) 282 *deviation*; translocation, transposition, transhipment, transfer 272 *transference*; mutual transfer 151 *interchange*; relief, replacement 150 *substitution*; uprooting, removal; taking away 304 *extraction*; unloading, unpacking; expulsion 300 *ejection*; weeding, eradication 300 *voidance*; exile, banishment 883 *seclusion*; refugee 268 *wanderer*; fish out of water, square peg in a round hole 25 *misfit*; docker, stevedore, removal man.

Vb. *displace,* disturb, disarrange, disorientate, derail, dislocate; dislodge, disestablish, unseat, unfix, unstick 46 *disunite*; dispel, scatter, send flying 75 *disperse*; shift, remove 265 *move*; cart away, transport 272 *transfer*; change round; transpose 151 *interchange*; dispatch, post 272 *send*; relegate, banish, exile, kick upstairs 300 *dismiss*; set aside, supersede 150 *substitute*, 752 *depose*; turn out, evict, unhouse 300 *eject*; wipe out, eradicate, uproot 165 *destroy*; discharge, unload, off-load, unship, tranship; clear away, rake, sweep, sweep up 648 *clean*; take away, take off, cart off; lift, raise, uplift 310 *elevate*; draw, draw out, pull o. 304 *extract*.

misplace, mislay, lose, lose touch with, lose track of.

189 Presence – N. *presence,* being there, existence; whereabouts 186 *situation*; being somewhere, ubiety; being everywhere, ubiquity, ubiquitousness, omnipresence; permeation, pervasion, diffusion; availability, bird in the hand; attendance; residence, occupancy, occupation, sit-in 773 *possession*; visit, descent, stay; nowness, present moment 121 *present time*; man on the spot; spectator, attendee, bystander 441 *onlookers*.

Adj. *ubiquitous,* omnipresent, permeating, pervading, pervasive 79 *universal*.

Vb. *be present,* exist, be; take up space, occupy; colonize, inhabit 192 *dwell*; hold 773 *possess*; stand, lie 186 *be situated*; look on, stand by, observe, witness 441 *watch*; frequent, haunt; occur 154 *happen*; stay, sojourn, summer, winter, revisit 882 *visit*; attend, assist at, grace the occasion, honour with one's presence; take part; show up, turn up, present oneself, announce o. 295 *arrive*; be in evidence, show one's face, put in an appearance, look in on; face, confront 711 *defy*.

pervade, permeate, fill 54 *make complete*; be diffused through, be disseminated, imbue, impregnate, soak, saturate, run through; overrun, swarm over, spread, filter through, meet one at every turn 297 *infiltrate*; make one's presence felt 178 *influence*.

190 Absence – N. *absence,* nonpresence, disappearing trick 446 *disappearance*; lack 636 *scarcity*; deprivation 772 *loss*; being nowhere; inexistence 2 *nonexistence*; being elsewhere, alibi; nonresidence, living out; leave of absence, sick leave, compassionate leave, vacation, holiday, sabbatical, furlough; nonattendance, nonappearance, truancy, skiving, bunking off, absenteeism, French leave 620 *avoidance*; absentee, truant 620 *avoider*; absentee landlord; backwoodsman, nonvoter, postal voter.

emptiness, bareness, empty space, void, vacuity, inanity, vacancy; blank 201 *gap*; nothing inside, hollowness,

shell; vacuum, air pocket; empties, dead men (empty bottles); blank cartridge, blank paper, clean sheet, tabula rasa; virgin territory, no-man's-land; waste, desolation, wilderness 172 *desert*; vacant lot, bomb site 183 *room*.

nobody, no one, nobody present, nobody on earth; not a soul, not a single person, not a living thing; empty seats.

Adj. *absent,* not present, not found, unrepresented; away, not resident; gone from home, on tour, on location; out, not at home; gone, flown, disappeared; lacking, wanting, missing, wanted; absent without leave, AWOL; truant, absentee; unavailable, unobtainable, off the menu, off 636 *unprovided*; lost, mislaid, missing, nowhere to be found; inexistent 2 *nonexistent*; exempt from, spared, exempted; on leave, on holiday, on vacation, on sabbatical, on furlough; omitted, left out.

empty, vacant, vacuous, inane; void, devoid, bare; blank, clean; characterless, featureless; hollow; vacant, unoccupied, unlived-in, uninhabited, untenanted, tenantless; unstaffed, crewless; depopulated; desert, deserted; unpeopled, unsettled, uncolonized; godforsaken, lonely; bleak, desolate 172 *unproductive*; uninhabitable.

Vb. *be absent,* have no place in, take no part in; absent oneself, not show up, stay away, keep away, keep out of the way, cut, skip, skive, play truant *or* hookey, bunk off, take French leave 620 *avoid*; be missed, leave a gap, be conspicuous by one's absence.

go away, withdraw, leave 296 *depart*; make oneself scarce, slip out, slip away, be off, naff off, retreat 296 *decamp*, 667 *escape*; vanish 446 *disappear*; vacate.

191 Inhabitant – N. *dweller,* inhabitant, habitant, denizen; sojourner, migrant, expatriate 59 *foreigner*; mainlander, Continental; islander; boat-dweller, water gipsy; landsman *or* -woman, hill-dweller, dalesman, daleswoman, highlander, lowlander, plains-dweller, fenman, fenwoman, forest-dweller,

bush-d.; frontiersman *or* -woman, borderer; city-dweller, town-d., urbanite, suburbanite, commuter; metropolitan, provincial; country-dweller, countryman *or* -woman, ruralist, villager, parishioner; peasant 370 *farmer*; desert-dweller, tent-d., bedouin; cave-dweller, troglodyte; slum-dweller 801 *poor person*. See *native*.

resident, householder, ratepayer; housewife, hausfrau, chatelaine, housekeeper; cottager, crofter, addressee, owner-occupier, occupier, occupant, incumbent, residentiary 776 *possessor*; locum tenens 150 *substitute*; tenant, sitting t., protected t., renter, lessee, leaseholder; inmate, in-patient; house surgeon, house physician, house officer 658 *doctor*; garrison, crew 686 *personnel*; lodger, boarder, au pair, paying guest, p.g.; guest, visitor, commensal; cuckoo, squatter 59 *intruder*; parasite 659 *bane*.

native, aboriginal, abo (derog), aborigines, autochthones, indigenes, first-comers 66 *precursor*; people, tribe, clan 371 *nation*; local, local inhabitant; parishioner, villager, townsperson, townee, city person, urbanite, city slicker, cockney, suburbanite, weekender, holiday-homer; yokel, rustic 869 *country-dweller*; fellow countryman *or* -woman, fellow citizen; national, patrial, citizen, burgher, burgess, voter; John Bull, Uncle Sam; Briton, Britisher, Brit; Celt, Gael, Scot, North Briton, Caledonian; Welshman *or* -woman, Irishman *or* -woman, Hibernian; Jock, Jimmy, Taffy, Paddy; Englishman *or* -woman, Northerner, Southerner, Midlander, East Anglian, Westcountryman *or* -woman; Londoner, Brummie, Bristolian, Mancunian, Liverpudlian, Scouse, Geordie, Glaswegian, Aberdonian; New Yorker, Parisian, Muscovite 59 *foreigner*; earth-dweller, terrestrial, tellurian; extraterrestrial, ET, space-dweller, Martian, Venusian, little green men.

settler, pioneer, Pilgrim Fathers 66 *precursor*; immigrant, colonist, colonial; planter 370 *farmer*; resident alien 59 *foreigner*.

Adj. *native,* vernacular, popular, national, ethnic; indigenous, autochthonous, aboriginal; earthbound, terrestrial, tellurian; home, home-made; domestic, domiciliary, domesticated; settled, domiciled, naturalized; resident.

occupied, occupied by, inhabited, lived in, tenanted, populated; garrisoned by, taken over by, manned, staffed.

192 Abode: place of habitation or resort –
N. *abode,* habitat, haunt, station 186 *situation;* place of residence 187 *locality;* habitation, street, house, home, second h.; address, house number, number; domicile, residence, residency; town, city, postal district 184 *district;* headquarters, base, seat 76 *focus;* temporary abode, hangout, camp, pad, pied-à-terre; weekend cottage, country seat, holiday home, timeshare flat *or* apartment, watering place, hill station 837 *pleasure ground;* cantonment, lines 187 *station;* bivouac, encampment; camp, refugee c.; campsite, caravan park; home from home.

quarters, living q., married q., accommodation, lodging, billet, berth, squat; barrack, lodgings, rooms, chambers, digs; residential hotel, guest house, boarding h., lodging h., pension; boarding school, hostel, dormitory, dorm; hall of residence; convent 986 *monastery.*

dwelling, roof over one's head 226 *roof;* prehistoric dwelling, lake d., pile d., crannog; tower, keep; cave, hut, kraal, igloo; wigwam, tepee, wickiup, tent, 226 *canopy;* lair, den, hole, form, burrow, warren, earth, sett 662 *shelter.*

nest, nidus; drey; branch 366 *tree;* aerie, eyrie, perch, roost; covert, heronry, rookery, swannery, hatchery, aviary, apiary, beehive, skep; bike, wasp's nest, antheap, anthill.

home, home-sweet-home, hearth and home, place where one hangs one's hat, hearth, fireside, fireplace, chimney corner, inglenook, rooftree, roof, paternal r., ancestral halls; homestead, household; bosom of one's family, family circle, cradle, birthplace, 'house where I

was born' 68 *origin;* native land, la patrie, motherland, fatherland, homeland, one's country, God's own country, the Old Country, Blighty, Albion; native soil, native sod, native ground, native heath, home ground, home town, own backyard.

house, building 164 *edifice;* abode, home, residence, dwelling, dwelling house; country house, town h.; villa, detached house, semidetached h., semi, terraced house; Queen Anne house, Georgian h., Regency h.; council h., council flat, high-rise f., prefab; ranch house, chalet, bungalow, chalet-b.; seat, place, mansion, hall, stately home; palace, dome, alcazar; chateau, castle, keep, tower; manor house, dower h., manor, grange, lodge, priory, abbey; vicarage 986 *parsonage;* farmhouse, farmstead, croft, hacienda 370 *farm;* official residence, Buckingham Palace, Holyrood P., Chequers, Mansion House, White House, embassy, consulate.

small house, bijou residence; two-up two-down, back-to-back; chalet, lodge, cottage, thatched c., cot, but and ben; cabin, log c., hut, Nissen h., shanty, bothy; hovel, dump, hole, slum dwelling; box, hunting-box *or* -lodge; shed, shack, lean-to, outhouse, outbuilding; shelter, tent 226 *canopy;* kiosk, booth, stall, shieling; houseboat 275 *boat;* mobile home, Dormobile (tdmk), caravan, trailer 274 *vehicle.* See *flat.*

housing, high-density h.; bricks and mortar 631 *building material;* built-up area, urban sprawl; asphalt jungle, concrete j., urban blight; urbanization, conurbation; town, satellite t., new t., commuter t., dormitory t., burgh, suburb, garden city 184 *city;* housing estate, residential area 184 *district;* villadom, suburbia; crescent, close, terrace, circus, square, avenue, street 624 *road;* block, court, row, mansions, villas, buildings; houses, tenements, high-rise flats; inner city, ghetto, slum; shanty town; hamlet, village, community.

flat, flatlet, granny flat, tenement f., high-rise f., council f., furnished f., service f., mews f., penthouse; apartment, suite, chambers; bedsitting room, bedsitter, bed-sit 194 *chamber*; maisonette, duplex; block of flats, apartment block, tower b.; mews, tenements.

stable, byre, cowshed; kennel, doghouse; sty, pigpen, fold, sheepfold 235 *enclosure*; dovecote, pigeon loft; stall, cage, coop, hencoop, hutch, battery; stabling, mews, coach-house, garage, carport, hangar; boathouse; marina, dock, dry d., graving d., floating d.; basin, wharf, roads, roadstead, port 662 *shelter*; berth, quay, jetty, pier.

inn, hotel, boarding house, guesthouse, hostelry, roadhouse, motel, bed and breakfast (see *quarters*); doss-house, bunk-h., kip, flophouse; youth hostel; auberge, trattoria.

tavern, alehouse, pothouse, boozer; public house, pub, local; free house, tied h.; gin palace, saloon; speakeasy, dive, joint, honky-tonk; shebeen; wine cellar, wine bar, bodega; beer cellar, beer hall, beer garden; bar, public b., spit-and-sawdust b., lounge b., saloon b., snug; taproom.

café, restaurant, self-service r., cafeteria; eating-house, eatery, steakhouse, diner, brasserie, bistro, pizzeria, kebab house, creperie, spaghetti house, trattoria, grill room, rotisserie; coffee bar, milk b., ice-cream parlour, soda fountain; lunch counter, fast-food c., snack bar, sandwich bar; teahouse, teashop, tearoom; buffet, canteen, Naafi; fish and chip shop, fish and chicken bar, chippie, baked potato shop, pancake house, takeaway; coffee stall, pull-in, transport café.

meeting place, conventicle, meeting house 990 *church*; day centre, community c., village hall; assembly rooms, pump r.; club, clubhouse, night club, working men's c., holiday camp 837 *place of amusement*; football ground, racecourse, dog track 724 *arena*; theatre, concert hall, opera house, stadium, stand 441 *onlookers*; astrodome, sports centre, gymnasium, drill hall, parade ground;

piazza, quadrangle, quad, campus, village green, town square 76 *focus*; shopping centre, shopping mall 796 *market*.

park, park, grounds, pleasure g., pleasance, gardens, green; walk, mall, avenue, parade, promenade, boulevard; national park, theme p., adventure p., safari p.; parkland, chase 837 *pleasure ground*.

pavilion, kiosk, stand, bandstand, rotunda, folly, bower, grotto 194 *arbour*; stoa, colonnade, arcade, peristyle; tent, marquee 226 *canopy*.

retreat, sanctuary, sanctum sanctorum, refuge, asylum, haven, ark 662 *shelter*; priesthole, hidey-hole 527 *hiding-place*; cubbyhole, den, snuggery, snug, sanctum, study 194 *chamber*; cell, hermitage 883 *seclusion*; cloister 986 *monastery*; almshouse, grace and favour house; workhouse, poorhouse; orphanage, home, old people's h., rest h., hostel, hospice, halfway house, sheltered housing.

Adj. *provincial,* parochial, parishpump, local, domestic, vernacular; upcountry, countrified, rural, rustic.

architectural, architect-d., designer 243 *formed*; Gothic 990 *churchlike*; classical, Byzantine, Romanesque, Norman, Tudor, Renaissance, Elizabethan, Jacobean, baroque, neo-classical, Palladian, Queen Anne, rococo, Georgian, Victorian, neo-gothic, Bauhaus 127 *olden*.

Vb. *dwell,* dwell in, inhabit, populate, people 189 *be present*; settle, colonize 786 *appropriate*; frequent, haunt 882 *visit*; take up one's abode, take up residence, hang up one's hat, move in; reside, remain, abide, sojourn, live 186 *be situated*; take rooms, put up at, stay, keep, lodge, lie, sleep at; live in, board out, be in digs; have an address, hang out at; tenant, occupy, squat 773 *possess*; nestle, perch, roost, nest, hive, burrow, stable; camp, encamp, bivouac, squat, doss down, pitch one's tent, make one's quarters 187 *place oneself*; tent, shelter 662 *seek refuge*; berth, dock, anchor 266 *come to rest*.

193 Contents: things contained – N. *contents*, ingredients, items, components, constituents, parts 58 *component*; inventory 87 *list*; furnishings, equipment 633 *provision*; load, payload, cargo, lading, freight, shipment, cartload, shipload, containerful 272 *thing transferred*; enclosure, inside 224 *insides*; stuffing, filling, stopping, wadding 227 *lining*; fistful, handful, cupful, quiverful 33 *small quantity*, 32 *great quantity*.

Vb. *load,* lade, freight, charge, burden; palletize, containerize; take in, take on board, ship; overload, overburden 322 *weigh*; pack, package, pack in, fit in, tuck in 303 *insert*; pack tight, squeeze in, cram, stuff 54 *fill*.

194 Receptacle – N. *receptacle,* container, holder; frame 218 *prop*; hutch, cage 748 *prison*; folder, wrapper, envelope, cover, file 235 *enclosure*; net, safety n., fishing n. 222 *network*; sheath, chrysalis, cocoon; packaging 226 *wrapping*; capsule, ampoule; pod, calyx, boll; mould 243 *form*; socket, mortise 255 *cavity*; groove, slot 262 *furrow*; pigeonhole, hole, cave, cavity 263 *opening*; bosom, lap 261 *fold*; pincushion; catch-all, trap; well, reservoir, hold, repository 632 *store*; drain, cesspit, sump 649 *sink*; crockery, chinaware, glassware 381 *pottery*.

stomach, maw, tummy, tum, abdomen, belly, corporation, pot belly, paunch 253 *swelling*; gizzard, gullet, crop, craw, jaws, mouth, oesophagus 263 *orifice*.

compartment, cell, cellule, loculus, follicle, ventricle; tray, cage; cubicle, carrel, booth, stall; sentry box; box 594 *theatre*; pew, choirstall 990 *church interior*; niche, nook, cranny, recess, bay, oriel; pigeonhole, cubbyhole; drawer, locker; shelving, rack 218 *shelf*; storey, floor, deck 207 *layer*.

cabinet, closet, commode, wardrobe, press, chest of drawers, chiffonier, tallboy; cupboard, corner c., built-in c., unit; whatnot, dresser, Welsh d., china cabinet; buffet, sideboard 218 *stand*; freezer, fridge-freezer 384 *refrigerator*; cocktail cabinet, dumbwaiter, lazy Susan, tea trolley; secretaire, escritoire, davenport, bureau, desk, writing d.; console; bookcase.

basket, creel; hamper, picnic basket; pannier; trug, punnet, skep, rush basket; crib, cradle, bassinet; clothesbasket, laundry basket; workbasket, workbox; wastepaper basket.

box, chest, ark; coffer, locker; case, canteen; safe, till, moneybox 799 *treasury*; coffin, sarcophagus 364 *tomb*; packing case, tea chest; tuckbox; attaché case, briefcase, dispatch box; suitcase, expanding s., overnight case, vanity c.; trunk, valise, portmanteau; sea chest, ditty-box; bandbox, hat box; ammunition chest, canister, caisson 723 *ammunition*; boxes, luggage, baggage, impedimenta, paraphernalia, bits and pieces, gear; boot, trunk, luggage van.

small box, pill b., snuff b., cigar b., pencil b., matchbox; cardboard box, carton, packet; plastic box; metal box, can, tin, caddy, tea-caddy, canister; casket, pyx 988 *ritual object*; salt cellar, pepper mill; castor; nest of boxes.

bag, sack, poke; handbag, vanity case, reticule, clutch bag, dorothy b., shoulder b., tote b.; shopping bag, carrier b., polythene b., poly b., plastic b., paper b.; cornet, twist, satchet; Gladstone bag, carpet b., travelling b., overnight b., flight b., sponge b.; sleeping bag; bedding-roll; holdall, grip; haversack, knapsack, rucksack, backpack; kitbag, ditty bag, duffle b.; pouch, sling; pannier, saddlebag, nosebag; school bag, satchel, sports bag.

case, étui, housewife; wallet, pocket book, notecase, billfold; spectacle case, cigarette c., compact; attaché case, briefcase, portfolio; file, box f.; scabbard, sheath; pistol case, holster; arrow case, quiver 632 *store*.

vat, butt, water b., cask, barrel, tun, tub, keg; drum 252 *cylinder*; wine cask, pipe, hogshead, firkin, kilderkin 465 *metrology*; hopper, cistern, tank 632 *store*.

vessel, vase, urn, jar, amphora, ampulla, cruse, crock, pot, water p.; pipkin, pitcher, ewer, jug, toby jug; gourd, calabash 366 *plant*; carafe, decanter, bottle; leather bottle, chagal *or* chagul, blackjack, wineskin; wine bottle, demijohn, magnum, jeroboam, rehoboam, methuselah, balthazar; flask, hip f., flagon, vial, phial; honeypot, jamjar; gallipot, carboy, crucible, retort, pipette, test tube, cupel 461 *testing agent*; chamber pot, bedpan, toilet bowl 649 *latrine*; pail, bucket, wooden b.; churn, can, watering c.; flowerpot, planter, jardinière; bin, litter b., rubbish b., dustbin 649 *sink*; scuttle, coal s., hod; skip, kibble; bath, tin b., tub.

pot 383 *heater;* boiler, copper, kettle, cauldron, cooking pot, skillet, pan, saucepan, stewpan, steamer, doubleboiler; frying pan, wok, omelette pan, grill p., girdle; casserole, Dutch oven, tandoor, bain-marie; mess tin, dixie, billycan; tea urn, teapot, samovar, coffeepot, percolator; vacuum flask, thermos f.; warming pan.

cup, eggcup, coffee cup, teacup, breakfast cup; tea service, tea set; chalice, goblet, beaker; drinking cup, loving c.; quaich; horn, drinking h., tankard, stoup, can, cannikin, pannikin, mug, stein, toby, noggin, rummer, schooner, tassie; tumbler, glass, liqueur g., wineglass, brandy balloon, pony.

bowl, basin, hand b., wash b., finger b.; toilet b.; pudding basin, mixing bowl, punch b., drinking b., jorum; porringer, ramekin; manger, trough; colander, strainer, vegetable dish, tureen, terrine, gravy boat; rose bowl, vase 844 *ornamentation.*

plate, salver, silver s., tray, platter, ashet, trencher, charger, dish; palette; saucer; pan, scale 322 *scales*; pallet; mortarboard, hod.

ladle, skimmer, dipper, baler, scoop, cupped hands; spoon, tablespoon, dessertspoon, teaspoon, eggspoon, soupspoon; spade, trowel, spatula, slice, shovel.

chamber, room, apartment 192 *flat*; cockpit, cubicle, cab; cabin, stateroom;

audience chamber, throne room; cabinet, closet, study, den, snug, snuggery, sanctum 192 *retreat*; library, studio, atelier, workroom, office 687 *workshop*; playroom, rumpus room, nursery; reception room, drawing room, front r., sitting r., living r., lounge, parlour, salon, boudoir; bedroom, dormitory; dressing room; bathroom, washroom, toilet, shower room, sauna; dining room, breakfast r., dinette; messroom, mess, hall, refectory, canteen 192 *café*; gunroom, wardroom; smoking room, billiard r.; bar, snug 192 *tavern*; cookhouse, galley, kitchen, kitchenette; scullery, pantry, larder, stillroom; dairy, laundry, utility room, offices, outhouse; coachhouse, garage 192 *stable*; storeroom, box room, lumber r., glory hole 632 *storage*; cloakroom, smallest room, lavatory 649 *latrine*. See *compartment.*

lobby, vestibule, foyer, anteroom, antechamber, waiting room; corridor, passage, hall, entrance h.; gallery, verandah, stoop, patio, piazza, loggia, balcony; portico, porch 263 *doorway*; extension, lean-to.

cellar, cellarage, vault, crypt, basement, garden flat 214 *base*; coalhole, bunker 632 *storage*; hold, dungeon 748 *prison.*

attic, loft, hayloft; penthouse, garret 213 *summit.*

arbour, alcove, bower, grotto, grot, summerhouse, gazebo, folly, pergola 192 *pavilion*; sun lounge, solarium, conservatory, orangery, greenhouse, glasshouse, hothouse 370 *garden.*

Section two: Dimensions

195 Size – N. *size,* magnitude, order of m.; proportions, dimensions, measurements 183 *measure*; extent, expanse, area 183 *space*; extension 203 *length,* 209 *height,* 211 *depth*; width, amplitude 205 *breadth*; volume; girth, circumference 233 *outline*; bulk, mass, weight 322 *gravity*; capacity, intake, tonnage; measured size, calibre 465 *measurement*;

real size, true dimensions 494 *accuracy*; greatest size, maximum 32 *greatness*; full size, life size 54 *plenitude*; large size, king s., queen s., magnum; largest portion 52 *chief part*; excessive size, hypertrophy, giantism, gigantism.

bulk, mass, weight, heaviness, avoirdupois 322 *gravity*; lump, dod, block, clod, boulder 324 *solid body*; hunk, chunk 53 *piece*; mound, heap 32 *great quantity*; mountain, pyramid 209 *high structure*; massiveness, bulkiness; turgidity 197 *dilation*; obesity, corpulence, fatness, stoutness, chubbiness, plumpness, embonpoint, chunkiness, fleshiness, meatiness, beefiness; flesh and blood, double chin, rotund figure, spare tyre, corporation 253 *swelling*; muscle man 162 *athlete*; fat person, fatty, tub, dumpling, mound of flesh, tub of lard, hulk; Billy Bunter, Bessie B., Falstaff.

giant, giantess, colossus 209 *tall creature*; mountain of a man *or* woman, young giant; ogre, monster, King Kong; leviathan, behemoth, Triton among the minnows; whale, hippopotamus, elephant, jumbo; mammoth, dinosaur; giantry, Titan, Titaness, Gargantua, Pantagruel, Brobdingnagian, Gog and Magog, Typhon, Atlas, Cyclops, Polyphemus, Goliath.

Adj. *large,* big 32 *great*; large size, economy s., king s., queen s., jumbo; fair-sized, considerable, sizable, good-sized; bulky, massive, massy 322 *weighty*; ample, capacious, voluminous, baggy; comprehensive 205 *broad*; vast, extensive 183 *spacious*; monumental, towering, mountainous 209 *tall*; fine, magnificent, spanking, thumping, thundering, whacking; man-size, life-s., large as life; well-grown, well-built, large-limbed, elephantine; macroscopic, large-scale, megalithic.

huge, immense, enormous, vast, mighty, grandiose, stupendous, monstrous 32 *prodigious*; record size; colossal, mammoth, dinosaurian, gigantic, giant, giant-like, mountainous; Brobdingnagian, titanic, Herculean, gargantuan; Cyclopean, megalithic; outsize, oversize,

overlarge, overweight 32 *exorbitant*; limitless 107 *infinite*.

fleshy, fat, stout, obese, overweight; well-covered, well-upholstered, Falstaffian; plump, ample, plumpish, sonsie, chubby, cuddly, fubsy, podgy, pudgy 205 *thick*; squat, squab, square, dumpy, chunky, stocky 205 *broad*; tubby, portly, corpulent, paunchy, pot-bellied 253 *convex*; puffy, bloated, bosomy, busty; round, rotund, roly-poly, full, full-faced, chubby-f.; double-chinned, dimpled, dimply, buxom, jolly, on the plump side; in condition, in good c., well-fed, well-grown, strapping, hunky, lusty, burly, beefy, brawny 162 *stalwart*; plump as a partridge, fat as butter, fat as a pig.

unwieldy, cumbersome, hulking, lumbering, gangling, lolloping; hulky, lumpy, lumpish, lubberly; too big, elephantine, whale-like, overweight; awkward, muscle-bound 695 *clumsy*.

196 Littleness – N. *littleness,* daintiness etc. adj.; small size 33 *smallness*; lack of height 204 *shortness*; diminutiveness, dwarfishness, stuntedness; scantiness, paucity, exiguity 105 *fewness*; meagreness 206 *thinness*.

minuteness, point; pinpoint, pinhead; crystal; atom, molecule, particle, electron, neutron, proton, quark; nucleus, cell; corpuscle; drop, droplet, dust, grain, g. of sand; seed, mustard s. 33 *small thing*; bubble, button, molehill 639 *trifle*.

miniature 553 *picture*; microphotograph, microdot, microfilm, microfiche 551 *photography*; pocket edition, duodecimo 589 *edition*; thumbnail sketch, epitome 592 *compendium*; model, microcosm; mini version.

dwarf, midget, minikin, pigmy, Lilliputian, halfling, hobbit; little people 970 *elf*; chit, slip, titch; teeny, mite, tot, tiddler 132 *child*; cocksparrow, bantam 33 *small quantity*; pipsqueak, squirt 639 *nonentity*; manikin, doll, puppet, Pinocchio; Tom Thumb, Thumbelina, Hop-o'-my-thumb, homunculus; shrimp, runt, weakling.

Adj. *little 33 small;* petite, dainty, dinky, dolly, elfin; diminutive, mini, pigmy, Lilliputian; no bigger than; wee, titchy, tiny, teeny, teeny-weeny, itsy-witsy; toy, baby, pocket, pocket-size, pocket-handkerchief, pint-size, duodecimo, mini-; miniature, model; portable, handy, compact, bijou; snug, cosy, poky, cramped, no room to swing a cat 206 *narrow*; puny 163 *weak*; petty 33 *inconsiderable*; one-horse 639 *unimportant.*

dwarfish, dwarf, dwarfed, Lilliputian, pigmy, undersized, stunted, wizened, shrunk; squat, dumpy 204 *short*; knee-high, knee-high to a grasshopper.

Vb. *be little,* take up no room, lie in a nutshell, roll up into a ball, fit on the head of a pin.

197 Expansion – N. *expansion,* enlargement, augmentation, aggrandizement 36 *increase*; amplification, supplementation, reinforcement 38 *addition*; hypertrophy, giantism, gigantism; hyperbole 546 *exaggeration*; stretching, extension, spread, deployment, fanning out 75 *dispersion*; ribbon development, urban sprawl 192 *housing*; increment, accretion 40 *adjunct*; upgrowth, overgrowth, development 157 *growth*, 171 *productiveness*; overstaffing, Parkinson's law 637 *superfluity.*

dilation, dilatation, distension, diastole; inflation, reflation, puffing, puff 352 *blowing*; swelling up, turgescence, turgidity, tumescence, intumescence, tumefaction; puffiness, dropsy, tumour 253 *swelling.*

Vb. *expand,* wax, grow larger, increase, snowball 36 *grow*; widen, broaden, flare, splay; spread, extend, sprawl; fan out, deploy, 75 *be dispersed*; spread over, spread like wildfire, overrun, straddle 226 *cover*; rise, prove (e.g. dough); gather, swell, distend, dilate, fill out; mushroom, balloon, belly; get fat, gain flesh, put on weight, put on the flab; burst at the seams; grow up, spring up, bud, burgeon, shoot, sprout, open, put forth, burst f., blossom, flower, blow, bloom, be out 171 *be fruitful.*

enlarge, aggrandize; make larger, expand; rarefy (by expansion); leaven 310 *elevate*; bore, ream; widen, broaden, let out; open, pull out; stretch, extend 203 *lengthen*; intensify, heighten, deepen, draw out; amplify, supplement, reinforce 38 *add*; double, redouble; develop, build up 36 *augment*; distend, inflate, reflate, pump up, blow up, puff, puff up, puff out 352 *blow*; bulk, thicken; stuff, pad 227 *line*; cram, fill to bursting 54 *fill*; feed up, fatten, plump up, bloat 301 *feed*; enlarge, blow up 551 *photograph*; magnify, overenlarge, overdevelop 546 *exaggerate.*

198 Contraction – N. *contraction,* reduction, abatement, lessening, deflation 37 *diminution*; decrease, shrinkage, diminuendo; curtailment, abbreviation, elision 204 *shortening*; consolidation 324 *condensation*; freezing 382 *refrigeration*; contracting, systole; contractions, labour pains 167 *obstetrics*; attenuation, emaciation, consumption, withering, atrophy; decline, retreat, recession, slump 655 *deterioration*; neck, isthmus, bottleneck, hourglass, wasp-waist 206 *narrowness*; epitome 592 *compendium.*

compression, pressure, compressure, compaction, squeeze, squeezing, stenosis, strangulation; constriction, constringency, astriction, astringency; contractility, contractibility, compressibility.

Vb. *become small,* grow less, lessen, dwindle, wane, ebb, fall away 37 *decrease*; shrivel, wither, waste away 51 *decompose*; lose weight, lose flesh 323 *be light*; level off, bottom out; contract, shrink, narrow, taper, taper off, draw in; condense 324 *be dense*; evaporate 338 *vaporize*; pucker, purse.

make smaller, lessen, reduce 37 *abate*; contract, shrink, abridge, take in, cut down to life size, dwarf, stunt 204 *shorten*; diet, slim, take off weight 323 *lighten*; taper, narrow, attenuate, thin, emaciate 206 *make thin*; puncture, deflate, rarefy; boil down, evaporate 338 *vaporize*; dehydrate 342 *dry*; cramp, constrict, pinch, nip, squeeze, bind,

bandage, corset; draw in, draw tight, strain, tauten 45 *tighten*; draw together, clench 264 *close*, 45 *join*; hug, crush, strangle, strangulate; compress, compact, constipate, condense, nucleate 324 *be dense*; huddle, crowd together; squeeze in, pack tight, pack like sardines, cram, jam 54 *fill*; squash 216 *flatten*; cramp, restrict 747 *restrain*; limit 232 *circumscribe*; chip away, whittle away, shave, shear, clip, trim, prune, pollard 46 *cut*; scrape, file, grind 332 *pulverize*; fold up, crumple 261 *fold*; roll, press, flatten 258 *smooth*.

199 Distance – N. *distance,* astronomical d., light years 183 *space*; measured distance, mileage, footage 203 *length*; focal distance; elongation, aphelion, apogee; far distance, horizon, skyline; background 238 *rear*; periphery, circumference 233 *outline*; drift, dispersion 282 *deviation*; reach, grasp, compass, span, stride, giant's s. 183 *range*; far cry, long way, fair w., tidy step, day's march, long long trail, marathon.

Adj. *distant,* distal, peripheral, terminal; far, farther; ulterior; ultimate, farthest, furthest, furthermost; long-distance, long-range; yon, yonder; not local, away, far away; outlying, peripheral; offshore, on the horizon; remote, aloof, far-flung, godforsaken; hyperborean, antipodean; out of range, telescopic; lost to sight, lost to view, out of sight 444 *invisible*; off-centre, wide, wide of the mark.

Vb. *be distant,* stretch to, reach to, extend to, spread to, go to, get to, stretch away to, carry to, carry on to 183 *extend*; carry, range; outdistance, outrange, outreach 306 *outdo*; keep one's distance, remain at a d., stay at arm's length, keep off, hold off, stand off, lie off; keep clear of, stand aloof, stand clear of, keep a safe distance, give a wide berth 620 *avoid*.

Adv. *beyond,* further, farther; further on, ahead, in front; clear of, wide of, wide of the mark; below the horizon; up over, down under, over the border, over the hills and far away.

too far, at the back of beyond, out of reach, out of range, out of sight, out of hearing, out of earshot, out of the sphere of, out of bounds.

200 Nearness – N. *nearness,* proximity, propinquity, closeness, near distance, foreground 237 *front*; vicinage, vicinity, neighbourhood 230 *surroundings*; brink, verge 234 *edge*; adjacency 202 *contiguity*; collision course 293 *convergence*; approximation 289 *approach*.

short distance, no d., shortest d., beeline, short cut; step, short s., no distance, walking d.; striking distance, close quarters, close grips; close range, earshot, stone's throw, spitting distance; short span, inch, millimetre, finger's breadth, hair's breadth 201 *gap*; close-up, close finish, photo f., needle race, near thing 716 *contest*.

Adj. *near,* proximate, proximal; very near, approximate; approximating, close, getting warm, warm 289 *approaching*; about to meet 293 *convergent*; nearby, wayside, roadside 289 *accessible*; not far, hard by, inshore; near at hand, close at hand, at hand, handy, at one's fingertips, present; near the surface 212 *shallow*; home, local, vicinal, in the neighbourhood; close to, next to, next-door to, neighbouring, bordering on, verging on, adjacent, adjoining, jostling, rubbing shoulders; fronting, facing 237 *frontal*; close, intimate, inseparable; bumper-to-bumper; on one's tail, breathing down one's neck; at close quarters, at close grips; close-run, neck-and-neck, nip and tuck, with nothing between, level, level-pegging; near in blood, related 11 *akin*.

Adv. *near,* not far, locally, in the neighbourhood, in the vicinity; nigh, hard by, fast by, close to, close up to, close upon, in the way, at close range, at close quarters; close behind, right b.; within call, within hearing, within earshot, within a stone's throw, only a step, at no great distance, not far from; on one's doorstep, in one's own backyard; at one's door, at one's feet, at one's

elbow, at one's side, under one's nose, at one's fingertips, within reach, close at hand; in the presence of, face to face, eyeball to eyeball; in juxtaposition, next door, side by side, cheek by jowl, tête-à-tête, arm in arm, beside, alongside; on the circumference, on the periphery, on *or* in the confines of, on the skirts of, on the outskirts, at the threshold; brinking on, verging on, on the brink of, on the verge of, on the tip of one's tongue.

nearly, practically, almost, all but; more or less, near enough, roughly, around, somewhere around; in the region of; about, much a., hereabouts, thereabouts, nearabouts, there or thereabouts, circa; closely, approximately, hard on, close on; well-nigh, as good as, on the way to; within an ace of, just about to.

201 Interval – N. *interval,* distance between, space; narrow interval, half-space, hairspace 200 *short distance*; interspace, daylight, head, length; clearance, margin, freeboard 183 *room*; interval of time, timelag; pause, break, intermission, breather, time out, truce 145 *lull*; hiatus 72 *discontinuity*; interruption, incompleteness, jump, leap; musical interval, tone, semitone, third, fourth, fifth 410 *musical note.*

gap, interstice, mesh 222 *network*; lacuna, cavity, hole, opening, aperture 263 *orifice*; pass, defile, ghat, wind-gap 305 *passage*; firebreak 662 *safeguard*; ditch, dike, trench 351 *drain*; water jump, ha-ha, sunk fence 231 *partition*; ravine, gorge, gully, couloir, chimney, crevasse, canyon 255 *valley*; cleft, crevice, chink, crack, rift, cut, gash, tear, rent, slit 46 *scission*; flaw, fault, breach, break, split, fracture, rupture, fissure, chap 46 *separation*; slot, groove 262 *furrow*; indentation 260 *notch*; seam, join 45 *joint*; leak 298 *outlet*; abyss, chasm 211 *depth*; yawning gulf, void 190 *emptiness*; inlet, creek, gulch 345 *gulf.*

Vb. *space,* interval, space out, place at intervals 46 *set apart*; crack, split, start, gape, dehisce 263 *open*; win by a head,

win by a length; clear, show daylight between; lattice, mesh, reticulate.

202 Contiguity – N. *contiguity,* juxtaposition, apposition, proximity, close p. 200 *nearness*; touching 378 *touch*; no interval 71 *continuity*; contact, tangency; abuttal, abutment; intercommunication, osculation; meeting, encounter, confrontation, interface 293 *convergence*; conjunction, syzygy (astronomy) 45 *union*; close contact, adhesion, cohesion 48 *coherence*; coexistence, coincidence, concomitance 89 *accompaniment*; grazing contact, tangent; border, fringe 234 *edge*; borderland, frontier 236 *limit*; buffer state 231 *interjacency.*

Vb. *be contiguous,* overlap 378 *touch*; make contact, come in c., brush, rub, skim, scrape, graze, kiss; join, meet 293 *converge*; stick, adhere 48 *cohere*; lie end to end, abut; abut on, adjoin, reach to, extend to 183 *extend*; sit next to, rub shoulders with, crowd, jostle, elbow; be bumper to bumper, be elbow to elbow, border with, march w., skirt 234 *hem*; coexist, coincide 89 *accompany*; osculate, intercommunicate 45 *connect*; get in touch, contact.

203 Length – N. *length,* longitude; extent, extension; reach, long arm; full length, overall l.; stretch, span, mileage, footage 199 *distance*; perspective 211 *depth.*

line, bar, rule, tape, measuring tape, strip, stripe, streak; spoke, radius; single file, line ahead, crocodile, queue 65 *sequence*; straight line, right l. 249 *straightness*; bent line, fractal 248 *curvature.*

long measure, linear m., measurement of length, micrometry 465 *measurement*; unit of length, finger, hand, hand's breadth, palm, span, cubit; arm's length, fathom; head, length; pace, step; inch, foot, yard; rod, pole, perch; chain, furlong; mile, statute m., geographical m., nautical m., knot, league; millimetre, centimetre, metre, kilometre; degree of latitude, degree of longitude; micro-

inch, micron, wavelength; astronomical unit, light year, parsec.

Adj. *long,* lengthy, extensive, a mile long; long-drawn out; lengthened, elongated, outstretched, extended, strung out; shoulder-length, ankle-length, down to ...; wire-drawn, lank 206 *lean*; lanky, leggy, long-legged 209 *tall*; as long as my arm, long as a wet week; interminable, no end to 838 *tedious*; polysyllabic, sesquipedalian 570 *diffuse*; uncut, full-length 54 *complete*.

longitudinal, oblong, linear; one-dimensional.

Vb. *lengthen,* stretch, elongate, draw out, wiredraw 206 *make thin*; pull out, stretch o., spreadeagle 197 *expand*; spread oneself out, sprawl 216 *be horizontal*; spread out, string o., deploy 75 *disperse*; extend, pay out, uncoil, unfurl, unroll, unfold 316 *evolve*; let down, drop the hem; produce, continue; prolong, protract; drawl 580 *stammer*.

Adv. *longwise,* longways, lengthwise; along, longitudinally, radially, in line ahead, in single file, in Indian f.; one in front and one behind, in tandem; in a crocodile; in a line, in perspective; at full length, end to end, overall; fore and aft; head to foot, head to tail, stem to stern, top to toe, head to heels, from the crown of the head to the sole of the foot.

204 Shortness – N. *shortness,* squatness etc. adj.; brevity, briefness; transience 114 *brief span*; inch, centimetre 200 *short distance*; low stature, dwarfishness, short legs, duck's disease 196 *littleness*; lack of inches, no height 210 *lowness*; shrinkage; scantiness, exiguity; scarceness 636 *insufficiency*; slippage; concision 569 *conciseness*; short hair, short back and sides, bob, crew cut; shorts, miniskirt.

shortening, abridgment, abbreviation; précis, summary 592 *compendium*; curtailment, cutback, cut, reduction 37 *diminution*; contraction 198 *compression*.

Adj. *short,* brief 114 *transient*; not big, dwarfish, stunted 196 *little*; knee-high to a grasshopper, not tall, squab, squabby,

squat, dumpy, fubsy, stumpy, stocky, thickset, stubby 195 *fleshy*, 205 *thick*; not high 210 *low*; pug-nosed, snub-n.; snub, retroussé, blunt; not long, inch-long; skimpy, scanty 636 *insufficient*; foreshortened 246 *distorted*; abbreviated, abridged; shortened, sawn-off; cut, curtailed, docked, beheaded, decapitated, truncated, topless, headless; shaven, shorn, mown; sparing of words, terse 569 *concise*; elliptical (of style); half-finished 55 *unfinished*; epitomized, potted, compact; compacted, compressed.

Vb. *shorten,* abridge, abbreviate, cut; pot, epitomize, boil down, summarize 592 *abstract*; sum up, recapitulate 569 *be concise*; compress, contract, telescope 198 *make smaller*; reduce, diminish 37 *abate*; foreshorten 246 *distort*; take up, put a tuck in, raise the hem, turn up, tuck up, kilt; behead, decapitate, guillotine, axe, chop up 46 *sunder*; cut short, dock, curtail, truncate; cut back, cut down, slash, lop, prune; shear, shave, trim, crop, clip, bob, shingle 46 *cut*; mow, scythe; nip in the bud, stunt, check the growth of 278 *retard*; scrimp, skimp.

205 Breadth. Thickness – N. *breadth,* width, latitude; width across, span, fingerspan, wingspan, wingspread; diameter, radius, gauge, broad g., bore, calibre; broadness, expanse; superficial extent, amplitude 183 *range*; wideness, fullness, bagginess.

Adj. *broad,* wide, expansive, unspanned 183 *spacious*; wide-cut, full, flared, ample, baggy; fan-like, umbelliferous; outspread, outstretched, splayed out; bell-bottomed, broad-b., broad-based; callipygian, steatopygous, wide-hipped; broad in the beam, beamy, wide-bodied; wide as a church door; broad-brimmed, wide-angle (lens); wide-mouthed 263 *open*; broad-shouldered, broad-chested 162 *stalwart*; wide-ranging, global 79 *general*.

thick, stout, dumpy, squat 204 *short*; thickset, tubby, beefy, stubby 195 *fleshy*; thick-lipped, full-l.; thick-necked, bull-

n.; thick-skinned, pachydermatous; thick-ribbed, barrel-chested, broad-shouldered 162 *strong*; thick as a rope; pyknic, endomorphic; solidly built 324 *dense*; semiliquid, ropy, lumpy, to be cut with a knife 354 *viscid*.

Adv. *broadways,* broadwise, breadthways, breadthwise; widthways, widthwise; broadways on 239 *sideways*.

206 Narrowness. Thinness – N. *narrowness,* tightness etc. adj.; narrow interval, closeness, tight squeeze, crack, chink, hair's breadth, finger's b. 200 *short distance*; lack of breadth, length without b., line, strip, stripe, streak; vein, capillary 208 *filament*; knife-edge, razor's edge, tightrope, wire; narrow gauge; bottleneck, narrows, strait 345 *gulf*; ridge, col, saddle 209 *high land*; ravine, gully 255 *valley*; pass, defile 305 *passage*; neck, isthmus, land-bridge 624 *bridge*.

thinness, tenuity, fineness 325 *rarity*; slenderness, gracility; skinniness, emaciation, anorexia (nervosa), consumption; scrag, skin and bone, skeleton; miserable specimen, scarecrow, rake, beanpole, broomstick, shadow, spindle-shanks, barebones; haggardness, lantern jaws, hatchet face, sunken cheeks; thread, paper, tissue 422 *transparency*; shaving, splinter 33 *small thing*; slip, wisp 208 *filament*.

Adj. *narrow,* not wide, single track; strait, tight, close; compressed, pinched, unexpanded; not thick, fine, thin, wafer-thin 422 *transparent*; attenuated, spun, fine-s., wire-drawn 203 *long*; thread-like, capillary; tapering 293 *convergent*; slight, slightly-built, wispy, delicate 163 *weak*; gracile, attenuate, slender, slim, svelte, slinky, sylph-like; willowy, rangy, skinny; long-legged, leggy, lanky, gangling; narrow-waisted, wasp-w.; isthmian; bottlenecked.

lean, thin, ectomorphic, spare, rangy, wiry, meagre, skinny, bony; cadaverous, fleshless, skin-and-bone, skeletal, rawboned, haggard, gaunt, drawn, lantern-jawed, sunken-eyed, hatchet-faced;

twiggy, spindly, spindle-shanked, spidery; undersized, weedy, scrawny, scrubby, scraggy; consumptive, emaciated, anorexic, wasted, withered, wizened, pinched, peaky 651 *sick*; sere, shrivelled 131 *ageing*; starved, starveling 636 *underfed*; wraith-like, scarecrow-like, worn to a shadow, thin as a rake, thin as a lath, without an ounce of flesh to spare.

Vb. *make thin,* contract, compress, pinch, nip 198 *make smaller*; starve, diet, reduce, lose weight; slim; draw, wiredraw, spin, spin fine 203 *lengthen*; attenuate 325 *rarefy*.

207 Layer – N. *layer,* stratum, substratum, underlay, floor 214 *base*; outcrop 254 *projection*; bed, course, range, row; zone, vein, seam, lode; thickness, ply; storey, tier, floor, mezzanine f., entresol, landing; stage, planking, platform 218 *frame*; deck, top d., lower d., upper d., orlop d., quarterdeck, bridge 275 *ship*; film 423 *opacity*; bloom, dross, scum; patina, coating, coat, undercoat, veneer, top layer, top-dressing, topcoat 226 *covering*; scale, scab, membrane, peel, pellicle, sheathe, bark, integument 226 *skin*; level, water l., water table 216 *horizontality*; atmospheric layer 340 *atmosphere*.

208 Filament – N. *filament,* flagellum, cilium, lash, eyelash, beard, down 259 *hair*; barb, feather, harl 259 *plumage*; flock, lock, shred of wool, thread, lock of hair, strand, wisp, curl; fringe 234 *edging*; fibre, fibril, fibrilla, rootlet, stalk, tendril 366 *plant*; whisker, antenna, antennule 378 *feeler*; gossamer, cobweb, web 222 *network*; capillary, vein, venule, veinlet 351 *conduit*; ramification, branch; wire, element, wick 420 *torch*.

fibre, natural f., animal f., hair, camel h., rabbit h.; Angora, goat's hair, mohair, cashmere; llama hair, alpaca, vicuna; wool, Shetland w., botany w., merino; silk, real s., wild silk, tussore, floss; vegetable fibre, cotton, cotton wool, silk cotton, kapok; linen, flax; manila, hemp;

jute, sisal, coir; hards; tow, oakum; bast, raffia; worsted, yarn; spun yarn, continuous filament y.; thread, twine, twist, strand, cord, string, line, rope 47 *cable*; artificial fibre, man-made f., acrylic f., rayon, nylon 222 *textile*; staple, denier 331 *texture*.

strip, fascia, band, bandage; belt, cord, thong, braid, tape, strap, ribbon, ribband; fillet; lath, slat, batten, stave; shaving, wafer; splinter, shiver, shred 53 *piece*; streak, stripe, strake 203 *line*.

209 Height – N. *height*, perpendicular length; altitude, elevation, ceiling, pitch 213 *summit*; loftiness, steepness, dizzy height; tallness, stature; eminence, sublimity; sky, stratosphere 340 *atmosphere*; zenith.

high land, height, highlands, heights, steeps, uplands, moor, moorland, downs, rolling country; rising ground, rise, bank, ben, brae, slope, climb 220 *incline*; hill, eminence, mount, mountain; fell, scar, tor, alp, Mont Blanc, Everest, mountain range, chain, sierra, cordillera, massif, Alps, Himalayas, Andes, Rockies; ridge, col, saddle, spur, headland, foothill 254 *projection*; crest, peak, pike, hilltop 213 *summit*; steepness, precipice, cliff, white cliffs of Dover; crag, scar, bluff, steep, escarpment; gorge, canyon, ravine 255 *valley*; summit level, mesa; plateau, tableland 216 *horizontality*.

high structure, column, pillar, turret, tower, pile, noble p., skyscraper, highrise flats, tower block 164 *edifice*; chimney stack, steeple, spire, flèche, belfry, campanile 990 *church exterior*; minaret; obelisk, Cleopatra's Needle; dome, cupola 226 *roof*; colossus 554 *sculpture*; mausoleum, pyramid 364 *tomb*; pagoda 990 *temple*; ziggurat, Tower of Babel; Eiffel Tower; mast, topmast; flagstaff, pikestaff; pole, maypole; lamppost, standard; pylon, radio mast; masthead 213 *summit*; watchtower, lookout, crow's nest, eyrie 438 *view*; column of smoke, mushroom cloud.

tall creature, giraffe, elephant, mammoth, ostrich, longlegs, beanpole, sixfooter, grenadier, colossus 195 *giant*.

Adj. *high*, high-up, sky-high; eminent, uplifted, exalted, lofty, sublime, supernal; highest 213 *topmost*; perching, hanging (gardens); aerial, airborne, flying; soaring, aspiring; towering, skyscraping; steep, dizzy, giddy; knee-high, thigh-h., breast-h., shoulder-h..

tall, lanky, leggy, rangy 206 *narrow*; long-legged, ostrich-necked, giraffelike, beanpole-like; colossal.

Vb. *be high*, - tall etc. adj.; tower, rear, soar; surmount, clear, overtop, overlook, dominate, command 34 *be superior*; overhang, overshadow 226 *cover*; beetle, impend 254 *jut*; hover, hang over 217 *hang*; culminate, peak, be at the zenith 725 *climax*; mount, bestride, bestraddle; grow taller, shoot up, add to one's inches; rise 308 *ascend*; stand on tiptoe, stand on another's shoulders 310 *lift oneself*.

make higher, heighten, build up, raise, hold aloft 310 *elevate*.

210 Lowness – N. *lowness*, debasement 311 *lowering*; prostration; sea level, flatness 216 *horizontality*; flats, levels 347 *marsh*; levelness, steppe 348 *plain*; low elevation, lowlands, pimple 196 *littleness*; gentle slope, nursery s., slight gradient 220 *incline*; lower level, foothill 35 *inferiority*; bottom, hollow, depression 255 *valley*; sea-floor 343 *ocean*; depths, cellar, nether regions, basement, well, mine 211 *depth*; floor, foot 214 *base*; underside 240 *contraposition*; nadir, lowest point, the pits; low water, low ebb, low tide 350 *current*.

Adj. *low*, not high, squat 204 *short*; crouched, crouching, stooping, slouching, bending; recumbent, laid low, prostrate 216 *supine*; low-lying, flat, at sea level 216 *flat*; low-level, single-storey; lower, under, nether, 35 *inferior*; sunken, lowered 255 *concave*; flattened, rounded, blunt; subterranean, subterraneous, underground, below the surface,

submarine 523 *latent*, 211 *deep*; underfoot 745 *subjected*.

Adv. *under*, beneath, underneath, neath; below, at the foot of; underfoot, underground, downstairs; below stairs; at a low ebb; below par.

211 Depth – N. *depth*, drop, fall; deepness etc. adj.; perspective 203 *length*; vertical range, profundity, lowest point, nadir; deeps, deep water 343 *ocean*; unknown depths, unfathomable d. 663 *pitfall*; depression, bottom 255 *valley*; hollow, pit, shaft, mine, well 255 *cavity*; abyss, abysm, chasm 201 *gap*; vault, crypt, dungeon 194 *cellar*; cave, pothole, catacomb, bowels of the earth 210 *lowness*; pot-holing, deep-sea diving 309 *descent*; caisson disease, the bends, underworld, bottomless pit 972 *hell*; diving bell, submarine.

Adj. *deep*, steep, plunging, profound; abysmal, yawning, cavernous; abyssal, deep-sea; deep-seated, deep-rooted 153 *fixed*; unplumbed, bottomless, fathomless; unsounded, unfathomed, subterranean, underground, underwater, undersea, submarine; buried, deep in, immersed, submerged; drowned; kneedeep, ankle-d.; infernal; benthic; depthmeasuring, bathymetric.

Vb. *be deep*, - profound etc. adj.; deepen, hollow, fathom, sound, take soundings, plumb, heave the lead; drop, lower 311 *let fall*; go deep, plumb the depths, touch bottom, reach rock bottom, be on one's knees; reach one's nadir; sink to the bottom, plunge 313 *founder*.

212 Shallowness – N. *shallowness*, no depth, superficiality 4 *insubstantiality*; film 223 *exteriority*; veneer, thin coat 226 *skin*; superficial wound, scratch, pinprick, graze 639 *trifle*; shoals, shallows; pond, puddle 346 *lake*; light soil, stony ground 344 *soil*.

Adj. *shallow*, slight, superficial 4 *insubstantial*; surface, skin-deep; shoaly, light, thin 206 *narrow*.

213 Summit – N. *summit*, sky, heaven, seventh h., cloud nine; pole, north p., south p.; top, peak, crest, apex, pinnacle, crown; maximum height, pitch; zenith, meridian, high noon, culmination, apogee; culminating point, crowning p.; acme, ne plus ultra, peak of perfection 646 *perfection*; crest of the wave, top of the tree 730 *prosperity*; highwater mark 236 *limit*; climax, turning point 137 *crisis*; dividing line, watershed, Great Divide 231 *partition*; copingstone, keystone; lintel, pediment, entablature, architrave, epistyle; capital, cornice.

vertex, apex, crown, top, cap, brow, head; tip, cusp, spike, point, nib, end 69 *extremity*; spire, finial 990 *church exterior*; stairhead, landing 308 *ascent*; acropolis 713 *fort*; summit level, hilltop, mountaintop, plateau, tableland 209 *high land*; treetop, housetop, rooftop; gable, gable-end; leads, ceiling 226 *roof*; upper chamber, garret, loft 194 *attic*; top storey; topside, upper deck, bridge 275 *ship*; topmast, masthead, crow's nest 209 *high structure*.

head, headpiece, pate, poll, sconce; noddle, nob, nut, noggin, coco, conk, bonce, crumpet, bean, block, chump; upper storey, belfry; brow, dome, temple, forehead; loaf, brain, grey matter 498 *intelligence*; epicranium, pericranium; scalp, crown, double c.; skull, cranium, brainpan 255 *cavity*; fontanelle; craniology, craniometry, cranioscopy, craniotomy; phrenology; brain scanning, brain scan, neuroradiology, brain surgery, neurosurgery.

Adj. *topmost*, top, highest 209 *high*; uppermost, upmost 34 *supreme*; polar, apical, crowning; capital, head; culminating, meridian; tiptop, super 644 *best*.

Vb. *crown*, cap, head, top, pinnacle, tip, surmount, crest, overtop 209 *be high*; culminate, consummate 725 *climax*; go up top, take top place, go into the lead 34 *be superior*; top out, put the finishing touches to 54 *make complete*.

214 Base – N. *base*, foot, toe, skirt 210 *lowness*; bottom, fundus, root; lowest

point, the depths, rock bottom, nadir, low water; footing, foundation 218 *basis*; the nitty gritty; fundamental 68 *origin*; groundwork, substructure, infrastructure, chassis 218 *frame*; baseboard, plinth, pedestal 218 *stand*; substratum, floor, underlayer, bed, bedrock; subsoil, pan, hardpan; ground, earth, foundations; footing, sill; damp course, dampproof course; basement, ground floor 194 *cellar*; flooring, pavement, pavingstone, flagstone; carpet 226 *floor-cover*; skirting board, wainscot, plinth, dado; keel, keelson; hold, bilge; sump, drain 649 *sink*.

foot, feet, tootsies, dogs, plates; beetlecrusher; forefoot, hindfoot; sole, heel, Achilles' tendon, instep, arch; toe, toenail, big toe, hallux; trotter, hoof, cloven h.; paw, pad; claw, talon 778 *pincers*; ankle, ankle-bone, tarsus, metatarsus, fetlock, pastern.

215 Verticality – N. *verticality,* the vertical, erectness, uprightness, upright carriage; steepness, sheerness, precipitousness 209 *height*; perpendicularity, right angle, square; elevation, azimuth circle; vertical line, plumbline, plummet; vertical structure, upright, pole, stalagmite 218 *pillar*; precipice, cliff, bluff, scarp, steep 209 *high land*; perpendicular drop, vertical height, rise.

Adj. *vertical,* upright, erect, standing; perpendicular, rectangular, sheer, abrupt, steep, precipitous 209 *high*; straight, plumb; straight up, straight down; upstanding, standing up, on one's feet, on one's legs, on one's hindlegs; bolt upright, stiff as a ramrod, unbowed; rampant, rearing; on end.

Vb. *be vertical,* stick up, cock up, bristle, stand on end; stand erect, stand upright, hold oneself straight; sit up, stand up, straighten up; rise, stand, be upstanding, rise to one's feet, get to one's feet, ramp, rear; keep standing, have no seat, sit on one's thumb.

216 Horizontality – N. *horizontality,* horizontalness; horizontal angle, azimuth; horizontal line, rule; horizontal course, strike; flatness 258 *smoothness*; level, plane, level plane; sea level, water l., water table; stratum; slab, tablet, table 207 *layer*; level stretch, steppe 348 *plain*; flats 347 *marsh*; platform, ledge 254 *projection*; terrace, esplanade; plateau, tableland 209 *high land*; billiard table, bowling green, cricket ground, croquet lawn 724 *arena*; gridiron, platter 194 *plate*; spirit level, T square 465 *gauge*; skyline, horizon, false h., horizon line 236 *limit*.

flattener, iron, flatiron, steam iron, mangle, press, trouser p.; rolling pin, roller, garden r., steamroller 258 *smoother*; bulldozer, juggernaut 168 *destroyer*.

Adj. *flat,* horizontal, two-dimensional, level, plane, even, flush 258 *smooth*; trodden, flat as a pancake; unwrinkled, smooth, smooth as a baby's bottom, smooth as glass, calm, calm as a millpond.

supine, flat on one's back, flat out; prone, face down, prostrate; recumbent; lying down, couchant; abed, laid up, laid out; stretched out, sprawling, spreadeagled, lolling.

Vb. *be horizontal,* lie, lie down, lie flat, lie prostrate, lie on one's back; measure one's length, recline, couch, sprawl, spread-eagle, loll 311 *sit down*; straighten out, level out, bottom o.

flatten, lay out, roll o., lay down, spread; lay flat, beat f., tread f., stamp down, trample d., squash; make flush, align, level, even, grade, plane 28 *equalize*; iron, iron out, roll out 258 *smooth*; pat down, smooth d, prostrate, knock down, floor, ground 311 *fell*.

217 Pendency – N. *pendency,* suspension, hanging, dangle; set, hang, drape; droop.

hanging object, hanging ornament, mobile, pendant, dangler, drop, eardrop, earring, dangling e. 844 *jewellery*; tassel, bobble, tag 844 *trimming*; hangings,

draperies, drapes, curtains, arras, tapestry 226 *covering*; train, skirt, coat-tails; flap, lappet, tippet 228 *headgear*; pigtail, tail 67 *sequel*, 259 *hair*; dewlap, lobe, appendix 40 *adjunct*; pendulum, bob, swing, hammock 317 *oscillation*; chandelier 420 *lamp*; icicle, stalactite.

hanger, coat h., curtain rod, curtain ring, runner, rack; hook, coathook, peg, knob, nail, hatstand 218 *prop*; suspender, braces, suspender belt 228 *underwear*; clothesline 47 *cable*; clotheshorse, airer 218 *frame*; crane; spar, mast 218 *pillar*; gallows, gibbet 964 *pillory*.

Adj. *hanging,* pendent, pendulous, pensile; hanging from, dependent, suspended, dangling etc.vb.; hanging the head, nodding, drooping, lowering, overhanging; beetling 254 *projecting*.

Vb. *hang,* be pendent, drape, set; hang down, draggle, trail, flow; hang on to, swing from; swing, sway, dangle, bob; hang the head, nod, loll, droop, sag, swag; hang in the wind, hang over, hover; overhang, lour; suspend, hang up, append 45 *join*.

218 Support – N. *support,* support, mounting, bearing; carriage, undercarriage, carrier, underframe, chassis; buttress, flying b., abutment, bulwark, embankment, wall, retaining w.; underpinning, shore, jack; flagstaff, jackstaff, stanchion, rod, bar, transom, brace, strut, stay, mainstay, guy, shrouds, rigging; sprit, boom, spar, mast, yard, yardarm, crosstree 254 *projection*; trunk, stem, stalk, caudex, pedicle, pedicel, peduncle 366 *plant*; arch, ogive 248 *curve*; keystone, headstone, cornerstone, springer; cantilever; pier (see *pillar*); strapping, bandage, elastic b., jockstrap, truss, splint; stiffener, whalebone; corset 228 *underwear*; yoke 217 *hanger*; rest, headrest, backrest, footrest, stirrup; banisters, handrail (see *handle*); foothold 778 *retention*; wedge 702 *obstacle*; staff, baton, stick, cane, alpenstock, crutch, crook, shepherd's c.; leg support, splint, calliper, irons; bracket (see *shelf*);

trivet, hob (see *stand*); life-support machine, collarbone, worldbearer, patron.

handle, holder, pen h., cigarette h. 194 *receptacle*; hilt, pommel, haft; knob, doorhandle; lug, ear, loop; railing, handrail, rail, poop r., taffrail, banisters, balustrade; shaft; handlebar, tiller; winder, crank, crankhandle; lever, trigger 630 *tool*.

basis, foundation, footings, deck; pallet, sleeper; substratum 207 *layer*; ground, groundwork, floor, bed, bedrock, rock bottom 214 *base*; sill *or* cill; flooring, pavement 226 *paving*; terra firma 344 *land*.

stand, tripod, trivet, hob; table mat, coaster; anvil, block, bench; trolley, tea trolley; table, console t., coffee t., card t., gateleg t., drop-leaf t., refectory t., board; sideboard, dresser, Welsh d. 194 *cabinet*; work table, desk, counter; pedestal, plinth, podium; platform, launching pad, launchpad, gantry; emplacement; footplate; landing; landing stage, pier; dais, pulpit, stage; doorstep, threshold; step, stair, tread, rung.

seat, throne, woolsack; bank, bench, form, settle; bucket seat, box s., rumble s., dicky; pew, choirstall, misericord 990 *church interior*; stall, fauteuil 594 *theatre*; chair, armchair, easy chair, wing c., club c., rocking c., revolving c., basket c., Windsor c., high c., deck c., lounger; chaise longue; sofa, settee, futon, divan, couch, studio c., ottoman, chesterfield, loveseat, windowseat; pouffe, stool, footstool, kitchen stool, campstool; priedieu, hassock; saddle, pillion, pad, howdah; ducking-stool 964 *pillory*; electric chair; lap; mat 226 *floor-cover*.

bed, cot, crib, cradle, bassinet; marriage bed, bridal b., double b., single b., king-size b., bunk b., bunk; bed settee, daybed, couch; tester, four-poster; charpoy, truckle bed, trundle b., camp b., pallet, airbed, futon, bedroll, shakedown; hammock 217 *hanging object*; sick bed, litter, hurdle, stretcher 658 *hospital*; bier 364 *funeral*; bedding, duvet 226 *coverlet*; bedstead, divan; headboard.

cushion, pillow; bolster; mattress, palliasse; squab, hassock, kneeler.

beam, balk, joist, girder, box g., rafter, purlin, tie beam, truss 47 *bond*; summer, bressummer; wall-plate 226 *roof*; crossbeam, transom, crossbar, traverse; architrave, lintel.

pillar, shaft, pier, pile, pole, stake, stud 331 *structure*; post, king post, queen p., crown p.; jamb, door j., doorpost; stanchion, puncheon; newelpost, banister, baluster; mullion; pilaster, column, Doric c., Ionic c., Corinthian c., Tuscan c.; caryatid, telamon, atlantes; spinal column, spine, backbone, vertebral column, vertebrae; neck, cervix.

pivot, fulcrum, lever, purchase; hinge 45 *joint*; pole, axis; gimbals; axle, swivel, spindle, arbor, pintle 315 *rotator*; bearing, gudgeon, trunnion; rowlock, tholepin; centreboard, keel.

shelf, bookshelf, ledge 254 *projection*; corbel, bracket, console; retable, niche 194 *compartment*; sill, windowsill, mantelpiece, mantelshelf, rack, dresser 194 *cabinet*; desktop, counter, worktop, plank, board, table, leaf, slab.

frame, skeleton, ribs; framework, infrastructure, staging, scaffolding 331 *structure*; trellis, espalier; chassis, fuselage, body (of a car), undercarriage; trestle; easel, clotheshorse; housing 235 *enclosure*; picture frame, window f., sash 233 *outline*.

Vb. *support,* sustain, bear, carry, hold, shoulder; uphold, hold up, bear up, buoy up; prop, shore up, underprop, underpin, jack up 310 *elevate*; buttress, bolster, bolster up, cushion; reinforce, underset 162 *strengthen*; bandage, brace, truss 45 *tighten*; steady, stay; cradle, pillow, cup, cup one's chin; maintain, give aliment, give alimony 633 *provide*; give one a hand, back up, give support, lend s., furnish s., afford s., supply s. 703 *aid*; frame, set, mount 235 *enclose*; be the infrastructure, bottom, ground, found, base 153 *stabilize*; stand, endure, survive, stand up to, stand the strain, take the s. 635 *suffice*.

219 Parallelism – **N.** *parallelism,* nonconvergence, nondivergence, equidistance, coextension, collimation, concentricity; parallel, correspondence 28 *equality*; parallel lines, lines of latitude; tramlines, rails, railway lines; parallel bars; parallelogram, parallelepiped.

220 Obliquity – **N.** *obliquity,* obliqueness, skewness; diagonal; rhomboid 247 *angular figure*; oblique angle, inclination 247 *angularity*; indirection, indirectness, squint; curvature, camber, bend, z-bend, chicane, humpback 248 *curve*; crookedness, zigzag, chevron; switchback 251 *meandering*; oblique motion, circumlocution, digression, swerve, lurch, stagger 282 *deviation*; splay, bias, twist, warp 246 *distortion*; leaning, list, tip, cant; slope, slant, tilt, pitch, rakish angle; sloping face; sloping edge, bevel, bezel; inclined plane, ramp, chute, slide; Tower of Pisa, leaning tower; measurement of inclination 247 *angular measure*.

incline, rise, ascent; ramp, acclivity, gradient; hill, rising ground, hillock; hillside 239 *laterality*; declivity, fall, dip, downhill 309 *descent*; gentle slope, nursery s.; escarpment, steepness, cliff, precipice 215 *verticality*; scarp 713 *fortification*; talus, bank, scree, landslip, landslide.

Adj. *sloping,* uphill, rising; downhill, falling, declining, dipping; anticlinal, synclinal; declivitous, steep, abrupt, sheer, precipitous, vertiginous, breakneck 215 *vertical.*

Vb. *be oblique,* be askew, be awry, be agley; incline, lean, tilt; pitch, slope, slant, shelve, dip, decline 309 *descend*; rise, climb 308 *ascend*; cut, cut across, transect 222 *cross*; lean, list, tip, lean over, bank, heel, careen, cant; bend, sag, give; bend over 311 *stoop*; walk sideways, edge, sidle, sidestep; look sideways, squint; zigzag; jink, dodge, duck, swerve; diverge, converge.

221 Inversion – **N.** *inversion,* turning back to front, palindrome; turning inside

out, eversion; turning backwards, retroversion, reversal 148 *reversion*; turning inward, introversion; turning over, capsizal (see *overturning*); turn of the tide, return 286 *regression*; oppositeness 14 *contrariety*, 240 *contraposition*; transposition, metathesis 151 *interchange*; inverted order, chiasmus 519 *trope*; spoonerism.

overturning, capsizal, upset, purler, spill; somersault, summerset, cartwheel, handspring; subversion, undermining, overthrowing 149 *revolution*.

Vb. *be inverted,* turn round, go r., wheel r., swing r., turn about, face a., right about turn 286 *turn back*; turn over, heel o., keel o., capsize, turn head over heels, turn turtle, turn topsy-turvy, be arsy-versy; tilt over 220 *be oblique*; go over, topple o. 309 *tumble*; do a handstand, stand on one's head; loop the loop; reverse, back, back away, go backwards 286 *regress*; be back to front, be inside out.

invert, transpose, put the cart before the horse 151 *interchange*; reverse, turn the tables; turn back; turn down 261 *fold*; introvert, turn inside out, upend, upturn, overturn, tip over, spill, upset, overset, capsize; turn topsy-turvy.

Adv. *inversely,* vice versa; contrariwise, quite the reverse, just the opposite, on the contrary, other way round; back to front, upside down; arsy-versy, topsy-turvy, head over heels; face down, face downwards, bottom side up.

222 Crossing: intertexture – N. *crossing,* crisscross, transection, intersection; decussation, X-shape; intertexture, interlacement, intertwinement, interweaving 844 *pattern*; braid, wreath, plait, pigtail 251 *convolution*; entanglement, intricacy, skein, cat's cradle 61 *complexity*; crossroads, intersection, roundabout, interchange, road junction 624 *road*; level crossing 624 *railway*; viaduct, flyover, overpass, underpass, subway 624 *bridge*, 305 *traffic control*.

cross, crux, rood, crucifix 988 *ritual object*; pectoral 989 *vestments*; ankh, ansate cross, tau c., Latin c., c. of Lorraine, Greek c., Maltese c., Celtic c., St Anthony's C., St Andrew's C.; saltire, crosslet 547 *heraldry*; gammadion, swastika, fylfot; crossbones, skull and c. 547 *flag*; crossbar, transom 218 *beam*.

network, reticulation, meshwork, netting, wire n., chicken wire; webbing, matting, wickerwork, basketwork, trellis, wattle; honeycomb, lattice, grating, grid, grille, gridiron; craquelure; tracery, fretwork, filigree 844 *ornamental art*; lace, crochet, knitting, darning, tatting, macramé 844 *needlework*; web, cobweb; net, fishnet, seine, purse-s., drag-net, trawl, beam t. 235 *enclosure*; plexus, mesh, reticle; chain, group, interconnection.

textile, weave, web, loom; woven stuff; bolt, roll, length, piece, cloth, stuff, material; broadcloth, fabric, tissue, suiting; batik 844 *ornamental art*; jute, hessian, gunny, sacking, hopsack, canvas, sailcloth, duck; ticking, crash, huckaback, towelling, terry t., candlewick; chintz, cretonne, damask, brocade, brocatelle, grosgrain, rep, chenille, tapestry 226 *covering*; mohair, cashmere; alpaca, vicuna, angora 208 *fibre*; wool, worsted, grogram; frieze, felt, baize; homespun, khadar, duffel, kersey, tweed, serge, shalloon, bombazine, gabardine, doeskin; flannel, swanskin, swansdown; paisley, jacquard 844 *pattern*; stockinette, jersey, tricot, nainsook, flannelette, winceyette; velvet, velveteen, velour; corduroy, needlecord; cotton, denim, drill, nankeen, cavalry twill, khaki; fustian, moleskin, sharkskin; poplin, calico, dimity, gingham, madras, seersucker, piqué; batiste, organdie, organza; silesia, cheesecloth, muslin, mull, voile, percale; cambric, lawn, toile, holland, linen; silk, surah, foulard, georgette, crêpe de chine, chiffon, mousseline; satin, sateen, taffeta, moire; tussore *or* tussah, shantung, pongee; ninon; tulle, net, gauze; lace, guipure; rayon, nylon, Terylene (tdmk); Crimplene (tdmk), polyester, Courtelle

(tdmk), Acrilan (tdmk), fibreglass 208 *fibre*.

weaving, texture; web, warp, weft, woof, selvedge; nap, pile 259 *hair*; frame, loom, shuttle; weaver, knitter; knitting machine, sewing m.; spinning wheel, distaff, whorl; spinner, spider, weaverbird; Arachne, Penelope.

Adj. *crossed,* crossing, cross, crisscross; quadrivial; diagonal, transverse, cross-eyed, squinting; decussate, X-shaped, quincunxial; cross-legged, cruciform, crucial, cruciate, forked, furcate 247 *angular*; plexiform; knotted, matted, tangled, balled-up, ravelled 61 *complex*; pleached, plashed, plaited, braided, interlaced, interwoven; textile, loomed, woven, handwoven, tweedy; twill, herringbone; trellised, latticed, honeycombed, mullioned, barred; corded, ribbed, streaked, striped 437 *variegated*.

Vb. *cross,* cross over, cross under 305 *pass*; intersect, cut 220 *be oblique*; decussate, inosculate, interdigitate; splice, dovetail, link 45 *join*; reticulate, mesh, net, knot; fork, bifurcate.

weave, loom; pleach, plash, plait, braid; felt, twill, knit, crochet, darn; spin, slub.

223 Exteriority – N. *exteriority,* the external; outwardness, externality 230 *surroundings*; periphery, circumference, sidelines 233 *outline*; exterior, outward appearance 445 *appearance*; superficiality, surface, superstratum, crust, cortex, shell, integument 226 *skin*; outer side, face, facet, facade 237 *front*; other side 240 *contraposition*; externalism; externalization, extroversion, extrovert 6 *extrinsicality*; outside, out of doors, open air; outer space 199 *distance*; extraterritoriality 57 *exclusion*; foreignness 59 *extraneousness*; eccentricity 84 *nonconformity*; outsider 84 *nonconformist*.

Adj. *exterior,* exoteric, outward; external 10 *unrelated*; peripheral; outer, outermost, outlying, extraterrestrial 199

distant; outside, outboard; outdoor, extramural; foreign 59 *extraneous*; extraterrestrial, extraterritorial 57 *excluding*; extrovert, outward-looking 6 *extrinsic*; centrifugal; exogenous; eccentric; surface, superficial, epidermal, cortical; skin-deep 212 *shallow*; facial 237 *frontal*.

Adv. *externally,* outwardly, outwards, superficially, on the surface; on the face of it, to the outsider; outside, out, out of doors, in the cold, in the sun, in the open, in the open air, al fresco.

224 Interiority – N. *interiority,* interior, inside, indoors; inner surface, undersurface; endoderm 226 *skin*; sapwood, heartwood 366 *wood*; inmost being, heart's blood, soul; heart, centre, breast, bosom 225 *centrality*; inland, Midlands, heartland, hinterland, up-country; the nitty gritty, pith, marrow 3 *substance*; substratum 214 *base*; pervasion 189 *presence*, 231 *interjacency*; deepness, cave, pit, pothole, recesses 211 *depth*; introversion 5 *intrinsicality*; self-absorption, egocentrism 932 *selfishness*.

insides 193 *contents;* inner man *or* woman, viscera, vitals; heart; lungs; lights; liver, kidneys, spleen; offal 301 *meat*; bowels, entrails, innards, guts, tripe; intestines, colon, rectum; abdomen, belly, paunch, underbelly; womb, uterus; stomach, tummy 194 *stomach*; chest, breast, bosom, solar plexus.

Adj. *interior,* internal, inward 5 *intrinsic*; inside, inner, innermost 225 *central*; inland; domestic, home; intimate, familiar 490 *known*; indoor, intramural, shut in, enclosed; built-in, inwrought; endemic; deep-seated, deep-rooted, ingrown 153 *fixed*; intestinal, visceral; intravenous, subcutaneous; interstitial 231 *interjacent*; inward-looking, introvert 5 *intrinsic*; endogamous; endogenous.

Adv. *inside,* within, in, deep down; inwardly, intimately; deeply, profoundly, at heart; within doors, indoors, at home, en famille, chez, at the sign of.

225 Centrality – N. *centrality,* centralness; concentricity; centralization, focalization, concentration 324 *condensation*; central position 231 *interjacency*; midriff, waistline, centreline.

centre, dead c.; centroid, centre of gravity, centre of pressure, metacentre; nerve centre, ganglion; centre of activity, focal point 76 *focus*; epicentre; storm centre; heart, core, kernel 5 *essential part*; nub, hub; nucleus, nucleolus; navel, umbilicus; spine, backbone, vertebrae, midrib; marrow, pith 224 *interiority*; pole, axis, fulcrum, centreboard 218 *pivot*; centre point, mid p. 70 *middle*; fess-point 547 *heraldry*; eye, pupil; bull's-eye, target 617 *objective*.

Adj. *central,* centric, centrical; nuclear, nucleolar; centremost, midmost 70 *middle*; axial, focal, pivotal; umbilical; concentric; geocentric; spinal, vertebral; centripetal; metropolitan, chief, head 34 *supreme*.

Vb. *centralize,* centre, focus; zero in on, centre upon; concentrate, nucleate, consolidate 324 *be dense*.

226 Covering – N. *covering,* capping etc. vb.; superimposition, overlaying; overlap, overlapping; coating, stratification 207 *layer*; veneer, top layer, top dressing, mulch, topsoil 344 *soil*; topping, icing, frosting 844 *ornamentation*; cover, lid; ledger 364 *tomb*; hatch, trapdoor; flap, shutter; film 423 *opacity*; glass, watch glass, crystal 422 *transparency*; cap, top, plug, bung, cork 264 *stopper*; plaster, Elastoplast (tdmk), Band-Aid (tdmk) 658 *surgical dressing*; carapace, shell, tortoiseshell 326 *hardness*; mail, plate 713 *armour*; shield, cowl, bonnet, hood (of a car); scab; crust, fur 649 *dirt*; capsule, ferrule, sheath, involucre, envelope 194 *receptacle*; pillowcase, pillowslip, cushion cover; table cloth, tray c.; chair cover, antimacassar; soft furnishings, loose covers; hangings, curtains, drapes 217 *hanging object*; wallpaper 227 *lining*.

roof, cupola 253 *dome*; mansard roof, hipped r., pitched r., gable r., flat r.,

housetop, rooftop 213 *vertex*; leads, slates, slating, tiles, tiling, pantile, shingle, thatch, thatching, corrugated iron 631 *building material*; eaves 234 *edge*; ceiling, deck; vaulting, vault; rafters 218 *beam*.

canopy, tilt, awning, sunblind 421 *screen*; marquee, pavilion, big top; tent, bell tent, ridge t., frame t.; tepee 192 *dwelling*; tentcloth, canvas, tarpaulin, fly sheet; mosquito net 222 *network*.

shade, hood, eyelid, eyelash; blind, venetian b., jalousie, shutters, slats; curtain, veil; umbrella, gamp, brolly; parasol, sunshade; sun hat, sun helmet, topee 228 *headgear*; visor, eye shade 421 *screen*; peak (of a cap); dark glasses, sunglasses, shades 442 *eyeglass*.

wrapping, wrapper, paper, tissue p., cellophane, polythene; polystyrene 227 *lining*; packaging, blister pack, bubble pack, gift box, shrinkpack 194 *receptacle*; bandage, roller; plaster cast 658 *surgical dressing*; book cover, binding, boards, dust jacket *or* cover 589 *bookbinding*; tunic, coat 228 *jacket*; mantle 228 *cloak*; comforter, scarf 228 *neckwear*; life belt, life jacket 662 *safeguard*; lagging; cocoon, chrysalis; shroud, winding sheet 364 *grave clothes*.

skin, epithelium; outer skin, scarf s., epidermis, cuticle; true skin, cutis, dermis, derma, corium; tegument 223 *exteriority*; integument, peel, bark, crust, rind, coat, cortex; pericarp, husk, hull, shell, pod, jacket; pellicle, membrane, film; scalp 213 *head*; scale; pelt, fleece, fell, fur; leather, hide, rawhide, imitation leather, leatheroid; shagreen, patent leather; crocodile, alligator; pigskin, morocco, calf, kid, chamois, suede, buff, buckskin, doeskin; rabbitskin, moleskin, sealskin; sheepskin, lamb, Persian l., astrakhan; mink, sable, ermine, miniver, cony; chinchilla 208 *fibre*; feathers, coverts 259 *plumage*.

paving, flooring, floor, parquet, quarry tiles; deck, floorboards, duckboards; pavement, sidewalk, pavé; flags, paving

stone, crazy paving; sett, cobble, cobblestone; gravel, chippings, asphalt, tarmac 624 *road.*

coverlet, bedspread, counterpane, bedding, bedclothes, bed linen; sheet, quilt, eiderdown, duvet, continental quilt, Downie (tdmk); blanket, rug; caparison, housings, trappings; saddlecloth, horsecloth; pall.

floor-cover, carpeting, carpet, fitted c., wall-to-wall; broadloom, pile carpet, Persian c.; mat, doormat, bath mat, prayer m.; rug, hearth r.; linoleum, lino, vinyl, tiles; matting, coconut m.; red carpet 875 *formality.*

facing, cladding; veneer, coating, varnish, japan, lacquer, enamel, glaze; roughcast, pebbledash; ashlar, weatherboarding 631 *building material;* stucco, compo, plaster, pargeting, rendering, screed; wash, whitewash, distemper, emulsion, paint; stain, polish, smearing, anointment; coat of paint 425 *pigment.*

Vb. *cover,* superimpose; roof, cork, cap, tip; ice, frost, decorate (a cake); spread, lay (a table); overlay, smother; insulate, lag 227 *line;* lap, wrap up, enfold, envelope 235 *enclose;* blanket, shroud, mantle, muffle; hood, veil 525 *conceal;* case, bind, cover (books); box, pack, vacuum-pack; wrap, shrink-w.; bandage, swathe, wrap round, dress 658 *doctor;* sheathe, encapsulate, encase 303 *insert;* wall in, wall up; cover up, keep under cover.

coat, revet, face, front; grout, roughcast, encrust, shingle; stucco, plaster, pebbledash, render, parget 844 *decorate;* thatch, tile; veneer, varnish, lacquer, japan, enamel, glaze, size; paint, whitewash, colourwash, distemper, emulsion, stain 425 *colour;* creosote; tar, pitch, pay; daub, bedaub, scumble, overpaint, grease, lard, lay it on thick; smear, butter, anoint, powder, sprinkle, gild, plate, silver; electroplate, silverplate; waterproof, fireproof, damp-proof 660 *safeguard.*

227 Lining – N. *lining,* liner, coating, inner c.; stuffing, wadding, padding,

quilting; kapok, foam, polystyrene 631 *materials;* lagging, insulation, doubleglazing, damp-proofing, soundproofing; backing, facing; doublure 589 *bookbinding;* upholstery; papering, wallpaper; wainscotting, panelling, wainscot, skirting board, dado, brattice; metal lining; brake lining; packing, dunnage; packaging 226 *wrapping;* filling, stopping (dentistry); washer.

Vb. *line,* encrust 226 *coat;* insulate 226 *cover;* interlard, inlay; back, face, paper, wallpaper; upholster, cushion; stuff, pad, wad; fill, pack.

228 Dressing – N. *dressing,* investment, investiture; clothing, covering, dressing up, toilet, toilette; overdressing, foppishness; underdressing, casualness 848 *fashion;* vesture, dress, garb, attire, rig, gear, clobber; panoply, array; garniture, trim, accoutrements, caparison, harness, housing, trappings; traps, paraphernalia, accessories; rig-out, turn-out; tailoring, dressmaking, millinery; haute couture; the rag trade, the fashion world.

clothing, wear, apparel, raiment, linen; clothes, garments, vestments, habiliments; togs, gear, kit, clobber; outfit, wardrobe, trousseau; maternity wear; layette, baby clothes, swaddling c., Babygro (tdmk); old clothes, duds, reach-me-downs, cast-offs, rags, tatters; working clothes, hand-me-downs, second-hand clothes, uniform; leisure wear, sportswear, tracksuit, casual clothes; best c.; Sunday best, best bib and tucker; party dress, glad rags; ostrich feathers, frippery 844 *finery;* fancy dress, masquerade; motley; national costume.

garment, article of clothing; neck, collar (**see** *neckwear, neckline*); top, bodice, bosom; corsage, bib, stomacher; shirtfront, dickey; waistline (**see** *belt*); peplum, bustle, train; crutch, codpiece; arms (**see** *sleeve*); flaps, coat tails 217 *hanging object;* placket, fly 263 *opening;* patch pocket; flap, gusset, gore, pleat, kick pleat; lapel, turn-up 261 *fold;* cuff, hemline 234 *edging.*

formal dress, correct d., court d., full d. 875 *formality*; grande toilette, evening dress, tails, white tie and tails; dinner jacket, black tie, tuxedo; morning dress; academic dress, academicals, cap and gown, subfusc; mourning, black, widow's weeds.

uniform, regimentals; dress uniform, undress, mess kit; battledress, fatigues, khaki; school uniform, academic dress; robes, vestments, clerical dress 989 *canonicals.*

informal dress, undress, mufti, civvies; casual clothes, leisure wear, slacks, jeans; déshabillé, dishabille; dressing gown, loungewear, peignoir, bathrobe, robe, wrapper, housecoat; smoking jacket, slippers.

robe, gown, robes, sari; kimono, caftan; jubbah, djellaba, toga, cassock 989 *canonicals.*

dress, frock, gown; creation, number, ballgown, cocktail dress, little black d.; sheath d., tube d., cheongsam, chemise, shift, sack; shirtwaister, coatdress, overdress, pinafore dress, jumper, gymslip; sundress.

suit, outfit, ensemble; coordinates, separates; lounge suit, zoot s., drape s., pinstripe s.; costume, tweeds, trouser suit, pantsuit; jumpsuit, catsuit, leotard, body-suit, body stocking; overalls, dungarees, boiler suit, siren s., tracksuit, leisure suit, skinsuit, wetsuit, G-suit, spacesuit.

jacket, coat, tail c., dinner jacket, tuxedo; monkey jacket, mess j., Eton j.; blazer, reefer, sports jacket, Norfolk j., hacking j., riding habit, hunting pink; donkey jacket, lumber j. (see *overcoat*); parka, windcheater, anorak, kagoule; bomber jacket, blouson; jerkin, tunic, tabard, surcoat, waistcoat, vest, gilet, spencer; bolero, coatee, matinee jacket.

jersey, pullover, woolly, knit, homeknit, handknit, jumper, sweater, V-neck, polo neck, turtle neck, crew neck, sloppy joe, sweatshirt, guernsey, Fair Isle, cardigan, cardi, tank top, twin set.

trousers, pants, trews, breeks; cords, flannels, pinstripes; hipsters, drainpipes,

bell-bottoms, flares; slacks, bags, Oxford b., plus fours; breeches, britches, jodhpurs, knickerbockers, pedal-pushers, leggings, tights; chaps, dungarees, denims, jeans, blue j., Levi's (tdmk); shorts, Bermuda s., hot pants; lederhosen; bloomers, pantaloons, rompers.

skirt, maxi s., midi s., miniskirt; pleated s., flared s., A-line s., gored s., full s., dirndl, bubble skirt, kilt, kirtle, filibeg; sarong; straight skirt, slit s., hobble s.; sports s., divided s., culottes; ballet skirt, tutu; crinoline, farthingale, hoop.

shirt, smock, angel top; polo neck, tee shirt, sweatshirt; blouse, camisole, top.

underwear, underclothes, undies, linen; lingerie, smalls, unmentionables; underpants, shorts, pants, Y-fronts, boxer shorts; briefs, panties, scanties, French knickers, camiknickers, teddy, knickers, bloomers, drawers; combinations, long johns, thermal underwear; singlet, vest, string v., undershirt, semmit; camisole, chemise, slip, half-slip, underskirt, petticoat; foundation garment, body stocking, corset, stays, girdle, pantie-g., roll-on; brassiere, bra; suspender belt, braces.

nightwear, nightclothes, sleeping suit; nightgown, nightdress, nightie, negligee; nightshirt, pyjamas; bedsocks, bed jacket, nightcap.

beachwear, sunsuit, sundress; bikini, bankini, monokini; swimming costume, swimsuit, one-piece s., bathing suit, trunks, bathers; beach robe.

overcoat, coat (see *jacket*); fur coat 226 *skin*; topcoat, greatcoat, frock coat; ulster, car coat, duffel c.; waterproof, oilskins; mac, mackintosh, raincoat, gabardine; Burberry (tdmk), trench coat; light coat, duster; fitted coat.

cloak, cape, cycling c.; poncho.

neckwear, scarf, fichu; stole, boa, tippet; comforter, muffler; neckerchief, jabot, cravat, necktie, tie, bow t.; necklace 844 *jewellery*; ruff, collar, dog c. 989 *canonicals*; Eton collar, mandarin c., Peter Pan c., Vandyke c., Bertha, sailor c., shawl c.; button-down c., stand-up c. See *neckline.*

headgear, millinery; hat, cap, lid, titfer, tile; headdress, mantilla; plumes, ribbons 844 *finery;* crown, coronet, tiara 743 *regalia;* fillet, snood; juliet cap, skull c., coif; headscarf, kerchief, bandanna, headband, sweatband, Alice band; turban; hood, cowl, wimple; veil, yashmak 421 *screen;* fez, tarboosh; kepi, busby, bearskin, helmet 713 *armour;* tin hat, crash helmet, safety h. 662 *safeguard;* woolly hat, bobble h., ski h.; rainhat, sou'wester; cap, cloth c., beret, tam-o'-shanter, tammy; Balmoral, glengarry, deerstalker; Homburg, trilby, pork-pie hat, billycock, fedora, beaver, bowler, derby; slouch hat, stetson, ten-gallon hat, sombrero, shovel hat, picture h., straw h., boater, panama, coolie hat, bush h., sunhat, pith helmet 226 *shade;* bonnet, Easter b., poke b., mob cap, toque, cloche, pillbox; top hat, topper, silk hat, stovepipe h.; cocked h., mortarboard; biretta 989 *canonicals;* witch's hat, wizard's h., dunce's cap.

neckline, boat neck, crew n., cowl n., turtle n., roll n., polo n., halter n., V-n., round n.; low n. 229 *bareness.*

belt, waistband; cummerbund, sash, obi; bandolier, baldric.

sleeve, arm, armhole; leg-of-mutton sleeve, raglan s., dolman s., batwing s., magyar s., puff s., cap s., short s., long s.; wristband, cuff.

glove, gauntlet, driving gloves, long g.; evening g.; mitten, mitt, muff.

legwear, hosiery; stockings, nylons, tights, fleshings; trunks, hose; socks, knee-length s., over-the-knee s., ankle s., bootees; leggings, gaiters, spats, puttees; garter, suspender 47 *fastening.*

footwear, footgear; slipper, carpet s., mule; patten, clog, sabot; flipflops, sandals, Jesus boots, chappals; rope-soled shoes, espadrilles, rubber-soled shoes, crepe-soled s., creepers, brothel creepers, sneakers, plimsolls, gym shoes, trainers, tennis shoes; pumps, ballet shoes; moccasins, slip-ons, casuals; winklepickers, beetlecrushers, clodhoppers; shoe, court s., high heels, stiletto h., platform h., Cuban h., wedge h.; peep-toed shoes, slingbacks, flat shoes, driving s., laceups, buckled shoes; Oxfords, brogues; boots, fashion b., high b., cowboy b.; thigh b., waders, wellingtons, wellies; gumboots; skiboots 274 *sled;* running shoes, spikes.

clothier, outfitter, costumier; tailor, couturier, couturière; fashion designer 848 *fashion;* dressmaker, seamstress, modiste; shoemaker, bootmaker; cobbler 686 *artisan;* hosier, hatter, milliner, draper, haberdasher; Savile Row, Carnaby Street; boutique; valet, batman 742 *domestic;* dresser, mistress of the wardrobe.

Adj. *tailored,* tailor-made, bespoke, made-to-measure, custom-made; designer, ready-to-wear, off-the-peg; fully fashioned.

Vb. *dress,* clothe, array, garb, attire; robe, drape, sheet, mantle; invest, put in uniform, equip, rig out, fit o., harness 669 *make ready;* dress up, deck, prink 843 *primp;* envelop, wrap, lap, enfold, wrap up, fold up, muffle up, roll up in, swaddle, swathe, shroud, sheathe 226 *cover.*

wear, put on, don, slip on, slip into; clothe oneself, attire o., get dressed, get one's clothes on; have on, dress in, dress up 875 *be ostentatious.*

229 Uncovering – N. *uncovering,* divestment, undressing etc. vb.; opening, openness, glasnost; exposure, indecent e. 526 *disclosure;* nudism, naturism; stripping, dance of the seven veils, striptease 594 *stage show;* undress, dishabille, déshabillé 228 *informal dress;* moulting, ecdysis, shedding; decortication, exfoliation, abscission, excoriation, peeling, desquamation; depilation, shaving; denudation, devastation.

bareness, décolleté, décolletage, bare neck, plunging neckline; nudity, nakedness, birthday suit, the altogether, the buff, the raw, starkers, not a stitch on, streaking.

stripper, ecdysiast, striptease artiste, flasher, dirty old man in a raincoat, streaker; nudist, naturist; nude model,

hair-remover, depilatory, wax, electrolysis.

Adj. *uncovered,* bared; exposed, unveiled 522 *manifest*; divested; debagged; stripped; unclad, unclothed, undressed, unattired; décolleté(e), bare-necked, off-the-shoulder, topless; bare-backed, bare-armed, barelegged; barefoot, unshod, hatless, bareheaded; en déshabillé, in one's shirt-sleeves; miniskirted, bikini-clad, swimsuited; indecently dressed; bare, naked, nude, raw; mother naked, in a state of undress, in the buff, in one's birthday suit, with nothing on, without a stitch on; stark, stark naked, starkers; unsheathed.

hairless, bald, baldheaded, beardless, shaved, shaven, clean-s., tonsured; bald as a coot, bald as an egg, bald as a billiard ball; threadbare; thin on top.

Vb. *uncover,* unveil, undress, unclothe; divest, debag; strip, skin, scalp, flay, tear off; pluck, peel, pare, bark, excoriate; hull, pod, shell, stone; bone, fillet 300 *empty*; denude, expose, bare, lay open 526 *disclose*; unsheathe, draw (a sword) 304 *extract*; unwrap, unpack; uncap, uncork 263 *open*; abrade 333 *rub*.

230 Surroundings – N. *surroundings* 223 *exteriority*; ambience, atmosphere, aura; medium, matrix; encompassment, containment, surrounding 235 *enclosure*; compass, circuit, circumference, periphery, perimeter 233 *outline*; milieu, environment, entourage; background, setting, scene, scenario 186 *situation*; neighbourhood, vicinity; outskirts, environs, suburbs, precincts 192 *housing*; sticks, outpost, cordon.

Vb. *surround,* lie around, encompass, lap; encircle 314 *circle*; begird 235 *enclose*; twine around; embrace, cuddle, hug 889 *caress*; contain, keep in, cloister, shut in, close round, hem in 232 *circumscribe*; blockade 712 *besiege*.

Adv. *around,* about, on every side, round about, all round; on all sides; outside, in the outskirts.

231 Interjacency – N. *interjacency,* intermediacy, intervention, penetration, permeation, infiltration 189 *presence*; dovetailing 45 *union*.

partition, curtain, Iron C., bamboo c. 421 *screen*; Great Wall of China 713 *defences*; Berlin Wall 57 *exclusion*; wall, party w., garden fence 235 *fence*; divide, watershed, parting 46 *separation*; division, panel 53 *subdivision*; hedge, ditch 201 *gap*.

intermediary, medium, link 47 *bond*; negotiator, go-between, pander, broker 720 *mediator*; agent 755 *deputy*; middleman, retailer 794 *merchant*; advocate 707 *patron*; buffer, bumper, fender, crumple zone, cushion, air bag 662 *safeguard*; air lock, buffer state, no-man's-land, no-go area, halfway house 70 *middle*.

interjection, sandwiching; interpolation 303 *insertion*; embolism 264 *closure*; interruption, intrusion, chipping in, butting in 72 *discontinuity*; interference, meddling 702 *hindrance*; episode, parenthesis 40 *adjunct*; insert.

interjector, interpolator; intruder, interloper.

Adj. *interjacent,* sandwiched; episodic, parenthetical, in brackets, in parentheses; intermediary, intervening etc. vb.; mediating; intrusive 59 *extraneous*; interplanetary; intermediate 303 *inserted*; median, medium, mean 70 *middle*; partitioning, dividing.

Vb. *lie between,* come b., stand b.; mediate, intervene.

introduce, let in 299 *admit*; throw in, work in, edge in, force in, thrust in 303 *insert*; ingrain; splice, dovetail, mortise 45 *join*; smuggle in, worm in, insinuate 297 *infiltrate*.

interfere, come between, intercept 702 *hinder*; step in, intervene, intercede 720 *mediate*; interrupt, put in, chip in, get a word in; obtrude, thrust in, poke one's nose in, horn in, butt in 297 *intrude*; invade, trespass 306 *encroach*; put one's oar in; have a finger in the pie 678 *meddle*.

Adv. *between,* betwixt, 'twixt, betwixt and between; among, amongst, amid, amidst, mid, midst; in the middle of; in the thick of; parenthetically.

232 Circumscription – N. *circumscription,* enclosing 235 *enclosure;* encircling, encompassing, circle, balloon; ringing round, hedging r., fencing r.; surrounding, framing, girdling; siege, blockade 712 *attack;* envelopment, encirclement, containment, confinement, limitation 747 *restriction;* ring 235 *fence.*

Vb. *circumscribe,* describe a circle, ring round, circle, encircle, encompass; envelop, close in, cut off, cordon off, rope off, mark off, invest, beleaguer, blockade, picket 712 *besiege;* beset, hem in, pen in; enclose, rail in, hedge in, fence in; box, cage, wall in, immure, cloister 747 *imprison;* frame 230 *surround;* encase, enfold, enshrine, edge, border 236 *limit;* clasp 889 *caress,* embrace.

233 Outline – N. *outline,* circumference, perimeter, periphery; surround, frame, rim 234 *edge;* compass, circuit 250 *circle;* delineation, configuration, features 445 *feature;* profile, relief 239 *laterality;* silhouette, skyline, horizon 553 *picture;* sketch, rough s., draft 623 *plan;* figure, diagram, layout; trace, tracing; skeleton, framework 331 *structure;* contour, contour line, shape 243 *form,* coastline, bounds 236 *limit.*

Vb. *outline,* describe a circle 232 *circumscribe;* frame 230 *surround;* delineate, draw, silhouette, profile, trace 551 *represent;* etch 555 *engrave;* map, block out, rough o., sketch o., sketch; diagrammatize.

234 Edge – N. *edge,* verge, brim; tip, brink, skirt, fringe, margin 69 *extremity;* confines, bounds, boundary, frontier, border 236 *limit;* coast, beach, strand, seaside, seashore, water's edge, waterfront 344 *shore;* wharf, quay, dock 192 *stable;* sideline, side, brim, kerb *or* curb, wayside, roadside, bank 239 *laterality;* hedge 235 *fence;* lip, ledge, eave, cornice,

rim, welt, flange 254 *projection;* horizon, skyline; knife edge, razor e.; sharpness, acrimony; advantage, upper hand.

threshold, sill, doorstep, door, portal, porch 263 *doorway;* mouth.

edging, frame 233 *outline;* selvedge; hem, border; binding, piping; fringe, frill, ruffle, flounce, furbelow, valance 844 *trimming;* scallop.

Adj. *marginal,* border, coastal; riverside, roadside, wayside; labial, edged, trimmed, bordered; borderline, peripheral.

Vb. *hem,* edge, lower e., border, trim, piping, fringe; crenellate 260 *notch;* bound, confine 236 *limit.*

235 Enclosure – N. *enclosure,* envelope, case 194 *receptacle;* wrapper, packaging 226 *wrapping;* ring, perimeter, circumference, periphery 233 *outline;* surround, frame; cloister, courtyard 185 *place;* reserve 883 *seclusion;* lot, holding, claim 184 *territory;* fold, pen, sheepfold, sty 369 *cattle pen;* park 370 *garden;* compound, yard, pound, paddock, field; car park, parking lot 192 *stable;* corral, stockade, lines 713 *defences;* net, trawl 222 *network;* cell, cage 748 *prison.*

fence, ring f., barbed-wire f., razor-wire fence, electric f. 222 *network;* hurdle, wooden fence, picket f., sunk f., ha-ha, hedge, privet h., quickset h., hedgerow, espalier; rails, balustrade, banisters, paling, railing; pale, wall, boundary w.; moat, dike, ditch, fosse, trench 713 *defences.*

barrier, wall, cavity w., brick w., drystone w. 231 *partition;* soundproofing, double-glazing, damp-proofing 660 *protection;* barricade, cordon, pale; balustrade, parapet; turnstile 702 *obstacle;* palisade, stockade 713 *fort;* portcullis, gate, door, bolt, bar, padlock 264 *closure.*

Vb. *enclose,* fence in, cordon off, rope off, surround, wall; pen, hem, ring, corral, 232 *circumscribe;* cloister, immure, wall up, confine, cage 747 *imprison;* wrap, enfold 261 *fold;* hug, embrace, cuddle 889 *caress;* frame.

236 Limit – N. *limit,* limitation, constraint 747 *restriction,* 468 *qualification;* delimitation, demarcation 783 *apportionment;* parameter; upper limit, ceiling, high-water mark 213 *summit;* lower limit, threshold 214 *base;* legal limit, Plimsoll line; saturation point 54 *completeness;* utmost, uttermost, extreme, ne plus ultra, pole 69 *extremity;* ends of the earth; terminus, terminal 69 *end;* goal, target, winning post, touch, touchline, home, base 617 *objective;* turning point, watershed 137 *crisis;* point of no return 599 *resolution;* Rubicon, threshold of pain, tolerance, capacity, end of one's tether; outside edge, perimeter, periphery, circumference 233 *outline;* tidemark, sea line 344 *shore;* landmark, boundary stone; milestone 27 *degree;* kerb *or* curb, kerbstone 624 *road;* boundary, verge; frontier, border, marches 234 *edge;* demarcation l., international date l., divide, parting 231 *partition;* skyline, horizon, equator; deadline, time limit, term 110 *period;* ultimatum 900 *threat;* speed limit 278 *slowness;* sound barrier.

Vb. *limit,* bound, border, edge 234 *hem;* top 213 *crown;* confine; restrict 747 *restrain;* encompass 232 *circumscribe;* delimit, demarcate; rope off, mark out 547 *mark.*

237 Front – N. *front,* fore, forefront 64 *precedence;* prefix, frontispiece, preface, foreword, front matter; forelock 259 *hair;* forecourt, anteroom, entrance, hall 263 *doorway;* foreground 200 *nearness;* front rank, front line; leading edge; forward line, centre forward; avant-garde, vanguard, advance guard; spearhead; outpost, scout, reconnaissance party; forerunner, pioneer 66 *precursor;* prequel.

face, frontage, façade, fascia; face of a coin, obverse, head; right side, outer s., recto; front view, front elevation; physiognomy, features, visage, countenance, phiz, phizog, mug, mush, dial, clock 445 *feature.*

Adj. *frontal,* fore, forward, front, obverse; full frontal, head-on, oncoming,

facing 240 *opposite;* anterior, prefixed 64 *preceding.*

Vb. *be in front,* stand in front etc. adv.; front, confront, face, eyeball, face up to 240 *be opposite;* breast; come to the fore, forge ahead, take the lead, head 283 *precede.*

Adv. *in front,* before, in advance, in the lead, in the van; ahead, ahead of one's time, further on 199 *beyond;* far ahead, before one's eyes; face to face, eyeball to eyeball, in the foreground, in the forefront, in the limelight.

238 Rear – N. *rear,* back end, rear end, tail end, stern 69 *extremity;* tailpiece, heel, colophon; coda 412 *musical piece;* tail, brush, scut 67 *sequel;* wake, train 67 *retinue;* booby prize, wooden spoon, back seat 35 *inferiority;* rearguard 67 *successor;* background, backdrop 594 *stage set;* hinterland, far corner 199 *distance;* behind, backstage, back side; reverse side, wrong s., verso 240 *contraposition;* reverse, other side, flip side, B-side; back door, back entrance, tradesmen's e., postern 263 *doorway;* back (of the body), dorsum; spine 218 *prop;* back of the neck, scruff of the n., nape; back of the head.

buttocks, backside, behind, rear end, derrière, posterior; bottom, btm, seat, sit-upon; bum, arse (vulg), ass, butt, fanny; rear, stern, tail; hindquarters; hips, haunches, hams, hunkers; rump; lower back, coccyx; anus.

Adj. *back,* rear; posterior, after, hind, hinder, hindermost, rearmost, tail-end; backswept 253 *convex;* reverse 240 *opposite;* placed last 35 *inferior;* spinal, vertebral, dorsal, lumbar; anal; caudal, caudate.

Vb. *be behind,* back on, back; back up 703 *aid;* follow, bring up the rear 65 *come after;* lag, trail, drop behind 278 *move slowly;* trail, tail, shadow, dog 619 *pursue;* follow at heel 284 *follow;* bend backwards 220 *be oblique.*

Adv. *rearward,* behind; in the rear, at the end; at the back, in the background; behind one's back; behind the scenes,

offstage; after; aft, abaft, astern, aback; to the rear, hindward, backward, above; overleaf; hard on the heels of, at the back of, close behind; one behind the other, back to back.

239 Laterality – N. *laterality,* side movement 317 *oscillation;* sidestep 282 *deviation;* sideline, side, bank 234 *edge;* coast 344 *shore;* siding, side entrance, side door; broadside; beam; quarter; flank, ribs; wing, fin, arm, hand; cheek, jowl; gills; side whiskers 259 *hair;* temples; profile, side elevation; lee side, leeward; windward 281 *direction;* off side, on s., near s. 241 *dextrality,* 242 *sinistrality.*

Adj. *lateral,* side 234 *marginal;* sidelong; winglike; flanking, skirting; flanked, sided; manysided, multilateral, unilateral, bilateral, trilateral, quadrilateral; collateral; edging, sidling.

Vb. *flank,* side, edge, skirt, border 234 *hem;* coast, move sideways, sidle; sidestep 282 *deviate.*

Adv. *sideways,* crabwise, laterally; askance, asquint; in profile, sideways on; sidelong, broadside on; aside; side by side, cheek by jowl 200 *near.*

240 Contraposition – N. *contraposition,* antithesis, opposition, antipodes 14 *contrariety;* opposite side, other s., other s. of the fence; reverse, back 238 *rear;* polarity, polarization; opposite poles, poles apart, North and South; crosscurrent, headwind 704 *opposition;* reversal, inverse 221 *inversion.*

Adj. *opposite,* contrapositive, reverse, inverse; contrary 14 *contrary;* facing, face to face, vis-à-vis, eyeball to eyeball, confronting 237 *frontal;* diametrically opposed, antipodean, antithetical; polarized, polar.

Vb. *be opposite,* - facing, etc. adj.; stand opposite, lie o.; subtend; face, confront 237 *be in front;* run counter 182 *counteract;* oppose, contrapose.

Adv. *against,* poles apart; facing, face to face, eyeball to eyeball, vis-à-vis; back to back; on the other side, on the other side of the fence, overleaf; contrariwise, vice versa.

241 Dextrality – N. *dextrality,* right hand, right-handedness; ambidextrousness 694 *skill;* right, offside, starboard; right-hand page, recto; right wing, right-winger; dextral, ambidexter.

242 Sinistrality – N. *sinistrality,* left hand, left-handedness, cack-handedness; left, near side, on s.; larboard, port; left-hand page, verso; left wing, left-winger; sinistral, southpaw.

Section three: Form

243 Form – N. *form,* idea; essence 3 *substance;* art form 551 *art,* 593 *verse form;* word form; shape, turn, lines, architecture; formation, conformation, configuration, fashion, style, trend, design 331 *structure;* contour, silhouette, relief, profile, frame, outline; figure, cut, set, trim, build, cut of one's jib, lineament 445 *feature;* physiognomy 237 *face;* look, expression, appearance 445 *mien;* posture, attitude, stance; get-up, turnout, rig, gear; type, kind, pattern, stamp, cast, mould, blank 23 *prototype;* format; morphology.

formation, forming, shaping, creation 164 *production;* formulation 62 *arrangement;* designing 844 *ornamental art;* weaving, knitting 222 *network;* tailoring 844 *needlework;* throwing 381 *pottery;* moulding 554 *sculpture;* joinery 694 *skill;* word-formation.

Adj. *formed,* created etc. vb.; sculptured, carved, moulded, thrown, turned; shaped, fashioned, fully f., styled; designer, tailor-made, custom-built; readymade, off the peg; matured, ready 669 *prepared;* solid, concrete 324 *dense.*

Vb. *form,* create, make 164 *produce;* formalize, shape, fashion; throw (pots), blow (glass); turn; cut, tailor; cut out, silhouette 233 *outline;* sketch, draft, draw 551 *represent;* model, carve, whittle, chisel 554 *sculpt;* hew, rough-h. 46

cut; mould, cast; stamp, coin, mint; hammer out, block o., punch o.; forge; knead, work, work up into; construct, build, frame 310 *elevate*; express, put into words, verbalize, formulate, put into shape, lick into s., knock into s.

244 Amorphism: absence of form – N. *amorphism*, formlessness; chaos 61 *disorder*; amorphousness, shapelessness; vagueness, fuzziness; uncouthness 670 *undevelopment*; raw material 631 *materials*; rough diamond; disfigurement, defacement, deformity 246 *distortion*.

Adj. *amorphous*, formless, unformed, unstructured, structureless; liquid 335 *fluid*; shapeless, characterless; chaotic; undefined, ill-defined, indistinct, nondescript, nebulous, vague, fuzzy, blurred 419 *shadowy*; unformed; embryonic 68 *beginning*; raw, callow 670 *immature*; unhewn 55 *incomplete*; rude, uncouth, barbaric 699 *artless*; rugged 259 *rough*; unshapely 842 *unsightly*; malformed, misshapen 246 *deformed*.

Vb. *deform*, deprive of form 165 *destroy*; melt 337 *liquefy*; knock out of shape, batter 46 *break*; grind, pulp 332 *pulverize*; warp, twist 246 *distort*; deface, disfigure 842 *make ugly*; mutilate 655 *impair*; jumble 63 *derange*.

245 Symmetry: regularity of form – N. *symmetry*, proportion 12 *correlation*; balance 28 *equilibrium*; regularity, evenness 16 *uniformity*; branching, ramification 219 *parallelism*; shapeliness, regular features, classic f. 841 *beauty*; harmony, congruity 24 *agreement*; rhythm 141 *periodicity*; finish 646 *perfection*.

Adj. *symmetrical*, balanced, well-balanced 28 *equal*; proportioned, well-p. 12 *correlative*; rhythmical, harmonious, congruous 24 *agreeing*; congruent; corresponding; analogous 18 *similar*; smooth, even 16 *uniform*; squared, rounded; evensided, isosceles, equilateral 81 *regular*; arborescent.

246 Distortion: irregularity of form – N. *distortion*, asymmetry, disproportion, disproportionateness 10 *unrelatedness*; fractal; imbalance, disequilibrium 29 *inequality*; lop-sidedness, crookedness, skewness 220 *obliquity*; projection 551 *map*; contortion, twisting; thrust, stress, strain, shear; bias, warp; buckle, bend, screw, twist 251 *convolution*; grimace, moue, snarl 547 *gesture*.

deformity, malformation, disfigurement, monstrosity, mutation, abortion 84 *abnormality*; curvature of the spine 248 *curvature*; clubfoot, knock knees, bow legs, rickets, hunchback 845 *blemish*; ugliness 842 *eyesore*; teratology.

Adj. *distorted*, contorted etc. vb.; irregular, asymmetric, scalene, unsymmetrical, disproportionate 17 *nonuniform*; weighted, biased; not true, not straight; out of shape, warped, mutative 244 *amorphous*; mangled, buckled, twisted, gnarled 251 *convoluted*; wry, awry, askew, crazy, crooked, cock-eyed, on one side; grimacing.

deformed, ugly 842 *unsightly*; ill-proportioned; defective 647 *imperfect*; mutative, ill-made, malformed, misshapen; hunchbacked, bandy-legged, bowlegged, knock-kneed; pigeon-toed, splayfooted, club-footed, web-footed; round-shouldered, pigeon-chested; harelipped; stunted 204 *short*.

Vb. *distort*, weight, bias; contort, screw, twist, knot 251 *twine*; bend, warp 251 *crinkle*; buckle, crumple; strain, sprain, skew, wrest, rack 63 *derange*; misshape, botch 244 *deform*; mangle, batter, knock out of shape 655 *impair*; pervert 552 *misrepresent*; misconstrue 521 *misinterpret*; grimace 547 *gesticulate*; frown.

247 Angularity – N. *angularity*, crotchet, bracket, crook, hook; bend, scythe, sickle, scimitar 248 *curvature*; chevron, zigzag 220 *obliquity*; V-shape, elbow, knee; withers 253 *camber*; knuckle, ankle, groin 45 *joint*; crotch 222 *cross*; fork, branching 222 *crossing*; corner, cranny, nook, niche, recess 194 *compartment*;

nose, Roman n., hook n. 254 *protuberance*; flexure 261 *fold*; indentation 260 *notch*.

angle, right a., acute a., obtuse a., salient a., solid a.

angular measure, trigonometry, altimetry; angular elevation, angular distance; zenith distance; second, degree, minute; radian; altimeter; clinometer, level, theodolite; transit circle; sextant, quadrant; protractor, set square.

angular figure, triangle, isosceles t., equilateral t., scalene t.; parallelogram, rectangle, square, quadrangle; quadrilateral, diamond; rhomb; trapezium, tetragon, polygon, pentagon, hexagon, heptagon, octagon, nonagon, decagon, dodecahedron, icosahedron; cube, pyramid, wedge; prism.

Adj. *angular,* hooked, Roman-nosed, aquiline; angled, sharp-a., cornered; staggered, crooked, zigzag; jagged, serrated, crinkled; bony, jointed; akimbo; knock-kneed; forked, bifurcate, V-shaped.

248 Curvature – N. *curvature,* curvation; inward curve 255 *concavity*; outward curve 253 *convexity*; flexure, inflexion, bending 261 *fold*; stooping 311 *obeisance*; bending down; turning away, swerve, detour 282 *deviation*; downward bend 309 *descent*; curliness, sinuosity 251 *convolution*; curvature of the spine 246 *deformity*.

curve, elbow 247 *angularity*; turn, bend, Z-bend, hairpin b., U-turn; horseshoe; bay, bight 345 *gulf*; figure of eight 250 *loop*; S-shape; curl 251 *convolution*; bow, Cupid's b., rainbow 250 *arc*; arch, ogee a., arcade, vault 253 *dome*; sickle, scimitar, crescent, half-moon, lens; trajectory, parabola, hyperbola, conic section; cone biopsy; arch (of the foot), instep; swan neck.

Adj. *curved,* cambered etc. vb.; bent; bowed, stooping; bowlike, curvilinear; rounded, curvaceous, curvy, bosomy, busty, wavy, billowy 251 *undulatory*; aquiline, hook-nosed 247 *angular*; beaked, beaklike; bent back, retroussé, turned-

up; circumflex; ogival, vaulted 253 *arched*; bow-legged, bandy-legged 246 *deformed*; hooked, semicircular 250 *round*; crescent, lunate, lunar; heart-shaped, bell-s., pear-s., hour-glass.

Vb. *be curved,* - bent etc. adj.; curve, swerve, bend, loop, wind, arch, sweep, sag, give 217 *hang*; bend, crook; turn, round; bend in, bend back, bend over, bend down, bow, incline 311 *stoop*; turn over 261 *fold*; turn away 282 *deflect*; arch; coil 251 *twine*; loop, curl, kink, wave, perm 251 *crinkle*; loop the loop.

249 Straightness – N. *straightness,* directness; perpendicularity 215 *verticality*; inflexibility, intransigence, rigidity 326 *hardness*; chord, radius, tangent 203 *line*; straight line, beeline; Roman road; straight stretch; short cut 200 *short distance*.

Adj. *straight,* direct, even, right, true; in a line, linear; straight-lined, rectilinear, rectilineal; perpendicular 215 *vertical*; stiff, inflexible 326 *rigid*; straightened, dead straight, undeviating, unswerving, undeflected, on the beam, straight as an arrow; straight as a die 929 *honourable*; not bent, heterosexual 83 *typical*.

Vb. *straighten,* align; iron out 216 *flatten*; unbend (a bow); uncross (legs), unfold (arms); uncurl 258 *smooth*; uncoil, unroll, unfurl, unfold 316 *evolve*.

250 Circularity: simple circularity – N. *circularity,* roundness 252 *rotundity*.

circle, full c., circumference 233 *outline*; equator, orb; areola; plate, saucer; round, disc, disk, discus; coin, button, sequin; washer, hoop, ring, bracelet, quoit; eye, iris; eyelet, loophole, keyhole 263 *orifice*; circuit, circus, roundabout; zodiac; fairy ring; smoke ring.

loop, figure of eight 251 *convolution*; bow; ringlet, curl, kink 259 *hair*; bracelet, armlet, torque 844 *finery*; crown, coronet 743 *regalia*; halo; wreath, garland 228 *headgear*; collar, neckband, necklace, choker 228 *neckwear*; band,

cordon, sash, girdle, cummerbund 228 *belt*; lasso.

wheel, pulley, castor 315 *rotator*; hub, tyre; spare t., radial t., roller 252 *rotundity*.

arc, semicircle; half-moon, crescent, rainbow 248 *curve*; sector, quadrant, sextant; ellipse, oval.

orbit, cycle; circuit; circulation 314 *circuition*.

Adj. *round*, rounded, circular, cyclic, discoid; orbicular, ringlike, annular; semicircular, hemicyclic; oval; elliptic, ovoid, egg-shaped, crescent-s., pear-s. 248 *curved*; cycloidal, spherical 252 *rotund*.

251 Convolution: complex circularity – N. *convolution*, involution, circumvolution; intricacy; sinuosity, sinuousness; tortuosity, tortuousness, reticulation 222 *network*; twist 208 *fibre*; ripple 350 *wave*; kink, wrinkle, corrugation 261 *fold*; indentation, scallop 260 *notch*; waviness, undulation, ogee 248 *curve*.

coil, roll, twist; turban 228 *headgear*; spiral, helix; screw, worm, corkscrew; spring, coiled s.; intrauterine device 172 *contraception*; whorl, snailshell, whirlpool 350 *eddy*, 315 *vortex*; tendril 366 *plant*; scalloped edge 234 *edging*; kink, curl; ringlet, lovelock 259 *hair*; scroll, flourish, twirl, curlicue, squiggle 844 *ornamentation*.

meandering, winding, twists and turns 282 *deviation*; labyrinth, maze 61 *complexity*; switchback, zigzag 220 *obliquity*.

serpent, snake, eel, worm 365 *reptile*; wriggler.

Adj. *convoluted*, twisted, contorted 246 *distorted*; cranky; winding, looping, twining, sinuous, tortuous, indented, ragged; crumpled, buckled.

snaky, serpentine, eel-like, wormlike, vermiform, undulating, curvy, sinuous, squirming, wriggling, S-shaped.

undulatory, undulating, rolling, heaving; up-and-down, switchback; wavy, curly, frizzy, kinky, crinkly; crimped, curled, permed; scolloped, wrinkled, corrugated, indented.

coiled, spiral, helical, cochlear; convolute, involute, turbinate, whorled, coiling, spiralling.

intricate, involved, complicated, knotted 61 *complex*.

Vb. *twine*, twist, twirl, roll, coil, spiral 315 *rotate*; entwine; be convoluted, - twisted etc. adj.; turn and twist, bend 248 *be curved*.

crinkle, crimp, frizz, perm, curl; wave, undulate, ripple, wrinkle, corrugate 261 *fold*; indent 260 *notch*; crumple 246 *distort*.

meander, loop, snake, twist and turn, zigzag, corkscrew. See *twine*.

wriggle, writhe, squirm, shimmy, shake; worm.

252 Rotundity – N. *rotundity*, roundness 250 *circularity*; sphericality, globularity, cylindricality.

sphere, globe, spheroid, ellipsoid, globoid, bladder; balloon 276 *airship*; soap bubble 355 *bubble*; ball, football, pelota, billiard ball, marble; crystal ball; cannonball, bullet, shot, pellet; bead, pearl, pill, pea, boll, globule; drop, droplet, dewdrop, blot; vesicle, bulb, onion, knob, pommel 253 *swelling*; boulder; round head.

cylinder, roll; roller, rolling pin; round, rung; round tower, martello t., column; trunk, stalk, stem; pipe, drainpipe 263 *tube*; funnel, chimneypot; hat b., pillbox; drum, barrel, cask.

cone, conoid; penumbra; cornet, horn 194 *cup*; top, spinning t.; pear shape.

Adj. *rotund*, 250 *round*; spherical, globular, global; round-headed, bullet-headed, beadlike, hemispherical; spheroidal, ovoid, egg-shaped; pot-bellied 195 *fleshy*.

253 Convexity – N. *convexity*, convexness; arching 248 *curvature*; sphericality 252 *rotundity*; bulginess, lumpiness, humpiness, bulge, bump, lump; projection, protrusion, protuberance 254 *prominence*; tumescence, swelling 197 *dilation*; pot-belliedness 195 *bulk*; pimpliness, wartiness.

swelling, bump, lump, bulge, growth, excrescence, gall, knot, node, nodule; knuckle; oedema, emphysema; sarcoma, tumour, neoplasm, carcinoma 651 *cancer*; goitre; Adam's ápple; bunion, corn, wart, verruca; cyst, boil, carbuncle, stye, pimple, blister, vesicle; polyp, adenoids, haemorrhoids, piles; proud flesh, weal, welt; cauliflower ear; drop 252 *sphere*; air bubble 355 *bubble*; knob; bulb, button, bud; belly, potbelly, paunch 195 *bulk*; billow, swell 350 *wave.*

bosom, bust, breasts; boobs, bristols, knockers, tits; mamma, mamilla, papilla, nipple, pap, dug, teat, udder; thorax, chest; breastplate; breast-feeding; breastcancer, mammogram.

dome, cupola, vault 226 *roof*; beehive; brow, forehead 237 *face*; skull 213 *head*; hemisphere, mound; hillock; molehill, anthill, mushroom, umbrella.

earthwork, tumulus; barrow, hill fort 713 *defences*; embankment.

camber, 248 *curve*; arch, bow, rainbow; hump, humpback 246 *deformity.*

Adj. *convex,* protruding 254 *projecting*; hemispheric, domelike 252 *rotund*; lentiform, lenticular; humpy, lumpy, bumpy; curvaceous, bosomy, busty, billowy 248 *curved*; bulging, bouffant; swelling, swollen; bloated, potbellied, barrel-chested 195 *fleshy*; turgid, tumid, tumescent, tumorous, tuberous; nubbly 259 *rough*; warty, pimply, spotty, acned; blistery, vesicular.

arched, cambered, bowed 248 *curved*; rounded.

254 Prominence – N. *prominence,* eminence 209 *high land*; conspicuousness 443 *visibility.*

projection, salient; outstretched arm, forefinger, index f.; bowsprit; tongue of land, point, mull, promontory, foreland, headland, ness 344 *land*; peninsula 349 *island*; spur, foothill; jetty, breakwater, pier 662 *shelter*; outwork 713 *fortification*; buttress 218 *prop*; shelf, sill, ledge, balcony; eaves 226 *roof*; overhang 220 *obliquity*; lip 234 *edge*; nozzle, spout;

tongue; tenon 45 *joint*; stump, outcrop; landmark 209 *high structure.*

protuberance, bump 253 *swelling*; nose, snout, schnozz, schnozzle, conk, hooter; neb, pecker, bill, beak, rostrum; muzzle, proboscis, trunk; antenna 378 *feeler*; chin, jaw, forehead, brow, beetle brow 237 *face*; figurehead; horn, antler 256 *sharp point.*

Adj. *projecting,* jutting, prominent, salient, bold; protuberant, protruding, bulging, popping etc. vb.; bug-eyed, goggle-e., pop-e., with eyes out on stalks; toothy; beetle-browed; raised, embossed, in relief, ridged, nobbly 259 *rough.*

Vb. *jut,* project, protrude, pout, pop, pop out; stand out, stick o., stick out like a sore thumb, hang o. 443 *be visible*; prick up, cock up 259 *roughen*; shoot up, swell up 197 *expand*; overhang 217 *hang.*

255 Concavity – N. *concavity,* concaveness 248 *curvature*; hollowness 190 *emptiness*; depression, dint, dimple, dent; impression, stamp, imprint, footprint 548 *trace*; intaglio 555 *engraving*; furrowing 262 *furrow*; indentation 260 *notch*; gap, lacuna 201 *interval.*

cavity, hollow, niche, nook, cranny 194 *compartment*; hole, den, burrow, warren; chasm, abyss 211 *depth*; cave, cavern; grotto, alcove 194 *arbour*; bowl, cup, saucer, basin, trough 194 *vessel*; sump 649 *sink*; cell, follicle, pore 263 *orifice*; dimple, pockmark; saltcellar, armpit; honeycomb, sponge 263 *porosity*; funnel, tunnel 263 *tube*; groove, socket 262 *furrow*; sinus; bay, bight, cove, creek, inlet 345 *gulf*; channel, ditch, moat, canal 351 *conduit*; shaft, dip, depression, pothole, crater, pit.

valley, vale, dell, dingle, corrie, strath; glen, dip, depression, ravine, gorge, canyon, gully 201 *gap.*

excavation, dugout, grave, gravepit 364 *tomb*; opencast mining; shaft, borehole, well, mine, coal m., shale m., diamond m., pit, coal p., colliery, quarry

632 *store*; trench, burrow, warren; underground railway, tube 263 *tunnel*; archaelogical excavation, dig; cutting.

Adj. *concave,* hollow, cavernous; vaulted, arched 248 *curved*; hollowed out, dug o.; caved in; depressed, sunk, sunken; spoonlike, cup-shaped; funnel-shaped; bell-shaped; cellular, dented, dimpled, pockmarked; full of holes, pincushion-like, honeycombed; spongy, porous.

Vb. *make concave,* depress, press in, stamp, impress; buckle, dent, dint, stave in; crush, push in, beat in; excavate, hollow, dig, canalize 262 *groove*; mine, undermine, burrow, tunnel, bore; perforate 263 *pierce*; scoop out, hollow o., dig o. 300 *eject*; pockmark; indent 260 *notch*.

256 Sharpness – N. *sharpness,* acuity, acuteness, pointedness, sting; serration 260 *notch*; thorniness, prickliness; acridity 388 *pungency*.

sharp point, sting, thorn, prick, point, cusp 213 *vertex*; nail, tack, drawing pin, staple 47 *fastening*; nib, tag, pin, needle, knitting-needle, stylus, bodkin, skewer, spit; awl, gimlet, drill, auger 263 *perforator*; arrow, shaft, bolt, arrowhead; barb, swordpoint, rapier, lance, pike 723 *spear*; gaff, harpoon; dagger, dirk, stiletto 723 *side arms*; spike, barbed wire 713 *defences*; spur; goad 612 *incentive*; fork, prong, tine, pick, horn, antler; claw, talon, nails 778 *pincers*; spire, steeple; peak 213 *summit*.

prickle, thorn, brier, bramble, thistle, nettle, cactus; bristle 259 *hair*; beard; spine, needle, quill.

tooth, tusk, fang; milktooth; canine-tooth, eyetooth, incisor, grinder, molar, wisdom tooth; dentition; front tooth, back t., set of teeth, denture, false teeth, gold t., plate, bridge; comb, saw; cog, ratchet, sprocket.

sharp edge, cutting e.; jagged edge, broken glass; cutlery, steel, razor; blade,

razor blade; ploughshare 370 *farm tool*; spade, mattock, trowel, shovel; scythe, sickle, hook, billhook; cutter, lawn mower; scissors, shears, clippers, secateurs, pruners, scalpel; chisel, plane, scraper 258 *smoother*; knife, bread-k., kitchen-k., cook's k., carving k., fish k., penknife, pocketknife, flick-knife, sheath knife, jack k., hunting k., bowie k.; machete; chopper, cleaver, wedge; hatchet, axe, adze; battleaxe 723 *axe*; sword, broadsword, cutlass, scimitar 723 *side arms*.

Adj. *sharp,* stinging, keen, acute; edged, cutting; swordlike; pointed; sharp-pointed, barbed; spiky, spiny, spinose, thorny, thistly; needlelike, needlesharp, acicular; prickly, bristly; spearlike, bayonet-like; craggy, jagged 259 *rough*; comblike, serrated; sharp-edged, knife-e., razor-e.; sharp as a razor, sharp as a needle; sharpened, whetted etc. vb.; razor-sharp.

toothed, toothy; tusky, fanged, dental, denticulate, dentiform; cogged, serrated, saw-edged.

Vb. *be sharp,* - stinging etc. adj.; have a point, prick, sting; bristle with; have an edge, bite, pierce 46 *cut*; taper, come to a point, end in a point 293 *converge*.

sharpen, edge, put an edge on, whet, hone, grind, file, strop; barb, point.

257 Bluntness – N. *bluntness,* obtuseness, flatness, bluffness; curves 258 *smoothness*; rustiness, dullness; toothlessness, toothless tiger, lack of bite; blunt instrument, foil; blunt edge, blade, flat.

Vb. *blunt,* make blunt; take off the point, bate (a foil); obtund, dull, rust; draw the teeth 161 *disable*; be blunt.

258 Smoothness – N. *smoothness,* evenness etc. adj.; silkiness; silk, satin, velvet, velour; fleeciness, down, swansdown 327 *softness*; sleekness; baby's bottom; millpond; marble, glass, ice; dance floor,

ice rink; flatness, levelness, lawn, bowling green, billiard table 216 *horizontality*; tarmac 226 *paving*; polish, wax, varnish, gloss, glaze, shine, finish; slipperiness, slipway, slide, chute; lubricity, oiliness, greasiness 334 *lubrication*; calm, dead c. 266 *quiescence*.

smoother, roller, garden r., road r., steamroller; bulldozer; rolling pin 216 *flattener*; iron, electric i., smoothing-i., flatiron; mangle, wringer; press, trouser p.; plane 256 *sharp edge*; rake, harrow; card, comb, brush; sandpaper, glasspaper, emery paper, emery board; file, nail f.; polish, French p., varnish, enamel 226 *facing*; lubricator, grease, oil, grease gun, oilcan 334 *lubricant*.

Adj. *smooth,* streamlined; slippery; lubricious, oily, greasy, buttery, soapy; greased, oiled 334 *lubricated*; polished, shiny, gleaming, varnished, waxed, enamelled, lacquered, glazed; soft, suave, bland, soothing; silky, satiny, velvety; peachlike, downy, woolly; marble, glassy; bald 229 *hairless*; sleek, slick, brushed; combed, carded; rolled, even, level, flush 216 *flat*; glassy, calm, c. as a millpond 266 *still*; blunt; smoothskinned; smooth-haired; smooth as glass, smooth as a baby's bottom, smooth as velvet, satin-smooth; slippery as an eel.

Vb. *smooth,* streamline; oil, grease 334 *lubricate*; smoothen, plane, even, level; rake, comb; file, rub down 333 *rub*; roll, calender, press, iron 216 *flatten*; mow, shave, cut 204 *shorten*; smooth over, slick down, plaster d.; iron out; shine, burnish 417 *make bright*; buff, polish, glaze, wax, varnish 226 *coat*.

259 Roughness – **N.** *roughness,* asperity, harshness; broken ground; rough water, choppiness 350 *wave*; turbulence 352 *wind*; brokenness, jaggedness, broken glass, barbed wire 256 *sharp edge*; serration, saw edge, scalloped e. 260 *notch*; ruggedness, cragginess; sierra 209 *high land*; rough going, dirt road, dirt track; unevenness 17 *nonuniformity*; kink, corrugation, ripple, corrugated iron 261

fold; rut 262 *furrow*; coarseness, coarse grain 253 *convexity*; washboard, grater, file, sandpaper, glasspaper, emery paper, emery board; sackcloth, tweed, homespun 222 *textile*; gooseflesh, goose pimples; chap, hack, crack; shagginess; hairiness; stubble, five o'clock shadow, burr, bristle, scrubbing brush, nailbrush.

hair 208 filament; head of h., shock of h., matted h., thatch, fuzz, wool; crop, mop, mane, fleece, shag; bristle, stubble, five o'clock shadow; locks, flowing l.; crowning glory, tresses, curls, ringlet; kiss curl; strand, plait, braid; pigtail, ponytail, bunches, rat's tails; topknot, forelock, lovelock, dread locks; fringe, bangs, cowlick, quiff, widow's peak; roll, French pleat, bun, chignon 843 *hairdressing*; false hair, hairpiece, hair extension, switch, wig, toupee 228 *headgear*; wisp; beard, full b., beaver, goatee, imperial, Van Dyke, Abe Lincoln; whiskers, sideboards, sideburns, mutton-chops; moustache, moustachio, toothbrush, handlebars; facial hair; eyebrows, eyelashes; woolliness, fleeciness, downiness, fluffiness; down, pubic hair, wool, fur 226 *skin*; tuft, flock; mohair, cashmere, Angora 208 *fibre*; fluff, fuzz; horsehair 227 *lining*.

plumage, feathering; quill, feathers; neck feathers, hackle; ruff, frill, plume, crest; peacock's feathers, ostrich f. 844 *finery*.

Adj. *rough,* irregular, uneven; rippling, choppy, storm-tossed; stony, rocky, rutted, pitted, potholed, bumpy; roughcast; lumpy, stony, nodular, studded, roughened, frosted; nubbly, slubbed, bouclé; crinkled 251 *undulatory*; knotted, gnarled, coarse-grained, coarse; cracked, hacked, chapped; lined, wrinkled, corrugated, ridged; rough-edged; craggy, jagged; scabby, pockmarked, acned, warty, scaly, blistered; ruffled, unkempt, unpolished; unsifted.

hairy, woolly, fleecy, furry; hirsute, shaggy, matted; bristly 256 *sharp*; wispy, straggly, fringed, bearded, moustached; unshaven, unshorn; curly, frizzy, fuzzy, permed, woolly.

Vb. *be rough,* - hairy etc. adj.; bristle 254 *jut*; creep (of flesh); scratch; jolt, bump, jerk 278 *move slowly.*

roughen, roughcast, rough-hew; serrate, indent 260 *notch*; stud, boss; corrugate, wrinkle, ripple, kink 251 *crinkle*; disorder, ruffle, tousle, tangle 63 *derange*; rumple, crumple, crease 261 *fold*; rub up the wrong way, set on edge; chap, crack, hack.

260 Notch – N. *notch,* serration, ragged edge 256 *sharpness*; indentation, deckle edge; crenellation 713 *fortification*; nick, snip, cut, gash, crenation 201 *gap*; indent, dent, dint, dimple 255 *concavity*; scallop, dogtooth 844 *pattern*; sprocket, cog, ratchet, cogwheel; saw, hacksaw, chain saw, circular saw 256 *tooth*; battlement.

Vb. *notch,* serrate, tooth, cog; nick, score, scratch, scarify, bite, slice 46 *cut*; crenellate, indent, scallop, jag, pink, slash; dent, knurl 259 *roughen*; pinch, snip, crimp 261 *fold.*

261 Fold – N. *fold,* flexure, doubling; facing, revers, hem; lapel, cuff, turnup; plait, braid, ply, pleat, box p., accordion p.; knife-edge p.; tuck, gather, pucker, ruche, ruffle; flounce, frill; wrinkle, ruck, frown, lines, wrinkles, age zones, crow's feet 131 *age*; joint.

Vb. *fold,* double, turn over, bend over, roll; corrugate, furrow, wrinkle 262 *groove*; pucker; ruffle, gather, frill, ruck, shirr, smock; hem, cuff; turn up; enfold, wrap, swathe 235 *enclose*; fold up, furl.

262 Furrow – N. *furrow,* groove, slot, slit, rabbet, mortise; crack, split, chink, cranny 201 *gap*; trough, hollow 255 *cavity*; flute, fluting, goffering; chamfer, bezel, incision, gash, slash, scratch, score 46 *scission*; streak, striation 437 *stripe*; rut 548 *trace*; gutter, ditch, dike, trench, dugout, moat, channel 351 *conduit*; ravine 255 *valley*; wrinkle, corrugation; corduroy, corrugated iron, washboard, ploughed field; ripple.

Vb. *groove,* slot, flute, chamfer; gash, scratch, score, incise 46 *cut*; claw, tear 655 *wound*; striate, streak 437 *variegate*; carve, bite in, etch 555 *engrave*; furrow, plough, channel, rut, wrinkle, line; corrugate, goffer 261 *fold.*

263 Opening – N. *opening,* throwing open, openness, glasnost; uncorking, uncapping 229 *uncovering*; yawn, yawning, splitting; gaping; hiatus, lacuna, space, interval 201 *gap*; aperture, split, crack, leak 46 *disunion*; hole, potato; hollow 255 *cavity*; placket.

porosity, porousness, sponge; sieve, sifter, riddle, screen 62 *sorting*; strainer, tea s., colander; grater; honeycomb, pincushion.

orifice, aperture, slot; oral cavity, mouth, gob, trap, kisser, mush, moosh, jaws, muzzle; throat, gullet 194 *stomach*; sucker; vagina, anus; flue pipe 353 *air pipe*; nozzle, spout, vent, vent-hole 298 *outlet*; blowhole, air-hole; nostril, rivermouth, pore; hole, crater, pothole 255 *cavity*; manhole, armhole, keyhole, buttonhole, punch hole, pin h.; pigeonhole 194 *compartment*; eye, eye of a needle, eyelet; ring 250 *loop*.

window, fenestration; shop window, plate-glass w., glass front; embrasure 713 *fortification*; lattice, grille; casement window, leaded w., sash w., bay w., oriel w., dormer w., French w., picture w.; rose window, lancet w. 990 *church interior*; light, fanlight, skylight, sunshine roof; companion, cabin window, port, porthole; peephole, keyhole; car window, windscreen, windshield; window frame, casement, sash, mullion, transom; window pane 422 *transparency*.

doorway, archway; doorstep, threshold 68 *entrance*; approach, drive, driveway, entry 297 *way in*; exit, way out; passage, corridor, gangway, drawbridge 624 *access*; gate, gateway; portal, porch; door, front d., Dutch d.; swing doors, revolving d., double d.; church d., lychgate; back door, tradesmen's d., postern 238 *rear*; small door, wicket; cat-flap;

hatch, hatchway; trapdoor, companion-way; stairwell; door jamb, gatepost, lintel; concierge 264 *doorkeeper*, entryphone.

open space 183 *space*; yard, court 185 *place*; opening, clearing, glade; panorama, vista 438 *view*; landscape, open country 348 *plain*.

tunnel, boring; subway, underpass, underground railway, underground, tube, metro; Channel Tunnel, chunnel; mine, shaft, pit, gallery, adit 255 *excavation*; cave 255 *cavity*; bolthole, rabbit hole, fox h., mouse h. 192 *dwelling*; funnel 252 *cone*; sewer 351 *drain*; qanat.

tube, pipe, duct 351 *conduit*; tubule, pipette, cannula; catheter, tubing, piping, pipeline, hose; artery, vein, capillary; colon, gut 224 *insides*; funnel, fistula.

opener, key, master k., skeleton k.; doorknob, handle; corkscrew, tin opener, can o., bottle o.; aperient, purgative; password, open sesame; passport.

perforator, piercer, borer, corer; gimlet, corkscrew; auger, drill, pneumatic d.; bit, brace and b.; trepan; probe, lancet, lance, bodkin, needle, hypodermic n.; awl, bradawl 256 *sharp point*; pin, nail 47 *fastening*; skewer, spit, broach, stiletto 723 *weapon*; punch, card p., stapler; dibble; pickaxe, pick, ice p.

Adj. *open*, exposed to view, on view 522 *manifest*; uncapped, uncorked, ajar; unbolted, unlocked, unbarred, unobstructed 289 *accessible*; wide-open, gaping; yawning, open-mouthed, gaping; opening, aperient; in bloom, out.

porous, permeable, spongy, percolating, leachy, leaky, leaking.

Vb. *open*, declare open, give the open sesame, give a passport to, unfold, unwrap, unpack, unpackage, undo, unlock, unlatch, unbolt, open the door, fling wide the gates 299 *admit*; uncover, bare; unplug, unstop, uncap, uncork; lay open, throw o. 522 *show*; force open 176 *force*; cut open, tear o., crack o.; fly open, split, gape, yawn; burst, explode; open out, fan o., deploy 75 *be dispersed*; unclench, bloom, be out.

pierce, transfix, impale; gore, run through, stick, pink, lance, bayonet, spear 655 *wound*; spike, skewer, spit; prick, puncture, tattoo; probe, stab, poke; inject; perforate, hole, riddle, pepper, honeycomb; knock holes in, punch, punch full of holes; bore, drill, trepan; burrow, tunnel, mine 255 *make concave*; cut through, penetrate 297 *enter*.

Adv. *openly*, frankly, unguardedly, out in the open.

264 Closure – N. *closure*, closing, closing down, shutting etc. vb.; occlusion, stoppage; contraction, strangulation 198 *compression*; sealing off, blockade 232 *circumscription*; 235 *enclosure*; embolism, obstruction, infarction, constipation, strangury; dead end, cul-de-sac, impasse, blank wall, road block 702 *obstacle*; caecum.

stopper, cork, plug, bung, peg; ramrod, piston; valve; wedge, tampon; wadding, padding, stuffing, stopping 227 *lining*; gag, muzzle 748 *fetter*; shutter 421 *screen*; tourniquet; damper, choke; tap, faucet, stopcock, top, lid, cap, cover, seal 226 *covering*; lock, Yale (tdmk) lock, mortise l., key, bolt, latch, bar 47 *fastening*.

doorkeeper, doorman, gatekeeper, porter, janitor, commissionaire, concierge; sentry, sentinel, night watchman 660 *protector*; warden, guard, guard dog, vigilante, 749 *keeper*; jailer, prison warder, turnkey, Cerberus 749 *gaoler*.

Adj. *closed*, unopened, shut etc. vb.; shuttered, bolted, barred, locked; stoppered, corked, unpierced, nonporous, impervious, impermeable 324 *dense*; impenetrable, impassable 470 *impracticable*; dead-end; clogged up, stuffed up, bunged up; strangulated.

Vb. *close*, shut, occlude, seal; clinch, fix, bind, make tight 45 *tighten*; put the lid on, cap 226 *cover*; batten down the hatches; slam, bang (a door); lock, fasten, plug, bung up, cork, stopper, button, zip up, do up 45 *join*; knit, furrow, clench (fist); block, dam, staunch, choke, throttle, strangle, smother, asphyxiate 702

obstruct; blockade 712 *besiege*; enclose, surround, shut in, seal off 232 *circumscribe*; trap, bolt, latch, bar, lock in 747 *imprison*; shut down, clamp d., batten d., ram d., tamp d., put up the shutters; close down, go out of business, flop, go bust, fail.

Section four: Motion

265 Motion: successive change of place –
N. *motion*, movement, move, march; speed, acceleration, pace, tempo; locomotion, motility, mobility, movableness; kinetic energy, motive power; forward motion, advance, progress, headway 285 *progression*; backward motion 286 *regression*, 290 *recession*; motion towards 289 *approach*, 293 *convergence*; motion away, shift 294 *divergence*, 282 *deviation*; motion into 297 *ingress*; motion out of 298 *egress*; upward motion, rising 308 *ascent*; downward motion, sinking, plummeting 309 *descent*, 313 *plunge*; motion round, circumnavigation 314 *circuition*; axial motion 315 *rotation*, 316 *evolution*; to and fro movement, fluctuation 317 *oscillation*; irregular motion 318 *agitation*; stir, bustle, unrest, restlessness 678 *activity*; rapid motion 277 *velocity*; slow motion 278 *slowness*; regular motion 16 *uniformity*, 71 *continuity*; recurring movement, cycle, rhythm 141 *periodicity*; motion in front 283 *preceding*; motion after 284 *following*, 619 *pursuit*; conduction, conductivity 272 *transference*; current, flow, flux, drift 350 *stream*; course, career, run; traffic, flow of traffic; transit 305 *passage*; transportation 272 *transport*; running, jogging, walking, foot-slogging, marathoning 267 *pedestrianism*; riding 267 *equitation*; travel 267 *land travel*, 269 *water travel*, 271 *air travel*; dancing, tangoing, gliding, sliding, skating, rolling, skipping; manoeuvre, manoeuvring, footwork; exercise, aerobics, gymnastics 162 *athletics*; gesticulation 547 *gesture*; motion picture, film 445 *cinema*; laws of motion, kinetics, dynamics.

gait, walk, carriage 688 *conduct*; pace, step, stride; run, lope, jog; hop, skip, jump 312 *leap*; skid, slide, slip; waddle, shuffle; undulate, swagger, stalk, strut, goosestep 875 *formality*; march; trot, amble, canter, gallop 267 *equitation*.

Adj. *moving*, rolling etc. vb.; in motion, under way; motive, motor; motile, movable, mobile; progressive, regressive; locomotive, automotive; transitional, shifting; mercurial 152 *changeful*; restless 678 *active*; nomadic; drifting, erratic, meandering, runaway; kinetic; cinematographic.

Vb. *be in motion*, move, go, hie, gang, wend, trail; budge, stir; flutter, wave, flap 217 *hang*; march, tramp 267 *walk*; tread; trip, dance 312 *leap*; shuffle, waddle 278 *move slowly*; toddle, patter; run, jog 277 *move fast*; run on wheels, roll, taxi; stream, roll on, drift 350 *flow*; paddle 269 *row*; skitter, slide, slither, skate, ski, sledge, toboggan, glide; fly, frisk, flit, dart, hover; climb 308 *ascend*; sink, plunge, plummet 309 *descend*; coast, cruise, steam, chug, proceed 146 *go on*; make one's way, push one's w., elbow one's w., shoulder one's w. 285 *progress*; pass through, wade t., pass by 305 *pass*; make a move, shift, dodge, duck, shift about, jink, jouk, tack, manoeuvre 282 *deviate*; twist 251 *wriggle*; creep, crawl, worm one's way, go on all fours; hover about, hang a. 136 *wait*; move house, flit, relocate; change places 151 *interchange*; move over, make room 190 *go away*; travel, stray 267 *wander*.

move, put in m.; set going; put skates under; put a bomb under, galvanize, actuate, switch on, put into operation 173 *operate*; stir up, jerk 318 *agitate*; budge, shift, trundle, roll, wheel 188 *displace*; push, shove 279 *impel*; move on, drive, hustle 680 *hasten*; tug, pull 288 *draw*; fling, throw 287 *propel*; convey, transport 272 *transfer*; dispatch 272 *send*; mobilize 74 *bring together*; scatter 75 *disperse*; raise, uplift 310 *elevate*; throw down, drop 311 *let fall*; motion, gesture 547 *gesticulate*; transpose 151 *interchange*.

266 Quiescence – N. *quiescence,* motionlesness; subsidence 145 *cessation*; rest, stillness; deadness; stagnation, 679 *inactivity*; pause, truce, standstill 145 *lull*; stoppage, halt; deadlock; full stop, dead s. 145 *stop*; embargo, freeze 757 *prohibition*; immobility, rigidity, stiffness 326 *hardness*; equilibrium 153 *stability*; trance.

quietude, quiet, quietness, stillness, hush 399 *silence*; tranquillity, peacefulness 717 *peace*; rest 683 *repose*; eternal rest 361 *death*; sleepiness, slumber 679 *sleep*; calm, millpond 258 *smoothness*; not a breath of air; dead quiet, not a mouse stirring; composure, cool 823 *inexcitability*; passivity, quietism; tranquillizer, sedation 177 *moderator*.

Adj. *quiescent,* quiet, still; asleep 679 *sleepy*; resting, at rest, becalmed; at anchor, anchored, moored, docked; at a standstill, stopped, idle 679 *inactive*; unemployed, disemployed, out of commission, inoperative; dormant, stagnant, vegetating, static, stationary 175 *inert*; sedentary; on one's back 216 *supine*; disabled, housebound, confined to bed 747 *restrained*; settled; unmoved 860 *indifferent*.

tranquil, undisturbed, sequestered 883 *secluded*; peaceful, restful; unhurried, easy-going 681 *leisurely*; uneventful 16 *uniform*; calm, like a millpond, airless; glassy 258 *smooth*; sunny, halcyon 730 *palmy*; at ease, comfortable, relaxed 683 *reposeful*; tranquillized, sedated, under sedation; cool, unruffled, serene 823 *inexcitable*.

still, unmoving, unstirring, not fizzy, flat 387 *tasteless*; immobile, motionless, expressionless, deadpan, poker-faced 820 *impassive*; steady, unblinking 153 *unchangeable*; rooted to the ground *or* spot 153 *fixed*; transfixed, spellbound; immovable, becalmed, stuck; stiff, frozen 326 *rigid*; paralysed 375 *insensible*; quiet, so quiet you could hear a pin drop, hushed, soundless 399 *silent*; stock-still, still as a statue, still as death; quiet as a mouse.

Vb. *be quiescent,* - still etc.adj.; subside, die down 37 *decrease*; pipe down 399 *be silent*; stand still, lie s., keep quiet; stagnate, vegetate; stand, mark time 136 *wait*; stay put, sit tight, remain in situ, remain 144 *stay*; ride at anchor; tarry 145 *pause*; rest, sit down, take a breather, rest on one's laurels, rest on one's oars 683 *repose*; retire, go to bed, doss down, turn in 679 *sleep*; settle down 187 *place oneself*; stick fast; jam; stand firm; not move a muscle, not stir a step; be at a standstill 145 *cease*.

come to rest, stop, stop short, stop in one's tracks, stop dead in one's tracks, freeze 145 *halt*; pull up, draw up; anchor, alight 295 *land*; relax, cool it, rest, pause 683 *repose*.

bring to rest, quiet, quieten, quell, hush 399 *silence*; lull, soothe, calm down, tranquillize, sedate 177 *assuage*; lull to sleep, cradle, rock; let alone, let well alone, let sleeping dogs lie 620 *avoid*; bring to a standstill, bring to, heave to; brake, put the brake on 278 *retard*; stay, immobilize 679 *make inactive*.

Int. stop! stay! halt! whoa! hold hard! hold on! hold it! don't move! freeze!

267 Land travel – N. *land travel,* travel, travelling; globe-trotting, tourism; walking, hiking, riding, driving, motoring, cycling, biking; journey, voyage, odyssey; course, passage; pilgrimage, quest, expedition, safari, trek, field trip; reconnaissance, exploration, orienteering, youth hostelling, backpacking; visit, trip, business t., tour, grand t., coach t.; package t.; circuit, turn, round, patrol, commuting; round trip, day t. 314 *circuition*; jaunt, hop, spin; ride, bike r., joy r., drive, lift; excursion, outing, airing; ramble, constitutional, promenade. See *pedestrianism.*

pedestrianism, walking, going on foot, footing it, Shanks's pony; foot-slogging, striding, tramping, marching, backpacking; perambulation; walkabout 314 *circuition*; walk, promenade, constitutional; stroll, saunter, amble, ramble;

hike, tramp, march, walking tour; run, cross-country run, jog, trot, jog t., lope 265 *gait*; foot race, racewalking, marathon 716 *racing*; sleepwalking, somnambulism.

marching, marching and countermarching; march, forced m., route m., quick march, slow m.; march past, parade, cavalcade, procession 875 *formality.*

equitation, equestrianism, horsemanship *or* horsewomanship, manège, dressage 694 *skill*; show jumping, eventing, gymkhana, steeplechasing, point-to-point racing 716 *contest*; horse racing; riding, bareback r. 162 *athletics.*

conveyance, lift, elevator, escalator, travelator 274 *conveyor*; feet, own two f. 214 *foot*; legs, Shanks's pony; horseback, mount 273 *horse*; bicycle, moped, scooter, motor cycle, car, bus, train, coach, taxi, ambulance 274 *vehicle*; traffic.

leg, limb, foreleg, hindleg; shank, shin, calf; thigh, ham, hamstrings; knee, kneecap 247 *angularity*; tibia, fibula, legs, pegs, pins 218 *prop*; stumps, stilts; stump, wooden leg, artificial l., prosthesis 150 *substitute*; bow legs, bandy l., knock-knees 845 *blemish*; thick legs, piano l., legs like tree stumps; long legs, spindle shanks.

itinerary, route 624 *way*; course 281 *direction*; route map, road m., plan, chart 551 *map*; guide, Baedeker, timetable, Bradshaw, A-Z 524 *guidebook*; milestone, fingerpost 547 *signpost.*

Vb. *travel,* journey, tour, see the world, go globetrotting, go on a world cruise, visit, explore 484 *discover*; get around, knock about, go places, sightsee, rubberneck; go on a pilgrimage; go on a trip, go on a journey; go on safari, trek, hump bluey; hike, backpack; be always on the move, live out of a suitcase; set out, take wing 296 *depart*; migrate, emigrate, immigrate, settle 187 *place oneself*; shuttle, commute; take oneself off, swan off, slope o.; go to, hie to, repair to, resort to, betake oneself to 295 *arrive*, 882 *visit*; go 265 *be in motion*; wend one's way, stir

one's stumps, bend one's steps, shape one's course, tread a path, follow the road; make one's way, pick one's way, thread one's w., elbow one's w., force a w., plough through; jog on, trudge on, shuffle on, pad on, plod on, tramp on, march on, chug on 146 *sustain*; course, race, post 277 *move fast*; proceed, advance 285 *progress*; coast, free-wheel, glide, slide, skate, ski, skim, roll along, bowl a., fly a.

traverse, cross, range, pass through, range t. 305 *pass*; go round, beat the bounds 314 *circle*; go the rounds, make one's rounds, patrol; scout, reconnoitre 438 *scan*; scour, sweep, sweep through.

wander, migrate; rove, roam, bum around; ramble, amble, stroll, saunter, mosey along, potter, dawdle, walk about, trail around; gad, traipse, gallivant, gad about, hover, flit about, dart a. 265 *be in motion*; prowl, skulk 523 *lurk*; straggle, trail 75 *be dispersed*; lose the way, get lost, wander away 282 *stray.*

walk, step, tread, pace, stride; stride out 277 *move fast*; strut, stalk, prance, mince 871 *be proud*; tread lightly, tiptoe, trip, skip, dance, curvet 312 *leap*; tread heavily, lumber, clump, stamp, tramp, goosestep; toddle, patter, pad; totter, stagger, lurch, reel, stumble 317 *oscillate*; limp, hobble, waddle, shuffle, shamble, dawdle 278 *move slowly*; paddle, wade; go on foot, go by Shanks's pony, foot it, hoof it, hike, footslog, wear out shoe leather; plod, stump, trudge, jog; go, go for a walk, perambulate, pace up and down; go for a run *or* a jog, take the air, take one's constitutional; march, troop; file, file past, defile, march in procession 65 *come after*; walk behind 284 *follow*; walk in front 283 *precede.*

ride, mount, hack; trot, amble, canter, gallop; prance, caper; cycle, bicycle, bike, motorcycle; freewheel, coast; drive, motor; go by bike, go by car, go by bus, bus it, go by coach, go by taxi, go by cab; go by road, go by tube, go by train; go by air 271 *fly*; take a lift, take a ride, cadge a lift, thumb a l., hitchhike.

Int. come along! move along there! move it! get along! get going! get out! git! go away! be off! buzz off! piss off (vulg)! hop it! skedaddle! scram!

268 Traveller – N. *traveller,* itinerant, wayfarer; explorer, adventurer, voyager 270 *mariner*; air traveller, spaceman *or*-woman, astronaut 271 *aeronaut*; pioneer, pathfinder, explorer 66 *precursor*; alpinist, mountaineer, cragsman 308 *climber*; pilgrim; walker, hiker, rambler, trekker; backpacker, camper, caravanner, youth hosteller; globe-trotter, tourist, rubberneck, sightseer 441 *spectator*; tripper, day-t., excursionist; sunseeker, holidaymaker, visitor; roundsman, hawker 794 *pedlar*; doorstepper, canvasser; travelling salesman, commercial traveller, rep 793 *seller*; messenger, errandboy 529 *courier*; daily traveller, commuter.

wanderer, migrant, bird of passage, visitant 365 *bird*; floating population, nomad, bedouin; gypsy, didicoi, Romany; rover, ranger, rambler, promenader, stroller; strolling player, wandering minstrel, touring company 594 *entertainer*; rolling stone, drifter, vagrant, vagabond, tramp, knight of the road, bag lady; swagman, sundowner, hobo, bum; loafer, beachcomber 679 *idler*; emigrant, émigré, refugee, deportee, exile 59 *foreigner*; runaway, fugitive, escapee 620 *avoider*; waif, stray, the homeless 801 *poor person*.

pedestrian, foot passenger, walker, tramper; jogger, sprinter, runner 716 *contender*; toddler; wader, paddler; skater, skier; skateboarder, roller-skater; hiker, hitch-h., foot-slogger; marcher 722 *infantry*; somnambulist, sleepwalker; prowler, loiterer; footpad 789 *robber*.

rider, horse-rider, camel-r., cameleer; elephant-rider, mahout; horseman, horsewoman, equestrian; postilion, postboy 529 *courier*; mounted police, Mounties; cavalier, knight, knight errant 722 *cavalry*; hunt, huntsman 619 *hunter*; jockey, steeplechaser, show jumper,

eventer 716 *contender*; trainer, breaker 369 *breeder*; roughrider, bareback r., broncobuster, cowboy, cowgirl, cowpuncher, gaucho, rodeo rider; cyclist, bicyclist, biker; circus rider, trick rider 162 *athlete*; motorcyclist, moped rider, scooterist;

driver, coachman; carter, waggoner, drayman; car driver, chauffeur, motorist, roadhog; joy rider; L-driver 538 *beginner*; taxi driver, cab d., cabby; bus driver, coach d.; lorry d., truck d., van d., trucker, routier, teamster; tractor d.; motorman, train driver, engine d.; pilot 271 *aeronaut.*

269 Water travel – N. *water travel,* seafaring, life on the ocean wave; navigation, voyaging, sailing, cruising; coasting, longshore sailing; boating, yachting, rowing (see *aquatics*); voyage, navigation, cruise, sail; course, run, passage, crossing, ferry c.; circumnavigation 314 *circuition*; sea trip, river t., canal t., breath of sea air 685 *refreshment*; way, headway, steerage way, sternway, seaway 265 *motion*; leeway, driftway 282 *deviation*; wake, track, wash, backwash 350 *eddy*; sea-path, sea lane, approaches 624 *route*; boat, sailing ship 275 *ship*; sailor 270 *mariner.*

navigation, piloting, steering, pilotage 689 *directorship*; astronavigation; plane sailing, plain s., spherical s., great-circle s., parallel s.; compass reading, dead reckoning 465 *measurement*; pilotship, seamanship 694 *skill.*

aquatics, boating, sailing, yachting, cruising; rowing, sculling, canoeing; yacht racing, speedboat r., ocean r. 716 *racing*; water skiing, surf riding, surfing, wind s., boardsailing, watersports 837 *sport*; natation, swimming, floating; stroke, breast s., side s., back s., crawl, back c., front c., butterfly, dogpaddle; diving, plunging 313 *plunge*; wading, paddling; swimsuit 228 *beachwear.*

sailing aid, navigational instrument, sextant, quadrant 247 *angular measure*; chronometer, ship's c. 117 *timekeeper*; log, line; lead, plummet 211 *depth*;

anchor 662 *safeguard*; compass, astrocompass, magnetic c., ship's c.; needle, magnetic n.; card, compass c. *or* rose; binnacle; gyrocompass 689 *directorship*; radar 484 *detector*; helm, wheel, tiller, rudder, steering oar; sea mark, buoy, lighthouse, pharos, lightship 547 *signpost*; chart, Admiralty c., portolano 551 *map*; nautical almanac, ephemeris 524 *guidebook*.

propeller, screw, twin screw, blade, rotor 287 *propellant*; paddle wheel, stern w., floatboard; oar, sweep, paddle, scull; pole, punt p., barge p.; fin, flipper, fish's tail 53 *limb*; sails 275 *sail.*

Vb. *go to sea,* join the navy; become a sailor, get one's sea legs; sail before the mast; go sailing, boat, yacht, cruise.

voyage, sail, go by sea, go by ship, go by boat, take the ferry, take the sea route; work one's passage; embark, go on board, put to sea, set sail,up anchor 296 *start out*; disembark, land 295 *arrive*; cruise; steam, ply, run, tramp, ferry; coast, hug the shore; roll, pitch, toss.

navigate, man a ship, work a s., crew; put to sea, set sail; launch, push off, boom off; unmoor, cast off, weigh anchor; get up steam; hoist sail, spread canvas; get under way, gather w., make w., carry sail 265 *be in motion*; drop the pilot; set a course, make for, head for 281 *steer for*; read the chart, go by the card 281 *orientate*; pilot, steer, hold the helm, captain 689 *direct*; stroke, cox, coxswain; trim the sails, square, square away; change course, veer, gybe, yaw 282 *deviate*; put about, wear ship 282 *turn round*; run before the wind, scud 277 *move fast*; put the helm up, fall to leeward, pay off; put the helm down, luff, bring into the wind; beat to windward, tack, weather; back and fill; round, double a point, circumnavigate 314 *circle*; be caught amidships 700 *be in difficulty*; careen, list, heel over 220 *be oblique*; turn turtle, capsize, overturn 221 *invert*; ride out the storm, weather the s., keep afloat 667 *escape*; run for port 662 *seek refuge*; lie to, lay to, heave to 266 *bring to rest*; take soundings, heave the

lead 465 *measure*; tide over 507 *await*; tow, haul, warp, kedge, clubhaul 288 *draw*; ground, run aground, wreck, be cast away 165 *destroy*; sight land, make a landfall, take on a pilot 289 *approach*; make port; cast anchor, drop a.; moor, tie up, dock, disembark 295 *land*; cross one's bows, take the wind out of one's sails, outmanoeuvre, gain the weather gauge 702 *obstruct*; foul 279 *collide*; back, go astern 286 *regress*; surface, break water 298 *emerge*; flood the tanks, dive 313 *plunge*; shoot, shoot a bridge, shoot the rapids 305 *pass.*

row, ply the oar, get the sweeps out; pull, stroke, scull; feather; catch a crab; ship oars; punt; paddle, canoe; boat; shoot the rapids.

swim, go swimming, do the breast stroke, do the crawl (**see** aquatics); aquaplane; strike out, breast the current, stem the stream; tread water; dive 313 *plunge*; bathe, dip, duck; wade, paddle.

270 Mariner – N. *mariner,* sailor, seaman, seafaring man; salt, old s., seadog, shellback; tar, Jack Tar, limey, matelot; bad sailor, fairweather s., landlubber 697 *bungler*; skipper, master mariner, master, ship m.; mate, boatswain, bosun; coxswain; able seaman, A.B. 696 *expert*; deckhand, swabbie; ship's steward, cabin boy 742 *servant*; shipmates, hearties; crew, complement, ship's c., men, watch 686 *personnel*; trawler, whaler, deep-sea fisherman; sea rover, privateer, buccaneer, sea king, Viking, pirate 789 *robber*; sea scout, sea cadet.

navigator, pilot, sailing master, helmsman, steersman, wheelman, man at the wheel, quartermaster; coxswain, cox 690 *leader*; leadsman, lookout man; foretopman, reefer; boatswain, bosun's mate; circumnavigator; compass 269 *sailing aid.*

nautical personnel, marine, submariner, naval cadet, bluejacket, rating 722 *naval man*; petty officer, midshipman, middy, lieutenant, sub-l., commander, captain, commodore, admiral 741 *naval officer*; Admiralty, Sea Lord;

Trinity House, lighthouse keeper, coastguard 660 *protector*; lifeboatman 703 *aider*; river police, naval patrol, harbour p., harbourmaster.

boatman, waterman, rowing man, wet bob; gigsman; galley slave; oar, oarsman, sculler, rower, punter; paddler, canoeist; yachtsman *or* -woman; gondolier, ferryman; wherryman, bargeman, bargee, lighterman; stevedore, docker, longshoreman; lock keeper.

271 Aeronautics – N. *aeronautics,* aeromechanics, aerodynamics, aerostatics; aerostation, ballooning; aerospace, astronautics; aeroballistics, rocketry 276 *rocket*; volitation, flight, vertical f., horizontal f.; subsonic f., supersonic f. 277 *velocity*; stratospheric flight, hypersonic f., space f.; aviation, flying, night f., blind f., instrument f.; shoran, teleran; gliding, powered g., hang-g.; parachuting, skydiving, free fall; flypast, formation flying, stunt f., aerobatics 875 *ostentation*; skywriting, vapour trail; planing, volplaning, looping the loop; spin, roll, side-slip; volplane, nose dive, pull-out; crash dive, crash, prang 309 *descent*; pancake, landing, belly l., crash l., forced l.; talkdown, touchdown 295 *arrival*; takeoff, vertical t. 296 *departure*.

air travel, air transport, airlift 272 *transport*; air service, airline; shuttle service, scheduled flight, charter f.; airlane, airway, air route 624 *route*; flight path, glide p., line of flight 281 *direction*; airspace 184 *territory*; takeoff, touchdown, landing; airbase; airstrip, runway, tarmac, airfield, aerodrome, airport, heliport, helipad; terminal, air t., check-in desk, luggage carousel, baggage reclaim, airside, landside 295 *goal*; hangar 192 *stable*; fear of flying, aerophobia; jetlag.

space travel, space flight, manned s.f., spacefaring 276 *spaceship*; lift-off, blast-off; orbit, flyby; docking, space walk; reentry, splashdown, soft landing; cosmodrome, spaceport, space station, space platform, space shuttle; launching pad, silo; spacesuit.

aeronaut, balloonist; glider, hang g., sky diver, parachutist; paratrooper 722 *soldier*; aviator, aviatrix, airwoman, airman, birdman; astronaut, cosmonaut, spaceman, spacewoman, space traveller; air traveller, air passenger, jet set 268 *traveller*; air hostess, steward, stewardess, cabin personnel 742 *servant*; flier, pilot, test p., jet p., copilot; automatic pilot, autopilot; navigator, air crew; pilot officer, flying o. 741 *air officer*; aircraftman 722 *air force*; air personnel, ground crew 686 *personnel*.

wing, pinion, feathers, flight f., wing feather, wing spread 259 *plumage*; sweptback wing, deltawing, swingwing, variable w.; aerofoil, aileron, flaps.

Vb. *fly,* wing, be on the w.; wing one's way, be wafted; soar, rise 308 *ascend*; hover, hang over 217 *hang*; flutter, flit 265 *be in motion*; taxi, take off, leave the ground, climb, circle 296 *depart*; be airborne, have lift-off; aviate, glide, plane; float, drift 323 *be light*; hit an air pocket, experience turbulence, stunt, spin, roll, side-slip, loop the loop, volplane; hedgehop, skim the rooftops, buzz; stall, dive, power-dive, nose-d., spiral 313 *plunge*; crash, prang, force-land, crash-land, pancake, ditch 309 *tumble*; pull out, flatten o.; touch down 295 *land*; bale out, jump, parachute, eject; blast off, lift o., take o.; orbit, go into o. 314 *circle*.

272 Transference – N. *transference,* relocation, transplantation, transhipment, transfer, bussing, commuting, shuttling; shifting, shift, drift, longshore d., continental d. 282 *deviation*; posting 751 *mandate*; transposition, metathesis 151 *interchange*; removal, moving house, flitting, relegation, deportation, expulsion 300 *ejection*; unpacking, unloading, airdrop 188 *displacement*; exportation, export 791 *trade*; trade-off, mutual transfer 791 *barter*; importation, import 299 *reception*; distribution, logistics 633 *provision*; transmittal, forwarding, sending, remittance, dispatch; recalling, recall, extradition 304 *extraction*; recovery, retrieval 771 *acquisition*; handing

over, delivery; takeover 792 *purchase*; conveyance, transfer of property, donation 780 *transfer*; committal, trust 751 *commission*; gaol delivery, habeas corpus, release 746 *liberation*; transition, metastasis; passing over, ferry, ferriage 305 *passage*; transmigration 143 *transformation*; transmission, throughput; conduction, convection; transfusion; decantation; diffusion, dispersal 75 *dispersion*; communication, contact 378 *touch*; contagion, infection, contamination 178 *influence*; transcription, transumption, copying, transliteration 520 *translation*.

transport, transportation; conveyance, carriage, shipping, shipment; carrying, humping, portage, porterage, haulage, draught 288 *traction*; carting; freightage, air freight, airlift; rail, road 274 *vehicle*; sea, canal 275 *ship*; pipeline, conveyor belt 274 *conveyor*. flotsam, jetsam, trust 767 *security*; legacy, bequest 781 *gift*; lease 777 *property*; cargo, load, payload, freight; consignment, shipment 193 *contents*; goods, mails; luggage, baggage, impedimenta; container, container-load, lorryload, trainload, coachload, busload; person transferred, passenger, rider, commuter 268 *traveller*.

Vb. *transfer*, hand over, deliver 780 *assign*; leave 780 *bequeath*; commit, entrust 751 *commission*; transmit, hand down, hand on, pass on; make over, turn over, hand to, pass to; transfer responsibility to, delegate, pass the buck; export, transport, convey, ship, airlift, fly, ferry 273 *carry*; infect, contaminate 178 *influence*; conduct, convect; carry over 38 *add*; transfer itself to, come off on, adhere, stick 48 *cohere*.

transpose, shift, move 188 *displace*; transfer, relocate, switch, shunt, shuffle, castle (chess) 151 *interchange*; detach, detail, draft; relegate, deport, expel, sack 300 *eject*; drag, pull 288 *draw*; push, shove 279 *impel*; containerize 193 *load*; channel, funnel, pour in *or* out, transfuse, decant, strain off, siphon off 300 *empty*; unload, remove 188 *displace*; download, upload; shovel, ladle, spoon

out, bail out 255 *make concave*; transliterate 520 *translate*.

send, remit, transmit, dispatch; direct, consign, address; post, mail; redirect, readdress, post on, forward; send by hand, deliver in person, send by post; send for, order, mail-order, tele-order 627 *require*; send away, detach, detail 287 *propel*.

Adv. *in transit*, en route, on the way; in the post; in the pipeline.

273 Carrier – N. *carrier*, haulier, carter, waggoner; shipper, transporter, exporter, importer; ferryman 270 *boatman*; lorry driver, truck d., van d., bus d. 268 *driver*; delivery boy; delivery van, lorry, truck, juggernaut, cart, goods train 274 *vehicle*; barge, cargo vessel, freighter, tramp 275 *ship*; chassis, undercarriage 218 *prop*; pallet, container; carrier bag, plastic b., poly b. 194 *bag*; conveyor belt, escalator 274 *conveyor*.

beast of burden, packhorse, packmule; ass, she-a., donkey, moke, Neddy, cuddy, burro; ox, oxen, bullock, draught animals 365 *cattle*; sledge dog, husky; camel, dromedary, ship of the desert; elephant 365 *mammal*.

horse, equine species, quadruped, horseflesh; dobbin, gee-gee; nag; Rosinante; mount, steed, trusty s.; stallion, gelding, mare, colt, filly, foal; stud horse, brood mare, stud, stable; carthorse; circus horse, liberty h.; roan, strawberry r., grey, dapple g., bay, chestnut, sorrel, black, piebald, skewbald, pinto, dun, palomino; purebred, blood-horse, bloodstock; Arab, Barbary horse; pacer, stepper, high-s., trotter; courser, racehorse, racer, goer, stayer; sprinter; steeplechaser, hurdler, fencer, jumper, hunter, foxhunter; warhorse, charger, courser, steed 722 *cavalry*, winged horse, Pegasus; Houyhnhnm.

draught horse, carthorse, dray h.; shaft-horse, trace-h.; carriage-horse, coach-h., post-h.; plough-h., shire-h., Clydesdale, punch, Suffolk P., Percheron, pit pony.

saddle horse, mount, hack, roadster; jade, screw, nag; pad, pad-nag, ambler; mustang, bronco; palfrey, jennet.

pony, cob, galloway, garron, sheltie; Shetland pony, fell p., Welsh p., Dartmoor p., Exmoor p., New Forest p.

Adj. *equine,* horsy, horse-faced; neighing; roan, grey etc. n.; asinine; mulish.

Vb. *carry,* bear 218 *support*; hump, humf, lug, heave, tote; caddy; shoulder, bear on one's back, carry on one's shoulders; fetch, bring, reach; fetch and carry; transport, cart, truck, railroad; ship, waft, raft; lift, fly 272 *transfer*; carry over, carry across, traject, ferry; convey, conduct, convoy, escort 89 *accompany*; be saddled with, be lumbered with, be burdened w.; be loaded with, be fraught 54 *be complete*.

274 Vehicle – N. *vehicle,* conveyance, public c.; public service vehicle, transport, public t.; vehicular traffic, motorised t., road t., wheeled t.; pedal power, horse p.; sedan chair, palanquin; litter, horse l.; brancard, stretcher, hurdle, crate; ambulance, bloodwagon, fire engine; Black Maria, paddy wagon; tumbril, hearse; snowplough, snowmobile, weasel; breakdown van, recovery vehicle; tractor, caterpillar t., tracked vehicle, bulldozer, JCB (tdmk); amphibian, moon buggy, space vehicle; rollercoaster, switchback, dodgem car; time machine.

sled, sledge, sleigh, dogsleigh; bobsleigh, bobsled, toboggan, sand yacht, surfboard, sailboard; skate, ice s., roller s., skateboard; snowshoes, skis.

bicycle, cycle, pedal c., bike, push b.; wheel, gridiron, crate; velocipede, hobbyhorse, boneshaker, penny-farthing, sit-up-and-beg; folding bicycle, sports model, racer, tourist, roadster, mountain bicycle *or* bike; ladies' bicycle, man's b.; five-speed, ten-s.; BMX (tdmk), Chopper (tdmk); stabilized bicycle; small-wheeler; tandem, randem;

monocycle, unicycle, tricycle, fairy cycle, trike, quadricycle; motorized bicycle, moped; scooter, motor s., motorcycle, motorbike, trail bike, scrambler; motorcycle combination, sidecar; invalid carriage; cycle-rickshaw, trishaw.

pushcart, perambulator, pram, baby buggy, buggy, pushchair, stroller; bath chair, wheelchair, invalid c.; rickshaw; barrow, wheelbarrow, handcart, cart, gocart; trolley, truck, float.

cart, ox-c., bullock-c., horse-and-cart; dray, milk float; farm cart, haywain, hay waggon; wain, waggon, covered w., prairie schooner; caravan, mobile home, trailer, horse-box, loose-b.; dustcart, watercart. See *lorry*.

carriage, horse-drawn c., equipage, turnout, rig; chariot, coach, state c., coach and four; barouche, landau, landaulet, berlin, victoria, brougham, phaeton, clarence; surrey, buckboard, buggy, wagonette; travelling carriage, chaise, shay, calèche, calash, britzka, droshky, troika; racing chariot, quadriga; four-inhand, drag, brake, charabanc; two-wheeler, cabriolet, curricle, tilbury, whisky, jaunting car; trap, gig, ponycart, dogcart, governess cart; carriole, sulky; shandrydan, rattletrap.

war chariot, scythed c.; gun carriage, caisson, limber, ammunition waggon; tank, armoured car 722 *cavalry*; jeep, staff car.

cab, hackney carriage, horsecab, fourwheeler, hansom, fly; fiacre, droshky; gharry, tonga; taxicab, taxi, minicab; rickshaw, jinrickisha, pedicab, cyclerickshaw.

bus, horsebus, motorbus; omnibus, double-decker, single-d.; autobus, trolleybus, motor coach, coach, postbus, minibus; airbus.

tram, horse t., tramcar, trolley, streetcar, cablecar.

automobile, horseless carriage, car, motor car; motor, auto; limousine, limo, gas guzzler; saloon, two-door s., four-d. s.; tourer, roadster, runabout, buggy; hard-top, soft-t., convertible; coupé, sports car; racing car, stock c., dragster,

hot-rod; go-kart, go-cart, kart; fastback, hatchback, estate car, station waggon, shooting brake; Land Rover (tdmk), jeep; police car, patrol c., panda c.; veteran car, vintage car, model T; tin Lizzie, banger, bus, jalopy, old crock, rattletrap; beetle, bubble car, minicar; invalid car, three-wheeler; minibus, camper, Dormobile (tdmk).

lorry, truck, pickup t., dump t.; refuse lorry, dustcart; container lorry, articulated l., roadliner, juggernaut; tanker, bowser; car transporter, low-loader; van, delivery v., removal v., pantechnicon; breakdown van; electric van, float.

train, railway t., passenger t., excursion t., boat t., motorail; express train, through t., intercity t., high-speed t., HST, slow train, stopping t.; goods train, freight t., freightliner; milk train, mail t., night mail; rolling stock; coach, carriage, compartment, first-class c., second-class c., smoker, nonsmoker; Pullman, wagon-lit, sleeping car, sleeper; restaurant car, dining c., buffet c., observation c.; guard's van, luggage v., brake v., caboose; truck, waggon, tank w., hopper w., trolley; bogie; steam train, diesel t., electric t., tube t., model t.; live rail, third r., overhead wires, pantograph; cable railway, electric r., underground r. 624 *railway.*

locomotive, diesel engine, steam engine, tender; choo-choo, puff-puff, traction engine, steam roller.

conveyor; conveyor belt, escalator, moving staircase, moving pavement, moving walkway, travelator; shovel, hod 194 *ladle*; fork, trowel 370 *farm tool*; crane.

275 Ship – N. *ship,* vessel, boat, craft; bark, barque; great ship, tall s.; little ship, cockleshell; bottom, keel, sail; hooker, tub, hull; hulk, prisonship; Argo, Golden Hind, Noah's Ark; steamer, screw s., steamship, steamboat, motor vessel; paddle steamer, paddleboat, stern-wheeler, riverboat, showboat; passenger ship, liner, luxury l., cruise ship;

channel steamer, ferry; hovercraft, hydrofoil; rotor ship; mail-boat, packet, steam p.; dredger, hopper, icebreaker; transport, hospital ship; storeship, tender, escort vessel; pilot vessel; tug, launch; lightship, weather ship; underwater craft, submarine, U-boat 722 *warship*; aircraft carrier.

merchant ship, galleon, argosy, Indiaman; banana boat, tea clipper; slave ship; cargo boat, freighter, tramp; coaster; lugger, collier, tanker, oil t., supertanker; containership.

fishing boat, inshore f. boat.; fishing smack, drifter, trawler, purse-seiner; factory ship; whaler, whale-catcher.

sailing ship, sailing boat, sailboat, sailer; windjammer, clipper, tall ship; square-rigged ship; four-masted ship, three-masted s., threemaster; barque, barquentine; two-masted ship, brig, hermaphrodite b., brigantine, schooner, pinnace; frigate, corvette 722 *warship*; cutter, sloop, ketch, yawl; wherry; yacht, racing y.; sailing dinghy, catamaran, smack; xebec, felucca, caïque, dhow, junk, sampan.

sail, sailcloth, canvas; square sail, lugsail, lug, lateen sail, fore-and-aft s., leg-of-mutton s., spanker; course, mainsail, foresail, topsail, topgallant sail, royal, skysail; jib, staysail, spinnaker, balloon sail, studding s.; rigging; mast, foremast, mainmast, mizzenmast 218 *prop.*

boat, skiff, foldboat, cockboat; lifeboat; ship's boat, tender, dinghy, pram; longboat, jolly boat; whaleboat, dory; pinnace, cutter, gig; bumboat, surf boat; barge, lighter, pontoon; ferry, ferryboat, canalboat, narrowboat; houseboat; towboat, tugboat, tug; sailing boat, sailboat, sailing dinghy, yacht, catamaran; powerboat, motorboat, motor launch; pleasure-boat, cabin cruiser; speedboat.

rowing boat, galley; eight, racing e.; sculler, shell, randan; skiff, dinghy, rubber dinghy; coracle, currach; punt, gondola; canoe, outrigger, dugout; pirogue, proa, kayak, umiak.

shipping, craft; argosy, fleet, armada, flotilla, squadron 722 *navy*; marine,

mercantile marine, merchant navy, shipping line; flag of convenience 547 *flag*.

Adj. *marine,* maritime, naval, nautical, sea-going, ocean-g.; sea-worthy, snug, shipshape, shipshape and Bristol fashion.

276 Aircraft – N. *aircraft* 271 *aeronautics*; flying machine; aeroplane, airplane, crate; plane, monoplane, biplane, triplane; amphibian; hydroplane, seaplane, flying boat; airliner, airbus, transport, freighter; warplane, fighter, bomber 722 *air force*; stratocruiser, jet plane, jet, jumbo j., jump j., supersonic j., turbojet, turboprop, turbofan, propfan; VTOL, STOL, HOTOL; microlight; helicopter, autogyro, whirlybird, chopper, copter; ornithopter; hovercraft 275 *ship*; glider, sailplane; flying instruments, controls, flight recorder, black box, autopilot, automatic pilot, joystick, rudder; aerofoil, fin, tail; flaps, aileron 271 *wing*; prop 269 *propeller*; cockpit, flight deck; undercarriage, landing gear; safety belt, life jacket, parachute, ejection seat; test bed, wind tunnel; flight simulator; aerodrome, airport 271 *air travel*.

airship, aerostat, balloon, Montgolfier b., hot-air b.; captive balloon, barrage b.; observation b., weather b., blimp; dirigible, Zeppelin; kite, box-k.; parachute, chute; hang glider; magic carpet; balloon-basket, nacelle, car, gondola.

rocket, rocketry; step rocket, multistage r.; booster; nose cone, warhead; guided missile, intercontinental ballistic m., ICBM, Exocet (tdmk), nuclear missile, Cruise m. 723 *missile weapon*; V2; Star Wars, Strategic Defence Initiative, SDI.

spaceship, spacecraft, space probe, space shot, space capsule, space shuttle, spaceplane, aerospaceplane; space lab; lunar module; space tug, orbital manoeuvring vehicle; space platform, space station, sputnik 321 *satellite*; flying saucer, UFO, unidentified flying object.

277 Velocity – N. *velocity,* celerity, rapidity, speed, swiftness, fleetness, quickness, liveliness, alacrity, agility; speed of thought 116 *instantaneity*; promptness, expedition, dispatch; speed, tempo, rate, pace, bat 265 *motion*; speed-rate, miles per hour, mph, knots; mach number; speed of light, speed of sound, supersonic speed; lightning speed; maximum speed, full s., full steam; utmost speed, press of sail, full s.; precipitation, hurry, flurry 680 *haste*; breakneck speed 857 *rashness*; streak of lightning, flash, lightning f.; flight, jet f., supersonic f.; gale, hurricane, tempest, torrent; electricity, telegraph, lightning, greased l.; speed measurement, tachometer, speedometer 465 *gauge*; wind gauge; log, logline; speed trap, radar t. 542 *trap*.

spurt, acceleration, speed-up, overtaking; burst of speed; thrust, drive, impetus 279 *impulse*; jump, spring, bound, pounce 312 *leap*; whizz, swoop, swoosh, vroom, zip, zing, zap, uprush, zoom; down rush, dive, power d.; flying start, rush, dash, scamper, run, sprint, gallop.

Adj. *speedy,* swift, fast, quick, rapid, nimble, volant; darting, dashing, lively, brisk, smart, snappy, nifty, zippy 174 *vigorous*; expeditious, hustling 680 *hasty*; double-quick, rapid-fire; prompt 135 *early*; immediate 116 *instantaneous*; high-speed, streamlined, souped-up, go-go; speeding, racing, ton-up; running, charging, runaway; flying, whizzing, hurtling, pelting; whirling, tempestuous; breakneck, headlong, precipitate 857 *rash*; fleet, fleet of foot, light-footed, nimble-f.; darting, starting, flashing; swift-moving, agile, nimble, mercurial, like quicksilver 152 *changeful*; like a bird; arrowy, like an arrow; like a shot; like a flash, like greased lightning, like the wind, quick as lightning, quick as thought, quick as a flash, quick as the wind, like a bat out of hell; meteoric, jet-propelled.

Vb. *move fast,* move, shift, travel, speed; drive, pelt, streak, flash, shoot; scorch, burn up the miles, tear up the road; scud, career; skim, nip, cut; bowl

along; sweep along, tear a., rattle a., thunder a., storm a.; tear, rip, vroom, zip, zing, zap, rush, dash; fly, wing, whizz, skirr; hurtle, zoom, dive; dash off, tear o., dart o., dash on, dash forward; plunge, lunge, swoop; run, trot, double, lope, spank, gallop; bolt, cut and run, hotfoot it, leg it, scoot, skedaddle, scamper, scurry, skelter, scuttle; show a clean pair of heels, be unable to be seen for dust 620 *run away*; hare, run like a h., run like the wind, run like mad, run like the clappers; start, dart, dartle, flit; frisk, whisk; spring, bound, leap, jump, pounce; ride hard, put one's best foot forward, stir one's stumps, get cracking, get a move on, get one's finger out; hie, hurry, post, haste 680 *hasten*; chase, charge, stampede, career, go full tilt, go full pelt, go full lick, go full steam, go all out; break the speed limit, break the sound barrier.

accelerate, speed up, raise the tempo; gather momentum, gather speed, spurt, sprint, put on speed, pick up s., step on it, step on the gas, put one's foot down, open the throttle, open up, let it rip; crowd on sail; quicken one's speed, get a move on; put on one's running shoes, set off at a run, get off to a flying start; make up time, make up for lost time, make forced marches; quicken, step up, drive, spur, urge forward, urge on; lend wings to, put a bomb under, hustle, expedite 680 *hasten*.

outstrip, overtake, overhaul, catch up, catch up with; lap, outpace, outrun 306 *outdo*; gain on, outdistance, leave behind, leave standing, leave at the starting post; lose, shake off; make the running, romp home, win the race, outclass 34 *be superior*.

Adv. *swiftly,* rapidly etc. adj.; trippingly, apace; posthaste, at full speed, at full tilt; in full gallop, all out, flat out; helter-skelter, headlong, lickety-split, hell for leather; pronto, smartish, p.d.q.; like greased lightning, like a shot, like the clappers, in a flash, before you could say Jack Robinson; in full sail, under press of sail *or* canvas, full speed ahead; on eagle's wings, with giant strides; nineteen to the dozen, hand over fist; at a rate of knots, at the double, in double-quick time, as fast as one's legs would carry one; at full speed, for all one is worth; by leaps and bounds, like wildfire.

278 Slowness – N. *slowness,* slackness, languor 679 *sluggishness*; inertia 175 *inertness*; deliberation 823 *inexcitability*; tentativeness, Fabian tactics; hesitation 858 *caution*; reluctance 598 *unwillingness*; go-slow, working to rule 145 *strike*; slowing down, slow-down, deceleration, retardation 113 *protraction*; drag 333 *friction*; brake, curb 747 *restraint*; leisureliness, no hurry, time to spare, time on one's hands, all the time in the world, easy stages 681 *leisure*; slow motion, low gear; slow march, dead m.; slow time, andante; slow pace, foot p., snail's p., crawl, creep, dawdle; dragging one's feet; amble 265 *gait*; limping, hobbling; standing start, slow s.; lag, time lag 136 *delay*.

slowcoach, snail, tortoise, tardigrade; stopping train, slow t.; funeral procession, dawdler, loiterer, lingerer; slow learner, late developer; laggard, sluggard, sleepyhead, slouch; drone 679 *idler*.

Adj. *slow,* painfully s.; low-geared, slow-motion, time-lapse; snail-like, tortoise-l., creeping, crawling, dragging; tardigrade, slow-moving 695 *clumsy*; limping, halting; taking one's time, dragging one's feet, hanging fire, tardy, dilatory, lagging 136 *late*; unhurried 681 *leisurely*; sedate 875 *formal*; deliberate 823 *patient*; painstaking 457 *careful*; Fabian 858 *cautious*; groping, tentative 461 *experimental*; languid, slack, sluggish 679 *lazy*; apathetic, phlegmatic 375 *insensible*; gradual, imperceptible.

Vb. *move slowly,* go slow, amble, crawl, creep, inch; trickle, dribble 350 *flow*; drift 282 *deviate*; hover; slouch, shuffle; toddle, waddle, mince; plod, trudge, lumber, wobble, totter, teeter, stagger, lurch; struggle, toil, labour,

chug, limp, hobble; drag one's steps, flag, falter 684 *be fatigued*; trail, lag, fall behind 284 *follow*; hang fire, drag one's feet, drag oneself 598 *be unwilling*; tarry, be long about it, take one's time 136 *be late*; laze, idle 679 *be inactive*; take it easy, linger, stroll, saunter, dawdle 267 *walk*; march in slow time, tick over; grope, feel one's way 461 *be tentative*; soft-pedal, hesitate 858 *be cautious*; speak slowly, drawl, spin something out 580 *stammer*.

decelerate, slow down, slow up, ease up, let up, lose momentum; reduce speed, slacken s., slacken one's pace, slacken off; relax, slacken, ease off 145 *pause*; lose ground, flag, falter, waver 684 *be fatigued*.

retard, check, curb, rein in, throttle down 177 *moderate*; reef, shorten sail, take in s., strike s 269 *navigate*; brake, put on the b., put on the drag 747 *restrain*; backpedal, backwater, backpaddle, put the engines astern, reverse 286 *regress*; handicap, impair, clip the wings 702 *hinder*.

Adv. *slowly,* deliberately etc. adj.; lazily, sluggishly; at low speed, in low gear, in bottom g.; at a snail's p., at a funeral p.; with leaden step; in one's own good time; in slow time, adagio, largo; by easy stages, by degrees, little by little, step by step.

279 Impulse – **N.** *impulse,* impulsion, pressure; impetus, momentum; boost 174 *stimulant*; encouragement 612 *incentive*; thrust, push, shove, heave; stroke; throw, fling 287 *propulsion*; lunge, kick 712 *attack*; beating, tapping, drumming; beat, drumbeat 403 *roll*; thud; ramming, bulldozing, hammering; butting, butt (**see** *collision*); shaking, rattling; shock, impact; slam, bang; flick, clip, tap 378 *touch*; shake, jerk, wrench 318 *agitation*; pulsation, pulse 318 *spasm*; mechanics, dynamics.

knock, dint, dent 255 *concavity*; rap, tap, clap; dab, pat, fillip, flip, flick; nudge, dig 547 *gesture*; smack, slap; cuff,

clip on *or* round the ear, clout, buffet, box on the ears; blow, fourpenny one; bunch of fives, knuckle sandwich; lash, stroke, hit, crack; cut, drive (cricket); thwack, thump, biff, bang, slug; punch, rabbit p., left, right, straight left, uppercut, jab, hook; body blow, swipe; knockout blow; stamp, kick; swat; spanking, trouncing, dusting, pasting, licking, leathering, whipping, flogging, thrashing, beating, bashing, hammering, pummelling, rain of blows; hiding 963 *corporal punishment*; assault, assault and battery 712 *attack*; exchange of blows, fisticuffs, cut and thrust, hammer and tongs 61 *turmoil*.

collision, encounter, meeting, confrontation; head-on collision; bird strike; graze, scrape 333 *friction*; clash 14 *contrariety*; cannon; impact, bump, shock, crash, smash, smashup, accident; brunt, charge, force 712 *attack*; collision course 293 *convergence*; multiple collision, pileup 74 *accumulation*; motorway madness.

hammer, sledge h., steam h., trip h.; hammerhead, peen; punch, puncher; beetle, maul, mallet; flail; cosh, blackjack, knuckle-duster, cudgel, club, sandbag 723 *weapon*; pestle, anvil.

ram, battering r., bulldozer; JCB (tdmk); piledriver, monkey; ramrod; rammer, tamper; cue, billiard c., pusher 287 *propellant*.

Vb. *impel,* fling, heave, throw 287 *propel*; give an impetus, impart momentum; slam, bang 264 *close*; press, press in, press up, press down; push, thrust, shove; ram down, tamp; shove off, push off, pole, punt; hustle, prod, urge, spur, railroad, pressurize 277 *accelerate*; fillip, flip, flick; jerk, shake, rattle, shock, jog, jolt, jostle 318 *agitate*; shoulder, elbow, push out of the way, push around 282 *deflect*; throw out, run out, expel 300 *eject*; frogmarch; drive forward, flog on, whip on; goad 612 *incite*; drive, start, run, set going, set moving 173 *operate*; raise 310 *elevate*; plunge, dip, douse 311 *lower*.

collide, impinge 306 *encroach*; come into collision 293 *converge*; meet, encounter, confront, clash; cross swords, fence 712 *strike at*; ram, butt, batter, bash, dint, dent; bulldoze 165 *demolish*; cannon into, bump into, bump against; graze 333 *rub*; butt against; drive into, crash i., smash i., run i., run down, run over; clash with, collide w., fall foul of; run one's head against, run into a brick wall, run against, dash a.; bark one's shins, stub one's toe; trip over 309 *tumble*; knock together, knock heads t., clash the cymbals, clap one's hands.

strike, smite, hit, land a blow, fetch one a b.; aim a blow, hit out at; lunge at; lash out at, lace into, let fly; hit wildly, swing, flail; strike hard, slam, bang, knock; knock for six, knock into the middle of next week, send flying; knock down, floor 311 *fell*; tap, rap; slap, smack; bop, clock, clout, bash, clobber, box the ears of, clip one's ear; box, spar, fisticuff 716 *fight*; buffet, punch, paste, thump, thwack, whack, wham, rain blows, pummel, trounce, beat up, sock it to, let one have it; give one a black eye *or* a bloody nose, make one see stars; pound, batter, bludgeon 332 *pulverize*; biff, bash, dash, slosh, sock, slog, slug, cosh, cudgel, club, mug, spifflicate; blackjack, sandbag, hit over the head, crown; concuss, stun, knock out, leave senseless; spank, wallop, thrash, lash, lam, lambast, beat, whip, cane 963 *flog*; leather, strap, belt, tan one's hide, give a hiding 963 *punish*; thresh, flail; hammer, drum; swat 216 *flatten*; maul 655 *wound*; throw stones at, stone, pelt; head (a football); bat, swipe, lob, smash, volley 287 *propel.*

280 Recoil – N. *recoil,* revulsion, reaction, retroaction, reflux 148 *reversion*; repercussion, reverberation, echo 404 *resonance*; reflex 417 *reflection*; kick, kickback, backlash; ricochet, cannon; rebound, bounce, spring, springboard, trampoline 328 *elasticity*; ducks and drakes; swing-back, swing of the pendulum 317 *oscillation*; volley, return (at

tennis), boomerang; rebuff, repulse 292 *repulsion*; riposte, return fire.

Vb. *recoil,* react 182 *counteract*; shrink, wince, blench, quail, start, flinch, jib, shy, jump back 620 *avoid*; kick back, hit b.; ricochet, cannon, cannon off; uncoil, spring back, fly b., rebound; return, swing back 148 *revert*; have repercussions; reverberate, echo 404 *resound*; be reflected, reflect 417 *shine*; boomerang 714 *retaliate.*

281 Direction – N. *direction,* bearing, compass reading; lie of the land 186 *situation*; orientation, collimation, alignment; set, drift 350 *current*; tenor, trend, bending 179 *tendency*; aim; course, beam; beeline, straight shot, line of sight, optical axis 249 *straightness*; course, tack; line, line of march, track, way, path, road 624 *route*; steering, steerage; aim, target 295 *goal*; compass, pelorus 269 *sailing aid*; collimator, sights; fingerpost 547 *signpost*; direction finder, range f. 465 *gauge*; orienteering.

Adj. *directed,* orientated, directed towards, signposted; aimed, well-directed, well-placed 187 *located*; bound for; aligned with; axial, diagonal; sideways 239 *lateral*; facing 240 *opposite*; direct, undeviating 249 *straight*; unswerving, straightforward, one-way, directive, guiding.

Vb. *orientate,* orientate oneself, box the compass, take one's bearings, shoot the sun, plot one's c. 269 *navigate*; find which way the wind blows, see how the land lies; ask the way, ask for directions; signpost, direct, show the way, put on the right track 547 *indicate*; pinpoint, locate 187 *place.*

steer for, shape a course for, be bound f., head f., make f., aim f.; make towards, bend one's steps to, go to, go towards, go straight for, direct oneself towards, make a beeline for; go straight to the point, hold the line, keep on the beam, keep the nose down.

point to, point out, point, show, point towards, signpost 547 *indicate*; incline towards.

aim, level, point; take aim, aim at; train one's sights, draw a bead on, level at; have one covered; collimate, set one's sights; hit the mark, get a bull's-eye.

Adv. *towards,* versus, facing; on the way, on the road to, through, via, en route for, by way of; straight, direct, straight forwards; point blank, straight as an arrow; in a direct line, in a straight line, in a line with, in a line for; directly, full tilt at, as the crow flies; upstream, downstream; upwind, downwind; before the wind, close to the w., near the w.; against the w., in the wind's eye, seaward, landward, homeward; downtown; cross-country; up-country; in all directions 183 *widely*; from *or* to the four winds; hither, thither; clockwise, anticlockwise, counterclockwise, widdershins.

282 Deviation – N. *deviation,* disorientation, misdirection, wrong course, wrong turning; aberration, deflection, refraction; diversion, digression; shift, veer, slew, swing; departure, declension 220 *obliquity*; flection, flexion, swerve, bend 248 *curvature*; branching off 294 *divergence*; deviousness, detour, long way round, scenic route, tourist r. 626 *circuit*; vagrancy; fall, lapse 495 *error*; wandering mind 456 *abstractedness*; drift, leeway; sidestep, sideslip; break, leg b., off b., googly (cricket); knight's move (chess); yaw, tack; zigzag, slalom course.

Vb. *deviate,* digress, make a detour, go a roundabout way, go the long way round; branch out 294 *diverge*; turn, filter, turn a corner, turn aside, swerve, slew; go out of one's way, depart from one's course; step aside, make way for; alter course, change direction, yaw, tack; veer, back (wind); bend, curve 248 *be curved*; zigzag, twist 251 *meander*; swing 317 *oscillate*; steer clear of, give a wide berth, sheer off; sidle, skid, sideslip; break (cricket); fly off at a tangent 220 *be oblique*; sidestep 620 *avoid*.

turn round, turn about, about turn, wheel, wheel about, face a., face the other way, do a U-turn, change one's mind; reverse, reverse direction, return 148 *revert*; go back 286 *turn back*.

stray, err, ramble, maunder, straggle 267 *wander*; go astray, go adrift, lose one's way, get lost; miss one's footing, lose one's bearings, lose one's sense of direction, take the wrong turning 495 *blunder*; lose track of, lose the place, lose the thread 456 *be inattentive*.

deflect, bend, crook; warp, skew; put off the scent, lead astray, draw a red herring, throw dust in one's eyes, set off on a wild-goose chase, misdirect, misaddress 495 *mislead*; avert; divert; change the course of; sidetrack, draw aside, push a., pull a.; elbow a., bias, slice, pull, hook, glance, bowl a break, bowl wide (cricket); shift, switch, shunt 151 *interchange*.

283 Preceding: going before – N. *preceding* 119 *priority*, 64 *precedence*; going before, going ahead of, leading, heading, flying start; preemption, queue-jumping; pride of place, head of the table, head of the river (bumping races); lead, leading role, star role 34 *superiority*; pioneer 66 *precursor*; van, vanguard, avant-garde 237 *front*; prequel, foreword, prelude.

Vb. *precede,* go before, go ahead of, be the forerunner of, herald, be the precursor of, be the prelude to; usher in, introduce; head, spearhead, lead, be in the vanguard, head the queue; go in front, go in advance, clear the way, light the w., lead the w.; lead the dance, guide, conduct 689 *direct*; take the lead, have a head start; steal a march on, preempt, steal one's thunder; get in front, jump the queue; get ahead of, lap 277 *outstrip*; be beforehand 135 *be early*; take precedence over, take priority over, have right of way 64 *come before*.

284 Following: going after – N. *following* 65 *sequence*; run, suit 71 *series*; subsequence 120 *posteriority*; pursuit, pursuance 619 *chase*; succession, reversion 780 *transfer*; last place 238 *rear*.

follower, attendant, suitor, hanger-on, camp follower, groupie 742 *dependant*; train, tail, wake, cortege, suite, followers

67 *retinue*; following, party, adherent, supporter, fan 703 *aider*; satellite, moon, artificial satellite, space station 276 *spaceship*; trailer, caravan 274 *cart*; tender 275 *ship*.

Vb. *follow,* come behind, succeed, follow on, follow after, follow close upon, sit on one's tail, breathe down one's neck, be bumper to bumper, follow in the wake of, tread on the heels of, tread in the steps of, follow the footprints of, come to heel 65 *come after*; stick like a shadow, tag after, hang on the skirts of, beset; attend, wait on, dance attendance on 742 *serve*; tag along 89 *accompany*; dog, shadow, trail, tail, track, chase 619 *pursue*; trail, dawdle 278 *move slowly*; bring up the rear 238 *be behind*.

285 Progression: motion forwards – N. *progression,* going forward; procession, march, way, course, career; march of time 111 *course of time*; progress, steady p., forward march 265 *motion*; giant strides, leap, quantum l., jump, leaps and bounds 277 *spurt*; irresistible progress, relentless p., majestic p., flood, tide 350 *current*; gain, ground gained, advance, headway 654 *improvement*; getting ahead, overtaking 283 *preceding*; encroachment 306 *overstepping*; next step, development, evolution 308 *ascent,* 71 *continuity*; furtherance, promotion, step up the ladder, advancement, preferment; rise, raise, lift, leg-up 310 *elevation*; progressiveness; enterprise, go-getting, go-go 672 *undertaking*; achievement 727 *success*; economic progress 730 *prosperity*.

Adj. *progressive,* enterprising, resourceful, go-ahead, go-go, go-getting, forward-looking, reformist; advancing etc. vb.; flowing on 265 *moving*; advanced 126 *modern*.

Vb. *progress,* proceed 265 *be in motion*; advance, go forward, take a step forward, come on, develop 316 *evolve*; show promise, promise well 654 *get better*; get on, get ahead, do well 730 *prosper*; march on, run on, flow on, pass on, jog on, wag on, rub on, hold on, keep on,

slog on 146 *go on*; move with the times 126 *modernize*; never look back, hold one's lead; press on, push on, drive on, push forward, press f., press onwards 680 *hasten*; make a good start, make good progress; gain, gain ground, make headway, make strides 277 *move fast*; get a move on, get ahead, forge a., advance by leaps and bounds; gain on, distance, outdistance, overtake, leave behind 277 *outstrip*; rise, climb the ladder 308 *climb*; reach out to, make up leeway, recover lost ground 31 *recoup*; gain time, make up t.

promote, further, contribute to, advance 703 *aid*; upgrade, move up, raise, lift 310 *elevate*; bring forward, develop 174 *invigorate*; speed up 277 *accelerate*; put ahead 64 *put in front*; favour, make for 156 *cause*.

Adv. *forward,* forwards, onward, forth, on, ahead, forrard; progressively, by leaps and bounds, with giant strides.

286 Regression: motion backwards – N. *regression,* regress; reverse direction, retroflexion, retrocession, retrogression, retrogradation, retroaction, backward step 148 *reversion*; retreat, withdrawal, retirement, disengagement 290 *recession*; regurgitation 300 *voidance*; reversing, backing; falling away, decline, drop, fall, downward trend, slump 655 *deterioration*.

return, remigration, homeward journey; homecoming 295 *arrival*; reentrance, reentry 297 *ingress*; going back, turn of the tide, reflux, ebb, regurgitation 350 *current*; veering, backing; relapse, backsliding 603 *change of mind*; U-turn, volte-face, about turn 148 *reversion*; countermarch, countermovement, countermotion 182 *counteraction*; turn, turning point 137 *crisis*; resilience 328 *elasticity*; reflex 280 *recoil*.

Vb. *regress,* recede, retrogress, retreat, sound a r., beat a r.; retire, withdraw, fall back, draw b.; turn away, turn tail 620 *run away*; back out, back down 753 *resign*; backtrack, backpedal; give way, give ground; recede into the distance 446

disappear; fall behind 278 *move slowly*; reverse, back, go backwards; run back, regurgitate; slip back; ebb, slump, fall, drop, decline 309 *descend*; bounce back 280 *recoil*.

turn back, retrace one's steps; remigrate, go back, go home, return 148 *revert*; look back, look over one's shoulder, hark back 505 *retrospect*; turn one's back, turn on one's heel; veer round, wheel r., about face, execute a volte-face, do a U-turn 603 *tergiversate*; double back, countermarch.

287 Propulsion – N. *propulsion*, jet p., drive; impulsion, push, forward thrust 279 *impulse*; projection, throwing, tossing, hurling, pelting, slinging, stone-throwing; precipitation; cast, throw, chuck, toss, fling, sling, shy, cock-shy; pot shot, pot, shot, long s.; shooting, firing, discharge, volley 712 *bombardment*; bowling, pitching, throw-in, full toss, yorker, lob (cricket); kick, punt, dribble (football); stroke, drive, swipe 279 *knock*; pull, slice (golf); rally, volley, smash (tennis); ballistics, gunnery, musketry, sniping, pea-shooting; archery, toxophily; marksmanship 694 *skill*; gunshot, bowshot, stone's throw 199 *distance*.

missile, projectile, shell, rocket, cannonball, grapeshot, ball, bullet, shot, small s.; pellet, brickbat, stone, snowball; arrow, dart 723 *missile weapon*; ball, tennis b., golf b., cricket b., hockey b.; football, rugby ball; bowl, boule, wood, jack, puck, curling stone; quoit, discus; javelin; hammer, caber.

propellant, thrust, driving force, jet, steam 160 *energy*; spray, aerosol; thruster, pusher, shover 279 *ram*; tail wind, following w. 352 *wind*; lever, treadle, pedal, bicycle p.; oar, sweep, paddle; screw, blade, paddlewheel 269 *propeller*; coal, petrol, diesel oil 385 *fuel*; gunpowder, dynamite 723 *explosive*; shotgun, rifle 723 *firearm*; revolver 723 *pistol*; airgun, pop gun, water pistol; blowpipe, pea-shooter; catapult, sling, bow 723 *missile weapon*.

Vb. *propel*, launch, project, set on its way; throw, cast, deliver, heave, pitch, toss, cant, chuck, shy, bung; bowl, lob, york; hurl, fling, sling, catapult; dart, flick; pelt, stone, shower, snowball; precipitate, get moving, send flying, send headlong; expel, pitchfork 300 *eject*; blow up, explode, put dynamite under, put a bomb under; serve, return, volley, smash, kill (tennis); bat, slam, slog, wham; sky, loft; drive, cut, pull, hook, glance (cricket); slice 279 *strike*; kick, dribble, punt (football); putt, push, shove, shoulder, ease along 279 *impel*; wheel, pedal, roll, bowl, trundle 315 *rotate*; move on, drive, hustle 265 *move*; sweep, sweep before one, carry before one; put to flight 727 *defeat*.

shoot, fire, open fire; fire a volley; discharge, explode, let off, set off; let fly, draw a bead on, pull the trigger; bombard 712 *fire at*; snipe, pot, take a potshot at, pepper 263 *pierce*.

288 Traction – N. *traction*, drawing etc. vb.; retraction; retractability; magnetism 291 *attraction*; haulage; pull, haul, tug, tow; towrope; rake, harrow; trawl, dragnet; hauler, haulier; retractor; lugsail, square sail 275 *sail*; windlass; tug 275 *ship*; tractor, traction engine 274 *locomotive*; loadstone; rowing; tug of war 716 *contest*; trailer, caravan 274 *cart*.

Vb. *draw*, pull, haul, kedge 269 *navigate*; tug, tow, take in tow; lug, drag, trail, trawl; rake, harrow; winch, reel in, wind in, lift, heave, hitch 310 *elevate*; drag down 311 *lower*; suck in 299 *absorb*; pluck, pull out 304 *extract*; wrench, twist 246 *distort*; yank, jerk, twitch, tweak, pluck at 318 *agitate*; pull towards 291 *attract*; pull back, draw in, retract.

289 Approach: motion towards – N. *approach*, advance 285 *progression*; approximation 200 *nearness*; meeting, confluence 293 *convergence*; access, accession, advent, coming 295 *arrival*, 189 *presence*; overtaking, overlapping 619 *pursuit*; onset 712 *attack*; advances,

pass, overture 759 *offer*; way in 624 *access*.

Adj. *approaching,* nearing, getting warm etc. vb.; close 200 *near*; meeting 293 *convergent*; closing in, imminent 155 *impending*; advancing, oncoming.

accessible, approachable, get-at-able; within easy reach; attainable 469 *possible*; available, obtainable, on tap; nearby 200 *near*; welcoming, inviting; 882 *sociable*; well-paved, made-up, metalled.

Vb. *approach,* draw near; approximate; come within range 295 *arrive*; come into view 443 *be visible*; come closer, meet 293 *converge*; near, draw n., go n., walk up to, run up to; roll up 74 *congregate*; come in 297 *enter*; accost 884 *greet*; make overtures, make passes 889 *court*; lean towards, incline 179 *tend*; move towards 265 *be in motion*; advance 285 *progress*; advance upon, bear down on 712 *attack*; close in, close in on 232 *circumscribe*; hover 155 *impend*; overtake 277 *outstrip*; narrow the gap, breathe down one's neck, tread on one's heels, sit on one's tail, drive bumper to bumper, run one close; be in sight of, be within shouting distance of.

290 Recession: motion from – N. *recession,* retirement, withdrawal, retreat, stepping back 286 *regression*; emigration, evacuation 296 *departure*; resignation 621 *relinquishment*; flight 667 *escape*; shrinking, shying, flinching 620 *avoidance*; revulsion 280 *recoil*.

Vb. *recede,* retire, withdraw, fall back, draw b., retreat 286 *regress*; ebb, subside, shrink, decline 37 *decrease*; fade from view 446 *disappear*; go, go away, leave, clear out, evacuate, emigrate 296 *depart*; move from, move away, put space between, widen the gap 199 *be distant*; stand aside, make way, sheer off 282 *deviate*; drift away 282 *stray*; back away, flinch 620 *avoid*; flee 620 *run away*; get away 667 *escape*; go back 286 *turn back*; jump back 280 *recoil*; come unstuck 46 *separate*.

291 Attraction – N. *attraction,* pull, drag, draw, tug; suction; magnetism, magnetic field; force of gravity; itch for 859 *desire*; affinity, sympathy, empathy; attractiveness, seductiveness, allure, appeal, sex a., it; allurement, seduction, temptation, lure, bait, decoy, charm, siren song 612 *inducement*; charmer, temptress, siren, Circe 612 *motivator*; centre of attraction, cynosure, honeypot 890 *favourite*.

Vb. *attract,* magnetize, pull, drag, tug 288 *draw*; adduct, exercise a pull, draw towards, pull t., drag t.; appeal, charm, move, pluck at one's heartstrings 821 *impress*; lure, allure, bait, seduce 612 *tempt*; decoy 542 *ensnare*.

292 Repulsion – N. *repulsion,* repulsiveness 842 *ugliness*; reflection 280 *recoil*; driving off, beating o. 713 *defence*; repulse, rebuff, snub, refusal, the cold shoulder, the bird 607 *rejection*; brushoff, dismissal 300 *ejection*.

Adj. *repellent,* repelling etc. vb.; repulsive, off-putting, antipathetic.

Vb. *repel,* put off, make sick 861 *cause dislike*; push away, butt a. 279 *impel*; drive away, repulse, beat off, stonewall, talk out; dispel 75 *disperse*; head off, turn away, reflect 282 *deflect*; be deaf to 760 *refuse*; rebuff, snub, brush off, reject one's advances 607 *reject*; give one the bird, cold-shoulder, keep at arm's length, make one keep his distance; show the door to, shut the door in one's face, send one off with a flea in his ear, send packing, send one about his business, give one his marching orders; boot out, give the boot, kick out, sack 300 *dismiss*.

293 Convergence – N. *convergence,* narrowing gap; confrontation, collision course 279 *collision*; concourse, confluence, conflux, meeting 45 *union*; congress, concurrence, concentration, resort, assembly 74 *assemblage*; closing in 232 *circumscription*; centering, focalization, zeroing in 76 *focus*; narrowing, tapering, taper 206 *narrowness*; tangent; perspective, vanishing point 438 *view*.

Adj. *convergent,* converging etc. vb.; focusing, zeroing in on, focused; centering; confluent, concurrent 45 *conjunctive*; tangential; pointed, conical, pyramidal; knock-kneed.

Vb. *converge,* come closer, close in; narrow the gap; come together 295 *meet*; unite, gather together, get t. 74 *congregate*; enter in 297 *enter*; close with, intercept, close in upon 232 *circumscribe*; concentrate, focus, bring into f.; centre on, zero in on 225 *centralize*; taper, come to a point, narrow down.

294 Divergence – N. *divergence,* divergency 15 *difference*; contradiction 14 *contrariety*; moving apart, drifting a., parting 46 *separation*; aberration, declination 282 *deviation*; spread, fanning out, deployment 75 *dispersion*; parting of the ways, fork, bifurcation, crossroads, watershed, points 222 *crossing*; radiation, ramification, branching out; Y-shape 247 *angularity*.

Adj. *divergent,* diverging etc. vb.; separated; radiating, radiant, palmate, stellate; centrifugal, centrifuge; aberrant.

Vb. *diverge* 15 differ; radiate; ramify, branch off, branch out; split off, fork, bifurcate; part, part company, come to the parting of the ways 46 *separate*; file off, go one's own way; change direction, switch; glance off, fly off, fly off at a tangent 282 *deviate*; deploy, fan out, spread, scatter 75 *be dispersed*; straddle, spread-eagle; splay, splay apart.

295 Arrival – N. *arrival,* advent, accession, appearance, entrance 289 *approach,* 189 *presence*; onset 68 *beginning*; coming, reaching, making; landfall, landing, touchdown, docking, mooring 266 *quiescence*; debarkation, disembarkation 298 *egress*; rejoining, meeting, encounter 154 *event*; greeting, handshake, golden hello, formalities 884 *courteous act*; homecoming 286 *return*; prodigal's return, reception, welcome 876 *celebration*; guest, visitor, visitant, new arrival, nouveau arrivé, recent a., homing pigeon 297 *incomer*; finish,

close f., neck-and-neck f., needle f., photo f. 716 *contest*; last lap, home stretch.

goal 617 objective; journey's end, point of no return, terminus 69 *extremity*; stop, halt 145 *stopping place*; pier; harbour, haven, anchorage, roadstead 662 *shelter*; aerodrome, airport, airfield, heliport, terminal, air t. 271 *air travel*; terminus, railway t., railway station, bus s., depot, rendezvous 192 *meeting place.*

Vb. *arrive,* come, reach, fetch up at, end up at, get there 189 *be present*; reach one's destination, make port; dock, moor, drop anchor 266 *come to rest* (see *land*); draw up, pull up, park; come home, return h. 286 *regress*; hit, make, win to, gain, attain; finish the race, breast the tape; achieve one's aim, reach one's goal 725 *carry through*; be on the doorstep 297 *enter*; make an entrance; appear, show up, pop up, turn up, roll up, drop in, blow in 882 *visit*; put in, pull in, stop 145 *pause*; clock in 135 *be early*; arrive at, find 484 *discover*; arrive at the top 727 *be successful,* 730 *prosper*; be brought, come to hand.

land, beach, run aground; touch down, make a landing; step ashore, disembark, get off, get out, get down, alight, light on, perch 309 *descend*; dismount.

meet, join, see again; receive, greet, welcome, shake hands 882 *be sociable*; go to meet, come to m.; rendezvous; come upon, encounter, come in contact, run into, meet by chance; hit, bump into, knock i., collide with 279 *collide*; upon, light upon, gather, assemble 74 *congregate.*

Int. welcome! greetings! hullo! hi! pleased to meet you! aloha! shalom! salaam!

296 Departure – N. *departure,* leaving, parting, removal, going away; walk-out, exit 298 *egress*; pulling out, emigration 290 *recession*; migration, exodus, general e., Hegira; flight, moonlight flit, decampment, elopement, getaway 667 *escape*; embarkation 297 *ingress*; saddling 267 *equitation*; setting out, outset 68

start; takeoff, blast-off 308 *ascent*; zero hour, time of departure, moment of leave-taking; point of departure.

valediction, farewell, valedictory, funeral oration, epitaph, obituary 364 *obsequies*; leave-taking, congé, dismissal; goodbyes, goodnights, farewells, adieus; last handshake, waving goodbye, wave of the handkerchief 884 *courteous act*; send-off, farewell address; last post, last words, final goodbye, parting shot; stirrup cup, doch-an-dorris, one for the road, nightcap.

Vb. *depart,* quit, leave, abandon 621 *relinquish*; retire, withdraw, retreat 286 *turn back*; remove, move house, flit, leave the neighbourhood, leave the country, leave home, emigrate, absent o. 190 *go away*; fly the nest, take one's leave, take one's departure, be going, be getting along; bid farewell, say goodbye, say good night, make one's adieus, tear oneself away, part, part company; receive one's congé, get one's marching orders; leave work, cease w. 145 *cease*; clock out, go home 298 *emerge*; quit the scene, leave the stage, bow out, give one's swan song, exit, make one's e. 753 *resign*; depart this life 361 *die*.

decamp, up sticks, strike tents, break camp, break up; walk out, march out, pack up, clear off; clear out, pull out, evacuate; make tracks; be off, beetle o., buzz o., slope o., swan o., push o., shove o., make oneself scarce; take wing 271 *fly*; vamoose, skedaddle, beat it, hop it, scram, bolt, scuttle, skip, slip away, cut and run 277 *move fast*; flee, take flight, make a break for it 620 *run away*; flit, make a moonlight f., make one's getaway 446 *disappear*; elope, abscond, give one the slip 667 *escape*.

start out, be off, get going, get on one's way, set out 68 *begin*; set forth, sally f., take up one's bed and walk, issue f., strike out, light out, march out 298 *emerge*; gird oneself, be ready to start, warm up 669 *make ready*; take ship, embark, go on board 297 *enter*; hoist the Blue Peter, unmoor, cast off, weigh anchor, push off, get under way, set sail,

put out to sea 269 *navigate*; mount, bridle, harness, saddle 267 *ride*; hitch up, pile in, hop on; catch a train, catch a plane, catch a bus; pull out, drive off, take off, be on one's way, see off.

Int. goodbye! farewell! adieu! au revoir! auf Wiedersehen! arrivederci! adios! be seeing you! see you later! cheerio! ciao! bye-bye! ta-ta! so long! pleasant journey! have a good trip! bon voyage! God be with you!

297 Ingress: motion into – N. *ingress,* incoming, entry, entrance; reentry 286 *return*; inflow, influx, flood 350 *stream*; inpouring, inrush; intrusion, trespass 306 *overstepping*; invasion, forced entry, inroad, raid, irruption, incursion 712 *attack*; immersion, diffusion, osmosis; penetration, infiltration, insinuation 231 *interjacency*, 303 *insertion*; immigration; intake 299 *reception*; import, importation 272 *transference*; right of entry, admission, admittance, access, entrée 756 *permission*; free trade 791 *trade*.

way in, way, path 624 *access*; entrance, entrance hall, entry, door 263 *doorway*; mouth, opening 263 *orifice*; inlet 345 *gulf*; channel 351 *conduit*; open door, free port 796 *market*.

incomer, newcomer, Johnny-come-lately; new arrival, nouveau arrivé, new member, new face; new boy, new girl 538 *beginner*; visitant, visitor, caller 882 *sociable person*; immigrant, migrant, colonist, settler 59 *foreigner*; stowaway, unwelcome guest 59 *intruder*; invader, raider 712 *attacker*; house-breaker, burglar 789 *thief*; entrant, competitor 716 *contender*.

Vb. *enter,* turn into, go in, come in, move in, drive in, run in, breeze in, venture in, sidle in, step in, walk in, file in; follow in 65 *come after*; set foot in, cross the threshold, darken the doors; let oneself in; unlock the door, turn the key 263 *open*; gain admittance, have entrée to, be invited; look in, drop in, pop in, blow in, call 882 *visit*; mount, board, get aboard; get in, hop in, jump in, pile in;

squeeze into, creep in, slip in, edge in, slink in, sneak in, steal in; work one's way into, buy one's way into, insinuate oneself; worm into, bore i. 263 *pierce*; bite into, eat i., cut i. 260 *notch*; put one's foot in, tread in, fall into, drop i. 309 *tumble*; sink into, plunge i., dive i. 313 *plunge*; join, enlist in, enroll oneself; immigrate, settle in 187 *place oneself*; let in 299 *admit*; put in 303 *insert*; enter oneself, enter for 716 *contend*.

infiltrate, percolate, seep, soak through; leak into, sink in, penetrate, permeate, mix in, taint, infect 655 *impair*; filter in, worm one's way in.

intrude, trespass, gatecrash, outstay one's welcome, be de trop; horn in, barge in, push in, muscle in, break in upon, burst in u., interrupt 63 *derange*; break in, burgle 788 *steal*.

298 Egress: motion out of – N. *egress,* egression, going out; exit; walkout, exodus, general e., evacuation 296 *departure*; emigration, expatriation, exile 883 *seclusion*; emergence, emerging, debouchment; emersion, surfacing; emanation, efflux, issue; evaporation 388 *evaporation*; eruption, outburst 176 *outbreak*; sortie, breakout 667 *escape*; export, exportation 272 *transference*.

outflow, effluence, efflux, effusion; emission 300 *ejection*; issue, outpouring, gushing, streaming; exudation, oozing, dribbling, weeping; bleeding 302 *haemorrhage*; perspiration, sweating, sweat; percolation, filtration; leak, escape, leakage, seepage 634 *waste*; drain, running sore 772 *loss*; discharge, drainage, draining 300 *voidance*; overflow, spill, flood 350 *waterfall*; jet, fountain, spring 156 *source*; gush, squirt 350 *stream*; geyser; streaming eyes, runny nose, postnasal drip.

outlet, vent, chute; spout, nozzle, tap, faucet; pore, blowhole 263 *orifice*, 352 *respiration*; sluice, floodgate 351 *conduit*; exhaust pipe; drainpipe, overflow, gargoyle; exit, way out, path 624 *access*; escape, loophole 667 *means of escape*.

Vb. *emerge,* pop out, stick out, project 254 *jut*; peep out, peer out 443 *be visible*; surface 308 *ascend*; emanate, transpire 526 *be disclosed*; egress, issue, debouch, make a sortie; issue forth, sally f., come f., go f.; issue out of, go out, come o., creep o., sneak o., march o, flounce o., fling o. 267 *walk*; jump out, bale o. 312 *leap*; clear out, evacuate 296 *decamp*; emigrate 267 *travel*; exit, walk off 296 *depart*; erupt, break out 667 *escape*.

exude, perspire, sweat, steam 379 *be hot*; ooze, seep through, soak t., leak t.; percolate, strain, strain out, filter, filtrate, distil; run, dribble, drip, drop, drivel, drool, slaver, slobber, salivate, water at the mouth 341 *be wet*; exhale 352 *breathe*.

299 Reception – N. *reception,* admission, admittance, entrance, entrée, access 297 *ingress*; invitation 759 *offer*; receptivity, acceptance; open arms, welcome, liberty hall 876 *celebration*; enlistment, enrolment 78 *inclusion*; initiation, baptism, baptismal fire 68 *debut*; asylum, sanctuary, shelter, refuge 660 *protection*; introduction; importation, import 272 *transference*; radio receiver, telephone r. 531 *telecommunication*; inhalation 352 *respiration*; sucking, suction; assimilation, digestion, absorption, resorption; engulfing, engulfment, swallowing, ingurgitation; ingestion (of food) 301 *eating*; imbibition, fluid intake 301 *drinking*; intake, consumption 634 *waste*; infusion 303 *insertion*; interjection 231 *interjacency*; admissibility.

Vb. *admit,* receive, accept, take in; grant asylum, afford sanctuary, shelter, give refuge 660 *safeguard*; welcome; invite, call in 759 *offer*; enlist, enrol, take on 622 *employ*; give entrance *or* admittance to, allow in, allow access, give a ticket to, grant a visa to; throw open, open the door 263 *open*; bring in, import, land 272 *transfer*; let in, show in, usher in, introduce 64 *come before*; send in 272 *send*; initiate, baptize 534 *teach*.

absorb, incorporate, engross, assimilate, digest; suck in; soak up, sponge,

mop up, blot 342 *dry*; take in, ingest, imbibe; lap up, swallow, engulf, gulp, gobble, devour 301 *eat, drink*; breathe in, inhale 352 *breathe*; sniff 394 *smell*; get the taste of 386 *taste*.

300 Ejection – N. *ejection*, ejaculation, expulsion; precipitation 287 *propulsion*; disbarment, striking off, disqualification, excommunication 57 *exclusion*; throwing out, chucking o., bum's rush; drumming out, marching orders; the heave ho, dismissal, discharge, redundancy, golden handshake, sack, boot, push, kick upstairs 607 *rejection*; deportation, extradition; relegation, downgrading, exile, banishment 883 *seclusion*; eviction, dislodgment 188 *displacement*; dispossession, deprivation 786 *expropriation*; jettison, throwing overboard 779 *nonretention*; clean sweep, elimination 165 *destruction*; emission, effusion, shedding, spilling 298 *outflow*; libation 981 *oblation*; secretion, salivation 302 *excretion*; radioactivity 417 *radiation*.

voidance, clearance, clearage, drainage, curettage, aspiration; eruption, eruptiveness 176 *outbreak*; egestion, regurgitation, disgorgement; vomiting, throwing up, nausea, vomit, puke; gas, wind, burp, belch, fart; breaking wind, belching; elimination, evacuation 302 *excretion*.

vomiting, sick, sickened, nauseated, sick to one's stomach, throwing up, green, g. around the gills; seasick, airsick, carsick; sick as a dog.

Vb. *eject*, expel, send down 963 *punish*; strike off, strike off the register, disbar, excommunicate 57 *exclude*; export, send away 272 *transfer*; deport, expatriate; exile, banish, transport 883 *seclude*; throw up, cast up, wash up; spit out, cough up, spew out; put out, push o., turf o., throw o., chuck o., fling o., bounce 287 *propel*; kick out, boot o., give the bum's rush, throw out on one's ear, give the heave-ho, bundle out, hustle o.; drum out; precipitate 287 *propel*; pull

out 304 *extract*; unearth, root out, weed o., uproot, eradicate 165 *destroy*; rub out, scratch o., eliminate 550 *obliterate*; exorcise, rid, get rid of, rid oneself, get shot of; shake off, brush o.; dispossess, expropriate 786 *deprive*; out, oust, evict, dislodge, turn out, turn adrift, turn out of house and home 188 *displace*; smoke out 619 *hunt*; jettison, discard, throw away, throw overboard 779 *not retain*; blackball 607 *reject*.

dismiss, discharge, lay off, make redundant, drop 674 *stop using*; axe, sack, fire, give the sack, give the boot, give the push, give the heave-ho, give marching orders to 779 *not retain*; turn away, send one about his business, send one away with a flea in his ear, send packing 292 *repel*; see off, shoo away 854 *frighten*; show the door, show out; bowl out, run o., catch o.; exorcize, order off, order away 757 *prohibit*.

empty, drain, void; evacuate, eliminate 302 *excrete*; discharge; pour out, decant 272 *transpose*; drink up, drain to the dregs 301 *drink*; drain off, strain off, ladle out, bail o., pump o., suck o., run off, siphon o., open the sluices, open the floodgates, turn on the tap 263 *open*; draw off, tap, broach 263 *pierce*; milk, bleed, let blood, catheterize 304 *extract*; clear, sweep away, clear a., clean up, mop up, make a clean sweep of, clear the decks 648 *clean*; clean out, clear out; unload, unpack 188 *displace*; disembowel, eviscerate, gut, clean, bone, fillet 229 *uncover*; disinfest 648 *purify*; depopulate, desertize, 105 *render few*.

emit, let out, give vent to; send out 272 *send*; emit rays 417 *radiate*; emit a smell, give off, exhale, breathe out, perfume, scent 394 *smell*; vapour, fume, smoke, steam, puff 338 *vaporize*; spit, splutter; pour, spill, shed, sprinkle, spray; spurt, squirt, jet, gush 341 *moisten*; bleed, weep; drip, drop, ooze; dribble, drool, slobber 298 *exude*; sweat, perspire 379 *be hot*; secrete 632 *store*; egest, pass 302 *excrete*; drop (a foal), lay (an egg) 167 *generate*.

vomit, be sick, be sick to one's stomach, bring up, throw up, regurgitate, disgorge, retch, gag; spew, puke, cat, honk, poop, chunder, be seasick, feel nausea, heave, have a bilious attack.

eruct, belch, burp; break wind, blow off, fart; hiccup, cough, hawk, clear the throat, expectorate, spit, gob.

301 Food: eating and drinking - N. *eating,* munching etc. vb.; ingestion; alimentation, nutrition; feeding, drip-f., force-f., gavage; consumption, devouring; swallowing, downing, getting down, bolting; biting, chewing, mastication; rumination, digestion; chewing the cud; cropping; table, diet, dining, lunching, breakfasting, supping, having tea, snacking, grazing; dining out 882 *sociability*; partaking; tasting, nibbling, pecking, licking, playing with one's food, toying with one's f.; anorexia, anorexia nervosa; guzzling, gobbling; overeating, overindulgence, bingeing, bulimia nervosa, seesaw eating 944 *sensualism*, 947 *gluttony*; obesity 195 *bulk*; appetite, voracity, wolfishness 859 *hunger*; omnivorousness 464 *indiscrimination*; eating habits, table manners 610 *practice*; carnivorousness, man-eating, cannibalism; herbivorousness, vegetarianism, veganism; edibility, digestibility, food chain.

feasting, eating and drinking, gormandizing, guzzling, swilling; banqueting, eating out, dining out, having a meal out; regalement; orgy, bacchanalia, feast; reception, wedding breakfast, annual dinner, do 876 *celebration*; harvest supper, beanfeast, bunfight, thrash; Christmas dinner, blowout, spread (**see** *meal*); loaded table, festive cheer, festive board, groaning b.; fleshpots 635 *plenty*.

dieting, dietetics 658 *therapy*; weight-watching, slimming 206 *thinness*; reducing, losing weight 946 *fasting*; diet, balanced d., crash d., macrobiotic d.; nouvelle cuisine, cuisine minceur, lean cuisine; regimen, regime, course, diet sheet,

calorie counter; malnutrition 651 *disease*; calories, vitamins (**see** *food content*); vitamin pill; additive, E number.

gastronomy, epicureanism, epicurism 944 *sensualism*; gourmandism, foodism, good living, high l. 947 *gluttony*; refined palate 463 *discrimination*.

cookery, cooking, baking, cuisine, haute c., nouvelle c., lean c.; food preparation, dressing; domestic science, home economics, catering 633 *provision*; food processing (**see** *provisions*); baker, cook, chef, sous c., commis c., cuisinier, cordon bleu 633 *caterer*; bakery, rotisserie, delicatessen, restaurant 192 *café*; kitchen, cookhouse, galley; microwave, oven 383 *furnace*; recipe, cookery book, cookbook.

eater, feeder, consumer, partaker, taster etc. vb.; nibbler, picker, pecker; messmate; diner, banqueter, feaster, picnicker; diner-out, dining club 882 *sociability*; connoisseur, gourmet, epicure; gourmand, trencherman, trencherwoman, bon vivant, foodie 947 *glutton*; flesh-eater, meat-e., carnivore; man-eater, cannibal; vegetarian, vegan, veggie, herbivore; omnivore, hearty eater; wolf, gannet, vulture, hyena, locust.

provisions, stores, commissariat; provender, foodstuff, groceries; tinned *or* canned food, frozen f., convenience f., junk f., fast f.; keep, board, maintenance, aliment, sustenance 633 *provision*; self-sufficiency; commons, rations, iron r.; helping 783 *portion*.

provender, animal food, fodder, feed, pasture, pasturage, forage; corn, oats, barley, grain, hay, grass, clover, lucerne, silage; beechmast, acorns; foodstuffs; winter feed; chicken feed, pigswill, cattle cake; saltlick.

food, meat, bread, staff of life; aliment, nutriment, liquid n.; alimentation, nutrition; nurture, sustenance, nourishment, food and drink, pabulum; manna; nectar and ambrosia, amrita; daily bread, staple food, wheat, maize, rice, pulses, beans, potatoes; foodstuffs,

comestibles, eats, victuals, viands, provender; grub, tuck, tucker, nosh, scoff,
chow, chuck; biscuit, salt pork, pemmi-
can; stodge 391 *unsavouriness*;
processed food, carrion, offal;
wholefood, health food, organic foodstuff, high-fibre food, low-fat f.; good c.,
cakes and ale; titbits, snacks; garnish,
flavouring, herbs, sauce 389 *condiment*.

food content, vitamins; calories,
roughage, bulk, fibre; minerals, salts; calcium, iron; protein, amino acid; fat, oil,
cholesterol, saturated fats, polyunsaturates; carbohydrates, starch; sugar,
glucose, sucrose, lactose, fructose 392
sweet thing; additive, preservative, artificial flavouring; E numbers.

mouthful, bite, nibble, morsel 33 *small
quantity*; sop, sip, swallow; titbit; sandwich, open s., club s., snack, savoury,
tortilla, nacho; petit four, biscuit, chocolate, sweet, toffee, chewing gum (**see**
sweetmeat); popcorn, crisps, nuts.

meal, refreshment, fare; snack, bite to
eat; piece, butty, sandwich, open s., club
s., toasted s., toastie, hamburger, hot
dog, fish and chips; packed lunch,
ploughman's l.; square meal, three-
course m., sit-down meal, repast, collation, spread, feed, blowout, beanfeast
(**see** *feasting*); beano, thrash, junket 837
festivity; picnic, barbecue; bread and
cheese l.; potluck; breakfast, elevenses,
luncheon, lunch, brunch, tiffin; tea, afternoon t., high tea; dinner, supper, fork
s., buffet s.; table d'hôte, à la carte, cover,
helping 783 *portion*; seconds.

dish, course; main dish; salad, side
dish, entre-mets; dessert, pudding,
savoury; speciality, pièce de résistance,
plat du jour, dish of the day; meat and
two veg (**see** *meat*); casserole, stew, Irish
s., hotpot, Lancashire h., ragout 43 *a
mixture*; meat loaf, hamburger; goulash,
curry; moussaka; pilau, pilaff, paella, risotto, biryani; chop suey, chow mein,
stir-fry; dhal, bhaji; pasta, ravioli,
lasagne, macaroni, spaghetti, tagliatelle,
fettuccine, vermicelli, tortellini, penne,
cannelloni, noodles; pancake, pizza,
taco; pasty, pie, flan, quiche; fricassee,

fritters, croquettes, spring roll; fry-up,
mixed grill, fritto misto, kebabs;
tandoori; fondue, soufflé, omelette, fu
yung; Welsh rabbit *or* rarebit, buck r.;
scrambled eggs, poached e., boiled e.,
fried e.; bread and cheese, bread and
dripping; cauliflower cheese, ratatouille,
bubble and squeak; pease pudding,
baked beans, nut cutlet; leftovers.

hors-d'oeuvres, antipasto, smorgasbord; starter, appetiser, canapé; angels
on horseback, devils on h.; taramasalata,
hummus, raita, mezze; vol-au-vent;
blini, samosa, pakora; soup, cream s.,
clear s.; broth, brew, potage, consommé;
stock, bouillon, julienne, bisque, chowder, puree; cock-a-leekie, mulligatawny,
minestrone, borscht, gazpacho, bouillabaisse; cold meats, cooked m., cold cuts,
salami, pâté, terrine, galantine; salad,
side s., green s., mixed s., potato s.,
Russian s., Waldorf s., coleslaw, macedoine; mayonnaise, dressing, French d.
389 *sauce*.

fish food, fish 365 *marine life*; fish and
chips, fish pie, fish cakes, gefilte fish, fish
fingers, quenelles, kedgeree; white fish,
oily f., fresh f., smoked f.; freshwater
fish, trout, salmon, lox, gravlax, eel;
seafish, cod, coley, rock salmon, dogfish,
whiting, plaice, sole, skate, hake, halibut,
haddock, smoked h., finnan haddie, turbot, mullet, mackerel, herring, rollmops,
brisling, whitebait, sprats; sardine,
pilchard, anchovies, tuna, tunny; kippers, bloaters, Arbroath smoky; Bombay
duck; seafood, shellfish, oyster, lobster,
crayfish, crab, shrimp, prawn, scampi;
scallop, cockle, winkle, mussel, whelk,
jellied eel; roe, soft r., hard r., caviar;
sushi.

meat, flesh; red meat, white m.; beef,
mutton, lamb, veal, pork, venison,
game; pheasant, grouse, partridge,
chicken 365 *table bird*, *poultry*; soya
flour, textured vegetable protein, TVP
150 *substitute*; roast meat, Sunday roast,
S. joint, roast beef and Yorkshire pudding; boiled beef and carrots; haggis,
black pudding; shepherd's pie, cottage

p.; minced meat, mince; meatballs, rissoles, hamburgers; sausage, banger, chipolata, frankfurter, smoked sausage; toad in the hole, Cornish pasty, steak and kidney pudding; cut, joint, leg; baron of beef, sirloin; shoulder, hand of pork, skirt, scrag end, breast, brisket; shin, loin, flank, ribs, topside, silverside; cutlet, chop, loin c., chump c., gigot c., escalope; steak, fillet s., rump s., porterhouse s., entrecôte s., sirloin s.; pork pie, ham, bacon, bacon rasher, streaky b., back b., boiled b., gammon; tongue, knuckle, brawn, oxtail, cowheel, pig's trotters, sweetbreads, tripe, chitterlings; offal, kidney, liver 224 *insides.*

dessert, pudding, sweet; milk pudding, rice p., semolina, tapioca, bread-and-butter pudding; steamed p., suet p., Christmas p., plum p., summer p., rolypoly, spotted dick; jam tart, mince pies (see *pastries*); crumble, charlotte; stewed fruit, compôte, fool; fresh fruit, fruit salad; icecream, sorbet, mousse, soufflé, sundae, trifle, blancmange, jelly, custard 392 *sweet thing;* cheese board; yoghourt.

sweets, boiled s., confectionery; candy, chocolate, caramel, toffee, fudge, Turkish delight, marshmallows, mints, liquorice; acid drops, pear d., barley sugar, humbugs, butterscotch, nougat; gobstopper, aniseed ball, chewing gum, bubble g.; lolly, lollipop 392 *sweet thing;* sweetmeat, comfit, bonbon; crystallized fruit; toffee apple, candy floss.

fruit and vegetables, soft fruit, berry, gooseberry, strawberry, raspberry, loganberry, blackberry, tayberry, bilberry, mulberry; currant, redcurrant, blackcurrant, whitecurrant; apricot, peach, nectarine, plum, greengage, damson, cherry; apple, crab a., pippin, russet, pear; citrus fruit, orange, grapefruit, pomelo, lemon, lime, tangerine, clementine, mandarin; banana, pineapple, grape; rhubarb; date, fig; dried fruit, currant, raisin, sultana, prune; pomegranate, persimmon, Sharon fruit, passion fruit, guava, lichee, star fruit; mango, avocado; melon, water m., cantaloupe, honeydew; pawpaw, papaya; breadfruit; nut, coconut, Brazil

nut, cashew n., pecan, peanut, groundnut, monkey nut; almond, walnut, chestnut, pine nut, hazel n., cob n., filbert; bottled fruit, tinned f., preserves 392 *sweet thing. vegetable, greens 366 plant;* turnip, swede, parsnip, carrot, Jerusalem artichoke; potato, sweet p., yam; spud, baked potato, roast p., boiled p., mashed p., duchesse p., fried p., sauté p., French fries, chips; green vegetable, cabbage, Chinese c., red c., green c., white c., savoy, cauliflower, broccoli, calabrese, kohlrabi, kale, curly k., seakale; sprouts, Brussel s., spring greens; peas, petits pois, mangetout, beans, French b., broad b., runner b.; okra, lady's fingers, sorrel, spinach, chard, spinach beet, seakale b., asparagus, globe artichoke; leek, onion, shallots, garlic (see *herb*); marrow, courgette, zucchini, cucumber, pumpkin, squash; aubergine, eggplant, capsicum, pepper, green p., red p., yellow p., chilli; sweetcorn; salads, lettuce, cos l., chicory, endive; spring onion, scallion, radish, celery, beetroot; tomato, beef t., love-apple; beansprouts, bamboo shoots; cress, watercress, mustard and cress; pulses, lentils, split peas, chick p.; haricot beans, butter b., kidney b., soya b., adzuki b.; mushroom, boletus, truffle; laver, laverbread, samphire; tofu, bean curd.

herb, bouquet garni, fines herbes; marjoram, sweet m., oregano, rosemary, sage, mint, parsley, chervil, chives, thyme, basil, balm, bergamot, savory, tarragon, bayleaf, dill, fennel, borage, hops, seasoning 389 *condiment.*

spice, spicery; coriander, cumin, cardamom, pepper, cayenne, paprika, chilli, curry powder, turmeric, allspice, mace, cinnamon, ginger, nutmeg, clove, caraway, juniper berries, capers, vanilla pod 389 *condiment.*

cereals, grains, wheat, buckwheat, oats, rye, maize, mealies, corn; rice, brown r., unpolished r., wild r., long grain r., patna r., basmatti r., short grain r., pudding r., millet, sorghum; breakfast cereal, cornflakes, muesli, oatmeal, porridge, gruel, skilly, brose; flour, meal,

wholemeal, wheat germ, bran; bread, dough, flour, yeast; crust, crumb; white bread, sliced b., soda b., brown b., wholemeal b., malt b., granary b., black b., rye b., pumpernickel, corn b., pitta b.; toast, rusk, croûtons; loaf, pan l., cottage l., cob, tin, farmhouse, bloomer, baguette, French stick, bread s.; roll, breakfast r., bridge r., bap, bagel, croissant, brioche, bun, currant b.; crumpet, muffin, scone, drop s., pancake, crêpe; teacake, oatcake, bannock; pappadum, chapatti, nan, paratha, polenta, tortilla, taco, waffle, wafer, crispbread, cracker, cream c.

pastries and cakes, confectionery; patty, pasty, turnover, dumpling; tart, flan, quiche, puff, pie, piecrust; pastry, shortcrust p., flaky p., puff p., rough p. p., choux p.; patisserie, gateau, cake, lardy c., fruit c., Dundee c., seed c., sponge c., Madeira c., angel c., battenburg c., layer c., galette, cheesecake; brownies, fairy cakes, cup cakes, meringue, eclair, macaroon; Chelsea bun, Bath b., doughnut, flapjack, brandysnap, gingerbread, shortbread, cookies, biscuits, crackers, digestive biscuits, Nice b., tea b., garibaldi b., custard creams, gingernuts.

dairy product (see *milk*); cream, clotted c., curds, whey, junket, yoghourt, fruit y.; cheese, goat's c., cream c., cottage c., full-fat c., crowdie, ricotta; Cheddar, Cheshire, Leicestershire, Double Gloucester, Caerphilly, Lancashire, Wensleydale, sage Derby, red Windsor; Emmental, Gruyère, Gouda, Edam, Havarti, Camembert, Brie; Bel Paese, Parmesan; ripe cheese, blue c., blue vinny, Roquefort, Gorgonzola, Stilton, Danish blue, Dolcellate, Lymeswold (tdmk).

drinking, imbibing, sipping, wine-tasting 463 *discrimination*; gulping; swilling, alcoholism 949 *drunkenness*; libation 981 *oblation*.

draught, drink, beverage, dram, bevvy; gulp, swallow, sip, sup; bottle, bowl, glass 194 *cup*; cuppa, pinta; glassful, bumper; swig, nip, noggin, jigger, tot,

slug; peg, double peg, snorter, snifter, chaser; long drink; short; quick one, quickie, snort; sundowner, nightcap; loving cup, stirrup c., doch-an-dorris, one for the road; health, toast; mixed drink, concoction, cocktail, punch, spritzer 43 *mixture*; potion, decoction, infusion 658 *medicine*; nectar.

soft drink, nonalcoholic beverage; water, drinking w., spring water, fountain; soda water, soda, cream s., soda fountain, siphon; table water, carbonated w., mineral w., Perrier (tdmk), tonic w., barley w., squash, low calorie drink, mixer; iced drink, frappé; milk, milk shake; ginger beer, ginger ale, Coca Cola *or* Coke (tdmk), Pepsi (tdmk); fizz, pop, lemonade, orangeade; cordial, fruit juice, tomato j., vegetable j.; coconut milk; tea, iced t., lemon t., herbal t., char, pekoe, orange p., Indian t., China t., green t., black t., Russian t., herb t., tisane 658 *tonic*; coffee, café au lait, café noir, black coffee, Irish c., Turkish c., espresso, cappuccino; cocoa (see *milk*); sherbet, syrup, julep, hydromel.

alcoholic drink, strong d., booze, bevvy, tipple, poison; brew, intoxicating l. (see *wine*); alcohol; malt liquor, John Barleycorn, beer, small b.; draught beer, keg b., bottled b.; strong beer; heavy, export; ale, real ale; barley wine; stout, lager, bitter, porter, mild, home brew; shandy; cider, scrumpy; perry, mead, Athole brose; palm wine, rice beer, toddy, sake, mescal, tequila; distilled liquor, spirituous l., spirits, ardent s., raw s., aqua vitae, firewater, hooch, moonshine, mountain dew, rotgut, hard stuff; brandy, cognac, eau-de-vie, armagnac, marc, applejack, Calvados, kirsch, slivovitz, jambava; gin, mother's ruin, geneva, sloe gin, schnapps; whisky, usquebaugh, Scotch whisky, scotch; rye, bourbon; Irish whiskey, poteen; vodka, aquavit, ouzo, raki, arrack; rum, white r., Bacardi (tdmk), margarita; aperitif, Pernod (tdmk), absinthe; liqueur, cassis, Cointreau (tdmk), Drambuie (tdmk), curaçao, crème de menthe, grog, hot toddy, punch, rum p.; spiced wine, mulled w.,

negus, posset, claret cup; Pimms (tdmk), gin and tonic, pink gin, highball, brandy and soda, whisky and s.; mint julep; cocktail, Manhattan, Bloody Mary.

wine, the grape, ampelology, ampelography; red wine, white w., vin rosé; vermouth; spumante, sparkling wine, sweet w., dry w., full-bodied w., vintage w.; vin ordinaire, vin de table, vin du pays; vino, plonk; table wine, dessert w.; fortified w., sack, sherry, port, vintage p., ruby p., white p., tawny p., madeira, marsala; champagne, champers, fizz, bubbly; claret, Bordeaux; burgundy, Beaujolais; Muscadet, hock, Sauternes, Moselle, Riesling; Spätlese, Auslese, Beerenauslese, Trockenbeerenauslese; Tokay, retsina, chianti; vintage wine, first great growth, premier cru.

milk, top of the m., cream; cow's milk, beestings; goat's milk, mare's m., koumiss; mother's milk, breast m.; buttermilk, dried m., skimmed m., semi-skimmed m., condensed m., evaporated m., pasteurized m.; milk drink, m. shake, malted m., cocoa, chocolate, hot c., Horlicks (tdmk); curdled milk, curds, junket. See *dairy product.*

Adj. *feeding,* eating, grazing etc. vb.; flesh-eating, meat-e.; carnivorous, creophagous, cannibalistic; omophagic, omophagous; insectivorous; herbivorous, graminivorous, frugivorous; vegetarian, vegan; omnivorous 464 *indiscriminating.*

edible, eatable; kosher; digestible; potable, drinkable; palatable, succulent, moreish, delicious 386 *tasty.*

nourishing, sustaining, nutritious, nutritive, nutritional; protein-rich, body-building; wholesome 652 *salubrious.*

culinary, dressed, oven-ready, ready-to-cook, made-up, ready-to-serve; cooked, done to a turn, well-done; al dente; underdone, red, rare, raw; overcooked, burnt, b. to a cinder; roasted etc. vb. (see *cook*); à la meunière, au gratin, au naturel, mornay, au fromage, à la campagne, à la mode, à la maison, à la meunière; gastronomic, epicurean; prandial, post-p., after-dinner; meal-time.

Vb. *eat,* feed, mess; partake 386 *taste*; take a meal, have a feed, break one's fast, break bread; breakfast, have brunch, snack, graze, eat between meals, lunch, have tea, take tea, dine, sup; dine out, feast, banquet, carouse 837 *revel*; do justice to, be a good trencherman *or* woman, ask for more; water at the mouth, drool, raven 859 *be hungry*; fall to, set to, tuck in, lay into; stuff oneself, binge 863 *sate*; guzzle, gormandize 947 *gluttonize*; eat up, leave a clean plate; lick the platter clean 165 *consume*; swallow, gulp down, devour, dispatch, bolt, wolf, make short work of; feed on, live on, fatten on, batten on, prey on; nibble, peck, lick, play with one's food, toy with one's f., be anorexic; nibble at, peck at, sniff at; be a seesaw eater; ingest, digest 299 *absorb.*

chew, masticate, champ, chomp, munch, crunch, scrunch; gnaw, grind 332 *pulverize*; chew up 46 *cut.*

graze, browse, crop, feed; ruminate, chew the cud; nibble.

drink, imbibe, suck 299 *absorb*; quaff, drink up, drink one's fill, drain, drink like a fish, slake one's thirst, lap, sip, gulp; wet one's lips, wet one's whistle; crack a bottle; lap up, soak up, wash down; booze, swill, swig, tipple, tope 949 *get drunk*; drain one's glass, knock it back; raise one's glass, pledge 876 *toast*; take one for the road, have one over the eight; refill one's glass 633 *replenish.*

feed, nourish, nurture, sustain, cater 633 *provide*; nurse, breast-feed, give suck; pasture, graze, put out to grass; fatten, fatten up 197 *enlarge*; dine, wine and dine, feast, fête, banquet 882 *be hospitable.*

cook, pressure-cook; microwave, bake, brown; roast, spit-roast, pot-r., braise; broil, grill, charcoal-grill, barbecue, spatchcock, griddle, devil, curry; sauté, fry, deep-f., shallow-f., stir-f.; fry sunny side up, scramble, poach; boil, parboil; coddle, simmer, steam, casserole, stew; baste, lard, bard; whip, whisk, beat, blend, liquidize, stir; draw, gut, bone, fillet; stuff, dress, garnish; dice, shred,

mince, grate; sauce, flavour, herb, spice 388 *season.*

Int. bon appétit! here's health! here's to you! here's mud in your eye! bottoms up! down the hatch! slàinte! prosit! skol! cheers!

302 Excretion – N. *excretion,* discharge, secretion 300 *ejection*; emanation 298 *egress*; exhalation, breathing out 352 *respiration*; exudation, perspiration, sweating 298 *outflow*; suppuration 651 *infection*; cold, common c., coryza, catarrh, hay fever, allergic rhinitis, allergy; salivation, expectoration, spitting; coughing, hawking, cough; urination, micturition, peeing, pissing (vulg), slashing; waterworks, plumbing; incontinence.

haemorrhage, bleeding, haemophilia 335 *blood*; menses, menarche, period, time of the month, curse; dysmenorrhoea, menorrhagia.

defecation, evacuation, elimination, clearance 300 *voidance*; bowel movement, shit (vulg), crap (vulg), motion; bodily functions; diarrhoea, the trots 651 *digestive disorders*; constipation.

excrement, waste matter; faeces, stool, shit (vulg), crap (vulg), excreta, ordure; dung, cowpat, manure, muck; droppings, guano; urine, piss (vulg), water; sweat; spittle, spit, gob, sputum; saliva, slaver, slobber; rheum, phlegm; catarrh, mucus, snot; matter, pus; afterbirth, lochia.

Vb. *excrete,* secrete; pass, move; move one's bowels, defecate, shit (vulg), crap (vulg); be taken short, have the trots; relieve oneself, answer the call of nature, go, go to the lavatory; urinate, micturate, piddle, pee; have a pee, piss (vulg), have a p. (vulg), have a slash, take a leak; make water, spend a penny; wet oneself; sweat, perspire 379 *be hot*; salivate, slobber, snivel; cough, hawk, spit, gob 300 *eruct*; weep 298 *exude.*

303 Insertion: forcible ingress – N. *insertion,* interpolation, parenthesis 231 *interjection*; adding 38 *addition*; introduction, insinuation 297 *ingress*; impaction;

planting 370 *agriculture*; inoculation, injection, jab, shot; infusion, enema, catheter; insert, inset; stuffing 227 *lining.*

Vb. *insert,* introduce; weave into; put into, thrust i., intrude; poke into, jab i., stick i.; transfix, run through 263 *pierce*; ram into, jam i., stuff i., pack i., push i., shove i., tuck i., press i., pop i. 193 *load*; pocket; ease into place, slide in, fit in; knock into, hammer i., drive i. 279 *impel*; put in, inlay, inset 227 *line*; subjoin 38 *add*; interpose 231 *put between*; drop in, put in the slot 311 *let fall*; pot, hole; bury 364 *inter.*

implant, plant, transplant, plant out, prick o., bed o., dibble; graft, engraft, bud; inoculate, vaccinate; embed, bury.

immerse, bathe, steep, souse, marinate, soak 341 *drench*; baptize, duck, dip 311 *lower*; submerge; immerse oneself 313 *plunge.*

304 Extraction: forcible egress – N. *extraction,* withdrawal, removal 188 *displacement*; elimination, eradication 300 *ejection*; abortion 172 *unproductiveness*; extermination 165 *destruction*; extrication, unravelment, disengagement, liberation 668 *deliverance*; tearing out, ripping o.; cutting out, excision; Caesarian birth, forceps delivery; expression, squeezing out; suction, sucking out, aspiration; vacuuming, pumping; drawing out, pull, tug, wrench 288 *traction*; digging out 255 *excavation*; mining, quarrying; fishery; distillation 338 *vaporization*; drawing off, tapping, milking; thing extracted, essence, extract.

Vb. *extract,* remove, pull 288 *draw*; draw out, elicit; unfold 316 *evolve*; pull out, take o., get o., pluck; withdraw, excise, cut out, rip o., tear o., whip o.; excavate, mine, quarry, dig out, unearth; dredge, dredge up; expel, lever out, winkle o., smoke o. 300 *eject*; extort, wring from; express, press out, squeeze o., gouge o.; force out, wring o., wrench o., drag o.; draw off, milk, tap; syphon off, aspirate, suck, void, pump; wring from, squeeze f., drag f.; pull up, dig up, grub up, rake up; eliminate, weed out, root up,

uproot, eradicate, extirpate 165 *destroy*; prune, thin out 105 *render few*; distil 338 *vaporize*; extricate, unravel, free 746 *liberate*; unpack, unload 188 *displace*; eviscerate, gut 300 *empty*; unwrap 229 *uncover*; pick out 605 *select*.

305 Passage: motion through – N. *passage,* transmission 272 *transference*; transportation 272 *transport*; passing, passing through, traversing; traverse, crossing, journey, patrol 267 *land travel*; penetration, permeation, infiltration; osmosis, 297 *ingress*; intervention 231 *interjacency*; right of way 624 *access*; stepping-stone, flyover, underpass, subway 624 *bridge*; track, route, orbit 624 *path*; intersection, junction 222 *crossing*; waterway, channel 351 *conduit*.

traffic control, flow of traffic; traffic jam, tailback; rush hour; highway code, Green Cross C., green man 693 *precept*; traffic lane, motorway l., bus l., cycle l., one-way street, carriageway, dual c., clearway 624 *road*; diversion, alternative route 282 *deviation*; contraflow, lane closure; white lines, yellow l., double yellow l., cat's-eyes (tdmk), sleeping policemen; traffic lights, lampposts, roundabout; pedestrian crossing, zebra c., pelican c., subway (see *passage*); Belisha beacon, bollard, refuge, island; parking, zone p., off-street p.; car park, parking lot, parking place, parking zone; parking meter, parking ticket, waiting, loading, unloading; lay-by; point duty, road patrol, speed trap, radar t.; traffic police, traffic cop; traffic warden, meter maid; lollipop man *or* lady; road user 268 *pedestrian*.

Vb. *pass,* pass by, leave on one side, skirt, coast; flash by 277 *move fast*, 114 *be transient*; go past, not stop 146 *go on*, 265 *be in motion*; pass along, circulate, weave; pass through, transit, traverse; shoot through, shoot the rapids 269 *navigate*; pass out, come out the other side 298 *emerge*; go through, soak t., seep t., percolate, permeate 189 *pervade*; pass and repass, patrol, walk up and down, work over, beat, scour, go over the

ground; pass into, penetrate, infiltrate 297 *enter*; bore, perforate 263 *pierce*; thread, thread through, string 45 *connect*; rake; force a passage; worm one's way, squeeze through, elbow t., clear the way 285 *progress*; cross, go across, cross over, make a crossing, reach the other side 295 *arrive*; wade across, ford; get through, get past, negotiate; pass beyond 306 *overstep*; pass in front, cut across 702 *obstruct*; step over, straddle; bridge 226 *cover*; carry over, carry across, transmit 272 *send*; pass to, hand, reach, pass from hand to hand, hand over 272 *transfer*.

306 Overstepping: motion beyond – N. *overstepping,* going beyond, overstepping the mark, stretching a point 305 *passage*; transcendence 34 *superiority*; digression 282 *deviation*; transgression 936 *guilty act*; encroachment 916 *arrogation*; infringement, intrusion 916 *undueness*; expansionism, greediness 859 *desire*; excessiveness 637 *redundance*; overdoing it, going overboard 546 *exaggeration*; overindulgence 943 *intemperance*.

Vb. *overstep,* overstep the mark; go too far, throw out the baby with the bathwater; exceed, exceed the limit; overrun, overshoot the mark, aim too high; overlap; cross the Rubicon, pass the point of no return, burn one's boats; overfill, spill o. 54 *fill*; overgrow 637 *superabound*; overdo 546 *exaggerate*; strain, stretch a point; overbid, have one's bluff called, overestimate 482 *overrate*; overindulge 943 *be intemperate*; outstay one's welcome, oversleep 136 *be late*.

encroach, invade, make inroads on 712 *attack*; infringe, transgress, trespass 954 *be illegal*; poach 788 *steal*; squat, usurp 786 *appropriate*; barge in, horn in, butt in 297 *intrude*; impinge; eat away, erode 655 *impair*; infest, overrun; overflow, flood 341 *drench*.

outdo, exceed, surpass, outclass; transcend, rise above, soar a., outrival 34 *be superior*; go one better, outbid; outwit;

outmanoeuvre, outflank, steal a march on, steal one's thunder; outpace, outrun, outride, outdistance; overtake; leave standing, leave at the starting post 277 *outstrip*; leave behind, beat hollow 727 *defeat*.

307 Shortfall – N. *shortfall*, falling short etc. vb.; inadequacy 636 *insufficiency*; a minus, deficit, short measure, shortage, slippage, loss; leeway, drift 282 *deviation*; unfinished state 55 *incompleteness*; nonfulfilment, 726 *noncompletion*; half measures 641 *lost labour*; shortcoming 647 *imperfection*; something missing, want, lack, need 627 *requirement*.

Adj. *deficient*, short, short of, minus, wanting, lacking, missing; underpowered, substandard; undermanned, short-staffed, half-done 55 *incomplete*; inadequate 636 *insufficient*; failing, running short 636 *scarce*; below par 647 *imperfect*;

Vb. *fall short*, run s. 636 *not suffice*; not reach to; lack, want, be without 627 *require*; underachieve, not make the grade, not come up to scratch; miss the mark; lag 136 *be late*; stop short, fall by the way, fall out, not stay the course; break down, get bogged down; fall behind, lose ground, slip back; slump, collapse 286 *regress*; fall through, come to nothing, fizzle out, fail 728 *miscarry*; labour in vain 641 *waste effort*; not come up to expectations 509 *disappoint*.

308 Ascent: motion upwards – N. *ascent*, ascension, lift, upward motion; levitation; taking off, takeoff, lift-off, blast-off 296 *departure*; soaring, spiral; zoom 271 *aeronautics*; culmination 213 *summit*; surfacing; going up, rising; rise, upturn, upward trend; uprush, upsurge, crescendo 36 *increase*; updraught, thermal; sunrise, sun-up, dawn 128 *morning*; mounting, climbing; hill-climbing, rock-c., mountaineering, alpinism; ladder-scaling, escalade 712 *attack*; jump, vault, pole v., pole jump 312 *leap*; bounce 280 *recoil*; rising ground, hill 209

high land; gradient, slope, ramp 220 *incline*; rising pitch 410 *musical note*; stairs, steps, stile, flight of stairs, staircase, spiral s., stairway, landing; ladder, step l., accommodation l., Jacob's l., companionway; rope ladder, ratlines; stair, step, tread, rung; lift, ski l., chair l., elevator, escalator; fire escape 667 *means of escape*.

climber, mountaineer, rock-climber, alpinist, cragsman or -woman, fell walker; steeplejack.

Vb. *ascend*, rise, rise up, go up, leave the ground; defy gravity, levitate; take off, become airborne, have lift-off, fly up 271 *fly*; gain height, mount, soar, spiral, zoom, climb; reach the top, get to the top of the ladder, reach the zenith, culminate; float up, bob up, surface, break water; jump up, spring, vault 312 *leap*; bounce 280 *recoil*; push up, grow up, shoot up 36 *grow*; curl upwards; tower, aspire, spire 209 *be high*; gush, spirt, spout, jet, play; get up, start up, stand up, rear, rear up, ramp 215 *be vertical*; rise to one's feet, get up 310 *lift oneself*; slope upwards 220 *be oblique*.

climb, walk up, struggle up; mount, make one's way up, work one's way up; go climbing, go mountaineering, mountaineer; clamber, scramble, swarm up, shin up, go up hand over fist; surmount, top, breast, conquer, scale, scale the heights 209 *be high*; go over the top, escalade 712 *attack*; go upstairs, climb a ladder; mount (a horse).

Adv. *up*, uphill, upstairs; upwards 209 *aloft*.

309 Descent – N. *descent*, declension 282 *deviation*; falling, dropping; cadence; downward trend, decline, drop, slump 37 *decrease*; sunset, moonset; comedown, demotion 286 *regression*; downfall, collapse, setback 165 *ruin*; trip, stumble; lurch, capsize 221 *overturning*; tumble, crash, spill, fall; cropper, purler; downrush, swoop, stoop, pounce; dive, header, bellyflop 313 *plunge*; nosedive, power-dive 271 *aeronautics*; landing, crash l., splashdown 295 *arrival*; sliding

down, glissade; subsidence, landslide, avalanche; downdraught 352 *wind*; downpour, shower 350 *rain*; cascade 350 *waterfall*; downthrow (geology); declivity, slope, tilt, dip 220 *incline*; chute, slide, helter-skelter; precipice, sheer drop 215 *verticality*; submergence, sinkage, slippage 311 *lowering*; burrowing, mining, undermining 255 *excavation*; speleology, pot-holing, caving.

Vb. *descend,* come down, go d., dip d.; decline, abate, ebb 37 *decrease*; slump, plummet, fall, drop, sink; sink like a lead balloon, sink without trace 322 *weigh*; soak in, seep down 297 *infiltrate*; reach the depths, touch bottom; bottom out, reach one's nadir 35 *be inferior*; sink to the bottom, gravitate, precipitate, settle, set; fall down, fall in, cave in, fall to the ground, collapse; sink in, subside, slip, give way; hang down, prolapse, droop, sag, swag 217 *hang*; go under water, draw; submerge, dive 313 *plunge*; drown 313 *founder*; go underground, dig down, burrow, mine, undermine 255 *make concave*; parachute; swoop, stoop, pounce; fly down, flutter d., float d.; lose height, drop down, swing low; touch down, alight, light, perch 295 *land*; lower oneself, abseil; get down, climb d., step d.; get off, fall o., dismount; coast down, slide down, glissade, toboggan; fall like rain, shower, cascade, drip 350 *rain*; bow down, dip, duck 311 *stoop*; flop, plop, splash down.

tumble, fall; topple, keel over, overbalance, capsize, tumble head over heels 221 *be inverted*; miss one's footing, trip, stumble; lose one's balance; take a header, dive 313 *plunge*; fall off, take a fall, be thrown, come a cropper, fall heavily, crash to the ground, fall flat on one's face, fall prostrate, bite the dust, measure one's length; plummet, plump down 311 *sit down*; slump, nosedive.

Adv. *down,* downwards; downhill, downstairs, downstream.

310 Elevation – N. *elevation,* raising etc. vb.; erection, uplift, upheaval; picking up, lift; hoist, boost; leg-up 703 *aid*;

levitation; exaltation, Assumption; uprising, uptrend, growth, upswing 308 *ascent*; eminence 209 *high land*, 254 *prominence*; height above sea level 209 *height*.

Vb. *elevate,* heighten 209 *make higher*; puff up, blow up, swell, leaven 197 *enlarge*; raise, erect, set up, put up, run up, rear up, build up, build; lift, lift up, raise up, heave up; uplift; jack up, lever up, hike up, prop 218 *support*; stand on end; hold up, bear up; buoy up; raise aloft, hold a., hold up, wave; hoist, haul up; pick up, take up; pull up, wind up; weigh; fish up, drag up, dredge up, pump up 304 *extract*; chair, shoulder, carry shoulder-high; exalt, put on a pedestal 866 *honour*; mount 213 *crown*; jump up, bounce up 285 *promote*; give a lift, give a leg-up 703 *aid*; throw in the air, throw up, cast up, toss up; loft; send up, shoot up, lob 287 *propel*; perk up (one's head), prick up (one's ears); bristle, bristle up 215 *be vertical*.

lift oneself, arise, rise 308 *ascend*; stand up, get up, get to one's feet, pick oneself up, jump up, leap up, spring up, spring to one's feet; pull oneself up; hold oneself up, hold one's head up, draw oneself up to one's full height, stand on tiptoe 215 *be vertical*.

311 Lowering – N. *lowering,* depression, hauling down etc. vb.; pushing down 279 *impulse*; ducking, sousing 313 *plunge*; debasement, demotion, reduction 872 *humiliation*; subversion 149 *revolution*; overthrow, prostration; overturn, upset 221 *overturning*; precipitation, defenestration 287 *propulsion*; suppression; a depression, dent, dip, dimple, hollow 255 *cavity*; low pressure 340 *weather*.

obeisance, reverence, bow, salaam, kowtow 884 *courtesy*; curtsy, bob, duck, nod, salute 884 *courteous act*; kneeling, genuflexion 920 *respect*.

Vb. *lower,* depress, push down, thrust d. 279 *impel*; shut down (a lid) 264 *close*; hold down, keep d., hold under 165 *suppress*; lower, let down, take d.; lower a flag, dip; haul down, strike; deflate, puncture, flatten, squash, crush 198

make smaller; let drop (see *let fall*); sink, scuttle, drown 309 *descend*; duck, souse, douse, dip 313 *plunge*; weigh on, press on 322 *weigh*; tip, hollow 255 *make concave*.

let fall, drop, shed; let go 779 *not retain*; let slip *or* slide through one's fingers; pour, pour out, decant 300 *empty*; spill, slop 341 *moisten*; sprinkle, shower, scatter, dust, dredge; sow, broadcast 75 *disperse*; lay down, put d., set d., throw d., fling d. (see *fell*); pitch *or* chuck overboard, jettison, drop over the side; precipitate, send headlong 287 *propel*.

fell, overthrow; prostrate; lay low, lay one on his back 216 *flatten*; knock down, bowl over; floor, raze to the ground, trample in the dust 165 *demolish*; hew down, cut d., axe 46 *cut*; bring down; shoot down 287 *shoot*.

abase, debase, lower one's sights; demote, reduce to the ranks, cashier 752 *depose*; humble, deflate, puncture, debunk, take down a peg, cut down to size, take the wind out of one's sails 872 *humiliate*; crush, squash, grind down 165 *suppress*.

sit down, sit, sit oneself down, be seated, squat, hunker; sink, lower oneself; take a seat, seat oneself, take a pew, park oneself; perch, alight 309 *descend*.

stoop, bend, bend down; bend over, bend forward, bend backward; lean forward, lean over backwards; cringe, crouch, cower 721 *knuckle under*; slouch, hunch one's back 248 *make curved*; bow, scrape, duck, bob, curtsy, bob a c. 884 *pay one's respects*; nod, incline one's head, bow down, make obeisance, kiss hands, salaam, prostrate oneself, kowtow 920 *show respect*; kneel, kneel to, genuflect, kiss the ground.

312 Leap – N. *leap*, leapfrogging; jump, hop, skip; spring, bound, vault, pole v.; high jump, long j., running j.; triple j., hop, skip and jump; caper, gambol, frolic; kick, cancan; jeté, entrechat; prance; dance step; dance, breakdance, reel, jig, Highland fling 837 *dancing*.

Vb. *leap*, jump, take a running j.; spring, bound, vault, pole-v., hurdle, steeplechase, take one's fences; skip, hop, leapfrog, bob, bounce, rebound, buck, bob up and down 317 *oscillate*; stamp 837 *dance*; caper, cut capers, gambol, frisk, romp; prance; start, give a jump; jump on, pounce; jump up, leap up, spring up 308 *ascend*; jump over, clear.

313 Plunge – N. *plunge*, swoop, pounce, stoop, plummet 309 *descent*; nosedive, power dive 271 *aeronautics*; dive, header, bellyflop; swallow dive, duck d.; dip, ducking; immersion, submergence; crash dive.

diver, skin d., scuba d., deepsea d., frogman; underwater swimmer, aquanaut; the bends, caisson disease.

Vb. *plunge*, dip, duck 341 *be wet*; fall in, jump in, plump, plop, plummet; dive, take a header, go headfirst; souse, douse, immerse, submerse, drown; submerge, crash-dive 309 *descend*; sink, scuttle, send to Davy Jones's locker 311 *lower*.

founder, go down 309 *descend*; get out of one's depth; drown, go to the bottom, go down like a stone 211 *be deep*; plummet, sink, sink without trace, sink like lead 322 *weigh*.

314 Circuition: curvilinear motion – N. *circuition*, circulation, circumnavigation, circling, wheeling, spiral 315 *rotation*; turning, cornering, turn, U-turn 286 *return*; orbit; lap; circuit, milk round, tour, round trip, full circle; figure of eight 250 *loop*; helix 251 *coil*; circuitousness, roundabout way, scenic route, tourist r. 626 *circuit*.

Adj. *circuitous*, turning etc. vb.; peripatetic; devious 626 *roundabout*.

Vb. *circle*, circulate, go the rounds, make the round of; circuit, make a c., lap; do the round trip; go round, skirt; circumnavigate, go round the world, go globetrotting; turn, round, weather a point; round a corner, turn a c.; revolve, orbit; wheel, spiral, come full circle, chase one's tail 315 *rotate*; do a U-turn,

turn round, bend r.; put about, wheel a., face a., turn on one's heel 286 *turn back*; draw a circle, describe a circle 232 *circumscribe*; curve, wind, twist, wind one's way 251 *meander*; make a detour 626 *circuit*.

315 Rotation: motion in a continued circle
– N. *rotation,* revolving, orbiting; revolution, full circle; gyration, circling, wheeling, spiralling; circulation; circumrotation; rolling 285 *progression*; spiral, roll, spin, flat s.; turn, twirl, pirouette, waltz 837 *dance*; whirl; dizzy round, rat race, milk round 678 *overactivity.*

vortex, whirl; whirlwind, tornado, cyclone 352 *gale*; waterspout, whirlpool, swirl 350 *eddy*; whirlpool bath, Jacuzzi (tdmk); maelstrom, Charybdis; smoke ring 250 *loop.*

rotator, rotor, spinner; whirligig, top, spinning t., humming t.; merry-go-round; churn, whisk; potter's wheel, lathe, circular saw; spinning wheel, spinning jenny; catherine wheel; flywheel, roulette w., wheel of Fortune 250 *wheel*; Hula Hoop; gyroscope, turntable; gramophone record, disc, magnetic tape, cassette, compact disc; wind pump, windmill, fan, sail; propeller, prop, screw; turbine; winder, capstan; swivel, hinge; spit, jack; spindle, axle, axis, shaft 218 *pivot*; spool, reel, roller 252 *cylinder*; rolling stone, planet, satellite 268 *wanderer.*

Vb. *rotate,* revolve, orbit, go into orbit 314 *circle*; turn right round, chase one's own tail; spin, twirl, pirouette; corkscrew 251 *twine*; gyrate, waltz, wheel; whirl, hum 404 *resound*; mill around, swirl, eddy 350 *flow*; bowl, trundle; roll, roll along; twirl, twiddle, twizzle; churn, whisk 43 *mix*; turn, crank, wind, reel, spool, spin; slew, slew round, swing round, swivel r.; roll up, furl 261 *fold*; roll itself up, curl up.

316 Evolution: motion in a reverse circle –
N. *evolution,* unrolling, unfolding, unfurling; development 157 *growth*; evolutionism, Darwinism 358 *biology.*

Vb. *evolve,* unfold, unfurl, unroll, unwind, uncoil, uncurl, untwist, untwine, disentangle; develop, grow into 147 *be turned to*, 1 *become*; roll back 263 *open.*

317 Oscillation: reciprocating motion –
N. *oscillation,* harmonic motion, pendular m., swing of the pendulum; vibration, tremor; vibrancy, resonance 141 *periodicity*; pulsation, rhythm; throbbing, drumming, pulse, beat, throb; pitter-patter, flutter, palpitation 318 *agitation*; breathing 352 *respiration*; undulation, wave motion, frequency, frequency band, wavelength 417 *radiation*; sound wave, radio w.; tidal w. 350 *wave*; seismic disturbance, earthquake, tremor 176 *violence*; seismology, seismograph; oscillator, vibrator; metronome; pendulum, bob, yoyo 217 *hanging object.* See *fluctuation.*

fluctuation, wave motion (**see** *oscillation*); alternation, reciprocation 12 *correlation*; to and fro movement, coming and going, shuttling; ups and downs, boom and bust, ebb and flow, flux and reflux; night and day 14 *contrariety*; rolling, pitching; roll, pitch, lurch, shake, nod, wag; swing, seesaw; shuttle; wavering, vacillation 601 *irresolution.*

Vb. *oscillate,* emit waves 417 *radiate*; wave, undulate; vibrate, pulsate, pulse, beat, drum; tick, throb, palpitate; pant, heave 352 *breathe*; play, sway, nod; swing, dangle 217 *hang*; seesaw, rock; lurch, stagger, totter, teeter, waddle, wobble, wiggle, waggle, wag; bob, bounce, bob up and down, dance 312 *leap*; toss, roll, pitch; rattle, chatter, shake; flutter, quiver, shiver 318 *be agitated*; flicker 417 *shine*; echo 404 *resound.* See *fluctuate.*

fluctuate, alternate, reciprocate 12 *correlate*; ebb and flow, come and go, pass and repass, shuttle.

brandish, wave, wag, waggle, shake, flourish; wave to and fro, shake up and down; flutter 318 *agitate.*

Adv. *to and fro,* backwards and forwards, back and forth; in and out, up and

down, side to side; zigzag, seesaw, like a yoyo; shuttlewise.

318 Agitation: irregular motion – N. *agitation,* jerkiness, fits and starts, unsteadiness, shakiness 152 *changeableness*; joltiness, bumpiness, choppiness, pitching, rolling 259 *roughness*; flicker, twinkle 417 *flash*; start, jump 508 *lack of expectation*; hop 312 *leap*; shake, toss 287 *propulsion*; shock, jar, jolt, jerk, judder, bounce, bump 279 *impulse*; nudge, dig, jog 547 *gesture*; vibration, thrill, throb, pulse, pit-a-pat, palpitation, flutter 317 *oscillation*; shuddering, shudder, shiver, frisson; quiver, quaver, tremor; tremulousness, trembling (**see** *spasm*); restlessness, feverishness, fever; tossing, turning; jiving, rock 'n roll, breakdancing 678 *activity,* 837 *dancing*; itchiness, itch 378 *formication*; twitchiness, twitch, grimacing, grimace; perturbation, disquiet 825 *worry*; trepidation, jumpiness, twitter, flap, butterflies, collywobbles 854 *nervousness*; delirium tremens, dt's, the shakes; Parkinson's disease, Parkinsonism; shivers, jumps, jitters, fidgets.

spasm, ague, shivering, chattering; twitch, tic, nervous t.; chorea, St Vitus' dance; lockjaw, tetanus; cramp, the cramps; throe 377 *pang*; convulsion, paroxysm, orgasm 503 *frenzy*; fit, epilepsy 651 *nervous disorders*; pulse, throb 317 *oscillation*; attack, seizure, stroke.

commotion, turbulence, tumult 61 *turmoil*; hurly-burly, hubbub, brouhaha, hassle; fever, flurry, rush, bustle 680 *haste*; furore 503 *frenzy*; fuss, to-do, bother, kerfuffle, shemozzle 678 *restlessness*; racket, din 400 *loudness*; stir, ferment 821 *excitation*; boiling, fermentation, ebullition, effervescence 355 *bubble*; ground swell, heavy sea 350 *wave*;

squall, tempest, thunderstorm, magnetic storm 176 *storm*; whirlpool 315 *vortex*; whirlwind 352 *gale*; disturbance, atmospherics.

Vb. *be agitated,* ripple, boil 355 *bubble*; stir, move, dash; shake, tremble, quiver, quaver, shiver; have a fever, throw a fit, be all of a doodah, be all of a dither; be in a flap; be like a cat on hot bricks; writhe, squirm, twitch 251 *wriggle*; toss, turn, toss about, thresh a.; kick, plunge, rear; flounder, flop, wallow, roll, reel, pitch 317 *fluctuate*; sway 220 *be oblique*; pulse, beat, thrill, vibrate, judder, shudder; wag, waggle, wobble, stagger, lurch, dodder, totter, teeter, dither 317 *oscillate*; whirr, whirl 315 *rotate*; jig around, jig up and down, jump about, hop, bob, bounce, dance 312 *leap*; flicker, twinkle, gutter, sputter 417 *shine*; flap, flutter, twitter, start, jump; throb, pant, palpitate, miss a beat, go pit-a-pat 821 *be excited*; bustle, rush, mill around 61 *rampage*; ramp, roar 891 *be angry*.

agitate, disturb, rumple, ruffle, untidy 63 *derange*; discompose, perturb, worry, hassle, throw into a panic 827 *trouble*; ripple, muddy; stir, stir up 43 *mix*; whisk, whip, beat, churn 315 *rotate*; shake up, shake; wag, waggle, wave, flourish 317 *brandish*; flutter, fly (a flag); jog, joggle, jolt, jounce, nudge, dig; jerk, pluck, twitch.

effervesce, froth, spume, foam, foam at the mouth, bubble up 355 *bubble*; boil, boil over, seethe, simmer, sizzle, spit 379 *be hot*; ferment, work.

Class three

MATTER

Section one: Matter in general

319 Materiality – N. *materiality,* materialness; corporeality, bodiliness; world of nature 3 *substantiality*; physical condition 1 *existence*; plenum 321 *world*; concreteness, tangibility, palpability, solidity 324 *density*; weight 322 *gravity*; personality, individuality 80 *speciality*; embodiment, incarnation, reincarnation, realization, materialization; materialism; worldliness, sensuality 944 *sensualism.*

matter, stuff; prime matter; mass, material, fabric, body, frame 331 *structure*; substance, corpus; flesh, flesh and blood, plasma, protoplasm 358 *organism.*

object, bird in the hand; inanimate object; body, flesh and blood, real person 371 *person*; thing, gadget, gizmo, something, commodity, article, item.

element, principle, nitty-gritty 68 *origin*; the four elements, earth, air, fire, water; factor, ingredient, nuts and bolts 58 *component*; isotope; atom, molecule; elementary particle, electron, neutron, meson, proton, quark 196 *minuteness*; nucleus, nucleon; photon; quantum; ion.

physics, physical science, natural s.; natural history 358 *biology*; chemistry, organic c., inorganic c., physical c.; mechanics, theory of relativity; thermodynamics; electromagnetism; atomic physics, nuclear physics 160 *nucleonics*; applied physics, technology 694 *skill*; natural philosophy 490 *science.*

Adj. *material,* real, natural; solid, concrete, palpable, tangible, weighty; physical, objective, impersonal, clinical, neuter; substantial; incarnate, embodied; corporeal, bodily, fleshly, of flesh and blood, in the flesh, carnal; reincarnated, realized, materialized; materialistic, worldly, unspiritual 944 *sensual.*

Vb. *materialize,* substantiate, objectify 223 *externalize*; realize, body forth; embody, incarnate, personify.

320 Immateriality – N. *immateriality,* unreality 4 *insubstantiality*; incorporeality, disembodiment, intangibility, impalpability, ghostliness, shadowiness; immaterialism, idealism, Platonism; spirituality, otherworldliness; animism; spiritualism 984 *occultism.*

subjectivity, personality, myself, me, yours truly 80 *self*; me generation; ego, id, superego; Conscious, Unconscious; psyche 447 *spirit.*

Adj. *immaterial,* incorporeal; abstract 447 *mental*; aery, ethereal, ghostly, shadowy 4 *insubstantial*; intangible; bodiless, disembodied; unearthly; psychic, astral 984 *psychical*; spiritual, otherworldly 973 *religious.*

321 Universe – N. *universe,* whole; matter; world, globe, creation; cosmos, macrocosm, microcosm; outer space, intergalactic s.; void; big bang theory, steady state t. 68 *start.*

world, wide w., four corners of the earth; earth, mother e.; planet earth, space, globe, sphere; geosphere, biosphere, ecosphere; continental drift 344 *land*; waters of the earth 343 *ocean*; atlas 551 *map*; Old World, New World 184 *region*; Ptolemaic system; personal world 8 *circumstance.*

heavens, sky, ether, celestial sphere, hemisphere; firmament; music of the spheres; aurora borealis, northern lights, aurora australis.

star, heavenly body, celestial b. 420 *luminary*; constellation, Great Bear, Little B., Plough, Big Dipper, Charles' Wain, Cassiopeia's Chair, Pleiades, Orion, Orion's belt, Southern Cross; starlight; blue star, white s., yellow s., red s; double star, binary; multiple star; variable star, cepheid; giant, supergiant, red giant; subgiant, dwarf, red d., white d.; X-ray star, radio s. 417 *radiation*; quasistellar object, quasar, pulsar, neutron star, black hole, white h.; nova, supernova; Pole Star, North Star, Polaris; Pointers; Dog star, Sirius; Star of David,

Star of Bethlehem; Milky Way, Galaxy; star cluster, globular c., galaxy, radio g.; island universe; nebula.

zodiac, signs of the z., Aries (the Ram), Taurus (the Bull), Gemini (the Twins), Cancer (the Crab), Leo (the Lion), Virgo (the Virgin), Libra (the Balance), Scorpio (the Scorpion), Sagittarius (the Archer), Capricornus (the Goat), Aquarius (the Watercarrier), Pisces (the Fishes); cusp.

planet, asteroid, planetoid; Mercury; Venus, morning star, evening s., Lucifer, Vesper, Hesperus; Mars, red planet; Earth, Jupiter, Saturn, Uranus, Neptune, Pluto; comet, wandering star, Halley's comet.

meteor, falling star, shooting s., fireball, bolide; meteorite, aerolite, siderite, chondrite; chondrule; meteoroid; micrometeorite.

sun, day-star, eye of heaven; midnight sun; sunlight, sunshine, sun spot, solar flare, corona; solar wind; Phoebus, Apollo; solar system, Copernican s.

moon, satellite; new moon, waxing moon, waning m., half-m., crescent m., horned m., full m., harvest m., hunter's m.; mock moon; moonscape, crater, mare, rill; Queen of the night, Diana, Phoebe, man in the moon; moonlight, moonshine.

satellite, moon; earth satellite, artificial s., sputnik, weather satellite, communications s., comsat; space station, skylab, space lab; space shuttle 276 *spaceship.*

astronomy, stargazing; satellite tracking; radioastronomy; astrophysics; uranography; astrology, horoscope 511 *divination*; observatory, planetarium; tracking station; telescope, refracting t., reflecting t., Newtonian t., Cassegrainian t., Gregorian t. 442 *telescope*; astronomical telescope, altazimuth, equatorial; transit instrument; radio telescope, parabolic reflector, dish; spectroscope 551 *photography.*

earth sciences, geography, orography, oceanography, physiography, geomorphology, speleology; geology, geodesy, geodetics; hydrology, hydrography.

Adj.*cosmic,* universal, cosmological; interplanetary; galactic, intragalactic; extragalactic.

celestial, heavenly, ethereal, empyreal; starry; sidereal, astral, stellar; solar, zodiacal; lunar, lunate; nebular, nebulous; heliocentric, geocentric; meteoric; equinoctial.

astronomic, astronomical, astrophysical, stargazing, star-watching; astrological, telescopic, spectroscopic.

geographic, geographical, oceanographic, orographical; geological, geomorphic, speleological; geodesic, geodetic, pysiographic; hydrographic, hydrological.

322 Gravity – N.*gravity,* gravitation, force of gravity, gravitational pull; gravity feed; weight, weightiness, heaviness, ponderousness 195 *bulk*; specific gravity; pressure, displacement, sinkage, draught; encumbrance, load, lading, freight; burden; ballast, makeweight, counterpoise; mass, lump 324 *solid body*; plummet 313 *diver.*

weighing, balancing, equipoise 28 *equalization;* weights, avoirdupois weight, troy w., apothecaries' w.; grain, carat, scruple, pennyweight, drachm; ounce, pound, stone, quarter, quintal, hundredweight, ton; milligram, gram, kilogram, kilo; megaton, kiloton; axle load, laden weight.

scales, weighing machine; steelyard, weighbeam; balance, spring b.; bathroom scales, kitchen s., pan, scale, weight; calibrator; platform scale, weighbridge.

Adj. *weighty,* heavy, heavyweight, ponderous; leaden; weighing etc. vb.; cumbersome, cumbrous 195 *unwieldy*; massive 324 *dense*; heavy-handed, heavy-footed, pressing, incumbent, oppressive; weighing, with a weight of; weighted, loaded, laden, charged, burdened; overburdened, overloaded, top-heavy 29 *unequal.*

Vb. *weigh,* balance 28 *be equal*; counterpoise, counterweigh 31 *compensate*; outweigh 34 *predominate*; tip the scales,

turn the s., tip the balance; settle 313 *founder*, 309 *descend*; lie heavy; press, weigh on, weigh one down, oppress, hang like a millstone 311 *lower*; load, cumber 702 *hinder*; find the weight of, put on the scales, lay in the scale 465 *measure*; weigh oneself, stand on the scales.

make heavy, weight, hang weights on; charge, burden, overweight, overburden, overload 193 *load*.

323 Lightness – N. *lightness,* portability; thinness, air, ether 325 *rarity*; buoyancy; volatility 338 *vaporization*; weightlessness; levitation 308 *ascent*; feather, thistledown, cobweb, gossamer; fluff, oose, dust, straw 4 *insubstantial thing*; cork, buoy, lifebelt, life jacket; balloon, bubble; hot air, helium.

leaven, raising agent; ferment, enzyme, barm, yeast, baking-powder, self-raising flour.

Adj. *light,* underweight 307 *deficient*; lightweight, featherweight; portable, handy 196 *little*; light-footed; light on one's feet; having a light touch; weightless, lighter than air; ethereal, airy, gaseous, volatile 325 *rare*; doughy, barmy, yeasty, fermenting, zymotic, enzymic; aerated, frothy, bubbly, sparkling, pétillant, foamy, whipped; floating, buoyed up, buoyant, feathery, cobwebby, fluffy; light as a feather.

Vb. *be light,* buoyant, etc. adj.; levitate, surface, float, swim; drift, waft, glide, be airborne 271 *fly*; soar, hover 308 *ascend*.

lighten, make light, make lighter, lose weight; ease 701 *disencumber*; jettison 300 *empty*; vaporize 340 *aerate*; leaven; raise, levitate 310 *elevate*.

Section two: Inorganic matter

324 Density – N. *density,* solidity, consistency; compactness, solidness, concreteness, thickness, concentration; incompressibility 326 *hardness*; impenetrability, impermeability; indissolubility, indivisibility; coalescence, cohesion, inseparability 48 *coherence*; relative density, specific gravity.

condensation, consolidation, concentration; constipation; thickening etc. vb.; concretion; solidification, consolidation; coagulation, thrombosis; congealment, gelatinization; glaciation; ossification, petrifaction, fossilization; crystallization; sedimentation, precipitation.

solid body, solid; block, mass 319 *matter*; knot, nugget, lump, chunk, dod, burl; condensation, nucleus, hard core; aggregate, conglomerate, concretion; concrete, cement; stone, crystal, hardpan 344 *rock*; precipitate, deposit, sediment, silt, clay, cake, clod, clump; bone, ossicle; gristle, cartilage 329 *toughness*; coagulum, curd, clot, blood-c.; solid mass.

Adj. *dense,* thick; close, heavy, stuffy (air); foggy, murky, smoky, to be cut with a knife; lumpy, clotted, coagulated, curdled; caked, matted, knotted, tangled 48 *cohesive*; consistent, monolithic; firm, close-textured, knotty, gnarled; substantial, massy, massive 322 *weighty*; concrete, solid, set, gelled or jelled, frozen, solidified etc. vb.; crystalline, crystallized; condensed, nucleated; costive, constipated; compact, close-packed, firm-p. 54 *full*; thick, bushy, luxuriant 635 *plentiful*; serried, massed; impenetrable, impermeable, impervious; indivisible.

indissoluble, insoluble, infusible; precipitated, sedimentary.

Vb. *be dense,* - solid etc. adj.; become solid, solidify, consolidate; conglomerate, cement 48 *cohere*; condense, nucleate, thicken; precipitate, deposit; freeze, glaciate 380 *be cold*; set, gell or jell; congeal, coagulate, clot, curdle; cake,

crust; crystallize; fossilize, petrify, ossify 326 *harden*; compact, compress, firm down, contract, squeeze 198 *make smaller*; crowd 74 *bring together*.

325 Rarity – N. *rarity,* low pressure, vacuum, near v. 190 *emptiness*; compressibility, sponginess 327 *softness*; tenuity, fineness 206 *thinness*; lack of substance 4 *insubstantiality*, 323 lightness; incorporeality, ethereality 320 *immateriality*; airiness, ether, gas 336 *gaseousness*, 340 *air*; rarefaction, expansion, dilatation, attenuation.

Adj. *rare,* tenuous, thin, fine, subtle, flimsy, airy, airy-fairy, slight 4 *insubstantial*; low-pressure, uncompressed; spongy 328 *elastic*; rarefied, aerated 336 *gaseous*; void, hollow 190 *empty*; ethereal, aery 323 *light*; incorporeal 320 *immaterial*; wispy, straggly 75 *unassembled*.

Vb. *rarefy,* reduce the pressure, expand, dilate; make a vacuum, hermetically seal, pump out, exhaust 300 *empty*; attenuate, refine, thin; dilute, adulterate 163 *weaken*; gasify 338 *vaporize*.

326 Hardness – N. *hardness,* intractability, intransigence, resistance 329 *toughness*; starchiness, stiffness, rigour, rigidity, inflexibility; inelasticity; firmness, callosity, callousness, lumpiness, nodosity, nodularity; grittiness, stoniness, rockiness, cragginess; grit, stone, pebble, boulder; flint, silica, quartz, granite, marble, diamond 344 *rock*; adamant, metal, duralumin; steel, iron, wrought i., cast i.; nails, hardware, stoneware; cement, concrete, reinforced c., brick; block, board, heartwood, duramen; hardwood, teak, oak, heart of o. 366 *wood*; bone, gristle, cartilage; spine, backbone; lump, nodule, callosity, callus, corn, wart; horn, ivory; crust, shell, hard s.; hard core, hard centre, jaw-breaker; brick wall; stiffener, starch, wax; whalebone, corset, splint 218 *prop*; ossification, sclerosis, hardening of the arteries.

Adj. *hard,* adamantine; indestructible, unbreakable 162 *strong*; shatterproof, fortified, armoured, armour-plated; steeled, proof; iron, cast-i.; steel, steely; hard as iron, hard as steel, hard as stone, rock-hard; sun-baked; stony, rocky, flinty; gritty, gravelly, pebbly; granitic; crystalline, vitreous, glassy; horny; calloused; bony; gristly 329 *tough*; hardened, tempered, case-hardened; vitrified, petrified, fossilized, ossified; icy, frozen.

rigid, stubborn, resistant, intractable, unmalleable, intransigent; firm, inflexible, unbending 162 *unyielding*; starchy, starched; boned, reinforced; muscle-bound 695 *clumsy*; braced, tense, taut, tight, set, solid; crisp 330 *brittle*; stiff, stiff as a poker, stiff as a board.

Vb. *harden,* render hard etc. adj.; steel 162 *strengthen*; temper, vulcanize, toughen; crisp, bake 381 *heat*; petrify, fossilize, ossify; calcify, vitrify, crystallize 324 *be dense*; set, gell *or* jell, glaciate, freeze 382 *refrigerate*; stiffen, back, bone, starch, wax (a moustache), tauten 45 *tighten*.

327 Softness – N. *softness,* tenderness; pliableness etc. adj.; compliance 739 *obedience*; pliancy, pliability, flexibility, plasticity, ductility, tractability; malleability, adaptability; suppleness, litheness; springiness, suspension 328 *elasticity*; impressibility, doughiness 356 *pulpiness*; sponginess, flaccidity, flabbiness, floppiness; laxity, looseness 354 *semiliquidity*; sogginess, squelchiness, marshiness, bogginess 347 *marsh*; downiness; velvetiness; butter, grease, oil, wax, putty, paste, Plasticine (tdmk), clay, dough, soap, plastic; padding, foam-filling, wadding, pad 227 *lining*; cushion, pillow, armchair, feather bed 376 *euphoria*; velvet, plush, down, thistledown, fluff, fleece 259 *hair*; feathers 259 *plumage*; snow, snowflake 323 *lightness*.

Adj. *soft,* tender 301 *edible*; melting 335 *fluid*; giving, yielding, compressible; springy, sprung 328 *elastic*; pneumatic, foam-filled, cushiony, padded, podgy;

impressible, waxy, doughy, spongy, soggy, mushy, squelchy, boggy 347 *marshy*; juicy, overripe; fleecy; turfy, mossy, grassy; velvety, silky 258 *smooth*; unstiffened, unstarched, limp; flaccid, flabby, floppy; unstrung, relaxed, slack, loose; soft as butter, soft as wax, soft as soap, soft as down, soft as velvet, soft as silk; tender as a chicken; softening, emollient.

flexible, bendable; pliant, pliable, putty-like; ductile, tractile, malleable, tractable, mouldable, plastic; stretchable 328 *elastic*; lithe, willowy, supple, lissom, limber, loose-limbed, double-jointed; acrobatic.

Vb. *soften*, tenderize; mellow 669 *mature*; oil, grease 334 *lubricate*; knead, massage, mash, pulp, squash 332 *pulverize*; macerate, marinade, steep 341 *drench*; melt, thaw 337 *liquefy*; cushion, featherbed; relax, unstring 46 *disunite*; yield, give, give way, relax, loosen up, hang loose 328 *be elastic*.

328 Elasticity – N. *elasticity*, give, stretch; spring, springiness; suspension; stretchability, tensibility; resilience, bounce 280 *recoil*; buoyancy, rubber, india r., foam r.; caoutchouc, guttapercha; elastic; elastic band, rubber band, rubber ball; stretch jeans; gum, chewing g., bubble g.

Adj. *elastic*, stretchy, stretchable, tensile; rubbery, springy, bouncy, resilient; buoyant; flexible; sprung, well-s.; ductile 327 *soft*.

329 Toughness – N. *toughness*, durability, survivability, infrangibility 162 *strength*; tenacity, cohesion 48 *coherence*; viscidity 354 *semiliquidity*; leatheriness, inedibility, indigestibility; leather, gristle, cartilage 326 *hardness*.

Adj. *tough*, durable; strong-fibred 162 *strong*; tenacious, retentive, clinging, sticky 48 *cohesive*; viscid 354 *semiliquid*; infrangible, unbreakable, indestructible, shockproof, shatter-proof; vulcanized,

toughened, strengthened; weather-beaten; hardboiled, overdone; stringy, sinewy, woody, fibrous; gristly, cartilaginous; rubbery, leathery, tough as old boots *or* shoe leather; chewy, indigestible, inedible; stubborn 326 *rigid*.

330 Brittleness – N. *brittleness*, crispness etc. adj.; frangibility; friableness, crumbliness 332 *powderiness*; fissility 46 *scission*; laminability, flakiness; fragility, frailty, flimsiness 163 *weakness*; eggshell, matchwood, shale, slate; glass, porcelain 381 *pottery*. greenhouse,

Adj. *brittle*, breakable, frangible; inelastic 326 *rigid*; fragile, papery, parchment like; splintery; friable, crumbly 332 *powdery*; crisp, flaky, laminable; fissile, splitting; frail, flimsy, eggshell 163 *weak*.

331 Structure. Texture – N. *structure*, organization, pattern, plan; complex, syndrome 52 *whole*; build 243 *form*; constitution, make-up, set-up, content, substance 56 *composition*; construction, make, works, workings, nuts and bolts; architecture; fabric, brickwork, stonework, woodwork, timberwork 631 *materials*; infrastructure, superstructure 164 *edifice*; scaffold, framework, chassis, shell 218 *frame*; infilling 303 *insertion*; lamination, cleavage; body, carcass, physique, anatomy 358 *organism*; skeleton, anatomy, physiology, histology 358 *biology*.

texture, tissue, fabric, stuff 222 *textile*; staple, denier 208 *fibre*; web, weave, warp and woof, warp and weft 222 *weaving*; nap, pile 259 *hair*; grain, grit; fineness of grain 258 *smoothness*; coarseness of grain 259 *roughness*; surface 223 *exteriority*; feel 378 *touch*.

Adj. *textural*, textile, woven 222 *crossed*; fine-woven, close-w.; ribbed, twilled; grained, granular; fine-grained, silky, satiny 258 *smooth*; coarse-grained, gritty 259 *rough*; fine, cobwebby, filmy; coarse, rough, homespun, tweedy 259 *hairy*.

332 Powderiness – N. *powderiness,* friability, crumbliness 330 *brittleness*; dustiness 649 *dirt*; sandiness, grittiness; granulation; friability, crumbliness 330 *brittleness*; pulverization, attrition, attenuation, disintegration, erosion 51 *decomposition*; grinding, milling; abrasion, filing 333 *friction*; fragmentation 46 *disunion*; sprinkling, dusting, powdering, frosting.

powder, face p., foot p., talcum p.; talc, chalk; pollen, spore; dust, coaldust, soot, ash 649 *dirt*; icing sugar, flour, cornflour, farina, arrowroot, starch; grist, meal, bran; sawdust, filings; efflorescence, flowers; scurf, dandruff; debris, detritus 41 *leavings*; sand, grit, gravel, shingle; grain, seed, crumb 53 *piece*; granule, speck 33 *small thing*; flake, snowflake; smut, smoke; dust cloud; fog, smog 355 *cloud*; sandstorm, dust storm 176 *storm*.

pulverizer, miller, grinder; roller, crusher, masher, atomizer; mill, millstone, muller, quern, quernstone; pestle, pestle and mortar; hand mill, coffee m., pepper m.; grater, grindstone, file; abrasive, sandpaper, emery paper, emery board; molar 256 *tooth*; chopper 256 *sharp edge*; sledgehammer 279 *hammer*; bulldozer 279 *ram*.

Adj. *powdery,* chalky, dusty, sooty, smoky 649 *dirty*; sandy 342 *dry*; farinaceous, floury; granulated, granular; gritty, gravelly; flaky, efflorescent; ground, sifted, sieved; crumbly, friable 330 *brittle*.

Vb. *pulverize,* powder, reduce to p.; granulate; crush, mash, smash, shatter, fragment, disintegrate 46 *break*; grind, mill, mince, beat, bruise, pound; crumble; crunch, scrunch 301 *chew*; abrade 333 *rub*; erode 51 *decompose*.

333 Friction – N. *friction,* frictional force, drag 278 *slowness*; rubbing etc. vb.; attrition, rubbing against, rubbing together 279 *collision*; rubbing out, erasure 550 *obliteration*; abrasion, excoriation, scraping; filing 332 *powderiness*; wearing away, erosion 165 *destruction*; scrape, graze, scratch; brushing, rub; polish, elbow grease; massage, facial m., cosmetic scrub, exfoliator, exfoliant, facial 843 *beautification*; pumice stone; eraser, rubber, rosin; whetstone.

Vb. *rub,* rub against, strike (a match); gnash, grind; fret, fray, chafe; graze, scratch, bark, take the skin off 655 *wound*; rub off, abrade, excoriate; skin, flay; scuff, scrape, scrub, scour, burnish; brush, rub down, towel, curry, currycomb 648 *clean*; polish, buff 258 *smooth*; rub out, erase 550 *obliterate*; erode, wear away 165 *consume*; rasp, file, grind 332 *pulverize*; shampoo, massage; rub in; anoint 334 *lubricate*; wax, rosin, chalk (one's cue); catch, stick; rub gently, stroke 889 *caress*; iron 258 *smooth*.

334 Lubrication – N. *lubrication,* greasing; anointment, unction, oiling etc. vb.; lubricity 357 *unctuousness*; nonfriction 258 *smoothness*.

lubricant, graphite, plumbago, black lead; glycerine, wax, grease, axle g. 357 *oil*; soap, lather 648 *cleanser*; saliva, spit, spittle; ointment, salve 658 *balm*; emollient, lenitive 357 *unguent*; lubricator, oil-can, grease-gun.

Vb. *lubricate,* oil, grease, wax, soap, lather; butter 357 *grease*; anoint.

335 Fluidity – N. *fluidity,* fluidness, liquidity, liquidness; wateriness, rheuminess 339 *water*; juiciness, sappiness 356 *pulpiness*; haemophilia; solubility, solubleness, liquescence 337 *liquefaction*; gaseous character 336 *gaseousness*; viscosity 354 *semiliquidity*; fluid mechanics.

fluid, liquid; water, running w. 339 *water*; drink 301 *draught*; milk, whey; juice, sap, latex; humour, chyle, rheum, mucus, saliva 302 *excrement*; serum, lymph, plasma; pus, matter, gore (see *blood*); hydrocele, dropsy 651 *disease*.

blood, lifeblood 360 *life*; bloodstream, circulation; red blood 162 *vitality*; blue blood 868 *nobility*; blood of the gods; gore; clot, blood c., coagulation 324 *solid*

body; corpuscle, red c., white c., platelet; lymph, plasma, serum, blood s.; haemoglobin, haematosis; blood group, Rhesus factor; blood count; haematology; blood transfusion; haemophilia, anaemia, leukaemia, AIDS.

Adj. liquid, in suspension; uncoagulated, unclotted, clarified; soluble, liquescent, melting; viscous 354 *viscid*; fluent, running 350 *flowing*; runny, rheumy 339 *watery*; serous; suppurating 653 *toxic*. *haematic*, sanguineous, haemic, haemal; serous, lymphatic, plasmatic; bloody, sanguinary; gory, bleeding; haemophilic, haemolytic.

336 Gaseousness – N. *gaseousness,* vaporousness etc adj.; windiness, flatulence 352 *wind*; aeration, gasification; volatility 338 *vaporization*; aerostatics, aerodynamics.

gas, vapour, ether 340 *air*; effluvium, exhalation, miasma 298 *egress*; flatus 352 *wind*; fumes, reek, smoke; steam, water vapour 355 *cloud*; laughing gas, coal g., natural g., North Sea g., methane 385 *fuel*; marsh gas, poison g. 659 *poison*; damp, after-d., black d., choke d., fire d.; gasbag; balloon 276 *airship*; gasworks, gas plant, gasification p. 687 *workshop*; gasometer 632 *storage*; gaslight, neon light 420 *lamp*; gas stove, gas cooker 383 *furnace*; gas meter 465 *meter*.

Adj. gaseous, gasiform; vaporous, steamy, volatile 338 *vaporific*; aerial, airy, aeriform, ethereal 340 *airy*; carbonated, effervescent, pétillant 355 *bubbly*; gassy, windy, flatulent; effluvial, miasmic; pneumatic, aerostatic, aerodynamic.

Vb. gasify, steam, emit vapour 338 *vaporize*; let off steam, blow off s. 300 *emit*; oxygenate 340 *aerate*; carbonate; hydrogenate, hydrogenize.

337 Liquefaction – N. *liquefaction,* liquidization; fluidization; solubility, deliquescence 335 *fluidity*; fusion 43 *mixture*; dissolution; thaw, melting 381

heating; solvent, dissolvent, flux; liquefier, liquefacient; liquidizer; anticoagulant 658 *antidote*.

solution, decoction, infusion; aqua; suspension; flux, lye.

Vb. liquefy, liquidize, unclot, clarify; liquate, dissolve, deliquesce, run 350 *flow*; unfreeze, thaw, melt, smelt 381 *heat*; render, clarify; leach; fluidize.

338 Vaporization – N. *vaporization,* gasification; exhalation 355 *cloud*; evaporation, volatilization, distillation, sublimation; steaming, fumigation, vapourability, volatility; atomization.

vaporizer, evaporater; atomizer, spray, aerosol; retort, still, distillery, vaporimeter.

Adj. vaporific, volatilized etc. vb.; reeking; vapouring, steaming etc. vb.; vaporous, vapoury, vapourish; steamy, gassy, smoky; evaporable, volatile.

Vb. vaporize, evaporate; 336 *gasify*; volatilize, distil, sublimate, exhale, transpire, emit vapour, blow off steam 300 *emit*; smoke, fume, reek, steam; fumigate, spray; atomize.

339 Water – N. *water,* H_2O; heavy water D_2O; hard water, soft w.; drinking water, tap w., Adam's ale; mineral w., soda w. 301 *soft drink*; water vapour, steam 355 *cloud*; rain water 350 *rain*; spring water, running w., fresh w. 350 *stream*; holy water 988 *ritual object*; weeping, tears 836 *lamentation*; sweat, saliva 335 *fluid*; high water, high tide, spring t., neap t., low water 350 *wave*; standing water, still w., stagnant w. 346 *lake*; sea water, salt w., brine, briny 343 *ocean*; water cure, taking the waters, hydrotherapy, hydropathy 658 *therapy*; bath water, bath, tub, Jacuzzi (tdmk), shower, douche, splash 648 *ablutions*; lotion, lavender water 843 *cosmetic*; diluent, adulteration, dilution 655 *impairment*; wateriness, damp, humidity, wet; watering; jug, ewer 194 *vessel*; tap, faucet, standpipe, hydrant 351 *conduit*; waterer, hose 341 *irrigator*; water supply, waterworks;

hot spring, geyser; well, Artesian w., borehole 632 *store*; hydrometry.

Adj. *watery,* aqueous, aquatic, lymphatic 335 *fluid*; hydrated, hydrous; hydrological, hydrographic 321 *geographic*; adulterated, diluted, 163 *weak*; wet, moist, drenching 341 *humid*; hydrotherapeutic; sudorific 658 *medical.*

340 Air – **N.** *air 336 gas;* thin air, ether 325 *rarity*; air pocket 190 *emptiness*; blast 352 *wind*; oxygen, nitrogen, argon; welkin, blue, blue sky 355 *cloud*; open air, open, out of doors, exposure 183 *space*; sea air, ozone; fresh air, country a., smokeless zone 648 *cleanness*; airing 342 *desiccation*; aeration 338 *vaporization*; fanning 352 *ventilation*; air-conditioning, air-cooling 382 *refrigeration*; ventilator, blower, fan, air-conditioner 384 *refrigerator*; air-filter 648 *cleanser*; humidifier, vaporizer, atomizer, ionizer 341 *moisture.*

atmosphere, troposphere, tropopause, stratosphere, ionosphere; mesosphere, exosphere; aerosphere; aerospace; greenhouse effect 381 *heating.*

weather, the elements; fine weather; balmy days, halcyon days; dry spell, heat wave, Indian summer 379 *heat*; doldrums; atmospheric pressure, anticyclone, high pressure; cyclone, depression, low pressure; rough weather 176 *storm*, 352 *gale*; bad weather, foul w., wet w. 350 *rain*; cold weather 380 *wintriness*; changeable weather; meteorology; weather forecast 511 *prediction*; isobar; glass, mercury, barometer; vane, weathervane, weathercock; hygrometer; weather ship, weather station, rain gauge; weatherman *or* -woman, meteorologist; climate, microclimate; climatology, climatography; climatologist.

Adj. *airy,* ethereal 4 *insubstantial*; aerial; pneumatic, aerated, oxygenated; inflated, blown up; flatulent 336 *gaseous*; breezy 352 *windy*; well-ventilated, fresh,

air-conditioned 382 *cooled*; meteorological, weather-wise; atmospheric, barometric; cyclonic, anticyclonic; high-pressure 324 *dense*; low-pressure 325 *rare*; climatic, climatological.

Vb. *aerate,* oxygenate; air, expose 342 *dry*; ventilate, freshen 648 *clean*; fan, winnow, make a draught 352 *blow*; take the air 352 *breathe.*

Adv. *alfresco,* out of doors, in the open air, en plein air, in the open.

341 Moisture – **N.** *moisture,* humidity, sap, juice 335 *fluid*; dampness, wetness, moistness, dewiness; dew point; dankness, condensation, rising damp; sogginess, swampiness, marshiness, bogginess; saturation, saturation point 54 *plenitude*; leakiness 298 *outflow*; raininess, showeriness; rainfall, high r., wet weather 350 *rain*; damp, wet; spray, spindrift, froth, foam 355 *bubble*; mist, haar, fog, fog bank 355 *cloud*; Scotch mist, drizzle, smirr, drip, dew, morning d.; drop, droplet, raindrop, dewdrop, teardrop; tears 836 *lamentation*; saliva, salivation, slabber, slobber, spit, spittle 302 *excrement*; ooze, slime, mud, squelch, fen, bog 347 *marsh*; sop.

irrigator, sprinkler, waterer, watercart; watering can; spray, rose; hose, garden h., syringe, squirt; pump, fire engine; shadoof, Archimedes' screw; water butt, dam, reservoir 632 *store*; catheter; sluice, water pipe, qanat 351 *conduit.*

Adj. *humid,* moistened, wet 339 *watery*; pluvial; drizzling, drizzly; damp, moist, dripping; dank, muggy, foggy, misty 355 *cloudy*; steaming, reeking; undrained, oozy, muddy, slimy, sloppy, slushy, squashy, squelchy, splashy, plashy, fenny, boggy 347 *marshy*; dewy, fresh, bedewed; juicy, sappy 335 *fluid*; dribbling, seeping, percolating; wetted, steeped, soaked, sprinkled.

Vb. *be wet,* - moist etc. adj.; be soaking wet, be wringing wet; be soaking, be sopping; squelch; slobber, salivate, sweat, perspire 298 *exude*; steam, reek 300 *emit*; percolate, seep 297 *infiltrate*; weep, bleed, stream; ooze, drip, leak;

trickle, smirr, drizzle, smirr, rain, pour, rain cats and dogs 350 *rain*; get wet, get wet through, get drenched, dip, duck; bathe, wash, shower, douche; paddle.

moisten, humidify, wet, dampen; dilute, hydrate; lick, lap, wash; splash, splatter; spill, slop; flood, spray, shower, spatter, bespatter, sprinkle, besprinkle, syringe; bedew.

drench, saturate, imbue; soak, deluge, wet through; leach; wash, bathe, shower, douche; hose down, sluice, slosh, rinse 648 *clean*; baptize 988 *perform ritual*; plunge, dip, duck, submerge, drown 303 *immerse*; swamp, flood, inundate, flood out, waterlog; dunk, douse, souse, steep; macerate, marinate.

irrigate, water, hose, pump; flood, submerge; percolate 297 *infiltrate*; squirt, inject, douche.

342 Dryness – N. *dryness,* aridity; thirst 859 *hunger*; drought, drouth, low rainfall, sandiness, desertification, desertization 172 *desert*; dry climate, dry season; sun, sunniness 379 *heat*.

desiccation, drying, drying up; airing, evaporation 338 *vaporization*; draining, drainage, catheterization; dehydration, sunning 381 *heating*; withering, searing 426 *achromatism*.

dryer, dehydrator, desiccator, evaporator; dehydrant, siccative, silica gel, sand, blotting paper; absorbent; mop, swab, sponge, towel, towelling; paper towel, kitchen t., tissue, toilet roll; hair drier, hand d., spin d., tumble d.; wringer, mangle; airer, clotheshorse 217 *hanger*; airing cupboard.

Adj. *dry,* thirsty 859 *hungry*; arid; sandy, dusty, desertized 332 *powdery*; bare, brown; desert, Saharan; dehydrated, desiccated; shrivelled, withered, seared, sere; dried up, parchment-like; sunned; aired; sun-dried, wind-d.; burnt, scorched, baked, parched 379 *hot*; sunny, fine, cloudless, fair; dried out, drained, evaporated; squeezed dry,

wrung out, mangled; waterproofed, waterproof, rainproof, showerproof, dampproof; watertight; high and dry; dry as a bone.

Vb. *dry,* dehumidify, desiccate, freezedry; dehydrate; drain, catheterize, pump out, suck dry 300 *empty*; wring out, mangle; spin-dry, tumble-d., drip-d.; hang out, peg o., air, evaporate 338 *vaporize*; sun, expose to sunlight, solarize, sundry; smoke, kipper, cure; parch, scorch, bake, burn 381 *heat*; sere, sear, shrivel, wither; mummify 666 *preserve*; dry up, stop the flow, apply a tourniquet 350 *staunch*; blot, blot up, mop, mop up, soak up, sponge 299 *absorb*; swab, wipe, wipe up, wipe dry.

343 Ocean – N. *ocean,* sea, blue, salt water, brine, briny; waters, billows, waves, tide 350 *wave*; Davy Jones's locker; main, deep, deep sea; high seas, great waters; trackless deep, watery waste; herring pond, drink; sea lane, shipping lane; ocean floor, sea bed, sea bottom, ooze, benthos; the seven seas; Atlantic Ocean, Pacific O., Indian O., Arctic O., Antarctic O., Red Sea, Mediterranean, Baltic, North Sea, Irish S., Caspian S., Black S., Caribbean S., Tasman S., Bering S., Dead S., Barents S., Beaufort S., Tethys.

sea god, Oceanus, Neptune, Poseidon, Triton; Nereus, merman 970 *mythical being*.

sea nymph, Oceanid, Nereid, siren; Amphitrite, Thetis; Calypso, Undine; mermaid; bathing beauty; water sprite 970 *fairy*.

344 Land – N. *land,* dry l., terra firma; earth, ground, earth's crust 321 *world*; continent, mainland; heartland, hinterland; midland, inland, interior 224 *interiority*; peninsula, delta, promontory 254 *projection*; isthmus; terrain, heights, highlands 209 *high land*; lowlands 210 *lowness*; reclaimed land, polder; steppe, fields 348 *plain*; wilderness 172 *desert*; oasis; isle 349 *island*; zone, clime; country, district, tract 184 *region*; territory,

possessions, acres, estate, real e. 777 *lands*; landscape.

shore, coastline 233 *outline*; coast 234 *edge*; strand, beach, sands, shingle; seaboard, seashore, seaside; sea cliff, sea wall; plage, lido, riviera; marina; bank, river bank, riverside; continental shelf.

soil, farmland, arable land 370 *farm*; pasture 348 *grassland*; deposit, moraine, loess, silt, alluvium; topsoil, sand, dust, subsoil; mould, leaf m., humus; loam, clay, bole, marl; Fuller's earth; argil, potter's clay, china clay, kaolin 381 *pottery*; gravel; stone, pebble, flint; turf, sod, clod 53 *piece*.

rock, cliff, scar, crag; stone, boulder; reef; stack, skerry; dyke, sill; igneous rock, plutonic r., granite, basalt; volcanic rock; lava; sedimentary rock, sandstone, shale, limestone, chalk; schist, marble; ore 359 *mineralogy*; precious stone, semi-p. s. 844 *gem*.

345 Gulf: inlet – N. *gulf,* bay, bight, cove, creek, lagoon; slough; natural harbour, road, roadstead; inlet, outlet, fleet, bayou; fjord, sea loch; ria; mouth, estuary; firth, frith, kyle; sound, strait, channel.

346 Lake – N. *lake,* lagoon; loch, lough, linn; fresh-water lake, salt l.; Dead Sea; oxbow lake, bayou l.; broads; sheet of water, standing w., stagnant w., backwater; mud flat, wash 347 *marsh*; pool, tarn, mere, pond, dewpond; fishpond, stew; millpond; artificial lake, dam, reservoir 632 *storage*; well 339 *water*; waterhole, puddle.

347 Marsh – N. *marsh,* morass; marshland; flat, mud f., salt marsh; fen, fenland, bog, peat b., quagmire, quicksand; saltpan; mudhole, slough, mire, mud; swamp, swampland, mangrove swamp; Slough of Despond.

Adj. *marshy,* paludal; swampy, boggy, fenny; quaggy; squelchy, spongy 327 *soft*; slushy; muddy, miry 649 *dirty*; waterlogged.

348 Plain – N. *plain,* peneplain; dale, levels 216 *horizontality*; lowlands 255 *valley*; flats 347 *marsh*; delta, alluvial plain; sands, desert s., waste 172 *desert*; tundra; ice field, ice floe 380 *ice*; grasslands, steppe, prairie, pampas, savanna, llanos, campos; heath, common, wold, downland, downs, moor, moorland, fell; upland, plateau, tableland 209 *high land*; bush, veld, range 183 *space*; fields, green belt, parkland, national park, safari p. 263 *open space*; lowlands, low countries 210 *lowness*.

grassland, pasture, pasturage, grazing 369 *animal husbandry*; sheeprun, sheep track, sheep walk; field, meadow, mead, lea; chase, park, grounds; green, greensward, lawn, turf.

349 Island – N. *island,* isle, islet, skerry; eyot, inch, holm; atoll, reef, coral r.; cay, key; sandbank; iceberg, ice floe; peninsula; archipelago; insularity.

350 Stream: water in motion – N. *stream,* running water, watercourse, river, subterranean r.; waterway; tributary, branch, streamlet, rivulet, brook, bourne, burn, rill, beck, gill, runnel, runlet; freshet, torrent; wadi; spring, fountain, fountainhead, headwaters 156 *source*; jet, spout, gush; geyser, hot spring, well 632 *store*.

current, flow, flux 285 *progression*; effluence 298 *egress*; confluence 293 *convergence*; inflow 297 *ingress*; outflow, reflux 286 *regression*; undercurrent, undertow, crosscurrent 182 *counteraction*; tide, spring t., neap t.; tidal flow, tidal current, ebb and flow 317 *fluctuation*; bore, eagre; tidal race; millrace, millstream; bloodstream.

eddy, whirlpool, swirl, maelstrom 315 *vortex*; whirlpool bath, Jacuzzi (tdmk); wake 67 *sequel*.

waterfall, falls, cataract, Niagara, Victoria; linn, cascade, rapids, weir; water power 160 *sources of energy*.

wave, bow w.; wash, backwash; ripple, cat's-paw 262 *furrow*; swell, ground s.; billow, roller, comber; breaker, surf,

spume, white horses; tidal wave; bore, eagre; choppiness 259 *roughness*; sea, choppy s., waviness, undulation.

rain, rainfall 341 *moisture*; precipitation; drizzle, mizzle, Scotch mist, smirr; sleet, hail 380 *wintriness*; shower, downpour, deluge, cloudburst, thunderstorm 176 *storm*; flurry 352 *gale*; pouring rain, teeming r., driving r., torrential r., sheets of rain; raininess, wet spell, foul weather; rainy season, the rains, monsoon; lovely weather for ducks; patter; dripping etc. vb.; rain-making, cloud-seeding; rain gauge.

Adj. *flowing,* falling etc. vb.; runny 335 *fluid*; fluent, riverine, fluvial, tidal; running, coursing, racing; streaming; in flood, overflowing, in spate; flooding, inundatory, cataclysmic; pouring, lashing, driving, dripping, gushing.

VB. *flow,* run, course, pour; ebb 286 *regress*; surge, gush, rush, spirt, spout, spew, play, squirt; well, well up, bubble up, issue 298 *emerge*; pour, stream; trickle, dribble 298 *exude*; drip, drop 309 *descend*; wash, slosh, splash 341 *moisten*; trill, murmur, babble, bubble, burble, gurgle; flow over, cascade, fall, flood, inundate, deluge 341 *drench*; flow into, drain i. 297 *enter*; run off; leak, percolate, pass through 305 *pass*; ooze.

rain, shower, stream, pour, pelt; snow, sleet, hail; fall, come down, bucket, piss down, rain hard, pour with rain, rain cats and dogs; come down in torrents, come down in sheets, come down in stair-rods, rain pitchforks; patter, drizzle, mizzle, smirr, drip, spit, sprinkle; be wet, rain and rain.

staunch, apply a tourniquet; plug 264 *close*; stem, dam, dam up 702 *obstruct*.

351 Conduit – N. *conduit,* water channel, tideway, riverbed; arroyo, wadi; trough, basin, river b.; canyon, ravine, gorge, gully 255 *valley*; inland waterways, canal system; canal, channel, watercourse, qanat; ditch, dike; trench, moat; gutter, mill race; duct, aqueduct; water pipe, water main; pipe, hose, garden h.; standpipe, hydrant, siphon, tap, spout, funnel

263 *tube*; valve, flume, sluice, weir, lock, floodgate, watergate, spillway; chute 350 *waterfall*; oilpipe, pipeline; vein, artery.

drain, gully, gutter, gargoyle, waterspout; overflow, wastepipe, drainpipe 298 *outlet*; culvert; ditch, sewer 649 *sink*; alimentary canal; catheter 300 *voidance*.

352 Wind: air in motion – N. *wind* 340 *air;* draught, downdraught, updraught; blast, blow (see *breeze*, *gale*); air stream, jet s.; current, air c., crosswind, headwind 182 *counteraction*; tailwind, following wind 287 *propellant*; air flow, slip stream; air pocket; cold draught, icy blast; hot wind, sirocco, monsoon, etesian winds; prevailing w., trade w., Roaring Forties; north wind, Boreas, mistral, tramontano; south wind, föhn, chinook; east wind, levanter; west wind, Zephyr, wind god, Aeolus.

breeze, zephyr; breath of air, waft, whiff, puff, gust, light breeze, sough, gentle b., fresh b., sea breeze, cooling b.

gale, high wind; blow, blast, gust, flurry; squall; nor'wester, sou'wester, hurricane, whirlwind, cyclone, tornado, twister, typhoon, simoom 315 *vortex*; thunderstorm, dust storm, sandstorm, dust devil, blizzard 176 *storm*; microburst; gale force.

blowing, insufflation, inflation 197 *dilation*; blowing up, pumping up; pumping out 300 *voidance*; pump, air p., stirrup p., bicycle p.; bellows, windbag, bagpipe; woodwind, brass 414 *musical instrument*; blowpipe; exhaust pipe, exhaust 298 *outlet*.

ventilation, airing 340 *air*; draught; fanning, cooling; ventilator 353 *air pipe*; blower, fan, extractor f., electric f., punkah, air-conditioner, air-conditioning 384 *refrigerator*.

respiration, breathing, inhalation, exhalation, expiration, inspiration; gills, lungs, bellows; respirator, iron lung, oxygen tent; windpipe 353 *air pipe*; sigh, sob, gulp, hiccup, catching of the breath, yawn; panting, gasping, huffing and puffing.

Adj. *windy,* airy, exposed, draughty, breezy, blowy; ventilated, fresh; blowing, gusty, gusting, squally; blustery, stormy, tempestuous, boisterous 176 *violent*; windswept, windblown; storm-tossed, storm-bound; flatulent; fizzy, gassy 336 *gaseous*; aeolian, boreal, zephyrous; cyclonic; gale-force, hurricane f.

Vb. *blow,* puff, blast; insufflate, blow up, get up, blow hard, blow great guns, blow a hurricane, rage, storm; howl, roar 409 *ululate*; screech, scream, whistle, pipe, sing in the shrouds 407 *shrill*; hum, moan, mutter, sough, sigh 401 *sound faint*; wave, flap, shake, flutter, flourish 318 *agitate*; draw, ventilate, fan 382 *refrigerate*; waft 287 *propel*; veer, back 282 *deviate*; die down, subside, drop, abate.

breathe, respire, breathe in, inhale; draw *or* take a deep breath, fill one's lungs; breathe out, exhale; aspirate, puff, huff, huff and puff, whiff; sniff, sniffle, snuffle, snort; breathe hard; gasp, pant, heave; wheeze, sneeze, cough 407 *rasp*; sigh, catch one's breath.

blow up, pump up, inflate, dilate 197 *enlarge*; pump out, exhaust 300 *empty*.

353 Air pipe – **N.** *air pipe,* airway, air shaft, air well; wind tunnel; blowpipe, peashooter 287 *propellant*; windpipe, trachea, larynx; bronchia, bronchus; throat, gullet, oesophagus; nose, nostril, spiracle, blowhole, nozzle, vent, mouthpiece 263 *orifice*; flue pipe, mouth organ 414 *organ*; gas main, gas pipe; tobacco pipe, pipe, briar, hookah 388 *tobacco*; funnel, flue, exhaust pipe.

354 Semiliquidity – **N.** *semiliquidity,* mucosity, viscidity; thickness, stodginess; semiliquid, colloid, emulsion, gore, albumen, mucus, phlegm, clot 324 *solid body*; pus, matter; juice, sap 335 *fluidity*; soup, slop, gruel, cream, curds 356 *pulpiness*; molten lava; oil slick; mud, glaur, slush, sludge, thaw, ooze, slime; silt 347 *marsh*.

thickening, coagulation, clotting 324 *condensation*; gelatinization; emulsification; thickener, starch, arrowroot, flour, cornflour; gelatine, isinglass, pectin.

viscidity, viscosity, glutinousness, stickiness, adhesiveness 48 *coherence*; glue, gluten, gum 47 *adhesive*; emulsion, colloid; glair, size, paste, glaze; gel, jelly; treacle, jam, syrup, honey, goo; wax, mastic 357 *resin*; flypaper.

Adj. *viscid,* viscous, gummy, gooey 48 *cohesive*; slimy, sticky, tacky; jammy, treacly, syrupy, gluey; glairy, glaireous; mucous.

Vb. *thicken,* inspissate, congeal 324 *be dense*; coagulate 48 *cohere*; emulsify; gelatinize, gel, jelly, jell; starch 326 *harden*; curdle, clot; churn, whip up, beat up, mash, pulp 332 *pulverize*.

355 Bubble. Cloud: air and water mixed – **N.** *bubble,* suds, soapsuds, lather, foam, froth; head; sea foam, spume, surf, spray, spindrift 341 *moisture*; mousse, soufflé, meringue, candyfloss; yeast, barm 323 *leaven*; scum 649 *dirt*.

cloud, scud; cloudbank; rain cloud, storm c.; woolpack, cumulus, altocumulus, cirrus, cirrocumulus, stratus, cirrostratus, nimbostratus; mackerel sky, mare's tail; vapour, steam 338 *vaporization*; brume, haze, mist, haar, fog, smog, pea-souper; cloudiness, film 419 *dimness*; nebulosity; nephology, nephoscope.

Adj. *bubbly,* bubbling etc. vb.; effervescent, fizzy, sparkling, pétillant 336 *gaseous*; mousseux, foamy; spumy, spumous; frothy, soapy, lathery; yeasty, aerated 323 *light*; scummy 649 *dirty*.

cloudy, clouded, overcast, nebulous; cirrose, foggy, hazy, misty, filmy, brumous 419 *dim*; steamy 338 *vaporific*.

Vb. *bubble,* spume, foam, froth, cream, form a head; boil, simmer, seethe, fizzle, gurgle 318 *effervesce*; work, ferment, fizz, sparkle; aerate, carbonate; steam 338 *vaporize*.

cloud, cloud over, be cloudy etc. adj.; befog, mist up 419 *be dim*.

356 Pulpiness – N. *pulpiness,* doughiness, sponginess; fleshiness, juiciness, 327 *softness*; poultice, pulp, pith, paste, putty, porridge, pap, puree; mush, mash, squash; dough, batter, sponge; jam 354 *viscidity*; puree, mousse 355 *bubble*; slush, papier mâché, wood pulp.

357 Unctuousness – N. *unctuousness,* unctuosity, oiliness, greasiness, lubricity, soapiness 334 *lubrication*; fattiness; saponification; anointment, unction.

oil, volatile o., essential o.; animal oil, whale o., sperm o., train o., cod-liver o.; vegetable oil, corn o., sunflower o., olive o., coconut o., almond o., linseed o., cotton-seed o., castor o., rape o., groundnut o., palm o., jojoba o.; mineral oil, shale o., rock o., crude o., petroleum; refined oil, coal o.; fuel oil, paraffin, kerosene, petrol, gasoline, gas 385 *fuel*; lubricating oil 334 *lubricant*; bath oil, suntan o.

fat, animal f., grease, adipocere; blubber, tallow, spermaceti; sebum, wax, beeswax; suet, lard, dripping, bacon fat 301 *cookery*; glycerine, stearin, olein; margarine, butter, ghee, spread; cream, Devonshire c., Cornish c.; top of the milk; buttermilk; soap, carbolic s., soft s., toilet s., liquid s., soap flakes, washcream 648 *cleanser*.

unguent, salve, unction, ointment, liniment, embrocation, lanolin; pomade, brilliantine; cream, cold cream 843 *cosmetic*.

resin, rosin, gum, gum arabic, tragacanth, myrrh, frankincense, camphor; lac, amber, ambergris; pitch, tar, bitumen, asphalt; varnish, mastic, shellac, lacquer, japan; epoxy resin; polyurethane, plastics.

Adj. *fatty,* fat, adipose, blubbery, flabby 195 *fleshy*; sebaceous, waxy, waxen; lardaceous; saponaceous, soapy; buttery, creamy, milky, rich 390 *savoury*.

Vb. *grease,* oil, anoint 334 *lubricate*; baste, lard; butter; saponify; resin, rosin.

Section three: Organic matter

358 Organisms: living matter – N. *organism,* organic matter; living beings; animal and vegetable kingdom, flora and fauna, biota; ecosystem; ecotype, biotype 77 *breed*; living matter 360 *life*; microscopic life; cell, protoplasm, cytoplasm, nucleus, nucleolus; nucleic acid, RNA, DNA; chromatin, chromosome, chromatid, gene 5 *heredity*; albumen, protein; enzyme, globulin; organic remains 125 *fossil*.

biology, microbiology; natural history, nature study; biochemistry, biophysics, molecular biology, cell b., cytology; histology; morphology, embryology; anatomy, physiology 331 *structure*; zoography 367 *zoology*; phytography 368 *botany*; ecology, marine biology; genetics, eugenics, genetic engineering; biomedicine; evolution, natural selection, survival of the fittest; Darwinism; biogenesis.

Adj. *biological,* physiological, zoological, palaeontological; biogenetic; evolutionary, Darwinian.

359 Mineral: inorganic matter – N. *mineral,* inorganic matter, earth's crust 344 *rock*; ore, metal, precious m., base m.; alloy 43 *a mixture*; mineralogical deposit, coal measures 632 *store*.

mineralogy, geology, lithology, petrography, petrology; metallurgy, metallography; speleology, glaciology 321 *earth sciences*.

360 Life – N. *life,* living, being 1 *existence*; the living, living being, being, soul, spirit; plant life 366 *vegetable life*; animal life 365 *animality*; human life 371 *humankind*; gift of life, birth, nativity 68 *origin*; renaissance 656 *revival*; life to come, the hereafter 124 *future state*; immortal life 971 *heaven*; animation; vitality, vital force, élan vital, life force; soul 447 *spirit*; will to live, survival, cat's nine lives, longevity 113 *long duration*;

liveliness, animation 819 *moral sensibility*; breathing 352 *respiration*; lifeblood, heart's blood 5 *essential part*; vital spark; heart, artery; staff of life 301 *food*; biological function, parenthood 167 *propagation*; sex, sexual activity 45 *coition*; living matter, protoplasm, living tissue; cell, unicellular organism 358 *organism*; symbiosis 706 *association*; life-support system; lifetime, one's born days; life expectancy, allotted span, life cycle; survivability, viability, viableness 469 *possibility*.

Adj. *alive,* living, quick, live, animate; breathing, alive and kicking; animated 819 *lively*; incarnate, in the flesh; surviving, in the land of the living, above ground, with us, on this side of the grave; long-lived 113 *lasting*; survivable, viable; vital, enlivened.

born, begotten, fathered, sired; mothered, dammed; foaled, dropped; out of, by 11 *akin*; spawned, littered; laid, new-l., hatched.

Vb. *live,* be alive, have life, have being; draw breath 352 *breathe*; exist 1 *be*; come to life, come to, liven up, quicken, revive 656 *be restored*; be spared, survive 41 *be left*; cheat death, have nine lives; live in 192 *dwell*.

be born, come into the world, come into existence, first see the light 68 *begin*; have one's nativity; draw breath; be begotten, be conceived.

vitalize, give birth to, beget, conceive, support life 167 *generate*; vivify, enliven, breathe life into, bring to life 174 *invigorate*; revitalize, give a new lease of life, put new life into, ginger, put zest into, reanimate 656 *revive*; maintain, provide for, keep body and soul together, make ends meet, keep the wolf from the door 301 *feed*.

361 Death – **N.** *death,* no life 2 *extinction*; dying (see *decease*); mortality, ephemerality 114 *transience*; sentence of death, doom, death knell; execution, martyrdom; curtains, deathblow, quietus 362 *killing*; necrosis, mortification 51 *decay*; the beyond, the great divide, crossing the Styx *or* Lethe; eternal rest, long sleep 266 *quietude*; Abraham's bosom 971 *heaven*; the grave 364 *tomb*; jaws of death, shadow of d.; nether regions, Stygian darkness, Hades 972 *hell*; Death, the Grim Reaper, the Great Leveller; Angel of Death; post mortem, autopsy, necroscopy 364 *inquest*; mortuary, charnel house, morgue 364 *cemetery*.

decease, clinical death, brain d., cerebral d.; extinction, exit, demise, curtains 69 *end*; departure, passing, passing away, passing over; natural death, quiet end, euthanasia 376 *euphoria*; welcome end; loss of life, fatality; sudden death, violent d., untimely end; death by drowning, watery grave; death on the roads; accidental death, death by misadventure; fatal disease, terminal illness *or* disease 651 *disease*; dying day, last hour; valley of the shadow of death; deathbed, deathbed repentance, death scene; last gasp, dying breath; swan song, death rattle, rigor mortis 69 *finality*; extreme unction; passing bell 364 *obsequies*.

the dead, forefathers 66 *precursor*; dear departed, souls 968 *saint*; the shades, ghosts, phantoms 970 *ghost*; dead body 363 *corpse*; next world 124 *future state*; world of spirits, netherworld, Styx; Hades, Stygian shore 972 *mythic hell*; Elysian fields, happy hunting grounds, Davy Jones's locker 971 *mythic heaven*.

death roll, mortality, fatality, death toll, death rate; casualty list; death register 87 *list*; death certificate 548 *record*; martyrology; obituary, obit, deaths column, death notice; the dead, the fallen, the lost; casualties, the dead and dying.

Adj. *dying,* expiring etc. vb.; mortal, ephemeral, perishable 114 *transient*; moribund, with one foot in the grave, deathly; all over with, all up with, not long for this world, not long to go; done for, had it; going, slipping away, sinking fast; sick unto death 651 *sick*; on the danger list, in a critical condition, terminally ill, on one's deathbed, at death's door; life hanging by a thread; at the last

gasp; on one's last legs, at the point of death; under sentence of death, doomed.

dead, deceased; passed over, passed away, departed, gone, gone before; dead and gone, dead and buried, in the grave, six feet under; stillborn; lifeless; extinct, bereft of life; cold, stiff; dead as a doornail, dead as a dodo; kaput, done for, gone for a burton; out of one's misery; departed this life, called to one's eternal rest, gathered to one's fathers, in Abraham's bosom, on the other side, beyond the grave; gone to join one's forefathers, gone to the happy hunting-grounds; defunct, late, late-lamented, gone but not forgotten, of sainted memory; martyred, slaughtered, massacred, killed.

Vb. *die (*see *perish);* be dead, lie in the grave, be gone, be no more, cease to be, lose one's life 2 *pass away;* die young, not make old bones; die a natural death, die in one's sleep, die in bed; end one's life, decease; expire, give up the ghost, breathe one's last; close one's eyes, sleep one's last sleep; pass over, be taken; depart this life 296 *depart;* ring down the curtain, shuffle off this mortal coil, go the way of all flesh, go to one's last home; cross the Styx, join the angels, meet one's Maker, reach a better world; croak, peg out, snuff it, cop it, have bought it; cash in one's chips, conk out, pop off, go west, go for a burton, hop the twig, kick the bucket, bite the dust, turn up one's toes, push up the daisies.

perish, die out, become extinct 2 *pass away;* go to the wall 165 *be destroyed;* wither, come to dust 51 *decompose;* meet one's end, meet one's fate; die in harness, die with one's boots on; get killed, be killed, fall in action, lose one's life, be lost; lay down one's life; become a martyr, make the supreme sacrifice; die young, drop down dead; meet a sticky end, die a violent death, break one's neck; bleed to death; drown, go to Davy Jones's locker 313 *founder;* be put to death, walk the plank; commit suicide 362 *kill oneself.*

362 Killing: destruction of life – N. *killing,* slaying 165 *destruction;* taking life; blood sports, hunting, shooting 619 *chase;* blood-shedding, blood-letting; vivisection; cull; mercy killing, euthanasia; murder, assassination, bumping off (**see** *homicide*); poisoning, drowning, suffocation, strangulation, hanging; immolation, sacrifice; martyrdom; crucifixion, execution 963 *capital punishment;* judicial murder, auto da fé, burning alive, the stake; deathblow, coup de grace, quietus; death by misadventure, violent death, fatal accident, death on the roads, car crash, train c., plane crash.

homicide, manslaughter; murder, premeditated m., capital m.; assassination; thuggery; crime passionel 911 *jealousy;* regicide, tyrannicide, parricide, patricide, matricide, uxoricide, fratricide; infanticide, genocide (**see** *slaughter*).

suicide, self-destruction, felo de se; suttee, hara-kiri; parasuicide, attempted suicide; mass suicide, Gadarene swine, lemmings.

slaughter, bloodshed, butchery, carnage; bloodbath, massacre, fusillade, holocaust; pogrom, purge, liquidation, decimation, extermination, annihilation 165 *destruction;* genocide; war, battle 718 *warfare;* Roman holiday, gladiatorial combat 716 *duel.*

killer, slayer; mercy killer 905 *pity;* soldier, guerrilla, urban g. 722 *combatant;* slaughterer, butcher; huntsman 619 *hunter;* trapper, mole-catcher, rat-catcher, pest exterminator; toreador, picador, matador 162 *athlete;* executioner, hangman; homicide (**see** *murderer*); lynch mob; homicidal maniac, psychopath; head-hunter, cannibal; predator, bird of prey, beast of prey, man-eater, insecticide.

murderer, homicide, killer, Cain; assassin, terrorist; poisoner, strangler, garrotter, thug; hatchet man, hitman, gangster, contract killer, gunman; cut-throat 904 *ruffian.*

Adj. *deadly,* killing, lethal; fell, mortal, fatal, deathly; life-threatening, capital; death-bringing, malignant, poisonous

653 *toxic*; asphyxiant, suffocating, stifling; miasmic 653 *insalubrious*; inoperable, incurable, terminal.

murderous, homicidal, genocidal; suicidal, self-destructive; internecine, death-dealing, trigger-happy; sanguinary, bloody, gory, bloodstained, redhanded; bloodthirsty 898 *cruel*; headhunting, man-eating, cannibalistic.

Vb. *kill,* slay, take life, deprive of l.; do in, do for 165 *destroy*; nip in the bud, shorten one's life; put down, put to sleep; hasten one's end, drive to one's death, work to d., put to d., send to the scaffold, hang, behead, guillotine, electrocute, send to the electric chair 963 *execute*; stone to death; string up, lynch; make away with, do away w., dispatch, get rid of; deal a deathblow, give the coup de grace, put one out of his misery, give one his quietus; shed blood, knife, put to the sword, lance, bayonet, stab, run through 263 *pierce*; shoot down, pick off, blow the brains out 287 *shoot*; strangle, garrotte, choke, suffocate, smother, stifle, drown; wall up, bury alive; brain, poleaxe, sandbag 279 *strike*; send to the stake 381 *burn*; immolate, sacrifice, offer up; martyr, condemn to death, sign the death warrant, ring the knell 961 *condemn*.

slaughter, butcher, poleaxe, cut the throat of; massacre, put to the sword; decimate, scupper, wipe out; cut to pieces, cut to ribbons, cut down, shoot d., mow d.; give no quarter, spare none 906 *be pitiless*; annihilate, exterminate, liquidate, purge, send to the gas chamber, commit genocide 165 *destroy*.

murder, commit m., commit homicide, commit manslaughter, assassinate, finish off, make away with, do in, do to death, do for, fix, settle, bump off, wipe out, liquidate, rub out; make to walk the plank; smother, suffocate, strangle, poison, gas.

kill oneself, do oneself in, do away with oneself, make away with oneself, commit suicide, suicide; commit hara-kiri, commit suttee; hang oneself, shoot o.,

blow out one's brains, cut one's throat, slash one's wrists; fall on one's sword, die Roman fashion; put one's head in the oven, gas oneself; take poison, take an overdose; jump overboard, drown oneself.

363 Corpse – N. *corpse,* dead body, body; dead man *or* woman, victim; stiff; cadaver, carcass, skeleton, dry bones; death's-head, skull; mummy; mortal remains, relics, ashes; carrion, food for worms, food for fishes.

364 Interment – N. *interment,* burial, entombment; inhumation, cremation, incineration; scattering of the ashes; embalming, mummification; embalmment, myrrh, spices, coffin, cist, shell, casket, urn; sarcophagus; pyre, funeral pile, crematorium; mortuary, morgue, charnel house; undertaker's, funeral parlour; sexton, gravedigger; undertaker, funeral director; mortician; embalmer.

obsequies, mourning, weeping and wailing, wake 836 *lamentation*; lying-in-state; last rites, burial service; funeral rites, cortege; knell; dead march, muffled drum, last post; memorial service, requiem, funeral hymn, funeral oration; elegy, dirge 836 *lament*; inscription, epitaph, obituary; tombstone, gravestone, headstone; cross, war memorial; cenotaph 548 *monument*; necrologist, obituary-writer.

funeral, hearse, bier, pall, coffin; mourner, weeper, keener; pallbearer; lychgate (see *obsequies*).

grave clothes, shroud, winding sheet.

cemetery, burial place, golgotha; churchyard, graveyard, God's Acre; catacombs, cinerarium; necropolis, city of the dead; garden of remembrance, garden of rest.

tomb, vault, crypt; burial chamber; pyramid; mausoleum, sepulchre; pantheon; grave, long home; cist; barrow 253 *earthwork*; cromlech, dolmen, menhir 548 *monument*; shrine, memorial, cenotaph.

inquest 459 enquiry; necropsy, autopsy, post-mortem; exhumation, disinterment, disentombment.

Adj. *funereal,* funebrial; sombre, sad 428 *black*; mourning; elegiac, mortuary, cinerary, crematory, sepulchral; obsequial, obituary; epitaphic; necrological, dirgelike 836 *lamenting.*

Vb. *inter,* inhume, bury; lay out; embalm, coffin; urn, entomb; lay in the grave, consign to earth, lay to rest; cremate, incinerate 381 *burn*; pay one's last respects, go to a funeral, toll the knell, sound the last post; mourn, keen, hold a wake 836 *lament.*

exhume, disinter; disentomb; unearth, dig up.

365 Animality. Animal − N. *animality,* animal life, wild life; animal kingdom, fauna; physique, flesh, flesh and blood; anthropomorphism; zoomorphism, Pan; animalism 944 *sensualism*; animal liberation movement, animal rights m.; antivivisectionist, animalist, animal liberationist.

animal, living thing; birds, beasts and fishes; creature, brute, beast, dumb animal, creeping thing; protozoon, metazoon; zoophyte; mammal, amphibian, fish, bird, reptile; worm, mollusc, arthropod; crustacean, insect, arachnid; invertebrate, vertebrate; biped, quadruped; carnivore, herbivore, insectivore, ruminant, man-eater; wild animal, game, big game; prey, beast of prey; pack, flock, herd 74 *group*; stock, livestock 369 *stock farm*; tame animal, domestic a.; pet a., household pet, goldfish, cagebird, hamster, gerbil, guinea pig, tortoise; young animal 132 *young creature*; draught animal 273 *horse, beast of burden*; endangered species, blue whale, onyx; extinct animal, dodo, auk, aurochs, prehistoric animal, pterodactyl, ichthyosaur, plesiosaur, dinosaur, brontosaurus, tyrannosaurus rex, megathere, mammoth, mastodon, sabre-toothed tiger; fabulous beast, heraldic b., unicorn, griffin 84 *rara avis.*

mammal, viviparous animal; man 371 *humankind*; primate, ape, anthropoid ape, gorilla, orang-outang, chimpanzee, gibbon, baboon, mandrill, monkey; marmoset, lemur; marsupial, kangaroo, wallaby, wombat, koala bear, opossum; rodent, rat, mouse, field m., dormouse, shrew, vole, porcupine, mongoose, chipmunk, skunk, polecat, squirrel; aardvark, ant-eater, mole; bat, bush baby, raccoon, badger, hedgehog; stoat, weasel, ferret; fox, dog f., vixen, Reynard; jackal, hyena, lion (**see** *cat*); herbivorous mammal (**see** *sheep* etc.); hare, mountain h., rabbit, bunny; otter, beaver, water rat, water vole; walrus, seal, sea lion; cetacean, dolphin, porpoise, whale, sperm w., right w.; pachyderm, elephant, rhinoceros, hippopotamus; bear, polar b., black b., brown b., grizzly b; giant panda; ungulate, giraffe, zebra (**see** *cattle*); deer, stag, hart, buck, doe, fawn, pricket; red deer, fallow d., roe d., muntjac; reindeer, caribou; elk, moose; gazelle, antelope, chamois, springbok, eland, hartebeest, wildebeest, gnu; horse, donkey, camel 273 *beast of burden.*

bird, winged thing, fowls of the air; fledgling, squab 132 *young creature*; avifauna, birdlife; cagebird, canary, budgerigar; parrot, polly, macaw, mynah bird; songbird, songster, warbler, nightingale, philomel, bulbul, lark, thrush, throstle, mavis, blackbird, linnet; curlew, plover, lapwing, peewit; dove, turtle d., ring d., pigeon, wood p.; woodpecker, jay, magpie, pie; jackdaw, rook, raven, crow; finch, goldfinch, greenfinch, chaffinch; tit, blue t., great t., wren, robin, sparrow, hedge s., house s.; yellowhammer, wagtail; humming b., sunbird, weaver b., b. of paradise, lyrebird; hoopoe, golden oriole; migrant, cuckoo, swallow, swift, martin; redwing, fieldfare, snow bunting; emu, ostrich, rhea, cassowary, kiwi, penguin; nightbird, owl, tawny o., barn o., screech o., nightjar; vulture, marabou, carrion crow; bird of prey, eagle, golden e; kite, kestrel,

harrier, osprey, buzzard, hawk, sparrowhawk, falcon, peregrine f., merlin, shrike; fishing bird, pelican, kingfisher, gannet, cormorant, shag, skua, Arctic s.; gull, herring g., kittiwake, tern, oystercatcher, puffin, guillemot; ocean bird, albatross, petrel, stormy p., Mother Carey's chickens; marsh bird, wader, stork, crane, heron, bittern; spoonbill, ibis, flamingo; water bird, waterfowl, swan, cob, pen, cygnet; duck, drake, duckling; goose, gander, gosling; merganser, pintail, teal, mallard, widgeon; moorhen, coot, lily-trotter, diver, dipper, grebe, dabchick.

table bird, game b., woodcock, wood pigeon, squab; peafowl, peacock, peahen; grouse, ptarmigan, capercaillie, pheasant, partridge, quail; goose, duck, snipe; turkey, guinea fowl, guinea hen.

poultry, fowl, hen; cock, cockerel, rooster; chicken, pullet; boiler, broiler, roaster, capon; Rhode Island Red, Leghorn, bantam.

cattle, kine, livestock 369 *stock farm*; bull, cow, calf, heifer, yearling; bullock, steer; beef cattle, highland c., Aberdeen Angus, Luing cattle, Hereford, Charolais; dairy cattle, milch cow, Guernsey, Jersey, Friesian; Simmental, dual-purpose cattle, Redpoll, shorthorn; zebu, brahmin, zho; ox, oxen; buffalo, beefalo, bison; yak, musk ox.

goat, billy g., nanny g., mountain g., ibex.

sheep, ram, tup, wether, bell w., ewe, lamb; teg; Southdown, Lincoln, Cheviot, Herdwick, Merino; mountain sheep, mouflon.

pig, swine, boar, warthog; hog, sow, piglet, pigling, sucking pig, porker; Large White, Wessex Saddleback, Berkshire, Tamworth.

dog, canine, bow-wow, man's best friend; bitch, whelp, pup, puppy; cur, hound, tyke, pooch, mutt; mongrel, pariah dog, pye-d.; guide dog, house d., watch d., police dog, bloodhound, mastiff; sheepdog, Old English S., collie, Border c.; Dobermann pinscher, bull terrier; bulldog, boxer; wolfhound, borzoi,

Afghan hound, Alsatian, Dalmatian; Great Dane; St Bernard; greyhound, courser, whippet; foxhound, staghound, beagle; basset, dachshund; gun dog, retriever, golden r., Labrador r., Labrador, golden l., pointer, setter, Irish s.; terrier, smooth-haired t., wire-h. t., fox t., sealyham, Scottish t., Scottie, West Highland terrier, Yorkshire t.; spaniel, cocker s., springer s., King Charles s.; show dog, fancy d., toy d., chihuahua, Pomeranian, chow; lap dog, Pekinese, peke, pug; Welsh corgi; poodle, French p., miniature p., toy p.; husky, sledge dog; wild dog, dingo; wolf, coyote.

cat, feline; grimalkin, moggie, puss, pussy, kitten, pussycat; tom, tom cat, tabby; mouser; Cheshire Cat; Persian c., Siamese c., Manx c., calico c., tortoiseshell c., marmalade c., tabby c.

big cat, lion, lioness, King of Beasts; tiger, tigress, tigon, leopard, leopardess, cheetah, panther, puma, jaguar, cougar, ocelot; wildcat, bobcat, lynx.

amphibian, frog, bullfrog, tree frog, platanna f.; frogspawn, tadpole; paddock, puddock, toad, natterjack; newt, eft; salamander, axolotl.

reptile, ophidian, serpent, sea s.; snake, water s.; grass s., venomous s., viper, adder, asp; cobra, king c., hamadryad; puff adder, mamba, horned viper, rattlesnake; anaconda, boa constrictor, python; crocodile, alligator, cayman; lizard, slowworm, blindworm; chameleon, iguana, monitor, gecko; turtle, tortoise, terrapin.

marine life, denizens of the deep; marine organisms, nekton, benthos; cetacean (see *mammal*); sea urchin, sea horse, sea anemone, coral, coral reef, jellyfish, Portuguese man of war, starfish, brittle-star; shellfish, mollusc, bivalve, clam, oyster, mussel, cockle; whelk, winkle, limpet; cephalopod, cuttlefish, squid, octopus; crustacean, crab, lobster, crayfish, shrimp; barnacle.

fish, flying f., swordfish, angelfish, dogfish, shark; piranha, barracuda; stingray, electric ray; tunny fish, turbot,

bass, conger eel 301 *fish food*; coelacanth; blenny; pike, roach, perch, bream, carp; trout, grayling; salmon, grilse; eel, elver, lamprey; minnow, gudgeon, stickleback.

insect, larva, pupa, imago; fly, house f., horse f., gadfly, cleg, bluebottle; mayfly, caddis fly; gnat, midge, tsetse fly, mosquito; greenfly, blackfly, aphid; thunder fly; ladybird, lacewing, hoverfly; firefly, glow-worm; dragonfly, crane fly, daddy longlegs; butterfly, cabbage white, red admiral, moth, hawk m., clothes m.; bee, bumble bee, humble b., honey b., queen b., worker b., drone; wasp, hornet; beetle, stag b., dung b., cockroach; vermin, parasites, bug, bed bug, flea, louse, nit, mite, tick; jigger; woodworm, weevil, borer, cockchafer, deathwatch beetle 659 *blight*; emmet, ant, soldier a., worker a., white a., termite; stick insect, praying mantis; locust, grasshopper, cicada, cricket.

creepy-crawly, grub, maggot, caterpillar, looper, inchworm; worm, earthworm, lugworm, wireworm, roundworm, flatworm, tapeworm, fluke; myriapod, centipede, millipede; slug, snail; earwig, woodlouse; spider, money s.; black widow s., tarantula; scorpion.

Adj. *animal,* brutish, beastly, bestial; feral, domestic; human, manly, subhuman; therianthropic, theriomorphic, anthromorphic zoomorphic; zoological; vertebrate, invertebrate; mammalian; anthropoid, simian; equine, asinine, mulish; deerlike, cervine; bovine, taurine, ruminant; ovine, sheepish; goatlike, goatish; porcine, piggy; bearish, ursine; elephantine; canine, doggy; lupine, wolfish; feline, catlike, cattish, tigerish; leonine; vulpine, foxy; avian, birdlike; aquiline, vulturine; passerine; owlish; dovelike; gallinaceous, anserine; cold-blooded, fishy, piscine, molluscan, molluscoid; amphibian, amphibious, salientian; reptilian, saurian, ophidian, snaky, serpentine, viperish; vermicular, wormy, weevilly; verminous; lepidopterous, entomological.

366 Vegetable life – N. *vegetable life,* vegetable kingdom; flora, vegetation; biomass; flowering, blooming, florescence; lushness, rankness, luxuriance 635 *plenty,* 171 *abundance*; wood nymph 967 *nymph*.

wood, timber, lumber, softwood, hardwood, heartwood, sapwood; forest, virgin f., primeval f.; rain f., jungle; coniferous forest, taiga; bush, heath, scrub, maquis, chapparal; woods, timberland, greenwood, woodland, bocage, copse, coppice, spinney; thicket, bosk, brake, covert; park, chase, game preserve; hurst, holt; plantation, arboretum, pinetum, pinery; orchard, orangery 370 *garden*; grove, clump; clearing, glade; brushwood, underwood, undergrowth; bushiness, bushes, shrubbery, windbreak, hedge, hedgerow.

forestry, dendrology, silviculture, tree-planting, afforestation; forester, woodcutter, dendrologist 370 *gardener*.

tree, shrub, bush, sapling, scion, stock; pollard; bonsai; shoot, sucker, trunk, bole; limb, branch, bough, twig; conifer, greenwood t., evergreen t., deciduous t., softwood t., hardwood t.; fruit tree, timber t.; mahogany, ebony, teak, walnut, oak, elm, ash, beech, sycamore, maple, plane, lime, linden; horse chestnut, copper beech; cedar of Lebanon, redwood, larch, fir, Douglas fir, spruce, pine, Scots p., lodgepole p.; poplar, Lombardy p., aspen, alder, sallow, willow, weeping w., pussy w.; birch, silver b., rowan, mountain ash; crab apple, sweet chestnut; hazel, elder, spindle, hawthorn, may, blackthorn, sloe; privet, yew, holly, ivy, box, bay, laurel; rhododendron, camellia, azalea; magnolia, laburnum, lilac; wisteria, Virginia creeper; acacia, jacaranda; palm, date p., coconut p., oil p.; baobab, banyan, mangrove; gum tree, eucalyptus, rubber tree 370 *agriculture*.

foliage, foliation, frondescence; greenery, verdure; leafiness, leafage; herbage; umbrage; limb, branch, bough, twig, shoot; spray, sprig; treetop; leaf, simple l., compound l.; frond, flag, blade; leaflet, foliole; pine needle; seed-leaf,

cotyledon; leaf-stalk, petiole, stipule, node, stalk, stem; tendril, prickle, thorn.

plant, herb, wort, weed; root, tuber, rhizome, bulb, corm 156 *source*; stolon, rootstock, cutting 132 *young plant*; culinary herb 301 *herb*; medicinal herb 658 *remedy*; fodder 301 *vegetable, fruit, provender*; national plant, rose, leek, daffodil, thistle, shamrock, fleur-de-lis; garden plant, pansy, primula, marigold, lupin, iris, dahlia, gladiolus, hyacinth, chrysanthemum, snapdragon, sweet william, pink, carnation, lily; lavender, honeysuckle 396 *fragrance*; wild plant, daisy, dandelion, buttercup, poppy, primrose, snowdrop, bluebell, harebell, foxglove, cowslip, forget-me-not, clover, heather; water lily, marsh marigold, flag; cactus, succulent; prickly plant, bramble, gorse, whin; insectivorous plant, Venus's flytrap, sundew; deadly nightshade 659 *poisonous plant*; creeper, climber, twiner, vine, bine, convolvulus, bindweed, liane; parasite, mistletoe; horsetail, fern, bracken; moss, clubmoss, bog m., sphagnum; liverwort; lichen, fungus, mushroom, toadstool, agaric, puffball; mould, penicillin; seaweed, wrack, bladderwrack, kelp, gulfweed; algae.

flower, floweret, floret, blossom, bloom, bud, burgeon; inflorescence, head, corymb, panicle, cyme, umbel, spike, catkin; petal, sepal; corolla, calyx; ovary, ovule, receptacle; pistil, style, stigma, stamen, anther, pollen; nectary; fruit, berry, nut, drupe; seed vessel, pod, capsule, cone; pip, spore, seed 156 *source*; annual, biennial, perennial; house plant, pot p.; hothouse p., exotic; garden flower, wild flower; flowerbed, seedbed, propagator, growbag; gardening, horticulture, floriculture 370 *garden*.

grass, hay; pasture, pasturage, herbage 348 *grassland*; verdure, turf, sod, lawn; meadow grass, rye g., couch g., bent g., fescue; sedge, rush, bulrush, reed, papyrus; marram grass, esparto g.; Pampas grass, elephant g., bamboo, sugar cane;

grain plant, wheat, oats, barley, rye, millet, sorghum, rice 301 *cereals*; grain, husk, bran, chaff, stubble, straw.

Adj. *wooden,* wood, treen, woody, ligneous, ligniform.

Vb. *vegetate,* germinate, sprout, shoot 36 *grow*; plant, garden 370 *cultivate*; afforest.

367 Zoology: the science of animals – N. *zoology,* morphology 331 *structure*; embryology 358 *biology*; animal behaviour; anthropography 371 *anthropology*; ornithology, bird watching, twitching; ichthyology, herpetology, ophiology, mammalogy, primatology, cetology, malacology, helminthology, nematology, entomology, lepidopterology, arachnology, conchology; palaeontology.

zoologist, ornithologist, ichthyologist, entomologist, lepidopterist, anthropologist etc. n.

368 Botany: the science of plants – N. *botany,* taxonomy; plant ecology; dendrology 366 *forestry*; mycology, fungology, bryology, algology; palaeobotany; botanical garden 370 *garden*; herbarium; botanist, herbalist, taxonomist etc. n.

369 Animal husbandry – N. *animal husbandry,* manège; breeding, stock-b.; veterinary science; horse-breeding, cattle-raising; dairy farming, beef f. 365 *cattle*; sheep farming, hill f., pig-f., bee-keeping, poultry farming; stirpiculture, pisciculture, aviculture, apiculture, sericulture; veterinary surgeon, vet, veterinarian, animal doctor, horse d. 658 *doctor*; groom 742 *servant*.

stock farm, stud f., dairy farm, cattle f., rancho, hacienda, ranch; fish farm, trout f., hatchery; fish pond, fish tank; duck pond; pig farm, piggery; beehive, hive, apiary; pasture, grazing, sheep farm, hill f., sheeprun, sheepwalk 348 *grassland*; poultry farm, chicken run, hen r., broiler house, battery, deep litter; factory farm; game preserve.

cattle pen, byre, cowshed 192 *stable*; sheepfold 235 *enclosure*; hutch, coop, hencoop, hen run, henhouse; cowshed, pigsty; swannery; bird cage, aviary.

zoo, zoological gardens, menagerie, circus; Noah's Ark; aviary, vivarium, terrarium, aquarium, dolphinarium; reptile house, monkey temple; bear pit; wildlife park, safari p.; game park, game reserve.

breeder, apiarist; fancier, pigeon-f.

herdsman, herd; cowherd, stockman, cattleman, byreman, cowman, rancher; cowboy, cowgirl, cowpuncher; broncobuster, gaucho; shepherd, shepherdess; swineherd; goatherd; goosegirl; milkmaid, dairymaid; kennel maid.

Vb. *break in,* tame, domesticate, acclimatize 610 *habituate*; train 534 *teach*; mount, whip, spur 267 *ride*; yoke, harness, hitch, bridle, saddle; round up, herd, corral, cage 235 *enclose*.

breed stock, breed, rear, raise, grow, hatch, culture, incubate, nurture, fatten; farm 370 *cultivate*.

groom, currycomb, rub down.

370 Agriculture – N. *agriculture,* agronomy, agronomics; Common Agricultural Policy, decerealization; butter mountain, grain m., wine lake; agribusiness, agro-industry, agrochemical i. 622 *business*; cultivation, ploughing, sowing, reaping; growth, harvest, produce, crop, vintage 632 *store*; cash crop, fodder c.; husbandry, farming, mixed f., factory f.; cattle farming, dairy f. 369 *animal husbandry*; cereal farming, arable f.; hydroponics, tank farming; irrigation; tillage, tilth; green fingers; floriculture, flower-growing; horticulture, gardening, market g.; bonsai; vegetable growing, fruit g., soft-fruit g., mushroom g.; viticulture, viniculture, wine-growing; arboriculture, silviculture, afforestation 366 *forestry*; landscape gardening, landscape architecture.

farm, home f., grange; arable farm, dairy f., sheep f., hill f., cattle f. 369 *stock farm*; ranch, rancho, hacienda; model farm; farmstead, steading, farmhouse;

farmyard, barnyard 235 *enclosure*; state farm, collective f., kolkhoz, kibbutz; farmland, arable land, ploughed land, fallow 344 *soil*; rice paddy, paddyfield; pasturage, pasture, fields, meadows 348 *grassland*; demesne, manor farm, estate, holding, smallholding, croft 777 *lands*; allotment, kitchen garden; market garden, herb g.; nursery; vineyard, vinery; fruit farm, orchard; tea garden, tea estate, coffee e., sugar plantation, rubber p.

garden, botanical g., flower g., rose g., Dutch g., herb g., rock g., alpine g., indoor g., winter g.; vegetable garden, cabbage patch, kitchen garden, allotment; fruit garden, orchard; arboretum, pinetum, pinery 366 *wood*; patch, plot, lawn, park 235 *enclosure*; shrubbery, border, herbaceous b., bed, flowerbed, parterre 844 *ornamental art*; seedbed, frame, cold f., propagator 167 *propagation*; cloche, conservatory, hothouse, greenhouse, glasshouse, orangery; grow bag, growing-bag; jardinière, planter, flowerpot.

farmer, husbandman, farm manager, grieve, factor, farm agent, bailiff; cultivator, planter, tea p., coffee p.; agronomist, agriculturalist; peasant, paysan; serf; villein; tenant farmer; gentleman farmer, yeoman; hill farmer; smallholder, crofter, allotment-holder; fruit grower; wine-grower, vigneron; farm hand, farm labourer, orraman, agricultural worker; land girl; ploughman, tractor driver, sower, reaper, harvester, gleaner; thresher; potato picker, hop p., fruit p.

gardener, horticulturist, flower grower; topiarist, landscape gardener; seedsman, nurseryman *or* -woman; market gardener; fruit-grower, vine-grower, vigneron; arborist, arboriculturalist, silviculturist 366 *forestry*.

farm tool, plough, ploughshare; harrow; cultivator, rotary c., spade, fork, farm f., graip, hoe, Dutch h., rake, trowel; dibble, drill; hayfork, pitchfork; scythe, sickle, shears, pruners, secateurs 256 *sharp edge*; flail; winepress, ciderpress; mowing machine, mower, Flymo

(tdmk), rotary m., cylinder m., trimmer, binder, baler, combine harvester, pea viner.

Vb. *cultivate,* bring under cultivation 171 *make fruitful*; farm, ranch, garden, grow; till, till the soil, dig, trench, dibble; sow, scatter the seed, set, plant, prick out, dibble in, transplant, plant out, bed o.; plough, harrow, rake, hoe; weed, prune, thin out, deadhead 204 *shorten*; graft 303 *implant*; layer, take cuttings; force; fertilize, topdress, mulch, manure 174 *invigorate*; grass over, rotate the crop; leave fallow 674 *not use*; harvest 632 *store*; glean, reap, mow, cut, scythe, cut a swathe; bind, bale, stook, sheaf; flail, thresh, winnow, sift, bolt 46 *separate*; crop, pluck, pick, gather; tread out the grapes; ensilage; ditch, drain, reclaim; water 341 *irrigate*.

371 Humankind – N. *humankind,* mankind, homo sapiens, womankind; humanity, human nature; flesh, mortality, human frailty; human race, human species, man; earthling; human being, Adam, Eve, civilized world 654 *civilization*; barbarians, savages; bushmen, aborigines; Stone-Age man, Cro-Magnon man, Neanderthal man, cavemen and -women, troglodytes; apemen and -women, Pithecanthropus, Australopithecus, Peking man, Java man, ethnic type 11 *race*.

anthropology, anthropography; somatology; ethnology, ethnography, folklore; social anthropology, demography; social science, humanitarianism 901 *sociology*; humanism; anthroposophy; anthropomorphism, pathetic fallacy; anthropologist, craniologist, ethnographer, demographer, folklorist, humanist.

person, individual, human being, everyman, everywoman; creature, mortal, body, bod; a being, soul, living s.; one, somebody, someone, so and so, such a one; party, customer, character, type, element; chap, customer, fellow 372 *male*; girl, female, bird 373 *woman*; personage, figure, person of note, VIP 638 *bigwig*; celebrity, star 890 *favourite*; dramatis

personae, all those concerned 686 *personnel*; unit, head, hand, nose.

social group, society, community, ethnic group, ghetto 74 *group*; kinship group 11 *family*; primitive society, tribalism; organized society; people, persons, folk; public, general p., man *or* woman in the street, joe soap, the average punter, everyman, you and me, the 'me' generation 79 *generality*; population, populace, citizenry 191 *inhabitants*; the masses 869 *commonalty*; social classes 869 *lower classes, middle c.,* 868 *upper class, aristocracy.*

nation, nationality, statehood, nationalism; chauvinism, jingoism, gung-ho nationalism, expansionism, imperialism, colonialism; Lebensraum; body politic, people, demos; state; realm, commonwealth 733 *political organization*; democracy, republic 733 *government*.

Adj. *national,* state, civic, general, communal, tribal, social, societal; cosmopolitan, international.

372 Male – N. *male,* male sex, man, he, him; Adam; manliness, masculinity, manhood; virility, machismo; male chauvinism, male-dominated society, patriarchy; mannishness, virilism; gentleman, sir, esquire, master; lord, my l., his lordship; Mr, mister, monsieur, Herr, señor, don, dom, senhor, signor, sahib; tovarich, comrade, citoyen; squire, guvnor, guv; buster, Mac, Jock, Jimmy; mate, buddy, butty, pal 880 *chum*; goodman, wight, swain; gaffer, buffer 133 *old man*; fellow, guy, scout, bloke, chap, chappie, johnny, gent; codger, card, cove, joker; blade, rake, gay dog 952 *libertine*; he-man, caveman, macho, Alpha Man; male chauvinist pig, MCP; sissy, mummy's boy 163 *weakling*; homosexual, homo, queer 84 *nonconformist*; eunuch, castrato; escort, beau, boy friend; bachelor, widower; bridegroom 894 *bridal party*; married man, husband, house h., man, live-in 894 *spouse*; family man, paterfamilias, patriarch; father 169 *paternity*; uncle,

brother, nephew; lad, stripling, boy 132 *youngster*; blue-eyed boy, son; spear side; stag party, menfolk.

male animal, jack, cock, cockerel, rooster; drake, gander, cob; buck, stag, hart; horse, stallion, stud horse, colt; bull, bull-calf, bullock, ox, steer; boar, hog; ram, tup; he-goat, billy g.; dog, dog fox, tom cat; gelding, capon.

Adj. *male,* he, masculine, manly, gentlemanly, chivalrous; virile, macho; mannish, manlike, butch, unfeminine, unwomanly.

373 Female – **N.** *female,* feminine sex, woman, she, her, -ess; Eve, femininity, feminineness; womanhood 134 *adultness*; womanliness, girlishness; feminism, gynography, women's rights, Women's Lib *or* Liberation, Women's Movement; matriarchy, gynocracy, regiment of women; girl, little g. 132 *youngster*; virgin, maiden; nun, unmarried woman, old maid 895 *spinster*; bachelor girl, career woman; feminist, sister, women's libber, bra burner; suffragette; bride, married woman, wife, 'trouble and strife', woman, live-in, squaw, widow, matron 894 *spouse*; dowager 133 *old woman*; mother, grandmother 169 *maternity*; unmarried mother, working wife *or* mother, superwoman, housewife; aunt, auntie, niece, sister, daughter; wench, lass, lassie, nymph; colleen, damsel; petticoat, skirt, doll, chick, bird; honey, hinny, baby; brunette, blonde, platinum b., redhead; girl friend, sweetheart 887 *loved one*; moll, bint, crumpet, bit of fluff; broad, courtesan 952 *loose woman*; lesbian, dyke *or* dike 84 *nonconformist*; minx, hussy, baggage, jade; shrew, virago, stramullion, Amazon, lady, gentlewoman; dame; milady, her ladyship, donna; madam, ma'am, marm, mistress, Mrs, missus, Ms, miss, madame, mademoiselle, Frau, Fraulein; signora, signorina, señora, señorita, memsahib; goodwife; gynaecology; obstetrics 167 *propagation.*

womankind, second sex, female s., fair s., gentle s., weaker s.; the distaff side,

womenfolk, women; hen party; women's quarters, purdah, seraglio, harem.

female animal, hen, bitch; mare, filly; cow, heifer; sow; ewe, ewelamb; nanny goat; hind, doe; vixen, tigress, lioness, leopardess.

Adj. *female,* she, feminine, petticoat, girlish, womanly, ladylike, maidenly, matronly; child-bearing; feminist, feministic; Amazonian; lesbian, lez *or* les, dykey *or* dikey; womanish, effeminate, unmanly, pansy.

374 Physical sensibility – **N.** *sensibility,* sensitivity; sensitiveness, soreness, tenderness, delicateness, threshold of pain; exposed nerve; perceptivity, awareness, consciousness 819 *moral sensibility*; susceptibility; allergy; funny bone; sensuousness, aestheticism, aesthetics; aesthete 846 *people of taste*; touchy person, sensitive plant, thin skin.

sense, sense organ, nervous system, sensorium; five senses; touch, hearing, taste, smell, sight; sensation, impression 818 *feeling*; effect, response, reaction, reflex, autosuggestion; sixth sense, feyness, second sight, extrasensory perception, ESP; telepathy, thought-transference 984 *psychics.*

Adj. *sentient,* perceptive, sensitive, sensitized; sensible, susceptible; sensory, perceptual; sensuous, aesthetic 818 *feeling*; percipient, aware, conscious 490 *knowing*; acute, sharp, keen 377 *painful*; ticklish, itchy; tender, raw, sore, exposed; impressionable, alive, alive to, warm, responsive; allergic, oversensitive, hypersensitive 819 *impressible.*

Vb. *have feeling,* sense, become aware; come to one's senses, awaken, wake up; perceive, realize 490 *know*; be sensible of 818 *feel*; react, tingle 819 *be sensitive*; have all one's senses, hear, see, touch, taste, smell; be alert, have one's wits about one, be on the ball, be on the qui vive.

cause feeling, stir the senses, stir the blood; arouse, awaken, excite, make *or* produce an impression 821 *impress*; cause a sensation 508 *surprise*; sensitize.

375 Physical insensibility – N. *insensibility,* insensitiveness; imperceptiveness, obtuseness 499 *unintelligence*; impassivity 820 *moral insensibility*; anaesthesia; analgesia; hypnosis, hypnotism, autosuggestion; suspended animation; apoplexy, paralysis, palsy; numbness; catalepsy, stupor, coma, trance, freak-out; faint, swoon, blackout, unconsciousness, senselessness; narcolepsy, narcotism, sleeping sickness 651 *disease*; narcosis 679 *sleep*.

anaesthetic, dope 658 *drug*; local anaesthetic, general a.; ether, chloroform, morphine, cocaine; gas, nitrous oxide, laughing gas; gas and air, epidural, pethidene; narcotic, sleeping tablets, Mogadon (tdmk), draught; opium, laudanum; painkiller, analgesic 177 *moderator*.

Adj. *insensible,* insensitive, insentient; obtuse, imperceptive 499 *unintelligent*; unaware, oblivious; unhearing 416 *deaf*; unseeing 439 *blind*; senseless, unconscious; inert 679 *inactive*; out cold, out for the count, dead 266 *quiescent*; numb, frozen; paralysed, paralytic, palsied; doped, dopy, drugged; freaked out, spaced o.; stoned 949 *dead drunk*; anaesthetized, hypnotized; dazed, stupefied; semiconscious, in a trance; catatonic, cataleptic, comatose.

unfeeling, cold, callous, insensitive, inured, toughened, hardened; pachydermatous, thick-skinned; stony, shockproof 820 *impassive*.

Vb. *render insensible,* blunt, deaden; paralyse, benumb; freeze 382 *refrigerate*; put to sleep, send to sleep, hypnotize, mesmerize 679 *make inactive*; anaesthetize, put under, gas, chloroform; drug, dope; dull, stupefy; stun, concuss, brain, knock out, render unconscious 279 *strike*.

376 Physical pleasure – N. *pleasure,* thrill 821 *excitation*; enjoyment, gratification, sensuousness, sensuality; self-indulgence, luxuriousness, hedonism 944 *sensualism*; dissipation 943 *intemperance*; treat, diversion, entertainment, divertissement 837 *amusement*; feast, thrash 301 *feasting*; epicurism, epicureanism, relish 386 *taste*; gusto, zest, delight, happiness, ecstasy 824 *joy*.

euphoria, well-being, contentment 828 *content*, 824 *happiness*; quiet.

Adj. *pleasant,* pleasure-giving 826 *pleasurable*; pleasing, titillating, arousing; delightful; welcome, gratifying, satisfying 685 *refreshing*; genial, congenial, friendly, matey, cordial, heart-warming; nice, agreeable, enjoyable 837 *amusing*; palatable, delicious 386 *tasty*; tuneful 410 *melodious*; lovely 841 *beautiful*.

comfortable, affording comfort, comfy, homely, snug, cosy, warm, comforting, restful 683 *reposeful*; convenient, cushy; downy 327 *soft*; luxurious; in comfort, at one's ease; pampered, featherbedded, in clover, on a bed of roses, on velvet; happy, gratified 828 *content*; relieved.

sensuous, appealing to the s.; bodily, physical 319 *material*; voluptuous, pleasure-loving, luxuriating, enjoying, epicurean, hedonistic 944 *sensual*.

Vb. *enjoy,* relish, like, love, adore; feel pleasure, experience p., take p. in 824 *be pleased*; thrill to 821 *be excited*; luxuriate in, revel in, bask in, roll in, wallow in; gloat over, get a kick out of; lick one's lips, smack one's l. 386 *taste*; live on the fat of the land, live comfortably, live in clover, rest on a bed of roses 730 *prosper*; give pleasure 826 *please*.

Adv. *in comfort,* at one's ease; in clover, on velvet, on a bed of roses.

377 Physical pain – N. *pain,* threshold of pain; discomfort, malaise; distress, hell 731 *adversity*; strain, stress 684 *fatigue*; hurt, bruise, sprain, break, fracture; cut, gash 655 *wound*; aching, smarting, throbbing; heartache, anguish, agony 825 *suffering*; torment, torture; crucifixion, martyrdom, vivisection; rack, wheel, thumbscrew 964 *instrument of torture*; painfulness, soreness, tenderness.

pang, throes; stab, labour pangs, hunger p., twinge, nip, pinch; pins and needles 378 *formication*; stitch, crick, cramp, convulsion 318 *spasm*; smart, sting, sharp pain, shooting p.; ache, headache, splitting head, migraine; toothache, earache; stomachache, bellyache, colic, collywobbles; neuritis, neuralgia, angina; arthritis, rheumatoid a., rheumatism, fibrositis; sciatica, lumbago, backache 651 *ill health.*

Adj. *painful,* aching, agonizing, excruciating, harrowing, racking, tormenting; burning, biting, searing, stabbing, shooting, tingling, smarting, throbbing; sore, raw, tender, exposed, grazed; bittersweet 393 *sour*; disagreeable.

Vb. *give pain,* hurt, pain, sting, graze; excruciate, lacerate, torment, twist the arm of 963 *torture*; flog, whip, crucify, martyr 963 *punish*; vivisect, tear, lacerate 46 *cut*; prick, stab 263 *pierce*; gripe, nip, pinch, tweak, twinge, shoot, throb; bite, gnaw; grate, jar, set on edge; fret, chafe, gall 333 *rub*; irritate 832 *aggravate*; put on the rack, break on the wheel; grate on the ear 411 *discord*; annoy, distress 827 *trouble.*

feel pain, feel the pangs 825 *suffer*; agonize, ache, smart, chafe; twitch, wince, flinch, writhe, squirm, creep, shiver, quiver 318 *be agitated*; tingle, get pins and needles; be a martyr, go through it 731 *have trouble*, groan 408 *cry.*

378 Touch: sensation of touch – **N.** *touch,* tactility, palpability; handling, feeling, palpation, manipulation; massage, kneading, squeeze, pressure 333 *friction*; graze, contact 202 *contiguity*; stroke, pat, caress; flick, flip, tap 279 *knock*; precision 494 *accuracy*; artistry 694 *skill.*

tingling, tingle, pins-and-needles, formication; creeps, gooseflesh *or* -bumps *or* -pimples, someone walking over one's grave; scratchiness, itchiness, itch; urticaria, nettlerash, hives, allergic reaction; rash, prickly heat 651 *skin disease.*

feeler, antenna, whisker, tentacle; proboscis, tongue; digit, forefinger, thumb (see *finger*); hand, paw, flipper.

finger, forefinger, index, middle finger, ring f., little f., pinkie; thumb, pollex; big toe 214 *foot*; five fingers, bunch of fives, knuckle sandwich, dukes, fingernail, talon, claw.

Adj. *tactual,* tactile; prehensile; touching, licking, grazing etc. vb.; touchable, tangible, palpable 319 *material.*

handed, right-handed; left-handed; manual.

Vb. *touch,* make contact, come into c.; graze, scrape, shave, brush, glance; kiss 202 *be contiguous*; impinge; hit, meet 279 *collide*; feel, palpate; finger, thumb, pinch, nip, massage 333 *rub*; palm, run the hand over; stroke 258 *smooth*; tap, tip, pat, dab, flick, flip, tickle, scratch; lick; nuzzle, rub noses; paw, fondle 889 *caress*; handle, twiddle, fiddle with, play with; manipulate, wield, ply, manhandle 173 *operate*; jab, poke, goose, bruise, crush 377 *give pain*; grope; put out a feeler 461 *be tentative.*

379 Heat – **N.** *heat,* radiant heat; convected heat; emission of heat, incandescence, flame, glow, flush, hot flush, blush; warmth, fervour, ardour; tepidity, lukewarmness; specific heat, blood h.; body h.; sweat, perspiration, swelter; pyrexia, fever, inflammation 651 *disease*; high temperature, white heat; ebullition, boiling point, flash p., melting p.; tropical heat, sweltering h., high summer, flaming June, Indian summer; dog days, heat haze 128 *summer*; heat wave, scorcher, sizzler; hot wind, simoom, sirocco; hot springs, thermal s., geyser, hot water, steam; tropics, torrid zone; sun, midday s., sunshine, solar heat 381 *heating.*

fire, flames; bonfire, beacon fire; St Elmo's f. 417 *glow*; hellfire; pyre 364 *obsequies*; coal fire, gas f., electric f., wood-burning stove 383 *furnace*; Greek fire, wild f. 723 *bomb*; conflagration, holocaust; forest fire, bush f.; fireball, blaze, flame, tongue of f., sheet of f., wall

of f.; spark, scintillation, flicker, arc 417 *flash*; flare 420 *torch*; eruption, volcano; pyrotechnics; arson 381 *incendiarism*; fire worship 981 *worship*.

thermometry, thermometer, clinical t., Fahrenheit t., centigrade *or* Celsius t., Réaumur t.; feverscan; thermostat; calorimeter; British Thermal Unit, BTU, therm, calorie; thermodynamics; thermography.

Adj. *hot,* heated, superheated; inflamed, fervent, fervid; flaming, glowing, fiery, red-hot, white-h.; hot as hell; piping hot; feverish, febrile, fevered; sweltering, sweating, perspiring; steaming, smoking; dripping with sweat; on the boil, boiling, seething, ebullient, scalding; tropical, torrid, scorching, grilling, broiling, searing, blistering, baking, toasting, roasting etc. vb.; scorched, scalded 381 *heated*; thirsty, burning, parched 342 *dry*.

fiery, burning, blazing, flaming; smoking, smouldering; ablaze, afire, on fire, aflame; candescent, incandescent, glowing, aglow 431 *red*; pyrogenic, igneous; ignited, lit, alight, kindled, volcanic, erupting.

warm, tepid, lukewarm; temperate, mild, genial, balmy; fair, set f., sunny, sunshiny 417 *undimmed*; summery; tropical, equatorial; torrid, sultry; stuffy, close, muggy; overheated, unventilated; oppressive, suffocating, stifling, like a hothouse 653 *insalubrious*; warm as toast; snug 376 *comfortable*; at room temperature, at blood heat.

Vb. *be hot,* be warm, get warm etc. adj.; incandesce; burn, kindle, catch fire, draw; blaze, flare, flame, burst into flame, go up in flames; glow, flush; smoke, smoulder, reek, fume, steam 300 *emit*; boil, seethe 318 *effervesce*; toast, grill, broil, roast, sizzle, crackle, fry, bake 381 *burn*; get burnt, scorch, boil dry; bask, sun oneself, sunbathe; get sunburnt, tan; swelter, sweat, perspire, glow; thaw 337 *liquefy*; parch; suffocate, stifle, pant, gasp for breath, fight for air; be in a fever, be feverish, have a fever, run a temperature; keep warm, wrap up, insulate, keep out the cold.

380 Cold – **N.** *coldness,* low temperature, drop in t.; cool, coolness, freshness; cold, freezing c., absolute zero; freezing point; frigidity; iciness, frostiness; chilliness, windchill factor, hypothermia, shivering, shivers, chattering of the teeth, chittering, gooseflesh, goose pimples, frostbite, chilblains, chap, hack; chill, common cold, coryza, a cold in the head; cold climate, Siberia, North Pole, South P.; Arctic, Antarctica; snowline, permafrost; Ice Age.

wintriness, winter, hard winter; nip in the air, cold snap; cold front; arctic conditions, degrees of frost; snowstorm, hailstorm, blizzard; frost, touch of f., Jack Frost, rime, hoarfrost, hard frost; sleet, hail, hailstone, black ice, freeze.

snow, snowfall, snowflake; avalanche, snowdrift, snowfield; snowstorm; snow line, snowcap, snowfield, snowball, snowman; snowplough, snowshoe, snowmobile, snow tyre; winter sports 837 *sport*; snow blindness; snowbound.

ice, ice cube; icicle; ice cap, ice field, ice sheet, ice shelf, floe, ice f., iceberg, tip of the iceberg, glacier, icefall; pack ice; icebreaker, ice yacht; ice house, icebox 384 *refrigerator*; glaciation 382 *refrigeration*.

Adj. *cold,* cool; shady, chilly, parky, nippy, perishing; unheated; fresh, raw, keen, bitter, biting, piercing; freezing, ice-cold; frigid 129 *wintry*; winterbound, frosty, snowy, snow-covered; sleety, icy; glacial, ice-capped, glaciated; boreal, polar, arctic, Siberian.

chilly, shivering, chattering, chittering, shivery, blue with cold; perishing, starved with cold, chilled to the bone, hypothermic, frozen, frostbitten, like ice, cold as charity, cold as marble, stone-cold, cold as death.

Vb. *be cold,* - chilly etc. adj.; grow cold, lose heat, drop in temperature; feel cold, chatter, chitter, shiver, tremble, shake, quake, quiver, shudder; freeze, starve,

perish with cold, suffer from hypothermia; catch cold, get a chill; chill 382 *refrigerate*.

381 Heating – N. *heating,* superheating, warming, keeping warm; space heating, central heating 383 *heater*; solar heating, sunning 342 *desiccation*; greenhouse effect; melting, thawing 337 *liquefaction*; smelting, boiling, seething, simmering, ebullition; baking, cooking 301 *cookery*.

burning, combustion; inflammation, kindling, ignition; afterburning; conflagration 379 *fire*; incineration, roasting; cremation 364 *interment*; suttee, self-burning 362 *suicide*; holocaust 981 *oblation*; cauterization, branding; scorching, singeing, charring, inflammability, flammability, combustibility; burner 383 *furnace*; vitriol; branding iron; match, touchpaper 385 *lighter*; burn, scorch mark, brand, sunburn, tan, sunstroke.

arson, fire-raising, pyromania, incendiarism; incendiary, arsonist, fire-raiser, fire-bug.

pottery, ceramics; earthenware, stoneware, lustre ware, glazed w.; majolica, faience, chinaware, porcelain; crockery, china, bone c., Wedgwood (tdmk) c., Spode c., Worcester c., Doulton c., Chelsea c., Staffordshire c., Derby c., Sèvres c., Dresden c.; delft, willow pattern, terracotta; tile, brick, adobe; pot, urn 194 *vessel*; potter's wheel.

Adj. *heated,* superheated 379 *hot*; centrally-heated, winterized, insulated; fired; cooked; warmed up; overheated; steamy, smoky.

heating, warming etc. vb.; calefactory, calorific, solid-fuel, coal-burning, oil-fired, gas-fired; incendiary, inflammatory; inflammable, flammable; antifreeze.

Vb. *heat,* raise the temperature, warm; winterize, insulate; keep the cold out, take the chill off; hot up, warm up, stoke up; rub one's hands, stamp one's feet; thaw, thaw out; inflame, foment; overheat, stifle, suffocate; parch, shrivel, sear 342 *dry*; roast 301 *cook*; defrost 337 *liquefy*.

kindle, ignite, light, strike a l.; set fire to, light the touchpaper, light the fuse, touch off; add fuel to the fire, poke the f.; lay the fire, rub two sticks together.

burn, burn up, burn out; consign to the flames; make a bonfire of, send to the stake; fire, set fire to, set on fire, set alight; cremate, incinerate; boil dry 342 *dry*; char, singe, sear, scorch; cauterize, brand; scald.

382 Refrigeration – N. *refrigeration,* cooling, reduction of temperature; icing etc. vb.; freezing, freezing up, glaciation 380 *ice*; solidification 324 *condensation*; exposure; cold storage 384 *refrigerator*; cryonic suspension 364 *interment*; cryogenics, cryosurgery.

extinguisher, fire e.; foam, water, hose, sprinkler, hydrant, standpipe; fire engine, fire truck, fire brigade, fire tender, fire station; fireman, firefighter.

Adj. *cooled,* chilled etc. vb.; ventilated, air-conditioned; iced up; frozen, deep-frozen, freeze-dried; frosted, iced, glacé, frappé; with ice, on the rocks 380 *cold*; cooling etc. vb.; refrigeratory.

Vb. *refrigerate,* cool, air-cool, water-c.; reduce the temperature, turn off the heat; freeze, deep-freeze, freeze-dry; ice up, ice over; chill, benumb, starve, nip, pinch, bite, pierce, chill to the marrow, make one's teeth chatter; expose to the cold, frost-bite.

extinguish, quench, put out, blow o., snuff out; choke, suffocate, stifle, smother 165 *suppress*; damp, douse, damp down, bank d.; stamp out; stub o.; go out, burn o., die down.

383 Furnace – N. *furnace,* fiery f.; the stake 964 *means of execution*; volcano, touchhole, gun barrel; forge, blast furnace; kiln; oasthouse; incinerator,, crematorium; brazier, stove, kitchen s., wood-burning s., gas s., electric s.; primus s., oil s.; oven, gas o., electric o.; microwave o.; range, kitchen r.; cooker, gas c., electric c., split-level c., turbo-fan c., ceramic hob; gas ring, burner, bunsen b.; blowlamp, oxyacetylene lamp; fire,

open f., coal f., log f. 379 *fire*; brand 385 *lighter*; fireplace, grate, hearth, ingle; fire-irons, andirons, firedog; poker, tongs, shovel; hob, trivet; fireguard, fender; flue.

heater, space h., paraffin h., radiator, solar panel; hot-air duct, hot-water pipe, immersion heater, geyser, boiler, back b., copper, kettle, electric k. 194 *pot*; hotplate; warming pan, hot-water bottle; electric blanket; still, retort, crucible 461 *testing agent*; blowpipe, bellows, damper; hot baths, Turkish bath, sauna, Jacuzzi (tdmk) 648 *ablutions*; hotbed, hothouse, greenhouse, conservatory 370 *garden*; sun trap, solarium; kitchen, galley, cookhouse; grill, frying pan, saucepan; toaster, electric t.; iron, flat i., electric i., steam i., soldering i., curling tongs; flame, sunlight 381 *heating*; gas, electricity, solar energy, greenhouse effect 160 *sources of energy*; steam, hot air; wood, coal, peat 385 *fuel*.

384 Refrigerator – N. *refrigerator*, cooler; frigidarium; refrigerating plant, fridge, chiller, wine cooler, ice bucket; coolant, snow, ice; icehouse, icebox, ice pack, ice cubes, rocks; cold storage, freezer, fridge-freezer, cooler cupboard, deep-freeze 382 *refrigeration*.

385 Fuel – N. *fuel*, inflammable material, flammable m., combustible; kindling; wood, brushwood, firewood, faggot, log, Yule l.; turf, peat; lignite, brown coal, charcoal; coal, natural gas, petroleum 357 *oil*, 336 *gas*; nuclear fuel 160 *nucleonics*; petrol, high octane p., two-star, three-s, four-s.; juice, gasoline, gas; diesel oil, derv; paraffin, kerosene; methylated spirit, North Sea gas, coal g., acetylene, propane, butane, methane.

coal, black diamond, anthracite, briquette; coal dust, slack; coal seam, coal deposit, coalfield 632 *store*; embers; coke; smokeless fuel.

lighter, fire-l., cigarette l., igniter, light, pilot l., illuminant, taper, spill, candle 420 *torch*; fire ship, incendiary bomb 723 *bomb*; touchpaper, match, percussion cap, detonator; safety match, lucifer, vesta, fusee; flint, steel, tinder, touchwood.

386 Taste – N. *taste*, savour; flavour, flavouring; smack, tang, aftertaste; relish, gusto, zest, appetite 859 *liking*; palate, tastebuds.

Adj. *tasty*, palatable, mouth-watering, tempting, appetizing 390 *savoury*; well-seasoned, tangy 388 *pungent*; flavoured, spiced, spicy, herbed, herby, rich, strong, full-bodied, fruity, well-matured, mellow, vintage.

Vb. *taste*, lick one's lips, lick one's fingers 376 *enjoy*; savour, sample; sip, lick, sup, nibble 301 *eat*; have a taste, taste of, savour of, smack of 18 *resemble*; taste good, tickle the palate, tempt the appetite, stimulate the tastebuds 390 *make appetizing*.

387 Insipidity – N. *insipidity*, vapidity, vapidness, tastelessness, wateriness, wershness etc. adj., pap.

Adj. *tasteless*, wersh; vapid, insipid, watery; adulterated 163 *weakened*; wishy-washy; unappetizing 391 *unsavoury*; flavourless, unspiced, unseasoned.

388 Pungency – N. *pungency*, piquancy, poignancy, sting, kick, bite, edge; causticity; spiciness; acridity, sharpness, acerbity, acidity 393 *sourness*; roughness, harshness; strength, tang; bad taste 391 *unsavouriness*; salt, brine, pepper, pickle, spice 389 *condiment*; sal volatile, smelling salts 656 *revival*.

tobacco, baccy, snout, nicotine; the weed; tobacco leaf, Virginia tobacco, Turkish t., smoking mixture; snuff; plug, quid, twist; chewing tobacco, nicotine chew, tobacco sachet, tobacco teabag; pipe tobacco, shag; cigar, cigarillo, cheroot, panatella, Havana, corona; smoke, cigarette, cig, ciggie, fag, gasper, coffin-nail; reefer, joint 949 *drug-taking*; filter tip, cork tip, low-tar cigarette, menthol c., roll-up; butt, stub, fag-end, dog-end;

tobacco pipe, clay p., churchwarden; briar, corncob; meerschaum; water pipe, hubble-bubble, hookah, narghile; pipe of peace, calumet; bowl, stem; smoker's cough; snuff taker; smoker, pipe s., cigarette s., cigar s., chain s.; smoking, passive s.; tobacconist, cigarette machine; snuff box, cigarette case, cigar c., cigarette box, cigar b.; pipe rack; pipe cleaner, tobacco pouch, tobacco jar; smokeroom; smoker, non-smoker, smoking compartment, smoking zone; smoke-free zone or area.

Adj. *pungent*, strong; stinging, biting 256 *sharp*; caustic, smoky; harsh 259 *rough*; bitter, acrid, tart, astringent 393 *sour*; strong-flavoured, high, gamy, off; highly-seasoned, hot, gingery, peppery, fiery; zesty, tangy, piquant, aromatic 390 *savoury*.

salty, salt, brackish, briny, saline, pickled.

Vb. *season,* salt, marinade, souse, pickle; flavour; spice, herb, season, pepper, devil, curry; smoke, kipper 666 *preserve*.

smoke, smoke a pipe, pull, draw, suck, inhale; puff, blow smoke rings; chainsmoke, smoke like a chimney; chew a quid, suck tobacco sachets; take a pinch.

389 Condiment – N. *condiment,* seasoning, flavouring, dressing, relish, garnish; aspic; salt, garlic s., celery s.; mustard, French m., German m., English m.; pepper, black p., white p., peppercorn; onion, garlic 301 *herb*; curry powder 301 *spice*.

sauce, roux; gravy, stock; brown sauce, white s., béchamel; parsley sauce, bread s., tartar s., mint s., horseradish s., sauce piquante; bearnaise sauce; apple sauce, cranberry s. 392 *sweet thing*; tomato sauce, ketchup; chilli sauce, Tabasco s. (tdmk), soy s., Worcester s.; chutney, sweet c., mango c., pickles, piccalilli, pickled onions, gherkins; salad dressing, French d., Thousand Island d., mayonnaise, vinaigrette.

Vb. *spice* 388 *season*.

390 Savouriness – N. *savouriness,* tastiness, palatability; gaminess; body, bouquet; savoury, relish, appetizer; delicacy, dainty, titbit 301 *mouthful*; hors d'oeuvre.

Adj. *savoury,* seasoned, flavoured, spicy, herby 386 *tasty*; tempting, appetizing, aromatic, piquant 388 *pungent*; palatable, toothsome; delectable, delicious, choice, epicurean; ambrosial, fit for the gods, fit for a king; scrumptious, yummy, moreish; succulent; gamy, high; full-flavoured.

Vb. *make appetizing,* garnish, spice, pep up 388 *season*; tempt the appetite, tickle the palate, stimulate the tastebuds; smell good, taste good.

391 Unsavouriness – N. *unsavouriness,* unpalatability, sourness, rankness, rottenness, over-ripeness, unwholesomeness 653 *insalubrity*; acerbity, acridity 393 *sourness*; austerity, prison fare, bread and water, nursery fare, iron rations; aloes, rue; bitter pill, gall and wormwood.

Adj. *unsavoury,* tasteless; unpalatable, unappetizing, wersh; underdone, undressed 670 *uncooked*; overdone, burnt, burnt to a cinder; uneatable, inedible; stale, leathery 329 *tough*; soggy 327 *soft*; bitter, acrid, acid 393 *sour*; undrinkable, corked; overripe, rank, rancid, putrid, rotten, gone off, high, stinking 397 *fetid*; revolting, disgusting, loathsome 827 *unpleasant*; nauseating; poisonous 653 *toxic*.

Vb. *be unpalatable,* - unappetizing etc. adj.; disgust, repel, sicken, nauseate, turn the stomach 861 *cause dislike*; poison; pall.

392 Sweetness – N. *sweetness,* sweetening, sugariness, sweet tooth.

sweet thing, sweetening, honey, honeycomb, honeypot; saccharin, sucrose, glucose, dextrose, fructose, lactose, galactose; sugar, cane s., beet s., invert s.; granulated s., castor s., icing s., demerara; molasses, syrup, maple s., treacle; artificial sweetener; custard, condensed

milk; julep, nectar, hydromel, mead; conserve, preserve; candied peel, glacé cherries; jam, marmalade, jelly; marzipan, icing, fondant, sugar coating; fudge, candy, sugar c. 301 *sweets*; jujube, cachou, lozenge, pastille; lollipop, ice cream, candyfloss, rock; confectionery, confection, cake 301 *pastries*, *dessert*.

Adj. *sweet,* sweetened, honeyed, candied, crystallized; iced, glacé; sugared, sugary, saccharine, melliferous; ambrosial, luscious, delicious 376 *pleasant*; sweet as a nut; cloying; 390 *savoury*.

Vb. *sweeten,* sugar, add sugar, candy, crystallize, ice, glaze; sugar the pill; mull.

393 Sourness – N. *sourness,* acerbity; astringency; tartness, bitterness, vinegariness; sharpness 388 *pungency*; acidity, acidosis; acid, tartar; lemon, lime, vinegar; sloe, crab apple; alum, bitter aloes, bitters; gall, wormwood, absinth.

Adj. *sour,* sourish, acid, acidy, acidulous, acidulated, acetic, tartaric; acerbic, crabbed, tart, bitter; sharp, astringent 388 *pungent*; vinegary 391 *unsavoury*; unripe, green 670 *immature*; sugarless; unsweetened, dry.

Vb. *be sour, -* acid etc. adj.; sour, turn, turn sour; acetify, acidify, acidulate; ferment; set one's teeth on edge.

394 Odour – N. *odour,* smell, aroma, bouquet, nose; perfume, scent, essence 396 *fragrance*; pong, niff, stink 397 *stench*; smoke, fume, reek; whiff; odorousness, redolence; tang, scent 548 *trace*; olfaction, sense of smell; olfactories.

Adj. *odorous,* odoriferous, smelling; scented, perfumed 396 *fragrant*; smelly, redolent, reeking; malodorous, whiffy, niffy, ponging 397 *fetid*.

Vb. *smell,* have an odour, smell of, reek of, reek, pong of, pong; exhale; smell a mile off; smell out, scent, get wind of 484 *detect*; get a whiff of, get a niff of; sniff, inhale 352 *breathe*.

395 Inodorousness – N. *inodorousness,* odourlessness, scentlessness; absence of smell, loss of s.; deodorant, deodorizer, incense, mouthwash; deodorization, fumigation, purification.

Adj. *odourless,* inodorous, scentless; unscented, unperfumed; deodorized; deodorizing.

396 Fragrance – N. *fragrance,* sweet smell, perfume; redolence, aroma, bouquet 394 *odour*; flower garden, rose g. 370 *garden*; buttonhole, nosegay; fumigation; perfumery, perfumer.

scent, perfume, aromatic gum; balm, myrrh, incense, frankincense, spikenard; spicery 389 *condiment*; cloves, cachou; musk, civet, ambergris, camphor; sandalwood, patchouli; essential oil, otto, attar; lavender, thyme, spearmint, chypre, citronella oil; frangipani, bergamot, orris root, tonka bean; honeysuckle, toilet water, eau-de-toilette, lavender water, rose w., attar of roses, eau-de-cologne; scented soap 843 *cosmetic*; lavender bag, pomander, potpourri, scent bottle, joss stick, censer, thurible.

Adj. *fragrant,* redolent, odorous, odoriferous, aromatic, scented, perfumed 376 *pleasant*; balmy; sweet-scented; musky, spicy, fruity.

397 Stench – N. *stench,* fetidity, fetidness; bad smell, bad odour; body odour, BO, armpits; bad breath, halitosis; stink, pong, niff, reek; mephitis; fumes, miasma 336 *gas*; rancidity, putrefaction 51 *decay*; foulness 649 *dirt*; mustiness, fustiness, staleness, fug; fungus, stinkhorn, garlic, asafoetida; hydrogen sulphide; ammonia; skunk, polecat; stink bomb, bad egg; dung 302 *excrement*; latrine, sewer, septic tank 649 *sink*.

Adj. *fetid,* reeking, ill-smelling, malodorous, smelly, whiffy, niffy, pongy, humming; stinking, rank; high; bad, gone b., rancid; putrid; stale, musty, fusty, fuggy, smoky, stuffy, suffocating; foul, noisome, noxious, sulphurous, ammoniacal, miasmic 653 *toxic*; acrid 388 *pungent*.

Vb. *stink,* smell, reek, pong, niff, hum; fart, blow off; have bad breath, have halitosis; have a bad smell, smell bad 51

decompose; stink to high heaven; smell like a bad egg, stink out.

398 Sound – N.
sound, audibility, reception 415 *hearing*; sounding, sonancy; audio, mono, monophonic sound, binaural s., stereophonic s., stereo, quadraphonic sound, surround-sound system; sound waves, vibrations 417 *radiation*; sound effect; sound track, voice-over; sonority, sonorousness 404 *resonance*; noise, loud sound 400 *loudness*; softness 401 *faintness*; tone, pitch, level, cadence; accent, intonation, twang, timbre 577 *voice*; tune, strain 410 *melody*, 412 *music*; types of sound 402 *bang*, 403 *roll*, 404 *resonance*, 405 *nonresonance*, 406 *sibilation*, 407 *stridor*, 408 *cry*, 409 *ululation*, 411 *discord*; transmission, telephone, cellular t., radio 531 *telecommunication*; recorded sound, high fidelity, hi-fi; record-player 414 *gramophone*; ghetto blaster, personal stereo; loudspeaker 415 *hearing aid*; decibel, phon, sone; sonic barrier, sound b.

speech sound, phone, syllable, polysyllable; consonant, fricative, plosive, sibilant; dental, alveolar, labial, nasal, palatal, guttural, glottal stop; click; aspirate, surd; semivowel; glide; vowel, diphthong 577 *voice*; ablaut; umlaut; vocable 559 *word*; International Phonetic Alphabet, IPA 586 *script*.

Adj. *sounding,* sonic; supersonic; audible, distinct; resounding, sonorous 404 *resonant*; stentorian 400 *loud*; auditory, acoustic; monaural, monophonic, mono; binaural, stereophonic, stereo, high fidelity, hi-fi; audio, audiovisual; phonic, phonetic; voiced; unvoiced, voiceless.

399 Silence – N.
silence, soundlessness, inaudibility, total silence, not a sound, not a squeak; stillness, hush, lull, rest, peace, quiet 266 *quiescence*; taciturnity, muteness, speechlessness 578 *voicelessness*; solemn silence, dead s., perfect s., uncanny s., deathly hush.

Adj. *silent,* still, hushed; calm, peaceful, quiet 266 *quiescent*; soft, faint 401 *muted*; noiseless, soundless, inaudible; soundproof; speechless, taciturn, mute 578 *voiceless*; unspoken; silent as the grave.

Vb. *be silent,* not open one's mouth, not say a word, hold one's tongue 582 *be taciturn*; not speak 578 *be mute*; make not a sound, not utter a squeak; become silent, relapse into silence, pipe down, be quiet, lose one's voice, fall silent.

silence, still, lull, hush, quiet, quieten, make silent; soft-pedal; stifle, muffle, gag, stop, stop someone's mouth, muzzle; drown the noise.

Int. hush! sh! silence! quiet! peace! soft! whist! hold your tongue! keep your mouth shut! shut up! keep your trap shut! dry up! pipe down! cut the cackle! stow it! mum's the word!

400 Loudness – N.
loudness, audibility; noise; high volume; broken silence, shattered s., knock, knocking; burst of sound, report; sonic boom, slam, clap, thunderclap, burst, shell b., explosion 402 *bang*; siren, alarm, honk, toot 665 *danger signal*; reverberation, boom, rattle 403 *roll*; thunder 176 *storm*; war in heaven, hissing 406 *sibilation*; gunfire, artillery, blitz 712 *bombardment*; shrillness, blast, blare, bray, fanfare, flourish 407 *stridor*; trumpet blast, clarion call, view halloo 547 *call*; sonority, clang 404 *resonance*; bells, peal, chimes; crescendo, fortissimo, full blast; clamour, outcry, roaring, shouting, bawling, yelling, screaming, whoop, shout, howl, shriek, scream, roar 408 *cry*, 409 *ululation*; cachinnation 835 *laughter*; stertorousness 352 *respiration*; noisiness, din, row; racket, crash, clash, clatter, hubbub, hullabaloo, ballyhoo, song and dance, slamming, banging, stamping, chanting, hooting, uproar, stramash, shemozzle, tumult, bedlam, pandemonium, all hell let loose 61 *turmoil*.

megaphone, amplifier, loud pedal; public address system, loudhailer, loudspeaker, speaker, microphone, mike; ear

trumpet 415 *hearing aid*; loud instrument, whistle, siren, ghetto blaster; town crier.

Adj. *loud,* audible; at full volume, at full pitch, at the top of one's voice; noisy, uproarious, rowdy, rumbustious 61 *disorderly*; clamorous, shouting, yelling, whooping, screaming, bellowing; sonorous, booming, full-throated, stentorian, ringing, carrying; deafening, dinning; piercing, ear-splitting, thunderous, rattling, crashing; pealing, shrill 407 *strident*; blaring; crescendo; fortissimo, enough to waken the dead.

Vb. *be loud,* - noisy etc. adj.; break the silence; raise the voice, caterwaul; skirl, scream, whistle 407 *shrill*; shout 408 *cry*; cachinnate 835 *laugh*; clap, stamp, raise the roof, raise the rafters; roar, bellow, howl 409 *ululate*; din, sound, boom; rattle, thunder, fulminate, storm, clash; ring, peal, clang, crash; bray, blare; slam 402 *bang*; explode, detonate; knock, hammer, drill; deafen, stun; shatter the eardrums, ring in the ear; waken the dead; raise Cain, kick up a shindy 61 *rampage*.

Adv. *loudly,* distinctly etc. adj.; noisily, aloud, at the top of one's voice; in full cry, full blast; fortissimo, crescendo.

401 Faintness – N. *faintness,* softness, indistinctness, inaudibility; low volume, sound-proofing, noise abatement; thud, thump, bump 405 *nonresonance*; whisper, bated breath; muffled tones 578 *voicelessness*; undertone; murmur, hum, drone 403 *roll*; sigh, sough, moan; scratch, squeak, creak, tick, click; tinkle, clink, chink; buzz, whirr; purr, swish; burble, gurgle; rustle, frou-frou; patter, pitter-p., pit-a-pat; soft footfall, pad; quiet tone, hushed tones, conversation level.

Adj. *muted,* distant, faint, inaudible, barely audible, sotto voce; half-heard; weak, feeble, unemphatic, unstressed, unaccented; soft, low, gentle; piano, subdued, hushed, stealthy, whispered; dull; muffled, suppressed, stifled, bated 407 *hoarse*.

Vb. *sound faint,* lower one's voice, whisper, breathe, murmur, mutter; hum, croon, purr; buzz, drone; babble, ripple, lap, gurgle 350 *flow*; tinkle, chime; moan, sigh, sough 352 *blow*; rustle, swish; tremble, melt; float on the air; fade away; squeak, creak; tick, click; clink, chink; thud, thump.

mute, soften, dull, deaden, dampen, soft-pedal; turn down the volume; hush, muffle, stifle 399 *silence*.

402 Bang: sudden and violent noise – N. *bang,* report, explosion, detonation, blast, blowout, backfire, sonic boom; peal, thunderclap, crash 400 *loudness*; crackle; smack, crack, snap; slap, clap, tap, rap, rat-tat-tat; thump, knock, slam; pop; burst, burst of fire, firing, volley, round, salvo; shot, pistol-s.; cracker, banger, squib.

Vb. *crackle,* sizzle, spit 318 *effervesce*; crack, split; click, rattle; snap, clap, rap, tap, slap, smack.

bang, slam, wham, clash, crash, boom; explode, blast, detonate; pop, go p.; backfire; burst.

403 Roll: repeated and protracted sounds – N. *roll,* rumbling, grumbling; mutter, witter, murmur, background m., rhubarb rhubarb, blahblah; din, rattle, racket, clack, clatter, chatter; booming, clang, ping, reverberation 404 *resonance*; chugging; knocking, drumming, tattoo, rub-a-dub, rat-a-tat, pit-a-pat; peal, carillon; dingdong, tick-tock, cuckoo 106 *repetition*; trill, tremolo, vibrato 410 *musical note*; quaver; hum, whirr, buzz, drone; ringing, singing; drumfire, barrage, cannonade.

Vb. *roll,* drum, tattoo, beat a t.; tap, thrum; chug, rev up, vroom; drum in the ear; boom, roar, din in the ear; grumble, rumble, drone, hum, whirr; trill, chime, peal, toll; tick, beat 317 *oscillate*; rattle, chatter, clatter, clack; reverberate, clang, ping, ring, sing, sing in the ear; quaver, shake, tremble, vibrate; patter 401 *sound faint.*

404 Resonance – N. *resonance,* sonorousness; vibration 317 *oscillation*; reverberation; echo 106 *recurrence*; twanging; ringing, ringing in the ear, tinnitus; singing, bell ringing, tintinnabulation; peal, carillon; sonority, boom; clang, peal, blare, bray; sounding brass, tinkling cymbal; tinkle, jingle; chink, clink; ping, ring, ting-a-ling, chime; low note 410 *musical note*; bass, baritone, basso profondo, bass b., contralto.

Adj. *resonant,* vibrant, reverberant, reverberative; carrying 400 *loud*; resounding etc. vb.; booming, echoing, lingering; sonorous; ringing, tintinnabulary; deeptoned; booming, hollow, sepulchral.

Vb. *resound,* vibrate, reverberate, echo 403 *roll*; whirr, buzz; hum, ring in the ear, sing; ping, ring, ding; jingle, jangle, chink, clink, clank, clunk; ting, tinkle; twang, thrum; gong, chime, tintinnabulate; tootle, toot, trumpet, blare, bray 400 *be loud.*

405 Nonresonance – N. *nonresonance,* nonvibration, thud, thump, bump; plump, plop, plonk, plunk; cracked bell 411 *discord*; muffled sound, muffled drums 401 *faintness*; mute, damper.

406 Sibilation: hissing sound – N. *sibilation,* sibilance, hissing, hiss; sibilant; sputter, splutter; splash, rustle, frou-frou 407 *stridor*; squelch, squish; swish, swoosh.

Vb. *hiss,* sibilate; snort, wheeze, snuffle, whistle; buzz, fizz, fizzle, sizzle, sputter, splutter, spit; splash 318 *effervesce*; swish, swoosh, whizz; squelch, squish; suck; rustle 407 *rasp.*

407 Stridor: harsh sound – N. *stridor,* stridency, discordance, cacophony 411 *discord*; roughness, raucousness, hoarseness, huskiness, gruffness; guttural; squeakiness, rustiness 333 *friction*; scrape, scratch, jarring, creak, squeak; stridulation; shriek, screech, squawk; yawp, yelp, braying 409 *ululation*; high pitch, shrillness, piping, whistling, wolf whistle; bleep; piercing note, sharp n.

410 *musical note*; soprano, treble, falsetto, tenor, countertenor; nasality, twang, drone; skirl, brass, blare.

Adj. *strident,* grating, rusty, creaky, creaking, jarring (see *hoarse*); harsh, metallic; high-pitched, acute, shrill, bleeping; piercing, tinny, ear-splitting 400 *loud*; blaring, braying; reedy, squeaky, squawky, screechy, scratchy; cracked; cacophonous 411 *discordant*.

hoarse, husky, throaty, guttural, raucous, rough, gruff; rasping, jarring, scraping, creaking; grunting, growling; hollow, deep, sepulchral; snoring, stertorous.

Vb. *rasp,* grate, crunch, scrunch, grind, saw, scrape, scratch, squeak; snore, snort, cough, hawk, clear the throat, hem, choke, gasp, sob; bray, croak, caw, screech 409 *ululate*; grunt, burr, break (of the voice); jar, grate on the ear, set the teeth on edge, clash, jangle, twang, clank, clink 411 *discord*.

shrill, bleep; drone, skirl; trumpet, blare 400 *be loud*; whistle, catcall, caterwaul 408 *cry*; scream, squeal, yelp, yawl, screech, squawk; buzz, hum, whine 409 *ululate*; go right through one, strain one's vocal chords.

408 Human cry – N. *cry,* animal cry 409 *ululation*; exclamation, ejaculation 577 *voice*; utterances 579 *speech*; talk, chat, chitchat, conversation 584 *interlocution*; raised voice, vociferousness, shouting, clamour, hullabaloo 400 *loudness*; yodel, song, chant, chorus 412 *vocal music*; shout, yell, whoop, bawl; howl, scream, shriek, screech 407 *stridor*, 377 *pain*; halloo, hail 547 *call*; view halloo, tallyho, hue and cry 619 *chase*; cheer, hurrah, hip-hip-hurrah, hooray 835 *rejoicing*; laugh, giggle, titter 835 *laughter*; hoot, boo, guffaw 924 *disapprobation*; sob, sigh 836 *lamentation*; caterwaul, yawl, squeal, wail, whine, boohoo; grunt, gasp 352 *respiration*; cheerleader; barker; town crier.

Vb. *cry,* cry out, exclaim, ejaculate, pipe up 579 *speak*; call, call out, hail 884 *greet*; whoop; hoot, boo, whistle 924

191

disapprove; cheer, hurrah (see *vociferate*); scream, screech, yawl, yowl, howl, groan 377 *feel pain*; snigger, titter, giggle 835 *laugh*; caterwaul, squall, boohoo, whine, whimper, wail, fret, mewl, pule 836 *weep*; yammer, moan, sob, sigh 836 *lament*; mutter, grumble 401 *sound faint*, 829 *be discontented*; gasp, grunt, snort, snore 352 *breathe*; squeak, squawk, yap, bark 409 *ululate*.

vociferate, clamour, shout, bawl, yell, yawl, yowl, holler; chant, chorus 413 *sing*; cheer, give three cheers, hurrah, hooray, huzza, exult 835 *rejoice*; hiss, hoot, boo, shout down 924 *disapprove*; roar, bellow 409 *ululate*; yell, cry out, sing o., thunder o.; raise the voice, give v., strain one's voice, make oneself hoarse, shout at the top of one's voice.

409 Ululation: animal sounds – N. *ululation*, howling, wailing, yowling, yawling; barking, baying; buzzing, humming, drone; chattering, twittering, chirping, chirruping; warble, call, cry, note, woodnote, birdsong; squeak, cheep, twitter, tweet-tweet; buzz, hum; croak, caw, coo, hiss, quack, cluck, squawk, screech, yawp; baa, moo, neigh, whinny, heehaw; cock-a-doodle-doo, cuckoo, tuwhit tu-whoo; miaow, mew, bark, yelp, yap, snap, snarl, growl. See *ululate*.

Vb. *ululate*, cry, call, give tongue; squawk, screech, yawp; caterwaul, yowl, yawl, howl, wail; roar, bellow, bell; hum, drone, buzz, spit 406 *hiss*; woof, bark, bay; yelp, yap; snap, snarl, growl, whine; trumpet, bell, troat; bray, neigh, whinny, whicker; bleat, baa; low, moo; miaow, mew, mewl, purr; quack, cackle, gaggle; gobble, gabble, cluck, clack; grunt, gruntle, snort, squeal; pipe, pule; chatter, sing, chirp, chirrup, cheep, peep, tweet, twitter, chuckle, churr, whirr, coo; caw, croak; hoot, honk, boom; grate, squeak 407 *rasp*; warble, carol, whistle 413 *sing*.

410 Melody: concord – N. *melody*, musicalness, melodiousness, tonality,

euphony, euphoniousness; harmoniousness, chime, harmony, concord, concert 24 *agreement*; assonance; unison; resolution (of a discord), cadence, perfect c.; harmonics, harmonization, counterpoint; part, second, chorus; orchestration, instrumentation; tone; phrasing; passage, theme, leit-motiv, coda; movement 412 *musical piece*.

musical note, note, keys, keyboard, manual; black notes, white n., sharp, flat, double f., double sharp, accidental, natural, tone, semitone; keynote, fundamental note; tonic, supertonic, mediant, subdominant, dominant, submediant, subtonic, leading note; interval, second, third, fourth, fifth, sixth, seventh, octave, ninth; diatesseron, diapason; gamut, scale (see *key*); chord, common c., triad, tetrachord, arpeggio; grace note, grace, ornament, crush note, appoggiatura, acciaccatura, mordent, turn, shake, trill, tremolo, vibrato, cadenza; tone, tonality, register, pitch, concert p., high p., low p.; high note 407 *stridor*; low note 404 *resonance*; undertone, overtone, harmonic, upper partial; sustained note, monotone, drone.

notation, musical n., tonic solfa; score; signature, key s., clef, treble c., bass c., tenor c., alto c.; bar, stave, staff; line, ledger l., space, brace; rest, pause, interval; breve, semibreve, minim, crotchet, quaver, semiquaver, demisemiquaver, hemidemisemiquaver.

tempo, time, beat; rhythm 593 *prosody*; measure, timing; syncopation; upbeat, downbeat; suspension, long note, short n., suspended n.; prolonged n.; tempo rubato; rallentando, andante, adagio; metronome.

key, signature, clef, modulation, transposition, major key, minor k.; scale, gamut, major scale, minor s., diatonic s., chromatic s., harmonic s., melodic s., enharmonic s., twelve-tone s.; series, tone row; mode, Lydian m., Phrygian m., Dorian m., mixolydian; ´ Indian mode, raga.

Adj. *melodious,* melodic, musical, lyrical, lilting, tuneful, catchy, tripping; dulcet, mellifluous, sweet-sounding; chiming; silver-toned; golden-toned; euphonious, euphonic.

harmonious, harmonizing, consonant 24 *agreeing*; in pitch; in chorus; assonant, rhyming, matching 18 *similar*; symphonic, symphonious.

Vb. *harmonize,* blend 24 *accord*; chorus 413 *sing*; attune, tune, tune up, pitch, string 24 *adjust*; be in key, be in unison, be on the beat; compose, put to music, set to music, score, symphonize, orchestrate 413 *compose music*; modulate, transpose.

411 Discord – N. *discord,* discordance, dissonance, disharmony, jangle 25 *disagreement*; atonality, twelve-tone scale; imperfect cadence; preparation (of a discord); harshness, hoarseness, jarring, cacophony; Babel, cat's concert, caterwauling, yowling 400 *loudness*; row, din, noise, pandemonium, bedlam, tumult, racket 61 *turmoil*; atmospherics, wow.

Adj. *discordant,* dissonant, jangling, discording 25 *disagreeing*; conflicting 14 *contrary*; jarring, grating, scraping, rasping, harsh, raucous, cacophonous 407 *strident*; inharmonious; unmelodious, unmusical; untuned, cracked; off pitch, off key, out of tune, sharp, flat; atonal, toneless, tuneless, droning, singsong.

Vb. *discord,* lack harmony 25 *disagree*; jangle, jar, grate, clash, crash; saw, scrape 407 *rasp*; be harsh, be out of tune, be off key; play sharp, play flat; thrum, drone, whine; prepare a discord.

412 Music – N. *music,* harmony; 410 *melody*; musicianship 413 *musical skill*; minstrelsy, music-making, playing; strumming, thrumming, vamping; improvisation; orchestration, instrumentation, composing, composition; instrumental music, pipe m., military m.; counterpoint, contrapuntal music; classical music, chamber m., organ m., choral m., operatic m., ballet m., sacred m., soul m.; light music, popular m., pop m., pop;

descriptive music, programme m.; electronic m., musique concrète; live music, recorded music, canned m., piped m., musical wallpaper, wall-to-wall m., muzak; disco music, dance m., waltztime; hot music, syncopation, jazz, progressive j., modern j., cool j., blue note, blues, mainstream jazz, traditional j., trad, Dixieland, ragtime, swing, doowop, bebop, bop, boogie-woogie; skiffle, jive, rock'n roll, rock music, hard r., soft r., heavy metal, hip-hop, new wave, mod, punk; ska, reggae; soul; rhythm'n blues, country and western, blue grass, folk; sheet music, the music, score, full s.; concert, orchestral c., choral c., promenade c., prom; singsong; music festival, eisteddfod, mod; conservatoire; Tin Pan Alley, Nashville.

tune, melody, strain; theme song, signature tune; descant; reprise, refrain; melodic line; air, popular a., aria, solo; peal, chime, carillon; phrase, passage, measure.

musical piece, piece, composition, opus, work; tape, cassette, recording 414 *gramophone*; orchestration, instrumentation; arrangement, adaptation, setting, transcription; accompaniment, obbligato; voluntary, prelude, overture, intermezzo, finale; incidental music, background m., wallpaper m., wall-to-wall m.; romance, rhapsody, extravaganza, impromptu, fantasia, caprice, divertissement, variations, raga; medley, potpourri; étude, study; suite, fugue, canon, toccata; sonata, sonatina, concerto, symphony, sinfonietta; symphonic poem, tone p.; pastorale, scherzo, rondo, gigue, jig, reel, strathspey; gavotte, minuet, tarantella, mazurka, polonaise, polka, waltz 837 *dance*; march, grand m., bridal m., wedding m., dead m., funeral m., dirge, pibroch; nocturne, serenade, berceuse, lullaby; introductory phrase, anacrusis; statement, exposition, development, recapitulation, variation; theme, motive, leitmotiv; movement; passage, phrase; chord 410 *musical note*; cadenza, coda.

vocal music, singing, vocalism, lyricism; vocalization; part; opera, operetta,

light opera, comic o., musical comedy, musical 594 *stage play*; choir-singing, oratorio, cantata, chorale; hymn-singing, psalmody, hymnology; descant, chant, plain c., Gregorian c., Ambrosian c., plainsong; cantus, c. firmus, recitative; bel canto, coloratura, bravura; solfège, solfa; introit, anthem, canticle, psalm 981 *hymn*; song, lay, roundelay, carol, lyric, lilt; canzonet, cavatina, lieder, lied, ballad; folk song, popular *or* pop s., rap, top twenty, hit parade, the charts; ditty, shanty, calypso; spiritual, blues; part song, glee, madrigal, round, catch, canon; chorus, refrain, burden; choral hymn, antiphony, dithyramb; boat song, barcarole; lullaby, cradle song, berceuse; serenade, aubade; bridal hymn, wedding h., epithalamium, prothalamium; love song, amorous ditty; song, birdsong, bird call, dawn chorus; requiem, dirge, threnody, coronach 836 *lament*; musical declamation, recitative; lyrics, libretto; songbook, hymnbook, psalter.

Adj. *musical 410 melodious;* philharmonic, symphonic; melodic; vocal, hummable; operatic, recitative; lyric; choral; hymnal, psalmodic; harmonized 410 *harmonious*; contrapuntal; orchestrated, scored; set to music, arranged; instrumental, orchestral, for strings; syncopated; doo-wop.

Adv. *adagio,* lento, largo, larghetto, andante, andantino, maestoso, moderato; allegro, allegretto; spiritoso, vivace, accelerando, presto, prestissimo; piano, mezzo-p., pianissimo, forte, mezzo-f., fortissimo, sforzando, con brio, capriccioso, scherzando; glissando, legato, sostenuto; staccato; crescendo, diminuendo, rallentando; affettuoso, cantabile, parlante; tremolo, pizzicato, vibrato; rubato; da capo.

413 Musician – N. *musician,* artiste, virtuoso, soloist; bravura player 696 *proficient person*; player, performer, concert artist; bard, minstrel, troubadour,

trovatore, minnesinger; street musician, busker; composer, symphonist, contrapuntist; scorer, arranger, harmonist; syncopator, jazzman; librettist, lyricist, liederwriter, hymnwriter, hymnographer, psalmist; musical director, music teacher, music master, kapellmeister, master of the music, bandmaster, conductor (see *orchestra*); musicologist, musicotherapist, music critic, concertgoer, operagoer 504 *enthusiast*.

instrumentalist, pianist, accompanist; organist, cembalist, harpsichordist, accordionist, concertina player, harmonica p.; violinist, fiddler; violist, cellist; harpist, lyre player, lute p., lutanist, sitarist, guitarist, bassist, mandolinist, banjoist; strummer, thrummer; piper, fifer, piccolo player, flautist, flutist, clarinettist, oboist, bassoonist; saxophonist, horn player, trumpeter, bugler; cornetist; bell ringer, carilloneur, campanologist; drummer, drummer boy, drum major; percussionist, timpanist; organ-grinder, hurdy-gurdy man.

orchestra, symphony o., chamber o., sinfonietta, quartet, quintet; ensemble, wind e.; strings, brass, woodwind, percussion, drums; band, string b., jazz b., ragtime b.; brass b., military b., pipe b.; skiffle group, steel band; rock b. *or* group, punk b. *or* g., pop g.; conductor, maestro, bandmaster; bandleader, leader, first violin; orchestra player, bandsman.

vocalist, singer, songster, caroller; chanteuse, songstress; troubadour, madrigal singer, minstrel, busker; ballad singer, folk s., pop s.; crooner, jazz singer, blues s.; opera singer, prima donna, diva; castrato, treble, soprano, mezzo-s., contralto, alto, tenor, countertenor, baritone, bass b., bass, basso, basso profondo.

choir, chorus, waits, wassailers, carol singers, glee club, barbershop quartet; massed choirs, eisteddfod; chorister, choirboy *or* -girl; precentor, cantor, choirmaster, choirleader.

Vb. *compose music*, compose; set to music, score, arrange, transpose, orchestrate, harmonize, improvise, extemporize.

play music, play, perform, execute, render, interpret; pick out a tune; conduct, wield the baton, beat time, syncopate; play the piano, accompany; pedal, vamp, strum; tickle the ivories; harp, pluck, pick, strike the lyre, pluck the guitar, bottleneck; thrum, twang; fiddle, bow, scrape, saw; play the concertina, squeeze the box, grind the organ; play the harmonica; wind, wind the horn, blow, bugle, blow the b., sound the horn, sound, trumpet, sound the t., toot, tootle; pipe, flute, whistle; clash the cymbals; drum, tattoo, beat, tap, ruffle, beat the drum 403 *roll*; ring, peal the bells, ring a change; toll, knell; tune, string, set to concert pitch; practise, do scales, improvise, jam, extemporise, play a voluntary, prelude; strike up.

sing, chant; intone, descant; warble, carol, lilt, trill, croon, hum, whistle, yodel; belt out; harmonize; chorus; serenade; chirp, chirrup, twitter, pipe 409 *ululate*; purr 401 *sound faint*.

414 Musical instruments – N. *musical instrument*, band, concert 413 *orchestra*; strings, brass, wind, woodwind, percussion; sounding board, diaphragm, sound box; synthesizer.

stringed instrument, harp, Aeolian harp; lyre, lute, sitar; theorbo; cithara, cithern, zither, gittern, guitar, acoustic g., semi-acoustic g., electric g., mandolin, ukulele, banjo, balalaika, zither; psaltery, vina; plectrum, fret.

viol, violin, Cremona, Stradivarius, fiddle, kit, crowd, rebec; viola *or* tenor violin, viola d'amore, viola da gamba *or* bass viol, cello *or* violoncello, double bass *or* contrabasso; musical saw; bow, fiddlestick; string, catgut; bridge; resin.

piano, pianoforte, grand piano, concert grand, baby g.; upright piano, cottage p.; virginals, dulcimer, harpsichord, cembalo, spinet, clavichord, celesta; piano-organ, player piano, Pianola (tdmk);

clavier, keyboard, manual, keys, ivories; loud pedal, soft p., damper.

organ, pipe o., church o., Hammond o., electric *or* electronic o., steam o., calliope; reed organ, harmonium, American organ, melodeon; mouth organ, harmonica; kazoo, comb; accordion, piano a., concertina; barrel organ, hurdy-gurdy; great organ, swell o., choir o.; organ pipe, flue p., organ stop, flue s.; manual, keyboard.

flute, fife, piccolo, flageolet, cornetto, recorder; woodwind, reed instrument, clarinet, bass c., basset horn; saxophone, sax, tenor s.; shawm, hautboy, oboe, tenor o., cor Anglais; bassoon, double b.; ocarina; pipe, oaten p., reed, straw; chanter, bagpipes, musette; pan pipes, Pandean p., syrinx; nose flute; whistle, penny w., tin w.; pitch-pipe; bazooka; mouthpiece, embouchure.

horn, brass; bugle horn, post h., hunting h.; bugle, trumpet, clarion; alpenhorn, French horn, flugelhorn, saxhorn, althorn, helicon horn, bass h., sousaphone; euphonium, ophicleide, serpent, bombardon; cornet, trombone, sackbut, tuba, saxtuba, bass tuba; conch, shell.

gong, bell, tintinnabulum; treble bell, tenor b.; church bell, alarm bell, tocsin 665 *danger signal*; tintinnabulation, peal, carillon, chimes, bells; bones, rattle, clappers, castanets, maracas; cymbals; xylophone, marimba, vibraphone, vibes; musical glasses, harmonica; tubular bell, glockenspiel; triangle; tuning fork; Jew's harp; sounding board; percussion instrument.

drum, big d., bass d., tenor d., side d., snare d., kettle d., timpani, steel drum; war drum, tomtom, bongo; tabor, tambourine; tabla.

gramophone, record player, phonograph, radiogram; tape recorder, cassette r., high-fidelity system, hi-fi, stereo set, stereo system, music centre, stack system, stereo tower, hi-fi t.; personal stereo, personal hi-fi, personal headset, Walkman (tdmk), ghetto blaster, compact disc player; playback; recording,

tape r., tape, cassette; gramophone record, disc, compact d., laser d., platter, long-playing record, LP, EP, 33, 45, 78; album, single, track; jukebox; head, needle, stylus, pickup, cartridge; deck, turntable; amplifier, speaker, tweeter, woofer.

415 Hearing – **N.** *hearing,* audition; sense of hearing, acute hearing; good ear, sharp e., ear for music; audibility, good reception; earshot, range, reach.

listening, hearkening 455 *attention*; aural examination 459 *enquiry*; listening-in; lip-reading 520 *interpretation*; eavesdropping, wire-tapping, bugging 523 *latency*; sound recording 548 *record*; audition, voice testing 461 *experiment*; interview, audience, hearing 584 *conference*; legal hearing 959 *legal trial*.

listener, hearer, audience, auditorium; stalls, pit, gallery, the gods 441 *spectator*; radio listener, radio ham, CB user; hi-fi enthusiast, audiophile; disciple, lecturegoer 538 *learner*; monitor, auditor, examiner 459 *questioner*; eavesdropper, listener-in, little pitcher.

ear, lug, lobe, earhole, lughole; external ear, middle e., internal e.; aural cavity, cochlea, eardrum, tympanum; auditory canal, labyrinth; otology; aurist, otologist, otolaryngologist, otorhinolaryngologist, ENT specialist, ear, nose and throat s.; Ménière's disease.

hearing aid, deaf-aid, ear trumpet; stethoscope, otoscope, auriscope; loudspeaker, loudhailer, tannoy, public address system 528 *publication*; microphone, mike, amplifier 400 *megaphone*; speaking tube; telephone, phone, cellular telephone, car t., blower; receiver, earpiece, extension, headphones, headset, earphones; walkie-talkie 531 *telecommunication*; sound recorder, asdic, sonar, magnetic tape, Dictaphone (tdmk), Dictograph (tdmk) 549 *recording instrument*; radiogram 414 *gramophone*, 531 *broadcasting*.

Adj. *auditory,* hearing, auricular, aural; audiovisual 398 *sounding*; otic, otological, stethoscopic; auditive, acoustic,

audile, within earshot, within hearing distance, audible.

Vb. *hear,* catch; list, listen, lip-read 520 *interpret*; listen in, switch on, tune in, tune to; lift the receiver, answer the phone; overhear, eavesdrop, listen at keyholes, keep one's ears open; intercept, bug, tap; hearken, lend an ear, give audience, interview, grant an interview 459 *interrogate*; hear confession 526 *confess*; be all ears, hang on the lips of, lap up 455 *be attentive*; strain one's ears, prick up one's e.; hear it said, hear it on *or* through the grapevine, come to one's ears 524 *be informed*.

416 Deafness – **N.** *deafness,* defective hearing, imperfect h., hardness of hearing; deaf-mutism; deaf-and-dumb speech, sign language, dactylogy; deaf-and-dumb person, deaf-mute; inaudibility 399 *silence*.

Adj. *deaf,* hard of hearing, dull of h., hearing-impaired, stone-deaf, deaf as a post, deaf and dumb, deaf-mute; deafened, unable to hear, with ears bunged up; deaf to, not listening 456 *inattentive*; tone-deaf; inaudible, out of earshot, out of hearing 399 *silent*.

Vb. *be deaf,* hear nothing, fail to catch; not listen, shut one's ears, close one's e., plug one's e. 458 *disregard*; turn a deaf ear to 760 *refuse*; have hearing difficulties, have impaired hearing, be hard of hearing, use a hearing aid; lip-read, use lip-reading 520 *translate*; talk with one's fingers, use sign language.

deafen, make deaf, split the eardrum, drown one's voice 400 *be loud*.

417 Light – **N.** *light,* daylight, light of day, noon, high n., broad daylight 128 *morning*; sunbeam, sunlight, sun 420 *luminary*; starlight, moonlight, moonshine, half-light, twilight, gloaming 419 *dimness*; artificial light, electric light, gaslight, candlelight, firelight 420 *lighting*; floodlight, son et lumière; illumination, irradiation, splendour, resplendence, effulgence, refulgence, intensity,

brightness, vividness, brilliance; luminousness, luminosity, luminance, candle power, magnitude; incandescence, radiance; sheen, shine, gloss, polish, lustre (see *reflection*); blaze, blaze of light; glare, dazzle; flare, flame 379 *fire*; halo, nimbus, aureole; spectrum, iridescence, rainbow 437 *variegation*.

flash, lightning; beam, stream, shaft, ray; streak, meteor flash; scintillation, sparkle, spark; glint, glitter, glisten, play of light; blink, twinkle, twinkling, flicker, flickering, glimmer, gleam, shimmer, shimmering; spangle, tinsel; strobe light, searchlight, torchlight 420 *lamp*; firefly.

glow, flush, afterglow, dawn, rosy-fingered d., sunset; lambent light; aurora, aurora borealis, aurora australis; northern lights; zodiacal light 321 *heavens*; radiance, incandescence 379 *heat*; luminescence, fluorescence, phosphorescence, thermoluminescence; will-o'-thewisp.

radiation, emission, absorption; radioactivity, irradiation 160 *nucleonics*; radioisotope; Geiger counter; fallout, nuclear f., mushroom cloud 659 *poison*; radiation belt, Van Allen layer 340 *atmosphere*; radio wave, frequency w.; long w., short w., medium w. 317 *oscillation*; wavelength, waveband; high frequency, VHF, UHF; interference, static 160 *electricity*; electromagnetic radiation, microwave; infrared radiation, radiant heat *or* energy; ultraviolet radiation; X-ray, gamma r., cosmic radiation; magnetic storm; photon; photoelectric cell; curie, millicurie, roentgen, rem, rad; half-life, radiology, industrial r., medical r., diagnostic r., radiotherapy.

reflection, refraction; diffraction, dispersion, scattering, interference, polarization; polish, gloss, sheen, shine, glisten, gleam, lustre; glare, dazzle, blink.

Adj. *luminous*, lucid; light; lit, well-lit, floodlit, bright, gay, shining, fulgent, resplendent, splendid, brilliant, flamboyant, vivid; colourful; radiant, effulgent, refulgent; dazzling, blinding, glaring, lurid, garish; incandescent, flaring, flaming, aflame, aglow, afire, ablaze 379

fiery; glowing, blushing, auroral 431 *red*; luminescent, fluorescent, phosphorescent; soft, lambent, beaming; glittery, flashing, glinting etc. vb.; scintillating, sparkling; lustrous, chatoyant, shimmering, shiny, sheeny, glossy, polished; reflecting; refractive; optical, photosensitive.

undimmed, clear, bright, fair; cloudless, unclouded, sunny, sunshiny; moonlit, starlit, starry; burnished, polished, glassy, gleaming; lucid, pellucid.

Vb. *shine*, burn, blaze, flame, flare 379 *be hot*; glow, incandesce, luminesce, phosphoresce; glare, dazzle, bedazzle, blind; dance; flash, glisten, glister, blink; glimmer, flicker, twinkle; glitter, shimmer, glance; scintillate, sparkle, spark; come up, gleam, glint.

radiate, beam, shoot, shoot out rays, send out r. 300 *emit*; reflect, refract; be radioactive, bombard; X-ray.

make bright, lighten, dawn, rise, wax (moon); clear, clear up, lift, brighten; light, ignite 381 *kindle*; light up; shed lustre, throw light on; shine upon, flood with light, irradiate, illuminate, illume; transilluminate; burnish, rub up 648 *clean*.

418 Darkness – N. *darkness*, dark; black 428 *blackness*; night, dark n., night-time, nightfall; dead of night, witching time 129 *midnight*; pitch darkness; Stygian gloom; murk, murkiness, gloom, dusk, gloaming, twilight, half-dark, semi-darkness; shadiness, shadows 419 *dimness*; shade, shadow; penumbra; silhouette, negative, radiograph; darkroom.

darkening, obfuscation 419 *dimness*; blackout; fadeout, eclipse, total e. 446 *disappearance*; lights out; sunset, sundown 129 *evening*; blackening, shading; chiaroscuro; dark lantern; dimmer, dip switch,

Adj. *dark*, sombre, dark-coloured, swarthy, dusky 428 *black*; poorly lit, obscure, pitch-dark, sooty, inky, jetblack, black as night; black as ink, black as hell, black as pitch, black as the ace of

197

spades, murky; funereal, gloomy, sombre; louring; shady 419 *shadowy*; darkened; nocturnal; hidden, secret 523 *occult.*

unlit, unlighted, unilluminated; sunless, moonless, starless; eclipsed, overcast; hazy, cloudy 423 *opaque*; extinguished; dimmed, blacked out; obscured.

Vb. *be dark,* grow d., get d., lour; cloud over, look black.

darken, black out; lower the light, dim the l., put out the l., switch off the l.; eclipse 226 *cover*; curtain, shutter, veil 421 *screen*; obscure, obfuscate; cloud, dim, tone down 419 *bedim*; overcast, overshadow, spread gloom; cast a shadow; silhouette 551 *represent*; shade, underexpose 428 *blacken.*

419 Dimness – N. *dimness,* indistinctness, vagueness, fuzziness, blur, lack of definition, soft focus; loom; faintness, paleness 426 *achromatism*; grey 429 *greyness*; dullness, lacklustre; matt finish; leaden skies; cloudiness, smokiness, poor visibility, impaired v., white-out 423 *opacity*; mistiness, fogginess; murk, gloom 418 *darkness*; fog, mist, haar 355 *cloud*; shadowiness, shadow, shade.

half-light, semidarkness, half-dark, bad light; waning light, gloaming 129 *evening*; twilight, dusk; daybreak, break of day, penumbra, half-shadow, partial eclipse.

Adj. *dim,* darkish, sombre, dusky, dusk, twilight, wan, dun, grey, pale 426 *colourless*; faint, faded, waning; imperceptible, indistinct, blurred, bleary; dull, lustreless, lacklustre, leaden; flat, matt; filmy, hazy, fuzzy, foggy, fogbound, misty, nebulous 355 *cloudy*; thick, smoky, sooty, muddy 423 *opaque*; dingy, grimy, rusty, rusted, mildewed, unpolished, unburnished 649 *dirty.*

shadowy, shady, shaded, overshadowed, overcast; vague, indistinct, undefined, ill-defined, obscure, confused, fuzzy, blurry; deceptive; half-glimpsed, half-hidden 444 *invisible*; half-lit 418 *unlit*; dreamlike, ghostly 4 *insubstantial*; coming and going.

Vb. *be dim,* - faint etc. adj.; be indistinct; lose definition, fade, wane, grow p. 426 *lose colour*; lour; glimmer, flicker, gutter.

dim, dip; bedim; lower *or* turn down the lights, fade out; obscure, blur; smear, besmirch, sully; rust, mildew, muddy, dirty 649 *make unclean*; fog, mist; becloud; overcast; shade, shadow, veil 226 *cover.*

420 Luminary: source of light – N. *luminary,* naked light, flame 379 *fire*; flare; sun; moon; starlight 321 *star*; bright star, first magnitude s., Sirius, Aldebaran, Betelgeuse, Canopus, Alpha Centauri; evening star, Hesperus, Vesper, Venus; morning star, Lucifer; shooting star, fireball 321 *meteor*; galaxy, Milky Way, northern lights 321 *heavens*; lightning, bolt of l., sheet l., forked l., ball l., summer l., lightning flash, levin; scintilla, spark, sparkle 417 *flash.*

torch, brand; torchlight, flambeau, match 385 *lighter*; candle, bougie, tallow candle, wax c.; flower c., cake c., christmas c; taper, wax t.; spill, wick, dip, rushlight, nightlight, naked light, flare, gas jet, burner, Bunsen b.

lamp, lamplight; lantern; safety lamp, Davy l., acetylene l.; oil lamp, hurricane l., paraffin l., spirit l.; gas lamp, Calor gas (tdmk) lamp, gas mantle; electric lamp, flash gun, torch, pocket t., penlight, flashlight, searchlight, arc light, floodlight; headlamp, headlight, side light; foglamp; tail light, brake l., reflector; bulb, flashbulb, photoflood, electric bulb, light b.; strobe light, stroboscope, strobe; vapour light, neon l., strip l., fluorescent l.; street l., mercury vapour lamp, sodium l.; Chinese lantern, fairy lights, Christmas tree l.; magic lantern, projector; light fitting, chandelier, candelabra; standard lamp, table l., desk l., reading l., Anglepoise (tdmk) l.; sun l., sunray l.; lamppost; candle holder, candlestick.

lighting, illumination, irradiation 417 *light*; artificial lighting, street l.; indirect lighting; gas lighting, electric l., neon l., fluorescent l.; floodlighting, son et lumière, limelight, spotlight, footlights, houselights.

signal light, warning l. 665 *danger signal*; traffic light, red l., green l., amber l., trafficator, indicator; Very light, Bengal l., rocket, star shell, parachute flare, flare; flare path, beacon, beacon fire, balefire 547 *signal*; lighthouse, lightship.

421 Screen – N. *screen,* shield 660 *protection*; shelter; bower 194 *arbour*; shady nook 418 *darkness*; sunshade, parasol; sun hat, sola topee 226 *shade*; awning 226 *canopy*; sunscreen, visor; lampshade; eyeshade, blinkers; eyelid, eyelashes 438 *eye*; dark glasses, tinted g., sun g., shades 442 *eyeglass*; smoked glass, frosted g., opaque g., polarized g. 424 *semitransparency*; stained glass 437 *variegation*; double glazing, soundproofing, partition, wall, hedge 235 *fence*; filter 57 *exclusion*; mask 527 *disguise*; hood, veil, mantle 228 *cloak*; cloud; mist; smokescreen.

curtain 226 shade; window curtain, net c., bead c.; drapes, shade, blind, sunblind; persienne, jalousie, venetian blind, roller b.; shutter.

Vb. *screen,* shield, shelter 660 *safeguard*; protect 713 *defend*; ward off, fend off, keep at bay; keep off, keep out, filter out 57 *exclude*; cover up, veil, hood 226 *cover*; mask, hide, shroud 525 *conceal*; intercept 702 *obstruct*; blinker, blindfold 439 *blind*; shade, shadow, darken; curtain, curtain off, canopy, draw the curtains, pull down the blind; put up the shutters, close the s. 264 *close*; cloud, fog.

422 Transparency – N. *transparency,* transmission of light; transparence, translucence; thinness; lucidity, pellucidity, limpidity; clearness, clarity; glassiness; water, ice, crystal, Perspex (tdmk), cellophane, shrink-wrapping, bubble pack, blister p., glass, plate g., magnifying g., lens, eyepiece 442 *eyeglass*; pane, window g.; sheer silk, gossamer, gauze, lace, chiffon 4 *insubstantial thing.*

Adj. *transparent,* diaphanous, revealing, sheer, see-through; thin, fine, filmy, gauzy, pellucid, translucent; lucent 424 *semitransparent*; liquid, limpid; crystal, crystalline, glassy; clear, lucid; crystal-clear.

423 Opacity – N. *opacity,* opaqueness; thickness, solidity 324 *density*; filminess, frost; turbidity, muddiness, dirtiness 649 *dirt*; fog, mist, haar, dense fog, smog, pea-souper 355 *cloud*; film, scale 421 *screen*; smoke-scree.

Adj. *opaque,* nontransparent, thick, impervious to light, blank, windowless; not clear, unclarified, cloudy, milky; filmy, turbid, muddy, muddied; foggy, hazy, misty, murky, smoky, sooty 419 *dim*; frosted, misted, clouded.

424 Semitransparency – N. *semitransparency,* milkiness; pearliness, opalescence; smoked glass, ground g., frosted g., tinted spectacles, dark glasses; gauze, muslin, net; pearl, opal 437 *variegation.*

Adj. *semitransparent,* gauzy, filmy; translucent, opalescent; milky, pearly; frosted; smoked 419 *dim*, 355 *cloudy.*

425 Colour – N. *colour,* primary c.; three primaries; chromatism, chromatic aberration; chromatic scale; prism, spectrum, rainbow 437 *variegation*; colour scheme, palette; coloration 553 *painting*; colour photography, Technicolor (tdmk); heraldic colour, tincture, chromatics; spectroscope, prism.

hue, chromaticity, tone; brilliance, intensity, warmth, loudness; softness, deadness, dullness; coloration, livery; pigmentation, colouring, complexion; flush, blush, glow; rosy cheek, ruddiness 431 *redness*; sickly hue, pallor 426 *achromatism*; discoloration; tint, shade, nuance, cast, dye; tinge, patina; half-tone, half-light, mezzotint.

pigment, colouring matter, rouge, blusher, dye, warpaint 843 *cosmetic*; dyestuff, dye, fast d.; natural d., vegetable d., madder, cochineal 431 *red pigment*; indigo 436 *purpleness*; woad 435 *blueness*; artificial dye, synthetic d., aniline d.; stain, fixative, mordant; wash, colourwash, whitewash, distemper; paint, emulsion p., gloss p., undercoat; oil paints, acrylic p., watercolours.

Adj. *florid,* colourful, high-coloured; over-stated; ruddy 431 *red*; intense, deep, strong, emphatic; unfaded, vivid, brilliant 417 *luminous*; warm, glowing, rich, painted, gay, bright; gaudy, garish, showy, flashy; glaring, flaring, flaunting, spectacular; harsh, stark, raw, crude; lurid, loud, screaming, shrieking; clashing, discordant 25 *disagreeing*.

soft-hued, soft, quiet, under-stated, tender, delicate, refined, discreet; pearly, creamy 427 *whitish*; light, pale, pastel, muted; simple; faded; weathered, mellow; harmonious 24 *agreeing*.

Vb. *colour,* colour in, block in, crayon, daub 553 *paint*; rouge 431 *redden*, 843 *primp*; pigment, tattoo; dye, tie-dye, dip, imbue; tint, touch up; shade; tincture, tinge; wash, colourwash, distemper, lacquer 226 *coat*; stain, run, discolour; come off (e.g. on one's fingers); tan, weather, mellow; illuminate, emblazon; whitewash; enamel 437 *variegate*.

426 Achromatism: absence of colour – N. *achromatism,* achromaticity, colourlessness; discoloration, etiolation, weathering, fading, bleaching 427 *whiteness*; overexposure 551 *photography*; pallor, pallidity, paleness; lightness, faintness etc. adj.; absence of colour, anaemia, bloodlessness; pigment deficiency, albinism, albinoism; neutral tint; monochrome; black and white; albino, blond(e), platinum b., peroxide b., artificial b.

bleacher, decolorant, peroxide, bleaching powder, bleach, lime.

Adj. *colourless,* neutral; uncoloured; achromatic; bleached, etiolated, overexposed, weathered; faint, faded, fading;

unpigmented, albino, light-skinned, fair-s., fair, blond(e) 433 *yellow*, 427 *whitish*; lustreless, mousy; bloodless, anaemic; without colour, drained of colour, washed out, wishy-washy, peaky; pale, pallid 427 *white*; ashen, livid, whey-faced; pasty, doughy, sallow, sickly 651 *unhealthy*; dingy, dull 429 *grey*; lacklustre; wan 419 *dim*; deathly, deathly pale, white as a sheet, ghostlike.

Vb. *lose colour* 419 *be dim*; pale, fade, bleach, blanch, turn pale, change countenance, go as white as a sheet 427 *whiten*; run.

427 Whiteness – N. *whiteness,* etiolation; albinism, albinoism 426 *achromatism*; whitishness, creaminess, off-whiteness, pearliness; hoariness; white light 417 *light*; white heat 379 *heat*; white, Caucasian, paleface; albino.

white thing, alabaster, marble; hoar frost, snow, new-fallen s.; chalk, paper, milk, flour, salt, ivory, lily, swan; albino; silver, pewter, platinum; pearl, teeth.

Adj. *white,* pure; light, bright 417 *luminous*; silvery, silver, alabaster, marble; chalky, snowy, snow-capped, snow-covered; hoary, frosty, frosted; foaming, spumy, foam-flecked; soapy, lathery; white hot 379 *hot*; white as a sheet, white as the driven snow; pure white, lily-white, milk-w., snow-w., white-skinned, Caucasian; whitened, whitewashed, bleached 648 *clean*.

whitish, pearly, milky, creamy 424 *semitransparent*; ivory, waxen, sallow, pale 426 *colourless*; off-white, oyster-w., mushroom, magnolia; ecru, beige 430 *brown*; hoary, grizzled 429 *grey*; pepper-and-salt 437 *mottled*; blond(e), fair, Nordic; ash-blond(e), platinum b., fair-haired, golden-h., flaxen-h., tow-headed.

Vb. *whiten,* white, blanco, pipeclay, whitewash, wash 648 *clean*; blanch, bleach; pale, fade; frost, silver, grizzle.

428 Blackness – N. *blackness,* 418 *darkness*; inkiness, lividity, black, sable; melanism, swarthiness, duskiness, pigmentation, dark colouring, colour; depth,

deep tone; black and white; blackening, darkening 418 *obscuration*; black, Negro, Negress; coloured.

black thing, coal, charcoal, soot, pitch, tar; ebony, jet, ink, smut; blacklead; burnt cork; melanin; sable; bruise, black eye; blackberry, sloe; crow, raven, blackbird; black clothes, mourning.

Adj. *black,* sable; inky, black as thunder 418 *dark*; sooty, smoky, smudgy, smutty 649 *dirty*; blackened, singed, charred; black-haired, raven-haired, dark-headed; black-eyed, sloe-e.; dark, brunette; black-skinned, Negroid; pigmented, coloured; sombre, gloomy, mourning 364 *funereal*; coal-black, jet-b., pitch-b.; blue-b.; black as ink, black as pitch, black as the ace of spades, black as hell; black as night.

blackish, swarthy, dusky, dark, dark-skinned, tanned, sun-t.; coloured, pigmented; livid, black and blue.

Vb. *blacken,* black, blacklead, japan, ink, ink in; dirty, blot; char 381 *burn*.

429 Greyness – **N.** *greyness,* neutral, greige, grisaille; pepper and salt, grey hairs, hoary head; pewter, silver; gunmetal, ashes, slate; grey, dove g. etc. adj.; oyster, taupe.

Adj. *grey,* neutral, dull, sombre, leaden, livid; greying, grizzled, grizzly, hoary; silvery, pearly, frosted 427 *whitish*; greige; light-grey, pale-g., ash-g., dove-g., pearl-g.; mouse-coloured, mousy, dun, drab, donkey-grey; steely, charcoal-g.; slate-coloured; greyish, ashen, smoky; dapple-grey.

430 Brownness – **N.** *brownness,* brown, bronze, copper, amber; tobacco leaf, autumn colours; cinnamon, coffee, chocolate; butterscotch, caramel, toffee, burnt almond; walnut, mahogany; dark skin *or* complexion, suntan; brunette.

brown pigment, bistre, ochre, sepia, burnt sienna, burnt umber, Vandyke brown.

Adj. *brown,* bronze, mahogany etc. n.; browned, toasted; bronzed, tanned, sunburnt; dark, brunette; nut-brown, hazel; light brown, ecru, oatmeal, beige, buff, fawn, biscuit, mushroom, café-au-lait; brownish, greyish-brown, dun, mud-coloured; yellowish-brown, snuff-coloured; khaki; tawny, tan; reddish-brown, bay, roan, sorrel, chestnut, auburn, copper-coloured; russet, rust-coloured; maroon; puce; dark brown, peat-b., mocha, chocolate, coffee-coloured etc. n.; brown as a berry, brown as a nut.

Vb. *brown,* bronze, tan, sunburn; singe, char, toast 381 *burn*.

431 Redness – **N.** *redness,* blush, flush, hectic f.; sunset, dawn, rosy-fingered d. 417 *glow*; reddening, warmth; rosiness, ruddiness, bloom, red cheeks, rosy c., cherry lips; high colour, floridness; red colour, crimson, scarlet, red etc. adj.; carnation, rose, geranium, poppy; cherry, tomato; burgundy, port, claret; gore 335 *blood*; ruby, garnet, cornelian; flame 379 *fire*; red ink, rubric; red planet, Mars; redbreast, robin r.; redskin, Red Indian; redhead, carrot-top, gingernob.

red pigment, red dye, cochineal, carmine, kermes; cinnabar, vermilion; madder; crimson lake, Venetian red, red ochre, red lead, rouge, blusher, lipstick 843 *cosmetic*.

Adj. *red,* reddish; ruddy, sanguine, florid, blowzy; warm, hot, fiery, glowing, red-hot 379 *hot*; flushed, fevered; flushing, blushing; red-cheeked, rosy-c.; bright red, red as a lobster, red as a beetroot; red-haired, ginger-h.; carroty, sandy, auburn, titian-red, flame-coloured; russet, rusty, rust-coloured; pink, roseate, rosy, rose-coloured, peach-c., flesh-c., salmon-p., shocking-p.; coral, carnation, damask, crushed strawberry; crimson, cherry-red, cerise, carmine, cramoisy; fuchsia, magenta, maroon 436 *purple*; wine-coloured; oxblood, sanguine; scarlet, cardinal-red, vermillion, pillarbox red; reddened, rouged, painted.

Vb. *redden,* rouge, apply blusher, raddle 843 *primp*; dye red, flush, blush,

glow; colour, colour up, crimson, go red, go pink.

432 Orange – N. *orange,* red and yellow, gold, old gold; amber; sunflower, marigold; apricot, tangerine; marmalade; ochre, cadmium orange, henna.

Adj. *orange,* apricot etc. n.; coppery, ginger; orangeish, orangey, orange-coloured, flame-c., copper-c., brass-c., brassy.

433 Yellowness – N. *yellowness,* yellow, sunshine y. etc. adj.; brass, gold, old gold, topaz, amber, old ivory; sulphur, brimstone; buttercup, daffodil, primrose, dandelion; lemon, honey; saffron, mustard; jaundice, yellow fever; sallow skin, fair hair, golden hair; blond(e), ash b., platinum b., strawberry b.; yellow rain, cadmium yellow, chrome y., lemon y., yellow ochre, xanthin.

Adj. *yellow,* gold, amber etc. n.; tawny, sandy; fair-haired, golden-h., yellow-h. 427 *whitish*; honey-coloured, straw-c.; pale yellow, acid y., lemon y.; primrose y., jasmine, chartreuse, champagne; canary yellow, sunshine y., bright y.; sulphur y., mustard y.; golden, gilded; deep yellow, yellowy, yellowish, flavescent, xanthic; sallow, jaundiced, bilious; yellow with age.

434 Greenness – N. *greenness,* green etc. adj.; verdancy, greenery, greenwood; verdure; grass, moss, turf, green leaf 366 *foliage*; lime, greengage; jade, emerald, beryl, aquamarine, olivine; verdigris; Lincoln green.

Adj. *green,* verdant; grassy, leafy; bright green, deep g., dark g., pale g.; grass-green, leaf-g., moss-g.; emerald, sea-green 435 *blue*; jade-green, bottle-g.; sage-g., willow-g.; pea-g., acid-g., apple-g., lime-g., chartreuse; eau-de-Nil, avocado, olive, olive-green; greenish.

435 Blueness – N. *blueness,* blue, azure; blue sky, blue sea; sapphire, aquamarine, turquoise, lapis lazuli; bluebell, cornflower, forget-me-not; gentian blue etc. adj.; bluishness, cyanosis; lividness.

blue pigment, blue dye, indigo, woad; cobalt blue; bluebag.

Adj. *blue,* cyanic, azure; sky-blue; duck-egg blue, eggshell b., turquoise; light blue, pale blue, ice-b., powder-b., Cambridge-b.; air-force b., Saxe-b., slate-b., steel-b., electric-b.; sapphire, aquamarine, peacock-b., kingfisher-b., bright b., royal-b., ultramarine, deep blue, dark b., Oxford-b., midnight-b., navy-b., navy, French n.; indigo; blueblack, black and blue, livid; cold, steely, bluish.

436 Purpleness – N. *purpleness,* purple, blue and red; imperial purple; amethyst; lavender, violet, heliotrope, heather, foxglove; plum, damson, aubergine; gentian violet; amaranth, lilac, mauve.

Adj. *purple,* plum etc. n.; purplish, violet, mauve, pale purple, lavender, lilac; bright purple, fuchsia, magenta, plum-coloured, damson-coloured, puce; heliotrope; deep purple, dark purple, mulberry; purple with rage.

437 Variegation – N. *variegation,* variety, diversification, diversity 15 *difference*; dancing light; play of colour, shot colours, iridescence, chatoyance; tiger's eye, opal, nacre, mother-of-pearl; shot silk, moire; peacock's tail, tortoiseshell, chameleon; Joseph's coat, motley, harlequin, patchwork, patchwork quilt; enamelwork; stained glass, kaleidoscope; rainbow, spectrum, prism; collage.

chequer, check, Prince of Wales c., hound's tooth, pepper-and-salt; plaid, tartan; chessboard, draughtboard; marquetry, inlay, inlaid work 844 *ornamental art*; mosaic, crazy paving 43 *medley*.

stripe, striation; line, streak, band, bar, bar code; agate; zebra, tiger; streakiness, mackerel sky; crack, craze; reticulation 222 *network*.

mottle, maculation; dappling, stippling, marbling; spottiness, patchiness

17 *nonuniformity*; patch, speck, speckle, macula, spots, pimples, pockmarks 845 blemish; freckle, fleck, dot, polka d.; blotch, splotch, splodge, splash; leopard, Dalmatian.

Adj. *variegated,* fretted etc. vb.; diversified; patterned, embroidered, worked 844 *ornamental*; colourful 425 *florid*; multi-coloured, parti-c., motley, patched; tortoiseshell, chameleon, harlequin, kaleidoscopic 82 *multiform*; plaid, tartan; rainbow-coloured, prismatic; mosaic, tessellated, parquet.

pied, parti-coloured, black-and-white, pepper-and-salt, grizzled, piebald, skewbald, roan, pinto, chequered, check, dappled, patchy.

mottled, marbled, veined, reticulated; studded, maculose, spotted, patchy; speckled, freckled; streaked, striated, lined, barred, banded, striped 222 *crossed*; brindled, tabby; pocked, pockmarked.

Vb. *variegate,* diversify, pattern; chequer; patch 656 *repair*; embroider, work 844 *decorate*; braid, quilt; inlay, tessellate; stud, pepper, dot with, mottle, speckle, freckle, spangle, spot; tattoo, stipple, dapple; streak, stripe, striate; craze, crack; marble, vein; discolour 649 *make unclean*; make iridescent.

438 Vision – N. *vision,* sight, power of s; eyesight; seeing, visualization, mind's eye 513 *imagination*; perception, recognition; acuity (of vision), good eyesight; long sight, far s.; defective vision, short sight 440 *dim sight*; second sight 984 *occultism*; double vision, binocular v.; magnification; winking, blinking, tic, squint; eye-testing; oculist, optician, ophthalmologist, optometrist; optometer, ophthalmoscope.

eye, eyeball, iris, pupil, white, cornea, retina, optic nerve; optics, orbs, sparklers, peepers; saucer eyes, goggle e.; eyelashes, eyelid 421 *screen*; lashes; naked eye; sharp e., gimlet e., X-ray e.; weak eyes 440 *dim sight*; glass e. 439 *blindness*; evil eye 983 *sorcery*; hawk, eagle, cat, lynx; basilisk, cockatrice.

look, glance, sideways look, squint; tail or corner of the eye; glint, blink, flash; gaze, steady g.; observation, close o., contemplation, watch; stare, fixed s.; come-hither look, glad eye, sheep's eyes, ogle, leer 889 *wooing*; wink 524 *hint*; grimace, dirty look, scowl, evil eye; peep, peek, glimpse, rapid g., brief g.

inspection, examination, autopsy 459 *enquiry*; view, preview, sneak p. 522 *manifestation*; supervision 689 *management*; survey, overview, bird's-eye view; reconnaissance, reconnoitre, recce, surveillance; sight-seeing, rubbernecking, gawping; look, butcher's, lookaround, look-see, dekko, once-over, shufti, second glance, double take; review, revision; viewing, home v. 445 *cinema*, 531 *broadcasting*; discernment, espial, view, first sight; looking round, observation, prying, spying; espionage; peeping, voyeurism, peeping Tom.

view, eyeful; vista, prospect, outlook, perspective; aspect 445 *appearance*; panorama, bird's-eye view; horizon, false h.; line of vision; range of view; field of view; scene, setting, stage 594 *theatre*; angle of vision, point of view, viewpoint, standpoint; vantage point, lookout, crow's nest, watchtower 209 *high structure*; camera obscura; astrodome, conning tower; observatory; grandstand, ringside seat 441 *onlookers*; peephole 263 *window*.

Adj. *seeing,* glimpsing etc. vb.; visual, perceptible 443 *visible*; panoramic, ocular, ophthalmic; optical, optometric; stereoscopic, binocular; orthoptic, perspicacious, sharp-eyed, gimlet-e., eagle-e., vigilant, with eyes in the back of one's head.

Vb. *see,* behold, visualize; perceive, discern, distinguish, make out, pick o., recognize; take in, see at a glance 498 *be wise*; descry, discover 484 *detect*; sight, espy, spy, spot, observe 455 *notice*; lay or set eyes on, catch sight of, sight; catch a glimpse of, glimpse; view, command a view of, have in sight; look on 441 *watch*.

gaze, quiz, gaze at, look, look at; look straight at, look in the eyes; look intently,

eye, stare, peer; stare at, stare hard, goggle, gape, gawk, gawp; focus, rivet one's eyes, fix one's gaze; glare, glower, look daggers, give a black look, look black 891 *be angry*; glance, glance at; squint, look askance, look down one's nose; wink, blink 524 *hint*; make eyes at, give the glad eye, give a come-hither look, ogle, leer 889 *court*; feast one's eyes on, gloat over 824 *be pleased*; steal a glance, peep, peek, take a peep; direct one's gaze, turn one's eyes on; notice, take n., look upon 455 *be attentive*; lift up one's eyes, look up; look down, look round, look behind, look in front; look ahead 858 *be cautious*; look away, avert one's gaze 439 *be blind*; exchange glances.

scan, scrutinize, inspect, examine, take stock of, look one up and down; contemplate, pore over 536 *study*; look over, look through, read t., riffle t., leaf t., skim t.; have *or* take a look at, have a dekko, have a butcher's, take a shufti at, take a gander *or* a squint at, run one's eye over, give the once-over; see, go and see, take in, sight-see, rubberneck, gawp; go to see 882 *visit*; view, survey, sweep, reconnoitre; scout, spy out the land, take a recce; peep, peek 453 *be curious*; spy, pry, snoop; observe, keep under observation, keep under surveillance, watch 457 *invigilate*; hold in view, keep in sight; watch out for, look out f. 507 *await*; keep watch, look out, keep a lookout for, keep an eye out for, keep a weather eye open for, keep cave, keep looking, keep one's eyes skinned *or* peeled; strain one's eyes, peer; squint at, squinny; crane, crane one's neck, stand on tiptoe.

439 Blindness – N. *blindness,* unawareness 491 *ignorance*; sightlessness; glaucoma, river blindness, cataract; night blindness, snow b., colour b.; dimsightedness 440 *dim sight*; blind spot 444 *invisibility*; tunnel vision; blind eye 456 *inattention*; word blindness, dyslexia; glass eye, artificial e.; blind man *or* woman, the blind; Braille, talking book; white stick, guide dog.

Adj. *blind,* sightless, unsighted, visually challenged, dark; unseeing, undiscerning, unperceiving, unobserving 456 *inattentive*; blinded, blindfold, blinkered; in the dark, benighted; 440 *dim-sighted*; stone-blind; blind as a bat.

Vb. *be blind,* not use one's eyes; go blind, lose one's sight, not see; grope in the dark, feel one's way 461 *be tentative*; be blindfolded, wear blinkers; be blind to 491 *not know*; ignore, have a blind spot, not see for looking, not see what is under one's nose; not see the wood for the trees; shut the eyes to, turn a blind eye, avert one's gaze, look the other way 458 *disregard*; blink, squint 440 *be dim-sighted*.

blind, gouge one's eyes out; dazzle; obscure 419 *bedim*; screen from sight; blinker, blindfold, bandage 421 *screen*; throw dust in one's eyes 495 *mislead*.

440 Dim-sightedness: imperfect vision – N. *dim sight,* failing sight, defective eyesight, dim-sightedness, purblindness 439 *blindness*; defective v., impaired v.; eyestrain; short s., near s., near-sightedness, myopia; hypermetropia, presbyopia, long sight, far s.; double vision; astigmatism; cataract; glaucoma; colourblindness; snow-blindness, night-blindness; ophthalmitis; conjunctivitis, pink eye; cast; strabismus, squint, cross-eye; wall-eye; wink, blink, nictitation, nervous tic; eyeshade, blinker 421 *screen*; tunnel vision, blind spot 444 *invisibility*.

visual fallacy, refraction 417 *reflection*; aberration of light 282 *deviation*; false light 552 *misrepresentation*; optical illusion, trick of light, mirage 542 *deception*; spectre, apparition 970 *ghost*; vision, dream 513 *fantasy*; distorting mirror, hall of mirrors, magic lantern.

Adj. *dim-sighted,* purblind, half-blind, semi-b.; visually impaired, bespectacled; myopic, short-sighted, near-s.; hypermetropic, presbyopic, long-sighted, farsighted, astigmatic; colour-blind; walleyed, squinting; strabismal, strabismic, cross-eyed; boss-eyed, bug-e.; nystagmic; blinking, dazzled; blinded, temporarily b. 439 *blind*; cataractous, glaucomatous.

Vb. *be dim-sighted,* - myopic etc. adj.; not see well, need spectacles; have a mist before the eyes; get something in one's e.; peer, screw up the eyes, squint; blink, wink, nictitate, have a nervous tic; see double, be blinded by, dazzle; grow blurred, dim, fail; see through a glass darkly.

blur, confuse; dim, mist, fog, smudge; be indistinct, be hazy.

441 Spectator – **N.** *spectator,* beholder; viewer, observer, watcher, invigilator; inspector, examiner, scrutinizer, overseer 690 *manager*; witness, eyewitness; bystander, onlooker; gazer, starer, gaper, gawper, goggler; ogler, voyeur, Peeping Tom; window shopper; sightseer, rubberneck, tourist, globetrotter 268 *traveller*; stargazer, astronomer; bird watcher, twitcher, train spotter, lookout 484 *detector*; watchman, night-w., security officer, security man, sentinel, sentry, 664 *warner*; patrolman, patrol; scout, spy, mole, spook, snoop 459 *detective*; filmgoer, cinemagoer 445 *cinema*; theatregoer 594 *playgoer*; televiewer, viewer, TV addict, square-eyes; captive audience.

onlookers, audience, auditorium, sea of faces; box office, gate; house, gallery, gods, circle, dress c., pit, stalls; stadium, grandstand, terraces; crowd, supporters, followers, aficionados, fans 707 *patron*, 504 *enthusiast*.

Vb. *watch,* spectate, look on, look at, view 438 *see*; witness 189 *be present*; follow with the eyes, observe 455 *be attentive*; attend, eye, ogle, give the glad eye, quiz; gape, gawk, stare; spy, spy out, scout, scout out, reconnoitre 438 *scan*.

442 Optical instrument – **N.** *eyeglass,* spectacles, specs, goggles, glasses, reading g., pince-nez, sunglasses, shades, dark glasses, Polaroid (tdmk) g., bifocals; pebble glasses; contact lens, hard c. l., soft c. l.; lorgnette, monocle; magnifying glass.

telescope, terrestrial telescope, astronomical t. 321 *astronomy*; collimator; sight, finder, viewfinder, rangefinder; periscope; spyglass, night glass; binoculars, prism b., field glasses, opera g.

microscope, electron m., photomicroscope, ultramicroscope.

mirror, reflector; concave mirror, speculum; rear-view mirror, wing m.; glass, looking g., cheval g., full-length mirror, dressing-table m., hand m.

camera, camera lucida, camera obscura, spectrograph 321 *astronomy*; box camera, disc c.; instant c., Polaroid (tdmk) c.; cinecamera; television camera, videopack, camcorder; electric eye, closed-circuit television 484 *detector*; shutter, aperture, stop; flashgun 420 *lamp*; film 551 *photography*; telephoto lens, zoom l., wide-angle l.; light meter; slide projector, overhead p., magic lantern 455 *cinema*.

443 Visibility – **N.** *visibility,* perceptibility; 445 *appearance*; sight, exposure; distinctness, clearness, clarity, definition, conspicuousness, prominence; eyewitness, visible evidence, object lesson 522 *manifestation*; visual aid 534 *teaching*; scene, field of view, field of vision 438 *view*; seeing, impaired visibility, reduced v.; horizon, skyline, visible distance 183 *range*; landmark 547 *signpost*; symptom.

Adj. *visible,* perceptible, perceivable, discernible, observable, detectable; noticeable, remarkable; recognizable, unmistakable, palpable, tangible; symptomatic; apparent 445 *appearing*; showing 522 *manifest*; exposed, open, naked; exposed to view, in full view; before one's eyes, under one's nose, for all to see; visible to the naked eye; telescopic, panoramic.

obvious, showing, for all to see 522 *shown*; plain, clear, clear-cut, crystal-clear, as clear as day; definite, well-defined, well-marked; distinct, unblurred; undisguised; conspicuous, pointed, prominent; eye-catching, striking, shining 417 *luminous*; glaring, staring; pronounced, highlighted, spotlit; vivid, eidetic; under one's nose, before one's very

eyes, staring one in the face, plain to see, plain as plain, plain as a pikestaff, plain as the nose on your face.

Vb. *be visible,* be seen, - obvious etc. adj.; show, shine through; attract attention, ask to be noticed 455 *attract notice*; strike, catch the eye, stand out, act as a landmark; come to light, dawn upon; heave in sight, come into view, show its face 445 *appear*; pop up, crop up, turn up, show up 295 *arrive*; spring up, start up, arise 68 *begin*; surface, break s. 308 *ascend*; come out, creep out 298 *emerge*; stick out, project 254 *jut*; show, materialize, develop; manifest itself, expose i., betray i. 522 *be plain*; symptomize 547 *indicate*; make one's entry, make an entrance 297 *enter*; step forward, advance; dazzle; break through the clouds 417 *shine*; stay in sight; make visible, expose 522 *manifest.*

444 Invisibility – N. *invisibility,* imperceptibility, indistinctness, poor definition; poor visibility, reduced v., obscurity 419 *dimness*; distance 199 *farness*; smallness 196 *minuteness*; privacy 883 *seclusion*; submergence 523 *latency*; hiding 525 *concealment*; mystery 525 *secrecy*; smoke screen, mist, fog, haar, veil, curtain; blind spot, blind eye 439 *blindness*; blind corner, 663 *pitfall*; hidden menace 661 *danger*.

Adj. *invisible,* imperceptible, indiscernible; indistinguishable, unrecognizable; unseen; sightless; unnoticed 458 *neglected*; out of sight; not in sight, remote 199 *distant*; sequestered 883 *secluded*; lurking 523 *latent*; camouflaged 525 *concealed*; shadowy, mysterious; obscured, eclipsed.

indistinct, unclear, poorly-defined, indefinite, indistinct 419 *dim*; faint, microscopic; confused, vague, blurred, out of focus; fuzzy, misty, hazy 424 *semitransparent.*

Vb. *be unseen,* hide, lie low, go to earth, go to ground, lie in ambush 523 *lurk*; escape notice, blush unseen 872 *be humble*; pale, fade, die 419 *be dim*; be

lost to view, vanish 446 *disappear*; hide away, submerge 525 *conceal*; veil 421 *screen*; darken, eclipse 419 *bedim.*

445 Appearance – N. *appearance,* first appearance 68 *beginning*; materialization, bodying forth, presence 1 *existence*; exhibition, display, view, demonstration 522 *manifestation*; 471 *probability*; revelation 484 *discovery*; outside 223 *exteriority*; appearances, look of things; visual impact, face value; first impressions, effect; image, front, public persona, façade 541 *duplicity*; veneer, show, seeming, semblance; side, aspect, facet; guise 228 *dressing*; shape, dimension 243 *form*; look; emanation; vision 513 *fantasy*; mirage, hallucination, illusion 440 *visual fallacy*; spectre 970 *ghost*; reflection, image; likeness 551 *representation.*

spectacle, impression, effect, something to write home about; decoration 844 *ornamentation*; eyeful, vision, sight, sight for sore eyes, scene; scenery, landscape, seascape, townscape, estatescape; panorama, bird's-eye view 438 *view*; display, pageantry, pageant, parade, review 875 *ostentation*; revue, extravaganza, pantomime, floor show 594 *stage show*; television, video 531 *broadcasting*; illuminations, son et lumière; pyrotechnics; presentation, show, demonstration, exhibition, exposition 522 *exhibit*; art exhibition 553 *picture*; visual entertainment, in-flight e., peep show, slide s., film s., picture s., home movies; kaleidoscope 437 *variegation*; panorama, staging, tableau; set, decor, scenario 594 *stage set.*

cinema, cinematography; big screen, silver s., Hollywood, film industry; film studio, film production, film-making, shooting 551 *photography*; direction, continuity, editing, cutting, montage, projection; photoplay, screenplay, scenario, script, shooting s.; credits, titles; special effects, animation; voiceover, sound effects, soundtrack; cinematograph, projector; picture house, drive-in

cinema, flea pit 594 *theatre*; film director, film star 594 *actor*; filmgoer 504 *enthusiast*.

film, films, pictures, motion p., movies, flicks; Technicolor (tdmk), 3-D, Cinerama (tdmk), Cinemascope (tdmk); silent film, talkie; 15, 18, PG, U; big picture, B p., B movie, supporting film, newsreel, trailer; cartoon, animated c., travelogue, documentary, docu-drama, feature film; art film, nouvelle vague; epic, blockbuster, musical; low-budget movie; weepie, bodice-ripper, thriller, cliffhanger, war film, horror film; blue movie, skinflick; Western, spaghetti w.; space odyssey; oldie, remake; rush, preview; general release.

look, mien, face; expression; countenance, looks; complexion, colour, cast; air, demeanour, carriage, bearing, deportment, poise, presence; gesture, posture, behaviour 688 *conduct*.

feature, trait, mark, lineament; lines, cut, shape, fashion, figure 243 *form*; outline, contour, relief, elevation, profile, silhouette; visage, physiognomy, cut of one's jib 237 *face*.

Adj. *appearing*, apparent; seeming, ostensible; deceptive; outward, external, superficial 223 *exterior*; on view 443 *visible*; visual, showing, exhibited, hung 522 *shown*; impressive, effective, spectacular 875 *showy*; revealed 522 *manifest*; dreamlike 513 *imaginary*.

Vb. *appear*, show 443 *be visible*; seem 18 *resemble*; have the look of, have an air of, take the shape of; figure in, cut a figure 875 *be ostentatious*; be on show; be showing; appear on television, star in; exhibit 522 *manifest*; arise; dawn, break 68 *begin*; materialize, pop up 295 *arrive*.

446 Disappearance – **N.** *disappearance*, loss, vanishing; disappearing trick, escapology 542 *sleight*; flight 667 *escape*; exit 296 *departure*; evaporation 338 *vaporization*; dissipation, dissolution 51 *decomposition*; extinction 2 *nonexistence*; occultation, eclipse 418 *obscuration*; fadeout; thin air 444 *invisibility*.

Vb. *disappear*, vanish, do the vanishing trick; dematerialize, melt into thin air; evaporate 338 *vaporize*; dissolve, melt away 337 *liquefy*; dwindle to vanishing point 37 *decrease*; fade away 114 *be transient*; suffer an eclipse 419 *be dim*; disperse, dissipate, diffuse, scatter 75 *be dispersed*; fail to appear, play truant, bunk off, take French leave, go AWOL 190 *be absent*; go, be gone, depart 296 *decamp*; run away, get a. 667 *escape*; hide, lie low, be in hiding 523 *lurk*; leave no trace 525 *conceal*; be lost to sight 444 *be unseen*; become extinct 2 *pass away*; erase, dispel 550 *obliterate*.

Class four

INTELLECT: *THE EXER-CISE OF THE MIND*

4.1 FORMATION OF IDEAS

Section one: General

447 Intellect – N. *intellect,* mind, psyche, mentality; understanding, conception; powers of thought; rationality, reasoning power; reason, association of ideas 475 *reasoning*; philosophy 449 *thought*; awareness, sense, consciousness, self-c., stream of c. 455 *attention*; cognition, perception, percipience, insight; extrasensory perception, ESP, instinct, sixth sense 476 *intuition*; flair, judgment 463 *discrimination*; intellectualism; mental capacity, brains, wits, senses, sense, grey matter, IQ, intelligence quotient 498 *intelligence*; genius; brain.

spirit, soul, inner mind; inner sense, inner being; heart, breast, bosom, inner man 5 *essential part*; double, genius 80 *self*; psyche, id, ego, superego, animus, self, the unconscious, the subconscious; personality, dual p., multiple p., split p. 503 *personality disorder*; spiritualism, psychical research 984 *occultism*; spiritualist, occultist.

psychology, parapsychology 984 *psychics*; Freudian psychology, Jungian p., Adlerian p.; Gestalt psychology, behaviourism; psychopathology, psychiatry, psychotherapy, psychodrama, psychoanalysis 658 *therapy*; psycholinguistics.

psychologist, psychoanalyst, psychiatrist, psychotherapist 658 *doctor*; analyst, head shrinker, shrink, trick cyclist.

Adj. *mental,* thinking, reasoning 475 *rational*; cerebral, intellectual, conceptual; theoretical; perceptual, perceptive; cognizant 490 *knowing.*

perceive, perceive 490 *know*; realize, sense, become aware of, become conscious of; note 438 *see*; mark 455 *notice*; reason; use one's head, understand 498 *be wise*; conceptualize, intellectualize 449 *think*; conceive, invent 484 *discover*; imagine.

448 Absence of intellect – N. *absence of intellect,* stocks and stones; brainlessness, mindlessness 450 *absence of thought*; brain damage, unsound mind, insanity 503 *mental disorder.*

Adj. *mindless,* unintelligent; inanimate; unreasoning; brainless, emptyheaded, vacuous 499 *foolish*; moronic, wanting 503 *mentally disordered.*

449 Thought – N. *thought,* mental process, thinking, thought processes; intellectual exercise, mental e., cogitation, cerebration, thinking cap; brainwork; hard thought, concentration 455 *attention*; deep thought, profundity 498 *wisdom*; thoughts, ideas 451 *idea*; conception, inmost thoughts 513 *ideality*; train of thought; association of ideas, reason 475 *reasoning*; brown study, deep thought, reverie 456 *abstractedness*; thinking out; second thoughts, afterthought 67 *sequel*; retrospection, hindsight, wisdom after the event 505 *memory*; forethought, forward planning, telepathy 984 *psychics*.

meditation, thoughtfulness, speculation 459 *enquiry*; lateral thinking; reflection, deep thought, brooding, rumination, consideration, pondering; contemplation 438 *inspection*; absorption, pensiveness; introspection, self-communing; transcendental meditation; retreat, mysticism 979 *piety*; deliberation, thinking out 480 *judgment*; application 536 *study.*

philosophy, metaphysics, ethics; speculation, abstract thought, scientific thought, natural philosophy; philosophical system, philosophical theory 512 *supposition*; school of philosophy 485 *opinion*; idealism, conceptualism, transcendentalism; phenomenalism, phenomenology, realism, nominalism, positivism, analytic philosophy 475 *reasoning*;

existentialism, voluntarism; determinism, mechanism; vitalism; holism, organicism, structuralism, functionalism, reductionism, reductivism; rationalism, humanism, hedonism; utilitarianism, materialism; empiricism, pragmatism; relativism, relativity; agnosticism, scepticism, irrationalism 486 *doubt*; eclecticism; atheism 974 *irreligion*; nihilism, fatalism 596 *fate*; Pythagoreanism, Platonism, Aristotelianism; Scepticism, Stoicism, Epicureanism, Cynicism; Neo-Platonism, gnosticism; scholasticism, Thomism; Cartesianism, Kantianism, Hegelianism, Neo-H., dialectical materialism, Marxism; anthroposophy, theosophy; Hinduism, Buddhism, Sufism, Yoga, Zen 973 *religion*.

Adj. *thoughtful,* speculative; cogitative, deliberative; pensive, meditative, ruminative, contemplative, reflective; introspective; wrapt in thought; absorbed 455 *obsessed*; musing, daydreaming, dreamy 456 *abstracted*; concentrated 455 *attentive*; studying 536 *studious*; considerate 901 *philanthropic*; prudent 510 *foreseeing*.

Vb. *think,* ween 512 *suppose*; form ideas, fancy 513 *imagine*; ponder, cogitate (see *meditate*); put on one's thinking cap, use one's grey matter; concentrate, collect one's thoughts 455 *be attentive*; apply the mind, trouble one's head about, cerebrate, mull over, puzzle over 536 *study*; think hard, rack one's brains; think through, reason out 475 *reason*; think up, invent 484 *discover*; devise 623 *plan*; take into one's head, harbour a notion, have a sudden fancy, have an idea, toy with an i., kick an i. around; cherish an i. 485 *believe*; become obsessed, get a bee in one's bonnet, have a hang-up about 481 *be biased*; bear in mind, take account of, think on 505 *remember*.

meditate, ruminate; wonder about, enquire into 459 *enquire*; reflect, contemplate, study; speculate, philosophize, theorize; think about, consider, take into account, take into consideration; take stock of, ponder, weigh 480 *estimate*;

think over, run over in the mind 505 *memorize*; reconsider, have second thoughts; think better of; take counsel, sleep on it 691 *consult*; brood, brood upon, muse, fall into a brown study.

dawn upon, occur to, cross the mind; come into one's head, come to one in a blinding flash, strike one.

cause thought, provoke thought, make one think, make one stop and think 821 *impress*; sink in, become a hang-up, obsess 481 *bias*.

absorb, engross, absorb, preoccupy, monopolize; be never out of one's thoughts, go round and round in one's head, occupy the mind, be uppermost in one's mind; prey on one's mind, obsess 481 *bias*; fascinate 983 *bewitch*.

450 Absence of thought – N. *absence of thought,* blank mind, abstraction 456 *abstractedness*; inanity, vacuity, blankness, fatuity, empty head 499 *unintelligence*; thoughtlessness 456 *inattention*; conditioned reflex; knee-jerk response, gut reaction; instinct 476 *intuition*.

451 Idea – N. *idea,* notion, a thought; abstract idea, concept; theory 512 *supposition*; mental image; Platonic idea; conception, perception, apprehension 447 *intellect*; observation 449 *thought*; impression, fancy 513 *imagination*; figment of imagination; associated ideas, complex; stream of consciousness, free association of ideas; invention, brainchild; brain wave, happy thought 484 *discovery*; wheeze, device 623 *contrivance*; point of view, slant, way of thinking, attitude 485 *opinion*; principle, main idea; obsession, hang-up 481 *prejudgment*.

452 Topic – N. *topic,* food for thought; gossip, rumour 529 *news*; subject matter, subject; contents, chapter, section 53 *subdivision*; what it is about, argument, plot, theme, message; text, commonplace, burden, motif; musical topic, statement, leitmotiv 412 *musical piece*;

concern, interest, human i.; matter, affair; shop 622 *business*; topic for discussion, business on hand, agenda, any other business, AOB, order paper 623 *policy*; item on the agenda, motion 761 *request*; resolution 480 *judgment*; problem; problematics, gist, drift; theorem, proposition 512 *supposition*; thesis, case, point 475 *argument*; issue, moot point, debatable p., point at issue; field of enquiry, field of study 536 *study*.

Adj. *topical,* thematic; thought about, uppermost in the mind, fit for consideration, worthy of discussion.

Adv. *in question,* in one's thoughts; afoot, on the agenda, on the table; before the house, before the committee, under consideration, under discussion.

Section two: Precursory conditions and operations

453 Curiosity: desire for knowledge – N. *curiosity,* intellectual c., speculativeness, enquiring mind, thirst *or* itch for knowledge 536 *study*; interest, inquisitiveness, curiousness; zeal, meddlesomeness, officiousness, nosiness 678 *overactivity*; quizzing 459 *question*; sightseeing, rubbernecking 267 *land travel*; morbid curiosity, ghoulishness; voyeurism 951 *impurity*.

Adj. *inquisitive,* curious, interested; speculating, searching, seeking, avid for knowledge, hungry for information 536 *studious*; morbidly curious, ghoulish, prurient; newsmongering, agog, all ears 455 *attentive*; burning with curiosity, consumed with c., eaten up with c.; itching, hungry for; overcurious, nosy, snoopy, prying, spying, peeping, peeking; questioning, inquisitorial 459 *enquiring*; meddlesome, interfering, officious.

Vb. *be curious,* want to know; look for 459 *search*; research 461 *experiment*; be interested, take an interest; show interest, show curiosity, prick up one's ears, be all agog 455 *be attentive*; mosey

around, dip into; dig up, nose out; peep, peek, spy 438 *scan*; snoop, pry, nose into 459 *enquire*; eavesdrop, tap the line, intercept, bug, listen, listen in, eavesdrop 415 *hear*; poke *or* stick one's nose in, be nosy, interfere, act the busybody 678 *meddle*; quiz, question, bombard with questions 459 *interrogate*; stand and stare, gape, gawk 438 *gaze*.

454 Incuriosity – N. *incuriosity,* lack of curiosity; mental inertia; uninterest, unconcern 860 *indifference*; apathy, phlegmatism 820 *moral insensibility*.

Adj. *incurious,* uninquisitive; uninterested; aloof, distant, blasé; unconcerned, uninvolved 860 *indifferent*; inert, apathetic 820 *impassive*.

Vb. *be incurious,* - indifferent etc. adj.; have no curiosity, take no interest 456 *be inattentive*; feel no concern, couldn't care less, not trouble oneself, not bother with 860 *be indifferent*; mind one's own business, go one's own way 820 *be insensitive*; look the other way 458 *disregard*.

455 Attention – N. *attention,* notice, regard 438 *look*; consideration 449 *thought*; heed, alertness, readiness, attentiveness, solicitude, observance 457 *carefulness*; observation, watchfulness, vigilance, watch, guard, invigilation 457 *surveillance*; wariness, circumspection 858 *caution*; contemplation, introspection 449 *meditation*; intentness, earnestness, seriousness 599 *resolution*; undivided attention; concentration, application, studiousness, close study 536 *study*; examination, scrutiny, checkup, review 438 *inspection*; close attention; meticulousness, attention to detail, minuteness, pernicketiness; diligence, trouble 678 *assiduity*; rapt attention; single-mindedness; absorption, preoccupation 456 *inattention*; interest 453 *curiosity*; one-track mind, fixation, obsession, hang-up.

Adj. *attentive,* intent, diligent, assiduous 678 *industrious*; considerate, caring, thoughtful 884 *courteous*; heedful, mindful; alert, ready, on one's toes, on

the qui vive, on the ball, with it; wakeful, awake, wide-a.; awake to, alive to, sensing 819 *sensitive*; aware, conscious, thinking 449 *thoughtful*; observant, sharp-eyed, watching, watchful 457 *vigilant*; attending, rapt, missing nothing; all eyes, all agog 438 *seeing*; all ears; concentrating; serious, earnest; eager to learn 536 *studious*; meticulous, punctilious 494 *accurate*; on the lookout 507 *expectant*.

obsessed, single-minded, engrossed, preoccupied, wrapped up in, taken up with, into, hooked on, addicted to, hung up; haunted by 854 *fearing*; monomaniacal 503 *crazy*.

Vb. *be attentive,* attend, pay attention; heed, pay h., take notice of, mind 457 *be careful*; care, take trouble, take pains, put oneself out for, bother 682 *exert oneself*; listen, prick up one's ears, sit up and take notice; take seriously; devote *or* give one's attention to, bend the mind to, direct one's thoughts to 449 *think*; think of nothing else, be obsessed with, be preoccupied with 481 *be biased*; keep one's eye on the ball, concentrate, miss nothing; watch, be all eyes, be all agog 438 *gaze*; be all ears, drink in, hang on the lips of 415 *hear*; focus one's mind on, rivet one's attention to, concentrate on, fix on; scrutinize; study closely.

be mindful, keep in mind, bear in m., have in m., be thinking of 505 *remember*; not forget, think of, spare a thought for, regard, look on 438 *see*; lend an ear to 415 *hear*; take care of, see to 457 *look after*; have regard to, have an eye to.

notice, note, take n., register; mark, recognize, spot; take cognizance of, take into consideration, take into account, review, reconsider 449 *meditate*; take account of, consider, weigh 480 *judge*; comment upon, remark on, talk about 584 *converse*; mention, just m., mention in passing, refer to en passant, touch on 524 *hint*; think worthy of attention, have time for, spare time f.; acknowledge.

attract notice, draw the attention, hold the a., engage the a., focus the a., rivet the a., be the cynosure of all eyes, draw the

crowds, cut a figure 875 *be ostentatious*; stick out like a sore thumb, arouse notice, interest 821 *impress*; excite attention, demand a.; catch the eye 443 *be visible*; bring to one's notice *or* attention 522 *show*; call attention to, advertise, publicize 528 *publish*; point out, point to, show 547 *indicate*; stress, underline 532 *emphasize*; fascinate; warn 665 *raise the alarm*; call to attention 737 *command*.

456 Inattention – N. *inattention,* inadvertence, forgetfulness 506 *oblivion*; oversight; lapse 495 *error*; lack of interest 454 *incuriosity*; unconcern, apathy 860 *indifference*; disregard 458 *negligence*; thoughtlessness, heedlessness 857 *rashness*; carelessness, inconsiderateness 481 *misjudgment*, 932 *selfishness*; deaf ears 416 *deafness*; unseeing eyes, blind spot, tunnel vision 439 *blindness*; diversion, distraction, dust in the eyes, wild-goose chase, red herring 612 *inducement*; absent-mindedness 450 *absence of thought*; stargazer, daydreamer, woolgatherer, head in the clouds, Johnny-head-in-air, Walter Mitty; scatterbrain, grasshopper mind, butterfly.

abstractedness, abstraction, absent-mindedness, wandering attention; woolgathering, daydreaming, stargazing, doodling; reverie; distraction, divided attention.

Adj. *inattentive,* careless 458 *negligent*; off one's guard, with one's trousers *or* pants down 508 *inexpectant*; unobservant, unnoticing 454 *incurious*; unseeing 439 *blind*; unhearing 416 *deaf*; undiscerning 464 *indiscriminating*; unmindful, unheeding, inadvertent, not thinking, unreflecting; half asleep; uninterested 860 *indifferent*; apathetic, unaware 820 *impassive*; oblivious 506 *forgetful*; inconsiderate, thoughtless, tactless, heedless; regardless 857 *rash*; cavalier, offhand, cursory, superficial 212 *shallow*.

abstracted, distrait(e), absent-minded, not with it, miles away; lost in thought;

rapt, with one's head in the c., stargazing; bemused, sunk in a brown study, deep in reverie, pensive, dreamy, daydreaming, mooning, woolgathering; half-awake 679 *sleepy*.

distracted, preoccupied, engrossed; diverted; put off, put off one's stroke; unnerved 854 *nervous*.

light-minded, desultory, trifling; frivolous, flippant, light-headed; mercurial, bird-witted, flighty, giddy; grasshopperminded, scatty, scatterbrained, harebrained, featherbrained; harum-scarum, inconstant 604 *capricious*.

Vb. *be inattentive,* pay no attention, pay no heed; turn a blind eye 439 *be blind*; stop one's ears 416 *be deaf*; not register, not use one's eyes; not get the message, not click; overlook 495 *blunder*; be off one's guard, be caught with one's trousers *or* pants down, let the cat out of the bag, let slip, be caught out; lose track of, lose sight of; not remember 506 *forget*; dream, nod 679 *sleep*; trifle, play at, toy with; be abstracted, let one's thoughts wander; go woolgathering, build castles in Spain, build castles in the air 513 *imagine*; fall into a brown study, muse, be lost in thought, moon, stargaze, have one's head in the clouds; idle, doodle 679 *be inactive*; be distracted, digress, lose the thread, lose the train of thought, fluff one's lines 282 *stray*; be disconcerted, be rattled 854 *be nervous*; be put off, be put off one's stroke 702 *hinder* (see *distract)*; disregard, ignore 458 *neglect*.

distract, divert, divert one's attention; put out one's head, drive out of one's mind; entice, throw a sop to Cerberus 612 *tempt*; muddle 63 *derange*; disturb, interrupt 72 *discontinue*; disconcert, upset, perplex, hassle, fluster, bother, flurry, rattle 318 *agitate*; put one off his stroke 702 *obstruct*; bewilder, flummox, throw off the scent, draw a red herring 474 *puzzle*; fuddle.

457 Carefulness – **N.** *carefulness,* attentiveness, diligence, pains 678 *assiduity*;

heed, care, utmost c. 455 *attention*; anxiety, solicitude 825 *worry*; loving care 897 *benevolence*; orderliness, neatness 60 *order*; attention to detail, thoroughness, meticulousness; exactitude 494 *accuracy*; perfectionism 862 *fastidiousness*; scruples 929 *probity*; vigilance, watchfulness, alertness, readiness; wariness 858 *caution*; forethought 510 *foresight*.

surveillance, watching, guarding, neighbourhood watch, home w. 660 *protection*; houseminding, homesitting, caretaking, vigilance, invigilation, inspection; baby-sitting, childminding, chaperonage; lookout, weather eye, Hoolivan, electronic surveillance; vigil, watch, deathwatch; doomwatch; guard; watchful e. 438 *eye*; chaperon, babysitter, childminder, sentry, sentinel 660 *protection*, 749 *keeper*.

Adj. *careful,* thoughtful, considerate, heedful 455 *attentive*; painstaking; solicitous, anxious; cautious; conscientious, scrupulous; diligent, assiduous 678 *industrious*; meticulous; nice, exact 494 *accurate*; pedantic, perfectionist 862 *fastidious*; neat 60 *orderly*; miserly 816 *parsimonious*.

vigilant, alert, ready 669 *prepared*; on the alert, on guard, on the qui vive, on one's toes; keeping cave, watchful, wideawake; observant, sharp-eyed; eagleeyed 438 *seeing*; prudent, far-sighted 510 *foreseeing*; circumspect, guarded, wary 858 *cautious*.

Vb. *be careful,* heed, beware 455 *be attentive*; take precautions, think twice; be on the qui vive, be on the alert, have one's eyes open, have one's wits about one, keep a lookout, keep cave, watch one's step, mind how one goes; look before one leaps; feel one's way 461 *be tentative*; be on one's guard, mind one's Ps and Qs; dot one's i's and cross one's t's.

look after, look to, see to, take care of, caretake, homesit 689 *manage*; take charge of; care for, mind, tend, keep 660 *safeguard*; baby-sit, childmind; nurse, foster, take into care, cherish 889 *pet*;

keep a sharp eye on, keep tabs on, monitor; escort, chaperon.

invigilate, keep vigil, watch; stand sentinel; keep watch, keep a sharp lookout, watch out for; keep one's wits about one, keep one's eyes peeled, keep one's weather-eye open, sleep with one eye o., keep one's ear to the ground; mount guard, post sentries.

458 Negligence – N. *negligence,* carelessness 456 *inattention*; forgetfulness 506 *oblivion*; neglect, oversight, omission; default 918 *undutifulness*; unwariness, unguarded hour *or* minute, unpreparedness 670 *nonpreparation*; disregard; unconcern, don't-care attitude, couldn't-care-less a. 860 *indifference*; recklessness 857 *rashness*; procrastination 136 *delay*; laziness 679 *inactivity*; slovenliness, sluttishness, untidiness 61 *disorder*; sloppiness, inexactitude 495 *inexactness*; offhandedness, casualness, laxness 734 *laxity*; perfunctoriness, superficiality 212 *shallowness*; trifling, scamping, skipping, dodging, botching 695 *bungling*; scamped work, skimped w., botched job, loose ends 728 *failure*.

Adj. *negligent,* neglectful, careless 456 *inattentive*; remiss 918 *undutiful*; thoughtless; oblivious 506 *forgetful*; uncaring; reckless 857 *rash*; heedless 769 *nonobservant*; casual, offhand 734 *lax*; sloppy, slipshod, slapdash, couldn't care less, perfunctory, superficial, with a lick and a promise; hit- and-miss, hurried 680 *hasty*; inaccurate 495 *inexact*; slack 679 lazy; procrastinating 136 *late*; sluttish, untidy, slovenly 649 *dirty*; unwary, unguarded, off guard 508 *inexpectant*; improvident 670 *unprepared*; disregarding, ignoring, lapsed 974 *irreligious*.

neglected, uncared for, untended; unkempt 649 *dirty*; unprotected, unguarded, unchaperoned; deserted; unattended, left alone; unheeded 860 *unwanted*; disregarded, ignored, out in the cold; overlooked, omitted; unnoticed, unmarked 444 *invisible*; shelved, pigeonholed, put aside, mothballed, on the back-burner 136 *late*; unread, unexplored; skimped, perfunctory 726 *uncompleted*; hid under a bushel.

Vb. *neglect,* omit; pass over; lose sight of, overlook 456 *be inattentive*; leave undone, leave half-done, leave loose ends, do by halves 726 *not complete*; botch, bungle 695 *be clumsy*; skimp, scamp 204 *shorten*; skip; skate over, gloss over 525 *conceal*.

disregard, ignore, pass over, give the go-by, dodge, shirk 620 *avoid*; let pass, connive at, take no notice 734 *be lax*; pay no attention to, turn a blind eye to, dismiss 439 *be blind*; excuse, overlook 909 *forgive*; discount 483 *underestimate*; pass by 282 *deviate*; turn one's back on, slight, cold-shoulder, cut, cut dead, send to Coventry 885 *be rude*; turn a deaf ear to 416 *be deaf*; take lightly, not take seriously, not trouble one's head about 860 *be indifferent*; have no time for, laugh off, pooh-pooh 922 *hold cheap*; leave out in the cold 57 *exclude*; leave to their own devices, leave in the lurch, desert, abandon 621 *relinquish*.

be neglectful, doze, nod 679 *sleep*; be off one's guard; be caught napping, oversleep; be caught with one's pants *or* trousers down 508 *not expect*; procrastinate, put off until tomorrow, let slide, let slip, let the grass grow under one's feet 677 *not act*; take it easy, coast 679 *be inactive*; shelve, pigeonhole, lay aside, mothball, put on the back-burner, put aside.

459 Enquiry – N. *enquiry,* asking, questioning (see *interrogation*); challenge (see *question*); asking about 524 *information*; close enquiry, witch-hunt (see *search*); inquisition, examination, investigation; checkup, medical; inquest, post mortem, autopsy, audit, trial 959 *legal trial*; public enquiry; commission of enquiry, working party (see *enquirer*); census, canvass, survey, market research; poll, public opinion poll, Gallup p. (tdmk), straw p. *or* vote 605 *vote*; probe, test, means t., check, spot c., trial run 461 *experiment*; review, scrutiny 438

inspection; IQ test; introspection; personality testing, Rorschach *or* inkblot test; research 536 *study*; analysis, dissection; exploration, reconnaissance, recce, reconnoitre, survey 484 *discovery*; discussion, canvassing, consultation 584 *conference*; scientific enquiry 449 *philosophy*.

interrogation, questioning; forensic examination, leading question, cross-examination; quiz, brains trust; catechism; inquisition, third degree, grilling; dialogue; question time, Prime Minister's question t.

question, question mark, interrogation m. 547 *punctuation*; query; questions, questionnaire 87 *list*; question paper, examination p.; Parliamentary question; challenge; trick question, catch, loaded q.; indirect question, feeler, leading question; rhetorical q.; moot point; point at issue 452 *topic*; crucial question, burning q., sixty-four-thousand-dollar q.; vexed question, controversy, bone of contention 475 *argument*; problem, brain-teaser, poser, mind-boggler, unsolved mystery 530 *enigma*.

exam, examination, oral e., viva voce e., viva; interview, audition 415 *hearing*; practical examination, written e., multiple choice e.; test, series of tests, battery; intelligence test, IQ test; 11-plus, qualifying examination, entrance e., common entrance, matriculation; Certificate of Secondary Education, CSE, 16-plus, General Certificate of Education, GCE, General Certificate of Secondary Education, GCSE; 'O' level, 'A' level, 'S' level, 'A/S' level; 'O' grade, Standard g., Higher, SYS, baccalaureate; prelims, pre-Meds, Responsions; tripos, Moderations, Mods., Greats, finals, degree exams; doctorate examination, bar e.; degree level, pass l., honours l.

search, probe, investigation, enquiry; quest, hunt, witch-h., treasure h. 619 *pursuit*; house-to-house search; frisking, skin-search, strip-search; rummaging, turning over; exploration, excavation, dig; speleology, potholing; searchparty; search warrant.

police enquiry, investigation, criminal i., detection 484 *discovery*; detective work, shadowing, tailing, house-watching; grilling, third degree; Criminal Investigation Department, CID, Federal Bureau of Investigation, FBI, Interpol; secret police, Gestapo.

secret service, espionage, counter-e., spying, intelligence, MI5, CIA, KGB; informer, spy, operative, mole, sleeper, spook, 007, undercover agent, secret a., cloak-and-dagger man; double agent, inside a.; counterspy; spy ring.

detective, investigator, criminologist; plain-clothes man; enquiry agent, private detective, private investigator, private eye; hotel detective, store d.; amateur detective; Federal agent, FBI a., G-man, CID man; tec, sleuth, bloodhound, gumshoe, dick, snooper, nose, spy 524 *informer*; graphologist, handwriting expert; Sherlock Holmes; forensic expert.

enquirer, investigator; journalist 529 *news reporter*; student, seeker for truth; search party; water diviner 484 *detector*; prospector, gold-digger; talent scout; scout, spy, surveyor, reconnoitrer; inspector; checker screener, scrutineer, censor, ombudsperson 480 *estimator*; scanner, examiner, board of examiners; tester, test pilot, researcher, research worker, analyst, dissector 461 *experimenter*; market researcher, sampler, pollster, canvasser; explorer 268 *traveller*.

questioner, cross-q., cross-examiner, interrogator, inquisitor, Grand I.; interviewer; challenger, heckler; question *or* quiz master.

Adj. *enquiring*, curious, prying, nosy 453 *inquisitive*; quizzing, quizzical; interrogatory, interrogative; examining, inquisitional; probing, poking, digging, investigative; testing, searching, fact-finding, exploratory, empirical, tentative 461 *experimental*; analytic, diagnostic.

Vb. *enquire*, ask 491 *not know*; demand 761 *request*; canvass, query, bring in question 475 *argue*; ask for, look for, enquire for, seek (see *search*); hunt for

215

619 *pursue*; enquire into, make enquiries, probe, delve into, dig i., sound, look into, investigate, throw open to enquiry, hold *or* conduct an enquiry, call in Scotland Yard; try, hear 959 *try a case*; review, overhaul, audit, scrutinize, monitor, screen; analyse, dissect, sift; research 536 *study*; examine 449 *meditate*; check, check on; take the temperature, put a toe in the water, take soundings; follow up an enquiry, pursue an e., get to the bottom of, fathom, X-ray 438 *scan*; ferret out, nose out; peer, peep, peek, snoop, spy, pry, nose around 453 *be curious*; survey, reconnoitre, case, sus out; explore, feel one's way 461 *be tentative*; test, try, sample, taste 461 *experiment*.

interrogate, ask questions; question; cross-question, cross-examine, badger, challenge, heckle; interview, hold a viva; examine, subject to questioning, sound out, probe, quiz, catechize, grill, give the third degree; put to the question 963 *torture*; pump, pick one's brains; move the question, put the q., pop the q.; pose, propose a question; frame a q., raise a q., moot, postulate a question.

search, seek, look for; conduct a search, rummage, ransack, comb; scrabble, forage, fossick, root about; scour, clean out, turn over, rake o., pick o., turn out, turn inside out, rake through, rifle t., go t., search t., look into every nook and corner; look high and low; sift through, winnow, go over with a fine-tooth comb; pry into, peer i., peep i., overhaul, frisk, strip-search, skin-search, go over, search one's pockets, search for, feel for, grope for, hunt for, drag for, fish, fish for, dig for; leave no stone unturned, explore every avenue 682 *exert oneself*; cast about, seek a clue, follow the trail 619 *pursue*; probe, explore, go in quest of 461 *be tentative*; dig, excavate, prospect, embark on a treasure-hunt.

460 Answer – N. *answer*, reply, response; reaction; answer by return of post, acknowledgment, return 588 *correspondence*; official reply; returns, results 548 *record*; feedback 524 *information*; echo

106 *repetition*; password 547 *identification*; keyword, open sesame; answering back, backchat, repartee; retort, counterblast, riposte 714 *retaliation*; give and take, question and answer, dialogue, discussion 584 *interlocution*; last word, final answer; Parthian shot; clue, key, right answer, explanation 520 *interpretation*; solution 658 *remedy*; oracle 530 *enigma*.

rejoinder, counterstatement, reply, counterblast, rebuttal; defence, reply; refutation, contradiction 533 *negation*, 467 *counterevidence*; countercharge, counterclaim.

respondent, defendant; answerer, responder, replier, correspondent; examinee; candidate, applicant, entrant, sitter, examinee 716 *contender*.

Vb. *answer*, reply, reply by return of post, reply to an invitation, RSVP, write back, acknowledge, respond, echo; answer back, retort, riposte 714 *retaliate*; say in reply, rejoin, rebut, counter 479 *confute*; field; parry 620 *avoid*; contradict 533 *negate*; defend; get the right answer, solve the riddle 520 *interpret*; settle, decide 480 *judge*; suit the requirements, suit one down to the ground 642 *be expedient*; answer to, correspond to 12 *correlate*.

461 Experiment – N. *experiment*, practical e., scientific e., controlled e.; experimentalism, experimentation, experimental method, verification, verification by experiment; exploration, probe; analysis, examination 459 *enquiry*; object lesson, proof 478 *demonstration*; assay 480 *estimate*; testability; check, test, crucial t., acid t., test case; probation; double-blind test; practical test, trial, trials, try-out, trial run, practice r., dry r., test flight 671 *attempt*; audition, voice test; pilot scheme.

empiricism, speculation, guesswork, guesstimation 512 *conjecture*; tentativeness; experience, practice, rule of thumb, trial, trial and error, hit and miss; random shot, shot in the dark, leap in the d.,

gamble 618 *gambling*; instinct 476 *intuition*; sampling, random sample, straw vote; feeler 459 *question*; straw to show which way the wind is blowing, kite-flying, toe in the water, trial balloon.

experimenter, experimentalist, empiricist, researcher, research worker, analyst, vivisector; assayer, chemist; tester; test driver, test pilot; speculator, prospector; prober, explorer.

testing agent, criterion, touchstone; standard, yardstick 465 *gauge*; breathalyser, sniffer torch; control; indicator, reagent, litmus paper, retort, test tube; proving ground, wind tunnel; simulator, flight s., test track; laboratory.

Adj. *experimental,* analytical, probationary; provisional, tentative 618 *speculative*; trial, exploratory 459 *enquiring*; empirical; in the experimental stage 474 *uncertain*.

Vb. *experiment,* experimentalize; put to the proof; assay, analyse; research; experiment upon, vivisect, make a guinea pig of, practise upon; test, put to the t., run a t. on, put through a battery of tests 459 *enquire*; give something a try; try out, give a trial to 671 *attempt*.

be tentative, feel one's way, proceed by trial and error; feel 378 *touch*; grope, fumble; get the feel of 536 *learn*; put out a feeler, dip a toe in, put a toe in the water, fly a kite, feel the pulse, consult the barometer, take the temperature, see how the land lies, see how the wind blows; fish for, angle for, cast one's net; wait and see, see what happens; try it on, see how far one can go; try one's fortune, try one's luck, speculate 618 *gamble*; venture, explore, prospect 672 *undertake*; probe, sound 459 *enquire*.

462 Comparison – N. *comparison,* comparing, likening; juxtaposition 202 *contiguity*; comparability, points of comparison, analogy, parallel, likeness, similitude 18 *similarity*; identification 13 *identity*; antithesis 14 *contrariety*; contrast 15 *differentiation*; simile, allegory 519 *metaphor*; criterion, pattern, model, check list, control 23 *prototype*.

Adj. *compared,* compared with, in comparison with, likened, measured against, contrasted; comparative, comparable, analogical; relative, correlative; allegorical, metaphorical 519 *figurative*.

Vb. *compare,* collate, confront; set side by side, bring together; draw a comparison 18 *liken*, 13 *identify*; parallel; contrast 15 *differentiate*; compare and contrast 463 *discriminate*; match, pair, balance 28 *equalize*; view together, check with 12 *correlate*; draw a parallel; compare to, compare with; compare notes.

463 Discrimination – N. *discrimination,* distinction 15 *differentiation*; discernment, discretion, connoisseurship 480 *judgment*; insight, perception, acumen, flair 498 *intelligence*; appreciation, critique 480 *estimate*; sensitivity 494 *accuracy*; sensibility 819 *moral sensibility*; tact, delicacy, kid gloves, refinement 846 *good taste*; timing, sense of t.; nicety, particularity 862 *fastidiousness*; sublety, hair-splitting 475 *reasoning*; sorting out 62 *sorting*; selection 605 *choice*; nuance 15 *difference*.

Adj. *discriminating,* discriminative, selective, judicious, discerning, discreet; sensitive 494 *accurate*; fine, delicate, nice, particular 862 *fastidious*; thoughtful, tactful 513 *imaginative*; tasting, appraising, critical 480 *judicial*; distinguishing 15 *distinctive*.

Vb. *discriminate,* distinguish 15 *differentiate*; compare and contrast 462 *compare*; sort out, sieve, sift; separate, separate the sheep from the goats, winnow, sort the wheat from the chaff 46 *set apart*; pick out 605 *select*; exercise discretion, make a distinction, make an exception, draw the line 468 *qualify*; make a value judgment 480 *judge*; have a feel for, have an eye *or* an ear for; know what's what, know how many beans make five, know one's way about, know one's stuff, know a hawk from a handsaw 490 *know*.

464 Indiscrimination – N. *indiscrimination,* lack of discrimination, promiscuity

79 *generality*; lack of judgment, simplicity, naiveté; obtuseness 499 *unintelligence*; indiscretion 857 *rashness*; imperceptivity 439 *blindness*; insensitiveness, insensibility; lack of refinement, coarseness, vulgarity 847 *bad taste*.

Adj. *indiscriminate*, unsorted; undistinguished, undifferentiated, same for everybody 16 *uniform*; random, unaimed, undirected; confused, undefined, unmeasured 474 *uncertain*; promiscuous, haphazard, wholesale, blanket, global 79 *general*.

indiscriminating, unselective, undiscerning, uncritical 499 *unintelligent*; imperceptive, obtuse; tactless, insensitive, unimaginative 820 *impassive*; unrefined, tasteless, coarse 847 *vulgar*; indiscreet, ill-judged 857 *rash*; tone-deaf 416 *deaf*; colour-blind 439 *blind*; inaccurate 495 *inexact*.

465 Measurement – N. *measurement*, quantification; mensuration, surveying; geodetics, geodesy; dose, dosage 26 *finite quantity*; rating, valuation, evaluation; appraisal, assessment, appreciation, estimation 480 *estimate*; calculation, computation, reckoning 86 *numeration*; gauging; checking, check; reading; trigonometry; second, degree, minute, quadrant 247 *angular measure*.

geometry, plane g., planimetry; solid geometry, stereometry; altimetry, hypsometry; Euclidean geometry, non-Euclidean g.; geometer.

metrology, dimensions, length, breadth, height, depth, thickness 195 *size*; weights and measures, avoirdupois, metric system, unit of measurement; weights 322 *weighing*; axle load; linear measure 203 *long measure*; measure of capacity, volume, cubic contents 183 *measure*; liquid measure, gill, pint, imperial p., quart, gallon, imperial g.; barrel, pipe, hogshead 194 *vessel*; litre; apothecaries' fluid measure, minim, dram; dry measure, peck, bushel, quarter; unit of energy, ohm, watt 160 *electricity*; horse power 160 *energy*; candlepower 417 *light*; decibel, sone.

gauge, measure, scale, graduated s.; time scale 117 *chronometry*; balance 322 *scales*; vernier, micrometer; footrule, yardstick, metre bar; yard measure, tape m., measuring tape, metal rule; chain, link, pole, perch, rod; lead, log, log-line; echo sounder; ruler, slide rule; straightedge, T-square, try s., set sq.; dividers, callipers, compass, protractor; sextant, quadrant 269 *sailing aid*; theodolite; astrolabe 321 *astronomy*; index, Plimsoll line, Plimsoll mark, bench m. 547 *indication*; high-water mark, tidemark, floodmark, water line 236 *limit*; axis, coordinate; rule of thumb, standard, criterion, norm 23 *prototype*; milestone 547 *signpost*.

meter, measuring instrument; altimeter; bathometer 211 *depth*; thermometer 379 *thermometry*; barometer, anemometer; dynamometer; hygrometer, fluviometer; gas etc. meter; speedometer, tachometer, tachymeter, tachograph, spy-in-the-cab, odometer, milometer 277 *velocity*; cyclometer, pedometer 267 *land travel*; metronome, time switch, parking meter 117 *timekeeper*; micrometer; Geiger counter; seismograph.

Adj. *metrical*, mensural; imperial, metric; metrological; dimensional, three-d.; cubic, volumetric, linear, micrometric; cadastral, topographical; geodetic.

Vb. *measure*, mensurate, survey, triangulate; compute, calculate, count, reckon 86 *number*; quantify, take the measurements, measure the length and breadth, measure up; size up, estimate the average 30 *average out*; beat the bounds, pace out; tape, span; calliper, use the dividers; probe, sound, fathom, plumb 313 *plunge*; take soundings, heave the lead; pace, check the speed 117 *time*; balance 322 *weigh*.

gauge, meter, take a reading, read, read off; standardize 16 *make uniform*; grade, mark off, mark out, calibrate 27 *graduate*; reduce to scale, draw to s., map 551 *represent*.

appraise, gauge, value, cost, fix the price of 809 *price*; evaluate, estimate,

make an e., form an e.; appreciate, assess, assay 480 *estimate*; form an opinion 480 *judge*; tape, have taped, have the measure of, size up.

mete out, mete, measure out, weigh, weigh out, dole o., allocate, divide, share, share out, portion out 775 *participate*, 783 *apportion*.

Section three: *Materials for reasoning*

466 Evidence – N. *evidence,* facts, data, biodata, curriculum vitae, case history; grounds 475 *reasons*; premises 475 *premise*; hearsay 524 *report*; circumstantial evidence 8 *circumstance*; constructive evidence 512 *supposition*; prima facie evidence; proof 478 *demonstration*; corroboration; verification, confirmation 473 *certainty*; 467 *counterevidence*; fact, relevant f.; document, exhibit, fingerprints, DNA fingerprinting, genetic f. 548 *record*; clue 524 *hint*; symptom, syndrome, sign, sure s. 547 *indication*; mention, reference, quotation, citation, chapter and verse; one's authorities, documentation.

testimony, witness; statement 524 *information*; admission, confession 526 *disclosure*; one's case, plea 614 *pretext*; word, assertion, allegation 532 *affirmation*; evidence on oath; legal evidence; deposition, affidavit, attestation 532 *oath*; State's evidence, King's *or* Queen's evidence; word of mouth, verbal; documentary evidence; character reference, compurgation 927 *vindication*; case record, dossier 548 *record*; written contract, contract of employment 765 *compact*; deed, testament 767 *security*.

credential, testimonial, chit, character, recommendation, references; seal, signature, countersignature, endorsement, docket, counterfoil; voucher, warranty, warrant, certificate, diploma 767 *security*; ticket, passport, visitor's p., visa 756 *permit*; authority, scripture.

witness, eye w. 441 *spectator*; indicator, informant, telltale, grass, supergrass 524 *informer*; deponent, testifier, swearer, attestor 765 *signatory*; witness to character, referee; sponsor 707 *patron*.

Adj. *evidential,* suggesting, significant 514 *meaningful*; indicative, symptomatic, identifying, diagnostic; deducible, verifiable 471 *probable*; corroborative, confirmatory; damning; presumptive, reliable 473 *certain*; proving, demonstrative, conclusive; factual, documented, well-documented 473 *positive*; well-grounded, well-founded 494 *true*; authoritative 178 *influential*; testified, attested, witnessed; in evidence, on the record.

Vb. *evidence,* show, evince, furnish evidence; show signs of, betray symptoms of, have the makings of; betoken 551 *represent*; breathe of, declare witness to 522 *manifest*; lend colour to 471 *make likely*; tell its own tale, speak for itself, speak volumes; carry weight 178 *influence*; suggest 547 *indicate*; argue, involve 523 *imply*.

testify, witness; take one's oath, swear, be sworn, speak on oath 532 *affirm*; bear witness, take the stand, give testimony, give evidence, witness for *or* against, swear to, vouch for, give one's word; authenticate, validate, give credence, certify 473 *make certain*; attest, subscribe, countersign, endorse, sign; plead, state one's case 475 *argue*; admit, avow, acknowledge 526 *confess*; give a character reference, act as referee.

corroborate, support, buttress 162 *strengthen*; sustain, uphold in evidence, substantiate 927 *vindicate*; bear out, verify; validate, confirm, ratify, establish, make a case for 473 *make certain*; lead evidence; produce one's witnesses; produce the evidence; document, give credence; collect evidence; cite the evidence, refer to a precedent, quote one's authorities, give chapter and verse.

467 Counterevidence – N. *counterevidence,* contraindication 14 *contrariety*;

evidence against, defence, rebuttal, rejoinder 460 *answer*; refutation 479 *confutation*; denial 533 *negation*; justification 927 *vindication*; one word against another; counteroath, counterclaim; conflicting evidence, contradictory e.; mitigating evidence 468 *qualification*; hostile witness.

Vb. *tell against,* weigh against, countervail; contravene, run counter, contradict, contraindicate; rebut 479 *confute*; oppose, point the other way 14 *be contrary*; cancel out 182 *counteract*; cut both ways 518 *be equivocal*; lead for the other side; fail to confirm, alter the case; weaken, damage, spoil; undermine, subvert 165 *destroy*; demolish the case, turn the tables, contradict oneself, turn hostile.

Adv. *conversely,* on the other hand; in rebuttal.

468 Qualification – N. *qualification,* specification 80 *speciality*; prerequisite 627 *requirement*; assumption 512 *supposition*; leaven, colouring, tinge; modification 143 *change*; mitigation 177 *moderation*; stipulation, condition, sine qua non 766 *conditions*; limitation 747 *restriction*; proviso, reservation; exception, salvo, escape clause, letout c., penalty clause, exemption 919 *nonliability*; demur, objection, but 704 *opposition*; consideration, concession, allowance; extenuating circumstances; redeeming feature.

Adj. *qualifying,* restricting, limiting; modifying; mitigatory; extenuating, palliative, excusing, weakening, colouring, leavening; contingent, provisional 766 *conditional*; discounting, allowing for, taking into account; saving, excepting, exempting; qualified, not absolute; exceptional, exempted, exempt 919 *nonliable*.

Vb. *qualify,* condition, limit, restrict 747 *restrain*; colour, shade; leaven, alter 143 *modify*; temper, season, palliate, mitigate 177 *moderate*; adulterate 163 *weaken*; excuse 927 *extenuate*; grant, concede, make allowance for, take into account, take cognizance of; lessen 37 *abate*; make exceptions 919 *exempt*; alter the case; insert a qualifying clause; insist on 627 *require*; relax 734 *be lax*; take exception, object, demur, raise an objection 762 *deprecate*.

Adv. *provided,* provided always, with the proviso that, according as, subject to, conditionally, with the understanding that, so *or* as long as; granting, admitting, supposing; allowing for; with a pinch of salt; not absolutely, not invariably; if, if not, unless 8 *if*; though, although, even if.

nevertheless, even so, all the same, for all that, after all; despite, in spite of; but, yet, still, at all events; whether, whether or no.

469 Possibility – N. *possibility,* potentiality; capacity, viability, viableness, workability 160 *ability*; what might be; best one can do, all in one's power, contingency, eventuality, a possibility, chance, off-chance 159 *fair chance*; good chance 137 *opportunity*; bare possibility, ghost of a chance, outside c.; likelihood 471 *probability*; conceivability; practicability; practicableness, feasibility; availability, accessibility; risk of.

Adj. *possible,* potential, hypothetical; able, capable, viable; arguable, reasonable; feasible, practicable, negotiable 701 *easy*; workable, achievable; doable, operable; attainable, approachable, accessible, obtainable, realizable; surmountable; within the bounds *or* realms of possibility; available, still open, not excluded, not too late; conceivable, imaginable; practical; allowable; contingent 124 *future*; on the cards 471 *probable*; liable, tending.

Vb. *be possible,* - feasible etc. adj.; may, might,'; be a possibility, depend, be contingent, lie within the bounds *or* realms of possibility; stand a chance 471 *be likely*.

make possible, enable; allow 756 *permit*; give the green light, clear the path, smoothe the way, remove the obstacles.

Adv. *possibly,* conceivably; perhaps, perchance, for all one knows; within reach, within one's grasp; may be, could be; if possible, if humanly possible; wind and weather permitting, God willing, Deo volente, D.V.

470 Impossibility – N. *impossibility,* inconceivability etc. adj.; unthinkableness, no chance, no way, not a chance of, not a cat's chance, not a snowball's chance in hell, not a hope 853 *hopelessness*; irrevocability; impasse, deadlock, logjam 702 *obstacle*; impracticability 643 *inexpedience*; unavailability, inaccessibility, sour grapes; impossible task, no go 700 *hard task.*

Adj. *impossible,* not possible; ruled out, excluded; not to be thought of, out of the question, hopeless; unreasonable; incompatible with the facts 495 *erroneous*; inconceivable, unthinkable, unimaginable, unheard of; miraculous 864 *wonderful*; unrealistic 513 *imaginary.*

impracticable, not feasible; unworkable; out of the question, unattainable, insoluble, inextricable, beyond one 700 *difficult*; insuperable, insurmountable, impenetrable, unnavigable, inaccessible, unobtainable, not within one's grasp; elusive.

Vb. *be impossible,* - impracticable etc. adj., have no chance whatever.

make impossible, rule out, exclude; put out of reach, set an impossible task; eat one's hat if 533 *negate.*

attempt the impossible, labour in vain 641 *waste effort*; have nothing to go upon, grasp at shadows, clutch at straws; be in two places at once, square the circle, discover the philosopher's stone, find the elixir of life, find a needle in a haystack; weave a rope of sand, gather grapes from thorns *or* figs from thistles, get blood from a stone, fetch water in a sieve; make bricks without straw, make a silk purse out of a sow's ear, change a leopard's spots; have one's cake and eat it; walk on water, set the Thames on fire.

Adv. *impossibly,* nohow, no way.

471 Probability – N. *probability,* likelihood 159 *chance*; good chance, fair c., sporting c., odds-on c. 469 *possibility*; excellent prospect 511 *prediction*; fair expectation 507 *expectation*; well-grounded hope 852 *hope*; safe bet, sure thing 473 *certainty*; credibility; likely belief 485 *belief*; plausibility, good reason 475 *reasons*; verisimilitude, semblance 445 *appearance*; theory of probability.

Adj. *probable,* likely 180 *liable*; on the cards, in a fair way; to be expected, foreseeable, foreseen; presumptive; promising 507 *expected*; on the horizon, in the wind 155 *impending*; highly possible 469 *possible.*

plausible, specious; to all intents and purposes, to all appearances 445 *appearing*; reasonable 475 *rational*; convincing, persuasive 485 *credible*; well-grounded, well-founded 494 *true.*

Vb. *be likely,* - probable etc. adj.; have a chance, be on the cards, stand a chance, be in with a c., run a good c. 469 *be possible*; bid fair to, be in danger of 179 *tend*; show signs, have the makings of, promise.

make likely, make probable, increase the chances; involve 523 *imply*; entail; put in the way to, promote 703 *aid*; point to 466 *evidence.*

assume, presume, take for granted; conjecture, guess, dare say 512 *suppose*; think likely; count upon 473 *be certain*; gather, deduce, infer 475 *reason.*

Adv. *probably,* presumably; in all probability, in all likelihood, doubtless, as is to be expected, all things considered; very likely, most l., ten to one, by all odds, a pound to a penny; seemingly, apparently, on the face of it, to all intents and purposes, to all appearances; like enough, as likely as not.

472 Improbability – N. *improbability,* doubt, real d. 474 *uncertainty*; little chance, little or no c., chance in a million, off-chance, small c., poor c., slim c., outside c., long shot; not a ghost of a

chance, no c., not a hope 470 *impossibil-ity*; long odds, barest of possibilities; pious hopes, forlorn hope, poor prospect 508 *lack of expectation*; rare occurrence, rarity 140 *infrequency*; implausibility, traveller's tale, fisherman's yarn 541 *falsehood*.

Adj. *improbable*, unlikely, more than doubtful, dubious 474 *uncertain*; hard to believe, fishy, unconvincing, implausible; rare 140 *infrequent*; inconceivable 470 *impossible*; incredible, too good to be true.

Vb. *be unlikely*, - improbable, look impossible etc. adj.; have the barest of chances, show little hope, be implausible, not wash, be hard to believe, strain one's credulity 486 *cause doubt*; think unlikely, whistle for 508 *not expect*.

Int. not likely! no fear! no way! not on your life! not on your nelly! not a hope! some hopes!

473 Certainty – **N.** *certainty*, certain knowledge 490 *knowledge*; certainness, assuredness, sureness; inevitability, inexorability, irrevocability, necessity 596 *fate*; infallibility; reliability, unimpeachability 494 *truth*; unambiguity, unequivocalness; incontrovertibility, irrefutability, indisputability, proof 478 *demonstration*; authentication, ratification, validation; certification, verification, confirmation; attestation 466 *testimony*; check 459 *enquiry*; ascertainment 484 *discovery*; dead certainty, cert, dead c., sure thing, safe bet, cinch, open and shut case, foregone conclusion; fact; matter of fact, fait accompli 154 *event*; settled decision 480 *judgment*.

positiveness, moral certainty; assurance, confidence, conviction, persuasion 485 *belief*; unshakable opinion 485 *opinion*; idée fixe, obsession 481 *bias*; dogmatism; infallibility, self-confidence; pontification, laying down the law.

dogmatist, self-opinionated person; bigot, fanatic, zealot; oracle, knowall, smarty-pants 500 *wiseacre*.

Adj. *certain*, sure, solid, unshakable, well-founded, well-grounded 3 *substantial*; reliable 929 *trustworthy*; authoritative, official 494 *genuine*; factual, historical 494 *true*; authenticated, ascertained, certified, attested, guaranteed, warranted; tested, tried, foolproof 660 *safe*; infallible, unerring 540 *veracious*; axiomatic, dogmatic, taken for granted; self-evident, evident, apparent; unequivocal, unambiguous; unmistakable, clear, clear as day 443 *obvious*; inevitable, irrevocable, inexorable 596 *fated*; bound, bound to be, in the bag; sure as fate, sure as death; inviolable, safe as houses, safe as the Bank of England 660 *invulnerable*; verifiable, demonstrable.

positive, confident, assured, self-assured, self-confident, certain in one's mind, undoubting, convinced, persuaded, certified, sure; opinionated, self-o; pontificating, oracular 532 *assertive*; dogmatic, doctrinaire 976 *orthodox*; obsessed, bigoted, fanatical 481 *biased*; unshaken, set in one's ways, fixed in one's opinions 153 *unchangeable*; clear-cut; definite, decisive, defined, unambiguous, unambivalent, unequivocal; convincing 485 *credible*; affirmative, categorical, absolute, unqualified, unreserved; conclusive.

undisputed, beyond doubt, beyond all reasonable d., without a shadow of doubt, axiomatic, uncontroversial; unquestioned, undoubted, uncontested, unarguable, undebatable, indubitable, unquestionable, incontrovertible, incontestable, unimpeachable, undeniable; irrefutable.

Vb. *be certain*, - sure etc. adj.; leave no doubt, be clear as day, be plain as the nose on your face, stand to reason, be axiomatic; be positive, be assured, satisfy oneself, convince o., feel sure, be clear in one's mind, have no doubts; know for certain 490 *know*; stick to one's guns, have made up one's mind, dismiss all doubt; depend on it, rely on, bank on, trust in, swear by; put one's shirt on, lay one's bottom dollar.

dogmatize, pontificate, lay down the law 532 *affirm*; know all the answers.

make certain, certify, authenticate, ratify, seal, sign 488 *endorse*; guarantee, warrant, assure; finalize, settle, decide 480 *judge*; remove doubt, persuade 485 *convince*; make sure, ascertain, check, run a check, double-check, verify, confirm, confirm in writing, clinch 466 *corroborate*; reassure oneself, take a second look, do a double take; insure against 660 *safeguard*; reinsure 858 *be cautious*; ensure, make inevitable 596 *necessitate*.

Adv. *certainly,* definitely, for sure, to be sure, no doubt, doubtless, indubitably, as sure as anything, as sure as eggs is eggs, as sure as God made little green apples, as night follows day, of course, as a matter of c., no question; no two ways about it, no ifs or buts; without fail, sink or swim, rain or shine, come hell or high water, come what may, whatever happens.

474 Uncertainty – N. *uncertainty,* doubtfulness, dubiousness; ambiguity, ambivalence 518 *equivocalness*; vagueness, haziness, obscurity 418 *darkness*; mist, haze, fog 423 *opacity*; grey area; yes and no, don't know, floating voter, vacillation, indeterminacy, borderline case; indefiniteness, roving commission; query, question mark 459 *question*; open question, anybody's guess, a matter of tossing a coin; nothing to go on, guesswork, guestimate 512 *conjecture*; contingency 159 *chance*; gamble, toss-up, wager 618 *gambling*; leap *or* shot in the dark, bow at a venture, pig in a poke, blind date; something or other, this or that.

dubiety, 486 *doubt*; open verdict, a verdict of not proven; suspense, waiting 507 *expectation*; doubt, indecision, hesitancy, shilly-shallying, vacillation 317 *fluctuation*; seesaw, floating vote 601 *irresolution*; bafflement, quandary; dilemma, cleft stick, Morton's fork.

unreliability, fallibility 495 *error*; precariousness, unstable condition, touch and go 661 *danger*; untrustworthiness, treacherousness; variability, changeability 152 *changeableness*; unpredictability, unexpectedness 508 *lack of expectation*; fickleness, capriciousness; slipperiness; lack of security, no guarantee, no collateral, gentleman's agreement, handshake deal.

Adj. *uncertain,* unsure, doubtful, dubious; chancy, risky 661 *unsafe*; treacherous **(see** *unreliable*); subject to chance, at the mercy of events; sporadic 140 *infrequent*; fluid; contingent, depending on 766 *conditional*; unpredictable, unforeseeable 508 *unexpected*; indeterminate, undefined; random; indecisive, undecided, vacillating, in suspense; in question, under enquiry; open to question, questionable; arguable, debatable, disputable, controvertible, controversial; suspicious 472 *improbable*; problematical, hypothetical, speculative; undefinable, borderline, grey-area, marginal; ambiguous 518 *equivocal*; paradoxical 477 *illogical*; oracular, enigmatic, cryptic, obscure 517 *puzzling*; vague, hazy, misty, cloudy 419 *shadowy*; mysterious, veiled 523 *occult*; unresolved, unexplained 517 *unintelligible*; perplexing, bewildering.

unreliable, undependable, untrustworthy; treacherous 930 *dishonest*; unsteady, unstable, variable, vacillating, changeable 152 *changeful*; unpredictable, unforeseeable; fickle 604 *capricious*; fallible, open to error 495 *erroneous*; precarious, touch and go.

doubting, in doubt, doubtful, dubious, full of doubt, riddled with d., plagued by uncertainty; agnostic, sceptical; sitting on the fence, hedging one's bets, in two minds; in suspense, open-minded; distrustful, mistrustful 858 *cautious*; uncertain, diffident; hesitant, undecided, wavering, vacillating, unsure which way to jump 601 *irresolute*; unable to say; baffled 517 *puzzled*; in a cleft stick, on the horns of a dilemma; disorientated; clueless 491 *ignorant*.

Vb. *be uncertain,* be contingent, lie in the lap of the gods; hinge on, be dependent on 157 *depend*; be touch and go,

hang by a thread, tremble in the balance; be open to question, be ambiguous 518 *be equivocal*; have one's doubts 486 *doubt*; wait and see 507 *await*; have a suspicion, suspect, wonder, wonder whether; dither, be in two minds, hover, float, be a don't know, sit on the fence, sway, seesaw, waver, teeter, vacillate, shilly-shally, falter, pause, hesitate 601 *be irresolute*; demur; flounder; be in the dark, have nothing to go on, grope 461 *be tentative*; cast about, lose the thread, miss one's way, get lost 282 *stray*; lose the scent, lose track of; not know which way to turn, be at one's wits' end, be at a loss, not know what to make of, be in a dilemma, be in a quandary; wouldn't swear, could be wrong.

puzzle, perplex, confuse, daze, bewilder, baffle, boggle the mind, nonplus, flummox, stump, floor 727 *defeat*; mystify, keep one guessing; bamboozle; fox, throw off the scent 495 *mislead*; plague *or* riddle with d. 486 *cause doubt*; make one think.

Adv. *in suspense,* in a state of uncertainty, on the horns of a dilemma, in a maze, in a daze.

Section four: Reasoning processes

475 Reasoning – **N.** *reasoning,* force of argument; reason, discursive r.; lateral thinking 476 *intuition*; sweet reason, reasonableness, rationality; dialectics, logic; logical process, logical sequence, inference, generalization; distinction 463 *discrimination*; deductive reasoning, deduction; inductive reasoning, empirical reasoning; rationalism, dialectic 449 *philosophy*; modern maths 86 *mathematics*; simple arithmetic.

premise, postulate, basis of reasoning; principle, general p., first p.; lemma, starting point; assumption, stipulation 512 *supposition*; axiom, self-evident truth 496 *maxim*; datum, data; hypothesis.

argument, discussion, symposium, dialogue; exchange of views, cut and thrust; disputation, controversy, debate 489 *dissent*; set *or* formal argument, plea, pleading; thesis, case; reasons, submission; defence; polemics; war of words, paper war 709 *quarrel*; propaganda, pamphleteering 534 *teaching*; controversialism, argumentativeness; hair-splitting, logic-chopping, contentiousness, wrangling, jangling 709 *dissension*; sophism 477 *sophistry*; legal argument, pleadings 959 *litigation*.

reasons, grounds; arguments, pros and cons; case, good c., case to answer; sound argument, conclusive argument 478 *demonstration*; point, valid p., point well taken.

Adj. *rational,* clear-headed, reasoning, reasonable; rationalistic, logical; cogent, acceptable, admissible, to the point, pointed, well-grounded, well-argued 9 *relevant*; sensible, fair 913 *just*; analytic; consistent, systematic, methodological; dialectic, discursive, deductive, inductive, axiomatic 473 *certain*; tenable 469 *possible*.

Vb. *be reasonable* 471 *be likely;* stand to reason, follow, hang together, hold water; appeal to reason; listen to reason, be guided by r.; yield to argument; admit, concede; have a case, have a case to be answered, have logic on one's side.

reason, philosophize 449 *think*; syllogize, rationalize; apply reason, bring reason to bear, use one's grey matter, put two and two together; infer, deduce, induct; explain 520 *interpret*.

argue, argufy, argy-bargy, bandy arguments, cut and thrust; hold a symposium; exchange opinions, have an exchange of views, discuss; debate, dispute; quibble, split hairs, chop logic; argue the case, argue the point; stick to one's guns; work an argument to death 532 *emphasize*; put one's case, plead; pamphleteer 534 *teach*; take up the case, defend; attack; cross swords, take up a point with, join issue, demur, cavil 489 *dissent*; analyse, pull to pieces; out-argue; have words, have a confrontation,

wrangle; answer back, make a rejoinder 460 *answer*; start an argument, move a motion, open a discussion *or* debate.

postulate, posit, stipulate, lay down, assume 512 *suppose*; take for granted, refer to first principles.

476 Intuition: absence of reason – N. *intuition,* instinct, association, Pavlovian response, automatic reaction, gut r., knee-jerk r. 450 *absence of thought*; sixth sense, extrasensory perception, ESP; telepathy; insight, second sight, clairvoyance 984 *psychics*; id, subconscious; intuitiveness; divination; inspiration, presentiment, impulse 818 *feeling*; feminine logic; rule of thumb; hunch.

Adj. *intuitive,* instinctive, impulsive; devoid of logic 477 *illogical*; impressionistic, subjective; involuntary 609 *spontaneous*; subconscious 447 *psychic*; beyond reason; inspirational, inspired, clairvoyant, ESP, telepathic.

Vb. *intuit,* know by instinct, have a sixth sense; sense, feel in one's bones, have a funny feeling, have a hunch; have a gut reaction, react instinctively; play it by ear, go by impressions, rely on intuition, dispense with reason, use feminine logic; use guesswork, work on a hunch.

477 Sophistry: false reasoning – N. *sophistry,* illogicalness, illogic; feminine logic 476 *intuition*; sophistical reasoning; false r., rationalization; double think, self-deception; mental reservation 525 *concealment*; equivocation, blinding with science, casuistry; subtlety, over-subtlety; hair-splitting, logic-chopping; claptrap, mere words 515 *empty talk*; quibbling; chicanery, subterfuge; evasion 614 *pretext*.

sophism, a sophistry, specious argument; illogicality, fallacy; loose thinking, sloppy t.; solecism, flaw in the argument; begging the question, circular reasoning; non sequitur, irrelevancy, contradiction in terms; weak case.

Adj. *illogical,* contrary to reason, irrational, unreasonable; unreasoned, arbitrary; fallacious, fallible; contradictory, self-c., inconsistent, incongruous; unwarranted, invalid, untenable, unsound; unfounded, ungrounded, groundless; irrelevant, inconsequent, inconsequential; incorrect, unscientific, false 495 *erroneous*.

poorly reasoned, unrigorous, inconclusive; unproved; weak, feeble; flimsy; loose, woolly, muddled, confused.

Vb. *reason badly,* argue in a circle, beg the question, fail to get to the point, not see the wood for the trees, strain at a gnat and swallow a camel; not have a leg to stand on; talk at random.

sophisticate, mislead 535 *misteach*; mystify, quibble, cavil, split hairs 475 *argue*; equivocate 518 *be equivocal*; dodge, shuffle, fence; not come to the point, beat about the bush 570 *be diffuse*; evade 667 *elude*; draw a veil over, varnish, gloss over, whitewash; colour 552 *misrepresent*; pervert, misapply 675 *misuse*; pervert reason, twist the argument, torture logic; prove that white is black.

478 Demonstration – N. *demonstration,* documentation, authentication 466 *evidence*; proven fact 494 *truth*; proof; conclusive proof; conclusiveness 473 *certainty*; verification, ascertainment 461 *experiment*; deduction, inference, argument, triumph of a. 475 *reasoning*; exposition, clarification 522 *manifestation*; burden of proof, onus.

V. *demonstrate,* prove; show, evince 522 *manifest*; justify 927 *vindicate*; bear out 466 *corroborate*; produce the evidence, document, provide documentation, substantiate, establish, verify 466 *evidence*; infer, deduce, draw, draw a conclusion 475 *reason*; settle the question, satisfy 473 *make certain*; make out a case, prove one's point, clinch an argument, have the best of an a., win an a. 485 *convince*.

be proved, prove to be true, stand to reason 475 *be reasonable*; stand up to

225

investigation, hold water, hold good 494 *be true.*

Adv. *of course,* undeniably, without doubt; as already proved.

479 Confutation – N. *confutation,* refutation, disproof, invalidation; conviction 961 *condemnation*; rebuttal, rejoinder, clincher, knock-down argument; last word, retort, repartee 839 *witticism*; contradiction, denial, denunciation 533 *negation*; exploded argument.

Vb. *confute,* refute, disprove, invalidate; rebut, rejoin, retort, have an answer, explain away; deny, contradict 533 *negate*; give the lie to, force to withdraw; prove the contrary, show the fallacy of; cut the ground from under, leave someone without a leg to stand on; confound, rout, silence, reduce to s., stop the mouth, shut up, floor, gravel, nonplus; condemn one out of his own mouth; show up, expose; convict 961 *condemn*; defeat one's logic; blow sky-high, shoot full of holes, puncture, riddle, destroy, explode, demolish one's arguments, drive a coach and horses through, knock the bottom out of 165 *demolish*; have, have in one's hand, have one on the hip; overthrow, squash, crush, overwhelm 727 *defeat*; riddle the defence, outargue, have the better of the argument, get the better of, score off; parry, avoid the trap; stand, stand up to argument; dismiss, override, sweep aside, brush a.; brook no denial, affirm the contrary 532 *affirm*.

Section five: Results of reasoning

480 Judgment: conclusion – N. *judgment,* judging (see *estimate*); good judgment, discretion 463 *discrimination*; bad judgment, lack of discretion 464 *indiscrimination*; arbitration, umpirage; verdict, finding; sentence 963 *punishment*; summing-up, pronouncement; act of judgment, decision, adjudication, award; order, court order, ruling; order of the court 737 *decree*; decree nisi; decree absolute; judgment in appeal, irrevocable decision; settled decision; final judgment, conclusion, result, upshot; moral 496 *maxim*; value judgment 476 *intuition*; reasoned judgment, deduction, inference, corollary 475 *reasoning*; wise judgment, j. of Solomon 498 *wisdom*; fair judgment, unclouded eye 913 *justice*; vox populi, voting, referendum, plebiscite, poll 605 *vote*.

estimate, estimation, view 485 *opinion*; assessment, valuation, evaluation, calculation 465 *measurement*; consideration, comparing, contrasting 462 *comparison*; appreciation, appraisal, appraisement 520 *interpretation*; criticism, constructive c. 703 *aid*; destructive criticism 702 *hindrance*; critique, crit, review, notice, press n., comment, comments, observations, remarks, profile 591 *article*; summing-up; survey 438 *inspection*; favourable report 923 *approbation*; unfavourable report, censure 924 *disapprobation*.

estimator, judge, adjudicator; arbitrator, umpire, referee; surveyor, valuer, valuator; inspector, inspecting officer, reporter, examiner, ombudsman, ACAS (=Advisory, Conciliation and Arbitration Service) 459 *enquirer*; counsellor 691 *adviser*; censor, critic, reviewer 591 *dissertator*; commentator, observer 520 *interpreter*; juror, assessor 957 *jury*; voter, elector 605 *electorate*.

Adj. *judicial,* judicious 463 *discriminating*; shrewd 498 *wise*; unbiased, dispassionate 913 *just*; arbitral; judicatory, conclusive; sententious.

Vb. *judge,* sit in judgment, hold the scales; arbitrate, referee, umpire; hear, try, hear the case, try the cause; uphold an objection, disallow an o.; rule, pronounce; find, find for, find against; decree, award, adjudicate; decide, settle, conclude; confirm, make absolute; pass judgment, deliver j.; sentence, pass s., doom 961 *condemn*; agree on a verdict, return a v., bring in a v.; sum up.

estimate, form an e., make an e., measure, calculate, make 465 *gauge*; value,

evaluate, appraise; rate, rank; sum up, size up; conjecture, guess 512 *suppose*; take stock 808 *account*; consider, weigh, ponder, weigh the pros and cons, take everything into consideration 449 *meditate*.

Adv. *sub judice,* under investigation, under trial, under sentence.

481 Misjudgment. Prejudice – N. *misjudgment,* miscalculation, misreckoning, misconception, wrong impression 495 *error*; loose thinking, sloppy t. 495 *inexactness*; bad judgment, poor j. 464 *indiscrimination*; fallibility, gullibility 499 *unintelligence*; misconstruction 521 *misinterpretation*; wrong verdict, miscarriage of justice 914 *injustice*; overvaluation 482 *overestimation*; undervaluation 483 *underestimation*; autosuggestion, self-deception, self-delusion, wishful thinking 542 *deception*; fool's paradise 513 *fantasy*; false dawn 509 *disappointment*.

prejudgment, foregone conclusion 608 *predetermination*; preconception, mind made up; preconceived idea; idée fixe, obsession, hang-up, fixation, bee in the bonnet, monomania 503 *personality disorder*.

prejudice, predilection; partiality, favouritism 914 *injustice*; penchant, bias, biased judgment, warped j., jaundiced eye; blind spot, blind side, tunnel vision, mote in the eye, beam in the e. 439 *blindness*; onesidedness, party spirit 708 *party*; partisanship, clannishness, cliquishness, esprit de corps; parochialism, provincialism, insularity; 978 *sectarianism*; gung-ho attitude, chauvinism, xenophobia, my country right or wrong; snobbishness, class war, class prejudice, classism; ageism; sexism, heterosexism, sex prejudice, sex discrimination; race prejudice, racialism, racism; colour prejudice, colour bar, apartheid, segregation, discrimination 57 *exclusion*; intolerance, persecution, anti-Semitism 888 *hatred*.

narrow mind, narrow-mindedness, small-m.; insularity, parochialism, provincialism; closed mind, one-track m., tunnel vision; one-sidedness; legalism, pedantry 735 *severity*; intolerance, dogmatism 473 *positiveness*; bigotry, fanaticism 602 *opinionatedness*; pedant, stickler 862 *perfectionist*; faddist 504 *crank*; zealot, bigot, fanatic 473 *dogmatist*; racialist, racist, white supremacist; chauvinist, sexist.

bias, unbalance, disequilibrium 29 *inequality*; warp, bent, slant, liability, penchant 179 *tendency*; angle, point of view 485 *opinion*; mind made up (see *prejudgment*).

Adj. *misjudging,* misconceiving, misinterpreting etc. vb.; miscalculating, in error, out 495 *mistaken*; fallible, gullible 499 *foolish*; wrong, wrong-headed; unseeing 439 *blind*; myopic, purblind, short-sighted 440 *dim-sighted*; misguided, superstitious 487 *credulous*; subjective, unrealistic, visionary, impractical; crankish, faddy, faddish, whimsical 503 *crazy*; besotted, infatuated 887 *enamoured*; haunted, obsessed, hung up, eaten up with.

narrow-minded, petty-m., narrow, hidebound; short-sighted, tunnel-visioned; parochial, provincial, insular; pedantic, donnish 735 *severe*; legalistic, literal, literal-minded, unimaginative, matter-of-fact; hypercritical, overscrupulous, fiky, fussy 862 *fastidious*; stiff, unbending 602 *obstinate*; dictatorial, dogmatic 473 *positive*; opinionated, opinionative; self-opinioned, self-conceited 871 *proud*.

biased, warped, twisted, swayed; jaundiced, prejudiced; snobbish, clannish, cliquish; partisan, one-sided, party-minded 978 *sectarian*; nationalistic, chauvinistic, gung-hoish, jingoistic, xenophobic; racist, racialist; sexist, ageist, classist; class-prejudiced, colour-p.; predisposed, preconceived; prejudging 608 *predetermined*; discriminatory 914 *unjust*; intolerant 735 *oppressive*; bigoted, fanatic 602 *obstinate*; blinded 439 *blind*.

Vb. *misjudge,* miscalculate, miscount 495 *blunder*; not take into account, reckon without; undervalue, minimize 483 *underestimate*; overestimate, overvalue 482 *overrate*; guess wrong, come to the wrong conclusion, misconceive 521 *misinterpret*; overreach oneself, overplay one's hand; get the wrong end of the stick 695 *act foolishly*; not see the wood for the trees; not see beyond one's nose 499 *be foolish*; fly in the face of facts 477 *reason badly.*

prejudge, judge beforehand, make up one's mind in advance 608 *predetermine*; prejudice the issue, precondemn; preconceive, presuppose, presume 475 *postulate*; jump to conclusions 857 *be rash.*

bias, warp, twist, bend; jaundice, prejudice; predispose 178 *influence.*

be biased, - prejudiced etc. adj.; be one-sided, see one side only, show favouritism, favour one side 914 *do wrong*; lean, favour, take sides, have a down on, have it in for, hold it against one, be unfair, discriminate against 735 *oppress*; lose one's sense of proportion; suffer from tunnel vision, blind oneself to, have a blind side, have a blind spot 439 *be blind.*

482 Overestimation – **N.** *overestimation,* overestimate, overenthusiasm, overvaluation 481 *misjudgment*; overstatement 546 *exaggeration*; boasting 877 *boast*; ballyhoo, hype, buildup, overkill 528 *publicity*; overpraise, panegyric, gush, hot air 515 *empty talk*; storm in a teacup, much ado about nothing; megalomania, vanity 871 *pride*; overconfidence 857 *rashness*; egotism 932 *selfishness*; overoptimism; defeatism 853 *hopelessness*; optimist 852 *hope*; pessimist, prophet of doom, doom-watcher, doomster, Jonah, defeatist; exaggerator, puffer, barker, advertiser, promoter 528 *publicizer.*

Adj. *optimistic,* upbeat, sanguine, overconfident; overpitched; overenthusiastic, raving.

Vb. *overestimate,* overrate, count all one's geese swans; overvalue, overprice, set too high a value on 811 *overcharge*; rave, idealize, overpraise, think too much of; make too much of 546 *exaggerate*; overemphasize, overstress, overdo, play up, overpitch, inflate, magnify 197 *enlarge*; boost, puff, panegyrize, hype 923 *praise*; attach too much importance to, make mountains out of molehills; maximize, make the most of; whitewash, paper over the cracks.

483 Underestimation – **N.** *underestimation,* underestimate, undervaluation, minimization; conservative estimate, modest calculation 177 *moderation*; depreciation 926 *detraction*; understatement, litotes, meiosis; euphemism 950 *prudery*; self-depreciation, self-effacement, overmodesty 872 *humility*; false modesty, mock m., irony 850 *affectation*; pessimism 853 *hopelessness*; pessimist, minimizer, cynic 926 *detractor.*

Vb. *underestimate,* underrate, undervalue, underprice; mark down, discount 812 *cheapen*; depreciate, underpraise, run down, cry d., disparage 926 *detract*; slight, pooh-pooh 922 *hold cheap*; not do justice to, do less than justice 481 *misjudge*; understate; play down, soft-pedal; shrug off 458 *disregard*; make little of, minimize; make light of, set no store by, think too little of 922 *despise.*

484 Discovery – **N.** *discovery,* finding; invention; exploration, archaeology, speleology, potholing; excavation 459 *search*; detection 438 *inspection*; radiolocation 187 *location*; water divining; exposure, revelation 522 *manifestation*; illumination, realization, disenchantment; hitting upon, serendipity; strike, find, lucky f., treasure trove; eye-opener 508 *lack of expectation*; open sesame 263 *opener.*

detector, probe; space p., spy satellite 276 *spaceship*; asdic, sonar; early warning system; radar, radar trap, speed trap; breathalyser, sniffer torch; finder 442 *telescope*; lie detector; Geiger counter 465 *meter*; metal detector; divining rod; water diviner; talent scout; discoverer,

inventor; explorer 268 *traveller*; archaeologist, speleologist, potholer 459 *enquirer*; prospector 461 *experimenter*; gastroscope, auriscope, ophthalmoscope, colposcope 658 *diagnostic*.

Vb. *discover*, invent, explore; find out; strike, hit, hit upon; come upon, happen on, stumble on; meet, encounter 154 *meet with*; tumble to, awake to, see the truth, see the light, see in its true colours 516 *understand*; find, locate 187 *place*; recognize, identify 490 *know*; unearth, uncover, bring to light 522 *manifest*; elicit, worm out, ferret o., nose o., sniff o., smell o. 459 *search*; get wind of 524 *be informed*.

detect, find a clue, be on the track, be getting warm, see daylight; put one's finger on the spot, hit the nail on the head; discern, perceive, notice, spot, catch sight of 438 *see*; sense, trace; smell a rat; nose, scent out; follow, tail, trail, trace, track down 619 *hunt*.

Int. eureka! got it!

485 Belief – N. *belief,* suspension of disbelief; credence, credit; assurance, conviction, persuasion; dependence on, trust, faith; religious belief 973 *religious faith*; implicit belief, firm b., unshakable b. 473 *certainty*; obsession, self-conviction; expectation 852 *hope*; folklore; popular belief, public opinion; one's word of honour 929 *probity*.

creed, credo, what one believes; dogma 976 *orthodoxy*; precepts, principles, tenets, articles; catechism, articles of faith; rubric, canon, rule 496 *maxim*; declaration of faith, confession of faith 526 *disclosure*; doctrine, system, school.

opinion, sentiment, mind, view; point of view, viewpoint, stand, position, attitude, angle 438 *view*; impression 818 *feeling*; conception, thought 451 *idea*; thinking, way of thinking, outlook on life 449 *philosophy*; assumption, presumption, principle 475 *premise*; theory, hypothesis 512 *supposition*; surmise, guess 512 *conjecture*; conclusion 480 *judgment*.

Adj. *credible,* plausible, believable, tenable, reasonable 469 *possible*; likely, to be expected 471 *probable*; reliable, trustworthy, trusty; persuasive, convincing 178 *influential*; trusted, believed; held, maintained; accepted, credited, accredited.

creedal, taught, doctrinal, dogmatic, confessional; canonical, orthodox, authoritative, accredited, ex cathedra; of faith, accepted on trust; sacrosanct, unquestioned, God-given; undeniable, absolute, unshakable 473 *undisputed*.

Vb. *believe,* be a believer; credit, put faith in; hold, hold to be true; maintain, declare 532 *affirm*; believe religiously, perceive as true, take for gospel; take on trust, take on credit; buy, swallow, swallow whole 487 *be credulous*; have no doubt, know for certain, be convinced, be sold on; rest assured, be easy in one's mind about, be secure in the belief, believe implicitly; have confidence in, trust, rely on, depend on, take one at his *or* her word; give one credit for, pin one's faith on, pin one's hopes on; have faith in, believe in, swear by, reckon on, count on, bank on; come to believe, be converted; realize 484 *discover*; take as proven.

be of the opinion that, opine, think, conceive, fancy; have a hunch, surmise, guess 512 *suppose*; suspect, be under the impression, have the i. 818 *feel*; deem, assume, presume, take it, hold; get hold of an idea, get it into one's head; have views, have a point of view, view as, take as, regard as, consider as, look upon as, set down as; cherish an opinion; express an opinion; hazard an o. 532 *affirm*; change one's mind 603 *recant*.

convince, make believe, assure, persuade, satisfy; bring home to 478 *demonstrate*; make confident, restore one's faith; convert, win over, bring o., bring round, wean from; evangelize, spread the gospel; propagandize, indoctrinate, din into 534 *teach*; cram down one's throat; sell an idea to, put over, put across; gain one's confidence, sway one's

belief 178 *influence*, mesmerize, hypnotize.

be believed, be widely b., be received, gain wide acceptance; go down well, be swallowed; find willing ears; carry conviction; find credence, pass for truth.

486 Unbelief. Doubt – N. *unbelief,* disbelief, incredulity, discredit; disagreement 489 *dissent*; agnosticism; denial 533 *negation*; want of faith; misbelief 977 *heresy*; atheism 974 *irreligion*; derision, scorn, mockery 851 *ridicule*; loss of faith, lapse of f., crisis of conscience, retraction 603 *recantation*; incredibility 472 *improbability*.

doubt 474 *dubiety*; hesitation, wavering, vacillation, shilly-shallying, uncertainty; misgiving, distrust, mistrust; suspiciousness, scepticism, agnosticism; reserve, reservation, second thoughts 468 *qualification*; demur, objection 704 *opposition*; scruple, qualm, suspicion 854 *nervousness*.

unbeliever, disbeliever; heathen, infidel 977 *heretic*; atheist; sceptic, agnostic; doubter, doubting Thomas; dissenter 489 *dissentient*; retractor, recanter 603 *tergiversator*; denier 533 *negation*; cynic, pessimist; scoffer, mocker, scorner 926 *detractor*.

Vb. *disbelieve,* be incredulous, find hard to believe, explain away, discredit; greet with scepticism, withhold assent, disagree 489 *dissent*; not fall for, not buy; mock, scoff at 851 *ridicule*; deny, deny outright 533 *negate*; refuse to admit, ignore; retract, lapse 603 *recant*.

doubt, half-believe 474 *be uncertain*; demur, object, cavil, question, scruple, boggle, have reservations 468 *qualify*; pause; hesitate, waver 601 *be irresolute*; distrust, mistrust, suspect, have fears 854 *be nervous*; shy at; be sceptical, doubt the truth of, take leave to doubt; not trust, set no store by; have one's doubts, take with a pinch of salt, harbour doubts, cherish scruples; entertain suspicions, smell a rat; hold back, not go all the way with one 598 *be unwilling*.

cause doubt, cast d., raise questions; cast a shadow over, render suspect; call in question, discredit 926 *defame*; shake, shake one's faith, undermine one's belief; pass belief 472 *be unlikely*; keep one guessing 517 *be unintelligible*.

487 Credulity – N. *credulity,* credulousness; simplicity, gullibility, naiveté; blind faith 612 *persuadability*; self-delusion, self-deception, wishful thinking 481 *misjudgment*; superstition, superstitiousness; sucker, mug 544 *dupe*.

Adj. *credulous,* believing, persuadable, amenable; easily taken in, easily deceived, easily duped; unworldly; naive, simple, unsophisticated, green; overcredulous; infatuated; confiding, trustful, unsuspecting.

Vb. *be credulous,* be easily persuaded; kid oneself, fool o.; suspend one's judgment 477 *reason badly*; follow implicitly, believe every word, fall for, buy it, take on trust, take for granted, take for gospel 485 *believe*; accept 299 *absorb*; rise to the bait, swallow, swallow hook, line and sinker 544 *be duped*; run away with an idea *or* a notion, rush *or* jump to a conclusion; be superstitious, touch wood, keep one's fingers crossed; think the moon is made of green cheese, not hear a word against.

488 Assent – N. *assent,* yes, aye, uh-huh, yea, amen; hearty assent; welcome; agreement, concurrence 758 *consent*; acceptance, agreement in principle 597 *willingness*; acquiescence 721 *submission*; acknowledgment, admission, clean breast, plea of guilty 939 *penitence*; confession; declaration of faith, profession 532 *affirmation*; sanction, nod, OK, imprimatur, thumbs up, go-ahead, green light 756 *permission*; approval 923 *approbation*; corroboration 466 *evidence*; confirmation, verification 478 *demonstration*; ratification; authentication, certification, endorsement, seal, signature, mark, cross; visa, passport, pass 756 *permit*; stamp, rubber s. 547 *label*; support 703 *aid*.

consensus, same mind 24 *agreement*; concordance, harmony, unison 710 *concord*; unanimity, common consent; universal agreement; popular belief, public opinion; single voice; likemindedness, same wavelength, two minds with but a single thought 18 *similarity*; mutual understanding, bargain 765 *compact*.

assenter, follower 83 *conformist*; fellow traveller, ally 707 *collaborator*; yesman 925 *flatterer*; the ayes; upholder, supporter, active s., abettor 703 *aider*; seconder 707 *patron*; subscriber, endorser 765 *signatory*; consenting party, covenanter.

Adj. *assenting,* concurring, party to 24 *agreeing*; aiding and abetting, supporting, collaborating 706 *cooperative*; likeminded, sympathetic, on the same wavelength, welcoming 880 *friendly*; unanimous, with one voice, in chorus; acquiescent 597 *willing*; granting 756 *permitting*; sanctioning, ratificatory; not opposed, conceding.

Vb. *assent,* concur, agree with 24 *accord*; welcome, acclaim 923 *applaud*; have no reservations 473 *be certain*; accept, agree in principle, like the idea, buy it; not deny, concede, own, acknowledge, grant, allow 475 *be reasonable*; plead guilty, avow 526 *confess*; signify assent, nod, say aye, say yes, raise one's hand in assent, agree to, give one's assent, go along with 758 *consent*; sanction 756 *permit*; ratify (**see** *endorse*); agree with, see eye to eye, be on the same wavelength; echo, say amen, say hear hear; back up; be a yes-man, rubber-stamp 925 *flatter*; side with 708 *join a party*; collaborate 706 *cooperate*; tolerate (**see** *acquiesce*); agree upon, come to an understanding, have a mutual agreement 765 *contract*.

acquiesce, accept, abide by 739 *obey*; tolerate, put up with, suffer, bear, endure, wear it; sign on the dotted line, toe the l. 721 *submit*; yield, defer to, withdraw one's objections; let the ayes have it, allow 756 *permit*; let it happen, look on 441 *watch*; go with the stream *or*

crowd, float with the current, join in the chorus, follow the fashion *or* trend, run with the pack, jump on the bandwagon 83 *conform*.

endorse, second, support, back up, vote for, give one's vote to 703 *patronize*; subscribe to, attest 547 *sign*; rubber-stamp, ratify, sanction, authorize 758 *consent*; authenticate 473 *make certain*; countersign.

Int. amen! hear, hear! aye, aye! well said! you can say that again! how right you are! I couldn't agree more! yes indeed! yes! absolutely!

489 Dissent – N. *dissent,* agreement to disagree *or* differ; dissidence, difference 704 *opposition*; difference of opinion, a vote against, disagreement, controversy 709 *dissension*; faction 708 *party*; disaffection 829 *discontent*; dissatisfaction, disapproval 924 *disapprobation*; repudiation 607 *rejection*; protestantism, nonconformism, schism 978 *sectarianism*; alternative life style, alternative medicine 84 *nonconformity*; withdrawal, secession 621 *relinquishment*; walkout 145 *strike*; reluctance 598 *unwillingness*; recusancy 738 *disobedience*; noncompliance 769 *nonobservance*; denial 760 *refusal*; contradiction 533 *negation*; recantation, retraction 603 *change of mind*; doubtfulness 486 *doubt*; demur, objection, reservation 468 *qualification*; protest; challenge 711 *defiance*; passive resistance 738 *sedition*.

dissentient, objector, critic 926 *detractor*; interrupter, heckler, obstructor; dissident, dissenter, protester; sectary 978 *sectarian*; separatist, seceder 978 *schismatic*; rebel 738 *revolter*; dropout 84 *nonconformist*; grouser 829 *malcontent*; odd man out, minority; splinter group, breakaway party, cave, faction 708 *party*; the noes, the opposition 704 *opposition*; conscientious objector, peace women, CND, green party 705 *opponent*; agitator, revolutionary, contra 149 *revolutionist*.

Adj. *dissenting,* differing, dissident 709 *quarrelling*; agnostic, sceptical; separatist, schismatic 978 *sectarian*; nonconformist 84 *unconformable*; malcontent, dissatisfied 829 *discontented*; recanting; not consenting; noncompliant 769 *nonobservant*; loath, reluctant 598 *unwilling*; obstructive; challenging 711 *defiant*; resistant 704 *opposing*.

Vb. *dissent,* differ, agree to d. 25 *disagree*; beg to differ, pick a bone with, take one up on 479 *confute*; demur, object, raise objections, have reservations, cavil, boggle; protest, raise one's voice against, demonstrate a. 762 *deprecate*; resist 704 *oppose*; challenge 711 *defy*; show reluctance 598 *be unwilling*; withhold assent, say no, shake one's head, not wear it 760 *refuse*; shrug one's shoulders, wash one's hands of it 860 *be indifferent*; disallow 757 *prohibit*; negative, contradict 533 *negate*; repudiate, hold no brief for; look askance at, not hold with 924 *disapprove*; secede, form a breakaway party, form a splinter group, withdraw 621 *relinquish*; recant, retract 603 *apostatize*; argue, wrangle, bicker 709 *quarrel*.

Adv. *no,* on the contrary, no way; in the negative.

Int. God forbid! not on your life! not on your nelly! over my dead body! tell that to the marines! not likely!

490 Knowledge – **N.** *knowledge,* ken; knowing, cognition, cognizance, recognition, realization, apprehension, comprehension, perception, understanding, grasp, mastery 447 *intellect*; conscience, consciousness, awareness; insight 476 *intuition*; precognition 510 *foresight*; illumination 975 *revelation*; enlightenment 498 *wisdom*; learning, lore (see *erudition*); folklore; occult lore 983 *sorcery*; education, background; experience, practical e., hands-on e., acquaintance, nodding a., acquaintanceship, familiarity, intimacy; private knowledge, being in the know, sharing the secret 524

information; public knowledge, common knowledge, open secret 528 *publicity*; omniscience; intimation, glimpse, glimmering, inkling, suggestion 524 *hint*; suspicion, scent; self-knowledge, introspection; detection, clue 484 *discovery*; expert knowledge, specialization savoir faire, savvy, know-how, expertise 694 *skill*; smattering 491 *sciolism*; epistemology.

erudition, lore, wisdom, scholarship, letters, literature 536 *learning*; acquired knowledge, general k., practical k.; professional k., encylopaedic k., universal k.; profound learning; smattering, dilettantism 491 *sciolism*; reading, wide r.; learning by rote, book-learning, bookishness, bibliomania; pedantry, donnishness; information; mine of information, store of knowledge, encyclopaedia 589 *library*.

culture, letters 557 *literature*; the humanities, the arts, the visual a.; education, instruction 534 *teaching*; literacy, numeracy; liberal education, scientific e.; self-education, self-instruction; civilization; attainments, accomplishments, proficiency, mastery.

science, natural s., the life sciences; natural philosophy; scientific knowledge; applied science, technology, computer science; ologies and isms.

Adj. *knowing,* all-k., encyclopaedic, comprehensive, omniscient 498 *wise*; cognizant, cognitive 447 *mental*; conscious, aware, mindful of 455 *attentive*; alive to, sensible of 819 *impressible*; experienced, competent, no stranger to, at home with, acquainted, familiar with, au fait with 610 *habituated*; intimate, privy to, wise to, on to, in the know, in on 524 *informed*; fly, canny, shrewd 498 *intelligent*; conversant, practised, versed in, proficient 694 *expert*; having hands-on experience.

known, perceived, seen, heard; ascertained, verified 473 *certain*; discovered, explored; noted, celebrated, famous 866 *renowned*; no secret, open s., public; familiar, intimate, dear; hackneyed, stale,

trite; proverbial, household, common-place 610 *usual*; prevalent 79 *general*; memorized, learnt off 505 *remembered*.

Vb. *know,* savvy; ken; have a nodding acquaintance with, be acquainted; apprehend, conceive, catch, grasp, twig, click, have, take in, get 516 *understand*; comprehend, master; come to know, latch on, get the hang of, get into one's head, realize; get to know, acquaint oneself, familiarize o., become au fait with; know again, recognize; be conscious of, be aware, be cognizant 447 *perceive*; discern 463 *discriminate*; perceive 438 *see*; know well, know full w., be thoroughly acquainted with, see through, read one like a book, have one's measure, have one taped, have one sized up, know inside out; know down to the ground, know from A to Z, know like the back of one's hand; know for a fact 473 *be certain*; know of, have knowledge of, know something; be in the know, be in the secret, have the lowdown 524 *be informed*; know by heart, know by rote 505 *memorize*; know backwards, have it pat, have at one's finger tips, be master of, know one's stuff 694 *be expert*; have a little knowledge of 491 *not know*; know by experience; get the picture, see the light; know all the answers, be omniscient; know what's what, see one's way, know one's way about 498 *be wise*.

be known, become k., come to one's knowledge, be brought to one's notice, come to one's ears; be a well-known fact, be public knowledge, be an open secret, be no secret 528 *be published*.

491 Ignorance – **N.** *ignorance,* no news, no word of; unawareness, unconsciousness 375 *insensibility*; incognizance, nonrecognition, nonrealization; incomprehension, incapacity, backwardness 499 *unintelligence*; inappreciation, Philistinism 439 *blindness*; obstacle to knowledge, superstition 495 *error*; crass ignorance; lack of knowledge; lack of education, no schooling; blank mind, tabula rasa; unfamiliarity, inexperience,

greenness, rawness; gaucherie, awkwardness; inexpertness, amateurishness 695 *unskilfulness*; innocence, simplicity, naivety 699 *artlessness*; nothing to go on, no lead, lack of information, general ignorance, anybody's guess, bewilderment 474 *uncertainty*; moral ignorance, unwisdom 499 *folly*; darkness, benightedness, unenlightenment; savagery, heathenism, paganism 982 *idolatry*; Age of Ignorance, Dark Ages; imperfect knowledge, semi-ignorance (see *sciolism*); ignorant person, illiterate 493 *ignoramus*; layman, autodidact, amateur, no expert 697 *bungler*; obscurantist; Philistine.

unknown thing, obstacle to knowledge; unknown quantity, matter of ignorance; prehistory 125 *antiquity*; sealed book, closed b., Greek; Dark Continent, terra incognita, unknown country, unexplored ground, virgin soil, lion country; frontiers of knowledge; dark horse, wild card, enigma, mystery 530 *secret*; unidentified flying object, UFO; unidentified body; unknown person, mystery p., Mr *or* Miss X., anonymity 562 *no name*.

sciolism, smattering, smatter, a little learning; glimmering, glimpse, half-glimpse 524 *hint*; vagueness, half-knowledge 495 *inexactness*; unreal knowledge 495 *error*; superficiality 212 *shallowness*; dilettantism, dabbling; affectation of knowledge, pedantry, quackery, charlatanism, bluff 850 *affectation*, smatterer 493 *dabbler*.

Adj. *ignorant,* unknowing; uncomprehending; unwitting; unaware, unconscious, oblivious 375 *insensible*; unfamiliar with, not au fait with, unacquainted, a stranger to, not at home with; in the dark (see *uninstructed*); mystified 474 *uncertain*; clueless, with nothing to go on; blindfolded 439 *blind*; groping 461 experimental; amateurish, inexpert, ham 695 *unskilful*; unversed, inexperienced, uninitiated, green, raw, wet behind the ears; innocent of, guiltless 935 *innocent*; naive, simple, unworldly 699 *artless*; unenlightened, benighted; savage, uncivilized; pagan, heathenish;

backward, dull, dense, dumb 499 *unintelligent*; empty-headed, foolish 499 *unwise*; half-baked, out of touch, behind the times 125 *retrospective*; wilfully ignorant, indifferent 454 *incurious*.

uninstructed, uninformed, kept in the dark; ill-informed, vague about 474 *uncertain*; untaught, untutored, untrained; illiterate, innumerate, uneducated; uncultivated, uncultured, lowbrow; unscholarly, unread, Philistine; dense, dumb (see *ignorant*).

unknown, unbeknown, untold, unheard; unspoken, unsaid, unvoiced, unuttered; unseen 444 *invisible*; hidden, veiled 525 *concealed*; unrecognized 525 *disguised*; unperceived; unexplained 517 *unintelligible*; dark, enigmatic, mysterious 523 *occult*; strange, new, newfangled, unfamiliar, unprecedented; unnamed 562 *anonymous*; unidentified, unclassified, uninvestigated 458 *neglected*; undiscovered, unexplored, uncharted, untravelled, unplumbed, unfathomed; untried, untested; virgin, novel 126 *new*; unforeseeable, unpredictable 124 *future*; unheard of, obscure 639 *unimportant*.

dabbling, unqualified; shallow, superficial, dilettante.

Vb. *not know,* be ignorant, be in the dark, have nothing to go on, have no lead; be unacquainted, not know from Adam; be green, be wet behind the ears, know no better; cannot say; not know the half of, have no conception, have no notion, have no clue, have no idea, have not the remotest i., not have the foggiest, not have an inkling, be reduced to guessing 512 *suppose*; know nothing of, not hear 416 *be deaf*; not see, suffer from tunnel vision 439 *be blind*; be at a loss, be stumped, not know what to make of 474 *be uncertain*; not know the first thing about, have to start at the bottom 695 *be unskilful*; not know chalk from cheese; misunderstand 517 *not understand*; misconstrue 481 *misjudge*; half know, know a little, have a smattering, dabble in; suspect 486 *doubt*; ignore 458 *disregard*; profess ignorance, shrug one's shoulders,

not want to know 860 *be indifferent*; grope, fumble 461 *be tentative*.

492 Scholar – **N.** *scholar,* savant(e), learned person, erudite p., educated p., man *or* woman of learning, man *or* woman of letters, bookman, bookwoman, bibliophile; don, reader, professor, pedagogue 537 *teacher*; pedant, bookworm, bluestocking; encyclopaedist; mine of information, walking encyclopaedia; talking dictionary; student, serious student 538 *learner*; degree-holder, graduate, diploma-holder; academic circles, academia, groves of academe; professoriate.

intellectual, academic, scholastic; genius, gifted child, prodigy 500 *sage*; know-all, brainbox; highbrow, egghead, bluestocking, intelligentsia, literati, illuminati, intellectual snob; academician.

collector, connoisseur, dilettante 846 *people of taste*; bibliophile, book-collector; librarian, curator 749 *keeper*; antiquary 125 *antiquarian*; numismatist, phillumenist, philatelist, stamp-collector 504 *enthusiast*; lexicographer, philologist 557 *linguist*.

493 Ignoramus – **N.** *ignoramus,* illiterate, lowbrow; philistine; duffer, thickhead, numskull 501 *dunce*; bonehead, blockhead, goof, goose, bungler 501 *fool*; greenhorn, novice, raw recruit 538 *beginner*; simpleton 544 *dupe*.

dabbler, dilettante; quack, charlatan 545 *impostor*.

494 Truth – **N.** *truth,* verity, rightness; basic truth; truism, platitude 496 *axiom*; accordance with fact; truth of the matter, honest truth, plain t., simple t.; gospel, Holy Writ, Bible 975 *revelation*; facts, lowdown, the heart of the matter; actuality; factualness, fact, matter of f. 3 *substantiality*; home truth, candour, frankness 929 *probity*; naked truth, unvarnished t.; the t., the whole t. and nothing but the t.; truthfulness 540 *veracity*; appearance of truth, verisimilitude 471 *probability*.

authenticity, validity, realness, genuineness; the real McCoy, the real thing, the genuine article, it 13 *identity*; no illusion, not a fake 21 *no imitation.*

accuracy, attention to fact; verisimilitude, local colour, realism, 'warts and all'; fidelity, high f., exactitude, exactness, preciseness, precision, mathematical p., clockwork p.; micrometry 465 *measurement*; mot juste, hitting the nail on the head, aptness 24 *adaptation*; meticulousness, punctiliousness 455 *attention*; letter of the law, acting according to the book 735 *severity*; literalness 514 *meaning*; true report, the very words, a verbatim account 540 *veracity*; chapter and verse, facts, statistics 466 *evidence.*

Adj. *true,* correct, right, so; real, tangible 3 *substantial*; actual, factual, historical; well-grounded, well-founded, well-thought-out; well-argued, well-taken; literal, truthful 540 *veracious*; true to the facts, true to scale, true to the letter, according to the book (**see** *accurate*); unquestionable 473 *undisputed*; reasonable 475 *rational*; true to life, true to nature, faithful, verbatim; realistic; unromantic, down to earth; candid, honest, warts and all.

genuine, authentic, bona fide, valid, guaranteed, authenticated, official; sound, solid, reliable, honest 929 *trustworthy*; natural, pure, sterling, hallmarked; fair dinkum; true-born; rightful, legitimate; unadulterated, unvarnished, uncoloured, straight from the shoulder, undisguised, undistorted, unexaggerated.

accurate, exact, precise, definite, defined; well-adjusted, well-pitched, high-fidelity, dead-on 24 *adjusted*; well-aimed, direct, straight, dead-centre 281 *directed*; unerring, undeviating; constant, regular 16 *uniform*; punctual, right, correct, true, spot on, on the button, on the mark; infallible; close, faithful; fine, nice, delicate, sensitive; micrometric; mathematically exact, scientifically e.; scrupulous, punctilious, meticulous, strict, severe 455 *attentive*; word

for word, verbatim, literal; literal-minded, just so 862 *fastidious.*

Vb. *be true,* be so, be just so, be the case, happen, exist 1 *be*; hold, hold true, hold good, hold water, wash, stand the test, ring true; conform to fact, prove true, hold together; speak the truth, omit nothing 540 *be truthful*; seem real, copy nature 551 *represent*; square, set, trim 24 *adjust*; substantiate 466 *corroborate*; prove 478 *demonstrate*; be right, be correct, have the right answer; get at the truth, hit the nail on the head, hit the mark, be spot on 484 *detect.*

Adv. *truly,* undeniably, indubitably, certainly, undoubtedly, really, genuinely, indeed; as a matter of fact 1 *actually*; to tell the truth 540 *truthfully*; strictly speaking; sic, literally, to the letter, word for word, verbatim; exactly, accurately, precisely, right, to an inch, to a nicety, to a turn, to a T, just right, spot on; in every detail, in all respects, tout à fait.

495 Error – N. *error,* erroneousness, wrongness, unsoundness; silliness 497 *absurdity*; untruth, falsity; straying from the truth, inexactitude 282 *deviation*; inaccuracy, fallacy, self-contradiction 477 *sophism*; unorthodoxy 977 *heterodoxy*; old wives' tales, superstition, popular misconception 491 *ignorance*; fallibility 481 *misjudgment*; mistaken belief, wishful thinking, doublethink, self-deception; misunderstanding, misconception, misconstruction, cross-purposes 521 *misinterpretation*; falseness, untruthfulness 541 *falsehood*; illusion, hallucination, mirage 440 *visual fallacy*; false pregnancy, pseudocyesis; false light, false dawn 509 *disappointment*; delusion 503 *mental disorder*; dream 513 *fantasy*; false impression; prejudice 481 *bias.*

inexactness, inexactitude, inaccuracy, imprecision, nonadjustment; faultiness; looseness, laxity, generalization 79 *generality*; loose thinking, sloppy t. 477 *sophistry*; carelessness 458 *negligence*;

mistiming 118 *anachronism*; misinformation 552 *misrepresentation*; misquotation (see *mistake*); malapropism 565 *solecism*.

mistake, miscalculation 481 *misjudgment*; blunder, botch-up 695 *bungling*; mistaken identity, wrong address; glaring error, bloomer, clanger, howler, gaffe, bull, Irish b. 497 *absurdity*; oversight 456 *inattention*; bungle, foul-up, louse-up, screw-up, balls-up, cock-up, boo-boo, slip-up, boob, goof, blooper; fluff, muff; leak, slip, slip of the pen, slip of the tongue, spoonerism 565 *solecism*; typist's error; typographical error, printer's e., misprint, typo, literal, erratum, corrigendum; human error, computer e.; inadvertency; bad tactics, faux pas; solecism 847 *bad taste*; blot, flaw 845 *blemish*.

Adj. *erroneous,* erring, wrong; in error (see *mistaken*); unfactual, unhistorical, mythical 2 *unreal*; aberrant; wide of the mark, wide of the truth, devoid of t. 543 *untrue*; unsound, unscientific, unreasoned, cock-eyed, ill-reasoned, self-contradictory 477 *illogical*; implausible 472 *improbable*; unsubstantiated, uncorroborated, unfounded, ungrounded, groundless, disproved; exploded, discredited 924 *disapproved*; fallacious, misleading; unauthentic, apocryphal; perverted, unorthodox, heretical; untruthful, lying 541 *false*; flawed, fake, simulated, bogus 542 *spurious*; hallucinatory, illusive, illusory, delusive, deceptive; unrealistic, fantastical 513 *imaginary*; wild, crackpot 497 *absurd*; fallible, perverse, prejudiced 481 *biased*; superstitious 491 *ignorant*.

mistaken, misunderstood, misconceived; misrepresented, perverted; misinterpreted, misconstrued, misread, misprinted; miscalculated, misjudged; in error, misled, misguided; misinformed, ill-informed, deluded 491 *uninstructed*; slipping, blundering 695 *clumsy*; straying, wandering; wide, misdirected, off-target, off-beam, out to lunch 25 *unapt*; at fault, cold, off the scent, off the track, off the beam, wide of

the mark, on the wrong tack, on the wrong scent, off the rails, at sea 474 *uncertain.*

inexact, inaccurate; loose; broad, generalized 79 *general*; incorrect, misreported, garbled; imprecise, erratic, wild, hit-or-miss; wildly out, maladjusted; untuned, out of tune, out of gear; out of synch, unsynchronized, slow, losing, fast, gaining; uncorrected, unrevised; faulty, full of holes, flawed, botched, mangled 695 *bungled*; misprinted, misread, mistranslated.

Vb. *err,* commit an error, go wrong, stray from the straight and narrow, mistake, make a m.; labour under a misapprehension, bark up the wrong tree, be on the wrong scent; be in the wrong, be mistaken; delude oneself, suffer hallucinations 481 *misjudge*; be misled, be misguided; receive a wrong impression, get hold of the wrong end of the stick, be at cross-purposes, misunderstand, misconceive, misapprehend, get it wrong 517 *not understand*; miscount, misreckon 482 *overrate*, 483 *underestimate*; go astray 282 *stray*; gain, be fast 135 *be early*; lose, be slow, stop 136 *be late*.

blunder, trip, stumble, miss, fault 695 *be clumsy*; slip, slip up, drop a brick, drop a clanger, boob, goof, foul up, screw up, mess up, make a hash of; commit a faux pas, put one's foot in it; betray oneself, give oneself away 526 *disclose*; blot one's copybook, blot, flaw; fluff, muff, botch, bungle; blow it 728 *fail*; play into one's hands 695 *act foolishly*; miscount, miscalculate 481 *misjudge*; misread, misquote, misprint, misapprehend, mistranslate 521 *misinterpret.*

mislead, misdirect 282 *deflect*; misinform, lead astray, pervert; beguile, lead one a dance, lead one up the garden path 542 *deceive*; give a false impression, create a false i., falsify, garble 541 *dissemble*; gloss over, whitewash, cover up 525 *conceal.*

496 Maxim – **N.** *maxim,* adage, saw, proverb, byword, aphorism; dictum, tag,

saying, stock s., common s., truth; epigram, mot 839 *witticism*; wise maxim; truism, cliché, commonplace, platitude, banality, hackneyed saying, trite remark, statement of the obvious, bromide; motto, watchword, slogan, catchword; formula, mantra; text, canon, sutra, rule, golden r. 693 *precept*; gloss, comment, note, remark, observation 520 *commentary*; moral, edifying story, fable, cautionary tale 590 *narrative*.

axiom, self-evident truth, truism; principle, postulate, theorem, formula; Sod's Law, Murphy's Law.

Adj. *aphoristic*, proverbial, moralizing, holier than thou 498 *wise*; epigrammatic, pithy 839 *witty*; snappy 569 *concise*; enigmatic 517 *puzzling*; common, banal, trite, corny, hackneyed, platitudinous, clichéd, commonplace, stock 610 *usual*; axiomatic.

Adv. *proverbially*, as the saying goes, as they say, as the old adage has it, to coin a phrase; in a nutshell; epigrammatically, by way of moral.

497 Absurdity – N. *absurdity*, height of a., height of nonsense, absurdness 849 *ridiculousness*; inconsequence 10 *irrelevance*; false logic 477 *sophistry*; foolishness, silliness, silly season 499 *folly*; senselessness, futility, fatuity 641 *lost labour*; nonsense verse, doggerel; talking through one's hat; rot, rubbish, nonsense, stuff and nonsense, gibberish, jargon, twaddle 515 *silly talk*; Irish bull, malapropism, howler 495 *mistake*; limerick 839 *witticism*; pun, play upon words 518 *equivocalness*; riddle, riddle-me-ree 530 *enigma*; anticlimax, bathos, descent from the sublime to the ridiculous.

foolery, antics, capers, fooling about, horsing around, silliness, tomfoolery, shenanigans, high jinks, skylarking 837 *revel*; vagary, whimsy, whimsicality 604 *whim*; extravagance, extravaganza; escapade, scrape 700 *predicament*; practical joke, monkey trick, piece of nonsense;

drollery 849 *ridiculousness; clowning, buffoonery, burlesque, parody, caricature 851 ridicule*; farce, mummery, pretence 850 *affectation*; showing off 875 *ostentation*.

Adj. *absurd,* ludicrous, laughable, risible, farcical, comical, grotesque 849 *ridiculous*; rash, silly, asinine, idiotic, cock-eyed, moronic, tomfool 499 *foolish*; nonsensical, senseless 515 *meaningless*; preposterous, without rhyme or reason 477 *illogical*; wild; pretentious 850 *affected*; frantic 503 *frenzied*; mad, crazy, crackpot, harebrained 495 *erroneous*; fanciful, fantastic 513 *imaginative*; futile, fatuous 641 *useless*; punning 518 *equivocal*.

Vb. *be absurd,* play the fool, play the clown, act like a fool, behave like an idiot 499 *be foolish*; fool, fool about, lark about, muck a., horse a., monkey around, play practical jokes 837 *amuse oneself*; be a laughingstock 849 *be ridiculous*; clown, clown about, parody, caricature, mimic, guy, make a fool of 851 *ridicule*; talk rot, talk nonsense, talk through one's hat, talk gibberish 515 *mean nothing*; rave 503 *be insane*.

498 Intelligence. Wisdom – N. *intelligence*, powers of thought, intellectualism 447 *intellect*; brains, brain, grey matter, head, loaf, upper storey, upstairs, noddle; nous, wit, commonsense; understanding, sense, good s., horse s., savvy, gumption, knowhow; wits, sharp w., ready w., quick thinking; ability, capacity, mental c., mental grasp; calibre, mental c., intelligence quotient, IQ; high IQ, Mensa, forwardness, brightness; braininess, cleverness 694 *aptitude*; mental gifts, giftedness, brilliance, talent, genius; ideas, inspiration, sheer i. 476 *intuition*; brainwave, bright idea 451 *idea*.

sagacity, judgment, sound j., discretion, discernment 463 *discrimination*; perception, perspicacity, clear thinking, clear-headedness; acumen, sharpness,

acuteness, acuity, penetration; shrewdness; level-headedness, balance 502 *sanity*; prudence, forethought, farsightedness 510 *foresight*; craftiness 698 *cunning*; worldly wisdom; vigilance, alertness, awareness 457 *carefulness*; tact, statesmanship, strategy 688 *tactics*.

wisdom, sapience; profundity of thought 449 *thought*; breadth of mind; experience, lifelong e.; soundness; mental balance, enlightenment.

Adj. *intelligent,* brainy, clever, forward, bright, bright as a button; brilliant, scintillating, talented 694 *gifted*; capable, able 694 *skilful*; apt, ready, quick, quick on the uptake, receptive; acute, sharp, sharp as a needle, sharp-witted, quick-w., nimble-w.; aware, on one's toes, streetwise, with it 455 *attentive*; astute, shrewd, fly, smart, canny, not born yesterday, all there, on the ball; knowing, sophisticated, worldly-wise; too smart for one's own good, too clever by half; sagacious, prudent, watchful 457 *careful*; farseeing, farsighted 510 *foreseeing*; discerning 463 *discriminating*; penetrating, perspicacious, clear-headed; politic, statesmanlike.

wise, sage, sagacious, sapient; thinking, reflecting 449 *thoughtful*; reasoning 475 *rational*; knowledgeable; highbrow, intellectual, profound, deep; sound, sensible, reasonable 502 *sane*; not born yesterday, experienced; level-headed, judicious 913 *just*; enlightened, prudent, tactful, politic 698 *cunning*; wise as a serpent, wise as an owl, wise as Solomon, like a Daniel come to judgment; well-advised, well-considered, well-judged.

Vb. *be wise,* - intelligent etc. adj.; use one's head, use one's loaf *or* noddle, use one's intelligence; have a fund of wisdom 490 *know*; have brains, have plenty of grey matter, have a head on one's shoulders, have one's wits about one, know how many beans make five, see with half an eye, see at a glance; have one's head screwed on the right way, know a thing or two, know what's what, know the score; be up on, be in the know,

be au courant; show foresight 510 *foresee*; know which side one's bread is buttered on, be prudent, take care 858 *be cautious*; have sense, listen to reason 475 *be reasonable*; be politic 623 *plan*; have tact 698 *be cunning*; learn from one's mistakes, come to one's senses.

499 Unintelligence. Folly - N. *unintelligence,* lack of intelligence, want of intellect 448 *absence of intellect*; feeblemindedness, low IQ, low mental age, brain damage, dementia, mental deficiency; mental handicap, arrested development, retardation, backwardness; imbecility, idiocy; stupidity, slowness, dullness, obtuseness, thickheadedness, denseness; oafishness; no head for; incapacity, incompetence 695 *unskilfulness*; gullibility 481 *misjudgment*; inanity, vacuity, vacuousness, superficiality 212 *shallowness.*

folly, foolishness, eccentricity 849 *ridiculousness*; tomfool idea, tomfoolery, act of folly 497 *foolery*; giddiness 456 *inattention*; irrationality, illogic 477 *sophistry*; indiscretion, tactlessness; fatuity, fatuousness, pointlessness; wildgoose chase 641 *lost labour*; silliness; idiocy, lunacy, utter folly; recklessness, wildness 857 *rashness*; infatuation 481 *misjudgment*; puerility, childishness 130 *nonage*; second childhood, senility, dotage, senile dementia 131 *old age*; drivelling, babbling, maundering, wandering.

Adj. *unintelligent,* unintellectual, lowbrow; talentless, no genius; incompetent 695 *clumsy*; dull; subnormal, ESN, mentally handicapped, mentally disadvantaged, mentally deficient; backward, retarded, feeble-minded, moronic, cretinous, imbecile 503 *mentally disordered*; deficient, wanting, not all there, vacant, not quite the full pound note, not right in the head; limited, weak, weak in the upper storey; slow, slow on the uptake, slow to learn; stupid, obtuse, dense, thick, gormless, bovine, blockish, oafish, doltish; dumb, dopey, dim, dim-witted, dull-w., slow-w., half-w.; pig thick *or* ignorant, dead from the neck up, thick as

two short planks; thick-skulled, bone-headed, muddle-h.; cracked, barmy 503 *crazy*; unteachable; muddled, addled.

foolish, silly, idiotic, imbecile, asinine; nonsensical, senseless, fatuous, futile, inane 497 *absurd*; ludicrous, laughable, risible 849 *ridiculous*; like a fool, like an idiot 544 *gullible*; inexperienced 491 *ignorant*; tactless, impolitic; soft, wet, soppy, sappy, gormless; goofy, dopey; puerile, infantile; gaga, senile, away with the fairies; besotted, doting; spoony 887 *enamoured*; dazed, fuddled, maudlin 949 *drunk*; babbling, burbling, drivelling, maundering, wandering; mindless (see *unintelligent*); bird-witted, feather-brained, crack-b., scatter-b., hare-b. 456 *light-minded*; eccentric, unstable, wild, madcap, scatty, nutty, dotty, daft 503 *crazy.*

unwise, unenlightened; unintellectual; irrational 477 *illogical*; indiscreet 464 *indiscriminating*; injudicious; short-sighted 439 *blind*; unteachable; thoughtless; impatient 680 *hasty*; foolhardy, reckless 857 *rash*; unbalanced; unreasonable; unseemly, improper 643 *inexpedient*; ill-considered, ill-advised, ill-judged 495 *mistaken.*

Vb. *be foolish,* maunder, dote, drivel, babble, burble, wander, talk through one's hat 515 *mean nothing*; go haywire, lose one's wits, take leave of one's senses, go off one's head, go off one's rocker 503 *be insane*; have no sense, not have the sense one was born with; not see farther than one's nose, not see the wood for the trees; never learn; invite ridicule, look like a fool, look foolish 849 *be ridiculous*; make a fool of oneself, play the fool, act the f., act the giddy goat 497 *be absurd*; burn one's fingers 695 *act foolishly*; go on a fool's errand 641 *waste effort*; miscalculate 481 *misjudge.*

500 Sage – N. *sage,* nobody's fool; learned person 492 *scholar*; wise man, wise woman, statesman *or* - woman; elder statesman *or* -woman, consultant, authority 691 *adviser*; expert 696 *proficient person*; genius, master mind;

master, mentor, guide, guru, pundit 537 *teacher*; Buddha 973 *religious teacher*; seer, prophet 511 *oracle*; yogi 945 *ascetic*; leading light, shining l., luminary; mahatma; doctor, thinker; egghead, boffin, highbrow, blue stocking 492 *intellectual*; wizard, witch doctor 983 *sorcerer*; magus, Magi, wise men from the East; Solomon, Daniel, Daniel come to judgment, learned judge; Grand Old Man.

wiseacre, wise guy, know-all, smarty-pants, smart ass 873 *vain person*; smart alec, clever dick.

501 Fool – N. *fool,* silly f., tomfool 504 *madman*; buffoon, clown, comic, jester, zany 594 *entertainer*; perfect fool, complete idiot, ninny, nincompoop, ass, jackass, donkey, goose, cuckoo; zombie, idiot, born fool; cretin, moron, imbecile; half-wit, dimwit, silly, silly-billy, twerp; stooge, butt 851 *laughingstock*; fathead, pinhead, muddle-head, incompetent, twit, clot, wally 697 *bungler*; birdbrain, featherbrain, dingbat; flibbertigibbet; crackpot, eccentric 504 *crank*; babbler, burbler, driveller; dotard 133 *old man.*

ninny, simpleton, Simple Simon; charley; nincompoop, juggins, muggins, booby, sap, big stiff, dope, jerk, gowk, galoot, goof; greenhorn 538 *beginner*; wet, weed, drip, milksop, wimp 163 *weakling*; sucker, mug 544 *dupe.*

dunce, dullard; blockhead, wooden-head, numskull, duffer, dummkopf, dolt, dumb cluck 493 *ignoramus*; fathead, bonehead, pinhead, blockhead, dunderhead, nitwit, dimwit; chump, clot, clod.

502 Sanity – N. *sanity,* saneness, soundness of mind; rationality, reason; balance of the mind, mental equilibrium; common sense; coherence 516 *intelligibility*; lucidity, lucid moment; proper mind, right m., senses; sound mind.

Adj. *sane,* of sound mind, all there; compos mentis, in one's right mind, in possession of one's faculties, with all

one's wits about one; rational, reasonable 498 *intelligent*; coherent 516 *intelligible*; lucid, clear-headed.

503 Insanity – N. *mental disorder,* insanity, lunacy, madness, certifiability; mental illness; mental instability; mental derangement, unsound mind, delirium, brain damage; Alzheimer's disease, softening of the brain 131 *age*; dementia, senile d., psychiatry, clinical psychology 447 *psychology*; psychotherapy 658 *therapy*; psychoanalyst, analyst, psychiatrist, shrink 658 *doctor.*

psychosis, paranoia, delusions, hallucinations; catatonia, schizophrenia; confusion; melancholia 834 *melancholy*; clinical depression, manic d., mania, megalomania, mental deficiency, idiocy, imbecility, cretinism, mongolism, Down's syndrome, feeblemindedness; autism 84 *abnormality.*

personality disorder, psychopathology, psychopathy, maladjustment; split personality, dual p.; persecution mania; kleptomania; nymphomania, satyriasis; inferiority c.

neurosis, psychoneurosis, anxiety neurosis, nerves, nervous disorder; hysteria; nervous breakdown, brainstorm; shellshock, combat fatigue; obsession, compulsion, phobia, claustrophobia, agorophobia 854 *phobia*; hypochondria; depression, depressed state, blues.

frenzy, furore; ecstasy, raving, hysteria; distraction 456 *abstractedness*; incoherence 517 *unintelligibility*; delirium tremens, DT's; epilepsy, fit, epileptic f., epileptic frenzy, paroxysm 318 *spasm.*

eccentricity, craziness, crankiness; queerness, oddness, weirdness; oddity, twist, quirk, kink, craze, fad 84 *abnormality*; a screw loose, bats in the belfry; fixation, hang-up; obsession, infatuation, bee in one's bonnet 604 *whim.*

mental hospital, psychiatric h., psychiatric unit, mental institution; mental home, madhouse, lunatic asylum, Bedlam; loony-bin, nuthouse, bughouse, funny farm; locked ward, padded cell 658 *hospital.*

Adj. *mentally disordered,* insane, mad, lunatic, of unsound mind, not in one's right m., non compos mentis, out of one's mind, deranged, demented; certifiable, mental; psychologically abnormal, mentally disturbed, mentally ill, of diseased *or* disordered *or* distempered mind; unbalanced; brain-damaged; raving mad, stark staring mad, mad as a hatter, mad as a March hare, off one's rocker (see *frenzied*); gaga, loony, certified; locked up, put away.

mentally handicapped, imbecile, moronic, cretinous, mongoloid, defective, feebleminded, subnormal 499 *unintelligent*; autistic.

psychotic, paranoiac, paranoid, schizophrenic, schizoid; manic, maniacal; catatonic, depressive, clinically depressed 834 *melancholic*; hyperactive.

neurotic, hypochondriac; kleptomaniac; nymphomaniac, claustrophobic, agoraphobic.

maladjusted, psychopathic, psychopathological.

crazy, bewildered, wandering, bemused, pixilated, moidered 456 *abstracted*; not all there, not right in the head; off one's head *or* one's nut, off one's trolley, round the bend *or* the twist, up the pole; crazed, demented, driven mad, maddened (see *frenzied*); unhinged, unbalanced, off one's rocker; deluded; infatuated, possessed; besotted 887 *enamoured*; drivelling, gaga, in one's second childhood, away with the fairies; touched, wanting; idiotic, scatterbrained, crack-brained 499 *foolish*; crackers, cracked, scatty, screwy, nutty, nutty as a fruit cake, nuts, bananas, batty, bats, cuckoo, barmy, bonkers, meshuga; daft, dippy, loony, loopy, goofy, potty, dotty; cranky, wacky, flaky, eccentric, erratic, funny, queer, odd, peculiar 84 *abnormal*; crotchety, whimsical 604 *capricious*; dizzy, giddy 456 *light-minded.*

frenzied, rabid, maddened; furious, foaming at the mouth 891 *angry*; wild,

distraught 825 *suffering*; possessed; frantic, frenetic, demented, like one possessed, out of one's mind, beside oneself, uncontrollable; berserk, seeing red, running amok, running wild 176 *violent*; having fits; hysterical, delirious, hallucinating, raving, rambling, wandering, incoherent, fevered.

Vb. *be insane,* - mad, - crazy etc. adj.; have bats in the belfry, have a screw loose; drivel 499 *be foolish*; ramble, wander; babble, rave; foam at the mouth; be delirious, see things.

go mad, go off one's head, go off one's rocker *or* nut, go crackers, lose one's marbles, go out of one's mind, crack up; go berserk, run amok, see red, foam at the mouth, lose one's head 891 *get angry*.

make mad, drive m., drive insane, madden; derange; send one off his head *or* out of his mind; send round the bend *or* the twist, drive up the wall; turn one's brain; blow one's mind 821 *excite*; unhinge, unbalance, send off one's rocker; infuriate, make one see red 891 *enrage*; possess; go to one's head, turn one's h.

504 Madman – N. *madman,* madwoman, lunatic; raving lunatic, maniac; screwball, nut, nutcase, loon, loony, kook, meshuggenah.

psychotic, paranoiac, schizoid, schizophrenic, manic depressive; megalomaniac; catatonic.

neurotic, hysteric; neuropath; hypochondriac; obsessive; phobic, claustrophobic, agoraphobic; depressive, melancholic; kleptomaniac, pyromaniac.

the mentally handicapped, idiot, congenital i., natural, cretin, moron 501 *fool*.

the maladjusted, psychopath, psycho, psychopathic personality, sociopath, unstable personality, aggressive p., antisocial p.; dipsomaniac 949 *drunkard*; dope addict, dope fiend, junkie; drug addict 949 *drug-taking*. crank, crackpot, nut, nutter, crackbrain; eccentric, oddball 851 *laughingstock*; freak 84 *nonconformist*; fanatic, extremist, lunatic fringe.

enthusiast, zealot; devotee, aficionado, addict, freak, buff; fan, supporter 707 *patron*; connoisseur, fancier 846 *people of taste*; fitness freak, radio ham, balletomane, opera buff, film b.; bibliophile 492 *collector*.

Section six: Extension of thought

505 Memory – N. *memory,* good m., retentiveness; photographic m.; tribal m., atavism.

remembrance, recollection, recall, total r.; commemoration, evocation, mind's eye; recapitulation 106 *repetition*; memorization, remembering, learning by heart, committing to memory, learning by rote 536 *learning*; reminiscence, retrospection, review, retrospect, hindsight; flashback, recurrence, voice from the past; déjà vu 984 *psychics*; afterthought 67 *sequel*; nostalgia, regrets 830 *regret*; memorabilia, memoirs, reminiscences, recollections; place in history 866 *famousness*; memoranda.

reminder, memorial, testimonial, commemoration; souvenir, keepsake, relic, memento, autograph; trophy, bust, statue 548 *monument*; prompter; testifier 466 *witness*; memorandum, memo, chit, note, notebook, memo pad, aide-mémoire, diary, engagement d., telephone book; album, autograph a., photograph a., scrapbook, commonplacebook, promptbook; leading question, prompt, prompting, suggestion, cue 524 *hint*; mnemonic, aid to memory, knotted handkerchief.

Adj. *remembered,* recollected etc. vb.; retained, not forgotten, green, fresh, fresh in one's memory, of recent memory, as clear as if it were yesterday; uppermost in one's thoughts; of blessed memory, missed, regretted; memorable, unforgettable; haunting, persistent, undying; deep-rooted, indelible, inscribed

upon the mind, stamped on one's memory; got by heart, memorized 490 *known*.

remembering, mindful, keeping in mind; evocative, commemorative 876 *celebratory*; reminiscent, recollecting; living in the past, dwelling upon the past, nostalgic; haunted; recalling, reminding, mnemonic, prompting, suggesting.

Vb. *remember,* bring to m., call to m.; recognize, know again 490 *know*; recollect; not forget, bottle up 778 *retain*; hold in mind; enshrine in one's memory, store in one's mind, cherish the memory; never forget, be unable to f.; recall, call to mind, return to thoughts of, think of; reflect, review, think back, muse upon, keep in mind 455 *be mindful*; recapture, hark back, cast one's mind b.; conjure up, rake up the past, reminisce; live in the past; reopen old wounds, recapture old times; remind oneself, make a note of, tie a knot in one's handkerchief; rack one's brains, tax one's memory.

remind, jog one's memory, refresh one's m.; renew one's m.; put one in mind of, take one back; drop a hint, cue, prompt, suggest 524 *hint*; not allow one to forget, haunt; not let sleeping dogs lie, fan the embers, keep the wounds open 821 *excite*; turn another's mind back, make one think of, awake memories of; commemorate, keep the memory green, toast 876 *celebrate*; recount, recapitulate 106 *repeat*.

memorize, commit to memory; get by heart, learn by rote 536 *learn*; fix in one's memory, implant in one's m., impress on one's m., engrave on the m., hammer into one's head, din into one's h.; cram the mind with.

be remembered, linger in the memory, stick in the mind, make a lasting impression; recur 106 *reoccur*; flash across one's mind, ring a bell; run in one's mind, haunt one's t. or mind, be at the back of one's mind, lurk in one's mind, make history; live on 115 *be eternal*.

Adv. *in memory,* in memory of, to the memory of, as a memorial to, in memoriam, lest we forget; by heart, by rote, from memory.

506 Oblivion – N. *oblivion,* blankness, no recollection, no memory; obliviousness, forgetfulness, absent-mindedness 456 *abstractedness*; loss of memory, amnesia, blackout, total blank, mental block; insensibility of the past; dim memory, hazy recollection; short memory, poor m., defective m., failing m.; lapse of memory, memory like a sieve; effacement 550 *obliteration*; Lethe, waters of oblivion; good riddance.

amnesty, letting bygones be bygones, burial of grievances, burial of the hatchet, shaking of hands; pardon, free p., absolution 909 *forgiveness*.

Adj. *forgotten,* clean f., beyond recall; not missed; unremembered; in limbo 458 *neglected*; misremembered etc. vb.; on the tip of one's tongue; in the recesses of one's mind, gone out of one's head; buried, suppressed; out of mind, over and done with, dead and buried, sunk in oblivion, amnestied.

forgetful, forgetting, oblivious; sunk in oblivion; unconscious of the past; unable to remember, suffering from amnesia, amnesic; unmindful, heedless, mindless 458 *negligent*; absent-minded 456 abstracted; conveniently forgetting 918 *undutiful*.

Vb. *forget,* clean f., not remember, have no recollection of; not give another thought to, think no more of; suppress the memory, consign to oblivion, be oblivious; amnesty, let bygones be bygones, bury the hatchet 909 *forgive*; break with the past; suffer from amnesia, lose one's memory, remember nothing; misremember; be forgetful, have a poor memory, need reminding; lose sight of, leave behind, overlook; be absent-minded, fluff one's notes 456 *be inattentive*; forget one's lines, dry; have a memory like a sieve, go in one ear and out of the other, forget one's own name; have on the tip of one's tongue, not quite recall, draw a blank.

be forgotten, slip one's memory; sink into oblivion, be consigned to o.; become passé, be overlooked.

507 Expectation – N. *expectation,* state of e., expectancy 455 *attention;* contemplation 617 *intention;* confidence, trust 473 *certainty;* presumption 475 *premise;* foretaste 135 *anticipation;* eager expectation 859 *desire;* breathless expectation 852 *hope;* waiting, suspense 474 *uncertainty;* dread, feelings of doom, doom watching, apprehension, apprehensiveness 854 *fear;* anxiety 825 *worry;* expectance, one's expectations 471 *probability;* prospect, lookout, outlook, forecast 511 *prediction;* contingency 469 *possibility;* destiny 596 *fate;* unfulfilled expectation 509 *disappointment;* what is expected, the usual thing 610 *practice.*

Adj. *expectant,* expecting, in expectation, in hourly e.; in suspense, on the waiting list, on the short l., on the short leet; sure, confident 473 *certain;* anticipatory, anticipating, banking on, putting all one's money on; presuming, taking for granted; predicting 510 *foreseeing;* forewarned, forearmed, ready 669 *prepared;* waiting, waiting for, awaiting; on the lookout, keeping cave, on the watch for, standing by, on call 457 *vigilant;* keyed up 821 *excited;* on tenterhooks, on the rack, in agonies of expectation, agog; hopeful, sanguine 852 *hoping;* dreading, anxious 854 *nervous;* doom-watching 853 *hopeless;* expecting a baby, expecting a happy event, parturient 167 *fertilized.*

expected, long e.; up to expectation, as one expected; anticipated, presumed, predicted, on the cards, foreseen 471 *probable;* prospective, future, on the horizon 155 *impending;* promised, intended, in prospect; longed for 859 *desired;* dreaded, feared 854 *frightening.*

Vb. *expect,* look for, face the prospect; have in mind; calculate 480 *estimate;* forecast 510 *foresee;* see it coming 865 *not wonder;* think likely, presume 471 *assume;* bank on, count upon, put one's money on 473 *be certain;* count one's chickens before they are hatched 509 *be disappointed;* anticipate 669 *prepare oneself;* look out for, watch out f., be waiting f., be ready f. 457 *be careful;*

stand by, be on call; hang around (**see** *await*); dread, doomwatch 854 *fear;* look forward to, hope for 852 *hope,* 859 *desire.*

await, be on the waiting list; stand and wait, watch and pray 136 *wait;* queue up, line up, mark time, bide one's t.; stand by, hold oneself ready, be on call; keep one waiting; have in store for, be in store for.

Adv. *expectantly,* in suspense, with bated breath, on edge, on the edge of one's chair.

508 Lack of expectation – N. *lack of expectation,* false expectation 509 *disappointment;* resignation, no hope 853 *hopelessness;* apathy 454 *incuriosity;* unpreparedness 670 *nonpreparation;* unexpectedness, unforeseen contingency; miscalculation 495 *error;* surprise; the unexpected, the unforeseen, surprise packet; windfall, gift from the gods, something to one's advantage 615 *benefit;* shock, nasty s., jolt; blow, sudden b.; bolt from the blue, thunderbolt, thunderclap, bombshell; revelation, eyeopener; culture shock; reversal; amazement 864 *wonder.*

Adj. *unexpected,* unanticipated, unlooked for; unpredicted, unforeseen; unheralded, unannounced; without warning; astounding, mind-boggling, eyeopening, staggering, amazing 864 *wonderful;* shocking, startling 854 *frightening;* sudden 116 *instantaneous;* like a bombshell, like a thunderbolt, like a bolt from the blue, dropped from the clouds; unbargained for, uncatered for 670 *unprepared;* contrary to expectation; beyond one's wildest dreams, unprecedented 84 *unusual;* freakish 84 *abnormal;* unaccountable 517 *puzzling.*

unexpecting, unexpectant, unsuspecting, off guard 456 *inattentive;* uninformed 491 *ignorant;* not forewarned; surprised, disconcerted, taken by surprise, taken aback, caught napping, caught with one's pants *or* trousers down, caught on the hop, on the wrong foot 670 *unprepared;* astonished,

amazed, thunderstruck, dumbfounded, dazed, stunned 864 *wondering*; startled, jolted, shocked; without expectations.

Vb. *not expect,* not look for, think unlikely, not foresee 472 *be unlikely*; not hope for 853 *despair*; be caught out, fall into the trap; be taken aback, be taken by surprise, be caught with one's pants *or* trousers down, not bargain for 670 *be unprepared*; get a shock, start, jump out of one's skin; have one's eyes opened; look surprised, goggle, stare, gawp.

surprise, take by s., spring something on one, catch, trap, ambush 542 *ensnare*; catch unawares, catch napping, catch off one's guard, catch with one's pants *or* trousers down; startle, make one jump, give one a turn, make one jump out of one's skin; take aback, leave speechless, stagger, stun; take one's breath away, knock one down with a feather, bowl one over, strike one all of a heap; be one in the eye for 509 *disappoint*; give one a surprise, pull out of the hat; astonish, amaze, astound, dumbfound 864 *be wonderful*; shock, electrify 821 *impress*; flutter the dovecotes, set the cat among the pigeons, let all hell loose 63 *derange*; drop from the clouds, come out of the blue; fall upon, spring u., pounce on; steal upon, creep up on; come up from behind, appear from nowhere.

509 Disappointment – N. *disappointment,* sad d., bitter d., cruel d.; regrets 830 *regret*; frustration, bafflement; blighted hopes 853 *hopelessness*false expectation 482 *overestimation*; bad news 529 *news*; not what one expected, disenchantment, disillusionment 829 *discontent*; miscalculation 481 *misjudgment*; mirage, trick of the light, false dawn, fool's paradise; shock, blow, setback, balk 702 *hitch*; nonfulfilment 726 *noncompletion*; bad luck, slip 'twixt the cup and the lip 731 *misfortune*; one in the eye for, letdown 872 *humiliation*; damp squib 728 *failure*.

Adj. *disappointed,* expecting otherwise 508 *inexpectant*; frustrated, thwarted, balked 702 *hindered*; baffled, foiled 728

defeated; crestfallen, chagrined, humiliated; disgruntled, dischuffed, soured 829 *discontented*; sick with disappointment 853 *hopeless*; let down; refused, turned away.

disappointing, unsatisfying, unsatisfactory 636 *insufficient*; not up to expectation 829 *discontenting*; abortive 728 *unsuccessful*.

Vb. *be disappointed,* - unsuccessful etc. adj.; try in vain 728 *fail*; have hoped for something better, not realize one's expectations 307 *fall short*; expect otherwise, be let down, be left in the lurch, be jilted, laugh on the wrong side of one's face, be crestfallen, look blue; be sick with disappointment.

disappoint, not come up to expectations 307 *fall short*; dash one's hopes; burst the bubble, disillusion; let one down, leave one in the lurch, not come up to scratch; balk, foil, thwart, frustrate 702 *hinder*; amaze, dumbfound, boggle one's mind 508 *surprise*; betray, play one false 930 *be dishonest*; jilt; dash the cup from one's lips, leave unsatisfied, spoil one's pleasure, dissatisfy, turn away 607 *reject*.

510 Foresight – N. *foresight,* anticipation, foretaste; foreknowledge, second sight, clairvoyancy; premonition, presentiment, foreboding, forewarning 511 *omen*; prognosis, prognostication 511 *prediction*; foregone conclusion 473 *certainty*; programme, prospectus 623 *plan*; forward planning, forethought, vision, longsightedness 498 *sagacity*; premeditation 608 *predetermination*; prudence, providence 858 *caution*; provision 669 *preparation*.

Adj. *foreseeing,* prospective, prognostic, predictive 511 *predicting*; clairvoyant, second-sighted, prophetic; farsighted, sagacious 498 *wise*; provident, prudent 858 *cautious*; anticipatory 507 *expectant*.

Vb. *foresee,* divine, prophesy, forecast 511 *predict*; forewarn 664 *warn*; see *or* peep *or* pry into the future, look into one's crystal ball, read one's palm, have

second sight; be forewarned, know in advance 524 *be informed*; look ahead, see it coming, scent, feel in one's bones; look for 507 *expect*; be prepared, anticipate, forestall 135 *be early*; make provision 669 *prepare*; surmise, make a good guess 512 *suppose*; forejudge 608 *predetermine*; plan ahead 623 *plan*; look to the future, have an eye to the f., see how the cat jumps, see how the wind blows 124 *look ahead*; have an eye on the main chance 498 *be wise*; feel one's way, keep a sharp lookout 455 *be attentive*; lay up for a rainy day 633 *provide*; take precautions, provide against 858 *be cautious*.

511 Prediction – N. *prediction,* foretelling, forewarning, prophecy; apocalypse 975 *revelation*; forecast; prognostication, prognosis; presentiment, foreboding 510 *foresight*; 1984; programme, prospectus, forward planning 623 *plan*; announcement, advance notice 528 *publication*; warning, preliminary w., warning shot 665 *danger signal*; prospect 507 *expectation*; shape of things to come, horoscope, fortune, palm-reading, palmistry, crystal-gazing.

divination, clairvoyancy; augury; soothsaying; astrology, horoscopy, casting nativities; fortune-telling, palmistry; crystal gazing; casting lots; dowsing 484 *discovery*.

omen, portent, writing on the wall; symptom, syndrome, sign 547 *indication*; forewarning, caution 664 *warning*; harbinger, herald 529 *messenger*; ominousness, portentousness, gathering clouds, signs of the times 661 *danger*; luck-bringer, black cat, horseshoe 983 *talisman*; portent of bad luck, broken mirror, spilt salt, shooting star, walking under a ladder; bird of ill omen, owl, raven.

oracle, consultant 500 *sage*; meteorologist, weatherman *or* woman; doom merchant, doomster, doomwatcher, Cassandra 664 *warner*; prophet, prophetess, seer, futurologist, forecaster; soothsayer 983 *sorcerer*; clairvoyant, medium 984 *occultist*; Delphic oracle;

Sibyl; Nostradamus; cards, tarot c., dice; crystal ball, tea leaves, palm.

diviner, water d., dowser; tipster 618 *gambler*; astrologer; fortune-teller, palmist, crystal-gazer.

Adj. *predicting,* predictive, foretelling; clairvoyant 510 *foreseeing*; fortune-telling; weather-forecasting; prophetic, apocalyptic; oracular; foreboding; heralding 66 *precursory*; ominous, portentous; auspicious, promising, favourable 730 *prosperous*; inauspicious, sinister 731 *adverse*.

Vb. *predict,* forecast, make a prediction, make a prognosis; foretell, prophesy, forebode, bode, augur, spell; foretoken, presage, portend; foreshow, foreshadow, prefigure, shadow forth, forerun, herald, be harbinger, usher in 64 *come before*; point to, betoken, typify, signify 547 *indicate*; announce, give notice, notify 528 *advertise*; forewarn, give warning 664 *warn*; look black, look ominous, lour, menace 900 *threaten*; promise, augur well, bid fair to, give hopes of, hold out hopes, build up h., raise expectations, excite e.

divine, auspicate, haruspicate; read the entrails, take the auspices, take the omens; soothsay, vaticinate; cast a horoscope, cast a nativity; cast lots 618 *gamble*; tell fortunes; read the future, read the signs, read the stars; read the cards, read one's hand, read one's palm.

Section Seven: Creative thought

512 Supposition – N. *supposition,* notion 451 *idea*; fancy; pretence, pretending 850 *affectation*; presumption, assumption, presupposition, postulation, postulate 475 *premise*; condition, stipulation, sine qua non 766 *conditions*; proposal, proposition 759 *offer*; submission 475 *argument*; hypothesis, working h., theory; thesis; basis of supposition, datum 466 *evidence*; association of ideas 449 *thought*; supposability, conjecturability 469 *possibility*.

conjecture, guess, surmise, suspicion; bare supposition, vague suspicion, rough guess, crude estimate, guesstimate; shrewd idea 476 *intuition*; guesswork, guessing, speculation; gamble, shot, shot in the dark 618 *gambling.*

Adj. *supposed,* conjectured etc. vb.; assumed, presumed, taken as read, postulated; proposed, mooted 452 *topical*; given, granted, granted for the sake of argument; putative, presumptive; so-called, quasi; not real 2 *unreal*; alleged.

Vb. *suppose,* just s., fancy; think, conceive, take into one's head, get into one's head 485 *opine*; surmise, conjecture, guess, hazard a g., make a g.; suppose so, dare say; presume, assume, presuppose; posit; take for granted, take it, postulate 475 *reason*; speculate, have a theory, theorize 449 *meditate*; rely on supposition 618 *gamble.*

propound, propose 759 *offer*; put on the agenda, moot, move, propose a motion, postulate 761 *request*; put a case, submit, make one's submission 475 *argue*; put forth, make a suggestion, venture to say, put forward a notion, throw out an idea, throw something into the melting-pot 691 *advise*; suggest.

513 Imagination – N. *imagination,* vivid i., fertile i., wild i.; imaginativeness, creativeness; inventiveness, creativity 21 *originality*; ingenuity, resourcefulness 694 *skill*; fancifulness, fantasy, stretch of the imagination; understanding, insight, empathy, sympathy 819 *moral sensibility*; poetic imagination, ecstasy, inspiration, fancy, the mind's eye, recollection, recollection in tranquillity, visualization, image-building, imagery, word-painting; artistry, creative work.

ideality, conception 449 *thought*; idealization; mental image, projection 445 *appearance*; concept, image, conceit, fancy, notion 451 *idea*; whim, whimsy 497 *absurdity*; vagary 604 *caprice*; figment, f. of the imagination, fiction 541 *falsehood*; work of fiction, story 590 *novel*; science fiction, space odyssey, fairy tale; flight of fancy, uncontrolled

imagination, romance, fantasy, extravaganza, rhapsody 546 *exaggeration*; poetic licence 593 *poetry*; skiamachy.

fantasy, wildest dreams; vision, dream, nightmare, night terror; Jabberwocky 84 *rara avis*; bogey, phantom 970 *ghost*; shadow, vapour 419 *dimness*; mirage 440 *visual fallacy*; delusion, hallucination, chimera 495 *error*; reverie, daydream, brown study 456 *abstractedness*; trance, somnambulism 375 *insensibility*; delirium 503 *frenzy*; autosuggestion; wishful thinking 477 *sophistry*; make-believe, vapourware, golden dream, pipe d. 859 *desire*; romance, stardust; romanticism, escapism, idealism, Utopianism; Utopia, Erewhon; promised land, El Dorado, the end of the rainbow; Happy Valley, Fortunate Isles, Isles of the Blest; land of Cockaigne, Ruritania, Shangrila, Atlantis, Lyonesse, Middle Earth, Narnia, San Serif; fairyland, wonderland; cloud-cuckoo-land, dream l., dream world, castles in Spain, castles in the air; pie in the sky, good time coming, millennium 124 *future state*; idle fancy, myth 543 *fable*; fantasy fiction.

visionary, seer 511 *diviner*; dreamer, day-d.; fantasist; idealist, Utopian 901 *philanthropist*; escapist; romantic, romancer, romanticist, rhapsodist, mythmaker; creative worker 556 *artist.*

Adj. *imaginative,* creative, lively, original, inventive, fertile, ingenious; resourceful 694 *skilful*; romancing, romantic; high-flown, rhapsodical, carried away; poetic, fictional; Utopian, idealistic; rhapsodic, enthusiastic; dreaming, daydreaming, in a trance; extravagant, grotesque, bizarre, fantastical, unreal, whimsical, airy-fairy, preposterous, impractical, Heath Robinson 497 *absurd*; visionary.

imaginary, unreal, unsubstantial 4 *insubstantial*; notional, chimerical, illusory 495 *erroneous*; dreamy, visionary, not of this world, of another world, ideal; vaporous 419 *shadowy*; fictitious, fabulous, fabled, legendary, mythological 543 *untrue*; fanciful, fancied, imagined, fabricated; thought-up,

dreamed-up; hypothetical; pretended, make-believe.

Vb. *imagine,* fancy, dream; think of, think up, conjure up, dream up; make up, devise, invent, originate, create, have an inspiration 609 *improvise;* coin, hatch, concoct, fabricate 164 *produce;* visualize, envisage, see in the mind's eye 438 *see;* conceive, form an image of; picture to oneself; paint, write a pen portrait of, conjure up a vision, capture, recapture 551 *represent;* use one's imagination, give reins to one's i., run riot in imagination 546 *exaggerate;* pretend, make-believe, daydream 456 *be inattentive;* build castles in the air, build castles in Spain; see visions, dream dreams; fantasize, idealize, romanticize, fictionalize, rhapsodize 546 *exaggerate;* enter into, empathize, sympathize 516 *understand.* 4.2 COMMUNICATION OF IDEAS

Section one: Nature of ideas communicated

514 Meaning – **N.** *meaning,* substance, essence, spirit, sum and substance, gist, pith, nitty-gritty; contents, text, matter, subject m. 452 *topic;* semantic content, sense, drift, tenor, purport, import, implication; relevance, bearing; meaningfulness, context; semantics.

connotation, denotation, signification, significance, reference, application; construction 520 *interpretation;* context; derivation, etymology 156 *source;* semantic field, comprehension; extended meaning, core m., leading sense; specialized meaning, idiom 80 *speciality;* usage, accepted meaning 610 *practice;* single meaning 516 *intelligibility;* double meaning, ambiguity 518 *equivocalness;* many meanings, polysemy; same meaning; synonym, synonymousness, synonymity, equivalence 13 *identity;* opposite meaning, antonym, antonymy 14

contrariety; contradictory meaning, countersense; changed meaning, semantic shift; level of meaning, literal meaning, literality 573 *plainness;* metaphorical meaning 519 *metaphor;* hidden meaning, esoteric sense 523 *latency;* constructive sense, implied s.; no sense 497 *absurdity.*

Adj. *meaningful,* significant, of moment 638 *important;* substantial, pithy, meaty, full of meaning, packed with m., pregnant; meaning etc. vb.; importing, purporting, indicative; telling 516 *expressive;* pointed, epigrammatic 839 *witty;* suggestive.

semantic, semiological, philological, etymological 557 *linguistic;* connotational, connotative; denotational, denotative; literal, verbal 573 *plain;* metaphorical 519 *figurative;* univocal, unambiguous 516 *intelligible;* polysemous, ambiguous 518 *equivocal;* synonymous, homonymous 13 *identical;* tantamount, equivalent 18 *similar;* tautologous 106 *repeated;* antonymous 14 *contrary;* idiomatic 80 *special;* paraphrastic 520 *interpretive;* obscure 568 *unclear;* clear; implied, constructive 523 *tacit;* nonsensical 497 *absurd;* without meaning 515 *meaningless.*

Vb. *mean,* mean something; convey a meaning, get across 524 *communicate;* symbolize 547 *indicate;* signify, denote, connote; purport; point to, add up to, boil down to, spell, involve 523 *imply;* convey, express, declare, assert 532 *affirm;* bespeak, tell of, speak of, breathe of, savour of, speak volumes 466 *evidence;* be getting at, be driving at, have in mind; be synonymous, have the same meaning; say it in other words, put it another way; mean the same thing, be the same thing in the end.

515 Lack of meaning – **N.** *lack of meaning,* meaninglessness, nonsignificance 639 *unimportance;* inanity, emptiness, triteness; truism, platitude, cliché 496 *maxim;* mere words, empty w.; illogicality 477 *sophistry;* invalidity, dead letter; illegibility, scribble, scribbling, scrawl

586 *script*; daub 552 *misrepresentation*; empty sound, strumming; sounding brass, tinkling cymbal 400 *loudness*; jargon, rigmarole, gobbledygook, galimatias, psychobabble; abracadabra, hocus-pocus, mumbo jumbo; gibberish, gabble, double dutch, Greek, Babel 517 *unintelligibility*; incoherence, raving, delirium 503 *frenzy*; double-talk.

silly talk, nonsense 497 *absurdity*; stuff and nonsense, balderdash, rubbish, load of r., rot, tommyrot; drivel, twaddle, fiddle-faddle, bosh, tosh, tripe, piffle, bilge, bull.

empty talk, sweet nothings; wind, gas, hot air, verbiage 570 *diffuseness*; rant, bombast 877 *boasting*; blether, blather, blah-blah, flimflam; guff, pi-jaw, eyewash, claptrap, poppycock 543 *fable*; humbug 541 *falsehood*; moonshine, malarkey, hokum, bunkum, bunk, boloney, hooey; flannel, flummery, blarney 925 *flattery*; sales talk, patter, sales p., spiel; talk, chatter, prattle, prating, yammering, babble, gabble, jabber, jabber jabber, jaw, yackety yack, yak yak, rhubarb rhubarb 581 *chatter*.

Adj. *meaningless,* nonsensical 497 *absurd*; senseless; unexpressive; insignificant, inane, empty, trivial, trite 639 *unimportant*; fatuous, piffling; waffling; incoherent, raving, gibbering 503 *frenzied*.

Vb. *mean nothing,* make no sense, be irrelevant; scribble, daub, talk bunkum 497 *be absurd*; babble, prattle, prate, gabble, gibber, jabber, yak 581 *be loquacious*; talk double dutch, talk gibberish; rant 546 *exaggerate*; rave, drivel, blether, waffle, talk hot air; not mean what one says; be Greek to, pass over one's head 474 *puzzle*.

516 Intelligibility – N. *intelligibility,* cognizability; explicability; comprehensibility; readability, legibility; clearness, clarity, coherence, limpidity, lucidity 567 *perspicuity*; precision, unambiguity 473 *certainty*; simplicity, straightforwardness, plain speaking, plain speech, plain words, plain English, no gobbledygook; simplification 701 *facility*.

Adj. *intelligible,* understandable, comprehensible; coherent 502 *sane*; audible, recognizable, distinguishable, unmistakable; cognizable 490 *known*; unambiguous, unequivocal 514 *meaningful*; explicit; distinct, clear-cut, precise 80 *definite*; articulate, eloquent; plain-spoken, downright, forthright 573 *plain*; straightforward, simple 701 *easy*; obvious, self-explanatory; explained, simplified; clear, limpid 422 *transparent*; lucid; readable, legible, decipherable, crystal clear, plain as a pikestaff 443 *visible*.

expressive, telling, meaningful, informative, striking, vivid, graphic, emphatic; illustrative, explicatory 520 *interpretive*.

Vb. *be intelligible,* - clear, - easy etc. adj.; be readable, be an easy read, read easily; make sense, add up 475 *be reasonable*; tell its own tale, speak for itself, be self-explanatory 466 *evidence*; have no secrets 443 *be visible*; be understood, come over, get across, sink in, dawn on; clarify, clear up, open one's eyes, elucidate 520 *interpret*; simplify.

understand, comprehend, apprehend 490 *know*; master 536 *learn*; have, hold, retain 505 *remember*; have understanding 498 *be wise*; see through, penetrate, fathom, get to the bottom of 484 *detect*; spot, descry, discern, distinguish, make out, see at a glance, see with half an eye 438 *see*; recognize, make no mistake 473 *be certain*; grasp, get hold of, be on to it, cotton on to, dig; get the hang of, take in, register; be with one, follow, savvy; collect, get, catch on, latch on to, twig; catch one's drift, get the idea, get the picture; realize, get wise to, tumble to, rumble; have one's eyes opened, see the light, see through, see it all; get to know, get the hang of.

517 Unintelligibility – N. *unintelligibility,* incomprehensibility, unaccountability, inconceivability; inexplicability; difficulty 474 *uncertainty*; obscurity 568 *imperspicuity*; ambiguity 518 *equivocalness*; mystification 515 *lack of meaning*; incoherence 503

mental disorder; double dutch, gibberish; jargon, psychobabble, foreign tongue, idiolect 560 *dialect, slang*; stammering 580 *speech defect*; undecipherability, illegibility; scribble, scrawl 586 *lettering*; inaudibility 401 *faintness*; Greek, sealed book 530 *secret*; paradox, knotty point, riddle 530 *enigma*; mysterious behaviour, Sphinx-like attitude.

Adj. *unintelligible,* incomprehensible, inconceivable, inexplicable, unaccountable; unrecognizable, as Greek to one, like double Dutch 491 *unknown*; unfathomable, inscrutable, impenetrable; blank, poker-faced, expressionless 820 *impassive*; inaudible 401 *muted*; illegible, scrawly, scribbled, undecipherable; undiscernible 444 *invisible*; arcane 523 *occult*; cryptic; esoteric 80 *private*; Sphinx-like, enigmatic.

puzzling, complex 700 *difficult*; hard, beyond one, over one's head, recondite, abstruse, elusive; sphinxian, enigmatic, mysterious 523 *occult*; nebulous, obscure 419 *shadowy*; clear as mud, clear as ditch water 568 *unclear*; ambiguous 518 *equivocal*; paradoxical 508 *unexpected*; fishy, strange, odd 84 *abnormal*; unexplained, insoluble, unsolvable.

inexpressible, unspeakable, untranslatable; unpronounceable, unutterable, ineffable; incommunicable, indefinable.

puzzled, mystified, out of one's depth, flummoxed, stumped, baffled, perplexed, nonplussed 474 *uncertain*.

Vb. *be unintelligible,* - puzzling, - inexpressible etc. adj.; be hard, be difficult, make one's head ache *or* swim 474 *puzzle*; talk in riddles 518 *be equivocal*; talk double dutch, talk gibberish 515 *mean nothing*; speak badly 580 *stammer*; write badly, scribble, scrawl; keep one guessing 486 *cause doubt*; perplex; require explanation, have no answer, need an interpreter; go over one's head; elude one's grasp, escape one; pass comprehension, baffle understanding.

not understand, not get it, not grasp it; find unintelligible, not make out, not know what to make of, make nothing of, make neither head nor tail of, be unable

to account for; puzzle over, rack one's brains over, be floored by, be stumped by, give up; be out of one's depth 491 *not know*; be at sea 474 *be uncertain*; have no grasp of 695 *be unskilful*; have a blind spot 439 *be blind*; be on different wavelengths, be at cross-purposes 495 *blunder*; get one wrong 481 *misjudge*.

518 Equivocalness – **N.** *equivocalness,* ambiguity, ambivalence 517 *unintelligibility*; vagueness 474 *uncertainty*; newspeak, doubletalk, weasel word 515 *lack of meaning*; conundrum, riddle 530 *enigma*; prevarication; equivocation, white lie 543 *untruth*; quibble, quibbling 477 *sophistry*; word-play, play upon words; pun, double entendre 839 *witticism*; faux ami, confusible; anagram, acrostic; synonymy, homonymy; homonym, homophone 18 *analogue*.

Adj. *equivocal,* ambiguous, ambivalent; two-edged; left-handed, back-h.; equivocating, prevaricating; evasive; anagrammatic.

Vb. *be equivocal,* cut both ways; play upon words, pun; have two meanings; speak with two voices 14 *be contrary*; fudge, waffle, stall, not give a straight answer, beat about the bush, sit on the fence 620 *avoid*; equivocate, prevaricate.

519 Metaphor: figure of speech – **N.** *metaphor,* mixed m.; transference; allusion; extended metaphor, allegory; fable, parable 534 *teaching*; symbol; symbolism, figurativeness, imagery 513 *imagination*; simile, likeness 462 *comparison*; personification.

trope, figure of speech, turn of s., flourish; manner of speech; irony, sarcasm 851 *satire*; rhetorical figure 574 *ornament*; metonymy, antonomasia, synecdoche, transferred epithet; anaphora; litotes 483 *underestimation*; hyperbole; stress, emphasis; circumlocution, euphuism, euphemism, dysphemism 850 *affectation*; anacoluthon, colloquialism 573 *plainness*; contrast, antithesis 462 *comparison*; metathesis 221 *inversion*;

paradox, epigram, paronomasia, word-play 518 *equivocalness.*

Adj. *figurative,* metaphorical, allusive, symbolical, allegorical; parabolical; euphemistic 850 *affected*; hyperbolic 546 *exaggerated*; flowery.

520 Interpretation – N. *interpretation,* explanation, explication, exposition; elucidation, clarification, illumination; illustration, exemplification 83 *example*; solution, key, clue 460 *answer*; decipherment, decoding, cracking 484 *discovery*; construction, reading; allegorization 519 *metaphor*; accepted reading, vulgate; alternative reading, variant r.; criticism, textual c., literary c., practical c., appreciation 557 *literature*; critique, review, notice 480 *estimate*; insight.

commentary, comment, editorial c., gloss, footnote; caption, legend 563 *phrase*; motto; annotation, notes, marginalia; exposition 591 *dissertation*; critical edition, variorum; glossary, lexicon 559 *dictionary.*

translation, version, rendering, free translation; literal translation; key, crib; paraphrase; précis, abridgment; adaptation; decoding, decipherment.

interpreter, explainer, exponent, expounder 537 *teacher*, 973 *religious teacher*; demythologizer; editor, copy e. 528 *publicizer*; textual critic; emender, emendator; commentator, annotator; glossarist, critic, reviewer; medium 984 *spiritualism*; translator, paraphraser; cryptographer, encoder; code-breaker; decoder; cryptanalyst, cryptologist; lip-reader; spokesman, mouthpiece; public relations officer, PR consultant, press officer 524 *informant*; executant, performer 413 *musician*; player 594 *actor.*

guide, precedent 83 *example*; light, guiding l., star, guiding s.; courier 690 *director*; demonstrator 522 *exhibitor.*

Adj. *intrepretative,* interpretive, constructive; explanatory, explicatory, elucidatory; expository 557 *literary*; defining; illuminating, illustrative, exemplary; glossarial, annotative, editorial;

lip-reading; mediumistic; literal; faithful; free 495 *inexact.*

Vb. *interpret,* define, clarify; explain, expound, elucidate 516 *be intelligible*; illustrate 83 *exemplify*; demonstrate 522 *show*; act as guide; comment on, edit, write notes for, add footnotes to, annotate, gloss; read, spell out; construe, put a construction on, understand by, make sense of; illuminate, throw light on, enlighten 524 *inform*; deduce, infer 475 *reason*; act as interpreter, be spokesman or -woman or -person 755 *deputize.*

translate, render, do into, turn i.; reword, paraphrase; abridge, précis, adapt; transliterate, transcribe; encode; lip-read.

decipher, crack, decode; read, spell out, puzzle o., make o., work o.; piece together, find the sense of; solve, resolve, unravel, disentangle, read between the lines.

Adv. *in plain words,* in plain English; by way of explanation; that is, i.e.; in other words, to put it another way, to wit, namely, viz.; to explain.

521 Misinterpretation – N. *misinterpretation,* misunderstanding, misconstruction, misapprehension, wrong end of the stick; cross-purposes; different wavelengths, crossed lines 495 *mistake*; mistranslation, misconstrue; wrong interpretation, false construction; false reading; dark glasses, rose-coloured spectacles; falsification 552 *misrepresentation*; travesty 851 *ridicule*; misapplication 565 *solecism.*

Vb. *misinterpret,* misunderstand; get wrong, get one wrong, get hold of the wrong end of the stick 495 *blunder*; misread, misspell 495 *err*; mistranslate, misconstrue, put a false sense or construction on; give a twist or turn, strain the sense; twist, twist the words 246 *distort*; equivocate, play upon words 518 *be equivocal*; read into, write i. 38 *add*; misquote; garble 552 *misrepresent*; parody, caricature; misrepresent 926 *defame.*

Section two: Modes of communication

522 Manifestation – N. *manifestation,* revelation, unfolding, discovery, daylight, exposure 526 *disclosure*; expression; proof 466 *evidence*; presentation; sign, token 547 *signal*; symptom, syndrome 511 *omen*; press conference, prerelease, preview 438 *view*; demonstration, exhibition; display, showing off 875 *ostentation*; proclamation 528 *publication*; candour; conspicuousness 443 *visibility*; apparition, vision, materialization 445 *appearance*; séance 984 *occultism*; incarnation.

exhibit, specimen, sample 83 *example*; piece of evidence, quotation, citation 466 *evidence*; model, mock-up 551 *image*; show piece, museum p., collector's item, antique, curio; display, show, dress s., mannequin parade 445 *spectacle*; scene 438 *view*; exhibition hall, exhibition centre, showplace, showroom, showcase, placard, hoarding, bill 528 *advertisement*; sign 547 *label*; shop window, museum, gallery 632 *collection*; exhibition, exposition; fair 796 *market*.

exhibitor, advertiser, publicist, promotion manager 528 *publicizer*; displayer, demonstrator; showman; impresario 594 *stage manager*; exhibitionist; model, male m., mannequin; flaunter.

Adj. *manifest,* apparent, ostensible 445 *appearing*; plain, clear, defined 80 *definite*; explained, plain as a pikestaff, plain as the nose on one's face, clear as daylight 516 *intelligible*; unconcealed, showing 443 *visible*; conspicuous, noticeable, notable, prominent, pronounced, signal, marked, striking, in relief, in the foreground, in the limelight 443 *obvious*; open, evident; gross, crass, palpable; self-evident, written all over one, for all to see, unmistakable, recognizable, identifiable, incontestable, staring one in the face 473 *certain*; public, famous, notorious, infamous; catching the eye, eye-catching, gaudy 875 *showy*; arrant, glaring, stark staring, flagrant, loud, on the rooftops, shouting from the r.

shown, manifested etc. vb.; declared, divulged, made public; unconcealed, overt, explicit, in the open, public; showing, featured, on show, on display, on view, on 443 *visible*; exhibited, shown off; brought forth, produced; mentioned, brought to one's notice; adduced, cited, quoted; confronted, brought face to face; worn, sported; paraded; unfurled, flaunted, waved, brandished; naked and unashamed; advertised, publicized, promoted 528 *published*; expressible, producible, showable.

Vb. *manifest,* reveal, divulge, give away, betray 526 *disclose*; evince, betoken, show signs of 466 *evidence*; bring to light, unearth 484 *discover*; explain, make plain, make obvious 520 *interpret*; expose, lay bare, unroll, unfurl, unsheathe 229 *uncover*; open up, throw open, lay o. 263 *open*; elicit, draw forth, drag out 304 *extract*; invent, bring forth 164 *produce*; bring out, shadow forth, body f.; incorporate, incarnate, personify; typify, symbolize, exemplify 547 *indicate*; point up, accentuate, enhance, develop 36 *augment*; throw light on; highlight, spotlight, throw into relief 532 *emphasize*; express, formulate 532 *affirm*; bring, bring up, make reference to, mention, cite, quote; bring to the fore, place in the foreground; bring to notice, produce, trot out, come out with, proclaim, publicize, promote 528 *publish*; show for what it is (see *show*).

show, exhibit, display; set out, put on display, put on show, put on view, expose to v., offer to the v., set before one's eyes; flourish 317 *brandish*; sport 228 *wear*; flaunt, parade 875 *be ostentatious*; make a show of, affect 850 *be affected*; present, feature, enact 551 *represent*; put on, stage, release 594 *dramatize*; televise, screen, film; stage an exhibition, put on show *or* display, hang (a picture); show off, set o., model (garments); put one through his paces; demonstrate 534 *teach*; show round, show over, give a guided tour, point out, draw attention

to, bring to notice 547 *indicate*; confront, force a confrontation, bring face to face, bring eyeball to eyeball; reflect, image, mirror, hold up the mirror to 20 *imitate*; tear off the mask, show up, expose 526 *disclose.*

be plain, - explicit etc. adj.; show one's face, unveil, unmask; show one's true colours, have no secrets, make no mystery, not try to hide, wear one's heart on one's sleeve; have no shame, wash one's dirty linen in public; speak one's mind, speak out, tell to one's face, make no secret of, give straight from the shoulder, make no bones about 573 *speak plainly*; speak for itself, tell its own story, require no explanation 516 *be intelligible*; be obvious, stand to reason, go without saying 478 *be proved*; be conspicuous, be as plain as the nose on one's face, stand out, stand out a mile 443 *be visible*; show the flag, be seen, show up, show up well, hold the stage, be in the limelight, have the spotlight on one, stand in full view 455 *attract notice*; loom large, stare one in the face; appear on the horizon, rear its head, show its face, transpire, emanate, come to light 445 *appear.*

523 Latency – N. *latency,* insidiousness; dormancy, potentiality 469 *possibility*; esotericism; occultness, mysticism; hidden meaning; symbolism, allegory 519 *metaphor*; implication, mystery 530 *secret*; inmost recesses 224 *interiority*; dark 418 *darkness*; shadowiness 419 *dimness*; imperceptibility 444 *invisibility*; more than meets the eye; deceptive appearance, hidden fires, hidden depths; iron hand in a velvet glove; slumbering volcano, sleeping dog, sleeping giant 661 *danger*; dark horse, mystery man; red under the bed, nigger in the woodpile, snake in the grass, mole 663 *pitfall*; manipulator, puppeteer, hidden hand, wirepuller, strings, friends in high places, friend at court, power behind the throne, éminence grise 178 *influence*; old-boy

network, networking; subconscious; subliminal influence, subliminal advertising; something rotten; innuendo, insinuation, suggestion 524 *hint*; sealed lips 582 *taciturnity*; undercurrent, undertone, aside 401 *faintness*; clandestineness, secret society, cabal, intrigue 623 *plot*; code, cryptography.

Adj. *latent,* lurking, skulking 525 *concealed*; dormant, sleeping 679 *inactive*; passive 266 *quiescent*; in abeyance 175 *inert*; undeveloped 469 *possible*; unsuspected; subconscious, subliminal, underlying; in the background, behind the scenes, backroom, undercover; unmanifested, unseen, undetected, unexposed 444 *invisible*; arcane, impenetrable 517 *unintelligible*; sequestered 883 *secluded*; undiscovered, unexplored.

tacit, unsaid, unspoken, unpronounced, unexpressed, unvoiced, unmentioned, unarticulated, untold of, unsung; undivulged, unproclaimed, unprofessed, undeclared; unwritten, unpublished; understood, implied, inferred, implicit, between the lines; allusive.

occult, mysterious, mystic; symbolic, allegorical 519 *figurative*; cryptic, esoteric; veiled, masked, covert; clandestine, secret; insidious 930 *perfidious*; underhand 525 *stealthy*; undiscovered, hush-hush, top-secret; off the record 80 *private*; cryptographic 525 *disguised.*

Vb. *lurk,* hide, be latent, lie dormant, be a stowaway; burrow, stay underground; lie hidden; lie low, lie doggo; evade detection, escape recognition; act behind the scenes; creep, slink; pull the strings, stage-manage, underlie, be at the bottom of 156 *cause*; smoulder; be subliminal.

imply, insinuate, whisper, murmur, suggest 524 *hint*; understand, infer, allude; connote, carry a suggestion, involve, spell 514 *mean.*

524 Information – N. *information,* informatics; information technology, data

base, viewdata 86 *data processing*; mailing list, distribution l. 588 *correspondence*; hearsay, word of mouth; enlightenment, instruction, briefing 534 *teaching*; thought-transference; communication; mass media 528 *the press*, 531 *broadcasting*; notification, announcement, intimation, warning, advice, notice, mention, tip, tip-off (see *hint*); newspaper announcement, hatch, match and dispatch, obit, small ad, advertisement, circular 528 *publicity*; common knowledge, gen, info; background, facts, the goods, documentary 494 *truth*; material, literature 589 *reading matter*; inside information, king's *or* queen's evidence, dope, lowdown, undisclosed source, confidence 530 *secret*; scoop; the know 490 *knowledge*; file, dossier 548 *record*; word, report, intelligence, item of news 529 *news*; wire, telegram, telemessage, telex, cable, cablegram 529 *message*; communicativeness; leak, disinformation 526 *disclosure*.

report, review, annual report; paper, Green Paper, White P., Black P.; account, eyewitness a. 590 *narrative*; statement, return, annual r., tax r. 86 *statistics*; specification, estimates 480 *estimate*; progress report, confidential r.; dispatch, bulletin, communiqué, handout, press release 529 *news*; presentation, case; petition 761 *entreaty*; round robin 762 *deprecation*; letters, letters to the editor, dispatches 588 *correspondence*.

hint, gentle h., whisper, aside 401 *faintness*; intimation; broad hint, signal, nod, a nod is as good as a wink to a blind horse, wink, look, nudge, kick, kick under the table, gesticulation 547 *gesture*; prompt, cue 505 *reminder*; suggestion; caution 664 *warning*; tip, tip-off (see *information*); word in the ear, word to the wise; insinuation, innuendo; clue, symptom 520 *interpretation*; sidelight, glimpse, inkling; suspicion, inference.

informant, teller; spokesman *or* -woman *or* -person 579 *speaker*; mouthpiece, representative 754 *delegate*; announcer, radio a., television a., weatherforecaster, weatherman *or* -woman 531 *broadcaster*; notifier, advertiser, promoter 528 *publicizer*; harbinger, herald 529 *messenger*; testifier 466 *witness*; one in the know, authority, source; quarter, channel, circle, grapevine; pander, go-between, contact 231 *intermediary*; informed circles, information centre; news agency, wire service, Reuter, TASS 528 *the press*; communicator, correspondent, special c., reporter, newshound, chequebook journalist, commentator, columnist, gossip writer 529 *news reporter*; tipster 691 *adviser*; guide; little bird.

informer, spy, spook, snoop, sleuth 459 *detective*; undercover agent, inside a., mole; stool pigeon, nark, copper's n., snitch, sneak, nose, squealer, whistle-blower, grass, supergrass; eavesdropper, telltale, talebearer, clype, tattler, tattle-tale, gossip 581 *chatterer*.

guidebook, Baedeker; travelogue; handbook, book of words, manual, vade mecum, ABC, A-Z; timetable, Bradshaw; roadbook, itinerary, route map, chart, plan 551 *map*; gazetteer 589 *reference book*; nautical almanac; telephone directory, phone book, Yellow Pages; index, catalogue 87 *directory*; courier 520 *guide*.

Adj. *informative,* communicative, newsy; instructive, documentary 534 *educational*; oral, verbal, spoken; explicit; indiscreet 581 *loquacious*.

informed, well-i., kept i., au fait; posted, primed, briefed, instructed 490 *knowing*; au courant, genned-up, clued-up, wised-up; in the know, in on, in the picture; brought up to date.

Vb. *inform,* certify, advise, beg to a.; intimate, impart, convey (see *communicate*); apprise, acquaint, have one know, give to understand; give one the facts, brief, instruct 534 *teach*; let one know, put one in the picture, fill one in on; enlighten 534 *educate*; point out, direct one's attention 547 *indicate*; insinuate (see *hint*); confide, mention privately; put one wise, put right, correct, disabuse,

disillusion; be specific, state, name, signify 80 *specify*; mention, mention en passant, refer to, touch on, speak of 579 *speak*; gossip, spread rumours; be indiscreet, open one's mouth, let the cat out of the bag, blurt out, talk 581 *be loquacious*; leak information, give disinformation, break the news, reveal 526 *disclose*; tell, clype, blab, split, grass, snitch, squeal, blow the gaff 526 *confess*; rat, turn Queen's evidence, turn State's e.; betray one, blow the whistle on, sell one down the river; tell tales, tell on, clype on; inform against, shop, denounce 928 *accuse*.

communicate, transmit, pass on, pass on information; dispatch news 588 *correspond*; report, cover, make a report, submit a r.; report progress, keep posted; get through, get across, put it over; contact, get in touch; convey, bring word, send w., leave w., write 588 *correspond*; beam; send a message, speak, semaphore 547 *signal*; wire, telegraph, send a telemessage, send a singing telegram, send a kissogram, etc., telex, radio; telephone, phone, call, dial, ring, ring up, give one a ring *or* a tinkle *or* a buzz; disseminate, broadcast, telecast, televise; announce, notify, give notice, serve n. 528 *advertise*; give out, put out, carry a report, issue a press notice *or* release, publicize 528 *publish*; retail, recount, narrate 590 *describe*; commune 584 *converse*; swap news, exchange information, pool one's knowledge.

hint, drop a h., suggest, throw out a suggestion; put an idea in one's head; prompt, give the cue 505 *remind*; caution 664 *warn*; tip off 691 *advise*; wink, tip the wink; nudge 547 *gesticulate*; insinuate, breathe, whisper, say in one's ear, touch upon, just mention, mention in passing *or* en passant, say by the way, let fall, imply, allude, leave one to gather, intimate.

be informed, be in possession of the facts 490 *know*; have it on good authority; keep one's ear to the ground, hear it on the grapevine, be a fly on the wall, overhear 415 *hear*; be told by a little

bird, get wind of; have a line on, have the dope, have the gen *or* info.

525 Concealment – N. *concealment*, confinement, purdah 883 *seclusion*; hiding 523 *latency*; covering up; cache 527 *hiding-place*; disguise, camouflage 542 *deception*; masquerade, anonymity, incognito 562 *no name*; smoke screen 421 *screen*; reticence, reserve; mental reservation, ulterior motive; evasion, evasiveness 518 *equivocalness*; misinformation, disinformation; white lie; subterfuge 542 *trickery*; suppression, D notice, Official Secrets Act; cover-up 543 *untruth*; deceitfulness, dissimulation 541 *duplicity*.

secrecy, secretness, mystery 530 *secret*; seal of secrecy, hearing in camera; secret society, clandestineness, secretiveness, furtiveness, stealthiness; underhand dealing 930 *improbity*; conspiracy 623 *plot*; cipher, code 517 *unintelligibility*.

Adj. *concealed*, crypto-, hidden, closet; hiding, in ambush; confined; mysterious, recondite, arcane 517 *unintelligible*; cryptic 523 *occult*; private 883 *secluded*; confidential, off the record; secret, top secret, restricted, hush-hush; unrevealed, ex-directory; undisclosed; unsigned, unnamed 562 *anonymous*; covert, behind the scenes; covered; hooded, masked, veiled, eclipsed; smothered, stifled, suppressed, clandestine, undercover, underground, subterranean 211 *deep*.

disguised, camouflaged; incognito 562 *anonymous*; unrecognizable 491 *unknown*; masked 421 *screened*; codified, cryptographic 517 *unintelligible*.

stealthy, silent, furtive, catlike, on tiptoe; prowling, skulking, loitering, lurking; clandestine, hugger-mugger, conspiratorial, cloak-and-dagger; hole-and-corner, backdoor, underhand, surreptitious 930 *dishonest*.

reticent, reserved, shy, self-contained, withdrawn; noncommittal, uncommunicative, uninformative, cagey, evasive; vague, studiously v.; keeping one's own counsel, discreet, silent 582 *taciturn*;

tight-lipped, poker-faced; close, secretive, buttoned-up, close as an oyster, clamlike; in one's shell 883 *unsociable*.

Vb. *conceal,* hide, hide away, plank, secrete, ensconce, confine, keep in purdah 883 *seclude*; stow away, lock up, seal up, bottle up 632 *store*; hide underground, bury 364 *inter*; put out of sight, sweep under the carpet, cover up, paper over, whitewash 226 *cover*; gloss over; blot out 550 *obliterate*; slur over, not mention 458 *disregard*; smother, stifle 165 *suppress*; veil, muffle, mask, disguise, camouflage; shroud, draw a veil over 421 *screen*; obscure, eclipse 418 *darken*; obfuscate 419 *bedim*; go incognito, masquerade 541 *dissemble*; encode.

keep secret, keep it dark, keep under wraps, keep close, keep under one's hat; look blank, look poker-faced, give nothing away, keep a straight face, keep mum, keep one's mouth shut, hold one's tongue, not breathe a word, not utter a syllable, not talk, keep one's counsel, make no sign 582 *be taciturn*; be discreet, neither confirm nor deny, make no comment; keep back, reserve, withhold, keep it to oneself, let it go no further; hush up, cover up, suppress; keep a low profile, keep in the background, stay in the shadows; let not one's right hand know what one's left hand does; blindfold, bamboozle, keep in the dark 542 *deceive*.

be stealthy, - furtive, - evasive etc. adj.; hugger-mugger, conspire 623 *plot*; snoop, sneak, slink, creep; glide, steal, steal along, steal by, steal past; tiptoe, go on t., pussyfoot; prowl, skulk, loiter; lie doggo 523 *lurk*; dodge 620 *avoid*.

Adv. *secretly,* hugger-mugger; confidentially, sotto voce, with bated breath; entre nous, between ourselves, between you and me and the gatepost, aside, to oneself; not for publication, privately, in private, in camera, behind closed doors, anonymously, incognito.

stealthily, furtively, like a thief in the night; under cloak of darkness; underhand, by the back door, in a hole-and-corner way, under-the-counter; on the sly, on the quiet, on the QT.

526 Disclosure – **N.** *disclosure,* revelation, apocalypse; daylight, cold light of day; discovery, uncovering; unwelcome discovery, disillusionment 509 *disappointment*; denouement; lid off, exposé, divulgence 528 *publication*; exposure, showing up 522 *manifestation*; telling all, explanations, showdown; communication, leak, indiscretion 524 *hint*; betrayal, giveaway; tell-tale sign; State's evidence, Queen's e. 603 *change of mind*; acknowledgment, admission, avowal, confession, coming clean; confessional 939 *penitence*; clean breast, whole truth, cards on the table 494 *truth*.

Vb. *disclose,* reveal, expose, take the wraps off, disinter 522 *manifest*; bare, lay b., strip b., denude; unfold, unroll, unfurl, unpack, unwrap 229 *uncover*; unveil, lift the veil, raise the curtain, let some light in; break the seal, unclose 263 *open*; lay open, open up 484 *discover*; catch out 484 *detect*; not hide; make known, give away, betray, blow one's cover; unmask, tear off the mask; expose oneself, betray o., give oneself away 495 *blunder*; declare oneself, drop the mask; show oneself in one's true colours, show for what it is, debunk; disabuse, set right, undeceive, disillusion, open the eyes 524 *inform*; take the lid off, unleash, let the cat out of the bag (see *divulge*).

divulge, declare, bring into the open, express, vent, give vent to 579 *speak*; ventilate, air, canvass, publicize 528 *publish*; tell all, let on, blurt out, blow the gaff, talk out of turn, spill the beans, let the cat out of the bag, give the show *or* the game away; speak of, talk; utter, breathe; let out, leak 524 *communicate*; let drop, let fall 524 *hint*; come out with, spit it out 573 *speak plainly*; get it off one's chest, unburden oneself; confide, let one into the secret, open one's mind *or* heart to; declare one's intentions, show one's hand, put one's cards on the table; report, tell, tell tales out of school,

tell on, clype, name names 928 *accuse*; split, squeal, blab, grass 524 *inform*; rat.

confess, admit, avow, acknowledge; concede, grant, allow, own 488 *assent*; own up, cough up; plead guilty; talk, sing, sing like a canary; come out with, come across with, come clean, tell all, speak the truth 540 *be truthful*; make a clean breast of it, go to confession; turn Queen's evidence 603 *tergiversate*.

be disclosed, come out, break 445 *appear*; come to light 478 *be proved*; show the cloven hoof, show its face, show its true colours, stand revealed 522 *be plain*; transpire, become known, become public knowledge 490 *be known*; leak out 298 *emerge*; show 443 *be visible*; show through; come as a revelation, break through the clouds, come with a blinding flash, flash on the mind 449 *dawn upon*; give oneself away, there speaks . . .

527 Hiding. Disguise – N. *hiding-place,* hide, hideout, hideaway, hidey-hole, priesthole, safe house 662 *refuge*; lair, den 192 *retreat*; cache, secret place, oubliette; crypt, vault 194 *cellar*; closet, secret drawer, hidden panel, safe place, safe, safe deposit 632 *storage*; recess, corner, nook, cranny, niche, holes and corners, secret passage, underground p.; cover, underground 662 *shelter*; inmost recesses 224 *interiority*.

ambush, spider's web 542 *trap*; catch 663 *pitfall*; stalking horse, Trojan h., decoy, stool pigeon 545 *impostor*; agent provocateur 663 *troublemaker*.

disguise, blind, masquerade 542 *deception*; camouflage 20 *mimicry*; veneer 226 *covering*; mask, visor, veil, domino 228 *cloak*; fancy dress; smoke screen, cover 421 *screen*.

Vb. *ambush,* set an a., lie in wait 523 *lurk*; set a trap for 542 *ensnare*; waylay.

528 Publication – N. *publication,* dissemination 526 *disclosure*; proclamation; edict; beat of drum, flourish of trumpets

400 *loudness*; press conference, press release, advance publicity (**see** *advertisement*); notification, public notice, official bulletin; announcement, press a., pronouncement, manifesto, programme, platform; the media, mass m.; publishing, book trade, book-selling 589 *book*; broadcasting, narrowcasting, televising 531 *telecommunication*; broadcast, telecast, newscast 529 *news*; kite-flying; circulation, circular, encyclical.

publicity, limelight, spotlight, public eye; common knowledge 490 *knowledge*; open discussion, seminar, ventilation, canvassing; blatancy 522 *manifestation*; open secret; notoriety, fame 866 *famousness*; currency, wide c.; circulation, wide c.; readership, audience, viewership; viewing figures, listening f., ratings; public relations, PR, promotion, sales p., propaganda; photocall, photo-opportunity; display, showmanship, salesmanship, window dressing 875 *ostentation*; sensationalism, ballyhoo, hype 546 *exaggeration*; publicization, advertising, skywriting; medium of publicity, television, radio 531 *broadcasting*; public address system, loudspeaker, loud hailer 415 *hearing aid*; public comment, journalism, reporting, rapportage, coverage, report, notice, write-up (**see** *the press*); investigative journalism 459 *enquiry*; newsreel, newsletter, news round-up 529 *news*; sounding board, correspondence column, open letter, letters to the editor; editorial 591 *article*; pulpit, platform, hustings, soapbox; printing press 587 *print*; blaze of publicity, letters a foot high; name in lights.

advertisement, notice, insertion, advert, ad, small a., classified a., advertorial; personal column; agony column; headline, banner h., streamer; puff, blurb, buildup, hype, ballyhoo; promotional literature, unsolicited mail, handout, handbill; bill, poster, flyer 522 *exhibit*; billboard, hoarding, placard, sandwich board, display b., notice b., bulletin b.; yellow pages; advertising copy, slogan, jingle; plug, teaser, trailer, commercial 531 *broadcasting*; hard sell,

soft s., subliminal advertising; cold-calling.

the press, fourth estate, Fleet Street, the papers; newspaper, newssheet, freesheet, paper, rag, tabloid, comic; underground press, gutter p., yellow p., tabloid p.; organ, journal, daily paper, daily, quality d., broadsheet, heavy; morning paper, evening p., Sunday p., local p.; issue, edition, stop-press e., sports e., extra; magazine section, supplement, colour s.; insert, leaflet, handbill, pamphlet, brochure, newsletter.

journal, review, magazine, glossy m., specialist m., women's m., male-interest m., pulp m.; part-work, periodical, serial, daily, weekly, monthly, quarterly, annual; gazette, trade journal, house magazine, trade publication 589 *reading matter.*

publicizer, notifier, announcer; herald, trumpet 529 *messenger;* proclaimer, crier, town crier; barker, tout; bill sticker, bill poster, sandwichman; demonstrator, promoter, publicist, publicity agent, press a., advertising a.; adman, advertiser, hidden persuader; copywriter, blurb writer, commercial artist, public relations officer, PRO, propagandist, pamphleteer 537 *preacher;* printer, publisher 589 *bookperson;* reporter, journalist, investigative j., chequebook j. 529 *news reporter.*

Vb. *publish,* make public; report, cover, write up; bring into the open, reveal 526 *divulge;* highlight, spotlight 532 *emphasize;* radio, broadcast, narrowcast, tape, telecast, televise, relay, diffuse 524 *inform;* spread, circulate, distribute, disseminate, circularize; canvass, ventilate, discuss 475 *argue;* pamphleteer, propagate, propagandize 534 *teach;* use the press 587 *print;* syndicate, serialize, edit, subedit, sub; issue, release, get out, put o., give o., send forth, lay before the public; bring to public notice, let it be known; spread a rumour, fly a kite; spread abroad; talk about, pass round, put about, bandy a.; voice, broach, talk of, speak of, utter, emit 579 *speak.*

proclaim, announce, herald, notify; pronounce, declare, go on record 532 *affirm;* make one's views public, make a proclamation, issue a public statement; publish a manifesto; noise, trumpet, blaze abroad, declaim, shout from the rooftops; beat the big drum, announce with a flourish of trumpets.

advertise, publicize; place an ad, bill, post, put up a poster; tell the world, put on the map, headline; make a cynosure of, put in lights, spotlight, build up, promote; make much of, feature; sell, boost, puff, hype up, write up, extol, rave about 482 *overrate;* plug 106 *repeat.*

be published, become public, come out; hit the headlines, make the front page; become the talk of the town, circulate, pass from mouth to mouth, go the rounds, get about, be bruited abroad, spread like wildfire, find a publisher, see oneself in print, get printed, get into the papers; sell well, go like a best-seller, become a blockbuster 793 *be sold.*

529 News – N. *news,* good n., no news is good n.; bad news 509 *disappointment;* tidings, glad t.; gospel, evangel 973 *religion;* dispatches, diplomatic bag; intelligence, report, dispatch, word, intimation, advice; titbit 524 *information;* bulletin, communiqué, handout, press release; newspaper report, press notice; news item, news flash 531 *broadcast;* latest news, stop-press n.; sensation, scoop, exclusive; old news, stale n.; copy, filler; yarn, story, tall s.; newscast, newsreel 528 *publicity;* news value, newsworthiness.

rumour, unconfirmed report; hearsay, gossip, talk, talk of the town, tittle-tattle 584 *chat;* scandal 926 *calumny;* whisper, buzz, noise; false report, hoax; grapevine, bush telegraph.

message, word of mouth, word, tip 524 *information;* communication 547 *signal;* wireless message, cable, telegram, telemessage, wire, fax, electronic mail 531 *telecommunication;* postcard, pc, note, letters, dispatches 588 *correspondence,* 531 *postal communications;* ring,

phone call, buzz, tinkle; errand 751 *commission*.

news reporter, newspaperman *or* -woman, reporter, cub r., journalist, correspondent, legman, stringer 589 *author*; gentleman *or* lady of the press, pressman *or* -woman, press representative 524 *informant*; newsreader, newscaster 531 *broadcaster*; chequebook journalist, muckraker, scandalmonger.

messenger, forerunner 66 *precursor*; harbinger 511 *omen*; announcer, town crier 528 *publicizer*; ambassador, spokesman *or* -woman *or* -person 754 *envoy*; apostle, emissary; herald; go-between, pander, contact, contact man *or* woman 231 *intermediary*.

courier, runner, Queen's Messenger, express m., dispatch rider, delivery-man *or* -woman; postman *or* -woman 531 *postal communications*; telegraph boy *or* girl, messenger b. *or* girl, errand b. *or* girl, office b. *or* girl; call-boy, bellhop, page, buttons, commissionaire; carrier pigeon 273 *carrier*; Mercury.

530 Secret – N. *secret,* esotericism; mystery 984 *occultism*; confidential information, sealed orders, top-secret file, state secret, affairs of state; confidential communication; sphinx, man *or* woman of mystery, enigmatic personality, Gioconda smile, inscrutable s.; Mr X 562 *no name*; dark horse, unknown quantity; unknown warrior; skeleton in the cupboard; sealed book; unknown country, terra incognita 491 *unknown thing*.

enigma, mystery, puzzle, Chinese p., Rubik's cube (tdmk), Rubik's magic (tdmk); problem, poser, brain-teaser; hard nut to crack, vexed question; cipher, code, cryptogram, hieroglyphics 517 *unintelligibility*; word-puzzle, anagram, acrostic, crossword; riddle, riddle-me-ree, conundrum; charade; intricacy, labyrinth, maze 61 *complexity*.

531 Communications – N. *telecommunication*; teleinformatics; long-distance communication, telephony, telegraphy,

radio *or* wireless t.; signalling, semaphore, morse 547 *signal*; cable, cablegram, telegram, telemessage, wire, fax, electronic mail 529 *message*; bush telegraph, grapevine; radar 484 *discovery*; telex, teleprinter, tape machine, ticker; teleconferencing; videoconferencing; intercom, walkie-talkie, bleeper, bleep; microphone 400 *megaphone*; headset 415 *hearing aid*; telephone, radio t., cellular t., cellphone, cordless telephone, car t., videophone; line, party l., hot l.; extension; telephone exchange, switchboard; telephonist, telephone receptionist, wireless operator, radio ham, telegrapher.

postal communications, postal services, Postal Union, GPO; post, first class p., second class p., mail, letters 588 *correspondence*; air letter, aerogramme, surface mail, sea m., air m.; parcel post, registered p., recorded delivery, express d., red star d.; postcode, postage stamp, first class s., second class s.; pillarbox, postbox, letterbox; post office, sorting o., mailbag; postmaster *or* -mistress, postman *or* -woman 529 *messenger*; pigeon post; diplomatic bag, dispatch box.

broadcasting, the media 528 *publicity*; broadcasting authority, BBC, Beeb, Auntie; IBA, ITA; independent television *or* radio; commercial t. *or* r., local t. *or* r., cable t. *or* r., satellite t., pirate r., Citizens' Band r., CB r.; transmitter, booster, communications satellite; aerial, antenna; radio waves, wave lengths, modulation, AM, FM 417 *radiation*; radio station, television channel, network; wireless, radio, cellular r., mobile r., steam r., cat's whisker, crystal set; radio-paging; portable, transistor, tranny *or* trannie, ghetto blaster, personal stereo; television, telly, TV, the box, gogglebox, small screen, talking head; colour television, black-and-white t., monochrome t.; closed-circuit t. 442 *camera*; videorecorder, videocassette, videocassette recorder, VCR, video, videotape, video nasty, video game 549 *recording instrument*; Teleprompter (tdmk), autocue; teletext, Ceefax (tdmk), Oracle (tdmk),

Prestel (tdmk) 524 *information*; Open University; radio listener 415 *listener*; viewer, televiewer, TV addict 441 *spectator*.

broadcast, outside b., telecast, transmission, relay, live r. 528 *publication*; recording, repeat, transcription 548 *record*; programme, request p., phone-in, telethon, quiz, chat show, music 837 *amusement*; news, newsflash, news roundup 529 *news*; time signal, pips; talk, feature, documentary 524 *report*; series, soap opera, situation comedy, sitcom, saga, docudrama, faction 594 *drama*; cartoon, film 445 *cinema*; commercial, commercial break 528 *advertisement*.

broadcaster, announcer, commentator, talking head, newsreader, newscaster 524 *informant*; presenter, frontman or -woman, anchorman or -woman, linkman or -woman, compere, question master; disc jockey, DJ, deejay; media personality 866 *person of repute*.

532 Affirmation – N. *affirmation,* saying, dictum 496 *maxim*; statement; submission, thesis 512 *supposition*; expressed opinion, conclusion 480 *judgment*; voice, suffrage, ballot 605 *vote*; expression, formulation; written statement, prepared text; one's position, one's stand *or* stance; declaration, profession; allegation 928 *accusation*; assertion, ipse dixit, say-so; averment; admission, confession, avowal 526 *disclosure*; corroboration, confirmation, assurance, one's word, warrant 466 *testimony*; insistence, vehemence, peremptoriness 571 *vigour*; stress, accent, emphasis, protesting too much; observation 579 *speech*; comment, criticism 480 *estimate*; assertiveness, self-assertion, pontification 473 *positiveness*.

oath, swearing, swearing on the Bible, statement on oath, deposition, affidavit 466 *testimony*; promissory oath, word of a gentleman, word of honour, pledge, promise, warrant, guarantee 764 *promise*.

Adj. *affirmative,* affirming, professing etc. vb.; not negative 473 *positive*; declaratory; pronouncing; unretractable 473 *undisputed*; committed, promised; earnest; solemn, sworn, formal.

assertive, telling; assured, dogmatic, pontificating, confident, self-assured 473 *positive*; pushing, trenchant, incisive, pointed, decisive; peremptory, categorical, absolute, brooking no denial, emphatic, insistent; vehement; making no bones, blunt, outspoken, strongly-worded, straight from the shoulder 573 *plain*.

Vb. *affirm,* state, express, formulate, set down; declare, pronounce, deliver, enunciate 528 *proclaim*, 579 *orate*; give expression to, voice 579 *speak*; remark, comment, observe, say; state with conviction, be bound, dare swear 485 *opine*; mean what one says, vow, protest; make a statement, make a verbal, assert; maintain, hold, contend 475 *argue*; make one's point 478 *demonstrate*; urge 512 *propound*; put one's case, put forward, submit; appeal, claim 761 *request*; allege, aver; bear witness 466 *testify*; certify, confirm, warrant, guarantee 466 *corroborate*; commit oneself, go as far as; pledge; hold out 759 *offer*; profess, avow; admit 526 *confess*; abide by, stick to one's guns 599 *stand firm*; speak up, speak out, put it bluntly, make no bones about 573 *speak plainly*; brook no denial, shout, shout down; lay down the law, pontificate 473 *dogmatize*; get on one's soapbox, hold the floor, have one's say, have the last word.

swear, take one's o.; attest, confirm by oath 466 *corroborate*; cross one's heart; kiss the book, swear on the Bible.

emphasize, stress, lay stress on, accent, accentuate; underline, italicize, dot the i's and cross the t's, put in bold letters; raise one's voice, speak up, shout, thunder, roar, bellow, fulminate 400 *be loud*; bang one's fist down, thump the table; urge; insist 737 *command*; drive home, impress on, din in, rub in; plug, dwell on, labour 106 *repeat*; highlight, enhance, point up.

533 Negation – N. *negation,* negative, nay, no; denial 760 *refusal;* disbelief 486 *unbelief;* disagreement 489 *dissent;* rebuttal, appeal 460 *rejoinder;* refutation 479 *confutation;* emphatic denial, contradiction, gainsaying; challenge 711 *defiance;* demurrer 468 *qualification;* protest 762 *deprecation;* repudiation, disclaimer, dissociation 607 *rejection;* abnegation, renunciation 621 *relinquishment;* abjuration 603 *recantation;* negativism, negative attitude, noncorroboration; contravention 738 *disobedience;* cancellation, invalidation, nullification, revocation.

Adj. *negative,* denying, negating, contradictory 14 *contrary;* contravening 738 *disobedient;* protesting; abnegating, renunciatory; denied, disowned, dissociated.

Vb. *negate,* negative; contravene 738 *disobey;* deny, gainsay, give the lie to, belie, contradict; eat one's hat if 470 *make impossible;* repudiate, disclaim, disown 607 *reject;* refuse to corroborate; hold no brief for 860 *be indifferent;* demur, object 468 *qualify;* disagree 489 *dissent;* dissociate oneself 704 *oppose;* impugn, question, call in q., express doubts, refute, rebut, disprove 479 *confute;* protest, appeal against 762 *deprecate;* challenge 711 *defy;* thwart 702 *obstruct;* say no, decline, shake one's head, disallow 760 *refuse;* not allow 757 *prohibit;* revoke, invalidate, nullify 752 *abrogate;* abnegate, renounce 621 *relinquish;* abjure, forswear, swear off 603 *recant;* go back on one's word, do a U-turn 603 *tergiversate.*

534 Teaching – N. *teaching,* pedagogy, pedagogics, tutoring; education, schooling; tutelage; direction, guidance, instruction, edification; dictation; chalk and talk; programmed instruction, direct method, immersion m., induction 475 *reasoning;* tuition, preparation, coaching, cramming; seminar, teach-in, workshop, tutorial; initiation, introduction; training, discipline, drill 682 *exercise;* inculcation, indoctrination, preaching; propagandism; conversion; conditioning, brainwashing; pamphleteering, propaganda, agitprop 528 *publicity.*

education, liberal e. 490 *culture;* classical education, scientific e., technical e.; moral training; technical training, technological training, vocational t.; coeducation, progressive education, Froebel system, Froebelism, kindergarten method, Montessori system; elementary education, grounding; nursery education, pre-school e., primary e., secondary e., further e., higher e., tertiary e., university e., adult e.; day release, block r.; sandwich course, refresher c.; advanced studies, postgraduate s.; remedial education; physical education, PE.

curriculum, course of study 536 *learning;* core curriculum, common core; ABC, the three R's 68 *beginning;* foundation course; set books, prescribed text; module, project, exercise, homework, prep; Open University course, correspondence c., in-service c.

lecture, talk, illustrated t., documentary 531 *broadcasting;* reading, discourse; sermon, homily 579 *oration;* lesson, parable.

Adj. *educational,* pedagogic, tutorial; scholastic, scholarly, academic; instructional, informational; audiovisual, instructive 524 *informative;* educative, didactic, doctrinal; edifying, moralizing, primary, secondary etc. n.; single-sex, coeducational, comprehensive, all-ability, all-in; set, streamed, creamed, mixed-ability; extramural, intramural; extracurricular; redbrick, Oxbridge, Ivy League; cultural.

Vb. *educate,* edify (**see** *teach*); rear, nurture, bring up, develop, form, mould, shape, lick into shape; send to school, tutor, teach, school; ground, coach, cram, prime 669 *prepare;* guide 689 *direct;* instruct 524 *inform;* enlighten; sharpen the wits, open the eyes; stuff with knowledge, cram with facts; impress on the memory, din in, inculcate, indoctrinate, imbue, impregnate, infuse,

instil, infix, implant, engraft, sow the seeds of.

teach, give lessons, take a class, lecture, deliver lectures; tutor, give tutorials, hold seminars; dictate, read out; preach, harangue, sermonize, pontificate; discourse, hold forth; moralize; expound 520 *interpret*; indoctrinate; pamphleteer, disseminate propaganda, condition, brainwash 178 *influence.*

train, coach 669 *prepare*; take on, take in hand, initiate, tame 369 *break in*; foster, cultivate; inure, keep one's nose to the grindstone; drill, exercise, practise, familiarize, accustom, groom one for 610 *habituate*; show one the ropes; make fit, qualify; house-train, teach manners, teach etiquette.

535 Misteaching – N. *misteaching,* misdirection; a case of the blind leading the blind; misinformation, disinformation 552 *misrepresentation*; propaganda, brainwashing 541 *falsehood*; perversion 246 *distortion*; false logic.

536 Learning – N. *learning,* lore, scholarship, attainments 490 *erudition*; tutelage, apprenticeship, initiation 669 *preparation*; basic training, basics, first steps, teething troubles 68 *beginning*; teachability 694 *aptitude*; self-improvement; culture, cultivation; self-c.

study, studying; application, studiousness; cramming, swotting, grind, mugging up, burning the midnight oil; studies, course of s., lessons, class, classwork, deskwork; homework, prep, preparation; revision, refresher course, further reading, further study; crash course; perusal, reading 455 *attention*; research, research work, field w., investigation 459 *enquiry.*

Adj. *studious,* academic; bookish, well-read, scholarly, erudite, learned, scholastic 490 *knowing*; diligent 678 *industrious*; receptive, teachable, self-taught, immersed in one's books 455 *attentive.*

Vb. *learn,* pursue one's education, go to school, attend college, take lessons, sit at the feet of, take a course; acquire knowledge, glean information, drink in, cram oneself with facts, know one's f. 490 *know*; apprentice oneself, learn one's trade, serve an apprenticeship, article oneself 669 *prepare oneself*; train, practise, exercise 610 *be wont*; learn the basics, get the feel of, get the hang of, master; get by heart, learn by rote 505 *memorize*; finish one's education, graduate.

study, apply oneself, burn the midnight oil; do, take up; research into 459 *enquire*; specialize, major in; swot, cram, mug, get up; revise, go over, run over, brush up, take a refresher course; read, peruse, pore over, wade through; thumb, browse, skip, flip through, turn the leaves, dip into; be studious, be bookish, always have one's nose in a book; bury oneself in one's books, become a polymath.

Adv. *studiously,* at one's books; under training, in articles.

537 Teacher – N. *teacher,* mentor 520 *guide*; minister 986 *pastor*; guru 500 *sage*; instructor, educator; tutor, crammer, coach; governor, governess, nursemaid 749 *keeper*; educationist, educationalist, pedagogue; pedant 500 *wiseacre*; dominie, beak, schoolmarm; master *or* mistress, school teacher, supply t., class t., form t.; house master *or* mistress; assistant teacher, deputy head, head teacher, head, headmaster *or* -mistress, principal, rector; pupil teacher, trainee t., proctor; dean, don, fellow; lecturer, demonstrator, exponent 520 *interpreter*; reader, professor, Regius p., professor emeritus; consultant 691 *adviser*; teaching staff, faculty, professoriate.

trainer, instructor; coach, choirmaster; dancing-master *or* mistress; animal trainer; breaker-in, lion-tamer 369 *breeder.*

preacher, lay p. 986 *pastor*; pulpiteer; hot gospeller, evangelist; apostle, missionary; prophet.

538 Learner – N. *learner,* disciple, follower; proselyte, convert, initiate; mature student; self-taught person; do-it-yourself fan; swot, mugger, bookworm 492 *scholar*; pupil, scholar, schoolboy *or* -girl, student; day pupil, boarder; sixthformer; schoolfellow, schoolmate, classmate, fellow student; gifted child, high flier; slow learner, late developer, underachiever, remedial pupil; school-leaver; old boy, old girl, former pupil.

beginner, novice, debutant; new boy *or* girl, tyro, greenhorn, tenderfoot, neophyte; rabbit, amateur 987 *lay person*; raw recruit, rookie; colt, cadet, trainee, apprentice, articled clerk; probationer, L-driver, examinee.

student, university s., college s.; undergraduate, undergrad, freshman, fresher, sophomore; former student, alumnus, alumna; foundationer, exhibitioner; scholarship-holder, bursary-h., Rhodes Scholar; honours student; graduand, graduate, post-g., fellow; mature student, research worker.

class, form, grade, remove; set, band, stream; age group; house; lower form, upper f.; workshop; seminar.

539 School – N. *academy,* institute, educational i.; college, lycée, gymnasium, senior secondary school; conservatoire, ballet school, art s., academy of dramatic art; finishing school; correspondence college; university, campus; Open University; redbrick university, Oxbridge, varsity; sixth-form college, FE c., college of further *or* higher education; polytechnic, poly; alma mater, old school, groves of academe.

school, nursery s., crèche, playgroup, kindergarten; infant school; private school, independent s., public s., stateaided s., state s.; preparatory school, prep s., crammer; primary school, middle s., secondary school, high s., secondary modern s., grammar s., senior secondary s.; comprehensive s., sixth form college, FE c.; boarding school, day s.; night s., evening classes; Sunday s.; special s.; approved school, List D s.; reform s.,

Borstal; remand home, detention centre; catchment area, parents' charter.

540 Veracity – N. *veracity,* truthfulness; truth, the whole truth and nothing but the truth, fidelity, verisimilitude, realism, exactitude 494 *accuracy*; candour; honour bright, scout's honour, no kidding; honesty, sincerity 929 *probity*; ingenuousness 699 *artlessness*; plain speaking, speaking straight from the shoulder 573 *plainness*; plain words, words of one syllable, home truth, honest truth 494 *truth*; clean breast 526 *disclosure.*

Adj. *veracious,* truthful 494 *true*; as good as one's word, reliable 929 *trustworthy*; factual, ungarbled, unembroidered, exact, just 494 *accurate*; full 570 *diffuse*; ingenuous 699 *artless*; bona fide; unaffected, unpretentious, open, above-board; frank, candid; blunt, forthright, outspoken, straightforward, straight from the shoulder, honest to God 573 *plain*; honest, sincere, on the level 929 *honourable.*

Vb. *be truthful,* tell the truth, tell the truth and shame the devil, tell the whole truth and nothing but the truth, stick to the facts, play it according to the letter 494 *be true*; mean it; weigh one's words 834 *be serious*; speak one's mind, keep nothing back 522 *show*; come clean, make a clean breast of it; appear in one's true colours 526 *disclose*; be prophetic 511 *predict.*

541 Falsehood – N. *falsehood,* falseness, spuriousness, falsity; treachery, bad faith 930 *perfidy*; untruthfulness, mendacity, deceitfulness; lie, terminological inexactitude; lying, pathological l., perjury 543 *untruth*; fabrication, fiction; faking, forgery, falsification 542 *deception*; invention 513 *imagination*; prevarication, equivocation, ambivalence, evasion, double-talk 518 *equivocalness*; economy of truth, whitewashing, coverup; overstatement 546 *exaggeration*; perversion 246 *distortion*; misrepresentation; humbug, bunkum, boloney,

hooey, rubbish, bull, flimflam 515 *empty talk*; cant, eyewash, hogwash (**see** *duplicity*), blarney.

duplicity, double life, double-dealing 930 *improbity*; guile 542 *trickery*; front, facade, mask, show, window-dressing, fanfaronade 875 *ostentation*; pretence, hollow p., bluff, act, fake, counterfeit, imposture 542 *sham*; hypocrisy; play-acting, dissimulation, dissembling, insincerity, tongue in cheek, cant; lip service, cupboard love; false piety; outward show, crocodile tears; Judas kiss; fraud, sting, diplomatic illness; cheating, sharp practice; collusion, nod and a wink; put-up job, frame-up; quackery, charlatanism 850 *pretension*.

Adj. *false,* not true; imagined, made-up; untruthful, lying, mendacious 543 *untrue*; perfidious, treacherous, perjured; disingenuous, dishonest; falsified, garbled; touched up; overdone; imitation, simulated, counterfeit, fake, phoney, sham, pseudo, quack, bogus 542 *spurious*; cheating, deceptive, deceitful, fraudulent; fiddled, fixed, engineered, rigged, packed; trumped up.

hypocritical, insincere, diplomatic; put on, imitated, pretended, simulated, feigned; make-believe, play-acting; two-faced, shifty, sly, treacherous, double-dealing, designing, Machiavellian 930 *perfidious*; sanctimonious; plausible, smooth, smooth-tongued, oily; creepy, goody-goody; mealy-mouthed, euphemistic 850 *affected*.

Vb. *be false,* - perjured, - forsworn etc. adj.; perjure oneself, bear false witness, swear that black is white; lie, tell lies, lie in one's teeth *or* one's throat; swing the lead, malinger; stretch the truth, tell a tall story 546 *exaggerate*; tell a white lie, fib, tell a fib, tell a whopper; invent, make believe, make up, romance 513 *imagine*; put a false construction on 521 *misinterpret*; garble, doctor, tamper with, falsify 246 *distort*; misquote, misinform, cry wolf 535 *misteach*; play false; run with the hare and hunt with the hounds, have a foot in both camps; break faith, betray 603 *tergiversate*.

dissemble, dissimulate, disguise 525 *conceal*; simulate, counterfeit 20 *imitate*; put on, assume, affect, dress up, play-act, play a part, go through the motions, make a show of 594 *act*; feign, pass off for, sham, pretend, be under false pretences, sail under false colours; malinger 542 *deceive*; be less than honest, say one thing and mean another; keep something back, fail to declare; fudge the issue, prevaricate, beat about the bush, dodge.

fake, fudge, fabricate, forge, plagiarize, counterfeit 20 *imitate*; get up, trump up, frame; manipulate, fiddle, fix, wangle, rig, pack (a jury); spin, weave, cook, cook up, concoct, hatch, invent 623 *plot*; touch-up, embroider; gloss over.

542 Deception – **N.** *deception,* kidding, kidology, tongue in cheek; self-deception, wishful thinking 487 *credulity*; fallacy 477 *sophistry*; illusion, delusion, hallucination; deceptiveness; false appearance, mockery, mirage, will-o'-the-wisp 440 *visual fallacy*; false show, meretriciousness, paint (**see** *sham*); feet of clay; bubble 4 *insubstantiality*; falseness, deceit, quackery, imposture, lie, terminological inexactitude, pious fraud 541 *falsehood*; deceitfulness, guile, craft, artfulness 698 *cunning*; hypocrisy, insincerity 541 *duplicity*; treachery, betrayal 930 *perfidy*; machination, hanky-panky, jiggery-pokery, monkey business, wheeler-dealing, collusion 623 *plot*; fraudulence, cozenage, cheating, cheat, diddling; cheat 545 *deceiver*.

trickery, dupery, swindling, skulduggery, shenanigan; sharp practice, wheeler-dealing, chicanery, pettifoggery; swindle, ramp, racket, wangle, fix, fiddle, diddle, swizzle, swiz, sell, fraud, cheat; cardsharping; trick, dirty t., bag of tricks, tricks of the trade, confidence trick, con trick, fast one, wiles, ruse, shift, dodge, artful d., blind, feint 698 *stratagem*; wrinkle 623 *contrivance*; bait, gimmick, diversion, red herring, smoke screen, hoax, bluff, spoof, leg-

pull; game, sport, joke, practical j., rag 839 *witticism*; April fooling.

sleight, sleight of hand, legerdemain, conjuring, hocus-pocus, illusion, ventriloquism; juggling, three-card trick; magic 983 *sorcery*.

trap, deathtrap 527 *ambush*; catch 530 *enigma*; plant, frame-up; snare, gin, man trap; net, meshes, web; blind, decoy, decoy duck, bait, lure, sprat to catch a mackerel; baited trap, mouse t., flypaper, birdlime; booby trap, mine, tripwire, pit 663 *pitfall*; car bomb, letter b., parcel b.; trapdoor, sliding panel, false bottom 530 *secret*; poisoned apple, Trojan horse, Greek gift.

sham, false front, veneer 541 *duplicity*; lip service, tokenism; make-believe, pretence 850 *affectation*; whitewash, gloss; whited sepulchre, man of straw, paper tiger; wolf in sheep's clothing 545 *impostor*; dummy, scarecrow, tattie bogle; imitation, simulacrum, facsimile 22 *copy*; mockery; counterfeit, forgery, fake; masquerade, mummery, mask, veil, cloak, disguise, borrowed plumes, false colours 525 *concealment*; imitation ware, tinsel, paste.

Adj. *spurious,* false, faked, fake; sham, counterfeit 541 *false*; trumped-up, pretended; make-believe, mock, ersatz, bogus, phoney; pseudo-, so-called; cosmetic; artificial, simulated, man-made, plastic, paste, cultured, imitation; shoddy, rubbishy 641 *useless*; tinsel, meretricious, flash, gaudy, pasteboard 330 *brittle*; whitewashed, varnished.

Vb. *deceive,* delude; beguile, sugar the pill, gild the p., give a false impression, belie; let down 509 *disappoint*; pull the wool over one's eyes, blindfold 439 *blind*; kid, bluff, bamboozle, hoodwink, hoax; throw dust in the eyes, create a smoke screen, lead up the garden path 495 *mislead*; spoof, mystify 535 *misteach*; play false, leave in the lurch, betray, two-time, double-cross 930 *be dishonest*; steal a march on 135 *be early*; pull a fast one, take one for a ride, outsmart 698 *be cunning*; trick, dupe; cheat, cozen, con, swindle, sell, rook, do;

diddle, do out of, bilk, fleece, rip off, shortchange, obtain money by false pretences 788 *defraud*; juggle, conjure, palm off, foist o.; fob, fob off with; live on one's wits, try it on; tinker with, fiddle, wangle, fix; load the dice, mark the cards; counterfeit 541 *fake*.

fool, make a fool of, make an ass of, make a wally of, make one look silly; mock, make fun of 851 *ridicule*; play tricks on, play practical jokes on, pull one's leg, have one on, make an April fool of, play a joke on 497 *be absurd*; throw over, jilt; take in, have, have on, put on, dupe, bull, victimize, gull, outwit, outsmart; trick, trap, catch out, take advantage of, manipulate, twist round one's little finger; kid, spoof, bamboozle, string along, lead one on (see *deceive*); cajole, wheedle, get round; play fast and loose with, leave in the lurch, leave one holding the baby 509 *disappoint*; send on a fool's errand, send on a wild-goose chase 495 *mislead*; make one an apple-pie bed.

ensnare, snare, trap, set a trap for, lay a trap for; entangle, net; trip, trip up, catch, catch out, hook; bait, bait the trap, bait the hook, lure, decoy, lead astray, entice, inveigle 612 *tempt*; lie in wait, waylay 527 *ambush*; nab, nick, kidnap, shanghai, hijack, take hostage 788 *steal*.

543 Untruth – N. *untruth,* more than the truth, lie, downright l., barefaced l.; white lie, fib, diplomatic excuse, whopper; false statement, terminological inexactitude; breach of promise 930 *perfidy*; perjury; pack of lies, tissue of l., trumped-up story, frame-up 466 *evidence*; fabrication, invention 513 *ideality (*see *fable*)*; false excuse; misinformation, disinformation; misrepresentation, perversion 246 *distortion*; gloss, varnish, falsification 521 *misinterpretation*; disingenuousness, economy of truth.

fable, invention, fiction, story, tale 590 *narrative*; tall story, shaggy dog story, fisherman's yarn, traveller's tale 546 *exaggeration*; fairy tale, nursery t., romance, tale, yarn, story, cock-and-bull

s., all my eye and Betty Martin 497 *absurdity*; claptrap, gossip, guff, bull; old wives' tales; myth; moonshine, farce, mare's nest, sell, swiz, hoax, humbug, flummery 515 *empty talk*.

Adj. *untrue,* lying, mendacious 541 *false*; trumped-up, framed, cooked, fixed, hatched, concocted; mythological, fabulous; unfounded, ungrounded, empty; fictitious, imagined, hallucinatory, make-believe; artificial, synthetic, simulated; phoney, bogus, so-called 542 *spurious*; perjured, forsworn 930 *perfidious*.

Vb. *be untrue,* not hold water, not stand up in court, be wide of the mark; not ring true 472 *be unlikely*; lie, be a liar 541 *be false*; spin a yarn, tell a tall story, draw the long bow 546 *exaggerate*; make-believe 513 *imagine*; be phoney, pretend, sham, counterfeit, forge, falsify 541 *dissemble*.

544 Dupe – N. *dupe,* fool, April f. 851 *laughingstock*; Simple Simon; easy prey, sitting duck, soft touch, soft mark, pushover, cinch; fair game, victim, schlemiel, fall guy, patsy, stooge, mug, sap, sucker, schmuck, schnook, dude, greenhorn, innocent 538 *beginner*; puppet, cat's-paw, pawn 628 *instrument*; admass.

Vb. *be duped,* be had, be done, be taken in; be sold a pup, be sold a pig in a poke, be diddled; fall for, walk into the trap, rise, nibble, swallow the bait, swallow hook line and sinker; get taken for a ride; carry the can; catch a Tartar 508 *not expect*.

545 Deceiver – N. *deceiver,* leg-puller; practical joker; dissembler; whited sepulchre, false friend, fair-weather f.; rat, two-timer, double-crosser, double agent; traitor, Judas 938 *knave*; seducer 952 *libertine*; serpent, snake in the grass, joker in the pack 663 *troublemaker*; plotter, Guy Fawkes, intriguer, conspirator 623 *planner*; counterfeiter, forger.

liar, pathological l.; fibber, storyteller; romancer; yarn-spinner; fabricator.

impostor, shammer, malingerer, adventurer, carpetbagger; usurper; cuckoo in the nest 59 *intruder*; wolf in sheep's clothing; pretender, charlatan, quack, mountebank; fake, fraud, con man, humbug; pseud, pseudo, phoney; masquerader.

trickster, hoaxer, spoofer, hoodwinker, bamboozler; cheat, cozener; sharper, cardsharp; shyster; fraudster, swindler, bilker, diddler, shark 789 *defrauder*; twister, rogue 938 *knave*; confidence trickster, con man; decoy, decoyduck, agent provocateur; fiddler, manipulator, rigger, fixer.

546 Exaggeration – N. *exaggeration,* overemphasis, inflation, magnification, enlargement 197 *expansion*; straining; extravagance, exaggerated lengths, gilding the lily, extremes, immoderation, extremism; overkill; excess, excessiveness, violence 943 *intemperance*; inordinacy, exorbitance, overdoing it, piling it on; overacting, histrionics 875 *ostentation*; sensationalism, ballyhoo, hype 528 *publicity*; overstatement, hyperbole 519 *trope*; embroidery 38 *addition*; disproportion 246 *distortion*; caricature, burlesque 851 *satire*; exacerbation 832 *aggravation*; big talk, 877 *boasting*; grandiloquence 574 *grandiloquence*; overpraise, chauvinism 481 *prejudice*; tall story 543 *fable*; flight of fancy, stretch of the imagination 513 *imagination*; fuss, storm in a teacup, much ado about nothing 318 *commotion*.

Vb. *exaggerate,* maximize, magnify, expand, inflate, blow up, blow up out of all proportion 197 *enlarge*; overamplify, overelaborate; add to, pile up, pile it on 38 *add*; touch up, enhance, heighten, add a flourish, touch up, embroider, varnish 844 *decorate*; lay it on thick *or* with a trowel, depict in glowing terms, overvalue; overdo, overcolour; overemphasize; overpraise, puff, hype up, oversell; make too much of 925 *flatter*; stretch, strain, labour 246 *distort*; caricature 851 *satirize*; go to all lengths, gild the lily, not know when to stop, protest too much;

overact, dramatize, out-Herod Herod; talk big, bull 877 *boast*; run riot, go to extremes; draw the long bow, overshoot the mark, overstep the m., go too far 306 *overstep*; spin a yarn, tell a tall tale; make mountains out of molehills, make a storm in a tea cup; exacerbate 832 *aggravate*; overcompensate, lean over backwards.

Section three: Means of communicating ideas

547 Indication – N. *indication,* signification, meaning 514 *connotation*; notification 524 *information*; symbolization, symbolism 551 *representation*; symbol; rune, hieroglyph 530 *enigma*; cross; pentacle 983 *talisman*; image, type, figure; token, emblem, figurehead (see *badge*); symptom, syndrome, sign 466 *evidence*; tell-tale sign, blush 526 *disclosure*; nudge, wink, kick 524 *hint* (see *gesture*); kite-flying, straw in the wind, sign of the times 511 *omen*; clue, scent, whiff, trace 484 *discovery*; noise, footfall 398 *sound*; semiology, semiotics; pointer, finger, forefinger, index finger (see *indicator*); guide, index, thumb i. 87 *directory*; key 520 *interpretation*; marker, mark; blaze; nick, scratch 260 *notch*; stamp, print, impression; stigma, stigmata; tattoo mark; scar 845 *blemish*; wrinkle, line, score, stroke; note, catchword (see *punctuation*); legend, caption 590 *description*; inscription, epitaph; motto, cipher, monogram.

identification, naming 561 *nomenclature*, 77 *classification*; brand, earmark, trademark, imprint (see *label*); name and address; autograph, signature, hand 586 *script*; fingerprint, footprint, spoor, track, trail, scent 548 *trace*; dental record; genetic fingerprinting, DNA f.; password, open sesame, watchword, shibboleth; markings, colouring; characteristic, trait, lineament, outline, form, shape 445 *feature*; personal characteristic, mannerism, idiolect; mole, scar,

birthmark, strawberry mark 845 *blemish*.

gesture, gesticulation, sign language; deaf-and-dumb language; sign 524 *hint*; pantomime, dumb show, charade, mime; body language, kinesics; demeanour, tone of one's voice 445 *mien*; motion, move; tic, twitch 318 *spasm*; shrug, shrug of the shoulders; raising of the eyebrows, nod, beck, wink, flicker of the eyelash, batting of the eyelids *or* eyelashes, twinkle, glance, ogle, leer, grimace 438 *look*; smile, laugh 835 *laughter*; touch, kick, kick under the table, nudge, jog, dig in the ribs 279 *knock*; hug; squeeze of the hand, handshake, grip; push, shove 279 *impulse*; pointing, signal, waving, wave, hand-signal, wave of the hand; raising one's hand; drumming one's fingers, tapping one's foot, stamp of the foot 822 *excitable state*; clenching one's teeth, gritting one's t. 599 *resolution*; gnashing *or* grinding one's teeth; wringing one's hands, tearing one's hair 836 *lamentation*; clenched fist 711 *defiance*; V-sign, flag-waving 876 *celebration*; clapping, cheer 923 *applause*; hissing, hooting, booing, catcall, Bronx cheer, raspberry 924 *disapprobation*; two-finger gesture, Harvey Smith salute; stuck-out tongue 878 *sauciness*; frown, scowl 893 *sullenness*; pout, moue, pursing of the lips 829 *discontent*.

signal 529 *message*; sign, symptom, syndrome 522 *manifestation*; flash, rocket; railway signal, smoke s., heliograph, semaphore, tick-tack; telegraph, morse 531 *telecommunication*; flashlamp, signal lamp 420 *lamp*; warning light, beacon 379 *fire*; red flag, warning light, red l., Belisha beacon, green light, all clear 420 *signal light*; alarum, alarm, fire a., burglar a., warning signal, distress s., SOS 665 *danger signal*; whistle, police w.; siren, hooter; bleeper, bleep; buzzer, knocker, doorknocker 414 *gong*; bell, doorbell, alarm bell; church bells, angelus, carillon; time signal, pip, dinner gong, dinner bell 117 *chronometry*; passing bell, knell, muffled drum 364 *obsequies*.

indicator, index, pointer, arrow, needle; arm, finger, index-f.; hand, hour h., minute h. 117 *timekeeper*; Plimsoll line 465 *gauge*; traffic indicator, trafficator; direction finder, radar; cursor; white line, cat's-eyes (tdmk) 305 *traffic control*; weathercock, wind sock 340 *weather.*

signpost, fingerpost; milestone, waymark; lighthouse, buoy 662 *safeguard*; compass 269 *sailing aid*; lodestar, guiding star, Southern Cross 321 *star*; landmark; cairn 253 *earthwork*; benchmark.

call, hue-and-cry 528 *publication*; shout, hail; call to prayer, church bell 981 *worship*; summons 737 *command*; call for help, cry of help, distress call, Mayday; bugle, trumpet; reveille, rally; last post; peal, flourish; drum, drumbeat, drum-roll, tattoo 403 *roll*; call to arms, fiery cross; battle cry, war c., rallying c.

badge, token, emblem, symbol, sign, totem (see *indication*); insignia (see *heraldry*); markings; throne, sceptre, orb, crown 743 *regalia*; badge of office, robes of o., Black Rod, mace 743 *badge of rule*; pips, stripes, epaulette 743 *badge of rank*; medal, cross, Victoria Cross, George C., Iron C., Croix de Guerre; order, star, garter, sash, ribbon 729 *decoration*; badge of merit, laurels, wreath 729 *trophy*; colours, blue, half-b., cap; favour, rosette; black armband, widow's weeds 228 *clothing.*

heraldry, armory, blazonry; heraldic register, Roll of Arms; armorial bearings, coat of arms, blazon; achievement, funereal a., hatchment; shield, escutcheon; crest, torse, wreath, helmet, crown, coronet, mantling, lambrequin; supporters, motto; field, quarter, dexter, sinister, chief, base; charge, device, bearing; ordinary, fess, bar, label, pale, bend, bend sinister, chevron, pile, saltire, cross; canton; inescutcheon, bordure, lozenge, fusil, gyron, flanches; marshalling, quartering, impaling, dimidiation; differencing; fess point, honour p., nombril p.; animal charge, lion, lion rampant, lion couchant, unicorn, griffin, cockatrice, eagle, falcon, martlet; floral charge, Tudor rose, cinquefoil, trefoil, planta genista; badge, rebus, antelope, bear and ragged staff, portcullis; national emblem, rose, thistle, leek, daffodil, shamrock, lilies, fleur-de-lis; device, national d., lion and unicorn, spread eagle, bear, hammer and sickle, triskelion; swastika, fylfot; skull and crossbones; heraldic tincture, colour, gules, azure, vert, sable, purpure, tenné, murrey; metal, or, argent; fur, ermine, ermines, erminois, pean, vair, potent; heraldic personnel, College of Arms, Earl Marshal, King of Arms, Lord Lyon K. of A.; herald, herald extraordinary, pursuivant, Bluemantle, Rouge Croix, Rouge Dragon, Portcullis.

flag, ensign, white e., blue e.; red ensign, Red Duster; jack, pilot j., merchant j.; flag of convenience; colours, ship's c., regimental c., King's Colour, Queen's C.; guidon, standard, vexillum, labarum, banner, gonfalon; bannerette, bannerol, banderole, oriflamme; pennon, streamer, pennant, swallowtail, triple tail; pendant, broad p., burgee; bunting; Blue Peter, yellow flag; white flag 721 *submission*; eagle, Roman e.; tricolour; Union Jack; Stars and Stripes, Old Glory, star-spangled banner; Red Flag; black flag, pirate f., Jolly Roger, skull and crossbones; parts of a flag, hoist, fly, canton; flagpole, flagstaff.

label, tattoo, caste mark (see *identification*); ticket, bus t., raffle t., cloakroom t., bill, docket, chit, counterfoil, stub, duplicate; counter, chip; mark, countermark; luggage label, sticky l., sticker; tie-on label, tab, tag; name badge, name tape, nameplate, signboard; numberplate, cherished n.; sign, inn s., barber's pole, three balls 522 *exhibit*; brass plate, trademark, logotype, logo, hallmark; earmark, brand; dunce's cap; seal, signet, stamp, impression; letterhead, masthead, caption, heading, title, headline, superscription, rubric; imprint, colophon, watermark; bookplate, name, name and address, personal details; card, visiting c.; birth certificate, marriage c., death c., identification papers,

identity card; passport, pass 756 *permit*; endorsement 466 *credential*; signature, autograph, cipher, mark, cross, initials, monogram; fingerprint, thumbprint, footprint 548 *trace*; genetic fingerprint.

punctuation, punctuation mark, point, stop, full s., period; comma, colon, semicolon; inverted commas, quotation marks, quotes, apostrophe; exclamation mark, question mark, query; parentheses, brackets, square b., crotchet, crook, brace; hyphen, hyphenation; en rule, em r., dash, swung d., dot, caret, omission mark, ellipsis, blank; asterisk; dagger, grave accent, acute a., circumflex a.; diaeresis, cedilla, tilde; macron, breve, umlaut; paragraph; plus sign, minus s., multiplication s., division s., equals s., decimal point; italics 587 *print-type.*

Adj. *heraldic,* emblematic; crested, armorial, blazoned, emblazoned etc. vb.; paly, barry; dexter, sinister; gules, azure, vert, purpure, sable, tenné, murrey, or, argent, ermine; fleury, semé, pommé; rampant, gardant, regardant, couchant, statant, sejant, passant.

Vb. *indicate,* point 281 *point to*; point out, exhibit 522 *show*; blazon; delineate, demarcate, mark out, blaze, signpost; register 548 *record*; name, give a name to, identify, classify 80 *specify*; index, supply references, refer; point the way, show the w., guide 689 *direct*; signify, denote, connote, suggest, imply, involve, spell, bespeak, argue 514 *mean*; symbolize, typify, betoken, stand for, be the sign of 551 *represent*; declare 532 *affirm*; highlight 532 *emphasize*; show signs of, bear the stamp of, give evidence of, witness to 466 *evidence*; smack of, smell of, hint at 524 *hint*; reveal 526 *disclose*; herald, prefigure, forebode, presage 511 *predict.*

mark, mark off, mark out, demarcate, delineate, delimit 236 *limit*; label, ticket, docket, tag, tab; earmark, designate; annotate, score, underline; number, letter, page, paginate, index; tick, tick off; nick, scribe 260 *notch*; chalk, chalk up; scratch, scribble, cover 586 *write*; blot, stain, blacken 649 *make unclean*; scar,

disfigure 842 *make ugly*; punctuate, dot, dash, cross, cross out, asterisk; put one's mark on, leave fingerprints *or* footprints; blaze, brand, earmark, burn in; tattoo 263 *pierce*; stamp, seal, punch, impress, emboss; imprint, overprint 587 *print*; etch 555 *engrave*; emblazon, blazon.

sign, autograph, write one's signature, inscribe; subscribe, undersign; initial; put one's cross.

gesticulate, mime, mimic, suit the action to the word 20 *imitate*; wave one's hands, talk with one's h.; wave 318 *agitate*; wave to, hold out one's hand 884 *greet*; stamp 923 *applaud*; wave one's arms, gesture, motion, sign; point, beckon, raise one's hand, bat one's eyelashes 455 *attract notice*; nod, wink, shrug; jog, nudge, kick, poke, prod, dig in the ribs, clap on the back; look, look volumes, look daggers, glance, leer, ogle 438 *gaze*; twinkle, smile 835 *laugh*; raise one's eyebrows, wag one's finger, shake one's head, purse one's lips 924 *disapprove*; wring one's hands, tear one's hair 836 *lament*; grit one's teeth, clench one's t. 599 *be resolute*; gnash one's teeth 891 *be angry*; snap, bite; grimace, pout, scowl, frown 829 *be discontented*; shrug one's shoulders, curl one's lip 922 *despise*; shuffle, pat, stroke 889 *caress.*

signal, send a s., send smoke s., speak 524 *communicate*; tap out a message, semaphore, heliograph; flag down, thumb; wave on; unfurl the flag, fly the f., dip the f., salute; alert, sound the alarm, cry help, send an SOS, dial 999 665 *raise the alarm*; beat the drum, sound the trumpets; fire a warning shot 664 *warn.*

548 Record – N. *record,* recording, documentation; historical record, memoir, chronicle, annals, history 590 *narrative*; case history, case notes, curriculum vitae 590 *biography*; photograph, portrait, sketch 551 *representation*; file, dossier, rogues' gallery; public record, gazette, official journal, Hansard; official publication, blue book, White Paper; minutes, transactions; notes, annotations,

marginalia, jottings, cuttings, press c.; memorabilia, memorandum, memo 505 *reminder*; reports, annual report, returns, tax r., statements 524 *report*; tally, scoresheet, scoreboard; document; voucher, certificate, diploma, charter 466 *credential*; birth certificate, death c., marriage c., marriage lines 767 *title deed*; copy, spare c., carbon c., Xerox (tdmk) 22 *duplicate*; records, files, archives, papers, correspondence; record, book, roll, register, registry; notebook, memo pad, logbook, log, diary, journal, commonplace book, scrapbook, album; ledger, cashbook, chequebook; catalogue, index, waiting list 87 *list*; card, index c., microfilm, microfiche 196 *miniature*; tape, computer t. 86 *data processing*; magnetic tape, pressing 414 *gramophone*; inscription, legend, caption, heading 547 *indication*; graffiti 586 *script*.

monument, memorial, war m. 505 *reminder*; mausoleum 364 *tomb*; statue, bust 551 *image*; brass, tablet, inscription 364 *obsequies*; pillar, memorial arch, obelisk, monolith; national monument, ancient m., cromlech, dolmen, menhir, megalith 125 *antiquity*; cairn, barrow 253 *earthwork*.

trace, vestige, relic, remains 41 *leavings*; track, tracks, footstep, footprint, footmark, hoofmark, clawmark, tread; spoor; scent, smell; wake, wash, trail, vapour t.; furrow, swathe, path; scuffmark, skidmark, tyremark, fingermark 547 *indication*; fingerprint, dabs 466 *evidence*; mark, tidemark, stain, scar, scratch, weal 845 *blemish*.

Vb. *record,* tape-record, telerecord, tape, videotape, video; store in a database, input, film 551 *photograph*; paint 551 *represent*; document, put *or* place on record; docket, file, index, catalogue; inscribe, carve; take down, note down, set down in black and white, commit to writing 586 *write*; capture on film, preserve for posterity; log, write down, jot d.; note, make a note of; take minutes of, minute; chronicle 590 *describe*.

register, mark up, chalk up, cross off, notch up, score; tabulate, enrol 87 *list*; enter 808 *account*; reserve, put on the waiting l.; inscribe, log.

549 Recorder – N. *recorder,* registrar, record-keeper, archivist; Master of the Rolls; amanuensis, stenographer, scribe; secretary; writer, clerk, filing c., bookkeeper 808 *accountant*; photographer, cameraman 551 *photography*; Record Office; Recording Angel.

chronicler, annalist, diarist, historian, historiographer, biographer, autobiographer; archaeologist 125 *antiquarian*; reporter, journalist.

recording instrument, recorder, tape r., videotape r., VTR, videocassette recorder, VCR; record, disc, compact d., laser d. 414 *gramophone*; dictaphone, teleprinter, tape machine 531 *telecommunication*; cash register, till, checkout; turnstile; speedometer, tachograph 465 *gauge*; flight recorder, black box; timerecorder, stopwatch 117 *timekeeper*; hygrometer; anemometer; camera, photocopier, Xerox (tdmk); pen, pencil, Biro (tdmk) 586 *stationery*.

550 Obliteration – N. *obliteration,* wiping out etc. vb.; erasure, effacement; defacement; deletion; crossing out, cancellation; annulment, 752 *abrogation*; oblivion 506 *amnesty*; blot 649 *dirt*; clean sweep 149 *revolution*; rubber, eraser.

Vb. *obliterate,* remove the traces, cover, cover up 525 *conceal*; deface; efface, eliminate, erase, scratch out, rub o.; expunge, wipe out; blot out; wipe off, wash o.; brush o.; cancel, delete; cross out, score o., censor, blue-pencil; raze 165 *demolish*; cover 364 *inter*; submerge 311 *lower*; drown 399 *silence*.

551 Representation – N. *representation,* personification, incarnation, embodiment, bodying forth; typifying, typification, symbolization 547 *indication*; diagram, hieroglyphics, runes 586 *writing*;

presentation; impersonation; enactment, performance; role-playing, psychodrama 658 *therapy*; mimicry, charade, mime, dumb show 20 *imitation*; depiction, characterization 590 *description*; delineation, drawing, illustration, artwork, graphics 553 *painting*; creation, work of art 164 *product*; impression, likeness, identikit, Photofit (tdmk) 18 *similarity*; exact likeness, double, spitting image, look-alike, facsimile 22 *duplicate*; tracing 233 *outline*; reflection (see *image*); portrayal; striking likeness, realism 553 *picture*; bad likeness 552 *misrepresentation*; reproduction, copy, Xerox (tdmk), lithograph; etching 555 *engraving*; design, blueprint, draft, cartoon, sketch, outline 623 *plan*.

image, spitting i. 22 *duplicate*; mental image, after-image 451 *idea*; reflected image, hologram, silhouette 417 *reflection*; pixel; visual aid 445 *spectacle*; idol, graven image 982 *idolatry*; icon; cherub; statue, colossus; statuette, bust, torso, head 554 *sculpture*; effigy, figure, figurine, figurehead; gargoyle; wax figure, waxwork; dummy, tailor's d., manikin; model; doll, china d., rag d., Cabbage Patch (tdmk) d., Cindy (tdmk) d., golliwog, teddy bear; marionette, puppet, finger p., glove p.; snowman, gingerbread man; scarecrow, tattie bogle, guy, Guy Fawkes; robot, Dalek, automaton; type, symbol.

art, architecture 243 *formation*; fine arts; graphic art 553 *painting*; plastic art 554 *sculpture*; classical art, Byzantine a., Renaissance a., Baroque, Rococo; art nouveau, art deco, modern art, abstract art; Surrealism, Expressionism 553 *school of painting*; op art, pop a.; kitsch, camp, high c. 847 *bad taste*; aestheticism, functionalism, De Stijl, Bauhaus; functional art, commercial a.; useful arts; decorative a. 844 *ornamental art*; the minor arts, illumination, calligraphy, weaving, tapestry, collage, embroidery, pottery.

photography, radiography, scanning; time-lapse photography, aerial p., telephotography, microphotography,

macrophotography; cinematography 445 *cinema*; photograph, photo, picture, snapshot, snap; plate, film; exposure, negative, print, sepia p., colour p., slide, transparency; frame, still; reel, spool, cassette; filmstrip, microfilm, microfiche, movie, home m. 445 *film*; hologram; radiograph, X-ray, scan 417 *radiation*; photocopy, Xerox (tdmk) 22 *copy*; shot, close-up, mug shot, pan, zoom, fade; lens 442 *camera*; cameraman, photographer, lensman, paparazzo; radiographer.

map, chart, plan, town p., outline 86 *statistics*; sketch map, relief m., survey m., Ordnance S. m., road m., star m.; Admiralty chart; ground plan, elevation; projection, Mercator's p.; atlas; globe; map-making, cartography, computerized c.

Vb. *represent*, stand for, denote, symbolize 514 *mean*; typify, embody, body forth, personify; act the part of, assume the role of, role-play; impersonate, pose as 542 *deceive*; pose, model, sit for 23 *be an example*; enact 594 *dramatize*; suggest; reflect, hold the mirror up to nature; mimic, mime, copy 20 *imitate*; depict, characterize 590 *describe*; delineate, draw, picture, portray; illustrate 553 *paint*; catch a likeness, capture; carve, cast 554 *sculpt*; cut 555 *engrave*; mould, shape 243 *form*; fashion upon; design, draft, sketch out, rough o.; block o. 623 *plan*; make a diagram, construct a figure, describe a circle 233 *outline*; sketch; map, chart, survey, plot.

photograph, photo, take a p. *or* a picture; snap; take, shoot, film; X-ray, scan; expose, develop, process, print, enlarge, blow up, reduce.

552 Misrepresentation – N. *misrepresentation*, not a true picture 19 *dissimilarity*; false light 541 *falsehood*; bad likeness, poor l. 914 *injustice*; travesty, parody 546 *exaggeration*; caricature; flattering portrait 925 *flattery*; nonrepresentational art 551 *art*; daub, botch; distorted image 246 *distortion*; misinformation, disinformation.

Vb. *misrepresent,* give a twist *or* turn, tone down 925 *flatter;* overdramatize 546 *exaggerate;* gild the lily, overembellish, caricature; parody, daub, botch, lie 541 *be false.*

553 Painting – N. *painting,* graphic art, colouring, illumination; daubing, finger painting; washing, colourwashing, tinting, touching up; ·depicting, drawing, sketching 551 *representation;* artistry, composition, design, technique, draughtsmanship, brushwork; line, perspective, golden section; treatment, tone, values, atmosphere, ambience; highlight, local colour, shading, contrast; monotone, monochrome, polychrome 425 *colour;* black and white, chiaroscuro, grisaille.

art style, style of painting, grand style, grand manner 243 *form;* intimate style, genre painting (**see** *art subject*); pasticcio, pastiche; trompe l'oeil; iconography, portrait-painting, portraiture; scenography, scene painting, sign p., poster p., miniature p.; oil painting, watercolour, tempera, gouache; fresco painting, mural p., encaustic p., impasto, secco.

school of painting, the Primitives, Byzantine school, Renaissance s., Sienese s., Florentine s., Venetian s., Dutch s., Flemish s., French s., Spanish s.; Mannerism, Baroque, Rococo, Pre-Raphaelitism, Neo-Classicism, Realism, Romanticism, Impressionism, Post-Impressionism, Neo-I., Pointillism, Symbolism, Fauvism, Dada, Cubism, Expressionism, Die Brücke, Der Blaue Reiter, Vorticism, Futurism, Surrealism, Abstract Expressionism, Tachism, action painting; minimal art, Minimalism, Conceptualism;

art subject, modernism 551 *art;* landscape, seascape, skyscape, cloudscape; scene, prospect, diorama, panorama 438 *view;* interior, conversation piece, still life, pastoral, nocturne, nude.

picture, pictorial equivalent 551 *representation;* tableau, mosaic, tapestry; collage, montage, photomontage; frottage; brass rubbing; painting, pastiche; icon,

triptych, diptych, panel; fresco, mural, wall painting, poster; canvas, daub; drawing, line d.; sketch, outline, cartoon; oil painting, oleograph, gouache, watercolour, aquarelle, pastel, wash drawing, pen-and-ink d., pencil d., charcoal d.; design, pattern, doodle; cartoon, chad, caricature, silhouette; miniature, vignette, thumbnail sketch, illuminated initial; old master, masterpiece; study, portrait, full-length p., half-l. p., kit-cat, head, profile, full-face portrait; studio portrait, snap, Polaroid (tdmk), pin-up 551 *photography;* rotogravure, photogravure, chromolithograph, reproduction, photographic r., halftone; aquatint, woodcut 555 *engraving;* print, plate; illustration, fashion plate, picture postcard, cigarette card, tea c., stamp, transfer, scrap, sticker; picture book, illustrated b., scrapbook, photograph album, illustrated work 589 *book.*

Adj. *painted,* graphic, pictorial, scenic, picturesque, decorative 844 *ornamental;* pastel, in paint, in oils, in watercolours, in tempera; linear, black-and-white, chiaroscuro, shaded, stippled, sfumato; grisaille 429 *grey;* painterly, paintable.

Vb. *paint,* wash 425 *colour;* tint, touch up; lay on the colour 226 *coat;* slap on paint; paint a picture, do a portrait, portray, draw, sketch, limn, cartoon 551 *represent;* illuminate; do in oils *or* watercolours *or* tempera, do in black-and-white; ink, chalk, crayon, pencil, stencil, shade, stipple; block in.

554 Sculpture – N. *sculpture,* plastic art 551 *representation;* modelling 243 *formation;* carving, stone cutting, wood carving; moulding; paper modelling, origami; rock carving; toreutics 844 *ornamental art;* constructivism 553 *school of painting;* kinetic art; statuary; statue; statuette, figurine, bust, torso, head; model, cast, plaster c., death mask, waxwork 551 *image;* ceramics 381 *pottery;* medallion, cameo, intaglio; relief, bas-relief; stone, marble; bronze, clay, modelling c., wax, Plasticine (tdmk), papier-mâché.

Vb. *sculpt,* sculpture, rough-hew 243 *form*; cut, carve, whittle, chisel, chip; chase, engrave, emboss; model, mould, cast.

555 Engraving. Printing – N. *engraving,* etching, line engraving, plate e., steel e., copper e.; photogravure, photoengraving; zincography, cerography, glyptography, gem cutting, gem engraving; glass engraving; mezzotint, aquatint; wood engraving, xylography, lignography, woodcut; linoprinting, linocut; scraperboard; silverpoint; drypoint; steel plate, copper p.; stone, block, wood-b.; chisel, graver, burin, burr, needle, dry-point, etching-p., style.

printing, type-p., typography 587 *print*; laser printing; plate printing, copper-plate p., intaglio p.; lithography, photolithography, photogravure, chromolithography, colour printing; fabric printing, batik; silk-screen printing, stereotype; impression.

Vb. *engrave,* grave, cut; etch, stipple, scrape; bite, bite in, eat in; sandblast; impress, stamp; lithograph 587 *print*.

556 Artist – N. *artist,* craftsman *or -* woman 686 *artisan*; architect 164 *producer*; art-master *or* mistress, designer, graphic d., draughtsman *or* -woman; dress-designer, couturier; drawer, sketcher, delineator; caricaturist; cartoonist; illustrator; commercial artist; painter, colourist; pavement artist, scene-painter, sign-p.; oil-painter, watercolourist, pastellist; miniaturist; portrait painter, landscape p., marine p., genre p., still-life p.; Academician, RA, old master, primitive; Pre-Raphaelite, Impressionist, Fauve, Dadaist, Cubist, Vorticist, Surrealist, action painter, Minimalist 553 *school of painting*; art historian.

557 Language – N. *language,* tongue, speech, idiom, parlance, talk, dialect; spoken language, living l.; patter, lingo

560 *dialect*; idiolect; mother tongue, native t.; vernacular, common speech, vulgar tongue; colloquial speech, English as she is spoken 579 *speech*; Queen's English; correct speech, idiomatic s., slang, jargon, vulgarism; lingua franca, pidgin English, sign language 547 *gesture*; Basic English; Esperanto; official language, Mandarin, Hindi; Received Pronunciation, Standard English, BBC English; officialese 560 *neology*; machine language 86 *data processing*; dead language, Latin, Greek, Sanskrit; metalanguage; Babel, babble 61 *confusion*.

literature, creative writing, belles lettres; letters, classics, humanities; literary genre, fiction, metafiction, faction, nonfiction 590 *narrative, description*; lyricism, poetry 593 *poem*; plays 594 *drama*; criticism 480 *estimate*; literary criticism 520 *interpretation*; literary movement, Classicism, Neo-classicism, Sturm und Drang, Romanticism, Symbolism, Idealism, Expressionism, Surrealism, Realism, Naturalism; literary history; Golden Age, Silver A., Augustan A., Classical A. 110 *era*.

linguist, philologist, etymologist, lexicographer; semanticist; grammarian 564 *grammar*; phonetician.

Adj. *linguistic,* philological, etymological, grammatical, morphological; lexicographical, lexicological, semantic; monosyllabic; inflected; written, literary, standard; spoken, living, idiomatic; vulgar, colloquial, vernacular, slangy, jargonistic 560 *dialectal*; current, common, demotic; bilingual, multilingual.

literary, written, polished; humanistic; classical, romantic, naturalistic, surrealistic, futuristic, decadent; learned; formal; critical 520 *interpretive*.

558 Letter – N. *letter,* sign, symbol, character 586 *writing*; alphabet, ABC; International Phonetic Alphabet, IPA; Chinese character; pictogram, cuneiform, hieroglyph 586 *lettering*; ogham alphabet, runic a., futhorc; Greek alphabet, Roman a., Cyrillic a., Hebrew a.,

Arabic a.; Pinyin; Devanagari; runic letter, rune, wen; lettering, Gothic, italic; ampersand; capital letter, cap, majuscule; small letter, minuscule; block letter, uncial; cursive; printed letter, letterpress, type, bold t. 587 *print-type.*

spelling, misspelling; orthography; phonography; spelling game, spelling bee; transliteration 520 *translation.*

Vb. *spell,* spell out, read, syllabify; alphabetize; transliterate; form letters 586 *write;* initial 547 *sign.*

559 Word – **N.** *word,* term 561 *name;* phoneme, syllable 398 *speech sound;* synonym 13 *identity;* homonym, homograph, homophone, palindrome, pun, weasel word 518 *equivocalness;* antonym 14 *contrariety;* etymon, root, back-formation; folk etymology; derivation, derivative, doublet; morpheme, stem, inflexion; part of speech 564 *grammar;* diminutive, intensive; contraction, abbreviation, acronym, portmanteau word 569 *conciseness;* cliché, catchword, vogue word, buzz w., nonce w., neologism, loan w. 560 *neology;* rhyming word; four-letter word 573 *plainness;* swearword, oath 899 *malediction;* hard word, long word, polysyllable; short word, monosyllable, word of one syllable; verbiage, wordiness, verbal diarrhoea, loquacity, verbosity 570 *pleonasm.*

dictionary, rhyming d., reverse word d., monolingual d., learners' d., school d., illustrated d., bilingual d., multilingual d.; lexicon, wordbook, word list, glossary, vocabulary; thesaurus 632 *store;* concordance.

Adj. *verbal,* literal; etymological, lexical; philological, lexicographical; derivative, conjugate, cognate; synonymous; verbose.

Adv. *verbally,* verbatim, word for word.

560 Neology – **N.** *neology,* neologism 126 *newness;* coinage, new word, nonce w., vogue w., buzz w., catch phrase, cliché;

borrowing, loan word; newfangled expression, slang e.; technical language, jargon, technical term, psychobabble, technospeak; barbarism, hybrid; corruption, dog Latin; novelese, journalese, officialese, telegraphese; baby talk; gobbledygook, newspeak, doubletalk; archaism; malapropism 565 *solecism;* wordplay, spoonerism 839 *witticism.*

Adj. *dialect,* idiom, lingo, patois, vernacular 557 *language;* idiolect, burr, brogue, accent 577 *pronunciation;* cockney, Geordie, Doric, broad Scots, Lallans; broken English, pidgin E., pidgin; lingua franca, hybrid language; Briticism, Strine, Franglais; anglicism, Americanism, Hibernicism, Irishism.

slang, vulgarism, colloquialism; jargon, psychobabble, technospeak, argot, cant, patter; Romany; thieves' Latin, rhyming slang; Billingsgate 899 *scurrility;* gobbledygook 515 *empty talk.*

dialectal, vernacular; Doric, Cockney, broad; local; colloquial; nonstandard, slangy, cant; jargonistic, journalistic.

561 Nomenclature – **N.** *nomenclature,* naming etc. vb.; eponymy; terminology; description, designation, appellation, denomination; addressing, roll-call 583 *allocution;* christening, baptism 988 *Christian rite;* study of place names, toponymy.

name, first name, forename, Christian name; middle name(s), surname, family name, patronymic, matronymic; maiden name, married n.; appellation, moniker; nickname, pet name, diminutive; sobriquet, epithet, description; handle, style 870 *title;* heading, caption 547 *indication;* designation; name and address, signature 547 *label;* term, technical t., trade name 560 *neology;* namesake, synonym, eponym; pen name, pseudonym 562 *misnomer;* noun, proper n. 564 *part of speech.*

Adj. *named,* called etc. vb.; entitled, christened; known as, alias, under the name of; so-called, soi-disant, self-styled; named after, eponymous.

Vb. *name,* call, christen, baptize 988 *perform ritual*; give one's name to; nickname, dub; address, sir; entitle, style, term 80 *specify*; call by name, call the roll, call out the names, announce.

562 Misnomer – **N.** *misnomer,* malapropism 565 *solecism*; false name, alias, assumed title; nom de guerre, nom de plume, pen name; stage name, pseudonym; nickname, pet name 561 *name*.

no name, anon, certain person, so-and-so, what's his name, what's his face; N or M, Miss X, A. N. Other; what d'you call it, thingummy, thingummyjig, thingamabob, whatsit, oojakapivvy; this or that; and co., etc.; some, any, what-have-you.

Adj. *anonymous,* unknown, faceless, nameless; incognito, unnamed, unsigned; a certain, certain, such; some, any, this or that.

Vb. *misname,* misterm, mistitle; nickname; assume an alias, go under a false name; be anonymous; write under an assumed name, pass oneself off as 541 *dissemble*.

563 Phrase – **N.** *phrase,* form of words; collocation; expression; idiom, mannerism 80 *speciality*; fixed expression; set phrase; euphemism, metaphor; catch phrase, slogan; hackneyed expression, cliché, commonplace 610 *habit*; saying, proverb, motto, moral, epigram, adage 496 *maxim*; epitaph 364 *obsequies*; inscription, legend, caption 548 *record*; empty phrases, words, empty w., compliments 515 *empty talk*; terminology 561 *nomenclature*; phraseology, phrasing, diction, wording, turn of phrase; well-turned phrase; circumlocution 570 *diffuseness*; paraphrase 520 *translation*; epigrammatist.

Vb. *phrase,* word, verbalize, voice, articulate, syllable; reword, rephrase 520 *translate*; express, formulate, put in words, clothe in w., find words for, state 532 *affirm*; sloganize, talk in clichés; put words together, turn a sentence, round a period 566.

564 Grammar – **N.** *grammar,* comparative g., philology; analysis, parsing, construing; accidence, inflection, case, declension; conjugation, mood, voice, tense; number, gender; punctuation; pointing 547 *punctuation*; syntax, word order, ellipsis, bad grammar 565 *solecism*; good grammar, grammaticalness, Standard English, good E.

part of speech, substantive, noun, common n., proper n., collective n.; pronoun; adjective; verb, reflexive v., transitive v., intransitive v.; adverb, preposition, conjunction, interjection; subject, object, direct o., indirect o.; predicate, copula, complement; article, definite a., indefinite a., particle, affix, suffix, infix, prefix; inflexion, case-ending; formative, morpheme, semanteme; diminutive, intensive, augmentative.

Adj. *grammatical,* correct; syntactic, inflectional; irregular, anomalous; masculine, feminine, neuter; singular, dual, plural; substantival, adjectival, attributive, predicative; verbal, adverbial; participial; prepositional; conjunctive; comparative, superlative.

565 Solecism – **N.** *solecism,* bad grammar, incorrectness, misusage; faulty syntax; barbarism 560 *neology*; malapropism, slip of the pen, slip of the tongue; mispronunciation, dropping one's aitches 580 *speech defect*; misspelling.

566 Style – **N.** *style,* fashion, mode, tone, manner, vein, strain, idiom; idiosyncrasy, mannerism 80 *speciality*; mode of expression, diction, phrasing, phraseology 563 *phrase*; idiolect, vocabulary; literary style, command of language *or* idiom, raciness, power 571 *vigour*; feeling for words; literary charm, grace 575 *elegance*; word power; vernacular s. 573 *plainness*; elaborate style 574 *ornament*.

Adj. *stylistic,* mannered, literary; elegant, ornate, rhetorical; expressive, eloquent, fluent; racy, idiomatic; plain, perspicuous, forceful.

567 Perspicuity – N. *perspicuity,* perspicuousness, clearness, clarity, lucidity, limpidity 422 *transparency*; lucid prose 516 *intelligibility*; directness 573 *plainness*; definition, definiteness, exactness 494 *accuracy.*

568 Imperspicuity – N. *imperspicuity,* obscurity, obfuscation 517 *unintelligibility*; fogginess 423 *opacity*; abstraction, abstruseness; complexity, involved style 574 *ornament*; purple prose, hard words, Johnsonese 700 *difficulty*; imprecision, impreciseness, vagueness 474 *uncertainty*; inaccuracy 495 *inexactness*; ambiguity 518 *equivocalness*; mysteriousness 530 *enigma*; profundity 211 *depth*; ellipsis 569 *conciseness*; verbiage 570 *diffuseness.*

Adj. *unclear,* not transparent, muddied, clear as mud, cloudy 423 *opaque*; obscure 418 *dark*; mysterious, enigmatic 517 *unintelligible*; abstruse, profound 211 *deep*; allusive, indirect 523 *latent*; vague, imprecise, indefinite 474 *uncertain*; ambiguous 518 *equivocal*; muddled, confused, tortuous, convoluted, involved 61 *complex*; hard, Johnsonian 700 *difficult.*

569 Conciseness – N. *conciseness,* succinctness, brevity; pithiness 496 *maxim*; aphorism, epigram, clerihew 839 *witticism*; economy of words, terseness, words of one syllable, laconicism; compression, telegraphese; overconciseness; ellipsis, abbreviation, contraction 204 *shortening*; epitome, précis, outline, brief sketch 592 *compendium*; compactness, portmanteau word; clipped speech, monosyllabism 582 *taciturnity*; nutshell.

Adj. *concise,* brief, not long in telling, short and sweet 204 *short*; laconic, monosyllabic, sparing of words 582 *taciturn*; succinct; crisp, brisk, to the point; trenchant, mordant, incisive; terse, curt, brusque; condensed, tight-knit, compact; pithy, neat, exact, epigrammatic; elliptic, telegraphic, contracted, compressed; summary, cut short, abbreviated, truncated.

Vb. *be concise,* - brief etc. adj.; need few words, not beat about the bush, pull no punches, come straight to the point, cut the cackle, cut a long story short, get down to brass tacks, talk turkey; telescope, compress, condense, contract, abridge, abbreviate, truncate 204 *shorten*; summarize; be short with, be curt with, cut short, cut off; waste no words.

Adv. *concisely,* in brief, in short, in a word, in a nutshell; to put it succinctly, to cut a long story short; to sum up.

570 Diffuseness – N. *diffuseness,* verboseness etc. adj.; profuseness, copiousness; amplification 197 *expansion*; expatiation, minuteness, blow-by-blow account; productivity 171 *productiveness*; inspiration, vein, flow, outpouring; abundance, superabundance, exuberance, redundancy 637 *redundance*; richness, verbosity, wordiness, verbiage; fluency, verbal diarrhoea 581 *loquacity*; long-windedness, prolixity, epic length; repetitiveness, reiteration 106 *repetition*; twice-told tale 838 *tedium*; gush, rigmarole, waffle, blah 515 *empty talk*; effusion, tirade, harangue, sermon, speeches 579 *oration*; superfluity, redundancy 637 *redundance*; tautology; circumlocution, periphrasis; beating about the bush 518 *equivocalness*; padding, filler 40 *extra*; digression 10 *irrelevance.*

Adj. *diffuse,* verbose, nonstop, in love with one's own voice 581 *loquacious*; profuse, copious, ample, rich; fertile, abundant, superabundant, voluminous, scribacious 171 *prolific*; fluent; exuberant, overflowing 637 *redundant*; expatiating, detailed, minute; gushing, effusive; windy, turgid, bombastic; polysyllabic, redundant, excessive, repetitious, repetitive; tautological; padded out.

prolix, long-winded, wordy, prosy; spun out, long-drawn-out; boring 838 *tedious*; lengthy, epic, never-ending, going on and on 203 *long*; discursive, digressing, episodic; rambling, wandering; loose-knit, incoherent; desultory, waffling, pointless 10 *irrelevant*; indirect,

circumlocutory, periphrastic, round-about.

Vb. *be diffuse,* - prolix etc. adj.; expatiate, amplify, particularize, detail, go into detail, expand, enlarge upon; descant, discourse at length; repeat; pad out, draw o., spin o., protract 203 *lengthen*; gush, be effusive 350 *flow*; let oneself go, rant, rant and rave, harangue 579 *orate*; have swallowed the dictionary; launch out on, spin a long yarn 838 *be tedious*; blether on, rabbit on, go on and on 581 *be loquacious*; wander, waffle, digress 282 *deviate*; ramble, drivel, beat about the bush, not come to the point 518 *be equivocal*.

Adv. *diffusely,* on and on, ad nauseam.

571 Vigour – **N.** *vigour* 174 *vigorousness*; power, strength, vitality, drive, force, forcefulness, oomph, go, get-up-and-go 160 *energy*; vim, punch, pep, guts, smeddum; verve, élan, panache, vivacity, liveliness, gusto, pizzazz, raciness; spirit, fire, ardour, glow, warmth, fervour, vehemence, enthusiasm, passion 818 *feeling*; stress, underlining, emphasis 532 *affirmation*; gravity, weight; impressiveness; declamation 574 *grandiloquence*; rhetoric 579 *eloquence*.

Adj. *forceful,* powerful, strenuous 162 *strong*; energetic, peppy, zingy, punchy 174 *vigorous*; racy; bold, dashing, spirited, vivacious 819 *lively*; fiery, ardent, enthusiastic, impassioned 818 *fervent*; vehement, emphatic, insistent, positive 532 *affirmative*; grave, sententious, strongly-worded, pulling no punches 834 *serious*; heavy, meaty, solid; weighty, forcible, cogent 740 *compelling*; vivid, graphic, effective; inspired 579 *eloquent*.

572 Feebleness – **N.** *feebleness* 163 *weakness*; ineffectiveness, flatness, staleness, vapidity 387 *insipidity*; jejuneness, poverty, thinness; enervation, flaccidity; anticlimax.

Adj. *feeble,* weak, thin, flat, vapid, insipid 387 *tasteless*; wishy-washy, watery, wersh; sloppy, sentimental, schmaltzy, novelettish; meagre, jejune,

exhausted, spent; wan, colourless, bald 573 *plain*; languid, flaccid, nerveless, emasculated; uninspired, unimpassioned; ineffective, prosaic, uninspiring; monotonous, pedestrian, dull, dry, boring 838 *tedious*; hackneyed, platitudinous, stale; inane, empty, pointless; juvenile, childish; limping; lame, unconvincing 477 *poorly reasoned*; limp, loose, lax, inexact; poor, trashy 847 *vulgar*.

573 Plainness – **N.** *plainness,* naturalness, simplicity 699 *artlessness*; austerity, severity, baldness, spareness, bareness, starkness; matter-of-factness, plain English 516 *intelligibility*; home truths 540 *veracity*; homespun, vernacular, common speech, vulgar parlance; unaffectedness 874 *modesty*; bluntness, frankness, speaking straight from the shoulder, mincing no words, coarseness, four-letter word.

Adj. *plain,* simple 699 *artless*; austere, severe; bald, spare, stark, bare, unfussy; neat 648 *clean*; pure, unadulterated 44 *unmixed*; unadorned, unvarnished, unembellished 540 *veracious*; played down; unassuming, unpretentious 874 *modest*; chaste, restrained; unaffected, honest, natural, straightforward; homely, homey, homespun; prosaic, sober 834 *serious*; workaday, everyday, commonplace 610 *usual*; uninspired.

Vb. *speak plainly,* call a spade a spade, use plain English 516 *be intelligible*; moderate one's language; say outright, tell it like it is, spell it out, tell one straight *or* to his *or* her face; not mince words, speak straight from the shoulder, not beat about the bush, come to the point, come down to brass tacks, talk turkey.

574 Ornament – **N.** *ornament,* embellishment, colour, decoration, embroidery, frills, flourish 844 *ornamentation*; floridness, floweriness, flowers/ of speech, arabesques 563 *phrase*; euphuism; preciousness, euphemism; rhetoric, purple patch *or* passage; figure of speech 519 *trope*; alliteration, assonance; paralipsis,

aposiopesis; inversion, chiasmus; zeugma; metaphor, simile, antithesis.

grandiloquence, high tone 579 *eloquence*; declamation, rhetoric 571 *vigour*; overstatement, extravagance, hyperbole 546 *exaggeration*; turgidity; pretentiousness, affectation, pomposity 875 *ostentation*; talking big 877 *boasting*; highfalutin, bombast, rant 515 *empty talk*; Johnsonese, long words.

Adj. *ornate,* beautified; rich, luxuriant, florid, flowery; precious, euphuistic, euphemistic; pretentious 850 *affected*; meretricious, flashy, flamboyant, frothy 875 *showy*; alliterative 519 *figurative*; stiff, stilted; pedantic, long-worded, Latinate, Johnsonian.

Vb. *ornament,* beautify, grace, adorn, enrich, gild 844 *decorate*; charge, overlay; elaborate, smell of the lamp, overelaborate, overembellish, gild the lily.

575 Elegance – **N.** *elegance,* style, grace, gracefulness 841 *beauty*; refinement, taste 846 *good taste*; propriety; classicism; harmony, euphony, balance, proportion 245 *symmetry*; rhythm, ease, fluency, felicity, the right word in the right place, the mot juste; neatness, polish, finish; well-turned phrase; flourish.

Adj. *elegant,* majestic, stately 841 *beautiful*; graceful; stylish 846 *tasteful*; dignified; expressive; unaffected 573 *plain*; unlaboured, fluid, fluent, rhythmic, mellifluous, euphonious; harmonious, balanced, well-proportioned 245 *symmetrical*; neat, felicitous, happy, right, neatly put, well-turned; artistic; polished, finished, soigné; flawless 646 *perfect*; classic, classical, Attic, Ciceronian, Augustan.

576 Inelegance – **N.** *inelegance,* awkwardness, roughness, uncouthness 699 *artlessness*; coarseness 647 *imperfection*; harshness; stiltedness 326 *hardness*; unwieldiness; impropriety, barbarism; vulgarity 847 *bad taste*; artificiality 850 *affectation*; lack of style; anti-chic; turgidity, pomposity 574 *grandiloquence*.

Adj. *inelegant,* ungraceful, graceless 842 *ugly*; unpolished, unrefined 647 *imperfect*; coarse, crude, barbarous 699 *artless*; tasteless 847 *vulgar*; meretricious; turgid; forced, laboured, artificial; jarring, grating; insensitive; harsh; halting, unfluent; clumsy, awkward, gauche; wooden, stiff, stilted 875 *formal*.

577 Voice – **N.** *voice,* vocal sound; speaking voice 579 *speech*; singing voice; tongue, vocal organs, vocal cords; lungs, bellows; larynx, voice box; phoneme, vowel, diphthong; open vowel, closed v., voiced consonant, syllable 398 *speech sound*; articulation; utterance, enunciation, delivery, articulation; exclamation, ejaculation, gasp; mutter, whisper, stage w., aside 401 *faintness*; tone of voice, accents, timbre, pitch, tone, intonation, modulation.

pronunciation, articulation, elocution, enunciation, inflection, accentuation, stress, emphasis; accent; broad accent; foreign a.; burr, brogue, drawl, twang 560 *dialect*; trill; aspiration, glottal stop; nasality; lisping, stammer 580 *speech defect*; mispronunciation 565 *solecism*.

Vb. *voice,* pronounce, verbalize, put into words 579 *speak*; mouth, give tongue, give voice, express, utter, enunciate, articulate; vocalize; inflect, modulate; breathe, aspirate, sound one's aitches; trill, roll, burr, roll one's r's; accent, stress 532 *emphasize*; raise the voice, lower the v., whisper, stage-w., make an aside, speak sotto voce; exclaim, ejaculate, rap out 408 *cry*; drone, intone, chant, warble, carol, hum 413 *sing*; bellow, shout, roar, vociferate, use one's voice 400 *be loud*; mispronounce, lisp, drawl, swallow one's consonants, speak thickly 580 *stammer*.

578 Voicelessness – **N.** *voicelessness,* no voice, loss of v.; difficulty in speaking, dysphonia, inarticulation; thick speech, hoarseness, huskiness, raucousness; muteness 399 *silence*; dumbness, mutism, deaf-m.; childish treble, falsetto; breaking voice; sob, sobbing; undertone,

aside, low voice, muffled tones, whisper, bated breath 401 *faintness*; surd, unvoiced consonant; sign language, deaf and dumb language 547 *gesture*; meaningful look; body language, kinesics.

Adj. *voiceless,* aphonic, dysphonic; unvoiced, surd; breathed, whispered, muffled, low-voiced, inaudible 401 *muted*; mute, dumb, deaf and dumb; speechless, at a loss for words; inarticulate, tonguetied; silent, mum 582 *taciturn*; silenced, gagged; croaking, hoarse as a raven 407 *hoarse*; breathless.

Vb. *be mute,* keep mum 582 *be taciturn*; be silent, keep quiet, hold one's tongue 525 *keep secret*; bridle one's tongue, dry up, shut up, ring off, hang up; lose one's voice, be struck dumb, lose the power of speech; make sign language, exchange meaningful glances 547 *gesticulate*; have difficulty in speaking 580 *stammer.*

make mute, strike dumb, dumbfound, take one's breath away, rob one of words; stick in one's throat, choke on; muffle, hush, deaden 401 *mute*; shout down, make one inaudible, drown one's voice; muzzle, gag, stifle 165 *suppress*; stop one's mouth, reduce one to silence, shut one up, cut one short, hang up on; still, hush, put to silence 399 *silence.*

579 Speech – N. *speech,* faculty of s., gift of s., tongue, lips 577 *voice*; parlance 557 *language*; word of mouth, personal account 524 *report*; spoken word, accents, tones 559 *word*; discourse, colloquy, conversation, talk, chat, rap, palaver, prattle, chinwag 584 *interlocution*; address; fluency, talkativeness, volubility 581 *loquacity*; prolixity; elocution, voice production; articulation, utterance, delivery, enunciation 577 *pronunciation*; ventriloquism; sign language, eye l., meaningful glance *or* look 547 *gesture*; body language; speech, dictum, utterance, remark, observation, comment, interjection 532 *affirmation*; fine words 515 *empty talk*; spiel, patter 542 *trickery*.

oration, speech; one's say, a word in edgeways; public speech, formal s., discourse, disquisition, address, talk; welcoming address 876 *celebration*; panegyric, eulogy; valedictory, funeral oration 364 *obsequies*; after-dinner speech, toast, vote of thanks; broadcast, commentary 534 *lecture*; recitation, recital, reading; set speech, declamation; sermon, homily, exhortation; harangue, ranting, tub-thumping, tirade, diatribe, invective; monologue 585 *soliloquy*; written speech, dictation, paper, screed 591 *dissertation*; preamble, prologue, foreword, narration, account, digression, peroration.

oratory, art of speaking, rhetoric, public speaking, stump oratory, tub-thumping; speech-making, speechifying; declamation, rhetoric, elocution, ranting, rant; vituperation, invective; soapbox; Hyde Park Corner.

eloquence, gift of the gab, fluency, articulacy; blarney; way with words, word power 566 *style*; power of speech; grandiloquence; elocution, good delivery; peroration, purple passage.

speaker, utterer; talker, prattler, gossiper 581 *chatterer*; conversationalist; speechifier, speech-maker, speechwriter, rhetorician, elocutionist; orator, public speaker, after-dinner s., toastmaster *or* -mistress; improviser, adlibber; declaimer, ranter, soap-box orator, tubthumper, haranguer 738 *agitator*; lecturer; pulpiteer 537 *preacher*; presenter, announcer 531 *broadcaster*; narrator, chorus 594 *actor*; mouthpiece, spokesman *or* -woman, spokesperson 754 *delegate*; advocate, pleader, mediator 231 *intermediary*; salesman *or* -woman, salesperson, rep 793 *seller*; Cicero.

Adj. *speaking,* talking; with a tongue in one's head, vocal; bilingual, polyglot; articulate, fluent, talkative 581 *loquacious*; oral; well-spoken, soft-s.; audible, spoken, verbal; elocutionary.

eloquent, spellbinding, silver-tongued; smooth-t. 925 *flattering*; elocutionary, oratorical; grandiloquent, declamatory

571 *forceful*; tub-thumping, fire-and-brimstone, ranting, rousing 821 *exciting*.

Vb. *speak,* mention, say; utter, articulate 577 *voice*; pronounce, declare 532 *affirm*; let out, blurt out, come clean, tell all 526 *divulge*; whisper, breathe 524 *hint*; talk 584 *converse*; give utterance, deliver oneself of; break silence, open one's mouth *or* lips, find one's tongue; pipe up, speak up, raise one's voice; give tongue, rattle on, gossip, prattle, chatter, rap 581 *be loquacious*; patter, give a spiel, jabber, gabble; sound off, speak one's mind, tell a thing or two, have one's say, expatiate 570 *be diffuse*; trot out, reel off, recite; read, read aloud, read out, dictate; have a tongue in one's head, speak for oneself; use sign language 547 *gesticulate*.

orate, speechify; declaim, deliver a speech; hold forth, spout, be on one's hind legs; take the floor *or* the stand, rise to speak; preach, harangue; lecture, address 534 *teach*, perorate, mouth, rant, rail, sound off, tub-thump; spellbind, hold enthralled, be eloquent, have the gift of the gab, have kissed the Blarney Stone, 925 *flatter*; talk to oneself 585 *soliloquize*; speak off the top of one's head, ad-lib 609 *improvise*.

580 Speech defect – N. *speech defect,* aphasia, loss of speech, aphonia; paraphasia, paralalia; idiolalia; stammering, stammer, stutter, lallation, lisp; sigmatism 406 *sibilation*; dysphonia, speech impediment, hesitation, drawl, slur; indistinctness, inarticulateness, thick speech, cleft palate; burr, brogue 560 *dialect*; accent, twang, nasal t. 577 *pronunciation*; affectation, plum in one's mouth, marble in one's m., Oxford accent, haw-haw 246 *distortion*; speech therapy.

Vb. *stammer,* stutter, trip over one's tongue; drawl, hesitate, falter, quaver, hem and ha, hum and haw; um and ah, mumble, mutter; lisp; splutter; speak through the nose, drone; clip one's words, swallow one's w., gabble, slur; mispronounce.

581 Loquacity – N. *loquacity,* loquaciousness, garrulity, talkativeness, communicativeness, yak, yackety-yack; volubility, runaway tongue, flow of words, fluency 570 *diffuseness*; verbosity, wordiness, prolixity; running on, spate of words, logorrhoea, verbal diarrhoea, inexhaustible vocabulary; patter, spiel, gab, gift of the g. 579 *eloquence*.

chatter, chattering, gossiping, gabble, jabber, rap, palaver, jaw-jaw, yackety-yack; clack, cackle, babble, prattle; small talk, gossip, idle g., tittle-tattle; waffle, blether, gush, guff, gas, hot air 515 *empty talk*.

chatterer, chatterbox; gossip, tittle-tattler 529 *news reporter*; haverer, ranter; preacher, sermonizer; windbag, gas-bag, conversationalist.

Adj. *loquacious,* talkative, garrulous, gossiping, tattling, tittle-tattling, yakking; communicative, rapping, chatty, gossipy, newsy 524 *informative*; gabbing, babbling, gabbling, gabby, gassy, windy, verbose, long-winded 570 *prolix*; nonstop, voluble, going on and on, fluent, glib; conversational.

Vb. *be loquacious,* - talkative etc. adj.; have a long tongue, chatter, rattle, go on and on, run on, bang on, reel off, talk nineteen to the dozen; gossip, tattle 584 *converse*; clack, gabble, jabber 515 *mean nothing*; talk, jaw, yak, go yackety-yack, gab, prate, gas, waffle, haver, blether, twitter, ramble on, rabbit on; rap; drone, drivel; launch into speech, start talking, give tongue, shoot; have one's say, talk at length; expatiate, spout 570 *be diffuse*; talk down; filibuster, stonewall; talk one's head off, talk the hind leg off a donkey; talk shop, bore 838 *be tedious*; engage in conversation, buttonhole; monopolize the conversation, hold the floor, not let one get a word in edgeways, never stop talking.

582 Taciturnity – N. *taciturnity,* incommunicativeness, reserve, reticence 525 *secrecy*; few words, brusqueness, curtness, gruffness 885 *rudeness*; muteness 578 *voicelessness*; economy of words; no

orator; person of few words; clam; Trappist.

Adj. *taciturn,* mute, mum 399 *silent*; sparing of words, monosyllabic, short, curt, laconic, brusque, gruff 569 *concise*; not talking, incommunicative; withdrawn, reserved, keeping oneself to oneself, guarded, with sealed lips 525 *reticent*; close, tight-lipped; not to be drawn, keeping one's counsel, discreet 858 *cautious*; inarticulate, tongue-tied 578 *voiceless.*

Vb. *be taciturn,* - laconic etc. adj.; spare one's words 569 *be concise*; not talk, say nothing, have little to say; observe silence, make no answer; not be drawn, refuse comment, neither confirm nor deny; keep one's counsel 525 *keep secret*; hold one's tongue, put a bridle on one's t., keep one's mouth *or* one's trap shut; fall silent, relapse into s., pipe down, dry up 145 *cease*; be speechless, lose one's tongue 578 *be mute*; waste no words on, save one's breath to cool one's porridge; not mention, leave out, pass over, omit 458 *disregard.*

Int. hush! sh! shut up! mum's the word! no comment! a word to the wise!

583 Allocution – **N.** *allocution,* apostrophe; address, lecture, talk, speech, pep talk, sermon 579 *oration*; greeting, salutation; invocation, appeal, interjection, buttonholing, word in the ear, aside.

Vb. *speak to,* address, talk to, lecture to; turn to, direct one's words at, appeal to, pray to; sir; approach, accost; hail, call to, salute, say good morning 884 *greet*; pass the time of day, parley with 584 *converse*; take aside, buttonhole.

584 Interlocution – **N.** *interlocution,* parley, colloquy, converse, conversation, talk, chat, rap; dialogue, question and answer; exchange, repartee, banter, badinage; slanging match 709 *quarrel*; confab, social intercourse 882 *fellowship*; commerce, communion, communication, intercommunication 524 *information*; tête-à-tête.

chat, chinwag, natter; chit-chat, talk, small t., rap; gossip; tattle, tittle-tattle, tongue-wagging 581 *chatter*; fireside chat, cosy chat, tête-à-tête, heart-to-heart.

conference, colloquy, talks, parley, pow-wow; discussion, debate, forum, symposium, seminar, teach-in, talk-in; controversy; exchange of views, high-level talks, summit meeting, summit conference, summit; negotiations, bargaining 765 *treaty*; conclave, convention, meeting, gathering 74 *assembly*; working lunch; reception 882 *social gathering*; audience, interview; consultation, huddle, council, war c., family c., round-table conference 691 *advice.*

Vb. *converse,* parley, talk together (**see** *confer*); pass the time of day, exchange pleasantries; draw one out; buttonhole, engage in conversation, carry on a c., join in a c., butt in, put in a word, bandy words, exchange w.; chat, have a chat *or* a natter *or* a good talk; be drawn out 579 *speak*; natter, chinwag, chew the fat, rap, gossip, tattle 581 *be loquacious*; commune with; be closeted with; whisper together, talk tête-à-tête, go into a huddle, indulge in pillow talk.

confer, talk it over, sit in council *or* in conclave, sit in committee, hold a council of war, pow-wow; discuss, debate 475 *argue*; parley, negotiate, hold talks, hold a summit, get round the table; consult with 691 *consult.*

585 Soliloquy – **N.** *soliloquy,* monologue; stream of consciousness; apostrophe; aside; one-man *or* one-woman show.

Vb. *soliloquize,* say to oneself, make an aside, think aloud; apostrophize; talk to the wall, address an empty house, have an audience of one.

586 Writing – **N.** *writing,* creative w., literary composition, authorship, journalism 590 *description*; literary output 557 *literature*; script, copy, works, books

589 *reading matter*; pen-pushing, hackwork, Grub Street; paperwork 548 *record*; copying, transcribing, transcription, rewriting, editing; holography; handwriting; longhand, shorthand, stenography; speedwriting, typewriting, typing 587 *print*; braille; cipher, code 530 *secret*; hieroglyphics; sign-writing, skywriting 528 *advertisement*; inscribing, carving; graphology.

lettering, stroke of the pen, up-stroke, down-s.; line, dot, point; flourish, scroll; handwriting; calligraphy, penmanship; fair hand; script, italic, copperplate; printing, block letters; scribble, scrawl; letters, characters, alphabet 558 *letter*; runes, pictogram, hieroglyph; palaeography.

script, written matter, illuminated address; calligraph; writing, screed, scrawl, scribble; manuscript, MS; original, one's own hand, autograph, holograph; signature; copy, transcript, transcription, fair copy 22 *duplicate*; typescript, stencil; newsprint; printed matter; letter, epistle, written reply 588 *correspondence*; inscription, graffito 548 *record*; superscription, caption, heading; illuminated letters.

stationery, writing materials, pen and paper, pen and ink; pen, quill-p., fountain p., cartridge p., felt-tip p., ballpoint p., Biro (tdmk); nib; stylo; pencil, propelling p., lead p., coloured p.; crayon, chalk; papyrus, parchment, vellum; foolscap 631 *paper*; writing paper, notepaper, lined p., blank p., notebook, pad, jotter; slate, blackboard; inkstand, inkwell; pencil sharpener, penknife; blotting paper, blotter; typewriter, ribbon, daisy wheel; stencil.

stenographer, shorthand writer, typist, shorthand t., stenotypist, audiotypist, secretary, personal s., personal assistant, PA, Girl Friday.

Adj. *written,* inscribed, in black and white; in writing, in longhand, in shorthand; handwritten, manuscript, signed; penned, pencilled, scrawled, scribbled etc. vb.; copybook, copperplate; italic,

calligraphic; hieroglyphic, lettered, alphabetic; runic, roman, italic 558 *literal*; upright, sloping, bold, spidery.

Vb. *write,* form characters, inscribe; letter, block, print; write well; write badly, scribble, scrawl; put in writing, confirm in writing, set down in black and white, commit to paper, write down, jot d., note 548 *record*; transcribe, copy out, make a fair copy, rewrite, write out; take down, take dictation, take down in shorthand, type, key; take down longhand, write in full; draft; compose; pen, pencil, dash off; write letters 588 *correspond*; write one's name 547 *sign*; take pen in hand, put pen to paper, be an author.

587 Print – N. *print,* printing, laser p., typing, typewriting 586 *writing*; typography, lithography, litho, photolithography, photolitho 555 *printing*; photocopying 551 *photography*; photocomposition, phototypesetting, computer typesetting, cold type; composition, typesetting, make-up; monotype, linotype, stereotype, electrotype; impression, printout; proof, galley p., bromide, page proof, revise; proofcopy.

print-type, type, stereotype, plate; flong, matrix; broken type, pie; upper case, lower c., capitals, small c., caps; fount, face, typeface, boldface, bold, clarendon, lightface, old face, bastard type; roman, italic, Gothic, black letter 558 *letter*; body, bevel, shoulder, shank, beard, ascender, descender, serif, sanserif; lead, rule, en, em; space, hairspace, quad; type bar, slug, logotype.

press, printing p., printing works, printers; composing room; machining r.; handpress, flatbed, platen press, rotary press, Linotype (tdmk), Monotype (tdmk), offset press.

Adj. *printed,* in print 528 *published*; cold-type, hot-metal; set, composed, machined etc. vb.; in type, in italic, in bold, in roman; typographic; leaded, spaced, justified; solid, tight, crowded.

Vb. *print,* stamp; typeset, key, compose, photocompose; align, register, justify; set up in type, make ready, impose, machine, run off, pull off, print off; collate, foliate; paginate, lithograph, litho, offset, stereotype; put to bed; proofread; bring out 528 *publish.*

588 Correspondence – N. *correspondence,* barrage of c., exchange of letters, backlog of correspondence; communication 524 *information*; mailing list, distribution l.; letters, mail, post, postbag 531 *postal communications*; letter, epistle, missive, dispatch, bulletin; love letter, billet doux, greetings card, Christmas c., Easter c., birthday c., Valentine 889 *endearment*; postcard, pc, picture p., card, letter c., notelet; air letter, aerogramme, air mail, sea m.; business letter, bill, account, enclosure; open letter 528 *publicity*; unsolicited mail, junk m., circular, round robin, chain letter, begging l.; note, line, chit; answer, acknowledgment; envelope, cover, stamp, seal; postcode.

correspondent, letter writer, penfriend, penpal, poison pen; foreign correspondent, contributor 529 *news reporter.*

Vb. *correspond,* correspond with, exchange letters, maintain *or* keep up a correspondence, keep in touch with 524 *communicate*; write to, send a letter to, drop a line; report 524 *inform*; deal with one's correspondence, catch up on one's c., acknowledge, reply, write back, reply by return 460 *answer*; circularize 528 *publish.*

589 Book – N. *book,* title, volume, tome, roll, scroll, document; codex, manuscript, MS; script, typescript; published work, publication, best-seller, potboiler, blockbuster; sleeper, remainder; standard work, classic, definitive work, collected works; major work, monumental w., magnum opus; slim volume; booklet; illustrated work, picture book, coffeetable b. 553 *picture*; magazine, periodical, rag 528 *journal*; brochure, pamphlet, leaflet 528 *the press*; bound book, cased book, hardback, softback, limpback, paperback (see *edition*).

reading matter, printed word, written w. 586 *writing*; forms, papers, bumf, literature, 548 *record*; circular, junk mail; script, copy; text, the words, libretto, lyrics, scenario, screenplay, book of words; proof, revise, pull; writings, prose literature 593 *prose*; poetical literature 593 *poetry*; classical literature, serious l., light l. 557 *literature*; books for children, children's books, juveniles; history, biography, travel 590 *description*; work of fiction 590 *novel*; biographical work, memoirs, memorabilia 590 *biography*; addresses, speeches 579 *oration*; essay, tract, treatise 591 *dissertation*; piece, occasional pieces 591 *article*; miscellanea, marginalia, jottings, thoughts, pensées; poetical works 593 *poem*; selections, flowers 592 *anthology*; dedicatory volume, Festschrift; early works, juvenilia; posthumous works, literary remains; complete works, oeuvre, corpus; newspaper, magazine 528 *journal*; issue, number, back n.; fascicle, part, instalment, serial, sequel, prequel.

reference book, encyclopaedia, cyclopaedia 490 *erudition*; lexicon, thesaurus 559 *dictionary*; biographical dictionary, dictionary of quotations, rhyming dictionary, dictionary of reverse words, technical dictionary, gazetteer, yearbook, annual 87 *directory*; calendar 117 *chronology*; guide 524 *guidebook*; notebook, diary, album 548 *record*; bibliography, reading list.

edition, impression, issue, run; series, set, collection, library; bound edition, library e., de luxe e., school e., trade e., standard e., definitive e., omnibus e., complete e., collected e., complete works; first edition, new e., revised e.; reissue, reprint; illustrated edition, special e., limited e., expurgated e.; critical e., annotated e., variorum e.; adaptation, abridgment 592 *compendium*; quarto, folio; layout, format; house style; front matter, prelims, preface, prefatory note; dedication, acknowledgments; title,

half-t.; flyleaf, title page, endpaper, colophon 547 *label*; contents, errata, corrigenda, addenda; back matter, appendix, supplement, index, thumb i., bibliography; caption, heading, headline, running h., footnote; guide word, catchword; margin; gutter; folio, page, leaf, recto, verso; sheet, forme, signature; chapter, section; inset; plate, print, illustration, halftone, line drawing 553 *picture*.

bookbinding, binding, spiral b., perfect b., stitching, casing; case, slip c., cover, jacket, dust j. 226 *wrapping*; boards 631 *paper*; cloth, limp c., linen, scrim, buckram, leather, pigskin, calf, morocco, vellum, parchment; spine, headband; tooling, gilding, marbling.

library, national library, public l., local l., reference l., mobile l., lending l., circulating l.

bookperson, man *or* woman of letters, bluestocking; reader, bookworm 492 *scholar*; bibliophile, book lover, book collector; bibliographer; librarian; stationer, bookseller, antiquarian b., secondhand b., publisher; editor, book reviewer, critic, reviewer 480 *estimator*.

author, authoress, writer, creative w., wordsmith; man *or* woman of letters; fiction-writer, novelist, crime writer, historian, biographer; essayist 591 *dissertator*; prose writer; verse writer 593 *poet*; playwright, librettist, script writer 594 *dramatist*; freelance; copywriter 528 *publicizer*; pressman *or* -woman, journalist 529 *news reporter*; editor; subeditor, copy editor, contributor, correspondent, special c., war c., sports c., columnist, gossip writer, diarist; agony aunt; scribbler, penpusher, hack, Grub Street h.; ghost writer.

590 Description – N. *description,* account, detailed a.; statement, exposé, summary 524 *report*; brief, abstract, inscription, caption, subtitle, legend 592 *compendium*; narration, relation, recital, version (see *narrative*); documentary account; specification, characterization, details, particulars 87 *list*; portrayal, delineation, depiction; portrait, word p.,

sketch, character s., profile; case history 548 *record*; faction, documentary drama, docu-drama; picture, true p., realism; travelogue 524 *guidebook*; vignette, cameo, thumbnail sketch, outline; idyll, parody 851 *satire*; epitaph 364 *obsequies*.

narrative, storyline, plot, subplot, scenario 594 *stage play*; episode 154 *event*; dénouement 725 *completion*; dramatic irony, comic relief; catharsis; stream of consciousness; fantasia 513 *fantasy*; fiction, faction, story, tale, romance, fairytale, folk tale; tradition, legend, myth, saga, river s., soap opera, serial, epic; ballad 593 *poem*; allegory, parable, cautionary tale; yarn 543 *fable*; anecdote, reminiscence 505 *remembrance*; annals, chronicle, history, historiography 548 *record*.

biography, real-life story, human interest; life, curriculum vitae, cv, biodata, life story *or* history; experiences, adventures, fortunes; hagiology, hagiography, martyrology; obituary, obit; autobiography, confessions, memoirs 505 *remembrance*; diary, journals 548 *record*; letters 588 *correspondence*.

novel, fiction; roman fleuve; anti-novel, metafiction; historical novel, novelization; short story, novelette, novella; light reading, bedside r. 589 *reading matter*; romance, love story, fairy s., adventure s., Western, science fiction, sci-fi; gothic novel, ghost story; picaresque novel; crime story, detective s., spy s., whodunit, whydunit; cliffhanger, thriller, horror story, shocker, bodice ripper, penny dreadful, horror comic; paperback, pulp literature, airport fiction; potboiler, trash; popular novel, blockbuster, best-seller 589 *book*.

Adj. *descriptive,* graphic, colourful, vivid; well-drawn, sharp; true-to-life, realistic, real-life, photographic, impressionistic, evocative, emotive, full, detailed 570 *diffuse*; documentary.

Vb. *describe,* delineate, draw, picture, depict, paint 551 *represent*; evoke, bring to life, capture; characterize, detail;

sketch 233 *outline*; relate, recount, recite, report, give an account 524 *communicate*; write, write about 548 *record*; narrate, tell, spin a yarn, unfold a tale; make a story out of; recapitulate 106 *repeat*; reminisce, relive the past 505 *retrospect*.

591 Dissertation – N. *dissertation,* treatise, tract, exposition, summary 592 *compendium*; theme, thesis 475 *argument*; disquisition, essay, examination, survey 459 *enquiry*; discourse, discussion; paper, monograph, study; homily, sermon 534 *lecture*. commentary.

article, news a., column; leader, editorial; essay; literary composition; comment, review, rave r., notice, critique, criticism, write-up 480 *estimate*.

dissertator, essayist; pamphleteer, publicist 528 *publicizer*; editor, leader writer; writer, contributor 589 *author*; reviewer, critic, commentator, pundit 520 *interpreter*.

Vb. *dissertate,* treat, handle, write about, deal with; discourse upon 475 *argue*; develop a thesis; go into, go into in depth, conduct an in-depth-enquiry, survey; set out, discuss, ventilate, air one's views; criticize, comment upon; write an essay, write a treatise, do a paper, write an article, do a piece; annotate, commentate 520 *interpret*.

592 Compendium – N. *compendium,* epitome, résumé, summary, brief; contents, heads, analysis; abstract, sum and substance, gist, drift; consolidation, digest, pandect; multum in parvo, précis; aperçu, conspectus, synopsis, bird's-eye view, survey; review, recapitulation, recap; rundown, runthrough; draft, minute, note 548 *record*; sketch, thumbnail s., outline, brief o., skeleton; blueprint 623 *plan*; syllabus, prospectus, brochure 87 *list*; abridgment, abbreviation, concise version 204 *shortening*; contraction, compression 569 *conciseness*.

anthology, treasury, flowers, gems; selections, extracts 589 *textbook*; collection, compilation, miscellany; ephemera; gleanings; cuttings, album, scrapbook, sketchbook, commonplace book.

Vb. *abstract,* sum up, resume, summarize, run over; epitomize, make a synopsis of, reduce, abbreviate, abridge 204 *shorten*; capsulize, encapsulate; docket 548 *record*; condense, pot, give an outline 569 *be concise*; compile 87 *list*; collect 74 *bring together*; conflate 50 *combine*; excerpt, select; sketch out 233 *outline*.

593 Poetry. Prose – N. *poetry,* poesy, balladry; versification (**see** *prosody*); poetic art, poetics; verse, rhyme; poetic licence; poetic inspiration, muse, Muses.

poem, versification, piece of verse, lines, verses, stanzas, strains; narrative verse, heroic poem, epic, dramatic poem, dramatic monologue, verse drama; light verse, lyric verse; comic verse, nonsense v., limerick; ode; dirge, elegy; idyll; occasional poem; song, shanty, lay, ballad 412 *vocal music*; warsong, marching song; love song, drinking s., collected poems 592 *anthology*; cycle, sequence.

doggerel, jingle, ditty, nursery rhyme; nonsense verse, comic v.; clerihew, limerick; burlesque.

verse form, sonnet, sestet, Petrarchan *or* Italian sonnet, Shakespearean *or* English s.; ballade, rondeau, virelay, triolet, villanelle, bouts rimés; burden, refrain, envoi; couplet, distich, sloka; haiku, tanka; triplet, tercet, terza rima, quatrain, ghazal; sestina, rhyme royal, ottava rima, Spenserian stanza; accentual verse, syllabic v., metrical v., blank v.; concrete poetry; Sapphics, Alcaics; limping iambics, scazon; free v., vers libre; verse, versicle, stanza, stave, laisse, strophe, antistrophe; stichomythia; broken line, half l., hemistich. See *prosody*.

prosody, versification, metre; scansion; rhyme, masculine r., feminine r., internal r., eye r.; rhyme scheme; assonance, alliteration; cadence, rhythm;

metrical unit, foot; iamb, trochee, spondee, pyrrhic; dactyl, anapaest; tetrameter, pentameter, hexameter, heptameter, octameter; iambic pentameters, blank verse; alexandrine, heroic couplet; beat, stress, accent; elision; caesura.

poet, poet laureate; Lake poet, Georgian p., Metaphysical p., beat p., modern p.; versemonger, poetaster; versifier, rhymer, bard, minstrel, balladeer, troubadour, Meistersinger; epic poet, lyric p., dramatic p., elegiac p.; sonneteer, ballad-monger; songwriter, librettist.

prose, prose poem; piece of prose, prose composition, prosaicness, prose-writing, everyday language 573 *plainness*; prose writer 589 *author.*

Adj. *poetic,* poetical; Parnassian, satiric; elegiac, lyrical, lyric, rhyming, jingling, etc. vb.; doggerel, prosodic, metrical, measured, rhythmic, scanning; iambic.

prosaic, pedestrian, uninspired, unpoetical, in prose, matter-of-fact 573 *plain.*

Vb. *poetize,* scan; rhyme; versify, put into verse; write poetry, compose an epic, write a lyric, write a sonnet; make up a limerick; celebrate in verse; lampoon 851 *satirize.*

594 Drama. Ballet – N. *drama,* the theatre, the stage, the boards, the footlights; theatreland, Broadway, West End; silver screen, Hollywood 445 *cinema*; show business, show biz, dramatic entertainment, straight drama, legitimate theatre, live t.; intimate t., theatre in the round, total theatre, alternative t., street t., the Fringe, off-off-Broadway; repertory, rep; theatricals, amateur dramatics, dressing-up; masque, charade, dumb show, puppetry, tableau, t. vivant 551 *representation*; tragic mask, comic m., sock, buskin; Thespis.

dramaturgy, dramatic form 590 *narrative*; dramatic unities; dramatization, theatricals, dramatics; melodramatics, histrionics; theatricality, staginess; good theatre, bad t., good cinema, good television; play writing, script w., libretto w.;

stagecraft; action, plot, subplot 590 *narrative*; characterization 551 *representation*; production, new p.; revival; auditions, casting; walkthrough, rehearsal, dress r.; direction, stage management; continuity; staging, stage directions; choreography; dialogue, soliloquy, stage whisper, aside, cue; entrance, exit (**see** *acting*); rising of the curtain, prologue, chorus; act, scene, opening s., coup de théâtre, deus ex machina, alarums and excursions; curtain, drop of the c., blackout; finale, final curtain, epilogue; curtain call, encore; interval, intermission, break; enactment, performance, command p., première, preview, first night, gala n.; matinée, first house, second h.; one-night stand, road show; sell-out, hit, smash h., box-office h., long run; flop.

stage play, play, drama, work; show, libretto, scenario, script, text, prompt book; part, lines 579 *speech*; dramatic representation 551 *representation*; five-act play, one-act p., playlet; sketch, skit; double bill; curtain-raiser, monologue, duologue, two-hander; masque, mystery play, miracle play, morality p., passion p., Oberammergau; commedia dell'arte; No, Kabuki; Greek drama, trilogy, tetralogy, cycle; poetic drama, verse d.; melodrama, gothic drama, blood and thunder; tragedy; tragicomedy, comedy, comedy of manners, Restoration comedy; situation comedy, sit-com; kitchen-sink drama, theatre of the absurd, t. of cruelty; black comedy, farce, slapstick, burlesque 849 *ridiculousness*; pantomime, panto, musical comedy, musical, light opera, comic o., grand opera 412 *vocal music*; television play 531 *broadcast*; screenplay 445 *cinema*; mime, puppet show, Punch and Judy show.

stage show 445 *spectacle*; live show; ice show, circus 837 *amusement*; variety, music hall, vaudeville; review, revue, intimate r., late-night r.; Follies, leg show, strip s.; floor show, cabaret; song and dance, act, turn; star turn; tableau.

ballet, dance, ballet dancing 837 *dancing*; choreography; classical ballet, modern dance; toe dance 837 *dance*; solo, pas

seul, pas de deux; chassé, glissade; arabesque; fouetté, plié, pirouette 315 *rotation*; pas de chat, entrechat, jeté 312 *leap.*

stage set, set, setting, décor, scenery, scene 445 *spectacle*; drop curtain, backdrop, backcloth; screen, wings; background, foreground, front stage, upstage, down stage, stage, boards; apron, proscenium, proscenium arch, apron stage, picture-frame stage; stage in the round, curtain; prompt box (see *theatre*); properties, props, costume; make-up, greasepaint.

theatre, amphitheatre, stadium 724 *arena*; circus, hippodrome; fleapit, picture house, movie theatre 445 *cinema*; theatre in the round, open-air t.; pavilion; big top; playhouse, opera house, music hall, vaudeville theatre, variety t.; night club, cabaret; stage, boards, proscenium, wings, flies; dressing room, green r.; footlights, spotlight, limelight, houselights; auditorium, orchestra; seating, stalls, front s., back s., orchestra s., front rows; pit, box, circle, dress c., upper c., gallery, balcony, gods; front of house, foyer, box office, stage door.

acting, impersonation; interpretation, improvisation, pantomime, miming, taking off 20 *mimicry*; histrionics, play-acting, the Method; hamming, barnstorming; overacting, camping it up, staginess, theatricality; repertoire; character, personage, role; leading role; part, fat p.; vignette, cameo; supporting part, bit p., speaking p.; walk-on p.; stock part, stereotype, ingenue, heavy father, injured husband, merry widow, stage villain, stage Irishman; principal boy *or* girl; Harlequin, Columbine, Pierrot, pantomime dame; hero, heroine, antihero; stage fever; stage fright, first-night nerves.

actor, actress, Thespian; mimic, mime 20 *imitator*; mummer, play-actor, player, strolling p., trouper, ham; rep player, character actor; actor-manager, star, star of stage and screen, film star,

starlet, tragedian, tragedienne; comedian, comedienne, comedy actor *or* actress; opera singer, prima donna, diva; ballet dancer, ballerina, prima b., protagonist, lead, leading man, leading lady, juvenile lead, understudy; extra, bit player; chorus, gentlemen *or* ladies of the chorus; corps de ballet, troupe, company, repertory c., dramatis personae, characters, cast.

entertainer, performer; artiste, artist, drag a., striptease a.; impressionist, impersonator, female i.; troubadour, minstrel; busker; crooner, pop singer 413 *vocalist*; comic, stand-up c., comedian, comedienne 839 *humorist*; ventriloquist, fire-eater, juggler; ropewalker, acrobat 162 *athlete*; clown; pierrot, Punch, hoofer, dancer, show girl, chorus g., can-can dancer, belly d., gogo d.; dancing girl.

stage manager, producer, director, actor manager, business m., press agent *or* officer; impresario, showman; backer, sponsor, angel.

dramatist, playwright, scenario writer, script w., librettist; choreographer.

playgoer, theatregoer, operagoer; film fan, opera buff, balletomane 504 *enthusiast*; first-nighter; stage-door Johnny; audience, house, packed h., full h., sell-out; stalls, pit, gods, gallery; dramatic critic, play *or* film reviewer.

Adj. *dramatic,* theatrical, stagy; operatic, balletic, Terpsichorean, choreographic; live, legitimate; Thespian; histrionic, camp; tragic, comic, tragicomic; farcical, burlesque, knockabout, slapstick 849 *funny*; melodramatic, sensational, horrific, blood and thunder 821 *exciting*; avant-garde; released, showing, running 522 *shown*; dramatized; camped up; barnstorming; on the stage; stagestruck, film-struck.

Vb. *dramatize,* write plays, write for the stage; make a play of, adapt for the stage *or* for radio; stage, mount, produce, direct, stage-manage; cast; star, feature; present, put on, release 522 *show*; open, raise *or* ring up the curtain.

act, go on the stage, tread the boards; face the cameras; perform, enact, play, playact, do a play; impersonate; take the part; mime, take off 20 *imitate*; create a role, play a part, play the lead; play opposite, support; star, co-star, get one's name in lights, steal the show, upstage, take all the limelight; play to the gallery, ham, camp it up, send up, barnstorm, overact 546 *exaggerate*; underact, throw away; walk on; understudy, stand in 150 *substitute*; rehearse, say one's lines; cue in; fluff, forget one's lines, dry; ad-lib, gag; take a curtain call, do an encore, receive a standing ovation.

Class five

VOLITION: *THE EXER-CISE OF THE WILL*

5.1 INDIVIDUAL VOLITION

Section one: Volition in general

595 Will – N. *will,* volition; disposition, inclination, mind, cast of mind, fancy, preference 597 *willingness*; act of will; strength of will, willpower, determination, firmness of purpose, 599 *resolution*; self-control 942 *temperance*; purpose 617 *intention*; decision 608 *predetermination*; one's own sweet will 932 *selfishness*; iron will, wilfulness 602 *obstinacy*; whimsicality 604 *caprice*; free will, self-determination 744 *independence*; free choice, option, discretion 605 *choice*; voluntariness, spontaneousness, spontaneity 597 *voluntary work*.

Adj. *volitional,* willing; unprompted, unasked, unbidden, freewill, spontaneous, original 597 *voluntary*; discretionary, optional; self-willed, iron-willed, wayward, wilful 602 *obstinate*; arbitrary, autocratic, dictatorial 735 *authoritarian*; independent; determined, hell-bent 599 *resolute*; intentional, willed, intended 608 *predetermined*.

Vb. *will,* exercise the will; impose one's will, have one's way, have it all one's own w. 737 *command*; do what one chooses, do as one likes 744 *be free*; be so minded, have a mind to, see fit, think f., think best 605 *choose*; determine 617 *intend*; wish 859 *desire*; have a mind of one's own, be independent, go one's own way, do as one chooses, be one's own man *or* woman; exercise one's discretion, judge for oneself 480 *judge*; take the responsibility, take it upon oneself; be hell-bent on, take the law into one's own hands, take the bit between one's

teeth 602 *be obstinate*; know one's own mind 599 *be resolute*; volunteer, offer, do of one's own accord, do without prompting 597 *be willing*.

596 Necessity – N. *necessity,* stern n., no alternative, no escape, no option, zero o., Hobson's choice 606 *no choice*; last shift, last resort 700 *predicament*; inevitability, the inevitable, inescapability, sure thing, what must be 155 *destiny*; determinism, fatalism 608 *predetermination*; pressure of events, pressure of work, force of circumstances, c. beyond one's control, act of God, fatality 154 *event*; no freedom 745 *subjection*; law of nature; superior force 740 *compulsion*; logical necessity, necessary conclusion, proof 478 *demonstration*; force of law 953 *law*; obligation, conscience 917 *duty*; indispensability, sine qua non, a necessity, a must, matter of life and death 627 *requirement*; want, lack 801 *poverty*; involuntariness, reflex action; instinct, impulse, blind i. 476 *intuition*.

fate, inexorable f., lot, portion; weird, karma, kismet; doom, die, predestination, destiny; book of fate, God's will, will of Allah; fortune, wheel of f., 159 *chance*; stars, planets, astral influence; Dame Fortune, the Fates; Destinies; Weird S., Lachesis, Clotho, Atropos.

Adj. *necessary,* indispensable, essential, vital, important, requisite 627 *required*; imperative; overriding, irresistible; compulsory, mandatory, binding 917 *obligatory*; necessitated, inevitable, unavoidable, inescapable, inexorable, life-and-death 473 *certain*; sure thing, leaving no choice, deterministic.

involuntary, instinctive 476 *intuitive*; unpremeditated, unintended 618 *unintentional*; unconscious, subliminal, unthinking, gut, unwitting, blind, impulsive 609 *spontaneous*; under a spell 983 *bewitched*; conditioned, reflex, automatic, mechanical.

fated, karmic, fatal; predestined, preordained 608 *predetermined*; doomed, precondemned 961 *condemned*.

Vb. *be forced,* compelled etc. adj.; incur the necessity; submit to the n. 721 *submit*; be fated, bow to fate, dree one's

weird; be cornered, be driven into a corner, be pushed to the wall 700 *be in difficulty*; be faced with a sine qua non, have no choice, have no option, have zero o., needs must; make a virtue of necessity; be unable to help it.

necessitate, dictate, impose, oblige 740 *compel*; bind by fate, destine, doom, foredoom, predetermine 155 *predestine*; brook no denial, not take no for an answer; leave no choice, face with a sine qua non, impose the necessity, drive into a corner, bulldoze; demand 627 *require.*

597 Willingness – N. *willingness,* voluntariness, volunteering; spontaneousness 609 *spontaneity*; free choice, option 605 *choice*; disposition; inclination, fancy, leaning, bent, bias, penchant, propensity 179 *tendency*; facility 694 *aptitude*; predisposition, readiness, right mood, receptive frame of mind; acquiescence 488 *assent*; compliance 758 *consent*; cheerful consent, alacrity, gameness, eagerness, enthusiasm; initiative, impatience, overeagerness; dedication, sacrifice 931 *disinterestedness*; helpfulness 706 *cooperation*; loyalty 739 *obedience*; pliancy, putty in one's hands, docility, tractability 612 *persuadability*; submissiveness 721 *submission*; obsequiousness 879 *servility.*

voluntary work, voluntary service 901 *philanthropy*; honorary employment, unpaid labour, labour of love, self-appointed task.

volunteer, unpaid worker, willing horse; no slouch; do-gooder 901 *philanthropist.*

Adj. *willing,* ungrudging, acquiescent 488 *assenting*; compliant, game for; in the mood, feeling like, receptive, inclined, disposed, well-d., predisposed, amenable; cordial; happy, pleased, glad, delighted; ready 669 *prepared*; ready and willing, prompt, quick 678 *active*; forward; eager, enthusiastic, dedicated, overeager, impatient, raring to go; doing one's best; helpful 706 *cooperative*; docile, biddable, easy-going 24 *agreeing*;

submissive 721 *submitting*; obsequious 879 *servile*; desirous, dying to.

voluntary, unprompted, unsought, unasked, unbidden 609 *spontaneous*; unsolicited, uncalled for, self-imposed; beyond the call of duty; discretionary, optional 605 *chosen*; volunteering, on one's own initiative, off one's own bat, of one's own free will; gratuitous, honorary, unpaid 812 *uncharged.*

Vb. *be willing,* - ready etc. adj.; have half a mind to; feel like, have a fancy to, have a good mind to 595 *will*; agree, acquiesce 488 *assent*; show willing, be ready and waiting, comply 758 *consent*; be found willing 739 *obey*; try, do one's best 671 *attempt*; go out of one's way to, lean over backwards; collaborate 706 *cooperate*; meet halfway; jump at, leap at; can't wait, be burning to, be thrilled at the idea; not hesitate; volunteer, sacrifice oneself 759 *offer oneself.*

Adv. *willingly,* with a will, with relish, cordially; voluntarily, spontaneously, without being asked; like a shot, at the drop of a hat; with open arms, with all one's heart, heart and soul, with a good grace, without demur, nothing loath; gladly, with pleasure.

598 Unwillingness – N. *unwillingness,* disinclination, reluctance; disagreement 489 *dissent*; demur, objection 468 *qualification*; protest 762 *deprecation*; recalcitrance 704 *opposition*; rejection 760 *refusal*; unhelpfulness, noncooperation 702 *hindrance*; dissociation; faintheartedness, lack of zeal 860 *indifference*; backwardness 278 *slowness*; hesitation 858 *caution*; scruple, repugnance 861 *dislike*; recoil, aversion, bashfulness 874 *modesty*; noncompliance 738 *disobedience*; refractoriness; grudging service; unreliability 474 *uncertainty*; shelving, postponement, procrastination, laziness 679 *sluggishness*; neglect, remissness 458 *negligence.*

Adj. *unwilling,* indisposed, loath, reluctant, averse; not prepared, not so minded, not in the mood, not feeling like; unconsenting, opposed; demurring;

regretful, with regret 830 *regretting*; hesitant 858 *cautious*; shy, bashful 874 *modest*; unenthusiastic, half-hearted, lukewarm; backward; uncooperative; recalcitrant; perfunctory, remiss 458 *negligent*; grudging; unspontaneous, forced, begrudged, with bad grace.

Vb. *be unwilling,* - reluctant etc. adj.; not have the heart to, not stomach 861 *dislike*; disagree, boggle, scruple 489 *dissent*; object, demur, protest 762 *deprecate*; resist 704 *oppose*; reject, give the thumbs down, give the red light 760 *refuse*; recoil, blench, fight shy, duck, shirk 620 *avoid*; drag one's feet, hold back, hesitate, tread warily, hang fire, go slow 278 *move slowly*; not play ball, abstain 702 *obstruct*; grudge, begrudge, turn up one's nose; force o.; have regrets 830 *regret*; tear oneself away 296 *depart*.

599 Resolution – **N.** *resolution,* sticking point, resoluteness, determination, grim d.; zeal, ardour, earnestness, seriousness; resolve, mind made up, decision 608 *predetermination*; drive, vigour 174 *vigorousness*; energy; concentration, iron will, willpower 595 *will*; strength of character, self-control, self-restraint, self-possession; tenacity 600 *perseverance*; aplomb, mettle, daring, dash, élan 712 *attack*; guts, pluck, spunk, grit, backbone, spirit; fortitude, stiff upper lip, gritted teeth, moral fibre 855 *courage*; single-mindedness, commitment, total c., devotedness, devotion, dedication; reliability, staunchness, steadiness, constancy, firmness 153 *stability*; insistence, pressure 740 *compulsion*; sternness, relentlessness, ruthlessness, inexorability, implacability 906 *pitilessness*; inflexibility, steeliness 326 *hardness*; iron, steel, rock; clenched teeth, hearts of oak, bulldog breed 600 *stamina*.

Adj. *resolute,* resolved, made up, determined 597 *willing*; desperate, stopping at nothing, all out; serious, earnest, concentrated; intent upon, set u., bent u.; insistent, pressing, urgent, driving, forceful, energetic, heroic 174 *vigorous*;

firm, staunch, reliable, constant 153 *unchangeable*; iron-willed, strong-w., strong-minded, decisive, unbending, immovable, unyielding, inflexible, uncompromising, intransigent 602 *obstinate*; stern, grim, inexorable, implacable, relentless, ruthless, merciless 906 *pitiless*; iron, steely; undaunted, nothing daunted; steadfast, unwavering, unshaken, unshakable, unflinching, game, tenacious; indomitable; steeled, armoured, proof; self-controlled, self-restrained 942 *temperate*; self-possessed, self-reliant, self-confident; purposeful, single-minded, whole-hearted, committed, devoted, dedicated.

Vb. *be resolute,* - determined etc. adj.; steel oneself, brace o.; clench one's teeth, grit one's t. (**see** *stand firm*); make up one's mind, take a resolution, will, resolve, determine, purpose 617 *intend*; decide, fix, seal, conclude, finish with 69 *terminate*; take on oneself, accept responsibility 595 *will*; know one's own mind, insist, press, urge, not take no for an answer 532 *emphasize*; cut through, override, put one's foot down, stand no nonsense; mean business, stick at nothing, not stop at trifles, go to all lengths, go to any length, push to extremes; go the whole hog, see it through 725 *carry through*; face, face the odds, take on all-comers, 661 *face danger*; bell the cat, outface, dare 711 *defy*; endure, go through fire and water 825 *suffer*; face the issue, bring to a head, take the bull by the horns; take the plunge, cross the Rubicon, burn one's boats, burn one's bridges, throw down the gauntlet, nail one's colours to the mast; be single-minded, set one's heart on, take up, go in for, take up in earnest, devote *or* dedicate oneself, commit oneself, give oneself to, give up everything for; set to, buckle to, go to it, put one's shoulder to the wheel, put one's heart into, grapple, strain 682 *exert oneself.*

stand firm, not be moved, dig one's toes *or* heels in, stand one's ground, stay put; not budge, not yield, not compromise, not give an inch; never despair,

stand fast, hold out 600 *persevere*; be hell-bent on, bear the brunt, have what it takes, fight on, soldier on, stick it out, grin and bear it, endure 825 *suffer*; fight to the death, die with one's boots on; go down with colours flying.

600 Perseverance – N. *perseverance*, persistence, tenacity, pertinacity, stubbornness 602 *obstinacy*; staunchness, constancy, steadfastness 599 *resolution*; single-mindedness, commitment, singleness of purpose, concentration 455 *attention*; sedulousness, application, tirelessness, indefatigability, assiduousness, industriousness 678 *assiduity*; doggedness, plodding, hard work 682 *exertion*; endurance, patience, fortitude 825 *suffering*; maintenance 146 *continuance*; ceaselessness 144 *permanence*; repeated efforts, unflagging e. 106 *repetition*.

stamina, endurance, staying power, indefatigability, fortitude 162 *strength*; grit, true g., backbone, gameness, guts, gutsiness, pluck; bulldog courage 855 *courage*.

Vb. *persevere*, persist, keep at it, not take no for an answer, hold out for; not despair, never d., never say die, never give up hope, hope on 852 *hope*; endure, have what it takes, come up for more 825 *suffer*; try, keep on trying, try and try again, renew one's efforts 671 *attempt*; maintain, keep up, follow up 146 *sustain*; plod, slog away, peg a., plug a., hammer away at, work at 682 *work*; continue, go on, keep on, keep the pot boiling, keep the ball rolling, rally, keep going; not let go, cling, hold fast, maintain one's grip, hang on like grim death 778 *retain*; hang on, stick it out, sweat it out, stay the course, stick with it, see it through, stay till the end; be in at the death, survive 41 *be left*; maintain one's ground, not budge, dig in one's heels, grit one's teeth 602 *be obstinate*; stick to one's guns, hold out, hold out to the last, die at one's post 599 *stand firm*; work till one drops, die with one's boots on, die in harness; spare no pains, move heaven and earth 682 *exert oneself*; bring to

conclusion, see the end of, complete 725 *carry through*.

601 Irresolution – N. *irresolution*, faint-heartedness, squeamishness, loss of nerve, spinelessness, no backbone, no grit 856 *cowardice*; nonperseverance, broken promise 603 *change of mind*; indecision, uncertainty, doubt, floating vote 474 *dubiety*; hesitation; inconstancy, fluctuation, vacillation, variability, blowing hot and cold 152 *changeableness*; levity, fickleness, whimsicality, irresponsibility 604 *caprice*; passivity 679 *inactivity*; compromise 734 *laxity*; lukewarmness, apathy 860 *indifference*; weak will 163 *weakness*; suggestibility 612 *persuadability*; pliancy, putty in one's hands, obsequiousness 879 *servility*; submissiveness.

Adj. *irresolute*, undecided, indecisive, of two minds, wavering, vacillating; unable to make up one's mind, stalling, undetermined, unresolved, uncertain 474 *doubting*; hesitating 598 *unwilling*; faint-hearted; lukewarm 860 *indifferent*; infirm of purpose 474 *unreliable*; characterless; compromising, weak-willed, weak-kneed, spineless 163 *weak*; flexible, pliant, putty-like 327 *soft*; inconstant, variable; whimsical, mercurial, not to be pinned down, grasshopper-like 604 *capricious*; restless, unsteady; uncommitted, giddy; superficial 456 *inattentive*.

Vb. *be irresolute*, - undecided etc. adj.; back away, shy, shirk 620 *avoid*; shilly-shally 518 *be equivocal*; fluctuate, vacillate, seesaw, waver, sway, hover, teeter, stall, dither 317 *oscillate*; not know one's own mind, blow hot and cold, back and fill, hum and haw, be in two minds, go round in circles, not know what to do, be at one's wits' end 474 *be uncertain*; leave in suspense, delay, put off a decision, put off until tomorrow 136 *put off*; dilly-dally 136 *wait*; debate, balance, weigh up the pros and cons, seesaw 475 *argue*; have second thoughts, hesitate 858 *be cautious*; falter, not persevere, give up 621 *relinquish*; make a compromise,

take half measures 770 *compromise*; yield, give way 721 *submit*; change sides.

602 Obstinacy – N. *obstinacy,* mind of one's own; determination, will, single-mindedness 599 *resolution*; doggedness, tenacity, bulldog t., pertinacity 600 *perseverance*; stubbornness, obduracy, obdurateness; pigheadedness; inflexibility, immovability, toughness 326 *hardness*; intransigence, hard line, hard core, no compromise; constancy, irreversibility, fixity 153 *stability*; stiff neck; incorrigibility 940 *impenitence*; intractability, mulishness, dourness, sulkiness 893 *sullenness*; perversity, wrongheadedness, cussedness, bloody-mindedness.

opinionatedness, dogmatism, bigotry, zealotry; intolerance, fanaticism 735 *severity*; ruling passion, obsession, idée fixe 481 *bias*; old school.

Adj. *obstinate,* stubborn, obdurate; pig-headed, mulish; pertinacious, unyielding, firm, determined 599 *resolute*; dogged, bulldog-like, tenacious; adamant, inflexible, unbending; obdurate, hard-nosed, hardened, case-h.; uncompromising, hard-core, intransigent; unrelenting, immovable 153 *unchangeable*; inexorable, implacable; set in one's ways, hidebound; impervious; opinionated, dogmatic, pedantic 473 *positive*; obsessed, bigoted, fanatical 481 *biased*; dour, grim 893 *sullen*; stiff-necked; perverse, incorrigible, bloody-minded, plain cussed; persistent, incurable, chronic 113 *lasting*.

wilful, self-willed, pig-headed, bull-headed, mulish, wayward; headstrong, perverse; unruly, refractory; unmanageable, intractable, uncontrollable 738 *disobedient*; incorrigible.

Vb. *be obstinate,* - stubborn etc. adj.; persist 600 *persevere*; brazen it out 940 *be impenitent*; stick to one's guns, dig in one's heels, stand out, not budge, stay put 599 *stand firm*; insist, brook no denial, not take no for an answer; must have one's way; not change one's mind 473 *dogmatize*; stay in a rut, cling to custom 610 *be wont*; not listen, stop up

one's ears, take no advice, take the bit between one's teeth, damn the consequences 857 *be rash*; not yield to treatment, become chronic 113 *last*.

603 Tergiversation: Change of mind – N. *change of mind,* tergiversation, better thoughts; afterthought, second thoughts 67 *sequel*; change of allegiance, conversion; new resolve; break with the past, repentance 939 *penitence*; revulsion 280 *recoil*; backsliding; shifting ground, change of direction 282 *deviation*; reversal, back-pedalling, veering round, about-face, about-turn, U-turn, volte-face, looking back 286 *return*; apostasy, turning renegade *or* traitor, defection, desertion 918 *undutifulness*; ratting, going over, treachery 930 *perfidy*; secession; abandonment 621 *relinquishment*; change of mood.

recantation, eating one's words, retraction, withdrawal, apology; renunciation, forswearing; disclaimer, denial 533 *negation*; revocation.

recanter, tergiversator, turncoat, rat; back-pedaller; opportunist, timeserver, Vicar of Bray 518 *equivocalness*; double-dealer, two-faced person 545 *deceiver*; jilt; apostate, renegade; traitor, Judas, betrayer 938 *knave*; quisling, fifth columnist, collaborationist 707 *collaborator*; deserter, defector, quitter, ratter; grass 524 *informer*; strike-breaker, blackleg, scab; seceder 978 *schismatic*; runaway; backslider 904 *offender*; convert.

Vb. *change one's mind,* tergiversate, think again, think better of it 601 *be irresolute*; change one's tune, shift one's ground 152 *vary*; get cold feet, back out, scratch, withdraw 753 *resign*; back down, crawl 872 *be humbled*; apologize (**see** *recant*); change round, swerve, tack, veer round, do a U-turn, backpedal, wheel about 282 *turn round*; turn one's back on 286 *turn back*; turn over a new leaf, repent 939 *be penitent*; reform, mend one's ways 654 *get better*; backslide 657 *relapse*; ditch, jilt, throw over,

desert, walk out on 918 *fail in duty*; turn against.

apostatize, turn one's coat, change sides, change one's allegiance, turn renegade *or* traitor; switch over, join the opposition, cross over, cross the floor, go over, desert, defect; blackleg, rat; betray, collaborate 930 *be dishonest*; be off with the old love, follow the rising star.

recant, unsay, eat one's words, eat one's hat; eat humble pie, apologize; take back, go back on, backpedal, backtrack, do a U-turn; withdraw 769 *not observe*; retract, disclaim, repudiate, deny 533 *negate*; renounce, abjure, forswear; recall, revoke, rescind 752 *abrogate*.

604 Caprice – N. *caprice,* capriciousness, arbitrariness; whimsicality, freakishness; faddishness; inconsistency 25 *disagreement*; fitfulness, changeability, variability, fickleness, unreliability, levity, giddiness, irresponsibility 152 *changeableness*; inconstancy, coquettishness, flirtatiousness.

whim, whimsy, caprice, fancy; passing fancy, impulse 609 *spontaneity*; vagary, humour, mood, fit, bee in the bonnet, quirk, kink, fad, craze, freak, idiosyncrasy 503 *eccentricity*; escapade, prank; coquetry, flirtation.

Adj. *capricious,* whimsical, fanciful, fantastic; eccentric, temperamental, crotchety, freakish, fitful; mad 503 *crazy*; mischievous; wayward, perverse; faddy; arbitrary, unreasonable; fretful, moody, contrary 892 *irascible*; refractory 602 *wilful*; erratic, uncertain, unpredictable 508 *unexpected*; volatile, mercurial, skittish, giddy, frivolous 456 *light-minded*; inconsistent, inconstant, variable; irresponsible, unreliable, fickle, feckless; coquettish.

Vb. *be capricious,* - whimsical etc. adj.; take it into one's head, have a sudden fancy for; chop and change, blow hot and cold 152 *vary*; be fickle; vacillate 601 *be irresolute*; flirt.

605 Choice – N. *choice,* election 463 *discrimination*; picking and choosing,

finickiness 862 *fastidiousness*; picking out, selection; co-option, adoption; nomination, appointment 751 *commission*; option; freedom of choice, discretion, pick; decision 480 *judgment*; preference, predilection, partiality, inclination, leaning, bias 179 *tendency*; taste 859 *liking*; availability 759 *offer*; selection, short list; short leet; alternative, embarras de choix; difficult choice, dilemma 474 *dubiety*; limited choice, no real alternative; Hobson's c., zero option; nothing for it but 606 *no choice*; preferability, desirability; favour, fancy, first choice, top seed; selection, excerpts; the best of; literary selection 592 *anthology*; deselection.

vote, voice 485 *opinion*; representation, proportional r.; majority vote, first past the post; casting v.; ballot, secret b., postal vote; vote of confidence; vote of no confidence, blackballing, vote-counting, show of hands, division, poll, straw p., plebiscite, referendum; suffrage, universal s.; franchise, votes for women, women's suffrage, suffragettism; electoral system, ballot box, vox populi; polling, counting heads; straw vote, Gallup poll (tdmk), Mori p. (tdmk), opinion p.; election, general e.; by-election; local election, local-government e.; primary; polls, voting, electioneering, whistle-stop tour, canvassing, doorstepping, polling, hustings, candidature; return; psephology, psephologist; suffragette.

electorate, voters, elector, electoral college; quorum; electoral roll; constituent, constituency, marginal c.; borough, pocket b., rotten b.; polling booth, ballot box, voting paper; ticket, manifesto.

Adj. *chosen,* well-c.; select, choice, hand-picked 644 *excellent*; seeded 62 *arranged*; elect, designate; elected; adopted, selected; deselected; on approval, on appro; favourite, pet; God's own; by appointment.

Vb. *choose,* make one's choice, make one's bed; shop around, be choosy, be picky; exercise one's discretion, accept, opt for, take up an option; elect, co-opt; adopt; favour, fancy; incline, lean, have

a bias 179 *tend*; prefer, have a preference; think it best to, make up one's mind 480 *judge*; settle on, fix on, plump fur; take sides, back, support, embrace, espouse, throw in one's lot with 703 *patronize.*

select, pick, single out; pass 923 *approve*; nominate, appoint 751 *commission*; designate, detail, mark out; preselect, earmark, reserve 46 *set apart*; recommend, put up, propose, second 703 *patronize*; cull; glean, winnow, sift 463 *discriminate*; separate; skim off, cream, pick the best; take one's pick, pick and choose 862 *be fastidious.*

vote, have a v., have a voice, have a say; be enfranchised, be on the electoral roll; poll, go to the polls; cast a vote, register one's v., raise one's hand; vote for, elect, return; deselect, vote with one's feet 607 *reject*; electioneer, canvass; stand 759 *offer oneself*; put to the vote, hold a referendum; count heads, count noses, count straws; hold an election, go to the country, appeal to the electorate, ask for a vote of confidence.

606 Absence of choice – N. *no choice,* Hobson's c., no alternative, zero option 596 *necessity*; any, the first that comes 464 *indiscrimination*; neutrality; no difference, six of one and half a dozen of the other, 'a plague on both your houses' 28 *equality.*

Vb. *be neutral,* take no sides, not vote, be a don't know, abstain; sit on the fence 601 *be irresolute*; not know.

have no choice, have no alternative, have Hobson's choice; have zero option; take it or leave it, make a virtue of necessity, make the best of a bad job 596 *be forced*; have no say.

Adv. *neither,* neither . . . nor.

607 Rejection – N. *rejection,* nonacceptance; repudiation; denial 533 *negation*; rebuff, frozen mitt, cold shoulder 760 *refusal*; spurning, kick, more kicks than ha'pence, more bricks than bouquets; electoral defeat; elimination 300 *ejection*; exemption 57 *exclusion*; discarding, deselection, disemployment 674 *nonuse*; reject, wallflower; no-hoper, lost cause.

Vb. *reject,* decline, say no to, draw the line at, rebuff, repulse, spurn, dismiss out of hand 760 *refuse*; send back; pass over, ignore 458 *disregard*; vote against; scrap, discard, deselect, ditch, junk, throw away, throw aside, lay a., give up 674 *stop using*; disallow, revoke 752 *abrogate*; set aside; expel, cast out, throw o., chuck o., sling o., kick o., fling o. 300 *eject*; kick upstairs; sort out 44 *eliminate*; exempt 57 *exclude*; blackball, cold-shoulder, hand the frozen mitt to, turn one's back on, give the brush-off 885 *be rude*; disclaim, deny 533 *negate*; abnegate, repudiate; disdain, deride 851 *ridicule*; turn up one's nose at, sniff at, look a gift horse in the mouth 922 *hold cheap.*

608 Predetermination – N. *predetermination,* predestination 596 *necessity*; preordination 155 *destiny*; decree 595 *will*; premeditation; prearrangement 669 *preparation*; order of the day, order paper, agenda 622 *business*; frame-up, put-up job, packed jury 623 *plot*; closed mind 481 *prejudice*; foregone conclusion.

Adj. *predetermined,* decreed, premeditated etc. vb.; predestined, preordained; deliberate, aforethought; with a motive, studied, calculated, measured; weighed, considered, advised; devised, controlled, contrived 623 *planned*; put-up, framed, stacked, packed, prearranged 669 *prepared.*

Vb. *predetermine,* predestine, preordain; premeditate, preconceive; agree beforehand; fix; contrive, arrange, prearrange 623 *plan*; frame, put up, pack a jury, stack the cards 541 *fake.*

609 Spontaneity – N. *spontaneity,* ad hoc measures, improvisation; extemporization, ad-libbing, impromptu thinking on

one's feet 670 *nonpreparation*; involuntariness, reflex, automatic r.; impulsiveness, impulse, blind i., instinct 476 *intuition*; spur of the moment; snap decision; burst of confidence 526 *disclosure*; inspiration, sudden thought, hunch, flash 451 *idea*.

Adj. *spontaneous,* off-the-cuff, ad hoc, improvised, ad-libbing, extemporaneous, extempory, sudden, snap; makeshift; impromptu, unpremeditated, unrehearsed 618 *unintentional*; unprompted, unmotivated, unprovoked; instinctive, involuntary, automatic, knee-jerk; impulsive.

Vb. *improvise,* extemporize, think on one's feet, vamp, ad-lib 670 *be unprepared*; obey an impulse, act on the spur of the moment 604 *be capricious*; blurt, come out with, say whatever comes into one's head, have a sudden brainwave; rise to the occasion.

Adv. *extempore,* impromptu, ad hoc, on the spur of the moment, off the cuff, off the top of one's head.

610 Habit – **N.** *habit,* disposition; force of habit; second nature; occupation; addiction, confirmed habit, constitutional; trait, idiosyncrasy; knack, trick, mannerism; instinct, leaning 179 *tendency*; bad habit; usage, custom, old c., mores; use, wont 146 *continuance*; inveteracy; tradition, law, precedent; way, ways, the old w.; lifestyle, way of life; beaten track, tramlines, groove, rut; fixed ways, daily round, daily grind, regularity 141 *periodicity*; routine, drill, system 60 *order*; red tape, bureaucracy, conventionalism, traditionalism, conservatism, old school 83 *conformity*.

practice, common p., matter of course; conventionality 83 *conformity*; mores, behaviour patterns; institution, ritual, observance 988 *rite*; religious observance; mode, vogue, craze, in-thing; order of the day 848 *fashion*; convention, protocol, unwritten law, done thing, the usual thing; recognized procedure, drill; form, good f. 848 *etiquette*; manners,

table m., eating habits; rules and regulations, house rules, standing order, routine 688 *conduct*.

habituation, training, indoctrination 534 *teaching*; inurement, hardening; naturalization, acclimatization; conditioning, reflex, conditioned r., drill, routine.

habitué, creature of habit, addict; traditionalist, conventionalist 83 *conformist*; regular, client 792 *purchaser*; frequenter, devotee, fan, groupie, camp follower 504 *enthusiast*.

Adj. *habitual,* customary; routine; conventional, traditional 976 *orthodox*; inveterate, time-honoured; habit-forming; ingrained, dyed-in-the-wool, bred in the bone 5 *intrinsic*; rooted, deep-r., deep-seated; imbued, soaked, permeated.

usual, accustomed, wonted, traditional; in character, natural; household, familiar, well-known 490 *known*; unoriginal, hackneyed; banal, commonplace, common, ordinary 79 *general*; set, stock, stereotyped 83 *typical*; widespread 79 *universal*; monthly, daily, everyday 139 *frequent*; practised, done; acknowledged, received, accepted, understood; established, official, hallowed by custom; de rigueur 740 *compelling*; invariable 153 *unchangeable*; in, in vogue 848 *fashionable*.

habituated, in the habit of, accustomed to, given to, addicted to; devoted to, wedded to; used to, familiar with, conversant w., au fait w., at home in 490 *knowing*; inveterate, confirmed; practised, inured, seasoned, incorrigible, hardened 669 *prepared*; broken in, trained, tame 369 *tamed*; naturalized, acclimatized.

Vb. *be wont,* be used to, be a creature of habit; haunt, frequent; make a habit of, take up, embrace, go in for; be set in one's ways, be in a rut, stick in a groove, become a habit, catch on, grow on one, take hold of o., stick; take root; be the rule, obtain, hold good 178 *prevail*; acquire the force of custom.

habituate, accustom oneself, get used to, get into the way of, get the knack of, get the feel of, get the hang of, warm up, get into one's stride; take to, acquire the habit; get into a habit, catch oneself doing; keep one's hand in, practise 106 *repeat*; accustom, inure, season, train; domesticate, tame 369 *break in*; naturalize, acclimatize; imbue 534 *teach*; condition, brainwash 178 *influence*.

611 Desuetude – N. *desuetude,* discontinuance, disuse 674 *nonuse*; rust, decay 655 *deterioration*; rustiness, lack of practice 695 *unskilfulness*; discarded custom; 550 *obliteration*; weaning 134 *adultness*; not the thing, not etiquette, unconventionality 84 *nonconformity*; inexperience, unfamiliarity 491 *ignorance*.

Adj. *unwonted,* not customary, not done; not de rigueur; unfashionable, bad form, non-U 847 *vulgar*; out of fashion, old hat, defunct 125 *past*; discarded 674 *disused*; unconventional 84 *unconformable*; untraditional, unprecedented,

unhabituated, unaccustomed, not in the habit of 769 *nonobservant*; untrained, undomesticated; unfamiliar, inexperienced, new, raw, fresh, callow, green 491 *uninstructed*; weaned; out of the habit, rusty 695 *unskilful*.

Vb. *disaccustom,* wean from, cure of 656 *cure*; break a habit, kick the h.; dry out; wean oneself from, outgrow; give up, throw off, slough off, shed.

612 Motive – N. *motive,* cause of action, what is behind it; rationale, reasons, grounds 156 *reason why*; motivation, driving force, impetus, mainspring, what makes one tick, what turns one on 156 *causation*; intention 617 *objective*; ideal, principle, guiding p.; aspiration 852 *hope*; ambition 859 *desire*; calling, call 622 *vocation*; conscience, dictate of c., personal reasons, ulterior motive 932 *selfishness*; impulse.

inducement, pressure, urgency, insistence; lobbying 178 *influence*; indirect

influence; provocation, urging, incitement, encouragement, incitation, instigation, prompting; support, abetment 703 *aid*; solicitation, invitation 761 *request*; temptation, enticement, carrot, allurement, seduction, seductiveness, fascination, charm, sex appeal, it, attractiveness, magnetism 291 *attraction*; blandishment 925 *flattery*; coaxing, wheedling 889 *endearment*; persuasion, persuasiveness, salesmanship, sales talk, spiel, patter 579 *eloquence*; pep talk, rallying cry 547 *call*; exhortation 534 *lecture*; pleading, advocacy 691 *advice*; propaganda, agitprop; advertising, sales promotion, soft sell, hard s. 528 *advertisement*; promises, election p.; bribery, b. and corruption, graft, palm-greasing, back-scratching 962 *reward*; honeyed words, winning ways.

persuadability, docility, tractability, willingness; pliancy, pliability, putty in one's hands 327 *softness*; susceptibility, impressibility; credulousness 487 *credulity*.

incentive, inducement; stimulus, fillip, tickle, prod, spur, goad, lash, whip; rod, big stick, crack of the whip 900 *threat*; energizer, tonic, carrot, carrot and stick, jam tomorrow, sop, sop to Cerberus 174 *stimulant*; charm 983 *spell*; attraction, magnet; lure, decoy, decoy duck, bait 542 *trap*; come-on, loss leader, special offer; profit 771 *gain*; cash, gold 797 *money*; pay, salary, perks, pay increase, increment, rise, raise, bonus 804 *payment*; donation, handout, freebie 781 *gift*; gratuity, tip, bribe, hush money, slush fund 962 *reward*; forbidden fruit; tempting offer, offer one cannot refuse 759 *offer*.

motivator, prime m. 156 *cause*; manipulator, wire-puller 178 *influence*; manoeuvrer, tactician, strategist 623 *planner*; instigator, prompter; inspirer; aider and abettor 703 *aider*; agent provocateur 545 *deceiver*; tempter, seducer; seductress, temptress, vamp, femme fatale,

siren; Circe, Lorelei; hypnotizer, hypnotist; orator, rhetorician 579 *speaker*; advocate; wheedler 925 *flatterer*; advertiser, promotion manager, propagandist 528 *publicizer*; ringleader 690 *leader*; firebrand, rabble-rouser 738 *agitator*; lobbyist, lobby, pressure group, ginger g.

Vb. *motivate,* move, actuate, manipulate 173 *operate*; work upon, play u., act u., operate u. 178 *influence*; weigh, count, be a consideration, sway 178 *prevail*; call the tune, override 34 *predominate*; work on the feelings, appeal, challenge, shame into; infect, inject with, infuse into 534 *educate*; interest, intrigue 821 *impress*; charm, fascinate, captivate, hypnotize, spellbind 983 *bewitch*; turnon; pull 291 *attract*; push 279 *impel*; force, enforce 740 *compel*; bend, incline, dispose; predispose, prejudice 481 *bias*; predestine 608 *predetermine*; lead, direct 689 *manage*; lead astray 495 *mislead*; give a lead, set the fashion, be a trend-setter, set an example, set the pace 283 *precede*.

incite, energize, galvanize, stimulate 174 *invigorate*; encourage, cheer on, act as cheer-leader, root for 855 *give courage*; inspire, animate, provoke, rouse, rally 821 *excite*; evoke, call forth, challenge; exhort, invite, urge, exert pressure, bring pressure to bear on, lobby; nag, needle, goad, prod, jog, jolt; spur, prick; whip, lash, flog; spur on, egg on; drive, hurry up 680 *hasten*; instigate, prompt, put up to; abet, aid and a. 703 *aid*; start, kindle 68 *initiate*.

induce, instigate, bring about 156 *cause*; persuade, carry with one 485 *convince*; prevail upon, talk into, push i., drive i., nag i., bully i., browbeat (see *motivate*); twist one's arm 740 *compel*; wear down, soften up; get round, bring r., talk r. 147 *convert*; bring over, win o., procure, enlist, engage; talk over, sweet-talk into, coax into, cajole 925 *flatter*; entice, seduce.

tempt, lead into temptation; entice, hold out a carrot to, dangle before one's eyes, make one's mouth water; tantalize,

tease; allure, lure, inveigle 542 *ensnare*; coax, wheedle.

bribe, offer an inducement, hold out a carrot 759 *offer*; suborn, seduce, corrupt; square, buy off; oil, grease the palm, give a sop to Cerberus; tip 962 *reward*.

613 Dissuasion – **N.** *dissuasion,* caution 664 *warning*; discouragement, setback 702 *hindrance*; deterrence 854 *intimidation*; objection, expostulation, remonstrance, reproof; admonition 762 *deprecation*; rebuff 715 *resistance*; disincentive; deterrent, red light 665 *danger signal*; contraindication; cold water, damper, wet blanket; killjoy, spoilsport.

Vb. *dissuade,* persuade against, convince to the contrary, talk out of 479 *confute*; caution 664 *warn*; remonstrate; expostulate, protest against 762 *deprecate*; make one stop in one's tracks, give one pause 486 *cause doubt*; head off, steer one away from, turn one aside 282 *deflect*; keep back; disenchant, disillusion, disincline; set against, turn a., put off, repel; dishearten, discourage; throw cold water on, dampen, quench, cool, damp the ardour, be a wet blanket; take the edge off 257 *blunt*.

614 Pretext – **N.** *pretext,* ostensible motive, alleged m., reason given; statement, allegation, profession, claim 532 *affirmation*; plea, excuse, defence, apology, rationale, justification 927 *vindication*; alibi 667 *means of escape*; peg to hang something on 218 *prop*; shallow pretext, lame excuse, quibble 477 *sophism*; proviso 468 *qualification*; subterfuge 698 *stratagem*; pretence, Bunbury, previous engagement, diplomatic illness 543 *untruth*; blind, red herring, dust thrown in the eyes; stalking horse, smoke screen, cloak, cover 421 *screen*; apology for, pale imitation of; colour, guise 445 *appearance*; bluff.

Adj. *ostensible,* alleged, pretended; seeming.

Vb. *plead,* allege, claim, give as one's reason *or* rationale, profess 532 *affirm*; make one's pretext, make a plea of 475

argue; make excuses, offer an excuse, excuse oneself, defend o. 927 *justify*; gloss over; shelter behind, use as a stalking horse; make capital out of, cash in on 137 *profit by*; find a loophole, wriggle out of 667 *escape*; bluff; varnish, colour; blind, throw dust in the eyes, draw a red herring across.

615 Good – N. *good,* one's g., what is good for one; advantage, benefit; the best; common good; lesser evil, utilitarianism 642 *good policy*; well-being, welfare 730 *prosperity*; riches 800 *wealth*; luck, good l., fortune, good f.; happy days, happy ending 824 *happiness*; blessing, world of good; well-wishing.

benefit, something to one's advantage, advantage, interest; convenience; crop, harvest, return 771 *acquisition*; profit, increment, gain; edification, betterment 654 *improvement*; boon 781 *gift*; good turn; favour, blessing, blessing in disguise; turn-up for the book, godsend, windfall, legacy, piece of luck, treasure trove, find, prize; good thing.

Adj. *good,* goodly, fine; blessed, happy; advantageous, heaven-sent 644 *beneficial*; worthwhile 644 *valuable*; helpful 706 *cooperative*; praiseworthy, commendable, recommended 923 *approved*; edifying, moral 933 *virtuous*; pleasure-giving 826 *pleasurable*.

Vb. *benefit,* do good, help, avail, be of service; edify, advantage, profit; repay 771 *be profitable*; do one a power of good 654 *make better*; turn out well, be all for the best, come right in the end.

flourish, thrive, do well, be on top of the world, be on the crest of a wave; rise, rise in the world 730 *prosper*; arrive 727 *succeed*; benefit by, gain by, be the better for, improve 654 *get better*; turn to good account, cash in on 137 *profit by*; make a profit 771 *gain*; make money 800 *get rich*.

Adv. *well,* satisfactorily, favourably, profitably, happily, healthily, not amiss, all to the good; to one's advantage, to one's benefit, for the best, in one's best interests; in fine style, on the up and up.

616 Evil – N. *evil,* wickedness, iniquity, mischievousness, injuriousness, disservice, injury, putting the boot in, dirty trick; wrong, injury, outrage 914 *injustice*; crying shame, shame, abuse; curse, scourge, poison, pest, plague, sore, running s. 659 *bane*; ill, ills that flesh is heir to, Pandora's box; sad world, vale of tears; trouble, troubles 731 *adversity*; affliction, misery, distress 825 *suffering*; grief, woe 825 *sorrow*; unease, malaise, angst, discomfort 825 *worry*; nuisance 827 *annoyance*; hurt, bodily harm, wound, bruise, cut, gash 377 *pain*; blow, mortal b., death b., buffet, stroke 279 *knock*; outrageous fortune, slings and arrows, calamity, bad luck 731 *misfortune*; casualty, accident 154 *event*; fatality 361 *death*; catastrophe 165 *ruin*; tragedy, sad ending 655 *deterioration*; mischief, devilry, harm, damage 772 *loss*; ill effect, bad result; disadvantage 35 *inferiority*; drawback, fly in the ointment 647 *defect*; setback 702 *hitch*; indigence 801 *poverty*; sense of injury, grievance 829 *discontent*; vindictiveness 910 *revengefulness*.

Adj. *evil,* wicked, iniquitous 934 *vicious*; black, foul, shameful 914 *wrong*; bad, too bad 645 *damnable*; unlucky, inauspicious, sinister 731 *adverse*; insidious, injurious, prejudicial, disadvantageous 645 *harmful*; trouble-making; troublous 827 *distressing*; fatal, fell, mortal, deathly 362 *deadly*; ruinous, disastrous 165 *destructive*; catastrophic, calamitous, tragic 731 *unfortunate*; all wrong, awry, out of joint, out of kilter.

Adv. *amiss,* wrong, awry, sour.

Section two: Prospective volition

617 Intention – N. *intention,* intent, meaning; deliberateness; calculation, calculated risk 480 *estimate*; purpose, determination, predetermination, resolve 599 *resolution*; mind 447 *intellect*; criminal intent 936 *guilt*; good intentions 897 *benevolence*; view, prospect; proposal; design 623 *plan*; enterprise

672 *undertaking*; ambition 859 *desire*; decision 480 *judgment*; ultimatum 766 *conditions*; bid, bid for 671 *attempt*; destination 69 *end*.

objective, destination, object, end, end in view, aim; axe to grind; butt, target, bull's-eye 225 *centre*; tape, winning post 295 *goal*; Mecca 76 *focus*; quarry, game, prey 619 *chase*; prize, crown, wreath, laurels 729 *trophy*; dream, aspiration, vision 513 *ideality*; heart's desire, Promised Land, El Dorado, Land flowing with milk and honey, pot *or* crock of gold at the end of the rainbow, Holy Grail 859 *desired object*.

Vb. *intend,* propose; have in mind, have in view, have an eye to, contemplate, think of; study, meditate; reckon on, calculate, look for 507 *expect*; foresee the necessity of 510 *foresee*; have a mind to, mean to, have every intention 599 *be resolute*; resolve, determine, premeditate 608 *predetermine*; project, design, plan for 623 *plan*; intend for, destine f. 155 *predestine*; earmark 547 *mark*; put aside for, reserve f.; intend for oneself (see *aim at*).

aim at, make one's target; go after, go all out for, work towards, strive after 619 *pursue*; try for 671 *attempt*; be after, have an eye on, have designs on, promise oneself, aspire to; take aim, zero in on, focus on, point at, level at, train one's sights on, aim high, hitch one's wagon to a star 281 *aim*.

Adv. *purposely,* on purpose, in cold blood, deliberately, intentionally; knowingly, wittingly; with forethought, with malice aforethought; in order to; with the intention of, with a view to, with the object of, by design, as planned, according to plan, as arranged.

618 Nondesign. Gamble – **N.** *nondesign,* indeterminacy; involuntariness, instinct 609 *spontaneity*; coincidence; accident, fluke, luck; good luck, windfall, stroke of luck; bad luck, hard l. 616 *evil*; lottery, luck of the draw (see *gambling*); potluck; wheel of Fortune 596 *fate*.

gambling, risk-taking; flier, risk, hazard, Russian roulette 661 *danger*; gamble, potluck 159 *chance*; venture, speculation, flutter 461 *experiment*; shot, shot in the dark, leap in the d., pig in a poke, blind bargain 474 *uncertainty*; bid, throw; toss of a coin, turn of a card; wager, bet, stake, ante; dice, die; element of risk, game of chance; bingo; fruit machine, gaming m., one-armed bandit; roulette, rouge et noir 837 *gambling game*; betting, turf, horse-racing, dog-r. 716 *racing*; football pool, treble chance, pools; draw, lottery, raffle, tombola, sweepstake. premium bond.

gaming-house, gambling den; betting shop, bookie's, bookmaker's, turf accountant's; casino, pool room, bingo hall, amusement arcade; racecourse, turf; tote.

stock exchange, exchange, share shop, bucket shop.

gambler, gamester, player, better, backer, punter; turf accountant, bookmaker, bookie, tout, tipster; risk-taker; venture capitalist, adventurer, entrepreneur 672 *undertaking*; speculator; bear, bull, stag; arbitrageur.

Adj. *unintentional,* inadvertent, unintended, unmeant 596 *involuntary*; unpremeditated; accidental, coincidental 159 *casual*.

speculative, experimental 474 *uncertain*; hazardous, risky, chancy, dicey; risk-taking, adventurous, enterprising.

Vb. *gamble,* do the pools; bet, stake, wager; call one's hand; play for high stakes; take bets, offer odds, make a book; back, punt; cover a bet; play the market, speculate, arbitrage, have a flutter 461 *experiment*; run a risk, take risks, push one's luck, tempt Providence; buy a pig in a poke 857 *be rash*; venture, chance it, chance one's arm, tempt fortune, tempt fate, try one's luck, trust to chance; raffle, draw lots, cut straws, cut for aces, spin a coin, toss up.

619 Pursuit – **N.** *pursuit,* pursuance, follow-up 65 *sequence*; hunting, seeking, looking for, quest 459 *search*; tracking,

spooring, trailing, tailing, dogging; hounding, persecution, witch-hunt; affairs 622 *business*.

chase, run; steeplechase, paperchase 716 *racing*; hunt, hunting, hounding, hue and cry, tally-ho; beat, drive; shooting, gunning, hunting, shooting and fishing 837 *sport*; blood sport, fox hunt, stag h.; big-game h., lion h., tiger h.; elephant h., boar h.; pigsticking; stalking, deer s.; hawking, fowling, falconry; fishing, angling, fly fishing, coarse f., sea f.; inshore f., deep-sea f., whaling; beagling, coursing, ratting, trapping, ferreting, rabbiting, mole-catching; fishing tackle, rod and line, bait, fly, fly-tying; fowling-piece 723 *firearm*; fishtrap, rat-trap 542 *trap*; manhunt, dragnet; game, quarry, prey, victim 617 *objective*; catch 771 *acquisition*.

hunter, quester, seeker, searcher 459 *enquirer*; search party; pursuer, tracker, trailer, sleuth, tail, shadow; huntsman, huntress; beater; Diana; sportsman, sportswoman, sportsperson 837 *player*; gun, shot, marksman *or* -woman; headhunter 362 *killer*; big-game hunter, fox h., deer stalker; poacher, guddler, trout-tickler; trapper, rat-catcher, rodent officer, mole-catcher; bird catcher, fowler, falconer, hawker; fisherman, angler; shrimper; trawler, trawlerman, whaler; pack, hounds; hound, foxhound, otterhound, bloodhound 365 *dog*; hawk 365 *bird*; beast of prey, man-eater 365 *mammal*; mouser 365 *cat*.

Vb. *pursue,* seek, look for, cast about for; be gunning for, hunt for, fish for, dig for 459 *search*; send out a search party; stalk; shadow, dog, track, trail, sleuth, tail, dog one's footsteps, follow the scent 284 *follow*; scent out 484 *discover*; witch-hunt, harry, persecute 735 *oppress*; chase, give c., hunt; raise the hunt, raise the hue and cry; mark as one's prey, make one's quarry 617 *aim at*; run after, set one's cap at, throw oneself at, woo 889 *court*; be after; pursue one's own interests 622 *busy oneself*; follow up.

hunt, go hunting, go big-game h., go shooting, ride to hounds; go fishing, fish,

angle, fly-fish; trawl; whale; shrimp; net, catch 542 *ensnare*; mouse; stalk, deer-s., fowl, hawk; course; flush, beat; set snares, poach, guddle.

620 Avoidance – N. *avoidance,* prevention 702 *hindrance*; abstinence, abstention 942 *temperance*; forbearance, refraining 177 *moderation*; nonintervention, noninvolvement; evasiveness 518 *equivocalness*; evasive action, dodge, duck, sidestep; delaying action; evasion, flight 667 *escape*; shrinking 854 *fear*; shunning, wide berth, safe distance 199 *distance*; shirking 458 *negligence*; nonattendance 190 *absence*; escapism.

avoider, abstainer; dodger, evader, tax e., moonlighter, bilker, welsher 545 *trickster*; shrinker, quitter 856 *coward*; shirker, skiver, slacker, sloucher, leadswinger 679 *idler*; skulker; draft-dodger, truant, deserter 918 *undutifulness*; runaway, fugitive, escapee 667 *escaper*; escapist, dreamer 513 *visionary*; head in the sand, ostrich.

Vb. *avoid,* not go near, keep off, keep away; bypass, circumvent 282 *deviate*; turn aside, look the other way, turn a blind eye, cold-shoulder; stand apart, have no hand in, play no part in, not soil one's fingers, keep one's hands clean, wash one's hands of, shun, eschew, leave, let alone, have nothing to do with, not touch with a bargepole; give a miss, give the go-by; fight shy, back away, draw back 290 *recede*; hold off, stand aloof, keep one's distance, keep a respectful d., keep at arm's length, give a wide berth; keep out of the way, keep clear, stand c., get out of the way; forbear; refrain, abstain, forswear; hold back, hang b., balk at 598 *be unwilling*; pass the buck, get out of; cop out, funk, shirk 458 *neglect*; shrink, flinch, jib, refuse, shy; take evasive action, lead one a dance, draw a red herring, throw dust in one's eyes, throw one off the scent, play hide-and-seek; sidestep, dodge, duck; deflect, ward off; duck the issue, fudge the i., get round, obviate, skirt round, fence, hedge, pussyfoot 518 *be equivocal*;

evade, escape, give one the slip 667 *elude*; hide 523 *lurk*; bury one's head in the sand, be ostrich-like; deny 533 *negate*.

run away, desert, play truant, jump bail, take French leave, go AWOL 918 *fail in duty*; abscond, welsh, flit, elope 667 *escape*; absent oneself 190 *be absent*; withdraw, retire, retreat, beat a r., turn tail, turn one's back 282 *turn round*; flee, flit, fly, take to flight, run for one's life; make off, slope o., bolt, run, run for it, cut and run, show a clean pair of heels, take to one's h., beat it, make oneself scarce, scoot, scram, skedaddle 277 *move fast*; slip the cable, break away 296 *decamp*; shake the dust from one's feet, steal away, sneak off, slink o., scuttle, do a bunk.

621 Relinquishment – N. *relinquishment*, abandonment; leaving, evacuation 296 *departure*; desertion, truancy, defection 918 *undutifulness*; withdrawal, secession 978 *schism*; walk-out 145 *strike*; cop-out 620 *avoidance*; yielding, giving up; abnegation, renunciation 779 *nonretention*; abdication, retirement 753 *resignation*; disuse 674 *nonuse*; discontinuance 611 *desuetude*; cancellation, annulment 752 *abrogation*;

Vb. *relinquish,* drop, let go, leave hold of; surrender, resign, give up, yield; waive, forgo; cede, hand over, transfer 780 *assign*; forfeit 772 *lose*; renounce, abnegate, recant, change one's mind 603 *tergiversate*; not proceed with, drop the idea, forget it 506 *forget*; wean oneself 611 *disaccustom*; forswear, abstain 620 *avoid*; shed, slough, cast off, divest; drop, discard, get rid of, jettison, write off 674 *stop using*; lose interest, have other fish to fry 860 *be indifferent*; abdicate, back down, scratch, stand down, withdraw, retire, drop out 753 *resign*; jack it in, give in, throw in the sponge *or* the towel, throw in one's hand 721 *submit*; leave, quit, move out, vacate, evacuate 296 *depart*; forsake, abandon, run out on, leave stranded, quit one's post, desert 918 *fail in duty*; play truant 190 *be*

absent; down tools, strike, come out 145 *cease*; walk out, secede; throw over, ditch, jilt, break it off, go back on one's word 542 *deceive*; pass on to the next, shelve, postpone 136 *put off*; annul, cancel 752 *abrogate*.

622 Business – N. *business,* affairs, business interests, irons in the fire; occupation, concern; business on hand, case, agenda 154 *affairs*; enterprise, venture, undertaking, pursuit 678 *activity*; office routine, daily round 610 *practice*; daily work; business circles, business world, City, world of commerce; technology, industry, light i., heavy i., sunrise i., commerce, big business; multinational, business company 708 *corporation*; cottage industry; industrialism, industrialization, industrial arts, manufacture 164 *production*; trade, craft, handicraft; guild, union, chamber of commerce, business association 706 *association*; employment, work.

vocation, calling, life work, mission; life, lifestyle, walk of life, career, chosen career, labour of love; living, livelihood, daily bread, one's bread and butter; profession, métier, craft, trade; line, line of country (see *function*); ministry; cloth, veil, habit 985 *the church*; military profession, arms 718 *war*; naval profession, sea; legal profession 953 *law*; teaching profession, education 534 *teaching*; medical profession, medicine, practice; industry, commerce 791 *trade*; diplomatic service, civil s., administration 689 *management*; public service, public life; social service 901 *sociology*.

job, chores, odd jobs, work, task, exercise 682 *labour*; duty, charge, commission, mission, errand; employ, service, employment, self-employment; hours of work, working day, working week, manhour; occupation, situation, position, appointment, post, office; full-time job, permanency; temporary job, part-time j., freelance work; situation wanted; situation vacant, opening, vacancy; labour exchange, employment agency, Job Centre, Department of Employment.

function, capacity, office, duty; area of interest, realm, province, domaine, orbit, sphere; scope, field, terms of reference 183 *range*; department, line, line of country; role, part; business, job; responsibility, brief, concern, care, look-out, baby, pigeon.

Vb. *employ,* busy, occupy, take up one's time, fill one's t.; give employment, engage, recruit, hire, enlist, appoint, post 751 *commission*; take on, take on the payroll 804 *pay*; offer a job to, fill a vacancy, staff.

busy oneself, work, work for 742 *serve*; have a career, be employed, be self-employed, be free-lance, work from home, do a job, hold down a j., earn, earn one's living; earn an honest crust, turn an honest penny, keep the wolf from the door 771 *acquire*; take on a job, apply for a j.; be up and doing, bustle 678 *be busy*; concern oneself with, make it one's business, take a hand in 678 *meddle*; work at, ply; engage in, turn one's hand to, take up, engage in, go in for; have one's hands full, take on oneself, bear the burden, assume responsibility, bear the brunt, take on one's shoulders 917 *incur a duty*; work with one's hands, work with one's brains; pursue one's hobby 837 *amuse oneself*.

function, work, go 173 *operate*; fill a role, play one's part, carry on; officiate, act, discharge one's duties, serve as, do duty for, perform the duties, do the work of; substitute, stand in for 755 *deputize*; hold office, hold down a job, have a brief.

do business, transact, negotiate 766 *make terms*; ply a trade, follow a career; have a business, engage in, carry on a trade, keep shop; do business with, deal w., enter into trade relations 791 *trade*; transact business, go about one's business; pursue one's vocation, earn one's living (see *busy oneself*); be self-employed, work from home, run a cottage industry, freelance, set up in business, go into b.

623 Plan – N. *plan,* scheme, design; planning; organization, systematization, rationalization, centralization 60 *order*; programme, project, proposal 617 *intention*; proposition, suggestion, motion, resolution (see *policy*); master plan, five-year p., ground p., scale drawing, blueprint 551 *map*; diagram, flow chart 86 *statistics*; sketch, outline, draft, first d., schedule; skeleton; model, pattern, pilot scheme 23 *prototype*; drawing board, planning office.

policy, forethought 510 *foresight*; statesmanship 498 *wisdom*; course of action, procedure, strategy 688 *tactics*; approach, attack 624 *way*; steps, measures 676 *action*; proposed line of action, programme, prospectus, platform, outline, ticket, slate; party line; formula 81 *rule*; schedule, agenda, order of the day, any other business, AOB 622 *business*.

contrivance, expedient, resource, recourse, resort, last r., card, trump c., card up one's sleeve 629 *means*; recipe; loophole, escape clause, way out, alternative, artifice, device, gimmick, dodge, ploy, flag of convenience 698 *stratagem*; wangle, fiddle; trick 694 *skill*; stunt; inspiration, brainwave, brainstorm, happy thought, bright idea; notion, invention; tool, weapon, contraption, gadget, gizmo 628 *instrument*; improvisation 609 *spontaneity*; feat, tour de force; bold move, masterstroke 676 *deed*.

plot, intrigue; web of intrigue; cabal, conspiracy, inside job, insider trading *or* dealing; scheme, racket, game 698 *stratagem*; frame-up, put-up job, fit-up, machination; manipulation, wire-pulling 612 *motive*.

planner, inventor, originator, deviser; proposer; founder, author, architect, designer, town-planner; backroom boy, boffin 696 *expert*; brains, mastermind; organizer, systems analyst; strategist, tactician; statesman *or* -woman, politician; wheeler-dealer, axe-grinder; plotter, intriguer; conspirator 545 *deceiver*.

Adj. *planned,* under consideration, at the planning stage, on the stocks, strategic, tactical.

Vb. *plan,* form a p.; make a plan, draw up, design, draft, blueprint; frame, shape 243 *form*; project, plan out, sketch o., map o., lay o., design a prototype; draw up a programme, lay the foundation; shape a course, mark out a c.; organize, systematize, rationalize; schedule, draw up a s., phase; invent, think up 484 *discover*; conceive a plan 513 *imagine*; devise, engineer; hatch, concoct; prearrange 608 *predetermine*; calculate, think ahead, look a. 498 *be wise*; follow a plan, work to a schedule; have an axe to grind.

plot, scheme, have designs, be up to something, wheel and deal; manipulate, pull strings 178 *influence*; conspire, intrigue; cook up; hatch a plot 698 *be cunning*; undermine; work against; frame 541 *fake*.

624 Way – N. *way,* route 267 *itinerary*; manner, guise; fashion, style 243 *form*; method, mode, line, approach, address, attack; procedure, process, way of, way of doing things, modus operandi 688 *tactics*; operation, treatment; routine 610 *practice*; technique, know-how 694 *skill*; gait 265 *motion*; progress 285 *progression*; primrose path; way of life, lifestyle.

access, right of way, communications; way to 289 *approach*; entrance, door 263 *doorway*; side-entrance, back-e., tradesman's e.; drive, driveway, gangway; porch, hall, hallway, corridor, vestibule 194 *lobby*; way through, pass, passageway 305 *passage*; intersection, junction, crossing; zebra crossing, pedestrian c., pelican c. 305 *traffic control*; strait, sound 345 *gulf*; channel, fairway, canal 351 *conduit*; lock, stile, turnstile, tollgate; stairs, flight of s., stairway, ladder 308 *ascent*.

bridge, brig; footbridge, flyover, road bridge, aqueduct; suspension bridge, swing b., Bailey b., humpback b.; viaduct, span; railway bridge; pontoon bridge, floating b., transporter b.; drawbridge; causeway, stepping-stone, gangway, gangplank, catwalk, duckboards;

ford, ferry 305 *passage*; way under, subway, underpass 263 *tunnel*; isthmus.

route, direction, way to or from, course, march, tack, track; trajectory, orbit; carriageway, lane, bus l. 305 *traffic control*; air lane, sea-l., seaway, fairway, waterway 351 *conduit*; short cut, bypass; detour; line of communication.

path, pathway, footpath, pavement, sidewalk; towpath, bridlepath; lane, track, sheep t., trail; right of way, public footpath; walk, promenade, esplanade, front, avenue, drive, boulevard, mall; pedestrian precinct, arcade, colonnade, aisle, cloister, ambulatory; racetrack, running track, speed t. 724 *arena*; fairway, runway.

road, high r., highway, Queen's h., highways and byways; main road, A road, minor r., B r., dirt r., cinder track; side road; toll road, turnpike, route nationale; thoroughfare, trunk r., artery, bypass, ring road; motorway, M-way, autoroute, autobahn, autostrada; expressway, throughway, clearway; sliproad, fast lane; crossroads, junction, T-junction, turn-off; intersection, roundabout, cloverleaf; crossing, pedestrian c., zebra c, pelican c. 305 *traffic control*; roadway, carriageway, dual c.; central reservation, crash barrier; cycle track, cycleway; street, high s., one-way s., side s., back s.; alleyway, wynd, alley, blind a., cul de sac; close, avenue 192 *housing*; pavement, sidewalk, kerb; paving, cobbles, setts, paving stone, flagstones; hard shoulder, verge; macadam, tarmac, asphalt, road metal; surface.

railway, railroad, line; permanent way, track, lines, railway l., electrified l., main line, branch l.; tramlines, tramway; monorail; funicular; overhead railway, elevated r., underground r., electric r., subway, tube, metro 274 *train*; light railway, narrow gauge, standard g.; junction, crossover, level crossing, tunnel, cutting, embankment; siding, marshalling yard, goods y., shunting y.; station, halt; platform 145 *stopping place*; signal; rails, points, sleepers.

Adv. *via,* by way of, in transit.

625 Middle way – N. *middle way,* middle course, middle of the road; balance, golden mean, happy medium 30 *average*; halfway, halfway house, midstream 30 *middle point*; half tide; neutrality 177 *moderation*; half measures 601 *irresolution*; mutual concession 770 *compromise.*

moderate, nonextremist, wet, Girondist, Menshevik; neutral, don't know; Laodicean.

Adj. *neutral,* impartial 913 *just*; uncommitted, unattached, free-floating, don't know; detached 860 *indifferent*; moderate, wet, nonextreme, middle-of-the-road 225 *central*; sitting on the fence, lukewarm, half-and-half, shilly-shallying 601 *irresolute*; neither one thing nor the other, grey.

626 Circuit – N. *circuit,* roundabout way, circuitous route, scenic r., bypass, detour, ring road, loop, diversion; orbit, round, lap 314 *circuition*; circumference 250 *circle.*

Adj. *roundabout,* circuitous, indirect, meandering; circumlocutory 570 *diffuse*; skirting.

Vb. *circuit,* lap, beat the bounds, go round, make a circuit, loop the loop 314 *circle*; make a detour, go a roundabout way, go out of one's way 282 *deviate*; short-circuit 620 *avoid*; encircle, encompass 230 *surround*; skirt.

Adv. *round about,* round the world, in a roundabout way, circuitously, indirectly, from pillar to post.

627 Requirement – N. *requirement,* essential, sine qua non, a must 596 *necessity*; needs, necessities; indent, order, requisition, shopping list; stipulation, prerequisite; need 636 *insufficiency*; gap, lacuna 190 *absence*; demand, call for, run on, seller's market, bearish m., bullish m. 792 *purchase*; consumption, input, intake; shortage 307 *shortfall*; slippage; balance due, what is owing 803 *debt*; claim 761 *request*; ultimatum, injunction 737 *command.*

needfulness, necessity for, indispensability, desirability; necessitousness, want, breadline, poverty level 801 *poverty*; exigency, urgency, emergency 137 *crisis*; matter of life and death 638 *important matter*; bare minimum.

Adj. *required,* requisite, prerequisite, needful, needed; necessary, essential, vital, indispensable; called for, in demand 859 *desired.*

necessitous, in want, in need, feeling the pinch, on the breadline, in the poverty trap; lacking, deprived of; destitute 801 *poor*; starving 636 *underfed*; disadvantaged.

Vb. *require,* need, have need of, want, lack 636 *be unsatisfied*; be without, feel the need for, have occasion for; have a vacancy for; miss; crave 859 *desire*; cry out f.; claim, put in a claim for, apply for 761 *request*; find necessary, be unable to do without, must have; create a need, necessitate; make demands 737 *demand*; order, tele-order, indent, requisition; reserve, book.

628 Instrumentality – N. *instrumentality,* operation 173 *agency*; occasion 156 *cause*; result 157 *effect*; pressure 178 *influence*; efficacy 160 *power*; services 703 *aid*; intervention, interference 678 *activity*; medium 629 *means*; use; instrumentation, mechanization, automation, computerization 630 *machine.*

instrument, hand, organ, sense o.; amanuensis, scribe, lackey, slave 742 *servant*; agent, midwife, medium, help, assistant 703 *aider*; go-between, pander 720 *mediator*; catalyst; vehicle; pawn; robot 630 *machine*; cat's paw, stooge, puppet, creature 707 *auxiliary*; weapon, implement, appliance, lever 630 *tool*; magic ring, Aladdin's lamp 983 *spell*; key, skeleton k., master k., passkey 263 *opener*; open sesame, watchword, password, slogan, shibboleth, passport 756 *permit*; stepping-stone 624 *bridge*; highway 624 *road*; controls; device, gadget, gizmo 623 *contrivance.*

Adj. *instrumental,* working 173 *operative*; manual; automatic, computerized,

electronic, push-button 630 *mechanical*; effective 160 *powerful*; conducive; applied; serviceable, promoting, assisting, helpful 703 *aiding*; functional.

Vb. *be instrumental,* work, act 173 *operate*; perform 676 *do*; serve, work for, lend oneself *or* itself to; help, assist 703 *aid*; advance, promote 703 *patronize*; have a hand in 775 *participate*; be to blame for 156 *cause*; be the creature of, be a cat's paw, pull another's chestnuts out of the fire; use one's influence, pull strings 178 *influence.*

Adv. *through,* per, by the hand of, by means of, with the help of, thanks to.

629 Means – N. *means,* ways and m., wherewithal; power, capacity 160 *ability*; conveniences, facilities; appliances, tools, tools of the trade, bag of tricks 630 *tool*; technology, new t., high t., high tech 490 *knowledge*; technique, know-how 694 *skill*; equipment, supplies, ammunition 633 *provision*; resources, raw material 631 *materials*; nuts and bolts 630 *machine*; workforce, manpower 686 *personnel*; cash flow 797 *money*; capital, working c. 628 *instrument*; assets, stock-in-trade 777 *property*; stocks and shares, investments; revenue, income; borrowing capacity; reserves, something in reserve, shot in one's locker, card up one's sleeve, two strings to one's bow 662 *safeguard*; method, measures, steps 624 *way*; expedient, device, resort, recourse 623 *contrivance*; last resort.

Adv. *by means of,* with, by, using, through; with the aid of; by dint of.

630 Tool – N. *tool,* precision t., machine t., hand t, implement 628 *instrument*; apparatus, appliance, utensil; weapon, arm 723 *arms*; device, contraption, gadget, gizmo 623 *contrivance*; doodah, thingummy, whatsit; screw, screwdriver, drill, electric d. 263 *perforator*; wrench, monkey w., pipe w., mole w., Stillson (tdmk), spanner; pliers, pincers, tweezers 778 *pincers*; chisel, wedge, knife, Stanley (tdmk) k. 256 *sharp edge*; rope

47 *cable*; peg, nail 217 *hanger,* 218 *support*; leverage, lever, jemmy, crowbar, jack 218 *pivot*; grip, haft, shaft, tiller, helm, rudder 218 *handle*; pulley, sheave 250 *wheel*; switch, stopcock; trigger; pedal, pole, punt-p. 287 *propulsion*; ram 279 *hammer*; prehistoric tool, flint; tools of the trade, tool-kit, do-it-yourself k., bag of tricks.

machine, machinery, mechanism, works; clockwork, wheels within wheels; nuts and bolts 58 *component*; spring, mainspring, hairspring; gears, gearing, bevel gears, syncromesh, automatic gear change; motor, engine, internal combustion e., lean-burn e., diesel e., steam e.; turbine, dynamo 160 *sources of energy*; servomechanism, servomotor; robot, automaton; computer 86 *data processing.*

equipment, gear, tackle; outfit, kit; furnishing; trappings, accoutrement 228 *dress*; utensils, impedimenta, paraphernalia, chattels 777 *property*; wares, stock-in-trade 795 *merchandise*; plant 687 *workshop.*

machinist, operator, operative; driver; engineer, technician, mechanic, fitter; craftsman, skilled worker 686 *artisan.*

Adj. *mechanical,* mechanized, motorized, powered, power-driven; labour-saving, automatic 628 *instrumental*; automated, computerized, electronic.

631 Materials – N. *materials,* resources 629 *means*; material, stuff; raw material; meat, fodder 301 *food*; ore, mineral, metal, pig-iron, ingot; clay, adobe, china clay, potter's c., gypsum 344 *soil*; glass 422 *transparency*; plastic, polythene, polyethylene, polypropylene, polystyrene, polyvinyl chloride, PVC, polytetrafluoroethylene, latex, celluloid, fibreglass; rope, yarn, wool 208 *fibre*; leather, hide 226 *skin*; timber 366 *wood*; rafter, board 218 *beam*; plank, plywood, lath; stuffing 227 *lining*; cloth, fabric 222 *textile.*

building material, building block, breeze b., brick 381 *pottery*; bricks and mortar, lath and plaster, wattle and

daub; thatch, slate, tile 226 *roof*; stone, marble, granite, flint, ashlar, masonry; rendering 226 *facing*; cement, concrete, reinforced c., flag, cobble 226 *paving*; gravel, tarmac, asphalt 624 *road*.

paper, pulp, newsprint; card, art paper, cartridge p., carbon p., tissue p., crepe p., tracing p., cellophane; papier mâché, cardboard, pasteboard; sheet, foolscap, quarto, imperial, A1, A2, A3, A4, A5; quire, ream; notepaper 586 *stationery*.

632 Store – N. *store,* mass, heap, load, stack, stockpile, mountain, butter m., lake, wine l., buildup 74 *accumulation*; packet, bundle, bagful, bucketful 26 *quantity*; harvest, crop, vintage, mow 771 *acquisition*; haystack, haycock, hayrick; stock, stock-in-trade 795 *merchandise*; assets, capital, holding, investment 777 *property*; fund, reserves, something in reserve, backlog; savings, savings account, nest egg; deposit, hoard, treasure; buried treasure, cache 527 *hiding-place*; bottom drawer, hope chest, trousseau 633 *provision*; pool, kitty; appeal fund; quarry, mine, gold-m.; natural resources, mineral deposit, coal d.; coalfield, gasfield, oilfield; coal mine, colliery, working, shaft; coalface, seam, lode; vein; well, oil w., gusher; fountain, fount 156 *source*; supply, stream; tap, pipeline, artesian well 341 *irrigator*; milch cow, the goose that lays the golden eggs, cornucopia, abundance 635 *plenty*.

storage, stowage, gathering, garnering 74 *accumulation*; conservation, bottling 666 *preservation*; safe deposit 660 *protection*; stabling, warehousing; mountain, butter m., lake, wine l.; storage space, shelf-room, space, accommodation 183 *room*; boxroom, loft; hold, bunker 194 *cellar*; storehouse, storeroom, stockroom; warehouse, goods shed; depot, dock, wharf 192 *stable*; magazine, arsenal, armoury, gunroom; treasure house 799 *treasury*; exchequer, strongroom, vault, coffer, moneybox, moneybag, till, safe, night s., bank; blood b., sperm b.; data b. 86 *data processing*;

store of memories 505 *memory*; hive, honeycomb; granary, garner, barn, silo; water tower, reservoir, cistern, tank, gasholder, gasometer; battery, garage, petrol station, gas s., filling s., petrol pump; dump, sump, drain, cesspool, sewage farm 649 *sink*; pantry, larder, buttery, stillroom 194 *chamber*; cupboard, shelf 194 *cabinet*; refrigerator, fridge, deep freeze, freezer, fridge-freezer; portmanteau, holdall, packing case 194 *box*; container, holder, quiver 194 *receptacle*.

collection, set, complete s.; archives, file 548 *record*; portfolio 74 *accumulation*; museum 125 *antiquity*; gallery, art g., art museum; library, thesaurus 559 *dictionary*; menagerie, aquarium 369 *zoo*; waxworks, Madame Tussaud's; exhibition 522 *exhibit*; repertory, repertoire, bag of tricks.

Vb. *store,* stow, pack, bundle 193 *load*; roll up, fold up; lay up, stow away, mothball; dump, garage, stable, warehouse; gather, harvest, reap, mow, pick, glean 370 *cultivate*; stack, heap, pile, amass, accumulate 74 *bring together*; stock up, stock up one's cupboards *or* larder, lay in, bulk-buy, panic buy, stockpile, pile up, build up; take on, take in, fuel; fill, fill up, top up, refill, refuel 633 *replenish*; put by, save, keep, hold, file, hang on to 778 *retain*; bottle, pickle, conserve 666 *preserve*; leave, set aside, put a., lay by, put b., reserve; bank, deposit, invest; hoard, treasure; bury, stash away, secrete 525 *conceal*; husband, save up, salt away, make a nest egg, prepare for a rainy day 814 *economize*; equip oneself, put in the bottom drawer 669 *prepare oneself*; pool, put in the kitty.

633 Provision – N. *provision,* furnishing, equipment; catering; service, delivery, distribution; self-service; procuring; feeding, entertainment, bed and breakfast, board and lodging, maintenance; assistance, lending 703 *subvention*; supply, food s., water s., feed; pipeline 272 *transference*; commissariat, provisioning, supplies, stores, rations, iron r.,

reserves 632 *store*; refill, filling-up 54 *plenitude*; food, provender 301 *provisions*; helping, portion 301 *meal*; grist to the mill, fuel to the flame; produce 164 *product*; budgeting.

caterer, purveyor, hotelier, hotel-keeper, hotel manager, restauranteur, head waiter, maître d'hôtel; innkeeper, landlord, landlady, licensee, mine host, publican; housekeeper, housewife; cook, chef; pastrycook, confectioner.

Vb. *provide,* afford, offer, lend 781 *give*; equip, furnish, arm, man, fit out, kit o. 669 *make ready*; supply; yield 164 *produce*; cater, purvey; procure, pander, pimp; service, service an order, meet an o. 793 *sell*; distribute, deliver, deliver the goods; hand out, hand round, serve, serve up, dish up; feed, do for, board, put up, maintain, keep, clothe; stock; budget, make provision, make due p.; provide for oneself, do for o.; stock up, lay in a stock 632 *store*; fuel; forage, water.

replenish, reinforce, top up, refill 54 *fill*; restock, refuel.

634 Waste – **N.** *waste,* wastage; leakage; depletion, exhaustion, drainage 300 *voidance*; dissipation 75 *dispersion*; evaporation 338 *vaporization*; melting 337 *liquefaction*; damage 772 *loss*; wear and tear, built-in obsolescence 655 *deterioration*; wastefulness, improvidence, lavishness, extravagance, overspending, squandering; overproduction 637 *superfluity*; misapplication, frittering away; vandalism, sabotage 165 *destruction*; waste product, litter, refuse 641 *rubbish*.

Adj. *wasteful,* extravagant, uneconomic 815 *prodigal*; time-consuming; damaging 165 *destructive*.

Vb. *waste,* deplete, drain 300 *empty*; dissipate, scatter; abuse, overwork, overfish, overgraze; wear out, erode, damage 655 *impair*; misapply, fritter away, cast pearls before swine; make no use of 674 *not use*; labour in vain 641 *waste effort*; be extravagant, overspend, squander, throw away, pour down the drain, throw out the baby with the bath

water 815 *be prodigal*; be careless, spill; be destructive, destroy, sabotage, vandalize; be wasted, decay 37 *decrease*; leak; melt, melt away 337 *liquefy*; evaporate 338 *vaporize*; run to seed 655 *deteriorate*; go down the drain.

635 Sufficiency – **N.** *sufficiency,* elegant s., right amount; right number, quorum; adequacy, enough; assets, competence, living wage; subsistence farming; self-sufficiency; exact requirement, no surplus; breadline; minimum, bare minimum, least one can do; full measure; fulfilment 725 *completion*; one's fill.

plenty, horn of p., cornucopia 171 *abundance*; showers of, flood, spate, oceans, streams 350 *stream*; lots, lashings, oodles, galore 32 *great quantity*; copiousness 54 *plenitude*; affluence, riches 800 *wealth*; fat of the land, luxury, groaning board, feast, banquet 301 *feasting*; orgy, profusion 815 *prodigality*; richness, fat; fertility, productivity, luxuriance, lushness 171 *productiveness*; harvest, rich h., vintage h., bumper crop; bonanza, endless supply; more than enough, too much, superabundance, embarras de choix, embarras de richesses 637 *redundance*.

Adj. *sufficient,* sufficing; self-sufficient 54 *complete*; enough, adequate, competent; enough to go round; satisfactory; up to the mark; just right, not too much not too little; only just enough.

plentiful, plenteous, ample, enough and to spare, more than enough 637 *superfluous*; lavish 813 *liberal*; without stint, unsparing, inexhaustible 32 *great*; luxuriant, riotous, lush, fertile, fat 171 *prolific*; profuse, abundant, copious, overflowing 637 *redundant*; rich, opulent, affluent 800 *moneyed*.

filled, full up, chock-full, chock-a-block, replete, satiated, had it up to here, ready to burst 863 *sated*; satisfied; teeming, overflowing with.

Vb. *suffice,* be enough, do. just do, do and no more, serve; qualify, make the grade 727 *be successful*; pass, pass muster, measure up to, meet requirements,

fill the bill; rise to the occasion; stand up to, take the strain 218 *support*; do what is required 725 *carry out*; satisfy 828 *content*; more than satisfy, satiate; make adequate provision 633 *provide*.

abound, proliferate, teem, swarm, bristle with, crawl w. 104 *be many*; riot, luxuriate 171 *be fruitful*; flow, shower, snow, pour, stream, sheet 350 *rain*; brim, overflow, flow with milk and honey 637 *superabound*.

have enough, be satisfied 828 *be content*; eat one's fill 301 *eat*; drink one's fill 301 *drink*; be sated, be chock-full, have had enough, have had it up to here, have had one's bellyful, be fed up 829 *be discontented*; have the means 800 *afford*.

Adv. *enough,* sufficiently, amply, to the full, to one's heart's content; on tap, on demand; abundantly.

636 Insufficiency – N. *insufficiency,* not enough, drop in the bucket; nonsatisfaction 829 *discontent*; inadequacy, incompetence; minginess, nothing to spare, too few; deficiency, imperfection 647 *defect*; deficit 55 *incompleteness*; nonfulfilment 726 *noncompletion*; half measures, failure, weakness, slippage 307 *shortfall*; bankruptcy 805 *insolvency*; subsistence level, breadline, poverty level, pittance, dole, mite; stinginess, meanness 816 *parsimony*; short commons, iron rations, starvation r., half r.; austerity, Spartan fare, starvation diet, bread and water 945 *asceticism*; malnutrition, vitamin deficiency 651 *disease*.

scarcity, scarceness, paucity 105 *fewness*; dearth, seven lean years; drought, famine, starvation; shortage 307 *shortfall*; slippage; power cut 37 *decrease*; short supply, seller's market, bearish m.; scantiness, meagreness, deprivation 801 *poverty*; lack, want, need 627 *needfulness*.

Adj. *insufficient,* disappointing 829 *discontenting*; inadequate, not enough, too little; scant, scanty, skimpy, slender; deficient, light on, low on, lacking 55 *incomplete*; wanting, poor 35 *inferior*;

incompetent, unequal to, not up to it 695 *unskilful*; weak, thin, watery, wersh, jejune, unnourishing 4 *insubstantial*; niggardly, miserly; stingy 816 *parsimonious*.

unprovided, unfurnished, illequipped, bare; unfilled, unsated 829 *discontented*; unprovided for, unaccommodated; lacking in, hard up 801 *poor*; undercapitalized, underfinanced, understaffed, undermanned, shorthanded, unavailable, off the menu, off 190 *absent*.

underfed, undernourished; halfstarved, on short commons; famished, starved, starving ravening, ravenous 946 *fasting*; skin and bone, anorexic, emaciated.

scarce, rare 140 *infrequent*; sparse 105 *few*; in short supply, at a premium, hard to get, hard to come by, not to be had for love or money, not to be had at any price, unavailable, unobtainable, out of season, out of stock.

Vb. *not suffice,* be insufficient, - inadequate etc. adj.; not meet requirements 647 *be imperfect*; want, lack; fail 509 *disappoint*; fall below 35 *be inferior*; come short, default 307 *fall short*; run out, dry up; paper over the cracks 726 *not complete*.

be unsatisfied, ask for more, come again, take a second helping; feel dissatisfied; spurn an offer, reject; miss, feel the lack, stand in need of; be a glutton for, be unable to have enough of 947 *gluttonize*.

637 Redundance – N. *redundance,* redundancy, overspill, overflow; superabundance; embarras de richesses, avalanche, spate 32 *great quantity*; too many, mob 74 *crowd*; saturation, saturation point 54 *plenitude*; excess 634 *waste*; excessiveness, exorbitance, extremes, too much 546 *exaggeration*; overdoing it, overstretching oneself, overextension, too many irons in the fire 678 *overactivity*; officiousness, red tape; overpraise, overoptimism 482 *overestimation*; overweight; overload, last straw 322 *gravity*;

lion's share; overindulgence 943 *intemperance*; plethora, congestion 863 *satiety*; more than enough; glut; obesity 651 *disease*.

superfluity, more than is needed, luxury; frills, luxuries, nonessentials; overkill, duplication; something over, bonus, spare cash, money to burn 40 *extra*; margin, overlap, excess, surplus, balance 41 *remainder*; superfluousness, accessory, fifth wheel, parasite 641 *uselessness*; padding; tautology 570 *diffuseness*; redundancy; overmanning 678 *activity*; too much of a good thing, embarras de richesses, glut, drug on the market; surfeit, overdose 863 *satiety*.

Adj. *redundant,* one too many, one over the eight 104 *many*; overmuch, overabundant, excessive, immoderate 32 *exorbitant*; overdone, overflowing, overfull, running over, brimming over 54 *full*; flooding; snowed under, overwhelmed; cloying; replete, stuffed, overfed; overstretched; overloaded; congested.

superfluous, redundant, supernumerary; needless, unnecessary, uncalled for 641 *useless*; excessive; luxurious; surplus, extra, over and above 41 *remaining*; spare 38 *additional*; de trop, on one's hands, left over, going begging 860 *unwanted*; dispensable, expendable.

Vb. *superabound,* luxuriate 635 *abound*; run riot 171 *be fruitful*; bristle with, swarm w., teem m., hotch w., crawl w.; overflow, brim over, burst at the seams 54 *be complete*; flood, inundate, burst its banks, deluge, overwhelm 350 *flow*; engulf 299 *absorb*; know no bounds, spread far and wide 306 *overstep*; overlap 183 *extend*; saturate 341 *drench*; stuff, gorge, cram 54 *fill*; congest, choke, suffocate; overdose, glut, cloy, satiate, sate; pamper oneself, overindulge o., overeat, overdrink 943 *be intemperate*; oversubscribe, do more than enough; oversell, flood the market; overstock; overdo, go over the top, overstep the mark, pile it on, lay it on thick, lay it on with a trowel 546 *exaggerate*;

overload, overburden; overcharge; lavish upon 813 *be liberal*; be lavish, make a splash 815 *be prodigal*; roll in, stink of 800 *be rich*.

be superfluous, - redundant etc. adj.; go begging, remain on one's hands 41 *be left*; have time on one's hands 679 *be inactive*; do twice over, duplicate; carry coals to Newcastle, gild the lily, teach one's grandmother to suck eggs; labour the obvious, take a sledgehammer to crack a nut, break a butterfly on a wheel, hold a candle to the sun; exceed requirements.

638 Importance – N. *importance,* priority, urgency 64 *precedence*; paramountcy, supremacy 34 *superiority*; essentialness; import, consequence, significance, weight, weightiness, gravity, seriousness; substance, moment 3 *substantiality*; interest, consideration, concern 622 *business*; notability, memorability, mark, prominence, distinction, eminence 866 *repute*; influence 866 *prestige*; size, magnitude 32 *greatness*; rank; value, merit 644 *goodness*; stress, emphasis.

important matter, vital concern; crucial moment, turning point 137 *crisis*; be-all and end-all; no joke, no laughing matter, matter of life and death; big news 529 *news*; exploit 676 *deed*; landmark, milestone; red-letter day, great d. 876 *special day*.

chief thing, what matters, the thing, great t., main t.; supreme issue, crux 452 *topic*; fundamentals, bedrock, nitty-gritty; nuts and bolts, sine qua non 627 *requirement*; priority 605 *choice*; substance 5 *essential part*; highlight; cream, crème de la crème, pick 644 *elite*; keynote, cornerstone, mainstay, linchpin, kingpin; head, spearhead; sum and substance, heart of the matter, heart, core, kernel, nucleus, nub 225 *centre*; hub 218 *pivot*; chief hope, trump card, main chance.

bigwig, personage, notable, personality, heavyweight, somebody 866 *person*

of repute; local worthy, pillar of the community; great man *or* woman, VIP, brass hat; his *or* her nibs, big gun, big shot, big noise, big wheel, big white chief, Mr Big; leading light; kingpin; prima donna, star, lion, catch 890 *favourite*; head, chief, godfather, Big Brother 34 *superior*; the greatest 644 *exceller*; grandee 868 *aristocrat*; magnate, mogul, mandarin; baron, tycoon 741 *autocrat*; captains of industry, big battalions, top brass, top people, establishment 733 *authority*; superpower 178 *influence*.

Adj. *important,* weighty, grave, serious; pregnant; of consequence, of importance, of concern; considerable; world-shattering, earth-shaking, momentous, critical, fateful 137 *timely*; chief, capital, cardinal, staple, major, main, paramount 34 *supreme*; crucial, essential; pivotal 225 *central*; basic, fundamental, bedrock, radical, grass-roots; primary, prime, foremost, leading; worthwhile, not to be sneezed at 644 *valuable*; necessary, vital, indispensable, key 627 *required*; significant, telling; imperative, urgent, high-priority; high-level; hush-hush 523 *latent*; high, grand, noble 32 *great*.

notable, memorable, signal, unforgettable 505 *remembered*; first-rate, A1, outstanding, superior; top-rank, top-flight 644 *excellent*; conspicuous, prominent, eminent, distinguished, exalted, august 866 *noteworthy*; imposing 821 *impressive*; formidable, powerful 178 *influential*; newsworthy, front-page; eventful, world-shattering, earth-shaking, epoch-making.

639 Unimportance – N. *unimportance,* inconsequence, insignificance 35 *inferiority*; immateriality, lack of substance 4 *insubstantiality*; nothingness; pettiness 33 *smallness*; triviality; worthlessness 812 *cheapness*; uselessness 641 *uselessness*; irrelevance, red herring 10 *unrelatedness*.

trifle, inessential, triviality; nothing, mere n., no great matter, secondary matter, nothing of note, matter of indifference, not the end of the world; no great shakes, nothing to speak of, nothing to write home about, nothing to worry about, storm in a teacup 482 *overestimation*; bagatelle, tinker's cuss, fig, damn, toss, straw, chaff, pin, button, feather, dust; tuppence, small change, small beer; paltry sum, peanuts, chickenfeed, fleabite; pinprick, scratch; nothing to it, child's play 701 *easy thing*; peccadillo; trifles, trivia, minutiae, petty detail 80 *particulars*; whit, jot, the least bit, drop in the ocean 33 *small quantity*; cent, brass farthing 33 *small quantity*; nonsense.

bauble, toy 837 *plaything*; geegaw, doodad, knick-knack, bric-a-brac; novelty, trinket; tinsel, trumpery, frippery, trash, gimcrack.

nonentity, nobody, nonperson; man of straw 4 *insubstantial thing*; figurehead, cipher, sleeping partner; lightweight, small beer; small fry, small game; other ranks, lower orders 869 *commonalty*; second fiddle 35 *inferior*; underling; pawn in the game, cat's paw, stooge, puppet 628 *instrument*; poor relation 801 *poor person*.

Adj. *unimportant,* immaterial 4 *insubstantial*; inconsequential, of no consequence, of no great weight; insignificant 515 *meaningless*; inessential, nonessential, fringe; unnecessary, expendable; small, petty, trifling, paltry 33 *inconsiderable*; negligible, inappreciable, not worth considering; weak; measly; obscure; beneath contempt 922 *contemptible*; jumped-up, no-account, tinpot; low-level, secondary, minor, subsidiary, peripheral 35 *inferior*.

trivial, trifling, piffling, piddling; pettifogging, nit-picking; footling, frivolous, puerile, childish 499 *foolish*; airy 4 *insubstantial*; superficial 212 *shallow*; slight 33 *small*; lightweight 323 *light*; parish-pump, small-time; twopenny-halfpenny, one-horse, second-rate, third-r.; grotty, rubbishy, trashy, tawdry,

shoddy, gimcrack 645 *bad*; two-a-penny 812 *cheap*; worthless, valueless 641 *useless*; not worth a second thought 922 *contemptible*; token, nominal, symbolic; mediocre, nondescript, eminently forgettable; commonplace, ordinary, uneventful 610 *usual*.

640 Utility – N. *utility*, use, usefulness; employability, serviceability, handiness 628 *instrumentality*; efficacy, efficiency 160 *ability*; adequacy 635 *sufficiency*; applicability, suitability 642 *good policy*; availability 189 *presence*; service, avail, help; value, worth, merit 644 *goodness*; virtue, function, capacity, potency, clout 160 *power*; advantage, commodity; profitability, bottom line, earning capacity, productivity 171 *productiveness*; profit, mileage 771 *gain*; convenience, benefit, common weal, public good 615 *good*; utilitarianism, functionalism; employment, utilization 673 *use*.

Adj. *useful*, of use, helpful, of service 703 *aiding*; sensible, practical, applied, functional; versatile, multipurpose, all-purpose, of all work; practicable, convenient, expedient 642 *advisable*; handy; at hand, available, on tap; serviceable, fit for, good for, applicable; ready for use, operative, on stream, usable, employable; valid, current; able, competent, efficacious, effective, effectual, efficient 160 *powerful*; conducive; adequate 635 *sufficient*; pragmatic, utilitarian.

profitable, paying, remunerative 771 *gainful*; beneficial, advantageous, to one's advantage, edifying, worthwhile 615 *good*; worth one's salt, worth one's keep, worth one's weight in gold, invaluable, priceless 644 *valuable*.

find useful, find a use for, make use of, utilize 673 *use*; turn to good account, make capital out of 137 *profit by*; reap the benefit of 771 *gain*; be the better for 654 *get better*.

641 Inutility – N. *uselessness;* inutility, superfluousness 637 *superfluity*; futility, inanity; worthlessness; inadequacy 636 *insufficiency*; inefficacy, ineffectualness,

inability 161 *impotence*; inefficiency, incompetence, ineptitude 695 *unskilfulness*; unserviceableness, unfitness 643 *inexpedience*; inapplicability, no benefit 172 *unproductiveness*; unhelpfulness.

lost labour, wasted effort 728 *failure*; game not worth the candle; waste of breath, waste of time, dead loss; labour in vain, wild-goose chase, fool's errand; labour of Sisyphus.

rubbish, trash, load of old rubbish; waste, refuse, lumber, junk, scrap, litter; wastage, bilge, wastepaper; scourings, sweepings, shavings 41 *leavings*; chaff, husks, bran; scraps; crumbs; offal, carrion; dust, muck, debris, slag, clinker; dross, scum 649 *dirt*; peel, orange p., banana skin, dead wood, stubble, weeds; rags and bones, old clothes, cast-offs; reject; midden, rubbish heap, tip, slag heap, dump.

Adj. *useless*, functionless, purposeless, pointless; naff; futile 497 *absurd*; unpractical, impracticable, unworkable, no go; nonfunctional 844 *ornamental*; redundant; expendable, dispensable; unfit, inapplicable 643 *inexpedient*; fit for nothing, unusable, unemployable; inefficient, incompetent 695 *unskilful*; unable, ineffective, feckless, ineffectual 161 *impotent*; nonfunctioning, inoperative, dud, kaput; invalid; out of order; broken down, worn out, hors de combat, past it, obsolete; hopeless, vain.

profitless, loss-making, unprofitable, wasteful, ill-spent; vain, abortive 728 *unsuccessful*; nothing to show for; unrewarding, thankless; fruitless; valueless; not worth the effort, not worth the paper it is written on 645 *bad*; unsalable, dear at any price 811 *dear*.

make useless, disqualify, unfit, disarm, render harmless, take the sting out of 161 *disable*; castrate, emasculate 161 *unman*; cripple, lame, clip the wings 655 *impair*; put out of commission, lay up 679 *make inactive*; sabotage, throw a spanner in the works, put a spoke in one's wheel, cramp one's style 702 *obstruct*; take to pieces, break up 46 *disunite*; deface.

waste effort, labour the obvious; waste one's breath, waste one's time, talk to a brick wall, beat one's head against a b. w.; preach to the converted 637 *be superfluous*; be on a hiding to nothing, get nowhere, labour in vain; flog a dead horse, beat the air, tilt at windmills; cry for the moon 470 *attempt the impossible.*

642 Good policy – N. *good policy,* expediency, expedience; right answer, advisability, desirability, worthwhileness, suitability 640 *utility*; fitness, propriety 915 *dueness*; proper time, opportunity 137 *occasion*; convenience, pragmatism, utilitarianism, opportunism; profit, advantage 615 *benefit*; facilities.

Adj. *advisable,* commendable; as well to, better to, desirable; fitting, seemly, proper 913 *right*; well-timed, opportune 137 *timely*; prudent, politic, judicious 498 *wise*; expedient, advantageous; practical, pragmatic; applicable.

Vb. *be expedient,* not come amiss, come in useful, suit the occasion; be to the purpose, help 703 *aid*; forward, advance, promote; have the desired effect, produce results; work, do, serve, be better than nothing, deliver the goods, fill *or* fit the bill 635 *suffice*; achieve one's aim 727 *succeed*; fit, be just the thing 24 *accord*; profit, advantage, benefit 644 *do good.*

643 Inexpedience – N. *inexpedience,* inexpediency; not the answer, lack of planning; inadvisability, undesirability; unsuitability, unfitness 25 *inaptitude*; impropriety, unfittingness, unseemliness 916 *undueness*; wrongness 914 *wrong*; inopportuneness 138 *untimeliness*; inconvenience, disadvantage; mixed blessing, two-edged weapon, last resort 596 *necessity.*

Adj. *inexpedient,* better not, as well not to, inadvisable, undesirable, not recommended; ill-advised, impolitic, imprudent, injudicious 499 *unwise*; inappropriate, unfitting, out of place, unseemly; improper; unfit, inadmissible,

unsuitable, unhappy, inept 25 *unapt*; unseasonable, inopportune, untimely 138 *ill-timed*; unsatisfactory 636 *insufficient*; inconvenient; detrimental, disadvantageous; unhealthy, unwholesome 653 *insalubrious*; unprofitable 641 *useless*; unhelpful; untoward 731 *adverse*; awkward 695 *clumsy*; cumbersome.

644 Goodness – N. *goodness,* soundness 650 *health*; virtuosity 694 *skill*; quality, vintage; good points, redeeming feature; merit, desert, claim to fame; excellence, eminence; virtue, worth, value 809 *price*; pricelessness; flawlessness 646 *perfection*; quintessence 1 *essence.*

elite, chosen few; pick, prime, flower; cream, crème de la crème, salt of the earth, pick of the bunch, meritocracy; crack troops; top people 638 *bigwig*; charmed circle, top drawer, upper crust, aristocracy, Sloane Rangers 868 *upper class*; titbit, prime cut, pièce de résistance; plum, prize 729 *trophy.*

exceller, nonpareil; prodigy, gifted child, genius; superman, wonderwoman, wonder, wonder of the world 864 *prodigy*; Admirable Crichton 646 *paragon*; one in a thousand, one in a million, treasure; jewel, pearl, ruby, diamond 844 *gem*; gem of the first water, pure gold, chef-d'oeuvre, pièce de résistance, collector's item, museum piece 694 *masterpiece*; record-breaker, best-seller, chart-topper, best ever, last word in, ne plus ultra, best thing since sliced bread; bee's knees, cat's whiskers, cat's pyjamas; the goods, winner, corker, humdinger, wow, knockout, hit, smash h.; smasher, charmer 841 *a beauty*; star, idol 890 *favourite*; best of its kind, the tops, the greatest, top of the pops; topnotcher, top seed, first-rater; cock of the walk, toast of the town, Queen of the May; champion, title-holder, worldbeater, prizewinner 727 *victor.*

Adj. *excellent,* fine, braw; exemplary; good, good as gold 933 *virtuous*; above par, preferable, better 34 *superior*; very good, first-rate, ace, A1, alpha plus; prime, quality, fine, superfine; God's

own, superlative, in a class by itself; all-star, of the first water, rare, vintage, classic 646 *perfect*; choice, select, hand-picked, exquisite, recherché 605 *chosen*; exclusive, pure 44 *unmixed*; worthy, meritorious; admired, admirable, estimable, praiseworthy, creditable; famous, great; lovely 841 *beautiful*; glorious, dazzling, splendid, splendiferous, magnificent, marvellous, wonderful, terrific, sensational, superb.

super, superduper, fantastic, way-out, fabulous, fab, groovy, brill, magic, wizard, wizzo; spot-on, bang-on; top-notch, top-flight (see *best*); lovely, glorious, gorgeous, heavenly, out of this world 32 *prodigious*; smashing, stunning, spiffing, ripping, topping, swell, great, grand, famous, capital, dandy, bully, hunky-dory; scrumptious, delicious, juicy, plummy, jammy 826 *pleasurable.*

best, optimum, A1, champion, tiptop, top-notch, ace; first-rate, crack; second to none 34 *supreme*; unequalled, unparalleled, unmatched, peerless, unbeatable, unsurpassable 646 *perfect*; best-ever, record, record-breaking, best-selling, chart-topping.

valuable, invaluable, inestimable, priceless, costly, rich 811 *of price*; rare, precious, worth its weight in gold, worth a king's ransom; sterling, gilt-edged, blue-chip.

beneficial, wholesome, healthy, salutary; edifying, worthwhile, advantageous, profitable 640 *useful*; favourable, propitious 730 *prosperous.*

not bad, tolerable, so-so, passable, respectable, fair; all right, okay, OK; indifferent, middle-of-the-road, middling, mediocre, ordinary, fifty-fifty, average 30 *median.*

Vb. *be good,* - sound etc. adj.; have merit, deserve well 915 *deserve*; stand the test, pass muster 635 *suffice*; equal the best 28 *be equal*; excel, transcend, take the prize 34 *be superior.*

do good, have a good effect, improve, edify; do a world of good; be the making of, make a man of 654 *make better*; help 615 *benefit*; do a favour, do a good turn.

645 Badness – **N.** *badness,* obnoxiousness, nastiness, beastliness, foulness, grossness, rottenness; unworthiness, worthlessness; second-rateness, inferiority; flaw 647 *imperfection*; shoddiness 641 *uselessness*; unsoundness, decay, corruption 655 *deterioration*; disruption; morbidity 651 *disease*; harmfulness, hurtfulness, ill, hurt, harm, injury, detriment, damage, mischief 616 *evil*; noxiousness, poisonousness, deadliness, virulence 653 *insalubrity*; poison, blight, canker, cancer 659 *bane*; pestilence, sickness 651 *plague*; contamination, plague spot, trouble s., hotbed 651 *infection*; affair, scandal 867 *slur*; abomination, filth 649 *uncleanness*; sewer 649 *sink*; bitterness; painfulness, sting, ache, pang, thorn in the flesh 377 *pain*; angst, anguish 825 *suffering*; maltreatment, oppression, persecution; unkindness, cruelty, malignancy, spitefulness, spite 898 *malevolence*; depravity, vice 934 *wickedness*; sin 936 *guilt*; bad influence, evil genius; ill wind; black magic, evil eye, hoodoo, jinx, gremlin 983 *sorcery*; curse 899 *malediction*; snake in the grass 663 *troublemaker.*

Adj. *bad,* vile, base, evil; gross, black; irredeemable; poor, mean, wretched, grotty, gungy, gruesome, measly, low-grade, second-rate, execrable, awful 35 *inferior*; worthless, shoddy, tacky, naff, crummy, ropy, punk, pathetic 641 *useless*; unsatisfactory, faulty, flawed 647 *imperfect*; incompetent, inefficient; mangled, spoiled 695 *bungled*; scruffy, filthy, mangy, manky 649 *dirty*; foul; gone bad, rank, tainted; corrupt, decaying, rotten to the core; infected, poisoned, septic 651 *diseased*; incurable; depraved, vicious, villainous, accursed 934 *wicked*; heinous, sinful 936 *guilty*; mean, wrongful, unjust 914 *wrong*; sinister 616 *evil* (see *harmful*); contemptible; shameful, scandalous, disgraceful 867 *discreditable*; lamentable, deplorable, grievous, heavy, burdensome; too bad 827 *annoying.*

harmful, hurtful, injurious, damaging, detrimental, prejudicial, disadvantageous 643 *inexpedient*; deleterious, corrosive, destructive; pernicious, fatal 362 *deadly*; disastrous, ruinous, calamitous 731 *adverse*; degenerative, noxious, malign, malignant, unhealthy, unwholesome, infectious 653 *insalubrious*; polluting, poisonous, risky 661 *dangerous*; sinister, ominous, dire, dreadful, accursed, devilish 616 *evil*; mischievous, spiteful, malicious, malevolent, ill-disposed; mischief-making; inhuman 898 *cruel*; outrageous, rough, harsh, intolerant, persecuting 735 *oppressive*; monstrous 32 *exorbitant.*

not nice, obnoxious, nasty, beastly, horrid, horrific, horrible, terrible, gruesome, grim, ghastly, awful, dreadful; foul, rotten, lousy, putrid, putrefying, stinking, sickening, revolting, nauseous, nauseating; loathsome, detestable, abominable 888 *hateful*; vulgar, sordid, low, indecent, improper, gross, filthy, pornographic, obscene 951 *impure*; shocking, disgusting, reprehensible, monstrous, horrendous.

damnable, damned, darned, blasted, bloody, confounded, blinking, dratted, blankety-blank; execrable, accursed, cursed, hellish, infernal, devilish, diabolical.

Vb. *harm,* do h., do one a mischief; disagree with, make one ill, make one sick; injure, damage, pollute 655 *impair*; corrupt 655 *pervert*; play havoc with 63 *derange*; do no good; have a deleterious effect on; molest; plague; land one in trouble, queer one's pitch, do for; be unkind 898 *be malevolent.*

ill-treat, maltreat, abuse 675 *misuse*; ill-use, put upon, tyrannize, trample on, victimize, prey upon; persecute 735 *oppress*; wrong, distress 827 *torment*; outrage, violate, force; savage, maul, bite, scratch, tear 655 *wound*; stab 263 *pierce*; batter, bruise, buffet 279 *strike*; crucify 963 *torture*; take one's spite out on; crush 165 *destroy.*

Adv. *badly,* amiss, wrong, ill.

646 Perfection – **N.** *perfection,* sheer p.; finish; the ideal; immaculateness, faultlessness, flawlessness, mint condition; correctness, irreproachability; impeccability, infallibility; transcendence 34 *superiority*; quintessence, essence; peak, zenith, pinnacle 213 *summit*; height of perfection, acme of p.; ne plus ultra, last word; chef d'oeuvre, flawless performance 694 *masterpiece.*

paragon, nonpareil, flower, prince of 644 *exceller*; ideal, knight in shining armour, saint, plaster s.; classic, pattern of perfection, model, shining example 23 *prototype*; superman, superwoman, wonderwoman, demigod 864 *prodigy.*

Adj. *perfect,* perfected, finished; just right, ideal, flawless, faultless, impeccable, infallible, correct, irreproachable; immaculate, spotless, blemish-free, without a stain; uncontaminated, pure 44 *unmixed*; sound as a bell, right as rain, in perfect condition; one hundred per cent, A1; complete 52 *intact*; consummate, unsurpassable 34 *supreme*; brilliant, masterly 694 *skilful*; model, classical.

undamaged, safe and sound, unhurt, unscathed, no harm done; unmarked; without blemish, unspoilt; without loss, intact; in the pink 650 *healthy.*

Vb. *perfect,* consummate, bring to perfection; put the finishing touch 213 *crown*; complete, leave nothing to be desired 725 *carry through.*

647 Imperfection – **N.** *imperfection,* imperfectness; room for improvement; faultiness, erroneousness, fallibility 495 *error*; patchiness, unevenness, curate's egg 17 *nonuniformity*; defectiveness, bit missing 55 *incompleteness*; deficiency, inadequacy 636 *insufficiency*; unsoundness 661 *vulnerability*; failure, weakness 307 *shortfall*; second best, third rate, makeshift 150 *substitute*; mediocrity; adulteration 43 *mixture.*

defect, fault 495 *error*; flaw, rift, leak, loophole, crack lacuna 201 *gap*; deficiency, limitation 307 *shortfall*; kink, foible, screw loose 503 *eccentricity*; weak

point, soft spot, tragic flaw, chink in one's armour, Achilles' heel 661 *vulnerability*; feet of clay, weak link in the chain 163 *weakness*; stain, blot, spot, smudge 845 *blemish*; snag.

Adj. *imperfect*, not quite right, less than perfect, fallible, uneven, patchy, good in parts, like the curate's egg 17 *nonuniform*; faulty, botched 695 *bungled*; flawed, cracked; leaky; wobbly, rickety 163 *flimsy*; unsound 661 *vulnerable*; shop-soiled, tainted, stained, spotted, marked, scratched; below par, off form; unfit, not good enough, not up to the mark, inadequate, deficient, wanting, lacking 636 *insufficient*; defective 55 *incomplete*; broken 53 *fragmentary*; crippled; half-finished 55 *unfinished*; perfunctory 456 *inattentive*; warped, twisted, distorted 246 *deformed*; mutilated, maimed, lame 163 *weakened*; undeveloped, makeshift, jerry-built, rough and ready, provisional 150 *substituted*; second-rate, third-rate 35 *inferior*; no great shakes, nothing to boast of, nothing to write home about.

Vb. *be imperfect*, fall short of perfection, be flawed; not bear inspection, not pass muster, fail the test, dissatisfy 636 *not suffice*; not make the grade 924 *incur blame*; have feet of clay.

648 Cleanness – N. *cleanness*, immaculateness 950 *purity*; freshness, whiteness; spit and polish; cleanliness, daintiness 862 *fastidiousness*.

cleansing, clean, spring-cleaning, dry-c.; washing, cleaning up, mopping up, washing up, wiping up, scrubbing; refining, purification; purgation; washing out, flushing, dialysis; purging, enema, defecation 302 *excretion*; airing, ventilation, fumigation 338 *vaporization*; deodorization 395 *inodorousness*; sterilization, disinfection, decontamination, delousing; sanitation, drainage, sewerage, plumbing 652 *hygiene*; water closet, flush 649 *latrine*.

ablutions, washing; hygiene, oral h.; douche, flush; wash, lick and a promise;

soaking, bathing, dipping; soaping, lathering, scrubbing, sponging, rinsing, shampoo; dip 313 *plunge*; bath, tub; bathtub, hipbath, bidet; washbasin, wash-hand basin, washstand; Turkish b., sauna, Jacuzzi (tdmk), hot tub; shower; bathroom, washroom, public baths; swimming bath, swimming pool; wash, laundry; washtub, washboard, dolly; copper, boiler, washing machine, washer, twin tub, launderette.

cleanser, purifier; disinfectant, carbolic, deodorant; detergent, soap, soap flakes; washing powder, soap p., washing-up liquid, water, soap and w., shampoo; mouth wash, gargle; cleansing cream; toothpaste; pumice stone; furniture polish, boot p., blacking; wax, varnish; whitewash, paint; blacklead; aperient 658 *purgative*.

cleaning utensil, broom, besom, mop, sponge, swab, scourer; loofah; duster, feather d.; brush, scrubbing b., nailbrush, toothbrush, toothpick, dental floss; comb, hair brush, clothes b.; dustpan and brush, waste bin, dustbin, wastepaper basket, litter bin, waste disposal unit, compactor; poop-scoop; carpet sweeper, vacuum cleaner, Hoover (tdmk); doormat, foot-scraper; pipe cleaner, windscreen wiper; sieve, riddle; filter; dishwasher.

cleaning cloth, duster; dishcloth, tea towel; wash-leather; chamois, shammy; face f., facecloth, towel, bath t., hand t.; handkerchief, paper h., tissue; toilet tissue, toilet paper, lavatory p., toilet roll.

cleaner, laundryman, laundress, washerwoman; washer-up, dish-washer; charwoman, char, charlady, cleaner, help, daily help, daily, home help; Mrs Mop; dustman, refuse collector; lavatory attendant, sanitary engineer; chimneysweep, window cleaner; bootblack.

Adj. *clean*, dirt-free; snowy 427 *white*; polished, clean, shining 417 *undimmed*; cleanly; fresh; bright as a new pin, fresh as a daisy; cleaned, scrubbed, polished etc. vb.; cleaned up, laundered; spruce, spick and span, well-groomed 60 *orderly*; deodorized, disinfected, hygienic,

sterilized; purified, immaculate, spotless, clean as a whistle 646 *perfect*; ritually clean, kosher 301 *edible*.

Vb. *clean,* spring-clean, clean up, clear up; groom, valet, spruce; wash, wipe, wipe clean, wash up, sponge, mop, mop up, swab, wash down; scrub, scour; scrape 333 *rub*; do the washing, launder; bleach, dry-clean; soap, lather, shampoo; bathe, dip, dunk, rinse, swill down, sluice, douche, shower 341 *drench*; dust, sweep, sweep up, beat, vacuum, hoover; brush, brush up; buff, polish; blacklead 417 *make bright*; whitewash 427 *whiten*; erase 550 *obliterate*; clean out, clear out, make a clean sweep 300 *eject*.

purify, purge, clean up; bowdlerize, censor, blue-pencil, expurgate; elevate 654 *make better*; cleanse, freshen, ventilate, deodorize, fumigate; desalinate; decontaminate, disinfect, sterilize, chlorinate, pasteurize 652 *make sanitary*; refine, distil, clarify, skim, scum, decarbonize; strain, filter, percolate, leach; sift, sieve; dialyse, catheterize, clean out, wash o., drain.

649 Uncleanness – N. *uncleanness,* uncleanliness; soiling, dirtiness (see *dirt*); muckiness; scruffiness, grottiness, filthiness; lousiness; squalor; untidiness, sluttishness, slovenliness 61 *disorder*; stink 397 *stench*; pollution, defilement; corruption, taint, putrefaction 51 *decomposition*; contamination 651 *infection*; unwashed body.

dirt, filth, stain, blot; crud, yuk, gunge, gunk, muck, mud, sludge, slime; bog 347 *marsh*; dung, droppings, ordure, faeces 302 *excrement*; snot, mucus; dust, mote 332 *powder*; cobweb, grime, smut, smudge, soot, smoke; grounds, dregs; scourings 41 *leavings*; sediment, deposit, precipitate, residuum, fur; scum, dross, froth; ashes, cinders, ash; drainage, sewerage; slough; scurf, dandruff; tartar, plaque; pus, matter, refuse, garbage, litter 641 *rubbish*; rot, rust, mildew, mould, fungus 51 *decay*; vermin.

latrine, privy, heads, jakes, bog, john, loo; closet, earth c., water closet, WC;

cloakroom, powder room, rest r., washroom, lavatory, toilet; urinal, public convenience, comfort station, Ladies, Gents; toilet bowl, lavatory b., commode, bedpan, chamber pot, potty 302 *defecation*.

sink, kitchen sink, draining board; cesspit, cesspool, sump, septic tank; gutter, sewer 351 *drain*; dunghill, midden, tip, rubbish heap, dust-h., compost-h.; dustbin, trashcan 194 *vessel*; pigsty; slum, spittoon.

dirty person, sloven, slattern, slut; litterbug, litter lout; street arab; scavenger 648 *cleaner*; pig, ratbag, fleabag.

Adj. *unclean,* smutty, obscene, corrupt 951 *impure*; coarse, unpurified; septic, festering; nonsterile 653 *infectious*; sordid, squalid, slummy, insanitary, unhygienic 653 *insalubrious*; foul, offensive, nasty, grotty, manky, yukky; disgusting, repulsive 645 *not nice*; nauseous, nauseating, stinking, ponging; uncleanly; grubby, scruffy, scabby, mangy; flea-ridden, lousy, crawling; faecal, rotting, tainted, high; flyblown, maggoty.

dirty, filthy; dusty, grimy, sooty, smoky, fuggy; polluted, littered; untidy, unkempt, slatternly, sleazy, slovenly, sluttish, bedraggled; unwashed; black, dingy, tarnished, stained, soiled; greasy, oily; caked, matted, muddied; messy, mucky, muddy, slimy 347 *marshy*; turbid; furred up, scummy; musty, fusty, cobwebby; mouldy, rotten 655 *dilapidated*.

Vb. *be unclean,* - dirty etc. adj.; collect dust, foul up, clog; rust, mildew, moulder, rot, go bad, go off 51 *decompose*; smell 397 *stink*.

make unclean, foul, dirty, soil; stain, blot, sully, tarnish; muck up, make a mess, untidy 61 *be disordered*; besmirch, smudge, blur, smoke 419 *bedim*; spot; streak, smear, besmear, grease; cake, clog, muddy, bespatter, splash; taint, infect, pollute, contaminate 655 *impair*; defile, profane, desecrate.

650 Health – N. *health,* rude h., good h.; healthiness, iron constitution, health

and strength 162 *vitality*; fitness, good condition, pink of c.; bloom, rosy cheeks, ruddy complexion; well-being, physical w.; soundness; clean bill of health.

Adj. *healthy,* wholesome, sanitary 652 *salubrious*; in good health, bursting with h., blooming, ruddy, rosy; lusty, bouncing, strapping, hale, hearty, hale and hearty, sound, fit, well, full of beans 174 *vigorous*; robust, hardy, strong, vigorous 162 *stalwart*; fighting fit, in peak condition, in tip-top c., in the pink, in good nick, in good shape, in fine fettle; feeling great; sound in wind and limb, sound as a bell, fit as a fiddle, fit as a flea, strong as a horse, A1; a picture of health, feeling good; getting well, convalescent, on the mend, on the up and up, up and about.

Vb. *be healthy,* - well etc. adj.; look after oneself, take care of o.; feel fine, bloom, thrive, flourish, enjoy good health; be in the pink, have never felt better; wear well, be well-preserved; keep fit, keep well, have a clean bill of health.

get healthy, - fit etc. adj.; recuperate, return to health, recover one's health, get the colour back in one's cheeks; mend, convalesce, get back on one's feet, take a fresh lease of life, become a new man *or* woman 656 *revive*.

651 Ill health. Disease – **N.** *ill health,* poor h., delicate h.; weak constitution; unhealthiness, weakliness, infirmity, debility 163 *weakness*; seediness; indisposition; allergy; chronic ill health, invalidism, valetudinarianism, hypochondria; nerves 503 *neurosis*.

illness, loss of health 655 *deterioration*; affliction, disability, handicap, infirmity 163 *weakness*; sickness, indisposition, ailment, complaint, virus, complication; condition, history of; bout of sickness, attack; spasm, stroke, seizure, apoplexy, fit; shock; poisoning, food p.; nausea, queasiness, vomiting; dizziness, vertigo; headache, migraine 377 *pain*; symptom, syndrome 547 *indication*; temperature, feverishness, fever, ague, shivers, shakes 318 *spasm*; hypothermia,

hyperthermia; pyrexia; delirium 503 *frenzy*; breakdown, collapse; fainting 375 *insensibility*; prostration, coma; terminal disease, fatal illness 361 *decease*.

disease, malady, disorder; epidemic disease, endemic d.; infectious d., contagious d., communicable d., notifiable d.; debilitating d., killer d.; congenital d.; occupational d., industrial d.; alcoholism, drug addiction; obesity; malnutrition, anorexia nervosa, bulimia n., avitaminosis, kwashiorkor, beri-beri, pellagra, rickets, scurvy; degenerative disease, wasting d., atrophy; trauma; organic disease; neurological d., nervous d., epilepsy; heart d., cardiac d.; diabetes; venereal d.; cancer; respiratory disease; gastro-intestinal d.; virus; bacterial d., fibrosis; brain disease 503 *mental disorder*.

plague, pest, scourge 659 *bane*; pestilence, infection, contagion; epidemic; bubonic p., Black Death.

infection, contagion, bug; pollution; infectiousness, contagiousness 653 *insalubrity*; suppuration, festering, purulence, gangrene; toxicity, sepsis, poisoning 659 *poison*; vector, carrier, host; parasite, worm, toxocara canis 659 *bane*; virus, parvovirus, retrovirus, lentivirus, bacillus, bacteria, germ, pathogen; blood-poisoning, toxaemia, septicaemia; food-poisoning, botulism; gastroenteritis, cholera; parasitical disease, toxocariasis, toxoplasmosis, bilharzia (**see** *tropical disease*); infectious disease, common cold, influenza, flu; diphtheria, pneumonia, viral p.; infective hepatitis; tuberculosis, consumption; measles, German measles, rubella; whooping-cough, pertussis, mumps; chickenpox, smallpox, variola; scarlet fever, scarlatina, roseola; fever, malaria (**see** *tropical disease*); typhus; typhoid; glandular fever, infectious mononucleosis; poliomyelitis, polio; encephalitis, meningitis; sleepy sickness; tetanus, lockjaw; rabies, hydrophobia.

tropical disease, malaria; cholera; yellow fever, blackwater f., Lassa f., dengue;

green monkey disease; kala-azar; sleeping sickness; bilharzia; hookworm; trachoma, glaucoma, river blindness 439 *blindness*; yaws; leprosy; beri-beri, kwashiorkor.

digestive disorders, indigestion, dyspepsia, liverishness; biliousness, nausea, sickness, vomiting, retching; colic, gripes; stomach ache; stomach upset, tummy u., collywobbles, gippy tummy, diarrhoea, travellers' d., dreaded lurgy, Montezuma's revenge; the runs, the trots 302 *defecation*; diarrhoea and vomiting, D and V, gastroenteritis; dysentery, cholera, typhoid; food poisoning, botulism; flatulence, wind, belching 300 *voidance*; acidosis, heartburn; hiatus hernia; ulcer, peptic u., gastric u., duodenal u.; gastritis, enteritis, colitis, peritonitis, appendicitis; cancer of the stomach; jaundice, hepatitis, cirrhosis, cystitis, nephritis; gallstones, haemorrhoids, piles; constipation; cancer of the bowel.

respiratory disease, cough, cold, common c., coryza; sore throat, catarrh, rhinitis, allergic r., sinusitis, adenoids, tonsilitis, pharyngitis; laryngitis, tracheitis, croup, bronchitis; emphysema, asthma; pleurisy, pneumonia, legionnaire's disease; pneumoconiosis, silicosis, asbestosis; diphtheria; whooping cough; lung cancer; smoker's cough; cystic fibrosis; tuberculosis, consumption.

cardiovascular disease, cardiac d.; angina; chest-pain; bradycardia, tachycardia; palpitation; heart murmur; enlarged heart; heart condition, bad heart, weak h., heart trouble; congenital heart disease, hole in the heart; rheumatic heart disease, coronary h. d.; heart failure, cardiac arrest; heart attack, coronary thrombosis, coronary; cerebral thrombosis, brain haemorrhage, stroke; blood pressure, hypertension; hypotension, high b. p., low blood pressure; vascular disease, atheroma, aneurysm; arteriosclerosis; phlebitis; varicose veins; thrombosis, coronary t., embolism, pulmonary e., infarction, myocardial i.

blood disease, anaemia, aplastic a., pernicious a., sickle-cell a.; leukaemia, Hodgkin's disease; haemophilia, AIDS; haemorrhage.

cancer, neoplasm, growth; primary g., secondary g., tumour, benign t., innocent t.; malignant t., cancerous growth; carcinoma, sarcoma, melanoma.

skin disease, skin lesion; mange; yaws; leprosy; erythema, prickly heat; erysipelas; impetigo, herpes, herpes zoster, shingles; dermatitis, eczema; serpigo, ringworm; pruritis, itch 378 *formication*; hives, urticaria, nettlerash; thrush; athlete's foot; rash, eruption, acne, rosacea, spots, blackheads; pustule, papula, pimple; goitre, cyst, blister, wart, verruca 253 *swelling*; macula, mole, freckle, birthmark, pockmark 845 *blemish*; skin cancer, melanoma.

venereal disease, VD, sexually-transmitted disease, social d., pox; syphilis, gonorrhoea, the clap; herpes.

ulcer, ulceration, gathering, festering, purulence; inflammation, lesion 655 *wound*; scald, burn, first-degree b.; sore, boil, abscess, fistula; cyst; chilblain, corn 253 *swelling*; gangrene.

rheumatism, rheumatics; rheumatic fever; fibrositis; frozen shoulder, tennis elbow, housemaid's knee, pulled muscle; arthritis, rheumatoid a.; gout 377 *pang*; osteoarthritis; lumbago, sciatica; slipped disc.

nervous disorders, nervous breakdown 503 *psychopathy*; brain tumour; cerebral haemorrhage, stroke, seizure; general paralysis, atrophy 375 *insensibility*; partial paralysis, paresis; cerebral palsy, spasticity; tic 318 *spasm*; petit mal, grand mal, epilepsy; poliomyelitis, polio; spina bifida; Parkinson's disease; Huntington's chorea, St Vitus's dance; multiple sclerosis, MS; muscular dystrophy.

animal disease, distemper, foot-and-mouth disease, swine fever, swine vesicular disease; myxomatosis; rinderpest, murrain; anthrax, sheeprot, bloat; liver fluke, worms; megrims, staggers; glanders, farcy, sweeny, spavin, thrush; Newcastle disease, fowl pest; psittacosis; hard pad; mange; rabies.

sick person, patient, in-p., out-p.; stretcher case, hospital c.; mental case 504 *madman*; invalid, chronic i.; valetudinarian, hypochondriac, malingerer, leadswinger, martyr to ill health; consumptive, asthmatic, bronchitic, dyspeptic, diabetic; haemophiliac, insomniac; addict, alcoholic; spastic, arthritic, paralytic; paraplegic, disabled person; crock, old c., cripple 163 *weakling.*

Adj. *unhealthy,* sickly; infirm, weakly 163 *weak*; delicate, of weak constitution, in poor health, out of kilter, in poor condition; anorexic, malnourished 636 *underfed*; peaky, emaciated, skin and bones; sallow, pale, anaemic 426 *colourless*; bilious 434 *green*; jaundiced 433 *yellow.*

sick, ill, unwell, indisposed, out of sorts, under the weather, off-colour, below par, one degree under, out of kilter; queasy, nauseated, green around the gills; in a bad way, poorly, seedy, squeamish, groggy, grotty, queer, ailing; sickening for; feverish, headachy, off one's food, off one's oats; confined, laid up, bedridden, on one's back, in bed, in hospital, on the sick list, invalided, hospitalized; run down, exhausted 684 *fatigued*; taken ill, taken bad; prostrate, collapsed; in a coma 375 *insensible*; on the danger list, in intensive care; critical, serious; chronic, incurable, inoperable; terminally ill 361 *dying.*

diseased, pathological; infected, contaminated, tainted, rotten, gangrenous; morbid, pathogenic; iatrogenic; psychosomatic 447 *mental*; infectious, contagious; poisonous, festering, purulent 653 *toxic*; degenerative, consumptive, tubercular; diabetic, hydrocephalic; anaemic, bloodless, leukaemic, haemophilic; arthritic, rheumatic, rheumatoid; palsied, paralysed, spastic, epileptic; leprous; cancerous, oncogenic, carcinogenic; syphilitic, venereal; swollen, oedematous; gouty; bronchial, bronchitic, asthmatic; allergic; pyretic, febrile, fevered, shivering, feverish, delirious; ulcerated, inflamed; erythematous, erysipelatous.

Vb. *be ill,* - sick etc. adj.; enjoy poor health; ail, suffer, undergo treatment; have a complaint *or* an affliction, be a chronic invalid; not feel well, complain of; feel queer etc. adj., come over all queer; feel sick 300 *vomit*; sicken, fall sick, fall ill; become infected, catch a bug, contract a disease; go down with; be seized, be stricken, be taken bad, not feel so good; have a stroke, collapse; be laid up, take to one's bed; be invalided out; go into a decline; fail, sink, weak 163 *be weak.*

652 Salubrity – **N.** *salubrity,* healthiness, state of health; well-being 650 *health*; salubriousness, wholesomeness; fresh air.

hygiene, sanitation, cleanliness 648 *cleanness*; cordon sanitaire 660 *protection*; pasteurization; antisepsis, sterilization, disinfection, chlorination.

Adj. *salubrious,* healthful, healthy, wholesome; pure, fresh 648 *clean*; ventilated; hygienic, sanitary, disinfected, chlorinated, pasteurized, sterilized, aseptic, antiseptic; good for, salutary, what the doctor ordered 644 *beneficial*; nutritious; body-building, health-giving.

make sanitary, disinfect, boil, sterilize, chlorinate, pasteurize; put in quarantine; ventilate 340 *aerate*; decontaminate 648 *purify*; cleanse 648 *clean.*

653 Insalubrity – **N.** *insalubrity,* unhealthiness, unwholesomeness; uncleanliness, lack of hygiene, dirty habits 649 *uncleanness*; slum; bad air, fug, smog; infectiousness, contagiousness; sewer 649 *sink*; contagion 651 *infection*; pollution, radioactivity, fallout; poisonousness 659 *bane.*

Adj. *insalubrious,* unwholesome, unhealthy; insanitary, unhygienic 649 *unclean*; noxious; injurious 645 *harmful*; radioactive, carcinogenic; verminous, rat-infested, flea-ridden, flyblown; stagnant, polluted, undrinkable, inedible; unnutritious; stale, gone bad, gone off; unventilated; stuffy; overheated, underheated.

infectious, pathogenic; infective, germ-carrying; contagious, catching, communicable; pestilent, plague-stricken; epidemic, pandemic, endemic; infected 649 *dirty.*

toxic, poisonous, germ-laden; venomous, poisoned; festering, septic, purulent, suppurating; lethal 362 *deadly.*

654 Improvement – N. *improvement,* betterment, amelioration, uplift, regeneration; good influence, the making of 178 *influence*; a turn for the better, change for the b., sea change, transfiguration 143 *transformation*; conversion, new leaf 939 *penitence*; revival, recovery 656 *restoration*; evolution; enrichment; advance, progress 285 *progression*; promotion, rise, lift; upturn, upward mobility, upswing 310 *elevation*; enhancement 36 *increase.*

amendment, mending etc. vb.; renovation 656 *repair*; reorganization 62 *arrangement*; reformation, reform; rectification; correction, revision, red ink, blue pencil; emendation, revised edition, new e., improved version 589 *edition*; revise, proof; second thoughts, review; polish, finishing touch 725 *completion.*

reformer, repairer, restorer 656 *mender*; emender, corrector, editor, proofreader, reviser; progressive, gradualist, Fabian 625 *moderate*; liberal, radical, feminist, masculinist; extremist, revolutionary 738 *agitator*; socialist, communist, Marxist, Red; reformist; idealist, Utopian 513 *visionary*; sociologist, social worker 901 *philanthropist.*

Adj. *improving,* reformatory, remedial; reforming, progressive, radical; civilizing, cultural; idealistic, perfectionist, Utopian, perfectionist 862 *fastidious.*

Vb. *get better,* improve, mend, take a turn for the better, turn the corner; pick up, rally, revive, recover 656 *be restored*; make progress, make headway, advance, develop, evolve 285 *progress*; mellow, ripen 669 *mature*; bear fruit 171 *be fruitful*; rise 308 *ascend*; graduate 727 *succeed*; rise in the world, prosper; better oneself, be upwardly mobile, mend one's

ways, reform, turn over a new leaf, go straight 939 *be penitent*; improve oneself, learn by experience 536 *learn.*

make better, better, improve, refine, ameliorate, reform; make improvements, improve upon, polish, enrich, enhance; work a miracle on, do one a power of good 644 *do good*; improve out of all recognition, transfigure 147 *transform*; make, be the making of, have a good influence, leaven 178 *influence*; uplift, regenerate; refine, elevate, sublimate 648 *purify*; civilize, socialize, teach manners; mend 656 *repair*; restore 656 *cure*; revive, infuse fresh blood into 685 *refresh*; forward, advance, upgrade 285 *promote*; foster, encourage, hype, bring to fruition 669 *mature*; make the most of, get the best out of 673 *use*; develop, open up; tidy up, make shipshape, neaten 62 *arrange*; spruce up, freshen up 648 *clean*; do up, vamp up, rationalize; renovate, refurbish, renew, give a face lift; bring up to date 126 *modernize*; touch up 841 *beautify*; improve on nature, gild the lily, make up, titivate 843 *primp*; embellish, adorn, ornament 844 *decorate.*

rectify, put right, set right, straighten, straighten out 24 *adjust*; mend, patch 656 *repair*; correct, debug, decontaminate, blue-pencil, proofread; revise, edit, subedit, amend, emend; rewrite, redraft; remould, refashion, remodel, reform; reorganize 62 *regularize*; streamline, finetune, rationalize; review; have second thoughts.

655 Deterioration – N. *deterioration,* debasement; cheapening, devaluation; retrogression, losing ground 286 *regression*; decline, ebb 37 *decrease*; twilight, fading 419 *dimness*; falling off, downturn, slump, depression, recession; impoverishment 801 *poverty*; exhaustion 634 *waste*; corruption, perversion, prostitution, depravation, degeneration, degeneracy, decadence, depravity 934 *wickedness*; downward course, primrose path 309 *descent*; setback 657 *relapse.*

dilapidation, collapse, ruination 165 *destruction*; planning blight; inner city deprivation, disrepair, neglect 458 *negligence*; slum 801 *poverty*; ravages of time, wear and tear, erosion, corrosion, rust, rot, canker, corruption, putrefaction, cancer, concrete cancer 51 *decay*; mouldiness, mildew 659 *blight*; decrepitude, senility 131 *old age*; atrophy 651 *disease*; ruin, wreck.

impairment, spoiling 675 *misuse*; detriment, damage, spoilage, waste 772 *loss*; discoloration; pollution, contamination, defilement 649 *uncleanness*; adulteration; ruination, demolition 165 *destruction*; injury, mischief, harm; disablement, crippling, laming, nobbling, disabling, mutilation, weakening 163 *weakness*; sprain, strain, pulled muscle, dislocation; sabotage.

wound, injury, trauma; sore, running s. 651 *ulcer*; laceration, lesion; cut, gash, incision, abrasion, nick, scratch 46 *scission*; stab, prick, jab, puncture; contusion, bruise, bump, discoloration, black eye, shiner, cauliflower ear 253 *swelling*; burn, scald; rupture, hernia; broken bones, fracture; scar, mark, scab.

Adj. *dilapidated,* the worse for wear, falling to pieces, in disrepair, in ruins; broken, kaput, cracked, leaking; battered, weather-beaten, storm-tossed; decrepit, ramshackle, tottery, wonky, shaky, rickety, tumbledown, run-down, on its last legs 163 *weakened*; condemned; worn, well-w., frayed, shabby, tatty, dingy, in tatters, in rags, out-at-elbows; worn out, done for 641 *useless*; seedy, down at heel, down and out 801 *poor*; rusty, rotten, mildewed, mouldering, moth-eaten, dog-eared.

Vb. *deteriorate,* worsen, get worse, go from bad to worse, take a turn for the worse; slip, slide, go downhill; have seen better days; fall off, slump, decline, wane, ebb, sink, fail 37 *decrease*; revert 286 *regress*; lapse; degenerate, let oneself go, go to pieces, run to seed; tread the primrose path, go to the bad 934 *be wicked*; disintegrate, fall apart, collapse,

break down, fall, totter, droop 309 *tumble*; contract, shrink 198 *become small*; wear out, age; fade, wither, wilt, shrivel, perish, crumble, moulder, mildew; go to rack and ruin; weather, rust, rot, decay 51 *decompose*; spoil, go flat, go off, go sour, turn 391 *be unpalatable*; go bad, smell, pong 397 *stink*; corrupt, putrefy, rankle, fester, suppurate 51 *decompose*; sicken 651 *be ill*; make things worse, jump from the frying pan into the fire.

pervert, deform, warp, twist 246 *distort*; prostitute 675 *misuse*; deprave 951 *debauch*; corrupt 934 *make wicked*; lower, degrade, debase 311 *abase*; brutalize, dehumanize; brainwash.

impair, damage, make inoperative, hurt, injure 645 *harm*; mess up, muck up 63 *jumble*; play havoc with 63 *derange*; disorganize; spoil, mar, botch, cock up, make a balls-up of 695 *be clumsy*; tinker, tamper, meddle with, fool w., monkey w. 678 *meddle*; deteriorate; degrade, devalue, debase 812 *cheapen*; stain; scar, mark; deface, disfigure, deform, warp 246 *distort*; mutilate, maim, lame, cripple 161 *disable*; cramp, hamper 702 *hinder*; castrate 161 *unman*; curtail; adulterate; deactivate 679 *make inactive*; subvert, sap, undermine, demoralize 163 *weaken*; erode, corrode, rust, rot, mildew 51 *decompose*; blight, blast; ravage, rape, waste, scorch; vandalize, wreck, ruin 165 *destroy*; crumble 332 *pulverize*; dilapidate, wear out; exhaust, deplete, drain; infect, contaminate; taint, pollute 649 *make unclean*; defile, desecrate, profane 980 *be impious*.

wound, draw blood; tear, lacerate, slit, mangle, rip 46 *disunite*; maul, savage, traumatize; black one's eye, bloody one's nose; bite, scratch, claw; slash, gash, hack, incise 46 *cut*; scarify, score 262 *groove*; nick 260 *notch*; sting, prick, stab, puncture 263 *pierce*; bruise, contuse; crush, grind 332 *pulverize*; chafe 333 *rub*; smash 46 *break*; graze, wing.

656 Restoration – N. *restoration,* giving back 787 *restitution*; redress, amends,

reparation 941 *atonement*; retrieval, recovery; reestablishment, recall, replacement, reinstatement; rehabilitation; reclamation, gentrification, recycling; rescue, salvage, redemption, ransom, salvation 668 *deliverance*; reconstitution, rebuilding, reformation, reconstruction, reorganization; readjustment; remodelling 654 *amendment*; resumption.

repair, reparation, repairs, running r., service, servicing, renovation, renewal, reconditioning; overhauling, DIY; rectification, emendation; restoration, mending, invisible m., darning, patching; cobbling, tinkering etc. vb.; reinforcement; new look, face-lift 843 *beautification*.

revival, recovery 685 *refreshment*; renewal, reawakening, resurgence, rally, comeback; economic miracle, boom 730 *prosperity*; reactivation, resuscitation, rejuvenation; face-lift, new look; rebirth, renaissance; regeneration; new life, resurrection.

recuperation, recovery, pulling through, rallying, perking up, taking a turn for the better, turning the corner, cure; healing, mending; healing over; convalescence 658 *remedy*; easing 831 *relief*; curability.

mender, repairer, renovator, painter, decorator, interior d., DIYer; mechanic; restorer; cobbler; shoe-repairer; plumber, handyman; healer, bone-setter, osteopath 658 *doctor*.

Vb. *be restored,* recover, come round, come to, revive, pick up, rally 685 *be refreshed*; pull through, get over, get well, convalesce, recuperate; turn the corner 654 *get better*; weather the storm, survive, live through; come to life again, arise from the dead, return from the grave; reappear, make a comeback, take on a new lease of life; be oneself again, bounce back, snap out of it, come up smiling; pick oneself up, find one's feet again; return to normal, get back to n.

restore, give back, hand b., yield up 787 *restitute*; make amends 941 *atone*;

replace; recall, reappoint, reinstall, reestablish, rehabilitate; reconstitute, reconstruct, reform, reorganize 654 *make better*; renovate, renew, rebuild, remake, redo; overhaul, service, refit, refurbish, make like new 126 *modernize*; make whole; reclaim; recycle; build up one's strength 162 *strengthen*; rally, reassemble 74 *bring together*; redeem, rescue, salvage 668 *deliver*.

revive, revitalize, resuscitate, regenerate, resurrect, rekindle; breathe fresh life into, give a new lease of life, rejuvenate; freshen 685 *refresh*.

cure, heal, make well, cure of, break of; nurse; bandage, put a plaster on, nurse through, work a cure, snatch from the grave, restore to health, set on one's feet again; set (a bone); heal over; knit together; right itself.

repair, do repairs; amend, emend, right, set to rights, put right, put back into operation, remedy 654 *rectify*; overhaul, DIY, mend, fix; cobble, resole, heel; recover, resurface, thatch 226 *cover*; reline 227 *line*; darn, patch, fill (teeth); make over, do up, touch up, freshen up, retouch, revamp, fill in the cracks, paper over; seal, plug a hole 350 *staunch*; caulk 264 *close*; splice, bind 45 *tie*; piece together, reassemble, cannibalize 45 *join*; give a face-lift, upgrade, gentrify, refurbish, recondition, renovate, renew, remodel, reform.

retrieve, get back, recover, regain, retake, recapture; find again, reclaim, claim back, compensate oneself 31 *recoup*; make up for, make up time, make up leeway.

657 Relapse – N. *relapse,* lapse, falling back; throwback, return 148 *reversion*; retrogression 286 *regression*; sinking, falling off, fall 655 *deterioration*; backsliding; reinfection, recurrence, fresh outbreak.

Vb. *relapse,* slip back, slide b., sink b., fall b., lose ground; return, retrogress 286 *regress*; degenerate 655 *deteriorate*; backslide, lapse, fall from grace 603

apostatize; revert to 148 *revert*; have a relapse, suffer a recurrence.

658 Remedy – N. *remedy,* succour, help 703 *aid*; oil on troubled waters 177 *moderator*; corrective 654 *amendment*; redress, amends 787 *restitution*; expiation 941 *atonement*; cure 656 *recuperation*; healing quality *or* property; sovereign remedy, specific, answer, solution; prescription, recipe, formula, nostrum; quack remedy, patent medicine; panacea, cure-all, elixir.

medicine, pharmacopoeia; herbal remedy; medicinal herb; balm, balsam; medication, medicament, patent medicine, proprietary drug, generic d., ethical d.; placebo; pill, bolus, tablet, capsule, caplet, lozenge; draught, potion, elixir; infusion; dose, booster d.; drops, drip; injection, jab, shot; preparation, mixture, powder, linctus; plaster (see *surgical dressing*); spray, inhaler.

diagnostic, symptom, syndrome; sample, urine s., semen s.; battery of tests, test, laboratory t., lab t., blood t., serotest, sputum t., stool t., eye t., hearing t.; pregnancy t.; amniocentesis, alphafetoprotein test, chorionic villus sampling; cervical smear, smear test, Pap t.; mammogram, angiogram, arteriogram, cardiogram, ECG, lymphogram, pyelogram, venogram; radiograph; chest X-ray; barium meal, barium enema; ultrasound, screening, scanning, CAT s., body s., brain s., EEG; biopsy, cone b.; stethoscope, bronchoscope, ophthalmoscope, auriscope; endoscope, colposcope, ureteroscope, bronchoscopy, colonoscopy, endoscopy, gastroscopy, laparoscopy; forensic test; DNA fingerprinting, genetic f.

prophylactic, preventive; cordon sanitaire, quarantine 652 *hygiene*; prophylaxis, immunization, inoculation, vaccination; vaccine, triple v., BCG, TAB; quinine; antisepsis, disinfection, sterilization; antiseptic, disinfectant, iodine, carbolic, boric acid, boracic a.; bactericide, germicide, insecticide 659 *poison*; fumigant; fluoridation, fluoride.

antidote, counterirritant, antihistamine; antiserum, antitoxin; antiemetic; febrifuge, quinine; vermifuge, anthelmintic; antigen, antibody, interferon; antibiotic; immunosuppressant; antispasmodic, anticonvulsant; sedative; anticoagulant; antacid, analgesic, painkiller.

purgative, purge, cathartic, laxative, aperient; castor oil, Epsom salts, health s., senna pods; cascara, milk of magnesia; diuretic; expectorant, emetic, nauseant, ipecacuanha; carminative, digestive, liquorice, dill water; douche, enema.

tonic, restorative; tonic wine; reviver, refresher, pick-me-up 174 *stimulant*; caffeine, nicotine, alcohol; spirits, smelling salts, sal volatile; infusion, tisane, herb tea; betel nut, ginseng, royal jelly; vitamin tablet, iron pill.

drug, wonder drug; antibiotic, sulphonamide; penicillin; aureomycin, streptomycin, insulin, cortisone; hormone, steroid; progesterone, oestrogen; contraceptive pill 172 *contraception*; analgesic, aspirin, codeine, paracetamol, 375 *anaesthetic*; tranquillizer, diazepam, Valium (tdmk), antidepressant, sedative; barbiturate, sleeping pill; narcotic, dope, morphia, morphine, opium, cocaine, heroin; stimulant 949 *drug-taking*.

balm, balsam, oil, emollient 177 *moderator*; salve, ointment; cream 843 *cosmetic*; lanolin, liniment, embrocation; lotion, wash; eyewash.

surgical dressing, dressing, lint, gauze; swab; bandage, sling, splint, cast, plaster of Paris; tourniquet; fingerstall; patch; plaster, sticking p., Elastoplast (tdmk), Band-Aid (tdmk) corn plaster; fomentation, poultice, compress; tampon; pessary, suppository.

medical art, therapeutics; medical advice, medical practice; homoeopathy, naturopathy; medicine, clinical m., preventive m., fringe m., alternative m., complementary m., holistic m., unorthodox m., folk m.; iridology, reflexology, radiesthesia; acupuncture, acupressure;

radiography, radiology, tomography; diagnosis, prognosis; healing, laying on of hands, faith healing, Christian Science; sexology, gynaecology, midwifery 167 *obstetrics*; gerontology, geriatrics, paediatrics; orthopaedics, orthotics, ophthalmology, orthoptics, neurology, dermatology, ear, nose and throat, ENT, cardiology, oncology; nuclear medicine; radiotherapy; psychopathology, bacteriology, microbiology, virology, immunology; pharmaceutics, pharmacology; veterinary medicine.

surgery, general surgery, brain s., heart s., cardiac s., open-heart s., by-pass s., transplant s.; plastic surgery, cosmetic s., rhinoplasty, prosthesis, prosthetics; chiropractic; operation, surgical o., op.; phlebotomy, venesection; tranfusion; dialysis; D and C, dilatation and curettage; transplant; cauterization; amputation, trephination, trepanning, lobotomy, tonsillectomy, appendicectomy, appendectomy, colostomy, laparotomy; mastectomy, radical m., lumpectomy; hysterectomy; vasectomy; dentistry, extracting, filling.

therapy, therapeutics; medical treatment; nursing, bedside manner; first aid, aftercare; cure, faith c.; hydrotherapy; regimen; bone-setting, orthopaedics, osteopathy, osteotherapy; hypnotherapy; hormone therapy; immunotherapy; chemotherapy; gene therapy; physiotherapy, occupational therapy; radiotherapy; heat treatment; electrotherapy, ECT; clinical psychology; child psychology; psychotherapy, psychiatry, psychoanalysis 447 *psychology*; group therapy, behaviour t., cognitive behaviour t., aversion t., Gestalt t., primal t.; acupuncture, acupressure; catheterization; intravenous injection, dripfeed; fomentation, poulticing.

hospital, infirmary, general hospital, maternity h., children's h.; 503 *mental hospital*; dispensary, clinic, antenatal c.; nursing home, convalescent h.; hospice; hospital ship, hospital train; stretcher, ambulance; ward, hospital w., casualty w., isolation w., sick bay, sickroom, sickbed; hospital bed; oxygen tent, iron lung; respirator, life-support system, heart-lung machine, kidney m.; incubator, intensive care unit; x-ray machine, scanner, body s., brain s., head s., CAT s.; first-aid station; operating theatre, operating table; consulting room, surgery, clinic, community health centre; sanatorium, spa, hydro; pump room, baths, hot springs, thermae.

doctor, physician; quack; veterinary surgeon, vet, horse-doctor; herbalist; faith healer, Christian Scientist; homoeopath, naturopath; acupuncturist; hakim, barefoot doctor, flying d.; witchdoctor, medicine man 983 *sorcerer*; medic, medical student; houseman, intern, registrar; medical practitioner, general p., GP, family doctor; locum tenens, locum; clinician, therapeutist; surgeon, general s., plastic s., neurosurgeon; medical officer, environmental health o., sanitary inspector; medical adviser, consultant, specialist; diagnostician, pathologist; alienist, psychiatrist, psychoanalyst, shrink, neurologist; paramedic, anaesthetist, radiologist, radiographer; physiotherapist, occupational therapist, speech t.; paediatrician, geriatrician; obstetrician, midwife; gynaecologist; sexologist; dermatologist, haematologist; biochemist, microbiologist; radiotherapist; orthopaedist, orthotist, osteopath, chiropractor, podiatrist, chiropodist; ophthalmologist, optician, ophthalmic optician, oculist, orthoptist; aurist; dentist, dental surgeon, orthodontist; dietician; medical profession, private medicine, Harley Street, National Health Service; Red Cross, St. John Ambulance; Hippocratic oath.

druggist, apothecary, chemist, pharmacist; dispenser, pharmacologist; chemist's, pharmacy.

nurse, male n., student n., staff n.; charge n., sister, night s., ward s., theatre s., nursing officer, senior n. o.; matron; state-enrolled nurse, SEN; state-registered nurse, SRN; special nurse, day n.,

night n.; district nurse; health visitor; nursing auxiliary, ward orderly, ambulanceman; almoner, hospital social worker 901 *sociology*; Florence Nightingale, lady with a lamp, ministering angel.

Adj. *remedial,* corrective, curative, restorative; helpful 644 *beneficial*; therapeutic, medicinal, healing, curing; soothing, emollient, palliative; anodyne, analgesic, narcotic, hypnotic, anaesthetic 375 *insensible*; digestive; purging; cathartic, emetic, laxative; antidotal; prophylactic, disinfectant, antiseptic; antipyretic, febrifugal; tonic; nutritional.

medical, pathological, homoeopathic, herbal; surgical, rhinoplastic, orthopaedic, orthotic; obstetric, obstetrical; clinical; operable, curable.

Vb. *remedy,* fix, put right, correct 656 *restore*; help 703 *aid*; treat, heal; soothe 831 *relieve*.

doctor, practise medicine; treat, prescribe; attend 703 *minister to*; tend, nurse; give first aid, give the kiss of life 656 *revive*; hospitalize, medicate; inject, give a jab, give a shot; dress, bandage, put a plaster on; apply a tourniquet 350 *staunch*; poultice, plaster; set, put in splints; drug, anaesthetize; operate, amputate; trepan, trephine; curette; cauterize; bleed, phlebotomize; transfuse; manipulate; extract, pull, fill; immunize, vaccinate, inoculate; sterilize.

659 Bane – **N.** *bane,* curse, plague; scourge, ruin 616 *evil*; malady 651 *disease*; bad habit, besetting sin 934 *vice*; hell, affliction 731 *adversity*; woe, funeral 825 *sorrow*; cross, cross to bear, trial; bore 838 *tedium*; bugbear, bête noire 827 *annoyance*; burden, imposition, white elephant; thorn in the flesh, stone round one's neck; stress, strain, perpetual worry, constant anxiety, angst, torment, nagging pain 825 *worry*; running sore 651 *ulcer*; bitterness 393 *sourness*; bite, sting, poison dart, fang, nettle 256 *sharp point*; trouble spot, hornet's nest 663 *pitfall*; viper, adder, serpent 365 *reptile*; snake, snake in the grass 663 *troublemaker*; parasite, tapeworm 365

insect, *creepy-crawly*; mosquito, mozzie, wasp; locust 168 *destroyer*; oppressor 735 *tyrant*.

blight, rot, dry r., wet r.; mildew, mould, rust, fungus; moth, woodworm, canker, cancer 51 *decay*; nuclear winter; visitation 651 *plague*; frost 380 *coldness*; drought 342 *desiccation*.

poison, poisonousness, virulence, venomousness, toxicity; pollution; bacteria, salmonella, bacillus, germ, virus 651 *infection*; teratogen, carcinogen, oncogene; biological weapon; venom, toxin; deadly poison, snake p., rat p.; germicide, insecticide, pesticide; fungicide, herbicide, weed-killer, defoliant, dioxin, paraquat, derris, DDT; hemlock, arsenic, strychnine, cyanide, prussic acid, vitriol; asphyxiant, poison gas, nerve g., mustard gas, tear g., CS gas; carbon monoxide, carbon dioxide; miasma, sewer gas 653 *insalubrity*; atmospheric pollution, acid rain, smog; lead pollution; uranium, plutonium; radioactivity, nuclear fallout, strontium 90 417 *radiation*; heroin 658 *drug*, 949 *drugtaking*; lethal dose, overdose; toxicology.

poisonous plant, hemlock, deadly nightshade, belladonna, datura, henbane, monkshood, aconite, hellebore; nux vomica, upas tree.

660 Safety – **N.** *safety,* safeness, security; immunity; safety in numbers 104 *multitude*; secure position, safe job; social security, welfare state 901 *sociology*; safe distance, wide berth 620 *avoidance*; all clear, coast c.; guarantee, warrant 473 *certainty*; sense of security, assurance, confidence 855 *courage*; safety valve 667 *means of escape*; rescue 668 *deliverance*.

protection, conservation 666 *preservation*; insurance, surety 858 *caution*; patronage, care, sponsorship, good offices, auspices, aegis, fatherly eye 703 *aid*; protectorate, guardianship, wardenship, wardship, tutelage, custody, surrogacy 747 *restraint*; safekeeping, keeping, charge, safe hands; ward, watch, electronic surveillance, Big Brother, vetting,

positive v. 457 *surveillance*; safeguard, precaution, security system, alarm s., preventive measure 713 *defence*; immunization, prophylaxis, quarantine, cordon sanitaire 652 *hygiene*; cushion, buffer; screen, cover; umbrella 662 *shelter*; deterrent 723 *weapon*; safe-conduct, passport, pass 756 *permit*; escort, convoy, guard 722 *armed force*; defence, bastion, bulwark, tower of strength 713 *defences*; haven, sanctuary, asylum 662 *refuge*; anchor 662 *safeguard*; moat, ditch, palisade, stockade 235 *fence*; shield, breastplate, armour plate 713 *armour*.

protector, protectress, guardian; guardian angel, patron saint, liege lord, feudal l., fairy godmother 707 *patron*; defender, preserver, shepherd; bodyguard, lifeguard, strongarm man, bouncer; vigilante 713 *defender*; custodian, curator, warden; warder, guard, security g., coastguard; chaperon, duenna, governess, nursemaid, nanny, baby-sitter 749 *keeper*; lookout, watch, watchman, night w. 664 *warner*; firewatcher, fire fighter, fireman; policeman *or* -woman, police constable, police sergeant, sheriff; copper, cop 955 *police*; private eye 459 *detective*; sentry, sentinel, garrison, security forces 722 *soldiery*; watchdog, guard dog, police d. 365 *dog*; Cerberus 457 *surveillance*.

Adj. *safe,* secure, sure; safe and sound, spared 666 *preserved*; intact, unharmed 646 *undamaged*; garrisoned, well-defended; insured; immunized, vaccinated, inoculated; disinfected; in safety, on sure ground, home and dry, on home ground, on the home stretch, on terra firma; in harbour; out of the wood, out of danger, out of harm's way; clear, in the clear, sheltered, shielded, screened, protected etc. vb.; under the protection of, under the wing of; in safe hands, in custody, behind bars, under lock and key 747 *imprisoned*; reliable, guaranteed; harmless 615 *good*.

invulnerable, immune, impregnable, sacrosanct; unassailable, unbreakable; tenable 162 *strong*; proof, foolproof;

weatherproof, waterproof, showerproof, leakproof, gasproof, fireproof, bulletproof, bombproof, shatterproof; seaworthy, airworthy; shrink-wrapped, vacuum sealed, hermetically s.; armoured.

Vb. *be safe,* - invulnerable etc. adj.; reach safety; come through, save one's bacon 667 *escape*; land on one's feet, keep one's head above water, weather the storm, ride it out; bear a charmed life, have nine lives; have a roof over one's head; be under cover 523 *lurk*; keep a safe distance, give a wide berth 620 *avoid*.

safeguard, keep safe, guard, protect; stand surety for, go bail for 713 *defend*; shield; grant asylum, afford sanctuary; keep, conserve 666 *preserve*; hoard 632 *store*; keep in custody 747 *imprison*; ward, watch over, care for, mother, take under one's wing; nurse, foster, cherish; have charge of, keep an eye on, chaperon 457 *look after*; hide, put in a safe place 525 *conceal*; cushion, cocoon 218 *support*; insulate; cover, shade 421 *screen*; keep under cover, garage, lock up; take in, house, shelter; enfold, make safe, secure, fortify 162 *strengthen*; entrench, fence in, fence round 232 *circumscribe*; arm, armour; shepherd, convoy, escort; flank, support; garrison, mount guard; immunize, inoculate, vaccinate; pasteurize, chlorinate, fluoridate, fluoridize, disinfect; give assurances, warrant, guarantee 473 *make certain*; keep order, police, patrol.

661 Danger – **N.** *danger,* peril; dangerousness, perilousness, shadow of death, jaws of d., lion's mouth, dragon's lair; dangerous situation, parlous state, dire straits, forlorn hope 700 *predicament*; emergency 137 *crisis*; jeopardy, risk, hazard, banana skin, precariousness, razor's edge 474 *uncertainty*; black spot, snag 663 *pitfall*; trap, death t. 527 *ambush*; endangerment, imperilment, hazarding, dangerous course; daring, overdaring 857 *rashness*; venture 672 *undertaking*; leap in the dark 618 *gambling*; slippery slope, road to ruin 655

deterioration; sword of Damocles, menace 900 *threat*; cause for alarm, rocks ahead, storm brewing, gathering clouds, gathering storm 665 *danger signal*; narrow escape, close shave, near thing 667 *escape*.

vulnerability, danger of 180 *liability*; security risk; exposure, nakedness, defencelessness, naivety 161 *helplessness*; insecurity 152 *changeableness*; easy target, sitting duck; chink in the armour, Achilles' heel 163 *weakness*; soft underbelly 327 *softness*; feet of clay, human error, tragic flaw, fatal f. 647 *imperfection*; weaker brethren, weaker sex.

Adj. *dangerous,* perilous, fraught with danger, treacherous, beset with perils; risky, hazardous, venturesome, dicey, dodgy, chancy 618 *speculative*; serious, nasty, critical; at stake; menacing, ominous, foreboding, alarming; toxic, poisonous 645 *harmful*; unhealthy, infectious 653 *insalubrious*; inflammable, flammable, explosive, radioactive.

unsafe, slippery, treacherous, untrustworthy 474 *unreliable*; insecure, precarious, dicky; unsteady; shaky, tottering, crumbling, ramshackle, rickety, frail 655 *dilapidated*; jerry-built, gimcrack, crazy 163 *weak*; built on sand; critical, touch and go, hanging by a thread, trembling in the balance, teetering on the edge, on the edge, on the brink, on the verge.

vulnerable, in danger of 180 *liable*; exposed, naked, bare 229 *uncovered*; undefended, unprotected, at the mercy of; shelterless, helpless; unguarded, unescorted; unsupported, out on a limb; off one's guard 508 *inexpectant*.

endangered, in danger, in peril etc. n.; in a bad way; on the rocks, on slippery ground, on thin ice; in a tight corner, surrounded, trapped, under fire; in the lion's den, be thrown to the lions, on the razor's edge; out of the frying pan into the fire; between the devil and the deep blue sea, between Scylla and Charybdis; on the run, not out of the wood; at bay, with one's back to the wall, awaiting execution 961 *condemned*.

Vb. *be in danger,* run the risk of 180 *be liable*; enter the lion's den, walk into a trap; tread on dangerous ground, skate on thin ice, get out of one's depth, sail too near the wind, play with fire, sit on a powder barrel, sleep on a volcano; lean on a broken reed, feel the ground give way, be up against it, have to run for it; hang by a thread, tremble in the balance, hover on the brink, teeter on the edge 474 *be uncertain*;

face danger, dice with death, have one's back to the wall; take one's life in one's hands 855 *be courageous*; lay oneself open to; bell the cat, look danger in the face, look down a gun barrel; face heavy odds, have the odds against one; engage in a forlorn hope, be on a hiding to nothing, tempt providence, court disaster; take a tiger by the tail, put one's head in the lion's mouth 857 *be rash*; run the gauntlet, come under fire; take a chance, stick one's neck out 618 *gamble*.

endanger, be dangerous, spell danger, expose to d., put at risk, put in jeopardy; imperil, jeopardize; risk 618 *gamble*; run on the rocks, drive dangerously, drive without due care and attention, put one in fear of his *or* her life; loom, forebode, bode ill, menace 900 *threaten*.

662 Refuge. Safeguard – N. *refuge,* sanctuary, asylum, retreat, safe house; traffic island, zebra crossing, pedestrian crossing, pelican c., green man; last resort, bolthole, burrow; trench, dugout, air-raid shelter, fallout s.; earth, hole, den, lair; hearth 192 *home*; sanctum 194 *chamber*; cloister, ivory tower 192 *retreat*; sanctum sanctorum, temple; bastion; stronghold 713 *fort*; keep; secret place 527 *hiding-place*; tower of strength, mainstay 218 *prop*.

shelter, cover, roof, roof over one's head; earth, hole, fold, sheepfold; lee; windbreak, hedge 235 *fence*; camp, stockade 235 *enclosure*; shield; fireguard, fender, bumper, mudguard, windscreen 421 *screen*; umbrella, oilskins; sunglasses, goggles, ear muffs, ear

plugs; shinguard, pads; protective clothing, overalls; haven, harbour, port; harbourage, anchorage, quay, jetty, marina, dock 192 *stable*; halfway house, sheltered housing; old people's home, children's home, dog's h., hospice, Welfare State.

safeguard, protection 660 *safety*; precautions 702 *hindrance*; crush barrier, guardrail, railing; mail 713 *armour*; arms, deterrent, Star Wars, SDI 723 *weapon*; respirator, gas mask; air-bag, dead man's handle, safety catch, safety valve; crash helmet, safety h. 228 *headgear*; seat belt, safety b., safety harness; ejector-seat, parachute; safety net; lifeboat, rubber dinghy, life raft; life belt, life jacket, lifeline, breeches buoy; reins, brake 748 *fetter*; bolt, lock 264 *stopper*; ballast; breakwater, sea wall, embankment; lighthouse, lightship 269 *sailing aid*; spare parts 40 *extra*.

Vb. *seek refuge,* take refuge; take to the hills; shelter under the wing of, pull the blankets over one's head; seek political asylum; clasp the knees of, hide behind the skirts of; reach safety, find shelter; let down the portcullis, raise the drawbridge, batten down the hatches.

663 Pitfall: source of danger – **N.** *pitfall,* pit, trap for the unwary, banana skin, catch, Catch-22; snag 702 *obstacle*; booby trap, death t., minefield 542 *trap*; lying in wait 527 *ambush*; sleeping dog; thin ice; quagmire 347 *marsh*; quicksands; reef, coral r., rock; chasm, abyss, crevasse, precipice 209 *high land*; rapids, crosscurrent, undertow 350 *current*; vortex, maelstrom, whirlpool 350 *eddy*; tidal wave, flash flood; volcano 383 *furnace*; dynamite, time bomb, powder keg 723 *explosive*; trouble spot 661 *danger*; hotbed 651 *infection*; hornet's nest, hazard 659 *bane*.

troublemaker, mischiefmaker, agent provocateur 738 *agitator*; ugly customer, vandal, delinquent 904 *ruffian*; nigger in the woodpile, snake in the grass, viper in the bosom; a wolf in sheep's clothing; yellow peril.

664 Warning – **N.** *warning,* caution, caveat; example, lesson, object l.; notice, advance n. 524 *information*; word, word in the ear, word to the wise, tip, tip-off, wink, nudge 524 *hint*; whistle-blowing 528 *publication*; final warning, final notice, ultimatum 737 *demand*; admonition, admonishment 924 *reprimand*; deterrent 613 *dissuasion*; warning shot, s. across the bows; foreboding, premonition 511 *prediction*; warning voice 917 *conscience*; alarm, siren, foghorn, red alert 665 *danger signal*; stormy petrel, bird of ill omen 511 *omen*; gathering cloud, war cloud 661 *danger*; writing on the wall, symptom, sign 547 *indication*; death knell 364 *obsequies*; beacon.

warner, prophet, Cassandra 511 *diviner*; signaller; lighthouse-keeper; watchman, lookout, security man *or* woman, watch 457 *surveillance*; scout, spy; picket, sentinel, sentry 660 *protector*; advanced guard, rearguard; watchdog.

Vb. *warn,* caution; give fair warning, give notice, notify 524 *inform*; drop a hint, tip off, blow the whistle on 524 *hint*; admonish 924 *reprove*; forewarn 511 *predict*; forearm, put someone on their guard, alert 669 *prepare*; lour, menace 900 *threaten*; issue a caveat; sound the alarm 665 *raise the alarm*.

665 Danger signal – **N.** *danger signal,* warning; writing on the wall, evil omen 511 *omen*; gale warning; alarm bell, burglar alarm, fire alarm, foghorn, motor horn, bicycle bell, police whistle; alarm, curfew, siren, red alert; war cry, battle c., rallying cry; fiery cross; warning light, red l., beacon; red flag, SOS 547 *signal*.

false alarm, cry of 'wolf', scare, hoax; hoax call; bad dream 854 *intimidation*; flash in the pan 4 *insubstantiality*; scaremonger 854 *alarmist*.

Vb. *raise the alarm,* sound the a., give the a., dial 999, alert, arouse, scare, startle 854 *frighten*; sound one's horn, honk, toot; turn out the guard, call the police, raise a hue and cry, cry blue murder 528 *proclaim*; give a false alarm, cry wolf, cry too soon; sound a warning, toll, knell.

666 Preservation – N. *preservation,* safekeeping; safe conduct 660 *protection;* saving, salvation 668 *deliverance;* conservation, conservancy; perpetuation 144 *permanence;* support 633 *provision;* self-preservation 932 *selfishness;* game reserve, nature r., bird sanctuary, conservation area, green belt, listed building; protected species; taxidermy, mummification, embalming 364 *interment;* cold storage, deep-freezing, freeze-drying 382 *refrigeration;* UHT, dehydration 342 *desiccation;* canning, processing; preventive medicine, quarantine, cordon sanitaire.

preserver, life-saver, rescuer, deliverer 668 *deliverance;* preservative, ice, formaldehyde; camphor, mothball; pickle, marinade, brine 389 *condiment;* freezer 384 *refrigerator;* thermos flask (tdmk); canning factory, bottling plant; safety device, seat belt, airbag, gas mask 662 *safeguard;* incubator, respirator, iron lung, life support system; embalmer, mummifier; canner, bottler; preservationist, conservationist, environmentalist, green; green peace movement, green m.

Adj. *preserved,* well-p., long-life; frozen, on ice; pickled, marinated, salted, canned, bottled; mummified, embalmed; mothballed; conserved, protected 660 *safe.*

Vb. *preserve,* conserve, freeze, freeze-dry, keep on ice 382 *refrigerate;* embalm, mummify, stuff; pickle, salt 388 *season;* marinate; cure, smoke, kipper, dehydrate 342 *dry;* bottle, tin, can, process; protect, varnish, creosote, waterproof; maintain, keep in good repair, service 656 *repair;* prop up, shore up 218 *support;* sustain; keep safe; hold 778 *retain;* prolong; save, rescue 668 *deliver.*

667 Escape – N. *escape,* leak, leakage; extrication, delivery, rescue 668 *deliverance;* riddance, good r. 831 *relief;* getaway, breakout; decampment, flight, flit, moonlight f., French leave 296 *departure;* withdrawal, retreat, hasty r. 286

regression; disappearing trick 446 *disappearance;* elopement; evasion, truancy, bunking off, tax-dodging black economy, moonlighting 620 *avoidance;* narrow escape, close shave, narrow squeak, near thing 661 *danger;* let-off, discharge, reprieve 960 *acquittal;* setting free 746 *liberation;* immunity, exemption 919 *nonliability;* escapology, escapism.

means of escape, exit, emergency e., way out, back door, secret passage 298 *egress;* ladder, fire escape, escape hatch; drawbridge 624 *bridge;* vent, safety valve 662 *safeguard;* dodge; loophole, escape clause, technicality, let-out.

escaper, escapee, runaway; truant, escaped prisoner, prison-breaker; fugitive, refugee; survivor; escapist; escapologist, Houdini.

Vb. *escape,* find *or* win freedom 746 *achieve liberty;* make good one's escape, make a getaway, vamoose, break gaol, break out of prison; abscond, jump bail, flit, elope, skip, take flight, take French leave, go AWOL 620 *run away;* steal away, sneak off, duck and run, make oneself scarce, beat a hasty retreat 296 *decamp;* slip through, break t., break out, break loose, break away, get free, break one's chains, go over the wall, slip one's lead, shake one's yoke; get out, bluff one's way o., sneak o. 298 *emerge;* get away, slip through one's fingers; get off, get off lightly, secure an acquittal, go scot-free; get off on a technicality, save one's bacon, weather the storm, survive; get away with it, secure exemption, wriggle out of 919 *be exempt;* rid oneself, be well rid of; leak.

elude, evade, welsh, abscond, dodge 620 *avoid;* lie low 523 *lurk;* give one the slip, shake off, throw off the scent, throw dust in one's eye, draw a red herring, give one a run for one's money; escape notice, be found to be missing 190 *be absent.*

668 Deliverance – N. *deliverance,* delivery, extrication 304 *extraction;* riddance 831 *relief;* liberation, rescue, life-saving; salvage, retrieval 656 *restoration;* salvation, redemption 965 *divine function;*

ransom, buying off 792 *purchase*; release, amnesty; discharge, reprieve 960 *acquittal*; day of grace, respite 136 *delay*; truce; way out, let-out 667 *escape*; dispensation, exemption 919 *nonliability*.

Vb. *deliver,* save, rescue, come to the r., save by the bell, snatch from the jaws of death, throw a lifeline; get one out of 304 *extract*; extricate; untie, unbind 46 *disunite*; rid, save from 831 *relieve*; release; free, set free 746 *liberate*; let one off, get one off 960 *acquit*; deliver oneself 667 *escape*; save one's skin, rid oneself, get rid of; snatch a brand from the burning, be the salvation of; redeem, ransom, buy off 792 *purchase*; salvage, retrieve, recover; spare, excuse, dispense from 919 *exempt*.

669 Preparation – N. *preparation,* preparing, making ready; premedication; clearing the decks; preliminaries, priming; mobilization 718 *war measures*; trial run, trial, trials 461 *experiment*; practice, rehearsal, dress r.; brief, briefing; training 534 *teaching*; prep, homework 536 *learning*; spadework 682 *labour*; groundwork, foundation 218 *basis*; planning, first draft, outline, blueprint, prototype, pilot scheme 623 *plan*; advance factory; prearrangement, premeditation 608 *predetermination*; consultation 691 *advice*; precautions 510 *foresight*; bottom drawer, nest egg 632 *store*.

ripening, maturation, bringing to a head; seasoning, acclimatization; brewing, hatching, gestation, incubation 167 *propagation*; nurture; cultivation, tillage, sowing, planting 370 *agriculture*; bloom, efflorescence; fruition 725 *completion*.

Adj. *preparatory,* preparing etc. adj.; precautionary, preliminary 64 *preceding*; provisional, stopgap 150 *substituted*; marinating, brewing, cooking; brooding, hatching, incubating, maturing; in embryo; in preparation, afoot, on

the stocks; in store, in the offing, forthcoming 155 *impending*; under consideration, at the committee stage, mooted 623 *planned*; under training.

prepared, ready, alert 457 *vigilant*; made ready, in readiness, at the ready; mobilized, standing by, on call; all set, ready to go, raring to go; teed up, keyed up, psyched up, spoiling for; trained, qualified, well-prepared, practised, in practice, at concert pitch, word-perfect; primed, briefed, instructed 524 *informed*; forewarned, forearmed; saddled; battened down; groomed, in one's best bib and tucker, dressed to kill, in full war-paint; accoutred, armed, in harness, armed to the teeth; rigged, rigged out, equipped, furnished, fully f., well-appointed, provided; in store, in hand; in reserve, to hand, ready for use; ready for anything; in working order, operational.

matured, ripened, cooked, hatched etc. vb.; ripe, mellow, mature, seasoned, weathered, hardened; tried, experienced, veteran 694 *expert*; adult, full-grown, full-fledged 134 *grown-up*; out, in flower, florescent, flowering, fruiting; overripe; elaborated, worked up, laboured, smelling of the lamp; perfected 725 *completed*.

ready-made, ready-mixed, cut and dried, ready to use, ready-to-wear, off the peg; prefabricated; processed, ovenready; precooked, instant.

Vb. *prepare,* take steps, take measures; make preparations, make ready, pave the way, show the w., bridge, build a b., lead up to, pioneer 64 *come before*; choose one's ground, lay the foundations, do the groundwork, provide the basis; soften up; prepare the ground, sow the seed 370 *cultivate*; set to work, address oneself to 68 *begin*; cut out, block o.; sketch, outline, blueprint 623 *plan*; plot, prearrange 608 *predetermine*; prepare for, forearm, insure, take precautions, prepare for a rainy day; anticipate 507 *expect*.

make ready, set in order, make operational; batten down the hatches; put in commission; put one's house in order,

331

put in working order, bring up to scratch, wind up, tune, adjust 62 *arrange*; set the stage; clear the decks; mobilize 74 *bring together*; whet the knife, shuffle the cards, tee up; set, cock, prime, load; warm up, crank up, rev up, get into gear; equip, man; fit out, furnish, kit out, rig out, dress; arm 633 *provide*; rehearse, drill, groom, exercise, lick into shape 534 *train*; inure, acclimatize 610 *habituate*; coach, brief, bring one up to date 524 *inform*.

mature, mellow, ripen, bring to fruition 646 *perfect*; force, bring on 174 *invigorate*; bring to a head 725 *climax*; brew 301 *cook*; gestate, hatch, incubate, breed 369 *breed stock*; grow, farm 370 *cultivate*; nurture; elaborate, work out 725 *carry through*; season, weather, smoke, dry, cure; temper, harden, season.

prepare oneself, brace o.; serve an apprenticeship; study, brief oneself, do one's homework; train, exercise, go for the burn, rehearse, practise 536 *learn*; gird up one's loins, roll up one's sleeves; limber up, warm up, gear oneself up, psych oneself up, flex one's muscles; buckle on one's armour, take up one's sword, take sword in hand, shoulder arms; be prepared, get ready for action, stand by, hold oneself in readiness, keep one's powder dry.

Adv. *in preparation,* in hand, in train, under way, under construction.

670 Nonpreparation – N. *nonpreparation,* potluck; unpreparedness, unreadiness; want of practice, rustiness; unfitness; rawness, immaturity, greenness, unripeness 126 *newness*; belatedness 136 *lateness*; neglect 458 *negligence*; hastiness; improvisation 609 *spontaneity*; imperfection 55 *incompleteness*.

undevelopment, virgin soil; untilled ground 458 *negligence*; raw material, unlicked cub, rough diamond; late developer; rough copy; embryo, abortion.

Adj. *unprepared,* not ready, behindhand 136 *late*; unorganized; unpremeditated, without preparation, ad hoc, ad lib, extemporized, improvised, impromptu, snap, off the top of one's head, off the cuff 609 *spontaneous*; careless 458 *negligent*; overhasty 680 *hasty*; unguarded, with one's trousers down 661 *vulnerable*; caught unawares, taken off guard, caught napping, on the wrong foot 508 *inexpectant*; at sixes and sevens; scratch, untrained 491 *uninstructed*; unrehearsed 611 *unhabituated*; untilled, virgin.

immature, half-grown, unripe, green, underripe; unseasoned; unfledged, callow, wet behind the ears; adolescent, juvenile, childish, puerile, boyish, girlish 130 *young*; undeveloped, half-baked, raw 647 *imperfect*; underdeveloped, backward, retarded 136 *late*; unhatched, unborn, embryonic, rudimentary 68 *beginning*; half-formed, unformed, rough-hewn, uncut, unpolished, half-finished, unfinished; premature, abortive, at half-cock 728 *unsuccessful*; untrained, apprentice 695 *unskilled*; crude; forced.

uncooked, raw, rare, underdone; cold; ungarnished.

unequipped, unrigged, undressed 229 *uncovered*; unfurnished, ill-provided 307 *deficient*; unfitted, unqualified.

Vb. *be unprepared,* - unready etc. adj.; want practice; make no preparations, offer potluck, extemporize 609 *improvise*; live from day to day, take one day at a time, let tomorrow take care of itself; be premature, go off at half-cock 135 *be early*; take no precautions, drop one's guard 456 *be inattentive*; catch unawares 508 *surprise*.

Adv. *unreadily,* extempore, off the cuff, ad hoc.

671 Attempt – N. *attempt,* essay, bid; step, move, gambit 676 *deed*; endeavour, effort 682 *exertion*; tackle, try, some attempt; good try; valiant effort; one's level best, best one can do; catch-as-catch-can; determined effort, dead s. 712 *attack*; trial, probation 461 *experiment*; go at, shot at, stab at, crack at, bash at; first attempt, first go, first shot, first

offence, first strike 68 *debut*; final attempt, swan song, last bid, last throw; venture; speculation; aim, goal 617 *objective*; straining after, high endeavour.

Vb. *attempt*, essay, try; seek to, aim, make it one's a. 617 *intend*; angle for, fish for, seek 459 *search*; offer, bid, make a b.; make an attempt, make shift to, make the effort, do something about, not just stand there; endeavour, struggle, strive, try hard, try and try again 599 *be resolute*; do one's best, do one's damnedest, go all out, redouble one's efforts 682 *exert oneself*; push hard, strain, sweat 682 *work*; tackle, take on, try one's hand at, have a go, give it a try, give it a whirl, have a shot at, have a crack at, have a stab at 672 *undertake*; take the bull by the horns; chance one's arm, try one's luck, venture, speculate 618 *gamble*; put out a feeler, dip in a toe, put a toe in the water, fly a kite 461 *be tentative*; bite off more than one can chew; die in the attempt 728 *fail*.

Int. Here goes! nothing venture, nothing gain;

672 Undertaking – **N.** *undertaking*, job, task, assignment; self-imposed task, labour of love, pilgrimage 597 *voluntary work*; contract, engagement, obligation 764 *promise*; operation, exercise; programme, project, design 623 *plan*; tall order, big undertaking 700 *hard task*; enterprise, quest, search, adventure 459 *enquiry*; venture, speculation 618 *gambling*; occupation, matter in hand 622 *business*; campaign 671 *attempt*.

Adj. *enterprising*, pioneering, adventurous, venturesome, daring; go-ahead, go-go, progressive, innovative; opportunist, with an eye to the main chance; ambitious.

Vb. *undertake*, engage in, apply oneself to, address o. to, take up, go in for, devote oneself to; venture on, take on, tackle 671 *attempt*; go about, take in hand, turn *or* put *or* set one's hand to; set going 68 *initiate*; proceed to, embark on, launch into, plunge into, fall to, set to, get one's head down, buckle to, put one's

best foot forward, set one's shoulder to the wheel, set one's hand to the plough 68 *begin*; grasp the nettle 855 *be courageous*; assume responsibility, take charge of 689 *manage*; execute 725 *carry out*; set up shop, have irons in the fire 622 *busy oneself*; shoulder, take on one's shoulders, take upon oneself 917 *incur a duty*; commit oneself 764 *promise*; get involved, let oneself in for, volunteer 597 *be willing*; take on too much, bite off more than one can chew, have too many irons in the fire 678 *be busy*.

673 Use – **N.** *use*, utilization, exploitation; employment, application, appliance; exercise 610 *practice*; usage; treatment, proper treatment 457 *carefulness*; ill-treatment; misuse; abuse; wear, wear and tear 655 *dilapidation*; exhaustion, consumption 634 *waste*; reuse, recycling; usefulness, benefit, service 642 *good policy*; practicality, applicability 640 *utility*.

Adj. *used*, applied, employed etc. vb.; in service, in use, in constant u., in practice; used up, consumed, worn, threadbare, down-at-heel, second-hand, well-used, well-thumbed, dog-eared, well-worn 655 *dilapidated*; beaten, well-trodden 490 *known*; hackneyed, stale; available, usable, employable, utilizable, convertible 640 *useful*; at one's service, consumable, disposable.

Vb. *use*, employ, exercise, practise, put into practice, put into operation; apply, exert, bring to bear, administer; spend on, give to, devote to, dedicate to; assign to, allot; utilize, make use of, convert, convert to use 640 *find useful*; reuse, recycle, exploit, get a lot of mileage out of, use to the full, get the best out of, make the most of, maximize, exhaust the possibilities; milk, drain 304 *extract*; put to good use, turn to good account, capitalize on, make capital out of, use to advantage, profit by; play on, trade on, cash in on; play off against; make a pawn *or* cat's-paw of, take advantage of; put to use, wear, wear out, use up, consume 634 *waste*; work, manipulate 173 *operate*;

wield, ply, brandish; overwork, tax 684 *fatigue*.

avail oneself of, take up, adopt, try; resort to, have recourse to, fall back on, turn to, draw on; impose on, presume on; press into service, enlist in one's s.

dispose of, have at one's disposal, control, have at one's command, do what one likes with; allot, assign 783 *apportion*; requisition; call into play, set in motion, set going, deploy 612 *motivate*; enjoy 773 *possess*; consume, expend, absorb, use up 634 *waste*.

674 Nonuse – N. *nonuse,* abeyance, suspension 677 *inaction*; nonavailability 190 *absence*; stagnation, unemployment 679 *inactivity*; abstinence 620 *avoidance*; disuse, obsolescence 611 *desuetude*; redundancy, dismissal 300 *ejection*; surrender, throwing in the towel 621 *relinquishment*; withdrawal, cancellation 752 *abrogation*; unsuitability 643 *inexpedience*; uselessness, write-off 641 *uselessness*.

Adj. *disused,* derelict, discarded, castoff, jettisoned, scrapped, written off; sacked, discharged, laid off etc. vb.; laid up, mothballed, put on the back burner, out of commission, rusting; in limbo 458 *neglected*; worn out; on the shelf, retired; out of use, superseded, superannuated, obsolete, discredited 127 *antiquated*.

Vb. *not use,* not utilize, hold in abeyance; not touch, have no use for; abstain, forbear, hold off, do without 620 *avoid*; dispense with; reserve, keep in hand 632 *store*.

stop using, leave off 145 *cease*; outgrow 611 *disaccustom*; lay up, put in mothballs, put on the back burner, put out of commission; have done with, lay aside, put on the shelf; pension off, put out to grass; discard, dump, ditch, scrap, write off; jettison, throw away, throw overboard 300 *eject*; slough, cast off; give up, relinquish, resign 779 *not retain*; suspend, withdraw, cancel 752 *abrogate*; discharge, lay off, pay off, make redundant 300 *dismiss*; drop, supersede, replace 150 *substitute*.

675 Misuse – N. *misuse,* abuse, wrong use; misapplication; mismanagement, maladministration 695 *bungling*; misappropriation, malpractice 788 *peculation*; perversion 246 *distortion*; prostitution, violation; desecration 980 *impiety*; malapropism 565 *solecism*; pollution 649 *uncleanness*; overuse, overgrazing, overfishing; extravagance 634 *waste*; misusage, mishandling, mistreatment, maltreatment, ill-treatment.

Vb. *misuse,* abuse; use wrongly, misemploy, put to bad use, misdirect; manipulate, misappropriate 788 *defraud*; violate, desecrate, take in vain 980 *profane*; prostitute 655 *pervert*; pollute 649 *make unclean*; do violence to 176 *force*; take advantage of, exploit 673 *use*; manhandle, knock about 645 *ill-treat*; maltreat 735 *oppress*; misgovern, misrule, mishandle, mismanage 695 *be unskilful*; squander, fritter away 634 *waste*; misapply, use a sledgehammer to crack a nut 641 *waste effort*.

Section three: Voluntary action

676 Action – N. *action,* doing, performance; steps, measures, move 623 *policy*; transaction, enactment, commission; execution, accomplishment 725 *completion*; procedure, routine 610 *practice*; behaviour 688 *conduct*; movement, play, swing 265 *motion*; operation, working, interaction 173 *agency*; force, pressure 178 *influence*; work, labour 682 *exertion*; militancy, activeness; effort, endeavour, campaign, crusade, battle 671 *attempt*; implementation, administration, handling 689 *management*.

deed, act; action, piece of the a., exploit, feat, achievement 855 *prowess*; crime; stunt, tour de force, stroke of genius 875 *ostentation*; gesture, measure, step, move 623 *policy*; manoeuvre 688 *tactics*; stroke, blow, coup, coup d'état 623 *contrivance*; job, task, operation, exercise 672 *undertaking*; proceeding, transaction, deal, doings, dealings 154 *affairs*; work, handiwork.

doer, man *or* woman of action, go-getter, activist 678 *busy person*; practical person; achiever; hero, heroine 855 *brave person*; practitioner 696 *expert*; stunt man *or* woman, player 594 *actor*; executant, performer; perpetrator, committer; mover, controller, manipulator 612 *motivator*; operator 686 *agent*; contractor, undertaker, entrepreneur, intrapreneur; campaigner, canvasser; executor, executive, administrator, manager 690 *director*; hand, workman, operative 686 *worker*;

Vb. *do,* act, perform, get in on the act; be in action, come into operation 173 *operate*; militate, act upon 178 *influence*; manipulate 612 *motivate*; use tactics, manoeuvre 698 *be cunning*; do something, lift a finger; proceed, proceed with, get on with, get going, move, take action, take steps; try 671 *attempt*; tackle, take on 672 *undertake*; adopt a measure, enact, legislate 953 *make legal*; do the deed, perpetrate, commit, achieve, accomplish, complete 725 *carry through*; do the needful, take care of, dispatch, execute, implement, fulfil, put into practice 725 *carry out*; do great deeds, make history, win renown 866 *have a reputation*; practise, exercise, carry on, discharge, prosecute, pursue, wage, ply, ply one's trade, employ oneself 622 *busy oneself*; officiate, do one's stuff 622 *function*; transact, proceed 622 *do business*; administer, administrate, manage, control 689 *direct*; have to do with 688 *deal with*; sweat, labour, campaign, canvass 682 *work*; exploit 673 *use*; have a hand in, be active in, play a part in 775 *participate*; deal in, have a finger in, get mixed up in 678 *meddle*; conduct oneself, indulge in 688 *behave.*

677 Inaction – N. *inaction,* nothing doing, inertia 175 *inertness*; impotence; failure to act, neglect 458 *negligence*; abstention, refraining 620 *avoidance*; passive resistance 711 *defiance*; suspension, abeyance, dormancy 674 *nonuse*; deadlock, stalemate, logjam 145 *stop*; immobility, paralysis, impassivity 375

insensibility; passivity, stagnation, vegetation, doldrums, stillness, quiet, calm 266 *quiescence*; time on one's hands, idle hours 681 *leisure*; rest 683 *repose*; nonemployment, underemployment, unemployment, joblessness; no work, sinecure; loafing, idleness, indolence, twiddling one's thumbs 679 *inactivity*; Fabian policy, Fabian tactics 136 *delay*; lack of progress 655 *deterioration*; noninterference, nonintervention 860 *indifference*; head in the sand, defeatism 856 *cowardice.*

Adj. *nonactive,* inoperative, idle, suspended, in abeyance 679 *inactive*; passive, dull, sluggish 175 *inert*; unoccupied, leisured 681 *leisurely*; do-nothing, unprogressive, ostrich-like; Fabian, cunctative, delaying, procrastinating; stationary, motionless, immobile, becalmed 266 *quiescent*; cold, extinct; not stirring, without a sign of life, dead-and-alive 361 *dead*; laid off, unemployed, jobless, out of work, on the dole, without employment; incapable of action 161 *impotent*; benumbed, paralysed 375 *insensible*; apathetic, phlegmatic 820 *impassive.*

Vb. *not act,* hang fire 598 *be unwilling*; refrain, abstain, pass the buck 620 *avoid*; look on, stand by 441 *watch*; let the world go by, wait and see, bide one's time 136 *wait*; procrastinate 136 *put off*; let things take their course, laisser faire, let sleeping dogs lie, let well alone; hold no brief for, stay neutral, not take sides, sit on the fence 860 *be indifferent*; do nothing, turn a blind eye 458 *disregard*; sit tight, not move, not budge, not lift a finger, not even attempt 175 *be inert*; rest on one's oars, rest on one's laurels; drift, slide, coast, free-wheel; have no hope 853 *despair*; let pass, let go by, leave alone, let a., give it a miss 458 *neglect*; stay still, keep quiet 266 *be quiescent*; sit back, relax 683 *repose*; have no function; have nothing to do, kick one's heels, twiddle one's thumbs, sit on one's hands; pause, desist 145 *cease*; rust, lie idle, stay on the shelf, lie fallow

674 *not use*; have no life, lie dead 361 *die*.

678 Activity – N. *activity,* activeness, activism, militancy 676 *action*; scene; interest, active i. 775 *participation*; social activity, group a. 882 *sociability*; activation 612 *motive*; excitation 174 *stimulation*; agitation, movement, mass m. 738 *sedition*; life, stir 265 *motion*; nimbleness, briskness, smartness, alacrity, promptitude 597 *willingness*; readiness 135 *punctuality*; quickness, dispatch, expedition 277 *velocity*; spurt, burst, fit 318 *spasm*; hurry, flurry, hurryskurry, hustle, bustle 680 *haste*; hussle, fuss, bother, botheration, ado, to-do, tumult, frenzy 61 *turmoil*; whirl, scramble, mad s., rat race, maelstrom 315 *vortex*; drama, much ado, thick of things, thick of the action, the fray; plenty to do, a piece of the action, irons in the fire 622 *business*; call on one's time; pressure of work, no sinecure; hum, hive of industry 687 *workshop*.

restlessness, fiddling; fidgets, fidgetiness 318 *agitation*; fret 503 *frenzy*; energy, dynamism, aggressiveness, militancy, enterprise, initiative, push, drive, go, get-up-and-go, pep 174 *vigorousness*; vivacity, spirit, animation, liveliness, vitality 360 *life*; watchfulness, wakefulness, vigilance 457 *carefulness*; sleeplessness, insomnia.

assiduity, application, concentration, intentness 455 *attention*; industriousness, industry, laboriousness; determination, earnestness, empressement 599 *resolution*; tirelessness, indefatigability 600 *perseverance*; studiousness, painstaking, diligence; whole-heartedness, devotedness.

overactivity, overextension, overexpansion, excess 637 *redundance*; Parkinson's law; displacement activity; chasing one's own tail 641 *lost labour*; song and dance 318 *commotion*; hyperthyroidism, overexertion; officiousness, interference, finger in every pie.

busy person, new broom, enthusiast, hustler, jet-setter; workaholic 686

worker; factotum, jack-of-all-trades, maid-of-all-work, galley slave, Trojan; eager beaver, busy bee, workhorse, willing horse; man *or* woman of action, activist, militant 676 *doer*; live wire, human dynamo; powerhouse, whiz kid, go-getter, pusher, careerist.

meddler, stirrer, interferer, troublemaker, nosy parker, busybody; back-seat driver 691 *adviser*.

Adj. *active,* stirring 265 *moving*; going, working, incessant; expeditious; able, able-bodied 162 *strong*; quick, brisk, nippy, spry, smart 277 *speedy*; nimble, energetic, forceful 174 *vigorous*; pushing, go-getting, up-and-coming 672 *enterprising*; frisky, sprightly, mettlesome, live, alive and kicking, full of beans, animated, bright-eyed and bushy-tailed, vivacious 819 *lively*; eager 818 *fervent*; enthusiastic, zealous, prompt, on one's toes 597 *willing*; awake, alert, watchful, wakeful, on the qui vive 457 *vigilant*; sleepless, restless, feverish, fretful, tossing, fidgety, jumpy, nervy, like a cat on hot bricks, like a hen on a hot griddle; frantic 503 *frenzied*; hyperactive, overactive 822 *excitable*; involved; aggressive, militant, up in arms 718 *warlike*.

busy, bustling, humming, lively, eventful; coming and going, rushing to and fro; up and doing, stirring, astir, afoot, on the move, on the go, on the trot, in full swing; rushed off one's feet, hard at it, up to one's eyes; at work, at one's desk; occupied, fully o., employed; busy as a bee.

industrious, studious, sedulous, assiduous; hardworking; slogging 682 *laborious*; tireless, indefatigable, burning the candle at both ends, efficient, workmanlike.

Vb. *be active,* interest oneself in, join in 775 *participate*; be stirring, rush to and fro 265 *move*; run riot 61 *rampage*; rouse oneself, bestir o., stir one's stumps, rub the sleep from one's eyes, be up and doing; hum, thrive 730 *prosper*; make progress 285 *progress*; keep moving, keep on the go, keep the pot boiling 146 *go on*; push, shove, thrust, drive 279

impel; elbow one's way, thrust oneself forward 174 *be vigorous*; rush, surge 350 *flow*; roar, rage, bluster 352 *blow*; explode, burst; dash, fly, run 277 *move fast*; make the effort, do one's best 671 *attempt*; take pains 455 *be attentive*; buckle to, put one's shoulder to the wheel, put one's hand to the tiller 682 *exert oneself*; persist, beaver away 600 *persevere*; polish off, dispatch, make short work of, not let the grass grow under one's feet; rise to the occasion, work wonders 727 *be successful*; jump to it, show willing, make things hum 676 *do*; be on one's toes, anticipate 457 *be careful*; seize the opportunity, take one's chance, take the bull by the horns 137 *profit by*; assert oneself, not take it lying down, be up in arms, react, react sharply, show fight 711 *defy*; protest, agitate, demonstrate, kick up a shindy, raise the dust 762 *deprecate*; be busy, keep b.; have irons in the fire 622 *busy oneself*; be always on the go, bustle, hurry, hassle, scurry 680 *hasten*; live in a whirl, join the rat race, run round in circles; chase one's own tail 641 *waste effort*; not know which way to turn 700 *be in difficulty*; have one's hands full, be rushed off one's feet, have not a moment to spare *or* to call one's own, have no time to lose, burn the midnight oil, burn the candle at both ends; stamp with impatience 822 *be excitable*; have other fish to fry 138 *be engaged*; slave, slog 682 *work*; never stop, improve the shining hour.

meddle, intervene, interfere, be officious, not mind one's own business, have a finger in every pie; pry into, poke one's nose in, shove one's oar in, butt in 297 *intrude*; pester, bother, annoy 827 *trouble*; be bossy, boss, boss one around, tyrannize 735 *oppress*; tinker, tamper.

Adv. *actively,* on the go, on one's toes; full tilt, full belt, whole hog, like a bomb, on all cylinders; with might and main, for all one is worth, for dear life, as if one's life depended on it.

679 Inactivity – N. *inactivity,* inactiveness 677 *inaction*; inertia, torpor 175

inertness; lull, suspension 145 *cessation*; immobility, stillness, slack period, doldrums, morgue 266 *quiescence*; logjam, putting off till tomorrow, stagnation 655 *deterioration*; rustiness 674 *nonuse*; slump, recession 37 *decrease*; unemployment, shutdown; absenteeism 598 *unwillingness*; procrastination, laissez-faire, mañana 136 *delay*; idleness, indolence, loafing.

sluggishness, lethargy, laziness, indolence, sloth; dawdling 278 *slowness*; debility 163 *weakness*; lifelessness; languor, listlessness 820 *moral insensibility*; stupor, torpor 375 *insensibility*; apathy 860 *indifference*; phlegm, impassivity 823 *inexcitability*; supineness, line of least resistance 721 *submission*.

sleepiness, tiredness, weariness, lassitude 684 *fatigue*; drowsiness, heaviness, nodding; yawning; tired eyes, heavy lids, sand in the eyes; dreaminess 513 *fantasy*.

sleep, slumber, kip, bye-byes; beauty sleep; sleep of the just; drowse; nap, catnap, forty winks, shut-eye, snooze, doze, siesta 683 *repose*; hibernation; unconsciousness, coma, oblivion, trance, catalepsy, hypnosis 375 *insensibility*; sleepwalking, somnambulism; sleepy sickness 651 *disease*; dreams; Land of Nod.

soporific, sleeping draught, nightcap; sleeping pill, sedative, barbiturate; opiate, opium, morphine 375 *anaesthetic*; lullaby, cradlesong, bedtime story.

idler, drone, lazybones, loafer, sloucher, sluggard; slacker, skiver, clock-watcher; sleepyhead; dawdler 278 *slowcoach*; hobo, bum, tramp 268 *wanderer*; mendicant 763 *beggar*; parasite, cadger, sponger, scrounger, moocher, freeloader; layabout, good-for-nothing, ne'er-do-well; drifter, free-wheeler; lotus-eater; passenger, sleeping partner; idle rich, Sloane Ranger, leisured classes; dreamer.

Adj. *inactive,* motionless, stationary, at a standstill, still 266 *quiescent*; suspended, discontinued, not working, not operating, not in use, laid up, out of commission 674 *disused*; inanimate,

lifeless 175 *inert*; torpid, unconscious, drugged 375 *insensible*; sluggish, rusty 677 *nonactive*; listless, lackadaisical 834 *dejected*; tired, faint, languid, languorous 684 *fatigued*; dull, heavy, leaden, lumpish, stolid 820 *impassive*; unresisting, supine, submissive 721 *submitting*; uninterested 454 *incurious*; apathetic 860 *indifferent*; lethargic 823 *inexcitable*; nonparticipating, sleeping 190 *absent*; idle, unoccupied 681 *leisurely*; on strike, out, locked o.

lazy, bone-l.; slothful, sluggish, workshy, indolent, idle, bone-idle, parasitical; idling, loafing 681 *leisurely*; dawdling 278 *slow*; tardy, procrastinating 136 *late*; slack 458 *negligent*.

sleepy, ready for bed, tired 684 *fatigued*; half-awake, half-asleep; somnolent, heavy-eyed; drowsy, dozy, dopey, groggy, nodding, yawning; napping, dozing; asleep, dreaming, snoring, fast asleep, sound a., dead to the world; unconscious, out, out cold; dormant, hibernating, comatose; in dreamland, in the land of Nod, in the arms of Morpheus, in bed.

Vb. *be inactive,* do nothing, rust, stagnate, vegetate, smoulder, hang fire 677 *not act*; let the grass grow under one's feet, let the world go by, delay 136 *put off*; not bother, take it easy, let things go, laisser faire 458 *be neglectful*; hang about, kick one's heels 136 *wait*; slouch, lag, loiter, dawdle 278 *move slowly*; dally, drag one's feet 136 *be late*; stand, sit, lie, loll, lounge, laze, rest, take it easy 683 *repose*; lie down on the job, slack, skive, shirk 620 *avoid*; not work, fold one's arms, sit around; have nothing to do, loaf, idle, mooch about, moon a., while away the time, kill t., sit on one's hands, twiddle one's thumbs; waste time, trifle, dabble, fritter away the time, piddle, potter 641 *waste effort*; come to a standstill 278 *decelerate*; dilly-dally, hesitate 474 *be uncertain*; droop, faint, fail, languish, slacken 266 *come to rest*; slump 37 *decrease*; be still, be hushed 266 *be quiescent*; discontinue, stop,

come to an end 145 *cease*; strike, come out, take industrial action.

sleep, slumber, snooze, nap, catnap; hibernate; sleep like a log, sleep like a top, sleep the sleep of the just; dream; snore, drive pigs to market; go to sleep, nod off, drop off, fall asleep, take a nap, have a kip, have forty winks; close one's eyes, feel sleepy, yawn, nod, doze, drowse; go to bed, turn in, doss down, kip d., shake d., hit the hay; settle down, bed d.

make inactive, put to sleep; send to sleep, lull, rock, cradle; soothe 177 *assuage*; deaden, paralyse, benumb, anaesthetize, dope, drug 375 *render insensible*; cramp, immobilize 747 *fetter*; lay up, put out of commission 674 *stop using*; dismantle 641 *make useless*; lay off 300 *dismiss*.

680 Haste – **N.** *haste,* hurry, scurry, hurry-scurry, hustle, bustle, hassle, flurry, whirl, scramble 678 *activity*; flap, flutter, fidget, fuss 318 *agitation*; rush, rush job 670 *nonpreparation*; feverish haste, tearing hurry, race against time, no time to lose 136 *lateness*; immediacy, urgency 638 *importance*; push, drive, expedition, dispatch 277 *velocity*; hastening, acceleration, forced march, dash 277 *spurt*; precipitateness, impetuosity 857 *rashness*; hastiness, impatience 822 *excitability*; the more haste the less speed.

Adj. *hasty,* impetuous, impulsive, hotheaded 857 *rash*; feverish, impatient; pushing, shoving, elbowing; boisterous, furious 176 *violent*; precipitate, headlong, breakneck 277 *speedy*; without delay; hastening, making speed; in haste, in all h., hotfoot, running, racing; in a hurry, unable to wait, pressed for time, hard-pressed, driven; done in haste, hurried, scamped, slapdash, cursory 458 *negligent*; rough and ready, forced, rushed, rush, last-minute 670 *unprepared*; rushed into, railroaded; stampeded; allowing no time, brooking no delay, urgent, immediate 638 *important*.

Vb. *hasten,* expedite; urge, drive, stampede, spur, goad, whip, lash, flog 612 *incite*; bundle off, hustle away; rush, allow no time, railroaded, brook no delay; be hasty, be precipitate, rush headlong 857 *be rash*; haste, make haste; race, run, dash off, tear off 277 *move fast*; make up for lost time, overtake 277 *outstrip*; spurt, dash, make a forced march 277 *accelerate*; hurry, scurry, hustle, bustle, fret, fume, fidget, rush to and fro, dart to and fro 678 *be active*; be in a hurry, have no time to spare, have no time to lose, act without ceremony, cut short the preliminaries, brush aside; cut corners, rush one's fences; rush through, dash through, make short work of; be pressed for time, work against time *or* to a deadline, work under pressure, think on one's feet; do at the last moment 136 *be late*; lose no time, lose not a moment, make every minute count; hasten away, cut and run, make oneself scarce, not be seen for dust 296 *decamp*.

Int. hurry up! be quick! buck up! look lively! look sharp! get a move on! step on it! quick march! at the double!

681 Leisure – N. *leisure,* spare time, free t.; idle moments; time on one's hands, time to kill; sinecure; idleness, breathing space, off duty, time off, day off, holiday, half-h., break, vacation, leave, sabbatical, furlough 679 *inactivity*; time to spare, no hurry, ample time, all the time in the world; rest, ease, relaxation 683 *repose*; redundancy, retirement 753 *resignation*.

Adj. *leisurely,* unhurried 278 *slow*; at one's convenience, in one's own time, at any odd moment; leisured, at leisure, unoccupied 683 *reposeful*; at a loose end; off duty, on holiday, on vacation, on leave, on furlough, on sabbatical; retired, in retirement, redundant; labour-saving.

682 Exertion – N. *exertion,* effort, struggle 671 *attempt*; strain, stress, might and main; tug, pull, stretch, heave, lift, throw; drive, force, pressure, applied energy 160 *energy*; ergonomics; ado, hassle, trouble, the hard way; muscle, elbow grease, sweat of one's brow; pains 678 *assiduity*; overwork 678 *overactivity*.

exercise, practice, drill, training, workout, the bar (ballet) 669 *preparation*; physical education, PE, keeping fit, jogging, jarming, cycling, constitutional, daily dozen; gymnastics 162 *athletics*; weight-lifting, body-building; yoga, isometrics, eurhythmics, callisthenics, aerobics; games, sports, races 837 *sport*.

labour, industry, work, hard w., long haul; spadework, donkeywork; legwork; manual labour, sweat of one's brow; housework, chores, daily grind, toil, drudgery, slavery, sweat, fag, grind, strain, treadmill, grindstone; hack work; bull; hard labour 963 *penalty*; forced labour, fatigue, spell of d. 917 *duty*; piecework, taskwork, homework, outwork; task, chore, job, operation, exercise 676 *deed*; shift, stint, stretch, bout, spell of work 110 *period*; job of work, stroke of w., hand's turn; working life, working week, working day, man-hours, woman-h.

Adj. *labouring,* horny-handed; working, drudging, etc. vb.; on the go, hard at it 678 *busy*; hardworking, laborious 678 *industrious*; slogging, plodding; strenuous, energetic 678 *active*; painstaking.

laborious, backbreaking; gruelling, punishing, unremitting, exhausting; weary, wearisome, painful, burdensome; heroic, Herculean; arduous, hard, heavy, uphill 700 *difficult*; hard-fought, hard-won; thorough, painstaking, laboured; effort-wasting 641 *useless*.

Vb. *exert oneself,* apply oneself, put one's best foot forward, make an effort, try 671 *attempt*; struggle, strain, strive, sweat blood; trouble oneself, put oneself out, bend over backwards; spare no effort, turn every stone, leave no stone unturned, do one's utmost, try one's best, use one's best endeavours, do all one can, go to any lengths, move heaven and earth; go all out, pull out all the stops, put one's heart and soul into it,

put one's back into it, strain every nerve 678 *be active*; force one's way, elbow one's way, drive through, wade t.; hammer at, slog at 600 *persevere*; take action 676 *do*.

work, labour, toil, drudge, grind, slog, sweat, work up a sweat, work up a lather; sweat blood; pull, haul, tug, shove, hump, heave, ply the oar; dig, lumber; get down to it, set to, roll up one's sleeves 68 *begin*; keep at it, plod 600 *persevere*; work hard, work overtime, moonlight, work all hours, be firing on all cylinders, burn the midnight oil 678 *be busy*; slave away, beaver away, work one's fingers to the bone, work like a galley slave, work like a horse, work like a Trojan; work oneself to death; overdo it; work for, serve 703 *minister to*; put to work, tax 684 *fatigue*.

683 Repose – N. *repose*, rest 679 *inactivity*; restfulness, ease, comfort 376 *euphoria*; peace and quiet, tranquillity 266 *quiescence*; happy dreams 679 *sleep*; relaxation, breathing space, breather 685 *refreshment*; pause, respite, let-up, recess, break 145 *lull*; interval; holiday, vacation, leave, furlough, day off, sabbatical, sabbatical year 681 *leisure*; day of rest, Sabbath, Lord's day.

Adj. *reposeful*, restful, relaxing; carefree, relaxed, laid-back, at ease 828 *content*; peaceful, quiet 266 *tranquil*; leisured, holiday 681 *leisurely*.

Vb. *repose*, rest, take a rest, take it easy, take one's ease, sit back, put one's feet up; recline, lie down, loll, lounge, laze, sprawl 216 *be horizontal*; perch, roost 311 *sit down*; go to bed, kip down, go to sleep 679 *sleep*; relax, unwind, unbend; take a breather 685 *be refreshed*; slack off, let up, slow down; rest on one's oars 266 *come to rest*; take time off *or* out.

684 Fatigue – N. *fatigue*, tiredness, weariness, lassitude, languor, lethargy; exhaustion, collapse, prostration; strain 682 *exertion*.

Adj. *fatigued*, tired, ready for bed 679 *sleepy*; asleep on one's feet, tired out, exhausted, spent; done, done up, done in, pooped, fagged out, knocked up, washed out, worn to a frazzle; stressed, strained, overworked, overtired, burned out; dog-tired, bone-weary, tired to death, ready to drop, on one's last legs, all in, dead beat, whacked, knackered, flaked out, flat o.; more dead than alive, prostrate; stiff, aching, sore, footsore, walked off one's feet; heavy-eyed, hollow-e.; tired-looking, haggard, worn; drooping, flagging.

Vb. *be fatigued*, - fagged etc. adj.; tire oneself out, overdo it, overtax one's strength; get weary, ache in every muscle *or* limb, gasp, pant, puff, blow, grunt 352 *breathe*; languish, droop, drop, sink, flag, fail 163 *be weak*; stagger, faint, swoon, feel giddy; yawn, nod, drowse 679 *sleep*; succumb, drop, collapse, flake out, crack up, pack up; be at the end of one's tether; can go no further; overwork, need a rest, need a break; be burned out.

fatigue, tire, tire out, wear, wear out, exhaust, do up, fag, whack, knock up, prostrate; wind; tax, strain, stress, overwork, overtax, overtask, overburden, overstrain, burn out; enervate, drain, take it out of; tire to death, weary 838 *be tedious*.

685 Refreshment – N. *refreshment*, breather, breath of air 683 *repose*; break, recess 145 *lull*; recreation, recuperation 656 *restoration*; revival; easing 831 *relief*; refresher, reviver, stimulant, refreshments.

Adj. *refreshing*, thirst-quenching; comforting; bracing, reviving.

Vb. *refresh*, freshen, freshen up 648 *clean*; air, fan, ventilate 340 *aerate*; cool, cool off, cool one down 382 *refrigerate*; brace, stimulate 174 *invigorate*; revive; offer food 301 *feed*.

be refreshed, draw breath, get one's breath back, regain *or* recover one's breath; clear one's head; come to, perk up, get one's second wind, feel like a new

man *or* woman; revive 656 *be restored*; mop one's brow, stretch one's legs, refresh oneself, take a breather, sleep it off.

686 Agent – N. *agent,* operator, actor, performer, player, executant, practitioner; perpetrator 676 *doer*; minister, tool 628 *instrument*; functionary 741 *officer*; representative 754 *delegate*; spokesman 755 *deputy*; proxy 150 *substitute*; executor, executrix, executive, administrator, dealer; middleman 794 *merchant.*

worker, voluntary w. 597 *volunteer*; social worker 901 *philanthropist*; freelance, self-employed person; organization man 83 *conformist*; trade unionist 775 *participator*; toiler, drudge, dogsbody, fag, hack; flunkey, menial, factotum, maid-of-all-work, domestic servant 742 *servant*; hewer of wood and drawer of water, beast of burden 742 *slave*; professional person, business man, business woman, career w., executive, breadwinner, salary e., wage earner, wage slave, employee; boffin; clerical worker, desk w., white-collar w., black-coat w.; office w., girl Friday, man Friday; shop assistant 793 *seller*; charwoman, dustman 648 *cleaner*; labourer, casual l., agricultural l., farm worker 370 *farmer*; pieceworker, manual w., blue-collar w.; working man *or* woman, working girl, workman, hand, operative, factory worker, factory hand; navvy, roadman; ganger, plate-layer; docker, stevedore, packer; porter.

artisan, tradesman; skilled worker, semi-skilled w., master 696 *proficient person*; journeyman, apprentice 538 *learner*; craftsman *or* -woman, potter, turner, joiner, cabinet-maker, carpenter, carver, woodworker, cooper; wheelwright; coach-builder; shipwright, boatbuilder; builder, architect, master mason, mason, housebuilder, bricklayer, plasterer, tiler, thatcher, painter, decorator; forger, metalworker, smith, blacksmith, tinsmith, goldsmith, silversmith, gunsmith, locksmith; tinker, knifegrinder; collier, miner, face-worker, steelworker, foundryman; mechanic, machinist, fitter; engineer, civil e., mining e., computer e., television e.; plumber, welder, electrician, gas-fitter; weaver, spinner, tailor, needlewoman 228 *clothier*; watchmaker, clockmaker; jeweller; glass-blower.

personnel, staff, force, company, team, gang, squad, crew; dramatis personae 594 *actor*; workpeople, hands, men, payroll; labour; workforce, labour force, manpower.

687 Workshop – N. *workshop,* studio; workroom, study, den, library; laboratory; works, factory; workshop, yard; mill, loom; sawmill, paper mill; foundry, metalworks; steelyard, steelworks, smelter; blast furnace, forge, smithy 383 *furnace*; power station, gasworks 160 *energy*; quarry, mine 632 *store*; colliery, coalmine, pit, coalface; tin mine; mint; arsenal, armoury; dockyard, shipyard, slips; wharf, dock 192 *stable*; construction site, building s.; refinery, distillery, brewery, shop, shopfloor, bench, production line; nursery 370 *farm*; dairy, creamery 369 *stock farm*; kitchen, laundry; office, bureau.

688 Conduct – N. *conduct,* behaviour, deportment; bearing, comportment, carriage; demeanour, attitude, posture 445 *mien*; aspect, look 445 *appearance*; tone of voice, delivery 577 *voice*; motion, action, gesticulation 547 *gesture*; mode of behaviour, fashion, style; manner, guise, air; poise, savoir faire, dignity, presence; breeding, graciousness, good manners 884 *courtesy*; ungraciousness, boorishness, rudeness, bad manners 885 *discourtesy*; pose, role-playing 850 *affectation*; outlook 485 *opinion*; mood 818 *feeling*; good behaviour 933 *virtue*; misbehaviour, misconduct 934 *wickedness*; past behaviour, track record, history; reward of conduct, deserts 915 *dueness*; way of life, ethos, morals, principles, ideals, customs, mores, manners, lifestyle 610 *habit*; line of action 623 *policy*; career, course, race, walk, walk of life

622 *vocation*; observance, routine 610 *practice*; procedure, process, method, modus operandi 624 *way*; organization, orchestration, treatment, handling, manipulation, direction, masterminding 689 *management*; gentle handling, kid gloves, velvet glove 736 *leniency*; rough handling, putting the boot in, jackboot, iron hand 735 *severity*; dealings, transactions 154 *affairs*; deeds 676 *deed*; behaviourism.

tactics, strategy, campaign, plan of c., logistics; programme 623 *plan*; line, party l. 623 *policy*; politics, diplomacy, statesmanship 733 *governance*; lifemanship, gamesmanship, one-upmanship 698 *cunning*; brinkmanship, generalship, seamanship 694 *skill*; jockeying for position; tactical advantage, vantage ground 34 *advantage*; playing for time 136 *delay*; manoeuvre; move, gambit 676 *deed*; stratagem.

Vb. *behave*, act 676 *do*; behave well, mind one's p's and q's, play the game 933 *be virtuous*; behave badly, break all the rules, misbehave, try it on 934 *be wicked*; keep out of mischief, be on one's best behaviour, keep a low profile; gesture 547 *gesticulate*; posture, pose, affect 850 *be affected*; conduct oneself, behave o., acquit o., comport o.; set an example; conduct one's affairs 622 *busy oneself*; follow a course, steer a c. 281 *steer for*; paddle one's own canoe, be master of one's own ship, shift for oneself 744 *be free*; employ tactics; behave towards, treat.

deal with, have on one's plate, have to do with 676 *do*; handle, manipulate 173 *operate*; carry on, conduct, run 689 *manage*; see to, cope with, do the needful; transact, enact, execute, dispatch, carry through, put into practice 725 *carry out*; work out 623 *plan*; work at, work through, wade t. 682 *work*; go through, read 536 *study*.

689 Management – N. *management*, conduct of affairs, running, handling; managership, agency 751 *commission*;

care, charge, control 733 *authority*; superintendence, oversight 457 *surveillance*; art of management, tact 694 *skill*; business management, work study, management s., time and motion s.; organization, masterminding, decision-making 623 *policy*; housekeeping, husbandry, economics, political economy; statesmanship; government 733 *governance*; ménage, regime; regulation, lawmaking 953 *legislation*; reins of government, ministry, cabinet; administration; bureaucracy.

directorship, direction, responsibility, control 737 *command*; dictatorship, leadership, premiership, chairmanship, captaincy 34 *superiority*; guidance.

Vb. *manage*, organize; influence; handle, conduct, run, carry on; administer; supervise, superintend, oversee, caretake 457 *invigilate*; have charge of; hold the purse strings, hold the reins 612 *motivate*; *keep order, police; legislate; control, govern, rule*.

direct, lead; boss, dictate 737 *command*; be in charge, head up, wear the trousers; hold office; mastermind, have overall responsibility; assume command; preside, take the chair, be in the chair; head, captain, skipper; steer, take the helm, show the way 547 *indicate*; guide, conduct, compère; channel.

690 Director – N. *director*, governing body 741 *governor*; steering committee, quango, select committee; cabinet, inner c. 692 *council*; board of directors, board, chair; staff, top brass, VIPs, management; manager, controller; legislator; employer, boss 741 *master*; headman, chief, head of state 34 *superior*; principal, head, headmaster *or* -mistress, rector, moderator, dean, vice-chancellor, chancellor; president; chairperson, chairman, chairwoman, speaker; premier, prime minister; captain, skipper; master 270 *mariner*; pilot 520 *guide*; director of studies 537 *teacher*.

leader, judge (Old Testament) 741 *governor*; messiah; ayatollah, guru; leader of the House, leader of the opposition;

spearhead, centre forward; shepherd, drover 369 *herdsman*; bell-wether; pacemaker; pacesetter, master of ceremonies, MC; high priest; chorus-leader; conductor, leader of the orchestra, first violin; drum major; Führer, Duce 741 *autocrat*; ringleader; captain.

manager, man *or* woman in charge, key person, kingpin 638 *bigwig*; administrator, executive, executor 676 *doer*; statesman *or* -woman, politician; housekeeper, chatelaine, housewife, house husband; steward, bailiff, farm manager, agent, factor 754 *consignee*; superintendent, supervisor, inspector, overseer, foreman *or* -woman, ganger, gaffer; warden, matron, senior nursing officer; party manager, whip, chief whip; custodian, caretaker, curator 749 *keeper*; master of hounds; ringmaster; compère.

official, office-bearer; steward; shop steward; MP, Member of Parliament, public servant, civil s., apparatchik; minister, cabinet m., secretary of state, secretary-general; permanent secretary, bureaucrat, Eurocrat, Euro-MP; magistrate 733 *position of authority*; commissioner, prefect; consul, praetor; first secretary; alderman, mayor 692 *councillor*; party official.

691 Advice – N. *advice,* word of a., piece of a., counsel; words of wisdom. counselling 658 *therapy*; criticism 480 *estimate*; didacticism, prescription 693 *precept*; caution 664 *warning*; recommendation, proposition, proposal, motion 512 *supposition*; suggestion; tip, word to the wise 524 *hint*; guidance, briefing, instruction 524 *information*; taking counsel, consultation, huddle, heads together, tête-à-tête, powwow, parley 584 *conference*.

adviser, counsellor, consultant, troubleshooter; referee, arbiter, arbitrator 480 *estimator*; advocate, prompter 612 *motivator*; medical adviser, therapist 658 *doctor*; legal adviser, advocate, counsel 958 *lawyer*; guide, mentor, confidant(e) 537 *teacher*; Dutch uncle; oracle, wise man 500 *sage*; backseat driver;

public enquiry, consultative body 692 *council*.

Vb. *advise,* give advice, counsel; recommend, prescribe, advocate, commend; propose, move, submit, suggest 512 *propound*; prompt 524 *hint*; urge, exhort 612 *incite*; advise against 613 *dissuade*; admonish 664 *warn*.

consult, seek advice, refer; call in, call on; refer to arbitration, ask for a second opinion, hold a public enquiry; confide in, be closeted with; take advice; take one's cue from, follow advice; sit in conclave, put heads together, hold a council of war, have a powwow with, parley, sit round a table.

692 Council – N. *council,* round table; council chamber, board room; court 956 *tribunal*; Privy Council; ecclesiastical council, Bench of Bishops; vestry; cabinet; panel, quango, think tank, board, advisory b., consultative body, Royal Commission; assembly, conventicle, congregation 74 *assembly*; conclave, convocation 985 *synod*; convention, congress, meeting, top-level m., summit; League of Nations, UNO, Security Council; municipal council, county c., regional c., district c., town c., parish c.; community c; soviet; council of elders; sitting, session, séance.

parliament, European P., Mother of Parliaments, Westminster, Upper House, House of Lords, Lower House, House of Commons; senate, senatus; legislative assembly; Reichsrat, Reichstag; States-General, National Assembly, Chambre des Députés, Bundesrat, Bundestag; Supreme Soviet; Congress, Senate; House of Representatives; quorum.

councillor, privy councillor; senator, peer; Lords Spiritual, L. Temporal; representative, deputy, congressman *or* -woman, member of Parliament, MP, Euro-MP 754 *delegate*; backbencher, parliamentarian; mayor, alderman 690 *official*.

693 Precept – N. *precept,* firm advice 691 *advice;* direction, instruction, injunction, charge 737 *command;* commission 751 *mandate;* order, writ 737 *warrant;* prescription, ordinance, regulation 737 *decree;* canon, form, formula, formulary; guidelines 81 *rule;* principle, rule, golden r., moral 496 *maxim;* recipe, receipt 658 *remedy;* commandment, statute, enactment, act, code, penal c. 953 *legislation;* tenet, article, set of rules, constitution; ticket, party line; Ten Commandments, Twelve Tables; canon law, common l., unwritten l. 953 *law;* habit and repute, convention 610 *practice.*

694 Skill – N. *skill,* skilfulness, dexterity, handiness, ambidexterity; style 575 *elegance;* deftness, adroitness; ease 701 *facility;* proficiency, competence; faculty, capability, capacity 160 *ability;* versatility; adaptability, flexibility; mastery, wizardry, virtuosity, excellence, prowess 644 *goodness;* strong point, métier, forte; attainment, accomplishment, skills; seamanship, airmanship, horsemanship, marksmanship; experience, expertise, professionalism; specialism; know-how, technique 490 *knowledge;* deft fingers; craftsmanship, art, artistry; finish, execution 646 *perfection;* ingenuity, resourcefulness, craft, craftiness 698 *cunning;* cleverness, sharpness, worldly wisdom; savoir faire, finesse 463 *discrimination;* feat of skill, trick, dodge 623 *contrivance;* sleight of hand.

aptitude, innate ability, good head for; bent, natural b. 179 *tendency;* faculty, endowment, gift, flair; knack, green fingers; talent, natural t., genius, genius for; aptness, fitness.

masterpiece, chef-d'oeuvre, a beauty, a creation; pièce de résistance, masterwork, magnum opus; stroke of genius, masterstroke, coup, feat, exploit, hat trick 676 *deed;* smash hit; tour de force; ace, trump 644 *exceller;* work of art, objet d'art, collector's piece *or* item.

Adj. *skilful,* good, good at, top-flight, top-notch, first-rate, ace 644 *excellent;* skilled, crack; handy, dexterous, ambidextrous, deft, slick, adroit, agile, nimble; nimble-fingered, green-f.; surefooted; cunning, clever, quick, quickwitted, shrewd, smart, ingenious 498 *intelligent;* politic, diplomatic, statesmanlike 498 *wise;* flexible, resourceful; versatile; sound, able, competent; wizard, masterly, accomplished.

gifted, of many parts, talented, endowed, well-e.

expert, experienced, veteran, seasoned, tried, versed in, up in, well up in, au fait; skilled, trained, practised, well-p. 669 *prepared;* finished, specialized 669 *matured;* proficient, qualified, competent, up to the mark; professional.

Vb. *be skilful,* - deft etc. adj.; be good at, do well 644 *be good;* shine, excel 34 *be superior;* have a gift for, show aptitude, show a talent for; have the knack; be on form, be in good f., have one's eye *or* hand in, play one's cards well, not put a foot wrong, know what one is about; live by one's wits, know all the answers, know what's what, have one's wits about one 498 *be wise.*

be expert, be at the top of one's profession, be good at one's job, be a topnotcher, know one's stuff *or* one's onions, have the know-how; have experience, be an old hand, know the ropes, know all the ins and outs, know backwards; display one's skill.

Adv. *skilfully,* craftily, artfully etc. adj.; well, with skill, with aplomb; knowledgeably, expertly; faultlessly, as to the manner born.

695 Unskilfulness – N. *unskilfulness,* lack of practice, rustiness 674 *nonuse;* inexperience, inexpertness 491 *ignorance;* inability, incompetence, inefficiency; lack of proficiency; clumsiness, awkwardness, gaucherie (see *bungling*); backwardness, slowness 499 *unintelligence;* booby prize, wooden spoon.

bungling, botching, half-measures, pale imitation, travesty 726 *noncompletion;* bungle, botch, dog's breakfast, pig's ear, cock-up, balls-up, shambles; off day,

poor show, bad job, flop 728 *failure*; hamhandedness, dropped catch, butterfingers, fumble, muff, fluff, miss, mishit, slice, misfire, own goal 495 *mistake*; tactlessness, heavy-handedness; indiscretion 464 *indiscrimination*; mishandling, misapplication 675 *misuse*; too many cooks; mismanagement, misrule, misgovernment, maladministration 481 *misjudgment*; wild-goose chase 641 *lost labour*.

Adj. unskilful, talentless, unendowed, unaccomplished; unversatile 679 *inactive*; unfit, inept 25 *unapt*; unable, incapable 161 *impotent*; incompetent, inefficient, ineffectual; unpractical, unbusinesslike, stupid, foolish 499 *unwise*; feckless; not up to scratch, failed 728 *unsuccessful*; inadequate 636 *insufficient*.

unskilled, raw, green, undeveloped 670 *immature*; uninitiated, under training, untrained, apprentice, half-skilled, semi-s. 670 *unprepared*; unqualified, inexpert, inexperienced, ignorant, unversed 491 *uninstructed*; nonprofessional, ham, amateurish, amateur, self-taught; unsound, quack.

clumsy, awkward, uneasy, gauche, gawky, boorish, uncouth 885 *discourteous*; stuttering; tactless, indiscreet 464 *indiscriminating*; bumbling, bungling; maladroit, all thumbs, butter-fingered; cack-h., heavy-h., ham-h., heavy-footed; ungainly, lumbering, hulking, gangling, shambling; out of practice, out of training 611 *unhabituated*; slovenly, slatternly, slapdash 458 *negligent*; fumbling, groping, tentative 461 *experimental*; graceless 576 *inelegant*; top-heavy, lopsided 29 *unequal*; cumbersome, ungainly.

bungled, botched, messed up, fouled up, screwed up, mismanaged, mishandled etc. vb.; ill-considered; ill-prepared 670 *unprepared*; ill-contrived, ill-devised, cobbled together; crude, rough and ready, inartistic, amateurish, jerrybuilt, slapdash, perfunctory 458 *neglected*; half-baked 726 *uncompleted*.

Vb. *be unskilful,* - inept, unqualified etc. adj.; not know how 491 *not know*; show one's ignorance, be handless, be clueless, go the wrong way about it; paper over the cracks 726 *not complete*; burn one's fingers, catch a Tartar 508 *not expect*; mismanage, misgovern; misapply 675 *misuse*; misdirect 495 *blunder*; forget one's words, fluff one's lines, miss one's cue 506 *forget*; ham; go rusty, get out of practice 611 *disaccustom*.

act foolishly, not know what one is about, cut one's own throat, cut off one's nose to spite one's face, throw out the baby with the bath water, make a fool of oneself, make an ass of oneself, lose face, be left with egg all over one's face 497 *be absurd*; bite the hand that feeds one, kill the goose that lays the golden eggs; spoil the ship for a ha'porth of tar; bring one's house about one's ears, knock one's head against a brick wall, put the cart before the horse; have too many eggs in one basket; bite off more than one can chew, have too many irons in the fire; put a square peg in a round hole, put new wine into old bottles 495 *blunder*; labour in vain 470 *attempt the impossible*; go on a fool's errand 641 *waste effort*; strain at a gnat and swallow a camel.

be clumsy, lumber, bumble, galumph, hulk, get in the way, be de trop, stand in the light; trip, trip over, stumble, blunder, boob; not look where one is going 456 *be inattentive*; stutter 580 *stammer*; fumble, grope, flounder 461 *be tentative*; muff, fluff; slice, mishit, misthrow, misfire; spill, slop, drop, drop a catch, drop a sitter 311 *let fall*; catch a crab; let the cat out of the bag, bungle, drop a brick, put one's foot in it, make a faux pas, get egg on one's face 495 *blunder*; botch, spoil, mar, blot 655 *impair*; fool with 678 *meddle*; make a mess of it, make a hash of it 728 *miscarry*; do a bad job, make a poor fist at 728 *fail*.

696 Proficient person – N. *proficient person,* sound player, expert, adept, dab hand, dabster; do-it-yourself type, allrounder, Jack of all trades, handyman,

admirable Crichton 646 *paragon*; Renaissance man, person of many parts; maître, master, past m., graduate, cordon bleu; intellectual, mastermind 500 *sage*; genius, wizard, gifted child 864 *prodigy*; magician; maestro, virtuoso; bravura player 413 *musician*; prima donna, first fiddle, top sawyer, prizewinner, gold-medallist, champion, titleholder, cup-h., dan, black belt, ace 644 *exceller*; picked man, capped player, star p., seeded p., white hope; crack shot; acrobat, gymnast 162 *athlete*.

expert, professional, pro, specialist, authority, doyen, professor 537 *teacher*; pundit, guru, walking encyclopaedia 492 *scholar*; veteran, old hand, old stager, old dog, old soldier, warhorse, sea dog; practised hand, practised eye; man *or* woman of the world, businessman *or -* woman, career woman, careerist; tactician, strategist, politician; diplomat, diplomatist; artist, craftsman *or* -woman; technician, skilled worker 686 *artisan*; experienced hand, right person for the job, key man *or* -woman; consultant 691 *adviser*; boffin 623 *planner*; cognoscente, connoisseur.

697 Bungler – N. *bungler*, failure 728 *loser*; one's despair; incompetent, botcher; bumbler, blunderer; fumbler, muffer, butterfingers; clumsy l.; hulk, bull in a china shop; duffer, buffoon, booby, galoot, clot, clod, hick, oaf, ass 501 *fool*; slob, sloven, slattern 61 *slut*; hack, dauber; poor shot; amateur, ham; jack of all trades and master of none; novice, greenhorn, raw recruit 538 *beginner*; landlubber; fish out of water, square peg in a round hole 25 *misfit*.

698 Cunning – N. *cunning*, craft 694 *skill*; know-how; resourcefulness, inventiveness, ingenuity 513 *imagination*; guile, gamesmanship, cunningness, craftiness, artfulness, subtlety, wiliness, slyness; stealthiness, stealth 523 *latency*; cageyness 525 *concealment*; slipperiness; sleight of hand, cheating, monkey business 542 *deception*; double-dealing,

imposture 541 *duplicity*; wheeling and dealing, manoeuvring 688 *tactics*; diplomacy, Machiavellism, realpolitik; gerrymandering 930 *improbity*; underhand dealing, under-the-counter dealing, sharp practice.

stratagem, ruse, wile, artifice, device, ploy, dodge 623 *contrivance*; machination, game, little g. 623 *plot*; subterfuge, evasion; excuse 614 *pretext*; white lie; cheat 542 *deception*; trick, old t., box of tricks, tricks of the trade, rules of the game 542 *trickery*; feint; ambush, Greek gift, Trojan horse, stalking h. 542 *trap*; ditch, pit 663 *pitfall*; Parthian shot; web of cunning, web of deceit; blind, dust thrown in the eyes, red herring; thin end of the wedge, manoeuvre, move 688 *tactics*.

slyboots, artful dodger, wily person, serpent, snake, fox; fraud, wolf in sheep's clothing, double-crosser 545 *deceiver*; cheat, sharper 545 *trickster*; juggler; smoothie 925 *flatterer*; Machiavelli, intriguer, plotter, schemer 623 *planner*; strategist, tactician, manoeuvrer, wheeler-dealer.

Adj. *cunning*, crafty, disingenuous, artful, sly, wily, subtle; tricksy; scheming, plotting, intriguing, Machiavellian; knowing, fly, slick, smart, sophisticated, urbane; canny, pawky, sharp, astute, shrewd, acute; too clever for, too clever by half, too smart for his *or* her own good, up to everything, not to be caught napping, no flies on, not born yesterday 498 *intelligent*; not to be drawn, cagey 525 *reticent*; experienced 694 *skilful*; resourceful, ingenious; tactical; insidious 930 *perfidious*; shifty, slippery 518 *equivocal*; deceitful, crooked, devious 930 *dishonest*.

Vb. *be cunning*, - sly etc. adj.; dodge, juggle, manoeuvre, jockey, double-cross; intrigue, scheme, weave a plot, have an ulterior motive, have an axe to grind, have an eye to the main chance 623 *plot*; contrive, wangle, devise 623 *plan*; monkey about with, gerrymander; pull a fast one, steal a march on, trick, cheat 542 *deceive*; sweet-talk 925 *flatter*; play for

time; be too clever for, be one up on, outsmart, outwit, go one better, know a trick worth two of that 306 *outdo*; be too quick for, snatch from under one's nose, pip at the post; waylay, dig a pit for, undermine, bait the trap 527 *ambush*; get one's foot in the door; have a card up one's sleeve, have a shot in one's locker; know all the answers, live by one's wits.

699 Artlessness – N. *artlessness,* simplicity, simple-mindedness; naivety, ingenuousness, guilelessness 935 *innocence*; inexperience, unworldliness; unaffectedness, unsophistication, naturalness 573 *plainness*; sincerity, candour, frankness; truth, honesty 929 *probity*.

Adj. *artless,* without artifice; unstudied; uncomplicated, uncontrived 44 *simple*; unadorned, unvarnished 573 *plain*; native, natural, unartificial, homespun, homemade; do-it-yourself 695 *unskilled*; in a state of nature, primitive; unsophisticated, ingenuous, naive, childlike 935 *innocent*; green, unworldly, simpleminded, callow, wet behind the ears; guileless, unsuspicious, confiding; unaffected 609 *spontaneous*; candid, frank, open, undissembling, straightforward 540 *veracious*; true, honest, sincere 929 *honourable*; above-board, on the level; transparent; shy, unassuming, unpretentious 874 *modest*.

Vb. *be artless,* - natural etc. adj.; have no guile 935 *be innocent*; have no affectations; wear one's heart upon one's sleeve; look one in the face, look one straight in the eyes, call a spade a spade, say what is in one's mind, speak one's mind 573 *speak plainly*; not mince one's words 540 *be truthful*.

Section four: Antagonism

700 Difficulty – N. *difficulty,* hardness, arduousness, laboriousness 682 *exertion*; impracticability, no go, nonstarter 470 *impossibility*; intricacy, perplexity, inextricability, involvement 61 *complexity*; complication 832 *aggravation*; obscurity, impenetrability 517 *unintelligibility*; inconvenience, awkwardness 643 *inexpedience*; difficult terrain, rough ground, hard going, bad patch 259 *roughness*; quagmire, slough 347 *marsh*; knot, Gordian k. 251 *coil*; problem, thorny p., crux, hard nut to crack, poser, teaser, puzzle, the sixty-four- thousand-dollar question, headache 530 *enigma*; impediment, handicap, obstacle, snag, rub, where the shoe pinches 702 *hindrance*; teething troubles 702 *hitch*; maze, crooked path 251 *convolution*; cul-de-sac, dead end, impasse, no-go area, blank wall 264 *closure*; deadlock, standstill, logjam, stoppage 145 *stop*; stress, brunt, burden 684 *fatigue*; trial, ordeal, temptation, tribulation, vexation 825 *suffering*; trouble, sea of troubles 731 *adversity*; difficult person, handful, one's despair, hot potato.

hard task, test, trial of strength; Herculean task, superhuman t., thankless t., never-ending t., Sisyphean labour; work cut out, hard row to hoe, hard furrow to plough, no picnic; handful, tall order, tough assignment, impossible task, hard work, uphill struggle 682 *labour*.

predicament, embarrassment, delicate situation; quandary, dilemma, cleft stick; catch-22 situation; fix, jam, hole, scrape, hot water, trouble, fine kettle of fish, pickle, stew, soup, imbroglio, mess, muddle; straits, pretty pass; slippery slope, sticky wicket, tight corner, painting oneself into a corner, diplomatic incident, ticklish situation, tricky s., hot seat 661 *danger*; emergency 137 *crisis*.

Adj. *difficult,* hard, tough, formidable; steep, arduous, uphill; inconvenient, onerous, burdensome, irksome 682 *laborious*; exacting, demanding; insuperable, impracticable 470 *impossible*; problematic; delicate, ticklish, tricky; unwieldy, unmanageable; intractable, refractory 738 *disobedient*; recalcitrant, stubborn, unyielding, perverse 602 *obstinate*; ill-behaved, naughty 934 *wicked*; perplexing, obscure 517 *unintelligible*; knotty, complex, complicated, inextricable, labyrinthine 251 *intricate*; impenetrable,

impassable, unnavigable; thorny, rugged, craggy 259 *rough*; sticky, critical 661 *dangerous*.

in difficulties, hampered 702 *hindered*; labouring under difficulties; in a quandary, in a dilemma, in a cleft stick, between two stools, between Scylla and Charybdis, between the devil and the deep blue sea 474 *doubting*; baffled, clueless, nonplussed 517 *puzzled*; in a jam, in a fix, on the hook, up a gum tree, up the creek, in a spot, in a hole, in a scrape, in hot water, in the soup, in a pickle; in deep water, out of one's depth, under fire, not out of the wood, in danger, on the danger list, on a hit list, in the hot seat 661 *endangered*; worried, beset with difficulties 825 *suffering*; under pressure, up against it, in a catch-22 situation, hard pressed, sore p., hard put to it, driven to extremities; in dire straits, in distressed circumstances; left holding the baby, left in the lurch; at one's wits end, at the end of one's tether, cornered, at bay, with one's back against the wall; stuck, stuck fast, aground.

Vb. *be difficult,* - hard etc. adj.; complicate matters 63 *bedevil*; put one on the spot, inconvenience, bother, irk, try one's patience, lead one a merry dance, be a thorn in one's flesh, be one's bête noire, go against the grain 827 *trouble*; present difficulties, set one a problem, pose, perplex, baffle, nonplus, stump 474 *puzzle*; hamper, obstruct 702 *hinder*; make things worse 832 *aggravate*; lead to an impasse, create deadlock 470 *make impossible*.

be in difficulty, have a problem; tread on eggs 461 *be tentative*; have one's hands full 678 *be busy*; not know which way to turn, be at a loss 474 *be uncertain*; have difficulties, have one's work cut out, be hard put to it, have trouble with; run into trouble, strike a bad patch; be asking for trouble, fish in troubled waters; let oneself in for, cop it, catch it, catch a packet, catch a Tartar, have a tiger by the tail, stir up a hornet's nest; have a hard time of it 731 *have trouble*; bear the brunt, feel the pinch 825 *suffer*;

sink under the burden 684 *be fatigued*; bring it on oneself, make heavy weather of, flounder; come unstuck 728 *miscarry*; do it the hard way, swim upstream, fight 716 *contend*; live dangerously 661 *face danger*; labour under difficulties, be disadvantaged, labour under a disadvantage, have one hand tied behind one's back, be handicapped by.

Adv. *with difficulty,* with much ado; the hard way, uphill, against the stream, against the wind, against the grain; in the teeth of; at a pinch.

701 Facility – **N.** *facility,* easiness, ease, convenience, comfort; flexibility, pliancy 327 *softness*; capability, capacity, feasibility 469 *possibility*; comprehensibility 516 *intelligibility*; facilitation, easing, making easy, simplification, smoothing disentanglement 746 *liberation*; free hand, full scope, blank cheque, clean slate 744 *scope*; facilities, provision for 703 *aid*; leave 756 *permission*; simplicity, no complication 44 *simpleness*; straightforwardness, no difficulty, no competition; an open-and-shut case; no friction, easy going, calm seas 258 *smoothness*; fair wind, clear coast, clear road 137 *opportunity*; straight road.

easy thing, no trouble, no sweat, a pleasure, child's play, kid's stuff; soft option, short work, light work, cushy number, sinecure 679 *inactivity*; picnic, doddle 837 *amusement*; chickenfeed, peanuts, piece of cake, money for jam *or* old rope; easy money, fast buck; smooth sailing, plain s., easy ride; nothing to it, easy target, sitting duck; easy meat, soft touch; pushover, walkover 727 *victory*; cinch, sure thing, dead cert 473 *certainty*.

Adj. *easy,* facile, undemanding, cushy; effortless, painless; light; uncomplicated 44 *simple*; not hard, not difficult, easy as pie, easily done, no sooner said than done; as easy as falling off a log, as simple as ABC; feasible 469 *possible*; facilitating 703 *aiding*; downhill, with the current, with the tide, with the

crowd; convenient 376 *comfortable*; approachable, within reach, within easy reach 289 *accessible*; open to all 263 *open*; comprehensible 516 *intelligible*.

tractable, manageable 597 *willing*; submissive 721 *submitting*; yielding, malleable, pliant 327 *flexible*; manoeuvrable.

Vb. *be easy,* - simple etc. adj.; be trouble-free, require no effort, present no difficulties, give no trouble, make no demands; be one's for the asking; be easily solved, have a simple answer 516 *be intelligible*; go like clockwork.

do easily, have no trouble; make light of, make no bones about, make short work of, do it standing on one's head, do it with one hand tied behind one's back; have it all one's own way, carry all before one, have it in the bag, hold all the trumps, win hands down, have a walkover 727 *win*; sail home, coast h., freewheel; be at ease, be at home, be in one's element, take in one's stride, take to like a duck to water; not strain oneself, drift with the tide, swim with the stream 721 *submit*; take the easy way out, take the line of least resistance.

facilitate, ease, make easy; iron out 258 *smooth*; oil 334 *lubricate*; explain, gloss, simplify 520 *interpret*; enable; make way for, allow 756 *permit*; put one in the way of 469 *make possible*; help, speed, accelerate, expedite 703 *aid*; clear the way, blaze a trail 64 *come before*; pave the way, bridge the gap; make an opening for 744 *give scope*.

disencumber, free, set free, liberate, unshackle, unfetter 668 *deliver*; clear, clear the ground, weed, clear away, unclog 648 *clean*; derestrict, cut through red tape; disentangle, extricate; untie 46 *disunite*; cut the knot, cut the Gordian k. 46 *cut*; ease, lighten, unload, unhamper, unburden, ease the burden, alleviate, obviate 831 *relieve*.

Adv. *easily,* smoothly, like clockwork; swimmingly; effortlessly, with one's eyes closed, with one hand tied behind one's back, just like that; without a hitch.

702 Hindrance – N. *hindrance,* let or h., impediment; inhibition, block; stalling, thwarting, obstruction, frustration; hampering, shackling, clogging etc. vb.; blockage, logjam, blocking 264 *closure*; blockade, siege 712 *attack*; limitation, restriction, control, squeeze 747 *restraint*; arrest 747 *detention*; check, retardation, deceleration 278 *slowness*; drag 333 *friction*; interference, meddling 678 *overactivity*; interruption, interception, intervention 231 *interjacency*; obtrusion 303 *insertion*; objection 762 *deprecation*; obstructiveness, picketing, secondary p., sabotage 704 *opposition*; lockout 182 *counteraction*; defence 715 *resistance*; discouragement, disincentive 613 *dissuasion*; hostility 924 *disapprobation*; blacking, boycott 620 *avoidance*; forestalling, prevention; prophylaxis 652 *hygiene*; sterilization, birth control 172 *contraception*; ban, embargo, no-no 757 *prohibition*; nuisance value.

obstacle, impediment, hindrance, nuisance, drawback, inconvenience, handicap 700 *difficulty*; hazard; bottleneck, blockage, road block, contraflow, traffic jam, logjam; a hindrance, wheel clamp, tie, tether 47 *bond*; previous engagement 138 *untimeliness*; red tape, regulations; snag, block; stumbling block, tripwire, hurdle, hedge, ditch, moat; water-jump; something in the way, barrier, bulkhead, wall, brick w., stone w., sea w., dam, weir, dike, embankment 662 *safeguard*; bulwark, buffer, parapet, portcullis, barbed wire 713 *defences*; fence, blockade 235 *enclosure*; curtain, iron c., bamboo c. 231 *partition*; stile, gate, turnstile, tollgate; crosswind, headwind, crosscurrent; impasse, deadlock, stalemate, vicious circle, catch-22; cul-de-sac, blind alley, dead end, blank wall.

hitch, unexpected obstacle, snag, catch; contretemps; teething troubles; technical hitch, breakdown, engine failure; puncture, flat; leak, burst pipe; fuse, short circuit; stoppage, holdup, setback 145 *stop*; something wrong, computer malfunction, screw loose, spanner in the works, fly in the ointment.

encumbrance, handicap; drag, shackle, chain 748 *fetter*; trammels; impedimenta, cross, millstone, albatross round one's neck, weight on one's shoulders, dead weight 322 *gravity*; burden, overload, last straw; onus, Old Man of the Sea; family commitments; mortgage, debts 803 *debt*.

Adj. *hindered*, waterlogged, handicapped, disadvantaged, encumbered, burdened with, lumbered w., saddled w., stuck w.; frustrated, thwarted, stymied etc. vb.; up against a brick wall; held up, delayed, stuck, becalmed, fogbound, snowbound, snowed-up 747 *restrained*; stopped, prevented 757 *prohibited*; heavy-laden, overburdened 684 *fatigued*; marooned, stranded, left high and dry, up the creek.

Vb. *hinder*, hamper, obstruct, impede; delay, use Fabian tactics; inconvenience 827 *trouble*; upset 63 *derange*; trip up, get under one's feet; entangle 542 *ensnare*; get in the way; come between, intervene, interpose 678 *meddle*; intercept, head off, undermine, stop one in the act, cut the ground from under one's feet, pull the rug from under one's f.; nip in the bud, stifle, choke; gag, muzzle 578 *make mute*; suffocate, repress 165 *suppress*; quell; hamper, burden, encumber; hang like a millstone round one's neck 322 *weigh*; load with, saddle w. 193 *load*; handicap; shackle, trammel, tie one's hands, tie hand and foot 747 *fetter*; put under house arrest, put under curfew; restrict 236 *limit*; check, brake, be a drag on, hold back 747 *restrain*; hold up, slow down, set one back 278 *retard*; lame, cripple, hobble, hamstring, paralyse 161 *disable*; wing 655 *wound*; clip the wings, cramp the style of, take the wind out of one's sails; deter 854 *frighten*; damp down, throw cold water on.

obstruct, intervene, interfere 678 *meddle*; obtrude 297 *intrude*; stymie, snooker, stand in the way 231 *lie between*; buzz, jostle, crowd, elbow, squeeze; sit on one's tail 284 *follow*; stop, intercept, occlude, stop up, block, block up, wall up 264 *close*; jam, jam tight, foul up, cause a stoppage, bring to a standstill; bind 350 *staunch*; dam, dam up; divert 495 *mislead*; fend off, stave off; barricade 235 *enclose*; fence, hedge in, blockade 232 *circumscribe*; deny access, keep out 57 *exclude*; prevent, inhibit, ban, bar, debar 757 *prohibit*.

be obstructive, make it hard for, play up 700 *be difficult*; put off, stall, stonewall; not play ball 598 *be unwilling*; baffle, foil, stymie, balk, be a dog in the manger; counter 182 *counteract*; thwart, frustrate; object, raise objections 704 *oppose*; interrupt, heckle, barrack; shout down 400 *be loud*; take evasive action 620 *avoid*; filibuster 581 *be loquacious*; play for time, use Fabian tactics, protract; strike 145 *halt*; picket; sabotage, throw a spanner in the works, gum up the works, spike the guns, put a spoke in one's wheel; take the wind out of one's sails.

703 Aid – **N.** *aid*, assistance, help, helping hand, leg-up, lift, boost; succour, rescue 668 *deliverance*; support, backing, seconding, abetment, encouragement; reinforcement; helpfulness 706 *cooperation*; service, ministration; good offices; patronage, auspices, sponsorship; favour 660 *protection*, 178 *influence*; good will, charity 897 *benevolence*; intercession 981 *prayers*; championship; good advice, constructive criticism 691 *advice*; spoonfeeding, featherbedding; first aid, medical assistance 658 *medical art*; favourable circumstances 730 *prosperity*; fair wind; self-help.

subvention, economic aid, monetary help; donation 781 *gift*; charity 901 *philanthropy*; social security, welfare benefit, unemployment b., sickness b., supplementary b., child b.; loan 802 *credit*; subsidy, hand-out, bounty, grant, allowance, expense account; stipend, bursary, scholarship 962 *reward*; maintenance, alimony, aliment, support, keep, upkeep 633 *provision*.

aider, help, helper, assistant, lieutenant, henchman, aide, right-hand man *or* woman, man Friday, girl F., backing

group; stand-by, support, mainstay; tower of strength, rock 660 *protector*; district nurse, social worker, counsellor 691 *adviser*; good neighbour, Good Samaritan; ally, brother-in-arms 707 *collaborator*; reinforcements 707 *auxiliary*; fairy godmother 903 *benefactor*; sponsor 707 *patron*; abettor.

Adj. *aiding,* helpful, obliging 706 *cooperative*; kind 897 *benevolent*; supporting, seconding, abetting; supportive, encouraging; of service, of help, of great assistance 640 *useful*; constructive, well-meant; morale-boosting; assistant, auxiliary, subsidiary, ancillary; contributory, assisting 628 *instrumental*.

Vb. *aid,* help, assist, lend a hand, give a helping hand 706 *cooperate*; render assistance; hold out a hand to, take under one's wing, take in tow, give a lift to; hold one's hand, spoonfeed, featherbed; be kind to, do one a good turn, give a leg up, help a lame duck, help a lame dog over a stile; help one out, tide one over, see one through; oblige, accommodate, lend money to 784 *lend*; put up the money, finance, subsidize; pitch in, chip in, send the hat round; facilitate, boost 285 *promote*; abet, fan the flame 612 *induce*; contribute to, be accessory to; lend support to, boost one's morale, back up, stand by, bolster, prop up 218 *support*; comfort, sustain, hearten, encourage, rally 855 *give courage*; succour, send help to, bail out, help o. 668 *deliver*; step into the breach, reinforce; set one on his *or* her feet 656 *restore*.

patronize, sponsor, back, guarantee, go bail for, stand surety for; recommend, put up for; propose, second; contribute to, subscribe to 488 *endorse*; take an interest in 880 *befriend*; champion, take up the cudgels for, stick up for, stand up f., stand by 713 *defend*; canvass for, root f., vote f. 605 *vote*; bestow one's custom, buy from 792 *purchase*.

minister to, wait on, do for, help, oblige 742 *serve*; give first aid to, nurse 658 *doctor*; squire, valet, mother; be of service to, make oneself useful to; anticipate the wishes of 597 *be willing*; pander

to, toady, humour, be a cat's paw to, scratch one's back, suck up to 925 *flatter*; slave, do all one can for, wait hand and foot on, do everything for 682 *work*; be assistant to, make oneself the tool of 628 *be instrumental*.

704 Opposition – N. *opposition,* antagonism, hostility 881 *enmity*; conflict, friction 709 *dissension*; noncooperation 598 *unwillingness*; contrariness, recalcitrance 602 *obstinacy*; counterargument 479 *confutation*; contradiction, denial 533 *negation*; challenge 711 *defiance*; stout opposition, stand 715 *resistance*; infringement 738 *revolt*; going against, siding a., voting a. canvassing a. 924 *disapprobation*; headwind, crosscurrent 702 *obstacle*; cross purposes, tug of war, tug of love, battle of wills; faction, rivalry, emulation, competition 716 *contention*; political opposition, the Opposition, Her Majesty's O., the other side.

opposites, contraries, extremes, opposite poles 14 *contrariety*; rivals, duellists, competitors 716 *contender*; opposite parties, factions, black and white, cat and dog; town and gown, the right and the left, management and workers, Labour and Conservative, Democrat and Republican.

Adj. *opposing,* opposed; in opposition; anti, against, agin; antagonistic, hostile, unfriendly, antipathetic, unsympathetic 881 *hostile*; unfavourable, unpropitious 731 *adverse*; cross, thwarting; contradictory 14 *contrary*; cussed, bloody-minded, bolshie 602 *obstinate*; refractory, recalcitrant 738 *disobedient*; resistant; clashing, conflicting, at variance, at odds with 709 *quarrelling*; militant, up in arms, at daggers drawn; face to face, eyeball to eyeball 237 *frontal*; at opposite extremes 240 *opposite*; rival, competitive 911 *jealous*.

Vb. *oppose,* go against, militate a. 14 *be contrary*; side against, stand a., hold out a., fight a., dig one's heels in, refuse to budge, stand one's ground 715 *resist*; set one's face against, make a dead set a. 607 *reject*; object, kick, protest, protest

against 762 *deprecate*; vote against 924 *disapprove*; canvass against, dissociate oneself; contradict, belie 533 *negate*; counter 479 *confute*; work against 182 *counteract*; countermine, thwart, baffle, foil 702 *be obstructive*; be at cross purposes; stand up to, challenge, dare 711 *defy*; vie with, compete with, bid against 716 *contend*.

withstand, confront, face, stand against, stand up to 661 *face danger*; rise against 738 *revolt*; take on, meet, encounter, cross swords with 716 *fight*; struggle against, breast the tide, stem the t., swim against the stream; cope with, grapple w., wrestle w. 678 *be active*; not be beaten 599 *stand firm*; hold one's own, bear the brunt 715 *resist*.

Adv. *in opposition,* against, versus, agin; in conflict with, against the crowd, against the tide, against the wind, against the grain, in the teeth of, in the face of, in defiance of.

705 Opponent – N. *opponent,* opposer, adversary, challenger, antagonist, foe 881 *enemy*; assailant 712 *attacker*; opposing party, opposition p., the opposition, opposite camp; cross benches; objector 489 *dissentient*; resister, dissident 829 *malcontent*; challenger, rival, competitor, combatant, contestant, duellist; entrant, the field, all comers 716 *contender*.

706 Cooperation – N. *cooperation,* helpfulness 597 *willingness*; interaction; duet, tandem; collaboration, joint effort, combined operation; team work, working together, concerted effort; relay race; team spirit, esprit de corps; unanimity, agreement 710 *concord*; clannishness, party spirit, cliquishness, partisanship; connivance, collusion, abetment 612 *inducement*; conspiracy 623 *plot*; complicity, participation, worker p.; sympathy 880 *friendliness*; fraternity, sorority, solidarity, fellowship, freemasonry, fellow feeling, comradeship, fellow-travelling; common cause, mutual assistance, networking, back-scratching, aiding and abetting; reciprocity, give and take, mutual concession 770 *compromise*.

association, co-ownership, partnership 775 *participation*; nationalization 775 *joint possession*; pool, kitty; affiliation 78 *inclusion*; tie-up 9 *relation*; combination 45 *union*; solidarity 52 *whole*; unification 88 *unity*; amalgamation, fusion, merger; coalition, alliance, league, federation, confederacy, umbrella organization; united front 708 *political party*; an association, fellowship, club, fraternity, sorority 708 *community*; set, clique, coterie, cell 708 *party*; workers' association, trade union, chapel; business association, company, joint-stock c., syndicate, combine, consortium, trust, cartel, ring 708 *corporation*; workers' cooperative, commune 708 *community*.

Adj. *cooperative,* helpful 703 *aiding*; collaborating, married, associating, associated, in league, back-scratching, hand in glove with; bipartisan; federal 708 *corporate*.

Vb. *cooperate,* collaborate, work together, pull t., work as a team; hunt in pairs, run in double harness; team up, join forces, pool resources, go into partnership 775 *participate*; show willing, play ball, reciprocate, respond; join in, take part, enter into, pitch in; rally round 703 *aid*; stand shoulder to shoulder, stand by each other, sink or swim together; be in league with, be in cahoots with, make common cause with; network, band together, gang up, associate, ally; coalesce, merge, unite; combine, make common cause, club together; conspire 623 *plot*; collude, connive, negotiate 766 *make terms*.

707 Auxiliary – N. *auxiliary,* reinforcement; back-up; second line 722 *soldiery*; paramedic, auxiliary nurse; assistant, helper 703 *aider*; right-hand man; adjutant, lieutenant, aide-de-camp; amanuensis, secretary, girl Friday; dogsbody 742 *servant*; acolyte; best man, bridesmaid; henchman, follower 742 *dependant*; disciple, adherent 978 *sectarian*;

loyalist, flunkey, stooge, cat's-paw, puppet 628 *instrument*; shadow.

collaborator, cooperator, co-author, co-worker, fellow w.; team-mate; fellow traveller, fifth column, fifth columnist, quisling, traitor, mole, conspirator, conniver.

colleague, associate, fellow-worker, peer, brother, sister; co-director, partner 775 *participator*; comrade, companion, boon c., playmate; alter ego, faithful companion; mate, chum, pal, buddy, oppo, crony 880 *friend*; helpmate, better half 894 *spouse*; stalwart; ally, confederate; accomplice, accessory, abettor, aider and abettor, fellow conspirator, partner in crime.

patron, guardian angel 660 *protector*; champion, friend at court; supporter, sponsor, backer, angel, guarantor; fan 887 *lover*; good friend, friend in need, deus ex machina; fairy godmother, rich uncle, sugar daddy 903 *benefactor*; promoter, founder; customer, client 792 *purchaser*.

708 Party – **N.** *party,* group, class 77 *classification*; denomination, church 978 *sect*; faction, cabal, cave, splinter group, breakaway movement 489 *dissentient*; circle, inner c., charmed c., kitchen cabinet; set, clique, in-crowd, coterie; caucus, committee, quango, club, cell, cadre; ring, closed shop; eight, eleven, fifteen; crew, team, complement 686 *personnel*; troupe, company 594 *actor*; gang, outfit 74 *band*; side, camp.

political party, right, left, centre; Conservative, Tories, Unionists, National Front; Liberals, Radicals, Whigs; Socialists, Labour, Liblab, Social Democrats, SDP; Democrats, Republicans; Nationalists; Ecologists, Greens; Militant Tendency, Workers' Revolutionary Party, International Socialists, Trotskyists, Marxists, Communists, Bolsheviks, Mensheviks; Fascists, Nazis; coalition, popular front, bloc; comrade; socialist,

Fabian; anarchist 738 *revolter*; right-winger, true blue; left-winger, leftist, leftie, pinko; populist, democrat; moderate; wet, dry; party worker, canvasser, party member, politician; militant, activist 676 *doer*.

society, partnership, coalition, combination, combine 706 *association*; league, alliance; federation, confederacy; cooperative, union, EEC, Common Market, free trade area; club 76 *focus*; secret society, Ku Klux Klan, Freemasonry, lodge, cell; trades union; chapel; youth movement, Boy Scouts, Cubs, Rovers, Rangers, Girl Guides, Brownies; Women's Institute, Townswomen's Guild, Mother's Union; fellow, associate, member, asociate m.; party m., paid-up m., card-carrying m.; trade unionist.

community, fellowship, brotherhood, congregation, fraternity, sorority, sisterhood; clique, coterie; guild; race, tribe, clan, sect 11 *family*; order 77 *classification*; social class 371 *social group*; state, nation.

corporation, body; company, joint-stock c., limited liability c., public limited c., holding c.; multinational c.; firm, concern; partnership; business house; establishment, organization, institute; trust, combine, monopoly, cartel, syndicate, conglomerate 706 *association*; trade association, chamber of commerce, guild, cooperative society; consumers' association.

Vb. *join a party,* subscribe; join, swell the ranks, become one of, become a member, take out membership; sign on, enlist, enrol oneself, get elected; align oneself, side with, range oneself with, team up w. 706 *cooperate*; associate, ally.

709 Dissension – **N.** *dissension,* disagreement 489 *dissent*; noncooperation 704 *opposition*; disharmony, jar, jangle, jarring note, discordant n. 411 *discord*; wrangling, quarrelling, bickering, sniping, cat-and-dog life; differences, odds, variance, friction, tension, unpleasantness, scenes; hostility 888 *hatred*; disunity, internal dissension, muttering in

the ranks, house divided against itself 25 *disagreement*; rift, cleavage, parting of the ways, separation 294 *divergence*; split 978 *schism*; cross purposes 481 *misjudgment*; breach, rupture, severance of relations; declaration of war, open war 718 *war*.

quarrelsomeness, factiousness, litigiousness; aggressiveness, combativeness, pugnacity, belligerence, warlike behaviour 718 *bellicosity*; provocativeness, inviting trouble, trailing one's coat 711 *defiance*; contentiousness 716 *contention*; rivalry 911 *jealousy*; apple of discord.

quarrel, feud, blood f., vendetta 910 *revenge*; war 718 *warfare*; strife 716 *contention*; conflict, clash 279 *collision*; legal battle 959 *litigation*; controversy, dispute, wrangle, argy-bargy; paper war 475 *argument*; words, war of w., raised voices, stormy exchange, confrontation, altercation, set-to, slanging match 899 *scurrility*; spat, tiff, squabble, wrangle, barney, hassle, squall, storm in a teacup; rumpus, dustup, disturbance, hubbub, racket, row, shindig, stramash, commotion, scrimmage, fracas, brawl, fisticuffs, breach of the peace 61 *turmoil*; gang warfare, street fighting, riot 716 *fight*.

Adj. *quarrelling,* clashing, conflicting 14 *contrary*; on bad terms, feuding, at odds, at loggerheads, at variance, at daggers drawn, up in arms 881 *hostile*; divided, factious, schismatic 489 *dissenting*; mutinous, rebellious 738 *disobedient*; cantankerous 892 *irascible*; litigious; quarrelsome, bellicose 718 *warlike*; pugnacious, combative, spoiling for a fight, trailing one's coat, inviting trouble, asking for it, belligerent, aggressive, militant; argumentative, contentious, disputatious, wrangling.

Vb. *quarrel,* clash, conflict 279 *collide*; cross swords with, be at one another's throats; be at cross purposes, be at variance, have differences, have a bone to pick 15 *differ*; fall out, go one's separate ways, part company, split, break with; break away; break off relations, break off diplomatic r., declare war 718 *go to war*;

go to law, take it to court 959 *litigate*; squabble, row with, go at it hammer and tongs, brawl; have a feud with, carry on a vendetta 910 *be revengeful*.

make quarrels, pick q., pick a fight; look for trouble, ask for it, be spoiling for a fight, trail one's coat, challenge 711 *defy*; rub up the wrong way, tread on one's toes, get up one's nose, provoke 891 *enrage*; have a bone to pick; estrange, set at odds, set at variance, set by the ears; sound a discordant note 411 *discord*; sow dissension, stir it, make mischief, make trouble, kick up a shindy, disturb the peace; put the cat among the pigeons; come between, drive a wedge b. 46 *sunder*; widen the breach, fan the flame 832 *aggravate*; set against.

710 Concord – N. *concord,* harmony 410 *melody*; unison, unity, duet 24 *agreement*; unanimity, bipartisanship 488 *consensus*; understanding, mutual u., rapport; solidarity, team spirit 706 *cooperation*; reciprocity 12 *correlation*; sympathy, fellow feeling 887 *love*; compatibility, coexistence 880 *friendship*; détente, reunion, reconciliation, conciliation, peacemaking 719 *pacification*; arbitration 720 *mediation*; entente cordiale, happy family, picture of content, the best of friends, sweetness and light, love and peace 717 *peace*; goodwill, honeymoon period.

Vb. *concord* 410 *harmonize;* bring into concord 719 *pacify*; agree 24 *accord*; hit it off, see eye to eye, play a duet, chime in with, pull together 706 *cooperate*; reciprocate, respond, run parallel 181 *concur*; fraternize 880 *be friendly*; keep the peace, remain at peace 717 *be at peace*.

711 Defiance – N. *defiance,* dare, daring, challenge, gage, gauntlet, hat in the ring; bold front, belling the cat, brave face 855 *courage*; war dance, war cry, war whoop, war song, battle cry, declaration of war 900 *threat*; brazenness 878 *insolence*; demonstration, display, bravura 875 *ostentation*.

Adj. *defiant,* defying, challenging, provocative, belligerent, bellicose, militant 718 *warlike*; saucy, insulting 878 *insolent*; mutinous, rebellious 738 *disobedient*; greatly daring 855 *courageous*; stiffnecked 871 *proud*; reckless, triggerhappy 857 *rash*.

Vb. *defy,* challenge, take one up on 489 *dissent*; stand up to 704 *oppose*; caution 664 *warn*; throw in one's teeth, throw down the gauntlet, throw one's hat in the ring; demand satisfaction, call out, send one's seconds; dare, outdare, beard; brave, run the gauntlet 661 *face danger*; laugh to scorn, laugh in one's face, laugh in one's beard, set at naught, snap one's fingers at 922 *hold cheap*; bid defiance to, set at d., hurl d.; call one's bluff, double the bid; show fight, bare one's teeth, show one's fangs, double one's fist, clench one's f., shake one's f. 900 *threaten*; refuse to bow down to 871 *be proud*; look big, throw out one's chest, beat one's c., show a bold front; wave a banner 317 *brandish*; march, demonstrate, hold a demonstration, stage a sit-in, not be moved; cock a snook 878 *be insolent*; ask for trouble 709 *make quarrels*; crow over, shout 727 *triumph*; crow, bluster, brag 877 *boast*.

Adv. *defiantly,* challengingly, in defiance of, in one's teeth, to one's face, under the very nose of; in open rebellion.

Int. do your worst! come on if you dare!

712 Attack – **N.** *attack,* hostile a., best method of defence; pugnacity, combativeness, aggressiveness 718 *bellicosity*; belligerence, aggression, unprovoked a. 914 *injustice*; stab in the back; mugging, assault, assault and battery, grievous bodily harm 176 *violence*; armed attack, offensive, drive, push, thrust, pincer movement 688 *tactics*; dead set at; onslaught, onset, rush, charge; sally, sortie, breakthrough; counterattack 714 *retaliation*; shock tactics, blitzkrieg, surprise; infringement 306 *overstepping*; invasion, incursion, overrunning 297 *ingress*; raid, foray 788 *brigandage*; blitz,

air raid; taking by storm, boarding; siege, blockade 230 *surroundings*.

terror tactics, guerrilla warfare, sniping, war of attrition, war of nerves 854 *intimidation*; shot across the bows; bloodbath 362 *slaughter*; laying waste.

bombardment, cannonade, barrage, strafe, blitz; broadside, volley, salvo; bomb-dropping, bombing, saturation b.; firing, shooting, gunfire, fusillade, cross-f.; antiaircraft fire, flak; sniping.

attacker, assailant, aggressor, mugger; storm troops, strike force; fighter pilot, bomber 722 *armed force*; sniper; terrorist, guerrilla; invader, raider; besieger.

Vb. *attack,* be spoiling for a fight; start a fight, declare war 718 *go to war*; strike the first blow, open fire on, fire the first shot; assault, go for, set on, pounce upon, fall u., pitch into, sail i.; attack tooth and nail, savage, maul, draw blood 655 *wound*; launch out at, let fly at, let one have it, lay into, tear into, lace into, round on; take by surprise, blitz, overwhelm; invade 306 *encroach*; raid, foray, overrun, infest; take the offensive; make a sortie; board, grapple; take by storm, capture 727 *overmaster*; ravage, make havoc; harry, drive 619 *hunt*; take up the cudgels 716 *fight*.

besiege, lay siege to, beleaguer, surround, beset, blockade 235 *enclose*.

strike at, raise one's hand against; lay about one, swipe, flail, hammer 279 *strike*; go berserk, run amok; lash out at; beat up, mug, lunge; grapple with, fight hand to hand, cut and thrust; push, butt, thrust, poke at, thrust at; stab, spear, lance, bayonet, run through, cut down 263 *pierce*; lay low, bring down 311 *abase*.

fire at, shoot at; fire a shot at, take a potshot, snipe, pick off 287 *shoot*; shoot down; torpedo; strafe, bombard, blitz, shell, pepper; bomb, drop b.; open fire; rake; take aim, pull the trigger, level, draw a bead on 281 *aim*.

713 Defence – **N.** *defence,* the defensive, self-defence 715 *resistance*; art of self-

defence, boxing 716 *pugilism*; judo, ju-jitsu, karate 716 *wrestling*; parry, warding off 182 *counteraction*; defensiveness 854 *nervousness*; guard; self-protection 660 *protection*; a defence, rampart, bulwark, screen, buffer, fender, bumper 662 *safeguard*.

defences, lines, entrenchment; earthwork, embankment, mound; boom; wall, barricade, fence 235 *barrier*; palisade, paling, stockade; moat, ditch, dike; trench, dugout; tripwire, booby trap 542 *trap*; barbed wire; spike; antitank obstacles, Maginot Line, Siegfried L., Hadrian's Wall, Antonine W., Great Wall of China; airraid shelter, fallout s., bunker 662 *shelter*; barrage, antiaircraft fire, flak; barrage balloon; minefield, mine; smokescreen 421 *screen*.

fortification (see *fort*); bulwark, rampart, wall; parapet, battlement, emplacement; escarp; bastion; outwork; buttress, abutment.

fort, fortress, stronghold, fastness; citadel, capitol, acropolis 662 *refuge*; castle, keep, tower, turret; portcullis, drawbridge; gate, postern; Martello tower, pillbox; laager, encampment 235 *enclosure*; Roman camp.

armour, panoply; mail, chain m.; breastplate; cuirass; hauberk, coat of mail, corslet; helmet, casque, visor, beaver; steel helmet, tin hat; bearskin 228 *headgear*; gauntlet; shield, buckler; protective clothing, riot shield, gas mask 662 *safeguard*.

defender, champion; patron 703 *aider*; knight-errant; loyalist, patriot; bodyguard, lifeguard 722 *soldier*; watch, sentry, sentinel; vigilante; patrol, patrolman; security man *or* woman; garrison, picket, guard, escort, rearguard; Home Guard, Territorials, Territorial Army, militia, thin red line 722 *soldiery*; fireman; Civil Defence; guardian, warden 660 *protector*; warder, custodian 749 *keeper*.

Vb. *defend,* guard, protect, keep, watch 660 *safeguard*; fence, hedge 232 *circumscribe*; barricade 235 *enclose*; block 702 *obstruct*; cushion, pad, shield,

curtain, cover 421 *screen*; cloak 525 *conceal*; arm 669 *make ready*; armour; reinforce, fortify 162 *strengthen*; entrench, dig in 599 *stand firm*; stand in front, stand by; garrison, man, stop the gap; plead for, hold a brief for, argue for, take up the cause of, champion 927 *vindicate*; fight for, take up arms for, take up the cudgels for, rescue.

714 Retaliation – N. *retaliation,* reprisal 910 *revenge*; requital, recompense, comeuppance 962 *reward*; deserts, just deserts 915 *dueness*; punitive action, poetic justice, retribution, Nemesis 963 *punishment*; reaction, boomerang, backlash 280 *recoil*; counterstroke, counterblast, counterplot, countermine 182 *counteraction*; counterattack, sally, sortie 712 *attack*; recrimination, answering back, riposte, retort 460 *rejoinder*; heaping coals of fire; reciprocation, like for like, tit for tat, quid pro quo, measure for measure, blow for blow, an eye for an eye and a tooth for a tooth, a taste of one's own medicine, a Roland for an Oliver, biter bit, a game at which two can play; what is coming to one; deterrent 854 *intimidation*.

Vb. *retaliate,* exact compensation 31 *recoup*; take reprisals 963 *punish*; counter, riposte; pay off old scores, square the account, be quits, get even with, get upsides with, get one's own back 910 *avenge*; teach one a lesson; reciprocate, give and take, return like for like; return the compliment, give as good as one got, pay one in his own coin, get one's pound of flesh; retort, cap, answer back 460 *answer*; round on, kick back, hit b., not take it lying down 715 *resist*; turn the tables on, hoist one with his *or* her own petard, make one laugh on the other side of his face, make one take back his *or* her own words, have the last laugh.

715 Resistance – N. *resistance,* stand, brave front 704 *opposition*; intractability 602 *obstinacy*; objection, demur 468 *qualification*; recalcitrance, protest 762

deprecation; noncooperation, passive resistance, civil disobedience; rising, insurrection, backlash 738 *revolt*; self-defence 713 *defence*; repulsion, rebuff 760 *refusal*.

Adj. *resisting,* opposing; protesting, reluctant 598 *unwilling*; recalcitrant, mutinous 738 *disobedient*; stubborn 602 *obstinate*; unyielding, indomitable; resistant, tough, proofed, bulletproof, waterproof, showerproof.

Vb. *resist,* offer resistance, stand against 704 *withstand*; obstruct 702 *hinder*; challenge, stand out against 711 *defy*; confront 661 *face danger*; struggle against, contend with, stem the tide 704 *oppose*; kick against the pricks, protest 762 *deprecate*; demur, object 468 *qualify*; down tools, vote with one's feet, walk out, come out 145 *cease*; call out 145 *halt*; mutiny, rise, not take it lying down 738 *revolt*; make a stand, fight off, keep at arm's length, keep at bay, hold off; make a fight of it 716 *contend*; hold out, not submit, stand one's ground, not give way 599 *stand firm*; endure 825 *suffer*; repel, rebuff 760 *refuse*; resist temptation, not be tempted.

716 Contention – N. *contention,* strife, tussle, conflict, clash, running battle 709 *dissension*; combat, fighting, war 718 *warfare*; debate, dispute, controversy, polemics, ink-slinging 475 *argument*; altercation, words, war of w. 709 *quarrel*; bone of contention; competition, rivalry, emulation 911 *jealousy*; competitiveness, gamesmanship, survival of the fittest, rat race; cut-throat competition, war to the knife, no holds barred; sports, athletics 837 *sport*.

contest, trial, trial of strength, marathon, pentathlon, decathlon, tug-of-war, tug of love 682 *exertion*; tussle, struggle 671 *attempt*; needle match; nothing in it, close finish, photo f. 200 *short distance*; competition, free-for-all; pro-am, knock-out competition, tournament; prize competition, stakes, Ashes; match, test m.; rally; event, handicap, run-off; heat, final, semifinal, quarterfinal, Cup tie,

Cup final; set, game, rubber; sporting event, wager, bet 837 *sport*; field day 837 *amusement*; Derby day (**see** *racing*); athletics, gymnastics; gymkhana, horseshow, rodeo; games, Highland Games, Commonwealth G., Olympic G., Olympics; Wimbledon, Wembley, Lords 724 *arena*.

racing, races, race, foot r., flat r., sprint; racewalking, road race, marathon, fun run; long-distance race, cross-country r., orienteering; slalom, obstacle race; hare and hounds r., treasure hunt; sack race, egg and spoon r.; relay r., team r.; the Turf, horse racing, sport of kings; the Derby, the Oaks; point-to-point, steeplechase, hurdles, sticks 312 *leap*; motor race, motor rally, dirt-track racing, stockcar r., speedway, motocross; cycle race, Tour de France, cyclocross; dog racing, the dogs; boat race, yacht r.; regatta, eights, Ascot, racecourse, track, stadium 724 *arena*.

pugilism, noble art of self-defence, boxing, sparring, jabbing, socking, slugging, pummeling, lambasting, fisticuffs; fighting, prize f., boxing match, prizefight; round, bout; the ring, the fancy 837 *sport*.

wrestling, jujitsu, judo, aikido, karate, kyokushinkai, taekwondo, kungfu, ninjutsu; all-in wrestling, catch-as-catch-can, no holds barred; catch, hold; wrestle, grapple, wrestling match.

duel, affair of honour, seconds out; jousting, tilting, tournament; fencing, iaido, swordplay, kendo; hand-to-hand fighting; bullfight; cockfight; bullring, cockpit, lists 724 *arena*.

fight, hostilities, blow-up, appeal to arms 718 *warfare*; battle royal, free fight, free-for-all, showdown, rough and tumble, roughhouse, horseplay, shindig, stramash, scuffle, scrum, scrimmage, scramble, dogfight, mêlée, fracas, uproar, rumpus, ruction 61 *turmoil*; gang warfare, street fight, riot, brawl, broil 709 *quarrel*; fisticuffs, blows, hard knocks; give and take, cut and thrust; affray, set-to, tussle; running fight, hand-to-hand fighting; combat, fray, clash,

conflict 279 *collision*; encounter, dustup, scrap, brush; skirmish; engagement, action, pitched battle, stand-up fight, shoot-out 718 *battle*; campaign, struggle; war to the knife, fight to the death; Armageddon.

contender, fighter, gladiator; duellist; candidate, entrant, examinee; competitor, rival; challenger, front runner, favourite, top seed; the field, all comers; contestant; racer, runner, marathoner 162 *athlete*; sprinter.

Vb. *contend,* combat, strive, struggle, battle, fight, tussle, wrestle, grapple 671 *attempt*; oppose, put up a fight 715 *resist*; argue for, stick out for, insist 532 *emphasize*; contest, compete, challenge, stake, wager, bet; play, play against, match oneself, vie with, race, run a race; emulate, rival; outrival 306 *outdo*; enter, enter for, take on, enter the lists, descend into the arena, take up the challenge, pick up the gauntlet; cross swords with; take on, grapple with, lock horns w. 712 *strike at*; have a hard fight, fight to a finish.

fight, scuffle, row, scrimmage, scrap, set to; pitch into, sail i. 712 *attack*; lay about one 712 *strike at*; mix it, join in the mêlée; square up to, come to blows, exchange b., put up one's fists; box, spar, pummel, jostle, hit, kick, scratch, bite 279 *strike*; quarrel; duel; encounter, have a brush with, scrap w., skirmish; take on, engage, fight a pitched battle; come to grips, close with, grapple, lock horns; fence, cross swords; fight hand to hand, combat, campaign, fight the good fight 718 *wage war*; fight it out, fight to the last man 599 *be resolute.*

717 Peace – **N.** *peace,* peacefulness, peace and quiet, a quiet life, the line of least resistance 266 *quiescence*; harmony 710 *concord*; peacetime; law and order 60 *order*; truce, armistice 145 *lull*; coexistence; neutrality; nonalignment; noninvolvement 860 *indifference*; nonintervention 620 *avoidance*; peaceableness, nonaggression 177 *moderation*;

cordial relations 880 *friendship*; pacifism, peace at any price, peace in our time, nonviolence; disarmament, peacemaking 719 *pacification*; pipe of peace; peace treaty, burial of the hatchet 506 *amnesty.*

pacifist, man *or* woman of peace, peace women, peace-lover, peacemonger, dove; peace camp, CND 177 *moderator*; neutral, noncombatant; passive resister, conscientious objector, conchie; peacemaker 720 *mediator.*

Adj. *peaceful,* quiet, halcyon 266 *tranquil*; bloodless; harmless, dovelike 935 *innocent*; easy-going 884 *amiable*; uncompetitive; peaceable, law-abiding, peace-loving, pacific, unaggressive, pacifist, nonviolent; unarmed, noncombatant; passive, submissive 721 *submitting*; peacemaking, conciliatory; without enemies, at peace; not at war, neutral; postwar, prewar, interwar; peacetime.

Vb. *be at peace,* stay at p., observe neutrality, keep out of trouble; mean no harm, forget one's differences, be pacific 935 *be innocent*; keep the peace, make p. 720 *mediate*; beat swords into ploughshares, make the lion lie down with the lamb, smoke the pipe of peace.

718 War – **N.** *war,* arms, the sword; cold w., armed neutrality; paper war, war of words, polemic 709 *quarrel*; war of nerves, sabre-rattling, gunboat diplomacy 854 *intimidation*; uneasy peace, phoney w.; armed intervention, police action; civil w., war of revolution, war of independence; wars of religion, holy war, crusade; war of expansion; all-out war; world w., total w., blitzkrieg, atomic war, nuclear w.; war of attrition, war to the death, no holds barred; war to end all wars, Armageddon; the panoply of war, martial music; call to arms, bugle call 547 *call*; battle cry, rallying cry, Mars.

belligerency, state of war; declaration of war, militancy, hostilities; wartime.

bellicosity, war fever; pugnacity, combativeness, aggressiveness, hawkishness,

militancy 709 *quarrelsomeness*; militarism, expansionism; jingoism, chauvinism, gung-ho 481 *prejudice*.

war measures, war preparations, arming 669 *preparation*; call to arms, clarion call, fiery cross 547 *call*; war effort, war work, call-up, rally, mobilization, recruitment, conscription, national service, military duty; volunteering, doing one's duty, for king *or* queen and country, joining up, enlisting.

warfare, war, open w., warpath, waging w.; bloodshed, battles, sieges 176 *violence*; fighting, campaigning, soldiering, active service; military s., naval s., air s.; bombing, saturation b. 712 *bombardment*; raiding; besieging, blockading 235 *enclosure*; aerial warfare, naval w., chemical w., gas w., germ w., atomic w., nuclear w.; economic w., blockade, attrition, scorched earth policy; psychological warfare, propaganda; offensive warfare 712 *attack*; defensive warfare 713 *defence*; trench w., desert w., jungle w.; bush-fighting, guerrilla warfare, sniping; campaign, expedition; operations; incursion, invasion, raid; order, orders 737 *command*; battle cry; plan of campaign, strategy 623 *plan*.

battle, pitched b., battle royal 716 *fight*; line of battle, array; line, firing l., front l., front, battle f., battle station; armed conflict, action, scrap, skirmish, brush, collision, clash, shoot-out; offensive, blitz 712 *attack*; defensive battle, stand 713 *defence*; engagement, naval e., sea fight, air f., dogfight; battlefield, theatre of war 724 *battleground*.

Adj. *warring,* on the warpath; campaigning, battling etc. vb.; at war; belligerent, aggressive, bellicose, militant, mobilized, under arms, in the army, at the front, on active service; militant, up in arms; armed, sword in hand 669 *prepared*; arrayed, embattled; engaged, at loggerheads 709 *quarrelling*; on the offensive.

warlike, militaristic, bellicose, hawkish, militant, aggressive, belligerent, pugnacious, pugilistic, combative; war-loving, warmongering; bloodthirsty, war-fevered; military, paramilitary, martial, battle-scarred.

Vb. *go to war,* resort to arms; declare war, open hostilities, let slip the dogs of war; appeal to arms, unsheathe the sword, throw away the scabbard, whet the sword, take up the cudgels 716 *fight*; fly to arms, rise, rebel 738 *revolt*; raise one's banner, call to arms, send round the fiery cross; arm, militarize, mobilize, put on a war footing; rally, call up, call to the colours, recruit, conscript; join the army, join up, enlist; make w., go on the warpath, march to war, engage in hostilities, war against; open a campaign; go on active service, take the offensive, invade 712 *attack*; act on the defensive 713 *defend*; march, countermarch; blockade, besiege 230 *surround*; shed blood, put to the sword 362 *slaughter*; ravage, burn, scorch; give battle; cross swords with, take issue with; join battle, engage, stage a shoot-out, call for a show-down, combat, confront, fight it out 716 *fight*; beat the drum, go over the top; open fire 712 *fire at*.

719 Pacification – N. *pacification,* pacifying, peacemaking; conciliation, appeasement, mollification 177 *moderation*; reconciliation, reconcilement, détente, rapprochement; accommodation, adjustment 24 *agreement*; good offices 720 *mediation*; entente, understanding, peace treaty, nonaggression pact, SALT 765 *treaty*; truce, armistice, cease-fire 145 *lull*; disarmament, CND, peace movement, demobilization, disbanding; nuclear-free zone, peace camp.

peace offering, appeasement 736 *leniency*; dove of peace, olive branch, overture, hand of friendship, outstretched hand 880 *friendliness*; flag of truce, white flag, pipe of peace 717 *peace*; blood money, compensation 787 *restitution*; plea for peace 506 *amnesty*.

Vb. *pacify,* make peace; allay, tranquillize, mollify, soothe 177 *assuage*; smooth one's ruffled feathers, pour balm into one's wounds, heal 656 *cure*; hold out the olive branch, hold out one's

hand, coo like a dove 880 *be friendly*; conciliate, propitiate, disarm, reconcile, placate, appease, satisfy 828 *content*; pour oil on troubled waters 266 *bring to rest*; restore harmony 410 *harmonize*; win over, meet halfway 770 *compromise*; settle differences; bring together 720 *mediate*; grant peace 766 *give terms*; keep the peace 717 *be at peace*.

make peace, stop fighting, cry quits, break it up 145 *cease*; bury the hatchet, let bygones be bygones, forgive and forget 506 *forget*; shake hands, make it up, make friends, kiss and make up, patch up a quarrel, come to an understanding, agree to differ; lay down one's arms, sheathe the sword, put up one's sword, beat swords into ploughshares; make a truce, suspend hostilities, demilitarize, disarm, demobilize; smoke the pipe of peace.

720 Mediation – N. *mediation,* good offices, mediatorship, intercession; umpirage, refereeship, arbitration; intervention, stepping-in, diplomacy; parley, negotiation 584 *conference*.

mediator, mutual friend, middleman, matchmaker, go-between, pander, Pandarus, negotiator 231 *intermediary*; arbitrator, umpire, referee 480 *estimator*; diplomat, diplomatist, representative, agent, spokesperson 754 *delegate*; peace movement 177 *moderator*; pacifier, troubleshooter, ombudsman, ACAS; marriage guidance counsellor, family conciliation service 691 *adviser*; peacemaker.

Vb. *mediate,* intervene 678 *meddle*; step in, interpose; proffer one's good offices, intercede for, propitiate; run messages for, be a go-between, act as a pander for; bring together, negotiate, act as agent; arbitrate, umpire 480 *judge*.

721 Submission – N. *submission,* submissiveness 739 *obedience*; subservience 745 *servitude*; acquiescence, compliance, consent 488 *assent*; supineness,

peace at any price, line of least resistance, nonresistance, passiveness, resignation, fatalism 679 *inactivity*; yielding, giving way, giving in, white flag, capitulation, surrender, unconditional s. 621 *relinquishment*; deference 872 *humility*; homage 739 *loyalty*; genuflexion, prostration 311 *obeisance*.

Adj. *submitting,* surrendering etc. vb.; meek, unresisting, law-abiding 717 *peaceful*; submissive 739 *obedient*; fatalistic, resigned, acquiescent 488 *assenting*; pliant, accommodating, malleable 327 *soft*; crawling, cringing, supine, prostrate; boot-licking, bowing and scraping; kneeling, on bended knees, sycophantic, Uriah Heepish, toadying 872 *humble*.

Vb. *submit,* yield, give in; defer to; bow to, make a virtue of necessity, admit defeat 728 *be defeated*; be resigned 488 *acquiesce*; accept 488 *assent*; shrug one's shoulders 860 *be indifferent*; withdraw, make way for, draw in one's horns 286 *turn back*; not contest 679 *be inactive*; stop fighting, have no fight left, have all the fight knocked out of one, give up, cry quits, have had enough, throw up the sponge, throw in the towel, surrender, hold up one's hands, show the white flag, ask for terms; surrender, capitulate; throw oneself on another's mercy; give oneself up, throw down one's arms, hand over one's sword, hang up one's sword, haul down the flag, strike one's colours.

knuckle under, succumb, cave in, collapse; show no fight, take the line of least resistance, bow before the inevitable, bow before the storm; be submissive, bow one's neck to the yoke, do homage 745 *be subject*; take one's medicine, swallow the pill 963 *be punished*; eat humble pie, eat dirt 872 *be humble*; take it, take it from one, take it lying down, grin and bear it, stomach, put up with 825 *suffer*; bend, bow, kneel, kowtow, toady, crouch, cringe, crawl, bow and scrape 311 *stoop*; grovel, lick the dust, lick the boots of, kiss the rod; fall on one's knees, throw oneself at the feet of,

clasp someone's knees, beg for mercy, cry *or* howl for m.

722 Combatant. Army. Navy. Air Force –
N. **combatant,** fighter 716 *contender*; aggressor, assailant, mugger 712 *attacker*; besieger; stormtroops; belligerent, fighting man, man-at-arms, warrior, brave; bodyguard 713 *defender*; gunman, strongarm man, hitman 362 *killer*; bully, rough, rowdy, bovver boy, boot boy 904 *ruffian*; duellist; swordsman, fencer; gladiator 162 *athlete*; fighting cock; bullfighter, toreador, matador, picador; wrestler, jujitsuist, judoist, karate expert 716 *wrestling*; competitor 716 *contender*; jouster, knight; wrangler; barrister, advocate 959 *litigant*.

pugilist, boxer, champion, champ, sparring partner; flyweight, bantamweight, featherweight, welterweight, middleweight, cruiserweight, heavyweight; slogger, pummeler 716 *pugilism*.

militarist, jingoist, chauvinist, gungho, expansionist, militant, warmonger, hawk; crusader; Samurai; mercenary; soldier of fortune; freebooter, pirate, buccaneer 789 *robber*.

soldier, army man, military man, regular; soldiery, troops (see *armed force*); old campaigner, veteran, Chelsea pensioner; fighting man, warrior, brave; man-at-arms, redcoat, legionnaire, centurion; standard-bearer, colour sergeant, ensign; sniper; territorial, Home Guard, militiaman; yeomanry, yeoman; irregular troops; raider, guerrilla, partisan, freedom fighter; resistance fighter, Maquis; guards 660 *protector*; enlisted man; reservist; volunteer; mercenary; conscript, recruit, rookie; serviceman, Tommy, Jock, GI, Anzac, sepoy, Gurkha; female warrior, Amazon, Boadicea; valkyrie; Wren, WRAF, WRAC.

soldiery, cannon fodder, gallant company, heroes; rank and file, other ranks; private, common soldier, man-at-arms; archer, crossbowman; spearman, pikeman, halberdier, lancer; musketeer, fusilier, rifleman, grenadier, bombardier, gunner, artilleryman; sapper, engineer;

signalman; corporal, sergeant, lieutenant 741 *army officer*.

army, host; legion; cohorts, big battalions; horde 104 *multitude*; National Guard, Home G.; militia, yeomanry; vigilantes; regular army, standing a., professional a., mercenary a., territorial a., draft; the services, armed forces.

armed force, forces, troops, contingents, men, personnel; armada; guards; Household Cavalry, Life Guards, crack troups; reconnaissance party, expeditionary force, flying column; paratroops, Commandoes, task force, raiding party, guerrilla force; combat troops, field army, line, thin red l., front l.; vanguard, rearguard; reserves, recruits, reinforcements, draft, levy 707 *auxiliary*; detachment, party, detail; patrol; sentry; garrison, army of occupation.

formation, line; legion; column; file; unit, detachment, corps, division, armoured d.; brigade, light b.; battery; regiment, cavalry r., squadron, troop; battalion, company, platoon, section, squad, detail, party 74 *band*.

infantry, foot regiment, infantryman, foot soldier; light infantry.

cavalry, yeomanry; cavalry regiment; horseman; mounted troops, mounted police, cavalryman, yeoman; trooper; knight; man-at-arms, hussar, dragoon; Cossack; armoured car; tank, Panzer; charger.

navy, admiralty; senior service, sail; fleet arm, armada; fleet, flotilla, squadron; argosy; merchant marine.

naval man, admiral, Sea Lord 741 *naval officer*; sailor 270 *mariner*; able seaman, rating; cabin boy; swabbie; marine, limey; submariner 270 *nautical personnel*; Royal Navy, RN, WRNS; Royal Marines; Royal Naval Reserve RNR.

warship, galleon 275 *ship*; pirate ship; man-o'-war, ship of the line, battleship, dreadnought; cruiser; frigate, corvette; gunboat, E-boat; destroyer; fire ship; minesweeper; submarine, nuclear s., U-boat; Q-ship; aircraft carrier; landing craft, troopship; hospital s.; flagship.

air force, RAF, WRAF; flying corps; fleet air arm; squadron, flight, group, wing; warplane 276 *aircraft*; battle plane, bomber, fighter; troop-carrier; Zeppelin, barrage balloon 276 *airship*; paratroopers; ground staff; fighter pilot, navigator, observer, air crew.

723 Arms – N. *arms (see weapon)*; armament, munitions; armaments, arms race; nuclear deterrent, Star Wars, Strategic Defence Initiative, SDI 713 *defence*; gun-running; ballistics, rocketry, missilery, gunnery, musketry, archery.

arsenal, armoury, gun room; magazine, powder keg; caisson; cartridge belt, bandolier; quiver; scabbard, sheath; holster 194 *receptacle.*

weapon, deterrent; conventional weapon, nuclear w.; secret weapon, death ray, laser; germ warfare, chemical w.; poison gas, mustard g., nerve g. 659 *poison*; teeth, claws, nails 256 *sharp point.*

missile weapon, javelin, harpoon, dart; lasso; boomerang; arrow, poisoned a., shaft, bolt; arrowhead, barb; stone, brick; shot, ball, bullet, pellet, shell, shrapnel, rocket, MIRV (see *ammunition*); bow, longbow, crossbow, catapult, sling; blowpipe; bazooka, rocketthrower; cruise missile, guided m., ballistic m., ICBM, intercontinental ballistic missile, surface-to-air m., Exocet (tdmk) 287 *missile*; Star Wars.

club, mace, hammer; battering ram 279 *ram*; bat, staff, stave, stick, switch; life-preserver, bludgeon, truncheon, cudgel, shillelagh, sandbag, knuckleduster, cosh, bicycle chain, blunt instrument.

spear, harpoon, gaff; lance, javelin, pike, assegai; halberd 256 *sharp point.*

axe, battleaxe, tomahawk, hatchet, halberd, poleaxe, chopper 256 *sharp edge.*

sidearms, sword; broadsword, claymore; cutlass, swordstick; sabre, scimitar; blade, trusty b.; rapier; épée, foil;

dagger, bayonet, dirk, skean, skean-dhu, poniard, dudgeon, stiletto 256 *sharp point*; machete, kukri, kris, parang, panga; knife, bowie k., flick k. 256 *sharp edge.*

firearm, small arms, hand gun; matchlock, flintlock, fusil, musket; blunderbuss, carbine; rifle, Winchester; fowling piece, shotgun, sawn-off s., double-barrelled g., elephant g.; Enfield rifle, bore, calibre; muzzle; trigger, lock; magazine; breech, butt; sight, ramrod.

pistol, duelling p.; six-shooter, colt, revolver, repeater, rod, shooting iron, automatic.

gun, guns, cannonry, artillery; battery, broadside; cannon, bombard, carronade; mortar; field gun; great gun; Big Bertha; howitzer, minethrower, trench gun; antiaircraft gun; Bofors gun, bazooka; Gatling gun, Lewis gun, machine g., Bren g., submachine g., tommy g.; flamethrower; caisson; gun emplacement, rocket site, launching pad, silo.

ammunition, live a., ammo; round of ammunition; shot, grape s., buckshot; cannonball, bullet, soft-nosed b., dumdum b., rubber b., plastic b., baton round; projectile 287 *missile*; slug, stone, pellet; shell, shrapnel; flak, ack-ack; wad, cartridge; spent cartridge, dud; blank cartridge, blank; cartridge belt, cartridge case.

explosive, gunpowder; saltpetre, high explosive, lyddite, melinite, cordite, gun cotton, dynamite, gelignite, TNT, nitroglycerine; cap, detonator, fuse; priming, charge, warhead, atomic w.; fissionable material; fireworks.

bomb, shell, bombshell; grenade, hand g., Molotov cocktail; megaton bomb, atom b., A-bomb, nuclear b., hydrogen b., H-bomb; neutron b., enhanced radiation b.; mushroom cloud, fallout; blockbuster; cluster bomb, fragmentation b.; firebomb, incendiary bomb, napalm b.; mine, landmine; booby trap 542 *trap*; depth charge, torpedo; flying bomb, doodlebug; time bomb;

724 Arena – N. *arena,* field; ground; terrain; centre, scene, stage, theatre; hustings, platform, floor; amphitheatre, coliseum, stadium, stand, grandstand; campus, parade ground, training g.; forum, marketplace 76 *focus*; hippodrome, circus, course, racecourse, turf; racetrack, track, running t., cinder t., indoor t., dog t.; ring, bullring, boxing r., ropes; rink, skating r., ice r.; gymnasium, gym, exercise room, work-out r.; range, shooting r., rifle r., butts; playground, beach, swimming complex, lido, marina, pier, fairground 837 *pleasure ground*; leisure centre, recreation ground, playing field, football f., pitch, cricket p.; court, tennis c., badminton c., squash c.; putting green, bowling g., bowling alley, skittle a.; snooker club; beargarden; chessboard; bridge table; snooker t., pool t.; auction room.

battleground, battlefield, field of conflict, scene of action; theatre of war, combat zone, no-go area; front, front line, firing l., trenches, no-man's-land; disputed territory 718 *battle*.

Section five: Results of action

725 Completion – N. *completion,* finish, termination, conclusion, end of the matter 69 *end*; terminus 295 *goal*; issue, upshot 154 *event*; result, end r., final r., end product 157 *effect*; fullness 54 *completeness*; fulfilment 635 *sufficiency*; maturity, maturation, fruition, readiness; consummation, culmination, ne plus ultra 646 *perfection*; exhaustiveness, thoroughness 455 *attention*; elaboration, rounding off, finishing off, mopping up, winding up; topping out; top, crown 213 *summit*; missing link 627 *requirement*; last touch, crowning glory, final stroke, coup de grace; the icing on the cake, achievement, fait accompli, finished product; boiling point, danger p., breaking p., last straw 236 *limit*; climax, payoff; resolution, solution, dénouement, catastrophe, last act, final curtain, swansong, finale, finis 69 *finality*; execution,

implementation, accomplishment, achievement.

Adj. *completed,* full 54 *complete*; accomplished etc. vb.; elaborate 646 *perfect*; sewn up, buttoned up, in the can, in the bag, under one's belt, secured 727 *successful*.

Vb. *carry through,* follow t., follow up; drive home, clinch, seal, set the seal on; clear up, mop up, wipe up, finish off, polish off; dispose of, dispatch; complete, consummate, put the finishing touch, put the icing on the cake, top out 54 *make complete*; elaborate, hammer out, work o. 646 *perfect*; ripen, bring to a head, bring to the boil 669 *mature*; sit out, see out, see it through; get through, get shot of, dispose of, bring to its close drive a nail into the coffin 69 *terminate*; set at rest 266 *bring to rest*.

carry out, see through, effect, enact 676 *do*; dispatch, execute, discharge, implement, realize, bring about, accomplish, fulfil, consummate, achieve 727 *succeed*; make short work of; leave no loose ends, leave no stone unturned, not do by halves, go the whole hog, be in at the death; deliver the goods, bring home the bacon, be as good as one's word, fill the bill.

climax, cap, crown all 213 *crown*; culminate, peak, reach its peak; reach the zenith, reach a climax, scale the heights, conquer Everest; have an orgasm, come; reach boiling point, come to a crisis; reach the limit, put the lid on; come to fruition, achieve one's goal 295 *arrive*.

726 Noncompletion – N. *noncompletion,* neglect 458 *negligence*; nonfulfilment 636 *insufficiency*; deficit 307 *shortfall*; lack 55 *incompleteness*; immaturity 670 *undevelopment*; never-ending task, painting the Forth Bridge, a woman's work, Sisyphean labour, going round in circles, recurring decimal 71 *continuity*; superficiality, a lick and a promise 456 *inattention*; work undone, job half-done, loose ends; no result, drawn game, draw; stalemate, deadlock.

Adj. *uncompleted,* fragmentary 55 *incomplete*; unaccomplished; unrealized, half-done, half-finished, scamped 458 *neglected*; unripe 670 *immature*; superficial; left hanging, left in the air; lacking finish, not worked out, not thought through, sketchy 647 *imperfect*; unprocessed.

Vb. *not complete,* leave undone, leave in the air, leave hanging 458 *neglect*; skip, skive, scamp, do by halves, scotch the snake not kill it 655 *wound*; give up, not follow through; fall out, drop o., not stay the course; fall short of one's goal, fall down on 728 *fail*; defer, postpone.

727 Success – N. *success,* sweet smell of s., coming up roses, glory 866 *famousness*; happy ending; success story, progress 285 *progression*; breakthrough, quantum leap; one's day, landing on one's feet, run of luck, good fortune 730 *prosperity*; lead 34 *advantage*; flash in the pan; feat, achievement 676 *deed*; accomplishment, goal 725 *completion*; a success, feather in one's cap, triumph, hit, smash h., box-office h., top of the charts, chart-topper, best-seller, sell-out, howling success, succès fou, rave reviews; good shot 694 *skill*; beginner's luck, lucky stroke, fluke 618 *nondesign*; hat trick, stroke of genius, coup, tour de force, masterstroke 694 *masterpiece*; trump, trump card; pass, qualification.

victory, beating, licking, trouncing 728 *defeat*; conquest; taking by storm 712 *attack*; the best of it; win, game, set and match; outright win, checkmate; narrow win, Pyrrhic victory; runaway victory, love game, walkover, pushover, picnic 701 *easy thing*; crushing victory, slam, grand s.; knockout, KO; upper hand, whip h., advantage, edge, pole position; triumph, ovation, standing o., bouquets.

victor, winner, champion, medallist, prizewinner, dux, first, double f. 644 *exceller*; winning side, the winners; conquering hero; conqueror, vanquisher; master *or* mistress of the field, master *or* mistress of the situation; a success, man

or woman to watch, whiz kid, rising star 730 *prosperous person.*

Adj. *successful,* effective, efficacious; fruitful 640 *profitable*; felicitous 694 *skilful*; foolproof; home and dry 725 *completed*; prizewinning, victorious, world-beating, chart-topping 644 *excellent*; winning, leading; on top, in the ascendant, rising, on the up and up, going places, sitting pretty 730 *prosperous*; triumphant; triumphal, victorious; crowned with success, flushed with victory.

Vb. *succeed,* succeed in, effect, accomplish, achieve; be successful, make out, win one's spurs; make a success of, make a go of, make short work of, rise to the occasion; make good, rise, do well, pull oneself up by one's bootstraps, become a self-made man *or* woman, get promotion, work one's way up the ladder, come to the top 730 *prosper*; pass, make the grade, qualify, graduate, come off well, land on one's feet, give a good account of oneself, come well out of it, come off with flying colours, come out on top, have the best of it 34 *be superior*; advance, break through, make a breakthrough 285 *progress*; reach one's goal, obtain one's objective; pull it off, bring it off, be as good as one's word, bring home the bacon; have a success, score a s.; make the big time, make a hit, top the charts, make a kill, go over big; hit the jackpot, break the bank; score a point, win a p., carry a p.; carry the day; arrive, be a success, make one's mark, click.

be successful, do the trick, fill the bill; turn up trumps, rise to the occasion; do the job, do wonders, do marvels, work miracles; work, work like magic, act like a charm 173 *operate*; take effect 178 *influence*; pay off, pay dividends, bear fruit 171 *be fruitful*; hit it, hit the nail on the head, find the mot juste; play one's hand well, not put a foot wrong, never go w., not be wrong-footed; keep on the right side of; have the ball at one's feet, hold all the trumps; have the world in his *or* her hand; be irresistible, not know the meaning of failure, brush obstacles aside

701 *do easily*; not know when one is beaten, land on one's feet, come up smiling, come up smelling of roses 599 *be resolute*; hold one's own 599 *stand firm*.

triumph, have one's day, be crowned with success, wear the laurels of victory 876 *celebrate*; crow, crow over 877 *boast*; score, score off, be one up on; triumph over difficulties, manage, make it, win through; overcome obstacles; find a loophole, find a way out, find a way round 667 *escape*; make headway against, stem the tide, weather the storm 715 *resist*; reap the fruits 771 *gain.*

overmaster, be too much for, be more than a match for 34 *be superior*; master, overcome, overpower, overthrow, overturn, override 306 *outdo*; have the advantage, seize the a., prevail 34 *predominate*; have one on the hip, have someone where one wants him *or* her, have one by the short hairs; have at one's mercy; checkmate, trump; conquer, vanquish, quell, subdue, subject, suppress, put down, crush 745 *subjugate*; capture, take by s.

defeat, discomfit, dash, put another's nose out of joint, settle one's hash, cook one's goose; repulse, rebuff 292 *repel*; best, be too good for, get the better of, get the upper hand, get the whip h. 34 *be superior*; worst, outplay, outpoint, outflank, outmanoeuvre, outclass, outwit, outshine 306 *outdo*; disconcert, cut the ground from under one's feet, lay by the heels 702 *obstruct*; baffle, nonplus 474 *puzzle*; knock spots off, wipe the floor with; beat, lick, thrash, trounce, crush, give a drubbing, trample underfoot, beat hollow, rout, put to flight, scatter 75 *disperse*; silence, put the lid on 165 *suppress*; flatten, knock the stuffing out of, put out for the count, knock out; knock for six, hit for s.; bowl out; drive to the wall, check, put in check 661 *endanger*; put an end to, wipe out, do for, settle, fix, dish 165 *destroy*; sink; break, bankrupt, beggar 801 *impoverish.*

win, win the battle, carry the day, achieve victory, defeat the enemy; be victorious, claim the victory; come off

best, come off with flying colours; win hands down, carry all before one, have it all one's own way, romp home, have a walkover, walk off with, waltz away with, walk it 701 *do easily*; win on points, win by a short head, win by a whisker, scrape home; win the last battle, win the last round; win the match, take the prize, gain the palm, wear the laurel wreath; become champion, beat all comers, sweep the board, rule OK 34 *be superior.*

728 Failure – N. *failure,* lack of success; no luck, off day 731 *misfortune*; nonfulfilment 726 *noncompletion*; frustration 702 *hindrance*; vain attempt, abortive a., wild-goose chase, futile effort, no result 641 *lost labour*; bungle 695 *bungling*; abortion, miscarriage 172 *unproductiveness*; damp squib, washout, fiasco, flop; slip, omission, faux pas 495 *mistake*; no go, halt 145 *stop*; engine failure, electrical fault, computer f., machine malfunction, gremlin, bug, breakdown 702 *hitch*; collapse, fall 309 *descent*; losses 772 *loss*; bankruptcy 805 *insolvency.*

defeat, bafflement 474 *uncertainty*; deadlock, stalemate 145 *stop*; repulse, rebuff, bloody nose, check, reverse; checkmate; the worst of it, discomfiture, stick, flak, beating, drubbing, hiding, licking, thrashing, trouncing; retreat; flight 290 *recession*; stampede; rout, landslide; fall, downfall, collapse, débâcle; lost cause, losing battle; deathblow, nail in the coffin, quietus; Waterloo.

loser, also-ran, nonstarter; has-been, dud, failure, flop, no-hoper, lemon; born loser 731 *unlucky person*; underdog 35 *inferior*; dropout 25 *misfit*; bankrupt 805 *nonpayer*; losing side.

Adj. *unsuccessful,* vain, fruitless; dud, misfired; miscarried, stillborn, aborted, abortive; ditched; manqué, failed, bombed, ploughed, flunked; out of one's depth, losing one's grip 474 *uncertain.*

defeated, beaten, bested, worsted, done for; baffled, thwarted, foiled 702 *hindered*; dashed, discomfited, hoist

with one's own petard; outmanoeuvred, outplayed, outvoted; outwitted, outclassed, outshone 35 *inferior*; thrashed, licked; on the losing side, out of the running; in retreat; routed, put to flight; sunk; overthrown, had it, knocked out, kaput, brought low, fallen; captured.

Vb. *fail,* have no success; be unsuccessful, - beaten etc. adj.; bomb, flop; fall down on, botch, bungle 495 *blunder*; flunk, not make the grade, be found wanting 636 *not suffice*; miss the boat 138 *lose a chance*; go wide, miss, hit the wrong target, fall between two stools, miss an opportunity 282 *deviate*; get nothing out of it, get no change out of it, draw a blank, back the wrong horse, return empty-handed, labour in vain, have shot one's bolt 641 *waste effort*; kiss goodbye to 772 *lose*; overreach oneself, bite off more than one can chew, come a cropper, fall, collapse, slide 309 *tumble*; break down, malfunction, come to pieces, fall to bits, come unstuck; falter, stall, seize up, pack up, conk out; stop, come to a dead stop, come up against a blank wall, come to a dead end; stick, get bogged down 145 *cease*; come to a sticky end, come to a bad e. 655 *deteriorate*; go on the rocks, run aground, be left high and dry, make a loss, crash, go bust, go bankrupt 805 *not pay*.

miscarry, be stillborn, abort; misfire; crash 309 *tumble*; not come off, come to naught, come to nothing, go by the board; fall flat, come to grief; blow up, go up in smoke; flop, bomb, prove a fiasco; go wrong, go awry, gang agley, take a turn for the worse, take an ugly turn; do no good, make things worse 832 *aggravate*.

be defeated, lose, lose out, suffer defeat, take a beating, lose the day, lose the battle, lose the match; lose the election, concede defeat, lose one's seat, lose the vote, be outvoted; lose by a whisker, get pipped at the post; be in a catch-22 situation; be on a hiding to nothing; get the worst of it, come off second best, go off with one's tail between one's legs, lick one's wounds; be taken to the cleaner's; lose hands down, come in last; bite the

dust; fall; be captured, fall a prey to; retreat, lose ground 290 *recede*; take to flight 620 *run away*; admit defeat, had enough, cry quits 721 *submit*; have not a leg to stand on, have the ground cut from under one's feet; go to the wall.

729 Trophy – **N.** *trophy,* spoils of war, captives 790 *booty*; scalp, battle, scars, wounds 655 *wound*; memorial, war m., memento 505 *reminder*; triumphal arch 548 *monument*; triumph, ovation, standing o. 876 *celebration*; plum, glittering prizes; benefit match; prize, consolation p., booby p., wooden spoon 962 *reward*; sports trophy, Ashes, cup, shield; award, Oscar a., Tony a., Emmy a., golden disc, laurels, crown, garland, wreath, palm of victory; pat on the back; bouquet; feather in one's cap.

decoration, battle honours, spurs 866 *honours*; citation, mention in dispatches; rosette, ribbon, sash, cordon bleu; blue, oar, cap; medal, cross, garter, order; service stripe, long-service medal, war m., campaign m.; Victoria Cross, VC, Military C., Croix de Guerre, Iron Cross; Distinguished Service Cross, Congressional Medal, Medal of Honour; George Cross, Legion of Honour, civic crown; honours list.

730 Prosperity – **N.** *prosperity,* thriving, health and wealth; well-being, welfare; economic prosperity, booming economy, boom; roaring trade, seller's market, bullish m., luxury, affluence, Easy Street 800 *wealth*; golden touch, Midas t.; fleshpots, fat of the land, milk and honey 635 *plenty*; auspiciousness, good fortune; bonanza, winning streak, luck, run of l., good l., break, lucky b., lucky gamble, lucky shot, luck of the draw 159 *chance*.

palmy days, heyday, prime, peak, zenith, halcyon days, summer, fair weather, Indian summer; life of Riley, place in the sun, clover, velvet, bed of roses, roses all the way 376 *euphoria*; Golden Age 824 *happiness*.

prosperous person, man *or* woman of substance, man *or* woman of property, fat cat 800 *rich person*; whiz kid; entrepreneur, nouveau riche, profiteer; celebrity.

Adj. *prosperous,* thriving, flourishing, booming 727 *successful*; rising, doing well, up and coming, on the up and up, in the ascendant, going up in the world; on the make, profiteering; well set-up, established, well-to-do, well-off, well-heeled, rolling in it, affluent, comfortable, comfortably off 800 *moneyed*; riding on the crest of a wave, buoyant, bullish; fortunate, lucky, born with a silver spoon in one's mouth, born under a lucky star; in clover, on velvet; on easy street, in the money, fat.

palmy, balmy, halcyon, golden, rosy; blissful; providential, favourable, promising, auspicious, propitious, cloudless, clear, fine, fair, set f.; glorious, euphoric.

Vb. *prosper,* thrive, flourish, do well, have a good time of it 376 *enjoy*; bask in sunshine, make hay, live in clover, lie on velvet, have it easy, live on easy street, have it made, live on milk and honey, live on the fat of the land, 'never have had it so good'; be in the money, be rolling in it; be well-heeled, batten on, grow fat; blossom, bloom, flower 171 *be fruitful*; boom, drive a roaring trade, enjoy a seller's market; profiteer 771 *gain*; get on, go far, rise in the world, work one's way up, make it, arrive 727 *succeed*; make money, make a fortune, strike it rich, make one's pile, feather one's nest line one's pockets, 800 *get rich*; run smoothly; go on swimmingly.

have luck, have all the l., have a stroke of l., have a lucky break, have a run of luck; strike lucky, strike oil, be on to a good thing, get on the gravy train; fall on one's feet, bear a charmed life, be born under a lucky star, be born with a silver spoon in one's mouth, have the ball at one's feet.

be auspicious, - propitious etc. adj.; promise well, augur well, set fair; look kindly on, smile on, bless.

Int. good luck! all the best! best of British!

731 Adversity – **N.** *adversity,* adverse circumstances, misfortune; continual struggle; hardship, hard life, tough time 825 *suffering*; travail 377 *pain*; hard times, hell upon earth, vale of sorrows 616 *evil*; burden, load, pressure, pressure of the times; ups and downs of life, vicissitude 154 *event*; troubles, sea of t., trials, cares, worries 825 *worry*; wretchedness, misery, despondency, Slough of Despond 834 *dejection*; bitter pill 872 *humiliation*; cross 825 *sorrow*; curse, blight, plague, scourge, infliction, visitation 659 *bane*; bleakness, cold wind, draught, chill, cold, winter 380 *coldness*; gloom 418 *darkness*; ill wind; blow, hard b. 704 *opposition*; setback, check, rebuff, reverse 728 *defeat*; pinch, plight, poor lookout, trouble ahead; trough, bad patch, rainy day 655 *deterioration*; slump, recession, depression 679 *inactivity*; storm clouds, gathering c. 900 *threat*; decline, downfall 165 *ruin*; want, need, distress, extremity 801 *poverty*.

misfortune, bad luck, hard luck; no luck 728 *failure*; evil star 645 *badness*; raw deal; hard lines; ill hap, mishap, misadventure, contretemps, accident, casualty 159 *chance*; disaster, calamity, catastrophe, the pits.

unlucky person, no-hoper, poor risk; star-crossed lover, plaything of the gods, Jonah; down-and-out 728 *loser*; underdog 35 *inferior*; lame dog, lame duck 163 *weakling*; scapegoat, victim.

Adj. *adverse,* hostile, ominous, sinister, inauspicious, unfavourable; disadvantageous, antipathetic, bleak, cold, hard; opposed, contrary, opposing; malign 645 *harmful*; ruinous 165 *destructive*; disastrous, calamitous, catastrophic.

unprosperous, in poor shape, out of kilter; not doing well, badly off 801 *poor*; in trouble, up against it, in adverse circumstances, with one's back to the wall, declining, on the wane, on the down

grade, on the slippery slope, on the road to ruin; in a bad way, in dire straits.

unfortunate, ill-fated, unlucky, ill-starred, star-crossed; luckless, hapless, poor, wretched, forlorn, miserable, unhappy; stricken, doomed, accursed; out of luck, down on one's luck; born under an evil star; accident-prone.

Vb. *have trouble,* be in t.; have no luck, get more kicks than ha'pence; get more bricks than bouquets; be in for it, go through it, be hard pressed, be up against it, strike a bad patch 825 *suffer*; come to grief 728 *miscarry*; feel the pinch, feel the draught, fall on evil days, have seen better d. 801 *be poor*; go downhill, go down in the world, decline 655 *deteriorate*; sink 313 *founder*; come to a bad end 728 *fail*; go to rack and ruin, go to the dogs 165 *be destroyed.*

732 Averageness – N. *averageness,* mediocrity 30 *average*; golden mean, neither too much nor too little; middle class; suburbia, common man, everyman, man in the street, joe soap 869 *commoner*; hoi polloi

Adj. *middling,* average, mediocre; neither good nor bad, ordinary, commonplace 30 *median*; middle-of-the-road 177 *moderate*; undistinguished, nothing special, fair, fair to middling; so-so, comme ci comme ça, adequate; tolerable, passable, fifty-fifty, much of a muchness; medium, middle, grey 625 *neutral.*

Vb. *be middling,* - mediocre etc. adj.; jog on, manage well enough, never set the Thames on fire, never set the heather on fire.

5.2 SOCIAL VOLITION

Section one: General social volition

733 Authority – N. *authority,* power;

368

powers that be, 'they', the Establishment, ruling classes, Big Brother 741 *master*; the Government, the Administration, Whitehall 690 *director*; right, divine r., prerogative, royal p.; law, rightful power; legislative assembly 692 *parliament*; regency, committee 751 *commission*; office, place; portfolio 955 *jurisdiction*; power behind the throne 178 *influence*; credit; leadership 689 *directorship*; ascendance, supremacy 34 *superiority*; pride of place, seniority, priority 64 *precedence*; majesty, royalty, crown 868 *nobility*; authoritativeness.

governance, rule, sway, reins of government, direction, command 689 *directorship*; control; hold, grip, clutches 778 *retention*; domination, mastery, whip hand, long arm; ascendancy, dominion, sovereignty, raj, overlordship, presidency, supremacy 34 *superiority*; reign, regency, dynasty; foreign rule, empire 745 *subjection*; imperialism, colonialism, white supremacy, black power; regime, regiment, regimen; state control, paternalism; bureaucracy, apparat, civil service, officialism, beadledom, bumbledom, red tape, bumf; Parkinson's law 197 *expansion.*

despotism, paternalism; tyranny; dictatorship, Caesarism, tsarism, Stalinism; autocracy, absolute monarchy; totalitarianism; police state, rule of terror 735 *brute force.*

government, direction 689 *management*; politics; constitutionalism, rule of law 953 *legality*; misgovernment 734 *anarchy*; theocracy, papal rule, hierocracy, clericalism 985 *ecclesiasticism*; monarchy, constitutional m.; republicanism, federalism; tribal system, tribalism, clan system; patriarchy, matriarchate; feudalism; benevolent despotism, paternalism; aristocracy, meritocracy, oligarchy, elitism; gynocracy 373 *womankind*; gerontocracy; triumvirate; plutocracy; representative government, parliamentary g., government by the ballot box, party system 708 *political party*, 605 *vote*; democracy, egalitarianism, government of

the people, by the people, for the people; demagogy, vox populi; majority rule, one man one vote, proportional representation; pluralism, collectivism, proletarianism; communism, Leninism, Maoism; Bolshevism, Fascism, Nazism; committee rule, sovietism; military government, martial law; mob rule, anarchy; socialism, Fabianism; bureaucracy, technocracy; self-government, autonomy, home rule 744 *independence*; puppet government 628 *instrument*; caretaker government, regency, interregnum; mandate.

position of authority, high office, kingship, tsardom, royalty, regency, protectorship; chieftainship, sheikhdom, emirate, lordship, sultanate, caliphate, governorship, viceroyalty; consulate, consulship, proconsulate, prefecture, tribunate, magistracy; mayoralty, aldermanship; headship, presidency, premiership, chairmanship 689 *directorship*; overlordship, superintendency, inspectorship; mastership; Big Brother; government post, Cabinet seat; seat of government.

political organization, body politic; state, commonwealth; country, realm, kingdom, republic, city state, city; federation, confederation; principality, duchy, archduchy, dukedom; empire, dominion, colony, dependency, protectorate, mandate, mandated territory 184 *territory*; communist bloc, Third World 184 *region*; superpower 34 *superiority*; banana republic 35 *inferiority*; buffer state 231 *interjacency*; province, county 184 *district*; welfare state.

Adj. *authoritative,* empowered, sanctioned, approved, competent; in office, in authority, magisterial, official, ex officio; mandatory, binding, compulsory 740 *compelling*; magistral, masterful, domineering; commanding, lordly, dignified, majestic; overruling, imperious, bossy; peremptory, arbitrary, absolute, autocratic, tyrannical, dictatorial, totalitarian 735 *authoritarian*; powerful 162

strong; leading 178 *influential*; preeminent, preponderant, predominant, dominant, paramount 34 *supreme*; Big Brotherish.

ruling, reigning; sovereign, on the throne; royal, regal, majestic, kinglike, kingly, queenly, princely, lordly; imperial; magisterial; governing, controlling, dictating etc. vb.

governmental, gubernatorial, political, constitutional; administrative, ministerial, official, bureaucratic, centralized; technocratic; matriarchal, patriarchal; monarchical, feudal, aristocratic, oligarchic, plutocratic, democratic, popular, classless, republican; self-governing, autonomous 744 *independent*; anarchy.

Vb. *rule,* hold sway, reign, reign supreme, wear the crown, wield the sceptre; govern, control 737 *command*; manage, hold the reins, hold office 689 *direct*; be in power, have authority, wield power, exercise authority, exert a., use one's a.; rule absolutely, tyrannize 735 *oppress*; dictate, lay down the law; keep order, police.

take authority, ascend the throne, succeed to the t., take office, assume command; take over the reigns; assume authority, form a government; gain power, take control; seize power, usurp.

dominate, turn the scale, hold all the aces, hold all the cards 34 *predominate*; lord it over, boss, rule the roost, be queen bee, wear the trousers, be in the driving seat, be in the saddle 737 *command*; have the upper hand, have the whip h., call the tune, call the shots 727 *overmaster*; have in one's power, have over a barrel; lead by the nose, twist round one's little finger, have under one's thumb, have one by the short hairs, bend to one's will, hold in the palm of one's hand 178 *influence*; drive 735 *be severe*; dictate, coerce 740 *compel*; hold down, ride roughshod over 745 *subjugate*; override, overrule, have it all one's own way.

734 Laxity: absence of authority – N. *laxity,* slackness, remissness, indifference 458 *negligence;* laissez-faire 744 *scope;* informality, lack of ceremony 769 *nonobservance;* looseness, relaxation, derestriction 746 *liberation;* decentralization 46 *disunion;* indulgence, toleration, licence, permissiveness 736 *leniency;* line of least resistance 721 *submission;* weak will, feeble grasp, weak administration, crumbling power 163 *weakness;* no drive, no push, inertia 175 *inertness;* no control, policy of nonintervention, abdication of authority, surrender of control 753 *resignation;* renunciation 621 *relinquishment.*

anarchy, breakdown of law and order; free-for-all, every man for himself, dog-eat-dog; disorder, disorganization, chaos 61 *turmoil;* anarchism 769 *nonobservance;* mob rule, mob law, lynch l. 954 *lawlessness.*

Adj. *lax,* loose, slack; disorganized; feeble, soft, wet, wimpish 163 *weak;* slipshod, remiss 458 *negligent;* relaxed, informal, free-and-easy; permissive, tolerant, undemanding 736 *lenient;* unassertive.

Vb. *be lax,* give one his *or* her head, give rope enough 744 *give scope;* waive the rules, stretch a point; tolerate, put up with; laisser faire, laisser aller 756 *permit;* let one get away with, not say boo to a goose; spoonfeed, featherbed, indulge, spoil 736 *be lenient;* make concessions 770 *compromise;* relax 46 *disunite;* lose control. reduce to chaos 63 *derange.*

735 Severity – N. *severity,* rigorousness, strictness, stringency; formalism; rigidity, inflexibility 326 *hardness;* discipline, strong hand, iron h., tight grasp 733 *authority;* rod of iron, heavy hand, Draconian laws; harshness, rigour, extremity, extremes; letter of the law, pound of flesh; intolerance, rigorism; censorship; puritanism 950 *prudery;* infliction, visitation, inquisition, persecution, exploitation, harassment, oppression; callousness, inclemency, mercilessness, pitilessness; harsh treatment, the hard way, tender mercies, cruelty 898 *inhumanity;* austerity 945 *asceticism.*

brute force, show of force; big battalions, gunboat diplomacy 160 *power;* coercion, bludgeoning 740 *compulsion;* violence; subjugation 745 *subjection;* autocracy, dictatorship 733 *despotism;* tyranny; Fascism, Nazism, totalitarianism; Prussianism, militarism; martial law, iron rule, iron hand, mailed fist, jackboot, bludgeon.

tyrant, petty tyrant; disciplinarian, martinet, sergeant major; militarist, jackboot; hanging judge; heavy father, Dutch uncle; Big Brother, authoritarian, despot, dictator 741 *autocrat;* boss, inquisitor, persecutor; oppressor, bully, taskmaster, slave-driver; bloodsucker; ogre, brute 938 *monster.*

Adj. *severe,* austere, Spartan 945 *ascetic;* strict, rigorous, extreme; strait-laced, puritanical, prudish, old-maidish; donnish, pedagogic, hide-bound; formalistic, pedantic; bigoted, fanatical; hypercritical 862 *fastidious;* intolerant, censorious 924 *disapproving;* unbending, stiff-necked, rigid 326 *hard;* hard as nails, hard-headed, hard-boiled, flinty, dour; inflexible, obdurate, uncompromising 602 *obstinate;* inexorable, relentless, merciless, unsparing, implacable, unforgiving 906 *pitiless;* heavy, stern, stiff; punitive; stringent, Draconian, drastic, savage.

authoritarian, masterful, domineering, lordly, arrogant, haughty 878 *insolent;* despotic, absolute, arbitrary; totalitarian, Fascist; dictatorial, Big Brotherish, autocratic; undemocratic; coercive, compulsive 740 *compelling;* bossy, nannyish.

oppressive, hard on 914 *unjust;* tyrannical, despotic; tyrannous, harsh, exigent, exacting, extortionate, persecuting, inquisitorial, unsparing; high-handed, overbearing, domineering; heavy-handed, Draconian, brutal, ogreish 898 *cruel.*

Vb. *be severe,* - harsh, - strict etc. adj.; be cruel to be kind; bear hard on; keep a tight rein on 747 *restrain;* be down on,

have a down on; come down on, come down like a ton of bricks, crack down on, stamp on, put a stop to, clamp down on 165 *suppress*; persecute, hunt down 619 *pursue*; ill-treat, mishandle, abuse 675 *misuse*; get tough with, pull no punches; take off the gloves, rule with an iron hand, inflict; mete out stern punishment; have one's pound of flesh; harden one's heart, show no mercy, take Draconian measures 906 *be pitiless*; give no quarter, put to the sword 362 *slaughter*.

oppress, tyrannize, play the tyrant, be despotic, abuse one's authority; domineer, lord it; overawe, intimidate, terrorize 854 *frighten*; bludgeon 740 *compel*; boss around, put upon; bully, be always on one's back, harass, plague, hassle 827 *torment*; persecute, victimize 898 *be malevolent*; break, crush the spirit, take the heart out of, tame 369 *break in*; tax 684 *fatigue*; overtax, exploit, extort, suck, squeeze, grind, grind the faces of the poor; trample, tread down, tread underfoot, stamp on, hold down 165 *suppress*; enslave 745 *subjugate*; ride roughshod, inflict injustice 914 *do wrong*; rule with an iron hand, rule with a rod of iron; take Draconian measures; whip, scourge, put the screws on 963 *torture*; shed blood 362 *murder*; be heavy, weigh on, burden, crush 322 *weigh*.

736 Leniency – N. *leniency*, lenience; mildness, gentleness, tenderness; forbearance, easygoingness, longsuffering 823 *patience*; pardon 909 *forgiveness*; quarter, mercy, lenity, clemency, mercifulness, compassion 905 *pity*; humanity, kindness 897 *benevolence*; indulgence, toleration; moderation; light rein, velvet glove, kid gloves.

Adj. *lenient*, soft, gentle, mild; indulgent, tolerant; moderate, easy, easy-going, undemanding 734 *lax*; longsuffering 823 *patient*; clement, merciful; tender 905 *pitying*.

Vb. *be lenient*, make few demands; go easy, handle with kid gloves 177 *moderate*; featherbed, spoonfeed, spoil, indulge, play the fond parent, humour 889

pet; stretch a point; forbear 823 *be patient*; pity, spare, give quarter 905 *show mercy*; pardon 909 *forgive*; relax.

737 Command – N. *command,* royal c., summons; commandment, ordinance; injunction, imposition; dictation, bidding, behest; dictum, say-so 532 *affirmation*; charge, commission, appointment 751 *mandate*; instructions, manifesto, rules, regulations, code of practice; brief 524 *information*; directive, order, order of the day, marching orders; word of command, word; beck, nod, sign 547 *gesture*; signal, bugle call, trumpet c. 547 *call*; whip, three-line w.; dictate 740 *compulsion*; ban, embargo; counterorder 752 *abrogation*.

decree, edict, ipse dixit; law, canon, prescript 693 *precept*; bull, papal decree; circular, encyclical; ordinance; decree nisi, decree absolute; decision 480 *judgment*; enactment, act 953 *legislation*; plebiscite, manifesto, electoral mandate 605 *vote*; dictate, diktat.

demand, claim, requisition 761 *request*; notice, warning n., final n., final demand, ultimatum; blackmail 900 *threat*; imposition, exaction, levy, tax demand 809 *tax*.

warrant, search w., authorization, written authority, passport 756 *permit*; writ, summons, subpoena, citation, habeas corpus 959 *legal process*.

Adj. *commanding,* imperative, categorical, dictatorial; mandatory, obligatory, peremptory, compulsive 740 *compelling*; authoritative; decisive, conclusive, final; demanding, insistent, hectoring.

Vb. *command,* bid, invite; order, tell, issue a command, give an order, lay down the law; signal, call, nod, beck, motion, sign, make a s. 547 *gesticulate*; wink, give a cue, tip the wink 524 *hint*; direct, give a directive, instruct, brief, circularize; rule, lay down, enjoin; give a mandate, charge, call upon 751 *commission*; impose, lay upon, set a task, make obligatory 917 *impose a duty*; detail; call

together, rally, convene 74 *bring together*; send for, summon; cite, subpoena, issue a writ 959 *litigate*; remand; dictate, take a strong line, put one's foot down 740 *compel*; countermand 752 *abrogate*; lay an embargo, ban, impose a ban, taboo, declare t., proscribe 757 *prohibit*.

decree, promulgate 528 *proclaim*; declare, say so, lay down the law 532 *affirm*; signify one's will and pleasure, prescribe, ordain 608 *predetermine*; enact, pass a law, legislate, decriminalize 953 *make legal*; pass judgment, give j., give a ruling 480 *judge*.

demand, require, requisition 627 *require*; order, indent 761 *request*; make demands on, send a final demand, issue a final warning, give final notice, present an ultimatum, demand with threats, blackmail 900 *threaten*; present one's claim, make claims upon, demand payment, dun, sue, bill, invoice; charge 809 *price*; exact, levy 809 *tax*.

738 Disobedience – N. *disobedience,* indiscipline, recalcitrance, refractoriness 598 *unwillingness*; naughtiness, misbehaviour, mischief-making, monkey tricks; delinquency 934 *wickedness*; insubordination, mutinousness, mutineering; defiance; noncompliance 769 *nonobservance*; disloyalty, defection, desertion 918 *undutifulness*; infraction, infringement, criminality, crime, sin 936 *guilty act*; civil disobedience, passive resistance 715 *resistance*; conscientious objection 704 *opposition*; obstructionism 702 *hindrance*; seditiousness; wildness 954 *lawlessness*.

revolt, mutiny; strike; faction 709 *dissension*; breakaway, secession 978 *schism*; defection 603 *change of mind*; restiveness 318 *agitation*; sabotage 165 *destruction*; breach of the peace, riot, street r., rioting, gang warfare, streetfighting, tumult 61 *turmoil*; rebellion, insurrection, rising, uprising 176 *outbreak*; putsch, coup d'état; resistance movement, insurgency 715 *resistance*; subversion 149 *revolution*; terrorism

954 *lawlessness*; civil war 718 *war*; anarchy; regicide, tyrannicide 362 *homicide*.

sedition, seditiousness; intrigue 623 *plot*; agitprop, subversion, infiltration, fifth-columnism; spying, espionage, underground activities 523 *latency*; terrorism, anarchism, nihilism; treason, high t., lese-majesty 930 *perfidy*.

revolter, mutineer, rebel; demonstrator, striker, picketer 705 *opponent*; secessionist, seceder, splinter group, rebel g. 978 *schismatic*; dissident 829 *malcontent*; blackleg, scab 84 *nonconformist*; maverick, lone wolf; seditionary, seditionist; traitor, Quisling, fifth columnist, infiltrator, spy, industrial spy 603 *tergiversator*; insurrectionist, insurgent; guerrilla, urban g., partisan; resistance, underground, Maquis; Black Panther, Black Muslim, Rastafarian; Provisional, Provo; extremist, Jacobin, Bolshevist, Trotskyist, red 149 *revolutionist*; counter-revolutionary, reactionary, monarchist, White Russian, terrorist, anarchist, nihilist; mafia.

agitator, agent provocateur; agitprop, protester, demonstrator, marcher; soapbox orator, tub-thumper, ranter, rabblerouser; firebrand, mischief-maker 663 *troublemaker*; seditionist; ringleader.

rioter, street r., urban guerrilla, bovver boy, boot boy, brawler, rowdy 904 *ruffian*; saboteur, Luddite.

Adj. *disobedient,* undisciplined; naughty, mischievous, misbehaving; unbiddable, difficult, self-willed, wayward, unruly, unmanageable 176 *violent*; intractable, ungovernable 598 *unwilling*; insubordinate, mutinous, rebellious, bolshie, bloody-minded; contrary 704 *opposing*; nonconformist 84 *unconformable*; uncompliant 769 *nonobservant*; recalcitrant 715 *resisting*; challenging 711 *defiant*; refractory, perverse 602 *obstinate*; subversive, revolutionary, reactionary; seditious; traitorous, treasonous; untamed.

Vb. *disobey,* be disobedient, misbehave, get into mischief; flout authority, not comply with 769 *not observe*; not do

as one is told, disobey orders, show insubordination 711 *defy*; defy the whip; cock a snook, snap one's fingers, fly in the face of 704 *oppose*; break the law, commit a crime 954 *be illegal*; violate, infringe, transgress, trespass 306 *encroach*; kick, chafe, fret, champ at the bit, play up; kick over the traces, take the bit between one's teeth, bolt, take French leave, go AWOL, go walkabout, take the law into one's own hands, be a law unto oneself.

revolt, rebel, mutiny; down tools, strike, take industrial action, come out 145 *cease*; sabotage 702 *obstruct*; undermine, work underground; secede, break away; betray 603 *tergiversate*; agitate, demonstrate, protest 762 *deprecate*; create, create a row, kick up a stink, raise Cain, start a riot, stage a revolt, lead a rebellion 715 *resist*; rise up, rise in arms, throw off the yoke, throw off one's shackles, overthrow.

739 Obedience – N. *obedience*, compliance 768 *observance*; meekness, biddability, tractability, pliancy, malleability 327 *softness*; willingness; nonresistance, submissiveness, acquiescence 721 *submission*; passiveness 679 *inactivity*; dutifulness, discipline 917 *duty*; deference, obsequiousness, slavishness 879 *servility*; tameness, docility.

loyalty, constancy, devotion, fidelity, faithfulness, good faith 929 *probity*; allegiance, fealty.

Adj. *obedient*, compliant, cooperating, conforming 768 *observant*; loyal, faithful, steadfast, constant; devoted, dedicated, sworn; submissive 721 *submitting*; law-abiding 717 *peaceful*; amenable, docile; good, well-behaved; daughterly; acquiescent, passive 679 *inactive*; meek, sheep-like, biddable, like putty in one's hands, dutiful; at one's beck and call, on a string, on a lead, puppet-like, under one's thumb, under control; disciplined, regimented 917 *obliged*; trained, manageable, tame; obsequious 879 *servile*.

Vb. *obey*, comply, act upon 768 *observe*; do the needful, sign on the dotted line, toe the l., come to heel 83 *conform*; assent 758 *consent*; listen, heed, obey orders, do as one is told; put oneself at one's service 597 *be willing*; obey the whip, follow the party line; do one's bidding, wait upon, follow, follow like a sheep, follow to the world's end 742 *serve*; be loyal, bear allegiance, pay homage 768 *keep faith*; pay tribute 745 *be subject*; make oneself useful, do sterling service 703 *minister to*; defer to, be submissive 721 *submit*.

740 Compulsion – N. *compulsion*, needs must 596 *necessity*; law of nature 953 *law*; act of God; moral compulsion 917 *conscience*; Hobson's choice 606 *no choice*; carrot and stick; coercion, regimentation; arm-twisting, blackmail 900 *threat*; sanctions 963 *penalty*; constraint, duress, force, physical f.; big stick, strongarm tactics 735 *brute force*; force-feeding; pressgang, conscription, call-up, draft 718 *war measures*; extortion; slavery, forced labour.

Adj. *compelling*, compulsive, of necessity, unavoidable, inevitable 596 *necessary*; imperative 737 *commanding*; compulsory, mandatory, binding 917 *obligatory*; urgent, pressing; coercive; forceful, cogent.

Vb. *compel*, constrain, coerce 176 *force*; enforce, put into force; dictate, necessitate, oblige, bind; order 737 *command*; impose 917 *impose a duty*; make one, leave no option; leave no escape, pin down, tie d.; impress, draft, conscript; drive, dragoon, regiment, discipline; force one's hand, apply pressure, bulldoze, steamroller, railroad, stampede, pressgang, bully into; bludgeon 735 *oppress*; take by force, requisition, commandeer, extort, exact, wring from, drag f. 786 *take*; apply pressure, lean on, squeeze, take the gloves off, turn the heat on, put the screws on, twist one's arm 963 *torture*; blackmail, hijack, hold to ransom 900 *threaten*; be peremptory, insist, make a point of, press, urge 532

emphasize; brook no denial, not take no for an answer 532 *affirm*; force upon, ram down one's throat, inflict, foist, fob off on; force-feed; hold back 747 *restrain*.

Adv. *by force,* under pressure, under protest, under duress; forcibly, willy-nilly, at gunpoint, at knifepoint.

741 Master – N. *master,* mistress; master *or* mistress of, captor, possessor 776 *owner*; sire, lord, lady, dame; liege, lord, overlord; protector 707 *patron*; seigneur, lord *or* lady of the manor, squire, laird 868 *aristocrat*; lord and master, man of the house 372 *male*; lady of the house, landlady 373 *lady*; senator; sir, madam 870 *title*; patriarch, matriarch 169 *parentage*; senior, head, principal, provost 34 *superior*; schoolmaster *or* -mistress 537 *teacher*; president, chairman *or* -woman, chairperson, speaker 690 *director*; employer, captain of industry, boss, governor, guvnor, guv 690 *manager*; leader, duce, führer (see *autocrat*); bigwig; ruling class, ruling party, vested interest, the Establishment; the authorities, the powers that be, 'them', Big Brother, Westminster, the Government, Whitehall, White House, Pentagon, Kremlin 733 *government*.

autocrat, absolute ruler, despot, tyrant, dictator, duce, führer, Big Brother; tycoon, boss, shogun, VIP, big gun, big shot 638 *bigwig*; petty tyrant, tin god, little Hitler 690 *official*.

sovereign, crowned head, anointed king *or* queen; Majesty, Highness, Royal H., Excellence; dynasty, house, royal line, royal blood; royalty, monarch, king, queen, rex, regina; divine king, Pharaoh; emperor, empress; Caesar, Kaiser, Kaiserin, Tsar *or* Czar, Tsarina *or* Czarina, Tsarevitch *or* Czarevich; prince, princess, Infante, Infanta, Dauphin, Prince of Wales, Crown Prince *or* Princess, King of Kings, Shah; khan; Mikado; Mogul, Sultan, Sultana; pope, pontiff, Dalai Lama, Aga Khan; caliph.

potentate, ruler; chief, chieftain, headman, sheikh; prince, princeling, rajah, rani, maharajah, maharani; emir, sherif; nawab, begum; archduke, duke, duchess; Elector, Electress; regent, Prince Regent.

governor, military g., High Commissioner, Governor-General, Crown Representative, viceroy, vicereine, khedive; proconsul; grand vizier, bey, pasha, bashaw; ecclesiastical governor, Prince Bishop; patriarch, archbishop, cardinal 986 *ecclesiarch*; ayatollah 690 *leader*.

officer, person in authority; functionary, mandarin, nabob, bureaucrat, apparatchik 690 *official*; civil servant, public s. 742 *servant*; commissar; prime minister, premier, grand vizier, chancellor, vice-c., Pooh-bah; constable, marshal, warden; mayor, lord m., lady m., mayoress, alderman, provost, bailie, city father, councillor; dignitary, local worthy 866 *person of repute*; sheriff, bailiff; justice of the peace, judge; magistrate, chief m., president, doge; consul; prefect, district officer; commissioner, deputy c.; headman; mace-bearer, beadle; sexton, verger 986 *church officer*; party official, whip, chief whip; powers that be.

naval officer, Sea Lord; admiral, vice-a., rear-a., commodore, captain, commander, lieutenant-c., lieutenant, sub-l., petty officer, leading seaman.

army officer, staff, High Command, staff officer, brass hat; commissioned officer; marshal, field m., commander-in-chief, general, lieutenant-g., major-g.; brigadier, colonel, lieutenant-c., major, captain, lieutenant, second l., subaltern; ensign; warrant officer, noncommissioned o., NCO, sergeant major, regimental s. m., staff s., colour s., sergeant, corporal, lance corporal; adjutant, aide-de-camp, quartermaster; war minister, warlord, commanding officer, commander, commandant.

air officer, air marshal, air commodore, group captain, wing commander, squadron leader, flight lieutenant, flying

officer, pilot o., warrant o., flight sergeant 722 *air force.*

742 Servant – N. *servant,* public s., civil s. 690 *official;* fag, slave; general servant, factotum, skivvy, maid-of-all work, chief cook and bottle washer 678 *busy person;* humble servant, menial; orderly, attendant; verger 986 *church officer;* subordinate, underling 35 *inferior;* subaltern, helper, assistant, right-hand man, girl Friday 703 *aider;* mercenary, hireling, employee, hand, hired man; odd-job man, handyman, worker, labourer; hewer of wood and drawer of water, hack, drudge, dogsbody; farmhand 370 *farmer;* shepherd, cowherd, milkmaid 369 *herdsman;* shop assistant, salesperson 793 *seller;* steward, stewardess, air hostess, cabin personnel, cabin boy; waiter, waitress, head waiter, wine w.; bartender, barman, barmaid, pot boy, tapster 192 *tavern;* stableman, ostler, groom, stable boy *or* lad, postilion; errand boy, messenger, runner 529 *courier;* doorman, commissionaire, janitor, concierge 264 *doorkeeper;* porter, night p.; caddy; callboy, page boy, bellboy, bellhop, buttons; boots, sweeper 648 *cleaner;* caretaker, house-minder, house-sitter, housekeeper; help, daily, daily help, char, charwoman, cleaning lady; universal aunt; baby-sitter, baby-minder; nurse, nursemaid, nanny 749 *keeper;* companion, confidante.

domestic, domestic servant, general s., manservant, man, serving m.; footman, flunkey, lackey; servant girl, maid, maidservant, handmaid, parlour maid, housemaid, chambermaid; maid of all work, tweeny, skivvy, slavey; kitchen maid, scullery m., dairy m., laundry m.; scullion, washer-up, dishwasher, housekeeper, butler, cook; steward, governess, tutor, nurse, nanny, nursemaid; personal servant, page, valet, gentlemen's gentleman, batman; lady's maid, waiting woman; mother's help, ayah, amah, au pair; scout, bed-maker; gardener, underg., groom; coachman, chauffeur 268 *driver.*

retainer, follower, train, cortege 67 *retinue;* court, courtier; attendant, usher, gillie; bodyguard, henchman, squire, page, train-bearer; majordomo, chamberlain, equerry, steward, bailiff; chatelaine, housekeeper; butler, cup-bearer; chaplain, beadsman; lady's maid, lady-in-waiting, companion, confidante; governess, nurse, nursemaid, mother's help, nanny 749 *keeper.*

dependant, hanger-on, parasite, satellite, camp follower, groupie, creature, jackal 284 *follower;* stooge, puppet 628 *instrument;* minion, lackey, flunkey; henchman, vassal; apprentice, protégé(e), ward, charge.

subject, national, citizen, patrial 191 *native;* liege, vassal; people, citizenry 869 *commonalty.*

slave, bondman, bondmaid, slave girl; serf, villein; galley slave, wage s., sweated labour 686 *worker;* eunuch; chattel, puppet, pawn; captive, chaingang 750 *prisoner.*

Adj. *serving,* ministering 703 *aiding;* in service, in domestic s., menial; working, in employment, on the payroll; on the staff; at one's beck and call 739 *obedient;* in servitude, in slavery, in captivity 745 *subject.*

Vb. *serve,* be in service, wait upon, wait on hand and foot 703 *minister to;* live in 89 *accompany;* follow 739 *obey;* tend, squire, valet; char, do chores, do housework, clean for, do for, oblige; fag for, do service; be part of the workforce, work for 622 *function.*

743 Badge of rule – N. *regalia,* insignia of royalty; crown, orb, sceptre; coronet, tiara, diadem; sword of state 733 *authority;* coronation robes, royal robe; ermine, royal purple; throne, seat of kings; ensign 547 *flag;* royal standard, royal arms 547 *heraldry;* lion, eagle, fleur-de-lis; Prince of Wales's feathers.

badge of rule, badge of office, chain of o.; emblem of authority, staff, wand, verge, rod, Black Rod, baton, truncheon, gavel; signet, seal, privy s., keys, ring; sword of state, sword of justice, mace;

crosier; woolsack, chair, bench; triple crown, mitre, bishop's hat, cardinal's hat., biretta; bishop's apron, gaiters 989 *canonicals*; judge's cap, black c. 961 *condemnation*; robe, mantle, toga.

badge of rank, sword, belt, sash, spurs, cocked hat, epaulette, tab 547 *badge*; uniform; brass, star, pips, crown, gold braid; chevron, stripe, anchor, armlet; garter, order 729 *decoration*.

744 Freedom – N. *freedom,* liberty; freedom of action; free will 595 *will*; free speech, freedom of the press, academic f., the four freedoms; civil rights, equal r. 915 *dueness*; privilege, prerogative, exemption, immunity, diplomatic i. 919 *nonliability*; liberalism; licence, poetic l.; free love 951 *illicit love*; laisser faire, nonintervention; neutralism 860 *indifference*; nonalignment, cross benches; isolationism; emancipation 746 *liberation*; women's liberation, women's lib; gay l.; enfranchisement.

independence, freedom of action; freedom of choice 605 *choice*; floating vote, don't know; freedom of thought, emancipation 84 *nonconformity*; bachelorhood 895 *celibacy*; self-expression, individuality 80 *speciality*; self-determination, national status 371 *nation*; autonomy, self-government, self-rule, home r.; self-sufficiency 635 *sufficiency*; freehold 777 *property*; independent means, private means.

scope, free play, full p. 183 *range*; swing, rope; manoeuvrability, leverage; field, room, lebensraum, living space, elbowroom, room to swing a cat, wide berth, leeway, margin, clearance 183 *room*; latitude, liberty; permissive society; informality; fling, licence, excess 734 *laxity*; one's head, one's own way, nothing in one's way; a free hand, ball at one's feet 137 *opportunity*; the run of, free hand, blank cheque, carte blanche; free-for-all, free enterprise, free trade, free port, free market.

free person, freeman, citizen, free c., patrial; freedman, freedwoman; ex-convict; escapee 667 *escaper*; free agent, freelance, free spirit; independent, crossbencher; neutral 625 *moderate*; free-trader; freethinker, libertarian, bohemian, individualist, eccentric 84 *nonconformist*.

Adj. *free,* freeborn, enfranchised; heart-whole, fancy-free, unattached; scot-free 960 *acquitted*; on the loose, at large; released, freed; free as air, free as the wind, free as a bird; footloose, go-as-you-please; privileged; exempt, immune; free-speaking 573 *plain*; freethinking, emancipated, broadminded; independent, uninfluenced 913 *just*; free and easy 882 *sociable*; loose, licentious, unbridled, at leisure, retired; relaxed, at ease 681 *leisurely*; free of cost, gratis, freebie, on the house, for free, unpaid for 812 *uncharged*; going begging 860 *unwanted*; free for all, unreserved, vacant, unoccupied, up for grabs 289 *accessible*.

independent, uncontrolled; unilateral 609 *spontaneous*; unforced, uninfluenced; unattached 860 *indifferent*; uncommitted, uninvolved; unaffiliated 625 *neutral*; isolationist 883 *unsociable*; unconquered, unbowed, irrepressible; autonomous, self-governing, self-sufficient, self-supporting, self-contained, self-motivated; self-reliant; anarchic; self-employed, one's own boss, freelance; unofficial, cowboy, wildcat; free-minded, free-spirited, maverick; single, bachelor; individualistic, unconventional 84 *unconformable*; breakaway 489 *dissenting*.

Vb. *be free,* enjoy liberty; go free, save oneself 667 *escape*; take French leave 738 *disobey*; have the run of, have the freedom of, range, have scope, have room to swing a cat, have room to breathe, have a free hand, have elbowroom; have plenty of rope, have one's head; feel at home, make oneself at home; feel free, let oneself go, let it all hang out, let one's hair down 683 *repose*; have one's fling, have one's way, have it one's own w., cut loose, drop out, follow one's bent, do one's own thing; go as you please, roam 282 *stray*; go one's own way, go it alone, be one's own boss, shift

for oneself, fend for oneself, paddle one's own canoe, stand alone; have a will of one's own 595 *will*; be independent, call no man master, be one's own man; stand up for one's rights, defy the whip 711 *defy*; stand on one's own feet, be self-sufficient; take liberties, make free with, go too far, presume on 878 *be insolent*; dare, make bold to.

give scope, give one his *or* her head, allow full play, give free rein to, allow enough rope 734 *be lax*; give a free hand, not cramp one's style, give the run of 701 *facilitate*; release, set free 746 *liberate*; live and let live, laissez aller, laissez faire.

745 Subjection – N. *subjection,* subordination; inferior rank, inferior status 35 *inferiority*; dependence, tutelage, guardianship, wardship, apron strings, leading s.; apprenticeship 536 *learning*; mutual dependence, symbiosis 12 *correlation*; allegiance; subjugation, conquest; loss of freedom, disfranchisement, bondage, enslavement 721 *submission*; constraint 747 *restraint*; oppression 735 *severity*; yoke 748 *fetter*; slavishness 879 *servility*.

servitude, slavery; captivity, bondage, yoke; serfdom.

Adj. *subjected,* dominated etc. vb.; subjugated, overwhelmed 728 *defeated*; subdued; taken prisoner, in chains 747 *restrained*; discriminated against, disadvantaged, disfranchised; colonized, reduced to slavery, sold into s.; in harness 742 *serving*; under the yoke, under the heel; oppressed, brought to one's knees, downtrodden; treated like dirt, henpecked, browbeaten; the sport of, the plaything of, kicked around like a football; brought to heel, quelled; eating out of one's hand, like putty in one's hands, submissive 721 *submitting*; subservient, slavish 879 *servile*.

subject, satellite; tributary; liege, vassal, feudal 739 *obedient*; subordinate, of lower rank, junior, cadet 35 *inferior*; dependent, in chancery; tied to one's

apron strings; subject to, liable to, exposed to 180 *liable*; a slave to 610 *habituated*; in the hands of, in the clutches of, under the control of, in the power of, at the mercy of, under the sway of, under one's thumb; not able to call one's soul one's own; puppet-like, like a puppet on a string; having no say in; parasitical, hanging on 879 *servile*; in the pay of; mortgaged 917 *obliged*.

Vb. *be subject,* pay tribute 739 *obey*; obey the whip; depend on 35 *be inferior*; be a doormat, let oneself be trampled on, let oneself be kicked around, be the stooge of; serve, be a slave; lose one's independence 721 *submit*; sacrifice one's freedom, have no will of one's own, be unable to stand on one's own two feet, be a cat's-paw, be a tool 628 *be instrumental*.

subjugate, subdue 727 *overmaster*; colonize, annex; take captive, drag at one's chariot wheels 727 *triumph*; take, capture, lead captive, sell into slavery; fetter, bind, hold in bondage 747 *imprison*; disfranchise; trample on, tread on, treat like dirt, treat like scum 735 *oppress*; keep under, hold down, repress, sit on, stamp out 165 *suppress*; enthral, captivate 821 *impress*; enchant 983 *bewitch*; dominate, lead by the nose 178 *influence*; tame, quell 369 *break in*; have eating out of one's hand, bring to heel, bring to his *or* her knees, have at one's beck and call; make one's plaything, make a stooge of, do what one likes with 673 *dispose of*.

746 Liberation – N. *liberation,* setting free, release, discharge 960 *acquittal*; abreaction, catharsis 818 *feeling*; unravelling, disentanglement, extrication, disinvolvement 46 *separation*; riddance, good r. 831 *relief*; rescue, redemption, salvation 668 *deliverance*; emancipation, enfranchisement; parole, bail; liberalization, relaxation (of control); derationing, deregulation 752 *abrogation*; demobilization 75 *dispersion*; absolution 909 *forgiveness*; acquittance.

Vb. *liberate,* rescue, save 668 *deliver*; pardon 909 *forgive*; discharge, absolve, let off the hook 960 *acquit*; make free, emancipate; enfranchise, give the vote; grant equal rights; introduce positive discrimination, adopt a policy of affirmative action, release, free, set free, set at liberty, let out; bail, parole 766 *give terms*; unfetter, unshackle, unchain; unlock 263 *open*; loosen, unloose, loose, unbind, untie, disentangle, extricate, disengage, clear; unstop, unplug, uncork; unleash, let off the lead; let loose, turn adrift; give play to, give free rein 744 *give scope*; give vent to 300 *empty*; leave hold, let go 779 *not retain*; relax 734 *be lax*; lift 831 *relieve*; decontrol, deregulate, deration 752 *abrogate*; demobilize, disband 75 *disperse*; unyoke, unharness, unload 701 *disencumber*.

achieve liberty, gain one's freedom; free oneself, shake oneself free; stand on one's own two feet; break loose, burst one's bonds, throw off the yoke, cast off one's shackles, throw off one's ball and chain, slip the collar, kick over the traces, get away 667 *escape*.

747 Restraint – N. *restraint,* self-r., self-control 942 *temperance*; reserve, shyness, inhibitions; suppression, repression, coercion, constraint, straitjacket 740 *compulsion*; cramp, check, obstacle, stumbling-block 702 *hindrance*; curb, drag, brake, clamp, bridle 748 *fetter*; arrest, retardation, deceleration 278 *slowness*; prevention, veto, ban, bar, embargo 757 *prohibition*; legal restraint, Official Secrets Act, D-notice 953 *law*; control, discipline 733 *authority*; censorship 550 *obliteration*; press laws 735 *severity*.

restriction, limitation 236 *limit*; keeping within limits 232 *circumscription*; speed limit, restricted area; exclusion order, no-go area, curfew; constriction, squeeze 198 *compression*; duress, pressure 740 *compulsion*; control, rationing; restrictive practice, exclusive rights, exclusivity 57 *exclusion*; monopoly, price ring, cartel, closed shop; charmed circle;

protectionism, intervention, interventionism, tariff wall; retrenchment, cuts 814 *economy*; economic pressure, freeze, price freeze, price control, credit squeeze; rate-capping; blockade.

detention, custody, protective c. 660 *protection*; arrest, house a., curfew; custodianship, keeping, guarding, keep, care, charge, ward; quarantine, internment; remand; captivity, duress; bondage, slavery 745 *servitude*; entombment, burial 364 *interment*; immurement, confinement, solitary c., incarceration, imprisonment; sentence, time, a stretch, bird, lag, porridge; penology, penologist.

Adj. *restraining,* checking etc. vb.; restrictive, conditional; limiting, custodial; cramping, hidebound; unbending, unyielding, strict 735 *severe*; stiff 326 *rigid*; tight 206 *narrow*; confining, close 198 *compressive*; confined, poky; coercive; repressive, inhibiting; monopolistic, protectionist, mercantilist.

restrained, self-controlled 942 *temperate*; pent up, bottled up; reserved, shy; disciplined, controlled, under control 739 *obedient*; kept on a leash, under the thumb; pinned down, kept under 745 *subjected*; on parole 917 *obliged*; protected, rationed; limited, restricted; cramped, hampered, trammelled, shackled 702 *hindered*; tied, bound, gagged; held up, weatherbound, fogbound, snowbound, housebound, bedridden, confined to bed.

imprisoned, confined, detained, kept in; landlocked; entombed, confined; quarantined, in quarantine; interned, in internment; under detention, under house arrest, incommunicado; under arrest, in custody; on remand; behind bars, incarcerated, locked up 750 *captive*; inside, in jug, in clink, in quod, in the slammer, in stir, in the cooler, in a cell; gated, confined to barracks; corralled, penned up, impounded; in irons, fettered, shackled; pilloried, in the stocks; serving a sentence, doing time, doing bird, doing porridge; caged, in captivity, trapped.

Vb. *restrain,* hold back; arrest, check, curb, rein in, brake, put a brake on, put clamps on, act as a brake 278 *retard;* cramp, clog, hamper 702 *hinder;* bind, tie hand and foot 45 *tie;* call a halt, stop, put a stop to 145 *halt;* inhibit, veto, ban, bar, embargo 757 *prohibit;* bridle, discipline, control 735 *be severe;* subdue 745 *subjugate;* restrain oneself, keep one's cool, keep one's hair *or* shirt on, 823 *keep calm;* grip, hold, pin, keep a tight hold *or* rein on, hold in check 778 *retain;* hold in, keep in, fight back, bottle up, choke back; restrict, tighten, hem in, limit, keep within bounds, cordon off, declare a no-go area, draw the line 232 *circumscribe;* damp down, pour water on 177 *moderate;* hold down, clamp down on, crack down on, keep under, sit on, jump on, repress 165 *suppress;* muzzle, gag, silence 578 *make mute;* censor, black out 550 *obliterate;* debar from, rope off, keep out 57 *exclude;* withhold, keep back, stint; ration, be sparing, cut back, retrench 814 *economize;* resist 704 *oppose;* police, patrol, keep order.

arrest, make an a., apprehend, lay by the heels, catch, cop, nab, collar, pinch, nick, pick up; haul in, run in; fetter, handcuff, put the handcuffs on; take, make a prisoner, take prisoner, capture, lead captive; kidnap, seize, snatch, take hostage; put under arrest, run in, take into custody, clap in jail, hold.

fetter, manacle, bind, pinion, tie up, handcuff, put in irons; pillory, put in the stocks, tether 45 *tie;* shackle, trammel, hobble; chain up, put a ball and chain on.

imprison, confine, immure, quarantine, intern; hold, detain, keep in, gate; keep in detention, keep under arrest, hold incommunicado; cloister 883 *seclude;* entomb, bury 364 *inter;* wall up, seal up; coop up, cage, impound, corral, pen up, box up, shut up, shut in, trap 235 *enclose;* put in a straitjacket; incarcerate, throw into prison, send to p., commit to p., remand, run in; lock up; turn the key on, keep under lock and key, keep behind bars, clap in irons; keep prisoner,

keep in captivity, keep in custody; hold hostage.

748 Prison – N. *prison,* prison-house, jail-house, jail, gaol, house of correction; quod, clink, jug, can, stir, slammer, cooler; glasshouse, brig; open prison, prison without bars, halfway house; penitentiary, reformatory, Borstal; approved school, List D school, remand home, community h.; assessment centre, detention c.; sin bin; dungeon, oubliette; Bastille, Tower; debtor's prison; Newgate, Wormwood Scrubs, Barlinnie, Holloway; Sing Sing, Alcatraz; criminal lunatic asylum, Broadmoor, Carstairs.

lockup, choky, calaboose, nick, police station; guardroom, guardhouse; cooler, slammer, peter, cell, prison c., condemned c., Death Row; dungeon, oubliette, torture chamber; prison van, Black Maria; dock, bar; pound, pen, cage, coop, kennel 235 *enclosure;* reserve; stocks, pillory.

prison camp, detention c., internment c., Stalag, Colditz; concentration camp, Belsen, Auschwitz, Buchenwald; labour camp, Gulag; penal settlement *or* colony, Botany Bay, Devil's Island.

fetter, shackle, trammel, bond, chain, ball and c., irons, hobble; manacle, pinion, handcuff; straitjacket; muzzle, gag, bit, bridle, halter; rein, bearing r., checkrein, leading rein, reins, traces; yoke, collar, harness; curb, brake, clamp 702 *hindrance;* lead, tether, rope, leading string, apron strings.

749 Keeper – N. *keeper,* custodian, curator; archivist, record keeper 549 *recorder;* officer in charge; caretaker, house-minder, janitor, concierge, housekeeper; chatelaine, warden; ranger, gamekeeper; guard, escort; garrison 713 *defender;* watchdog, sentry, sentinel, lookout, watchman, night w., security man *or* woman, security officer, watch, house-minder, house-sitter, vigilante, coastguard, lighthouse keeper 660 *protector;* invigilator, tutor, chaperon, duenna, governess, nurse, foster n., wet n.,

nanny, nursemaid, baby-sitter, baby-minder 742 *domestic*; foster parent, adoptive p.; guardian, legal g.; probation officer 901 *philanthropist*.

gaoler, jailer, turnkey, warder, wardress, prison guard, prison officer, screw; prison governor.

750 Prisoner – N. *prisoner,* captive, prisoner of war, POW; ticket-of-leave man; political prisoner, prisoner of conscience; detainee; prisoner at the bar, defendant, accused 928 *accused person*; persistent offender, old lag, jailbird 904 *offender*; guest of Her Majesty; condemned prisoner, convict; lifer; galley slave 742 *slave*; hostage, kidnap victim 767 *security*.

Adj. *captive,* imprisoned, in chains, in irons, behind bars, under lock and key; jailed, in prison, inside 747 *imprisoned*; in custody, under arrest, remanded; under detention, detained at her Majesty's pleasure; held hostage.

751 Commission: vicarious authority – N. *commission,* vicarious authority; committal, delegation; devolution, decentralization; deputation, legation, mission, embassy 754 *envoy*; regency 733 *authority*; representation, proxy; card vote; agency, factorage, trusteeship, executorship 689 *management*; clerkship.

mandate, trust, charge 737 *command*; commission, assignment, appointment, office, task, errand, mission; enterprise 672 *undertaking*; nomination, return, election 605 *vote*; posting, translation, transfer 272 *transference*; investment, induction, inauguration, ordination, coronation; power of attorney, written authority, charter, writ 737 *warrant*; diploma 756 *permit*; terms of reference 766 *conditions*; responsibility, care, cure (of souls); ward, charge.

Vb. *commission,* empower, authorize, charge, sanction, charter, license 756 *permit*; post, appoint, detail, assign, nominate; engage, hire, staff 622 *employ*; invest, induct, install, ordain; crown, anoint; commit, turn over to,

leave it to; consign, entrust, trust with, grant powers of attorney; delegate, depute, send on a mission, send on an errand, send out, return, elect, give a mandate 605 *vote*.

752 Abrogation – N. *abrogation,* annulment, invalidation; nullification; cancellation, suppression; repeal, revocation, rescinding; abolition, dissolution; repudiation 533 *negation*; recantation; suspension, discontinuance, disuse, undoing 148 *reversion*; counterorder.

deposal, deposition, dethronement; demotion, degradation; disestablishment, discharge, congé, dismissal, sack, redundancy, removal 300 *ejection*; unfrocking 963 *punishment*; ousting, deprivation, divestment 786 *expropriation*.

Vb. *abrogate,* annul, cancel; scrub, wipe out 550 *obliterate*; invalidate, abolish, dissolve, nullify, void, render null and void, declare null and void; quash, set aside, reverse, overrule; repeal, revoke, recall; rescind, tear up; undo 148 *revert*; countermand, counterorder; disclaim, disown, deny 533 *negate*; repudiate, retract 603 *recant*; ignore 458 *disregard*; call off, call a halt 747 *restrain*; suspend, discontinue, write off 674 *stop using*.

depose, dethrone; unseat; divest 786 *deprive*; unfrock; disbar, strike off the register, strike off 57 *exclude*; disestablish; suspend 300 *dismiss*; ease out, edge out, elbow out, oust 300 *eject*; demote, degrade, reduce to the ranks, take down a peg or two, kick upstairs; remove 272 *transfer*.

753 Resignation – N. *resignation,* retirement, retiral; leaving, withdrawal 296 *departure*; pension, compensation, golden handshake 962 *reward*; waiver, surrender, abandonment, abdication, renunciation 621 *relinquishment*; abjuration, disclaimer 533 *negation*; state of retirement 681 *leisure*.

Vb. *resign,* tender one's resignation, hand in one's notice, give n.; hand over, vacate office; apply for the Chiltern

Hundreds; stand down, stand aside, make way for; sign off, declare (cricket); scratch, withdraw, back out, give a walk-over, retire from the contest, throw in one's hand, surrender, give up 721 *submit*; quit, throw up, chuck it; ask for one's cards; sign away, give a. 780 *assign*; abdicate, abandon, renounce 621 *relinquish*; retire, go into retirement, take early retirement, accept redundancy, be superannuated, be put out to grass; be pensioned off.

754 Consignee – N. *consignee,* committee, steering c., panel, quango 692 *council*; counsellor, team of experts, think tank, brains trust, working party 691 *adviser*; nominee, licensee; trustee, executor 686 *agent*; factor, one's man of business, bailiff, steward 690 *manager*; caretaker, curator 749 *keeper*; representative; legal representative, attorney, counsel, advocate 958 *law agent*; proxy, surrogate 755 *deputy*; negotiator, middleman, broker, stockbroker 231 *intermediary*; underwriter, insurer; purser, bursar 798 *treasurer*; rent collector, tax c., revenue c., income-tax officer; office-bearer, secretary of state 741 *officer*; functionary 690 *official.*

delegate, shop steward; nominee, representative; correspondent, special c. 588 *correspondent*; emissary, special messenger 529 *messenger*; delegation, mission.

envoy, emissary, legate, papal nuncio, representative, ambassador, ambassadress, High Commissioner, chargé d'affaires; ambassador at large; diplomatic corps; minister, diplomat; consul, vice-c.; attaché; embassy, legation, mission, consulate, High Commission; diplomatist, negotiator.

755 Deputy – N. *deputy,* surrogate, alternate, proxy; scapegoat, substitute, locum tenens, locum, understudy, stand-in, temp 150 *substitution*; viceroy, vice-president, vice-chairman, vice-chancellor, vice-admiral, vice-captain, vice-consul; vicar; second-in-command, number

two 741 *officer*; right-hand man, lieutenant, secretary 703 *aider*; alter ego, power behind the throne, éminence grise 612 *motivator*; caretaker government; heir, heir apparent 776 *beneficiary*; spokesperson, spokesman *or* -woman, mouthpiece, herald 529 *messenger*; second, advocate, champion 707 *patron*; agent, factor, attorney 754 *consignee.*

Vb. *deputize,* act for 622 *function*; act on behalf of, represent, hold a proxy f., appear for, speak f., answer f., hold a brief f.; hold in trust, be executor 689 *manage*; negotiate, act as go-between for, be broker for, replace, stand in for, understudy, do duty for 150 *substitute*; act as scapegoat.

Section two: Special social volition

756 Permission – N. *permission,* liberty 744 *freedom*; leave, sanction, clearance; grant; licence, authorization, warrant; allowance, sufferance, tolerance, indulgence 736 *leniency*; acquiescence 758 *consent*; blessing, approval 923 *approbation*; grace and favour 897 *benevolence*; concession, dispensation, exemption 919 *nonliability*; release 746 *liberation*.

permit, written permission; authority, law 737 *warrant*; commission 751 *mandate*; charter, pass, password; passport, passbook, visa, safe-conduct; ticket, chit; licence, driving l.; free hand, carte blanche, blank cheque 744 *scope*; leave, compassionate l., sick l., leave of absence, furlough, holiday, vacation, sabbatical; parole; clearance, all clear, green light, go-ahead; imprimatur.

Adj. *permitting,* permissive, indulgent, complaisant, laissez faire, easy-going.

Vb. *permit,* let 469 *make possible*; give permission, grant leave, accord, vouchsafe 781 *give*; nod, say yes 758 *consent*;

give one's blessing; sanction 923 *approve*; entitle, authorize, warrant, charter, patent, license, enable; ratify, legalize, decriminalize 953 *make legal*; decontrol; lift a ban, raise an embargo, dispense, release 919 *exempt*; clear, give clearance 746 *liberate*; give the go-ahead, give the all clear, give the green light, tip the wink, let off the hook; recognize, concede, allow 488 *assent*; give one a chance, let one try; leave the way open, open the door to 263 *open*; suffer, tolerate, put up with, brook 736 *be lenient*; connive at, shut one's eyes to, turn a blind eye, wink at 734 *be lax*; laisser faire, laisser aller, allow a free hand, give carte blanche, issue a blank cheque 744 *give scope*; permit oneself, allow o., take the liberty.

ask leave, beg l., ask if one may, ask one's blessing; ask to be excused; petition 761 *request.*

757 Prohibition – N. *prohibition,* inhibition, injunction; counterorder; intervention, interference; interdict, veto, ban, embargo; restriction, curfew 747 *restraint*; proscription, taboo; rejection, red light, thumbs down 760 *refusal*; intolerance 924 *disapprobation*; licensing laws 942 *temperance*; censorship, press laws, repression, suppression 735 *severity*; abolition, cancellation, suspension 752 *abrogation*; blackout 550 *obliteration*; forbidden fruit.

Adj. *prohibited,* forbidden, verboten; barred, banned, under ban; censored, blue-pencilled, blacked-out; contraband, illicit, unlawful, outlawed, against the law 954 *illegal*; taboo; frowned on, not done; unmentionable, unprintable; out of bounds; blackballed, ostracized.

Vb. *prohibit,* forbid; disallow, veto, withhold permission, refuse leave, give the thumbs down, give the red light, forbid the banns 760 *refuse*; withdraw permission, cancel leave; countermand, counterorder, revoke, suspend 752 *abrogate*; prevent 702 *hinder*; restrict, stop 747 *restrain*; ban, taboo, proscribe, outlaw; black; impose a ban, place out of

bounds; bar, debar, warn off, shut the door on, blackball, ostracize 57 *exclude*; excommunicate 300 *eject*; repress, stifle, kill 165 *suppress*; censor, blue-pencil 550 *obliterate*; put one's foot down 735 *be severe*; frown on, not countenance, not brook 924 *disapprove*; discourage, crack down on 613 *dissuade*; cramp 232 *circumscribe*; draw the line; intervene, interfere.

758 Consent – N. *consent,* willingness; agreement 488 *assent*; compliance 768 *observance*; accord; acquiescence, acceptance 756 *permission*; sanction, endorsement, ratification, confirmation.

Vb. *consent,* say yes, nod; give consent, give the go-ahead, give the green light, set one's seal on, ratify, confirm 488 *endorse*; sanction, pass 756 *permit*; give one's approval 923 *approve*; tolerate, recognize, allow, connive 736 *be lenient*; agree, fall in with, go along with, accede 488 *assent*; have no objection 488 *acquiesce*; be persuaded, come round; yield, give way 721 *submit*; comply; grant, concede 781 *give*; go halfway to meet 597 *be willing*; do all one is asked 828 *content*; accept, take up an offer, jump at; clinch a deal, seal a bargain 766 *make terms*.

759 Offer – N. *offer,* fair o., proffer; bribe 612 *inducement*; tender, bid, takeover b., green mail, buy-out, merger, proposal; motion, proposition, proposal; approach, overture, advance, invitation; feeler; final offer; present, presentation, offering, sacrifice 781 *gift*; dedication.

Vb. *offer,* proffer, hold out, make an offer, bid, tender; present, lay at one's feet 781 *give*; dedicate, consecrate; sacrifice to; introduce, broach, move, propose, make a proposition, put forward, suggest 512 *propound*; make overtures, leave the door open, keep one's offer open; bribe; invite, send an invitation, ask one in 882 *be hospitable*; hawk, invite tenders, put up for sale 793 *sell*; auction; make a present of 469 *make possible*.

offer oneself, stand, be a candidate, compete, run for, be in the running for, enter 716 *contend;* volunteer, come forward 597 *be willing;* apply, put in for 761 *request.*

760 Refusal – N. *refusal,* nonacceptance, declining, turning down, thumbs down, red light 607 *rejection;* denial, no, nay 533 *negation;* disclaimer, flat refusal 711 *defiance;* repulse, rebuff, slap in the face 292 *repulsion;* withholding 778 *retention;* recalcitrance 738 *disobedience;* noncompliance 769 *nonobservance;* recusancy 598 *unwillingness;* objection, protest 762 *deprecation;* renunciation, abnegation 621 *relinquishment.*

Vb. *refuse,* say no, shake one's head; excuse oneself, send one's apologies; disagree 489 *dissent;* deny, repudiate, disclaim 533 *negate;* decline, turn down, pass up, spurn 607 *reject;* repulse, rebuff 292 *repel;* turn away 300 *dismiss;* dig in one's heels, be unmoved, harden one's heart 602 *be obstinate;* not hear, not listen, turn a deaf ear 416 *be deaf;* close one's purse; turn one's back on; hang fire, hang back 598 *be unwilling;* beg off, back down; turn from, have nothing to do with, shy at, jib at 620 *avoid;* debar, keep out, shut the door 57 *exclude;* not allow 757 *prohibit;* set one's face against 715 *resist;* oppose 704 *withstand;* kick, protest 762 *deprecate;* not comply 769 *not observe;* grudge, begrudge, withhold, keep from 778 *retain.*

761 Request – N. *request,* asking, first time of a.; canvassing, hawking 793 *sale;* requisition; final demand, last time of asking, ultimatum 737 *demand;* blackmail 900 *threat;* claim, counterclaim 915 *dueness;* consumer demand, seller's market 627 *requirement;* postulate 475 *premise;* proposition, proposal, motion; overture, approach 759 *offer;* bid, application; petition, round robin; prayer, appeal, plea; insistence 740 *compulsion;* cri de coeur; importunity; soliciting, accosting, invitation, temptation; mendicancy,

begging, busking, bumming; begging letter, flag day, bazaar, charity performance, benefit match.

entreaty, imploring, begging, beseeching; submission, clasped hands, bended knees; supplication, prayer 981 *prayers;* appeal 583 *allocution;* solemn entreaty, imprecation.

Adj. *supplicatory,* entreating, suppliant, on bended knees, with folded hands, cap in hand; imploring, beseeching.

Vb. *request,* ask, invite, solicit; make overtures, approach, accost 759 *offer;* woo, pop the question 889 *court;* seek, look for 459 *search;* fish for, angle for; need, call for, clamour f. 627 *require;* crave, make a request, beg a favour, ask a f., have a request to make, make bold to ask, trouble one for 859 *desire;* apply, make application, put in for, bid, bid for, make a bid f.; apply to, call on, appeal to, run to, address oneself to, go cap in hand to; tout, hawk, doorstep, canvass, solicit orders 793 *sell;* petition, press a suit, press a claim, expect 915 *claim;* make demands 737 *demand;* blackmail, put the bite on 900 *threaten;* coax, wheedle, cajole; importune, dun; touch 785 *borrow;* requisition 786 *take;* send an ultimatum 766 *give terms.*

beg, cadge, crave, sponge, freeload; bum, scrounge, mooch; thumb a lift, hitchhike; hold out one's hand, go from door to door, doorstep, knock at doors; appeal for funds, pass the hat, launch an appeal 786 *levy.*

entreat, supplicate, be a suppliant; pray, implore, beseech, appeal, invoke, appeal to, call on 583 *speak to;* address one's prayers to, pray to 981 *offer worship;* kneel to, go down on one's knees, go down on bended knee, fall at one's feet.

762 Deprecation: negative request – N. *deprecation,* dissuasion; plea for mercy; intercession, mediation 981 *prayers;* counterclaim 761 *request;* murmur, complaint 829 *discontent;* exception, demur, expostulation, remonstrance, protest 704 *opposition;* reaction, backlash

182 *counteraction*; tut-tut, raised eyebrows, groans, jeers, sniffs of disapproval 924 *disapprobation*; petition, open letter, round robin; demonstration, march, protest m., hunger m., hunger strike, industrial action, sit-in; noncompliance 760 *refusal*.

Vb. *deprecate*, ask one not to, advise against, have a better idea, make a counterproposal 613 *dissuade*; touch wood, knock on w., cross one's fingers, keep one's fingers crossed; beg off, intercede 720 *mediate*; pray, appeal 761 *entreat*; cry for mercy 905 *ask mercy*; tut-tut, shake one's head, raise one's eyebrows, sniff 924 *disapprove*; remonstrate, expostulate 924 *reprove*; jeer, groan, stamp 926 *detract*; murmur, beef, complain 829 *be discontented*; object, take exception to; demur, jib, kick, squeak, protest against, appeal a., petition a., lobby a., campaign a., raise one's voice a., cry out a. 704 *oppose*; demonstrate, organize a protest march, hold a protest meeting, go on hunger strike; strike, take industrial action, come out, walk o. 145 *cease*.

763 Petitioner – **N.** *petitioner*, suppliant, supplicant; appealer, appellant; claimant, pretender; postulant, aspirant; solicitor, asker, seeker, enquirer, advertiser; customer, bidder, tenderer; suitor, courter, wooer; canvasser, hawker, tout, barker; dunner; pressure group, ginger g., lobby, lobbyist; applicant, candidate, entrant; competitor 716 *contender*.

beggar, busker, mendicant; tramp, bum 268 *wanderer*; cadger, borrower, moocher, scrounger, hitch-hiker; sponger, freeloader, ligger, parasite 879 *toady*.

Section three: Conditional social volition

764 Promise – **N.** *promise*, offer; undertaking, commitment; affiance, betrothal, engagement 894 *marriage*; troth, plight, word, word of honour, vow, marriage v.

532 *oath*; declaration 532 *affirmation*; declared intention 617 *intention*; profession, fair words; assurance, pledge, warranty, guarantee, insurance 767 *security*; bargain, gentlemen's agreement, unwritten a., mutual a. 765 *compact*; covenant, bond, promise to pay 803 *debt*; debt of honour 917 *duty*.

promised, covenanted, guaranteed, secured; bespoke, reserved; pledged, affianced; committed, bound 917 *obliged*.

Vb. *promise*, say one will 532 *affirm*; hold out, proffer 759 *offer*; make a promise, give one's word, pledge one's w.; vow, take one's oath on it 532 *swear*; vouch for, go bail for, warrant, guarantee, assure, insure, underwrite 767 *give security*; pledge, stake; pledge one's honour, stake one's credit; engage, enter into an engagement 672 *undertake*; make a gentleman's agreement, strike a bargain, sign on the dotted line, shake on it, commit oneself, bind oneself, be bound, covenant 765 *contract*; take on oneself, accept responsibility 917 *incur a duty*; accept a liability, promise to pay, incur a debt of honour 785 *borrow*; plight one's troth, exchange vows 894 *wed*.

take a pledge, demand security 473 *make certain*; put on oath, swear, make one s. 466 *testify*; exact a promise; take one's word 485 *believe*; rely on, expect 473 *be certain*.

Adv. *as promised*, according to contract, as agreed, duly.

765 Compact – **N.** *compact*, contract, bargain, concordat, agreement, mutual undertaking 672 *undertaking*; gentleman's agreement, unwritten a., debt of honour 764 *promise*; exchange of vows; engagement, betrothal 894 *marriage*; covenant, bond 767 *security*; league, alliance, cartel 706 *cooperation*; pact, understanding 24 *agreement*; private u., something between them; conspiracy 623 *plot*; negotiation 766 *conditions*; deal 770 *compromise*; arrangement, settlement; seal, signature, countersignature; deed of agreement, indenture 767 *title deed*.

treaty, international agreement; Treaty of Rome, Warsaw Pact; peace treaty, nonaggression pact 719 *pacification*; convention, concordat; Geneva Convention.

signatory, signer, countersigner, subscriber, the undersigned; swearer, attestor 466 *witness*; endorser, ratifier; adherent, consenting party 488 *assenter*; covenanter, contractor, contracting party; treaty-maker, negotiator 720 *mediator.*

Adj. *contractual,* bilateral, multilateral; agreed to, negotiated, signed, countersigned, sworn, ratified; covenanted, signed, signed on the dotted line, sealed and delivered.

Vb. *contract,* enter into a contract, engage 672 *undertake*; promise; covenant, strike a bargain, sign a pact, shake hands on, do a deal, clinch a d.; ally 706 *cooperate*; treat, negotiate 791 *bargain*; agree, come to terms 766 *make terms*; conclude, close, settle; indent, execute, sign, sign on the dotted line, subscribe, ratify, attest, confirm 488 *endorse*; insure, underwrite 767 *give security.*

766 Conditions – N. *conditions,* treaty-making, diplomacy, summitry, negotiation, bargaining, collective b.; hard bargaining, trade-off, horse-trading 791 *barter*; formula, terms, terms for agreement; ultimatum, time limit 900 *threat*; part of the bargain, set of terms, basis for negotiation, frame of reference; articles of agreement; provision, clause, escape c., let-out c., proviso, limitation, strings, reservation, exception, small print 468 *qualification*; stipulation, sine qua non, essential clause 627 *requirement*; rule 693 *precept*; terms of reference 751 *mandate.*

Adj. *conditional,* with strings attached, stipulatory, qualificatory, provisory 468 *qualifying*; limiting, subject to terms, contingent, provisional.

Vb. *give terms,* propose conditions; attach strings; hold out for, insist on, make demands 737 *demand*; stipulate, make it a sine qua non 627 *require*; allow

no exception 735 *be severe*; insert a proviso, leave a loophole 468 *qualify*; fix the terms, impose the conditions, write the articles, draft the clauses; add a let-out c., write in; keep one's options open, hedge one's bets.

make terms, negotiate, be in treaty, parley, powwow, hold conversations 584 *confer*; deal with, treat w., negotiate w.; make overtures, throw out a feeler 461 *be tentative*; haggle 791 *bargain*; make proposals 759 *offer*; compromise; negotiate a treaty, hammer out a formula, work something out, do a deal 765 *contract.*

Adv. *on terms,* on one's own t.; conditionally, provisionally, subject to, with a reservation.

767 Security – N. *security,* guarantee, warranty, authorization, writ 737 *warrant*; word of honour 764 *promise*; sponsorship, patronage 660 *protection*; surety, bail, parole; gage, pledge, pawn, hostage; stake, deposit, earnest, handsel, token, instalment; colour of one's money, earnest m.; down payment 804 *payment*; indemnity, insurance, underwriting 660 *safety*; transfer of security, mortgage 780 *transfer*; collateral.

title deed, deed, instrument; deed poll; indenture; charter, covenant, bond, bearer b.; receipt, IOU, voucher, counterfoil, certificate, authentication, marriage lines; verification, seal, stamp, signature, endorsement, acceptance 466 *credential*; banknote, treasury note, promissory n., note of hand, bill, treasury bill, bill of exchange; blue chip, gilt-edged security; portfolio, scrip, share, debenture; insurance policy; will, last will and testament, codicil, certificate of probate; archives 548 *record.*

Vb. *give bail,* go b., bail one out, go surety; take bail, release on bail; hold in pledge, keep in pawn 764 *take a pledge.*

give security, offer collateral, mortgage; pledge, pawn, pop, hock 785 *borrow*; guarantee, act as guarantor, stand surety for, warrant 473 *make certain*;

authenticate, verify 466 *corroborate*; execute, endorse, seal, stamp, sign, sign on the dotted line, countersign, subscribe, give one's signature 488 *endorse*; vouch for 764 *promise*; secure, indemnify, insure, assure, underwrite 660 *safeguard*.

768 Observance – N. *observance*, practice; fulfilment 635 *sufficiency*; diligence, conscientiousness; adherence to, attention to; acknowledgment; performance, discharge 676 *action*; compliance 739 *obedience*; conformance 83 *conformity*; fidelity; dependability, reliability 929 *probity*.

Adj. *observant*, practising; heedful, watchful, careful of, attentive to 455 *attentive*; conscientious, diligent, religious, punctilious; meticulous; exact 494 *accurate*; responsible, reliable, dependable 929 *trustworthy*; loyal 739 *obedient*; adhering to, sticking to 83 *conformable*; faithful 929 *honourable*.

Vb. *observe*, heed, respect, regard, have regard to, pay respect to, acknowledge, pay attention to, attend to 455 *be attentive*; keep, practise, adhere to, stick to, cling to, follow, hold by, abide by, be loyal to 83 *conform*; comply 739 *obey*; fulfil, discharge, perform, execute, carry out, carry out to the letter 676 *do*; satisfy 635 *suffice*.

keep faith, be faithful *or* loyal to, discharge one's functions 917 *do one's duty*; honour one's obligations, meet one's o., be as good as one's word, make good one's promise, keep one's p., fulfil one's engagement, be true to the spirit of, stand by; come up to scratch, pay one's debt, pay up 804 *pay*; give one his due.

769 Nonobservance – N. *nonobservance*, informality, indifference 734 *laxity*; inattention, omission 458 *negligence*; nonadherence 84 *nonconformity*; nonperformance; nonfulfilment, shortcoming 726 *noncompletion*; infringement, violation; noncompliance, disloyalty

738 *disobedience*; protest 762 *deprecation*; disregard, discourtesy 921 *disrespect*; breach of faith, repudiation, denial 533 *negation*.

Adj. *nonobservant*, nonpractising, lapsed; nonconforming, blacklegging, nonadhering, nonconformist 84 *unconformable*; inattentive to, disregarding, neglectful 458 *negligent*; informal 734 *lax*; noncompliant 738 *disobedient*; infringing, unlawful 954 *lawbreaking*; disloyal 918 *undutiful*; unfaithful 930 *perfidious*.

Vb. *not observe*, not practise; not conform, not adhere, stand out 84 *be unconformable*; discard 674 *stop using*; set aside 752 *abrogate*; omit, ignore 458 *neglect*; disregard, show no respect for, cock a snook, snap one's fingers at 921 *not respect*; stretch a point 734 *be lax*; violate, do violence to, drive a coach and horses through, ride roughshod over, trample underfoot 176 *force*; transgress 306 *overstep*; not comply with 738 *disobey*; desert 918 *fail in duty*; fail, not qualify, not come up to scratch 636 *not suffice*; break one's word; renege on, go back on, back out, cancel; give the go-by, cut, shirk, dodge, parry, evade, elude 620 *avoid*.

770 Compromise – N. *compromise*, mutual concession, give and take, trade-off, adjustment; commutation; second best, half a loaf 35 *inferiority*; working arrangement 624 *way*; splitting the difference 30 *average*; halfway 625 *middle way*; balancing act, swings and roundabouts.

Vb. *compromise*, find a formula; make mutual concessions, strike a balance, find a happy medium, steer a middle course, give and take, meet one halfway; live and let live, stretch a point 734 *be lax*; take the mean, go half and half, go Dutch, split the difference 30 *average out*; commute 150 *substitute*; compose differences, go to arbitration; patch up 719 *pacify*; take the good with the bad, take what is offered, make a virtue of

necessity, make the best of a bad job; sit on the fence.

Section four: Possessive relations

771 Acquisition – N. *acquisition,* getting, winning; earning; acquirement, obtainment, procurement; collection 74 *assemblage*; realization, profit-taking 793 *sale*; encashment 780 *transfer*; fund-raising; exploitation, profiteering; money-grubbing 816 *avarice*; heap, stack, pile, mountain, pool, scoop, jackpot 74 *accumulation*; finding 484 *discovery*; recovery, retrieval, recoupment 656 *restoration*; redemption 792 *purchase*; appropriation; theft 788 *stealing*; inheritance, patrimony; find, windfall, treasure trove; something for nothing, free gift, freebie, giveaway 781 *gift*; legacy, bequest; gratuity, baksheesh 962 *reward*; benefit match, prize 729 *trophy*; gravy 615 *benefit*; easy money 701 *facility*; lucre 797 *money*; plunder 790 *booty*.

earnings, income, earned i., wage, salary, screw, pay packet, take-home pay, productivity bonus 804 *pay*; rate for the job, pay scale, differential; fee for service, honorarium; pension, superannuation, compensation, golden handshake; remuneration, emolument 962 *reward*; allowance, expense account; pickings, perquisite, perks, fringe benefits, extras; commission, rake-off 810 *discount*; return, receipts, proceeds, turnover, takings, revenue, taxes 807 *receipt*; harvest, crop, gleanings.

gain, savings 814 *economy*; credit side, profit, net p., capital gain, winnings; dividend, share-out 775 *participation*; usury, interest, high i., compound i., simple i. 36 *increment*; profitable transaction; pay increase, rise, raise 36 *increase*; advantage, benefit.

Adj. *acquiring,* acquisitive, accumulative; on the make, gold-digging, getting, winning 730 *prosperous*.

gainful, paying, money-making, money-spinning, lucrative, remunerative; advantageous 640 *profitable*; fruitful.

Vb. *acquire,* get, come by; earn, gain, obtain, procure; find, strike, come across, come by, pick up, light upon 484 *discover*; get hold of, get possession of, lay one's hands on, make one's own, annex 786 *appropriate*; win, secure, capture, catch, land, net, bag 786 *take*; pick, glean, fill one's pockets; gather, reap, crop, harvest; derive, draw, tap, milk, mine 304 *extract*; collect, accumulate, heap, pile up 74 *bring together*; scrape together, rake t.; collect funds, launch an appeal, raise, levy, raise the wind; save, save up, hoard 632 *store*; buy, preempt 792 *purchase*; reserve, book, engage 135 *be early*; beg, borrow or steal; earn a living, turn an honest penny, keep the wolf from the door 622 *busy oneself*; make money, draw a salary, draw a pension, receive one's wages; have an income, be in receipt of, have a turnover, gross, take 782 *receive*; convert, cash, encash, realize, clear, make; get back, recover, salvage, recycle, regain, redeem, recapture, reconquer 656 *retrieve*; take back, resume, reclaim; recover one's losses 31 *recoup*; recover one's costs, break even, balance the books, practise creative accounting, balance accounts 28 *equalize*; attain, reach; come in for, catch, incur.

inherit, come into, be left, be willed, be bequeathed, fall heir to, come by, come in for, receive a legacy; succeed, succeed to, step into the shoes of, be the heir of.

gain, make a profit, earn a dividend; make; make money, coin m., coin it, line one's pockets 730 *prosper*; make a fortune, make a killing, make one's pile, rake in the shekels, rake it in, turn a pretty penny 800 *get rich*; make a scoop, win, win the jackpot, break the bank; sell at a profit.

be profitable, profit, repay, be worthwhile; pay, pay well; yield 164 *produce*; bring in a return, pay a dividend, show a profit 730 *prosper*.

387

772 Loss – N. *loss,* deprivation, privation, bereavement; dispossession, eviction 786 *expropriation*; sacrifice, forfeit, lapse 963 *penalty*; dead loss, irretrievable l., perdition 165 *ruin*; depreciation 655 *deterioration*; diminishing returns; setback, check, reverse; loss of profit, loss leader; overdraft, bankruptcy 805 *insolvency*; consumption 806 *expenditure*; nonrecovery, spilt milk, wastage, wear and tear, leakage 634 *waste*; dissipation, evaporation, drain 37 *decrease*; good riddance 746 *liberation*; losing battle 728 *defeat.*

Adj. *lost,* long l., gone, gone for ever; gone by the board, out of sight out of mind, consigned to oblivion 458 *neglected*; vanished, flown out of the window; missing, astray, adrift, mislaid; untraceable, lost, stolen or strayed 190 *absent*; lacking 307 *deficient*; irrecoverable, irretrievable, irredeemable, unsalvageable, nonreturnable, nonrecyclable; spent, gone down the drain, squandered; forfeited.

Vb. *lose,* be unable to find, look in vain for; mislay 188 *misplace*; miss, let slip through one's fingers, kiss *or* say goodbye to 138 *lose a chance*; meet one's Waterloo; squander, throw away 634 *waste*; deserve to lose, forfeit, sacrifice; spill; fritter away, throw good money after bad, sink 806 *expend*; be a loser, draw a blank, burn one's fingers 731 *have trouble*; lose one's bet, pay out; be out of pocket; be set back, incur losses, sell at a loss; be unable to pay, go broke, go bankrupt 805 *not pay*; be overdrawn, be in the red, be minus.

be lost, be missing, be declared m. 190 *be absent*; go down the drain, go down the spout, go up in smoke, go to pot 165 *be destroyed.*

773 Possession – N. *possession,* ownership, proprietorship, lawful possession, enjoyment; occupancy, nine points of the law, bird in the hand; mastery, hold, grasp, grip 778 *retention*; haves and have-nots 776 *possessor*; a possession

777 *property*; tenancy, holding 777 *estate*; tenure, feu, fief; monopoly, ring; preoccupancy, preemption, squatting; expectations, inheritance, heritage, patrimony, taking possession, appropriation, laying claim to.

Adj. *possessed,* held etc. vb.; in the possession of, in one's hand, in one's grasp, in the bag; in the bank, to one's name; at one's disposal, on hand; one's own, exclusive; monopolized by, engrossed by, taken up by; booked, reserved, engaged, occupied; included in, attaching.

Vb. *possess,* be possessed of, be the proud possessor of, number among one's possessions, own, have; hold, have and hold, hold in one's grasp, grip 778 *retain*; have at one's command, have absolute disposal of; call one's own, boast of 915 *claim*; contain, include 78 *comprise*; fill, occupy; squat, settle upon, inhabit; enjoy, have for one's own 673 *use*; monopolize, have exclusive rights to, hog, corner the market; get, take possession, make one's own 786 *take*; preoccupy; reserve, engage 135 *be early.*

belong, be vested in, belong to; go with, be included in.

774 Nonownership – N. *nonownership,* nonpossession, vacancy; tenancy, temporary lease; pauperism 801 *poverty*; deprivation 772 *loss*; no-man's-land, debatable territory 190 *emptiness.*

Adj. *unpossessed,* unattached; masterless, ownerless, nobody's, no man's; common; unclaimed; disowned; up for grabs, anybody's; unoccupied, untenanted; vacant 190 *empty*; abandoned 779 *not retained*; untaken, free, going begging 860 *unwanted.*

775 Joint possession – N. *joint possession,* joint tenancy; joint ownership; common land, common; public property, public domain 777 *property*; condominium 733 *political organization*; joint stock, pool, kitty 632 *store*; cooperative system; nationalization, public

ownership, state o., socialism, communism, collectivism; collective farm, collective, commune, kolkhoz, kibbutz 370 *farm*; time-sharing.

participation, membership, affiliation 78 *inclusion*; partnership, profit-sharing, time-sharing 706 *association*; Dutch treat, bottle party, byob, share-out; involvement, sympathy; fellow feeling, empathy, sympathetic strike, joint action.

participator, member, partner, joint heir; shareholder, stockholder 776 *possessor*; co-tenant, flat-mate, room-m., housing association; cooperator; trade unionist; collectivist, socialist, communist; commune-dweller, kolkhoznik, kibbutznik; sympathizer, contributor 707 *patron*.

Vb. *participate,* have a hand in, have a say in, join in, pitch in, sit in, be in on, have a finger in the pie 706 *cooperate*; partake of, share in, come in for a s.; share, go shares, go halves, go fifty-fifty, pull one's weight, share and share alike 783 *apportion*; share expenses, go Dutch 804 *defray*.

776 Possessor – N. *possessor,* holder, taker, captor, conqueror; squatter; monopolizer, dog in the manger; occupant, lodger, occupier, incumbent; mortgagee; renter, hirer, lessee, leaseholder, rent-payer; tenantry, tenant; house-owner, owner-occupier, householder, free-holder.

owner, monarch, monarch of all one surveys; master, mistress, proprietor, proprietress, proprietrix; purchaser, buyer 792 *purchaser*; lord, lord *or* lady of the manor, landed gentry, landed interest; squire, laird 868 *aristocracy*; man *or* woman of property, property-holder, shareholder, stockholder, landowner, landlord, landlady; mortgagor; testator, testatrix, bequeather 781 *giver*.

beneficiary, grantee; incumbent 986 *cleric*; legatee; inheritor, successor, successor apparent; next of kin 11 *kinsman*; heir *or* heiress, heir apparent, heir presumptive; crown prince 741 *sovereign*.

777 Property – N. *property,* possession, possessions, one's all; stake; personal property, public p., common p.; church property; chattel, immovables; movables, personal estate, goods and chattels, worldly goods, appurtenances, belongings, paraphernalia, accoutrements, effects, personal e., impedimenta, baggage, bag and baggage, things, gear, what one stands up in; goods, stock 795 *merchandise*; plant, fixtures, furniture.

estate, estate and effects, assets, frozen a., liquid a., assets and liabilities; circumstances, what one is worth, resources 629 *means*; substance, capital, one's money, one's fortune 800 *wealth*; revenue, income 807 *receipt*; valuables, securities, stocks and shares, portfolio; stake, holding, investment; debts; title, interest; living 985 *benefice*; lease, tenure, freehold, copyhold, fee.

lands, land, acres, broad a., acreage, tract, grounds; estate, property, landed p.; real estate, realty; holding, tenure, freehold, copyhold, fief, manor; lordship, domain; plot 184 *territory*; farm, home f., manor f., homestead, plantation, ranch, hacienda; crown lands, common land, common 775 *joint possession*; dependency, dominion 733 *political organization*.

dower, dowry, marriage portion, jointure, marriage settlement; allowance, pin money; alimony, aliment, maintenance, palimony; patrimony, birthright 915 *dueness*; heritage; inheritance, legacy, bequest; heirloom; expectations, entail.

Adj. *proprietary,* branded, patented; landed, feudal, freehold, leasehold, copyhold; hereditary, heritable, entailed; endowed.

Vb. *endow,* endow, bless w. 781 *give*; bequeath; grant, allot 780 *assign*; put in possession, instal 751 *commission*; found.

778 Retention – N. *retention,* prehensility, tenacity; stickiness 354 *viscidity*; tenaciousness, retentiveness, holding on,

hanging on, clinging to, handhold, foothold, toehold 218 *support*; beachhead 34 *advantage*; clutches, grip, vice-like g., grasp, hold, firm h., stranglehold, half-nelson; squeeze 198 *compression*; clinch, lock; hug, bear h., embrace, clasp, cuddle 889 *endearment*; keeping in 747 *detention*; finders keepers 760 *refusal*; containment 235 *enclosure*.

pincers, nippers; tweezers, pliers, snub-nosed p., wrench, tongs, forceps, vice, clamp 47 *fastening*; talon, claw, nails 256 *sharp point*; tentacle, hook, tendril 378 *feeler*; teeth, fangs 256 *tooth*; paw, hand, fingers 378 *finger*; fist, clenched f., duke.

Adj. *retentive*, tenacious, prehensile; vice-like, retaining 747 *restraining*; clinging, adhesive, sticky, gummy, gluey, gooey 48 *cohesive*; firm, unshakable 45 *tied*; tight, strangling.

Vb. *retain*, hold; grab, buttonhole, hold back 702 *obstruct*; hold up, catch, steady 218 *support*; hold on, hold fast, hold tight, keep a firm hold of, maintain one's hold, not let go; cling to, hang on to, freeze on to, stick to, adhere; fasten on, grip, grasp, grapple, clench, clinch, lock; hug, clasp, clutch, embrace; pin, pin down, hold d.; have by the throat, throttle, strangle, keep a stranglehold on, get a half-nelson on, tighten one's grip 747 *restrain*; dig one's nails in, dig one's toes in, hang on like a bulldog, hang on with all one's might, hang on for dear life; keep in, detain 747 *imprison*; contain, keep within limits, draw the line 235 *enclose*; keep to oneself, keep in one's own hands, keep back, keep to one side, withhold 525 *keep secret*; not dispose of 632 *store*; save, keep 666 *preserve*; not part with, keep back, withhold 760 *refuse*.

779 Nonretention – **N.** *nonretention*, parting with, disposal, alienation 780 *transfer*; selling off 793 *sale*; letting go, leaving hold of, release 746 *liberation*; dispensation; dissolution (of a marriage) 896 *divorce*; abandonment, renunciation 621 *relinquishment*; cancellation

752 *abrogation*; disuse 611 *desuetude*; leak 298 *outflow*; incontinence.

derelict, jetsam, flotsam 641 *rubbish*; cast-off; waif, stray, foundling, orphan, outcast, pariah; down-and-out, vagrant.

Adj. *not retained*, under notice to quit; alienated, disposed of, sold off; left behind 41 *remaining*; dispensed with, abandoned; released; fired, made redundant, given the sack *or* the chop, given the heave-ho; derelict, unclaimed; disowned, divorced, disinherited; for sale 793 *salable*.

Vb. *not retain*, part with, alienate, transfer 780 *assign*; sell off, dispose of 793 *sell*; be open-handed 815 *be prodigal*; free, let go, let slip, unhand, leave hold of, relax one's grip, release one's hold; unlock, unclench 263 *open*; unbind, untie, disentangle 46 *disunite*; forego, dispense with, do without, spare, give up, waive, abandon, cede, yield 621 *relinquish*; renounce, abjure 603 *recant*; cancel, revoke 752 *abrogate*; lift restrictions, derestrict, raise an embargo, decontrol, deregulate, deration 746 *liberate*; supersede, replace 150 *substitute*; wash one's hands of, turn one's back on, disown, disclaim 533 *negate*; dissolve (a marriage) 896 *divorce*; disinherit, cut off without a penny, cut off with a shilling 801 *impoverish*; marry off 894 *marry*; get rid of, cast off, ditch, jettison, throw overboard 300 *eject*; cast away, abandon, maroon; pension off, put out to grass, invalid out, retire; discharge, give notice to quit, declare redundant, give the heave-ho, ease out, edge out, elbow out, kick o. 300 *dismiss*; lay off; drop, discard 674 *stop using*; withdraw, abandon one's position 753 *resign*; estrange; leak 300 *emit*.

780 Transfer (of property) – **N.** *transfer*, transmission, consignment, delivery, handover 272 *transference*; settlement; conveyancing; bequeathal; assignment; bequest 781 *gift*; lease, let, rental, hire; buying 793 *sale*; trade, trade-off 791

barter; conversion, exchange 151 *interchange*; nationalization, privatization; change of hands, changeover 150 *substitution*; devolution, delegation 751 *commission*; succession, inheritance; pawn.

Vb. *assign,* convey; transfer by will; grant, sign away, give a. 781 *give*; let, rent, hire 784 *lease*; sell; negotiate, barter 791 *trade*; change over 150 *substitute*; exchange, convert 151 *interchange*; confer ownership, put in possession, invest with; devolve, delegate, entrust 751 *commission*; give away, marry off 894 *marry*; deliver, transmit, hand over, unload on, pass to, pass the buck 272 *transfer*; pawn 784 *lend*; transfer ownership, nationalize, privatize.

bequeath, will; grant, assign; leave, leave by will, make a bequest, leave a legacy; make a will, make one's last will and testament, put in one's will, add a codicil; leave a fortune.

change hands, be under new management; change places, be transferred, pass, shift; revert to, devolve upon; pass from hand to hand, circulate, go the rounds 314 *circle.*

781 Giving – N. *giving,* bestowal, donation; alms-giving, charity 901 *philanthropy*; liberality; contribution, subscription; prize-giving, presentation, award 962 *reward*; delivery, consignment, conveyance 780 *transfer*; endowment, settlement 777 *dower*; grant, conferment; investment, investiture; bequeathal.

gift, souvenir, memento, keepsake, token; gift token, gift voucher; present, birthday p., Christmas p.; good-luck present, handsel; Christmas box, whip-round, tip, fee, honorarium, baksheesh, gratuity, pourboire, trinkgeld 962 *reward*; token, consideration; bribe, sweetener, douceur, slush fund 612 *inducement*; prize, award, presentation 729 *trophy*; benefit, benefit match, benefit performance; alms, maundy money, dole, charity 901 *philanthropy*; food parcel,

free meal; freebie, giveaway; bounty, manna from heaven; largesse, donation, hand-out; bonus; extras; perks, perquisites, expense account; grant, allowance, subsidy, aid 703 *subvention*; boon, grace, favour, service, labour of love 597 *voluntary work*; free gift, ex gratia payment; piece of luck, windfall 771 *acquisition*; conscience money 804 *payment*; tribute 809 *tax*; bequest, legacy 780 *transfer.*

offering, dedication, consecration; peace offering, offertory, collection, sacrifice 981 *oblation*; Peter's pence; widow's mite; contribution, subscription, flag day, appeal; stake.

giver, donor, bestower; rewarder, tipper, briber; grantor; presenter, awarder, prize-giver; bequeather; subscriber, contributor; sacrificer 981 *worshipper*; almsgiver, blood donor, kidney d., organ d. 903 *benefactor*; Lady Bountiful, fairy godmother, rich uncle, sugar daddy, Santa Claus, Father Christmas 813 *good giver*; backer, angel.

Adj. *given,* gratuitous, gratis, for nothing, free, freebie, giveaway 812 *uncharged*; concessional.

Vb. *give,* bestow, lend, render; afford, provide; vouchsafe, honour w.; grant, accord 756 *permit*; gift, donate, make a present of; leave 780 *bequeath*; endow; present, award 962 *reward*; confer, bestow upon, invest with; dedicate, consecrate; offer; devote, offer up, sacrifice 981 *offer worship*; make time for; give a present, tip, remember, cross one's palm with silver; grease the palm 612 *bribe*; bestow alms, give to charity 897 *do good*; give freely, open one's purse, put one's hand in one's pocket, lavish, pour out, shower upon 813 *be liberal*; spare, give away; stand, treat 882 *be hospitable*; give out, dispense, dole out, allot, deal out 783 *apportion*; contribute, subscribe, subsidize, help 703 *aid*; have a whip-round, pass round the hat, launch an appeal; pay one's share *or* whack, chip in 775 *participate*; part with, fork out, shell o. 804 *pay*; impart 524 *communicate*; pay tribute; yield 621 *relinquish*; hand

over, give o., deliver 780 *assign*; commit, entrust 751 *commission*; dispatch 272 *send*.

782 Receiving – N. *receiving,* admittance 299 *reception*; getting 771 *acquisition*; acceptance; inheritance; collection; a receipt, windfall 781 *gift*; toll, tribute, dues, receipts, proceeds, winnings, takings 771 *earnings*; receiving end.

recipient, acceptor, receiver, taker; trustee 754 *consignee*; addressee 588 *correspondent*; buyer 792 *purchaser*; grantee, assignee, licensee, patentee, lessee; legatee, inheritor, heir, successor 776 *beneficiary*; payee, earner, wage-earner; pensioner, old-age p., remittance man 742 *dependant*; winner, prize-w.; exhibitioner; one at the receiving end 825 *sufferer*.

receiver, official r., liquidator 798 *treasurer*; payee, collector, debt-c., rent-c., tax-c., publican; income-tax officer, excise o., customs officer; booking clerk.

Vb. *receive,* be given, have from; get 771 *acquire*; collect, take up; gross, net, clear, pocket, be in receipt of, get one's share; accept, take in 299 *admit*; accept from, draw, encash, be paid; have an income, draw a pension; inherit, come into, come in for, be left.

783 Apportionment – N. *apportionment,* assignment, allotment, allocation, earmarking; division, job-sharing, job-splitting, sharing out, parcelling out, div-vying up, doling out; shares, distribution, deal; dispensing, administration; demarcation, delimitation 236 *limit*; assigned place, seat 27 *degree*.

portion, share, share-out, split; dividend, interim d., final d., divvy, divi; allocation, allotment; lot; proportion, ratio; quota; halves 53 *part*; deal, hand (at cards); modicum, pittance, allowance; ration, iron rations; dose, dosage, measure, dollop, whack, helping, slice, slice of the cake, piece of the action 53 *piece*; rake-off, cut, commission 810 *discount*; stake, ante; task, stint 682 *labour*.

Vb. *apportion,* allot, allocate, earmark; appoint, assign; cast; assign a place, detail, billet; partition, zone; demarcate, delimit 236 *limit*; divide up, subdivide, carve up, split, cut; halve 92 *bisect*; go shares 775 *participate*; share out, divvy up, distribute, spread around; dispense, administer, serve, deal out, dole out, parcel out, dish out 781 *give*; mete out, measure, ration.

Adv. *pro rata,* to each according to his share; proportionately, respectively, each to each, per capita.

784 Lending – N. *lending,* hiring, leasing, farming out; letting, subletting, renting out, lending at interest, on-lending, usury, giving credit 802 *credit*; investment; mortgage, bridging loan; advance, loan; pawnbroking; lease; let, sublet.

pawnshop, pawnbroker's, one's uncle's, pop-shop, hock s.; bank, credit company, building society, International Monetary Fund, IMF, World Bank.

lender, creditor; investor, financier, banker; moneylender, usurer, Shylock; pawnbroker, uncle; mortgagee, lessor, hirer, renter, letter; backer, angel; tallyman; hire-purchase dealer.

Vb. *lend,* loan, on-lend; advance, accommodate, give one a loan 802 *credit*; lend on security, lend on collateral; put up the money, back, finance; invest, risk one's money, play the stockmarket 791 *speculate*.

lease, let, hire out, rent out, farm out; sublet.

785 Borrowing – N. *borrowing,* touching; request for credit, mortgage 803 *debt*; credit account, credit card, plastic money, plastic; hire purchase, HP, tick; instalment plan, the never-never; pawning; loan, bank loan; forced loan, Morton's fork *or* crutch; infringement, plagiarism, piracy, copying 20 *imitation*; borrowed plumes 542 *deception*.

Vb. *borrow,* cadge from, scrounge from, bum from, mooch from, touch for 761 *request*; mortgage, pawn, pop, hock;

provide collateral 767 *give security*; take a loan, exact a forced loan; use a credit card, use plastic money, use plastic, get credit, take on loan, take on credit, take on tick; buy in instalments, buy on hire purchase *or* the never-never 792 *purchase*; ask for credit, apply for a loan, raise a loan, raise the wind; issue debentures; beg, borrow, or steal 771 *acquire*; crib, plagiarize, pirate, infringe 20 *copy*.

786 Taking – N. *taking,* snatching; seizure, capture, rape; taking hold, grasp, apprehension 778 *retention*; taking possession, appropriation, assumption 916 *arrogation*; requisition, earmarking, commandeering, compulsory purchase 771 *acquisition*; exaction, taxation, levy 809 *tax*; taking away, removal 188 *displacement*; stealing; cadging, scrounging, mooching, bumming, touching one for money, abduction, kidnapping, hijacking, piracy; raid; hostage, take, haul, catch, bag, prize, plum 790 *booty*; receipts, takings, winnings, pickings, ill-gotten gains, gleanings 771 *earnings*.

expropriation, dispossession; attachment, foreclosure; eviction 300 *ejection*; takeover, deprivation; hiving off, asset-stripping; disinheritance 780 *transfer*; confiscation; extortion; swindle, rip-off; impounding, sequestration.

rapacity, rapaciousness, avidity, thirst 859 *hunger*; greed, insatiability 816 *avarice*; extortion, blackmail.

taker, appropriator, remover; seizer, snatcher, grabber; raider, pillager, marauder, ransacker, sacker, looter 789 *robber*; kidnapper, hijacker, abductor, press gang; captor, capturer 741 *master*; usurper, extortioner, blackmailer; devourer 168 *destroyer*; bloodsucker, leech, parasite, vampire, harpy, vulture, wolf, shark; beast *or* bird of prey, predator; confiscator, sequestrator 782 *receiver*; expropriator, asset-stripper.

Vb. *take,* accept, be given 782 *receive*; take over, take back; take in, let in 299 *admit*; take up; anticipate 135 *be early*; take hold, fasten on, stick to, clutch, grip,

cling 778 *retain*; lay hands upon, seize, snatch, grab, pounce on; snatch at, reach out for, make a long arm; grasp at, clutch at, grab at, make a grab, scramble for, rush f.; capture, rape, storm, take by s. 727 *overmaster*; conquer, captive 745 *subjugate*; catch, overtake, intercept 277 *outstrip*; apprehend, take into custody, make an arrest, run in, nab, nobble, collar, lay by the heels 747 *arrest*; make sure of, fasten, pinion 747 *fetter*; hook, trap, snare, lime 542 *ensnare*; net, land, bag, pocket; gross, have a turnover 771 *acquire*; gather, accumulate, amass, collect 74 *bring together*; cull, pick, pluck; reap, crop, harvest, glean 370 *cultivate*; scrounge, cadge, mooch, bum, ransack 459 *search*; pick up, snap up, snaffle; knock off, help oneself 788 *steal*; pick clean, strip 229 *uncover*; remove; deduct 39 *subtract*; draw off, milk, tap, mine 304 *extract*.

appropriate, take to or for oneself, make one's own, annex; pirate, plagiarize 20 *copy*; take possession, lay claim to, stake one's claim; take over, assume ownership, possess; enter into, come i., succeed 771 *inherit*; instal oneself, seat o. 187 *place oneself*; overrun, occupy, settle, colonize; win, conquer; recover 656 *retrieve*; reclaim 915 *claim*; earmark, commandeer, requisition 737 *demand*; usurp, trespass, squat 916 *be undue*; treat as one's own, make free with; monopolize, hog, engulf, swallow up 299 *absorb*; devour, eat up.

levy, raise, extort, exact, wrest from 304 *extract*; compel to lend 785 *borrow*; exact tribute, extort protection money, raise taxes 809 *tax*; fleece; wring, squeeze dry, squeeze till the pips squeak 735 *oppress*; sequestrate.

take away, remove, shift, unload, disburden 188 *displace*; hive off, relieve of 788 *steal*; escort 89 *accompany*; kidnap, shanghai, pressgang, abduct, take hostage, hijack, carry off; run away w., elope w. 296 *decamp*.

deprive, bereave, orphan, widow; divest, denude, strip 229 *uncover*; unfrock 752 *depose*; dispossess, usurp 916

393

disentitle; oust, elbow out, evict, expel 300 *eject*; confiscate, sequester, foreclose; disinherit, cut out of one's will, cut off with a shilling.

fleece, pluck, skin, shear, clip; strip, denude 229 *uncover*; take to the cleaners, rip off; take one for a ride, swindle, bilk, welsh, con, cheat 542 *deceive*; blackmail, bleed, bleed white, sponge, suck dry; soak, sting; mulct 788 *defraud*; devour, eat out of house and home 301 *eat*; rook, bankrupt, leave one without a penny *or* cent 801 *impoverish*.

787 Restitution – N. *restitution,* giving back, return, reversion; bringing back, repatriation; reinstatement; rehabilitation 656 *restoration*; ransom, rescue 668 *deliverance*; recuperation, recovery; compensation, repayment, recoupment; refund, reimbursement; indemnity, damages 963 *penalty*; amends, reparation 941 *atonement*.

Vb. *restitute,* make restitution 656 *restore*; return, give back 779 *not retain*; refund, repay, give one one's money back, recoup, reimburse; indemnify, compensate, make it up to; pay compensation, make reparation, make redress, make amends 941 *atone*; repatriate; redeem 668 *deliver*; reinstate, rehabilitate, restore one to favour; recover 656 *retrieve*.

788 Stealing – N. *stealing,* thieving, lifting, robbing etc. vb.; theft, larceny, petty l.; pilfering, snitching, swiping, nicking, filching, putting one's fingers in the till, pickpocketing, shoplifting, kleptomania; burglary, house-breaking, breaking and entering; safe-breaking, robbery, highway r., robbery with violence, stickup, holdup, bag-snatching, mugging, jumping, smash and grab raid; autocrime; poaching, cattle-rustling; rape, abduction, kidnapping, dognapping, hijack, skyjack; body-snatching; cribbing, plagiarism, pirating 20 *imitation*; joyride 785 *borrowing*; thievery, job, fiddle.

plundering, looting, pillage, sacking, ravaging; banditry, outlawry, piracy, buccaneering; raiding, foray 712 *attack*.

swindling, embezzlement, misappropriation; blackmail, extortion, protection racket; daylight robbery, rip-off; moonlighting, tax evasion, black economy, fraud, computer crime, fiddle, swindle, cheating; confidence trick.

thievishness, thievery, light-fingeredness, sticky fingers, kleptomania; dishonesty, crookedness 930 *improbity*.

Adj. *thieving,* light-fingered, sticky-fingered; kleptomaniac; larcenous, predatory, raptorial; piratical, buccaneering, raiding, marauding; scrounging, foraging; fraudulent, on the fiddle 930 *dishonest*.

Vb. *steal,* lift, thieve, pilfer, shoplift, help oneself; be light-fingered, be sticky-fingered, pick pockets, have a finger in the till; pick locks, blow a safe; burgle, burglarize, house-break; rob, relieve of; rifle, sack, clean out; swipe, nobble, nick, pinch, pocket, snaffle, snitch, knock off 786 *take*; forage, scrounge; rustle, make off with; abduct, kidnap, shanghai; purloin, filch; walk off with, spirit away; crib, copy, lift, plagiarize, pirate 20 *copy*; smuggle, bootleg, poach, hijack, skyjack.

defraud, embezzle, misappropriate, purloin, fiddle, cook the books, practise creative accounting, obtain money on false pretences; commit a computer crime; con, swindle, cheat, diddle, do out of, bilk 542 *deceive*; rook, gull, dupe; rip off 786 *fleece*.

rob, mug; hold up, stick up; maraud, raid; foray, forage; ransack, rifle; plunder, pillage, loot, sack, despoil, ravage; blackmail, demand money with menaces; extort protection money, screw, squeeze 735 *oppress*.

789 Thief – N. *thief,* den of thieves; crook, Artful Dodger; light fingers, sticky fingers; kleptomaniac, stealer, lifter, filcher, purloiner, pilferer, petty thief, larcenist; sneak thief, shoplifter; pickpocket, cutpurse, bag-snatcher; cattle thief, rustler; burglar, cat b., house-

breaker, safe-b., safe-blower, picklock, poacher, bootlegger, smuggler, gun runner; abductor, kidnapper 786 *taker*; hijacker, skyjacker; body-snatcher, resurrectionist; fence, plagiarist, pirate.

robber, forty thieves; brigand, bandit, outlaw, Robin Hood; footpad, highwayman, Dick Turpin, mugger, thug, gangster, racketeer; gunman, hijacker, skyjacker, terrorist; pirate, buccaneer; raider, freebooter, plunderer, pillager, sacker, ravager.

defrauder, embezzler, fiddler, creative accountant, diddler; defaulter, welsher; fraudster, swindler, sharper, cheat, computer criminal, shark, con man 545 *trickster*; forger, counterfeiter.

790 Booty – N. *booty,* spoils; spoils of war, plunder, loot, pillage; find, strike, prize, haul, catch 771 *gain*; pickings, gleanings, stolen goods, swag; contraband; ill-gotten gains, graft, blackmail.

791 Barter – N. *barter,* exchange, fair e., swap 151 *interchange*; payment in kind, traffic, trading, dealing, trade-off, buying and selling; factorage, brokerage, agiotage, jobbing; negotiation, bargaining, hard b., haggling, horse-trading.

trade, trading, exporting 272 *transference*; visible trade, invisible t.; protection, trade restrictions, intervention, interventionism 747 *restriction*; free trade, open market, economic zone, EEC, OPEC 796 *market*; traffic, drug t., white slave t., slave trade; smuggling, black market; retail trade 793 *sale*; capitalism, free enterprise, laisser faire 744 *scope*; boom and bust 317 *fluctuation*; commerce 622 *business*; private enterprise, privatization, nationalization; private sector, public s.; business venture 672 *undertaking*; speculation 618 *gambling*; transaction, commercial t., deal, business d., bargain, trade-off, negotiation 765 *compact*.

Vb. *trade,* exchange 151 *interchange*; barter, haggle, swap, do a s.; traffic in; vend, buy and sell, export and import; drive a trade, peddle, do business; trade in, deal in, handle; deal in stolen property, fence; turn over 793 *sell*; commercialize, put on a business footing; trade with, do business w., deal w., have dealings w., open an account w.

speculate, venture, risk 618 *gamble*; invest, sink one's capital in, put one's money to work, make one's money work for one; profiteer; deal in the black market, sell under the counter; play the market.

bargain, negotiate, push up, beat down; haggle, argy-bargy 766 *make terms*; bid for, make a takeover bid, propose a merger, act as white knight; raise the bid, outbid 759 *offer*; underbid 483 *underestimate*; stick out for, hold out for, ask for, charge 766 *give terms*; settle for; drive a hard bargain, do a deal, shake hands on, sign on the dotted line 765 *contract*.

792 Purchase – N. *purchase,* buying; buying up, takeover, buy-out, green mail, cornering, preemption; hire purchase, HP, the never-never, tick 785 *borrowing*; shopping, window s., spending, shopping spree 806 *expenditure*; shopping by post, mail order, teleshopping, tele-ordering; consumer demand 627 *requirement*; bid, take-over b. 759 *offer*; buy, purchase on appro, on approval, good buy, bargain, real b.; shopping list, shopping basket.

purchaser, buyer; consignee; shopper; customer, patron, client, clientele, consumer; bidder; bargainer, haggler; share-buyer, bull, stag.

Vb. *purchase,* make a p., complete a p.; buy 771 *acquire*; shop, market, be in the market for, go shopping, purchase by mail order, purchase by tele-ordering, teleshop; get one's money's worth; buy outright, pay cash for, pay on the spot; buy on credit, buy on hire purchase; buy on the never-never, buy on an instalment plan, pay by instalment, buy on tick 785 *borrow*; pay by cheque *or* by Giro, pay by credit card, buy in 632 *store*; buy up; buy out, make a take-over bid, propose a merger, act as a white knight for; buy

over, bribe; buy back, redeem; pay for, bear the cost of 804 *defray*; buy oneself in, invest in, sink one's money in 791 *speculate*; rent; bid for 759 *offer*; buy shares.

793 Sale – N. *sale,* selling, putting on sale, putting on the market, marketing, distribution; disposal 779 *nonretention*; sell-out; clearance sale, stock-taking s., end-of-season s., closing-down s., white s., jumble s., sale of work, charity sale, car boot s., garage s., bazaar; monopoly; auction, sale by a., roup, Dutch auction, good market, market for; boom 730 *prosperity*; salesmanship, sales talk, pitch, sales patter, spiel; hard sell, soft s. 528 *advertisement*; market research 459 *enquiry*; salability, marketability.

seller, vendor, share-seller, bear; auctioneer; market trader, barrow boy, costermonger, hawker 794 *pedlar*; shopkeeper, dealer 633 *caterer*; wholesaler, retailer 794 *tradespeople*; sales representative, rep, door-to-door salesman, doorstepper; traveller, commercial t., travelling salesman *or* -woman; agent, canvasser, tout; shop assistant, salesman, saleswoman, salesperson; booking clerk, ticket agent; roundsman.

Adj. *salable,* marketable, on sale, for sale; in demand, sought after; on the market, up for sale; bearish, up for grabs; on auction, under the hammer.

Vb. *sell,* make a sale; flog, dispose of; market, put on sale, offer for s., have for s., have on offer, vend; hawk, peddle, push; canvass, tout; put up for sale, auction, auction off, sell by a., bring under the hammer, sell to the highest bidder, knock down to; wholesale; retail, sell under the counter, sell on the black market; turn over one's stock 791 *trade*; sell at a profit 771 *gain*; sell at a loss 772 *lose*; undercut 812 *cheapen*; sell off, remainder; sell up, sell out, wind up 145 *cease*; hold a sale.

be sold, be on sale, come under the hammer 780 *change hands*; sell, have a market, meet a demand, sell well, sell

like hot cakes; be a best-seller, be a loss-leader.

794 Merchant – N. *merchant,* guild, chamber of commerce, firm 708 *corporation*; business person, man *or* woman of business; entrepreneur, speculator, operator 618 *gambler*; trafficker, fence; importer, exporter; wholesaler; retailer, merchandiser, dealer; middleman, broker, stockbroker; estate agent, house a.; financier, banker 784 *lender*.

tradespeople, tradesman, retailer, middleman, tallyman; shopkeeper 793 *seller*; ironmonger, haberdasher, grocer, greengrocer, butcher, tobacconist, newsagent 633 *caterer*.

pedlar, seller; hawker, tinker, gipsy, bagman; costermonger, barrow boy; market trader, stall-keeper.

795 Merchandise – N. *merchandise,* line, staple; article, commodity, stock, range 632 *store*; freight, cargo 193 *contents*; wares, goods, consumer durables; perishable goods, dry g., white g., sundries.

796 Market – N. *market,* mart; free trade area, Common Market, EEC, OPEC, free market, economic zone 791 *trade*; black market, black economy; grey market; seller's market, buyer's m.; marketplace, market cross; street market, flea m., Petticoat Lane; auction room, Christie's, Sotheby's; fair, world f., international f., trade f.; exhibition, exposition, shop window 522 *exhibit*; exchange, corn e., Stock E., bourse; share shop, bucket shop; Wall Street.

emporium, free port; warehouse 632 *storage*; trading centre, trading post; bazaar, arcade, covered market, shopping mall, pedestrian precinct, shopping centre.

shop, retailer's; store, multiple s., department s., chain s.; emporium, bazaar, boutique, bargain basement, supermarket, hypermarket, superstore, cash and carry; trading house; corner shop, stall, booth, stand, newsstand, kiosk, barrow, vending machine, slot m.

797 Money – N. *money,* Lsd, pounds, shillings and pence; wealth; lucre, filthy l., root of all evil; currency, decimal c., hard c., soft c.; legal tender; money of account, sterling, pound s.; precious metal, gold, bullion, gold bar, ingot; silver, ready money, the ready, cash, spot c., hard c., petty c.; change, small c., coppers 33 *small quantity*; pocket money, pin m., allowance; spending money; paltry sum, chickenfeed, peanuts.

shekels, brass, dough, lolly, bread; loot, gravy.

funds, hot money; liquidity, bank account, current a., deposit a., savings a., money in the bank, liquid assets; wherewithal, the needful 629 *means*; ready money, the ready, finances, exchequer, cash flow, monies, treasure 633 *provision*; remittance 804 *payment*; capital; reserves, balances; sum of money, amount, figure, sum, round s., lump s.; quid, smacker, oncer, buck; fiver, tenner, pony, monkey, ton, century, grand; mint of money, wads, scads, pile, packet, stacks, heaps, mountains, millions, billions, zillions 32 *great quantity*.

finance, high finance, IMF; financial control, purse strings, almighty dollar; zaitech, cash transaction; money market, Eurodollar m., exchange, stock exchange, Big Bang 796 *market*; exchange rate, bank r., minimum lending r., effective r., sterling effective r.; APR, annual percentage rate; agio, agiotage, snake; floating pound; devaluation, depreciation; strong pound, rallying 654 *improvement*; gold standard; green pound; managed currency, sinking f., inflation; deflation; stagflation; reflation.

coinage, minting, issue; metallic currency, stamped coinage, gold c., silver c., electrum c., copper c., nickel c., billon c., bronze c.; specie, minted coinage, coin, piece, coin of the realm; guinea, sovereign, half s.; pound, quid, nicker; crown, half c., florin, shilling, bob, sixpence, tanner, threepenny bit, penny, bun p., copper, halfpenny, ship h.; farthing; decimal coinage, pound coin, fifty p., twenty

p., ten p., five p., two p., one p., half p.; dollar, buck; half dollar, quarter, dime, nickel, jitney, cent; ten-dollar piece, eagle; napoleon, louis d'or; franc, new f.; mark, Deutschmark, guilder, krona, krone, lira, drachma, peseta, escudo, peso, dinar, rupee, rand, yuan, yen, zloty, rouble; obol, talent, shekel, solidus, bezant, ducat, angel, noble, real, pistole, piece of eight; change, small c., groat, bawbee, obolus, centime, sou, pfennig, piastre, kopek, cash 33 *small quantity*; shell money, cowrie, wampum; numismatics, numismatology.

paper money, fiduciary currency; bankroll, wad; note, banknote, treasury note, pound n., five-p. n., ten-p. n., bill, dollar b., greenback, buck, ten-dollar bill; bill of exchange; draft, money order, postal o., cheque, certified c., giro c., traveller's c., Eurocheque, letter of credit; promissory note, note of hand, IOU; standing order, direct debit; scrip, premium bond 767 *security*.

Adj. *monetary,* numismatic; pecuniary, financial, fiscal, budgetary; coined, stamped, minted, issued; fiduciary; gold-based, sterling, solvent 800 *rich*; inflationary, deflationary, floating; devalued, depreciated.

Vb. *mint,* coin, stamp; issue, circulate; forge, counterfeit.

draw money, cash, encash, realize, draw upon, cash a cheque, endorse a c., write a c. 804 *pay*.

798 Treasurer – N. *treasurer,* honorary t.; bursar, purser; cashier, teller, croupier; trustee, steward 754 *consignee*; liquidator 782 *receiver*; bookkeeper 808 *accountant*; banker, financier; keeper of the purse, paymaster, controller, comptroller, Chancellor of the Exchequer, Secretary of the Treasury, Governor of the Bank of England.

799 Treasury – N. *treasury,* exchequer, fisc, public purse; reserves, fund 632 *store*; counting house; bursary; bank, Bank of England, Old Lady of Threadneedle Street; savings bank, Post

Office savings b., building society; credit union, coffer, chest 194 *box*; treasure chest, depository 632 *storage*; strongroom, strongbox, safe, safe deposit, cash box, moneybox, piggybank, stocking, mattress; till, cash register, cash desk, slot machine; cash dispenser, automated teller machine, ATM; personal identification number, PIN; box office, gate, turnstile; purse 194 *pocket*; wallet, pocket book, billfold.

800 Wealth – N. *wealth,* lucre, brass 797 *money*; moneymaking, golden touch, Midas t., philosopher's stone; riches, fleshpots 635 *plenty*; luxury 637 *superfluity*; opulence, affluence 730 *prosperity*; ease, comfort, easy street 376 *euphoria*; solvency, credit-worthiness 802 *credit*; substance 3 *substantiality*; independence, competence, self-sufficiency 635 *sufficiency*; high income; gains 771 *gain*; resources, well-lined pockets, capital 629 *means*; liquid assets, bank account, building society a., Post Office savings a.; bottomless purse, goose that lays golden eggs; nest egg 632 *store*; tidy sum, pots of money, pile, heap, mountain, scads, wads, packet, cool million, zillions 32 *great quantity*; fortune; broad acres 777 *property*; bonanza, gold mine; El Dorado, pot of gold, the end of the rainbow, riches of Solomon, king's ransom.

rich person, wealthy p., well-to-do p., man *or* woman of means; baron, tycoon, magnate, moneybags, millionaire, multim., millionairess; Croesus, Midas; moneymaker, fat cat, capitalist, plutocrat, bloated p.; heir, heiress, poor little rich girl 776 *beneficiary*; the haves, the privileged, moneyed class, propertied c., leisured c., the well-to-do, the well-off, the well-heeled, jet set, glitterati 848 *beau monde*; new rich, nouveau riche, self-made man 730 *prosperous person.*

Adj. *rich,* richly endowed, lush, fertile 171 *prolific*; abundant 635 *plentiful*; luxurious, upholstered, plush, ritzy; glittering, glitzy 875 *ostentatious*; wealthy,

well-endowed, born in the purple, born with a silver spoon in one's mouth; opulent, affluent 730 *prosperous*; well-off, well-to-do, well-heeled, in easy circumstances, comfortably off, well-paid.

moneyed, propertied, worth a packet, worth millions; made of money, rolling in m., rolling in it, dripping, loaded; stinking rich, filthy r.; rich as Croesus; on easy street, in clover, in funds, in cash, in credit, in the black; well-heeled, flush, in the money; quids in, doing nicely thank you; credit-worthy, solvent.

Vb. *be rich,* have money, have means; be rolling in money, wallow in riches; be in clover, be on easy street, be on velvet, be born in the purple, be born with a silver spoon in one's mouth; be sitting on a goldmine, be raking it in; be flush, be in funds etc. adj.; have money to burn.

afford, have the means, have the wherewithal, be solvent, make both ends meet, keep one's head above water, keep the wolf from the door, keep up with the Joneses 635 *have enough.*

get rich, come into money 771 *inherit*; do all right for oneself 730 *prosper*; make a profit, make money, coin it, rake in the shekels, rake it in, laugh all the way to the bank; make a packet, make a pile, make a bomb, make a fortune, make a mint, make a killing, clean up, feather one's nest, line one's pocket, strike it rich, hit the jackpot, turn up trumps, win the pools, have one's ship come home, find one's Eldorado, find the pot of gold at the end of the rainbow 771 *gain.*

801 Poverty – N. *poverty,* asceticism; financial embarrassment, difficulties, Queer Street 805 *insolvency*; impoverishment, beggary, penury, pennilessness, pauperism, destitution; privation, indigence, neediness, necessity, dire n., need, want, pinch 627 *requirement*; empty larder 636 *scarcity*; wolf at the door, famine 946 *fasting*; empty purse, slender means, straitened circumstances, insufficiency, dire straits, belt-tightening 825 *suffering*; grinding poverty, subsistence level, breadline, poverty line, poverty trap,

hand-to-mouth existence; poorness, meagreness, shabbiness, seediness, raggedness; recession, slump, depression 655 *deterioration*; squalor, slum; workhouse, poorhouse.

poor person, broken man *or* woman, bankrupt, insolvent 805 *nonpayer*; pauper, indigent, beggar, vagrant, tramp, bum, down-and-out 763 *beggar*; the poor, new poor, the have-nots, the disadvantaged, the underprivileged 869 *lower classes*; Cinderella; poor relation 35 *inferior*.

Adj. *poor,* as poor as a church-mouse; not well-off, badly o., hard up; lowpaid, underprivileged; hard up, impecunious, short of cash, out of pocket, in the red; skint, cleaned out, bust, broke, flat b., stony b., bankrupt, insolvent 805 *nonpaying*; on the breadline, below the poverty line, in the poverty trap, on the dole; impoverished, beggared; deprived, robbed; poverty-stricken; needy, indigent, in want, in need 627 *necessitous*; homeless; hungry 636 *underfed*; in distress, hard put to it, down at heel, down and out, out at elbow, on one's uppers, on one's beam ends, on the rocks, up against it, not knowing which way to turn 700 *in difficulties*; unable to make both ends meet, unable to pay one's way, unable to keep the wolf from the door; unprovided for, penniless, destitute; down to one's last penny, without a bean, without a cent, without a sou.

Vb. *be poor,* live on a pittance, eke out a livelihood, scratch a living, live from hand to mouth; feel the pinch, fall on hard times, be in dire straits, be on one's uppers, be on the breadline, be below the poverty line, be caught in the poverty trap, have to watch the pennies; sing for one's supper; starve 859 *be hungry*; want, lack 627 *require*; not have a penny, not have two halfpennies to rub together; have no prospects; go broke 805 *not pay*; lose one's money, come down in the world 655 *deteriorate*; go on the dole, claim supplementary benefit.

impoverish, reduce to poverty, leave destitute, beggar, ruin 165 *destroy*; rob,

strip 786 *fleece*; disinherit, cut off without a penny 786 *deprive*.

802 Credit – N. *credit,* repute, reputation 866 *prestige*; creditworthiness; borrowing capacity, tick; letter of credit, credit card, charge card, plastic money, plastic, phonecard, credit note, the black; APR, annual percentage rate (of charge); credits, balances, credit balance 807 *receipt*; unpaid bill, account, budget a., score, tally, bill 808 *accounts*; trading deficit, floating debt 803 *debt*; loan, mortgage.

Vb. *credit,* give *or* furnish c., extend c.; credit one's account; grant, vote; charge to one's account, charge to one's budget a.; sell on tick, take credit, open an account, run up an account, run up a bill 785 *borrow*.

803 Debt – N. *debt,* indebtedness 785 *borrowing*; liability, obligation, commitment; mortgage 767 *security*; debit, charge; debts, bills, hire-purchase debt; national debt, floating d.; debt of honour, unsecured debt 764 *promise*; gearing, leverage; bad debt, write-off 772 *loss*; tally, account; deficit, overdraft 307 *shortfall*; insolvency, frozen assets 805 *nonpayment*; deferred payment 802 *credit*; arrears, back pay; foreclosure.

interest, simple i., compound i., usury, pound of flesh; premium, rate of interest, minimum lending rate, discount rate, bank rate.

Vb. *be in debt,* owe, owe money; be debited with; get credit, overdraw (one's account); get on tick, buy on hire purchase *or* the never-never 785 *borrow*; use a credit card, use a charge card, use plastic money, use plastic, keep an account with, have charged to one's account; charge to one's budget a., run up an a., run into debt; be in the red, be overdrawn; leave one's bills unpaid, bilk, welsh.

804 Payment – N. *payment,* bearing the cost; defraying the cost, paying off, satisfaction, liquidation, clearance, settlement, settlement on account; receipt;

cash payment, down p., ready money 797 *money*; earnest money, deposit; instalment, standing order, direct debit; deferred payment, hire purchase 785 *borrowing*; subscription, tribute 809 *tax*; contribution, whip-round, appeal, collection 781 *offering*; compensation, indemnity 787 *restitution*; remittance 806 *expenditure.*

pay, payout, payoff, pay packet, pay cheque, take-home pay, pay day, wages, salary 771 *earnings*; grant, subsidy 703 *subvention*; salary, pension, annuity, remuneration, emolument, fee, honorarium, bribe 962 *reward*; cut, commission 810 *discount*; contribution, subscription, collection, tribute 809 *tax*; damages, indemnity 963 *penalty*; back pay, compensation, redundancy pay, severance pay, golden handshake, ex gratia payment.

Vb. *pay,* disburse 806 *expend*; contribute 781 *give*; negotiate a trade-off, barter 791 *trade*; pay out, shell o., fork o., dole out, dish out, stump up, cough up; come across, do the needful, put one's hand in one's pocket, open one's wallet; pay a high price, pay an exorbitant price, pay through the nose; pay back, repay, reimburse, compensate 787 *restitute*; grease the palm, cross one's palm with silver 612 *bribe*; pay wages, remunerate, tip 962 *reward*; pay in advance, put money up front, ante up, pay on sight, pay on delivery, C.O.D., pay on demand; pay by cheque *or* by giro; pay by banker's order, pay by standing o., pay by direct debit; pay on the nail, pay cash; honour (a bill), pay up, meet, discharge, get a receipt; settle an account, square accounts with 808 *account*; settle accounts with, settle a score.

defray, pay for, bear the cost, put up funds; pay one's way, pay one's share; foot the bill, pick up the tab, pay the piper; stand a round, treat 781 *give*; go Dutch 775 *participate.*

805 Nonpayment – N. *nonpayment,* default; deduction 963 *penalty*; moratorium, embargo, freeze; refusal to pay,

repudiation 760 *refusal*; tax avoidance, tax evasion, creative accounting, black economy 620 *avoidance*; deferred payment, hire purchase 785 *borrowing*; dishonoured cheque, dud c., bouncing c.

insolvency, inability to pay, failure to meet one's obligations; crash; failure of credit, cash-flow crisis; bankruptcy; nothing in the kitty, overdraft 636 *insufficiency.*

nonpayer, defaulter, embezzler, tax dodger 789 *defrauder*; bilker, welsher; bankrupt.

Adj. *nonpaying,* in arrears; insolvent, bankrupt; up to one's ears in debt, ruined 801 *poor.*

Vb. *not pay,* default; fall into arrears, get behindhand; withhold p., freeze; refuse payment; fiddle one's income tax, practise tax evasion, moonlight, be part of the black economy 930 *be dishonest*; divert, sequester 786 *deprive*; have one's cheque bounce, dishonour; have a cash-flow crisis, become insolvent, go bankrupt, go to the wall; sink, fail, go bust, crash, wind up, go into liquidation; welsh, bilk 542 *deceive*, be unable to pay 801 *be poor.*

806 Expenditure – N. *expenditure,* spending, disbursement 804 *payment*; cost of living; outgoings, overheads, costs, expenses, out-of-pocket e., extras, expense account; expense, outlay, investment; spending spree 815 *prodigality.*

Vb. *expend,* spend; buy 792 *purchase*; lay out, invest, sink money; be out of pocket, incur expenses; afford, stand, bear the cost, defray the c., bankroll, meet charges, disburse, pay out 804 *pay*; draw on one's savings; open one's wallet, put one's hand in one's pocket; donate 781 *give*; spare no expense, go on a spree, do one proud, be lavish 813 *be liberal*; fling money around, splash out, blow, blow one's cash 815 *be prodigal*; use up, consume, get through 634 *waste.*

807 Receipt – N. *receipt,* voucher, counterfoil; credits, revenue, royalty, rents,

rates, dues; customs, taxes 809 *tax*; turnover, takings, proceeds, returns, receipts, gross r., net r., box-office r., gate money; income, private i., privy purse; emolument, regular income, pay, half p., salary, wages 771 *earnings*; remuneration 962 *reward*; pension, annuity; allowance, personal a.; pin money, pocket money, spending m.; alimony, aliment, palimony, maintenance; bursary, scholarship 771 *acquisition*; interest, return, rake-off, cut; winnings, profits, gross p., net p., capital gain 771 *gain*; bonus, premium 40 *extra*; legacy, inheritance 777 *dower*.

Vb. see 771 *acquire,* 782 *receive,* 786 *take.*

808 Accounts – N. *accounts,* accountancy, accounting; book-keeping, entry; audit; account, profit and loss a., balance sheet, debit and credit; budgeting, budget, zero-based budgeting; current account, cash a., deposit a., savings a., expense a.; account rendered, statement, bill, invoice 87 *list*; account settled 804 *payment*; reckoning, computation, score, tally, facts and figures 86 *numeration.*

accountant, chartered a., bookkeeper; cashier 798 *treasurer*; auditor; actuary, statistician.

Adj. *accounting,* actuarial, computing, inventorial, budgetary.

Vb. *account,* keep the books, keep accounts; make up an account, budget, prepare a b.; cost, value, write up, write down 480 *estimate*; enter, carry over, debit, credit 548 *register*; prepare a cash-flow forecast, prepare a balance sheet, balance accounts; settle accounts, square a., finalize a., wind up a.; prepare a statement, present an account, charge, bill, invoice; practise creative accounting, cook the accounts *or* the books, falsify the a., fiddle, doctor 788 *defraud*; audit, go through the books; take stock.

809 Price – N. *price,* selling p., market p., retail p., wholesale p., discount p., list p.; rate, going r., rate for the job, fee for service; piece rate, flat r.; price control, fixed price 747 *restraint*; value, face v.; worth, what it will fetch; premium, scarcity value; price list, tariff; quoted price, quotation; amount, figure, sum asked for; ransom, fine 963 *penalty*; demand, dues, charge; surcharge, supplement 40 *extra*; rip-off; fare, flat f., hire, rental, rent, ground r.; fee, entrance *or* admission fee; refresher, commission, cut, rake-off; charges, freightage, wharfage; postage; cover charge, service c., corkage.

cost, purchase p.; damage, costs, expenses 806 *expenditure*; running costs, overheads; wage bill, salary b.; legal costs, damages 963 *penalty*; cost of living.

tax, taxes, dues; taxation, Inland Revenue, tax return, tax form, tax demand 737 *demand*; rating, assessment, rateable value; rates, community charge *or* tax, poll tax, water rate; levy, toll, duty; imposition; charge; exaction, forced loan, Morton's fork *or* crutch; punitive tax 963 *penalty*; tribute, danegeld, blackmail, protection money, ransom 804 *payment*; ecclesiastical tax, Peter's pence, tithe; national insurance; poll tax, capitation t.; estate duty, death duty, inheritance tax; direct taxation, income tax, PAYE, surtax, supertax, company tax, corporation t.; capital levy, capital gains tax 786 *expropriation*; indirect taxation, excise, customs, tariff; local tax, purchase tax, sales t., value-added tax, VAT, zero-rated goods.

Vb. *price,* cost, assess, value, rate 480 *estimate*; put a price on; place a value on, fix a price for; raise a price, lower a p.; fix the p.; ask a p., charge 737 *demand*.

cost, be worth, fetch, bring in; amount to, come to, mount up to; be priced at, be valued at; bear a price; sell for, go f., set one back, change hands for, realize.

tax, impose a tax; fix a tariff, levy a rate, assess for tax, value; subject to duty, raise taxes, collect t., levy t.

810 Discount – N. *discount,* something off, reduction, rebate, cut; concession,

special price; cut price, cut rate, special offer, loss leader 612 *incentive*; bargain price, knock-down p., bargain sale 812 *cheapness*; one's cut, commission, rake-off.

Vb. *discount,* deduct 39 *subtract*; allow a margin, reduce, depreciate, give a rebate; offer a discount; mark down, take off, cut, slash 812 *cheapen*; take a discount, take one's cut, take one's percentage.

811 Dearness – N. *dearness,* costliness, expensiveness; value, pricelessness; scarcity value, rarity; exorbitance, extortion, rack rents, rip-off; overcharge, daylight robbery; bad bargain, high price, fancy p.; cost, high c., pretty penny; ruinous charge; rising costs, sellers' market; bull m., soaring prices; inflation.

Adj. *dear,* high-priced, pricy, expensive, exclusive, ritzy, upmarket; costly, multimillion; extravagant, dearly-bought; dear at the price, overpriced, overpaid; exorbitant, excessive, extortionate; steep, stiff, sky-high; beyond one's means, prohibitive; dear at any price 641 *useless*; rising in price, soaring, mounting, going through the ceiling, inflationary; bullish.

of value, of worth 644 *valuable*; priceless, beyond price; invaluable 640 *useful*; inestimable, worth a king's ransom, worth its weight in gold, worth a fortune; precious, rare, scarce, like gold dust 140 *infrequent*; at a premium, not to be had for love or money.

Vb. *be dear,* cost a lot, cost a packet, cost a pretty penny, be high-priced, hurt one's pocket, make a hole in one's p.; rise in price, harden; go up, appreciate, escalate, soar, go through the ceiling; be out of one's price range, price itself out of the market; prove expensive, cost one dear, cost a fortune, cost the earth.

overcharge, overprice, sell dear, ask too much; profiteer, soak, sting, bleed, skin, extort, charge rack rents, rip off, do, short-change, hold to ransom 786 *fleece*; put up prices, inflate p., mark up; bull, raise the price, raise the bid.

pay too much, pay through the nose, be stung, be ripped off, be had, be done; pay dear, buy a white elephant; achieve a Pyrrhic victory; ruin oneself.

812 Cheapness – N. *cheapness,* inexpensiveness, affordability; good value, value for money, snip, steal, bargain, sale goods, seconds, rejects; low price; cheap rate, off-peak r., off-season r., concessional r., excursion fare, railcard 810 *discount*; reduced price, knock-down p., cut p., bargain p., budget p., competitive p., sale p., giveaway p., rockbottom p., loss leader; peppercorn rent, easy terms; buyers' market, sluggish m.; Dutch auction; falling prices, bearishness; depreciation, fall, slump; deflation; glut, drug on the market 635 *plenty.*

no charge, nominal c. 781 *gift*; gratuitousness, labour of love 597 *voluntary work*; free trade, free port; free entry, free admission, free seats, free pass, free ticket, freebie, complimentary ticket; free quarters, grace and favour; free board, free service, free delivery; everything for nothing.

Adj. *cheap,* inexpensive, reasonable; affordable, within one's means, easy on the pocket; low-budget; substandard; economical, economy, economy size; not dear, worth the money; low-priced, cheap at the price; dirt-cheap, going cheap, going for a song, for peanuts; bargain-rate, bargain-basement, downmarket, cut-price, concessional, sale-price, reduced, r. to clear; marked down, half-price; tourist-class, off-season; two-a-penny; cheapjack, jerry-built; cheapening, bearish, falling; underpaid, underpriced.

uncharged, gratuitous, complimentary, courtesy, gratis, for nothing, for love, for kicks, for the asking; costing nothing, free, scot-f., free of charge, for free, giveaway; zero-rated, untaxed, tax-free, rent-f., post-f.; given away, as a gift 781 *given*; free, gratis and for nothing.

Vb. *be cheap,* - inexpensive etc. adj.; cost little, be economical, be within anyone's reach, be easy on the pocket; be

cheap at the price; be bought for a song, go dirt-cheap; cost nothing, be free, be had for the asking; cheapen, get cheaper, fall in price, depreciate.

cheapen, lower the price, reduce the p.; keep cheap, lower one's charges, trim one's prices, mark down, cut, slash; undercharge, let go for a song, give away 781 *give*; beat down, haggle, undercut, undersell.

Adv. *cheaply,* on the cheap; at cost price, at wholesale prices, at a discount, for a song.

813 Liberality – **N.** *liberality,* bountifulness, munificence, generosity 931 *disinterestedness*; open-handedness, open hand, open purse, hospitality, open house 882 *sociability*; free hand, blank cheque, carte blanche 744 *scope*; lavishness 815 *prodigality*; bounty, largesse 781 *gift*; charity.

good giver, generous g.; donor, blood d., organ d., kidney d.; good tipper; fairy godmother, Lady Bountiful, Father Christmas, Santa Claus, sugar daddy, rich uncle 903 *benefactor.*

Adj. *liberal,* free-spending, open-handed, lavish 815 *prodigal*; bountiful, charitable 897 *benevolent*; hospitable 882 *sociable*; handsome, generous, munificent, slap-up; lordly, princely, royal, right royal; unstinting, unsparing; in liberal quantities, abundant, ample, overwhelming, bounteous, profuse, full, plenteous; overflowing 637 *redundant.*

Vb. *be liberal,* - generous etc. adj.; lavish, shower largesse, shower upon 781 *give*; put one's hand in one's pocket, open one's wallet; give generously, give one's last penny, give the shirt off one's back; pay well, tip w.; keep open house 882 *be hospitable*; do one proud, spare no expense; give carte blanche, give a blank cheque 744 *give scope*; spend freely, not ask for the change, throw money about like water, throw one's money around 815 *be prodigal.*

814 Economy – **N.** *economy,* thrift, thriftiness, frugality; prudence, care, carefulness; husbandry, good housekeeping, sound stewardship, good management, terotechnology; credit squeeze 747 *restriction*; economy drive, economy measures; time-saving, labour-s., time and motion study, management s.; husbanding of resources, economizing, saving, sparing, pinching, cheese-paring; retrenchment, economies, cuts, cut-backs; savings 632 *store*; conservation, energy-saving.

Adj. *economical,* time-saving, labour-s., energy-s., money-s., cost-cutting; money-conscious, counting every penny 816 *parsimonious*; thrifty, careful, prudent, canny, frugal, cheese-paring, saving, sparing; meagre, Spartan.

Vb. *economize,* be economical, - sparing etc. adj.; husband one's resources, keep costs down, waste nothing, recycle, reuse; keep within one's budget, cut one's coat according to one's cloth, make both ends meet; cut costs, trim expenditure, cut back, make economies, retrench, tighten one's belt; pinch, scrape, look after the pennies 816 *be parsimonious*; save 632 *store*; make one's money work for one.

815 Prodigality – **N.** *prodigality,* lavishness, profusion, profuseness 637 *redundance*; extravagance; wastefulness, profligacy, dissipation, squandering, spending spree, splurge 634 *waste*; improvidence; misuse of funds 675 *misuse*; money burning a hole in one's pocket.

prodigal, prodigal son, big spender; wastrel, profligate, spendthrift, spendaholic, squanderer.

Adj. *prodigal,* lavish 813 *liberal*; profuse, extravagant, wasteful, squandering, profligate; uneconomic, uneconomical, thriftless, spendthrift, improvident, reckless, dissipated.

Vb. *be prodigal,* blow one's money, blue one's m.; overspend, pour out money, splash money around, throw one's money around, flash pound notes; splurge, go on a spending spree, spend

money like water; burn one's money, run through one's savings, exhaust one's resources, spend up to the hilt, splurge out, lash out, blow everything, waste one's inheritance, squander 634 *waste*; burn the candle at both ends, fritter away, throw a., dissipate, scatter to the winds, pour down the drain; not count the cost, have no money sense, think money grows on trees; misspend, throw good money after bad; have no thought for the morrow, overdraw; eat up one's capital; put nothing by, have no nest-egg, have nothing to fall back on, keep nothing for a rainy day.

Int. hang the expense! a short life and a merry one! easy come easy go! you can't take it with you!

816 Parsimony – N. *parsimony,* parsimoniousness; false economy; cheese-paring, scrimping, pinching, scraping, penny-pinching; tightfistedness, niggardliness, meanness, minginess, stinginess, miserliness; uncharitableness; moths in one's wallet 932 *selfishness*.

avarice, cupidity, acquisitiveness, covetousness, green-eyed monster, possessiveness; money-grubbing, itching palm;

rapacity, avidity, greed 859 *desire*; mercenariness.

niggard, skinflint, penny pincher, cheese-parer, tightwad, meanie; miser, money-grubber, cadger; hoarder, magpie; Scrooge.

Adj. *parsimonious,* careful 814 *economical*; money-conscious, pennywise, miserly, mean, mingy, stingy, near, close, tight; tight-fisted, close-f. 778 *retentive*; grudging, cheese-paring, ungenerous, uncharitable; sparing, pinching, scraping, scrimping.

avaricious, grasping, monopolistic 932 *selfish*; possessive, acquisitive 771 *acquiring*; hoarding; penny-pinching; miserly; money-grubbing, money-mad, covetous 859 *greedy*; rapacious; mercenary,

Vb. *be parsimonious,* - niggardly etc. adj.; begrudge; stint, skimp; scrape, scrimp, pinch 814 *economize*; fleece; be penny-wise, spoil the ship for a ha'porth of tar; starve oneself, live on a shoestring, live like a pauper; grudge every farthing, haggle 791 *bargain*; sit on, keep for oneself 932 *be selfish*.

Class six

EMOTION, RELIGION AND MORALITY

Section one: General

817 Affections – N. *affections,* qualities, instincts; passions, feelings, inner f., emotions; nature, disposition 5 *character*; spirit, temper, mettle 5 *temperament*; cast of mind, trait 7 *state*; personality, psychology, psyche, mentality, outlook, inherited characteristics 5 *heredity*; being, innermost b., breast, bosom, heart, soul, core, inmost soul, inner man, cockles of the heart, heart of hearts 5 *essential part,* 447 *spirit*; animus, attitude, frame of mind, state of m., vein, strain, humour, mood; predilection, predisposition, inclinations, turn, bent, bias 179 *tendency*; passion, ruling p.; prejudice; heartstrings 818 *feeling.*

Adj. *with affections,* affected, characterized, formed, moulded, shaped, cast, tempered, framed; imbued with, permeated w., devoured w.; obsessed w., hung up about, ingrained, inborn, inbred, congenital 5 *genetic*; deep-rooted, deep-set, emotional, demonstrative 818 *feeling.*

818 Feeling – N. *feeling,* experience, emotional life, sensation, sense of 374 *sense*; emotion, sentiment; sincerity 540 *veracity*; impulse 609 *spontaneity*; intuition, instinct; responsiveness, response, reaction, fellow feeling, sympathy, involvement, personal i. 880 *friendliness*; vibrations, vibes, bad v., good v.; empathy, appreciation, understanding 490 *knowledge*; impression, deep feeling, deep sense of 819 *moral sensibility*; religious feeling, piety; finer feelings 897 *benevolence*; tender feelings 887 *love*; hard feelings 891 *resentment*; thrill, kick 318

spasm; shock, turn 508 *lack of expectation*; pathos 825 *suffering*; cathartsis, abreaction; animus, emotionalism 822 *excitability*; sentimentality, romanticism; show of feeling, demonstration, demonstrativeness; expression, facial e., play of features 547 *gesture*; blush, reddening, going pink, flush, hectic f., suffusion; tingling, gooseflesh, creeps, tremor, trembling, nervous tension, quiver, flutter, flurry, palpitation, pulsation, heaving, panting, throbbing 318 *agitation*; ferment 318 *commotion*; lump in one's throat, tears in one's eyes; stoicism, endurance, stiff upper lip 823 *patience.*

warm feeling, glow; cordiality, effusiveness, heartiness; hot head, impatience; unction, earnestness 834 *seriousness*; eagerness, keenness, fervour, ardour, vehemence, enthusiasm, dash, fire 174 *vigorousness*; vigour, zeal 678 *activity*; fanaticism, mania 481 *prejudice*; emotion, passion, ecstasy, inspiration, hwyl, transports of delight 822 *excitable state.*

Adj. *feeling,* sensory 374 *sentient*; spirited, vivacious, lively 819 *sensitive*; sensuous 944 *sensual*; intuitive, sensitive, vibrant, responsive; involved, sympathetic, empathetic; tenderhearted 819 *impressible*; emotional, passionate, red-blooded, full of feeling; unctuous, soulful; intense, tense 821 *excited*; cordial, hearty; gushing, effusive; sentimental, romantic; mawkish, maudlin, schmaltzy, soppy; thrilling, tingling, throbbing.

impressed, affected, influenced; stirred, aroused, moved, touched 821 *excited*; struck, awed, awestruck, overwhelmed, struck all of a heap; imbued with, aflame w., consumed w., devoured by, inspired by; rapt, enraptured, enthralled, ecstatic; lyrical, raving 822 *excitable.*

fervent, fervid, passionate, red-blooded, ardent, tense, intense; eager, breathless, panting, throbbing, pulsating, palpitating; impassioned, vehement, earnest, zealous; enthusiastic, exuberant, bubbling, bubbly; hot-headed, warm-blooded, impetuous, impatient 822 *excitable*; warm, fiery, glowing,

405

burning, red-hot, flaming, white-hot, boiling 379 *hot*; frenzied; strong, uncontrollable, overwhelming, furious 176 *violent.*

Vb. *feel,* sense, receive an impression, get the feeling, have a funny feeling, feel in one's bones, have a hunch; entertain feelings, have f., cherish f., harbour f., feel deeply, take to heart 819 *be sensitive*; know the feeling, experience, live, live through, go t., pass t., taste; bear, endure, undergo, smart under 825 *suffer*; sympathize, empathize, share 775 *participate*; respond, react, tingle, warm to, fire, kindle, catch.

show feeling, show signs of emotion; be demonstrative, not hide one's feelings 522 *manifest*; enthuse, go into ecstasies, go into transports of delight 824 *be pleased*; fly into a passion, fly off the handle 891 *get angry*; change colour, colour up; go purple 428 *blacken*; blench, turn pale, go white, look ashen 427 *whiten*; colour, blush, flush, go pink, turn red, turn crimson, go red in the face 431 *redden*; quiver, tremble, shudder, wince; shake, quake 318 *be agitated*; tingle, thrill, vibrate, throb, pulsate, beat faster 317 *oscillate*; palpitate, pant, heave, draw a deep breath 352 *breathe*; reel, lurch, stagger; stutter 580 *stammer.*

819 Sensibility – **N.** *moral sensibility,* sensitivity, sensitiveness, soul; over-sensitivity, touchiness, prickliness, irritability 892 *irascibility*; thin skin, soft spot, Achilles' heel; sore point, where the shoe pinches 891 *resentment*; susceptibility; finer feelings, sentiments; sentimentality, mawkishness; tenderness, affection 887 *love*; spirit, spiritedness, vivacity, vivaciousness, liveliness, verve 571 *vigour*; emotionalism, over-emotionalism, ebullience, effervescence 822 *excitability*; fastidiousness, finickiness, fikiness, aestheticism 463 *discrimination*; temperament, mood, changeability 152 *changeableness.*

Adj. *impressible,* malleable, plastic, putty-like 327 *soft*; sensible, aware, conscious of, mindful of, awake to, alive to,

responsive 374 *sentient*; impressed with, touched, moved, moved to tears, touched to the quick 818 *impressed*; impressionable 822 *excitable*; susceptible; romantic, sentimental; mawkish, maudlin, schmaltzy, soppy, wet, sentimentalizing, gushing; emotional; tender-hearted, soft-h., compassionate 905 *pitying.*

sensitive, sensitized; tingling, sore, raw, tender 374 *sentient*; aesthetic, fastidious 463 *discriminating*; oversensitive, hypersensitive, with one's heart on one's sleeve 822 *excitable*; touchy, irritable, thin-skinned.

lively, vital, vivacious, animated, fun-loving; irrepressible, ebullient, effervescent, bubbly; spirited, high-s.; alert, on one's toes 455 *attentive*; highly-strung; expressive, racy 571 *forceful.*

Vb. *be sensitive,* - sentimental etc. adj.; be tender-hearted, have a soft heart, take it to heart, weep for, break one's heart for 905 *pity*; tingle 318 *be agitated.*

820 Insensibility – **N.** *moral insensibility,* insensitiveness; numbness, stupor 375 *insensibility*; inertia 175 *inertness*; lethargy 679 *inactivity*; stagnation, vegetation 266 *quiescence*; woodenness, blockishness, obtuseness, stupidity, dullness; slowness, delayed reaction 456 *inattention*; uninterest 454 *incuriosity*; nonchalance, insouciance, unconcern, lack of care, detachment, apathy 860 *indifference*; phlegm, stolidness, calmness, steadiness, coolness, sangfroid 823 *inexcitability*; aloofness, impassivity; repression, stoicism, stiff upper lip 823 *patience*; inscrutability, poker face, deadpan expression 834 *seriousness*; insensitivity, coarseness, Philistinism 699 *artlessness*; thick skin, rhinoceros hide, elephant h.; frigidity; dourness; unsentimentality, cynicism; callousness 326 *hardness*; lack of feeling, dry eyes, no heart, heart of stone, brutishness, brutality 898 *inhumanity.*

unfeeling person, iceberg, icicle, cold fish; stoic, ascetic; vegetable, stone, block.

Adj. *impassive,* unconscious 375 *insensible*; unsusceptible, insensitive, unimaginative, uninspired; unresponsive, unimpressionable; phlegmatic, stolid, vegetable-like; wooden, blockish; bovine; dull, slow, slow-witted 499 *unintelligent*; unemotional, passionless; proof against, stoical, with stiff upper lip, ascetic, controlled, undemonstrative; aloof, distant, detached 860 *indifferent*; unaffected, calm 266 *tranquil*; steady, unruffled, unshaken, unshockable; imperturbable, without a nerve in one's body; cool; inscrutable, blank, expressionless, deadpan, poker-faced; unseeing 439 *blind*; unhearing 416 *deaf*; unsentimental, cynical; impersonal, dispassionate, reserved, unforthcoming, stony, frigid, frozen, icy, cold; unfeeling, heartless, soulless, inhuman; fancy-free, heart-whole; undemonstrative.

apathetic, unenthusiastic, unambitious; unimpassioned, uninspired, unexcited, unmoved; half-hearted, lukewarm, Laodicean; uninterested 454 *incurious*; insouciant, neglectful 458 *negligent*; spiritless, lackadaisical, couldn't care less; stagnant, bovine, cow-like 266 *quiescent*; sluggish, supine 679 *inactive*; passive 175 *inert*.

thick-skinned, impenetrable, impervious, impermeable; blind to, deaf to, dead to, closed to; obtuse, unimaginative, insensitive, uninspired; callous, insensate, tough, hard, case-hardened, hard-bitten, hard-boiled, inured 669 *matured*; shameless, brazen.

Vb. *be insensitive,* - impassive etc. adj.; have no feelings; miss the point of, be blind to 439 *be blind*; lack animation, lack spirit; steel oneself, harden one's heart against, be pitiless; feel indifference; feel no emotion, have no finer feelings, be a Philistine; show no regard for 922 *despise*; take no interest 454 *be incurious*; ignore 458 *disregard*; keep a stiff upper lip 942 *be temperate*; stagnate, vegetate 679 *be inactive*; not turn a hair, not bat an eyelid 599 *be resolute*.

821 Excitation – N. *excitation,* rousing, arousal, stirring up, waking up, working up, whipping up; igniting, galvanization, electrification 174 *stimulation*; inspiration, muse, exhilaration, intoxication, headiness; evocation, calling forth; encouragement, animation, incitement, invitation, appeal 612 *inducement*; provocation, irritation; impact 178 *influence*; enchantment 983 *sorcery*; rapture 824 *joy*; sentiment, sob-stuff, pathos; sensationalism; excitement, tension 160 *energy*; perturbation, effervescence, ebullience 318 *agitation*; shock, thrill, kicks 318 *spasm*; ferment, tizzy, flurry, furore 318 *commotion*; fever pitch, orgasm 503 *frenzy*; climax 137 *crisis*, passion, emotion, enthusiasm 818 *feeling*; fuss, hassle, drama 822 *excitable state*; temper, fury, rage 891 *anger*; amazement 864 *wonder*; awe 854 *fear*.

excitant, stimulator, agent provocateur, rabble-rouser, tub-thumper 738 *agitator*; sensationalist, sob sister, muckraker, chequebook journalist; headline, banner h. 528 *publicity*; fillip, ginger, tonic, pick-me-up 174 *stimulant*; upper, pep pill 949 *drug-taking*; sting, prick, goad, spur, whip, lash, stick, carrot and stick 612 *incentive*; fan; irritant, gadfly.

Adj. *excited,* activated, stimulated, stung etc. vb.; busy, astir, bustling, rushing 678 *active*; ebullient, effervescent, boiling, seething 355 *bubbly*; tense, wrought up, uptight, strung up, keyed up, wound up; feverish; frantic 503 *frenzied*; flushed 379 *hot*; violent 176 *furious*; hot under the collar, hot and bothered; seeing red, wild, mad, livid, fuming, foaming at the mouth, frothing, roaring, raging 891 *angry*; avid, eager, itching, agog, watering at the mouth; tingling 818 *feeling*; flurried, atwitter, all of a flutter, all of a doodah; restless, restive, overexcited, overwrought, distraught, distracted, distrait(e); freaked out, on a high, on a trip, on an ego-trip; beside oneself, hysterical, out of control, uncontrollable, running amok, carried away; turned on, hyped up; crazy about

887 *enamoured*; possessed, impassioned, enthusiastic.

exciting, stimulating, intoxicating, heady, exhilarating; provocative, teasing, piquant, tantalizing; spicy, appetizing; alluring; evocative, emotive, suggestive; cliff-hanging, hair-raising, spine-chilling; thrilling, agitating; moving, affecting, inspiring; rousing, stirring; sensational, dramatic, melodramatic, mind-boggling; gripping.

impressive, imposing, grand, stately; dignified, august, lofty, majestic, regal, royal, kingly, queenly 868 *noble*; awe-inspiring, overwhelming, overpowering; picturesque, scenic; striking, arresting, dramatic; telling, forceful 178 *influential*.

Vb. *excite,* affect, infect 178 *influence*; cheer; touch, move; touch the heart-strings, strike a chord; quicken the pulse, startle, electrify, galvanize; raise to fever pitch 381 *heat*; inflame, set on fire, light the touchpaper 381 *burn*; sting, goad, pique, irritate 891 *enrage*; tease 827 *torment*; cut to the quick, work up, whip up 612 *incite*; enthuse; stir, rouse, arouse, wake, awaken, kindle, turn on (see *animate*); touch off, evoke, elicit, summon up, call forth; thrill, exhilarate, intoxicate; send into ecstasies 826 *delight*.

animate, enliven, breathe life into, quicken 360 *vitalize*; revive, resuscitate; inspire; encourage, hearten, buoy up 855 *give courage*; give an edge, put teeth into, whet 256 *sharpen*; urge, nag, egg on, spur, goad, lash 277 *accelerate*; jolt, jog, shake up; buck up, pep up, give a fillip to, stimulate, ginger 174 *invigorate*; cherish, foster, foment 162 *strengthen*; fuel, intensify, fan the flame, blow on the coals, add fuel to the fire, stir the embers.

impress, sink in, leave an impression; project *or* present an image; interest, hold, grip, absorb; intrigue, rouse curiosity, make one sit up; claim attention 455 *attract notice*; affect 178 *influence*; let sink in, bring home to, drive home 532 *emphasize*; penetrate, pierce 516 *be intelligible*; arrest, shake, amaze, astound, stagger 508 *surprise*; stupefy; dazzle;

take one's breath away, overwhelm, overpower; upset, unsettle, distress, worry 827 *trouble*.

be excited, lose one's cool, lose control of oneself; flare up, burn 379 *be hot*; sizzle, seethe, simmer, boil, explode 318 *effervesce*; thrill to 818 *feel*; tingle, tremble 822 *be excitable*; quiver, flutter, palpitate, pulsate 318 *be agitated*; squirm, writhe 251 *wriggle*; dance; jump, leap up and down with excitement 312 *leap*; toss and turn.

822 Excitability – N. *excitability,* excitableness, inflammability; instability, emotionalism; hot temper, irritability, touchiness 892 *irascibility*; impatience, impetuosity, recklessness 857 *rashness*; effervescence, turbulence; restlessness, fidgets, nerves, butterflies in the stomach, collywobbles, flap 318 *agitation*.

excitable state, exhilaration, elation, euphoria, intoxication; thrill, trip, high, ecstasy; fever, fret, perturbation, trepidation, bother, fuss, hassle, flurry, whirl 318 *agitation*; ferment, pother, stew; storm, tempest 352 *gale*; effervescence, outburst, explosion, scene, song and dance 318 *commotion*; hysterics, fit, apoplectic f., frenzy; madness 503 *mental disorder*; passion, rage, towering r., fury 176 *violence*; temper, tantrums, rampage 891 *anger*.

Adj. *excitable,* passionate, emotional; inflammable, like tinder, like touchpaper; unstable, impressionable; temperamental, moody, mercurial, volatile 152 *changeful*; fitful 604 *capricious*; restless, nervy, fidgety, edgy, on edge, agitated; nervous, skittish 819 *lively*; irritable, fiery, hot-tempered, hot-headed 892 *irascible*; impatient, trigger-happy 680 *hasty*; impetuous, impulsive, madcap 857 *rash*; tempestuous, turbulent, stormy 176 *violent*; restive; effervescent, seething, boiling, volcanic, explosive; unbalanced; rabid 176 *furious*; feverish, hysterical 503 *frenzied*; like a cat on hot bricks, like a hen on a hot girdle *or* griddle, like a cat on a hot tin roof; tense, electric; elated.

Vb. *be excitable*, - impatient etc. adj.; drum one's fingers, tap one's foot, fret, fume, stamp; shuffle, fidget, champ at the bit; be itching to, be dying to; be on edge, be in a stew, flap 318 *be agitated*; start, jump 854 *be nervous*; be on the verge of a breakdown; have a temper; fume, foam, froth, throw fits, have hysterics 503 *go mad*; throw a tantrum, go wild, run riot, run amok, go berserk, see red; rush about 61 *rampage*; rage, rant; fly into a temper, fly off the handle, explode; kindle; flare up 821 *be excited*.

823 Inexcitability – **N.** *inexcitability*, imperturbability, calmness, steadiness, composure; coolness, cool, sangfroid, nonchalance; frigidity; tranquillity 266 *quietude*; serenity, placidity 828 *content*; equanimity, poise, equilibrium; self-control 942 *temperance*; stoicism 945 *asceticism*; detachment, dispassionateness 860 *indifference*; staidness, sobriety 834 *seriousness*; lack of fire.

patience, patience of Job; forbearance, endurance, longsuffering, tolerance, stoicism; resignation 721 *submission*.

Adj. *inexcitable,* dispassionate, cold, frigid, impassive; stable 153 *unchangeable*; cool, imperturbable, unflappable; level-headed; composed, controlled; moderate 942 *temperate*; inscrutable, deadpan, poker-faced; unhurried; equable 16 *uniform*; even-tempered, easygoing; staid, sedate, reserved, grave 834 *serious*; placid, unruffled, calm, peaceful, serene 266 *tranquil*; spiritless, lackadaisical, torpid, passive, vegetable-like 175 *inert*; earthbound 593 *prosaic*.

patient, meek, like patience on a monument, tolerant, longsuffering, forbearing, enduring; stoic, stoical, philosophical, uncomplaining.

Vb. *keep calm,* compose oneself, keep cool, keep a cool head, swallow one's resentment, control one's temper, keep one's cool, not rise to the bait, keep one's hair *or* shirt on; not turn a hair, not bat an eyelid 820 *be insensitive*; relax, not excite oneself, not worry, stop worrying, take things easy, take things as they come

683 *repose*; resign oneself, take in good part, take philosophically, have patience, be resigned 721 *submit*.

be patient, show patience, show forbearance; show restraint, put up with, stand, tolerate, bear, endure, support, suffer, abide; resign oneself, grin and bear it, accept the situation with good grace, put a brave face on it; brook, take, take it from, swallow, digest, stomach, pocket 721 *knuckle under*; turn the other cheek 909 *forgive*; be tolerant, live and let live, condone 736 *be lenient*; turn a blind eye, overlook 734 *be lax*; allow 756 *permit*; not rise to the bait, coexist 770 *compromise*.

tranquillize, steady, moderate, assuage; calm, lull 266 *bring to rest*; cool down, compose 719 *pacify*; set one's mind at rest 831 *relieve*; control, restrain.

Section two: Personal emotion

824 Joy – **N.** *joy 376 pleasure;* enjoyment, thrill, kick 826 *pleasurableness*; joyfulness 835 *rejoicing*; delight, gladness, rapture, exaltation, exhilaration, transports of delight; abandonment, euphoria, ecstasy; gloating; life of pleasure, joys of life, roses all the way; halcyon days, days of wine and roses.

happiness, felicity, good fortune, well-being, ease 376 *euphoria*; golden age, age of Aquarius 730 *prosperity*; blessedness, bliss; seventh heaven, cloud nine, nirvana, Paradise, Elysium, the happy hunting-ground in the sky, Garden of Eden, Isles of the Blessed, Arcadia 513 *fantasy*; happy valley, bower of bliss, home sweet home.

enjoyment, gratification, satisfaction, fulfilment 828 *content*; delectation, relish, lip-smacking, zest, gusto; indulgence, luxuriation, wallowing 943 *intemperance*; full life, hedonism, Epicureanism 944 *sensualism*; merry-making, merriment; fun, treat, excursion, outing 837 *amusement*; feast, bean-feast,

thrash; refreshment, good cheer, cakes and ale, beer and skittles 301 *eating*.

Adj. *pleased,* well-p., glad, welcoming; satisfied, happy 828 *content*; gratified, flattered, chuffed, pleased as Punch; over the moon, on top of the world; enjoying, loving it, tickled to death, tickled pink; exhilarated 833 *merry*; euphoric, walking on air, with feet not touching the ground; euphoric, elated, overjoyed 833 *jubilant*; delighted, transported; approving; ravished, in raptures, in transports, in the seventh heaven, on cloud nine; captivated, charmed, enchanted 818 *impressed*; gloating.

happy, happy as a king, happy as a sandboy, happy as a lark, happy as Larry, happy as the day is long, happy as a pig in muck; blithe, joyful, joyous, gladsome 833 *merry*; beaming, smiling 835 *laughing*; radiant, starry-eyed; felicitous, lucky, fortunate 730 *prosperous*; blissful, blessed; in paradise.

Vb. *be pleased,* - glad etc. adj.; hug oneself, congratulate o., purr with pleasure, be like a cat with a dish of cream, be like a dog with two tails, jump *or* dance for joy 833 *be cheerful*; laugh, smile 835 *rejoice*; get pleasure from, get a kick out of, take pleasure in, delight in, rejoice in; go into ecstasies, be in a state of euphoria, rave about 818 *show feeling*; luxuriate in, bask in, wallow; enjoy; have fun 837 *amuse oneself*; gloat; savour, relish, smack one's lips 386 *taste*; take a fancy to, like 887 *love*; think well of 923 *approve*.

825 Suffering – N. *suffering,* heartache, weltschmerz 834 *melancholy*; longing, homesickness, nostalgia 859 *desire*; discontent, weariness 684 *fatigue*; nightmare, waking nightmare, pain, affliction, distress, dolour, anguish, angst, agony, torture, torment, mental t.; twinge, stab, smart, sting, thorn 377 *pang*; painfulness; Passion, Crucifixion, Calvary, martyrdom; rack, the stake 963 *punishment*; purgatory, hell, damnation, eternal d. 961 *condemnation*; bed of nails, bed of thorns 700 *difficulty*; unpleasantness, setback, inconvenience, disagreeableness, discomfort, malaise; the hard way, trial, ordeal; shock, trauma, blow, infliction, visitation, tribulation 659 *bane*; extremity, death's door 651 *illness*; living death, fate worse than death 616 *evil*; evil days, unhappy times.

sorrow, grief, sadness, mournfulness, gloom 834 *dejection*; woe, wretchedness, misery, depths of m.; prostration, despair, despondency, desolation 853 *hopelessness*; unhappiness, tale of woe 731 *adversity*; heavy heart, broken h.; displeasure, dissatisfaction 829 *discontent*; vexation, bitterness, mortification, chagrin, fretting, remorse 830 *regret*.

worry, worrying, worriedness, uneasiness, disquiet, fretting 318 *agitation*; dismay, distress 63 *derangement*; phobia, hang-up, obsession; something on one's mind, weight on one's m., anxiety, concern, solicitude, care; responsibility, load, burden; strain, stress, tension; a worry, worries, business w., cares, cares of the world; trouble, troubles 616 *evil*; bother, annoyance, irritation, bête noire, pest, thorn in the flesh; headache, teaser, puzzle, problem 530 *enigma*.

sufferer, victim, scapegoat, sacrifice; prey; martyr; patient 651 *sick person*.

Adj. *suffering,* ill, indisposed 651 *sick*; writhing, aching, in pain, on a bed of p., in agony, bleeding, harrowed, on the rack, in torment, in hell; inconvenienced, uncomfortable, ill at ease; anguished, distressed, anxious, unhappy about, worried, troubled, apprehensive, dismayed 854 *nervous*; sick with worry, out of one's mind with w., cut up about, in a state 316 *agitated*; discomposed, disconcerted; ill-used, maltreated, abused; longsuffering, downtrodden 745 *subjected*; martyred, victimized, sacrificed; stricken, wounded; heavy-laden, crushed, prostrate 684 *fatigued*; careworn; woeful, woebegone, haggard.

unhappy, infelicitous, unlucky, accursed 731 *unfortunate*; despairing 853

hopeless; doomed 961 *condemned*; pitiable, poor, wretched, miserable; sad, melancholy, despondent, disconsolate; cut up, heart-broken, broken-hearted, heavy-h., sick at heart; sorrowful, sorrowing, grieved, grieving, grief-stricken, woebegone 834 *dejected*; sunk in misery, weeping, sobbing, tearful, in tears 836 *lamenting*; disappointed 829 *discontented*; offended, vexed, peeved, miffed, annoyed, pained 924 *disapproving*; piqued, mortified, humiliated 891 *resentful*; sickened, disgusted, nauseated; sorry, remorseful, regretful 830 *regretting*.

Vb. *suffer,* undergo, endure, go through, experience 818 *feel*; bear, put up with, grin and bear it; suffer torments, bleed; hurt oneself, be hurt, do harm to oneself, smart, chafe, ache 377 *feel pain*; wince, flinch, writhe, squirm 251 *wriggle*; take up one's cross, become a martyr, sacrifice oneself; take one's punishment, take it on the chin 599 *stand firm*; have a thin time, have a bad t., go through it, have trouble enough 731 *have trouble*; distress oneself, fuss, hassle, worry, worry to death, fret, be on pins and needles, be on tenterhooks 318 *be agitated*; mind, be upset, take it badly, take it ill, take it to heart; sorrow, grieve, weep, sigh 836 *lament*.

826 Pleasurableness – N. *pleasurableness,* pleasures of, pleasantness, niceness, delectableness, delectability, delightfulness, amenity, sunny side, bright s.; attractiveness, appeal, sex a., it, comehither look 291 *attraction*; winning ways 925 *flattery*; amiability, winsomeness, charm, fascination, enchantment, witchery, loveliness, sight for sore eyes 841 *beauty*; joyfulness, honeymoon 824 *joy*; a real tonic, a little of what one fancies, a delight, a treat, a joy; novelty, pastime, fun 837 *amusement*; melody, harmony 412 *music*; tastiness, deliciousness 390 *savouriness*; spice, zest, relish, je ne sais quoi; dainty, titbit, sweet 392 *sweetness*; manna in the wilderness, balm 685 *refreshment*; land flowing with milk and honey 635 *plenty*; peace, peace and quiet, tranquillity 266 *quietude*, 681 *leisure*; idyll; pipedream 513 *fantasy*.

Adj. *pleasurable,* pleasant, nice, good; pleasure-giving 837 *amusing*; pleasing, agreeable, gratifying; acceptable, welcome, welcome as the flowers in May; well-liked, to one's taste, to one's liking, just what the doctor ordered; wonderful, marvellous, fabulous, splendid 644 *excellent*; easeful, refreshing 683 *reposeful*; peaceful, quiet 266 *tranquil*; luxurious, voluptuous 376 *sensuous*; genial, warm, sunny; delightful, delectable, delicious, exquisite, choice; luscious, juicy; delicate, tasty 390 *savoury*; sugary 392 *sweet*; dulcet, musical, harmonious 410 *melodious*; picturesque, scenic, lovely 841 *beautiful*; amiable, dear, winning, disarming, endearing; attractive, fetching, appealing, alluring, interesting; seductive, enticing, inviting, captivating; charming, enchanting, bewitching, ravishing; haunting, thrilling, heart-melting, heart-warming 821 *exciting*; homely, cosy; pastoral, idyllic; heavenly, out of this world; beatific, blessed, blissful 824 *happy*.

Vb. *please,* give pleasure, agree with; lull, soothe, calm 177 *assuage*; comfort 833 *cheer*; put at ease, make comfortable 831 *relieve*; give a golden hello to, give a sweetener to, sugar, gild *or* sugar the pill 392 *sweeten*; stroke, pat, pet, baby, coddle, nurse, cuddle 889 *caress*; indulge, pander to 734 *be lax*; charm, interest 837 *amuse*; rejoice, gladden, make happy; gratify, satisfy, leave one walking on air, leave nothing more to be desired 828 *content*; raise to the seventh heaven.

delight, rejoice, exhilarate, elate, elevate, uplift; rejoice one's heart, warm the cockles of one's h., do one's heart good, bring tears of joy *or* happiness; thrill, intoxicate, ravish; transport, turn on, send, send one into raptures *or* ecstasies 821 *excite*; be music to one's ears 925 *flatter*; take one's fancy, tickle one's f.; tickle one's palate 390 *make appetizing*; regale, refresh; tickle, tickle one to death, titillate; entrance, enrapture; enchant,

411

charm 983 *bewitch*; take one's breath away 821 *impress*; allure, seduce 291 *attract*.

827 Painfulness – N. *painfulness,* harshness, roughness, abuse, child a., sexual a., harassment, sexual h., persecution 735 *severity*; hurtfulness, harmfulness 645 *badness*; disagreeableness, unpleasantness; loathsomeness, hatefulness, beastliness 616 *evil*; grimness 842 *ugliness*; friction, chafing, irritation, ulceration, inflammation, exacerbation 832 *aggravation*; soreness, tenderness 377 *pain*; irritability, inflammability 822 *excitability*; sore point; sore, running s., ulcer, thorn in the flesh, pinprick, where the shoe pinches 659 *bane*; shock 508 *lack of expectation*; unpalatability, disgust, nausea, sickener 391 *unsavouriness*; sharpness, bitterness, bitter pill, gall and wormwood, vinegar 393 *sourness*; affliction, adversity; tribulation, trials and tribulations, ordeal, cross 825 *suffering*; trouble, care 825 *worry*; pathos; sorry sight, sad spectacle, object of pity 731 *unlucky person*; sorrow.

annoyance, vexation, death of, pest, bête noire, curse, plague, pain in the neck 659 *bane*; botheration, hassle, embarrassment 825 *worry*; nuisance, pinprick; burden, drag 702 *encumbrance*; grievance, complaint; hardship, troubles 616 *evil*; last straw, limit, the end; offence, affront, insult, provocation 921 *indignity*; molestation, infestation, persecution, malignity 898 *malevolence*; displeasure, mortification 891 *resentment*; menace, enfant terrible.

Adj. *paining,* hurting, aching, painful, sore, tender; agonizing 377 *painful*; searing, scalding, burning, sharp, shooting, biting, nipping, gnawing, throbbing; caustic, corrosive, vitriolic; harsh, hard, rough, cruel 735 *severe*; grinding, gruelling, punishing, excruciating, extreme; hurtful, harmful, poisonous.

unpleasant, unpleasing, disagreeable; uncomfortable, comfortless, joyless, dreary, dreich, dismal, depressing 834 *cheerless*; unattractive; hideous 842

ugly; unwelcome, unacceptable 860 *unwanted*; thankless, unpopular, displeasing; disappointing, unsatisfactory; distasteful, unpalatable, off 391 *unsavoury*; foul, nasty, beastly, horrible, ghastly 645 *not nice*; malodorous, stinking 397 *fetid*; bitter, sharp 393 *sour*; invidious, obnoxious, offensive, objectionable, undesirable, odious, hateful, loathsome, nauseous, slimy, disgusting, revolting, repellent; execrable, accursed 645 *damnable*.

annoying, too bad; troublesome, embarrassing, discomfiting, worrying; bothersome, wearisome, irksome, tiresome, boring 838 *tedious*; burdensome, onerous, oppressive 322 *weighty*; disappointing, unlucky, unfortunate, untoward 731 *adverse*; awkward, unaccommodating, impossible, harassing, hassling; importunate, pestering; trying, irritating, aggravating, provoking, maddening, infuriating; galling, mortifying.

distressing, afflicting, crushing, prostrating, grievous, traumatic; moving, affecting, touching; harrowing, heartbreaking, heart-rending, tear-jerking; pathetic, tragic, tragical, sad, woeful, rueful, mournful, pitiful, lamentable, deplorable; ghastly, grim, dreadful, shocking, appalling, horrifying, horrific 854 *frightening*.

intolerable, insufferable, impossible, insupportable, unbearable 32 *exorbitant*; past enduring, not to be borne; extreme, beyond the limits of tolerance, more than flesh and blood can stand, enough to make a parson swear, enough to try the patience of Job, enough to provoke a saint.

Vb. *hurt,* injure 645 *harm*; pain, cause p. 377 *give pain*; bite, cut, tear, rend 655 *wound*; hurt the feelings, gall, pique, nettle, mortify 891 *huff*; rub up the wrong way, tread on one's corns; cut to the quick, pierce the heart, rend the heartstrings, bring tears to one's eyes, draw tears, grieve, afflict, cause trauma, distress 834 *sadden*; plant a thorn in one's side; corrode, embitter, exacerbate, make matters worse, rub salt in the wound, gnaw, chafe, rankle, fester 832

aggravate; offend, aggrieve (**see** *displease*); insult, affront 921 *not respect*.

torment, martyr; harrow, rack, put to the r., break on the wheel 963 *torture*; give the third degree, give one the works; put one through it, put through the hoop, give one a bad time, maltreat, abuse, bait, bully, rag, bullyrag, persecute 735 *oppress*; be offensive, snap at, bark at 885 *be rude*; importune, dun, doorstep, beset, besiege 737 *demand*; haunt, obsess; annoy; tease, pester, plague, nag, henpeck, badger, worry, try, chivvy, harass, hassle, harry, heckle; molest, bother, vex, provoke, peeve, miff, ruffle, irritate, needle, sting, chafe, fret, bug, gall, irk, roil, rile 891 *enrage*.

trouble, disquiet, disturb, agitate, discompose, disconcert, discomfit, put one out, upset, incommode 63 *derange*; worry, embarrass, perplex 474 *puzzle*; tire 684 *fatigue*; weary, bore 838 *be tedious*; obsess, haunt, bedevil; weigh upon one, prey on the mind, weigh on the spirits, act as a damper, deject 834 *depress*; infest, get in one's hair, dog one's footsteps, get under one's feet, get in one's way, thwart 702 *obstruct*.

displease, find no favour 924 *incur blame*; disagree with, grate on, jar on, strike a jarring note, get on one's nerves, set the teeth on edge, go against the grain, give one the pip, give one a pain, get one's goat, get on one's wick, get up one's nose, get under one's skin; disenchant, disillusion 509 *disappoint*; dissatisfy, aggrieve 829 *cause discontent*; offend, shock, horrify, scandalize, disgust, revolt, repel, put one off, turn one off, sicken, nauseate, fill one with loathing, stick in the throat, make one's gorge rise, turn one's stomach, make one sick, make one sick to one's stomach, make one vomit, make one throw up 861 *cause dislike*; make one's hair curl, make one's flesh creep, make one's blood run cold, curdle the blood, make one's hair stand on end, appal 854 *frighten*.

828 Content – **N.** *content*, contentment, satisfaction, complacency; self-complacency, self-satisfaction, smugness 873 *vanity*; half-smile, purr of content, ray of comfort; serenity, tranquillity 266 *quietude*; peace of mind, heart's ease 376 *euphoria*; reconciliation 719 *pacification*; snugness, cosiness, comfort, sitting pretty; dreams come true 730 *prosperity*.

Adj. *content*, contented, satisfied 824 *happy*; appeased, pacified 717 *peaceful*; cosy, snug 376 *comfortable*; at ease 683 *reposeful*; smiling 833 *cheerful*; pleased; with nothing left to wish for, having nothing to grumble at 863 *sated*; uncomplaining, with no regrets, without complaints; philosophic, resigned 721 *submitting*; easily pleased, easygoing, easyosy 736 *lenient*; secure 660 *safe*; untroubled, blessed with contentment.

Vb. *be content*, - satisfied etc. adj.; purr with content 824 *be pleased*; rest and be thankful, count one's blessings; be thankful, have much to be thankful for 907 *be grateful*; have all one could ask for, have one's wish, make one's dreams come true, fulfil one's ambition 730 *prosper*; congratulate oneself, rejoice; be at ease, be in one's element, sit pretty 376 *enjoy*; be reconciled 719 *make peace*; get over it, take comfort; rest content; take things as they come, make the best of, have no complaints, have nothing to grumble about, have no regrets; acquiesce 721 *submit*.

content, satisfy, make one's day 826 *please*; meet with approval, go down well, go down a treat; make happy, bless with contentment; grant a boon 781 *give*; make one's dreams come true, comfort 833 *cheer*; bring comfort to; lull, set at ease, set at rest; propitiate, reconcile, conciliate, appease 719 *pacify*.

829 Discontent – **N.** *discontent*, discontentment; displeasure, pain, dissatisfaction 924 *disapprobation*; cold comfort 509 *disappointment*; irritation, chagrin, pique, mortification, bitterness, spleen 891 *resentment*; uneasiness, disquiet 825 *worry*; grief 825 *sorrow*; unrest, state

of u., restiveness 738 *disobedience*; agitation 318 *commotion*; finickiness, faddiness, fikiness, hypercriticism, nit-picking 862 *fastidiousness*; querulousness 709 *quarrelsomeness*; chip on one's shoulder, grievance, grudge, complaint 709 *quarrel*; weariness, world-w., weltschmerz, melancholy, ennui 834 *dejection*; sulkiness, sulks, the hump, dirty look, grimace, scowl, frown 893 *sullenness*; groan, curse 899 *malediction*; murmuring, whispering campaign, smear c. 762 *deprecation*.

malcontent, grumbler, grouch, grouser, sniper, complainer, whiner, bleater, bellyacher, Jonah 834 *moper*; plaintiff 763 *petitioner*; faultfinder, nit-picker, critic, censurer; person with a grievance, someone with a chip on their shoulder, angry young man; dissident, dropout 738 *revolter*; seditionist 738 *agitator*; protest meeting, sit-in; conscientious objector.

Adj. *discontented,* displeased, not best pleased; dissatisfied 924 *disapproving*; frustrated 509 *disappointed*; defeated 728 *unsuccessful*; malcontent, dissident 489 *dissenting*; restive 738 *disobedient*; disgruntled, dischuffed, weary, browned off, cheesed o., hacked off, gutted, fed up to the back teeth 838 *bored*, 825 *unhappy*; sad, disconsolate 834 *dejected*; ill-disposed, grudging, jealous, envious; embittered, soured 393 *sour*; peevish, testy, crabbed, crabbit, cross, sulky, sulking, pouting 893 *sullen*; grouchy, grumbling, grousing, whining, swearing 899 *cursing*; protesting; smarting, mortified, insulted, affronted, piqued, vexed, miffed, put out, annoyed 891 *resentful*; fretful, querulous, petulant, complaining; difficult, hard to please, never satisfied, exigent, exacting 862 *fastidious*; faultfinding, critical, hypercritical, censorious; resisting 704 *opposing*.

Vb. *be discontented,* - dissatisfied etc. adj.; carp, criticize, give flak, find fault 862 *be fastidious*; lack, miss 627 *require*; jeer 924 *disapprove*; take offence, take amiss, take ill, take to heart, take on, be offended, be miffed 891 *resent*; get the hump, sulk; look blue, look glum; moan, whine, whinge, winge, bleat, beef, protest, complain, object 762 *deprecate*; bellyache, grumble, grouse, grouch, gripe; wail 836 *lament*; be aggrieved, have a grievance, nurse a grudge, have a chip on one's shoulder; join the opposition 704 *oppose*; rise up, be up in arms about 738 *revolt*; grudge 912 *envy*; quarrel; not know when one is well off, look a gift horse in the mouth; ask for one's money back, demand a refund, return 607 *reject*.

cause discontent, dissatisfy 636 *not suffice*; leave room for complaint 509 *disappoint*; spoil one's pleasure, get one down 834 *depress*; dishearten, discourage 613 *dissuade*; sour, embitter, disgruntle, dischuff; upset, miff, chafe, niggle, put out of humour, irritate 891 *huff*; mortify 872 *humiliate*; offend, cause resentment 827 *displease*; disgust 861 *cause dislike*; sow the seeds of discontent, make trouble, stir up t., mix it, agitate 738 *revolt*.

830 Regret – N. *regret,* regretfulness; mortification 891 *resentment*; harking back, crying over spilt milk; soul-searching, remorse, contrition, repentance, compunction, qualms, pangs of conscience, regrets, apologies 939 *penitence*; disillusion, second thoughts 67 *sequel*; longing, homesickness, nostalgia 859 *desire*; sense of loss 737 *demand*; matter of regret, pity of it.

Adj. *regretting,* homesick, nostalgic; regretful, remorseful, rueful, conscience-stricken, sorry, apologetic, penitent, contrite 939 *repentant*; disillusioned, sadder and wiser.

Vb. *regret,* rue, deplore, rue the day; curse one's folly, never forgive oneself, blame o., reproach o., kick o., bite one's tongue; wish undone, wring one's hands, cry over spilt milk, spend time in vain regrets 836 *lament*; want one's time over again, sigh for the good old days, fight one's battles over again, relive the past, reopen old wounds, hark back; look back, look over one's shoulder; miss,

sadly m., regret the loss; long for, hanker after, be homesick 859 *desire*; express regrets, apologize, be full of remorse, feel contrite, feel remorse, be sorry 939 *be penitent*; ask for another chance 905 *ask mercy*; lament 924 *disapprove*; feel mortified, gnash one's teeth 891 *resent*; have cause for regret, have had one's lesson 963 *be punished*.

831 Relief – N. *relief,* welcome r., rest 685 *refreshment*; easing, alleviation, mitigation, palliation, abatement 177 *moderation*; good riddance; exemption 668 *deliverance*; solace, consolation, comfort, ray of c., crumb of c.; silver lining, break in the clouds 852 *hope*; load off one's mind, sigh of relief 656 *revival*; lulling; soothing, salve 658 *balm*; pain-killer, analgesic 375 *anaesthetic*; sedative, tranquillizer.

Vb. *relieve,* ease, soften, cushion; relax, lessen the strain; temper 177 *moderate*; lift, raise, take off, lighten, relieve the burden, take a load off one's mind 701 *disencumber*; spare, exempt from 919 *exempt*; save 668 *deliver*; console, solace, comfort, bring c., offer a crumb of c.; cheer up, buck up, encourage, hearten 833 *cheer*; refresh; restore, repair 656 *cure*; put a plaster on, bandage, bind up, apply a tourniquet, poultice, kiss it better 658 *doctor*; calm, soothe, palliate, mitigate, moderate, alleviate 177 *assuage*; smooth the brow, take out the wrinkles, iron out the difficulties 258 *smooth*; lull; kill the pain 375 *render insensible*; take pity on, put one out of one's misery.

832 Aggravation – N. *aggravation,* exacerbation, exasperation, irritation; enhancement, augmentation 36 *increase*; intensification; heightening, deepening, adding to 482 *overestimation*; making worse 655 *deterioration*; complication 700 *difficulty*.

Vb. *aggravate,* intensify 162 *strengthen*; enhance, heighten, deepen; increase 36 *augment*; worsen, make

things w., not improve matters 655 *deteriorate*; add insult to injury, rub salt in the wound, rub it in, rub one's nose in it, exacerbate, inflame 821 *excite*; exasperate, irritate 891 *enrage*; add fuel to the flame, fan the embers; complicate, make bad worse, escalate the war, go from bad to worse, jump from the frying pan into the fire.

833 Cheerfulness – N. *cheerfulness,* alacrity 597 *willingness*; optimism, hopefulness 852 *hope*; happiness 824 *joy*; geniality, smiles, good humour; vitality, high spirits, youthful h. s., joie de vivre 360 *life*; light-heartedness, spring in one's step, optimistic outlook 828 *content*; liveliness, sparkle, vivacity, animation, elation, euphoria, exhilaration, elevation 822 *excitable state*; life and soul of the party, party spirit, conviviality 882 *sociability*.

merriment, good cheer; high spirits, gay abandon; jollity, joviality, jocularity, gaiety, glee, mirth, hilarity 835 *laughter*; levity, frivolity 499 *folly*; merry-making, fun, fun and games, amusement; jubilation, jubilee 876 *celebration*.

Adj. *cheerful,* cheery, blithe 824 *happy*; hearty, genial, convivial 882 *sociable*; sanguine, optimistic, rose-coloured; smiling, sunny, bright, beaming, radiant 835 *laughing*; breezy, of good cheer, in high spirits, in a good humour; in good heart, optimistic, upbeat, hopeful, buoyant; irrepressible; carefree, light-hearted, happy-go-lucky; bouncing; pert, jaunty, bright-eyed and bushy-tailed, perky, chirpy, chipper, spry, spirited, peppy, sprightly, vivacious, animated, vital, sparkling, all lit up, full of beans, on the top of one's form 819 *lively*.

merry, joyful, happy as a sandboy, happy as a king, happy as the day is long, happy as Larry; ebullient, effervescent, bubbly, sparkling, laughter-loving, jocular 839 *witty*; gay, frivolous 456 *light-minded*; playful, sportive, frisky, frolicsome, kittenish 837 *amusing*; roguish,

arch, sly; merry-making, mirthful, jovial, jolly, joking, dancing, laughing, singing, drinking; hilarious, uproarious, rip-roaring, rollicking, splitting one's sides, helpless with laughter, tickled pink.

jubilant, overjoyed, gleeful, delighted 824 *pleased*; chuffed, elated, euphoric, flushed, exultant, triumphant, cock-a-hoop, dancing on air 727 *successful*; celebratory.

Vb. *be cheerful,* be in good spirits, be in good humour, be in a good mood, be in good heart; keep cheerful, look on the bright side, keep one's spirits up 852 *hope*; keep one's pecker up, grin and bear it, make the best of it, put a good face upon it 599 *be resolute*; take heart, snap out of it, cheer up, perk up, buck up; brighten, liven up, grow animated, let oneself go, let one's hair down, abandon oneself; radiate good humour, smile, grin from ear to ear, beam, sparkle; dance, sing, carol, lilt, chirrup, chirp, whistle, laugh 835 *rejoice*; whoop, cheer 876 *celebrate*; have fun, frisk, frolic, rollick, romp, gambol, sport, disport oneself, enjoy o., have a good time 837 *amuse oneself*; throw a party, make whoopee 882 *be sociable*.

cheer, gladden, warm the cockles of the heart 828 *content*; comfort, console 831 *relieve*; rejoice the heart, put in a good humour 826 *please*; enliven 821 *animate*; exhilarate, elate 826 *delight*; encourage, uplift, hearten, raise the spirits, buck up, perk up, jolly along, bolster up 855 *give courage*; act like a tonic, put new life into 174 *invigorate*.

834 Dejection. Seriousness – **N.** *dejection,* joylessness, unhappiness, cheerlessness, dreariness, dejectedness, low spirits, blues, dumps, doldrums; dispiritedness, low spirits, sinking heart; disillusion 509 *disappointment*; defeatism, pessimism, cynicism, depression, despair, death wish, suicidal tendency 853 *hopelessness*; weariness, oppression, enervation, exhaustion 684 *fatigue*; oppression of spirit, heartache, heaviness,

sadness, misery, wretchedness, disconsolateness, dolefulness 825 *sorrow*; despondency, prostration; Slough of Despond, grey dawn; gloom; glumness, long face, face as long as a fiddle; funereal aspect, lacklustre eye; gloom and doom, trouble 825 *worry*.

melancholy, melancholia, depression, clinical d., endogenous d., exogenous d., black mood, blues, moping, sighing, sigh; vapours, spleen 829 *discontent*; weariness of life, world-weariness, Weltschmerz, angst, nostalgia, homesickness 825 *suffering*.

seriousness, earnestness; gravity, solemnity, sobriety, demureness, staidness, grimness 893 *sullenness*; primness, humourlessness; straight face, poker f., dead pan; sternness; no laughing matter, no cause for mirth.

moper, complainer, Jonah 829 *malcontent*; sourpuss, crosspatch, bear with a sore head; pessimist, damper, wet blanket, killjoy, spoilsport; Job's comforter, misery, sobersides; death's-head, skeleton at the feast, gloom and doom merchant, doomwatcher, doomster, ecodoomster; hypochondriac, malade imaginaire.

Adj. *dejected,* joyless, dreary, dreich, cheerless, unhappy, sad; gloomy, despondent, downbeat, unhopeful, pessimistic, defeatist, despairing 853 *hopeless*; discouraged, disheartened; dispirited; troubled, worried 825 *suffering*; downcast, downhearted, low, down, down in the mouth, low-spirited, depressed; out of sorts, not oneself, out of spirits; sluggish, listless, spiritless, lackadaisical 679 *inactive*; lacklustre 419 *dim*; crestfallen 509 *disappointed*; browned off, cheesed off, pissed off, hacked off, gutted, sick as a parrot 829 *discontented*; down in the dumps, in the doldrums; sadder and wiser 830 *regretting*; subdued, disillusioned 509 *disappointed*.

melancholic, hypochondriacal; blue, down in the dumps; jaundiced, sour, pensive, deep in thought; melancholy, sad, triste; saddened, cut up, heavy-

hearted, sick at heart, heart-sick 825 *unhappy*; sorry, rueful 830 *regretting*; mournful, doleful, woeful, tearful 836 *lamenting*; cheerless, joyless, dreary, comfortless; forlorn, miserable, broken up, wretched, disconsolate; self-pitying; moody, sulky 893 *sullen*; dismal, gloomy, morose, glum, sunk in gloom; down in the mouth, woebegone.

serious, sober, sober as a judge, sober-sided, solemn, sedate, stolid, staid, demure, muted, grave, stern, Puritanical 735 *severe*; dour, grim, forbidding 893 *sullen*; unsmiling; inscrutable, straight-faced, po-f., poker-f., deadpan; prim; humourless; unfunny, heavy-going, dull, solid 838 *tedious*.

cheerless, comfortless; uncongenial, unwelcoming; depressing, dreary, dreich, dull 838 *tedious*; dismal, lugubrious, funereal, gloomy, dark, forbidding; drab, grey, sombre; ungenial.

Vb. *be dejected*, become despondent, lose heart, admit defeat 853 *despair*; succumb 728 *be defeated*; languish, sink, droop, sag, wilt, flag, give up 684 *be fatigued*; look downcast, look down in the mouth, look blue, hang one's head, pull a long face, laugh on the wrong side of one's face; mope, brood 449 *think*; take to heart, sulk; eat one's heart out, sigh, grieve 829 *be discontented*; groan 825 *suffer*; weep 836 *lament*.

be serious, keep a straight face, keep one's countenance, maintain one's gravity; look grave; lack humour, not see the joke, have no sense of humour, take oneself seriously, be a bore 838 *be tedious*.

sadden, grieve; turn one's hair grey, break one's heart, pluck at one's heart-strings, make one's heart bleed; draw tears, bring tears to one's eyes, touch the heart, leave not a dry eye 821 *impress*; pain, spoil one's pleasure 829 *cause discontent*; drive to despair; prostrate.

depress, deject, get one down; cause alarm and despondency, dishearten, discourage, dispirit, take the heart out of, unman, unnerve 854 *frighten*; spoil the fun, take the joy out of, cast a shadow,

cast a gloom over 418 *darken*; damp, dampen, damp the spirits, put a damper on, be a wet blanket, throw cold water, frown upon 613 *dissuade*; dash one's hopes 509 *disappoint*; weigh heavy on one's heart; make the heart sick, weary 684 *fatigue*; sober 534 *teach*.

835 Rejoicing – N. *rejoicing*, jubilation, exultation 876 *celebration*; congratulations, felicitation, pat on the back, bouquets, self-congratulation, mutual c. 886 *congratulation*; plaudits, clapping, applause, shout, cheers, rousing c., three c., huzza, hurrah, hosannah, hallelujah 923 *praise*; thanksgiving 907 *thanks*; paean; raptures, elation, euphoria 824 *joy*; revelling 837 *revel*; merrymaking, gay abandon 833 *merriment*.

laughter, risibility; loud laughter, hearty l., shout of laughter, peal of l., shrieks of l., hoots of l., gales of l., cachinnation; derision 851 *ridicule*; laugh, belly l., horse l., guffaw, chuckle, chortle, gurgle, cackle, crow, coo; giggle, snigger, snicker, titter, tee-hee; fit of laughing, the giggles; forced laugh; smile, simper, smirk, grin, broad g., grin from ear to ear, Cheshire cat grin; twinkle, half-smile; humour, sense of h. 839 *wit*; laughableness, laughing matter, comedy, farce 497 *absurdity*.

Adj. *rejoicing*, revelling, cheering, shouting etc. vb.; exultant, elated, euphoric 833 *jubilant*; lyrical, ecstatic 923 *approving*.

laughing, guffawing etc. vb.; splitting one's sides, laughing one's head off, creased, doubled up, convulsed with laughter, dying with l., shrieking with mirth, rolling in the aisles; humorous; mocking; laughable, risible, derisory 849 *ridiculous*; comic, comical, funny, farcical 497 *absurd*.

Vb. *rejoice*, be joyful, jump for j., dance for j., dance, skip 312 *leap*; clap, clap one's hands, throw one's cap in the air, whoop, cheer, huzza, hurrah 923 *applaud*; shout 408 *vociferate*; carol 413 *sing*; sing paeans, shout hosannas, sound the trumpet 923 *praise*; exult, crow 876

417

celebrate; felicitate 886 *congratulate*; give thanks, thank one's lucky stars 907 *thank*; abandon oneself, let oneself go, loosen up, let one's hair down, paint the town red, go mad for joy, dance in the streets; make merry 833 *be cheerful*; have a good time, frolic, frisk 837 *revel*; have a party, go on a spree, celebrate 882 *be sociable*; feel pleased, congratulate oneself, hug o., give oneself a pat on the back, rub one's hands, smack one's lips, gloat 824 *be pleased*; purr, coo, gurgle; sigh for pleasure, cry for joy.

laugh, burst out laughing, crack up, break up, get the giggles, get a fit of the g.; hoot, chuckle, chortle, cackle; giggle, snigger, snicker, titter, tee-hee, ha-ha, haw-haw; laugh at, laugh in one's sleeve *or* one's beard, mock, deride 851 *ridicule*; cachinnate; shake with mirth, fall about, split one's sides, be in stitches, double up, shriek with laughter, hoot with l., roar with l., kill oneself laughing, laugh fit to burst, laugh one's head off.

smile, break into a s., grin, grin from ear to ear, grin like a Cheshire cat; give a half-smile, smirk; twinkle, beam, flash a smile.

Int. cheers! three c.! huzza! hurrah! hooray! hosannah! hallelujah! glory be! hail the conquering hero!

836 Lamentation – N. *lamentation*, lamenting, ululation, wail, groaning, weeping, wailing, keening; weeping and wailing, beating the breast, tearing one's hair, wringing one's hands; mourning 364 *obsequies*; sackcloth and ashes; widow's weeds, crepe, black; Wailing Wall; crying, sobbing, sighing, blubbering, whimpering, whining, snivelling etc. vb.; tears, tearfulness, dolefulness 834 *dejection*; tears of pity 905 *pity*; red eyes, eyes swimming *or* brimming with tears; floods of tears, hysterics; cry, good c.; tear, teardrop; heaving breast, sob, sigh, groan, moan, bawl, boo-hoo.

lament, plaint, dirge, knell, requiem, elegy, swansong, funeral oration 364 *obsequies*; keen, wake 905 *condolence*; howl 409 *ululation*; tears of grief; tale of woe; show of grief, crocodile tears 542 *sham*.

Adj. *lamenting*, crying etc. vb.; in tears, bathed in t.; tearful, lachrymose; red-eyed, with moist eyes; close to tears, on the verge of t., ready to cry; mournful, doleful, lugubrious 825 *unhappy*; woeful, woebegone, wringing one's hands, beating one's breast 834 *dejected*; plaintive, singing the blues; elegiac, dirgelike 364 *funereal*; in mourning, in black, in widow's weeds, in sackcloth and ashes; at half-mast; with a tale of woe; pathetic, pitiful, lamentable, tear-jerking.

Vb. *lament*, grieve, sorrow, sigh, heave a s. 825 *suffer*; deplore 830 *regret*; condole, commiserate 905 *pity*; grieve for, sigh for, weep over, cry o., bewail, bemoan, elegize; sing the dirge, sing a requiem, toll the knell 364 *inter*; mourn, wail, weep and wail, keen; express grief, go into mourning; put on sackcloth and ashes, wring one's hands, beat one's breast, tear one's hair; take on, carry on, take it badly; tell one's tale of woe 829 *be discontented*.

weep, wail, greet; shed tears, burst into t., dissolve in t.; give way to tears, break down, cry, cry like a baby, boo-hoo, bawl, cry one's eyes out; howl, yell, scream, shriek 409 *ululate*; sob, sigh, moan, groan 825 *suffer*; snivel, grizzle, blubber, pule, mewl, whine, whinge, whimper; be on the verge of tears; cry out before one is hurt.

837 Amusement – N. *amusement*, pleasure, delight 826 *pleasurableness*; diversion, divertissement, entertainment, light e., popular e.; dramatic entertainment 594 *drama*; radio, television 531 *broadcasting*; video, video game; pop music, personal stereo, ghetto blaster; pastime, hobby, labour of love 597 *voluntary work*; solace, recreation 685 *refreshment*; relaxation 683 *repose*; holiday, Bank h. 681 *leisure*; April Fool's Day, rag day, gala day, red-letter d. 876 *special day*; play, sport, fun, good clean f., high jinks, merriment; do, show,

thrash, junket, Gaudy night 876 *celebration*; outing, excursion, jaunt, day out, pleasure trip; treat, Sunday school t., picnic; social gathering, get-together, at-home, conversazione, garden party, bunfight, beanfeast, fête, flower show, gymkhana, jamboree 74 *assembly*; whist drive, bridge party (see *card game*); party games (see *indoor game*).

festivity, holiday-making, vacationing; visiting 882 *social round*; fun 835 *laughter*; beer and skittles 824 *enjoyment*; social whirl, round of pleasure; high life, night l.; good time; living it up, painting the town red, burning the candle at both ends, a short life and a merry one 943 *intemperance*; festival, fair, funfair, fun of the fair, carnival, fiesta, gala; masque; festivities, fun and games, merrymaking, revels, Mardi Gras 833 *merriment*; feast day, special d; carousal, wassail 301 *feasting*; conviviality, house-warming, party, bottle p., byob (=bring your own bottle) p. 882 *social gathering*; drinking bout, spree, bender 301 *drinking*; orgy, carouse 949 *drunkenness*; binge, beano, thrash, blowout; barbecue, beanfeast, bunfight, dinner, annual d., banquet 301 *meal*.

revel, rave-up, knees-up, jollification, whoopee, fun, high old time; fun fast and furious, high jinks, spree, junket, junketing; night out, night on the tiles; bonfire; play, game, romp, frolic, lark, skylarking, escapade, antic, prank, rag, trick, monkey t. 497 *foolery*.

pleasure ground, park, theme p., adventure p., deer p., wildlife p., safari p., national p., grouse moor; village green, gardens, pleasure g., winter g. 192 *park*; seaside, Riviera, lido, marina, bathing beach, holiday camp; playground, adventure p., recreation ground, playing field, links, golf course; rink, skating r., ice r.; tennis court, petanque c., bowling green, croquet lawn 724 *arena*; circus, fair.

place of amusement, fairground, funfair, shooting gallery, amusement arcade; skittle alley, bowling a., billiard room, pool r.; concert hall, music h., cinema, movie theatre; theatre, ballroom; dance hall, discothèque, disco; cabaret, night club, strip joint, clip j.; bingo hall, casino 618 *gaming-house*.

sport, outdoor life; sportsmanship, gamesmanship 694 *skill*; sports, field s., track events; games, gymnastics 162 *athletics*, 312 *leap*, 716 *contest, racing, pugilism, wrestling*; weight-lifting, weight-training, pumping iron, outdoor sports, cycling, hiking, rambling, orienteering, camping, picnicking; running, jogging, racewalking, marathon; riding, pony-trekking; archery, shooting, clay-pigeon s.; hunting, shooting and fishing 619 *chase*; water sports, swimming, bathing, surf-riding, wind-surfing, boardsailing; skin diving, subaqua, water skiing, aquaplaning, boating, rowing, yachting, sailing 269 *aquatics*; rock-climbing, mountaineering 308 *ascent*; exploring, caving, speleology, pot-holing 309 *descent*; winter sports, skiing, ski-jumping, bobsleighing, tobogganning, skating, ice s., ice hockey; curling; flying, gliding, hang g. 271 *aeronautics*.

ball game, bat and ball game; cricket, French c.; baseball, rounders; tennis, lawn t., real t., table t., pingpong; badminton; squash, rackets; handball, volleyball; fives, pelota; netball, basketball; football, Association f., soccer; rugby, Rugby football, R. Union, R. League, rugger; lacrosse, hockey, ice h.; polo, water polo; croquet, putting, golf, clock g., crazy g.; skittles, ninepins, bowls, petanque, boules, curling; marbles; quoits, deck q., hoop-la; billiards, snooker, pool; bagatelle, pinball, shove ha'penny.

indoor game, parlour g., panel g., party g.; musical bumps, musical chairs, hunt the thimble, hunt the slipper, pass the parcel, postman's knock, kiss in the ring, oranges and lemons, nuts in May; sardines, rabbits, murder; forfeits, guessing game; quiz, twenty questions; charades; parson's *or* minister's cat, I-spy; word game, spelling bee, riddles, crosswords,

acrostics, pangrams; paper game, consequences, noughts and crosses, battleships, hangman; darts, dominoes, mah jong, tiddly-winks, jigsaw puzzle.

board game, chess; draughts, checkers, Chinese c., halma; backgammon; Scrabble (tdmk), ludo, snakes and ladders, Monopoly (tdmk), Trivial Pursuit (tdmk), go.

children's games, ring-a-ring-o'-roses; leapfrog, hopscotch, peever 312 *leap*; touch, tag, tig, he, hide-and-seek, follow-my-leader, Simon says, blind man's buff, hares and hounds, cowboys and Indians, cops and robbers.

card game, cards, game of cards, rubber of whist, rubber of bridge; whist, solo w., auction w.; auction bridge, contract b.; nap, napoleon; picquet, cribbage, bezique; rummy, gin r., canasta, hearts, Newmarket, speculation, solitaire, patience; snap, beggar-my-neighbour, old maid, Happy Families; lotto, housey-housey, bingo; vingt-et-un, pontoon, black jack; poker, strip p., stud p.; banker, baccarat, chemin de fer, chemmy.

gambling game, dice g.; roulette, rouge et noir; coin-spinning, heads and tails, raffle, tombola, sweepstake, lottery, football pool 618 *gambling.*

dancing, dance, ball; masquerade; fancy dress dance; thé dansant, tea dance, ceilidh, square dance, hoe-down; hop, jam session, disco, disco dancing, breakdancing, body-popping; ballet dancing; tap dancing, clog d., folk d., country d., Scottish c. d., Highland d., Irish d., morris d., old-time d., sequence d., ballroom dancing; choreography; eurhythmics, aerobics.

dance, war dance, sword d., corroboree; soft-shoe shuffle, cakewalk; clog dance, step d., tap d., toe d.; fan dance, dance of the seven veils, hula-hula; high kicks, cancan; belly dance; flamenco; country dance, morris d., barn d., square d., sailor's dance, hornpipe; folk dance, polonaise, mazurka, czardas; jig, Irish j.;

Highland fling; reel, eightsome r., foursome r., strathspey, Gay Gordons, Petronella, Duke of Perth, Strip the Willow, Dashing White Sergeant, Sir Roger de Coverley; tarantella, bolero, fandango, galliard, écossaise, gavotte, quadrille, cotillion, minuet, pavane, allemande, schottische, polka; waltz, last w., Viennese w., hesitation w., St Bernard; valeta, Lancers; foxtrot, turkey trot, quickstep; Charleston, black bottom, blues, one-step, two-s., Boston t-s., military t-s., paso-doble, tango, rumba, samba, mambo, bossa nova, beguine, conga, conga line, cha-cha; boomps-a-daisy, hokey-cokey, Lambeth Walk, Palais Glide; stomp, bop, bebop, shimmy, jive, breakdancing, bodypopping, disco dancing, Lindy-hopping, rock 'n' roll, twist; excuse-me dance, Paul Jones, snowball.

plaything, toy 639 *bauble*; children's toy, rattle, bricks, building b., meccano (tdmk), Lego (tdmk); Jack-in-the-box, teddy bear, puppet, golliwog, doll, china d., rag d., Cabbage Patch (tdmk) d., Cindy (tdmk) d., doll's house, doll's pram; top, whipping t., yo-yo; marbles; ball, balloon 252 *sphere*; hoop, Hula-Hoop (tdmk), skipping rope, stilts, pogo stick, rocking horse, hobby h., tricycle; roller skates, skateboard, surfboard; popgun, airgun, water pistol; toy soldier, tin s., lead s.; model, model aeroplane, clockwork train, model railway; magic lantern, toy theatre 522 *exhibit*; puppet show, marionettes, Punch and Judy 551 *image*; billiard table; cards; domino, tile; draught, counter, chip; tiddly-wink; chess piece, pawn, knight, bishop, castle *or* rook, queen, king.

player, sportsman *or* -woman, sportsperson; competitor 716 *contender*; all-rounder; ball-player, footballer, forward, striker, winger, defence, sweeper, goalkeeper; cricketer, batsman, fielder, wicket-keeper, bowler; hockey-player, tennis-p.; marksman, archer; shot-putter; gambler; card-player, chess-p.

Adj. *amusing,* entertaining, diverting etc. vb.; fun-making, full of fun 833

merry; pleasant 826 *pleasurable*; recreational 685 *refreshing*.

Vb. *amuse,* entertain, divert, tickle, make one laugh, take one out of oneself; tickle the fancy, titillate, please 826 *delight*; enliven 833 *cheer*; raise a smile, convulse with laughter, have them rolling in the aisles, wow, slay, be the death of 849 *be ridiculous*; humour, keep amused, put in a good humour, put in a cheerful mood; give a party, have a get-together, play the host *or* hostess 882 *be hospitable*.

amuse oneself, kill time, while away the t., pass the t.; pursue one's hobby, dabble in; play, play at, have fun, enjoy oneself 833 *be cheerful*; take a holiday, have a break, go on vacation, go on an outing, have a field day, have a ball; disport oneself; take one's pleasure; frolic, romp, gambol, caper; play tricks, play pranks, lark around, fool about, play the fool 497 *be absurd*; jest 839 *be witty*; play cards; game, dice 618 *gamble*; play games, be a fitness freak; live the outdoor life, camp, caravan, take a holiday home, timeshare; picnic; sail, yacht, surf, windsurf, sailboard, fly; hunt, shoot, fish; play golf; ride, trek, hike, ramble; run, jog, race, jump; bathe, swim, dive; skate, roller-skate, ski, toboggan; work out, pump iron.

dance, go dancing; tap-dance, waltz, foxtrot, quickstep, Charleston, tango, rumba, jive, jitterbug, stomp, bop, twist, rock 'n' roll, disco-dance, breakdance, bodypop; whirl 315 *rotate*; cavort, caper, jig about, bob up and down; shuffle, hoof, tread a measure, trip the light fantastic 312 *leap*.

revel, make merry, make whoopee, have a ball, celebrate 835 *rejoice*; drive dull care away, make it a party, have a good time; let oneself go, let one's hair down, let off steam; go on a bender, go on a spree, have a night out, have a night on the tiles, live it up, paint the town red; junket, roister; feast, banquet, carouse, make the rafters ring; go on a binge, go pub-crawling 301 *drink*; drown one's sorrows 949 *get drunk*; sow one's wild

oats, burn the candle at both ends; stay up till all hours, go home in the wee sma' hours, never go home till morning, go home with the cows.

838 Tedium – N. *tedium,* ennui, world-weariness, Weltschmerz 834 *melancholy*; lack of interest 860 *indifference*; weariness, languor 684 *fatigue*; tediousness, irksomeness; dryness, stodginess, heaviness; flatness, staleness 387 *insipidity*; stuffiness 840 *dullness*; prolixity 570 *diffuseness*; sameness 16 *uniformity*; monotony 106 *repetition*; time to kill 679 *inactivity*; doodling, thumb-twiddling.

bore, utter b., no fun; drag, bind, chore; beaten track, daily round, rut 610 *habit*; grindstone, treadmill 682 *labour*; pub bore.

Adj. *tedious,* uninteresting, unexciting, unentertaining; slow, dragging, leaden, heavy; dry, arid; flat, stale, insipid 387 *tasteless*; bald 573 *plain*; humdrum, soulless, suburban, depressing, dreary, dreich, stuffy, bourgeois 840 *dull*; stodgy, prosaic, uninspired; long-winded, drawn out 570 *prolix*; soporific, boring, wearisome, tiresome, irksome; wearing; repetitive; unvarying, monotonous 16 *uniform*; cloying, satiating.

bored, twiddling one's thumbs, doodling, kicking one's heels 679 *inactive*; fed up to the back teeth, browned off, cheesed off, hacked off, had it up to here 829 *discontented*; jaded 684 *fatigued*; world-weary 834 *melancholic*; blasé 860 *indifferent*; satiated, cloyed 863 *sated*; sick of, sick and tired, fed up.

Vb. *be tedious,* pall, lose its novelty, cloy, jade, satiate 863 *sate*; bore, irk, try, weary 684 *fatigue*; bore to death, bore to tears, bore the pants off, bore stiff; weary to distraction, get one down, get on one's nerves, outstay one's welcome; make one yawn, send one to sleep; drag 278 *move slowly*; go on and on, never end; drone on, bang on, harp on; be prolix 570 *be diffuse*.

Adv. *boringly,* ad nauseam, to death.

839 Wit – N. *wit,* wittiness, pointedness, point; ready wit, badinage, repartee; Attic salt, elegance; sparkle, scintillation, brightness 498 *intelligence*; humour, sense of h.; wry humour, pawkiness, dryness; drollery, pleasantry, waggishness, facetiousness; jocularity 833 *merriment*; comicalness, absurdity 849 *ridiculousness*; flippancy 456 *inattention*; fun, joking, practical j., jesting, tomfoolery, buffoonery, clowning, funny business 497 *foolery*; comic turn, laugh a minute; broad humour, low h., vulgarity 847 *bad taste*; farce, broad f., knockabout comedy, slapstick, custard-pie humour, ham, high camp 594 *dramaturgy*; whimsicality, fancy 604 *whim*; cartoon, comic strip, caricature; biting wit, cruel humour, satire, sarcasm 851 *ridicule*; irony, spoof 850 *affectation*; black comedy, black humour, sick h.; wordplay, play upon words, punning.

witticism, witty remark; sally, mot, bon mot; epigram; pun, play upon words; punch line, throwaway l.; banter, chaff, badinage; repartee, quid pro quo, backchat 460 *answer*; sarcasm 851 *satire*; joke, standing j., private j., family j., in-joke; jest, good one, rib-tickler, side-splitter; quip; gag, one-liner; old joke, corny j., chestnut; practical joke, hoax, spoof, legpull; dirty joke, blue j., sick j.; story, funny s., shaggy-dog s.; limerick, clerihew.

humorist, wit, epigrammatist; life and soul of the party, wag, joker; jokesmith, funny man, gagster, punster; banterer, leg-puller, ragger, teaser; practical joker, hoaxer, spoof artist 545 *deceiver*; satirist, lampooner 926 *detractor*; comedian, comedienne, comic, standup c., slapstick c. 594 *entertainer*; comic writer, cartoonist, caricaturist; impersonator, parodist 20 *imitator*; raconteur, raconteuse; jester, court j., clown, zany, buffoon, stooge 501 *fool.*

Adj. *witty,* nimble-witted, quick; elegant; pointed, pithy, epigrammatic; brilliant, sparkling, smart, clever, too clever by half 498 *intelligent*; salty, racy, piquant; fruity, risqué; snappy, biting, pungent, keen, sharp, sarcastic; ironic, dry, sly, pawky; facetious, flippant 456 *light-minded*; jocular, joking, jokey, waggish, roguish; comic, funny ha-ha, rib-tickling 849 *funny*; comical, humorous, droll; whimsical 604 *capricious*; playful, sportive, fooling 497 *absurd.*

Vb. *be witty,* scintillate, sparkle; jest, joke, crack a j., quip, wisecrack; tell a good story, raise a laugh, have the audience in stitches 837 *amuse*; pun, make a p., play upon words; pull one's leg, have one on, put one on, make fun of, poke fun at, get a rise out of 851 *ridicule*; caricature 851 *satirize.*

840 Dullness – N. *dullness,* heaviness 834 *dejection*; stuffiness, dreariness, dreichness, deadliness; monotony, boringness 838 *tedium*; colourlessness, drabness; lack of sparkle, lack of fire, lack of inspiration, want of originality; stodginess, turgidity; staleness, flatness 387 *insipidity*; banality; lack of humour, prosaicness.

Adj. *dull,* uninteresting, uninspiring; deadly dull, dull as ditchwater; stuffy, dreary, deadly; boring, tedious; colourless, drab; flat, bland, vapid, insipid 387 *tasteless*; unimaginative, uninventive, unoriginal, derivative; stupid 499 *unintelligent*; humourless, frumpish 834 *serious*; inelegant; heavy, heavy-footed, clod-hopping, ponderous, sluggish 278 *slow*; stodgy, turgid, prosaic, matter-of-fact, pedestrian; stale, banal, commonplace, hackneyed, trite, platitudinous 610 *usual.*

841 Beauty – N. *beauty,* pulchritude; perfection; the sublime, splendour, gorgeousness; radiance; transfiguration 843 *beautification*; polish, gloss, ornament 844 *ornamentation*; scenic beauty, picturesqueness, scenery, view, landscape, seascape, snowscape, cloudscape 445 *spectacle*; regular features, classic f. 245 *symmetry*; physical beauty, loveliness, comeliness, fairness, handsomeness, bonniness, prettiness, chocolate-box p.,

picture-postcard p.; attraction, attractiveness, agreeableness, charm 826 *pleasurableness*; appeal, glamour, glitz, sex appeal, it, cuteness, attractions, physical a., charms; good looks, pretty face, beaux yeux; eyes of blue, ruby lips, schoolgirl complexion, peaches and cream c.; shapeliness, trim figure, curves, curvaceousness, vital statistics; gracefulness, grace 575 *elegance*; chic, style, dress sense 848 *fashion*; delicacy, refinement 846 *good taste*; aesthetics.

a beauty, thing of beauty, work of art; garden, beauty spot; masterpiece 644 *exceller*; bijou, jewel, jewel in the crown, pearl, treasure 646 *paragon*; peacock, swan, flower, rosebud, rose, lily; belle, raving beauty, toast of the tour, idol 890 *favourite*; dream girl; jolie laide; beauty queen, Miss World, bathing belle, pin-up girl, cover girl, page 3 girl, centre-fold g., pin-up, cheesecake; beefcake, hunk, muscleman, Mr Universe; fine figure of a man *or* woman; blond(e), brunette, redhead; English rose; dream, a dream walking, vision, poem, picture, sight for sore eyes; angel, charmer, dazzler; knockout, eyeful, good-looker, looker; doll, dolly bird; glamour puss, glamour girl *or* boy; heartthrob, dreamboat; enchantress, femme fatale, vamp, seductress, siren, witch 983 *sorceress*; smasher, lovely, cutie, honey, beaut, peach, dish; Venus, Aphrodite, Helen of Troy; Adonis, Narcissus.

Adj. *beautiful,* pulchritudinous, beauteous; lovely, fair, radiant; comely, bonny, pretty; pretty-pretty, pretty in a chocolate box way, picture-postcard, good enough to eat; pretty as a picture, photogenic; handsome, good-looking; well-built, husky, manly; tall, dark and handsome; statuesque, Junoesque; godlike, goddess-like, divine, pleasing to the eye, lovely to behold; picturesque, scenic, ornamental; aesthetic 846 *tasteful*; exquisite, perfect.

splendid, superb, fine 644 *excellent*; grand 868 *noble*; glorious, rich, gorgeous; resplendent, magnificent.

shapely, well-proportioned, of classic proportions 245 *symmetrical*; well-formed, well-turned; well-rounded, well-stacked, well-endowed, buxom, bosomy, curvaceous 248 *curved*; slinky; clean-limbed, straight, slender, slim, lissom, svelte, willowy 206 *lean*; graceful, elegant, chic; petite, dainty, delicate; perfect.

personable, prepossessing, agreeable; buxom, sonsy; attractive, dishy, fetching, appealing 826 *pleasurable*; sexy, cute; charming, entrancing, alluring, enchanting, glamorous; winsome; fresh-faced, clean-cut, wholesome, blooming; rosy-cheeked, apple-c., cherry-lipped, fresh-complexioned, bright-eyed; sightly, becoming, easy on the eye; presentable, natty, trim; spruce, dapper, glossy, sleek; well-dressed, well turned out, smart, stylish, classy, chic, soigné(e) 848 *fashionable*; elegant, dainty, delicate, refined 846 *tasteful*.

Vb. *be beautiful,* - splendid etc. adj.; be entrancing 983 *bewitch*; take one's breath away, beggar all description; be photogenic, photograph well; have good looks, bloom, dazzle 417 *shine*; be dressed to kill.

beautify, trim, improve; prettify, decorate; ornament; set off, grace, suit, become, go well, show one off, flatter; bring out the highlights, enhance one's looks, glamorize, transfigure; give a face-lift, smarten up; prink, titivate, do oneself up, do one's face, powder, rouge 843 *primp*.

842 Ugliness – N. *ugliness,* unsightliness, hideousness, repulsiveness; gracelessness, lumpishness, clumsiness 576 *inelegance*; asymmetry 246 *distortion*; unshapeliness 246 *deformity*; disfigurement 845 *blemish*; defacement; squalor, filth, grottiness, yuk 649 *uncleanness*; homeliness, plainness, ugly face; not much to look at, no beauty, no oil painting, wry face, forbidding countenance, haggardness; fading beauty, dim eyes, wrinkles, crowsfeet, hand of time, ravages of time 131 *age.*

eyesore, hideosity; blemish; offence to the eyes; blot on the landscape, architectural monstrosity, satanic mills; ugly person, fright, sight, frump; scarecrow, horror, death's-head, gargoyle; monster; harridan, witch; toad, gorilla, baboon, crow; plain Jane, ugly duckling; satyr, Caliban; Gorgon, Medusa; Beast.

Adj. *ugly,* ugly as sin, hideous, foul 649 *unclean;* frightful, shocking, monstrous; repulsive, repellent, odious, loathsome; beastly; not much to look at, short on looks, unprepossessing, homely, plain, plain-looking, without any looks; mousy, frumpish; ill-favoured, saturnine 893 *sullen.*

unsightly, ravaged, wrinkled 131 *ageing;* not fit to be seen, unseemly; marred; shapeless, formless 244 *amorphous;* grotesque, twisted, deformed, disfigured 246 *distorted;* defaced, vandalized, litter-strewn; ill-proportioned, misshapen; dumpy, squat 196 *dwarfish;* bloated 195 *fleshy;* ghastly; gruesome.

graceless, ungraceful 576 *inelegant;* unaesthetic; unattractive; badly dressed; tawdry; crude, uncouth 699 *artless;* clumsy, awkward, ungainly, cumbersome, hulky, hulking, slouching, clodhopping 195 *unwieldy.*

Vb. *be ugly,* be short on looks, lose one's l.; show one's age; look a wreck, look a mess, look a fright.

make ugly, uglify; sully 649 *make unclean;* deface, disfigure, mar, blemish; grimace; twist 246 *distort;* mutilate, vandalize 655 *impair.*

843 Beautification – N. *beautification,* beautifying 844 *ornamentation;* transfiguration 143 *transformation;* landscape gardening 844 *ornamental art;* plastic surgery, cosmetic s., nose-job, skin-grafting, face-lift 658 *surgery;* beauty treatment, face-lifting, eyebrow-plucking, waxing, electrolysis; face mask, mud pack, facial, facial scrub; massage, body m.; manicure, buffing; pedicure, chiropody; tattooing 844 *ornamental art;* ear-piercing; sun-tanning; sun lamp, sun bed; toilet, grooming,

make-up, cosmetology; cleansing, moisturizing, toning, creaming, rouging, painting, dyeing, powdering; soaping, shampooing; wash and brush up 648 *ablutions.*

hairdressing, trichology; shaving, clipping, trimming, thinning, singeing; depilation; cutting, haircut, bobbing, shingling; shave, hair cut, razor c., clip, trim, singe, short back and sides; hair style, coiffure, crop, Eton c., bob, shingle, pageboy, crewcut, urchin cut, bouffant c., coupe sauvage, spike; styling, hair-s., curling, frizzing, waving, setting, hair-straightening, defrizzing; hairdo, restyle, shampoo and set, set; blow-dry, finger-dry, scrunching; wave, blow w., marcel w., cold w.; permanent w., perm; curl 251 *coil;* bang, fringe, ponytail, bunches, pigtail, plaits, chignon, bun; pompadour, beehive, Afro 259 *hair;* hairpiece, toupee, switch, hair extension, hair weaving, hair implant; curling iron, tongs, curl papers, curlers, rollers, heated r.; bandeau, Alice band; comb, hairpin, hairgrip, bobby pin, Kirbigrip (tdmk); slide; hairnet, snood 228 *headgear.*

hairwash, shampoo, conditioner, rinse, highlights, bleach, tint, dye, henna, peroxide; hair mousse, hair gel, setting lotion, hair spray, lacquer, haircream, brilliantine; hair-restorer.

cosmetic, beauty aid, beauty spot; make-up, stick m.; greasepaint, warpaint, rouge, blusher, highlighter, cream, face c., cold c., cleansing c., vanishing c., moisturizing c., night c., lanolin 357 *unguent;* lipstick, lip gloss; nail polish, nail varnish, powder, face p., talcum p.; eye make-up, kohl, mascara, eye shadow, eyeliner, eyebrow pencil; hand lotion, skin toner, aftershave lotion, suntan l.; bath salts, bath oil, bath essence, bubble bath, foam b. 648 *cleanser;* antiperspirant, deodorant; scent, perfume, essence, cologne, eau de c., lavender water, toilet w.; false eyelashes; powder puff, compact; vanity case, manicure set, nail file, nail scissors, clippers; shaver, razor, electric r., depilatory, strip wax; toiletry, toiletries.

beautician, plastic surgeon; make-up artist; cosmetician; barber, hairdresser, hair stylist, coiffeur, coiffeuse; trichologist; manicurist, pedicurist, chiropodist.

Vb. *primp,* prettify, doll up, do up, dress up, ornament 844 *decorate*; prink, trick out; preen; titivate, make up, apply cosmetics, rouge, paint, powder; shave, pluck one's eyebrows, wax one's e., varnish one's nails, dye *or* tint one's hair; curl, wave, perm; have a hairdo, have a facial, have a manicure 841 *beautify.*

844 Ornamentation – N. *ornamentation,* decoration, adornment, garnish; ornateness 574 *ornament*; art deco, art nouveau, baroque, rococo; chinoiserie; richness, gilt, gaudiness 875 *ostentation*; enhancement, enrichment, embellishment; table decoration, centrepiece, silver, china, glass; floral decoration, flower arrangement, wreath, garland, bouquet, nosegay, posy, buttonhole; objet d'art, bric-a-brac, curio, bibelot.

ornamental art, landscape gardening, topiarism; architecture; interior decoration; statuary 554 *sculpture*; frieze, dado, triglyph; figurehead; boss, cornice, gargoyle; astragal, moulding, beading, fluting; fretting, tracery; varnishing 226 *facing*; veneering, panelling; ormolu, gilt, gold leaf; illumination, illustration, signpainting, graphic art 551 *art*; stained glass; tie-dyeing, batik; heraldic art 547 *heraldry*; tattooing; etching 555 *engraving*; handiwork, handicraft, fancywork, woodwork, fretwork, open-work, filigree; whittling, carving, embossing, chasing, intaglio; inlay, inset, enamelling, mosaic, marquetry 437 *variegation*; metalwork; gem-cutting, setting; cut glass, engraved g.; wrought iron.

pattern, motif, print, design, composition 331 *structure*; detail; geometrical style, rose window, spandrel, cyma, ogee, fleuron, cusp, trefoil, fleur-de-lis; tracery, scrollwork, arabesque, flourish, curlicue 251 *coil*; weave 331 *texture*; argyle, Arran, paisley 222 *textile*; chevron; tartan, check 437 *chequer*; pin-stripe 437 *stripe*; spot, dot, polka d. 437 *maculation*; herringbone, zigzag, dogtooth, hound's tooth 220 *obliquity*; watermark, logo 547 *identification*.

needlework, cross-stitch; patchwork, appliqué; open work, drawn-thread w.; embroidery, smocking; crochet, lace, broderie anglaise; tatting, knitting 222 *network*; stitch, purl, plain, stocking stitch, garter s., moss s.; gros point, petit p., needle p.; chain stitch, cable s., hem s., stem s., blanket s., feather s., back s., satin s., herringbone s., French knot, lazy-daisy.

trimming, piping, valance, border, fringe, frieze, frill, flounce 234 *edging*; binding 589 *bookbinding*; trappings; braid, frog, lapel, epaulette, star, rosette, cockade 547 *badge*; bow 47 *fastening*; bobble, pompom; tassel, bead; ermine, fur 259 *hair*; feather, ostrich f., osprey, plume 259 *plumage*; streamer, ribbon.

finery, togs, gear, glad rags, Sunday best, best bib and tucker 228 *clothing*; frippery, frills and furbelows, ribbons, froufrou; trinket, knick-knack, gewgaw, fandangle; tinsel, spangle, sequin, diamante, costume jewellery, glass, paste, marcasite, rhinestone 639 *bauble*.

jewellery, bijouterie; crown jewels, diadem, tiara 743 *regalia*; costume jewellery; drop, pendant, locket 217 *hanging object*; crucifix; amulet, charm 983 *talisman*; rope, string, necklet, necklace, beads, pearls, choker, chain, watch c. 250 *loop*; armlet, anklet, bracelet, bangle; ring, earring, drop e., signet ring, wedding r., eternity r., engagement r., dress r. 250 *circle*; cameo, brooch, clasp, badge, crest; stud, pin, gold p., tie p., collar stud, cufflinks 47 *fastening*; medal, medallion.

gem, jewel, bijou; stone, precious s., semiprecious s.; uncut gem, cut g., cabochon; diamond, rock, ice; solitaire; ruby, pearl, cultured p., seed p.; opal, black o., fire o.; sapphire, turquoise, emerald, beryl, aquamarine; garnet, amethyst, topaz, chalcedony, cornelian, jasper, agate,

onyx; heliotrope, bloodstone, moonstone, cat's-eye, zircon, jacinth, hyacinth, chrysolite; coral, ivory, mother of pearl, jet, amber, jade, lapis lazuli.

Adj. *ornamental,* decorative, fancy, arty-crafty; intricate, elaborate; picturesque, pretty-pretty, chocolate-box pretty; scenic; geometric; Doric, Ionic, Corinthian, Moresque, Romanesque, Decorated; baroque, rococo.

Vb. *decorate,* adorn, embellish, enhance, enrich; set off 574 *ornament;* paint, bejewel; tart up, glamorize, prettify 841 *beautify;* garnish, trim; array, bedeck 228 *dress;* deck out, trick o., preen, titivate 843 *primp;* add the finishing touches; freshen, smarten, spruce up, furbish, burnish 648 *clean;* beribbon; stud, bespangle 437 *variegate;* whitewash, varnish, japan, lacquer 226 *coat;* enamel, gild, silver; emblazon, illuminate, illustrate 553 *paint,* 425 *colour;* trim 234 *hem;* work, pick out, embroider; inlay, engrave; encrust, emboss, bead, mould; fret, carve 262 *groove,* 260 *notch;* wreathe.

845 Blemish – N. *blemish,* scar, cicatrice, weal, welt, mark, pockmark; flaw, crack, defect 647 *imperfection;* disfigurement, deformity 246 *distortion;* stigma, blot, blot on the landscape 842 *eyesore;* graffiti; blotch, splotch, smudge 550 *obliteration;* smut, patch, smear, stain, tarnish, rust, patina 649 *dirt;* spot, speck, speckle, macula, spottiness 437 *maculation;* freckle, mole, birthmark, strawberry mark; excrescence, pimple, plook, zit, blackhead, whitehead, carbuncle, sebaceous cyst, wen, wart 253 *swelling;* acne, rosacea, eczema 651 *skin disease;* harelip, cleft palate; cast, squint; scratch, bruise, black eye, shiner, cauliflower ear, broken nose 655 *wound.*

Vb. *blemish,* flaw, crack, injure, damage 655 *impair;* blot, smudge, stain, smear, sully, soil 649 *make unclean;* stigmatize, brand 547 *mark;* scar, pit, pockmark; mar, spoil, spoil the look of 842 *make ugly;* deface, vandalize, disfigure, scratch 244 *deform.*

846 Good Taste – N. *good taste,* tastefulness, taste; simplicity 573 *plainness;* refinement, delicacy 950 *purity;* discernment, palate 463 *discrimination;* daintiness, finickiness, fikiness, kid gloves 862 *fastidiousness;* decency, seemliness 848 *etiquette;* tact, consideration, dignity, manners, table m., breeding, civility, social graces 884 *courtesy;* propriety, decorum; grace, polish, finish, sophistication, gracious living 575 *elegance;* cultivation, culture, connoisseurship; epicureanism, epicurism; aesthetics 480 *judgment;* artistry, virtuosity.

people of taste, connoisseur, cognoscente; epicurean, epicure, gourmet; aesthete, art critic 480 *estimator;* arbiter of taste; purist.

Adj. *tasteful,* in good taste, in the best of t.; exquisite 644 *excellent;* simple 573 *plain;* graceful, classical 575 *elegant;* refined, delicate 950 *pure;* aesthetic, artistic 819 *sensitive;* discerning, epicurean 463 *discriminating;* nice, dainty 862 *fastidious;* decent, seemly, becoming 24 *apt;* proper, correct, comme il faut 848 *fashionable;* mannerly 848 *well-bred.*

Vb. *have taste,* show good t., reveal fine feelings 463 *discriminate;* appreciate, value 480 *judge;* settle for nothing less than the best, be a perfectionist 862 *be fastidious.*

847 Bad Taste – N. *bad taste,* tastelessness, poor taste 645 *badness;* no taste; kitsch; commercialization; yellow press, gutter p.; unrefinement, coarseness, barbarism, vulgarism, philistinism 699 *artlessness;* vulgarity, gaudiness, garishness, loudness; tawdriness, shoddiness; paste, ersatz, imitation 639 *bauble;* insensitivity, crassness, grossness, coarseness; tactlessness, indelicacy, impropriety, unseemliness; bad joke, sick j., obscenity 951 *impurity;* dowdiness.

ill-breeding, vulgarity, commonness; loudness; provinciality, suburbanism,

unfashionableness; bad form, lack of etiquette; bad manners, boorishness, impoliteness 885 *discourtesy*; ungentlemanliness; unladylikeness; misbehaviour, indecorum; rowdyism 61 *disorder*.

Adj. *vulgar,* unrefined 576 *inelegant*; tasteless, in bad taste, in the worst possible t.; gross, crass, coarse; philistine, yobbish, barbarian 699 *artless*; commercial, commercialized; tawdry, cheap, cheap and nasty, naff, kitschy, ersatz; flashy; blatant, loud, gaudy, garish; flaunting, shameless; excessive; schmaltzy; overdressed; common, common as muck, low, gutter, sordid 867 *disreputable*; improper, indelicate, indecorous; beyond the pale, scandalous, indecent, ribald 951 *impure*.

ill-bred, badly brought up; unpresentable, not to be taken anywhere; ungentlemanly, unladylike; hoydenish; ungenteel, non-U 869 *plebeian*; loud; tactless, insensitive, blunt; impolite, unmannerly, ill-mannered 885 *discourteous*; provincial, gone native; crude, rude, boorish, churlish, yobbish, loutish, clodhopping, uncouth, uncultured, unrefined 491 *ignorant*; unsophisticated, knowing no better 699 *artless*; uncivilized, barbaric; gauche 695 *clumsy*; rowdy 61 *disorderly*.

848 Fashion. Etiquette – N. *fashion,* style, mode, cut 243 *form*; method 624 *way*; vogue, cult 610 *habit*; prevailing taste, current fashion, trend 126 *modernism*; rage, fad, craze; new look, the latest, latest fashion, what's new 126 *newness*; dernier cri, last word, ne plus ultra; height of fashion; dash 875 *ostentation*; fashionableness; stylishness, flair, chic, anti-chic; dress sense; fashion show, mannequin parade 522 *exhibit*; haute couture, elegance; foppery 850 *affectation*.

etiquette, point of e. 875 *formality*; protocol, convention, custom, conventionality 610 *practice*; done thing, good form, what is expected; proprieties, appearances, Mrs Grundy; decorum, propriety, right note, correctness 846 *good* *taste*; courtesy; breeding, good b.; gentility, gentlemanliness, ladylike behaviour; manners, table m., good m.; best behaviour; savoir faire, savvy 688 *conduct*.

beau monde, society, high s., civilization; Mayfair; St James's, court; top drawer, right people, smart set, upper ten 868 *nobility*; upper crust, cream of society 644 *elite*; beautiful people, glitterati, jet set; fashionable person; Sloane Ranger, Sloane; yuppy; man *or* woman about town, man *or* woman of fashion, slave to fashion, trend-setter; man *or* woman of the world, socialite, playboy 882 *sociable person*.

fop, buck; dandy, beau, Beau Brummel; popinjay, peacock, clothes-horse, fashion plate; coxcomb; swell, toff, dude, nob, His Nibs, Lady Muck; lounge lizard, gigolo, gallant; ladykiller.

Adj. *fashionable,* modish, stylish, voguish; in, in vogue, in fashion, à la mode, chichi; chic, elegant, colour-supplement, well-dressed, well-groomed 846 *tasteful*; clothes-conscious, foppish, dressy; dashing, snazzy, flashy 875 *showy*; smart, classy, ritzy, swanky, swish, posh; up-to-the-minute, bang up-to-date, ultrafashionable, new-fangled, all the rage 126 *modern*; hip, hep, groovy, trendy, with it; dressed up to the nines, dressed to kill; from the top drawer, moving in the best circles, knowing the right people; in the swim 83 *conformable*.

well-bred, thoroughbred, blue-blooded 868 *noble*; civilized, urbane; well brought up, house-trained; U, gentlemanly, ladylike 868 *genteel*; civil, well-mannered, well-spoken 884 *courteous*; courtly 875 *formal*; poised; correct, conventional, decorous, proper; considerate 884 *amiable*; punctilious 929 *honourable*.

Vb. *be in fashion,* be done, catch on 610 *be wont*; be all the rage, be the latest, be the latest craze, be trendy 126 *modernize*; get with it, follow the fashion, jump on the band wagon, change with the times 83 *conform*; move in the best circles, be seen in the right places; keep

427

up with the Jones's, keep up appearances; cut a dash, be a trend-setter, set the tone; have style.

849 Ridiculousness – N. *ridiculousness,* ludicrousness, risibility, laughability, height of nonsense, height of absurdity 497 *absurdity*; funniness, pricelessness, drollery 839 *wit*; quaintness, oddness, queerness, eccentricity 84 *nonconformity*; bathos, anticlimax 509 *disappointment*; extravagance, bombast 546 *exaggeration*; light relief, comic r.; light verse, comic v., nonsense v., doggerel, limerick 839 *witticism*; spoonerism, malapropism, bull; comic turn, comedy, farce, burlesque, slapstick, knockabout, clowning, buffoonery 594 *stage play*.

Adj. *ridiculous,* ludicrous, preposterous, monstrous, grotesque, fantastic, inappropriate 497 *absurd*; clownish 695 *clumsy*; silly 499 *foolish*; derisory 639 *unimportant*; laughable, risible; bizarre, rum, quaint, odd, queer 84 *unusual*; strange, outlandish 59 *extraneous*; stilted 850 *affected*; bombastic, extravagant, outré; crazy, crackpot.

funny, funny-peculiar 84 *abnormal*; funny-ha-ha, good for a laugh 837 *amusing*; comical, droll, humorous 839 *witty*; rich, priceless, side-splitting, wildly amusing, hilarious, a real hoot, a scream, too funny for words; light, comic; ironical, satirical; burlesque; doggerel; farcical, slapstick, clownish, custard-pie, knockabout.

Vb. *be ridiculous,* make one laugh, excite laughter, raise a laugh; tickle, make one fall about, give one the giggles; entertain 837 *amuse*; look silly, be a figure of fun, cut a ridiculous figure, be a laughingstock, fool, play the fool 497 *be absurd*; pass from the sublime to the ridiculous; make an exhibition of oneself 695 *act foolishly*.

850 Affectation – N. *affectation,* fad 848 *fashion*; affectedness, pretentiousness 875 *ostentation*; putting on airs, grand a.

873 *airs*; posing, posturing, attitudinizing; pose, public image, façade; artificiality, mannerism, literary affectation, grandiloquence; preciosity, euphuism 574 *ornament*; foppery, foppishness, dandyism 873 *vanity*; euphemism, mock modesty 874 *modesty*; theatricality, camp, histrionics.

pretension, pretensions, false p.; artifice, sham, humbug, quackery, charlatanism, fraud 542 *deception*; superficiality; stiltedness; pedantry 735 *severity*; prudery; sanctimony, sanctimoniousness 979 *pietism*.

Adj. *affected,* self-conscious; studied, mannered, euphuistic, precious, chichi 574 *ornate*; artificial, unnatural, stilted 875 *formal*; prim, priggish, prudish, goody-goody, mealy-mouthed, euphemistic, sanctimonious, self-righteous, holier than thou, smug, demure 979 *pietistic*; arch, sly, nudging, winking 833 *merry*; coquettish, coy, cute, twee, tootoo, namby-pamby, mincing, simpering; hypocritical, tongue-in-cheek, ironical; bluffing; shallow, hollow, specious, pretentious, high-sounding; gushing, fulsome, stagy, theatrical, camp, overdramatized 875 *ostentatious*; dandified, foppish, poncy, camp; conceited, la-dida, giving oneself airs, putting on a., showing off, swanking, posturing, posing, striking poses, attitudinizing 873 *vain*; stuck up 871 *prideful*; name-dropping, keeping up appearances 847 *illbred*; bogus 541 *false*; for effect, assumed, put on, insincere, phoney; overdone.

Vb. *be affected,* affect, put on, assume; pretend, feign, go through the motions, make a show of, bluff 541 *dissemble*; make as if 20 *imitate*; act a part, play-act, role-play 594 *act*; overact, ham, barnstorm 546 *exaggerate*; do for effect, camp it up, play to the gallery; dramatize oneself, attitudinize, strike attitudes, posture, strike a p., prance, mince, ponce about 875 *be ostentatious*; put on airs, give oneself a., put on side, swank, show off, make an exhibition of oneself 873 *be*

vain; air one's knowledge 490 *know*; euphuize.

851 Ridicule – N. *ridicule,* derision, derisiveness, poking fun; mockery, mimicry, scoffing; sniggering, grinning 835 *laughter*; teasing, making fun of, ribbing, banter, badinage, leg-pulling, chaff, leg-pull; buffoonery, horseplay, clowning, practical joke 497 *foolery*; snigger, scoff, mock; irony, sarcasm, barbed shaft, backhanded compliment; catcall, hoot, hiss 924 *censure*; ribaldry 839 *witticism*.

satire, parody, burlesque, travesty, caricature, cartoon 552 *misrepresentation*; skit, spoof, send-up, take-off 20 *mimicry*; lampoon 926 *detraction*.

laughingstock, object of ridicule, figure of fun, butt; sport, game, fair g.; Aunt Sally; April fool, silly f.; buffoon, clown, zany 501 *fool*; stooge, foil, feed, straight man; guy, caricature, travesty, mockery of, apology for; eccentric 504 *crank*; original, card, caution, queer fish, odd f.; fall guy, victim 728 *loser*.

Vb. *ridicule,* deride, pour scorn on, laugh at, smirk at; snigger, laugh in *or* up one's sleeve; banter, chaff, twit, rib, tease, rag, pull one's leg, poke fun, make fun of, make sport of, make game of, take the mickey out of, have one on, put one on, kid, fool, make a fool of, make a laughing-stock of, take the piss out of (vulg), make an April fool of; mock, scoff, jeer 926 *detract*; make a joke of 922 *hold cheap*; take down, deflate, debunk, take the wind out of one's sails, make one look silly, make one laugh on the other side of his face 872 *humiliate*.

satirize, lampoon 921 *not respect*; mock; mimic, send up, take off 20 *imitate*; parody, travesty, spoof, burlesque, caricature 552 *misrepresent*; pillory 928 *accuse*.

852 Hope – N. *hope,* hopes, expectations, presumption 507 *expectation*; high hopes, conviction 485 *belief*; reliance, trust, confidence, faith, assurance 473 *certainty*; reassurance 831 *relief*; security, anchor, mainstay, staff 218 *support*; last hope, ray of hope, glimmer of h. 469 *possibility*; good omen, favourable auspices, promise, bright prospect 511 *omen*; blue sky, silver lining, a break in the clouds; hopefulness; buoyancy, optimism 833 *cheerfulness*; wishful thinking, self-deception; rose-coloured spectacles, rosy picture.

aspiration, ambition, purpose 617 *intention*; pious hope, fond h.; vision, pipe dream, heart's desire; castles in the air, castles in Spain, El Dorado, fool's paradise 513 *fantasy*; the end of the rainbow, promised land, utopia, millennium, the day 617 *objective*.

Adj. *hoping,* aspiring, starry-eyed; ambitious, go-getting, would-be; dreaming, day-dreaming 513 *imaginative*; hopeful, in hopes 507 *expectant*; happy in the hope, in sight of, on the verge of; sanguine, confident 473 *certain*; buoyant, optimistic; hoping for the best, everhoping.

promising, full of promise, favourable, auspicious, propitious 730 *prosperous*; bright, fair, golden, rosy; hopeful, encouraging; likely 471 *probable*; utopian, millennial; visionary 513 *imaginary*.

Vb. *hope,* trust, have faith; rest assured, feel confident, put one's trust in, rely, bank on, count on, pin one's hopes on, hope and believe 485 *believe*; assume; look forward 507 *expect*; hope for, dream of, aspire, promise oneself, aim high 617 *intend*; have hopes, have high h., have expectations, live in hopes, keep one's fingers crossed; nurse hope; take hope, recover h., see light at the end of the tunnel; refuse to give up hope, see no cause for despair, hope against hope, keep hope alive, never say die; catch at straws, keep one's spirits up, look on the bright side, hope for the best 833 *be cheerful*; keep smiling 600 *persevere*; see life through rose-coloured spectacles; delude oneself 477 *reason badly*; anticipate, count one's chickens before they are hatched 135 *be early*; indulge in wishful thinking, dream 513 *imagine*.

Int. nil desperandum! never say die! while there's life there's hope! hope springs eternal!

853 Hopelessness – N. *hopelessness,* no hope, defeatism, despondency 834 *dejection*; pessimism, cynicism, despair, desperation, no way out, last hope gone; dashed hopes, hope extinguished 509 *disappointment*; resignation 508 *lack of expectation*; not a hope 470 *impossibility*; vain hope, forlorn h. 513 *fantasy*; poor lookout, no prospects; hopeless case, dead duck; hopeless situation, catch-22, bad business 700 *predicament*; Job's comforter.

Adj. *hopeless,* bereft of hope, devoid of h., despairing, in despair, desperate, suicidal; unhopeful, pessimistic, cynical, looking on the black side; defeatist, fearing the worst, sunk in despair, inconsolable, disconsolate 834 *dejected*; wringing one's hands 836 *lamenting*; disappointed; desolate, forlorn; ruined, undone, 731 *unfortunate*.

unpromising, hopeless 834 *cheerless*; desperate 661 *dangerous*; unpropitious, inauspicious 731 *adverse*; ill-omened, ominous 511 *presageful*; irremediable, incurable, inoperable, terminal; beyond hope, past recall, despaired of; incorrigible, irreparable, irrecoverable, irrevocable, irreversible, inevitable; out of the question 470 *impossible*.

Vb. *despair,* lose heart, lose hope; become despondent, give way to despair, wring one's hands 834 *be dejected*; have shot one's last bolt, have no cards up one's sleeves, give up hope; abandon h., hope for nothing more from, write off 674 *stop using*; give up, turn one's face to the wall 721 *submit*.

854 Fear – N. *fear,* healthy f., dread, awe 920 *respect*; abject fear 856 *cowardice*; fright, stage f.; wind up, funk, blue funk; terror, mortal t.; state of terror, intimidation, trepidation, alarm, false a.; shock, flutter, flap, flat spin 318 *agitation*; fit, fit of terror, scare, stampede, panic, panic attack 318 *spasm*; flight, sauve qui

peut; the creeps, horror, hair on end, cold sweat; dismay 853 *hopelessness*; defence mechanism, fight or flight.

nervousness, lack of confidence 856 *cowardice*; diffidence 874 *modesty*; timidity, timorousness, fearfulness, hesitation 620 *avoidance*; loss of nerve, cold feet, second thoughts, fears, suspicions, misgivings, qualms, mistrust, apprehension, apprehensiveness, uneasiness, disquiet, anxiety, angst, care 825 *worry*; perturbation, trepidation, fear and trembling, flutter, tremor, palpitation, trembling, quaking, shaking, shuddering, shivering, stuttering; nerves, willies, butterflies, collywobbles, creeps, shivers, jumps, jitters, heebie-jeebies 318 *agitation*; gooseflesh, hair on end, knees knocking, teeth chattering.

phobia, claustrophobia, agoraphobia, aerophobia, acrophobia, pyrophobia, frigophobia, pogonophobia, autophobia, phobophobia, acrophobia, zoophobia, algophobia, monophobia, aquaphobia, astrophobia, nyctophobia, triskaidekaphobia, homophobia, ailurophobia, canophobia; thanatophobia, fear of death; technophobia, cyberphobia, technofear; antisemitism, racial prejudice, xenophobia 888 *hatred*; McCarthyism, Reds under the beds, witch-hunting.

intimidation, deterrence, war of nerves, sabre-rattling, arms build up, fee faw fum; threatening 900 *threat*; caution 664 *warning*; terror, terrorism, reign of terror 735 *severity*; alarmism, scaremongering; sword of Damocles; suspended sentence 963 *punishment*; deterrent 723 *weapon*; object of terror, goblin, hobgoblin 970 *demon*; spook, spectre 970 *ghost*; Gorgon, Medusa, scarecrow, tattie bogle, nightmare; bugbear, ogre 938 *monster*; skeleton, death's head, skull and crossbones.

alarmist, scaremonger, doom merchant, gloom and doom m., doomwatcher, doomster, ecodoomster, Cassandra, Calamity Jane; pessimist; terrorist; sabre-rattler.

Adj. *fearing,* afraid, frightened, funky, panicky; overawed 920 *respectful*; intimidated, terrorized; in mortal fear, in trepidation, in a cold sweat, in a flap, in a flat spin, in a panic, in a frenzy; panic-stricken; stampeding, scared, alarmed, startled; hysterical, having fits, in hysterics, in the grip of a panic attack; dismayed; frozen, petrified, stunned; aghast, horror-struck, unmanned, scared out of one's wits, trembling with fear, paralysed by f., rooted to the spot with fear, frightened to death, white as a sheet, ashen-faced.

nervous, tense, uptight; waiting for the axe to fall; timid, timorous, shy, diffident, self-conscious 874 *modest*; wary, shrinking, treading warily 858 *cautious*; doubtful, distrustful, suspicious 474 *doubting*; windy, faint-hearted 601 *irresolute*; disturbed; apprehensive, uneasy, fearful, dreading, anxious, worried 825 *unhappy*; a prey to fears; highly-strung, afraid of one's own shadow, jittery, jumpy, nervy, on edge; shaking, trembling, quaking, cowering, cringing 856 *cowardly*; with one's heart in one's mouth, shaking like a leaf *or* a jelly; on pins and needles, palpitating, breathless.

frightening, shocking, startling, alarming etc. vb.; formidable, redoubtable; hazardous, hairy 661 *dangerous*; dreadful, awe-inspiring, fearsome, awesome 821 *impressive*; grim, grisly, hideous, ghastly, lurid, frightful, revolting, petrifying, horrifying, horrific, horrible, terrible, awful; mind-boggling, mind-blowing; hair-raising, flesh-creeping, blood-curdling; weird, eerie, creepy, scary, ghoulish, nightmarish, gruesome, macabre, sinister; portentous, ominous; intimidating, sabre-rattling, bullying, hectoring 735 *oppressive*; menacing; nerve-racking 827 *distressing*.

Vb. *fear,* funk, be afraid, - frightened etc. adj.; stand in fear *or* awe, go in fear and tembling, dread 920 *respect*; flap, be in a f., be in a bit of a state, have the wind up, have the willies; get the wind up, take fright, take alarm; panic, fall into p.,

have a panic attack, press the panic button, stampede, take to flight, fly 620 *run away*; start, jump 318 *be agitated*; faint, collapse.

quake, shake, tremble, quiver, shiver, shudder, stutter, quaver; quake in one's shoes, shake like a jelly, fear for one's life, be frightened to death, be scared out of one's wits; change colour, blench, pale, go white as a sheet, turn ashen; wince, flinch, shrink, shy, jib 620 *avoid*; quail, cower, crouch; stand aghast, be horrified, be petrified, be chilled with fear, freeze, freeze with horror, be rooted to the spot with terror, feel one's blood run cold, feel one's hair stand on end.

be nervous, - apprehensive etc. adj.; have misgivings; shrink, quail, funk it, put off the evil day; be anxious, dread, have qualms; hesitate, get cold feet, think twice, have second thoughts, think better of it, not dare 858 *be cautious*; get the wind up, start at one's own shadow, be on edge, be all of a doodah 318 *be agitated*.

frighten, scare, panic, stampede; intimidate, menace 900 *threaten*; hang over 155 *impend*; alarm, cause a., raise the a., press the panic button, cry wolf; frighten to death, scare the living daylights out of, scare stiff, scare half to death; make one jump, give one a fright, give one a turn, startle, make one all of a doodah 318 *agitate*; disquiet, disturb, perturb, prey on the mind 827 *trouble*; put the wind up, make nervous, set on edge, rattle, shake, unnerve; play on one's nerves, throw into a nervous state; unman, make a coward of; put the fear of God into, overawe 821 *impress*; cow 727 *overmaster*; disconcert 63 *derange*; frighten off, daunt, deter; terrorize 735 *oppress*; browbeat, bully 827 *torment*; terrify; chill, freeze, paralyse, petrify, turn to stone, mesmerize 375 *render insensible*; make one's blood run cold; make one's hair stand on end *or* curl, make one's flesh creep, make one's knees knock, make one's teeth chatter, frighten out of one's wits, reduce one to a quivering jelly.

431

855 Courage – N. *courage,* bravery, valour, derring-do; courage of one's convictions 929 *probity*; courage in the face of the enemy, heroism, gallantry, chivalry; fearlessness, intrepidity, daring, nerve; boldness, audacity 857 *rashness*; spirit, mettle, dash, go, élan, panache 174 *vigorousness*; enterprise 672 *undertaking*; tenacity, survivability, bulldog courage 600 *perseverance*; stoutness of heart, resoluteness 599 *resolution*; gameness, pluck, smeddum, spunk, guts, heart, stout h., heart of oak, backbone, grit 600 *stamina*; Dutch courage; courage of despair; brave face, bold front 711 *defiance*; fresh courage, new heart, encouragement 612 *inducement.*

manliness, manhood, machismo 929 *probity*; chivalry; manly spirit; endurance, stiff upper lip 599 *resolution.*

prowess, derring-do, chivalry, heroism, act of courage, courage in the face of the enemy; feat, exploit, bold stroke, coup de grâce 676 *deed*; desperate venture 857 *rashness*; heroics.

brave person, hero, heroine, VC, GC, Croix de Guerre; knight; brave, warrior 722 *soldier*; man *or* woman of mettle, man *or* woman of spirit, plucky fellow, bulldog; daredevil, stunt man *or* woman; fire-eater; Galahad, Lionheart; Joan of Arc, Boadicea, Amazon; knight-errant; the bravest of the brave; band of heroes, gallant company, SAS; forlorn hope 644 *elite*; lion, tiger, fighting cock, bulldog.

Adj. *courageous,* brave, valiant, gallant, heroic; chivalrous, knightly; soldierly, martial, Amazonian 718 *warlike*; stout, manly, tough, macho, Ramboesque, red-blooded; aggressive, fire-eating; fierce; bold 711 *defiant*; audacious, daring, venturesome, bold as brass 857 *rash*; adventurous 672 *enterprising*; mettlesome, spirited, stout-hearted, brave-h., lion-hearted, bold as a lion; full of courage, spunky; unbowed, firm, indomitable, never say die; determined 599 *resolute*; game, plucky, sporting; ready for the fray, ready for anything, unflinching 597 *willing.*

Vb. *be courageous,* - bold etc. adj.; have what it takes, have guts, come up to scratch, show spirit, show one's mettle 716 *fight*; venture, bell the cat, take the plunge, take the bull by the horns 672 *undertake*; dare 661 *face danger*; show fight, brave, face, outface, outdare, beard, defy; confront, look straight in the face, look in the eyes, be eyeball to eyeball with, eyeball; speak out, speak one's mind, speak up, stand up and be counted 532 *affirm*; face the music, stick one's neck out, show a bold front 599 *stand firm*; laugh at danger, mock at d. 857 *be rash*; grin and bear it, take one's medicine 825 *suffer.*

take courage, pluck up c., muster c., nerve *or* steel oneself, take one's courage in both hands; put a brave face on it, screw up one's courage 599 *be resolute.*

give courage, infuse c.; put heart into, hearten, make a man of; embolden 612 *incite*; buck up, rally 833 *cheer*; raise morale, bolster up, give confidence.

856 Cowardice – N. *cowardice,* abject fear, funk, blue f. 854 *fear*; cowardliness, no guts 601 *irresolution*; timidity; faint-heartedness, chicken-heartedness; unmanliness, defeatism 853 *hopelessness*; leaving the sinking ship, desertion, quitting, shirking 918 *undutifulness*; white feather, yellow streak, faint heart, chicken liver; Dutch courage; cowering, skulking; overcaution 858 *caution*; moral cowardice.

coward, funk, poltroon, craven, lily-liver, chickenheart, wheyface; scaredy-cat, fraidycat, cowardly custard; coward at heart, sissy, milksop, mummy's boy, baby, big b., cry-b. 163 *weakling*; quitter, shirker, deserter; cur, chicken, rabbit, mouse, jellyfish, invertebrate, doormat; scaremonger.

Adj. *cowardly,* coward, craven, poltroonish; pusillanimous, timid, timorous, fearful, afraid of one's own shadow, unable to say boo to a goose, of a nervous disposition 854 *nervous*; soft, womanish, babyish, unmanly, sissy 163 *weak*;

spiritless, spunkless, without grit, without guts, lacking smeddum, with no backbone, faint-hearted, chicken-livered, yellow-l., lily-l., chicken; cowering, quailing; yellow, abject, base; unwarlike, cowed, defeatist 853 *hopeless*; unheroic, uncourageous 858 *cautious*; shy, coy 874 *modest*; infirm of purpose 601 *irresolute*.

Vb. *be cowardly,* lack courage, have no fight, have no pluck, have no grit, have no guts, lack smeddum, have no backbone, have no heart *or* stomach for, not dare 601 *be irresolute*; lose one's nerve, get the jitters, have cold feet 854 *be nervous*; shrink, funk, shy from, back out, chicken o. 620 *avoid*; hide, skulk, quail, cower, cringe 721 *knuckle under*; show a yellow streak, show the white feather, show fear, turn tail, cut and run, run for cover, panic, press the panic button, stampede, scuttle, show one's back, desert 620 *run away*; lead from behind, keep well to the rear 858 *be cautious*.

857 Rashness – N. *rashness,* lack of caution, incautiousness, unwariness, heedlessness 456 *inattention*; carelessness, neglect 458 *negligence*; imprudence, improvidence, indiscretion 499 *folly*; lack of consideration, irresponsibility; wildness, indiscipline 738 *disobedience*; daredevilry, recklessness, foolhardiness, temerity, audacity, presumption, overconfidence; hotheadedness, impatience 822 *excitability*; rushing into things, impetuosity, precipitance, hastiness, overhastiness 680 *haste*; quixotry; playing with fire, brinkmanship, game of chicken; desperation, courage of despair 855 *courage*; needless risk, leap in the dark 661 *danger*; too many eggs in one basket, underinsurance, counting one's chickens before they are hatched 661 *vulnerability*; reckless gamble, last throw 618 *gambling*; reckless expenditure 815 *prodigality*.

desperado, daredevil, madcap, hothead, adventurer, inveterate gambler 618 *gambler*; harum-scarum, ne'er-do-well; one who sticks at nothing, gunman, terrorist, contra, guerrilla; bully 904 *ruffian*.

Adj. *rash,* ill-considered, ill-conceived, ill-advised, harebrained, foolhardy, wildcat, injudicious, indiscreet, imprudent 499 *unwise*; careless, hit-and-miss, slapdash, free-and-easy 458 *negligent*; uncircumspect, lemming-like, incautious, unwary, heedless, thoughtless, inconsiderate, uncalculating 456 *inattentive*; frivolous, flippant, giddy, devil-may-care, harum-scarum, slaphappy, trigger-happy 456 *light-minded*; irresponsible, reckless, regardless, couldn't-care-less, don't-care, damning the consquences, lunatic, wanton, wild, cavalier; bold, daring, audacious; overdaring, madcap, daredevil, do-or-die, breakneck, suicidal; overambitious, over the top, oversanguine, oversure, overconfident 852 *hoping*; overweening, presumptuous, arrogant 878 *insolent*; precipitate, headlong, hell-bent, desperate 680 *hasty*; unchecked, headstrong 602 *wilful*; 491 *ignorant*; impulsive, impatient, hot-blooded, hot-headed 822 *excitable*; venturesome 618 *speculative*; adventurous, thrill-seeking, risk-taking 672 *enterprising*; improvident 815 *prodigal*.

Vb. *be rash,* - reckless etc. adj.; lack caution, want judgment, lean on a broken reed; expose oneself, drop one's guard, stick one's neck out, take unnecessary risks, put one's head in the lion's cage, ride the tiger; go bull-headed at, charge at, rush at, rush into, rush one's fences 680 *hasten*; take a leap in the dark, leap before one looks, buy a pig in a poke, take something on trust; ignore the consequences, damn the c.; gamble, put all one's eggs into one basket, underinsure; not care 456 *be inattentive*; play fast and loose 634 *waste*; spend to the hilt 815 *be prodigal*; play the fool, play with fire, burn one's fingers; go out on a limb, risk one's neck, dice with death 661 *face danger*; play a desperate game, court disaster, ask for trouble, tempt providence, push one's luck, rush in where angels fear to tread; count one's

chickens before they are hatched, aim too high 695 *act foolishly*.

Adv. *rashly*, incautiously; headlong, recklessly, like Gadarene swine, like lemmings.

858 Caution – N. *caution*, cautiousness, wariness, heedfulness, care, heed 457 *carefulness*; hesitation, doubt, second thoughts 854 *nervousness*; instinct of self-preservation 932 *selfishness*; looking before one leaps, looking twice, looking round, circumspection; guardedness, secretiveness, reticence 525 *secrecy*; calculation, counting the risk, safety first; nothing left to chance 669 *preparation*; deliberation, due d., mature consideration 480 *judgment*; sobriety, balance, level-headedness 834 *seriousness*; prudence, discretion, worldly wisdom 498 *wisdom*; insurance, precaution 662 *safeguard*; forethought 510 *foresight*; Fabian policy 823 *patience*; going slow, taking one's time, watching one's step, one step at a time, festina lente 278 *slowness*; wait-and-see policy, waiting game, cat-and-mouse 136 *delay*.

Adj. *cautious*, wary, watchful 455 *attentive*; heedful 457 *careful*; hesitating, doubtful, suspicious 854 *nervous*; taking no risks, insured, hedging; guarded, secret, secretive, incommunicative, cagey 525 *reticent*; experienced, taught by experience, once bitten, twice shy 669 *prepared*; on one's guard, circumspect, looking round, looking all ways, gingerly, stealthy, feeling one's way, taking one's time, watching one's step, tentative 461 *experimental*; conservative 660 *safe*; responsible 929 *trustworthy*; prudent, discreet 498 *wise*; noncommittal 625 *neutral*; frugal, counting the cost 814 *economical*; canny, timid, slow-moving, overcautious, unenterprising, unadventurous; slow, deliberate, Fabian 823 *patient*; sober, cool-headed, level-h., cool; cold-blooded, calm, self-possessed 823 *inexcitable*.

Vb. *be cautious*, beware 457 *be careful*; take no risks, play it by the book, play safe, play a waiting game, play a cat-and-mouse g. 498 *be wise*; ca' canny, go slow, festina lente 278 *move slowly*; cover up, cover one's tracks 525 *conceal*; not talk 525 *keep secret*; keep under cover, keep on the safe side, keep in the rear, keep in the background, keep out of the limelight, hide 523 *lurk*; look out, see how the land lies 438 *scan*; see how the wind blows, feel one's way, play it by ear, put a toe in the water 461 *be tentative*; be on one's guard, tread warily, watch one's step, pussyfoot 525 *be stealthy*; think twice 455 *be mindful*; calculate, reckon 480 *judge*; consider the risk factor, count the cost, cut one's coat according to one's cloth 814 *economize*; know when to stop, take one's time; let well alone, let sleeping dogs lie, keep well out of 620 *avoid*; consider the consequences 511 *predict*; take precautions; look a gift horse in the mouth 480 *estimate*; make sure 473 *make certain*; cover oneself, insure, hedge; leave nothing to chance 669 *prepare*.

Adv. *cautiously*, gingerly; softly softly.

859 Desire – N. *desire*, wish, will and pleasure 595 *will*; summons, call, cry 737 *command*; demand; wanting, want, need, exigency 627 *requirement*; claim 915 *dueness*; nostalgia, nostalgie de la boue, homesickness 830 *regret*; wistfulness, longing, hankering, yearning, sheep's eyes; wishing, thinking, daydreaming, daydream, castles in the air 513 *fantasy*; ambition, aspiration 852 *hope*; yen, urge 279 *impulse*; itch; thrill-seeking, rubber-necking, curiousness, thirst for knowledge, intellectual curiosity 453 *curiosity*; avidity, eagerness, zeal 597 *willingness*; passion, ardour, warmth, impetuosity, impatience 822 *excitability*; rage, fury 503 *frenzy*; mania 503 *personality disorder*; craving, lust for, appetite, hunger, thirst; expansionism, a place in the sun; covetousness, cupidity, itching palm 816 *avarice*; graspingness, greediness, greed 786 *rapacity*; voracity, wolfishness, insatiability 947 *gluttony*; concupiscence, lust (see *libido*); incontinence 943 *intemperance*.

hunger, starvation, famine, famished condition, empty stomach 946 *fasting*; appetite, good a., keen a., voracious a., edge of a.; thirst, thirstiness 342 *dryness*; dipsomania 949 *alcoholism.*

liking, fancy, fondness, infatuation 887 *love*; stomach, appetite, zest, craving; relish, tooth, sweet t. 386 *taste*; leaning, penchant, propensity, trend 179 *tendency*; weakness, partiality; affinity; sympathy, involvement 775 *participation*; inclination, mind 617 *intention*; predilection, favour 605 *choice*; whim, whimsy 604 *caprice*; hobby, craze, fad, mania 481 *bias*; fascination, allurement, attraction, temptation, titillation, seduction 612 *inducement.*

libido, sexual urge; erotism, eroticism; concupiscence, sexual desire, carnal d., passion, rut, heat, oestrus; mating season; libidinousness, prurience, lust, lecherousness, letch, the hots 951 *unchastity*; nymphomania, priapism, satyriasis 84 *abnormality.*

desired object, one's heart's desire, wish, desire 627 *requirement*; catch, prize, plum 729 *trophy*; cynosure 890 *favourite*; forbidden fruit, torment of Tantalus; envy, temptation; magnet, lure, draw 291 *attraction*; the unattainable; aim, goal, star, ambition, aspiration, dream 617 *objective*; ideal 646 *perfection*; height of one's ambition.

Adj. *greedy,* acquisitive 932 *selfish*; ambitious, status-seeking; voracious, omnivorous, open-mouthed 947 *gluttonous*; unsated, unsatisfied, unslaked; insatiable, rapacious, grasping, retentive 816 *avaricious.*

hungry, hungering; unfilled, empty, supperless, dinnerless 946 *fasting*; half-starved, starving, famished 636 *underfed*; peckish, ready for, ravenous, hungry as a hunter, ready to eat a horse; thirsty, dry, drouthy, parched, dehydrated.

desired, wanted, liked; likable, desirable, worth having, enviable, coveted, in

demand; acceptable, welcome; appetizing 826 *pleasurable*; fetching, catchy, attractive, appealing; wished, self-sought, invited 597 *voluntary.*

Vb. *desire,* want, miss, feel the lack of 627 *require*; ask for, cry out f., clamour f. 737 *demand*; call, summon, send for, ring for 737 *command*; invite 882 *be hospitable*; wish, make a w., pray; wish otherwise, unwish 830 *regret*; covet 912 *envy*; have a mind to, set one's heart on, set one's mind on, have designs on, set one's sights on, aim at, have at heart 617 *intend*; plan for, angle f., fish f. 623 *plan*; aspire, dream of, dream, daydream 852 *hope*; aim high; look for, expect 915 *claim*; wish in vain, whistle for, cry for the moon 695 *act foolishly*; pray for, intercede, invoke, wish on, call down on; wish ill 899 *curse*; wish one well; welcome, be glad of, jump at, catch at, grasp at, clutch at 786 *take*; lean towards 179 *tend*; favour, prefer, select 605 *choose*; crave, itch for, hanker after, have a yen for, long for; long, yearn, pine, languish; pant for, gasp f., burn f., die f., be dying f. 636 *be unsatisfied*; thirst for, hunger f.; can't wait, must have; like, have a liking, have a taste for, care for 887 *love*; take to, warm to, take a fancy to, fall in love with, dote, dote on, be infatuated with, moon after, be in love, ogle, make eyes at, make passes, solicit, woo 889 *court*; set one's cap at, make a dead set at, run after, chase 619 *pursue*; lust, lust for, lust after, letch after, have the hots for 951 *be impure*; rut, be on heat.

be hungry, hunger, famish, starve, be ravenous, have an empty stomach, have an aching void, be ready to eat a horse 636 *be unsatisfied*; have a good appetite, lick one's chops, salivate, water at the mouth 301 *eat*; thirst, be dry, be dying for a drink, be parched, be dehydrated.

860 Indifference – **N.** *indifference,* unconcern, uninterestedness 454 *incuriosity*; lack of interest, half-heartedness, want of zeal, lukewarmness 598 *unwillingness*; coolness, coldness, faint praise;

lovelessness, mutual indifference, nothing between them; anorexia, no appetite, loss of a.; no desire for; inertia, apathy 679 *inactivity*; nonchalance, insouciance 458 *negligence*; perfunctoriness, carelessness 456 *inattention*; don't-care attitude 734 *laxity*; recklessness, heedlessness 857 *rashness*; promiscuousness 464 *indiscrimination*; amorality; open mind, unbiased attitude, impartiality, equity 913 *justice*; neutrality 625 *middle way*; nothing to choose between, six of one and half a dozen of the other.

Adj. *indifferent,* unconcerned, uninterested 454 *incurious*; lukewarm, Laodicean, half-hearted 598 *unwilling*; impersonal, uninvolved, phlegmatic 820 *impassive*; unimpressed, blasé; calm, cool, cold 823 *inexcitable*; nonchalant, insouciant, careless, perfunctory 458 *negligent*; supine, lackadaisical, listless 679 *inactive*; unambitious, unaspiring; don't-care, easy-going 734 *lax*; unresponsive, unmoved, insensible to; fancy-free, uninvolved; disenchanted, disillusioned, out of love, cooling off; impartial; noncommittal 625 *neutral*.

unwanted, unwelcome, de trop, in the way; unwished for, unasked, uninvited; unvalued 458 *neglected*; on the shelf; unattractive, undesirable.

Vb. *be indifferent,* - unconcerned etc. adj.; be uninvolved, take no interest 456 *be inattentive*; not mind, care little for, not lose any sleep over, damn with faint praise; care nothing for, not give a fig *or* a thankyou for, not care a straw about, couldn't care less, take it or leave it; not think twice about, not care, not give a hoot, shrug off, dismiss, let go, make light of 922 *hold cheap*; not defend, hold no brief for, take neither side, sit on the fence 606 *be neutral*; grow indifferent, fall out of love, lose interest, cool off.

Int. Never mind! what does it matter! who cares? so what?

861 Dislike – **N.** *dislike,* disinclination, no inclination for, no fancy for, no stomach for; reluctance, backwardness 598

unwillingness; displeasure 891 *resentment*; dissatisfaction 829 *discontent*; disagreement 489 *dissent*; shyness, aversion 620 *avoidance*; sudden *or* instant dislike, antipathy, allergy; rooted dislike, distaste, repugnance, repulsion, disgust, abomination, abhorrence, detestation, loathing; shuddering, horror, mortal h. 854 *fear*; xenophobia 854 *phobia*; prejudice 481 *bias*; animosity, bad blood, ill feeling, mutual hatred, common h. 888 *hatred*; nausea, queasiness, turn, heaving stomach, vomit 300 *voidance*; object of dislike, not one's type, bête-noire, pet aversion, a red rag to a bull.

Vb. *dislike,* find not to one's taste; not care for, have no liking f., have no desire for; have no stomach for, have no heart for 598 *be unwilling*; not choose, prefer not to 607 *reject*; object 762 *deprecate*; mind 891 *resent*; take a dislike to, feel an aversion for, have a down on, have one's knife in, have it in for 481 *be biased*; react against 280 *recoil*; feel sick at 300 *vomit*; shun, turn away, shrink from, have no time for 620 *avoid*; look askance at 924 *disapprove*; turn up the nose at, sniff at, sneer at 922 *despise*; make a face, grimace; be unable to abide, not endure, can't stand, can't bear, detest, loathe, abominate, abhor 888 *hate*; not like the look of, shudder at 854 *fear*; unwish, wish undone 830 *regret*.

cause dislike, disincline, deter 854 *frighten*; go against the grain, rub the wrong way, antagonize, put one's back up 891 *enrage*; set against, set at odds, make bad blood; satiate, pall, jade 863 *sate*; disagree with, upset 25 *disagree*; put off, revolt 292 *repel*; offend, grate, jar 827 *displease*; get one's goat, get up one's nose, get on one's nerves 827 *torment*; disgust, stick in one's throat, nauseate, sicken, make one's gorge rise, turn one's stomach, make one sick; shock, scandalize, make a scandal 924 *incur blame*.

862 Fastidiousness – **N.** *fastidiousness,* niceness, nicety, daintiness, finicalness,

finicality, fikiness, pernicketiness, delicacy; discernment, perspicacity, sublety 463 *discrimination*; refinement 846 *good taste*; connoisseurship, epicurism; meticulousness, preciseness 457 *carefulness*; idealism, overdeveloped conscience 917 *conscience*; perfectionism, fussiness, nit-picking, over-refinement, hypercriticalness, pedantry, hair-splitting; prudishness, Puritanism 950 *prudery*.

perfectionist, idealist, purist, rigorist, fusspot, pedant, nit-picker, stickler, hard taskmaster; picker and chooser, gourmet, epicure.

Adj. *fastidious,* nice, dainty, delicate, epicurean; perspicacious, discerning 463 *discriminating*; particular, demanding, choosy, finicky, finical, fiky; overnice, overparticular, scrupulous, meticulous, squeamish 455 *attentive*; punctilious, painstaking, conscientious, overconscientious, critical, hypercritical, overcritical, fussy, pernickety, hard to please, fault-finding, censorious 924 *disapproving*; pedantic, donnish, precise, rigorous, exacting, difficult 735 *severe*; prim, puritanical 950 *prudish*.

Vb. *be fastidious,* - choosy etc. adj.; settle for nothing less than the best; pick and choose 605 *choose*; over-refine, split hairs, mince matters 475 *argue*; draw distinctions 463 *discriminate*; find fault 924 *dispraise*; fuss, turn up one's nose, wrinkle one's n.; look a gift horse in the mouth, feel superior, disdain 922 *despise*; keep oneself to oneself.

863 Satiety – N. *satiety,* jadedness, fullness, repletion 54 *plenitude*; overfulness, plethora, overabundance, stuffing, engorgement, saturation, saturation point 637 *redundance*; glut, surfeit, too much of a good thing 838 *tedium*; overdose, excess 637 *superfluity*; spoiled child, spoilt brat.

Adj. *sated,* satiated, satisfied, replete, saturated, brimming 635 *filled*; overfull, surfeited, gorged, glutted, cloyed, sick of; jaded, blasé 838 *bored*.

Vb. *sate,* satiate; satisfy, quench, slake 635 *suffice*; fill up, overfill, saturate 54 *fill*; soak 341 *drench*; stuff, gorge, glut, surfeit, cloy, jade, pall; overdose, overfeed; sicken 861 *cause dislike*; spoil, overindulge, kill with kindness; bore, weary 838 *be tedious*.

864 Wonder – N. *wonder,* state of wonder, wonderment, raptness; admiration, hero worship 887 *love*; awe, fascination; cry of wonder, gasp of admiration, whistle, wolf w., exclamation, exclamation mark; shocked silence 399 *silence*; open mouth, popping eyes, eyes on stalks; shock, surprise, surprisal 508 *lack of expectation*; astonishment, amazement; stupor, stupefaction; bewilderment, bafflement 474 *uncertainty*; consternation 854 *fear*.

miracle-working, wonder-working, spellbinding, magic 983 *sorcery*; stroke of genius, feat, exploit 676 *deed*; transformation scene, coup de théâtre 594 *dramaturgy*.

prodigy, portent, sign, eye-opener 511 *omen*; quite something, phenomenon, miracle, marvel, wonder; drama, sensation, cause célèbre, nine-days' wonder; object of wonder *or* admiration, wonderland, fairyland 513 *fantasy*; seven wonders of the world; sight 445 *spectacle*; infant prodigy, genius, man *or* woman of genius 696 *proficient person*; miracleworker, thaumaturge, wizard, witch, fairy godmother 983 *sorcerer*; hero, heroine, wonder boy, superman, dream girl, superwoman, whiz kid 646 *paragon*; freak, sport, curiosity, oddity, guy, monster, monstrosity 84 *rara avis*; puzzle 530 *enigma*.

Adj. *wonderful,* to wonder at, wondrous, marvellous, miraculous, monstrous, prodigious, phenomenal; stupendous, fearful 854 *frightening*; admirable, exquisite 644 *excellent*; record-breaking 644 *best*; striking, overwhelming, awesome, awe-inspiring, breathtaking 821 *impressive*; dramatic, sensational; shocking, scandalizing; rare, exceptional, extraordinary, unprecedented 84

unusual; remarkable, noteworthy; strange, passing s., odd, very odd, outré, weird, weird and wonderful, unaccountable, mysterious, enigmatic 517 *puzzling*; exotic, outlandish, unheard of 59 *extraneous*; fantastic 513 *imaginary*; impossible, hardly possible, too good *or* bad to be true 472 *improbable*; unbelievable, incredible, inconceivable, unimaginable, indescribable; unutterable, unspeakable, ineffable 517 *inexpressible*; surprising 508 *unexpected*; mind-boggling, mind-blowing, astounding, amazing, shattering, bewildering etc. vb.; wonder-working; magic, like m. 983 *magical*.

Vb. *wonder,* marvel, admire, whistle; hold one's breath, gasp, gasp with admiration; stare, goggle at, gawk, open one's eyes wide, rub one's e., not believe one's e.; gape, gawp, open one's mouth, stand in amazement, look aghast 508 *not expect*; be awestruck, be overwhelmed 854 *fear*; have no words to express, not know what to say, be reduced to silence, be struck dumb 399 *be silent*.

be wonderful, - marvellous etc. adj.; do wonders, work miracles, achieve marvels; surpass belief, stagger b., boggle the mind 486 *cause doubt*; beggar all description, baffle d., beat everything; spellbind, enchant 983 *bewitch*; dazzle, strike with admiration, turn one's head; strike dumb, awe, electrify 821 *impress*; make one's eyes open, make one sit up and take notice, take one's breath away; bowl over, stagger; blow one's mind, stun, daze, stupefy, petrify, dumbfound, confound, astound, astonish, amaze, flabbergast 508 *surprise*; baffle, bewilder 474 *puzzle*; startle 854 *frighten*; shock, scandalize 924 *incur blame*.

865 Lack of wonder – N. *lack of wonder,* irreverence, refusal to be impressed, blankness, stony indifference 860 *indifference*; composure, calmness, serenity, tranquillity 266 *quietude*; imperturbability, impassiveness, cold blood 820 *moral insensibility*; taking for granted 610 *habituation*; lack of imagination,

unimaginativeness; disbelief 486 *unbelief*; matter of course, just what one thought, nothing to wonder at, nothing to write home about, nothing in it.

Vb. *not wonder,* see nothing remarkable 820 *be insensitive*; treat as a matter of course, not raise an eyebrow, take for granted, take as one's due; see it coming 507 *expect*.

866 Repute – N. *repute,* good r., high r.; reputation, good r.; report, good r.; title to fame, name, great n., good n., fair n., character, good c., high c., reputability, respectability 802 *credit*; regard, esteem 920 *respect*; opinion, good o., good odour, favour, high f., popular f., good books; popularity, vogue 848 *fashion*; acclaim, applause, approval, stamp of a., seal of a., cachet 923 *approbation*.

prestige, aura, mystique, magic; glamour, glitz, dazzle, éclat, lustre, splendour; brilliance, prowess; illustriousness, glory, honour, honour and glory, kudos, claim to fame, succès d'estime (see *famousness*); esteem, estimation, account, high a., worship 638 *importance*; face, izzat, caste; degree, rank, ranking, standing, footing, status, honorary s.; condition, position, position in society; top of the ladder *or* the tree, precedence 34 *superiority*; conspicuousness, prominence, eminence 443 *visibility*; distinction, greatness, high rank, exaltedness, majesty 868 *nobility*; impressiveness, dignity, stateliness, solemnity, grandeur, sublimity, awesomeness; name to conjure with 178 *influence*; paramountcy, ascendancy, hegemony, primacy 733 *authority*; leadership, acknowledged l. 689 *directorship*; prestigiousness, snob value.

famousness, title to fame, celebrity, notability, remarkability; illustriousness, renown, stardom, fame, name, note; household name, synonym for; glory 727 *success*; notoriety 867 *disrepute*; talk of the town 528 *publicity*; claim to fame, place in history, posthumous fame 505 *memory*; undying name, immortal n., immortality, deathlessness;

remembrance, commemoration, niche in the hall of fame.

honours, honour, blaze of glory, crown of g.; crown, martyr's c.; halo, aureole, nimbus, glory; blushing honours, battle h.; laurels, bays, wreath, garland, favour; feather, feather in one's cap 729 *trophy*; order, star, garter, ribbon, medal 729 *decoration*; spurs, sword, shield, arms 547 *heraldry*; an honour, signal h., distinction, accolade, award 962 *reward*; compliment, bouquet, flattery, incense, laud, eulogy 923 *praise*; memorial, statue, bust, picture, portrait, niche, plaque, temple, monument 505 *reminder*; title of honour, dignity, handle 870 *title*; patent of nobility, knighthood, baronetcy, peerage 868 *nobility*; academic honour, baccalaureate, doctorate, degree, academic d., honours d., pass d., ordinary d., aegrotat d., honorary d., diploma, certificate 870 *academic title*; sports trophy, cup, cap, blue; source of honour, fount of h., College of Arms; honours list, birthday honours, roll of honour 87 *list*.

person of repute, honoured sir *or* madam, gentle reader; worthy, sound person, good citizen, loyal subject, pillar of society, pillar of the church, pillar of the state; man *or* woman of honour; knight, dame, peer 868 *person of rank*; somebody, great man, great woman, big shot, big noise, big gun, big name, big wheel, VIP 638 *bigwig*; someone of mark, notable, celebrity, notability, figure, public f.; champion 644 *exceller*; lion, star, rising star, luminary; man *or* woman of the hour, heroine of the hour, hero of the day, popular hero; pop singer, idol 890 *favourite*; cynosure, model, mirror 646 *paragon*; cream, cream of society, crême de la crême 644 *elite*; choice spirit, master s., leading light 690 *leader*; grand old man, GOM 500 *sage*; noble army, great company, bevy, galaxy, constellation 74 *band*.

Adj. *reputable,* reputed, of repute, of good *or* sound reputation, of credit;

creditworthy 929 *trustworthy*; gentlemanly 929 *honourable*; worthy, creditable, meritorious, prestigious 644 *excellent*; esteemed, respectable, regarded, well-r., well thought of; edifying, moral 933 *virtuous*; in good odour, in the good books, in favour, in high f. 923 *approved*; popular, modish 848 *fashionable*; sanctioned, allowed, admitted.

worshipful, reverend, honourable; admirable 864 *wonderful*; heroic 855 *courageous*; imposing, dignified, august, stately, grand, sublime 821 *impressive*; lofty, high; high and mighty, mighty 32 *great*; lordly, princely, kingly, queenly, majestic, royal, regal 868 *noble*; aristocratic, well-born, high-caste, heaven-born; glorious, in glory, full of g., full of honours, honoured, titled, ennobled; time-honoured, ancient, age-old 127 *immemorial*; sacrosanct, sacred, holy 979 *sanctified*; honorific, dignifying.

noteworthy, notable, remarkable, extraordinary 84 *unusual*; wonderful; of mark, of distinction, distinguished, distingué(e) 638 *important*; conspicuous, prominent, public, in the public eye, in the limelight 443 *obvious*; eminent, pre-eminent, supereminent; peerless, nonpareil, foremost, in the forefront 34 *superior*; ranking, starring, leading, commanding; brilliant, bright, lustrous 417 *luminous*; illustrious, splendid, glorious 875 *ostentatious*.

renowned, celebrated, acclaimed; of renown, of glorious name, of fame; famous, fabled, legendary, famed, far-f.; historic, illustrious, great, noble, glorious 644 *excellent*; notorious 867 *disreputable*; known as, well-known, on the map 490 *known*; of note, noted (**see** *noteworthy*); talked of, resounding, on all lips, on every tongue, in the news; lasting, unfading, never-fading, evergreen, imperishable, deathless, immortal, eternal 115 *perpetual*.

Vb. *have a reputation,* enjoy a r., wear a halo; have a good name; rank, stand high, have status *or* standing, be looked up to, have a name for, be praised f. 920 *command respect*; stand well with, do

oneself credit, win honour, win renown, gain prestige, gain recognition, build a reputation, earn a name; be somebody, make one's mark, set the heather on fire 730 *prosper*; win one's spurs, gain one's laurels, take one's degree, graduate 727 *succeed*; cut a figure, cut a dash, cover oneself with glory 875 *be ostentatious*; rise to fame, get to the top of the ladder *or* tree, flash to stardom; shine, excel 644 *be good*; outshine, eclipse, steal the show, throw into the shade, overshadow 34 *be superior*; have precedence, play first fiddle, take the lead, play the l., star 64 *come before*; bask in glory, have fame, have a great name, hand down one's name to posterity; make history, live in h., be sure of immortality, carve a niche for oneself in the hall of fame 505 *be remembered*.

honour, revere, regard, look up to, hold in respect, hold in reverence, hold in honour 920 *respect*; stand in awe of 854 *fear*; bow down to, recognize as superior 981 *worship*; know how to value, appreciate, prize, value, tender, treasure 887 *love*; show honour, pay respect, pay due regard, pay one's respects to 920 *show respect*; be polite to 884 *be courteous*; compliment 925 *flatter*; grace with, honour w., dedicate to, inscribe to; praise, sing the praises, laud, glorify, acclaim 923 *applaud*; crown, grant the palm, deck with laurels, make much of, eulogize, lionize, chair, ask for one's autograph; credit, give c., honour for 907 *thank*; glorify, immortalize, eternize, commemorate, memorialize 505 *remember*; celebrate, renown, blazon 528 *proclaim*; reflect honour, redound to one's honour *or* one's credit, lend distinction *or* lustre to, do credit to, be a credit to.

dignify, glorify, exalt; canonize, beatify, deify, consecrate, dedicate 979 *sanctify*; install, enthrone, crown 751 *commission*; signalize, mark out, distinguish 547 *indicate*; aggrandize, advance, upgrade 285 *promote*; honour, delight to h., confer an h.; bemedal, beribbon 844 *decorate*; bestow a title, create, elevate, raise

to the peerage, ennoble; confer a knighthood, dub, knight, give the accolade; give one his *or* her title, sir, bemadam 561 *name*; take a title, take a handle to one's name, accept a knighthood.

867 Disrepute – N. *disrepute,* disreputableness, bad reputation, bad name, bad character, shady reputation, past; disesteem 921 *disrespect*; notoriety, infamy, ill repute, ill fame, succès de scandale; no reputation, no standing, ingloriousness, obscurity; bad odour, ill favour, disfavour, bad books, discredit, black books, bad light; derogation, dishonour, disgrace, shame (see *slur*), smear campaign 926 *detraction*; ignominy, loss of honour, loss of reputation, faded r., withered laurels, tarnished honour; departed glory, Ichabod; loss of face, loss of rank, demotion, degradation, reduction to the ranks, dishonourable discharge; debasement, abasement, comedown 872 *humiliation*; abjectness, baseness, vileness, turpitude 934 *wickedness*.

slur, reproach 924 *censure*; imputation, brick-bat, aspersion, reflection, slander, opprobrium, abuse 926 *calumny*; slight, insult, put-down 921 *indignity*; scandal, shocking s., disgrace, shame, burning s., crying s.; defilement, pollution 649 *uncleanness*; stain, smear, smudge 649 *dirt*; stigma, brand, mark, black m., spot, blot, tarnish, taint 845 *blemish*; dirty linen; bar sinister, blot on one's scutcheon, badge of infamy, scarlet letter, mark of Cain.

Adj. *disreputable,* not respectable, disrespectable, louche, shifty, shady; notorious, infamous, of ill fame, of ill repute, nefarious; arrant 645 *bad*; doubtful, dubious, questionable, objectionable 645 *not nice*; risqué, ribald, improper, indecent, obscene 951 *impure*; not thought much of, held in contempt, despised 922 *contemptible*; characterless, without references, of no repute *or* reputation; petty, pitiful 639 *unimportant*; outcast; down-and-out, degraded, base, abject, despicable, odious 888 *hateful*; mean, cheap, low 847 *vulgar*; shabby, squalid,

dirty, scruffy 649 *unclean*; poor, down at heel, out at elbows 655 *dilapidated*; in a bad light, under a cloud, in one's bad *or* black books, in the doghouse, in Coventry, unable to show one's face; discredited, disgraced, in disgrace (**see** *inglorious*); reproached; unpopular.

discreditable, no credit to, bringing discredit, reflecting upon one, damaging, compromising; ignoble, unworthy; improper, unbecoming 643 *inexpedient*; dishonourable 930 *dishonest*; despicable 922 *contemptible*; censurable 924 *blameworthy*; shameful, shame-making, disgraceful, infamous, scandalous, shocking, outrageous, unmentionable, disgusting; too bad 645 *not nice.*

degrading, lowering, demeaning, ignominious, opprobrious, mortifying, humiliating; derogatory, hurting one's dignity; beneath one, beneath one's dignity, infra dig.

inglorious, without repute, without prestige, without note; without a name, nameless 562 *anonymous*; unheroic 879 *servile*; unaspiring, unambitious 874 *modest*; unnoted, unremarked, unnoticed, unmentioned 458 *neglected*; unrenowned, unknown to fame, unheard of, obscure 491 *unknown*; unseen, unheard 444 *invisible*; unhymned, unsung, unglorified, unhonoured, undecorated; titleless 869 *plebeian*; deflated, put down, cut down to size, debunked, humiliated, mortified; sunk low, shorn of glory, faded, withered, tarnished; stripped of reputation, discredited, creditless, disgraced, dishonoured, out of favour, in the bad *or* black books, in eclipse; degraded, demoted, reduced to the ranks.

Vb. *have no repute,* have no reputation, have no character, have no name to lose, have a past; have no credit, rank low, stand low in estimation, have no standing, have little status, be a nobody, cut no ice; be out of favour, be in the bad *or* black books, be in bad odour, be unpopular, be discredited, be in disgrace, stink in the nostrils; play second fiddle, take a back seat, stay in the background 35 *be inferior*; blush unseen, hide one's light 444 *be unseen.*

lose repute, fall *or* go out of fashion, pass from the public eye, fall out of favour; come down in the world, fall, sink 309 *descend*; fade, wither; fall into disrepute, incur discredit, incur dishonour, incur disgrace, achieve notoriety, get a bad name for oneself 924 *incur blame*; spoil one's record, blot one's copybook, disgrace oneself, compromise one's name, risk one's reputation, lose one's r., outlive one's r.; tarnish one's glory, forfeit one's honour, lose one's halo, lose one's good name, earn no credit, earn no honour, win no glory 728 *fail*; come down in the eyes of, forfeit one's good opinion, sink in estimation, suffer in reputation, lose prestige, lose face, lose rank; admit defeat, slink away, crawl, crouch 721 *knuckle under*; look silly, look foolish, be a laughing-stock, cut a sorry figure, blush for shame, laugh on the wrong side of one's mouth 497 *be absurd*; be exposed, be brought to book 963 *be punished.*

demean oneself, lower o., degrade o.; condescend, stoop, marry beneath one; make oneself cheap, cheapen oneself, disgrace o., behave unworthily, have no sense of one's position; sacrifice one's pride, forfeit self-respect; have no pride, feel no shame, think no s.

shame, put to s., hold up to s.; pillory, expose, show up, post; scorn, mock 851 *ridicule*; snub, put down, take down a peg or two 872 *humiliate*; discompose, disconcert, discomfit, put out of countenance, put one's nose out of joint, deflate, cut down to size, debunk; strip of one's honours, strip of rank, deplume, degrade, downgrade, demote, disrate, reduce to the ranks, cashier, disbar, defrock, deprive, strip 963 *punish*; blackball, ostracize 57 *exclude*; vilify, malign, disparage 926 *defame*; destroy one's reputation, take away one's good name, ruin one's credit; put in a bad light, reflect upon, taint; sully, mar, blacken, tarnish, stain, blot, besmear, smear, bespatter

649 *make unclean*; debase, defile, desecrate, profane 980 *be impious*; stigmatize, brand, cast a slur upon, tar 547 *mark*; dishonour, disgrace, discredit, give a bad name, bring into disrepute, bring shame upon, scandalize, be a public scandal 924 *incur blame*; heap shame upon, dump on, heap dirt u., drag through the mire *or* mud; trample, tread underfoot, ride roughshod over, outrage 735 *oppress*; contemn, disdain 922 *despise*; make one blush, outrage one's modesty 951 *debauch*; not spare one's blushes, eulogize, overpraise.

868 Nobility – N. *nobility,* nobleness, distinction, rank, high r., titled r., station, order 27 *degree*; royalty, kingliness, queenliness, princeliness, majesty, prerogative 733 *authority*; birth, high b., gentle b., gentility, noblesse; descent, high d., noble d., ancestry, long a., line, unbroken l., lineage, pedigree, ancient p. 169 *genealogy*; noble family, noble house, ancient h., royal h., dynasty, royal d. 11 *family*; blood, blue b., best b.; bloodstock, caste, high c.; badge of rank, patent of nobility, coat of arms, crest 547 *heraldry*.

aristocracy, patriciate, patrician order; nobility, hereditary n., lesser n., noblesse, ancien régime; lordship, lords, peerage, House of Lords, lords spiritual and temporal; dukedom, earldom, viscountcy, baronetcy; baronage, knightage; landed interest, squirearchy, squiredom; county family, county set, gentry, landed g., gentlefolk; the great, great folk, the high and the mighty, notables; life peerage.

upper class, upper classes, upper ten, upper crust, top layer, top drawer; first families, the quality, best people, better sort, chosen few 644 *elite*; high society, social register, high life, fashionable world 848 *beau monde*; ruling class, the twice-born, the Establishment 733 *authority*; high-ups, Olympians; the haves 800 *rich person*; salaried class, salariat.

aristocrat, patrician, nobleman *or* -woman; person of high caste, Brahman;

bloodstock, thoroughbred; senator, magnifico, magnate, dignitary; don, grandee, caballero, hidalgo; gentleman, gentlewoman; squire, laird; boyar, Junker; emperor, king, queen, prince 741 *sovereign*; nob, swell, gent, toff 848 *fop*; panjandrum, superior person 638 *bigwig*.

person of rank, titled person, noble, nobleman *or* -woman, noble lord *or* lady, seigneur; princeling, lordling, aristo; lordship, milord; ladyship, milady; peer, hereditary p., life p.; peer of the realm, peeress; Prince of Wales, princess royal, duke, grand d., archduke, duchess; marquis, marquess, marquise, marchioness, margrave, margravine, count, countess, contessa; earl, belted e.; viscount, viscountess, baron, baroness, thane, baronet, knight, banneret, knight-bachelor, knight-banneret; rajah, bey, nawab, begum, emir, khan, sheikh 741 *potentate, governor*.

Adj. *noble,* chivalrous, knightly; gentlemanly, gentlemanlike, ladylike (see *genteel*); majestic, royal, regal, every inch a king *or* queen; kingly, queenly, princely, lordly; ducal, baronial, seigneurial; of royal blood, of high birth, of gentle b., of good family, pedigreed, well-born, high-b., born in the purple, born with a silver spoon in one's mouth; thoroughbred, blue-blooded; of rank, ennobled, titled, in Debrett, in Burke's Peerage; haughty, high, exalted, high-up, grand 32 *great*.

genteel, patrician, senatorial; aristocratic; superior, top-drawer, upper-crust, high-class, upper-c., cabin-c., classy, posh, U, highly respectable, comme il faut; of good breeding 848 *well-bred*.

869 Commonalty – N. *commonalty,* commons, third estate, bourgeoisie, middle classes, lower c.; plebs, plebeians; citizenry, democracy; townsfolk, countryfolk; silent majority, grass roots; the public, general public; people at large, populace, the people, the common p.; vulgar herd, great unwashed; the many, the multitude, hoi polloi; the masses, mass

of society, mass of the people, admass, proletariat; the general, rank and file, rag, tag and bobtail, Tom Dick and Harry 79 *everyman*.

rabble, mob, horde 74 *crowd*; clamjamphrie, rout, rabble r., varletry; riffraff, scum, off-scourings, dregs of society, the flotsam and jetsam, canaille, cattle, vermin.

lower classes, lower orders, one's inferiors 35 *inferior*; common sort, small fry, humble folk; working class, blue-collar workers, wage earners, servant class; steerage class, lower deck; second-class citizens, the have-nots, the underprivileged, the disadvantaged; proletariat, proles; down-and-outs, depressed class, outcasts, outcasts of society, poor whites, white trash; demi-monde, underworld, low company, low life.

middle classes, bourgeoisie 732 *averageness*; professional classes, salaried c., white-collar workers; Brown, Jones and Robinson.

commoner, bourgeois(e), plebeian, pleb; untitled person, plain Mr *or* Mrs; citizen, mere citizen, John Citizen, Joe Bloggs, joe soap; one of the people, man *or* woman of the p., democrat, republican; proletarian, prole; working man *or* woman 686 *worker*; town-dweller, country-d. 191 *native*; little man, man *or* woman in the street, everyman, everywoman, common type, average t. 30 *common man*; common person, groundling, pittite, galleryite 35 *inferior*; backbencher, private; underling 742 *servant*; ranker, upstart, parvenu, social climber, arriviste, nouveau riche, Philistine; a nobody, nobody one knows, nobody knows who 639 *nonentity*; low-caste person, outcaste; Untouchable; villein, serf 742 *slave*.

country-dweller, countryman *or* -woman, yeoman, rustic, swain, gaffer, peasant, son *or* daughter of the soil, tiller of the soil, ploughman, teuchter 370 *farmer*; boor, churl, bog-trotter; yokel, hind, clod, clodhopper, rube, redneck, hayseed, hick, backwoodsman; bumpkin, country b., Tony Lumpkin, country cousin, provincial, hillbilly; village idiot 501 *ninny*.

low fellow, fellow, varlet 938 *cad*; slum-dweller 801 *poor person*; guttersnipe, mudlark, street arab, gamin, ragamuffin, down-and-out, tramp, bag lady, bum, vagabond 268 *wanderer*; gaberlunzie, panhandler 763 *beggar*; low type, rough t., bully, ugly customer, plug ugly, ruffian, rowdy, rough, boot boy, bovver boy, roughneck 904 *ruffian*; rascal 938 *knave*; gangster, hood, crook; criminal, delinquent, juvenile d. 904 *offender*; barbarian, savage, Goth, Vandal, Yahoo.

Adj. *plebeian,* common, simple, untitled, unennobled, without rank, titleless; ignoble, below the salt; below-stairs, servant-class; lower-deck, rank and file 732 *middling*; mean, low, low-down, street-corner 867 *disreputable*; lowly, base-born, low-born, low-caste, of low birth, of low origin, of mean parentage, of mean extraction; slave-born, servile; humble, of low estate, of humble condition 35 *inferior*; unaristocratic, middle-class, lower m.-c., working-c., cloth-cap, non-U, proletarian, homely, homespun 573 *plain*; obscure 867 *inglorious*; coarse, brutish, uncouth, unpolished 847 *ill-bred*; unfashionable, cockney, bourgeois, Main Street, suburban, provincial, rustic; parvenu, risen from the ranks 847 *vulgar*; boorish, churlish, loutish, yobbish.

barbaric, barbarous, barbarian, wild, savage, brutish, yobbish; uncivilized, uncultured, without arts, philistine, primitive, neolithic 699 *artless*.

870 Title – N. *title,* title to fame, entitlement, claim 915 *dueness*; title of honour, courtesy title, handle, handle to one's name; honour, distinction, order, knighthood 866 *honours*; royal we, editorial we 875 *formality*; mode of address, style of a., Royal Highness, Serene H., Excellency, Grace, Lordship, Ladyship, noble, most n., my liege, my lord, my lady, dame; the Honourable, Right Honourable; Reverend, Very R., Right R., Most R., Monsignor, His Holiness;

dom, padre; your reverence, your honour, your worship; sire, esquire, sir, dear s., madam, ma'am, master, mister, mistress, miss, Ms; monsieur, madame, mademoiselle; don, señor, señora, señorita; signore, signora, signorina; Herr, mynheer, Frau, Fraulein; babu, sahib, memsahib; bwana, effendi, mirza; citoyen, comrade, tovarich.

academic title, doctor, doctor honoris causa; doctor of philosophy, D Phil, PhD; doctor of literature, D Litt.; doctor of divinity, DD; doctor of laws, LLD; doctor of medicine, MD; doctor of music, Mus D; bachelor of arts, BA; bachelor of literature, B Litt; bachelor of science, BSc; bachelor of medicine and surgery, MBChB, MBBS; bachelor of education, B Ed; bachelor of law, BL; bachelor of music, Mus B; master of arts, MA; master of science, MSc; M Ed; M Litt, M Phil; Professor, Professor Emeritus; reader, lecturer; doctorate, baccalaureate.

871 Pride – N. *pride,* self-esteem, amour propre; self-respect, self-confidence; conceit, self-c., swelled *or* swollen head, swank, side 873 *vanity*; snobbery, inverted s. 850 *affectation*; false pride, touchiness 819 *moral sensibility*; dignity, reputation 866 *prestige*; stateliness, loftiness; condescension, hauteur, haughtiness, uppitiness, unapproachability, disdain 922 *contempt*; overweening pride, bumptiousness, arrogance, hubris 878 *insolence*; swelling pride, pomp, pomposity, grandiosity, show, display 875 *ostentation*; egoism, self-praise, vainglory 877 *boasting*; class-consciousness, race-prejudice, sexism 481 *prejudice*.

proud person, vain p., snob, parvenu; swelled head, swank; lady muck, lord of creation 638 *bigwig*; fine gentleman, grande dame 848 *fop*; peacock, turkey cock, cock of the walk, swaggerer, bragger; purse-proud plutocrat 800 *rich person*; class-conscious person 868 *aristocrat*.

Adj. *proud,* elevated, haughty, lofty, sublime 209 *high*; plumed, crested 875 *showy*; fine, grand 848 *fashionable*; grandiose, dignified, stately, statuesque 821 *impressive*; majestic, royal, kingly, queenly, lordly, aristocratic 868 *noble*; self-respecting, self-confident, proud-hearted, high-souled 855 *courageous*; high-stepping, high-spirited 819 *lively*; stiff-necked 602 *obstinate*; mighty, overmighty 32 *great*; imperious, commanding 733 *authoritative*; high-handed 735 *oppressive*; overweening, overbearing, hubristic, arrogant 878 *insolent*; puffed-up, inflated, swelling, swollen, big-headed; overproud, high and mighty, stuck-up, toffee-nosed, snobbish, nose-in-the-air, snooty; upstage, uppish, uppity; on one's dignity, on one's high horse; haughty, disdainful, superior, holier than thou, supercilious, hoity-toity, high-hat, patronizing, condescending; standoffish, aloof; taking pride in, house-proud; proud of, bursting with pride, inches taller; strutting, swaggering, vainglorious; pleased with oneself, pleased as Punch, pleased as a dog with two tails, like the cat that got the cream; cocky, bumptious, conceited 873 *vain*; pretentious 850 *affected*; swanky, swanking, pompous 875 *showy*; proud as Lucifer, proud as a peacock.

Vb. *be proud,* have one's pride, have one's self-respect, be jealous of one's honour, guard one's reputation, hold one's head high, stand erect, refuse to stoop, bow to no one, stand on one's dignity, mount one's high horse; give oneself airs, toss one's head, hold one's nose in the air, think it beneath one, be too proud to, be too grand to; be stuck-up, be snooty, swank, show off, swagger, strut 875 *be ostentatious*; condescend, patronize; look down on, disdain 922 *despise*; display hauteur 878 *be insolent*; lord it, queen it, come it over, throw one's weight about, pull rank, overween 735 *oppress*.

872 Humility. Humiliation – N. *humility,* humbleness, humble spirit 874 *modesty*;

abasement, lowness, lowliness; unpretentiousness, quietness; harmlessness, inoffensiveness 935 *innocence*; meekness, resignation, submissiveness, servility 721 *submission*; self-depreciation, self-effacement, self-abasement, mortification 931 *disinterestedness*; condescension, stooping 884 *courtesy*; mouse, violet, shrinking v.

humiliation, abasement, humbling, letdown, climbdown, comedown, slap in the face 921 *indignity*; crushing retort; rebuke 924 *reprimand*; shame, disgrace 867 *disrepute*; sense of shame, sense of disgrace, blush, suffusion, confusion; shamefaced look, hangdog expression, tail between the legs; chastening thought, mortification, hurt pride, injured p., offended dignity 891 *resentment*.

Adj. **humble,** humble-minded, self-deprecating, poor in spirit, lowly; meek, submissive, resigned, unprotesting, servile 721 *submitting*; self-effacing 931 *disinterested*; self-abasing, stooping, condescending 884 *courteous*; mouse-like, harmless, inoffensive, unoffending 935 *innocent*; unassuming, unpretentious, without airs, without side 874 *modest*; mean, low 639 *unimportant*; of lowly birth 869 *plebeian*.

Vb. **be humble,** - lowly etc. adj.; have no sense of pride, have no self-conceit, humble oneself 867 *demean oneself*; play second fiddle, take a back seat 874 *be modest*; put others first, not think of oneself 931 *be disinterested*; condescend, unbend 884 *be courteous*; stoop, bow down, crawl, be a sycophant, sing small, eat humble pie, eat crow 721 *knuckle under*; turn the other cheek.

be humbled, - humiliated etc. adj.; receive a snub, be cold-shouldered, get a slap in the face, be put in one's place, be taken down a peg; be ashamed, be ashamed of oneself, feel shame; blush, colour up 431 *redden*; feel small, hide one's face, hang one's head, avert one's eyes, have nothing to say for oneself, wish to sink through the floor, wish the earth would swallow one up; stop swanking, come off it.

humiliate, humble, chasten, abash, disconcert, put to the blush; lower, take down a peg, put down, debunk, deflate; make one feel small, make one sing small, make one feel this high, teach one his place, make one crawl, rub one's nose in the dirt, rub one's nose in it; snub, cut, crush, squash, sit on, send away with a flea in their ear 885 *be rude*; slight 921 *not respect*; mortify, hurt one's pride, offend one's dignity, lower in all men's eyes, put to shame 867 *shame*; score off, put one's nose out of joint, make a fool of, make one look silly; put in the shade 306 *outdo*; outstare, outfrown, frown down, daunt 854 *frighten*; get the better of, gain the upper hand, triumph over, crow o. 727 *overmaster*.

873 Vanity – **N.** *vanity,* emptiness 4 *insubstantiality*; empty pride 871 *pride*; immodesty, conceit, conceitedness, self-importance, megalomania; swank, side, puffed-up chest, swelled head; cockiness, bumptiousness, assurance, self-a.; good opinion of oneself, self-conceit, self-esteem, amour propre; self-satisfaction, smugness; self-love, self-admiration, narcissism; self-complacency, self-approbation, self-praise, self-applause, self-flattery, self-congratulation, self-glorification, vainglory 877 *boasting*; self-sufficiency, self-centredness, egotism, me-ism 932 *selfishness*; exhibitionism, showing off, self-display 875 *ostentation*.

airs, fine a., airs and graces, mannerisms, pretensions, absurd p. 850 *affectation*; swank, side, pompousness 875 *ostentation*; coxcombry, priggishness, foppery.

vain person, self-admirer, Narcissus; self-centred person, me generation, egotist, coxcomb 848 *fop*; exhibitionist, peacock, turkey cock, show-off; know-all, bighead, God's gift to women; smartypants, smart alec, smart ass, cleverstick, clever dick, Mr Clever, Miss Clever 500 *wiseacre*; stuffed shirt, pompous twit 4 *insubstantial thing*.

Adj. *vain,* conceited, overweening, stuck-up, snooty, proud 871 *prideful*;

egotistic, egocentric, self-centred, self-satisfied, self-complacent, full of oneself, self-important 932 *selfish*; smug, pleased with oneself; self-loving, narcissistic, stuck on oneself; wise in one's own conceit, dogmatic, opinionated, oversubtle, overclever, clever clever, too clever by half, too smart for one's own good 498 *intelligent*; swollen-headed, puffed-up, too big for one's boots, bigheaded, bumptious, cocky, perky, smart-ass 878 *insolent*; immodest, blatant; showing off, swaggering, vainglorious, self-glorious; pompous 875 *ostentatious*; pretentious, soi-disant, so-called, self-styled; coxcombical, fantastical, putting on airs 850 *affected*.

Vb. *be vain,* - conceited etc. adj.; have a swelled head, have one's head turned; have a high opinion of oneself, set a high value on o., think a lot of o., think too much of o., think oneself the cat's pyjamas, think o. God Almighty, regard oneself as God's gift; exaggerate one's own merits, blow one's own trumpet 877 *boast*; admire oneself, hug o., flatter o., give oneself a pat on the back; plume oneself, preen o., pride o.; swank, strut, show off, put on airs, put on side, show one's paces, display one's talents, talk for effect, talk big, not hide one's light under a bushel, push oneself forward 875 *be ostentatious*; lap up flattery, fish for compliments; get above oneself, have pretentions, give oneself airs 850 *be affected*; play the fop, be overconcerned with one's appearance, dress up, doll oneself up, dandify 843 *primp*.

874 Modesty – N. *modesty,* lack of ostentation, shyness, retiring disposition; diffidence, timidness, timidity 854 *nervousness*; overmodesty, prudishness 950 *prudery*; bashfulness, blushing, blush; shamefacedness, shockability; chastity 950 *purity*; deprecation, self-depreciation, self-effacement, hiding one's light 872 *humility*; unobtrusiveness, unpretentiousness, unassuming nature; demureness, reserve; shrinking violet, mouse.

Adj. *modest,* without vanity, free from pride; self-effacing, unobtrusive, unseen, unheard 872 *humble*; self-deprecating, unboastful; unassertive, unpushing, unthrustful, unambitious; quiet, unassuming, unpretentious, unpretending; unimposing, unimpressive, moderate, mediocre 639 *unimportant*; shy, retiring, shrinking, timid, mouse-like, diffident, unselfconfident, unsure of oneself 854 *nervous*; overshy, awkward, constrained, embarrassed, inarticulate; deprecating, demurring; bashful, blushing, rosy; shamefaced, sheepish; reserved, demure, coy; shockable, overmodest, prudish 850 *affected*; chaste 950 *pure*.

Vb. *be modest,* show moderation; not blow one's trumpet, not push oneself forward, efface oneself, yield precedence 872 *be humble*; play second fiddle, keep in the background, merge into the background, take a back seat, be a back-room boy *or* girl, know one's place; blush unseen, shun the limelight, shrink from the public gaze, hide one's light under a bushel 456 *escape notice*; not look for praise, do good by stealth and blush to find it fame; retire, creep into one's shell, shrink, hang back, be coy 620 *avoid*; show bashfulness, blush, colour, go red, crimson 431 *redden*; preserve one's modesty 933 *be virtuous*.

875 Ostentation. Formality – N. *ostentation,* demonstration, display, parade, show 522 *manifestation*; unconcealment, blatancy, flagrancy, shamelessness, brazenness, exhibitionism 528 *publicity*; ostentatiousness, showiness, magnificence, delusions of grandeur, grandiosity; splendour, brilliance; self-consequence, self-importance 873 *vanity*; pomposity, fuss, swagger, showing off, pretension, pretensions, airs and graces 873 *airs*; swank, side, thrown-out chest, strut; machismo, bravado, heroics 877 *boast*; theatricality, camp, histrionics, dramatization, dramatics, sensationalism 546 *exaggeration*; demonstrativeness, back-slapping, bonhomie 882 *sociability*; showmanship, effect, window-

dressing; solemnity (see *formality*); grandeur, dignity, stateliness, impressiveness; declamation, rhetoric 574 *grandiloquence*; flourish, flourish of trumpets, fanfaronade, big drum 528 *publication*; pageantry, pomp, circumstance, pomp and c., bravery, pride, panache, waving plumes, fine feathers, flying colours, dash, splash, splurge 844 *finery*; frippery, gaudiness, glitter, tinsel 844 *ornamentation*; idle pomp, idle show, false glitter, unsubstantial pageant, mummery, mockery, idle m., hollow m., solemn m. 4 *insubstantiality*; tomfoolery 497 *foolery*; travesty 20 *mimicry*; exterior, gloss, veneer, polish, varnish 223 *exteriority*; pretence, profession 614 *pretext*; insincerity, lip service, tokenism 542 *deception*; formality, state, stateliness, dignity; ceremoniousness, stiffness, starchiness; royal we, editorial we 870 *title*; ceremony, ceremonial 988 *ritual*; drill, smartness, spit and polish, military bull; correctness, correctitude, protocol, form, good f., right f. 848 *etiquette*; punctilio, punctiliousness, preciseness 455 *attention*; routine, fixed r. 610 *practice*; solemnity, formal occasion, ceremonial o., state o., function, grand f., official f., red carpet 876 *celebration*; full dress, court d., robes, regalia, finery, black tie 228 *formal dress*; correct dress 228 *uniform*.

pageant, show 522 *exhibit*; fete, gala, gala performance, tournament, tattoo; field day, great doings 876 *celebration*; son et lumière 445 *spectacle*; set piece, tableau, scene, transformation s., stage effect 594 *stage set*; display, bravura, stunt; pyrotechnics; carnival, Lord Mayor's Show 837 *festivity, revel*; procession, promenade, march-past, flypast; changing the guard, trooping the colour; turnout, review, grand r., parade, array 74 *assembly*.

Adj. *ostentatious,* showy, pompous; done for effect; window-dressing, for show, for the sake of appearance; for prestige, for the look of the thing; specious, seeming, hollow 542 *spurious*;

consequential, self-important; pretentious, would-be 850 *affected*; showing off, swanking, swanky 873 *vain*; inflated, turgid, orotund, pontificating, windy, magniloquent, declamatory, high-sounding, high-flown; grand, highfalutin, splendiferous, splendid, brilliant, magnificent, grandiose, posh; superb, royal 813 *liberal*; sumptuous, diamond-studded, luxurious, de luxe, plushy, ritzy, glitzy, costly, expensive, expense-account 811 *dear*; painted, glorified, tarted up.

showy, flashy, dressy, dressed to kill, all dolled up, foppish 848 *fashionable*; colourful, lurid, gaudy, gorgeous 425 *florid*; tinsel, glittering, garish, tawdry 847 *vulgar*; flaming, flaring, flaunting, flagrant, blatant, public; brave, dashing, gallant, gay, jaunty, rakish, sporty; spectacular, scenic, dramatic, histrionic, theatrical, camp, stagy; sensational, daring; exhibitionist, stunting.

formal, dignified, solemn, stately, majestic, grand, fine; ceremonious, standing on ceremony, punctilious, stickling, correct, precise, stiff, starchy; black-tie, white-tie, full-dress; of state, public, official; ceremonial, ritual 988 *ritualistic*; for a special occasion, for a gala o.

Vb. *be ostentatious, -* showy etc. adj.; observe the formalities, stand on ceremony; splurge, splash out, cut a dash, make a splash, make a figure; glitter, dazzle 417 *shine*; flaunt, sport 228 *wear*; dress up 843 *primp*; wave, flourish 317 *brandish*; blazon, trumpet, sound the t., beat the big drum 528 *proclaim*; stage a demonstration, wave banners 711 *defy*; demonstrate, exhibit 522 *show*; act the showman, make a display, put on a show; make the most of, put on a front, window-dress, stage-manage; see to the outside, paper the cracks, polish, veneer 226 *coat*; intend for effect, strive for e., sensationalize, camp up; talk for effect, shoot a line 877 *boast*; take the centre of the stage, grab *or* hog the limelight 455 *attract notice*; put oneself forward, advertise oneself, dramatize o.; play to the

gallery, fish for compliments 850 *be affected*; show off, flaunt oneself, show one's paces, prance, promenade, swan around; parade, march, march past, fly past; peacock, strut, swank, put on side 873 *be vain*; make an exhibition of oneself, make a public spectacle of oneself, make people stare.

876 Celebration – N. *celebration,* performance, solemnization 676 *action*; commemoration 505 *remembrance*; observance, solemn o. 988 *ritual*; ceremony, ceremonial, function, occasion, do; formal occasion, coronation, enthronement, inauguration, installation, presentation 751 *commission*; debut, coming out 68 *beginning*; reception, welcome, hero's w., tickertape w., red-carpet treatment 875 *formality*; official reception 923 *applause*; festive occasion, fete, jubilee, diamond j. 837 *festivity*; jubilation, cheering, ovation, standing o., triumph, salute, salvo, tattoo, roll, roll of drums, fanfare, fanfaronade, flourish of trumpets, flying colours, flag waving, mafficking 835 *rejoicing*; flags, banners, bunting, streamers, decorations, Chinese lanterns, illuminations; firework display; bonfire 379 *fire*; triumphal arch 729 *trophy*; harvest home, thanksgiving, Te Deum 907 *thanks*; paean, hosannah, hallelujah 886 *congratulation*; health, toast.

special day, day to remember, great day, red-letter d., gala d., flag d., field d.; Saint's day, feast d., fast d. 988 *holy day*; Armistice Day, D-Day, Remembrance Sunday; Fourth of July, Independence Day, Republic D., Bastille D.; birthday, name-day; wedding anniversary, silver wedding, golden w., diamond w., ruby w.; centenary, bicentenary, sesquicentenary 141 *anniversary*.

Vb. *celebrate,* solemnize; hallow, keep holy, keep sacred 979 *sanctify*; commemorate 505 *remember*; honour, observe; make it an occasion, mark the o.; make much of, welcome, kill the fatted calf, do one proud 882 *be hospitable*; do honour to, fete; chair, carry shoulder-

high 310 *elevate*; mob, rush 61 *rampage*; garland, deck with flowers, wreathe, crown 962 *reward*; lionize, give a hero's welcome, fling wide the gates, roll out the red carpet, hang out the flags, put out the bunting, beat a tattoo, blow the trumpets, clash the cymbals, fire a salute, fire a salvo, fire a feu de joie 884 *pay one's respects*; cheer, jubilate, triumph, rejoice; make holiday 837 *revel*.

toast, pledge, clink glasses; drink to, raise one's glass to, drink a health 301 *drink*.

877 Boasting – N. *boasting,* bragging, boastfulness, fanfaronade; ostentation; self-glorification, swagger, swank 873 *vanity*; advertisement, hype 528 *publicity*; puffery 482 *overestimation*; grandiloquence, fine talk 515 *empty talk*; swaggering, swashbuckling, heroics, bravado; flag-wagging *or* -waving, chauvinism, jingoism 481 *bias*; defensiveness, blustering, bluster 854 *nervousness*; sabre-rattling, intimidation 900 *threat*.

boast, brag; hype 528 *advertisement*; flourish, fanfaronade, bravado, bombast, rant, tall talk 546 *exaggeration*; hot air, gas, bunkum 515 *empty talk*; bluff 542 *deception*; big talk, bluster, hectoring, idle threat 900 *threat*.

Vb. *boast,* brag, crow, vaunt, talk big, have a big mouth, shoot one's mouth, shoot a line, bluff, huff and puff, bluster, hector, shout; bid defiance 711 *defy*; vapour, prate, rant, gas 515 *mean nothing*; enlarge, magnify, lay it on thick, draw the longbow 546 *exaggerate*; trumpet, parade, flaunt, show off 528 *publish*; puff, crack up, cry one's wares 528 *advertise*; sell oneself, advertise o., be a self-publicist, blow one's own trumpet, blow hard, sing one's own praises, bang the big drum 875 *be ostentatious*; flourish, wave 317 *brandish*; play the jingo, rattle the sabre 900 *threaten*; show off, strut, swagger, prance, swank, throw out one's chest 873 *be vain*; gloat, pat oneself on the back, hug oneself 824 *be pleased*; boast of, plume oneself on 871 *be proud*; glory

in, crow over 727 *triumph*; exult 835 *rejoice.*

878 Insolence – N. *insolence,* arrogance, haughtiness, loftiness 871 *pride*; domineering, tyranny 735 *severity*; bravado 711 *defiance*; bluster 900 *threat*; disdain 922 *contempt*; sneer, sneering 926 *detraction*; contumely 899 *scurrility*; assurance, self-a., self-assertion, bumptiousness, cockiness, brashness; presumption 916 *arrogation*; audacity, hardihood, boldness, effrontery, chutzpah, shamelessness, brazenness, brass neck, blatancy, flagrancy; face, front, hardened f., brazen face.

sauciness, disrespect, impertinence, impudence, pertness, freshness, sassiness; flippancy, nerve, gall, brass, cheek, cool c., neck; lip, mouth, sauce, crust, sass, snook, V-sign 547 *gesture*; taunt, personality, insult, affront 921 *indignity*; rudeness, incivility, throwaway manner 885 *discourtesy*; petulance, defiance, answer, provocation, answering back, backtalk, backchat 460 *rejoinder*; raillery, banter 851 *ridicule.*

insolent person, minx, hussy, baggage, madam; whippersnapper, pup, puppy; upstart, Jack-in-office, tin god 639 *nonentity*; blusterer, swaggerer, braggart; bantam-cock; bully, swashbuckler.

Adj. *insolent,* rebellious 711 *defiant*; sneering; insulting 921 *disrespectful*; injurious, scurrilous 899 *cursing*; lofty, supercilious, disdainful, contemptuous; undemocratic, snobbish, haughty, snooty, up-stage, high-hat, high and mighty 871 *proud*; arrogant, presumptuous, assuming; brash, bumptious, bouncing 873 *vain*; flagrant, blatant; shameless, brazen, brazen-faced, brass-necked, bold as brass; bold, hardy, audacious 857 *rash*; overweening, overbearing, domineering, imperious, lordly, dictatorial, arbitrary, high-handed, harsh, tyrannical 735 *oppressive.*

impertinent, pert, forward, fresh; impudent, saucy, sassy, cheeky, smart-mouth, cool, cocky, cocksure, flippant, flip; cavalier, offhand, presumptuous, out of line, familiar, overfamiliar, free-and-easy 921 *disrespectful*; impolite, rude, uncivil, ill-mannered 885 *discourteous*; defiant, answering back, offensive.

Vb. *be insolent,* - arrogant etc. adj.; forget one's manners, get personal 885 *be rude*; have a nerve, cheek, sauce, sass, give lip, taunt, provoke 891 *enrage*; have the audacity to, have the brass neck to, have the cheek to; retort, answer back 460 *answer*; shout down 479 *confute*; get above oneself, get above one's station, teach one's grandmother to suck eggs; not know one's place, presume, be out-of-line, arrogate, assume, take on oneself, make bold to, make free with, get fresh; put on airs, hold one's nose in the air, look one up and down 871 *be proud*; look down on, sneer at 922 *despise*; banter, rally 851 *ridicule*; express contempt, sniff, snort; not give a fig 860 *be indifferent*; cock a snook, put one's tongue out, give the V-sign 711 *defy*; outstare, outface, brazen it out, brave it o.; take a high tone, lord it, queen it, lord it over; lay down the law, throw one's weight around; hector, bully, browbeat, grind down, trample on, ride roughshod over, treat with a high hand 735 *oppress*; swank, swagger, swell, look big 873 *be vain*; brag, talk big 877 *boast*; be a law unto oneself 738 *disobey*; tempt providence *or* fate.

879 Servility – N. *servility,* slavishness, no pride, lack of self-respect 856 *cowardice*; subservience 721 *submission*; submissiveness, obsequiousness, compliance, pliancy 739 *obedience*; time-serving 603 *change of mind*; abasement 872 *humility*; prostration, genuflexion, stooping, bent back, bow, scrape, bowing and scraping, duck, bob 311 *obeisance*; cringing, crawling, fawning, bootlicking, bumsucking, toadyism, sycophancy, ingratiation, soft soap 925 *flattery*; flunkeyism; servile condition, slavery 745 *servitude.*

toady, collaborator, Uncle Tom; yesman, rubber stamp 488 *assenter*; lickspittle, bootlicker, backscratcher, bumsucker, apple-polisher, kow-tower, groveller, crawler, creep; hypocrite, creeping Jesus, Uriah Heep; spaniel, fawner, courtier, fortune-hunter, lion-h. 925 *flatterer*; sycophant, parasite, leech, sponger, freeloader; jackal, hanger-on, gigolo 742 *dependant*; flunkey, lackey 742 *retainer*; born slave, slave; doormat, footstool, lapdog, poodle; tool, creature, puppet, dupe, cat's-paw 628 *instrument*.

Adj. *servile,* not free, dependent 745 *subject*; slavish 856 *cowardly*; meanspirited, mean, abject, base, tame 745 *subjected*; subservient, submissive, deferential 721 *submitting*; pliant, puttylike, compliant, supple 739 *obedient*; time-serving, bowed, stooping, prostrate, bootlicking, backscratching, bumsucking, grovelling, kow-towing, bowing, scraping, cringing, cowering, crawling, sneaking, fawning; begging, whining; toadying, toadyish, sycophantic, parasitical; creepy, obsequious, unctuous, soapy, oily, slimy, overattentive, soft-soaping, ingratiating 925 *flattering*.

Vb. *be servile,* forfeit one's self-respect, stoop to anything 867 *demean oneself*; crawl, grovel, kiss the hands of, kiss the feet of, kiss the hem of one's garment, lick the boots of 721 *knuckle under*; bow and scrape, bend, kowtow, touch the forelock, make obeisance, kneel 311 *stoop*; swallow insults 872 *be humble*; make up to, toady to, suck up to, fawn, ingratiate oneself, soft-soap, pay court to, curry favour, worm oneself into f. 925 *flatter*; squire, attend, dance attendance on, fetch and carry for 742 *serve*; comply 739 *obey*; be the tool of, do one's dirty work, pander to, stooge for 628 *be instrumental*; let oneself be walked all over, be a doormat, act as a footstool; beg for favours, beg for crumbs 761 *beg*; play the parasite, batten on, sponge, sponge on; jump on the band wagon, run with the hare and hunt with the hounds 83 *conform*; serve the times 603 *tergiversate*.

Section three: Interpersonal emotion

880 Friendship – **N.** *friendship,* bonds of f., amity 710 *concord*; compatibility, mateyness, chumminess, palliness; friendly relations, social intercourse, hobnobbing 882 *fellowship*; companionship, belonging, togetherness; alignment, fellowship, comradeship, sodality, freemansonry, brotherhood, sisterhood 706 *association*; solidarity, mutual support 706 *cooperation*; acquaintanceship, acquaintance, mutual a., familiarity, intimacy 490 *knowledge*; close friendship 887 *love*.

friendliness, amicability, kindliness, kindness, neighbourliness 884 *courtesy*; heartiness, cordiality, warmth 897 *benevolence*; fraternization, camaraderie, palliness, mateyness; hospitality 882 *sociability*; greeting, welcome, open arms, handclasp, handshake, hand-kissing, kissing, peck on the cheek, hug, rubbing noses 884 *courteous act*; regard, mutual r. 920 *respect*; goodwill, mutual g.; fellow feeling, sympathy, response 775 *participation*; understanding, same wavelength, entente, entente cordiale, hands across the sea.

friend, girlfriend, boyfriend 887 *loved one*; one's friends and acquaintances, one's circle of friends, acquaintance, intimate a.; friend of the family, lifelong friend, mutual f., friend of a friend; crony, old c. (see *chum*); neighbour, good n., fellow townsman *or* -woman, fellow countryman *or* -woman; cousin, clansman 11 *kinsman*; well-wisher, backer, angel 707 *patron*; second 660 *protector*; fellow, sister, brother, partner, associate 707 *colleague*; ally, brother-in-arms 707 *auxiliary*; collaborator, helper, friend in need 703 *aider*; guest, welcome g., frequent visitor, persona grata; young friend, protégé(e); host, kind h. 882 *sociable person*; former friend, fairweather f. 603 *tergiversator*.

close friend, best f.; soul mate, kindred spirit; best man, bridesmaid 894 *bridal*

party; dear friend, good f., close f., f. in need; intimate, bosom friend, bosom pal, confidant(e), alter ego, other self, shadow; comrade, companion, boon c., drinking c.; good friends all, happy family; mutual friends, inseparables, band of brothers *or* sisters, Three Musketeers, David and Jonathan, Ruth and Naomi, Castor and Pollux; two minds with but a single thought, birds of a feather.

chum, crony; pal, mate, amigo, cobber, buddy, butty, marrow, sidekick, oppo; fellow, comrade, shipmate, messmate, roommate, stable companion 707 *colleague*; teammate, playmate, classmate, schoolmate, schoolfellow; pen friend, pen pal.

Adj. *friendly,* nonhostile, amicable, devoted 887 *loving*; loyal, faithful, staunch, fast, firm, tried and true 929 *trustworthy*; fraternal, brotherly, sisterly, cousinly; natural, unstrained, easy, harmonious; compatible, congenial, sympathetic, understanding; well-wishing, well-meaning, well-intentioned, philanthropic 897 *benevolent*; hearty, cordial, warm, welcoming, hospitable 882 *sociable*; effusive, demonstrative, back-slapping, hail-fellow-well-met; comradely, chummy, pally, matey, buddy-buddy, palsy-walsy; friendly with, good friends w., at home w.; acquainted 490 *knowing*; free and easy, on familiar terms, on visiting t., on intimate t., on the best of t., well in with, intimate, inseparable, thick, thick as thieves, hand in glove.

Vb. *be friendly,* be friends with, get on well w., be on friendly terms w.; have dealings w., rub along w., be palsy-walsy w., be buddy-buddy w.; fraternize, hobnob, keep company with, keep up w., keep in w., go about together, be inseparable 882 *be sociable*; have friends, make f., win f., have a wide circle of friends, have a large acquaintance; shake hands, clasp h., embrace 884 *greet*; welcome, entertain 882 *be hospitable*; sympathize 516 *understand*; like, warm to, become fond of 887 *love*; mean well, have the best intentions, have the friendliest feelings.

befriend, take up, take in tow, protect 703 *patronize*; gain one's friendship; extend the right hand of fellowship, make welcome; strike an acquaintance, scrape an a.; break the ice, make overtures 289 *approach*; seek one's friendship, cultivate one's f., pay one's addresses to 889 *court*; take to, warm to, click with, hit it off; fraternize with, frat, hobnob, get pally with, get matey w., get chummy w., chum up w., make friends w.

881 Enmity – **N.** *enmity,* inimicality, hostility, antagonism 704 *opposition*; no love lost, unfriendliness, incompatibility, antipathy 861 *dislike*; loathing 888 *hatred*; animosity, spite, grudge, ill feeling, ill will, bad blood, intolerance, persecution 898 *malevolence*; jealousy 912 *envy*; coolness, coldness 380 *ice*; estrangement, alienation, strain, tension, dissension; bitterness, hard feelings, rancour, soreness 891 *resentment*; unfaithfulness, disloyalty 930 *perfidy*; breach, open b., breach of friendship 709 *quarrel*; hostile act; conflict, hostilities, breaking off of diplomatic relations, state of war 718 *belligerency*; vendetta, feud, blood f.

enemy, no friend; ex-friend 603 *tergiversator*; traitor, viper in one's bosom 663 *troublemaker*; bad neighbour, illwisher; antagonist, opposite side, other s., them 705 *opponent*; competitor, rival 716 *contender*; open enemy, foe, foeman, hostile force 722 *combatant*; aggressor 712 *attacker*; enemy within the gates, fifth column, Trojan Horse; public enemy; sworn enemy, bitter e.; arch enemy; misanthropist, misogynist 902 *misanthrope*; xenophobe, Anglophobe, Francophobe, racialist, anti-Semite 481 *narrow mind*; persona non grata, pet aversion, bête-noire 888 *hateful object*.

Adj. *hostile,* inimical, unfriendly, illdisposed, disaffected; disloyal, unfaithful 930 *perfidious*; aloof, distant, unwelcoming 883 *unsociable*; cool, chilly,

frigid, icy 380 *cold*; antipathetic, incompatible, unsympathetic; loathing; hostile, antagonistic, warring, conflicting, actively opposed 704 *opposing*; antagonized, estranged, alienated, unreconciled, irreconcilable; bitter, embittered, rancorous 891 *resentful*; jealous, grudging 912 *envious*; spiteful 898 *malevolent*; bad friends with, on bad terms, not on speaking t.; at variance, at loggerheads, at daggers drawn 709 *quarrelling*; aggressive, militant, belligerent, at war with 718 *warring*; intolerant, persecuting 735 *oppressive*; dangerous, venomous, virulent, deadly, fell.

Vb. *be hostile,* - unfriendly etc. adj.; show hostility; harden one's heart, bear ill will, bear malice 898 *be malevolent*; grudge, nurse a g. 912 *envy*; hound, persecute 735 *oppress*; chase, hunt down 619 *hunt*; battle 716 *fight*; make war 718 *wage war*; take offence, take something the wrong way, take umbrage 891 *resent*; fall out, come to blows 709 *quarrel*; be incompatible, have nothing in common, be on different wavelengths, conflict, collide, clash 14 *be contrary*; withstand 704 *oppose*.

882 Sociality – **N.** *fellowship,* membership, membership of society, intercommunity, consociation 706 *association*; making one of, being one of, belonging; team spirit, esprit de corps; comradeship, companionship, society; camaraderie, fraternization, hobnobbing; social intercourse, familiarity, intimacy, palliness, mateyness, togetherness 880 *friendship*; social circle, home c., family c., one's friends and acquaintances 880 *friend*; social ambition, social climbing; society, the world.

sociability, group activity; compatibility 83 *conformity*; sociableness, gregariousness, sociable disposition 880 *friendliness*; social success, popularity; social tact; social graces, savoir vivre, good manners, easy m. 884 *courtesy*; urbanity 846 *good taste*; clubbability; affability 584 *interlocution*; acceptability, welcome, smiling reception, open door;

greeting, glad hand, handshake, handclasp, embrace 884 *courteous act*; hospitality, entertaining, home from home, open house, Liberty Hall, pot luck 813 *liberality*; good company, good fellowship, geniality, cordiality, heartiness, back-slapping, bonhomie; conviviality, joviality, jollity, merrymaking 824 *enjoyment*; gaiety 837 *revel*; good cheer 301 *food*; festive board, the cup that cheers.

social gathering, forgathering, meeting 74 *assembly*; reunion, get-together, social; reception, at home, soirée, levee; entertainment 837 *amusement*; singsong, camp fire; party, do, shindig, thrash, hen party, stag p., tête-à-tête; housewarming, house party, weekend p., birthday p., coming-out p.; feast, banquet, orgy 301 *feasting*; communion, love feast 988 *ritual act*; coffee morning, tea party, bun fight, drinks, cocktail party, dinner p., supper p., garden p., picnic, barbecue, bottle party, byob (=bring your own bottle) p. 837 *festivity*; dance, ball, ceilidh, hop, disco 837 *dancing*.

social round, social activities, social whirl, season, social s., social entertainment; social calls, round of visits; seeing one's friends, visiting, calling, dropping in; weekending, stay, visit, formal v., call, courtesy c.; visiting terms, haunting 880 *friendship*; social demands, engagement, something on; dating, trysting, rendezvous, assignation, date, blind d.; meeting place, club, pub, local 76 *focus*.

sociable person, active member, keen m.; caller, visitor, dropper-in, frequenter, haunter, habitué; convivial person, bon vivant, bon viveur; good mixer, good company, life and soul of the party; social success, catch, lion 890 *favourite*; boon companion, hobnobber, clubman, club woman; good neighbour 880 *friend*; hostess, host, mine h.; guest, welcome g., one of the family; parasite, freeloader, ligger, gatecrasher; gadabout, social butterfly; socialite, social climber 848 *beau monde*.

Adj. *sociable*, gregarious, social, sociably disposed, extrovert, outgoing, fond of company, party-minded; companionable, fraternizing, affable, conversable, chatty, gossipy; clubbable; couthie, cosy, folksy; neighbourly, matey, chummy, pally, palsy-walsy, buddy-buddy 880 *friendly*; hospitable, welcoming, smiling, cordial, warm, hearty, back-slapping, hail-fellow-well-met; convivial, jolly, jovial 833 *merry*; lively, witty 837 *amusing*; urbane 884 *courteous*; easy, free-and-easy.

Vb. *be sociable*, - gregarious etc. adj.; like company, have friends, make friends easily, hobnob, fraternize, socialize, mix with 880 *be friendly*; mix well, be a good mixer, get around, mix in society, go out, dine o.; freeload, lig, gate-crash; have fun, live it up, be the life and soul of the party 837 *amuse oneself*; join in, get together, make it a party, club together, go Dutch, share, go shares 775 *participate*; take pot luck 301 *eat*; join in a bottle, crack a b. 301 *drink*; toast; carouse 837 *revel*; make oneself at home, become one of the family; relax, unbend 683 *repose*; chat to 584 *converse*; make engagements, date, make a date; make friends, make friendly overtures 880 *befriend*; introduce oneself, exchange names, exchange telephone numbers; enlarge one's circle of acquaintances; keep up with, keep in touch w., write to 588 *correspond*.

visit, go visiting, pay a visit, be one's guest, sojourn, stay, weekend; see one's friends; go and see, look one up, call, call in, look in, drop in; leave a card; exchange visits, be on visiting terms.

be hospitable, keep open house 813 *be liberal*; invite, have round, ask in, be at home to, receive, open one's home to, keep open house; welcome, welcome with open arms; act the host, do the honours, preside; do proud, kill the fatted calf 876 *celebrate*; have company, entertain 301 *feed*; give a party, throw a p. 837 *revel*; cater for, provide entertainment 633 *provide*.

883 Unsociability. Seclusion – **N.** *unsociability*, unsociableness, unsocial habits, shyness 620 *avoidance*; introversion, autism; keeping one's own company, keeping oneself to oneself; staying at home; inhospitality 816 *parsimony*; standoffishness, unapproachability, distance, aloofness 871 *pride*; unfriendliness, coolness, coldness, moroseness, 893 *sullenness*; silence, lack of conversation 582 *taciturnity*; ostracism, boycott 57 *exclusion*; blacklist 607 *rejection*.

seclusion, privacy, private world, world of one's own; island universe 321 *star*; peace and quiet 266 *quietude*; home life, domesticity; loneliness, solitariness, solitude; retreat, retirement, withdrawal; hiddenness 523 *latency*; confinement, solitary c., purdah 525 *concealment*; isolation, splendid i. 744 *independence*; division, estrangement 46 *separation*; renunciation 621 *relinquishment*; renunciation of the world, monasticism; self-exile, expatriation; sequestration, segregation, ghettoization, rustication, excommunication, house arrest, quarantine, deportation, banishment, exile 57 *exclusion*; reserve, reservation, ghetto, harem; gaol 748 *prison*; sequestered nook, godforsaken hole, back of beyond; island, desert, wilderness; hide-out, hideaway 527 *hiding-place*; den, study, sanctum, inner s., cloister, cell, hermitage 192 *retreat*; ivory tower, private quarters, shell; backwater.

solitary, unsocial person, iceberg; lonely heart; loner, lone wolf, rogue elephant; isolationist; introvert; stay-at-home, home-body; ruralist, recluse, anchorite, hermit; stylite; maroon, castaway 779 *derelict*; Robinson Crusoe.

outcast, pariah, leper, outsider; outcaste, untouchable; expatriate, alien 59 *foreigner*; exile, evictee, deportee, evacuee, refugee, political r., displaced person, homeless p., stateless p.; nonperson, unperson; proscribed person, outlaw, bandit; reject, flotsam and jetsam, the dregs 641 *rubbish*.

Adj. *unsociable,* unsocial, antisocial, introverted, morose; unassimilated, foreign 59 *extraneous*; unclubbable, stay-at-home, domestic; inhospitable, unwelcoming, forbidding, hostile, unneighbourly, unfriendly, uncongenial, unaffable, misanthropic; distant, aloof, unbending, stiff; stand-offish, haughty 871 *prideful*; unwelcoming, frosty, icy, cold 893 *sullen*; unforthcoming, in one's shell; unconversational, uncommunicative, close, silent 582 *taciturn*; cool, impersonal 860 *indifferent*; solitary, lonely, lone 88 *alone*; shy, reserved, retiring, withdrawn; wild, feral; celibate, unmarried; by the world forgot.

secluded, private, sequestered, cloistered, shut away, hidden, buried, tucked away 523 *latent*; veiled, in purdah; quiet, lonely, isolated, enisled, marooned; remote, out of the way; godforsaken, unfrequented, unexplored, unseen, unfamiliar, off the beaten track, far from the madding crowd 491 *unknown*; uninhabited, deserted 190 *empty*.

Vb. *seclude,* sequester, isolate, quarantine, segregate, ghettoize; keep in purdah; confine, shut up 747 *imprison*.

884 Courtesy – N. *courtesy,* chivalry, knightliness, gallantry; common courtesy, deference 920 *respect*; consideration, condescension 872 *humility*; graciousness, politeness, civility, urbanity, mannerliness, manners, good m., good behaviour; good breeding, gentlemanliness, ladylikeness, gentility 846 *good taste*; tactfulness, diplomacy; courtliness, correctness, correctitude, etiquette 875 *formality*; amiability, niceness, obligingness, kindness, kindliness 897 *benevolence*; gentleness, mildness 736 *leniency*; agreeableness, affability, social tact 882 *sociability*.

courteous act, act of courtesy, graceful gesture, courtesy, common c., civility, favour, kindness; compliment, bouquet 886 *congratulation*; kind words, fair w., sweet w. 889 *endearment*; introduction 880 *friendliness*; welcome, reception, invitation; acknowledgment, recognition,

nod, salutation, salute, greeting, smile, kiss, hug, squeeze, handclasp, handshake 920 *respects*; salaam, kowtow, bow, curtsy 311 *obeisance*; respects, regards, kind r., best r., remembrances, love, best wishes; love and kisses, farewell 296 *valediction*.

Adj. *courteous,* chivalrous, knightly, generous 868 *noble*; courtly, gallant, old-world, correct 875 *formal*; polite, civil, urbane, gentle, gentlemanly, ladylike, dignified, well-mannered, fine-m. 848 *well-bred*; gracious, mannerly 920 *respectful*; on one's best behaviour, minding one's P's and Q's 455 *attentive*; obliging, kind 897 *benevolent*; agreeable, suave; well-spoken.

amiable, nice, sweet, winning; affable, friendly, amicable 882 *sociable*; considerate, kind 897 *benevolent*; inoffensive, harmless 935 *innocent*; gentle, easy, mild, soft-spoken 736 *lenient*; good-tempered, sweet-t., good-natured, unruffled 823 *inexcitable*; well-behaved, good 739 *obedient*; peaceable 717 *peaceful*.

Vb. *be courteous,* be on one's best behaviour, mind one's P's and Q's; mind one's manners; show courtesy; make time for 455 *be attentive*; not forget one's manners, keep a civil tongue in one's head, make oneself agreeable, be all things to all men; take no offence, take in good part, 823 *be patient*; mend one's manners.

pay one's respects, give one's regards, send one's r., send one's compliments, do one the honour; pay compliments 925 *flatter*; drink to, toast; pay homage, show one's respect, kneel, kiss hands 920 *show respect*; honour 876 *celebrate*.

greet, send greetings (see *pay one's respects*); acknowledge, recognize, hold out one's hand 455 *notice*; shout or call out one's greeting, hail 408 *vociferate*; nod, wave, smile, kiss one's fingers, blow a kiss; say hallo, bid good morning 583 *speak to*; salute, raise one's hat; touch one's cap, tug one's forelock; bow, bob, curtsy, salaam, make obeisance, kiss hands, prostrate oneself, kowtow 311 *stoop*; shake hands, clasp h., shake the

hand, press *or* squeeze *or* wring *or* pump the hand; escort 89 *accompany*; make a salute, fire a s., present arms, parade 876 *celebrate*; receive, do the honours, be mother; welcome 882 *be sociable*; welcome with open arms 824 *be pleased*; embrace, hug, kiss, kiss on both cheeks 889 *caress*; usher in, present, introduce 299 *admit*.

885 Discourtesy – N. *discourtesy,* impoliteness, bad manners, disgraceful table m.; no manners, want of courtesy, lack of politeness, lack of manners, incivility; churlishness, uncouthness, boorishness, yobbishness 847 *ill-breeding*; unpleasantness, nastiness, misbehaviour, misconduct, unbecoming conduct; tactlessness, want of consideration, stepping on one's toes.

rudeness, ungraciousness, gruffness, bluntness; sharpness, tartness, acerbity, acrimony, asperity; roughness, harshness 735 *severity*; offhandedness 456 *inattention*; shortness; sarcasm 851 *ridicule*; unparliamentary language, bad l., rude words, virulence 899 *scurrility*; rebuff, insult 921 *indignity*; impertinence, pertness, sauce, sassiness, lip, cheek, truculence 878 *insolence*; interruption, shouting 822 *excitability*; black look, sour l., scowl, frown, pulling faces, sticking out the tongue 893 *sullenness*; act of discourtesy, display of bad manners.

rude person, no gentleman, no lady; savage, barbarian, brute, lout, boor, yob, loudmouth; crab, bear; sourpuss, crosspatch, grouch, grouser, fault-finder, bellyacher, beefer, sulker 829 *malcontent*.

Adj. *discourteous,* unchivalrous; unceremonious, ungentlemanly, unladylike; impolite, uncivil, rude; mannerless, unmannerly, ill-mannered, bad-m., boorish, loutish, yobbish, uncouth, brutish, beastly, savage, barbarian 847 *ill-bred*; insolent, impudent; cheeky, saucy, sassy, pert, forward 878 *impertinent*; unpleasant, disagreeable, unaccommodating 860 *indifferent*; offhanded, cavalier, tactless, inconsiderate 456 *inattentive*.

Vb. *be rude,* - mannerless etc. adj.; have no manners, flout etiquette; know no better 699 *be artless*; forget one's manners, show discourtesy 878 *be insolent*; show no thought for others, step on everyone's toes, ride roughshod over everyone 921 *not respect*; have no time for 456 *be inattentive*; treat rudely, snub, turn one's back on, cold-shoulder, hand one the frozen mitt, cut, ignore, look right through, cut dead; show one the door, send away with a flea in their ear 300 *eject*; cause offence, miff, ruffle one's feelings 891 *huff*; insult, abuse; take liberties, make free with, make bold; stare, ogle 438 *gaze*; make one blush 867 *shame*; lose one's temper, shout, interrupt 891 *get angry*; curse, swear; snarl, growl, frown, scowl, lour, pout, sulk.

886 Congratulation – N. *congratulation,* congratulations, felicitations, compliments, bouquets, compliments of the season; good wishes, best w.; salute, toast; welcome, hero's w., official reception 876 *celebration*; thanks 907 *gratitude*.

Vb. *congratulate,* compliment, proffer bouquets; offer one's congratulations, wish one joy, wish many happy returns, wish a merry Christmas and a happy New Year, offer the season's greetings; send one's congratulations, send one's compliments 884 *pay one's respects*; give one a hero's welcome, give a standing ovation, give three cheers, clap 923 *applaud*; fete, lionize 876 *celebrate*; congratulate oneself, give oneself a pat on the back.

887 Love – N. *love,* affection, friendship, charity; brotherly love, sisterly l., Christian l.; true love, real thing; parental affection, paternal a., maternal a., mother-love; possessiveness 911 *jealousy*; conjugal love, uxoriousness; closeness, intimacy, sentiment 818 *feeling*; tenderness 897 *benevolence*; Platonic love 880 *friendship*; two hearts that beat as one, mutual love, mutual affection,

mutual attraction, compatibility, sympathy, fellow feeling, understanding; fondness, liking, predilection, inclination 179 *tendency*; preference 605 *choice*; fancy 604 *caprice*; attachment, sentimental a.; devotion, patriotism 739 *loyalty*; courtly love, gallantry; sentimentality, susceptibility, amorousness 819 *moral sensibility*; power of love, fascination, enchantment, bewitchment 983 *sorcery*; lovesickness, yearning, longing 859 *desire*; eroticism, lust 859 *libido*; regard 920 *respect*; admiration, hero-worship, worship from afar 864 *wonder*; first love, calf l., puppy l., young l.; crush, pash, infatuation; worship 982 *idolatry*; romantic love, l. at first sight, coup de foudre, passion, tender p., flames of love, enthusiasm, rapture, ecstasy, transports of love 822 *excitable state*; narcissism, Oedipus complex; love-hate.

love affair, romantic a., affair of the heart, affaire de coeur; romance, love and the world well lost; flirtation, amour, entanglement; free love; liaison, intrigue, seduction, adultery 951 *illicit love*; falling in love, something between them; course of love, the old old story; betrothal, engagement, wedding bells 894 *marriage*.

lovemaking, flirting, spooning, canoodling, necking, billing and cooing 889 *endearment*; courting, walking out, going with, going steady, pressing one's suit, laying siege 889 *wooing*; pursuit of love, flirting, coquetry, philandering; dalliance.

lover, love, true l., sweetheart; young man, boyfriend, Romeo; young woman, girlfriend, bird; swain, beau, gallant, cavalier, squire, escort, date; steady, fiancé(e); wooer, courter, suitor, follower, admirer, hero-worshipper, adorer, votary, worshipper; aficionado, fan, devoted following, fan club; sugar daddy; gigolo, ladies' man, lady-killer, seducer, Lothario, Don Juan, Casanova; paramour, flirt, coquette, philanderer; gold-digger, vamp, cohabitee, common-law husband *or* wife, man, woman, live-in,

bidie-in, POSSLQ (=person of opposite sex sharing living quarters).

loved one, beloved, love, true love, soul mate, heart's desire, light of one's life, one's own 890 *darling*; intimate 880 *close friend*; lucky man, intended, betrothed, affianced, fiancé(e), bride-to-be 894 *spouse*; conquest, inamorata, ladylove, girlfriend, girl, bird, bit, honey, baby, sweetie; angel, princess, goddess; sweetheart, valentine, flame, old f.; idol, hero; heartthrob, maiden's prayer, dream man, Alpha man, dream girl 859 *desired object*; favourite, mistress, concubine 952 *kept woman*; femme fatale.

Adj. *loving,* brotherly, sisterly; loyal, patriotic 931 *disinterested*; wooing, courting, cuddling, making love; affectionate, demonstrative; tender, motherly, wifely, conjugal; loverlike, gallant, romantic, sentimental, lovesick; mooning, moping, lovelorn, languishing 834 *dejected*; attached to, fond of, fond, mad about, uxorious, doting; possessive 911 *jealous*; admiring, adoring, devoted, enslaved (see *enamoured*); flirtatious, coquettish 604 *capricious*; amorous, ardent, passionate 818 *fervent*; yearning, lustful, libidinous 951 *lecherous*.

enamoured, in love, inclined to, sweet on, soft on, keen on, set on, stuck on, gone on, sold on; struck with, taken w., smitten, bitten, caught, hooked; charmed, enchanted, fascinated 983 *bewitched*; mad on, infatuated, besotted, crazy about, wild a., head over heels in love 503 *crazy*.

erotic, aphrodisiac, erogenous; sexy, page 3, pornographic 951 *impure*.

Vb. *love,* like, care, rather care for, quite like, take pleasure in, be partial to, take an interest in; sympathize with, feel w., be fond of, have a soft spot for; be susceptible, have a heart, have a warm h.; bear love towards, hold in affection, hold dear, care for, cherish, cling to, embrace; appreciate, value, prize, treasure, think the world of, regard, admire, revere 920 *respect*; adore, worship, idolize, only have eyes for; live for, live only f.; burn with love, be on fire with passion

(**see** *be in love*); make love, bestow one's favours 45 *unite with*; make much of, spoil, indulge, pet, fondle, drool over, slobber o. 889 *caress*.

be in love, burn with love, dote 503 *be insane*; take a fancy to, take a shine to, cotton on to, take to, warm to, be taken with, be sweet on, dig, have a crush on, have a pash for; carry a torch for 859 *desire*; form an attachment, fall for, fall in love, get infatuated, get hooked on, have it bad; go crazy over, be nuts on 503 *go mad*; set one's heart on, lose one's heart, bestow one's affections; declare one's love, offer one's heart to, woo, sue, sigh, press one's suit, make one's addresses 889 *court*; set one's cap at, chase 619 *pursue*; enjoy one's favours; honeymoon 894 *wed*.

888 Hatred – N. *hatred,* hate, no love lost; love-hate; disillusion; aversion, antipathy, allergy, nausea 861 *dislike*; intense dislike, repugnance, detestation, loathing, abhorrence, abomination; disfavour, displeasure; disaffection, estrangement, alienation 709 *dissension*; hostility, antagonism 881 *enmity*; animosity, ill feeling, bad blood, bitterness, acrimony, rancour 891 *resentment*; malice, ill will, evil eye, spite, grudge, ancient g. 898 *malevolence*; jealousy 912 *envy*; wrath 891 *anger*; execration 899 *malediction*; scowl, black looks, snap, snarl, baring one's fangs 893 *sullenness*; phobia, xenophobia, Anglophobia, anti-Semitism, racialism, racism, colour prejudice 481 *prejudice*; misogyny 902 *misanthropy*. odium, disfavour, unpopularity 924 *disapprobation*; discredit, bad odour, bad books, black books 867 *disrepute*; odiousness, hatefulness, loathsomeness, beastliness, obnoxiousness; despicability, despisedness 922 *contemptibility*.

hateful object, anathema; unwelcome necessity, bitter pill; abomination; object of one's hate 881 *enemy*; not one's type, pet aversion, bête-noire, bugbear, Dr Fell, nobody's darling; pest, menace, public nuisance, good riddance 659 *bane*; blackleg.

Adj. *hateful,* odious, unlovable, unloved; invidious, antagonizing, obnoxious, pestilential; beastly, nasty, horrid 645 *not nice*; abhorrent, loathsome, abominable; accursed, execrable; offensive, repulsive, repellent, nauseous, nauseating, revolting, disgusting; bitter, sharp 393 *sour*; unwelcome 860 *unwanted*.

Vb. *hate,* bear hatred, have no love for; hate one's guts; loathe, abominate, detest, abhor; turn away from, shrink f. 620 *avoid*; revolt from, recoil at 280 *recoil*; can't bear, can't stand, can't stomach 861 *dislike*; reject; spurn 922 *despise*; denounce 899 *curse*; bear malice, have a down on 898 *be malevolent*; bear a grudge, nurse resentment, have it in for 910 *be revengeful*, 891 *resent*; conceive a hatred for, fall out of love, become disenchanted with, turn to hate.

889 Endearment – N. *endearment,* blandishments, compliments, bouquets 925 *flattery*; loving words, pretty speeches, pet name; sweet nothings, lovers' vows; billing and cooing, holding hands, slap and tickle, footsie; fondling, cuddling, canoodling, lovemaking, petting, necking, smooching, snogging, kissing; caress, embrace, clasp, hug, bear h., cuddle, squeeze; salute, kiss, butterfly k., French k., smacker; nibble, bite, love b.; stroke, tickle, pat.

wooing, courting, spooning, flirting; love-play, lovemaking; flirtation, philandering, coquetry; courtship, suit, love s., addresses, advances 887 *lovemaking*; serenade, love song, love lyric, amorous ditty; love letter, billet-doux; love poem, sonnet; proposal, engagement, betrothal 894 *marriage*.

love token, true lover's knot, favour, ribbon, glove; ring, engagement r., wedding r., eternity r.; valentine, love letter, billet-doux; language of flowers, posy, red roses; arrow, heart; tattoo.

Vb. *pet,* pamper, spoil, indulge, overindulge, spoonfeed, featherbed, mother,

smother, kill with kindness; cosset, coddle; make much of, be all over one; nurse, rock, cradle, baby; sing to, croon over; coax, wheedle 925 *flatter*.

caress, fondle, dandle, take in one's lap; play with, stroke, smooth, pat, paw, pinch one's cheek, pat one on the head, chuck under the chin; kiss, brush one's cheek; embrace, enfold, fold in one's arms, press to one's bosom, hang on one's neck, fly into the arms of; open one's arms, clasp, hug, hold one tight, cling 778 *retain*; squeeze, cuddle; snuggle, nestle, nuzzle, nibble, give love bites; play, romp, wanton, toy, trifle, dally, spark; make love, carry on, canoodle, spoon, bill and coo, hold hands, pet, neck, snog, smooch, play footsie.

court, make advances, give the glad eye; make eyes, make sheep's e., ogle, leer, eye 438 *gaze*; get off with, try to get off with, get fresh, make a pass, make passes, pat one's bottom, goose; philander, flirt, coquette; be sweet on 887 *be in love*; set one's cap at, run after, do all the running, chase 619 *pursue*; squire, escort 89 *accompany*; hang round, wait on 284 *follow*; date, make a date, take out; walk out with, go steady, go out with, go with; sue, woo, go a-wooing, go courting, pay court to, pay one's addresses to, pay suit to, press one's suit; lay siege to one's affections, whisper sweet nothings; serenade; sigh, pine, languish 887 *love*; offer one's heart, offer one's hand; ask for the hand of, propose, propose marriage, pop the question, plight one's troth, become engaged, announce one's engagement, publish the banns, make a match 894 *wed*.

890 Darling. Favourite – N. *darling,* dear, my dear; dear friend; dearest, dear one, only one; one's own, one's all; truelove, love, beloved 887 *loved one*; heart, dear h.; sweetheart, fancy, valentine; sweeting, sweetie, sugar, honey, honeybaby, honeybunch; flower, precious, jewel, treasure; chéri(e), chou, mavourneen; angel, angel child, cherub; poppet, popsy, moppet, mopsy; pet, lamb, precious l., chick, chicken, duck, ducks, ducky, hen, dearie, lovey.

favourite, spoiled darling, spoiled child, mother's darling, teacher's pet; jewel, jewel in the crown, apple of one's eye, blue-eyed boy; persona grata, someone after one's own heart, one of the best, Mr *or* Miss Right; flavour of the month, the tops, salt of the earth; first choice, front runner, top seed, only possible choice 644 *exceller*; someone to be proud of, pride and joy; favourite son, man *or* woman of the hour 866 *person of repute*; idol, pop i., hero, heroine, golden girl *or* boy; screen goddess, media personality, star, film s.; universal favourite, toast of the town; world's sweetheart, pinup girl 841 *a beauty*; centre of attraction, cynosure 291 *attraction*; catch, lion 859 *desired object*.

891 Resentment. Anger – N. *resentment,* dissatisfaction 829 *discontent*; huffiness, ill humour, the hump, sulks 893 *sullenness*; sternness 735 *severity*; rankling, rancour, soreness, painful feelings; growing impatience, indignation (see *anger*); umbrage, offence, taking o., huff, tiff, pique; bile, spleen, gall; acerbity, acrimony, bitterness, bitter resentment, smouldering r., hard feelings, daggers drawn; virulence, hate 888 *hatred*; animosity, grudge, ancient g., bone to pick 881 *enmity*; vindictiveness, revengefulness, spite 910 *revenge*; malice 898 *malevolence*; impatience, fierceness, hot blood 892 *irascibility*; cause of offence, red rag to a bull, sore point; pinprick, irritation 827 *annoyance*; provocation, aggravation, insult, affront, last straw 921 *indignity*; wrong, injury 914 *injustice*.

anger, wrathfulness, irritation, exasperation, vexation, indignation; dudgeon, high d., wrath, ire; rage, fury, raging f., passion, towering p. 822 *excitable state*; crossness, temper, tantrum, tizzy, paddy, fume, fret, pet, fit of temper, burst of anger, outburst, explosion, storm, stew, ferment, taking, paroxysm,

tears of rage 318 *agitation*; rampage, fire and fury, gnashing the teeth, stamping the foot; shout, roar 400 *loudness*; fierceness, angry look, glare, frown, scowl, black look; growl, snarl, bark, bite, snap, snappishness, asperity 892 *irascibility*; warmth, heat, words, high words, angry w. 709 *quarrel*; box on the ear, rap on the knuckles, slap in the face 921 *indignity*; blows, fisticuffs 716 *fight*.

Adj. *resentful,* piqued, stung, galled, huffed, miffed; hurt, sore, smarting 829 *discontented*; surprised, pained, hurt, offended; warm, indignant; unresigned, reproachful 924 *disapproving*; bitter, embittered, acrimonious, full of hate, rancorous, virulent; splenetic, spiteful 898 *malevolent*; full of revenge, vindictive; jealous, green with envy 912 *envious*; grudging 598 *unwilling*.

angry, displeased, not amused, stern, frowning 834 *serious*; impatient, cross, crabbit, waxy, ratty, wild, mad, livid; wroth, wrathy, wrathful, ireful, irate; peeved, nettled, rattled, annoyed, irritated, vexed, provoked, stung; worked up, wrought up, het up, hot, hot under the collar; angry with, mad at; indignant, angered, incensed, infuriated, beside oneself with rage, leaping up and down in anger; shirty, in a temper, in a paddy, in a wax, in a huff, in a rage, in a boiling r., in a fury, in a taking, in a passion; warm, fuming, boiling, burning; speechless, stuttering, gnashing, spitting with fury, crying with rage, stamping one's foot in rage; raging, foaming, savage, violent 176 *furious*; apoplectic, rabid, foaming at the mouth, mad as a hornet, hopping m., dancing, rampaging, rampageous 503 *frenzied*; seeing red, berserk; roaring, ramping, rearing; snarling, snapping, glaring, glowering 893 *sullen*; red with anger, flushed with rage, purple with r., red-eyed, bloodshot 431 *red*; blue in the face; pale with anger; dangerous, fierce 892 *irascible*.

Vb. *resent,* be piqued, - offended etc. adj.; find intolerable, not bear, be unable to stomach 825 *suffer*; mind, have a chip on one's shoulder, feel resentment, smart under 829 *be discontented*; take amiss, take ill, take the wrong way, not see the joke; feel insulted, take offence, take on the nose, take umbrage, take exception to 709 *quarrel*; jib, take in ill part, take in bad p., get sore, cut up rough; burn, smoulder, sizzle, simmer, boil with indignation; express resentment, vent one's spleen, indulge one's spite 898 *be malevolent*; take to heart, let it rankle, remember an injury, cherish a grudge, nurse resentment, bear malice 910 *be revengeful*; go green with envy 912 *envy*.

get angry, get cross, get wild, get mad; get peeved, get sore, get in a pet, go spare; kindle, grow warm, grow heated, colour, redden, go purple, flush with anger; take fire, flare up, start up, rear up, ramp; bridle, bristle, raise one's hackles, arch one's back; lose patience, lose one's temper, lose control of one's t., forget oneself; throw a tantrum, stamp, shout, throw things; get one's dander up, get one's monkey up, fall into a passion, fly into a temper, fly off the handle; let fly, burst out, let off steam, boil over, blow up, flip one's lid, blow one's top, explode; see red, go berserk, go mad, foam at the mouth 822 *be excitable*.

be angry, - impatient etc. adj.; show impatience, interrupt, chafe, fret, fume, fuss, flounce, dance, ramp, stamp, champ, champ the bit, paw the ground; carry on, create, perform, make a scene, make an exhibition of oneself, make a row, go on the warpath 61 *rampage*; turn nasty, cut up rough, raise Cain; rage, rant, roar, bellow, bluster, storm, thunder, fulminate 400 *be loud*; look like thunder, look black, look daggers, glare, glower, frown, scowl, growl, snarl; spit, snap, lash out; gnash one's teeth, grind one's t., weep with rage, boil with r., quiver with r., shake with passion, swell with fury, burst with indignation, stamp with rage, dance with fury, lash one's tail 821 *be excited*; breathe fire and fury, out-Lear Lear; let fly, express one's feelings, vent one's spleen.

huff, miff, pique, sting, nettle, rankle, smart; ruffle the dignity, ruffle one's feathers, wound, wound the feelings 827 *hurt;* antagonize, put one's back up, rub up the wrong way, get across, give umbrage, offend, cause offence, cause lasting o., put one's nose out of joint, embitter; stick in the throat, raise one's gorge 861 *cause dislike;* affront, insult, outrage 921 *not respect.*

enrage, upset, discompose, ruffle, disturb one's equanimity, ruffle one's temper, irritate, rile, peeve, miff; annoy, vex, pester, bug, bother 827 *trouble;* get on one's nerves, get under one's skin, get up one's nose, get one's goat, give one the pip; do it to annoy, tease, bait, pinprick, needle 827 *torment;* bite, fret, nag, gnaw; put in an ill humour, try one's patience, exasperate; push too far, make one lose one's temper, put into a temper, work into a passion; anger, incense, infuriate, madden, drive mad; goad, sting, taunt, trail one's coat, invite a quarrel, throw down the gauntlet; drive into a fury, lash into f., whip up one's anger, rouse one's ire, kindle one's wrath, excite indignation, stir the blood, stir one's bile, make one's gorge rise, raise one's hackles, get one's dander up; make one's blood boil, make one see red; cause resentment, embitter, poison; exasperate, add fuel to the fire *or* flame, fan the flame 832 *aggravate;* embroil, set at loggerheads, set by the ears 709 *make quarrels.*

892 Irascibility – N. *irascibility,* irritability, impatience 822 *excitability;* grumpiness, gruffness 883 *unsociability;* sharpness, tartness, asperity, gall 393 *sourness;* sensitivity 819 *moral sensibility;* huffness, touchiness, prickliness, readiness to take offence, pugnacity, bellicosity 709 *quarrelsomeness;* temperament, testiness, pepperiness, peevishness, petulance; captiousness, uncertain temper, doubtful t., sharp t., short t., quick t.; hot temper, fierce t., fiery t.; limited patience, snappishness, fierceness, dangerousness, hot blood, fieriness, inflammable nature; bad temper, dangerous t., foul t., nasty t., evil t.

Adj. *irascible,* impatient, choleric, irritable, peppery, testy, crusty, peevish, crotchety, cranky, cross-grained; short-tempered, hot-t., sharp-t.; prickly, touchy, tetchy, huffy, thin-skinned 819 *sensitive;* inflammable, like tinder; hot-blooded, fierce, fiery, passionate 822 *excitable;* quick, warm, hasty, overhasty, trigger-happy 857 *rash;* quick-tempered, easily roused 709 *quarrelling;* scolding, shrewish, vixenish; sharp-tongued 899 *cursing;* petulant, cantankerous, crabbed, crabbit, snarling, querulous; captious, bitter, vinegary 393 *sour;* splenetic, liverish; snappy, waspish; tart, sharp, short; uptight, edgy; fractious, fretful, moody, temperamental, changeable; gruff, grumpy, ratty, like a bear with a sore head 829 *discontented;* ill-humoured, cross, stroppy 893 *sullen.*

893 Sullenness – N. *sullenness,* sternness, grimness 834 *seriousness;* sulkiness, ill humour, pettishness; morosity, surliness, churlishness, crabbedness, crustiness, unsociableness 883 *unsociability;* vinegar 393 *sourness;* grumpiness, grouchiness, pout, grimace 829 *discontent;* gruffness 885 *discourtesy;* crossness, peevishness, ill temper, bad t., savage t., shocking t. 892 *irascibility;* spleen, bile, liver; sulks, fit of the s., the hump, the pouts, mulligrubs, dumps, grouch, bouderie, moodiness, temperament; cafard, the blues, blue devils 834 *melancholy;* black look, hangdog l.; glare, glower, lour, frown, scowl; snort, growl, snarl, snap, bite.

Adj. *sullen,* forbidding, ugly; gloomy, saturnine, overcast, cloudy, sunless 418 *dark;* glowering, scowling, stern, frowning, unsmiling, grim 834 *serious;* sulky, sulking, cross, cross as two sticks, out of temper, out of humour, out of sorts, misanthropic 883 *unsociable;* surly, morose, dyspeptic, crabbed, crabbit, crusty,

cross-grained, difficult; snarling, snapping, snappish, shrewish, vixenish, cantankerous, quarrelsome, stroppy 709 *quarrelling*; refractory, jibbing 738 *disobedient*; grouchy, grumbling, grousing, belly-aching, beefing, grumpy 829 *discontented*; acid, tart, vinegary 393 *sour*; gruff, rough, abrupt, brusque 885 *discourteous*; temperamental, moody, up and down 152 *changeful*; jaundiced, dyspeptic; blue, down, down in the dumps, depressed, melancholy 834 *melancholic*; petulant, pettish, peevish, shirty, ill-tempered, bad-t. 892 *irascible*; smouldering, sultry.

894 Marriage – N. *marriage,* matrimony, holy m., sacrament of m., one flesh; wedlock, wedded state, married s., state of matrimony, wedded bliss; match, union, alliance, partnership; conjugality, conjugal knot, nuptial bond, marriage tie, marriage bed, bed and board, cohabitation, living as man and wife, living together by habit and repute, living together, life together; banns, marriage certificate, marriage lines.

type of marriage, matrimonial arrangement, monogamy, monandry, bigamy, polygamy, Mormonism, polygyny, polyandry; digamy, deuterogamy, second marriage, remarriage, levirate; endogamy, exogamy; arranged match, marriage of convenience, mariage de convenance, mariage blanc; love-match; mixed marriage, intermarriage, miscegenation 43 *mixture*; mismarriage, mésalliance, misalliance, morganatic marriage, left-handed m.; companionate marriage, temporary m., trial m., open m., common-law m., marriage by habit and repute; free union, free love, concubinage; compulsory marriage, forcible wedlock, shotgun wedding; abduction, Sabine rape.

wedding, getting married, match, match-making, betrothal, engagement; nuptial vows, marriage v., ring, wedding r.; bridal, nuptials; leading to the altar, tying the knot, getting spliced, getting

hitched; marriage rites, marriage ceremony; wedding service, nuptial mass, nuptial benediction 988 *Christian rite*; church wedding, white w., civil marriage, registry-office m.; Gretna Green marriage, run-away match, elopement; solemn wedding, quiet w.; wedding day, wedding bells; marriage feast, wedding breakfast, reception; honeymoon; silver wedding, golden w., wedding anniversary 876 *special day*.

bridal party, groomsman, best man, maid *or* matron of honour, bridesmaid, best maid, page, train-bearer; attendant, usher.

spouse, one's promised, one's betrothed 887 *loved one*; man, wife; spouses, man and wife, Mr and Mrs, Darby and Joan; married couple, young marrieds, bridal pair, newlyweds, honeymooners; bride, blushing b.; bridegroom; consort, partner, mate, helpmate, helpmeet, better half, soul-mate; married man, husband, hubbie, man, old man, lord and master; much-married man, henpecked husband; injured husband; married woman, wife, wedded wife, lawful w., lady, matron, feme covert, partner of one's bed and board; wife of one's bosom, woman, old w., missus, wifey, better half, old dutch, rib, trouble and strife, squaw; common-law husband *or* wife, 887 *lover*.

Vb. *marry,* marry off, find a husband *or* wife for, match, mate; matchmake, make a match, arrange a m., arrange a marriage; betroth, affiance, publish the banns, announce the engagement; give in marriage, give away; join in marriage, declare man and wife; join, couple, splice, hitch, tie the knot.

wed, marry; take a wife, find a husband; ask for the hand of 889 *court*; give up one's freedom, renounce bachelorhood, take the plunge, get married, get hitched, get spliced, mate with, marry oneself to, unite oneself with, give oneself in marriage, bestow one's hand, accept a proposal, plight one's troth, become engaged, put up the banns; lead to the altar, walk down the aisle, say 'I do',

take for better or worse, be made one 45 *unite with*; pair off, mate, couple; honeymoon, cohabit, live together, set up house together, share bed and board, live as man and wife; marry well, make a good match, make a marriage of convenience; mismarry, make a bad match, repent at leisure; make a love match 887 *be in love*; marry in haste, run away, elope; contract marriage, make an honest woman of, go through a form of marriage; marry again, remarry; commit bigamy; intermarry, miscegenate.

895 Celibacy – N. *celibacy*, singleness, single state, unmarried s., single blessedness 744 *independence*; bachelorhood, bachelorship, bachelordom; misogamy, misogyny 883 *unsociability*; spinsterhood, spinsterdom, the shelf; monkhood, the veil 985 *monasticism*; maidenhood, virginity 950 *purity*.

celibate, unmarried man, single m., bachelor; confirmed bachelor, born b., old b., gay b., not the marrying kind; misogamist, misogynist 902 *misanthrope*; monk; hermit 883 *solitary*.

spinster, unmarried woman, bachelor girl; maid, maiden, virgo intacta; maiden aunt, old maid; Vestal Virgin 986 *nun*.

896 Divorce. Widowhood – N. *divorce,* dissolution of marriage, putting away, repudiation; divorce decree, decree nisi, decree absolute; separation, legal s., judicial s.; annulment; nonconsummation; nullity, impediment, prohibited degree, consanguinity, affinity; desertion, living apart; alimony, aliment, palimony; marriage on the rocks, breakup, split-up, broken marriage, broken engagement, forbidding the banns; divorce court, divorce case; divorced person, divorcee, divorcé(e); corespondent; single parent.

Vb. *divorce,* separate, split up, break up, go one's separate ways, live separately, live apart, desert 621 *relinquish*; untie the knot 46 *disunite*; put away, sue for divorce, file a divorce suit; bring a charge of adultery; get a divorce, revert to bachelorhood, revert to the single state, regain one's freedom; put asunder, dissolve marriage, annul a m., grant a decree of nullity, grant a divorce, pronounce a decree absolute.

897 Benevolence – N. *benevolence,* good will, helpfulness 880 *friendliness*; ahimsa, harmlessness 935 *innocence*; benignity, kindly disposition, heart of gold; amiability, bonhomie 882 *sociability*; milk of human kindness, goodness of nature, warmth of heart, warm-heartedness, kind-heartedness, kindliness, kindness, loving-k., goodness and mercy, charity, Christian c. 887 *love*; godly love, brotherly l., brotherliness, fraternal feeling 880 *friendship*; tenderness, consideration 736 *leniency*; understanding, responsiveness, caring, concern, fellow feeling, empathy, sympathy, overflowing s. 818 *feeling*; condolence 905 *pity*; decent feeling, humanity, humaneness, humanitarianism 901 *philanthropy*; utilitarianism 901 *sociology*; charitableness, hospitality, unselfishness, generosity, magnanimity 813 *liberality*; gentleness, softness, mildness, tolerance, toleration 734 *laxity*; placability, mercy 909 *forgiveness*; God's love, grace of God; blessing, benediction.

Adj. *benevolent,* well meant, well-intentioned, with the best intentions, for the best 880 *friendly*; out of kindness, to oblige; out of charity, eleemosynary; kind of one, good of one, so good of; sympathetic, wishing well, well-wishing, favouring, praying for; kindly disposed, benign, benignant, kindly, kind-hearted, overflowing with kindness, full of the milk of human k., warm-hearted, large-h., golden-h.; kind, good, human, decent, Christian; affectionate 887 *loving*; fatherly, paternal; motherly, maternal; brotherly, fraternal; sisterly, cousinly; good-humoured, good-natured, easy, sweet, gentle 884 *amiable*; placable, merciful; tolerant, indulgent 734 *lax*; humane, considerate 736 *lenient*; soft-hearted, tender, pitiful, sympathizing, condolent 905 *pitying*; genial, hospitable

882 *sociable*; bounteous, bountiful 813 *liberal*; generous, magnanimous, unselfish, selfless, unenvious, unjealous, altruistic 931 *disinterested*; beneficent, charitable, humanitarian, doing good 901 *philanthropic*; obliging, accommodating, helpful 703 *aiding*; tactful, complaisant, gracious, gallant, chivalrous, chivalric 884 *courteous*.

do good, philanthropize, do good works, be a caring person, have a social conscience, serve the community, show public spirit, be a good Samaritan, do a good turn, do one a favour, render a service; care; get involved 678 *be active*; reform; relieve the poor, visit, nurse 703 *minister to*; mother 889 *pet*.

898 Malevolence – N. *malevolence*, ill will 881 *enmity*; truculence, cussedness, bitchiness, beastliness, evil intent, bad intention, worst intentions, cloven hoof; spite, gall, spitefulness, viciousness, despite, malignity, malignancy, malice, malice aforethought; bad blood, hate 888 *hatred*; venom, virulence, deadliness, balefulness 659 *bane*; bitterness, acrimony, acerbity 393 *sourness*; mordacity 388 *pungency*; rancour, spleen 891 *resentment*; gloating, unholy joy 912 *envy*; evil eye 983 *spell*.

inhumanity, misanthropy, inconsiderateness, lack of concern; uncharitableness; intolerance, persecution 735 *severity*; harshness, mercilessness, implacability, hardness of heart, obduracy, heart of stone 906 *pitilessness*; cold feelings, unkindness; callousness 326 *hardness*; cruelty, barbarity, bloodthirstiness; barbarism, savagery, ferocity, barbarousness, savageness, ferociousness; outrageousness; sadism, fiendishness, devilishness 934 *wickedness*; truculence, brutality, ruffianism; destructiveness, vandalism 165 *destruction*.

cruel act, brutality; ill-treatment, ill usage 675 *misuse*; abuse, child a., sexual a., disservice, ill turn; victimization, harassment, sexual h., bullying 735 *severity*; foul play, bloodshed 176 *violence*; act of inhumanity, atrocity, outrage; cruelty, torture, barbarities; cannibalism, murder 362 *homicide*; mass murder, genocide 362 *slaughter*.

Adj. *malevolent*, ill-wishing, ill-willed, evil-intentioned, ill-disposed, meaning harm 661 *dangerous*; ill-natured, churlish 893 *sullen*; nasty, bloody-minded, bitchy, cussed 602 *wilful*; malicious, catty, spiteful; mischievous, mischief-making; baleful, squint-eyed, malign, malignant 645 *harmful*; vicious, viperous, venomous 362 *deadly*; blackhearted, full of spite; jealous 912 *envious*; disloyal, treacherous 930 *perfidious*; bitter, rancorous 891 *resentful*; implacable, unforgiving, merciless 906 *pitiless*; vindictive, gloating; hostile, fell 881 *hostile*; intolerant, persecuting 735 *oppressive*.

unkind, ill-natured 893 *sullen*; unkindly; unchristian; cold, unfriendly, hostile, misanthropic 881 *hostile*; inhospitable 883 *unsociable*; unhelpful, disobliging; uncharitable; mean, nasty; unsympathetic, unmoved 820 *impassive*; stern 735 *severe*; inhuman.

cruel, grim, fell; hard-hearted, flint-h., stony-h.; callous, cold-blooded; heartless, ruthless, merciless 906 *pitiless*; tyrannical 735 *oppressive*; sadistic; bloodthirsty, cannibalistic 362 *murderous*; bloody 176 *violent*; atrocious, outrageous; feral, tigerish, wolfish; unnatural, subhuman, dehumanized, brutalized, brutish; brutal, rough, fierce, ferocious; savage, barbarous, wild, untamed; inhuman, ghoulish, fiendish, devilish, diabolical, demoniacal, satanic, hellish, infernal.

Vb. *be malevolent*, bear malice, cherish a grudge, nurse resentment, have it in for 888 *hate*; show ill will, spite, do one a bad turn; do one's worst, wreak one's spite, break a butterfly on a wheel, have no mercy 906 *be pitiless*; take one's revenge, exact r., victimize; take it out of one, bully, maltreat, abuse 645 *ill-treat*; molest, hurt, injure, annoy 645 *harm*; malign, run down, throw stones at 926 *detract*; tease, harass, harry, hound, persecute, tyrannize, torture 735 *oppress*;

thirst for blood 362 *slaughter*; rankle, fester, poison, be a thorn in the flesh; create havoc, blight; blast, cast the evil eye 983 *bewitch*.

899 Malediction – N. *malediction,* curse, imprecation, anathema; evil eye; ill wishes, execration, denunciation; fulmination, thunder; ban, proscription, excommunication; exorcism, bell, book and candle.

scurrility, ribaldry, vulgarity; profanity, swearing, profane s., cursing and swearing, blasting, effing and blinding, effing and ceeing; bad language, foul l., filthy l., blue l., shocking l., strong l., unparliamentary l., Limehouse, Billingsgate; naughty word, four-letter w., expletive, swearword, oath, swear, damn, curse, cuss, tinker's c.; invective, vituperation, abuse, volley of a.; mutual abuse, slanging match, stormy exchange; vain abuse, empty curse, more bark than bite 900 *threat*; no compliment, aspersion, reflection, vilification, slander 926 *calumny*; cheek, sauce 878 *sauciness*; personal remarks, epithet, insult 921 *indignity*; contumely, scorn 922 *contempt*; scolding, rough edge of one's tongue, lambasting, tongue-lashing 924 *reproach*.

Adj. *cursing,* evil-speaking, swearing, damning, blasting; profane, foul-mouthed, foul-tongued, foul-spoken, effing and ceeing, unparliamentary, scurrilous, scurrile, ribald 847 *vulgar*; blue; vituperative, abusive, vitriolic, injurious; scornful.

Vb. *curse,* cast the evil eye 983 *bewitch*; accurse, wish ill 898 *be malevolent*; wish on, call down on; wish one joy of; curse with bell, book and candle, curse up hill and down dale; anathematize, imprecate, invoke curses on, execrate, hold up to execration; fulminate, thunder against, rant and rail against, inveigh 924 *reprove*; denounce 928 *accuse*; excommunicate, damn 961 *condemn*; round upon, confound, send to the devil, send to blazes; abuse, vituperate, revile, rail, chide, heap abuse, pour vitriol 924 *reproach*.

cuss, curse, swear, damn, blast; blaspheme 980 *be impious*; swear like a trooper, use expletives, use Billingsgate, curse and swear, use four-letter words, eff and blind, eff and cee, turn the air blue; slang, abuse; rail at, scold, lash out at, give the rough edge of one's tongue, slag off.

Int. curse! a curse on! a plague on! woe to! woe betide! ill betide! confound it! devil take it! blast! damn! darn! drat! hang! the deuce! the dickens!

900 Threat – N. *threat,* menace; fulmination 899 *malediction*; minacity, ominousness; challenge, dare 711 *defiance*; blackmail 737 *demand*; battle cry, war whoop, sabre-rattling, war of nerves 854 *intimidation*; deterrent, big stick 723 *weapon*; black cloud, gathering clouds 511 *omen*; hidden fires, secret weapon 663 *pitfall*; impending danger, sword of Damocles 661 *danger*; danger signal, fair warning, writing on the wall 664 *warning*; bluster, idle threat, hollow t. 877 *boast*; bark, growl, snarl, bared teeth 893 *sullenness*.

Vb. *threaten,* menace, use threats, hold out t., utter t.; demand with menaces, blackmail 737 *demand*; hijack, hold to ransom, take hostage; frighten, deter, intimidate, bully, wave the big stick 854 *frighten*; roar, bellow 408 *vociferate*; fulminate, thunder 899 *curse*; bark, talk big, bluster, hector 877 *boast*; shake, wave, flaunt 317 *brandish*; rattle the sabre, clench the fist, draw one's sword 711 *defy*; bare the fangs, snarl, growl, mutter; bristle, spit, look daggers, grow nasty 891 *get angry*; pull a gun on, hold at gunpoint; draw a bead on, cover, have one covered, keep one c. 281 *aim*; gather, mass, lour, hang over, hover 155 *impend*; bode ill, presage, disaster, mean no good, promise trouble, spell danger 511 *predict*; serve notice, caution, forewarn 664 *warn*; breathe revenge, threaten reprisals 910 *be revengeful*.

901 Philanthropy – N. *philanthropy,* humanitarianism, humanity, humaneness, the golden rule 897 *benevolence*; humanism, cosmopolitanism, internationalism; altruism 931 *disinterestedness*; idealism, ideals 933 *virtue*; the greatest happiness of the greatest number, utilitarianism, Benthamism; common good, socialism, communism; reformism; chivalry, knight-errantry; dedication, crusading spirit, missionary s., social conscience; good works, mission; Holy War, jihad, crusade, campaign, cause, good c.

sociology, social science, social planning; poor relief, social security, benefit, dole; social services, Welfare State; community service, social service, social work, good works.

patriotism, civic ideals, good citizenship, public spirit, concern for the community, love of one's country; parochialism; nationalism, chauvinism, gung-hoism, my country right or wrong.

philanthropist, humanitarian, dogooder, benefactor, social worker; community service worker, VSO, Peace Corps 597 *volunteer*; paladin, champion, crusader, knight, knight errant; Messiah 690 *leader*; missionary; idealist, altruist, flower people 513 *visionary*; reformist 654 *reformer*; utilitarian, Benthamite; Utopian, millenarian; humanist.

patriot, lover of one's country; nationalist, chauvinist.

Adj. *philanthropic,* humanitarian, humane, human 897 *benevolent*; charitable, aid-giving 703 *aiding*; enlightened, humanistic, liberal; idealistic, altruistic 931 *disinterested*; visionary, dedicated; socialistic, communistic; utilitarian.

patriotic, public-spirited, communityminded; nationalistic, chauvinistic; loyal, true, true-blue.

902 Misanthropy – N. *misanthropy,* cynicism 883 *unsociability*; misandry, misogyny; moroseness 893 *sullenness*; inhumanity.

misanthrope, misanthropist, manhater, woman-h., misandrist, misogynist; cynic, Diogenes; world-hater.

903 Benefactor – N. *benefactor,* benefactress 901 *philanthropist*; Lady Bountiful, Father Christmas, Santa Claus 781 *giver*; fairy godmother, guardian angel, good genius 660 *protector*; founder, foundress, supporter, angel, backer 707 *patron*; protector of the people 901 *patriot*; saviour, redeemer, rescuer 668 *deliverance*; champion 713 *defender*; Good Samaritan; good neighbour 880 *friend*; helper, present help in time of trouble 703 *aider*; saint 937 *good person*.

904 Evildoer – N. *evildoer,* malefactor, wrongdoer, sinner 934 *wickedness*; villain, blackguard, bad lot, baddy; one up to no good, mischief-maker 663 *troublemaker*; slanderer 926 *detractor*; snake in the grass, viper in the bosom, traitor 545 *deceiver*; saboteur; despoiler, wrecker, defacer, vandal, Hun, iconoclast 168 *destroyer*; terrorist, nihilist, anarchist 738 *revolter*; incendiary, arsonist 381 *incendiarism*; disturber of the peace 738 *rioter*.

ruffian, blackguard, rogue, scoundrel 938 *knave*; lout, hooligan, hoodlum, boot boy, bovver boy, larrikin 869 *low fellow*; Hell's Angel, skinhead, yob, yobbo, punk; bully, terror, terror of the neighbourhood; rough, tough, rowdy, ugly customer, hard man, plug-ugly, bruiser, thug, bravo, desperado, assassin, hired a.; cutthroat, hatchet man, hit man, gunman, contract man, killer, butcher 362 *murderer*; genocide, mass murderer; plague, scourge, scourge of the human race, Attila 659 *bane*; petty tyrant; molester, brute, savage b., beast, savage, barbarian; homicidal maniac 504 *madman*.

offender, sinner, black sheep 938 *bad person*; suspect; culprit, guilty person, law-breaker; criminal, villain, crook, malefactor, wrongdoer, felon; delinquent, juvenile d., first offender; recidivist, backslider, old offender, hardened

o., lag, old l., convict, ex-c., jailbird; lifer, gallowsbird, parolee, probationer, ticket-of-leave man; mafioso, mobster, gangster, racketeer; housebreaker 789 *thief, robber*; forger 789 *defrauder*; blackmailer, bloodsucker; poisoner 362 *murderer*; outlaw, public enemy 881 *enemy*; intruder, trespasser; criminal world, underworld, Mafia 934 *wickedness*.

905 Pity – N. *pity,* ruth; remorse, compunction 830 *regret*; charity, compassion, compassionateness, humanity 897 *benevolence*; soft heart, tender h., bleeding h.; gentleness, softness 736 *leniency*; commiseration, touched feelings, melting mood, tears of sympathy 825 *sorrow*; Weltschmerz 834 *dejection*; sympathy, empathy, understanding, fellow feeling; self-pity.

condolence, commiseration, sympathy, fellow feeling 775 *participation*; consolation, comfort 831 *relief*; keen, coronach, wake 836 *lament*.

mercy, tender mercies, quarter, grace; second chance; mercifulness, clemency, lenity, placability, forbearance, long-suffering 909 *forgiveness*; light sentence 963 *penalty*; let-off, pardon 960 *acquittal*.

Adj. *pitying,* compassionate, sympathetic, understanding, commiserating; sorry for, feeling for; merciful, clement, full of mercy 736 *lenient*; tender, tender-hearted, soft, soft-hearted 819 *impressible*; disposed to mercy; humane, charitable 897 *benevolent*; forbearing 823 *patient*.

Vb. *pity,* feel p; show compassion, show pity, take pity on; sympathize, sympathize with, empathize, feel for, feel with, share the grief of 775 *participate*; sorrow, grieve, bleed for, feel sorry for, weep f., lament f., commiserate, condole, express one's condolences, send one's c.; yearn over 836 *lament*; console, comfort, offer consolation, wipe away one's tears 833 *cheer*; have pity, have compassion.

show mercy, have m., spare, spare the life of, give quarter; commute (a sentence), pardon, grant a p.; forget one's anger 909 *forgive*; be slow to anger, forbear; give one a break, give one a second chance 736 *be lenient*; relent, not be too hard upon, go easy on, let one down gently; put out of their misery.

ask mercy, plead for m., appeal for m., pray for m., beg for m., throw oneself upon another's mercy, fall at one's feet, cry mercy, ask for quarter, plead for one's life.

906 Pitilessness – N. *pitilessness,* lack of pity, heartlessness, ruthlessness, mercilessness; inclemency, intolerance, rigour 735 *severity*; callousness, hardness of heart 898 *inhumanity*; inflexibility 326 *hardness*; inexorability, relentlessness, remorselessness, unforgivingness 910 *revengefulness*; letter of the law, pound of flesh; no pity, no heart, no feelings, short shrift, no quarter.

Adj. *pitiless,* unfeeling 820 *impassive*; unsympathetic; unmoved, dry-eyed; hard-hearted, stony-h.; callous 326 *hard*; harsh, rigorous, intolerant, persecuting 735 *severe*; brutal, sadistic 898 *cruel*; merciless, ruthless, heartless; inclement, unmerciful, unrelenting, relentless, remorseless, inflexible, inexorable, implacable.

Vb. *be pitiless,* - ruthless etc. adj.; have no heart, have no compassion, have no pity; not be moved, turn a deaf ear; show no pity, show no mercy, give no quarter; harden one's heart, be deaf to appeal; stand on the letter of the law, insist on one's pound of flesh 735 *be severe*; take one's revenge 910 *avenge*.

907 Gratitude – N. *gratitude,* gratefulness, thankfulness, grateful heart, sense of obligation; appreciativeness, appreciation.

thanks, hearty t., grateful t.; vote of t., thankyou; thanksgiving, eucharist, benediction, blessing; praises, Te Deum 876 *celebration*; grace; thankyou letter, bread-and-butter l.; credit, credit title,

acknowledgment, due a., grateful a., recognition, grateful r.; tribute 923 *praise*; parting present, leaving p., recognition of one's services, golden handshake, token of one's gratitude, tip 962 *reward*.

Adj. *grateful,* thankful, appreciative; thanking; crediting, giving credit; obliged, under obligation, in one's debt, owing a favour, beholden, indebted.

Vb. *be grateful,* thank one's lucky stars; feel an obligation; accept gratefully, receive with open arms, not look a gift horse in the mouth.

thank, give thanks, express t.; acknowledge, credit, give c., give due c., give full c. 158 *attribute*; show appreciation, tip 962 *reward*; return a favour.

Int. thanks! many t.! much obliged! thank you! ta! cheers! thank goodness! thank Heaven! Heaven be praised!

908 Ingratitude – N. *ingratitude,* lack of appreciation, ungratefulness, thanklessness; grudging thanks; taking everything as one's due, thankless task; ingrate.

Adj. *ungrateful,* unthankful 885 *discourteous*; unbeholden; unmindful of favours.

Vb. *be ungrateful,* take for granted, take as one's due; omit to thank; not give a thankyou for; look a gift horse in the mouth; forget a kindness, return evil for good.

Int. thank you for nothing! no thanks to.

909 Forgiveness – N. *forgiveness,* pardon, free p., full p., reprieve 506 *amnesty*; indemnity, grace, indulgence, plenary i. 905 *mercy*; cancellation, remission, absolution 960 *acquittal*; justification, exculpation, exoneration, excuse 927 *vindication*; conciliation, reconciliation 719 *pacification*; mercifulness, placability, lenity 905 *pity*; longsuffering, forbearance 823 *patience*.

Vb. *forgive,* pardon, reprieve, forgive and forget, think no more of, not give another thought 506 *forget*; remit, absolve, shrive; cancel, blot out, wipe the slate clean 550 *obliterate*; relent, unbend, accept an apology 736 *be lenient*; be merciful, not be too hard upon, let one down gently, let one off the hook 905 *show mercy*; bear with, put up w., forbear, tolerate, make allowances 823 *be patient*; take no offence, bear no malice, take in good part, pocket, stomach, not hold it against one; forget an injury, ignore a wrong, overlook, pass over, not punish, leave unavenged, turn the other cheek; return good for evil; connive, wink at, condone, not make an issue of, turn a blind eye 458 *disregard*; excuse, find excuses for 927 *justify*; intercede 720 *mediate*; exculpate, exonerate 960 *acquit*; be ready to forgive, make the first move, bury the hatchet, let bygones be bygones, make it up, extend the hand of forgiveness, shake hands, kiss and be friends, kiss and make up, be reconciled 880 *be friendly*; restore to favour, kill the fatted calf 876 *celebrate*.

910 Revenge – N. *revengefulness,* thirst for revenge; vengefulness, vindictiveness, spitefulness, spite 898 *malevolence*; ruthlessness 906 *pitilessness*; remorselessness, relentlessness, implacability, irreconcilability, unappeasability; resentment.

revenge, sweet r.; crime passionel 911 *jealousy*; vengeance, day of reckoning 963 *punishment*; reprisal, reprisals, punitive expedition 714 *retaliation*; tit for tat, a Roland for an Oliver, measure for measure, eye for an eye, tooth for a tooth; vendetta, feud, blood f. 881 *enmity*.

Vb. *avenge,* avenge oneself, revenge o., take one's revenge, exact r., take vengeance, wreak v., take the law into one's own hands; exact retribution, get one's own back, repay, pay out, pay off *or* settle old scores, square an account, give someone what was coming to them, give someone his *or* her come-uppance; get back at, give tit for tat 714 *retaliate*; enjoy one's revenge, gloat.

be revengeful, get one's knife into 898
be malevolent; bear malice, promise vengeance 888 hate; nurse one's revenge,
harbour a grudge, carry on a feud, conduct a blood feud, have a rod in pickle,
have a bone to pick, have a score or
accounts to settle 881 be hostile; let it
rankle, remember an injury, refuse to
forget 891 resent.

911 Jealousy – N. jealousy, pangs of j.,
jealousness; jaundiced eye, green-eyed
monster; distrust, mistrust 486 doubt;
resentment; enviousness 912 envy; hate
888 hatred; inferiority complex, emulation, competitiveness, competitive
spirit, competition, rivalry, jealous r.
716 contention; possessiveness 887 love;
sexual jealousy, eternal triangle, crime
passionel 910 revenge; competitor, rival,
hated r., the other man, the other woman; Othello.
   Adj. jealous, green-eyed, yellow-e.,
jaundiced, envying 912 envious; devoured with jealousy, consumed with j.,
eaten up with j.; possessive 887 loving;
suspicious, mistrusting, distrustful 474
doubting; emulative, competitive, rival,
competing.

912 Envy – N. envy, envious eye, enviousness, covetousness 859 desire; rivalry
716 contention; jealousy; ill will, spite,
spleen; mortification, unwilling admiration, grudging praise.
   Adj. envious, envying, envious-eyed,
green with envy 911 jealous; greedy, unsatisfied 829 discontented; covetous,
longing; grudging.
   Vb. envy, view with e., cast envious
looks, cast covetous l., turn green with e.,
resent; covet, crave, lust after, must have
for oneself, long to change places with
859 desire.

Section four: Morality

913 Right – N. right, rightfulness, rightness, fitness, what is fitting, what ought
to be, what should be; obligation 917

duty; fittingness, seemliness, propriety,
decency 848 etiquette; normality 83 conformity; rules, rules and regulations 693
precept; ethicalness, morality, moral
code, good morals 917 morals; righteousness 933 virtue; rectitude, uprightness, honour 929 probity; one's right,
one's due, one's prerogative, deserts,
merits, claim 915 dueness.
   justice, freedom from wrong, justifia-
bility; righting wrong, redress; reform
654 reformism; even-handed justice, impartial j.; scales of justice, justice under
the law, process of l. 953 legality; retribution, retributive justice, poetic j. 962
reward; give and take, retaliation; fair-
mindedness, objectivity, lack of bias,
disinterestedness, detachment, impartiality, equalness 28 equality; equity, equi-
tableness, reasonableness, fairness; fair
deal, square d., fair treatment, fair play;
no discrimination, equal opportunity;
fair society; good law, Queensberry
rules.
   Adj. right, rightful, proper, right and
p., fitting, suitable, appropriate 24 fit;
good 917 ethical; put right, redressed,
reformed; normal, standard, classical 83
conformable.
   just, upright, righteous, right-minded,
high-principled, on the side of the angels
933 virtuous; fair-minded, disinterested,
unprejudiced, unbiased, unswerving,
undeflected 625 neutral; detached, impersonal, dispassionate, objective, open-
minded; equal, egalitarian, impartial,
even-handed; fair, square, fair and s.,
equitable, reasonable, fair enough; in the
right, justifiable, justified, unchallengeable, unchallenged, unimpeachable;
above-board, legitimate, according to
law 953 legal; sporting, sportsmanlike
929 honourable; deserved, well-d.,
earned, merited, well-m., 915 due; overdue, demanded, claimed, rightly c.,
claimable 627 required.

914 Wrong – N. wrong, wrongness,
something wrong, something amiss,
oddness, queerness 84 abnormality;
something rotten, curse, bane, scandal

645 *badness*; disgrace, shame, crying s., dishonour 867 *slur*; impropriety, indecorum 847 *bad taste*; wrongheadedness, unreasonableness 481 *misjudgment*; unjustifiability, what ought not to be, what must not be 916 *undueness*; inexcusability, culpability, guiltiness 936 *guilt*; immorality, vice, sin 934 *wickedness*; dishonesty, unrighteousness 930 *improbity*; irregularity, illegitimacy, criminality, crime, lawlessness 954 *illegality*; wrongfulness, misdoing, transgression, trespass, encroachment; misdeed, offence 936 *guilty act*; a wrong, injustice, mischief, outrage, foul; sense of wrong, complaint, charge 928 *accusation*; grievance, just g. 891 *resentment*; wrong-doer, unjust judge 938 *bad person*.

injustice, no justice; miscarriage of justice, wrong verdict 481 *misjudgment*; warped judgment, packed jury 481 *bias*; one-sidedness, inequity, unfairness; discrimination, race d., sex d., racism, sexism, heterosexism, ageism, classism; partiality, leaning, favouritism, favour, nepotism; preferential treatment, positive discrimination, affirmative action; partisanship, party spirit, old school tie 481 *prejudice*; unlawfulness, no law 954 *illegality*; justice denied, right withheld, privilege curtailed 916 *undueness*; unfair advantage, 'heads I win, tails you lose'; no equality, wolf and the lamb 29 *inequality*; not cricket; imposition, robbing Peter to pay Paul.

Adj. *wrong,* not right 645 *bad*; odd, queer, suspect 84 *abnormal*; unfitting, inappropriate, unseemly, improper 847 *vulgar*; wrongheaded, unreasonable; wrong from the start, out of court, inadmissible; irregular, against the rules, foul, unauthorized, unwarranted 757 *prohibited*; wrongful, illegitimate, illicit, felonious, criminal 954 *illegal*; condemnable, culpable, in the wrong, offside 936 *guilty*; unwarrantable, inexcusable, unpardonable, unforgivable, unjustifiable

(see *unjust*); open to objection, objectionable, reprehensible, scandalous; injurious, mischievous 645 *harmful*; unrighteous 930 *dishonest*; iniquitous, sinful, vicious, immoral 934 *wicked*.

unjust, unjustifiable; uneven, weighted 29 *unequal*; inequitable, iniquitous, unfair; hard, hard on 735 *severe*; foul, not playing the game, not keeping to the rules, below the belt, unsportsmanlike; discriminatory, favouring, one-sided, leaning to one side, partial, partisan, prejudiced 481 *biased*; selling justice 930 *venal*; wresting the law 954 *illegal*.

do wrong, wrong, hurt, injure, do an injury 645 *harm*; be hard on, have a down on 735 *be severe*; not play the game, not play cricket, hit below the belt; break the rules, commit a foul; commit a crime, break the law, pervert the course of justice, be illegal; transgress, infringe, trespass 306 *encroach*; wink at, connive at, turn a blind eye; do less than justice, withhold justice, deny j., deny one's rights; weight, load the scales, pack the jury, rig the jury; lean, lean to one side, discriminate against, show partiality, show favouritism, discriminate 481 *be biased*; favour 703 *patronize*; go too far, overcompensate, lean over backwards; commit, perpetrate.

915 Dueness – N. *dueness,* what is due, what is owing; accountability, responsibility, obligation 917 *duty*; from each according to his ability and to each according to his need; the least one can do, bare minimum; what one looks for, expectations; dues 804 *payment*; something owed, indebtedness 803 *debt*; tribute, credit 158 *attribution*; recognition, acknowledgment 907 *thanks*; something to be said for, something in favour of, case for; qualification, merits, deserts, just d. 913 *right*; justification 927 *vindication*; entitlement, claim, title 913 *right*; birthright, patriality, patrimony 777 *dower*; interest, vested i., prescriptive right, absolute r., inalienable r.; legal right, prescription, ancient lights;

human rights, women's r., animal r. 744 *freedom*; constitutional right, civil rights, bill of r., Magna Carta; privilege, exemption, immunity 919 *nonliability*; prerogative, privilege; charter, warrant, licence 756 *permit*; liberty, franchise; bond, security 767 *title deed*; patent, copyright; recovery of rights, restoration, compensation 787 *restitution*; owner, title-holder 776 *possessor*; heir 776 *beneficiary*; claimant, plaintiff, pursuer, appellant; person with a grievance 763 *petitioner*.

Adj. *due,* owing, payable; ascribable, attributable, assignable; merited, well-m., deserved, well-d., richly-d., earned, well-e., coming to one; admitted, allowed, sanctioned, warranted, licit, lawful; constitutional, entrenched, untouchable, uninfringeable, unchallengeable, unimpeachable, inviolable; privileged, sacrosant; confirmed, vested, prescriptive, inalienable, imprescriptible; secured by law, legalized, legitimate, rightful, of right, de jure, by habit and repute 953 *legal*; claimable, heritable, inheritable, earmarked, reserved, set aside; expected, fit, fitting, befitting 913 *right*; proper, en règle 642 *advisable*.

Vb. *claim,* claim as a right, lay claim to, stake a c., take possession 786 *appropriate*; claim unduly, arrogate; demand one's rights, assert one's r., stand up for one's r., vindicate one's r., insist on one's r., stand on one's r.; draw on, come down on for, take one's toll 786 *levy*; call in (debts), reclaim 656 *retrieve*; publish one's claims, declare one's right; sue, demand redress 761 *request*; enforce a claim, exercise a right; establish a right, patent, copyright.

deserve, merit, be worthy, be found w., have a claim on; have a right to, have right on one's side; earn, receive one's due, meet with one's deserts, get one's d.; have it coming to one, get one's comeuppance, have only oneself to thank; sow the wind and reap the whirlwind.

916 Undueness – N. *undueness,* not what one expects *or* would expect 508 *lack of*

expectation; not the thing, not quite the t., impropriety, unseemliness, indecorum 847 *bad taste*; inappropriateness, unfittingness 643 *inexpedience*; unworthiness, demerit 934 *vice*; illicitness, illegitimacy, bastardy 954 *illegality*; no thanks to 908 *ingratitude*; absence of right, want of title, failure of t., nonentitlement; no claim, no right, no title, false t., courtesy t.; gratuitousness, gratuity, bonus, grace marks, unearned increment; inordinacy, excessiveness, too much, overpayment 637 *redundance*; imposition, exaction 735 *severity*; unfair share, lion's s.; violation, breach, infraction, infringement, encroachment 306 *overstepping*; profanation, desecration 980 *impiety*.

arrogation, assumption, unjustified a., presumption, unwarranted p.; pretendership, usurpation, tyranny; misappropriation 786 *expropriation*; encroachment, inroad, trespass 306 *overstepping*.

loss of right, disentitlement, disfranchisement, disqualification; denaturalization, detribalization 147 *conversion*; forfeiture 772 *loss*; deportation, dismissal, deprivation, dethronement 752 *deposal*; ouster, dispossession 786 *expropriation*; seizure, forcible s., robbery 788 *stealing*; cancellation 752 *abrogation*; waiver, abdication 621 *relinquishment*.

usurper, pretender 545 *impostor*; desecrator; violator, infringer, encroacher, trespasser, squatter, cuckoo in the nest.

Adj. *unwarranted,* unwarrantable; unauthorized, unsanctioned, unlicensed, unchartered, unconstitutional; unrightful, unlegalized, illicit, illegitimate, ultra vires 954 *illegal*; arrogated, usurped, stolen, borrowed; excessive, presumptuous, assuming 878 *insolent*; unjustified, unjustifiable 914 *wrong*; undeserved, unmerited, unearned; overpaid, underpaid; invalid, weak; forfeited, forfeit; false, bastard 542 *spurious*; fictitious, would-be, self-styled 850 *affected*.

Vb. *disentitle,* uncrown, dethrone 752 *depose*; disqualify, unfrock, disfranchise, alienize, denaturalize, detribalize, denationalize; invalidate 752 *abrogate*; disallow 757 *prohibit*; dispossess, expropriate 786 *deprive*; forfeit, declare f.; defeat a claim, mock the claims of; make illegitimate, illegalize, criminalize 954 *make illegal*; bastardize, debase 655 *impair.*

917 Duty – N. *duty,* what ought to be done, what is up to one, the right thing, the proper t., the decent t.; one's duty, bounden d., inescapable d.; obligation, liability, onus, responsibility, accountability 915 *dueness*; fealty, allegiance, loyalty 739 *obedience*; sense of duty, dutifulness, duteousness 597 *willingness*; discharge of duty, performance, acquittal, discharge 768 *observance*; call of duty, claims of conscience, case of c.; bond, tie, engagement, commitment, word, pledge 764 *promise*; task, office, charge 751 *commission*; walk of life, station, profession 622 *vocation.*

conscience, tender c., inner voice, 'still, small voice',

code of duty, code of honour, unwritten code, professional c.; Ten Commandments, Hippocratic oath 693 *precept.*

morals, morality 933 *virtue*; honour 929 *probity*; moral principles, high p., ideals, high i., standards, high s., professional s.; ethics, religious e., humanist e., professional e.; ethology, deontology, casuistry, ethical philosophy, moral p., moral science, idealism, humanism, utilitarianism, behaviourism 449 *philosophy.*

Adj. *obliged,* duty-bound, on duty, bound by duty, called by d.; under duty, in duty bound, in the line of duty; obligated, beholden, under obligation; tied, bound, sworn, pledged, committed, engaged; unexempted, liable, chargeable, answerable, responsible, accountable; in honour bound, bound in conscience, answerable to God; plagued by conscience,

conscience-stricken 939 *repentant*; conscientious, punctilious 768 *observant*; duteous, dutiful 739 *obedient*; vowed, under a vow.

obligatory, incumbent, imposed, behoving, up to one; binding, de rigueur, compulsory, mandatory, peremptory, operative 740 *compelling*; inescapable, unavoidable; strict, unconditional, categorical.

ethical, moral, principled 933 *virtuous*; honest, decent 929 *honourable*; moralistic, ethological, casuistical; moralizing; humanistic, idealistic; utilitarian.

Vb. *be one's duty,* be incumbent, behove, become, befit 915 *be due*; devolve on, belong to, be up to, pertain to, fall to, arise from one's functions, be part of the job; lie with, lie at one's door, rest with, rest on one's shoulders.

incur a duty, make it one's d., take on oneself, accept responsibility, shoulder one's r.; make oneself liable, commit oneself, pledge o., engage for 764 *promise*; assume one's functions, enter upon one's office, receive a posting; have the office, have the function, have the charge, have the duty; owe it to oneself, feel it up to one, feel it incumbent upon one; feel duty's call, accept the c., answer the c., submit to one's vocation.

do one's duty, fulfil one's d. 739 *obey*; discharge, acquit, perform, do the needful 676 *do*; do one's bit, play one's part; perform one's office, discharge one's functions 768 *observe*; be on duty, stay at one's post, go down with one's ship; come up to what is expected of one, come up to expectation, not be found wanting; keep faith with one's conscience, meet one's obligations, discharge an obligation, make good one's promise, redeem a pledge, be as good as one's word; honour, meet, pay up 804 *pay.*

impose a duty, require, oblige, look to, call upon; devolve, call to office, swear one in, offer a post, post 751 *commission*; assign a duty, saddle with, detail, order, enjoin, decree 737 *command*; tax,

overtax, task, overtask 684 *fatigue*; exact 735 *be severe*; demand obedience, expect it of one, expect too much of one 507 *expect*; bind, condition 766 *give terms*; bind over, take security 764 *take a pledge*.

Adv. *on duty*, at one's post; under an obligation; in the line of duty, as in duty bound; with a clear conscience; for conscience' sake.

918 Undutifulness – **N.** *undutifulness*, default, want of duty, dereliction of d.; neglect, wilful n., culpable negligence 458 *negligence*; disrespect; malingering, evasion of duty, cop-out 620 *avoidance*; nonpractice, nonperformance 769 *nonobservance*; idleness, laziness 679 *sluggishness*; forgetfulness 506 *oblivion*; noncooperation, want of alacrity 598 *unwillingness*; truancy, absenteeism 190 *absence*; absconding 667 *escape*; infraction, violation, breach of orders, indiscipline, mutiny, rebellion 738 *disobedience*; incompetence, mismanagement 695 *bungling*; obstruction, sabotage 702 *hindrance*; desertion, defection 603 *change of mind*; disloyalty, treachery, treason 930 *perfidy*; secession, breakaway 978 *schism*; irresponsibility, escapism; truant, absentee, malingerer, defaulter 620 *avoider*; slacker 679 *idler*; deserter, absconder 667 *escaper*; betrayer, traitor 603 *tergiversator*; saboteur; mutineer, rebel 738 *revolter*; seceder, splinter group 978 *schismatic*.

Adj. *undutiful*, wanting in duty, uncooperative 598 *unwilling*; unfilial, undaughterly 921 *disrespectful*; mutinous, rebellious, seceding, breakaway 738 *disobedient*; disloyal, treacherous, treasonous 930 *perfidious*; irresponsible, unreliable; truant, absentee 190 *absent*; absconding.

Vb. *fail in duty*, neglect one's d., be wilfully negligent 458 *neglect*; ignore one's obligations 458 *disregard*; oversleep, sleep in 679 *sleep*; default, let one down, leave one in the lurch 509 *disappoint*; mismanage, bungle 495 *blunder*; not remember 506 *forget*; shirk, evade,

wriggle out of, malinger, 620 *avoid*; wash one's hands of, pass the buck 919 *be exempt*; play truant, overstay leave 190 *be absent*; abscond 667 *escape*; quit, scuttle, scarper 296 *decamp*; abandon, abandon one's post, desert, desert the colours 621 *relinquish*; break orders, disobey o., violate o., exceed one's instructions 738 *disobey*; mutiny, rebel 738 *revolt*; be disloyal, prove treacherous, betray, commit treason 603 *tergiversate*; sabotage 702 *obstruct*; noncooperate, withdraw, walk out, break away, form a splinter group, secede.

919 Nonliability – **N.** *nonliability*, nonresponsibility, exemption, dispensation; conscience clause, escape c., let-out c., force majeure 468 *qualification*; immunity, impunity, privilege, special treatment, special case, benefit of clergy; extraterritoriality, diplomatic immunity; franchise, charter 915 *dueness*; independence, liberty, the four freedoms 744 *freedom*; licence, leave 756 *permission*; compassionate leave, aegrotat, certificate of exemption 756 *permit*; excuse, exoneration, exculpation 960 *acquittal*; absolution, pardon, amnesty 909 *forgiveness*; discharge, release 746 *liberation*; renunciation 621 *relinquishment*; evasion of responsibility, escapism, self-exemption, washing one's hands, passing the buck 753 *resignation*.

Vb. *exempt*, set apart, set aside; eliminate, count out, rule o. 57 *exclude*; excuse, exonerate, exculpate 960 *acquit*; grant absolution, absolve, pardon 909 *forgive*; spare 905 *show mercy*; grant immunity, privilege, charter 756 *permit*; license, dispense, give dispensation, grant impunity; amnesty, declare an amnesty 506 *forget*; enfranchise, set free, set at liberty, release 746 *liberate*; pass over, stretch a point 736 *be lenient*.

be exempt, - exempted etc. adj.; owe no responsibility, be free from r., have no liability, not come within the scope of; enjoy immunity, enjoy diplomatic i., enjoy impunity, enjoy a privileged position, enjoy independence 744 *be free*;

spare oneself the necessity, exempt oneself, excuse oneself, absent oneself, take leave, go on leave 190 *go away*; transfer the responsibility, pass the buck, shift the blame 272 *transfer*; evade *or* escape liability, get away with 667 *escape*; own *or* admit no responsibility, wash one's hands of 918 *fail in duty.*

920 Respect – N. *respect,* regard, consideration, esteem 923 *approbation*; high standing, honour, favour 866 *repute*; polite regard, attention, attentions, flattering a. 884 *courtesy*; due respect, respectfulness, deference, humbleness 872 *humility*; obsequiousness 879 *servility*; devotion 739 *loyalty*; admiration, awe 864 *wonder*; terror 854 *fear*; reverence, veneration, adoration 981 *worship.*

respects, regards, duty, kind regards, kindest r., greetings 884 *courteous act*; red carpet, guard of honour, address of welcome, illuminated address, salutation, salaam; nod, bob, duck, bow, scrape, curtsy, genuflexion, prostration, kowtow 311 *obeisance*; reverence, homage; salute, presenting arms; honours of war, flags flying.

Adj. *respectful,* deferential, knowing one's place 872 *humble*; obsequious, boot-licking, kowtowing 879 *servile*; submissive 721 *submitting*; reverent, reverential; admiring, awestruck; polite 884 *courteous*; ceremonious, at the salute, saluting, cap in hand, bare-headed, forelock-tugging; kneeling, on one's knees, prostrate; bobbing, bowing, scraping, bowing and s., bending; showing respect, rising, standing, on one's feet, all standing.

Vb. *respect,* hold in r., hold in honour, hold in high regard, hold in high esteem, think well of, rank high, place h., look up to, esteem, regard, value; admire 864 *wonder*; reverence, venerate, exalt 866 *honour*; adore 981 *worship*; idolize; revere, stand in awe of, have a wholesome respect for 854 *fear*; know one's place, defer to, take a back seat to 721 *submit*; pay tribute to, take one's hat off to 923 *praise*; do homage to, make much of,

lionize, chair, carry shoulder-high 876 *celebrate.*

show respect, render honour, pay homage, do the honours 884 *pay one's respects*; make way for, leave room for, keep one's distance, take a back seat to, know one's place; welcome, hail, salute, present arms, turn out the guard, roll out the red carpet, put out the bunting 884 *greet*; cheer, drink to 876 *toast*; bob, bow, bow and scrape, curtsy, kneel, kowtow, prostrate oneself 311 *stoop*; observe decorum, stand on ceremony, stand, rise, rise to one's feet, rise from one's seat, uncover, remove one's hat *or* cap, stand bareheaded; humble oneself, condescend 872 *be humble.*

command respect, inspire r., awe, strike with a., overawe, impose 821 *impress*; enjoy a reputation, rank high, stand h., stand well in the eyes of all 866 *have a reputation*; compel respect, demand r., command admiration 864 *be wonderful*; dazzle, bedazzle 875 *be ostentatious*; receive respect, gain honour, gain a reputation, receive bouquets 923 *be praised.*

921 Disrespect – N. *disrespect,* want of respect, scant r., disrespectfulness, irreverence, impoliteness, incivility, discourtesy 885 *rudeness*; dishonour, disfavour 924 *disapprobation*; neglect, undervaluation 483 *underestimation*; low esteem 867 *disrepute*; depreciation, disparagement 926 *detraction*; scorn 922 *contempt*; mockery 851 *ridicule*; desecration 980 *impiety.*

indignity, humiliation, mortification, affront, insult, slight, snub, slap in the face, outrage 878 *insolence*; snook, V-sign, Harvey Smith salute 878 *sauciness*; gibe, taunt, jeer 922 *contempt*; quip, sarcasm, mock, flout 851 *ridicule*; hiss, hoot, boo, catcall, brickbat, rotten eggs 924 *disapprobation.*

Adj. *disrespectful,* wanting in respect, slighting, neglectful 458 *negligent*; insubordinate 738 *disobedient*; irreverent, irreverential, aweless; sacrilegious 980 *profane*; outspoken, overcandid 573

plain; rude, impolite 885 *discourteous*; airy, breezy, offhand, offhanded, cavalier, familiar, cheeky, saucy 878 *impertinent*; insulting, outrageous 878 *insolent*; flouting, jeering, gibing, scoffing, mocking, satirical, cynical, sarcastic; injurious, contumelious, scurrilous 899 *cursing*; denigratory, depreciative, pejorative; snobbish, supercilious, disdainful, scornful; unflattering, uncomplimentary 924 *disapproving*.

Vb. *not respect,* be disrespectful; have no respect for, have no regard f., have no use f. 924 *disapprove*; misprize, undervalue, underrate 483 *underestimate*; look down on, have a low opinion of, disdain, scorn 922 *despise*; run down, denigrate, disparage 926 *defame*; spit on, toss aside 607 *reject*; show disrespect, show no respect, lack courtesy, remain seated, remain covered, keep one's hat on, push aside, shove a., elbow a., crowd, jostle 885 *be rude*; ignore, turn one's back 458 *disregard*; snub, slight, insult, affront, outrage 872 *humiliate*; dishonour, disgrace, put to shame, drag in the mud 867 *shame*; trifle with, treat lightly 922 *hold cheap*; cheapen, lower, degrade; have no awe, not reverence, desecrate, profane 980 *be impious*; call names, abuse 899 *curse*; taunt, twit, cock a snook 878 *be insolent*; laugh at, guy, scoff, mock, flout, deride 851 *ridicule*; make mouths at, make faces at, jeer, hiss, hoot, heckle, boo, point at, spit at 924 *reproach*; mob, hound, chase 619 *pursue*; pelt, stone, heave a brick.

922 Contempt – **N.** *contempt,* utter c.; scorn, disdain, disdainfulness, superiority, loftiness 871 *pride*; contemptuousness, sniffiness; snootiness, superciliousness, snobbishness 850 *affectation*; superior airs, side, smile of contempt, curl of the lip, snort, sniff; slight, humiliation 921 *indignity*; sneer, dig at 926 *detraction*; derision, scoffing 851 *ridicule*; snub, rebuff 885 *discourtesy*.

contemptibility, unworthiness, despisedness, insignificance, puerility,

pitiability, futility 639 *unimportance*; pettiness, meanness, littleness, paltriness 33 *smallness*; cause for shame, byword of reproach.

Adj. *contemptible,* despicable, beneath contempt; abject, worthless 645 *bad*; petty, paltry, little, mean 33 *small*; spurned, spat on; scorned, despised, contemned, low in one's estimation; trifling, pitiable, futile, of no account 639 *unimportant*.

Vb. *despise,* hold in contempt, feel utter contempt for, have no use for 921 *not respect*; look down on, consider beneath one, be too good for, be too grand for 871 *be proud*; disdain, spurn, sniff at, snort at 607 *reject*; come it over, turn up one's nose, wrinkle the n., curl one's lips, toss one's head, snort; snub, turn one's back on 885 *be rude*; scorn, whistle, hiss, boo, give a slow handclap, point at, point the finger of scorn 924 *reproach*; laugh at, have a dig at, laugh to scorn, scoff, scout, flout, gibe, jeer, mock, deride 851 *ridicule*; trample on, ride roughshod over 735 *oppress*; disgrace, roll in the mire 867 *shame*.

hold cheap, have a low opinion of 921 *not respect*; ignore, dismiss, discount, take no account of 458 *disregard*; belittle, disparage, fail to appreciate, underrate, undervalue 483 *underestimate*; decry 926 *detract*; set no value on, set no store by, think nothing of, think small beer of, not care a rap for, not care a straw, not give a hoot *or* a damn, not give that for, laugh at, treat as a laughing matter, snap one's fingers at, shrug away, pooh-pooh; slight, trifle with, treat lightly, treat like dirt, denigrate, lower, degrade 872 *humiliate*.

923 Approbation – **N.** *approbation,* approval, modified rapture; satisfaction 828 *content*; appreciation, recognition, acknowledgement 907 *gratitude*; good opinion, golden opinions, kudos, credit 866 *prestige*; regard, admiration, esteem 920 *respect*; good books, good graces, grace, favour, popularity, affection 887

love; adoption, acceptance, welcome, favourable reception 299 *reception*; sanction 756 *permission*; nod of approval, seal of a., blessing; nod, wink, thumbs up, consent 488 *assent*; countenance, patronage, championship, advocacy, backing 703 *aid*; friendly notice, favourable review, rave r. 480 *estimate*; good word, kind w., testimonial, written t., reference, commendation, recommendation 466 *credential*.

praise, loud p., praise and glory, laudation, benediction, blessing; compliment, eulogy, panegyric, glorification, adulation, idolatry 925 *flattery*; hero worship 864 *wonder*; overpraise 482 *overestimation*; faint praise, two cheers; shout of praise, hosanna, alleluia; praises, song of praise, hymn of p., paean of p., Te Deum; tribute, credit, due credit 907 *thanks*; complimentary reference, bouquet, accolade, citation, honourable mention, commendation, glowing terms; official biography, hagiography; self-praise, self-glorification 877 *boasting*; name in lights, letters of gold; puff, blurb 528 *advertisement*.

applause, clamorous a., acclaim, universal a.; enthusiasm, excitement 821 *excitation*; warm reception, hero's welcome 876 *celebration*; acclamation, plaudits, clapping, stamping, whistling, cheering; clap, three cheers, paean, hosannah; thunderous applause, shout of a., chorus of a., round of a., salvo of a., storm of a., ovation, standing o., shouts of 'encore', shouts of 'more, more'; encore, curtain call; bouquet, pat on the back.

commender, praiser, eulogist, panegyrist; clapper, applauder, shouter; approver, friendly critic, admirer, devoted a., hero-worshipper, fan club, supporters' c.; advocate, recommender, supporter, speaker for the motion 707 *patron*; inscriber, dedicator; advertiser, blurb-writer, puffer, promotions manager, booster; agent, tout, touter, barker 528 *publicizer*; canvasser, electioneer, election agent.

Adj. *approving*, uncensorious, uncomplaining, satisfied 828 *content*; favouring, supporting, advocating 703 *aiding*; appreciative 907 *grateful*; approbatory, favourable, friendly, well-inclined; complimentary, commendatory, laudatory, eulogistic, panegyrical, lyrical; admiring, hero-worshipping, idolatrous; lavish, generous; fulsome, overpraising, uncritical, undiscriminating; acclamatory, clapping, applauding, thunderous 400 *loud*; ecstatic, rapturous, in raptures 821 *excited*.

approved, passed, tested, tried; uncensured, free from blame, stamped with approval, blessed; popular, in favour, in high f., in one's good books, in the good graces of, in good odour, in high esteem, thought well of 866 *reputable*; praised etc. vb.; commended, highly c.; favoured, backed, odds on 605 *chosen*.

Vb. *approve*, see nothing wrong with, sound pleased, have no fault to find, be unable to fault, have nothing but praise for, think highly of 920 *respect*; like well 887 *love*; think well of, admire, esteem, value, prize, treasure, cherish, set store by 866 *honour*; appreciate, give credit, give full c., give credit where credit is due, salute, take one's hat off to, hand it to, give full marks; think no worse of, think the better of; count it to one's credit, see the good points, see the good in one, think good, think perfect; think desirable 912 *envy*; think the best, award the palm; pronounce good, mark with approbation, give the seal *or* stamp of approval; accept, pass, tick, give marks for, give points for; nod, wink, nod one's approval, give one's assent 488 *assent*; sanction, bless, give one's blessing 756 *permit*; ratify 488 *endorse*; commend, recommend, advocate, support, back, favour, countenance, stand up for, speak up f., put in a good word for, give one a reference *or* a testimonial, act as referee for 703 *patronize*.

praise, compliment, pay compliments 925 *flatter*; speak well of, speak highly, swear by; bless 907 *thank*; salute, pay tribute to, hand it to, take one's hat off

to; commend, give praise, hand out bouquets to, laud, eulogize, praise to the skies, sound the praises, sing the p., exalt, extol, glorify, magnify; wax lyrical, get carried away; not spare one's blushes 546 *exaggerate*; puff, inflate, overpraise, overestimate 482 *overrate*; lionize, hero-worship, idolize; trumpet, write up, cry up, puff up, hype up, crack up, boost 528 *advertise*; praise oneself, glorify o. 877 *boast*.

applaud, welcome, hail; acclaim, receive with acclamation, clap, clap one's hands, give a big hand, stamp, whistle, bring the house down, raise the roof; give a standing ovation; cheer, raise a c., give three cheers, give three times three; cheer to the echo, shout for, root for; clap on the back, pat on the back, hand out bouquets to; welcome, congratulate, garland, chair 876 *celebrate*; drink to 876 *toast*.

Int. bravo! well done! hear hear! encore! more, more! bis! three cheers! hurrah! hosannah! olé!

924 Disapprobation – N. *disapprobation,* disapproval, dissatisfaction 829 *discontent*; nonapproval, return 607 *rejection*; refusal; disfavour, displeasure, unpopularity 861 *dislike*; low opinion 921 *disrespect*; bad books, black b. 867 *disrepute*; disparagement, decrial, carping, niggling 926 *detraction*; censoriousness, faultfinding 862 *fastidiousness*; hostility 881 *enmity*; objection, exception, cavil 468 *qualification*; complaint, clamour, outcry, protest, tut-tut, sniffing 762 *deprecation*; indignation 891 *anger*; sibilation, hissing, hiss, boo, slow handclap, whistle, catcall; brickbats 851 *ridicule*; ostracism, boycott, bar, colour b., ban, nonadmission 57 *exclusion*; blackball, blacklist, Index.

censure, blame, impeachment, inculpation 928 *accusation*; home truth, no compliment, left-handed c., backhanded c.; criticism, stricture, lambasting, hypercriticism, fault-finding; onslaught 712 *attack*; brickbats, bad press,

critical review, hostile r., slashing r., slating, panning; open letter, tirade, jeremiad, philippic, diatribe 704 *opposition*; conviction 961 *condemnation*; false accusation 928 *false charge*; slur, slander, aspersions, insinuation, innuendo 926 *calumny*; brand, stigma.

reproach, reproaches; recriminations 709 *quarrel*; home truths, invective, vituperation, calling names, bawling out, shouting down 899 *scurrility*; execration 899 *malediction*; personal remarks, aspersion, reflection 921 *indignity*; taunt, sneer 878 *insolence*; sarcasm, irony, satire, biting wit, biting tongue, dig, cut, hit, brickbat 851 *ridicule*; rough side of one's tongue, tongue-lashing, lambasting, hard words, cutting w., bitter w. (see *reprimand*); silent reproach, disapproving look, dirty l., black l. 893 *sullenness*.

reprimand, remonstrance 762 *deprecation*; stricture, animadversion, reprehension, reprobation; censure, rebuke, flea in one's ear, reproof, snub; rocket, raspberry; piece of one's mind, expression of displeasure, mark of d., black mark; castigation, correction, rap over the knuckles, smack *or* slap on the wrist, box on the ears 963 *punishment*; inculpation, admonition, admonishment, tongue-lashing, chiding, talking-to, upbraiding, scolding, slating, strafing, trouncing, lambasting, dressing down, blowing up, roasting, wigging, carpeting; talking to, lecture, curtain l.

Adj. *disapproving,* unapproving, not amused; shocked, scandalized; unimpressed; disillusioned 509 *disappointed*; sparing of praise, grudging; silent 582 *taciturn*; unfavourable, hostile 881 *hostile*; objecting, protesting, deprecatory; reproachful, chiding, scolding, upbraiding, vituperative, lambasting; critical, unflattering, uncomplimentary; withering, hard-hitting, pulling no punches, strongly worded; overcritical, hypercritical, captious, fault-finding, niggling, carping, cavilling; disparaging, defamatory, damaging; caustic, sharp, bitter, venomous, trenchant, mordant; sarcastic, sardonic, cynical; censorious, holier

than thou; blaming, faulting, censuring, reprimanding, recriminative, denunciatory, accusatory, condemning, damning, damnatory.

blameworthy, blamable, open to criticism, censurable, condemnable 645 *bad*; reprehensible, dishonourable, unjustifiable 867 *discreditable*; unpraiseworthy, uncommendable, not to be thought of; reprobate, culpable, to blame.

Vb. *disapprove,* hold no brief for, have no regard for, not think much of, think little of, take a dim view of; think the worse of, think ill of 922 *despise*; not pass, fail, plough; return 607 *reject*; disallow 757 *prohibit*; cancel 752 *abrogate*; censor 550 *obliterate*; withhold approval, look grave, shake one's head, not hold with 489 *dissent*; disfavour, reprehend, lament, deplore 830 *regret*; abhor, reprobate 861 *dislike*; wash one's hands of, turn one's back on, disown, look askance, avoid, ignore; keep at a distance, draw the line, ostracize, ban, bar, blacklist 57 *exclude*; protest, tut-tut, sniff, remonstrate, object, take exception to, demur 762 *deprecate*; discountenance, show disapproval, exclaim, shout down, bawl d., hoot, boo, bay, heckle, hiss, whistle, give a slow handclap, give the bird, drive off the stage; hand out brickbats, throw mud, throw rotten eggs, throw bricks *or* stones; hound, chase, mob, lynch; make a face, grimace, make a moue, make mouths at, spit; look black; sullen; look daggers 891 *be angry*.

criticize, not recommend, give no marks *or* points to, damn with faint praise, damn 961 *condemn*; fault, find f., pick holes, niggle, cavil, carp, nitpick, deprecate, run down, belittle 926 *detract*; oppose, tilt at, shoot at, throw the book at 712 *attack*; weigh in, pitch into, hit out at, let fly, lay into, lam into, savage, maul, slash, slate, lambast, scourge, flay, put the boot in; inveigh, thunder, fulminate, storm against, rage a. 61 *rampage*; shout down, cry shame, slang, call names; gird, rail, revile, abuse, heap a., pour vitriol, objurgate, execrate 899 *curse*; vilify, blacken, denigrate 926

defame; stigmatize, brand, pillory; expose, denounce, recriminate 928 *accuse*; sneer, twit, taunt 921 *not respect*.

reprove, reprehend, reproach, rebuke, administer a r., snub, rebuff, send away with a flea in the ear; call to order, caution, wag one's finger, read the Riot Act 664 *warn*; book, give one a black mark; censure, reprimand, take to task, rap over the knuckles, smack *or* slap the wrist, box the ears; tick off, tell off, have one's head for, carpet, have on the carpet, haul over the coals, send before the beak; remonstrate, expostulate, admonish, castigate, chide, correct; lecture, read one a lecture, give one a talking to, give one a wigging, give one a dressing-down, lambast, trounce, roast, browbeat, blow up, tear strips off, come down hard on, come down on like a ton of bricks, chastise 963 *punish*.

blame, find fault, carp, cavil, nitpick, pick holes in; get at, henpeck; reprehend, hold to blame, pick on, put the blame on, hold responsible; throw the first stone, inculpate, incriminate, complain against, impute, impeach, charge, criminate 928 *accuse*; round on, return the charge, recriminate 714 *retaliate*; think the worst of 961 *condemn*.

reproach, heap reproaches on; upbraid, slate, rate, berate, rail, slag, strafe, shend, lambast, revile, abuse, denigrate, blackguard 899 *curse*; go for, inveigh against, bawl out, scold, tongue-lash, lash, give the rough edge of one's tongue, rail in good set terms against, give one a piece of one's mind, give one what for, give it to one straight from the shoulder, give to one straight, not mince matters, not pull one's punches, let it rip.

incur blame, take the blame, take the rap, carry the can, catch it; be held responsible, have to answer for; be open to criticism, blot one's copy book, get a bad name 867 *lose repute*; be up on a charge, be carpeted, be up before the beak, be court-martialled, stand accused; stand corrected; be an example, be a scandal, scandalize, shock, revolt 861 *cause dislike*.

925 Flattery – N. *flattery,* cajolery, wheedling, getting round, blarney, blandishments, sweet talk; flannel, soft soap; adulation; voice of the charmer, honeyed words, sweet nothings 889 *endearment*; compliment, pretty speeches, bouquets; coquetry, winning ways; fawning, backscratching; obsequiousness, flunkeyism, sycophancy, toadying 879 *servility*; unctuousness, smarminess, euphemism, insincerity, hypocrisy, tongue in cheek, lip-homage 542 *sham.*

flatterer, adulator, cajoler, wheedler; coquette, charmer; tout, puffer, hyper, promoter, booster, claqueur, claque 923 *commender*; courtier, yes-man 488 *assenter*; creep, fawner, backscratcher, sycophant, parasite, minion, hanger-on 879 *toady*; fair-weather friend, hypocrite 545 *deceiver.*

Adj.   *flattering,*   overpraising, overdone; boosting, puffing, hyping, overpromoting;   complimentary, overcomplimentary, full of compliments; fulsome, adulatory; sugary, saccharine; cajoling, wheedling, coaxing, blarneying, mealy-mouthed, glozing; canting;   smooth-tongued,   honey-t., bland; smooth, oily, unctuous, soapy, slimy, smarmy; obsequious, all over one, courtly, fawning, crawling, back-scratching, sycophantic 879 *servile*; specious, plausible, beguiling, ingratiating, insinuating; lulling, soothing; vote-catching, vote-snatching; false, insincere, tongue-in-cheek, unreliable 541 *hypocritical.*

Vb. *flatter,* deal in flattery, have kissed the Blarney Stone; compliment, hand out bouquets 923 *praise*; overpraise, overdo it, lard it on, lay it on thick, lay it on with a trowel, not spare one's blushes; puff, hype, promote, boost, cry up 482 *overrate*; adulate, burn incense to, assail with flattery, turn one's head; butter up, soften up, soft-soap; blarney, flannel; sweet-talk, sugar; wheedle, coax, cajole, coo; lull, soothe, beguile 542 *deceive*; humour, jolly along, pander to; gild the pill, sugar the p., make things pleasant, tell people what they want to hear; blandish, smooth, smarm; make much of; be

all over one 889 *caress*; fawn, fawn on, cultivate, court, pay court to, play the courtier, massage one's ego; smirk 835 *smile*; scratch one's back, backscratch, curry favour, make up to, suck up to; toady to, pander to 879 *be servile*; insinuate oneself, worm oneself into favour, get on the right side of, creep into one's good graces; flatter oneself, have a swelled head 873 *be vain.*

926 Detraction – N. *detraction,* faint praise, two cheers, understatement 483 *underestimation*; criticism, hostile c., destructive c., flak, bad review, slating r., bad press 924 *disapprobation*; onslaught 712 *attack*; hatchet job; impeachment 928 *accusation*; exposure, bad light 867 *disrepute*; decrial, disparagement, depreciation, running down; lowering, derogation; slighting language, scorn 922 *contempt*; vilification, abuse, invective 899 *scurrility*; defamation 543 *untruth*; backbiting, cattiness, spite 898 *malevolence*; aspersion, reflection, snide remark (see *calumny*); whisper, innuendo, insinuation, imputation, whispering campaign; smear campaign, mud-slinging, smirching, denigration, character assassination; brand, stigma; muck-raking, scandal-mongering; disillusionment, cynicism 865 *lack of wonder.*

calumny, slander, libel, aspersion, false report, roorback 543 *untruth*; a defamation, defamatory remark, damaging report; smear, smear-word, dirty word 867 *slur*; offensive remark, personal r., insult, taunt, dig at, brickbat 921 *indignity*; scoff, sarcasm 851 *ridicule*; sneer, sniff; caricature 552 *misrepresentation*; skit, lampoon 851 *satire*; scandal, scandalous talk, malicious gossip, bad mouth.

detractor, decrier, disparager, slighter; debunker, deflater, cynic; mocker, scoffer, satirizer, satirist, lampooner; castigator, denouncer, reprover, censurer, censor; no respecter of persons, no flatterer, candid friend, candid critic; critic, hostile c., destructive c., attacker; arch-critic, chief accuser, impeacher 928

accuser; captious critic, knocker, fault-finder, carper, caviller, niggler, nit-picker, hair-splitter; heckler, barracker; Philistine; defamer, destroyer of reputations, hatchet man; smircher, smearer, slanderer, libeller; backbiter, gossiper, scandal-monger, muck-raker; gossip columnist, gutter press, chequebook journalist; denigrator, mud-slinger; brander, stigmatizer; vituperator, reviler; scold, poison pen.

Vb. *detract,* deprecate, disparage, run down, sell short; debunk, deflate, puncture, cut down to size 921 *not respect*; minimize 483 *underestimate*; belittle, slight 922 *hold cheap*; sneer at, sniff at 922 *despise*; decry, cry down, rubbish, damn with faint praise, fail to appreciate 924 *disapprove*; find nothing to praise, criticize, knock, bad mouth, slam, fault, find f., pick holes in, slate, pull to pieces, tear to ribbons 924 *criticize*; caricature, guy 552 *misrepresent*; lampoon, dip one's pen in gall 851 *satirize*; scoff, mock 851 *ridicule*; make catty remarks, get in a dig at; whisper, insinuate, cast aspersions.

defame, dishonour, damage, compromise, scandalize, degrade, lower, put to shame 867 *shame*; give a dog a bad name, lower *or* lessen one's reputation, destroy one's good name; denounce, expose, pillory, stigmatize, brand 928 *accuse*; libel, slander, traduce, malign; vilify, denigrate, blacken, tarnish, sully; reflect upon, put in a bad light; speak ill of, speak evil, gossip, badmouth, make scandal, talk about, backbite, talk behind one's back; discredit 486 *cause doubt*; smear, start a smear campaign, besmear, smirch, besmirch, spatter, bespatter, throw mud, fling dirt, drag in the gutter 649 *make unclean*; hound, witch-hunt 619 *hunt*; look for scandal, smell evil, muckrake, rake about in the gutter 619 *pursue*.

927 Vindication – N. *vindication,* restoration, rehabilitation 787 *restitution*; triumph of justice, wrong righted; exoneration, exculpation, clearance 960 *acquittal*; justification, good grounds, just cause, every excuse; apologetics, self-defence, apologia, defence, legal d., good d.; alibi, plea, excuse, whitewash, gloss 614 *pretext*; fair excuse, good e. 494 *truth*; extenuation, palliation, mitigation, mitigating circumstance, extenuating c., palliative 468 *qualification*; counterargument 479 *confutation*; reply, reply for the defence, rebuttal 460 *rejoinder*; recrimination, countercharge; accusation; bringing to book, poetic justice, just punishment 963 *punishment*.

Vb. *vindicate,* revenge 910 *avenge*; do justice to, give the devil his due; set right, restore, rehabilitate 787 *restitute*; maintain, speak up for, argue f., contend f., advocate 475 *argue*; undertake to prove, bear out, confirm, make good, prove the truth of, prove 478 *demonstrate*; champion, stand up for, stick up for 713 *defend*; support, offer moral support 703 *patronize*.

justify, warrant, justify by the event, give grounds for, provide justification, furnish an excuse, give one cause; put one in the right, put one in the clear, clear, clear one's name, free from blame, exonerate, exculpate, acquit; whitewash, varnish, gloss; salve one's conscience, justify oneself, defend o. 614 *plead*; plead one's own cause, say in defence, rebut the charge, plead ignorance.

extenuate, excuse, make excuses for, make allowances; palliate, mitigate, soften, mince one's words, soft-pedal, slur, slur over, play down, downplay, gloss, gloss over, varnish, whitewash; take the will for the deed 736 *be lenient*.

928 Accusation – N. *accusation,* complaint, charge, home truth; censure, blame, stricture 924 *reproach*; challenge 711 *defiance*; countercharge, recrimination 460 *rejoinder*; twit, taunt 921 *indignity*; imputation, allegation, information, denunciation; plaint, suit, action

959 *litigation*; prosecution, impeachment, arraignment, indictment, citation, summons; bill of indictment, true bill; gravamen, substance of a charge; case, case to answer, case for the prosecution 475 *reasons*; evidence.

false charge, trumped-up c., put-up job, frame-up; false information, perjured testimony, false evidence; counterfeit evidence, plant; illegal prosecution; lie, libel, slander, scandal, stigma 926 *calumny*.

accuser, complainant, plaintiff, pursuer, petitioner, appellant, libellant, litigant; challenger, denouncer, charger; grass, supergrass, nark, copper's n. 524 *informer*; common informer, delator, relator; impeacher, indicter, prosecutor, public p., procurator fiscal; libeller, slanderer, calumniator, stigmatizer; hostile witness 881 *enemy*; the finger of suspicion.

accused person, the accused, prisoner, prisoner at the bar; defendant, respondent, corespondent; culprit; suspect, victim of suspicion, marked man; slandered person, libellee, victim.

Vb. *accuse*, challenge 711 *defy*; taunt; point a finger at, finger, cast the first stone, throw in one's teeth, reproach 924 *reprove*; stigmatize, brand, pillory, cast a slur on, cast aspersions, defame; impute, charge with, saddle w., tax w., hold against, lay to one's charge, lay at one's door, hold responsible, make r.; pick on, fix on, hold to blame, put the blame on, pin on, stick on, bring home to 924 *blame*; point at, expose, show up, name, name names 526 *divulge*; denounce, inform against, tell, tell on, clype, blab, squeal, sing, rat on, split on, turn Queen's evidence 524 *inform*; involve, implicate, incriminate; countercharge, rebut the charge, turn the tables upon 479 *confute*; make one a scapegoat, shift the blame; admit the charge, plead guilty 526 *confess*; implicate oneself, lay oneself open.

indict, impeach, arraign, inform against, lodge a complaint, lay information against; complain, charge, bring a charge, file charges, swear an indictment 959 *litigate*; book, cite, summon, serve with a writ, prosecute, sue; bring an action, bring a suit, bring a case; haul up, send before the beak, have up, put on trial, put in the dock; throw the book at 712 *attack*; charge falsely, lie against 541 *be false*; frame, trump up a charge, cook the evidence, use false e., fake the e., plant the e. 541 *fake*.

Adv. *accusingly*, censoriously.

929 Probity – N. *probity*, rectitude, uprightness, goodness, sanctity 933 *virtue*; stainlessness 950 *purity*; good character, moral fibre, honesty, soundness, incorruptibility, integrity; high character, nobleness, nobility; honourableness, decent feelings, finer f., tender conscience; honour, personal h., sense of h., principles, high p.; conscientiousness 768 *observance*; scrupulousness, scrupulosity, punctiliousness, meticulousness 457 *carefulness*; ingenuousness, singleheartedness; trustworthiness, reliability, sense of responsibility; truthfulness 540 *veracity*; candour, plain-speaking 573 *plainness*; sincerity, good faith 494 *truth*; fidelity, faith, troth, faithfulness, trustiness, constancy 739 *loyalty*; clean hands, clear conscience 935 *innocence*; impartiality, fairness, sportsmanship 913 *justice*; respectability 866 *repute*; gentlemanliness, ladylikeness, chivalry; principle, point of honour, punctilio, code, code of honour, bushido 913 *right*; court of justice, court of honour, field of h.

Adj. *honourable*, upright, erect, of integrity, of honour 933 *virtuous*; correct, strict; law-abiding, honest, on the level; principled, high-p., above-board, on the up-and-up; scrupulous, conscientious, soul-searching; incorruptible, not to be bought off; incorrupt, immaculate 935 *innocent*; stainless, unstained, untarnished, unsullied 648 *clean*; noble, high-minded, pure-m. 950 *pure*; ingenuous, unworldly 699 *artless*; good, straight, straight as a die, square, on the square, one hundred per cent; fair, fair-

dealing, equitable, impartial 913 *just*; sporting, sportsmanlike, playing the game; gentlemanly, chivalrous, knightly, jealous of one's honour; careful of one's reputation, respectable 866 *reputable*; saintly 979 *pious*.

trustworthy, creditworthy, reliable, dependable, tried, tested, proven; trusty, true-hearted, true-blue, true to the core, sure, staunch, single-hearted, constant, unchanging, faithful, loyal 739 *obedient*; responsible, duteous, dutiful 768 *observant*; conscientious, religious, scrupulous, meticulous, punctilious 457 *careful*; candid, frank, open, open and above-board, open-hearted, transparent, ingenuous, without guile, guileless 494 *true*; straightforward, truthful, truthspeaking, as good as one's word 540 *veracious*; unperjured, unperfidious, untreacherous.

930 Improbity – N. *improbity,* dishonesty; lack of principle; laxity; unconscientiousness 456 *inattention*; unscrupulousness, opportunism; insincerity, disingenuousness, unstraightforwardness, untrustworthiness, unreliability, undependability, untruthfulness 541 *falsehood*; unfairness, partiality, bias 914 *injustice*; shuffling, slipperiness, artfulness; suspiciousness, shadiness, deviousness, crookedness; corruption, corruptibility, venality, bribability, graft, palm-greasing, nepotism, simony, baseness, shabbiness, abjectness, debasement, shamefulness, disgrace, dishonour, shame 867 *disrepute*; worthlessness, good-for-nothingness, villainousness, villainy, knavery, roguery, rascality, spivvery, skulduggery, racketeering, black market, under-the-counter dealings; criminality, crime, complicity, aiding and abetting 954 *lawbreaking*; turpitude, moral t. 934 *wickedness*.

perfidy, perfidiousness, faithlessness, unfaithfulness, infidelity, unfaith 543 *untruth*; bad faith, divided allegiance, wavering loyalty, sitting on the fence, disloyalty 738 *disobedience*; running with the hare and hunting with the hounds, double-dealing, double-crossing, Judas kiss 541 *duplicity*; volte face, U-turn 603 *change of mind*; defection, desertion 918 *undutifulness*; betrayal, treachery, stab in the back, sell-out; treason, high t. 738 *sedition*; fifth column, Trojan horse; breach of faith, broken word, broken promise, breach of p., cry of treason, dirty trick, stab in the back; not playing the game, foul, hitting below the belt 914 *wrong*; professional foul 623 *contrivance*; trick, shuffle, chicanery 542 *trickery*; sharp practice, heads I win tails you lose; dirty work, job, deal, racket; under-the-counter dealing, fiddle, wangle, manipulation, gerrymandering, hanky-panky, monkey business; tax evasion 620 *avoidance*; malversation 788 *peculation*; crime, felony 954 *lawbreaking*.

Adj. *dishonest,* not on the level 914 *wrong*; unprincipled, unscrupulous; shameless, dead to honour, lost to shame; unethical, immoral 934 *wicked*; untrustworthy, unreliable, undependable, not to be trusted; disingenuous, untruthful 543 *untrue*; two-faced, insincere 541 *hypocritical*; creeping, crawling; artful, dodging, opportunist, slippery, foxy 698 *cunning*; shifty, shuffling, prevaricating 518 *equivocal*; designing, scheming; sneaking, underhand 523 *latent*; up to something, on the fiddle, wangling; not straight, bent, crooked, devious, tortuous, winding; insidious, dark, sinister; shady, fishy, suspicious, doubtful, questionable; fraudulent 542 *spurious*; illicit 954 *illegal*; foul 645 *bad*; unclean 649 *dirty*; mean, shabby, dishonourable, infamous 867 *disreputable*; derogatory, unworthy, undignified; inglorious, ignominious 867 *degrading*; ignoble, unchivalrous, ungentlemanly; unsporting, unsportsmanlike, unfair.

venal, corruptible, bribable, mercenary; palm-greasing, corrupt, grafting, nepotistic.

perfidious, treacherous, unfaithful, inconstant, faithless 541 *false*; double-dealing, double-crossing; disloyal; false-hearted, traitorous, treasonous, untrue

738 *disobedient*; plotting, scheming, intriguing; Machiavellian; cheating; fraudulent 542 *spurious*.

Vb. *be dishonest,* have no morals, yield to temptation, be lost to shame; lack honesty, live by one's wits, lead a life of crime 954 *be illegal*; fiddle, finagle, wangle, gerrymander, racketeer; defraud; cheat, swindle 542 *deceive*; betray, play false, do the dirty on, stab in the back; run with the hare and hunt with the hounds, double-cross 541 *dissemble*; fawn 925 *flatter*; break faith, break one's word, go back on one's promises, tell lies 541 *be false*; shuffle, dodge, prevaricate 518 *be equivocal*; sell out, sell down the river 603 *apostatize*; sink into crime, sell one's honour 867 *lose repute*; smack of dishonesty, smell fishy.

931 Disinterestedness – N. *disinterestedness,* impartiality, lack of bias 913 *justice*; selflessness, self-effacement 872 *humility*; self-sacrifice, martyrdom; loftiness of purpose, idealism; magnanimity; quixotry; purity of motive, labour of love; altruism, thought for others; charity 887 *love*.

Adj. *disinterested,* impartial, without self-interest, without bias 913 *just*; incorruptible, uncorrupted; unselfish, selfless, self-sacrificing; altruistic, philanthropic; undesigning; sacrificial, unmercenary, for love, non-profitmaking; idealistic, quixotic, lofty, elevated; magnanimous.

Vb. *be disinterested,* - unselfish etc. adj.; sacrifice, sacrifice oneself; think of others, put oneself last, take a back seat 872 *be humble*; rise above petty considerations; have no axe to grind, have nothing to gain, have no ulterior motive, do for its own sake.

932 Selfishness – N. *selfishness,* self-love, self-admiration, narcissism, self-worship, self-praise 873 *vanity*; self-pity, self-indulgence, ego trip 943 *intemperance*; egocentricity; egoism, egotism;

self-preservation, everyone for themselves; axe to grind, personal considerations, personal motives, private ends, personal advantage; self-seeking, self-aggrandizement, self-interest, looking after number one; no thought for others, 'I'm all right, Jack'; charity that begins at home, cupboard love; meanness 816 *parsimony*; greed, acquisitiveness 816 *avarice*; possessiveness 911 *jealousy*; 'heads I win tails you lose' 914 *injustice*; selfish ambition; power politics.

egotist, egoist, self-centred person, narcissist 873 *vain person*; self-seeker; go-getter, adventurer; monopolist, dog in the manger, hog, road h.; opportunist.

Adj. *selfish,* egocentric, self-centred, wrapped up in oneself; egoistic, egotistic, egotistical; personal, concerned with number one; self-interested, self-seeking; self-indulgent 943 *intemperate*; narcissistic 873 *vain*; not altruistic; uncharitable, mean, acquisitive, mercenary 816 *avaricious*; covetous 912 *envious*; hogging, monopolistic 859 *greedy*; possessive, dog-in-the-manger; designing, axe-grinding; go-getting, on the make, on the gravy train, opportunist; materialistic.

Vb. *be selfish,* - egoistic etc. adj.; put oneself first, think only of oneself, take care of number one; indulge oneself, spoil o.; have only oneself to please; feather one's nest, look out for oneself, have an eye to the main chance, know on which side one's bread is buttered; keep for oneself, hog, monopolize, be a dog in the manger 778 *retain*; have personal motives, have an axe to grind; pursue one's interests, advance one's own i., sacrifice the interests of others.

933 Virtue – N. *virtue,* virtuousness; goodness; saintliness, holiness, spirituality, odour of sanctity 979 *sanctity*; righteousness 913 *justice*; uprightness, rectitude, moral r., character, integrity, principles, high principle, honour 929 *probity*; guiltlessness 935 *innocence*; morality, ethics 917 *morals*; temperance, chastity 950 *purity*; straight and narrow path, virtuous conduct, christian c.,

good behaviour, well-spent life, duty done; clear conscience.

virtues, cardinal v., moral v.; theological virtues, faith, hope, charity; natural virtues, prudence, justice, temperance, fortitude; qualities, saving grace; merits; perfections 646 *perfection*; nobleness, magnanimity.

Adj. *virtuous,* moral 917 *ethical*; good, good as gold 644 *excellent*; stainless 950 *pure*; guiltless 935 *innocent*; irreproachable, above reproach, impeccable, above temptation 646 *perfect*; saint-like, seraphic, angelic, saintly, holy 979 *sanctified*; high-principled, right-minded, on the side of the angels 913 *right*; righteous 913 *just*; upright, honest 929 *honourable*; dutiful 739 *obedient*; generous, magnanimous, philanthropic 897 *benevolent*; sober 942 *temperate*; chaste, virginal; proper, exemplary; meritorious, worthy, praiseworthy, commendable 923 *approved*.

Vb. *be virtuous,* - good etc. adj.; have all the virtues, be a shining light 644 *be good*; behave, be on one's good *or* best behaviour; resist temptation 942 *be temperate*; have a soul above; keep to the straight and narrow path, follow one's conscience, fight the good fight; discharge one's obligations 917 *do one's duty*; go straight; hear no evil, see no evil, speak no evil; set a good example, be a shining e., shame the devil 644 *do good*.

934 Wickedness – **N.** *wickedness,* principle of evil 645 *badness*; Devil, cloven hoof 969 *Satan*; fallen nature, Old Adam; iniquity, sinfulness, sin 914 *wrong*; loss of innocence 936 *guilt*; ungodliness 980 *impiety*; amorality 860 *indifference*; hardness of heart 898 *malevolence*; naughtiness, bad behaviour 738 *disobedience*; immorality, turpitude, moral t.; loose morals, profligacy 951 *impurity*; degeneracy, degradation 655 *deterioration*; vice, corruption, depravity 645 *badness*; heinousness, flagrancy; bad character, viciousness, unworthiness, baseness, vileness; villainy; dishonesty 930 *improbity*; crime, criminality

954 *lawbreaking*; devilry, hellishness 898 *inhumanity*; devil worship 982 *idolatry*; scandal, abomination, enormity, infamy 867 *disrepute*; infamous conduct, misbehaviour, delinquency, wrongdoing, evil-doing, transgression, wicked ways, career of crime; primrose path, slippery slope; low life, criminal world, underworld, demi-monde; den of vice, sink of iniquity 649 *sink*.

vice, fault, demerit, unworthiness; human weakness, moral w., infirmity, frailty, human f., foible 163 *weakness*; imperfection, shortcoming, defect, deficiency, limitation, failing, flaw, fatal f., weak point, weakness of the flesh; transgression, trespass, injury, outrage, enormity 914 *wrong*; sin, besetting s., deadly s.; seven deadly sins, pride, covetousness, lust, anger, gluttony, envy, sloth; venial sin, small fault, slight transgression, peccadillo, scrape; impropriety, indecorum 847 *bad taste*; offence 936 *guilty act*; crime, felony, deadly crime, capital c., hanging matter 954 *illegality*.

Adj. *wicked,* unvirtuous, immoral, amoral, amoralistic 860 *indifferent*; unprincipled, unscrupulous 930 *dishonest*; callous; ungodly, irreligious, profane 980 *impious*; iniquitous 914 *unjust*; evil 645 *bad*; evil-minded, black-hearted 898 *malevolent*; evil-doing; misbehaving, bad, naughty 738 *disobedient*; erring, sinning, transgressing, sinful 936 *guilty*; unworthy; not in a state of grace, reprobate; unredeemed, irredeemable; accursed, godforsaken; hellish, infernal, devilish, fiendish, Mephistophelian, satanic 969 *diabolic*.

vicious, steeped in vice, sunk in iniquity; good-for-nothing, ne'er-do-well; past praying for; unworthy, graceless; villainous, miscreant; improper, indecent 847 *vulgar*; immoral; unvirtuous, intemperate 951 *unchaste*; profligate, dissolute, abandoned; corrupt, debauched, depraved, perverted, degenerate, sick, rotten, rotten to the core; brutalized, brutal 898 *cruel*.

frail, infirm, feeble 163 *weak*; having one's foibles, having a touch of human

frailty, human, only h.; easily tempted 661 *vulnerable*; not above temptation, not perfect, fallen 647 *imperfect*; slipping, sliding, recidivous.

heinous, grave, serious, deadly; abysmal, hellish, infernal; sinful, immoral, wicked 914 *wrong*; criminal, nefarious, felonious 954 *lawbreaking*; monstrous, flagrant, scandalous, shocking, outrageous, obscene; gross, foul, rank; base, vile, abominable, accursed; despicable 645 *bad*; blameworthy, culpable; reprehensible, indefensible, unjustifiable 916 *unwarranted*; atrocious, brutal 898 *cruel*; unforgivable, unpardonable, inexcusable.

Vb. *be wicked,* - vicious, - sinful etc. adj.; not be in a state of grace; fall from grace, spoil one's record, blot one's copybook, lapse, relapse, backslide; fall into evil ways, go to the bad *or* to the dogs 655 *deteriorate*; do wrong, transgress, misbehave, carry on, be naughty, sow one's wild oats, kick over the traces; trespass, offend, sin, commit s.; leave *or* stray from the straight and narrow, deviate from the paths of virtue, err, stray, slip, trip, stumble, fall.

make wicked, corrupt, deform one's character, brutalize 655 *pervert*; mislead, lead astray, seduce 612 *tempt*; set a bad example, dehumanize.

935 Innocence – **N.** *innocence,* guiltlessness, clean hands; clear conscience, irreproachability; nothing to confess; blamelessness, freedom from blame, every excuse; declared innocence 960 *acquittal*; inexperience, unworldliness 699 *artlessness*; playfulness, harmlessness, inoffensiveness; freedom from sin, unfallen state, saintliness, purity of heart, state of grace 933 *virtue*; undefilement 950 *purity*; incorruptibility 929 *probity*; impeccability 646 *perfection*; days of innocence, golden age 824 *happiness.*

innocent, Holy Innocents, babe, newborn babe, babe unborn, babes and sucklings; child, ingénue; lamb, dove; angel,

pure soul; milksop, goody-goody; one in the right, innocent party, injured p.

Adj. *innocent,* pure, unspotted, stainless, unblemished, spotless, immaculate 648 *clean*; uncorrupted, undefiled; unfallen, free from sin, unerring, impeccable 646 *perfect*; green, inexperienced, callow, naive, unversed in crime 491 *ignorant*; unworldly, guileless 699 *artless*; innocuous, harmless, inoffensive, playful, gentle, lamb-like, dove-like, child-like, angelic, saintly; wide-eyed, looking as if butter would not melt in one's mouth; innocent as a lamb *or* a dove, innocent as a babe unborn, innocent as a child; Arcadian.

guiltless, free from guilt, not responsible, not guilty 960 *acquitted*; more sinned against than sinning; falsely accused, wrongly a., misunderstood; clean-handed, bloodless; blameless, faultless, unblameworthy, not culpable; irreproachable, above reproach, above suspicion; unobjectionable, unexceptionable, unimpeachable; pardonable, forgivable, excusable, venial.

Vb. *be innocent,* know no wrong; live in a state of grace, not fall from g. 933 *be virtuous*; have every excuse, have no need to blush, have clean hands, have a clear conscience, have nothing to be ashamed of, have nothing to confess; know no better.

936 Guilt – **N.** *guilt,* guiltiness, redhandedness; culpability; criminality, delinquency 954 *illegality*; sinfulness, original sin 934 *wickedness*; involvement, complicity, aiding and abetting; liability, one's fault; burden of guilt 702 *encumbrance*; blame, censure 924 *reproach*; guilt complex 503 *eccentricity*; guilty feelings, guilty conscience, bad c.; guilty behaviour, suspicious conduct, blush, stammer, embarrassment; confession 526 *disclosure*; twinge of conscience, remorse, shame 939 *penitence.*

guilty act, sin, deadly s., venial s. 934 *vice*; misdeed, wicked deed, misdoing, sinning, transgression, trespass, offence,

crime 954 *illegality*; misdemeanour, felony; misconduct, misbehaviour, malpractice; unprofessional conduct; indiscretion, impropriety, peccadillo; naughtiness, scrape; lapse, slip, faux pas, blunder 495 *mistake*; omission, sin of o. 458 *negligence*; fault, failure, dereliction of duty 918 *undutifulness*; injustice, injury 914 *wrong*; enormity, atrocity, outrage 898 *cruel act*.

Adj. *guilty,* found g., convicted 961 *condemned*; suspected, blamed, censured 924 *disapproved*; responsible 180 *liable*; in the wrong, at fault, to blame, culpable, chargeable; reprehensible, censurable 924 *blameworthy*; deadly 934 *heinous*; trespassing, transgressing, sinful 934 *wicked*; criminal 954 *illegal*; redhanded, caught in the act, flagrante delicto, caught with one's pants *or* trousers down; caught with one's hand in the till; hangdog, sheepish, shamefaced, blushing, ashamed.

Vb. *be guilty,* be at fault, be in the wrong, be to blame; have crimes to answer for, have blood on one's hands; be caught in the act, be caught red-handed, be caught with one's hand in the till; have nothing to say for oneself, plead guilty 526 *confess*; have no excuse, stand condemned; trespass, transgress, sin 934 *be wicked*.

937 Good person– N. *good person,* sterling character; pillar of society, model of virtue, salt of the earth, shining light 646 *paragon*; Christian, true C.; saint 979 *pietist*; angel 935 *innocent*; heart of gold; good neighbour, Good Samaritan 903 *benefactor*; one of the best, one in a million, the tops 890 *favourite*; hero, heroine 855 *brave person*; goody, good guy, good sort, good old boy, stout fellow, brick, trump, sport.

938 Bad person – N. *bad person,* no saint, sinner, hardened s., limb of Satan, Antichrist 904 *evildoer*; fallen angel, lost sheep, lost soul; reprobate, scapegrace, good-for-nothing, ne'er-do-well, black sheep, the despair of; scallywag, scamp;

rake, roué, profligate 952 *libertine*; wanton, hussy 952 *loose woman*; wastrel, waster, prodigal son 815 *prodigal*; scum; nasty type, ugly customer, undesirable, bad 'un, wrong 'un, thug, bully, boot boy, bovver boy, hitman, terrorist, roughneck 904 *ruffian*; bad lot, bad egg, bad hat, bad character, bad guy, baddy, villain; rotten apple; bad influence, bad example; bad child, naughty c., terror, holy t., enfant terrible, monkey, little devil 663 *troublemaker*; knave, wretch, rascal, 869 *low fellow*; rogue, criminal 904 *offender*; thief, pirate, freebooter 789 *robber*; villain, blackguard, scoundrel, miscreant; cheat, liar, crook; impostor, twister, conman 545 *trickster*; sneak, grass, supergrass, squealer, canary, rat 524 *informer*; renegade, recreant 603 *tergiversator*; betrayer, traitor, Quisling, Judas.

cad, utter cad, nasty bit of work, scoundrel, blackguard; rotter, out-and-out r., blighter, bastard, bounder, jerk, heel, slob, scab, son of a bitch; stinker, skunk, dirty dog, filthy beast; pervert, degenerate; swine, rat, worm; louse, insect, vermin; pig, beast, cat, bitch.

monster, unspeakable villain; brute, savage, sadist; ogre 735 *tyrant*; fiend, demon, ghoul 969 *devil*; hellhound, fury; devil incarnate, ape-man, King Kong, Frankenstein's monster, bogy.

939 Penitence – N. *penitence,* repentance, contrition, attrition, compunction, remorse, self-reproach 830 *regret*; confession 988 *Christian rite*; weight on one's mind, voice of conscience, uneasy c., guilty c., bad c., twinge of c. 936 *guilt*; deathbed repentance, sackcloth and ashes, stool of repentance 941 *penance*; apology 941 *atonement*.

penitent, confessor; returned prodigal, a sadder and a wiser man; reformed character.

Adj. *repentant,* contrite, remorseful, regretful, sorry, apologetic 830 *regretting*; ashamed; weeping 836 *lamenting*; conscience-stricken, plagued by c.; self-condemned; confessing; penitent, doing penance 941 *atoning*; chastened,

sobered; reclaimed, reformed, converted, born again.

Vb. *be penitent,* repent, show compunction, feel remorse, feel shame, blush for s., feel sorry, say one is s., express regrets, apologize; reproach oneself, blame o.; go to confession 526 *confess*; do penance, repent in sackcloth and ashes 941 *atone*; bewail one's sins; beat one's breast, prostrate oneself; eat humble pie 721 *knuckle under*; rue, have regrets, wish undone 830 *regret*; have second thoughts, think better of; learn one's lesson, find out from bitter experience 536 *learn*; reform, be reformed, be a reformed character, be reclaimed, turn over a new leaf 654 *get better*; see the light, see the error of one's ways, be converted, return to the straight and narrow 147 *be turned to*.

940 Impenitence – **N.** *impenitence,* lack of contrition; refusal to recant, obduracy, stubbornness 602 *obstinacy*; hardness of heart 326 *hardness*; no apologies, no regrets, no remorse, no compunction 906 *pitilessness*; hardened sinner, despair of 938 *bad person*.

Adj. *impenitent,* unregretting; obdurate, inveterate, stubborn 602 *obstinate*; unrepentant; without regrets; unrelenting, relentless; without compunction, without remorse, remorseless, heartless 898 *cruel*; hard, hardened; conscienceless, unashamed, unblushing, brazen; incorrigible, irreclaimable, irredeemable, hopeless, despaired of, lost 934 *wicked*; unshriven; unreformed, unreconciled; unconverted.

Vb. *be impenitent,* make no excuses, offer no apologies, have no regrets, not wish things otherwise, would do it again; not see the light, not see the error of one's ways, refuse to recant 602 *be obstinate*; make no confession; stay unreconciled, want no forgiveness; feel no compunction, feel no remorse, harden one's heart, steel one's h. 906 *be pitiless*.

941 Atonement – **N.** *atonement,* making amends, amends, apology, satisfaction;

reparation, compensation, indemnity, indemnification, blood money, conscience money 787 *restitution*; repayment, quits.

propitiation, expiation, satisfaction, reconciliation, conciliation 719 *pacification*; reclamation, redemption; sacrifice, offering, burnt o., peace o. 981 *oblation*; scapegoat, whipping boy 150 *substitute*.

penance, shrift, confession, acknowledgment 939 *penitence*; sacrament of penance, fasting, flagellation 945 *asceticism*; purgation; purgatory; penitent form, stool of repentance, cutty stool, corner 964 *pillory*; sackcloth and ashes, breast-beating 836 *lamentation*.

Adj. *atoning,* making amends 939 *repentant*; reparatory, compensatory, indemnificatory; conciliatory, apologetic; expiatory, purgatorial; sacrificial; penitential, penitentiary, doing penance 963 *punitive*.

Vb. *atone,* salve one's conscience, make amends, make reparation, indemnify, compensate, pay compensation, make it up to; apologize, make apologies, offer one's a.; propitiate, conciliate 719 *pacify*; give satisfaction, offer s. 787 *restitute*; make up for, make *or* put matters right; sacrifice to, offer sacrifice; expiate, pay the penalty, pay the forfeit, pay the cost; become the whipping boy, make oneself the scapegoat 931 *be disinterested*.

do penance, undergo p.; pray, fast, flagellate oneself, scourge o.; suffer purgatory; put on sackcloth and ashes, don a hair-shirt, rend one's garments, stand in the corner, sit on the stool of repentance; take one's punishment, swallow one's medicine 963 *be punished*; salve one's conscience, go to confession 526 *confess*.

942 Temperance – **N.** *temperance,* temperateness, nothing in excess 177 *moderation*; self-denial 931 *disinterestedness*; self-restraint, self-control, self-discipline, keeping a stiff upper lip, stoicism 747 *restraint*; continence, chastity 950 *purity*; soberness 948 *sobriety*; forbearance 620 *avoidance*; renunciation 621

relinquishment; abstemiousness, abstinence, abstention, total abstinence, teetotalism; prohibition, prohibitionism 747 *restriction*; vegetarianism, veganism; dieting 946 *fasting*; frugality 814 *economy*; plain living, simple life, self-sufficiency, getting away from it all; frugal diet 945 *asceticism*.

abstainer, total a., teetotaller 948 *sober person*; prohibitionist; nonsmoker; vegetarian, vegan, demi-veg; dropout, dieter, faster; Spartan 945 *ascetic*.

Adj. *temperate,* not excessive, within bounds, within reasonable limits; tempered 177 *moderate*; plain, Spartan, sparing 814 *economical*; frugal 816 *parsimonious*; forbearing, abstemious, abstinent; dry, teetotal 948 *sober*; vegan, vegetarian, not self-indulgent, self-controlled, self-disciplined, continent 747 *restrained*; chaste 950 *pure*; self-denying 945 *ascetic*.

Vb. *be temperate,* - moderate etc. adj.; moderate, temper, keep within bounds, avoid excess, know when one has had enough, know when to stop; keep sober 948 *be sober*; forbear, refrain, abstain 620 *avoid*; control oneself, contain o. 747 *restrain*; deny oneself 945 *be ascetic*; take the pledge, go on the wagon; give up, swear off; ration oneself, restrict o., tighten one's belt, draw in one's b. 946 *starve*; diet, go on a d. 206 *make thin*.

943 Intemperance – **N.** *intemperance,* immoderation, abandon; excess, excessiveness, luxury 637 *redundance*; too much 637 *superfluity*; wastefulness, extravagance, profligacy, waste 815 *prodigality*; indiscipline, incontinence 734 *laxity*; indulgence, self-i., overindulgence; addiction, bad habit 610 *habit*; drug habit 949 *drug-taking*; high living, dissipation, licentiousness, debauchery 944 *sensualism*; overeating 947 *gluttony*; intoxication.

Adj. *intemperate,* immoderate, excessive 637 *redundant*; unlimited 635 *plentiful*; wasteful, extravagant, profligate, spendthrift 815 *prodigal*; luxurious 637

superfluous; hedonistic, indulgent, self-i., overindulgent, denying oneself nothing; unrestrained, uncontrolled, lacking self-control, undisciplined; incontinent 951 *unchaste*.

Vb. *be intemperate,* - immoderate etc. adj.; roll in, luxuriate, wallow; lack self-control, want discipline, lose control 734 *be lax*; deny oneself nothing, indulge oneself, give oneself up to; kick over the traces, have one's fling, sow one's wild oats 815 *be prodigal*; run to excess, run riot, exceed 306 *overstep*; observe no limits, go to any lengths, stick at nothing, not know when to stop, overindulge, burn the candle at both ends 634 *waste*; live it up, go on a spree, go on a binge, go on a bender 837 *revel*; drink like a fish, drink to excess, be a heavy drinker 949 *get drunk*; eat to excess, gorge, overeat, binge, make oneself sick 947 *gluttonize*; be incontinent, grow dissipated 951 *be impure*.

944 Sensualism – **N.** *sensualism,* earthiness, materialism 319 *materiality*; sensuality, carnality, sexuality, the flesh; grossness, beastliness, bestiality, wallowing; craze for excitement 822 *excitability*; love of pleasure, search for p., hedonism, epicurism, epicureanism 376 *pleasure*; voluptuousness, voluptuosity, softness, luxuriousness, dolce vita; luxury, lap of l. 637 *superfluity*; full life, life of pleasure, high living, fast l., wine, women and song 824 *enjoyment*; dissipation, abandon 943 *intemperance*; licentiousness, dissoluteness, debauchery 951 *impurity*; indulgence, self-i., overindulgence, greediness 947 *gluttony*; eating and drinking 301 *feasting*; bingeing, orgy, Bacchanalia 837 *revel*.

sensualist, pig, swine, hog, wallower; hedonist, playboy *or* -girl, pleasure-lover, thrill-seeker; luxury-lover, epicurean, bon vivant, bon viveur; epicure, gourmet, gourmand 947 *glutton*; hard drinker 949 *drunkard*; loose liver, profligate, rake 952 *libertine*; drug addict 949 *drug-taking*; degenerate, decadent.

Adj. *sensual,* earthy, gross, unspiritual 319 *material*; fleshly, carnal, bodily; sexual, venereal 887 *erotic*; bestial, beastly, brutish, swinish, hoggish, wallowing; pleasure-giving 826 *pleasurable*; voluptuous, pleasure-loving, thrill-seeking, living for kicks; hedonistic, epicurean, luxury-loving, luxurious; pampered, indulged, spoilt, self-i., overindulged, featherbedded; overfed 947 *gluttonous*; high-living, fast-l., incontinent 943 *intemperate*; licentious, dissipated, debauched 951 *impure*; riotous, orgiastic, bingeing, Bacchanalian 949 *drunken.*

Vb. *be sensual,* - voluptuous etc. adj.; live for pleasure, wallow in luxury, live off the fat of the land 730 *prosper*; indulge oneself, pamper o., spoil o., do oneself proud; run riot, live in the fast lane, burn the candle at both ends 943 *be intemperate.*

945 Asceticism – N. *asceticism,* austerity, mortification, flagellation 941 *penance*; ascetic practice, yoga; anchoritism 883 *seclusion*; holy poverty 801 *poverty*; plain living, simple fare, Spartan fare 946 *fasting*; fast day 946 *fast*; self-denial 942 *temperance*; frugality 814 *economy*; Puritanism, sackcloth, hair shirt.

ascetic, yogi, fakir, dervish, fire-walker; hermit, anchorite, recluse 883 *solitary*; flagellant 939 *penitent*; faster 942 *abstainer*; Puritan, Plymouth Brethren.

Adj. *ascetic,* yogic, self-mortifying, fasting, flagellating; hermit-like, anchoretic; puritanical; austere, rigorous 735 *severe*; Spartan.

Vb. *be ascetic,* live like a Spartan, live the simple life; fast 946 *starve*; live like a hermit, wear a hair shirt, put on sackcloth; lie on nails, walk through fire.

946 Fasting – N. *fasting,* abstinence from food; no appetite, anorexia, a. nervosa 651 *ill health*; cutting down 301 *dieting*; strict fast, hunger strike; lenten fare, bread and water, meagre diet, starvation d.; iron rations, short commons 636 *scarcity*; no food, starvation 859 *hunger*.

fast, fast day, Good Friday, Lent, Ramadan; day of abstinence; hunger strike 145 *strike*.

Adj. *fasting,* not eating, off one's food; abstinent 942 *temperate*; on hunger strike; without food, unfed, empty, with an empty stomach, supperless; poorly fed, half-starved 636 *underfed*; starved, starving, famished, famishing, ravenous, wasting away 206 *lean*; wanting food 859 *hungry*.

Vb. *starve,* famish 859 *be hungry*; waste with hunger, be a bag of bones; have no food, have nothing to eat, live on water, live on air 801 *be poor*; fast, go without food, abstain from f., eat no meat; keep Lent, keep Ramadan; give up eating, refuse one's food, go on hunger strike; eat less, diet, go on a d., go on a crash d., reduce, take off weight 37 *abate*; tighten one's belt, go on short commons, live on iron rations; eat sparingly, make a little go a long way, control one's appetite 942 *be temperate*; keep a poor table 816 *be parsimonious*.

947 Gluttony – N. *gluttony,* greediness, greed, insatiability, voracity, voraciousness, wolfishness, hoggishness, piggishness; insatiable appetite 859 *hunger*; good living, high l., indulgence, overeating, overfeeding 943 *intemperance*; guzzling, gorging, bingeing, gormandizing, gluttonizing, epicureanism, epicurism, foodism, pleasures of the table 301 *gastronomy*; bust, binge, blowout, masses of food, groaning table 301 *feasting*.

glutton, glutton for food, guzzler, gormandizer, bolter, gorger, crammer, stuffer, binger; locust, wolf, vulture, cormorant, pig, hog; trencherman *or* -woman, good eater, hearty e. 301 *eater*; greedy-guts, greedy pig; gourmand, gastronome, gourmet, epicure, bon vivant, bon viveur.

Adj. *gluttonous,* greedy; devouring, voracious, wolfish; omnivorous 464 *indiscriminating*; insatiable, never full 859 *hungry*; eating one's fill 301 *feeding*; guzzling, gorging, bingeing, stuffing, cramming, licking one's lips, licking

one's chops, drooling, watering at the mouth; gastronomic, epicurean.

Vb. *gluttonize,* guzzle, bolt, wolf, gobble, gobble up, devour, gulp down; fill oneself, gorge, cram, stuff, binge; overeat 301 *eat*; eat one's head off, eat out of house and home; have a good appetite, be a good trencherman *or* -woman; eat like a trooper, eat like a horse, eat like a pig, have eyes bigger than one's stomach; make oneself sick; tickle one's palate; lick one's lips, lick one's chops, water at the mouth, drool at the sight of food; keep a good table; like one's food, live to eat, not eat to live, live only for eating.

948 Sobriety – N. *sobriety,* soberness 942 *temperance*; teetotalism; clear head, unfuddled brain, no hangover; dry area.

sober person, moderate drinker; teetotaller, total abstainer 942 *abstainer*; temperance society, Alcoholics Anonymous; prohibitionist.

Adj. *sober,* abstinent, abstemious; off drink, drying out, on the wagon; teetotal, strictly TT, prohibitionist, dry; clearheaded, with a clear head, sober as a judge, stone-cold sober; sobered up, without a hangover; dried out, off the bottle.

Vb. *be sober,* - abstemious, etc. adj.; not drink, never touch drink, drink moderately 942 *be temperate*; give up drinking, dry out, come off (drugs), go on the wagon, give up alcohol, become teetotal, sign the pledge; go dry; hold one's liquor, keep a clear head, be sober as a judge; sober up, clear one's head, sleep it off.

949 Drunkenness. Drug-taking – N. *drunkenness,* excessive drinking 943 *intemperance*; insobriety; weakness for liquor, fondness for the bottle; Dutch courage 855 *courage*; intoxication, inebriation; thick speech, slurred s. 580 *speech defect*; tipsiness, wooziness, staggering 317 *oscillation*; getting drunk, one for the road, one over the eight, drop too much, hard drinking; libations; hair of the dog that bit one; booze, liquor 301 *alcoholic drink, wine*; drinking bout, jag,

lush, blind, binge, spree, bender, pub-crawl.

crapulence, crapulousness; morning after the night before, hangover, thick head, sick headache.

alcoholism, alcoholic addiction, dipsomania; delirium tremens, dt's, the horrors, heebiejeebies, jimjams, pink elephants.

drug-taking, smoking, snorting, sniffing, glue-s., hitting up, shooting up, injecting, main-lining; pill-popping, chasing the dragon; hard drug, soft d.; joint, reefer, spliff, roach; shot, fix; narcotic, dope; designer drug; nicotine 388 *tobacco*; cannabis, marijuana, ganja, hemp, hashish, hash, bhang, kef, pot, grass, Acapulco gold, sinsemilla; cocaine, coke, snow, crack, rock, free-base; heroin, horse, junk, smack, scag; methadone; downers, barbiturates, barbs, morphia, morphine, opium 658 *drug*; stimulant, pep pill, amphetamine, speed, purple hearts, dexies, uppers 821 *excitant*; intoxicant, hallucinogen, LSD, acid, phencyclidine, PCP, angel dust, STP, mescalin, peyote, magic mushroom; drug addiction, drug abuse, solvent a., drug dependence, habit 943 *intemperance*; acid trip, bad t., freak-out; drying out, withdrawal symptoms, cold turkey; drug addict, dope fiend, freak; head, acidhead, junkie, mainliner, acid-scorer, drug-s.; dope-peddler, drug-pusher, pusher.

drunkard, drunk, sot, lush; slave to drink, wino, alcoholic, dipsomaniac, dipso; drinker, social d., hard d., secret d.; tippler, toper, boozer, swiller, old soak; tosspot, barfly; pub-crawler.

Adj. *drunk,* inebriated, intoxicated, under the influence, having had a drop too much; in one's cups, in liquor, the worse for l.; half-seas over, three sheets in the wind, one over the eight; boozed up, ginned up, liquored up, lit up, flushed, merry, happy, high; full, fou, tanked up, bevvied up; roaring drunk, drunk and disorderly 61 *disorderly*.

tipsy, tiddly, squiffy, tight, half-cut, pissed, Brahms and Liszt; well-oiled,

pickled, canned, bottled, stewed, well-lubricated; pixilated, fuddled; maudlin; drunken, boozy, muzzy, woozy; pie-eyed; reeling, staggering; hiccupping.

dead drunk, smashed, sloshed, sozzled, soaked, soused, plastered; stinko, stoned; blind drunk, blind, blotto; legless, paralytic, stocious; in a drunken stupor; under the table; drunk as a lord; pissed as a newt, fou as a coot, fou as a wulk, etc.

crapulous, crapulent, with a hangover, with a thick head; dizzy, giddy, sick.

drugged, doped, high, zonked, spaced out, freaked o., in a trance; stoned 375 *insensible*; turned on, hooked on drugs, addicted.

drunken, never sober; gin-sodden; boozy, beery; fond of a drink, having a drink problem; tippling, boozing, toping, swilling, hard-drinking; pub-crawling; gouty, given to drink, a slave to d., addicted to d., on the bottle, alcoholic, dipsomaniac.

intoxicating, inebriating; exhilarating, going to the head, heady, winy, like wine 821 *exciting*; stimulant, intoxicant; opiate, narcotic; hallucinatory, psychedelic, psychotropic, mind-bending, mind-blowing; addictive, habit-forming; alcoholic, spirituous, vinous, beery; hard, potent, double-strength, overproof 162 *strong*; neat 44 *unmixed.*

Vb. *be drunk,* - tipsy etc. adj.; be under the influence of liquor, be under the influence, have had too much, have had one too many; have a weak head, not hold one's liquor, not walk straight, lurch, stagger, reel 317 *oscillate.*

get drunk, have too much, have one over the eight, drink like a fish; liquor up, tank up, crack a bottle, knock back a few, bend one's elbow, lush, bib, tipple, fuddle, booze, tope, swill, souse, hit the bottle 301 *drink*; go on the spree, go on a blind *or* a bender, go pub-crawling; drown one's sorrows; quaff, carouse, wassail.

drug oneself, smoke, sniff, snort, inject oneself, shoot, mainline; turn on, take a trip, blow one's mind; freak out.

950 Purity – N. *purity,* faultlessness 646 *perfection*; innocence; moral purity, morals, morality 933 *virtue*; decency, propriety, delicacy 846 *good taste*; shame, bashfulness 874 *modesty*; chastity 942 *temperance*; frigidity 820 *moral insensibility*; honour, one's h.; virginity, maidenhood, maidenhead 895 *celibacy*; prudery, prudishness; false modesty 874 *modesty*; demureness, gravity 834 *seriousness*; priggishness, primness, coyness 850 *affectation*; sanctimoniousness 979 *pietism*; Puritanism; euphemism, Grundyism, genteelism, mealy-mouthedness; censorship, expurgation, bowdlerization 550 *obliteration.*

virgin, maiden, vestal virgin, virgo intacta, maid, old maid, spinster 895 *celibate*; religious celibate 986 *monk, nun*; virtuous woman.

prude, prig, Victorian, euphemist; Puritan, wowser; guardian of morality, censor, Watch Committee, Mrs Grundy.

Adj. *pure,* faultless 646 *perfect*; undefiled, unfallen 935 *innocent*; maidenly, virgin, virginal, vestal, untouched; modest; coy, shy; chaste 942 *temperate*; impregnable, incorruptible 929 *honourable*; frigid 380 *cold*; immaculate, spotless, snowy 427 *white*; good, moral 933 *virtuous*; Platonic, purified; decent, decorous, delicate, refined 846 *tasteful*; censored, bowdlerized, expurgated.

prudish, squeamish, shockable, Victorian; prim 850 *affected*; straitlaced, narrow-minded, puritan, priggish; holy, sanctimonious 979 *pietistic.*

951 Impurity – N. *impurity,* impure thoughts, filthiness, defilement 649 *uncleanness*; indelicacy 847 *bad taste*; indecency, immodesty, shamelessness, exhibitionism; coarseness, grossness, nastiness; ribaldry, bawdiness, salaciousness; blue joke; double entendre; smut, dirt, filth, obscenity, obscene literature, adult l., erotic l., erotica; pornography, hard-core p., porn, soft porn, page 3, girlie magazine; blue film, skin flick, video nasty; prurience.

unchastity, promiscuity, wantonness; easy virtue, amorality; permissive society 734 *laxity*; vice, immorality; prurience, lust 859 *libido*; carnality, sexuality, eroticism, the flesh 944 *sensualism*; sexiness, lasciviousness, lewdness, salacity, lubricity; dissoluteness, dissipation, debauchery, licentiousness, licence, libertinism; seduction, defloration; lechery, fornication, womanizing, whoring, screwing around, sleeping a.; harlotry, whorishness.

illicit love, unlawful desires, forbidden fruit; extramarital relations; incest; perversion, pederasty, buggery, sodomy, bestiality; satyriasis, priapism, nymphomania; adultery, unfaithfulness, infidelity, marital i., cuckolding, cuckoldry; eternal triangle, liaison, intrigue, amour, seduction 887 *love affair*; free love, living together; wife-swapping.

rape, ravishment, violation, indecent assault, grope; gang bang; sexual abuse, sex crime.

social evil, harlotry, whoredom; oldest profession, Mrs Warren's p.; streetwalking, prostitution, soliciting, hooking; indecent exposure, exposing oneself, flashing; pimping, pandering, brothel-keeping, living on immoral earnings, white slave traffic; vice squad.

brothel, bordello, whorehouse, bawdyhouse, cathouse, disorderly h., house of ill fame, house of ill repute; knockingshop; red-light district.

Adj. *impure,* defiled, unclean; unwholesome 653 *insalubrious*; vulgar, coarse, gross; ribald, loose; strong, racy, bawdy, Rabelaisian; uncensored, unexpurgated, unbowdlerized; suggestive, provocative, piquant, titillating, near the knuckle, near the bone; spicy; immoral, risqué, nudge-nudge, winkwink; naughty, wicked, blue; unmentionable, unquotable, unprintable; smutty, filthy, scatogological, offensive; indecent, obscene, lewd, salacious; licentious, pornographic; prurient, erotic, priapic; sexual, sexy, hot.

unchaste, unvirtuous 934 *vicious*; fallen, seduced; of easy virtue, of loose morals, amoral, immoral; light, wanton, loose, fast, naughty; wild, rackety; immodest, daring, revealing; unblushing, shameless, brazen, flaunting, scarlet, meretricious, whorish, tarty; promiscuous, sleeping around, screwing a.; streetwalking, on the game.

lecherous, carnal; libidinous, lustful, goatish; prurient; on *or* in heat, rutting; turned-on, hot, randy; oversexed, sexmad, sex-crazy, nymphomaniac; perverted, bestial; lewd, licentious, libertine; depraved, debauched, dissolute, dissipated, profligate 934 *vicious*.

Vb. *be impure,* - unchaste etc. adj.; have no morals; be unfaithful, commit adultery, cuckold; be dissipated 943 *be intemperate*; fornicate, womanize, whore, keep a mistress, have a lover; lech, lust, rut, be on heat, be hot, have the hots 859 *desire*; be promiscuous, sleep around, screw a.; become a prostitute, become a hooker, become a rentboy, street-walk, be on the streets; pimp, pander, procure, keep a brothel.

debauch, defile, smirch 649 *make unclean*; proposition, seduce, lead astray; have one's way with; dishonour, deflower, disgrace 867 *shame*; prostitute, make a whore of; lay, screw, knock off, bed, go to bed with, lie with, sleep w. 45 *unite with*; rape, ravish, violate, molest, abuse, interfere with, assault, indecently a., sexually abuse.

952 Libertine – **N.** *libertine,* philanderer, flirt; free-lover, fast man *or* woman, gay dog, rip, rake, roué, debauchee 944 *sensualist*; lady-killer, gallant; fancy-man, gigolo, sugar daddy; seducer, deceiver, gay d., Lothario; corespondent, adulterer; cuckolder, bed-hopper, wife-swapper; Don Juan, Casanova; wolf, kerbcrawler; womanizer, fornicator, stud; whoremonger, whoremaster; voyeur, lecher, flasher, satyr, goat, dirty old man, DOM; sex maniac; rapist; male prostitute, rent-boy; pederast, sodomite, pervert 84 *nonconformist*.

loose woman, wanton, easy lay, anybody's; fast woman, sexpot, hot stuff;

woman of easy virtue, one no better than she should be; flirt, bit, bint, wench, floozy, jade, hussy, minx, nymphet, sex kitten, Lolita, groupie; baggage, trash, trollop, slut; tart, chippy, scrubber, pick-up; vamp, adventuress, temptress, seductress, femme fatale, scarlet woman, painted w., Jezebel, Delilah; adultress, other woman; nymphomaniac, nympho.

kept woman, fancy w., mistress, paramour, concubine; bit of fluff, bit on the side, floozie, doxy, moll.

prostitute, pro; white slave, fallen woman; harlot, trollop, whore, strumpet; streetwalker, woman of the streets, broad, hustler, hooker, scrubber; pickup, callgirl; courtesan; male prostitute, rent-boy, gigolo.

bawd, go-between, pimp, ponce, pander, procurer, procuress, brothel-keeper, madam; white slaver.

953 Legality – N. *legality,* due process 959 *litigation*; letter of the law, four corners of the l.; respect for law, constitutionalism; judgment according to the law 480 *judgment*; keeping within the law, lawfulness, legitimateness, legitimacy, validity.

legislation, legislature, legislatorship, law-giving, law-making, constitutionm.; legalization, legitimization, validation, ratification, confirmation 532 *affirmation*; passing into law, enacting, enactment, regulation; plebiscite 605 *vote*; law, statute, ordinance, order, bylaw 737 *decree*; canon, rule, edict 693 *precept*.

law, the law; body of law, constitution, written c., unwritten c.; charter, institution; statute book, legal code; Ten Commandments, penal code, civil c., Napoleonic c.; written law, common l., unwritten l., natural l.; canon law, ecclesiastical l.; international law, law of nations, law of the sea, law of the air; law of commerce, commercial law, law of contract, criminal law, civil l., constitutional l., law of the land; arm of the law, legal process 955 *jurisdiction*; writ, summons, lawsuit 959 *legal trial*.

Adj. *legal,* lawful 913 *just*; law-abiding 739 *obedient*; legitimate, competent; licit, licensed, permissible, allowable; within the law, sanctioned by law, according to l., legally sound; statutory, constitutional; law-giving, legislative; legislated, enacted, passed, voted, made law, ordained, decreed, ordered, by order; legalized, legitimized, decriminalized, brought within the law; actionable; pertaining to law, jurisprudential.

Vb. *be legal,* - legitimate etc. adj.; stand up in law *or* court; come within the law, keep within the l., stay the right side of the l.

make legal, legalize, legitimize, decriminalize, validate, confirm, ratify, formalize 488 *endorse*; vest, establish 153 *stabilize*; legislate, make laws, give l.; pass, enact, ordain, enforce 737 *decree*.

954 Illegality – N. *illegality,* legal flaw, loophole, let-out, irregularity, error of law; wrong verdict, bad judgment 481 *misjudgment*; contradictory law; miscarriage of justice 914 *injustice*; wrong side of the law, unlawfulness; incompetence, illicitness, illegitimacy 757 *prohibition*.

lawbreaking, breach of law, violation of l., transgression, contravention, infringement, encroachment 306 *overstepping*; trespass, offence, offence against the law, civil wrong; malpractice; dishonesty 930 *improbity*; criminality 936 *guilt*; criminal activity, criminal offence, indictable o., crime, capital c., misdemeanour, felony; wrongdoing 914 *wrong*; criminology.

lawlessness, outlawry; breakdown of law and order, crime wave 734 *anarchy*; summary justice, vigilantism; kangaroo court, gang rule, mob law, lynch l.; riot, race r., rioting, hooliganism, ruffianism, rebellion 738 *revolt*; coup d'état, usurpation 916 *arrogation*; arbitrary rule, abolition of law; martial law; mailed fist, jackboot 735 *brute force*.

bastardy, bar *or* bend *or* baton sinister; bastardization, illegitimacy; bastard, illegitimate child, natural c., love c., byblow.

Adj. *illegal,* illegitimate, illicit; contraband, black-market, hot; impermissible, verboten 757 *prohibited*; unauthorized, incompetent, without authority, unwarrantable, informal, unofficial; unlawful, wrongful 914 *wrong*; unlegislated, exceeding the l.; unchartered, unconstitutional, unstatutory; suspended, null and void, nullified, annulled; irregular; extrajudicial; on the wrong side of the law, against the l.; outside the law, outwith the l., outlawed, out of bounds; actionable, punishable.

lawbreaking, trespassing, transgressing, infringing, encroaching; sinning 934 *wicked*; offending 936 *guilty*; criminal, felonious; fraudulent, shady 930 *dishonest*.

lawless, chaotic; ungovernable, licentious; violent, summary; arbitrary, irresponsible, unanswerable, unaccountable; without legal backing, unofficial, cowboy; above the law; despotic, tyrannical 735 *oppressive*.

bastard, illegitimate, spurious; born out of wedlock, born on the wrong side of the blanket; without a father, without a name, without benefit of clergy; bastardized.

Vb. *be illegal,* be against the law, break the law; circumvent the l.; be lawless, defy the law, drive a coach and horses through the l. 914 *do wrong*; take the law into one's own hands, exceed one's authority, encroach; stand above the law; stand outside the law.

make illegal, - unlawful etc. adj.; outlaw; criminalize 757 *prohibit*; forbid by law, penalize 963 *punish*; bastardize; suspend, annul, cancel, make the law a dead letter 752 *abrogate*.

955 Jurisdiction – N. *jurisdiction,* portfolio 622 *function*; judicature, magistracy, commission of the peace; mayoralty; competence, legal c., legal authority, arm of the law 733 *authority*; administration

of justice, legal administration, Home Office; local authority, corporation, municipality, county council, regional c., district c., parish c., community c., bailiwick 692 *council*; vigilance committee, watch c. 956 *tribunal*; office, bureau, secretariat 687 *workshop*; legal authority, competence, cognizance 751 *mandate*.

law officer, legal administrator, Lord Chancellor, Attorney General, Lord Advocate, Solicitor General, Queen's Proctor; Crown Counsel, public prosecutor; judge advocate, procurator fiscal, district attorney 957 *judge*; mayor, lord m., provost, lord p., sheriff 733 *position of authority*; court officer, clerk of the court, bailiff; summoner, Bow-street runner; beadle, mace-bearer 690 *official*.

police, forces of law and order, long arm of the law; police force, the force, the fuzz, Old Bill, the boys in blue; Scotland Yard; constabulary, gendarmerie, military police, transport p.; police officer, limb of the law, policeman *or* -woman, constable, special c., copper, cop, traffic c., patrolman *or* -woman; bobby, flatfoot, rozzer, pig, smokey bear, flic; police sergeant, police inspector, police superintendent, commissioner of police, chief constable, provost marshal; watch, posse comitatus; special patrol group, SPG; plain-clothes man, dick 459 *detective*.

956 Tribunal – N. *tribunal,* seat of justice, woolsack, throne; judgment seat, bar; confessional, Judgment Day; forum 692 *council*; public opinion, vox populi, electorate; judicatory, bench, board, bench of judges, panel of j., judge and jury; judicial assembly; Justices of the Peace.

lawcourt, court, open c.; court of law, court of justice, criminal court, civil c.; Federal Court, High Court, Court of Justiciary; Sheriff C., District Court, County Court; Supreme Court, appellate court, Court of Appeal; Court of Exchequer, Star Chamber; House of Lords 692 *parliament*; High Court of Justice,

Queen's Bench, Queen's Bench Division, Court of Criminal Appeal; Admiralty Division; Probate Court, Divorce C.; Court of Chancery, court of equity, c. of arbitration; Court of Common Pleas; circuit court; assizes; Court of Session, sessions, quarter s., petty s.; Central Criminal Court, Old Bailey; magistrate's court, juvenile c., police c.; coroner's court; court of record, feudal c., manorial c., Stannary C., court baron, court leet; guild court, hustings; court-martial, summary court.

957 Judge – N. *judge*, justice, your Lordship, my lud, m'lud; justiciary, Lord Chancellor, Lord Chief Justice, Master of the Rolls, Lords of Appeal; military judge, Judge Advocate General; chief justice, puisné judge, county court j., recorder, Common Serjeant; sessions judge, assize j., circuit j.; district judge, subordinate j.; sheriff, sheriff substitute; magistrate, district m., city m., police m., stipiendary m.; coroner; honorary magistrate, justice of the peace, JP; bench, judiciary; hanging judge.

magistracy, the beak, his *or* her Worship, his *or* her Honour, his nibs, her nibs; arbiter, umpire, referee, assessor, arbitrator, Ombudsman 480 *estimator*; Recording Angel 549 *recorder*; Solomon, Daniel come to judgment.

jury, twelve good men and true; grand jury, special j., common j., petty j., trial j., coroner's j.; rigged j.; hung j.; juror's panel, jury list; juror, juryman *or* -woman, jurat; foreman *or* forewoman of the jury.

958 Lawyer – N. *lawyer,* legal practitioner, solicitor, member of the legal profession, man *or* woman of law; civil lawyer, criminal l.; one called to the bar, barrister, barrister-at-law, devil, advocate, counsel, learned c.; junior barrister, junior counsel; senior barrister, bencher, bencher of the Inns of Court; silk, leading counsel, King's C., K.C., Queen's C., Q.C.; serjeant, serjeant-at-law; circuit barrister; Philadelphia lawyer 696 *expert*; shyster, pettifogger, crooked lawyer.

law agent, attorney, public a., attorney at law, proctor, procurator; Writer to the Signet, solicitor before the Supreme Court; solicitor, legal adviser; legal representative, legal agent, pleader, advocate; conveyancer.

notary, notary public, commissioner for oaths; scrivener, petition-writer; clerk of the court 955 *law officer*; solicitor's clerk, barrister's c., barrister's devil.

jurist, legal adviser, legal expert; pundit, legalist; student of law.

bar, civil b., criminal b., English bar, Scottish b., junior b., senior b.; Inns of Chancery, Inns of Court, Gray's I., Lincoln's I., Inner Temple, Middle T.; barristership, advocacy.

Vb. *do law,* study l., go in for l., take up l.; be called to the bar; take silk; practise at the bar, accept a brief, take a case, advocate, plead; practise law; devil.

959 Litigation – N. *litigation,* going to law, litigiousness 709 *quarrelsomeness*; legal dispute 709 *quarrel*; issue, legal i.; lawsuit, suit at law, suit, case, cause, action; prosecution, arraignment, impeachment, charge 928 *accusation*; test case 461 *experiment*; claim, counter c. 915 *dueness*; plea, petition 761 *request*; affidavit, written statement, averment, pleading, demurrer 532 *affirmation*.

legal process, proceedings, legal procedure, arm of the law 955 *jurisdiction*; citation, subpoena, summons, search warrant 737 *warrant*; arrest, apprehension, detention, committal 747 *restraint*; habeas corpus, bail, surety, security; injunction; writ.

legal trial, trial, justice seen to be done; trial by law, trial by jury, trial at the bar, trial in court, assize, sessions 956 *lawcourt*; inquest, inquisition, examination 459 *enquiry*; hearing, prosecution, defence; hearing of evidence, taking of e., recording of e. 466 *evidence*;

examination, cross-e., objection sustained, objection overruled 466 *testimony*; pleadings, arguments 475 *reasoning*; counterargument, rebutter, rebuttal 460 *rejoinder*; proof 478 *demonstration*; disproof 479 *confutation*; summing-up, charge to the jury; ruling, finding, decision, verdict 480 *judgment*; majority verdict, hung jury; favourable verdict 960 *acquittal*; unfavourable verdict 961 *condemnation*; execution of judgment 963 *punishment*; appeal, motion of a.; successful appeal, reversal of judgment, retrial; precedent, case law; law reports; case record, dossier 548 *record*.

litigant, litigator, party, party to a suit, suitor 763 *petitioner*; claimant, plaintiff, pursuer, defendant, appellant, respondent, objector, intervener; accused, prisoner at the bar 928 *accused person*; prosecutor 928 *accuser*.

Vb. *litigate,* go to law, appeal to l., set the law in motion, institute legal proceedings, bring a suit, file a s., petition 761 *request*; prepare a brief, brief counsel; file a claim, contest at law 915 *claim*; have the law on one, take one to court, haul before the c., have one up, sue, arraign, impeach, accuse, charge, prefer charges, press c. 928 *indict*; cite, summon, serve notice on; prosecute, put on trial, bring to justice, bring to trial; call evidence 475 *argue*.

try a case, put down for hearing; call witnesses, examine, cross-examine, take statements; sit in judgment, rule, find, decide, adjudicate 480 *judge*; sum up, charge the jury; bring in a verdict, pronounce sentence; commit for trial.

stand trial, come up for trial, be put on t., stand in the dock; plead guilty, plead not guilty; submit to judgment, hear sentence; defend an action.

960 Acquittal – **N.** *acquittal,* favourable verdict, verdict of not guilty, verdict of not proven, benefit of the doubt; clearance, exculpation, exoneration 935 *innocence*; absolution, discharge; let-off, thumbs up 746 *liberation*; whitewashing, justification, compurgation

927 *vindication*; successful defence; case dismissed; no case, withdrawal of the charge, quashing, quietus; reprieve, pardon 909 *forgiveness*; nonprosecution, exemption, impunity 919 *nonliability*.

Adj. *acquitted,* not guilty, not proven 935 *guiltless*; clear, cleared, in the clear, exonerated, exculpated, vindicated; immune, exempted, exempt; let off, let off the hook, discharged, without a stain on one's character; reprieved; recommended for mercy.

Vb. *acquit,* find *or* pronounce not guilty, prove innocent, find that the case is not proven, justify, whitewash, get one off 927 *vindicate*; clear, absolve, exonerate, exculpate; find there is no case to answer, not press charges, not prosecute 919 *exempt*; discharge, let go, let off 746 *liberate*; reprieve, respite, pardon, remit the penalty 909 *forgive*; quash, quash the conviction, set aside the sentence, allow an appeal 752 *abrogate*.

961 Condemnation – **N.** *condemnation,* unfavourable verdict; conviction; successful prosecution; damnation, perdition; blacklist, Index 924 *disapprobation*; excommunication 899 *malediction*; doom, judgment, sentence 963 *punishment*; writing on the wall 511 *omen*; outlawry, price on one's head, proscription, attainder; death warrant, condemned cell, execution chamber, electric chair, Death Row; black cap, thumbs down.

Adj. *condemned,* found guilty, made liable; convicted, sentenced; sentenced to death; proscribed, outlawed, with a price on one's head; having no case, without a leg to stand on; damned, in hell.

Vb. *condemn,* prove guilty, bring home the charge; find liable, find against; find guilty, pronounce g., convict, sentence; sentence to death, put on the black cap, sign one's death warrant; reject one's defence, reject one's appeal 607 *reject*; proscribe, outlaw, bar, put a price on one's head 954 *make illegal*;

blacklist 924 *disapprove*; damn, excommunicate 899 *curse*; stand condemned out of one's own mouth 936 *be guilty*; plead guilty, sign a confession, be verballed 526 *confess*.

962 Reward – N. *reward,* remuneration, recompense; meed, deserts, just d. 913 *justice*; recognition, due r., acknowledgment, thanks 907 *gratitude*; tribute, bouquets 923 *praise*; prize-giving, award, presentation, prize, Nobel P.; crown, cup, shield, certificate, medal 729 *trophy*; consolation prize, booby p.; honour 729 *decoration*; birthday honours 866 *honours*; letters after one's name, peerdom 870 *title*; prize money, cash p., jackpot; prize fellowship, scholarship, bursary, stipend, exhibition 703 *subvention*; reward for service, fee, retainer, refresher, honorarium, payment, payment in kind, remuneration, emolument, pension, salary, wage, wages, increment 804 *pay*; productivity bonus, overtime pay 612 *incentive*; perquisite, perks, expense account, fringe benefits; income, turnover 771 *earnings*; return, profit, margin of p., bottom line 771 *gain*; compensation, indemnification, satisfaction; consideration, quid pro quo; comeuppance 714 *retaliation*; reparation 787 *restitution*; bounty, gratuity, golden handshake, golden parachute, redundancy money; commission, rake-off; golden handcuffs; tip, douceur, sweetener, pourboire, trinkgeld, baksheesh 781 *gift*; tempting offer 759 *offer*; golden hello, bait, lure, bribe 612 *incentive*; slush fund, hush money, protection m., blackmail.

Vb. *reward,* recompense; award, give a prize, offer a reward; bestow a medal, honour with a title 866 *honour*; recognize, acknowledge, pay tribute, hand out bouquets, thank, show one's gratitude 907 *be grateful*; remunerate 804 *pay*; satisfy, tip 781 *give*; repay, requite 714 *retaliate*; compensate, indemnify, make reparation 787 *restitute*; offer a bribe, grease the palm, win over 612 *bribe*.

be rewarded, win a prize, get a medal, receive a title; be given an honorarium, get paid, draw a salary, earn an income, have a gainful occupation 771 *acquire*; accept payment 782 *receive*; take a bribe, have one's palm greased; have one's reward, get one's deserts, receive one's due 915 *deserve*; get one's comeuppance; reap a profit 771 *gain*.

963 Punishment – N. *punishment,* sentence 961 *condemnation*; execution of sentence; chastisement, heads rolling; castigation, carpeting 924 *reprimand*; disciplinary action; dose, pill, bitter p., infliction, trial, visitation, carrying the can 731 *adversity*; just deserts, meet reward, comeuppance 915 *dueness*; doom, judgment, day of j., day of reckoning, divine justice 913 *justice*; poetic justice, retribution, Nemesis; reckoning, repayment 787 *restitution*; requital, reprisal 714 *retaliation*; penance 941 *atonement*; hara-kiri 362 *suicide*; penology.

corporal punishment, smacking, slapping, trouncing, hiding, beating, thrashing, kicking; caning, whipping, flogging, birching; scourging, flagellation; ducking, keel-hauling; slap, smack, rap over the knuckles, box on the ear; drubbing, blow, buffet, cuff, clout, stroke, stripe 279 *knock*; kick; third degree, torture, breaking on the wheel.

capital punishment, extreme penalty 361 *death*; death sentence, death warrant; execution 362 *killing*; decapitation, beheading, guillotining; hanging, drawing and quartering; strangulation, garrotte; hanging, long drop; electrocution, hot seat, electric chair; stoning; crucifixion, impalement, flaying alive; burning, burning at the stake; drowning; massacre, mass murder, mass execution, purge, genocide 362 *slaughter*; martyrdom, martyrization; lynching, lynch law, contract; judicial murder.

penalty, injury, damage 772 *loss*; imposition, task, lines, punishment exercise; sentence, penalization; penal code, penology; devil to pay, liability, legal l.

915 *dueness*; damages, costs, compensation, restoration 787 *restitution*; fining, fine, compulsory payment 804 *payment*; ransom 809 *price*; forfeit, forfeiture, sequestration, confiscation, deprivation 786 *expropriation*; keeping in, gating, imprisonment 747 *detention*; suspension, rustication; binding over 747 *restraint*; penal servitude, hard labour; transportation, expulsion, deportation 300 *ejection*; ostracism, sending to Coventry, banishment, exile, proscription, ban, outlawing, blackballing 57 *exclusion*; reprisal 714 *retaliation*.

Adj. *punitive*, penal, punitory; castigatory, disciplinary, corrective; vindictive, retributive; in reprisal; penalizing, fining; confiscatory, expropriatory; scourging, flagellatory, torturing 377 *painful*.

Vb. *punish*, afflict 827 *hurt*; persecute, victimize, make an example of 735 *be severe*; inflict punishment, take disciplinary action; give *or* teach one a lesson, discipline, correct, chastise, castigate; reprimand, rebuke, tell off, rap across the knuckles, smack on the wrist; throw the book at, come down hard on, come down on like a ton of bricks, give one what for; penalize, impose a penalty, sentence 961 *condemn*; exact retribution, settle with, get even w., pay one out *or* back 714 *retaliate*; settle, fix, bring to book, give one what was coming to him, give one his/her come-uppance; fine, forfeit, deprive, sequestrate, confiscate 786 *take away*; unfrock, demote, degrade, downgrade, reduce to the ranks, suspend 867 *shame*; stand in a corner, send out of the room; tar and feather; pillory, set in the stocks; duck, keelhaul; lock up 747 *imprison*; transport.

spank, slap, smack; cuff, clout, box on the ears, rap over the knuckles, smack on the wrist; drub, trounce, beat, belt, strap, leather, lather, wallop, tan, cane, birch, whack, tan one's hide, give one a hiding, beat black and blue 279 *strike*.

flog, whip, horsewhip, thrash, hide, give a hiding, cudgel 279 *strike*; scourge,

give one the cat; lash, birch, give one the birch, flay; flagellate.

torture, give the third degree; put on the rack, break on the wheel, kneecap, persecute, martyrize 827 *torment*.

execute, put to death 362 *kill*; lynch 362 *murder*; tear limb from limb; crucify; stone to death; shoot, fusillade; burn at the stake, send to the s.; necklace, give one a n.; garrotte, strangle; hang, hang by the neck, string up, bring to the gallows; hang, draw and quarter; send to the scaffold, behead, decapitate, guillotine; electrocute, send to the chair, send to the hot seat; gas, put in the gas chamber; commit genocide, hold mass executions, purge, massacre, decimate 362 *slaughter*.

be punished, suffer punishment, take the consequences, be for the high jump, have it coming to one, get one's come-uppance, catch it, catch *or* get it in the neck; take the rap, face the music; take one's medicine; get what one was asking for, get one's deserts; pay the ultimate price; lay one's head on the block; come to the gallows, swing; die the death.

964 Means of punishment – N. *scourge*, birch, cat, cat-o'-nine-tails, rope's end; whip, horsewhip, switch; lash, strap, tawse, thong, belt; cane, rattan; stick, big s., rod, ferule, cudgel, ruler, cosh 723 *club*; rubber hose, bicycle chain, sandbag.

pillory, stocks, whipping post, ducking stool; corner, dunce's cap; stool of repentance, cutty stool; chain, irons 748 *fetter*; prison house 748 *prison*.

instrument of torture, rack, thumbscrew, iron boot; Iron Maiden, wheel; treadmill; torture chamber.

means of execution, scaffold, block, gallows, gibbet; cross; stake; hemlock 659 *poison*; bullet; axe, guillotine, maiden, widow-maker; rope, noose; garrotte; necklace; electric chair, hot seat; death chamber, gas c.; condemned cell, Death Row 961 *condemnation*.

Section five: Religion

965 Divineness – N. *divineness,* divinity, deity; godhead; divine principle, Brahma; mana; divine essence, the Good the True and the Beautiful; love, Fatherhood; Brahmahood, nirvana; world soul; divine nature, God's ways, Providence.

divine attribute, omnipresence 189 *presence*; omniscience, wisdom 490 *knowledge*; omnipotence, almightiness 160 *power*; timelessness, eternity 115 *perpetuity*; changelessness 153 *stability*; truth, sanctity, holiness, goodness, justice, mercy; transcendence, sublimity, supremacy, sovereignty, majesty, glory, light; glory of the Lord.

the Deity, God, Supreme Being, Alpha and Omega; the Almighty; the All-holy, the All-merciful; Ruler of Heaven and Earth, Judge of all men, Maker of all things, Creator, Preserver; Allah; Elohim, Yahweh, Jehovah, Adonai, ineffable name, I AM; name of God, Tetragrammaton; God of Abraham, God of Moses, Lord of Hosts, God of our fathers; our Father; All-Father, Great Spirit; Krishna.

God the Son, Son of God, the Only Begotten; Messiah, Son of David, the Lord's Anointed, Christ; Immanuel; Lamb of God, Son of Man; Son of Mary, Jesus, Jesu, Jesus Christ; Holy Infant, Christ Child, Child of Bethlehem; Jesus of Nazareth; the Good Shepherd, Saviour, Redeemer, Friend; Lord, Master; Rock of Ages, Bread of Life; the Way the Truth and the Life; Light of the World, Sun of Righteousness; King of Kings, Prince of Peace.

Adj. *divine,* holy, hallowed, sanctified, sacred, sacrosanct, heavenly, celestial; transcendental, sublime, ineffable; mystical, religious, spiritual, superhuman, supernatural, unearthly, not of this world.

godlike, divine, superhuman; omnipresent 189 *ubiquitous*; immortal 115 *perpetual*; immutable, changeless 144

permanent; almighty, all-powerful, omnipotent 160 *powerful*; creative 160 *dynamic*; all-wise, all-seeing, all-knowing, omniscient 490 *knowing*; all-merciful, merciful; compassionate 905 *pitying*; holy, all-h., worshipped 979 *sanctified*; sovereign 34 *supreme*; incarnate, in the image of God, deified; messianic, anointed; Christly, Christlike.

966 Deities in general – N. *deity,* god, goddess, deva, devi; the gods, the immortals; Olympian 967 *Olympian deity*; false god, idol; petty god, inferior g.; demigod, half-god, divine hero, divine king; fetish, totem 982 *idol*; mumbo jumbo.

mythic deity, nature god *or* goddess, Pan, Flora; earth goddess, Gaia; mother earth, mother goddess, earth mother; fertility god, Adonis, Marduk, Atys; god of the underworld, Pluto, Dis 967 *Chthonian deity*; sky god, Zeus, Jupiter; storm god, Indra, wind god, Aeolus; sun god, Apollo, Hyperion, Helios, Ra, Mithras; river god, sea g., Poseidon, Neptune; war god *or* goddess, Mars, Bellona; god *or* goddess of love, Cupid, Eros, Venus, Aphrodite; household gods, Lares, Penates; the Fates 596 *fate*.

967 Pantheon: classical and nonclassical deities – N. *classical deities,* gods and goddesses of Greece and Rome, Graeco-Roman pantheon; Homeric deities, Hesiodic theogony; primeval deities, Erebus, Nox; Ge, Gaia, Tellus, Uranus, Cronus, Saturn, Rhea, Ops; Pontus, Oceanus, Tethys; Helios, Sol, Hyperion, Phaëthon; Titan, Atlas, Prometheus; Giant, Enceladus; the Fates, Parcae, Clotho, Lachesis, Atropos.

Olympian deity, Olympian, Zeus, Jupiter, Jove, president of the immortals; Pluto, Hades; Poseidon, Neptune; Apollo, Phoebus; Hermes, Mercury; Ares, Mars; Hephaestus, Vulcan; Dionysus, Bacchus; Hera, Juno; Demeter, Ceres; Persephone, Proserpina; Athena, Minerva; Aphrodite, Venus; Artemis, Diana; Eros, Cupid; Iris; Hebe.

Chthonian deity, Ge, Gaia, Dis Pater, Orcus, Hades, Pluto, Persephone; Erectheus, Trophonius, Pytho; Eumenides, Erinyes, Furies.

lesser deity, Pan, Silvanus, Flora, Faunus, Silenus; Aurora, Eos; Luna, Selene; Aeolus, Boreas 352 *wind*; Triton, Nereus, Proteus, Glaucus; Ate, Eris, Bellona, Nike; Astraea; Muses, tuneful Nine, Erato, Euterpe, Terpsichore, Polyhymnia, Clio, Calliope, Melpomene, Thalia, Urania; Asclepius, Aesculapius; Hypnos, Somnus, Morpheus; Hymen; Hestia, Vesta; Lares, Penates; local god, genius loci.

nymph, wood n., tree n., dryad, hamadryad; mountain nymph, oread; water nymph, naiad; sea nymph, nereid; Oceanid; Thetis, Calypso, Callisto; Pleiades, Maia; Latona, Leto; siren 970 *mythical being.*

demigod, divine offspring, divine hero; Heracles, Hercules; Dioscuri, Castor and Pollux, Castor and Polydeuces; Perseus, Achilles, Aeneas, Memnon.

Hindu deities, Brahmanic d., Vedic d.; Dyaus Pitar, Prithivi; Varuna (sky), Mitra (light), Indra (thunder), Agni (fire), Surya (sun); Trimurti, Brahma, Siva, Vishnu; Sakti, Uma *or* Parvat, Kali *or* Durga; Ganesha (luck-bringer), Karttikeya (fertility), Sarasvati (learning), Hanuman (monkey-god), Sitala (smallpox), Manasa (snakes), Lakshmi (wealth and fortune).

Egyptian deities, Nun, Atum; Shu (air), Tefnut (moisture), Nut (sky), Geb (earth), Osiris, Isis, Set, Nephthys; Ra *or* Re, Amon- *or* Amun-Ra, Atum-ra, Aton; Horus, elder Horus, Ra-Harakhte, Khepera; Amon, Min (all-father), Hathor (all-mother), Neith, Anata; Ptah (creator), Ma'at (truth), Imhotep (peace), Bes (dancing), Serapis (underworld); theriomorphic deity, theriocephalous d.; Apis (sacred bull), Thoth (ibis), Anubis (jackal), Sekhmet (lioness), Sebek (crocodile), Bast (cat), Setekh (hound), Uadjit (cobra), Taurt (hippopotamus).

Semitic deities, Nammu, Anu, Enlil, Enki *or* Ea; Shamash, Sin, Adad; Bel, Marduk; El, Baal, Aleyan-Baal; Moloch, Rimmon, Asshur; great mother, Ishtar, Ashtoreth, Astarte, Asherah, Inanna, Anat; fertility god, Tammuz, Atys; Mot, Allatu.

Nordic deities, Aesir, Vanir; Odin *or* Wotan, Frigg his wife; Thor (thunder god), his wife Sif, his son Ull; Tiu *or* Tyr (war), Heimdall, Balder the beautiful, Vidar the silent, Hoder the blind, Bragi (god of poetry), Hermoder (messenger), Vali (youngest son of Odin); Frey *or* Freyr (peace, fertility), Freya *or* Freyja (goddess of love), Njord *or* Nerthus (wealth and ships), Hoenir, Odmir; Skadi; Loki (evil and strife), Hel (goddess of the dead); Aegir (ocean), his wife Ran, Mimir (guardian of the spring of wisdom), Ymir (father of the Giants).

Celtic deities, Dagda, Math, Magog, Oengus *or* Dwyn; Ogma, Belinus, Esos, Teutates, Taranis; Mabon, Borvo *or* Bormo; Epona; Bilé *or* Beli, Govannon *or* Goibniu (smith), Diancecht (medecine), Lludd *or* Nudd *or* Nuada (sun); Gwydion, Amaethon; Lleu *or* Lug (light), Dylan (darkness); sea gods, Ler *or* Llyr, Bran *or* Branwen, Manannan *or* Manawydan; Dana *or* Don, Morrigan (war), Brigit, Blathnat, Arianrod, Blodeuwedd, Creirwy (love), Keridwen (poetry), Rhiannon (underworld).

Aztec deities, Nahuan d.; Cipactli (earth dragon); Coatlicue (ancient earth goddess); Red Tezcatlipoca, Black T., White T., Blue T., Xipe Topec (spring), Quetzalcoatl (culture), Huitzilopochti (warrior); god and goddess of creation, Tonacatecuhtli, Tonicacihuatl; deities of fertility, Cihuacoatl, Chicomecoatl, Centeotl, Tlazolteotl, Xochipilli; Tlaloc (rain), Chalcihuitlicue (water); Xiuhtecuhtli (fire), Tonatiuh (sun), Teccuciztecutl, Metztli (moon), Mixcoatl (sky), Mictlantecuhtli (death).

968 Angel. Saint. Madonna – N. *angel,* archangel, heavenly host; seraph, seraphim, cherub, cherubim; Michael,

Gabriel, Raphael, Uriel, Zadkiel; Israfel, Azrael, angel of death; guardian angel.

saint, patron s., the blessed ....

Madonna, Our Lady, Blessed Virgin Mary, Mother of God; Mariolatry.

Adj. *angelic,* seraphic, cherubic; saintly.

969 Devil – N. *Satan,* Lucifer, fallen angel; Archfiend, Prince of Darkness; serpent, Tempter, Adversary, Antichrist, Common Enemy, Enemy of mankind; evil genie, Shaitan, Eblis; King of Hell, angel of the bottomless pit, Apollyon, Abaddon; the foul fiend, the Devil, the Evil One, Wicked O., Auld Nick, cloven hoof; Ahriman, Angra Mainyu.

Mephisto, Mephistopheles, His Satanic Majesty, the old one, the Old Gentleman, Old Nick, Auld N., Old Harry, Old Scratch, Auld Hornie, Clootie.

devil, fiend; familiar, imp of Satan 938 *bad person*; Tutivillus, Asmodeus, Azazel 970 *demon*; malevolent spirit; powers of darkness; fallen angel, lost soul, sinner, dweller in Pandemonium, denizen of Hell; Mammon, Belial, Beelzebub, Lord of the Flies; horns, cloven hoof.

diabolism, devilry, demonry, diablerie 898 *inhumanity*; Satanism, devilism; devil worship, demonism, demonolatry; demonomania, demoniac possession; witchcraft, black magic, Black Mass 983 *sorcery*; Satanology, demonology; demonization.

diabolist, Satanist, devil-worshipper, demonolater, demonist; demonologist, demonologer.

Adj. *diabolic,* diabolical, devil-like, satanic, Mephistophelean, fiendish, demonic, demoniacal, devilish 898 *malevolent*; infernal, hellish, hell-born; devil-worshipping; demoniac, possessed; demonological.

970 Fairy – N. *fairy,* elfland, fairyland, faerie; fairy folk, little people; fay, peri; good fairy, fairy godmother 903 *benefactor*; bad fairy, witch 983 *sorceress*; fairy queen, Mab, Queen M., Titania; fairy

king, Oberon, Erl King; Puck, Robin Goodfellow; spirit of air, Ariel; sylph, sylphid; fairy ring; fairy tales; A Midsummer Night's Dream, The Faerie Queene.

elf, elves, elfin folk, pixie, brownie; gnome, dwarf, Nibelung; troll, trow; orc, goblin, flibbertigibbet; imp, sprite, hobgoblin; changeling; leprechaun; poltergeist, gremlin; Puck, Hob, Robin Goodfellow.

ghost, spirit, departed s.; shades, souls of the dead, Manes; zombie; revenant, haunter, poltergeist; spook, spectre, apparition, phantom, shade, wraith, presence, doppelganger 440 *visual fallacy*; White Lady, Grey L.

demon, flibbertigibbet; imp, familiar 969 *devil*; she-demon, banshee; kelpie, troll; ogre, ogress, giant, giantess; bugbear, bugaboo, bogle, bogy, bogyman 938 *monster*; ghoul, vampire, lycanthrope, werewolf; incubus, succubus, nightmare; fury, harpy; Gorgon.

mythical being 968 angel, 969 *devil*; demon, genie, jinn; houri; Valkyrie; centaur, satyr, faun; sea nymph, river n., water n., Oceanid, Naiad, kelpie, nix, nixie; merman, mermaid; Lorelei, Siren; water spirit, Undine 967 *nymph*; Lady of the Lake, Old Man of the Sea; Merlin 983 *sorcerer*; Wayland Smith, Green Man, Wodwose; Yeti, Abominable Snowman, Leviathan, Phoenix 84 *rara avis*.

Adj. *fairylike,* fairy, sylph-like 206 *lean*; dwarf-like 196 *dwarfish*; elf-like, elfin, elvish, impish, Puckish; magic 983 *magical*.

spooky, ghostly, ghoulish; haunted, hagridden; nightmarish, macabre 854 *frightening*; weird, uncanny, unearthly, eldritch 84 *abnormal*; eerie, supernatural; spectral, wraith-like; disembodied 320 *immaterial*; spiritualistic 984 *psychical*.

Vb. *haunt,* visit, walk.

971 Heaven – N. *heaven,* abode of G., kingdom of G., kingdom of heaven,

heavenly kingdom, kingdom come; Paradise, abode of the saints, land of the leal, gates of St Peter; Abraham's bosom, eternal home, happy h.; eternal rest, blessed state; nirvana, seventh heaven; the Millennium, earthly Paradise, heaven on earth, Zion, Land of Beulah, New Jerusalem, Holy City, Celestial C.; afterlife, the hereafter, eternal life, eternity 124 *future state*; resurrection; assumption, glorification; deification, apotheosis.

mythic heaven, Olympus; Valhalla, Asgard; Elysium, Elysian fields, happy hunting grounds, the happy hunting grounds in the skies; Earthly Paradise, Eden, Garden of E., garden of the Hesperides, Islands of the Blest, the Happy Isles, Isle of Avalon 513 *fantasy.*

972 Hell – N. *hell,* place of the dead, nether regions, underworld; grave, limbo, Hades; purgatory; perdition, place of the damned, abode of evil spirits, inferno, Pandemonium; abyss, bottomless pit, Abaddon; place of torment, Gehenna, lake of fire and brimstone; hellfire.

mythic hell, Hel, Niflheim; realm of Pluto, Hades, Tartarus, Avernus, Erebus; river of hell, Acheron, Styx, Cocytus, Phlegethon, Lethe; Stygian Ferryman, Charon; infernal watchdog, Cerberus; infernal judge, Minos, Rhadamanthus; nether gods, Chthonians, Pluto, Osiris 967 *Chthonian deity.*

973 Religion – N. *religion,* religious belief, creed, dogma; deism; primitive religion; paganism 982 *idolatry*; dharma, revealed religion, incarnational r., sacramental r.; mysticism, Sufism; yoga, hathayoga, dharmayoga, jnanayoga, karmayoga, bhaktiyoga; Eightfold Path; theosophy 449 *philosophy*; theolatry 981 *worship*; religious cult, state religion 981 *cult*; atheism 974 *irreligion.*

deism, belief in a god, theism; animism, pantheism, polytheism, henotheism, monotheism, dualism; gnosticism.

religious faith, faith 485 *belief*; Christianity, the Cross; Judaism; Islam, Muhammedanism, the Crescent; Baha'ism, Zoroastrianism, Mazdaism; Vedic religion, Dharma; Hinduism, Brahmanism, Vedantism, Tantrism; Vaishnavism 978 *sectarianism*; Sikhism; Jainism; Buddhism, Theravada, Hinayana, Mahayana, Zen; Shintoism; Taoism, Confucianism; Theosophy; Scientology.

theology, natural theology, revealed t.; religious knowledge, religious learning, divinity; scholastic theology, scholasticism, Thomism; Rabbinism; demythologization; eschatology; hagiology, hagiography, iconology; dogmatics; symbolics, creedal theology; deposit of faith; religious doctrine, received d., defined d.; definition, canon; doxy, dogma, tenet; articles of faith, credo 485 *creed*; confession, Thirty-nine Articles; fundamentalism 976 *orthodoxism*; Bibliology; comparative religion.

theologian, divinity student, divine; rabbi, scribe, mufti, mullah; schoolman, scholastic, scholastic theologian, Thomist, Talmudist, canonist; theogonist, hagiologist, hagiographer, iconologist; psalmist, hymnographer, hymnwriter; textualist; scripturalist, fundamentalist, rabbinist.

religious teacher, prophet, rishi, inspired writer; guru, maharishi 500 *sage*; evangelist, apostle, missionary; reformer, religious r.; expected leader, Messiah, Mahdi, Invisible Imam, twelfth avatar of Vishnu; founder of Christianity, Christ, Jesus Christ; Prophet of God, Muhammad, Mohammed *or* Mahomet; Zoroaster *or* Zarathustra; Ramakrishna, Baha'ullah; Buddha, Gautama; Confucius, Lao-tzu; Joseph Smith, Mary Baker Eddy, Madame Blavatsky; expounder, hierophant, gospeller, catechist 520 *interpreter.*

religionist, deist, theist; monotheist, polytheist, pantheist; animist, fetishist; pagan, gentile 974 *heathen*; adherent, believer, orthodoxist; believer 979

zealot; Christian, Nazarene; Jew; Muslim, Moslem, Islamite, Mussulman, Muhammedan; Sunnite, Shi'ite 978 *non-Christian sect*; Sufi, dervish; Baha'i; Parsee, Zoroastrian; Hindu, gymnosophist, Brahmanist; Sikh; Jain; Buddhist, Zen B.; Tantrist; Taoist; Confucianist; Shintoist; Theosophist; Mormon 978 *sect*; Rosicrucian 984 *occultist*; gnostic 977 *heretic*.

Adj. *religious,* divine, holy, sacred, spiritual, sacramental; deistic, theistic, pantheistic, monotheistic, dualistic; Christian, Islamic, Moslem, Jewish, Judaistic, Mosaic; Baha'i, Zoroastrian, Avestan; Confucian, Taoistic; Buddhistic, Hinduistic, Vedic, Brahminical, Upanashadic, Vedantic; yogic, mystic, Sufic; devotional, devout, practising.

974 Irreligion – N. *irreligion,* profaneness, ungodliness 980 *impiety*; heathenism 982 *idolatry*; atheism, disbelief 486 *unbelief*; humanism; agnosticism, scepticism; lack of faith; lapse from faith, recidivism, backsliding 603 *change of mind*; paganization; apathy 860 *indifference*.

heathen, non-Christian, pagan, paynim; misbeliever, infidel, giaour; gentile, the uncircumcised, the unbaptized, the unconverted; apostate, backslider, lapsed Christian 603 *tergiversator*.

Adj. *irreligious,* godless, profane 980 *impious*; atheistic, atheistical; humanistic; agnostic, doubting, sceptical, Pyrrhonic; free-thinking, rationalistic, nonpractising; ungodly 934 *wicked*; amoral 860 *indifferent*; secular, worldly, materialistic, Mammonistic 944 *sensual*; lacking faith, backsliding, recidivous, lapsed, paganized; unchristian, non-Christian; anticlerical.

heathenish, unholy, unhallowed, unsanctified, unblest, unconsecrated 980 *profane*; unchristian, unbaptized, unconfirmed; gentile, uncircumcised; heathen, pagan, infidel; pre-Christian, unconverted, in darkness 491 *uninstructed*.

Vb. *be irreligious,* - atheistic etc. adj.; have no religion, lack faith; serve Mammon; lose one's faith, suffer a lapse of faith, give up the Church 603 *apostatize*; demythologize, rationalize; deny God, blaspheme 980 *be impious*.

975 Revelation – N. *revelation,* divine r., apocalypse 526 *disclosure*; illumination 417 *light*; inspiration, divine i.; prophecy; intuition, mysticism; Mosaic Law, Ten Commandments; God's word, gospel; God revealed, theophany, burning bush, epiphany, incarnation, Word made flesh; avatar, emanation, divine e.

scripture, word of God, sacred writings; Holy Scripture, Holy Writ, Bible, Holy B., the Book, the Good Book, the Word; Wyclif's Bible, Geneva *or* Breeches B., King James's Bible, Authorized Version, Revised V., Revised Standard Version, Jerusalem Bible, New English B., Good News B.; Vulgate, Douai Version, Greek version, Septuagint; canonical writings, canonical books, canon; Old Testament, Pentateuch, Hexateuch, Octateuch, Major Prophets, Minor P.; Torah, the Law and the Prophets, Hagiographa; New Testament, Gospels, Synoptic G., Epistles, Pastoral E., Pauline E., Johannine E., Petrine E.; Acts of the Apostles, Revelation, Apocalypse; noncanonical writings, Apocrypha, agrapha, logia, sayings, noncanonical gospel; patristic writings; psalter, psalmbook, breviary, missal; prayer book, Book of Common Prayer 981 *prayers*; hymn book, hymnal 981 *hymn*; post-Biblical writings (Hebrew), Targum, Talmud, Mishnah, Gemara; textual commentary, Masorah, Higher Criticism; fundamentalism, scripturalism.

non-Biblical scripture, Koran, the Glorious Koran, Qur'an; Hadith, Sunna; Hindu scripture, Veda, the Four Vedas, Rigveda, Yajurveda, Samaveda, Atharvaveda; Brahmana, Upanishad, Purana; Bhagavad Gita; sruti, smriti, shastra, sutra, tantra; Granth; Buddhist scripture, Pitaka, Tripitaka, Nikaya,

Dhammapada; Iranian and Zoroastrian scripture, Avesta, Zend-Avesta; Book of the Dead (Egyptian); Book of Mormon.

Adj. *revelational,* inspirational, mystic; inspired, prophetic, revealed; visional; apocalyptic; prophetic, evangelical.

scriptural, sacred, holy; hierographic; revealed, inspired, prophetic; canonical 733 *authoritative*; biblical, Mosaic; gospel, evangelistic, apostolic; patristic, homiletic; Talmudic, Mishnaic; Koranic, uncreated; Vedic, Upanishadic, Puranic; textuary, textual, Masoretic.

976 Orthodoxy – N. *orthodoxy,* orthodoxness, correct opinion; sound theology, religious truth, gospel t., pure Gospel 494 *truth*; scripturality, canonicity; the Faith, the true faith; early Church, Apostolic age; ecumenicalism, catholicity, Catholicism; formulated faith, credo 485 *creed*; Apostles' Creed, Nicene C., Athanasian C.; Thirty-nine Articles, Tridentine decrees; textuary, catechism, Church Catechism.

orthodoxism, strictness, strict interpretation; scripturalism, textualism, fundamentalism, literalism, precisianism; Karaism (Jewish); traditionalism, institutionalism, ecclesiasticism, churchianity 985 *the church*; sound churchmanship 83 *conformity*; Christian practice 768 *observance*; intolerance, heresy-hunting, persecution; suppression of heresy, extermination of error, Counter-Reformation; religious censorship, Holy Office 956 *tribunal*; Inquisition 459 *interrogation*; Index, Index Expurgatorius, Index Librorum Prohibitorum 924 *disapprobation*; guaranteed orthodoxy, imprimatur 923 *approbation*.

Christendom, Christian world, the Church; undivided Church; Holy Church, Mother C.; Bride of Christ; Body of Christ, universal Church; Church Militant, Church on earth, visible Church; invisible Church, Church Triumphant; established Church, recognized C., denominational C.; Orthodox C., Eastern Orthodox C., Armenian C., Coptic C.; Church of Rome, Roman Catholic and Apostolic C.; Church of England, Episcopalian C.; Church of Scotland; United Free Church, Free Church; Church of South India; Reformed Church, Protestant C., Lutheran C., Calvinist C.; Ecumenical Council, World Council of Churches.

Catholicism, Orthodoxy, Eastern O.; Roman Catholicism, Romanism, popery, papistry, ultramontanism, Scarlet Woman; Counter-Reformation; Old Catholicism; Anglicanism, Episcopalianism, prelacy; Anglo-Catholicism, High Church; Tractarianism, Oxford Movement.

Protestantism, the Reformation, Anglicanism, Lutheranism, Zwinglianism, Calvinism; Presbyterianism, Congregationalism, United Reformed Church, Baptists; Quakerism, Society of Friends; Wesleyanism, Methodism, Primitive M. 978 *sect*.

Catholic, Orthodox, Eastern O.; Greek O., Russian O., Coptic; Roman Catholic, Romanist, papist, ultramontanist; Old Catholic, Anglo-C., Anglican, Episcopalian, High-Churchman, Tractarian.

Protestant, reformer, Anglican, Lutheran, Zwinglian, Calvinist, Huguenot, Anabaptist; Presbyterian, Wee Free, Congregationalist, United Reformist, Baptist, Wesleyan, Methodist, Wesleyan M., Primitive M.; Quaker, Friend; Plymouth Brother.

Adj. *orthodox,* right-minded; nonheretical, unschismatical 488 *assenting*; undivided 52 *whole*; unswerving, undeviating, loyal, devout 739 *obedient*; practising, conforming, conventional 83 *conformable*; churchy 979 *pietistic*; strict, pedantic; holier than thou, bible-thumping *or* bashing; intolerant, witch-hunting, inquisitional 459 *enquiring*; correct 494 *accurate*; doctrinal 485 *creedal*; authoritative, defined, canonical, biblical, scriptural, evangelical, gospel 494 *genuine*; textual, literal, fundamentalist,

fundamentalistic; Trinitarian; Athanasian; catholic, ecumenical, universal; accepted, held, widely h., believed, generally b. 485 *credible*; traditional, customary 610 *usual*.

Roman Catholic, Catholic, Roman, Romish, Romanist, Romanizing, ultramontanist; popish, papistic.

Anglican, episcopalian; tractarian, Anglo-Catholic, High-Church, high; Low-Church; Broad-C., Latitudinarian.

Protestant, reformed; denominational 978 *sectarian*; Lutheran, Zwinglian, Calvinist, Calvinistic; Presbyterian, Congregational, United Reformed, Baptist, Methodist, Wesleyan, Quaker; bishopless, nonepiscopal.

977 Heterodoxy – N. *heterodoxy,* unorthodoxy; erroneous opinion, wrong belief, false creed, superstition 495 *error*; new teaching; perversion of the truth; heretical tendency, latitudinarianism, modernism, Higher Criticism; unscripturality, noncatholicity, partial truth; heresy, rank h.

heresy, heathen theology, Gnosticism; Monarchianism, Arianism; Socinianism; Unitarianism; Apollinarianism, Nestorianism; Monophysitism, Monothelitism; Pelagianism; Montanism, Donatism, Manichaeism, Albigensianism, Antinomianism; Lollardy; Erastianism, antipapalism.

heretic, arch-h., heresiarch; Gnostic, Manichee; Monarchian, Unitarian; Arius, Arian; Socinus, Socinian; Nestorius, Nestorian; Eutyches, Apollinaris, Apollinarian; Monophysite, Monothelite; Pelagius; Montanus, millenarian; Donatist; Manichaean, Cathar, Paulician, Albigensian; Antinomian; Wycliffite, Lollard, Hussite; Waldenses.

Adj. *heretical,* heretic; heathen, Gnostic, Manichean, Monarchian, Unitarian, Socinian; Arian, Eutychian, Apollinarian, Nestorian, Monophysitic, Monothelite; Pelagian; Montanist; Manichaean, Albigensian; Antinomian, Waldensian, Wycliffite, Lollard, Hussite.

978 Sectarianism – N. *sectarianism,* exclusiveness, clannishness, cliqueishness, sectionalism 481 *prejudice*; bigotry 481 *bias*; party spirit, factiousness 709 *quarrelsomeness*; separatism, schismatical tendency 738 *disobedience*; denominationalism, nonconformism, nonconformity 489 *dissent*; Lutheranism, Calvinism, Anabaptism, Pietism, Moravianism, Puritanism 976 *Protestantism*; Puseyism, Tractarianism 976 *Catholicism*.

schism, division, differences 709 *quarrel*; dissociation, breakaway, splintering, secession, withdrawal 46 *separation*; nonrecognition, mutual excommunication 883 *seclusion*; recusancy 769 *nonobservance*; religious schism, Great Schism.

sect, division, off-shoot, branch, group, faction, splinter group 708 *party*; order, religious o., brotherhood, sisterhood 708 *community*; nonconformist sect, chapel, conventicle 976 *Protestantism*; Society of Friends, Friends, Quakers; Unitarians; Moravians; Plymouth Brethren; Churches of Christ; Sabbatarians, Seventh-day Adventists; Church of Christ Scientist; Church of Jesus Christ of the Latter-Day Saints, Mormons; Jehovah's Witnesses; Salvation Army, Salvationists; Oxford Group, Moral Rearmament.

non-Christian sect, Jewish s.; Orthodox Jews, Reform J.; Pharisees, Sadducees; Hasidim, Rabbinists; Karaites; Nazarites, Essenes; pagano-christian sect, Gnostics, Mandaeans, Euchites; Islamic sect, Sunnis, Shi'ites, Sufis, Wahhabis; Black Muslims; Rastafarians, Rastas; Hindu sect, Vedantists, Vaishnavas, Saivas, Shaktas; Brahmoists, Hare Krishna sect; Tantrists, Pure Land sect, Jodo s. 973 *religious faith*.

sectarian, particularist; follower, adherent, devotee; Sectary, Nonconformist, Independant; Puritan, Shaker; Quaker, Friend; Pentecostalist; Presbyterian, Wee Free, Covenanter 976 *Protestant*; Salvationist; Christian Scientist;

Jehovah's Witness; Unitarian; Seventh-day Adventist, Mennonite; Mormon; Moonie; Christadelphian, Scientologist, Gnostic 977 *heretic*.

schismatic, separated brother; schismatics, separated brethren; separatist, separationist; seceder, secessionist; splinter group; factionary, factionist; rebel, mutineer 738 *revolter*; recusant, nonjuror; dissident, dissenter, nonconformist 489 *dissentient*; wrong believer 977 *heretic*; apostate 603 *tergiversator*.

Adj. *sectarian*, particularist; party-minded, partisan 481 *biased*; clannish, exclusive; Judaizer, Ebionite; Gallican; Erastian; High-Church, episcopalian 976 *Anglican*; Low-Church, evangelical 976 *Protestant*; Puritan, Independant, Presbyterian, Covenanting; revivalist, Pentecostalist; Vaishnavite, Saiva, Shakta, Tantrist; Ramakrishna; Rastafarian; Sunni, Shi'ite, Sufic; Essene, Pharisaic, Sadducean, Hasidic; Gnostic.

schismatical, schismatic, secessionist, seceding, breakaway; divided, separated 46 *separate*; excommunicated, excommunicable 977 *heretical*; dissentient, nonconformist 489 *dissenting*; recusant 769 *nonobservant*; rebellious, rebel, contumacious 738 *disobedient*; apostate.

979 Piety – N. *piety*, piousness, goodness 933 *virtue*; reverence, veneration, honour, decent respect 920 *respect*; dutifulness, attendance at worship, regular churchgoing 768 *observance*; churchmanship 976 *orthodoxy*; religiousness, religion, theism 973 *deism*; religious feeling; fear of God 854 *fear*; pious belief, faith, trust in God 485 *belief*; devotion, dedication 931 *disinterestedness*; devoutness, sincerity, earnestness, unction; enthusiasm, fervour, zeal; inspiration, exaltation, speaking in tongues, glossolalia 821 *excitation*; adoration, prostration 981 *worship*; meditation, retreat; contemplation, mysticism, communion with God, mystic communion 973 *religion*; faith healing 656 *restoration*; act of piety; good works; pilgrimage, hajj.

sanctity, sanctitude, holiness, hallowedness, sacredness, sacrosanctity; goodness, cardinal virtues 933 *virtue*; state of grace, odour of sanctity 950 *purity*; godliness, saintliness; spirituality, unworldliness, otherworldiness; spiritual life; sainthood, blessedness, blessed state; enlightenment; conversion, regeneration, rebirth, new birth 656 *revival*; sanctification; canonization, beatification, consecration, dedication.

pietism, show of piety, sanctimony; sanctimoniousness, unction, cant 542 *sham*; religionism, religiosity, religious mania; bible-thumping *or* bashing; tender conscience; austerity 945 *asceticism*; formalism, Puritanism 481 *narrow mind*; literalness, fundamentalism, Bible-worship, bibliolatry 494 *accuracy*; sabbatarianism 978 *sectarianism*; churchiness, sacerdotalism, ritualism 985 *ecclesiasticism*; preachiness, unctuousness; bigotry, fanaticism 481 *prejudice*; persecution, witch-hunting, heresy-h. 735 *severity*.

pietist, pious person, real saint 937 *good person*; children of God, c. of light; the good, the righteous, the just; conformist 488 *assenter*; practising Christian, communicant 981 *worshipper*; confessor, martyr; saint, bodhissattva, marabout; man *or* woman of prayer, contemplative, mystic, sufi; holy man, sadhu, sannyasi, bhikshu, fakir, dervish 945 *ascetic*; hermit, anchorite 883 *solitary*; monk, nun, religious 986 *clergy*; devotee; convert, neophyte, catechumen, ordinand 538 *learner*; believer, the faithful; the chosen people, the elect; pilgrim, palmer, hajji; votary.

zealot, religionist, enthusiast, wowser, fanatic, bigot, image-breaker, iconoclast; formalist, precisian, Puritan; Pharisee, scribe, scribes and Pharisees; the unco guid, goody-goody; fundamentalist, inerrantist, Bible-worshipper, bibliolater, Sabbatarian 978 *sectarian*; bible-puncher *or* thumper *or* basher; pulpiteer 537 *preacher*; evangelical, salvationist,

hot-gospeller; missionary 901 *philanthropist*; revivalist, speaker in tongues, faith healer; champion of the faith, crusader; militant Christian; militant Islamite, ghazi; persecutor 735 *tyrant*.

Adj. *pious*, good, 933 *virtuous*; decent, reverent 920 *respectful*; faithful 739 *obedient*; conforming; believing 976 *orthodox*; sincere; pure, pure in heart, holyminded; unworldly, otherworldly, spiritual; godly, God-fearing, religious, devout; praying, psalm-singing; in retreat, meditative, contemplative, mystic; holy, saintly, saintlike; Christian.

pietistic, ardent, fervent, seraphic; enthusiastic, inspired; austere 945 *ascetic*; hermit-like, anchoretic 883 *unsociable*; earnest, pi, religiose, overreligious, overpious, self-righteous, holier than thou; overstrict, precise, Puritan; formalistic, Pharisaic, ritualistic 978 *sectarian*; priest-ridden, churchy; psalm-singing, hymn-s.; preachy, bible-thumping *or* bashing, sanctimonious, canting 850 *affected*; goody-goody, too good to be true 933 *virtuous*; crusading, evangelical, missionary-minded.

sanctified, consecrated, dedicated, enshrined; reverend, holy, sacred, solemn, sacrosanct 866 *worshipful*; haloed, sainted, canonized, beatified; chosen; saved, redeemed, ransomed; renewed, reborn, born again.

Vb. *be pious*, - religious etc. adj.; have one's mind on higher things; fear God 854 *fear*; have faith 485 *believe*; keep the faith, fight the good fight 162 *be strong*; walk humbly with one's God; go to church, be a regular churchgoer; pray, say one's prayers 981 *worship*; kneel, genuflect, bow 311 *stoop*; cross oneself, make the sign of the cross; make offering, sacrifice, devote 759 *offer*; give alms and oblations, lend to God 781 *give*; give to charity; glorify God 923 *praise*; give God the glory 907 *thank*; revere, show reverence 920 *show respect*; sermonize, preach at 534 *teach*; set a good example.

become pious, be converted, get religion; see the light, see the error of one's

ways 603 *recant*; mend one's ways, reform, repent, repent of one's evil ways, receive Christ 939 *be penitent*; enter the church, become ordained, take holy orders, take vows, take the veil 986 *take orders*.

make pious, bring religion to, proselytize, convert 485 *convince*; Christianize, win for Christ, baptize, receive into the church 299 *admit*; Islamize, Judaize; spiritualize 648 *purify*; confirm in the faith 162 *strengthen*; inspire, fill with grace; redeem 656 *restore*.

sanctify, hallow, make holy, keep h. 866 *honour*; consecrate, dedicate, enshrine 866 *dignify*; make a saint of, canonize, beatify, invest with a halo; bless, make the sign of the cross.

980 Impiety – **N.** *impiety*, impiousness; irreverence; godlessness 974 *irreligion*; scoffing, mockery, derision 851 *ridicule*; scorn, pride 922 *contempt*; sacrilegiousness, profanity; blasphemy, cursing, swearing 899 *malediction*; sacrilege, desecration, violation, profanation, perversion, abuse 675 *misuse*; immorality, sin, pervertedness 934 *wickedness*; lapse of faith, backsliding, apostasy; profaneness, unholiness, worldliness, materialism 319 *materiality*; paganism, heathenism.

false piety, sham p. 541 *falsehood*; sanctimoniousness, Pharisaism 979 *pietism*; hypocrisy, lip service 541 *duplicity*; cant 850 *affectation*.

impious person, blasphemer, curser, swearer 899 *malediction*; defamer 926 *detractor*; desecrator, violator, profaner 904 *offender*; gentile, pagan, infidel, unbeliever 974 *heathen*; atheist, sceptic; materialist, immoralist 944 *sensualist*; sinner, reprobate, children of darkness 938 *bad person*; recidivist, backslider, apostate; fallen angel 969 *Satan*.

Adj. *impious*, ungodly, anti-Christian; dissenting 977 *heretical*; unbelieving, nonbelieving, atheistical, godless 974 *irreligious*; nonpractising 769 *nonobservant*; scoffing, mocking, deriding;

blasphemous, swearing 899 *cursing*; irreligious, irreverent; sacrilegious, profaning, desecrating, violating, iconoclastic 954 *lawless*; sinning, sinful, impure, perverted, reprobate 934 *wicked*; lapsing, backsliding, apostate.

profane, unholy, unhallowed, unsanctified, unblest; accursed; unconsecrated; infidel, pagan.

Vb. *be impious,* - sacrilegious etc. adj.; sin 934 *be wicked*; swear, blaspheme, take the name of the Lord in vain 899 *curse*; profane, desecrate, violate 675 *misuse*; commit sacrilege, defile, sully 649 *make unclean*; worship false gods; play false 541 *dissemble*; lapse, backslide 603 *apostatize.*

981 Worship – **N.** *worship,* honour, reverence, homage 920 *respect*; awe 854 *fear*; veneration, adoration; humbleness 872 *humility*; devotion, devotedness 979 *piety*; prayer, one's devotions, one's prayers; retreat, meditation, contemplation, communion with God.

cult, mystique; service of God, supreme worship, latria; inferior worship, dulia, hyperdulia; Christolatry, Mariolatry; iconolatry, image-worship; false worship 982 *idolatry.*

act of worship, rites; praises; glorification; hymn-singing, psalm-s., psalmody, plainsong, chanting 412 *vocal music*; thanksgiving, blessing, benediction 907 *thanks*; offering, oblation, almsgiving, sacrifice, offering (**see** *oblation*); praying, saying one's prayers, reciting the rosary; self-examination 939 *penitence*; self-denial, self-discipline 945 *asceticism*; keeping fast 946 *fasting*; hajj, pilgrimage.

prayers, orisons, devotions; retreat, contemplation 449 *meditation*; prayer; petition, petitionary prayer 761 *request*; invocation, invocatory prayer 583 *allocution*; intercession, intercessory prayer, arrow p. 762 *deprecation*; suffrage, prayers for the dead, vigils; special

prayer, intention; rogation, supplication, solemn s., litany, solemn l.; comminatory prayer, commination, denunciation 900 *threat*; imprecation, imprecatory prayer 899 *malediction*; excommunication, ban 883 *seclusion*; exorcism 300 *ejection*; benediction, benedicite, benison, grace 907 *thanks*; prayer for the day, collect; liturgical prayer, the Lord's Prayer, Paternoster, Our Father; Ave, Ave Maria, Hail Mary; Kyrie Eleison, Sursum Corda, Sanctus; Nunc Dimittis; dismissal, blessing; rosary, beads, beadroll; prayer-wheel; prayer book, missal, breviary, book of hours; call to prayer, muezzin's cry 547 *call.*

hymn, song, psalm, metrical p.; religious song, spiritual; processional hymn, recessional; introit; plainsong, Gregorian chant, Ambrosian c., descant 412 *vocal music*; anthem, cantata, motet; antiphon, response; canticle, Te Deum, Benedicite; song of praise, paean, Magnificat; doxology, Gloria; greater doxology, Gloria in Excelsis; lesser doxology, Gloria Patri; paean, Hallelujah, Hosanna; Homeric hymn; Vedic hymn; hymn-singing, hymnody; psalm-singing, psalmody; hymnbook, hymnal, hymnary, psalter; Vedic hymns, Rigveda, Samaveda; hymnology, hymnography.

oblation, offertory, collection, alms and oblations 781 *offering*; pew rent, pewage; libation, incense; dedication, consecration; votive offering; scapegoat 150 *substitute*; burnt offering, holocaust; sacrifice, devotion; immolation, hecatomb 362 *slaughter*; human sacrifice 362 *homicide*; self-sacrifice 931 *disinterestedness*; self-immolation, suttee 362 *suicide*; expiation, propitiation 941 *atonement*; a humble and a contrite heart 939 *penitence.*

public worship, common prayer, intercommunion; agape, love-feast; service, divine service, divine office, mass, matins, evensong, benediction 988 *church service*; psalm-singing, psalmody, hymn-singing 412 *vocal music*; church, church-going, chapel-g. 979 *piety*; meeting for

prayer, gathering for worship 74 *assembly*; prayer meeting, revival m.; open-air service, mission s., street evangelism, revivalism; temple worship, state religion 973 *religion*.

worshipper, fellow w., coreligionist; adorer, venerator; votary, devotee, oblate 979 *pietist*; glorifier, hymner, praiser, idolizer, admirer, ardent a., humble a. 923 *commender*; follower, server 742 *servant*; image-worshipper, iconolater; sacrificer, offerer 781 *giver*; invocator, invoker, caller 583 *allocution*; supplicator, supplicant, suppliant 763 *petitioner*; man *or* woman of prayer, beadsman, intercessor; contemplative, mystic, sufi, visionary; dervish, marabout, enthusiast, revivalist, prophet 973 *religious teacher*; celebrant, officiant 986 *clergy*; communicant, churchgoer, chapelgoer, temple worshipper; congregation, the faithful; psalm-singer, hymn-s., psalmodist, chanter, cantor; psalmist, hymn-writer, hymnologist; pilgrim, palmer, hajji 268 *traveller*.

Vb. *worship*, honour, revere, venerate, adore 920 *respect*; honour and obey 854 *fear*; pay homage to, acknowledge 917 *do one's duty*; make a god of one, deify; bow down before, kneel to, genuflect, prostrate oneself. lift up one's heart; extol, laud, magnify, glorify, give glory to 923 *praise*; celebrate 413 *sing*; light candles to, burn incense before, offer sacrifice to; pray, say a prayer, say one's prayers, recite the rosary; commune with God 979 *be pious*.

offer worship, celebrate, officiate, minister, administer the sacraments 988 *perform ritual*; lead the congregation, lead in prayer; sacrifice, make s., offer up 781 *give*; sacrifice to, propitiate, appease 719 *pacify*; vow, make vows 764 *promise*; dedicate, consecrate 979 *sanctify*; take vows, enter holy orders 986 *take orders*; go to church, go to chapel, go to meeting, meet for prayer 979 *be pious*; go to service, hear Mass, take the sacraments, receive the Eucharist, take Holy Communion; observe Lent 946 *starve*; deny oneself 945 *be ascetic*; go into retreat 449

meditate; chant psalms, sing hymns, sing praises.

982 Idolatry – N. *idolatry*, idolatrousness, false worship, superstition 981 *worship*; heathenism, paganism 973 *religion*; fetishism, anthropomorphism, zoomorphism; iconolatry, image worship; mumbo jumbo, hocus-pocus 983 *sorcery*; cult; sacrifice, human s. 981 *oblation*; heliolatry, sun worship; star worship, Sabaism; pyrolatry, fire worship; zoolatry, animal worship; ophiolatry, snake worship; necrolatry, worship of the dead, demonolatry, devil worship 969 *diabolism*; Mammonism, worship of wealth.

idol, image, graven i., fetish, totem pole; lingam, yoni; golden calf 966 *deity*; godling, joss; teraphim, lares et penates, totem; Mumbo-Jumbo; Juggernaut, Baal, Moloch.

983 Sorcery – N. *sorcery*, witchery, magic arts, enchantments; witchcraft; magic lore 490 *knowledge*; wizardry; wonderworking, thaumaturgy 864 *miracleworking*; magic, jugglery, illusionism 542 *sleight*; white magic; black magic, black art, necromancy; witch-doctoring, shamanism; obeah, obi, voodooism, voodoo, hoodoo; spirit-raising 511 *divination*, 984 *occultism*; spirit-laying, ghost-l., exorcism 988 *rite*; magic rite, incantation; coven, witches' sabbath, witches' coven; Walpurgisnacht, Hallowe'en; witching hour.

spell, charm, enchantment, cantrip, hoodoo, curse; evil eye, jinx, hex, influence; bewitchment, fascination 291 *attraction*; obsession, possession, demoniacal p.; incantation; magic sign; magic word, magic formula, abraxas, open sesame, abracadabra; hocus pocus, mumbo jumbo, fee faw fum 515 *lack of meaning*; philtre, love potion.

talisman, charm, countercharm; cross, phylactery; St Christopher medal 662 *safeguard*; juju, obeah, mojo, fetish 982 *idol*; periapt, amulet, mascot, lucky charm; rabbit's foot, four-leaf clover,

horseshoe, black cat; pentacle, pentagram 547 *indication*; swastika, fylfot, gammadion; scarab; birthstone; emblem; relic, holy r.

magic instrument, bell, book and candle, broomstick; witches' brew, hellbroth, witches' cauldron; philtre, potion, moly; wand, magic w., fairy w.; magic ring, wishing cap; Aladdin's lamp, flying carpet, magic c.; seven-league boots; Excalibur; wishing well, wishbone, merrythought.

sorcerer, wise man, seer, soothsayer; astrologer, alchemist 984 *occultist*; Druid, magus, the Magi; thaumaturgist, wonder-worker, miracle-w. 864 *miracleworking*; shaman, witchdoctor, medicine man, fetishist; obi-man, voodooist, hoodooist, spirit-raiser 984 *occultist*; conjuror, exorcist; snakecharmer; juggler, illusionist; enchanter, wizard, warlock; magician, theurgist; necromancer 969 *diabolist*; familiar, imp, evil spirit 969 *devil*; sorcerer's apprentice; Merlin, Prospero, Gandalf; Faust, Pied Piper.

sorceress, wise woman, Sibyl 511 *diviner*; Druidess; enchantress, witch, weird sister; hag, hellcat; succubus, succuba; lamia; fairy godmother, wicked fairy, Morgan le Fay 970 *fairy*; Witch of Endor, Hecate, Circe, Medea; three witches in 'Macbeth'.

Adj. *magical,* otherworldly, supernatural, uncanny, eldritch, weird 970 *fairylike*; spell-like; voodooistic; talismanic, phylacteric; magic, charmed, enchanted 178 *influential*.

bewitched, enchanted, charmed, fey; hypnotized, fascinated, spellbound, under the evil eye; under a curse, cursed; blighted, blasted, withered; hag-ridden, haunted.

Vb. *bewitch,* charm, enchant, fascinate 291 *attract*; hypnotize; magic; spellbind, cast a spell on, weave a spell over, lay under a spell; put a voodoo on; cast the evil eye, blight, blast 898 *be malevolent*; put a curse on, lay under a curse 899 *curse*; taboo, make t. 757 *prohibit*; hagride.

984 Occultism – N. *occultism,* esotericism, hermeticism, mysticism, transcendentalism 973 *religion*; cabbalism, cabbala, gematria; theosophy, reincarnationism; yogism; sciosophy, hyperphysics, metapsychics; supernaturalism, psychicism, pseudopsychology; secret art, esoteric science, occult lore, alchemy, astrology, psychomancy, spiritualism, magic 983 *sorcery*; sortilege 511 *divination*; fortune-telling, crystal-gazing, palmistry, chiromancy, tea-leaf reading 511 *prediction*; clairvoyance, feyness, second sight 438 *vision*; sixth sense 476 *intuition*; animal magnetism, mesmerism, hypnotism; hypnosis, hypnotic trance 375 *insensibility*.

psychics, parapsychology, psychism 447 *psychology*; psychic science, psychical research; paranormal perception, extrasensory p., ESP; telaesthesia, clairvoyance, feyness, second sight 476 *intuition*; psychokinesis, fork-bending; telepathy, telergy; thought-reading, mind-r., thought transference; precognition, psi faculty; déjà vu.

spiritualism, spiritism; spirit communication, psychomancy 983 *sorcery*; sciomancy 511 *divination*; mediumism; séance; astral body, spirit b., ethereal b. 320 *immateriality*; spirit manifestation, materialization, ectoplasm 319 *materiality*; apport, telekinesis; poltergeists; spirit-rapping, table-tapping, table-turning; automatism, automatic writing, spirit w., psychography 586 *writing*; spirit message, psychogram; spiritualistic apparatus, psychograph, planchette, ouija board; control 970 *ghost*; ghost-hunting; psychical research; exorcism.

occultist, mystic; cabbalist; theosophist, yogi; spiritualist; astrologer, fortune-teller, spaewife *or* man, crystalgazer, palmist 511 *diviner*.

psychic, clairvoyant; telepathist; mind reader, thought r.; mesmerist, hypnotist; medium, spirit-rapper, automatist, psychographer, spirit-writer; seer, prophet 511 *oracle*.

psychical, psychic, fey, second-sighted; prophetic 511 *predicting*; tele-pathic, clairvoyant; thought-reading, mind-r.; spiritualistic, mediumistic; ectoplasmic, telekinetic, spirit-rapping; mesmeric, hypnotic.

paranormal, parapsychological, meta-psychological, supernatural, preternatu-ral, supranormal, supranatural.

985 The Church – N. *the church,* theocracy 733 *authority*; church government, Canterbury, Vatican 733 *government*; ecclesiastical order; papalism, papacy, popedom; popishness, ultramontanism; prelatism, prelacy; episcopacy, episcopalianism; presbytery, presbyterianism, congregationalism, ecclesiology.

ecclesiasticism, clericalism, sacerdotalism; priestliness, priesthood, brahminhood; priestdom, priestcraft; Brahminism; benefit of clergy 919 *nonliability*; Holy Office, Index Expurgatorious 757 *prohibition.*

monasticism, monastic life, mona-chism 895 *celibacy*; cenobitism 883 *seclusion*; monkhood, monkishness 945 *asceticism.*

holy orders, orders, minor o. 986 *cleric*; apostolic succession, ordination, consecration; induction, reading in; installation, enthronement; nomination, presentation, appointment 751 *commission*; preferment, translation, elevation 285 *progression.*

church office 689 *management*; ecclesiastical rank; priesthood; apostolate, apostleship; pontificate, papacy, Holy See, Vatican; cardinalate, cardinalship; patriarchate, exarchate, metropolitanate; primacy, primateship; archiepiscopate, archbishopric; see, bishopric, episcopate, episcopacy, prelacy, prelature; abbotship, abbacy, abbotric; priorate, priorship; archdeaconry, archdeaconate, archdeaconship; deanery, deanship; canonry, canonicate; prebendaryship; deaconate, deaconship; diaconate, subdiaconate; presbyterate,

presbytership, eldership, moderator-ship, ministership, pastorship, pastorate; rectorship, vicarship, vicariate; curacy, cure of souls; chaplainship, chaplaincy, chaplainry; incumbency, tenure, benefice 773 *possession.*

parish, deanery; presbytery; diocese, bishopric, see, archbishopric; metropolitanate, patriarchate, province 184 *district.*

benefice, incumbency, tenure; living, rectorship, parsonage; glebe, tithe; prebend, prebendal stall, canonry; temporalities, church lands, church endowments 777 *property*; patronage, advowson, right of presentation.

synod, provincial s., convocation, general council, ecumenical c. 692 *council*; college of cardinals, consistory, conclave; bench of bishops, episcopal bench; chapter, vestry; kirk session, presbytery, synod, Sanhedrim 956 *tribunal*; consistorial court, Court of Arches.

Adj. *ecclesiastical,* ecclestiastic, churchly, ecclesiological, theocratic; infallible 733 *authoritative*; priest-ridden, ultramontane 976 *orthodox*; apostolic; hierarchical, pontifical, papal 976 *Roman Catholic*; patriarchal, metropolitan; episcopal, prelatic; episcopalian, presbyterian, Wee Free 978 *sectarian*; prioral, abbatial; conciliar, synodic, presbyteral, capitular; sanhedral, consistorial; provincial, diocesan, parochial.

986 Clergy – N. *clergy,* hierarchy; clerical order, parsondom, the cloth, the pulpit, the ministry; sacerdotal order, priesthood, secular clergy, regular clergy, religious.

cleric, clerk in holy orders, priest, deacon, subdeacon, acolyte, exorcist, lector, ostiary; churchman *or* -woman, ecclesiastic, divine; Doctor of Divinity; clergyman, man *or* woman of the cloth, minister of the Gospel, servant of God; reverend, father, father in God; padre, sky pilot, Holy Joe; beneficed clergyman, beneficiary, pluralist, parson, minister,

rector, incumbent, residentiary 776 *possessor*; hedgepriest, priestling 639 *nonentity*; ordinand, seminarist 538 *learner*.

pastor, shepherd, father in God, minister, woman m., parish priest, rector, vicar, perpetual curate, curate, abbé; chaplain; confessor, father c., penitentiary; spiritual director, spiritual adviser; pardoner; friar; preaching order, predicant; pulpiteer, lay preacher 537 *preacher*; field preacher, missioner, missionary 901 *philanthropist*; evangelist, revivalist, salvationist, hot-gospeller.

ecclesiarch, ecclesiastical potentate, hierarch, dignitary 741 *governor*; pope, Supreme Pontiff, Holy Father, Vicar of Christ, Bishop of Rome; cardinal, prince of the church; patriarch, exarch, metropolitan, primate, archbishop; prelate, diocesan, bishop; suffragan, assistant bishop, 'episcopal curate'; bench of bishops, episcopate, Lords Spiritual; episcopi vagantes; archpriest, archpresbyter; archdeacon, deacon, subdeacon; dean, subdean, rural dean; canon, canon regular, canon secular, residentiary; prebendary, capitular; archimandrite; Superior, Mother S.; abbot, abbess; prior, prioress, Grand Prior; elder, presbyter, moderator.

monk, monastic 895 *celibate*; hermit, cenobite, Desert Father 883 *solitary*; Orthodox monk, caloyer; Islamic monk, santon, marabout; sufi 979 *pietist*; dervish, fakir 945 *ascetic*; Buddhist monk, pongye, bonze; brother, regular, conventual; superior, archimandrite, abbot, prior; novice, lay brother; friar, begging f., mendicant f., discalced f., barefoot f.; monks, religious; fraternity, brotherhood, lay b., friary; order, religious o. 708 *community*; Black Monk, Benedictine, Cistercian, Bernardine, Trappist; Carthusian; Cluniac; Gilbertine; Premonstratensian, Mathurin, Trinitarian; Dominicans, Friars Majors, Black Friars; Franciscans, Poverelli, Grey Friars, Friars Minors, Capuchins; Augustines, Austin Friars; Carmelites, White Friars; Crutched Friars; Beghards; teaching order, missionary o., Society of Jesus, Jesuits; crusading order, Templars, Knights Templars; Hospitallers, Knights Hospitallers, Knights of the Hospital of St John of Jerusalem, Knights of Malta.

nun, clergywoman; anchoress, recluse; religious, bride of Christ; sister, mother; novice, postulant; lay sister; Superioress, Mother Superior, abbess, prioress, canoness, deaconess; sisterhood, lay s., beguinage, Beguine; Carmelites, Ursulines, Poor Clares, Little Sisters of the Poor, Sisters of Mercy.

church officer, elder, presbyter, deacon 741 *officer*; priest, chantry p., chaplain; curate in charge, minister; lay preacher, lay reader; acolyte, server, altar boy; crucifer, thurifer; chorister, choirboy, precentor, succentor, cantor 413 *choir*; sidesman *or* -woman; churchwarden; clerk, vestry c., parish c.; beadle, verger, pew-opener; sacristan, sexton; grave digger, bellringer.

priest, chief p., high p., archpriest, hierophant; priestess, Vestal, Pythia, Pythoness, prophetess, prophet 511 *oracle*; Levite; rabbi; imam, mufti; Brahmin; bonze, lama, Dalai L., Panchen L.; pontifex, pontiff, flamen, archflamen; Druid, Druidess; shaman, witch doctor.

church title, Holy Father; Eminence; Monsignor, Monseigneur; Lordship, Lord Spiritual; Most Reverend, Right R., Very R.; the Reverend; parson, rector, vicar; father, brother, Dom; mother, sister.

monastery, monkery, bonzery, lamasery; friary; priory, abbey; cloister, convent, nunnery, beguinage; ashram, hermitage 192 *retreat*; community house 192 *abode*; theological college, seminary; cell 194 *chamber*.

parsonage, presbytery, rectory, vicarage; manse; deanery, archdeaconry 192 *abode*; palaee, bishop's p., patriarchate; Lambeth, Vatican; close, cathedral c., precincts 235 *enclosure*.

Adj. *monastic,* cloistered, enclosed; monkish, celibate; contemplative, in retreat; cowled, veiled; tonsured, shaven and shorn.

Vb. *take orders,* take holy orders, be ordained, enter the church, enter the ministry, become a minister *or* vicar, wear the cloth; take vows, take the tonsure, take the cowl; take the veil, become a nun; enter a monastery *or* a nunnery; renounce the world.

987 Laity – N. *laity,* temporalty, lay people, people, civilians 869 *commonalty*; cure, charge, parish; flock, sheep, fold; diocesans, parishioners; brethren, congregation, society; lay brethren, lay sisterhood, lay community 708 *community*.

lay person, laic; lay rector, lay deacon; lay brother, lay sister; catechumen, ordinand, seminarist, novice, postulant 538 *learner*; lay preacher, lay reader; elder, deacon, deaconess 986 *church officer*; parishioner, diocesan, member of the flock; laicizer, secularizer.

988 Ritual – N. *ritual,* procedure, way of doing things, method, routine 624 *way*; prescribed procedure, due order 60 *order*; form, order, liturgy 610 *practice*; ceremonial, ceremony 875 *formality*.

rite, mode of worship 981 *cult*; observance, ritual practice 610 *practice*; form, order, ordinance, rubric, formula, formulary 693 *precept*; ceremony, solemnity, sacrament, mystery 876 *celebration*; rites, mysteries 551 *representation*; initiatory rite, rite of passage, circumcision, initiation, initiation rites, baptism 299 *reception*; christening; salat, puja.

ministration, functioning, officiation, performance 676 *action*; administration, celebration, solemnization; the pulpit, sermon, address, preaching 534 *teaching*; homily 534 *lecture*; homiletics 579 *oratory*; pastoral care, cure of souls; pastoral epistle, pastoral letter; confession, auricular c.; shrift, absolution, penance.

Christian rite, rites of the Church; sacrament, the seven sacraments; baptism, christening 299 *reception*; immersion, total i. 303 *immersion*; laying on of hands, confirmation, First Communion;

Holy Communion, Eucharist, reservation of the sacraments; penitential rites 941 *penance*; absolution 960 *acquittal*; Holy Matrimony 894 *marriage*; Holy Orders 985 *the church*; Holy Unction, chrism; visitation of the sick, extreme unction, last rites, viaticum; burial of the dead; requiem mass; liturgy, order of service, order of baptism, marriage service, solemnization of matrimony, nuptial mass; churching of women; ordination, ordering of deacons, ordering of priests; consecration, consecration of bishops; exorcism 300 *ejection*; excommunication, ban, bell, book and candle; canonization, beatification; dedication, undedication.

Holy Communion, Eucharist, Blessed E.; mass, high m., missa solemnis; sung m., missa cantata; low mass; public mass, private m.; communion, the Lord's Supper; preparation, confession, asperges; service of the book, introit, the Kyries, the Gloria, the Lesson, the Gradual, the Collects, the Gospel, the creed; service of the Altar, the offertory, offertory sentence, offertory prayers, the biddings; the blessing, the thanksgiving, Sursum Corda, Preface, Sanctus, Great Amen; the breaking of the bread, the commixture; the Pax; consecration; elevation of the Host; Angus Dei; the Communion; kiss of peace; prayers of thanksgiving, the dismissal; the blessing.

the sacrament, the Holy Sacrament, the Blessed Eucharist; Corpus Christi; body and blood of Christ; real presence, transubstantiation, consubstantiation, impanation; the elements, bread and wine, altar bread; consecrated bread, host; reserved sacrament; viaticum.

church service, office, duty, service 981 *act of worship*; liturgy, celebration, concelebration; canonical hours, matins, lauds, prime, terce, sext, none, vespers, compline; the little hours; morning prayer, matins; evening prayer, evensong, benediction; Tenebrae; vigil, midnight mass, watchnight service; devotional service, three-hour s.; novena.

ritual act, symbolical act, sacramental, symbolism 551 *representation*; lustration, purification; thurification, incense-burning 338 *vaporization*; sprinkling, aspersion, asperges; circumambulation 314 *circuition*; procession 285 *progression*; stations of the cross 981 *act of worship*; obeisance, bowing, kneeling, genuflexion, prostration, homage 920 *respects*; crossing oneself, signation, sign of the cross 547 *gesture*; eucharistic rite, breaking the bread; intinction; elevating of the Host; kiss of peace; sacrifice.

ritual object, cross, rood, Holy Rood, crucifix; altar, Lord's table, communion t.; altar furniture, altar cloth, candle, candlestick; communion wine, communion bread; cup, chalice, grail, Holy Grail, Sangrail; cruet; paten, ciborium, pyx, pyx chest, tabernacle; monstrance, chrism, chrismatory; collection plate, salver; incense, incensory, censer, thurible; holy water; aspergillum; aspersorium; piscina; sacring bell, Sanctus bell; font, baptismal f., baptistery; baptismal garment, chrisom, christening gown; wedding garment, wedding dress, bridal veil, wedding ring; devotional object, relics, sacred relics; reliquary, shrine, casket 194 *box*; icon, Pietà, Holy Sepulchre, stations of the cross 551 *image*; osculatory, pax; Agnus Dei, rosary, beads, beadroll 981 *prayers*; votive candle; non-Christian objects; Ark of the Covenant, Mercy-seat; seven-branched candlestick; shewbread; laver; hyssop; sackcloth and ashes; libation dish, patina; joss stick; prayer wheel; altar of incense; urim, thummim; temple veil.

hymnal, hymn book, hymnary; psalter, psalm-book, book of psalms 981 *hymn.*

holy day, feast, feast day, festival 837 *festivity*; fast day, meatless d. 946 *fast*; high day, day of observance, day of obligation 876 *celebration*; sabbath, sabbath-day, day of rest 681 *leisure*; Lord's Day, Sunday; saint's day 141 *anniversary*; All Hallows, All Saints, All Souls, Lady Day, Feast of the Annunciation; Candlemas, Feast of the Purification;

Feast of the Assumption; Lammas, Martinmas, Michaelmas; Advent; Christmas, Christmastide, Yuletide, Noel, Nativity, Epiphany, Twelfth Night; Lent, Shrove Tuesday, Ash Wednesday, Maundy Thursday, Good Friday; Holy Week, Passion Week; Easter, Eastertide, Easter Sunday; Ascension Day; Whitsuntide, Whitsun, Pentecost; Corpus Christi; Trinity Sunday; Passover; Feast of Weeks, Pentecost; Feast of Tabernacles, Feast of Ingathering; Feast of the Dedication, Hanukkah; Day of Atonement, Yom Kippur; Ramadan, Bairam; Muharram.

Adj. *ritual,* procedural; formal, solemn, ceremonial, liturgical; processional, recessional; symbolic, symbolical.

ritualistic, ceremonious, ceremonial, formulistic.

Vb. *perform ritual,* perform the rites, say office, celebrate, concelebrate, officiate; take the service, lead worship 981 *offer worship*; baptize, christen, confirm, ordain, lay on hands; minister, administer the sacraments, give communion; sacrifice, offer s., make s.; offer prayers, bless, give benediction; anathematize, ban, ban with bell, book and candle; excommunicate, unchurch, unfrock; dedicate, consecrate, deconsecrate; purify, lustrate, asperge; cense, burn incense; anoint, give extreme unction; confess, absolve, pronounce absolution, shrive; take communion, partake of Holy Communion, receive the sacraments; bow, kneel, genuflect, prostrate oneself; sign oneself, cross o., make the sign of the cross; take holy water; tell one's beads, say one's rosary; make one's stations; process, go in procession; circumambulate; fast, flagellate oneself, do penance.

989 Canonicals – N. *canonicals,* clericals, clerical dress, cloth, clerical black 228 *dress*; frock, soutane, cassock, scapular; cloak, gown, Geneva g. 228 *cloak*; robe, cowl, hood, capuche; lappet, bands, Geneva b.; clerical collar, dog c.; chimere,

lawn sleeves; apron, gaiters, shovel hat; cardinal's hat; priests' cap, biretta, black b., purple b., red b.; skullcap, calotte, zucchetto; Salvation Army bonnet 228 *headgear*; tonsure, shaven crown 229 *bareness*; prayer-cap; tallith.

vestments, ephod, priestly vesture, canonical robes; pontificalia, pontificals; cassock, surplice, rochet; cope, tunicle, dalmatic, alb 228 *robe*; amice, chasuble; stole, deacon's s.; scarf, tippet, pallium; cingulum; maniple, fanon; mitre, tiara, triple crown 743 *regalia*; papal vestment, orale; crosier, crook, staff, pastoral s. 743 *badge of rank*; pectoral 222 *cross*; episcopal ring; orphrey *or* orfray, ecclesiastical embroidery 844 *ornamentation.*

990 Temple – N. *temple,* pantheon; shrine; joss house; house of God, tabernacle, the Temple, House of the Lord; place of worship 981 *worship*; masjid, mosque; house of prayer, oratory; pagoda, stupa, tope, dagoba, ziggurat 164 *edifice*; torii, toran, gopuram 263 *doorway.*

holy place, holy ground, sacred g.; sanctuary, adytum, cella, naos; Ark of the Covenant, Mercy-seat, Sanctum, Holy of Holies, oracle; martyry, sacred tomb, marabout, sepulchre, Holy Sepulchre; graveyard, God's Acre 364 *cemetery*; place of pilgrimage; Holy City, Zion, Jerusalem; Mecca, Benares.

church, God's house; parish church, daughter c., chapel of ease; cathedral, minster, procathedral; basilica; abbey; kirk, chapel, tabernacle, temple, bethel, ebenezer; conventicle, meeting house, prayer h.; house of prayer, oratory, chantry, chantry chapel; synagogue, mosque.

altar, high a., sacrarium, sanctuary; altar stone, altar slab; altar table, Lord's

t., communion t.; altar bread 988 *the sacrament*; altar pyx; prothesis, credence, credence table 988 *ritual object*; canopy, baldachin, altarpiece, diptych, triptych, altar screen, reredos; altar cloth, altar frontal, antependium; predella, altar rails.

church utensil, font, baptistry; ambry, stoup, piscina; chalice, paten 988 *ritual object*; pulpit, lectern; bible, chained b.; hymnal, hymnary, prayer book 981 *prayers*; hassock, kneeler; salver, collection plate, offertory bag; organ, harmonium; bell, church b., carillon.

church interior, nave, aisle, apse, ambulatory, transept; chancel, chevet, choir, sanctuary; hagioscope, squint; chancel screen, rood screen, jube, rood loft, gallery, organ loft; stall, choir s., sedile, sedilia, misericorde; pew, box pew; pulpit, ambo; lectern; chapel, side c., Lady c., feretory; confessional; clerestory, triforium; spandrel; stained glass, stained-glass window, rose w., jesse w.; calvary, stations of the cross, Easter sepulchre; baptistry, font; aumbry, sacristy, vestry; undercroft, crypt, vault; rood, cross, crucifix.

church exterior, porch, narthex, galilee; tympanum 263 *doorway*; tower, steeple, spire 209 *high structure*; bell tower, bellcote, belfry, campanile; buttress, flying b. 218 *prop*; cloister, ambulatory; chapterhouse, presbytery 692 *council*; churchyard, kirkyard, lychgate; close 235 *enclosure.*

Adj. *churchlike,* basilican, cathedrallike, cathedralesque; cruciform 222 *crossed*; apsidal 248 *curved*; Romanesque, Norman, Gothic, Early English, Decorated, Perpendicular, baroque, Puginesque, Gothic revival.

INDEX

For a note on how to use the index, see p. xiii

miscarry 728 vb.
abortion
  abnormality 84 n.
  propagation 167 n.
  unproductiveness
    172 n.
  deformity 246 n.
  extraction 304 n.
  undevelopment
    670 n.
  failure 728 n.
abortive
  unproductive
    172 adj.
  disappointing
    509 adj.
  profitless 641 adj.
  immature 670 adj.
  unsuccessful
    728 adj.
about
  concerning 9 adv.
  about 33 adv.
  nearly 200 adv.
  around 230 adv.
about-turn
  reversion 148 n.
  change of mind
    603 n.
above
  before 64 adv.
  rearward 238 adv.
above all
  eminently 34 adv.
above-board
  veracious 540 adj.
  artless 699 adj.
  just 913 adj.
  honourable
    929 adj.
above-mentioned
  preceding 64 adj.
  repeated 106 adj.
  prior 119 adj.
abracadabra
  lack of meaning
    515 n.
  spell 983 n.
abrasion
  diminution 37 n.
  subtraction 39 n.
  powderiness 332 n.
  friction 333 n.
  wound 655 n.
abrasive
  pulverizer 332 n.

abreaction
  liberation 746 n.
  feeling 818 n.
abreast
  equal 28 adj.
abridge
  abate 37 vb.
  subtract 39 vb.
  make smaller
    198 vb.
  shorten 204 vb.
  be concise 569 vb.
  abstract 592 vb.
abridged
  small 33 adj.
  short 204 adj.
abridgment
  smallness 33 n.
  diminution 37 n.
  shortening 204 n.
  translation 520 n.
  edition 589 n.
  compendium
    592 n.
abrogate
  abrogate 752 vb.
abrupt
  instantaneous
    116 adj.
  vertical 215 adj.
  sloping 220 adj.
  sullen 893 adj.
abscess
  ulcer 651 n.
abscission
  scission 46 n.
  uncovering 229 n.
abscond
  decamp 296 vb.
  run away 620 vb.
  elude 667 vb.
  escape 667 vb.
  fail in duty 918 vb.
abseil
  descend 309 vb.
absence
  absence 190 n.
absent
  absent 190 adj.
absenteeism
  absence 190 n.
  inactivity 679 n.
  undutifulness
    918 n.
absent-minded
  abstracted 456 adj.
  forgetful 506 adj.

absent oneself
  be absent 190 vb.
  depart 296 vb.
  run away 620 vb.
  be exempt 919 vb.
absinth, absinthe
  alcoholic drink
    301 n.
  sourness 393 n.
absolute
  existing 1 adj.
  unrelated 10 adj.
  absolute 32 adj.
  complete 54 adj.
  one 88 adj.
  positive 473 adj.
  creedal 485 adj.
  assertive 532 adj.
  authoritative
    733 adj.
  authoritarian
    735 adj.
absoluteness
  unrelatedness 10 n.
  simpleness 44 n.
  unity 88 n.
absolute zero
  coldness 380 n.
absolution
  amnesty 506 n.
  liberation 746 n.
  forgiveness 909 n.
  nonliability 919 n.
  acquittal 960 n.
  Christian rite
    988 n.
  ministration 988 n.
absolve
  liberate 746 vb.
  forgive 909 vb.
  exempt 919 vb.
  acquit 960 vb.
  perform ritual
    988 vb.
absorb
  combine 50 vb.
  contain 56 vb.
  absorb 299 vb.
  absorb 449 vb.
  dispose of 673 vb.
  impress 821 vb.
absorption
  identity 13 n.
  combination 50 n.
  reception 299 n.
  radiation 417 n.
  meditation 449 n.

attention 455 n.
abstain
  be unwilling
    598 vb.
  be neutral 606 vb.
  avoid 620 vb.
  relinquish 621 vb.
  not use 674 vb.
  not act 677 vb.
  be temperate
    942 vb.
abstemious
  temperate 942 adj.
  sober 948 adj.
abstention
  avoidance 620 n.
  inaction 677 n.
  temperance 942 n.
abstinence
  avoidance 620 n.
  nonuse 674 n.
  temperance 942 n.
abstract
  subtract 39 vb.
  immaterial
    320 adj.
  description 590 n.
  abstract 592 vb.
  compendium
    592 n.
abstracted
  separate 46 adj.
  abstracted 456 adj.
abstraction
  insubstantial thing
    4 n.
  subtraction 39 n.
  absence of thought
    450 n.
  abstractedness
    456 n.
  imperspicuity
    568 n.
abstruse
  puzzling 517 adj.
  unclear 568 adj.
absurd
  absurd 497 adj.
abundance
  greatness 32 n.
  great quantity
    32 n.
  increase 36 n.
  abundance 171 n.
  diffuseness 570 n.
  store 632 n.

abundant
  great 32 adj.
  many 104 adj.
  diffuse 570 adj.
  plentiful 635 adj.
  rich 800 adj.
  liberal 813 adj.
abuse
  force 176 vb.
  evil 616 n.
  waste 634 vb.
  ill-treat 645 vb.
  use 673 n.
  misuse 675 n.
  misuse 675 vb.
  be severe 735 vb.
  painfulness 827 n.
  torment 827 vb.
  slur 867 n.
  be rude 885 vb.
  be malevolent
    898 vb.
  cruel act 898 n.
  curse 899 vb.
  cuss 899 vb.
  scurrility 899 n.
  not respect 921 vb.
  criticize 924 vb.
  reproach 924 vb.
  detraction 926 n.
  debauch 951 vb.
  impiety 980 n.
abusive
  cursing 899 adj.
abut
  be contiguous
    202 vb.
abyss
  space 183 n.
  gap 201 n.
  depth 211 n.
  cavity 255 n.
  pitfall 663 n.
  hell 972 n.
acacia
  tree 366 n.
academic
  irrelevant 10 adj.
  intellectual 492 n.
  educational
    534 adj.
  studious 536 adj.
academic dress
  formal dress 228 n.
  uniform 228 n.

academic title
  academic title
    870 n.
academy
  academy 539 n.
accede
  consent 758 vb.
accelerate
  accelerate 277 vb.
  facilitate 701 vb.
acceleration
  increase 36 n.
  motion 265 n.
  haste 680 n.
accent
  sound 398 n.
  affirmation 532 n.
  emphasize 532 vb.
  dialect 560 adj.
  pronunciation
    577 n.
  voice 577 vb.
  speech defect
    580 n.
  prosody 593 n.
accentuate
  manifest 522 vb.
  emphasize 532 vb.
accept
  admit 299 vb.
  be credulous
    487 vb.
  acquiesce 488 vb.
  assent 488 vb.
  choose 605 vb.
  submit 721 vb.
  consent 758 vb.
  receive 782 vb.
  take 786 vb.
  approve 923 vb.
acceptance
  reception 299 n.
  assent 488 n.
  consent 758 n.
  title deed 767 n.
  receiving 782 n.
  approbation 923 n.
access
  approach 289 n.
  ingress 297 n.
  reception 299 n.
  access 624 n.
accessible
  accessible 289 adj.
  possible 469 adj.
accession
  increment 36 n.

addition 38 n.
accessory
  extrinsic 6 adj.
  extrinsicality 6 n.
  adjunct 40 n.
  concomitant 89 n.
  superfluity 637 n.
  colleague 707 n.
accidence
  extrinsicality 6 n.
  grammar 564 n.
accident
  extrinsicality 6 n.
  event 154 n.
  chance 159 n.
  collision 279 n.
  evil 616 n.
  nondesign 618 n.
  misfortune 731 n.
accidental
  extrinsic 6 adj.
  casual 159 adj.
  musical note
    410 n.
  unintentional
    618 adj.
accidental death
  decease 361 n.
acclaim
  assent 488 vb.
  honour 866 vb.
  repute 866 n.
  applaud 923 vb.
  applause 923 n.
acclamation
  conformity 83 n.
acclimatize
  make conform
    83 vb.
  break in 369 vb.
  habituate 610 vb.
  make ready
    669 vb.
acclivity
  incline 220 n.
accolade
  honours 866 n.
  praise 923 n.
accommodate
  adjust 24 vb.
  equalize 28 vb.
  comprise 78 vb.
  make conform
    83 vb.
  place 187 vb.
  aid 703 vb.
  lend 784 vb.

accommodation
  adaptation 24 n.
  inclusion 78 n.
  conformity 83 n.
  room 183 n.
  quarters 192 n.
  storage 632 n.
  pacification 719 n.
accompaniment
  accompaniment
    89 n.
  concomitant 89 n.
  musical piece
    412 n.
accompanist
  concomitant 89 n.
  instrumentalist
    413 n.
accompany
  accompany 89 vb.
  play music 413 vb.
accomplice
  concomitant 89 n.
  colleague 707 n.
accomplish
  produce 164 vb.
  do 676 vb.
  carry out 725 vb.
  succeed 727 vb.
accomplishment
  production 164 n.
  action 676 n.
  skill 694 n.
  completion 725 n.
  success 727 n.
accord
  accord 24 vb.
  agreement 24 n.
  attribute 158 vb.
  permit 756 vb.
  consent 758 n.
  give 781 vb.
accordance
  uniformity 16 n.
  agreement 24 n.
according to
  agreeing 24 adj.
accordion
  organ 414 n.
accost
  approach 289 vb.
  speak to 583 vb.
  request 761 vb.
account
  statistics 86 n.
  list 87 n.
  report 524 n.

ACC

oration 579 n.
correspondence
588 n.
description 590 n.
credit 802 n.
debt 803 n.
account 808 vb.
accounts 808 n.
prestige 866 n.
accountable
liable 180 adj.
obliged 917 adj.
accountancy
numeration 86 n.
accounts 808 n.
accountant
accountant 808 n.
account for
account for 158 vb.
accounts
accounts 808 n.
accoutrements
adjunct 40 n.
dressing 228 n.
property 777 n.
accredited
credible 485 adj.
creedal 485 adj.
accretion
increment 36 n.
addition 38 n.
adjunct 40 n.
extraneousness
59 n.
expansion 197 n.
accrue
augment 36 vb.
accrue 38 vb.
result 157 vb.
accumulate
grow 36 vb.
join 45 vb.
bring together
74 vb.
store 632 vb.
acquire 771 vb.
take 786 vb.
accurate
accurate 494 adj.
accursed
bad 645 adj.
damnable 645 adj.
harmful 645 adj.
unfortunate
731 adj.
unhappy 825 adj.

ACH

unpleasant
827 adj.
hateful 888 adj.
heinous 934 adj.
wicked 934 adj.
profane 980 adj.
accusation
vindication 927 n.
accusation 928 n.
accuse
accuse 928 vb.
litigate 959 vb.
accused
prisoner 750 n.
accused person
928 n.
litigant 959 n.
accustom
train 534 vb.
habituate 610 vb.
accustomed
usual 610 adj.
accustomed to
habituated 610 adj.
AC/DC
abnormal 84 adj.
double 91 adj.
ace
unit 88 n.
best 644 adj.
excellent 644 adj.
masterpiece 694 n.
skilful 694 adj.
proficient person
696 n.
acerbity
pungency 388 n.
unsavouriness
391 n.
sourness 393 n.
rudeness 885 n.
resentment 891 n.
malevolence 898 n.
acetic
sour 393 adj.
acetylene
fuel 385 n.
ache
feel pain 377 vb.
pang 377 n.
badness 645 n.
suffer 825 vb.
achieve
produce 164 vb.
do 676 vb.
carry out 725 vb.
succeed 727 vb.

ACK

achievement
production 164 n.
progression 285 n.
heraldry 547 n.
deed 676 n.
completion 725 n.
success 727 n.
Achilles' heel
weakness 163 n.
defect 647 n.
vulnerability 661 n.
moral sensibility
819 n.
Achilles' tendon
foot 214 n.
aching
pain 377 n.
painful 377 adj.
fatigued 684 adj.
suffering 825 adj.
paining 827 adj.
achromatic
colourless 426 adj.
acid
destroyer 168 n.
keen 174 adj.
unsavoury 391 adj.
sour 393 adj.
sourness 393 n.
sullen 893 adj.
drug-taking 949 n.
acidity
pungency 388 n.
sourness 393 n.
acidosis
sourness 393 n.
digestive disorders
651 n.
acid rain
poison 659 n.
acid test
experiment 461 n.
acidulous
sour 393 adj.
acknowledge
attribute 158 vb.
notice 455 vb.
answer 460 vb.
testify 466 vb.
assent 488 vb.
confess 526 vb.
correspond 588 vb.
observe 768 vb.
greet 884 vb.
thank 907 vb.
reward 962 vb.
worship 981 vb.

ACQ

acknowledged
usual 610 adj.
acknowledgment
attribution 158 n.
answer 460 n.
assent 488 n.
disclosure 526 n.
correspondence
588 n.
observance 768 n.
courteous act
884 n.
thanks 907 n.
dueness 915 n.
approbation 923 n.
penance 941 n.
reward 962 n.
acme
summit 213 n.
acme of perfection
perfection 646 n.
acne
skin disease 651 n.
blemish 845 n.
acolyte
auxiliary 707 n.
church officer
986 n.
cleric 986 n.
aconite
poisonous plant
659 n.
acoustic
sounding 398 adj.
auditory 415 adj.
acquaint
inform 524 vb.
acquaintance
knowledge 490 n.
friend 880 n.
friendship 880 n.
acquiesce
concur 181 vb.
acquiesce 488 vb.
be willing 597 vb.
be content 828 vb.
acquiescence
conformity 83 n.
concurrence 181 n.
assent 488 n.
willingness 597 n.
submission 721 n.
obedience 739 n.
permission 756 n.
consent 758 n.
acquire
acquire 771 vb.

ACQ

acquired
extrinsic 6 adj.
acquisition
acquisition 771 n.
acquisitive
acquiring 771 adj.
avaricious 816 adj.
greedy 859 adj.
selfish 932 adj.
acquit
do one's duty
917 vb.
justify 927 vb.
acquit 960 vb.
acquittal
duty 917 n.
acquittal 960 n.
acreage
measure 183 n.
lands 777 n.
acres
measure 183 n.
land 344 n.
lands 777 n.
acrid
keen 174 adj.
pungent 388 adj.
unsavoury 391 adj.
fetid 397 adj.
acrimonious
keen 174 adj.
resentful 891 adj.
acrimony
edge 234 n.
rudeness 885 n.
hatred 888 n.
resentment 891 n.
malevolence 898 n.
acrobat
athlete 162 n.
entertainer 594 n.
proficient person
696 n.
acrobatics
athletics 162 n.
acronym
word 559 n.
across-the-board
extensive 32 adj.
comprehensive
52 adj.
inclusive 78 adj.
general 79 adj.
acrostic
equivocalness
518 n.
enigma 530 n.

ACT

act
imitate 20 vb.
operate 173 vb.
duplicity 541 n.
act 594 vb.
dramaturgy 594 n.
stage show 594 n.
function 622 vb.
be instrumental
628 vb.
deed 676 n.
do 676 vb.
behave 688 vb.
precept 693 n.
decree 737 n.
act for
substitute 150 vb.
deputize 755 vb.
acting
substituted 150 adj.
acting 594 n.
action
dramaturgy 594 n.
action 676 n.
deed 676 n.
conduct 688 n.
fight 716 n.
battle 718 n.
accusation 928 n.
litigation 959 n.
actionable
legal 953 adj.
illegal 954 adj.
activate
invigorate 174 vb.
active
active 678 adj.
active service
warfare 718 n.
activist
doer 676 n.
busy person 678 n.
political party
708 n.
activity
activity 678 n.
act of God
ruin 165 n.
necessity 596 n.
compulsion 740 n,
act of worship
act of worship
981 n.
actor
imitator 20 n.
actor 594 n.
agent 686 n.

ADA

actress
actor 594 n.
act the fool
be foolish 499 vb.
actual
real 1 adj.
substantial 3 adj.
present 121 adj.
true 494 adj.
actuality
reality 1 n.
truth 494 n.
actuary
accountant 808 n.
actuate
operate 173 vb.
influence 178 vb.
move 265 vb.
motivate 612 vb.
acuity
sharpness 256 n.
sagacity 498 n.
acumen
discrimination
463 n.
sagacity 498 n.
acupressure
medical art 658 n.
therapy 658 n.
acupuncture
medical art 658 n.
therapy 658 n.
acute
keen 174 adj.
violent 176 adj.
sharp 256 adj.
sentient 374 adj.
strident 407 adj.
intelligent 498 adj.
cunning 698 adj.
acute accent
punctuation 547 n.
acute angle
angle 247 n.
acuteness
sharpness 256 n.
sagacity 498 n.
ad
advertisement
528 n.
adage
maxim 496 n.
phrase 563 n.
adagio
slowly 278 adv.
tempo 410 n.
adagio 412 adv.

ADD

adamant
hardness 326 n.
obstinate 602 adj.
Adam's ale
water 339 n.
Adam's apple
swelling 253 n.
adapt
adjust 24 vb.
modify 143 vb.
translate 520 vb.
adaptable
conformable
83 adj.
adaptation
adaptation 24 n.
conformity 83 n.
transformation
143 n.
musical piece
412 n.
translation 520 n.
edition 589 n.
add
add 38 vb.
added
additional 38 adj.
addendum
addition 38 n.
adjunct 40 n.
extra 40 n.
adder
reptile 365 n.
bane 659 n.
add fuel to the
fire/flames
augment 36 vb.
kindle 381 vb.
animate 821 vb.
aggravate 832 vb.
enrage 891 vb.
addict
enthusiast 504 n.
habitué 610 n.
sick person 651 n.
addiction
habit 610 n.
intemperance
943 n.
addictive
influential 178 adj.
intoxicating
949 adj.
add insult to injury
aggravate 832 vb.
addition
addition 38 n.

adjunct 40 n.

additive
  addition 38 n.
  additional 38 adj.
  adjunct 40 n.
  extra 40 n.
  component 58 n.
  dieting 301 n.
  food content 301 n.

add-on
  addition 38 n.
  adjunct 40 n.
  join 45 vb.
  exaggerate 546 vb.

address
  place 185 n.
  situation 186 n.
  locality 187 n.
  abode 192 n.
  send 272 vb.
  name 561 vb.
  orate 579 vb.
  oration 579 n.
  speech 579 n.
  allocution 583 n.
  speak to 583 vb.
  way 624 n.
  ministration 988 n.

addressee
  resident 191 n.
  recipient 782 n.

addresses
  reading matter
    589 n.
  wooing 889 n.

add up
  add 38 vb.
  be intelligible
    516 vb.

add up to
  number 86 vb.
  mean 514 vb.

adenoids
  swelling 253 n.
  respiratory disease
    651 n.

adept
  proficient person
    696 n.

adequate
  powerful 160 adj.
  sufficient 635 adj.
  useful 640 adj.
  middling 732 adj.

adhere
  unite with 45 vb.
  cohere 48 vb.

be contiguous
  202 vb.
  transfer 272 vb.
  retain 778 vb.

adherent
  cohesive 48 adj.
  follower 284 n.
  auxiliary 707 n.
  signatory 765 n.
  religionist 973 n.
  sectarian 978 n.

adhere to
  observe 768 vb.

adhesive
  conjunctive 45 adj.
  adhesive 47 n.
  cohesive 48 adj.
  retentive 778 adj.

ad hoc
  specially 80 adv.
  extempore
    609 adv.
  spontaneity 609 n.
  spontaneous
    609 adj.
  unprepared
    670 adj.
  unreadily 670 adv.

adieu
  goodbye 296 int.

ad infinitum
  infinitely 107 adv.

adipose
  fatty 357 adj.

adjacent
  near 200 adj.

adjective
  adjunct 40 n.
  part of speech
    564 n.

adjoin
  be contiguous
    202 vb.

adjourn
  put off 136 vb.
  pause 145 vb.

adjudicate
  judge 480 vb.
  try a case 959 vb.

adjudicator
  estimator 480 n.

adjunct
  adjunct 40 n.

adjust
  adjust 24 vb.
  make ready
    669 vb.

adjustment
  adaptation 24 n.
  equalization 28 n.
  conformity 83 n.
  change 143 n.
  moderation 177 n.
  pacification 719 n.
  compromise 770 n.

adjust oneself
  conform 83 vb.

adjutant
  auxiliary 707 n.
  army officer 741 n.

ad lib
  unprepared
    670 adj.

ad-lib
  orate 579 vb.
  act 594 vb.
  improvise 609 vb.

administer
  use 673 vb.
  do 676 vb.
  manage 689 vb.
  apportion 783 vb.

administer the sacra-
ments
  offer worship
    981 vb.
  perform ritual
    988 vb.

administration
  arrangement 62 n.
  vocation 622 n.
  action 676 n.
  management
    689 n.
  apportionment
    783 n.
  ministration 988 n.

administrative
  governmental
    733 adj.

admirable
  excellent 644 adj.
  proficient person
    696 n.
  wonderful 864 adj.
  worshipful 866 adj.

admiral
  nautical personnel
    270 n.
  naval man 722 n.
  naval officer 741 n.

admiralty
  navy 722 n.

admiration
  wonder 864 n.
  love 887 n.
  respect 920 n.
  approbation 923 n.

admire
  wonder 864 vb.
  love 887 vb.
  respect 920 vb.
  approve 923 vb.

admirer
  lover 887 n.
  commender 923 n.
  worshipper 981 n.

admissible
  apt 24 adj.
  included 78 adj.
  rational 475 adj.

admission
  inclusion 78 n.
  ingress 297 n.
  reception 299 n.
  testimony 466 n.
  assent 488 n.
  disclosure 526 n.
  affirmation 532 n.

admit
  admit 299 vb.
  testify 466 vb.
  be reasonable
    475 vb.
  confess 526 vb.
  affirm 532 vb.

admit defeat
  submit 721 vb.
  be defeated 728 vb.
  be dejected 834 vb.
  lose repute 867 vb.

admittance
  ingress 297 n.
  reception 299 n.
  receiving 782 n.

admonish
  warn 664 vb.
  advise 691 vb.
  reprove 924 vb.

admonition
  dissuasion 613 n.
  warning 664 n.
  reprimand 924 n.

ad nauseam
  diffusely 570 adv.
  boringly 838 adv.

ado
  activity 678 n.
  exertion 682 n.

adolescence
  youth 130 n.
adolescent
  young 130 adj.
  youngster 132 n.
  immature 670 adj.
Adonis
  a beauty 841 n.
  mythic deity 966 n.
adopt
  be akin 11 vb.
  choose 605 vb.
  avail oneself of
    673 vb.
adoption
  parentage 169 n.
  choice 605 n.
  approbation 923 n.
adore
  enjoy 376 vb.
  love 887 vb.
  respect 920 vb.
  worship 981 vb.
adorn
  ornament 574 vb.
  make better
    654 vb.
  decorate 844 vb.
adornment
  ornamentation
    844 n.
adroit
  skilful 694 adj.
adulation
  praise 923 n.
  flattery 925 n.
adult
  adult 134 n.
  grown-up 134 adj.
  matured 669 adj.
adulterate
  mix 43 vb.
  modify 143 vb.
  weaken 163 vb.
  rarefy 325 vb.
  qualify 468 vb.
  impair 655 vb.
adulterer
  libertine 952 n.
adultery
  love affair 887 n.
  illicit love 951 n.
adultress
  loose woman
    952 n.
advance
  augment 36 vb.

grow 36 vb.
part 53 n.
elapse 111 vb.
go on 146 vb.
happen 154 vb.
motion 265 n.
travel 267 n.
progress 285 vb.
progression 285 n.
promote 285 vb.
approach 289 n.
approach 289 vb.
be visible 443 vb.
be instrumental
  628 vb.
be expedient
  642 vb.
get better 654 vb.
improvement
  654 n.
make better
  654 vb.
succeed 727 vb.
offer 759 n.
lend 784 vb.
lending 784 n.
dignify 866 vb.
advanced
  modern 126 adj.
  progressive
    285 adj.
advanced in years
  ageing 131 adj.
advancement
  increase 36 n.
  progression 285 n.
advances
  approach 289 n.
  wooing 889 n.
advancing
  progressive
    285 adj.
  approaching
    289 adj.
advantage
  advantage 34 n.
  edge 234 n.
  benefit 615 n.
  benefit 615 vb.
  good 615 vb.
  utility 640 n.
  be expedient
    642 vb.
  good policy 642 n.
  victory 727 n.
  gain 771 n.

Advent
  holy day 988 n.
advent
  futurity 124 n.
  event 154 n.
  approach 289 n.
  arrival 295 n.
adventure
  event 154 n.
  undertaking 672 n.
adventure play-
  ground
  pleasure ground
    837 n.
adventurer
  traveller 268 n.
  impostor 545 n.
  gambler 618 n.
  desperado 857 n.
  egotist 932 n.
adventuress
  loose woman
    952 n.
adventurous
  speculative
    618 adj.
  enterprising
    672 adj.
  courageous
    855 adj.
  rash 857 adj.
adverb
  adjunct 40 n.
  part of speech
    564 n.
adversary
  opponent 705 n.
adverse
  contrary 14 adj.
  adverse 731 adj.
adversity
  adversity 731 n.
  painfulness 827 n.
advert
  advertisement
    528 n.
advertise
  attract notice
    455 vb.
  advertise 528 vb.
  boast 877 vb.
advertisement
  information 524 n.
  advertisement
    528 n.
  boasting 877 n.

advertising
  publicity 528 n.
  inducement 612 n.
advice
  information 524 n.
  news 529 n.
  advice 691 n.
advise
  inform 524 vb.
  advise 691 vb.
adviser
  adviser 691 n.
advocate
  intermediary
    231 n.
  speaker 579 n.
  motivator 612 n.
  advise 691 vb.
  adviser 691 n.
  combatant 722 n.
  consignee 754 n.
  deputy 755 n.
  approve 923 vb.
  commender 923 n.
  vindicate 927 vb.
  do law 958 vb.
  law agent 958 n.
  lawyer 958 n.
adze
  sharp edge 256 n.
aegis
  protection 660 n.
aeon
  era 110 n.
aerated
  light 323 adj.
  rare 325 adj.
  airy 340 adj.
  bubbly 355 adj.
aerial
  high 209 adj.
  gaseous 336 adj.
  airy 340 adj.
  broadcasting
    531 n.
aerie
  nest 192 n.
aerobatics
  aeronautics 271 n.
aerobics
  athletics 162 n.
  motion 265 n.
  exercise 682 n.
  dancing 837 n.
aerodrome
  air travel 271 n.
  aircraft 276 n.

goal 295 n.
aerodynamics
  aeronautics 271 n.
  gaseousness 336 n.
aerofoil
  wing 271 n.
  aircraft 276 n.
aerogramme
  postal communica-
    tions 531 n.
  correspondence
    588 n.
aeronautics
  aeronautics 271 n.
aeroplane
  aircraft 276 n.
aerosol
  propellant 287 n.
  vaporizer 338 n.
aerospace
  space 183 n.
  aeronautics 271 n.
  atmosphere 340 n.
aery
  immaterial
    320 adj.
  rare 325 adj.
aesthetic
  sentient 374 adj.
  sensitive 819 adj.
  beautiful 841 adj.
  tasteful 846 adj.
aesthetics
  sensibility 374 n.
  beauty 841 n.
  good taste 846 n.
aetherial
  insubstantial 4 adj.
aetiology
  causation 156 n.
  attribution 158 n.
affable
  sociable 882 adj.
  amiable 884 adj.
affair
  topic 452 n.
  badness 645 n.
affaire de coeur
  love affair 887 n.
affair of honour
  duel 716 n.
affair of the heart
  love affair 887 n.
affairs
  affairs 154 n.
  event 154 n.
  pursuit 619 n.

business 622 n.
affairs of state
  secret 530 n.
affect
  be related 9 vb.
  influence 178 vb.
  show 522 vb.
  dissemble 541 vb.
  behave 688 vb.
  excite 821 vb.
  impress 821 vb.
  be affected 850 vb.
affectation
  grandiloquence
    574 n.
  speech defect
    580 n.
  affectation 850 n.
affected
  changeable
    143 adj.
  with affections
    817 adj.
  impressed 818 adj.
  affected 850 adj.
affection
  moral sensibility
    819 n.
  love 887 n.
  approbation 923 n.
affectionate
  loving 887 adj.
  benevolent 897 adj.
affianced
  promised 764 n.
  loved one 887 n.
affidavit
  testimony 466 n.
  oath 532 n.
  litigation 959 n.
affiliation
  relation 9 n.
  consanguinity
    11 n.
  attribution 158 n.
  association 706 n.
  participation
    775 n.
affinity
  relation 9 n.
  consanguinity
    11 n.
  similarity 18 n.
  tendency 179 n.
  attraction 291 n.
  liking 859 n.
  divorce 896 n.

affirm
  affirm 532 vb.
affirmative
  positive 473 adj.
  affirmative
    532 adj.
affirmative action
  equalization 28 n.
  injustice 914 n.
affix
  add 38 vb.
  adjunct 40 n.
  affix 45 vb.
  sequel 67 n.
  part of speech
    564 n.
afflict
  hurt 827 vb.
  punish 963 vb.
affliction
  evil 616 n.
  illness 651 n.
  bane 659 n.
  suffering 825 n.
  painfulness 827 n.
affluence
  plenty 635 n.
  prosperity 730 n.
  wealth 800 n.
afford
  provide 633 vb.
  give 781 vb.
  afford 800 vb.
  expend 806 vb.
afforestation
  forestry 366 n.
  agriculture 370 n.
affray
  turmoil 61 n.
  fight 716 n.
affront
  annoyance 827 n.
  hurt 827 vb.
  sauciness 878 n.
  huff 891 vb.
  resentment 891 n.
  indignity 921 n.
  not respect 921 vb.
aficionado
  enthusiast 504 n.
  lover 887 n.
afoot
  operative 173 adj.
  in question
    452 adv.
  preparatory
    669 adj.

busy 678 adj.
aforementioned
  prior 119 adj.
afraid
  fearing 854 adj.
afresh
  again 106 vb.
aft
  rearward 238 adv.
after
  similar 18 adj.
  after 65 adv.
  subsequent
    120 adj.
  subsequently
    120 adv.
  back 238 adj.
  rearward 238 adv.
after a fashion
  partially 33 adv.
  subsequently
    120 adv.
after all
  nevertheless
    468 adv.
afterbirth
  sequel 67 n.
  obstetrics 167 n.
  excrement 302 n.
aftercare
  therapy 658 n.
aftereffect
  sequel 67 n.
afterglow
  remainder 41 n.
  sequel 67 n.
  glow 417 n.
afterlife
  sequel 67 n.
  future state 124 n.
  heaven 971 n.
aftermath
  sequel 67 n.
  posteriority 120 n.
  effect 157 n.
  abundance 171 n.
afternoon
  evening 129 n.
afternoon tea
  evening 129 n.
  meal 301 n.
afters
  sequel 67 n.
aftertaste
  sequel 67 n.
  taste 386 n.

afterthought
sequel 67 n.
lateness 136 n.
thought 449 n.
remembrance
505 n.
change of mind
603 n.
after time
late 136 adv.
afterwards
after 65 adv.
subsequently
120 adv.
afterworld
destiny 155 n.
again
again 106 vb.
again and again
often 139 adv.
against
although 182 adv.
against 240 adv.
in opposition
704 adv.
opposing 704 adj.
against the grain
disagreeing 25 adj.
with difficulty
700 adv.
in opposition
704 adv.
against the law
prohibited 757 adj.
illegal 954 adj.
agate
stripe 437 n.
gem 844 n.
age
date 108 n.
pass time 108 vb.
era 110 n.
chronology 117 n.
be old 127 vb.
oldness 127 n.
age 131 n.
deteriorate 655 vb.
age, an
long duration
113 n.
aged
ageing 131 adj.
age group
group 74 n.
classification 77 n.
contemporary
123 n.

class 538 n.
ageing
ageing 131 adj.
ageism
prejudice 481 n.
injustice 914 n.
ageless
perpetual 115 adj.
young 130 adj.
agelong
lasting 113 adj.
perpetual 115 adj.
agency
agency 173 n.
management
689 n.
commission 751 n.
agenda
affairs 154 n.
topic 452 n.
predetermination
608 n.
business 622 n.
policy 623 n.
agent
inferior 35 n.
substitute 150 n.
cause 156 n.
intermediary
231 n.
instrument 628 n.
agent 686 n.
manager 690 n.
mediator 720 n.
deputy 755 n.
seller 793 n.
commender 923 n.
agent provocateur
ambush 527 n.
trickster 545 n.
motivator 612 n.
troublemaker
663 n.
agitator 738 n.
excitant 821 n.
age of consent
adultness 134 n.
**Age of Enlighten-
ment**
era 110 n.
age-old
antiquated 127 adj.
worshipful 866 adj.
ages
long duration
113 n.

agglomeration
accumulation 74 n.
agglutination
addition 38 n.
union 45 n.
coherence 48 n.
aggrandizement
greatness 32 n.
increase 36 n.
expansion 197 n.
aggravate
aggravate 832 vb.
aggravating
annoying 827 adj.
aggregate
all 52 n.
bring together
74 vb.
numerical result
85 n.
number 86 vb.
solid body 324 n.
aggression
attack 712 n.
aggressive
vigorous 174 adj.
violent 176 adj.
active 678 adj.
quarrelling
709 adj.
warlike 718 adj.
warring 718 adj.
courageous
855 adj.
hostile 881 adj.
aggressiveness
vitality 162 n.
vigorousness 174 n.
restlessness 678 n.
quarrelsomeness
709 n.
attack 712 n.
bellicosity 718 n.
aggressor
attacker 712 n.
combatant 722 n.
enemy 881 n.
aggrieved, be
be discontented
829 vb.
aggro
counteraction
182 n.
aghast
fearing 854 adj.
agile
speedy 277 adj.

skilful 694 adj.
agility
velocity 277 n.
agin
in opposition
704 adv.
opposing 704 adj.
agiotage
barter 791 n.
finance 797 n.
agitate
agitate 318 vb.
be active 678 vb.
revolt 738 vb.
trouble 827 vb.
cause discontent
829 vb.
agitation
agitation 318 n.
activity 678 n.
discontent 829 n.
agitator
dissentient 489 n.
agitator 738 n.
agitprop
teaching 534 n.
inducement 612 n.
agitator 738 n.
sedition 738 n.
agley, be
be oblique 220 vb.
aglow
fiery 379 adj.
luminous 417 adj.
agnosticism
philosophy 449 n.
doubt 486 n.
unbelief 486 n.
irreligion 974 n.
ago
formerly 125 adv.
agog
inquisitive 453 adj.
expectant 507 adj.
excited 821 adj.
agonizing
painful 377 adj.
paining 827 adj.
agony
pain 377 n.
suffering 825 n.
agony aunt
author 589 n.
agony column
advertisement
528 n.

agoraphobia
  neurosis 503 n.
  phobia 854 n.
agree
  accord 24 vb.
  concur 181 vb.
  be willing 597 vb.
  concord 710 n.
  consent 758 vb.
  contract 765 vb.
agreeable
  agreeing 24 adj.
  pleasant 376 adj.
  pleasurable
    826 adj.
  personable 841 adj.
  courteous 884 adj.
agreement
  agreement 24 n.
  assent 488 n.
  cooperation 706 n.
  consent 758 n.
  compact 765 n.
agree to differ
  dissent 489 vb.
  make peace
    719 vb.
agriculture
  agriculture 370 n.
aground
  in difficulties
    700 adj.
ague
  spasm 318 n.
  illness 651 n.
ahead
  superior 34 adj.
  future 124 adj.
  beyond 199 adv.
  in front 237 adv.
  forward 285 adv.
AID
  propagation 167 n.
aid
  concur 181 vb.
  aid 703 n.
  aid 703 vb.
  gift 781 n.
aid and abet
  concur 181 vb.
  incite 612 vb.
aide
  aider 703 n.
aide-mémoire
  reminder 505 n.
AIDS
  blood 335 n.

blood disease
  651 n.
aikido
  wrestling 716 n.
aileron
  equilibrium 28 n.
  wing 271 n.
  aircraft 276 n.
ailing
  sick 651 adj.
ailment
  illness 651 n.
aim
  range 183 n.
  aim 281 vb.
  direction 281 n.
  objective 617 n.
  attempt 671 n.
  attempt 671 vb.
  desired object
    859 n.
aim high
  aim at 617 vb.
  hope 852 vb.
  desire 859 vb.
aim too high
  overstep 306 vb.
  be rash 857 vb.
air
  insubstantial thing
    4 n.
  element 319 n.
  lightness 323 n.
  aerate 340 vb.
  air 340 n.
  dry 342 vb.
  tune 412 n.
  look 445 n.
  divulge 526 vb.
  refresh 685 vb.
  conduct 688 n.
air-bag
  intermediary
    231 n.
  safeguard 662 n.
  preserver 666 n.
air base
  station 187 n.
  airtravel 271 n.
airbed
  bed 218 n.
airborne
  high 209 adj.
air commodore
  air officer 741 n.
air-conditioning
  air 340 n.

ventilation 352 n.
aircraft
  aircraft 276 n.
aircraft carrier
  ship 275 n.
  warship 722 n.
air crew
  aeronaut 271 n.
  air force 722 n.
air current
  wind 352 n.
airfield
  air travel 271 n.
  goal 295 n.
air force
  air force 722 n.
air freight
  transport 272 n.
airgun
  propellant 287 n.
  plaything 837 n.
air hostess
  aeronaut 271 n.
  servant 742 n.
airiness
  rarity 325 n.
airing
  land travel 267 n.
  air 340 n.
  desiccation 342 n.
  ventilation 352 n.
  cleansing 648 n.
air lane
  route 624 n.
airline
  air travel 271 n.
airliner
  aircraft 276 n.
air mail
  postal communica-
    tions 531 n.
  correspondence
    588 n.
air marshal
  air officer 741 n.
airport
  air travel 271 n.
  aircraft 276 n.
  goal 295 n.
air raid
  attack 712 n.
air-raid shelter
  refuge 662 n.
  defences 713 n.
airs
  airs 873 n.

airship
  airship 276 n.
airside
  air travel 271 n.
airspace
  space 183 n.
  territory 184 n.
  air travel 271 n.
air terminal
  stopping place
    145 n.
  air travel 271 n.
  goal 295 n.
airway
  air travel 271 n.
  air pipe 353 n.
airy
  light 323 adj.
  rare 325 adj.
  gaseous 336 adj.
  airy 340 adj.
  windy 352 adj.
  trivial 639 adj.
  disrespectful
    921 adj.
airy-fairy
  rare 325 adj.
  imaginative
    513 adj.
aisle
  path 624 n.
  church interior
    990 n.
ajar
  open 263 adj.
akimbo
  angular 247 adj.
akin
  akin 11 adj.
alabaster
  white 427 adj.
  white thing 427 n.
à la carte
  meal 301 n.
alacrity
  velocity 277 n.
  willingness 597 n.
  activity 678 n.
  cheerfulness 833 n.
Aladdin's lamp
  instrument 628 n.
  magic instrument
    983 n.
alarm
  loudness 400 n.
  signal 547 n.
  warning 664 n.

danger signal
665 n.
fear 854 n.
frighten 854 vb.
alarming
dangerous 661 adj.
frightening
854 adj.
alarums and excursions
dramaturgy 594 n.
alb
vestments 989 n.
albatross
bird 365 n.
encumbrance
702 n.
albino
nonconformist
84 n.
achromatism
426 n.
colourless 426 adj.
whiteness 427 n.
white thing 427 n.
album
gramophone 414 n.
reminder 505 n.
record 548 n.
reference book
589 n.
anthology 592 n.
albumen
semiliquidity
354 n.
organism 358 n.
alchemy
conversion 147 n.
occultism 984 n.
alcohol
stimulant 174 n.
alcoholic drink
301 n.
tonic 658 n.
alcoholic
strong 162 adj.
sick person 651 n.
drunkard 949 n.
drunken 949 adj.
intoxicating
949 adj.
alcoholism
drinking 301 n.
disease 651 n.
alcoholism 949 n.
alcove
arbour 194 n.

cavity 255 n.
al dente
culinary 301 adj.
alder
tree 366 n.
alderman
official 690 n.
councillor 692 n.
officer 741 n.
ale
alcoholic drink
301 n.
alert
attentive 455 adj.
vigilant 457 adj.
signal 547 vb.
warn 664 vb.
raise the alarm
665 vb.
prepared 669 adj.
active 678 adj.
lively 819 adj.
'A' level
exam 459 n.
alexandrine
prosody 593 n.
alfresco
alfresco 340 adv.
algae
plant 366 n.
algebra
mathematics 86 n.
algorithm
number 85 n.
mathematics 86 n.
numeration 86 n.
alias
named 561 adj.
misnomer 562 n.
alibi
absence 190 n.
pretext 614 n.
vindication 927 n.
Alice band
headgear 228 n.
hairdressing 843 n.
alien
unrelated 10 adj.
disagreeing 25 adj.
misfit 25 n.
separate 46 adj.
extraneous 59 adj.
foreigner 59 n.
intruder 59 n.
unconformable
84 adj.
outcast 883 n.

alienate
set apart 46 vb.
not retain 779 vb.
alienist
doctor 658 n.
alight
place oneself
187 vb.
come to rest
266 vb.
land 295 vb.
descend 309 vb.
sit down 311 vb.
fiery 379 adj.
align
make uniform
16 vb.
adjust 24 vb.
arrange 62 vb.
flatten 216 vb.
straighten 249 vb.
print 587 vb.
alignment
direction 281 n.
friendship 880 n.
alike
similar 18 adj.
aliment
food 301 n.
provisions 301 n.
subvention 703 n.
dower 777 n.
receipt 807 n.
divorce 896 n.
alimentary canal
drain 351 n.
alimony
subvention 703 n.
dower 777 n.
receipt 807 n.
divorce 896 n.
A-line skirt
skirt 228 n.
alive
alive 360 adj.
sentient 374 adj.
all
great quantity
32 n.
all 52 n.
universal 79 adj.
Allah
the Deity 965 n.
all along
while 108 adv.
all along 113 adv.

all and sundry
everyman 79 n.
allay
abate 37 vb.
assuage 177 vb.
pacify 719 vb.
all but
almost 33 adv.
on the whole
52 adv.
nearly 200 adv.
all clear
signal 547 n.
safety 660 n.
permit 756 n.
all comers
opponent 705 n.
contender 716 n.
allegation
testimony 466 n.
affirmation 532 n.
pretext 614 n.
accusation 928 n.
allege
affirm 532 vb.
plead 614 vb.
allegiance
loyalty 739 n.
subjection 745 n.
duty 917 n.
allegory
analogue 18 n.
assimilation 18 n.
comparison 462 n.
metaphor 519 n.
latency 523 n.
narrative 590 n.
allegro
adagio 412 adv.
alleluia
praise 923 n.
allergic
sentient 374 adj.
diseased 651 adj.
allergy
excretion 302 n.
sensibility 374 n.
ill health 651 n.
dislike 861 n.
hatred 888 n.
alleviate
abate 37 vb.
assuage 177 vb.
disencumber
701 vb.
relieve 831 vb.

alley
  road 624 n.
All Hallows
  holy day 988 n.
all hands
  everyman 79 n.
alliance
  relation 9 n.
  consanguinity
    11 n.
  union 45 n.
  combination 50 n.
  concurrence 181 n.
  association 706 n.
  society 708 n.
  compact 765 n.
  marriage 894 n.
alligator
  skin 226 n.
  reptile 365 n.
all in
  impotent 161 adj.
  fatigued 684 adj.
all-in
  complete 54 adj.
  inclusive 78 adj.
  educational
    534 adj.
all in all
  on the whole
    52 adv.
all-inclusive
  inclusive 78 adj.
all-in wrestling
  wrestling 716 n.
alliteration
  assimilation 18 n.
  recurrence 106 n.
  ornament 574 n.
  prosody 593 n.
all-knowing
  knowing 490 adj.
  godlike 965 adj.
all manner of
  different 15 adj.
allocate
  arrange 62 vb.
  mete out 465 vb.
  apportion 783 vb.
allocution
  allocution 583 n.
all one
  equivalent 28 adj.
allot
  arrange 62 vb.
  disperse 75 vb.
  dispose of 673 vb.

  use 673 vb.
  endow 777 vb.
  give 781 vb.
  apportion 783 vb.
allotment
  piece 53 n.
  arrangement 62 n.
  farm 370 n.
  garden 370 n.
  apportionment
    783 n.
  portion 783 n.
allotted span
  old age 131 n.
  life 360 n.
all out
  completely 54 adv.
  swiftly 277 adv.
  resolute 599 adj.
all over
  widely 183 adv.
all over, be
  be complete 54 vb.
  end 69 vb.
all over one, be
  pet 889 vb.
  flatter 925 vb.
all over with, be
  be destroyed
    165 vb.
allow
  subtract 39 vb.
  attribute 158 vb.
  make possible
    469 vb.
  acquiesce 488 vb.
  assent 488 vb.
  confess 526 vb.
  facilitate 701 vb.
  permit 756 vb.
  consent 758 vb.
  be patient 823 vb.
allowance
  extra 40 n.
  qualification 468 n.
  subvention 703 n.
  permission 756 n.
  earnings 771 n.
  dower 777 n.
  gift 781 n.
  portion 783 n.
  money 797 n.
  receipt 807 n.
  due 915 adj.
allowing
  thus 8 adv.

allowing for
  provided 468 adv.
  qualifying 468 adj.
alloy
  a mixture 43 n.
  mix 43 vb.
  compound 50 n.
  mineral 359 n.
all right
  not bad 644 adj.
all-rounder
  athlete 162 n.
  proficient person
    696 n.
  player 837 n.
All Saints
  holy day 988 n.
all set
  prepared 669 adj.
all sorts
  medley 43 n.
  everyman 79 n.
All Souls
  holy day 988 n.
all talk
  insubstantial thing
    4 n.
all the best
  good luck 730 int.
all the rage
  fashionable
    848 adj.
all there
  intelligent 498 adj.
  sane 502 adj.
all the same
  nevertheless
    468 adv.
all the time
  while 108 adv.
**all the time in the
  world**
  slowness 278 n.
  leisure 681 n.
all the way
  throughout 54 adv.
all together
  collectively 52 adv.
  together 74 adv.
all told
  completely 54 adv.
all to the good
  well 615 adv.
allude
  imply 523 vb.
  hint 524 vb.

all up with, be
  be destroyed
    165 vb.
allure
  attract 291 vb.
  attraction 291 n.
  tempt 612 vb.
  delight 826 vb.
alluring
  exciting 821 adj.
  pleasurable
    826 adj.
  personable 841 adj.
allusion
  referral 9 n.
  metaphor 519 n.
alluvium
  leavings 41 n.
  soil 344 n.
ally
  join 45 vb.
  combine 50 vb.
  assenter 488 n.
  aider 703 n.
  cooperate 706 vb.
  colleague 707 n.
  join a party
    708 vb.
  contract 765 vb.
  friend 880 n.
alma mater
  academy 539 n.
almanac
  directory 87 n.
  chronology 117 n.
almighty
  powerful 160 adj.
  godlike 965 adj.
Almighty, the
  the Deity 965 n.
almoner
  nurse 658 n.
almost
  almost 33 adv.
  on the whole
    52 adv.
  nearly 200 adv.
alms
  gift 781 n.
almshouse
  retreat 192 n.
aloes
  unsavouriness
    391 n.
alone
  alone 88 adj.
  singly 88 adv.

along
longwise 203 adv.
alongside
near 200 adv.
along with
in addition 38 adv.
with 89 adv.
aloof
distant 199 adj.
incurious 454 adj.
impassive 820 adj.
proud 871 adj.
hostile 881 adj.
unsociable 883 adj.
aloud
loudly 400 adv.
alp
high land 209 n.
alpaca
fibre 208 n.
textile 222 n.
alpha
beginning 68 n.
Alpha and Omega
the Deity 965 n.
alphabet
beginning 68 n.
list 87 n.
letter 558 n.
lettering 586 n.
alphabetical order
order 60 n.
alpha-fetoprotein test
obstetrics 167 n.
diagnostic 658 n.
alphanumeric
computerized 86 adj.
alpha plus
excellent 644 adj.
Alps
high land 209 n.
already
before 119 adv.
at present 121 adv.
Alsatian
dog 365 n.
also
in addition 38 adv.
also-ran
inferior 35 n.
loser 728 n.
altar
ritual object 988 n.
altar 990 n.

altar boy
church officer 986 n.
altarpiece
altar 990 n.
alter
change 143 vb.
modify 143 vb.
qualify 468 vb.
alteration
difference 15 n.
change 143 n.
transition 147 n.
altercation
quarrel 709 n.
contention 716 n.
alter ego
identity 13 n.
analogue 18 n.
colleague 707 n.
deputy 755 n.
close friend 880 n.
alternate
correlate 12 vb.
correlative 12 adj.
come after 65 vb.
sequential 65 adj.
be discontinuous 72 vb.
discontinuous 72 adj.
periodical 141 adj.
substitute 150 n.
vary 152 vb.
fluctuate 317 vb.
deputy 755 n.
alternately
correlatively 12 adv.
alternating
correlative 12 adj.
sequential 65 adj.
discontinuous 72 adj.
periodical 141 adj.
alternative
changeable 143 adj.
substitute 150 n.
choice 605 n.
contrivance 623 n.
alternative medicine
dissent 489 n.
medical art 658 n.
alternative reading
interpretation 520 n.

alternator
electronics 160 n.
although
although 182 adv.
provided 468 adv.
altimeter
angular measure 247 n.
meter 465 n.
altitude
quantity 26 n.
degree 27 n.
height 209 n.
alto
vocalist 413 n.
altogether
completely 54 adv.
altogether, the
bareness 229 n.
altruism
philanthropy 901 n.
disinterestedness 931 n.
altruistic
benevolent 897 adj.
philanthropic 901 adj.
disinterested 931 adj.
alumnus
student 538 n.
always
while 108 adv.
Alzheimer's disease
old age 131 n.
helplessness 161 n.
mental disorder 503 n.
a.m.
o'clock 117 adv.
morning 128 n.
amah
domestic 742 n.
amalgam
a mixture 43 n.
compound 50 n.
amalgamation
mixture 43 n.
combination 50 n.
association 706 n.
amanuensis
recorder 549 n.
instrument 628 n.
auxiliary 707 n.
amass
join 45 vb.

bring together 74 vb.
store 632 vb.
take 786 vb.
amateur
ignorance 491 n.
beginner 538 n.
unskilled 695 adj.
bungler 697 n.
amateur dramatics
drama 594 n.
amateurish
ignorant 491 adj.
bungled 695 adj.
unskilled 695 adj.
amaze
surprise 508 vb.
disappoint 509 vb.
impress 821 vb.
be wonderful 864 vb.
amazing
prodigious 32 adj.
unexpected 508 adj.
wonderful 864 adj.
Amazon
violent creature 176 n.
female 373 n.
soldier 722 n.
brave person 855 n.
ambassador
messenger 529 n.
envoy 754 n.
amber
resin 357 n.
brownness 430 n.
orange 432 n.
yellow 433 adj.
yellowness 433 n.
gem 844 n.
ambidextrous
dual 90 adj.
double 91 adj.
skilful 694 adj.
ambience
surroundings 230 n.
painting 553 n.
ambiguity
disagreement 25 n.
uncertainty 474 n.
connotation 514 n.
unintelligibility 517 n.

similar 18 adj.
 symmetrical
  245 adj.
analogue
 analogue 18 n.
 computerized
  86 adj.
analogue computer
 counting instru-
  ment 86 n.
analogue watch
 timekeeper 117 n.
analogy
 relativeness 9 n.
 similarity 18 n.
 comparison 462 n.
analyse
 sunder 46 vb.
 decompose 51 vb.
 class 62 vb.
 enquire 459 vb.
 experiment 461 vb.
 argue 475 vb.
analysis
 separation 46 n.
 decomposition
  51 n.
 arrangement 62 n.
 enquiry 459 n.
 experiment 461 n.
 grammar 564 n.
 compendium
  592 n.
analyst
 psychologist 447 n.
 enquirer 459 n.
 experimenter
  461 n.
 mental disorder
  503 n.
anaphora
 repetition 106 n.
 trope 519 n.
anarchism
 anarchy 734 n.
 sedition 738 n.
anarchist
 anarchist 61 n.
 revolutionist 149 n.
 destroyer 168 n.
 political party
  708 n.
 revolter 738 n.
 evildoer 904 n.
anarchy
 government 733 n.

governmental
  733 adj.
 anarchy 734 n.
 revolt 738 n.
anathema
 hateful object
  888 n.
 malediction 899 n.
anatomy
 structure 331 n.
 biology 358 n.
ancestor
 precursor 66 n.
 source 156 n.
 paternity 169 n.
ancestral
 parental 169 adj.
ancestry
 heredity 5 n.
 consanguinity
  11 n.
 origin 68 n.
 source 156 n.
 genealogy 169 n.
 nobility 868 n.
anchor
 affix 45 vb.
 place 187 vb.
 place oneself
  187 vb.
 dwell 192 vb.
 come to rest
  266 vb.
 sailing aid 269 n.
 protection 660 n.
 badge of rank
  743 n.
 hope 852 n.
anchorite
 solitary 883 n.
 ascetic 945 n.
 pietist 979 n.
anchovies
 fish food 301 n.
ancien régime
 archaism 127 n.
 aristocracy 868 n.
ancient
 great 32 adj.
 past 125 adj.
 olden 127 adj.
 worshipful 866 adj.
ancient monument
 antiquity 125 n.
 archaism 127 n.
 edifice 164 n.
 monument 548 n.

ancients, the
 precursor 66 n.
 antiquity 125 n.
ancillary
 inferior 35 adj.
 aiding 703 adj.
and
 in addition 38 adv.
andante
 slowness 278 n.
 tempo 410 n.
 adagio 412 adv.
andantino
 adagio 412 adv.
and co.
 no name 562 n.
Andes
 high land 209 n.
androgynous
 abnormal 84 adj.
and so forth
 in addition 38 adv.
and so on
 in addition 38 adv.
anecdote
 narrative 590 n.
anemometer
 meter 465 n.
 recording instru-
  ment 549 n.
aneurysm
 cardiovascular dis-
  ease 651 n.
anew
 again 106 vb.
angel
 stage manager
  594 n.
 patron 707 n.
 giver 781 n.
 lender 784 n.
 coinage 797 n.
 a beauty 841 n.
 friend 880 n.
 loved one 887 n.
 darling 890 n.
 benefactor 903 n.
 innocent 935 n.
 good person 937 n.
 angel 968 n.
angel dust
 drug-taking 949 n.
angelfish
 fish 365 n.
angelic
 virtuous 933 adj.
 innocent 935 adj.

angelic 968 adj.
angelus
 signal 547 n.
anger
 anger 891 n.
 enrage 891 vb.
 vice 934 n.
angina
 pang 377 n.
 cardiovascular dis-
  ease 651 n.
angiogram
 diagnostic 658 n.
angle
 angle 247 n.
 bias 481 n.
 opinion 485 n.
 hunt 619 vb.
Anglican
 Anglican 976 adj.
 Catholic 976 n.
 Protestant 976 n.
angling
 chase 619 n.
angry
 angry 891 adj.
angry young man
 nonconformist
  84 n.
 malcontent 829 n.
angst
 evil 616 n.
 badness 645 n.
 bane 659 n.
 suffering 825 n.
 melancholy 834 n.
 nervousness 854 n.
anguish
 pain 377 n.
 badness 645 n.
 suffering 825 n.
angular
 angular 247 adj.
aniline dye
 pigment 425 n.
animal
 organism 358 n.
 animal 365 adj.
 animal 365 n.
animal behaviour
 animality 365 n.
 zoology 367 n.
animalism
 animality 365 n.
animal liberationist
 animality 365 n.

hatred 888 n.
antagonist
  opponent 705 n.
  enemy 881 n.
antagonistic
  contrary 14 adj.
  disagreeing 25 adj.
  opposing 704 adj.
  hostile 881 adj.
antagonize
  counteract 182 vb.
  cause dislike
    861 vb.
  huff 891 vb.
ante
  before 64 adv.
  gambling 618 n.
  portion 783 n.
antecedent
  precursor 66 n.
  prior 119 adj.
  priority 119 n.
antedate
  come before 64 vb.
antediluvian
  prior 119 adj.
  antiquated 127 adj.
  primal 127 adj.
antelope
  mammal 365 n.
  heraldry 547 n.
antenatal
  prior 119 adj.
antenna
  filament 208 n.
  protuberance
    254 n.
  feeler 378 n.
  broadcasting
    531 n.
antependium
  altar 990 n.
anterior
  prior 119 adj.
  frontal 237 adj.
anteroom
  lobby 194 n.
  front 237 n.
anthelmintic
  antidote 658 n.
anthem
  vocal music 412 n.
  hymn 981 n.
anther
  flower 366 n.
anthill
  nest 192 n.

dome 253 n.
anthology
  assemblage 74 n.
  anthology 592 n.
anthracite
  coal 385 n.
anthrax
  animal disease
    651 n.
anthropoid
  animal 365 adj.
anthropologist
  zoologist 367 n.
  anthropology
    371 n.
anthropology
  anthropology
    371 n.
anthropomorphism
  animality 365 n.
  anthropology
    371 n.
  idolatry 982 n.
anti-
  contrary 14 adj.
  opposing 704 adj.
anti-aircraft fire
  bombardment
    712 n.
antibiotic
  antidote 658 n.
  drug 658 n.
antibody
  antidote 658 n.
antic
  revel 837 n.
anti-chic
  inelegance 576 n.
  fashion 848 n.
Antichrist
  bad person 938 n.
  Satan 969 n.
anticipate
  do before 119 vb.
  expect 507 vb.
  foresee 510 vb.
  prepare 669 vb.
  be active 678 vb.
  take 786 vb.
  hope 852 vb.
anticipation
  precursor 66 n.
  anticipation 135 n.
  foresight 510 n.
anticlimax
  absurdity 497 n.
  feebleness 572 n.

ridiculousness
  849 n.
anticlockwise
  towards 281 adv.
anticoagulant
  liquefaction 337 n.
  antidote 658 n.
anticonvulsant
  antidote 658 n.
antics
  foolery 497 n.
anticyclone
  weather 340 n.
antidepressant
  drug 658 n.
antidote
  contrariety 14 n.
  compensation 31 n.
  antidote 658 n.
antifreeze
  heating 381 adj.
antigen
  antidote 658 n.
antihero
  acting 594 n.
antihistamine
  antidote 658 n.
antimacassar
  covering 226 n.
antipasto
  hors-d'oeuvres
    301 n.
antipathy
  contrariety 14 n.
  difference 15 n.
  counteraction
    182 n.
  dislike 861 n.
  enmity 881 n.
  hatred 888 n.
antiperspirant
  cosmetic 843 n.
antiphony
  vocal music 412 n.
antipodes
  contrariety 14 n.
  extremity 69 n.
  contraposition
    240 n.
antiquarian
  antiquarian 125 n.
  olden 127 adj.
antiquary
  antiquarian 125 n.
  collector 492 n.
antiquated
  antiquated 127 adj.

antique
  great 32 adj.
  archaism 127 n.
  olden 127 adj.
  exhibit 522 n.
antiquity
  time 108 n.
  long duration
    113 n.
  antiquity 125 n.
  past time 125 n.
antisemitism
  phobia 854 n.
antiseptic
  salubrious 652 adj.
  prophylactic 658 n.
  remedial 658 adj.
antisocial
  unsociable 883 adj.
antistrophe
  verse form 593 n.
antithesis
  contrariety 14 n.
  difference 15 n.
  contraposition
    240 n.
  comparison 462 n.
  trope 519 n.
  ornament 574 n.
antivivisectionist
  animality 365 n.
antler
  protuberance
    254 n.
  sharp point 256 n.
antonym
  contrariety 14 n.
  connotation 514 n.
  word 559 n.
anus
  buttocks 238 n.
  orifice 263 n.
anvil
  stand 218 n.
  hammer 279 n.
anxiety
  carefulness 457 n.
  expectation 507 n.
  worry 825 n.
  nervousness 854 n.
anxious
  careful 457 adj.
  expectant 507 adj.
  suffering 825 adj.
  nervous 854 adj.
any
  quantitative 26 adj.

universal 79 adj.
anonymous
562 adj.
no name 562 n.
no choice 606 n.
anybody's
unpossessed
774 adj.
loose woman
952 n.
anybody's guess
uncertainty 474 n.
ignorance 491 n.
anyone
everyman 79 n.
any other business
topic 452 n.
policy 623 n.
anything
everyman 79 n.
anything but
contrary 14 adj.
AOB
topic 452 n.
policy 623 n.
apace
swiftly 277 adv.
apart
apart 46 adv.
separate 46 adj.
apart from
in addition 38 adv.
exclusive of 57 adv.
apartheid
separation 46 n.
exclusion 57 n.
prejudice 481 n.
apartment
flat 192 n.
chamber 194 n.
apathetic
inert 175 adj.
slow 278 adj.
incurious 454 adj.
inattentive 456 adj.
nonactive 677 adj.
inactive 679 adj.
apathetic 820 adj.
apathy
inertness 175 n.
incuriosity 454 n.
inattention 456 n.
lack of expectation
508 n.
irresolution 601 n.
sluggishness 679 n.

moral insensibility
820 n.
indifference 860 n.
irreligion 974 n.
ape
imitate 20 vb.
imitator 20 n.
mammal 365 n.
aperient
open 263 adj.
opener 263 n.
cleanser 648 n.
purgative 658 n.
aperitif
prelude 66 n.
stimulant 174 n.
alcoholic drink
301 n.
aperture
gap 201 n.
opening 263 n.
orifice 263 n.
camera 442 n.
apex
summit 213 n.
vertex 213 n.
aphasia
speech defect
580 n.
aphid
insect 365 n.
aphorism
maxim 496 n.
conciseness 569 n.
aphrodisiac
stimulant 174 n.
erotic 887 adj.
Aphrodite
a beauty 841 n.
mythic deity 966 n.
Olympian deity
967 n.
apiary
nest 192 n.
stock farm 369 n.
apiculture
animal husbandry
369 n.
apiece
severally 80 adv.
aplastic anaemia
blood disease
651 n.
aplomb
stability 153 n.
resolution 599 n.

apocalypse
ruin 165 n.
prediction 511 n.
disclosure 526 n.
revelation 975 n.
scripture 975 n.
apocryphal
erroneous 495 adj.
apogee
distance 199 n.
summit 213 n.
Apollo
sun 321 n.
mythic deity 966 n.
Olympian deity
967 n.
apologetic
regretting 830 adj.
repentant 939 adj.
atoning 941 adj.
apologia
vindication 927 n.
apologize
change one's mind
603 vb.
See **recant**
recant 603 vb.
regret 830 vb.
be penitent 939 vb.
atone 941 vb.
apology
recantation 603 n.
pretext 614 n.
penitence 939 n.
atonement 941 n.
apoplectic
angry 891 adj.
apoplectic fit
excitable state
822 n.
apoplexy
helplessness 161 n.
insensibility 375 n.
illness 651 n.
apostasy
change of mind
603 n.
impiety 980 n.
apostle
messenger 529 n.
preacher 537 n.
religious teacher
973 n.
apostolic
scriptural 975 adj.
ecclesiastical
985 adj.

apostrophe
punctuation 547 n.
allocution 583 n.
soliloquy 585 n.
apothecary
druggist 658 n.
apotheosis
heaven 971 n.
appal
displease 827 vb.
appalling
distressing 827 adj.
apparat
governance 733 n.
apparatchik
official 690 n.
officer 741 n.
apparatus
tool 630 n.
apparel
clothing 228 n.
apparent
visible 443 adj.
appearing 445 adj.
certain 473 adj.
manifest 522 adj.
apparition
visual fallacy
440 n.
manifestation
522 n.
ghost 970 n.
appeal
attract 291 vb.
attraction 291 n.
affirm 532 vb.
negation 533 n.
allocution 583 n.
motivate 612 vb.
entreat 761 vb.
entreaty 761 n.
request 761 n.
deprecate 762 vb.
offering 781 n.
payment 804 n.
excitation 821 n.
pleasurableness
826 n.
beauty 841 n.
legal trial 959 n.
appeal against
negate 533 vb.
deprecate 762 vb.
appealing
pleasurable
826 adj.
personable 841 adj.

desired 859 adj.
appeal to
  speak to 583 vb.
  entreat 761 vb.
  request 761 vb.
appear
  begin 68 vb.
  happen 154 vb.
  arrive 295 vb.
  appear 445 vb.
appearance
  form 243 n.
  arrival 295 n.
  appearance 445 n.
appearances
  circumstance 8 n.
  appearance 445 n.
  etiquette 848 n.
appear for
  deputize 755 vb.
appease
  assuage 177 vb.
  pacify 719 vb.
  content 828 vb.
  offer worship
    981 vb.
appellant
  petitioner 763 n.
  dueness 915 n.
  accuser 928 n.
  litigant 959 n.
appellation
  name 561 n.
  nomenclature
    561 n.
appendage
  addition 38 n.
  adjunct 40 n.
  limb 53 n.
  sequel 67 n.
  concomitant 89 n.
appendectomy
  surgery 658 n.
appendicectomy
  surgery 658 n.
appendicitis
  digestive disorders
    651 n.
appendix
  addition 38 n.
  adjunct 40 n.
  sequel 67 n.
  extremity 69 n.
  hanging object
    217 n.
  edition 589 n.

appertain
  be related 9 vb.
appertaining
  relative 9 adj.
appertain to
  be included 78 vb.
appetite
  eating 301 n.
  taste 386 n.
  desire 859 n.
  hunger 859 n.
  liking 859 n.
appetizer
  prelude 66 n.
  stimulant 174 n.
  hors-d'oeuvres
    301 n.
  savouriness 390 n.
appetizing
  tasty 386 adj.
  savoury 390 adj.
  exciting 821 adj.
  desired 859 adj.
applaud
  applaud 923 vb.
applause
  rejoicing 835 n.
  repute 866 n.
  applause 923 n.
apple
  fruit and vegetables
    301 n.
applejack
  alcoholic drink
    301 n.
apple of discord
  quarrelsomeness
    709 n.
apple of one's eye
  sauce 389 n.
  favourite 890 n.
appliance
  instrument 628 n.
  tool 630 n.
  use 673 n.
applicable
  relevant 9 adj.
  apt 24 adj.
  useful 640 adj.
  advisable 642 adj.
applicant
  respondent 460 n.
  petitioner 763 n.
application
  referral 9 n.
  relevance 9 n.
  meditation 449 n.

attention 455 n.
  connotation 514 n.
  study 536 n.
  perseverance 600 n.
  use 673 n.
  assiduity 678 n.
  request 761 n.
appliqué
  needlework 844 n.
apply
  relate 9 vb.
  use 673 vb.
  offer oneself
    759 vb.
  request 761 vb.
apply for
  require 627 vb.
apply for a job
  busy oneself
    622 vb.
apply oneself
  think 449 vb.
  study 536 vb.
  exert oneself
    682 vb.
apply to
  request 761 vb.
appoggiatura
  musical note
    410 n.
appoint
  select 605 vb.
  employ 622 vb.
  commission
    751 vb.
  apportion 783 vb.
appointment
  choice 605 n.
  job 622 n.
  command 737 n.
  mandate 751 n.
  holy orders 985 n.
apportion
  apportion 783 vb.
apposite
  relevant 9 adj.
appraise
  appraise 465 vb.
  estimate 480 vb.
appreciate
  grow 36 vb.
  appraise 465 vb.
  be dear 811 vb.
  have taste 846 vb.
  honour 866 vb.
  love 887 vb.
  approve 923 vb.

appreciation
  discrimination
    463 n.
  measurement
    465 n.
  estimate 480 n.
  interpretation
    520 n.
  feeling 818 n.
  gratitude 907 n.
  approbation 923 n.
appreciative
  grateful 907 adj.
  approving 923 adj.
apprehend
  know 490 vb.
  understand 516 vb.
  arrest 747 vb.
  take 786 vb.
apprehension
  idea 451 n.
  knowledge 490 n.
  expectation 507 n.
  taking 786 n.
  nervousness 854 n.
  legal process 959 n.
apprehensive
  suffering 825 adj.
  nervous 854 adj.
apprentice
  beginner 538 n.
  immature 670 adj.
  artisan 686 n.
  unskilled 695 adj.
  dependant 742 n.
apprise
  inform 524 vb.
approach
  doorway 263 n.
  approach 289 n.
  approach 289 vb.
  speak to 583 vb.
  policy 623 n.
  way 624 n.
  offer 759 n.
  request 761 n.
  request 761 vb.
approachable
  accessible 289 adj.
  possible 469 adj.
  easy 701 adj.
approaching
  relative 9 adj.
  approaching
    289 adj.
approbation
  approbation 923 n.

appropriate
  circumstantial
    8 adj.
  relevant 9 adj.
  apt 24 adj.
  special 80 adj.
  appropriate
    786 vb.
  right 913 adj.
approval
  assent 488 n.
  permission 756 n.
  repute 866 n.
  approbation 923 n.
approve
  approve 923 vb.
approved
  authoritative
    733 adj.
  approved 923 adj.
approximate
  liken 18 vb.
  similar 18 adj.
  near 200 adj.
  approach 289 vb.
approximately
  almost 33 adv.
  nearly 200 adv.
approximation
  relativeness 9 n.
  similarity 18 n.
  nearness 200 n.
  approach 289 n.
appurtenance(s)
  addition 38 n.
  adjunct 40 n.
  component 58 n.
  concomitant 89 n.
  property 777 n.
APR
  finance 797 n.
  credit 802 n.
après
  similar 18 adj.
April fool
  dupe 544 n.
  laughingstock
    851 n.
April shower
  brief span 114 n.
apron
  stage set 594 n.
  canonicals 989 n.
apron stage
  stage set 594 n.
apron strings
  subjection 745 n.

fetter 748 n.
apropos
  concerning 9 adv.
  apt 24 adj.
  incidentally
    137 vb.
apse
  church interior
    990 n.
apt
  apt 24 adj.
  intelligent 498 adj.
aptitude
  aptitude 694 n.
aptness
  fitness 24 n.
  tendency 179 n.
  accuracy 494 n.
  aptitude 694 n.
aptness vitae
  alcoholic drink
    301 n.
apt to
  liable 180 adj.
aquamarine
  greenness 434 n.
  blue 435 adj.
  blueness 435 n.
  gem 844 n.
aquarium
  accumulation 74 n.
  zoo 369 n.
  collection 632 n.
aquatic
  watery 339 adj.
aquavit
  alcoholic drink
    301 n.
aqua vitae
  alcoholic drink
    301 n.
aqueduct
  conduit 351 n.
  bridge 624 n.
aquiline
  angular 247 adj.
  curved 248 adj.
  animal 365 adj.
arabesque
  ballet 594 n.
  pattern 844 n.
Arabic alphabet
  letter 558 n.
Arabic numerals
  number 85 n.
arable farm
  farm 370 n.

arachnid
  animal 365 n.
arbiter
  adviser 691 n.
  magistracy 957 n.
arbitrage
  gamble 618 vb.
arbitrageur
  gambler 618 n.
arbitrary
  unrelated 10 adj.
  illogical 477 adj.
  volitional 595 adj.
  capricious 604 adj.
  authoritative
    733 adj.
  authoritarian
    735 adj.
  insolent 878 adj.
  lawless 954 adj.
arbitrate
  judge 480 vb.
  mediate 720 vb.
arbitration
  judgment 480 n.
  concord 710 n.
  mediation 720 n.
arbitrator
  estimator 480 n.
  adviser 691 n.
  mediator 720 n.
  magistracy 957 n.
arbor
  pivot 218 n.
arboretum
  wood 366 n.
  garden 370 n.
arboriculture
  agriculture 370 n.
arbour
  arbour 194 n.
Arbroath smoky
  fish food 301 n.
arc
  part 53 n.
  arc 250 n.
  fire 379 n.
arcade
  pavilion 192 n.
  curve 248 n.
  path 624 n.
  emporium 796 n.
Arcadia
  happiness 824 n.
arcane
  unintelligible
    517 adj.

  latent 523 adj.
  concealed 525 adj.
arch
  consummate
    32 adj.
  supreme 34 adj.
  bond 47 n.
  foot 214 n.
  support 218 n.
  be curved 248 vb.
  curve 248 n.
  camber 253 n.
  merry 833 adj.
  affected 850 adj.
archaeologist
  antiquarian 125 n.
  detector 484 n.
  chronicler 549 n.
archaeology
  antiquity 125 n.
  palaeology 125 n.
  discovery 484 n.
archaic
  antiquated 127 adj.
  olden 127 adj.
archaism
  archaism 127 n.
  neology 560 n.
archangel
  angel 968 n.
archbishop
  governor 741 n.
  ecclesiarch 986 n.
archdeacon
  ecclesiarch 986 n.
archduke
  potentate 741 n.
  person of rank
    868 n.
arched
  arched 253 adj.
  concave 255 adj.
arch enemy
  enemy 881 n.
archery
  propulsion 287 n.
  arms 723 n.
  sport 837 n.
archetypal
  original 21 adj.
archetype
  prototype 23 n.
Archimedes' screw
  irrigator 341 n.
archipelago
  island 349 n.

architect
  producer 164 n.
  artist 556 n.
  planner 623 n.
  artisan 686 n.
architecture
  composition 56 n.
  form 243 n.
  structure 331 n.
  art 551 n.
  ornamental art
    844 n.
archives
  record 548 n.
  collection 632 n.
  title deed 767 n.
archivist
  recorder 549 n.
  keeper 749 n.
archpriest
  ecclesiarch 986 n.
  priest 986 n.
archway
  doorway 263 n.
arc light
  lamp 420 n.
ardent
  forceful 571 adj.
  fervent 818 adj.
  loving 887 adj.
  pietistic 979 adj.
ardour
  heat 379 n.
  vigour 571 n.
  resolution 599 n.
  warm feeling
    818 n.
  desire 859 n.
arduous
  laborious 682 adj.
  difficult 700 adj.
area
  quantity 26 n.
  greatness 32 n.
  measure 183 n.
  space 183 n.
  region 184 n.
  place 185 n.
  size 195 n.
arena
  range 183 n.
  arena 724 n.
areola
  circle 250 n.
argent
  heraldic 547 adj.
  heraldry 547 n.

argil
  soil 344 n.
argon
  air 340 n.
argosy
  merchant ship
    275 n.
  shipping 275 n.
  navy 722 n.
argot
  slang 560 adj.
arguable
  possible 469 adj.
  uncertain 474 adj.
argue
  evidence 466 vb.
  argue 475 vb.
  dissent 489 vb.
  indicate 547 vb.
argue for
  defend 713 vb.
  contend 716 vb.
  vindicate 927 vb.
argue the point
  argue 475 vb.
argument
  number 85 n.
  topic 452 n.
  argument 475 n.
  demonstration
    478 n.
argumentative
  quarrelling
    709 adj.
argy-bargy
  argue 475 vb.
  quarrel 709 n.
  bargain 791 vb.
aria
  tune 412 n.
Arian
  heretic 977 n.
  heretical 977 adj.
arid
  unproductive
    172 adj.
  dry 342 adj.
  tedious 838 adj.
aridity
  desert 172 n.
  unproductiveness
    172 n.
  dryness 342 n.
aridness
  desert 172 n.
  unproductiveness
    172 n.

Ariel
  fairy 970 n.
arise
  begin 68 vb.
  happen 154 vb.
  lift oneself 310 vb.
  be visible 443 vb.
  appear 445 vb.
arise from
  result 157 vb.
aristocracy
  superior 34 n.
  superiority 34 n.
  social group 371 n.
  elite 644 n.
  government 733 n.
  aristocracy 868 n.
aristocrat
  aristocrat 868 n.
aristocratic
  governmental
    733 adj.
  worshipful 866 adj.
  genteel 868 adj.
  proud 871 adj.
arithmetic
  mathematics 86 n.
arithmetical
  numerical 85 adj.
  statistical 86 adj.
ark
  retreat 192 n.
  box 194 n.
Ark of the Covenant
  ritual object 988 n.
  holy place 990 n.
arm
  adjunct 40 n.
  limb 53 n.
  extremity 69 n.
  sleeve 228 n.
  laterality 239 n.
  indicator 547 n.
  tool 630 n.
  provide 633 vb.
  safeguard 660 vb.
  make ready
    669 vb.
  defend 713 vb.
  go to war 718 vb.
armada
  shipping 275 n.
  armed force 722 n.
  navy 722 n.
Armageddon
  fight 716 n.
  war 718 n.

armagnac
  alcoholic drink
    301 n.
armament
  arms 723 n.
arm and a leg
  greatness 32 n.
armchair
  seat 218 n.
  softness 327 n.
armed
  strong 162 adj.
  prepared 669 adj.
  warring 718 adj.
armed forces
  army 722 n.
armhole
  sleeve 228 n.
  orifice 263 n.
armistice
  lull 145 n.
  peace 717 n.
  pacification 719 n.
Armistice Day
  special day 876 n.
armlet
  loop 250 n.
  badge of rank
    743 n.
  jewellery 844 n.
arm of the law
  law 953 n.
  jurisdiction 955 n.
  legal process 959 n.
armorial
  heraldic 547 adj.
armory
  heraldry 547 n.
armour
  safeguard 660 vb.
  armour 713 n.
  defend 713 vb.
armoured
  hard 326 adj.
  resolute 599 adj.
  invulnerable
    660 adj.
armoured car
  war chariot 274 n.
  cavalry 722 n.
armoury
  accumulation 74 n.
  storage 632 n.
  workshop 687 n.
  arsenal 723 n.
armpit
  cavity 255 n.

arms
garment 228 n.
See **sleeve**
vocation 622 n.
safeguard 662 n.
war 718 n.
arms 723 n.
See **weapon**
honours 866 n.
arm's length
long measure
203 n.
arms race
arms 723 n.
army
army 722 n.
army officer
army officer 741 n.
aroma
odour 394 n.
fragrance 396 n.
aromatic
pungent 388 adj.
savoury 390 adj.
fragrant 396 adj.
around
nearly 200 adv.
around 230 adv.
around the clock
continuously
71 adv.
arouse
cause 156 vb.
cause feeling
374 vb.
raise the alarm
665 vb.
excite 821 vb.
arpeggio
musical note
410 n.
arraign
indict 928 vb.
litigate 959 vb.
arrange
arrange 62 vb.
compose music
413 vb.
predetermine
608 vb.
arranged
arranged 62 adj.
musical 412 adj.
arranged match
type of marriage
894 n.

arrangement
arrangement 62 n.
musical piece
412 n.
compact 765 n.
arranger
musician 413 n.
arras
hanging object
217 n.
array
order 60 n.
arrange 62 vb.
arrangement 62 n.
series 71 n.
multitude 104 n.
place 187 vb.
dress 228 vb.
dressing 228 n.
battle 718 n.
decorate 844 vb.
pageant 875 n.
arrears
debt 803 n.
arrest
cessation 145 n.
halt 145 vb.
hindrance 702 n.
arrest 747 n.
detention 747 n.
restrain 747 vb.
restraint 747 n.
impress 821 vb.
legal process 959 n.
arrival
intruder 59 n.
arrival 295 n.
arrive
arrive 295 vb.
flourish 615 vb.
succeed 727 vb.
prosper 730 vb.
arrivederci
goodbye 296 int.
arrogant
authoritarian
735 adj.
rash 857 adj.
proud 871 adj.
insolent 878 adj.
arrow
sharp point 256 n.
missile 287 n.
indicator 547 n.
missile weapon
723 n.
love token 889 n.

arrowhead
sharp point 256 n.
missile weapon
723 n.
arrowroot
powder 332 n.
thickening 354 n.
arsenal
storage 632 n.
workshop 687 n.
arsenal 723 n.
arsenic
poison 659 n.
arson
destruction 165 n.
fire 379 n.
arson 381 n.
art
art 551 n.
skill 694 n.
art critic
people of taste
846 n.
art deco
art 551 n.
ornamentation
844 n.
arteriogram
diagnostic 658 n.
arteriosclerosis
cardiovascular dis-
ease 651 n.
artery
essential part 5 n.
tube 263 n.
conduit 351 n.
life 360 n.
road 624 n.
Artesian well
water 339 n.
store 632 n.
art exhibition
spectacle 445 n.
artful
cunning 698 adj.
dishonest 930 adj.
artful dodger
slyboots 698 n.
thief 789 n.
artfulness
deception 542 n.
cunning 698 n.
improbity 930 n.
art gallery
collection 632 n.
art historian
artist 556 n.

arthritic
impotent 161 adj.
crippled 163 adj.
diseased 651 adj.
sick person 651 n.
arthritis
pang 377 n.
rheumatism 651 n.
arthropod
animal 365 n.
article
unit 88 n.
product 164 n.
object 319 n.
part of speech
564 n.
article 591 n.
precept 693 n.
merchandise
795 n.
articled clerk
beginner 538 n.
articles
creed 485 n.
articles of agreement
conditions 766 n.
articles of faith
creed 485 n.
theology 973 n.
articulate
join 45 vb.
intelligible 516 adj.
phrase 563 vb.
voice 577 vb.
speak 579 vb.
speaking 579 adj.
articulated lorry
lorry 274 n.
articulation
pronunciation
577 n.
voice 577 n.
speech 579 n.
artifact
product 164 n.
artifice
contrivance 623 n.
stratagem 698 n.
pretension 850 n.
artificer
producer 164 n.
artificial
simulating 18 adj.
imitative 20 adj.
spurious 542 adj.
untrue 543 adj.
inelegant 576 adj.

affected 850 adj.
artificial eye
  blindness 439 n.
artificial insemina-
  tion
  propagation 167 n.
artificiality
  inelegance 576 n.
  affectation 850 n.
artificial limb
  substitute 150 n.
artillery
  loudness 400 n.
  gun 723 n.
artisan
  artisan 686 n.
artist
  artist 556 n.
  entertainer 594 n.
  expert 696 n.
artiste
  musician 413 n.
  entertainer 594 n.
artistic
  elegant 575 adj.
  tasteful 846 adj.
artistry
  touch 378 n.
  imagination 513 n.
  painting 553 n.
  skill 694 n.
  good taste 846 n.
artless
  artless 699 adj.
art-master or mis-
  tress
  artist 556 n.
art museum
  collection 632 n.
art nouveau
  art 551 n.
  ornamentation
    844 n.
arts, the
  culture 490 n.
artwork
  representation
    551 n.
arty-crafty
  ornamental
    844 adj.
as
  similarly 18 adv.
asafoetida
  stench 397 n.

as agreed
  as promised
    764 adv.
as arranged
  purposely 617 adv.
asbestosis
  respiratory disease
    651 n.
ascend
  ascend 308 vb.
ascendance
  authority 733 n.
ascendancy
  superiority 34 n.
  power 160 n.
  influence 178 n.
  governance 733 n.
  prestige 866 n.
ascending order
  series 71 n.
ascension
  ascent 308 n.
ascent
  incline 220 n.
  ascent 308 n.
ascertain
  make certain
    473 vb.
ascetic
  impassive 820 adj.
  unfeeling person
    820 n.
  ascetic 945 adj.
  ascetic 945 n.
Ascot
  racing 716 n.
ascribe
  attribute 158 vb.
asdic
  hearing aid 415 n.
  detector 484 n.
aseptic
  salubrious 652 adj.
as follows
  after 65 adv.
as good as
  on the whole
    52 adv.
  nearly 200 adv.
ash
  powder 332 n.
  tree 366 n.
  dirt 649 n.
ashamed
  guilty 936 adj.
  repentant 939 adj.

ash-blond(e)
  whitish 427 adj.
  yellowness 433 n.
ashen
  colourless 426 adj.
  grey 429 adj.
Ashes
  contest 716 n.
  trophy 729 n.
ashes
  remainder 41 n.
  corpse 363 n.
  greyness 429 n.
  dirt 649 n.
ashet
  plate 194 n.
ashlar
  facing 226 n.
  building material
    631 n.
ashram
  monastery 986 n.
Ashtoreth
  Semitic deities
    967 n.
Ash Wednesday
  holy day 988 n.
aside
  sideways 239 adv.
  latency 523 n.
  hint 524 n.
  secretly 525 adv.
  voice 577 n.
  voicelessness 578 n.
  allocution 583 n.
  soliloquy 585 n.
  dramaturgy 594 n.
as if
  similarly 18 adv.
asinine
  equine 273 adj.
  animal 365 adj.
  absurd 497 adj.
  foolish 499 adj.
as it were
  be identical 13 vb.
  similarly 18 adv.
ask
  enquire 459 vb.
  request 761 vb.
ask a favour
  request 761 vb.
askance
  sideways 239 adv.
askew
  distorted 246 adj.

ask for
  enquire 459 vb.
  bargain 791 vb.
  desire 859 vb.
ask for it
  make quarrels
    709 vb.
ask for more
  eat 301 vb.
  be unsatisfied
    636 vb.
ask for the hand of
  court 889 vb.
  wed 894 vb.
ask for trouble
  defy 711 vb.
  be rash 857 vb.
ask in
  be hospitable
    882 vb.
asking
  enquiry 459 n.
  request 761 n.
asking for it
  quarrelling
    709 adj.
asking for trouble, be
  be in difficulty
    700 vb.
ask leave
  ask leave 756 vb.
ask one's blessing
  ask leave 756 vb.
ask the way
  orientate 281 vb.
asleep
  quiescent 266 adj.
  sleepy 679 adj.
as likely as not
  probably 471 adv.
Asmodeus
  devil 969 n.
as one
  together 74 adv.
asp
  reptile 365 n.
asparagus
  fruit and vegetables
    301 n.
aspect
  modality 7 n.
  circumstance 8 n.
  situation 186 n.
  view 438 n.
  appearance 445 n.
  conduct 688 n.

aspen
tree 366 n.

asperges
Holy Communion
988 n.
ritual act 988 n.

asperity
roughness 259 n.
rudeness 885 n.
anger 891 n.
irascibility 892 n.

aspersion(s)
slur 867 n.
scurrility 899 n.
censure 924 n.
reproach 924 n.
calumny 926 n.
detraction 926 n.
ritual act 988 n.

asphalt
paving 226 n.
resin 357 n.
road 624 n.
building material
631 n.

asphyxiate
close 264 vb.

aspic
condiment 389 n.

aspirant
petitioner 763 n.

aspirate
extract 304 vb.
breathe 352 vb.
speech sound
398 n.
voice 577 vb.

aspiration
voidance 300 n.
extraction 304 n.
pronunciation
577 n.
motive 612 n.
objective 617 n.
aspiration 852 n.
desire 859 n.
desired object
859 n.

aspire
ascend 308 vb.
hope 852 vb.
desire 859 vb.

aspire to
aim at 617 vb.

aspirin
drug 658 n.

aspiring
new 126 adj.
high 209 adj.
hoping 852 adj.

as regards
concerning 9 adv.

ass
buttocks 238 n.
beast of burden
273 n.
fool 501 n.
bungler 697 n.

assailant
opponent 705 n.
attacker 712 n.
combatant 722 n.

assassin
destroyer 168 n.
violent creature
176 n.
murderer 362 n.
ruffian 904 n.

assassinate
murder 362 vb.

assassination
homicide 362 n.
killing 362 n.

assault
knock 279 n.
attack 712 n.
attack 712 vb.
debauch 951 vb.

assault and battery
knock 279 n.
attack 712 n.

assay
experiment 461 n.
experiment 461 vb.
appraise 465 vb.

assegai
spear 723 n.

assemblage
assemblage 74 n.

assemble
compose 56 vb.
bring together
74 vb.
congregate 74 vb.
produce 164 vb.
meet 295 vb.

assembly
combination 50 n.
assembly 74 n.
convergence 293 n.
council 692 n.

assembly line
continuity 71 n.

assent
assent 488 n.
assent 488 vb.
obey 739 vb.

assert
mean 514 vb.
affirm 532 vb.

assertion
testimony 466 n.
affirmation 532 n.

assertive
assertive 532 adj.

assert oneself
influence 178 vb.
be active 678 vb.

assess
appraise 465 vb.
price 809 vb.

assessment
measurement
465 n.
estimate 480 n.
tax 809 n.

assessor
estimator 480 n.
magistracy 957 n.

assets
means 629 n.
store 632 n.
sufficiency 635 n.
estate 777 n.

asset-stripping
expropriation
786 n.

assiduity
assiduity 678 n.

assiduous
frequent 139 adj.
attentive 455 adj.
careful 457 adj.
industrious
678 adj.

assign
arrange 62 vb.
dispose of 673 vb.
commission
751 vb.
assign 780 vb.
bequeath 780 vb.
apportion 783 vb.

assignation
social round 882 n.

assignee
recipient 782 n.

assignment
undertaking 672 n.
mandate 751 n.

transfer 780 n.
apportionment
783 n.

assign to
attribute 158 vb.
use 673 vb.

assimilate
identify 13 vb.
make uniform
16 vb.
combine 50 vb.
make conform
83 vb.
absorb 299 vb.

assimilation
assimilation 18 n.
combination 50 n.
inclusion 78 n.
conformity 83 n.
reception 299 n.

assist
be instrumental
628 vb.
aid 703 vb.

assistance
provision 633 n.
aid 703 n.

assistant
inferior 35 n.
instrument 628 n.
aider 703 n.
aiding 703 adj.
auxiliary 707 n.
servant 742 n.

assist at
be present 189 vb.

assisting
instrumental
628 adj.
aiding 703 adj.

assize
legal trial 959 n.

assizes
lawcourt 956 n.

as... so...
correlatively
12 adv.

associate
join 45 vb.
combine 50 vb.
congregate 74 vb.
concomitant 89 n.
cooperate 706 vb.
colleague 707 n.
join a party
708 vb.
society 708 n.

friend 880 n.
associated
relative 9 adj.
combined 50 adj.
cooperative
706 adj.
associate member
society 708 n.
associate with
unite with 45 vb.
accompany 89 vb.
associating
cooperative
706 adj.
association
intuition 476 n.
association 706 n.
Association football
ball game 837 n.
assonance
assimilation 18 n.
recurrence 106 n.
melody 410 n.
ornament 574 n.
prosody 593 n.
assorted
different 15 adj.
uniform 16 adj.
assortment
uniformity 16 n.
arrangement 62 n.
series 71 n.
accumulation 74 n.
bunch 74 n.
sort 77 n.
assuage
assuage 177 vb.
tranquillize
823 vb.
assume
account for 158 vb.
assume 471 vb.
postulate 475 vb.
be of the opinion
that 485 vb.
suppose 512 vb.
dissemble 541 vb.
be affected 850 vb.
hope 852 vb.
be insolent 878 vb.
assumed
supposed 512 adj.
affected 850 adj.
assumed title
misnomer 562 n.
assuming
thus 8 adv.

insolent 878 adj.
unwarranted
916 adj.
Assumption
elevation 310 n.
assumption
attribution 158 n.
qualification 468 n.
premise 475 n.
opinion 485 n.
supposition 512 n.
taking 786 n.
arrogation 916 n.
heaven 971 n.
assurance
positiveness 473 n.
belief 485 n.
affirmation 532 n.
safety 660 n.
promise 764 n.
hope 852 n.
vanity 873 n.
insolence 878 n.
assure
make certain
473 vb.
convince 485 vb.
promise 764 vb.
give security
767 vb.
assured
positive 473 adj.
assertive 532 adj.
Astarte
Semitic deities
967 n.
asterisk
mark 547 vb.
punctuation 547 n.
astern
rearward 238 adv.
asteroid
planet 321 n.
as... they say
proverbially
496 adv.
asthma
respiratory disease
651 n.
asthmatic
diseased 651 adj.
sick person 651 n.
astigmatic
dim-sighted
440 adj.
astigmatism
dim sight 440 n.

astir
busy 678 adj.
excited 821 adj.
as... to
concerning 9 adv.
astonish
surprise 508 vb.
be wonderful
864 vb.
astonishing
prodigious 32 adj.
unusual 84 adj.
astonishment
wonder 864 n.
astound
surprise 508 vb.
impress 821 vb.
be wonderful
864 vb.
astounding
prodigious 32 adj.
unexpected
508 adj.
wonderful 864 adj.
astrakhan
skin 226 n.
astral
immaterial
320 adj.
celestial 321 adj.
astral body
spiritualism 984 n.
astray
unrelated 10 adj.
lost 772 adj.
astringent
conjunctive 45 adj.
pungent 388 adj.
sour 393 adj.
astrodome
athletics 162 n.
meeting place
192 n.
view 438 n.
astrolabe
gauge 465 n.
astrologer
diviner 511 n.
sorcerer 983 n.
occultist 984 n.
astrological
astronomic
321 adj.
astrology
influence 178 n.
astronomy 321 n.
divination 511 n.

occultism 984 n.
astronaut
traveller 268 n.
aeronaut 271 n.
astronomer
spectator 441 n.
astronomic
astronomic
321 adj.
astronomical
exorbitant 32 adj.
astronomic
321 adj.
astronomy
astronomy 321 n.
astrophysics
astronomy 321 n.
astute
intelligent 498 adj.
cunning 698 adj.
asunder
apart 46 adv.
separate 46 adj.
as... well as
in addition 38 adv.
as... well not to
inexpedient
643 adj.
as... well to
advisable 642 adj.
asylum
retreat 192 n.
reception 299 n.
protection 660 n.
refuge 662 n.
asymmetric
distorted 246 adj.
asymmetrical
unrelated 10 adj.
nonuniform 17 adj.
unequal 29 adj.
abnormal 84 adj.
asymmetry
unrelatedness 10 n.
nonuniformity
17 n.
disagreement 25 n.
inequality 29 n.
distortion 246 n.
ugliness 842 n.
at a guess
about 33 adv.
at all times
perpetually
139 adv.
at a loose end
leisurely 681 adj.

539

at a loss, be
be uncertain
474 vb.
not know 491 vb.
be in difficulty
700 vb.
at a loss for words
voiceless 578 adj.
at a pinch
with difficulty
700 adv.
at a standstill
quiescent 266 adj.
inactive 679 adj.
atavism
consanguinity
11 n.
recurrence 106 n.
reversion 148 n.
reproduction
166 n.
memory 505 n.
at bay
endangered
661 adj.
in difficulties
700 adj.
at close range
near 200 adv.
at cross purposes
disagreeing 25 adj.
at daggers drawn
opposing 704 adj.
quarrelling
709 adj.
hostile 881 adj.
at death's door
dying 361 adj.
at ease
tranquil 266 adj.
reposeful 683 adj.
free 744 adj.
content 828 adj.
atelier
chamber 194 n.
at fault
mistaken 495 adj.
guilty 936 adj.
at full pitch
loud 400 adj.
at full speed
swiftly 277 adv.
at gunpoint
by force 740 adv.
at half-cock
immature 670 adj.

at half-mast
lamenting 836 adj.
at hand
early 135 adj.
impending 155 adj.
near 200 adj.
useful 640 adj.
Atharvaveda
non-Biblical scrip-
ture 975 n.
at heart
inside 224 adv.
atheism
philosophy 449 n.
unbelief 486 n.
religion 973 n.
irreligion 974 n.
atheroma
cardiovascular dis-
ease 651 n.
athlete
athlete 162 n.
athlete's foot
skin disease 651 n.
athletics
athletics 162 n.
contention 716 n.
contest 716 n.
at home
apt 24 adj.
assembly 74 n.
inside 224 adv.
at home in
habituated 610 adj.
at intervals
periodically
141 adv.
at its height
great 32 adj.
beyond 34 adv.
at knifepoint
by force 740 adv.
Atlantis
fantasy 513 n.
at large
free 744 adj.
Atlas
athlete 162 n.
giant 195 n.
classical deities
967 n.
atlas
directory 87 n.
world 321 n.
map 551 n.
at last
finally 69 adv.

at last 113 adv.
late 136 adv.
at least
slightly 33 adv.
at length
late 136 adv.
at long last
finally 69 adv.
at last 113 adv.
late 136 adv.
ATM
treasury 799 n.
atmosphere
surroundings
230 n.
atmosphere 340 n.
painting 553 n.
atmospheric
airy 340 adj.
atmospheric pressure
weather 340 n.
atmospherics
commotion 318 n.
discord 411 n.
at no time
never 109 adv.
at odds
disagreeing 25 adj.
quarrelling
709 adj.
atoll
island 349 n.
atom
small thing 33 n.
unit 88 n.
minuteness 196 n.
element 319 n.
atomic
dynamic 160 adj.
atomizer
pulverizer 332 n.
vaporizer 338 n.
air 340 n.
atonal
discordant 411 adj.
at one
agreeing 24 adj.
atone
atone 941 vb.
at one's beck and call
obedient 739 adj.
serving 742 adj.
at one's convenience
leisurely 681 adj.
at one's disposal
possessed 773 adj.

at one's ease
comfortable
376 adj.
in comfort
376 adj.
at one's feet
near 200 adv.
at one's fingertips
near 200 adv.
near 200 adv.
at one's peak
strong 162 adj.
at one's service
used 673 adj.
at one's wits end
in difficulties
700 adj.
at present
at present 121 adv.
at rest
fixed 153 adj.
quiescent 266 adj.
atrocious
cruel 898 adj.
heinous 934 adj.
atrocity
cruel act 898 n.
guilty act 936 n.
atrophy
helplessness 161 n.
contraction 198 n.
disease 651 n.
nervous disorders
651 n.
dilapidation 655 n.
at sea
mistaken 495 adj.
at sixes and sevens
unprepared
670 adj.
attach
add 38 vb.
affix 45 vb.
connect 45 vb.
attaché
envoy 754 n.
attaché case
box 194 n.
case 194 n.
attached
tied 45 adj.
attached to
loving 887 adj.
attachment
adjunct 40 n.
part 53 n.

expropriation
786 n.
love 887 n.
attack
begin 68 vb.
spasm 318 n.
argue 475 vb.
policy 623 n.
way 624 n.
illness 651 n.
attack 712 n.
attack 712 vb.
attacker
attacker 712 n.
detractor 926 n.
attain
arrive 295 vb.
acquire 771 vb.
attainable
accessible 289 adj.
possible 469 adj.
attainder
condemnation
961 n.
attainments
culture 490 n.
learning 536 n.
attar
scent 396 n.
attempt
attempt 671 n.
attempt 671 vb.
attend
be present 189 vb.
follow 284 vb.
watch 441 vb.
be attentive 455 vb.
doctor 658 vb.
be servile 879 vb.
attendance
accompaniment
89 n.
presence 189 n.
attendant
concomitant 89 n.
follower 284 n.
retainer 742 n.
servant 742 n.
bridal party 894 n.
attend to
observe 768 vb.
attention
attention 455 n.
respect 920 n.
attentive
attentive 455 adj.

attentiveness
attention 455 n.
carefulness 457 n.
attentive to
observant 768 adj.
attenuate
make smaller
198 vb.
make thin 206 vb.
narrow 206 adj.
rarefy 325 vb.
attest
testify 466 vb.
endorse 488 vb.
swear 532 vb.
contract 765 vb.
attested
evidential 466 adj.
certain 473 adj.
at the double
swiftly 277 adv.
hurry up 680 int.
at the drop of a hat
suddenly 135 adv.
willingly 597 adv.
at the end of one's
tether
in difficulties
700 adj.
at the last minute
late 136 adv.
at the present time
at present 121 adv.
at the ready
near 200 adv.
prepared 669 adj.
at the top of one's
voice
beyond 34 adv.
loud 400 adj.
loudly 400 adv.
at the very least
slightly 33 adv.
at the very start
beyond 34 adv.
initially 68 adv.
at present 121 adv.
be high 209 vb.
at this moment in
time
at present 121 adv.
at this stage
at present 121 adv.
at this time
at present 121 adv.
Attic
elegant 575 adj.

attic
attic 194 n.
Attic salt
wit 839 n.
Attila
ruffian 904 n.
at times
sometimes
139 adv.
attire
dress 228 vb.
dressing 228 n.
attitude
state 7 n.
situation 186 n.
form 243 n.
idea 451 n.
opinion 485 n.
conduct 688 n.
affections 817 n.
attitudinize
be affected 850 vb.
attorney
consignee 754 n.
deputy 755 n.
law agent 958 n.
Attorney General
law officer 955 n.
attract
attract 291 vb.
attraction
attraction 291 n.
incentive 612 n.
beauty 841 n.
liking 859 n.
attractions
beauty 841 n.
attractive
influential 178 adj.
pleasurable
826 adj.
personable 841 adj.
desired 859 adj.
attractiveness
attraction 291 n.
inducement 612 n.
pleasurableness
826 n.
beauty 841 n.
attributable
due 915 adj.
attribute
essential part 5 n.
speciality 80 n.
concomitant 89 n.
attribute 158 vb.
attribution 158 n.

ability 160 n.
attributed to
caused 157 adj.
attributive
grammatical
564 adj.
attrition
powderiness 332 n.
friction 333 n.
warfare 718 n.
penitence 939 n.
attune
adjust 24 vb.
harmonize 410 vb.
Atum
Egyptian deities
967 n.
Atum-ra
Egyptian deities
967 n.
at variance
disagreeing 25 adj.
opposing 704 adj.
quarrelling
709 n.
hostile 881 adj.
at war
disagreeing 25 adj.
warring 718 adj.
at work
operative 173 adj.
busy 678 adj.
atypical
nonuniform 17 adj.
dissimilar 19 adj.
inimitable 21 adj.
abnormal 84 adj.
Atys
mythic deity 966 n.
Semitic deities
967 n.
aubade
vocal music 412 n.
auberge
inn 192 n.
auburn
brown 430 adj.
red 431 adj.
au courant
be wise 498 vb.
informed 524 adj.
auction
offer 759 vb.
sale 793 n.
sell 793 vb.
auction bridge
card game 837 n.

auctioneer
seller 793 n.
audacious
courageous
855 adj.
rash 857 adj.
insolent 878 adj.
audacity
courage 855 n.
rashness 857 n.
insolence 878 n.
audibility
sound 398 n.
loudness 400 n.
hearing 415 n.
audible
sounding 398 adj.
loud 400 adj.
auditory 415 adj.
intelligible 516 adj.
speaking 579 adj.
audience
listener 415 n.
listening 415 n.
onlookers 441 n.
publicity 528 n.
conference 584 n.
playgoer 594 n.
audio
sound 398 n.
sounding 398 adj.
audiotypist
stenographer
586 n.
audiovisual
sounding 398 adj.
auditory 415 adj.
educational
534 adj.
audit
number 86 vb.
enquire 459 vb.
enquiry 459 n.
account 808 vb.
accounts 808 n.
audition
hearing 415 n.
listening 415 n.
exam 459 n.
experiment 461 n.
dramaturgy 594 n.
auditorium
listener 415 n.
onlookers 441 n.
theatre 594 n.
auf Wiedersehen
goodbye 296 int.

auger
sharp point 256 n.
perforator 263 n.
augment
augment 36 vb.
augmentation
increase 36 n.
increment 36 n.
expansion 197 n.
aggravation 832 n.
augur
predict 511 vb.
augury
divination 511 n.
august
great 32 adj.
notable 638 adj.
impressive 821 adj.
worshipful 866 adj.
Augustan Age
literature 557 n.
auk
animal 365 n.
auld lang syne
past time 125 n.
aumbry
church interior
990 n.
aunt
kinsman 11 n.
female 373 n.
Auntie
broadcasting
531 n.
auntie
kinsman 11 n.
female 373 n.
Aunt Sally
laughingstock
851 n.
au pair
resident 191 n.
domestic 742 n.
aura
surroundings
230 n.
prestige 866 n.
aural
auditory 415 adj.
aureole
light 417 n.
honours 866 n.
aureomycin
drug 658 n.
au revoir
goodbye 296 int.

auricular
auditory 415 adj.
auriscope
hearing aid 415 n.
detector 484 n.
diagnostic 658 n.
Aurora
morning 128 n.
aurora
glow 417 n.
aurora australis
heavens 321 n.
glow 417 n.
aurora borealis
heavens 321 n.
glow 417 n.
auspices
protection 660 n.
aid 703 n.
auspicious
opportune 137 adj.
predicting 511 adj.
palmy 730 adj.
promising 852 adj.
austere
plain 573 adj.
severe 735 adj.
ascetic 945 adj.
pietistic 979 adj.
austerity
unsavouriness
391 n.
plainness 573 n.
insufficiency 636 n.
severity 735 n.
asceticism 945 n.
pietism 979 n.
authentic
genuine 494 adj.
authenticate
testify 466 vb.
make certain
473 vb.
endorse 488 vb.
give security
767 vb.
title deed 767 n.
authenticity
authenticity 494 n.
author
cause 156 n.
author 589 n.
planner 623 n.
authoritarian
authoritarian
735 adj.
tyrant 735 n.

authoritative
evidential 466 adj.
certain 473 adj.
creedal 485 adj.
authoritative
733 adj.
commanding
737 adj.
orthodox 976 adj.
authorities, the
master 741 n.
authority
credential 466 n.
sage 500 n.
informant 524 n.
expert 696 n.
authority 733 n.
permit 756 n.
authorization
warrant 737 n.
permission 756 n.
security 767 n.
authorize
endorse 488 vb.
commission
751 vb.
permit 756 vb.
Authorized Version
scripture 975 n.
authorship
composition 56 n.
causation 156 n.
production 164 n.
writing 586 n.
autism
intrinsicality 5 n.
psychosis 503 n.
unsociability
883 n.
autistic
intrinsic 5 adj.
mentally handi-
capped 503 adj.
auto
automobile 274 n.
autobahn
road 624 n.
autobiography
biography 590 n.
autobus
bus 274 n.
autochthones
native 191 n.
autocrat
autocrat 741 n.
autocratic
volitional 595 adj.

authoritative
733 adj.
authoritarian
735 adj.
autocrime
stealing 788 n.
autocue
broadcasting
531 n.
auto da fé
killing 362 n.
autograph
no imitation 21 n.
reminder 505 n.
identification
547 n.
label 547 n.
sign 547 vb.
script 586 n.
automated
dynamic 160 adj.
mechanical
630 adj.
automated teller machine
treasury 799 n.
automatic
intrinsic 5 adj.
computerized
86 adj.
involuntary
596 adj.
spontaneous
609 adj.
instrumental
628 adj.
mechanical
630 adj.
pistol 723 n.
automatic pilot
aeronaut 271 n.
aircraft 276 n.
automatic reflex
spontaneity 609 n.
automation
uniformity 16 n.
electronics 160 n.
instrumentality
628 n.
automatism
spiritualism 984 n.
automaton
image 551 n.
machine 630 n.
automobile
automobile 274 n.

automotive
moving 265 adj.
autonomous
governmental
733 adj.
independent
744 adj.
autonomy
government 733 n.
independence
744 n.
autopilot
aeronaut 271 n.
aircraft 276 n.
autopsy
death 361 n.
inquest 364 n.
inspection 438 n.
enquiry 459 n.
autoroute
road 624 n.
autostrada
road 624 n.
autosuggestion
sense 374 n.
insensibility 375 n.
misjudgment
481 n.
fantasy 513 n.
autumn
period 110 n.
autumn 129 n.
auxiliary
inferior 35 adj.
additional 38 adj.
aiding 703 adj.
auxiliary 707 n.
avail
benefit 615 vb.
utility 640 n.
available
accessible 289 adj.
possible 469 adj.
useful 640 adj.
used 673 adj.
avalanche
revolution 149 n.
descent 309 n.
snow 380 n.
redundance 637 n.
avant-garde
precursor 66 n.
modern 126 adj.
modernist 126 n.
front 237 n.
preceding 283 n.
dramatic 594 adj.

avarice
avarice 816 n.
avaricious
avaricious 816 adj.
avatar
transformation
143 n.
revelation 975 n.
Ave
prayers 981 n.
avenge
avenge 910 vb.
avenue
housing 192 n.
park 192 n.
path 624 n.
road 624 n.
aver
affirm 532 vb.
average
average 30 n.
average out 30 vb.
median 30 adj.
general 79 adj.
typical 83 adj.
not bad 644 adj.
middling 732 adj.
averageness
averageness 732 n.
average punter, the
social group 371 n.
averages
statistics 86 n.
averment
affirmation 532 n.
litigation 959 n.
Avernus
mythic hell 972 n.
averse
unwilling 598 adj.
aversion
unwillingness
598 n.
dislike 861 n.
hatred 888 n.
avert
deflect 282 vb.
Avesta
non-Biblical scripture 975 n.
avian
animal 365 adj.
aviary
nest 192 n.
cattle pen 369 n.
zoo 369 n.

aviation
aeronautics 271 n.
aviator
aeronaut 271 n.
aviculture
animal husbandry
369 n.
avid
excited 821 adj.
avidity
rapacity 786 n.
avarice 816 n.
desire 859 n.
avitaminosis
disease 651 n.
avocado
fruit and vegetables
301 n.
green 434 adj.
avoid
avoid 620 vb.
disapprove 924 vb.
avoidance
avoidance 620 n.
avoirdupois
finite quantity
26 n.
bulk 195 n.
metrology 465 n.
avoirdupois weight
weighing 322 n.
avow
testify 466 vb.
assent 488 vb.
confess 526 vb.
affirm 532 vb.
avowal
disclosure 526 n.
affirmation 532 n.
avuncular
akin 11 adj.
await
await 507 vb.
awake
attentive 455 adj.
active 678 adj.
awaken
cause 156 vb.
cause feeling
374 vb.
have feeling
374 vb.
excite 821 vb.
awake to
attentive 455 adj.
discover 484 vb.

AWA

impressible
819 adj.
award
judge 480 vb.
judgment 480 n.
trophy 729 n.
gift 781 n.
give 781 vb.
giving 781 n.
honours 866 n.
reward 962 n.
reward 962 vb.
aware
sentient 374 adj.
attentive 455 adj.
knowing 490 adj.
intelligent 498 adj.
impressible
819 adj.
awareness
sensibility 374 n.
intellect 447 n.
knowledge 490 n.
sagacity 498 n.
away
absent 190 adj.
distant 199 adj.
away with the fairies
foolish 499 adj.
crazy 503 adj.
awe
excitation 821 n.
fear 854 n.
be wonderful
864 vb.
wonder 864 n.
command respect
920 vb.
respect 920 n.
worship 981 n.
awesome
frightening
854 adj.
wonderful 864 adj.
awful
bad 645 adj.
not nice 645 adj.
frightening
854 adj.
awfully
extremely 32 vb.
awkward
young 130 adj.
unwieldy 195 adj.
inelegant 576 adj.
inexpedient
643 adj.

AYA

clumsy 695 adj.
annoying 827 adj.
graceless 842 adj.
modest 874 adj.
awl
sharp point 256 n.
perforator 263 n.
awning
canopy 226 n.
screen 421 n.
AWOL
absent 190 adj.
awry
unequal 29 adj.
distorted 246 adj.
amiss 616 adv.
evil 616 adj.
awry, be
be oblique 220 vb.
axe
destroy 165 vb.
shorten 204 vb.
sharp edge 256 n.
dismiss 300 vb.
fell 311 vb.
axe 723 n.
means of execution
964 n.
axe to grind
affairs 154 n.
objective 617 n.
selfishness 932 n.
axial
central 225 adj.
directed 281 adj.
axiom
premise 475 n.
axiom 496 n.
axiomatic
certain 473 adj.
undisputed
473 adj.
rational 475 adj.
aphoristic 496 adj.
axis
pivot 218 n.
centre 225 n.
rotator 315 n.
gauge 465 n.
axle
pivot 218 n.
rotator 315 n.
ayah
domestic 742 n.
ayatollah
leader 690 n.
governor 741 n.

BAB

aye
assent 488 n.
aye, aye
amen 488 int.
ayes, the
assenter 488 n.
A-Z
list 87 n.
itinerary 267 n.
guidebook 524 n.
azalea
tree 366 n.
Azazel
devil 969 n.
azimuth
horizontality
216 n.
azimuth circle
verticality 215 n.
Azrael
angel 968 n.
azure
blue 435 adj.
blueness 435 n.
heraldic 547 adj.
heraldry 547 n.

B

BA
academic title
870 n.
baa
ululate 409 vb.
ululation 409 n.
Baal
Semitic deities
967 n.
idol 982 n.
babble
flow 350 vb.
sound faint 401 vb.
be foolish 499 vb.
be insane 503 vb.
empty talk 515 n.
mean nothing
515 vb.
language 557 n.
chatter 581 n.
babe
child 132 n.
innocent 935 n.
Babel
disorder 61 n.
discord 411 n.
lack of meaning
515 n.

BAC

language 557 n.
babes and sucklings
innocent 935 n.
baboon
mammal 365 n.
eyesore 842 n.
baby
child 132 n.
weakling 163 n.
little 196 adj.
female 373 n.
function 622 n.
please 826 vb.
coward 856 n.
loved one 887 n.
pet 889 vb.
baby boom
productiveness
171 n.
baby buggy
pushcart 274 n.
baby grand
piano 414 n.
Babygro (tdmk)
clothing 228 n.
babyhood
beginning 68 n.
youth 130 n.
helplessness 161 n.
babyish
weak 163 adj.
cowardly 856 adj.
baby-minder
servant 742 n.
keeper 749 n.
baby-sit
look after 457 vb.
baby-sitter
surveillance 457 n.
protector 660 n.
servant 742 n.
keeper 749 n.
baby talk
neology 560 n.
baccalaureate
exam 459 n.
honours 866 n.
academic title
870 n.
baccarat
card game 837 n.
bacchanalia
feasting 301 n.
Bacchus
Olympian deity
967 n.

baccy
tobacco 388 n.
bachelor
unit 88 n.
male 372 n.
independent
744 adj.
celibate 895 n.
bachelor girl
unit 88 n.
female 373 n.
spinster 895 n.
bachelor of arts etc.
academic title
870 n.
bacillus
infection 651 n.
poison 659 n.
back
be inverted 221 vb.
line 227 vb.
back 238 adj.
be behind 238 vb.
contraposition
240 n.
navigate 269 vb.
regress 286 vb.
harden 326 vb.
blow 352 vb.
choose 605 vb.
gamble 618 vb.
patronize 703 vb.
lend 784 vb.
approve 923 vb.
backache
pang 377 n.
back and forth
to and fro 317 adv.
back away
be inverted 221 vb.
recede 290 vb.
be irresolute
601 vb.
avoid 620 vb.
backbencher
inferior 35 n.
councillor 692 n.
commoner 869 n.
backbite
defame 926 vb.
backbiter
detractor 926 n.
backbiting
detraction 926 n.
backbone
essential part 5 n.
vitality 162 n.

vigorousness 174 n.
pillar 218 n.
centre 225 n.
hardness 326 n.
resolution 599 n.
stamina 600 n.
courage 855 n.
backchat
answer 460 n.
witticism 839 n.
sauciness 878 n.
backcloth
stage set 594 n.
back door
rear 238 n.
means of escape
667 n.
doorway 263 n.
backdoor
stealthy 525 adj.
back down
revert 148 vb.
regress 286 vb.
change one's mind
603 vb.
relinquish 621 vb.
refuse 760 vb.
backdown
reversion 148 n.
backdrop
rear 238 n.
stage set 594 n.
backer
stage manager
594 n.
gambler 618 n.
patron 707 n.
giver 781 n.
lender 784 n.
friend 880 n.
benefactor 903 n.
backfire
reversion 148 n.
revert 148 vb.
counteraction
182 n.
bang 402 n.
bang 402 vb.
back-formation
word 559 n.
backgammon
board game 837 n.
background
concomitant 89 n.
distance 199 n.
surroundings
230 n.

rear 238 n.
knowledge 490 n.
information 524 n.
stage set 594 n.
back-handed
equivocal 518 adj.
back-handed compliment
ridicule 851 n.
censure 924 n.
back number
archaism 127 n.
reading matter
589 n.
backing
lining 227 n.
regression 286 n.
return 286 n.
aid 703 n.
approbation 923 n.
backlash
reversion 148 n.
effect 157 n.
counteraction
182 n.
recoil 280 n.
retaliation 714 n.
resistance 715 n.
deprecation 762 n.
backlog
store 632 n.
back of beyond
district 184 n.
seclusion 883 n.
back of the head
rear 238 n.
back on
be behind 238 vb.
back out
regress 286 vb.
change one's mind
603 vb.
resign 753 vb.
not observe 769 vb.
be cowardly
856 vb.
backpack
bag 194 n.
travel 267 vb.
backpacking
land travel 267 n.
pedestrianism
267 n.
back pay
debt 803 n.
pay 804 n.

backpedal
retard 278 vb.
regress 286 vb.
change one's mind
603 vb.
recant 603 vb.
back-pedaller
recanter 603 n.
back-pedalling
change of mind
603 n.
backrest
support 218 n.
backroom
latent 523 adj.
backroom boy
planner 623 n.
back-scratching
inducement 612 n.
cooperation 706 n.
cooperative
706 adj.
servile 879 adj.
flattering 925 adj.
flattery 925 n.
back seat
inferiority 35 n.
rear 238 n.
back-seat driver
meddler 678 n.
adviser 691 n.
back side
rear 238 n.
backside
buttocks 238 n.
back-slapping
ostentation 875 n.
friendly 880 adj.
sociability 882 n.
sociable 882 adj.
backslide
revert 148 vb.
change one's mind
603 vb.
relapse 657 vb.
be wicked 934 vb.
be impious 980 vb.
backstage
rear 238 n.
back stalls
theatre 594 n.
back street
road 624 n.
back stroke
aquatics 269 n.
back to back
rearward 238 adv.

against 240 adv.
back-to-back
　small house 192 n.
back to front
　inversely 221 adv.
backtrack
　regress 286 vb.
　recant 603 vb.
back up
　support 218 vb.
　be behind 238 vb.
　assent 488 vb.
　endorse 488 vb.
　aid 703 vb.
back-up
　auxiliary 707 n.
backward
　late 136 adj.
　rearward 238 adv.
　ignorant 491 adj.
　unintelligent
　　499 adj.
　unwilling 598 adj.
　immature 670 adj.
backward-looking
　retrospective
　　125 adj.
backwardness
　lateness 136 n.
　ignorance 491 n.
　unintelligence
　　499 n.
　unwillingness
　　598 n.
　unskilfulness
　　695 n.
　dislike 861 n.
backwards and for-
　wards
　to and fro 317 adv.
backwash
　effect 157 n.
　water travel 269 n.
　wave 350 n.
backwater
　retard 278 vb.
　lake 346 n.
　seclusion 883 n.
backwoods
　district 184 n.
backwoodsman
　absence 190 n.
　country-dweller
　　869 n.
backyard
　place 185 n.

bacon
　meat 301 n.
bacteria
　infection 651 n.
　poison 659 n.
bacteriology
　medical art 658 n.
bad
　fetid 397 adj.
　evil 616 adj.
　bad 645 adj.
　wicked 934 adj.
bad blood
　dislike 861 n.
　enmity 881 n.
　hatred 888 n.
　malevolence 898 n.
bad books
　disrepute 867 n.
　hatred 888 n.
　disapprobation
　　924 n.
bad breath
　stench 397 n.
baddy
　evildoer 904 n.
　bad person 938 n.
bad egg
　stench 397 n.
　bad person 938 n.
bad form
　unwonted 611 adj.
　ill-breeding 847 n.
badge
　badge 547 n.
　heraldry 547 n.
　jewellery 844 n.
badge of office
　badge 547 n.
　badge of rule
　　743 n.
badger
　mammal 365 n.
　interrogate 459 vb.
　torment 827 vb.
bad hat
　bad person 938 n.
badinage
　interlocution
　　584 n.
　wit 839 n.
　witticism 839 n.
　ridicule 851 n.
bad language
　rudeness 885 n.
　scurrility 899 n.

bad lot
　evildoer 904 n.
　bad person 938 n.
badly
　slightly 33 adv.
　badly 645 adv.
badly brought up
　ill-bred 847 adj.
badly off
　unprosperous
　　731 adj.
　poor 801 adj.
bad manners
　conduct 688 n.
　ill-breeding 847 n.
　discourtesy 885 n.
badminton
　ball game 837 n.
bad mouth
　news 529 n.
　calumny 926 n.
　detract 926 vb.
badness
　badness 645 n.
bad patch
　difficulty 700 n.
　adversity 731 n.
bad press
　censure 924 n.
　detraction 926 n.
bad reputation
　disrepute 867 n.
bad smell
　stench 397 n.
bad-tempered
　sullen 893 adj.
Baedeker
　itinerary 267 n.
　guidebook 524 n.
baffle
　puzzle 474 vb.
　be difficult 700 vb.
　be obstructive
　　702 vb.
　oppose 704 vb.
　defeat 727 vb.
　be wonderful
　　864 vb.
bag
　bunch 74 n.
　bag 194 n.
　acquire 771 vb.
　take 786 vb.
　taking 786 n.
bag and baggage
　property 777 n.

bagatelle
　trifle 639 n.
　ball game 837 n.
bagel
　cereals 301 n.
bagful
　finite quantity
　　26 n.
　store 632 n.
baggage
　youngster 132 n.
　box 194 n.
　transport 272 n.
　female 373 n.
　property 777 n.
　insolent person
　　878 n.
　loose woman
　　952 n.
baggage reclaim
　air travel 271 n.
baggy
　spacious 183 adj.
　large 195 adj.
　broad 205 adj.
bag lady
　nonconformist
　　84 n.
　wanderer 268 n.
　low fellow 869 n.
bagman
　pedlar 794 n.
bag of tricks
　trickery 542 n.
　means 629 n.
　tool 630 n.
　collection 632 n.
bagpipes
　flute 414 n.
bags
　great quantity
　　32 n.
　trousers 228 n.
bag-snatching
　stealing 788 n.
baguette
　cereals 301 n.
Baha'ism
　religious faith
　　973 n.
Baha'ullah
　religious teacher
　　973 n.
bail
　liberate 746 vb.
　liberation 746 n.
　security 767 n.

legal process 959 n.
Bailey bridge
  bridge 624 n.
bailie
  officer 741 n.
bailiff
  farmer 370 n.
  manager 690 n.
  officer 741 n.
  retainer 742 n.
  consignee 754 n.
  law officer 955 n.
bail one out
  give bail 767 vb.
bail out
  transpose 272 vb.
  empty 300 vb.
  aid 703 vb.
bain-marie
  pot 194 n.
Bairam
  holy day 988 n.
bait
  attract 291 vb.
  attraction 291 n.
  ensnare 542 vb.
  trap 542 n.
  trickery 542 n.
  incentive 612 n.
  chase 619 n.
  torment 827 vb.
  enrage 891 vb.
  reward 962 n.
baize
  textile 222 n.
bake
  cook 301 vb.
  harden 326 vb.
  dry 342 vb.
  be hot 379 vb.
baked
  dry 342 adj.
baked beans
  dish 301 n.
baker
  cookery 301 n.
baker's dozen
  over five 99 n.
bakery
  cookery 301 n.
baking
  cookery 301 n.
  hot 379 adj.
  heating 381 n.
baking-powder
  leaven 323 n.

baksheesh
  acquisition 771 n.
  gift 781 n.
  reward 962 n.
balalaika
  stringed instrument
    414 n.
balance
  relate 9 vb.
  correlate 12 vb.
  adjust 24 vb.
  equality 28 n.
  equalize 28 vb.
  equilibrium 28 n.
  average 30 n.
  remainder 41 n.
  number 86 vb.
  stability 153 n.
  stabilize 153 vb.
  symmetry 245 n.
  scales 322 n.
  weigh 322 vb.
  compare 462 vb.
  gauge 465 n.
  measure 465 vb.
  sagacity 498 n.
  elegance 575 n.
  be irresolute
    601 vb.
  middle way 625 n.
  superfluity 637 n.
  caution 858 n.
balanced
  adjusted 24 adj.
  equal 28 adj.
  fixed 153 adj.
  symmetrical
    245 adj.
  elegant 575 adj.
balance of power
  equilibrium 28 n.
balance of the mind
  sanity 502 n.
balance of trade
  equilibrium 28 n.
balance sheet
  accounts 808 n.
balancing act
  compromise 770 n.
balcony
  lobby 194 n.
  projection 254 n.
  theatre 594 n.
bald
  hairless 229 adj.
  smooth 258 adj.
  feeble 572 adj.

plain 573 adj.
  tedious 838 adj.
balderdash
  silly talk 515 n.
baldric
  belt 228 n.
bale
  bunch 74 n.
  cultivate 370 vb.
baleful
  malevolent
    898 adj.
bale out
  fly 271 vb.
  emerge 298 vb.
balk
  beam 218 n.
  disappoint 509 vb.
  disappointment
    509 n.
  be obstructive
    702 vb.
balk at
  avoid 620 vb.
ball
  sphere 252 n.
  missile 287 n.
  missile weapon
    723 n.
  dancing 837 n.
  plaything 837 n.
  social gathering
    882 n.
ballad
  vocal music 412 n.
  narrative 590 n.
  poem 593 n.
ballade
  verse form 593 n.
ball and chain
  fetter 748 n.
ballast
  compensate 31 vb.
  stabilizer 153 n.
  gravity 322 n.
  safeguard 662 n.
balled up
  complex 61 adj.
  crossed 222 adj.
ballerina
  actor 594 n.
ballet
  ballet 594 n.
ballet dancing
  ballet 594 n.
  dancing 837 n.

balletomane
  enthusiast 504 n.
  playgoer 594 n.
ballet shoes
  footwear 228 n.
ball game
  ball game 837 n.
ballgown
  dress 228 n.
ballistics
  propulsion 287 n.
  arms 723 n.
balloon
  expand 197 vb.
  circumscription
    232 n.
  sphere 252 n.
  airship 276 n.
  lightness 323 n.
  gas 336 n.
  plaything 837 n.
ballot
  affirmation 532 n.
  vote 605 n.
ballot box
  electorate 605 n.
  vote 605 n.
ballpoint pen
  stationery 586 n.
ballroom
  place of amuse-
    ment 837 n.
ballroom dancing
  dancing 837 n.
balls-up
  mistake 495 n.
  bungling 695 n.
ball up
  bedevil 63 vb.
ballyhoo
  loudness 400 n.
  overestimation
    482 n.
  advertisement
    528 n.
  publicity 528 n.
  exaggeration
    546 n.
balm
  herb 301 n.
  scent 396 n.
  balm 658 n.
  medicine 658 n.
  pleasurableness
    826 n.
balmy
  warm 379 adj.

fragrant 396 adj.
palmy 730 adj.
balsam
balm 658 n.
medicine 658 n.
balthazar
vessel 194 n.
balustrade
handle 218 n.
barrier 235 n.
fence 235 n.
bambino
child 132 n.
bamboo
grass 366 n.
bamboo curtain
exclusion 57 n.
partition 231 n.
obstacle 702 n.
bamboo shoots
fruit and vegetables
301 n.
bamboozle
puzzle 474 vb.
keep secret 525 vb.
deceive 542 vb.
fool 542 vb.
ban
exclude 57 vb.
exclusion 57 n.
hindrance 702 n.
obstruct 702 vb.
command 737 n.
command 737 vb.
restrain 747 vb.
restraint 747 n.
prohibit 757 vb.
prohibition 757 n.
malediction 899 n.
disapprobation
924 n.
disapprove 924 vb.
penalty 963 n.
prayers 981 n.
Christian rite
988 n.
perform ritual
988 vb.
banal
aphoristic 496 adj.
usual 610 adj.
dull 840 adj.
banana
fruit and vegetables
301 n.

banana republic
political organiza-
tion 733 n.
bananas
crazy 503 adj.
banana skin
rubbish 641 n.
danger 661 n.
pitfall 663 n.
band
bond 47 n.
ligature 47 n.
band 74 n.
strip 208 n.
loop 250 n.
orchestra 413 n.
musical instrument
414 n.
stripe 437 n.
class 538 n.
bandage
tie 45 vb.
ligature 47 n.
make smaller
198 vb.
strip 208 n.
support 218 n.
support 218 vb.
cover 226 vb.
wrapping 226 n.
blind 439 vb.
cure 656 vb.
doctor 658 vb.
surgical dressing
658 n.
relieve 831 vb.
Band-Aid (tdmk)
adhesive 47 n.
substitute 150 n.
covering 226 n.
bandanna
headgear 228 n.
bandbox
box 194 n.
bandeau
hairdressing 843 n.
bandit
robber 789 n.
outcast 883 n.
bandleader
living model 23 n.
orchestra 413 n.
bandolier
belt 228 n.
arsenal 723 n.
bandstand
pavilion 192 n.

band together
combine 50 vb.
congregate 74 vb.
cooperate 706 vb.
bandy about
publish 528 vb.
bandy-legged
deformed 246 adj.
curved 248 adj.
bandy words
interchange
151 vb.
converse 584 vb.
bane
bane 659 n.
wrong 914 n.
bang
impel 279 vb.
impulse 279 n.
knock 279 n.
strike 279 vb.
bang 402 n.
bang 402 vb.
hairdressing 843 n.
banger
automobile 274 n.
meat 301 n.
bang 402 n.
bangle
jewellery 844 n.
bang on
be tedious 838 vb.
bangs
hair 259 n.
banish
exclude 57 vb.
displace 188 vb.
eject 300 vb.
banisters
handle 218 n.
support 218 n.
fence 235 n.
banjo
stringed instrument
414 n.
bank
high land 209 n.
seat 218 n.
be oblique 220 vb.
incline 220 n.
edge 234 n.
laterality 239 n.
shore 344 n.
storage 632 n.
store 632 vb.
pawnshop 784 n.
treasury 799 n.

bank account
funds 797 n.
wealth 800 n.
banker
lender 784 n.
merchant 794 n.
treasurer 798 n.
card game 837 n.
Bank holiday
amusement 837 n.
banknote
title deed 767 n.
paper money
797 n.
Bank of England
treasury 799 n.
bank on
be certain 473 vb.
believe 485 vb.
expect 507 vb.
hope 852 vb.
bank rate
finance 797 n.
interest 803 n.
bankroll
paper money
797 n.
expend 806 vb.
bankrupt
defeat 727 vb.
loser 728 n.
fleece 786 vb.
poor 801 adj.
poor person 801 n.
nonpayer 805 n.
nonpaying 805 adj.
bankruptcy
insufficiency 636 n.
failure 728 n.
loss 772 n.
insolvency 805 n.
banner
flag 547 n.
bannock
cereals 301 n.
banns
marriage 894 n.
banquet
eat 301 vb.
feed 301 vb.
plenty 635 n.
festivity 837 n.
revel 837 vb.
social gathering
882 n.
banshee
demon 970 n.

bantam
dwarf 196 n.
poultry 365 n.
bantamweight
pugilist 722 n.
banter
interlocution
584 n.
witticism 839 n.
ridicule 851 n.
ridicule 851 vb.
be insolent 878 vb.
sauciness 878 n.
banyan
tree 366 n.
baobab
tree 366 n.
bap
cereals 301 n.
baptism
reception 299 n.
nomenclature
561 n.
Christian rite
988 n.
rite 988 n.
baptism of fire
debut 68 n.
Baptist
Protestant 976 adj.
Protestant 976 n.
baptistry
church interior
990 n.
church utensil
990 n.
baptize
auspicate 68 vb.
admit 299 vb.
immerse 303 vb.
drench 341 vb.
name 561 vb.
make pious 979 vb.
perform ritual
988 vb.
bar
degree 27 n.
fastening 47 n.
exclude 57 vb.
exclusion 57 n.
exclusive of 57 adv.
tavern 192 n.
chamber 194 n.
line 203 n.
support 218 n.
barrier 235 n.
close 264 vb.

stopper 264 n.
notation 410 n.
stripe 437 n.
heraldry 547 n.
obstruct 702 vb.
restrain 747 vb.
restraint 747 n.
lockup 748 n.
prohibit 757 vb.
disapprobation
924 n.
disapprove 924 vb.
tribunal 956 n.
bar 958 n.
condemn 961 vb.
barb
filament 208 n.
sharpen 256 vb.
sharp point 256 n.
missile weapon
723 n.
barbarian
extraneous 59 adj.
destroyer 168 n.
violent creature
176 n.
vulgar 847 adj.
barbaric 869 adj.
low fellow 869 n.
discourteous
885 adj.
rude person 885 n.
ruffian 904 n.
barbaric
amorphous
244 adj.
ill-bred 847 adj.
barbaric 869 adj.
barbarous
violent 176 adj.
inelegant 576 adj.
barbaric 869 adj.
cruel 898 adj.
barbecue
cook 301 vb.
meal 301 n.
festivity 837 n.
social gathering
882 n.
barbed
sharp 256 adj.
barbed wire
sharp point 256 n.
roughness 259 n.
obstacle 702 n.
defences 713 n.

barbed-wire fence
fence 235 n.
barber
beautician 843 n.
barbershop quartet
choir 413 n.
barbiturate
moderator 177 n.
drug 658 n.
soporific 679 n.
barbiturates
drug-taking 949 n.
barcarole
vocal music 412 n.
bar code
stripe 437 n.
bard
cook 301 vb.
musician 413 n.
poet 593 n.
bare
unproductive
172 adj.
empty 190 adj.
uncover 229 vb.
uncovered 229 adj.
open 263 vb.
dry 342 adj.
disclose 526 vb.
plain 573 adj.
unprovided
636 adj.
vulnerable 661 adj.
bareback rider
athlete 162 n.
bared teeth
threat 900 n.
barefaced lie
untruth 543 n.
barefoot
uncovered 229 adj.
bareheaded
uncovered 229 adj.
barely
slightly 33 adv.
bareness
emptiness 190 n.
bareness 229 n.
plainness 573 n.
bare one's teeth
defy 711 vb.
bargain
consensus 488 n.
promise 764 n.
compact 765 n.
bargain 791 vb.
trade 791 n.

purchase 792 n.
cheapness 812 n.
bargain basement
shop 796 n.
cheap 812 adj.
bargaining
conference 584 n.
conditions 766 n.
barter 791 n.
barge
carrier 273 n.
boat 275 n.
barge in
intrude 297 vb.
encroach 306 vb.
barge pole
propeller 269 n.
bar graph
statistics 86 n.
baritone
resonance 404 n.
vocalist 413 n.
barium enema
diagnostic 658 n.
barium meal
diagnostic 658 n.
bark
layer 207 n.
skin 226 n.
uncover 229 vb.
ship 275 n.
rub 333 vb.
cry 408 vb.
ululate 409 vb.
ululation 409 n.
anger 891 n.
threat 900 n.
threaten 900 vb.
barker
cry 408 n.
overestimation
482 n.
publicizer 528 n.
petitioner 763 n.
commender 923 n.
**bark up the wrong
tree**
err 495 vb.
barley
provender 301 n.
grass 366 n.
barley sugar
sweets 301 n.
barm
leaven 323 n.
bubble 355 n.

barmaid
  servant 742 n.
barmy
  light 323 adj.
  unintelligent
    499 adj.
  crazy 503 adj.
barn
  storage 632 n.
barnacle
  marine life 365 n.
barn dance
  dance 837 n.
barney
  quarrel 709 n.
barn owl
  bird 365 n.
barnstorming
  acting 594 n.
  dramatic 594 adj.
barometer
  prototype 23 n.
  weather 340 n.
  meter 465 n.
baron
  bigwig 638 n.
  rich person 800 n.
  person of rank
    868 n.
baronet
  person of rank
    868 n.
baronetcy
  honours 866 n.
  aristocracy 868 n.
Baroque
  architectural
    192 adj.
  art 551 n.
  school of painting
    553 n.
  ornamental
    844 adj.
  ornamentation
    844 n.
  churchlike 990 adj.
barque
  sailing ship 275 n.
  ship 275 n.
barrack
  quarters 192 n.
  be obstructive
    702 vb.
barracks
  station 187 n.
barracuda
  fish 365 n.

barrage
  roll 403 n.
  bombardment
    712 n.
  defences 713 n.
barrage balloon
  airship 276 n.
  defences 713 n.
  air force 722 n.
barrel
  vat 194 n.
  cylinder 252 n.
  metrology 465 n.
barren
  impotent 161 adj.
  unproductive
    172 adj.
barricade
  exclusion 57 n.
  barrier 235 n.
  obstruct 702 vb.
  defences 713 n.
  defend 713 vb.
barrier
  barrier 235 n.
  obstacle 702 n.
barrier contraceptive
  contraception
    172 n.
barring
  exclusive of 57 adv.
barrister
  combatant 722 n.
  lawyer 958 n.
barrow
  earthwork 253 n.
  pushcart 274 n.
  tomb 364 n.
  monument 548 n.
  shop 796 n.
barrow boy
  seller 793 n.
  pedlar 794 n.
barry
  heraldic 547 adj.
bar sinister
  slur 867 n.
barter
  correlate 12 vb.
  interchange
    151 vb.
  assign 780 vb.
  barter 791 vb.
  trade 791 vb.
  pay 804 vb.
basalt
  rock 344 n.

base
  situation 186 n.
  place 187 vb.
  station 187 n.
  abode 192 n.
  base 214 n.
  support 218 vb.
  limit 236 n.
  heraldry 547 n.
  bad 645 adj.
  cowardly 856 adj.
  disreputable
    867 adj.
  servile 879 adj.
  heinous 934 adj.
baseball
  ball game 837 n.
baseboard
  base 214 n.
baseline
  place 185 n.
basement
  cellar 194 n.
  lowness 210 n.
  base 214 n.
base metal
  mineral 359 n.
baseness
  disrepute 867 n.
  improbity 930 n.
  wickedness 934 n.
bash
  collide 279 vb.
  strike 279 vb.
bashful
  unwilling 598 adj.
  modest 874 adj.
bashing
  knock 279 n.
basic
  simple 44 adj.
  fundamental
    156 adj.
  important 638 adj.
basics
  reality 1 n.
  learning 536 n.
basic training
  learning 536 n.
basil
  herb 301 n.
basilica
  church 990 n.
basilisk
  rara avis 84 n.
  eye 438 n.

basin
  stable 192 n.
  bowl 194 n.
  cavity 255 n.
  conduit 351 n.
basis
  reason why 156 n.
  basis 218 n.
bask
  be hot 379 vb.
basket
  basket 194 n.
basketball
  ball game 837 n.
basket chair
  seat 218 n.
basketwork
  network 222 n.
bask in
  enjoy 376 vb.
  be pleased 824 vb.
basmatti rice
  cereals 301 n.
bas-relief
  sculpture 554 n.
bass
  fish 365 n.
  resonance 404 n.
  vocalist 413 n.
basset
  dog 365 n.
bassinet
  basket 194 n.
  bed 218 n.
bassoon
  flute 414 n.
bastard
  unwarranted
    916 adj.
  cad 938 n.
  bastard 954 adj.
  bastardy 954 n.
bastardize
  disentitle 916 vb.
  make illegal
    954 vb.
baste
  tie 45 vb.
  cook 301 vb.
  grease 357 vb.
Bastille Day
  anniversary 141 n.
  special day 876 n.
bastion
  protection 660 n.
  refuge 662 n.
  fortification 713 n.

bat
velocity 277 n.
strike 279 vb.
propel 287 vb.
mammal 365 n.
club 723 n.

batch
finite quantity
26 n.
bunch 74 n.
group 74 n.

batch processing
data processing
86 n.

bated breath
faintness 401 n.
voicelessness 578 n.

bath
vessel 194 n.
water 339 n.
ablutions 648 n.

bath chair
pushcart 274 n.

bathe
swim 269 vb.
immerse 303 vb.
be wet 341 vb.
drench 341 vb.
clean 648 vb.
amuse oneself
837 vb.

bathing beauty
sea nymph 343 n.

bathing suit
beachwear 228 n.

bathos
absurdity 497 n.
ridiculousness
849 n.

bathrobe
informal dress
228 n.

bathroom
chamber 194 n.
ablutions 648 n.

bathroom scales
scales 322 n.

bath salts
cosmetic 843 n.

bathtub
ablutions 648 n.

bathymetric
deep 211 adj.

batik
textile 222 n.
printing 555 n.

ornamental art
844 n.

batman
clothier 228 n.
domestic 742 n.

baton
support 218 n.
badge of rule
743 n.

bat one's eyelashes
gesticulate 547 vb.

bats
crazy 503 adj.

bats in the belfry
eccentricity 503 n.

batsman
player 837 n.

battalion(s)
multitude 104 n.
formation 722 n.

batten
fastening 47 n.
strip 208 n.

battenburg cake
pastries and cakes
301 n.

**batten down the
hatches**
close 264 vb.
seek refuge 662 vb.
make ready
669 vb.

batten on
eat 301 vb.
prosper 730 vb.
be servile 879 vb.

batter
demolish 165 vb.
deform 244 vb.
distort 246 vb.
collide 279 vb.
strike 279 vb.
pulpiness 356 n.
ill-treat 645 vb.

battering ram
ram 279 n.
club 723 n.

battery
accumulation 74 n.
electronics 160 n.
stable 192 n.
stock farm 369 n.
exam 459 n.
storage 632 n.
formation 722 n.
gun 723 n.

battery of tests
diagnostic 658 n.

battle
slaughter 362 n.
action 676 n.
contend 716 vb.
battle 718 n.
trophy 729 n.
be hostile 881 vb.

battleaxe
sharp edge 256 n.
axe 723 n.

battle cry
call 547 n.
danger signal
665 n.
defiance 711 n.
war 718 n.
warfare 718 n.
threat 900 n.

battledress
uniform 228 n.

battlefield
battle 718 n.
battleground
724 n.

battle front
battle 718 n.

battleground
battleground
724 n.

battlement
notch 260 n.
fortification 713 n.

battle royal
fight 716 n.
battle 718 n.

battleship(s)
warship 722 n.
indoor game 837 n.

battle station
battle 718 n.

batty
crazy 503 adj.

batwing sleeve
sleeve 228 n.

bauble
insubstantial thing
4 n.
bauble 639 n.

Bauhaus
architectural
192 adj.
art 551 n.

bawbee
coinage 797 n.

bawdy
impure 951 adj.

bawl
cry 408 n.
vociferate 408 vb.
lamentation 836 n.
weep 836 vb.

bawl out
reproach 924 vb.

bay
compartment
194 n.
curve 248 n.
cavity 255 n.
horse 273 n.
gulf 345 n.
tree 366 n.
ululate 409 vb.
brown 430 adj.
disapprove 924 vb.

bayleaf
herb 301 n.

bayonet
pierce 263 vb.
kill 362 vb.
strike at 712 vb.
sidearms 723 n.

bayou
gulf 345 n.

bay window
window 263 n.

bazaar
request 761 n.
sale 793 n.
emporium 796 n.
shop 796 n.

bazooka
flute 414 n.
gun 723 n.
missile weapon
723 n.

BBC
broadcasting
531 n.

be
be 1 vb.
be situated 186 vb.
be present 189 vb.

beach
edge 234 n.
land 295 vb.
shore 344 n.
arena 724 n.

beachcomber
wanderer 268 n.

beacon
signal light 420 n.

signal 547 n.
warning 664 n.
danger signal
665 n.
bead
sphere 252 n.
decorate 844 vb.
trimming 844 n.
beading
ornamental art
844 n.
beadle
officer 741 n.
law officer 955 n.
church officer
986 n.
beads
jewellery 844 n.
prayers 981 n.
ritual object 988 n.
beagle
dog 365 n.
beak
protuberance
254 n.
teacher 537 n.
beak, the
magistracy 957 n.
beaker
cup 194 n.
be-all and end-all
all 52 n.
important matter
638 n.
beam
beam 218 n.
laterality 239 n.
direction 281 n.
flash 417 n.
radiate 417 vb.
communicate
524 vb.
be cheerful 833 vb.
smile 835 vb.
beaming
luminous 417 adj.
happy 824 adj.
cheerful 833 adj.
bean
head 213 n.
bean curd
fruit and vegetables
301 n.
beanfeast
feasting 301 n.
meal 301 n.
enjoyment 824 n.

amusement 837 n.
festivity 837 n.
beanpole
thinness 206 n.
tall creature 209 n.
beans
food 301 n.
fruit and vegetables
301 n.
beansprouts
fruit and vegetables
301 n.
bear
reproduce itself
167 vb.
be fruitful 171 vb.
support 218 vb.
carry 273 vb.
mammal 365 n.
acquiesce 488 vb.
heraldry 547 n.
gambler 618 n.
seller 793 n.
feel 818 vb.
be patient 823 vb.
suffer 825 vb.
rude person 885 n.
bear a grudge
hate 888 vb.
beard
filament 208 n.
prickle 256 n.
hair 259 n.
print-type 587 n.
defy 711 vb.
be courageous
855 vb.
bearded
hairy 259 adj.
bear down on
approach 289 vb.
bearer bond
title deed 767 n.
bear fruit
reproduce itself
167 vb.
get better 654 vb.
be successful
727 vb.
beargarden
turmoil 61 n.
arena 724 n.
bear hug
retention 778 n.
endearment 889 n.
bear ill will
be hostile 881 vb.

bearing
relation 9 n.
pivot 218 n.
support 218 n.
direction 281 n.
look 445 n.
meaning 514 n.
heraldry 547 n.
conduct 688 n.
bear in mind
think 449 vb.
be mindful 455 vb.
bearish
animal 365 adj.
salable 793 adj.
cheap 812 adj.
bearnaise sauce
sauce 389 n.
bear no malice
forgive 909 vb.
bear out
corroborate 466 vb.
demonstrate
478 V.
vindicate 927 vb.
bear pit
zoo 369 n.
bearskin
headgear 228 n.
armour 713 n.
bear the brunt
stand firm 599 vb.
busy oneself
622 vb.
be in difficulty
700 vb.
withstand 704 vb.
bear the mark of
be intrinsic 5 vb.
bear up
support 218 vb.
elevate 310 vb.
bear upon
be related 9 vb.
influence 178 vb.
bear with
forgive 909 vb.
bear with a sore head
moper 834 n.
bear witness
testify 466 vb.
affirm 532 vb.
beast
violent creature
176 n.
animal 365 n.
eyesore 842 n.

ruffian 904 n.
cad 938 n.
beastly
animal 365 adj.
not nice 645 adj.
unpleasant
827 adj.
ugly 842 adj.
discourteous
885 adj.
hateful 888 adj.
sensual 944 adj.
beast of burden
beast of burden
273 n.
animal 365 n.
worker 686 n.
beat
be superior 34 vb.
periodicity 141 n.
territory 184 n.
place 185 n.
impulse 279 n.
strike 279 vb.
cook 301 vb.
pass 305 vb.
oscillate 317 vb.
oscillation 317 n.
agitate 318 vb.
be agitated 318 vb.
pulverize 332 vb.
roll 403 vb.
tempo 410 n.
play music 413 vb.
prosody 593 n.
chase 619 n.
hunt 619 vb.
clean 648 vb.
defeat 727 vb.
spank 963 vb.
beat about the bush
sophisticate
477 vb.
be equivocal
518 vb.
dissemble 541 vb.
be diffuse 570 vb.
beat a retreat
regress 286 vb.
run away 620 vb.
beat a tattoo
roll 403 vb.
celebrate 876 vb.
beat down
demolish 165 vb.
bargain 791 vb.
cheapen 812 vb.

beaten
inferior 35 adj.
used 673 adj.
defeated 728 adj.

beaten track
habit 610 n.
bore 838 n.

beater
hunter 619 n.

beatific
pleasurable
826 adj.

beatify
dignify 866 vb.
sanctify 979 vb.

beating
periodical 141 adj.
impulse 279 n.
knock 279 n.
victory 727 n.
defeat 728 n.
*corporal punish-
ment* 963 n.

beat it
decamp 296 vb.
run away 620 vb.

beatnik
nonconformist
84 n.
unconformable
84 adj.

beat one's breast
lament 836 vb.
be penitent 939 vb.

**beat one's head
against a brick
wall**
waste effort
641 adj.

**beat swords into
ploughshares**
be at peace 717 vb.
make peace
719 vb.

beat the big drum
proclaim 528 vb.
be ostentatious
875 vb.

beat the record
be superior 34 vb.

beat time
time 117 vb.
play music 413 vb.

beat up
force 176 vb.
strike 279 vb.
thicken 354 vb.

strike at 712 vb.

beau
male 372 n.
fop 848 n.
lover 887 n.

Beau Brummel
fop 848 n.

Beaujolais
wine 301 n.

beau monde
beau monde 848 n.

beaut
a beauty 841 n.

beautician
beautician 843 n.

beautiful
beautiful 841 adj.

beautify
ornament 574 vb.
beautify 841 vb.

beauty
beauty 841 n.

beauty, a
masterpiece 694 n.

beauty queen
a beauty 841 n.

beauty sleep
sleep 679 n.

beauty spot
a beauty 841 n.
cosmetic 843 n.

beaux yeux
beauty 841 n.

beaver
headgear 228 n.
hair 259 n.
mammal 365 n.
armour 713 n.

beaver away
be active 678 vb.
work 682 vb.

becalmed
quiescent 266 adj.
still 266 adj.
nonactive 677 adj.
hindered 702 adj.

because
hence 158 adv.

béchamel
sauce 389 n.

beck
stream 350 n.
gesture 547 n.
command 737 n.
command 737 vb.

beckon
gesticulate 547 vb.

become
become 1 vb.
be turned to
147 vb.
happen 154 vb.
beautify 841 vb.
be one's duty
917 vb.

become one of
join a party
708 vb.

**become one of the
family**
be sociable 882 vb.

**become public
knowledge**
be disclosed
526 vb.

becoming
agreeing 24 adj.
converted 147 adj.
personable 841 adj.
tasteful 846 adj.

bed
unite with 45 vb.
place 187 vb.
layer 207 n.
base 214 n.
basis 218 n.
bed 218 n.
garden 370 n.
debauch 951 vb.

bed and breakfast
inn 192 n.
provision 633 n.

bedaub
coat 226 vb.

bedazzle
shine 417 vb.
command respect
920 vb.

bed bug
insect 365 n.

bedclothes
coverlet 226 n.

bedding
bed 218 n.
coverlet 226 n.

bed down
place 187 vb.
sleep 679 vb.

bedevil
bedevil 63 vb.
trouble 827 vb.

bed jacket
nightwear 228 n.

bedlam, Bedlam
disorder 61 n.
turmoil 61 n.
loudness 400 n.
discord 411 n.
mental hospital
503 n.

bed linen
coverlet 226 n.

bed of nails
suffering 825 n.

bed of roses
palmy days 730 n.

bedouin
dweller 191 n.
wanderer 268 n.

bed out
implant 303 vb.
cultivate 370 vb.

bedpan
vessel 194 n.
latrine 649 n.

bedraggled
dirty 649 n.

bedridden
sick 651 adj.
restrained 747 adj.

bedrock
reality 1 n.
permanence 144 n.
fixture 153 n.
source 156 n.
base 214 n.
basis 218 n.
chief thing 638 n.
important 638 adj.

bedroom
chamber 194 n.

bed settee
bed 218 n.

bedside manner
therapy 658 n.

bed-sitter
flat 192 n.

bedspread
coverlet 226 n.

bedstead
bed 218 n.

bedtime
clock time 117 n.
evening 129 n.

bedtime story
soporific 679 n.

bee
insect 365 n.

Beeb
broadcasting
531 n.
beech
tree 366 n.
beechmast
provender 301 n.
beef
meat 301 n.
deprecate 762 vb.
be discontented
829 vb.
beefcake
a beauty 841 n.
beefiness
vitality 162 n.
bulk 195 n.
beef up
strengthen 162 vb.
beefy
stalwart 162 adj.
fleshy 195 adj.
thick 205 adj.
beehive
nest 192 n.
dome 253 n.
stock farm 369 n.
hairdressing 843 n.
bee in one's bonnet
prejudgment 481 n.
eccentricity 503 n.
whim 604 n.
bee-keeping
animal husbandry
369 n.
beeline
short distance
200 n.
straightness 249 n.
direction 281 n.
Beelzebub
devil 969 n.
beer
alcoholic drink
301 n.
beer and skittles
enjoyment 824 n.
festivity 837 n.
beery
drunken 949 adj.
intoxicating
949 adj.
bee's knees
exceller 644 n.
beestings
milk 301 n.

554

beeswax
fat 357 n.
beetle
be high 209 vb.
automobile 274 n.
hammer 279 n.
insect 365 n.
beetle-browed
projecting 254 adj.
beetle off
decamp 296 vb.
beetroot
fruit and vegetables
301 n.
beet sugar
sweet thing 392 n.
befall
happen 154 vb.
befitting
fit 24 adj.
due 915 adj.
before
before 64 adv.
before 119 adv.
in front 237 adv.
beforehand
before 119 adv.
beforehand
135 adv.
before long
betimes 135 adv.
before-mentioned
preceding 64 adj.
before now
before 119 adv.
before one's eyes
in front 237 adv.
obvious 443 adj.
visible 443 adj.
before the Flood
antiquated 127 adj.
primal 127 adj.
before then
before 119 adv.
before you could say
Jack Robinson
swiftly 277 adv.
beg
beg 761 vb.
acquire 771 vb.
beg a favour
request 761 vb.
beg, borrow, or steal
borrow 785 vb.
beget
cause 156 vb.
generate 167 vb.

vitalize 360 vb.
beg for mercy
knuckle under
721 vb.
ask mercy 905 vb.
beggar
defeat 727 vb.
beggar 763 n.
impoverish 801 vb.
poor person 801 n.
beggar-my-neigh-
bour
card game 837 n.
begging letter
correspondence
588 n.
request 761 n.
begin again
repeat 106 vb.
begin at the begin-
ning
begin 68 vb.
beginning
beginning 68 adj.
beginning 68 n.
beg, leave
ask leave 756 vb.
beg off
refuse 760 vb.
deprecate 762 vb.
begotten
born 360 adj.
begrudge
be unwilling
598 vb.
refuse 760 vb.
be parsimonious
816 vb.
beg the question
reason badly
477 vb.
beg to differ
dissent 489 vb.
beguile
mislead 495 vb.
deceive 542 vb.
flatter 925 vb.
Beguine
nun 986 n.
beguine
dance 837 n.
begum
potentate 741 n.
person of rank
868 n.
behave
behave 688 vb.

be virtuous 933 vb.
behave oneself
behave 688 vb.
behaviour
look 445 n.
action 676 n.
conduct 688 n.
behaviourism
psychology 447 n.
conduct 688 n.
morals 917 n.
behaviour therapy
therapy 658 n.
behead
subtract 39 vb.
sunder 46 vb.
shorten 204 vb.
kill 362 vb.
execute 963 vb.
behemoth
giant 195 n.
behest
command 737 n.
behind
buttocks 238 n.
rear 238 n.
rearward 238 adv.
behind, be
be behind 238 vb.
behind closed doors
secretly 525 adv.
behindhand
late 136 adv.
unprepared
670 adj.
behind one
past 125 adj.
behind one's back
rearward 238 adv.
behind the scenes
rearward 238 adv.
latent 523 adj.
concealed 525 adj.
behind the times
antiquated 127 adj.
ignorant 491 adj.
behold
see 438 vb.
beholden
grateful 907 adj.
obliged 917 adj.
behove
be one's duty
917 vb.
beige
whitish 427 adj.
brown 430 adj.

being
existence 1 n.
self 80 n.
life 360 n.
person 371 n.
affections 817 n.
Bel
Semitic deities
967 n.
belated
late 136 adj.
belay
tie 45 vb.
bel canto
vocal music 412 n.
belch
eruct 300 vb.
voidance 300 n.
beleaguer
circumscribe
232 vb.
besiege 712 vb.
belfry
high structure
209 n.
head 213 n.
church exterior
990 n.
belie
negate 533 vb.
deceive 542 vb.
oppose 704 vb.
belief
belief 485 n.
believable
credible 485 adj.
believe
believe 485 vb.
believe in
believe 485 vb.
believer
religionist 973 n.
pietist 979 n.
Belisha beacon
traffic control
305 n.
signal 547 n.
belittle
abate 37 vb.
hold cheap 922 vb.
criticize 924 vb.
detract 926 vb.
bell
timekeeper 117 n.
ululate 409 vb.
gong 414 n.
signal 547 n.

church utensil
990 n.
belladonna
poisonous plant
659 n.
bell, book and candle
malediction 899 n.
magic instrument
983 n.
Christian rite
988 n.
bell-bottoms
trousers 228 n.
bellboy
servant 742 n.
belle
a beauty 841 n.
belle époque
era 110 n.
belles lettres
literature 557 n.
bellhop
courier 529 n.
servant 742 n.
bellicose
violent 176 adj.
quarrelling
709 adj.
defiant 711 adj.
warlike 718 adj.
warring 718 adj.
belligerent
quarrelling
709 adj.
defiant 711 adj.
warlike 718 adj.
warring 718 adj.
combatant 722 n.
hostile 881 adj.
bellow
be loud 400 vb.
vociferate 408 vb.
ululate 409 vb.
emphasize 532 vb.
voice 577 vb.
be angry 891 vb.
threaten 900 vb.
bellows
blowing 352 n.
respiration 352 n.
heater 383 n.
voice 577 n.
bell ringer
instrumentalist
413 n.
bell tent
canopy 226 n.

bell the cat
be resolute 599 vb.
face danger 661 vb.
be courageous
855 vb.
bell tower
church exterior
990 n.
bell wether
sheep 365 n.
leader 690 n.
belly
stomach 194 n.
expand 197 vb.
insides 224 n.
swelling 253 n.
bellyache
pang 377 n.
be discontented
829 vb.
belly dancer
entertainer 594 n.
bellyful
plenitude 54 n.
belly landing
aeronautics 271 n.
belly laugh
laughter 835 n.
belong
be related 9 vb.
accord 24 vb.
be included 78 vb.
accompany 89 vb.
belong 773 vb.
belonging
relative 9 adj.
component 58 adj.
included 78 adj.
friendship 880 n.
fellowship 882 n.
belongings
property 777 n.
belong to
constitute 56 vb.
belong 773 vb.
be one's duty
917 vb.
beloved
loved one 887 n.
darling 890 n.
below
after 65 adv.
under 210 adv.
below par
unequal 29 adj.
abnormal 84 adj.
weakly 163 adj.

under 210 adv.
deficient 307 adj.
imperfect 647 adj.
sick 651 adj.
below the belt
unjust 914 adj.
below the salt
inferior 35 adj.
plebeian 869 adj.
Belsen
prison camp 748 n.
belt
region 184 n.
strip 208 n.
belt 228 n.
strike 279 vb.
badge of rank
743 n.
spank 963 vb.
scourge 964 n.
belted earl
person of rank
868 n.
belt out
sing 413 vb.
bemused
abstracted 456 adj.
crazy 503 adj.
ben
high land 209 n.
Benares
holy place 990 n.
bench
seat 218 n.
stand 218 n.
workshop 687 n.
badge of rule
743 n.
tribunal 956 n.
judge 957 n.
bench mark
prototype 23 n.
gauge 465 n.
signpost 547 n.
bend
break 46 vb.
ligature 47 n.
derange 63 vb.
conform 83 vb.
make conform
83 vb.
modify 143 vb.
be oblique 220 vb.
obliquity 220 n.
distort 246 vb.
distortion 246 n.
angularity 247 n.

555

be curved 248 vb.
curve 248 n.
twine 251 vb.
deflect 282 vb.
deviate 282 vb.
deviation 282 n.
stoop 311 vb.
bias 481 vb.
heraldry 547 n.
motivate 612 vb.
knuckle under
  721 vb.
be servile 879 vb.
bend down
be curved 248 vb.
stoop 311 vb.
bended knees
entreaty 761 n.
bender
festivity 837 n.
drunkenness 949 n.
bend forward
stoop 311 vb.
bend over
be oblique 220 vb.
be curved 248 vb.
fold 261 vb.
stoop 311 vb.
bend over backwards
exert oneself
  682 vb.
bend sinister
heraldry 547 n.
bends, the
depth 211 n.
diver 313 n.
bend the mind to
be attentive 455 vb.
beneath
less 35 adv.
under 210 adv.
beneath one
degrading 867 adj.
Benedicite
hymn 981 n.
prayers 981 n.
Benedictine
monk 986 n.
benediction
benevolence 897 n.
thanks 907 n.
praise 923 n.
act of worship
  981 n.
prayers 981 n.
public worship
  981 n.

church service
  988 n.
benefactor
philanthropist
  901 n.
benefactor 903 n.
benefice
benefice 985 n.
church office 985 n.
beneficial
profitable 640 adj.
beneficial 644 adj.
beneficiary
beneficiary 776 n.
cleric 986 n.
benefit
benefit 615 n.
benefit 615 vb.
good 615 n.
utility 640 n.
be expedient
  642 vb.
use 673 n.
gain 771 n.
gift 781 n.
sociology 901 n.
benefit match
trophy 729 n.
request 761 n.
acquisition 771 n.
gift 781 n.
benefit of clergy
nonliability 919 n.
ecclesiasticism
  985 n.
benefit of the doubt
acquittal 960 n.
benefit performance
gift 781 n.
benevolence
benevolence 897 n.
benevolent
benevolent 897 adj.
benighted
late 136 adj.
blind 439 adj.
ignorant 491 adj.
benign
benevolent 897 adj.
benign tumour
cancer 651 n.
benison
prayers 981 n.
bent
abnormal 84 adj.
tendency 179 n.
curved 248 adj.

bias 481 n.
willingness 597 n.
aptitude 694 n.
affections 817 n.
dishonest 930 adj.
Benthamism
philanthropy
  901 n.
benthos
ocean 343 n.
marine life 365 n.
bent upon
resolute 599 adj.
benumbed
nonactive 677 adj.
bequeath
endow 777 vb.
bequeath 780 vb.
bequest
transport 272 n.
acquisition 771 n.
dower 777 n.
transfer 780 n.
gift 781 n.
berate
reproach 924 vb.
berceuse
musical piece
  412 n.
vocal music 412 n.
bereavement
loss 772 n.
bereft of hope
hopeless 853 adj.
beret
headgear 228 n.
beri-beri
disease 651 n.
tropical disease
  651 n.
Berlin Wall
partition 231 n.
Bermuda shorts
trousers 228 n.
berry
product 164 n.
fruit and vegetables
  301 n.
flower 366 n.
berserk
furious 176 adj.
frenzied 503 adj.
angry 891 adj.
berth
place 187 vb.
dwell 192 vb.
quarters 192 n.

stable 192 n.
beryl
greenness 434 n.
gem 844 n.
beseech
entreat 761 vb.
beset
circumscribe
  232 vb.
follow 284 vb.
besiege 712 vb.
torment 827 vb.
besetting sin
bane 659 n.
vice 934 n.
beside
near 200 adv.
beside oneself
frenzied 503 adj.
excited 821 adj.
besides
in addition 38 adv.
beside the mark
irrelevant 10 adj.
beside the point
irrelevant 10 adj.
besiege
besiege 712 vb.
go to war 718 vb.
torment 827 vb.
besmirch
dim 419 vb.
make unclean
  649 vb.
defame 926 vb.
besom
cleaning utensil
  648 n.
besotted
misjudging
  481 adj.
foolish 499 adj.
crazy 503 adj.
enamoured
  887 adj.
bespatter
moisten 341 vb.
make unclean
  649 vb.
shame 867 vb.
defame 926 vb.
bespoke
adjusted 24 adj.
tailored 228 adj.
promised 764 n.
Bessie Bunter
bulk 195 n.

best
be superior 34 vb.
best 644 adj.
defeat 727 vb.
best behaviour
etiquette 848 n.
best bib and tucker
clothing 228 n.
finery 844 n.
best ever
best 644 adj.
exceller 644 n.
best friend
concomitant 89 n.
close friend 880 n.
bestial
animal 365 adj.
sensual 944 adj.
lecherous 951 adj.
best maid
bridal party 894 n.
best man
auxiliary 707 n.
close friend 880 n.
bridal party 894 n.
best of British
good luck 730 int.
best of friends, the
concord 710 n.
bestow
place 187 vb.
give 781 vb.
bestraddle
be high 209 vb.
best regards
courteous act
884 n.
bestride
influence 178 vb.
extend 183 vb.
be high 209 vb.
best-seller
book 589 n.
novel 590 n.
exceller 644 n.
success 727 n.
best wishes
courteous act
884 n.
congratulation
886 n.
bet
gamble 618 vb.
gambling 618 n.
contend 716 vb.
contest 716 n.

betake oneself to
travel 267 vb.
betel nut
tonic 658 n.
bête noire
bane 659 n.
worry 825 n.
annoyance 827 n.
dislike 861 n.
enemy 881 n.
hateful object
888 n.
bethel
church 990 n.
betide
happen 154 vb.
betimes, be
be early 135 vb.
betoken
evidence 466 vb.
predict 511 vb.
manifest 522 vb.
indicate 547 vb.
betray
disappoint 509 vb.
manifest 522 vb.
disclose 526 vb.
be false 541 vb.
deceive 542 vb.
apostatize 603 vb.
revolt 738 vb.
fail in duty 918 vb.
be dishonest
930 vb.
betrayal
disclosure 526 n.
deception 542 n.
perfidy 930 n.
betrothal
promise 764 n.
compact 765 n.
love affair 887 n.
wooing 889 n.
wedding 894 n.
betrothed
promised 764 n.
loved one 887 n.
better
be superior 34 vb.
superior 34 adj.
gambler 618 n.
excellent 644 adj.
make better
654 vb.
better half
analogue 18 n.

colleague 707 n.
spouse 894 n.
betterment
benefit 615 n.
improvement
654 n.
better oneself
get better 654 vb.
**better than nothing,
be**
change of mind
603 n.
be expedient
642 vb.
better to
advisable 642 adj.
betting
gambling 618 n.
between
correlatively
12 adv.
between 231 adv.
between ourselves
secretly 525 adv.
**between Scylla and
Charybdis**
endangered
661 adj.
in difficulties
700 adj.
**between the devil and
the deep blue
sea**
endangered
661 adj.
in difficulties
700 adj.
between the lines
tacit 523 adj.
between two stools
in difficulties
700 adj.
**between you and me
and the gatepost**
secretly 525 adv.
betwixt
between 231 adv.
betwixt and between
middle 70 adj.
between 231 adv.
bevel
cut 46 vb.
obliquity 220 n.
print-type 587 n.
beverage
draught 301 n.

bevvy
alcoholic drink
301 n.
draught 301 n.
bevy
group 74 n.
person of repute
866 n.
bewail
lament 836 vb.
beware
be careful 457 vb.
be cautious 858 vb.
bewilder
distract 456 vb.
puzzle 474 vb.
be wonderful
864 vb.
bewitched
converted 147 adj.
bewitched 983 adj.
bey
governor 741 n.
person of rank
868 n.
beyond
beyond 34 adv.
beyond 199 adv.
**beyond all reasona-
ble doubt**
undisputed
473 adj.
beyond compare
extremely 32 vb.
supreme 34 adj.
beyond description
unspeakable
32 adj.
beyond one
impracticable
470 adj.
puzzling 517 adj.
**beyond one's wildest
dreams**
unexpected
508 adj.
beyond price
of value 811 adj.
beyond recall
forgotten 506 adj.
**beyond the call of
duty**
voluntary 597 adj.
beyond the pale
exorbitant 32 adj.
vulgar 847 adj.

bezel
obliquity 220 n.
furrow 262 n.
bezique
card game 837 n.
bhaji
dish 301 n.
bhaktiyoga
religion 973 n.
bhang
drug-taking 949 n.
bhikshu
pietist 979 n.
bias
tendency 179 n.
obliquity 220 n.
distort 246 vb.
distortion 246 n.
deflect 282 vb.
bias 481 n.
bias 481 vb.
prejudice 481 n.
willingness 597 n.
choice 605 n.
affections 817 n.
improbity 930 n.
bib
garment 228 n.
get drunk 949 vb.
Bible
truth 494 n.
scripture 975 n.
church utensil
990 n.
biblical
scriptural 975 adj.
orthodox 976 adj.
bibliography
list 87 n.
edition 589 n.
reference book
589 n.
bibliolatry
pietism 979 n.
Bibliology
theology 973 n.
bibliophile
collector 492 n.
scholar 492 n.
enthusiast 504 n.
bookperson 589 n.
bicameral
dual 90 adj.
bicentenary
anniversary 141 n.
special day 876 n.

bicentennial
seasonal 141 adj.
biceps
vitality 162 n.
bickering
disagreeing 25 adj.
disagreement 25 n.
dissension 709 n.
bicuspid
bisected 92 adj.
bicycle
conveyance 267 n.
ride 267 vb.
bicycle 274 n.
bicycle chain
club 723 n.
scourge 964 n.
bicycle pump
blowing 352 n.
bicyclist
rider 268 n.
bid
intention 617 n.
gambling 618 n.
attempt 671 n.
attempt 671 vb.
command 737 vb.
offer 759 n.
offer 759 vb.
request 761 n.
request 761 vb.
purchase 792 n.
biddable
willing 597 adj.
obedient 739 adj.
bidder
petitioner 763 n.
purchaser 792 n.
bide one's time
wait 136 vb.
await 507 vb.
not act 677 vb.
bidet
ablutions 648 n.
bid fair to
be likely 471 vb.
predict 511 vb.
bid farewell
depart 296 vb.
bid for
intention 617 n.
request 761 vb.
bargain 791 vb.
purchase 792 vb.
bidie-in
lover 887 n.

biennial
periodic 110 adj.
seasonal 141 adj.
flower 366 n.
bier
bed 218 n.
funeral 364 n.
biff
knock 279 n.
strike 279 vb.
bifid
bisected 92 adj.
bifocal
dual 90 adj.
bifurcate
bifurcate 92 vb.
cross 222 vb.
angular 247 adj.
diverge 294 vb.
big
great 32 adj.
large 195 adj.
bigamy
type of marriage
894 n.
Big Apple, the
city 184 n.
Big Bang
finance 797 n.
big bang theory
universe 321 n.
big battalions
bigwig 638 n.
army 722 n.
brute force 735 n.
Big Ben
timekeeper 117 n.
Big Brother
influence 178 n.
bigwig 638 n.
protection 660 n.
authority 733 n.
position of author-
ity 733 n.
tyrant 735 n.
autocrat 741 n.
master 741 n.
big business
business 622 n.
big drum
drum 414 n.
ostentation 875 n.
big fish in a small
pool
superior 34 n.
big game
animal 365 n.

big gun
bigwig 638 n.
autocrat 741 n.
person of repute
866 n.
big-headed
proud 871 adj.
bight
curve 248 n.
cavity 255 n.
gulf 345 n.
big noise
influence 178 n.
bigwig 638 n.
person of repute
866 n.
bigot
dogmatist 473 n.
narrow mind
481 n.
zealot 979 n.
big shot
influence 178 n.
bigwig 638 n.
autocrat 741 n.
person of repute
866 n.
Big Smoke, the
city 184 n.
big stick
incentive 612 n.
compulsion 740 n.
threat 900 n.
scourge 964 n.
big toe
foot 214 n.
finger 378 n.
big top
canopy 226 n.
theatre 594 n.
big wheel
bigwig 638 n.
person of repute
866 n.
big white chief
bigwig 638 n.
bigwig
bigwig 638 n.
master 741 n.
bijou
little 196 adj.
a beauty 841 n.
gem 844 n.
bijou residence
small house 192 n.
bike
nest 192 n

ride 267 vb.
bicycle 274 n.
bikini
beachwear 228 n.
bilateral
dual 90 adj.
lateral 239 adj.
contractual
765 adj.
bilberry
fruit and vegetables
301 n.
bile
resentment 891 n.
sullenness 893 n.
Bilé or Beli
Celtic deities
967 n.
bilge
leavings 41 n.
base 214 n.
silly talk 515 n.
rubbish 641 n.
bilharzia
infection 651 n.
See **tropical disease**
tropical disease
651 n.
bilingual
linguistic 557 adj.
speaking 579 adj.
bilious
yellow 433 adj.
unhealthy 651 adj.
bilk
deceive 542 vb.
fleece 786 vb.
defraud 788 vb.
be in debt 803 vb.
not pay 805 vb.
bill
numerical result
85 n.
list 87 n.
protuberance
254 n.
exhibit 522 n.
advertise 528 vb.
advertisement
528 n.
label 547 n.
correspondence
588 n.
demand 737 vb.
title deed 767 n.

paper money
797 n.
credit 802 n.
account 808 vb.
accounts 808 n.
bill and coo
caress 889 vb.
billboard
advertisement
528 n.
billet
stopping place
145 n.
place 185 n.
place 187 vb.
quarters 192 n.
apportion 783 vb.
billet-doux
correspondence
588 n.
love token 889 n.
wooing 889 n.
billfold
case 194 n.
treasury 799 n.
billhook
sharp edge 256 n.
billiard ball
sphere 252 n.
billiards
ball game 837 n.
Billingsgate
slang 560 adj.
scurrility 899 n.
billion
over one hundred
99 n.
billions
funds 797 n.
bill of exchange
title deed 767 n.
paper money
797 n.
bill of fare
list 87 n.
bill of lading
list 87 n.
bill of rights
dueness 915 n.
billow(s)
swelling 253 n.
ocean 343 n.
wave 350 n.
Billy Bunter
bulk 195 n.
billycan
pot 194 n.

billy goat
goat 365 n.
male animal
372 n.
bin
vessel 194 n.
binary
computerized
86 adj.
dual 90 adj.
star 321 n.
binary system
number 85 n.
bind
tie 45 vb.
combine 50 vb.
bring together
74 vb.
stabilize 153 vb.
make smaller
198 vb.
cover 226 vb.
close 264 vb.
cultivate 370 vb.
repair 656 vb.
obstruct 702 vb.
compel 740 vb.
subjugate 745 vb.
fetter 747 vb.
restrain 747 vb.
bore 838 n.
impose a duty
917 vb.
binder
bond 47 n.
farm tool 370 n.
binding
ligature 47 n.
wrapping 226 n.
edging 234 n.
bookbinding 589 n.
necessary 596 adj.
authoritative
733 adj.
compelling
740 adj.
trimming 844 n.
obligatory 917 adj.
bind oneself
promise 764 vb.
bind over
impose a duty
917 vb.
bindweed
plant 366 n.
bine
plant 366 n.

bin-ends
leavings 41 n.
piece 53 n.
binge
eat 301 vb.
festivity 837 n.
be intemperate
943 vb.
gluttonize 947 vb.
gluttony 947 n.
drunkenness 949 n.
bingo
gambling 618 n.
card game 837 n.
binnacle
sailing aid 269 n.
binocular
seeing 438 adj.
binoculars
telescope 442 n.
bint
female 373 n.
loose woman
952 n.
biochemistry
biology 358 n.
biodata
evidence 466 n.
biography 590 n.
biogenetic
biological 358 adj.
biography
reading matter
589 n.
biography 590 n.
biological
biological 358 adj.
biology
biology 358 n.
biomass
vegetable life
366 n.
biomedicine
biology 358 n.
biophysics
biology 358 n.
biopsy
diagnostic 658 n.
biorhythm
regular return
141 n.
biosphere
world 321 n.
biota
organism 358 n.
biotype
situation 186 n.

559

organism 358 n.
bipartisan
dual 90 adj.
cooperative
706 adj.
bipartite
bisected 92 adj.
biped
animal 365 n.
biplane
aircraft 276 n.
birch
tree 366 n.
flog 963 vb.
spank 963 vb.
scourge 964 n.
bird
young creature
132 n.
animal 365 n.
bird 365 n.
person 371 n.
female 373 n.
detention 747 n.
loved one 887 n.
lover 887 n.
bird, the
repulsion 292 n.
bird cage
cattle pen 369 n.
bird in the hand
presence 189 n.
object 319 n.
possession 773 n.
birdlife
bird 365 n.
birdlike
animal 365 adj.
birdman
aeronaut 271 n.
bird of ill omen
omen 511 n.
warning 664 n.
bird of paradise
bird 365 n.
bird of passage
brief span 114 n.
wanderer 268 n.
bird of prey
killer 362 n.
bird 365 n.
birds
animal 365 n.
bird sanctuary
preservation 666 n.
birds and the bees
propagation 167 n.

bird's-eye view
combination 50 n.
whole 52 n.
generality 79 n.
inspection 438 n.
view 438 n.
spectacle 445 n.
compendium
592 n.
birds of a feather
analogue 18 n.
coherence 48 n.
close friend 880 n.
birdsong
ululation 409 n.
vocal music 412 n.
bird strike
collision 279 n.
bird watching
zoology 367 n.
spectator 441 n.
bird-witted
light-minded
456 adj.
foolish 499 adj.
biretta
headgear 228 n.
badge of rule
743 n.
canonicals 989 n.
Biro (tdmk)
recording instru-
ment 549 n.
stationery 586 n.
birth
beginning 68 n.
origin 68 n.
obstetrics 167 n.
propagation 167 n.
genealogy 169 n.
life 360 n.
nobility 868 n.
birth certificate
label 547 n.
record 548 n.
birth control
contraception
172 n.
hindrance 702 n.
birthday
date 108 n.
anniversary 141 n.
special day 876 n.
birthday card
correspondence
588 n.

birthday honours
honours 866 n.
reward 962 n.
birthday party
social gathering
882 n.
birthday present
gift 781 n.
birthday suit
bareness 229 n.
birthmark
identification
547 n.
skin disease 651 n.
blemish 845 n.
birthplace
source 156 n.
place 185 n.
home 192 n.
birth rate
statistics 86 n.
propagation 167 n.
birthright
priority 119 n.
dower 777 n.
dueness 915 n.
birthstone
talisman 983 n.
biryani
dish 301 n.
bis
bravo 923 int.
biscuit
food 301 n.
mouthful 301 n.
pastries and cakes
301 n.
brown 430 adj.
bisect
bisect 92 vb.
bisexual
abnormal 84 adj.
dual 90 adj.
double 91 adj.
bishop
plaything 837 n.
ecclesiarch 986 n.
bishopric
district 184 n.
church office 985 n.
parish 985 n.
bison
cattle 365 n.
bisque
hors-d'oeuvres
301 n.

bissextile
seasonal 141 adj.
bistre
brown pigment
430 n.
bistro
café 192 n.
bit
finite quantity
26 n.
small quantity
33 n.
piece 53 n.
component 58 n.
data processing
86 n.
perforator 263 n.
fetter 748 n.
loved one 887 n.
loose woman
952 n.
bit by bit
by degrees 27 adv.
severally 80 adv.
bitch
dog 365 n.
female animal
373 n.
cad 938 n.
bitchy
malevolent
898 adj.
bite
small quantity
33 n.
cut 46 vb.
piece 53 n.
vigorousness 174 n.
be sharp 256 vb.
notch 260 vb.
mouthful 301 n.
give pain 377 vb.
refrigerate 382 vb.
pungency 388 n.
gesticulate 547 vb.
engrave 555 vb.
ill-treat 645 vb.
wound 655 vb.
bane 659 n.
fight 716 vb.
hurt 827 vb.
endearment 889 n.
anger 891 n.
enrage 891 vb.
sullenness 893 n.
bite into
enter 297 vb.

**bite off more than
  one can chew**
attempt 671 vb.
undertake 672 vb.
act foolishly
  695 vb.
fail 728 vb.
biter bit
retaliation 714 n.
bite the dust
be destroyed
  165 vb.
tumble 309 vb.
die 361 vb.
be defeated 728 vb.
biting
keen 174 adj.
eating 301 n.
painful 377 adj.
cold 380 adj.
pungent 388 adj.
paining 827 adj.
witty 839 adj.
bit on the side
kept woman 952 n.
bit part
acting 594 n.
bits and pieces
piece 53 n.
box 194 n.
bitten
enamoured
  887 adj.
bitter
alcoholic drink
  301 n.
cold 380 adj.
pungent 388 adj.
unsavoury 391 adj.
sour 393 adj.
unpleasant
  827 adj.
hostile 881 adj.
hateful 888 adj.
resentful 891 adj.
irascible 892 adj.
malevolent
  898 adj.
disapproving
  924 adj.
bittern
bird 365 n.
bitterness
sourness 393 n.
badness 645 n.
bane 659 n.
sorrow 825 n.

painfulness 827 n.
discontent 829 n.
enmity 881 n.
hatred 888 n.
resentment 891 n.
malevolence 898 n.
bitters
sourness 393 n.
bittersweet
contrary 14 adj.
painful 377 adj.
bitty
fragmentary
  53 adj.
incomplete 55 adj.
bitumen
resin 357 n.
bivalve
marine life 365 n.
bivouac
place oneself
  187 vb.
station 187 n.
abode 192 n.
dwell 192 vb.
biweekly
seasonal 141 adj.
bizarre
unusual 84 adj.
imaginative
  513 adj.
ridiculous 849 adj.
blab
inform 524 vb.
divulge 526 vb.
accuse 928 vb.
black
set apart 46 vb.
exclude 57 vb.
formal dress 228 n.
horse 273 n.
darkness 418 n.
black 428 adj.
blacken 428 vb.
blackness 428 n.
evil 616 adj.
bad 645 adj.
dirty 649 adj.
prohibit 757 vb.
lamentation 836 n.
black and blue
blackish 428 adj.
blue 435 adj.
black and white
polarity 14 n.
antiquated 127 adj.

achromatism
  426 n.
blackness 428 n.
pied 437 adj.
painted 553 adj.
painting 553 n.
opposites 704 n.
**black-and-white tele-
  vision**
broadcasting
  531 n.
black armband ⌐
badge 547 n.
black art
sorcery 983 n.
blackball
exclude 57 vb.
exclusion 57 n.
eject 300 vb.
reject 607 vb.
prohibit 757 vb.
shame 867 vb.
disapprobation
  924 n.
black belt
proficient person
  696 n.
blackberry
fruit and vegetables
  301 n.
black thing 428 n.
blackbird
bird 365 n.
black thing 428 n.
blackboard
stationery 586 n.
black books
disrepute 867 n.
hatred 888 n.
disapprobation
  924 n.
black bottom
dance 837 n.
black box
aircraft 276 n.
*recording instru-
  ment* 549 n.
black cap
badge of rule
  743 n.
condemnation
  961 n.
black cat
omen 511 n.
talisman 983 n.
black cloud
threat 900 n.

black coffee
soft drink 301 n.
black comedy
stage play 594 n.
wit 839 n.
blackcurrant
fruit and vegetables
  301 n.
Black Death
plague 651 n.
black diamond
coal 385 n.
black economy
escape 667 n.
swindling 788 n.
market 796 n.
nonpayment 805 n.
blacken
blacken 428 vb.
mark 547 vb.
shame 867 vb.
criticize 924 vb.
defame 926 vb.
black eye
black 428 adj.
black thing 428 n.
wound 655 n.
blemish 845 n.
blackfly
insect 365 n.
blackguard
evildoer 904 n.
ruffian 904 n.
reproach 924 vb.
bad person 938 n.
cad 938 n.
blackhead
skin disease 651 n.
blemish 845 n.
black hole
star 321 n.
black ice
wintriness 380 n.
blacking
cleanser 648 n.
hindrance 702 n.
blackjack
vessel 194 n.
hammer 279 n.
strike 279 vb.
black lead
lubricant 334 n.
blacklead
blacken 428 vb.
black thing 428 n.
clean 648 vb.
cleanser 648 n.

blackleg
nonconformist
84 n.
apostatize 603 vb.
recanter 603 n.
revolter 738 n.
hateful object
888 n.
blacklist
set apart 46 vb.
list 87 n.
unsociability
883 n.
disapprobation
924 n.
disapprove 924 vb.
condemn 961 vb.
condemnation
961 n.
black look
rudeness 885 n.
anger 891 n.
sullenness 893 n.
reproach 924 n.
black magic
badness 645 n.
diabolism 969 n.
sorcery 983 n.
blackmail
demand 737 n.
demand 737 vb.
compel 740 vb.
compulsion 740 n.
request 761 n.
request 761 vb.
fleece 786 vb.
rapacity 786 n.
rob 788 vb.
swindling 788 n.
booty 790 n.
tax 809 n.
threat 900 n.
threaten 900 vb.
reward 962 n.
Black Maria
vehicle 274 n.
lockup 748 n.
black mark
slur 867 n.
reprimand 924 n.
black market
trade 791 n.
market 796 n.
improbity 930 n.
illegal 954 adj.
Black Muslim
revolter 738 n.

non-Christian sect
978 n.
blackness
blackness 428 n.
blackout
insensibility 375 n.
darkening 418 n.
oblivion 506 n.
dramaturgy 594 n.
prohibition 757 n.
black pepper
condiment 389 n.
black pudding
meat 301 n.
Black Rod
badge 547 n.
badge of rule
743 n.
black sheep
offender 904 n.
bad person 938 n.
blacksmith
artisan 686 n.
black spot
danger 661 n.
blackthorn
tree 366 n.
black tie
formal dress 228 n.
ostentation 875 n.
blackwater fever
tropical disease
651 n.
bladder
sphere 252 n.
blade
sharp edge 256 n.
bluntness 257 n.
propeller 269 n.
propellant 287 n.
foliage 366 n.
male 372 n.
sidearms 723 n.
blah-blah
empty talk 515 n.
blame
blame 924 vb.
censure 924 n.
accusation 928 n.
guilt 936 n.
blameless
guiltless 935 adj.
blanch
lose colour 426 vb.
whiten 427 vb.
blancmange
dessert 301 n.

blanco
whiten 427 vb.
bland
smooth 258 adj.
dull 840 adj.
flattering 925 adj.
blandishment(s)
inducement 612 n.
endearment 889 n.
flattery 925 n.
blank
nonexistence 2 n.
insubstantial 4 adj.
uniform 16 adj.
zero 103 n.
emptiness 190 n.
empty 190 adj.
form 243 n.
opaque 423 adj.
unintelligible
517 adj.
punctuation 547 n.
ammunition 723 n.
impassive 820 adj.
blank cartridge
emptiness 190 n.
ammunition 723 n.
blank cheque
facility 701 n.
scope 744 n.
permit 756 n.
liberality 813 n.
blanket
inclusive 78 adj.
general 79 adj.
suppress 165 vb.
moderate 177 vb.
cover 226 vb.
coverlet 226 n.
indiscriminate
464 adj.
blanket coverage
inclusion 78 n.
blankety-blank
damnable 645 adj.
blankness
absence of thought
450 n.
oblivion 506 n.
lack of wonder
865 n.
blank verse
prosody 593 n.
verse form 593 n.
blank wall
closure 264 n.
difficulty 700 n.

obstacle 702 n.
blare
be loud 400 vb.
loudness 400 n.
resonance 404 n.
resound 404 vb.
shrill 407 vb.
stridor 407 n.
blaring
loud 400 adj.
strident 407 adj.
blarney
empty talk 515 n.
falsehood 541 n.
eloquence 579 n.
flatter 925 vb.
flattery 925 n.
blasé
incurious 454 adj.
bored 838 adj.
indifferent 860 adj.
sated 863 adj.
blaspheme
cuss 899 vb.
be irreligious
974 vb.
be impious 980 vb.
blasphemy
impiety 980 n.
blast
demolish 165 vb.
outbreak 176 n.
air 340 n.
blow 352 vb.
gale 352 n.
wind 352 n.
loudness 400 n.
bang 402 n.
bang 402 vb.
impair 655 vb.
be malevolent
898 vb.
curse 899 int.
cuss 899 vb.
bewitch 983 vb.
blasting
cursing 899 adj.
scurrility 899 n.
blast off
fly 271 vb.
blast-off
space travel 271 n.
departure 296 n.
ascent 308 n.
blatant
flagrant 32 adj.
vulgar 847 adj.

vain 873 adj.
showy 875 adj.
insolent 878 adj.
blather
empty talk 515 n.
Blathnat
Celtic deities
967 n.
blaze
be hot 379 vb.
fire 379 n.
light 417 n.
shine 417 vb.
indicate 547 vb.
indication 547 n.
mark 547 vb.
blazer
jacket 228 n.
blazing
fiery 379 adj.
blazon
heraldry 547 n.
indicate 547 vb.
mark 547 vb.
honour 866 vb.
be ostentatious
875 vb.
bleach
bleacher 426 n.
lose colour 426 vb.
white 427 adj.
whiten 427 vb.
clean 648 vb.
hairwash 843 n.
bleak
wintry 129 adj.
unproductive
172 adj.
empty 190 adj.
adverse 731 adj.
bleakness
adversity 731 n.
bleary
dim 419 adj.
bleat
ululate 409 vb.
be discontented
829 vb.
bleed
emit 300 vb.
empty 300 vb.
be wet 341 vb.
doctor 658 vb.
fleece 786 vb.
overcharge 811 vb.
suffer 825 vb.

bleed for
pity 905 vb.
bleeding
outflow 298 n.
haemorrhage
302 n.
haematic 335 adj.
suffering 825 adj.
bleed to death
perish 361 vb.
bleed white
fleece 786 vb.
bleep
shrill 407 vb.
stridor 407 n.
telecommunication
531 n.
signal 547 n.
bleeper
telecommunication
531 n.
signal 547 n.
blemish
eyesore 842 n.
make ugly 842 vb.
blemish 845 n.
blemish 845 vb.
blench
recoil 280 vb.
be unwilling
598 vb.
show feeling
818 vb.
quake 854 vb.
blend
a mixture 43 n.
mix 43 vb.
combine 50 vb.
compound 50 n.
produce 164 vb.
cook 301 vb.
harmonize 410 vb.
blenny
fish 365 n.
bless
be auspicious
730 vb.
approve 923 vb.
praise 923 vb.
sanctify 979 vb.
perform ritual
988 vb.
blessed
good 615 adj.
happy 824 adj.
pleasurable
826 adj.

approved 923 adj.
blessedness
happiness 824 n.
sanctity 979 n.
blessed state
heaven 971 n.
sanctity 979 n.
blessing
benefit 615 n.
good 615 n.
permission 756 n.
benevolence 897 n.
thanks 907 n.
approbation 923 n.
praise 923 n.
act of worship
981 n.
prayers 981 n.
blessing, the
Holy Communion
988 n.
blessing in disguise
benefit 615 n.
blether
empty talk 515 n.
mean nothing
515 vb.
be loquacious
581 vb.
chatter 581 n.
blight
destroyer 168 n.
badness 645 n.
impair 655 vb.
blight 659 n.
adversity 731 n.
be malevolent
898 vb.
bewitch 983 vb.
blighter
cad 938 n.
Blighty
home 192 n.
blimp
airship 276 n.
blind
shade 226 n.
shine 417 vb.
curtain 421 n.
blind 439 adj.
blind 439 vb.
disguise 527 n.
trap 542 n.
trickery 542 n.
involuntary
596 adj.
plead 614 vb.

pretext 614 n.
stratagem 698 n.
dead drunk
949 adj.
drunkenness 949 n.
blind alley
stopping place
145 n.
road 624 n.
obstacle 702 n.
blind chance
chance 159 n.
blind corner
invisibility 444 n.
blind date
uncertainty 474 n.
social round 882 n.
blind drunk
dead drunk
949 adj.
blind eye
blindness 439 n.
invisibility 444 n.
blindfold
screen 421 vb.
blind 439 adj.
blind 439 vb.
keep secret 525 vb.
deceive 542 vb.
blinding
luminous 417 adj.
blind man's buff
children's games
837 n.
blindness
blindness 439 n.
blind spot
blindness 439 n.
dim sight 440 n.
invisibility 444 n.
inattention 456 n.
prejudice 481 n.
blini
hors-d'oeuvres
301 n.
blink
flash 417 n.
reflection 417 n.
shine 417 vb.
gaze 438 vb.
look 438 n.
be blind 439 vb.
be dim-sighted
440 vb.
dim sight 440 n.
blinker(s)
screen 421 n.

563

screen 421 vb.
blind 439 vb.
dim sight 440 n.
blinking
vision 438 n.
dim-sighted
440 adj.
damnable 645 adj.
bliss
happiness 824 n.
blissful
palmy 730 adj.
happy 824 adj.
pleasurable
826 adj.
blister
swelling 253 n.
skin disease 651 n.
blistering
hot 379 adj.
blithe
happy 824 adj.
cheerful 833 adj.
blitz
demolish 165 vb.
loudness 400 n.
attack 712 n.
attack 712 vb.
bombardment
712 n.
fire at 712 vb.
battle 718 n.
blitzkrieg
attack 712 n.
war 718 n.
blizzard
storm 176 n.
gale 352 n.
wintriness 380 n.
bloat
enlarge 197 vb.
animal disease
651 n.
bloaters
fish food 301 n.
bloc
political party
708 n.
block
housing 192 n.
bulk 195 n.
head 213 n.
stand 218 n.
close 264 vb.
solid body 324 n.
hardness 326 n.
engraving 555 n.

write 586 vb.
hindrance 702 n.
obstacle 702 n.
obstruct 702 vb.
defend 713 vb.
unfeeling person
820 n.
means of execution
964 n.
blockade
surround 230 vb.
circumscribe
232 vb.
circumscription
232 n.
close 264 vb.
closure 264 n.
hindrance 702 n.
obstacle 702 n.
obstruct 702 vb.
attack 712 n.
besiege 712 vb.
go to war 718 vb.
warfare 718 n.
restriction 747 n.
blockage
stop 145 n.
hindrance 702 n.
obstacle 702 n.
blockbuster
destroyer 168 n.
film 445 n.
book 589 n.
novel 590 n.
bomb 723 n.
blockhead
ignoramus 493 n.
dunce 501 n.
block in
colour 425 vb.
paint 553 vb.
block letters
lettering 586 n.
block out
outline 233 vb.
form 243 vb.
represent 551 vb.
prepare 669 vb.
block up
obstruct 702 vb.
bloke
male 372 n.
blond(e)
achromatism
426 n.
colourless 426 adj.
whitish 427 adj.

yellowness 433 n.
a beauty 841 n.
blood
consanguinity
11 n.
kinsman 11 n.
auspicate 68 vb.
breed 77 n.
genealogy 169 n.
vigorousness 174 n.
blood 335 n.
nobility 868 n.
blood bank
storage 632 n.
blood-clot
solid body 324 n.
blood 335 n.
blood count
blood 335 n.
blood-curdling
frightening
854 adj.
blood disease
blood disease
651 n.
blood donor
giver 781 n.
good giver 813 n.
blood feud
quarrel 709 n.
enmity 881 n.
revenge 910 n.
blood group
classification 77 n.
blood 335 n.
blood heat
heat 379 n.
bloodhound
dog 365 n.
detective 459 n.
hunter 619 n.
bloodless
colourless 426 adj.
diseased 651 adj.
peaceful 717 adj.
guiltless 935 adj.
blood-letting
killing 362 n.
blood money
blood 335 n.
peace offering
719 n.
atonement 941 n.
blood-poisoning
infection 651 n.

blood pressure
cardiovascular dis-
ease 651 n.
bloodshed
slaughter 362 n.
warfare 718 n.
cruel act 898 n.
bloodshot
angry 891 adj.
blood sport
killing 362 n.
chase 619 n.
bloodstock
horse 273 n.
aristocrat 868 n.
nobility 868 n.
bloodstream
blood 335 n.
current 350 n.
blood test
diagnostic 658 n.
bloodthirsty
furious 176 adj.
murderous 362 adj.
warlike 718 adj.
cruel 898 adj.
blood transfusion
blood 335 n.
bloody
violent 176 adj.
haematic 335 adj.
murderous 362 adj.
damnable 645 adj.
cruel 898 adj.
Bloody Mary
alcoholic drink
301 n.
bloody-minded
obstinate 602 adj.
opposing 704 adj.
disobedient
738 adj.
malevolent
898 adj.
bloody nose
defeat 728 n.
bloom
reproduce itself
167 vb.
be fruitful 171 vb.
expand 197 vb.
layer 207 n.
open 263 vb.
flower 366 n.
redness 431 n.
be healthy 650 vb.
health 650 n.

ripening 669 n.
prosper 730 vb.
be beautiful
841 vb.
bloomer
cereals 301 n.
mistake 495 n.
bloomers
trousers 228 n.
underwear 228 n.
blooming
young 130 adj.
vigorous 174 adj.
vegetable life
366 n.
healthy 650 adj.
personable 841 adj.
blossom
grow 36 vb.
growth 157 n.
product 164 n.
be fruitful 171 vb.
expand 197 vb.
flower 366 n.
prosper 730 vb.
blot
sphere 252 n.
absorb 299 vb.
dry 342 vb.
blacken 428 vb.
blunder 495 vb.
mistake 495 n.
mark 547 vb.
obliteration 550 n.
defect 647 n.
dirt 649 n.
make unclean
649 vb.
be clumsy 695 vb.
blemish 845 n.
blemish 845 vb.
shame 867 vb.
slur 867 n.
blotch
mottle 437 n.
blemish 845 n.
blot one's copy book
blunder 495 vb.
lose repute 867 vb.
incur blame
924 vb.
be wicked 934 vb.
blot out
subtract 39 vb.
destroy 165 vb.
conceal 525 vb.
obliterate 550 vb.

forgive 909 vb.
blotter
stationery 586 n.
blotting paper
dryer 342 n.
stationery 586 n.
blotto
dead drunk
949 adj.
blot up
dry 342 vb.
blouse
shirt 228 n.
blouson
jacket 228 n.
blow
expand 197 vb.
knock 279 n.
blow 352 vb.
gale 352 n.
wind 352 n.
See **breeze**
play music 413 vb.
lack of expectation
508 n.
disappointment
509 n.
evil 616 n.
deed 676 n.
be fatigued 684 vb.
adversity 731 n.
expend 806 vb.
suffering 825 n.
*corporal punish-
ment* 963 n.
**blow-by-blow ac-
count**
diffuseness 570 n.
blow-dry
hairdressing 843 n.
blower
air 340 n.
ventilation 352 n.
hearing aid 415 n.
blow hard
be strong 162 vb.
blow 352 vb.
boast 877 vb.
blowhole
orifice 263 n.
outlet 298 n.
air pipe 353 n.
blow hot and cold
change 143 vb.
vary 152 vb.
be irresolute
601 vb.

be capricious
604 vb.
blow it
blunder 495 vb.
blowlamp
furnace 383 n.
blow one's cover
disclose 526 vb.
blow one's mind
make mad 503 vb.
be wonderful
864 vb.
drug oneself
949 vb.
**blow one's own trum-
pet**
be vain 873 vb.
boast 877 vb.
blow one's top
get angry 891 vb.
blowout
feasting 301 n.
meal 301 n.
bang 402 n.
festivity 837 n.
gluttony 947 n.
blow over
be past 125 vb.
cease 145 vb.
blowpipe
propellant 287 n.
blowing 352 n.
air pipe 353 n.
heater 383 n.
missile weapon
723 n.
blows
fight 716 n.
anger 891 n.
blow sky-high
demolish 165 vb.
confute 479 vb.
blow the brains out
kill 362 vb.
blow the gaff
inform 524 vb.
divulge 526 vb.
blow the whistle on
inform 524 vb.
warn 664 vb.
blow up
augment 36 vb.
be dispersed 75 vb.
demolish 165 vb.
force 176 vb.
enlarge 197 vb.
propel 287 vb.

elevate 310 vb.
blow 352 vb.
blow up 352 vb.
exaggerate 546 vb.
photograph 551 vb.
get angry 891 vb.
reprove 924 vb.
blowy
windy 352 adj.
blowzy
red 431 adj.
blubber
fat 357 n.
weep 836 vb.
bludgeon
strike 279 vb.
club 723 n.
brute force 735 n.
oppress 735 vb.
compel 740 vb.
Blue
athlete 162 n.
blue
air 340 n.
ocean 343 n.
blue 435 adj.
blueness 435 n.
badge 547 n.
decoration 729 n.
melancholic
834 adj.
honours 866 n.
sullen 893 adj.
cursing 899 adj.
impure 951 adj.
bluebell
plant 366 n.
blueness 435 n.
blue blood
genealogy 169 n.
blood 335 n.
nobility 868 n.
bluebottle
insect 365 n.
blue-chip
valuable 644 adj.
blue-collar worker
worker 686 n.
lower classes 869 n.
blue devils
sullenness 893 n.
blue dye
blue pigment
435 n.
blue ensign
flag 547 n.

blue-eyed boy
male 372 n.
favourite 890 n.
blue funk
fear 854 n.
cowardice 856 n.
blue grass
music 412 n.
blue in the face
angry 891 adj.
blue jeans
trousers 228 n.
blue joke
witticism 839 n.
impurity 951 n.
blue moon
neverness 109 n.
blue movie
film 445 n.
blue-pencil
moderate 177 vb.
obliterate 550 vb.
purify 648 vb.
rectify 654 vb.
prohibit 757 vb.
Blue Peter
flag 547 n.
blueprint
prototype 23 n.
representation
551 n.
compendium
592 n.
plan 623 n.
plan 623 vb.
preparation 669 n.
prepare 669 vb.
blues
music 412 n.
vocal music 412 n.
neurosis 503 n.
dejection 834 n.
melancholy 834 n.
dance 837 n.
blues, the
sullenness 893 n.
blue sky
air 340 n.
blueness 435 n.
hope 852 n.
bluestocking
intellectual 492 n.
scholar 492 n.
sage 500 n.
bookperson 589 n.
blue tit
bird 365 n.

bluff
high land 209 n.
verticality 215 n.
sciolism 491 n.
duplicity 541 n.
deceive 542 vb.
trickery 542 n.
plead 614 vb.
pretext 614 n.
be affected 850 vb.
boast 877 n.
boast 877 vb.
bluff one's way out
escape 667 vb.
bluish
blue 435 adj.
blunder
blunder 495 vb.
mistake 495 n.
be clumsy 695 vb.
guilty act 936 n.
blunderbuss
firearm 723 n.
blunt
short 204 adj.
low 210 adj.
blunt 257 vb.
smooth 258 adj.
render insensible
375 vb.
assertive 532 adj.
veracious 540 adj.
ill-bred 847 adj.
blunt instrument
bluntness 257 n.
club 723 n.
bluntness
bluntness 257 n.
plainness 573 n.
rudeness 885 n.
blur
dim 419 vb.
dimness 419 n.
blur 440 vb.
make unclean
649 vb.
blurb
advertisement
528 n.
praise 923 n.
blurred
amorphous
244 adj.
dim 419 adj.
indistinct 444 adj.
blurt
improvise 609 vb.

blurt out
inform 524 vb.
divulge 526 vb.
speak 579 vb.
blush
heat 379 n.
hue 425 n.
redden 431 vb.
redness 431 n.
indication 547 n.
feeling 818 n.
show feeling
818 vb.
be humbled
872 vb.
humiliation 872 n.
be modest 874 vb.
modesty 874 n.
guilt 936 n.
blusher
pigment 425 n.
red pigment 431 n.
cosmetic 843 n.
blushing
luminous 417 adj.
red 431 adj.
modest 874 adj.
modesty 874 n.
guilty 936 adj.
bluster
be active 678 vb.
defy 711 vb.
boast 877 n.
boast 877 vb.
boasting 877 n.
insolence 878 n.
be angry 891 vb.
threat 900 n.
threaten 900 vb.
blustery
violent 176 adj.
windy 352 adj.
Blu-tack (tdmk)
adhesive 47 n.
fastening 47 n.
BMX (tdmk)
bicycle 274 n.
BO
stench 397 n.
boa
neckwear 228 n.
boa constrictor
reptile 365 n.
Boadicea
soldier 722 n.
brave person 855 n.

boar
pig 365 n.
male animal
372 n.
board
shelf 218 n.
stand 218 n.
enter 297 vb.
provisions 301 n.
hardness 326 n.
materials 631 n.
provide 633 vb.
director 690 n.
council 692 n.
attack 712 vb.
tribunal 956 n.
board and lodging
provision 633 n.
boarder
resident 191 n.
learner 538 n.
board game
board game 837 n.
boarding
attack 712 n.
boarding house
inn 192 n.
quarters 192 n.
boarding school
quarters 192 n.
school 539 n.
board of directors
director 690 n.
board of examiners
enquirer 459 n.
board out
dwell 192 vb.
board room
council 692 n.
boards
wrapping 226 n.
bookbinding 589 n.
stage set 594 n.
theatre 594 n.
boards, the
drama 594 n.
boar hunt
chase 619 n.
boast
comprise 78 vb.
boast 877 n.
boast 877 vb.
boastfulness
boasting 877 n.
boasting
overestimation
482 n.

boasting 877 n.
boast of
possess 773 vb.
boast 877 vb.
boat
go to sea 269 vb.
row 269 vb.
water travel 269 n.
boat 275 n.
ship 275 n.
boat-builder
artisan 686 n.
boater
headgear 228 n.
boating
aquatics 269 n.
water travel 269 n.
sport 837 n.
boatman
boatman 270 n.
boat neck
neckline 228 n.
boat race
racing 716 n.
boatswain
mariner 270 n.
navigator 270 n.
bob
shorten 204 vb.
shortness 204 n.
hang 217 vb.
hanging object 217 n.
obeisance 311 n.
stoop 311 vb.
leap 312 vb.
oscillate 317 vb.
oscillation 317 n.
be agitated 318 vb.
coinage 797 n.
hairdressing 843 n.
servility 879 n.
greet 884 vb.
respects 920 n.
show respect 920 vb.
bobble
hanging object 217 n.
trimming 844 n.
bobby
police 955 n.
bobsled
sled 274 n.
bobsleigh
sled 274 n.

bob up
ascend 308 vb.
bob up and down
leap 312 vb.
oscillate 317 vb.
dance 837 vb.
bod
person 371 n.
bode
predict 511 vb.
bodega
tavern 192 n.
bode ill
endanger 661 vb.
threaten 900 vb.
bodice
garment 228 n.
bodily
material 319 adj.
sensuous 376 adj.
sensual 944 adj.
bodkin
sharp point 256 n.
perforator 263 n.
body
quantity 26 n.
chief part 52 n.
band 74 n.
matter 319 n.
object 319 n.
structure 331 n.
corpse 363 n.
person 371 n.
savouriness 390 n.
print-type 587 n.
corporation 708 n.
body and blood of Christ
the sacrament 988 n.
body blow
knock 279 n.
body-builder
athlete 162 n.
body-building
athletics 162 n.
nourishing 301 adj.
salubrious 652 adj.
exercise 682 n.
body forth
materialize 319 vb.
manifest 522 vb.
represent 551 vb.
bodyguard
concomitant 89 n.
protector 660 n.
defender 713 n.

combatant 722 n.
retainer 742 n.
body heat
heat 379 n.
body language
gesture 547 n.
voicelessness 578 n.
speech 579 n.
bodypopping
dance 837 n.
body scanner
hospital 658 n.
body-snatcher
thief 789 n.
body stocking
suit 228 n.
underwear 228 n.
body-suit
suit 228 n.
boffin
sage 500 n.
planner 623 n.
worker 686 n.
expert 696 n.
bog
moisture 341 n.
marsh 347 n.
dirt 649 n.
latrine 649 n.
bogey
fantasy 513 n.
bogged down
late 136 adj.
boggle
puzzle 474 vb.
doubt 486 vb.
dissent 489 vb.
disappoint 509 vb.
be unwilling 598 vb.
be wonderful 864 vb.
boggy
soft 327 adj.
humid 341 adj.
marshy 347 adj.
bogle
demon 970 n.
bogus
erroneous 495 adj.
false 541 adj.
spurious 542 adj.
untrue 543 adj.
affected 850 adj.
bogy
monster 938 n.
demon 970 n.

Bohemian
nonconformist 84 n.
unconformable 84 adj.
free person 744 n.
boil
swelling 253 n.
cook 301 vb.
be agitated 318 vb.
effervesce 318 vb.
bubble 355 vb.
be hot 379 vb.
ulcer 651 n.
make sanitary 652 adj.
be excited 821 vb.
boil down
abate 37 vb.
make smaller 198 vb.
shorten 204 vb.
boil down to
be intrinsic 5 vb.
mean 514 vb.
boil dry
be hot 379 vb.
burn 381 vb.
boiler
pot 194 n.
poultry 365 n.
heater 383 n.
ablutions 648 n.
boiler suit
suit 228 n.
boiling
furious 176 adj.
commotion 318 n.
hot 379 adj.
heating 381 n.
fervent 818 adj.
excited 821 adj.
excitable 822 adj.
angry 891 adj.
boiling point
heat 379 n.
completion 725 n.
boil over
effervesce 318 vb.
get angry 891 vb.
boisterous
disorderly 61 adj.
violent 176 adj.
windy 352 adj.
hasty 680 adj.
bold
projecting 254 adj.

567

BOL

forceful 571 adj.
written 586 adj.
print-type 587 n.
courageous
 855 adj.
rash 857 adj.
insolent 878 adj.
boldface
print-type 587 n.
boldness
courage 855 n.
insolence 878 n.
bold type
letter 558 n.
bole
chief part 52 n.
soil 344 n.
tree 366 n.
bolero
jacket 228 n.
dance 837 n.
boletus
fruit and vegetables
 301 n.
boll
receptacle 194 n.
sphere 252 n.
bollard
fastening 47 n.
traffic control
 305 n.
boloney
empty talk 515 n.
falsehood 541 n.
Bolsheviks
political party
 708 n.
bolshie
opposing 704 adj.
disobedient
 738 adj.
bolster
cushion 218 n.
support 218 vb.
aid 703 vb.
bolster up
support 218 vb.
cheer 833 vb.
give courage
 855 vb.
bolt
affix 45 vb.
fastening 47 n.
bunch 74 n.
textile 222 n.
barrier 235 n.
sharp point 256 n.

BOM

close 264 vb.
stopper 264 n.
move fast 277 vb.
decamp 296 vb.
eat 301 vb.
cultivate 370 vb.
run away 620 vb.
safeguard 662 n.
missile weapon
 723 n.
disobey 738 vb.
gluttonize 947 vb.
bolt from the blue
lack of expectation
 508 n.
bolthole
tunnel 263 n.
refuge 662 n.
bolt of lightning
luminary 420 n.
bolt upright
vertical 215 adj.
bolus
medicine 658 n.
bomb
demolish 165 vb.
fire at 712 vb.
bomb 723 n.
fail 728 vb.
miscarry 728 vb.
bombard
demolish 165 vb.
shoot 287 vb.
radiate 417 vb.
fire at 712 vb.
gun 723 n.
bombardier
soldiery 722 n.
**bombard with ques-
tions**
be curious 453 vb.
bombast
empty talk 515 n.
grandiloquence
 574 n.
ridiculousness
 849 n.
boast 877 n.
Bombay duck
fish food 301 n.
bomb-dropping
bombardment
 712 n.
bomber
aircraft 276 n.
attacker 712 n.
air force 722 n.

BON

bomber jacket
jacket 228 n.
bombshell
lack of expectation
 508 n.
bomb 723 n.
bomb site
emptiness 190 n.
bona fide
genuine 494 adj.
veracious 540 adj.
bonanza
plenty 635 n.
prosperity 730 n.
wealth 800 n.
bon appétit
bon appétit 301 int.
bonbon
sweets 301 n.
bond
bond 47 n.
fetter 748 n.
promise 764 n.
compact 765 n.
title deed 767 n.
dueness 915 n.
duty 917 n.
bondage
servitude 745 n.
subjection 745 n.
detention 747 n.
bone
uncover 229 vb.
empty 300 vb.
cook 301 vb.
solid body 324 n.
harden 326 vb.
hardness 326 n.
bone china
pottery 381 n.
bonehead
ignoramus 493 n.
dunce 501 n.
bone-idle
lazy 679 adj.
bone-lazy
lazy 679 adj.
bonemeal
fertilizer 171 n.
bone of contention
question 459 n.
contention 716 n.
bones
remainder 41 n.
gong 414 n.
boneshaker
bicycle 274 n.

BOO

bone to pick
resentment 891 n.
bonfire
fire 379 n.
revel 837 n.
celebration 876 n.
bongo
drum 414 n.
bonhomie
ostentation 875 n.
sociability 882 n.
benevolence 897 n.
bonk
unite with 45 vb.
bonkers
crazy 503 adj.
bon mot
witticism 839 n.
bonnet
covering 226 n.
headgear 228 n.
bonny
beautiful 841 adj.
bonsai
tree 366 n.
agriculture 370 n.
bonus
extra 40 n.
incentive 612 n.
superfluity 637 n.
gift 781 n.
receipt 807 n.
undueness 916 n.
bon vivant
eater 301 n.
sociable person
 882 n.
sensualist 944 n.
glutton 947 n.
bon viveur
sociable person
 882 n.
sensualist 944 n.
glutton 947 n.
bon voyage
goodbye 296 int.
bony
lean 206 adj.
angular 247 adj.
hard 326 adj.
boo
cry 408 n.
cry 408 n.
vociferate 408 vb.
indignity 921 n.
not respect 921 vb.
despise 922 vb.

disapprobation
924 n.
disapprove 924 vb.
boob
blunder 495 vb.
mistake 495 vb.
be clumsy 695 vb.
boo-boo
mistake 495 n.
boobs
bosom 253 n.
booby
ninny 501 n.
bungler 697 n.
booby prize
rear 238 n.
unskilfulness
695 n.
trophy 729 n.
reward 962 n.
booby trap
trap 542 n.
pitfall 663 n.
defences 713 n.
bomb 723 n.
boogie-woogie
music 412 n.
boohoo
cry 408 n.
cry 408 vb.
lamentation 836 n.
weep 836 vb.
booing
gesture 547 n.
book
list 87 vb.
be early 135 vb.
record 548 n.
book 589 n.
require 627 vb.
acquire 771 vb.
reprove 924 vb.
indict 928 vb.
Book, the
scripture 975 n.
book and candle
perform ritual
988 vb.
bookbinding
bookbinding 589 n.
bookcase
cabinet 194 n.
bookie
gambler 618 n.
bookie's
gaming-house
618 n.

bookish
studious 536 adj.
bookkeeper
treasurer 798 n.
accountant 808 n.
bookkeeping
accounts 808 n.
booklet
book 589 n.
book lover
bookperson 589 n.
bookmaker
gambler 618 n.
**Book of Common
Prayer**
scripture 975 n.
book of days
list 87 n.
chronology 117 n.
book of psalms
hymnal 988 n.
book of words
guidebook 524 n.
reading matter
589 n.
books
list 87 n.
writing 586 n.
bookseller
bookperson 589 n.
book-selling
publication 528 n.
bookshelf
shelf 218 n.
bookworm
scholar 492 n.
learner 538 n.
bookperson 589 n.
boom
grow 36 vb.
be fruitful 171 vb.
productiveness
171 n.
support 218 n.
be loud 400 vb.
loudness 400 n.
bang 402 vb.
roll 403 vb.
resonance 404 n.
ululate 409 vb.
revival 656 n.
defences 713 n.
prosper 730 vb.
prosperity 730 n.
sale 793 n.
boomerang
revert 148 vb.

recoil 280 n.
recoil 280 vb.
retaliation 714 n.
missile weapon
723 n.
boomerang effect
reversion 148 n.
effect 157 n.
counteraction
182 n.
boon
benefit 615 n.
gift 781 n.
boon companion
concomitant 89 n.
colleague 707 n.
close friend 880 n.
sociable person
882 n.
boor
country-dweller
869 n.
rude person 885 n.
boorish
clumsy 695 adj.
ill-bred 847 adj.
plebeian 869 adj.
discourteous
885 adj.
boost
augment 36 vb.
increase 36 n.
invigorate 174 vb.
stimulation 174 n.
impulse 279 n.
elevation 310 n.
overestimate
482 vb.
advertise 528 vb.
aid 703 n.
aid 703 vb.
praise 923 vb.
flatter 925 vb.
booster
stimulant 174 n.
rocket 276 n.
broadcasting
531 n.
commender 923 n.
flatterer 925 n.
boot
box 194 n.
ejection 300 n.
bootblack
cleaner 648 n.

boot boy
violent creature
176 n.
combatant 722 n.
rioter 738 n.
low fellow 869 n.
ruffian 904 n.
bad person 938 n.
bootees
legwear 228 n.
booth
small house 192 n.
compartment
194 n.
shop 796 n.
bootlegger
thief 789 n.
boot-licking
submitting 721 adj.
respectful 920 adj.
bootmaker
clothier 228 n.
boot out
repel 292 vb.
eject 300 vb.
boots
footwear 228 n.
servant 742 n.
booty
booty 790 n.
booze
alcoholic drink
301 n.
drink 301 vb.
drunkenness 949 n.
get drunk 949 vb.
bop
strike 279 vb.
music 412 n.
dance 837 n.
dance 837 vb.
borage
herb 301 n.
bordello
brothel 951 n.
border
entrance 68 n.
contiguity 202 n.
circumscribe
232 vb.
edge 234 n.
edging 234 n.
hem 234 vb.
marginal 234 adj.
limit 236 n.
limit 236 vb.
flank 239 vb.

BOR

garden 370 n.
trimming 844 n.
borderline
marginal 234 adj.
uncertain 474 adj.
bore
enlarge 197 vb.
breadth 205 n.
make concave
255 vb.
pierce 263 vb.
pass 305 vb.
current 350 n.
wave 350 n.
be loquacious
581 vb.
bane 659 n.
firearm 723 n.
trouble 827 vb.
be tedious 838 vb.
bore 838 n.
sate 863 vb.
borehole
excavation 255 n.
water 339 n.
borer
perforator 263 n.
insect 365 n.
bore stiff
be tedious 838 vb.
boring
tunnel 263 n.
prolix 570 adj.
feeble 572 adj.
annoying 827 adj.
tedious 838 adj.
dull 840 adj.
born
born 360 adj.
born, be
be born 360 vb.
born again
converted 147 adj.
repentant 939 adj.
sanctified 979 adj.
born fool
fool 501 n.
born in the purple
rich 800 adj.
noble 868 adj.
born on the wrong side of the blanket
bastard 954 adj.
born out of wedlock
bastard 954 adj.

BOS

born with a silver spoon in one's mouth
prosperous 730 adj.
rich 800 adj.
noble 868 adj.
borough
district 184 n.
electorate 605 n.
borrow
copy 20 vb.
borrow 785 vb.
borrowed plumes
sham 542 n.
borrowing 785 n.
borscht
hors-d'oeuvres
301 n.
Borstal
school 539 n.
prison 748 n.
Borvo or Bormo
Celtic deities
967 n.
borzoi
dog 365 n.
bosh
silly talk 515 n.
bosom
receptacle 194 n.
insides 224 n.
interiority 224 n.
garment 228 n.
bosom 253 n.
spirit 447 n.
affections 817 n.
bosom friend
close friend 880 n.
bosom pal
close friend 880 n.
boss
superior 34 n.
roughen 259 vb.
meddle 678 vb.
direct 689 vb.
director 690 n.
dominate 733 vb.
tyrant 735 n.
autocrat 741 n.
master 741 n.
ornamental art
844 n.
bossa nova
dance 837 n.
boss-eyed
dim-sighted
440 adj.

BOT

bossy
authoritative
733 adj.
authoritarian
735 adj.
Boston two-step
dance 837 n.
bosun
mariner 270 n.
botanical garden
botany 368 n.
garden 370 n.
botanist
botany 368 n.
botany
botany 368 n.
botch
distort 246 vb.
neglect 458 vb.
blunder 495 vb.
misrepresent
552 vb.
misrepresentation
552 vb.
impair 655 vb.
be clumsy 695 vb.
bungling 695 n.
fail 728 vb.
botch-up
mistake 495 n.
both
dual 90 adj.
bother
commotion 318 n.
be attentive 455 vb.
distract 456 vb.
activity 678 n.
meddle 678 vb.
be difficult 700 vb.
excitable state
822 n.
worry 825 n.
torment 827 vb.
enrage 891 vb.
bothy
small house 192 n.
bottle
vessel 194 n.
draught 301 n.
store 632 vb.
preserve 666 vb.
bottleneck
contraction 198 n.
narrowness 206 n.
play music 413 vb.
obstacle 702 n.

BOU

bottle party
participation
775 n.
festivity 837 n.
social gathering
882 n.
bottle up
remember 505 vb.
conceal 525 vb.
restrain 747 vb.
bottom
extremity 69 n.
lowness 210 n.
depth 211 n.
base 214 n.
support 218 vb.
buttocks 238 n.
ship 275 n.
bottom dollar
extremity 69 n.
bottom drawer
store 632 n.
preparation 669 n.
bottomless
deep 211 adj.
bottomless pit
depth 211 n.
hell 972 n.
bottom line
utility 640 n.
reward 962 n.
bottom out
decrease 37 vb.
become small
198 vb.
be horizontal
216 vb.
descend 309 vb.
bottoms up
bon appétit 301 int.
botulism
digestive disorders
651 n.
infection 651 n.
bouclé
rough 259 adj.
boudoir
chamber 194 n.
bouffant
convex 253 adj.
bough
branch 53 n.
foliage 366 n.
tree 366 n.
bouillabaisse
hors-d'oeuvres
301 n.

bouillon
  hors-d'oeuvres
    301 n.
boulder
  bulk 195 n.
  sphere 252 n.
  hardness 326 n.
  rock 344 n.
boules
  ball game 837 n.
boulevard
  park 192 n.
  path 624 n.
bounce
  recoil 280 n.
  eject 300 vb.
  ascend 308 vb.
  ascent 308 n.
  leap 312 vb.
  oscillate 317 vb.
  agitation 318 n.
  be agitated 318 vb.
  elasticity 328 n.
bounce back
  regress 286 vb.
  be restored 656 vb.
bouncer
  protector 660 n.
bouncing
  vigorous 174 adj.
  healthy 650 adj.
  cheerful 833 adj.
  insolent 878 adj.
bound
  tied 45 adj.
  hem 234 vb.
  limit 236 vb.
  move fast 277 vb.
  spurt 277 n.
  leap 312 n.
  leap 312 vb.
  certain 473 adj.
  restrained 747 adj.
  promised 764 n.
  obliged 917 adj.
bound, be
  affirm 532 vb.
boundaries
  region 184 n.
boundary
  extremity 69 n.
  edge 234 n.
  limit 236 n.
bounden duty
  duty 917 n.
bounder
  cad 938 n.

bound for
  directed 281 adj.
boundless
  infinite 107 adj.
  spacious 183 adj.
bounds
  region 184 n.
  place 185 n.
  outline 233 n.
  edge 234 n.
bound to be
  certain 473 adj.
bounteous
  liberal 813 adj.
  benevolent 897 adj.
bountiful
  liberal 813 adj.
  benevolent 897 adj.
bounty
  subvention 703 n.
  gift 781 n.
  liberality 813 n.
  reward 962 n.
bouquet
  bunch 74 n.
  savouriness 390 n.
  odour 394 n.
  fragrance 396 n.
  trophy 729 n.
  ornamentation
    844 n.
  honours 866 n.
  courteous act
    884 n.
  applause 923 n.
  praise 923 n.
bouquet garni
  herb 301 n.
bouquets
  victory 727 n.
  rejoicing 835 n.
  congratulation
    886 n.
  endearment 889 n.
  flattery 925 n.
  reward 962 n.
bourbon
  alcoholic drink
    301 n.
bourgeois
  tedious 838 adj.
  plebeian 869 adj.
bourgeois(e)
  commonalty 869 n.
  commoner 869 n.
  middle classes
    869 n.

bourse
  market 796 n.
bout
  period 110 n.
  labour 682 n.
  pugilism 716 n.
boutique
  clothier 228 n.
  shop 796 n.
bovine
  animal 365 adj.
  unintelligent
    499 adj.
  apathetic 820 adj.
  impassive 820 adj.
bovver boy
  violent creature
    176 n.
  combatant 722 n.
  rioter 738 n.
  low fellow 869 n.
  ruffian 904 n.
  bad person 938 n.
bow
  be curved 248 vb.
  curve 248 n.
  loop 250 n.
  camber 253 n.
  propellant 287 n.
  obeisance 311 n.
  stoop 311 vb.
  play music 413 vb.
  viol 414 n.
  knuckle under
    721 vb.
  missile weapon
    723 n.
  trimming 844 n.
  servility 879 n.
  courteous act
    884 n.
  greet 884 vb.
  respects 920 n.
  show respect
    920 vb.
  be pious 979 vb.
  perform ritual
    988 vb.
bow at a venture
  uncertainty 474 n.
bowdlerize
  exclude 57 vb.
  purify 648 vb.
bow down
  descend 309 vb.
  stoop 311 vb.
  be humble 872 vb.

bow down before
  worship 981 vb.
bowel movement
  defecation 302 n.
bowels
  insides 224 n.
bowels of the earth
  depth 211 n.
bower
  pavilion 192 n.
  arbour 194 n.
  screen 421 n.
bowie knife
  sharp edge 256 n.
bowing
  servile 879 adj.
  respectful 920 adj.
  ritual act 988 n.
bowing and scraping
  submitting 721 adj.
  servility 879 n.
  respectful 920 adj.
bowl
  bowl 194 n.
  cavity 255 n.
  missile 287 n.
  propel 287 vb.
  draught 301 n.
  rotate 315 vb.
  tobacco 388 n.
bowl along
  travel 267 vb.
  move fast 277 vb.
bow-legged
  deformed 246 adj.
  curved 248 adj.
bowler
  headgear 228 n.
  player 837 n.
bowling
  propulsion 287 n.
bowling alley
  arena 724 n.
  place of amuse-
    ment 837 n.
bowling green
  horizontality
    216 n.
  smoothness 258 n.
  arena 724 n.
  pleasure ground
    837 n.
bowl one over
  surprise 508 vb.
bowl out
  dismiss 300 vb.
  defeat 727 vb.

bowl over
　disable 161 vb.
　fell 311 vb.
　be wonderful
　　864 vb.
bowls
　ball game 837 n.
bow out
　depart 296 vb.
bowsprit
　projection 254 n.
Bow-street runner
　law officer 955 n.
bow tie
　neckwear 228 n.
bow to
　be inferior 35 vb.
　submit 721 vb.
bow-wow
　dog 365 n.
box
　small house 192 n.
　box 194 n.
　compartment
　　194 n.
　cover 226 vb.
　circumscribe
　　232 vb.
　strike 279 vb.
　tree 366 n.
　theatre 594 n.
　fight 716 vb.
box, the
　broadcasting
　　531 n.
box camera
　camera 442 n.
boxer
　dog 365 n.
　pugilist 722 n.
boxer shorts
　underwear 228 n.
box girder
　beam 218 n.
boxing
　defence 713 n.
　pugilism 716 n.
boxing match
　pugilism 716 n.
box-kite
　airship 276 n.
box office
　onlookers 441 n.
　theatre 594 n.
　treasury 799 n.
box-office hit
　dramaturgy 594 n.

　success 727 n.
box of tricks
　stratagem 698 n.
box on the ear
　knock 279 n.
　anger 891 n.
　reprimand 924 n.
　corporal punish-
　　ment 963 n.
　spank 963 vb.
box pleat
　fold 261 n.
boxroom
　storage 632 n.
box the compass
　orientate 281 vb.
boy
　youngster 132 n.
　male 372 n.
boycott
　separation 46 n.
　set apart 46 vb.
　exclude 57 vb.
　exclusion 57 n.
　hindrance 702 n.
　unsociability
　　883 n.
　disapprobation
　　924 n.
boyfriend
　male 372 n.
　friend 880 n.
　lover 887 n.
boyhood
　youth 130 n.
boyish
　young 130 adj.
　immature 670 adj.
Boy Scouts
　band 74 n.
　society 708 n.
boys in blue, the
　police 955 n.
bra
　underwear 228 n.
brace
　fastening 47 n.
　group 74 n.
　duality 90 n.
　strengthen 162 vb.
　support 218 n.
　support 218 vb.
　notation 410 n.
　punctuation 547 n.
　refresh 685 vb.
brace and bit
　perforator 263 n.

bracelet
　circle 250 n.
　loop 250 n.
　jewellery 844 n.
brace oneself
　be resolute 599 vb.
　prepare oneself
　　669 vb.
braces
　fastening 47 n.
　hanger 217 n.
　underwear 228 n.
bracing
　vigorous 174 adj.
　refreshing 685 adj.
bracken
　plant 366 n.
bracket
　equalize 28 vb.
　join 45 vb.
　bond 47 n.
　classification 77 n.
　pair 90 vb.
　shelf 218 n.
　support 218 n.
　　See **shelf**
　angularity 247 n.
brackets
　punctuation 547 n.
bracket with
　liken 18 vb.
brackish
　salty 388 adj.
bradawl
　perforator 263 n.
Bradshaw
　directory 87 n.
　itinerary 267 n.
　guidebook 524 n.
brae
　high land 209 n.
brag
　defy 711 vb.
　boast 877 n.
　boast 877 vb.
　be insolent 878 vb.
braggart
　insolent person
　　878 n.
Bragi
　Nordic deities
　　967 n.
Brahma
　divineness 965 n.
　Hindu deities
　　967 n.

Brahman
　aristocrat 868 n.
Brahmana
　non-Biblical scrip-
　　ture 975 n.
Brahmin
　priest 986 n.
Brahminism
　ecclesiasticism
　　985 n.
braid
　tie 45 vb.
　ligature 47 n.
　strip 208 n.
　crossing 222 n.
　weave 222 vb.
　hair 259 n.
　fold 261 n.
　variegate 437 vb.
　trimming 844 n.
Braille
　blindness 439 n.
　writing 586 n.
brain
　head 213 n.
　kill 362 vb.
　render insensible
　　375 vb.
　intellect 447 n.
　intelligence 498 n.
brain-child
　product 104 n.
　idea 451 n.
brain death
　decease 361 n.
brainless
　mindless 448 adj.
brains
　intellect 447 n.
　intelligence 498 n.
　planner 623 n.
brain scanner
　hospital 658 n.
brainstorm
　neurosis 503 n.
　contrivance 623 n.
brains trust
　interrogation
　　459 n.
　consignee 754 n.
brain surgery
　head 213 n.
　surgery 658 n.
brain-teaser
　question 459 n.
　enigma 530 n.

brainwash
convert 147 vb.
influence 178 vb.
teach 534 vb.
habituate 610 vb.
pervert 655 vb.
brainwave
product 164 n.
idea 451 n.
intelligence 498 n.
contrivance 623 n.
brainy
intelligent 498 adj.
braise
cook 301 vb.
brake
halt 145 vb.
moderator 177 n.
bring to rest
  266 vb.
carriage 274 n.
retard 278 vb.
slowness 278 n.
wood 366 n.
safeguard 662 n.
hinder 702 vb.
restrain 747 vb.
restraint 747 n.
fetter 748 n.
brake light
lamp 420 n.
bramble
prickle 256 n.
plant 366 n.
bran
cereals 301 n.
powder 332 n.
grass 366 n.
rubbish 641 n.
branch
branch 53 n.
be dispersed 75 vb.
classification 77 n.
descendant 170 n.
extend 183 vb.
nest 192 n.
filament 208 n.
stream 350 n.
foliage 366 n.
tree 366 n.
sect 978 n.
branch off
bifurcate 92 vb.
diverge 294 vb.
branch out
be dispersed 75 vb.
deviate 282 vb.

diverge 294 vb.
brand
sort 77 n.
burn 381 vb.
burning 381 n.
furnace 383 n.
torch 420 n.
identification
  547 n.
label 547 n.
mark 547 vb.
blemish 845 vb.
shame 867 vb.
slur 867 n.
censure 924 n.
criticize 924 vb.
defame 926 vb.
detraction 926 n.
accuse 928 vb.
branded
proprietary
  777 adj.
brandish
brandish 317 vb.
use 673 vb.
brand-new
new 126 adj.
brandy
alcoholic drink
  301 n.
brandysnap
pastries and cakes
  301 n.
brash
piece 53 n.
insolent 878 adj.
brass
a mixture 43 n.
blowing 352 n.
stridor 407 n.
orchestra 413 n.
horn 414 n.
musical instrument
  414 n.
yellowness 433 n.
monument 548 n.
badge of rank
  743 n.
shekels 797 n.
wealth 800 n.
sauciness 878 n.
brass band
band 74 n.
orchestra 413 n.
brasserie
café 192 n.

brass farthing
trifle 639 n.
brass hat
bigwig 638 n.
army officer 741 n.
brassiere
underwear 228 n.
brass-necked
insolent 878 adj.
brass plate
label 547 n.
brass rubbing
picture 553 n.
brass tacks
reality 1 n.
brat
child 132 n.
bravado
ostentation 875 n.
boast 877 n.
boasting 877 n.
insolence 878 n.
brave
defy 711 vb.
combatant 722 n.
soldier 722 n.
be courageous
  855 vb.
brave person 855 n.
courage 855 n.
courageous
  855 adj.
showy 875 adj.
brave it out
be insolent 878 vb.
bravery
courage 855 n.
ostentation 875 n.
bravo
ruffian 904 n.
bravo 923 int.
bravura
vocal music 412 n.
defiance 711 n.
pageant 875 n.
brawl
turmoil 61 n.
quarrel 709 n.
quarrel 709 vb.
fight 716 n.
brawn
vitality 162 n.
meat 301 n.
brawny
stalwart 162 adj.
fleshy 195 adj.

bray
be loud 400 vb.
loudness 400 n.
resonance 404 n.
resound 404 vb.
rasp 407 vb.
ululate 409 vb.
brazen
thick-skinned
  820 adj.
insolent 878 adj.
impenitent
  940 adj.
unchaste 951 adj.
brazen-faced
insolent 878 adj.
brazen it out
be obstinate
  602 vb.
be insolent 878 vb.
brazier
furnace 383 n.
breach
disagreement 25 n.
disunion 46 n.
gap 201 n.
dissension 709 n.
enmity 881 n.
undueness 916 n.
breach of promise
untruth 543 n.
perfidy 930 n.
breach of the peace
turmoil 61 n.
quarrel 709 n.
revolt 738 n.
bread
cereals 301 n.
food 301 n.
shekels 797 n.
bread and wine
the sacrament
  988 n.
bread-knife
sharp edge 256 n.
breadline
needfulness 627 n.
sufficiency 635 n.
insufficiency 636 n.
poverty 801 n.
Bread of Life
God the Son 965 n.
breadth
breadth 205 n.
metrology 465 n.

breadthways
broadways
205 adv.
breadthwise
broadways
205 adv.
breadwinner
worker 686 n.
break
break 46 vb.
disunion 46 n.
separate 46 vb.
incompleteness
55 n.
discontinue 72 vb.
discontinuity 72 n.
opportunity 137 n.
change 143 n.
lull 145 n.
continuance 146 n.
disable 161 vb.
gap 201 n.
interval 201 n.
deviation 282 n.
pain 377 n.
appear 445 vb.
be disclosed
526 vb.
dramaturgy 594 n.
leisure 681 n.
repose 683 n.
refreshment 685 n.
defeat 727 vb.
prosperity 730 n.
oppress 735 vb.
breakable
brittle 330 adj.
break a law
be unconformable
84 vb.
break all the rules
behave 688 vb.
break away
be dispersed 75 vb.
run away 620 vb.
escape 667 vb.
quarrel 709 vb.
revolt 738 vb.
fail in duty 918 vb.
breakaway
revolt 738 n.
independent
744 adj.
undutiful 918 adj.
undutifulness
918 n.
schism 978 n.

schismatical
978 adj.
break bread
eat 301 vb.
break camp
decamp 296 vb.
breakdancing
agitation 318 n.
dance 837 n.
dancing 837 n.
break down
decompose 51 vb.
simplify 44 vb.
disunite 46 vb.
demolish 165 vb.
fall short 307 vb.
deteriorate 655 vb.
fail 728 vb.
weep 836 vb.
breakdown
separation 46 n.
decomposition
51 n.
stop 145 n.
helplessness 161 n.
ruin 165 n.
illness 651 n.
hitch 702 n.
failure 728 n.
breaker
rider 268 n.
wave 350 n.
break even
be equal 28 vb.
acquire 771 vb.
break faith
be false 541 vb.
be dishonest
930 vb.
breakfast
eat 301 vb.
meal 301 n.
breakfasting
eating 301 n.
break in
intrude 297 vb.
break in 369 vb.
breaking
separation 46 n.
**breaking and enter-
ing**
stealing 788 n.
breaking-off
stop 145 n.
breaking-off point
completion 725 n.

break in two
break 46 vb.
break in upon
discontinue 72 vb.
intrude 297 vb.
break it up
make peace
719 vb.
breakneck
sloping 220 adj.
speedy 277 adj.
hasty 680 adj.
rash 857 adj.
break off
be incomplete
55 vb.
discontinue 72 vb.
cease 145 vb.
break one's fast
eat 301 vb.
break one's heart
sadden 834 vb.
break one's neck
perish 361 vb.
break one's word
not observe 769 vb.
be dishonest
930 vb.
break out
emerge 298 vb.
escape 667 vb.
breakout
egress 298 n.
escape 667 n.
break the ice
initiate 68 vb.
befriend 880 vb.
break the law
disobey 738 vb.
do wrong 914 adj.
be illegal 954 vb.
break the news
inform 524 vb.
break through
escape 667 vb.
succeed 727 vb.
breakthrough
attack 712 n.
success 727 n.
break up
break 46 vb.
disunite 46 vb.
separate 46 vb.
sunder 46 vb.
decompose 51 vb.
be disordered
61 vb.

be dispersed 75 vb.
disperse 75 vb.
be destroyed
165 vb.
demolish 165 vb.
make useless
641 vb.
laugh 835 vb.
divorce 896 vb.
breakup
disunion 46 n.
decomposition
51 n.
finality 69 n.
dispersion 75 n.
ruin 165 n.
divorce 896 n.
break water
navigate 269 vb.
ascend 308 vb.
breakwater
projection 254 n.
safeguard 662 n.
break wind
eruct 300 vb.
break with
quarrel 709 vb.
break with custom
be unconformable
84 vb.
bream
fish 365 n.
breast
insides 224 n.
interiority 224 n.
be in front 237 vb.
meat 301 n.
climb 308 vb.
spirit 447 n.
affections 817 n.
breast-feeding
bosom 253 n.
breasts
bosom 253 n.
breast stroke
aquatics 269 vb.
breast the tide
withstand 704 vb.
breath
small quantity
33 n.
instant 116 n.
breathalyser
testing agent
461 n.
detector 484 n.

breathe
be 1 vb.
pass time 108 vb.
breathe 352 vb.
sound faint 401 vb.
hint 524 vb.
divulge 526 vb.
voice 577 vb.
speak 579 vb.
breathe in
absorb 299 vb.
breathe 352 vb.
breathe one's last
die 361 vb.
breathe out
emit 300 vb.
breathe 352 vb.
breather
lull 145 n.
interval 201 n.
repose 683 n.
refreshment 685 n.
breathing
periodical 141 adj.
oscillation 317 n.
respiration 352 n.
alive 360 adj.
life 360 n.
breathless
voiceless 578 adj.
fervent 818 adj.
nervous 854 adj.
breath of air
breeze 352 n.
refreshment 685 n.
breathtaking
prodigious 32 adj.
wonderful 864 adj.
breed
character 5 n.
race 11 n.
grow 36 vb.
group 74 n.
breed 77 n.
produce 164 vb.
reproduce 166 vb.
generate 167 vb.
reproduce itself
167 vb.
posterity 170 n.
breed stock 369 vb.
mature 669 vb.
breeder
breeder 369 n.
breeding
production 164 n.
propagation 167 n.

animal husbandry
369 n.
conduct 688 n.
good taste 846 n.
etiquette 848 n.
breeze
breeze 352 n.
breezy
airy 340 adj.
windy 352 adj.
cheerful 833 adj.
disrespectful
921 adj.
breve
notation 410 n.
punctuation 547 n.
breviary
scripture 975 n.
prayers 981 n.
brevity
smallness 33 n.
brief span 114 n.
shortness 204 n.
conciseness 569 n.
brew
a mixture 43 n.
mix 43 vb.
alcoholic drink
301 n.
hors-d'oeuvres
301 n.
mature 669 vb.
brewery
workshop 687 n.
brewing
impending 155 adj.
production 164 n.
preparatory
669 adj.
ripening 669 n.
bribe
compensate 31 vb.
bribe 612 vb.
incentive 612 n.
offer 759 n.
offer 759 vb.
gift 781 n.
purchase 792 vb.
pay 804 n.
reward 962 n.
bribery
inducement 612 n.
bribery and corruption
inducement 612 n.
bric-a-brac
bauble 639 n.

ornamentation
844 n.
brick
hardness 326 n.
pottery 381 n.
building material
631 n.
missile weapon
723 n.
good person 937 n.
brickbat
missile 287 n.
slur 867 n.
indignity 921 n.
reproach 924 n.
calumny 926 n.
bricks and mortar
housing 192 n.
building material
631 n.
brickwork
structure 331 n.
bridal
wedding 894 n.
bride
female 373 n.
spouse 894 n.
bridegroom
male 372 n.
spouse 894 n.
bridesmaid
auxiliary 707 n.
close friend 880 n.
bridal party 894 n.
bridge
connect 45 vb.
layer 207 n.
vertex 213 n.
tooth 256 n.
pass 305 vb.
viol 414 n.
bridge 624 n.
prepare 669 vb.
bridle
affix 45 vb.
start out 296 vb.
break in 369 vb.
restrain 747 vb.
restraint 747 n.
fetter 748 n.
get angry 891 vb.
brief
small 33 adj.
brief 114 adj.
short 204 adj.
inform 524 vb.
concise 569 adj.

description 590 n.
compendium
592 n.
function 622 n.
make ready
669 vb.
preparation 669 n.
command 737 n.
command 737 vb.
briefcase
box 194 n.
case 194 n.
briefing
information 524 n.
preparation 669 n.
advice 691 n.
briefs
underwear 228 n.
brigade
bring together
74 vb.
group 74 n.
formation 722 n.
brigadier
army officer 741 n.
brigand
robber 789 n.
bright
modernist 126 n.
luminous 417 adj.
undimmed
417 adj.
luminary 420 n.
florid 425 adj.
white 427 adj.
yellow 433 adj.
green 434 adj.
intelligent 498 adj.
contrivance 623 n.
active 678 adj.
cheerful 833 adj.
promising 852 adj.
noteworthy
866 adj.
brighten
make bright
417 vb.
be cheerful 833 vb.
brightness
light 417 n.
intelligence 498 n.
wit 839 n.
brilliance
light 417 n.
hue 425 n.
intelligence 498 n.
prestige 866 n.

ostentation 875 n.

brilliant
  luminous 417 adj.
  florid 425 adj.
  intelligent 498 adj.
  perfect 646 adj.
  witty 839 adj.
  noteworthy
    866 adj.
  ostentatious
    875 adj.

brim
  fill 54 vb.
  edge 234 n.
  abound 635 vb.

brim over
  superabound
    637 vb.

brine
  water 339 n.
  ocean 343 n.
  pungency 388 n.
  preserver 666 n.

bring
  happen 154 vb.
  cause 156 vb.
  produce 164 vb.
  carry 273 vb.
  manifest 522 vb.
  induce 612 vb.
  carry out 725 vb.
  divorce 896 vb.
  indict 928 vb.

bring down
  fell 311 vb.
  strike at 712 vb.

bring forth
  reproduce itself
    167 vb.
  manifest 522 vb.

bring in
  admit 299 vb.
  cost 809 vb.

bring it off
  succeed 727 vb.

bring on
  cause 156 vb.
  mature 669 vb.

bring out
  cause 156 vb.
  manifest 522 vb.
  print 587 vb.

bring round
  assuage 177 vb.
  convince 485 vb.
  induce 612 vb.

bring to
  bring to rest
    266 vb.

bring to bear
  use 673 vb.

bring to book
  punish 963 vb.

bring together
  bring together
    74 vb.
  compare 462 vb.
  pacify 719 vb.
  mediate 720 vb.

bring to light
  discover 484 vb.
  manifest 522 vb.

bring up
  produce 164 vb.
  generate 167 vb.
  vomit 300 vb.
  manifest 522 vb.
  educate 534 vb.

brink
  extremity 69 n.
  nearness 200 n.
  edge 234 n.

brinkmanship
  tactics 688 n.
  rashness 857 n.

briquette
  coal 385 n.

brisk
  brief 114 adj.
  vigorous 174 adj.
  speedy 277 adj.
  concise 569 adj.
  active 678 adj.

bristle
  be vertical 215 vb.
  prickle 256 n.
  be rough 259 vb.
  hair 259 n.
  roughness 259 n.
  elevate 310 vb.
  get angry 891 vb.
  threaten 900 vb.

bristle with
  be many 104 vb.
  be sharp 256 vb.
  abound 635 vb.
  superabound
    637 vb.

brittle
  brittle 330 adj.

broach
  initiate 68 vb.
  cause 156 vb.

perforator 263 n.
  empty 300 vb.
  publish 528 vb.
  offer 759 vb.

B road
  road 624 n.

broad
  general 79 adj.
  spacious 183 adj.
  broad 205 adj.
  female 373 n.
  inexact 495 adj.
  dialectal 560 adj.
  prostitute 952 n.

broadcast
  disperse 75 vb.
  generalize 79 vb.
  let fall 311 vb.
  communicate
    524 vb.
  publication 528 n.
  publish 528 vb.
  broadcast 531 n.
  oration 579 n.

broadcasting
  dispersion 75 n.
  publication 528 n.
  broadcasting
    531 n.

broad daylight
  light 417 n.

broaden
  augment 36 vb.
  generalize 79 vb.
  enlarge 197 vb.
  expand 197 vb.

broadminded
  free 744 adj.

broadside
  laterality 239 n.
  bombardment
    712 n.
  gun 723 n.

Broadway
  drama 594 n.

Brobdingnagian
  giant 195 n.
  huge 195 adj.

brocade
  textile 222 n.

broccoli
  fruit and vegetables
    301 n.

brochure
  the press 528 n.
  book 589 n.

compendium
    592 n.

brogue
  speciality 80 n.
  dialect 560 adj.
  pronunciation
    577 n.
  speech defect
    580 n.

brogues
  footwear 228 n.

broil
  cook 301 vb.
  be hot 379 vb.
  fight 716 n.

broke
  poor 801 adj.

broken
  fragmentary
    53 adj.
  discontinuous
    72 adj.
  imperfect 647 adj.
  dilapidated
    655 adj.

broken-hearted
  unhappy 825 adj.

broken in
  habituated 610 adj.

broken thread
  discontinuity 72 n.

broker
  intermediary
    231 n.
  consignee 754 n.
  merchant 794 n.

brokerage
  barter 791 n.

bromide
  moderator 177 n.
  maxim 496 n.
  print 587 n.

bronchitis
  respiratory disease
    651 n.

bronze
  a mixture 43 n.
  brown 430 adj.
  brown 430 vb.
  brownness 430 n.
  sculpture 554 n.

brooch
  fastening 47 n.
  jewellery 844 n.

brood
  group 74 n.

BRO

young creature
132 n.
posterity 170 n.
meditate 449 vb.
be dejected 834 vb.
brood upon
meditate 449 vb.
brook
stream 350 n.
permit 756 vb.
be patient 823 vb.
broom
cleaning utensil
648 n.
broomstick
thinness 206 n.
magic instrument
983 n.
broth
hors-d'oeuvres
301 n.
brothel
brothel 951 n.
brother
compeer 28 n.
male 372 n.
colleague 707 n.
friend 880 n.
church title 986 n.
monk 986 n.
brotherhood
family 11 n.
group 74 n.
community 708 n.
friendship 880 n.
sect 978 n.
monk 986 n.
brouhaha
violence 176 n.
commotion 318 n.
brow
head 213 n.
vertex 213 n.
dome 253 n.
protuberance
254 n.
browbeat
induce 612 vb.
See **motivate**
frighten 854 vb.
be insolent 878 vb.
reprove 924 vb.
brown
cook 301 vb.
dry 342 adj.
brown 430 adj.
brown 430 vb.

BRU

brownness 430 n.
browned off
discontented
829 adj.
dejected 834 adj.
bored 838 adj.
brownie
elf 970 n.
brownies
pastries and cakes
301 n.
browse
graze 301 vb.
study 536 vb.
bruise
force 176 vb.
pulverize 332 vb.
pain 377 n.
touch 378 vb.
black thing 428 n.
evil 616 n.
ill-treat 645 vb.
wound 655 n.
wound 655 vb.
blemish 845 n.
bruited abroad, be
be published
528 vb.
brunch
meal 301 n.
brunette
female 373 n.
black 428 adj.
brown 430 adj.
brownness 430 n.
a beauty 841 n.
brunt
collision 279 n.
difficulty 700 n.
brush
district 184 n.
be contiguous
202 vb.
rear 238 n.
smoother 258 n.
rub 333 vb.
touch 378 vb.
clean 648 vb.
cleaning utensil
648 n.
fight 716 n.
battle 718 n.
brush aside
confute 479 vb.
hasten 680 vb.
brush-off
repulsion 292 n.

BUB

brush up
study 536 vb.
clean 648 vb.
brushwood
wood 366 n.
fuel 385 n.
brushwork
painting 553 n.
brusque
concise 569 adj.
taciturn 582 adj.
sullen 893 adj.
brutal
violent 176 adj.
oppressive 735 adj.
cruel 898 adj.
pitiless 906 adj.
heinous 934 adj.
vicious 934 adj.
brutalize
pervert 655 vb.
make wicked
934 vb.
brute
violent creature
176 n.
animal 365 n.
tyrant 735 n.
rude person 885 n.
ruffian 904 n.
monster 938 n.
B-side
rear 238 n.
bubble
insubstantial thing
4 n.
brief span 114 n.
minuteness 196 n.
lightness 323 n.
flow 350 VB.
bubble 355 n.
bubble 355 vb.
deception 542 n.
bubble gum
sweets 301 n.
elasticity 328 n.
bubble pack
wrapping 226 n.
transparency
422 n.
bubbly
wine 301 n.
light 323 adj.
bubbly 355 adj.
fervent 818 adj.
lively 819 adj.
merry 833 adj.

BUD

buccaneer
mariner 270 n.
militarist 722 n.
robber 789 n.
buck
leap 312 vb.
mammal 365 n.
male animal
372 n.
coinage 797 n.
funds 797 n.
paper money
797 n.
bucket
vessel 194 n.
rain 350 VB.
bucket shop
stock exchange
618 n.
market 796 n.
buckle
join 45 vb.
break 46 vb.
fastening 47 n.
distort 246 vb.
distortion 246 n.
make concave
255 vb.
buckler
armour 713 n.
buckle to
be resolute 599 vb.
undertake 672 vb.
be active 678 vb.
buckshot
ammunition 723 n.
buck up
hurry up 680 int.
animate 821 vb.
relieve 831 vb.
be cheerful 833 vb.
cheer 833 vb.
give courage
855 vb.
bud
grow 36 vb.
origin 68 n.
source 156 n.
growth 157 n.
result 157 vb.
generate 167 vb.
expand 197 vb.
swelling 253 n.
implant 303 vb.
flower 366 n.
Buddhism
philosophy 449 n.

religious faith
973 n.
budding
beginning 68 adj.
young 130 adj.
buddy
male 372 n.
colleague 707 n.
chum 880 n.
budge
be in motion
265 vb.
move 265 vb.
budget
provide 633 vb.
account 808 vb.
accounts 808 n.
budget account
credit 802 n.
budgetary
monetary 797 adj.
accounting
808 adj.
buff
skin 226 n.
smooth 258 vb.
rub 333 vb.
brown 430 adj.
enthusiast 504 n.
clean 648 vb.
buff, the
bareness 229 n.
buffer
intermediary
231 n.
male 372 n.
protection 660 n.
obstacle 702 n.
defence 713 n.
buffet
café 192 n.
cabinet 194 n.
knock 279 n.
strike 279 vb.
evil 616 n.
ill-treat 645 vb.
corporal punish-
ment 963 n.
buffoon
fool 501 n.
bungler 697 n.
humorist 839 n.
laughingstock
851 n.
bug
insect 365 n.
hear 415 vb.

be curious 453 vb.
infection 651 n.
failure 728 n.
torment 827 n.
enrage 891 vb.
bugbear
bane 659 n.
intimidation
854 n.
hateful object
888 n.
demon 970 n.
buggery
illicit love 951 n.
Buggin's turn
sequence 65 n.
buggy
automobile 274 n.
carriage 274 n.
pushcart 274 n.
bugle
play music 413 vb.
horn 414 n.
call 547 n.
build
compose 56 vb.
composition 56 n.
produce 164 vb.
form 243 n.
form 243 vb.
elevate 310 vb.
structure 331 n.
builder
producer 164 n.
artisan 686 n.
building
edifice 164 n.
place 185 n.
house 192 n.
building site
workshop 687 n.
building society
pawnshop 784 n.
treasury 799 n.
build up
augment 36 vb.
make complete
54 vb.
bring together
74 vb.
strengthen 162 vb.
enlarge 197 vb.
make higher
209 vb.
elevate 310 vb.
buildup
increase 36 n.

overestimation
482 n.
advertisement
528 n.
store 632 n.
built-in
intrinsic 5 adj.
component 58 adj.
interior 224 adj.
built-up area
district 184 n.
housing 192 n.
bulb
source 156 n.
sphere 252 n.
swelling 253 n.
plant 366 n.
lamp 420 n.
bulge
grow 36 vb.
increment 36 n.
convexity 253 n.
swelling 253 n.
bulging
full 54 adj.
convex 253 adj.
projecting 254 adj.
bulimia nervosa
eating 301 n.
disease 651 n.
bulk
quantity 26 n.
chief part 52 n.
bulk 195 n.
size 195 n.
enlarge 197 vb.
food content 301 n.
bulky
substantial 3 adj.
great 32 adj.
large 195 adj.
bull
cattle 365 n.
male animal
372 n.
mistake 495 n.
silly talk 515 n.
falsehood 541 n.
fool 542 vb.
fable 543 n.
exaggerate 546 vb.
gambler 618 n.
labour 682 n.
decree 737 n.
purchaser 792 n.
overcharge 811 vb.

ridiculousness
849 n.
bulldog
dog 365 n.
brave person 855 n.
bulldoze
demolish 165 vb.
collide 279 vb.
necessitate 596 vb.
compel 740 vb.
bulldozer
destroyer 168 n.
flattener 216 n.
smoother 258 n.
vehicle 274 n.
ram 279 n.
pulverizer 332 n.
bullet
sphere 252 n.
missile 287 n.
ammunition 723 n.
missile weapon
723 n.
means of execution
964 n.
bulletin
report 524 n.
news 529 n.
correspondence
588 n.
bulletproof
strong 162 adj.
invulnerable
660 adj.
resisting 715 adj.
bull in a china shop
bungler 697 n.
bullion
money 797 n.
bullish
prosperous 730 adj.
dear 811 adj.
bullock
beast of burden
273 n.
cattle 365 n.
male animal
372 n.
bullring
duel 716 n.
arena 724 n.
bull's-eye
centre 225 n.
objective 617 n.
bull terrier
dog 365 n.

bully
 violent creature
  176 n.
 super 644 adj.
 combatant 722 n.
 oppress 735 vb.
 tyrant 735 n.
 torment 827 vb.
 frighten 854 vb.
 desperado 857 n.
 low fellow 869 n.
 be insolent 878 vb.
 insolent person
  878 n.
 be malevolent
  898 vb.
 threaten 900 vb.
 ruffian 904 n.
 bad person 938 n.
bulwark
 support 218 n.
 protection 660 n.
 obstacle 702 n.
 defence 713 n.
 fortification 713 n.
bum
 buttocks 238 n.
 wanderer 268 n.
 idler 679 n.
 beg 761 vb.
 beggar 763 n.
 take 786 vb.
 poor person 801 n.
 low fellow 869 n.
bum around
 wander 267 vb.
bumble
 be clumsy 695 vb.
bumble bee
 insect 365 n.
bumf
 reading matter
  589 n.
 governance 733 n.
bump
 convexity 253 n.
 swelling 253 n.
 protuberance
  254 n.
 be rough 259 vb.
 collision 279 n.
 agitation 318 n.
 faintness 401 n.
 nonresonance
  405 n.
 wound 655 n.

bumper
 plenitude 54 n.
 intermediary
  231 n.
 draught 301 n.
 shelter 662 n.
 defence 713 n.
bumper-to-bumper
 near 200 adj.
bump into
 chance 159 vb.
 collide 279 vb.
 meet 295 vb.
bumpkin
 country-dweller
  869 n.
bump off
 murder 362 vb.
bumptious
 proud 871 adj.
 vain 873 adj.
 insolent 878 adj.
bumpy
 nonuniform 17 adj.
 discontinuous
  72 adj.
 convex 253 adj.
 rough 259 adj.
bun
 hair 259 n.
 cereals 301 n.
 hairdressing 843 n.
bunch
 cohere 48 vb.
 band 74 n.
 bring together
  74 vb.
 bunch 74 n.
 congregate 74 vb.
 crowd 74 n.
bunfight
 feasting 301 n.
 amusement 837 n.
 festivity 837 n.
bung
 covering 226 n.
 stopper 264 n.
 propel 287 vb.
bungalow
 house 192 n.
bungle
 lose a chance
  138 vb.
 neglect 458 vb.
 blunder 495 vb.
 mistake 495 n.
 be clumsy 695 vb.

bungling 695 n.
 fail 728 vb.
 failure 728 n.
 fail in duty 918 vb.
bunion
 swelling 253 n.
bunk
 bed 218 n.
 empty talk 515 n.
bunker
 cellar 194 n.
 storage 632 n.
 defences 713 n.
bunkum
 empty talk 515 n.
 falsehood 541 n.
 boast 877 n.
bunting
 flag 547 n.
 celebration 876 n.
buoy
 sailing aid 269 n.
 lightness 323 n.
 signpost 547 n.
buoyancy
 lightness 323 n.
 elasticity 328 n.
 hope 852 n.
buoyant
 be light 323 vb.
 light 323 adj.
 elastic 328 adj.
 prosperous 730 adj.
 cheerful 833 adj.
 hoping 852 adj.
burble
 flow 350 VB.
 faintness 401 n.
 be foolish 499 vb.
burden
 load 193 vb.
 gravity 322 n.
 make heavy
  322 vb.
 vocal music 412 n.
 topic 452 n.
 verse form 593 n.
 bane 659 n.
 difficulty 700 n.
 encumbrance
  702 n.
 hinder 702 vb.
 adversity 731 n.
 oppress 735 vb.
 worry 825 n.
 annoyance 827 n.

burden of proof
 demonstration
  478 n.
bureau
 cabinet 194 n.
 workshop 687 n.
 jurisdiction 955 n.
bureaucracy
 delay 136 n.
 habit 610 n.
 management
  689 n.
 governance 733 n.
 government 733 n.
bureaucrat
 official 690 n.
 officer 741 n.
burgeoning
 young 130 adj.
burglar
 incomer 297 n.
 thief 789 n.
burglary
 stealing 788 n.
burgle
 intrude 297 vb.
 steal 788 vb.
burial
 interment 364 n.
 detention 747 n.
buried
 deep 211 adj.
 forgotten 506 adj.
 secluded 883 adj.
burlesque
 imitate 20 vb.
 imitative 20 adj.
 mimicry 20 n.
 foolery 497 n.
 exaggeration
  546 n.
 doggerel 593 n.
 dramatic 594 adj.
 stage play 594 n.
 funny 849 adj.
 ridiculousness
  849 n.
 satire 851 n.
 satirize 851 vb.
burly
 stalwart 162 adj.
 fleshy 195 adj.
burn
 dry 342 vb.
 stream 350 n.
 be hot 379 vb.
 burn 381 vb.

burning 381 n.
shine 417 vb.
ulcer 651 n.
wound 655 n.
go to war 718 vb.
be excited 821 vb.
resent 891 vb.
burned out
fatigued 684 adj.
burner
burning 381 n.
furnace 383 n.
torch 420 n.
burning
painful 377 adj.
fiery 379 adj.
hot 379 adj.
burning 381 n.
fervent 818 adj.
paining 827 adj.
angry 891 adj.
capital punishment
  963 n.
burnish
smooth 258 vb.
rub 333 vb.
make bright
  417 vb.
decorate 844 vb.
burn one's boats
overstep 306 vb.
be resolute 599 vb.
burn out
burn 381 vb.
extinguish 382 vb.
fatigue 684 vb.
burnt
culinary 301 adj.
dry 342 adj.
unsavoury 391 adj.
burn the candle at
  both ends
be late 136 vb.
be active 678 vb.
be active 678 vb.
work 682 vb.
be prodigal 815 vb.
revel 837 vb.
be intemperate
  943 vb.
be sensual 944 vb.
burp
eruct 300 vb.
voidance 300 n.
burr
roughness 259 n.
rasp 407 vb.

engraving 555 n.
dialect 560 adj.
pronunciation
  577 n.
voice 577 vb.
speech defect
  580 n.
burrow
place oneself
  187 vb.
dwell 192 vb.
dwelling 192 n.
cavity 255 n.
excavation 255 n.
make concave
  255 vb.
pierce 263 vb.
descend 309 vb.
lurk 523 vb.
refuge 662 n.
burst
break 46 vb.
rend 46 vb.
be dispersed 75 vb.
instant 116 n.
outbreak 176 n.
open 263 vb.
loudness 400 n.
bang 402 n.
bang 402 vb.
activity 678 n.
be active 678 vb.
burst into tears
weep 836 vb.
bury
implant 303 vb.
insert 303 vb.
inter 364 vb.
conceal 525 vb.
store 632 n.
imprison 747 vb.
bury one's head in
  the sand
avoid 620 vb.
bury the hatchet
forget 506 vb.
make peace
  719 vb.
forgive 909 vb.
bus
conveyance 267 n.
automobile 274 n.
bus 274 n.
busby
headgear 228 n.
bush
desert 172 n.

district 184 n.
plain 348 n.
tree 366 n.
wood 366 n.
bush telegraph
rumour 529 n.
telecommunication
  531 n.
bushy
dense 324 adj.
business
business 622 n.
function 622 n.
business end
essential part 5 n.
business man, -wo-
  man
worker 686 n.
expert 696 n.
busker
musician 413 n.
vocalist 413 n.
entertainer 594 n.
beggar 763 n.
bust
break 46 vb.
bosom 253 n.
reminder 505 n.
monument 548 n.
image 551 n.
sculpture 554 n.
poor 801 adj.
honours 866 n.
gluttony 947 n.
bustling
busy 678 adj.
excited 821 adj.
busy
influential 178 adj.
employ 622 vb.
busy 678 adj.
excited 821 adj.
busybody
meddler 678 n.
but
nevertheless
  468 adv.
qualification 468 n.
butane
fuel 385 n.
butch
male 372 adj.
butcher
killer 362 n.
slaughter 362 vb.
tradespeople 794 n.
ruffian 904 n.

butler
domestic 742 n.
retainer 742 n.
butt
vat 194 n.
buttocks 238 n.
collide 279 vb.
impulse 279 n.
  See **collision**
tobacco 388 n.
fool 501 n.
objective 617 n.
strike at 712 vb.
firearm 723 n.
laughingstock
  851 n.
butter
coat 226 vb.
softness 327 n.
lubricate 334 vb.
fat 357 n.
grease 357 vb.
buttercup
plant 366 n.
yellowness 433 n.
butterfingers
bungling 695 n.
bungler 697 n.
butterflies
agitation 318 n.
nervousness 854 n.
butterfly
aquatics 269 n.
insect 365 n.
inattention 456 n.
butter up
flatter 925 vb.
buttery
smooth 258 adj.
fatty 357 adj.
storage 632 n.
butt in
discontinue 72 vb.
interfere 231 vb.
encroach 306 vb.
converse 584 vb.
meddle 678 vb.
buttocks
buttocks 238 n.
button
fastening 47 n.
minuteness 196 n.
circle 250 n.
swelling 253 n.
close 264 vb.
trifle 639 n.

buttoned-up
 reticent 525 adj.
 completed 725 adj.
buttonhole
 fastening 47 n.
 orifice 263 n.
 fragrance 396 n.
 be loquacious
  581 vb.
 speak to 583 vb.
 converse 584 vb.
 retain 778 vb.
 ornamentation
  844 n.
buttress
 stabilizer 153 n.
 support 218 n.
 support 218 vb.
 projection 254 n.
 corroborate 466 vb.
 fortification 713 n.
 church exterior
  990 n.
buxom
 fleshy 195 adj.
 personable 841 adj.
 shapely 841 adj.
buy
 believe 485 vb.
 acquire 771 vb.
 purchase 792 n.
 purchase 792 vb.
 expend 806 vb.
buy a pig in a poke
 gamble 618 vb.
 be rash 857 vb.
buyer
 owner 776 n.
 recipient 782 n.
 purchaser 792 n.
buy it
 be credulous
  487 vb.
 assent 488 vb.
buy-out
 offer 759 n.
 purchase 792 n.
buzz
 fly 271 vb.
 faintness 401 n.
 sound faint 401 vb.
 roll 403 n.
 resound 404 vb.
 hiss 406 vb.
 shrill 407 vb.
 ululate 409 vb.
 ululation 409 n.

 message 529 n.
 rumour 529 n.
 obstruct 702 vb.
buzzard
 bird 365 n.
buzzer
 signal 547 n.
buzz off
 come along
  267 int.
 decamp 296 vb.
buzz word
 word 559 n.
 neology 560 n.
by
 akin 11 adj.
 before 119 adv.
 caused 157 adj.
 born 360 adj.
 by means of
  629 adv.
bye-bye
 goodbye 296 int.
by-election
 vote 605 n.
bygone
 past 125 adj.
 archaism 127 n.
by heart
 in memory
  505 adv.
bylaw
 rule 81 n.
 legislation 953 n.
by leaps and bounds
 swiftly 277 adv.
 forward 285 adv.
by oneself
 alone 88 adj.
 singly 88 adv.
bypass
 avoid 620 vb.
 road 624 n.
 route 624 n.
 circuit 626 n.
by-pass surgery
 surgery 658 n.
by-product
 extra 40 n.
 sequel 67 n.
 concomitant 89 n.
 effect 157 n.
 product 164 n.
by proxy
 instead 150 adv.

by rote
 in memory
  505 adv.
bystander
 presence 189 n.
 spectator 441 n.
byte
 data processing
  86 n.
by the by(e)
 concerning 9 adv.
 incidentally
  137 vb.
by the way
 concerning 9 adv.
 incidentally
  137 vb.
byword
 maxim 496 n.

C

cab
 chamber 194 n.
 cab 274 n.
cabal
 combination 50 n.
 latency 523 n.
 plot 623 n.
 party 708 n.
cabaret
 stage show 594 n.
 theatre 594 n.
 place of amuse-
  ment 837 n.
cabbage
 fruit and vegetables
  301 n.
Cabbage Patch
 (tdmk) doll
 image 551 n.
 plaything 837 n.
caber
 missile 287 n.
cabin
 small house 192 n.
 chamber 194 n.
cabin boy
 mariner 270 n.
 naval man 722 n.
 servant 742 n.
cabinet
 cabinet 194 n.
 chamber 194 n.
 management
  689 n.
 director 690 n.

 council 692 n.
cabinet-maker
 artisan 686 n.
cable
 cable 47 n.
 information 524 n.
 message 529 n.
 telecommunication
  531 n.
cablegram
 information 524 n.
 telecommunication
  531 n.
cable railway
 train 274 n.
cable stitch
 needlework 844 n.
cable television or ra-
 dio
 broadcasting
  531 n.
caboodle
 great quantity
  32 n.
cache
 concealment 525 n.
 hiding-place 527 n.
 store 632 n.
cachet
 repute 866 n.
cack-handed
 clumsy 695 adj.
cack-handedness
 sinistrality 242 n.
cackle
 ululate 409 vb.
 chatter 581 n.
 laugh 835 vb.
 laughter 835 n.
cacophony
 stridor 407 n.
 discord 411 n.
cactus
 prickle 256 n.
 plant 366 n.
cad
 cad 938 n.
cadaver
 corpse 363 n.
caddy
 small box 194 n.
 carry 273 vb.
 servant 742 n.
cadence
 descent 309 n.
 sound 398 n.
 melody 410 n.

prosody 593 n.

cadet
posteriority 120 n.
subsequent
120 adj.
young 130 adj.
beginner 538 n.
subject 745 adj.

cadge
beg 761 vb.
take 786 vb.

cadre
party 708 n.

caecum
closure 264 n.

Caesar
sovereign 741 n.

Caesarian birth
extraction 304 n.

Caesarian (section)
obstetrics 167 n.

caesura
discontinuity 72 n.
prosody 593 n.

café
café 192 n.

cafeteria
café 192 n.

caffeine
tonic 658 n.

caftan
robe 228 n.

cage
stable 192 n.
compartment
194 n.
receptacle 194 n.
circumscribe
232 vb.
enclose 235 vb.
enclosure 235 n.
break in 369 vb.
imprison 747 vb.
lockup 748 n.

cagey
reticent 525 adj.
cunning 698 adj.
cautious 858 adj.

cairn
signpost 547 n.
monument 548 n.

caisson disease
depth 211 n.
diver 313 n.

cajole
fool 542 vb.
induce 612 vb.

request 761 vb.
flatter 925 vb.

cake
cohere 48 vb.
pastries and cakes
301 n.
be dense 324 vb.
solid body 324 n.
sweet thing 392 n.
make unclean
649 vb.

cakewalk
dance 837 n.

calamity
evil 616 n.
misfortune 731 n.

calcify
harden 326 vb.

calcium
food content 301 n.

calculate
number 86 vb.
measure 465 vb.
estimate 480 vb.
expect 507 vb.
intend 617 vb.
plan 623 vb.
be cautious 858 vb.

calculated
predetermined
608 adj.

calculated risk
intention 617 n.

calculation
numeration 86 n.
measurement
465 n.
estimate 480 n.
intention 617 n.
caution 858 n.

calculator
counting instru-
ment 86 n.

calendar
directory 87 n.
list 87 n.
chronology 117 n.
time 117 vb.
reference book
589 n.

calendar month
period 110 n.

calender
smooth 258 vb.

calends
date 108 n.

calf
young creature
132 n.
skin 226 n.
leg 267 n.
cattle 365 n.
bookbinding 589 n.

calf love
love 887 n.

calibrate
graduate 27 vb.
gauge 465 vb.

calibre
sort 77 n.
size 195 n.
breadth 205 n.
intelligence 498 n.
firearm 723 n.

calico
textile 222 n.

caliph
sovereign 741 n.

call
enter 297 vb.
cry 408 vb.
ululate 409 vb.
ululation 409 n.
communicate
524 vb.
call 547 vb.
name 561 vb.
motive 612 n.
command 737 vb.
desire 859 n.
desire 859 vb.
social round 882 n.
visit 882 vb.

called to the bar, be
do law 958 vb.

caller
incomer 297 n.
sociable person
882 n.
worshipper 981 n.

callgirl
prostitute 952 n.

calligraphy
art 551 n.
lettering 586 n.

call in
bring together
74 vb.
admit 299 vb.
consult 691 vb.
visit 882 vb.

calling
motive 612 n.

vocation 622 n.
social round 882 n.

call in question
cause doubt
486 vb.
negate 533 vb.

calliper
support 218 n.
measure 465 vb.

callipers
gauge 465 n.

call it a day
terminate 69 vb.
cease 145 vb.

call of duty
duty 917 n.

call off
halt 145 vb.
abrogate 752 vb.

call one's bluff
defy 711 vb.

callosity
hardness 326 n.

callous
unfeeling 375 adj.
thick-skinned
820 adj.
cruel 898 adj.
pitiless 906 adj.
wicked 934 adj.

call out
halt 145 vb.
cry 408 vb.
defy 711 vb.
resist 715 vb.

callow
new 126 adj.
young 130 adj.
amorphous
244 adj.
unhabituated
611 adj.
immature 670 adj.
artless 699 adj.
innocent 935 adj.

call the shots
dominate 733 vb.

call the tune
motivate 612 vb.
dominate 733 vb.

call to arms
remember 505 vb.
call 547 n.
go to war 718 vb.
war 718 n.
war measures
718 n.

call to mind
remember 505 vb.
call up
bring together
74 vb.
go to war 718 vb.
call upon
command 737 vb.
impose a duty
917 vb.
callus
hardness 326 n.
calm
assuage 177 vb.
moderate 177 adj.
moderation 177 n.
flat 216 adj.
smooth 258 adj.
smoothness 258 n.
quietude 266 n.
tranquil 266 adj.
silent 399 adj.
inaction 677 n.
impassive 820 adj.
inexcitable
823 adj.
tranquillize
823 vb.
please 826 vb.
relieve 831 vb.
cautious 858 adj.
indifferent 860 adj.
calm as a millpond
flat 216 adj.
smooth 258 adj.
calm before the
storm
reversion 148 n.
calorie(s)
energy 160 n.
dieting 301 n.
food content 301 n.
thermometry
379 n.
calumny
calumny 926 n.
Calvary
suffering 825 n.
Calvinistic
Protestant 976 adj.
calypso
vocal music 412 n.
calyx
receptacle 194 n.
flower 366 n.
camaraderie
friendliness 880 n.

fellowship 882 n.
camber
obliquity 220 n.
camber 253 n.
camcorder
camera 442 n.
camel
beast of burden
273 n.
mammal 365 n.
camel hair
fibre 208 n.
camellia
tree 366 n.
cameo
sculpture 554 n.
description 590 n.
acting 594 n.
jewellery 844 n.
camera
camera 442 n.
recording instru-
ment 549 n.
camisole
shirt 228 n.
underwear 228 n.
camouflage
assimilation 18 n.
imitate 20 vb.
mimicry 20 n.
transform 147 vb.
conceal 525 vb.
concealment 525 n.
disguise 527 n.
camp
place oneself
187 vb.
station 187 n.
abode 192 n.
dwell 192 vb.
art 551 n.
dramatic 594 adj.
shelter 662 n.
party 708 n.
amuse oneself
837 vb.
affectation 850 n.
affected 850 adj.
ostentation 875 n.
showy 875 adj.
campaign
undertaking 672 n.
action 676 n.
do 676 vb.
tactics 688 n.
fight 716 n.
fight 716 vb.

warfare 718 n.
philanthropy
901 n.
campanologist
instrumentalist
413 n.
camper
traveller 268 n.
automobile 274 n.
camp follower(s)
retinue 67 n.
concomitant 89 n.
follower 284 n.
habitué 610 n.
dependant 742 n.
camphor
resin 357 n.
scent 396 n.
preserver 666 n.
camping
sport 837 n.
camp it up
act 594 vb.
be affected 850 vb.
campsite
station 187 n.
abode 192 n.
campus
focus 76 n.
meeting place
192 n.
academy 539 n.
arena 724 n.
can
be able 160 vb.
cup 194 n.
small box 194 n.
vessel 194 n.
preserve 666 vb.
prison 748 n.
canaille
rabble 869 n.
canal
cavity 255 n.
transport 272 n.
conduit 351 n.
access 624 n.
canapé
hors-d'oeuvres
301 n.
canary
bird 365 n.
bad person 938 n.
canasta
card game 837 n.
cancan
leap 312 n.

dance 837 n.
cancel
nullify 2 vb.
exclude 57 vb.
destroy 165 vb.
counteract 182 vb.
obliterate 550 vb.
relinquish 621 vb.
stop using 674 vb.
abrogate 752 vb.
not observe 769 vb.
not retain 779 vb.
forgive 909 vb.
disapprove 924 vb.
make illegal
954 vb.
cancellation
extinction 2 n.
counteraction
182 n.
negation 533 n.
obliteration 550 n.
relinquishment
621 n.
nonuse 674 n.
abrogation 752 n.
prohibition 757 n.
nonretention
779 n.
forgiveness 909 n.
loss of right 916 n.
cancer
badness 645 n.
cancer 651 n.
disease 651 n.
dilapidation 655 n.
blight 659 n.
candelabra
lamp 420 n.
candescent
fiery 379 adj.
candid
true 494 adj.
veracious 540 adj.
artless 699 adj.
trustworthy
929 adj.
candidate
respondent 460 n.
contender 716 n.
petitioner 763 n.
candle
lighter 385 n.
torch 420 n.
ritual object 988 n.
candlelight
evening 129 n.

wealth 800 n.
capital gains tax
  tax 809 n.
capitalist
  rich person 800 n.
capitalize
  profit by 137 vb.
capitalize on
  use 673 vb.
capital letter
  letter 558 n.
capital punishment
  capital punishment
   963 n.
capitals
  print-type 587 n.
capitation
  numeration 86 n.
  statistics 86 n.
capitol
  fort 713 n.
capitulate
  submit 721 vb.
capon
  poultry 365 n.
  male animal
   372 n.
cappuccino
  soft drink 301 n.
caprice
  musical piece
   412 n.
  caprice 604 n.
  whim 604 n.
capricious
  capricious 604 adj.
capsicum
  fruit and vegetables
   301 n.
capsize
  be unequal 29 vb.
  derange 63 vb.
  be inverted 221 vb.
  invert 221 vb.
  navigate 269 vb.
  descent 309 n.
  tumble 309 vb.
capsule
  receptacle 194 n.
  covering 226 n.
  flower 366 n.
  medicine 658 n.
captain
  navigate 269 vb.
  nautical personnel
   270 n.
  direct 689 vb.

director 690 n.
leader 690 n.
army officer 741 n.
naval officer 741 n.
captain of industry
  bigwig 638 n.
  master 741 n.
caption
  commentary 520 n.
  indication 547 n.
  label 547 n.
  record 548 n.
  name 561 n.
  phrase 563 n.
  script 586 n.
  edition 589 n.
  description 590 n.
captious
  irascible 892 adj.
  disapproving
   924 adj.
captivate
  motivate 612 vb.
  subjugate 745 vb.
captive
  slave 742 n.
  captive 750 adj.
  prisoner 750 n.
  take 786 vb.
captivity
  servitude 745 n.
  detention 747 n.
captor
  master 741 n.
  possessor 776 n.
  taker 786 n.
capture
  imagine 513 vb.
  represent 551 vb.
  describe 590 vb.
  attack 712 vb.
  overmaster 727 vb.
  subjugate 745 vb.
  arrest 747 vb.
  acquire 771 vb.
  take 786 vb.
  taking 786 n.
car
  conveyance 267 n.
  automobile 274 n.
  airship 276 n.
carafe
  vessel 194 n.
caramel
  sweets 301 n.
  brownness 430 n.

carapace
  covering 226 n.
carat
  weighing 322 n.
caravan
  small house 192 n.
  cart 274 n.
  follower 284 n.
  traction 288 n.
  amuse oneself
   837 vb.
caravan site
  station 187 n.
caraway
  spice 301 n.
carbine
  firearm 723 n.
carbohydrates
  food content 301 n.
carbolic
  cleanser 648 n.
  prophylactic 658 n.
carbonate
  gasify 336 vb.
  bubble 355 vb.
carbonated
  gaseous 336 adj.
carbon copy
  duplicate 22 n.
  duplication 91 n.
  record 548 n.
carbon dioxide
  poison 659 n.
carbon monoxide
  poison 659 n.
carbon paper
  paper 631 n.
carbuncle
  swelling 253 n.
  blemish 845 n.
carcass
  structure 331 n.
  corpse 363 n.
carcinogenic
  diseased 651 adj.
  insalubrious
   653 adj.
carcinoma
  growth 157 n.
  swelling 253 n.
  cancer 651 n.
card
  nonconformist
   84 n.
  smoother 258 n.
  sailing aid 269 n.
  male 372 n.

label 547 n.
record 548 n.
correspondence
  588 n.
contrivance 623 n.
paper 631 n.
laughingstock
  851 n.
cardamom
  spice 301 n.
cardboard
  paper 631 n.
card game
  card game 837 n.
cardiac arrest
  cardiovascular dis-
   ease 651 n.
cardiac disease
  cardiovascular dis-
   ease 651 n.
cardigan
  jersey 228 n.
cardinal
  intrinsic 5 adj.
  supreme 34 adj.
  numerical 85 adj.
  important 638 adj.
  governor 741 n.
  ecclesiarch 986 n.
cardinal number
  number 85 n.
card index
  sorting 62 n.
  list 87 n.
cardiology
  medical art 658 n.
cardiovascular dis-
  ease
  cardiovascular dis-
   ease 651 n.
cards
  oracle 511 n.
  card game 837 n.
  plaything 837 n.
cards on the table
  disclosure 526 n.
card up one's sleeve
  advantage 34 n.
  contrivance 623 n.
  means 629 n.
care
  be attentive 455 vb.
  carefulness 457 n.
  function 622 n.
  protection 660 n.
  management
   689 n.

detention 747 n.
mandate 751 n.
economy 814 n.
worry 825 n.
painfulness 827 n.
nervousness 854 n.
caution 858 n.
love 887 vb.
do good 897 adj.
career
continuity 71 n.
motion 265 n.
move fast 277 vb.
progression 285 n.
vocation 622 n.
conduct 688 n.
career woman
female 373 n.
worker 686 n.
expert 696 n.
care for
look after 457 vb.
safeguard 660 vb.
desire 859 vb.
love 887 vb.
carefree
reposeful 683 adj.
cheerful 833 adj.
careful
careful 457 adj.
economical
  814 adj.
parsimonious
  816 adj.
careless
inattentive 456 adj.
negligent 458 adj.
unprepared
  670 adj.
rash 857 adj.
indifferent 860 adj.
caress
touch 378 n.
caress 889 vb.
endearment 889 n.
caret
punctuation 547 n.
caretaker
manager 690 n.
servant 742 n.
keeper 749 n.
consignee 754 n.
careworn
suffering 825 adj.
cargo
contents 193 n.
transport 272 n.

merchandise
  795 n.
caribou
mammal 365 n.
caricature
imitate 20 vb.
mimicry 20 n.
copy 22 n.
be absurd 497 vb.
foolery 497 n.
misinterpret
  521 vb.
exaggerate 546 vb.
exaggeration
  546 n.
misrepresent
  552 vb.
misrepresentation
  552 n.
picture 553 n.
be witty 839 vb.
wit 839 n.
laughingstock
  851 n.
satire 851 n.
satirize 851 vb.
calumny 926 n.
detract 926 vb.
caricaturist
imitator 20 n.
artist 556 n.
humorist 839 n.
caries
decay 51 n.
carillon
roll 403 n.
resonance 404 n.
tune 412 n.
gong 414 n.
signal 547 n.
church utensil
  990 n.
carmine
red 431 adj.
red pigment 431 n.
Carnaby Street
clothier 228 n.
carnage
slaughter 362 n.
carnal
material 319 adj.
sensual 944 adj.
lecherous 951 adj.
carnal knowledge
coition 45 n.
carnation
plant 366 n.

red 431 adj.
redness 431 n.
carnival
festivity 837 n.
pageant 875 n.
carnivorous
feeding 301 adj.
carol
ululate 409 vb.
vocal music 412 n.
sing 413 vb.
voice 577 vb.
be cheerful 833 vb.
rejoice 835 vb.
carol singers
choir 413 n.
carouse
eat 301 vb.
festivity 837 n.
revel 837 vb.
be sociable 882 vb.
get drunk 949 vb.
carp
fish 365 n.
be discontented
  829 vb.
blame 924 vb.
criticize 924 vb.
car park
accumulation 74 n.
station 187 n.
enclosure 235 n.
traffic control
  305 n.
carpenter
artisan 686 n.
carpet
base 214 n.
floor-cover 226 n.
reprove 924 vb.
carpetbagger
impostor 545 n.
carpeted, be
incur blame
  924 vb.
carpet slipper
footwear 228 n.
carport
stable 192 n.
carrel
compartment
  194 n.
carriage
support 218 n.
gait 265 n.
transport 272 n.
carriage 274 n.

train 274 n.
look 445 n.
conduct 688 n.
carriageway
traffic control
  305 n.
road 624 n.
route 624 n.
carried away
imaginative
  513 adj.
excited 821 adj.
carried over
remaining 41 adj.
carrier
support 218 n.
carrier 273 n.
infection 651 n.
carrier bag
bag 194 n.
carrier 273 n.
carrier pigeon
courier 529 n.
carrion
decay 51 n.
food 301 n.
corpse 363 n.
rubbish 641 n.
carrion crow
bird 365 n.
carrot
fruit and vegetables
  301 n.
incentive 612 n.
inducement 612 n.
carrot and stick
incentive 612 n.
compulsion 740 n.
excitant 821 n.
carroty
red 431 adj.
carry
reproduce itself
  167 vb.
range 183 n.
be distant 199 vb.
support 218 vb.
carry 273 vb.
carry all before one
do easily 701 vb.
win 727 vb.
carry a torch for
be in love 887 vb.
**carry coals to New-
castle**
be superfluous
  637 vb.

carry off
  take away 786 vb.
carry on
  go on 146 vb.
  function 622 vb.
  do 676 vb.
  deal with 688 vb.
  manage 689 vb.
  lament 836 vb.
  caress 889 vb.
  be angry 891 vb.
  be wicked 934 vb.
carry out
  make complete
    54 vb.
  carry out 725 vb.
  observe 768 vb.
carry over
  add 38 vb.
  transfer 272 vb.
  carry 273 vb.
  pass 305 vb.
  account 808 vb.
carry the can
  be duped 544 vb.
  incur blame
    924 vb.
carry the day
  succeed 727 vb.
  win 727 vb.
carry through
  deal with 688 vb.
  carry through
    725 vb.
carry weight
  influence 178 vb.
  evidence 466 vb.
cart
  carrier 273 n.
  carry 273 vb.
  cart 274 n.
  pushcart 274 n.
cart away
  displace 188 vb.
carte blanche
  scope 744 n.
  permit 756 n.
  liberality 813 n.
cartel
  association 706 n.
  corporation 708 n.
  restriction 747 n.
  compact 765 n.
carter
  driver 268 n.
  carrier 273 n.

cartilage
  solid body 324 n.
  hardness 326 n.
  toughness 329 n.
cartography
  map 551 n.
carton
  small box 194 n.
cartoon
  copy 22 n.
  film 445 n.
  broadcast 531 n.
  representation
    551 n.
  paint 553 vb.
  picture 553 n.
  wit 839 n.
  satire 851 n.
cartoonist
  artist 556 n.
  humorist 839 n.
cartridge
  gramophone 414 n.
  ammunition 723 n.
cartwheel
  overturning 221 n.
carve
  cut 46 vb.
  sunder 46 vb.
    See **cut**
  produce 164 vb.
  form 243 vb.
  groove 262 vb.
  record 548 vb.
  represent 551 vb.
  sculpt 554 vb.
  decorate 844 vb.
carve up
  apportion 783 vb.
carving knife
  sharp edge 256 n.
Casanova
  lover 887 n.
  libertine 952 n.
cascade
  descend 309 vb.
  descent 309 n.
  flow 350 VB.
  waterfall 350 n.
cascara
  purgative 658 n.
case
  example 83 n.
  event 154 n.
  box 194 n.
  case 194 n.
  cover 226 vb.

  enclosure 235 n.
  topic 452 n.
  enquire 459 vb.
  argument 475 n.
  reasons 475 n.
  report 524 n.
  grammar 564 n.
  bookbinding 589 n.
  business 622 n.
  accusation 928 n.
  litigation 959 n.
case, be the
  be 1 vb.
  happen 154 vb.
  be true 494 vb.
case history
  evidence 466 n.
  record 548 n.
  description 590 n.
casement
  window 263 n.
cash
  incentive 612 n.
  acquire 771 vb.
  coinage 797 n.
  draw money
    797 vb.
  money 797 n.
cash and carry
  shop 796 n.
cash dispenser
  treasury 799 n.
cash flow
  means 629 n.
  funds 797 n.
cashier
  abase 311 vb.
  treasurer 798 n.
  accountant 808 vb.
  shame 867 vb.
cash in on
  profit by 137 vb.
  plead 614 vb.
  flourish 615 vb.
  use 673 vb.
cash in one's chips
  die 361 vb.
cashmere
  fibre 208 n.
  textile 222 n.
  hair 259 n.
cash register
  counting instru-
    ment 86 n.
  recording instru-
    ment 549 n.
  treasury 799 n.

casino
  gaming-house
    618 n.
  place of amuse-
    ment 837 n.
cask
  vat 194 n.
  cylinder 252 n.
casket
  small box 194 n.
  interment 364 n.
  ritual object 988 n.
casserole
  pot 194 n.
  cook 301 vb.
  dish 301 n.
cassette
  rotator 315 n.
  musical piece
    412 n.
  gramophone 414 n.
  photography 551 n.
cassette recorder
  gramophone 414 n.
cassock
  robe 228 n.
  canonicals 989 n.
  vestments 989 n.
cast
  character 5 n.
  copy 22 n.
  band 74 n.
  number 86 vb.
  produce 164 vb.
  tendency 179 n.
  form 243 n.
  form 243 vb.
  propel 287 vb.
  propulsion 287 n.
  hue 425 n.
  dim sight 440 n.
  look 445 n.
  represent 551 vb.
  sculpt 554 vb.
  sculpture 554 n.
  actor 594 n.
  dramatize 594 vb.
  surgical dressing
    658 n.
  apportion 783 vb.
  with affections
    817 adj.
  blemish 845 n.
cast about (for)
  search 459 vb.
  be uncertain
    474 vb.

pursue 619 vb.

cast anchor
  navigate 269 vb.

castanets
  gong 414 n.

cast a spell on
  bewitch 983 vb.

cast aspersions
  detract 926 vb.
  accuse 928 vb.

castaway
  solitary 883 n.

caste
  degree 27 n.
  serial place 73 n.
  breed 77 n.
  classification 77 n.
  prestige 866 n.
  nobility 868 n.

caste mark
  label 547 n.
  See **identifica-
tion**

castigate
  reprove 924 vb.
  punish 963 vb.

casting vote
  influence 178 n.

cast-iron
  hard 326 adj.

castle
  house 192 n.
  fort 713 n.

castle (chess)
  interchange
    151 vb.
  transpose 272 vb.

castle in the air
  insubstantial thing
    4 n.

castles in Spain
  fantasy 513 n.
  aspiration 852 n.

castles in the air
  fantasy 513 n.
  aspiration 852 n.
  desire 859 n.

cast lots
  divine 511 vb.

cast off
  decrease 37 vb.
  separate 46 vb.
  navigate 269 vb.
  start out 296 vb.
  relinquish 621 vb.

cast of mind
  tendency 179 n.

588

will 595 n.
  affections 817 n.

cast-offs
  clothing 228 n.
  rubbish 641 n.

castor
  small box 194 n.
  wheel 250 n.

castrate
  subtract 39 vb.
  unman 161 vb.
  make useless
    641 adj.
  impair 655 vb.

cast up
  eject 300 vb.
  elevate 310 vb.

casual
  casual 159 adj.
  negligent 458 adj.

casualty
  event 154 n.
  chance 159 n.
  evil 616 n.
  misfortune 731 n.

casuistry
  sophistry 477 n.
  morals 917 n.

cat
  vomit 300 vb.
  cat 365 n.
  eye 438 n.
  cad 938 n.
  scourge 964 n.

cataclysmic
  revolutionary
    149 adj.
  destructive 165 adj.
  violent 176 adj.
  flowing 350 adj.

catacomb
  depth 211 n.
  cemetery 364 n.

catalepsy
  insensibility 375 n.
  sleep 679 n.

catalogue
  arrangement 62 n.
  class 62 vb.
  list 87 n.
  list 87 vb.
  guidebook 524 n.
  record 548 n.
  record 548 vb.

catalyst
  stimulant 174 n.
  instrument 628 n.

catamaran
  boat 275 n.
  sailing ship 275 n.

cat and dog
  opposites 704 n.
  dissension 709 n.

cat-and-mouse
  caution 858 n.

catapult
  propel 287 vb.
  propellant 287 n.
  missile weapon
    723 n.

cataract
  waterfall 350 n.
  blindness 439 n.
  dim sight 440 n.

catarrh
  excrement 302 n.
  excretion 302 n.
  respiratory disease
    651 n.

catastrophe
  revolution 149 n.
  event 154 n.
  ruin 165 n.
  evil 616 n.
  completion 725 n.
  misfortune 731 n.

catatonic
  impotent 161 adj.
  insensible 375 adj.
  psychotic 503 adj.
  psychotic 504 n.

cat burglar
  thief 789 n.

catcall
  shrill 407 vb.
  gesture 547 n.
  ridicule 851 n.
  indignity 921 n.
  disapprobation
    924 n.

catch
  copy 20 vb.
  joint 45 n.
  fastening 47 n.
  bring together
    74 vb.
  halt 145 vb.
  rub 333 vb.
  vocal music 412 n.
  hear 415 vb.
  question 459 n.
  know 490 vb.
  surprise 508 vb.
  ambush 527 n.

ensnare 542 vb.
  trap 542 n.
  chase 619 n.
  hunt 619 vb.
  bigwig 638 n.
  pitfall 663 n.
  hitch 702 n.
  wrestling 716 n.
  arrest 747 vb.
  acquire 771 vb.
  retain 778 vb.
  take 786 vb.
  taking 786 n.
  booty 790 n.
  feel 818 vb.
  desired object
    859 n.
  sociable person
    882 n.
  favourite 890 n.

catch-22
  pitfall 663 n.
  predicament 700 n.
  obstacle 702 n.
  hopelessness 853 n.

catch a crab
  row 269 vb.
  be clumsy 695 vb.

catch-as-catch-can
  attempt 671 n.
  wrestling 716 n.

catch at
  desire 859 vb.

catch at straws
  hope 852 vb.

catch cold
  be cold 380 vb.

catching
  infectious 653 adj.

catch it
  be in difficulty
    700 vb.
  incur blame
    924 vb.
  be punished
    963 vb.

catchment area
  territory 184 n.
  school 539 n.

catch napping
  be early 135 vb.
  surprise 508 vb.

catch on
  prevail 178 vb.
  understand 516 vb.
  be wont 610 vb.

be in fashion
848 vb.

catch out
dismiss 300 vb.
disclose 526 vb.
ensnare 542 vb.
fool 542 vb.

catch phrase
neology 560 n.
phrase 563 n.

catch up
outstrip 277 vb.

catch up with
outstrip 277 vb.

catchword
maxim 496 n.
indication 547 n.
See **punctuation**
word 559 n.
edition 589 n.

catchy
melodious 410 adj.
desired 859 adj.

catechism
interrogation
459 n.
creed 485 n.
orthodoxy 976 n.

categorical
positive 473 adj.
assertive 532 adj.
commanding
737 adj.
obligatory 917 adj.

category
state 7 n.
classification 77 n.

cater
feed 301 vb.
provide 633 vb.

catering
cookery 301 n.
provision 633 n.

caterpillar
young creature
132 n.
creepy-crawly
365 n.

caterwauling
discord 411 n.

catgut
viol 414 n.

catharsis
narrative 590 n.
liberation 746 n.

cathedral
church 990 n.

catherine wheel
rotator 315 n.

catheter
tube 263 n.
insertion 303 n.
irrigator 341 n.
drain 351 n.

catheterize
empty 300 vb.
dry 342 vb.
purify 648 vb.

cathode
electricity 160 n.

Catholic
Catholic 976 n.
Roman Catholic
976 adj.

catholic
universal 79 adj.
orthodox 976 adj.

Catholicism
Catholicism 976 n.
orthodoxy 976 n.

catholicism
generality 79 n.

catkin
flower 366 n.

catnap
sleep 679 n.
sleep 679 vb.

cat-o'-nine-tails
scourge 964 n.

CAT scanner
hospital 658 n.

cat's-paw
wave 350 n.
dupe 544 n.
instrument 628 n.
nonentity 639 n.
auxiliary 707 n.
toady 879 n.

cattle
cattle 365 n.
rabble 869 n.

catty
malevolent
898 adj.

catwalk
bridge 624 n.

Caucasian
white 427 adj.
whiteness 427 n.

caucus
assemblage 74 n.
party 708 n.

caudal
ending 69 adj.

back 238 adj.

caught
enamoured
887 adj.

caught in the act, be
be guilty 936 vb.

caught napping, be
be neglectful
458 vb.

caught on the hop
unexpecting
508 adj.

**caught red-handed,
be**
be guilty 936 vb.

caught unawares
unprepared
670 adj.

**caught with one's
pants/trousers
down, be**
be inattentive
456 vb.
be neglectful
458 vb.
not expect 508 vb.

cauldron
pot 194 n.

cauliflower
fruit and vegetables
301 n.

cauliflower ear
swelling 253 n.
wound 655 n.
blemish 845 n.

caulk
repair 656 vb.

causation
causation 156 n.

cause
cause 156 n.
cause 156 vb.
reason why 156 n.
philanthropy
901 n.
litigation 959 n.

cause and effect
relativeness 9 n.
causation 156 n.

cause célèbre
prodigy 864 n.

causeway
bond 47 n.
bridge 624 n.

caustic
keen 174 adj.
pungent 388 adj.

paining 827 adj.
disapproving
924 adj.

cauterize
burn 381 vb.
doctor 658 vb.

caution
nonconformist
84 n.
omen 511 n.
hint 524 n.
hint 524 n.
dissuade 613 vb.
dissuasion 613 n.
warn 664 vb.
warning 664 n.
advice 691 n.
defy 711 vb.
laughingstock
851 n.
intimidation
854 n.
caution 858 n.
threaten 900 vb.
reprove 924 vb.

cautious
careful 457 adj.
cautious 858 adj.

cavalcade
marching 267 n.

cave
dwelling 192 n.
receptacle 194 n.
depth 211 n.
interiority 224 n.
cavity 255 n.
tunnel 263 n.
dissentient 489 n.
party 708 n.

caveat
warning 664 n.

cave in
break 46 vb.
descend 309 vb.
knuckle under
721 vb.

cavemen and -women
antiquity 125 n.
humankind 371 n.

cavern
cavity 255 n.

caviar
fish food 301 n.

cavil
argue 475 vb.
sophisticate
477 vb.

doubt 486 vb.
dissent 489 vb.
blame 924 vb.
criticize 924 vb.
disapprobation
924 n.
cavity
receptacle 194 n.
gap 201 n.
cavity 255 n.
cavort
dance 837 vb.
caw
rasp 407 vb.
ululate 409 vb.
ululation 409 n.
cayenne
spice 301 n.
CB radio
broadcasting
531 n.
cease
cease 145 vb.
cease-fire
lull 145 n.
pacification 719 n.
ceaseless
continuous 71 adj.
perpetual 115 adj.
cede
be inferior 35 vb.
relinquish 621 vb.
not retain 779 vb.
cedilla
punctuation 547 n.
Ceefax (tdmk)
data processing
86 n.
broadcasting
531 n.
ceilidh
assembly 74 n.
dancing 837 n.
social gathering
882 n.
ceiling
finite quantity
26 n.
superiority 34 n.
height 209 n.
vertex 213 n.
roof 226 n.
limit 236 n.
celebrate
rejoice 835 vb.
revel 837 vb.
honour 866 vb.

celebrate 876 vb.
offer worship
981 vb.
worship 981 vb.
perform ritual
988 vb.
celebrated
known 490 adj.
renowned 866 adj.
celebration
celebration 876 n.
church service
988 n.
ministration 988 n.
celebrity
person 371 n.
prosperous person
730 n.
famousness 866 n.
person of repute
866 n.
celerity
velocity 277 n.
celestial
celestial 321 adj.
divine 965 adj.
celestial body
star 321 n.
celibate
alone 88 adj.
unproductive
172 adj.
unsociable 883 adj.
celibate 895 n.
monastic 986 adj.
cell
electronics 160 n.
retreat 192 n.
compartment
194 n.
minuteness 196 n.
enclosure 235 n.
cavity 255 n.
organism 358 n.
life 360 n.
association 706 n.
party 708 n.
society 708 n.
lockup 748 n.
seclusion 883 n.
monastery 986 n.
cellar
cellar 194 n.
lowness 210 n.
cellist
instrumentalist
413 n.

cello or violoncello
viol 414 n.
cellophane
wrapping 226 n.
transparency
422 n.
paper 631 n.
cellular
concave 255 adj.
cellular radio
broadcasting
531 n.
cellular telephone
sound 398 n.
hearing aid 415 n.
telecommunication
531 n.
celluloid
materials 631 n.
Celt
native 191 n.
cembalo
piano 414 n.
cement
join 45 vb.
adhesive 47 n.
bond 47 n.
See **adhesive**
be dense 324 vb.
solid body 324 n.
hardness 326 n.
building material
631 n.
cementation
coherence 48 n.
cemetery
cemetery 364 n.
cenotaph
obsequies 364 n.
tomb 364 n.
censer
scent 396 n.
ritual object 988 n.
censor
subtract 39 vb.
exclude 57 vb.
enquirer 459 n.
estimator 480 n.
obliterate 550 vb.
purify 648 vb.
restrain 747 vb.
prohibit 757 vb.
disapprove 924 vb.
detractor 926 n.
prude 950 n.
censorious
severe 735 adj.

discontented
829 adj.
fastidious 862 adj.
disapproving
924 adj.
censure
estimate 480 n.
censure 924 n.
reprimand 924 n.
reprove 924 vb.
accusation 928 n.
guilt 936 n.
census
numeration 86 n.
statistics 86 n.
list 87 n.
enquiry 459 n.
cent
trifle 639 n.
coinage 797 n.
centaur
rara avis 84 n.
mythical being
970 n.
centenarian
hundred 99 n.
centenary
hundred 99 n.
anniversary 141 n.
special day 876 n.
centennial
hundred 99 n.
periodic 110 adj.
seasonal 141 adj.
centering
assemblage 74 n.
location 187 n.
convergence 293 n.
convergent 293 adj.
centigrade or Celsius
thermometer
thermometry
379 n.
centillion
over one hundred
99 n.
centime
coinage 797 n.
centimetre
long measure
203 n.
shortness 204 n.
centipede
hundred 99 n.
creepy-crawly
365 n.

central
fundamental
156 adj.
central 225 adj.
central heating
heating 381 n.
centralization
uniformity 16 n.
combination 50 n.
arrangement 62 n.
accumulation 74 n.
centrality 225 n.
plan 623 n.
centralize
combine 50 vb.
regularize 62 vb.
focus 76 vb.
centralize 225 vb.
central reservation
road 624 n.
centre
essence 1 n.
bring together
74 vb.
place 185 n.
place 187 vb.
interiority 224 n.
centralize 225 vb.
centre 225 n.
political party
708 n.
arena 724 n.
centre forward
front 237 n.
leader 690 n.
centre of gravity
centre 225 n.
centre on
congregate 74 vb.
focus 76 vb.
depend 157 vb.
be situated 186 vb.
converge 293 vb.
centrepiece
ornamentation
844 n.
centre upon
centralize 225 vb.
centrifugal
exterior 223 adj.
divergent 294 adj.
centurion
hundred 99 n.
soldier 722 n.
century
hundred 99 n.
period 110 n.

funds 797 n.
cephalopod
marine life 365 n.
cepheid
star 321 n.
ceramics
pottery 381 n.
sculpture 554 n.
Cerberus
three 93 n.
doorkeeper 264 n.
protector 660 n.
mythic hell 972 n.
cereals
cereals 301 n.
cerebral
mental 447 adj.
cerebral death
decease 361 n.
cerebral palsy
nervous disorders
651 n.
cerebrate
think 449 vb.
**cerebrovascular acci-
dent**
helplessness 161 n.
ceremonial
formal 875 adj.
ostentation 875 n.
celebration 876 n.
ritual 988 adj.
ritual 988 n.
ritualistic 988 adj.
ceremonious
formal 875 adj.
respectful 920 adj.
ritualistic 988 adj.
ceremony
ostentation 875 n.
celebration 876 n.
rite 988 n.
ritual 988 n.
Ceres
Olympian deity
967 n.
cerise
red 431 adj.
cerography
engraving 555 n.
cert
certainty 473 n.
certain
quantitative 26 adj.
definite 80 adj.
certain 473 adj.

anonymous
562 adj.
certain, a
one 88 adj.
anonymous
562 adj.
certain age, a
middle age 131 n.
certainly
certainly 473 adv.
truly 494 adv.
certain person
no name 562 n.
certainty
certainty 473 n.
certifiable
*mentally disor-
dered* 503 adj.
certificate
credential 466 n.
record 548 n.
title deed 767 n.
honours 866 n.
reward 962 n.
certify
testify 466 vb.
make certain
473 vb.
inform 524 vb.
affirm 532 vb.
cervical smear
diagnostic 658 n.
cervix
genitalia 167 n.
pillar 218 n.
cessation
cessation 145 n.
cesspit
receptacle 194 n.
sink 649 n.
cesspool
storage 632 n.
sink 649 n.
cetacean
mammal 365 n.
marine life 365 n.
See **mammal**
cetology
zoology 367 n.
cha-cha
dance 837 n.
chafe
rub 333 vb.
feel pain 377 vb.
give pain 377 vb.
wound 655 vb.
disobey 738 vb.

suffer 825 vb.
hurt 827 vb.
torment 827 vb.
cause discontent
829 vb.
be angry 891 vb.
chaff
leavings 41 n.
grass 366 n.
trifle 639 n.
rubbish 641 n.
witticism 839 n.
ridicule 851 n.
ridicule 851 vb.
chaffinch
bird 365 n.
chagrin
sorrow 825 n.
discontent 829 n.
chain
bond 47 n.
cable 47 n.
coherence 48 n.
continuity 71 n.
series 71 n.
long measure
203 n.
high land 209 n.
network 222 n.
gauge 465 n.
encumbrance
702 n.
fetter 748 n.
jewellery 844 n.
pillory 964 n.
chaingang
slave 742 n.
chain letter
continuity 71 n.
correspondence
588 n.
chain mail
armour 713 n.
chain of office
badge of rule
743 n.
chain reaction
continuity 71 n.
chain-smoke
smoke 388 vb.
chain smoker
tobacco 388 n.
chain stitch
needlework 844 n.
chain store
shop 796 n.

chair
seat 218 n.
elevate 310 vb.
director 690 n.
badge of rule
  743 n.
honour 866 vb.
celebrate 876 vb.
respect 920 vb.
applaud 923 vb.
chair cover
covering 226 n.
chair lift
ascent 308 n.
**chairman, chairwo-
  man**
director 690 n.
master 741 n.
chairperson
director 690 n.
master 741 n.
chaise longue
seat 218 n.
chalcedony
gem 844 n.
chalet
house 192 n.
small house 192 n.
chalice
cup 194 n.
ritual object 988 n.
church utensil
  990 n.
chalk
powder 332 n.
rock 344 n.
white thing 427 n.
mark 547 vb.
paint 553 vb.
stationery 586 n.
chalk and cheese
polarity 14 n.
chalk up
mark 547 vb.
register 548 vb.
chalky
powdery 332 adj.
white 427 adj.
challenge
disagreement 25 n.
enquiry 459 n.
  See **question**
interrogate 459 vb.
question 459 n.
dissent 489 n.
dissent 489 vb.
negate 533 vb.

negation 533 n.
incite 612 vb.
motivate 612 vb.
oppose 704 vb.
opposition 704 n.
make quarrels
  709 vb.
defiance 711 n.
defy 711 vb.
resist 715 vb.
contend 716 vb.
threat 900 n.
accusation 928 n.
accuse 928 vb.
challenger
questioner 459 n.
opponent 705 n.
contender 716 n.
accuser 928 n.
challenging
dissenting 489 adj.
defiant 711 adj.
disobedient
  738 adj.
chamber
chamber 194 n.
chambermaid
domestic 742 n.
chamber pot
vessel 194 n.
latrine 649 n.
chambers
flat 192 n.
quarters 192 n.
chameleon
changeable thing
  152 n.
reptile 365 n.
variegated 437 adj.
variegation 437 n.
chamois
skin 226 n.
mammal 365 n.
cleaning cloth
  648 n.
champ
chew 301 vb.
pugilist 722 n.
be angry 891 vb.
champagne
wine 301 n.
yellow 433 adj.
champ at the bit
disobey 738 vb.
be excitable
  822 vb.
be angry 891 vb.

champion
superior 34 n.
supreme 34 adj.
athlete 162 n.
best 644 adj.
exceller 644 n.
proficient person
  696 n.
patronize 703 vb.
patron 707 n.
defend 713 vb.
defender 713 n.
pugilist 722 n.
victor 727 n.
deputy 755 n.
person of repute
  866 n.
philanthropist
  901 n.
benefactor 903 n.
vindicate 927 vb.
championship
superiority 34 n.
aid 703 n.
approbation 923 n.
chance
casual 159 adj.
chance 159 n.
chance 159 vb.
possibility 469 n.
chance it
chance 159 vb.
gamble 618 vb.
chancel
church interior
  990 n.
chancellor
director 690 n.
officer 741 n.
**Chancellor of the
  Exchequer**
treasurer 798 n.
chance one's arm
gamble 618 vb.
attempt 671 vb.
chance upon
meet with 154 vb.
chance 159 vb.
chancy
casual 159 adj.
uncertain 474 adj.
speculative
  618 adj.
dangerous 661 adj.
chandelier
hanging object
  217 n.

lamp 420 n.
change
correlation 12 n.
change 143 n.
change 143 vb.
coinage 797 n.
money 797 n.
change, the
middle age 131 n.
unproductiveness
  172 n.
changeable
multiform 82 adj.
transient 114 adj.
changeable
  143 adj.
unreliable 474 adj.
irascible 892 adj.
change colour
change 143 vb.
show feeling
  818 vb.
quake 854 vb.
change direction
deviate 282 vb.
diverge 294 vb.
change for the better
change 143 n.
improvement
  654 n.
change hands
change hands
  780 vb.
change into
become 1 vb.
changeless
unchangeable
  153 adj.
godlike 965 adj.
changeling
child 132 n.
  See **young crea-
  ture**
substitute 150 n.
elf 970 n.
change of heart
change 143 n.
change of life
middle age 131 n.
unproductiveness
  172 n.
change one's mind
vary 152 vb.
turn round 282 vb.
*be of the opinion
  that* 485 vb.

change one's mind
603 vb.
relinquish 621 vb.
change one's tune
differ 15 vb.
change 143 vb.
change one's mind
603 vb.
changeover
transfer 780 n.
change round
modify 143 vb.
displace 188 vb.
change one's mind
603 vb.
change sides
be irresolute
601 vb.
apostatize 603 vb.
changing
changeful 152 adj.
channel
bond 47 n.
cavity 255 n.
furrow 262 n.
groove 262 vb.
transpose 272 vb.
way in 297 n.
passage 305 n.
gulf 345 n.
conduit 351 n.
informant 524 n.
access 624 n.
direct 689 vb.
Channel Tunnel
tunnel 263 n.
chant
cry 408 n.
vociferate 408 vb.
vocal music 412 n.
sing 413 vb.
voice 577 vb.
chanter
flute 414 n.
worshipper 981 n.
chanting
loudness 400 n.
act of worship
981 n.
chantry
church 990 n.
chaos
noncoherence 49 n.
decomposition
51 n.
disorder 61 n.
amorphism 244 n.

anarchy 734 n.
chaotic
amorphous
244 adj.
lawless 954 adj.
chap
gap 201 n.
roughen 259 vb.
roughness 259 n.
person 371 n.
male 372 n.
coldness 380 n.
chapel
association 706 n.
society 708 n.
sect 978 n.
church 990 n.
church interior
990 n.
chaperon
accompany 89 vb.
concomitant 89 n.
look after 457 vb.
surveillance 457 n.
protector 660 n.
safeguard 660 vb.
keeper 749 n.
chaplain
retainer 742 n.
church officer
986 n.
pastor 986 n.
chaplaincy
church office 985 n.
chapped
rough 259 adj.
chappie
male 372 n.
chaps
trousers 228 n.
chapter
subdivision 53 n.
topic 452 n.
edition 589 n.
synod 985 n.
chapter and verse
evidence 466 n.
accuracy 494 n.
chapterhouse
church exterior
990 n.
char
soft drink 301 n.
burn 381 vb.
blacken 428 vb.
brown 430 vb.
cleaner 648 n.

servant 742 n.
serve 742 vb.
charabanc
carriage 274 n.
character
character 5 n.
modality 7 n.
composition 56 n.
nonconformist
84 n.
number 85 n.
person 371 n.
credential 466 n.
letter 558 n.
acting 594 n.
repute 866 n.
virtue 933 n.
characteristic
characteristic
5 adj.
intrinsic 5 adj.
special 80 adj.
speciality 80 n.
tendency 179 n.
identification
547 n.
characteristics
character 5 n.
characterization
representation
551 n.
description 590 n.
dramaturgy 594 n.
characterize
make uniform
16 vb.
represent 551 vb.
describe 590 vb.
characters
lettering 586 n.
actor 594 n.
charade
enigma 530 n.
gesture 547 n.
representation
551 n.
drama 594 n.
charades
indoor game 837 n.
charcoal
fuel 385 n.
black thing 428 n.
chard
fruit and vegetables
301 n.
charge
fill 54 vb.

energy 160 n.
load 193 vb.
move fast 277 vb.
collision 279 n.
make heavy
322 vb.
heraldry 547 n.
ornament 574 vb.
job 622 n.
protection 660 n.
management
689 n.
precept 693 n.
attack 712 n.
explosive 723 n.
command 737 n.
command 737 vb.
demand 737 vb.
dependant 742 n.
detention 747 n.
commission
751 vb.
mandate 751 n.
bargain 791 vb.
debt 803 n.
account 808 vb.
price 809 n.
price 809 vb.
tax 809 n.
wrong 914 n.
duty 917 n.
blame 924 vb.
accusation 928 n.
indict 928 vb.
litigate 959 vb.
litigation 959 n.
laity 987 n.
charge at
be rash 857 vb.
charge card
credit 802 n.
charged
weighty 322 adj.
chargé d'affaires
envoy 754 n.
charge nurse
nurse 658 n.
charger
plate 194 n.
horse 273 n.
cavalry 722 n.
accuser 928 n.
charges
price 809 n.
charge with
attribute 158 vb.
accuse 928 vb.

chariot
 carriage 274 n.
charisma
 power 160 n.
 influence 178 n.
charismatic
 influential 178 adj.
charitable
 liberal 813 adj.
 benevolent 897 adj.
 philanthropic
  901 adj.
 pitying 905 adj.
charity
 aid 703 n.
 subvention 703 n.
 gift 781 n.
 giving 781 n.
 liberality 813 n.
 love 887 n.
 benevolence 897 n.
 pity 905 n.
 disinterestedness
  931 n.
 virtues 933 n.
charity that begins at
 home
 selfishness 932 n.
charlatan
 dabbler 493 n.
 impostor 545 n.
charlatanism
 sciolism 491 n.
 duplicity 541 n.
 pretension 850 n.
Charleston
 dance 837 n.
 dance 837 vb.
Charles' Wain
 star 321 n.
charley
 ninny 501 n.
charlotte
 dessert 301 n.
charm
 attract 291 vb.
 attraction 291 n.
 incentive 612 n.
 inducement 612 n.
 motivate 612 vb.
 delight 826 vb.
 please 826 vb.
 pleasurableness
  826 n.
 beauty 841 n.
 jewellery 844 n.
 bewitch 983 vb.

 spell 983 n.
 talisman 983 n.
charmer
 attraction 291 n.
 exceller 644 n.
 a beauty 841 n.
 flatterer 925 n.
charming
 pleasurable
  826 adj.
 personable 841 adj.
charms
 beauty 841 n.
charnel house
 death 361 n.
 interment 364 n.
Charolais
 cattle 365 n.
Charon
 mythic hell 972 n.
charpoy
 bed 218 n.
chart
 list 87 n.
 situation 186 n.
 itinerary 267 n.
 sailing aid 269 n.
 guidebook 524 n.
 map 551 n.
 represent 551 vb.
charter
 record 548 n.
 commission
  751 vb.
 mandate 751 n.
 permit 756 n.
 permit 756 vb.
 title deed 767 n.
 dueness 915 n.
 exempt 919 vb.
 nonliability 919 n.
 law 953 n.
chartered accountant
 accountant 808 n.
charter flight
 air travel 271 n.
chartreuse
 yellow 433 adj.
 green 434 adj.
charts, the
 vocal music 412 n.
chart-topping
 best 644 adj.
 successful 727 adj.
charwoman
 cleaner 648 n.
 worker 686 n.

 servant 742 n.
Charybdis
 vortex 315 n.
chase
 park 192 n.
 move fast 277 vb.
 follow 284 vb.
 grassland 348 n.
 wood 366 n.
 sculpt 554 vb.
 chase 619 n.
 pursue 619 vb.
 desire 859 vb.
 be hostile 881 vb.
 be in love 887 vb.
 court 889 vb.
 not respect 921 vb.
 disapprove 924 vb.
chaser
 draught 301 n.
chasing
 ornamental art
  844 n.
chasing the dragon
 drug-taking 949 n.
chasm
 disunion 46 n.
 gap 201 n.
 depth 211 n.
 cavity 255 n.
 pitfall 663 n.
chassé
 ballet 594 n.
chassis
 base 214 n.
 frame 218 n.
 support 218 n.
 carrier 273 n.
 structure 331 n.
chaste
 plain 573 adj.
 modest 874 adj.
 virtuous 933 adj.
 temperate 942 adj.
 pure 950 adj.
chasten
 moderate 177 vb.
 humiliate 872 vb.
chastened
 repentant 939 adj.
chastise
 reprove 924 vb.
 punish 963 vb.
chastity
 contraception
  172 n.
 modesty 874 n.

 virtue 933 n.
 temperance 942 n.
 purity 950 n.
chasuble
 vestments 989 n.
chat
 cry 408 n.
 speech 579 n.
 chat 584 n.
 converse 584 vb.
 interlocution
  584 n.
chateau
 house 192 n.
chatelaine
 resident 191 n.
 manager 690 n.
 retainer 742 n.
 keeper 749 n.
chatoyance
 variegation 437 n.
chatoyant
 luminous 417 adj.
chat show
 broadcast 531 n.
chattel
 slave 742 n.
 property 777 n.
chattels
 equipment 630 n.
chatter
 oscillate 317 vb.
 be cold 380 vb.
 roll 403 n.
 roll 403 vb.
 ululate 409 vb.
 empty talk 515 n.
 speak 579 vb.
 be loquacious
  581 vb.
 chatter 581 n.
chatterbox
 chatterer 581 n.
chat to
 be sociable 882 vb.
chatty
 loquacious 581 adj.
 sociable 882 adj.
chauffeur
 driver 268 n.
 domestic 742 n.
chauvinism
 nation 371 n.
 prejudice 481 n.
 exaggeration
  546 n.
 bellicosity 718 n.

boasting 877 n.
patriotism 901 n.
chauvinist
narrow mind
481 n.
militarist 722 n.
patriot 901 n.
cheap
cheap 812 adj.
vulgar 847 adj.
disreputable
867 adj.
cheapen
be cheap 812 vb.
cheapen 812 vb.
not respect 921 vb.
cheapen oneself
demean oneself
867 vb.
cheapjack
cheap 812 adj.
cheat
deceive 542 vb.
deception 542 n.
trickery 542 n.
trickster 545 n.
be cunning 698 vb.
slyboots 698 n.
stratagem 698 n.
fleece 786 vb.
defraud 788 vb.
defrauder 789 n.
be dishonest
930 vb.
bad person 938 n.
cheating
duplicity 541 n.
false 541 adj.
deception 542 n.
cunning 698 n.
swindling 788 n.
perfidious 930 adj.
check
number 86 vb.
halt 145 vb.
stop 145 n.
moderate 177 vb.
moderation 177 n.
counteraction
182 n.
retard 278 vb.
chequer 437 n.
pied 437 adj.
enquire 459 vb.
enquiry 459 n.
experiment 461 n.

measurement
465 n.
certainty 473 n.
make certain
473 vb.
hinder 702 vb.
hindrance 702 n.
defeat 727 vb.
defeat 728 n.
adversity 731 n.
restrain 747 vb.
restraint 747 n.
loss 772 n.
pattern 844 n.
checkers
board game 837 n.
checking
measurement
465 n.
restraining
747 adj.
checklist
list 87 n.
comparison 462 n.
checkmate
halt 145 vb.
stop 145 n.
overmaster 727 vb.
victory 727 n.
defeat 728 n.
check on
enquire 459 vb.
checkout
recording instru-
ment 549 n.
checkup
attention 455 n.
enquiry 459 n.
check with
compare 462 vb.
cheek
laterality 239 n.
be insolent 878 vb.
sauciness 878 n.
rudeness 885 n.
scurrility 899 n.
cheek by jowl
with 89 adv.
near 200 adv.
sideways 239 adv.
cheeky
impertinent
878 adj.
discourteous
885 adj.
disrespectful
921 adj.

cheep
ululate 409 vb.
ululation 409 n.
cheer
cry 408 n.
cry 408 vb.
vociferate 408 vb.
gesture 547 n.
excite 821 vb.
be cheerful 833 vb.
cheer 833 vb.
rejoice 835 vb.
celebrate 876 vb.
show respect
920 vb.
applaud 923 vb.
cheerful
cheerful 833 adj.
cheerio
goodbye 296 int.
cheerleader
cry 408 n.
cheerless
cheerless 834 adj.
dejected 834 adj.
melancholic
834 adj.
cheers
bon appétit 301 int.
cheers 835 int.
rejoicing 835 n.
thanks 907 int.
cheer up
relieve 831 vb.
be cheerful 833 vb.
cheery
cheerful 833 adj.
cheese
dairy product
301 n.
cheesecake
pastries and cakes
301 n.
a beauty 841 n.
cheesed off
discontented
829 adj.
dejected 834 adj.
bored 838 adj.
cheese-paring
economical
814 adj.
economy 814 n.
parsimonious
816 adj.
parsimony 816 n.

cheetah
big cat 365 n.
chef
cookery 301 n.
caterer 633 n.
chef d'oeuvre
perfection 646 n.
masterpiece 694 n.
Chelsea pensioner
soldier 722 n.
chemise
dress 228 n.
underwear 228 n.
chemist
experimenter
461 n.
druggist 658 n.
chemistry
conversion 147 n.
physics 319 n.
chemotherapy
therapy 658 n.
chenille
textile 222 n.
cheongsam
dress 228 n.
cheque
paper money
797 n.
chequebook
record 548 n.
chequer
chequer 437 n.
variegate 437 vb.
chequered
changeable
143 adj.
pied 437 adj.
Chequers
house 192 n.
chéri(e)
darling 890 n.
cherish
look after 457 vb.
safeguard 660 vb.
animate 821 vb.
love 887 vb.
approve 923 vb.
**cherished number-
plate**
label 547 n.
cheroot
tobacco 388 n.
cherry
fruit and vegetables
301 n.
redness 431 n.

595

cherub
child 132 n.
image 551 n.
darling 890 n.
angel 968 n.
cherubim
angel 968 n.
Cheshire cat grin
laughter 835 n.
chess
board game 837 n.
chessboard
chequer 437 n.
arena 724 n.
chess piece
plaything 837 n.
chest
box 194 n.
insides 224 n.
bosom 253 n.
treasury 799 n.
chesterfield
seat 218 n.
chestnut
repetition 106 n.
horse 273 n.
fruit and vegetables
301 n.
brown 430 adj.
witticism 839 n.
chest of drawers
cabinet 194 n.
cheval glass
mirror 442 n.
chevet
church interior
990 n.
chevron
obliquity 220 n.
angularity 247 n.
heraldry 547 n.
badge of rank
743 n.
pattern 844 n.
chew
chew 301 vb.
chewing
eating 301 n.
chewing gum
mouthful 301 n.
See sweetmeat
sweets 301 n.
elasticity 328 n.
chew the cud
graze 301 vb.
chewy
tough 329 adj.

chez
inside 224 adv.
chianti
wine 301 n.
chiaroscuro
darkening 418 n.
painted 553 adj.
painting 553 n.
chiasmus
inversion 221 n.
ornament 574 n.
chic
beauty 841 n.
personable 841 adj.
shapely 841 adj.
fashion 848 n.
fashionable
848 adj.
chicanery
sophistry 477 n.
trickery 542 n.
perfidy 930 n.
chichi
fashionable
848 adj.
affected 850 adj.
chick
young creature
132 n.
youngster 132 n.
female 373 n.
darling 890 n.
chicken
young creature
132 n.
weakling 163 n.
meat 301 n.
poultry 365 n.
coward 856 n.
cowardice 856 n.
cowardly 856 adj.
darling 890 n.
chickenfeed
small quantity
33 n.
trifle 639 n.
easy thing 701 n.
money 797 n.
chicken-livered
cowardly 856 adj.
chicken out
be cowardly
856 vb.
chickenpox
infection 651 n.

chicory
fruit and vegetables
301 n.
chide
curse 899 vb.
reprove 924 vb.
chief
superior 34 n.
supreme 34 adj.
first 68 adj.
central 225 adj.
heraldry 547 n.
bigwig 638 n.
important 638 adj.
director 690 n.
potentate 741 n.
chief constable
police 955 n.
chieftain
potentate 741 n.
chiffon
textile 222 n.
transparency
422 n.
chiffonier
cabinet 194 n.
chignon
hair 259 n.
hairdressing 843 n.
chihuahua
dog 365 n.
chilblain(s)
coldness 380 n.
ulcer 651 n.
child
child 132 n.
innocent 935 n.
child abuse
painfulness 827 n.
cruel act 898 n.
child-bearing
female 373 adj.
child benefit
subvention 703 n.
childbirth
obstetrics 167 n.
childhood
youth 130 n.
childish
young 130 adj.
feeble 572 adj.
trivial 639 adj.
immature 670 adj.
childless
unproductive
172 adj.

childlike
young 130 adj.
artless 699 adj.
innocent 935 adj.
childminder
surveillance 457 n.
child psychology
therapy 658 n.
children
kinsman 11 n.
child 132 n.
posterity 170 n.
children's home
shelter 662 n.
child's play
trifle 639 n.
easy thing 701 n.
chill
moderate 177 vb.
be cold 380 vb.
coldness 380 n.
refrigerate 382 vb.
adversity 731 n.
frighten 854 vb.
chilli
fruit and vegetables
301 n.
spice 301 n.
chilly
chilly 380 adj.
cold 380 adj.
hostile 881 adj.
chime
sound faint 401 vb.
roll 403 vb.
resonance 404 n.
resound 404 vb.
melody 410 n.
tune 412 n.
chime in
accord 24 vb.
chimera
insubstantial thing
4 n.
rara avis 84 n.
fantasy 513 n.
chimney
gap 201 n.
chimneypot
cylinder 252 n.
chimney stack
high structure
209 n.
chimneysweep
cleaner 648 n.
chimpanzee
mammal 365 n.

chin
  protuberance
    254 n.
china
  weak thing 163 n.
  pottery 381 n.
  ornamentation
    844 n.
china doll
  image 551 n.
  plaything 837 n.
chinaware
  receptacle 194 n.
  pottery 381 n.
chinchilla
  skin 226 n.
chinese lantern
  lamp 420 n.
  celebration 876 n.
chink
  gap 201 n.
  narrowness 206 n.
  furrow 262 n.
  faintness 401 n.
  sound faint 401 vb.
  resonance 404 n.
  resound 404 vb.
chink in one's ar-
    mour
  defect 647 n.
  vulnerability 661 n.
chinoiserie
  ornamentation
    844 n.
chinook
  wind 352 n.
chintz
  textile 222 n.
chinwag
  speech 579 n.
  chat 584 n.
  converse 584 vb.
chip
  small thing 33 n.
  break 46 vb.
  cut 46 vb.
  piece 53 n.
  label 547 n.
  sculpt 554 vb.
chip away
  make smaller
    198 vb.
chip in
  discontinue 72 vb.
  interfere 231 vb.
  aid 703 vb.
  give 781 vb.

chipmunk
  mammal 365 n.
chip off the old block
  analogue 18 n.
  descendant 170 n.
chipolata
  meat 301 n.
chip on one's shoul-
    der
  discontent 829 n.
chipper
  cheerful 833 adj.
chippy
  loose woman
    952 n.
chips
  fruit and vegetables
    301 n.
chips are down, the
  crisis 137 n.
chiromancy
  occultism 984 n.
chiropodist
  doctor 658 n.
  beautician 843 n.
chiropractor
  doctor 658 n.
chirp
  ululate 409 vb.
  sing 413 vb.
  be cheerful 833 vb.
chirpy
  cheerful 833 adj.
chirrup
  ululate 409 vb.
  sing 413 vb.
  be cheerful 833 vb.
chisel
  cut 46 vb.
  produce 164 vb.
  form 243 vb.
  sharp edge 256 n.
  sculpt 554 vb.
  engraving 555 n.
  tool 630 n.
chit
  youngster 132 n.
  dwarf 196 n.
  credential 466 n.
  reminder 505 n.
  label 547 n.
  correspondence
    588 n.
  permit 756 n.
chit-chat
  chat 584 n.

chitter
  be cold 380 vb.
chitterlings
  meat 301 n.
chivalrous
  male 372 adj.
  courageous
    855 adj.
  noble 868 adj.
  courteous 884 adj.
  benevolent 897 adj.
  honourable
    929 adj.
chivalry
  courage 855 n.
  manliness 855 n.
  prowess 855 n.
  courtesy 884 n.
  philanthropy
    901 n.
  probity 929 n.
chives
  herb 301 n.
chlorinate
  purify 648 vb.
  make sanitary
    652 vb.
  safeguard 660 vb.
chloroform
  anaesthetic 375 n.
  render insensible
    375 vb.
chock-a-block
  full 54 adj.
  filled 635 adj.
chock-full
  full 54 adj.
  filled 635 adj.
chocolate
  milk 301 n.
  mouthful 301 n.
  sweets 301 n.
  brown 430 adj.
  brownness 430 n.
choice
  unusual 84 adj.
  savoury 390 adj.
  choice 605 n.
  chosen 605 adj.
  excellent 644 adj.
  pleasurable
    826 adj.
choir
  choir 413 n.
  church interior
    990 n.

choirboy or -girl
  choir 413 n.
  church officer
    986 n.
choirmaster
  choir 413 n.
  trainer 537 n.
choirstall
  compartment
    194 n.
  seat 218 n.
  church interior
    990 n.
choke
  close 264 vb.
  stopper 264 n.
  kill 362 vb.
  extinguish 382 vb.
  rasp 407 vb.
  superabound
    637 vb.
  hinder 702 vb.
choke back
  restrain 747 vb.
choker
  loop 250 n.
  jewellery 844 n.
choky
  lockup 748 n.
cholera
  digestive disorders
    651 n.
  infection 651 n.
  tropical disease
    651 n.
choleric
  irascible 892 adj.
cholesterol
  food content 301 n.
chomp
  chew 301 vb.
choose
  choose 605 vb.
choosy
  fastidious 862 adj.
chop
  cut 46 vb.
  piece 53 n.
  meat 301 n.
chop and change
  change 143 vb.
  vary 152 vb.
  be capricious
    604 vb.
Chopper (tdmk)
  bicycle 274 n.

chopper
  sharp edge 256 n.
  aircraft 276 n.
  pulverizer 332 n.
  axe 723 n.
choppy
  rough 259 adj.
chop suey
  dish 301 n.
choral
  musical 412 adj.
chorale
  vocal music 412 n.
choral music
  music 412 n.
chord
  straightness 249 n.
  musical note
    410 n.
  musical piece
    412 n.
chore
  labour 682 n.
  bore 838 n.
chorea
  spasm 318 n.
choreography
  composition 56 n.
  arrangement 62 n.
  ballet 594 n.
  dramaturgy 594 n.
  dancing 837 n.
chores
  job 622 n.
  labour 682 n.
chorionic villus sampling
  diagnostic 658 n.
chorister
  choir 413 n.
  church officer
    986 n.
chortle
  laugh 835 vb.
  laughter 835 n.
chorus
  be uniform 16 vb.
  do likewise 20 vb.
  accord 24 vb.
  agreement 24 n.
  combination 50 n.
  repetition 106 n.
  synchronize
    123 vb.
  periodicity 141 n.
  cry 408 n.
  vociferate 408 vb.

  harmonize 410 vb.
  melody 410 n.
  vocal music 412 n.
  choir 413 n.
  sing 413 vb.
  speaker 579 n.
  actor 594 n.
  dramaturgy 594 n.
chorus girl
  entertainer 594 n.
chosen
  chosen 605 adj.
  sanctified 979 adj.
chosen few
  elite 644 n.
  upper class 868 n.
chou
  darling 890 n.
choux pastry
  pastries and cakes
    301 n.
chow
  food 301 n.
  dog 365 n.
chowder
  hors-d'oeuvres
    301 n.
chow mein
  dish 301 n.
chrismatory
  ritual object 988 n.
Christ
  God the Son 965 n.
  religious teacher
    973 n.
christen
  auspicate 68 vb.
  name 561 vb.
  perform ritual
    988 vb.
christening
  nomenclature
    561 n.
  Christian rite
    988 n.
  rite 988 n.
christening gown
  ritual object 988 n.
Christian
  benevolent 897 adj.
  good person 937 n.
  religionist 973 n.
  religious 973 adj.
  pious 979 adj.
Christianity
  religious faith
    973 n.

Christian name
  name 561 n.
Christian Scientist
  doctor 658 n.
  sectarian 978 n.
Christmas
  winter 129 n.
  holy day 988 n.
Christmas box
  gift 781 n.
Christmas candle
  torch 420 n.
Christmas card
  correspondence
    588 n.
Christmas dinner
  feasting 301 n.
Christmas present
  gift 781 n.
Christmas pudding
  dessert 301 n.
Christmas tree lights
  lamp 420 n.
chromatics
  colour 425 n.
chromatin
  organism 358 n.
chromatism
  colour 425 n.
chrome yellow
  yellowness 433 n.
chromosome
  heredity 5 n.
  organism 358 n.
chronic
  lasting 113 adj.
  obstinate 602 adj.
  sick 651 adj.
chronicle
  chronology 117 n.
  time 117 vb.
  record 548 n.
  record 548 vb.
  narrative 590 n.
chronicler
  chronologist 117 n.
  chronicler 549 n.
chronograph
  timekeeper 117 n.
chronology
  chronology 117 n.
chronometry
  chronometry
    117 n.
chronoscope
  timekeeper 117 n.

chronoscopy
  chronometry
    117 n.
chrysalis
  young creature
    132 n.
  source 156 n.
  receptacle 194 n.
  wrapping 226 n.
chrysanthemum
  plant 366 n.
chrysolite
  gem 844 n.
chubby
  fleshy 195 adj.
chuck
  propel 287 vb.
  propulsion 287 n.
  food 301 n.
chuck it
  resign 753 vb.
chuckle
  ululate 409 vb.
  laugh 835 vb.
  laughter 835 n.
chuck out
  eject 300 vb.
  reject 607 vb.
chuck under the chin
  caress 889 vb.
chuffed
  pleased 824 adj.
  jubilant 833 adj.
chug
  be in motion
    265 vb.
  move slowly
    278 vb.
  roll 403 vb.
chum
  colleague 707 n.
  chum 880 n.
chummy
  friendly 880 adj.
  sociable 882 adj.
chump
  head 213 n.
  dunce 501 n.
chump chop
  meat 301 n.
chunder
  vomit 300 vb.
chunk
  piece 53 n.
  bulk 195 n.
  solid body 324 n.

chunky
  fleshy 195 adj.
chunnel
  tunnel 263 n.
church
  edifice 164 n.
  party 708 n.
  public worship
    981 n.
  church 990 n.
church bell
  gong 414 n.
  call 547 n.
  church utensil
    990 n.
churchgoer
  worshipper 981 n.
church-going
  public worship
    981 n.
churchman or -wo-
    man
  cleric 986 n.
church officer
  Christendom
    976 n.
  church officer
    986 n.
Church of Rome
  Christendom
    976 n.
church organ
  organ 414 n.
church service
  church service
    988 n.
churchwarden
  tobacco 388 n.
  church officer
    986 n.
churchy
  orthodox 976 adj.
  pietistic 979 adj.
churchyard
  cemetery 364 n.
  church exterior
    990 n.
churlish
  ill-bred 847 adj.
  plebeian 869 adj.
  malevolent
    898 adj.
churn
  vessel 194 n.
  rotate 315 vb.
  rotator 315 n.
  agitate 318 vb.

thicken 354 vb.
churn out
  produce 164 vb.
chute
  obliquity 220 n.
  smoothness 258 n.
  airship 276 n.
  outlet 298 n.
  descent 309 n.
  conduit 351 n.
chutney
  sauce 389 n.
chutzpah
  insolence 878 n.
chyle
  fluid 335 n.
chypre
  scent 396 n.
CIA
  secret service
    459 n.
ciao
  goodbye 296 int.
ciborium
  ritual object 988 n.
cicada
  insect 365 n.
cicatrice
  blemish 845 n.
Cicero
  speaker 579 n.
CID
  police enquiry
    459 n.
cider
  alcoholic drink
    301 n.
ci-devant
  prior 119 adj.
cigar
  tobacco 388 n.
cigar case
  tobacco 388 n.
cigarette
  tobacco 388 n.
cigarette card
  picture 553 n.
cigarette case
  case 194 n.
  tobacco 388 n.
cigarette holder
  handle 218 n.
cigarette machine
  tobacco 388 n.
cilium
  filament 208 n.

cinch
  certainty 473 n.
  dupe 544 n.
  easy thing 701 n.
Cinderella
  poor person 801 n.
Cindy (tdmk) doll
  image 551 n.
  plaything 837 n.
cinema
  cinema 445 n.
  place of amuse-
    ment 837 n.
Cinemascope (tdmk)
  film 445 n.
cinematography
  cinema 445 n.
  photography 551 n.
Cinerama (tdmk)
  film 445 n.
cinerarium
  cemetery 364 n.
cinerary
  funereal 364 adj.
cingulum
  vestments 989 n.
cinnabar
  red pigment 431 n.
cinnamon
  spice 301 n.
  brownness 430 n.
cinquefoil
  five 99 n.
  heraldry 547 n.
Cinque Ports
  five 99 n.
cipher
  nonexistence 2 n.
  insubstantial thing
    4 n.
  number 85 n.
  zero 103 n.
  secrecy 525 n.
  enigma 530 n.
  indication 547 n.
  label 547 n.
  writing 586 n.
  nonentity 639 n.
circa
  nearly 200 adv.
Circe
  attraction 291 n.
  motivator 612 n.
  sorceress 983 n.
circle
  continuity 71 n.
  assembly 74 n.

  group 74 n.
  region 184 n.
circumscribe
    232 vb.
circumscription
    232 n.
  circle 250 n.
  fly 271 vb.
  circle 314 vb.
  onlookers 441 n.
  informant 524 n.
  theatre 594 n.
  party 708 n.
circuit
  continuity 71 n.
  periodicity 141 n.
  regular return
    141 n.
  revolution 149 n.
  electricity 160 n.
  region 184 n.
  surroundings
    230 n.
  outline 233 n.
  circle 250 n.
  orbit 250 n.
  land travel 267 n.
  circle 314 vb.
  circuition 314 n.
  circuit 626 n.
  circuit 626 vb.
circuit judge
  judge 957 n.
circuitous
  circuitous 314 adj.
  roundabout
    626 adj.
circular
  continuous 71 adj.
  round 250 adj.
  information 524 n.
  publication 528 n.
  correspondence
    588 n.
  reading matter
    589 n.
  decree 737 n.
circularity
  circularity 250 n.
circularize
  publish 528 vb.
  correspond 588 vb.
  command 737 vb.
circular saw
  notch 260 n.
  rotator 315 n.

psychic 984 n.
psychical 984 n.
clam
marine life 365 n.
taciturnity 582 n.
clamber
climb 308 vb.
clamlike
reticent 525 adj.
clamour
loudness 400 n.
cry 408 n.
vociferate 408 vb.
disapprobation
924 n.
clamp
affix 45 vb.
fastening 47 n.
moderator 177 n.
restraint 747 n.
fetter 748 n.
pincers 778 n.
clamp down on
suppress 165 vb.
be severe 735 vb.
restrain 747 vb.
clan
family 11 n.
race 11 n.
group 74 n.
breed 77 n.
genealogy 169 n.
native 191 n.
community 708 n.
clandestine
occult 523 adj.
concealed 525 adj.
stealthy 525 adj.
clang
be loud 400 vb.
loudness 400 n.
roll 403 n.
roll 403 vb.
resonance 404 n.
clanger
mistake 495 n.
clank
resound 404 vb.
rasp 407 vb.
clannish
ethnic 11 adj.
excluding 57 adj.
biased 481 adj.
sectarian 978 adj.
clansman
kinsman 11 n.
friend 880 n.

clap
knock 279 n.
be loud 400 vb.
loudness 400 n.
bang 402 n.
crackle 402 vb.
rejoice 835 vb.
congratulate
886 vb.
applaud 923 vb.
applause 923 n.
clap, the
venereal disease
651 n.
clap in jail
arrest 747 vb.
clap one's hands
collide 279 vb.
rejoice 835 vb.
applaud 923 vb.
clap on the back
gesticulate 547 vb.
applaud 923 vb.
clapped out
impotent 161 adj.
clappers
gong 414 n.
clapping
gesture 547 n.
rejoicing 835 n.
applause 923 n.
approving 923 adj.
claptrap
sophistry 477 n.
empty talk 515 n.
fable 543 n.
claque
flatterer 925 n.
clarendon
print-type 587 n.
claret
wine 301 n.
redness 431 n.
clarification
demonstration
478 n.
interpretation
520 n.
clarify
liquefy 337 vb.
be intelligible
516 vb.
interpret 520 vb.
purify 648 vb.
clarinet
flute 414 n.

clarinettist
instrumentalist
413 n.
clarion
horn 414 n.
clarion call
loudness 400 n.
war measures
718 n.
clarity
transparency
422 n.
visibility 443 n.
intelligibility
516 n.
perspicuity 567 n.
clash
contrariety 14 n.
disagree 25 vb.
disagreement 25 n.
union 45 n.
violence 176 n.
counteract 182 vb.
counteraction
182 n.
collide 279 vb.
collision 279 n.
be loud 400 vb.
loudness 400 n.
bang 402 vb.
rasp 407 vb.
discord 411 vb.
quarrel 709 n.
quarrel 709 vb.
contention 716 n.
fight 716 n.
battle 718 n.
be hostile 881 vb.
clash with
collide 279 vb.
clasp
fastening 47 n.
cohere 48 vb.
circumscribe
232 vb.
retain 778 vb.
retention 778 n.
jewellery 844 n.
caress 889 vb.
endearment 889 n.
clasped hands
entreaty 761 n.
class
degree 27 n.
graduate 27 vb.
arrangement 62 n.
class 62 vb.

grade 73 vb.
group 74 n.
breed 77 n.
classification 77 n.
contemporary
123 n.
study 536 n.
class 538 n.
party 708 n.
class-consciousness
pride 871 n.
classes, the
group 74 n.
classic
elegant 575 adj.
book 589 n.
excellent 644 adj.
paragon 646 n.
classical
architectural
192 adj.
literary 557 adj.
elegant 575 adj.
perfect 646 adj.
tasteful 846 adj.
right 913 adj.
classical music
music 412 n.
classic example
relevance 9 n.
analogue 18 n.
example 83 n.
**Classicism, classi-
cism**
literature 557 n.
elegance 575 n.
classics
literature 557 n.
classification
relation 9 n.
subdivision 53 n.
arrangement 62 n.
classification 77 n.
classified
orderly 60 adj.
arranged 62 adj.
classified ad
advertisement
528 n.
classify
class 62 vb.
grade 73 vb.
indicate 547 vb.
classism
prejudice 481 n.
injustice 914 n.

classmate
learner 538 n.
chum 880 n.
class war
prejudice 481 n.
classwork
study 536 n.
classy
personable 841 adj.
fashionable
848 adj.
genteel 868 adj.
clatter
medley 43 n.
loudness 400 n.
roll 403 n.
roll 403 vb.
clause
part 53 n.
subdivision 53 n.
conditions 766 n.
claustrophobia
neurosis 503 adj.
phobia 854 n.
clavichord
piano 414 n.
clavier
piano 414 n.
claw
rend 46 vb.
foot 214 n.
sharp point 256 n.
groove 262 vb.
finger 378 n.
wound 655 vb.
pincers 778 n.
claws
weapon 723 n.
clay
adhesive 47 n.
changeable thing
152 n.
solid body 324 n.
softness 327 n.
soil 344 n.
sculpture 554 n.
materials 631 n.
claymore
sidearms 723 n.
clay pipe
tobacco 388 n.
clean
empty 190 adj.
empty 300 vb.
clean 648 adj.
clean 648 vb.
cleansing 648 n.

clean bill of health
health 650 n.
clean breast
assent 488 n.
disclosure 526 n.
veracity 540 n.
clean-cut
personable 841 adj.
cleaned out
poor 801 adj.
cleaner
cleaner 648 n.
cleaning lady
servant 742 n.
cleanliness
cleanness 648 n.
hygiene 652 n.
cleanly
clean 648 adj.
cleanness
cleanness 648 n.
clean out
empty 300 vb.
search 459 vb.
clean 648 vb.
purify 648 vb.
steal 788 vb.
cleanse
purify 648 vb.
make sanitary
652 adj.
cleanser
cleanser 648 n.
clean-shaven
hairless 229 adj.
cleansing
cleansing 648 n.
beautification
843 n.
cleansing cream
cleanser 648 n.
cosmetic 843 n.
clean slate
extinction 2 n.
newness 126 n.
revolution 149 n.
facility 701 n.
clean sweep
revolution 149 n.
ejection 300 n.
obliteration 550 n.
clean up
empty 300 vb.
clean 648 vb.
purify 648 vb.
get rich 800 vb.

clear
be great - large
32 vb.
unmixed 44 adj.
space 201 vb.
be high 209 vb.
empty 300 vb.
leap 312 vb.
make bright
417 vb.
undimmed
417 adj.
transparent
422 adj.
obvious 443 adj.
certain 473 adj.
semantic 514 adj.
intelligible 516 adj.
manifest 522 adj.
safe 660 adj.
disencumber
701 vb.
palmy 730 adj.
liberate 746 vb.
permit 756 vb.
acquire 771 vb.
receive 782 vb.
justify 927 vb.
acquit 960 vb.
acquitted 960 adj.
clearage
voidance 300 n.
clearance
subtraction 39 n.
room 183 n.
interval 201 n.
voidance 300 n.
defecation 302 n.
scope 744 n.
permission 756 n.
permit 756 n.
payment 804 n.
vindication 927 n.
acquittal 960 n.
clear as daylight
manifest 522 adj.
clear as ditch water
puzzling 517 adj.
clear as mud
puzzling 517 adj.
unclear 568 adj.
clear away
displace 188 vb.
empty 300 vb.
disencumber
701 vb.

clear conscience
probity 929 n.
virtue 933 n.
innocence 935 n.
clear-cut
definite 80 adj.
obvious 443 adj.
positive 473 adj.
intelligible 516 adj.
clear-headed
rational 475 adj.
intelligent 498 adj.
sane 502 adj.
sober 948 adj.
clearing
open space 263 n.
wood 366 n.
clearness
transparency
422 n.
visibility 443 n.
intelligibility
516 n.
perspicuity 567 n.
clear off
decamp 296 vb.
clear one's name
justify 927 vb.
clear out
recede 290 vb.
decamp 296 vb.
emerge 298 vb.
empty 300 vb.
clean 648 vb.
clear the decks
empty 300 vb.
make ready
669 vb.
clear the throat
eruct 300 vb.
rasp 407 vb.
clear the way
come before 64 vb.
precede 283 vb.
pass 305 vb.
facilitate 701 vb.
clear up
cease 145 vb.
make bright
417 vb.
be intelligible
516 vb.
clean 648 vb.
carry through
725 vb.

clearway
traffic control
305 n.
road 624 n.

cleat
fastening 47 n.

cleavage
disunion 46 n.
scission 46 n.
structure 331 n.
dissension 709 n.

cleave
break 46 vb.
cut 46 vb.
sunder 46 vb.
bisect 92 vb.

cleaver
sharp edge 256 n.

cleave to
cohere 48 vb.

clef
key 410 n.
notation 410 n.

cleft
disunion 46 n.
gap 201 n.

cleft palate
speech defect
580 n.
blemish 845 n.

cleft stick
dubiety 474 n.
predicament 700 n.

cleg
insect 365 n.

clemency
leniency 736 n.
mercy 905 n.

clementine
fruit and vegetables
301 n.

clench
make smaller
198 vb.
retain 778 vb.

clenched fist
gesture 547 n.

clench one's teeth
gesticulate 547 vb.
be resolute 599 vb.

clench the fist
threaten 900 vb.

Cleopatra's Needle
high structure
209 n.

clerestory
church interior
990 n.

clergy
clergy 986 n.

clergyman
cleric 986 n.

clergywoman
nun 986 n.

cleric
cleric 986 n.

clerical black
canonicals 989 n.

clerical collar
canonicals 989 n.

clerical dress
uniform 228 n.
canonicals 989 n.

clericalism
government 733 n.
ecclesiasticism
985 n.

clerical order
clergy 986 n.

clericals
canonicals 989 n.

clerihew
conciseness 569 n.
doggerel 593 n.
witticism 839 n.

clerk
recorder 549 n.
church officer
986 n.

clerk of the court
law officer 955 n.
notary 958 n.

clerkship
commission 751 n.

clever
intelligent 498 adj.
skilful 694 adj.
witty 839 adj.

clever clever
vain 873 adj.

clever dick
wiseacre 500 n.
vain person 873 n.

cleverness
intelligence 498 n.
skill 694 n.

cliché
uniformity 16 n.
maxim 496 n.
lack of meaning
515 n.
word 559 n.

neology 560 n.
phrase 563 n.

click
speech sound
398 n.
faintness 401 n.
sound faint 401 vb.
crackle 402 vb.
know 490 vb.
succeed 727 vb.

click with
befriend 880 vb.

client
habitué 610 n.
patron 707 n.
purchaser 792 n.

clientele
purchaser 792 n.

cliff
high land 209 n.
verticality 215 n.
incline 220 n.
rock 344 n.

cliffhanger
film 445 n.
novel 590 n.

climacteric
middle age 131 n.

climactic
crucial 137 adj.

climate
influence 178 n.
tendency 179 n.
region 184 n.
weather 340 n.

climatic
airy 340 adj.

climatology
weather 340 n.

climax
superiority 34 n.
summit 213 n.
climax 725 vb.
completion 725 n.
excitation 821 n.

climb
grow 36 vb.
high land 209 n.
be oblique 220 vb.
be in motion
265 vb.
fly 271 vb.
ascend 308 vb.
climb 308 vb.

climb down
descend 309 vb.

climbdown
humiliation 872 n.

climber
climber 308 n.
plant 366 n.

climbing
great 32 adj.
ascent 308 n.

climb the ladder
progress 285 vb.

clime
region 184 n.
land 344 n.

clinch
affix 45 vb.
unite with 45 vb.
ligature 47 n.
close 264 vb.
make certain
473 vb.
carry through
725 vb.
retain 778 vb.
retention 778 n.

clinch a deal
consent 758 vb.
contract 765 vb.

cling
cohere 48 vb.
persevere 600 vb.
take 786 vb.
caress 889 vb.

clinging
cohesive 48 adj.
tough 329 adj.
retentive 778 adj.

clinging to
retention 778 n.

cling to
observe 768 vb.
retain 778 vb.
love 887 vb.

clinic
hospital 658 n.

clinical
material 319 adj.
medical 658 adj.

clinical death
decease 361 n.

clinical depression
psychosis 503 n.
melancholy 834 n.

clinical medicine
medical art 658 n.

clinical psychology
mental disorder
503 n.

therapy 658 n.
clinical thermometer
  thermometry
    379 n.
clinician
  doctor 658 n.
clink
  faintness 401 n.
  sound faint 401 vb.
  resonance 404 n.
  resound 404 vb.
  rasp 407 vb.
  prison 748 n.
clinker
  rubbish 641 n.
clinometer
  angular measure
    247 n.
Clio
  lesser deity 967 n.
clip
  abate 37 vb.
  subtract 39 vb.
  connect 45 vb.
  cut 46 vb.
  fastening 47 n.
  make smaller
    198 vb.
  shorten 204 vb.
  impulse 279 n.
  fleece 786 vb.
  hairdressing 843 n.
clip joint
  place of amuse-
    ment 837 n.
clip on or round the
    ear
  knock 279 n.
clipped speech
  conciseness 569 n.
clipper
  sailing ship 275 n.
clippers
  sharp edge 256 n.
  cosmetic 843 n.
clipping
  small thing 33 n.
  diminution 37 n.
  hairdressing 843 n.
clip the wings
  disable 161 vb.
  retard 278 vb.
  make useless
    641 adj.
  hinder 702 vb.
clique
  band 74 n.

classification 77 n.
  association 706 n.
  community 708 n.
  party 708 n.
clitoris
  genitalia 167 n.
cloak
  cloak 228 n.
  sham 542 n.
  pretext 614 n.
  defend 713 vb.
  canonicals 989 n.
cloak-and-dagger
  stealthy 525 adj.
cloakroom
  chamber 194 n.
  latrine 649 n.
clobber
  clothing 228 n.
  dressing 228 n.
  strike 279 vb.
cloche
  headgear 228 n.
  garden 370 n.
clock
  time 117 vb.
  timekeeper 117 n.
  face 237 n.
  strike 279 vb.
clock in
  begin 68 vb.
  time 117 vb.
  arrive 295 vb.
clockmaker
  artisan 686 n.
clock out
  end 69 vb.
  time 117 vb.
  depart 296 vb.
clock radio
  timekeeper 117 n.
clockwise
  towards 281 adv.
clockwork
  machine 630 n.
clod
  piece 53 n.
  bulk 195 n.
  solid body 324 n.
  soil 344 n.
  dunce 501 n.
  bungler 697 n.
  country-dweller
    869 n.
clodhoppers
  footwear 228 n.

clod-hopping
  dull 840 adj.
  graceless 842 adj.
  ill-bred 847 adj.
clog
  footwear 228 n.
  be unclean 649 vb.
  make unclean
    649 vb.
  restrain 747 vb.
clog dance
  dance 837 n.
clogged up
  closed 264 adj.
cloister
  retreat 192 n.
  surround 230 vb.
  circumscribe
    232 vb.
  enclose 235 vb.
  enclosure 235 n.
  path 624 n.
  refuge 662 n.
  imprison 747 vb.
  seclusion 883 n.
  monastery 986 n.
  church exterior
    990 n.
cloistered
  secluded 883 adj.
  monastic 986 adj.
clone
  analogue 18 n.
  copy 22 n.
  reproduce 166 vb.
close
  similar 18 adj.
  firm 45 adj.
  cohesive 48 adj.
  end 69 n.
  end 69 vb.
  terminate 69 vb.
  cease 145 vb.
  impending 155 adj.
  region 184 n.
  place 185 n.
  housing 192 n.
  near 200 adj.
  narrow 206 adj.
  close 264 vb.
  approaching
    289 adj.
  dense 324 adj.
  warm 379 adj.
  accurate 494 adj.
  reticent 525 adj.
  taciturn 582 adj.

road 624 n.
  restraining
    747 adj.
  contract 765 vb.
  parsimonious
    816 adj.
  unsociable 883 adj.
  parsonage 986 n.
  church exterior
    990 n.
closed
  closed 264 adj.
closed book
  unknown thing
    491 n.
closed circuit
  electricity 160 n.
closed-circuit televi-
    sion
  camera 442 n.
  broadcasting
    531 n.
close down
  terminate 69 vb.
  close 264 vb.
closed shop
  uniformity 16 n.
  exclusion 57 n.
  party 708 n.
  restriction 747 n.
closed to
  thick-skinned
    820 adj.
close finish
  short distance
    200 n.
  arrival 295 n.
  contest 716 n.
close-fisted
  parsimonious
    816 adj.
close-fitting
  cohesive 48 adj.
close friend
  close friend 880 n.
close in
  circumscribe
    232 vb.
  approach 289 vb.
  converge 293 vb.
close in on
  approach 289 vb.
closely
  greatly 32 vb.
  nearly 200 adv.
closeness
  nearness 200 n.

narrowness 206 n.
love 887 n.
close on
nearly 200 adv.
close one's eyes
die 361 vb.
sleep 679 vb.
close quarters
short distance
200 n.
close range
short distance
200 n.
close-run
near 200 adj.
close season
lull 145 n.
close shave
danger 661 n.
escape 667 n.
closet
cabinet 194 n.
chamber 194 n.
concealed 525 adj.
hiding-place 527 n.
latrine 649 n.
closeted with, be
converse 584 vb.
close to
near 200 adj.
near 200 adv.
close to the wind
towards 281 adv.
close-up
short distance
200 n.
photography 551 n.
close with
cohere 48 vb.
converge 293 vb.
fight 716 vb.
closing
ending 69 adj.
closure 264 n.
closing down
stop 145 n.
closure 264 n.
closure
end 69 n.
closure 264 n.
clot
be dense 324 vb.
solid body 324 n.
blood 335 n.
semiliquidity
354 n.
thicken 354 vb.

dunce 501 n.
fool 501 n.
bungler 697 n.
cloth
product 164 n.
textile 222 n.
bookbinding 589 n.
vocation 622 n.
materials 631 n.
canonicals 989 n.
cloth, the
clergy 986 n.
cloth cap
headgear 228 n.
plebeian 869 adj.
clothe
dress 228 vb.
provide 633 vb.
clothes
clothing 228 n.
clothes brush
cleaning utensil
648 n.
clothes-conscious
fashionable
848 adj.
clotheshorse
hanger 217 n.
frame 218 n.
dryer 342 n.
fop 848 n.
clothier
clothier 228 n.
clothing
clothing 228 n.
dressing 228 n.
clotted
dense 324 adj.
clotting
thickening 354 n.
cloud
cloud 355 n.
cloud 355 vb.
darken 418 vb.
screen 421 n.
screen 421 vb.
cloudburst
storm 176 n.
rain 350 n.
cloud-cuckoo-land
fantasy 513 n.
cloudless
dry 342 adj.
undimmed
417 adj.
palmy 730 adj.

cloud nine
summit 213 n.
happiness 824 n.
cloudy
cloudy 355 adj.
unlit 418 adj.
opaque 423 adj.
uncertain 474 adj.
unclear 568 adj.
sullen 893 adj.
clout
advantage 34 n.
influence 178 n.
knock 279 n.
strike 279 vb.
utility 640 n.
corporal punish-
ment 963 n.
spank 963 vb.
clove(s)
spice 301 n.
scent 396 n.
cloven
bisected 92 adj.
cloven hoof
foot 214 n.
malevolence 898 n.
wickedness 934 n.
devil 969 n.
Satan 969 n.
clover
provender 301 n.
plant 366 n.
palmy days 730 n.
cloverleaf
road 624 n.
clown
be absurd 497 vb.
fool 501 n.
entertainer 594 n.
humorist 839 n.
laughingstock
851 n.
cloy
superabound
637 vb.
be tedious 838 vb.
sate 863 vb.
cloying
sweet 392 adj.
redundant 637 adj.
tedious 838 adj.
club
group 74 n.
focus 76 n.
meeting place
192 n.

hammer 279 n.
strike 279 vb.
association 706 n.
party 708 n.
society 708 n.
club 723 n.
social round 882 n.
clubbable
sociable 882 adj.
clubfoot
deformity 246 n.
clubhouse
meeting place
192 n.
club together
cooperate 706 vb.
be sociable 882 vb.
cluck
ululate 409 vb.
ululation 409 n.
clue
answer 460 n.
evidence 466 n.
knowledge 490 n.
interpretation
520 n.
hint 524 n.
indication 547 n.
clueless
doubting 474 adj.
ignorant 491 adj.
in difficulties
700 adj.
clump
bunch 74 n.
walk 267 vb.
solid body 324 n.
wood 366 n.
clumsy
inelegant 576 adj.
clumsy 695 adj.
graceless 842 adj.
clunk
resound 404 vb.
cluster
congregate 74 vb.
crowd 74 n.
group 74 n.
clutch
group 74 n.
young creature
132 n.
retain 778 vb.
take 786 vb.
clutch at
take 786 vb.
desire 859 vb.

clutches
governance 733 n.
retention 778 n.
clutter
disorder 61 n.
be many 104 vb.
clype
inform 524 vb.
informer 524 n.
divulge 526 vb.
accuse 928 vb.
CND
dissentient 489 n.
pacifist 717 n.
pacification 719 n.
coach
conveyance 267 n.
bus 274 n.
carriage 274 n.
train 274 n.
educate 534 vb.
train 534 vb.
teacher 537 n.
trainer 537 n.
make ready
669 vb.
coach-builder
artisan 686 n.
coaching
teaching 534 n.
coachman
driver 268 n.
domestic 742 n.
coach tour
land travel 267 n.
coagulate
cohere 48 vb.
be dense 324 vb.
thicken 354 vb.
coal
propellant 287 n.
heater 383 n.
coal 385 n.
fuel 385 n.
black thing 428 n.
coalesce
be identical 13 vb.
combine 50 vb.
cooperate 706 vb.
coalface
store 632 n.
workshop 687 n.
coalfield
coal 385 n.
store 632 n.
coal gas
gas 336 n.

fuel 385 n.
coalition
union 45 n.
association 706 n.
political party
708 n.
society 708 n.
coal mine
excavation 255 n.
store 632 n.
workshop 687 n.
coarse
rough 259 adj.
textural 331 adj.
indiscriminating
464 adj.
inelegant 576 adj.
unclean 649 adj.
vulgar 847 adj.
plebeian 869 adj.
impure 951 adj.
coarse fishing
chase 619 n.
coarseness
roughness 259 n.
indiscrimination
464 n.
plainness 573 n.
inelegance 576 n.
moral insensibility
820 n.
bad taste 847 n.
impurity 951 n.
coast
edge 234 n.
flank 239 vb.
laterality 239 n.
be in motion
265 vb.
ride 267 vb.
travel 267 vb.
voyage 269 vb.
pass 305 vb.
shore 344 n.
be neglectful
458 vb.
not act 677 vb.
coastal
marginal 234 adj.
coaster
stand 218 n.
merchant ship
275 n.
coastguard
nautical personnel
270 n.
protector 660 n.

keeper 749 n.
coast home
do easily 701 vb.
coasting
water travel 269 n.
coastline
outline 233 n.
shore 344 n.
coat
layer 207 n.
coat 226 vb.
skin 226 n.
wrapping 226 n.
jacket 228 n.
overcoat 228 n.
See **jacket**
coatee
jacket 228 n.
coating
layer 207 n.
covering 226 n.
facing 226 n.
lining 227 n.
coat of arms
heraldry 547 n.
nobility 868 n.
coat-tail(s)
extremity 69 n.
hanging object
217 n.
garment 228 n.
coax
tempt 612 vb.
request 761 vb.
pet 889 vb.
flatter 925 vb.
cob
pony 273 n.
cereals 301 n.
bird 365 n.
male animal
372 n.
cobber
chum 880 n.
cobble
paving 226 n.
building material
631 n.
repair 656 vb.
cobbler
clothier 228 n.
mender 656 n.
cobblestone
paving 226 n.
cobble together
produce 164 vb.

cob nut
fruit and vegetables
301 n.
cobra
reptile 365 n.
cobweb
weak thing 163 n.
filament 208 n.
network 222 n.
lightness 323 n.
dirt 649 n.
Coca Cola or Coke
(tdmk)
soft drink 301 n.
cocaine
anaesthetic 375 n.
drug 658 n.
drug-taking 949 n.
coccyx
buttocks 238 n.
cochineal
pigment 425 n.
red pigment 431 n.
cochlea
ear 415 n.
cock
poultry 365 n.
male animal
372 n.
make ready
669 vb.
cockade
trimming 844 n.
cock-a-hoop
jubilant 833 adj.
cock and bull story
insubstantial thing
4 n.
fable 543 n.
cock a snook
defy 711 vb.
disobey 738 vb.
not observe 769 vb.
be insolent 878 vb.
not respect 921 vb.
cockatrice
rara avis 84 n.
eye 438 n.
heraldry 547 n.
cockerel
poultry 365 n.
male animal
372 n.
cock-eyed
distorted 246 adj.
erroneous 495 adj.
absurd 497 adj.

606

cockfight
duel 716 n.
cockle
fish food 301 n.
marine life 365 n.
cockles of the heart
affections 817 n.
Cockney, cockney
native 191 n.
dialect 560 adj.
dialectal 560 adj.
plebeian 869 adj.
cockpit
chamber 194 n.
aircraft 276 n.
duel 716 n.
cockroach
insect 365 n.
cocktail
a mixture 43 n.
alcoholic drink
301 n.
draught 301 n.
cocktail party
social gathering
882 n.
cock-up
mistake 495 n.
cocky
proud 871 adj.
vain 873 adj.
impertinent
878 adj.
cocoa
milk 301 n.
soft drink 301 n.
See **milk**
coconut
fruit and vegetables
301 n.
cocoon
young creature
132 n.
source 156 n.
receptacle 194 n.
wrapping 226 n.
safeguard 660 vb.
C.O.D.
pay 804 vb.
cod
fish food 301 n.
coda
adjunct 40 n.
sequel 67 n.
end 69 n.
rear 238 n.
melody 410 n.

musical piece
412 n.
coddle
cook 301 vb.
please 826 vb.
pet 889 vb.
code
arrangement 62 n.
rule 81 n.
latency 523 n.
secrecy 525 n.
enigma 530 n.
writing 586 n.
precept 693 n.
probity 929 n.
codeine
drug 658 n.
codex
book 589 n.
codicil
adjunct 40 n.
sequel 67 n.
title deed 767 n.
codification
arrangement 62 n.
codpiece
garment 228 n.
coeducational
educational
534 adj.
coefficient
numerical element
85 n.
coerce
dominate 733 vb.
compel 740 vb.
coeval
contemporary
123 n.
synchronous
123 adj.
coexistence
accompaniment
89 n.
synchronism 123 n.
contiguity 202 n.
concord 710 n.
peace 717 n.
coffee
soft drink 301 n.
brownness 430 n.
coffee morning
social gathering
882 n.
coffee table
stand 218 n.

coffee-table book
book 589 n.
coffer
box 194 n.
storage 632 n.
treasury 799 n.
coffin
place 185 n.
box 194 n.
funeral 364 n.
inter 364 vb.
interment 364 n.
cog
tooth 256 n.
notch 260 n.
notch 260 vb.
cogent
powerful 160 adj.
rational 475 adj.
forceful 571 adj.
compelling
740 adj.
cogitate
think 449 vb.
See **meditate**
cognac
alcoholic drink
301 n.
cognate
relative 9 adj.
verbal 559 adj.
cognition
intellect 447 n.
knowledge 490 n.
cognitive
knowing 490 adj.
cognizance
knowledge 490 n.
jurisdiction 955 n.
cognoscente
expert 696 n.
people of taste
846 n.
cogwheel
notch 260 n.
cohabit
unite with 45 vb.
accompany 89 vb.
lover 887 n.
wed 894 vb.
cohere
cohere 48 vb.
coherent
sane 502 adj.
intelligible 516 adj.
cohesion
union 45 n.

coherence 48 n.
contiguity 202 n.
density 324 n.
toughness 329 n.
cohesive
cohesive 48 adj.
cohorts
army 722 n.
coiffure
hairdressing 843 n.
coil
complexity 61 n.
contraception
172 n.
be curved 248 vb.
coil 251 n.
twine 251 vb.
coin
produce 164 vb.
form 243 vb.
circle 250 n.
imagine 513 vb.
coinage 797 n.
mint 797 vb.
coinage
neology 560 n.
coinage 797 n.
coincide
be 1 vb.
be identical 13 vb.
accord 24 vb.
synchronize
123 vb.
be contiguous
202 vb.
coincidence
identity 13 n.
conformance 24 n.
equality 28 n.
accompaniment
89 n.
concomitant 89 n.
synchronism 123 n.
event 154 n.
chance 159 n.
concurrence 181 n.
contiguity 202 n.
nondesign 618 n.
coincidental
casual 159 adj.
unintentional
618 adj.
coincide with
be equal 28 vb.
Cointreau (tdmk)
alcoholic drink
301 n.

607

coir
fibre 208 n.

coitus
coition 45 n.

coke
coal 385 n.
drug-taking 949 n.

colander
bowl 194 n.
porosity 263 n.

cold
excretion 302 n.
dead 361 adj.
unfeeling 375 adj.
cold 380 adj.
coldness 380 n.
blue 435 adj.
mistaken 495 adj.
respiratory disease
 651 n.
uncooked 670 adj.
nonactive 677 adj.
adverse 731 adj.
adversity 731 n.
impassive 820 adj.
inexcitable
 823 adj.
indifferent 860 adj.
unsociable 883 adj.
unkind 898 adj.

cold-blooded
animal 365 adj.
cautious 858 adj.
cruel 898 adj.

cold-calling
advertisement
 528 n.

cold cream
unguent 357 n.
cosmetic 843 n.

cold cuts
hors-d'oeuvres
 301 n.

cold feet
nervousness 854 n.

cold fish
unfeeling person
 820 n.

cold front
coldness 380 n.
wintriness 380 n.

coldness
coldness 380 n.
indifference 860 n.
enmity 881 n.
unsociability
 883 n.

cold-shoulder
exclude 57 vb.
repel 292 vb.
disregard 458 vb.
reject 607 vb.
avoid 620 vb.
be rude 885 vb.

cold storage
delay 136 n.
refrigeration 382 n.
refrigerator 384 n.
preservation 666 n.

cold turkey
drug-taking 949 n.

cold water
moderator 177 n.
dissuasion 613 n.

coleslaw
hors-d'oeuvres
 301 n.

colic
pang 377 n.
digestive disorders
 651 n.

coliseum
arena 724 n.

colitis
digestive disorders
 651 n.

collaborate
assent 488 vb.
be willing 597 vb.
apostatize 603 vb.
cooperate 706 vb.

collaborator
collaborator 707 n.
toady 879 n.
friend 880 n.

collage
variegation 437 n.
art 551 n.
picture 553 n.

collapse
decrease 37 vb.
decomposition
 51 n.
cease 145 vb.
helplessness 161 n.
weakness 163 n.
ruin 165 n.
fall short 307 vb.
descend 309 vb.
descent 309 n.
be ill 651 vb.
illness 651 n.
deteriorate 655 vb.
dilapidation 655 n.

be fatigued 684 vb.
fatigue 684 n.
knuckle under
 721 vb.
defeat 728 n.
fail 728 vb.
failure 728 n.
fear 854 vb.

collar
garment 228 n.
 See **neckwear**
neckwear 228 n.
loop 250 n.
arrest 747 vb.
fetter 748 n.
take 786 vb.

collarbone
support 218 n.

collate
compare 462 vb.
print 587 vb.

collateral
relative 9 adj.
lateral 239 adj.
security 767 n.

collation
meal 301 n.

colleague
colleague 707 n.

collect
bring together
 74 vb.
congregate 74 vb.
understand 516 vb.
book 589 n.
abstract 592 vb.
acquire 771 vb.
receive 782 vb.
take 786 vb.
prayers 981 n.

collection
arrangement 62 n.
assemblage 74 n.
edition 589 n.
anthology 592 n.
collection 632 n.
acquisition 771 n.
offering 781 n.
receiving 782 n.
pay 804 n.
payment 804 n.
oblation 981 n.

collection plate
ritual object 988 n.
church utensil
 990 n.

collective
assemblage 74 n.
general 79 adj.
joint possession
 775 n.

collective bargaining
conditions 766 n.

collector
collector 492 n.
receiver 782 n.

collector's item
exhibit 522 n.
exceller 644 n.
masterpiece 694 n.

colleen
youngster 132 n.
female 373 n.

college
edifice 164 n.
academy 539 n.

collide
disagree 25 vb.
collide 279 vb.
be hostile 881 vb.

collide with
collide 279 vb.
meet 295 vb.

collie
dog 365 n.

collier
merchant ship
 275 n.
artisan 686 n.

colliery
excavation 255 n.
store 632 n.
workshop 687 n.

collimate
aim 281 vb.

collimation
parallelism 219 n.
direction 281 n.

collision
collision 279 n.
battle 718 n.

collocate
arrange 62 vb.
bring together
 74 vb.
place 187 vb.

collocation
assemblage 74 n.
location 187 n.
phrase 563 n.

colloid
semiliquidity
 354 n.

viscidity 354 n.
colloquial
  linguistic 557 adj.
  dialectal 560 adj.
collusion
  concurrence 181 n.
  duplicity 541 n.
  deception 542 n.
  cooperation 706 n.
collywobbles
  agitation 318 n.
  pang 377 n.
  digestive disorders
    651 n.
  excitability 822 n.
  nervousness 854 n.
cologne
  cosmetic 843 n.
colon
  insides 224 n.
  tube 263 n.
  punctuation 547 n.
colonel
  army officer 741 n.
colonial
  foreigner 59 n.
  settler 191 n.
colonize
  place oneself
    187 vb.
  be present 189 vb.
  dwell 192 vb.
  subjugate 745 vb.
  appropriate
    786 vb.
colonnade
  series 71 n.
  pavilion 192 n.
  path 624 n.
colonoscopy
  diagnostic 658 n.
colony
  crowd 74 n.
  descendant 170 n.
  territory 184 n.
  station 187 n.
  political organiza-
    tion 733 n.
colophon
  sequel 67 n.
  rear 238 n.
  label 547 n.
  edition 589 n.
coloration
  colour 425 n.
  hue 425 n.

coloratura
  vocal music 412 n.
colossal
  enormous 32 adj.
  stalwart 162 adj.
  huge 195 adj.
  tall 209 adj.
colossus
  giant 195 n.
  high structure
    209 n.
  tall creature 209 n.
  image 551 n.
colostomy
  surgery 658 n.
colour
  character 5 n.
  tincture 43 n.
  sort 77 n.
  colour 425 n.
  colour 425 vb.
  blackness 428 n.
  redden 431 vb.
  look 445 n.
  qualify 468 vb.
  sophisticate
    477 vb.
  heraldry 547 n.
  ornament 574 n.
  plead 614 vb.
  pretext 614 n.
  show feeling
    818 vb.
  be modest 874 vb.
  get angry 891 vb.
colour bar
  exclusion 57 n.
  prejudice 481 n.
  disapprobation
    924 n.
colour-blind
  dim-sighted
    440 adj.
  indiscriminating
    464 adj.
colour blindness
  blindness 439 n.
  dim sight 440 n.
coloured
  black 428 adj.
  blackish 428 adj.
  blackness 428 n.
colourful
  luminous 417 adj.
  florid 425 adj.
  variegated 437 adj.
  descriptive 590 adj.

  showy 875 adj.
colouring
  hue 425 n.
  qualification 468 n.
  qualifying 468 adj.
  identification
    547 n.
  painting 553 n.
colouring matter
  pigment 425 n.
colourless
  colourless 426 adj.
  feeble 572 adj.
  dull 840 adj.
colour print
  photography 551 n.
colours
  badge 547 n.
  flag 547 n.
colour scheme
  colour 425 n.
colposcope
  detector 484 n.
  diagnostic 658 n.
colt
  young creature
    132 n.
  horse 273 n.
  male animal
    372 n.
  beginner 538 n.
  pistol 723 n.
column
  high structure
    209 n.
  pillar 218 n.
  cylinder 252 n.
  article 591 n.
  formation 722 n.
columnist
  informant 524 n.
  author 589 n.
coma
  helplessness 161 n.
  insensibility 375 n.
  illness 651 n.
  sleep 679 n.
comatose
  impotent 161 adj.
  insensible 375 adj.
  sleepy 679 adj.
comb
  tooth 256 n.
  smooth 258 vb.
  smoother 258 n.
  organ 414 n.
  search 459 vb.

  cleaning utensil
    648 n.
  hairdressing 843 n.
combat
  contend 716 vb.
  contention 716 n.
  fight 716 n.
  fight 716 vb.
  go to war 718 vb.
combatant
  opponent 705 n.
  combatant 722 n.
comber
  wave 350 n.
combination
  combination 50 n.
  association 706 n.
  society 708 n.
combinations
  underwear 228 n.
combine
  combine 50 vb.
  association 706 n.
  cooperate 706 vb.
  corporation 708 n.
  society 708 n.
combine with
  accrue 38 vb.
combings
  leavings 41 n.
combustible
  fuel 385 n.
combustion
  burning 381 n.
come
  arrive 295 vb.
  climax 725 vb.
come about
  be 1 vb.
  happen 154 vb.
come across
  acquire 771 vb.
  pay 804 vb.
come across with
  confess 526 vb.
come and go
  fluctuate 317 vb.
come apart
  separate 46 vb.
comeback
  recurrence 106 n.
  revival 656 n.
come between
  interfere 231 vb.
  lie between 231 vb.
  hinder 702 vb.

make quarrels
709 vb.
come by
acquire 771 vb.
inherit 771 vb.
come clean
confess 526 vb.
be truthful 540 vb.
speak 579 vb.
**comedian, comedi-
enne**
actor 594 n.
entertainer 594 n.
humorist 839 n.
come down
decrease 37 vb.
descend 309 vb.
rain 350 vb.
comedown
descent 309 n.
disrepute 867 n.
humiliation 872 n.
come down on
be severe 735 vb.
comedy
stage play 594 n.
laughter 835 n.
ridiculousness
849 n.
come forward
offer oneself
759 vb.
come-hither look
look 438 n.
pleasurableness
826 n.
come home
arrive 295 vb.
come in
be included 78 vb.
approach 289 vb.
enter 297 vb.
come into
inherit 771 vb.
receive 782 vb.
appropriate
786 vb.
come it over
be proud 871 vb.
despise 922 vb.
comeliness
beauty 841 n.
comely
beautiful 841 adj.
come of
result 157 vb.

come off
cease 145 vb.
happen 154 vb.
come on
impend 155 vb.
progress 285 vb.
come-on
incentive 612 n.
come out
begin 68 vb.
cease 145 vb.
emerge 298 vb.
pass 305 vb.
be visible 443 vb.
be disclosed
526 vb.
be published
528 vb.
relinquish 621 vb.
be inactive 679 vb.
resist 715 vb.
revolt 738 vb.
deprecate 762 vb.
come out with
manifest 522 vb.
confess 526 vb.
divulge 526 vb.
improvise 609 vb.
come over
be intelligible
516 vb.
come round
be restored 656 vb.
consent 758 vb.
comestibles
food 301 n.
comet
planet 321 n.
come through
be safe 660 vb.
come to
number 86 vb.
be turned to
147 vb.
live 360 vb.
be restored 656 vb.
be refreshed
685 vb.
cost 809 vb.
come to a head
culminate 34 vb.
be complete 54 vb.
come together
congregate 74 vb.
converge 293 vb.
come to life
live 360 vb.

come to nothing
pass away 2 vb.
fall short 307 vb.
miscarry 728 vb.
come to one's ears
hear 415 vb.
be known 490 vb.
come to pass
happen 154 vb.
come under
be included 78 vb.
come upon
chance 159 vb.
meet 295 vb.
discover 484 vb.
comeuppance
retaliation 714 n.
reward 962 n.
punishment 963 n.
come what may
certainly 473 adv.
comfit
sweets 301 n.
comfort
assuage 177 vb.
repose 683 n.
facility 701 n.
aid 703 vb.
wealth 800 n.
please 826 vb.
content 828 n.
content 828 vb.
relief 831 n.
relieve 831 vb.
cheer 833 vb.
condolence 905 n.
pity 905 vb.
comfortable
tranquil 266 adj.
comfortable
376 adj.
prosperous 730 adj.
comforter
wrapping 226 n.
neckwear 228 n.
comfortless
unpleasant
827 adj.
cheerless 834 adj.
melancholic
834 adj.
comfy
comfortable
376 adj.
comic
fool 501 n.
the press 528 n.

dramatic 594 adj.
entertainer 594 n.
laughing 835 adj.
humorist 839 n.
witty 839 adj.
funny 849 adj.
comical
absurd 497 adj.
laughing 835 adj.
witty 839 adj.
funny 849 adj.
coming
future 124 adj.
approach 289 n.
arrival 295 n.
coming and going
reversion 148 n.
fluctuation 317 n.
shadowy 419 adj.
busy 678 adj.
coming out
debut 68 n.
celebration 876 n.
coming to one
due 915 adj.
comma
punctuation 547 n.
command
advantage 34 n.
be superior 34 vb.
be high 209 vb.
style 566 n.
governance 733 n.
command 737 n.
command 737 vb.
commandant
army officer 741 n.
commandeer
compel 740 vb.
appropriate
786 vb.
commander
superior 34 n.
nautical personnel
270 n.
army officer 741 n.
naval officer 741 n.
commander-in-chief
army officer 741 n.
commanding
superior 34 adj.
influential 178 adj.
authoritative
733 adj.
commanding
737 adj.

noteworthy
866 adj.
proud 871 adj.
commandment
precept 693 n.
command 737 n.
Commandoes
armed force 722 n.
tasteful 846 adj.
genteel 868 adj.
commemorate
remind 505 vb.
honour 866 vb.
celebrate 876 vb.
commence
begin 68 vb.
commend
advise 691 vb.
approve 923 vb.
praise 923 vb.
commendation
approbation 923 n.
praise 923 n.
commensal
resident 191 n.
commensurable
numerical 85 adj.
comment
estimate 480 n.
maxim 496 n.
commentary 520 n.
affirm 532 vb.
affirmation 532 n.
speech 579 n.
article 591 n.
commentary
commentary 520 n.
oration 579 n.
dissertation 591 n.
commentator
estimator 480 n.
interpreter 520 n.
informant 524 n.
broadcaster 531 n.
dissertator 591 n.
comment on
interpret 520 vb.
comment upon
notice 455 vb.
dissertate 591 vb.
commerce
interlocution
584 n.
business 622 n.
vocation 622 n.
trade 791 n.

commercial
advertisement
528 n.
broadcast 531 n.
bad taste 847 n.
vulgar 847 adj.
commercialize
trade 791 vb.
commercialized
vulgar 847 adj.
commination
prayers 981 n.
commiserate
lament 836 vb.
pity 905 vb.
commissar
officer 741 n.
commissariat
provisions 301 n.
provision 633 n.
commission
increment 36 n.
band 74 n.
job 622 n.
action 676 n.
precept 693 n.
command 737 n.
commission 751 n.
commission
751 vb.
mandate 751 n.
permit 756 n.
earnings 771 n.
portion 783 n.
pay 804 n.
price 809 n.
discount 810 n.
reward 962 n.
commissionaire
doorkeeper 264 n.
courier 529 n.
servant 742 n.
commissioned officer
army officer 741 n.
commissioner
official 690 n.
officer 741 n.
commit
transfer 272 vb.
do 676 vb.
commission
751 vb.
give 781 vb.
do wrong 914 adj.
commitment
resolution 599 n.
perseverance 600 n.

promise 764 n.
debt 803 n.
duty 917 n.
committal
transference 272 n.
commission 751 n.
legal process 959 n.
committee
band 74 n.
party 708 n.
authority 733 n.
consignee 754 n.
commode
cabinet 194 n.
latrine 649 n.
commodious
spacious 183 adj.
commodity
object 319 n.
utility 640 n.
merchandise
795 n.
commodore
nautical personnel
270 n.
naval officer 741 n.
common
general 79 adj.
typical 83 adj.
frequent 139 adj.
plain 348 n.
aphoristic 496 adj.
linguistic 557 adj.
usual 610 adj.
unpossessed
774 adj.
joint possession
775 n.
lands 777 n.
vulgar 847 adj.
plebeian 869 adj.
common cold
excretion 302 n.
coldness 380 n.
infection 651 n.
respiratory disease
651 n.
**common denomina-
tor**
relation 9 n.
numerical element
85 n.
common factor
numerical element
85 n.
common knowledge
knowledge 490 n.

information 524 n.
publicity 528 n.
common law
tradition 127 n.
precept 693 n.
law 953 n.
**common-law hus-
band or wife**
lover 887 n.
spouse 894 n.
common man
common man 30 n.
averageness 732 n.
Common Market
society 708 n.
market 796 n.
common or garden
typical 83 adj.
commonplace
median 30 adj.
general 79 adj.
typical 83 adj.
topic 452 n.
known 490 adj.
aphoristic 496 adj.
maxim 496 n.
phrase 563 n.
plain 573 adj.
usual 610 adj.
trivial 639 adj.
middling 732 adj.
dull 840 adj.
commonplace book
reminder 505 n.
record 548 n.
anthology 592 n.
common prayer
public worship
981 n.
commonsense
intelligence 498 n.
sanity 502 n.
commonwealth
territory 184 n.
nation 371 n.
*political organiza-
tion* 733 n.
commotion
commotion 318 n.
quarrel 709 n.
communal
national 371 adj.
commune
district 184 n.
communicate
524 vb.
association 706 n.

611

joint possession
775 n.
commune with
converse 584 vb.
communicable
infectious 653 adj.
communicant
pietist 979 n.
worshipper 981 n.
communicate
connect 45 vb.
communicate
524 vb.
communication
union 45 n.
transference 272 n.
information 524 n.
disclosure 526 n.
message 529 n.
interlocution
584 n.
correspondence
588 n.
communications
access 624 n.
communicative
informative
524 adj.
loquacious 581 adj.
communion
interlocution
584 n.
social gathering
882 n.
Holy Communion
988 n.
communiqué
report 524 n.
news 529 n.
communism
government 733 n.
joint possession
775 n.
philanthropy
901 n.
Communists
political party
708 n.
community
subdivision 53 n.
district 184 n.
housing 192 n.
social group 371 n.
community 708 n.
community centre
focus 76 n.

meeting place
192 n.
**community charge or
tax**
tax 809 n.
community council
council 692 n.
jurisdiction 955 n.
commutation
compensation 31 n.
substitution 150 n.
interchange 151 n.
compromise 770 n.
commutator
electronics 160 n.
commute
interchange
151 vb.
travel 267 vb.
compromise
770 vb.
show mercy
905 vb.
commuter
dweller 191 n.
traveller 268 n.
transport 272 n.
compact
small 33 adj.
case 194 n.
little 196 adj.
make smaller
198 vb.
short 204 adj.
be dense 324 vb.
dense 324 adj.
concise 569 adj.
compact 765 n.
cosmetic 843 n.
compact disc
rotator 315 n.
gramophone 414 n.
*recording instru-
ment* 549 n.
compaction
coherence 48 n.
compression 198 n.
companion
analogue 18 n.
concomitant 89 n.
window 263 n.
colleague 707 n.
retainer 742 n.
servant 742 n.
close friend 880 n.

companionship
accompaniment
89 n.
friendship 880 n.
fellowship 882 n.
companionway
doorway 263 n.
ascent 308 n.
company
component 58 n.
assembly 74 n.
band 74 n.
accompaniment
89 n.
actor 594 n.
personnel 686 n.
association 706 n.
corporation 708 n.
party 708 n.
formation 722 n.
comparable
relative 9 adj.
equivalent 28 adj.
compared 462 adj.
comparative
relative 9 adj.
distinctive 15 adj.
comparative 27 n.
compared 462 adj.
grammatical
564 adj.
compare
relate 9 vb.
graduate 27 vb.
compare 462 vb.
comparison
comparison 462 n.
compartment
subdivision 53 n.
compartment
194 n.
train 274 n.
compass
degree 27 n.
range 183 n.
region 184 n.
distance 199 n.
surroundings
230 n.
outline 233 n.
sailing aid 269 n.
navigator 270 n.
direction 281 n.
gauge 465 n.
signpost 547 n.
compassion
leniency 736 n.

pity 905 n.
compassionate
impressible
819 adj.
pitying 905 adj.
godlike 965 adj.
compatibility
adaptation 24 n.
concord 710 n.
friendship 880 n.
sociability 882 n.
love 887 n.
compatriot
kinsman 11 n.
compeer
compeer 28 n.
compel
compel 740 vb.
compendium
compendium
592 n.
compensate
be equal 28 vb.
compensate 31 vb.
restitute 787 vb.
pay 804 vb.
atone 941 vb.
reward 962 vb.
compensation
compensation 31 n.
peace offering
719 n.
resignation 753 n.
earnings 771 n.
restitution 787 n.
pay 804 n.
payment 804 n.
dueness 915 n.
atonement 941 n.
reward 962 n.
penalty 963 n.
compere
broadcaster 531 n.
direct 689 vb.
manager 690 n.
compete
contend 716 vb.
offer oneself
759 vb.
competence
ability 160 n.
sufficiency 635 n.
skill 694 n.
wealth 800 n.
jurisdiction 955 n.
competent
powerful 160 adj.

knowing 490 adj.
sufficient 635 adj.
useful 640 adj.
expert 694 adj.
skilful 694 adj.
authoritative
  733 adj.
legal 953 adj.
compete with
  oppose 704 vb.
competition
  opposition 704 n.
  contention 716 n.
  contest 716 n.
  jealousy 911 n.
competitive
  opposing 704 adj.
  jealous 911 adj.
competitor
  incomer 297 n.
  opponent 705 n.
  contender 716 n.
  combatant 722 n.
  petitioner 763 n.
  player 837 n.
  enemy 881 n.
  jealousy 911 n.
compile
  compose 56 vb.
  bring together
    74 vb.
  abstract 592 vb.
complacency
  content 828 n.
complain
  deprecate 762 vb.
  be discontented
    829 vb.
  indict 928 vb.
complain of
  be ill 651 vb.
complaint
  illness 651 n.
  deprecation 762 n.
  annoyance 827 n.
  discontent 829 n.
  wrong 914 n.
  disapprobation
    924 n.
  accusation 928 n.
complaisant
  permitting 756 adj.
  benevolent 897 adj.
complement
  analogue 18 n.
  adjunct 40 n.

make complete
  54 vb.
  plenitude 54 n.
  component 58 n.
  band 74 n.
  inclusion 78 n.
  numerical element
    85 n.
  concomitant 89 n.
  mariner 270 n.
  part of speech
    564 n.
  party 708 n.
complementary
  correlative 12 adj.
  complete 54 adj.
  numerical 85 adj.
complementary
  medicine
  medical art 658 n.
complete
  complete 54 adj.
  make complete
    54 vb.
  persevere 600 vb.
  perfect 646 adj.
  perfect 646 vb.
  do 676 vb.
  carry through
    725 vb.
completion
  plenitude 54 n.
  completion 725 n.
complex
  whole 52 n.
  complex 61 adj.
  structure 331 n.
  idea 451 n.
  puzzling 517 adj.
  difficult 700 adj.
complexion
  character 5 n.
  hue 425 n.
  look 445 n.
complexity
  complexity 61 n.
  imperspicuity
    568 n.
complex number
  number 85 n.
compliance
  concurrence 181 n.
  softness 327 n.
  willingness 597 n.
  submission 721 n.
  obedience 739 n.
  consent 758 n.

observance 768 n.
servility 879 n.
compliant
  willing 597 adj.
  obedient 739 adj.
  servile 879 adj.
complicate
  bedevil 63 vb.
  aggravate 832 vb.
complicated
  complex 61 adj.
  intricate 251 adj.
  difficult 700 adj.
complication
  complexity 61 n.
  illness 651 n.
  difficulty 700 n.
  aggravation 832 n.
compliment(s)
  phrase 563 n.
  honour 866 vb.
  honours 866 n.
  courteous act
    884 n.
  congratulate
    886 vb.
  congratulation
    886 n.
  endearment 889 n.
  praise 923 n.
  praise 923 vb.
  flatter 925 vb.
  flattery 925 n.
complimentary
  uncharged 812 adj.
  approving 923 adj.
  flattering 925 adj.
comply
  be willing 597 vb.
  obey 739 vb.
  consent 758 vb.
  observe 768 vb.
  be servile 879 vb.
comply with
  conform 83 vb.
component(s)
  component 58 adj.
  component 58 n.
  contents 193 n.
comport oneself
  behave 688 vb.
compose
  compose 56 vb.
  constitute 56 vb.
  produce 164 vb.
  harmonize 410 vb.

compose music
  413 vb.
  write 586 vb.
  print 587 vb.
  tranquillize
    823 vb.
composer
  producer 164 n.
  musician 413 n.
composite
  mixed 43 adj.
  compound 50 n.
  plural 101 adj.
compos mentis
  sane 502 adj.
compost
  fertilizer 171 n.
composure
  quietude 266 n.
  inexcitability
    823 n.
  lack of wonder
    865 n.
compound
  a mixture 43 n.
  compound 50 n.
  compose 56 vb.
  composition 56 n.
  substitute 150 vb.
  place 185 n.
  enclosure 235 n.
comprehend
  contain 56 vb.
  comprise 78 vb.
  know 490 vb.
  understand 516 vb.
comprehensible
  intelligible 516 adj.
  easy 701 adj.
comprehension
  inclusion 78 n.
  knowledge 490 n.
  connotation 514 n.
comprehensive
  extensive 32 adj.
  comprehensive
    52 adj.
  complete 54 adj.
  spacious 183 adj.
  large 195 adj.
  knowing 490 adj.
  educational
    534 adj.
compress
  abate 37 vb.
  tighten 45 vb.

make smaller
198 vb.
shorten 204 vb.
make thin 206 vb.
be dense 324 vb.
be concise 569 vb.
surgical dressing
658 n.

compressed
short 204 adj.
narrow 206 adj.
concise 569 adj.

compression
smallness 33 n.
diminution 37 n.
compression 198 n.
conciseness 569 n.
compendium
592 n.

comprise
be included 78 vb.
comprise 78 vb.

comprising
inclusion 78 n.
inclusive 78 adj.

compromise
irresolution 601 n.
make terms
766 vb.
compromise 770 n.
compromise
770 vb.
defame 926 vb.

compromising
irresolute 601 adj.
discreditable
867 adj.

compulsion
neurosis 503 n.
compulsion 740 n.

compulsive
powerful 160 adj.
strong 162 adj.
authoritarian
735 adj.
commanding
737 adj.
compelling
740 adj.

compulsory
necessary 596 adj.
authoritative
733 adj.
compelling
740 adj.
obligatory 917 adj.

compunction
regret 830 n.
pity 905 n.
penitence 939 n.

computation
data processing
86 n.
numeration 86 n.
measurement
465 n.
accounts 808 n.

compute
computerize 86 vb.
number 86 vb.
measure 465 vb.

computer
counting instru-
ment 86 n.
machine 630 n.

computerized
computerized
86 adj.
dynamic 160 adj.
instrumental
628 adj.
mechanical
630 adj.

computer language
data processing
86 n.

computer program
arrangement 62 n.
data processing
86 n.

comrade
concomitant 89 n.
male 372 n.
colleague 707 n.
political party
708 n.
title 870 n.
chum 880 n.
close friend 880 n.

con
deceive 542 vb.
fleece 786 vb.
defraud 788 vb.

concave
concave 255 adj.

conceal
conceal 525 vb.

concede
qualify 468 vb.
be reasonable
475 vb.
assent 488 vb.
confess 526 vb.

permit 756 vb.
consent 758 vb.

conceit
ideality 513 n.
pride 871 n.
vanity 873 n.

conceive
produce 164 vb.
reproduce itself
167 vb.
be fruitful 171 vb.
vitalize 360 vb.
perceive 447 adj.
be of the opinion
that 485 vb.
know 490 vb.
suppose 512 vb.
imagine 513 vb.

conceived, be
be born 360 vb.

concentrate
bring together
74 vb.
congregate 74 vb.
focus 76 vb.
centralize 225 vb.
converge 293 vb.
think 449 vb.
be attentive 455 vb.

concentration
increase 36 n.
accumulation 74 n.
assemblage 74 n.
centrality 225 n.
convergence 293 n.
condensation
324 n.
density 324 n.
thought 449 n.
attention 455 n.
resolution 599 n.
perseverance 600 n.
assiduity 678 n.

concentric
central 225 adj.

concept
idea 451 n.
ideality 513 n.

conception
origin 68 n.
product 164 n.
propagation 167 n.
intellect 447 n.
thought 449 n.
idea 451 n.
opinion 485 n.
ideality 513 n.

conceptual
mental 447 adj.

conceptualize
perceive 447 adj.

concern
be related 9 vb.
relation 9 n.
affairs 154 n.
topic 452 n.
business 622 n.
function 622 n.
importance 638 n.
corporation 708 n.
worry 825 n.
benevolence 897 n.

concerning
concerning 9 adv.
relative 9 adj.

concern oneself with
busy oneself
622 vb.

concert
agreement 24 n.
concurrence 181 n.
melody 410 n.
music 412 n.
musical instrument
414 n.

concerted
agreeing 24 adj.

concertina
organ 414 n.

concerto
musical piece
412 n.

concession
qualification 468 n.
permission 756 n.
discount 810 n.

concierge
doorway 263 n.
doorkeeper 264 n.
servant 742 n.
keeper 749 n.

conciliate
pacify 719 vb.
content 828 vb.
atone 941 vb.

conciliation
conformity 83 n.
concord 710 n.
pacification 719 n.
forgiveness 909 n.
propitiation 941 n.

concise
small 33 adj.
concise 569 adj.

conclave
 assembly 74 n.
 conference 584 n.
 council 692 n.
 synod 985 n.
conclude
 end 69 vb.
 terminate 69 vb.
 judge 480 vb.
 be resolute 599 vb.
 contract 765 vb.
conclusion
 sequel 67 n.
 end 69 n.
 finality 69 n.
 judgment 480 n.
 opinion 485 n.
 affirmation 532 n.
 completion 725 n.
conclusive
 ending 69 adj.
 evidential 466 adj.
 positive 473 adj.
 judicial 480 adj.
 commanding
  737 adj.
concoct
 imagine 513 vb.
 fake 541 vb.
 plan 623 vb.
concoction
 a mixture 43 n.
 production 164 n.
 draught 301 n.
concomitant
 concomitant 89 n.
 synchronous
  123 adj.
concord
 concurrence 181 n.
 melody 410 n.
 concord 710 n.
 concord 710 vb.
concordance
 agreement 24 n.
 consensus 488 n.
 dictionary 559 n.
concordat
 agreement 24 n.
 compact 765 n.
 treaty 765 n.
concourse
 union 45 n.
 assembly 74 n.
 convergence 293 n.
concrete
 real 1 adj.

substantial 3 adj.
 coherence 48 n.
 cohesive 48 adj.
 definite 80 adj.
 formed 243 adj.
 material 319 adj.
 dense 324 adj.
 solid body 324 n.
 hardness 326 n.
 building material
  631 n.
concrete poetry
 verse form 593 n.
concretion
 substance 3 n.
 union 45 n.
 condensation
  324 n.
 solid body 324 n.
concubine
 loved one 887 n.
 kept woman 952 n.
concupiscence
 desire 859 n.
 libido 859 n.
concur
 accord 24 vb.
 synchronize
  123 vb.
 concur 181 vb.
 assent 488 vb.
concurrence
 union 45 n.
 assembly 74 n.
 synchronism 123 n.
 concurrence 181 n.
 convergence 293 n.
 assent 488 n.
concuss
 strike 279 vb.
 render insensible
  375 vb.
condemn
 condemn 961 vb.
condemnation
 condemnation
  961 n.
condemned
 dilapidated
  655 adj.
 condemned
  961 adj.
condensation
 condensation
  324 n.
 solid body 324 n.
 moisture 341 n.

condense
 become small
  198 vb.
 make smaller
  198 vb.
 be dense 324 vb.
 be concise 569 vb.
 abstract 592 vb.
condescend
 demean oneself
  867 vb.
 be proud 871 vb.
 be humble 872 vb.
 show respect
  920 vb.
condescending
 proud 871 adj.
 humble 872 adj.
condiment
 condiment 389 n.
condition
 state 7 n.
 composition 56 n.
 qualification 468 n.
 qualify 468 vb.
 supposition 512 n.
 teach 534 vb.
 habituate 610 vb.
 illness 651 n.
 prestige 866 n.
 impose a duty
  917 vb.
conditional
 restraining
  747 adj.
 conditional
  766 adj.
conditioned
 involuntary
  596 adj.
conditioning
 teaching 534 n.
 habituation 610 n.
conditions
 circumstance 8 n.
 conditions 766 n.
condolence
 benevolent 897 adj.
 condolence 905 n.
condom
 contraception
  172 n.
condominium
 joint possession
  775 n.
condone
 be patient 823 vb.

forgive 909 vb.
conducive
 instrumental
  628 adj.
 useful 640 adj.
conduct
 come before 64 vb.
 accompany 89 vb.
 transfer 272 vb.
 carry 273 vb.
 precede 283 vb.
 play music 413 vb.
 conduct 688 n.
 deal with 688 vb.
 direct 689 vb.
 manage 689 vb.
conduction
 electricity 160 n.
 motion 265 n.
 transference 272 n.
conductivity
 motion 265 n.
conduct oneself
 do 676 vb.
 behave 688 vb.
conductor
 living model 23 n.
 electricity 160 n.
 musician 413 n.
  See orchestra
 orchestra 413 n.
 leader 690 n.
conduit
 conduit 351 n.
cone
 cone 252 n.
 flower 366 n.
confectionery
 pastries and cakes
  301 n.
 sweets 301 n.
 sweet thing 392 n.
confederacy
 association 706 n.
 society 708 n.
confederate
 colleague 707 n.
confer
 confer 584 vb.
 give 781 vb.
conference
 conference 584 n.
confess
 confess 526 vb.
 perform ritual
  988 vb.

confession
testimony 466 n.
assent 488 n.
disclosure 526 n.
affirmation 532 n.
guilt 936 n.
penitence 939 n.
penance 941 n.
theology 973 n.
Holy Communion
988 n.
ministration 988 n.

confessional
creedal 485 adj.
disclosure 526 n.
tribunal 956 n.
church interior
990 n.

confessor
penitent 939 n.
pietist 979 n.
pastor 986 n.

confetti
small thing 33 n.

confidant(e)
adviser 691 n.
retainer 742 n.
servant 742 n.
close friend 880 n.

confide
inform 524 vb.
divulge 526 vb.

confide in
consult 691 vb.

confidence
positiveness 473 n.
expectation 507 n.
information 524 n.
safety 660 n.
hope 852 n.

confidence trick
trickery 542 n.
swindling 788 n.

confident
positive 473 adj.
expectant 507 adj.
assertive 532 adj.
hoping 852 adj.

confidential
private 80 adj.
concealed 525 adj.

configuration
outline 233 n.
form 243 n.

confine
hem 234 vb.
enclose 235 vb.

limit 236 vb.
conceal 525 vb.
imprison 747 vb.
seclude 883 vb.

confinement
obstetrics 167 n.
circumscription
232 n.
concealment 525 n.
detention 747 n.
seclusion 883 n.

confines
region 184 n.
place 185 n.
edge 234 n.

confirm
stabilize 153 vb.
strengthen 162 vb.
corroborate 466 vb.
make certain
473 vb.
judge 480 vb.
affirm 532 vb.
consent 758 vb.
contract 765 vb.
vindicate 927 vb.
make legal 953 vb.
perform ritual
988 vb.

confirmation
evidence 466 n.
certainty 473 n.
assent 488 n.
affirmation 532 n.
consent 758 n.
legislation 953 n.
Christian rite
988 n.

confirmed
habituated 610 adj.
due 915 adj.

confiscate
deprive 786 vb.
punish 963 vb.

conflagration
fire 379 n.
burning 381 n.

conflate
abstract 592 vb.

conflict
contrariety 14 n.
differ 15 vb.
disagreement 25 n.
counteraction
182 n.
opposition 704 n.
quarrel 709 n.

quarrel 709 vb.
contention 716 n.
fight 716 n.
be hostile 881 vb.
enmity 881 n.

confluence
union 45 n.
approach 289 n.
convergence 293 n.
current 350 n.

conform
adjust 24 vb.
conform 83 vb.
make conform
83 vb.
modify 143 vb.

conformist
conformist 83 n.
pietist 979 n.

confound
bedevil 63 vb.
confute 479 vb.
be wonderful
864 vb.
curse 899 vb.

confounded
damnable 645 adj.

confront
disagree 25 vb.
be present 189 vb.
be in front 237 vb.
be opposite 240 vb.
collide 279 vb.
compare 462 vb.
show 522 vb.
withstand 704 vb.
resist 715 vb.
go to war 718 vb.
be courageous
855 vb.

confrontation
contrariety 14 n.
disagreement 25 n.
contiguity 202 n.
collision 279 n.
convergence 293 n.
quarrel 709 n.

confuse
derange 63 vb.
blur 440 vb.
puzzle 474 vb.

confused
mixed 43 adj.
shadowy 419 adj.
indistinct 444 adj.
indiscriminate
464 adj.

poorly reasoned
477 adj.
unclear 568 adj.

confusion
psychosis 503 n.
humiliation 872 n.

confute
confute 479 vb.

conga
dance 837 n.

congé
valediction 296 n.
deposal 752 n.

congeal
be dense 324 vb.
thicken 354 vb.

congenial
pleasant 376 adj.
friendly 880 adj.

congenital
genetic 5 adj.

congestion
crowd 74 n.
redundance 637 n.

conglomerate
cohere 48 vb.
bring together
74 vb.
congregate 74 vb.
be dense 324 vb.
solid body 324 n.
corporation 708 n.

conglomeration
medley 43 n.
coherence 48 n.
accumulation 74 n.

congratulate
congratulate
886 vb.
applaud 923 vb.

congratulate oneself
be pleased 824 vb.
be content 828 vb.
rejoice 835 vb.
congratulate
886 vb.

congratulations
rejoicing 835 n.
congratulation
886 n.

congregate
congregate 74 vb.

congregation
assembly 74 n.
council 692 n.
community 708 n.
worshipper 981 n.

laity 987 n.
congress
  union 45 n.
  convergence 293 n.
  council 692 n.
  parliament 692 n.
congruent
  identical 13 adj.
  agreeing 24 adj.
  equal 28 adj.
  symmetrical
    245 adj.
congruity
  similarity 18 n.
  conformance 24 n.
  symmetry 245 n.
conical
  convergent 293 adj.
conifer
  tree 366 n.
conjecture
  attribution 158 n.
  assume 471 vb.
  estimate 480 vb.
  conjecture 512 n.
  suppose 512 vb.
conjugal
  loving 887 adj.
conjugate
  verbal 559 adj.
conjugation
  differentiation
    15 n.
  arrangement 62 n.
  grammar 564 n.
conjunction
  union 45 n.
  concurrence 181 n.
  contiguity 202 n.
  part of speech
    564 n.
conjunctive
  additional 38 adj.
  conjunctive 45 adj.
  grammatical
    564 adj.
conjunctivitis
  dim sight 440 n.
conjure
  deceive 542 vb.
conjure up
  remember 505 vb.
  imagine 513 vb.
conjuror
  sorcerer 983 n.
conk
  head 213 n.

protuberance
    254 n.
conk out
  die 361 vb.
  fail 728 vb.
con man
  impostor 545 n.
  trickster 545 n.
  defrauder 789 n.
  bad person 938 n.
connect
  relate 9 vb.
  connect 45 vb.
connection
  relation 9 n.
  consanguinity
    11 n.
  union 45 n.
  bond 47 n.
  coherence 48 n.
connivance
  cooperation 706 n.
connive
  concur 181 vb.
  cooperate 706 vb.
  consent 758 vb.
  forgive 909 vb.
connive at
  disregard 458 vb.
  permit 756 vb.
  do wrong 914 adj.
connoisseur
  eater 301 n.
  collector 492 n.
  enthusiast 504 n.
  expert 696 n.
  people of taste
    846 n.
connotation
  connotation 514 n.
connote
  mean 514 vb.
  imply 523 vb.
  indicate 547 vb.
conquer
  climb 308 vb.
  overmaster 727 vb.
  appropriate
    786 vb.
  take 786 vb.
conqueror
  victor 727 n.
  possessor 776 n.
conquest
  victory 727 n.
  subjection 745 n.
  loved one 887 n.

consanguinity
  consanguinity
    11 n.
  divorce 896 n.
conscience
  knowledge 490 n.
  necessity 596 n.
  motive 612 n.
  conscience 917 n.
conscientious
  careful 457 adj.
  observant 768 adj.
  fastidious 862 adj.
  obliged 917 adj.
  honourable
    929 adj.
  trustworthy
    929 adj.
conscientious objector
  dissentient 489 n.
  pacifist 717 n.
  malcontent 829 n.
conscious
  sentient 374 adj.
  attentive 455 adj.
  knowing 490 adj.
conscript
  go to war 718 vb.
  soldier 722 n.
  compel 740 vb.
consecrate
  offer 759 vb.
  give 781 vb.
  dignify 866 vb.
  sanctify 979 vb.
  offer worship
    981 vb.
  perform ritual
    988 vb.
consecutive
  relative 9 adj.
  sequential 65 adj.
  continuous 71 adj.
  subsequent
    120 adj.
consensus
  concurrence 181 n.
  consensus 488 n.
consent
  agreement 24 n.
  submission 721 n.
  consent 758 n.
  consent 758 vb.
  approbation 923 n.
consentient
  agreeing 24 adj.

consequence
  conformance 24 n.
  sequence 65 n.
  sequel 67 n.
  event 154 n.
  effect 157 n.
  importance 638 n.
consequences
  indoor game 837 n.
consequential
  caused 157 adj.
  ostentatious
    875 adj.
conservation
  permanence 144 n.
  storage 632 n.
  protection 660 n.
  preservation 666 n.
  economy 814 n.
conservationist
  preserver 666 n.
Conservative
  political party
    708 n.
conservative
  antiquated 127 adj.
  permanent 144 adj.
  cautious 858 adj.
conservatoire
  music 412 n.
  academy 539 n.
conservatory
  arbour 194 n.
  garden 370 n.
conserve
  sweet thing 392 n.
  store 632 vb.
  safeguard 660 vb.
  preserve 666 vb.
consider
  meditate 449 vb.
  notice 455 vb.
  estimate 480 vb.
considerable
  substantial 3 adj.
  great 32 adj.
  many 104 adj.
  large 195 adj.
  important 638 adj.
considerate
  thoughtful 449 adj.
  attentive 455 adj.
  careful 457 adj.
  well-bred 848 adj.
  amiable 884 adj.
  benevolent 897 adj.

consideration
meditation 449 n.
attention 455 n.
qualification 468 n.
estimate 480 n.
importance 638 n.
gift 781 n.
good taste 846 n.
courtesy 884 n.
benevolence 897 n.
respect 920 n.
reward 962 n.

consider beneath one
despise 922 vb.

consign
send 272 vb.
commission 751 vb.

consignment
transport 272 n.
transfer 780 n.
giving 781 n.

consign to oblivion
forget 506 vb.

consistency
uniformity 16 n.
conformance 24 n.
density 324 n.

consistent
uniform 16 adj.
agreeing 24 adj.
dense 324 adj.
rational 475 adj.

consist of
contain 56 vb.
comprise 78 vb.

consolation
relief 831 n.
condolence 905 n.

console
cabinet 194 n.
shelf 218 n.
relieve 831 vb.
cheer 833 vb.
pity 905 vb.

consolidate
bring together 74 vb.
centralize 225 vb.
be dense 324 vb.

consonant
speech sound 398 n.
harmonious 410 adj.

consort
concomitant 89 n.

spouse 894 n.

consortium
agreement 24 n.
association 706 n.

conspectus
combination 50 n.
whole 52 n.
generality 79 n.
compendium 592 n.

conspicuous
obvious 443 adj.
manifest 522 adj.
notable 638 adj.
noteworthy 866 adj.

conspiracy
assemblage 74 n.
concurrence 181 n.
secrecy 525 n.
plot 623 n.
cooperation 706 n.
compact 765 n.

conspirator
deceiver 545 n.
planner 623 n.
collaborator 707 n.

conspire
combine 50 vb.
concur 181 vb.
be stealthy 525 vb.
plot 623 vb.
cooperate 706 vb.

constable
officer 741 n.
police 955 n.

constancy
uniformity 16 n.
regularity 81 n.
stability 153 n.
resolution 599 n.
perseverance 600 n.
obstinacy 602 n.
loyalty 739 n.
probity 929 n.

constant
identical 13 adj.
identity 13 n.
uniform 16 adj.
continuous 71 adj.
regular 81 adj.
number 85 n.
lasting 113 adj.
perpetual 115 adj.
frequent 139 adj.
periodical 141 adj.
fixture 153 n.

unchangeable 153 adj.
accurate 494 adj.
resolute 599 adj.
obedient 739 adj.
trustworthy 929 adj.

constellation
group 74 n.
star 321 n.
person of repute 866 n.

consternation
wonder 864 n.

constipation
closure 264 n.
defecation 302 n.
condensation 324 n.
digestive disorders 651 n.

constituency
district 184 n.
electorate 605 n.

constituent
part 53 n.
component 58 adj.
component 58 n.
included 78 adj.
electorate 605 n.

constitute
constitute 56 vb.
be included 78 vb.
produce 164 vb.

constitution
character 5 n.
composition 56 n.
beginning 68 n.
inclusion 78 n.
structure 331 n.
precept 693 n.
law 953 n.
legislation 953 n.

constitutional
intrinsic 5 adj.
land travel 267 n.
pedestrianism 267 n.
habit 610 n.
exercise 682 n.
governmental 733 adj.
due 915 adj.
legal 953 adj.

constraint
limit 236 n.
compulsion 740 n.

subjection 745 n.
restraint 747 n.

constrict
tighten 45 vb.
make smaller 198 vb.

constriction
compression 198 n.
restriction 747 n.

construct
make complete 54 vb.
compose 56 vb.
produce 164 vb.
form 243 vb.

construction
composition 56 n.
arrangement 62 n.
production 164 n.
structure 331 n.
connotation 514 n.
interpretation 520 n.

constructive
semantic 514 adj.
intrepretative 520 adj.
aiding 703 adj.

construe
interpret 520 vb.

consul
official 690 n.
officer 741 n.
envoy 754 n.

consulate
house 192 n.
position of authority 733 n.
envoy 754 n.

consult
consult 691 vb.

consultant
sage 500 n.
oracle 511 n.
teacher 537 n.
doctor 658 n.
adviser 691 n.
expert 696 n.

consultation
enquiry 459 n.
conference 584 n.
preparation 669 n.
advice 691 n.

consume
decompose 51 vb.
disable 161 vb.
consume 165 vb.

destroy 165 vb.
dispose of 673 vb.
use 673 vb.
expend 806 vb.
consumer
eater 301 n.
purchaser 792 n.
consumer durables
merchandise
  795 n.
consummate
consummate
  32 adj.
terminate 69 vb.
crown 213 vb.
perfect 646 adj.
perfect 646 vb.
consumption
contraction 198 n.
thinness 206 n.
reception 299 n.
eating 301 n.
requirement 627 n.
infection 651 n.
respiratory disease
  651 n.
use 673 n.
loss 772 n.
consumptive
lean 206 adj.
diseased 651 adj.
sick person 651 n.
contact
connect 45 vb.
union 45 n.
be contiguous
  202 vb.
contiguity 202 n.
transference 272 n.
touch 378 n.
communicate
  524 vb.
informant 524 n.
messenger 529 n.
contact lens
eyeglass 442 n.
contagious
diseased 651 adj.
infectious 653 adj.
contain
contain 56 vb.
surround 230 vb.
possess 773 vb.
retain 778 vb.
container
receptacle 194 n.
transport 272 n.

carrier 273 n.
storage 632 n.
containerize
load 193 vb.
transpose 272 vb.
contain oneself
be temperate
  942 vb.
contaminate
transfer 272 vb.
make unclean
  649 vb.
impair 655 vb.
contaminated
diseased 651 adj.
contemplate
scan 438 vb.
meditate 449 vb.
intend 617 vb.
contemplation
look 438 n.
meditation 449 n.
attention 455 n.
expectation 507 n.
piety 979 n.
prayers 981 n.
worship 981 n.
contemplative
thoughtful 449 adj.
pietist 979 n.
pious 979 adj.
worshipper 981 n.
monastic 986 adj.
contemporaneous
present 121 adj.
synchronous
  123 adj.
contemporary
present 121 adj.
contemporary
  123 n.
synchronous
  123 adj.
modern 126 adj.
contempt
contempt 922 n.
contemptible
bad 645 adj.
contemptible
  922 adj.
contemptuous
insolent 878 adj.
contend
affirm 532 vb.
contend 716 vb.
contender
contender 716 n.

contend with
resist 715 vb.
content
structure 331 n.
content 828 adj.
content 828 n.
content 828 vb.
contention
contention 716 n.
contentious
quarrelling
  709 n.
contentment
euphoria 376 n.
content 828 n.
contents
contents 193 n.
topic 452 n.
meaning 514 n.
edition 589 n.
compendium
  592 n.
contest
contend 716 vb.
contest 716 n.
contestant
opponent 705 n.
contender 716 n.
context
circumstance 8 n.
relation 9 n.
concomitant 89 n.
connotation 514 n.
meaning 514 n.
contiguous, be
be contiguous
  202 vb.
continence
temperance 942 n.
continent
region 184 n.
land 344 n.
temperate 942 adj.
continental
extraneous 59 adj.
continental quilt
coverlet 226 n.
contingency
extrinsicality 6 n.
juncture 8 n.
event 154 n.
possibility 469 n.
uncertainty 474 n.
expectation 507 n.
contingent
extrinsic 6 adj.

circumstantial
  8 adj.
part 53 n.
caused 157 adj.
liable 180 adj.
qualifying 468 adj.
possible 469 adj.
uncertain 474 adj.
conditional
  766 adj.
contingent, be
be possible 469 vb.
continual
continuous 71 adj.
perpetual 115 adj.
frequent 139 adj.
continuance
continuance 146 n.
continuation
adjunct 40 n.
sequence 65 n.
sequel 67 n.
continuity 71 n.
continuance 146 n.
continue
be 1 vb.
continue 71 adj.
continue 108 vb.
last 113 vb.
perpetuate 115 vb.
happen 154 vb.
lengthen 203 vb.
persevere 600 vb.
continuity
continuity 71 n.
cinema 445 n.
dramaturgy 594 n.
continuous
continuous 71 adj.
continuum
continuity 71 n.
space 183 n.
contort
distort 246 vb.
contour
outline 233 n.
form 243 n.
feature 445 n.
contra
nonconformist
  84 n.
dissentient 489 n.
desperado 857 n.
contraband
prohibited 757 adj.
booty 790 n.
illegal 954 adj.

contraception
impotence 161 n.
contraception
172 n.
counteraction
182 n.

contraceptive
contraception
172 n.

contract
abate 37 vb.
decrease 37 vb.
become small
198 vb.
make smaller
198 vb.
shorten 204 vb.
make thin 206 vb.
be dense 324 vb.
be concise 569 vb.
deteriorate 655 vb.
undertaking 672 n.
compact 765 n.
contract 765 vb.
capital punishment
963 n.

contract a disease
be ill 651 vb.

contraction
contraction 198 n.
shortening 204 n.
closure 264 n.
word 559 n.
conciseness 569 n.
compendium
592 n.

contractions
obstetrics 167 n.
contraction 198 n.

contractor
doer 676 n.
signatory 765 n.

contractual
contractual
765 adj.

contradict
be contrary 14 vb.
disagree 25 vb.
answer 460 vb.
tell against 467 vb.
confute 479 vb.
dissent 489 vb.
negate 533 vb.
oppose 704 vb.

contradiction
contrariety 14 n.
disagreement 25 n.

divergence 294 n.
rejoinder 460 n.
confutation 479 n.
dissent 489 n.
negation 533 n.
opposition 704 n.

**contradiction in
terms**
sophism 477 n.

contradictory
contrary 14 adj.
disagreeing 25 adj.
illogical 477 adj.
negative 533 adj.
opposing 704 adj.

contradistinction
contrariety 14 n.
differentiation
15 n.

contraflow
contrariety 14 n.
traffic control
305 n.
obstacle 702 n.

contraindication
contrariety 14 n.
counterevidence
467 n.
dissuasion 613 n.

contralto
resonance 404 n.
vocalist 413 n.

contraposition
contraposition
240 n.

contraption
contrivance 623 n.
tool 630 n.

contrapuntal
musical 412 adj.

contrariness
contrariety 14 n.
opposition 704 n.

contrary
contrary 14 adj.
opposite 240 adj.
capricious 604 adj.
adverse 731 adj.
disobedient
738 adj.

contrast
be contrary 14 vb.
contrariety 14 n.
differ 15 vb.
difference 15 n.
nonuniform 17 adj.

nonuniformity
17 n.
dissimilarity 19 n.
nonconformity
84 n.
compare 462 vb.
compared 462 adj.
comparison 462 n.
trope 519 n.
painting 553 n.

contrasting
contrary 14 adj.
different 15 adj.
estimate 480 n.

contravene
be contrary 14 vb.
tell against 467 vb.
negate 533 vb.

contravention
negation 533 n.
lawbreaking 954 n.

contretemps
untimeliness
138 n.
hitch 702 n.
misfortune 731 n.

contribute
concur 181 vb.
give 781 vb.
pay 804 vb.

contribute to
augment 36 vb.
add 38 vb.
promote 285 vb.
aid 703 vb.
patronize 703 vb.

contribution
increment 36 n.
addition 38 n.
adjunct 40 n.
giving 781 n.
offering 781 n.
pay 804 n.
payment 804 n.

contributor
cause 156 n.
correspondent
588 n.
author 589 n.
dissertator 591 n.
participator 775 n.
giver 781 n.

contributory
additional 38 adj.
aiding 703 adj.

contrite
regretting 830 adj.

repentant 939 adj.

contrivance
contrivance 623 n.

contrive
cause 156 vb.
produce 164 vb.
predetermine
608 vb.
be cunning 698 vb.

control
be able 160 vb.
power 160 n.
moderate 177 vb.
moderation 177 n.
influence 178 n.
prevail 178 vb.
testing agent
461 n.
comparison 462 n.
dispose of 673 vb.
do 676 vb.
directorship 689 n.
manage 689 vb.
management
689 n.
hindrance 702 n.
governance 733 n.
rule 733 vb.
restrain 747 vb.
restraint 747 n.
restriction 747 n.
tranquillize
823 vb.
spiritualism 984 n.

controller
doer 676 n.
director 690 n.
treasurer 798 n.

control oneself
be temperate
942 vb.

controls
aircraft 276 n.
instrument 628 n.

controversial
uncertain 474 adj.

controversy
disagreement 25 n.
question 459 n.
argument 475 n.
dissent 489 n.
conference 584 n.
quarrel 709 n.
contention 716 n.

controvertible
uncertain 474 adj.

contumacious
schismatical
978 adj.
contumely
insolence 878 n.
scurrility 899 n.
contusion
wound 655 n.
conundrum
equivocalness
518 n.
enigma 530 n.
conurbation
city 184 n.
housing 192 n.
convalesce
be strong 162 vb.
get healthy 650 vb.
be restored 656 vb.
convalescent
healthy 650 adj.
convect
transfer 272 vb.
convection
transference 272 n.
convene
bring together
74 vb.
command 737 vb.
convenience
opportunity 137 n.
benefit 615 n.
utility 640 n.
good policy 642 n.
facility 701 n.
convenience food
provisions 301 n.
conveniences
means 629 n.
convenient
circumstantial
8 adj.
comfortable
376 adj.
useful 640 adj.
easy 701 adj.
convent
quarters 192 n.
monastery 986 n.
conventicle
assembly 74 n.
meeting place
192 n.
council 692 n.
sect 978 n.
church 990 n.

convention
agreement 24 n.
assembly 74 n.
regularity 81 n.
conformity 83 n.
conference 584 n.
practice 610 n.
council 692 n.
precept 693 n.
treaty 765 n.
etiquette 848 n.
conventional
regular 81 adj.
conformable
83 adj.
typical 83 adj.
habitual 610 adj.
well-bred 848 adj.
orthodox 976 adj.
converge
be oblique 220 vb.
converge 293 vb.
convergent
convergent 293 adj.
conversant
knowing 490 adj.
conversation
cry 408 n.
speech 579 n.
interlocution
584 n.
conversational
loquacious 581 adj.
conversation piece
art subject 553 n.
converse
contrariety 14 n.
contrary 14 adj.
converse 584 vb.
interlocution
584 n.
conversely
contrarily 14 adv.
conversely 467 adv.
conversion
conversion 147 n.
teaching 534 n.
change of mind
603 n.
improvement
654 n.
transfer 780 n.
sanctity 979 n.
convert
convert 147 vb.
interchange
151 vb.

convince 485 vb.
learner 538 n.
recanter 603 n.
use 673 vb.
acquire 771 vb.
assign 780 vb.
make pious 979 vb.
pietist 979 n.
convertible
identical 13 adj.
automobile 274 n.
used 673 adj.
convex
convex 253 adj.
convey
move 265 vb.
transfer 272 vb.
carry 273 vb.
mean 514 vb.
communicate
524 vb.
inform 524 vb.
See **communi-
cate**
assign 780 vb.
conveyance
conveyance 267 n.
transference 272 n.
transport 272 n.
vehicle 274 n.
giving 781 n.
conveyancing
transfer 780 n.
conveyor
conveyor 274 n.
conveyor belt
uniform 16 adj.
uniformity 16 n.
continuity 71 n.
transport 272 n.
carrier 273 n.
conveyor 274 n.
convict
confute 479 vb.
prisoner 750 n.
offender 904 n.
condemn 961 vb.
conviction
positiveness 473 n.
confutation 479 n.
belief 485 n.
hope 852 n.
censure 924 n.
condemnation
961 n.
convince
convince 485 vb.

convince oneself
be certain 473 vb.
convincing
plausible 471 adj.
positive 473 adj.
credible 485 adj.
convivial
cheerful 833 adj.
sociable 882 adj.
convocation
assembly 74 n.
council 692 n.
synod 985 n.
convoluted
convoluted 251 adj.
unclear 568 adj.
convolvulus
plant 366 n.
convoy
accompany 89 vb.
concomitant 89 n.
carry 273 vb.
protection 660 n.
safeguard 660 vb.
convulse
derange 63 vb.
**convulse with laugh-
ter**
amuse 837 vb.
convulsion
turmoil 61 n.
derangement 63 n.
revolution 149 n.
outbreak 176 n.
spasm 318 n.
pang 377 n.
coo
ululate 409 vb.
ululation 409 n.
laughter 835 n.
rejoice 835 vb.
flatter 925 vb.
cook
cook 301 vb.
cookery 301 n.
fake 541 vb.
caterer 633 n.
domestic 742 n.
cooker
furnace 383 n.
cookery
cookery 301 n.
cookies
pastries and cakes
301 n.
cooking
impending 155 adj.

cookery 301 n.
heating 381 n.
preparatory
  669 adj.
cook one's goose
destroy 165 vb.
defeat 727 vb.
cook the books
defraud 788 vb.
cool
moderate 177 adj.
moderate 177 vb.
quietude 266 n.
tranquil 266 adj.
cold 380 adj.
coldness 380 n.
refrigerate 382 vb.
dissuade 613 vb.
refresh 685 vb.
impassive 820 adj.
inexcitability
  823 n.
inexcitable
  823 adj.
cautious 858 adj.
indifferent 860 adj.
impertinent
  878 adj.
hostile 881 adj.
unsociable 883 adj.
cool down
tranquillize
  823 vb.
cooler
moderator 177 n.
refrigerator 384 n.
lockup 748 n.
prison 748 n.
cooling-off period
delay 136 n.
lull 145 n.
cool it
come to rest
  266 vb.
coolness
coldness 380 n.
moral insensibility
  820 n.
inexcitability
  823 n.
indifference 860 n.
enmity 881 n.
unsociability
  883 n.
cool off
refresh 685 vb.

be indifferent
  860 vb.
coop
stable 192 n.
cattle pen 369 n.
lockup 748 n.
cooperate
cooperate 706 vb.
cooperation
cooperation 706 n.
cooperative
cooperative
  706 adj.
society 708 n.
co-opt
choose 605 vb.
coop up
imprison 747 vb.
coordinate
equal 28 adj.
gauge 465 n.
cop
protector 660 n.
arrest 747 vb.
police 955 n.
cope
vestments 989 n.
cope with
be equal 28 vb.
deal with 688 vb.
withstand 704 vb.
copious
prolific 171 adj.
diffuse 570 adj.
plentiful 635 adj.
cop it
be destroyed
  165 vb.
die 361 vb.
be in difficulty
  700 vb.
cop out
avoid 620 vb.
copper
pot 194 n.
heater 383 n.
brownness 430 n.
engraving 555 n.
ablutions 648 n.
protector 660 n.
coinage 797 n.
police 955 n.
copperplate
lettering 586 n.
written 586 adj.
coppice
wood 366 n.

copse
bunch 74 n.
wood 366 n.
copulate
unite with 45 vb.
generate 167 vb.
copulation
coition 45 n.
propagation 167 n.
copy
copy 20 vb.
copy 22 n.
prototype 23 n.
conform 83 vb.
duplication 91 n.
reproduction
  166 n.
news 529 n.
record 548 n.
represent 551 vb.
representation
  551 n.
script 586 n.
writing 586 n.
reading matter
  589 n.
steal 788 vb.
copycat
imitator 20 n.
conformist 83 n.
copyright
claim 915 vb.
dueness 915 n.
copywriter
publicizer 528 n.
author 589 n.
coquette
lover 887 n.
court 889 vb.
flatterer 925 n.
coral
fossil 125 n.
marine life 365 n.
red 431 adj.
gem 844 n.
coral reef
island 349 n.
marine life 365 n.
pitfall 663 n.
cor Anglais
flute 414 n.
cord
cable 47 n.
ligature 47 n.
fibre 208 n.
strip 208 n.

cordial
soft drink 301 n.
pleasant 376 adj.
willing 597 adj.
feeling 818 adj.
friendly 880 adj.
sociable 882 adj.
cordite
explosive 723 n.
cordless telephone
telecommunication
  531 n.
cordon
surroundings
  230 n.
barrier 235 n.
loop 250 n.
cordon bleu
cookery 301 n.
proficient person
  696 n.
decoration 729 n.
cordon off
circumscribe
  232 vb.
enclose 235 vb.
restrain 747 vb.
cordon sanitaire
hygiene 652 n.
prophylactic 658 n.
protection 660 n.
preservation 666 n.
corduroy
textile 222 n.
furrow 262 n.
core
essence 1 n.
substance 3 n.
essential part 5 n.
focus 76 n.
centre 225 n.
chief thing 638 n.
affections 817 n.
corespondent
divorce 896 n.
accused person
  928 n.
libertine 952 n.
coriander
spice 301 n.
cork
cover 226 vb.
covering 226 n.
close 264 vb.
stopper 264 n.
lightness 323 n.

corkage
price 809 n.
corked
closed 264 adj.
unsavoury 391 adj.
corkscrew
coil 251 n.
meander 251 vb.
See **twine**
opener 263 n.
perforator 263 n.
rotate 315 vb.
corn
swelling 253 n.
cereals 301 n.
provender 301 n.
hardness 326 n.
ulcer 651 n.
cornea
eye 438 n.
corner
circumstance 8 n.
place 185 n.
angularity 247 n.
hiding-place 527 n.
penance 941 n.
pillory 964 n.
cornered
angular 247 adj.
in difficulties
700 adj.
cornerstone
fixture 153 n.
support 218 n.
chief thing 638 n.
cornet
bag 194 n.
cone 252 n.
horn 414 n.
cornice
summit 213 n.
edge 234 n.
ornamental art
844 n.
cornucopia
abundance 171 n.
store 632 n.
plenty 635 n.
corollary
adjunct 40 n.
concomitant 89 n.
effect 157 n.
judgment 480 n.
corona
sun 321 n.
tobacco 388 n.

coronary
cardiovascular dis-
ease 651 n.
coronation
mandate 751 n.
celebration 876 n.
coroner
judge 957 n.
coronet
headgear 228 n.
loop 250 n.
heraldry 547 n.
regalia 743 n.
corporal
soldiery 722 n.
army officer 741 n.
corporal punishment
corpóral punish-
ment 963 n.
corporation
stomach 194 n.
bulk 195 n.
corporation 708 n.
jurisdiction 955 n.
corporeal
substantial 3 adj.
material 319 adj.
corps
band 74 n.
formation 722 n.
corpse
corpse 363 n.
corpulent
fleshy 195 adj.
corpus
great quantity
32 n.
whole 52 n.
assemblage 74 n.
matter 319 n.
reading matter
589 n.
corpuscle
minuteness 196 n.
blood 335 n.
corral
bring together
74 vb.
enclose 235 vb.
enclosure 235 n.
break in 369 vb.
imprison 747 vb.
correct
orderly 60 adj.
modify 143 vb.
moderate 177 vb.
accurate 494 adj.

true 494 adj.
inform 524 vb.
grammatical
564 adj.
perfect 646 adj.
rectify 654 vb.
remedy 658 vb.
tasteful 846 adj.
well-bred 848 adj.
formal 875 adj.
courteous 884 adj.
reprove 924 vb.
honourable
929 adj.
punish 963 vb.
orthodox 976 adj.
correction
moderation 177 n.
amendment 654 n.
reprimand 924 n.
correctness
perfection 646 n.
etiquette 848 n.
ostentation 875 n.
courtesy 884 n.
correlate
correlate 12 vb.
correspond
be related 9 vb.
correlate 12 vb.
accord 24 vb.
conform 83 vb.
correspond 588 vb.
correspondence
relativeness 9 n.
correlation 12 n.
uniformity 16 n.
similarity 18 n.
conformance 24 n.
parallelism 219 n.
record 548 n.
correspondence
588 n.
correspondent
respondent 460 n.
informant 524 n.
news reporter
529 n.
correspondent
588 n.
author 589 n.
delegate 754 n.
corresponding
relative 9 adj.
correlative 12 adj.
similar 18 adj.
agreeing 24 adj.

equivalent 28 adj.
symmetrical
245 adj.
correspond to
answer 460 vb.
correspond with
correspond 588 vb.
corridor
bond 47 n.
entrance 68 n.
region 184 n.
lobby 194 n.
doorway 263 n.
access 624 n.
corrigenda
edition 589 n.
corroborate
corroborate 466 vb.
corrode
impair 655 vb.
hurt 827 vb.
corrosion
dilapidation 655 n.
corrugated
undulatory
251 adj.
rough 259 adj.
corrugated iron
roof 226 n.
roughness 259 n.
furrow 262 n.
corrupt
decompose 51 vb.
bribe 612 vb.
bad 645 adj.
harm 645 vb.
unclean 649 adj.
deteriorate 655 vb.
pervert 655 vb.
venal 930 adj.
make wicked
934 vb.
vicious 934 adj.
corruption
decay 51 n.
neology 560 n.
badness 645 n.
uncleanness 649 n.
deterioration
655 n.
dilapidation 655 n.
improbity 930 n.
wickedness 934 n.
corset
make smaller
198 vb.
support 218 n.

imitative 20 adj.
substituted 150 adj.
dissemble 541 vb.
duplicity 541 n.
fake 541 vb.
false 541 adj.
deceive 542 vb.
sham 542 n.
spurious 542 adj.
be untrue 543 vb.
mint 797 vb.
counterfoil
credential 466 n.
label 547 n.
title deed 767 n.
receipt 807 n.
counterirritant
counteraction 182 n.
antidote 658 n.
countermand
command 737 vb.
abrogate 752 vb.
prohibit 757 vb.
counterpane
coverlet 226 n.
counterpart
analogue 18 n.
compeer 28 n.
counterpoint
contrariety 14 n.
combination 50 n.
melody 410 n.
music 412 n.
counter-revolution
reversion 148 n.
revolution 149 n.
countersign
testify 466 vb.
endorse 488 vb.
give security 767 vb.
countess
person of rank 868 n.
count for
substitute 150 vb.
count heads
number 86 vb.
vote 605 vb.
counting
inclusive 78 adj.
numeration 86 n.
countless
multitudinous 104 adj.
infinite 107 adj.

count on
believe 485 vb.
hope 852 vb.
count one's blessings
be content 828 vb.
count one's chickens before they are hatched
expect 507 vb.
hope 852 vb.
be rash 857 vb.
count out
exclude 57 vb.
exempt 919 vb.
country
region 184 n.
land 344 n.
political organization 733 n.
country and western
music 412 n.
country dancing
dancing 837 n.
country-dweller
dweller 191 n.
commoner 869 n.
country-dweller 869 n.
country house
house 192 n.
count the cost
be cautious 858 vb.
count upon
assume 471 vb.
expect 507 vb.
county
district 184 n.
political organization 733 n.
county council
council 692 n.
jurisdiction 955 n.
coup
instant 116 n.
deed 676 n.
masterpiece 694 n.
success 727 n.
coup de foudre
love 887 n.
coup de grace
end 69 n.
ruin 165 n.
killing 362 n.
completion 725 n.
prowess 855 n.
coup d'état
revolution 149 n.

deed 676 n.
revolt 738 n.
lawlessness 954 n.
coup de théâtre
dramaturgy 594 n.
miracle-working 864 n.
coupé
automobile 274 n.
couple
analogue 18 n.
join 45 vb.
unite with 45 vb.
duality 90 n.
pair 90 vb.
marry 894 vb.
wed 894 vb.
couplet
duality 90 n.
verse form 593 n.
courage
courage 855 n.
courage in the face of the enemy
courage 855 n.
prowess 855 n.
courage of one's convictions
courage 855 n.
courageous
courageous 855 adj.
courier
guide 520 n.
guidebook 524 n.
courier 529 n.
course
continuity 71 n.
time 108 n.
conversion 147 n.
tendency 179 n.
layer 207 n.
motion 265 n.
itinerary 267 n.
land travel 267 n.
travel 267 vb.
water travel 269 n.
sail 275 n.
direction 281 n.
progression 285 n.
dieting 301 n.
dish 301 n.
flow 350 VB.
curriculum 534 n.
hunt 619 vb.
route 624 n.
conduct 688 n.

arena 724 n.
course garment
underwear 228 n.
course of action
policy 623 n.
courser
horse 273 n.
dog 365 n.
court
concomitant 89 n.
place 185 n.
housing 192 n.
open space 263 n.
council 692 n.
arena 724 n.
retainer 742 n.
beau monde 848 n.
court 889 n.
flatter 925 vb.
lawcourt 956 n.
courteous
courteous 884 adj.
courter
petitioner 763 n.
lover 887 n.
courtesan
female 373 n.
prostitute 952 n.
courtesy
uncharged 812 adj.
etiquette 848 n.
courteous act 884 n.
courtesy 884 n.
courtesy call
social round 882 n.
courtesy title
insubstantial thing 4 n.
title 870 n.
undueness 916 n.
courtier
retainer 742 n.
toady 879 n.
flatterer 925 n.
courting
lovemaking 887 n.
loving 887 adj.
wooing 889 n.
courtliness
courtesy 884 n.
courtly
well-bred 848 adj.
courteous 884 adj.
flattering 925 adj.
courtly love
love 887 n.

625

court-martial
lawcourt 956 n.
court-martialled, be
incur blame
924 vb.
court officer
law officer 955 n.
court of justice
probity 929 n.
lawcourt 956 n.
Court of Session
lawcourt 956 n.
court order
judgment 480 n.
courtship
wooing 889 n.
courtyard
place 185 n.
enclosure 235 n.
cousin
kinsman 11 n.
friend 880 n.
couthie
sociable 882 adj.
couturier
clothier 228 n.
artist 556 n.
cove
cavity 255 n.
gulf 345 n.
male 372 n.
coven
assembly 74 n.
sorcery 983 n.
covenant
promise 764 n.
promise 764 vb.
compact 765 n.
contract 765 vb.
title deed 767 n.
Covenanter
sectarian 978 n.
cover
unite with 45 vb.
be dispersed 75 vb.
comprise 78 vb.
modify 143 vb.
suppress 165 vb.
extend 183 vb.
receptacle 194 n.
cover 226 vb.
covering 226 n.
stopper 264 n.
meal 301 n.
communicate
524 vb.
disguise 527 n.

hiding-place 527 n.
publish 528 vb.
mark 547 vb.
obliterate 550 vb.
correspondence
588 n.
bookbinding 589 n.
pretext 614 n.
protection 660 n.
safeguard 660 vb.
shelter 662 n.
defend 713 vb.
threaten 900 vb.
coverage
inclusion 78 n.
publicity 528 n.
covered
concealed 525 adj.
cover girl
a beauty 841 n.
covering
covering 226 n.
dressing 228 n.
covering up
concealment 525 n.
coverlet
coverlet 226 n.
cover oneself
be cautious 858 vb.
cover one's tracks
be cautious 858 vb.
covert
nest 192 n.
wood 366 n.
occult 523 adj.
concealed 525 adj.
cover up
cover 226 vb.
screen 421 vb.
mislead 495 vb.
conceal 525 vb.
keep secret 525 vb.
obliterate 550 vb.
be cautious 858 vb.
cover up for
substitute 150 vb.
covet
desire 859 vb.
envy 912 vb.
covetous
avaricious 816 adj.
envious 912 adj.
selfish 932 adj.
covey
group 74 n.
cow
cattle 365 n.

female animal
373 n.
frighten 854 vb.
coward
coward 856 n.
cowardly 856 adj.
cowardice
cowardice 856 n.
cowardly
cowardly 856 adj.
cowboy
rider 268 n.
herdsman 369 n.
independent
744 adj.
lawless 954 adj.
cowboys and Indians
children's games
837 n.
cowed
cowardly 856 adj.
cower
stoop 311 vb.
quake 854 vb.
be cowardly
856 vb.
cowering
nervous 854 adj.
cowardice 856 n.
cowardly 856 adj.
servile 879 adj.
cowgirl
rider 268 n.
herdsman 369 n.
cowherd
herdsman 369 n.
servant 742 n.
cowl
covering 226 n.
headgear 228 n.
canonicals 989 n.
cowman
herdsman 369 n.
co-worker
concomitant 89 n.
collaborator 707 n.
cowpat
excrement 302 n.
cowshed
stable 192 n.
cattle pen 369 n.
cowslip
plant 366 n.
cox
navigate 269 vb.
navigator 270 n.

coxcomb
fop 848 n.
vain person 873 n.
coxswain
navigate 269 vb.
mariner 270 n.
navigator 270 n.
coy
affected 850 adj.
cowardly 856 adj.
modest 874 adj.
pure 950 adj.
coyote
dog 365 n.
crab
fish food 301 n.
marine life 365 n.
rude person 885 n.
crab apple
fruit and vegetables
301 n.
tree 366 n.
sourness 393 n.
crabbed
sour 393 adj.
discontented
829 adj.
irascible 892 adj.
sullen 893 adj.
crabbit
discontented
829 adj.
angry 891 adj.
irascible 892 adj.
sullen 893 adj.
crabwise
sideways 239 adv.
crack
break 46 vb.
disunion 46 n.
separate 46 vb.
discontinuity 72 n.
instant 116 n.
weakness 163 n.
gap 201 n.
space 201 vb.
narrowness 206 n.
roughen 259 vb.
roughness 259 n.
furrow 262 n.
opening 263 n.
knock 279 n.
bang 402 n.
crackle 402 vb.
stripe 437 n.
variegate 437 vb.
decipher 520 vb.

best 644 adj.
defect 647 n.
skilful 694 adj.
blemish 845 n.
blemish 845 vb.
drug-taking 949 n.
crack a bottle
drink 301 vb.
be sociable 882 vb.
get drunk 949 vb.
crack a joke
be witty 839 vb.
crack down on
abate 37 vb.
be severe 735 vb.
restrain 747 vb.
prohibit 757 vb.
cracked
rough 259 adj.
strident 407 adj.
discordant 411 adj.
unintelligent
　499 adj.
crazy 503 adj.
imperfect 647 adj.
dilapidated
　655 adj.
cracker
cereals 301 n.
bang 402 n.
crackers
pastries and cakes
　301 n.
crazy 503 adj.
cracking
separation 46 n.
interpretation
　520 n.
crackle
be hot 379 vb.
bang 402 n.
crackle 402 vb.
crack of the whip
stimulant 174 n.
incentive 612 n.
crack open
open 263 vb.
crackpot
erroneous 495 adj.
absurd 497 adj.
fool 501 n.
the maladjusted
　504 n.
ridiculous 849 adj.
crack shot
proficient person
　696 n.

crack up
go mad 503 vb.
be fatigued 684 vb.
laugh 835 vb.
boast 877 vb.
praise 923 vb.
crack-up
ruin 165 n.
cradle
origin 68 n.
nonage 130 n.
assuage 177 vb.
place 187 vb.
home 192 n.
basket 194 n.
bed 218 n.
support 218 vb.
bring to rest
　266 vb.
make inactive
　679 vb.
pet 889 vb.
craft
ship 275 n.
shipping 275 n.
deception 542 n.
business 622 n.
vocation 622 n.
skill 694 n.
cunning 698 n.
craftily
skilfully 694 adv.
craftiness
sagacity 498 n.
skill 694 n.
cunning 698 n.
craftsman or -woman
producer 164 n.
artist 556 n.
machinist 630 n.
artisan 686 n.
expert 696 n.
crafty
cunning 698 adj.
crag
high land 209 n.
rock 344 n.
craggy
sharp 256 adj.
rough 259 adj.
difficult 700 adj.
cram
fill 54 vb.
bring together
　74 vb.
load 193 vb.
enlarge 197 vb.

make smaller
　198 vb.
educate 534 vb.
study 536 vb.
superabound
　637 vb.
gluttonize 947 vb.
cram down one's
　throat
convince 485 vb.
crammed
full 54 adj.
crammer
teacher 537 n.
school 539 n.
glutton 947 n.
cramoisy
red 431 adj.
cramp
fastening 47 n.
weaken 163 vb.
make smaller
　198 vb.
spasm 318 n.
pang 377 n.
impair 655 vb.
make inactive
　679 vb.
restrain 747 vb.
restraint 747 n.
prohibit 757 vb.
cramped
little 196 adj.
restrained 747 adj.
cramp one's style
disable 161 vb.
make useless
　641 adj.
cramps, the
spasm 318 n.
crane
hanger 217 n.
conveyor 274 n.
bird 365 n.
scan 438 vb.
crane fly
insect 365 n.
crane one's neck
scan 438 vb.
craniology
head 213 n.
craniotomy
head 213 n.
cranium
head 213 n.
crank
handle 218 n.

rotate 315 vb.
the maladjusted
　504 n.
crank up
make ready
　669 vb.
cranky
convoluted 251 adj.
crazy 503 adj.
irascible 892 adj.
cranny
place 185 n.
compartment
　194 n.
angularity 247 n.
cavity 255 n.
furrow 262 n.
hiding-place 527 n.
crapulence
crapulence 949 n.
crap (vulg)
defecation 302 n.
excrement 302 n.
excrete 302 vb.
crash
revolution 149 n.
ruin 165 n.
textile 222 n.
aeronautics 271 n.
fly 271 vb.
collision 279 n.
descent 309 n.
be loud 400 vb.
loudness 400 n.
bang 402 n.
bang 402 vb.
discord 411 vb.
fail 728 vb.
miscarry 728 vb.
insolvency 805 n.
not pay 805 vb.
crash barrier
road 624 n.
crash course
study 536 n.
crash diet
dieting 301 n.
crash dive
aeronautics 271 n.
plunge 313 n.
plunge 313 vb.
crash helmet
headgear 228 n.
safeguard 662 n.
crash into
collide 279 vb.

crash-land
fly 271 vb.
descent 309 n.
crass
consummate
32 adj.
manifest 522 adj.
vulgar 847 adj.
crate
bicycle 274 n.
vehicle 274 n.
aircraft 276 n.
crater
cavity 255 n.
orifice 263 n.
moon 321 n.
cravat
ligature 47 n.
neckwear 228 n.
crave
require 627 vb.
beg 761 vb.
request 761 vb.
desire 859 vb.
envy 912 vb.
craven
coward 856 n.
cowardly 856 adj.
craw
stomach 194 n.
crawl
elapse 111 vb.
be in motion
265 vb.
aquatics 269 n.
move slowly
278 vb.
slowness 278 n.
change one's mind
603 vb.
knuckle under
721 vb.
lose repute 867 vb.
be humble 872 vb.
be servile 879 vb.
crawler
toady 879 n.
crawling
multitudinous
104 adj.
slow 278 adj.
unclean 649 adj.
submitting 721 adj.
servile 879 adj.
servility 879 n.
flattering 925 adj.
dishonest 930 adj.

crawling with
full 54 adj.
crayfish
fish food 301 n.
marine life 365 n.
crayon
colour 425 vb.
paint 553 vb.
stationery 586 n.
craze
stripe 437 n.
variegate 437 vb.
eccentricity 503 n.
whim 604 n.
practice 610 n.
fashion 848 n.
liking 859 n.
crazy
distorted 246 adj.
absurd 497 adj.
crazy 503 adj.
unsafe 661 adj.
ridiculous 849 adj.
crazy about
excited 821 adj.
enamoured
887 adj.
crazy golf
ball game 837 n.
crazy paving
nonuniformity
17 n.
paving 226 n.
chequer 437 n.
creak
faintness 401 n.
sound faint 401 vb.
stridor 407 n.
creaking
hoarse 407 adj.
strident 407 adj.
cream
dairy product
301 n.
milk 301 n.
semiliquidity
354 n.
bubble 355 vb.
fat 357 n.
unguent 357 n.
select 605 vb.
chief thing 638 n.
elite 644 n.
balm 658 n.
cosmetic 843 n.
person of repute
866 n.

cream cracker
cereals 301 n.
creamed
educational
534 adj.
creamery
workshop 687 n.
creamy
fatty 357 adj.
soft-hued 425 adj.
whitish 427 adj.
crease
joint 45 n.
jumble 63 vb.
roughen 259 vb.
crease (cricket)
place 185 n.
create
cause 156 vb.
produce 164 vb.
form 243 vb.
imagine 513 vb.
revolt 738 vb.
dignify 866 vb.
be angry 891 vb.
create an opening
profit by 137 vb.
create a row
revolt 738 vb.
creation
existence 1 n.
beginning 68 n.
antiquity 125 n.
causation 156 n.
product 164 n.
production 164 n.
dress 228 n.
formation 243 n.
universe 321 n.
representation
551 n.
creative
original 21 adj.
prolific 171 adj.
imaginative
513 adj.
godlike 965 adj.
creative accounting
nonpayment 805 n.
creativity
imagination 513 n.
Creator
producer 164 n.
the Deity 965 n.
creator
cause 156 n.
producer 164 n.

creature
product 164 n.
animal 365 n.
person 371 n.
instrument 628 n.
dependant 742 n.
toady 879 n.
crèche
school 539 n.
credence
belief 485 n.
altar 990 n.
credential
credential 466 n.
credible
credible 485 adj.
credit
attribute 158 vb.
attribution 158 n.
belief 485 n.
believe 485 vb.
authority 733 n.
credit 802 n.
credit 802 vb.
account 808 vb.
honour 866 vb.
thank 907 vb.
thanks 907 n.
dueness 915 n.
approbation 923 n.
praise 923 n.
creditable
excellent 644 adj.
reputable 866 adj.
credit account
borrowing 785 n.
credit card
borrowing 785 n.
credit 802 n.
creditor
lender 784 n.
credits
cinema 445 n.
credit 802 n.
receipt 807 n.
credit union
treasury 799 n.
credit with
attribute 158 vb.
credit-worthy
moneyed 800 adj.
reputable 866 adj.
trustworthy
929 adj.
credo
creed 485 n.
theology 973 n.

rigid 326 adj.
brittle 330 adj.
concise 569 adj.
crispbread
cereals 301 n.
crisps
mouthful 301 n.
crisscross
crossed 222 adj.
crossing 222 n.
crit
estimate 480 n.
criterion
prototype 23 n.
testing agent
461 n.
comparison 462 n.
gauge 465 n.
critic
estimator 480 n.
dissentient 489 n.
interpreter 520 n.
bookperson 589 n.
dissertator 591 n.
malcontent 829 n.
detractor 926 n.
critical
circumstantial
8 adj.
crucial 137 adj.
discriminating
463 adj.
literary 557 adj.
important 638 adj.
sick 651 adj.
dangerous 661 adj.
unsafe 661 adj.
difficult 700 adj.
discontented
829 adj.
fastidious 862 adj.
disapproving
924 adj.
critical moment
juncture 8 n.
criticism
estimate 480 n.
interpretation
520 n.
affirmation 532 n.
literature 557 n.
article 591 n.
advice 691 n.
censure 924 n.
detraction 926 n.
criticize
dissertate 591 vb.

be discontented
829 vb.
criticize 924 vb.
detract 926 vb.
critique
discrimination
463 n.
estimate 480 n.
interpretation
520 n.
article 591 n.
croak
die 361 vb.
rasp 407 vb.
ululate 409 vb.
ululation 409 n.
crochet
tie 45 vb.
network 222 n.
weave 222 vb.
needlework 844 n.
crock
vessel 194 n.
sick person 651 n.
crockery
receptacle 194 n.
pottery 381 n.
crocodile
line 203 n.
skin 226 n.
reptile 365 n.
crocodile tears
duplicity 541 n.
lament 836 n.
Croesus
rich person 800 n.
croft
house 192 n.
farm 370 n.
croissant
cereals 301 n.
crone
old woman 133 n.
crony
colleague 707 n.
chum 880 n.
friend 880 n.
crook
support 218 n.
angularity 247 n.
be curved 248 vb.
deflect 282 vb.
punctuation 547 n.
thief 789 n.
low fellow 869 n.
offender 904 n.
bad person 938 n.

vestments 989 n.
crooked
distorted 246 adj.
angular 247 adj.
cunning 698 adj.
dishonest 930 adj.
croon
sound faint 401 vb.
sing 413 vb.
crooner
vocalist 413 n.
entertainer 594 n.
crop
great quantity
32 n.
growth 157 n.
product 164 n.
stomach 194 n.
shorten 204 vb.
hair 259 n.
graze 301 vb.
agriculture 370 n.
cultivate 370 vb.
benefit 615 n.
store 632 n.
acquire 771 vb.
earnings 771 n.
take 786 vb.
hairdressing 843 n.
cropped
incomplete 55 adj.
cropper
descent 309 n.
crop up
happen 154 vb.
chance 159 vb.
be visible 443 vb.
croquet
ball game 837 n.
croquettes
dish 301 n.
crosier
badge of rule
743 n.
vestments 989 n.
cross
hybrid 43 n.
mix 43 vb.
counteract 182 vb.
cross 222 n.
cross 222 vb.
crossed 222 adj.
traverse 267 vb.
pass 305 vb.
obsequies 364 n.
assent 488 n.
badge 547 n.

heraldry 547 n.
indication 547 n.
label 547 n.
mark 547 vb.
bane 659 n.
encumbrance
702 n.
opposing 704 adj.
decoration 729 n.
adversity 731 n.
painfulness 827 n.
discontented
829 adj.
angry 891 adj.
irascible 892 adj.
sullen 893 adj.
means of execution
964 n.
talisman 983 n.
ritual object 988 n.
church interior
990 n.
crossbeam
beam 218 n.
cross benches
opponent 705 n.
freedom 744 n.
crossbones
cross 222 n.
crossbow
missile weapon
723 n.
cross-breed
hybrid 43 n.
mix 43 vb.
cross-country
towards 281 adv.
cross-country race
racing 716 n.
crosscurrent
counteraction
182 n.
contraposition
240 n.
current 350 n.
pitfall 663 n.
obstacle 702 n.
opposition 704 n.
crossed
mixed 43 adj.
crossed 222 adj.
crossed lines
misinterpretation
521 n.
cross-examine
interrogate 459 vb.
try a case 959 vb.

cross-eyed
crossed 222 adj.
dim-sighted
440 adj.
cross-fertilization
mixture 43 n.
cross-fire
interchange 151 n.
crossing
crossed 222 adj.
crossing 222 n.
water travel 269 n.
passage 305 n.
access 624 n.
road 624 n.
cross-legged
crossed 222 adj.
crossness
anger 891 n.
sullenness 893 n.
cross off
register 548 vb.
cross one's fingers
deprecate 762 vb.
cross one's heart
swear 532 vb.
**cross one's palm with
silver**
give 781 vb.
pay 804 vb.
cross out
subtract 39 vb.
exclude 57 vb.
mark 547 vb.
obliterate 550 vb.
cross over
cross 222 vb.
pass 305 vb.
apostatize 603 vb.
crossover
railway 624 n.
crosspatch
moper 834 n.
rude person 885 n.
cross-purposes
error 495 n.
misinterpretation
521 n.
opposition 704 n.
dissension 709 n.
cross-question
interrogate 459 vb.
cross-reference
referral 9 n.
class 62 vb.
sorting 62 n.

crossroads
juncture 8 n.
joint 45 n.
focus 76 n.
crossing 222 n.
divergence 294 n.
road 624 n.
cross-section
example 83 n.
cross swords
collide 279 vb.
argue 475 vb.
withstand 704 vb.
quarrel 709 vb.
contend 716 vb.
fight 716 vb.
go to war 718 vb.
cross the Rubicon
overstep 306 vb.
be resolute 599 vb.
cross to bear
bane 659 n.
crosstree
support 218 n.
crosswind
wind 352 n.
obstacle 702 n.
cross with
unite with 45 vb.
crossword
enigma 530 n.
indoor game 837 n.
crotch
angularity 247 n.
crotchet
angularity 247 n.
notation 410 n.
punctuation 547 n.
crotchety
crazy 503 adj.
capricious 604 adj.
irascible 892 adj.
crouch
stoop 311 vb.
knuckle under
721 vb.
quake 854 vb.
lose repute 867 vb.
croup
respiratory disease
651 n.
croupier
treasurer 798 n.
croûtons
cereals 301 n.
crow
bird 365 n.

black thing 428 n.
defy 711 vb.
triumph 727 vb.
laughter 835 n.
rejoice 835 vb.
eyesore 842 n.
boast 877 vb.
crowbar
tool 630 n.
crowd
congregate 74 vb.
crowd 74 n.
be many 104 vb.
be contiguous
202 vb.
be dense 324 vb.
viol 414 n.
onlookers 441 n.
obstruct 702 vb.
not respect 921 vb.
crowded
firm 45 adj.
multitudinous
104 adj.
printed 587 adj.
crowds
great quantity
32 n.
crowd together
make smaller
198 vb.
crown
completeness 54 n.
crown 213 vb.
head 213 n.
summit 213 n.
vertex 213 n.
headgear 228 n.
loop 250 n.
strike 279 vb.
badge 547 n.
heraldry 547 n.
objective 617 n.
completion 725 n.
trophy 729 n.
authority 733 n.
badge of rank
743 n.
regalia 743 n.
commission
751 vb.
coinage 797 n.
dignify 866 vb.
honour 866 vb.
honours 866 n.
celebrate 876 vb.
reward 962 n.

crown all
culminate 34 vb.
climax 725 vb.
crowned head
sovereign 741 n.
crowning
complete 54 adj.
ending 69 adj.
topmost 213 adj.
crowning glory
hair 259 n.
completion 725 n.
crown jewels
jewellery 844 n.
**Crown Prince or
Princess**
sovereign 741 n.
crow over
defy 711 vb.
triumph 727 vb.
humiliate 872 vb.
boast 877 vb.
crow's feet
fold 261 n.
ugliness 842 n.
crow's nest
high structure
209 n.
vertex 213 n.
view 438 n.
crucial
circumstantial
8 adj.
crucial 137 adj.
fundamental
156 adj.
crossed 222 adj.
important 638 adj.
crucial moment
juncture 8 n.
crisis 137 n.
important matter
638 n.
cruciate
crossed 222 adj.
crucible
vessel 194 n.
heater 383 n.
crucifix
cross 222 n.
jewellery 844 n.
ritual object 988 n.
church interior
990 n.
crucifixion
killing 362 n.
pain 377 n.

suffering 825 n.
capital punishment
  963 n.
cruciform
crossed 222 adj.
churchlike 990 adj.
crucify
give pain 377 vb.
ill-treat 645 vb.
execute 963 vb.
crud
dirt 649 n.
crude
incomplete 55 adj.
florid 425 adj.
inelegant 576 adj.
immature 670 adj.
bungled 695 adj.
graceless 842 adj.
ill-bred 847 adj.
cruel
paining 827 adj.
cruel 898 adj.
cruelty
badness 645 n.
severity 735 n.
cruel act 898 n.
inhumanity 898 n.
cruet
ritual object 988 n.
cruise
be in motion
  265 vb.
go to sea 269 vb.
voyage 269 vb.
water travel 269 n.
cruise missile
rocket 276 n.
missile weapon
  723 n.
cruiser
warship 722 n.
cruise ship
ship 275 n.
crumb
small thing 33 n.
piece 53 n.
cereals 301 n.
powder 332 n.
crumble
abate 37 vb.
break 46 vb.
decompose 51 vb.
be weak 163 vb.
be destroyed
  165 vb.
dessert 301 n.

pulverize 332 vb.
deteriorate 655 vb.
impair 655 vb.
crumbling
decrease 37 n.
unsafe 661 adj.
crumbly
fragmentary
  53 adj.
brittle 330 adj.
powdery 332 adj.
crumb of comfort
relief 831 n.
crumbs
leavings 41 n.
rubbish 641 n.
crummy
inferior 35 adj.
bad 645 adj.
crumpet
head 213 n.
cereals 301 n.
female 373 n.
crumple
jumble 63 vb.
make smaller
  198 vb.
distort 246 vb.
crinkle 251 vb.
roughen 259 vb.
crunch
rend 46 vb.
chew 301 vb.
pulverize 332 vb.
rasp 407 vb.
crusade
action 676 n.
war 718 n.
philanthropy
  901 n.
crusader
militarist 722 n.
philanthropist
  901 n.
zealot 979 n.
cruse
vessel 194 n.
crush
jumble 63 vb.
crowd 74 n.
demolish 165 vb.
force 176 vb.
make smaller
  198 vb.
make concave
  255 vb.
abase 311 vb.

lower 311 vb.
pulverize 332 vb.
touch 378 vb.
confute 479 vb.
ill-treat 645 vb.
wound 655 vb.
defeat 727 vb.
overmaster 727 vb.
oppress 735 vb.
humiliate 872 vb.
love 887 n.
crush barrier
safeguard 662 n.
crushing
destruction 165 n.
destructive 165 adj.
distressing 827 adj.
crushing blow
ruin 165 n.
crust
piece 53 n.
exteriority 223 n.
covering 226 n.
skin 226 n.
cereals 301 n.
be dense 324 vb.
hardness 326 n.
sauciness 878 n.
crustacean
animal 365 n.
marine life 365 n.
crusty
irascible 892 adj.
sullen 893 adj.
crutch
support 218 n.
garment 228 n.
crux
crisis 137 n.
cross 222 n.
chief thing 638 n.
difficulty 700 n.
cry
cry 408 n.
cry 408 vb.
ululate 409 vb.
ululation 409 n.
lamentation 836 n.
weep 836 vb.
desire 859 n.
cry down
underestimate
  483 vb.
detract 926 vb.
cry for the moon
waste effort
  641 adj.

desire 859 vb.
crying
lamentation 836 n.
crying shame
evil 616 n.
slur 867 n.
wrong 914 n.
cryosurgery
refrigeration 382 n.
cry out
cry 408 vb.
vociferate 408 vb.
cry out against
deprecate 762 vb.
cry out for
require 627 vb.
desire 859 vb.
cry over spilt milk
regret 830 vb.
crypt
cellar 194 n.
depth 211 n.
tomb 364 n.
hiding-place 527 n.
church interior
  990 n.
cryptic
uncertain 474 adj.
unintelligible
  517 adj.
occult 523 adj.
concealed 525 adj.
cryptogram
enigma 530 n.
cryptologist
interpreter 520 n.
cry quits
make peace
  719 vb.
submit 721 vb.
be defeated 728 vb.
crystal
minuteness 196 n.
covering 226 n.
solid body 324 n.
transparency
  422 n.
transparent
  422 adj.
crystal ball
sphere 252 n.
oracle 511 n.
crystal-gazing
divination 511 n.
prediction 511 n.
occultism 984 n.

crystalline
  dense 324 adj.
  hard 326 adj.
  transparent
    422 adj.
crystallize
  be dense 324 vb.
  harden 326 vb.
  sweeten 392 vb.
crystal set
  broadcasting
    531 n.
cry wolf
  be false 541 vb.
  raise the alarm
    665 vb.
  frighten 854 vb.
CSE
  exam 459 n.
CS gas
  poison 659 n.
cub
  young creature
    132 n.
  youngster 132 n.
  reproduce itself
    167 vb.
cubbyhole
  retreat 192 n.
  compartment
    194 n.
cube
  three 93 n.
  treble 94 vb.
  angular figure
    247 n.
cube root
  numerical element
    85 n.
cubic
  metrical 465 adj.
cubicle
  chamber 194 n.
  compartment
    194 n.
cubit
  long measure
    203 n.
cuckold
  be impure 951 vb.
cuckoo
  resident 191 n.
  bird 365 n.
  roll 403 n.
  ululation 409 n.
  fool 501 n.
  crazy 503 adj.

cuckoo clock
  timekeeper 117 n.
cuckoo in the nest
  unrelatedness 10 n.
  intruder 59 n.
  impostor 545 n.
  usurper 916 n.
cuddle
  surround 230 vb.
  enclose 235 vb.
  retention 778 n.
  please 826 vb.
  caress 889 vb.
  endearment 889 n.
cuddly
  fleshy 195 adj.
cudgel
  hammer 279 n.
  strike 279 vb.
  club 723 n.
  flog 963 vb.
  scourge 964 n.
cue
  ram 279 n.
  remind 505 vb.
  reminder 505 n.
  hint 524 n.
  dramaturgy 594 n.
cue in
  act 594 vb.
cuff
  garment 228 n.
  sleeve 228 n.
  fold 261 n.
  fold 261 vb.
  knock 279 n.
  corporal punish-
    ment 963 n.
  spank 963 vb.
cufflinks
  jewellery 844 n.
cuirass
  armour 713 n.
Cuisenaire rods
  counting instru-
    ment 86 n.
cuisine
  cookery 301 n.
cul-de-sac
  stopping place
    145 n.
  closure 264 n.
  road 624 n.
  difficulty 700 n.
  obstacle 702 n.
culinary
  culinary 301 adj.

cull
  killing 362 n.
  select 605 vb.
  take 786 vb.
culminate
  culminate 34 vb.
  be complete 54 vb.
  be high 209 vb.
  crown 213 vb.
  ascend 308 vb.
  climax 725 vb.
culottes
  skirt 228 n.
culpable
  wrong 914 adj.
  blameworthy
    924 adj.
  heinous 934 adj.
  guilty 936 adj.
culprit
  offender 904 n.
  accused person
    928 n.
cult
  fashion 848 n.
  cult 981 n.
  idolatry 982 n.
cultivate
  cultivate 370 vb.
  train 534 vb.
  flatter 925 vb.
cultivation
  causation 156 n.
  agriculture 370 n.
  learning 536 n.
  ripening 669 n.
  good taste 846 n.
cultural
  educational
    534 adj.
  improving 654 adj.
culture
  breed stock 369 vb.
  culture 490 n.
  learning 536 n.
  good taste 846 n.
cultured
  spurious 542 adj.
cultured pearl
  gem 844 n.
culvert
  drain 351 n.
cumbersome
  unwieldy 195 adj.
  weighty 322 adj.
  inexpedient
    643 adj.

clumsy 695 adj.
  graceless 842 adj.
cummerbund
  belt 228 n.
  loop 250 n.
cumulative
  increasing 36 adj.
cumulus
  accumulation 74 n.
  cloud 355 n.
cunctative
  nonactive 677 adj.
cuneiform
  letter 558 n.
cunning
  skilful 694 adj.
  cunning 698 adj.
  cunning 698 n.
cup
  cup 194 n.
  support 218 vb.
  cavity 255 n.
  trophy 729 n.
  honours 866 n.
  reward 962 n.
  ritual object 988 n.
cup-bearer
  retainer 742 n.
cupboard
  cabinet 194 n.
  storage 632 n.
cupboard love
  duplicity 541 n.
  selfishness 932 n.
cupful
  finite quantity
    26 n.
  small quantity
    33 n.
  contents 193 n.
Cupid
  mythic deity 966 n.
  Olympian deity
    967 n.
cupidity
  avarice 816 n.
  desire 859 n.
cupola
  high structure
    209 n.
  roof 226 n.
  dome 253 n.
cup that cheers, the
  sociability 882 n.
Cup tie
  contest 716 n.

cur
  nonconformist
    84 n.
  dog 365 n.
  coward 856 n.
curable
  medical 658 adj.
curate
  pastor 986 n.
curate's egg
  imperfection 647 n.
curative
  remedial 658 adj.
curator
  collector 492 n.
  protector 660 n.
  manager 690 n.
  keeper 749 n.
  consignee 754 n.
curb
  moderate 177 vb.
  retard 278 vb.
  slowness 278 n.
  restrain 747 vb.
  restraint 747 n.
  fetter 748 n.
curd
  solid body 324 n.
curdle
  be dense 324 vb.
  thicken 354 vb.
curds
  dairy product
    301 n.
  milk 301 n.
  semiliquidity
    354 n.
cure
  counteract 182 vb.
  dry 342 vb.
  cure 656 vb.
  recuperation 656 n.
  remedy 658 n.
  therapy 658 n.
  preserve 666 vb.
  mature 669 vb.
  laity 987 n.
curettage
  voidance 300 n.
curfew
  evening 129 n.
  danger signal
    665 n.
  detention 747 n.
  restriction 747 n.
  prohibition 757 n.

curie
  radiation 417 n.
curio
  exhibit 522 n.
  ornamentation
    844 n.
curiosity
  nonconformist
    84 n.
  curiosity 453 n.
  prodigy 864 n.
curious
  unusual 84 adj.
  inquisitive 453 adj.
  enquiring 459 adj.
curl
  filament 208 n.
  be curved 248 vb.
  curve 248 n.
  loop 250 n.
  coil 251 n.
  crinkle 251 vb.
  hairdressing 843 n.
  primp 843 vb.
curlers
  fastening 47 n.
  hairdressing 843 n.
curlew
  bird 365 n.
curlicue
  coil 251 n.
  pattern 844 n.
curliness
  curvature 248 n.
curling
  ball game 837 n.
  sport 837 n.
  hairdressing 843 n.
curling stone
  missile 287 n.
curling tongs
  heater 383 n.
curl one's lip
  gesticulate 547 vb.
  despise 922 vb.
curls
  hair 259 n.
curl up
  ascend 308 vb.
  rotate 315 vb.
curly
  undulatory
    251 adj.
  hairy 259 adj.
currant
  fruit and vegetables
    301 n.

currency
  publicity 528 n.
  money 797 n.
current
  present 121 adj.
  motion 265 n.
  current 350 n.
  wind 352 n.
  linguistic 557 adj.
  useful 640 adj.
current account
  funds 797 n.
  accounts 808 n.
current affairs
  affairs 154 n.
curricle
  carriage 274 n.
curriculum
  curriculum 534 n.
curriculum vitae
  evidence 466 n.
  record 548 n.
  biography 590 n.
curry
  cook 301 vb.
  dish 301 n.
  rub 333 vb.
  season 388 vb.
currycomb
  rub 333 vb.
  groom 369 vb.
curry favour
  be servile 879 vb.
  flatter 925 vb.
curry powder
  spice 301 n.
  condiment 389 n.
curse
  influence 178 n.
  haemorrhage
    302 n.
  evil 616 n.
  badness 645 n.
  bane 659 n.
  adversity 731 n.
  annoyance 827 n.
  discontent 829 n.
  be rude 885 vb.
  curse 899 int.
  curse 899 vb.
  cuss 899 vb.
  malediction 899 n.
  scurrility 899 n.
  wrong 914 n.
  spell 983 n.
curse and swear
  cuss 899 vb.

cursed
  damnable 645 adj.
  bewitched 983 adj.
cursing
  cursing 899 adj.
  impiety 980 n.
cursing and swearing
  scurrility 899 n.
cursive
  letter 558 n.
cursor
  indicator 547 n.
cursory
  inconsiderable
    33 adj.
  transient 114 adj.
  inattentive 456 adj.
  hasty 680 adj.
curt
  concise 569 adj.
  taciturn 582 adj.
curtail
  abate 37 vb.
  subtract 39 vb.
  cut 46 vb.
    See **sunder**
  sunder 46 vb.
  shorten 204 vb.
  impair 655 vb.
curtain
  exclusion 57 n.
  end 69 n.
  shade 226 n.
  partition 231 n.
  darken 418 vb.
  curtain 421 n.
  screen 421 vb.
  invisibility 444 n.
  dramaturgy 594 n.
  stage set 594 n.
  obstacle 702 n.
  defend 713 vb.
curtain call
  recurrence 106 n.
  dramaturgy 594 n.
  applause 923 n.
curtain-raiser
  stage play 594 n.
curtains
  hanging object
    217 n.
  covering 226 n.
  death 361 n.
  decease 361 n.
curtsy
  obeisance 311 n.
  stoop 311 vb.

courteous act
884 n.
greet 884 vb.
respects 920 n.
show respect
920 vb.

curvaceous
curved 248 adj.
convex 253 adj.
shapely 841 adj.

curvature
obliquity 220 n.
curvature 248 n.

curvature of the spine
deformity 246 n.
curvature 248 n.

curve
be curved 248 vb.
curve 248 n.
deviate 282 vb.
circle 314 vb.

curved
curved 248 adj.

curves
bluntness 257 n.
beauty 841 n.

curvet
walk 267 vb.

curvy
curved 248 adj.
snaky 251 adj.

cushion
weaken 163 vb.
moderate 177 vb.
moderator 177 n.
cushion 218 n.
support 218 vb.
line 227 vb.
intermediary
231 n.
soften 327 vb.
softness 327 n.
protection 660 n.
safeguard 660 vb.
defend 713 vb.
relieve 831 vb.

cushy
comfortable
376 adj.
easy 701 adj.

cusp
extremity 69 n.
vertex 213 n.
sharp point 256 n.
zodiac 321 n.
pattern 844 n.

cuss
cuss 899 vb.
scurrility 899 n.

cussed
opposing 704 adj.
malevolent
898 adj.

cussedness
obstinacy 602 n.
malevolence 898 n.

custard
dessert 301 n.
sweet thing 392 n.

custard-pie
funny 849 adj.

custard-pie humour
wit 839 n.

custodian
protector 660 n.
manager 690 n.
defender 713 n.
keeper 749 n.

custody
protection 660 n.
detention 747 n.

custom
order 60 n.
continuity 71 n.
generality 79 n.
regularity 81 n.
tradition 127 n.
permanence 144 n.
habit 610 n.
etiquette 848 n.

customary
general 79 adj.
regular 81 adj.
habitual 610 adj.
orthodox 976 adj.

custom-built
one 88 adj.
formed 243 adj.

customer
person 371 n.
patron 707 n.
petitioner 763 n.
purchaser 792 n.

custom-made
tailored 228 adj.

customs
conduct 688 n.
receipt 807 n.
tax 809 n.

customs officer
receiver 782 n.

cut
adjust 24 vb.

small 33 adj.
decrease 37 n.
diminution 37 n.
subtract 39 vb.
cut 46 vb.
disunion 46 n.
piece 53 n.
discontinuity 72 n.
be absent 190 vb.
gap 201 n.
short 204 adj.
shorten 204 vb.
shortening 204 n.
be oblique 220 vb.
cross 222 vb.
form 243 n.
form 243 vb.
smooth 258 vb.
notch 260 n.
move fast 277 vb.
knock 279 n.
propel 287 vb.
meat 301 n.
cultivate 370 vb.
pain 377 n.
feature 445 n.
disregard 458 vb.
represent 551 vb.
sculpt 554 vb.
engrave 555 vb.
evil 616 n.
wound 655 n.
not observe 769 vb.
apportion 783 vb.
portion 783 n.
pay 804 n.
receipt 807 n.
price 809 n.
discount 810 n.
discount 810 vb.
cheapen 812 vb.
hurt 827 vb.
fashion 848 n.
humiliate 872 vb.
be rude 885 vb.
reproach 924 n.

cut above, a
superior 34 adj.

cut across
be oblique 220 vb.
pass 305 vb.

cut a dash
be in fashion
848 vb.
have a reputation
866 vb.

be ostentatious
875 vb.

cut adrift
separate 46 vb.
repeat 106 vb.

cut a long story short
be concise 569 vb.

cut and dried
arranged 62 adj.
definite 80 adj.
ready-made
669 adj.

cut and run
move fast 277 vb.
decamp 296 vb.
run away 620 vb.
hasten 680 vb.
be cowardly
856 vb.

cut back
abate 37 vb.
subtract 39 vb.
render few 105 vb.
shorten 204 vb.
restrain 747 vb.
economize 814 vb.

cutback
decrease 37 n.
shortening 201 n.
economy 814 n.

cut both ways
tell against 467 vb.
be equivocal
518 vb.

cut corners
hasten 680 vb.

cut dead
disregard 458 vb.
be rude 885 vb.

cut down
abate 37 vb.
subtract 39 vb.
cut 46 vb.
demolish 165 vb.
shorten 204 vb.
fell 311 vb.
slaughter 362 vb.
strike at 712 vb.

cut down to size
make conform
83 vb.
abase 311 vb.
inglorious 867 adj.
shame 867 vb.
detract 926 vb.

cute
personable 841 adj.

affected 850 adj.
cuteness
  beauty 841 n.
cut glass
  ornamental art
    844 n.
cuticle
  skin 226 n.
cut in two
  bisect 92 vb.
cutlass
  sharp edge 256 n.
  sidearms 723 n.
cutlery
  sharp edge 256 n.
cutlet
  piece 53 n.
  meat 301 n.
cut loose
  separate 46 vb.
  be free 744 vb.
cut no ice
  have no repute
    867 vb.
cut off
  cut 46 vb.
  set apart 46 vb.
  terminate 69 vb.
  suppress 165 vb.
  circumscribe
    232 vb.
  be concise 569 vb.
cut off one's nose to
    spite one's face
  act foolishly
    695 vb.
cut off without a
    penny
  not retain 779 vb.
  impoverish 801 vb.
cut of one's jib
  form 243 n.
  feature 445 n.
cut one's coat accord-
    ing to one's
    cloth
  economize 814 vb.
  be cautious 858 vb.
cut one short
  make mute 578 vb.
cut one's own throat
  act foolishly
    695 vb.
cut open
  cut 46 vb.
  open 263 vb.

cut out for
  fit 24 adj.
cut-price
  discount 810 n.
  cheap 812 adj.
  cheapness 812 n.
cuts
  restriction 747 n.
  economy 814 n.
cut short
  cut 46 vb.
  halt 145 vb.
  suppress 165 vb.
  shorten 204 vb.
  be concise 569 vb.
  concise 569 adj.
cut straws
  gamble 618 vb.
cut the Gordian knot
  disencumber
    701 vb.
cut the ground from
    under one's feet
  hinder 702 vb.
  defeat 727 vb.
cutter
  sharp edge 256 n.
  boat 275 n.
  sailing ship 275 n.
cut-throat
  destructive 165 adj.
cutthroat
  murderer 362 n.
  ruffian 904 n.
cut-throat competi-
    tion
  contention 716 n.
cut through
  cut 46 vb.
  pierce 263 vb.
  be resolute 599 vb.
cutting
  scission 46 n.
  excavation 255 n.
  sharp 256 adj.
  plant 366 n.
  cinema 445 n.
  railway 624 n.
  hairdressing 843 n.
cutting edge
  sharp edge 256 n.
cuttings
  record 548 n.
  anthology 592 n.
cuttlefish
  marine life 365 n.

cut to pieces
  slaughter 362 vb.
cut to the quick
  excite 821 vb.
  hurt 827 vb.
cut up
  cut 46 vb.
  unhappy 825 adj.
  melancholic
    834 adj.
cut up about
  suffering 825 adj.
cut up rough
  be angry 891 vb.
  resent 891 vb.
cv
  biography 590 n.
cyanide
  poison 659 n.
cyanosis
  blueness 435 n.
cybernetics
  data processing
    86 n.
cycle
  continuity 71 n.
  recurrence 106 n.
  era 110 n.
  periodicity 141 n.
  regular return
    141 n.
  orbit 250 n.
  motion 265 n.
  ride 267 vb.
  bicycle 274 n.
  poem 593 n.
  stage play 594 n.
cycle track
  road 624 n.
cyclic
  periodical 141 adj.
  round 250 adj.
cyclical
  continuous 71 adj.
cycling
  land travel 267 n.
  exercise 682 n.
  sport 837 n.
cyclist
  rider 268 n.
cyclometer
  meter 465 n.
cyclone
  storm 176 n.
  vortex 315 n.
  weather 340 n.
  gale 352 n.

Cyclops
  giant 195 n.
cyclostyle
  copy 20 vb.
cyclotron
  nucleonics 160 n.
cygnet
  young creature
    132 n.
  bird 365 n.
cylinder
  cylinder 252 n.
cyma
  pattern 844 n.
cymbals
  gong 414 n.
cyme
  flower 366 n.
cynic
  underestimation
    483 n.
  unbeliever 486 n.
  misanthrope 902 n.
  detractor 926 n.
cynical
  impassive 820 adj.
  hopeless 853 adj.
  disrespectful
    921 adj.
  disapproving
    924 adj.
cynicism
  philosophy 449 n.
  moral insensibility
    820 n.
  dejection 834 n.
  hopelessness 853 n.
  misanthropy 902 n.
  detraction 926 n.
cynosure
  focus 76 n.
  attraction 291 n.
  desired object
    859 n.
  person of repute
    866 n.
  favourite 890 n.
cyst
  swelling 253 n.
  skin disease 651 n.
  ulcer 651 n.
cystitis
  digestive disorders
    651 n.
cytology
  biology 358 n.

czardas
dance 837 n.

D

dab
small thing 33 n.
knock 279 n.
touch 378 vb.
dabble
be inactive 679 vb.
dabble in
not know 491 vb.
amuse oneself
837 vb.
dabchick
bird 365 n.
dab hand
proficient person
696 n.
dabs
trace 548 n.
dactyl
prosody 593 n.
dad
paternity 169 n.
Dada
school of painting
553 n.
Dadaist
artist 556 n.
daddy
paternity 169 n.
daddy longlegs
insect 365 n.
dado
base 214 n.
lining 227 n.
ornamental art
844 n.
daffodil
plant 366 n.
yellowness 433 n.
heraldry 547 n.
daft
foolish 499 adj.
crazy 503 adj.
dagger
sharp point 256 n.
punctuation 547 n.
sidearms 723 n.
daggers drawn
resentment 891 n.
dahlia
plant 366 n.
daily
often 139 adv.

periodically
141 adv.
seasonal 141 adj.
journal 528 n.
the press 528 n.
usual 610 adj.
cleaner 648 n.
servant 742 n.
daily dozen
exercise 682 n.
daily help
cleaner 648 n.
servant 742 n.
dainty
small 33 adj.
flimsy 163 adj.
little 196 adj.
savouriness 390 n.
pleasurableness
826 n.
personable 841 adj.
shapely 841 adj.
tasteful 846 adj.
fastidious 862 adj.
dairy
chamber 194 n.
workshop 687 n.
dairy farm
stock farm 369 n.
farm 370 n.
dairymaid
herdsman 369 n.
dais
stand 218 n.
daisy
plant 366 n.
daisy wheel
stationery 586 n.
Dalai Lama
sovereign 741 n.
priest 986 n.
dale
plain 348 n.
Dalek
image 551 n.
dalliance
lovemaking 887 n.
dally
be inactive 679 vb.
caress 889 vb.
Dalmatian
dog 365 n.
mottle 437 n.
dam
exclusion 57 n.
maternity 169 n.
close 264 vb.

irrigator 341 n.
lake 346 n.
staunch 350 VB.
obstacle 702 n.
obstruct 702 vb.
damage
break 46 vb.
derange 63 vb.
tell against 467 vb.
evil 616 n.
waste 634 n.
waste 634 vb.
badness 645 n.
harm 645 vb.
impair 655 vb.
impairment 655 n.
cost 809 n.
blemish 845 vb.
defame 926 vb.
penalty 963 n.
damages
compensation 31 n.
restitution 787 n.
pay 804 n.
cost 809 n.
penalty 963 n.
damaging
wasteful 634 adj.
harmful 645 adj.
discreditable
867 adj.
disapproving
924 adj.
damask
textile 222 n.
red 431 adj.
dame
female 373 n.
master 741 n.
person of repute
866 n.
title 870 n.
dammed
born 360 adj.
damn
trifle 639 n.
curse 899 int.
curse 899 vb.
cuss 899 vb.
scurrility 899 n.
criticize 924 vb.
condemn 961 vb.
damnable
damnable 645 adj.
damnably
extremely 32 vb.

damnation
future state 124 n.
suffering 825 n.
condemnation
961 n.
damned
damnable 645 adj.
condemned
961 adj.
damning
evidential 466 adj.
cursing 899 adj.
disapproving
924 adj.
**damn with faint
praise**
be indifferent
860 vb.
criticize 924 vb.
detract 926 vb.
damp
moderate 177 vb.
gas 336 n.
water 339 n.
humid 341 adj.
moisture 341 n.
extinguish 382 vb.
depress 834 vb.
damp course
base 214 n.
damp down
abate 37 vb.
extinguish 382 vb.
hinder 702 vb.
restrain 747 vb.
dampen
moderate 177 vb.
moisten 341 vb.
mute 401 vb.
dissuade 613 vb.
depress 834 vb.
damper
moderator 177 n.
stopper 264 n.
heater 383 n.
nonresonance
405 n.
piano 414 n.
dissuasion 613 n.
moper 834 n.
dampness
moisture 341 n.
damp-proof
strong 162 adj.
coat 226 vb.

damp squib
disappointment
509 n.
failure 728 n.

damsel
youngster 132 n.
female 373 n.

damson
fruit and vegetables
301 n.
purpleness 436 n.

damson-coloured
purple 436 adj.

dam up
staunch 350 VB.
obstruct 702 vb.

dan
proficient person
696 n.

dance
vary 152 vb.
be in motion
265 vb.
walk 267 vb.
leap 312 n.
oscillate 317 vb.
be agitated 318 vb.
shine 417 vb.
ballet 594 n.
be excited 821 vb.
be cheerful 833 vb.
rejoice 835 vb.
dance 837 n.
dance 837 vb.
dancing 837 n.
social gathering
882 n.
be angry 891 vb.

dance attendance on
follow 284 vb.
be servile 879 vb.

dance band
band 74 n.

dance floor
smoothness 258 n.

dance hall
place of amuse-
ment 837 n.

dance music
music 412 n.

dance of the seven
veils
uncovering 229 n.
dance 837 n.

dancer
entertainer 594 n.

dance step
leap 312 n.

dancing
motion 265 n.
merry 833 adj.
dancing 837 n.
angry 891 adj.

dancing girl
entertainer 594 n.

dandelion
plant 366 n.
yellowness 433 n.

dandle
caress 889 vb.

dandruff
powder 332 n.
dirt 649 n.

dandy
super 644 adj.
fop 848 n.

danegeld
tax 809 n.

danger
destiny 155 n.
danger 661 n.

danger of
vulnerability 661 n.

dangerous
dangerous 661 adj.
hostile 881 adj.
angry 891 adj.

danger signal
danger signal
665 n.
threat 900 n.

dangle
come unstuck
49 vb.
hang 217 vb.
pendency 217 n.
oscillate 317 vb.

Daniel come to judg-
ment
sage 500 n.
magistracy 957 n.

dank
humid 341 adj.

dapper
orderly 60 adj.
personable 841 adj.

dappled
mixed 43 adj.
pied 437 adj.

Darby and Joan
duality 90 n.
old couple 133 n.
spouse 894 n.

dare
be resolute 599 vb.
oppose 704 vb.
defiance 711 n.
defy 711 vb.
be free 744 vb.
be courageous
855 vb.
threat 900 n.

daredevil
brave person 855 n.
desperado 857 n.
rash 857 adj.

dare say
assume 471 vb.
suppose 512 vb.

daring
resolution 599 n.
danger 661 n.
enterprising
672 adj.
defiance 711 n.
courage 855 n.
courageous
855 adj.
rash 857 adj.
showy 875 adj.
unchaste 951 adj.

dark
evening 129 n.
dark 418 adj.
darkness 418 n.
black 428 adj.
blackish 428 adj.
brown 430 adj.
blind 439 adj.
unknown 491 adj.
latency 523 n.
cheerless 834 adj.
dishonest 930 adj.

Dark Ages
era 110 n.
antiquity 125 n.
ignorance 491 n.

darken
darken 418 vb.
screen 421 vb.
be unseen 444 vb.

darkening
darkening 418 n.
blackness 428 n.

darken the doors
enter 297 vb.

dark glasses
shade 226 n.
screen 421 n.

semitransparency
424 n.
eyeglass 442 n.
misinterpretation
521 n.

dark-headed
black 428 adj.

dark horse
unknown thing
491 n.
latency 523 n.
secret 530 n.

darkish
dim 419 adj.

darkness
darkness 418 n.
ignorance 491 n.

darkroom
darkness 418 n.

dark-skinned
blackish 428 adj.

darling
darling 890 n.

darn
join 45 vb.
modify 143 vb.
weave 222 vb.
repair 656 vb.
curse 899 int.

darned
damnable 645 adj.

darning
network 222 n.
repair 656 n.

dart
vary 152 vb.
be in motion
265 vb.
move fast 277 vb.
missile 287 n.
propel 287 vb.
missile weapon
723 n.

darting
speedy 277 adj.

darts
indoor game 837 n.

Darwinism
evolution 316 n.
biology 358 n.

dash
small quantity
33 n.
tincture 43 n.
bond 47 n.
vigorousness 174 n.
move fast 277 vb.

spurt 277 n.
strike 279 vb.
be agitated 318 vb.
mark 547 vb.
punctuation 547 n.
resolution 599 n.
be active 678 vb.
haste 680 n.
hasten 680 vb.
defeat 727 vb.
warm feeling
818 n.
fashion 848 n.
courage 855 n.
ostentation 875 n.
dash against
move fast 277 vb.
collide 279 vb.
dashed
defeated 728 adj.
dashing
speedy 277 adj.
forceful 571 adj.
fashionable
848 adj.
showy 875 adj.
dash off
move fast 277 vb.
write 586 vb.
hasten 680 vb.
dash one's hopes
disappoint 509 vb.
depress 834 vb.
data
data processing
86 n.
evidence 466 n.
premise 475 n.
data bank
data processing
86 n.
storage 632 n.
data base
data processing
86 n.
information 524 n.
data processing
data processing
86 n.
date
date 108 n.
fix the time 108 vb.
chronology 117 n.
time 117 vb.
fruit and vegetables
301 n.
be sociable 882 vb.

social round 882 n.
lover 887 n.
court 889 vb.
dated
antiquated 127 adj.
date line
dividing line 92 n.
dating
chronology 117 n.
chronometry
117 n.
social round 882 n.
datum
premise 475 n.
supposition 512 n.
datura
poisonous plant
659 n.
daub
coat 226 vb.
colour 425 vb.
lack of meaning
515 n.
mean nothing
515 vb.
misrepresent
552 vb.
misrepresentation
552 n.
picture 553 n.
daughter
descendant 170 n.
female 373 n.
daughterly
obedient 739 adj.
daunt
frighten 854 vb.
humiliate 872 vb.
Dauphin
sovereign 741 n.
davenport
cabinet 194 n.
David and Jonathan
close friend 880 n.
Davy Jones's locker
ocean 343 n.
the dead 361 n.
Davy lamp
lamp 420 n.
dawdle
walk 267 vb.
wander 267 vb.
move slowly
278 vb.
slowness 278 n.
follow 284 vb.
be inactive 679 vb.

dawn
begin 68 vb.
beginning 68 n.
morning 128 n.
ascent 308 n.
glow 417 n.
make bright
417 vb.
redness 431 n.
appear 445 vb.
dawn chorus
morning 128 n.
vocal music 412 n.
dawn on
be visible 443 vb.
dawn upon 449 vb.
be intelligible
516 vb.
day
date 108 n.
period 110 n.
day after day
perpetually
139 adv.
day and night
polarity 14 n.
perpetually
139 adv.
daybed
bed 218 n.
daybreak
morning 128 n.
half-light 419 n.
day by day
while 108 adv.
daydream
fantasy 513 n.
imagine 513 vb.
desire 859 n.
desire 859 vb.
daydreaming
abstracted 456 adj.
abstractedness
456 n.
imaginative
513 adj.
desire 859 n.
day in
perpetually
139 adv.
day in day out
all along 113 adv.
daylight
morning 128 n.
interval 201 n.
light 417 n.

manifestation
522 n.
disclosure 526 n.
daylight robbery
swindling 788 n.
dearness 811 n.
daylight saving time
clock time 117 n.
day off
lull 145 n.
leisure 681 n.
repose 683 n.
Day of Judgment
finality 69 n.
punishment 963 n.
day of obligation
holy day 988 n.
day of reckoning
revenge 910 n.
punishment 963 n.
day of the week
date 108 n.
day out
perpetually
139 adv.
amusement 837 n.
day release
education 534 n.
days
time 108 n.
era 110 n.
futurity 124 n.
delay 136 n.
days of old
past time 125 n.
days of wine and
roses
joy 824 n.
daystar
morning 128 n.
sun 321 n.
daytime
morning 128 n.
day to remember
special day 876 n.
daze
puzzle 474 vb.
be wonderful
864 vb.
dazzle
light 417 n.
reflection 417 n.
shine 417 vb.
blind 439 vb.
be dim-sighted
440 vb.
be visible 443 vb.

639

impress 821 vb.
be beautiful
821 vb.
be wonderful
864 vb.
prestige 866 n.
be ostentatious
875 vb.
command respect
920 vb.
dazzling
luminous 417 adj.
excellent 644 adj.
D-day
start 68 n.
date 108 n.
DDT
poison 659 n.
deacon
church officer
986 n.
cleric 986 n.
ecclesiarch 986 n.
lay person 987 n.
deaconess
nun 986 n.
lay person 987 n.
deactivate
weaken 163 vb.
assuage 177 vb.
counteract 182 vb.
impair 655 vb.
dead
inert 175 adj.
dead 361 adj.
insensible 375 adj.
dead-and-alive
nonactive 677 adj.
dead as a dodo
extinct 2 adj.
past 125 adj.
dead 361 adj.
dead-beat
impotent 161 adj.
fatigued 684 adj.
dead body
the dead 361 n.
corpse 363 n.
dead cert
certainty 473 n.
dead duck
hopelessness 853 n.
deaden
disable 161 vb.
assuage 177 vb.
render insensible
375 vb.

mute 401 vb.
make mute 578 vb.
make inactive
679 vb.
dead end
stopping place
145 n.
closure 264 n.
difficulty 700 n.
obstacle 702 n.
deadhead
cultivate 370 vb.
dead heat
draw 28 n.
synchronism 123 n.
deadline
finality 69 n.
limit 236 n.
deadlock
draw 28 n.
equilibrium 28 n.
stop 145 n.
quiescence 266 n.
impossibility
470 n.
inaction 677 n.
difficulty 700 n.
obstacle 702 n.
noncompletion
726 n.
defeat 728 n.
dead loss
lost labour 641 n.
loss 772 n.
deadly
deadly 362 adj.
dull 840 adj.
hostile 881 adj.
heinous 934 adj.
guilty 936 adj.
deadly nightshade
plant 366 n.
poisonous plant
659 n.
dead men (empty
bottles)
emptiness 190 n.
dead of night
midnight 129 n.
darkness 418 n.
dead-on
accurate 494 adj.
dead pan
seriousness 834 n.
deadpan
still 266 adj.
impassive 820 adj.

inexcitable
823 adj.
serious 834 adj.
dead ringer
identity 13 n.
analogue 18 n.
Dead Sea
ocean 343 n.
dead to
thick-skinned
820 adj.
dead to the world
sleepy 679 adj.
dead weight
rubbish 641 n.
encumbrance
702 n.
deaf
deaf 416 adj.
deaf-aid
hearing aid 415 n.
deaf and dumb
deaf 416 adj.
voiceless 578 adj.
deaf as a post
deaf 416 adj.
deaf ears
inattention 456 n.
deafen
be loud 400 vb.
deafen 416 vb.
deafening
loud 400 adj.
deaf-mute
deaf 416 adj.
deafness 416 n.
deaf to
deaf 416 adj.
thick-skinned
820 adj.
deal
great quantity
32 n.
arrange 62 vb.
disperse 75 vb.
deed 676 n.
compact 765 n.
apportionment
783 n.
portion 783 n.
trade 791 n.
perfidy 930 n.
deal, a
greatly 32 vb.
deal a deathblow
kill 362 vb.

dealer
agent 686 n.
seller 793 n.
merchant 794 n.
dealing
barter 791 n.
dealings
deed 676 n.
conduct 688 n.
deal out
disperse 75 vb.
give 781 vb.
apportion 783 vb.
deal with
be related 9 vb.
dissertate 591 vb.
do business 622 vb.
deal with 688 vb.
make terms
766 vb.
trade 791 vb.
dean
teacher 537 n.
director 690 n.
ecclesiarch 986 n.
dear
known 490 adj.
dear 811 adj.
pleasurable
826 adj.
darling 890 n.
dear departed
the dead 361 n.
dearest
darling 890 n.
dear heart
darling 890 n.
dearly
greatly 32 vb.
dearly-bought
dear 811 adj.
dearness
dearness 811 n.
dear sir
title 870 n.
dearth
unproductiveness
172 n.
scarcity 636 n.
death
death 361 n.
deathbed
late 136 adj.
decease 361 n.
deathbed repentance
decease 361 n.
penitence 939 n.

deathblow
end 69 n.
death 361 n.
killing 362 n.
evil 616 n.
defeat 728 n.
death certificate
death roll 361 n.
label 547 n.
record 548 n.
death chamber
means of execution
  964 n.
death duty
tax 809 n.
death knell
death 361 n.
warning 664 n.
deathless
perpetual 115 adj.
renowned 866 adj.
deathly
dying 361 adj.
deadly 362 adj.
colourless 426 adj.
evil 616 adj.
deathly pale
colourless 426 adj.
death mask
copy 22 n.
sculpture 554 n.
death rate
statistics 86 n.
death roll 361 n.
death rattle
decease 361 n.
death roll
death roll 361 n.
Death Row
lockup 748 n.
condemnation
  961 n.
means of execution
  964 n.
death's door
suffering 825 n.
Death sentence
capital punishment
  963 n.
death's-head
corpse 363 n.
moper 834 n.
eyesore 842 n.
intimidation
  854 n.
deathtrap
trap 542 n.

danger 661 n.
pitfall 663 n.
death warrant
condemnation
  961 n.
capital punishment
  963 n.
deathwatch
surveillance 457 n.
deathwatch beetle
insect 365 n.
death wish
dejection 834 n.
debacle
revolution 149 n.
ruin 165 n.
defeat 728 n.
debag
uncover 229 vb.
debar
exclude 57 vb.
obstruct 702 vb.
prohibit 757 vb.
refuse 760 vb.
debar from
restrain 747 vb.
debarkation
arrival 295 n.
debase
abase 311 vb.
impair 655 vb.
pervert 655 vb.
shame 867 vb.
disentitle 916 vb.
debasement
lowness 210 n.
lowering 311 n.
deterioration
  655 n.
disrepute 867 n.
improbity 930 n.
debatable
uncertain 474 adj.
debate
argue 475 vb.
argument 475 n.
confer 584 vb.
conference 584 n.
be irresolute
  601 vb.
contention 716 n.
debauched
vicious 934 adj.
sensual 944 adj.
lecherous 951 adj.
debenture
title deed 767 n.

debilitated
weakened 163 adj.
debility
old age 131 n.
weakness 163 n.
ill health 651 n.
sluggishness 679 n.
debit
debt 803 n.
account 808 vb.
debouchment
egress 298 n.
Debrett
directory 87 n.
debris
remainder 41 n.
piece 53 n.
accumulation 74 n.
powder 332 n.
rubbish 641 n.
debt
debt 803 n.
debt-collector
receiver 782 n.
debug
computerize 86 vb.
rectify 654 vb.
debunk
abase 311 vb.
disclose 526 vb.
ridicule 851 vb.
shame 867 vb.
humiliate 872 vb.
detract 926 vb.
debut
debut 68 n.
celebration 876 n.
debutant
beginner 538 n.
decade
over five 99 n.
period 110 n.
decadent
literary 557 adj.
sensualist 944 n.
decagon
over five 99 n.
angular figure
  247 n.
decahedron
over five 99 n.
Decalogue
over five 99 n.
decamp
decamp 296 vb.
decant
transpose 272 vb.

empty 300 vb.
let fall 311 vb.
decanter
vessel 194 n.
decapitate
subtract 39 vb.
sunder 46 vb.
shorten 204 vb.
execute 963 vb.
decathlon
contest 716 n.
decay
decrease 37 n.
decrease 37 vb.
disunion 46 n.
decay 51 n.
decompose 51 vb.
be dispersed 75 vb.
desuetude 611 n.
waste 634 n.
badness 645 n.
deteriorate 655 vb.
decease
decease 361 n.
die 361 vb.
deceased
dead 361 adj.
deceit
deception 542 n.
deceitful
false 541 adj.
cunning 698 adj.
deceive
deceive 542 vb.
deceiver
deceiver 545 n.
libertine 952 n.
deceleration
diminution 37 n.
delay 136 n.
slowness 278 n.
hindrance 702 n.
restraint 747 n.
decency
good taste 846 n.
right 913 n.
purity 950 n.
decennial
seasonal 141 adj.
decent
tasteful 846 adj.
benevolent 897 adj.
ethical 917 adj.
pure 950 adj.
pious 979 adj.

decentralization
decomposition
51 n.
arrangement 62 n.
dispersion 75 n.
laxity 734 n.
commission 751 n.
decentralize
decompose 51 vb.
disperse 75 vb.
deception
deception 542 n.
deceptive
simulating 18 adj.
shadowy 419 adj.
appearing 445 adj.
erroneous 495 adj.
false 541 adj.
decerealization
agriculture 370 n.
decibel
sound 398 n.
metrology 465 n.
decide
cause 156 vb.
answer 460 vb.
make certain
473 vb.
judge 480 vb.
be resolute 599 vb.
try a case 959 vb.
deciduous tree
tree 366 n.
decimal
numerical 85 adj.
numerical element
85 n.
multifid 100 adj.
decimal coinage
coinage 797 n.
decimal currency
money 797 n.
decimal fraction
fraction 102 n.
decimalize
multisect 100 vb.
decimal point
punctuation 547 n.
decimal system
number 85 n.
numeration 86 n.
decimate
abate 37 vb.
multisect 100 vb.
render few 105 vb.
weaken 163 vb.
destroy 165 vb.

slaughter 362 vb.
execute 963 vb.
decipher
decipher 520 vb.
decision
judgment 480 n.
will 595 n.
resolution 599 n.
choice 605 n.
intention 617 n.
decree 737 n.
legal trial 959 n.
decisive
crucial 137 adj.
influential 178 adj.
positive 473 adj.
assertive 532 adj.
resolute 599 adj.
commanding
737 adj.
deck
compartment
194 n.
layer 207 n.
basis 218 n.
paving 226 n.
roof 226 n.
dress 228 vb.
gramophone 414 n.
deck chair
seat 218 n.
deckhand
mariner 270 n.
deckle edge
notch 260 n.
declaim
proclaim 528 vb.
orate 579 vb.
declamation
vigour 571 n.
grandiloquence
574 n.
oration 579 n.
oratory 579 n.
ostentation 875 n.
declaration
affirmation 532 n.
promise 764 n.
declaration of faith
creed 485 n.
assent 488 n.
declaration of war
dissension 709 n.
defiance 711 n.
belligerency 718 n.
declare
believe 485 vb.

mean 514 vb.
divulge 526 vb.
proclaim 528 vb.
affirm 532 vb.
indicate 547 vb.
speak 579 vb.
decree 737 vb.
declare (cricket)
resign 753 vb.
declare oneself
disclose 526 vb.
declare war
quarrel 709 vb.
attack 712 vb.
go to war 718 vb.
declassify
derange 63 vb.
declension
differentiation
15 n.
decrease 37 n.
change 143 n.
deviation 282 n.
descent 309 n.
grammar 564 n.
decline
inferiority 35 n.
decrease 37 n.
decrease 37 vb.
be old 127 vb.
oldness 127 n.
be weak 163 vb.
weakness 163 n.
contraction 198 n.
be oblique 220 vb.
regress 286 vb.
regression 286 n.
recede 290 vb.
descend 309 vb.
descent 309 n.
negate 533 vb.
reject 607 vb.
deteriorate 655 vb.
deterioration
655 n.
adversity 731 n.
have trouble
731 n.
refuse 760 vb.
declining
small 33 adj.
decreasing 37 adj.
ageing 131 adj.
sloping 220 adj.
unprosperous
731 adj.
refusal 760 n.

declining years
old age 131 n.
declivity
incline 220 n.
descent 309 n.
decode
decipher 520 vb.
décolleté
bareness 229 n.
uncovered 229 adj.
decolorant
bleacher 426 n.
decompose
decompose 51 vb.
deconsecrate
perform ritual
988 vb.
decontaminate
purify 648 vb.
make sanitary
652 adj.
rectify 654 vb.
decontrol
liberate 746 vb.
permit 756 vb.
not retain 779 vb.
decor
spectacle 445 n.
stage set 594 n.
decorate
beautify 841 vb.
decorate 844 vb.
decoration
spectacle 445 n.
ornament 574 n.
decoration 729 n.
ornamentation
844 n.
decorations
celebration 876 n.
decorative
painted 553 adj.
ornamental
844 adj.
decorator
mender 656 n.
artisan 686 n.
decorous
fit 24 adj.
orderly 60 adj.
well-bred 848 adj.
pure 950 adj.
decortication
uncovering 229 n.
decorum
good taste 846 n.
etiquette 848 n.

decoy
  attract 291 vb.
  attraction 291 n.
  ambush 527 n.
  ensnare 542 vb.
  trap 542 n.
  trickster 545 n.
  incentive 612 n.
decoy duck
  trap 542 n.
  trickster 545 n.
  incentive 612 n.
decrease
  abate 37 vb.
  decrease 37 n.
  decrease 37 vb.
  subtract 39 vb.
  contraction 198 n.
decree
  judge 480 vb.
  predetermination
    608 n.
  decree 737 n.
  decree 737 vb.
  impose a duty
    917 vb.
decree absolute
  judgment 480 n.
  decree 737 n.
  divorce 896 n.
decree nisi
  judgment 480 n.
  decree 737 n.
  divorce 896 n.
decrepit
  ageing 131 adj.
  weak 163 adj.
  dilapidated
    655 adj.
decrier
  detractor 926 n.
decriminalize
  decree 737 vb.
  permit 756 vb.
  make legal 953 vb.
decry
  abate 37 vb.
  hold cheap 922 vb.
  detract 926 vb.
decussate
  cross 222 vb.
  crossed 222 adj.
dedicate
  offer 759 vb.
  give 781 vb.
  dignify 866 vb.
  sanctify 979 vb.

  offer worship
    981 vb.
  perform ritual
    988 vb.
dedicated
  willing 597 adj.
  resolute 599 adj.
  obedient 739 adj.
  philanthropic
    901 adj.
  sanctified 979 adj.
dedicate to
  use 673 vb.
  honour 866 vb.
dedication
  edition 589 n.
  willingness 597 n.
  resolution 599 n.
  offer 759 n.
  offering 781 n.
  philanthropy
    901 n.
  piety 979 n.
  sanctity 979 n.
  oblation 981 n.
  Christian rite
    988 n.
deduce
  assume 471 vb.
  reason 475 vb.
  demonstrate
    478 V.
  interpret 520 vb.
deducible
  evidential 466 adj.
deduction
  diminution 37 n.
  subtraction 39 n.
  decrement 42 n.
  reasoning 475 n.
  demonstration
    478 n.
  nonpayment 805 n.
deed
  testimony 466 n.
  deed 676 n.
  title deed 767 n.
deed poll
  title deed 767 n.
deeds
  conduct 688 n.
deejay
  broadcaster 531 n.
deem
  be of the opinion
    that 485 vb.

deep
  spacious 183 adj.
  deep 211 adj.
  ocean 343 n.
  hoarse 407 adj.
  florid 425 adj.
  wise 498 adj.
deep down
  intrinsic 5 adj.
  inside 224 adv.
deepen
  augment 36 vb.
  enlarge 197 vb.
  be deep 211 vb.
  aggravate 832 vb.
deep-freeze
  refrigerate 382 vb.
  refrigerator 384 n.
  storage 632 n.
deep-frozen
  cooled 382 adj.
deep-fry
  cook 301 vb.
deep in
  deep 211 adj.
deep in thought
  melancholic
    834 adj.
deeply
  greatly 32 vb.
  inside 224 adv.
deepness
  quantity 26 n.
  interiority 224 n.
deep-rooted
  intrinsic 5 adj.
  lasting 113 adj.
  fixed 153 adj.
  deep 211 adj.
  interior 224 adj.
  remembered
    505 adj.
  habitual 610 adj.
  with affections
    817 adj.
deep-sea
  deep 211 adj.
deep-sea diving
  depth 211 n.
deep-seated
  intrinsic 5 adj.
  lasting 113 adj.
  fixed 153 adj.
  deep 211 adj.
  interior 224 adj.
  habitual 610 adj.

deep water
  depth 211 n.
deer
  mammal 365 n.
deer stalking
  chase 619 n.
de-escalation
  decrease 37 n.
  diminution 37 n.
deface
  destroy 165 vb.
  deform 244 vb.
  obliterate 550 vb.
  make useless
    641 adj.
  impair 655 vb.
  make ugly 842 vb.
  blemish 845 vb.
defamation
  detraction 926 n.
defame
  defame 926 vb.
  accuse 928 vb.
default
  be incomplete
    55 vb.
  deficit 55 n.
  negligence 458 n.
  not suffice 636 vb.
  nonpayment 805 n.
  not pay 805 vb.
  fail in duty 918 vb.
  undutifulness
    918 n.
defaulter
  defrauder 789 n.
  nonpayer 805 n.
  undutifulness
    918 n.
defeat
  defeat 727 vb.
  defeat 728 n.
defeated
  defeated 728 adj.
  discontented
    829 adj.
defeatism
  overestimation
    482 n.
  inaction 677 n.
  dejection 834 n.
  hopelessness 853 n.
  cowardice 856 n.
defeatist
  overestimation
    482 n.
  dejected 834 adj.

hopeless 853 adj.
cowardly 856 adj.
defecate
excrete 302 vb.
defect
inferiority 35 n.
apostatize 603 vb.
defect 647 n.
blemish 845 n.
vice 934 n.
defection
change of mind
603 n.
relinquishment
621 n.
disobedience
738 n.
revolt 738 n.
undutifulness
918 n.
perfidy 930 n.
defective
unequal 29 adj.
inferior 35 adj.
incomplete 55 adj.
deformed 246 adj.
*mentally handi-
capped* 503 adj.
imperfect 647 adj.
defector
recanter 603 n.
defence
rejoinder 460 n.
counterevidence
467 n.
argument 475 n.
pretext 614 n.
protection 660 n.
hindrance 702 n.
defence 713 n.
player 837 n.
vindication 927 n.
legal trial 959 n.
defencelessness
helplessness 161 n.
vulnerability 661 n.
defences
defences 713 n.
defend
answer 460 vb.
argue 475 vb.
defend 713 vb.
defendant
respondent 460 n.
prisoner 750 n.
accused person
928 n.

litigant 959 n.
defender
protector 660 n.
defender 713 n.
defend oneself
counteract 182 vb.
plead 614 vb.
justify 927 vb.
defenestration
lowering 311 n.
defensiveness
defence 713 n.
boasting 877 n.
defer
put off 136 vb.
not complete
726 vb.
deference
submission 721 n.
obedience 739 n.
courtesy 884 n.
respect 920 n.
deferential
servile 879 adj.
respectful 920 adj.
deferment
delay 136 n.
deferred
late 136 adj.
defer to
acquiesce 488 vb.
submit 721 vb.
obey 739 vb.
respect 920 vb.
defiance
disagreement 25 n.
defiance 711 n.
disobedience
738 n.
sauciness 878 n.
deficiency
incompleteness
55 n.
insufficiency 636 n.
defect 647 n.
imperfection 647 n.
vice 934 n.
deficient
unequal 29 adj.
deficient 307 adj.
unintelligent
499 adj.
insufficient
636 adj.
imperfect 647 adj.
deficit
deficit 55 n.

shortfall 307 n.
insufficiency 636 n.
noncompletion
726 n.
debt 803 n.
defile
gap 201 n.
narrowness 206 n.
walk 267 vb.
make unclean
649 vb.
impair 655 vb.
shame 867 vb.
debauch 951 vb.
be impious 980 vb.
defilement
uncleanness 649 n.
impairment 655 n.
slur 867 n.
impurity 951 n.
define
arrange 62 vb.
specify 80 vb.
interpret 520 vb.
defined
positive 473 adj.
accurate 494 adj.
manifest 522 adj.
orthodox 976 adj.
definite
arranged 62 adj.
definite 80 adj.
obvious 443 adj.
positive 473 adj.
accurate 494 adj.
definite article
part of speech
564 n.
definitely
certainly 473 adv.
definition
visibility 443 n.
perspicuity 567 n.
theology 973 n.
definitive
ending 69 adj.
definite 80 adj.
definitive edition
edition 589 n.
deflate
abate 37 vb.
disable 161 vb.
make smaller
198 vb.
abase 311 vb.
lower 311 vb.
ridicule 851 vb.

shame 867 vb.
humiliate 872 vb.
detract 926 vb.
deflation
decrease 37 n.
contraction 198 n.
finance 797 n.
cheapness 812 n.
deflationary
monetary 797 adj.
deflect
deflect 282 vb.
avoid 620 vb.
deflower
unite with 45 vb.
debauch 951 vb.
defoliant
poison 659 n.
defoliation
unproductiveness
172 n.
deforestation
unproductiveness
172 n.
deform
modify 143 vb.
transform 147 vb.
force 176 vb.
deform 244 vb.
impair 655 vb.
pervert 655 vb.
deformed
abnormal 84 adj.
deformed 246 adj.
unsightly 842 adj.
deformity
amorphism 244 n.
deformity 246 n.
blemish 845 n.
defraud
defraud 788 vb.
be dishonest
930 vb.
defray
defray 804 vb.
defray the cost
expend 806 vb.
defrock
shame 867 vb.
defrost
heat 381 vb.
deft
skilful 694 adj.
defunct
extinct 2 adj.
dead 361 adj.
unwonted 611 adj.

defy
defy 711 vb.
be courageous
855 vb.
defying
defiant 711 adj.
degeneracy
deterioration
655 n.
wickedness 934 n.
degenerate
decrease 37 vb.
be turned to
147 vb.
deteriorate 655 vb.
relapse 657 vb.
vicious 934 adj.
cad 938 n.
sensualist 944 n.
degenerative
harmful 645 adj.
diseased 651 adj.
degradation
diminution 37 n.
deposal 752 n.
disrepute 867 n.
wickedness 934 n.
degrade
abate 37 vb.
impair 655 vb.
pervert 655 vb.
depose 752 vb.
shame 867 vb.
not respect 921 vb.
hold cheap 922 vb.
defame 926 vb.
punish 963 vb.
degrading
degrading 867 adj.
degree
degree 27 n.
angular measure
247 n.
measurement
465 n.
honours 866 n.
prestige 866 n.
degree of latitude
long measure
203 n.
degree of longitude
long measure
203 n.
dehumanize
pervert 655 vb.
make wicked
934 vb.

dehumidify
dry 342 vb.
dehydrate
make smaller
198 vb.
dry 342 vb.
preserve 666 vb.
dehydrated
dry 342 adj.
hungry 859 adj.
dehydration
desiccation 342 n.
preservation 666 n.
deification
heaven 971 n.
deism
deism 973 n.
religion 973 n.
deity
divineness 965 n.
deity 966 n.
Deity, the
the Deity 965 n.
déjà vu
remembrance
505 n.
psychics 984 n.
dejected
dejected 834 adj.
dejection
dejection 834 n.
de jure
due 915 adj.
dekko
inspection 438 n.
delay
delay 136 n.
put off 136 vb.
be irresolute
601 vb.
be inactive 679 vb.
hinder 702 vb.
delayed
late 136 adj.
hindered 702 adj.
delaying
nonactive 677 adj.
delaying tactics
delay 136 n.
delectable
savoury 390 adj.
pleasurable
826 adj.
delectation
enjoyment 824 n.
delegate
transfer 272 vb.

commission
751 vb.
delegate 754 n.
assign 780 vb.
delegation
decomposition
51 n.
dispersion 75 n.
commission 751 n.
delegate 754 n.
transfer 780 n.
delete
subtract 39 vb.
destroy 165 vb.
obliterate 550 vb.
deleterious
harmful 645 adj.
deletion
subtraction 39 n.
obliteration 550 n.
delft
pottery 381 n.
deliberate
slow 278 adj.
predetermined
608 adj.
cautious 858 adj.
deliberateness
intention 617 n.
deliberation
slowness 278 n.
meditation 449 n.
caution 858 n.
delicacy
weakness 163 n.
savouriness 390 n.
discrimination
463 n.
beauty 841 n.
good taste 846 n.
fastidiousness
862 n.
purity 950 n.
delicate
insubstantial 4 adj.
small 33 adj.
flimsy 163 adj.
weak 163 adj.
weakly 163 adj.
narrow 206 adj.
soft-hued 425 adj.
discriminating
463 adj.
accurate 494 adj.
unhealthy 651 adj.
difficult 700 adj.

pleasurable
826 adj.
personable 841 adj.
shapely 841 adj.
tasteful 846 adj.
fastidious 862 adj.
pure 950 adj.
delicatessen
cookery 301 n.
delicious
edible 301 adj.
pleasant 376 adj.
savoury 390 adj.
sweet 392 adj.
super 644 adj.
pleasurable
826 adj.
delight
pleasure 376 n.
joy 824 n.
delight 826 vb.
amusement 837 n.
delighted
willing 597 adj.
pleased 824 adj.
jubilant 833 adj.
delightful
pleasant 376 adj.
pleasurable
826 adj.
delight in
be pleased 824 vb.
Delilah
loose woman
952 n.
delineation
outline 233 n.
representation
551 n.
description 590 n.
delinquent
troublemaker
663 n.
low fellow 869 n.
offender 904 n.
deliquesce
liquefy 337 vb.
delirious
frenzied 503 adj.
diseased 651 adj.
delirium
mental disorder
503 n.
fantasy 513 n.
lack of meaning
515 n.
illness 651 n.

645

delirium tremens
agitation 318 n.
frenzy 503 n.
alcoholism 949 n.
deliver
transfer 272 vb.
propel 287 vb.
affirm 532 vb.
provide 633 vb.
deliver 668 vb.
assign 780 vb.
give 781 vb.
deliverance
deliverance 668 n.
deliver a speech
orate 579 vb.
deliver the goods
provide 633 vb.
be expedient
642 vb.
carry out 725 vb.
delivery
obstetrics 167 n.
transference 272 n.
voice 577 n.
speech 579 n.
provision 633 n.
escape 667 n.
deliverance 668 n.
conduct 688 n.
transfer 780 n.
giving 781 n.
delivery boy
carrier 273 n.
delivery van
carrier 273 n.
lorry 274 n.
dell
valley 255 n.
delousing
cleansing 648 n.
Delphic oracle
oracle 511 n.
delta
land 344 n.
plain 348 n.
deltoid
three 93 adj.
delude
deceive 542 vb.
deluded
mistaken 495 adj.
crazy 503 adj.
delude oneself
err 495 vb.
hope 852 vb.

deluge
crowd 74 n.
drench 341 vb.
flow 350 VB.
rain 350 n.
superabound
637 vb.
delusion
error 495 n.
fantasy 513 n.
deception 542 n.
delusions
psychosis 503 n.
delusions of grandeur
ostentation 875 n.
de luxe
ostentatious
875 adj.
delve into
enquire 459 vb.
demagogy
government 733 n.
demand
enquire 459 vb.
necessitate 596 vb.
requirement 627 n.
demand 737 n.
demand 737 vb.
price 809 n.
desire 859 n.
demanding
difficult 700 adj.
commanding
737 adj.
fastidious 862 adj.
demand satisfaction
defy 711 vb.
demarcation
limit 236 n.
apportionment
783 n.
dematerialize
pass away 2 vb.
disappear 446 vb.
demeaning
degrading 867 adj.
demean oneself
demean oneself
867 vb.
demeanour
look 445 n.
gesture 547 n.
conduct 688 n.
demented
crazy 503 adj.
frenzied 503 adj.

mentally disor-
dered 503 adj.
dementia
helplessness 161 n.
unintelligence
499 n.
mental disorder
503 n.
demerara
sweet thing 392 n.
demerit
undueness 916 n.
vice 934 n.
demesne
farm 370 n.
demigod
paragon 646 n.
deity 966 n.
demigod 967 n.
demilitarize
disable 161 vb.
make peace
719 vb.
demi-monde
lower classes 869 n.
wickedness 934 n.
demise
decease 361 n.
demi-veg
abstainer 942 n.
demobilization
dispersion 75 n.
impotence 161 n.
pacification 719 n.
liberation 746 n.
democracy
nation 371 n.
government 733 n.
commonalty 869 n.
democrat
political party
708 n.
commoner 869 n.
Democrat and Re-
publican
opposites 704 n.
democratic
governmental
733 adj.
Democrats
political party
708 n.
démodé
antiquated 127 adj.
demography
statistics 86 n.

anthropology
371 n.
demolish
demolish 165 vb.
demolition
destruction 165 n.
impairment 655 n.
demon
violent creature
176 n.
monster 938 n.
demon 970 n.
mythical being
970 n.
demoniac
diabolic 969 adj.
demoniacal
cruel 898 adj.
diabolic 969 adj.
demonist
diabolist 969 n.
demonolatry
diabolism 969 n.
idolatry 982 n.
demonological
diabolic 969 adj.
demonology
diabolism 969 n.
demonry
diabolism 969 n.
demonstrable
certain 473 adj.
demonstrate
demonstrate
478 V.
interpret 520 vb.
show 522 vb.
be active 678 vb.
defy 711 vb.
revolt 738 vb.
deprecate 762 vb.
be ostentatious
875 vb.
demonstrate against
dissent 489 vb.
demonstration
assemblage 74 n.
appearance 445 n.
spectacle 445 n.
demonstration
478 n.
manifestation
522 n.
defiance 711 n.
deprecation 762 n.
feeling 818 n.
ostentation 875 n.

demonstrative
  evidential 466 adj.
  with affections
  817 adj.
  friendly 880 adj.
  loving 887 adj.
demonstrator
  guide 520 n.
  exhibitor 522 n.
  publicizer 528 n.
  teacher 537 n.
  agitator 738 n.
  revolter 738 n.
demoralize
  impair 655 vb.
demos
  nation 371 n.
demote
  abate 37 vb.
  abase 311 vb.
  depose 752 vb.
  shame 867 vb.
  punish 963 vb.
demoted
  inglorious 867 adj.
demotic
  linguistic 557 adj.
demotion
  diminution 37 n.
  descent 309 n.
  lowering 311 n.
  deposal 752 n.
  disrepute 867 n.
demur
  qualification 468 n.
  qualify 468 vb.
  be uncertain
  474 vb.
  argue 475 vb.
  doubt 486 n.
  doubt 486 vb.
  dissent 489 n.
  dissent 489 vb.
  negate 533 vb.
  be unwilling
  598 vb.
  unwillingness
  598 n.
  resist 715 vb.
  resistance 715 n.
  deprecate 762 vb.
  deprecation 762 n.
  disapprove 924 vb.
demure
  serious 834 adj.
  affected 850 adj.
  modest 874 adj.

demureness
  seriousness 834 n.
  modesty 874 n.
  purity 950 n.
demurring
  unwilling 598 adj.
  modest 874 adj.
demythologize
  be irreligious
  974 vb.
den
  dwelling 192 n.
  retreat 192 n.
  chamber 194 n.
  cavity 255 n.
  hiding-place 527 n.
  refuge 662 n.
  workshop 687 n.
  seclusion 883 n.
denationalize
  disentitle 916 vb.
denaturalize
  disentitle 916 vb.
dendrochronology
  chronology 117 n.
dendrology
  forestry 366 n.
  botany 368 n.
dengue
  tropical disease
  651 n.
denial
  counterevidence
  467 n.
  confutation 479 n.
  unbelief 486 n.
  dissent 489 n.
  negation 533 n.
  recantation 603 n.
  rejection 607 n.
  opposition 704 n.
  refusal 760 n.
  nonobservance
  769 n.
denigrate
  not respect 921 vb.
  hold cheap 922 vb.
  criticize 924 vb.
  reproach 924 vb.
  defame 926 vb.
denim
  textile 222 n.
denims
  trousers 228 n.
denizen
  dweller 191 n.

denizens of the deep
  marine life 365 n.
den of thieves
  thief 789 n.
denomination
  classification 77 n.
  nomenclature
  561 n.
  party 708 n.
denominational
  Protestant 976 adj.
denominator
  numerical element
  85 n.
denotation
  connotation 514 n.
denotative
  semantic 514 adj.
denote
  mean 514 vb.
  indicate 547 vb.
  represent 551 vb.
denouement
  end 69 n.
  event 154 n.
  effect 157 n.
  disclosure 526 n.
  narrative 590 n.
  completion 725 n.
denounce
  inform 524 vb.
  hate 888 vb.
  curse 899 vb.
  criticize 924 vb.
  defame 926 vb.
  accuse 928 vb.
denouncer
  detractor 926 n.
  accuser 928 n.
de novo
  again 106 vb.
dense
  dense 324 adj.
  ignorant 491 adj.
  uninstructed
  491 adj.
  unintelligent
  499 adj.
denseness
  unintelligence
  499 n.
density
  density 324 n.
dent
  concavity 255 n.
  make concave
  255 vb.

  notch 260 n.
  notch 260 vb.
  collide 279 vb.
  knock 279 n.
  lowering 311 n.
dental
  toothed 256 adj.
  speech sound
  398 n.
dented
  concave 255 adj.
denticulate
  toothed 256 adj.
dentiform
  toothed 256 adj.
dentist
  doctor 658 n.
dentistry
  surgery 658 n.
dentition
  tooth 256 n.
denture
  tooth 256 n.
denude
  abate 37 vb.
  subtract 39 vb.
  uncover 229 vb.
  disclose 526 vb.
  deprive 786 vb.
  fleece 786 vb.
denunciation
  confutation 479 n.
  malediction 899 n.
  accusation 928 n.
  prayers 981 n.
deny
  exclude 57 vb.
  confute 479 vb.
  disbelieve 486 vb.
  negate 533 vb.
  recant 603 vb.
  reject 607 vb.
  avoid 620 vb.
  abrogate 752 vb.
  refuse 760 vb.
deny oneself nothing
  be intemperate
  943 vb.
deodorant
  inodorousness
  395 n.
  cleanser 648 n.
  cosmetic 843 n.
deodorized
  odourless 395 adj.
  clean 648 adj.

depart
  depart 296 vb.
  disappear 446 vb.
departed
  dead 361 adj.
department
  subdivision 53 n.
  classification 77 n.
  district 184 n.
  function 622 n.
department store
  shop 796 n.
departure
  deviation 282 n.
  departure 296 n.
  decease 361 n.
depend
  depend 157 vb.
  be possible 469 vb.
dependable
  observant 768 adj.
  trustworthy
    929 adj.
dependant
  dependant 742 n.
dependence
  relativeness 9 n.
  inferiority 35 n.
  subjection 745 n.
dependency
  territory 184 n.
  political organiza-
    tion 733 n.
  lands 777 n.
dependent
  inferior 35 adj.
  hanging 217 adj.
  subject 745 adj.
  servile 879 adj.
dependent on
  caused 157 adj.
  liable 180 adj.
depending
  caused 157 adj.
depending on
  uncertain 474 adj.
depend on
  believe 485 vb.
  be subject 745 vb.
depict
  represent 551 vb.
  describe 590 vb.
depicting
  painting 553 n.
depilatory
  stripper 229 n.
  cosmetic 843 n.

deplete
  weaken 163 vb.
  waste 634 vb.
  impair 655 vb.
deplorable
  bad 645 adj.
  distressing 827 adj.
deplore
  regret 830 vb.
  lament 836 vb.
  disapprove 924 vb.
deploy
  place 187 vb.
  expand 197 vb.
  lengthen 203 vb.
  open 263 vb.
  diverge 294 vb.
  dispose of 673 vb.
deployment
  expansion 197 n.
  divergence 294 n.
depopulated
  empty 190 adj.
deport
  exclude 57 vb.
  transpose 272 vb.
  eject 300 vb.
deportation
  exclusion 57 n.
  transference 272 n.
  ejection 300 n.
  seclusion 883 n.
  loss of right 916 n.
  penalty 963 n.
deportment
  look 445 n.
  conduct 688 n.
depose
  depose 752 vb.
deposit
  leavings 41 n.
  part 53 n.
  place 187 vb.
  be dense 324 vb.
  solid body 324 n.
  soil 344 n.
  store 632 n.
  store 632 vb.
  dirt 649 n.
  security 767 n.
  payment 804 n.
deposit account
  funds 797 n.
  accounts 808 n.
depository
  treasury 799 n.

depot
  focus 76 n.
  station 187 n.
  goal 295 n.
  storage 632 n.
depravation
  deterioration
    655 n.
depraved
  bad 645 adj.
  vicious 934 adj.
  lecherous 951 adj.
depravity
  badness 645 n.
  deterioration
    655 n.
  wickedness 934 n.
deprecate
  deprecate 762 vb.
  criticize 924 vb.
  detract 926 vb.
deprecatory
  disapproving
    924 adj.
depreciate
  abate 37 vb.
  underestimate
    483 vb.
  discount 810 vb.
  be cheap 812 vb.
depreciated
  monetary 797 adj.
depreciation
  decrease 37 n.
  underestimation
    483 n.
  loss 772 n.
  finance 797 n.
  cheapness 812 n.
  disrespect 921 n.
  detraction 926 n.
depress
  abate 37 vb.
  make concave
    255 vb.
  lower 311 vb.
  depress 834 vb.
depressed
  concave 255 adj.
  dejected 834 adj.
  sullen 893 adj.
depressing
  unpleasant
    827 adj.
  cheerless 834 adj.
  tedious 838 adj.

depression
  inferiority 35 n.
  lowness 210 n.
  depth 211 n.
  cavity 255 n.
  concavity 255 n.
  valley 255 n.
  lowering 311 n.
  weather 340 n.
  neurosis 503 n.
  deterioration
    655 n.
  adversity 731 n.
  poverty 801 n.
  dejection 834 n.
  melancholy 834 n.
depressive
  psychotic 503 adj.
  neurotic 504 n.
deprivation
  absence 190 n.
  ejection 300 n.
  scarcity 636 n.
  deposal 752 n.
  loss 772 n.
  nonownership
    774 n.
  expropriation
    786 n.
  loss of right 916 n.
  penalty 963 n.
deprive
  weaken 163 vb.
  deprive 786 vb.
  shame 867 vb.
  punish 963 vb.
deprived
  poor 801 adj.
depth
  depth 211 n.
  blackness 428 n.
  metrology 465 n.
depths
  lowness 210 n.
deputation
  commission 751 n.
deputize
  deputize 755 vb.
deputy
  councillor 692 n.
  deputy 755 n.
derailment
  displacement
    188 n.
deranged
  mentally disor-
    dered 503 adj.

derationing
liberation 746 n.
derby
headgear 228 n.
Derby, the
racing 716 n.
deregulate
liberate 746 vb.
not retain 779 vb.
deregulation
liberation 746 n.
derelict
disused 674 adj.
derelict 779 n.
not retained
779 adj.
dereliction of duty
undutifulness
918 n.
guilty act 936 n.
derestriction
laxity 734 n.
deride
reject 607 vb.
laugh 835 vb.
ridicule 851 vb.
not respect 921 vb.
despise 922 vb.
impious 980 adj.
de rigueur
usual 610 adj.
obligatory 917 adj.
derision
unbelief 486 n.
laughter 835 n.
ridicule 851 n.
contempt 922 n.
impiety 980 n.
derisory
laughing 835 adj.
ridiculous 849 adj.
derisory amount, a
fewness 105 n.
derivation
origin 68 n.
reversion 148 n.
source 156 n.
effect 157 n.
attribution 158 n.
connotation 514 n.
word 559 n.
derivative
imitative 20 adj.
numerical element
85 n.
caused 157 adj.
effect 157 n.

verbal 559 adj.
word 559 n.
dull 840 adj.
derive
acquire 771 vb.
derive from
result 157 vb.
attribute 158 vb.
dermatitis
skin disease 651 n.
dermatology
medical art 658 n.
derogatory
degrading 867 adj.
dishonest 930 adj.
derring-do
courage 855 n.
prowess 855 n.
derris
poison 659 n.
derv
fuel 385 n.
dervish
ascetic 945 n.
religionist 973 n.
pietist 979 n.
worshipper 981 n.
monk 986 n.
desalinate
purify 648 vb.
descant
tune 412 n.
vocal music 412 n.
sing 413 vb.
be diffuse 570 vb.
hymn 981 n.
descend
descend 309 vb.
descendant
successor 67 n.
posteriority 120 n.
descendant 170 n.
descender
print-type 587 n.
descend from
result 157 vb.
descending order
decrease 37 n.
series 71 n.
descent
consanguinity
11 n.
sequence 65 n.
continuity 71 n.
posteriority 120 n.
source 156 n.
genealogy 169 n.

presence 189 n.
descent 309 n.
nobility 868 n.
describe
describe 590 vb.
describe a circle
circumscribe
232 vb.
outline 233 vb.
circle 314 vb.
represent 551 vb.
description
literature 557 n.
name 561 n.
nomenclature
561 n.
description 590 n.
descriptive
descriptive 590 adj.
descry
see 438 vb.
understand 516 vb.
desecrate
make unclean
649 vb.
impair 655 vb.
misuse 675 vb.
shame 867 vb.
not respect 921 vb.
be impious 980 vb.
deselect
vote 605 vb.
reject 607 vb.
desert
desert 172 n.
unproductive
172 adj.
empty 190 adj.
dry 342 adj.
disregard 458 vb.
apostatize 603 vb.
change one's mind
603 vb.
run away 620 vb.
relinquish 621 vb.
goodness 644 n.
not observe 769 vb.
be cowardly
856 vb.
seclusion 883 n.
divorce 896 vb.
fail in duty 918 vb.
deserted
alone 88 adj.
empty 190 adj.
neglected 458 adj.
secluded 883 adj.

deserter
recanter 603 n.
avoider 620 n.
coward 856 n.
undutifulness
918 n.
desertification
unproductiveness
172 n.
dryness 342 n.
desertion
change of mind
603 n.
relinquishment
621 n.
disobedience
738 n.
cowardice 856 n.
divorce 896 n.
undutifulness
918 n.
perfidy 930 n.
desert island
desert 172 n.
desertization
unproductiveness
172 n.
dryness 342 n.
deserts
conduct 688 n.
retaliation 714 n.
right 913 n.
dueness 915 n.
reward 962 n.
deserve
deserve 915 vb.
deserved
just 913 adj.
due 915 adj.
déshabillé
informal dress
228 n.
uncovering 229 n.
desiccated
dry 342 adj.
desiccator
dryer 342 n.
design
correlation 12 n.
prototype 23 n.
composition 56 n.
produce 164 vb.
production 164 n.
form 243 n.
represent 551 vb.
representation
551 n.

painting 553 n.
picture 553 n.
intend 617 vb.
intention 617 n.
plan 623 n.
plan 623 vb.
undertaking 672 n.
pattern 844 n.
designate
subsequent
  120 adj.
future 124 adj.
mark 547 vb.
chosen 605 adj.
select 605 vb.
designation
classification 77 n.
name 561 n.
nomenclature
  561 n.
designer
producer 164 n.
architectural
  192 adj.
tailored 228 adj.
formed 243 adj.
artist 556 n.
planner 623 n.
designer drug
drug-taking 949 n.
designing
formation 243 n.
hypocritical
  541 adj.
dishonest 930 adj.
selfish 932 adj.
desirable
advisable 642 adj.
desired 859 adj.
desire
desire 859 n.
desire 859 vb.
desired object
  859 n.
desirous
willing 597 adj.
desist
discontinue 72 vb.
cease 145 vb.
not act 677 vb.
desk
cabinet 194 n.
stand 218 n.
desk-top computer
counting instru-
  ment 86 n.

deskwork
study 536 n.
desolate
unproductive
  172 adj.
empty 190 adj.
hopeless 853 adj.
desolation
desert 172 n.
emptiness 190 n.
sorrow 825 n.
despair
sorrow 825 n.
dejection 834 n.
despair 853 vb.
hopelessness 853 n.
despairing
unhappy 825 adj.
dejected 834 adj.
hopeless 853 adj.
despair of
impenitence 940 n.
desperado
desperado 857 n.
ruffian 904 n.
desperate
consummate
  32 adj.
furious 176 adj.
resolute 599 adj.
hopeless 853 adj.
unpromising
  853 adj.
rash 857 adj.
desperate venture
prowess 855 n.
desperation
hopelessness 853 n.
rashness 857 n.
despicable
discreditable
  867 adj.
disreputable
  867 adj.
contemptible
  922 adj.
heinous 934 adj.
despise
despise 922 vb.
despite
although 182 adv.
nevertheless
  468 adv.
malevolence 898 n.
despoil
rob 788 vb.

despondency
adversity 731 n.
sorrow 825 n.
dejection 834 n.
hopelessness 853 n.
despot
tyrant 735 n.
autocrat 741 n.
despotic
authoritarian
  735 adj.
oppressive 735 adj.
lawless 954 adj.
desquamation
uncovering 229 n.
dessert
sequel 67 n.
dessert 301 n.
dish 301 n.
sweet thing 392 n.
dessertspoon
ladle 194 n.
destination
stopping place
  145 n.
intention 617 n.
objective 617 n.
destine
necessitate 596 vb.
destine for
intend 617 vb.
destiny
finality 69 n.
destiny 155 n.
influence 178 n.
expectation 507 n.
fate 596 n.
destitute
necessitous
  627 adj.
poor 801 adj.
destitution
poverty 801 n.
destroy
destroy 165 vb.
confute 479 vb.
waste 634 vb.
destroyer
destroyer 168 n.
warship 722 n.
destruct
destroy 165 vb.
destruction
disorder 61 n.
destruction 165 n.
destructive
destructive 165 adj.

harmful 645 adj.
destructiveness
destruction 165 n.
violence 176 n.
inhumanity 898 n.
desultory
light-minded
  456 adj.
prolix 570 adj.
detach
disunite 46 vb.
disperse 75 vb.
send 272 vb.
transpose 272 vb.
detached
unrelated 10 adj.
neutral 625 adj.
impassive 820 adj.
just 913 adj.
detached house
house 192 n.
detachment
disunion 46 n.
part 53 n.
armed force 722 n.
formation 722 n.
moral insensibility
  820 n.
inexcitability
  823 n.
justice 913 n.
detail
small quantity
  33 n.
part 53 n.
specify 80 vb.
send 272 vb.
transpose 272 vb.
be diffuse 570 vb.
describe 590 vb.
select 605 vb.
armed force 722 n.
formation 722 n.
command 737 vb.
commission
  751 vb.
apportion 783 vb.
pattern 844 n.
impose a duty
  917 vb.
detailed
complete 54 adj.
definite 80 adj.
diffuse 570 adj.
descriptive 590 adj.
detailed account
description 590 n.

details
 particulars 80 n.
 description 590 n.
detain
 imprison 747 vb.
 retain 778 vb.
detainee
 prisoner 750 n.
detect
 detect 484 vb.
detectable
 visible 443 adj.
detection
 police enquiry
  459 n.
 discovery 484 n.
 knowledge 490 n.
detective
 detective 459 n.
detective story
 novel 590 n.
detector
 detector 484 n.
détente
 moderation 177 n.
 concord 710 n.
 pacification 719 n.
detention
 detention 747 n.
 legal process 959 n.
deter
 hinder 702 vb.
 frighten 854 vb.
 cause dislike
  861 vb.
 threaten 900 vb.
detergent
 cleanser 648 n.
deteriorate
 deteriorate 655 vb.
 impair 655 vb.
determinant
 numerical element
  85 n.
 cause 156 n.
determination
 will 595 n.
 resolution 599 n.
 obstinacy 602 n.
 intention 617 n.
 assiduity 678 n.
determine
 arrange 62 vb.
 specify 80 vb.
 cause 156 vb.
 will 595 vb.
 be resolute 599 vb.

intend 617 vb.
determined
 volitional 595 adj.
 resolute 599 adj.
 obstinate 602 adj.
 courageous
  855 adj.
determined effort
 attempt 671 n.
determinism
 philosophy 449 n.
 necessity 596 n.
deterrent
 counteraction
  182 n.
 dissuasion 613 n.
 protection 660 n.
 safeguard 662 n.
 warning 664 n.
 retaliation 714 n.
 weapon 723 n.
 intimidation
  854 n.
 threat 900 n.
detest
 dislike 861 vb.
 hate 888 vb.
detestation
 dislike 861 n.
 hatred 888 n.
dethrone
 depose 752 vb.
 disentitle 916 vb.
detonate
 be loud 400 vb.
 bang 402 vb.
detonator
 lighter 385 n.
 explosive 723 n.
detour
 curvature 248 n.
 deviation 282 n.
 route 624 n.
 circuit 626 n.
detract
 disunite 46 vb.
 detract 926 vb.
detract from
 abate 37 vb.
 subtract 39 vb.
detraction
 detraction 926 n.
detrimental
 inexpedient
  643 adj.
 harmful 645 adj.

detritus
 leavings 41 n.
 piece 53 n.
 accumulation 74 n.
 powder 332 n.
de trop
 intrude 297 vb.
 superfluous
  637 adj.
 be clumsy 695 vb.
 unwanted 860 adj.
deuce
 draw 28 n.
 duality 90 n.
deuce, the
 curse 899 int.
deucedly
 extremely 32 vb.
deuterogamy
 type of marriage
  894 n.
Deutschmark
 coinage 797 n.
devaluation
 deterioration
  655 n.
 finance 797 n.
devalue
 impair 655 vb.
devalued
 monetary 797 adj.
devastation
 uncovering 229 n.
develop
 become 1 vb.
 augment 36 vb.
 grow 36 vb.
 result 157 vb.
 produce 164 vb.
 enlarge 197 vb.
 progress 285 vb.
 promote 285 vb.
 evolve 316 vb.
 be visible 443 vb.
 manifest 522 vb.
 educate 534 vb.
 photograph 551 vb.
 get better 654 vb.
 make better
  654 vb.
developer
 producer 164 n.
developing
 young 130 adj.
 converted 147 adj.

develop into
 be turned to
  147 vb.
development
 increase 36 n.
 adultness 134 n.
 conversion 147 n.
 growth 157 n.
 production 164 n.
 propagation 167 n.
 expansion 197 n.
 progression 285 n.
 evolution 316 n.
 musical piece
  412 n.
deviant
 abnormal 84 adj.
 nonconformist
  84 n.
deviate
 deviate 282 vb.
deviation
 statistics 86 n.
 deviation 282 n.
device
 idea 451 n.
 heraldry 547 n.
 contrivance 623 n.
 instrument 628 n.
 means 629 n.
 tool 630 n.
 stratagem 698 n.
devil
 violent creature
  176 n.
 cook 301 vb.
 season 388 vb.
 wickedness 934 n.
 do law 958 vb.
 lawyer 958 n.
 devil 969 n.
Devil, the
 Satan 969 n.
devilish
 damnable 645 adj.
 harmful 645 adj.
 cruel 898 adj.
 wicked 934 adj.
 diabolic 969 adj.
devil-may-care
 rash 857 adj.
devilry
 evil 616 n.
 wickedness 934 n.
 diabolism 969 n.
devil-worshipping
 diabolic 969 adj.

devious
 circuitous 314 adj.
 cunning 698 adj.
 dishonest 930 adj.
devise
 think 449 vb.
 imagine 513 vb.
 plan 623 vb.
 be cunning 698 vb.
devitalize
 unman 161 vb.
 weaken 163 vb.
devoid
 empty 190 adj.
devolution
 decomposition
  51 n.
 commission 751 n.
 transfer 780 n.
devolve
 assign 780 vb.
 impose a duty
  917 vb.
devolve upon
 change hands
  780 vb.
devote
 give 781 vb.
 be pious 979 vb.
devoted
 resolute 599 adj.
 obedient 739 adj.
 friendly 880 adj.
 loving 887 adj.
devoted to
 habituated 610 adj.
devotee
 enthusiast 504 n.
 habitué 610 n.
 sectarian 978 n.
 pietist 979 n.
 worshipper 981 n.
devote oneself to
 undertake 672 vb.
devotion
 resolution 599 n.
 loyalty 739 n.
 love 887 n.
 respect 920 n.
 piety 979 n.
 oblation 981 n.
 worship 981 n.
devotional
 religious 973 adj.
devotions
 prayers 981 n.

devour
 consume 165 vb.
 destroy 165 vb.
 absorb 299 vb.
 eat 301 vb.
 appropriate
  786 vb.
 fleece 786 vb.
 gluttonize 947 vb.
devouring
 eating 301 n.
 gluttonous 947 adj.
devout
 religious 973 adj.
 orthodox 976 adj.
 pious 979 adj.
devoutness
 piety 979 n.
dew
 moisture 341 n.
dewlap
 hanging object
  217 n.
dewy
 new 126 adj.
 humid 341 adj.
dexterity
 skill 694 n.
dexterous
 skilful 694 adj.
dextrality
 dextrality 241 n.
dextrose
 sweet thing 392 n.
dhal
 dish 301 n.
dharma
 religion 973 n.
dhow
 sailing ship 275 n.
diabetes
 disease 651 n.
diabetic
 diseased 651 adj.
 sick person 651 n.
diablerie
 diabolism 969 n.
diabolical
 damnable 645 adj.
 cruel 898 adj.
 diabolic 969 adj.
diabolism
 diabolism 969 n.
diadem
 regalia 743 n.
 jewellery 844 n.

diaeresis
 punctuation 547 n.
diagnosis
 character 5 n.
 classification 77 n.
 medical art 658 n.
diagnostic
 distinctive 15 adj.
 separate 46 adj.
 special 80 adj.
 enquiring 459 adj.
 evidential 466 adj.
 diagnostic 658 n.
diagnostician
 doctor 658 n.
diagnostic radiology
 radiation 417 n.
diagonal
 dividing line 92 n.
 obliquity 220 n.
 crossed 222 adj.
 directed 281 adj.
diagram
 outline 233 n.
 representation
  551 n.
 plan 623 n.
dial
 timekeeper 117 n.
 face 237 n.
 communicate
  524 vb.
 signal 547 vb.
 raise the alarm
  665 vb.
dialect
 language 557 n.
 dialect 560 adj.
dialectal
 dialectal 560 adj.
dialectic
 rational 475 adj.
 reasoning 475 n.
dialectics
 reasoning 475 n.
dialogue
 interrogation
  459 n.
 answer 460 n.
 argument 475 n.
 interlocution
  584 n.
 dramaturgy 594 n.
dialyse
 purify 648 vb.
dialysis
 cleansing 648 n.

 surgery 658 n.
diamante
 finery 844 n.
diameter
 dividing line 92 n.
 breadth 205 n.
diamond
 angular figure
  247 n.
 hardness 326 n.
 exceller 644 n.
 gem 844 n.
diamond jubilee
 anniversary 141 n.
 celebration 876 n.
diamond wedding
 anniversary 141 n.
 special day 876 n.
Diana
 moon 321 n.
 hunter 619 n.
 Olympian deity
  967 n.
diaphanous
 transparent
  422 adj.
diaphragm
 middle 70 n.
 contraception
  172 n.
 musical instrument
  414 n.
diarist
 chronologist 117 n.
 chronicler 549 n.
 author 589 n.
diarrhoea
 defecation 302 n.
 digestive disorders
  651 n.
diary
 list 87 n.
 chronology 117 n.
 reminder 505 n.
 record 548 n.
 reference book
  589 n.
 biography 590 n.
diatonic scale
 key 410 n.
diatribe
 oration 579 n.
 censure 924 n.
diazepam
 drug 658 n.
dice
 cut 46 vb.

cook 301 vb.
oracle 511 n.
gambling 618 n.
amuse oneself
  837 vb.
dice game
  gambling game
  837 n.
dice with death
  face danger 661 vb.
  be rash 857 vb.
dicey
  casual 159 adj.
  speculative
    618 adj.
  dangerous 661 adj.
dichotomy
  disunion 46 n.
  scission 46 n.
  bisection 92 n.
dick
  detective 459 n.
  police 955 n.
dickens, the
  curse 899 int.
dickey
  garment 228 n.
dicky
  seat 218 n.
  unsafe 661 adj.
Dictaphone (tdmk)
  hearing aid 415 n.
  *recording instru-
    ment* 549 n.
dictate
  teach 534 vb.
  speak 579 vb.
  necessitate 596 vb.
  direct 689 vb.
  dominate 733 vb.
  rule 733 vb.
  command 737 n.
  command 737 vb.
  decree 737 n.
  compel 740 vb.
dictation
  teaching 534 n.
  oration 579 n.
  command 737 n.
dictator
  tyrant 735 n.
  autocrat 741 n.
dictatorial
  narrow-minded
    481 adj.
  volitional 595 adj.

authoritative
  733 adj.
authoritarian
  735 adj.
commanding
  737 adj.
insolent 878 adj.
dictatorship
  directorship 689 n.
  despotism 733 n.
  brute force 735 n.
diction
  phrase 563 n.
  style 566 n.
dictionary
  dictionary 559 n.
dictum
  maxim 496 n.
  affirmation 532 n.
  speech 579 n.
  command 737 n.
didactic
  educational
    534 adj.
diddled, be
  be duped 544 vb.
didicoi
  wanderer 268 n.
die
  mould 23 n.
  be past 125 vb.
  die 361 vb.
    See **perish**
  be unseen 444 vb.
  fate 596 n.
  gambling 618 n.
die down
  decrease 37 vb.
  be quiescent
    266 vb.
  blow 352 vb.
  extinguish 382 vb.
die for
  desire 859 vb.
diehard
  permanent 144 adj.
die out
  pass away 2 vb.
  end 69 vb.
  perish 361 vb.
diesel engine
  locomotive 274 n.
diet
  make smaller
    198 vb.
  make thin 206 vb.
  dieting 301 n.

eating 301 n.
be temperate
  942 vb.
starve 946 vb.
dietetics
  dieting 301 n.
die the death
  be punished
    963 vb.
dietician
  doctor 658 n.
differ
  differ 15 vb.
  disagree 25 vb.
  dissent 489 vb.
difference
  difference 15 n.
  numerical result
    85 n.
  dissent 489 n.
difference of opinion
  dissent 489 n.
differences
  dissension 709 n.
  schism 978 n.
different
  different 15 adj.
different ball game, a
  variant 15 n.
differentia
  difference 15 n.
differential
  difference 15 n.
  degree 27 n.
  numerical 85 adj.
  numerical element
    85 n.
  earnings 771 n.
differentiate
  differentiate 15 vb.
**different kettle of
fish**
  variant 15 n.
differing
  different 15 adj.
  dissenting 489 adj.
difficult
  difficult 700 adj.
  disobedient
    738 adj.
  discontented
    829 adj.
  fastidious 862 adj.
  sullen 893 adj.
difficulties
  poverty 801 n.

difficulty
  unintelligibility
    517 n.
  difficulty 700 n.
diffidence
  nervousness 854 n.
  modesty 874 n.
diffident
  doubting 474 adj.
  nervous 854 adj.
  modest 874 adj.
diffraction
  dispersion 75 n.
  reflection 417 n.
diffuse
  disperse 75 vb.
  generalize 79 vb.
  disappear 446 vb.
  publish 528 vb.
  diffuse 570 adj.
diffusion
  disunion 46 n.
  dispersion 75 n.
  presence 189 n.
  transference 272 n.
  ingress 297 n.
dig
  antiquity 125 n.
  excavation 255 n.
  make concave
    255 n.
  knock 279 n.
  agitate 318 vb.
  agitation 318 n.
  cultivate 370 vb.
  search 459 n.
  search 459 vb.
  understand 516 vb.
  work 682 vb.
  be in love 887 vb.
  reproach 924 n.
digamy
  type of marriage
    894 n.
dig at
  contempt 922 n.
  calumny 926 n.
dig down
  descend 309 vb.
digest
  arrangement 62 n.
  modify 143 vb.
  absorb 299 vb.
  eat 301 vb.
  compendium
    592 n.
  be patient 823 vb.

digestible
 edible 301 adj.
digestion
 combination 50 n.
 reception 299 n.
 eating 301 n.
digestive
 purgative 658 n.
 remedial 658 adj.
dig for
 search 459 vb.
 pursue 619 vb.
dig in
 place oneself
  187 vb.
 defend 713 vb.
dig in one's heels
 persevere 600 vb.
 be obstinate
  602 vb.
 refuse 760 vb.
dig into
 enquire 459 vb.
digit
 number 85 n.
 feeler 378 n.
digital
 numerical 85 adj.
 computerized
  86 adj.
 statistical 86 adj.
digital clock
 timekeeper 117 n.
digital computer
 counting instru-
  ment 86 n.
digital watch
 timekeeper 117 n.
digitize
 computerize 86 vb.
dignified
 elegant 575 adj.
 authoritative
  733 adj.
 impressive 821 adj.
 worshipful 866 adj.
 proud 871 adj.
 formal 875 adj.
 courteous 884 adj.
dignitary
 officer 741 n.
 aristocrat 868 n.
 ecclesiarch 986 n.
dignity
 conduct 688 n.
 good taste 846 n.
 honours 866 n.

prestige 866 n.
 pride 871 n.
 ostentation 875 n.
digress
 deviate 282 vb.
 be inattentive
  456 vb.
 be diffuse 570 vb.
digression
 obliquity 220 n.
 deviation 282 n.
 overstepping 306 n.
 diffuseness 570 n.
 oration 579 n.
digs
 quarters 192 n.
dig up
 extract 304 vb.
 exhume 364 vb.
 be curious 453 vb.
dike
 gap 201 n.
 fence 235 n.
 furrow 262 n.
 conduit 351 n.
 obstacle 702 n.
 defences 713 n.
diktat
 decree 737 n.
dilapidated
 dilapidated
  655 adj.
dilatation
 dilation 197 n.
 rarity 325 n.
dilatation and curet-
 tage
 surgery 658 n.
dilate
 grow 36 vb.
 expand 197 vb.
 rarefy 325 vb.
 blow up 352 vb.
dilatoriness
 delay 136 n.
dilatory
 late 136 adj.
 slow 278 adj.
dilemma
 circumstance 8 n.
 dubiety 474 n.
 choice 605 n.
 predicament 700 n.
dilettante
 dabbling 491 adj.
 collector 492 n.
 dabbler 493 n.

diligent
 attentive 455 adj.
 careful 457 adj.
 studious 536 adj.
 observant 768 adj.
dilly-dally
 be irresolute
  601 vb.
 be inactive 679 vb.
dilute
 abate 37 vb.
 weaken 163 vb.
 rarefy 325 vb.
 moisten 341 vb.
dim
 darken 418 vb.
 dim 419 adj.
 dim 419 vb.
 be dim-sighted
  440 vb.
 blur 440 vb.
 unintelligent
  499 adj.
dime
 small thing 33 n.
 coinage 797 n.
dimension
 quantity 26 n.
 measure 183 n.
 appearance 445 n.
dimensions
 quantity 26 n.
 greatness 32 n.
 size 195 n.
 metrology 465 n.
diminish
 abate 37 vb.
 subtract 39 vb.
 render few 105 vb.
 moderate 177 vb.
 shorten 204 vb.
diminuendo
 contraction 198 n.
 adagio 412 adv.
diminution
 smallness 33 n.
 diminution 37 n.
 subtraction 39 n.
diminutive
 small 33 adj.
 little 196 adj.
 word 559 n.
 name 561 n.
 part of speech
  564 n.
diminutiveness
 smallness 33 n.

littleness 196 n.
dimple
 cavity 255 n.
 concavity 255 n.
 notch 260 n.
 lowering 311 n.
dimwit
 dunce 501 n.
 fool 501 n.
dim-witted
 weak 163 adj.
 unintelligent
  499 adj.
din
 greatness 32 n.
 commotion 318 n.
 be loud 400 vb.
 loudness 400 n.
 roll 403 n.
 discord 411 n.
dinar
 coinage 797 n.
dine
 eat 301 vb.
 feed 301 vb.
dine out
 eat 301 vb.
 be sociable 882 vb.
diner
 café 192 n.
 eater 301 n.
ding
 resound 404 vb.
dingbat
 fool 501 n.
dingdong
 roll 403 n.
dinghy
 boat 275 n.
 rowing boat 275 n.
dingle
 valley 255 n.
dingo
 dog 365 n.
dingy
 dim 419 adj.
 colourless 426 adj.
 dirty 649 adj.
 dilapidated
  655 adj.
din in
 emphasize 532 vb.
 educate 534 vb.
dining
 eating 301 n.
dining room
 chamber 194 n.

dinky
little 196 adj.

dinner
meal 301 n.
festivity 837 n.

dinner jacket
formal dress 228 n.
jacket 228 n.

dinner party
social gathering
836 n.

dinosaur
fossil 125 n.
archaism 127 n.
giant 195 n.
animal 365 n.

dint
concavity 255 n.
make concave
255 vb.
notch 260 n.
collide 279 vb.
knock 279 n.

diocese
district 184 n.
parish 985 n.

Diogenes
misanthrope 902 n.

dioxin
poison 659 n.

dip
be oblique 220 vb.
incline 220 n.
cavity 255 n.
valley 255 n.
swim 269 vb.
impel 279 vb.
immerse 303 vb.
descend 309 vb.
descent 309 n.
lower 311 vb.
lowering 311 n.
plunge 313 n.
plunge 313 vb.
be wet 341 vb.
drench 341 vb.
dim 419 vb.
torch 420 n.
colour 425 vb.
ablutions 648 n.
clean 648 vb.

diphtheria
infection 651 n.
respiratory disease
651 n.

diphthong
speech sound
398 n.
voice 577 n.

dip into
be curious 453 vb.
study 536 vb.

diploma
credential 466 n.
record 548 n.
mandate 751 n.
honours 866 n.

diplomacy
tactics 688 n.
cunning 698 n.
mediation 720 n.
conditions 766 n.
courtesy 884 n.

diplomat
expert 696 n.
mediator 720 n.
envoy 754 n.

diplomatic
hypocritical
541 adj.
skilful 694 adj.

diplomatic excuse
untruth 543 n.

diplomatic immunity
freedom 744 n.
nonliability 919 n.

diplomatic incident
predicament 700 n.

diplomatic service
vocation 622 n.

diplomatist
expert 696 n.
mediator 720 n.
envoy 754 n.

dipper
ladle 194 n.
bird 365 n.

dippy
crazy 503 adj.

dipso
drunkard 949 n.

dipsomaniac
the maladjusted
504 n.
drunkard 949 n.
drunken 949 adj.

dip the flag
signal 547 vb.

diptych
list 87 n.
picture 553 n.
altar 990 n.

dire
harmful 645 adj.

direct
simple 44 adj.
orderly 60 adj.
straight 249 adj.
send 272 vb.
directed 281 adj.
orientate 281 vb.
towards 281 adv.
accurate 494 adj.
dramatize 594 vb.
motivate 612 vb.
direct 689 vb.
command 737 vb.

direct current
electricity 160 n.

direct debit
paper money
797 n.
payment 804 n.

direction
relation 9 n.
direction 281 n.
cinema 445 n.
teaching 534 n.
dramaturgy 594 n.
route 624 n.
conduct 688 n.
directorship 689 n.
precept 693 n.
governance 733 n.
government 733 n.

direction finder
direction 281 n.
indicator 547 n.

directive
directed 281 adj.
command 737 n.

directly
towards 281 adv.

directness
straightness 249 n.
perspicuity 567 n.

direct object
part of speech
564 n.

direct opposite
contrariety 14 n.

director
stage manager
594 n.
director 690 n.

director of studies
director 690 n.

directory
directory 87 n.

direct taxation
tax 809 n.

dire necessity
poverty 801 n.

dire straits
danger 661 n.
poverty 801 n.

dirge
obsequies 364 n.
musical piece
412 n.
vocal music 412 n.
poem 593 n.
lament 836 n.

dirigible
airship 276 n.

dirk
sharp point 256 n.
sidearms 723 n.

dirndl
skirt 228 n.

dirt
dirt 649 n.
impurity 951 n.

dirt-cheap
cheap 812 adj.

dirtiness
opacity 423 n.
uncleanness 649 n.
See dirt

dirt road
roughness 259 n.
road 624 n.

dirt-track racing
racing 716 n.

dirty
dim 419 vb.
blacken 428 vb.
dirty 649 adj.
make unclean
649 vb.
disreputable
867 adj.

dirty dog
cad 938 n.

dirty look
look 438 n.
discontent 829 n.
reproach 924 n.

dirty old man
libertine 952 n.

dirty trick
trickery 542 n.
evil 616 n.
perfidy 930 n.

dirty word
calumny 926 n.

dirty work
  perfidy 930 n.
disability
  illness 651 n.
disabled
  impotent 161 adj.
  crippled 163 adj.
  weakened 163 adj.
  quiescent 266 adj.
disabuse
  inform 524 vb.
  disclose 526 vb.
disaccustom
  disaccustom
    611 vb.
disadvantage
  evil 616 n.
  inexpedience
    643 n.
disadvantaged
  necessitous
    627 adj.
  hindered 702 adj.
  subjected 745 adj.
disadvantaged, be
  be in difficulty
    700 vb.
disadvantaged, the
  poor person 801 n.
  lower classes 869 n.
disadvantageous
  evil 616 adj.
  inexpedient
    643 adj.
  harmful 645 adj.
  adverse 731 adj.
disaffection
  dissent 489 n.
  hatred 888 n.
disagree
  disagree 25 vb.
  disbelieve 486 vb.
  negate 533 vb.
  be unwilling
    598 vb.
  refuse 760 vb.
disagreeable
  painful 377 adj.
  unpleasant
    827 adj.
  discourteous
    885 adj.
disagreement
  disagreement 25 n.
  unbelief 486 n.
  dissent 489 n.
  negation 533 n.

unwillingness
    598 n.
  dissension 709 n.
  dislike 861 n.
disagree with
  harm 645 vb.
  displease 827 vb.
  cause dislike
    861 vb.
disallow
  exclude 57 vb.
  dissent 489 vb.
  negate 533 vb.
  reject 607 vb.
  prohibit 757 vb.
  disentitle 916 vb.
  disapprove 924 vb.
disappear
  disappear 446 vb.
disappearance
  disappearance
    446 n.
disappoint
  disappoint 509 vb.
disappointed
  disappointed
    509 adj.
  unhappy 825 adj.
  hopeless 853 adj.
disappointing
  disappointing
    509 adj.
  insufficient
    636 adj.
  annoying 827 adj.
  unpleasant
    827 adj.
disappointment
  disappointment
    509 n.
disapprobation
  disapprobation
    924 n.
disapproval
  dissent 489 n.
  disapprobation
    924 n.
disapprove
  disapprove 924 vb.
disarm
  disable 161 vb.
  weaken 163 vb.
  assuage 177 vb.
  make useless
    641 adj.
  make peace
    719 vb.

pacify 719 vb.
disarmament
  impotence 161 n.
  peace 717 n.
  pacification 719 n.
disarming
  pleasurable
    826 adj.
disarrange
  derange 63 vb.
  displace 188 vb.
disarray
  disorder 61 n.
disaster
  ruin 165 n.
  misfortune 731 n.
  threaten 900 vb.
disastrous
  evil 616 adj.
  harmful 645 adj.
  adverse 731 adj.
disband
  disunite 46 vb.
  decompose 51 vb.
  disperse 75 vb.
  liberate 746 vb.
disbar
  exclude 57 vb.
  eject 300 vb.
  depose 752 vb.
  shame 867 vb.
disbarment
  exclusion 57 n.
  ejection 300 n.
disbelief
  unbelief 486 n.
  negation 533 n.
  lack of wonder
    865 n.
  irreligion 974 n.
disbelieve
  disbelieve 486 vb.
disburden
  take away 786 vb.
disburse
  pay 804 vb.
  expend 806 vb.
disc
  circle 250 n.
  rotator 315 n.
  gramophone 414 n.
  recording instru-
    ment 549 n.
discard
  leave over 41 vb.
  eject 300 vb.
  reject 607 vb.

relinquish 621 vb.
  stop using 674 vb.
  not observe 769 vb.
  not retain 779 vb.
discern
  see 438 vb.
  detect 484 vb.
  know 490 vb.
  understand 516 vb.
discernible
  visible 443 adj.
discerning
  discriminating
    463 adj.
  intelligent 498 adj.
  tasteful 846 adj.
  fastidious 862 adj.
discernment
  inspection 438 n.
  discrimination
    463 n.
  sagacity 498 n.
  good taste 846 n.
  fastidiousness
    862 n.
discharge
  displace 188 vb.
  propulsion 287 n.
  shoot 287 vb.
  outflow 298 n.
  dismiss 300 vb.
  ejection 300 n.
  empty 300 vb.
  excretion 302 n.
  escape 667 n.
  deliverance 668 n.
  stop using 674 vb.
  do 676 vb.
  carry out 725 vb.
  liberate 746 vb.
  liberation 746 n.
  deposal 752 n.
  observance 768 n.
  observe 768 vb.
  not retain 779 vb.
  pay 804 vb.
  do one's duty
    917 vb.
  duty 917 n.
  nonliability 919 n.
  acquit 960 vb.
  acquittal 960 n.
discharge an obliga-
    tion
  do one's duty
    917 vb.

dischuffed
disappointed
509 adj.
discontented
829 adj.
disciple
listener 415 n.
learner 538 n.
auxiliary 707 n.
disciplinarian
tyrant 735 n.
disciplinary
punitive 963 adj.
disciplinary action
punishment 963 n.
discipline
order 60 n.
teaching 534 n.
severity 735 n.
obedience 739 n.
compel 740 vb.
restrain 747 vb.
restraint 747 n.
punish 963 vb.
disc jockey
broadcaster 531 n.
disclaim
negate 533 vb.
recant 603 vb.
reject 607 vb.
abrogate 752 vb.
refuse 760 vb.
not retain 779 vb.
disclaimer
negation 533 n.
recantation 603 n.
resignation 753 n.
refusal 760 n.
disclose
disclose 526 vb.
disco
dancing 837 n.
place of amuse-
ment 837 n.
social gathering
882 n.
discoid
round 250 adj.
discoloration
hue 425 n.
achromatism
426 n.
impairment 655 n.
wound 655 n.
discolour
modify 143 vb.
colour 425 vb.

variegate 437 vb.
discomfit
defeat 727 vb.
trouble 827 vb.
shame 867 vb.
discomfiture
defeat 728 n.
discomfort
pain 377 n.
evil 616 n.
suffering 825 n.
discompose
derange 63 vb.
agitate 318 vb.
trouble 827 vb.
shame 867 vb.
enrage 891 vb.
discomposure
disorder 61 n.
derangement 63 n.
disconcert
derange 63 vb.
distract 456 vb.
defeat 727 vb.
trouble 827 vb.
frighten 854 vb.
shame 867 vb.
humiliate 872 vb.
disconcerted
unexpecting
508 adj.
suffering 825 adj.
disconnect
disunite 46 vb.
discontinue 72 vb.
disconsolate
unhappy 825 adj.
discontented
829 adj.
melancholic
834 adj.
hopeless 853 adj.
discontent
suffering 825 n.
discontent 829 n.
discontented
discontented
829 adj.
discontinue
terminate 69 vb.
discontinue 72 vb.
be inactive 679 vb.
abrogate 752 vb.
discord
contrariety 14 n.
difference 15 n.
discord 411 n.

discord 411 vb.
discordant
unrelated 10 adj.
contrary 14 adj.
different 15 adj.
discordant 411 adj.
florid 425 adj.
discordant note
dissension 709 n.
discothèque
place of amuse-
ment 837 n.
discount
disregard 458 vb.
underestimate
483 vb.
discount 810 n.
discount 810 vb.
hold cheap 922 vb.
discountenance
disapprove 924 vb.
discounting
qualifying 468 adj.
discourage
dissuade 613 vb.
prohibit 757 vb.
cause discontent
829 vb.
depress 834 vb.
discouragement
dissuasion 613 n.
hindrance 702 n.
discourse
lecture 534 n.
teach 534 vb.
oration 579 n.
speech 579 n.
dissertation 591 n.
discourse upon
dissertate 591 vb.
discourteous
discourteous
885 adj.
discourtesy
nonobservance
769 n.
discourtesy 885 n.
disrespect 921 n.
discover
see 438 vb.
discover 484 vb.
discoverer
precursor 66 n.
producer 164 n.
detector 484 n.
discovery
discovery 484 n.

manifestation
522 n.
disclosure 526 n.
discredit
cause doubt
486 vb.
disbelieve 486 vb.
unbelief 486 n.
disrepute 867 n.
shame 867 vb.
hatred 888 n.
defame 926 vb.
discredited
erroneous 495 adj.
disused 674 adj.
disreputable
867 adj.
inglorious 867 adj.
discreet
soft-hued 425 adj.
discriminating
463 adj.
reticent 525 adj.
taciturn 582 adj.
cautious 858 adj.
discrepancy
difference 15 n.
disagreement 25 n.
discrete
separate 46 adj.
discontinuous
72 adj.
discretion
discrimination
463 n.
judgment 480 n.
sagacity 498 n.
will 595 n.
choice 605 n.
caution 858 n.
discriminate
make unlike 19 vb.
discriminate
463 vb.
do wrong 914 adj.
discriminate against
be biased 481 vb.
do wrong 914 vb.
discriminating
discriminating
463 adj.
discrimination
inequality 29 n.
separation 46 n.
exclusion 57 n.
discrimination
463 n.

prejudice 481 n.
injustice 914 n.
discriminatory
biased 481 adj.
unjust 914 adj.
discursive
rational 475 adj.
prolix 570 adj.
discus
circle 250 n.
missile 287 n.
argue 475 vb.
publish 528 vb.
confer 584 vb.
dissertate 591 vb.
discussion
enquiry 459 n.
answer 460 n.
argument 475 n.
conference 584 n.
dissertation 591 n.
disdain
reject 607 vb.
be fastidious
  862 vb.
shame 867 vb.
be proud 871 vb.
pride 871 n.
insolence 878 n.
not respect 921 vb.
contempt 922 n.
despise 922 vb.
disdainful
proud 871 adj.
insolent 878 adj.
disrespectful
  921 adj.
disease
disease 651 n.
disembark
navigate 269 vb.
voyage 269 vb.
land 295 vb.
disembodied
immaterial
  320 adj.
spooky 970 adj.
disembowel
empty 300 vb.
disemployed
powerless 161 adj.
quiescent 266 adj.
disenchanted
indifferent 860 adj.
disenchantment
reversion 148 n.
discovery 484 n.

disappointment
  509 n.
disengage
disunite 46 vb.
separate 46 vb.
liberate 746 vb.
disentangle
simplify 44 vb.
disunite 46 vb.
evolve 316 vb.
decipher 520 vb.
disencumber
  701 vb.
liberate 746 vb.
not retain 779 vb.
disestablish
displace 188 vb.
depose 752 vb.
disfavour
disrepute 867 n.
hatred 888 n.
disrespect 921 n.
disapprobation
  924 n.
disapprove 924 vb.
disfigure
deform 244 vb.
mark 547 vb.
impair 655 vb.
make ugly 842 vb.
blemish 845 vb.
disfigured
unsightly 842 adj.
disfranchised
subjected 745 adj.
disgorge
vomit 300 vb.
disgrace
disrepute 867 n.
shame 867 vb.
slur 867 n.
humiliation 872 n.
wrong 914 n.
not respect 921 vb.
despise 922 vb.
improbity 930 n.
debauch 951 vb.
disgraceful
bad 645 adj.
discreditable
  867 adj.
disgrace oneself
demean oneself
  867 vb.
lose repute 867 vb.

disgruntled
disappointed
  509 adj.
discontented
  829 adj.
disguise
make unlike 19 vb.
mimicry 20 n.
modify 143 vb.
transform 147 vb.
conceal 525 vb.
concealment 525 n.
disguise 527 n.
dissemble 541 vb.
sham 542 n.
disgust
be unpalatable
  391 vb.
displease 827 vb.
painfulness 827 n.
cause discontent
  829 vb.
cause dislike
  861 vb.
dislike 861 vb.
disgusted
unhappy 825 adj.
disgusting
unsavoury 391 adj.
not nice 645 adj.
unclean 649 adj.
unpleasant
  827 adj.
discreditable
  867 adj.
hateful 888 adj.
dish
destroy 165 vb.
plate 194 n.
dish 301 n.
astronomy 321 n.
defeat 727 vb.
a beauty 841 n.
dishabille
informal dress
  228 n.
uncovering 229 n.
dishcloth
cleaning cloth
  648 n.
dishearten
dissuade 613 vb.
cause discontent
  829 vb.
depress 834 vb.
dishevel
jumble 63 vb.

dishonest
false 541 adj.
dishonest 930 adj.
dishonesty
thievishness 788 n.
wrong 914 n.
improbity 930 n.
wickedness 934 n.
lawbreaking 954 n.
dishonour
not pay 805 vb.
disrepute 867 n.
shame 867 vb.
wrong 914 n.
disrespect 921 n.
not respect 921 vb.
defame 926 vb.
improbity 930 n.
debauch 951 vb.
dish out
apportion 783 vb.
pay 804 vb.
dishwasher
cleaner 648 n.
cleaning utensil
  648 n.
domestic 742 n.
dishwater
weak thing 163 n.
dishy
personable 841 adj.
disillusion
disappoint 509 vb.
inform 524 vb.
disclose 526 vb.
dissuade 613 vb.
displease 827 vb.
regret 830 n.
dejection 834 n.
hatred 888 n.
disillusionment
disappointment
  509 n.
disclosure 526 n.
detraction 926 n.
disincentive
dissuasion 613 n.
hindrance 702 n.
disinclination
unwillingness
  598 n.
dislike 861 n.
disinfect
purify 648 vb.
make sanitary
  652 adj.
safeguard 660 vb.

disinfectant
cleanser 648 n.
prophylactic 658 n.
remedial 658 adj.
disinformation
information 524 n.
concealment 525 n.
misteaching 535 n.
untruth 543 n.
misrepresentation
552 n.
disingenuous
false 541 adj.
cunning 698 adj.
dishonest 930 adj.
disinherit
not retain 779 vb.
deprive 786 vb.
impoverish 801 vb.
disinheritance
expropriation
786 n.
disintegrate
break 46 vb.
disunite 46 vb.
separate 46 vb.
decompose 51 vb.
be dispersed 75 vb.
disperse 75 vb.
pulverize 332 vb.
deteriorate 655 vb.
disintegration
disunion 46 n.
separation 46 n.
decay 51 n.
decomposition
51 n.
dispersion 75 n.
powderiness 332 n.
disinter
exhume 364 vb.
disclose 526 vb.
disinterested
just 913 adj.
disinterested
931 adj.
disinterment
inquest 364 n.
disinvolvement
liberation 746 n.
disjunction
disunion 46 n.
disk
circle 250 n.
disk drive
data processing
86 n.

dislike
dislike 861 n.
dislike 861 vb.
dislocate
disunite 46 vb.
derange 63 vb.
disable 161 vb.
force 176 vb.
displace 188 vb.
dislocation
separation 46 n.
derangement 63 n.
displacement
188 n.
impairment 655 n.
dislodge
derange 63 vb.
displace 188 vb.
eject 300 vb.
disloyal
changeful 152 adj.
nonobservant
769 adj.
hostile 881 adj.
malevolent
898 adj.
undutiful 918 adj.
perfidious 930 adj.
dismal
unpleasant
827 adj.
cheerless 834 adj.
melancholic
834 adj.
dismantle
break 46 vb.
See **sunder**
sunder 46 vb.
demolish 165 vb.
destroy 165 vb.
make inactive
679 vb.
dismay
worry 825 n.
fear 854 n.
dismember
cut 46 vb.
rend 46 vb.
sunder 46 vb.
dismiss
exclude 57 vb.
disperse 75 vb.
dismiss 300 vb.
disregard 458 vb.
confute 479 vb.
be indifferent
860 vb.

hold cheap 922 vb.
dismissal
exclusion 57 n.
repulsion 292 n.
valediction 296 n.
ejection 300 n.
nonuse 674 n.
deposal 752 n.
loss of right 916 n.
prayers 981 n.
dismount
sunder 46 vb.
land 295 vb.
descend 309 vb.
disobedience
disobedience
738 n.
disobedient
disobedient
738 adj.
disobey
disobey 738 vb.
disobliging
unkind 898 adj.
disorder
be disordered
61 vb.
disorder 61 n.
derange 63 vb.
roughen 259 vb.
disease 651 n.
anarchy 734 n.
disorderly
disorderly 61 adj.
disorganize
derange 63 vb.
impair 655 vb.
disorientate
derange 63 vb.
displace 188 vb.
disorientated
doubting 474 adj.
disown
negate 533 vb.
abrogate 752 vb.
not retain 779 vb.
disapprove 924 vb.
disparage
abate 37 vb.
underestimate
483 vb.
shame 867 vb.
not respect 921 vb.
hold cheap 922 vb.
detract 926 vb.

disparaging
disapproving
924 adj.
disparate
unrelated 10 adj.
different 15 adj.
dissimilar 19 adj.
unequal 29 adj.
disparity
unrelatedness 10 n.
difference 15 n.
dissimilarity 19 n.
disagreement 25 n.
inequality 29 n.
dispassionate
judicial 480 adj.
impassive 820 adj.
inexcitable
823 adj.
just 913 adj.
dispatch
displace 188 vb.
move 265 vb.
send 272 vb.
transference 272 n.
velocity 277 n.
eat 301 vb.
kill 362 vb.
report 524 n.
news 529 n.
correspondence
588 n.
do 676 vb.
activity 678 n.
be active 678 vb.
haste 680 n.
deal with 688 vb.
carry out 725 vb.
carry through
725 vb.
give 781 vb.
dispatches
report 524 n.
message 529 n.
news 529 n.
dispel
disunite 46 vb.
disperse 75 vb.
destroy 165 vb.
displace 188 vb.
repel 292 vb.
disappear 446 vb.
dispensable
superfluous
637 adj.
useless 641 adj.

dispensary
hospital 658 n.
dispensation
exclusion 57 n.
deliverance 668 n.
permission 756 n.
nonretention
779 n.
nonliability 919 n.
dispense
exclude 57 vb.
disperse 75 vb.
permit 756 vb.
give 781 vb.
apportion 783 vb.
exempt 919 vb.
dispenser
druggist 658 n.
dispense with
not use 674 vb.
not retain 779 vb.
dispersal
disunion 46 n.
dispersion 75 n.
transference 272 n.
disperse
be dispersed 75 vb.
disperse 75 vb.
disappear 446 vb.
dispirited
dejected 834 adj.
displace
disunite 46 vb.
substitute 150 vb.
displace 188 vb.
displaced person
outcast 883 n.
display
accumulation 74 n.
appearance 445 n.
spectacle 445 n.
exhibit 522 n.
manifestation
522 n.
show 522 vb.
publicity 528 n.
defiance 711 n.
pride 871 n.
ostentation 875 n.
pageant 875 n.
displeased
discontented
829 adj.
angry 891 adj.
displeasure
sorrow 825 n.
annoyance 827 n.

discontent 829 n.
dislike 861 n.
hatred 888 n.
disapprobation
924 n.
disport oneself
be cheerful 833 vb.
amuse oneself
837 vb.
disposable
ephemeral 114 adj.
used 673 adj.
disposal
arrangement 62 n.
nonretention
779 n.
sale 793 n.
dispose
order 60 vb.
arrange 62 vb.
motivate 612 vb.
disposed
arranged 62 adj.
willing 597 adj.
disposed of
not retained
779 adj.
dispose of
dispose of 673 vb.
carry through
725 vb.
not retain 779 vb.
sell 793 vb.
disposition
temperament 5 n.
state 7 n.
arrangement 62 n.
location 187 n.
will 595 n.
willingness 597 n.
habit 610 n.
affections 817 n.
dispossess
eject 300 vb.
deprive 786 vb.
disentitle 916 vb.
disproportionate
unrelated 10 adj.
unequal 29 adj.
distorted 246 adj.
disprove
confute 479 vb.
negate 533 vb.
disputable
uncertain 474 adj.
disputation
argument 475 n.

dispute
disagree 25 vb.
argue 475 vb.
quarrel 709 n.
contention 716 n.
disputed territory
battleground
724 n.
disqualify
exclude 57 vb.
disable 161 vb.
make useless
641 adj.
disentitle 916 vb.
disquiet
changeableness
152 n.
agitation 318 n.
worry 825 n.
trouble 827 vb.
discontent 829 n.
frighten 854 vb.
nervousness 854 n.
disquisition
oration 579 n.
dissertation 591 n.
disregard
exclude 57 vb.
be inattentive
456 vb.
inattention 456 n.
disregard 458 vb.
negligence 458 n.
nonobservance
769 n.
not observe 769 vb.
disregarding
negligent 458 adj.
nonobservant
769 adj.
disrepair
dilapidation 655 n.
disreputable
disreputable
867 adj.
disrepute
disrepute 867 n.
disrespect
sauciness 878 n.
undutifulness
918 n.
disrespect 921 n.
disrespectful
disrespectful
921 adj.
disruption
separation 46 n.

discontinuity 72 n.
destruction 165 n.
badness 645 n.
dissatisfaction
incompleteness
55 n.
dissent 489 n.
sorrow 825 n.
discontent 829 n.
dislike 861 n.
resentment 891 n.
disapprobation
924 n.
dissatisfied
dissenting 489 adj.
discontented
829 adj.
dissatisfy
disappoint 509 vb.
be imperfect
647 vb.
displease 827 vb.
cause discontent
829 vb.
dissect
sunder 46 vb.
decompose 51 vb.
class 62 vb.
enquire 459 vb.
dissection
scission 46 n.
separation 46 n.
decomposition
51 n.
enquiry 459 n.
dissemblance
dissimilarity 19 n.
dissemble
make unlike 19 vb.
dissemble 541 vb.
disseminate
disperse 75 vb.
communicate
524 vb.
publish 528 vb.
dissemination
dispersion 75 n.
publication 528 n.
dissension
dissension 709 n.
enmity 881 n.
dissent
dissent 489 n.
dissent 489 vb.
dissenting
nonuniform 17 adj.
disagreeing 25 adj.

distribution
arrangement 62 n.
dispersion 75 n.
transference 272 n.
provision 633 n.
apportionment
   783 n.
sale 793 n.
distributor
electronics 160 n.
district
district 184 n.
land 344 n.
district nurse
nurse 658 n.
aider 703 n.
distrust
doubt 486 n.
doubt 486 vb.
jealousy 911 n.
distrustful
doubting 474 adj.
nervous 854 adj.
jealous 911 adj.
disturb
decompose 51 vb.
derange 63 vb.
mistime 138 vb.
displace 188 vb.
agitate 318 vb.
distract 456 vb.
trouble 827 vb.
frighten 854 vb.
disturbance
turmoil 61 n.
derangement 63 n.
untimeliness
   138 n.
commotion 318 n.
quarrel 709 n.
disturbed
violent 176 adj.
nervous 854 adj.
disunity
disagreement 25 n.
dissension 709 n.
disuse
desuetude 611 n.
relinquishment
   621 n.
nonuse 674 n.
abrogation 752 n.
nonretention
   779 n.
ditch
gap 201 n.
partition 231 n.

fence 235 n.
cavity 255 n.
furrow 262 n.
fly 271 vb.
conduit 351 n.
drain 351 n.
cultivate 370 vb.
change one's mind
   603 vb.
reject 607 vb.
relinquish 621 vb.
protection 660 n.
stop using 674 vb.
stratagem 698 n.
obstacle 702 n.
defences 713 n.
not retain 779 vb.
dither
be agitated 318 vb.
be uncertain
   474 vb.
be irresolute
   601 vb.
ditto
be identical 13 vb.
identically 13 adv.
identity 13 n.
do likewise 20 vb.
accord 24 vb.
again 106 vb.
repeat 106 vb.
repetition 106 n.
ditty
vocal music 412 n.
doggerel 593 n.
diuretic
purgative 658 n.
diurnal
seasonal 141 adj.
diva
vocalist 413 n.
actor 594 n.
divan
bed 218 n.
seat 218 n.
dive
tavern 192 n.
navigate 269 vb.
swim 269 vb.
fly 271 vb.
move fast 277 vb.
spurt 277 vb.
descend 309 vb.
descent 309 n.
tumble 309 vb.
plunge 313 n.
plunge 313 vb.

amuse oneself
   837 vb.
diver
diver 313 n.
bird 365 n.
diverge
disagree 25 vb.
be oblique 220 vb.
diverge 294 vb.
diverge from
differ 15 vb.
divergence
difference 15 n.
nonuniformity
   17 n.
dissimilarity 19 n.
disagreement 25 n.
divergence 294 n.
divergent
nonuniform 17 adj.
divergent 294 adj.
divers
multiform 82 adj.
many 104 adj.
diverse
different 15 adj.
nonuniform 17 adj.
dissimilar 19 adj.
multiform 82 adj.
diversification
variegation 437 n.
diversify
modify 143 vb.
variegate 437 vb.
diversion
irrelevance 10 n.
change 143 n.
deviation 282 n.
traffic control
   305 n.
pleasure 376 n.
inattention 456 n.
trickery 542 n.
circuit 626 n.
amusement 837 n.
diversity
unrelatedness 10 n.
difference 15 n.
nonuniformity
   17 n.
multiformity 82 n.
variegation 437 n.
divert
deflect 282 vb.
distract 456 vb.
obstruct 702 vb.
not pay 805 vb.

amuse 837 vb.
diverting
amusing 837 adj.
divertissement
pleasure 376 n.
musical piece
   412 n.
amusement 837 n.
divert one's attention
distract 456 vb.
divest
subtract 39 vb.
uncover 229 vb.
relinquish 621 vb.
depose 752 vb.
deprive 786 vb.
divide
sunder 46 vb.
part 53 vb.
class 62 vb.
bisect 92 vb.
partition 231 n.
limit 236 n.
mete out 465 vb.
divided
fragmentary
   53 adj.
quarrelling
   709 adj.
schismatical
   978 adj.
divided allegiance
perfidy 930 n.
divided skirt
skirt 228 n.
dividend
part 53 n.
numerical element
   85 n.
gain 771 n.
portion 783 n.
dividers
gauge 465 n.
divide up
sunder 46 vb.
apportion 783 vb.
dividing
separate 46 adj.
interjacent 231 adj.
divination
intuition 476 n.
divination 511 n.
divine
foresee 510 vb.
divine 511 vb.
beautiful 841 adj.
divine 965 adj.

godlike 965 adj.
religious 973 adj.
theologian 973 n.
cleric 986 n.

diviner
diviner 511 n.

divine right
authority 733 n.

divining rod
detector 484 n.

divinity
divineness 965 n.
theology 973 n.

divisible
numerical 85 adj.

division
scission 46 n.
decomposition
51 n.
subdivision 53 n.
arrangement 62 n.
discontinuity 72 n.
classification 77 n.
district 184 n.
partition 231 n.
vote 605 n.
formation 722 n.
apportionment
783 n.
seclusion 883 n.
schism 978 n.
sect 978 n.

divisor
numerical element
85 n.

divorce
disunite 46 vb.
separate 46 vb.
divorce 896 n.
divorce 896 vb.

divorcé(e)
divorce 896 n.

divorced
separate 46 adj.
not retained
779 adj.

divot
piece 53 n.

divulge
manifest 522 vb.
divulge 526 vb.

Dixieland
music 412 n.

DIY
repair 656 n.
repair 656 vb.

dizzy
unequal 29 adj.
changeful 152 adj.
high 209 adj.
crazy 503 adj.
crapulous 949 adj.

dizzy height
height 209 n.

DJ
broadcaster 531 n.

DNA
heredity 5 n.
organism 358 n.

DNA fingerprinting
evidence 466 n.
identification
547 n.
diagnostic 658 n.

D notice
restraint 747 n.

do
accord 24 vb.
unite with 45 vb.
feasting 301 n.
study 536 vb.
deceive 542 vb.
suffice 635 vb.
be expedient
642 vb.
do 676 vb.
overcharge 811 vb.
amusement 837 n.
celebration 876 n.
social gathering
882 n.

do a bunk
run away 620 vb.

do a favour
do good 644 vb.

do again
repeat 106 vb.

do away with
destroy 165 vb.
kill 362 vb.

dobbin
horse 273 n.

Dobermann pinscher
dog 365 n.

doch-an-dorris
valediction 296 n.
draught 301 n.

docile
willing 597 adj.
obedient 739 adj.

dock
subtract 39 vb.
cut 46 vb.

sunder 46 vb.
place 187 vb.
dwell 192 vb.
stable 192 n.
shorten 204 vb.
edge 234 n.
navigate 269 vb.
arrive 295 vb.
storage 632 n.
shelter 662 n.
workshop 687 n.
lockup 748 n.

docker
displacement
188 n.
boatman 270 n.
worker 686 n.

docket
list 87 n.
list 87 vb.
credential 466 n.
label 547 n.
mark 547 vb.
record 548 vb.
abstract 592 vb.

dockyard
workshop 687 n.

doctor
mix 43 vb.
modify 143 vb.
sage 500 n.
be false 541 vb.
doctor 658 n.
doctor 658 vb.
account 808 vb.
academic title
870 n.

doctorate
honours 866 n.
academic title
870 n.

**doctor of divinity,
literature,
medicine, phi-
losophy etc.**
academic title
870 n.

doctrinaire
positive 473 adj.

doctrinal
creedal 485 adj.
educational
534 adj.
orthodox 976 adj.

doctrine
creed 485 n.

document
corroborate 466 vb.
evidence 466 n.
demonstrate
478 V.
record 548 n.
record 548 vb.
book 589 n.

documentary
film 445 n.
information 524 n.
informative
524 adj.
broadcast 531 n.
lecture 534 n.
descriptive 590 adj.

documentation
evidence 466 n.
demonstration
478 n.
record 548 n.

documented
evidential 466 adj.

dod
bulk 195 n.
solid body 324 n.

doddering
ageing 131 adj.

doddle
easy thing 701 n.

dodecahedron
over five 99 n.
angular figure
247 n.

dodge
vary 152 vb.
be oblique 220 vb.
be in motion
265 vb.
disregard 458 vb.
sophisticate
477 vb.
be stealthy 525 vb.
dissemble 541 vb.
trickery 542 n.
avoid 620 vb.
avoidance 620 n.
contrivance 623 n.
elude 667 vb.
means of escape
667 n.
skill 694 n.
be cunning 698 vb.
stratagem 698 n.
not observe 769 vb.
be dishonest
930 vb.

dodgem car
  vehicle 274 n.
dodgy
  dangerous 661 adj.
dodo
  archaism 127 n.
  animal 365 n.
doe
  mammal 365 n.
  female animal
    373 n.
doer
  doer 676 n.
doeskin
  textile 222 n.
  skin 226 n.
do for
  destroy 165 vb.
  kill 362 vb.
  murder 362 vb.
  provide 633 vb.
  harm 645 vb.
  minister to 703 vb.
  defeat 727 vb.
  serve 742 vb.
do for oneself
  provide 633 vb.
dog
  accompany 89 vb.
  be behind 238 vb.
  follow 284 vb.
  dog 365 n.
  male animal
    372 n.
  pursue 619 vb.
dogcart
  carriage 274 n.
dog collar
  neckwear 228 n.
  canonicals 989 n.
doge
  officer 741 n.
dog-eared
  dilapidated
    655 adj.
  used 673 adj.
dog-eat-dog
  anarchy 734 n.
dog-end
  tobacco 388 n.
dogfight
  fight 716 n.
  battle 718 n.
dogfish
  fish food 301 n.
  fish 365 n.

dogged
  obstinate 602 adj.
doggedness
  perseverance 600 n.
  obstinacy 602 n.
doggerel
  absurdity 497 n.
  doggerel 593 n.
  poetic 593 adj.
  funny 849 adj.
  ridiculousness
    849 n.
doggy
  animal 365 adj.
doghouse
  stable 192 n.
dog in the manger
  possessor 776 n.
  egotist 932 n.
  selfish 932 adj.
dogma
  creed 485 n.
  religion 973 n.
  theology 973 n.
dogmatic
  certain 473 adj.
  positive 473 adj.
  narrow-minded
    481 adj.
  creedal 485 adj.
  assertive 532 adj.
  obstinate 602 adj.
  vain 873 adj.
do-gooder
  volunteer 597 n.
  philanthropist
    901 n.
dogs, the
  racing 716 n.
dogsbody
  worker 686 n.
  auxiliary 707 n.
  servant 742 n.
dog's breakfast
  bungling 695 n.
dog's home
  shelter 662 n.
dogsleigh
  sled 274 n.
Dog star
  star 321 n.
dog-tired
  fatigued 684 adj.
dogtooth
  notch 260 n.
  pattern 844 n.

dog track
  meeting place
    192 n.
  arena 724 n.
dog-watches
  evening 129 n.
do in
  destroy 165 vb.
  kill 362 vb.
  murder 362 vb.
doing
  agency 173 n.
  action 676 n.
doings
  affairs 154 n.
  deed 676 n.
do-it-yourself
  artless 699 adj.
do justice to
  eat 301 vb.
  vindicate 927 vb.
do one's duty
  do one's duty
    917 vb.
do one's utmost
  exert oneself
    682 vb.
doldrums
  weather 340 n.
  inaction 677 n.
  inactivity 679 n.
  dejection 834 n.
dole
  small quantity
    33 n.
  insufficiency 636 n.
  gift 781 n.
  sociology 901 n.
doleful
  melancholic
    834 adj.
  lamenting 836 adj.
dole out
  disperse 75 vb.
  mete out 465 vb.
  give 781 vb.
  apportion 783 vb.
  pay 804 vb.
doll
  dwarf 196 n.
  female 373 n.
  image 551 n.
  plaything 837 n.
  a beauty 841 n.
dollar
  coinage 797 n.

dollar bill
  paper money
    797 n.
dollop
  portion 783 n.
doll's house
  plaything 837 n.
doll up
  primp 843 vb.
dolly
  little 196 adj.
dolly bird
  a beauty 841 n.
dolman sleeve
  sleeve 228 n.
dolmen
  tomb 364 n.
  monument 548 n.
dolour
  suffering 825 n.
dolphin
  mammal 365 n.
dolt
  dunce 501 n.
dom
  male 372 n.
  title 870 n.
domain
  classification 77 n.
  territory 184 n.
  lands 777 n.
domaine
  function 622 n.
dome
  edifice 164 n.
  house 192 n.
  high structure
    209 n.
  head 213 n.
  dome 253 n.
Domesday Book
  list 87 n.
domestic
  native 191 adj.
  provincial 192 adj.
  interior 224 adj.
  animal 365 adj.
  domestic 742 n.
  unsociable 883 adj.
domesticate
  break in 369 vb.
  habituate 610 vb.
domicile
  abode 192 n.
domiciliary
  native 191 adj.

dominant
supreme 34 adj.
influential 178 adj.
musical note
410 n.
authoritative
733 adj.
dominate
influence 178 vb.
be high 209 vb.
dominate 733 vb.
subjugate 745 vb.
domination
superiority 34 n.
influence 178 n.
governance 733 n.
domineer
oppress 735 vb.
domineering
authoritative
733 adj.
authoritarian
735 adj.
oppressive 735 adj.
insolence 878 n.
insolent 878 adj.
dominie
teacher 537 n.
dominion
territory 184 n.
governance 733 n.
*political organiza-
tion* 733 n.
lands 777 n.
domino
disguise 527 n.
plaything 837 n.
dominoes
indoor game 837 n.
don
wear 228 vb.
male 372 n.
scholar 492 n.
teacher 537 n.
aristocrat 868 n.
title 870 n.
donate
give 781 vb.
expend 806 vb.
donation
transference 272 n.
incentive 612 n.
subvention 703 n.
gift 781 n.
giving 781 n.
done
past 125 adj.

caused 157 adj.
usual 610 adj.
fatigued 684 adj.
done, be
be duped 544 vb.
pay too much
811 vb.
be in fashion
848 vb.
done for
dead 361 adj.
dying 361 adj.
dilapidated
655 adj.
defeated 728 adj.
done in
fatigued 684 adj.
done thing
practice 610 n.
etiquette 848 n.
Don Juan
lover 887 n.
libertine 952 n.
donkey
beast of burden
273 n.
mammal 365 n.
fool 501 n.
donkey's years
long duration
113 n.
donkeywork
labour 682 n.
donor
propagation 167 n.
giver 781 n.
good giver 813 n.
don't-care
rash 857 adj.
indifferent 860 adj.
don't know
changeable thing
152 n.
uncertainty 474 n.
moderate 625 n.
neutral 625 adj.
independence
744 n.
doodad
bauble 639 n.
doodah
tool 630 n.
doodle
be inattentive
456 vb.
picture 553 n.

doom
finality 69 n.
ruin 165 n.
death 361 n.
judge 480 vb.
fate 596 n.
necessitate 596 vb.
condemnation
961 n.
punishment 963 n.
doomed
dying 361 adj.
fated 596 adj.
unfortunate
731 adj.
unhappy 825 adj.
doomsday
future state 124 n.
doomwatch
surveillance 457 n.
expect 507 vb.
door
threshold 234 n.
barrier 235 n.
doorway 263 n.
way in 297 n.
access 624 n.
doorbell
signal 547 n.
do-or-die
rash 857 adj.
doorhandle
handle 218 n.
doorkeeper
doorkeeper 264 n.
doorknob
opener 263 n.
doorknocker
signal 547 n.
doorman
doorkeeper 264 n.
servant 742 n.
doormat
weakling 163 n.
floor-cover 226 n.
cleaning utensil
648 n.
coward 856 n.
toady 879 n.
doorpost
pillar 218 n.
doorstep
stand 218 n.
threshold 234 n.
doorway 263 n.
beg 761 vb.
request 761 vb.

torment 827 vb.
doorstepping
vote 605 n.
doorway
doorway 263 n.
do out of
deceive 542 vb.
defraud 788 vb.
doo-wop
music 412 n.
musical 412 adj.
dope
anaesthetic 375 n.
render insensible
375 vb.
ninny 501 n.
information 524 n.
drug 658 n.
make inactive
679 vb.
drug-taking 949 n.
dope addict
the maladjusted
504 n.
dope-peddler
drug-taking 949 n.
dopey
foolish 499 adj.
unintelligent
499 adj.
sleepy 679 adj.
doppelgänger
analogue 18 n.
ghost 970 n.
Doppler effect
displacement
188 n.
dorm
quarters 192 n.
dormant
inert 175 adj.
quiescent 266 adj.
latent 523 adj.
sleepy 679 adj.
dormer window
window 263 n.
dormitory
quarters 192 n.
chamber 194 n.
dormitory town
housing 192 n.
Dormobile (tdmk)
small house 192 n.
automobile 274 n.
dormouse
mammal 365 n.

dorsal
back 238 adj.
dory
boat 275 n.
dosage
measurement
465 n.
portion 783 n.
dose
finite quantity
26 n.
piece 53 n.
measurement
465 n.
medicine 658 n.
portion 783 n.
punishment 963 n.
doss down
dwell 192 vb.
be quiescent
266 vb.
sleep 679 vb.
doss-house
inn 192 n.
dossier
bunch 74 n.
testimony 466 n.
information 524 n.
record 548 n.
legal trial 959 n.
dot
small thing 33 n.
place 185 n.
mottle 437 n.
mark 547 n.
punctuation 547 n.
lettering 586 n.
pattern 844 n.
dotage
old age 131 n.
folly 499 n.
dotard
old man 133 n.
fool 501 n.
dote
be foolish 499 vb.
desire 859 vb.
be in love 887 vb.
dote on
desire 859 vb.
doting
foolish 499 adj.
loving 887 adj.
**dot one's i's and
cross one's t's**
be careful 457 vb.
emphasize 532 vb.

dotted line
discontinuity 72 n.
dotty
foolish 499 adj.
crazy 503 adj.
double
identity 13 n.
analogue 18 n.
augment 36 vb.
double 91 adj.
double 91 vb.
substitute 150 n.
vary 152 vb.
invigorate 174 vb.
enlarge 197 vb.
fold 261 vb.
move fast 277 vb.
spirit 447 n.
representation
551 n.
double agent
secret service
459 n.
deceiver 545 n.
double back
turn back 286 vb.
double-barrelled
dual 90 adj.
**double bass or con-
trabasso**
viol 414 n.
double bed
bed 218 n.
double bill
stage play 594 n.
double-boiler
pot 194 n.
double-check
make certain
473 vb.
double chin
bulk 195 n.
double-cross
deceive 542 vb.
be cunning 698 vb.
be dishonest
930 vb.
double-dealing
duplicity 541 n.
hypocritical
541 adj.
cunning 698 n.
perfidious 930 adj.
perfidy 930 n.
double-decker
bus 274 n.

double dutch
lack of meaning
515 n.
unintelligibility
517 n.
double entendre
equivocalness
518 n.
impurity 951 n.
double figures
over five 99 n.
double-glazing
lining 227 n.
barrier 235 n.
screen 421 n.
double-jointed
flexible 327 adj.
double life
duality 90 n.
duplicity 541 n.
double meaning
connotation 514 n.
double-quick
speedy 277 adj.
double star
star 321 n.
double-strength
strong 162 adj.
intoxicating
949 adj.
double take
inspection 438 n.
doublet
substitute 150 n.
word 559 n.
doubletalk
lack of meaning
515 n.
equivocalness
518 n.
falsehood 541 n.
neology 560 n.
double up
laugh 835 vb.
double vision
vision 438 n.
dim sight 440 n.
double yellow lines
traffic control
305 n.
doublethink
error 495 n.
doublure
lining 227 n.
doubly
greatly 32 vb.

doubt
improbability
472 n.
dubiety 474 n.
doubt 486 n.
doubt 486 vb.
irresolution 601 n.
caution 858 n.
doubtful
doubting 474 adj.
uncertain 474 adj.
nervous 854 adj.
cautious 858 adj.
disreputable
867 adj.
dishonest 930 adj.
doubting
doubting 474 adj.
irreligious 974 adj.
doubting Thomas
unbeliever 486 n.
doubtless
probably 471 adv.
certainly 473 adv.
douche
water 339 n.
be wet 341 vb.
drench 341 vb.
irrigate 341 vb.
ablutions 648 n.
clean 648 vb.
purgative 658 n.
dough
cereals 301 n.
softness 327 n.
pulpiness 356 n.
shekels 797 n.
doughnut
pastries and cakes
301 n.
doughty
stalwart 162 adj.
doughy
light 323 adj.
soft 327 adj.
colourless 426 adj.
do up
join 45 vb.
tie 45 vb.
modernize 126 vb.
close 264 vb.
make better
654 vb.
repair 656 vb.
fatigue 684 vb.
primp 843 vb.

dour
  obstinate 602 adj.
  severe 735 adj.
  serious 834 adj.
douse
  impel 279 vb.
  lower 311 vb.
  plunge 313 vb.
  drench 341 vb.
  extinguish 382 vb.
dove
  bird 365 n.
  pacifist 717 n.
  innocent 935 n.
dovecote
  stable 192 n.
dovetail
  accord 24 vb.
  join 45 vb.
  joint 45 n.
  cross 222 vb.
  introduce 231 vb.
dowager
  old woman 133 n.
  female 373 n.
dowdiness
  bad taste 847 n.
dowel
  fastening 47 n.
do well
  progress 285 vb.
  flourish 615 vb.
  be skilful 694 vb.
  succeed 727 vb.
  prosper 730 vb.
dower house
  house 192 n.
do without
  not use 674 vb.
  not retain 779 vb.
down
  filament 208 n.
  smoothness 258 n.
  hair 259 n.
  down 309 adv.
  softness 327 n.
  dejected 834 adj.
  sullen 893 adj.
down-and-out
  dilapidated
   655 adj.
  unlucky person
   731 n.
  derelict 779 n.
  poor person 801 n.
  disreputable
   867 adj.

  low fellow 869 n.
down-at-heel
  dilapidated
   655 adj.
  used 673 adj.
  poor 801 adj.
  disreputable
   867 adj.
downbeat
  tempo 410 n.
  dejected 834 adj.
downcast
  dejected 834 adj.
downdraught
  descent 309 n.
  wind 352 n.
downers
  drug-taking 949 n.
downfall
  ruin 165 n.
  descent 309 n.
  defeat 728 n.
  adversity 731 n.
downhearted
  dejected 834 adj.
downhill
  incline 220 n.
  sloping 220 adj.
  down 309 adv.
  easy 701 adj.
Downie (tdmk)
  coverlet 226 n.
downiness
  hair 259 n.
  softness 327 n.
down in the mouth
  dejected 834 adj.
  melancholic
   834 adj.
download
  transpose 272 vb.
downmarket
  cheap 812 adj.
down on one's luck
  unfortunate
   731 adj.
down payment
  part 53 n.
  security 767 n.
  payment 804 n.
downpour
  storm 176 n.
  descent 309 n.
  rain 350 n.
downright
  consummate
   32 adj.

  complete 54 adj.
  completely 54 adv.
  intelligible 516 adj.
downright lie
  untruth 543 n.
downs
  high land 209 n.
  plain 348 n.
Down's syndrome
  psychosis 503 n.
down stage
  stage set 594 n.
downstairs
  under 210 adv.
  down 309 adv.
downstream
  towards 281 adv.
  down 309 adv.
downtime
  data processing
   86 n.
down to earth
  true 494 adj.
down tools
  cease 145 vb.
  relinquish 621 vb.
  resist 715 vb.
  revolt 738 vb.
downtown
  towards 281 adv.
downtrodden
  subjected 745 adj.
  suffering 825 adj.
downturn
  decrease 37 n.
  deterioration
   655 n.
down under
  beyond 199 adv.
downwards
  down 309 adv.
downward trend
  decrease 37 n.
  regression 286 n.
  descent 309 n.
downwind
  towards 281 adv.
downy
  smooth 258 adj.
  comfortable
   376 adj.
dowry
  dower 777 n.
dowsing
  divination 511 n.
doxology
  hymn 981 n.

doxy
  kept woman 952 n.
  theology 973 n.
doyen
  seniority 131 n.
  expert 696 n.
doze
  be neglectful
   458 vb.
  sleep 679 n.
  sleep 679 vb.
dozen
  over five 99 n.
dozy
  sleepy 679 adj.
drab
  grey 429 adj.
  cheerless 834 adj.
  dull 840 adj.
drachm
  weighing 322 n.
  coinage 797 n.
Draconian
  exorbitant 32 adj.
  oppressive 735 adj.
  severe 735 adj.
draft
  copy 22 n.
  prototype 23 n.
  compose 56 vb.
  disperse 75 vb.
  outline 233 n.
  form 243 n.
  transpose 272 vb.
  represent 551 vb.
  representation
   551 n.
  write 586 vb.
  compendium
   592 n.
  plan 623 n.
  plan 623 vb.
  armed force 722 n.
  army 722 n.
  compel 740 vb.
  compulsion 740 n.
  paper money
   797 n.
draft-dodger
  avoider 620 n.
drag
  influence 178 n.
  counteraction
   182 n.
  transpose 272 vb.
  carriage 274 n.
  slowness 278 n.

draw 288 vb.
attract 291 vb.
attraction 291 n.
friction 333 n.
encumbrance
    702 n.
hindrance 702 n.
restraint 747 n.
annoyance 827 n.
be tedious 838 vb.
bore 838 n.
drag artist
    nonconformist
    84 n.
    entertainer 594 n.
drag down
    draw 288 vb.
    compel 740 vb.
drag in the mud
    not respect 921 vb.
dragnet
    generality 79 n.
    network 222 n.
    traction 288 n.
    chase 619 n.
drag on
    continue 108 vb.
dragon
    rara avis 84 n.
    violent creature
    176 n.
drag one's feet
    be late 136 vb.
    move slowly
    278 vb.
    be unwilling
    598 vb.
    be inactive 679 vb.
dragonfly
    insect 365 n.
dragoon
    cavalry 722 n.
    compel 740 vb.
drag out
    extract 304 vb.
    manifest 522 vb.
drag up
    elevate 310 vb.
drain
    receptacle 194 n.
    base 214 n.
    outflow 298 n.
    empty 300 vb.
    drink 301 vb.
    dry 342 vb.
    drain 351 n.
    cultivate 370 vb.

storage 632 n.
waste 634 vb.
purify 648 vb.
impair 655 vb.
use 673 vb.
fatigue 684 vb.
loss 772 n.
drainage
    outflow 298 n.
    voidance 300 n.
    desiccation 342 n.
    waste 634 n.
    cleansing 648 n.
    dirt 649 n.
drained
    weakened 163 adj.
    dry 342 adj.
draining
    outflow 298 n.
    desiccation 342 n.
drainpipe
    cylinder 252 n.
    outlet 298 n.
    drain 351 n.
drainpipes
    trousers 228 n.
drake
    bird 365 n.
    male animal
    372 n.
dram
    draught 301 n.
    metrology 465 n.
drama
    drama 594 n.
    stage play 594 n.
    activity 678 n.
    excitation 821 n.
    prodigy 864 n.
dramatic
    dramatic 594 adj.
    exciting 821 adj.
    impressive 821 adj.
    wonderful 864 adj.
    showy 875 adj.
dramatics
    dramaturgy 594 n.
    ostentation 875 n.
dramatis personae
    list 87 n.
    person 371 n.
    actor 594 n.
    personnel 686 n.
dramatist
    dramatist 594 n.
dramatize
    exaggerate 546 vb.

dramatize 594 vb.
dramatize oneself
    be affected 850 vb.
    be ostentatious
    875 vb.
dramaturgy
    dramaturgy 594 n.
drape
    hang 217 vb.
    pendency 217 n.
    dress 228 vb.
draper
    clothier 228 n.
drapes
    hanging object
    217 n.
    covering 226 n.
    curtain 421 n.
drastic
    severe 735 adj.
drat
    curse 899 int.
dratted
    damnable 645 adj.
draught
    transport 272 n.
    draught 301 n.
    gravity 322 n.
    ventilation 352 n.
    wind 352 n.
    anaesthetic 375 n.
    medicine 658 n.
    adversity 731 n.
    plaything 837 n.
draught beer
    alcoholic drink
    301 n.
draughtboard
    chequer 437 n.
draught horse
    draught horse
    273 n.
draughts
    board game 837 n.
draughtsman or -wo-
    man
    artist 556 n.
draughty
    windy 352 adj.
draw
    be equal 28 vb.
    draw 28 n.
    compose 56 vb.
    bring together
    74 vb.
    displace 188 vb.
    make thin 206 vb.

outline 233 vb.
form 243 vb.
draw 288 vb.
attraction 291 n.
cook 301 vb.
descend 309 vb.
blow 352 vb.
be hot 379 vb.
smoke 388 vb.
demonstrate
    478 V.
represent 551 vb.
paint 553 vb.
describe 590 vb.
gambling 618 n.
noncompletion
    726 n.
acquire 771 vb.
receive 782 vb.
desired object
    859 n.
draw a blank
    forget 506 vb.
    fail 728 vb.
    lose 772 vb.
draw a red herring
    be unrelated 10 vb.
    deflect 282 vb.
    distract 456 vb.
    avoid 620 vb.
    elude 667 vb.
draw back
    regress 286 vb.
    recede 290 vb.
    avoid 620 vb.
drawback
    evil 616 n.
    obstacle 702 n.
drawbridge
    doorway 263 n.
    bridge 624 n.
    means of escape
    667 n.
    fort 713 n.
drawer
    compartment
    194 n.
    artist 556 n.
drawers
    underwear 228 n.
draw in
    become small
    198 vb.
    make smaller
    198 vb.
    draw 288 vb.

drawing
  copy 22 n.
  representation
    551 n.
  painting 553 n.
  picture 553 n.
drawing and quarter-
  ing
  capital punishment
    963 n.
drawing pin
  fastening 47 n.
  sharp point 256 n.
drawing room
  chamber 194 n.
draw in one's horns
  submit 721 vb.
drawl
  lengthen 203 vb.
  move slowly
    278 vb.
  pronunciation
    577 n.
  voice 577 vb.
  speech defect
    580 n.
  stammer 580 vb.
draw lots
  gamble 618 vb.
drawn
  equal 28 adj.
  lean 206 adj.
drawn game
  draw 28 n.
  noncompletion
    726 n.
drawn out
  tedious 838 adj.
draw on
  avail oneself of
    673 vb.
  claim 915 vb.
draw out
  cause 156 vb.
  displace 188 vb.
  enlarge 197 vb.
  lengthen 203 vb.
  extract 304 vb.
  be diffuse 570 vb.
drawstring
  fastening 47 n.
  ligature 47 n.
draw the line
  exclude 57 vb.
  discriminate
    463 vb.
  restrain 747 vb.

prohibit 757 vb.
  retain 778 vb.
  disapprove 924 vb.
draw up
  compose 56 vb.
  be in order 60 vb.
  cease 145 vb.
  come to rest
    266 vb.
  arrive 295 vb.
  plan 623 vb.
draw upon
  draw money
    797 vb.
dread
  expect 507 vb.
  expectation 507 n.
  be nervous 854 vb.
  fear 854 n.
  fear 854 vb.
dreadful
  prodigious 32 adj.
  harmful 645 adj.
  not nice 645 adj.
  distressing 827 adj.
  frightening
    854 adj.
dreading
  expectant 507 adj.
  nervous 854 adj.
dreadlocks
  hair 259 n.
dream
  insubstantial thing
    4 n.
  visual fallacy
    440 n.
  be inattentive
    456 vb.
  error 495 n.
  fantasy 513 n.
  imagine 513 vb.
  objective 617 n.
  sleep 679 n.
  a beauty 841 n.
  hope 852 vb.
  desire 859 vb.
  desired object
    859 n.
dreamer
  visionary 513 n.
  avoider 620 n.
  idler 679 n.
dreaming
  imaginative
    513 adj.
  sleepy 679 adj.

hoping 852 adj.
dreamlike
  shadowy 419 adj.
  appearing 445 adj.
dreams
  sleep 679 n.
dreams come true
  content 828 n.
dream up
  imagine 513 vb.
dreamy
  thoughtful 449 adj.
  abstracted 456 adj.
  imaginary 513 adj.
dreary
  unpleasant
    827 adj.
  cheerless 834 adj.
  dejected 834 adj.
  melancholic
    834 adj.
  tedious 838 adj.
  dull 840 adj.
dredge
  extract 304 vb.
  let fall 311 vb.
dredger
  ship 275 n.
dredge up
  bring together
    74 vb.
  extract 304 vb.
  elevate 310 vb.
dregs
  leavings 41 n.
  extremity 69 n.
  dirt 649 n.
dreich
  unpleasant
    827 adj.
  cheerless 834 adj.
  dejected 834 adj.
  tedious 838 adj.
drench
  drench 341 vb.
Dresden china
  pottery 381 n.
dress
  equalize 28 vb.
  cover 226 vb.
  dress 228 n.
  dress 228 vb.
  dressing 228 n.
  cook 301 vb.
  doctor 658 vb.
  make ready
    669 vb.

dressage
  equitation 267 n.
dressed
  culinary 301 adj.
dressed to kill
  prepared 669 adj.
  fashionable
    848 adj.
  showy 875 adj.
dresser
  cabinet 194 n.
  shelf 218 n.
  stand 218 n.
  clothier 228 n.
dressing
  dressing 228 n.
  cookery 301 n.
  hors-d'oeuvres
    301 n.
  condiment 389 n.
  surgical dressing
    658 n.
dressing down
  reprimand 924 n.
dressing gown
  informal dress
    228 n.
dressing room
  chamber 194 n.
  theatre 594 n.
dressmaking
  dressing 228 n.
dress rehearsal
  dramaturgy 594 n.
  preparation 669 n.
dress up
  dress 228 vb.
  wear 228 vb.
  dissemble 541 vb.
  primp 843 vb.
  be vain 873 vb.
  be ostentatious
    875 vb.
dressy
  fashionable
    848 adj.
  showy 875 adj.
drey
  nest 192 n.
dribble
  small quantity
    33 n.
  move slowly
    278 vb.
  propel 287 vb.
  exude 298 vb.
  emit 300 vb.

flow 350 vb.
dribble (football)
  propulsion 287 n.
dried out
  dry 342 adj.
  sober 948 adj.
dried up
  unproductive
   172 adj.
  dry 342 adj.
drift
  leavings 41 n.
  vary 152 vb.
  tendency 179 n.
  distance 199 n.
  be in motion
   265 vb.
  motion 265 n.
  fly 271 vb.
  transference 272 n.
  move slowly
   278 vb.
  direction 281 n.
  deviation 282 n.
  shortfall 307 n.
  be light 323 vb.
  topic 452 n.
  meaning 514 n.
  compendium
   592 n.
  not act 677 vb.
drift apart
  be dispersed 75 vb.
drifter
  wanderer 268 n.
  fishing boat 275 n.
  idler 679 n.
drill
  make uniform
   16 vb.
  regularity 81 n.
  make conform
   83 vb.
  textile 222 n.
  sharp point 256 n.
  perforator 263 n.
  pierce 263 vb.
  farm tool 370 n.
  be loud 400 vb.
  teaching 534 n.
  train 534 vb.
  habit 610 n.
  habituation 610 n.
  practice 610 n.
  tool 630 n.
  make ready
   669 vb.

exercise 682 n.
  ostentation 875 n.
drink
  absorb 299 vb.
  draught 301 n.
  drink 301 vb.
  fluid 335 n.
  ocean 343 n.
drink a health
  toast 876 vb.
drink in
  be attentive 455 vb.
  learn 536 vb.
drinks
  social gathering
   882 n.
drink to
  toast 876 vb.
  pay one's respects
   884 vb.
  show respect
   920 vb.
  applaud 923 vb.
drip
  weakling 163 n.
  exude 298 vb.
  emit 300 vb.
  descend 309 vb.
  be wet 341 vb.
  moisture 341 n.
  flow 350 VB.
  rain 350 VB.
  ninny 501 n.
  medicine 658 n.
drip-dry
  dry 342 vb.
drip-feeding
  eating 301 n.
dripping
  humid 341 adj.
  flowing 350 adj.
  fat 357 n.
  moneyed 800 adj.
dripping with
  full 54 adj.
drive
  energy 160 n.
  operate 173 vb.
  be vigorous 174 vb.
  vigorousness 174 n.
  doorway 263 n.
  move 265 vb.
  land travel 267 n.
  ride 267 vb.
  accelerate 277 vb.
  move fast 277 vb.
  spurt 277 n.

impel 279 vb.
  propel 287 vb.
  propulsion 287 n.
  vigour 571 n.
  resolution 599 n.
  incite 612 vb.
  chase 619 n.
  access 624 n.
  path 624 n.
  be active 678 vb.
  restlessness 678 n.
  haste 680 n.
  hasten 680 vb.
  exertion 682 n.
  attack 712 n.
  attack 712 vb.
  dominate 733 vb.
  compel 740 vb.
drive (cricket)
  knock 279 n.
drive a coach and
   horses through
  confute 479 vb.
  not observe 769 vb.
drive a hard bargain
  bargain 791 vb.
drive apart
  set apart 46 vb.
drive away
  repel 292 vb.
drive a wedge be-
   tween
  set apart 46 vb.
  make quarrels
   709 vb.
drive home
  emphasize 532 vb.
  carry through
   725 vb.
  impress 821 vb.
drive in
  affix 45 vb.
  enter 297 vb.
drivel
  exude 298 vb.
  be foolish 499 vb.
  be insane 503 vb.
  mean nothing
   515 vb.
  silly talk 515 n.
  be diffuse 570 vb.
  be loquacious
   581 vb.
drive mad
  derange 63 vb.
  make mad 503 vb.
  enrage 891 vb.

drive off
  start out 296 vb.
driver
  driver 268 n.
  machinist 630 n.
drive to despair
  sadden 834 vb.
drive up the wall
  make mad 503 vb.
driveway
  doorway 263 n.
  access 624 n.
driving
  land travel 267 n.
  flowing 350 adj.
  resolute 599 adj.
driving at, be
  mean 514 vb.
driving force
  power 160 n.
  propellant 287 n.
  motive 612 n.
driving licence
  permit 756 n.
drizzle
  be wet 341 vb.
  moisture 341 n.
  rain 350 n.
  rain 350 VB.
droit du seigneur
  fixture 153 n.
droll
  witty 839 adj.
  funny 849 adj.
dromedary
  beast of burden
   273 n.
drone
  slowcoach 278 n.
  insect 365 n.
  faintness 401 n.
  sound faint 401 vb.
  roll 403 n.
  roll 403 vb.
  shrill 407 vb.
  stridor 407 n.
  ululate 409 vb.
  ululation 409 n.
  musical note
   410 n.
  discord 411 vb.
  voice 577 vb.
  stammer 580 vb.
  be loquacious
   581 vb.
  idler 679 n.

drone on
  be tedious 838 vb.
drool
  exude 298 vb.
  emit 300 vb.
  eat 301 vb.
droop
  be weak 163 vb.
  hang 217 vb.
  pendency 217 n.
  descend 309 vb.
  deteriorate 655 vb.
  be inactive 679 vb.
  be fatigued 684 vb.
  be dejected 834 vb.
drop
  small thing 33 n.
  decrease 37 n.
  decrease 37 vb.
  tincture 43 n.
  terminate 69 vb.
  be weak 163 vb.
  reproduce itself
    167 vb.
  minuteness 196 n.
  be deep 211 vb.
  depth 211 n.
  hanging object
    217 n.
  sphere 252 n.
  swelling 253 n.
  move 265 vb.
  regress 286 vb.
  regression 286 n.
  exude 298 vb.
  dismiss 300 vb.
  emit 300 vb.
  descend 309 vb.
  descent 309 n.
  let fall 311 vb.
  moisture 341 n.
  flow 350 VB.
  blow 352 vb.
  relinquish 621 vb.
  stop using 674 vb.
  be fatigued 684 vb.
  be clumsy 695 vb.
  not retain 779 vb.
  jewellery 844 n.
drop a brick
  blunder 495 vb.
  be clumsy 695 vb.
drop anchor
  place oneself
    187 vb.
  navigate 269 vb.
  arrive 295 vb.

drop behind
  be behind 238 vb.
drop down dead
  perish 361 vb.
drop in
  arrive 295 vb.
  enter 297 vb.
  insert 303 vb.
  visit 882 vb.
droplet
  small thing 33 n.
  minuteness 196 n.
  sphere 252 n.
  moisture 341 n.
drop off
  sleep 679 vb.
drop out
  be unconformable
    84 vb.
  relinquish 621 vb.
  not complete
    726 vb.
  be free 744 vb.
dropout
  nonconformist
    84 n.
  dissentient 489 n.
  loser 728 n.
  malcontent 829 n.
  abstainer 942 n.
droppings
  excrement 302 n.
  dirt 649 n.
drops
  medicine 658 n.
dropsy
  dilation 197 n.
  fluid 335 n.
dross
  leavings 41 n.
  layer 207 n.
  rubbish 641 n.
  dirt 649 n.
drought
  dryness 342 n.
  scarcity 636 n.
  blight 659 n.
drouth
  dryness 342 n.
drove
  group 74 n.
drown
  fill 54 vb.
  destroy 165 vb.
  suppress 165 vb.
  descend 309 vb.
  lower 311 vb.

  founder 313 vb.
  plunge 313 vb.
  drench 341 vb.
  perish 361 vb.
  kill 362 vb.
  obliterate 550 vb.
drowned
  full 54 adj.
  deep 211 adj.
drowning
  plenitude 54 n.
  killing 362 n.
  capital punishment
    963 n.
drown one's sorrows
  revel 837 vb.
  get drunk 949 vb.
drowsy
  sleepy 679 adj.
drubbing
  defeat 728 n.
  corporal punish-
    ment 963 n.
drudge
  work 682 vb.
  worker 686 n.
  servant 742 n.
drug
  render insensible
    375 vb.
  doctor 658 vb.
  drug 658 n.
  make inactive
    679 vb.
drug abuse
  drug-taking 949 n.
drug addict
  the maladjusted
    504 n.
  sensualist 944 n.
  drug-taking 949 n.
druggist
  druggist 658 n.
drug-pusher
  drug-taking 949 n.
drug-taking
  drug-taking 949 n.
drug traffic
  trade 791 n.
Druid
  sorcerer 983 n.
  priest 986 n.
drum
  vat 194 n.
  cylinder 252 n.
  strike 279 vb.
  oscillate 317 vb.

  roll 403 vb.
  play music 413 vb.
  drum 414 n.
  call 547 n.
drumbeat
  periodicity 141 n.
  impulse 279 n.
  call 547 n.
drumfire
  roll 403 vb.
drum major
  instrumentalist
    413 n.
  leader 690 n.
drummer
  instrumentalist
    413 n.
drummer boy
  instrumentalist
    413 n.
drum one's fingers
  be excitable
    822 vb.
drum-roll
  call 547 n.
drums
  orchestra 413 n.
drunk
  drunk 949 adj.
  drunkard 949 n.
drunkard
  drunkard 949 n.
drunken
  drunken 949 adj.
  tipsy 949 adj.
drupe
  flower 366 n.
dry
  dry 342 adj.
  dry 342 vb.
  sour 393 adj.
  forget 506 vb.
  feeble 572 adj.
  act 594 vb.
  mature 669 vb.
  political party
    708 n.
  tedious 838 adj.
  witty 839 adj.
  hungry 859 adj.
  temperate 942 adj.
  sober 948 adj.
dryad
  nymph 967 n.
dry-cleaning
  cleansing 648 n.

dry dock
stable 192 n.
dryer
dryer 342 n.
dry goods
merchandise
795 n.
drying
desiccation 342 n.
dryness
desert 172 n.
dryness 342 n.
tedium 838 n.
wit 839 n.
dry out
disaccustom
611 vb.
be sober 948 vb.
dry rot
destroyer 168 n.
blight 659 n.
dry run
experiment 461 n.
dry up
cease 145 vb.
dry 342 vb.
hush 399 int.
be mute 578 vb.
be taciturn 582 vb.
not suffice 636 vb.
dry wine
wine 301 n.
DT's
agitation 318 n.
frenzy 503 n.
alcoholism 949 n.
dual
dual 90 adj.
grammatical
564 adj.
dual carriageway
traffic control
305 n.
road 624 n.
duality
duality 90 n.
dual personality
duality 90 n.
spirit 447 n.
personality disor-
der 503 n.
dual-purpose
double 91 adj.
dub
name 561 vb.
dignify 866 vb.

dubiety
dubiety 474 n.
dubious
improbable
472 adj.
doubting 474 adj.
uncertain 474 adj.
disreputable
867 adj.
ducal
noble 868 adj.
ducat
coinage 797 n.
duchess
potentate 741 n.
person of rank
868 n.
duck
zero 103 n.
be oblique 220 vb.
textile 222 n.
be in motion
265 vb.
swim 269 vb.
immerse 303 vb.
descend 309 vb.
lower 311 vb.
obeisance 311 n.
stoop 311 vb.
plunge 313 vb.
be wet 341 vb.
drench 341 vb.
bird 365 n.
table bird 365 n.
be unwilling
598 vb.
avoid 620 vb.
avoidance 620 n.
servility 879 n.
darling 890 n.
respects 920 n.
punish 963 vb.
ducking
lowering 311 n.
plunge 313 n.
corporal punish-
ment 963 n.
duckling
young creature
132 n.
bird 365 n.
duck pond
stock farm 369 n.
ducks and drakes
recoil 280 n.
duck's disease
shortness 204 n.

duck the issue
avoid 620 vb.
ducky
darling 890 n.
duct
tube 263 n.
conduit 351 n.
ductile
flexible 327 adj.
elastic 328 adj.
dud
powerless 161 adj.
useless 641 adj.
ammunition 723 n.
loser 728 n.
unsuccessful
728 adj.
dude
dupe 544 n.
fop 848 n.
dudgeon
sidearms 723 n.
anger 891 n.
duds
clothing 228 n.
due
future 124 adj.
impending 155 adj.
due 915 adj.
duel
duality 90 n.
duel 716 n.
fight 716 vb.
duenna
protector 660 n.
keeper 749 n.
dues
receiving 782 n.
receipt 807 n.
price 809 n.
tax 809 n.
dueness 915 n.
duet
duality 90 n.
cooperation 706 n.
concord 710 n.
due to
caused 157 adj.
duffer
ignoramus 493 n.
dunce 501 n.
bungler 697 n.
dug
bosom 253 n.
dugout
concave 255 adj.
excavation 255 n.

furrow 262 n.
rowing boat 275 n.
refuge 662 n.
defences 713 n.
duke
potentate 741 n.
pincers 778 n.
person of rank
868 n.
dukedom
political organiza-
tion 733 n.
aristocracy 868 n.
dulcet
melodious 410 adj.
pleasurable
826 adj.
dulcimer
piano 414 n.
dull
assuage 177 vb.
blunt 257 vb.
render insensible
375 vb.
mute 401 vb.
muted 401 adj.
dim 419 adj.
colourless 426 adj.
grey 429 adj.
ignorant 491 adj.
unintelligent
499 adj.
feeble 572 adj.
nonactive 677 adj.
inactive 679 adj.
impassive 820 adj.
cheerless 834 adj.
serious 834 adj.
dull 840 adj.
dullard
dunce 501 n.
dull of hearing
deaf 416 adj.
duly
as promised
764 adv.
dumb
ignorant 491 adj.
uninstructed
491 adj.
See **ignorant**
unintelligent
499 adj.
voiceless 578 adj.
dumbfound
surprise 508 vb.
disappoint 509 vb.

make mute 578 vb.
be wonderful
864 vb.
dumb show
gesture 547 n.
representation
551 n.
drama 594 n.
dummy
copy 22 n.
prototype 23 n.
substituted 150 adj.
moderator 177 n.
sham 542 n.
image 551 n.
dump
accumulation 74 n.
computerize 86 vb.
small house 192 n.
storage 632 n.
store 632 vb.
rubbish 641 n.
stop using 674 vb.
dumpling
bulk 195 n.
pastries and cakes
301 n.
dumps
dejection 834 n.
sullenness 893 n.
dump truck
lorry 274 n.
dumpy
fleshy 195 adj.
dwarfish 196 adj.
short 204 adj.
thick 205 adj.
unsightly 842 adj.
dun
horse 273 n.
dim 419 adj.
grey 429 adj.
brown 430 adj.
demand 737 vb.
request 761 vb.
torment 827 vb.
dunce
dunce 501 n.
dunderhead
dunce 501 n.
dung
fertilizer 171 n.
excrement 302 n.
stench 397 n.
dirt 649 n.
dungarees
suit 228 n.

trousers 228 n.
dungeon
cellar 194 n.
depth 211 n.
lockup 748 n.
prison 748 n.
dunghill
sink 649 n.
dunk
drench 341 vb.
clean 648 vb.
duo
duality 90 n.
duodenal ulcer
digestive disorders
651 n.
dupe
deceive 542 vb.
fool 542 vb.
dupe 544 n.
defraud 788 vb.
toady 879 n.
duplex
dual 90 adj.
double 91 adj.
flat 192 n.
duplicate
identity 13 n.
copy 20 vb.
duplicate 22 n.
augment 36 vb.
double 91 adj.
double 91 vb.
repeat 106 vb.
reproduce 166 vb.
label 547 n.
be superfluous
637 vb.
duplicity
duplicity 541 n.
durable
lasting 113 adj.
perpetual 115 adj.
permanent 144 adj.
unchangeable
153 adj.
tough 329 adj.
duration
time 108 n.
course of time
111 n.
permanence 144 n.
duress
compulsion 740 n.
detention 747 n.
restriction 747 n.

during
while 108 adv.
dusk
evening 129 n.
darkness 418 n.
dim 419 adj.
half-light 419 n.
dusky
dark 418 adj.
dim 419 adj.
blackish 428 adj.
dust
minuteness 196 n.
let fall 311 vb.
lightness 323 n.
powder 332 n.
soil 344 n.
trifle 639 n.
rubbish 641 n.
clean 648 vb.
dirt 649 n.
sink 649 n.
dustbin
vessel 194 n.
cleaning utensil
648 n.
sink 649 n.
dustbowl
desert 172 n.
dustcart
cart 274 n.
lorry 274 n.
duster
overcoat 228 n.
cleaning cloth
648 n.
cleaning utensil
648 n.
dusting
knock 279 n.
powderiness 332 n.
dust jacket
wrapping 226 n.
bookbinding 589 n.
dustman
cleaner 648 n.
worker 686 n.
dust of ages
oldness 127 n.
**dust thrown in the
eyes**
pretext 614 n.
stratagem 698 n.
dustup
turmoil 61 n.
quarrel 709 n.
fight 716 n.

dusty
powdery 332 adj.
dry 342 adj.
dirty 649 adj.
Dutch auction
sale 793 n.
cheapness 812 n.
Dutch cap
contraception
172 n.
Dutch courage
courage 855 n.
cowardice 856 n.
drunkenness 949 n.
Dutch hoe
farm tool 370 n.
Dutch oven
pot 194 n.
Dutch treat
participation
775 n.
Dutch uncle
adviser 691 n.
tyrant 735 n.
duteous
obliged 917 n.
trustworthy
929 adj.
dutiful
obedient 739 adj.
obliged 917 adj.
trustworthy
929 adj.
virtuous 933 adj.
duty
function 622 n.
job 622 n.
tax 809 n.
duty 917 n.
respects 920 n.
church service
988 n.
duty-bound
obliged 917 adj.
duvet
bed 218 n.
coverlet 226 n.
dux
victor 727 n.
dwarf
abate 37 vb.
dwarf 196 n.
dwarfish 196 adj.
make smaller
198 vb.
star 321 n.
elf 970 n.

assent 488 vb.
echoing
imitative 20 adj.
repeated 106 adj.
resonant 404 adj.
eclair
pastries and cakes
301 n.
éclat
vigorousness 174 n.
prestige 866 n.
eclectic
mixed 43 adj.
eclipse
be superior 34 vb.
darken 418 vb.
darkening 418 n.
be unseen 444 vb.
disappearance
446 n.
conceal 525 vb.
have a reputation
866 vb.
ecology
situation 186 n.
biology 358 n.
economical
cheap 812 adj.
economical
814 adj.
economics
management
689 n.
economize
economize 814 vb.
economy
cheap 812 adj.
economy 814 n.
economy of truth
falsehood 541 n.
untruth 543 n.
economy size
large 195 adj.
cheap 812 adj.
ecosphere
situation 186 n.
world 321 n.
ecosystem
situation 186 n.
organism 358 n.
ecotype
organism 358 n.
ecru
whitish 427 adj.
brown 430 adj.
ecstasy
pleasure 376 n.

frenzy 503 n.
imagination 513 n.
warm feeling
818 n.
excitable state
822 n.
joy 824 n.
love 887 n.
ecstatic
impressed 818 adj.
rejoicing 835 adj.
approving 923 adj.
ECT
therapy 658 n.
ectopic
unconformable
84 adj.
ectoplasm
spiritualism 984 n.
ecumenical
universal 79 adj.
orthodox 976 adj.
eczema
skin disease 651 n.
blemish 845 n.
eddy
changeable thing
152 n.
rotate 315 vb.
eddy 350 n.
Eden
mythic heaven
971 n.
edge
advantage 34 n.
be oblique 220 vb.
circumscribe
232 vb.
edge 234 n.
hem 234 vb.
limit 236 vb.
flank 239 vb.
sharpen 256 vb.
pungency 388 n.
victory 727 n.
edge in
introduce 231 vb.
enter 297 vb.
edge out
depose 752 vb.
not retain 779 vb.
edging
edging 234 n.
lateral 239 adj.
edgy
excitable 822 adj.
irascible 892 adj.

edible
edible 301 adj.
edict
publication 528 n.
decree 737 n.
legislation 953 n.
edification
teaching 534 n.
benefit 615 n.
edifice
edifice 164 n.
edify
educate 534 vb.
  See **teach**
benefit 615 vb.
do good 644 vb.
edit
modify 143 vb.
interpret 520 vb.
publish 528 vb.
rectify 654 vb.
edition
the press 528 n.
edition 589 n.
editor
interpreter 520 n.
author 589 n.
bookperson 589 n.
dissertator 591 n.
reformer 654 n.
editorial
intrepretative
520 adj.
publicity 528 n.
article 591 n.
EDP
data processing
86 n.
educate
produce 164 vb.
educate 534 vb.
education
culture 490 n.
knowledge 490 n.
education 534 n.
teaching 534 n.
vocation 622 n.
educational
educational
534 adj.
educationalist
teacher 537 n.
EEC
society 708 n.
trade 791 n.
market 796 n.

EEG
diagnostic 658 n.
eel
serpent 251 n.
fish food 301 n.
fish 365 n.
eerie
frightening
854 adj.
spooky 970 adj.
efface
destroy 165 vb.
obliterate 550 vb.
efface oneself
be modest 874 vb.
effect
cause 156 vb.
caused 157 adj.
effect 157 n.
produce 164 vb.
sense 374 n.
appearance 445 n.
spectacle 445 n.
carry out 725 vb.
succeed 727 vb.
ostentation 875 n.
effective
powerful 160 adj.
influential 178 adj.
appearing 445 adj.
forceful 571 adj.
instrumental
628 adj.
useful 640 adj.
successful 727 adj.
effects
property 777 n.
effectual
powerful 160 adj.
operative 173 adj.
useful 640 adj.
effeminate
weak 163 adj.
female 373 adj.
effervescent
vigorous 174 adj.
gaseous 336 adj.
bubbly 355 adj.
lively 819 adj.
excited 821 adj.
excitable 822 adj.
merry 833 adj.
effete
impotent 161 adj.
weakened 163 adj.
efficacious
powerful 160 adj.

operative 173 adj.
useful 640 adj.
successful 727 adj.
efficacy
  ability 160 n.
  instrumentality
    628 n.
  utility 640 n.
efficiency
  ability 160 n.
  agency 173 n.
  utility 640 n.
efficient
  operative 173 adj.
  useful 640 adj.
  industrious
    678 adj.
effigy
  copy 22 n.
  image 551 n.
efflorescence
  powder 332 n.
  ripening 669 n.
effluence
  outflow 298 n.
  current 350 n.
effluvial
  gaseous 336 adj.
effluvium
  gas 336 n.
efflux
  egress 298 n.
  outflow 298 n.
effort
  power 160 n.
  vigorousness 174 n.
  attempt 671 n.
  action 676 n.
  exertion 682 n.
effortless
  easy 701 adj.
effrontery
  insolence 878 n.
effulgence
  light 417 n.
effusion
  outflow 298 n.
  ejection 300 n.
  diffuseness 570 n.
effusive
  diffuse 570 adj.
  feeling 818 adj.
  friendly 880 adj.
eft
  amphibian 365 n.
egalitarian
  uniformist 16 n.

just 913 adj.
egest
  emit 300 vb.
egg
  origin 68 n.
  source 156 n.
  product 164 n.
  genitalia 167 n.
eggcup
  cup 194 n.
egghead
  intellectual 492 n.
  sage 500 n.
egg on
  invigorate 174 vb.
  incite 612 vb.
  animate 821 vb.
eggshell
  weak thing 163 n.
  brittle 330 adj.
  brittleness 330 n.
eggspoon
  ladle 194 n.
egg timer
  timekeeper 117 n.
ego
  intrinsicality 5 n.
  self 80 n.
  subjectivity 320 n.
  spirit 447 n.
egocentric
  vain 873 adj.
  selfish 932 adj.
egoistic
  selfish 932 adj.
egotism
  overestimation
    482 n.
  vanity 873 n.
  selfishness 932 n.
egotist
  vain person 873 n.
  egotist 932 n.
ego trip
  selfishness 932 n.
egress
  egress 298 n.
  emerge 298 vb.
eiderdown
  coverlet 226 n.
eidetic
  obvious 443 adj.
eight
  band 74 n.
  over five 99 n.
  rowing boat 275 n.
  party 708 n.

eights
  racing 716 n.
eighty
  twenty and over
    99 n.
eisteddfod
  assembly 74 n.
  music 412 n.
  choir 413 n.
ejaculate
  cry 408 vb.
  voice 577 vb.
eject
  fly 271 vb.
  eject 300 vb.
eke out
  make complete
    54 vb.
elaborate
  complex 61 adj.
  ornament 574 vb.
  mature 669 vb.
  carry through
    725 vb.
  completed 725 adj.
  ornamental
    844 adj.
elaboration
  completion 725 n.
élan
  vigorousness 174 n.
  vigour 571 n.
  resolution 599 n.
  courage 855 n.
elapse
  elapse 111 vb.
  be past 125 vb.
elastic
  elastic 328 adj.
  elasticity 328 n.
elastic band
  elasticity 328 n.
elasticity
  elasticity 328 n.
Elastoplast (tdmk)
  adhesive 47 n.
  covering 226 n.
  surgical dressing
    658 n.
elated
  excitable 822 adj.
  pleased 824 adj.
  jubilant 833 adj.
  rejoicing 835 adj.
elbow
  joint 45 n.

be contiguous
    202 vb.
  angularity 247 n.
  curve 248 n.
  impel 279 vb.
  obstruct 702 vb.
elbow grease
  friction 333 n.
  exertion 682 n.
elbows out
  depose 752 vb.
  not retain 779 vb.
  deprive 786 vb.
elbowroom
  room 183 n.
  scope 744 n.
elder
  prior 119 adj.
  older 131 adj.
  tree 366 n.
  church officer
    986 n.
  ecclesiarch 986 n.
  lay person 987 n.
elderly
  ageing 131 adj.
elders
  seniority 131 n.
**elder statesman or -
  woman**
  old man 133 n.
  sage 500 n.
eldest
  precursor 66 n.
  prior 119 adj.
  priority 119 n.
  older 131 adj.
El Dorado
  fantasy 513 n.
  objective 617 n.
  wealth 800 n.
  aspiration 852 n.
eldritch
  spooky 970 adj.
  magical 983 adj.
elect
  choose 605 vb.
  chosen 605 adj.
  vote 605 vb.
  commission
    751 vb.
election
  choice 605 n.
  vote 605 n.
  mandate 751 n.
electioneering
  vote 605 n.

677

elector
estimator 480 n.
electorate 605 n.
electoral college
electorate 605 n.
electoral roll
list 87 n.
electorate 605 n.
electoral system
vote 605 n.
electorate
electorate 605 n.
tribunal 956 n.
electric
dynamic 160 adj.
excitable 822 adj.
electrical
dynamic 160 adj.
electrical engineering
electronics 160 n.
electrical fault
failure 728 n.
electric blanket
heater 383 n.
electric bulb
lamp 420 n.
electric chair
seat 218 n.
condemnation 961 n.
capital punishment 963 n.
means of execution 964 n.
electric cooker
furnace 383 n.
electric current
electricity 160 n.
electric drill
tool 630 n.
electric fire
fire 379 n.
electric guitar
stringed instrument 414 n.
electrician
artisan 686 n.
electric iron
smoother 258 n.
heater 383 n.
electricity
electricity 160 n.
velocity 277 n.
heater 383 n.
electric kettle
heater 383 n.

electric lamp
lamp 420 n.
electric light
light 417 n.
electric or electronic organ
organ 414 n.
electric railway
train 274 n.
railway 624 n.
electric razor
cosmetic 843 n.
electric toaster
heater 383 n.
electric train
train 274 n.
electrify
invigorate 174 vb.
surprise 508 vb.
excite 821 vb.
be wonderful 864 vb.
electrocute
kill 362 vb.
execute 963 vb.
electrode
electricity 160 n.
electrodynamics
electricity 160 n.
electrolysis
decomposition 51 n.
stripper 229 n.
beautification 843 n.
electromagnetism
electricity 160 n.
physics 319 n.
electron
minuteness 196 n.
element 319 n.
electronic
computerized 86 adj.
dynamic 160 adj.
instrumental 628 adj.
mechanical 630 adj.
electronic calculator
counting instrument 86 n.
electronic mail
message 529 n.
telecommunication 531 n.

electronic music
music 412 n.
electronics
electronics 160 n.
electronic surveillance
surveillance 457 n.
protection 660 n.
electron microscope
microscope 442 n.
electroplate
coat 226 vb.
electrostatics
electricity 160 n.
electrotherapy
therapy 658 n.
electrotype
print 587 n.
elegance
elegance 575 n.
wit 839 n.
fashion 848 n.
elegant
stylistic 566 adj.
elegant 575 adj.
witty 839 adj.
personable 841 adj.
shapely 841 adj.
fashionable 848 adj.
elegiac
funereal 364 adj.
poetic 593 adj.
lamenting 836 adj.
elegy
obsequies 364 n.
poem 593 n.
lament 836 n.
element
tincture 43 n.
part 53 n.
component 58 n.
source 156 n.
filament 208 n.
element 319 n.
person 371 n.
elemental
intrinsic 5 adj.
simple 44 adj.
fundamental 156 adj.
elementary
simple 44 adj.
beginning 68 adj.
elements, the
weather 340 n.

elephant
giant 195 n.
tall creature 209 n.
beast of burden 273 n.
mammal 365 n.
elephantine
large 195 adj.
unwieldy 195 adj.
animal 365 adj.
elevate
elevate 310 vb.
purify 648 vb.
make better 654 vb.
delight 826 vb.
dignify 866 vb.
elevated
proud 871 adj.
disinterested 931 adj.
elevation
height 209 n.
verticality 215 n.
elevation 310 n.
feature 445 n.
map 551 n.
cheerfulness 833 n.
holy orders 985 n.
elevator
conveyance 267 n.
ascent 308 n.
eleven
band 74 n.
over five 99 n.
party 708 n.
elevenses
meal 301 n.
eleventh hour
late 136 adj.
lateness 136 n.
crisis 137 n.
elf
elf 970 n.
elfin
little 196 adj.
fairylike 970 adj.
elicit
cause 156 vb.
extract 304 vb.
discover 484 vb.
manifest 522 vb.
excite 821 vb.
eligible
included 78 adj.
eliminate
render few 105 vb.

678

eject 300 vb.
empty 300 vb.
extract 304 vb.
obliterate 550 vb.
exempt 919 vb.
elision
contraction 198 n.
prosody 593 n.
elite
elite 644 n.
elitism
government 733 n.
elixir
medicine 658 n.
remedy 658 n.
elk
mammal 365 n.
ellipse
arc 250 n.
ellipsis
punctuation 547 n.
grammar 564 n.
imperspicuity
568 n.
conciseness 569 n.
elliptic
round 250 adj.
concise 569 adj.
elm
tree 366 n.
elocution
pronunciation
577 n.
eloquence 579 n.
oratory 579 n.
speech 579 n.
elongate
lengthen 203 vb.
elope
decamp 296 vb.
run away 620 vb.
escape 667 vb.
wed 894 vb.
eloquence
eloquence 579 n.
eloquent
intelligible 516 adj.
stylistic 566 adj.
eloquent 579 adj.
else
in addition 38 adv.
elucidate
be intelligible
516 vb.
interpret 520 vb.
elude
elude 667 vb.

not observe 769 vb.
elusive
impracticable
470 adj.
puzzling 517 adj.
elves
elf 970 n.
Elysium
happiness 824 n.
mythic heaven
971 n.
em
print-type 587 n.
emaciated
lean 206 adj.
underfed 636 adj.
unhealthy 651 adj.
emanate
happen 154 vb.
result 157 vb.
emerge 298 vb.
be plain 522 vb.
emanation
egress 298 n.
excretion 302 n.
appearance 445 n.
revelation 975 n.
emancipated
free 744 adj.
emancipation
freedom 744 n.
independence
744 n.
liberation 746 n.
emasculated
impotent 161 adj.
feeble 572 adj.
embalm
inter 364 vb.
preserve 666 vb.
embankment
support 218 n.
earthwork 253 n.
railway 624 n.
safeguard 662 n.
obstacle 702 n.
defences 713 n.
embargo
exclusion 57 n.
quiescence 266 n.
hindrance 702 n.
command 737 n.
restrain 747 vb.
restraint 747 n.
prohibition 757 n.
nonpayment 805 n.

embark
voyage 269 vb.
start out 296 vb.
embarkation
start 68 n.
departure 296 n.
embark on
begin 68 vb.
undertake 672 vb.
embarras de
richesses
greatness 32 n.
productiveness
171 n.
plenty 635 n.
redundance 637 n.
superfluity 637 n.
embarrass
trouble 827 vb.
embarrassment
predicament 700 n.
annoyance 827 n.
guilt 936 n.
embassy
house 192 n.
commission 751 n.
envoy 754 n.
embed
place 187 vb.
implant 303 vb.
embellish
add 38 vb.
make better
654 vb.
decorate 844 vb.
embers
coal 385 n.
embezzle
defraud 788 vb.
embittered
discontented
829 adj.
hostile 881 adj.
resentful 891 adj.
emblazon
colour 425 vb.
mark 547 vb.
decorate 844 vb.
emblem
badge 547 n.
indication 547 n.
talisman 983 n.
emblematic
insubstantial 4 adj.
heraldic 547 adj.
embody
combine 50 vb.

contain 56 vb.
comprise 78 vb.
materialize 319 vb.
represent 551 vb.
embolism
interjection 231 n.
closure 264 n.
*cardiovascular dis-
ease* 651 n.
embonpoint
bulk 195 n.
emboss
mark 547 vb.
sculpt 554 vb.
decorate 844 vb.
embrace
join 45 vb.
unite with 45 vb.
cohere 48 vb.
contain 56 vb.
comprise 78 vb.
surround 230 vb.
circumscribe
232 vb.
enclose 235 vb.
choose 605 vb.
be wont 610 vb.
retain 778 vb.
retention 778 n.
be friendly 880 vb.
sociability 882 n.
greet 884 vb.
love 887 vb.
caress 889 vb.
endearment 889 n.
embrasure
window 263 n.
embrocation
unguent 357 n.
balm 658 n.
embroider
variegate 437 vb.
fake 541 vb.
exaggerate 546 vb.
decorate 844 vb.
embroidery
adjunct 40 n.
exaggeration
546 n.
art 551 n.
ornament 574 n.
needlework 844 n.
embroil
bedevil 63 vb.
enrage 891 vb.

embryo
young creature
132 n.
source 156 n.
undevelopment
670 n.

embryonic
beginning 68 adj.
converted 147 adj.
impending 155 adj.
amorphous
244 adj.
immature 670 adj.

emend
rectify 654 vb.
repair 656 vb.

emendation
amendment 654 n.
repair 656 n.

emerald
green 434 adj.
greenness 434 n.
gem 844 n.

emerge
begin 68 vb.
emerge 298 vb.

emergence
beginning 68 n.
egress 298 n.

emergency
crisis 137 n.
event 154 n.
needfulness 627 n.
danger 661 n.
predicament 700 n.

emeritus
prior 119 adj.
former 125 adj.

emersion
egress 298 n.

emery board
smoother 258 n.
roughness 259 n.
pulverizer 332 n.

emetic
purgative 658 n.
remedial 658 adj.

emigrant
foreigner 59 n.
wanderer 268 n.

emigrate
travel 267 vb.
recede 290 vb.
depart 296 vb.
emerge 298 vb.

emigration
recession 290 n.

emo
departure 296 n.
egress 298 n.

émigré
foreigner 59 n.
wanderer 268 n.

eminence
greatness 32 n.
superiority 34 n.
height 209 n.
high land 209 n.
prominence 254 n.
elevation 310 n.
importance 638 n.
goodness 644 n.
prestige 866 n.

éminence grise
latency 523 n.
deputy 755 n.

eminent
remarkable 32 adj.
high 209 adj.
notable 638 adj.
noteworthy
866 adj.

eminently
eminently 34 adv.

emir
potentate 741 n.
person of rank
868 n.

emissary
messenger 529 n.
delegate 754 n.
envoy 754 n.

emission
outflow 298 n.
ejection 300 n.

emit
emit 300 vb.
publish 528 vb.

emmet
foreigner 59 n.
insect 365 n.

Emmy award
trophy 729 n.

emollient
soft 327 adj.
lubricant 334 n.
balm 658 n.
remedial 658 adj.

emolument
earnings 771 n.
pay 804 n.
receipt 807 n.
reward 962 n.

emotion
feeling 818 n.

emp
warm feeling
818 n.
excitation 821 n.

emotional
with affections
817 adj.
feeling 818 adj.
impressible
819 adj.
excitable 822 adj.

emotions
affections 817 n.

emotive
descriptive 590 adj.
exciting 821 adj.

empathy
bond 47 n.
attraction 291 n.
imagination 513 n.
participation
775 n.
feeling 818 n.
benevolence 897 n.
pity 905 n.

emperor
sovereign 741 n.
aristocrat 868 n.

emphasis
trope 519 n.
affirmation 532 n.
vigour 571 n.
pronunciation
577 n.
importance 638 n.

emphasize
emphasize 532 vb.

emphatic
strong 162 adj.
florid 425 adj.
expressive 516 adj.
assertive 532 adj.
forceful 571 adj.

emphysema
swelling 253 n.
respiratory disease
651 n.

empire
territory 184 n.
governance 733 n.
*political organiza-
tion* 733 n.

empirical
enquiring 459 adj.
experimental
461 adj.

empiricism
philosophy 449 n.

emu
empiricism 461 n.

emplacement
place 185 n.
situation 186 n.
location 187 n.
station 187 n.
stand 218 n.
fortification 713 n.

employ
employ 622 vb.
job 622 n.
use 673 vb.

employee
worker 686 n.
servant 742 n.

employer
director 690 n.
master 741 n.

employment
business 622 n.
job 622 n.
utility 640 n.
use 673 n.

employment agency
job 622 n.

emporium
emporium 796 n.
shop 796 n.

empowered
powerful 160 adj.
authoritative
733 adj.

empress
sovereign 741 n.

emptiness
emptiness 190 n.
lack of meaning
515 n.
vanity 873 n.

empty
empty 190 adj.
empty 300 vb.
meaningless
515 n.
untrue 543 adj.
feeble 572 adj.
hungry 859 adj.
fasting 946 adj.

empty-headed
mindless 448 adj.
ignorant 491 adj.

empyreal
celestial 321 adj.

em rule
punctuation 547 n.

emu
bird 365 n.

emulate
do likewise 20 vb.
imitate 20 vb.
contend 716 vb.

emulsify
thicken 354 vb.

emulsion
coat 226 vb.
facing 226 n.
semiliquidity 354 n.
viscidity 354 n.

emulsion paint
pigment 425 n.

en
print-type 587 n.

enable
make possible 469 vb.
facilitate 701 vb.
permit 756 vb.

enact
show 522 vb.
represent 551 vb.
act 594 vb.
do 676 vb.
deal with 688 vb.
carry out 725 vb.
decree 737 vb.
make legal 953 vb.

enactment
representation 551 n.
dramaturgy 594 n.
action 676 n.
precept 693 n.
decree 737 n.
legislation 953 n.

enamel
coat 226 vb.
facing 226 n.
smoother 258 n.
colour 425 vb.
decorate 844 vb.

enamoured
enamoured 887 adj.

encampment
station 187 n.
abode 192 n.
fort 713 n.

encapsulate
comprise 78 vb.
cover 226 vb.
abstract 592 vb.

encase
cover 226 vb.

circumscribe 232 vb.

enceinte
fertilized 167 adj.

encephalitis
infection 651 n.

enchant
convert 147 vb.
subjugate 745 vb.
delight 826 vb.
be wonderful 864 vb.
bewitch 983 vb.

enchanted
pleased 824 adj.
enamoured 887 adj.
bewitched 983 adj.
magical 983 adj.

enchantress
a beauty 841 n.
sorceress 983 n.

encircle
comprise 78 vb.
surround 230 vb.
circumscribe 232 vb.
circuit 626 vb.

enclave
region 184 n.

enclose
circumscribe 232 vb.
enclose 235 vb.
close 264 vb.

enclosure
contents 193 n.
enclosure 235 n.
correspondence 588 n.

encode
translate 520 vb.
conceal 525 vb.

encompass
comprise 78 vb.
extend 183 vb.
surround 230 vb.
circumscribe 232 vb.
limit 236 vb.
circuit 626 vb.

encore
double 91 vb.
duplication 91 n.
again 106 vb.
repetition 106 n.
dramaturgy 594 n.

applause 923 n.
bravo 923 int.

encounter
synchronize 123 vb.
event 154 n.
meet with 154 vb.
contiguity 202 n.
collide 279 vb.
collision 279 n.
arrival 295 n.
meet 295 vb.
discover 484 vb.
withstand 704 vb.
fight 716 n.
fight 716 vb.

encourage
incite 612 vb.
make better 654 vb.
aid 703 vb.
animate 821 vb.
relieve 831 vb.
cheer 833 vb.

encouragement
causation 156 n.
impulse 279 n.
inducement 612 n.
aid 703 n.
excitation 821 n.
courage 855 n.

encroach
encroach 306 vb.
be illegal 954 vb.

encroachment
progression 285 n.
overstepping 306 n.
wrong 914 n.
arrogation 916 n.
undueness 916 n.
lawbreaking 954 n.

encrust
coat 226 vb.
line 227 vb.
decorate 844 vb.

encumbrance
gravity 322 n.
encumbrance 702 n.

encyclopaedia
erudition 490 n.
reference book 589 n.

encyclopaedic
general 79 adj.
knowing 490 adj.

end
end 69 n.
end 69 vb.
extremity 69 n.
cease 145 vb.
destroy 165 vb.
ruin 165 n.
vertex 213 n.
objective 617 n.

endangered
endangered 661 adj.

endangered species
animal 365 n.

endearment
endearment 889 n.

endeavour
power 160 n.
production 164 n.
attempt 671 n.
attempt 671 vb.
action 676 n.

endemic
interior 224 adj.
infectious 653 adj.

ending
adjunct 40 n.
end 69 n.
ending 69 adj.

endless
multitudinous 104 adj.
infinite 107 adj.
perpetual 115 adj.

endoderm
interiority 224 n.

end of one's tether
limit 236 n.

endogamy
type of marriage 894 n.

endogenous
interior 224 adj.

endomorphic
thick 205 adj.

endorse
testify 466 vb.
endorse 488 vb.
give security 767 vb.

endoscopy
diagnostic 658 n.

endow
endow 777 vb.
give 781 vb.

endowment
aptitude 694 n.

giving 781 n.
endpaper
edition 589 n.
end-product
product 164 n.
completion 725 n.
endurance
durability 113 n.
perpetuity 115 n.
permanence 144 n.
power 160 n.
strength 162 n.
perseverance 600 n.
stamina 600 n.
feeling 818 n.
patience 823 n.
manliness 855 n.
endure
be 1 vb.
continue 108 vb.
last 113 vb.
stay 144 vb.
go on 146 vb.
meet with 154 vb.
support 218 vb.
acquiesce 488 vb.
be resolute 599 vb.
stand firm 599 vb.
persevere 600 vb.
resist 715 vb.
feel 818 vb.
be patient 823 vb.
suffer 825 vb.
enema
insertion 303 n.
cleansing 648 n.
purgative 658 n.
enemy
enemy 881 n.
energetic
dynamic 160 adj.
vigorous 174 adj.
forceful 571 adj.
resolute 599 adj.
active 678 adj.
labouring 682 adj.
energy
energy 160 n.
strength 162 n.
vigorousness 174 n.
resolution 599 n.
restlessness 678 n.
enervate
weaken 163 vb.
fatigue 684 vb.
enfant terrible
firearm 723 n.

annoyance 827 n.
bad person 938 n.
enfold
cover 226 vb.
dress 228 vb.
circumscribe 232 vb.
enclose 235 vb.
fold 261 vb.
safeguard 660 vb.
caress 889 vb.
enforce
motivate 612 vb.
compel 740 vb.
make legal 953 vb.
enfranchise
liberate 746 vb.
exempt 919 vb.
engage
unite with 45 vb.
be early 135 vb.
induce 612 vb.
employ 622 vb.
fight 716 vb.
go to war 718 vb.
commission 751 vb.
promise 764 vb.
contract 765 vb.
acquire 771 vb.
possess 773 vb.
engage in
busy oneself 622 vb.
do business 622 vb.
undertake 672 vb.
engagement
undertaking 672 n.
fight 716 n.
battle 718 n.
promise 764 n.
compact 765 n.
social round 882 n.
love affair 887 n.
wooing 889 n.
wedding 894 n.
duty 917 n.
engagement book
list 87 n.
engagement ring
jewellery 844 n.
love token 889 n.
engender
generate 167 vb.
engine
strengthen 162 vb.
machine 630 n.

engine driver
driver 268 n.
engineer
cause 156 vb.
produce 164 vb.
producer 164 n.
plan 623 vb.
machinist 630 n.
artisan 686 n.
soldiery 722 n.
engineering
production 164 n.
English rose
a beauty 841 n.
engorgement
satiety 863 n.
engrave
memorize 505 vb.
sculpt 554 vb.
engrave 555 vb.
decorate 844 vb.
engraving
engraving 555 n.
engross
absorb 299 vb.
absorb 449 vb.
engulf
consume 165 vb.
destroy 165 vb.
absorb 299 vb.
superabound 637 vb.
appropriate 786 vb.
enhance
augment 36 vb.
manifest 522 vb.
emphasize 532 vb.
exaggerate 546 vb.
make better 654 vb.
aggravate 832 vb.
decorate 844 vb.
enigma
unknown thing 491 n.
enigma 530 n.
enigmatic
uncertain 474 adj.
unknown 491 adj.
aphoristic 496 adj.
puzzling 517 adj.
unintelligible 517 adj.
unclear 568 adj.
wonderful 864 adj.

enjoin
command 737 vb.
impose a duty 917 vb.
enjoy
unite with 45 vb.
enjoy 376 vb.
dispose of 673 vb.
possess 773 vb.
be pleased 824 vb.
enjoyable
pleasant 376 adj.
enjoyment
pleasure 376 n.
possession 773 n.
enjoyment 824 n.
joy 824 n.
enjoy oneself
be cheerful 833 vb.
amuse oneself 837 vb.
enlarge
be great - large 32 vb.
augment 36 vb.
enlarge 197 vb.
photograph 551 vb.
boast 877 vb.
enlarge upon
be diffuse 570 vb.
enlighten
interpret 520 vb.
inform 524 vb.
educate 534 vb.
enlightenment
knowledge 490 n.
wisdom 498 n.
information 524 n.
sanctity 979 n.
enlist
be included 78 vb.
list 87 vb.
admit 299 vb.
induce 612 vb.
employ 622 vb.
join a party 708 vb.
go to war 718 vb.
enliven
invigorate 174 vb.
vitalize 360 vb.
animate 821 vb.
cheer 833 vb.
amuse 837 vb.
en masse
collectively 52 adv.
together 74 adv.

enmeshed
complex 61 adj.
enmity
enmity 881 n.
ennoble
dignify 866 vb.
ennui
discontent 829 n.
tedium 838 n.
enormity
greatness 32 n.
vice 934 n.
wickedness 934 n.
guilty act 936 n.
enormous
enormous 32 adj.
huge 195 adj.
enough
greatly 32 vb.
enough 635 adv.
sufficiency 635 n.
sufficient 635 adj.
en passant
incidentally
137 vb.
enquire
enquire 459 vb.
enquirer
enquirer 459 n.
petitioner 763 n.
enquiry
enquiry 459 n.
search 459 n.
enrage
enrage 891 vb.
enrapture
delight 826 vb.
enrich
augment 36 vb.
ornament 574 vb.
make better
654 vb.
decorate 844 vb.
enrol
list 87 vb.
admit 299 vb.
register 548 vb.
enrolment
reception 299 n.
en route
in transit 272 adv.
ensconce
place 187 vb.
conceal 525 vb.
ensconce oneself
place oneself
187 vb.

ensemble
all 52 n.
whole 52 n.
suit 228 n.
orchestra 413 n.
enshrine
circumscribe
232 n.
sanctify 979 vb.
ensign
flag 547 n.
soldier 722 n.
army officer 741 n.
regalia 743 n.
enslave
oppress 735 vb.
ensnare
ensnare 542 vb.
ensue
come after 65 vb.
ensue 120 vb.
result 157 vb.
ensuing
sequential 65 adj.
subsequent
120 adj.
ensure
make certain
473 vb.
ENT
medical art 658 n.
entail
make likely
471 vb.
dower 777 n.
entailed
proprietary
777 adj.
entangle
bedevil 63 vb.
ensnare 542 vb.
hinder 702 vb.
entente
agreement 24 n.
pacification 719 n.
friendliness 880 n.
entente cordiale
concord 710 n.
friendliness 880 n.
enter
fill 54 vb.
list 87 vb.
enter 297 vb.
register 548 vb.
contend 716 vb.
offer oneself
759 vb.

account 808 vb.
enter for
enter 297 vb.
contend 716 vb.
enter into
constitute 56 vb.
be included 78 vb.
imagine 513 vb.
cooperate 706 vb.
appropriate
786 vb.
enteritis
digestive disorders
651 n.
enterprise
vigorousness 174 n.
progression 285 n.
intention 617 n.
business 622 n.
undertaking 672 n.
restlessness 678 n.
mandate 751 n.
courage 855 n.
enterprising
vigorous 174 adj.
progressive
285 adj.
speculative
618 adj.
enterprising
672 adj.
entertain
amuse 837 vb.
be ridiculous
849 vb.
be friendly 880 vb.
be hospitable
882 vb.
entertainer
entertainer 594 n.
entertainment
pleasure 376 n.
provision 633 n.
amusement 837 n.
social gathering
882 n.
enthral
subjugate 745 vb.
enthrone
dignify 866 vb.
enthuse
show feeling
818 vb.
excite 821 vb.
enthusiasm
vigorousness 174 n.
vigour 571 n.

willingness 597 n.
warm feeling
818 n.
excitation 821 n.
love 887 n.
applause 923 n.
piety 979 n.
enthusiastic
imaginative
513 adj.
forceful 571 adj.
willing 597 adj.
active 678 adj.
fervent 818 adj.
excited 821 adj.
pietistic 979 adj.
entice
distract 456 vb.
ensnare 542 vb.
induce 612 vb.
tempt 612 vb.
entire
consummate
32 adj.
simple 44 adj.
complete 54 adj.
entirely
greatly 32 vb.
completely 54 adv.
entirety
great quantity
32 n.
whole 52 n.
completeness 54 n.
entitle
name 561 vb.
permit 756 vb.
entity
existence 1 n.
substance 3 n.
whole 52 n.
unit 88 n.
entomb
inter 364 vb.
imprison 747 vb.
entomology
zoology 367 n.
entourage
concomitant 89 n.
surroundings
230 n.
entrails
insides 224 n.
entrance
entrance 68 n.
front 237 n.
arrival 295 n.

EPI

phrase 563 n.
description 590 n.
epithet
name 561 n.
scurrility 899 n.
epitome
miniature 196 n.
contraction 198 n.
conciseness 569 n.
compendium
592 n.
epitomize
shorten 204 vb.
abstract 592 vb.
epoch
era 110 n.
chronology 117 n.
eponym
name 561 n.
nomenclature
561 n.
equable
uniform 16 adj.
equal 28 adj.
inexcitable
823 adj.
equal
be equal 28 vb.
compeer 28 n.
equal 28 adj.
just 913 adj.
equality
equality 28 n.
equalize
equalize 28 vb.
equal opportunity
equality 28 n.
justice 913 n.
equals sign
punctuation 547 n.
equanimity
inexcitability
823 n.
equate
identify 13 vb.
equalize 28 vb.
equation
equalization 28 n.
equivalence 28 n.
number 85 n.
numerical result
85 n.
equator
middle 70 n.
dividing line 92 n.
limit 236 n.
circle 250 n.

EQU

equatorial
middle 70 adj.
astronomy 321 n.
warm 379 adj.
equerry
retainer 742 n.
equestrian
rider 268 n.
equidistant
equal 28 adj.
middle 70 adj.
equilateral
equal 28 adj.
symmetrical
245 adj.
equilateral triangle
angular figure
247 n.
equilibrium
equilibrium 28 n.
quiescence 266 n.
inexcitability
823 n.
equine
equine 273 adj.
animal 365 adj.
equinoctial
celestial 321 adj.
equip
dress 228 vb.
provide 633 vb.
make ready
669 vb.
equipage
carriage 274 n.
equipment
contents 193 n.
means 629 n.
equipment 630 n.
provision 633 n.
equipoise
equilibrium 28 n.
weighing 322 n.
equitable
equal 28 adj.
just 913 adj.
honourable
929 adj.
equitation
equitation 267 n.
equity
indifference 860 n.
justice 913 n.
equivalent
identical 13 adj.
analogue 18 n.
compeer 28 n.

ERM

equivalence 28 n.
equivalent 28 adj.
semantic 514 adj.
equivocal
equivocal 518 adj.
equivocate
sophisticate
477 vb.
be equivocal
518 vb.
misinterpret
521 vb.
era
era 110 n.
eradicate
subtract 39 vb.
exclude 57 vb.
revolutionize
149 vb.
destroy 165 vb.
displace 188 vb.
eject 300 vb.
extract 304 vb.
erase
destroy 165 vb.
rub 333 vb.
disappear 446 vb.
obliterate 550 vb.
clean 648 vb.
erasure
extinction 2 n.
friction 333 n.
obliteration 550 n.
ere
before 119 adv.
erect
stabilize 153 vb.
cause 156 vb.
produce 164 vb.
place 187 vb.
vertical 215 adj.
elevate 310 vb.
honourable
929 adj.
erection
edifice 164 n.
production 164 n.
elevation 310 n.
erg
energy 160 n.
ergo
hence 158 adv.
ergonomics
exertion 682 n.
ermine
skin 226 n.
heraldic 547 adj.

ERS

heraldry 547 n.
regalia 743 n.
trimming 844 n.
erode
abate 37 vb.
subtract 39 vb.
decompose 51 vb.
encroach 306 vb.
pulverize 332 vb.
rub 333 vb.
waste 634 vb.
impair 655 vb.
erogenous
erotic 887 adj.
erosion
decrease 37 n.
diminution 37 n.
subtraction 39 n.
decay 51 n.
destroyer 168 n.
unproductiveness
172 n.
powderiness 332 n.
friction 333 n.
dilapidation 655 n.
erotic
erotic 887 adj.
impure 951 adj.
err
stray 282 vb.
err 495 vb.
be wicked 934 vb.
errand
message 529 n.
job 622 n.
mandate 751 n.
errand boy or girl
courier 529 n.
erratic
nonuniform 17 adj.
fitful 142 adj.
moving 265 adj.
inexact 495 adj.
crazy 503 adj.
capricious 604 adj.
erratum
mistake 495 n.
erroneous
erroneous 495 adj.
error
error 495 n.
ersatz
simulating 18 adj.
imitative 20 adj.
substitute 150 n.
substituted 150 adj.
spurious 542 adj.

bad taste 847 n.
vulgar 847 adj.
erstwhile
prior 119 adj.
erudite
studious 536 adj.
erupt
emerge 298 vb.
eruption
revolution 149 n.
outbreak 176 n.
egress 298 n.
voidance 300 n.
fire 379 n.
skin disease 651 n.
erysipelas
skin disease 651 n.
erythema
skin disease 651 n.
escalate
grow 36 vb.
be dear 811 vb.
escalator
conveyance 267 n.
carrier 273 n.
conveyor 274 n.
ascent 308 n.
escalope
meat 301 n.
escapade
foolery 497 n.
whim 604 n.
revel 837 n.
escape
outflow 298 n.
outlet 298 n.
avoid 620 vb.
escape 667 n.
escape 667 vb.
escape clause
nonconformity
  84 n.
qualification 468 n.
contrivance 623 n.
means of escape
  667 n.
conditions 766 n.
nonliability 919 n.
escapism
fantasy 513 n.
avoidance 620 n.
escape 667 n.
undutifulness
  918 n.
nonliability 919 n.

escapology
disappearance
  446 n.
escape 667 n.
escarpment
high land 209 n.
incline 220 n.
eschatology
theology 973 n.
eschew
avoid 620 vb.
escort
accompany 89 vb.
concomitant 89 n.
carry 273 vb.
male 372 n.
look after 457 vb.
protection 660 n.
safeguard 660 vb.
defender 713 n.
keeper 749 n.
take away 786 vb.
greet 884 vb.
lover 887 n.
court 889 vb.
escritoire
cabinet 194 n.
escudo
coinage 797 n.
escutcheon
heraldry 547 n.
esoteric
private 80 adj.
unintelligible
  517 adj.
occult 523 adj.
ESP
sense 374 n.
intellect 447 n.
intuition 476 n.
intuitive 476 adj.
psychics 984 n.
espadrilles
footwear 228 n.
espalier
frame 218 n.
fence 235 n.
esparto grass
grass 366 n.
especially
eminently 34 adv.
specially 80 adv.
Esperanto
language 557 n.
espionage
inspection 438 n.

secret service
  459 n.
sedition 738 n.
esplanade
horizontality
  216 n.
path 624 n.
espouse
choose 605 vb.
espresso
soft drink 301 n.
esprit de corps
prejudice 481 n.
cooperation 706 n.
fellowship 882 n.
espy
see 438 vb.
esquire
male 372 n.
title 870 n.
essay
reading matter
  589 n.
article 591 n.
dissertation 591 n.
attempt 671 n.
attempt 671 vb.
essence
essence 1 n.
product 164 n.
form 243 n.
extraction 304 n.
odour 394 n.
meaning 514 n.
perfection 646 n.
cosmetic 843 n.
essential
existing 1 adj.
real 1 adj.
intrinsic 5 adj.
absolute 32 adj.
necessary 596 adj.
required 627 adj.
requirement 627 n.
important 638 adj.
establish
auspicate 68 vb.
perpetuate 115 vb.
stabilize 153 vb.
produce 164 vb.
place 187 vb.
corroborate 466 vb.
demonstrate
  478 V.
established
usual 610 adj.
prosperous 730 adj.

establisher
producer 164 n.
establishment
fixture 153 n.
production 164 n.
location 187 n.
bigwig 638 n.
corporation 708 n.
estate
land 344 n.
farm 370 n.
estate 777 n.
lands 777 n.
estate agent
merchant 794 n.
esteem
prestige 866 n.
repute 866 n.
respect 920 n.
respect 920 vb.
approbation 923 n.
approve 923 vb.
estimate
appraise 465 vb.
estimate 480 n.
estimate 480 vb.
estimation
measurement
  465 n.
estimate 480 n.
prestige 866 n.
estrange
set apart 46 vb.
make quarrels
  709 vb.
not retain 779 vb.
estuary
gulf 345 n.
ET
native 191 n.
et cetera
in addition 38 adv.
including 78 adv.
etch
outline 233 vb.
groove 262 vb.
mark 547 vb.
engrave 555 vb.
etching
representation
  551 n.
engraving 555 n.
ornamental art
  844 n.
eternal
existing 1 adj.
infinite 107 adj.

lasting 113 adj.
perpetual 115 adj.
renowned 866 adj.
eternal triangle
jealousy 911 n.
illicit love 951 n.
eternity
existence 1 n.
infinity 107 n.
time 108 n.
neverness 109 n.
perpetuity 115 n.
divine attribute
  965 n.
heaven 971 n.
eternity ring
jewellery 844 n.
love token 889 n.
ether
heavens 321 n.
lightness 323 n.
rarity 325 n.
gas 336 n.
air 340 n.
anaesthetic 375 n.
ethereal
immaterial
  320 adj.
celestial 321 adj.
light 323 adj.
rare 325 adj.
gaseous 336 adj.
airy 340 adj.
ethical
ethical 917 adj.
ethics
philosophy 449 n.
morals 917 n.
virtue 933 n.
ethnic
ethnic 11 adj.
native 191 adj.
ethos
character 5 n.
conduct 688 n.
etiolated
colourless 426 adj.
etiquette
etiquette 848 n.
courtesy 884 n.
Eton collar
neckwear 228 n.
Eton crop
hairdressing 843 n.
étude
musical piece
  412 n.

étui
case 194 n.
etymology
source 156 n.
attribution 158 n.
connotation 514 n.
eucalyptus
tree 366 n.
Eucharist
Christian rite
  988 n.
Holy Communion
  988 n.
Euclidean geometry
geometry 465 n.
eugenics
propagation 167 n.
biology 358 n.
eulogize
honour 866 vb.
shame 867 vb.
praise 923 vb.
eulogy
oration 579 n.
honours 866 n.
praise 923 n.
Eumenides
Chthonian deity
  967 n.
eunuch
male 372 n.
slave 742 n.
euphemism
underestimation
  483 n.
trope 519 n.
phrase 563 n.
ornament 574 n.
affectation 850 n.
flattery 925 n.
purity 950 n.
euphonic
melodious 410 adj.
euphonious
melodious 410 adj.
elegant 575 adj.
euphonium
horn 414 n.
euphony
melody 410 n.
elegance 575 n.
euphoria
euphoria 376 n.
excitable state
  822 n.
joy 824 n.
cheerfulness 833 n.

rejoicing 835 n.
euphoric
palmy 730 adj.
pleased 824 adj.
jubilant 833 adj.
rejoicing 835 adj.
euphuism
trope 519 n.
ornament 574 n.
affectation 850 n.
eureka
eureka 484 int.
eurhythmics
exercise 682 n.
dancing 837 n.
European parliament
parliament 692 n.
euthanasia
decease 361 n.
killing 362 n.
evacuate
recede 290 vb.
decamp 296 vb.
emerge 298 vb.
empty 300 vb.
relinquish 621 vb.
evacuation
recession 290 n.
egress 298 n.
voidance 300 n.
defecation 302 n.
relinquishment
  621 n.
evacuee
outcast 883 n.
evade
sophisticate
  477 vb.
avoid 620 vb.
elude 667 vb.
not observe 769 vb.
fail in duty 918 vb.
evaluate
class 62 vb.
appraise 465 vb.
estimate 480 vb.
evanescent
transient 114 adj.
evangelical
revelational
  975 adj.
orthodox 976 adj.
sectarian 978 adj.
pietistic 979 adj.
zealot 979 n.
evangelist
preacher 537 n.

religious teacher
  973 n.
pastor 986 n.
evaporate
pass away 2 vb.
decrease 37 vb.
be dispersed 75 vb.
be transient
  114 vb.
destroy 165 vb.
become small
  198 vb.
make smaller
  198 vb.
vaporize 338 vb.
dry 342 vb.
disappear 446 vb.
waste 634 vb.
evaporated
dry 342 adj.
evaporation
dispersion 75 n.
egress 298 n.
vaporization 338 n.
desiccation 342 n.
disappearance
  446 n.
waste 634 n.
loss 772 n.
evasion
sophistry 477 n.
concealment 525 n.
falsehood 541 n.
avoidance 620 n.
escape 667 n.
stratagem 698 n.
evasive
equivocal 518 adj.
reticent 525 adj.
evasive action
avoidance 620 n.
eve
precursor 66 n.
priority 119 n.
evening 129 n.
even
uniform 16 adj.
equal 28 adj.
regular 81 adj.
numerical 85 adj.
evening 129 n.
periodical 141 adj.
flat 216 adj.
flatten 216 vb.
symmetrical
  245 adj.
straight 249 adj.

smooth 258 adj.
smooth 258 vb.
even if
provided 468 adv.
evening
period 110 n.
evening 129 n.
evening dress
formal dress 228 n.
evening star
evening 129 n.
planet 321 n.
luminary 420 n.
even keel
equilibrium 28 n.
evenness
uniformity 16 n.
equality 28 n.
periodicity 141 n.
symmetry 245 n.
smoothness 258 n.
evensong
evening 129 n.
public worship
981 n.
church service
988 n.
event
event 154 n.
contest 716 n.
even-tempered
inexcitable
823 adj.
eventful
notable 638 adj.
busy 678 adj.
eventide home
gerontology 131 n.
eventing
equitation 267 n.
eventuality
juncture 8 n.
event 154 n.
possibility 469 n.
eventually
eventually 154 adv.
even up
equalize 28 vb.
ever and always
for ever 115 adv.
Everest
high land 209 n.
evergreen
lasting 113 adj.
perpetual 115 adj.
new 126 adj.

unchangeable
153 adj.
renowned 866 adj.
evergreen tree
tree 366 n.
everlasting
perpetual 115 adj.
evermore
for ever 115 adv.
ever since
all along 113 adv.
ever so
greatly 32 vb.
ever so little
partially 33 adv.
ever so many
many 104 adj.
ever so much
greatly 32 vb.
every
universal 79 adj.
everybody
all 52 n.
everyman 79 n.
everyday
typical 83 adj.
plain 573 adj.
usual 610 adj.
everyman
prototype 23 n.
everyman 79 n.
person 371 n.
social group 371 n.
averageness 732 n.
commoner 869 n.
every man Jack
everyman 79 n.
every now and again
sometimes
139 adv.
every now and then
periodically
141 adv.
every one
everyman 79 n.
everyone
all 52 n.
**everyone for them-
selves**
selfishness 932 n.
everywhere
widely 183 adv.
everywoman
common man 30 n.
everyman 79 n.
person 371 n.
commoner 869 n.

evict
displace 188 vb.
eject 300 vb.
deprive 786 vb.
eviction
exclusion 57 n.
ejection 300 n.
loss 772 n.
expropriation
786 n.
evidence
evidence 466 n.
evidence 466 vb.
accusation 928 n.
evident
certain 473 adj.
manifest 522 adj.
evil
evil 616 adj.
evil 616 n.
bad 645 adj.
wicked 934 adj.
evildoer
evildoer 904 n.
evince
evidence 466 vb.
demonstrate
478 V.
manifest 522 vb.
eviscerate
weaken 163 vb.
empty 300 vb.
extract 304 vb.
evocative
remembering
505 adj.
descriptive 590 adj.
exciting 821 adj.
evoke
cause 156 vb.
describe 590 vb.
incite 612 vb.
excite 821 vb.
evolution
existence 1 n.
conversion 147 n.
progression 285 n.
evolution 316 n.
biology 358 n.
improvement
654 n.
evolve
generate 167 vb.
evolve 316 vb.
get better 654 vb.

evolve into
be turned to
147 vb.
ewe
sheep 365 n.
female animal
373 n.
ewelamb
female animal
373 n.
ewer
vessel 194 n.
water 339 n.
exacerbate
augment 36 vb.
exaggerate 546 vb.
hurt 827 vb.
aggravate 832 vb.
exact
lifelike 18 adj.
definite 80 adj.
careful 457 adj.
accurate 494 adj.
veracious 540 adj.
concise 569 adj.
demand 737 vb.
compel 740 vb.
observant 768 adj.
levy 786 vb.
impose a duty
917 vb.
exacting
difficult 700 adj.
oppressive 735 adj.
discontented
829 adj.
fastidious 862 adj.
exactitude
carefulness 457 n.
accuracy 494 n.
veracity 540 n.
exact likeness
representation
551 n.
exactly
truly 494 adv.
exactness
accuracy 494 n.
perspicuity 567 n.
exaggerate
exaggerate 546 vb.
exaggeration
exaggeration
546 n.
exaltation
elevation 310 n.
joy 824 n.

piety 979 n.
exalted
  great 32 adj.
  high 209 adj.
  notable 638 adj.
  noble 868 adj.
exaltedness
  prestige 866 n.
examination
  inspection 438 n.
  attention 455 n.
  enquiry 459 n.
  exam 459 n.
  experiment 461 n.
  dissertation 591 n.
  legal trial 959 n.
examination paper
  question 459 n.
examine
  scan 438 vb.
  enquire 459 vb.
  interrogate 459 vb.
  try a case 959 vb.
examiner
  listener 415 n.
  spectator 441 n.
  enquirer 459 n.
  estimator 480 n.
example
  example 83 n.
  warning 664 n.
exasperate
  aggravate 832 vb.
  enrage 891 vb.
Excalibur
  magic instrument 983 n.
ex cathedra
  creedal 485 adj.
excavate
  make concave 255 vb.
  extract 304 vb.
  search 459 vb.
excavation
  antiquity 125 n.
  excavation 255 n.
  search 459 n.
  discovery 484 n.
exceed
  be great - large 32 vb.
  be superior 34 vb.
  grow 36 vb.
  outdo 306 vb.
  overstep 306 vb.

be intemperate 943 vb.
exceedingly
  extremely 32 vb.
excel
  be superior 34 vb.
  be good 644 vb.
  be skilful 694 vb.
  have a reputation 866 vb.
excellence
  superiority 34 n.
  precedence 64 n.
  goodness 644 n.
  skill 694 n.
Excellency
  title 870 n.
excellent
  great 32 adj.
  supreme 34 adj.
  excellent 644 adj.
except
  thus 8 adv.
  abate 37 vb.
  subtract 39 vb.
  exclude 57 vb.
  exclusive of 57 adv.
excepting
  exclusive of 57 adv.
  qualifying 468 adj.
exception
  nonuniformity 17 n.
  exclusion 57 n.
  speciality 80 n.
  nonconformity 84 n.
  qualification 468 n.
  deprecation 762 n.
  conditions 766 n.
  disapprobation 924 n.
exceptional
  remarkable 32 adj.
  extraneous 59 adj.
  abnormal 84 adj.
  qualifying 468 adj.
  wonderful 864 adj.
exceptionally
  greatly 32 vb.
excerpt
  part 53 n.
  abstract 592 vb.
excess
  greatness 32 n.
  superiority 34 n.

exaggeration 546 n.
  redundance 637 n.
  superfluity 637 n.
  overactivity 678 n.
  scope 744 n.
  satiety 863 n.
  intemperance 943 n.
excessive
  exorbitant 32 adj.
  violent 176 adj.
  diffuse 570 adj.
  redundant 637 adj.
  superfluous 637 adj.
  dear 811 adj.
  vulgar 847 adj.
  unwarranted 916 adj.
  intemperate 943 adj.
excessively
  extremely 32 vb.
exchange
  correlate 12 vb.
  correlation 12 n.
  equivalence 28 n.
  union 45 n.
  focus 76 n.
  substitute 150 vb.
  substitution 150 n.
  interchange 151 n.
  interchange 151 n.
  interlocution 584 n.
  stock exchange 618 n.
  assign 780 vb.
  transfer 780 n.
  barter 791 n.
  trade 791 vb.
  market 796 n.
  finance 797 n.
exchequer
  storage 632 n.
  funds 797 n.
  treasury 799 n.
excise
  subtract 39 vb.
  extract 304 vb.
  tax 809 n.
excise officer
  receiver 782 n.
excision
  subtraction 39 n.

extraction 304 n.
excitable
  excitable 822 adj.
excitation
  increase 36 n.
  activity 678 n.
  excitation 821 n.
excite
  cause feeling 374 vb.
  excite 821 vb.
excited
  excited 821 adj.
excitement
  stimulation 174 n.
  excitation 821 n.
  applause 923 n.
exciting
  exciting 821 adj.
exclaim
  cry 408 vb.
  voice 577 vb.
  disapprove 924 vb.
exclamation
  cry 408 n.
  voice 577 n.
  wonder 864 n.
exclamation mark
  punctuation 547 n.
  wonder 864 n.
exclude
  exclude 57 vb.
  make impossible 470 vb.
excluded, be
  be excluded 57 vb.
excluding
  unmixed 44 adj.
  excluding 57 adj.
exclusion
  exclusion 57 n.
exclusive
  excluding 57 adj.
  private 80 adj.
  news 529 n.
  excellent 644 adj.
  possessed 773 adj.
  dear 811 adj.
  sectarian 978 adj.
exclusivity
  restriction 747 n.
excommunicate
  exclude 57 vb.
  eject 300 vb.
  prohibit 757 vb.
  curse 899 vb.
  condemn 961 vb.

perform ritual
988 vb.
excommunicated
schismatical
978 adj.
excoriate
uncover 229 vb.
rub 333 vb.
excrement
excrement 302 n.
excrescence
swelling 253 n.
blemish 845 n.
excreta
excrement 302 n.
excrete
excrete 302 vb.
excretion
excretion 302 n.
excruciating
painful 377 adj.
paining 827 adj.
exculpate
forgive 909 vb.
exempt 919 vb.
justify 927 vb.
acquit 960 vb.
excursion
land travel 267 n.
enjoyment 824 n.
amusement 837 n.
excuse
exclude 57 vb.
reason why 156 n.
disregard 458 vb.
qualify 468 vb.
pretext 614 n.
deliver 668 vb.
stratagem 698 n.
forgive 909 vb.
forgiveness 909 n.
exempt 919 vb.
nonliability 919 n.
extenuate 927 vb.
vindication 927 n.
excuse oneself
plead 614 vb.
refuse 760 vb.
be exempt 919 vb.
ex-directory
concealed 525 adj.
execrable
bad 645 adj.
damnable 645 adj.
unpleasant
827 adj.
hateful 888 adj.

execration
hatred 888 n.
malediction 899 n.
reproach 924 n.
executant
interpreter 520 n.
doer 676 n.
agent 686 n.
execute
produce 164 vb.
operate 173 vb.
play music 413 vb.
undertake 672 vb.
do 676 vb.
deal with 688 vb.
carry out 725 vb.
contract 765 vb.
give security
767 vb.
observe 768 vb.
execute 963 vb.
execution
production 164 n.
agency 173 n.
death 361 n.
killing 362 n.
action 676 n.
skill 694 n.
completion 725 n.
capital punishment
963 n.
executioner
destroyer 168 n.
violent creature
176 n.
killer 362 n.
executive
producer 164 n.
doer 676 n.
agent 686 n.
worker 686 n.
manager 690 n.
executor
doer 676 n.
agent 686 n.
manager 690 n.
consignee 754 n.
executor, be
deputize 755 vb.
executrix
agent 686 n.
exemplar
prototype 23 n.
example 83 n.
exemplary
typical 83 adj.

intrepretative
520 adj.
excellent 644 adj.
virtuous 933 adj.
exemplify
exemplify 83 vb.
manifest 522 vb.
exempt
separate 46 adj.
set apart 46 vb.
exclude 57 vb.
qualifying 468 adj.
reject 607 vb.
free 744 adj.
exempt 919 vb.
acquitted 960 adj.
exempt from
absent 190 adj.
relieve 831 vb.
exemption
separation 46 n.
exclusion 57 n.
nonconformity
84 n.
qualification 468 n.
rejection 607 n.
escape 667 n.
deliverance 668 n.
freedom 744 n.
permission 756 n.
relief 831 n.
dueness 915 n.
nonliability 919 n.
acquittal 960 n.
exercise
agency 173 n.
motion 265 n.
curriculum 534 n.
train 534 vb.
learn 536 vb.
job 622 n.
make ready
669 vb.
prepare oneself
669 vb.
undertaking 672 n.
use 673 n.
use 673 vb.
deed 676 n.
do 676 vb.
exercise 682 n.
labour 682 n.
exert
use 673 vb.
exertion
vigorousness 174 n.
exertion 682 n.

exert oneself
exert oneself
682 vb.
exfoliation
uncovering 229 n.
ex gratia payment
gift 781 n.
pay 804 n.
exhale
exude 298 vb.
emit 300 vb.
vaporize 338 vb.
breathe 352 vb.
smell 394 vb.
exhaust
abate 37 vb.
disable 161 vb.
rarefy 325 vb.
blowing 352 n.
blow up 352 vb.
impair 655 vb.
fatigue 684 vb.
exhaustion
decrease 37 n.
helplessness 161 n.
weakness 163 n.
waste 634 n.
deterioration
655 n.
use 673 n.
fatigue 684 n.
dejection 834 n.
exhaustive
complete 54 adj.
exhaust pipe
outlet 298 n.
blowing 352 n.
air pipe 353 n.
exhibit
appear 445 vb.
evidence 466 n.
exhibit 522 n.
show 522 vb.
indicate 547 vb.
be ostentatious
875 vb.
exhibition
appearance 445 n.
spectacle 445 n.
exhibit 522 n.
manifestation
522 n.
collection 632 n.
market 796 n.
reward 962 n.
exhibition centre
exhibit 522 n.

exhibitionism
vanity 873 n.
ostentation 875 n.
impurity 951 n.
exhibitor
exhibitor 522 n.
exhilarate
excite 821 vb.
delight 826 vb.
cheer 833 vb.
exhort
incite 612 vb.
advise 691 vb.
exhortation
oration 579 n.
inducement 612 n.
exhume
exhume 364 vb.
exigency
needfulness 627 n.
desire 859 n.
exiguous
small 33 adj.
exile
exclude 57 vb.
exclusion 57 n.
foreigner 59 n.
displace 188 vb.
displacement
188 n.
wanderer 268 n.
egress 298 n.
eject 300 vb.
ejection 300 n.
outcast 883 n.
seclusion 883 n.
penalty 963 n.
exist
be 1 vb.
pass time 108 vb.
be present 189 vb.
live 360 vb.
be true 494 vb.
existence
existence 1 n.
presence 189 n.
existentialism
existence 1 n.
philosophy 449 n.
exit
doorway 263 n.
depart 296 vb.
departure 296 n.
egress 298 n.
emerge 298 vb.
outlet 298 n.
decease 361 n.

disappearance
446 n.
dramaturgy 594 n.
See **acting**
means of escape
667 n.
Exocet (tdmk)
rocket 276 n.
missile weapon
723 n.
exodus
departure 296 n.
egress 298 n.
ex officio
authoritative
733 adj.
exogamy
type of marriage
894 n.
exogenous
exterior 223 adj.
exonerate
forgive 909 vb.
exempt 919 vb.
justify 927 vb.
acquit 960 vb.
exorbitant
exorbitant 32 adj.
dear 811 adj.
exorcism
malediction 899 n.
prayers 981 n.
sorcery 983 n.
spiritualism 984 n.
Christian rite
988 n.
exorcize
dismiss 300 vb.
exoteric
exterior 223 adj.
exotic
unrelated 10 adj.
unrelatedness 10 n.
dissimilar 19 adj.
extraneous 59 adj.
unconformable
84 adj.
unusual 84 adj.
flower 366 n.
wonderful 864 adj.
expand
add 38 vb.
enlarge 197 vb.
expand 197 vb.
rarefy 325 vb.
exaggerate 546 vb.
be diffuse 570 vb.

expanse
greatness 32 n.
great quantity
32 n.
space 183 n.
size 195 n.
breadth 205 n.
expansion
growth 157 n.
space 183 n.
expansion 197 n.
rarity 325 n.
expansionism
overstepping 306 n.
nation 371 n.
bellicosity 718 n.
desire 859 n.
expansive
spacious 183 adj.
broad 205 adj.
expatiate
be diffuse 570 vb.
speak 579 vb.
be loquacious
581 vb.
expatriate
exclude 57 vb.
foreigner 59 n.
dweller 191 n.
eject 300 vb.
outcast 883 n.
expect
expect 507 vb.
request 761 vb.
take a pledge
764 vb.
desire 859 vb.
expectancy
expectation 507 n.
expectant
fertilized 167 adj.
expectant 507 adj.
expectant mother
maternity 169 n.
expectation
belief 485 n.
expectation 507 n.
expectations
possession 773 n.
dower 777 n.
hope 852 n.
dueness 915 n.
expecting
fertilized 167 adj.
expectant 507 adj.
expecting a baby
expectant 507 adj.

**expecting a happy
event**
fertilized 167 adj.
expectant 507 adj.
expectorant
purgative 658 n.
expectorate
eruct 300 vb.
expedience
good policy 642 n.
expediency
good policy 642 n.
expedient
substitute 150 n.
contrivance 623 n.
means 629 n.
useful 640 adj.
advisable 642 adj.
expedite
accelerate 277 vb.
hasten 680 vb.
facilitate 701 vb.
expedition
land travel 267 n.
velocity 277 n.
activity 678 n.
haste 680 n.
warfare 718 n.
expeditious
speedy 277 adj.
active 678 adj.
expel
subtract 39 vb.
disunite 46 vb.
transpose 272 vb.
impel 279 vb.
propel 287 vb.
eject 300 vb.
extract 304 vb.
reject 607 vb.
deprive 786 vb.
expendable
superfluous
637 adj.
unimportant
639 adj.
useless 641 adj.
expenditure
expenditure 806 n.
expense
expenditure 806 n.
expense account
subvention 703 n.
earnings 771 n.
gift 781 n.
expenditure 806 n.
accounts 808 n.

ostentatious
875 adj.
reward 962 n.
expenses
increment 36 n.
expenditure 806 n.
cost 809 n.
expensive
dear 811 adj.
ostentatious
875 adj.
experience
meet with 154 vb.
empiricism 461 n.
knowledge 490 n.
wisdom 498 n.
skill 694 n.
feel 818 vb.
feeling 818 n.
suffer 825 vb.
experienced
knowing 490 adj.
wise 498 adj.
matured 669 adj.
expert 694 adj.
cunning 698 adj.
cautious 858 adj.
experiences
biography 590 n.
experiment
experiment 461 n.
experiment 461 vb.
experimental
experimental
461 adj.
speculative
618 adj.
experimentation
experiment 461 n.
experiment upon
experiment 461 vb.
expert
sage 500 n.
expert 694 adj.
expert 696 n.
proficient person
696 n.
expertise
knowledge 490 n.
skill 694 n.
expiate
atone 941 vb.
expiration
end 69 n.
respiration 352 n.
expire
end 69 vb.

die 361 vb.
explain
specify 80 vb.
account for 158 vb.
reason 475 vb.
interpret 520 vb.
manifest 522 vb.
facilitate 701 vb.
explain away
confute 479 vb.
disbelieve 486 vb.
explanation
reason why 156 n.
attribution 158 n.
answer 460 n.
interpretation
520 n.
explanatory
intrepretative
520 adj.
expletive
scurrility 899 n.
explicit
definite 80 adj.
intelligible 516 adj.
shown 522 adj.
informative
524 adj.
explode
be dispersed 75 vb.
demolish 165 vb.
open 263 vb.
propel 287 vb.
shoot 287 vb.
be loud 400 vb.
bang 402 vb.
confute 479 vb.
be active 678 vb.
be excited 821 vb.
be excitable
822 vb.
get angry 891 vb.
exploit
profit by 137 vb.
produce 164 vb.
important matter
638 n.
use 673 vb.
misuse 675 vb.
deed 676 n.
do 676 vb.
masterpiece 694 n.
oppress 735 vb.
prowess 855 n.
miracle-working
864 n.

exploitation
use 673 n.
severity 735 n.
acquisition 771 n.
exploration
land travel 267 n.
enquiry 459 n.
search 459 n.
experiment 461 n.
discovery 484 n.
exploratory
precursory 66 adj.
enquiring 459 adj.
experimental
461 adj.
explore
travel 267 vb.
enquire 459 vb.
search 459 vb.
be tentative 461 vb.
discover 484 vb.
explorer
precursor 66 n.
traveller 268 n.
enquirer 459 n.
experimenter
461 n.
detector 484 n.
explosion
revolution 149 n.
outbreak 176 n.
loudness 400 n.
bang 402 n.
excitable state
822 n.
anger 891 n.
explosive
violent 176 adj.
dangerous 661 adj.
explosive 723 n.
excitable 822 adj.
exponent
numerical element
85 n.
interpreter 520 n.
teacher 537 n.
exponential
numerical 85 adj.
export
transfer 272 vb.
transference 272 n.
egress 298 n.
eject 300 vb.
alcoholic drink
301 n.
exporter
carrier 273 n.

merchant 794 n.
expose
uncover 229 vb.
aerate 340 vb.
be visible 443 vb.
confute 479 vb.
manifest 522 vb.
show 522 vb.
disclose 526 vb.
shame 867 vb.
criticize 924 vb.
defame 926 vb.
accuse 928 vb.
exposé
disclosure 526 n.
photograph 551 vb.
description 590 n.
exposed
uncovered 229 adj.
windy 352 adj.
sentient 374 adj.
painful 377 adj.
visible 443 adj.
vulnerable 661 adj.
expose oneself
disclose 526 vb.
be rash 857 vb.
exposition
musical piece
412 n.
spectacle 445 n.
demonstration
478 n.
commentary 520 n.
interpretation
520 n.
exhibit 522 n.
dissertation 591 n.
market 796 n.
expostulate
dissuade 613 vb.
deprecate 762 vb.
reprove 924 vb.
exposure
liability 180 n.
uncovering 229 n.
air 340 n.
refrigeration 382 n.
visibility 443 n.
discovery 484 n.
manifestation
522 n.
disclosure 526 n.
photography 551 n.
vulnerability 661 n.
detraction 926 n.

expound
interpret 520 vb.
teach 534 vb.
express
form 243 vb.
extract 304 vb.
mean 514 vb.
manifest 522 vb.
divulge 526 vb.
affirm 532 vb.
phrase 563 vb.
voice 577 vb.
expression
number 85 n.
form 243 n.
extraction 304 n.
look 445 n.
manifestation
522 n.
affirmation 532 n.
phrase 563 n.
feeling 818 n.
Expressionism
art 551 n.
school of painting
553 n.
literature 557 n.
expressionless
still 266 adj.
unintelligible
517 adj.
impassive 820 adj.
expressive
expressive 516 adj.
stylistic 566 adj.
elegant 575 adj.
lively 819 adj.
express train
train 274 n.
expressway
road 624 n.
expropriate
eject 300 vb.
disentitle 916 vb.
expulsion
separation 46 n.
exclusion 57 n.
energy 160 n.
displacement
188 n.
transference 272 n.
ejection 300 n.
penalty 963 n.
expunge
destroy 165 vb.
obliterate 550 vb.

expurgated
pure 950 adj.
expurgated edition
edition 589 n.
exquisite
excellent 644 adj.
pleasurable
826 adj.
beautiful 841 adj.
tasteful 846 adj.
wonderful 864 adj.
extant
existing 1 adj.
present 121 adj.
extemporary
spontaneous
609 adj.
extempore
extempore
609 adv.
unreadily 670 adv.
extemporize
compose music
413 vb.
play music 413 vb.
improvise 609 vb.
be unprepared
670 vb.
extend
augment 36 vb.
add 38 vb.
extend 183 vb.
enlarge 197 vb.
expand 197 vb.
lengthen 203 vb.
extended
long 203 adj.
extended family
family 11 n.
extension
quantity 26 n.
greatness 32 n.
increase 36 n.
adjunct 40 n.
protraction 113 n.
continuance 146 n.
space 183 n.
lobby 194 n.
size 195 n.
expansion 197 n.
length 203 n.
hearing aid 415 n.
telecommunication
531 n.
extensive
extensive 32 adj.
large 195 adj.

long 203 adj.
extent
quantity 26 n.
degree 27 n.
greatness 32 n.
time 108 n.
space 183 n.
size 195 n.
length 203 n.
extenuate
abate 37 vb.
weaken 163 vb.
moderate 177 vb.
extenuate 927 vb.
extenuating
qualifying 468 adj.
**extenuating circum-
stances**
qualification 468 n.
vindication 927 n.
exterior
exterior 223 adj.
exteriority 223 n.
ostentation 875 n.
exterminate
destroy 165 vb.
slaughter 362 vb.
external
extrinsic 6 adj.
separate 46 adj.
exterior 223 adj.
appearing 445 adj.
externalism
exteriority 223 n.
extinct
extinct 2 adj.
dead 361 adj.
nonactive 677 adj.
extinction
extinction 2 n.
decease 361 n.
disappearance
446 n.
extinguish
nullify 2 vb.
extinguish 382 vb.
extinguisher
destroyer 168 n.
extinguisher 382 n.
extirpate
destroy 165 vb.
extract 304 vb.
extol
advertise 528 vb.
praise 923 vb.
worship 981 vb.

extort
extract 304 vb.
oppress 735 vb.
compel 740 vb.
levy 786 vb.
overcharge 811 vb.
extortion
compulsion 740 n.
expropriation
786 n.
rapacity 786 n.
swindling 788 n.
dearness 811 n.
extortionate
exorbitant 32 adj.
oppressive 735 adj.
dear 811 adj.
extortioner
taker 786 n.
extra
additional 38 adj.
in addition 38 adv.
extra 40 n.
the press 528 n.
actor 594 n.
superfluous
637 adj.
extract
part 53 n.
product 164 n.
extract 304 vb.
extraction 304 n.
doctor 658 vb.
extraction
genealogy 169 n.
extraction 304 n.
extraction fan
ventilation 352 n.
extracts
anthology 592 n.
extracurricular
educational
534 adj.
extradite
exclude 57 vb.
extradition
transference 272 n.
ejection 300 n.
extragalactic
extraneous 59 adj.
cosmic 321 adj.
**extramarital rela-
tions**
illicit love 951 n.
extramural
extrinsic 6 adj.
exterior 223 adj.

educational
  534 adj.
extraneous
  extraneous 59 adj.
extraordinary
  remarkable 32 adj.
  unusual 84 adj.
  wonderful 864 adj.
  noteworthy
    866 adj.
extras
  earnings 771 n.
  gift 781 n.
  expenditure 806 n.
**extrasensory percep-
tion**
  sense 374 n.
  intellect 447 n.
  intuition 476 n.
  psychics 984 n.
extraterrestrial
  unrelated 10 adj.
  extraneous 59 adj.
  native 191 n.
  exterior 223 adj.
extravagance
  foolery 497 n.
  exaggeration
    546 n.
  grandiloquence
    574 n.
  waste 634 n.
  misuse 675 n.
  prodigality 815 n.
  ridiculousness
    849 n.
  intemperance
    943 n.
extravagant
  exorbitant 32 adj.
  violent 176 adj.
  imaginative
    513 adj.
  wasteful 634 adj.
  dear 811 adj.
  prodigal 815 adj.
  ridiculous 849 adj.
  intemperate
    943 adj.
extravaganza
  musical piece
    412 n.
  spectacle 445 n.
  foolery 497 n.
  ideality 513 n.
extreme
  exorbitant 32 adj.

complete 54 adj.
  ending 69 adj.
  extremity 69 n.
  violent 176 adj.
  limit 236 n.
  severe 735 adj.
  intolerable 827 adj.
  paining 827 adj.
extremes
  exaggeration
    546 n.
  redundance 637 n.
  opposites 704 n.
  severity 735 n.
extremist
  the maladjusted
    504 n.
  reformer 654 n.
  revolter 738 n.
extremity
  adjunct 40 n.
  extremity 69 n.
  crisis 137 n.
  adversity 731 n.
  severity 735 n.
  suffering 825 n.
extricate
  extract 304 vb.
  deliver 668 vb.
  disencumber
    701 vb.
  liberate 746 vb.
extrinsic
  extrinsic 6 adj.
extrovert
  extrinsicality 6 n.
  exterior 223 adj.
  exteriority 223 n.
  sociable 882 adj.
extroverted
  extrinsic 6 adj.
exuberant
  prolific 171 adj.
  diffuse 570 adj.
  fervent 818 adj.
exude
  exude 298 vb.
exult
  vociferate 408 vb.
  rejoice 835 vb.
  boast 877 vb.
exultant
  jubilant 833 adj.
  rejoicing 835 adj.
exultation
  rejoicing 835 n.

eye
  centre 225 n.
  circle 250 n.
  orifice 263 n.
  eye 438 n.
  gaze 438 vb.
  watch 441 vb.
  court 889 vb.
eyeball
  be in front 237 vb.
  eye 438 n.
  be courageous
    855 vb.
eyeball to eyeball
  near 200 adv.
  in front 237 adv.
  against 240 adv.
  opposite 240 adj.
  opposing 704 adj.
eyebrows
  hair 259 n.
eye-catching
  obvious 443 adj.
  manifest 522 adj.
eye for an eye
  interchange 151 n.
  retaliation 714 n.
  revenge 910 n.
eyeful
  view 438 n.
  spectacle 445 n.
  a beauty 841 n.
eyeglass
  eyeglass 442 n.
eyelash
  filament 208 n.
  shade 226 n.
eyelashes
  hair 259 n.
  screen 421 n.
  eye 438 n.
eyelet
  fastening 47 n.
  circle 250 n.
  orifice 263 n.
eyelid
  shade 226 n.
  screen 421 n.
  eye 438 n.
eye-opener
  discovery 484 n.
  lack of expectation
    508 n.
  prodigy 864 n.
eye-opening
  unexpected
    508 n.

eyesight
  vision 438 n.
eyesore
  eyesore 842 n.
eye test
  diagnostic 658 n.
eyetooth
  tooth 256 n.
eyewash
  empty talk 515 n.
  falsehood 541 n.
  balm 658 n.
eyewitness
  spectator 441 n.
  visibility 443 n.
  witness 466 n.
eyrie
  group 74 n.
  nest 192 n.
  high structure
    209 n.

F

fab
  super 644 adj.
Fabian
  late 136 adj.
  slow 278 adj.
  reformer 654 n.
  nonactive 677 adj.
  political party
    708 n.
  cautious 858 adj.
Fabian tactics
  slowness 278 n.
  inaction 677 n.
fable
  maxim 496 n.
  metaphor 519 n.
  fable 543 n.
fabric
  modality 7 n.
  product 164 n.
  textile 222 n.
  matter 319 n.
  structure 331 n.
  texture 331 n.
  materials 631 n.
fabricate
  compose 56 vb.
  produce 164 vb.
  imagine 513 vb.
  fake 541 vb.
fabrication
  production 164 n.
  falsehood 541 n.

untruth 543 n.
fabulous
　unreal 2 adj.
　prodigious 32 adj.
　imaginary 513 adj.
　untrue 543 adj.
　super 644 adj.
　pleasurable
　　826 adj.
façade
　exteriority 223 n.
　face 237 n.
　appearance 445 n.
　duplicity 541 n.
　affectation 850 n.
face
　timekeeper 117 n.
　impend 155 vb.
　be present 189 vb.
　exteriority 223 n.
　coat 226 vb.
　line 227 vb.
　be in front 237 vb.
　face 237 n.
　be opposite 240 vb.
　look 445 n.
　print-type 587 n.
　be resolute 599 vb.
　withstand 704 vb.
　be courageous
　　855 vb.
　prestige 866 n.
　insolence 878 n.
face about
　revert 148 vb.
　be inverted 221 vb.
　turn round 282 vb.
　circle 314 vb.
face down
　supine 216 adj.
　inversely 221 adv.
faceless
　anonymous
　　562 adj.
face-lift
　repair 656 n.
　revival 656 n.
　beautification
　　843 n.
face mask
　beautification
　　843 n.
facet
　exteriority 223 n.
　appearance 445 n.

face the music
　be courageous
　　855 vb.
　be punished
　　963 vb.
face the other way
　turn round 282 vb.
facetious
　witty 839 adj.
face to face
　near 200 adv.
　in front 237 adv.
　against 240 adv.
　opposite 240 adv.
　opposing 704 adj.
face up to
　be in front 237 vb.
face value
　appearance 445 n.
　price 809 n.
facial
　exterior 223 adj.
　friction 333 n.
　beautification
　　843 n.
facile
　easy 701 adj.
facilitate
　facilitate 701 vb.
　aid 703 vb.
facilities
　means 629 n.
　good policy 642 n.
　facility 701 n.
facility
　willingness 597 n.
　facility 701 n.
facing
　near 200 adj.
　facing 226 n.
　lining 227 n.
　frontal 237 adj.
　against 240 adv.
　opposite 240 adj.
　fold 261 n.
　directed 281 adj.
　towards 281 adv.
facsimile
　copy 22 n.
　sham 542 n.
　representation
　　551 n.
fact
　reality 1 n.
　event 154 n.
　evidence 466 n.
　certainty 473 n.

truth 494 n.
faction
　disagreement 25 n.
　part 53 n.
　dissent 489 n.
　dissentient 489 n.
　broadcast 531 n.
　literature 557 n.
　description 590 n.
　narrative 590 n.
　opposition 704 n.
　party 708 n.
　revolt 738 n.
　sect 978 n.
factions
　opposites 704 n.
factious
　quarrelling
　　709 adj.
fact of life
　reality 1 n.
factor
　part 53 n.
　component 58 n.
　numerical element
　　85 n.
　cause 156 n.
　influence 178 n.
　element 319 n.
　farmer 370 n.
　manager 690 n.
　consignee 754 n.
　deputy 755 n.
factorize
　simplify 44 vb.
　sunder 46 vb.
　decompose 51 vb.
factors
　circumstance 8 n.
factory
　workshop 687 n.
factory farming
　production 164 n.
　agriculture 370 n.
factory ship
　fishing boat 275 n.
factotum
　busy person 678 n.
　worker 686 n.
　servant 742 n.
facts
　evidence 466 n.
　accuracy 494 n.
　truth 494 n.
　information 524 n.
facts and figures
　accounts 808 n.

facts of life
　propagation 167 n.
factual
　real 1 adj.
　evidential 466 adj.
　certain 473 adj.
　true 494 adj.
　veracious 540 adj.
faculty
　classification 77 n.
　ability 160 n.
　teacher 537 n.
　aptitude 694 n.
　skill 694 n.
fad
　eccentricity 503 n.
　whim 604 n.
　fashion 848 n.
　affectation 850 n.
　liking 859 n.
faddy
　misjudging
　　481 adj.
　capricious 604 adj.
fade
　decrease 37 vb.
　be transient
　　114 vb.
　be old 127 vb.
　be weak 163 vb.
　be dim 419 vb.
　lose colour 426 vb.
　whiten 427 vb.
　be unseen 444 vb.
　photography 551 n.
　deteriorate 655 vb.
　lose repute 867 vb.
fade away
　cease 145 vb.
　sound faint 401 vb.
　disappear 446 vb.
faded
　dim 419 adj.
　soft-hued 425 adj.
　colourless 426 adj.
　inglorious 867 adj.
fade out
　cease 145 vb.
　dim 419 vb.
fading
　decrease 37 n.
　decreasing 37 adj.
　transient 114 adj.
　achromatism
　　426 n.
　colourless 426 adj.

deterioration
  655 n.
faeces
  excrement 302 n.
  dirt 649 n.
faerie
  fairy 970 n.
fag
  tobacco 388 n.
  labour 682 n.
  fatigue 684 vb.
  worker 686 n.
  servant 742 n.
fag end
  remainder 41 n.
  extremity 69 n.
  tobacco 388 n.
fag for
  serve 742 vb.
fagged out
  fatigued 684 adj.
faggot
  bunch 74 n.
  fuel 385 n.
faience
  pottery 381 n.
fail
  decrease 37 vb.
  be weak 163 vb.
  close 264 vb.
  fall short 307 vb.
  be dim-sighted
    440 vb.
  not suffice 636 vb.
  be ill 651 vb.
  deteriorate 655 vb.
  be inactive 679 vb.
  be fatigued 684 vb.
  fail 728 vb.
  not observe 769 vb.
  not pay 805 vb.
  disapprove 924 vb.
failed
  unskilful 695 adj.
  unsuccessful
    728 adj.
failing
  inferior 35 adj.
  ageing 131 adj.
  deficient 307 adj.
  vice 934 n.
failure
  inferiority 35 n.
  insufficiency 636 n.
  imperfection 647 n.
  bungler 697 n.
  failure 728 n.

loser 728 n.
  guilty act 936 n.
faint
  small 33 adj.
  helplessness 161 n.
  be weak 163 vb.
  weak 163 adj.
  weakly 163 adj.
  insensibility 375 n.
  silent 399 adj.
  muted 401 adj.
  dim 419 adj.
  colourless 426 adj.
  indistinct 444 adj.
  be inactive 679 vb.
  inactive 679 adj.
  be fatigued 684 vb.
  fear 854 vb.
faint-hearted
  irresolute 601 adj.
  nervous 854 adj.
  cowardly 856 adj.
fainting
  illness 651 n.
faintly
  slightly 33 adv.
faintness
  faintness 401 n.
  dimness 419 n.
faint praise
  indifference 860 n.
  praise 923 n.
  detraction 926 n.
fair
  dry 342 adj.
  warm 379 adj.
  undimmed
    417 adj.
  colourless 426 adj.
  whitish 427 adj.
  rational 475 adj.
  exhibit 522 n.
  not bad 644 adj.
  palmy 730 adj.
  middling 732 adj.
  market 796 n.
  festivity 837 n.
  pleasure ground
    837 n.
  beautiful 841 adj.
  promising 852 adj.
  just 913 adj.
  honourable
    929 adj.
fair and square
  just 913 adj.

fair enough
  just 913 adj.
fair exchange
  equivalence 28 n.
  barter 791 n.
fair game
  dupe 544 n.
  laughingstock
    851 n.
fairground
  arena 724 n.
  place of amuse-
    ment 837 n.
fairly
  greatly 32 vb.
  slightly 33 adv.
fair name
  repute 866 n.
fairness
  beauty 841 n.
  justice 913 n.
  probity 929 n.
fair offer
  offer 759 n.
fair play
  justice 913 n.
fair sex
  womankind 373 n.
fair-sized
  great 32 adj.
  large 195 adj.
fair-skinned
  colourless 426 adj.
fair to middling
  middling 732 adj.
fair treatment
  justice 913 n.
fair warning
  threat 900 n.
fairway
  access 624 n.
  path 624 n.
  route 624 n.
fair weather
  palmy days 730 n.
fair-weather friend
  deceiver 545 n.
  friend 880 n.
  flatterer 925 n.
fairy
  nonconformist
    84 n.
  fairy 970 n.
  fairylike 970 adj.
fairy cakes
  pastries and cakes
    301 n.

fairy cycle
  bicycle 274 n.
fairy godmother
  protector 660 n.
  aider 703 n.
  patron 707 n.
  giver 781 n.
  good giver 813 n.
  prodigy 864 n.
  benefactor 903 n.
  fairy 970 n.
  sorceress 983 n.
fairyland
  fantasy 513 n.
  prodigy 864 n.
  fairy 970 n.
fairy lights
  lamp 420 n.
fairylike
  fairylike 970 adj.
fairy queen
  fairy 970 n.
fairy tale
  ideality 513 n.
  fable 543 n.
  narrative 590 n.
  fairy 970 n.
fait accompli
  reality 1 n.
  certainty 473 n.
  completion 725 n.
faith
  belief 485 n.
  hope 852 n.
  probity 929 n.
  virtues 933 n.
  religious faith
    973 n.
  piety 979 n.
faithful
  lifelike 18 adj.
  conformable
    83 adj.
  accurate 494 adj.
  true 494 adj.
  intrepretative
    520 adj.
  obedient 739 adj.
  observant 768 adj.
  friendly 880 adj.
  trustworthy
    929 adj.
  pious 979 adj.
faithful, the
  pietist 979 n.
  worshipper 981 n.

faithfulness
conformity 83 n.
loyalty 739 n.
probity 929 n.
faith healing
medical art 658 n.
piety 979 n.
faithless
perfidious 930 adj.
fake
imitation 20 n.
copy 22 n.
erroneous 495 adj.
duplicity 541 n.
fake 541 vb.
false 541 adj.
sham 542 n.
spurious 542 adj.
impostor 545 n.
faked
spurious 542 adj.
fakir
ascetic 945 n.
pietist 979 n.
monk 986 n.
falcon
bird 365 n.
heraldry 547 n.
falconry
chase 619 n.
fall
decrease 37 n.
decrease 37 vb.
period 110 n.
autumn 129 n.
be weak 163 vb.
be destroyed
165 vb.
reproduce itself
167 vb.
depth 211 n.
incline 220 n.
deviation 282 n.
regress 286 vb.
regression 286 n.
descend 309 vb.
descent 309 n.
tumble 309 vb.
flow 350 vb.
rain 350 vb.
deteriorate 655 vb.
relapse 657 vb.
be defeated 728 vb.
defeat 728 n.
fail 728 vb.
failure 728 n.
cheapness 812 n.

lose repute 867 vb.
be wicked 934 vb.
fall about
laugh 835 vb.
fallacious
illogical 477 adj.
erroneous 495 adj.
fallacy
sophism 477 n.
error 495 n.
deception 542 n.
fall apart
separate 46 vb.
deteriorate 655 vb.
fall asleep
sleep 679 vb.
fall away
separate 46 vb.
become small
198 vb.
fall back
regress 286 vb.
recede 290 vb.
relapse 657 vb.
fall back on
avail oneself of
673 vb.
fall behind
be inferior 35 vb.
be dispersed 75 vb.
move slowly
278 vb.
regress 286 vb.
fall short 307 vb.
fall below
be inferior 35 vb.
not suffice 636 vb.
fall between two
stools
fail 728 vb.
fall by the way
fall short 307 vb.
fall down
descend 309 vb.
fallen
fertilized 167 adj.
defeated 728 adj.
frail 934 adj.
unchaste 951 adj.
fallen, the
death roll 361 n.
fallen angel
bad person 938 n.
devil 969 n.
Satan 969 n.
impious person
980 n.

fallen woman
prostitute 952 n.
fall flat
miscarry 728 vb.
fall for
be credulous
487 vb.
be duped 544 vb.
be in love 887 vb.
fall foul of
collide 279 vb.
fall from grace
relapse 657 vb.
be wicked 934 vb.
fall guy
dupe 544 n.
laughingstock
851 n.
fall heir to
inherit 771 vb.
fallible
unreliable 474 adj.
illogical 477 adj.
misjudging
481 adj.
erroneous 495 adj.
imperfect 647 adj.
fall ill
be ill 651 vb.
fall in
be uniform 16 vb.
descend 309 vb.
plunge 313 vb.
falling
unequal 29 adj.
sloping 220 adj.
descent 309 n.
cheap 812 adj.
falling star
meteor 321 n.
fall in love
be in love 887 vb.
fall into
be turned to
147 vb.
enter 297 vb.
fall into line
conform 83 vb.
fall into place
be in order 60 vb.
fall in with
conform 83 vb.
consent 758 vb.
fall off
separate 46 vb.
descend 309 vb.
tumble 309 vb.

deteriorate 655 vb.
fall on one's feet
have luck 730 vb.
fall on one's sword
kill oneself 362 vb.
Fallopian tubes
genitalia 167 n.
fall out
disagree 25 vb.
be dispersed 75 vb.
happen 154 vb.
result 157 vb.
fall short 307 vb.
quarrel 709 vb.
not complete
726 vb.
be hostile 881 vb.
fallout
sequel 67 n.
nucleonics 160 n.
radiation 417 n.
insalubrity 653 n.
bomb 723 n.
fall out of favour
lose repute 867 vb.
fall out of love
be indifferent
860 vb.
hate 888 vb.
fallow
unproductive
172 adj.
inert 175 adj.
farm 370 n.
fall prostrate
tumble 309 vb.
falls
waterfall 350 n.
fall short
be unequal 29 vb.
be inferior 35 vb.
fall short 307 vb.
fall through
fall short 307 vb.
fall to
eat 301 vb.
undertake 672 vb.
be one's duty
917 vb.
fall under
be included 78 vb.
fall upon
surprise 508 vb.
attack 712 vb.
false
substituted 150 adj.
illogical 477 adj.

false 541 adj.
spurious 542 adj.
unwarranted
  916 adj.
flattering 925 adj.
false alarm
  false alarm 665 n.
  fear 854 n.
false dawn
  misjudgment
    481 n.
  error 495 n.
  disappointment
    509 n.
false-hearted
  perfidious 930 adj.
falsehood
  falsehood 541 n.
false name
  misnomer 562 n.
falseness
  error 495 n.
  falsehood 541 n.
  deception 542 n.
false pregnancy
  error 495 n.
false pretensions
  pretension 850 n.
false teeth
  tooth 256 n.
falsetto
  stridor 407 n.
  voicelessness 578 n.
falsify
  mislead 495 vb.
  be false 541 vb.
  be untrue 543 vb.
Falstaff
  bulk 195 n.
falter
  decelerate 278 vb.
  move slowly
    278 vb.
  be uncertain
    474 vb.
  stammer 580 vb.
  be irresolute
    601 vb.
  fail 728 vb.
fame
  greatness 32 n.
  publicity 528 n.
  famousness 866 n.
familial
  genetic 5 adj.
familiar
  interior 224 adj.

known 490 adj.
usual 610 adj.
impertinent
  878 adj.
disrespectful
  921 adj.
devil 969 n.
demon 970 n.
sorcerer 983 n.
familiarity
  knowledge 490 n.
  friendship 880 n.
  fellowship 882 n.
familiar with
  knowing 490 adj.
  habituated 610 adj.
family
  akin 11 adj.
  consanguinity
    11 n.
  family 11 n.
  subdivision 53 n.
  breed 77 n.
  parental 169 adj.
family circle
  family 11 n.
  home 192 n.
  fellowship 882 n.
family doctor
  doctor 658 n.
family name
  name 561 n.
family planning
  contraception
    172 n.
family tree
  series 71 n.
  list 87 n.
  genealogy 169 n.
famine
  unproductiveness
    172 n.
  scarcity 636 n.
  poverty 801 n.
  hunger 859 n.
famish
  be hungry 859 vb.
  starve 946 vb.
famished
  underfed 636 adj.
  hungry 859 adj.
  fasting 946 adj.
famishing
  fasting 946 adj.
famous
  great 32 adj.
  known 490 adj.

manifest 522 adj.
excellent 644 adj.
super 644 adj.
renowned 866 adj.
fan
  bunch 74 n.
  follower 284 n.
  rotator 315 n.
  aerate 340 vb.
  air 340 n.
  blow 352 vb.
  ventilation 352 n.
  enthusiast 504 n.
  habitué 610 n.
  refresh 685 vb.
  patron 707 n.
  excitant 821 n.
  lover 887 n.
fanatic
  nonconformist
    84 n.
  dogmatist 473 n.
  biased 481 adj.
  narrow mind
    481 n.
  the maladjusted
    504 n.
  zealot 979 n.
fanatical
  positive 473 adj.
  obstinate 602 adj.
  severe 735 adj.
fanaticism
  narrow mind
    481 n.
  opinionatedness
    602 n.
  warm feeling
    818 n.
  pietism 979 n.
fancier
  breeder 369 n.
  enthusiast 504 n.
fanciful
  absurd 497 adj.
  imaginary 513 adj.
  capricious 604 adj.
fan club
  lover 887 n.
  commender 923 n.
fancy
  think 449 vb.
  idea 451 n.
  be of the opinion
    that 485 vb.
  suppose 512 vb.
  supposition 512 n.

ideality 513 n.
imagination 513 n.
imagine 513 vb.
will 595 n.
willingness 597 n.
whim 604 n.
choice 605 n.
choose 605 vb.
wit 839 n.
ornamental
  844 adj.
liking 859 n.
love 887 n.
darling 890 n.
fancy, the
  pugilism 716 n.
fancy dress
  clothing 228 n.
  disguise 527 n.
fancy-free
  free 744 adj.
  impassive 820 adj.
  indifferent 860 adj.
fancy-man
  libertine 952 n.
fancy woman
  kept woman 952 n.
fancywork
  ornamental art
    844 n.
fandango
  dance 837 n.
fanfare
  loudness 400 n.
  celebration 876 n.
fang
  tooth 256 n.
  bane 659 n.
fangs
  pincers 778 n.
fanlight
  window 263 n.
fan out
  be dispersed 75 vb.
  expand 197 vb.
  open 263 vb.
  diverge 294 vb.
fantasia
  musical piece
    412 n.
  narrative 590 n.
fantasize
  imagine 513 vb.
fantastic
  prodigious 32 adj.
  unusual 84 adj.
  absurd 497 adj.

capricious 604 adj.
super 644 adj.
ridiculous 849 adj.
wonderful 864 adj.
fantasy
  insubstantiality
    4 n.
  fantasy 513 n.
  ideality 513 n.
  imagination 513 n.
fantasy fiction
  fantasy 513 n.
far
  distant 199 adj.
far ahead
  in front 237 adv.
far and away
  eminently 34 adv.
far and near
  widely 183 adv.
far and wide
  widely 183 adv.
far away
  distant 199 adj.
farce
  foolery 497 n.
  fable 543 n.
  stage play 594 n.
  laughter 835 n.
  wit 839 n.
  ridiculousness
    849 n.
farcical
  absurd 497 adj.
  dramatic 594 adj.
  laughing 835 adj.
  funny 849 adj.
far cry from, a
  dissimilar 19 adj.
fare
  meal 301 n.
  price 809 n.
farewell
  goodbye 296 int.
  valediction 296 n.
  courteous act
    884 n.
far-fetched
  irrelevant 10 adj.
far-flung
  extensive 32 adj.
  spacious 183 adj.
  distant 199 adj.
far from it
  different 15 adj.
farinaceous
  powdery 332 adj.

farm
  produce 164 vb.
  breed stock 369 vb.
  cultivate 370 vb.
  farm 370 n.
  mature 669 vb.
  lands 777 n.
farmer
  farmer 370 n.
  servant 742 n.
farm hand
  farmer 370 n.
farmhouse
  house 192 n.
  cereals 301 n.
  farm 370 n.
farming
  agriculture 370 n.
farmland
  soil 344 n.
  farm 370 n.
farm out
  lease 784 vb.
farmyard
  place 185 n.
  farm 370 n.
farmyard manure
  fertilizer 171 n.
far-reaching
  extensive 32 adj.
  spacious 183 adj.
farrow
  young creature
    132 n.
  reproduce itself
    167 vb.
  posterity 170 n.
farseeing
  intelligent 498 adj.
farsighted
  dim-sighted
    440 adj.
  vigilant 457 adj.
  intelligent 498 adj.
  foreseeing 510 adj.
fart
  eruct 300 vb.
  voidance 300 n.
  stink 397 vb.
farther
  beyond 199 adv.
  distant 199 adj.
farthest
  distant 199 adj.
farthing
  quadrisection 98 n.
  coinage 797 n.

farthingale
  skirt 228 n.
fascia
  strip 208 n.
  face 237 n.
fascicle
  bunch 74 n.
  reading matter
    589 n.
fascinate
  absorb 449 vb.
  attract notice
    455 vb.
  motivate 612 vb.
  bewitch 983 vb.
fascination
  inducement 612 n.
  pleasurableness
    826 n.
  liking 859 n.
  wonder 864 n.
  love 887 n.
  spell 983 n.
fascine
  bunch 74 n.
Fascists
  political party
    708 n.
fashion
  modality 7 n.
  similarity 18 n.
  produce 164 vb.
  form 243 n.
  form 243 vb.
  feature 445 n.
  style 566 n.
  way 624 n.
  conduct 688 n.
  fashion 848 n.
fashionable
  fashionable
    848 adj.
fashion designer
  clothier 228 n.
fashion model
  living model 23 n.
fashion plate
  picture 553 n.
  fop 848 n.
fashion show
  fashion 848 n.
fast
  firm 45 adj.
  tied 45 adj.
  fixed 153 adj.
  speedy 277 adj.
  inexact 495 adj.

friendly 880 adj.
do penance 941 vb.
be ascetic 945 vb.
fast 946 n.
starve 946 vb.
unchaste 951 adj.
perform ritual
  988 vb.
fast asleep
  sleepy 679 adj.
fastback
  automobile 274 n.
fast buck
  easy thing 701 n.
fast day
  special day 876 n.
  asceticism 945 n.
  fast 946 n.
  holy day 988 n.
fasten
  affix 45 vb.
  join 45 vb.
  tighten 45 vb.
  close 264 vb.
  take 786 vb.
fastener
  fastening 47 n.
fastening
  fastening 47 n.
fasten on
  retain 778 vb.
  take 786 vb.
faster
  abstainer 942 n.
  ascetic 945 n.
fast food
  provisions 301 n.
fastidious
  sensitive 819 adj.
  fastidious 862 adj.
fasting
  penance 941 n.
  ascetic 945 adj.
  fasting 946 adj.
  fasting 946 n.
fast lane
  road 624 n.
fastness
  fort 713 n.
fast one
  trickery 542 n.
fat
  prolific 171 adj.
  fleshy 195 adj.
  food content 301 n.
  fat 357 n.
  fatty 357 adj.

699

plentiful 635 adj.
plenty 635 n.
prosperous 730 adj.
fatal
deadly 362 adj.
fated 596 adj.
evil 616 adj.
harmful 645 adj.
fatal flaw
weakness 163 n.
vulnerability 661 n.
vice 934 n.
fatalistic
submitting 721 adj.
fatality
death roll 361 n.
decease 361 n.
necessity 596 n.
evil 616 n.
fat cat
prosperous person
  730 n.
rich person 800 n.
fate
futurity 124 n.
cause 156 n.
fate 596 n.
fated
future 124 adj.
fated 596 adj.
fateful
important 638 adj.
Fates, the
fate 596 n.
fate worse than death
suffering 825 n.
fathead
dunce 501 n.
fool 501 n.
father
be akin 11 vb.
kinsman 11 n.
cause 156 n.
generate 167 vb.
paternity 169 n.
male 372 n.
church title 986 n.
cleric 986 n.
Father Christmas
giver 781 n.
good giver 813 n.
benefactor 903 n.
father confessor
pastor 986 n.
fathered
born 360 adj.

father figure
substitute 150 n.
paternity 169 n.
Fatherhood
divineness 965 n.
fatherhood
family 11 n.
parentage 169 n.
paternity 169 n.
father in God
cleric 986 n.
pastor 986 n.
father-in-law
paternity 169 n.
fatherland
paternity 169 n.
territory 184 n.
home 192 n.
fatherlike
parental 169 adj.
fatherly
parental 169 adj.
benevolent 897 adj.
fatherly eye
protection 660 n.
Father Time
time 108 n.
father upon
attribute 158 vb.
fathom
long measure
  203 n.
be deep 211 vb.
enquire 459 vb.
measure 465 vb.
understand 516 vb.
fathomless
deep 211 adj.
fatigue
labour 682 n.
fatigue 684 n.
fatigue 684 vb.
fatigued
fatigued 684 adj.
fatigued, be
be fatigued 684 vb.
fatigues
uniform 228 n.
fat in the fire
turmoil 61 n.
fat lot
great quantity
  32 n.
fatness
bulk 195 n.
fat of the land
plenty 635 n.

prosperity 730 n.
fatten
grow 36 vb.
enlarge 197 vb.
feed 301 vb.
breed stock 369 vb.
fatten on
eat 301 vb.
fatten up
feed 301 vb.
fattiness
unctuousness
  357 n.
fatty
bulk 195 n.
fatty 357 adj.
fatuity
insubstantiality
  4 n.
insubstantial thing
  4 n.
absence of thought
  450 n.
absurdity 497 n.
folly 499 n.
fatuous
absurd 497 adj.
foolish 499 adj.
meaningless
  515 adj.
fatuousness
folly 499 n.
faucet
stopper 264 n.
outlet 298 n.
water 339 n.
fault
discontinuity 72 n.
weakness 163 n.
gap 201 n.
blunder 495 vb.
defect 647 n.
criticize 924 vb.
detract 926 vb.
vice 934 n.
guilty act 936 n.
fault-finding
discontented
  829 adj.
fastidious 862 adj.
censure 924 n.
disapprobation
  924 n.
disapproving
  924 adj.
faultless
perfect 646 adj.

guiltless 935 adj.
pure 950 adj.
faultlessness
perfection 646 n.
purity 950 n.
faulty
inexact 495 adj.
bad 645 adj.
imperfect 647 adj.
faun
mythical being
  970 n.
fauna
animality 365 n.
Faust
sorcerer 983 n.
faute de mieux
instead 150 adv.
Fauvism ·
school of painting
  553 n.
faux pas
mistake 495 n.
failure 728 n.
guilty act 936 n.
favour
resemble 18 vb.
advantage 34 n.
influence 178 n.
promote 285 vb.
be biased 481 vb.
badge 547 n.
choice 605 n.
choose 605 vb.
benefit 615 n.
aid 703 n.
gift 781 n.
desire 859 vb.
liking 859 n.
honours 866 n.
repute 866 n.
courteous act
  884 n.
love token 889 n.
do wrong 914 adj.
injustice 914 n.
respect 920 n.
approbation 923 n.
approve 923 vb.
favourable
opportune 137 adj.
predicting 511 adj.
beneficial 644 adj.
palmy 730 adj.
promising 852 adj.
approving 923 adj.

favourable verdict
  legal trial 959 n.
  acquittal 960 n.
favourably
  well 615 adv.
favourite
  chosen 605 adj.
  contender 716 n.
  loved one 887 n.
  favourite 890 n.
favouritism
  prejudice 481 n.
  injustice 914 n.
fawn
  young creature
    132 n.
  mammal 365 n.
  brown 430 adj.
  be servile 879 vb.
  flatter 925 vb.
  be dishonest
    930 vb.
fawn on
  flatter 925 vb.
fax
  message 529 n.
  telecommunication
    531 n.
fay
  fairy 970 n.
FBI
  police enquiry
    459 n.
fealty
  loyalty 739 n.
  duty 917 n.
fear
  fear 854 n.
  fear 854 vb.
fear for one's life
  quake 854 vb.
fearful
  nervous 854 adj.
  cowardly 856 adj.
  wonderful 864 adj.
fearing
  fearing 854 adj.
fear of death
  phobia 854 n.
fear of God
  piety 979 n.
fears
  nervousness 854 n.
fearsome
  frightening
    854 adj.

feasibility
  possibility 469 n.
  facility 701 n.
feasible
  possible 469 adj.
  easy 701 adj.
feast
  eat 301 vb.
  feasting 301 n.
  feed 301 vb.
  pleasure 376 n.
  plenty 635 n.
  enjoyment 824 n.
  revel 837 vb.
  social gathering
    882 n.
  holy day 988 n.
feast day
  festivity 837 n.
  special day 876 n.
  holy day 988 n.
feat
  contrivance 623 n.
  deed 676 n.
  masterpiece 694 n.
  success 727 n.
  prowess 855 n.
  miracle-working
    864 n.
feather
  sort 77 n.
  filament 208 n.
  row 269 vb.
  lightness 323 n.
  trifle 639 n.
  trimming 844 n.
  honours 866 n.
feather bed
  softness 327 n.
featherbed
  soften 327 vb.
  aid 703 vb.
  be lax 734 vb.
  be lenient 736 vb.
  pet 889 vb.
featherbrain
  fool 501 n.
featherbrained
  light-minded
    456 adj.
  foolish 499 adj.
feather in one's cap
  success 727 n.
  trophy 729 n.
  honours 866 n.
feather one's nest
  prosper 730 vb.

  get rich 800 vb.
  be selfish 932 vb.
feathers
  skin 226 n.
  plumage 259 n.
  wing 271 n.
  softness 327 n.
featherweight
  light 323 adj.
  pugilist 722 n.
feathery
  light 323 adj.
feature
  component 58 n.
  speciality 80 n.
  feature 445 n.
  show 522 vb.
  advertise 528 vb.
  broadcast 531 n.
  dramatize 594 vb.
feature film
  film 445 n.
features
  character 5 n.
  outline 233 n.
  face 237 n.
febrifuge
  antidote 658 n.
febrile
  hot 379 adj.
  diseased 651 adj.
feckless
  capricious 604 adj.
  useless 641 adj.
  unskilful 695 adj.
FE college
  academy 539 n.
  school 539 n.
fecund
  prolific 171 adj.
fecundity
  propagation 167 n.
  productiveness
    171 n.
federal
  cooperative
    706 adj.
federalism
  government 733 n.
federation
  association 706 n.
  society 708 n.
  *political organiza-
    tion* 733 n.
fed up
  have enough
    635 vb.

  bored 838 adj.
fee
  estate 777 n.
  gift 781 n.
  pay 804 n.
  price 809 n.
  reward 962 n.
feeble
  small 33 adj.
  inferior 35 adj.
  impotent 161 adj.
  powerless 161 adj.
  weak 163 adj.
  muted 401 adj.
  poorly reasoned
    477 adj.
  feeble 572 adj.
  lax 734 adj.
  frail 934 adj.
feeble-minded
  weak 163 adj.
  unintelligent
    499 adj.
  *mentally handi-
    capped* 503 adj.
feebleness
  weakness 163 n.
  feebleness 572 n.
feed
  eat 301 vb.
  feed 301 vb.
  graze 301 vb.
  meal 301 n.
  provender 301 n.
  provide 633 vb.
  provision 633 n.
  laughingstock
    851 n.
feedback
  data processing
    86 n.
  reversion 148 n.
  answer 460 n.
feed on
  eat 301 vb.
fee faw fum
  intimidation
    854 n.
  spell 983 n.
feel
  texture 331 n.
  touch 378 vb.
  be tentative 461 vb.
  feel 818 vb.
feeler
  feeler 378 n.
  question 459 n.

empiricism 461 n.
offer 759 n.

feel for
search 459 vb.
pity 905 vb.

feeling
touch 378 n.
feeling 818 adj.
feeling 818 n.

feelings
affections 817 n.

feel like
be willing 597 vb.

feel sorry
be penitent 939 vb.

feel sorry for
pity 905 vb.

feel the pinch
be in difficulty 700 vb.
have trouble 731 vb.
be poor 801 vb.

feet
foot 214 n.
conveyance 267 n.

feet of clay
weakness 163 n.
deception 542 n.
defect 647 n.
vulnerability 661 n.

feign
imitate 20 vb.
dissemble 541 vb.
be affected 850 vb.

feint
trickery 542 n.
stratagem 698 n.

felicitations
congratulation 886 n.

felicitous
apt 24 adj.
elegant 575 adj.
successful 727 adj.
happy 824 adj.

felicity
elegance 575 n.
happiness 824 n.

feline
animal 365 adj.
cat 365 n.

fell
cut 46 vb.
high land 209 n.
skin 226 n.
fell 311 vb.

plain 348 n.
deadly 362 adj.
evil 616 adj.
hostile 881 adj.
cruel 898 adj.
malevolent 898 adj.

fellow
identity 13 n.
analogue 18 n.
compeer 28 n.
adjunct 40 n.
concomitant 89 n.
person 371 n.
male 372 n.
teacher 537 n.
student 538 n.
society 708 n.
low fellow 869 n.
chum 880 n.
friend 880 n.

fellow feeling
bond 47 n.
cooperation 706 n.
concord 710 n.
participation 775 n.
feeling 818 n.
friendliness 880 n.
love 887 n.
benevolence 897 n.
condolence 905 n.
pity 905 n.

fellowship
group 74 n.
association 706 n.
cooperation 706 n.
community 708 n.
friendship 880 n.
fellowship 882 n.

fellow traveller
assenter 488 n.
collaborator 707 n.

fell walker
climber 308 n.

felo de se
suicide 362 n.

felon
offender 904 n.

felony
perfidy 930 n.
vice 934 n.
guilty act 936 n.
lawbreaking 954 n.

felt
textile 222 n.
weave 222 vb.

felt-tip pen
stationery 586 n.

felucca
sailing ship 275 n.

female
person 371 n.
female 373 adj.
female 373 n.

female impersonator
imitator 20 n.
entertainer 594 n.

female sex
womankind 373 n.

feminine
female 373 adj.
grammatical 564 adj.

feminineness
female 373 n.

femininity
female 373 n.

feminism
female 373 n.

feminist
female 373 adj.
female 373 n.
reformer 654 n.

feministic
female 373 adj.

femme fatale
motivator 612 n.
a beauty 841 n.
loved one 887 n.
loose woman 952 n.

fen
moisture 341 n.
marsh 347 n.

fence
fence 235 n.
collide 279 vb.
sophisticate 477 vb.
avoid 620 vb.
obstacle 702 n.
obstruct 702 vb.
defences 713 n.
defend 713 vb.
fight 716 vb.
thief 789 n.
trade 791 vb.
merchant 794 n.

fence in
circumscribe 232 vb.
enclose 235 vb.
safeguard 660 vb.

fence off
exclude 57 vb.

fencing
duel 716 n.

fender
intermediary 231 n.
furnace 383 n.
shelter 662 n.
defence 713 n.

fend for oneself
be free 744 vb.

fend off
screen 421 vb.
obstruct 702 vb.

fenland
marsh 347 n.

feral
animal 365 adj.
unsociable 883 adj.
cruel 898 adj.

ferment
turmoil 61 n.
be turned to 147 vb.
convert 147 vb.
stimulation 174 n.
violence 176 n.
commotion 318 n.
effervesce 318 vb.
leaven 323 n.
bubble 355 vb.
be sour 393 vb.
feeling 818 n.
excitation 821 n.
excitable state 822 n.
anger 891 n.

fern
plant 366 n.

ferocious
furious 176 adj.
cruel 898 adj.

ferocity
violence 176 n.
inhumanity 898 n.

ferret
mammal 365 n.

ferret out
enquire 459 vb.
discover 484 vb.

ferrule
covering 226 n.

ferry
voyage 269 vb.
transfer 272 vb.
transference 272 n.

carry 273 vb.
boat 275 n.
ship 275 n.
bridge 624 n.

fertile
prolific 171 adj.
imaginative
  513 adj.
diffuse 570 adj.
plentiful 635 adj.
rich 800 adj.

fertility
propagation 167 n.
productiveness
  171 n.
plenty 635 n.

fertilize
make fruitful
  171 vb.
cultivate 370 vb.

fertilizer
propagation 167 n.
fertilizer 171 n.

fervent
hot 379 adj.
fervent 818 adj.
pietistic 979 adj.

fervid
hot 379 adj.
fervent 818 adj.

fervour
vigorousness 174 n.
heat 379 n.
vigour 571 n.
warm feeling
  818 n.
piety 979 n.

fess
heraldry 547 n.

fester
deteriorate 655 vb.
hurt 827 vb.
be malevolent
  898 vb.

festina lente
be cautious 858 vb.
caution 858 n.

festival
assembly 74 n.
festivity 837 n.
holy day 988 n.

festive cheer
feasting 301 n.

festivities
festivity 837 n.

festivity
festivity 837 n.

festschrift
accumulation 74 n.
reading matter
  589 n.

fetch
carry 273 vb.
cost 809 vb.

fetching
pleasurable
  826 adj.
personable 841 adj.
desired 859 adj.

fetch up at
arrive 295 vb.

fête
feed 301 vb.
amusement 837 n.
pageant 875 n.
celebrate 876 vb.
celebration 876 n.
congratulate
  886 vb.

fetid
fetid 397 adj.

fetish
deity 966 n.
idol 982 n.
talisman 983 n.

fetlock
foot 214 n.

fetter
bond 47 n.
subjugate 745 vb.
arrest 747 vb.
fetter 747 vb.
fetter 748 n.

fettle
state 7 n.

fettucine
dish 301 n.

feu
possession 773 n.

feud
quarrel 709 n.
enmity 881 n.
revenge 910 n.

feudal
olden 127 adj.
governmental
  733 adj.
subject 745 adj.
proprietary
  777 adj.

feudalism
government 733 n.

fever
agitation 318 n.

commotion 318 n.
heat 379 n.
illness 651 n.
infection 651 n.
excitable state
  822 n.

feverish
hot 379 adj.
diseased 651 adj.
sick 651 adj.
active 678 adj.
hasty 680 adj.
excited 821 adj.
excitable 822 adj.

fever pitch
excitation 821 n.

feverscan
thermometry
  379 n.

few
plurality 101 n.
few 105 adj.
fewness 105 n.

few and far between
discontinuous
  72 adj.
few 105 adj.
infrequent 140 adj.
seldom 140 adv.

fey
bewitched 983 adj.
psychical 984 n.

fez
headgear 228 n.

fiancé(e)
loved one 887 n.
lover 887 n.

fiasco
failure 728 n.

fib
be false 541 vb.
untruth 543 n.

fibre
essential part 5 n.
fibre 208 n.
filament 208 n.
food content 301 n.

fibreglass
textile 222 n.
materials 631 n.

fibril
filament 208 n.

fibrilla
filament 208 n.

fibrosis
disease 651 n.

fibrositis
pang 377 n.
rheumatism 651 n.

fibrous
tough 329 adj.

fibula
leg 267 n.

fichu
neckwear 228 n.

fickle
changeable
  143 adj.
changeful 152 adj.
unreliable 474 adj.
capricious 604 adj.

fiction
product 164 n.
ideality 513 n.
falsehood 541 n.
fable 543 n.
literature 557 n.
narrative 590 n.
novel 590 n.

fictional
imaginative
  513 adj.

fictitious
unreal 2 adj.
insubstantial 4 adj.
imaginary 513 adj.
untrue 543 adj.
unwarranted
  916 adj.

fiddle
play music 413 vb.
viol 414 n.
fake 541 vb.
deceive 542 vb.
trickery 542 n.
contrivance 623 n.
defraud 788 vb.
stealing 788 n.
swindling 788 n.
account 808 vb.
be dishonest
  930 vb.
perfidy 930 n.

fiddle-faddle
silly talk 515 n.

fiddler
instrumentalist
  413 n.
trickster 545 n.
defrauder 789 n.

fiddlestick
viol 414 n.

fiddle with
   touch 378 vb.
fidelity
   accuracy 494 n.
   veracity 540 n.
   loyalty 739 n.
   observance 768 n.
   probity 929 n.
fidget
   haste 680 n.
   hasten 680 vb.
   be excitable
      822 vb.
fiduciary
   monetary 797 adj.
fief
   possession 773 n.
   lands 777 n.
field
   classification 77 n.
   opportunity 137 n.
   range 183 n.
   region 184 n.
   place 185 n.
   enclosure 235 n.
   grassland 348 n.
   answer 460 vb.
   heraldry 547 n.
   function 622 n.
   arena 724 n.
   scope 744 n.
field, the
   opponent 705 n.
   contender 716 n.
field day
   contest 716 n.
   pageant 875 n.
   special day 876 n.
fielder
   player 837 n.
fieldfare
   bird 365 n.
field glasses
   telescope 442 n.
field marshal
   army officer 741 n.
field mouse
   mammal 365 n.
field of vision
   visibility 443 n.
fields
   land 344 n.
   plain 348 n.
   farm 370 n.
field sports
   sport 837 n.

field trip
   land travel 267 n.
fiend
   monster 938 n.
   devil 969 n.
fiendish
   cruel 898 adj.
   wicked 934 adj.
   diabolic 969 adj.
fierce
   furious 176 adj.
   courageous
      855 adj.
   angry 891 adj.
   irascible 892 adj.
   cruel 898 adj.
fiery
   fiery 379 adj.
   hot 379 adj.
   pungent 388 adj.
   red 431 adj.
   forceful 571 adj.
   fervent 818 adj.
   excitable 822 adj.
   irascible 892 adj.
fiery cross
   call 547 n.
   danger signal
      665 n.
   war measures
      718 n.
fiesta
   festivity 837 n.
fife
   flute 414 n.
fifteen
   band 74 n.
   party 708 n.
fifth
   interval 201 n.
   musical note
      410 n.
fifth column
   collaborator 707 n.
   enemy 881 n.
   perfidy 930 n.
fifty
   twenty and over
      99 n.
fifty-fifty
   equal 28 adj.
   mixed 43 adj.
   equal chance
      159 n.
   not bad 644 adj.
   middling 732 adj.

fifty per cent
   bisection 92 n.
fig
   small quantity
      33 n.
   fruit and vegetables
      301 n.
   trifle 639 n.
fight
   be in difficulty
      700 vb.
   contend 716 vb.
   fight 716 n.
   fight 716 vb.
fight against
   counteract 182 vb.
   oppose 704 vb.
fight back
   restrain 747 vb.
fighter
   aircraft 276 n.
   contender 716 n.
   air force 722 n.
   combatant 722 n.
fight for
   defend 713 vb.
fighting
   contention 716 n.
   pugilism 716 n.
   warfare 718 n.
fighting chance
   fair chance 159 n.
fighting fit
   healthy 650 adj.
fight it out
   fight 716 vb.
   go to war 718 vb.
fight off
   resist 715 vb.
fight or flight
   fear 854 n.
fight shy
   be unwilling
      598 vb.
   avoid 620 vb.
figment
   insubstantial thing
      4 n.
   ideality 513 n.
figurative
   figurative 519 adj.
figure
   number 85 n.
   outline 233 n.
   form 243 n.
   person 371 n.
   feature 445 n.

   indication 547 n.
   image 551 n.
   funds 797 n.
   price 809 n.
   person of repute
      866 n.
figurehead
   insubstantial thing
      4 n.
   powerless 161 adj.
   protuberance
      254 n.
   indication 547 n.
   See **badge**
   image 551 n.
   nonentity 639 n.
   ornamental art
      844 n.
figure of eight
   over five 99 n.
   curve 248 n.
   loop 250 n.
   circuition 314 n.
figure of fun
   laughingstock
      851 n.
figure of speech
   trope 519 n.
   ornament 574 n.
figures
   statistics 86 n.
figurine
   image 551 n.
   sculpture 554 n.
fiky
   narrow-minded
      481 adj.
   fastidious 862 adj.
filament
   filament 208 n.
filbert
   fruit and vegetables
      301 n.
filch
   steal 788 vb.
file
   abate 37 vb.
   arrangement 62 n.
   class 62 vb.
   sorting 62 n.
   bunch 74 n.
   list 87 n.
   list 87 vb.
   put off 136 vb.
   case 194 n.
   receptacle 194 n.

make smaller
198 vb.
sharpen 256 vb.
smooth 258 vb.
smoother 258 n.
roughness 259 n.
walk 267 vb.
pulverizer 332 n.
rub 333 vb.
information 524 n.
record 548 n.
record 548 vb.
collection 632 n.
store 632 vb.
formation 722 n.
file charges
indict 928 vb.
file down
subtract 39 vb.
file in
enter 297 vb.
file off
diverge 294 vb.
files
record 548 n.
filiated
relative 9 adj.
filibeg
skirt 228 n.
filibustering
protraction 113 n.
delay 136 n.
filigree
network 222 n.
ornamental art
844 n.
filing
powderiness 332 n.
friction 333 n.
filings
leavings 41 n.
powder 332 n.
filing system
sorting 62 n.
fill
grow 36 vb.
fill 54 vb.
pervade 189 vb.
line 227 vb.
store 632 vb.
doctor 658 vb.
possess 773 vb.
filled
filled 635 adj.
filler
news 529 n.
diffuseness 570 n.

fillet
ligature 47 n.
strip 208 n.
headgear 228 n.
uncover 229 vb.
empty 300 vb.
cook 301 vb.
fillet steak
meat 301 n.
fill in
augment 36 vb.
fill 54 vb.
filling
increasing 36 adj.
plenitude 54 n.
contents 193 n.
lining 227 n.
surgery 658 n.
filling station
storage 632 n.
fillip
stimulant 174 n.
impel 279 vb.
knock 279 n.
incentive 612 n.
excitant 821 n.
fill one in on
inform 524 vb.
fill out
augment 36 vb.
grow 36 vb.
be complete 54 vb.
expand 197 vb.
fill up
fill 54 vb.
store 632 vb.
sate 863 vb.
filly
young creature
132 n.
horse 273 n.
female animal
373 n.
film
layer 207 n.
shallowness 212 n.
covering 226 n.
skin 226 n.
motion 265 n.
cloud 355 n.
opacity 423 n.
camera 442 n.
film 445 n.
show 522 vb.
broadcast 531 n.
record 548 vb.
photograph 551 vb.

photography 551 n.
films
film 445 n.
film star
cinema 445 n.
actor 594 n.
favourite 890 n.
filmstrip
photography 551 n.
filmy
textural 331 adj.
cloudy 355 adj.
dim 419 adj.
transparent
422 adj.
opaque 423 adj.
semitransparent
424 adj.
filter
deviate 282 vb.
exude 298 vb.
screen 421 n.
cleaning utensil
648 n.
purify 648 vb.
filter through
pervade 189 vb.
filter tip
tobacco 388 n.
filth
badness 645 n.
dirt 649 n.
ugliness 842 n.
impurity 951 n.
filthy
bad 645 adj.
not nice 645 adj.
dirty 649 adj.
impure 951 adj.
filthy lucre
money 797 n.
filthy rich
moneyed 800 adj.
filtrate
exude 298 vb.
fin
equilibrium 28 n.
limb 53 n.
stabilizer 153 n.
laterality 239 n.
propeller 269 n.
aircraft 276 n.
final
ending 69 adj.
contest 716 n.
commanding
737 adj.

final curtain
dramaturgy 594 n.
completion 725 n.
final demand
demand 737 n.
request 761 n.
finale
end 69 n.
musical piece
412 n.
dramaturgy 594 n.
completion 725 n.
finality
finality 69 n.
finalize
make certain
473 vb.
final offer
offer 759 n.
finals
end 69 n.
exam 459 n.
final say
influence 178 n.
final warning
warning 664 n.
finance
aid 703 vb.
lend 784 vb.
finance 797 n.
financial
monetary 797 adj.
financier
lender 784 n.
merchant 794 n.
treasurer 798 n.
finch
bird 365 n.
find
meet with 154 vb.
arrive 295 vb.
judge 480 vb.
discover 484 vb.
discovery 484 n.
benefit 615 n.
acquire 771 vb.
acquisition 771 n.
booty 790 n.
try a case 959 vb.
find against
judge 480 vb.
condemn 961 vb.
finder
telescope 442 n.
detector 484 n.
finders keepers
retention 778 n.

fireguard
furnace 383 n.
shelter 662 n.
fire-irons
furnace 383 n.
firelight
light 417 n.
fire-lighter
lighter 385 n.
fireman
extinguisher 382 n.
protector 660 n.
defender 713 n.
fireplace
home 192 n.
furnace 383 n.
fireproof
strong 162 adj.
coat 226 vb.
invulnerable
660 adj.
fire-raiser
arson 381 n.
fire ship
lighter 385 n.
warship 722 n.
fireside
focus 76 n.
place 185 n.
home 192 n.
fireside chat
chat 584 n.
fire station
extinguisher 382 n.
fire tender
extinguisher 382 n.
firewatcher
protector 660 n.
firewood
fuel 385 n.
fireworks
explosive 723 n.
fire worship
fire 379 n.
idolatry 982 n.
firing
propulsion 287 n.
bang 402 n.
bombardment
712 n.
firing line
battle 718 n.
battleground
724 n.
firing on all cylinders, be
work 682 vb.

firkin
vat 194 n.
firm
firm 45 adj.
fixed 153 adj.
dense 324 adj.
rigid 326 adj.
resolute 599 adj.
obstinate 602 adj.
corporation 708 n.
retentive 778 adj.
merchant 794 n.
courageous
855 adj.
friendly 880 adj.
firmament
heavens 321 n.
firmness
permanence 144 n.
stability 153 n.
hardness 326 n.
resolution 599 n.
firmness of purpose
will 595 n.
first
original 21 adj.
supreme 34 adj.
first 68 adj.
initially 68 adv.
prior 119 adj.
victor 727 n.
first aid
therapy 658 n.
aid 703 n.
first and foremost
initially 68 adv.
firstborn
precursor 66 n.
prior 119 adj.
priority 119 n.
older 131 adj.
first-class
supreme 34 adj.
first class post
*postal communica-
tions* 531 n.
first cousin
kinsman 11 n.
first draft
plan 623 n.
preparation 669 n.
first edition
edition 589 n.
first great growth
wine 301 n.
first-hand
original 21 adj.

new 126 adj.
**first-hand impres-
sion**
beginning 68 n.
firstly
initially 68 adv.
first magnitude star
luminary 420 n.
first name
name 561 n.
first night
debut 68 n.
dramaturgy 594 n.
first of all
initially 68 adv.
first offender
offender 904 n.
first principles
beginning 68 n.
first-rate
supreme 34 adj.
notable 638 adj.
best 644 adj.
excellent 644 adj.
skilful 694 adj.
first-rater
exceller 644 n.
first secretary
official 690 n.
**first see the light of
day**
become 1 vb.
first strike
attempt 671 n.
first thing
betimes 135 adv.
firth
gulf 345 n.
fiscal
monetary 797 adj.
fiscal year
period 110 n.
fish
fish food 301 n.
animal 365 n.
fish 365 n.
search 459 vb.
hunt 619 vb.
amuse oneself
837 vb.
fish and chips
fish food 301 n.
meal 301 n.
fish cakes
fish food 301 n.
fisherman
hunter 619 n.

fisherman's yarn
improbability
472 n.
fable 543 n.
fishery
extraction 304 n.
fish farm
stock farm 369 n.
fish fingers
fish food 301 n.
fish for
search 459 vb.
be tentative 461 vb.
pursue 619 vb.
attempt 671 vb.
request 761 vb.
desire 859 vb.
fish for compliments
be vain 873 vb.
be ostentatious
875 vb.
fishing
chase 619 n.
fishing boat
fishing boat 275 n.
fishing net
receptacle 194 n.
fishing smack
fishing boat 275 n.
fishing tackle
chase 619 n.
fish knife
sharp edge 256 n.
fishnet
network 222 n.
fish out of water
unrelatedness 10 n.
misfit 25 n.
nonconformist
84 n.
displacement
188 n.
bungler 697 n.
fish's tail
propeller 269 n.
fish tank
stock farm 369 n.
fish up
elevate 310 vb.
fishy
animal 365 adj.
improbable
472 adj.
puzzling 517 adj.
dishonest 930 adj.
fissile
brittle 330 adj.

fission
separation 46 n.
decompose 51 vb.
decomposition
  51 n.
nucleonics 160 n.
fissure
disunion 46 n.
gap 201 n.
fist
pincers 778 n.
fistful
contents 193 n.
fisticuffs
turmoil 61 n.
violence 176 n.
knock 279 n.
quarrel 709 n.
fight 716 n.
pugilism 716 n.
anger 891 n.
fistula
tube 263 n.
ulcer 651 n.
fit
accord 24 vb.
adjust 24 vb.
fit 24 adj.
equalize 28 vb.
join 45 vb.
cohere 48 vb.
make conform
  83 vb.
violence 176 n.
spasm 318 n.
frenzy 503 n.
whim 604 n.
be expedient
  642 vb.
healthy 650 adj.
illness 651 n.
activity 678 n.
excitable state
  822 n.
fear 854 n.
due 915 adj.
fit as a fiddle
strong 162 adj.
healthy 650 adj.
fit for
useful 640 adj.
fit for nothing
useless 641 adj.
fitful
fitful 142 adj.
capricious 604 adj.
excitable 822 adj.

fit in
accord 24 vb.
conform 83 vb.
make conform
  83 vb.
load 193 vb.
insert 303 vb.
fit in with
conform 83 vb.
fit like a glove
accord 24 vb.
fitness
fitness 24 n.
vitality 162 n.
good policy 642 n.
health 650 n.
aptitude 694 n.
right 913 n.
fitness freak
enthusiast 504 n.
fit of laughing
laughter 835 n.
fit of temper
anger 891 n.
fit out
dress 228 vb.
provide 633 vb.
make ready
  669 vb.
fits and starts
fitfulness 142 n.
agitation 318 n.
fitter
machinist 630 n.
artisan 686 n.
fitting
relevant 9 adj.
adaptation 24 n.
adjusted 24 adj.
fit 24 adj.
opportune 137 adj.
advisable 642 adj.
right 913 adj.
due 915 adj.
fit to a T
accord 24 vb.
fit-up
plot 623 n.
five
five 99 n.
five-a-side
five 99 n.
five-day week
period 110 n.
five o'clock
evening 129 n.

five o'clock shadow
hair 259 n.
roughness 259 n.
five-pound note
coinage 797 n.
paper money
  797 n.
fiver
funds 797 n.
fives
ball game 837 n.
five senses
five 99 n.
sense 374 n.
five-year plan
plan 623 n.
fix
circumstance 8 n.
affix 45 vb.
arrange 62 vb.
stabilize 153 vb.
place 187 vb.
close 264 vb.
murder 362 vb.
fake 541 vb.
deceive 542 vb.
trickery 542 n.
be resolute 599 vb.
predetermine
  608 vb.
repair 656 vb.
remedy 658 vb.
predicament 700 n.
defeat 727 vb.
drug-taking 949 n.
punish 963 vb.
fixation
location 187 n.
attention 455 n.
prejudgment 481 n.
eccentricity 503 n.
fixative
adhesive 47 n.
pigment 425 n.
fixed
permanent 144 adj.
fixed 153 adj.
false 541 adj.
untrue 543 adj.
fixed calendar
chronology 117 n.
fixed price
price 809 n.
fixer
trickster 545 n.
fixity
permanence 144 n.

obstinacy 602 n.
fix on
be attentive 455 vb.
choose 605 vb.
accuse 928 vb.
fixture
adjunct 40 n.
concomitant 89 n.
fixture 153 n.
property 777 n.
fizz
vigorousness 174 n.
soft drink 301 n.
wine 301 n.
bubble 355 vb.
hiss 406 vb.
fizzle
bubble 355 vb.
hiss 406 vb.
fizzle out
fall short 307 vb.
fizzy
vigorous 174 adj.
windy 352 adj.
bubbly 355 adj.
fjord
gulf 345 n.
flabbergast
be wonderful
  864 vb.
flabby
weak 163 adj.
soft 327 adj.
fatty 357 adj.
flaccid
weak 163 adj.
inert 175 adj.
soft 327 adj.
feeble 572 adj.
flag
be weak 163 vb.
decelerate 278 vb.
move slowly
  278 vb.
foliage 366 n.
plant 366 n.
flag 547 n.
building material
  631 n.
be fatigued 684 vb.
be dejected 834 vb.
flag day
request 761 n.
offering 781 n.
special day 876 n.
flag down
signal 547 vb.

flagellate
do penance 941 vb.
flog 963 vb.
perform ritual
988 vb.
flagellation
penance 941 n.
asceticism 945 n.
corporal punish-
ment 963 n.
flagellum
filament 208 n.
flageolet
flute 414 n.
flagging
fatigued 684 adj.
flag of convenience
shipping 275 n.
flag 547 n.
contrivance 623 n.
flagon
vessel 194 n.
flagpole
flag 547 n.
flagrancy
ostentation 875 n.
insolence 878 n.
wickedness 934 n.
flagrant
flagrant 32 adj.
manifest 522 adj.
showy 875 adj.
insolent 878 adj.
heinous 934 adj.
flagrante delicto
guilty 936 adj.
flags
paving 226 n.
celebration 876 n.
flagship
warship 722 n.
flagstones
road 624 n.
flag-waving
gesture 547 n.
celebration 876 n.
flail
hammer 279 n.
strike 279 vb.
cultivate 370 vb.
farm tool 370 n.
strike at 712 vb.
flair
ability 160 n.
intellect 447 n.
discrimination
463 n.

aptitude 694 n.
fashion 848 n.
flak
bombardment
712 n.
defences 713 n.
ammunition 723 n.
defeat 728 n.
detraction 926 n.
flake
small thing 33 n.
piece 53 n.
powder 332 n.
flake out
be fatigued 684 vb.
flaky
brittle 330 adj.
powdery 332 adj.
crazy 503 adj.
flaky pastry
pastries and cakes
301 n.
flambeau
torch 420 n.
flamboyant
luminous 417 adj.
ornate 574 adj.
flame
be hot 379 vb.
fire 379 n.
heat 379 n.
heater 383 n.
light 417 n.
shine 417 vb.
luminary 420 n.
redness 431 n.
loved one 887 n.
flame-coloured
red 431 adj.
orange 432 adj.
flamen
priest 986 n.
flamenco
dance 837 n.
flames
fire 379 n.
flamethrower
gun 723 n.
flaming
violent 176 adj.
fiery 379 adj.
hot 379 adj.
luminous 417 adj.
fervent 818 adj.
showy 875 adj.
flamingo
bird 365 n.

flammability
burning 381 n.
flammable
heating 381 adj.
dangerous 661 adj.
flan
dish 301 n.
pastries and cakes
301 n.
flanches
heraldry 547 n.
flange
edge 234 n.
flank
flank 239 vb.
laterality 239 n.
meat 301 n.
safeguard 660 vb.
flannel
textile 222 n.
empty talk 515 n.
flatter 925 vb.
flattery 925 n.
flannelette
textile 222 n.
flannels
trousers 228 n.
flap
adjunct 40 n.
come unstuck
49 vb.
vary 152 vb.
hanging object
217 n.
covering 226 n.
garment 228 n.
be in motion
265 vb.
agitation 318 n.
be agitated 318 vb.
blow 352 vb.
haste 680 n.
be excitable
822 vb.
excitability 822 n.
fear 854 n.
fear 854 n.
flapjack
pastries and cakes
301 n.
flaps
garment 228 n.
wing 271 n.
aircraft 276 n.
flare
expand 197 vb.
be hot 379 vb.

fire 379 n.
light 417 n.
shine 417 vb.
luminary 420 n.
signal light 420 n.
torch 420 n.
flared
broad 205 adj.
flared skirt
skirt 228 n.
flares
trousers 228 n.
flare up
be excited 821 vb.
be excitable
822 vb.
get angry 891 vb.
flash
small quantity
33 n.
instant 116 n.
changeableness
152 n.
vary 152 vb.
move fast 277 vb.
velocity 277 n.
flash 417 n.
shine 417 vb.
look 438 n.
spurious 542 adj.
signal 547 n.
spontaneity 609 n.
flash across one's
mind
be remembered
505 vb.
flashback
remembrance
505 n.
flashbulb
lamp 420 n.
flasher
stripper 229 n.
libertine 952 n.
flashgun
lamp 420 n.
camera 442 n.
flashing
speedy 277 adj.
luminous 417 adj.
social evil 951 n.
flash in the pan
insubstantial thing
4 n.
brief span 114 n.
false alarm 665 n.
success 727 n.

flashlamp
 signal 547 n.
flashlight
 lamp 420 n.
flash point
 heat 379 n.
flashy
 florid 425 adj.
 ornate 574 adj.
 vulgar 847 adj.
 fashionable
  848 adj.
 showy 875 adj.
flask
 vessel 194 n.
flat
 flat 192 n.
 low 210 adj.
 flat 216 adj.
 bluntness 257 n.
 still 266 adj.
 marsh 347 n.
 musical note
  410 n.
 discordant 411 adj.
 dim 419 adj.
 feeble 572 adj.
 hitch 702 n.
 tedious 838 adj.
 dull 840 adj.
flatbed
 press 587 n.
flatfoot
 police 955 n.
flatiron
 flattener 216 n.
 smoother 258 n.
 heater 383 n.
flatlet
 flat 192 n.
flatness
 lowness 210 n.
 horizontality
  216 n.
 bluntness 257 n.
 smoothness 258 n.
 feebleness 572 n.
 tedium 838 n.
 dullness 840 n.
flat out
 supine 216 adj.
 swiftly 277 adv.
 fatigued 684 adj.
flat race
 racing 716 n.
flat rate
 price 809 n.

flats
 lowness 210 n.
 horizontality
  216 n.
 plain 348 n.
flat shoes
 footwear 228 n.
flat spin
 rotation 315 n.
 fear 854 n.
flatten
 make smaller
  198 vb.
 flatten 216 vb.
 lower 311 vb.
 defeat 727 vb.
flatten out
 destroy 165 vb.
 fly 271 vb.
flatter
 beautify 841 vb.
 flatter 925 vb.
flattering
 flattering 925 adj.
flatter oneself
 be vain 873 vb.
 flatter 925 vb.
flattery
 honours 866 n.
 flattery 925 n.
flatulence
 gaseousness 336 n.
 digestive disorders
  651 n.
flatus
 gas 336 n.
flatworm
 creepy-crawly
  365 n.
flaunt
 show 522 vb.
 be ostentatious
  875 vb.
 boast 877 vb.
 threaten 900 vb.
flaunt oneself
 be ostentatious
  875 vb.
flautist
 instrumentalist
  413 n.
flavescent
 yellow 433 adj.
flavour
 tincture 43 n.
 cook 301 vb.
 taste 386 n.

 season 388 vb.
flavouring
 food 301 n.
 taste 386 n.
 condiment 389 n.
flavourless
 tasteless 387 adj.
flavour of the month
 favourite 890 n.
flaw
 discontinuity 72 n.
 weakness 163 n.
 gap 201 n.
 blunder 495 vb.
 mistake 495 n.
 badness 645 n.
 defect 647 n.
 blemish 845 n.
 blemish 845 vb.
 vice 934 n.
flawed
 incomplete 55 adj.
 erroneous 495 adj.
 inexact 495 adj.
 bad 645 adj.
 imperfect 647 adj.
flawless
 consummate
  32 adj.
 elegant 575 adj.
 perfect 646 adj.
flax
 fibre 208 n.
flaxen-haired
 whitish 427 adj.
flay
 disunite 46 vb.
 uncover 229 vb.
 rub 333 vb.
 criticize 924 vb.
 flog 963 vb.
flaying alive
 capital punishment
  963 n.
flea
 small thing 33 n.
 insect 365 n.
fleabag
 dirty person 649 n.
fleabite
 trifle 639 n.
flea in one's ear
 reprimand 924 n.
flea market
 market 796 n.
fleapit
 cinema 445 n.

 theatre 594 n.
flea-ridden
 unclean 649 adj.
 insalubrious
  653 adj.
flèche
 high structure
  209 n.
fleck
 small thing 33 n.
 mottle 437 n.
fledgling
 young creature
  132 n.
 bird 365 n.
flee
 recede 290 vb.
 decamp 296 vb.
 run away 620 vb.
fleece
 subtract 39 vb.
 skin 226 n.
 hair 259 n.
 softness 327 n.
 deceive 542 vb.
 fleece 786 n.
 levy 786 vb.
 be parsimonious
  816 vb.
fleecy
 hairy 259 adj.
 soft 327 adj.
fleet
 multitude 104 n.
 elapse 111 vb.
 be transient
  114 vb.
 brief 114 adj.
 shipping 275 n.
 speedy 277 adj.
 gulf 345 n.
 navy 722 n.
fleet air arm
 air force 722 n.
fleet arm
 navy 722 n.
fleeting
 ephemeral 114 adj.
 transient 114 adj.
fleetness
 velocity 277 n.
fleet of foot
 speedy 277 adj.
Fleet Street
 the press 528 n.
Flemish bond
 joint 45 n.

Flemish school
  school of painting
    553 n.

flesh
  meat 301 n.
  matter 319 n.
  animality 365 n.
  humankind 371 n.

flesh, the
  sensualism 944 n.
  unchastity 951 n.

flesh and blood
  real 1 adj.
  bulk 195 n.
  matter 319 n.
  object 319 n.
  animality 365 n.

flesh-coloured
  red 431 adj.

flesh-eating
  feeding 301 adj.

fleshly
  material 319 adj.
  sensual 944 adj.

fleshpots
  feasting 301 n.
  prosperity 730 n.
  wealth 800 n.

fleshy
  fleshy 195 adj.

fleur-de-lis
  plant 366 n.
  heraldry 547 n.
  regalia 743 n.
  pattern 844 n.

fleuron
  pattern 844 n.

fleury
  heraldic 547 adj.

flex
  electronics 160 n.

flexible
  flexible 327 adj.
  elastic 328 adj.
  irresolute 601 adj.
  skilful 694 adj.

flexion
  deviation 282 n.

flex one's muscles
  prepare oneself
    669 vb.

flexure
  angularity 247 n.
  curvature 248 n.
  fold 261 n.

flibbertigibbet
  fool 501 n.

---

  demon 970 n.
  elf 970 n.

flic
  police 955 n.

flick
  impel 279 vb.
  impulse 279 n.
  knock 279 n.
  propel 287 vb.
  touch 378 n.
  touch 378 vb.

flicker
  small quantity
    33 n.
  be transient
    114 vb.
  vary 152 vb.
  oscillate 317 vb.
  agitation 318 n.
  be agitated 318 vb.
  fire 379 n.
  flash 417 n.
  shine 417 vb.
  be dim 419 vb.

flickering
  transient 114 adj.
  fitful 142 adj.
  flash 417 n.

flick knife
  sharp edge 256 n.
  sidearms 723 n.

flicks
  film 445 n.

flier
  aeronaut 271 n.
  gambling 618 n.

flies
  theatre 594 n.

flight
  group 74 n.
  aeronautics 271 n.
  velocity 277 n.
  recession 290 n.
  departure 296 n.
  disappearance
    446 n.
  avoidance 620 n.
  escape 667 n.
  air force 722 n.
  defeat 728 n.
  fear 854 n.

flight bag
  bag 194 n.

flight deck
  aircraft 276 n.

flight lieutenant
  air officer 741 n.

---

flight of fancy
  insubstantial thing
    4 n.
  ideality 513 n.
  exaggeration
    546 n.

flight of stairs
  ascent 308 n.
  access 624 n.

flight path
  air travel 271 n.

flight recorder
  aircraft 276 n.
  recording instru-
    ment 549 n.

flight sergeant
  air officer 741 n.

flighty
  changeful 152 adj.
  light-minded
    456 adj.

flimflam
  empty talk 515 n.
  falsehood 541 n.

flimsy
  small 33 adj.
  flimsy 163 adj.
  rare 325 adj.
  brittle 330 adj.
  poorly reasoned
    477 adj.

flinch
  recoil 280 vb.
  recede 290 vb.
  feel pain 377 vb.
  avoid 620 vb.
  suffer 825 vb.
  quake 854 vb.

fling
  move 265 vb.
  impel 279 vb.
  impulse 279 n.
  propel 287 vb.
  propulsion 287 n.
  scope 744 n.

fling out
  emerge 298 vb.
  eject 300 vb.
  reject 607 vb.

flint
  hardness 326 n.
  soil 344 n.
  lighter 385 n.
  tool 630 n.
  building material
    631 n.

---

flint-hearted
  cruel 898 adj.

flintlock
  firearm 723 n.

flinty
  hard 326 adj.
  severe 735 adj.

flip
  impel 279 vb.
  knock 279 n.
  touch 378 n.
  touch 378 vb.
  impertinent
    878 adj.

flipflops
  footwear 228 n.

flip one's lid
  get angry 891 vb.

flippant
  light-minded
    456 adj.
  witty 839 adj.
  rash 857 adj.
  impertinent
    878 adj.

flipper
  limb 53 n.
  propeller 269 n.
  feeler 378 n.

flip side
  rear 238 n.

flip through
  study 536 vb.

flirt
  be capricious
    604 vb.
  lover 887 n.
  court 889 vb.
  libertine 952 n.
  loose woman
    952 n.

flirtation
  whim 604 n.
  love affair 887 n.
  wooing 889 n.

flirtatious
  loving 887 adj.

flit
  elapse 111 vb.
  be transient
    114 vb.
  vary 152 vb.
  be in motion
    265 vb.
  fly 271 vb.
  move fast 277 vb.
  decamp 296 vb.

depart 296 vb.
run away 620 vb.
escape 667 n.
escape 667 vb.

flitting
transient 114 adj.
transference 272 n.

float
vary 152 vb.
stabilize 153 vb.
fly 271 vb.
lorry 274 n.
pushcart 274 n.
be light 323 vb.
be uncertain
    474 vb.

floatboard
propeller 269 n.

floating
unrelated 10 adj.
aquatics 269 n.
light 323 adj.
monetary 797 adj.

floating bridge
bridge 624 n.

floating debt
credit 802 n.
debt 803 n.

floating dock
stable 192 n.

floating population
wanderer 268 n.

floating pound
finance 797 n.

floating vote
dubiety 474 n.
irresolution 601 n.
independence
    744 n.

flock
group 74 n.
be many 104 vb.
filament 208 n.
hair 259 n.
animal 365 n.
laity 987 n.

flock together
congregate 74 vb.

floe
ice 380 n.

flog
give pain 377 vb.
incite 612 vb.
hasten 680 vb.
sell 793 vb.
flog 963 vb.

flog a dead horse
waste effort
    641 adj.

flogging
knock 279 n.
*corporal punish-
    ment* 963 n.

flog on
impel 279 vb.

flood
increase 36 n.
congregate 74 vb.
crowd 74 n.
be dispersed 75 vb.
be many 104 vb.
destroyer 168 n.
outbreak 176 n.
progression 285 n.
ingress 297 n.
outflow 298 n.
encroach 306 vb.
drench 341 n.
irrigate 341 vb.
moisten 341 vb.
flow 350 VB.
plenty 635 n.
superabound
    637 vb.

floodgate
outlet 298 n.
conduit 351 n.

flooding
flowing 350 adj.
redundant 637 adj.

floodlight
light 417 n.
lamp 420 n.

floodlit
luminous 417 adj.

floods
great quantity
    32 n.

floods of tears
lamentation 836 n.

floor
compartment
    194 n.
layer 207 n.
lowness 210 n.
base 214 n.
flatten 216 vb.
basis 218 n.
paving 226 n.
strike 279 vb.
fell 311 vb.
puzzle 474 vb.
confute 479 vb.

arena 724 n.

floorboards
paving 226 n.

floored by, be
not understand
    517 vb.

flooring
base 214 n.
basis 218 n.
paving 226 n.

floor show
spectacle 445 n.
stage show 594 n.

floozy
kept woman 952 n.
loose woman
    952 n.

flop
close 264 vb.
descend 309 vb.
be agitated 318 vb.
dramaturgy 594 n.
bungling 695 n.
fail 728 vb.
failure 728 n.
loser 728 n.
miscarry 728 vb.

flophouse
inn 192 n.

floppy
weak 163 adj.
soft 327 adj.

floppy disk
data processing
    86 n.

flora
vegetable life
    366 n.

flora and fauna
organism 358 n.

Florence Nightingale
nurse 658 n.

florescent
matured 669 adj.

floriculture
flower 366 n.
agriculture 370 n.

florid
florid 425 adj.
red 431 adj.
ornate 574 adj.

florin
coinage 797 n.

floss
fibre 208 n.

flotilla
shipping 275 n.

navy 722 n.

flotsam
transport 272 n.
derelict 779 n.

flotsam and jetsam
rabble 869 n.
outcast 883 n.

flounce
edging 234 n.
fold 261 n.
trimming 844 n.
be angry 891 vb.

flounder
be agitated 318 vb.
be uncertain
    474 vb.
be clumsy 695 vb.
be in difficulty
    700 vb.

flour
cereals 301 n.
powder 332 n.
thickening 354 n.
white thing 427 n.

flourish
grow 36 vb.
be fruitful 171 vb.
coil 251 n.
brandish 317 vb.
agitate 318 vb.
blow 352 vb.
loudness 400 n.
trope 519 n.
show 522 vb.
call 547 n.
ornament 574 n.
elegance 575 n.
lettering 586 n.
flourish 615 vb.
be healthy 650 vb.
prosper 730 vb.
pattern 844 n.
be ostentatious
    875 vb.
ostentation 875 n.
boast 877 n.
boast 877 vb.

flourishing
prosperous 730 adj.

flourish of trumpets
publication 528 n.
ostentation 875 n.
celebration 876 n.

floury
powdery 332 adj.

flout
indignity 921 n.

not respect 921 vb.
despise 922 vb.
flow
quantity 26 n.
continuity 71 n.
elapse 111 vb.
continuance 146 n.
hang 217 vb.
motion 265 n.
current 350 n.
flow 350 VB.
diffuseness 570 n.
abound 635 vb.
flow chart
statistics 86 n.
plan 623 n.
flower
essential part 5 n.
grow 36 vb.
product 164 n.
reproduce itself 167 vb.
expand 197 vb.
flower 366 n.
elite 644 n.
paragon 646 n.
prosper 730 vb.
a beauty 841 n.
darling 890 n.
flower arrangement
ornamentation 844 n.
flowerbed
flower 366 n.
garden 370 n.
floweret
flower 366 n.
flower garden
garden 370 n.
fragrance 396 n.
flowering
young 130 adj.
propagation 167 n.
vegetable life 366 n.
matured 669 adj.
flower people
philanthropist 901 n.
flowerpot
vessel 194 n.
garden 370 n.
flowers
powder 332 n.
reading matter 589 n.
anthology 592 n.

flowery
figurative 519 adj.
ornate 574 adj.
flowing
perpetual 115 adj.
flowing 350 adj.
flown
absent 190 adj.
flu
infection 651 n.
fluctuate
fluctuate 317 vb.
be irresolute 601 vb.
flue
air pipe 353 n.
furnace 383 n.
fluent
blood 335 adj.
flowing 350 adj.
stylistic 566 adj.
diffuse 570 adj.
elegant 575 adj.
speaking 579 adj.
loquacious 581 adj.
flue pipe
orifice 263 n.
air pipe 353 n.
organ 414 n.
fluff
hair 259 n.
lightness 323 n.
softness 327 n.
blunder 495 vb.
mistake 495 n.
act 594 vb.
be clumsy 695 vb.
bungling 695 n.
fluff one's lines
be inattentive 456 vb.
be unskilful 695 vb.
fluffy
light 323 adj.
flugelhorn
horn 414 n.
fluid
fluid 335 n.
uncertain 474 adj.
elegant 575 adj.
fluidity
fluidity 335 n.
fluidize
liquefy 337 vb.
fluke
chance 159 n.

creepy-crawly 365 n.
nondesign 618 n.
success 727 n.
fluky
casual 159 adj.
flummox
distract 456 vb.
puzzle 474 vb.
flunk
fail 728 vb.
flunkey
worker 686 n.
auxiliary 707 n.
dependant 742 n.
domestic 742 n.
toady 879 n.
fluorescent
luminous 417 adj.
fluorescent light
lamp 420 n.
fluoridate
safeguard 660 vb.
fluoride
prophylactic 658 n.
fluoridize
safeguard 660 vb.
flurry
derange 63 vb.
velocity 277 n.
commotion 318 n.
rain 350 n.
gale 352 n.
distract 456 vb.
activity 678 n.
haste 680 n.
feeling 818 n.
excitation 821 n.
excitable state 822 n.
flush
uniform 16 adj.
equal 28 adj.
flat 216 adj.
smooth 258 adj.
be hot 379 vb.
heat 379 n.
glow 417 n.
hue 425 n.
redden 431 vb.
redness 431 n.
hunt 619 vb.
ablutions 648 n.
cleansing 648 n.
moneyed 800 adj.
feeling 818 n.

show feeling 818 vb.
flush, be
be rich 800 vb.
flushed
red 431 adj.
excited 821 adj.
jubilant 833 adj.
drunk 949 adj.
flushed with rage
angry 891 adj.
flushed with victory
successful 727 adj.
flushing
red 431 adj.
cleansing 648 n.
flushness
uniformity 16 n.
flush with anger
get angry 891 vb.
fluster
derange 63 vb.
distract 456 vb.
flute
furrow 262 n.
groove 262 vb.
play music 413 vb.
flute 414 n.
fluting
furrow 262 n.
ornamental art 844 n.
flutist
instrumentalist 413 n.
flutter
vary 152 vb.
be in motion 265 vb.
fly 271 vb.
brandish 317 vb.
oscillate 317 vb.
oscillation 317 n.
agitate 318 vb.
agitation 318 n.
be agitated 318 vb.
blow 352 vb.
gambling 618 n.
haste 680 n.
feeling 818 n.
be excited 821 vb.
fear 854 n.
nervousness 854 n.
flutter down
descend 309 vb.
fluttering
fitful 142 adj.

flutter the dovecotes
surprise 508 vb.
fluvial
flowing 350 adj.
fluviometer
meter 465 n.
flux
conversion 147 n.
motion 265 n.
liquefaction 337 n.
solution 337 n.
current 350 n.
flux and reflux
fluctuation 317 n.
fluxion
numerical element
85 n.
fluxional
numerical 85 adj.
fluxions
mathematics 86 n.
fly
elapse 111 vb.
be transient
114 vb.
garment 228 n.
be in motion
265 vb.
fly 271 vb.
transfer 272 vb.
carry 273 vb.
cab 274 n.
move fast 277 vb.
insect 365 n.
knowing 490 adj.
intelligent 498 adj.
flag 547 n.
chase 619 n.
run away 620 vb.
be active 678 vb.
cunning 698 adj.
amuse oneself
837 vb.
fear 854 vb.
fly a kite
be tentative 461 vb.
publish 528 vb.
attempt 671 vb.
flyblown
unclean 649 adj.
insalubrious
653 adj.
flyer
advertisement
528 n.
fly fishing
chase 619 n.

flying
transient 114 adj.
high 209 adj.
aeronautics 271 n.
speedy 277 adj.
sport 837 n.
flying buttress
support 218 n.
church exterior
990 n.
flying carpet
magic instrument
983 n.
flying fish
fish 365 n.
flying machine
aircraft 276 n.
flying officer
aeronaut 271 n.
air officer 741 n.
flying saucer
spaceship 276 n.
flying start
advantage 34 n.
start 68 n.
priority 119 n.
spurt 277 n.
preceding 283 n.
fly in the face of
disobey 738 vb.
fly in the ointment
evil 616 n.
hitch 702 n.
fly into a temper
be excitable
822 vb.
get angry 891 vb.
flyleaf
edition 589 n.
fly off the handle
show feeling
818 vb.
be excitable
822 vb.
get angry 891 vb.
fly open
open 263 vb.
flyover
crossing 222 n.
passage 305 n.
bridge 624 n.
flypaper
adhesive 47 n.
viscidity 354 n.
trap 542 n.
fly past
elapse 111 vb.

be ostentatious
875 vb.
flypast
aeronautics 271 n.
pageant 875 n.
fly sheet
canopy 226 n.
fly the flag
signal 547 vb.
flyweight
pugilist 722 n.
flywheel
rotator 315 n.
FM
broadcasting
531 n.
foal
young creature
132 n.
reproduce itself
167 vb.
horse 273 n.
foam
lining 227 n.
effervesce 318 vb.
moisture 341 n.
bubble 355 n.
bubble 355 n.
extinguisher 382 n.
be excitable
822 vb.
foam at the mouth
effervesce 318 vb.
be insane 503 vb.
go mad 503 vb.
get angry 891 vb.
foam bath
cosmetic 843 n.
foam-filled
soft 327 adj.
foam rubber
elasticity 328 n.
fob
deceive 542 vb.
fob off with
substitute 150 vb.
deceive 542 vb.
fob-watch
timekeeper 117 n.
focal
central 225 adj.
focal point
focus 76 n.
centre 225 n.
focus
adjust 24 vb.

bring together
74 vb.
focus 76 n.
focus 76 vb.
centralize 225 vb.
converge 293 vb.
gaze 438 vb.
focusing
assemblage 74 n.
convergent 293 adj.
focus upon
focus 76 vb.
fodder
provender 301 n.
plant 366 n.
materials 631 n.
foe
opponent 705 n.
enemy 881 n.
foetus
young creature
132 n.
source 156 n.
fog
powder 332 n.
moisture 341 n.
cloud 355 n.
dim 419 vb.
dimness 419 n.
screen 421 vb.
opacity 423 n.
blur 440 vb.
invisibility 444 n.
uncertainty 474 n.
fogbound
dim 419 adj.
hindered 702 adj.
restrained 747 adj.
foggy
dense 324 adj.
humid 341 adj.
cloudy 355 adj.
dim 419 adj.
opaque 423 adj.
foghorn
warning 664 n.
danger signal
665 n.
föhn
wind 352 n.
foible
speciality 80 n.
defect 647 n.
vice 934 n.
foil
bluntness 257 n.
disappoint 509 vb.

be obstructive
 702 vb.
 oppose 704 vb.
 sidearms 723 n.
 laughingstock
 851 n.

foist
 compel 740 vb.

fold
 stable 192 n.
 enclosure 235 n.
 fold 261 n.
 fold 261 vb.
 shelter 662 n.
 laity 987 n.

folder
 sorting 62 n.
 receptacle 194 n.

fold one's arms
 be inactive 679 vb.

fold up
 cease 145 vb.
 make smaller
 198 vb.
 dress 228 vb.
 fold 261 vb.
 store 632 vb.

foliage
 foliage 366 n.

foliate
 print 587 vb.

folio
 part 53 n.
 edition 589 n.

foliole
 foliage 366 n.

folk
 social group 371 n.
 music 412 n.

folk dance
 dance 837 n.

folklore
 tradition 127 n.
 anthropology
 371 n.
 belief 485 n.
 knowledge 490 n.

folk medicine
 medical art 658 n.

folk singer
 vocalist 413 n.

folk tale
 narrative 590 n.

follicle
 compartment
 194 n.
 cavity 255 n.

Follies
 stage show 594 n.

follow
 be behind 238 vb.
 follow 284 vb.
 be reasonable
 475 vb.
 detect 484 vb.
 understand 516 vb.
 obey 739 vb.
 serve 742 vb.
 observe 768 vb.

follow after
 ensue 120 vb.
 follow 284 vb.

follower
 conformist 83 n.
 follower 284 n.
 assenter 488 n.
 learner 538 n.
 auxiliary 707 n.
 retainer 742 n.
 lover 887 n.
 sectarian 978 n.
 worshipper 981 n.

followers
 retinue 67 n.
 follower 284 n.
 onlookers 441 n.

following
 imitative 20 adj.
 adjunct 40 n.
 after 65 adv.
 sequential 65 adj.
 retinue 67 n.
 band 74 n.
 conformable
 83 adj.
 concomitant 89 n.
 subsequent
 120 adj.
 follower 284 n.
 following 284 n.

follow in the foot-
 steps of
 ensue 120 vb.

follow-my-leader
 do likewise 20 vb.
 children's games
 837 n.

follow on
 result 157 vb.
 follow 284 vb.

follow suit
 do likewise 20 vb.
 conform 83 vb.

follow through
 sustain 146 vb.
 carry through
 725 vb.

follow-up
 sequel 67 n.
 pursuit 619 n.

folly
 pavilion 192 n.
 arbour 194 n.
 folly 499 n.

fomentation
 causation 156 n.
 surgical dressing
 658 n.
 therapy 658 n.

fond
 loving 887 adj.

fondant
 sweet thing 392 n.

fond hope
 aspiration 852 n.

fondle
 touch 378 vb.
 love 887 vb.
 caress 889 vb.

fondness
 liking 859 n.
 love 887 n.

fondue
 dish 301 n.

fons et origo
 origin 68 n.

font
 ritual object 988 n.
 church interior
 990 n.
 church utensil
 990 n.

fontanelle
 head 213 n.

food
 food 301 n.
 provision 633 n.

food chain
 continuity 71 n.
 eating 301 n.

foodie
 eater 301 n.

foodism
 gastronomy 301 n.
 gluttony 947 n.

food poisoning
 digestive disorders
 651 n.
 illness 651 n.
 infection 651 n.

food processing
 cookery 301 n.
 See **provisions**

fool
 dessert 301 n.
 be absurd 497 vb.
 fool 501 n.
 fool 542 vb.
 dupe 544 n.
 be ridiculous
 849 vb.
 ridicule 851 vb.

fool about
 be absurd 497 vb.
 amuse oneself
 837 vb.

foolery
 foolery 497 n.

foolhardy
 unwise 499 adj.
 rash 857 adj.

foolish
 ignorant 491 adj.
 foolish 499 adj.
 unskilful 695 adj.

foolproof
 certain 473 adj.
 invulnerable
 660 adj.
 successful 727 adj.

foolscap
 stationery 586 n.
 paper 631 n.

fool's errand
 lost labour 641 n.

fool's paradise
 insubstantial thing
 4 n.
 misjudgment
 481 n.
 disappointment
 509 n.
 aspiration 852 n.

foot
 extremity 69 n.
 long measure
 203 n.
 lowness 210 n.
 base 214 n.
 foot 214 n.
 prosody 593 n.

footage
 distance 199 n.
 length 203 n.

foot-and-mouth dis-
 ease

animal disease
651 n.
football
sphere 252 n.
missile 287 n.
ball game 837 n.
footballer
player 837 n.
football pool
gambling 618 n.
gambling game
837 n.
footbridge
bridge 624 n.
footfall
indication 547 n.
foothill
high land 209 n.
lowness 210 n.
projection 254 n.
foothold
support 218 n.
retention 778 n.
footing
state 7 n.
circumstance 8 n.
degree 27 n.
serial place 73 n.
influence 178 n.
situation 186 n.
base 214 n.
prestige 866 n.
footlights
lighting 420 n.
drama 594 n.
theatre 594 n.
footling
trivial 639 adj.
footloose
free 744 adj.
footman
domestic 742 n.
footmark
trace 548 n.
footnote
adjunct 40 n.
commentary 520 n.
edition 589 n.
footpad
pedestrian 268 n.
robber 789 n.
footpath
path 624 n.
footplate
stand 218 n.
footprint
concavity 255 n.

identification
547 n.
label 547 n.
trace 548 n.
foot regiment
infantry 722 n.
footrest
support 218 n.
footrule
gauge 465 n.
footsie
endearment 889 n.
footsore
fatigued 684 adj.
footstep
trace 548 n.
footstool
seat 218 n.
toady 879 n.
foot the bill
defray 804 vb.
footwear
footwear 228 n.
footwork
motion 265 n.
fop
fop 848 n.
foppish
fashionable
848 adj.
affected 850 adj.
showy 875 adj.
for
hence 158 adv.
forage
provender 301 n.
search 459 vb.
provide 633 vb.
rob 788 vb.
steal 788 vb.
for all that
nevertheless
468 adv.
foray
attack 712 n.
attack 712 vb.
plundering 788 n.
rob 788 vb.
forbear
precursor 66 n.
paternity 169 n.
avoid 620 vb.
not use 674 vb.
be lenient 736 vb.
show mercy
905 vb.
forgive 909 vb.

be temperate
942 vb.
forbearance
avoidance 620 n.
leniency 736 n.
patience 823 n.
mercy 905 n.
forgiveness 909 n.
temperance 942 n.
forbearing
patient 823 adj.
pitying 905 adj.
temperate 942 adj.
for better for worse
for a long time
113 adv.
for ever 115 adv.
forbid
prohibit 757 vb.
forbidden
prohibited 757 adj.
forbidden fruit
incentive 612 n.
prohibition 757 n.
desired object
859 n.
illicit love 951 n.
forbidding
cheerless 834 adj.
serious 834 adj.
unsociable 883 adj.
sullen 893 adj.
force
be unrelated 10 vb.
quantity 26 n.
band 74 n.
make conform
83 vb.
cause 156 n.
be able 160 vb.
energy 160 n.
power 160 n.
strength 162 n.
agency 173 n.
vigorousness 174 n.
force 176 vb.
violence 176 n.
influence 178 vb.
collision 279 n.
cultivate 370 vb.
vigour 571 n.
motivate 612 vb.
ill-treat 645 vb.
mature 669 vb.
action 676 n.
exertion 682 n.
personnel 686 n.

compulsion 740 n.
force, the
police 955 n.
force apart
break 46 vb.
forced
irrelevant 10 adj.
inelegant 576 adj.
unwilling 598 adj.
immature 670 adj.
hasty 680 adj.
forced entry
ingress 297 n.
forced labour
labour 682 n.
compulsion 740 n.
forced loan
borrowing 785 n.
tax 809 n.
forced march
marching 267 n.
haste 680 n.
force-feed
compel 740 vb.
forceful
strong 162 adj.
vigorous 174 adj.
stylistic 566 adj.
forceful 571 adj.
resolute 599 adj.
active 678 adj.
compelling
740 adj.
impressive 821 adj.
forcefulness
vigour 571 n.
force-land
fly 271 vb.
force majeure
nonliability 919 n.
**force of circum-
stances**
necessity 596 n.
force of gravity
energy 160 n.
attraction 291 n.
gravity 322 n.
force of habit
habit 610 n.
forceps
pincers 778 n.
forceps delivery
obstetrics 167 n.
extraction 304 n.
forces
armed force 722 n.

forcible
violent 176 adj.
forceful 571 adj.
ford
pass 305 vb.
bridge 624 n.
fore
front 237 n.
frontal 237 adj.
forearmed
expectant 507 adj.
prepared 669 adj.
foreboding
foresight 510 n.
predicting 511 adj.
prediction 511 n.
dangerous 661 adj.
warning 664 n.
forecast
destiny 155 n.
impending 155 adj.
expect 507 vb.
expectation 507 n.
foresee 510 vb.
predict 511 vb.
prediction 511 n.
foreclose
deprive 786 vb.
foreclosure
expropriation
   786 n.
debt 803 n.
forecourt
front 237 n.
forefather
paternity 169 n.
the dead 361 n.
forefinger
projection 254 n.
feeler 378 n.
finger 378 n.
indication 547 n.
forefront
beginning 68 n.
front 237 n.
forego
not retain 779 vb.
foregoing
preceding 64 adj.
prior 119 adj.
foregoing 125 adj.
foregone conclusion
certainty 473 n.
prejudgment 481 n.
foresight 510 n.
predetermination
   608 n.

foreground
nearness 200 n.
front 237 n.
stage set 594 n.
forehead
head 213 n.
dome 253 n.
protuberance
   254 n.
foreign
extrinsic 6 adj.
unrelated 10 adj.
disagreeing 25 adj.
separate 46 adj.
extraneous 59 adj.
exterior 223 adj.
unsociable 883 adj.
foreign body
dissimilarity 19 n.
misfit 25 n.
extraneousness
   59 n.
foreigner
misfit 25 n.
foreigner 59 n.
foreleg
leg 267 n.
forelock
front 237 n.
hair 259 n.
forelock-tugging
respectful 920 adj.
foreman or -woman
superior 34 n.
manager 690 n.
**foreman or -woman
   of the jury**
jury 957 n.
foremost
supreme 34 adj.
first 68 adj.
important 638 adj.
noteworthy
   866 adj.
forename
name 561 n.
forenoon
morning 128 n.
forensic examination
interrogation
   459 n.
forensic test
diagnostic 658 n.
forerunner
precursor 66 n.
front 237 n.
messenger 529 n.

foresee
foresee 510 vb.
foreseeable
future 124 adj.
probable 471 adj.
foreseen
probable 471 adj.
expected 507 adj.
foreshadow
predict 511 vb.
foreshortened
short 204 adj.
foresight
foresight 510 n.
forest
multitude 104 n.
wood 366 n.
forestall
exclude 57 vb.
do before 119 vb.
be early 135 vb.
foresee 510 vb.
forester
forestry 366 n.
forest fire
fire 379 n.
forestry
forestry 366 n.
foretaste
precursor 66 n.
example 83 n.
priority 119 n.
expectation 507 n.
foresight 510 n.
forethought
thought 449 n.
carefulness 457 n.
sagacity 498 n.
foresight 510 n.
policy 623 n.
caution 858 n.
for ever
for a long time
   113 adv.
for ever 115 adv.
forewarned
expectant 507 adj.
prepared 669 adj.
foreword
prelude 66 n.
front 237 n.
preceding 283 n.
oration 579 n.
forfeit
relinquish 621 vb.
lose 772 vb.
loss 772 n.

disentitle 916 vb.
unwarranted
   916 adj.
penalty 963 n.
punish 963 vb.
forfeits
indoor game 837 n.
forfeiture
loss of right 916 n.
penalty 963 n.
forgather
congregate 74 vb.
forge
copy 20 vb.
produce 164 vb.
form 243 vb.
furnace 383 n.
fake 541 vb.
be untrue 543 vb.
workshop 687 n.
mint 797 vb.
forge ahead
be in front 237 vb.
progress 285 vb.
forgery
imitation 20 n.
falsehood 541 n.
sham 542 n.
forget
forget 506 vb.
forgetful
forgetful 506 adj.
forget-me-not
plant 366 n.
blueness 435 n.
forget one's anger
show mercy
   905 vb.
forget oneself
get angry 891 vb.
forgivable
guiltless 935 adj.
forgive
forgive 909 vb.
forgive and forget
make peace
   719 vb.
forgive 909 vb.
forgo
relinquish 621 vb.
for good
for a long time
   113 adv.
forgotten
forgotten 506 adj.
fork
bifurcate 92 vb.

717

bifurcation 92 n.
cross 222 vb.
angularity 247 n.
sharp point 256 n.
conveyor 274 n.
diverge 294 vb.
divergence 294 n.
farm tool 370 n.
forked
bisected 92 adj.
crossed 222 adj.
angular 247 adj.
forked lightning
luminary 420 n.
for keeps
for ever 115 adv.
fork out
give 781 vb.
pay 804 vb.
fork supper
meal 301 n.
forlorn
unfortunate
731 adj.
melancholic
834 adj.
hopeless 853 adj.
forlorn hope
improbability
472 n.
danger 661 n.
hopelessness 853 n.
brave person 855 n.
form
constitute 56 vb.
arrange 62 vb.
arrangement 62 n.
regularity 81 n.
rule 81 n.
conformity 83 n.
dwelling 192 n.
seat 218 n.
form 243 n.
form 243 vb.
educate 534 vb.
class 538 n.
identification
547 n.
practice 610 n.
precept 693 n.
ostentation 875 n.
rite 988 n.
ritual 988 n.
formal
affirmative
532 adj.
literary 557 adj.

formal 875 adj.
ritual 988 adj.
formaldehyde
preserver 666 n.
formal dress
formal dress 228 n.
formalism
conformity 83 n.
severity 735 n.
pietism 979 n.
formalities
arrival 295 n.
formality
ostentation 875 n.
formalize
form 243 vb.
make legal 953 vb.
format
form 243 n.
edition 589 n.
formation
composition 56 n.
form 243 n.
formation 243 n.
formation 722 n.
formation flying
aeronautics 271 n.
formative
part of speech
564 n.
forme
edition 589 n.
former
preceding 64 adj.
prior 119 adj.
former 125 adj.
formerly
before 119 adv.
formerly 125 adv.
former pupil
learner 538 n.
formication
tingling 378 n.
formidable
notable 638 adj.
difficult 700 adj.
frightening
854 adj.
formless
amorphous
244 adj.
unsightly 842 adj.
forms
reading matter
589 n.
formula
rule 81 n.

number 85 n.
axiom 496 n.
maxim 496 n.
policy 623 n.
remedy 658 n.
precept 693 n.
conditions 766 n.
rite 988 n.
formulate
arrange 62 vb.
form 243 vb.
manifest 522 vb.
affirm 532 vb.
phrase 563 vb.
fornicate
be impure 951 vb.
fornication
unchastity 951 n.
for now
while 108 adv.
at present 121 adv.
forsake
relinquish 621 vb.
forsaken
alone 88 adj.
for sale
not retained
779 adj.
salable 793 adj.
uncharged 812 adj.
forswear
negate 533 vb.
recant 603 vb.
avoid 620 vb.
relinquish 621 vb.
fort
fort 713 n.
forte
adagio 412 adv.
skill 694 n.
forth
forward 285 adv.
forthcoming
early 135 adj.
impending 155 adj.
preparatory
669 adj.
for the best
well 615 adv.
benevolent 897 adj.
for the nonce
singly 88 adv.
at present 121 adv.
for the time being
while 108 adv.
at present 121 adv.

forthright
intelligible 516 adj.
veracious 540 adj.
forthwith
suddenly 135 adv.
fortification
fortification 713 n.
See **fort**
fortified
strong 162 adj.
hard 326 adj.
fortified wine
wine 301 n.
fortify
mix 43 vb.
strengthen 162 vb.
safeguard 660 vb.
defend 713 vb.
fortiori, a
eminently 34 adv.
fortissimo
loud 400 adj.
loudly 400 adv.
loudness 400 n.
adagio 412 adv.
fortitude
resolution 599 n.
perseverance 600 n.
stamina 600 n.
virtues 933 n.
fortnight
period 110 n.
fortress
edifice 164 n.
fort 713 n.
fortuitous
extrinsic 6 adj.
casual 159 adj.
fortuity
chance 159 n.
fortunate
opportune 137 adj.
prosperous 730 adj.
happy 824 adj.
fortune
changeable thing
152 n.
event 154 n.
chance 159 n.
prediction 511 n.
fate 596 n.
good 615 n.
wealth 800 n.
fortunes
biography 590 n.
fortune-teller
diviner 511 n.

occultist 984 n.
forty
  twenty and over
    99 n.
forty thieves
  robber 789 n.
forty winks
  sleep 679 n.
forum
  conference 584 n.
  arena 724 n.
  tribunal 956 n.
forward
  early 135 adj.
  frontal 237 adj.
  send 272 vb.
  forward 285 adv.
  intelligent 498 adj.
  willing 597 adj.
  be expedient
    642 vb.
  make better
    654 vb.
  player 837 n.
  impertinent
    878 adj.
  discourteous
    885 adj.
forward line
  front 237 n.
forward-looking
  progressive
    285 adj.
forwardness
  intelligence 498 n.
forwards
  forward 285 adv.
fossil
  remainder 41 n.
  fossil 125 n.
  primal 127 adj.
fossilized
  past 125 adj.
  antiquated 127 adj.
  hard 326 adj.
foster
  be akin 11 vb.
  look after 457 vb.
  train 534 vb.
  make better
    654 vb.
  safeguard 660 vb.
  animate 821 vb.
foster-father
  paternity 169 n.
fostering
  parentage 169 n.

fosterling
  child 132 n.
foster-mother
  maternity 169 n.
fou
  drunk 949 adj.
fouetté
  ballet 594 n.
foul
  navigate 269 vb.
  fetid 397 adj.
  evil 616 adj.
  bad 645 adj.
  not nice 645 adj.
  make unclean
    649 vb.
  unclean 649 adj.
  unpleasant
    827 adj.
  ugly 842 adj.
  unjust 914 adj.
  wrong 914 adj.
  wrong 914 n.
  dishonest 930 adj.
  perfidy 930 n.
  heinous 934 adj.
foulard
  textile 222 n.
foul-mouthed
  cursing 899 adj.
foulness
  stench 397 n.
  badness 645 n.
foul play
  cruel act 898 n.
foul up
  bedevil 63 vb.
  blunder 495 vb.
  be unclean 649 vb.
  obstruct 702 vb.
foul weather
  weather 340 n.
  rain 350 n.
found
  initiate 68 vb.
  stabilize 153 vb.
  cause 156 vb.
  produce 164 vb.
  support 218 vb.
  endow 777 vb.
foundation
  beginning 68 n.
  permanence 144 n.
  source 156 n.
  base 214 n.
  basis 218 n.
  preparation 669 n.

foundationer
  student 538 n.
foundations
  fixture 153 n.
  base 214 n.
founder
  cause 156 n.
  producer 164 n.
  be destroyed
    165 vb.
  founder 313 vb.
  planner 623 n.
  patron 707 n.
  benefactor 903 n.
founder member
  producer 164 n.
founding father
  producer 164 n.
foundling
  derelict 779 n.
foundry
  workshop 687 n.
found wanting, be
  fail 728 vb.
fount
  origin 68 n.
  source 156 n.
  print-type 587 n.
  store 632 n.
fountain
  source 156 n.
  outflow 298 n.
  soft drink 301 n.
  stream 350 n.
  store 632 n.
fountainhead
  source 156 n.
  stream 350 n.
fountain pen
  stationery 586 n.
four
  four 96 adj.
  quaternity 96 n.
**four corners of the
  earth**
  world 321 n.
fourfold
  fourfold 97 adj.
four-footed
  four 96 adj.
four-leaf clover
  talisman 983 n.
four-letter word
  word 559 n.
  plainness 573 n.
  scurrility 899 n.

four-poster
  bed 218 n.
four score
  twenty and over
    99 n.
foursome
  quaternity 96 n.
foursquare
  four 96 adj.
  fixed 153 adj.
four-star
  fuel 385 n.
fourth
  quadrisection 98 n.
  interval 201 n.
  musical note
    410 n.
fourth estate
  the press 528 n.
Fourth of July
  anniversary 141 n.
  special day 876 n.
four winds
  quaternity 96 n.
fowl
  poultry 365 n.
  hunt 619 vb.
fowling-piece
  chase 619 n.
  firearm 723 n.
fox
  mammal 365 n.
  puzzle 474 vb.
  slyboots 698 n.
foxglove
  plant 366 n.
  purpleness 436 n.
foxhound
  dog 365 n.
  hunter 619 n.
fox hunt
  chase 619 n.
foxhunter
  horse 273 n.
fox terrier
  dog 365 n.
foxtrot
  dance 837 n.
  dance 837 vb.
foxy
  animal 365 adj.
  dishonest 930 adj.
foyer
  lobby 194 n.
  theatre 594 n.
fracas
  turmoil 61 n.

quarrel 709 n.
fight 716 n.
fractal
line 203 n.
distortion 246 n.
fraction
quantity 26 n.
small quantity
33 n.
part 53 n.
numerical element
85 n.
fraction 102 n.
fractional
fragmentary
53 adj.
numerical 85 adj.
fractional 102 adj.
fractionate
sunder 46 vb.
fractious
irascible 892 adj.
fracture
break 46 vb.
separation 46 n.
discontinuity 72 n.
disable 161 vb.
force 176 vb.
gap 201 n.
pain 377 n.
wound 655 n.
fragile
insubstantial 4 adj.
small 33 adj.
ephemeral 114 adj.
flimsy 163 adj.
brittle 330 adj.
fragment
small quantity
33 n.
small thing 33 n.
break 46 vb.
sunder 46 vb.
part 53 n.
See **piece**
part 53 vb.
piece 53 n.
fraction 102 n.
pulverize 332 vb.
fragmentary
fragmentary
53 adj.
uncompleted
726 adj.
fragmentation bomb
bomb 723 n.

fragrant
fragrant 396 adj.
frail
small 33 adj.
ephemeral 114 adj.
flimsy 163 adj.
weak 163 adj.
brittle 330 adj.
unsafe 661 adj.
frail 934 adj.
frailty
transience 114 n.
weakness 163 n.
brittleness 330 n.
vice 934 n.
frame
mould 23 n.
affix 45 vb.
sort 77 n.
produce 164 vb.
receptacle 194 n.
frame 218 n.
support 218 vb.
weaving 222 n.
circumscribe
232 vb.
outline 233 n.
outline 233 vb.
edging 234 n.
enclose 235 vb.
enclosure 235 n.
form 243 n.
form 243 vb.
matter 319 n.
garden 370 n.
fake 541 vb.
photography 551 n.
predetermine
608 vb.
plan 623 vb.
plot 623 vb.
indict 928 vb.
frame of mind
temperament 5 n.
state 7 n.
affections 817 n.
frame of reference
referral 9 n.
prototype 23 n.
conditions 766 n.
frame tent
canopy 226 n.
frame-up
duplicity 541 n.
trap 542 n.
untruth 543 n.

predetermination
608 n.
plot 623 n.
false charge 928 n.
framework
frame 218 n.
outline 233 n.
structure 331 n.
franc
coinage 797 n.
franchise
vote 605 n.
dueness 915 n.
nonliability 919 n.
Franciscans
monk 986 n.
frangible
brittle 330 adj.
frangipani
scent 396 n.
Franglais
dialect 560 adj.
frank
veracious 540 adj.
artless 699 adj.
trustworthy
929 adj.
Frankenstein's mon-
ster
monster 938 n.
frankfurter
meat 301 n.
frankincense
resin 357 n.
scent 396 n.
frankly
openly 263 adv.
frankness
truth 494 n.
plainness 573 n.
artlessness 699 n.
frantic
disorderly 61 adj.
furious 176 adj.
absurd 497 adj.
frenzied 503 adj.
active 678 adj.
excited 821 adj.
fraternal
akin 11 adj.
friendly 880 adj.
benevolent 897 adj.
fraternity
family 11 n.
association 706 n.
cooperation 706 n.
community 708 n.

monk 986 n.
fraternize
accord 24 vb.
combine 50 vb.
concord 710 vb.
be friendly 880 vb.
be sociable 882 vb.
fraternize with
befriend 880 vb.
fratricide
homicide 362 n.
Frau
female 373 n.
title 870 n.
fraud
duplicity 541 n.
trickery 542 n.
impostor 545 n.
slyboots 698 n.
swindling 788 n.
pretension 850 n.
fraudulent
false 541 adj.
thieving 788 adj.
dishonest 930 adj.
perfidious 930 adj.
lawbreaking
954 adj.
fraught, be
carry 273 vb.
fraught with danger
dangerous 661 adj.
Fraulein
female 373 n.
title 870 n.
fray
rend 46 vb.
rub 333 vb.
fight 716 n.
fray, the
activity 678 n.
freak
variant 15 n.
nonuniformity
17 n.
misfit 25 n.
nonconformist
84 n.
enthusiast 504 n.
the maladjusted
504 n.
whim 604 n.
prodigy 864 n.
drug-taking 949 n.
freakish
abnormal 84 adj.

unconformable
84 adj.
unexpected
508 adj.
capricious 604 adj.
freak out
be unconformable
84 vb.
drug oneself
949 vb.
freckle
mottle 437 n.
variegate 437 vb.
skin disease 651 n.
blemish 845 n.
free
disunite 46 vb.
extract 304 vb.
intrepretative
520 adj.
deliver 668 vb.
disencumber
701 vb.
free 744 adj.
liberate 746 vb.
unpossessed
774 adj.
not retain 779 vb.
given 781 adj.
uncharged 812 adj.
free agent
free person 744 n.
free-and-easy
lax 734 adj.
free 744 adj.
rash 857 adj.
impertinent
878 adj.
friendly 880 adj.
sociable 882 adj.
free-base
drug-taking 949 n.
freebie
extra 40 n.
incentive 612 n.
free 744 adj.
acquisition 771 n.
gift 781 n.
given 781 adj.
no charge 812 n.
freebooter
militarist 722 n.
robber 789 n.
bad person 938 n.
freeborn
free 744 adj.

Free Church
Christendom
976 n.
freedom
noncoherence 49 n.
freedom 744 n.
freedom fighter
soldier 722 n.
freedom of action
freedom 744 n.
independence
744 n.
freedom of choice
opportunity 137 n.
choice 605 n.
independence
744 n.
free fall
aeronautics 271 n.
free for all
turmoil 61 n.
contest 716 n.
fight 716 n.
anarchy 734 n.
free 744 adj.
scope 744 n.
free gift
extra 40 n.
acquisition 771 n.
gift 781 n.
**free, gratis and for
nothing**
uncharged 812 adj.
free hand
facility 701 n.
scope 744 n.
permit 756 n.
liberality 813 n.
free hand, a
scope 744 n.
freehold
independence
744 n.
estate 777 n.
lands 777 n.
proprietary
777 adj.
free house
tavern 192 n.
freelance
author 589 n.
do business 622 vb.
worker 686 n.
independent
744 adj.
free person 744 n.

freeloader
idler 679 n.
beggar 763 n.
toady 879 n.
sociable person
882 n.
free love
freedom 744 n.
love affair 887 n.
type of marriage
894 n.
illicit love 951 n.
Freemasonry
society 708 n.
free of charge
uncharged 812 adj.
free pardon
amnesty 506 n.
forgiveness 909 n.
free port
way in 297 n.
scope 744 n.
emporium 796 n.
no charge 812 n.
freesheet
the press 528 n.
free speech
freedom 744 n.
free spirit
free person 744 n.
free-thinking
free 744 adj.
irreligious 974 adj.
free time
leisure 681 n.
free trade
ingress 297 n.
scope 744 n.
trade 791 n.
no charge 812 n.
free verse
verse form 593 n.
freewheel
ride 267 vb.
travel 267 vb.
not act 677 vb.
do easily 701 vb.
free will
will 595 n.
freedom 744 n.
freewill
volitional 595 adj.
freeze
halt 145 vb.
come to rest
266 vb.
quiescence 266 n.

stop 266 int.
be dense 324 vb.
harden 326 vb.
render insensible
375 vb.
be cold 380 vb.
wintriness 380 n.
refrigerate 382 vb.
preserve 666 vb.
restriction 747 n.
nonpayment 805 n.
not pay 805 vb.
frighten 854 vb.
quake 854 vb.
freeze-dry
dry 342 vb.
refrigerate 382 vb.
preserve 666 vb.
freezer
cabinet 194 n.
refrigerator 384 n.
storage 632 n.
preserver 666 n.
freezing
contraction 198 n.
cold 380 adj.
refrigeration 382 n.
freezing point
coldness 380 n.
freight
fill 54 vb.
contents 193 n.
load 193 vb.
transport 272 n.
gravity 322 n.
merchandise
795 n.
freight train
train 274 n.
French beans
fruit and vegetables
301 n.
French cricket
ball game 837 n.
French dressing
hors-d'oeuvres
301 n.
sauce 389 n.
French fries
fruit and vegetables
301 n.
French horn
horn 414 n.
French kiss
endearment 889 n.
French knickers
underwear 228 n.

French leave
absence 190 n.
escape 667 n.
French letter
contraception
172 n.
French polish
smoother 258 n.
French poodle
dog 365 n.
French window
window 263 n.
frenetic
furious 176 adj.
frenzied 503 adj.
frenzied
frenzied 503 adj.
fervent 818 adj.
frenzy
turmoil 61 n.
violence 176 n.
frenzy 503 n.
activity 678 n.
excitable state
822 n.
frequency
degree 27 n.
frequency 139 n.
periodicity 141 n.
electricity 160 n.
oscillation 317 n.
frequency band
oscillation 317 n.
frequency wave
radiation 417 n.
frequent
frequent 139 adj.
recur 139 vb.
go on 146 vb.
be present 189 vb.
dwell 192 vb.
be wont 610 vb.
frequently
often 139 adv.
fresco
picture 553 n.
fresh
original 21 adj.
lasting 113 adj.
new 126 adj.
airy 340 adj.
humid 341 adj.
windy 352 adj.
cold 380 adj.
remembered
505 adj.

unhabituated
611 adj.
clean 648 adj.
salubrious 652 adj.
impertinent
878 adj.
fresh air
air 340 n.
salubrity 652 n.
freshen
invigorate 174 vb.
aerate 340 vb.
purify 648 vb.
revive 656 vb.
refresh 685 vb.
decorate 844 vb.
freshen up
make better
654 vb.
repair 656 vb.
refresh 685 vb.
fresher
student 538 n.
fresh-faced
personable 841 adj.
freshness
originality 21 n.
newness 126 n.
youth 130 n.
coldness 380 n.
cleanness 648 n.
sauciness 878 n.
fresh-water lake
lake 346 n.
fret
rend 46 vb.
rub 333 vb.
give pain 377 vb.
cry 408 vb.
stringed instrument
414 n.
restlessness 678 n.
hasten 680 vb.
disobey 738 vb.
be excitable
822 vb.
excitable state
822 n.
suffer 825 vb.
torment 827 vb.
decorate 844 vb.
anger 891 n.
be angry 891 vb.
enrage 891 vb.
fretful
capricious 604 adj.
active 678 adj.

discontented
829 adj.
irascible 892 adj.
fretwork
network 222 n.
ornamental art
844 n.
friable
brittle 330 adj.
powdery 332 adj.
friar
monk 986 n.
pastor 986 n.
friary
monastery 986 n.
monk 986 n.
fricassee
dish 301 n.
fricative
speech sound
398 n.
friction
counteraction
182 n.
friction 333 n.
opposition 704 n.
dissension 709 n.
painfulness 827 n.
fridge
refrigerator 384 n.
storage 632 n.
fridge-freezer
cabinet 194 n.
refrigerator 384 n.
storage 632 n.
friend
friend 880 n.
friend at court
influence 178 n.
latency 523 n.
patron 707 n.
friendly
pleasant 376 adj.
friendly 880 adj.
amiable 884 adj.
approving 923 adj.
friendship
friendship 880 n.
love 887 n.
Friesian
cattle 365 n.
frieze
textile 222 n.
ornamental art
844 n.
trimming 844 n.

frigate
sailing ship 275 n.
warship 722 n.
fright
eyesore 842 n.
fear 854 n.
frighten
frighten 854 vb.
threaten 900 vb.
frightened
fearing 854 adj.
frightening
frightening
854 adj.
frightful
prodigious 32 adj.
ugly 842 adj.
frightening
854 adj.
frigid
cold 380 adj.
impassive 820 adj.
inexcitable
823 adj.
hostile 881 adj.
pure 950 adj.
frigidity
coldness 380 n.
moral insensibility
820 n.
inexcitability
823 n.
purity 950 n.
frill
edging 234 n.
plumage 259 n.
fold 261 n.
fold 261 vb.
trimming 844 n.
fringe
adjunct 40 n.
extremity 69 n.
contiguity 202 n.
filament 208 n.
edge 234 n.
edging 234 n.
hem 234 vb.
hair 259 n.
unimportant
639 adj.
hairdressing 843 n.
trimming 844 n.
fringe benefits
earnings 771 n.
reward 962 n.
fringe medicine
medical art 658 n.

frippery
clothing 228 n.
bauble 639 n.
finery 844 n.
ostentation 875 n.

frisk
be in motion
 265 vb.
move fast 277 vb.
leap 312 vb.
search 459 vb.
be cheerful 833 vb.
rejoice 835 vb.

frisky
active 678 adj.
merry 833 adj.

frisson
agitation 318 n.

fritter away
waste 634 vb.
misuse 675 vb.
lose 772 vb.
be prodigal 815 vb.

fritters
dish 301 n.

frivolous
changeful 152 adj.
light-minded
 456 adj.
capricious 604 adj.
trivial 639 adj.
merry 833 adj.
rash 857 adj.

frizzy
undulatory
 251 adj.
hairy 259 adj.

frock
dress 228 n.
canonicals 989 n.

frock coat
overcoat 228 n.

Froebel system
education 534 n.

frog
fastening 47 n.
amphibian 365 n.
trimming 844 n.

frogman
diver 313 n.

frogmarch
impel 279 vb.

frolic
leap 312 n.
be cheerful 833 vb.
rejoice 835 vb.

amuse oneself
 837 vb.
revel 837 n.

frolicsome
merry 833 adj.

from A to Z
including 78 adv.

from pillar to post
round about
 626 adv.

from scratch
initially 68 adv.

from time to time
sometimes
 139 adv.

frond
foliage 366 n.

front
put in front 64 vb.
beginning 68 n.
first 68 adj.
impend 155 vb.
coat 226 vb.
be in front 237 vb.
front 237 n.
frontal 237 adj.
appearance 445 n.
duplicity 541 n.
path 624 n.
battle 718 n.
battleground
 724 n.
insolence 878 n.

frontage
situation 186 n.
face 237 n.

frontal
frontal 237 adj.

frontier
extremity 69 n.
contiguity 202 n.
edge 234 n.
limit 236 n.

fronting
near 200 adj.

frontispiece
prelude 66 n.
front 237 n.

frontman or -woman
broadcaster 531 n.

front of house
theatre 594 n.

front room
chamber 194 n.

front runner
contender 716 n.
favourite 890 n.

front tooth
tooth 256 n.

frost
cover 226 vb.
wintriness 380 n.
opacity 423 n.
whiten 427 vb.
blight 659 n.

frost-bite
coldness 380 n.
refrigerate 382 vb.

frosted
rough 259 adj.
cooled 382 adj.
opaque 423 adj.
semitransparent
 424 adj.
white 427 adj.
grey 429 adj.

frosted glass
screen 421 n.
semitransparency
 424 n.

frosting
covering 226 n.
powderiness 332 n.

frosty
cold 380 adj.
white 427 adj.
unsociable 883 adj.

froth
effervesce 318 vb.
moisture 341 n.
bubble 355 n.
bubble 355 vb.
dirt 649 n.
be excitable
 822 vb.

frothy
light 323 adj.
bubbly 355 adj.
ornate 574 adj.

frottage
picture 553 n.

frou-frou
faintness 401 n.
sibilation 406 n.
finery 844 n.

frown
distort 246 vb.
fold 261 n.
gesticulate 547 vb.
gesture 547 n.
discontent 829 n.
be rude 885 vb.
rudeness 885 n.
anger 891 n.

be angry 891 vb.
sullenness 893 n.

frown upon
depress 834 vb.

frozen
cohesive 48 adj.
fixed 153 adj.
still 266 adj.
dense 324 adj.
hard 326 adj.
insensible 375 adj.
chilly 380 adj.
cooled 382 adj.
preserved 666 adj.
impassive 820 adj.
fearing 854 adj.

frozen assets
estate 777 n.
debt 803 n.

frozen food
provisions 301 n.

frozen mitt
rejection 607 n.

frozen shoulder
rheumatism 651 n.

fructification
productiveness
 171 n.

fructose
food content 301 n.
sweet thing 392 n.

frugal
economical
 814 adj.
cautious 858 adj.
temperate 942 adj.

frugivorous
feeding 301 adj.

fruit
nonconformist
 84 n.
growth 157 n.
product 164 n.
reproduce itself
 167 vb.
flower 366 n.
plant 366 n.

fruitful
increasing 36 adj.
prolific 171 adj.
successful 727 adj.
gainful 771 adj.

fruit growing
agriculture 370 n.

fruition
propagation 167 n.
ripening 669 n.

completion 725 n.

fruit juice
　soft drink 301 n.

fruitless
　unproductive
　　172 adj.
　profitless 641 adj.
　unsuccessful
　　728 adj.

fruit machine
　gambling 618 n.

fruity
　tasty 386 adj.
　fragrant 396 adj.
　witty 839 adj.

frump
　eyesore 842 n.

frustrate
　disappoint 509 vb.
　be obstructive
　　702 vb.

frustration
　disappointment
　　509 n.
　hindrance 702 n.
　failure 728 n.

fry
　young creature
　　132 n.
　cook 301 vb.
　be hot 379 vb.

frying pan
　pot 194 n.
　heater 383 n.

fry-up
　dish 301 n.

fuchsia
　red 431 adj.
　purple 436 adj.

fuddled
　foolish 499 adj.
　tipsy 949 adj.

fuddy-duddy
　archaism 127 n.

fudge
　sweets 301 n.
　sweet thing 392 n.
　be equivocal
　　518 vb.
　fake 541 vb.

fudge the issue
　dissemble 541 vb.
　avoid 620 vb.

fuel
　fuel 385 n.
　store 632 vb.
　provide 633 vb.

animate 821 vb.

fuel to the flame
　provision 633 n.

fug
　stench 397 n.
　insalubrity 653 n.

fuggy
　fetid 397 adj.
　dirty 649 adj.

fugitive
　transient 114 adj.
　wanderer 268 n.
　avoider 620 n.
　escaper 667 n.

fugue
　musical piece
　　412 n.

Führer
　leader 690 n.
　autocrat 741 n.
　master 741 n.
　　See **autocrat**

fulcrum
　pivot 218 n.
　centre 225 n.

fulfil
　do 676 vb.
　carry out 725 vb.
　observe 768 vb.

fulfilment
　completeness 54 n.
　sufficiency 635 n.
　completion 725 n.
　observance 768 n.
　enjoyment 824 n.

fulgent
　luminous 417 adj.

full
　whole 52 adj.
　complete 54 adj.
　full 54 adj.
　fleshy 195 adj.
　broad 205 adj.
　veracious 540 adj.
　descriptive 590 adj.
　completed 725 adj.
　liberal 813 adj.
　drunk 949 adj.

full-blooded
　vigorous 174 adj.

full-blown
　complete 54 adj.
　grown-up 134 adj.

full-bodied
　wine 301 n.
　tasty 386 adj.

full circle
　revolution 149 n.
　circle 250 n.
　circuition 314 n.
　rotation 315 n.

Fuller's earth
　soil 344 n.

full-fledged
　grown-up 134 adj.
　matured 669 adj.

full frontal
　frontal 237 adj.

full-grown
　complete 54 adj.
　grown-up 134 adj.
　matured 669 adj.

full-length
　comprehensive
　　52 adj.
　plenitude 54 n.
　length 203 n.
　long 203 adj.

full moon
　moon 321 n.

fullness
　greatness 32 n.
　whole 52 n.
　plenitude 54 n.
　breadth 205 n.
　completion 725 n.
　satiety 863 n.

full of
　full 54 adj.

full of beans
　vigorous 174 adj.
　inexact 495 adj.
　healthy 650 adj.
　active 678 adj.
　cheerful 833 adj.

full of oneself
　vain 873 adj.

full out
　completely 54 adv.

full pardon
　forgiveness 909 n.

full play
　scope 744 n.

full sail
　velocity 277 n.

full-scale
　extensive 32 adj.

full size
　plenitude 54 n.
　size 195 n.

full skirt
　skirt 228 n.

full speed
　velocity 277 n.

full speed ahead
　swiftly 277 adv.

full stop
　quiescence 266 n.
　punctuation 547 n.

full tilt
　actively 678 adv.

full time
　period 110 n.

full up
　filled 635 adj.

full volume
　plenitude 54 n.

fully
　greatly 32 vb.
　completely 54 adv.

fully fashioned
　tailored 228 adj.
　formed 243 adj.

fully-fledged
　complete 54 adj.

fulminate
　be loud 400 vb.
　emphasize 532 vb.
　be angry 891 vb.
　curse 899 vb.
　threaten 900 vb.
　criticize 924 vb.

fulsome
　affected 850 adj.
　approving 923 adj.
　flattering 925 adj.

fumble
　be tentative 461 vb.
　not know 491 vb.
　be clumsy 695 vb.
　bungling 695 vb.

fume
　emit 300 vb.
　vaporize 338 vb.
　be hot 379 vb.
　odour 394 n.
　hasten 680 vb.
　be excitable
　　822 vb.
　anger 891 n.
　be angry 891 vb.

fumes
　gas 336 n.
　stench 397 n.

fumigate
　vaporize 338 vb.
　purify 648 vb.

fuming
　furious 176 adj.

excited 821 adj.
angry 891 adj.

fun
enjoyment 824 n.
pleasurableness
826 n.
merriment 833 n.
amusement 837 n.
festivity 837 n.
revel 837 n.
wit 839 n.

fun and games
merriment 833 n.
festivity 837 n.

function
number 85 n.
function 622 n.
function 622 vb.
utility 640 n.
ostentation 875 n.
celebration 876 n.

functional
operative 173 adj.
instrumental
628 adj.
useful 640 adj.

functionalism
philosophy 449 n.
art 551 n.
utility 640 n.

functionary
agent 686 n.
officer 741 n.
consignee 754 n.

fund
store 632 n.
treasury 799 n.

fundamental
simple 44 adj.
fundamental
156 adj.
base 214 n.
important 638 adj.

fundamentalist
theologian 973 n.
orthodox 976 adj.
zealot 979 n.

fundamentals
reality 1 n.
source 156 n.
chief thing 638 n.

fund-raising
acquisition 771 n.

funds
funds 797 n.

funebrial
funereal 364 adj.

funeral
funeral 364 n.
bane 659 n.

funeral director
interment 364 n.

funeral march
musical piece
412 n.

funeral parlour
interment 364 n.

funeral rites
obsequies 364 n.

funereal
funereal 364 adj.
dark 418 adj.
cheerless 834 adj.

funfair
festivity 837 n.
place of amuse-
ment 837 n.

fungicide
poison 659 n.

fungus
plant 366 n.
stench 397 n.
dirt 649 n.
blight 659 n.

funicular
railway 624 n.

funk
avoid 620 vb.
fear 854 n.
fear 854 vb.
be cowardly
856 vb.
coward 856 n.
cowardice 856 n.

funk it
be nervous 854 vb.

funnel
cylinder 252 n.
cavity 255 n.
tube 263 n.
tunnel 263 n.
transpose 272 vb.
conduit 351 n.
air pipe 353 n.

funny
unusual 84 adj.
crazy 503 adj.
laughing 835 adj.
funny 849 adj.

funny bone
sensibility 374 n.

funny business
wit 839 n.

funny farm
mental hospital
503 n.

funny ha-ha
witty 839 adj.
funny 849 adj.

funny-peculiar
funny 849 adj.

funny story
witticism 839 n.

fun of the fair
festivity 837 n.

fun run
racing 716 n.

fur
covering 226 n.
skin 226 n.
hair 259 n.
heraldry 547 n.
dirt 649 n.
trimming 844 n.

furbelow
edging 234 n.

furbish
decorate 844 vb.

furcate
crossed 222 adj.

fur coat
overcoat 228 n.

Furies
Chthonian deity
967 n.

furious
furious 176 adj.
violent 176 adj.
frenzied 503 adj.
hasty 680 adj.
fervent 818 adj.

furl
fold 261 vb.
rotate 315 vb.

furlong
long measure
203 n.

furlough
absence 190 n.
leisure 681 n.
repose 683 n.
permit 756 n.

furnace
furnace 383 n.

furnish
provide 633 vb.
make ready
669 vb.

furnished
prepared 669 adj.

furnished flat
flat 192 n.

furnishing
equipment 630 n.
provision 633 n.

furniture
property 777 n.

furniture polish
cleanser 648 n.

furore
violence 176 n.
commotion 318 n.
frenzy 503 n.
excitation 821 n.

furred up
dirty 649 adj.

furrow
fold 261 vb.
furrow 262 n.
groove 262 vb.
close 264 vb.
trace 548 n.

furry
hairy 259 adj.

further
additional 38 adj.
in addition 38 adv.
beyond 199 adv.
promote 285 vb.

furtherance
progression 285 n.

further education
education 534 n.

furthermore
in addition 38 adv.

furthermost
distant 199 adj.

furthest
distant 199 adj.

furtive
stealthy 525 adj.

fury
violence 176 n.
excitation 821 n.
excitable state
822 n.
desire 859 n.
anger 891 n.
monster 938 n.
demon 970 n.

fuse
mix 43 vb.
join 45 vb.
combine 50 vb.
hitch 702 n.
explosive 723 n.

fused
mixed 43 adj.
combined 50 adj.
fuselage
frame 218 n.
fusilier
soldiery 722 n.
fusillade
slaughter 362 n.
bombardment
712 n.
execute 963 vb.
fusion
a mixture 43 n.
mixture 43 n.
union 45 n.
combination 50 n.
nucleonics 160 n.
liquefaction 337 n.
association 706 n.
fuss
commotion 318 n.
exaggeration
546 n.
activity 678 n.
haste 680 n.
excitation 821 n.
excitable state
822 n.
suffer 825 vb.
be fastidious
862 vb.
ostentation 875 n.
be angry 891 vb.
fusspot
perfectionist 862 n.
fussy
narrow-minded
481 adj.
fastidious 862 adj.
fustian
textile 222 n.
fusty
fetid 397 adj.
dirty 649 adj.
futile
absurd 497 adj.
foolish 499 adj.
useless 641 adj.
contemptible
922 adj.
futon
bed 218 n.
seat 218 n.
future
future 124 adj.
futurity 124 n.

expected 507 adj.
future tense
futurity 124 n.
Futurism
school of painting
553 n.
futuristic
modern 126 adj.
literary 557 adj.
futurologist
oracle 511 n.
fu yung
dish 301 n.
fuzz
hair 259 n.
fuzz, the
police 955 n.
fuzzy
amorphous
244 adj.
hairy 259 adj.
dim 419 adj.
shadowy 419 adj.
indistinct 444 adj.
fylfot
quaternity 96 n.
cross 222 n.
heraldry 547 n.
talisman 983 n.

G

gabardine
textile 222 n.
overcoat 228 n.
gabble
ululate 409 vb.
empty talk 515 n.
lack of meaning
515 n.
mean nothing
515 vb.
speak 579 vb.
stammer 580 vb.
be loquacious
581 vb.
chatter 581 n.
gabbling
loquacious 581 adj.
gable
vertex 213 n.
gable end
extremity 69 n.
vertex 213 n.
Gabriel
angel 968 n.

gad
wander 267 vb.
gadabout
sociable person
882 n.
Gadarene swine
suicide 362 n.
gadfly
insect 365 n.
excitant 821 n.
gadget
object 319 n.
contrivance 623 n.
instrument 628 n.
tool 630 n.
Gael
native 191 n.
gaff
sharp point 256 n.
spear 723 n.
gaffe
mistake 495 n.
gaffer
old man 133 n.
male 372 n.
manager 690 n.
country-dweller
869 n.
gag
stopper 264 n.
vomit 300 vb.
silence 399 vb.
make mute 578 vb.
act 594 vb.
hinder 702 vb.
restrain 747 vb.
fetter 748 n.
witticism 839 n.
gaga
ageing 131 adj.
impotent 161 adj.
foolish 499 adj.
crazy 503 adj.
mentally disor-
dered 503 adj.
gage
defiance 711 n.
security 767 n.
gaggle
group 74 n.
ululate 409 vb.
gaiety
merriment 833 n.
sociability 882 n.
gain
grow 36 vb.
progress 285 vb.

progression 285 n.
arrive 295 vb.
err 495 vb.
benefit 615 n.
acquire 771 vb.
gain 771 n.
gain 771 vb.
gainful
gainful 771 adj.
gain on
outstrip 277 vb.
progress 285 vb.
gains
wealth 800 n.
gainsay
negate 533 vb.
gait
gait 265 n.
way 624 n.
gaiters
legwear 228 n.
badge of rule
743 n.
canonicals 989 n.
gala
festivity 837 n.
pageant 875 n.
galactic
cosmic 321 adj.
galactose
sweet thing 392 n.
gala day
amusement 837 n.
special day 876 n.
Galahad
brave person 855 n.
gala performance
pageant 875 n.
galaxy
group 74 n.
star 321 n.
luminary 420 n.
person of repute
866 n.
gale
velocity 277 n.
gale 352 n.
windy 352 adj.
gales of laughter
laughter 835 n.
gall
swelling 253 n.
give pain 377 vb.
sourness 393 n.
hurt 827 vb.
torment 827 vb.
sauciness 878 n.

resentment 891 n.
irascibility 892 n.
malevolence 898 n.
gallant
fop 848 n.
courageous
855 adj.
showy 875 adj.
courteous 884 adj.
lover 887 n.
loving 887 adj.
benevolent 897 adj.
libertine 952 n.
gallantry
courage 855 n.
courtesy 884 n.
love 887 n.
galleon
merchant ship
275 n.
warship 722 n.
gallery
lobby 194 n.
tunnel 263 n.
listener 415 n.
onlookers 441 n.
exhibit 522 n.
playgoer 594 n.
theatre 594 n.
collection 632 n.
church interior
990 n.
galley
chamber 194 n.
rowing boat 275 n.
cookery 301 n.
heater 383 n.
galley proof
print 587 n.
galley slave
boatman 270 n.
busy person 678 n.
slave 742 n.
prisoner 750 n.
galliard
dance 837 n.
gallimaufry
medley 43 n.
galling
annoying 827 adj.
gallivant
wander 267 vb.
gallon
metrology 465 n.
gallons
great quantity
32 n.

gallop
be transient
114 vb.
gait 265 n.
ride 267 vb.
move fast 277 vb.
spurt 277 n.
gallows
hanger 217 n.
means of execution
964 n.
gallstones
digestive disorders
651 n.
Gallup poll (tdmk)
statistics 86 n.
enquiry 459 n.
vote 605 n.
galoot
ninny 501 n.
bungler 697 n.
galore
great quantity
32 n.
many 104 adj.
plenty 635 n.
galumph
be clumsy 695 vb.
galvanize
invigorate 174 vb.
move 265 vb.
incite 612 vb.
excite 821 vb.
gambit
debut 68 n.
attempt 671 n.
tactics 688 n.
gamble
empiricism 461 n.
uncertainty 474 n.
conjecture 512 n.
gamble 618 vb.
gambling 618 n.
be rash 857 vb.
gambler
gambler 618 n.
player 837 n.
gambling
gambling 618 n.
gambling den
gaming-house
618 n.
gambol
leap 312 n.
leap 312 vb.
be cheerful 833 vb.

amuse oneself
837 vb.
game
crippled 163 adj.
meat 301 n.
animal 365 n.
trickery 542 n.
resolute 599 adj.
objective 617 n.
chase 619 n.
plot 623 n.
stratagem 698 n.
contest 716 n.
amuse oneself
837 vb.
revel 837 n.
laughingstock
851 n.
courageous
855 adj.
game bird
table bird 365 n.
gamekeeper
keeper 749 n.
gameness
willingness 597 n.
stamina 600 n.
courage 855 n.
**game not worth the
candle**
lost labour 641 n.
game preserve
wood 366 n.
stock farm 369 n.
games
exercise 682 n.
contest 716 n.
sport 837 n.
game, set and match
victory 727 n.
gamesmanship
tactics 688 n.
cunning 698 n.
contention 716 n.
sport 837 n.
gaming machine
gambling 618 n.
gamma ray
radiation 417 n.
gammer
old woman 133 n.
gammon
meat 301 n.
gammy
crippled 163 adj.
gamp
shade 226 n.

gamut
series 71 n.
key 410 n.
musical note
410 n.
gamy
pungent 388 adj.
savoury 390 adj.
gander
bird 365 n.
male animal
372 n.
gang
band 74 n.
be in motion
265 vb.
personnel 686 n.
party 708 n.
gang agley
miscarry 728 vb.
gang bang
rape 951 n.
ganger
worker 686 n.
manager 690 n.
gangling
unwieldy 195 adj.
narrow 206 adj.
clumsy 695 adj.
ganglion
centre 225 n.
gangplank
bridge 624 n.
gangrene
decay 51 n.
decompose 51 vb.
infection 651 n.
ulcer 651 n.
gangster
murderer 362 n.
robber 789 n.
low fellow 869 n.
offender 904 n.
gang up
congregate 74 vb.
cooperate 706 vb.
gangway
doorway 263 n.
access 624 n.
bridge 624 n.
gannet
eater 301 n.
bird 365 n.
gantry
stand 218 n.
gaol
prison 748 n.

seclusion 883 n.

gap
  incompleteness
    55 n.
  gap 201 n.
  concavity 255 n.
  requirement 627 n.

gape
  space 201 vb.
  open 263 vb.
  gaze 438 vb.
  watch 441 vb.
  be curious 453 vb.
  wonder 864 vb.

gaping
  open 263 adj.
  opening 263 n.

garage
  stable 192 n.
  chamber 194 n.
  storage 632 n.
  store 632 vb.
  safeguard 660 vb.

garage sale
  sale 793 n.

garb
  dress 228 vb.
  dressing 228 n.

garbage
  dirt 649 n.

garble
  mislead 495 vb.
  misinterpret
    521 vb.
  be false 541 vb.

garbled
  incomplete 55 adj.
  inexact 495 adj.
  false 541 adj.

garden
  vegetate 366 vb.
  cultivate 370 vb.
  garden 370 n.
  a beauty 841 n.

gardener
  producer 164 n.
  gardener 370 n.
  domestic 742 n.

garden flat
  cellar 194 n.

gardening
  flower 366 n.
  agriculture 370 n.

Garden of Eden
  happiness 824 n.
  mythic heaven
    971 n.

**garden of remem-
  brance**
  cemetery 364 n.

garden party
  amusement 837 n.
  social gathering
    882 n.

gardens
  park 192 n.
  pleasure ground
    837 n.

gargantuan
  huge 195 adj.

gargle
  cleanser 648 n.

gargoyle
  outlet 298 n.
  drain 351 n.
  image 551 n.
  eyesore 842 n.
  ornamental art
    844 n.

garish
  luminous 417 adj.
  florid 425 adj.
  vulgar 847 adj.
  showy 875 adj.

garland
  loop 250 n.
  trophy 729 n.
  ornamentation
    844 n.
  honours 866 n.
  celebrate 876 vb.
  applaud 923 vb.

garlic
  fruit and vegetables
    301 n.
  See **herb**
  condiment 389 n.
  stench 397 n.

garments
  clothing 228 n.

garner
  bring together
    74 vb.
  storage 632 n.

garnet
  redness 431 n.
  gem 844 n.

garnish
  adjunct 40 n.
  cook 301 vb.
  food 301 n.
  condiment 389 n.
  make appetizing
    390 vb.

decorate 844 vb.
  ornamentation
    844 n.

garret
  attic 194 n.
  vertex 213 n.

garrison
  resident 191 n.
  protector 660 n.
  safeguard 660 vb.
  defend 713 vb.
  defender 713 n.
  armed force 722 n.
  keeper 749 n.

garrotte
  kill 362 vb.
  capital punishment
    963 n.
  execute 963 vb.
  means of execution
    964 n.

garrulous
  loquacious 581 adj.

garter
  fastening 47 n.
  legwear 228 n.
  badge 547 n.
  decoration 729 n.
  badge of rank
    743 n.
  honours 866 n.

gas
  voidance 300 n.
  rarity 325 n.
  gas 336 n.
  oil 357 n.
  murder 362 vb.
  anaesthetic 375 n.
  render insensible
    375 vb.
  heater 383 n.
  fuel 385 n.
  empty talk 515 n.
  be loquacious
    581 vb.
  chatter 581 n.
  boast 877 n.
  boast 877 vb.
  execute 963 vb.

gas and air
  anaesthetic 375 n.

gasbag
  gas 336 n.

gas chamber
  means of execution
    964 n.

gaseous
  light 323 adj.
  gaseous 336 adj.

gas-fired
  heating 381 adj.

gas-fitter
  artisan 686 n.

gas guzzler
  automobile 274 n.

gash
  cut 46 vb.
  disunion 46 n.
  gap 201 n.
  notch 260 n.
  furrow 262 n.
  groove 262 vb.
  pain 377 n.
  evil 616 n.
  wound 655 n.
  wound 655 vb.

gas main
  air pipe 353 n.

gas mask
  safeguard 662 n.
  preserver 666 n.
  armour 713 n.

gasoline
  oil 357 n.
  fuel 385 n.

gasometer
  gas 336 n.
  storage 632 n.

gas oven
  furnace 383 n.

gasp
  breathe 352 vb.
  rasp 407 vb.
  cry 408 n.
  cry 408 vb.
  voice 577 n.
  be fatigued 684 vb.
  wonder 864 vb.

gasp for
  desire 859 vb.

gas ring
  furnace 383 n.

gas station
  storage 632 n.

gassy
  gaseous 336 adj.
  vaporific 338 adj.
  windy 352 adj.
  loquacious 581 adj.

gastritis
  digestive disorders
    651 n.

gastroenteritis
digestive disorders
651 n.
infection 651 n.
gastronomy
gastronomy 301 n.
gastroscopy
diagnostic 658 n.
gas warfare
warfare 718 n.
gasworks
gas 336 n.
workshop 687 n.
gate
barrier 235 n.
doorway 263 n.
onlookers 441 n.
obstacle 702 n.
fort 713 n.
imprison 747 vb.
treasury 799 n.
gateau
pastries and cakes
301 n.
gate-crash
intrude 297 vb.
be sociable 882 vb.
gated
imprisoned
747 adj.
gatekeeper
doorkeeper 264 n.
gate money
receipt 807 n.
gates of St Peter
heaven 971 n.
gateway
entrance 68 n.
doorway 263 n.
gather
join 45 vb.
bring together
74 vb.
congregate 74 vb.
expand 197 vb.
fold 261 n.
fold 261 vb.
meet 295 vb.
cultivate 370 vb.
assume 471 vb.
store 632 vb.
acquire 771 vb.
take 786 vb.
threaten 900 vb.
gathering
assemblage 74 n.
assembly 74 n.

conference 584 n.
storage 632 n.
ulcer 651 n.
gathering clouds
omen 511 n.
danger 661 n.
adversity 731 n.
threat 900 n.
gathering of the
clans
assembly 74 n.
gathering storm
danger 661 n.
gather momentum
accelerate 277 vb.
gather round
congregate 74 vb.
gather speed
accelerate 277 vb.
gather together
converge 293 vb.
gating
penalty 963 n.
gauche
inelegant 576 adj.
clumsy 695 adj.
ill-bred 847 adj.
gaucho
rider 268 n.
herdsman 369 n.
gaudy
florid 425 adj.
manifest 522 adj.
spurious 542 adj.
vulgar 847 adj.
showy 875 adj.
gauge
breadth 205 n.
appraise 465 vb.
gauge 465 n.
gauge 465 vb.
gaunt
unproductive
172 adj.
lean 206 adj.
gauntlet
glove 228 n.
defiance 711 n.
armour 713 n.
gauze
textile 222 n.
transparency
422 n.
semitransparency
424 n.
surgical dressing
658 n.

gavel
badge of rule
743 n.
gavotte
musical piece
412 n.
dance 837 n.
gawky
clumsy 695 adj.
gawp
gaze 438 vb.
scan 438 vb.
not expect 508 vb.
wonder 864 vb.
gay
abnormal 84 adj.
nonconformist
84 n.
luminous 417 adj.
florid 425 adj.
merry 833 adj.
showy 875 adj.
gay abandon
merriment 833 n.
rejoicing 835 n.
gay lib
freedom 744 n.
gaze
gaze 438 vb.
look 438 n.
gazebo
arbour 194 n.
gazelle
mammal 365 n.
gazette
journal 528 n.
record 548 n.
gazetteer
directory 87 n.
guidebook 524 n.
reference book
589 n.
gazpacho
hors-d'oeuvres
301 n.
GCE
exam 459 n.
GCSE
exam 459 n.
gear
accumulation 74 n.
sort 77 n.
box 194 n.
clothing 228 n.
dressing 228 n.
form 243 n.
equipment 630 n.

property 777 n.
finery 844 n.
gearing
machine 630 n.
debt 803 n.
gear oneself up
prepare oneself
669 vb.
gears
machine 630 n.
gecko
reptile 365 n.
geegaw
bauble 639 n.
gee-gee
horse 273 n.
gefilte fish
fish food 301 n.
Geiger counter
radiation 417 n.
meter 465 n.
detector 484 n.
gel
thicken 354 vb.
viscidity 354 n.
gelatine
thickening 354 n.
geld
subtract 39 vb.
unman 161 vb.
gelding
horse 273 n.
male animal
372 n.
gelignite
explosive 723 n.
gell or jell
be dense 324 vb.
harden 326 vb.
gem
gem 844 n.
gen
information 524 n.
gendarmerie
police 955 n.
gender
classification 77 n.
grammar 564 n.
gene
heredity 5 n.
organism 358 n.
genealogy
genealogy 169 n.
general
general 79 adj.
national 371 adj.
army officer 741 n.

general anaesthetic
 anaesthetic 375 n.
 synod 985 n.
general election
 vote 605 n.
generality
 generality 79 n.
generalization
 whole 52 n.
 generality 79 n.
 reasoning 475 n.
 inexactness 495 n.
general knowledge
 erudition 490 n.
generally
 generally 79 adv.
 often 139 adv.
general practitioner
 doctor 658 n.
general public
 social group 371 n.
 commonalty 869 n.
generalship
 tactics 688 n.
generate
 generate 167 vb.
generation
 coition 45 n.
 era 110 n.
generations
 long duration
 113 n.
generator
 electronics 160 n.
generic
 general 79 adj.
generic drug
 medicine 658 n.
generosity
 liberality 813 n.
 benevolence 897 n.
generous
 great 32 adj.
 many 104 adj.
 liberal 813 adj.
 courteous 884 adj.
 benevolent 897 adj.
 approving 923 adj.
 virtuous 933 adj.
genesis
 origin 68 n.
 source 156 n.
gene therapy
 therapy 658 n.
genetic
 genetic 5 adj.

genetic counselling
 heredity 5 n.
genetic engineering
 heredity 5 n.
 biology 358 n.
genetic fingerprint
 label 547 n.
**genetic fingerprint-
 ing**
 evidence 466 n.
 identification
 547 n.
 diagnostic 658 n.
genetics
 heredity 5 n.
 biology 358 n.
geneva
 alcoholic drink
 301 n.
Geneva Convention
 treaty 765 n.
genial
 pleasant 376 adj.
 warm 379 adj.
 pleasurable
 826 adj.
 cheerful 833 adj.
 benevolent 897 adj.
genie
 mythical being
 970 n.
genitalia
 genitalia 167 n.
genitals
 genitalia 167 n.
genius
 identity 13 n.
 analogue 18 n.
 tendency 179 n.
 intellect 447 n.
 spirit 447 n.
 intellectual 492 n.
 intelligence 498 n.
 sage 500 n.
 exceller 644 n.
 aptitude 694 n.
 proficient person
 696 n.
 prodigy 864 n.
genius loci
 lesser deity 967 n.
genned-up
 informed 524 adj.
genocide
 destruction 165 n.
 homicide 362 n.
 See **slaughter**

slaughter 362 n.
 cruel act 898 n.
 ruffian 904 n.
 capital punishment
 963 n.
genotype
 breed 77 n.
genre
 sort 77 n.
gent
 male 372 n.
 aristocrat 868 n.
genteel
 genteel 868 adj.
gentian violet
 purpleness 436 n.
gentile
 religionist 973 n.
 heathen 974 n.
 heathenish 974 adj.
 impious person
 980 n.
gentility
 etiquette 848 n.
 nobility 868 n.
 courtesy 884 n.
gentle
 muted 401 adj.
 lenient 736 adj.
 amiable 884 adj.
 courteous 884 adj.
 benevolent 897 adj.
 innocent 935 adj.
gentlefolk
 aristocracy 868 n.
gentleman
 adult 134 n.
 male 372 n.
 aristocrat 868 n.
gentlemanly
 male 372 adj.
 well-bred 848 adj.
 reputable 866 adj.
 noble 868 adj.
 courteous 884 adj.
 honourable
 929 adj.
**gentleman's agree-
 ment**
 unreliability 474 n.
 promise 764 n.
 compact 765 n.
gentleness
 moderation 177 n.
 leniency 736 n.
 courtesy 884 n.
 benevolence 897 n.

pity 905 n.
gentle sex
 womankind 373 n.
gentlewoman
 female 373 n.
 aristocrat 868 n.
gentrification
 restoration 656 n.
gentry
 aristocracy 868 n.
Gents
 latrine 649 n.
genuflexion
 obeisance 311 n.
 submission 721 n.
 servility 879 n.
 respects 920 n.
 ritual act 988 n.
genuine
 genuine 494 adj.
genuine article, the
 no imitation 21 n.
 authenticity 494 n.
genuineness
 identity 13 n.
 no imitation 21 n.
 authenticity 494 n.
genus
 group 74 n.
 breed 77 n.
geocentric
 central 225 adj.
 celestial 321 adj.
geodesy
 earth sciences
 321 n.
 measurement
 465 n.
geographic
 geographic
 321 adj.
geography
 situation 186 n.
 earth sciences
 321 n.
geology
 earth sciences
 321 n.
 mineralogy 359 n.
geometric
 ornamental
 844 adj.
geometrical
 statistical 86 adj.
**geometrical progres-
 sion**
 ratio 85 n.

geometry
mathematics 86 n.
geometry 465 n.

geomorphology
earth sciences
321 n.

George Cross
badge 547 n.
decoration 729 n.

georgette
textile 222 n.

Georgian
architectural
192 adj.

geranium
redness 431 n.

gerbil
animal 365 n.

geriatric
ageing 131 adj.

geriatrics
gerontology 131 n.
medical art 658 n.

germ
origin 68 n.
source 156 n.
infection 651 n.
poison 659 n.

germane
apt 24 adj.

German measles
infection 651 n.

germicide
prophylactic 658 n.
poison 659 n.

germinate
begin 68 vb.
result 157 vb.
reproduce itself
167 vb.
be fruitful 171 vb.
vegetate 366 vb.

germ warfare
warfare 718 n.
weapon 723 n.

gerontology
gerontology 131 n.
medical art 658 n.

gerrymandering
cunning 698 n.
perfidy 930 n.

Gestalt psychology
psychology 447 n.

Gestalt therapy
therapy 658 n.

Gestapo
police enquiry
459 n.

gestation
propagation 167 n.
See **obstetrics**
ripening 669 n.

gesticulate
gesticulate 547 vb.

gesture
move 265 vb.
look 445 n.
gesticulate 547 vb.
gesture 547 n.
deed 676 n.
behave 688 vb.

get
be turned to
147 vb.
generate 167 vb.
know 490 vb.
understand 516 vb.
acquire 771 vb.
possess 773 vb.
receive 782 vb.

get above oneself
be vain 873 vb.
be insolent 878 vb.

get across
mean 514 vb.
be intelligible
516 vb.
communicate
524 vb.
huff 891 vb.

get ahead
come before 64 vb.
progress 285 vb.

get a move on
accelerate 277 vb.
move fast 277 vb.
progress 285 vb.
hurry up 680 int.

get around
travel 267 vb.
be sociable 882 vb.

get at
blame 924 vb.

get away
recede 290 vb.
disappear 446 vb.
escape 667 vb.
achieve liberty
746 vb.

getaway
departure 296 n.
escape 667 n.

get back
recoup 31 vb.
retrieve 656 vb.
acquire 771 vb.

get back at
be restored 656 vb.
avenge 910 vb.

get better
get better 654 vb.

get cracking
begin 68 vb.
move fast 277 vb.

get down to it
be related 9 vb.
work 682 vb.

get in the way
be clumsy 695 vb.
hinder 702 vb.

get in touch
be contiguous
202 vb.
communicate
524 vb.

get nowhere
waste effort
641 adj.

get off
land 295 vb.
descend 309 vb.
escape 667 vb.

get off with
court 889 vb.

get on
progress 285 vb.
prosper 730 vb.

get one down
cause discontent
829 vb.
depress 834 vb.
be tedious 838 vb.

get one's come-up-
pance
deserve 915 vb.
be punished
963 vb.

get on one's nerves
displease 827 vb.
be tedious 838 vb.
cause dislike
861 vb.
enrage 891 vb.

get on with
accord 24 vb.
do 676 vb.

get out
come along
267 int.

land 295 vb.
extract 304 vb.
publish 528 vb.
escape 667 vb.

get over
be restored 656 vb.

get rid of
destroy 165 vb.
eject 300 vb.
kill 362 vb.
relinquish 621 vb.
deliver 668 vb.
not retain 779 vb.

get round
fool 542 vb.
induce 612 vb.
avoid 620 vb.

get shot of
eject 300 vb.
carry through
725 vb.

get the better of
be superior 34 vb.
confute 479 vb.
defeat 727 vb.
humiliate 872 vb.

get the picture
know 490 vb.
understand 516 vb.

get there
arrive 295 vb.

getting warm, be
approaching
289 adj.
detect 484 vb.

getting well
healthy 650 adj.

get-together
assembly 74 n.
amusement 837 n.
social gathering
882 n.

get to one's feet
be vertical 215 vb.
lift oneself 310 vb.

get up
produce 164 vb.
ascend 308 vb.
lift oneself 310 vb.
blow 352 vb.
study 536 vb.
fake 541 vb.

get-up
form 243 n.

get-up-and-go
vigour 571 n.
restlessness 678 n.

get wind of
  smell 394 vb.
  discover 484 vb.
  be informed
    524 vb.
get with it
  modernize 126 vb.
  be in fashion
    848 vb.
get worse
  be inferior 35 vb.
  deteriorate 655 vb.
gewgaw
  finery 844 n.
geyser
  outflow 298 n.
  water 339 n.
  stream 350 n.
  heat 379 n.
  heater 383 n.
gharry
  cab 274 n.
ghastly
  not nice 645 adj.
  distressing 827 adj.
  unpleasant
    827 adj.
  unsightly 842 adj.
  frightening
    854 adj.
ghat
  gap 201 n.
ghazal
  verse form 593 n.
ghazi
  zealot 979 n.
ghee
  fat 357 n.
gherkins
  sauce 389 n.
ghetto
  exclusion 57 n.
  housing 192 n.
  social group 371 n.
  seclusion 883 n.
ghetto blaster
  sound 398 n.
  megaphone 400 n.
  gramophone 414 n.
  broadcasting
    531 n.
  amusement 837 n.
ghettoization
  separation 46 n.
  seclusion 883 n.
ghettoize
  set apart 46 vb.

seclude 883 vb.
ghost
  insubstantial thing
    4 n.
  substitute 150 n.
  ghost 970 n.
ghost for
  substitute 150 vb.
ghost-hunting
  spiritualism 984 n.
ghost-laying
  sorcery 983 n.
ghostlike
  colourless 426 adj.
ghostliness
  immateriality
    320 n.
ghostly
  insubstantial 4 adj.
  immaterial
    320 adj.
  shadowy 419 adj.
  spooky 970 adj.
ghost of a chance
  possibility 469 n.
ghosts
  the dead 361 n.
ghost story
  novel 590 n.
ghost writer
  substitute 150 n.
  author 589 n.
ghoul
  monster 938 n.
  demon 970 n.
ghoulish
  inquisitive 453 adj.
  frightening
    854 adj.
  cruel 898 adj.
  spooky 970 adj.
ghoulishness
  curiosity 453 n.
GI
  soldier 722 n.
giant
  enormous 32 adj.
  giant 195 n.
  huge 195 adj.
  star 321 n.
giantess
  giant 195 n.
  demon 970 n.
giantism
  size 195 n.
  expansion 197 n.

giant panda
  mammal 365 n.
giaour
  heathen 974 n.
gibberish
  absurdity 497 n.
  lack of meaning
    515 n.
  unintelligibility
    517 n.
gibbet
  hanger 217 n.
  means of execution
    964 n.
gibbon
  mammal 365 n.
gibe
  indignity 921 n.
  despise 922 vb.
giddy
  unequal 29 adj.
  changeful 152 adj.
  high 209 adj.
  light-minded
    456 adj.
  crazy 503 adj.
  irresolute 601 adj.
  capricious 604 adj.
  rash 857 adj.
  crapulous 949 adj.
gift
  speciality 80 n.
  ability 160 n.
  tendency 179 n.
  aptitude 694 n.
  gift 781 n.
  give 781 vb.
gifted child
  intellectual 492 n.
  learner 538 n.
  exceller 644 n.
  proficient person
    696 n.
gift of the gab
  eloquence 579 n.
  loquacity 581 n.
gift token
  gift 781 n.
gift voucher
  gift 781 n.
gig
  carriage 274 n.
  boat 275 n.
gigantic
  enormous 32 adj.
  stalwart 162 adj.
  huge 195 adj.

giggle
  cry 408 n.
  cry 408 n.
  laugh 835 vb.
  laughter 835 n.
gigolo
  fop 848 n.
  toady 879 n.
  lover 887 n.
  libertine 952 n.
  prostitute 952 n.
gild
  coat 226 vb.
  ornament 574 vb.
  decorate 844 vb.
gild or sugar the pill
  deceive 542 vb.
  please 826 vb.
  flatter 925 vb.
gild the lily
  exaggerate 546 vb.
  misrepresent
    552 vb.
  ornament 574 vb.
  be superfluous
    637 vb.
  make better
    654 vb.
gill
  stream 350 n.
  metrology 465 n.
gillie
  retainer 742 n.
gills
  laterality 239 n.
  respiration 352 n.
gilt
  ornamental art
    844 n.
  ornamentation
    844 n.
gilt-edged
  valuable 644 adj.
gimcrack
  flimsy 163 adj.
  bauble 639 n.
  trivial 639 adj.
  unsafe 661 adj.
gimlet
  sharp point 256 n.
  perforator 263 n.
gimlet-eyed
  seeing 438 adj.
gimmick
  trickery 542 n.
  contrivance 623 n.

gin
  alcoholic drink
    301 n.
  trap 542 n.
ginger
  spice 301 n.
  vitalize 360 vb.
  orange 432 adj.
  animate 821 vb.
  excitant 821 n.
ginger ale
  soft drink 301 n.
ginger beer
  soft drink 301 n.
gingerbread
  pastries and cakes
    301 n.
ginger group
  motivator 612 n.
  petitioner 763 n.
ginger-haired
  red 431 adj.
gingerly
  cautious 858 adj.
  cautiously 858 adv.
ginger up
  invigorate 174 vb.
gingery
  pungent 388 adj.
gingham
  textile 222 n.
gin rummy
  card game 837 n.
ginseng
  tonic 658 n.
Gioconda smile
  secret 530 n.
giraffe
  tall creature 209 n.
  mammal 365 n.
gird
  tie 45 vb.
  criticize 924 vb.
girder
  bond 47 n.
  beam 218 n.
girdle
  tie 45 vb.
  pot 194 n.
  underwear 228 n.
  loop 250 n.
gird up one's loins
  prepare oneself
    669 vb.
girl
  youngster 132 n.
  person 371 n.

  female 373 n.
  loved one 887 n.
girl Friday
  stenographer
    586 n.
  worker 686 n.
  aider 703 n.
  auxiliary 707 n.
  servant 742 n.
girlfriend
  female 373 n.
  friend 880 n.
  loved one 887 n.
  lover 887 n.
girlhood
  youth 130 n.
girlish
  young 130 adj.
  female 373 adj.
  immature 670 adj.
giro cheque
  paper money
    797 n.
girth
  greatness 32 n.
  size 195 n.
gist
  chief part 52 n.
  topic 452 n.
  meaning 514 n.
  compendium
    592 n.
give
  be oblique 220 vb.
  be curved 248 vb.
  soften 327 vb.
  elasticity 328 n.
  give 781 vb.
give a miss
  avoid 620 vb.
give a name to
  indicate 547 vb.
give-and-take
  reversion 148 n.
  interchange 151 n.
give as good as one
    gets
  interchange
    151 vb.
  retaliate 714 vb.
give away
  manifest 522 vb.
  disclose 526 vb.
  resign 753 vb.
  assign 780 vb.
  give 781 vb.
  cheapen 812 vb.

  marry 894 vb.
giveaway
  extra 40 n.
  disclosure 526 n.
  acquisition 771 n.
  gift 781 n.
  given 781 adj.
  uncharged 812 adj.
give back
  restore 656 vb.
  restitute 787 vb.
give birth (to)
  reproduce itself
    167 vb.
  be fruitful 171 vb.
  vitalize 360 vb.
give grounds for
  justify 927 vb.
give in
  be inferior 35 vb.
  relinquish 621 vb.
  submit 721 vb.
give it a whirl
  attempt 671 vb.
given, be
  receive 782 vb.
  take 786 vb.
give notice
  predict 511 vb.
  communicate
    524 vb.
  warn 664 vb.
  resign 753 vb.
given that
  thus 8 adv.
given to
  liable 180 adj.
  habituated 610 adj.
given off
  emit 300 vb.
give oneself airs
  be affected 850 vb.
  be proud 871 vb.
  be vain 873 vb.
give oneself away
  blunder 495 vb.
  be disclosed
    526 vb.
  disclose 526 vb.
give one's word
  testify 466 vb.
  promise 764 vb.
give one the slip
  decamp 296 vb.
  avoid 620 vb.

give out
  communicate
    524 vb.
  publish 528 vb.
  give 781 vb.
give over
  cease 145 vb.
  give 781 vb.
give the bird
  disapprove 924 vb.
give the boot
  repel 292 vb.
  dismiss 300 vb.
give the go-by
  disregard 458 vb.
  avoid 620 vb.
  not observe 769 vb.
give the heave-ho
  dismiss 300 vb.
  eject 300 vb.
  not retain 779 vb.
give to
  use 673 vb.
give umbrage
  huff 891 vb.
give up
  cease 145 vb.
  not understand
    517 vb.
  be irresolute
    601 vb.
  reject 607 vb.
  disaccustom
    611 vb.
  relinquish 621 vb.
  stop using 674 vb.
  submit 721 vb.
  not complete
    726 vb.
  resign 753 vb.
  not retain 779 vb.
  be dejected 834 vb.
  despair 853 vb.
  be temperate
    942 vb.
give way
  be weak 163 vb.
  regress 286 vb.
  descend 309 vb.
  soften 327 vb.
  be irresolute
    601 vb.
  consent 758 vb.
giving
  weak 163 adj.
  soft 327 adj.
  giving 781 n.

gizmo
  object 319 n.
  contrivance 623 n.
  instrument 628 n.
  tool 630 n.
gizzard
  stomach 194 n.
glacé
  cooled 382 adj.
  sweet 392 adj.
glacial
  cold 380 adj.
glaciation
  condensation
    324 n.
  ice 380 n.
  refrigeration 382 n.
glacier
  ice 380 n.
glad
  willing 597 adj.
  pleased 824 adj.
gladden
  please 826 vb.
  cheer 833 vb.
glade
  open space 263 n.
  wood 366 n.
glad eye
  look 438 n.
gladiator
  contender 716 n.
  combatant 722 n.
gladiolus
  plant 366 n.
gladly
  willingly 597 adv.
glad rags
  clothing 228 n.
  finery 844 n.
gladsome
  happy 824 adj.
glairy
  viscid 354 adj.
glamorous
  personable 841 adj.
glamour
  beauty 841 n.
  prestige 866 n.
glance
  deflect 282 vb.
  touch 378 vb.
  shine 417 vb.
  gaze 438 vb.
  look 438 n.
  gesticulate 547 vb.
  gesture 547 n.

glance off
  diverge 294 vb.
glandular fever
  infection 651 n.
glare
  light 417 n.
  reflection 417 n.
  shine 417 vb.
  gaze 438 vb.
  anger 891 n.
  be angry 891 vb.
  sullenness 893 n.
glaring
  flagrant 32 adj.
  luminous 417 adj.
  florid 425 adj.
  obvious 443 adj.
  manifest 522 adj.
  angry 891 adj.
glasnost
  uncovering 229 n.
  opening 263 n.
glass
  weak thing 163 n.
  cup 194 n.
  covering 226 n.
  smoothness 258 n.
  draught 301 n.
  brittleness 330 n.
  weather 340 n.
  transparency
    422 n.
  mirror 442 n.
  materials 631 n.
  finery 844 n.
  ornamentation
    844 n.
glass-blower
  artisan 686 n.
glasses
  eyeglass 442 n.
glasshouse
  arbour 194 n.
  garden 370 n.
  prison 748 n.
glassware
  receptacle 194 n.
glassy
  smooth 258 adj.
  tranquil 266 adj.
  hard 326 adj.
  undimmed
    417 adj.
  transparent
    422 adj.
glaucoma
  blindness 439 n.

dim sight 440 n.
  tropical disease
    651 n.
glaur
  semiliquidity
    354 n.
glaze
  coat 226 vb.
  facing 226 n.
  smooth 258 vb.
  smoothness 258 n.
  viscidity 354 n.
  sweeten 392 vb.
gleam
  small quantity
    33 n.
  flash 417 n.
  reflection 417 n.
  shine 417 vb.
gleaming
  smooth 258 adj.
  undimmed
    417 adj.
glean
  cultivate 370 vb.
  select 605 vb.
  store 632 vb.
  acquire 771 vb.
  take 786 vb.
gleanings
  anthology 592 n.
  earnings 771 n.
  taking 786 n.
  booty 790 n.
glee
  vocal music 412 n.
  merriment 833 n.
glee club
  choir 413 n.
gleeful
  jubilant 833 adj.
glen
  valley 255 n.
glib
  loquacious 581 adj.
glide
  elapse 111 vb.
  be in motion
    265 vb.
  travel 267 vb.
  fly 271 vb.
  be light 323 vb.
  speech sound
    398 n.
  be stealthy 525 vb.
glider
  aeronaut 271 n.

aircraft 276 n.
glimmer
  flash 417 n.
  shine 417 vb.
  be dim 419 vb.
glimmer of hope
  hope 852 n.
glimpse
  look 438 n.
  see 438 vb.
  knowledge 490 n.
  sciolism 491 n.
  hint 524 n.
glint
  flash 417 n.
  shine 417 vb.
  look 438 n.
glisten
  flash 417 n.
  reflection 417 n.
  shine 417 vb.
glitter
  flash 417 n.
  shine 417 vb.
  be ostentatious
    875 vb.
  ostentation 875 n.
glitterati
  rich person 800 n.
  beau monde 848 n.
glitzy
  rich 800 adj.
  ostentatious
    875 adj.
gloaming
  evening 129 n.
  light 417 n.
  darkness 418 n.
  half-light 419 n.
gloat
  be pleased 824 vb.
  rejoice 835 vb.
  boast 877 vb.
  avenge 910 vb.
global
  extensive 32 adj.
  comprehensive
    52 adj.
  inclusive 78 adj.
  universal 79 adj.
  spacious 183 adj.
  broad 205 adj.
  rotund 252 adj.
  indiscriminate
    464 adj.
globe
  whole 52 n.

sphere 252 n.
universe 321 n.
world 321 n.
map 551 n.

globe-trotter
traveller 268 n.
spectator 441 n.

globular
rotund 252 adj.

globule
sphere 252 n.

glockenspiel
gong 414 n.

gloom
darkness 418 n.
dimness 419 n.
adversity 731 n.
sorrow 825 n.
dejection 834 n.

gloom and doom
dejection 834 n.

gloomy
dark 418 adj.
black 428 adj.
cheerless 834 adj.
dejected 834 adj.
melancholic
    834 adj.
sullen 893 adj.

glorified
ostentatious
    875 adj.

glorify
augment 36 vb.
dignify 866 vb.
honour 866 vb.
praise 923 vb.
worship 981 vb.

glorious
great 32 adj.
excellent 644 adj.
super 644 adj.
palmy 730 adj.
splendid 841 adj.
noteworthy
    866 adj.
renowned 866 adj.
worshipful 866 adj.

glory
success 727 n.
famousness 866 n.
honours 866 n.
prestige 866 n.
divine attribute
    965 n.

glory hole
chamber 194 n.

gloss
smoothness 258 n.
light 417 n.
reflection 417 n.
maxim 496 n.
commentary 520 n.
interpret 520 vb.
sham 542 n.
untruth 543 n.
facilitate 701 vb.
beauty 841 n.
ostentation 875 n.
extenuate 927 vb.
justify 927 vb.
vindication 927 n.

glossary
word list 87 n.
commentary 520 n.
dictionary 559 n.

glossolalia
piety 979 n.

gloss over
neglect 458 vb.
sophisticate
    477 vb.
mislead 495 vb.
conceal 525 vb.
fake 541 vb.
plead 614 vb.
extenuate 927 vb.

gloss paint
pigment 425 n.

glossy
luminous 417 adj.
personable 841 adj.

glossy magazine
journal 528 n.

glottal stop
speech sound
    398 n.
pronunciation
    577 n.

glove
glove 228 n.
love token 889 n.

glove puppet
image 551 n.

glow
be hot 379 vb.
heat 379 n.
glow 417 n.
shine 417 vb.
hue 425 n.
redden 431 vb.
vigour 571 n.
warm feeling
    818 n.

glower
gaze 438 vb.
be angry 891 vb.
sullenness 893 n.

glowering
angry 891 adj.
sullen 893 adj.

glowing terms
praise 923 n.

glow-worm
insect 365 n.

glucose
food content 301 n.
sweet thing 392 n.

glue
join 45 vb.
adhesive 47 n.
viscidity 354 n.

glue-sniffing
drug-taking 949 n.

glum
melancholic
    834 adj.

glut
productiveness
    171 n.
redundance 637 n.
superabound
    637 vb.
superfluity 637 n.
cheapness 812 n.
sate 863 vb.
satiety 863 n.

gluten
viscidity 354 n.

glutton
glutton 947 n.

gluttony
vice 934 n.
gluttony 947 n.

glycerine
lubricant 334 n.
fat 357 n.

G.M.T.
clock time 117 n.

gnarled
distorted 246 adj.
rough 259 adj.
dense 324 adj.

gnash
rub 333 vb.

gnash one's teeth
gesticulate 547 vb.
regret 830 vb.
be angry 891 vb.

gnat
small thing 33 n.

insect 365 n.

gnaw
abate 37 vb.
rend 46 vb.
chew 301 vb.
give pain 377 vb.
hurt 827 vb.
enrage 891 vb.

gnome
elf 970 n.

gnostic
religionist 973 n.
heretic 977 n.
heretical 977 adj.
sectarian 978 adj.
sectarian 978 n.

gnu
mammal 365 n.

go
pass away 2 vb.
period 110 n.
periodicity 141 n.
operate 173 vb.
vigorousness 174 n.
be in motion
    265 vb.
travel 267 vb.
walk 267 vb.
recede 290 vb.
excrete 302 vb.
disappear 446 vb.
vigour 571 n.
function 622 vb.
restlessness 678 n.
board game 837 n.
courage 855 n.

go about
undertake 672 vb.

goad
stimulant 174 n.
sharp point 256 n.
impel 279 vb.
incentive 612 n.
incite 612 vb.
hasten 680 vb.
animate 821 vb.
excitant 821 n.
excite 821 vb.
enrage 891 vb.

go against
counteract 182 vb.
oppose 704 vb.

go against the grain
be difficult 700 vb.
displease 827 vb.
cause dislike
    861 vb.

go-ahead
vigorous 174 adj.
progressive
285 adj.
assent 488 n.
enterprising
672 adj.
permit 756 n.
goal
limit 236 n.
goal 295 n.
attempt 671 n.
success 727 n.
desired object
859 n.
goalkeeper
player 837 n.
go along with
concur 181 vb.
assent 488 vb.
consent 758 vb.
goat
goat 365 n.
libertine 952 n.
go back
revert 148 vb.
turn round 282 vb.
turn back 286 vb.
recede 290 vb.
go back on
recant 603 vb.
not observe 769 vb.
gobbet
small thing 33 n.
gobbledygook
lack of meaning
515 n.
neology 560 n.
slang 560 adj.
gobble (up)
consume 165 vb.
absorb 299 vb.
ululate 409 vb.
gluttonize 947 vb.
go-between
intermediary
231 n.
informant 524 n.
messenger 529 n.
instrument 628 n.
mediator 720 n.
goblet
cup 194 n.
goblin
intimidation
854 n.
elf 970 n.

gobs
great quantity
32 n.
go by
elapse 111 vb.
go-cart
automobile 274 n.
pushcart 274 n.
God
cause 156 n.
the Deity 965 n.
god, goddess
deity 966 n.
godchild
family 11 n.
godfather
bigwig 638 n.
godforsaken
empty 190 adj.
distant 199 adj.
secluded 883 adj.
wicked 934 adj.
godhead
divineness 965 n.
godless
irreligious 974 adj.
impious 980 adj.
godlike
beautiful 841 adj.
godlike 965 adj.
godly
pious 979 adj.
go down
be destroyed
165 vb.
descend 309 vb.
founder 313 vb.
godparent
parentage 169 n.
godsend
benefit 615 n.
gods (the)
onlookers 441 n.
playgoer 594 n.
theatre 594 n.
go Dutch
compromise
770 vb.
participate 775 vb.
defray 804 vb.
be sociable 882 vb.
go easy (on)
be lenient 736 vb.
show mercy
905 vb.
goffer
groove 262 vb.

go for
attack 712 vb.
cost 809 vb.
reproach 924 vb.
go-getter
doer 676 n.
busy person 678 n.
egotist 932 n.
goggle
gaze 438 vb.
not expect 508 vb.
wonder 864 vb.
goggles
eyeglass 442 n.
shelter 662 n.
go-go
speedy 277 adj.
progression 285 n.
progressive
285 adj.
enterprising
672 adj.
gogo dancer
entertainer 594 n.
go in for
be resolute 599 vb.
be wont 610 vb.
busy oneself
622 vb.
undertake 672 vb.
going begging
superfluous
637 adj.
free 744 adj.
unpossessed
774 adj.
going beyond
overstepping 306 n.
going cheap
cheap 812 adj.
going down
decreasing 37 adj.
going for a song
cheap 812 adj.
going rate
price 809 n.
go into
dissertate 591 vb.
go it alone
be free 744 vb.
goitre
swelling 253 n.
skin disease 651 n.
gold
orange 432 n.
yellow 433 adj.
yellowness 433 n.

incentive 612 n.
money 797 n.
gold-digger
enquirer 459 n.
lover 887 n.
golden
yellow 433 adj.
palmy 730 adj.
promising 852 adj.
Golden Age
era 110 n.
literature 557 n.
palmy days 730 n.
happiness 824 n.
innocence 935 n.
golden girl or boy
favourite 890 n.
golden handcuffs
reward 962 n.
golden handshake
extra 40 n.
ejection 300 n.
resignation 753 n.
earnings 771 n.
pay 804 n.
thanks 907 n.
reward 962 n.
golden hello
extra 40 n.
arrival 295 n.
reward 962 n.
golden mean
average 30 n.
moderation 177 n.
middle way 625 n.
averageness 732 n.
golden oldie
archaism 127 n.
golden rule
maxim 496 n.
precept 693 n.
philanthropy
901 n.
golden wedding
period 110 n.
anniversary 141 n.
special day 876 n.
wedding 894 n.
goldfish
animal 365 n.
gold-medallist
proficient person
696 n.
gold-mine
store 632 n.
wealth 800 n.

gold standard
finance 797 n.
golf
ball game 837 n.
golf course
pleasure ground
837 n.
Goliath
athlete 162 n.
giant 195 n.
gondola
rowing boat 275 n.
airship 276 n.
gone
past 125 adj.
absent 190 adj.
dead 361 adj.
lost 772 adj.
gong
timekeeper 117 n.
resound 404 vb.
gong 414 n.
gonorrhoea
venereal disease
651 n.
goo
viscidity 354 n.
good
good 615 adj.
good 615 n.
excellent 644 adj.
skilful 694 adj.
obedient 739 adj.
pleasurable
826 adj.
amiable 884 adj.
benevolent 897 adj.
right 913 adj.
honourable
929 adj.
virtuous 933 adj.
pure 950 adj.
pious 979 adj.
good, be
be good 644 vb.
good behaviour
conduct 688 n.
courtesy 884 n.
virtue 933 n.
good books
repute 866 n.
approbation 923 n.
good breeding
etiquette 848 n.
courtesy 884 n.
goodbye
goodbye 296 int.

good cause
philanthropy
901 n.
good chance
fair chance 159 n.
possibility 469 n.
probability 471 n.
good cheer
enjoyment 824 n.
merriment 833 n.
sociability 882 n.
good company
sociability 882 n.
sociable person
882 n.
good faith
loyalty 739 n.
probity 929 n.
good form
practice 610 n.
etiquette 848 n.
ostentation 875 n.
good-for-nothing
powerless 161 adj.
idler 679 n.
vicious 934 adj.
bad person 938 n.
good fortune
chance 159 n.
good 615 n.
success 727 n.
prosperity 730 n.
happiness 824 n.
good graces
approbation 923 n.
good-humoured
benevolent 897 adj.
good in parts
imperfect 647 adj.
good intentions
intention 617 n.
good living
gastronomy 301 n.
gluttony 947 n.
good looks
beauty 841 n.
good luck
chance 159 n.
good 615 n.
nondesign 618 n.
good luck 730 int.
prosperity 730 n.
goodly
good 615 adj.
good management
economy 814 n.

good manners
conduct 688 n.
etiquette 848 n.
sociability 882 n.
courtesy 884 n.
good name
repute 866 n.
good-natured
amiable 884 adj.
benevolent 897 adj.
good neighbour
aider 703 n.
friend 880 n.
sociable person
882 n.
benefactor 903 n.
good person 937 n.
goodness
goodness 644 n.
probity 929 n.
virtue 933 n.
divine attribute
965 n.
piety 979 n.
sanctity 979 n.
good offices
protection 660 n.
aid 703 n.
pacification 719 n.
mediation 720 n.
good old days
past time 125 n.
good riddance
oblivion 506 n.
escape 667 n.
liberation 746 n.
loss 772 n.
relief 831 n.
hateful object
888 n.
goods
product 164 n.
transport 272 n.
property 777 n.
merchandise
795 n.
goods, the
information 524 n.
Good Samaritan
aider 703 n.
benefactor 903 n.
good person 937 n.
goods and chattels
property 777 n.
good sense
intelligence 498 n.

good taste
good taste 846 n.
good-tempered
amiable 884 adj.
good turn
benefit 615 n.
good vibes
feeling 818 n.
good will
aid 703 n.
concord 710 n.
friendliness 880 n.
benevolence 897 n.
good wishes
congratulation
886 n.
good works
philanthropy
901 n.
sociology 901 n.
piety 979 n.
goody-goody
hypocritical
541 adj.
affected 850 adj.
innocent 935 n.
pietistic 979 adj.
zealot 979 n.
gooey
viscid 354 adj.
retentive 778 adj.
go off
happen 154 vb.
be unclean 649 vb.
deteriorate 655 vb.
goofy
foolish 499 adj.
crazy 503 adj.
googly (cricket)
deviation 282 n.
go on
go on 146 vb.
persevere 600 vb.
go one better
be superior 34 vb.
outdo 306 vb.
be cunning 698 vb.
go one's own way
diverge 294 vb.
be incurious
454 vb.
will 595 vb.
be free 744 vb.
goose
bird 365 n.
table bird 365 n.
touch 378 vb.

ignoramus 493 n.
fool 501 n.
court 889 vb.
gooseberry
fruit and vegetables
301 n.
gooseberry bush
obstetrics 167 n.
gooseflesh
roughness 259 n.
coldness 380 n.
feeling 818 n.
nervousness 854 n.
goose pimples
roughness 259 n.
coldness 380 n.
goosestep
gait 265 n.
walk 267 vb.
**goose that lays
golden eggs**
wealth 800 n.
go out
emerge 298 vb.
extinguish 382 vb.
be sociable 882 vb.
**go out of one's way
(to)**
deviate 282 vb.
be willing 597 vb.
circuit 626 vb.
go over
number 86 vb.
repeat 106 vb.
be inverted 221 vb.
search 459 vb.
study 536 vb.
apostatize 603 vb.
Gordian knot
ligature 47 n.
complexity 61 n.
difficulty 700 n.
gore
garment 228 n.
pierce 263 vb.
blood 335 n.
fluid 335 n.
See **blood**
semiliquidity
354 n.
redness 431 n.
gorge
gap 201 n.
high land 209 n.
valley 255 n.
conduit 351 n.

superabound
637 vb.
sate 863 vb.
be intemperate
943 vb.
gluttonize 947 vb.
gorgeous
super 644 adj.
splendid 841 adj.
showy 875 adj.
gorgeousness
beauty 841 n.
gorgon
rara avis 84 n.
eyesore 842 n.
intimidation
854 n.
demon 970 n.
gorilla
mammal 365 n.
eyesore 842 n.
gormandizing
feasting 301 n.
gluttony 947 n.
gormless
foolish 499 adj.
unintelligent
499 adj.
go round
be inverted 221 vb.
traverse 267 vb.
circle 314 vb.
circuit 626 vb.
gorse
plant 366 n.
gory
haematic 335 adj.
murderous 362 adj.
gospel
truth 494 n.
news 529 n.
revelation 975 n.
scriptural 975 adj.
orthodox 976 adj.
gossamer
insubstantial 4 adj.
insubstantial thing
4 n.
flimsy 163 adj.
filament 208 n.
lightness 323 n.
transparency
422 n.
gossip
insubstantial thing
4 n.
topic 452 n.

inform 524 vb.
informer 524 n.
rumour 529 n.
fable 543 n.
speak 579 vb.
be loquacious
581 vb.
chatter 581 n.
chatterer 581 n.
chat 584 n.
converse 584 vb.
defame 926 vb.
go steady
court 889 vb.
go straight
get better 654 vb.
be virtuous 933 vb.
Gothic
architectural
192 adj.
letter 558 n.
print-type 587 n.
churchlike 990 adj.
go through
meet with 154 vb.
pass 305 vb.
search 459 vb.
deal with 688 vb.
feel 818 vb.
suffer 825 vb.
go to bed
be quiescent
266 vb.
sleep 679 vb.
repose 683 vb.
go to earth
be unseen 444 vb.
go together
accompany 89 vb.
go too far
overstep 306 vb.
exaggerate 546 vb.
be free 744 vb.
do wrong 914 adj.
go to one's head
invigorate 174 vb.
make mad 503 vb.
go to pieces
decompose 51 vb.
be destroyed
165 vb.
deteriorate 655 vb.
go to the wall
be destroyed
165 vb.
perish 361 vb.
be defeated 728 vb.

not pay 805 vb.
gouache
art style 553 n.
picture 553 n.
gouge out
extract 304 vb.
goulash
a mixture 43 n.
dish 301 n.
go under
be included 78 vb.
be destroyed
165 vb.
gourd
vessel 194 n.
gourmand
eater 301 n.
sensualist 944 n.
glutton 947 n.
gourmet
eater 301 n.
people of taste
846 n.
perfectionist 862 n.
sensualist 944 n.
glutton 947 n.
gout
rheumatism 651 n.
govern
order 60 vb.
moderate 177 vb.
manage 689 vb.
rule 733 vb.
governess
teacher 537 n.
protector 660 n.
domestic 742 n.
retainer 742 n.
keeper 749 n.
government
management
689 n.
government 733 n.
governor
paternity 169 n.
teacher 537 n.
governor 741 n.
master 741 n.
person of rank
868 n.
go walkabout
disobey 738 vb.
go west
be destroyed
165 vb.
die 361 vb.

go with
 accord 24 vb.
 accompany 89 vb.
 concur 181 vb.
 belong 773 vb.
 court 889 vb.
gowk
 ninny 501 n.
gown
 dress 228 n.
 robe 228 n.
 canonicals 989 n.
go wrong
 err 495 vb.
 miscarry 728 vb.
GP
 doctor 658 n.
grab
 retain 778 vb.
 take 786 vb.
Grace
 title 870 n.
grace
 musical note
  410 n.
 style 566 n.
 ornament 574 vb.
 elegance 575 n.
 gift 781 n.
 beautify 841 vb.
 beauty 841 n.
 good taste 846 n.
 mercy 905 n.
 thanks 907 n.
 forgiveness 909 n.
 approbation 923 n.
 prayers 981 n.
grace and favour
 permission 756 n.
 no charge 812 n.
graceful
 elegant 575 adj.
 shapely 841 adj.
 tasteful 846 adj.
grace note
 musical note
  410 n.
grace with
 honour 866 vb.
gracious
 courteous 884 adj.
 benevolent 897 adj.
gradation
 degree 27 n.
 order 60 n.
 arrangement 62 n.
 series 71 n.

 serial place 73 n.
grade
 make uniform
  16 vb.
 degree 27 n.
 arrange 62 vb.
 class 62 vb.
 grade 73 vb.
 serial place 73 n.
 sort 77 n.
 flatten 216 vb.
 gauge 465 vb.
 class 538 n.
gradient
 incline 220 n.
 ascent 308 n.
gradual
 slow 278 adj.
gradually
 by degrees 27 adv.
 slightly 33 adv.
graduand
 student 538 n.
graduate
 adjust 24 vb.
 graduate 27 vb.
 scholar 492 n.
 learn 536 vb.
 student 538 n.
 get better 654 vb.
 proficient person
  696 n.
 succeed 727 vb.
 have a reputation
  866 vb.
graduation
 degree 27 n.
 arrangement 62 n.
graffiti
 record 548 n.
 blemish 845 n.
graft
 extra 40 n.
 generate 167 vb.
 descendant 170 n.
 place 187 vb.
 implant 303 vb.
 cultivate 370 vb.
 inducement 612 n.
 booty 790 n.
 improbity 930 n.
grail
 ritual object 988 n.
grain
 small thing 33 n.
 tendency 179 n.
 minuteness 196 n.

 provender 301 n.
 weighing 322 n.
 texture 331 n.
 powder 332 n.
 grass 366 n.
grains
 cereals 301 n.
gram
 small quantity
  33 n.
 weighing 322 n.
grammar
 grammar 564 n.
grammarian
 linguist 557 n.
grammatical
 linguistic 557 adj.
 grammatical
  564 adj.
gramophone
 gramophone 414 n.
gramophone record
 rotator 315 n.
 gramophone 414 n.
granary
 storage 632 n.
grand
 great 32 adj.
 over one hundred
  99 n.
 sage 500 n.
 important 638 adj.
 super 644 adj.
 funds 797 n.
 impressive 821 adj.
 splendid 841 adj.
 person of repute
  866 n.
 worshipful 866 adj.
 noble 868 adj.
 proud 871 adj.
 formal 875 adj.
 ostentatious
  875 adj.
grandee
 bigwig 638 n.
 aristocrat 868 n.
grandeur
 greatness 32 n.
 prestige 866 n.
 ostentation 875 n.
grandfather
 old man 133 n.
 paternity 169 n.
grandiloquence
 exaggeration
  546 n.

 grandiloquence
  574 n.
 eloquence 579 n.
 affectation 850 n.
 boasting 877 n.
grandiose
 huge 195 adj.
 proud 871 adj.
 ostentatious
  875 adj.
grandmother
 old woman 133 n.
 maternity 169 n.
 female 373 n.
grand old man
 sage 500 n.
 person of repute
  866 n.
grand opera
 stage play 594 n.
grand piano
 piano 414 n.
grandstand
 view 438 n.
 onlookers 441 n.
 arena 724 n.
granite
 hardness 326 n.
 rock 344 n.
 building material
  631 n.
grant
 attribute 158 vb.
 qualify 468 vb.
 assent 488 vb.
 confess 526 vb.
 subvention 703 n.
 permission 756 n.
 consent 758 vb.
 endow 777 vb.
 assign 780 vb.
 bequeath 780 vb.
 gift 781 n.
 give 781 vb.
 giving 781 n.
 credit 802 vb.
 pay 804 n.
granted
 supposed 512 adj.
granular
 textural 331 adj.
 powdery 332 adj.
granulated
 powdery 332 adj.
granule
 small thing 33 n.
 powder 332 n.

grape, the
wine 301 n.
grapefruit
fruit and vegetables
301 n.
grape shot
ammunition 723 n.
grapevine
informant 524 n.
rumour 529 n.
telecommunication
531 n.
graphic
lifelike 18 adj.
expressive 516 adj.
painted 553 adj.
forceful 571 adj.
descriptive 590 adj.
graphite
lubricant 334 n.
graphology
writing 586 n.
graphs
mathematics 86 n.
grapple
join 45 vb.
unite with 45 vb.
be resolute 599 vb.
attack 712 vb.
contend 716 vb.
fight 716 vb.
wrestling 716 n.
retain 778 vb.
grapple with
withstand 704 vb.
strike at 712 vb.
contend 716 vb.
grasp
ability 160 n.
range 183 n.
distance 199 n.
know 490 vb.
knowledge 490 n.
understand 516 vb.
possession 773 n.
retain 778 vb.
retention 778 n.
taking 786 n.
grasping
avaricious 816 adj.
greedy 859 adj.
grass
provender 301 n.
grass 366 n.
greenness 434 n.
witness 466 n.
inform 524 vb.

informer 524 n.
divulge 526 vb.
recanter 603 n.
accuser 928 n.
bad person 938 n.
drug-taking 949 n.
grasshopper
insect 365 n.
grasshopper mind
changeable thing
152 n.
inattention 456 n.
grassland(s)
grassland 348 n.
plain 348 n.
grass-roots
important 638 adj.
commonalty 869 n.
grate
cook 301 vb.
give pain 377 vb.
furnace 383 n.
rasp 407 vb.
ululate 409 vb.
discord 411 vb.
cause dislike
861 vb.
grateful
grateful 907 adj.
grater
roughness 259 n.
porosity 263 n.
pulverizer 332 n.
gratification
pleasure 376 n.
enjoyment 824 n.
gratify
please 826 vb.
grating
disagreeing 25 adj.
network 222 n.
strident 407 adj.
discordant 411 adj.
inelegant 576 adj.
gratis
free 744 adj.
given 781 adj.
uncharged 812 adj.
gratitude
gratitude 907 n.
gratuitous
voluntary 597 adj.
given 781 adj.
uncharged 812 adj.
gratuity
extra 40 n.
incentive 612 n.

acquisition 771 n.
gift 781 n.
undueness 916 n.
reward 962 n.
grave
great 32 adj.
place 185 n.
excavation 255 n.
tomb 364 n.
engrave 555 vb.
forceful 571 adj.
important 638 adj.
inexcitable
823 adj.
serious 834 adj.
heinous 934 adj.
hell 972 n.
gravedigger
interment 364 n.
church officer
986 n.
gravel
paving 226 n.
powder 332 n.
soil 344 n.
confute 479 vb.
building material
631 n.
graveyard
cemetery 364 n.
holy place 990 n.
gravitate
descend 309 vb.
gravitation
tendency 179 n.
gravity 322 n.
gravity
gravity 322 n.
vigour 571 n.
importance 638 n.
seriousness 834 n.
purity 950 n.
gravlax
fish food 301 n.
gravy
sauce 389 n.
acquisition 771 n.
shekels 797 n.
graze
be contiguous
202 vb.
shallowness 212 n.
collide 279 vb.
collision 279 n.
eat 301 vb.
feed 301 vb.
graze 301 vb.

friction 333 n.
rub 333 vb.
give pain 377 vb.
touch 378 n.
touch 378 vb.
wound 655 vb.
grazing
eating 301 n.
feeding 301 adj.
grassland 348 n.
stock farm 369 n.
tactual 378 adj.
grease
adhesive 47 n.
coat 226 vb.
smooth 258 vb.
smoother 258 n.
soften 327 vb.
softness 327 n.
lubricant 334 n.
lubricate 334 vb.
fat 357 n.
grease 357 vb.
make unclean
649 vb.
greasepaint
stage set 594 n.
cosmetic 843 n.
grease the palm
bribe 612 vb.
greasy
smooth 258 adj.
dirty 649 adj.
great
great 32 adj.
excellent 644 adj.
super 644 adj.
renowned 866 adj.
Great Bear
star 321 n.
great day
important matter
638 n.
special day 876 n.
Greater London
city 184 n.
greatest
great 32 adj.
supreme 34 adj.
greatest, the
exceller 644 n.
Great Leveller, the
death 361 n.
great man or woman
bigwig 638 n.
person of repute
866 n.

greatness
  greatness 32 n.
  prestige 866 n.
great-uncle
  kinsman 11 n.
greed
  rapacity 786 n.
  avarice 816 n.
  desire 859 n.
  selfishness 932 n.
  gluttony 947 n.
greedy
  greedy 859 adj.
  envious 912 adj.
  gluttonous 947 adj.
Greek Calends
  neverness 109 n.
Greek gift
  trap 542 n.
  stratagem 698 n.
green
  new 126 adj.
  young 130 adj.
  park 192 n.
  vomiting 300 n.
  grassland 348 n.
  sour 393 adj.
  green 434 adj.
  credulous 487 adj.
  ignorant 491 adj.
  remembered
    505 adj.
  unhabituated
    611 adj.
  preserver 666 n.
  immature 670 adj.
  unskilled 695 adj.
  artless 699 adj.
  innocent 935 adj.
green belt
  space 183 n.
  district 184 n.
  plain 348 n.
  preservation 666 n.
greenery
  foliage 366 n.
  greenness 434 n.
green-eyed
  jealous 911 adj.
green fingers
  agriculture 370 n.
  aptitude 694 n.
greenfly
  insect 365 n.
greengrocer
  tradespeople 794 n.

greenhorn
  ignoramus 493 n.
  ninny 501 n.
  beginner 538 n.
  dupe 544 n.
  bungler 697 n.
greenhouse
  arbour 194 n.
  brittleness 330 n.
  garden 370 n.
  heater 383 n.
green light
  signal light 420 n.
  assent 488 n.
  signal 547 n.
  permit 756 n.
green mail
  offer 759 n.
  purchase 792 n.
green man
  traffic control
    305 n.
  refuge 662 n.
green party
  dissentient 489 n.
green room
  theatre 594 n.
greens
  fruit and vegetables
    301 n.
greet
  meet 295 vb.
  weep 836 vb.
  greet 884 vb.
greeting
  arrival 295 n.
  allocution 583 n.
  friendliness 880 n.
  sociability 882 n.
  courteous act
    884 n.
gregarious
  sociable 882 adj.
gremlin
  badness 645 n.
  failure 728 n.
  elf 970 n.
grenade
  bomb 723 n.
grey
  median 30 adj.
  horse 273 n.
  dim 419 adj.
  dimness 419 n.
  grey 429 adj.
  greyness 429 n.
  neutral 625 adj.

  middling 732 adj.
  cheerless 834 adj.
grey area
  uncertainty 474 n.
grey-haired
  ageing 131 adj.
greyhound
  dog 365 n.
grey matter
  head 213 n.
  intellect 447 n.
  intelligence 498 n.
grid
  correlation 12 n.
  electronics 160 n.
  network 222 n.
griddle
  cook 301 vb.
gridiron
  horizontality
    216 n.
  network 222 n.
  bicycle 274 n.
grief
  evil 616 n.
  sorrow 825 n.
  discontent 829 n.
grievance
  evil 616 n.
  annoyance 827 n.
  discontent 829 n.
  wrong 914 n.
grieve
  farmer 370 n.
  suffer 825 vb.
  hurt 827 vb.
  be dejected 834 vb.
  sadden 834 vb.
  lament 836 vb.
  pity 905 vb.
grievous
  bad 645 adj.
  distressing 827 adj.
grievous bodily harm
  attack 712 n.
griffin
  rara avis 84 n.
  animal 365 n.
  heraldry 547 n.
grill
  cook 301 vb.
  be hot 379 vb.
  heater 383 n.
  interrogate 459 vb.
grille
  network 222 n.
  window 263 n.

grim
  resolute 599 adj.
  obstinate 602 adj.
  not nice 645 adj.
  distressing 827 adj.
  serious 834 adj.
  frightening
    854 adj.
  sullen 893 adj.
  cruel 898 adj.
grimace
  distort 246 vb.
  distortion 246 n.
  agitation 318 n.
  look 438 n.
  gesticulate 547 vb.
  gesture 547 n.
  discontent 829 n.
  make ugly 842 vb.
  dislike 861 vb.
  sullenness 893 n.
  disapprove 924 vb.
grime
  dirt 649 n.
grin
  laughter 835 n.
  smile 835 vb.
grin and bear it
  stand firm 599 vb.
  knuckle under
    721 vb.
  be patient 823 vb.
  suffer 825 vb.
  be cheerful 833 vb.
  be courageous
    855 vb.
grind
  break 46 vb.
  rend 46 vb.
  demolish 165 vb.
  make smaller
    198 vb.
  deform 244 vb.
  sharpen 256 vb.
  chew 301 vb.
  pulverize 332 vb.
  rub 333 vb.
  rasp 407 vb.
  study 536 n.
  wound 655 vb.
  labour 682 vb.
  work 682 vb.
  oppress 735 vb.
grind down
  abase 311 vb.
  be insolent 878 vb.

grind one's teeth
 be angry 891 vb.
grindstone
 pulverizer 332 n.
 labour 682 n.
 bore 838 n.
grip
 join 45 vb.
 unite with 45 vb.
 fastening 47 n.
 vitality 162 n.
 vigorousness 174 n.
 influence 178 n.
 bag 194 n.
 gesture 547 n.
 tool 630 n.
 governance 733 n.
 restrain 747 vb.
 possess 773 vb.
 possession 773 n.
 retain 778 vb.
 retention 778 n.
 take 786 vb.
 impress 821 vb.
gripe
 give pain 377 vb.
 be discontented
  829 vb.
grisly
 frightening
  854 adj.
grist
 powder 332 n.
gristle
 solid body 324 n.
 hardness 326 n.
 toughness 329 n.
grist to the mill
 provision 633 n.
grit
 strength 162 n.
 vigorousness 174 n.
 hardness 326 n.
 texture 331 n.
 powder 332 n.
 resolution 599 n.
 stamina 600 n.
 courage 855 n.
grit one's teeth
 gesticulate 547 vb.
 be resolute 599 vb.
  See **stand firm**
 persevere 600 vb.
gritty
 hard 326 adj.
 textural 331 adj.
 powdery 332 adj.

grizzled
 whitish 427 adj.
 grey 429 adj.
 pied 437 adj.
grizzly
 grey 429 adj.
groan
 feel pain 377 vb.
 cry 408 vb.
 deprecate 762 vb.
 discontent 829 n.
 be dejected 834 vb.
 lamentation 836 n.
 weep 836 vb.
grocer
 tradespeople 794 n.
groceries
 provisions 301 n.
groggy
 weakly 163 adj.
 sick 651 adj.
 sleepy 679 adj.
groin
 angularity 247 n.
groom
 animal husbandry
  369 n.
 groom 369 vb.
 clean 648 vb.
 make ready
  669 vb.
 domestic 742 n.
 servant 742 n.
groom for
 fit 24 adj.
groomsman
 bridal party 894 n.
groove
 regularity 81 n.
 place 185 n.
 receptacle 194 n.
 gap 201 n.
 cavity 255 n.
 furrow 262 n.
 groove 262 vb.
 habit 610 n.
grope
 move slowly
  278 vb.
 touch 378 vb.
 be tentative 461 vb.
 be uncertain
  474 vb.
 not know 491 vb.
 be clumsy 695 vb.
 rape 951 n.

grope for
 search 459 vb.
gross
 consummate
  32 adj.
 whole 52 adj.
 manifest 522 adj.
 bad 645 adj.
 not nice 645 adj.
 acquire 771 vb.
 receive 782 vb.
 take 786 vb.
 vulgar 847 adj.
 heinous 934 adj.
 sensual 944 adj.
 impure 951 adj.
gross, a
 over one hundred
  99 n.
grotesque
 unusual 84 adj.
 absurd 497 adj.
 imaginative
  513 adj.
 unsightly 842 adj.
 ridiculous 849 adj.
grotto
 pavilion 192 n.
 arbour 194 n.
 cavity 255 n.
grotty
 trivial 639 adj.
 bad 645 adj.
 unclean 649 adj.
 sick 651 adj.
grouch
 be discontented
  829 vb.
 malcontent 829 n.
 rude person 885 n.
 sullenness 893 n.
ground
 fragmentary
  53 adj.
 reason why 156 n.
 region 184 n.
 territory 184 n.
 situation 186 n.
 base 214 n.
 flatten 216 vb.
 basis 218 n.
 support 218 vb.
 navigate 269 vb.
 powdery 332 adj.
 land 344 n.
 educate 534 vb.

 arena 724 n.
grounded
 fixed 153 adj.
ground floor
 base 214 n.
groundless
 unreal 2 adj.
 insubstantial 4 adj.
 illogical 477 adj.
 erroneous 495 adj.
grounds
 leavings 41 n.
 territory 184 n.
 park 192 n.
 grassland 348 n.
 evidence 466 n.
 reasons 475 n.
 motive 612 n.
 dirt 649 n.
 lands 777 n.
ground swell
 commotion 318 n.
 wave 350 n.
groundwork
 source 156 n.
 base 214 n.
 basis 218 n.
 preparation 669 n.
group
 combine 50 vb.
 part 53 n.
 subdivision 53 n.
 arrange 62 vb.
 arrangement 62 n.
 class 62 vb.
 bring together
  74 vb.
 group 74 n.
 network 222 n.
 party 708 n.
 air force 722 n.
 sect 978 n.
groupie
 concomitant 89 n.
 follower 284 n.
 habitué 610 n.
grouse
 meat 301 n.
 table bird 365 n.
 be discontented
  829 vb.
grout
 adhesive 47 n.
 coat 226 vb.
grove
 wood 366 n.

grovel
knuckle under
721 vb.
be servile 879 vb.
grow
become 1 vb.
augment 36 vb.
grow 36 vb.
produce 164 vb.
breed stock 369 vb.
cultivate 370 vb.
mature 669 vb.
growing
increasing 36 adj.
young 130 adj.
grow into
evolve 316 vb.
growl
ululate 409 vb.
ululation 409 n.
See **ululate**
be rude 885 vb.
anger 891 n.
be angry 891 vb.
sullenness 893 n.
threat 900 n.
threaten 900 vb.
grown-up
adult 134 n.
grown-up 134 adj.
grow on one
be wont 610 vb.
growth
increase 36 n.
growth 157 n.
production 164 n.
swelling 253 n.
elevation 310 n.
agriculture 370 n.
cancer 651 n.
grow up
grow 36 vb.
expand 197 vb.
ascend 308 vb.
grub
young creature
132 n.
food 301 n.
creepy-crawly
365 n.
grubby
unclean 649 adj.
grudge
be unwilling
598 vb.
refuse 760 vb.

be discontented
829 vb.
discontent 829 n.
be hostile 881 vb.
enmity 881 n.
hatred 888 n.
resentment 891 n.
gruelling
laborious 682 adj.
paining 827 adj.
gruesome
bad 645 adj.
not nice 645 adj.
unsightly 842 adj.
frightening
854 adj.
gruff
hoarse 407 adj.
taciturn 582 adj.
irascible 892 adj.
sullen 893 adj.
grumble
roll 403 vb.
cry 408 vb.
be discontented
829 vb.
grumpy
irascible 892 adj.
sullen 893 adj.
grunt
rasp 407 vb.
cry 408 n.
cry 408 vb.
ululate 409 vb.
be fatigued 684 vb.
G-suit
suit 228 n.
guarantee
make certain
473 vb.
affirm 532 vb.
oath 532 n.
safe 660 adj.
safeguard 660 vb.
safety 660 n.
patronize 703 vb.
promise 764 n.
promise 764 vb.
promised 764 n.
give security
767 vb.
security 767 n.
guarantor
patron 707 n.
guard
doorkeeper 264 n.
attention 455 n.

surveillance 457 n.
protection 660 n.
protector 660 n.
safeguard 660 vb.
defence 713 n.
defend 713 vb.
defender 713 n.
keeper 749 n.
guarded
vigilant 457 adj.
taciturn 582 adj.
cautious 858 adj.
guardian
parentage 169 n.
protector 660 n.
defender 713 n.
keeper 749 n.
guards
armed force 722 n.
soldier 722 n.
guava
fruit and vegetables
301 n.
guerrilla
killer 362 n.
attacker 712 n.
soldier 722 n.
revolter 738 n.
desperado 857 n.
guess
assume 471 vb.
estimate 480 vb.
*be of the opinion
that* 485 vb.
opinion 485 n.
conjecture 512 n.
suppose 512 vb.
guesstimate
uncertainty 474 n.
conjecture 512 n.
guest
resident 191 n.
arrival 295 n.
friend 880 n.
sociable person
882 n.
guff
empty talk 515 n.
fable 543 n.
chatter 581 n.
guffaw
cry 408 n.
laughter 835 n.
guidance
teaching 534 n.
directorship 689 n.
advice 691 n.

guide
prototype 23 n.
superior 34 n.
come before 64 vb.
precursor 66 n.
rule 81 n.
accompany 89 vb.
concomitant 89 n.
influence 178 n.
itinerary 267 n.
precede 283 vb.
sage 500 n.
guide 520 n.
informant 524 n.
educate 534 vb.
indicate 547 vb.
indication 547 n.
reference book
589 n.
direct 689 vb.
adviser 691 n.
guidebook
guidebook 524 n.
guidelines
precept 693 n.
guiding
precedence 64 n.
influential 178 adj.
directed 281 adj.
guild
group 74 n.
business 622 n.
community 708 n.
corporation 708 n.
merchant 794 n.
guile
duplicity 541 n.
deception 542 n.
cunning 698 n.
guillotine
end 69 n.
stop 145 n.
shorten 204 vb.
kill 362 vb.
execute 963 vb.
means of execution
964 n.
guilt
guilt 936 n.
guiltless
ignorant 491 adj.
virtuous 933 adj.
guiltless 935 adj.
guilty
guilty 936 adj.
guinea
table bird 365 n.

drug-taking 949 n.
habitat
place 185 n.
situation 186 n.
locality 187 n.
abode 192 n.
habitation
edifice 164 n.
abode 192 n.
habit-forming
habitual 610 adj.
intoxicating
949 adj.
habitual
typical 83 adj.
repeated 106 adj.
habitual 610 adj.
habitué
habitué 610 n.
sociable person
882 n.
hacienda
house 192 n.
stock farm 369 n.
farm 370 n.
lands 777 n.
hack
cut 46 vb.
roughen 259 vb.
roughness 259 n.
ride 267 vb.
saddle horse 273 n.
coldness 380 n.
author 589 n.
wound 655 vb.
worker 686 n.
bungler 697 n.
servant 742 n.
hackle
plumage 259 n.
hackneyed
imitative 20 adj.
known 490 adj.
aphoristic 496 adj.
feeble 572 adj.
usual 610 adj.
used 673 adj.
dull 840 adj.
hacksaw
notch 260 n.
had, be
be duped 544 vb.
pay too much
811 vb.
haddock
fish food 301 n.

had enough
be defeated 728 vb.
Hades
destiny 155 n.
death 361 n.
the dead 361 n.
hell 972 n.
mythic hell 972 n.
had it
dying 361 adj.
defeated 728 adj.
haematologist
doctor 658 n.
haematology
blood 335 n.
haemoglobin
blood 335 n.
haemophilia
haemorrhage
302 n.
blood 335 n.
fluidity 335 n.
blood disease
651 n.
haemorrhage
haemorrhage
302 n.
blood disease
651 n.
haemorrhoids
swelling 253 n.
digestive disorders
651 n.
hag
old woman 133 n.
sorceress 983 n.
haggard
lean 206 adj.
fatigued 684 adj.
suffering 825 adj.
haggis
meat 301 n.
haggle
make terms
766 vb.
bargain 791 vb.
trade 791 vb.
cheapen 812 vb.
be parsimonious
816 vb.
hagiography
biography 590 n.
praise 923 n.
theology 973 n.
ha-ha
gap 201 n.
fence 235 n.

laugh 835 vb.
haiku
verse form 593 n.
hail
crowd 74 n.
rain 350 n.
rain 350 VB.
wintriness 380 n.
cry 408 n.
cry 408 vb.
call 547 n.
speak to 583 vb.
greet 884 vb.
show respect
920 vb.
applaud 923 vb.
hail-fellow-well-met
friendly 880 adj.
sociable 882 adj.
hailstone
wintriness 380 n.
hair
small thing 33 n.
fibre 208 n.
hair 259 n.
hairdo
hairdressing 843 n.
hairdresser
beautician 843 n.
hairless
hairless 229 adj.
hair of the dog that
bit one
drunkenness 949 n.
hairpin bend
curve 248 n.
hair-raising
exciting 821 adj.
frightening
854 adj.
hair's breadth
short distance
200 n.
narrowness 206 n.
hair shirt
asceticism 945 n.
hair-splitting
discrimination
463 n.
argument 475 n.
sophistry 477 n.
fastidiousness
862 n.
hairy
hairy 259 adj.
frightening
854 adj.

hajj
piety 979 n.
act of worship
981 n.
halberd
axe 723 n.
spear 723 n.
halcyon
tranquil 266 adj.
peaceful 717 adj.
palmy 730 adj.
halcyon days
weather 340 n.
palmy days 730 n.
joy 824 n.
hale and hearty
healthy 650 adj.
half
part 53 n.
bisection 92 n.
half a chance
fair chance 159 n.
half-a-dozen
over five 99 n.
half a loaf
compromise 770 n.
half-and-half
equal 28 adj.
mixed 43 adj.
neutral 625 adj.
half-baked
ignorant 491 adj.
immature 670 adj.
bungled 695 adj.
half-caste
hybrid 43 n.
mixed 43 adj.
half crown
coinage 797 n.
half-hearted
incomplete 55 adj.
weak 163 adj.
unwilling 598 adj.
apathetic 820 adj.
indifferent 860 adj.
half-holiday
leisure 681 n.
half measures
incompleteness
55 n.
shortfall 307 n.
middle way 625 n.
insufficiency 636 n.
half pay
receipt 807 n.
halfpenny
edition 589 n.

coinage 797 n.
halfway
middle point 30 n.
middle way 625 n.
compromise 770 n.
half-witted
unintelligent
499 adj.
halibut
fish food 301 n.
halitosis
stench 397 n.
hall
edifice 164 n.
house 192 n.
chamber 194 n.
lobby 194 n.
front 237 n.
access 624 n.
hallelujah
cheers 835 int.
rejoicing 835 n.
celebration 876 n.
hymn 981 n.
Halley's comet
planet 321 n.
hallmark
label 547 n.
halloo
cry 408 n.
hallowed
divine 965 adj.
Hallowe'en
sorcery 983 n.
hallucination
insubstantiality
4 n.
appearance 445 n.
error 495 n.
fantasy 513 n.
deception 542 n.
hallway
access 624 n.
halo
loop 250 n.
light 417 n.
honours 866 n.
halt
end 69 n.
be discontinuous
72 vb.
cease 145 vb.
halt 145 vb.
stop 145 n.
stopping place
145 n.
be weak 163 vb.

crippled 163 adj.
quiescence 266 n.
stop 266 int.
goal 295 n.
railway 624 n.
failure 728 n.
halter
fetter 748 n.
halting
incomplete 55 adj.
fitful 142 adj.
slow 278 adj.
inelegant 576 adj.
halve
sunder 46 vb.
bisect 92 vb.
apportion 783 vb.
halves
portion 783 n.
ham
leg 267 n.
meat 301 n.
ignorant 491 adj.
act 594 vb.
actor 594 n.
be unskilful
695 vb.
unskilled 695 adj.
bungler 697 n.
wit 839 n.
be affected 850 vb.
hamburger
dish 301 n.
meal 301 n.
ham-handed
clumsy 695 adj.
hamlet
district 184 n.
housing 192 n.
hammer
hammer 279 n.
strike 279 vb.
missile 287 n.
be loud 400 vb.
strike at 712 vb.
club 723 n.
hammer and tongs
knock 279 n.
hammer away at
persevere 600 vb.
hammer in
affix 45 vb.
hammering
recurrence 106 n.
repeated 106 adj.
impulse 279 n.
knock 279 n.

hammock
hanging object
217 n.
bed 218 n.
hamper
basket 194 n.
impair 655 vb.
be difficult 700 vb.
hinder 702 vb.
restrain 747 vb.
hamster
animal 365 n.
hamstring
disable 161 vb.
hinder 702 vb.
hand
limb 53 n.
timekeeper 117 n.
long measure
203 n.
laterality 239 n.
pass 305 vb.
person 371 n.
feeler 378 n.
identification
547 n.
indicator 547 n.
instrument 628 n.
doer 676 n.
worker 686 n.
servant 742 n.
pincers 778 n.
hand (at cards)
group 74 n.
portion 783 n.
hand back
restore 656 vb.
handbag
bag 194 n.
handball
ball game 837 n.
handbook
guidebook 524 n.
handclasp
friendliness 880 n.
sociability 882 n.
courteous act
884 n.
handcuff
tie 45 vb.
bond 47 n.
arrest 747 vb.
fetter 747 vb.
fetter 748 n.
hand down
transfer 272 vb.

handful
small quantity
33 n.
bunch 74 n.
contents 193 n.
difficulty 700 n.
hard task 700 n.
handicap
equalize 28 vb.
advantage 34 n.
inferiority 35 n.
retard 278 vb.
illness 651 n.
difficulty 700 n.
encumbrance
702 n.
hinder 702 vb.
obstacle 702 n.
contest 716 n.
handicapped
crippled 163 adj.
hindered 702 adj.
handicraft
business 622 n.
ornamental art
844 n.
hand in glove (with)
cooperative
706 adj.
friendly 880 adj.
hand in hand
with 89 adv.
hand it to
be inferior 35 vb.
approve 923 vb.
praise 923 vb.
handiwork
effect 157 n.
product 164 n.
deed 676 n.
ornamental art
844 n.
handkerchief
cleaning cloth
648 n.
handle
handle 218 n.
opener 263 n.
touch 378 vb.
name 561 n.
dissertate 591 vb.
deal with 688 vb.
manage 689 vb.
trade 791 vb.
honours 866 n.
title 870 n.

handless
  crippled 163 adj.
handless, be
  be unskilful
  695 vb.
handle to one's name
  title 870 n.
hand-made
  nonuniform 17 adj.
hand-me-downs
  clothing 228 n.
hand on
  transfer 272 vb.
hand out
  provide 633 vb.
handout
  report 524 n.
  advertisement
  528 n.
  news 529 n.
  incentive 612 n.
  subvention 703 n.
  gift 781 n.
hand over
  transfer 272 vb.
  pass 305 vb.
  relinquish 621 vb.
  resign 753 vb.
  assign 780 vb.
  give 781 vb.
hand over fist
  swiftly 277 adv.
handsel
  initiate 68 vb.
  security 767 n.
  gift 781 n.
handshake
  arrival 295 n.
  gesture 547 n.
  friendliness 880 n.
  sociability 882 n.
  courteous act
  884 n.
handsome
  liberal 813 adj.
  beautiful 841 adj.
hand's turn
  labour 682 n.
hand-to-hand fighting
  duel 716 n.
  fight 716 n.
hand-to-mouth existence
  poverty 801 n.
handwriting
  lettering 586 n.

writing 586 n.
handy
  little 196 adj.
  near 200 adj.
  light 323 adj.
  useful 640 adj.
  skilful 694 adj.
handyman
  mender 656 n.
  proficient person
  696 n.
  servant 742 n.
hang
  hang 217 vb.
  pendency 217 n.
  kill 362 vb.
  curse 899 int.
  execute 963 vb.
hang (a picture)
  show 522 vb.
hang about
  wait 136 vb.
  be in motion
  265 vb.
  be inactive 679 vb.
hangar
  stable 192 n.
  air travel 271 n.
hang around
  expect 507 vb.
  See **await**
hang back
  be late 136 vb.
  avoid 620 vb.
  refuse 760 vb.
  be modest 874 vb.
hang by a thread
  be uncertain
  474 vb.
  be in danger
  661 vb.
hangdog
  guilty 936 adj.
hang down
  hang 217 vb.
  descend 309 vb.
hang, draw and quarter
  execute 963 vb.
hanger
  hanger 217 n.
hanger-on
  successor 67 n.
  concomitant 89 n.
  follower 284 n.
  dependant 742 n.
  toady 879 n.

flatterer 925 n.
hang fire
  wait 136 vb.
  pause 145 vb.
  move slowly
  278 vb.
  be unwilling
  598 vb.
  not act 677 vb.
  be inactive 679 vb.
  refuse 760 vb.
hang-gliding
  aeronautics 271 n.
  sport 837 n.
hanging
  hanging 217 adj.
  pendency 217 n.
  killing 362 n.
  capital punishment
  963 n.
hangings
  hanging object
  217 n.
  covering 226 n.
hangman
  destroyer 168 n.
  killer 362 n.
  indoor game 837 n.
hang on
  affix 45 vb.
  wait 136 vb.
  go on 146 vb.
  persevere 600 vb.
hang oneself
  kill oneself 362 vb.
hang on to
  hang 217 vb.
  store 632 vb.
  retain 778 vb.
hang out
  jut 254 vb.
  dry 342 vb.
hangout
  abode 192 n.
hang over
  impend 155 vb.
  be high 209 vb.
  hang 217 vb.
  fly 271 vb.
  frighten 854 vb.
  threaten 900 vb.
hangover
  sequel 67 n.
  crapulence 949 n.
hang together
  accord 24 vb.
  unite with 45 vb.

cohere 48 vb.
  concur 181 vb.
  be reasonable
  475 vb.
hang up
  terminate 69 vb.
  cease 145 vb.
  hang 217 vb.
hang-up
  idea 451 n.
  attention 455 n.
  prejudgment 481 n.
  eccentricity 503 n.
hang upon
  depend 157 vb.
hank
  bunch 74 n.
hanker after
  regret 830 vb.
  desire 859 vb.
hanky-panky
  deception 542 n.
  perfidy 930 n.
hansom
  cab 274 n.
haphazard
  nonuniform 17 adj.
  casual 159 adj.
  indiscriminate
  464 adj.
hapless
  unfortunate
  731 adj.
happen
  happen 154 vb.
  be true 494 vb.
happening
  event 154 n.
happiness
  pleasure 376 n.
  happiness 824 n.
  cheerfulness 833 n.
happy
  apt 24 adj.
  opportune 137 adj.
  comfortable
  376 adj.
  elegant 575 adj.
  willing 597 adj.
  good 615 adj.
  happy 824 adj.
  pleased 824 adj.
  drunk 949 adj.
happy ending
  good 615 n.
  success 727 n.

happy event
propagation 167 n.
happy-go-lucky
cheerful 833 adj.
happy medium
average 30 n.
middle way 625 n.
hara-kiri
suicide 362 n.
punishment 963 n.
harangue
teach 534 vb.
be diffuse 570 vb.
diffuseness 570 n.
orate 579 vb.
oration 579 n.
harass
oppress 735 vb.
torment 827 vb.
be malevolent
898 vb.
harbinger
precursor 66 n.
omen 511 n.
informant 524 n.
messenger 529 n.
harbour
stopping place
145 n.
goal 295 n.
shelter 662 n.
harbourage
shelter 662 n.
hard
hard 326 adj.
puzzling 517 adj.
unclear 568 adj.
laborious 682 adj.
difficult 700 adj.
adverse 731 adj.
thick-skinned
820 adj.
paining 827 adj.
unjust 914 adj.
impenitent
940 adj.
intoxicating
949 adj.
hard-bitten
thick-skinned
820 adj.
hard-boiled
severe 735 adj.
thick-skinned
820 adj.
hard by
near 200 adj.

near 200 adv.
hard cash
money 797 n.
hard-core
obstinate 602 adj.
hard drug
drug-taking 949 n.
harden
harden 326 vb.
mature 669 vb.
be dear 811 vb.
harden one's heart
be severe 735 vb.
refuse 760 vb.
be hostile 881 vb.
be pitiless 906 vb.
be impenitent
940 vb.
hard feelings
feeling 818 n.
enmity 881 n.
resentment 891 n.
hard frost
wintriness 380 n.
hard going
difficulty 700 n.
hard-headed
severe 735 adj.
hard-hearted
cruel 898 adj.
pitiless 906 adj.
hard-hitting
disapproving
924 adj.
hard labour
labour 682 n.
penalty 963 n.
hard lines
misfortune 731 n.
hard luck
nondesign 618 n.
misfortune 731 n.
hardly
slightly 33 adv.
seldom 140 adv.
hardly any
few 105 adj.
hardly ever
seldom 140 adv.
hardness
hardness 326 n.
difficulty 700 n.
hardness of hearing
deafness 416 n.
hard-nosed
obstinate 602 adj.

hard of hearing
deaf 416 adj.
hard on
nearly 200 adv.
oppressive 735 adj.
unjust 914 adj.
hard-pressed
hasty 680 adj.
in difficulties
700 adj.
hard put to it
in difficulties
700 adj.
poor 801 adj.
hard sell
advertisement
528 n.
inducement 612 n.
sale 793 n.
hardship
adversity 731 n.
annoyance 827 n.
hard shoulder
road 624 n.
hard stuff
alcoholic drink
301 n.
hard times
adversity 731 n.
hard up
unprovided
636 adj.
poor 801 adj.
hardware
data processing
86 n.
See **counting in-**
strument
product 164 n.
hardness 326 n.
hard way, the
exertion 682 n.
with difficulty
700 adv.
severity 735 n.
suffering 825 n.
hardworking
industrious
678 adj.
labouring 682 adj.
hardy
stalwart 162 adj.
healthy 650 adj.
insolent 878 adj.
hare
move fast 277 vb.
mammal 365 n.

harebrained
light-minded
456 adj.
absurd 497 adj.
foolish 499 adj.
rash 857 adj.
harelip
blemish 845 n.
harem
womankind 373 n.
seclusion 883 n.
hark back
revert 148 vb.
turn back 286 vb.
remember 505 vb.
regret 830 vb.
harlequin
variegated 437 adj.
variegation 437 n.
harlot
prostitute 952 n.
harm
evil 616 n.
badness 645 n.
harm 645 vb.
impairment 655 n.
harmful
harmful 645 adj.
paining 827 adj.
harmless
weak 163 adj.
safe 660 adj.
peaceful 717 adj.
humble 872 adj.
amiable 884 adj.
innocent 935 adj.
harmonica
gong 414 n.
organ 414 n.
harmonious
orderly 60 adj.
symmetrical
245 adj.
harmonious
410 adj.
soft-hued 425 adj.
elegant 575 adj.
pleasurable
826 adj.
friendly 880 adj.
harmonize
accord 24 vb.
mix 43 vb.
combine 50 vb.
be in order 60 vb.
concur 181 vb.
harmonize 410 vb.

compose music
413 vb.
sing 413 vb.

harmony
agreement 24 n.
a mixture 43 n.
combination 50 n.
completeness 54 n.
order 60 n.
concurrence 181 n.
symmetry 245 n.
melody 410 n.
music 412 n.
consensus 488 n.
elegance 575 n.
concord 710 n.
peace 717 n.
pleasurableness
826 n.

harness
affix 45 vb.
dress 228 vb.
dressing 228 n.
start out 296 vb.
break in 369 vb.
fetter 748 n.

harp
play music 413 vb.
stringed instrument
414 n.

harpist
instrumentalist
413 n.

harp on
sustain 146 vb.
be tedious 838 vb.

harpoon
sharp point 256 n.
missile weapon
723 n.
spear 723 n.

harpsichord
piano 414 n.

harridan
eyesore 842 n.

harrier
bird 365 n.

harrow
smoother 258 n.
draw 288 vb.
traction 288 n.
cultivate 370 vb.
farm tool 370 n.
torment 827 vb.

harrowing
painful 377 adj.
distressing 827 adj.

harry
pursue 619 vb.
attack 712 vb.
torment 827 vb.
be malevolent
898 vb.

harsh
exorbitant 32 adj.
pungent 388 adj.
strident 407 adj.
discordant 411 adj.
florid 425 adj.
inelegant 576 adj.
harmful 645 adj.
oppressive 735 adj.
paining 827 adj.
insolent 878 adj.
pitiless 906 adj.

harshness
roughness 259 n.
pungency 388 n.
discord 411 n.
inelegance 576 n.
severity 735 n.
painfulness 827 n.
rudeness 885 n.
inhumanity 898 n.

hart
mammal 365 n.
male animal
372 n.

harum-scarum
disorderly 61 adj.
light-minded
456 adj.
desperado 857 n.
rash 857 adj.

haruspicate
divine 511 vb.

harvest
assemblage 74 n.
autumn 129 n.
growth 157 n.
product 164 n.
abundance 171 n.
agriculture 370 n.
cultivate 370 vb.
benefit 615 n.
store 632 n.
store 632 vb.
plenty 635 n.
acquire 771 vb.
earnings 771 n.
take 786 vb.

harvest home
celebration 876 n.

has-been
past 125 adj.
archaism 127 n.
loser 728 n.

hash
disorder 61 n.
drug-taking 949 n.

hashish
drug-taking 949 n.

hasp
joint 45 n.
fastening 47 n.

hassle
agitate 318 vb.
commotion 318 n.
distract 456 vb.
be active 678 vb.
haste 680 n.
exertion 682 n.
quarrel 709 n.
oppress 735 vb.
excitation 821 n.
excitable state
822 n.
suffer 825 vb.
annoyance 827 n.
torment 827 vb.

hassock
cushion 218 n.
seat 218 n.
church utensil
990 n.

haste
move fast 277 vb.
haste 680 n.
hasten 680 vb.

hasten
hasten 680 vb.

hasty
hasty 680 adj.
irascible 892 adj.

hat
headgear 228 n.

hatch
group 74 n.
produce 164 vb.
generate 167 vb.
reproduce itself
167 vb.
covering 226 n.
doorway 263 n.
breed stock 369 vb.
imagine 513 vb.
fake 541 vb.
plan 623 vb.
mature 669 vb.

hatchet
sharp edge 256 n.
axe 723 n.

hatchet-faced
lean 206 adj.

hatchet job
destruction 165 n.
detraction 926 n.

hatchway
doorway 263 n.

hate
hate 888 vb.
hatred 888 n.
resentment 891 n.
malevolence 898 n.
jealousy 911 n.

hateful
unpleasant
827 adj.
hateful 888 adj.

hatpin
fastening 47 n.

hatred
hatred 888 n.

hatstand
hanger 217 n.

hatter
clothier 228 n.

hat trick
triplication 94 n.
masterpiece 694 n.
success 727 n.

hauberk
armour 713 n.

haughty
authoritarian
735 adj.
noble 868 adj.
proud 871 adj.
insolent 878 adj.
unsociable 883 adj.

haul
navigate 269 vb.
draw 288 vb.
traction 288 n.
work 682 vb.
taking 786 n.

haulage
transport 272 n.
traction 288 n.

haulier
carrier 273 n.
traction 288 n.

haunches
buttocks 238 n.

haunt
recur 139 vb.

go on 146 vb.
district 184 n.
locality 187 n.
be present 189 vb.
abode 192 n.
dwell 192 vb.
remind 505 vb.
be wont 610 vb.
torment 827 vb.
trouble 827 vb.
haunt 970 vb.

haunting
repeated 106 adj.
frequency 139 n.
frequent 139 adj.
remembered
  505 adj.
pleasurable
  826 adj.
social round 882 n.

hautboy
flute 414 n.

haute couture
dressing 228 n.
fashion 848 n.

haute cuisine
cookery 301 n.

hauteur
pride 871 n.

have
unite with 45 vb.
contain 56 vb.
comprise 78 vb.
confute 479 vb.
know 490 vb.
understand 516 vb.
fool 542 vb.
possess 773 vb.

have a ball
amuse oneself
  837 vb.
revel 837 vb.

have a facial
primp 843 vb.

have a fancy to
be willing 597 vb.

have a feed
eat 301 vb.

hvae a feel for
discriminate
  463 vb.

have a feud with
quarrel 709 vb.

have a fever
be agitated 318 vb.
be hot 379 vb.

have a field day
amuse oneself
  837 vb.

have a finger in
do 676 vb.

have a finger in every pie
meddle 678 vb.

have a finger in the pie
interfere 231 vb.
participate 775 vb.

have a finger in the till
steal 788 vb.

have a flutter
gamble 618 vb.

have a foot in both camps
be false 541 vb.

have a free hand
be free 744 vb.

have a fund of wisdom
be wise 498 vb.

have a funny feeling
intuit 476 vb.
feel 818 vb.

have a gainful occupation
be rewarded
  962 vb.

have a get-together
amuse 837 vb.

have a go
attempt 671 vb.

have a hold on
influence 178 vb.

have an eye to
be mindful 455 vb.
intend 617 vb.

have a say
vote 605 vb.

have had enough
have enough
  635 vb.
submit 721 vb.

have had it
be destroyed
  165 vb.

have it in for
be biased 481 vb.
dislike 861 vb.
hate 888 vb.
be malevolent
  898 vb.

haven
retreat 192 n.
goal 295 n.
protection 660 n.
shelter 662 n.

have no function
not act 677 vb.

have no grasp of
not understand
  517 vb.

have no grit
be cowardly
  856 vb.

have no guile
be artless 699 vb.

have no guts
be cowardly
  856 vb.

have no hand in
avoid 620 vb.

have no heart
be pitiless 906 vb.

have no heart for
dislike 861 vb.

have no heart or stomach for
be cowardly
  856 vb.

have no hope
not act 677 vb.

have no idea
not know 491 vb.

have no lead
not know 491 vb.

have no liability
be exempt 919 vb.

have no life
not act 677 vb.

have no liking for
dislike 861 vb.

have no love for
hate 888 vb.

have no luck
have trouble
  731 vb.

have no manners
be rude 885 vb.

have no mercy
be malevolent
  898 vb.

have no money sense
be prodigal 815 vb.

have no morals
be dishonest
  930 vb.
be impure 951 vb.

have no name to lose
have no repute
  867 vb.

have no need to blush
be innocent 935 vb.

have no nest-egg
be prodigal 815 vb.

have no notion
not know 491 vb.

have no objection
consent 758 vb.

have no option
be forced 596 vb.

have no pity
be pitiless 906 vb.

have no place in
be absent 190 vb.

have no pluck
be cowardly
  856 vb.

have no pride
demean oneself
  867 vb.

have no prospects
be poor 801 vb.

have no recollection of
forget 506 vb.

have no regard for
not respect 921 vb.
disapprove 924 vb.

have no regrets
be content 828 vb.
be impenitent
  940 vb.

have no religion
be irreligious
  974 vb.

have no reputation
have no repute
  867 vb.

have no repute
have no repute
  867 vb.

have nothing to do with
be unrelated 10 vb.
disagree 25 vb.
avoid 620 vb.
refuse 760 vb.

have-nots, the
poor person 801 n.
lower classes 869 n.

have on
wear 228 vb.
fool 542 vb.

have one's cake and eat it
attempt the impossible 470 vb.

have one's say
affirm 532 vb.
speak 579 vb.
be loquacious 581 vb.

have one's way
will 595 vb.
be free 744 vb.

have over a barrel
dominate 733 vb.

have power
be able 160 vb.

have precedence
come before 64 vb.
have a reputation 866 vb.

have pretentions
be vain 873 vb.

have qualms
be nervous 854 vb.

haver
be loquacious 581 vb.

have recourse to
avail oneself of 673 vb.

have reference to
be related 9 vb.

have regard to
be mindful 455 vb.
observe 768 vb.

have regrets
be unwilling 598 vb.
be penitent 939 vb.

have repercussions
recoil 280 vb.

have reservations
doubt 486 vb.
dissent 489 vb.

have right of way
precede 283 vb.

have right on one's side
deserve 915 vb.

have room to breathe
be free 744 vb.

have room to swing a cat
be free 744 vb.

have round
be hospitable 882 vb.

haversack
bag 194 n.

have run its course
end 69 vb.
be past 125 vb.

have scope
be free 744 vb.

have second sight
foresee 510 vb.

have second thoughts
meditate 449 vb.
be irresolute 601 vb.
rectify 654 vb.
be nervous 854 vb.
be penitent 939 vb.

have seen better days
deteriorate 655 vb.
have trouble 731 vb.

have sense
be wise 498 vb.

have sex with
unite with 45 vb.

have shot one's bolt
fail 728 vb.

have shot one's last bolt
despair 853 vb.

have someone where one wants him or her
overmaster 727 vb.

have status or standing
have a reputation 866 vb.

have style
be in fashion 848 vb.

have swallowed the dictionary
be diffuse 570 vb.

have tact
be wise 498 vb.

have taped
appraise 465 vb.

have taste
have taste 846 vb.

have tea
eat 301 vb.

have the advantage
be unequal 29 vb.
predominate 34 vb.
overmaster 727 vb.

have the audacity to
be insolent 878 vb.

have the audience in stitches
be witty 839 vb.

have the ball at one's feet
be successful 727 vb.
have luck 730 vb.

have the best of it
succeed 727 vb.

have the makings of
evidence 466 vb.
be likely 471 vb.

have up
indict 928 vb.

have words
argue 475 vb.

having
inclusive 78 adj.

haw-haw
speech defect 580 n.
laugh 835 vb.

hawk
eruct 300 vb.
excrete 302 vb.
bird 365 n.
rasp 407 vb.
eye 438 n.
hunt 619 vb.
hunter 619 n.
militarist 722 n.
offer 759 vb.
request 761 vb.
sell 793 vb.

hawker
traveller 268 n.
hunter 619 n.
petitioner 763 n.
seller 793 n.
pedlar 794 n.

hawkish
warlike 718 adj.

hawser
cable 47 n.

hawthorn
tree 366 n.

hay
provender 301 n.
grass 366 n.

hay fever
excretion 302 n.

hayloft
attic 194 n.

haymaking
summer 128 n.

haystack
store 632 n.

hazard
chance 159 n.
gambling 618 n.
danger 661 n.
pitfall 663 n.
obstacle 702 n.

hazard a guess
suppose 512 vb.

hazardous
speculative 618 adj.
dangerous 661 adj.
frightening 854 adj.

haze
cloud 355 n.
uncertainty 474 n.

hazel
tree 366 n.
brown 430 adj.

hazy
cloudy 355 adj.
unlit 418 adj.
dim 419 adj.
opaque 423 adj.
indistinct 444 adj.
uncertain 474 adj.

H-bomb
bomb 723 n.

he
male 372 adj.
male 372 n.
children's games 837 n.

head
come before 64 vb.
first 68 vb.
extremity 69 n.
classification 77 n.
energy 160 n.
interval 201 n.
long measure 203 n.
crown 213 vb.
head 213 n.
topmost 213 adj.
vertex 213 n.
central 225 adj.
be in front 237 vb.
face 237 n.
precede 283 vb.
bubble 355 n.
flower 366 n.
person 371 n.
gramophone 414 n.

intelligence 498 n.
teacher 537 n.
image 551 n.
picture 553 n.
sculpture 554 n.
bigwig 638 n.
chief thing 638 n.
direct 689 vb.
director 690 n.
master 741 n.
drug-taking 949 n.
headache
pang 377 n.
illness 651 n.
sick 651 adj.
difficulty 700 n.
worry 825 n.
headband
headgear 228 n.
bookbinding 589 n.
head-count
numeration 86 n.
headdress
headgear 228 n.
header
descent 309 n.
plunge 313 n.
head for
steer for 281 vb.
headgear
headgear 228 n.
head-hunter
killer 362 n.
heading
prelude 66 n.
beginning 68 n.
classification 77 n.
preceding 283 n.
label 547 n.
record 548 n.
name 561 n.
script 586 n.
edition 589 n.
headlamp
lamp 420 n.
headland
high land 209 n.
projection 254 n.
headless
short 204 adj.
headlight
lamp 420 n.
headline
beginning 68 n.
advertise 528 vb.
advertisement
528 n.

label 547 n.
edition 589 n.
excitant 821 n.
headlong
speedy 277 adj.
swiftly 277 adv.
hasty 680 adj.
rash 857 adj.
rashly 857 adv.
headmaster or -mis-
tress
teacher 537 n.
head off
hunter 619 n.
repel 292 vb.
dissuade 613 vb.
hinder 702 vb.
head-on
frontal 237 adj.
head over heels
completely 54 adv.
inversely 221 adv.
headphones
hearing aid 415 n.
headquarters
focus 76 n.
abode 192 n.
headrest
support 218 n.
headroom
room 183 n.
latrine 649 n.
head scanner
hospital 658 n.
headscarf
headgear 228 n.
headset
hearing aid 415 n.
telecommunication
531 n.
heads or tails
equal chance
159 n.
head start
advantage 34 n.
headstone
support 218 n.
obsequies 364 n.
headstrong
furious 176 adj.
wilful 602 adj.
rash 857 adj.
head teacher
teacher 537 n.
head up
direct 689 vb.

headway
room 183 n.
motion 265 n.
water travel 269 n.
progression 285 n.
headwind
contrariety 14 n.
counteraction
182 n.
contraposition
240 n.
wind 352 n.
obstacle 702 n.
opposition 704 n.
heady
strong 162 adj.
vigorous 174 adj.
exciting 821 adj.
intoxicating
949 adj.
heal
cure 656 vb.
remedy 658 vb.
pacify 719 vb.
healing
recuperation 656 n.
medical art 658 n.
remedial 658 adj.
health
draught 301 n.
health 650 n.
prosperity 730 n.
celebration 876 n.
health food
food 301 n.
health salts
purgative 658 n.
health visitor
nurse 658 n.
healthy
beneficial 644 adj.
healthy 650 adj.
salubrious 652 adj.
heap
great quantity
32 n.
chief part 52 n.
accumulation 74 n.
bring together
74 vb.
bunch 74 n.
bulk 195 n.
store 632 n.
store 632 vb.
acquire 771 vb.
acquisition 771 n.
wealth 800 n.

heaps
finite quantity
26 n.
great quantity
32 n.
multitude 104 n.
funds 797 n.
hear
have feeling
374 vb.
hear 415 vb.
enquire 459 vb.
judge 480 vb.
heard
known 490 adj.
hearer
listener 415 n.
hear, hear
amen 488 int.
bravo 923 int.
hearing
sense 374 n.
auditory 415 adj.
hearing 415 n.
listening 415 n.
legal trial 959 n.
hearing aid
hearing aid 415 n.
hearken
hear 415 vb.
hearsay
evidence 466 n.
information 524 n.
rumour 529 n.
hearse
vehicle 274 n.
funeral 364 n.
heart
essence 1 n.
essential part 5 n.
middle 70 n.
focus 76 n.
insides 224 n.
interiority 224 n.
centre 225 n.
life 360 n.
spirit 447 n.
chief thing 638 n.
affections 817 n.
courage 855 n.
love token 889 n.
darling 890 n.
heartache
pain 377 n.
suffering 825 n.
dejection 834 n.

heart attack
cardiovascular disease 651 n.
heartbreaking
distressing 827 adj.
heart-broken
unhappy 825 adj.
heartburn
digestive disorders 651 n.
heart condition
cardiovascular disease 651 n.
hearten
invigorate 174 vb.
aid 703 vb.
animate 821 vb.
relieve 831 vb.
cheer 833 vb.
give courage 855 vb.
heart failure
cardiovascular disease 651 n.
hearth
home 192 n.
furnace 383 n.
refuge 662 n.
heartily
greatly 32 vb.
heartland
district 184 n.
interiority 224 n.
land 344 n.
heartless
impassive 820 adj.
cruel 898 adj.
pitiless 906 adj.
impenitent 940 adj.
heart-melting
pleasurable 826 adj.
heart-rending
distressing 827 adj.
hearts
card game 837 n.
heart's blood
essential part 5 n.
interiority 224 n.
life 360 n.
heart's desire
objective 617 n.
aspiration 852 n.
loved one 887 n.
heart-shaped
curved 248 adj.

heartstrings
affections 817 n.
heartthrob
a beauty 841 n.
loved one 887 n.
heart-to-heart
chat 584 n.
heart trouble
cardiovascular disease 651 n.
heart-warming
pleasant 376 adj.
pleasurable 826 adj.
hearty
vigorous 174 adj.
healthy 650 adj.
feeling 818 adj.
cheerful 833 adj.
friendly 880 adj.
sociable 882 adj.
heat
part 53 n.
heat 379 n.
heat 381 vb.
contest 716 n.
libido 859 n.
anger 891 n.
heated
hot 379 adj.
heated 381 adj.
heater
heater 383 n.
heath
desert 172 n.
plain 348 n.
wood 366 n.
heathen
unbeliever 486 n.
heathen 974 n.
heathenish 974 adj.
heresy 977 n.
heretical 977 adj.
heather
plant 366 n.
purpleness 436 n.
Heath Robinson
imaginative 513 adj.
heating
heating 381 adj.
heating 381 n.
heave
carry 273 vb.
impel 279 vb.
impulse 279 n.
propel 287 vb.

draw 288 vb.
vomit 300 vb.
oscillate 317 vb.
breathe 352 vb.
exertion 682 n.
work 682 vb.
show feeling 818 vb.
heaven
summit 213 n.
heaven 971 n.
heavenly
celestial 321 adj.
super 644 adj.
pleasurable 826 adj.
divine 965 adj.
heaven-sent
opportune 137 adj.
good 615 adj.
heave to
bring to rest 266 vb.
navigate 269 vb.
heavy
substantial 3 adj.
great 32 adj.
strong 162 adj.
inert 175 adj.
alcoholic drink 301 n.
weighty 322 adj.
dense 324 adj.
the press 528 n.
forceful 571 adj.
bad 645 adj.
inactive 679 adj.
laborious 682 adj.
severe 735 adj.
tedious 838 adj.
dull 840 adj.
heavy-going
serious 834 adj.
heavy-handed
violent 176 adj.
weighty 322 adj.
oppressive 735 adj.
heavy-hearted
unhappy 825 adj.
melancholic 834 adj.
heavyweight
athlete 162 n.
weighty 322 adj.
bigwig 638 n.
pugilist 722 n.

heavy with
impending 155 adj.
fertilized 167 adj.
prolific 171 adj.
hecatomb
oblation 981 n.
heckle
interrogate 459 vb.
be obstructive 702 vb.
torment 827 vb.
not respect 921 vb.
disapprove 924 vb.
hector
boast 877 vb.
be insolent 878 vb.
threaten 900 vb.
hedge
partition 231 n.
edge 234 n.
fence 235 n.
wood 366 n.
screen 421 n.
avoid 620 vb.
shelter 662 n.
obstacle 702 n.
defend 713 vb.
be cautious 858 vb.
hedgehog
mammal 365 n.
hedgerow
fence 235 n.
wood 366 n.
hedonism
pleasure 376 n.
philosophy 449 n.
enjoyment 824 n.
sensualism 944 n.
heed
attention 455 n.
be attentive 455 vb.
be careful 457 vb.
carefulness 457 n.
obey 739 vb.
observe 768 vb.
caution 858 n.
heedless
inattentive 456 adj.
negligent 458 adj.
forgetful 506 adj.
rash 857 adj.
heel
foot 214 n.
be oblique 220 vb.
rear 238 n.
repair 656 vb.
cad 938 n.

hefty
  stalwart 162 adj.
Hegira
  departure 296 n.
heifer
  young creature
    132 n.
  cattle 365 n.
  female animal
    373 n.
height
  height 209 n.
  high land 209 n.
  metrology 465 n.
heighten
  augment 36 vb.
  enlarge 197 vb.
  make higher
    209 vb.
  elevate 310 vb.
  exaggerate 546 vb.
  aggravate 832 vb.
heinous
  bad 645 adj.
  heinous 934 adj.
heir
  successor 67 n.
  descendant 170 n.
  deputy 755 n.
  recipient 782 n.
  rich person 800 n.
  dueness 915 n.
heir apparent
  deputy 755 n.
  beneficiary 776 n.
heiress
  descendant 170 n.
  rich person 800 n.
heirloom
  archaism 127 n.
  dower 777 n.
held
  credible 485 adj.
  orthodox 976 adj.
held up
  late 136 adj.
  hindered 702 adj.
  restrained 747 adj.
helical
  coiled 251 adj.
helicopter
  aircraft 276 n.
heliograph
  signal 547 n.
  signal 547 vb.
heliotrope
  purple 436 adj.

purpleness 436 n.
  gem 844 n.
helium
  lightness 323 n.
helix
  coil 251 n.
  circuition 314 n.
hell
  pain 377 n.
  bane 659 n.
  suffering 825 n.
  hell 972 n.
hell-bent
  volitional 595 adj.
  rash 857 adj.
hellfire
  fire 379 n.
  hell 972 n.
hell for leather
  swiftly 277 adv.
hellish
  damnable 645 adj.
  cruel 898 adj.
  heinous 934 adj.
  wicked 934 adj.
  diabolic 969 adj.
helm
  sailing aid 269 n.
  tool 630 n.
helmet
  headgear 228 n.
  heraldry 547 n.
  armour 713 n.
help
  concur 181 vb.
  benefit 615 vb.
  be instrumental
    628 vb.
  instrument 628 n.
  utility 640 n.
  be expedient
    642 vb.
  do good 644 vb.
  cleaner 648 n.
  remedy 658 n.
  remedy 658 vb.
  facilitate 701 vb.
  aid 703 n.
  aid 703 vb.
  aider 703 n.
  minister to 703 vb.
  servant 742 n.
  give 781 vb.
helper
  aider 703 n.
  auxiliary 707 n.
  servant 742 n.

friend 880 n.
  benefactor 903 n.
helpful
  willing 597 adj.
  good 615 adj.
  instrumental
    628 adj.
  useful 640 adj.
  remedial 658 adj.
  aiding 703 adj.
  cooperative
    706 adj.
  benevolent 897 adj.
helpfulness
  willingness 597 n.
  aid 703 n.
  cooperation 706 n.
  benevolence 897 n.
helping
  meal 301 n.
  provisions 301 n.
  provision 633 n.
  portion 783 n.
helpless
  impotent 161 adj.
  vulnerable 661 adj.
help oneself
  take 786 vb.
  steal 788 vb.
help out
  aid 703 vb.
helter-skelter
  swiftly 277 adv.
  descent 309 n.
hem
  edging 234 n.
  hem 234 vb.
  enclose 235 vb.
  fold 261 n.
  fold 261 vb.
  rasp 407 vb.
he-man
  athlete 162 n.
  violent creature
    176 n.
  male 372 n.
hem and ha
  stammer 580 vb.
hem in
  surround 230 vb.
  circumscribe
    232 vb.
  restrain 747 vb.
hemiplegia
  helplessness 161 n.
hemisphere
  part 53 n.

bisection 92 n.
  region 184 n.
  dome 253 n.
  heavens 321 n.
hemline
  garment 228 n.
hemlock
  poison 659 n.
  poisonous plant
    659 n.
  means of execution
    964 n.
hemp
  fibre 208 n.
  drug-taking 949 n.
hen
  poultry 365 n.
  female animal
    373 n.
  darling 890 n.
henbane
  poisonous plant
    659 n.
hence
  hence 158 adv.
henceforth
  henceforth 124 vb.
henchman
  aider 703 n.
  auxiliary 707 n.
  dependant 742 n.
  retainer 742 n.
henhouse
  cattle pen 369 n.
henna
  orange 432 n.
  hairwash 843 n.
hen party
  womankind 373 n.
  social gathering
    882 n.
henpecked
  subjected 745 adj.
hepatitis
  digestive disorders
    651 n.
heptagon
  angular figure
    247 n.
Heptateuch
  over five 99 n.
herald
  come before 64 vb.
  precursor 66 n.
  initiate 68 vb.
  priority 119 n.
  precede 283 vb.

omen 511 n.
predict 511 vb.
informant 524 n.
proclaim 528 vb.
publicizer 528 n.
messenger 529 n.
heraldry 547 n.
indicate 547 vb.
deputy 755 n.
heraldic
heraldic 547 adj.
heraldry
heraldry 547 n.
herb
cook 301 vb.
herb 301 n.
plant 366 n.
garden 370 n.
season 388 vb.
herbaceous border
garden 370 n.
herbal
medical 658 adj.
herbalist
botany 368 n.
doctor 658 n.
herbal remedy
medicine 658 n.
herbicide
poison 659 n.
herbivorous
feeding 301 adj.
Herculean
stalwart 162 adj.
huge 195 adj.
laborious 682 adj.
Herculean task
hard task 700 n.
herd
bring together
74 vb.
group 74 n.
animal 365 n.
break in 369 vb.
herdsman 369 n.
herdsman
herdsman 369 n.
here
widely 183 adv.
hereabouts
nearly 200 adv.
hereafter
sequel 67 n.
future state 124 n.
destiny 155 n.

here and there
here and there
105 adv.
hereditary
genetic 5 adj.
parental 169 adj.
proprietary
777 adj.
heredity
heredity 5 n.
genealogy 169 n.
heresy
heresy 977 n.
heterodoxy 977 n.
heretic
heretic 977 n.
heretical 977 adj.
heritage
futurity 124 n.
posterity 170 n.
possession 773 n.
dower 777 n.
hermaphrodite
nonconformist
84 n.
double 91 adj.
hermetically seal
rarefy 325 vb.
hermit
nonconformist
84 n.
unit 88 n.
solitary 883 n.
celibate 895 n.
ascetic 945 n.
pietist 979 n.
monk 986 n.
hermitage
retreat 192 n.
seclusion 883 n.
monastery 986 n.
hernia
wound 655 n.
hero
acting 594 n.
doer 676 n.
brave person 855 n.
prodigy 864 n.
person of repute
866 n.
loved one 887 n.
favourite 890 n.
good person 937 n.
heroic
resolute 599 adj.
laborious 682 adj.

courageous
855 adj.
worshipful 866 adj.
heroin
drug 658 n.
poison 659 n.
drug-taking 949 n.
heroine
acting 594 n.
doer 676 n.
brave person 855 n.
prodigy 864 n.
favourite 890 n.
good person 937 n.
heron
bird 365 n.
heron zoster
skin disease 651 n.
hero worship
wonder 864 n.
love 887 n.
praise 923 n.
praise 923 vb.
Herr
male 372 n.
title 870 n.
herring
fish food 301 n.
herringbone
crossed 222 adj.
pattern 844 n.
hesitant
doubting 474 adj.
unwilling 598 adj.
hesitate
pause 145 vb.
vary 152 vb.
move slowly
278 vb.
be uncertain
474 vb.
doubt 486 vb.
stammer 580 vb.
be unwilling
598 vb.
be irresolute
601 vb.
be inactive 679 vb.
be nervous 854 vb.
hessian
textile 222 n.
heterodoxy
heterodoxy 977 n.
heterogeneous
different 15 adj.
nonuniform 17 adj.
mixed 43 adj.

multiform 82 adj.
heterosexual
straight 249 adj.
het up
angry 891 adj.
hew
cut 46 vb.
form 243 vb.
hexagon
over five 99 n.
angular figure
247 n.
hexameter
over five 99 n.
prosody 593 n.
heyday
salad days 130 n.
palmy days 730 n.
hi
welcome 295 int.
hiatus
discontinuity 72 n.
interval 201 n.
opening 263 n.
hiatus hernia
digestive disorders
651 n.
hibernate
sleep 679 vb.
hiccup
eruct 300 vb.
respiration 352 n.
hick
lesser 35 adj.
bungler 697 n.
country-dweller
869 n.
hidden
dark 418 adj.
unknown 491 adj.
concealed 525 adj.
secluded 883 adj.
hide
measure 183 n.
skin 226 n.
screen 421 vb.
be unseen 444 vb.
disappear 446 vb.
lurk 523 vb.
conceal 525 vb.
hiding-place 527 n.
avoid 620 vb.
materials 631 n.
safeguard 660 vb.
be cowardly
856 vb.
be cautious 858 vb.

flog 963 vb.
hide-and-seek
children's games
837 n.
hideaway
hiding-place 527 n.
seclusion 883 n.
hide-bound
narrow-minded
481 adj.
obstinate 602 adj.
severe 735 adj.
restraining
747 adj.
hideous
unpleasant
827 adj.
ugly 842 adj.
frightening
854 adj.
hide-out
hiding-place 527 n.
seclusion 883 n.
hiding
knock 279 n.
invisibility 444 n.
concealed 525 adj.
concealment 525 n.
defeat 728 n.
*corporal punish-
ment* 963 n.
hierarchy
degree 27 n.
order 60 n.
series 71 n.
clergy 986 n.
hieroglyphics
enigma 530 n.
representation
551 n.
writing 586 n.
hi-fi
sound 398 n.
sounding 398 adj.
gramophone 414 n.
high
superiority 34 n.
high 209 adj.
pungent 388 adj.
savoury 390 adj.
unsavoury 391 adj.
fetid 397 adj.
important 638 adj.
unclean 649 adj.
excitable state
822 n.
worshipful 866 adj.

noble 868 adj.
drugged 949 adj.
drunk 949 adj.
Anglican 976 adj.
high and dry
fixed 153 adj.
dry 342 adj.
high and low
throughout 54 adv.
widely 183 adv.
high and mighty
worshipful 866 adj.
proud 871 adj.
insolent 878 adj.
highbrow
intellectual 492 n.
wise 498 adj.
sage 500 n.
High-Church
Anglican 976 adj.
high-class
genteel 868 adj.
High Commissioner
governor 741 n.
envoy 754 n.
high dudgeon
anger 891 n.
higher
superior 34 adj.
highest
supreme 34 adj.
high 209 adj.
topmost 213 adj.
highfalutin
grandiloquence
574 n.
ostentatious
875 adj.
high fidelity
sound 398 n.
sounding 398 adj.
accuracy 494 n.
accurate 494 adj.
high flier
learner 538 n.
high-flown
imaginative
513 adj.
ostentatious
875 adj.
high frequency
radiation 417 n.
high-handed
oppressive 735 adj.
proud 871 adj.
insolent 878 adj.

high-hat
proud 871 adj.
insolent 878 adj.
high land
high land 209 n.
highlands
high land 209 n.
land 344 n.
high-level
superior 34 adj.
important 638 adj.
high life
festivity 837 n.
upper class 868 n.
highlight
manifest 522 vb.
publish 528 vb.
emphasize 532 vb.
indicate 547 vb.
painting 553 n.
chief thing 638 n.
high living
gastronomy 301 n.
intemperance
943 n.
highly-strung
lively 819 adj.
nervous 854 adj.
high mass
Holy Communion
988 n.
high-minded
honourable
929 adj.
high noon
noon 128 n.
high-pitched
strident 407 adj.
high priest
leader 690 n.
priest 986 n.
high-sounding
affected 850 adj.
ostentatious
875 adj.
high spirits
cheerfulness 833 n.
merriment 833 n.
respect 920 n.
high street
road 624 n.
high technology
means 629 n.
high tension
energy 160 n.
high tide
water 339 n.

grandiloquence
574 n.
high treason
sedition 738 n.
highway
road 624 n.
instrument 628 n.
hijack
ensnare 542 vb.
compel 740 vb.
take away 786 vb.
steal 788 vb.
stealing 788 n.
threaten 900 vb.
hike
pedestrianism
267 n.
travel 267 vb.
walk 267 vb.
amuse oneself
837 vb.
hiker
pedestrian 268 n.
traveller 268 n.
sport 837 n.
hilarious
merry 833 adj.
funny 849 adj.
hill
high land 209 n.
incline 220 n.
ascent 308 n.
hillbilly
country-dweller
869 n.
hillock
incline 220 n.
dome 253 n.
hillside
incline 220 n.
hilt
handle 218 n.
Hinayana
religious faith
973 n.
hind
back 238 adj.
female animal
373 n.
country-dweller
869 n.
hinder
back 238 adj.
hinder 702 vb.
hindmost
ending 69 adj.

give security
767 vb.
borrow 785 vb.

hockey
ball game 837 n.

hocus-pocus
lack of meaning
515 n.
sleight 542 n.
idolatry 982 n.
spell 983 n.

hod
plate 194 n.
vessel 194 n.
conveyor 274 n.

hodgepodge
medley 43 n.

Hodgkin's disease
blood disease
651 n.

hoe
cultivate 370 vb.
farm tool 370 n.

hoe-down
dancing 837 n.

hog
pig 365 n.
male animal
372 n.
possess 773 vb.
appropriate
786 vb.
be selfish 932 vb.
egotist 932 n.
sensualist 944 n.
glutton 947 n.

hoi polloi
crowd 74 n.
everyman 79 n.
averageness 732 n.
commonalty 869 n.

hoist
elevate 310 vb.
elevation 310 n.
flag 547 n.

**hoist with one's own
petard**
defeated 728 adj.

hoity-toity
proud 871 adj.

hold
fastening 47 n.
contain 56 vb.
comprise 78 vb.
stay 144 vb.
cease 145 vb.
go on 146 vb.

influence 178 n.
prevail 178 vb.
be present 189 vb.
cellar 194 n.
receptacle 194 n.
base 214 n.
support 218 vb.
believe 485 vb.
*be of the opinion
that* 485 vb.
be true 494 vb.
understand 516 vb.
affirm 532 vb.
storage 632 n.
store 632 vb.
preserve 666 vb.
wrestling 716 n.
governance 733 n.
arrest 747 vb.
imprison 747 vb.
restrain 747 vb.
possess 773 vb.
possession 773 n.
retain 778 vb.
retention 778 n.
impress 821 vb.

holdall
bag 194 n.
storage 632 n.

hold back
pause 145 vb.
doubt 486 vb.
be unwilling
598 vb.
avoid 620 vb.
hinder 702 vb.
compel 740 vb.
restrain 747 vb.
retain 778 vb.

holder
receptacle 194 n.
handle 218 n.
storage 632 n.
possessor 776 n.

hold fast
cohere 48 vb.
persevere 600 vb.
retain 778 vb.

hold forth
teach 534 vb.
orate 579 vb.

hold good
be 1 vb.
stay 144 vb.
be proved 478 V.
be true 494 vb.
be wont 610 vb.

holding
inclusive 78 adj.
territory 184 n.
enclosure 235 n.
farm 370 n.
store 632 n.
possession 773 n.
estate 777 n.
lands 777 n.

hold it
stay 144 vb.
stop 266 int.

hold off
be distant 199 vb.
avoid 620 vb.
not use 674 vb.
resist 715 vb.

hold on
wait 136 vb.
stay 144 vb.
stop 266 int.
progress 285 vb.
retain 778 vb.

hold one's own
be equal 28 vb.
withstand 704 vb.
be successful
727 vb.

hold out
affirm 532 vb.
stand firm 599 vb.
persevere 600 vb.
resist 715 vb.
offer 759 vb.
promise 764 vb.

hold over
put off 136 vb.

hold the whip hand
prevail 178 vb.

hold tight
retain 778 vb.

hold up
put off 136 vb.
halt 145 vb.
support 218 vb.
elevate 310 vb.
hinder 702 vb.
retain 778 vb.
rob 788 vb.

holdup
delay 136 n.
hitch 702 n.
stealing 788 n.

hold water
be reasonable
475 vb.
be proved 478 V.

be true 494 vb.

hole
circumstance 8 n.
disunion 46 n.
place 185 n.
dwelling 192 n.
small house 192 n.
receptacle 194 n.
gap 201 n.
cavity 255 n.
opening 263 n.
orifice 263 n.
pierce 263 vb.
insert 303 vb.
refuge 662 n.
shelter 662 n.
predicament 700 n.

hole-and-corner
stealthy 525 adj.

holiday
lull 145 n.
absence 190 n.
leisure 681 n.
repose 683 n.
reposeful 683 adj.
permit 756 n.
amusement 837 n.

holier than thou
aphoristic 496 adj.
affected 850 adj.
proud 871 adj.
disapproving
924 adj.
orthodox 976 adj.
pietistic 979 adj.

holiness
virtue 933 n.
divine attribute
965 n.
sanctity 979 n.

holistic medicine
medical art 658 n.

holler
vociferate 408 vb.

hollow
empty 190 adj.
lowness 210 n.
be deep 211 vb.
depth 211 n.
cavity 255 n.
concave 255 adj.
make concave
255 vb.
furrow 262 n.
opening 263 n.
lower 311 vb.
lowering 311 n.

rare 325 adj.
resonant 404 adj.
hoarse 407 adj.
affected 850 adj.
ostentatious
    875 adj.
hollow-eyed
    fatigued 684 adj.
Hollywood
    cinema 445 n.
    drama 594 n.
holocaust
    slaughter 362 n.
    fire 379 n.
    burning 381 n.
    oblation 981 n.
hologram
    image 551 n.
    photography 551 n.
holster
    case 194 n.
    arsenal 723 n.
holy
    worshipful 866 adj.
    virtuous 933 adj.
    prudish 950 adj.
    divine 965 adj.
    godlike 965 adj.
    religious 973 adj.
    scriptural 975 adj.
    pious 979 adj.
    sanctified 979 adj.
Holy Bible
    scripture 975 n.
Holy Communion
    Christian rite
        988 n.
    Holy Communion
        988 n.
holy day
    holy day 988 n.
Holy Grail
    objective 617 n.
    ritual object 988 n.
holy ground
    holy place 990 n.
Holy of Holies
    ritual object 988 n.
    holy place 990 n.
holy terror
    violent creature
        176 n.
    bad person 938 n.
Holy Week
    holy day 988 n.
homage
    submission 721 n.

respects 920 n.
worship 981 n.
ritual act 988 n.
home
    native 191 adj.
    abode 192 n.
    home 192 n.
    house 192 n.
    retreat 192 n.
    near 200 adv.
    interior 224 adj.
    limit 236 n.
    social gathering
        882 n.
homecoming
    return 286 n.
    arrival 295 n.
home economics
    cookery 301 n.
home help
    cleaner 648 n.
homeland
    territory 184 n.
    home 192 n.
homeless
    unrelated 10 adj.
    alone 88 adj.
    poor 801 adj.
homely
    comfortable
        376 adj.
    plain 573 adj.
    pleasurable
        826 adj.
    ugly 842 adj.
    plebeian 869 adj.
homemade
    artless 699 adj.
homesickness
    suffering 825 n.
    regret 830 n.
    melancholy 834 n.
    desire 859 n.
homespun
    textile 222 n.
    roughness 259 n.
    textural 331 adj.
    plain 573 adj.
    plainness 573 n.
    artless 699 adj.
    plebeian 869 adj.
homestead
    home 192 n.
    lands 777 n.
home truth
    truth 494 n.
    veracity 540 n.

censure 924 n.
accusation 928 n.
homework
    curriculum 534 n.
    study 536 n.
    preparation 669 n.
    labour 682 n.
homicidal
    murderous 362 adj.
homicide
    homicide 362 n.
    killer 362 n.
    See **murderer**
    murderer 362 n.
homily
    lecture 534 n.
    oration 579 n.
    dissertation 591 n.
    ministration 988 n.
homoeopathic
    small 33 adj.
    medical 658 adj.
homoeopathy
    medical art 658 n.
homoeostasis
    equilibrium 28 n.
    stability 153 n.
homogeneous
    identical 13 adj.
    uniform 16 adj.
    similar 18 adj.
    simple 44 adj.
homologous
    equal 28 n.
homonym
    identity 13 n.
    equivocalness
        518 n.
    word 559 n.
homo sapiens
    humankind 371 n.
homosexual
    abnormal 84 adj.
    nonconformist
        84 n.
    male 372 n.
hone
    sharpen 256 vb.
honest
    genuine 494 adj.
    true 494 adj.
    veracious 540 adj.
    plain 573 adj.
    artless 699 adj.
    ethical 917 adj.
    honourable
        929 adj.

virtuous 933 adj.
honey
    viscidity 354 n.
    female 373 n.
    sweet thing 392 n.
    yellowness 433 n.
    a beauty 841 n.
    loved one 887 n.
    darling 890 n.
honeycomb
    network 222 n.
    cavity 255 n.
    pierce 263 vb.
    porosity 263 n.
    sweet thing 392 n.
    storage 632 n.
honeyed words
    inducement 612 n.
    flattery 925 n.
honeymoon
    start 68 n.
    pleasurableness
        826 n.
    be in love 887 vb.
    wed 894 vb.
    wedding 894 n.
honeypot
    focus 76 n.
    vessel 194 n.
    attraction 291 n.
    sweet thing 392 n.
honk
    loudness 400 n.
    ululate 409 vb.
    raise the alarm
        665 vb.
honorarium
    earnings 771 n.
    gift 781 n.
    pay 804 n.
    reward 962 n.
honorary
    insubstantial 4 adj.
    voluntary 597 adj.
honour
    dignify 866 vb.
    honour 866 vb.
    honours 866 n.
    prestige 866 n.
    title 870 n.
    celebrate 876 vb.
    pay one's respects
        884 vb.
    right 913 n.
    do one's duty
        917 vb.
    morals 917 n.

759

respect 920 n.
probity 929 n.
virtue 933 n.
purity 950 n.
reward 962 n.
piety 979 n.
worship 981 n.
worship 981 vb.
honourable
worshipful 866 adj.
honourable
  929 adj.
honours
honours 866 n.
hooch
alcoholic drink
  301 n.
hood
cover 226 vb.
shade 226 n.
headgear 228 n.
screen 421 n.
screen 421 vb.
low fellow 869 n.
canonicals 989 n.
hoodlum
ruffian 904 n.
hood (of a car)
covering 226 n.
hoodoo
badness 645 n.
sorcery 983 n.
spell 983 n.
hoodwink
deceive 542 vb.
hooey
empty talk 515 n.
falsehood 541 n.
hoof
foot 214 n.
dance 837 vb.
hook
all 52 n.
completely 54 adv.
hanger 217 n.
angularity 247 n.
sharp edge 256 n.
knock 279 n.
deflect 282 vb.
propel 287 vb.
ensnare 542 vb.
pincers 778 n.
take 786 vb.
hookah
air pipe 353 n.
tobacco 388 n.

hook and eye
fastening 47 n.
hooked on
obsessed 455 adj.
enamoured
  887 adj.
hooker
ship 275 n.
prostitute 952 n.
hookup
union 45 n.
hooligan
violent creature
  176 n.
ruffian 904 n.
hoop
bond 47 n.
skirt 228 n.
circle 250 n.
plaything 837 n.
hooray
cry 408 n.
vociferate 408 vb.
cheers 835 int.
hoot
cry 408 n.
cry 408 vb.
vociferate 408 vb.
ululate 409 vb.
laugh 835 vb.
ridicule 851 n.
indignity 921 n.
not respect 921 vb.
disapprove 924 vb.
hooter
timekeeper 117 n.
protuberance
  254 n.
signal 547 n.
Hoover (tdmk)
cleaning utensil
  648 n.
hop
gait 265 n.
land travel 267 n.
leap 312 n.
leap 312 vb.
agitation 318 n.
be agitated 318 vb.
dancing 837 n.
social gathering
  882 n.
hope
hope 852 n.
hope 852 vb.
virtues 933 n.

hopeful
expectant 507 adj.
cheerful 833 adj.
hoping 852 adj.
promising 852 adj.
hopeless
impossible 470 adj.
useless 641 adj.
hopeless 853 adj.
unpromising
  853 adj.
impenitent
  940 adj.
hop it
come along
  267 int.
decamp 296 vb.
hops
herb 301 n.
hopscotch
children's games
  837 n.
horde
multitude 104 n.
army 722 n.
rabble 869 n.
horizon
distance 199 n.
horizontality
  216 n.
outline 233 n.
edge 234 n.
limit 236 n.
view 438 n.
visibility 443 n.
horizontal
flat 216 adj.
hormone
drug 658 n.
hormone therapy
therapy 658 n.
horn
cup 194 n.
cone 252 n.
protuberance
  254 n.
sharp point 256 n.
hardness 326 n.
horn 414 n.
hornet
insect 365 n.
hornet's nest
bane 659 n.
pitfall 663 n.
horn in
interfere 231 vb.
intrude 297 vb.

encroach 306 vb.
horny
hard 326 adj.
horoscope
destiny 155 n.
influence 178 n.
astronomy 321 n.
prediction 511 n.
horrendous
not nice 645 adj.
horrible
not nice 645 adj.
unpleasant
  827 adj.
frightening
  854 adj.
horrid
not nice 645 adj.
hateful 888 adj.
horrific
dramatic 594 adj.
not nice 645 adj.
distressing 827 adj.
frightening
  854 adj.
horrify
displease 827 vb.
horror
eyesore 842 n.
fear 854 n.
dislike 861 n.
hors de combat
useless 641 adj.
hors d'oeuvre
prelude 66 n.
savouriness 390 n.
hors-d'oeuvres
hors-d'oeuvres
  301 n.
horse
horse 273 n.
mammal 365 n.
male animal
  372 n.
drug-taking 949 n.
horse about
be absurd 497 vb.
horse-breeding
animal husbandry
  369 n.
horse chestnut
tree 366 n.
horsemanship
skill 694 n.
horseplay
fight 716 n.
ridicule 851 n.

horsepower
energy 160 n.
strength 162 n.
vehicle 274 n.
metrology 465 n.

horse racing
equitation 267 n.
gambling 618 n.
racing 716 n.

horse sense
intelligence 498 n.

horseshoe
curve 248 n.
omen 511 n.
talisman 983 n.

horse-trading
conditions 766 n.
barter 791 n.

horsewhip
flog 963 vb.
scourge 964 n.

horticulture
flower 366 n.
agriculture 370 n.

hosanna
cheers 835 int.
rejoicing 835 n.
celebration 876 n.
applause 923 n.
bravo 923 int.
praise 923 n.
hymn 981 n.

hose
legwear 228 n.
tube 263 n.
water 339 n.
irrigate 341 vb.
irrigator 341 n.
conduit 351 n.
extinguisher 382 n.

hosier
clothier 228 n.

hospice
retreat 192 n.
hospital 658 n.
shelter 662 n.

hospitable
liberal 813 adj.
friendly 880 adj.
sociable 882 adj.
benevolent 897 adj.

hospital
hospital 658 n.

hospitality
liberality 813 n.
friendliness 880 n.
sociability 882 n.

benevolence 897 n.

host
band 74 n.
multitude 104 n.
infection 651 n.
army 722 n.
friend 880 n.
sociable person 882 n.
the sacrament 988 n.

hostage
prisoner 750 n.
security 767 n.
taking 786 n.

hostel
station 187 n.
quarters 192 n.
retreat 192 n.

hostelry
inn 192 n.

hostess
sociable person 882 n.

hostile
contrary 14 adj.
disagreeing 25 adj.
separate 46 adj.
opposing 704 adj.
adverse 731 adj.
hostile 881 adj.
unsociable 883 adj.
malevolent 898 adj.
unkind 898 adj.
disapproving 924 adj.

hostile, be
be hostile 881 vb.

hostilities
fight 716 n.
belligerency 718 n.
enmity 881 n.

hostility
contrariety 14 n.
disagreement 25 n.
hindrance 702 n.
opposition 704 n.
dissension 709 n.
enmity 881 n.
hatred 888 n.
disapprobation 924 n.

hot
violent 176 adj.
hot 379 adj.
pungent 388 adj.

red 431 adj.
angry 891 adj.
impure 951 adj.
lecherous 951 adj.
illegal 954 adj.

hot air
insubstantial thing 4 n.
polarity 14 n.
lightness 323 n.
be hot 379 vb.
heater 383 n.
overestimation 482 n.
empty talk 515 n.
chatter 581 n.
excited 821 adj.
boast 877 n.

hotbed
abundance 171 n.
heater 383 n.
badness 645 n.
pitfall 663 n.

hotching with
full 54 adj.
multitudinous 104 adj.

hotchpotch
nonuniformity 17 n.
medley 43 n.
disorder 61 n.

hot dog
meal 301 n.

hotel
inn 192 n.

hotelier
caterer 633 n.

hotfoot
hasty 680 adj.

hot-headed
hasty 680 adj.
fervent 818 adj.
excitable 822 adj.
rash 857 adj.

hothouse
arbour 194 n.
garden 370 n.
heater 383 n.

hot line
telecommunication 531 n.

hotpot
dish 301 n.

hot potato
difficulty 700 n.

hot-rod
automobile 274 n.

hot seat
predicament 700 n.

hot toddy
alcoholic drink 301 n.

hot under the collar
excited 821 adj.
angry 891 adj.

hot up
heat 381 vb.

hot water
heat 379 n.
predicament 700 n.

Houdini
escaper 667 n.

hound
dog 365 n.
hunter 619 n.
be hostile 881 vb.
be malevolent 898 vb.
not respect 921 vb.
disapprove 924 vb.
defame 926 vb.

hour
juncture 8 n.
period 110 n.

hourglass
timekeeper 117 n.
contraction 198 n.
curved 248 adj.

house
race 11 n.
genealogy 169 n.
place 187 vb.
abode 192 n.
house 192 n.
onlookers 441 n.
class 538 n.
playgoer 594 n.
safeguard 660 vb.
sovereign 741 n.

house arrest
detention 747 n.
seclusion 883 n.

houseboat
small house 192 n.
boat 275 n.

house-breaking
stealing 788 n.

household
family 11 n.
group 74 n.
home 192 n.
known 490 adj.

usual 610 adj.
household name
famousness 866 n.
housekeeper
resident 191 n.
caterer 633 n.
manager 690 n.
domestic 742 n.
retainer 742 n.
servant 742 n.
keeper 749 n.
housekeeping
management
689 n.
housemaid
domestic 742 n.
houseman
doctor 658 n.
house of cards
weak thing 163 n.
House of Commons
parliament 692 n.
House of Lords
parliament 692 n.
housetop
vertex 213 n.
roof 226 n.
housewarming
start 68 n.
festivity 837 n.
social gathering
882 n.
housewife
resident 191 n.
case 194 n.
female 373 n.
caterer 633 n.
manager 690 n.
housework
labour 682 n.
housing
housing 192 n.
frame 218 n.
dressing 228 n.
hovel
small house 192 n.
hover
vary 152 vb.
impend 155 vb.
be high 209 vb.
hang 217 vb.
be in motion
265 vb.
wander 267 vb.
fly 271 vb.
move slowly
278 vb.

approach 289 vb.
be light 323 vb.
be uncertain
474 vb.
be irresolute
601 vb.
threaten 900 vb.
hovercraft
ship 275 n.
aircraft 276 n.
howdah
seat 218 n.
how-do-you-do
complexity 61 n.
howl
blow 352 vb.
be loud 400 vb.
loudness 400 n.
cry 408 n.
cry 408 vb.
ululate 409 vb.
lament 836 n.
weep 836 vb.
howler
mistake 495 n.
absurdity 497 n.
hoydenish
ill-bred 847 adj.
HP
strength 162 n.
borrowing 785 n.
purchase 792 n.
hub
middle 70 n.
focus 76 n.
centre 225 n.
wheel 250 n.
chief thing 638 n.
hubbub
turmoil 61 n.
commotion 318 n.
loudness 400 n.
quarrel 709 n.
huddle
congregate 74 vb.
crowd 74 n.
make smaller
198 vb.
conference 584 n.
advice 691 n.
hue
hue 425 n.
hue and cry
cry 408 n.
call 547 n.
chase 619 n.

huff
breathe 352 vb.
huff 891 vb.
resentment 891 n.
huffy
irascible 892 adj.
hug
cohere 48 vb.
make smaller
198 vb.
surround 230 vb.
enclose 235 vb.
gesture 547 n.
retain 778 vb.
retention 778 n.
friendliness 880 n.
courteous act
884 n.
greet 884 vb.
caress 889 vb.
endearment 889 n.
huge
huge 195 adj.
hugely
greatly 32 vb.
hugger-mugger
disorder 61 n.
be stealthy 525 vb.
secretly 525 adv.
stealthy 525 adj.
hulk
chief part 52 n.
bulk 195 n.
ship 275 n.
be clumsy 695 vb.
bungler 697 n.
hulking
stalwart 162 adj.
unwieldy 195 adj.
clumsy 695 adj.
graceless 842 adj.
hull
chief part 52 n.
skin 226 n.
uncover 229 vb.
ship 275 n.
hullabaloo
turmoil 61 n.
loudness 400 n.
cry 408 n.
hullo
welcome 295 int.
hum
rotate 315 vb.
blow 352 vb.
stink 397 vb.

faintness 401 n.
sound faint 401 vb.
roll 403 n.
roll 403 vb.
resound 404 vb.
shrill 407 vb.
ululate 409 vb.
ululation 409 n.
sing 413 vb.
voice 577 vb.
activity 678 n.
be active 678 vb.
human
animal 365 adj.
benevolent 897 adj.
philanthropic
901 adj.
frail 934 adj.
human being
humankind 371 n.
person 371 n.
hum and haw
stammer 580 vb.
be irresolute
601 vb.
humane
benevolent 897 adj.
philanthropic
901 adj.
pitying 905 adj.
humanism
anthropology
371 n.
philosophy 449 n.
philanthropy
901 n.
morals 917 n.
irreligion 974 n.
humanitarian
benevolent 897 adj.
philanthropic
901 adj.
philanthropist
901 n.
humanities
culture 490 n.
literature 557 n.
humanity
humankind 371 n.
leniency 736 n.
benevolence 897 n.
philanthropy
901 n.
pity 905 n.
humankind
humankind 371 n.

humble
inconsiderable
33 adj.
abase 311 vb.
plebeian 869 adj.
humble 872 adj.
humiliate 872 vb.
humbug
empty talk 515 n.
falsehood 541 n.
fable 543 n.
impostor 545 n.
pretension 850 n.
humdrum
tedious 838 adj.
humf
carry 273 vb.
humid
humid 341 adj.
humidifier
air 340 n.
humidify
moisten 341 vb.
humidity
water 339 n.
moisture 341 n.
humiliate
humiliate 872 vb.
humiliation
humiliation 872 n.
indignity 921 n.
contempt 922 n.
humility
humility 872 n.
humming
multitudinous
104 adj.
fetid 397 adj.
ululation 409 n.
busy 678 adj.
humorist
humorist 839 n.
humorous
laughing 835 adj.
witty 839 adj.
funny 849 adj.
humour
temperament 5 n.
state 7 n.
composition 56 n.
tendency 179 n.
fluid 335 n.
whim 604 n.
minister to 703 vb.
be lenient 736 vb.
affections 817 n.
laughter 835 n.

amuse 837 vb.
wit 839 n.
flatter 925 vb.
humourless
serious 834 adj.
dull 840 adj.
hump
camber 253 n.
carry 273 vb.
work 682 vb.
hump, the
discontent 829 n.
resentment 891 n.
sullenness 893 n.
humpback
obliquity 220 n.
camber 253 n.
humpy
convex 253 adj.
hunch
intuition 476 n.
spontaneity 609 n.
hundred
hundred 99 n.
district 184 n.
hung
appearing 445 adj.
hunger
be hungry 859 vb.
desire 859 n.
hunger 859 n.
hunger strike
deprecation 762 n.
fast 946 n.
fasting 946 n.
hungry
poor 801 adj.
hungry 859 adj.
hungry for
inquisitive 453 adj.
hunk
piece 53 n.
bulk 195 n.
a beauty 841 n.
hunkers
buttocks 238 n.
hunky-dory
super 644 adj.
hunt
rider 268 n.
search 459 n.
chase 619 n.
hunt 619 vb.
pursue 619 vb.
amuse oneself
837 vb.

hunter
timekeeper 117 n.
horse 273 n.
hunter 619 n.
hunting
killing 362 n.
chase 619 n.
pursuit 619 n.
hurdle
bed 218 n.
fence 235 n.
vehicle 274 n.
leap 312 vb.
obstacle 702 n.
hurl
propel 287 vb.
hurly-burly
turmoil 61 n.
commotion 318 n.
hurrah
cry 408 n.
cry 408 vb.
See **vociferate**
vociferate 408 vb.
cheers 835 int.
rejoice 835 vb.
rejoicing 835 n.
bravo 923 int.
hurricane
turmoil 61 n.
storm 176 n.
velocity 277 n.
gale 352 n.
hurry
move fast 277 vb.
velocity 277 n.
activity 678 n.
be active 678 vb.
haste 680 n.
hasten 680 vb.
hurt
weaken 163 vb.
give pain 377 vb.
pain 377 n.
evil 616 n.
badness 645 n.
impair 655 vb.
hurt 827 vb.
resentful 891 adj.
be malevolent
898 vb.
do wrong 914 adj.
hurtful
harmful 645 adj.
paining 827 adj.
hurtle
move fast 277 vb.

hurt the feelings
hurt 827 vb.
husband
male 372 n.
store 632 vb.
spouse 894 n.
husbandry
agriculture 370 n.
management
689 n.
economy 814 n.
hush
assuage 177 vb.
bring to rest
266 vb.
quietude 266 n.
hush 399 int.
silence 399 n.
silence 399 vb.
mute 401 vb.
make mute 578 vb.
hush-hush
occult 523 adj.
concealed 525 adj.
important 638 adj.
husk
remainder 41 n.
skin 226 n.
grass 366 n.
husky
stalwart 162 adj.
beast of burden
273 n.
dog 365 n.
hoarse 407 adj.
beautiful 841 adj.
hussy
female 373 n.
insolent person
878 n.
bad person 938 n.
loose woman
952 n.
hustings
publicity 528 n.
vote 605 n.
arena 724 n.
lawcourt 956 n.
hustle
move 265 vb.
accelerate 277 vb.
impel 279 vb.
propel 287 vb.
activity 678 n.
haste 680 n.
hasten 680 vb.

hustler
  busy person 678 n.
  prostitute 952 n.
hut
  dwelling 192 n.
  small house 192 n.
hutch
  stable 192 n.
  receptacle 194 n.
  cattle pen 369 n.
huzza
  vociferate 408 vb.
  cheers 835 int.
  rejoice 835 vb.
  rejoicing 835 n.
hyacinth
  plant 366 n.
  gem 844 n.
hybrid
  hybrid 43 n.
  mixed 43 adj.
  abnormal 84 adj.
  neology 560 n.
hydrant
  water 339 n.
  conduit 351 n.
  extinguisher 382 n.
hydro
  hospital 658 n.
hydrocephalic
  diseased 651 adj.
hydrofoil
  ship 275 n.
hydrogen bomb
  bomb 723 n.
hydrography
  earth sciences
    321 n.
hydrology
  earth sciences
    321 n.
hydrolysis
  decomposition
    51 n.
hydrometry
  water 339 n.
hydropathy
  water 339 n.
hydrophobia
  infection 651 n.
hydroplane
  aircraft 276 n.
hydroponics
  agriculture 370 n.
hydrotherapy
  water 339 n.
  therapy 658 n.

hydrous
  watery 339 adj.
hyena
  eater 301 n.
  mammal 365 n.
hygiene
  ablutions 648 n.
  hygiene 652 n.
hygrometer
  weather 340 n.
  meter 465 n.
  recording instru-
    ment 549 n.
hymn
  hymn 981 n.
hymnal
  musical 412 adj.
  scripture 975 n.
  hymn 981 n.
  hymnal 988 n.
  church utensil
    990 n.
hymnary
  hymn 981 n.
  hymnal 988 n.
  church utensil
    990 n.
hymnbook
  vocal music 412 n.
  hymn 981 n.
hype
  overestimate
    482 vb.
  overestimation
    482 n.
  advertisement
    528 n.
  publicity 528 n.
  exaggeration
    546 n.
  make better
    654 vb.
  boast 877 n.
  boasting 877 n.
  flatter 925 vb.
hyperactive
  psychotic 503 adj.
  active 678 adj.
hyperbola
  curve 248 n.
hyperbole
  expansion 197 n.
  trope 519 n.
  exaggeration
    546 n.
  grandiloquence
    574 n.

hypercritical
  narrow-minded
    481 adj.
  severe 735 adj.
  discontented
    829 adj.
  fastidious 862 adj.
  disapproving
    924 adj.
hypermarket
  shop 796 n.
hypersensitive
  sentient 374 adj.
  sensitive 819 adj.
hypertension
  cardiovascular dis-
    ease 651 n.
hyperthermia
  illness 651 n.
hyperthyroidism
  overactivity 678 n.
hypertrophy
  size 195 n.
  expansion 197 n.
hype up
  advertise 528 vb.
  exaggerate 546 vb.
  praise 923 vb.
hyphen
  bond 47 n.
  punctuation 547 n.
hyphenation
  punctuation 547 n.
hypnosis
  insensibility 375 n.
  sleep 679 n.
  occultism 984 n.
hypnotherapy
  therapy 658 n.
hypnotism
  influence 178 n.
  insensibility 375 n.
  occultism 984 n.
hypnotize
  influence 178 vb.
  render insensible
    375 vb.
  convince 485 vb.
  motivate 612 vb.
  bewitch 983 vb.
hypochondria
  neurosis 503 n.
  ill health 651 n.
hypocrisy
  duplicity 541 n.
  deception 542 n.
  flattery 925 n.

  false piety 980 n.
hypocrite
  imitator 20 n.
  toady 879 n.
  flatterer 925 n.
hypodermic needle
  perforator 263 n.
hypotension
  cardiovascular dis-
    ease 651 n.
hypothermia
  coldness 380 n.
  illness 651 n.
hypothesis
  attribution 158 n.
  premise 475 n.
  opinion 485 n.
  supposition 512 n.
hypothetical
  possible 469 adj.
  uncertain 474 adj.
  imaginary 513 adj.
hysterectomy
  contraception
    172 n.
  surgery 658 n.
hysteria
  frenzy 503 n.
  neurosis 503 n.
hysterical
  furious 176 adj.
  frenzied 503 adj.
  excited 821 adj.
  excitable 822 adj.
  fearing 854 adj.
hysterics
  violence 176 n.
  excitable state
    822 n.
  lamentation 836 n.

I

I
  self 80 n.
iaido
  duel 716 n.
iatrogenic
  diseased 651 adj.
ice
  cover 226 vb.
  smoothness 258 n.
  ice 380 n.
  refrigerator 384 n.
  sweeten 392 vb.
  transparency
    422 n.

ICE

preserver 666 n.
gem 844 n.

iceberg
island 349 n.
ice 380 n.
unfeeling person
820 n.
solitary 883 n.

icebox
ice 380 n.
refrigerator 384 n.

icecream
dessert 301 n.
sweet thing 392 n.

ice rink
smoothness 258 n.
arena 724 n.
pleasure ground
837 n.

ice skating
sport 837 n.

ichthyology
zoology 367 n.

icicle
hanging object
217 n.
ice 380 n.
unfeeling person
820 n.

icing
covering 226 n.
sweet thing 392 n.

icon
copy 22 n.
image 551 n.
picture 553 n.
ritual object 988 n.

iconoclast
destroyer 168 n.
violent creature
176 n.
evildoer 904 n.
zealot 979 n.

icy
hard 326 adj.
cold 380 adj.
impassive 820 adj.
hostile 881 adj.
unsociable 883 adj.

id
self 80 n.
subjectivity 320 n.
spirit 447 n.
intuition 476 n.

idea
reason why 156 n.
form 243 n.

IDE

idea 451 n.

ideal
prototype 23 n.
imaginary 513 adj.
motive 612 n.
paragon 646 n.
perfect 646 adj.
desired object
859 n.

idealism
existence 1 n.
immateriality
320 n.
philosophy 449 n.
fantasy 513 n.
fastidiousness
862 n.
philanthropy
901 n.
morals 917 n.
disinterestedness
931 n.

idealist
revolutionist 149 n.
visionary 513 n.
reformer 654 n.
perfectionist 862 n.
philanthropist
901 n.

idealistic
imaginative
513 adj.
improving 654 adj.
philanthropic
901 adj.
ethical 917 adj.
disinterested
931 adj.

idealize
overestimate
482 vb.
imagine 513 vb.

identical
identical 13 adj.

identification
identity 13 n.
assimilation 18 n.
comparison 462 n.
identification
547 n.

identify
identify 13 vb.
discover 484 vb.
indicate 547 vb.

identikit
representation
551 n.

IDL

identity
identity 13 n.
self 80 n.

ides
date 108 n.

idiocy
folly 499 n.
unintelligence
499 n.
psychosis 503 n.

idiolect
speciality 80 n.
unintelligibility
517 n.
identification
547 n.
language 557 n.
dialect 560 adj.
style 566 n.

idiom
speciality 80 n.
connotation 514 n.
language 557 n.
dialect 560 adj.
phrase 563 n.
style 566 n.

idiomatic
special 80 adj.
semantic 514 adj.
linguistic 557 adj.
stylistic 566 adj.

idiosyncrasy
temperament 5 n.
originality 21 n.
speciality 80 n.
nonconformity
84 n.
tendency 179 n.
style 566 n.
whim 604 n.
habit 610 n.

idiot
fool 501 n.
*the mentally handi-
capped* 504 n.

idle
quiescent 266 adj.
move slowly
278 vb.
be inattentive
456 vb.
nonactive 677 adj.
be inactive 679 vb.
inactive 679 adj.
lazy 679 adj.

IGN

idleness
unproductiveness
172 n.
inaction 677 n.
inactivity 679 n.
leisure 681 n.
undutifulness
918 n.

idol
image 551 n.
exceller 644 n.
a beauty 841 n.
person of repute
866 n.
loved one 887 n.
favourite 890 n.
deity 966 n.
idol 982 n.

idolatry
praise 923 n.
idolatry 982 n.

idolize
love 887 vb.
respect 920 vb.
praise 923 vb.
worshipper 981 n.

idyll
description 590 n.
poem 593 n.
pleasurableness
826 n.

idyllic
pleasurable
826 adj.

if
thus 8 adv.
provided 468 adv.

igloo
dwelling 192 n.

igneous
fiery 379 adj.

ignite
kindle 381 vb.
make bright
417 vb.

ignition
burning 381 n.

ignoble
discreditable
867 adj.
plebeian 869 adj.
dishonest 930 adj.

ignominious
degrading 867 adj.
dishonest 930 adj.

ignoramus
ignoramus 493 n.

ignorant
ignorant 491 adj.
unskilled 695 adj.
ignore
be blind 439 vb.
be inattentive
456 vb.
disregard 458 vb.
disbelieve 486 vb.
not know 491 vb.
reject 607 vb.
abrogate 752 vb.
not observe 769 vb.
be insensitive
820 vb.
be rude 885 vb.
not respect 921 vb.
hold cheap 922 vb.
disapprove 924 vb.
iguana
reptile 365 n.
ilk
sort 77 n.
ill
evil 616 n.
badly 645 adv.
badness 645 n.
sick 651 adj.
suffering 825 adj.
ill-assorted
disagreeing 25 adj.
ill at ease
suffering 825 adj.
ill-bred
ill-bred 847 adj.
ill-conceived
rash 857 adj.
ill-defined
amorphous
244 adj.
shadowy 419 adj.
illegal
illegal 954 adj.
illegible
unintelligible
517 adj.
illegitimate
wrong 914 adj.
unwarranted
916 adj.
bastard 954 adj.
illegal 954 adj.
ill-fated
unfortunate
731 adj.
ill-gotten gains
taking 786 n.

booty 790 n.
illicit
prohibited 757 adj.
wrong 914 adj.
unwarranted
916 adj.
dishonest 930 adj.
illegal 954 adj.
ill-informed
uninstructed
491 adj.
mistaken 495 adj.
illiterate
ignorance 491 n.
uninstructed
491 adj.
ignoramus 493 n.
ill-mannered
ill-bred 847 adj.
impertinent
878 adj.
discourteous
885 adj.
ill-natured
malevolent
898 adj.
unkind 898 adj.
illness
illness 651 n.
illogic
sophistry 477 n.
folly 499 n.
illogical
irrelevant 10 adj.
illogical 477 adj.
ill repute
disrepute 867 n.
ill-spent
profitless 641 adj.
ill-treat
ill-treat 645 vb.
be severe 735 vb.
illuminate
make bright
417 vb.
colour 425 vb.
interpret 520 vb.
paint 553 vb.
decorate 844 vb.
illumination
light 417 n.
lighting 420 n.
discovery 484 n.
knowledge 490 n.
interpretation
520 n.
art 551 n.

painting 553 n.
ornamental art
844 n.
revelation 975 n.
illusion
appearance 445 n.
error 495 n.
deception 542 n.
sleight 542 n.
illusory
erroneous 495 adj.
imaginary 513 adj.
illustrate
exemplify 83 vb.
interpret 520 vb.
represent 551 vb.
decorate 844 vb.
illustration
example 83 n.
interpretation
520 n.
representation
551 n.
picture 553 n.
edition 589 n.
ornamental art
844 n.
illustrator
artist 556 n.
illustrious
noteworthy
866 adj.
renowned 866 adj.
ill will
badness 645 n.
adversity 731 n.
enmity 881 n.
hatred 888 n.
malevolence 898 n.
envy 912 n.
image
copy 22 n.
appearance 445 n.
ideality 513 n.
show 522 vb.
indication 547 n.
image 551 n.
idol 982 n.
imagery
imagination 513 n.
metaphor 519 n.
imaginary
imaginary 513 adj.
imagination
imagination 513 n.

imaginative
imaginative
513 adj.
imagine
perceive 447 adj.
imagine 513 vb.
imbalance
inequality 29 n.
changeableness
152 n.
distortion 246 n.
imbecile
weak 163 adj.
foolish 499 adj.
unintelligent
499 adj.
fool 501 n.
*mentally handi-
capped* 503 adj.
imbibe
absorb 299 vb.
drink 301 vb.
imbroglio
medley 43 n.
complexity 61 n.
disorder 61 n.
predicament 700 n.
imbue
mix 43 vb.
combine 50 vb.
pervade 189 vb.
drench 341 vb.
colour 425 vb.
educate 534 vb.
habituate 610 vb.
imitate
imitate 20 vb.
imitation
imitation 20 n.
imitative 20 adj.
substituted 150 adj.
false 541 adj.
sham 542 n.
spurious 542 adj.
bad taste 847 n.
imitative
imitative 20 adj.
imitator
imitator 20 n.
immaculate
perfect 646 adj.
clean 648 adj.
honourable
929 adj.
innocent 935 adj.
pure 950 adj.

immanent
intrinsic 5 adj.
immaterial
irrelevant 10 adj.
immaterial
320 adj.
unimportant
639 adj.
immature
immature 670 adj.
immeasurable
infinite 107 adj.
immediacy
instantaneity
116 n.
punctuality 135 n.
haste 680 n.
immediate
instantaneous
116 adj.
early 135 adj.
impending 155 adj.
speedy 277 adj.
hasty 680 adj.
immemorial
great 32 adj.
immense
enormous 32 adj.
infinite 107 adj.
huge 195 adj.
immerse
immerse 303 vb.
plunge 313 vb.
immersion
ingress 297 n.
plunge 313 n.
Christian rite
988 n.
immigrant
extraneous 59 adj.
foreigner 59 n.
settler 191 n.
incomer 297 n.
immigrate
travel 267 vb.
enter 297 vb.
immigration
ingress 297 n.
imminent
future 124 adj.
early 135 adj.
impending 155 adj.
approaching
289 adj.
immobile
permanent 144 adj.
fixed 153 adj.

still 266 adj.
nonactive 677 adj.
immobilize
bring to rest
266 vb.
make inactive
679 vb.
immoderate
violent 176 adj.
redundant 637 adj.
intemperate
943 adj.
immodest
vain 873 adj.
unchaste 951 adj.
immolate
kill 362 vb.
immoral
wrong 914 adj.
dishonest 930 adj.
heinous 934 adj.
vicious 934 adj.
wicked 934 adj.
impure 951 adj.
unchaste 951 adj.
immorality
wrong 914 n.
wickedness 934 n.
unchastity 951 n.
impiety 980 n.
immortal
existing 1 adj.
perpetual 115 adj.
renowned 866 adj.
godlike 965 adj.
immortalize
perpetuate 115 vb.
honour 866 vb.
immovable
firm 45 adj.
fixed 153 adj.
still 266 adj.
resolute 599 adj.
obstinate 602 adj.
immune
invulnerable
660 adj.
free 744 adj.
acquitted 960 adj.
immunity
safety 660 n.
escape 667 n.
freedom 744 n.
dueness 915 n.
nonliability 919 n.
immunize
doctor 658 vb.

safeguard 660 vb.
immure
circumscribe
232 vb.
enclose 235 vb.
imprison 747 vb.
immutable
perpetual 115 adj.
permanent 144 adj.
unchangeable
153 adj.
godlike 965 adj.
imp
demon 970 n.
elf 970 n.
sorcerer 983 n.
impact
affix 45 vb.
influence 178 n.
collision 279 n.
impulse 279 n.
excitation 821 n.
impacted
firm 45 adj.
impaired
incomplete 55 adj.
crippled 163 adj.
impairment
incompleteness
55 n.
impairment 655 n.
impale
pierce 263 vb.
impalpability
insubstantiality
4 n.
immateriality
320 n.
impart
inform 524 vb.
give 781 vb.
impartial
equal 28 adj.
neutral 625 adj.
indifferent 860 adj.
just 913 adj.
honourable
929 adj.
disinterested
931 adj.
impassable
closed 264 adj.
difficult 700 adj.
impasse
stop 145 n.
closure 264 n.

impossibility
470 n.
difficulty 700 n.
obstacle 702 n.
impassioned
forceful 571 adj.
fervent 818 adj.
excited 821 adj.
impassive
impassive 820 adj.
inexcitable
823 adj.
impatient
unwise 499 adj.
willing 597 adj.
hasty 680 adj.
fervent 818 adj.
excitable 822 adj.
rash 857 adj.
angry 891 adj.
irascible 892 adj.
impeachment
censure 924 n.
detraction 926 n.
accusation 928 n.
litigation 959 n.
impeccable
perfect 646 adj.
virtuous 933 adj.
innocent 935 adj.
impecunious
poor 801 adj.
impede
hinder 702 vb.
impediment
difficulty 700 n.
hindrance 702 n.
obstacle 702 n.
divorce 896 n.
impel
impel 279 vb.
impending
impending 155 adj.
impenetrable
closed 264 adj.
dense 324 adj.
impracticable
470 adj.
unintelligible
517 adj.
latent 523 adj.
difficult 700 adj.
thick-skinned
820 adj.
impenitent
impenitent
940 adj.

imperative
necessary 596 adj.
important 638 adj.
commanding
737 adj.
compelling
740 adj.
imperceptible
inconsiderable
33 adj.
slow 278 adj.
dim 419 adj.
invisible 444 adj.
imperceptive
insensible 375 adj.
indiscriminating
464 adj.
imperfect
imperfect 647 adj.
imperfection
insufficiency 636 n.
imperfection 647 n.
nonpreparation
670 n.
vice 934 n.
imperial
great 32 adj.
hair 259 n.
metrical 465 adj.
paper 631 n.
ruling 733 adj.
imperialism
nation 371 n.
governance 733 n.
imperil
endanger 661 vb.
imperious
authoritative
733 adj.
proud 871 adj.
insolent 878 adj.
impermanence
transience 114 n.
changeableness
152 n.
impermeable
strong 162 adj.
closed 264 adj.
dense 324 adj.
thick-skinned
820 adj.
impersonal
general 79 adj.
material 319 adj.
impassive 820 adj.
indifferent 860 adj.
unsociable 883 adj.

just 913 adj.
impersonate
represent 551 vb.
act 594 vb.
imperspicuity
imperspicuity
568 n.
impertinent
irrelevant 10 adj.
impertinent
878 adj.
imperturbable
impassive 820 adj.
inexcitable
823 adj.
impervious
closed 264 adj.
dense 324 adj.
obstinate 602 adj.
thick-skinned
820 adj.
impetigo
skin disease 651 n.
impetuous
furious 176 adj.
hasty 680 adj.
fervent 818 adj.
excitable 822 adj.
impetus
energy 160 n.
vigorousness 174 n.
spurt 277 n.
impulse 279 n.
motive 612 n.
impiety
impiety 980 n.
impinge
collide 279 vb.
encroach 306 vb.
touch 378 vb.
impious
impious 980 adj.
impish
fairylike 970 adj.
implacable
resolute 599 adj.
obstinate 602 adj.
severe 735 adj.
malevolent
898 adj.
pitiless 906 adj.
implant
affix 45 vb.
place 187 vb.
implant 303 vb.
educate 534 vb.

implausible
improbable
472 adj.
erroneous 495 adj.
implement
produce 164 vb.
instrument 628 n.
tool 630 n.
do 676 vb.
carry out 725 vb.
implementation
action 676 n.
completion 725 n.
implicate
accuse 928 vb.
implication
relation 9 n.
complexity 61 n.
meaning 514 n.
latency 523 n.
implicit
intrinsic 5 adj.
tacit 523 adj.
implore
entreat 761 vb.
imploring
entreaty 761 n.
supplicatory
761 adj.
imply
comprise 78 vb.
imply 523 vb.
hint 524 vb.
indicate 547 vb.
impolite
ill-bred 847 adj.
impertinent
878 adj.
discourteous
885 adj.
disrespectful
921 adj.
impolitic
foolish 499 adj.
inexpedient
643 adj.
import
relation 9 n.
transference 272 n.
ingress 297 n.
admit 299 vb.
reception 299 n.
meaning 514 n.
importance 638 n.
importance
importance 638 n.

important
necessary 596 adj.
important 638 adj.
importation
transference 272 n.
ingress 297 n.
reception 299 n.
importer
carrier 273 n.
merchant 794 n.
importunate
annoying 827 adj.
importune
request 761 vb.
torment 827 vb.
impose
place 187 vb.
print 587 vb.
necessitate 596 vb.
command 737 vb.
compel 740 vb.
command respect
920 vb.
imposing
notable 638 adj.
impressive 821 adj.
worshipful 866 adj.
imposition
addition 38 n.
bane 659 n.
command 737 n.
demand 737 n.
tax 809 n.
injustice 914 n.
undueness 916 n.
penalty 963 n.
impossible
impossible 470 adj.
annoying 827 adj.
intolerable 827 adj.
wonderful 864 adj.
impostor
impostor 545 n.
bad person 938 n.
imposture
duplicity 541 n.
deception 542 n.
cunning 698 n.
impotent
impotent 161 adj.
powerless 161 adj.
unproductive
172 adj.
impound
imprison 747 vb.
impoverished
weakened 163 adj.

poor 801 adj.
impracticable
unapt 25 adj.
impracticable
470 adj.
useless 641 adj.
difficult 700 adj.
impractical
misjudging
481 adj.
imaginative
513 adj.
imprecation
entreaty 761 n.
malediction 899 n.
prayers 981 n.
imprecise
inexact 495 adj.
unclear 568 adj.
impregnable
strong 162 adj.
invulnerable
660 adj.
pure 950 adj.
impregnation
mixture 43 n.
propagation 167 n.
impresario
exhibitor 522 n.
stage manager
594 n.
impress
effect 157 n.
make concave
255 vb.
mark 547 vb.
engrave 555 vb.
compel 740 vb.
impress 821 vb.
impressible
soft 327 adj.
impressible
819 adj.
impression
copy 22 n.
concavity 255 n.
sense 374 n.
spectacle 445 n.
idea 451 n.
opinion 485 n.
indication 547 n.
label 547 n.
representation
551 n.
printing 555 n.
print 587 n.
edition 589 n.

feeling 818 n.
impressionable
sentient 374 adj.
impressible
819 adj.
excitable 822 adj.
Impressionism
school of painting
553 n.
impressive
appearing 445 adj.
impressive 821 adj.
impress on
emphasize 532 vb.
imprimatur
assent 488 n.
permit 756 n.
orthodoxism 976 n.
imprint
copy 22 n.
concavity 255 n.
identification
547 n.
See **label**
label 547 n.
mark 547 vb.
imprison
imprison 747 vb.
improbable
improbable
472 adj.
impromptu
musical piece
412 n.
extempore
609 adv.
spontaneity 609 n.
spontaneous
609 adj.
unprepared
670 adj.
improper
unapt 25 adj.
unwise 499 adj.
inexpedient
643 adj.
not nice 645 adj.
vulgar 847 adj.
discreditable
867 adj.
disreputable
867 adj.
wrong 914 adj.
vicious 934 adj.
improper fraction
numerical element
85 n.

impropriety
inaptitude 25 n.
inelegance 576 n.
inexpedience
643 n.
bad taste 847 n.
wrong 914 n.
undueness 916 n.
vice 934 n.
guilty act 936 n.
improve
grow 36 vb.
flourish 615 vb.
do good 644 vb.
get better 654 vb.
make better
654 vb.
beautify 841 vb.
improvement
improvement
654 n.
improve on
be superior 34 vb.
make better
654 vb.
improvident
negligent 458 adj.
prodigal 815 adj.
rash 857 adj.
improvise
compose music
413 vb.
play music 413 vb.
improvise 609 vb.
imprudent
inexpedient
643 adj.
rash 857 adj.
impudent
impertinent
878 adj.
discourteous
885 adj.
impugn
negate 533 vb.
impulse
impulse 279 n.
intuition 476 n.
necessity 596 n.
whim 604 n.
spontaneity 609 n.
motive 612 n.
feeling 818 n.
impulsive
intuitive 476 adj.
involuntary
596 adj.

spontaneous
609 adj.
hasty 680 adj.
excitable 822 adj.
rash 857 adj.
impunity
nonliability 919 n.
acquittal 960 n.
impure
impure 951 adj.
impious 980 adj.
impurity
impurity 951 n.
impute
attribute 158 vb.
blame 924 vb.
accuse 928 vb.
in
inside 224 adv.
usual 610 adj.
fashionable
848 adj.
inability
impotence 161 n.
uselessness 641 n.
unskilfulness
695 n.
inaccessible
impracticable
470 adj.
inaccurate
negligent 458 adj.
indiscriminating
464 adj.
inexact 495 adj.
inactive
inactive 679 adj.
inactivity
weakness 163 n.
inactivity 679 n.
inadequate
unequal 29 adj.
incomplete 55 adj.
powerless 161 adj.
deficient 307 adj.
insufficient
636 adj.
imperfect 647 adj.
unskilful 695 adj.
inadmissible
unapt 25 adj.
extraneous 59 adj.
inexpedient
643 adj.
wrong 914 adj.
inadvertent
inattentive 456 adj.

unintentional
618 adj.
inadvisable
inexpedient
643 adj.
inalienable
due 915 adj.
inane
insubstantial 4 adj.
empty 190 adj.
foolish 499 adj.
meaningless
515 adj.
feeble 572 adj.
inanimate
mindless 448 adj.
inactive 679 adj.
in a nutshell
proverbially
496 adv.
concisely 569 adv.
inapplicable
irrelevant 10 adj.
unapt 25 adj.
useless 641 adj.
inapposite
irrelevant 10 adj.
inappreciable
unimportant
639 adj.
inappropriate
unrelated 10 adj.
unapt 25 adj.
inexpedient
643 adj.
ridiculous 849 adj.
wrong 914 adj.
inaptitude
inaptitude 25 n.
in arrears
nonpaying 805 adj.
inarticulate
voiceless 578 adj.
taciturn 582 adj.
modest 874 adj.
inartistic
bungled 695 adj.
inasmuch
concerning 9 adv.
inattentive
inattentive 456 adj.
inaudible
silent 399 adj.
muted 401 adj.
deaf 416 adj.
unintelligible
517 adj.

voiceless 578 adj.
inaugural
precursory 66 adj.
beginning 68 adj.
inauguration
debut 68 n.
mandate 751 n.
celebration 876 n.
inauspicious
inopportune
138 adj.
predicting 511 adj.
evil 616 adj.
adverse 731 adj.
unpromising
853 adj.
in black and white
written 586 adj.
inborn
genetic 5 adj.
with affections
817 adj.
inbred
genetic 5 adj.
extrinsic 6 adj.
ethnic 11 adj.
combined 50 adj.
with affections
817 adj.
incalculable
multitudinous
104 adj.
infinite 107 adj.
casual 159 adj.
incandescent
fiery 379 adj.
luminous 417 adj.
incantation
sorcery 983 n.
spell 983 n.
incapable
powerless 161 adj.
unskilful 695 adj.
incapacitated
impotent 161 adj.
crippled 163 adj.
incarcerate
imprison 747 vb.
incarnate
material 319 adj.
materialize 319 vb.
alive 360 adj.
manifest 522 vb.
godlike 965 adj.
incarnation
essential part 5 n.
materiality 319 n.

manifestation
522 n.
representation
551 n.
revelation 975 n.
incendiary
destructive 165 adj.
violent 176 adj.
violent creature
176 n.
arson 381 n.
heating 381 adj.
evildoer 904 n.
incense
inodorousness
395 n.
scent 396 n.
honours 866 n.
enrage 891 vb.
oblation 981 n.
ritual object 988 n.
incentive
incentive 612 n.
inception
beginning 68 n.
incessant
continuous 71 adj.
repeated 106 adj.
perpetual 115 adj.
active 678 adj.
incest
illicit love 951 n.
inch
small quantity
33 n.
short distance
200 n.
long measure
203 n.
shortness 204 n.
move slowly
278 vb.
island 349 n.
inchworm
creepy-crawly
365 n.
incidence
event 154 n.
incident
event 154 n.
incidental
extrinsic 6 adj.
circumstantial
8 adj.
irrelevance 10 n.
irrelevant 10 adj.
unrelated 10 adj.

casual 159 adj.
liable 180 adj.
incinerate
destroy 165 vb.
inter 364 vb.
burn 381 vb.
incinerator;
furnace 383 n.
incipient
beginning 68 adj.
incise
cut 46 vb.
groove 262 vb.
wound 655 vb.
incisive
assertive 532 adj.
concise 569 adj.
incisor
tooth 256 n.
incite
cause 156 vb.
incite 612 vb.
inclement
pitiless 906 adj.
inclination
tendency 179 n.
obliquity 220 n.
will 595 n.
willingness 597 n.
choice 605 n.
liking 859 n.
love 887 n.
incline
tend 179 vb.
be oblique 220 vb.
incline 220 n.
be curved 248 vb.
approach 289 vb.
choose 605 vb.
motivate 612 vb.
include
join 45 vb.
contain 56 vb.
comprise 78 vb.
possess 773 vb.
including
in addition 38 adv.
including 78 adv.
inclusive 78 adj.
including out
exclusion 57 n.
exclusive of 57 adv.
inclusive
in addition 38 adv.
inclusive 78 adj.
incognito
concealment 525 n.

disguised 525 adj.
secretly 525 adv.
anonymous
562 adj.
incoherent
discontinuous
72 adj.
frenzied 503 adj.
meaningless
515 adj.
prolix 570 adj.
income
means 629 n.
earnings 771 n.
estate 777 n.
receipt 807 n.
reward 962 n.
incomer
incomer 297 n.
income tax
tax 809 n.
incoming
ingress 297 n.
incommode
trouble 827 vb.
incommunicable
inexpressible
517 adj.
incommunicado
imprisoned
747 adj.
incommunicative
taciturn 582 adj.
cautious 858 adj.
incomparable
inimitable 21 adj.
supreme 34 adj.
incompatible
unrelated 10 adj.
contrary 14 adj.
disagreeing 25 adj.
hostile 881 adj.
incompetent
unapt 25 adj.
powerless 161 adj.
unintelligent
499 adj.
fool 501 n.
insufficient
636 adj.
useless 641 adj.
bad 645 adj.
unskilful 695 adj.
bungler 697 n.
illegal 954 adj.
incomplete
incomplete 55 adj.

incomprehensible
infinite 107 adj.
unintelligible
517 adj.
inconceivable
impossible 470 adj.
improbable
472 adj.
unintelligible
517 adj.
wonderful 864 adj.
inconclusive
poorly reasoned
477 adj.
incongruous
different 15 adj.
disagreeing 25 adj.
unconformable
84 adj.
illogical 477 adj.
inconsequential
irrelevant 10 adj.
illogical 477 adj.
unimportant
639 adj.
inconsiderate
inattentive 456 adj.
rash 857 adj.
discourteous
885 adj.
inconsistent
contrary 14 adj.
nonuniform 17 adj.
illogical 477 adj.
capricious 604 adj.
inconstant
nonuniform 17 adj.
fitful 142 adj.
changeful 152 adj.
light-minded
456 adj.
irresolute 601 adj.
capricious 604 adj.
perfidious 930 adj.
incontestable
strong 162 adj.
undisputed
473 adj.
manifest 522 adj.
incontinent
impotent 161 adj.
intemperate
943 adj.
sensual 944 adj.
incontrovertible
undisputed
473 adj.

inconvenient
ill-timed 138 adj.
inexpedient
643 adj.
difficult 700 adj.
inconvertible
unchangeable
153 adj.
incorporate
join 45 vb.
combine 50 vb.
comprise 78 vb.
absorb 299 vb.
manifest 522 vb.
incorporating
inclusive 78 adj.
incorporeal
insubstantial 4 adj.
immaterial
320 adj.
rare 325 adj.
incorrect
illogical 477 adj.
inexact 495 adj.
incorrigible
obstinate 602 adj.
wilful 602 adj.
habituated 610 adj.
unpromising
853 adj.
impenitent
940 adj.
incorruptible
disinterested
931 adj.
pure 950 adj.
increase
augment 36 vb.
grow 36 vb.
increase 36 n.
product 164 n.
expand 197 vb.
aggravate 832 vb.
incredible
prodigious 32 adj.
unusual 84 adj.
improbable
472 adj.
wonderful 864 adj.
incredulous, be
disbelieve 486 vb.
increment
increase 36 n.
increment 36 n.
addition 38 n.
adjunct 40 n.
extra 40 n.

expansion 197 n.
incentive 612 n.
benefit 615 n.
reward 962 n.
incriminate
blame 924 vb.
accuse 928 vb.
incubate
generate 167 vb.
breed stock 369 vb.
mature 669 vb.
incubator
hospital 658 n.
preserver 666 n.
incubus
demon 970 n.
inculcate
educate 534 vb.
inculpate
blame 924 vb.
incumbent
resident 191 n.
weighty 322 adj.
beneficiary 776 n.
possessor 776 n.
obligatory 917 adj.
cleric 986 n.
incumbent, be
be one's duty
917 vb.
incur
meet with 154 vb.
be liable 180 vb.
acquire 771 vb.
incurable
deadly 362 adj.
obstinate 602 adj.
bad 645 adj.
sick 651 adj.
unpromising
853 adj.
incurious
incurious 454 adj.
incursion
ingress 297 n.
attack 712 n.
warfare 718 n.
indebted
grateful 907 adj.
indecent
not nice 645 adj.
vulgar 847 adj.
disreputable
867 adj.
vicious 934 adj.
impure 951 adj.

indecisive
uncertain 474 adj.
irresolute 601 adj.
indecorous
vulgar 847 adj.
indeed
truly 494 adv.
indefatigable
industrious
678 adj.
indefensible
heinous 934 adj.
indefinable
unspeakable
32 adj.
inexpressible
517 adj.
indefinite
general 79 adj.
infinite 107 adj.
indistinct 444 adj.
unclear 568 adj.
indefinite article
part of speech
564 n.
indelible
fixed 153 adj.
remembered
505 adj.
indelicate
vulgar 847 adj.
indemnify
compensate 31 vb.
give security
767 vb.
restitute 787 vb.
atone 941 vb.
reward 962 vb.
indemnity
security 767 n.
restitution 787 n.
pay 804 n.
payment 804 n.
forgiveness 909 n.
atonement 941 n.
indent
crinkle 251 vb.
make concave
255 vb.
roughen 259 vb.
notch 260 n.
notch 260 vb.
require 627 vb.
requirement 627 n.
demand 737 vb.
contract 765 vb.

indentation
gap 201 n.
angularity 247 n.
convolution 251 n.
concavity 255 n.
notch 260 n.
indenture
compact 765 n.
title deed 767 n.
independence
unrelatedness 10 n.
independence
744 n.
wealth 800 n.
nonliability 919 n.
Independence Day
anniversary 141 n.
special day 876 n.
independent
unrelated 10 adj.
volitional 595 adj.
free 744 adj.
free person 744 n.
independent
744 adj.
indescribable
unspeakable
32 adj.
wonderful 864 adj.
indestructible
existing 1 adj.
lasting 113 adj.
unchangeable
153 adj.
strong 162 adj.
hard 326 adj.
tough 329 adj.
indeterminate
uncertain 474 adj.
index
class 62 vb.
numerical element
85 n.
list 87 n.
list 87 vb.
finger 378 n.
gauge 465 n.
guidebook 524 n.
indicate 547 vb.
indication 547 n.
indicator 547 n.
mark 547 vb.
record 548 n.
record 548 vb.
edition 589 n.
india rubber
elasticity 328 n.

india summer
summer 128 n.
autumn 129 n.
weather 340 n.
heat 379 n.
palmy days 730 n.
indicate
indicate 547 vb.
indication
indication 547 n.
indicator
signal light 420 n.
testing agent
461 n.
witness 466 n.
indicator 547 n.
indict
indict 928 vb.
indictment
accusation 928 n.
indifferent
ignorant 491 adj.
not bad 644 adj.
indifferent 860 adj.
indigenous
intrinsic 5 adj.
native 191 adj.
indigent
poor 801 adj.
poor person 801 n.
indigestible
tough 329 adj.
indigestion
digestive disorders
651 n.
indignant
angry 891 adj.
resentful 891 adj.
indignity
indignity 921 n.
indigo
pigment 425 n.
blue 435 adj.
blue pigment
435 n.
indirect
unclear 568 adj.
prolix 570 adj.
roundabout
626 adj.
indirectly
round about
626 adv.
indiscernible
invisible 444 adj.

indiscipline
disobedience
738 n.
rashness 857 n.
undutifulness
918 n.
intemperance
943 n.
indiscreet
indiscriminating
464 adj.
unwise 499 adj.
informative
524 adj.
clumsy 695 adj.
rash 857 adj.
indiscriminate
indiscriminate
464 adj.
indispensable
intrinsic 5 adj.
necessary 596 adj.
required 627 adj.
important 638 adj.
indisposed
unwilling 598 adj.
sick 651 adj.
suffering 825 adj.
indissoluble
tied 45 adj.
indissoluble
324 adj.
indistinct
amorphous
244 adj.
dim 419 adj.
shadowy 419 adj.
indistinct 444 adj.
indistinguishable
identical 13 adj.
equivalent 28 adj.
invisible 444 adj.
individual
unrelated 10 adj.
nonuniform 17 adj.
original 21 adj.
special 80 adj.
one 88 adj.
unit 88 n.
person 371 n.
individualist
free person 744 n.
indivisible
simple 44 adj.
cohesive 48 adj.
indivisible 52 adj.
dense 324 adj.

indoctrinate
 convince 485 vb.
 educate 534 vb.
 teach 534 vb.
indolent
 lazy 679 adj.
indomitable
 strong 162 adj.
 resolute 599 adj.
 resisting 715 adj.
 courageous
  855 adj.
indoor
 interior 224 adj.
indoors
 inside 224 adv.
 interiority 224 n.
indubitable
 undisputed
  473 adj.
induce
 cause 156 vb.
 induce 612 vb.
induct
 reason 475 vb.
 commission
  751 vb.
inductance
 electricity 160 n.
induction
 electricity 160 n.
 teaching 534 n.
 mandate 751 n.
 holy orders 985 n.
inductive
 rational 475 adj.
indulge
 be lax 734 vb.
 be lenient 736 vb.
 please 826 vb.
 love 887 vb.
 pet 889 vb.
indulge in
 do 676 vb.
indulgent
 lenient 736 adj.
 permitting 756 adj.
 benevolent 897 adj.
 intemperate
  943 adj.
indulge oneself
 be selfish 932 vb.
 be intemperate
  943 vb.
 be sensual 944 vb.
industrial action
 strike 145 n.

industrialist
 producer 164 n.
industrialization
 business 622 n.
industrious
 industrious
  678 adj.
industry
 production 164 n.
 business 622 n.
 vocation 622 n.
 assiduity 678 n.
 labour 682 n.
inebriated
 drunk 949 adj.
inedible
 tough 329 adj.
 unsavoury 391 adj.
 insalubrious
  653 adj.
ineffable
 unspeakable
  32 adj.
 inexpressible
  517 adj.
 wonderful 864 adj.
 divine 965 adj.
ineffective
 powerless 161 adj.
 unproductive
  172 adj.
 feeble 572 adj.
 useless 641 adj.
ineffectual
 powerless 161 adj.
 useless 641 adj.
 unskilful 695 adj.
inefficacious
 powerless 161 adj.
inefficient
 powerless 161 adj.
 useless 641 adj.
 bad 645 adj.
 unskilful 695 adj.
inelegant
 inelegant 576 adj.
 dull 840 adj.
ineligible
 unapt 25 adj.
inept
 irrelevant 10 adj.
 unapt 25 adj.
 powerless 161 adj.
 inexpedient
  643 adj.
 unskilful 695 adj.

inequality
 inequality 29 n.
inequity
 injustice 914 n.
ineradicable
 fixed 153 adj.
inert
 inert 175 adj.
 insensible 375 adj.
 incurious 454 adj.
inertia
 energy 160 n.
 inertness 175 n.
 counteraction
  182 n.
 slowness 278 n.
 inaction 677 n.
 inactivity 679 n.
 laxity 734 n.
 moral insensibility
  820 n.
 indifference 860 n.
inescapable
 impending 155 adj.
 necessary 596 adj.
 obligatory 917 adj.
inestimable
 valuable 644 adj.
 of value 811 adj.
inevitable
 impending 155 adj.
 certain 473 adj.
 necessary 596 adj.
 compelling
  740 adj.
 unpromising
  853 adj.
inexact
 inexact 495 adj.
 feeble 572 adj.
inexcusable
 wrong 914 adj.
 heinous 934 adj.
inexhaustible
 multitudinous
  104 adj.
 infinite 107 adj.
 plentiful 635 adj.
inexorable
 certain 473 adj.
 necessary 596 adj.
 resolute 599 adj.
 obstinate 602 adj.
 severe 735 adj.
 pitiless 906 adj.
inexpensive
 cheap 812 adj.

inexperienced
 ignorant 491 adj.
 foolish 499 adj.
 unhabituated
  611 adj.
 unskilled 695 adj.
 innocent 935 adj.
inexpert
 ignorant 491 adj.
 unskilled 695 adj.
inexplicable
 unusual 84 adj.
 unintelligible
  517 adj.
inexpressible
 inexpressible
  517 adj.
inextinguishable
 unchangeable
  153 adj.
 violent 176 adj.
inextricable
 firm 45 adj.
 tied 45 adj.
 cohesive 48 adj.
 complex 61 adj.
 impracticable
  470 adj.
 difficult 700 adj.
infallible
 certain 473 adj.
 accurate 494 adj.
 perfect 646 adj.
 ecclesiastical
  985 adj.
infamous
 manifest 522 adj.
 discreditable
  867 adj.
 disreputable
  867 adj.
 dishonest 930 adj.
infamy
 disrepute 867 n.
 wickedness 934 n.
infancy
 beginning 68 n.
 nonage 130 n.
 youth 130 n.
 helplessness 161 n.
infant
 beginning 68 adj.
 young 130 adj.
 child 132 n.
 weakling 163 n.
 descendant 170 n.

infanticide
homicide 362 n.
infantile
foolish 499 adj.
infantry
infantry 722 n.
infarction
closure 264 n.
cardiovascular disease 651 n.
infatuated
misjudging
481 adj.
credulous 487 adj.
crazy 503 adj.
enamoured
887 adj.
infect
transfer 272 vb.
infiltrate 297 vb.
motivate 612 vb.
make unclean
649 vb.
impair 655 vb.
excite 821 vb.
infection
mixture 43 n.
transference 272 n.
infection 651 n.
plague 651 n.
infectious
harmful 645 adj.
diseased 651 adj.
infectious 653 adj.
dangerous 661 adj.
infective
infectious 653 adj.
infecundity
unproductiveness
172 n.
infer
assume 471 vb.
reason 475 vb.
demonstrate
478 vb.
interpret 520 vb.
imply 523 vb.
inference
sequence 65 n.
reasoning 475 n.
demonstration
478 n.
judgment 480 n.
hint 524 n.
inferior
be inferior 35 vb.
inferior 35 adj.

inferior 35 n.
inferiority
inferiority 35 n.
badness 645 n.
inferiority complex
personality disorder 503 n.
jealousy 911 n.
infernal
deep 211 adj.
damnable 645 adj.
cruel 898 adj.
heinous 934 adj.
wicked 934 adj.
diabolic 969 adj.
inferno
turmoil 61 n.
hell 972 n.
infertile
impotent 161 adj.
unproductive
172 adj.
infestation
crowd 74 n.
annoyance 827 n.
infidel
unbeliever 486 n.
heathen 974 n.
heathenish 974 adj.
impious person
980 n.
profane 980 adj.
infidelity
perfidy 930 n.
illicit love 951 n.
infilling
structure 331 n.
infiltrate
infiltrate 297 vb.
pass 305 vb.
infinite
infinite 107 adj.
infinitely
greatly 32 vb.
infinitely 107 adv.
infinitesimal
small 33 adj.
infinite space
infinity 107 n.
infinity
infinity 107 n.
infirm
weakly 163 adj.
unhealthy 651 adj.
frail 934 adj.
infirmary
hospital 658 n.

infirmity
old age 131 n.
weakness 163 n.
ill health 651 n.
illness 651 n.
vice 934 n.
infix
add 38 vb.
educate 534 vb.
part of speech
564 n.
inflame
invigorate 174 vb.
heat 381 vb.
excite 821 vb.
aggravate 832 vb.
inflamed
violent 176 adj.
hot 379 adj.
diseased 651 adj.
inflammable
heating 381 adj.
dangerous 661 adj.
excitable 822 adj.
irascible 892 adj.
inflammation
heat 379 n.
burning 381 n.
ulcer 651 n.
painfulness 827 n.
inflate
augment 36 vb.
enlarge 197 vb.
blow up 352 vb.
overestimate
482 vb.
exaggerate 546 vb.
praise 923 vb.
inflation
increase 36 n.
dilation 197 n.
blowing 352 n.
exaggeration
546 n.
finance 797 n.
dearness 811 n.
inflect
voice 577 vb.
inflexible
unchangeable
153 adj.
straight 249 adj.
rigid 326 adj.
resolute 599 adj.
obstinate 602 adj.
severe 735 adj.
pitiless 906 adj.

inflexion
adjunct 40 n.
sequel 67 n.
extremity 69 n.
change 143 n.
curvature 248 n.
word 559 n.
grammar 564 n.
part of speech
564 n.
pronunciation
577 n.
inflict
be severe 735 vb.
compel 740 vb.
inflorescence
flower 366 n.
influence
influence 178 n.
influence 178 vb.
importance 638 n.
manage 689 vb.
spell 983 n.
influential
influential 178 adj.
influenza
infection 651 n.
influx
ingress 297 n.
info
information 524 n.
inform
inform 524 vb.
inform against
inform 524 vb.
accuse 928 vb.
indict 928 vb.
informal
lax 734 adj.
nonobservant
769 adj.
illegal 954 adj.
informal dress
informal dress
228 n.
informality
laxity 734 n.
scope 744 n.
nonobservance
769 n.
informant
witness 466 n.
informant 524 n.
informatics
information 524 n.
information
erudition 490 n.

information 524 n.
accusation 928 n.
informative
expressive 516 adj.
informative
524 adj.
informer
secret service
459 n.
informer 524 n.
infraction
nonconformity
84 n.
disobedience
738 n.
undueness 916 n.
undutifulness
918 n.
infra dig
degrading 867 adj.
infrangible
tough 329 adj.
infrared radiation
radiation 417 n.
infrastructure
base 214 n.
frame 218 n.
structure 331 n.
infrequent
infrequent 140 adj.
infringement
nonconformity
84 n.
overstepping 306 n.
opposition 704 n.
attack 712 n.
disobedience
738 n.
nonobservance
769 n.
borrowing 785 n.
undueness 916 n.
lawbreaking 954 n.
infuriate
make mad 503 vb.
enrage 891 vb.
infuse
educate 534 vb.
infusion
a mixture 43 n.
mixture 43 n.
tincture 43 n.
reception 299 n.
draught 301 n.
insertion 303 n.
solution 337 n.
medicine 658 n.

tonic 658 n.
ingenious
imaginative
513 adj.
skilful 694 adj.
cunning 698 adj.
ingenue
acting 594 n.
innocent 935 n.
ingenuous
veracious 540 adj.
artless 699 adj.
honourable
929 adj.
trustworthy
929 adj.
ingest
absorb 299 vb.
eat 301 vb.
inglenook
home 192 n.
inglorious
inglorious 867 adj.
dishonest 930 adj.
ingrained
intrinsic 5 adj.
combined 50 adj.
fixed 153 adj.
habitual 610 adj.
with affections
817 adj.
ingrate
ingratitude 908 n.
ingratiate oneself
be servile 879 vb.
ingratitude
ingratitude 908 n.
ingredient
adjunct 40 n.
tincture 43 n.
part 53 n.
component 58 adj.
component 58 n.
element 319 n.
ingredients
contents 193 n.
ingress
ingress 297 n.
ingrown
firm 45 adj.
interior 224 adj.
inhabit
be present 189 vb.
dwell 192 vb.
possess 773 vb.
inhabitant
dweller 191 n.

inhalation
reception 299 n.
respiration 352 n.
inhale
absorb 299 vb.
breathe 352 vb.
smoke 388 vb.
smell 394 vb.
inharmonious
discordant 411 adj.
inherent
intrinsic 5 adj.
component 58 adj.
included 78 adj.
inherit
be intrinsic 5 vb.
come after 65 vb.
reproduce 166 vb.
inherit 771 vb.
receive 782 vb.
inheritance
sequel 67 n.
posterity 170 n.
acquisition 771 n.
possession 773 n.
dower 777 n.
transfer 780 n.
receiving 782 n.
receipt 807 n.
inhibit
counteract 182 vb.
obstruct 702 vb.
restrain 747 vb.
inhibition
hindrance 702 n.
prohibition 757 n.
inhospitable
unsociable 883 adj.
unkind 898 adj.
inhuman
harmful 645 adj.
impassive 820 adj.
cruel 898 adj.
unkind 898 adj.
inhumanity
inhumanity 898 n.
misanthropy 902 n.
inhume
inter 364 vb.
inimical
hostile 881 adj.
inimitable
inimitable 21 adj.
iniquitous
evil 616 adj.
unjust 914 adj.
wrong 914 adj.

wicked 934 adj.
initial
beginning 68 n.
first 68 adj.
sign 547 vb.
spell 558 vb.
initials
label 547 n.
initiate
auspicate 68 vb.
initiate 68 vb.
admit 299 vb.
train 534 vb.
learner 538 n.
initiative
beginning 68 n.
vigorousness 174 n.
willingness 597 n.
restlessness 678 n.
inject
pierce 263 vb.
irrigate 341 vb.
doctor 658 vb.
injection
insertion 303 n.
medicine 658 n.
injudicious
unwise 499 adj.
inexpedient
643 adj.
rash 857 adj.
injunction
requirement 627 n.
precept 693 n.
command 737 n.
prohibition 757 n.
legal process 959 n.
injure
weaken 163 vb.
harm 645 vb.
impair 655 vb.
hurt 827 vb.
blemish 845 vb.
be malevolent
898 vb.
do wrong 914 adj.
injury
evil 616 n.
badness 645 n.
impairment 655 n.
wound 655 n.
resentment 891 n.
vice 934 n.
guilty act 936 n.
penalty 963 n.
injustice
injustice 914 n.

INK

wrong 914 n.
guilty act 936 n.
ink
blacken 428 vb.
black thing 428 n.
inkling
knowledge 490 n.
hint 524 n.
inky
dark 418 adj.
black 428 adj.
inlaid work
chequer 437 n.
inland
interior 224 adj.
interiority 224 n.
land 344 n.
inlay
line 227 vb.
insert 303 vb.
chequer 437 n.
variegate 437 vb.
decorate 844 vb.
ornamental art 844 n.
inlet
entrance 68 n.
gap 201 n.
cavity 255 n.
way in 297 n.
gulf 345 n.
inmate
resident 191 n.
inmost thoughts
thought 449 n.
inn
inn 192 n.
innards
insides 224 n.
innate
genetic 5 adj.
inner
interior 224 adj.
inner being
essence 1 n.
spirit 447 n.
inner city
housing 192 n.
innermost
interior 224 adj.
innings
period 110 n.
innkeeper
caterer 633 n.
innocence
ignorance 491 n.
innocence 935 n.

INO

purity 950 n.
innocuous
moderate 177 adj.
innocent 935 adj.
innovation
originality 21 n.
beginning 68 n.
newness 126 n.
change 143 n.
production 164 n.
innovative
modern 126 adj.
new 126 adj.
enterprising 672 adj.
innuendo
latency 523 n.
hint 524 n.
censure 924 n.
detraction 926 n.
innumerable
many 104 adj.
multitudinous 104 adj.
infinite 107 adj.
innumerate
uninstructed 491 adj.
inoculate
combine 50 vb.
implant 303 vb.
doctor 658 vb.
safeguard 660 vb.
inoffensive
humble 872 adj.
amiable 884 adj.
innocent 935 adj.
inoperable
deadly 362 adj.
sick 651 adj.
unpromising 853 adj.
inoperative
powerless 161 adj.
unproductive 172 adj.
quiescent 266 adj.
useless 641 adj.
nonactive 677 adj.
inopportune
inopportune 138 adj.
inexpedient 643 adj.
inordinate
exorbitant 32 adj.

INS

input
data processing 86 n.
record 548 vb.
requirement 627 n.
inquest
inquest 364 n.
enquiry 459 n.
legal trial 959 n.
inquisition
enquiry 459 n.
interrogation 459 n.
severity 735 n.
legal trial 959 n.
inquisitive
inquisitive 453 adj.
inquisitor
questioner 459 n.
tyrant 735 n.
inroad
ingress 297 n.
arrogation 916 n.
inrush
ingress 297 n.
insalubrious
insalubrious 653 adj.
ins and outs of, the
particulars 80 n.
insane
mentally disordered 503 adj.
insanitary
unclean 649 adj.
insalubrious 653 adj.
insanity
absence of intellect 448 n.
mental disorder 503 n.
insatiable
greedy 859 adj.
gluttonous 947 adj.
inscription
obsequies 364 n.
indication 547 n.
monument 548 n.
record 548 n.
phrase 563 n.
script 586 n.
description 590 n.
inscrutable
unintelligible 517 adj.
impassive 820 adj.

INS

inexcitable 823 adj.
serious 834 adj.
insect
animal 365 n.
insect 365 n.
cad 938 n.
insecticide
killer 362 n.
prophylactic 658 n.
poison 659 n.
insectivorous
feeding 301 adj.
insecure
unsafe 661 adj.
insemination
propagation 167 n.
insensate
thick-skinned 820 adj.
insensible
insensible 375 adj.
insensitive
insensible 375 adj.
unfeeling 375 adj.
indiscriminating 464 adj.
inelegant 576 adj.
impassive 820 adj.
thick-skinned 820 adj.
ill-bred 847 adj.
insentient
insensible 375 adj.
inseparable
intrinsic 5 adj.
firm 45 adj.
cohesive 48 adj.
indivisible 52 adj.
concomitant 89 n.
near 200 adj.
friendly 880 adj.
insert
interjection 231 n.
insert 303 vb.
insertion 303 n.
the press 528 n.
insertion
adjunct 40 n.
piece 53 n.
insertion 303 n.
advertisement 528 n.
inset
insert 303 vb.
insertion 303 n.
edition 589 n.

ornamental art
844 n.
inshore
near 200 adj.
inside
contents 193 n.
inside 224 adv.
interior 224 adj.
interiority 224 n.
imprisoned
747 adj.
captive 750 adj.
inside information
information 524 n.
inside job
plot 623 n.
insider trading or
dealing
plot 623 n.
insides
component 58 n.
insides 224 n.
insidious
occult 523 adj.
evil 616 adj.
cunning 698 adj.
dishonest 930 adj.
insight
intellect 447 n.
discrimination
463 n.
intuition 476 n.
knowledge 490 n.
imagination 513 n.
interpretation
520 n.
insignia
badge 547 n.
See **heraldry**
insignificant
inconsiderable
33 adj.
meaningless
515 adj.
unimportant
639 adj.
insincere
hypocritical
541 adj.
affected 850 adj.
flattering 925 adj.
dishonest 930 adj.
insinuate
introduce 231 vb.
imply 523 vb.
hint 524 vb.

inform 524 vb.
See **hint**
detract 926 vb.
insinuate oneself
enter 297 vb.
flatter 925 vb.
insipid
weak 163 adj.
tasteless 387 adj.
feeble 572 adj.
tedious 838 adj.
dull 840 adj.
insist
emphasize 532 vb.
be resolute 599 vb.
be obstinate
602 vb.
contend 716 vb.
compel 740 vb.
insistent
assertive 532 adj.
forceful 571 adj.
resolute 599 adj.
commanding
737 adj.
insist on
qualify 468 vb.
give terms 766 vb.
insolent
insolent 878 adj.
discourteous
885 adj.
insoluble
indissoluble
324 adj.
impracticable
470 adj.
puzzling 517 adj.
insolvent
poor 801 adj.
poor person 801 n.
nonpaying 805 adj.
insomnia
restlessness 678 n.
insouciant
apathetic 820 adj.
indifferent 860 adj.
inspect
scan 438 vb.
inspection
inspection 438 n.
surveillance 457 n.
inspector
spectator 441 n.
enquirer 459 n.
estimator 480 n.
manager 690 n.

inspiration
causation 156 n.
influence 178 n.
respiration 352 n.
intuition 476 n.
intelligence 498 n.
imagination 513 n.
diffuseness 570 n.
spontaneity 609 n.
contrivance 623 n.
warm feeling
818 n.
excitation 821 n.
revelation 975 n.
piety 979 n.
inspire
cause 156 vb.
influence 178 vb.
incite 612 vb.
animate 821 vb.
make pious 979 vb.
instability
changeableness
152 n.
weakness 163 n.
excitability 822 n.
install
place 187 vb.
commission
751 vb.
dignify 866 vb.
installation
location 187 n.
celebration 876 n.
holy orders 985 n.
instance
example 83 n.
exemplify 83 vb.
instant
instant 116 n.
instantaneous
116 adj.
present 121 adj.
impending 155 adj.
ready-made
669 adj.
instantaneous
instantaneous
116 adj.
instead
instead 150 adv.
instep
foot 214 n.
curve 248 n.
instigate
incite 612 vb.
induce 612 vb.

instil
mix 43 vb.
combine 50 vb.
educate 534 vb.
instinct
intellect 447 n.
absence of thought
450 n.
empiricism 461 n.
intuition 476 n.
necessity 596 n.
spontaneity 609 n.
habit 610 n.
nondesign 618 n.
feeling 818 n.
instinctive
intrinsic 5 adj.
intuitive 476 adj.
involuntary
596 adj.
spontaneous
609 adj.
institute
cause 156 vb.
produce 164 vb.
academy 539 n.
corporation 708 n.
institution
beginning 68 n.
practice 610 n.
law 953 n.
institutionalize
make uniform
16 vb.
instruct
inform 524 vb.
educate 534 vb.
command 737 vb.
instruction
culture 490 n.
information 524 n.
teaching 534 n.
advice 691 n.
precept 693 n.
instructions
command 737 n.
instructive
influential 178 adj.
informative
524 adj.
educational
534 adj.
instrument
instrument 628 n.
title deed 767 n.
instrumental
musical 412 adj.

instrumental
628 adj.
instrumentalist
instrumentalist
413 n.
instrumentation
composition 56 n.
melody 410 n.
music 412 n.
musical piece
412 n.
instrumentality
628 n.
insubordinate
disobedient
738 adj.
disrespectful
921 adj.
insubstantial
insubstantial 4 adj.
insufferable
intolerable 827 adj.
insufficient
insufficient
636 adj.
insular
unrelated 10 adj.
separate 46 adj.
alone 88 adj.
narrow-minded
481 adj.
insulate
set apart 46 vb.
cover 226 vb.
line 227 vb.
be hot 379 vb.
heat 381 vb.
safeguard 660 vb.
insulated
heated 381 adj.
insulation
lining 227 n.
insulin
drug 658 n.
insult
annoyance 827 n.
hurt 827 vb.
slur 867 n.
sauciness 878 n.
be rude 885 vb.
rudeness 885 n.
huff 891 vb.
resentment 891 n.
scurrility 899 n.
indignity 921 n.
not respect 921 vb.
calumny 926 n.

insuperable
impracticable
470 adj.
difficult 700 adj.
insupportable
intolerable 827 adj.
insurance
protection 660 n.
promise 764 n.
security 767 n.
caution 858 n.
insurance policy
title deed 767 n.
insure
prepare 669 vb.
promise 764 vb.
contract 765 vb.
give security
767 vb.
be cautious 858 vb.
insurgent
revolter 738 n.
insurmountable
impracticable
470 adj.
insurrection
resistance 715 n.
revolt 738 n.
intact
intact 52 adj.
undamaged
646 adj.
safe 660 adj.
intaglio
mould 23 n.
concavity 255 n.
sculpture 554 n.
ornamental art
844 n.
intake
size 195 n.
ingress 297 n.
reception 299 n.
requirement 627 n.
intangible
unreal 2 adj.
immaterial
320 adj.
integer
whole 52 n.
number 85 n.
unit 88 n.
integral
intrinsic 5 adj.
whole 52 adj.
complete 54 adj.
numerical 85 adj.

numerical element
85 n.
integrate
combine 50 vb.
make complete
54 vb.
integrated circuit
electronics 160 n.
integration
mixture 43 n.
combination 50 n.
whole 52 n.
completeness 54 n.
inclusion 78 n.
unity 88 n.
integrity
whole 52 n.
probity 929 n.
virtue 933 n.
integument
layer 207 n.
exteriority 223 n.
skin 226 n.
intellect
intellect 447 n.
intellectual
mental 447 adj.
intellectual 492 n.
wise 498 adj.
proficient person
696 n.
intelligence
secret service
459 n.
intelligence 498 n.
information 524 n.
news 529 n.
intelligence quotient
intellect 447 n.
intelligence 498 n.
intelligent
intelligent 498 adj.
intelligentsia
intellectual 492 n.
intelligible
intelligible 516 adj.
intemperate
violent 176 adj.
vicious 934 adj.
intemperate
943 adj.
intend
intend 617 vb.
intended
impending 155 adj.
expected 507 adj.
volitional 595 adj.

loved one 887 n.
intense
great 32 adj.
vigorous 174 adj.
florid 425 adj.
feeling 818 adj.
fervent 818 adj.
intensify
augment 36 vb.
invigorate 174 vb.
enlarge 197 vb.
animate 821 vb.
aggravate 832 vb.
intensity
degree 27 n.
greatness 32 n.
vigorousness 174 n.
light 417 n.
hue 425 n.
intensive
increasing 36 adj.
word 559 n.
part of speech
564 n.
intensive care unit
hospital 658 n.
intent
attentive 455 adj.
intention 617 n.
intention
motive 612 n.
intention 617 n.
prayers 981 n.
intentional
volitional 595 adj.
intent upon
resolute 599 adj.
inter
correlative 12 adj.
inter 364 vb.
interact
correlate 12 vb.
inter alia
among 43 adv.
intercede
interfere 231 vb.
deprecate 762 vb.
desire 859 vb.
forgive 909 vb.
intercede for
mediate 720 vb.
intercept
interfere 231 vb.
converge 293 vb.
hear 415 vb.
screen 421 vb.
be curious 453 vb.

hinder 702 vb.
obstruct 702 vb.
take 786 vb.
intercession
aid 703 n.
mediation 720 n.
deprecation 762 n.
prayers 981 n.
interchange
interchange 151 n.
interchange
151 vb.
crossing 222 n.
interchangeable
correlative 12 adj.
identical 13 adj.
equivalent 28 adj.
substituted 150 adj.
intercom
telecommunication
531 n.
intercommunication
union 45 n.
contiguity 202 n.
interlocution
584 n.
intercourse
union 45 n.
interdict
prohibition 757 n.
interest
be related 9 vb.
relation 9 n.
extra 40 n.
product 164 n.
topic 452 n.
curiosity 453 n.
attention 455 n.
attract notice
455 vb.
motivate 612 vb.
benefit 615 n.
importance 638 n.
activity 678 n.
gain 771 n.
estate 777 n.
interest 803 n.
receipt 807 n.
impress 821 vb.
please 826 vb.
dueness 915 n.
interesting
pleasurable
826 adj.
interest oneself in
be active 678 vb.

interests
affairs 154 n.
interface
contiguity 202 n.
interfere
derange 63 vb.
counteract 182 vb.
interfere 231 vb.
be curious 453 vb.
meddle 678 vb.
obstruct 702 vb.
prohibit 757 vb.
interfere with
debauch 951 vb.
interior
component 58 n.
interior 224 adj.
interiority 224 n.
land 344 n.
art subject 553 n.
interior decoration
ornamental art
844 n.
interject
add 38 vb.
discontinue 72 vb.
interjection
addition 38 n.
interjection 231 n.
reception 299 n.
part of speech
564 n.
speech 579 n.
allocution 583 n.
interlaced
crossed 222 adj.
interleave
mix 43 vb.
interlocking
correlative 12 adj.
union 45 n.
interloper
intruder 59 n.
interjector 231 n.
interlude
adjunct 40 n.
lull 145 n.
intermarry
wed 894 vb.
intermediary
interjacent 231 adj.
intermediary
231 n.
intermediate
median 30 adj.
middle 70 adj.
interjacent 231 adj.

interment
interment 364 n.
intermezzo
adjunct 40 n.
musical piece
412 n.
interminable
infinite 107 adj.
perpetual 115 adj.
long 203 adj.
intermingle
mix 43 vb.
intermission
interval 201 n.
dramaturgy 594 n.
intermittent
discontinuous
72 adj.
infrequent 140 adj.
periodical 141 adj.
fitful 142 adj.
intern
doctor 658 n.
imprison 747 vb.
internal
intrinsic 5 adj.
interior 224 adj.
internal combustion
engine
machine 630 n.
international
correlative 12 adj.
comprehensive
52 adj.
universal 79 adj.
national 371 adj.
internecine
destructive 165 adj.
murderous 362 adj.
internment
detention 747 n.
interplay
correlate 12 vb.
correlation 12 n.
interchange 151 n.
Interpol
police enquiry
459 n.
interpolation
adjunct 40 n.
mixture 43 n.
interjection 231 n.
insertion 303 n.
interpose
add 38 vb.
discontinue 72 vb.
insert 303 vb.

hinder 702 vb.
mediate 720 vb.
interpret
play music 413 vb.
interpret 520 vb.
interpretation
interpretation
520 n.
acting 594 n.
interregnum
transience 114 n.
government 733 n.
interrogation
interrogation
459 n.
interrogation mark
question 459 n.
interrupt
be incomplete
55 vb.
derange 63 vb.
discontinue 72 vb.
cease 145 vb.
halt 145 vb.
interfere 231 vb.
intrude 297 vb.
distract 456 vb.
be obstructive
702 vb.
be rude 885 vb.
be angry 891 vb.
interruption
inaptitude 25 n.
derangement 63 n.
discontinuity 72 n.
stop 145 n.
interval 201 n.
interjection 231 n.
hindrance 702 n.
rudeness 885 n.
intersection
joint 45 n.
crossing 222 n.
passage 305 n.
access 624 n.
road 624 n.
intersperse
mix 43 vb.
interstice
gap 201 n.
intertwine
mix 43 vb.
tie 45 vb.
interval
degree 27 n.
disunion 46 n.
discontinuity 72 n.

period 110 n.
lull 145 n.
interval 201 n.
space 201 vb.
opening 263 n.
musical note
410 n.
notation 410 n.
dramaturgy 594 n.
repose 683 n.
intervene
discontinue 72 vb.
interfere 231 vb.
lie between 231 vb.
meddle 678 vb.
hinder 702 vb.
obstruct 702 vb.
mediate 720 vb.
prohibit 757 vb.
intervention
discontinuity 72 n.
interjacency 231 n.
passage 305 n.
instrumentality
628 n.
hindrance 702 n.
mediation 720 n.
restriction 747 n.
prohibition 757 n.
trade 791 n.
interview
hear 415 vb.
listening 415 n.
exam 459 n.
interrogate 459 vb.
conference 584 n.
intestinal
interior 224 adj.
intestines
insides 224 n.
in the clear
safe 660 adj.
acquitted 960 adj.
in the flesh
material 319 adj.
alive 360 adj.
in the red
poor 801 adj.
in the red, be
lose 772 vb.
be in debt 803 vb.
in the running for, be
offer oneself
759 vb.
in the same boat
with 89 adv.

in the teeth of
with difficulty
700 adv.
in opposition
704 adv.
in the thick of
between 231 adv.
in the way
near 200 adv.
unwanted 860 adj.
intimacy
relation 9 n.
coition 45 n.
knowledge 490 n.
friendship 880 n.
fellowship 882 n.
love 887 n.
intimate
conjunctive 45 adj.
private 80 adj.
near 200 adj.
interior 224 adj.
knowing 490 adj.
known 490 adj.
hint 524 vb.
inform 524 vb.
close friend 880 n.
friendly 880 adj.
loved one 887 n.
intimation
knowledge 490 n.
hint 524 n.
information 524 n.
news 529 n.
intimidate
oppress 735 vb.
frighten 854 vb.
threaten 900 vb.
intimidation
fear 854 n.
intimidation
854 n.
boasting 877 n.
into
obsessed 455 adj.
intolerable
intolerable 827 adj.
intolerant
biased 481 adj.
harmful 645 adj.
severe 735 adj.
hostile 881 adj.
malevolent
898 adj.
pitiless 906 adj.
orthodox 976 adj.

intonation
sound 398 n.
voice 577 n.
intoxicate
invigorate 174 vb.
excite 821 vb.
delight 826 vb.
intoxication
excitation 821 n.
excitable state
822 n.
intemperance
943 n.
drunkenness 949 n.
intractable
rigid 326 adj.
wilful 602 adj.
difficult 700 adj.
disobedient
738 adj.
intransigent
strong 162 adj.
rigid 326 adj.
resolute 599 adj.
obstinate 602 adj.
intrapreneur
doer 676 n.
intravenous
interior 224 adj.
intricacy
complexity 61 n.
crossing 222 n.
convolution 251 n.
enigma 530 n.
difficulty 700 n.
intricate
tied 45 adj.
complex 61 adj.
intricate 251 adj.
ornamental
844 adj.
intrigue
latency 523 n.
motivate 612 vb.
plot 623 n.
plot 623 vb.
be cunning 698 vb.
sedition 738 n.
impress 821 vb.
love affair 887 n.
illicit love 951 n.
intriguing
cunning 698 adj.
perfidious 930 adj.
intrinsic
intrinsic 5 adj.

introduce
add 38 vb.
come before 64 vb.
initiate 68 vb.
introduce 231 vb.
precede 283 vb.
admit 299 vb.
insert 303 vb.
offer 759 vb.
greet 884 vb.
introduction
prelude 66 n.
beginning 68 n.
reception 299 n.
insertion 303 n.
teaching 534 n.
courteous act
884 n.
introit
vocal music 412 n.
hymn 981 n.
Holy Communion
988 n.
introspective
intrinsic 5 adj.
thoughtful 449 adj.
introverted
intrinsic 5 adj.
unsociable 883 adj.
intrude
intrude 297 vb.
insert 303 vb.
intruder
unrelatedness 10 n.
intruder 59 n.
interjector 231 n.
offender 904 n.
intrusion
interjection 231 n.
ingress 297 n.
overstepping 306 n.
intrusive
unrelated 10 adj.
extraneous 59 adj.
interjacent 231 adj.
intuition
intuition 476 n.
feeling 818 n.
revelation 975 n.
intumescence
dilation 197 n.
inundate
drench 341 vb.
flow 350 vb.
superabound
637 vb.

inure
train 534 vb.
habituate 610 vb.
make ready
669 vb.
invade
congregate 74 vb.
interfere 231 vb.
encroach 306 vb.
attack 712 vb.
go to war 718 vb.
invader
intruder 59 n.
incomer 297 n.
attacker 712 n.
invalid
helplessness 161 n.
powerless 161 adj.
weakling 163 n.
illogical 477 adj.
useless 641 adj.
sick person 651 n.
unwarranted
916 adj.
invalidate
disable 161 vb.
weaken 163 vb.
destroy 165 vb.
confute 479 vb.
negate 533 vb.
abrogate 752 vb.
disentitle 916 vb.
invalided
sick 651 adj.
invalidity
impotence 161 n.
lack of meaning
515 n.
invaluable
profitable 640 adj.
valuable 644 adj.
of value 811 adj.
invariable
identical 13 adj.
uniform 16 adj.
unchangeable
153 adj.
usual 610 adj.
invasion
crowd 74 n.
ingress 297 n.
attack 712 n.
warfare 718 n.
invective
oration 579 n.
oratory 579 n.
scurrility 899 n.

reproach 924 n.
detraction 926 n.
inveigh
curse 899 vb.
criticize 924 vb.
inveigle
ensnare 542 vb.
tempt 612 vb.
invent
initiate 68 vb.
cause 156 vb.
produce 164 vb.
perceive 447 adj.
think 449 vb.
discover 484 vb.
imagine 513 vb.
manifest 522 vb.
be false 541 vb.
fake 541 vb.
plan 623 vb.
invention
beginning 68 n.
causation 156 n.
production 164 n.
idea 451 n.
discovery 484 n.
falsehood 541 n.
fable 543 n.
untruth 543 n.
contrivance 623 n.
inventive
original 21 adj.
new 126 adj.
imaginative
513 adj.
inventor
precursor 66 n.
cause 156 n.
producer 164 n.
detector 484 n.
planner 623 n.
inventory
all 52 n.
arrangement 62 n.
number 86 vb.
list 87 n.
list 87 vb.
contents 193 n.
inverse
contrariety 14 n.
contrary 14 adj.
contraposition
240 n.
opposite 240 adj.
invert
invert 221 vb.

invertebrate
animal 365 adj.
animal 365 n.
coward 856 n.
invest
place 187 vb.
dress 228 vb.
circumscribe
232 vb.
store 632 vb.
commission
751 vb.
lend 784 vb.
speculate 791 vb.
expend 806 vb.
investigate
enquire 459 vb.
investigation
enquiry 459 n.
police enquiry
459 n.
search 459 n.
study 536 n.
investiture
dressing 228 n.
giving 781 n.
investment
dressing 228 n.
store 632 n.
mandate 751 n.
estate 777 n.
giving 781 n.
lending 784 n.
expenditure 806 n.
inveterate
lasting 113 adj.
permanent 144 adj.
habitual 610 adj.
habituated 610 adj.
impenitent
940 adj.
invidious
unpleasant
827 adj.
hateful 888 adj.
invigilate
invigilate 457 vb.
invigilator
spectator 441 n.
keeper 749 n.
invigorate
invigorate 174 vb.
invincible
strong 162 adj.
inviolable
certain 473 adj.
due 915 adj.

invisible
invisible 444 adj.
invitation
reception 299 n.
inducement 612 n.
offer 759 n.
request 761 n.
excitation 821 n.
courteous act
884 n.
invite
admit 299 vb.
incite 612 vb.
command 737 vb.
offer 759 vb.
request 761 vb.
desire 859 vb.
be hospitable
882 vb.
inviting
accessible 289 adj.
pleasurable
826 adj.
invocation
allocution 583 n.
prayers 981 n.
invoice
list 87 n.
demand 737 vb.
account 808 vb.
accounts 808 n.
invoke
entreat 761 vb.
desire 859 vb.
involuntary
intuitive 476 adj.
involuntary
596 adj.
spontaneous
609 adj.
involution
convolution 251 n.
involve
be intrinsic 5 vb.
bedevil 63 vb.
comprise 78 vb.
evidence 466 vb.
make likely
471 vb.
mean 514 vb.
imply 523 vb.
indicate 547 vb.
accuse 928 vb.
involvement
relation 9 n.
union 45 n.
complexity 61 n.

irruption
ingress 297 n.
Islam
religious faith
973 n.
island
region 184 n.
traffic control
305 n.
island 349 n.
seclusion 883 n.
islander
dweller 191 n.
isle
land 344 n.
island 349 n.
isobar
weather 340 n.
isolate
set apart 46 vb.
seclude 883 vb.
isolation
unrelatedness 10 n.
disunion 46 n.
unity 88 n.
seclusion 883 n.
isometrics
exercise 682 n.
isosceles triangle
angular figure
247 n.
isotope
element 319 n.
I-spy
indoor game 837 n.
issue
kinsman 11 n.
subdivision 53 n.
event 154 n.
happen 154 vb.
effect 157 n.
result 157 vb.
posterity 170 n.
egress 298 n.
emerge 298 vb.
outflow 298 n.
flow 350 vb.
topic 452 n.
publish 528 vb.
the press 528 n.
edition 589 n.
reading matter
589 n.
completion 725 n.
coinage 797 n.
mint 797 vb.
litigation 959 n.

isthmus
bond 47 n.
contraction 198 n.
narrowness 206 n.
land 344 n.
bridge 624 n.
it
identity 13 n.
attraction 291 n.
authenticity 494 n.
inducement 612 n.
pleasurableness
826 n.
beauty 841 n.
italic
letter 558 n.
lettering 586 n.
written 586 adj.
print-type 587 n.
italicize
emphasize 532 vb.
itch
agitation 318 n.
tingling 378 n.
skin disease 651 n.
desire 859 n.
item
in addition 38 adv.
part 53 n.
component 58 n.
unit 88 n.
object 319 n.
itemize
specify 80 vb.
list 87 vb.
iteration
duplication 91 n.
repetition 106 n.
itinerant
traveller 268 n.
itinerary
itinerary 267 n.
guidebook 524 n.
ivory
hardness 326 n.
white thing 427 n.
whitish 427 adj.
gem 844 n.
ivory tower
refuge 662 n.
seclusion 883 n.
ivy
tree 366 n.

J

jab
knock 279 n.
insertion 303 n.
touch 378 vb.
wound 655 n.
medicine 658 n.
jabber
empty talk 515 n.
mean nothing
515 vb.
speak 579 vb.
be loquacious
581 vb.
chatter 581 n.
Jabberwocky
rara avis 84 n.
fantasy 513 n.
jabot
neckwear 228 n.
jack
support 218 n.
missile 287 n.
rotator 315 n.
male animal
372 n.
flag 547 n.
tool 630 n.
jackal
mammal 365 n.
dependant 742 n.
toady 879 n.
jackass
fool 501 n.
jackboot
conduct 688 n.
brute force 735 n.
tyrant 735 n.
lawlessness 954 n.
jackdaw
bird 365 n.
jacket
skin 226 n.
jacket 228 n.
bookbinding 589 n.
Jack-in-the-box
plaything 837 n.
jack-of-all-trades
busy person 678 n.
proficient person
696 n.
jackpot
acquisition 771 n.
reward 962 n.
Jacuzzi (tdmk)
vortex 315 n.
water 339 n.

eddy 350 n.
heater 383 n.
ablutions 648 n.
jade
saddle horse 273 n.
female 373 n.
greenness 434 n.
be tedious 838 vb.
gem 844 n.
cause dislike
861 vb.
sate 863 vb.
loose woman
952 n.
jaded
bored 838 adj.
sated 863 adj.
jag
notch 260 vb.
drunkenness 949 n.
jagged
angular 247 adj.
sharp 256 adj.
rough 259 adj.
jaguar
big cat 365 n.
jail
prison 748 n.
jailer
doorkeeper 264 n.
gaoler 749 n.
jalopy
automobile 274 n.
jam
circumstance 8 n.
affix 45 vb.
join 45 vb.
crowd 74 n.
halt 145 vb.
make smaller
198 vb.
be quiescent
266 vb.
viscidity 354 n.
pulpiness 356 n.
sweet thing 392 n.
play music 413 vb.
predicament 700 n.
obstruct 702 vb.
jamb
pillar 218 n.
jamboree
amusement 837 n.
jam in
fill 54 vb.
jam session
dancing 837 n.

jam tomorrow
neverness 109 n.
future state 124 n.
incentive 612 n.
jangle
resound 404 vb.
rasp 407 vb.
discord 411 n.
discord 411 vb.
dissension 709 n.
jar
disagree 25 vb.
misfit 25 n.
vessel 194 n.
agitation 318 n.
give pain 377 vb.
rasp 407 vb.
discord 411 n.
dissension 709 n.
cause dislike
  861 vb.
jargon
speciality 80 n.
absurdity 497 n.
lack of meaning
  515 n.
unintelligibility
  517 n.
language 557 n.
neology 560 n.
slang 560 adj.
jar on
displease 827 vb.
jasmine
yellow 433 adj.
jasper
gem 844 n.
jaundice
yellowness 433 n.
bias 481 n.
digestive disorders
  651 n.
jaunt
land travel 267 n.
amusement 837 n.
jaunty
cheerful 833 adj.
showy 875 adj.
javelin
missile 287 n.
missile weapon
  723 n.
spear 723 n.
jaw
protuberance
  254 n.
empty talk 515 n.

be loquacious
  581 vb.
jaws
stomach 194 n.
orifice 263 n.
jay
bird 365 n.
jazz
music 412 n.
JCB (tdmk)
vehicle 274 n.
jealous
discontented
  829 adj.
hostile 881 adj.
resentful 891 adj.
malevolent
  898 adj.
jealous 911 adj.
jeans
informal dress
  228 n.
trousers 228 n.
jeep
automobile 274 n.
war chariot 274 n.
jeer
deprecate 762 vb.
be discontented
  829 vb.
ridicule 851 vb.
indignity 921 n.
not respect 921 vb.
despise 922 vb.
jejune
feeble 572 adj.
insufficient
  636 adj.
Jekyll and Hyde
multiformity 82 n.
duality 90 n.
jell
thicken 354 vb.
jelly
dessert 301 n.
thicken 354 vb.
viscidity 354 n.
sweet thing 392 n.
jellyfish
weakling 163 n.
marine life 365 n.
coward 856 n.
je ne sais quoi
influence 178 n.
pleasurableness
  826 n.

jeopardy
danger 661 n.
jerk
be rough 259 vb.
move 265 vb.
impel 279 vb.
impulse 279 n.
draw 288 vb.
agitate 318 vb.
agitation 318 n.
ninny 501 n.
cad 938 n.
jerky
discontinuous
  72 adj.
fitful 142 adj.
jeroboam
vessel 194 n.
jerry-built
inferior 35 adj.
flimsy 163 adj.
imperfect 647 adj.
unsafe 661 adj.
bungled 695 adj.
cheap 812 adj.
jersey
textile 222 n.
jersey 228 n.
jest
amuse oneself
  837 vb.
be witty 839 vb.
witticism 839 n.
jet
aircraft 276 n.
propellant 287 n.
outflow 298 n.
emit 300 vb.
ascend 308 vb.
stream 350 n.
black thing 428 n.
gem 844 n.
jetlag
delay 136 n.
airtravel 271 n.
air travel 271 n.
aircraft 276 n.
jet-propelled
speedy 277 adj.
jetsam
transport 272 n.
derelict 779 n.
jet set
aeronaut 271 n.
rich person 800 n.
beau monde 848 n.

jettison
eject 300 vb.
ejection 300 n.
let fall 311 vb.
lighten 323 vb.
relinquish 621 vb.
stop using 674 vb.
not retain 779 vb.
jetty
stable 192 n.
projection 254 n.
shelter 662 n.
jewel
exceller 644 n.
a beauty 841 n.
gem 844 n.
darling 890 n.
favourite 890 n.
jewellery
jewellery 844 n.
Jewish
religious 973 adj.
jib
sail 275 n.
recoil 280 vb.
avoid 620 vb.
deprecate 762 vb.
quake 854 vb.
resent 891 vb.
jib at
refuse 760 vb.
jiffy
instant 116 n.
jig
leap 312 n.
musical piece
  412 n.
dance 837 n.
jiggle
derange 63 vb.
jigsaw puzzle
indoor game 837 n.
jilt
disappoint 509 vb.
fool 542 n.
change one's mind
  603 vb.
recanter 603 n.
relinquish 621 vb.
jingle
resonance 404 n.
resound 404 vb.
advertisement
  528 n.
doggerel 593 n.
jingoism
nation 371 n.

JIN

bellicosity 718 n.
boasting 877 n.
jinn
  mythical being
    970 n.
jinx
  badness 645 n.
  spell 983 n.
jitters
  agitation 318 n.
  nervousness 854 n.
jive
  music 412 n.
  dance 837 n.
  dance 837 vb.
job
  agency 173 n.
  function 622 n.
  job 622 n.
  undertaking 672 n.
  deed 676 n.
  labour 682 n.
  stealing 788 n.
  perfidy 930 n.
jobbing
  barter 791 n.
jobless
  nonactive 677 adj.
jockey
  rider 268 n.
  be cunning 698 vb.
jocular
  merry 833 adj.
  witty 839 adj.
jodhpurs
  trousers 228 n.
joe soap
  common man 30 n.
  everyman 79 n.
  social group 371 n.
  averageness 732 n.
  commoner 869 n.
jog
  be in motion
    265 vb.
  gait 265 n.
  pedestrianism
    267 n.
  walk 267 vb.
  impel 279 vb.
  agitate 318 vb.
  agitation 318 n.
  gesticulate 547 vb.
  gesture 547 n.
  incite 612 vb.
  animate 821 vb.

JOK

amuse oneself
    837 vb.
jogging
  motion 265 n.
  exercise 682 n.
  sport 837 n.
joie de vivre
  cheerfulness 833 n.
join
  accrue 38 vb.
  join 45 vb.
  unite with 45 vb.
  be included 78 vb.
  gap 201 n.
  be contiguous
    202 vb.
  meet 295 vb.
  enter 297 vb.
  join a party
    708 vb.
  marry 894 vb.
join a party
  join a party
    708 vb.
joiner
  artisan 686 n.
join forces
  cooperate 706 vb.
join forces with
  combine 50 vb.
join in
  be active 678 vb.
  cooperate 706 vb.
  participate 775 vb.
  be sociable 882 vb.
joint
  joint 45 n.
  tavern 192 n.
  fold 261 n.
  meat 301 n.
  tobacco 388 n.
  drug-taking 949 n.
jointed
  angular 247 adj.
join up
  go to war 718 vb.
joist
  beam 218 n.
joke
  trickery 542 n.
  be witty 839 vb.
  witticism 839 n.
joker
  misfit 25 n.
  nonconformist
    84 n.
  male 372 n.

JOU

humorist 839 n.
jolie laide
  a beauty 841 n.
jollification
  revel 837 n.
jolly
  fleshy 195 adj.
  merry 833 adj.
jolt
  stimulant 174 n.
  be rough 259 vb.
  impel 279 vb.
  agitate 318 vb.
  agitation 318 n.
  lack of expectation
    508 n.
  incite 612 vb.
  animate 821 vb.
Jonah
  overestimation
    482 n.
  unlucky person
    731 n.
  malcontent 829 n.
  moper 834 n.
joss
  idol 982 n.
joss stick
  scent 396 n.
  ritual object 988 n.
jostle
  be contiguous
    202 vb.
  impel 279 vb.
  obstruct 702 vb.
  fight 716 vb.
  not respect 921 vb.
jot
  small quantity
    33 n.
  trifle 639 n.
jot down
  record 548 vb.
  write 586 vb.
joule
  energy 160 n.
journal
  chronology 117 n.
  journal 528 n.
  the press 528 n.
  record 548 n.
journalism
  publicity 528 n.
  writing 586 n.
journalist
  enquirer 459 n.
  publicizer 528 n.

JUD

news reporter
    529 n.
  chronicler 549 n.
  author 589 n.
journey
  land travel 267 n.
  travel 267 vb.
  passage 305 n.
journeyman
  artisan 686 n.
jousting
  duel 716 n.
jovial
  merry 833 adj.
  sociable 882 adj.
jowl
  laterality 239 n.
joy
  joy 824 n.
joyful
  happy 824 adj.
  merry 833 adj.
joyous
  happy 824 adj.
jubilant
  jubilant 833 adj.
jubilation
  merriment 833 n.
  rejoicing 835 n.
  celebration 876 n.
jubilee
  twenty and over
    99 n.
  period 110 n.
  anniversary 141 n.
  merriment 833 n.
  celebration 876 n.
Judaism
  religious faith
    973 n.
judder
  agitation 318 n.
  be agitated 318 vb.
judge
  estimator 480 n.
  judge 480 vb.
  officer 741 n.
  judge 957 n.
judgment
  intellect 447 n.
  judgment 480 n.
  sagacity 498 n.
  condemnation
    961 n.
  punishment 963 n.
Judgment Day
  tribunal 956 n.

judgment seat
 tribunal 956 n.
judicial
 judicial 480 adj.
judicious
 discriminating
  463 adj.
 judicial 480 adj.
 wise 498 adj.
 advisable 642 adj.
judo
 defence 713 n.
 wrestling 716 n.
jug
 vessel 194 n.
 water 339 n.
 prison 748 n.
juggernaut
 destroyer 168 n.
 flattener 216 n.
 carrier 273 n.
 lorry 274 n.
 idol 982 n.
juggle
 deceive 542 vb.
 be cunning 698 vb.
juggler
 entertainer 594 n.
 slyboots 698 n.
 sorcerer 983 n.
jugular vein
 essential part 5 n.
juice
 fluid 335 n.
 moisture 341 n.
 semiliquidity
  354 n.
 fuel 385 n.
juicy
 new 126 adj.
 soft 327 adj.
 humid 341 adj.
 super 644 adj.
 pleasurable
  826 adj.
jujitsu
 defence 713 n.
 wrestling 716 n.
jujube
 sweet thing 392 n.
jukebox
 gramophone 414 n.
jumble
 medley 43 n.
 disorder 61 n.
 jumble 63 vb.
 deform 244 vb.

jumbo
 giant 195 n.
 large 195 adj.
jumbo jet
 aircraft 276 n.
jump
 interval 201 n.
 gait 265 n.
 fly 271 vb.
 move fast 277 vb.
 spurt 277 n.
 progression 285 n.
 ascent 308 n.
 leap 312 n.
 leap 312 vb.
 agitation 318 n.
 be agitated 318 vb.
 be excited 821 vb.
 be excitable
  822 vb.
 amuse oneself
  837 vb.
 fear 854 vb.
jump at
 be willing 597 vb.
 consent 758 vb.
 desire 859 vb.
jumped-up
 unimportant
  639 adj.
jumper
 dress 228 n.
 jersey 228 n.
 horse 273 n.
jump on the band
  wagon
 do likewise 20 vb.
 conform 83 vb.
 acquiesce 488 vb.
 be in fashion
  848 vb.
 be servile 879 vb.
jump the gun
 do before 119 vb.
 be early 135 vb.
jump the queue
 be disordered
  61 vb.
 come before 64 vb.
 do before 119 vb.
 precede 283 vb.
jump to conclusions
 prejudge 481 vb.
jump to it
 be active 678 vb.
jumpy
 active 678 adj.

 nervous 854 adj.
junction
 joint 45 n.
 union 45 n.
 bond 47 n.
 focus 76 n.
 passage 305 n.
 access 624 n.
 railway 624 n.
 road 624 n.
juncture
 juncture 8 n.
 joint 45 n.
 present time 121 n.
 occasion 137 n.
jungle
 wood 366 n.
junior
 inferior 35 adj.
 inferior 35 n.
 subsequent
  120 adj.
 young 130 adj.
 subject 745 adj.
junk
 sailing ship 275 n.
 reject 607 vb.
 rubbish 641 n.
 drug-taking 949 n.
junket
 dairy product
  301 n.
 meal 301 n.
 milk 301 n.
 amusement 837 n.
 revel 837 n.
 revel 837 vb.
junketing
 revel 837 n.
junk food
 provisions 301 n.
junkie
 the maladjusted
  504 n.
 drug-taking 949 n.
jurisdiction
 jurisdiction 955 n.
jury
 jury 957 n.
just
 veracious 540 adj.
 just 913 adj.
justice
 justice 913 n.
 virtues 933 n.
 judge 957 n.

 divine attribute
  965 n.
justification
 counterevidence
  467 n.
 pretext 614 n.
 forgiveness 909 n.
 dueness 915 n.
 vindication 927 n.
 acquittal 960 n.
justify
 demonstrate
  478 V.
 print 587 vb.
 justify 927 vb.
 acquit 960 vb.
just so
 accurate 494 adj.
jut
 jut 254 vb.
jute
 fibre 208 n.
 textile 222 n.
juvenile
 young 130 adj.
 youngster 132 n.
 feeble 572 adj.
 immature 670 adj.
juvenile delinquent
 low fellow 869 n.
 offender 904 n.
juvenilia
 reading matter
  589 n.
juxtaposition
 contiguity 202 n.
 comparison 462 n.

K

kagoule
 jacket 228 n.
kaleidoscope
 medley 43 n.
 multiformity 82 n.
 changeable thing
  152 n.
 variegation 437 n.
 spectacle 445 n.
kangaroo
 mammal 365 n.
kangaroo court
 lawlessness 954 n.
kaolin
 soil 344 n.
kapok
 fibre 208 n.

lining 227 n.

kaput
  powerless 161 adj.
  dead 361 adj.
  useless 641 adj.
  dilapidated
    655 adj.
  defeated 728 adj.

karate
  defence 713 n.
  wrestling 716 n.

karma
  effect 157 n.
  fate 596 n.

kart
  automobile 274 n.

kayak
  rowing boat 275 n.

kebabs
  dish 301 n.

kedge
  navigate 269 vb.
  draw 288 vb.

kedgeree
  fish food 301 n.

keel
  stabilizer 153 n.
  base 214 n.
  pivot 218 n.
  ship 275 n.

keelhaul
  punish 963 vb.

keen
  keen 174 adj.
  vigorous 174 adj.
  sharp 256 adj.
  inter 364 vb.
  sentient 374 adj.
  cold 380 adj.
  lament 836 n.
  lament 836 vb.
  witty 839 adj.
  condolence 905 n.

keening
  lamentation 836 n.

keep
  recur 139 vb.
  dwell 192 vb.
  dwelling 192 n.
  house 192 n.
  provisions 301 n.
  look after 457 vb.
  store 632 vb.
  provide 633 vb.
  safeguard 660 vb.
  refuge 662 n.
  subvention 703 n.

defend 713 vb.
fort 713 n.
detention 747 n.
observe 768 vb.
retain 778 vb.

keep abreast of
  concur 181 vb.

keep a low profile
  keep secret 525 vb.
  behave 688 vb.

keep an eye on
  safeguard 660 vb.

keep an eye out for
  scan 438 vb.

keep at arm's length
  repel 292 vb.
  avoid 620 vb.
  resist 715 vb.

keep back
  keep secret 525 vb.
  dissuade 613 vb.
  restrain 747 vb.
  retain 778 vb.

keep down
  suppress 165 vb.
  lower 311 vb.

keeper
  keeper 749 n.

keep faith
  keep faith 768 vb.

keep faith with one's
  conscience
  do one's duty
    917 vb.

keep fit
  be healthy 650 vb.

keep going
  go on 146 vb.
  persevere 600 vb.

keep in
  surround 230 vb.
  imprison 747 vb.
  restrain 747 vb.
  retain 778 vb.

keep in step
  conform 83 vb.

keep in touch with
  correspond 588 vb.
  be sociable 882 vb.

keep off
  be distant 199 vb.
  screen 421 vb.
  avoid 620 vb.

keep on
  recur 139 vb.
  stay 144 vb.
  sustain 146 vb.

progress 285 vb.
persevere 600 vb.

keep oneself to one-
  self
  be fastidious
    862 vb.

keep order
  order 60 vb.
  safeguard 660 vb.
  manage 689 vb.
  rule 733 vb.
  restrain 747 vb.

keep out
  exclude 57 vb.
  screen 421 vb.
  obstruct 702 vb.
  restrain 747 vb.
  refuse 760 vb.

keepsake
  reminder 505 n.
  gift 781 n.

keep time
  time 117 vb.
  synchronize
    123 vb.

keep up
  stay 144 vb.
  sustain 146 vb.
  persevere 600 vb.

keep up with
  be equal 28 vb.
  be friendly 880 vb.
  be sociable 882 vb.

keep up with the
  Joneses
  conform 83 vb.
  afford 800 vb.
  be in fashion
    848 vb.

keg
  vat 194 n.

ken
  know 490 vb.
  knowledge 490 n.

kennel
  group 74 n.
  stable 192 n.
  lockup 748 n.

kepi
  headgear 228 n.

kept woman
  kept woman 952 n.

kerb or curb
  edge 234 n.
  limit 236 n.
  road 624 n.

kerfuffle
  commotion 318 n.

kernel
  essential part 5 n.
  middle 70 n.
  focus 76 n.
  centre 225 n.
  chief thing 638 n.

kerosene
  oil 357 n.
  fuel 385 n.

ketchup
  sauce 389 n.

kettle
  pot 194 n.
  heater 383 n.

key
  degree 27 n.
  crucial 137 adj.
  reason why 156 n.
  influential 178 adj.
  opener 263 n.
  stopper 264 n.
  island 349 n.
  key 410 n.
  answer 460 n.
  interpretation
    520 n.
  translation 520 n.
  indication 547 n.
  write 586 vb.
  print 587 vb.
  instrument 628 n.
  important 638 adj.

keyboard
  computerize 86 vb.
  data processing
    86 n.
  musical note
    410 n.
  organ 414 n.
  piano 414 n.

keyed up
  expectant 507 adj.
  prepared 669 adj.
  excited 821 adj.

keyhole
  circle 250 n.
  orifice 263 n.
  window 263 n.

key in
  computerize 86 vb.

keynote
  prototype 23 n.
  rule 81 n.
  musical note
    410 n.

chief thing 638 n.
keypad
  data processing
    86 n.
keystone
  summit 213 n.
  support 218 n.
KGB
  secret service
    459 n.
khaki
  textile 222 n.
  uniform 228 n.
  brown 430 adj.
kibbutz
  farm 370 n.
  joint possession
    775 n.
kick
  vigorousness 174 n.
  impulse 279 n.
  knock 279 n.
  recoil 280 n.
  propel 287 vb.
  propulsion 287 n.
  leap 312 n.
  be agitated 318 vb.
  pungency 388 n.
  hint 524 n.
  gesticulate 547 vb.
  gesture 547 n.
  indication 547 n.
  rejection 607 n.
  oppose 704 vb.
  fight 716 vb.
  disobey 738 vb.
  refuse 760 vb.
  deprecate 762 vb.
  feeling 818 n.
  joy 824 n.
  *corporal punish-
    ment* 963 n.
kick oneself
  regret 830 vb.
kick one's heels
  not act 677 vb.
  be inactive 679 vb.
kick out
  repel 292 vb.
  eject 300 vb.
  reject 607 vb.
  not retain 779 vb.
kicks
  excitation 821 n.
kick the habit
  disaccustom
    611 vb.

kick upstairs
  displace 188 vb.
  ejection 300 n.
  reject 607 vb.
  depose 752 vb.
kid
  child 132 n.
  young creature
    132 n.
  skin 226 n.
  deceive 542 vb.
  fool 542 vb.
  ridicule 851 vb.
kid gloves
  discrimination
    463 n.
  conduct 688 n.
  leniency 736 n.
  good taste 846 n.
kidnap
  ensnare 542 vb.
  arrest 747 vb.
  take away 786 vb.
  steal 788 vb.
kidney
  sort 77 n.
  meat 301 n.
kidney donor
  giver 781 n.
  good giver 813 n.
kidney machine
  hospital 658 n.
kidology
  deception 542 n.
kid's stuff
  easy thing 701 n.
kill
  kill 362 vb.
  prohibit 757 vb.
killer
  destroyer 168 n.
  killer 362 n.
  murderer 362 n.
  ruffian 904 n.
killjoy
  moderator 177 n.
  dissuasion 613 n.
  moper 834 n.
kill oneself
  kill oneself 362 vb.
kill time
  pass time 108 vb.
  be inactive 679 vb.
  amuse oneself
    837 vb.
kiln
  furnace 383 n.

kilo
  weighing 322 n.
kilometre
  long measure
    203 n.
kilt
  shorten 204 vb.
  skirt 228 n.
kimono
  robe 228 n.
kin
  kinsman 11 n.
  breed 77 n.
  genealogy 169 n.
kind
  degree 27 n.
  sort 77 n.
  form 243 n.
  aiding 703 adj.
  amiable 884 adj.
  courteous 884 adj.
  benevolent 897 adj.
kindergarten
  nonage 130 n.
  school 539 n.
kind-hearted
  benevolent 897 adj.
kindle
  cause 156 vb.
  invigorate 174 vb.
  be hot 379 vb.
  kindle 381 vb.
  incite 612 vb.
  feel 818 vb.
  excite 821 vb.
  be excitable
    822 vb.
  get angry 891 vb.
kindliness
  friendliness 880 n.
  courtesy 884 n.
  benevolence 897 n.
kindly
  benevolent 897 adj.
kindness
  leniency 736 n.
  friendliness 880 n.
  courteous act
    884 n.
  courtesy 884 n.
  benevolence 897 n.
kindred
  relative 9 adj.
  akin 11 adj.
  consanguinity
    11 n.
  kinsman 11 n.

kinetics
  motion 265 n.
king
  sovereign 741 n.
  plaything 837 n.
  aristocrat 868 n.
kingdom
  breed 77 n.
  territory 184 n.
  *political organiza-
    tion* 733 n.
kingpin
  bigwig 638 n.
  chief thing 638 n.
  manager 690 n.
king size
  large 195 adj.
  size 195 n.
kink
  complexity 61 n.
  nonconformity
    84 n.
  be curved 248 vb.
  loop 250 n.
  coil 251 n.
  convolution 251 n.
  roughen 259 vb.
  roughness 259 n.
  eccentricity 503 n.
  whim 604 n.
  defect 647 n.
kinky
  abnormal 84 adj.
  undulatory
    251 adj.
kiosk
  pavilion 192 n.
  small house 192 n.
  shop 796 n.
kipper
  dry 342 vb.
  season 388 vb.
  preserve 666 vb.
kippers
  fish food 301 n.
kirk
  church 990 n.
kismet
  fate 596 n.
kiss
  be contiguous
    202 vb.
  touch 378 vb.
  courteous act
    884 n.
  greet 884 vb.
  caress 889 vb.

endearment 889 n.
kit
  accumulation 74 n.
  sort 77 n.
  unit 88 n.
  clothing 228 n.
  viol 414 n.
  equipment 630 n.
kitbag
  bag 194 n.
kitchen
  chamber 194 n.
  cookery 301 n.
  heater 383 n.
  workshop 687 n.
kitchen sink
  sink 649 n.
kitchen-sink drama
  stage play 594 n.
kite
  airship 276 n.
  bird 365 n.
kite-flying
  empiricism 461 n.
  publication 528 n.
  indication 547 n.
kith and kin
  kinsman 11 n.
kit out
  provide 633 vb.
kitsch
  inferiority 35 n.
  art 551 n.
  bad taste 847 n.
kitten
  young creature 132 n.
  weakling 163 n.
  reproduce itself 167 vb.
  cat 365 n.
kittenish
  merry 833 adj.
kitty
  store 632 n.
  association 706 n.
  joint possession 775 n.
kleptomaniac
  neurotic 503 adj.
  neurotic 504 n.
  thieving 788 adj.
  thief 789 n.
knack
  habit 610 n.
  aptitude 694 n.

knackered
  fatigued 684 adj.
knave
  bad person 938 n.
knead
  mix 43 vb.
  form 243 vb.
  soften 327 vb.
knee
  joint 45 n.
  angularity 247 n.
  leg 267 n.
knee-deep
  deep 211 adj.
knee-high to a grass-hopper
  dwarfish 196 adj.
  short 204 adj.
kneel
  stoop 311 vb.
  knuckle under 721 vb.
  be servile 879 vb.
  pay one's respects 884 vb.
  show respect 920 vb.
  be pious 979 vb.
  perform ritual 988 vb.
kneeler
  cushion 218 n.
  church utensil 990 n.
knees-up
  revel 837 n.
knell
  ruin 165 n.
  obsequies 364 n.
  play music 413 vb.
  signal 547 n.
  raise the alarm 665 vb.
  lament 836 n.
knickerbockers
  trousers 228 n.
knickers
  underwear 228 n.
knick-knack
  bauble 639 n.
  finery 844 n.
knife
  cut 46 vb.
  sharp edge 256 n.
  kill 362 vb.
  tool 630 n.
  sidearms 723 n.

knife-edge
  narrowness 206 n.
  edge 234 n.
knight
  rider 268 n.
  cavalry 722 n.
  combatant 722 n.
  plaything 837 n.
  brave person 855 n.
  dignify 866 vb.
  person of repute 866 n.
  person of rank 868 n.
  philanthropist 901 n.
knight errant
  rider 268 n.
  defender 713 n.
  brave person 855 n.
  philanthropist 901 n.
knighthood
  honours 866 n.
  title 870 n.
knit
  join 45 vb.
  tie 45 vb.
  compose 56 vb.
  produce 164 vb.
  weave 222 vb.
  jersey 228 n.
  close 264 vb.
knitting
  network 222 n.
  formation 243 n.
  needlework 844 n.
knob
  hanger 217 n.
  handle 218 n.
  sphere 252 n.
  swelling 253 n.
knock
  knock 279 n.
  strike 279 vb.
  be loud 400 vb.
  loudness 400 n.
  bang 402 n.
  detract 926 vb.
knock about
  travel 267 vb.
  misuse 675 vb.
knockabout
  dramatic 594 adj.
  funny 849 adj.
  ridiculousness 849 n.

knock down
  demolish 165 vb.
  flatten 216 vb.
  strike 279 vb.
  fell 311 vb.
knock-down price
  discount 810 n.
  cheapness 812 n.
knocker
  signal 547 n.
  detractor 926 n.
knocking
  loudness 400 n.
  roll 403 n.
knock it back
  drink 301 vb.
knock-kneed
  crippled 163 adj.
  deformed 246 adj.
  angular 247 adj.
  convergent 293 adj.
knock off
  subtract 39 vb.
  unite with 45 vb.
  cease 145 vb.
  take 786 vb.
  steal 788 vb.
  debauch 951 vb.
knock out
  disable 161 vb.
  destroy 165 vb.
  strike 279 vb.
  render insensible 375 vb.
  defeat 727 vb.
knockout
  end 69 n.
  exceller 644 n.
  victory 727 n.
  a beauty 841 n.
knot
  tie 45 vb.
  ligature 47 n.
  complexity 61 n.
  band 74 n.
  crowd 74 n.
  long measure 203 n.
  cross 222 vb.
  distort 246 vb.
  swelling 253 n.
  solid body 324 n.
  difficulty 700 n.
knots
  velocity 277 n.
knotty
  dense 324 adj.

difficult 700 adj.
know
  unite with 45 vb.
  know 490 vb.
know-all
  dogmatist 473 n.
  intellectual 492 n.
  wiseacre 500 n.
  vain person 873 n.
know-how
  knowledge 490 n.
  intelligence 498 n.
  way 624 n.
  means 629 n.
  skill 694 n.
  cunning 698 n.
knowing
  knowing 490 adj.
  knowledge 490 n.
  intelligent 498 adj.
  cunning 698 adj.
knowingly
  purposely 617 adv.
knowledge
  knowledge 490 n.
knowledgeable
  wise 498 adj.
know one's place
  be modest 874 vb.
  respect 920 vb.
  show respect
    920 vb.
know one's stuff
  discriminate
    463 vb.
  know 490 vb.
knuckle
  joint 45 n.
  angularity 247 n.
  swelling 253 n.
  meat 301 n.
knuckle under
  be inferior 35 vb.
  knuckle under
    721 vb.
Koran
  non-Biblical scrip-
    ture 975 n.
kosher
  edible 301 adj.
  clean 648 adj.
kowtow
  obeisance 311 n.
  stoop 311 vb.
  knuckle under
    721 vb.
  be servile 879 vb.

790

---

courteous act
  884 n.
  greet 884 vb.
  respects 920 n.
  show respect
    920 vb.
kraal
  dwelling 192 n.
Kremlin
  master 741 n.
kudos
  prestige 866 n.
  approbation 923 n.
Ku Klux Klan
  society 708 n.
kungfu
  wrestling 716 n.

L

laager
  station 187 n.
  fort 713 n.
labarum
  flag 547 n.
label
  class 62 vb.
  heraldry 547 n.
  label 547 n.
  mark 547 vb.
labial
  marginal 234 adj.
  speech sound
    398 n.
laboratory
  testing agent
    461 n.
  workshop 687 n.
laborious
  laborious 682 adj.
  labouring 682 adj.
Labour
  political party
    708 n.
labour
  be unrelated 10 vb.
  obstetrics 167 n.
  move slowly
    278 vb.
  emphasize 532 vb.
  exaggerate 546 vb.
  action 676 n.
  do 676 vb.
  labour 682 vb.
  work 682 vb.
  personnel 686 n.

---

labour camp
  prison camp 748 n.
laboured
  irrelevant 10 adj.
  inelegant 576 adj.
  matured 669 adj.
  laborious 682 adj.
labourer
  producer 164 n.
  worker 686 n.
  servant 742 n.
labour in vain
  fall short 307 vb.
  attempt the impos-
    sible 470 vb.
  waste 634 vb.
  lost labour 641 n.
  waste effort
    641 adj.
  act foolishly
    695 vb.
  fail 728 vb.
labour of love
  voluntary work
    597 n.
  vocation 622 n.
  undertaking 672 n.
  gift 781 n.
  no charge 812 n.
  amusement 837 n.
  disinterestedness
    931 n.
labour of Sisyphus
  lost labour 641 n.
labour-saving
  mechanical
    630 adj.
  leisurely 681 adj.
  economical
    814 adj.
  economy 814 n.
labour the obvious
  waste effort
    641 adj.
laburnum
  tree 366 n.
labyrinth
  complexity 61 n.
  meandering 251 n.
  ear 415 n.
  enigma 530 n.
labyrinthine
  difficult 700 adj.
lace
  mix 43 vb.
  join 45 vb.
  tie 45 vb.

---

ligature 47 n.
  network 222 n.
  textile 222 n.
  transparency
    422 n.
  needlework 844 n.
lace into
  strike 279 vb.
  attack 712 vb.
laceration
  scission 46 n.
  wound 655 n.
lachrymose
  lamenting 836 adj.
lack
  be inferior 35 vb.
  be incomplete
    55 vb.
  deficit 55 n.
  absence 190 n.
  fall short 307 vb.
  shortfall 307 n.
  necessity 596 n.
  require 627 vb.
  not suffice 636 vb.
  scarcity 636 n.
  noncompletion
    726 n.
  be poor 801 n.
  be discontented
    829 vb.
lackadaisical
  inactive 679 adj.
  apathetic 820 adj.
  inexcitable
    823 adj.
  dejected 834 adj.
  indifferent 860 adj.
lackey
  instrument 628 n.
  dependant 742 n.
  domestic 742 n.
  toady 879 n.
lacking
  incomplete 55 adj.
  absent 190 adj.
  deficient 307 adj.
  necessitous
    627 adj.
  insufficient
    636 adj.
  imperfect 647 adj.
  lost 772 adj.
lacklustre
  weakly 163 adj.
  dim 419 adj.
  dimness 419 n.

colourless 426 adj.
dejected 834 adj.

laconic
concise 569 adj.
taciturn 582 adj.

lacquer
coat 226 vb.
facing 226 n.
resin 357 n.
colour 425 vb.
hairwash 843 n.
decorate 844 vb.

lactose
food content 301 n.
sweet thing 392 n.

lacuna
incompleteness
55 n.
discontinuity 72 n.
gap 201 n.
concavity 255 n.
opening 263 n.
requirement 627 n.
defect 647 n.

lad
youngster 132 n.
male 372 n.

ladder
bond 47 n.
series 71 n.
discontinuity 72 n.
ascent 308 n.
access 624 n.
means of escape
667 n.

laden
full 54 adj.
weighty 322 adj.

la-di-da
affected 850 adj.

Ladies
latrine 649 n.

ladle
ladle 194 n.
transpose 272 vb.

lady
adult 134 n.
female 373 n.
master 741 n.
spouse 894 n.

Lady Bountiful
giver 781 n.
good giver 813 n.
benefactor 903 n.

lady-in-waiting
retainer 742 n.

lady-killer
lover 887 n.
libertine 952 n.

ladylike
female 373 adj.
well-bred 848 adj.
noble 868 adj.
See **genteel**
courteous 884 adj.

lag
be inferior 35 vb.
decrease 37 vb.
cover 226 vb.
be behind 238 vb.
move slowly
278 vb.
slowness 278 n.
fall short 307 vb.
be inactive 679 vb.
detention 747 n.
offender 904 n.

lager
alcoholic drink
301 n.

laggard
lateness 136 n.
slowcoach 278 n.

lagoon
gulf 345 n.
lake 346 n.

laid
born 360 adj.

laid-back
reposeful 683 adj.

laid low
weakened 163 adj.
low 210 adj.

laid off
disused 674 adj.
nonactive 677 adj.

laid up
powerless 161 adj.
supine 216 adj.
sick 651 adj.
disused 674 adj.
inactive 679 adj.

lair
dwelling 192 n.
hiding-place 527 n.
refuge 662 n.

laird
master 741 n.
owner 776 n.
aristocrat 868 n.

laisse
verse form 593 n.

laisser faire
not act 677 vb.
be inactive 679 vb.
inactivity 679 n.
be lax 734 vb.
laxity 734 n.
freedom 744 n.
give scope 744 vb.
permit 756 vb.
permitting 756 adj.
trade 791 n.

laity
laity 987 n.

lake
great quantity
32 n.
lake 346 n.
storage 632 n.
store 632 n.

lam
strike 279 vb.
criticize 924 vb.

lama
priest 986 n.

lamb
young creature
132 n.
reproduce itself
167 vb.
skin 226 n.
meat 301 n.
sheep 365 n.
darling 890 n.
innocent 935 n.

lambast
strike 279 vb.
criticize 924 vb.
reproach 924 vb.
reprove 924 vb.

lambent
luminous 417 adj.

lame
disable 161 vb.
crippled 163 adj.
feeble 572 adj.
make useless
641 adj.
imperfect 647 adj.
impair 655 vb.
hinder 702 vb.

lame duck
weakling 163 n.
unlucky person
731 n.

lament
regret 830 vb.
lament 836 vb.

lament 836 vb.
disapprove 924 vb.

lamentable
bad 645 adj.
distressing 827 adj.
lamenting 836 adj.

lamination
structure 331 n.

lamp
lamp 420 n.

lampoon
imitate 20 vb.
copy 22 n.
poetize 593 vb.
satire 851 n.
satirize 851 vb.
calumny 926 n.
detract 926 vb.

lamprey
fish 365 n.

lampshade
screen 421 n.

lance
sharp point 256 n.
perforator 263 n.
pierce 263 vb.
kill 362 vb.
strike at 712 vb.
spear 723 n.

lance corporal
army officer 741 n.

lancer
soldiery 722 n.

lancet
perforator 263 n.

land
voyage 269 vb.
land 295 vb.
admit 299 vb.
land 344 n.
acquire 771 vb.
lands 777 n.
take 786 vb.

land a blow
strike 279 vb.

landau
carriage 274 n.

landed
proprietary
777 adj.

landfall
arrival 295 n.

landing
layer 207 n.
vertex 213 n.
stand 218 n.
aeronautics 271 n.

LAN

air travel 271 n.
arrival 295 n.
ascent 308 n.
descent 309 n.

landlocked
imprisoned
747 adj.

landlord, landlady
caterer 633 n.
owner 776 n.

landmark
limit 236 n.
projection 254 n.
visibility 443 n.
signpost 547 n.
important matter
638 n.

land on one's feet
be safe 660 vb.
be successful
727 vb.
succeed 727 vb.

landowner
owner 776 n.

landscape
transform 147 vb.
open space 263 n.
land 344 n.
spectacle 445 n.
art subject 553 n.
beauty 841 n.

landscape gardening
agriculture 370 n.
beautification
843 n.
ornamental art
844 n.

landside
air travel 271 n.

landslide
revolution 149 n.
ruin 165 n.
incline 220 n.
descent 309 n.
defeat 728 n.

lane
path 624 n.
route 624 n.

language
language 557 n.

languid
inert 175 adj.
slow 278 adj.
feeble 572 adj.
inactive 679 adj.

languish
be weak 163 vb.

LAP

be inactive 679 vb.
be fatigued 684 vb.
be dejected 834 vb.
desire 859 vb.
court 889 vb.

languor
inertness 175 n.
slowness 278 n.
sluggishness 679 n.
fatigue 684 n.
tedium 838 n.

lank
long 203 adj.

lanky
long 203 adj.
narrow 206 adj.
tall 209 adj.

lanolin
unguent 357 n.
balm 658 n.
cosmetic 843 n.

lantern
lamp 420 n.

Laodicean
moderate 625 n.
apathetic 820 adj.
indifferent 860 adj.

lap
be superior 34 vb.
part 53 n.
period 110 n.
periodicity 141 n.
receptacle 194 n.
seat 218 n.
cover 226 vb.
dress 228 vb.
surround 230 vb.
outstrip 277 vb.
precede 283 vb.
drink 301 vb.
circle 314 vb.
circuition 314 n.
moisten 341 vb.
sound faint 401 vb.
circuit 626 n.
circuit 626 vb.

laparoscopy
diagnostic 658 n.

lap dog
dog 365 n.

lapel
adjunct 40 n.
garment 228 n.
fold 261 n.
trimming 844 n.

lapis lazuli
blueness 435 n.

LAR

gem 844 n.

lapse
end 69 n.
time 108 n.
elapse 111 vb.
conversion 147 n.
deviation 282 n.
inattention 456 n.
disbelieve 486 vb.
deteriorate 655 vb.
relapse 657 n.
relapse 657 vb.
loss 772 n.
be wicked 934 vb.
guilty act 936 n.
be impious 980 vb.

lapsed
past 125 adj.
negligent 458 adj.
nonobservant
769 adj.
irreligious 974 adj.

lap up
absorb 299 vb.
drink 301 vb.
hear 415 vb.

larceny
stealing 788 n.

lard
coat 226 vb.
cook 301 vb.
fat 357 n.
grease 357 vb.

larder
chamber 194 n.
storage 632 n.

lares et penates
idol 982 n.

large
large 195 adj.

largesse
gift 781 n.
liberality 813 n.

lark
bird 365 n.
revel 837 n.

lark about, around
be absurd 497 vb.
amuse oneself
837 vb.

larva
young creature
132 n.
insect 365 n.

laryngitis
respiratory disease
651 n.

LAS

larynx
air pipe 353 n.
voice 577 n.

lasagne
dish 301 n.

laser
weapon 723 n.

laser disc
gramophone 414 n.
recording instru-
ment 549 n.

lash
tie 45 vb.
stimulant 174 n.
filament 208 n.
knock 279 n.
strike 279 vb.
incentive 612 n.
incite 612 vb.
hasten 680 vb.
animate 821 vb.
excitant 821 n.
reproach 924 vb.
flog 963 vb.
scourge 964 n.

lashings
great quantity
32 n.
plenty 635 n.

lash out
be prodigal 815 vb.
be angry 891 vb.

lash up
tie 45 vb.

lass
youngster 132 n.
female 373 n.

lassitude
sleepiness 679 n.
fatigue 684 n.

lasso
loop 250 n.
missile weapon
723 n.

last
mould 23 n.
ending 69 adj.
last 113 vb.
foregoing 125 adj.

last gasp
end 69 n.
decease 361 n.

lasting
lasting 113 adj.
renowned 866 adj.

last lap
end 69 n.

arrival 295 n.
last minute
  lateness 136 n.
last post
  evening 129 n.
  valediction 296 n.
  obsequies 364 n.
  call 547 n.
last resort
  necessity 596 n.
  contrivance 623 n.
  means 629 n.
  inexpedience
    643 n.
  refuge 662 n.
last rites
  obsequies 364 n.
  Christian rite
    988 n.
last straw
  redundance 637 n.
  encumbrance
    702 n.
  completion 725 n.
  annoyance 827 n.
  resentment 891 n.
last throw
  attempt 671 n.
  rashness 857 n.
last word in
  supreme 34 adj.
  exceller 644 n.
last words
  end 69 n.
  valediction 296 n.
latch
  join 45 vb.
  joint 45 n.
  fastening 47 n.
  close 264 vb.
  stopper 264 n.
latch on
  know 490 vb.
  understand 516 vb.
late
  former 125 adj.
  modern 126 adj.
  late 136 adj.
  late 136 adv.
  dead 361 adj.
latecomer
  lateness 136 n.
lately
  formerly 125 adv.
latent
  latent 523 adj.

later
  after 65 adv.
  sequential 65 adj.
  subsequent
    120 adj.
  subsequently
    120 adv.
  future 124 adj.
lateral
  lateral 239 adj.
lateral thinking
  meditation 449 n.
  reasoning 475 n.
latest, the
  modernism 126 n.
  fashion 848 n.
lath
  strip 208 n.
  materials 631 n.
lathe
  district 184 n.
  rotator 315 n.
lather
  lubricant 334 n.
  lubricate 334 vb.
  bubble 355 n.
  clean 648 vb.
  spank 963 vb.
Latin
  language 557 n.
latitude
  range 183 n.
  room 183 n.
  region 184 n.
  breadth 205 n.
  scope 744 n.
latitudinarianism
  heterodoxy 977 n.
latrine
  stench 397 n.
  latrine 649 n.
latter
  sequential 65 adj.
  foregoing 125 adj.
latter-day
  present 121 adj.
  modern 126 adj.
lattice
  space 201 vb.
  network 222 n.
  window 263 n.
laud
  honour 866 vb.
  honours 866 n.
  praise 923 vb.
  worship 981 vb.

laudanum
  moderator 177 n.
  anaesthetic 375 n.
  praise 923 n.
laudatory
  approving 923 n.
laugh
  cry 408 n.
  gesture 547 n.
  be pleased 824 vb.
  be cheerful 833 vb.
  laugh 835 vb.
  laughter 835 n.
laughable
  inconsiderable
    33 adj.
  absurd 497 adj.
  foolish 499 adj.
  laughing 835 adj.
  ridiculous 849 adj.
laugh at
  laugh 835 vb.
  ridicule 851 vb.
  not respect 921 vb.
  despise 922 vb.
  hold cheap 922 vb.
laughingstock
  laughingstock
    851 n.
laugh off
  disregard 458 vb.
laughter
  laughter 835 n.
launch
  auspicate 68 vb.
  initiate 68 vb.
  cause 156 vb.
  navigate 269 vb.
  ship 275 n.
  propel 287 vb.
launching
  debut 68 n.
launching pad
  stand 218 n.
  space travel 271 n.
  gun 723 n.
launder
  clean 648 vb.
launderette
  ablutions 648 n.
laundry
  chamber 194 n.
  ablutions 648 n.
  workshop 687 n.
laurel
  tree 366 n.

laurels
  badge 547 n.
  objective 617 n.
  trophy 729 n.
  honours 866 n.
lava
  rock 344 n.
lavatory
  chamber 194 n.
  latrine 649 n.
lavender
  plant 366 n.
  scent 396 n.
  purple 436 adj.
  purpleness 436 n.
lavish
  many 104 adj.
  plentiful 635 adj.
  give 781 vb.
  be liberal 813 vb.
  liberal 813 adj.
  prodigal 815 adj.
  approving 923 adj.
law
  rule 81 n.
  fixture 153 n.
  habit 610 n.
  authority 733 n.
  decree 737 n.
  permit 756 n.
  law 953 n.
  legislation 953 n.
law-abiding
  peaceful 717 adj.
  submitting 721 adj.
  obedient 739 adj.
  honourable
    929 adj.
  legal 953 adj.
law and order
  peace 717 n.
law-breaker
  offender 904 n.
lawcourt
  lawcourt 956 n.
lawful
  due 915 adj.
  legal 953 adj.
lawless
  disorderly 61 adj.
  unconformable
    84 adj.
  lawless 954 adj.
lawn
  textile 222 n.
  smoothness 258 n.
  grassland 348 n.

grass 366 n.
garden 370 n.
lawyer
lawyer 958 n.
lax
feeble 572 adj.
lax 734 adj.
laxative
purgative 658 n.
remedial 658 adj.
laxity
softness 327 n.
inexactness 495 n.
laxity 734 n.
improbity 930 n.
laxness
negligence 458 n.
lay
unite with 45 vb.
place 187 vb.
vocal music 412 n.
poem 593 n.
debauch 951 vb.
layabout
idler 679 n.
lay aside
exclude 57 vb.
be neglectful
  458 vb.
reject 607 vb.
stop using 674 vb.
lay at one's door
attribute 158 vb.
accuse 928 vb.
lay by
store 632 vb.
lay-by
station 187 n.
traffic control
  305 n.
lay down
place 187 vb.
flatten 216 vb.
let fall 311 vb.
postulate 475 vb.
command 737 vb.
lay down the law
dogmatize 473 vb.
affirm 532 vb.
rule 733 vb.
command 737 vb.
decree 737 vb.
be insolent 878 vb.
layer
generate 167 vb.
layer 207 n.
cultivate 370 vb.

layette
clothing 228 n.
lay hands upon
acquire 771 vb.
take 786 vb.
lay in
store 632 vb.
laying on of hands
medical art 658 n.
Christian rite
  988 n.
laying waste
terror tactics 712 n.
lay into
eat 301 vb.
attack 712 vb.
criticize 924 vb.
lay low
fell 311 vb.
strike at 712 vb.
lay off
dismiss 300 vb.
stop using 674 vb.
make inactive
  679 vb.
not retain 779 vb.
lay open
uncover 229 vb.
open 263 vb.
manifest 522 vb.
disclose 526 vb.
lay out
arrange 62 vb.
flatten 216 vb.
inter 364 vb.
plan 623 vb.
expend 806 vb.
layout
arrangement 62 n.
outline 233 n.
edition 589 n.
lay person
lay person 987 n.
lay siege to
besiege 712 vb.
lay up
store 632 vb.
make useless
  641 adj.
stop using 674 vb.
make inactive
  679 vb.
laze
move slowly
  278 vb.
be inactive 679 vb.
repose 683 vb.

lazy
lazy 679 adj.
L-driver
driver 268 n.
beginner 538 n.
leach
liquefy 337 vb.
drench 341 vb.
purify 648 vb.
lead
advantage 34 n.
predominate 34 vb.
come before 64 vb.
prelude 66 n.
initiate 68 vb.
make conform
  83 vb.
accompany 89 vb.
do before 119 vb.
electronics 160 n.
sailing aid 269 n.
precede 283 vb.
preceding 283 n.
gauge 465 n.
print-type 587 n.
actor 594 n.
motivate 612 vb.
direct 689 vb.
success 727 n.
fetter 748 n.
lead astray
deflect 282 vb.
mislead 495 vb.
ensnare 542 vb.
motivate 612 vb.
make wicked
  934 vb.
debauch 951 vb.
leaden
weighty 322 adj.
dim 419 adj.
grey 429 adj.
inactive 679 adj.
tedious 838 adj.
leader
orchestra 413 n.
article 591 n.
leader 690 n.
master 741 n.
leadership
superiority 34 n.
precedence 64 n.
directorship 689 n.
authority 733 n.
prestige 866 n.
leading
supreme 34 adj.

precedence 64 n.
first 68 adj.
priority 119 n.
influential 178 adj.
preceding 283 n.
important 638 adj.
successful 727 adj.
authoritative
  733 adj.
noteworthy
  866 adj.
leading lady
actor 594 n.
leading light
sage 500 n.
bigwig 638 n.
person of repute
  866 n.
leading question
interrogation
  459 n.
question 459 n.
reminder 505 n.
lead one on
fool 542 vb.
  See **deceive**
leadswinger
avoider 620 n.
sick person 651 n.
lead the way
initiate 68 vb.
precede 283 vb.
lead to
tend 179 vb.
lead up to
prepare 669 vb.
leaf
branch 53 n.
part 53 n.
shelf 218 n.
foliage 366 n.
edition 589 n.
leaflet
foliage 366 n.
the press 528 n.
book 589 n.
leaf through
scan 438 vb.
leafy
prolific 171 adj.
green 434 adj.
league
combination 50 n.
concurrence 181 n.
long measure
  203 n.
association 706 n.

society 708 n.
compact 765 n.
leak
gap 201 n.
opening 263 n.
outflow 298 n.
be wet 341 vb.
flow 350 **VB.**
mistake 495 n.
information 524 n.
disclosure 526 n.
divulge 526 vb.
waste 634 vb.
defect 647 n.
escape 667 n.
escape 667 vb.
hitch 702 n.
nonretention
   779 n.
not retain 779 vb.
leakage
outflow 298 n.
waste 634 n.
escape 667 n.
loss 772 n.
leaky
porous 263 adj.
imperfect 647 adj.
lean
be unequal 29 vb.
small 33 adj.
tend 179 vb.
lean 206 adj.
be oblique 220 vb.
be biased 481 vb.
choose 605 vb.
do wrong 914 adj.
lean-burn engine
machine 630 n.
lean cuisine
cookery 301 n.
dieting 301 n.
leaning
unequal 29 adj.
tendency 179 n.
obliquity 220 n.
willingness 597 n.
choice 605 n.
habit 610 n.
liking 859 n.
injustice 914 n.
leanness
smallness 33 n.
lean on
compel 740 vb.
lean over backwards
compensate 31 vb.

stoop 311 vb.
exaggerate 546 vb.
be willing 597 vb.
do wrong 914 adj.
lean-to
small house 192 n.
lobby 194 n.
lean towards
approach 289 vb.
desire 859 vb.
leap
vary 152 vb.
interval 201 n.
move fast 277 vb.
progression 285 n.
leap 312 n.
leap 312 vb.
leap at
be willing 597 vb.
leapfrog
leap 312 vb.
children's games
   837 n.
leap in the dark
empiricism 461 n.
gambling 618 n.
danger 661 n.
rashness 857 n.
leap or shot in the
   dark
uncertainty 474 n.
leaps and bounds
progression 285 n.
leap year
period 110 n.
learn
learn 536 vb.
learned
studious 536 adj.
literary 557 adj.
learner
learner 538 n.
learning
knowledge 490 n.
learning 536 n.
lease
transport 272 n.
estate 777 n.
transfer 780 n.
lease 784 vb.
lending 784 n.
leasehold
proprietary
   777 adj.
leash
affix 45 vb.
group 74 n.

least
small 33 adj.
least one can do
sufficiency 635 n.
dueness 915 n.
leather
skin 226 n.
strike 279 vb.
toughness 329 n.
bookbinding 589 n.
materials 631 n.
spank 963 vb.
leathering
knock 279 n.
leathery
tough 329 adj.
unsavoury 391 adj.
leave
leave over 41 vb.
separate 46 vb.
cease 145 vb.
go away 190 vb.
transfer 272 vb.
recede 290 vb.
depart 296 vb.
avoid 620 vb.
relinquish 621 vb.
store 632 vb.
leisure 681 n.
repose 683 n.
facility 701 n.
permission 756 n.
permit 756 n.
bequeath 780 vb.
give 781 vb.
nonliability 919 n.
leave alone
not act 677 vb.
leave behind
be superior 34 vb.
leave over 41 vb.
outstrip 277 vb.
progress 285 vb.
outdo 306 vb.
forget 506 vb.
leave in the lurch
disregard 458 vb.
deceive 542 vb.
fool 542 vb.
leaven
component 58 n.
modify 143 vb.
conversion 147 n.
convert 147 vb.
cause 156 n.
stimulant 174 n.
enlarge 197 vb.

elevate 310 vb.
leaven 323 n.
lighten 323 vb.
qualification 468 n.
qualify 468 vb.
make better
   654 vb.
leave off
cease 145 vb.
stop using 674 vb.
leave out
subtract 39 vb.
leave over 41 vb.
set apart 46 vb.
exclude 57 vb.
be taciturn 582 vb.
leave out in the cold
disregard 458 vb.
leave over
leave over 41 vb.
leave-taking
valediction 296 n.
leave undone
be incomplete
   55 vb.
neglect 458 vb.
not complete
   726 vb.
leaving
departure 296 n.
relinquishment
   621 n.
resignation 753 n.
leavings
leavings 41 n.
Lebensraum
whole 52 n.
room 183 n.
nation 371 n.
scope 744 n.
lech
be impure 951 vb.
lecher
libertine 952 n.
lechery
unchastity 951 n.
lectern
church interior
   990 n.
church utensil
   990 n.
lector
cleric 986 n.
lecture
lecture 534 n.
teach 534 vb.
orate 579 vb.

leper
outcast 883 n.
lepidopterist
zoologist 367 n.
leprechaun
elf 970 n.
leprosy
skin disease 651 n.
tropical disease
651 n.
lesbian
abnormal 84 adj.
nonconformist
84 n.
female 373 adj.
female 373 n.
lese-majesty
sedition 738 n.
lesion
ulcer 651 n.
wound 655 n.
less
finite quantity
26 n.
small 33 adj.
less 35 adv.
lesser 35 adj.
lessee
resident 191 n.
possessor 776 n.
recipient 782 n.
lessen
abate 37 vb.
decrease 37 vb.
weaken 163 vb.
moderate 177 vb.
become small
198 vb.
make smaller
198 vb.
qualify 468 vb.
lesser
lesser 35 adj.
lesson
lecture 534 n.
warning 664 n.
lessons
study 536 n.
lessor
lender 784 n.
less than perfect
imperfect 647 adj.
let
permit 756 vb.
assign 780 vb.
transfer 780 n.
lease 784 vb.

lending 784 n.
let alone
in addition 38 adv.
exclusive of 57 adv.
bring to rest
266 vb.
avoid 620 vb.
not act 677 vb.
letch after
desire 859 vb.
let down
lengthen 203 vb.
lower 311 vb.
disappointed
509 adj.
deceive 542 vb.
letdown
disappointment
509 n.
humiliation 872 n.
let drop
lower 311 vb.
See let fall
divulge 526 vb.
let fall
let fall 311 vb.
hint 524 vb.
divulge 526 vb.
let fly
strike 279 vb.
shoot 287 vb.
be angry 891 vb.
get angry 891 vb.
criticize 924 vb.
let fly at
attack 712 vb.
let go
let fall 311 vb.
relinquish 621 vb.
liberate 746 vb.
not retain 779 vb.
be indifferent
860 vb.
acquit 960 vb.
lethal
deadly 362 adj.
toxic 653 adj.
lethargy
sluggishness 679 n.
fatigue 684 n.
moral insensibility
820 n.
Lethe
oblivion 506 n.
mythic hell 972 n.
let in
add 38 vb.

introduce 231 vb.
enter 297 vb.
admit 299 vb.
take 786 vb.
let it all hang out
be free 744 vb.
let it happen
acquiesce 488 vb.
let it rip
accelerate 277 vb.
reproach 924 vb.
let loose
liberate 746 vb.
let off
shoot 287 vb.
acquit 960 vb.
let off steam
gasify 336 vb.
revel 837 vb.
get angry 891 vb.
let off the hook
liberate 746 vb.
permit 756 vb.
acquitted 960 adj.
let on
divulge 526 vb.
let one down
disappoint 509 vb.
fail in duty 918 vb.
let oneself go
be diffuse 570 vb.
deteriorate 655 vb.
be free 744 vb.
be cheerful 833 vb.
rejoice 835 vb.
revel 837 vb.
let oneself in for
undertake 672 vb.
be in difficulty
700 vb.
let out
enlarge 197 vb.
emit 300 vb.
divulge 526 vb.
speak 579 vb.
means of escape
667 n.
deliverance 668 n.
illegality 954 n.
let pass
disregard 458 vb.
not act 677 vb.
let slide
be neglectful
458 vb.
letter
component 58 n.

mark 547 vb.
letter 558 n.
script 586 n.
write 586 vb.
correspondence
588 n.
lender 784 n.
letterhead
label 547 n.
lettering
letter 558 n.
lettering 586 n.
letter of the law
accuracy 494 n.
severity 735 n.
pitilessness 906 n.
legality 953 n.
letterpress
letter 558 n.
letters
culture 490 n.
erudition 490 n.
report 524 n.
message 529 n.
postal communica-
tions 531 n.
literature 557 n.
lettering 586 n.
correspondence
588 n.
biography 590 n.
let up
cease 145 vb.
decelerate 278 vb.
letup
lull 145 n.
moderation 177 n.
leukaemia
blood 335 n.
blood disease
651 n.
levee
social gathering
882 n.
level
make uniform
16 vb.
uniform 16 adj.
degree 27 n.
equal 28 adj.
equalize 28 vb.
serial place 73 n.
synchronous
123 adj.
demolish 165 vb.
near 200 adj.
layer 207 n.

flat 216 adj.
flatten 216 vb.
horizontality
216 n.
angular measure
247 n.
smooth 258 adj.
smooth 258 vb.
aim 281 vb.
sound 398 n.
fire at 712 vb.
level at
aim 281 vb.
aim at 617 vb.
level crossing
crossing 222 n.
railway 624 n.
level-headed
wise 498 adj.
inexcitable
823 adj.
cautious 858 adj.
leveller
uniformist 16 n.
destroyer 168 n.
levelness
uniformity 16 n.
lowness 210 n.
smoothness 258 n.
level off
decrease 37 vb.
become small
198 vb.
level out
be horizontal
216 vb.
level-pegging
draw 28 n.
equal 28 adj.
equivalence 28 n.
synchronism 123 n.
near 200 adj.
level stretch
horizontality
216 n.
lever
influence 178 n.
handle 218 n.
pivot 218 n.
propellant 287 n.
instrument 628 n.
tool 630 n.
leverage
advantage 34 n.
influence 178 n.
tool 630 n.
scope 744 n.

debt 803 n.
lever open
force 176 vb.
leviathan
rara avis 84 n.
giant 195 n.
mythical being
970 n.
levitate
ascend 308 vb.
be light 323 vb.
lighten 323 vb.
levity
irresolution 601 n.
caprice 604 n.
merriment 833 n.
levy
assemblage 74 n.
armed force 722 n.
demand 737 n.
demand 737 vb.
acquire 771 vb.
levy 786 vb.
taking 786 n.
tax 809 n.
lewd
impure 951 adj.
lecherous 951 adj.
lexicographer
collector 492 n.
linguist 557 n.
lez or les
abnormal 84 adj.
nonconformist
84 n.
female 373 adj.
liability
liability 180 n.
bias 481 n.
debt 803 n.
duty 917 n.
guilt 936 n.
penalty 963 n.
liable
liable 180 adj.
possible 469 adj.
obliged 917 adj.
liable to
subject 745 adj.
liaison
relation 9 n.
bond 47 n.
concurrence 181 n.
love affair 887 n.
illicit love 951 n.
liar
liar 545 n.

bad person 938 n.
libation
ejection 300 n.
drinking 301 n.
oblation 981 n.
libel
calumny 926 n.
defame 926 vb.
false charge 928 n.
liberal
reformer 654 n.
liberal 813 adj.
philanthropic
901 adj.
liberality
giving 781 n.
liberality 813 n.
Liberals
political party
708 n.
liberate
disencumber
701 vb.
liberate 746 vb.
libertarian
free person 744 n.
libertine
lecherous 951 adj.
libertine 952 n.
liberty
freedom 744 n.
scope 744 n.
permission 756 n.
sociability 882 n.
dueness 915 n.
nonliability 919 n.
libidinous
loving 887 adj.
lecherous 951 adj.
libido
libido 859 n.
librarian
collector 492 n.
bookperson 589 n.
library
chamber 194 n.
edition 589 n.
library 589 n.
collection 632 n.
workshop 687 n.
library edition
edition 589 n.
libretto
vocal music 412 n.
reading matter
589 n.
stage play 594 n.

licence
laxity 734 n.
freedom 744 n.
scope 744 n.
permission 756 n.
permit 756 n.
dueness 915 n.
nonliability 919 n.
unchastity 951 n.
license
commission
751 vb.
permit 756 vb.
exempt 919 vb.
licensee
caterer 633 n.
consignee 754 n.
recipient 782 n.
licentious
free 744 adj.
sensual 944 adj.
impure 951 adj.
lecherous 951 adj.
lawless 954 adj.
lichee
fruit and vegetables
301 n.
lichen
plant 366 n.
licit
due 915 adj.
legal 953 adj.
lick
small quantity
33 n.
eat 301 vb.
moisten 341 vb.
touch 378 vb.
taste 386 vb.
defeat 727 vb.
lick and a promise, a
incompleteness
55 n.
ablutions 648 n.
noncompletion
726 n.
licking
knock 279 n.
eating 301 n.
tactual 378 adj.
victory 727 n.
defeat 728 n.
lick into shape
form 243 vb.
educate 534 vb.
make ready
669 vb.

lick one's lips
  enjoy 376 vb.
  taste 386 vb.
  gluttonize 947 vb.
lickspittle
  toady 879 n.
lid
  covering 226 n.
  headgear 228 n.
  stopper 264 n.
lido
  shore 344 n.
  arena 724 n.
  pleasure ground
    837 n.
lie
  be 1 vb.
  be situated 186 vb.
  be present 189 vb.
  dwell 192 vb.
  be horizontal
    216 vb.
  be false 541 vb.
  falsehood 541 n.
  deception 542 n.
  be untrue 543 vb.
  untruth 543 n.
  misrepresent
    552 vb.
  be inactive 679 vb.
  false charge 928 n.
lieder
  vocal music 412 n.
lie detector
  detector 484 n.
lie doggo
  lurk 523 vb.
  be stealthy 525 vb.
lie down
  be horizontal
    216 vb.
  repose 683 vb.
lie flat
  be horizontal
    216 vb.
liege
  master 741 n.
  subject 742 n.
  subject 745 adj.
lie in wait
  ambush 527 vb.
  ensnare 542 vb.
lie low
  be unseen 444 vb.
  disappear 446 vb.
  lurk 523 vb.
  elude 667 vb.

lie of the land
  circumstance 8 n.
  direction 281 n.
lieutenant
  nautical personnel
    270 n.
  aider 703 n.
  auxiliary 707 n.
  soldiery 722 n.
  army officer 741 n.
  naval officer 741 n.
  deputy 755 n.
life
  essential part 5 n.
  time 108 n.
  affairs 154 n.
  vigorousness 174 n.
  life 360 n.
  biography 590 n.
  vocation 622 n.
  activity 678 n.
life-and-death
  necessary 596 adj.
life belt
  wrapping 226 n.
  safeguard 662 n.
  lightness 323 n.
lifeblood
  essential part 5 n.
  blood 335 n.
  life 360 n.
lifeboat
  boat 275 n.
  safeguard 662 n.
lifeguard
  protector 660 n.
  defender 713 n.
Life Guards
  armed force 722 n.
life jacket
  wrapping 226 n.
  aircraft 276 n.
  lightness 323 n.
  safeguard 662 n.
lifeless
  inert 175 adj.
  dead 361 adj.
  inactive 679 adj.
lifelike
  lifelike 18 adj.
lifeline
  bond 47 n.
  safeguard 662 n.
lifelong
  lasting 113 adj.

life peer
  person of rank
    868 n.
life-saving
  deliverance 668 n.
life sciences, the
  science 490 n.
life-size
  large 195 adj.
  size 195 n.
life story or history
  biography 590 n.
lifestyle
  state 7 n.
  habit 610 n.
  vocation 622 n.
  way 624 n.
  conduct 688 n.
life-support machine
  support 218 n.
lifetime
  time 108 n.
  long duration
    113 n.
  life 360 n.
life to come
  future state 124 n.
  life 360 n.
lift
  copy 20 vb.
  displace 188 vb.
  conveyance 267 n.
  land travel 267 n.
  carry 273 vb.
  progression 285 n.
  promote 285 vb.
  draw 288 vb.
  ascent 308 n.
  elevate 310 vb.
  elevation 310 n.
  make bright
    417 vb.
  improvement
    654 n.
  exertion 682 n.
  aid 703 n.
  liberate 746 vb.
  steal 788 vb.
  relieve 831 vb.
lift-off
  space travel 271 n.
  ascent 308 n.
ligament
  ligature 47 n.
ligature
  ligature 47 n.

light
  shallow 212 adj.
  window 263 n.
  descend 309 vb.
  light 323 adj.
  kindle 381 vb.
  lighter 385 n.
  light 417 n.
  luminous 417 adj.
  make bright
    417 vb.
  soft-hued 425 adj.
  white 427 adj.
  guide 520 n.
  easy 701 adj.
  funny 849 adj.
  unchaste 951 adj.
  divine attribute
    965 n.
lighten
  assuage 177 vb.
  lighten 323 vb.
  make bright
    417 vb.
  disencumber
    701 vb.
  relieve 831 vb.
lighter
  boat 275 n.
  lighter 385 n.
light-fingered
  thieving 788 adj.
light-headed
  light-minded
    456 adj.
light-hearted
  cheerful 833 adj.
lighthouse
  sailing aid 269 n.
  signal light 420 n.
  signpost 547 n.
  safeguard 662 n.
lighting
  lighting 420 n.
lightly
  slightly 33 adv.
light music
  music 412 n.
lightness
  lightness 323 n.
  achromatism
    426 n.
lightning
  electricity 160 n.
  velocity 277 n.
  flash 417 n.
  luminary 420 n.

light on
 land 295 vb.
light relief
 contrariety 14 n.
 ridiculousness
 849 n.
lights
 insides 224 n.
light upon
 chance 159 vb.
 meet 295 vb.
 acquire 771 vb.
lightweight
 inconsiderable
 33 adj.
 weak 163 adj.
 weakling 163 n.
 light 323 adj.
 nonentity 639 n.
 trivial 639 adj.
light year
 period 110 n.
 distance 199 n.
 long measure
 203 n.
ligneous
 wooden 366 adj.
lignite
 fuel 385 n.
likable
 desired 859 adj.
like
 relative 9 adj.
 similar 18 adj.
 similarly 18 adv.
 equal 28 adj.
 enjoy 376 vb.
 be pleased 824 vb.
 desire 859 vb.
 be friendly 880 vb.
 love 887 vb.
like lemmings
 rashly 857 adv.
likelihood
 liability 180 n.
 possibility 469 n.
 probability 471 n.
likely
 probable 471 adj.
 credible 485 adj.
 promising 852 adj.
like magic
 wonderful 864 adj.
like-minded
 agreeing 24 adj.
 assenting 488 adj.

liken
 liken 18 vb.
likeness
 analogue 18 n.
 similarity 18 n.
 equivalence 28 n.
 appearance 445 n.
 comparison 462 n.
 metaphor 519 n.
 representation
 551 n.
likes of, the
 analogue 18 n.
likewise
 similarly 18 adv.
 in addition 38 adv.
liking
 tendency 179 n.
 liking 859 n.
 love 887 n.
lilac
 tree 366 n.
 purple 436 adj.
 purpleness 436 n.
Lilliputian
 dwarf 196 n.
 dwarfish 196 adj.
 little 196 adj.
lilting
 melodious 410 adj.
lily
 plant 366 n.
 white thing 427 n.
 a beauty 841 n.
lily-livered
 weak 163 adj.
 cowardly 856 adj.
limb
 branch 53 n.
 limb 53 n.
 piece 53 n.
 leg 267 n.
 foliage 366 n.
 tree 366 n.
limber
 war chariot 274 n.
 flexible 327 adj.
limber up
 begin 68 vb.
 prepare oneself
 669 vb.
limbless
 crippled 163 adj.
limbo
 hell 972 n.
lime
 adhesive 47 n.

 fertilizer 171 n.
 fruit and vegetables
 301 n.
 tree 366 n.
 sourness 393 n.
 bleacher 426 n.
 greenness 434 n.
 take 786 vb.
limelight
 lighting 420 n.
 publicity 528 n.
 theatre 594 n.
limerick
 absurdity 497 n.
 doggerel 593 n.
 poem 593 n.
 witticism 839 n.
 ridiculousness
 849 n.
limestone
 rock 344 n.
limit
 abate 37 vb.
 moderate 177 vb.
 make smaller
 198 vb.
 limit 236 n.
 limit 236 vb.
 qualify 468 vb.
 restrain 747 vb.
 annoyance 827 n.
limit, the
 completeness 54 n.
limitation
 circumscription
 232 n.
 limit 236 n.
 qualification 468 n.
 defect 647 n.
 hindrance 702 n.
 restriction 747 n.
 conditions 766 n.
 vice 934 n.
limited
 small 33 adj.
 unintelligent
 499 adj.
 restrained 747 adj.
limitless
 infinite 107 adj.
 huge 195 adj.
limousine
 automobile 274 n.
limp
 be weak 163 vb.
 weak 163 adj.
 inert 175 adj.

 walk 267 vb.
 move slowly
 278 vb.
 soft 327 adj.
 feeble 572 adj.
limpback
 book 589 n.
limpet
 marine life 365 n.
limpid
 transparent
 422 adj.
 intelligible 516 adj.
limping
 crippled 163 adj.
 slow 278 adj.
 slowness 278 n.
 feeble 572 adj.
linch pin
 fastening 47 n.
 chief thing 638 n.
Lincoln's Inns
 bar 958 n.
linctus
 medicine 658 n.
line
 race 11 n.
 degree 27 n.
 cable 47 n.
 fill 54 vb.
 sequence 65 n.
 continuity 71 n.
 series 71 n.
 breed 77 n.
 posteriority 120 n.
 genealogy 169 n.
 line 203 n.
 narrowness 206 n.
 fibre 208 n.
 line 227 vb.
 groove 262 vb.
 sailing aid 269 n.
 direction 281 n.
 notation 410 n.
 stripe 437 n.
 telecommunication
 531 n.
 indication 547 n.
 painting 553 n.
 lettering 586 n.
 correspondence
 588 n.
 function 622 n.
 vocation 622 n.
 railway 624 n.
 way 624 n.
 tactics 688 n.

battle 718 n.
armed force 722 n.
formation 722 n.
merchandise
795 n.
nobility 868 n.
line, the
middle 70 n.
lineage
consanguinity
11 n.
sequence 65 n.
continuity 71 n.
series 71 n.
posteriority 120 n.
source 156 n.
genealogy 169 n.
nobility 868 n.
lineament
form 243 n.
feature 445 n.
identification
547 n.
linear
continuous 71 adj.
longitudinal
203 adj.
straight 249 adj.
metrical 465 adj.
painted 553 adj.
linen
fibre 208 n.
textile 222 n.
clothing 228 n.
underwear 228 n.
bookbinding 589 n.
liner
lining 227 n.
ship 275 n.
lines
station 187 n.
abode 192 n.
enclosure 235 n.
form 243 n.
fold 261 n.
feature 445 n.
poem 593 n.
stage play 594 n.
railway 624 n.
defences 713 n.
penalty 963 n.
line up
be in order 60 vb.
arrange 62 vb.
await 507 vb.
lineup
assemblage 74 n.

linger
be late 136 vb.
go on 146 vb.
move slowly
278 vb.
lingerie
underwear 228 n.
lingo
language 557 n.
dialect 560 adj.
lingua franca
language 557 n.
dialect 560 adj.
linguistic
linguistic 557 adj.
liniment
unguent 357 n.
balm 658 n.
lining
lining 227 n.
link
relate 9 vb.
relation 9 n.
connect 45 vb.
bond 47 n.
component 58 n.
cross 222 vb.
intermediary
231 n.
gauge 465 n.
linkage
union 45 n.
links
pleasure ground
837 n.
linkup
union 45 n.
lino
floor-cover 226 n.
linocut
engraving 555 n.
linoleum
floor-cover 226 n.
lint
surgical dressing
658 n.
lintel
summit 213 n.
beam 218 n.
doorway 263 n.
lion
big cat 365 n.
mammal 365 n.
See **cat**
heraldry 547 n.
bigwig 638 n.
regalia 743 n.

brave person 855 n.
person of repute
866 n.
sociable person
882 n.
favourite 890 n.
lioness
big cat 365 n.
female animal
373 n.
lion-hearted
courageous
855 adj.
lion-hunter
toady 879 n.
lionize
honour 866 vb.
celebrate 876 vb.
congratulate
886 vb.
respect 920 vb.
praise 923 vb.
lion's share
chief part 52 n.
redundance 637 n.
undueness 916 n.
lip
edge 234 n.
projection 254 n.
sauciness 878 n.
rudeness 885 n.
lip-reading
listening 415 n.
intrepretative
520 adj.
lip service
duplicity 541 n.
sham 542 n.
ostentation 875 n.
false piety 980 n.
liquefy
liquefy 337 vb.
liquescent
blood 335 adj.
liqueur
alcoholic drink
301 n.
liquid
amorphous
244 adj.
blood 335 adj.
fluid 335 n.
transparent
422 adj.
liquid assets
estate 777 n.
funds 797 n.

wealth 800 n.
liquidate
destroy 165 vb.
murder 362 vb.
slaughter 362 vb.
liquidator
receiver 782 n.
treasurer 798 n.
liquidity
fluidity 335 n.
funds 797 n.
liquidize
cook 301 vb.
liquefy 337 vb.
liquidizer
liquefaction 337 n.
liquidness
fluidity 335 n.
liquor
stimulant 174 n.
drunkenness 949 n.
liquorice
sweets 301 n.
purgative 658 n.
lira
coinage 797 n.
lisp
voice 577 vb.
speech defect
580 n.
stammer 580 vb.
lissom
flexible 327 adj.
shapely 841 adj.
list
be unequal 29 vb.
list 87 n.
list 87 vb.
be oblique 220 vb.
obliquity 220 n.
navigate 269 vb.
hear 415 vb.
listed building
archaism 127 n.
preservation 666 n.
listen
hear 415 vb.
be curious 453 vb.
be attentive 455 vb.
obey 739 vb.
listener
listener 415 n.
listen in
hear 415 vb.
be curious 453 vb.
listless
weakly 163 adj.

inactive 679 adj.
dejected 834 adj.
indifferent 860 adj.
lists
duel 716 n.
lit
fiery 379 adj.
luminous 417 adj.
litany
prayers 981 n.
literacy
culture 490 n.
literal
narrow-minded
481 adj.
accurate 494 adj.
true 494 adj.
mistake 495 n.
semantic 514 adj.
intrepretative
520 adj.
verbal 559 adj.
orthodox 976 adj.
literally
truly 494 adv.
literal-minded
narrow-minded
481 adj.
accurate 494 adj.
literary
linguistic 557 adj.
literary 557 adj.
stylistic 566 adj.
literature
erudition 490 n.
information 524 n.
literature 557 n.
reading matter
589 n.
lithe
flexible 327 adj.
lithography
printing 555 n.
print 587 n.
litigant
accuser 928 n.
litigant 959 n.
litigation
litigation 959 n.
litigious
quarrelling
709 adj.
litmus paper
testing agent
461 n.

litotes
underestimation
483 n.
trope 519 n.
litre
metrology 465 n.
litter
leavings 41 n.
disorder 61 n.
group 74 n.
be dispersed 75 vb.
young creature
132 n.
reproduce itself
167 vb.
posterity 170 n.
bed 218 n.
vehicle 274 n.
waste 634 n.
rubbish 641 n.
dirt 649 n.
litter lout
slut 61 n.
dirty person 649 n.
litter-strewn
unsightly 842 adj.
little
slightly 33 adv.
few 105 adj.
seldom 140 adv.
little 196 adj.
contemptible
922 adj.
little bird
informant 524 n.
little by little
by degrees 27 adv.
slightly 33 adv.
slowly 278 adv.
littleness
inferiority 35 n.
littleness 196 n.
contemptibility
922 n.
little pitcher
listener 415 n.
liturgy
Christian rite
988 n.
church service
988 n.
ritual 988 n.
live
be 1 vb.
at present 121 adv.
stay 144 vb.
be situated 186 vb.

dwell 192 vb.
alive 360 adj.
live 360 vb.
dramatic 594 adj.
active 678 adj.
feel 818 vb.
live and let live
give scope 744 vb.
compromise
770 vb.
be patient 823 vb.
lived in
occupied 191 adj.
live in
dwell 192 vb.
live 360 vb.
live-in
lover 887 n.
**live in a state of
grace**
be innocent 935 vb.
live in the past
remember 505 vb.
live it up
revel 837 vb.
be sociable 882 vb.
be intemperate
943 vb.
livelihood
vocation 622 n.
livelong
lasting 113 adj.
lively
speedy 277 adj.
imaginative
513 adj.
busy 678 adj.
feeling 818 adj.
lively 819 adj.
sociable 882 adj.
live music
music 412 n.
liven up
live 360 vb.
be cheerful 833 vb.
live on
eat 301 vb.
be remembered
505 vb.
liver
insides 224 n.
meat 301 n.
sullenness 893 n.
liverish
irascible 892 adj.
livery
hue 425 n.

livestock
animal 365 n.
cattle 365 n.
live theatre
drama 594 n.
live together
wed 894 vb.
live with
unite with 45 vb.
accompany 89 vb.
livid
colourless 426 adj.
blackish 428 adj.
grey 429 adj.
blue 435 adj.
excited 821 adj.
angry 891 adj.
living
existing 1 adj.
alive 360 adj.
life 360 n.
linguistic 557 adj.
vocation 622 n.
estate 777 n.
benefice 985 n.
living image
analogue 18 n.
duplication 91 n.
living room
chamber 194 n.
living soul
person 371 n.
lizard
reptile 365 n.
llanos
plain 348 n.
load
finite quantity
26 n.
addition 38 n.
fill 54 vb.
bunch 74 n.
contents 193 n.
load 193 vb.
transport 272 n.
gravity 322 n.
weigh 322 vb.
store 632 n.
make ready
669 vb.
adversity 731 n.
worry 825 n.
loaded
weighty 322 adj.
moneyed 800 adj.

loads
great quantity
32 n.
multitude 104 n.
loadstone
traction 288 n.
load the dice
deceive 542 vb.
load with
hinder 702 vb.
loaf
head 213 n.
cereals 301 n.
intelligence 498 n.
be inactive 679 vb.
loam
soil 344 n.
loan
subvention 703 n.
lend 784 vb.
lending 784 n.
borrowing 785 n.
credit 802 n.
loan word
word 559 n.
neology 560 n.
loath
dissenting 489 adj.
unwilling 598 adj.
loathe
dislike 861 vb.
hate 888 vb.
loathsome
unsavoury 391 adj.
not nice 645 adj.
unpleasant
827 adj.
ugly 842 adj.
hateful 888 adj.
lob
strike 279 vb.
propel 287 vb.
elevate 310 vb.
lob (cricket)
propulsion 287 n.
lobby
influence 178 n.
influence 178 vb.
lobby 194 n.
incite 612 vb.
motivator 612 n.
petitioner 763 n.
lobbyist
motivator 612 n.
petitioner 763 n.

lobe
hanging object
217 n.
ear 415 n.
lobotomy
surgery 658 n.
lobster
fish food 301 n.
marine life 365 n.
local
focus 76 n.
native 191 n.
provincial 192 adj.
tavern 192 n.
near 200 adj.
dialectal 560 adj.
social round 882 n.
local anaesthetic
anaesthetic 375 n.
locality
region 184 n.
place 185 n.
locality 187 n.
localize
place 187 vb.
locally
near 200 adv.
local time
clock time 117 n.
locate
specify 80 vb.
place 187 vb.
orientate 281 vb.
discover 484 vb.
location
place 185 n.
situation 186 n.
location 187 n.
loch
lake 346 n.
lochia
excrement 302 n.
lock
join 45 vb.
fastening 47 n.
all 52 n.
filament 208 n.
close 264 vb.
stopper 264 n.
conduit 351 n.
access 624 n.
safeguard 662 n.
firearm 723 n.
retain 778 vb.
retention 778 n.
lock and key
fastening 47 n.

locker
box 194 n.
compartment
194 n.
locket
jewellery 844 n.
lockjaw
spasm 318 n.
infection 651 n.
lockout
exclusion 57 n.
strike 145 n.
hindrance 702 n.
locks
hair 259 n.
locksmith
artisan 686 n.
lock stock and barrel
finite quantity
26 n.
lock up
conceal 525 vb.
safeguard 660 vb.
imprison 747 vb.
punish 963 vb.
lockup
lockup 748 n.
locomotive
dynamic 160 adj.
moving 265 adj.
locomotive 274 n.
locum
substitute 150 n.
doctor 658 n.
deputy 755 n.
locust
destroyer 168 n.
eater 301 n.
insect 365 n.
bane 659 n.
glutton 947 n.
lodestar
signpost 547 n.
lodge
place 187 vb.
place oneself
187 vb.
dwell 192 vb.
house 192 n.
small house 192 n.
society 708 n.
lodger
resident 191 n.
possessor 776 n.
lodgings
quarters 192 n.

loess
leavings 41 n.
soil 344 n.
loft
attic 194 n.
vertex 213 n.
propel 287 vb.
elevate 310 vb.
storage 632 n.
lofty
great 32 adj.
high 209 adj.
impressive 821 adj.
worshipful 866 adj.
proud 871 adj.
insolent 878 adj.
disinterested
931 adj.
log
sailing aid 269 n.
velocity 277 n.
fuel 385 n.
gauge 465 n.
record 548 n.
record 548 vb.
register 548 vb.
logarithms
mathematics 86 n.
log-book
chronology 117 n.
record 548 n.
logic
conformance 24 n.
reasoning 475 n.
logical
rational 475 adj.
logistics
transference 272 n.
tactics 688 n.
logjam
equilibrium 28 n.
stop 145 n.
impossibility
470 n.
inaction 677 n.
inactivity 679 n.
difficulty 700 n.
hindrance 702 n.
obstacle 702 n.
logo
label 547 n.
pattern 844 n.
log off
computerize 86 vb.
log on
computerize 86 vb.

loins
source 156 n.
genitalia 167 n.
parentage 169 n.

loiter
be late 136 vb.
be stealthy 525 vb.
be inactive 679 vb.

loll
be horizontal
  216 vb.
hang 217 vb.
be inactive 679 vb.
repose 683 vb.

lollipop
sweets 301 n.
sweet thing 392 n.

lollipop man or lady
traffic control
  305 n.

lone
nonuniform 17 adj.
alone 88 adj.
one 88 adj.
unsociable 883 adj.

lonely
separate 46 adj.
alone 88 adj.
empty 190 adj.
secluded 883 adj.
unsociable 883 adj.

loner
nonconformist
  84 n.
unit 88 n.
solitary 883 n.

lonesome
alone 88 adj.

lone wolf
unit 88 n.
revolter 738 n.
solitary 883 n.

long
for a long time
  113 adv.
long 203 adj.
desire 859 vb.

longbow
missile weapon
  723 n.

long drink
draught 301 n.

longevity
long duration
  113 n.
old age 131 n.
life 360 n.

long for
regret 830 vb.
desire 859 vb.

longhand
writing 586 n.

longing
suffering 825 n.
regret 830 n.
desire 859 n.
love 887 n.
envious 912 adj.

longitude
quantity 26 n.
length 203 n.

longlasting
perpetual 115 adj.

long-legged
long 203 adj.
narrow 206 adj.
tall 209 adj.

long odds
fair chance 159 n.
improbability
  472 n.

long shot
propulsion 287 n.
improbability
  472 n.

long sight
vision 438 n.
dim sight 440 n.

long standing
durability 113 n.
permanence 144 n.

longstanding
lasting 113 adj.
permanent 144 adj.

longsuffering
leniency 736 n.
lenient 736 adj.
patience 823 n.
patient 823 adj.
suffering 825 adj.
mercy 905 n.
forgiveness 909 n.

long-term
lasting 113 adj.

long wave
radiation 417 n.

long-winded
prolix 570 adj.
loquacious 581 adj.
tedious 838 adj.

loo
latrine 649 n.

loofah
cleaning utensil
  648 n.

look
similarity 18 n.
form 243 n.
gaze 438 vb.
inspection 438 n.
look 438 n.
appearance 445 n.
look 445 n.
hint 524 n.
gesticulate 547 vb.
conduct 688 n.

look after
look after 457 vb.

look ahead
gaze 438 vb.
foresee 510 vb.
plan 623 vb.

look-alike
identical 13 adj.
identity 13 n.
analogue 18 n.
duplication 91 n.
substitute 150 n.
representation
  551 n.

look at
gaze 438 vb.
watch 441 vb.

look back
turn back 286 vb.
regret 830 vb.

look down on
be proud 871 vb.
be insolent 878 vb.
not respect 921 vb.
despise 922 vb.

look for
be curious 453 vb.
enquire 459 vb.
search 459 vb.
expect 507 vb.
foresee 510 vb.
intend 617 vb.
pursue 619 vb.
request 761 vb.
desire 859 vb.

look forward
hope 852 vb.

look in
enter 297 vb.
visit 882 vb.

look-in
opportunity 137 n.

look in front
gaze 438 vb.

looking glass
mirror 442 n.

look into
enquire 459 vb.

look like
resemble 18 vb.

look on
be present 189 vb.
see 438 vb.
watch 441 vb.
be mindful 455 vb.
acquiesce 488 vb.
not act 677 vb.

look out
scan 438 vb.
be cautious 858 vb.

lookout
high structure
  209 n.
view 438 n.
spectator 441 n.
surveillance 457 n.
expectation 507 n.
function 622 n.
protector 660 n.
warner 664 n.
keeper 749 n.

look over
scan 438 vb.

look through
scan 438 vb.

look up to
honour 866 vb.
respect 920 vb.

loom
be great - large
  32 vb.
impend 155 vb.
textile 222 n.
weave 222 vb.
weaving 222 n.
dimness 419 n.
endanger 661 vb.
workshop 687 n.

loomed
crossed 222 adj.

loony
crazy 503 adj.
mentally disor-
  dered 503 adj.
madman 504 n.

loop
fastening 47 n.
contraception
  172 n.

LOO

handle 218 n.
be curved 248 vb.
loop 250 n.
meander 251 vb.
circuit 626 n.
loophole
circle 250 n.
outlet 298 n.
contrivance 623 n.
defect 647 n.
means of escape
   667 n.
illegality 954 n.
loose
disunite 46 vb.
general 79 adj.
weak 163 adj.
soft 327 adj.
poorly reasoned
   477 adj.
inexact 495 adj.
feeble 572 adj.
lax 734 adj.
free 744 adj.
liberate 746 vb.
impure 951 adj.
unchaste 951 adj.
loose-box
cart 274 n.
loose ends
negligence 458 n.
noncompletion
   726 n.
loose-limbed
flexible 327 adj.
loosely
generally 79 adv.
loosen
disunite 46 vb.
weaken 163 vb.
liberate 746 vb.
looseness
noncoherence 49 n.
softness 327 n.
inexactness 495 n.
laxity 734 n.
loose woman
loose woman
   952 n.
loot
rob 788 vb.
booty 790 n.
shekels 797 n.
lop
subtract 39 vb.
cut 46 vb.
shorten 204 vb.

LOR

lope
gait 265 n.
pedestrianism
   267 n.
move fast 277 vb.
lopsided
unequal 29 adj.
clumsy 695 adj.
loquacious
loquacious 581 adj.
loquacity
word 559 n.
loquacity 581 n.
Lord
God the Son 965 n.
lord
male 372 n.
master 741 n.
owner 776 n.
lord it over
dominate 733 vb.
be insolent 878 vb.
lordly
authoritative
   733 adj.
ruling 733 adj.
authoritarian
   735 adj.
liberal 813 adj.
worshipful 866 adj.
noble 868 adj.
proud 871 adj.
insolent 878 adj.
**lord or lady of the
   manor**
master 741 n.
Lords
contest 716 n.
Lords day
repose 683 n.
holy day 988 n.
lordship
*position of author-
   ity* 733 n.
lands 777 n.
aristocracy 868 n.
person of rank
   868 n.
title 870 n.
church title 986 n.
Lord's Prayer, the
prayers 981 n.
Lord's Supper, the
Holy Communion
   988 n.
lore
tradition 127 n.

LOS

erudition 490 n.
knowledge 490 n.
   See **erudition**
learning 536 n.
lorgnette
eyeglass 442 n.
lorry
carrier 273 n.
lorry 274 n.
lose
decrease 37 vb.
derange 63 vb.
be late 136 vb.
misplace 188 vb.
outstrip 277 vb.
err 495 vb.
be defeated 728 vb.
lose 772 vb.
lose face
be inferior 35 vb.
act foolishly
   695 vb.
lose repute 867 vb.
lose ground
decelerate 278 vb.
fall short 307 vb.
relapse 657 vb.
be defeated 728 vb.
lose heart
be dejected 834 vb.
despair 853 vb.
lose one's balance
tumble 309 vb.
lose one's cool
be excited 821 vb.
lose one's head
go mad 503 vb.
lose one's nerve
be cowardly
   856 vb.
lose one's temper
be rude 885 vb.
get angry 891 vb.
lose one's way
stray 282 vb.
lose out
be defeated 728 vb.
loser
loser 728 n.
lose sight of
be inattentive
   456 vb.
neglect 458 vb.
forget 506 vb.
lose the day
be defeated 728 vb.

LOT

lose the thread
be unrelated 10 vb.
stray 282 vb.
be inattentive
   456 vb.
be uncertain
   474 vb.
losing battle
defeat 728 n.
loss 772 n.
loss
ruin 165 n.
shortfall 307 n.
disappearance
   446 n.
loss 772 n.
loss leader
incentive 612 n.
loss 772 n.
discount 810 n.
cheapness 812 n.
lost
separate 46 adj.
incomplete 55 adj.
past 125 adj.
absent 190 adj.
lost 772 adj.
impenitent
   940 adj.
lost cause
rejection 607 n.
defeat 728 n.
lost sheep
bad person 938 n.
lot
state 7 n.
finite quantity
   26 n.
great quantity
   32 n.
all 52 n.
accumulation 74 n.
bunch 74 n.
group 74 n.
sort 77 n.
chance 159 n.
territory 184 n.
enclosure 235 n.
fate 596 n.
portion 783 n.
Lothario
lover 887 n.
libertine 952 n.
lotion
water 339 n.
balm 658 n.

lots
great quantity
32 n.
multitude 104 n.
plenty 635 n.
lottery
equal chance
159 n.
gambling 618 n.
nondesign 618 n.
gambling game
837 n.
lotus-eater
idler 679 n.
loud
loud 400 adj.
florid 425 adj.
manifest 522 adj.
ill-bred 847 adj.
vulgar 847 adj.
loud hailer
megaphone 400 n.
hearing aid 415 n.
publicity 528 n.
loudly
loudly 400 adv.
loudmouth
rude person 885 n.
loudness
loudness 400 n.
hue 425 n.
bad taste 847 n.
ill-breeding 847 n.
loudspeaker
sound 398 n.
megaphone 400 n.
hearing aid 415 n.
publicity 528 n.
lounge
chamber 194 n.
be inactive 679 vb.
repose 683 vb.
lounge bar
tavern 192 n.
lour
impend 155 vb.
hang 217 vb.
be dark 418 vb.
be dim 419 vb.
predict 511 vb.
warn 664 vb.
be rude 885 vb.
sullenness 893 n.
threaten 900 vb.
Lourdes
focus 76 n.

louse
insect 365 n.
cad 938 n.
louse-up
mistake 495 n.
lousy
not nice 645 adj.
unclean 649 adj.
lousy with
full 54 adj.
multitudinous
104 adj.
lout
rude person 885 n.
ruffian 904 n.
love
zero 103 n.
enjoy 376 vb.
courteous act
884 n.
love 887 n.
love 887 vb.
loved one 887 n.
lover 887 n.
darling 890 n.
divineness 965 n.
love affair
love affair 887 n.
love child
descendant 170 n.
bastardy 954 n.
loved one
loved one 887 n.
love letter
correspondence
588 n.
love token 889 n.
wooing 889 n.
lovelorn
loving 887 adj.
lovely
pleasant 376 adj.
excellent 644 adj.
super 644 adj.
pleasurable
826 adj.
a beauty 841 n.
beautiful 841 adj.
lovemaking
lovemaking 887 n.
endearment 889 n.
wooing 889 n.
love-play
wooing 889 n.
lover
concomitant 89 n.
lover 887 n.

lovesick
loving 887 adj.
loving cup
cup 194 n.
draught 301 n.
loving words
endearment 889 n.
low
small 33 adj.
inferior 35 adj.
inferiority 35 n.
weak 163 adj.
low 210 n.
muted 401 adj.
ululate 409 vb.
not nice 645 adj.
dejected 834 adj.
vulgar 847 adj.
disreputable
867 adj.
plebeian 869 adj.
humble 872 adj.
low-born
plebeian 869 adj.
lowbrow
uninstructed
491 adj.
ignoramus 493 n.
unintelligent
499 adj.
low-budget
cheap 812 adj.
lowdown
truth 494 n.
information 524 n.
low ebb
lowness 210 n.
lower
inferior 35 adj.
low 210 adj.
be deep 211 vb.
lower 311 vb.
pervert 655 vb.
humiliate 872 vb.
not respect 921 vb.
hold cheap 922 vb.
defame 926 vb.
Lower House
parliament 692 n.
lower level
lowness 210 n.
lower oneself
descend 309 vb.
sit down 311 vb.
demean oneself
867 vb.

lower one's sights
abase 311 vb.
lower the light
darken 418 vb.
lowest point
inferiority 35 n.
lowness 210 n.
depth 211 n.
base 214 n.
low-fat food
food 301 n.
low fellow
low fellow 869 n.
low gear
slowness 278 n.
low-key
moderate 177 adj.
lowlands
lowness 210 n.
land 344 n.
plain 348 n.
low-level
low 210 adj.
unimportant
639 adj.
lowly
inferior 35 adj.
plebeian 869 adj.
humble 872 adj.
lowness
lowness 210 n.
humility 872 n.
low on
insufficient
636 adj.
lowpaid
poor 801 adj.
lox
fish food 301 n.
loyal
conformable
83 adj.
obedient 739 adj.
observant 768 adj.
friendly 880 adj.
loving 887 adj.
patriotic 901 adj.
trustworthy
929 adj.
orthodox 976 adj.
loyalist
conformist 83 n.
auxiliary 707 n.
defender 713 n.
loyalty
willingness 597 n.
loyalty 739 n.

duty 917 n.

lozenge
sweet thing 392 n.
heraldry 547 n.
medicine 658 n.

LP
gramophone 414 n.

LSD
drug-taking 949 n.

Lsd
money 797 n.

lubricant
lubricant 334 n.

lubricate
lubricate 334 vb.

lubricating oil
oil 357 n.

lubrication
lubrication 334 n.

lubricator
smoother 258 n.
lubricant 334 n.

lubricious
smooth 258 adj.

lubricity
changeableness
  152 n.
smoothness 258 n.
lubrication 334 n.
unctuousness
  357 n.
unchastity 951 n.

lucent
transparent
  422 adj.

lucerne
provender 301 n.

lucid
orderly 60 adj.
luminous 417 adj.
undimmed
  417 adj.
transparent
  422 adj.
sane 502 adj.
intelligible 516 adj.

lucidity
transparency
  422 n.
sanity 502 n.
intelligibility
  516 n.
perspicuity 567 n.

lucid moment
sanity 502 n.

lucid prose
perspicuity 567 n.

Lucifer
planet 321 n.
luminary 420 n.
Satan 969 n.

lucifer
lighter 385 n.

luck
changeable thing
  152 n.
chance 159 n.
good 615 n.
nondesign 618 n.
prosperity 730 n.

luckless
unfortunate
  731 adj.

luck of the draw
chance 159 n.
nondesign 618 n.
  See **gambling**
prosperity 730 n.

lucky
opportune 137 adj.
prosperous 730 adj.
happy 824 adj.

lucky break
prosperity 730 n.

lucky charm
talisman 983 n.

lucky dip
nonuniformity
  17 n.
medley 43 n.
equal chance
  159 n.

lucrative
gainful 771 adj.

Luddite
destroyer 168 n.
rioter 738 n.

ludicrous
absurd 497 adj.
foolish 499 adj.
ridiculous 849 adj.

ludo
board game 837 n.

lug
handle 218 n.
carry 273 vb.
sail 275 n.
draw 288 vb.
ear 415 n.

luggage
box 194 n.
transport 272 n.

lugubrious
cheerless 834 adj.

lamenting 836 adj.

lugworm
creepy-crawly
  365 n.

lukewarm
median 30 adj.
warm 379 adj.
unwilling 598 adj.
irresolute 601 adj.
neutral 625 adj.
apathetic 820 adj.
indifferent 860 adj.

lull
lull 145 n.
assuage 177 vb.
bring to rest
  266 vb.
silence 399 n.
silence 399 vb.
inactivity 679 n.
make inactive
  679 vb.
tranquillize
  823 vb.
please 826 vb.
content 828 vb.
relieve 831 vb.
flatter 925 vb.

lullaby
moderator 177 n.
musical piece
  412 n.
vocal music 412 n.
soporific 679 n.

lumbago
pang 377 n.
rheumatism 651 n.

lumbar
back 238 adj.

lumber
leavings 41 n.
disorder 61 n.
walk 267 vb.
move slowly
  278 vb.
wood 366 n.
rubbish 641 n.
work 682 vb.
be clumsy 695 vb.

lumbered with
hindered 702 adj.

lumbering
unwieldy 195 adj.
clumsy 695 adj.

luminary
luminary 420 n.
sage 500 n.

person of repute
  866 n.

luminescent
luminous 417 adj.

luminous
luminous 417 adj.

lump
great quantity
  32 n.
piece 53 n.
bulk 195 n.
convexity 253 n.
swelling 253 n.
gravity 322 n.
solid body 324 n.
hardness 326 n.

lumpectomy
surgery 658 n.

lump in one's throat
feeling 818 n.

lumpish
inert 175 adj.
unwieldy 195 adj.
inactive 679 adj.

lump sum
funds 797 n.

lump together
join 45 vb.
combine 50 vb.
bring together
  74 vb.

lumpy
unwieldy 195 adj.
thick 205 adj.
convex 253 adj.
rough 259 adj.
dense 324 adj.

lunacy
folly 499 n.
mental disorder
  503 n.

lunar
curved 248 adj.
celestial 321 adj.

lunar month
period 110 n.

lunatic
mentally disor-
  dered 503 adj.
madman 504 n.
rash 857 adj.

lunch
eat 301 vb.
meal 301 n.

luncheon
meal 301 n.

lung cancer
  respiratory disease
    651 n.
lunge
  move fast 277 vb.
  impulse 279 n.
  strike at 712 vb.
lunge at
  strike 279 vb.
lungs
  insides 224 n.
  respiration 352 n.
  voice 577 n.
lupin
  plant 366 n.
lupine
  animal 365 adj.
lurch
  obliquity 220 n.
  walk 267 vb.
  move slowly
    278 vb.
  descent 309 n.
  fluctuation 317 n.
  oscillate 317 vb.
  be agitated 318 vb.
  show feeling
    818 vb.
  be drunk 949 vb.
lurching
  fitfulness 142 n.
lure
  attract 291 vb.
  attraction 291 n.
  ensnare 542 vb.
  trap 542 n.
  incentive 612 n.
  tempt 612 vb.
  desired object
    859 n.
  reward 962 n.
lurid
  luminous 417 adj.
  florid 425 adj.
  frightening
    854 adj.
  showy 875 adj.
lurk
  lurk 523 vb.
lurking
  invisible 444 adj.
  latent 523 adj.
  stealthy 525 adj.
luscious
  sweet 392 adj.
  pleasurable
    826 adj.

lush
  prolific 171 adj.
  vigorous 174 adj.
  plentiful 635 adj.
  rich 800 adj.
  drunkard 949 n.
  drunkenness 949 n.
  get drunk 949 vb.
lust
  desire 859 n.
    See **libido**
  desire 859 vb.
  libido 859 n.
  love 887 n.
  vice 934 n.
  be impure 951 vb.
  unchastity 951 n.
lust after
  desire 859 vb.
  envy 912 vb.
lustful
  loving 887 adj.
  lecherous 951 adj.
lustration
  ritual act 988 n.
lustre
  light 417 n.
    See **reflection**
  reflection 417 n.
  prestige 866 n.
lustrous
  luminous 417 adj.
  noteworthy
    866 adj.
lusty
  strong 162 adj.
  vigorous 174 adj.
  fleshy 195 adj.
  healthy 650 adj.
lute
  stringed instrument
    414 n.
luxuriant
  prolific 171 adj.
  dense 324 adj.
  ornate 574 adj.
  plentiful 635 adj.
luxuriate
  abound 635 vb.
  superabound
    637 vb.
  be intemperate
    943 vb.
luxurious
  comfortable
    376 adj.

superfluous
    637 adj.
  rich 800 adj.
  pleasurable
    826 adj.
  ostentatious
    875 adj.
  intemperate
    943 adj.
  sensual 944 adj.
luxury
  plenty 635 n.
  superfluity 637 n.
  prosperity 730 n.
  wealth 800 n.
  intemperance
    943 n.
  sensualism 944 n.
lycanthrope
  demon 970 n.
lychgate
  doorway 263 n.
  funeral 364 n.
    See **obsequies**
  church exterior
    990 n.
lyddite
  explosive 723 n.
lye
  solution 337 n.
lying
  erroneous 495 adj.
  false 541 adj.
  falsehood 541 n.
  untrue 543 adj.
lymph
  blood 335 n.
  fluid 335 n.
lymphatic
  haematic 335 adj.
  watery 339 adj.
lymphogram
  diagnostic 658 n.
lynch
  kill 362 vb.
  disapprove 924 vb.
  execute 963 vb.
lynx
  big cat 365 n.
  eye 438 n.
lyre
  stringed instrument
    414 n.
lyric
  musical 412 adj.
  vocal music 412 n.
  poetic 593 adj.

lyrical
  melodious 410 adj.
  poetic 593 adj.
  impressed 818 adj.
  rejoicing 835 adj.
  approving 923 adj.
lyrics
  vocal music 412 n.
  reading matter
    589 n.

M

ma'am
  female 373 n.
  title 870 n.
mac
  overcoat 228 n.
macabre
  frightening
    854 adj.
  spooky 970 adj.
macadam
  road 624 n.
macaroni
  dish 301 n.
macaroon
  pastries and cakes
    301 n.
macaw
  bird 365 n.
mace
  spice 301 n.
  badge 547 n.
  club 723 n.
  badge of rule
    743 n.
macedoine
  hors-d'oeuvres
    301 n.
macerate
  soften 327 vb.
  drench 341 vb.
machete
  sharp edge 256 n.
  sidearms 723 n.
Machiavellian
  hypocritical
    541 adj.
  cunning 698 adj.
  perfidious 930 adj.
machination
  deception 542 n.
  plot 623 n.
  stratagem 698 n.
machine
  produce 164 vb.

print 587 vb.
machine 630 n.
machine language
language 557 n.
machinery
component 58 n.
machine 630 n.
machinist
machinist 630 n.
artisan 686 n.
machismo
male 372 n.
manliness 855 n.
ostentation 875 n.
mach number
velocity 277 n.
macho
manly 162 adj.
male 372 adj.
male 372 n.
courageous
855 adj.
mackerel
fish food 301 n.
mackintosh
overcoat 228 n.
macramé
network 222 n.
macrobiotic diet
dieting 301 n.
macrocosm
generality 79 n.
universe 321 n.
macron
punctuation 547 n.
macroscopic
large 195 adj.
macula
mottle 437 n.
skin disease 651 n.
blemish 845 n.
mad
furious 176 adj.
absurd 497 adj.
*mentally disor-
dered* 503 adj.
capricious 604 adj.
excited 821 adj.
angry 891 adj.
mad about
loving 887 adj.
madam
female 373 n.
master 741 n.
title 870 n.
insolent person
878 n.

bawd 952 n.
madame
female 373 n.
title 870 n.
madcap
foolish 499 adj.
excitable 822 adj.
desperado 857 n.
rash 857 adj.
madden
make mad 503 vb.
enrage 891 vb.
maddening
annoying 827 adj.
madder
pigment 425 n.
red pigment 431 n.
madeira
wine 301 n.
Madeira cake
pastries and cakes
301 n.
made-to-measure
tailored 228 adj.
madhouse
disorder 61 n.
See **turmoil**
turmoil 61 n.
mental hospital
503 n.
madly
extremely 32 vb.
madman
madman 504 n.
madrigal
vocal music 412 n.
madwoman
madman 504 n.
maelstrom
vortex 315 n.
eddy 350 n.
pitfall 663 n.
activity 678 n.
maestro
orchestra 413 n.
proficient person
696 n.
mafficking
celebration 876 n.
mafia
revolter 738 n.
offender 904 n.
mafioso
offender 904 n.
magazine
accumulation 74 n.
journal 528 n.

book 589 n.
reading matter
589 n.
storage 632 n.
arsenal 723 n.
firearm 723 n.
magenta
red 431 adj.
purple 436 adj.
maggot
creepy-crawly
365 n.
Magi
sage 500 n.
magic
influence 178 n.
sleight 542 n.
super 644 adj.
miracle-working
864 n.
wonderful 864 adj.
prestige 866 n.
fairylike 970 adj.
bewitch 983 vb.
magical 983 adj.
sorcery 983 n.
occultism 984 n.
magic carpet
airship 276 n.
magic instrument
983 n.
magician
proficient person
696 n.
sorcerer 983 n.
magic lantern
lamp 420 n.
visual fallacy
440 n.
camera 442 n.
plaything 837 n.
magic mushroom
drug-taking 949 n.
magistrate
official 690 n.
officer 741 n.
judge 957 n.
Magna Carta
dueness 915 n.
magnanimous
benevolent 897 adj.
disinterested
931 adj.
virtuous 933 adj.
magnate
bigwig 638 n.
rich person 800 n.

aristocrat 868 n.
magnet
incentive 612 n.
desired object
859 n.
magnetic
dynamic 160 adj.
magnetic field
energy 160 n.
attraction 291 n.
magnetic tape
data processing
86 n.
rotator 315 n.
hearing aid 415 n.
record 548 n.
magnetism
influence 178 n.
traction 288 n.
attraction 291 n.
inducement 612 n.
magnetize
attract 291 vb.
magneto
electronics 160 n.
magnification
greatness 32 n.
vision 438 n.
exaggeration
546 n.
magnificent
large 195 adj.
excellent 644 adj.
splendid 841 adj.
ostentatious
875 adj.
magnifico
aristocrat 868 n.
magnify
augment 36 vb.
enlarge 197 vb.
overestimate
482 vb.
exaggerate 546 vb.
boast 877 vb.
praise 923 vb.
worship 981 vb.
magnifying glass
transparency
422 n.
magnitude
degree 27 n.
greatness 32 n.
size 195 n.
light 417 n.
importance 638 n.

magnolia
tree 366 n.
whitish 427 adj.
magnum
vessel 194 n.
size 195 n.
magnum opus
product 164 n.
book 589 n.
masterpiece 694 n.
magpie
bird 365 n.
niggard 816 n.
maharajah
potentate 741 n.
maharani
potentate 741 n.
maharishi
religious teacher
973 n.
mahatma
sage 500 n.
mah jong
indoor game 837 n.
mahogany
tree 366 n.
brown 430 adj.
brownness 430 n.
mahout
rider 268 n.
maid
youngster 132 n.
domestic 742 n.
spinster 895 n.
virgin 950 n.
maiden
first 68 adj.
new 126 adj.
youngster 132 n.
female 373 n.
spinster 895 n.
virgin 950 n.
means of execution
964 n.
maiden aunt
spinster 895 n.
maidenhead
purity 950 n.
maidenhood
celibacy 895 n.
purity 950 n.
maiden name
name 561 n.
maiden speech
debut 68 n.
maiden's prayer
loved one 887 n.

maiden voyage
debut 68 n.
maid or matron of honour
bridal party 894 n.
mail
covering 226 n.
send 272 vb.
postal communica-tions 531 n.
correspondence
588 n.
safeguard 662 n.
armour 713 n.
mailed fist
brute force 735 n.
lawlessness 954 n.
mailing list
information 524 n.
correspondence
588 n.
mail-order
send 272 vb.
purchase 792 n.
maim
disable 161 vb.
impair 655 vb.
main
great 32 adj.
supreme 34 adj.
ocean 343 n.
important 638 adj.
main chance
chief thing 638 n.
mainframe
counting instru-ment 86 n.
mainland
land 344 n.
mainline
drug oneself
949 vb.
mainly
greatly 32 vb.
on the whole
52 adv.
generally 79 adv.
main road
road 624 n.
mainsail
sail 275 n.
mainstay
support 218 n.
chief thing 638 n.
refuge 662 n.
aider 703 n.
hope 852 n.

maintain
stay 144 vb.
sustain 146 vb.
support 218 vb.
vitalize 360 vb.
believe 485 vb.
affirm 532 vb.
persevere 600 vb.
provide 633 vb.
preserve 666 vb.
vindicate 927 vb.
maintenance
continuance 146 n.
provisions 301 n.
perseverance 600 n.
provision 633 n.
subvention 703 n.
dower 777 n.
receipt 807 n.
maisonette
flat 192 n.
maître d'hôtel
caterer 633 n.
maize
cereals 301 n.
food 301 n.
majestic
elegant 575 adj.
authoritative
733 adj.
ruling 733 adj.
impressive 821 adj.
worshipful 866 adj.
noble 868 adj.
proud 871 adj.
formal 875 adj.
majesty
greatness 32 n.
superiority 34 n.
authority 733 n.
prestige 866 n.
nobility 868 n.
divine attribute
965 n.
major
great 32 adj.
first 68 adj.
older 131 adj.
important 638 adj.
army officer 741 n.
majordomo
retainer 742 n.
majority
finite quantity
26 n.
degree 27 n.
chief part 52 n.

plurality 101 n.
adultness 134 n.
majuscule
letter 558 n.
make
unite with 45 vb.
compose 56 vb.
constitute 56 vb.
sort 77 n.
convert 147 vb.
cause 156 vb.
produce 164 vb.
form 243 vb.
arrive 295 vb.
structure 331 n.
estimate 480 vb.
make better
654 vb.
acquire 771 vb.
gain 771 vb.
make a balls-up of
impair 655 vb.
make a beeline for
steer for 281 vb.
make a break for it
decamp 296 vb.
make a clean breast of it
confess 526 vb.
be truthful 540 vb.
make a clean sweep (of)
revolutionize
149 vb.
empty 300 vb.
clean 648 vb.
make a comeback
recoup 31 vb.
be restored 656 vb.
make a dead set at
desire 859 vb.
make advances
court 889 vb.
make a face
dislike 861 vb.
disapprove 924 vb.
make a fool of
be absurd 497 vb.
fool 542 vb.
ridicule 851 vb.
humiliate 872 vb.
make a go of
succeed 727 vb.
make a guinea pig of
experiment 461 vb.
make a killing
gain 771 vb.

get rich 800 vb.
make alterations
  differ 15 vb.
make a man of
  do good 644 vb.
  give courage
    855 vb.
make amends
  compensate 31 vb.
  restore 656 vb.
  restitute 787 vb.
  atone 941 vb.
make a mint
  get rich 800 vb.
make an aside
  voice 577 vb.
  soliloquize 585 vb.
make a packet
  get rich 800 vb.
make a pass
  court 889 vb.
make a point of
  compel 740 vb.
make a scene
  be angry 891 vb.
make a show of
  show 522 vb.
  dissemble 541 vb.
  be affected 850 vb.
make a stand
  resist 715 vb.
make a storm in a tea cup
  exaggerate 546 vb.
make away with
  destroy 165 vb.
  kill 362 vb.
  murder 362 vb.
make-believe
  fantasy 513 n.
  imaginary 513 adj.
  imagine 513 vb.
  hypocritical
    541 adj.
  sham 542 n.
  spurious 542 adj.
  be untrue 543 vb.
  untrue 543 adj.
make capital out of
  plead 614 vb.
  find useful 640 adj.
  use 673 vb.
make do with
  substitute 150 vb.
make ends meet
  vitalize 360 vb.

make fast
  tighten 45 vb.
  stabilize 153 vb.
make for
  congregate 74 vb.
  navigate 269 vb.
  promote 285 vb.
make free with
  be free 744 vb.
  appropriate
    786 vb.
  be insolent 878 vb.
  be rude 885 vb.
make fun of
  fool 542 vb.
  be witty 839 vb.
  ridicule 851 vb.
make good
  compensate 31 vb.
  succeed 727 vb.
  vindicate 927 vb.
make hay while the sun shines
  profit by 137 vb.
make headway
  progress 285 vb.
  get better 654 vb.
make inroads on
  encroach 306 vb.
make into
  convert 147 vb.
make it
  triumph 727 vb.
  prosper 730 vb.
make it up
  make peace
    719 vb.
  forgive 909 vb.
make light of
  underestimate
    483 vb.
  do easily 701 vb.
  be indifferent
    860 vb.
make love
  unite with 45 vb.
  love 887 vb.
  caress 889 vb.
make merry
  rejoice 835 vb.
  revel 837 vb.
make money
  flourish 615 vb.
  prosper 730 vb.
  acquire 771 vb.
  gain 771 vb.
  get rich 800 vb.

make off with
  steal 788 vb.
make one
  compel 740 vb.
make one jump
  surprise 508 vb.
  frighten 854 vb.
make one sit up
  impress 821 vb.
make or mar
  cause 156 vb.
make out
  see 438 vb.
  understand 516 vb.
  decipher 520 vb.
  succeed 727 vb.
make over
  transfer 272 vb.
  repair 656 vb.
make overtures
  approach 289 vb.
  offer 759 vb.
  request 761 vb.
  make terms
    766 vb.
  befriend 880 vb.
make public
  publish 528 vb.
make sense
  be intelligible
    516 vb.
makeshift
  inferior 35 adj.
  substitute 150 n.
  substituted 150 adj.
  flimsy 163 adj.
  spontaneous
    609 adj.
  imperfect 647 adj.
  imperfection 647 n.
make shipshape
  make better
    654 vb.
make short work of
  destroy 165 vb.
  eat 301 vb.
  be active 678 vb.
  hasten 680 vb.
  do easily 701 vb.
  carry out 725 vb.
  succeed 727 vb.
make sure
  stabilize 153 vb.
  make certain
    473 vb.
  be cautious 858 vb.

make terms
  make terms
    766 vb.
make the best of
  be content 828 vb.
make the grade
  be equal 28 vb.
  suffice 635 vb.
  succeed 727 vb.
make the most of
  overestimate
    482 vb.
  make better
    654 vb.
  use 673 vb.
  be ostentatious
    875 vb.
make the running
  outstrip 277 vb.
make things worse
  deteriorate 655 vb.
  be difficult 700 vb.
  miscarry 728 vb.
make to measure
  adjust 24 vb.
make too much of
  overestimate
    482 vb.
  exaggerate 546 vb.
make tracks
  decamp 296 vb.
make up
  compensate 31 vb.
  combine 50 vb.
  make complete
    54 vb.
  compose 56 vb.
  constitute 56 vb.
  produce 164 vb.
  imagine 513 vb.
  be false 541 vb.
  make better
    654 vb.
make-up
  character 5 n.
  mimicry 20 n.
  compensation 56 n.
  structure 331 n.
  print 587 n.
  stage set 594 n.
  beautification
    843 n.
  cosmetic 843 n.
make up for
  compensate 31 vb.
  retrieve 656 vb.
  atone 941 vb.

make up to
  be servile 879 vb.
  flatter 925 vb.
make use of
  find useful 640 vb.
  use 673 vb.
make way for
  deviate 282 vb.
  facilitate 701 vb.
  submit 721 vb.
  resign 753 vb.
  show respect
    920 vb.
maladjusted
  unapt 25 adj.
  inexact 495 adj.
  maladjusted
    503 adj.
maladroit
  clumsy 695 adj.
malady
  disease 651 n.
  bane 659 n.
malaise
  pain 377 n.
  evil 616 n.
  suffering 825 n.
malapropism
  inexactness 495 n.
  absurdity 497 n.
  neology 560 n.
  misnomer 562 n.
  solecism 565 n.
  misuse 675 n.
  ridiculousness
    849 n.
malaria
  infection 651 n.
    See **tropical disease**
  tropical disease
    651 n.
malcontent
  dissenting 489 adj.
  discontented
    829 adj.
  malcontent 829 n.
male
  male 372 adj.
  male 372 n.
male chauvinism
  male 372 n.
malediction
  malediction 899 n.
malefactor
  evildoer 904 n.
  offender 904 n.

malevolence
  malevolence 898 n.
malevolent
  harmful 645 adj.
  malevolent
    898 adj.
malformed
  amorphous
    244 adj.
  deformed 246 adj.
malfunction
  fail 728 vb.
malice
  hatred 888 n.
  resentment 891 n.
  malevolence 898 n.
malicious
  harmful 645 adj.
  malevolent
    898 adj.
malign
  harmful 645 adj.
  adverse 731 adj.
  shame 867 vb.
  be malevolent
    898 vb.
  malevolent
    898 adj.
  defame 926 vb.
malignant
  deadly 362 adj.
  harmful 645 adj.
  malevolent
    898 adj.
malinger
  be false 541 vb.
  dissemble 541 vb.
  fail in duty 918 vb.
mall
  park 192 n.
  path 624 n.
malleable
  conformable
    83 adj.
  changeful 152 adj.
  flexible 327 adj.
  tractable 701 adj.
  submitting 721 adj.
  impressible
    819 adj.
mallet
  hammer 279 n.
malnutrition
  dieting 301 n.
  insufficiency 636 n.
  disease 651 n.

malodorous
  odorous 394 adj.
  fetid 397 adj.
  unpleasant
    827 adj.
malpractice
  misuse 675 n.
  guilty act 936 n.
  lawbreaking 954 n.
maltreat
  ill-treat 645 vb.
  misuse 675 vb.
  torment 827 vb.
  be malevolent
    898 vb.
malversation
  perfidy 930 n.
mamba
  reptile 365 n.
mambo
  dance 837 n.
mamma
  maternity 169 n.
  bosom 253 n.
mammal
  animal 365 n.
  mammal 365 n.
mammogram
  bosom 253 n.
  diagnostic 658 n.
Mammon
  devil 969 n.
mammoth
  fossil 125 n.
  giant 195 n.
  huge 195 adj.
  tall creature 209 n.
  animal 365 n.
man
  adult 134 n.
  operate 173 vb.
  mammal 365 n.
  humankind 371 n.
  male 372 n.
  provide 633 vb.
  make ready
    669 vb.
  defend 713 vb.
  domestic 742 n.
  lover 887 n.
  spouse 894 n.
mana
  power 160 n.
  influence 178 n.
  divineness 965 n.
man or woman about
  town

  beau monde 848 n.
manacle
  tie 45 vb.
  fetter 747 vb.
  fetter 748 n.
manage
  be able 160 vb.
  do 676 vb.
  manage 689 vb.
  triumph 727 vb.
  rule 733 vb.
manageable
  tractable 701 adj.
  obedient 739 adj.
management
  management
    689 n.
  director 690 n.
manager
  doer 676 n.
  director 690 n.
  manager 690 n.
mañana
  neverness 109 n.
  future state 124 n.
  futurity 124 n.
  delay 136 n.
  inactivity 679 n.
man-at-arms
  cavalry 722 n.
  combatant 722 n.
  soldier 722 n.
  soldiery 722 n.
Mandarin
  language 557 n.
mandarin
  fruit and vegetables
    301 n.
  bigwig 638 n.
  officer 741 n.
mandate
  government 733 n.
  political organiza-
    tion 733 n.
  mandate 751 n.
mandatory
  necessary 596 adj.
  authoritative
    733 adj.
  commanding
    737 adj.
  compelling
    740 adj.
  obligatory 917 adj.
mandolin
  stringed instrument
    414 n.

mane
hair 259 n.
man-eater
eater 301 n.
killer 362 n.
animal 365 n.
hunter 619 n.
man-eating
eating 301 n.
murderous 362 adj.
manège
equitation 267 n.
animal husbandry
369 n.
man Friday
worker 686 n.
aider 703 n.
manful
manly 162 adj.
mange
animal disease
651 n.
skin disease 651 n.
manger
bowl 194 n.
mangetout
fruit and vegetables
301 n.
mangle
flattener 216 n.
distort 246 vb.
smoother 258 n.
dry 342 vb.
dryer 342 n.
wound 655 vb.
mangrove
tree 366 n.
mangy
bad 645 adj.
unclean 649 adj.
manhandle
touch 378 vb.
misuse 675 vb.
man-hater
misanthrope 902 n.
manhole
orifice 263 n.
manhood
adultness 134 n.
male 372 n.
manliness 855 n.
man-hours
labour 682 n.
manhunt
chase 619 n.
mania
psychosis 503 n.

warm feeling
818 n.
desire 859 n.
liking 859 n.
maniac
madman 504 n.
maniacal
psychotic 503 adj.
manic
psychotic 503 adj.
manic depression
psychosis 503 n.
Manichaeism
heresy 977 n.
manicure
beautification
843 n.
manicurist
beautician 843 n.
manifest
list 87 n.
manifest 522 adj.
manifest 522 vb.
manifestation
manifestation
522 n.
manifest itself
be visible 443 vb.
manifesto
publication 528 n.
electorate 605 n.
command 737 n.
decree 737 n.
manifold
multiform 82 adj.
many 104 adj.
manikin
small thing 33 n.
dwarf 196 n.
image 551 n.
manila
fibre 208 n.
man or woman in the
street
common man 30 n.
everyman 79 n.
social group 371 n.
commoner 869 n.
maniple
vestments 989 n.
manipulate
touch 378 vb.
fake 541 vb.
fool 542 vb.
motivate 612 vb.
plot 623 vb.
doctor 658 vb.

use 673 vb.
misuse 675 vb.
do 676 vb.
deal with 688 vb.
mankind
humankind 371 n.
manliness
male 372 n.
manliness 855 n.
manly
grown-up 134 adj.
manly 162 adj.
animal 365 adj.
male 372 adj.
beautiful 841 adj.
courageous
855 adj.
man-made
imitative 20 adj.
spurious 542 adj.
manna
food 301 n.
manna from heaven
gift 781 n.
manned
occupied 191 adj.
mannequin
living model 23 n.
exhibitor 522 n.
manner
modality 7 n.
sort 77 n.
style 566 n.
way 624 n.
conduct 688 n.
mannered
stylistic 566 adj.
affected 850 adj.
mannerism
speciality 80 n.
nonconformity
84 n.
identification
547 n.
phrase 563 n.
style 566 n.
habit 610 n.
affectation 850 n.
mannerly
tasteful 846 adj.
courteous 884 adj.
manners
practice 610 n.
conduct 688 n.
good taste 846 n.
etiquette 848 n.
courtesy 884 n.

mannish
male 372 adj.
manoeuvre
be in motion
265 vb.
motion 265 n.
deed 676 n.
do 676 vb.
tactics 688 n.
be cunning 698 vb.
stratagem 698 n.
man or woman of
means
rich person 800 n.
man or woman of the
world
expert 696 n.
beau monde 848 n.
manor
house 192 n.
lands 777 n.
man-o'-war
warship 722 n.
man of straw
insubstantial thing
4 n.
changeable thing
152 n.
sham 542 n.
nonentity 639 n.
manpower
band 74 n.
power 160 n.
means 629 n.
personnel 686 n.
manqué
unsuccessful
728 adj.
manse
parsonage 986 n.
mansion
edifice 164 n.
place 185 n.
house 192 n.
man-size
large 195 adj.
manslaughter
homicide 362 n.
mantelpiece
shelf 218 n.
mantilla
headgear 228 n.
mantissa
numerical element
85 n.
mantle
sequence 65 n.

cover 226 vb.
wrapping 226 n.
dress 228 vb.
screen 421 n.
badge of rule
   743 n.
mantra
maxim 496 n.
man trap
trap 542 n.
manual
handed 378 adj.
musical note
   410 n.
organ 414 n.
piano 414 n.
guidebook 524 n.
instrumental
   628 adj.
manual worker
worker 686 n.
manufacture
produce 164 vb.
product 164 n.
production 164 n.
business 622 n.
manufacturer
producer 164 n.
manure
fertilizer 171 n.
excrement 302 n.
cultivate 370 vb.
manuscript
no imitation 21 n.
prototype 23 n.
script 586 n.
written 586 adj.
book 589 n.
many
great 32 adj.
many 104 adj.
many-sided
multiform 82 adj.
plural 101 adj.
lateral 239 adj.
Maoism
government 733 n.
map
outline 233 vb.
gauge 465 vb.
map 551 n.
represent 551 vb.
maple
tree 366 n.
maple syrup
sweet thing 392 n.

map out
plan 623 vb.
Maquis
soldier 722 n.
revolter 738 n.
maquis
wood 366 n.
mar
derange 63 vb.
impair 655 vb.
be clumsy 695 vb.
make ugly 842 vb.
blemish 845 vb.
shame 867 vb.
maracas
gong 414 n.
marathon
lasting 113 adj.
distance 199 n.
pedestrianism
   267 n.
contest 716 n.
racing 716 n.
sport 837 n.
marauding
thieving 788 adj.
marble
sphere 252 n.
smooth 258 adj.
smoothness 258 n.
hardness 326 n.
rock 344 n.
white 427 adj.
white thing 427 n.
variegate 437 vb.
sculpture 554 n.
building material
   631 n.
marbled
mottled 437 adj.
marbles
ball game 837 n.
plaything 837 n.
marcasite
finery 844 n.
marcel wave
hairdressing 843 n.
march
assemblage 74 n.
be in motion
   265 vb.
gait 265 n.
motion 265 n.
marching 267 n.
pedestrianism
   267 n.
walk 267 vb.

progression 285 n.
musical piece
   412 n.
route 624 n.
defy 711 vb.
go to war 718 vb.
deprecation 762 n.
be ostentatious
   875 vb.
marcher
pedestrian 268 n.
agitator 738 n.
marches
region 184 n.
limit 236 n.
marching orders
ejection 300 n.
command 737 n.
marchioness
person of rank
   868 n.
march-past
pageant 875 n.
Mardi Gras
festivity 837 n.
mare
horse 273 n.
moon 321 n.
female animal
   373 n.
mare's tail
cloud 355 n.
margarine
fat 357 n.
margin
difference 15 n.
range 183 n.
room 183 n.
interval 201 n.
edge 234 n.
edition 589 n.
superfluity 637 n.
scope 744 n.
marginal
inconsiderable
   33 adj.
marginal 234 adj.
uncertain 474 adj.
**mariage de conve-
   nance**
type of marriage
   894 n.
marigold
plant 366 n.
orange 432 n.
marijuana
drug-taking 949 n.

marina
stable 192 n.
shore 344 n.
shelter 662 n.
arena 724 n.
pleasure ground
   837 n.
marinade
soften 327 vb.
season 388 vb.
preserver 666 n.
marinate
immerse 303 vb.
drench 341 vb.
preserve 666 vb.
marine
nautical personnel
   270 n.
marine 275 adj.
shipping 275 n.
naval man 722 n.
mariner
mariner 270 n.
Mariolatry
Madonna 968 n.
cult 981 n.
marionette
image 551 n.
maritime
marine 275 adj.
mark
degree 27 n.
serial place 73 n.
sort 77 n.
speciality 80 n.
effect 157 n.
feature 445 n.
perceive 447 adj.
notice 455 vb.
assent 488 n.
indication 547 n.
label 547 n.
mark 547 vb.
trace 548 n.
importance 638 n.
impair 655 vb.
wound 655 n.
coinage 797 n.
blemish 845 n.
slur 867 n.
mark down
underestimate
   483 vb.
discount 810 vb.
cheapen 812 vb.
marked
remarkable 32 adj.

special 80 adj.
manifest 522 adj.
imperfect 647 adj.
markedly
remarkably 32 vb.
marked man
accused person
928 n.
**marked with crow's
feet**
ageing 131 adj.
marker
indication 547 n.
market
purchase 792 vb.
sell 793 vb.
market 796 n.
marketable
salable 793 adj.
market gardening
agriculture 370 n.
marketing
sale 793 n.
market place
focus 76 n.
arena 724 n.
market 796 n.
market research
statistics 86 n.
enquiry 459 n.
sale 793 n.
markings
badge 547 n.
identification
547 n.
mark out
set apart 46 vb.
limit 236 vb.
gauge 465 vb.
indicate 547 vb.
mark 547 vb.
select 605 vb.
dignify 866 vb.
marksman, -woman
hunter 619 n.
player 837 n.
marksmanship
propulsion 287 n.
skill 694 n.
mark time
pass time 108 vb.
time 117 vb.
be quiescent
266 vb.
await 507 vb.
mark up
register 548 vb.

overcharge 811 vb.
marl
soil 344 n.
marm
female 373 n.
marmalade
sweet thing 392 n.
orange 432 n.
marmoset
mammal 365 n.
maroon
set apart 46 vb.
brown 430 adj.
red 431 adj.
not retain 779 vb.
solitary 883 n.
marquee
pavilion 192 n.
canopy 226 n.
marquess
person of rank
868 n.
marquetry
chequer 437 n.
ornamental art
844 n.
marquis
person of rank
868 n.
marquise
person of rank
868 n.
marred
unsightly 842 adj.
marriage
combination 50 n.
accompaniment
89 n.
marriage 894 n.
**marriage of conve-
nience**
type of marriage
894 n.
marriage service
Christian rite
988 n.
marrow
substance 3 n.
essential part 5 n.
interiority 224 n.
centre 225 n.
fruit and vegetables
301 n.
chum 880 n.
marry
unite with 45 vb.
combine 50 vb.

marry 894 vb.
wed 894 vb.
marry off
not retain 779 vb.
assign 780 vb.
marry 894 vb.
Mars
planet 321 n.
redness 431 n.
war 718 n.
mythic deity 966 n.
Olympian deity
967 n.
marsh
marsh 347 n.
marshal
arrange 62 vb.
army officer 741 n.
officer 741 n.
marshalling
arrangement 62 n.
heraldry 547 n.
marsh gas
gas 336 n.
marshland
marsh 347 n.
marshy
marshy 347 adj.
marsupial
mammal 365 n.
mart
market 796 n.
martial
warlike 718 adj.
courageous
855 adj.
martial law
government 733 n.
brute force 735 n.
lawlessness 954 n.
Martian
foreigner 59 n.
native 191 n.
martin
bird 365 n.
martinet
tyrant 735 n.
Martinmas
holy day 988 n.
martlet
heraldry 547 n.
martyr
kill 362 vb.
give pain 377 vb.
sufferer 825 n.
torment 827 vb.
pietist 979 n.

martyrdom
death 361 n.
killing 362 n.
pain 377 n.
suffering 825 n.
disinterestedness
931 n.
capital punishment
963 n.
martyred
dead 361 adj.
suffering 825 adj.
martyrology
list 87 n.
death roll 361 n.
biography 590 n.
marvel
prodigy 864 n.
wonder 864 vb.
marvellous
prodigious 32 adj.
excellent 644 adj.
pleasurable
826 adj.
wonderful 864 adj.
Marxists
political party
708 n.
marzipan
sweet thing 392 n.
mascara
cosmetic 843 n.
mascot
talisman 983 n.
masculine
manly 162 adj.
male 372 adj.
grammatical
564 adj.
masculinist
reformer 654 n.
masculinity
male 372 n.
mash
mix 43 vb.
soften 327 vb.
pulverize 332 vb.
thicken 354 vb.
pulpiness 356 n.
masjid
temple 990 n.
mask
modify 143 vb.
screen 421 n.
screen 421 vb.
conceal 525 vb.
disguise 527 n.

MAS

duplicity 541 n.
sham 542 n.

masked
occult 523 adj.
concealed 525 adj.
disguised 525 adj.

masochist
nonconformist
84 n.

mason
artisan 686 n.

masque
drama 594 n.
stage play 594 n.
festivity 837 n.

masquerade
imitate 20 vb.
clothing 228 n.
conceal 525 vb.
concealment 525 n.
disguise 527 n.
sham 542 n.
dancing 837 n.

mass
quantity 26 n.
extensive 32 adj.
great quantity
32 n.
chief part 52 n.
piece 53 n.
bring together
74 vb.
congregate 74 vb.
crowd 74 n.
general 79 adj.
be many 104 vb.
bulk 195 n.
size 195 n.
matter 319 n.
gravity 322 n.
solid body 324 n.
store 632 n.
threaten 900 vb.
public worship
981 n.
Holy Communion
988 n.

massacre
destruction 165 n.
slaughter 362 n.
slaughter 362 vb.
capital punishment
963 n.
execute 963 vb.

massage
soften 327 vb.
friction 333 n.

MAS

rub 333 vb.
touch 378 n.
touch 378 vb.
beautification
843 n.

massed
multitudinous
104 adj.
dense 324 adj.

masses, the
crowd 74 n.
everyman 79 n.
social group 371 n.
commonalty 869 n.

massif
high land 209 n.

massive
great 32 adj.
large 195 adj.
weighty 322 adj.
dense 324 adj.

mass media
information 524 n.
publication 528 n.

mass-produced
uniform 16 adj.

mast
high structure
209 n.
hanger 217 n.
support 218 n.
sail 275 n.

mastectomy
surgery 658 n.

master
prevail 178 vb.
mariner 270 n.
male 372 n.
know 490 vb.
sage 500 n.
understand 516 vb.
learn 536 vb.
artisan 686 n.
director 690 n.
proficient person
696 n.
overmaster 727 vb.
master 741 n.
owner 776 n.
title 870 n.

masterful
authoritative
733 adj.
authoritarian
735 adj.

master key
opener 263 n.

MAT

instrument 628 n.

masterly
perfect 646 adj.
skilful 694 adj.

mastermind
superior 34 n.
planner 623 n.
direct 689 vb.
proficient person
696 n.

master of ceremonies
leader 690 n.

masterpiece
picture 553 n.
masterpiece 694 n.
a beauty 841 n.

master plan
prototype 23 n.
plan 623 n.

masterstroke
contrivance 623 n.
masterpiece 694 n.
success 727 n.

mastery
culture 490 n.
knowledge 490 n.
skill 694 n.
governance 733 n.
possession 773 n.

masthead
high structure
209 n.
vertex 213 n.
label 547 n.

mastic
viscidity 354 n.
resin 357 n.

masticate
chew 301 vb.

mastiff
dog 365 n.

mat
seat 218 n.
floor-cover 226 n.

matador
killer 362 n.
combatant 722 n.

match
identify 13 vb.
identity 13 n.
analogue 18 n.
resemble 18 vb.
accord 24 vb.
be equal 28 vb.
compeer 28 n.
equalize 28 vb.
join 45 vb.

MAT

pair 90 vb.
burning 381 n.
lighter 385 n.
torch 420 n.
compare 462 vb.
contest 716 n.
marriage 894 n.
marry 894 vb.
wedding 894 n.

matchbox
small box 194 n.

matching
similar 18 adj.
adaptation 24 n.
agreeing 24 adj.
harmonious
410 adj.

matchless
dissimilar 19 adj.
supreme 34 adj.

matchlock
firearm 723 n.

matchmaker
mediator 720 n.

match-making
wedding 894 n.

matchstick
weak thing 163 n.

mate
analogue 18 n.
compeer 28 n.
unite with 45 vb.
combine 50 vb.
concomitant 89 n.
pair 90 n.
mariner 270 n.
male 372 n.
colleague 707 n.
chum 880 n.
marry 894 vb.
spouse 894 n.
wed 894 vb.

matelot
mariner 270 n.

mater
maternity 169 n.

material
substantiality 3 n.
textile 222 n.
material 319 adj.
matter 319 n.
information 524 n.
materials 631 n.

materialism
existence 1 n.
materiality 319 n.
philosophy 449 n.

sensualism 944 n.
impiety 980 n.
materialistic
material 319 adj.
selfish 932 adj.
irreligious 974 adj.
materialize
happen 154 vb.
materialize 319 vb.
be visible 443 vb.
appear 445 vb.
maternal
akin 11 adj.
parental 169 adj.
benevolent 897 adj.
maternity
propagation 167 n.
maternity 169 n.
parentage 169 n.
mate with
wed 894 vb.
matey
pleasant 376 adj.
friendly 880 adj.
sociable 882 adj.
mathematical
statistical 86 adj.
mathematics
mathematics 86 n.
matinée
evening 129 n.
dramaturgy 594 n.
matinee jacket
jacket 228 n.
mating
coition 45 n.
matins
morning 128 n.
public worship
981 n.
church service
988 n.
matriarchal
governmental
733 adj.
matriarchy
family 11 n.
female 373 n.
matriculation
exam 459 n.
matrimony
marriage 894 n.
matrix
mould 23 n.
number 85 n.
surroundings
230 n.

print-type 587 n.
matron
adult 134 n.
maternity 169 n.
female 373 n.
nurse 658 n.
manager 690 n.
spouse 894 n.
matronly
ageing 131 adj.
grown-up 134 adj.
parental 169 adj.
female 373 adj.
matt
dim 419 adj.
matted
crossed 222 adj.
hairy 259 adj.
dense 324 adj.
dirty 649 adj.
matter
excrement 302 n.
matter 319 n.
universe 321 n.
fluid 335 n.
semiliquidity
354 n.
topic 452 n.
meaning 514 n.
dirt 649 n.
matter of course
practice 610 n.
lack of wonder
865 n.
matter of fact
reality 1 n.
event 154 n.
certainty 473 n.
narrow-minded
481 adj.
truth 494 n.
mattock
sharp edge 256 n.
mattress
cushion 218 n.
treasury 799 n.
maturation
ripening 669 n.
completion 725 n.
mature
ageing 131 adj.
grown-up 134 adj.
mature 669 vb.
matured 669 adj.
maturity
oldness 127 n.
middle age 131 n.

adultness 134 n.
completion 725 n.
maudlin
foolish 499 adj.
feeling 818 adj.
impressible
819 adj.
tipsy 949 adj.
maul
hammer 279 n.
strike 279 vb.
ill-treat 645 vb.
wound 655 vb.
attack 712 vb.
criticize 924 vb.
maundering
folly 499 n.
foolish 499 adj.
mausoleum
edifice 164 n.
high structure
209 n.
tomb 364 n.
monument 548 n.
mauve
purple 436 adj.
purpleness 436 n.
maverick
nonconformist
84 n.
revolter 738 n.
independent
744 adj.
maw
stomach 194 n.
mawkish
feeling 818 adj.
impressible
819 adj.
maxim
prototype 23 n.
rule 81 n.
maxim 496 n.
maximize
augment 36 vb.
overestimate
482 vb.
exaggerate 546 vb.
use 673 vb.
maximum
great 32 adj.
greatness 32 n.
superiority 34 n.
plenitude 54 n.
size 195 n.
may
tree 366 n.

be possible 469 vb.
Mayday
call 547 n.
mayfly
brief span 114 n.
insect 365 n.
mayhem
disorder 61 n.
mayonnaise
hors-d'oeuvres
301 n.
sauce 389 n.
mayor
official 690 n.
councillor 692 n.
officer 741 n.
law officer 955 n.
mayoress
officer 741 n.
maypole
high structure
209 n.
maze
complexity 61 n.
meandering 251 n.
enigma 530 n.
difficulty 700 n.
mazurka
musical piece
412 n.
dance 837 n.
MC
leader 690 n.
MCP
male 372 n.
me
subjectivity 320 n.
mead
alcoholic drink
301 n.
grassland 348 n.
sweet thing 392 n.
meadow
grassland 348 n.
meagre
small 33 adj.
lean 206 adj.
feeble 572 adj.
economical
814 adj.
meal
cereals 301 n.
meal 301 n.
powder 332 n.
mealy-mouthed
hypocritical
541 adj.

817

affected 850 adj.
flattering 925 adj.
mean
  average 30 n.
  median 30 adj.
  middle 70 adj.
  middle 70 n.
  comprise 78 vb.
  statistics 86 n.
  interjacent 231 adj.
  mean 514 vb.
  bad 645 adj.
  parsimonious
    816 adj.
  disreputable
    867 adj.
  plebeian 869 adj.
  humble 872 adj.
  servile 879 adj.
  unkind 898 adj.
  contemptible
    922 adj.
  dishonest 930 adj.
  selfish 932 adj.
mean business
  be resolute 599 vb.
meandering
  meandering 251 n.
  moving 265 adj.
  roundabout
    626 adj.
meaning
  meaning 514 n.
  indication 547 n.
  intention 617 n.
meaningful
  substantial 3 adj.
  meaningful
    514 adj.
  expressive 516 adj.
meaningless
  meaningless
    515 adj.
mean it
  be truthful 540 vb.
meanness
  smallness 33 n.
  insufficiency 636 n.
  parsimony 816 n.
  contemptibility
    922 n.
  selfishness 932 n.
means
  means 629 n.
means test
  enquiry 459 n.

meantime
  while 108 adv.
mean to
  intend 617 vb.
mean well
  be friendly 880 vb.
meanwhile
  while 108 adv.
measles
  infection 651 n.
measly
  unimportant
    639 adj.
  bad 645 adj.
measure
  finite quantity
    26 n.
  graduate 27 vb.
  comprise 78 vb.
  measure 183 n.
  tempo 410 n.
  tune 412 n.
  gauge 465 n.
  measure 465 vb.
  estimate 480 vb.
  deed 676 n.
  apportion 783 vb.
  portion 783 n.
measured
  moderate 177 adj.
  poetic 593 adj.
  predetermined
    608 adj.
measurement
  measurement
    465 n.
measurements
  size 195 n.
measures
  policy 623 n.
  means 629 n.
  action 676 n.
measure up to
  be equal 28 vb.
  be able 160 vb.
  suffice 635 vb.
meat
  substance 3 n.
  food 301 n.
  meat 301 n.
  materials 631 n.
meat-eating
  feeding 301 adj.
meaty
  substantial 3 adj.
  meaningful
    514 adj.

forceful 571 adj.
Mecca
  focus 76 n.
  objective 617 n.
  holy place 990 n.
mechanic
  machinist 630 n.
  mender 656 n.
  artisan 686 n.
mechanical
  involuntary
    596 adj.
  mechanical
    630 adj.
mechanics
  impulse 279 n.
  physics 319 n.
mechanism
  philosophy 449 n.
  machine 630 n.
mechanized
  dynamic 160 adj.
  mechanical
    630 adj.
medal
  badge 547 n.
  decoration 729 n.
  jewellery 844 n.
  honours 866 n.
  reward 962 n.
medallion
  sculpture 554 n.
  jewellery 844 n.
medallist
  victor 727 n.
meddle
  meddle 678 vb.
meddlesome
  inquisitive 453 adj.
meddle with
  modify 143 vb.
  impair 655 vb.
meddling
  influential 178 adj.
  interjection 231 n.
  hindrance 702 n.
Medea
  sorceress 983 n.
media, the
  publication 528 n.
  broadcasting
    531 n.
medial
  middle 70 adj.
median
  average 30 n.
  median 30 adj.

interjacent 231 adj.
media personality
  broadcaster 531 n.
  favourite 890 n.
mediate
  lie between 231 vb.
  mediate 720 vb.
mediator
  speaker 579 n.
  mediator 720 n.
medical
  enquiry 459 n.
  medical 658 adj.
medical practitioner
  doctor 658 n.
medicament
  medicine 658 n.
medication
  medicine 658 n.
medicinal
  remedial 658 adj.
medicine
  vocation 622 n.
  medical art 658 n.
  medicine 658 n.
medicine man
  doctor 658 n.
  sorcerer 983 n.
medieval
  olden 127 adj.
mediocre
  median 30 adj.
  trivial 639 adj.
  not bad 644 adj.
  middling 732 adj.
  modest 874 adj.
mediocrity
  smallness 33 n.
  imperfection 647 n.
  averageness 732 n.
meditate
  meditate 449 vb.
  intend 617 vb.
meditation
  meditation 449 n.
  piety 979 n.
  worship 981 n.
Mediterranean
  ocean 343 n.
mediterranean
  middle 70 adj.
medium
  average 30 n.
  middle 70 n.
  surroundings
    230 n.
  interjacent 231 adj.

intermediary
231 n.
oracle 511 n.
interpreter 520 n.
instrument 628 n.
instrumentality
628 n.
middling 732 adj.
psychic 984 n.
medley
medley 43 n.
disorder 61 n.
musical piece
412 n.
Medusa
eyesore 842 n.
intimidation
854 n.
meed
reward 962 n.
meek
submitting 721 adj.
obedient 739 adj.
patient 823 adj.
humble 872 adj.
meerschaum
tobacco 388 n.
meet
accord 24 vb.
unite with 45 vb.
assembly 74 n.
congregate 74 vb.
be contiguous
202 vb.
collide 279 vb.
approach 289 vb.
meet 295 vb.
touch 378 vb.
discover 484 vb.
withstand 704 vb.
pay 804 vb.
do one's duty
917 vb.
meet a demand
be sold 793 vb.
meet halfway
be willing 597 vb.
pacify 719 vb.
meeting
union 45 n.
assembly 74 n.
event 154 n.
contiguity 202 n.
collision 279 n.
approach 289 n.
approaching
289 adj.

convergence 293 n.
arrival 295 n.
conference 584 n.
council 692 n.
social gathering
882 n.
meeting place
union 45 n.
place 185 n.
locality 187 n.
meeting place
192 n.
social round 882 n.
meet one's end
perish 361 vb.
meet with
meet with 154 vb.
megalithic
huge 195 adj.
large 195 adj.
megalomania
overestimation
482 n.
psychosis 503 n.
vanity 873 n.
megaphone
megaphone 400 n.
megaton
weighing 322 n.
meiosis
underestimation
483 n.
melancholia
psychosis 503 n.
melancholy 834 n.
melancholy
unhappy 825 adj.
discontent 829 n.
melancholic
834 adj.
melancholy 834 n.
sullen 893 adj.
mélange
a mixture 43 n.
melanin
black thing 428 n.
melanoma
cancer 651 n.
skin disease 651 n.
mêlée
turmoil 61 n.
fight 716 n.
mellifluous
melodious 410 adj.
elegant 575 adj.
mellow
ageing 131 adj.

be turned to
147 vb.
soften 327 vb.
tasty 386 adj.
colour 425 vb.
soft-hued 425 adj.
get better 654 vb.
mature 669 vb.
matured 669 adj.
melodeon
organ 414 n.
melodious
melodious 410 adj.
melodrama
stage play 594 n.
melodramatic
dramatic 594 adj.
exciting 821 adj.
melody
melody 410 n.
tune 412 n.
pleasurableness
826 n.
melt
come unstuck
49 vb.
decompose 51 vb.
be dispersed 75 vb.
be transient
114 vb.
deform 244 vb.
soften 327 vb.
liquefy 337 vb.
sound faint 401 vb.
waste 634 vb.
meltdown
ruin 165 n.
melting
soft 327 adj.
blood 335 adj.
liquefaction 337 n.
heating 381 n.
waste 634 n.
melting point
heat 379 n.
member
limb 53 n.
part 53 n.
component 58 n.
society 708 n.
participator 775 n.
**Member of Parlia-
ment**
official 690 n.
councillor 692 n.
membership
inclusion 78 n.

participation
775 n.
fellowship 882 n.
membrane
layer 207 n.
skin 226 n.
memento
reminder 505 n.
trophy 729 n.
gift 781 n.
memo
reminder 505 n.
record 548 n.
memoir
record 548 n.
memoirs
remembrance
505 n.
reading matter
589 n.
biography 590 n.
memorabilia
remainder 41 n.
remembrance
505 n.
record 548 n.
reading matter
589 n.
memorable
remembered
505 adj.
notable 638 adj.
memorandum
reminder 505 n.
record 548 n.
memorial
tomb 364 n.
reminder 505 n.
monument 548 n.
trophy 729 n.
honours 866 n.
memorize
memorize 505 vb.
memory
data processing
86 n.
memory 505 n.
men
component 58 n.
mariner 270 n.
personnel 686 n.
armed force 722 n.
menace
predict 511 vb.
danger 661 n.
endanger 661 vb.
warn 664 vb.

annoyance 827 n.
frighten 854 vb.
hateful object
888 n.
threat 900 n.
threaten 900 vb.
menacing
dangerous 661 adj.
frightening
854 adj.
ménage
management
689 n.
menagerie
accumulation 74 n.
zoo 369 n.
collection 632 n.
menarche
productiveness
171 n.
haemorrhage
302 n.
mend
join 45 vb.
get healthy 650 vb.
get better 654 vb.
make better
654 vb.
rectify 654 vb.
repair 656 vb.
mendacious
false 541 adj.
untrue 543 adj.
mendicant
idler 679 n.
beggar 763 n.
mending
amendment 654 n.
recuperation 656 n.
repair 656 n.
mend one's ways
change one's mind
603 vb.
get better 654 vb.
become pious
979 vb.
menhir
tomb 364 n.
monument 548 n.
menial
inferior 35 n.
worker 686 n.
servant 742 n.
serving 742 adj.
Ménière's disease
ear 415 n.

meningitis
infection 651 n.
Mennonite
sectarian 978 n.
menopause
middle age 131 n.
unproductiveness
172 n.
menorrhagia
haemorrhage
302 n.
Mensa
intelligence 498 n.
menses
regular return
141 n.
haemorrhage
302 n.
Mensheviks
political party
708 n.
menstrual
seasonal 141 adj.
mensurate
measure 465 vb.
mental
mental 447 adj.
*mentally disor-
dered* 503 adj.
mental block
oblivion 506 n.
mental disorder
mental disorder
503 n.
mental handicap
unintelligence
499 n.
mental hospital
mental hospital
503 n.
mental illness
mental disorder
503 n.
mentality
intellect 447 n.
affections 817 n.
mentally deficient
unintelligent
499 adj.
**mentally handi-
capped**
unintelligent
499 adj.
*mentally handi-
capped* 503 adj.
menthol cigarette
tobacco 388 n.

mention
referral 9 n.
relate 9 vb.
specify 80 vb.
notice 455 vb.
evidence 466 n.
manifest 522 vb.
inform 524 vb.
information 524 n.
speak 579 vb.
**mention in dis-
patches**
decoration 729 n.
mentor
sage 500 n.
teacher 537 n.
adviser 691 n.
menu
data processing
86 n.
list 87 n.
Mephistopheles
Mephisto 969 n.
mercenary
militarist 722 n.
soldier 722 n.
servant 742 n.
avaricious 816 adj.
venal 930 n.
selfish 932 adj.
merchandise
merchandise
795 n.
merchant
merchant 794 n.
merchant navy
shipping 275 n.
merciful
lenient 736 adj.
benevolent 897 adj.
pitying 905 adj.
godlike 965 adj.
merciless
destructive 165 adj.
resolute 599 adj.
severe 735 adj.
cruel 898 adj.
malevolent
898 adj.
pitiless 906 adj.
mercurial
changeful 152 adj.
moving 265 adj.
speedy 277 adj.
light-minded
456 adj.
irresolute 601 adj.

capricious 604 adj.
excitable 822 adj.
Mercury
planet 321 n.
courier 529 n.
Olympian deity
967 n.
mercury
changeable thing
152 n.
mercy
leniency 736 n.
benevolence 897 n.
mercy 905 n.
divine attribute
965 n.
mercy killing
killing 362 n.
mere
absolute 32 adj.
simple 44 adj.
lake 346 n.
mere nothing
trifle 639 n.
meretricious
spurious 542 adj.
ornate 574 adj.
inelegant 576 adj.
unchaste 951 adj.
merge
be identical 13 vb.
mix 43 vb.
join 45 vb.
combine 50 vb.
cooperate 706 vb.
merger
relation 9 n.
mixture 43 n.
union 45 n.
combination 50 n.
association 706 n.
offer 759 n.
meridian
noon 128 n.
region 184 n.
summit 213 n.
topmost 213 adj.
meringue
pastries and cakes
301 n.
bubble 355 n.
Merino
sheep 365 n.
merino
fibre 208 n.
merit
importance 638 n.

utility 640 n.
goodness 644 n.
deserve 915 vb.
meritocracy
elite 644 n.
government 733 n.
meritorious
excellent 644 adj.
reputable 866 adj.
virtuous 933 adj.
merits
right 913 n.
dueness 915 n.
virtues 933 n.
Merlin
mythical being
970 n.
sorcerer 983 n.
merlin
bird 365 n.
mermaid
rara avis 84 n.
sea nymph 343 n.
mythical being
970 n.
merman
rara avis 84 n.
sea god 343 n.
mythical being
970 n.
merriment
enjoyment 824 n.
merriment 833 n.
amusement 837 n.
merry
merry 833 adj.
drunk 949 adj.
merry-go-round
rotator 315 n.
merry-making
enjoyment 824 n.
merriment 833 n.
merry 833 adj.
rejoicing 835 n.
festivity 837 n.
sociability 882 n.
mésalliance
misfit 25 n.
type of marriage
894 n.
mescalin
drug-taking 949 n.
mesh
unite with 45 vb.
gap 201 n.
space 201 vb.
cross 222 vb.

network 222 n.
meshuga
crazy 503 adj.
mesmerism
influence 178 n.
occultism 984 n.
mesmerize
influence 178 vb.
render insensible
375 vb.
convince 485 vb.
frighten 854 vb.
mesolithic
primal 127 adj.
mess
disorder 61 n.
jumble 63 vb.
chamber 194 n.
eat 301 vb.
predicament 700 n.
message
topic 452 n.
message 529 n.
messenger
traveller 268 n.
messenger 529 n.
servant 742 n.
Messiah
philanthropist
901 n.
God the Son 965 n.
religious teacher
973 n.
messiah
leader 690 n.
mess up
jumble 63 vb.
blunder 495 vb.
impair 655 vb.
messy
dirty 649 adj.
metabolism
transformation
143 n.
metabolize
modify 143 vb.
metal
hardness 326 n.
mineral 359 n.
heraldry 547 n.
materials 631 n.
metalanguage
language 557 n.
metallic
strident 407 adj.
metallurgy
mineralogy 359 n.

metal rule
gauge 465 n.
metamorphosis
transformation
143 n.
revolution 149 n.
metaphor
analogue 18 n.
assimilation 18 n.
substitute 150 n.
metaphor 519 n.
phrase 563 n.
ornament 574 n.
metaphorical
compared 462 adj.
semantic 514 adj.
figurative 519 adj.
metaphysics
existence 1 n.
philosophy 449 n.
metasomatism
transformation
143 n.
metastasis
transference 272 n.
metathesis
interchange 151 n.
inversion 221 n.
transference 272 n.
trope 519 n.
metazoon
animal 365 n.
mete
mete out 465 vb.
meteor
brief span 114 n.
meteor 321 n.
meteoric
brief 114 adj.
speedy 277 adj.
celestial 321 adj.
meteorite
meteor 321 n.
meteorological
airy 340 adj.
meteorology
weather 340 n.
meter
gauge 465 vb.
meter 465 n.
meter maid
traffic control
305 n.
methadone
drug-taking 949 n.
methane
gas 336 n.

fuel 385 n.
method
uniformity 16 n.
order 60 n.
arrangement 62 n.
regularity 81 n.
way 624 n.
means 629 n.
conduct 688 n.
fashion 848 n.
ritual 988 n.
methodical
orderly 60 adj.
arranged 62 adj.
regular 81 adj.
Methodism
Protestantism
976 n.
methodology
order 60 n.
methylated spirit
fuel 385 n.
meticulous
attentive 455 adj.
careful 457 adj.
accurate 494 adj.
observant 768 adj.
fastidious 862 adj.
trustworthy
929 adj.
métier
vocation 622 n.
skill 694 n.
metonymy
trope 519 n.
metre
long measure
203 n.
prosody 593 n.
metric
metrical 465 adj.
metrical
metrical 465 adj.
poetic 593 adj.
metric system
metrology 465 n.
metro
tunnel 263 n.
railway 624 n.
metronome
prototype 23 n.
timekeeper 117 n.
oscillation 317 n.
tempo 410 n.
meter 465 n.
metropolis
city 184 n.

metropolitan
dweller 191 n.
central 225 adj.
ecclesiastical
985 adj.
ecclesiarch 986 n.

mettle
vigorousness 174 n.
resolution 599 n.
affections 817 n.
courage 855 n.

mettlesome
vigorous 174 adj.
active 678 adj.
courageous
855 adj.

mew
ululate 409 vb.
ululation 409 n.

mewl
cry 408 vb.
ululate 409 vb.
weep 836 vb.

mews
flat 192 n.
stable 192 n.

mezzanine floor
layer 207 n.

mezze
hors-d'oeuvres
301 n.

mezzo
middle 70 adj.

mezzo floor
middle 70 n.

mezzo-soprano
vocalist 413 n.

miaow
ululate 409 vb.
ululation 409 n.

miasma
gas 336 n.
stench 397 n.
poison 659 n.

miasmic
gaseous 336 adj.
deadly 362 adj.
fetid 397 adj.

Michaelmas
autumn 129 n.
holy day 988 n.

microbiology
biology 358 n.
medical art 658 n.

microcomputer
counting instru-
ment 86 n.

microcosm
small thing 33 n.
whole 52 n.
miniature 196 n.
universe 321 n.

microfiche
copy 22 n.
miniature 196 n.
record 548 n.
photography 551 n.

microfilm
copy 22 n.
miniature 196 n.
record 548 n.
photography 551 n.

microlight
aircraft 276 n.

micrometer
gauge 465 n.
meter 465 n.

micrometry
long measure
203 n.
accuracy 494 n.

micron
small quantity
33 n.
long measure
203 n.

microphone
megaphone 400 n.
hearing aid 415 n.
telecommunication
531 n.

microprocessor
counting instru-
ment 86 n.
electronics 160 n.

microscope
microscope 442 n.

microscopic
small 33 adj.
indistinct 444 adj.

microwave
cook 301 vb.
cookery 301 n.
furnace 383 n.
radiation 417 n.

micturate
excrete 302 vb.

mid
middle 70 adj.
between 231 adv.

Midas touch
prosperity 730 n.
wealth 800 n.

midday
noon 128 n.

midden
accumulation 74 n.
rubbish 641 n.
sink 649 n.

middle
middle 70 adj.
middle 70 n.
middling 732 adj.

middle age
middle age 131 n.

Middle Ages
era 110 n.
antiquity 125 n.

middle classes
social group 371 n.
commonalty 869 n.
middle classes
869 n.

middle course
middle point 30 n.
middle way 625 n.

middle ground
middle point 30 n.

middleman
intermediary
231 n.
agent 686 n.
mediator 720 n.
consignee 754 n.
merchant 794 n.
tradespeople 794 n.

middle-of-the-road
median 30 adj.
middle point 30 n.
moderate 177 adj.
middle way 625 n.
neutral 625 adj.
not bad 644 adj.
middling 732 adj.

middling
not bad 644 adj.
middling 732 adj.

midge
insect 365 n.

midget
small thing 33 n.
dwarf 196 n.

midline
middle 70 n.

midnight
midnight 129 n.

midpoint
middle point 30 n.
middle 70 n.
centre 225 n.

midriff
middle 70 n.
centrality 225 n.

midshipman
nautical personnel
270 n.

midst
middle 70 n.
between 231 adv.

midstream
middle 70 n.
middle way 625 n.

midsummer
summer 128 n.

midway
middle point 30 n.

midwife
obstetrics 167 n.
instrument 628 n.
doctor 658 n.

midwinter
middle 70 n.
winter 129 n.

mien
look 445 n.

miffed
unhappy 825 adj.
discontented
829 adj.
resentful 891 adj.

might
greatness 32 n.
power 160 n.
strength 162 n.
be possible 469 vb.

might and main
power 160 n.
exertion 682 n.

mighty
great 32 adj.
greatly 32 vb.
powerful 160 adj.
strong 162 adj.
influential 178 adj.
huge 195 adj.
worshipful 866 adj.
proud 871 adj.

migraine
pang 377 n.
illness 651 n.

migrant
foreigner 59 n.
dweller 191 n.
wanderer 268 n.
incomer 297 n.
bird 365 n.

migrate
  travel 267 vb.
  wander 267 vb.
migration
  departure 296 n.
mike
  megaphone 400 n.
  hearing aid 415 n.
mild
  alcoholic drink
    301 n.
  warm 379 adj.
  lenient 736 adj.
  amiable 884 adj.
mildew
  destroyer 168 n.
  dim 419 vb.
  be unclean 649 vb.
  dirt 649 n.
  deteriorate 655 vb.
  dilapidation 655 n.
  impair 655 vb.
  blight 659 n.
mildness
  moderation 177 n.
  leniency 736 n.
  courtesy 884 n.
  benevolence 897 n.
mile
  long measure
    203 n.
mileage
  distance 199 n.
  length 203 n.
  utility 640 n.
milestone
  degree 27 n.
  serial place 73 n.
  event 154 n.
  situation 186 n.
  limit 236 n.
  itinerary 267 n.
  gauge 465 n.
  signpost 547 n.
  important matter
    638 n.
milieu
  circumstance 8 n.
  relation 9 n.
  locality 187 n.
  surroundings
    230 n.
militant
  violent creature
    176 n.
  active 678 adj.
  busy person 678 n.

opposing 704 adj.
political party
  708 n.
quarrelling
  709 adj.
defiant 711 adj.
warlike 718 adj.
warring 718 adj.
militarist 722 n.
hostile 881 adj.
Militant Tendency
  political party
    708 n.
militaristic
  warlike 718 adj.
military
  warlike 718 adj.
militate
  influence 178 vb.
  counteract 182 vb.
  do 676 vb.
  oppose 704 vb.
militia
  defender 713 n.
  army 722 n.
milk
  moderator 177 n.
  empty 300 vb.
  milk 301 n.
  soft drink 301 n.
  extract 304 vb.
  fluid 335 n.
  white thing 427 n.
  use 673 vb.
  acquire 771 vb.
  take 786 vb.
milk and honey
  prosperity 730 n.
milk and water
  weak 163 adj.
  weak thing 163 n.
milkmaid
  herdsman 369 n.
  servant 742 n.
**milk of human kind-
  ness**
  benevolence 897 n.
milksop
  weakling 163 n.
  ninny 501 n.
  coward 856 n.
  innocent 935 n.
milky
  fatty 357 adj.
  opaque 423 adj.
  semitransparent
    424 adj.

whitish 427 adj.
Milky Way
  star 321 n.
  luminary 420 n.
mill
  produce 164 vb.
  pulverize 332 vb.
  pulverizer 332 n.
  workshop 687 n.
mill around
  congregate 74 vb.
  rotate 315 vb.
  be agitated 318 vb.
millennium
  over one hundred
    99 n.
  period 110 n.
  future state 124 n.
  fantasy 513 n.
  aspiration 852 n.
  heaven 971 n.
miller
  pulverizer 332 n.
millet
  cereals 301 n.
  grass 366 n.
milliard
  over one hundred
    99 n.
milligram
  weighing 322 n.
millimetre
  small quantity
    33 n.
  short distance
    200 n.
  long measure
    203 n.
millinery
  dressing 228 n.
  headgear 228 n.
million
  over one hundred
    99 n.
  multitude 104 n.
**millionaire, million-
  airess**
  rich person 800 n.
millions
  great quantity
    32 n.
  multitude 104 n.
  funds 797 n.
millpond
  smoothness 258 n.
  quietude 266 n.
  lake 346 n.

millstone
  pulverizer 332 n.
  encumbrance
    702 n.
mime
  imitate 20 vb.
  imitator 20 n.
  mimicry 20 n.
  gesticulate 547 vb.
  gesture 547 n.
  represent 551 vb.
  representation
    551 n.
  act 594 vb.
  actor 594 n.
  stage play 594 n.
mimesis
  imitation 20 n.
  mimicry 20 n.
mimic
  imitate 20 vb.
  imitative 20 adj.
  imitator 20 n.
  be absurd 497 vb.
  gesticulate 547 vb.
  represent 551 vb.
  actor 594 n.
  satirize 851 vb.
mimicry
  mimicry 20 n.
  representation
    551 n.
  ridicule 851 n.
minaret
  high structure
    209 n.
mince
  cut 46 vb.
  rend 46 vb.
  walk 267 vb.
  move slowly
    278 vb.
  cook 301 vb.
  meat 301 n.
  pulverize 332 vb.
  be affected 850 vb.
minced
  fragmentary
    53 adj.
mincing
  affected 850 adj.
mind
  intellect 447 n.
  be attentive 455 vb.
  look after 457 vb.
  opinion 485 n.
  will 595 n.

intention 617 n.
suffer 825 vb.
liking 859 n.
dislike 861 n.
resent 891 vb.
mind-blowing
frightening
854 adj.
wonderful 864 adj.
intoxicating
949 adj.
mind-boggling
unexpected
508 adj.
exciting 821 adj.
frightening
854 adj.
wonderful 864 adj.
mindful
attentive 455 adj.
remembering
505 adj.
mindless
mindless 448 adj.
foolish 499 adj.
See **unintelligent**
forgetful 506 adj.
mind one's Ps and
Qs
be careful 457 vb.
behave 688 vb.
be courteous
884 vb.
mind reader
psychic 984 n.
mind-reading
psychical 984 n.
psychics 984 n.
mind's eye
vision 438 n.
remembrance
505 n.
imagination 513 n.
mine
great quantity
32 n.
source 156 n.
produce 164 vb.
lowness 210 n.
depth 211 n.
excavation 255 n.
make concave
255 vb.
pierce 263 vb.
tunnel 263 n.
extract 304 vb.
descend 309 vb.

trap 542 n.
store 632 n.
workshop 687 n.
defences 713 n.
bomb 723 n.
acquire 771 vb.
take 786 vb.
minefield
pitfall 663 n.
defences 713 n.
miner
producer 164 n.
artisan 686 n.
mineral
mineral 359 n.
materials 631 n.
mineralogy
mineralogy 359 n.
mineral water
soft drink 301 n.
minestrone
hors-d'oeuvres
301 n.
minesweeper
warship 722 n.
mingle
mix 43 vb.
mingy
parsimonious
816 adj.
mini-
little 196 adj.
miniature
small 33 adj.
little 196 adj.
miniature 196 n.
picture 553 n.
miniaturization
smallness 33 n.
minibus
automobile 274 n.
bus 274 n.
minicab
cab 274 n.
minim
small quantity
33 n.
notation 410 n.
metrology 465 n.
minimal
small 33 adj.
Minimalism
school of painting
553 n.
minimize
abate 37 vb.
misjudge 481 vb.

underestimate
483 vb.
detract 926 vb.
minimum
small 33 adj.
small quantity
33 n.
inferiority 35 n.
sufficiency 635 n.
minion
dependant 742 n.
flatterer 925 n.
miniskirt
shortness 204 n.
skirt 228 n.
minister
teacher 537 n.
agent 686 n.
official 690 n.
envoy 754 n.
offer worship
981 vb.
church officer
986 n.
cleric 986 n.
pastor 986 n.
perform ritual
988 vb.
ministerial
governmental
733 adj.
minister to
minister to 703 vb.
ministry
vocation 622 n.
management
689 n.
ministry, the
clergy 986 n.
mink
skin 226 n.
minnesinger
musician 413 n.
minnow
small thing 33 n.
fish 365 n.
minor
inconsiderable
33 adj.
inferior 35 n.
lesser 35 adj.
young 130 adj.
youth 130 n.
unimportant
639 adj.
minority
inferiority 35 n.

fewness 105 n.
nonage 130 n.
helplessness 161 n.
dissentient 489 n.
minster
church 990 n.
minstrel
musician 413 n.
vocalist 413 n.
poet 593 n.
entertainer 594 n.
minstrelsy
music 412 n.
mint
mould 23 n.
great quantity
32 n.
form 243 vb.
herb 301 n.
workshop 687 n.
mint 797 vb.
mint condition
perfection 646 n.
minuet
musical piece
412 n.
dance 837 n.
minus
difference 15 n.
less 35 adv.
deficient 307 adj.
minuscule
letter 558 n.
minute
small 33 adj.
period 110 n.
brief span 114 n.
angular measure
247 n.
measurement
465 n.
record 548 vb.
diffuse 570 adj.
compendium
592 n.
minutiae
small quantity
33 n.
particulars 80 n.
trifle 639 n.
minx
female 373 n.
insolent person
878 n.
loose woman
952 n.

miracle
nonconformity
84 n.
prodigy 864 n.
miraculous
unusual 84 adj.
impossible 470 adj.
wonderful 864 adj.
mirage
insubstantial thing
4 n.
visual fallacy
440 n.
appearance 445 n.
error 495 n.
disappointment
509 n.
fantasy 513 n.
deception 542 n.
mire
marsh 347 n.
mirror
contrariety 14 n.
resemble 18 vb.
imitate 20 vb.
imitation 20 n.
copy 22 n.
mirror 442 n.
show 522 vb.
person of repute
866 n.
mirror image
contrariety 14 n.
mirth
merriment 833 n.
misadventure
event 154 n.
chance 159 n.
misfortune 731 n.
misalliance
type of marriage
894 n.
misandry
misanthropy 902 n.
misanthrope
misanthrope 902 n.
misanthropy
inhumanity 898 n.
misanthropy 902 n.
misapply
sophisticate
477 vb.
waste 634 vb.
misuse 675 vb.
be unskilful
695 vb.

misapprehension
misinterpretation
521 n.
misappropriate
misuse 675 vb.
defraud 788 vb.
misbehave
behave 688 vb.
disobey 738 vb.
be wicked 934 vb.
miscalculate
misjudge 481 vb.
blunder 495 vb.
be foolish 499 vb.
miscarriage
failure 728 n.
miscarriage of justice
misjudgment
481 n.
injustice 914 n.
illegality 954 n.
miscarry
miscarry 728 vb.
miscegenation
mixture 43 n.
type of marriage
894 n.
miscellaneous
nonuniform 17 adj.
mixed 43 adj.
miscellany
medley 43 n.
accumulation 74 n.
anthology 592 n.
mischief
evil 616 n.
badness 645 n.
impairment 655 n.
wrong 914 n.
mischievous
destructive 165 adj.
capricious 604 adj.
harmful 645 adj.
disobedient
738 adj.
malevolent
898 adj.
wrong 914 adj.
miscible
mixed 43 adj.
misconception
misjudgment
481 n.
error 495 n.
misconduct
conduct 688 n.
discourtesy 885 n.

guilty act 936 n.
misconstruction
misjudgment
481 n.
error 495 n.
misinterpretation
521 n.
misconstrue
distort 246 vb.
not know 491 vb.
misinterpret
521 vb.
misinterpretation
521 n.
misconstrued
mistaken 495 adj.
miscount
misjudge 481 vb.
blunder 495 vb.
err 495 vb.
miscreant
vicious 934 adj.
bad person 938 n.
misdeed
wrong 914 n.
guilty act 936 n.
misdemeanour
guilty act 936 n.
lawbreaking 954 n.
misdirect
derange 63 vb.
deflect 282 vb.
mislead 495 vb.
misuse 675 vb.
be unskilful
695 vb.
miser
niggard 816 n.
miserable
unfortunate
731 adj.
unhappy 825 adj.
melancholic
834 adj.
miserly
careful 457 adj.
insufficient
636 adj.
avaricious 816 adj.
parsimonious
816 adj.
misery
evil 616 n.
adversity 731 n.
sorrow 825 n.
dejection 834 n.
moper 834 n.

misfire
be clumsy 695 vb.
bungling 695 n.
miscarry 728 vb.
misfit
misfit 25 n.
misfortune
adversity 731 n.
misfortune 731 n.
misgiving(s)
doubt 486 n.
nervousness 854 n.
misguided
misjudging
481 adj.
mistaken 495 adj.
mishandle
misuse 675 vb.
be severe 735 vb.
mishap
untimeliness
138 n.
event 154 n.
misfortune 731 n.
mishmash
medley 43 n.
disorder 61 n.
misinform
mislead 495 vb.
be false 541 vb.
misinterpret
misinterpret
521 vb.
misjudge
misjudge 481 vb.
mislay
misplace 188 vb.
lose 772 vb.
mislead
sophisticate
477 vb.
mislead 495 vb.
make wicked
934 vb.
misleading
erroneous 495 adj.
mismanage
misuse 675 vb.
be unskilful
695 vb.
fail in duty 918 vb.
misnomer
misnomer 562 n.
misogamy
celibacy 895 n.
misogyny
hatred 888 n.

celibacy 895 n.
misanthropy 902 n.
misplace
misplace 188 vb.
misprint
blunder 495 vb.
mistake 495 n.
mispronounce
voice 577 vb.
stammer 580 vb.
misquote
blunder 495 vb.
misinterpret
521 vb.
be false 541 vb.
misremember
forget 506 vb.
misrepresent
misinterpret
521 vb.
misrepresent
552 vb.
misrepresentation
falsehood 541 n.
untruth 543 n.
misrepresentation
552 n.
misrule
misuse 675 vb.
bungling 695 n.
miss
be incomplete
55 vb.
youngster 132 n.
female 373 n.
blunder 495 vb.
require 627 vb.
be unsatisfied
636 vb.
bungling 695 n.
fail 728 vb.
lose 772 vb.
be discontented
829 vb.
regret 830 vb.
desire 859 vb.
title 870 n.
missal
scripture 975 n.
prayers 981 n.
misshapen
amorphous
244 adj.
deformed 246 adj.
unsightly 842 adj.
missile
missile 287 n.

missing
nonexistent 2 adj.
incomplete 55 adj.
absent 190 adj.
deficient 307 adj.
lost 772 adj.
missing link
deficit 55 n.
incompleteness
55 n.
discontinuity 72 n.
completion 725 n.
mission
job 622 n.
vocation 622 n.
commission 751 n.
mandate 751 n.
delegate 754 n.
envoy 754 n.
philanthropy
901 n.
missionary
preacher 537 n.
philanthropist
901 n.
religious teacher
973 n.
zealot 979 n.
pastor 986 n.
mission service
public worship
981 n.
missive
correspondence
588 n.
miss out
be incomplete
55 vb.
exclude 57 vb.
misspell
misinterpret
521 vb.
misspend
be prodigal 815 vb.
miss the boat
be late 136 vb.
lose a chance
138 vb.
fail 728 vb.
miss the mark
fall short 307 vb.
mist
insubstantial thing
4 n.
moisture 341 n.
cloud 355 n.
dim 419 vb.

dimness 419 n.
screen 421 n.
opacity 423 n.
blur 440 vb.
invisibility 444 n.
uncertainty 474 n.
mistake
err 495 vb.
mistake 495 n.
mistaken
mistaken 495 adj.
mistime
mistime 138 vb.
mistletoe
plant 366 n.
mistral
wind 352 n.
mistreatment
misuse 675 n.
mistress
female 373 n.
master 741 n.
owner 776 n.
title 870 n.
loved one 887 n.
kept woman 952 n.
mistrust
doubt 486 n.
doubt 486 vb.
nervousness 854 n.
jealousy 911 n.
misty
insubstantial 4 adj.
humid 341 adj.
cloudy 355 adj.
dim 419 adj.
opaque 423 adj.
indistinct 444 adj.
uncertain 474 adj.
misunderstand
not know 491 vb.
err 495 vb.
misinterpret
521 vb.
misunderstanding
error 495 n.
misinterpretation
521 n.
misuse
use 673 n.
misuse 675 n.
misuse 675 vb.
mite
small quantity
33 n.
small thing 33 n.
child 132 n.

dwarf 196 n.
insect 365 n.
insufficiency 636 n.
mitigate
abate 37 vb.
moderate 177 vb.
qualify 468 vb.
relieve 831 vb.
extenuate 927 vb.
mitre
join 45 vb.
joint 45 n.
badge of rule
743 n.
vestments 989 n.
mitt
glove 228 n.
mitten
glove 228 n.
mix
mix 43 vb.
mixed-ability
educational
534 adj.
mixed bag
nonuniformity
17 n.
medley 43 n.
accumulation 74 n.
mixed blessing
inexpedience
643 n.
mixed farming
agriculture 370 n.
mixed grill
dish 301 n.
mixer
soft drink 301 n.
mixing bowl
bowl 194 n.
mix it
fight 716 vb.
cause discontent
829 vb.
mixture
mixture 43 n.
medicine 658 n.
mix-up
disorder 61 n.
mnemonic
remembering
505 adj.
reminder 505 n.
moan
blow 352 vb.
faintness 401 n.
sound faint 401 vb.

MOA

cry 408 vb.
be discontented
  829 vb.
lamentation 836 n.
weep 836 vb.
moat
fence 235 n.
cavity 255 n.
furrow 262 n.
conduit 351 n.
protection 660 n.
obstacle 702 n.
defences 713 n.
mob
rampage 61 vb.
crowd 74 n.
multitude 104 n.
redundance 637 n.
rabble 869 n.
celebrate 876 vb.
not respect 921 vb.
disapprove 924 vb.
mobile
changeable thing
  152 n.
hanging object
  217 n.
moving 265 adj.
mobile home
small house 192 n.
cart 274 n.
mobility
changeableness
  152 n.
motion 265 n.
mobilize
bring together
  74 vb.
move 265 vb.
make ready
  669 vb.
go to war 718 vb.
mob law
anarchy 734 n.
lawlessness 954 n.
moccasins
footwear 228 n.
mocha
brown 430 adj.
mock
simulating 18 adj.
imitative 20 adj.
substituted 150 adj.
disbelieve 486 vb.
fool 542 vb.
spurious 542 adj.
laugh 835 vb.

MOD

ridicule 851 n.
ridicule 851 vb.
satirize 851 vb.
shame 867 vb.
indignity 921 n.
not respect 921 vb.
despise 922 vb.
detract 926 vb.
mockery
insubstantial thing
  4 n.
mimicry 20 n.
unbelief 486 n.
deception 542 n.
sham 542 n.
ridicule 851 n.
ostentation 875 n.
disrespect 921 n.
impiety 980 n.
mockingbird
imitator 20 n.
mock-up
prototype 23 n.
exhibit 522 n.
mod
assembly 74 n.
youngster 132 n.
music 412 n.
modality
modality 7 n.
mode
modality 7 n.
statistics 86 n.
key 410 n.
style 566 n.
practice 610 n.
way 624 n.
fashion 848 n.
model
copy 22 n.
be an example
  23 vb.
living model 23 n.
prototype 23 n.
composition 56 n.
rule 81 n.
example 83 n.
little 196 adj.
miniature 196 n.
form 243 vb.
comparison 462 n.
exhibit 522 n.
exhibitor 522 n.
image 551 n.
represent 551 vb.
sculpt 554 vb.
sculpture 554 n.

MOD

plan 623 n.
paragon 646 n.
perfect 646 adj.
plaything 837 n.
person of repute
  866 n.
modelling
sculpture 554 n.
mode of address
title 870 n.
moderate
median 30 adj.
small 33 adj.
decrease 37 vb.
moderate 177 adj.
moderate 625 n.
political party
  708 n.
lenient 736 adj.
inexcitable
  823 adj.
tranquillize
  823 vb.
relieve 831 vb.
modest 874 adj.
be temperate
  942 vb.
moderation
smallness 33 n.
moderation 177 n.
leniency 736 n.
modern
modern 126 adj.
modernism
modernism 126 n.
art subject 553 n.
heterodoxy 977 n.
modernize
modernize 126 vb.
modest
inconsiderable
  33 adj.
small 33 adj.
modest 874 adj.
pure 950 adj.
modesty
modesty 874 n.
modicum
small quantity
  33 n.
portion 783 n.
modification
difference 15 n.
change 143 n.
qualification 468 n.
modify
differ 15 vb.

MOL

make unlike 19 vb.
modify 143 vb.
modish
fashionable
  848 adj.
reputable 866 adj.
modulate
adjust 24 vb.
modify 143 vb.
harmonize 410 vb.
voice 577 vb.
module
prototype 23 n.
curriculum 534 n.
modus operandi
way 624 n.
modus vivendi
substitute 150 n.
mogul
bigwig 638 n.
mohair
fibre 208 n.
textile 222 n.
hair 259 n.
Mohammed or Ma-
  homet
religious teacher
  973 n.
moiety
bisection 92 n.
moire
textile 222 n.
variegation 437 n.
moist
watery 339 adj.
humid 341 adj.
moisten
moisten 341 vb.
moisture
moisture 341 n.
moisturizing
beautification
  843 n.
moke
beast of burden
  273 n.
molar
tooth 256 n.
pulverizer 332 n.
molasses
sweet thing 392 n.
mole
mammal 365 n.
spectator 441 n.
secret service
  459 n.
latency 523 n.

informer 524 n.
identification
  547 n.
skin disease 651 n.
collaborator 707 n.
blemish 845 n.
molecule
  minuteness 196 n.
  element 319 n.
molehill
  minuteness 196 n.
  dome 253 n.
molest
  harm 645 vb.
  torment 827 vb.
  be malevolent
   898 vb.
  debauch 951 vb.
moll
  female 373 n.
  kept woman 952 n.
mollify
  assuage 177 vb.
  pacify 719 vb.
mollusc
  animal 365 n.
  marine life 365 n.
moment
  juncture 8 n.
  small quantity
   33 n.
  date 108 n.
  brief span 114 n.
  instant 116 n.
  cause 156 n.
  importance 638 n.
momentary
  brief 114 adj.
momentous
  crucial 137 adj.
  influential 178 adj.
  important 638 adj.
momentum
  energy 160 n.
  impulse 279 n.
monad
  existence 1 n.
  unit 88 n.
monarch
  sovereign 741 n.
  owner 776 n.
  heretical 977 adj.
Monarchianism
  heresy 977 n.
monarchist
  revolter 738 n.

monarchy
  government 733 n.
monastery
  monastery 986 n.
monastic
  monastic 986 adj.
  monk 986 n.
monaural
  sounding 398 adj.
monetary
  monetary 797 adj.
money
  money 797 n.
moneybags
  rich person 800 n.
moneybox
  box 194 n.
  storage 632 n.
  treasury 799 n.
moneyed
  moneyed 800 adj.
**money for jam or old
  rope**
  easy thing 701 n.
moneylender
  lender 784 n.
money-making
  gainful 771 adj.
mongolism
  psychosis 503 n.
mongoloid
  *mentally handi-
   capped* 503 adj.
mongoose
  mammal 365 n.
mongrel
  hybrid 43 n.
  mixed 43 adj.
  abnormal 84 adj.
  nonconformist
   84 n.
  dog 365 n.
monies
  funds 797 n.
moniker
  name 561 n.
monism
  unity 88 n.
monitor
  reptile 365 n.
  listener 415 n.
  look after 457 vb.
  enquire 459 vb.
monk
  celibate 895 n.
  pietist 979 n.
  monk 986 n.

monkey
  ram 279 n.
  mammal 365 n.
  be cunning 698 vb.
  funds 797 n.
  bad person 938 n.
monkey business
  deception 542 n.
  cunning 698 n.
  perfidy 930 n.
monkey tricks
  foolery 497 n.
  disobedience
   738 n.
  revel 837 n.
monkey with
  impair 655 vb.
monkey wrench
  tool 630 n.
mono
  one 88 adj.
  sound 398 n.
  sounding 398 adj.
monochrome
  uniform 16 adj.
  achromatism
   426 n.
  painting 553 n.
monocle
  eyeglass 442 n.
monogamy
  type of marriage
   894 n.
monogram
  indication 547 n.
  label 547 n.
monograph
  dissertation 591 n.
**monolingual diction-
  ary**
  dictionary 559 n.
monolith
  uniformity 16 n.
  coherence 48 n.
  unit 88 n.
  monument 548 n.
monolithic
  identical 13 adj.
  uniform 16 adj.
  simple 44 adj.
  cohesive 48 adj.
  indivisible 52 adj.
  one 88 adj.
  dense 324 adj.
monologue
  uniformity 16 n.
  unit 88 n.

oration 579 n.
soliloquy 585 n.
stage play 594 n.
monomania
  prejudgment 481 n.
monophonic
  sounding 398 adj.
monoplane
  aircraft 276 n.
monopolize
  prevail 178 vb.
  absorb 449 vb.
  possess 773 vb.
  appropriate
   786 vb.
  be selfish 932 vb.
monopoly
  exclusion 57 n.
  corporation 708 n.
  restriction 747 n.
  possession 773 n.
  sale 793 n.
monorail
  railway 624 n.
monosyllable
  word 559 n.
monotheism
  unity 88 n.
  deism 973 n.
monotheist
  religionist 973 n.
monotone
  uniform 16 adj.
  uniformity 16 n.
  musical note
   410 n.
  painting 553 n.
monotonous
  identical 13 adj.
  uniform 16 adj.
  continuous 71 adj.
  repeated 106 adj.
  feeble 572 adj.
  tedious 838 adj.
monotony
  uniformity 16 n.
  continuity 71 n.
  tedium 838 n.
  dullness 840 n.
Monseigneur
  church title 986 n.
monsieur
  male 372 n.
  title 870 n.
monsoon
  rain 350 n.
  wind 352 n.

monster
abnormality 84 n.
nonconformist
84 n.
giant 195 n.
eyesore 842 n.
prodigy 864 n.
monster 938 n.
monstrosity
abnormality 84 n.
deformity 246 n.
prodigy 864 n.
monstrous
exorbitant 32 adj.
unusual 84 adj.
huge 195 adj.
harmful 645 adj.
not nice 645 adj.
ugly 842 adj.
ridiculous 849 adj.
wonderful 864 adj.
heinous 934 adj.
montage
cinema 445 n.
picture 553 n.
month
period 110 n.
monthly
periodically
141 adv.
seasonal 141 adj.
journal 528 n.
usual 610 adj.
month of Sundays
neverness 109 n.
long duration
113 n.
monument
monument 548 n.
honours 866 n.
monumental
enormous 32 adj.
large 195 adj.
moo
ululate 409 vb.
ululation 409 n.
mooch
beg 761 vb.
take 786 vb.
mood
temperament 5 n.
state 7 n.
tendency 179 n.
grammar 564 n.
whim 604 n.
conduct 688 n.
affections 817 n.

moral sensibility
819 n.
moody
fitful 142 adj.
changeful 152 adj.
capricious 604 adj.
excitable 822 adj.
melancholic
834 adj.
irascible 892 adj.
sullen 893 adj.
moon
changeable thing
152 n.
follower 284 n.
moon 321 n.
satellite 321 n.
luminary 420 n.
be inattentive
456 vb.
moon after
desire 859 vb.
moonlight
moon 321 n.
light 417 n.
work 682 vb.
not pay 805 vb.
moonlighting
escape 667 n.
swindling 788 n.
moonlit
undimmed
417 adj.
moonshine
insubstantial thing
4 n.
alcoholic drink
301 n.
moon 321 n.
light 417 n.
empty talk 515 n.
fable 543 n.
moonstone
gem 844 n.
moor
affix 45 vb.
tie 45 vb.
desert 172 n.
place 187 vb.
high land 209 n.
navigate 269 vb.
arrive 295 vb.
plain 348 n.
mooring
station 187 n.
arrival 295 n.

moose
mammal 365 n.
moot
interrogate 459 vb.
propound 512 vb.
moot point
topic 452 n.
question 459 n.
mop
hair 259 n.
dry 342 vb.
dryer 342 n.
clean 648 vb.
cleaning utensil
648 n.
mope
be dejected 834 vb.
moped
conveyance 267 n.
bicycle 274 n.
moped rider
rider 268 n.
mop up
destroy 165 vb.
absorb 299 vb.
empty 300 vb.
dry 342 vb.
clean 648 vb.
carry through
725 vb.
moraine
leavings 41 n.
piece 53 n.
soil 344 n.
moral
judgment 480 n.
maxim 496 n.
phrase 563 n.
good 615 adj.
precept 693 n.
reputable 866 adj.
ethical 917 adj.
virtuous 933 adj.
pure 950 adj.
moral certainty
positiveness 473 n.
morale
state 7 n.
morale-boosting
aiding 703 adj.
moralistic
ethical 917 adj.
morality
right 913 n.
morals 917 n.
virtue 933 n.
purity 950 n.

moralize
teach 534 vb.
moral philosophy
morals 917 n.
morals
conduct 688 n.
morals 917 n.
purity 950 n.
morass
marsh 347 n.
moratorium
delay 136 n.
lull 145 n.
nonpayment 805 n.
morbid
diseased 651 adj.
morbidity
badness 645 n.
mordant
keen 174 adj.
pigment 425 n.
concise 569 adj.
disapproving
924 adj.
more
finite quantity
26 n.
beyond 34 adv.
additional 38 adj.
in addition 38 adv.
bravo 923 int.
moreish
edible 301 adj.
savoury 390 adj.
more or less
about 33 adv.
nearly 200 adv.
moreover
in addition 38 adv.
mores
habit 610 n.
practice 610 n.
conduct 688 n.
morgue
death 361 n.
interment 364 n.
inactivity 679 n.
moribund
ageing 131 adj.
dying 361 adj.
Mori poll (tdmk)
vote 605 n.
Mormon
religionist 973 n.
sectarian 978 n.
morn
morning 128 n.

morning
period 110 n.
morning 128 n.
perpetually
139 adv.
morning after the
night before
crapulence 949 n.
morning dress
formal dress 228 n.
morning star
planet 321 n.
luminary 420 n.
morocco
skin 226 n.
bookbinding 589 n.
moron
fool 501 n.
the mentally handi-
capped 504 n.
moronic
mindless 448 adj.
absurd 497 adj.
unintelligent
499 adj.
mentally handi-
capped 503 adj.
morose
melancholic
834 adj.
unsociable 883 adj.
sullen 893 adj.
morpheme
word 559 n.
part of speech
564 n.
morphia
drug 658 n.
drug-taking 949 n.
morphine
anaesthetic 375 n.
drug 658 n.
soporific 679 n.
drug-taking 949 n.
morphology
form 243 n.
biology 358 n.
zoology 367 n.
morris dance
dance 837 n.
morse
fastening 47 n.
telecommunication
531 n.
signal 547 n.

morsel
small quantity
33 n.
piece 53 n.
mouthful 301 n.
mortal
ephemeral 114 adj.
destructive 165 adj.
dying 361 adj.
deadly 362 adj.
person 371 n.
evil 616 adj.
mortality
transience 114 n.
death 361 n.
death roll 361 n.
humankind 371 n.
mortar
adhesive 47 n.
gun 723 n.
mortgage
encumbrance
702 n.
give security
767 vb.
security 767 n.
lending 784 n.
borrow 785 vb.
borrowing 785 n.
credit 802 n.
debt 803 n.
mortification
decay 51 n.
death 361 n.
sorrow 825 n.
annoyance 827 n.
discontent 829 n.
regret 830 n.
humiliation 872 n.
humility 872 n.
envy 912 n.
indignity 921 n.
asceticism 945 n.
mortified
unhappy 825 adj.
discontented
829 adj.
inglorious 867 adj.
mortify
decompose 51 vb.
hurt 827 vb.
cause discontent
829 vb.
humiliate 872 vb.
mortise
join 45 vb.
receptacle 194 n.

introduce 231 vb.
furrow 262 n.
mortuary
death 361 n.
funereal 364 adj.
interment 364 n.
Mosaic
religious 973 adj.
scriptural 975 adj.
mosaic
nonuniformity
17 n.
medley 43 n.
multiform 82 adj.
chequer 437 n.
variegated 437 adj.
picture 553 n.
ornamental art
844 n.
mosey along
wander 267 vb.
mosey around
be curious 453 vb.
Moslem
religionist 973 n.
religious 973 adj.
mosque
church 990 n.
temple 990 n.
mosquito
insect 365 n.
bane 659 n.
moss
plant 366 n.
greenness 434 n.
mossy
soft 327 adj.
most
finite quantity
26 n.
great 32 adj.
mostly
greatly 32 vb.
mot
maxim 496 n.
witticism 839 n.
mote
small thing 33 n.
dirt 649 n.
mote in the eye
prejudice 481 n.
motel
inn 192 n.
moth
destroyer 168 n.
insect 365 n.
blight 659 n.

mothball
pause 145 vb.
be neglectful
458 vb.
store 632 vb.
preserver 666 n.
moth-eaten
dilapidated
655 adj.
mother
kinsman 11 n.
maternity 169 n.
female 373 n.
safeguard 660 vb.
minister to 703 vb.
pet 889 vb.
do good 897 adj.
church title 986 n.
nun 986 n.
motherhood
family 11 n.
maternity 169 n.
parentage 169 n.
mother-in-law
maternity 169 n.
motherland
territory 184 n.
home 192 n.
motherly
parental 169 adj.
loving 887 adj.
benevolent 897 adj.
mother-of-pearl
variegation 437 n.
gem 844 n.
Mother Superior
ecclesiarch 986 n.
nun 986 n.
mother-to-be
maternity 169 n.
mother tongue
language 557 n.
motif
topic 452 n.
pattern 844 n.
motility
motion 265 n.
motion
motion 265 n.
move 265 vb.
defecation 302 n.
topic 452 n.
gesticulate 547 vb.
gesture 547 n.
plan 623 n.
conduct 688 n.
advice 691 n.

command 737 vb.
offer 759 n.
request 761 n.
motionless
still 266 adj.
nonactive 677 adj.
inactive 679 adj.
motion pictures
film 445 n.
motivation
causation 156 n.
motive 612 n.
motive
reason why 156 n.
moving 265 adj.
musical piece
412 n.
motive 612 n.
mot juste
fitness 24 n.
accuracy 494 n.
elegance 575 n.
motley
nonuniformity
17 n.
medley 43 n.
mixed 43 adj.
multiform 82 adj.
clothing 228 n.
variegated 437 adj.
variegation 437 n.
motor
moving 265 adj.
ride 267 vb.
automobile 274 n.
machine 630 n.
motor car
automobile 274 n.
motoring
land travel 267 n.
motorist
driver 268 n.
motorized
mechanical
630 adj.
motorway
road 624 n.
mottled
mottled 437 adj.
motto
maxim 496 n.
commentary 520 n.
heraldry 547 n.
indication 547 n.
phrase 563 n.
moue
distortion 246 n.

gesture 547 n.
mould
modality 7 n.
uniformity 16 n.
mould 23 n.
decay 51 n.
sort 77 n.
convert 147 vb.
produce 164 vb.
receptacle 194 n.
form 243 n.
form 243 vb.
soil 344 n.
plant 366 n.
educate 534 vb.
represent 551 vb.
sculpt 554 vb.
dirt 649 n.
blight 659 n.
decorate 844 vb.
moulded
formed 243 adj.
with affections
817 adj.
mouldering
decay 51 n.
antiquated 127 adj.
dilapidated
655 adj.
moulding
cohesive 48 adj.
formation 243 n.
sculpture 554 n.
ornamental art
844 n.
mould oneself on
do likewise 20 vb.
mouldy
dirty 649 adj.
moulting
uncovering 229 n.
mound
bulk 195 n.
dome 253 n.
defences 713 n.
mount
be great - large
32 vb.
grow 36 vb.
unite with 45 vb.
be high 209 vb.
high land 209 n.
support 218 vb.
conveyance 267 n.
ride 267 vb.
horse 273 n.
saddle horse 273 n.

start out 296 vb.
enter 297 vb.
ascend 308 vb.
climb 308 vb.
elevate 310 vb.
break in 369 vb.
dramatize 594 vb.
mountain
great quantity
32 n.
bulk 195 n.
high land 209 n.
storage 632 n.
store 632 n.
acquisition 771 n.
wealth 800 n.
mountaineer
traveller 268 n.
climb 308 vb.
climber 308 n.
mountainous
huge 195 adj.
large 195 adj.
mountain range
high land 209 n.
mountebank
impostor 545 n.
mount guard
invigilate 457 vb.
safeguard 660 vb.
mounting
support 218 n.
ascent 308 n.
dear 811 adj.
mourn
inter 364 vb.
lament 836 vb.
mournful
distressing 827 adj.
melancholic
834 adj.
lamenting 836 adj.
mourning
formal dress 228 n.
funereal 364 adj.
obsequies 364 n.
black 428 adj.
black thing 428 n.
lamentation 836 n.
mouse
data processing
86 n.
mammal 365 n.
hunt 619 vb.
coward 856 n.
humility 872 n.
modesty 874 n.

mouse-coloured
grey 429 adj.
moussaka
dish 301 n.
mousse
dessert 301 n.
bubble 355 n.
pulpiness 356 n.
moustache
hair 259 n.
mousy
colourless 426 adj.
grey 429 adj.
ugly 842 adj.
mouth
entrance 68 n.
stomach 194 n.
threshold 234 n.
orifice 263 n.
way in 297 n.
gulf 345 n.
voice 577 n.
orate 579 n.
sauciness 878 n.
mouthful
small quantity
33 n.
mouthful 301 n.
mouth organ
air pipe 353 n.
organ 414 n.
mouthpiece
air pipe 353 n.
flute 414 n.
interpreter 520 n.
informant 524 n.
speaker 579 n.
deputy 755 n.
mouth-watering
tasty 386 adj.
movable
moving 265 adj.
move
displacement
188 n.
be in motion
265 vb.
motion 265 n.
move 265 vb.
transpose 272 vb.
move fast 277 vb.
attract 291 vb.
excrete 302 vb.
be agitated 318 vb.
propound 512 vb.
gesture 547 n.
motivate 612 vb.

attempt 671 n.
action 676 n.
deed 676 n.
do 676 vb.
tactics 688 n.
advise 691 vb.
stratagem 698 n.
offer 759 vb.
excite 821 vb.
moved
  impressed 818 adj.
  impressible
   819 adj.
move heaven and
  earth
  persevere 600 vb.
  exert oneself
   682 vb.
move in
  place oneself
   187 vb.
  dwell 192 vb.
  enter 297 vb.
move it
  come along
   267 int.
movement
  transition 147 n.
  motion 265 n.
  melody 410 n.
  musical piece
   412 n.
  action 676 n.
  activity 678 n.
move one's bowels
  excrete 302 vb.
move with the times
  modernize 126 vb.
  change 143 vb.
  progress 285 vb.
movies
  film 445 n.
moving
  influential 178 adj.
  moving 265 adj.
  exciting 821 adj.
  distressing 827 adj.
mow
  cut 46 vb.
  shorten 204 vb.
  smooth 258 vb.
  cultivate 370 vb.
  store 632 n.
  store 632 vb.
mow down
  demolish 165 vb.
  slaughter 362 vb.

mower
  farm tool 370 n.
MP
  official 690 n.
  councillor 692 n.
Mr or Miss Right
  favourite 890 n.
Mr or Miss X
  unknown thing
   491 n.
Mr or Mrs average
  everyman 79 n.
Mrs Grundy
  etiquette 848 n.
  prude 950 n.
Mrs Mop
  cleaner 648 n.
much
  greatly 32 vb.
  great quantity
   32 n.
  many 104 adj.
much of a muchness
  similar 18 adj.
  middling 732 adj.
muck
  excrement 302 n.
  rubbish 641 n.
  dirt 649 n.
muck about
  be absurd 497 vb.
muck-raking
  detraction 926 n.
muck up
  jumble 63 vb.
  make unclean
   649 vb.
  impair 655 vb.
mucky
  dirty 649 adj.
mucous
  viscid 354 adj.
mucus
  excrement 302 n.
  fluid 335 n.
  semiliquidity
   354 n.
  dirt 649 n.
mud
  moisture 341 n.
  marsh 347 n.
  semiliquidity
   354 n.
  dirt 649 n.
muddle
  disorder 61 n.
  derange 63 vb.

jumble 63 vb.
distract 456 vb.
predicament 700 n.
muddled
  poorly reasoned
   477 adj.
  unintelligent
   499 adj.
  unclear 568 adj.
muddy
  agitate 318 vb.
  humid 341 adj.
  marshy 347 adj.
  dim 419 adj.
  dim 419 vb.
  opaque 423 adj.
  dirty 649 adj.
  make unclean
   649 vb.
mud flat
  lake 346 n.
mudguard
  shelter 662 n.
mud-slinging
  detraction 926 n.
muesli
  cereals 301 n.
muff
  glove 228 n.
  blunder 495 vb.
  mistake 495 n.
  be clumsy 695 vb.
  bungling 695 n.
muffer
  bungler 697 n.
muffin
  cereals 301 n.
muffle
  weaken 163 vb.
  moderate 177 vb.
  cover 226 vb.
  silence 399 vb.
  mute 401 vb.
  conceal 525 vb.
  make mute 578 vb.
muffler
  neckwear 228 n.
mufti
  informal dress
   228 n.
  theologian 973 n.
  priest 986 n.
mug
  force 176 vb.
  cup 194 n.
  face 237 n.
  strike 279 vb.

credulity 487 n.
ninny 501 n.
study 536 vb.
dupe 544 n.
strike at 712 vb.
rob 788 vb.
mugging
  attack 712 n.
  stealing 788 n.
muggins
  ninny 501 n.
muggy
  humid 341 adj.
  warm 379 adj.
Muhammedanism
  religious faith
   973 n.
mulberry
  fruit and vegetables
   301 n.
  purple 436 adj.
mulch
  fertilizer 171 n.
  covering 226 n.
  cultivate 370 vb.
mule
  hybrid 43 n.
  footwear 228 n.
mulish
  equine 273 adj.
  animal 365 adj.
  obstinate 602 adj.
  wilful 602 adj.
mull
  textile 222 n.
  projection 254 n.
  sweeten 392 vb.
mullah
  theologian 973 n.
mullet
  fish food 301 n.
mullion
  pillar 218 n.
  window 263 n.
mull over
  think 449 vb.
multicoloured
  nonuniform 17 adj.
  variegated 437 adj.
multifarious
  unrelated 10 adj.
  different 15 adj.
  nonuniform 17 adj.
  multiform 82 adj.
  many 104 adj.
multifariousness
  unrelatedness 10 n.

multiformity 82 n.
multiform
  multiform 82 adj.
  plural 101 adj.
multimillion
  over one hundred
    99 n.
  dear 811 adj.
multi-millionaire
  rich person 800 n.
multinational
  influential 178 adj.
  business 622 n.
multiparous
  plural 101 adj.
multiple
  quantity 26 n.
  multiform 82 adj.
  numerical 85 adj.
  numerical element
    85 n.
  plural 101 adj.
  many 104 adj.
multiple sclerosis
  nervous disorders
    651 n.
multiplication
  greatness 32 n.
  increase 36 n.
  reproduction
    166 n.
  propagation 167 n.
  productiveness
    171 n.
multiplicity
  multiformity 82 n.
  plurality 101 n.
  multitude 104 n.
multiply
  augment 36 vb.
  grow 36 vb.
  repeat 106 vb.
  produce 164 vb.
  reproduce 166 vb.
  reproduce itself
    167 vb.
  be fruitful 171 vb.
multipurpose
  general 79 adj.
  plural 101 adj.
  useful 640 adj.
multiracial
  mixed 43 adj.
multitude
  multitude 104 n.

multitudes
  great quantity
    32 n.
mum
  maternity 169 n.
  voiceless 578 adj.
  taciturn 582 adj.
mumble
  stammer 580 vb.
mumbo jumbo
  lack of meaning
    515 n.
  deity 966 n.
  idol 982 n.
  idolatry 982 n.
  spell 983 n.
mummer
  actor 594 n.
mummify
  dry 342 vb.
  preserve 666 vb.
mummy
  maternity 169 n.
  corpse 363 n.
mummy's boy
  weakling 163 n.
  male 372 n.
  coward 856 n.
mumps
  infection 651 n.
mum's the word
  hush 399 int.
munch
  chew 301 vb.
municipality
  district 184 n.
  jurisdiction 955 n.
munificent
  liberal 813 adj.
munitions
  arms 723 n.
mural
  picture 553 n.
murder
  homicide 362 n.
  killing 362 n.
  murder 362 vb.
  indoor game 837 n.
  cruel act 898 n.
murderer
  murderer 362 n.
murderous
  murderous 362 adj.
murk
  darkness 418 n.
  dimness 419 n.

murky
  dense 324 adj.
  dark 418 adj.
  opaque 423 adj.
murmur
  flow 350 VB.
  faintness 401 n.
  sound faint 401 vb.
  roll 403 n.
  imply 523 vb.
  deprecate 762 vb.
  deprecation 762 n.
Murphy's law
  rule 81 n.
  axiom 496 n.
muscle
  ligature 47 n.
  power 160 n.
  vitality 162 n.
  exertion 682 n.
muscle in
  intrude 297 vb.
muscleman
  athlete 162 n.
  bulk 195 n.
  a beauty 841 n.
muscular
  stalwart 162 adj.
muscular dystrophy
  nervous disorders
    651 n.
muse
  meditate 449 vb.
  be inattentive
    456 vb.
  poetry 593 n.
  excitation 821 n.
Muses
  poetry 593 n.
  lesser deity 967 n.
museum
  accumulation 74 n.
  antiquity 125 n.
  exhibit 522 n.
  collection 632 n.
museum piece
  archaism 127 n.
  exhibit 522 n.
  exceller 644 n.
mush
  face 237 n.
  orifice 263 n.
  pulpiness 356 n.
mushroom
  grow 36 vb.
  new 126 adj.
  be fruitful 171 vb.

  expand 197 vb.
  dome 253 n.
  fruit and vegetables
    301 n.
  plant 366 n.
  whitish 427 adj.
  brown 430 adj.
mushy
  soft 327 adj.
music
  music 412 n.
  broadcast 531 n.
musical
  melodious 410 adj.
  musical 412 adj.
  vocal music 412 n.
  film 445 n.
  stage play 594 n.
  pleasurable
    826 adj.
musical chairs
  indoor game 837 n.
musical comedy
  vocal music 412 n.
  stage play 594 n.
musical instrument
  musical instrument
    414 n.
music centre
  gramophone 414 n.
musician
  musician 413 n.
music-making
  music 412 n.
musicologist
  musician 413 n.
music to one's ears,
be
  delight 826 vb.
musk
  scent 396 n.
musket
  firearm 723 n.
musketeer
  soldiery 722 n.
musky
  fragrant 396 adj.
Muslim
  religionist 973 n.
muslin
  textile 222 n.
  semitransparency
    424 n.
mussel
  fish food 301 n.
  marine life 365 n.

must, a
  necessity 596 n.
  requirement 627 n.
mustang
  saddle horse 273 n.
mustard
  condiment 389 n.
  yellowness 433 n.
mustard gas
  poison 659 n.
  weapon 723 n.
muster
  bring together
    74 vb.
  number 86 vb.
  statistics 86 n.
musty
  fetid 397 adj.
  dirty 649 adj.
mutable
  changeable
    143 adj.
  changeful 152 adj.
mutant
  nonconformist
    84 n.
mutation
  variant 15 n.
  nonuniformity
    17 n.
  misfit 25 n.
  abnormality 84 n.
  change 143 n.
  conversion 147 n.
  deformity 246 n.
mute
  silent 399 adj.
  mute 401 vb.
  nonresonance
    405 n.
  voiceless 578 adj.
  taciturn 582 adj.
muted
  muted 401 adj.
  soft-hued 425 adj.
  serious 834 adj.
mutilate
  subtract 39 vb.
  destroy 165 vb.
  deform 244 vb.
  impair 655 vb.
  make ugly 842 vb.
mutineer
  revolter 738 n.
  undutifulness
    918 n.
  schismatic 978 n.

mutinous
  quarrelling
    709 adj.
  defiant 711 adj.
  resisting 715 adj.
  disobedient
    738 adj.
  undutiful 918 adj.
mutiny
  strike 145 n.
  resist 715 vb.
  revolt 738 n.
  revolt 738 vb.
  fail in duty 918 vb.
  undutifulness
    918 n.
mutt
  dog 365 n.
mutter
  blow 352 vb.
  sound faint 401 vb.
  roll 403 n.
  cry 408 vb.
  voice 577 n.
  stammer 580 vb.
  threaten 900 vb.
mutton
  meat 301 n.
mutton-chops
  hair 259 n.
mutual
  relative 9 adj.
  correlative 12 adj.
muzak
  music 412 n.
muzzle
  disable 161 vb.
  protuberance
    254 n.
  orifice 263 n.
  stopper 264 n.
  silence 399 vb.
  make mute 578 vb.
  hinder 702 vb.
  firearm 723 n.
  restrain 747 vb.
  fetter 748 n.
muzzy
  tipsy 949 adj.
mycology
  botany 368 n.
myna bird
  imitator 20 n.
  bird 365 n.
myopia
  dim sight 440 n.

myriad
  over one hundred
    99 n.
  many 104 adj.
myrrh
  resin 357 n.
  interment 364 n.
  scent 396 n.
myself
  self 80 n.
  subjectivity 320 n.
mysterious
  unusual 84 adj.
  invisible 444 adj.
  uncertain 474 adj.
  unknown 491 adj.
  puzzling 517 adj.
  occult 523 adj.
  concealed 525 adj.
  unclear 568 adj.
  wonderful 864 adj.
mystery
  invisibility 444 n.
  unknown thing
    491 n.
  latency 523 n.
  secrecy 525 n.
  enigma 530 n.
  secret 530 n.
  rite 988 n.
mystery play
  stage play 594 n.
mystic
  occult 523 adj.
  religious 973 adj.
  revelational
    975 adj.
  pietist 979 n.
  pious 979 adj.
  worshipper 981 n.
  occultist 984 n.
mystical
  divine 965 adj.
mysticism
  meditation 449 n.
  latency 523 n.
  religion 973 n.
  revelation 975 n.
  piety 979 n.
  occultism 984 n.
mystify
  puzzle 474 vb.
  sophisticate
    477 vb.
  deceive 542 vb.
mystique
  prestige 866 n.

  cult 981 n.
myth
  fantasy 513 n.
  fable 543 n.
  narrative 590 n.
mythical
  erroneous 495 adj.
mythology
  tradition 127 n.
myxomatosis
  animal disease
    651 n.

N

n
  many 104 adj.
Naafi
  café 192 n.
nab
  ensnare 542 vb.
  arrest 747 vb.
  take 786 vb.
nabob
  officer 741 n.
nadir
  inferiority 35 n.
  extremity 69 n.
  zero 103 n.
  lowness 210 n.
  depth 211 n.
  base 214 n.
naff
  useless 641 adj.
  bad 645 adj.
  vulgar 847 adj.
naff off
  go away 190 vb.
nag
  horse 273 n.
  saddle horse 273 n.
  incite 612 vb.
  animate 821 vb.
  torment 827 vb.
  enrage 891 vb.
naiad
  nymph 967 n.
  mythical being
    970 n.
nail
  affix 45 vb.
  fastening 47 n.
  hanger 217 n.
  sharp point 256 n.
  perforator 263 n.
  tool 630 n.

nail file
smoother 258 n.
cosmetic 843 n.
naive
credulous 487 adj.
ignorant 491 adj.
artless 699 adj.
innocent 935 adj.
naked
simple 44 adj.
uncovered 229 adj.
visible 443 adj.
vulnerable 661 adj.
namby-pamby
weak 163 adj.
weakling 163 n.
affected 850 adj.
name
inform 524 vb.
indicate 547 vb.
label 547 n.
name 561 n.
name 561 vb.
famousness 866 n.
repute 866 n.
accuse 928 vb.
name-dropping
affected 850 adj.
nameless
anonymous
   562 adj.
inglorious 867 adj.
namely
namely 80 adv.
in plain words
   520 adv.
namesake
name 561 n.
nan
maternity 169 n.
cereals 301 n.
nancy
nonconformist
   84 n.
nanny
protector 660 n.
domestic 742 n.
retainer 742 n.
servant 742 n.
keeper 749 n.
nanny goat
goat 365 n.
female animal
   373 n.
nap
weaving 222 n.
texture 331 n.

sleep 679 n.
sleep 679 vb.
card game 837 n.
nape
rear 238 n.
narcissism
vanity 873 n.
love 887 n.
selfishness 932 n.
narcolepsy
insensibility 375 n.
narcotic
anaesthetic 375 n.
drug 658 n.
remedial 658 adj.
drug-taking 949 n.
intoxicating
   949 adj.
nark
informer 524 n.
accuser 928 n.
narrate
communicate
   524 vb.
describe 590 vb.
narrative
narrative 590 n.
narrator
speaker 579 n.
narrow
become small
   198 vb.
make smaller
   198 vb.
narrow 206 adj.
narrow-minded
   481 adj.
narrowboat
boat 275 n.
narrowcasting
publication 528 n.
narrow escape
danger 661 n.
escape 667 n.
narrow-minded
narrow-minded
   481 adj.
prudish 950 adj.
narrows
narrowness 206 n.
nasal
speech sound
   398 n.
nascent
beginning 68 adj.
nasty
not nice 645 adj.

unclean 649 adj.
dangerous 661 adj.
unpleasant
   827 adj.
hateful 888 adj.
malevolent
   898 adj.
unkind 898 adj.
natal
first 68 adj.
nation
race 11 n.
nation 371 n.
community 708 n.
national
universal 79 adj.
native 191 adj.
native 191 n.
national 371 adj.
subject 742 n.
national emblem
heraldry 547 n.
nationalism
nation 371 n.
patriotism 901 n.
nationalist
patriot 901 n.
nationalistic
biased 481 adj.
patriotic 901 adj.
nationality
consanguinity
   11 n.
nation 371 n.
nationalization
association 706 n.
joint possession
   775 n.
transfer 780 n.
trade 791 n.
national monument
monument 548 n.
national service
war measures
   718 n.
nationwide
universal 79 adj.
native
genetic 5 adj.
intrinsic 5 adj.
component 58 adj.
native 191 adj.
native 191 n.
artless 699 adj.
native heath
home 192 n.

native wit
ability 160 n.
Nativity
holy day 988 n.
nativity
origin 68 n.
propagation 167 n.
life 360 n.
natter
chat 584 n.
converse 584 vb.
natty
personable 841 adj.
natural
real 1 adj.
substantial 3 adj.
intrinsic 5 adj.
typical 83 adj.
material 319 adj.
musical note
   410 n.
genuine 494 adj.
*the mentally handi-
   capped* 504 n.
plain 573 adj.
usual 610 adj.
artless 699 adj.
friendly 880 adj.
natural gas
gas 336 n.
fuel 385 n.
naturalistic
literary 557 adj.
naturalized
converted 147 adj.
native 191 adj.
habituated 610 adj.
naturalness
plainness 573 n.
artlessness 699 n.
natural philosophy
physics 319 n.
philosophy 449 n.
science 490 n.
nature
essence 1 n.
character 5 n.
composition 56 n.
sort 77 n.
tendency 179 n.
affections 817 n.
nature study
biology 358 n.
naturism
uncovering 229 n.
naturist
stripper 229 n.

naturopathy
  medical art 658 n.
naught
  insubstantiality
    4 n.
  zero 103 n.
naughty
  difficult 700 adj.
  disobedient
    738 adj.
  wicked 934 adj.
  impure 951 adj.
  unchaste 951 adj.
nausea
  voidance 300 n.
  digestive disorders
    651 n.
  illness 651 n.
  painfulness 827 n.
  dislike 861 n.
  hatred 888 n.
nauseate
  be unpalatable
    391 vb.
  displease 827 vb.
  cause dislike
    861 vb.
nauseous
  not nice 645 adj.
  unclean 649 adj.
  unpleasant
    827 adj.
  hateful 888 adj.
nautical
  marine 275 adj.
nautical mile
  long measure
    203 n.
naval
  marine 275 adj.
nave
  middle 70 n.
  church interior
    990 n.
navel
  middle 70 n.
  centre 225 n.
navigate
  navigate 269 vb.
navigator
  navigator 270 n.
  aeronaut 271 n.
  air force 722 n.
navvy
  worker 686 n.
navy
  blue 435 adj.

navy 722 n.
nawab
  potentate 741 n.
  person of rank
    868 n.
nay
  negation 533 n.
  refusal 760 n.
Nazism
  government 733 n.
  brute force 735 n.
Neanderthal man
  antiquity 125 n.
  fossil 125 n.
  violent creature
    176 n.
  humankind 371 n.
neap tide
  water 339 n.
  current 350 n.
near
  akin 11 adj.
  be to come 124 vb.
  near 200 adj.
  near 200 adv.
  approach 289 vb.
  parsimonious
    816 adj.
nearby
  near 200 adj.
  accessible 289 adj.
nearly
  nearly 200 adv.
near-sighted
  dim-sighted
    440 adj.
near the bone
  impure 951 adj.
near thing
  short distance
    200 n.
  danger 661 n.
  escape 667 n.
neat
  unmixed 44 adj.
  orderly 60 adj.
  strong 162 adj.
  careful 457 adj.
  concise 569 adj.
  plain 573 adj.
  elegant 575 adj.
  intoxicating
    949 adj.
neaten
  arrange 62 vb.
  make better
    654 vb.

nebula
  star 321 n.
nebulous
  amorphous
    244 adj.
  celestial 321 adj.
  cloudy 355 adj.
  dim 419 adj.
  puzzling 517 adj.
necessary
  necessary 596 adj.
  required 627 adj.
  important 638 adj.
necessitate
  necessitate 596 vb.
  require 627 vb.
  compel 740 vb.
necessity
  certainty 473 n.
  necessity 596 n.
  poverty 801 n.
neck
  bond 47 n.
  contraction 198 n.
  narrowness 206 n.
  pillar 218 n.
  garment 228 n.
  sauciness 878 n.
  caress 889 vb.
neck and crop
  completely 54 adv.
neck-and-neck
  equal 28 adj.
  synchronism 123 n.
  synchronous
    123 adj.
  near 200 adj.
neckband
  loop 250 n.
neckerchief
  neckwear 228 n.
necking
  lovemaking 887 n.
  endearment 889 n.
necklace
  neckwear 228 n.
  loop 250 n.
  jewellery 844 n.
  execute 963 vb.
  means of execution
    964 n.
neck of the woods
  locality 187 n.
necromancy
  sorcery 983 n.
necrophilia
  abnormality 84 n.

necropolis
  cemetery 364 n.
necrosis
  decay 51 n.
  death 361 n.
nectar
  draught 301 n.
  sweet thing 392 n.
nectarine
  fruit and vegetables
    301 n.
need
  be incomplete
    55 vb.
  deficit 55 n.
  shortfall 307 n.
  require 627 vb.
  requirement 627 n.
  scarcity 636 n.
  adversity 731 n.
  request 761 vb.
  poverty 801 n.
  desire 859 n.
needful, the
  funds 797 n.
needing
  incomplete 55 adj.
needle
  prickle 256 n.
  sharp point 256 n.
  perforator 263 n.
  sailing aid 269 n.
  gramophone 414 n.
  indicator 547 n.
  incite 612 vb.
  torment 827 vb.
  enrage 891 vb.
needlecord
  textile 222 n.
needless
  superfluous
    637 adj.
needy
  poor 801 adj.
ne'er-do-well
  idler 679 n.
  desperado 857 n.
  vicious 934 adj.
  bad person 938 n.
nefarious
  disreputable
    867 adj.
  heinous 934 adj.
negate
  negate 533 vb.
negative
  nullify 2 vb.

mould 23 n.
numerical 85 adj.
electricity 160 n.
darkness 418 n.
dissent 489 vb.
negate 533 vb.
negation 533 n.
negative 533 adj.
photography 551 n.
neglect
  disorder 61 n.
  neglect 458 vb.
  negligence 458 n.
  unwillingness
    598 n.
  dilapidation 655 n.
  nonpreparation
    670 n.
  inaction 677 n.
  noncompletion
    726 n.
  rashness 857 n.
  undutifulness
    918 n.
  disrespect 921 n.
neglectful
  negligent 458 adj.
  nonobservant
    769 adj.
  apathetic 820 adj.
  disrespectful
    921 adj.
negligee
  nightwear 228 n.
negligent
  negligent 458 adj.
negligible
  inconsiderable
    33 adj.
  unimportant
    639 adj.
negotiable
  possible 469 adj.
negotiate
  accord 24 vb.
  pass 305 vb.
  confer 584 vb.
  do business 622 vb.
  cooperate 706 vb.
  mediate 720 vb.
  deputize 755 vb.
  contract 765 vb.
  make terms
    766 vb.
  assign 780 vb.
  bargain 791 vb.

negotiation
  adaptation 24 n.
  mediation 720 n.
  compact 765 n.
  conditions 766 n.
  barter 791 n.
  trade 791 n.
negus
  alcoholic drink
    301 n.
neigh
  ululate 409 vb.
  ululation 409 n.
neighbour
  friend 880 n.
neighbourhood
  district 184 n.
  locality 187 n.
  nearness 200 n.
  surroundings
    230 n.
neither
  neither 606 adv.
nematology
  zoology 367 n.
Nemesis
  retaliation 714 n.
  punishment 963 n.
Neo-Classicism
  school of painting
    553 n.
neolithic
  primal 127 adj.
  barbaric 869 adj.
neologism
  word 559 n.
  neology 560 n.
neon light
  gas 336 n.
neophyte
  beginner 538 n.
  pietist 979 n.
nephew
  kinsman 11 n.
  male 372 n.
nephritis
  digestive disorders
    651 n.
ne plus ultra
  superiority 34 n.
  completeness 54 n.
  extremity 69 n.
  summit 213 n.
  limit 236 n.
  exceller 644 n.
  perfection 646 n.
  completion 725 n.

fashion 848 n.
nepotism
  consanguinity
    11 n.
  injustice 914 n.
Neptune
  planet 321 n.
  sea god 343 n.
  mythic deity 966 n.
  Olympian deity
    967 n.
nereid
  nymph 967 n.
nerve
  stability 153 n.
  vitality 162 n.
  courage 855 n.
  sauciness 878 n.
nerve gas
  poison 659 n.
  weapon 723 n.
nerve-racking
  frightening
    854 adj.
nerves
  neurosis 503 n.
  ill health 651 n.
  excitability 822 n.
  nervousness 854 n.
nervous
  excitable 822 adj.
  nervous 854 adj.
nervous breakdown
  neurosis 503 n.
  nervous disorders
    651 n.
nervous system
  sense 374 n.
nervy
  active 678 adj.
  excitable 822 adj.
  nervous 854 adj.
nest
  origin 68 n.
  group 74 n.
  dwell 192 vb.
  nest 192 n.
nest egg
  store 632 n.
  preparation 669 n.
  wealth 800 n.
nestle
  dwell 192 vb.
  caress 889 vb.
nestling
  young creature
    132 n.

net
  remaining 41 adj.
  bring together
    74 vb.
  receptacle 194 n.
  cross 222 vb.
  network 222 n.
  textile 222 n.
  enclosure 235 n.
  semitransparency
    424 n.
  ensnare 542 vb.
  trap 542 n.
  hunt 619 vb.
  acquire 771 vb.
  receive 782 vb.
  take 786 vb.
netball
  ball game 837 n.
nether
  low 210 adj.
net profit
  gain 771 n.
netting
  network 222 n.
nettle
  prickle 256 n.
  bane 659 n.
  hurt 827 vb.
  huff 891 vb.
nettlerash
  tingling 378 n.
  skin disease 651 n.
network
  connect 45 vb.
  union 45 n.
  bond 47 n.
  network 222 n.
  broadcasting
    531 n.
  cooperate 706 vb.
networking
  latency 523 n.
  cooperation 706 n.
neuralgia
  pang 377 n.
neuritis
  pang 377 n.
neurology
  medical art 658 n.
neuropath
  neurotic 504 n.
neurosis
  neurosis 503 n.
neurosurgery
  head 213 n.

neurotic
  neurotic 503 adj.
  neurotic 504 n.
neuter
  unman 161 vb.
  material 319 adj.
  grammatical
    564 adj.
neutral
  inert 175 adj.
  colourless 426 adj.
  grey 429 adj.
  greyness 429 n.
  moderate 625 n.
  neutral 625 adj.
  pacifist 717 n.
  peaceful 717 adj.
  free person 744 n.
neutrality
  middle point 30 n.
  disunion 46 n.
  moderation 177 n.
  no choice 606 n.
  middle way 625 n.
  peace 717 n.
  indifference 860 n.
neutralize
  nullify 2 vb.
  disable 161 vb.
  weaken 163 vb.
  assuage 177 vb.
  counteract 182 vb.
neutron
  minuteness 196 n.
  element 319 n.
neutron bomb
  bomb 723 n.
never
  never 109 adv.
never-ending
  perpetual 115 adj.
  prolix 570 adj.
never-never, the
  borrowing 785 n.
  purchase 792 n.
nevertheless
  nevertheless
    468 adv.
new
  new 126 adj.
  unknown 491 adj.
  unhabituated
    611 adj.
new boy
  intruder 59 n.
  incomer 297 n.
  beginner 538 n.

new broom
  newness 126 n.
  busy person 678 n.
newcomer
  intruder 59 n.
  successor 67 n.
  incomer 297 n.
new departure
  originality 21 n.
newfangled
  unusual 84 adj.
  modern 126 adj.
  changeable
    143 adj.
  unknown 491 adj.
  fashionable
    848 adj.
new leaf
  newness 126 n.
  improvement
    654 n.
new look
  modernism 126 n.
  change 143 n.
  repair 656 n.
  revival 656 n.
  fashion 848 n.
newlyweds
  spouse 894 n.
new moon
  moon 321 n.
news
  news 529 n.
  broadcast 531 n.
newsagent
  tradespeople 794 n.
newscaster
  news reporter
    529 n.
  broadcaster 531 n.
news flash
  news 529 n.
  broadcast 531 n.
newsletter
  publicity 528 n.
  the press 528 n.
newspaper
  the press 528 n.
  reading matter
    589 n.
newspeak
  equivocalness
    518 n.
  neology 560 n.
newsprint
  script 586 n.
  paper 631 n.

newsreader
  news reporter
    529 n.
  broadcaster 531 n.
newsreel
  film 445 n.
  publicity 528 n.
  news 529 n.
newssheet
  the press 528 n.
newsworthy
  notable 638 n.
newsy
  informative
    524 adj.
  loquacious 581 adj.
newt
  amphibian 365 n.
new technology
  means 629 n.
next
  after 65 adv.
  sequential 65 adj.
  subsequent
    120 adj.
  subsequently
    120 adv.
next-door to
  near 200 adj.
next-of-kin
  akin 11 adj.
  kinsman 11 n.
  beneficiary 776 n.
nib
  vertex 213 n.
  sharp point 256 n.
  stationery 586 n.
nibble
  eat 301 vb.
  graze 301 vb.
  mouthful 301 n.
  taste 386 vb.
  be duped 544 vb.
  caress 889 vb.
  endearment 889 n.
nice
  pleasant 376 adj.
  careful 457 adj.
  discriminating
    463 adj.
  accurate 494 adj.
  pleasurable
    826 adj.
  tasteful 846 adj.
  fastidious 862 adj.
  amiable 884 adj.

niceness
  pleasurableness
    826 n.
  fastidiousness
    862 n.
  courtesy 884 n.
nicety
  differentiation
    15 n.
  discrimination
    463 n.
  fastidiousness
    862 n.
niche
  place 185 n.
  compartment
    194 n.
  shelf 218 n.
  angularity 247 n.
  cavity 255 n.
  hiding-place 527 n.
  honours 866 n.
nick
  small thing 33 n.
  cut 46 vb.
  notch 260 n.
  notch 260 vb.
  ensnare 542 vb.
  indication 547 n.
  mark 547 vb.
  wound 655 n.
  wound 655 vb.
  arrest 747 vb.
  lockup 748 n.
  steal 788 vb.
nickel
  coinage 797 n.
nicker
  coinage 797 n.
nickname
  name 561 n.
  name 561 vb.
  misname 562 vb.
  misnomer 562 n.
nick of time
  occasion 137 n.
nicotine
  tobacco 388 n.
  tonic 658 n.
  drug-taking 949 n.
nictitate
  be dim-sighted
    440 vb.
nidus
  nest 192 n.
niece
  kinsman 11 n.

female 373 n.
niff
  odour 394 n.
  stench 397 n.
  stink 397 vb.
nifty
  speedy 277 adj.
niggardly
  insufficient
    636 adj.
niggle
  cause discontent
    829 vb.
  criticize 924 vb.
nigh
  future 124 adj.
  near 200 adv.
night
  darkness 418 n.
night and day
  continuously
    71 adv.
  perpetually
    139 adv.
  fluctuation 317 n.
nightbird
  bird 365 n.
nightcap
  moderator 177 n.
  nightwear 228 n.
  valediction 296 n.
  draught 301 n.
  soporific 679 n.
nightclothes
  nightwear 228 n.
night club
  meeting place
    192 n.
  theatre 594 n.
  place of amuse-
    ment 837 n.
night cream
  cosmetic 843 n.
nightdress
  nightwear 228 n.
nightfall
  evening 129 n.
  darkness 418 n.
nightingale
  bird 365 n.
nightly
  seasonal 141 adj.
nightmare
  fantasy 513 n.
  suffering 825 n.
  intimidation
    854 n.

demon 970 n.
night-owl
  evening 129 n.
nightshirt
  nightwear 228 n.
night watchman
  doorkeeper 264 n.
  spectator 441 n.
  protector 660 n.
  keeper 749 n.
nihilism
  extinction 2 n.
  nonexistence 2 n.
  disorder 61 n.
  philosophy 449 n.
  sedition 738 n.
nihilistic
  disorderly 61 adj.
  violent 176 adj.
nil
  nonexistence 2 n.
  zero 103 n.
nimble
  speedy 277 adj.
  active 678 adj.
  skilful 694 adj.
nimbus
  light 417 n.
  honours 866 n.
nincompoop
  fool 501 n.
  ninny 501 n.
nine
  over five 99 n.
nine days' wonder
  insubstantial thing
    4 n.
  over five 99 n.
  brief span 114 n.
  prodigy 864 n.
ninepins
  ball game 837 n.
nineteen to the dozen
  swiftly 277 adv.
ninety
  twenty and over
    99 n.
ninety-nine per cent
  chief part 52 n.
ninjutsu
  wrestling 716 n.
ninny
  fool 501 n.
  ninny 501 n.
ninth
  musical note
    410 n.

nip
  make smaller
    198 vb.
  make thin 206 vb.
  move fast 277 vb.
  draught 301 n.
  give pain 377 vb.
  pang 377 n.
  touch 378 vb.
  refrigerate 382 vb.
nip and tuck
  equal 28 adj.
  synchronism 123 n.
  near 200 adj.
nip in the bud
  be early 135 vb.
  destroy 165 vb.
  suppress 165 vb.
  shorten 204 vb.
  kill 362 vb.
  hinder 702 vb.
nipper
  youngster 132 n.
nippers
  pincers 778 n.
nipple
  bosom 253 n.
nippy
  vigorous 174 adj.
  cold 380 adj.
  active 678 adj.
nirvana
  extinction 2 n.
  happiness 824 n.
  divineness 965 n.
  heaven 971 n.
Nissen hut
  small house 192 n.
nit
  insect 365 n.
nit-picking
  trivial 639 adj.
  discontent 829 n.
  fastidiousness
    862 n.
nitrates
  fertilizer 171 n.
nitrogen
  air 340 n.
nitroglycerine
  explosive 723 n.
nitty-gritty
  reality 1 n.
  substance 3 n.
  essential part 5 n.
  chief part 52 n.
  particulars 80 n.

source 156 n.
  base 214 n.
  interiority 224 n.
  element 319 n.
  meaning 514 n.
  chief thing 638 n.
nitwit
  dunce 501 n.
nix
  zero 103 n.
  mythical being
    970 n.
No
  stage play 594 n.
no
  no 489 adv.
  negation 533 n.
  refusal 760 n.
Noah's Ark
  ship 275 n.
  zoo 369 n.
nob
  head 213 n.
  fop 848 n.
  aristocrat 868 n.
nobble
  disable 161 vb.
  take 786 vb.
  steal 788 vb.
nobbly
  projecting 254 adj.
Nobel prize
  reward 962 n.
nobility
  aristocracy 868 n.
  nobility 868 n.
  probity 929 n.
noble
  important 638 adj.
  coinage 797 n.
  renowned 866 adj.
  noble 868 adj.
  person of rank
    868 n.
  title 870 n.
  honourable
    929 adj.
nobleman or -woman
  aristocrat 868 n.
  person of rank
    868 n.
noblesse
  aristocracy 868 n.
  nobility 868 n.
nobody
  zero 103 n.
  nobody 190 n.

nonentity 639 n.
nobody's
  unpossessed
    774 adj.
nobody's fool
  sage 500 n.
nocturnal
  dark 418 adj.
nocturne
  musical piece
    412 n.
  art subject 553 n.
nod
  hang 217 vb.
  obeisance 311 n.
  stoop 311 vb.
  fluctuation 317 n.
  oscillate 317 vb.
  be inattentive
    456 vb.
  be neglectful
    458 vb.
  assent 488 n.
  assent 488 vb.
  hint 524 n.
  gesticulate 547 vb.
  gesture 547 n.
  sleep 679 vb.
  be fatigued 684 vb.
  command 737 n.
  command 737 vb.
  permit 756 vb.
  consent 758 vb.
  courteous act
    884 n.
  greet 884 vb.
  respects 920 n.
  approbation 923 n.
  approve 923 vb.
nodding
  hanging 217 adj.
  sleepiness 679 n.
  sleepy 679 adj.
nodding acquain-
    tance
  knowledge 490 n.
noddle
  head 213 n.
  intelligence 498 n.
node
  joint 45 n.
  swelling 253 n.
  foliage 366 n.
nod off
  sleep 679 vb.
no doubt
  certainly 473 adv.

nodular
  rough 259 adj.
nodule
  swelling 253 n.
  hardness 326 n.
Noel
  holy day 988 n.
no fear
  not likely 472 int.
noggin
  cup 194 n.
  head 213 n.
  draught 301 n.
no-go area
  exclusion 57 n.
  territory 184 n.
  intermediary
    231 n.
  difficulty 700 n.
  battleground
    724 n.
  restriction 747 n.
no great shakes
  inconsiderable
    33 adj.
  trifle 639 n.
  imperfect 647 adj.
no-hoper
  rejection 607 n.
  loser 728 n.
  unlucky person
    731 n.
noise
  greatness 32 n.
  sound 398 n.
  loudness 400 n.
  discord 411 n.
  proclaim 528 vb.
  rumour 529 n.
  indication 547 n.
noiseless
  silent 399 adj.
noisome
  fetid 397 adj.
noisy
  great 32 adj.
  loud 400 adj.
no joke
  reality 1 n.
  important matter
    638 n.
nomad
  extraneous 59 adj.
  nonconformist
    84 n.
  wanderer 268 n.

no-man's land
  exclusion 57 n.
  territory 184 n.
  emptiness 190 n.
  intermediary
    231 n.
  battleground
    724 n.
  nonownership
    774 n.
nom de plume
  misnomer 562 n.
nomenclature
  nomenclature
    561 n.
nominal
  insubstantial 4 adj.
  powerless 161 adj.
  trivial 639 adj.
nominate
  select 605 vb.
  commission
    751 vb.
nomination
  choice 605 n.
  mandate 751 n.
  holy orders 985 n.
nominee
  consignee 754 n.
  delegate 754 n.
nonage
  nonage 130 n.
nonagon
  angular figure
    247 n.
nonce, the
  present time 121 n.
nonce word
  speciality 80 n.
  unit 88 n.
  word 559 n.
  neology 560 n.
nonchalance
  moral insensibility
    820 n.
  inexcitability
    823 n.
  indifference 860 n.
nonclassification
  disorder 61 n.
noncoherence
  noncoherence 49 n.
noncombatant
  pacifist 717 n.
  peaceful 717 adj.
noncommissioned of-
    ficer

  army officer 741 n.
noncommittal
  reticent 525 adj.
  cautious 858 adj.
  indifferent 860 adj.
nonconforming
  nonobservant
    769 adj.
Nonconformist
  sectarian 978 n.
nonconformist
  nonconformist
    84 n.
  unconformable
    84 adj.
  dissenting 489 adj.
  disobedient
    738 adj.
  nonobservant
    769 adj.
  schismatic 978 n.
  schismatical
    978 adj.
nonconformity
  nonconformity
    84 n.
  sectarianism
    978 n.
nondescript
  amorphous
    244 adj.
  trivial 639 adj.
none
  zero 103 n.
  church service
    988 n.
nonentity
  nonexistence 2 n.
  nonentity 639 n.
nones
  date 108 n.
nonfiction
  literature 557 n.
nonintervention
  avoidance 620 n.
  inaction 677 n.
  peace 717 n.
  freedom 744 n.
no-no
  hindrance 702 n.
nonpareil
  dissimilar 19 adj.
  supreme 34 adj.
  exceller 644 n.
  paragon 646 n.
  noteworthy
    866 adj.

nonperson
  nonexistence 2 n.
  nonentity 639 n.
  outcast 883 n.
nonplus
  puzzle 474 vb.
  confute 479 vb.
  be difficult 700 vb.
  defeat 727 vb.
nonsense
  absurdity 497 n.
  silly talk 515 n.
  trifle 639 n.
nonsensical
  absurd 497 adj.
  foolish 499 adj.
  semantic 514 adj.
  meaningless
    515 adj.
non sequitur
  irrelevance 10 n.
  discontinuity 72 n.
  sophism 477 n.
nonsmoker
  train 274 n.
  abstainer 942 n.
nonstarter
  difficulty 700 n.
  loser 728 n.
nonstop
  continuous 71 adj.
  perpetual 115 adj.
  diffuse 570 adj.
  loquacious 581 adj.
non-U
  unwonted 611 adj.
  plebeian 869 adj.
noodles
  dish 301 n.
nook
  place 185 n.
  compartment
    194 n.
  angularity 247 n.
  cavity 255 n.
  hiding-place 527 n.
noon
  noon 128 n.
  light 417 n.
noon and night
  perpetually
    139 adv.
no one
  nonexistence 2 n.
  insubstantiality
    4 n.
  nobody 190 n.

noose
  means of execution
    964 n.
norm
  prototype 23 n.
  average 30 n.
  rule 81 n.
  gauge 465 n.
normal
  uniform 16 adj.
  general 79 adj.
  regular 81 adj.
  typical 83 adj.
  right 913 adj.
normality
  regularity 81 n.
  right 913 n.
normalize
  order 60 vb.
  regularize 62 vb.
  make conform
    83 vb.
north and south
  polarity 14 n.
northern lights
  heavens 321 n.
  glow 417 n.
  luminary 420 n.
north pole
  summit 213 n.
  coldness 380 n.
North Sea
  ocean 343 n.
North Sea gas
  gas 336 n.
  fuel 385 n.
north wind
  wind 352 n.
nose
  angularity 247 n.
  protuberance
    254 n.
  air pipe 353 n.
  person 371 n.
  odour 394 n.
  detective 459 n.
  detect 484 vb.
  informer 524 n.
nose and throat
  medical art 658 n.
nosebag
  bag 194 n.
nose dive
  aeronautics 271 n.
  fly 271 vb.
  descent 309 n.
  tumble 309 vb.

  plunge 313 n.
nosegay
  bunch 74 n.
  fragrance 396 n.
  ornamentation
    844 n.
nose-job
  beautification
    843 n.
nose out
  be curious 453 vb.
  enquire 459 vb.
  discover 484 vb.
nose to tail
  continuously
    71 adv.
nosh
  food 301 n.
nostalgia
  remembrance
    505 n.
  suffering 825 n.
  regret 830 n.
  melancholy 834 n.
  desire 859 n.
Nostradamus
  oracle 511 n.
nostril
  orifice 263 n.
  air pipe 353 n.
nostrum
  remedy 658 n.
no sweat
  easy thing 701 n.
nosy
  inquisitive 453 adj.
  enquiring 459 adj.
nosy parker
  meddler 678 n.
not a bit
  in no way 33 adv.
notable
  manifest 522 adj.
  bigwig 638 n.
  notable 638 adj.
  noteworthy
    866 adj.
  person of repute
    866 n.
notably
  remarkably 32 vb.
not a jot
  in no way 33 adv.
not all there
  unintelligent
    499 adj.
  crazy 503 adj.

not a patch on
  inferior 35 adj.
notary
  notary 958 n.
not a soul
  insubstantiality
    4 n.
  zero 103 n.
  nobody 190 n.
not at all
  in no way 33 adv.
notation
  notation 410 n.
not a whit, jot
  insubstantiality
    4 n.
  in no way 33 adv.
not bad
  not bad 644 adj.
**not beat about the
  bush**
  be concise 569 vb.
  speak plainly
    573 vb.
not before time
  at last 113 adv.
  timely 137 adj.
not born yesterday
  intelligent 498 adj.
  wise 498 adj.
  cunning 698 adj.
not care
  be rash 857 vb.
  be indifferent
    860 vb.
notch
  degree 27 n.
  notch 260 n.
  notch 260 vb.
notch up
  number 86 vb.
  register 548 vb.
not come amiss
  be expedient
    642 vb.
not countenance
  prohibit 757 vb.
not counting
  exclusive of 57 adv.
not cricket
  injustice 914 n.
not done
  unconformable
    84 adj.
  unwonted 611 adj.
  prohibited 757 adj.

note
ululation 409 n.
musical note
410 n.
perceive 447 adj.
notice 455 vb.
maxim 496 n.
reminder 505 n.
message 529 n.
indication 547 n.
record 548 vb.
write 586 vb.
correspondence
588 n.
compendium
592 n.
paper money
797 n.
famousness 866 n.
notebook
reminder 505 n.
record 548 vb.
stationery 586 n.
reference book
589 n.
notecase
case 194 n.
noted
included 78 adj.
known 490 adj.
renowned 866 adj.
See **noteworthy**
note down
record 548 vb.
notelet
correspondence
588 n.
notepaper
stationery 586 n.
paper 631 n.
notes
commentary 520 n.
record 548 n.
not ever
never 109 adv.
noteworthy
unusual 84 adj.
wonderful 864 adj.
noteworthy
866 adj.
not fit to hold a candle to
inferior 35 adj.
not forgetting
in addition 38 adv.
not give an inch
stand firm 599 vb.

not have a leg to
stand on
reason badly
477 vb.
nothing
nonexistence 2 n.
insubstantiality
4 n.
zero 103 n.
trifle 639 n.
nothing but
simple 44 adj.
nothing doing
inaction 677 n.
nothing for it but
choice 605 n.
nothing in it
equivalence 28 n.
contest 716 n.
lack of wonder
865 n.
nothing loath
willingly 597 adv.
nothingness
nonexistence 2 n.
insubstantiality
4 n.
zero 103 n.
unimportance
639 n.
nothing to it
trifle 639 n.
easy thing 701 n.
nothing to write
home about
trifle 639 n.
imperfect 647 adj.
lack of wonder
865 n.
nothing venture
Here goes 671 int.
not hold with
dissent 489 vb.
disapprove 924 vb.
notice
gaze 438 vb.
attention 455 n.
notice 455 vb.
estimate 480 n.
detect 484 vb.
interpretation
520 n.
information 524 n.
advertisement
528 n.
publicity 528 n.
article 591 n.

warning 664 n.
demand 737 n.
noticeable
remarkable 32 adj.
visible 443 adj.
manifest 522 adj.
noticeably
remarkably 32 vb.
notice board
advertisement
528 n.
notification
information 524 n.
publication 528 n.
indication 547 n.
notify
predict 511 vb.
communicate
524 vb.
proclaim 528 vb.
warn 664 vb.
not in the least
in no way 33 adv.
notion
idea 451 n.
supposition 512 n.
ideality 513 n.
contrivance 623 n.
notional
imaginary 513 adj.
not knowing which
way to turn
poor 801 adj.
not know when one is
beaten
be successful
727 vb.
not last
be transient
114 vb.
not lift a finger
not act 677 vb.
not likely
not likely 472 int.
God forbid 489 int.
not many
inconsiderable
33 adj.
few 105 adj.
not mince words
speak plainly
573 vb.
not much
small 33 adj.
not now
different time
122 n.

not often
seldom 140 adv.
not oneself
dejected 834 adj.
not on your life
not likely 472 int.
God forbid 489 int.
notorious
manifest 522 adj.
renowned 866 adj.
disreputable
867 adj.
not out, be
go on 146 vb.
not proven
acquitted 960 adj.
not quite
almost 33 adv.
not right
wrong 914 adj.
not so much
finite quantity
26 n.
not take sides
not act 677 vb.
not the end of the
world
trifle 639 n.
not the thing
desuetude 611 n.
undueness 916 n.
not think much of
disapprove 924 vb.
not to mention
in addition 38 adv.
not trouble oneself
be incurious
454 vb.
not turn a hair
be insensitive
820 vb.
keep calm 823 vb.
not up to it
insufficient
636 adj.
not with it
antiquated 127 adj.
abstracted 456 adj.
notwithstanding
although 182 adv.
not worth the effort
profitless 641 adj.
nougat
sweets 301 n.
nought
zero 103 n.

noughts and crosses
indoor game 837 n.
noun
name 561 n.
part of speech
564 n.
nourish
feed 301 vb.
nourishment
food 301 n.
nous
intelligence 498 n.
nouveau riche
new 126 adj.
prosperous person
730 n.
rich person 800 n.
commoner 869 n.
nouvelle cuisine
cookery 301 n.
dieting 301 n.
nouvelle vague
film 445 n.
nova
star 321 n.
novel
dissimilar 19 adj.
original 21 adj.
new 126 adj.
unknown 491 adj.
novel 590 n.
novelette
novel 590 n.
novelist
author 589 n.
novelty
dissimilarity 19 n.
originality 21 n.
newness 126 n.
bauble 639 n.
pleasurableness
826 n.
novena
over five 99 n.
church service
988 n.
novice
ignoramus 493 n.
beginner 538 n.
bungler 697 n.
monk 986 n.
nun 986 n.
lay person 987 n.
now
at present 121 adv.
nowadays
at present 121 adv.

present time 121 n.
now and then
sometimes
139 adv.
no way
impossibility
470 n.
impossibly
470 adv.
not likely 472 int.
no 489 adv.
now or never
at present 121 adv.
noxious
fetid 397 adj.
harmful 645 adj.
insalubrious
653 adj.
nozzle
projection 254 n.
orifice 263 n.
outlet 298 n.
air pipe 353 n.
nuance
differentiation
15 n.
degree 27 n.
small quantity
33 n.
hue 425 n.
discrimination
463 n.
nub
substance 3 n.
essential part 5 n.
focus 76 n.
centre 225 n.
chief thing 638 n.
nubile
grown-up 134 adj.
nuclear
dynamic 160 adj.
central 225 adj.
nuclear bomb
bomb 723 n.
nuclear fallout
radiation 417 n.
poison 659 n.
nuclear family
family 11 n.
nuclear missile
nucleonics 160 n.
rocket 276 n.
nuclear reactor
nucleonics 160 n.
nuclear weapon
weapon 723 n.

nuclear winter
winter 129 n.
nucleonics 160 n.
blight 659 n.
nucleate
make smaller
198 vb.
centralize 225 vb.
be dense 324 vb.
nucleolus
centre 225 n.
organism 358 n.
nucleonics
nucleonics 160 n.
nucleus
essential part 5 n.
middle 70 n.
source 156 n.
minuteness 196 n.
centre 225 n.
element 319 n.
solid body 324 n.
organism 358 n.
chief thing 638 n.
nude
uncovered 229 adj.
art subject 553 n.
nudge
knock 279 n.
agitate 318 vb.
agitation 318 n.
hint 524 n.
hint 524 vb.
gesticulate 547 vb.
gesture 547 n.
indication 547 n.
warning 664 n.
nudge-nudge
impure 951 adj.
nudism
uncovering 229 n.
nudist
stripper 229 n.
nudity
bareness 229 n.
nugget
solid body 324 n.
nuisance
evil 616 n.
hindrance 702 n.
obstacle 702 n.
annoyance 827 n.
null
insubstantial 4 adj.
not one 103 adj.
null and void
nonexistent 2 adj.

powerless 161 adj.
unproductive
172 adj.
illegal 954 adj.
nullify
nullify 2 vb.
not be 4 vb.
negate 533 vb.
abrogate 752 vb.
numb
inert 175 adj.
insensible 375 adj.
number
subdivision 53 n.
number 85 n.
number 86 vb.
abode 192 n.
dress 228 n.
mark 547 vb.
grammar 564 n.
reading matter
589 n.
numbered
statistical 86 adj.
number one
self 80 n.
numberplate
label 547 n.
numbness
helplessness 161 n.
insensibility 375 n.
moral insensibility
820 n.
numeracy
culture 490 n.
numeral
number 85 n.
numerical 85 adj.
numeration
numeration 86 n.
numerator
numerical element
85 n.
numerical
numerical 85 adj.
numerous
many 104 adj.
numismatics
coinage 797 n.
numismatist
collector 492 n.
numskull
ignoramus 493 n.
dunce 501 n.
nun
female 373 n.
virgin 950 n.

pietist 979 n.
nun 986 n.
nunnery
monastery 986 n.
nuptials
wedding 894 n.
nurse
feed 301 vb.
look after 457 vb.
cure 656 vb.
doctor 658 vb.
nurse 658 n.
safeguard 660 vb.
minister to 703 vb.
domestic 742 n.
retainer 742 n.
servant 742 n.
keeper 749 n.
please 826 vb.
pet 889 vb.
do good 897 adj.
nurse a grudge
be discontented
829 vb.
be hostile 881 vb.
nursemaid
teacher 537 n.
protector 660 n.
domestic 742 n.
retainer 742 n.
servant 742 n.
keeper 749 n.
nursery
nonage 130 n.
abundance 171 n.
chamber 194 n.
farm 370 n.
workshop 687 n.
**nurseryman or -wo-
man**
gardener 370 n.
nursery rhyme
doggerel 593 n.
nursery slope
lowness 210 n.
incline 220 n.
nursing
therapy 658 n.
nurture
feed 301 vb.
food 301 n.
breed stock 369 vb.
educate 534 vb.
mature 669 vb.
ripening 669 n.
nut
fastening 47 n.

head 213 n.
fruit and vegetables
301 n.
flower 366 n.
madman 504 n.
the maladjusted
504 n.
nut-brown
brown 430 adj.
nutmeg
spice 301 n.
nutriment
food 301 n.
nutrition
eating 301 n.
food 301 n.
nutritious
nourishing 301 adj.
salubrious 652 adj.
nuts
mouthful 301 n.
crazy 503 adj.
nuts and bolts
reality 1 n.
essential part 5 n.
simple 44 adj.
chief part 52 n.
component 58 n.
source 156 n.
element 319 n.
structure 331 n.
means 629 n.
machine 630 n.
chief thing 638 n.
nutshell
small quantity
33 n.
conciseness 569 n.
nutty
foolish 499 adj.
crazy 503 adj.
nuzzle
touch 378 vb.
caress 889 vb.
nylon
fibre 208 n.
textile 222 n.
nylons
legwear 228 n.
nymph
young creature
132 n.
youngster 132 n.
female 373 n.
nymph 967 n.

nympho
loose woman
952 n.
nymphomaniac
neurotic 503 adj.
lecherous 951 adj.
loose woman
952 n.
nystagmic
dim-sighted
440 adj.

O

oaf
bungler 697 n.
oafish
unintelligent
499 adj.
oak
hardness 326 n.
tree 366 n.
Oaks, the
racing 716 n.
O.A.P.
old person 133 n.
oar
propeller 269 n.
boatman 270 n.
propellant 287 n.
decoration 729 n.
oasis
land 344 n.
oath
oath 532 n.
word 559 n.
scurrility 899 n.
oatmeal
cereals 301 n.
brown 430 adj.
oats
cereals 301 n.
provender 301 n.
grass 366 n.
obdurate
obstinate 602 adj.
severe 735 adj.
impenitent
940 adj.
obedience
obedience 739 n.
obedient
obedient 739 adj.
obeisance
obeisance 311 n.
ritual act 988 n.

obelisk
high structure
209 n.
monument 548 n.
Oberon
fairy 970 n.
obese
fleshy 195 adj.
obey
obey 739 vb.
obfuscate
darken 418 vb.
conceal 525 vb.
obi
belt 228 n.
sorcery 983 n.
obit
death roll 361 n.
information 524 n.
biography 590 n.
obituary
valediction 296 n.
death roll 361 n.
funereal 364 adj.
obsequies 364 n.
biography 590 n.
object
object 319 n.
qualify 468 vb.
doubt 486 vb.
dissent 489 vb.
negate 533 vb.
part of speech
564 n.
be unwilling
598 vb.
objective 617 n.
be obstructive
702 vb.
oppose 704 vb.
resist 715 vb.
deprecate 762 vb.
be discontented
829 vb.
dislike 861 vb.
disapprove 924 vb.
objectify
make extrinsic
6 vb.
materialize 319 vb.
objection
qualification 468 n.
doubt 486 n.
dissent 489 n.
unwillingness
598 n.
dissuasion 613 n.

hindrance 702 n.
resistance 715 n.
refusal 760 n.
disapprobation
  924 n.
objectionable
unpleasant
  827 adj.
disreputable
  867 adj.
wrong 914 adj.
objective
substantial 3 adj.
material 319 adj.
objective 617 n.
just 913 adj.
objectivity
substantiality 3 n.
extrinsicality 6 n.
justice 913 n.
object lesson
example 83 n.
visibility 443 n.
experiment 461 n.
warning 664 n.
object of pity
painfulness 827 n.
objet d'art
masterpiece 694 n.
ornamentation
  844 n.
oblation
act of worship
  981 n.
oblation 981 n.
obligation
liability 180 n.
necessity 596 n.
undertaking 672 n.
debt 803 n.
right 913 n.
dueness 915 n.
duty 917 n.
obligatory
commanding
  737 adj.
obligatory 917 adj.
oblige
necessitate 596 vb.
aid 703 vb.
minister to 703 vb.
compel 740 vb.
serve 742 vb.
impose a duty
  917 vb.
obliged
grateful 907 adj.

obliged 917 adj.
obliging
aiding 703 adj.
courteous 884 adj.
benevolent 897 adj.
oblique, be
be oblique 220 vb.
obliqueness
obliquity 220 n.
obliquity
obliquity 220 n.
obliterate
obliterate 550 vb.
oblivion
extinction 2 n.
oblivion 506 n.
obliteration 550 n.
sleep 679 n.
oblivious
insensible 375 adj.
inattentive 456 adj.
negligent 458 adj.
ignorant 491 adj.
forgetful 506 adj.
oblong
longitudinal
  203 adj.
obnoxious
not nice 645 adj.
unpleasant
  827 adj.
hateful 888 adj.
oboe
flute 414 n.
obscene
not nice 645 adj.
unclean 649 adj.
disreputable
  867 adj.
heinous 934 adj.
impure 951 adj.
obscenity
bad taste 847 n.
impurity 951 n.
obscurantist
ignorance 491 n.
obscure
dark 418 adj.
darken 418 vb.
dim 419 vb.
shadowy 419 adj.
blind 439 vb.
uncertain 474 adj.
unknown 491 adj.
semantic 514 adj.
puzzling 517 adj.
conceal 525 vb.

unclear 568 adj.
unimportant
  639 adj.
difficult 700 adj.
inglorious 867 adj.
plebeian 869 adj.
obscurity
inferiority 35 n.
invisibility 444 n.
uncertainty 474 n.
unintelligibility
  517 n.
imperspicuity
  568 n.
difficulty 700 n.
disrepute 867 n.
obsequies
obsequies 364 n.
obsequious
willing 597 adj.
obedient 739 adj.
servile 879 adj.
respectful 920 adj.
flattering 925 adj.
observance
attention 455 n.
practice 610 n.
conduct 688 n.
observance 768 n.
celebration 876 n.
rite 988 n.
observant
attentive 455 adj.
vigilant 457 adj.
observant 768 adj.
observation
inspection 438 n.
look 438 n.
idea 451 n.
attention 455 n.
maxim 496 n.
affirmation 532 n.
speech 579 n.
observatory
astronomy 321 n.
view 438 n.
observe
be present 189 vb.
scan 438 vb.
see 438 vb.
watch 441 vb.
affirm 532 vb.
observe 768 vb.
celebrate 876 vb.
observe decorum
show respect
  920 vb.

observer
spectator 441 n.
estimator 480 n.
air force 722 n.
observe the formalities
be ostentatious
  875 vb.
obsess
absorb 449 vb.
cause thought
  449 vb.
torment 827 vb.
trouble 827 vb.
obsessed
obsessed 455 adj.
positive 473 adj.
misjudging
  481 adj.
obstinate 602 adj.
obsessed with
with affections
  817 adj.
obsession
idea 451 n.
attention 455 n.
positiveness 473 n.
prejudgment 481 n.
belief 485 n.
eccentricity 503 n.
neurosis 503 n.
opinionatedness
  602 n.
worry 825 n.
spell 983 n.
obsessive
neurotic 504 n.
obsolescent
antiquated 127 adj.
obsolete
extinct 2 adj.
past 125 adj.
antiquated 127 adj.
powerless 161 adj.
useless 641 adj.
disused 674 adj.
obstacle
difficulty 700 n.
obstacle 702 n.
restraint 747 n.
obstetric
fertilized 167 adj.
medical 658 adj.
obstetrician
obstetrics 167 n.
doctor 658 n.

obstetrics
  obstetrics 167 n.
  female 373 n.
obstinacy
  obstinacy 602 n.
obstinate
  obstinate 602 adj.
obstreperous
  violent 176 adj.
obstruct
  be difficult 700 vb.
  hinder 702 vb.
  obstruct 702 vb.
  resist 715 vb.
obstruction
  derangement 63 n.
  closure 264 n.
  hindrance 702 n.
  undutifulness
    918 n.
obstructive
  dissenting 489 adj.
obtain
  be wont 610 vb.
  acquire 771 vb.
obtainable
  accessible 289 adj.
  possible 469 adj.
obtrude
  interfere 231 vb.
  obstruct 702 vb.
obtrusion
  hindrance 702 n.
obtuse
  insensible 375 adj.
  indiscriminating
    464 adj.
  unintelligent
    499 adj.
  thick-skinned
    820 adj.
obtuseness
  bluntness 257 n.
  insensibility 375 n.
  indiscrimination
    464 n.
  unintelligence
    499 n.
  moral insensibility
    820 n.
obverse
  face 237 n.
  frontal 237 adj.
obviate
  counteract 182 vb.
  avoid 620 vb.

disencumber
  701 vb.
obvious
  obvious 443 adj.
  intelligible 516 adj.
occasion
  occasion 137 n.
  happen 154 vb.
  cause 156 vb.
  reason why 156 n.
  instrumentality
    628 n.
  celebration 876 n.
occasional
  infrequent 140 adj.
  fitful 142 adj.
occasionally
  sometimes
    139 adv.
occlude
  close 264 vb.
  obstruct 702 vb.
occlusion
  closure 264 n.
occult
  occult 523 adj.
occultism
  occultism 984 n.
occupancy
  presence 189 n.
  possession 773 n.
occupant
  resident 191 n.
  possessor 776 n.
occupation
  presence 189 n.
  habit 610 n.
  business 622 n.
  job 622 n.
  undertaking 672 n.
occupational therapy
  therapy 658 n.
occupied
  occupied 191 adj.
  busy 678 adj.
  possessed 773 adj.
occupier
  resident 191 n.
  possessor 776 n.
occupy
  fill 54 vb.
  be present 189 vb.
  dwell 192 vb.
  employ 622 vb.
  possess 773 vb.
  appropriate
    786 vb.

occur
  be 1 vb.
  happen 154 vb.
  be present 189 vb.
occurrence
  event 154 n.
occur to
  dawn upon 449 vb.
ocean
  great quantity
    32 n.
  ocean 343 n.
oceanography
  earth sciences
    321 n.
oceans
  great quantity
    32 n.
  plenty 635 n.
ocelot
  big cat 365 n.
ochre
  brown pigment
    430 n.
  orange 432 n.
o'clock
  o'clock 117 adv.
octagon
  over five 99 n.
  angular figure
    247 n.
octameter
  prosody 593 n.
octave
  over five 99 n.
  musical note
    410 n.
octet
  over five 99 n.
octogenarian
  twenty and over
    99 n.
octopus
  marine life 365 n.
ocular
  seeing 438 adj.
oculist
  vision 438 n.
  doctor 658 n.
odd
  different 15 adj.
  disagreeing 25 adj.
  unequal 29 adj.
  remaining 41 adj.
  unusual 84 adj.
  numerical 85 adj.
  crazy 503 adj.

puzzling 517 adj.
  ridiculous 849 adj.
  wonderful 864 adj.
  wrong 914 adj.
oddball
  nonconformist
    84 n.
  the maladjusted
    504 n.
oddity
  misfit 25 n.
  nonconformist
    84 n.
  nonconformity
    84 n.
  eccentricity 503 n.
  prodigy 864 n.
odd-job man
  servant 742 n.
oddly
  remarkably 32 vb.
odd man out
  nonuniformity
    17 n.
  dissimilarity 19 n.
  misfit 25 n.
  nonconformist
    84 n.
  dissentient 489 n.
oddments
  piece 53 n.
oddness
  inequality 29 n.
  eccentricity 503 n.
  ridiculousness
    849 n.
  wrong 914 n.
odds
  difference 15 n.
  inequality 29 n.
  advantage 34 n.
  fair chance 159 n.
  dissension 709 n.
odds and ends
  nonuniformity
    17 n.
  extra 40 n.
  leavings 41 n.
  medley 43 n.
  piece 53 n.
odds on
  fair chance 159 n.
  approved 923 adj.
ode
  poem 593 n.

odious
unpleasant
827 adj.
ugly 842 adj.
disreputable
867 adj.
hateful 888 adj.
odium
hatred 888 n.
odometer
meter 465 n.
odoriferous
odorous 394 adj.
fragrant 396 adj.
odorous
odorous 394 adj.
fragrant 396 adj.
odour
odour 394 n.
odourless
odourless 395 adj.
odour of sanctity
virtue 933 n.
sanctity 979 n.
odyssey
land travel 267 n.
oedema
swelling 253 n.
Oedipus complex
love 887 n.
oesophagus
stomach 194 n.
air pipe 353 n.
oestrogen
drug 658 n.
oeuvre
product 164 n.
reading matter
589 n.
of a certain age
ageing 131 adj.
of age
grown-up 134 adj.
of a piece
similar 18 adj.
of course
certainly 473 adv.
of course 478 adv.
off
absent 190 adj.
pungent 388 adj.
unprovided
636 adj.
unpleasant
827 adj.

off, be
come along
267 int.
decamp 296 vb.
start out 296 vb.
offal
insides 224 n.
food 301 n.
meat 301 n.
rubbish 641 n.
offbeat
unconformable
84 adj.
off-chance
possibility 469 n.
improbability
472 n.
off-colour
sick 651 adj.
offcut
piece 53 n.
off day
bungling 695 n.
failure 728 n.
off duty
leisure 681 n.
leisurely 681 adj.
offence
annoyance 827 n.
resentment 891 n.
wrong 914 n.
vice 934 n.
guilty act 936 n.
lawbreaking 954 n.
offend
displease 827 vb.
hurt 827 vb.
cause discontent
829 vb.
cause dislike
861 vb.
huff 891 vb.
be wicked 934 vb.
offender
offender 904 n.
offensive
unclean 649 adj.
attack 712 n.
battle 718 n.
unpleasant
827 adj.
impertinent
878 adj.
hateful 888 adj.
impure 951 adj.
offer
will 595 vb.

provide 633 vb.
attempt 671 vb.
offer 759 n.
offer 759 vb.
promise 764 n.
give 781 vb.
offering
offer 759 n.
offering 781 n.
propitiation 941 n.
act of worship
981 n.
oblation 981 n.
offer one's hand
court 889 vb.
offertory
offering 781 n.
oblation 981 n.
off guard
negligent 458 adj.
unexpecting
508 adj.
offhand
inattentive 456 adj.
negligent 458 adj.
impertinent
878 adj.
disrespectful
921 adj.
offhanded
discourteous
885 adj.
disrespectful
921 adj.
office
agency 173 n.
chamber 194 n.
function 622 n.
job 622 n.
workshop 687 n.
authority 733 n.
mandate 751 n.
duty 917 n.
jurisdiction 955 n.
church service
988 n.
office-bearer
official 690 n.
consignee 754 n.
office boy or girl
courier 529 n.
officer
officer 741 n.
offices
chamber 194 n.
official
certain 473 adj.

genuine 494 adj.
usual 610 adj.
official 690 n.
authoritative
733 adj.
governmental
733 adj.
formal 875 adj.
officialese
language 557 n.
neology 560 n.
Official Secrets Act
concealment 525 n.
restraint 747 n.
officiate
function 622 vb.
do 676 vb.
offer worship
981 vb.
perform ritual
988 vb.
officious
inquisitive 453 adj.
officiousness
curiosity 453 n.
redundance 637 n.
overactivity 678 n.
off key
discordant 411 adj.
off-load
displace 188 vb.
off-peak rate
cheapness 812 n.
offprint
copy 22 n.
off-putting
repellent 292 adj.
off-season
cheap 812 adj.
offshoot
adjunct 40 n.
branch 53 n.
young plant 132 n.
descendant 170 n.
sect 978 n.
off side
laterality 239 n.
offside
dextrality 241 n.
wrong 914 adj.
offspring
kinsman 11 n.
effect 157 n.
product 164 n.
posterity 170 n.
off the beam
irrelevant 10 adj.

mistaken 495 adj.
off the beaten track
　secluded 883 adj.
off the cuff
　extempore
　　609 adv.
　spontaneous
　　609 adj.
　unprepared
　　670 adj.
　unreadily 670 adv.
off-the-peg
　tailored 228 adj.
　formed 243 adj.
　ready-made
　　669 adj.
off the rails
　unconformable
　　84 adj.
　mistaken 495 adj.
off the record
　private 80 adj.
　occult 523 adj.
　concealed 525 adj.
off-the-shoulder
　uncovered 229 adj.
off-white
　whitish 427 adj.
oft
　often 139 adv.
often
　often 139 adv.
of that ilk
　identical 13 adj.
of two minds
　irresolute 601 adj.
ogee
　convolution 251 n.
　pattern 844 n.
ogive
　support 218 n.
ogle
　gaze 438 vb.
　look 438 n.
　watch 441 vb.
　gesticulate 547 vb.
　gesture 547 n.
　desire 859 vb.
　be rude 885 vb.
　court 889 vb.
'O' grade
　exam 459 n.
ogre
　giant 195 n.
　tyrant 735 n.
　intimidation
　　854 n.

monster 938 n.
　demon 970 n.
ogress
　demon 970 n.
ohm
　electronics 160 n.
　metrology 465 n.
oil
　smooth 258 vb.
　smoother 258 n.
　food content 301 n.
　soften 327 vb.
　softness 327 n.
　lubricate 334 vb.
　grease 357 vb.
　oil 357 n.
　bribe 612 vb.
　balm 658 n.
　facilitate 701 vb.
oilfield
　store 632 n.
oil on troubled waters
　moderator 177 n.
　remedy 658 n.
oil painting
　art style 553 n.
　picture 553 n.
oilskins
　overcoat 228 n.
　shelter 662 n.
oil well
　store 632 n.
oily
　smooth 258 adj.
　hypocritical
　　541 adj.
　dirty 649 adj.
　servile 879 adj.
　flattering 925 adj.
ointment
　lubricant 334 n.
　unguent 357 n.
　balm 658 n.
OK
　assent 488 n.
　not bad 644 adj.
okra
　fruit and vegetables
　　301 n.
old
　antiquated 127 adj.
　olden 127 adj.
　ageing 131 adj.
　weak 163 adj.
old age
　old age 131 n.

helplessness 161 n.
Old Bailey
　lawcourt 956 n.
old boy
　old man 133 n.
　learner 538 n.
old-boy network
　latency 523 n.
old crony
　friend 880 n.
　　See **chum**
old dog
　expert 696 n.
olden
　olden 127 adj.
olden days
　past time 125 n.
older
　older 131 adj.
olde worlde
　antiquated 127 adj.
old-fashioned
　anachronistic
　　118 adj.
　antiquated 127 adj.
old flame
　loved one 887 n.
old fogy
　archaism 127 n.
　old man 133 n.
old girl
　old woman 133 n.
　learner 538 n.
old gold
　orange 432 n.
old hand
　old man 133 n.
　expert 696 n.
old hat
　antiquated 127 adj.
　unwonted 611 adj.
old lag
　prisoner 750 n.
　offender 904 n.
old maid
　female 373 n.
　card game 837 n.
　spinster 895 n.
　virgin 950 n.
old master
　picture 553 n.
　artist 556 n.
Old Nick
　Mephisto 969 n.
old offender
　offender 904 n.

old people's home
　gerontology 131 n.
　retreat 192 n.
　shelter 662 n.
old salt
　mariner 270 n.
old-school
　antiquated 127 adj.
　opinionatedness
　　602 n.
old-school tie
　injustice 914 n.
old stager
　old man 133 n.
　expert 696 n.
Old Testament
　scripture 975 n.
old wives' tales
　error 495 n.
　fable 543 n.
old-world
　antiquated 127 adj.
　courteous 884 adj.
oleograph
　picture 553 n.
'O' level
　exam 459 n.
olfaction
　odour 394 n.
oligarchy
　government 733 n.
olive
　green 434 adj.
olive branch
　peace offering
　　719 n.
olive oil
　oil 357 n.
Olympics
　contest 716 n.
ombudsman
　estimator 480 n.
　mediator 720 n.
　magistracy 957 n.
omega
　extremity 69 n.
omelette
　dish 301 n.
omen
　omen 511 n.
ominous
　predicting 511 adj.
　harmful 645 adj.
　dangerous 661 adj.
　adverse 731 adj.
　unpromising
　　853 adj.

frightening
854 adj.
omission
deficit 55 n.
incompleteness
55 n.
exclusion 57 n.
negligence 458 n.
failure 728 n.
nonobservance
769 n.
guilty act 936 n.
omission mark
punctuation 547 n.
omit
be incomplete
55 vb.
exclude 57 vb.
neglect 458 vb.
be taciturn 582 vb.
not observe 769 vb.
omnibus
comprehensive
52 adj.
bus 274 n.
omnibus edition
edition 589 n.
omnipotent
powerful 160 adj.
strong 162 adj.
godlike 965 adj.
omnipresent
ubiquitous 189 adj.
godlike 965 adj.
omniscient
knowing 490 adj.
godlike 965 adj.
omnivorous
feeding 301 adj.
greedy 859 adj.
gluttonous 947 adj.
omophagous
feeding 301 adj.
on
concerning 9 adv.
forward 285 adv.
shown 522 adj.
on account of
hence 158 adv.
**on a hiding to noth-
ing, be**
waste effort
641 adj.
face danger 661 vb.
be defeated 728 vb.
on all cylinders
actively 678 adv.

on and on
for ever 115 adv.
diffusely 570 adv.
on a par
equal 28 adj.
on appro, approval
chosen 605 adj.
purchase 792 n.
on call
expectant 507 adj.
prepared 669 adj.
once
singly 88 adv.
once (and) for all
singly 88 adv.
once bitten, twice shy
cautious 858 adj.
once in a blue moon
seldom 140 adv.
once-over
inspection 438 n.
once upon a time
when 108 adv.
formerly 125 adv.
oncology
medical art 658 n.
oncoming
frontal 237 adj.
approaching
289 adj.
on demand
enough 635 adv.
on display
shown 522 adj.
on duty
obliged 917 adj.
on duty 917 adv.
one
one 88 adj.
unit 88 n.
person 371 n.
one and only
identical 13 adj.
dissimilar 19 adj.
inimitable 21 adj.
one 88 adj.
one another
correlation 12 n.
correlatively
12 adv.
one-armed bandit
gambling 618 n.
one by one
severally 80 adv.
singly 88 adv.
one degree under
weakly 163 adj.

sick 651 adj.
on edge
expectantly
507 adv.
excitable 822 adj.
nervous 854 adj.
one for the road
valediction 296 n.
draught 301 n.
drunkenness 949 n.
one-horse
lesser 35 adj.
little 196 adj.
trivial 639 adj.
one in the eye for
disappointment
509 n.
on end
vertical 215 adj.
oneness
simpleness 44 n.
whole 52 n.
unity 88 n.
one-off
one 88 adj.
one over the eight
over five 99 n.
redundant 637 adj.
drunk 949 adj.
drunkenness 949 n.
one-piece
uniform 16 adj.
onerous
difficult 700 adj.
annoying 827 adj.
one's betters
superior 34 n.
oneself again, be
be restored 656 vb.
one-sided
biased 481 adj.
unjust 914 adj.
one's own
possessed 773 adj.
loved one 887 n.
darling 890 n.
one's own way
scope 744 n.
one's stars
destiny 155 n.
onetime
prior 119 adj.
one too many
redundant 637 adj.
one up
advantage 34 n.
superior 34 adj.

one-upmanship
superiority 34 n.
tactics 688 n.
one-way street
traffic control
305 n.
road 624 n.
one with, be
be identical 13 vb.
on form, be
be skilful 694 vb.
ongoing
continuous 71 adj.
on hand
possessed 773 adj.
on or in heat
lecherous 951 adj.
on heat, be
desire 859 vb.
be impure 951 vb.
on hold
late 136 adj.
on ice
late 136 adj.
preserved 666 adj.
onion
sphere 252 n.
fruit and vegetables
301 n.
condiment 389 n.
on its last legs
flimsy 163 adj.
weakened 163 adj.
dilapidated
655 adj.
on leave
absent 190 adj.
leisurely 681 adj.
on-lend
lend 784 vb.
on-line
computerized
86 adj.
onlooker
spectator 441 n.
only
one 88 adj.
singly 88 adv.
only just
slightly 33 adv.
on-off
discontinuous
72 adj.
fitful 142 adj.
onomatopoeia
mimicry 20 n.

on one's guard
cautious 858 adj.
on one's high horse
proud 871 adj.
on one's last legs
dying 361 adj.
fatigued 684 adj.
on one's own
alone 88 adj.
singly 88 adv.
on one's tod
alone 88 adj.
on-screen
computerized
86 adj.
onset
beginning 68 n.
approach 289 n.
arrival 295 n.
attack 712 n.
on show
shown 522 adj.
onslaught
attack 712 n.
censure 924 n.
detraction 926 n.
on stream
useful 640 adj.
on tap
accessible 289 adj.
enough 635 adv.
useful 640 adj.
on tenterhooks
expectant 507 adj.
on tenterhooks, be
suffer 825 vb.
on terra firma
safe 660 adj.
on the alert
vigilant 457 adj.
on the back-burner
unfinished 55 adj.
late 136 adj.
neglected 458 adj.
on the ball
attentive 455 adj.
intelligent 498 adj.
on the breadline
necessitous
627 adj.
poor 801 adj.
on the button
accurate 494 adj.
on the cards
impending 155 adj.
liable 180 adj.
possible 469 adj.

probable 471 adj.
expected 507 adj.
on the contrary
contrarily 14 adv.
inversely 221 adv.
no 489 adv.
on the dole
nonactive 677 adj.
poor 801 adj.
on the dot
timely 137 adj.
on the face of it
externally 223 adv.
probably 471 adv.
on the game
unchaste 951 adj.
on the go
actively 678 adv.
busy 678 adj.
labouring 682 adj.
on the horizon, be
impend 155 vb.
on the horns of a dilemma
doubting 474 adj.
in suspense
474 adv.
on the house
free 744 adj.
on the level
veracious 540 adj.
artless 699 adj.
honourable
929 adj.
on the loose
free 744 adj.
on the make
prosperous 730 adj.
acquiring 771 adj.
selfish 932 adj.
on the mend
healthy 650 adj.
on the move
busy 678 adj.
on the other hand
contrarily 14 adv.
conversely 467 adv.
on the QT
stealthily 525 adv.
on the quiet
stealthily 525 adv.
on the qui vive
attentive 455 adj.
vigilant 457 adj.
active 678 adj.
on the rocks
cooled 382 adj.

endangered
661 adj.
poor 801 adj.
on the run
endangered
661 adj.
on the same wavelength
combined 50 adj.
assenting 488 adj.
on the shelf
remaining 41 adj.
disused 674 adj.
unwanted 860 adj.
on the sick list
sick 651 adj.
on the spot
at present 121 adv.
on the table
in question
452 adv.
on the trot
continuously
71 adv.
busy 678 adj.
on the up and up
increasing 36 adj.
well 615 adv.
healthy 650 adj.
successful 727 adj.
prosperous 730 adj.
on the verge of
almost 33 adv.
near 200 adv.
hoping 852 adj.
on the wagon
sober 948 adj.
on the way
in transit 272 adv.
towards 281 adv.
on the whole
on the whole
52 adv.
on time
early 135 adj.
timely 137 adj.
on to
knowing 490 adj.
onus
demonstration
478 n.
encumbrance
702 n.
duty 917 n.
onward
forward 285 adv.

onyx
animal 365 n.
gem 844 n.
oodles
great quantity
32 n.
plenty 635 n.
oojakapivvy
no name 562 n.
oomph
vigorousness 174 n.
vigour 571 n.
ooze
exude 298 vb.
emit 300 vb.
be wet 341 vb.
moisture 341 n.
ocean 343 n.
flow 350 VB.
semiliquidity
354 n.
opacity
opacity 423 n.
opal
semitransparency
424 n.
variegation 437 n.
gem 844 n.
opalescent
semitransparent
424 adj.
opaque
opaque 423 adj.
op art
art 551 n.
open
apart 46 adv.
come before 64 vb.
auspicate 68 vb.
begin 68 vb.
initiate 68 vb.
cause 156 vb.
enlarge 197 vb.
expand 197 vb.
open 263 adj.
open 263 vb.
air 340 n.
visible 443 adj.
manifest 522 adj.
veracious 540 adj.
dramatize 594 vb.
artless 699 adj.
trustworthy
929 adj.
open air
exteriority 223 n.
air 340 n.

open and shut case
  certainty 473 n.
  facility 701 n.
open arms
  reception 299 n.
  friendliness 880 n.
open door
  way in 297 n.
  sociability 882 n.
opener
  opener 263 n.
open fire
  initiate 68 vb.
  shoot 287 vb.
open-handed
  not retain 779 vb.
  liberal 813 adj.
  liberality 813 n.
open-heart surgery
  surgery 658 n.
open hostilities
  go to war 718 vb.
open house
  liberality 813 n.
  sociability 882 n.
opening
  disunion 46 n.
  scission 46 n.
  prelude 66 n.
  debut 68 n.
  entrance 68 n.
  opportunity 137 n.
  room 183 n.
  gap 201 n.
  uncovering 229 n.
  open 263 adj.
  opening 263 n.
  open space 263 n.
  way in 297 n.
  job 622 n.
open letter
  publicity 528 n.
  correspondence 588 n.
  deprecation 762 n.
  censure 924 n.
openly
  openly 263 adv.
open-minded
  doubting 474 adj.
  just 913 adj.
open-mouthed
  open 263 adj.
  greedy 859 adj.
openness
  uncovering 229 n.
  opening 263 n.

open out
  open 263 vb.
open question
  uncertainty 474 n.
open secret
  knowledge 490 n.
  known 490 adj.
  publicity 528 n.
open sesame
  opener 263 n.
  answer 460 n.
  discovery 484 n.
  identification 547 n.
  instrument 628 n.
  spell 983 n.
open the eyes
  disclose 526 vb.
  educate 534 vb.
open to
  liable 180 adj.
open up
  cause 156 vb.
  accelerate 277 vb.
  manifest 522 vb.
  disclose 526 vb.
  make better 654 vb.
open verdict
  dubiety 474 n.
opera
  vocal music 412 n.
operable
  possible 469 adj.
  medical 658 adj.
operate
  produce 164 vb.
  operate 173 vb.
  doctor 658 vb.
operatic
  musical 412 adj.
  dramatic 594 adj.
operation
  agency 173 n.
  way 624 n.
  instrumentality 628 n.
  surgery 658 n.
  undertaking 672 n.
  action 676 n.
  deed 676 n.
  labour 682 n.
operational
  operative 173 adj.
  prepared 669 adj.
operations
  warfare 718 n.

operative
  powerful 160 adj.
  operative 173 adj.
  secret service 459 n.
  machinist 630 n.
  useful 640 adj.
  doer 676 n.
  worker 686 n.
  obligatory 917 adj.
operator
  number 85 n.
  machinist 630 n.
  doer 676 n.
  agent 686 n.
  merchant 794 n.
operetta
  vocal music 412 n.
ophthalmic
  seeing 438 adj.
ophthalmologist
  vision 438 n.
  doctor 658 n.
opiate
  moderator 177 n.
  soporific 679 n.
  intoxicating 949 adj.
opinion
  opinion 485 n.
  repute 866 n.
opinionated
  positive 473 adj.
  narrow-minded 481 adj.
  obstinate 602 adj.
  vain 873 adj.
opinion poll
  vote 605 n.
opium
  moderator 177 n.
  anaesthetic 375 n.
  drug 658 n.
  soporific 679 n.
  drug-taking 949 n.
opponent
  opponent 705 n.
opportune
  apt 24 adj.
  opportune 137 adj.
  advisable 642 adj.
opportunist
  recanter 603 n.
  enterprising 672 adj.
  dishonest 930 adj.

  egotist 932 n.
  selfish 932 adj.
opportunity
  juncture 8 n.
  present time 121 n.
  opportunity 137 n.
  good policy 642 n.
oppose
  be opposite 240 vb.
  tell against 467 vb.
  oppose 704 vb.
  contend 716 vb.
  refuse 760 vb.
  criticize 924 vb.
opposing
  opposing 704 adj.
  resisting 715 adj.
  adverse 731 adj.
opposite
  correlative 12 adj.
  difference 15 n.
  opposite 240 adj.
opposite number
  correlation 12 n.
  compeer 28 n.
opposites
  opposites 704 n.
opposition
  contraposition 240 n.
  opposition 704 n.
opposition party
  opponent 705 n.
oppress
  weigh 322 vb.
  oppress 735 vb.
oppression
  badness 645 n.
  severity 735 n.
  subjection 745 n.
  dejection 834 n.
oppressive
  weighty 322 adj.
  warm 379 adj.
  oppressive 735 adj.
  annoying 827 adj.
oppressor
  bane 659 n.
  tyrant 735 n.
opprobrium
  slur 867 n.
opt for
  choose 605 vb.
optical
  luminous 417 adj.
  seeing 438 adj.

optical illusion
  insubstantial thing
    4 n.
  visual fallacy
    440 n.
optician
  vision 438 n.
  doctor 658 n.
optics
  electronics 160 n.
  eye 438 n.
optimism
  cheerfulness 833 n.
  hope 852 n.
optimistic
  optimistic 482 adj.
  cheerful 833 adj.
  hoping 852 adj.
optimum
  best 644 adj.
option
  will 595 n.
  willingness 597 n.
  choice 605 n.
optional
  volitional 595 adj.
  voluntary 597 adj.
opulent
  plentiful 635 adj.
  rich 800 adj.
opus
  product 164 n.
  musical piece
    412 n.
or
  heraldic 547 adj.
  heraldry 547 n.
Oracle (tdmk)
  data processing
    86 n.
  broadcasting
    531 n.
oracle
  answer 460 n.
  dogmatist 473 n.
  oracle 511 n.
  adviser 691 n.
  holy place 990 n.
oral
  informative
    524 adj.
  speaking 579 adj.
orange
  fruit and vegetables
    301 n.
  orange 432 adj.
  orange 432 n.

orangeade
  soft drink 301 n.
orange peel
  rubbish 641 n.
oranges and lemons
  indoor game 837 n.
orang-outang
  mammal 365 n.
oration
  oration 579 n.
orator
  speaker 579 n.
  motivator 612 n.
oratorio
  vocal music 412 n.
oratory
  oratory 579 n.
  church 990 n.
  temple 990 n.
orb
  region 184 n.
  circle 250 n.
  badge 547 n.
  regalia 743 n.
orbit
  influence 178 n.
  orbit 250 n.
  fly 271 vb.
  space travel 271 n.
  passage 305 n.
  circle 314 vb.
  circuition 314 n.
  rotate 315 vb.
  function 622 n.
  route 624 n.
  circuit 626 n.
orchard
  wood 366 n.
  farm 370 n.
  garden 370 n.
orchestra
  orchestra 413 n.
  theatre 594 n.
orchestral
  musical 412 adj.
orchestrate
  compose 56 vb.
  arrange 62 vb.
  harmonize 410 vb.
  compose music
    413 vb.
ordain
  decree 737 vb.
  commission
    751 vb.
  make legal 953 vb.

  perform ritual
    988 vb.
ordained, be
  take orders 986 vb.
ordeal
  difficulty 700 n.
  suffering 825 n.
  painfulness 827 n.
order
  uniformity 16 n.
  order 60 n.
  order 60 vb.
  serial place 73 n.
  breed 77 n.
  sort 77 n.
  regularity 81 n.
  rule 81 n.
  be early 135 vb.
  send 272 vb.
  judgment 480 n.
  badge 547 n.
  require 627 vb.
  requirement 627 n.
  precept 693 n.
  community 708 n.
  warfare 718 n.
  decoration 729 n.
  command 737 n.
  command 737 vb.
  demand 737 vb.
  compel 740 vb.
  badge of rank
    743 n.
  honours 866 n.
  nobility 868 n.
  title 870 n.
  impose a duty
    917 vb.
  legislation 953 n.
  sect 978 n.
  monk 986 n.
  rite 988 n.
  ritual 988 n.
ordered
  orderly 60 adj.
  arranged 62 adj.
  legal 953 adj.
ordering
  arrangement 62 n.
orderly
  uniform 16 adj.
  orderly 60 adj.
  servant 742 n.
order of the day
  predetermination
    608 n.
  practice 610 n.

  policy 623 n.
  command 737 n.
orders
  warfare 718 n.
  holy orders 985 n.
ordinal
  numerical 85 adj.
ordinance
  precept 693 n.
  command 737 n.
  decree 737 n.
  legislation 953 n.
  rite 988 n.
ordinary
  median 30 adj.
  general 79 adj.
  typical 83 adj.
  heraldry 547 n.
  usual 610 adj.
  trivial 639 adj.
  not bad 644 adj.
  middling 732 adj.
ordination
  mandate 751 n.
  holy orders 985 n.
  Christian rite
    988 n.
ordure
  excrement 302 n.
  dirt 649 n.
ore
  source 156 n.
  rock 344 n.
  mineral 359 n.
  materials 631 n.
organ
  limb 53 n.
  organ 414 n.
  the press 528 n.
  instrument 628 n.
  church utensil
    990 n.
organdie
  textile 222 n.
organ-grinder
  instrumentalist
    413 n.
organic
  intrinsic 5 adj.
organic chemistry
  physics 319 n.
organic foodstuff
  food 301 n.
organism
  organism 358 n.
organization
  composition 56 n.

order 60 n.
  arrangement 62 n.
  production 164 n.
  structure 331 n.
  plan 623 n.
  conduct 688 n.
  management
   689 n.
  corporation 708 n.
organize
  compose 56 vb.
  order 60 vb.
  regularize 62 vb.
  produce 164 vb.
  plan 623 vb.
  manage 689 vb.
organizer
  planner 623 n.
orgasm
  spasm 318 n.
  excitation 821 n.
orgiastic
  disorderly 61 adj.
  sensual 944 adj.
orgy
  feasting 301 n.
  plenty 635 n.
  festivity 837 n.
  social gathering
   882 n.
  sensualism 944 n.
oriel
  compartment
   194 n.
orientate
  orientate 281 vb.
orientation
  situation 186 n.
  direction 281 n.
orienteering
  land travel 267 n.
  direction 281 n.
  racing 716 n.
  sport 837 n.
orifice
  orifice 263 n.
origami
  sculpture 554 n.
origin
  origin 68 n.
original
  intrinsic 5 adj.
  different 15 adj.
  dissimilar 19 adj.
  original 21 adj.
  prototype 23 n.
  special 80 adj.

nonconformist
  84 n.
  fundamental
   156 adj.
  imaginative
   513 adj.
  script 586 n.
  volitional 595 adj.
  laughingstock
   851 n.
originality
  originality 21 n.
  speciality 80 n.
originally
  initially 68 adv.
original sin
  heredity 5 n.
  guilt 936 n.
originate
  initiate 68 vb.
  cause 156 vb.
  produce 164 vb.
  imagine 513 vb.
originate from or in
  result 157 vb.
Orion
  star 321 n.
orisons
  prayers 981 n.
ormolu
  ornamental art
   844 n.
ornament
  add 38 vb.
  musical note
   410 n.
  ornament 574 n.
  ornament 574 vb.
  make better
   654 vb.
  beautify 841 vb.
  beauty 841 n.
  primp 843 vb.
ornamental
  beautiful 841 adj.
  ornamental
   844 adj.
ornate
  stylistic 566 adj.
  ornate 574 adj.
ornithology
  zoology 367 n.
orography
  earth sciences
   321 n.

orotund
  ostentatious
   875 adj.
orphan
  derelict 779 n.
  deprive 786 vb.
orphanage
  retreat 192 n.
orris root
  scent 396 n.
orthodontist
  doctor 658 n.
orthodox
  creedal 485 adj.
  orthodox 976 adj.
orthodoxy
  orthodoxy 976 n.
orthography
  spelling 558 n.
orthopaedics
  medical art 658 n.
  therapy 658 n.
orthoptics
  medical art 658 n.
orthotics
  medical art 658 n.
O.S.
  chronology 117 n.
oscillate
  oscillate 317 vb.
oscillator
  electronics 160 n.
  oscillation 317 n.
osculate
  be contiguous
   202 vb.
osier
  ligature 47 n.
osmosis
  ingress 297 n.
  passage 305 n.
osprey
  bird 365 n.
  trimming 844 n.
ossified
  antiquated 127 adj.
  hard 326 adj.
ossify
  be dense 324 vb.
  harden 326 vb.
ostensible
  appearing 445 adj.
  manifest 522 adj.
  ostensible 614 adj.
ostentation
  ostentation 875 n.
  boasting 877 n.

osteoarthritis
  rheumatism 651 n.
osteopathy
  therapy 658 n.
ostler
  servant 742 n.
ostracize
  exclude 57 vb.
  prohibit 757 vb.
  shame 867 vb.
  disapprove 924 vb.
ostrich
  tall creature 209 n.
  bird 365 n.
  avoider 620 n.
ostrich-like
  avoid 620 vb.
  nonactive 677 adj.
other
  different 15 adj.
other extreme
  contrariety 14 n.
other ranks
  inferior 35 n.
  nonentity 639 n.
  soldiery 722 n.
other side
  contrariety 14 n.
  exteriority 223 n.
  rear 238 n.
  contraposition
   240 n.
  enemy 881 n.
other way round, the
  contrarily 14 adv.
otherwise
  contrarily 14 adv.
otherworldly
  immaterial
   320 adj.
  pious 979 adj.
  magical 983 adj.
otic
  auditory 415 adj.
otology
  ear 415 n.
otoscope
  hearing aid 415 n.
otter
  mammal 365 n.
ottoman
  seat 218 n.
ouija board
  spiritualism 984 n.
ounce
  small quantity
   33 n.

weighing 322 n.
Our Father
prayers 981 n.
ourselves
self 80 n.
oust
substitute 150 vb.
eject 300 vb.
depose 752 vb.
deprive 786 vb.
out
absent 190 adj.
externally 223 adv.
open 263 adj.
eject 300 vb.
misjudging 481 adj.
matured 669 adj.
inactive 679 adj.
sleepy 679 adj.
out-and-out
revolutionary 149 adj.
outback
space 183 n.
district 184 n.
outbid
outdo 306 vb.
bargain 791 vb.
outboard
exterior 223 adj.
outbreak
disorder 61 n.
See **turmoil**
outbreak 176 n.
outbuilding
small house 192 n.
outburst
outbreak 176 n.
egress 298 n.
excitable state 822 n.
anger 891 n.
outcast
remaining 41 adj.
derelict 779 n.
disreputable 867 adj.
outcast 883 n.
outclass
be unequal 29 vb.
be superior 34 vb.
outstrip 277 vb.
outdo 306 vb.
defeat 727 vb.
out cold
insensible 375 adj.
sleepy 679 adj.
outcome
event 154 n.
effect 157 n.
outcrop
layer 207 n.
projection 254 n.
outcry
loudness 400 n.
disapprobation 924 n.
outdated
antiquated 127 adj.
outdistance
be distant 199 vb.
outstrip 277 vb.
progress 285 vb.
outdo 306 vb.
outdo
outdo 306 vb.
outdoor
exterior 223 adj.
outer
exterior 223 adj.
outermost
exterior 223 adj.
outer space
extrinsicality 6 n.
infinity 107 n.
space 183 n.
exteriority 223 n.
universe 321 n.
outface
be resolute 599 vb.
be courageous 855 vb.
be insolent 878 vb.
outfit
component 58 n.
unit 88 n.
clothing 228 n.
suit 228 n.
equipment 630 n.
party 708 n.
outfitter
clothier 228 n.
outflow
outflow 298 n.
current 350 n.
outgoing
preceding 64 adj.
former 125 adj.
sociable 882 adj.
outgrow
disaccustom 611 vb.
stop using 674 vb.
outhouse
adjunct 40 n.
small house 192 n.
chamber 194 n.
outing
land travel 267 n.
enjoyment 824 n.
amusement 837 n.
out in the open
openly 263 adv.
outlandish
extraneous 59 adj.
unconformable 84 adj.
ridiculous 849 adj.
wonderful 864 adj.
outlast
outlast 113 vb.
stay 144 vb.
outlaw
exclude 57 vb.
nonconformist 84 n.
prohibit 757 vb.
robber 789 n.
outcast 883 n.
offender 904 n.
make illegal 954 vb.
condemn 961 vb.
outlay
expenditure 806 n.
outlet
outlet 298 n.
gulf 345 n.
outline
copy 22 n.
prototype 23 n.
incompleteness 55 n.
outline 233 n.
outline 233 vb.
form 243 n.
feature 445 n.
identification 547 n.
map 551 n.
representation 551 n.
picture 553 n.
conciseness 569 n.
description 590 n.
compendium 592 n.
plan 623 n.
policy 623 n.
preparation 669 n.
prepare 669 vb.
outlive
outlast 113 vb.
outlook
futurity 124 n.
destiny 155 n.
view 438 n.
expectation 507 n.
conduct 688 n.
affections 817 n.
outlying
distant 199 adj.
exterior 223 adj.
outmanoeuvre
be superior 34 vb.
navigate 269 vb.
outdo 306 vb.
defeat 727 vb.
outmoded
antiquated 127 adj.
outnumber
be many 104 vb.
out of
akin 11 adj.
caused 157 adj.
born 360 adj.
out of action
unproductive 172 adj.
out of bounds
too far 199 adv.
prohibited 757 adj.
illegal 954 adj.
out of commission
quiescent 266 adj.
disused 674 adj.
inactive 679 adj.
out of control
disorderly 61 adj.
furious 176 adj.
excited 821 adj.
out of danger
safe 660 adj.
out of date
anachronistic 118 adj.
antiquated 127 adj.
out of doors
exteriority 223 n.
externally 223 adv.
air 340 n.
alfresco 340 adv.
out of favour
inglorious 867 adj.
out of focus
indistinct 444 adj.

overload
  load 193 vb.
  make heavy
    322 vb.
  redundance 637 n.
  superabound
    637 vb.
  encumbrance
    702 n.
overlook
  be superior 34 vb.
  be high 209 vb.
  be inattentive
    456 vb.
  disregard 458 vb.
  neglect 458 vb.
  forget 506 vb.
  be patient 823 vb.
  forgive 909 vb.
overlord
  superior 34 n.
  master 741 n.
overly
  extremely 32 vb.
overmanning
  superfluity 637 n.
over one's dead body
  never 109 adv.
overoptimism
  overestimation
    482 n.
  redundance 637 n.
overpaid
  dear 811 adj.
  unwarranted
    916 adj.
overparticular
  fastidious 862 adj.
overpass
  crossing 222 n.
overpower
  be strong 162 vb.
  overmaster 727 vb.
  impress 821 vb.
overpriced
  dear 811 adj.
overrate
  overestimate
    482 vb.
overreach oneself
  misjudge 481 vb.
  fail 728 vb.
overreligious
  pietistic 979 adj.
overriding
  supreme 34 adj.
  necessary 596 adj.

overripe
  ageing 131 adj.
  soft 327 adj.
  unsavoury 391 adj.
  matured 669 adj.
overruling
  supreme 34 adj.
  authoritative
    733 adj.
overrun
  fill 54 vb.
  full 54 adj.
  be many 104 vb.
  pervade 189 vb.
  expand 197 vb.
  encroach 306 vb.
  overstep 306 vb.
  attack 712 vb.
  appropriate
    786 vb.
overseas
  extraneous 59 adj.
oversee
  manage 689 vb.
overseer
  spectator 441 n.
  manager 690 n.
oversexed
  lecherous 951 adj.
overshadow
  be superior 34 vb.
  abate 37 vb.
  be high 209 vb.
  darken 418 vb.
  have a reputation
    866 vb.
overshoot the mark
  overstep 306 vb.
  exaggerate 546 vb.
oversight
  inattention 456 n.
  negligence 458 n.
  mistake 495 n.
  management
    689 n.
oversize
  huge 195 adj.
oversleep
  be late 136 vb.
  overstep 306 vb.
  be neglectful
    458 vb.
  fail in duty 918 vb.
overspill
  redundance 637 n.
overstaffing
  expansion 197 n.

over-stated
  florid 425 adj.
overstatement
  overestimation
    482 n.
  falsehood 541 n.
  exaggeration
    546 n.
  grandiloquence
    574 n.
overstep
  overstep 306 vb.
overstepping
  overstepping 306 vb.
overstepping the
  mark
  overstepping 306 n.
overstep the mark
  overstep 306 vb.
  exaggerate 546 vb.
  superabound
    637 vb.
overstretched
  redundant 637 adj.
oversubscribe
  superabound
    637 vb.
overt
  shown 522 adj.
overtake
  be superior 34 vb.
  outstrip 277 vb.
  progress 285 vb.
  approach 289 vb.
  outdo 306 vb.
  hasten 680 vb.
  take 786 vb.
overtaking
  sequence 65 n.
  spurt 277 n.
  progression 285 n.
  approach 289 n.
overtax
  fatigue 684 vb.
  oppress 735 vb.
  impose a duty
    917 vb.
over the moon
  pleased 824 vb.
over the top
  rash 857 adj.
overthrow
  change 143 n.
  revolution 149 n.
  demolish 165 vb.
  destruction 165 n.
  fell 311 vb.

  lowering 311 n.
  confute 479 vb.
  overmaster 727 vb.
  revolt 738 vb.
overtime
  addition 38 n.
  extra 40 n.
  protraction 113 n.
overtired
  fatigued 684 adj.
overtopping
  superior 34 adj.
overture
  prelude 66 n.
  approach 289 n.
  musical piece
    412 n.
  peace offering
    719 n.
  offer 759 n.
  request 761 n.
overturn
  derange 63 vb.
  revolutionize
    149 vb.
  demolish 165 vb.
  invert 221 vb.
  navigate 269 vb.
  lowering 311 n.
  overmaster 727 vb.
overvaluation
  misjudgment
    481 n.
  overestimation
    482 n.
overview
  whole 52 n.
  inspection 438 n.
overweening
  rash 857 adj.
  proud 871 adj.
  vain 873 adj.
  insolent 878 adj.
overweight
  be unequal 29 vb.
  unequal 29 adj.
  fleshy 195 adj.
  huge 195 adj.
  unwieldy 195 adj.
  make heavy
    322 vb.
  redundance 637 n.
overwhelm
  fill 54 vb.
  be many 104 vb.
  destroy 165 vb.
  confute 479 vb.

superabound
  637 vb.
attack 712 vb.
impress 821 vb.
overwhelming
  prodigious 32 adj.
  strong 162 adj.
  destructive 165 adj.
  violent 176 adj.
  liberal 813 adj.
  fervent 818 adj.
  impressive 821 adj.
  wonderful 864 adj.
overwork
  waste 634 vb.
  use 673 vb.
  exertion 682 n.
  be fatigued 684 vb.
  fatigue 684 vb.
overwrought
  excited 821 adj.
ovoid
  round 250 adj.
  rotund 252 adj.
ovule
  flower 366 n.
ovum
  genitalia 167 n.
owe
  be in debt 803 vb.
owing
  impending 155 adj.
  due 915 adj.
owing to
  caused 157 adj.
  hence 158 adv.
owl
  bird 365 n.
  omen 511 n.
owlish
  animal 365 adj.
own
  assent 488 vb.
  confess 526 vb.
  possess 773 vb.
owner
  owner 776 n.
  dueness 915 n.
ownership
  possession 773 n.
own goal
  bungling 695 n.
own up
  confess 526 vb.
ox
  beast of burden
  273 n.

cattle 365 n.
male animal
  372 n.
Oxbridge
  educational
  534 adj.
  academy 539 n.
oxen
  beast of burden
  273 n.
  cattle 365 n.
oxtail
  meat 301 n.
oxygen
  air 340 n.
oxygen tent
  respiration 352 n.
  hospital 658 n.
oyster
  fish food 301 n.
  marine life 365 n.
  greyness 429 n.
ozone
  air 340 n.

P

pabulum
  food 301 n.
pace
  synchronize
  123 vb.
  long measure
  203 n.
  gait 265 n.
  motion 265 n.
  walk 267 vb.
  velocity 277 n.
  measure 465 vb.
pacemaker
  living model 23 n.
  substitute 150 n.
  leader 690 n.
pacesetter
  leader 690 n.
pace up and down
  walk 267 vb.
pachyderm
  mammal 365 n.
pacific
  moderate 177 adj.
  peaceful 717 adj.
pacifier
  moderator 177 n.
  mediator 720 n.
pacifist
  pacifist 717 n.

peaceful 717 adj.
pacify
  pacify 719 vb.
pack
  fill 54 vb.
  bring together
  74 vb.
  bunch 74 n.
  group 74 n.
  load 193 vb.
  cover 226 vb.
  line 227 vb.
  animal 365 n.
  hunter 619 n.
  store 632 n.
pack (a jury)
  fake 541 vb.
  predetermine
  608 vb.
  do wrong 914 adj.
package
  bring together
  74 vb.
  bunch 74 n.
  inclusion 78 n.
  unit 88 n.
  load 193 vb.
package deal
  inclusion 78 n.
packaging
  receptacle 194 n.
  wrapping 226 n.
  lining 227 n.
  enclosure 235 n.
pack a punch
  be strong 162 vb.
packed
  firm 45 adj.
  full 54 adj.
  false 541 adj.
  predetermined
  608 adj.
packer
  worker 686 n.
packet
  bunch 74 n.
  small box 194 n.
  ship 275 n.
  store 632 n.
  funds 797 n.
  wealth 800 n.
packhorse
  beast of burden
  273 n.
packing
  lining 227 n.

pack-mule
  beast of burden
  273 n.
pack up
  decamp 296 vb.
  be fatigued 684 vb.
  fail 728 vb.
pact
  agreement 24 n.
  compact 765 n.
pad
  abode 192 n.
  enlarge 197 vb.
  foot 214 n.
  seat 218 n.
  line 227 vb.
  walk 267 vb.
  saddle horse 273 n.
  softness 327 n.
  faintness 401 n.
  stationery 586 n.
  defend 713 vb.
padded cell
  mental hospital
  503 n.
padding
  increment 36 n.
  adjunct 40 n.
  lining 227 n.
  stopper 264 n.
  softness 327 n.
  diffuseness 570 n.
  superfluity 637 n.
paddle
  be in motion
  265 vb.
  walk 267 vb.
  propeller 269 n.
  row 269 vb.
  swim 269 vb.
  propellant 287 n.
  be wet 341 vb.
paddle one's own ca-noe
  behave 688 vb.
  be free 744 vb.
paddle steamer
  ship 275 n.
paddlewheel
  propellant 287 n.
paddock
  place 185 n.
  enclosure 235 n.
  amphibian 365 n.
paddyfield
  farm 370 n.

padlock
  fastening 47 n.
  barrier 235 n.
pad out
  augment 36 vb.
  be diffuse 570 vb.
padre
  title 870 n.
  cleric 986 n.
paean
  rejoicing 835 n.
  celebration 876 n.
  applause 923 n.
  hymn 981 n.
paean of praise
  praise 923 n.
paediatrics
  medical art 658 n.
paella
  dish 301 n.
pagan
  ignorant 491 adj.
  religionist 973 n.
  heathen 974 n.
  heathenish 974 adj.
  impious person
    980 n.
  profane 980 adj.
page
  part 53 n.
  courier 529 n.
  mark 547 vb.
  edition 589 n.
  domestic 742 n.
  retainer 742 n.
  a beauty 841 n.
  erotic 887 adj.
  bridal party 894 n.
  impurity 951 n.
pageant
  spectacle 445 n.
  pageant 875 n.
pageantry
  spectacle 445 n.
  ostentation 875 n.
pageboy
  servant 742 n.
  hairdressing 843 n.
paginate
  number 86 vb.
  mark 547 vb.
  print 587 vb.
pagoda
  high structure
    209 n.
  temple 990 n.

pail
  vessel 194 n.
pain
  give pain 377 vb.
  pain 377 n.
  suffering 825 n.
  hurt 827 vb.
  discontent 829 n.
  sadden 834 vb.
painful
  painful 377 adj.
  laborious 682 adj.
  paining 827 adj.
pain in the neck
  annoyance 827 n.
painkiller
  anaesthetic 375 n.
  antidote 658 n.
  relief 831 n.
painless
  easy 701 adj.
painstaking
  slow 278 adj.
  careful 457 adj.
  assiduity 678 n.
  laborious 682 adj.
  labouring 682 adj.
  fastidious 862 adj.
paint
  coat 226 vb.
  facing 226 n.
  pigment 425 n.
  imagine 513 vb.
  deception 542 n.
    See **sham**
  record 548 vb.
  paint 553 vb.
  describe 590 vb.
  cleanser 648 n.
  primp 843 vb.
  decorate 844 vb.
painter
  cable 47 n.
  producer 164 n.
  artist 556 n.
  mender 656 n.
  artisan 686 n.
painterly
  painted 553 adj.
painting
  painting 553 n.
  picture 553 n.
  beautification
    843 n.
painting oneself into
  a corner
  predicament 700 n.

paint the town red
  rejoice 835 vb.
  revel 837 vb.
pair
  identify 13 vb.
  identity 13 n.
  analogue 18 n.
  liken 18 vb.
  compeer 28 n.
  adjunct 40 n.
  join 45 vb.
  unite with 45 vb.
  group 74 n.
  concomitant 89 n.
  duality 90 n.
  pair 90 vb.
  compare 462 vb.
pair off
  pair 90 vb.
  wed 894 vb.
paisley
  textile 222 n.
  pattern 844 n.
pakora
  hors-d'oeuvres
    301 n.
pal
  male 372 n.
  colleague 707 n.
  chum 880 n.
palace
  house 192 n.
palaeology
  palaeology 125 n.
palatable
  edible 301 adj.
  pleasant 376 adj.
  tasty 386 adj.
  savoury 390 adj.
palate
  taste 386 n.
  good taste 846 n.
palaver
  speech 579 n.
  chatter 581 n.
pale
  insubstantial 4 adj.
  fastening 47 n.
  exclusion 57 n.
  weak 163 adj.
  region 184 n.
  barrier 235 n.
  fence 235 n.
  dim 419 adj.
  soft-hued 425 adj.
  colourless 426 adj.
  lose colour 426 vb.

  whiten 427 vb.
  whitish 427 adj.
  be unseen 444 vb.
  heraldry 547 n.
  unhealthy 651 adj.
  quake 854 vb.
pale imitation
  pretext 614 n.
  bungling 695 n.
palette
  plate 194 n.
  colour 425 n.
palimony
  dower 777 n.
  receipt 807 n.
  divorce 896 n.
palindrome
  inversion 221 n.
  word 559 n.
paling
  fence 235 n.
  defences 713 n.
palisade
  barrier 235 n.
  protection 660 n.
  defences 713 n.
pall
  coverlet 226 n.
  funeral 364 n.
  be unpalatable
    391 vb.
  be tedious 838 vb.
  cause dislike
    861 vb.
  sate 863 vb.
pallbearer
  funeral 364 n.
pallet
  plate 194 n.
  basis 218 n.
  bed 218 n.
  carrier 273 n.
palliasse
  cushion 218 n.
palliate
  moderate 177 vb.
  qualify 468 vb.
  relieve 831 vb.
  extenuate 927 vb.
palliative
  moderator 177 n.
  qualifying 468 adj.
  remedial 658 adj.
  vindication 927 n.
pallid
  weakly 163 adj.
  colourless 426 adj.

pallor
hue 425 n.
achromatism
426 n.
friendly 880 adj.

pally
friendly 880 adj.
sociable 882 adj.

palm
long measure
203 n.
tree 366 n.
touch 378 vb.
oracle 511 n.

palmate
divergent 294 adj.

palmistry
divination 511 n.
prediction 511 n.
occultism 984 n.

palm off
substitute 150 vb.
deceive 542 vb.

palm-reading
prediction 511 n.

palomino
horse 273 n.
touch 378 n.

palpable
substantial 3 adj.
material 319 adj.
tactual 378 adj.
visible 443 adj.
manifest 522 adj.

palpate
touch 378 vb.

palpitate
oscillate 317 vb.
be agitated 318 vb.
show feeling
818 vb.
be excited 821 vb.

palpitation
oscillation 317 n.
agitation 318 n.
*cardiovascular dis-
ease* 651 n.
feeling 818 n.
nervousness 854 n.

palsy
insensibility 375 n.

paltry
inconsiderable
33 adj.
unimportant
639 adj.

contemptible
922 adj.

paludal
marshy 347 adj.

pampas
plain 348 n.

pamper
pet 889 vb.

pamphlet
the press 528 n.
book 589 n.

Pan
animality 365 n.
mythic deity 966 n.
lesser deity 967 n.

pan
plate 194 n.
pot 194 n.
base 214 n.
scales 322 n.

panacea
remedy 658 n.

panache
vigour 571 n.
courage 855 n.
ostentation 875 n.

panama
headgear 228 n.

panatella
tobacco 388 n.

pancake
aeronautics 271 n.
fly 271 vb.
cereals 301 n.
dish 301 n.

panda car
automobile 274 n.

pandemic
turmoil 61 n.
generality 79 n.
universal 79 adj.
loudness 400 n.
discord 411 n.
infectious 653 adj.

pandemonium
turmoil 61 n.
loudness 400 n.
discord 411 n.
hell 972 n.

pander
intermediary
231 n.
informant 524 n.
messenger 529 n.
instrument 628 n.
provide 633 vb.
mediator 720 n.

be impure 951 vb.
bawd 952 n.

pander to
minister to 703 vb.
please 826 vb.
be servile 879 vb.
flatter 925 vb.

Pandora's box
evil 616 n.

pane
transparency
422 n.

panegyric
overestimation
482 n.
oration 579 n.
praise 923 n.

panel
band 74 n.
list 87 n.
partition 231 n.
picture 553 n.
council 692 n.
consignee 754 n.

panel game
indoor game 837 n.

panelling
lining 227 n.
ornamental art
844 n.

pang
pang 377 n.
badness 645 n.

panic
fear 854 n.
fear 854 vb.
frighten 854 vb.
be cowardly
856 vb.

panjandrum
aristocrat 868 n.

pannier
bag 194 n.
basket 194 n.

panoply
dressing 228 n.
armour 713 n.

panorama
whole 52 n.
generality 79 n.
open space 263 n.
view 438 n.
spectacle 445 n.
art subject 553 n.

pan out
happen 154 vb.
result 157 vb.

pansy
nonconformist
84 n.
weakling 163 n.
plant 366 n.
female 373 adj.

pant
oscillate 317 vb.
be agitated 318 vb.
breathe 352 vb.
be hot 379 vb.
be fatigued 684 vb.
show feeling
818 vb.

pantaloons
trousers 228 n.

pantechnicon
lorry 274 n.

pant for
desire 859 vb.

pantheism
deism 973 n.

pantheon
tomb 364 n.
temple 990 n.

panther
big cat 365 n.

panties
underwear 228 n.

pantile
roof 226 n.

panto
stage play 594 n.

pantomime
mimicry 20 n.
spectacle 445 n.
gesture 547 n.
acting 594 n.
stage play 594 n.

pantry
chamber 194 n.
storage 632 n.

pants
trousers 228 n.
underwear 228 n.

Panzer
cavalry 722 n.

pap
bosom 253 n.
pulpiness 356 n.
insipidity 387 n.

papa
paternity 169 n.

papacy
church office 985 n.
the church 985 n.

papal
 ecclesiastical
  985 adj.
paparazzo
 photography 551 n.
papaya
 fruit and vegetables
  301 n.
paper
 weak thing 163 n.
 thinness 206 n.
 wrapping 226 n.
 line 227 vb.
 white thing 427 n.
 report 524 n.
 the press 528 n.
 oration 579 n.
 dissertation 591 n.
 paper 631 n.
paperback
 book 589 n.
 See **edition**
 novel 590 n.
paper bag
 bag 194 n.
paper over the cracks
 transform 147 vb.
 overestimate
  482 vb.
 not suffice 636 vb.
 be unskilful
  695 vb.
 be ostentatious
  875 vb.
papers
 record 548 n.
 reading matter
  589 n.
papers, the
 the press 528 n.
paper tiger
 sham 542 n.
paperwork
 writing 586 n.
papier mâché
 pulpiness 356 n.
 sculpture 554 n.
 paper 631 n.
papist
 Catholic 976 n.
papoose
 child 132 n.
pappadum
 cereals 301 n.
paprika
 spice 301 n.

Pap test
 diagnostic 658 n.
papyrus
 grass 366 n.
 stationery 586 n.
par
 equal 28 adj.
 equivalence 28 n.
 average 30 n.
 median 30 adj.
parable
 analogue 18 n.
 assimilation 18 n.
 metaphor 519 n.
 lecture 534 n.
 narrative 590 n.
parabola
 curve 248 n.
parachute
 fly 271 vb.
 aircraft 276 n.
 airship 276 n.
 descend 309 vb.
 safeguard 662 n.
parachutist
 aeronaut 271 n.
parade
 series 71 n.
 assemblage 74 n.
 park 192 n.
 marching 267 n.
 spectacle 445 n.
 show 522 vb.
 be ostentatious
  875 vb.
 ostentation 875 n.
 pageant 875 n.
 boast 877 vb.
 greet 884 vb.
paradigm
 prototype 23 n.
Paradise
 happiness 824 n.
 heaven 971 n.
paradox
 contrariety 14 n.
 unintelligibility
  517 n.
 trope 519 n.
paraffin
 oil 357 n.
 fuel 385 n.
paragon
 paragon 646 n.
paragraph
 part 53 n.
 subdivision 53 n.

 punctuation 547 n.
parallel
 correlative 12 adj.
 analogue 18 n.
 similar 18 adj.
 be equal 28 vb.
 compeer 28 n.
 equal 28 adj.
 equalize 28 vb.
 equivalent 28 adj.
 region 184 n.
 parallelism 219 n.
 compare 462 vb.
 comparison 462 n.
parallel lines
 parallelism 219 n.
parallelogram
 parallelism 219 n.
 angular figure
  247 n.
paralyse
 disable 161 vb.
 render insensible
  375 vb.
 make inactive
  679 vb.
 hinder 702 vb.
 frighten 854 vb.
paralysis
 helplessness 161 n.
 inertness 175 n.
 insensibility 375 n.
 inaction 677 n.
paralytic
 impotent 161 adj.
 insensible 375 adj.
 sick person 651 n.
 dead drunk
  949 adj.
parameter
 numerical element
  85 n.
 limit 236 n.
paramount
 supreme 34 adj.
 important 638 adj.
 authoritative
  733 adj.
paramour
 lover 887 n.
 kept woman 952 n.
paranoia
 psychosis 503 n.
paranoiac
 psychotic 503 adj.
 psychotic 504 n.

paranoid
 psychotic 503 adj.
parapet
 barrier 235 n.
 obstacle 702 n.
 fortification 713 n.
paraphernalia
 medley 43 n.
 box 194 n.
 dressing 228 n.
 equipment 630 n.
 property 777 n.
paraphrase
 copy 20 vb.
 copy 22 n.
 translate 520 vb.
 translation 520 n.
 phrase 563 n.
paraphrastic
 imitative 20 adj.
 semantic 514 adj.
paraplegia
 helplessness 161 n.
paraplegic
 sick person 651 n.
paraquat
 poison 659 n.
parasite
 concomitant 89 n.
 resident 191 n.
 plant 366 n.
 superfluity 637 n.
 infection 651 n.
 bane 659 n.
 idler 679 n.
 dependant 742 n.
 beggar 763 n.
 taker 786 n.
 toady 879 n.
 sociable person
  882 n.
 flatterer 925 n.
parasol
 shade 226 n.
 screen 421 n.
paratha
 cereals 301 n.
paratroops
 armed force 722 n.
parboil
 cook 301 vb.
parcel
 piece 53 n.
 bring together
  74 vb.
 bunch 74 n.

parcel out
 sunder 46 vb.
 arrange 62 vb.
 apportion 783 vb.
parched
 dry 342 adj.
 hot 379 adj.
 hungry 859 adj.
parchment
 stationery 586 n.
 bookbinding 589 n.
pardon
 amnesty 506 n.
 be lenient 736 vb.
 leniency 736 n.
 liberate 746 vb.
 mercy 905 n.
 show mercy
  905 vb.
 forgive 909 vb.
 forgiveness 909 n.
 exempt 919 vb.
 nonliability 919 n.
 acquit 960 vb.
 acquittal 960 n.
pardoner
 pastor 986 n.
pare
 abate 37 vb.
 subtract 39 vb.
 cut 46 vb.
 render few 105 vb.
 uncover 229 vb.
parent
 source 156 n.
 parentage 169 n.
parentage
 parentage 169 n.
parental
 parental 169 adj.
parenthesis
 irrelevance 10 n.
 discontinuity 72 n.
 interjection 231 n.
 insertion 303 n.
parenthood
 propagation 167 n.
 parentage 169 n.
 life 360 n.
par excellence
 eminently 34 adv.
pariah
 nonconformist
  84 n.
 derelict 779 n.
 outcast 883 n.

parings
 piece 53 n.
parish
 subdivision 53 n.
 district 184 n.
 parish 985 n.
 laity 987 n.
parishioner
 dweller 191 n.
 native 191 n.
 lay person 987 n.
parish-pump
 provincial 192 adj.
 trivial 639 adj.
parity
 similarity 18 n.
 equality 28 n.
park
 territory 184 n.
 place 187 vb.
 place oneself
  187 vb.
 park 192 n.
 enclosure 235 n.
 arrive 295 vb.
 grassland 348 n.
 wood 366 n.
 garden 370 n.
 pleasure ground
  837 n.
parka
 jacket 228 n.
parking
 traffic control
  305 n.
Parkinson's disease
 agitation 318 n.
 nervous disorders
  651 n.
Parkinson's law
 rule 81 n.
 expansion 197 n.
 overactivity 678 n.
 governance 733 n.
parlance
 language 557 n.
 speech 579 n.
parley
 confer 584 vb.
 conference 584 n.
 converse 584 vb.
 interlocution
  584 n.
 advice 691 n.
 consult 691 vb.
 mediation 720 n.

 make terms
  766 vb.
parliament
 parliament 692 n.
parlour
 chamber 194 n.
parlour game
 indoor game 837 n.
parochial
 provincial 192 adj.
 narrow-minded
  481 adj.
 ecclesiastical
  985 adj.
parody
 imitate 20 vb.
 mimicry 20 n.
 copy 22 n.
 be absurd 497 vb.
 foolery 497 n.
 misinterpret
  521 vb.
 misrepresent
  552 vb.
 misrepresentation
  552 n.
 description 590 n.
 satire 851 n.
 satirize 851 vb.
parole
 liberate 746 vb.
 liberation 746 n.
 permit 756 n.
 security 767 n.
paroxysm
 violence 176 n.
 spasm 318 n.
 frenzy 503 n.
 anger 891 n.
parquet
 paving 226 n.
 variegated 437 adj.
parrot
 imitate 20 vb.
 imitator 20 n.
 repeat 106 vb.
 bird 365 n.
parry
 answer 460 vb.
 confute 479 vb.
 defence 713 n.
 not observe 769 vb.
parse
 decompose 51 vb.
parsimonious
 parsimonious
  816 adj.

parsing
 decomposition
  51 n.
 grammar 564 n.
parsley
 herb 301 n.
parsnip
 fruit and vegetables
  301 n.
parson
 church title 986 n.
 cleric 986 n.
parsonage
 benefice 985 n.
 parsonage 986 n.
part
 disunite 46 vb.
 separate 46 vb.
 part 53 n.
 part 53 vb.
 subdivision 53 n.
 diverge 294 vb.
 depart 296 vb.
 melody 410 n.
 vocal music 412 n.
 reading matter
  589 n.
 acting 594 n.
 stage play 594 n.
 function 622 n.
partake
 eat 301 vb.
partake of
 participate 775 vb.
part and parcel
 intrinsic 5 adj.
 component 58 n.
Parthian shot
 answer 460 n.
 stratagem 698 n.
partial
 unequal 29 adj.
 fragmentary
  53 adj.
 incomplete 55 adj.
 fractional 102 adj.
 unjust 914 adj.
partiality
 inequality 29 n.
 prejudice 481 n.
 choice 605 n.
 liking 859 n.
 injustice 914 n.
 improbity 930 n.
partially
 partially 33 adv.

participate
  participate 775 vb.
particle
  small thing 33 n.
  minuteness 196 n.
  part of speech
    564 n.
parti-coloured
  pied 437 adj.
  variegated 437 adj.
particular
  part 53 n.
  special 80 adj.
  discriminating
    463 adj.
  fastidious 862 adj.
particularize
  specify 80 vb.
  be diffuse 570 vb.
particularly
  greatly 32 vb.
  eminently 34 adv.
particulars
  particulars 80 n.
  description 590 n.
parting
  separation 46 n.
  dividing line 92 n.
  partition 231 n.
  limit 236 n.
  divergence 294 n.
  departure 296 n.
partisan
  biased 481 adj.
  soldier 722 n.
  revolter 738 n.
  unjust 914 adj.
  sectarian 978 adj.
partition
  scission 46 n.
  sunder 46 vb.
  decomposition
    51 n.
  part 53 vb.
  exclusion 57 n.
  partition 231 n.
  screen 421 n.
  apportion 783 vb.
partly
  partially 33 adv.
partner
  unite with 45 vb.
  accompany 89 vb.
  concomitant 89 n.
  colleague 707 n.
  participator 775 n.
  friend 880 n.

spouse 894 n.
partnership
  accompaniment
    89 n.
  concurrence 181 n.
  association 706 n.
  corporation 708 n.
  society 708 n.
  participation
    775 n.
  marriage 894 n.
part of speech
  word 559 n.
  part of speech
    564 n.
partridge
  meat 301 n.
  table bird 365 n.
parts
  region 184 n.
  locality 187 n.
  contents 193 n.
parturition
  obstetrics 167 n.
part with
  not retain 779 vb.
  give 781 vb.
party
  assembly 74 n.
  band 74 n.
  follower 284 n.
  person 371 n.
  party 708 n.
  armed force 722 n.
  formation 722 n.
  festivity 837 n.
  social gathering
    882 n.
  litigant 959 n.
party games
  amusement 837 n.
  See **indoor game**
party line
  rule 81 n.
  telecommunication
    531 n.
  policy 623 n.
  tactics 688 n.
  precept 693 n.
parvenu
  new 126 adj.
  commoner 869 n.
  plebeian 869 adj.
  proud person
    871 n.
parvovirus
  infection 651 n.

pasha
  governor 741 n.
pass
  be superior 34 vb.
  entrance 68 n.
  continue 108 vb.
  elapse 111 vb.
  be past 125 vb.
  event 154 n.
  gap 201 n.
  narrowness 206 n.
  approach 289 n.
  emit 300 vb.
  excrete 302 vb.
  pass 305 vb.
  assent 488 n.
  label 547 n.
  select 605 vb.
  access 624 n.
  suffice 635 vb.
  protection 660 n.
  succeed 727 vb.
  success 727 n.
  permit 756 n.
  consent 758 vb.
  change hands
    780 vb.
  approve 923 vb.
  make legal 953 vb.
passable
  not bad 644 adj.
  middling 732 adj.
passage
  bond 47 n.
  part 53 n.
  lobby 194 n.
  doorway 263 n.
  land travel 267 n.
  water travel 269 n.
  passage 305 n.
  melody 410 n.
  musical piece
    412 n.
  tune 412 n.
passageway
  access 624 n.
pass away
  pass away 2 vb.
  not be 4 vb.
pass by
  elapse 111 vb.
  be in motion
    265 vb.
  pass 305 vb.
  disregard 458 vb.
passé
  past 125 adj.

antiquated 127 adj.
  ageing 131 adj.
passed
  approved 923 adj.
  legal 953 adj.
passenger
  transport 272 n.
  idler 679 n.
pass for
  resemble 18 vb.
passing
  transient 114 adj.
  passage 305 n.
  decease 361 n.
passing fancy
  whim 604 n.
passion
  vigour 571 n.
  affections 817 n.
  warm feeling
    818 n.
  excitation 821 n.
  excitable state
    822 n.
  suffering 825 n.
  desire 859 n.
  libido 859 n.
  love 887 n.
  anger 891 n.
passionate
  feeling 818 adj.
  fervent 818 adj.
  excitable 822 adj.
  loving 887 adj.
  irascible 892 adj.
passionless
  impassive 820 adj.
passion play
  stage play 594 n.
passive
  inert 175 adj.
  latent 523 adj.
  nonactive 677 adj.
  peaceful 717 adj.
  obedient 739 adj.
  apathetic 820 adj.
  inexcitable
    823 adj.
passive resistance
  inertness 175 n.
  dissent 489 n.
  inaction 677 n.
  resistance 715 n.
  disobedience
    738 n.
passive smoking
  tobacco 388 n.

863

passivity
inertness 175 n.
quietude 266 n.
irresolution 601 n.
inaction 677 n.
passkey
instrument 628 n.
pass muster
be equal 28 vb.
suffice 635 vb.
be good 644 vb.
pass on
transfer 272 vb.
progress 285 vb.
communicate
524 vb.
pass oneself off as
misname 562 vb.
pass out
pass 305 vb.
pass over
exclude 57 vb.
die 361 vb.
disregard 458 vb.
neglect 458 vb.
be taciturn 582 vb.
reject 607 vb.
forgive 909 vb.
exempt 919 vb.
passport
opener 263 n.
credential 466 n.
assent 488 n.
label 547 n.
instrument 628 n.
protection 660 n.
warrant 737 n.
permit 756 n.
pass the buck
transfer 272 vb.
avoid 620 vb.
not act 677 vb.
assign 780 vb.
fail in duty 918 vb.
be exempt 919 vb.
pass the hat
beg 761 vb.
pass the time
be 1 vb.
amuse oneself
837 vb.
pass up
refuse 760 vb.
password
opener 263 n.
answer 460 n.

identification
547 n.
instrument 628 n.
permit 756 n.
past
past 125 adj.
disrepute 867 n.
past, the
priority 119 n.
past time 125 n.
pasta
dish 301 n.
past behaviour
conduct 688 n.
paste
a mixture 43 n.
adhesive 47 n.
strike 279 vb.
softness 327 n.
viscidity 354 n.
pulpiness 356 n.
sham 542 n.
spurious 542 adj.
finery 844 n.
bad taste 847 n.
pasteboard
spurious 542 adj.
paper 631 n.
pastel
soft-hued 425 adj.
painted 553 adj.
picture 553 n.
pasteurize
purify 648 vb.
make sanitary
652 adj.
safeguard 660 vb.
pastiche
copy 22 n.
a mixture 43 n.
art style 553 n.
picture 553 n.
pastille
sweet thing 392 n.
pastime
pleasurableness
826 n.
amusement 837 n.
past it
ageing 131 adj.
weak 163 adj.
useless 641 adj.
past master
proficient person
696 n.
pastor
pastor 986 n.

pastoral
art subject 553 n.
pleasurable
826 adj.
pastorale
musical piece
412 n.
past recall
unpromising
853 adj.
pastry
pastries and cakes
301 n.
past tense
time 108 n.
past time 125 n.
pasture
feed 301 vb.
provender 301 n.
soil 344 n.
grassland 348 n.
grass 366 n.
stock farm 369 n.
farm 370 n.
pasty
dish 301 n.
pastries and cakes
301 n.
colourless 426 adj.
pat
apt 24 adj.
firm 45 adj.
fixed 153 adj.
knock 279 n.
touch 378 n.
touch 378 vb.
gesticulate 547 vb.
please 826 vb.
caress 889 vb.
endearment 889 n.
patch
adjunct 40 n.
join 45 vb.
piece 53 n.
modify 143 vb.
garden 370 n.
mottle 437 vb.
variegate 437 vb.
rectify 654 vb.
repair 656 vb.
surgical dressing
658 n.
blemish 845 n.
patch up a quarrel
make peace
719 vb.

patchwork
nonuniformity
17 n.
variegation 437 n.
needlework 844 n.
patchy
nonuniform 17 adj.
unequal 29 adj.
mixed 43 adj.
mottled 437 adj.
pied 437 adj.
imperfect 647 adj.
pate
head 213 n.
pâté
hors-d'oeuvres
301 n.
patent
permit 756 vb.
claim 915 vb.
dueness 915 n.
patented
proprietary
777 adj.
patent leather
skin 226 n.
paterfamilias
paternity 169 n.
male 372 n.
paternal
akin 11 adj.
parental 169 adj.
benevolent 897 adj.
paternalism
despotism 733 n.
governance 733 n.
government 733 n.
paternity
propagation 167 n.
parentage 169 n.
paternity 169 n.
path
direction 281 n.
way in 297 n.
outlet 298 n.
trace 548 n.
path 624 n.
pathetic
bad 645 adj.
distressing 827 adj.
lamenting 836 adj.
pathetic fallacy
anthropology
371 n.
pathogenic
diseased 651 adj.
infectious 653 adj.

pathological
  diseased 651 adj.
  medical 658 adj.
pathological liar
  liar 545 n.
pathologist
  doctor 658 n.
pathos
  feeling 818 n.
  excitation 821 n.
  painfulness 827 n.
pathway
  path 624 n.
patience
  perseverance 600 n.
  patience 823 n.
  card game 837 n.
patience of Job
  patience 823 n.
patient
  sick person 651 n.
  patient 823 adj.
  sufferer 825 n.
patio
  lobby 194 n.
patisserie
  pastries and cakes
    301 n.
patois
  speciality 80 n.
  dialect 560 adj.
pat oneself on the
    back
  boast 877 vb.
pat on the back
  trophy 729 n.
  rejoicing 835 n.
  applaud 923 vb.
  applause 923 n.
patrial
  native 191 n.
  subject 742 n.
  free person 744 n.
patriarch
  old man 133 n.
  paternity 169 n.
  male 372 n.
  governor 741 n.
  master 741 n.
  ecclesiarch 986 n.
patriarchy
  family 11 n.
  male 372 n.
  government 733 n.
patrician
  aristocrat 868 n.
  genteel 868 adj.

patricide
  homicide 362 n.
patrimony
  acquisition 771 n.
  possession 773 n.
  dower 777 n.
  dueness 915 n.
patriot
  defender 713 n.
  patriot 901 n.
patriotism
  love 887 n.
  patriotism 901 n.
patrol
  land travel 267 n.
  traverse 267 vb.
  pass 305 vb.
  passage 305 n.
  spectator 441 n.
  safeguard 660 vb.
  defender 713 n.
  armed force 722 n.
  restrain 747 vb.
patron
  support 218 n.
  patron 707 n.
  defender 713 n.
  purchaser 792 n.
patronage
  influence 178 n.
  protection 660 n.
  aid 703 n.
  security 767 n.
  approbation 923 n.
  benefice 985 n.
patronize
  patronize 703 vb.
  be proud 871 vb.
patron saint
  protector 660 n.
  saint 968 n.
patronymic
  name 561 n.
patter
  be in motion
    265 vb.
  walk 267 vb.
  rain 350 n.
  rain 350 VB.
  faintness 401 n.
  roll 403 vb.
  empty talk 515 n.
  language 557 n.
  slang 560 adj.
  speak 579 vb.
  speech 579 n.
  loquacity 581 n.

  inducement 612 n.
pattern
  correlation 12 n.
  uniformity 16 n.
  prototype 23 n.
  composition 56 n.
  order 60 n.
  arrangement 62 n.
  rule 81 n.
  example 83 n.
  form 243 n.
  structure 331 n.
  variegate 437 vb.
  comparison 462 n.
  picture 553 n.
  plan 623 n.
  pattern 844 n.
patty
  pastries and cakes
    301 n.
paucity
  smallness 33 n.
  fewness 105 n.
  littleness 196 n.
  scarcity 636 n.
paunch
  stomach 194 n.
  insides 224 n.
  swelling 253 n.
pauper
  poor person 801 n.
pause
  discontinuity 72 n.
  period 110 n.
  delay 136 n.
  lull 145 n.
  pause 145 vb.
  interval 201 n.
  come to rest
    266 vb.
  quiescence 266 n.
  notation 410 n.
  be uncertain
    474 vb.
  doubt 486 vb.
  not act 677 vb.
  repose 683 n.
pavement
  base 214 n.
  basis 218 n.
  paving 226 n.
  path 624 n.
  road 624 n.
pave the way
  prepare 669 vb.
  facilitate 701 vb.

pavilion
  pavilion 192 n.
  canopy 226 n.
  theatre 594 n.
paving
  paving 226 n.
  road 624 n.
paving stone
  paving 226 n.
  road 624 n.
Pavlovian response
  intuition 476 n.
paw
  foot 214 n.
  feeler 378 n.
  touch 378 vb.
  pincers 778 n.
  caress 889 vb.
pawky
  cunning 698 adj.
  witty 839 adj.
pawn
  inferior 35 n.
  dupe 544 n.
  instrument 628 n.
  slave 742 n.
  give security
    767 vb.
  security 767 n.
  assign 780 vb.
  transfer 780 n.
  borrow 785 vb.
  plaything 837 n.
pawnbroker
  lender 784 n.
pawpaw
  fruit and vegetables
    301 n.
pay
  compensate 31 vb.
  coat 226 vb.
  incentive 612 n.
  be profitable
    771 vb.
  pay 804 n.
  pay 804 vb.
  receipt 807 n.
pay attention
  be attentive 455 vb.
pay a visit
  visit 882 vb.
pay back
  compensate 31 vb.
  pay 804 vb.
pay court to
  be servile 879 vb.
  court 889 vb.

flatter 925 vb.
PAYE
tax 809 n.
pay homage
obey 739 vb.
pay one's respects
  884 vb.
show respect
  920 vb.
paying
prolific 171 adj.
profitable 640 adj.
gainful 771 adj.
paying guest
resident 191 n.
paymaster
treasurer 798 n.
payment
payment 804 n.
reward 962 n.
pay off
navigate 269 vb.
stop using 674 vb.
be successful
  727 vb.
payoff
end 69 n.
completion 725 n.
pay 804 n.
pay one's respects
honour 866 vb.
pay one's respects
  884 vb.
pay one's way
defray 804 vb.
payroll
list 87 n.
personnel 686 n.
pay the piper
defray 804 vb.
pay through the nose
pay 804 vb.
pay too much
  811 vb.
pay tribute
obey 739 vb.
be subject 745 vb.
give 781 vb.
respect 920 vb.
praise 923 vb.
reward 962 vb.
pay up
keep faith 768 vb.
pay 804 vb.
do one's duty
  917 vb.

pc
message 529 n.
correspondence
  588 n.
p.d.q.
swiftly 277 adv.
pea
sphere 252 n.
peace
agreement 24 n.
hush 399 int.
silence 399 n.
peace 717 n.
pleasurableness
  826 n.
peaceable
moderate 177 adj.
peaceful 717 adj.
amiable 884 adj.
peace camp
pacifist 717 n.
pacification 719 n.
peaceful
tranquil 266 adj.
silent 399 adj.
reposeful 683 adj.
peaceful 717 adj.
inexcitable
  823 adj.
pleasurable
  826 adj.
peacemaker
moderator 177 n.
pacifist 717 n.
mediator 720 n.
peace offering
peace offering
  719 n.
offering 781 n.
propitiation 941 n.
peacetime
peace 717 n.
peaceful 717 adj.
peach
fruit and vegetables
  301 n.
a beauty 841 n.
peacock
table bird 365 n.
a beauty 841 n.
fop 848 n.
proud person
  871 n.
vain person 873 n.
be ostentatious
  875 vb.

peak
superiority 34 n.
completeness 54 n.
extremity 69 n.
be high 209 vb.
high land 209 n.
summit 213 n.
sharp point 256 n.
perfection 646 n.
climax 725 vb.
palmy days 730 n.
peak of perfection
summit 213 n.
peaky
lean 206 adj.
colourless 426 adj.
unhealthy 651 adj.
peal
be loud 400 vb.
loudness 400 n.
bang 402 n.
roll 403 n.
roll 403 vb.
resonance 404 n.
tune 412 n.
gong 414 n.
call 547 n.
peanut
fruit and vegetables
  301 n.
peanuts
small quantity
  33 n.
trifle 639 n.
easy thing 701 n.
money 797 n.
pear
fruit and vegetables
  301 n.
pearl
sphere 252 n.
semitransparency
  424 n.
white thing 427 n.
exceller 644 n.
a beauty 841 n.
gem 844 n.
pearls
jewellery 844 n.
pearly
semitransparent
  424 adj.
soft-hued 425 adj.
whitish 427 adj.
grey 429 adj.
pear-shaped
curved 248 adj.

round 250 adj.
peas
fruit and vegetables
  301 n.
peasant
dweller 191 n.
farmer 370 n.
country-dweller
  869 n.
pea-souper
cloud 355 n.
opacity 423 n.
peat
heater 383 n.
fuel 385 n.
pebble
hardness 326 n.
soil 344 n.
pebbledash
coat 226 vb.
facing 226 n.
pebbly
hard 326 adj.
pecan
fruit and vegetables
  301 n.
peccadillo
trifle 639 n.
vice 934 n.
guilty act 936 n.
peck
great quantity
  32 n.
eat 301 vb.
metrology 465 n.
peck at
eat 301 vb.
peckish
hungry 859 adj.
pectin
thickening 354 n.
pectoral
cross 222 n.
vestments 989 n.
peculiar
special 80 adj.
unusual 84 adj.
crazy 503 adj.
peculiarity
temperament 5 n.
speciality 80 n.
nonconformity
  84 n.
pecuniary
monetary 797 adj.

pedagogic
educational
534 adj.
severe 735 adj.
pedagogy
teaching 534 n.
pedal
propel 287 vb.
propellant 287 n.
play music 413 vb.
tool 630 n.
pedantic
careful 457 adj.
narrow-minded
481 adj.
ornate 574 adj.
obstinate 602 adj.
severe 735 adj.
fastidious 862 adj.
orthodox 976 adj.
peddle
trade 791 vb.
sell 793 vb.
pederast
libertine 952 n.
pedestal
base 214 n.
stand 218 n.
pedestrian
pedestrian 268 n.
feeble 572 adj.
prosaic 593 adj.
dull 840 adj.
pedestrian crossing
traffic control
305 n.
access 624 n.
road 624 n.
refuge 662 n.
pedigree
list 87 n.
genealogy 169 n.
nobility 868 n.
pediment
summit 213 n.
pedlar
pedlar 794 n.
pedometer
meter 465 n.
peek
gaze 438 vb.
look 438 n.
scan 438 vb.
be curious 453 vb.
enquire 459 vb.
peel
abate 37 vb.

subtract 39 vb.
leavings 41 n.
disunite 46 vb.
layer 207 n.
skin 226 n.
uncover 229 vb.
rubbish 641 n.
peel off
come unstuck
49 vb.
peep
ululate 409 vb.
gaze 438 vb.
look 438 n.
scan 438 vb.
be curious 453 vb.
enquire 459 vb.
peeping
inspection 438 n.
inquisitive 453 adj.
peeping Tom
inspection 438 n.
spectator 441 n.
peep show
spectacle 445 n.
peer
compeer 28 n.
gaze 438 vb.
scan 438 vb.
be dim-sighted
440 vb.
enquire 459 vb.
councillor 692 n.
colleague 707 n.
person of repute
866 n.
person of rank
868 n.
peerage
honours 866 n.
aristocracy 868 n.
peer group
group 74 n.
contemporary
123 n.
peerless
dissimilar 19 adj.
supreme 34 adj.
best 644 adj.
noteworthy
866 adj.
peer out
emerge 298 vb.
peeved
unhappy 825 adj.
angry 891 adj.

peevish
discontented
829 adj.
irascible 892 adj.
sullen 893 adj.
peg
degree 27 n.
fastening 47 n.
hanger 217 n.
stopper 264 n.
draught 301 n.
tool 630 n.
peg out
dry 342 vb.
die 361 vb.
pejorative
disrespectful
921 adj.
peke
dog 365 n.
pelican
bird 365 n.
pelican crossing
traffic control
305 n.
access 624 n.
road 624 n.
refuge 662 n.
pellet
sphere 252 n.
missile 287 n.
ammunition 723 n.
missile weapon
723 n.
pellucid
undimmed
417 adj.
transparent
422 adj.
pelt
skin 226 n.
move fast 277 vb.
strike 279 vb.
propel 287 vb.
rain 350 VB.
not respect 921 vb.
pen
place 185 n.
enclose 235 vb.
enclosure 235 n.
bird 365 n.
recording instru-
ment 549 n.
stationery 586 n.
write 586 vb.
lockup 748 n.

penal
punitive 963 adj.
penal code
precept 693 n.
law 953 n.
penalty 963 n.
penalize
make illegal
954 vb.
punish 963 vb.
penalty
penalty 963 n.
penalty clause
qualification 468 n.
penance
penance 941 n.
punishment 963 n.
ministration 988 n.
penchant
tendency 179 n.
bias 481 n.
prejudice 481 n.
willingness 597 n.
liking 859 n.
pencil
recording instru-
ment 549 n.
paint 553 vb.
stationery 586 n.
write 586 vb.
pendant
hanging object
217 n.
flag 547 n.
jewellery 844 n.
pendent
hanging 217 adj.
pending
continuing 108 adj.
while 108 adv.
pendulous
hanging 217 adj.
pendulum
timekeeper 117 n.
hanging object
217 n.
oscillation 317 n.
penetrate
pierce 263 vb.
infiltrate 297 vb.
pass 305 vb.
understand 516 vb.
impress 821 vb.
penetration
mixture 43 n.
interjacency 231 n.
ingress 297 n.

passage 305 n.
sagacity 498 n.
penguin
bird 365 n.
penicillin
plant 366 n.
drug 658 n.
peninsula
region 184 n.
projection 254 n.
land 344 n.
island 349 n.
penis
genitalia 167 n.
penitent
regretting 830 adj.
penitent 939 n.
repentant 939 adj.
penitentiary
prison 748 n.
atoning 941 adj.
pastor 986 n.
penknife
sharp edge 256 n.
stationery 586 n.
pen name
name 561 n.
misnomer 562 n.
pennant
flag 547 n.
penne
dish 301 n.
penniless
poor 801 adj.
penny
coinage 797 n.
penny-farthing
bicycle 274 n.
penny whistle
flute 414 n.
penpal
correspondent
588 n.
pension
quarters 192 n.
resignation 753 n.
earnings 771 n.
pay 804 n.
receipt 807 n.
reward 962 n.
pensioner
old person 133 n.
recipient 782 n.
pension off
stop using 674 vb.
not retain 779 vb.

pensive
thoughtful 449 adj.
abstracted 456 adj.
melancholic
834 adj.
pentacle
indication 547 n.
talisman 983 n.
pentagon
five 99 n.
angular figure
247 n.
pentameter
five 99 n.
prosody 593 n.
pentathlon
five 99 n.
contest 716 n.
Pentecost
holy day 988 n.
penthouse
flat 192 n.
attic 194 n.
penumbra
cone 252 n.
darkness 418 n.
half-light 419 n.
penury
poverty 801 n.
people
race 11 n.
place oneself
187 vb.
native 191 n.
dwell 192 vb.
nation 371 n.
social group 371 n.
subject 742 n.
laity 987 n.
people, the
commonalty 869 n.
pep
energy 160 n.
vigorousness 174 n.
vigour 571 n.
restlessness 678 n.
pepper
pierce 263 vb.
shoot 287 vb.
fruit and vegetables
301 n.
spice 301 n.
pungency 388 n.
season 388 vb.
condiment 389 n.
variegate 437 vb.
fire at 712 vb.

pepper-and-salt
whitish 427 adj.
chequer 437 n.
pied 437 adj.
peppercorn
condiment 389 n.
peppercorn rent
cheapness 812 n.
peppery
pungent 388 adj.
irascible 892 adj.
peppy
dynamic 160 adj.
vigorous 174 adj.
forceful 571 adj.
cheerful 833 adj.
pep talk
stimulant 174 n.
allocution 583 n.
inducement 612 n.
peptic ulcer
digestive disorders
651 n.
per
through 628 adv.
perambulator
pushcart 274 n.
per annum
periodically
141 adv.
per capita
pro rata 783 adv.
perceive
have feeling
374 vb.
see 438 vb.
perceive 447 adj.
detect 484 vb.
know 490 vb.
per cent
ratio 85 n.
percentage
increment 36 n.
extra 40 n.
part 53 n.
ratio 85 n.
perceptible
seeing 438 adj.
visible 443 adj.
perception
vision 438 n.
intellect 447 n.
idea 451 n.
discrimination
463 n.
knowledge 490 n.
sagacity 498 n.

perceptive
sentient 374 adj.
mental 447 adj.
perceptual
sentient 374 adj.
mental 447 adj.
perch
place oneself
187 vb.
dwell 192 vb.
nest 192 n.
long measure
203 n.
land 295 vb.
descend 309 vb.
sit down 311 vb.
fish 365 n.
gauge 465 n.
repose 683 vb.
perchance
by chance 159 adv.
possibly 469 adv.
percipient
sentient 374 adj.
percolate
infiltrate 297 vb.
exude 298 vb.
pass 305 vb.
be wet 341 vb.
irrigate 341 vb.
flow 350 VB.
purify 648 vb.
percolator
pot 194 n.
percussion
orchestra 413 n.
musical instrument
414 n.
perdition
ruin 165 n.
loss 772 n.
condemnation
961 n.
hell 972 n.
peremptory
assertive 532 adj.
authoritative
733 adj.
commanding
737 adj.
obligatory 917 adj.
perennial
lasting 113 adj.
perpetual 115 adj.
unchangeable
153 adj.
flower 366 n.

perestroika
arrangement 62 n.
revolution 149 n.
perfect
past time 125 n.
perfect 646 adj.
perfect 646 vb.
beautiful 841 adj.
shapely 841 adj.
perfection
perfection 646 n.
beauty 841 n.
perfectionist
careful 457 adj.
improving 654 adj.
perfectionist 862 n.
perfidious
false 541 adj.
perfidious 930 adj.
perfidy
perfidy 930 n.
perforate
make concave
  255 vb.
pierce 263 vb.
pass 305 vb.
perform
produce 164 vb.
operate 173 vb.
play music 413 vb.
act 594 vb.
be instrumental
  628 vb.
do 676 vb.
observe 768 vb.
be angry 891 vb.
do one's duty
  917 vb.
performance
effect 157 n.
production 164 n.
representation
  551 n.
dramaturgy 594 n.
action 676 n.
observance 768 n.
celebration 876 n.
duty 917 n.
ministration 988 n.
performer
musician 413 n.
interpreter 520 n.
entertainer 594 n.
doer 676 n.
agent 686 n.
perfume
emit 300 vb.

odour 394 n.
fragrance 396 n.
scent 396 n.
cosmetic 843 n.
perfunctory
incomplete 55 adj.
neglected 458 adj.
negligent 458 adj.
unwilling 598 adj.
imperfect 647 adj.
bungled 695 adj.
indifferent 860 adj.
pergola
arbour 194 n.
perhaps
by chance 159 adv.
possibly 469 adv.
peril
danger 661 n.
perilous
dangerous 661 adj.
perimeter
surroundings
  230 n.
outline 233 n.
enclosure 235 n.
limit 236 n.
period
end 69 n.
era 110 n.
period 110 n.
periodic 110 adj.
haemorrhage
  302 n.
punctuation 547 n.
periodic
periodic 110 adj.
periodical 141 adj.
fitful 142 adj.
periodical
periodical 141 adj.
journal 528 n.
book 589 n.
periodically
periodically
  141 adv.
peripatetic
circuitous 314 adj.
peripheral
irrelevant 10 adj.
distant 199 adj.
exterior 223 adj.
marginal 234 adj.
unimportant
  639 adj.
periphery
distance 199 n.

exteriority 223 n.
surroundings
  230 n.
outline 233 n.
enclosure 235 n.
limit 236 n.
periphrastic
prolix 570 adj.
periscope
telescope 442 n.
perish
decompose 51 vb.
perish 361 vb.
deteriorate 655 vb.
perishing
chilly 380 adj.
cold 380 adj.
peritonitis
digestive disorders
  651 n.
perjury
falsehood 541 n.
untruth 543 n.
perk
extra 40 n.
perks
incentive 612 n.
earnings 771 n.
gift 781 n.
reward 962 n.
perk up
be refreshed
  685 vb.
be cheerful 833 vb.
cheer 833 vb.
perky
cheerful 833 adj.
vain 873 adj.
perm
be curved 248 vb.
crinkle 251 vb.
hairdressing 843 n.
primp 843 vb.
permanence
durability 113 n.
permanence 144 n.
permanent
continuing 108 adj.
lasting 113 adj.
permanent 144 adj.
permeable
porous 263 adj.
permeate
prevail 178 vb.
pervade 189 vb.
infiltrate 297 vb.
pass 305 vb.

permissible
legal 953 adj.
permission
permission 756 n.
permissive
lax 734 adj.
permitting 756 adj.
permissive society
scope 744 n.
unchastity 951 n.
permit
permit 756 n.
permit 756 vb.
permutation
change 143 n.
interchange 151 n.
pernicious
destructive 165 adj.
harmful 645 adj.
pernicious anaemia
blood disease
  651 n.
pernickety
fastidious 862 adj.
peroration
eloquence 579 n.
oration 579 n.
peroxide
bleacher 426 n.
hairwash 843 n.
perpendicular
vertical 215 adj.
straight 249 adj.
perpetrate
do 676 vb.
do wrong 914 adj.
perpetrator
doer 676 n.
agent 686 n.
perpetual
perpetual 115 adj.
perpetuate
perpetuate 115 vb.
perpetuity
perpetuity 115 n.
perplex
bedevil 63 vb.
distract 456 vb.
puzzle 474 vb.
be unintelligible
  517 vb.
be difficult 700 vb.
trouble 827 vb.
perquisite
extra 40 n.
earnings 771 n.
reward 962 n.

per se
singly 88 adv.
persecute
counteract 182 vb.
pursue 619 vb.
ill-treat 645 vb.
be severe 735 vb.
oppress 735 vb.
torment 827 vb.
be hostile 881 vb.
be malevolent
898 vb.
punish 963 vb.
torture 963 vb.
persecution
counteraction
182 n.
prejudice 481 n.
pursuit 619 n.
badness 645 n.
severity 735 n.
annoyance 827 n.
painfulness 827 n.
enmity 881 n.
inhumanity 898 n.
orthodoxism 976 n.
pietism 979 n.
persecutor
tyrant 735 n.
zealot 979 n.
persevere
persevere 600 vb.
persist
stay 144 vb.
go on 146 vb.
persevere 600 vb.
be obstinate
602 vb.
be active 678 vb.
persistent
lasting 113 adj.
strong 162 adj.
remembered
505 adj.
obstinate 602 adj.
person
person 371 n.
personable
personable 841 adj.
personage
person 371 n.
acting 594 n.
bigwig 638 n.
personal
private 80 adj.
special 80 adj.
selfish 932 adj.

personal assistant
stenographer
586 n.
personal details
label 547 n.
personal effects
property 777 n.
personal identification number
treasury 799 n.
personality
character 5 n.
self 80 n.
speciality 80 n.
influence 178 n.
materiality 319 n.
subjectivity 320 n.
spirit 447 n.
bigwig 638 n.
affections 817 n.
sauciness 878 n.
personalized
private 80 adj.
personally
specially 80 adv.
personal remark
scurrility 899 n.
reproach 924 n.
calumny 926 n.
personal stereo
sound 398 n.
gramophone 414 n.
broadcasting
531 n.
amusement 837 n.
persona non grata
enemy 881 n.
personification
metaphor 519 n.
representation
551 n.
personify
materialize 319 vb.
manifest 522 vb.
represent 551 vb.
personnel
personnel 686 n.
armed force 722 n.
perspective
relativeness 9 n.
range 183 n.
length 203 n.
depth 211 n.
convergence 293 n.
view 438 n.
painting 553 n.

perspicacity
sagacity 498 n.
fastidiousness
862 n.
perspicuous
stylistic 566 adj.
perspiration
outflow 298 n.
excretion 302 n.
heat 379 n.
perspire
exude 298 vb.
emit 300 vb.
excrete 302 vb.
be wet 341 vb.
be hot 379 vb.
persuade
influence 178 vb.
make certain
473 vb.
convince 485 vb.
induce 612 vb.
persuasion
classification 77 n.
influence 178 n.
positiveness 473 n.
belief 485 n.
inducement 612 n.
persuasive
influential 178 adj.
plausible 471 adj.
credible 485 adj.
pert
cheerful 833 adj.
impertinent
878 adj.
discourteous
885 adj.
pertain
be related 9 vb.
be included 78 vb.
pertain to
be one's duty
917 vb.
pertinacity
perseverance 600 n.
obstinacy 602 n.
pertinent
relevant 9 adj.
apt 24 adj.
included 78 adj.
perturb
derange 63 vb.
agitate 318 vb.
frighten 854 vb.
pertussis
infection 651 n.

peruse
study 536 vb.
pervade
pervade 189 vb.
pervasive
mixed 43 adj.
universal 79 adj.
influential 178 adj.
ubiquitous 189 adj.
perverse
erroneous 495 adj.
obstinate 602 adj.
wilful 602 adj.
capricious 604 adj.
difficult 700 adj.
disobedient
738 adj.
perversion
misteaching 535 n.
falsehood 541 n.
untruth 543 n.
deterioration
655 n.
misuse 675 n.
illicit love 951 n.
impiety 980 n.
pervert
nonconformist
84 n.
distort 246 vb.
sophisticate
477 vb.
mislead 495 vb.
pervert 655 vb.
cad 938 n.
libertine 952 n.
perverted
erroneous 495 adj.
mistaken 495 adj.
vicious 934 adj.
lecherous 951 adj.
impious 980 adj.
peseta
coinage 797 n.
pessary
surgical dressing
658 n.
pessimism
underestimation
483 n.
dejection 834 n.
hopelessness 853 n.
pessimistic
dejected 834 adj.
hopeless 853 adj.
pest
evil 616 n.

plague 651 n.
worry 825 n.
annoyance 827 n.
hateful object
  888 n.
pester
  recur 139 vb.
  meddle 678 vb.
  torment 827 vb.
  enrage 891 vb.
pesticide
  poison 659 n.
pestilence
  badness 645 n.
  plague 651 n.
pestilential
  hateful 888 adj.
pestle
  hammer 279 n.
  pulverizer 332 n.
pet
  chosen 605 adj.
  please 826 vb.
  love 887 vb.
  caress 889 vb.
  pet 889 vb.
  darling 890 n.
  anger 891 n.
petal
  flower 366 n.
pet aversion
  dislike 861 n.
  enemy 881 n.
  hateful object
    888 n.
peter out
  decrease 37 vb.
  cease 145 vb.
Peter Pan
  youth 130 n.
pétillant
  light 323 adj.
  gaseous 336 adj.
  bubbly 355 adj.
petite
  little 196 adj.
  shapely 841 adj.
petition
  report 524 n.
  ask leave 756 vb.
  request 761 n.
  request 761 vb.
  deprecation 762 n.
  litigate 959 vb.
  litigation 959 n.
  prayers 981 n.

petitioner
  petitioner 763 n.
  accuser 928 n.
petit mal
  nervous disorders
    651 n.
petrel
  bird 365 n.
petrified, be
  quake 854 vb.
petrify
  be dense 324 vb.
  harden 326 vb.
  frighten 854 vb.
  be wonderful
    864 vb.
petrol
  propellant 287 n.
  oil 357 n.
  fuel 385 n.
petroleum
  oil 357 n.
  fuel 385 n.
petrology
  mineralogy 359 n.
petticoat
  underwear 228 n.
  female 373 adj.
  female 373 n.
pettifogging
  trivial 639 adj.
pettishness
  sullenness 893 n.
petty
  inconsiderable
    33 adj.
  little 196 adj.
  unimportant
    639 adj.
  disreputable
    867 adj.
  contemptible
    922 adj.
petty cash
  money 797 n.
petty larceny
  stealing 788 n.
petty officer
  nautical personnel
    270 n.
  naval officer 741 n.
petulant
  discontented
    829 adj.
  irascible 892 adj.
  sullen 893 adj.

pew
  compartment
    194 n.
  seat 218 n.
  church interior
    990 n.
pewter
  a mixture 43 n.
  white thing 427 n.
  greyness 429 n.
peyote
  drug-taking 949 n.
pfennig
  coinage 797 n.
phalanx
  coherence 48 n.
phallus
  genitalia 167 n.
phantasmagoria
  medley 43 n.
phantom
  insubstantial thing
    4 n.
  fantasy 513 n.
  ghost 970 n.
Pharaoh
  sovereign 741 n.
Pharisee
  zealot 979 n.
pharmacist
  druggist 658 n.
pharmacologist
  druggist 658 n.
pharmacopoeia
  medicine 658 n.
pharmacy
  druggist 658 n.
pharyngitis
  respiratory disease
    651 n.
phase
  be identical 13 vb.
  time 117 vb.
  synchronize
    123 vb.
  plan 623 vb.
pheasant
  meat 301 n.
  table bird 365 n.
phenomenal
  substantial 3 adj.
  unusual 84 adj.
  wonderful 864 adj.
phenomenon
  event 154 n.
  prodigy 864 n.

phial
  vessel 194 n.
philanderer
  lover 887 n.
  libertine 952 n.
philanthropic
  friendly 880 adj.
  philanthropic
    901 adj.
  disinterested
    931 adj.
  virtuous 933 adj.
philanthropy
  philanthropy
    901 n.
philatelist
  collector 492 n.
philistine
  ignorance 491 n.
  uninstructed
    491 adj.
  ignoramus 493 n.
  vulgar 847 adj.
  barbaric 869 adj.
  commoner 869 n.
  detractor 926 n.
phillumenist
  collector 492 n.
philologist
  collector 492 n.
  linguist 557 n.
philology
  grammar 564 n.
philomel
  bird 365 n.
philosophic
  content 828 adj.
philosophical
  patient 823 adj.
philosophy
  intellect 447 n.
  philosophy 449 n.
phlebitis
  cardiovascular dis-
    ease 651 n.
phlegm
  excrement 302 n.
  semiliquidity
    354 n.
  sluggishness 679 n.
  moral insensibility
    820 n.
phlegmatic
  slow 278 adj.
  nonactive 677 adj.
  impassive 820 adj.
  indifferent 860 adj.

phobia
  neurosis 503 n.
  worry 825 n.
  phobia 854 n.
  hatred 888 n.
Phoenix
  rara avis 84 n.
  reproduction
  166 n.
  mythical being
  970 n.
phone
  speech sound
  398 n.
  hearing aid 415 n.
  communicate
  524 vb.
phone book
  directory 87 n.
  guidebook 524 n.
phonecard
  credit 802 n.
phoneme
  word 559 n.
  voice 577 n.
phonetic
  sounding 398 adj.
phoney
  false 541 adj.
  spurious 542 adj.
  untrue 543 adj.
  impostor 545 n.
  affected 850 adj.
phosphorescent
  luminous 417 adj.
photo
  photograph 551 vb.
  photography 551 n.
photocall
  publicity 528 n.
photocopier
  imitator 20 n.
  recording instru-
  ment 549 n.
photocopy
  copy 20 vb.
  copy 22 n.
  double 91 vb.
  duplication 91 n.
  photography 551 n.
photo finish
  draw 28 n.
  short distance
  200 n.
  arrival 295 n.
  contest 716 n.

Photofit (tdmk)
  representation
  551 n.
photogenic
  beautiful 841 adj.
photograph
  copy 22 n.
  duplicate 22 n.
  record 548 n.
  photograph 551 vb.
  photography 551 n.
photograph album
  reminder 505 n.
  picture 553 n.
photographer
  recorder 549 n.
  photography 551 n.
photographic
  descriptive 590 adj.
**photographic mem-
ory**
  memory 505 n.
photography
  photography 551 n.
photosensitive
  luminous 417 adj.
Photostat (tdmk)
  copy 22 n.
phrase
  subdivision 53 n.
  musical piece
  412 n.
  tune 412 n.
  phrase 563 n.
  phrase 563 vb.
phrasing
  melody 410 n.
  phrase 563 n.
  style 566 n.
phrenology
  head 213 n.
phylum
  breed 77 n.
physical
  real 1 adj.
  substantial 3 adj.
  material 319 adj.
  sensuous 376 adj.
physical education
  education 534 n.
  exercise 682 n.
physician
  doctor 658 n.
physics
  physics 319 n.
physiognomy
  face 237 n.

  form 243 n.
  feature 445 n.
physiography
  earth sciences
  321 n.
physiological
  biological 358 adj.
physiology
  structure 331 n.
  biology 358 n.
physiotherapy
  therapy 658 n.
physique
  vitality 162 n.
  structure 331 n.
  animality 365 n.
pianissimo
  adagio 412 adv.
piano
  muted 401 adj.
  adagio 412 adv.
  piano 414 n.
piano accordion
  organ 414 n.
pianoforte
  piano 414 n.
piastre
  coinage 797 n.
piazza
  meeting place
  192 n.
  lobby 194 n.
pibroch
  musical piece
  412 n.
picador
  killer 362 n.
  combatant 722 n.
piccolo
  flute 414 n.
pick
  subtract 39 vb.
  sharp point 256 n.
  perforator 263 n.
  cultivate 370 vb.
  play music 413 vb.
  choice 605 n.
  select 605 vb.
  store 632 vb.
  chief thing 638 n.
  elite 644 n.
  acquire 771 vb.
  take 786 vb.
pick a bone with
  dissent 489 vb.
pick and choose
  select 605 vb.

  be fastidious
  862 vb.
pickaxe
  perforator 263 n.
picket
  tie 45 vb.
  place 187 vb.
  circumscribe
  232 vb.
  warner 664 n.
  be obstructive
  702 vb.
  defender 713 n.
picketing
  hindrance 702 n.
picket line
  exclusion 57 n.
pickings
  earnings 771 n.
  taking 786 n.
  booty 790 n.
pickle
  circumstance 8 n.
  complexity 61 n.
  pungency 388 n.
  season 388 vb.
  store 632 vb.
  preserve 666 vb.
  preserver 666 n.
  predicament 700 n.
pickled
  salty 388 adj.
  preserved 666 adj.
  tipsy 949 adj.
pickled onions
  sauce 389 n.
pick-me-up
  stimulant 174 n.
  tonic 658 n.
  excitant 821 n.
pick off
  kill 362 vb.
  fire at 712 vb.
pick on
  blame 924 vb.
  accuse 928 vb.
pick one's brains
  interrogate 459 vb.
pick oneself up
  lift oneself 310 vb.
  be restored 656 vb.
pick out
  subtract 39 vb.
  extract 304 vb.
  see 438 vb.
  discriminate
  463 vb.

decorate 844 vb.
pickpocket
  thief 789 n.
pick up
  elevate 310 vb.
  get better 654 vb.
  be restored 656 vb.
  arrest 747 vb.
  acquire 771 vb.
  take 786 vb.
pick-up
  loose woman
    952 n.
  prostitute 952 n.
pick up the tab
  defray 804 vb.
pickup truck
  lorry 274 n.
picnic
  meal 301 n.
  easy thing 701 n.
  victory 727 n.
  amusement 837 n.
  amuse oneself
    837 vb.
  social gathering
    882 n.
pictorial
  painted 553 adj.
picture
  composition 56 n.
  photography 551 n.
  represent 551 vb.
  picture 553 n.
  describe 590 vb.
  description 590 n.
  a beauty 841 n.
  honours 866 n.
picture house
  cinema 445 n.
  theatre 594 n.
picture postcard
  picture 553 n.
pictures
  film 445 n.
picturesque
  painted 553 adj.
  impressive 821 adj.
  pleasurable
    826 adj.
  beautiful 841 adj.
  ornamental
    844 adj.
picture window
  window 263 n.
piddling
  trivial 639 adj.

pidgin English
  language 557 n.
  dialect 560 adj.
pie
  dish 301 n.
  pastries and cakes
    301 n.
  bird 365 n.
  print-type 587 n.
piebald
  horse 273 n.
  pied 437 adj.
piece
  piece 53 n.
  component 58 n.
  unit 88 n.
  product 164 n.
  textile 222 n.
  dish 301 n.
  meal 301 n.
  musical piece
    412 n.
  reading matter
    589 n.
  coinage 797 n.
pièce de résistance
  dish 301 n.
  elite 644 n.
  exceller 644 n.
  masterpiece 694 n.
piece of cake
  easy thing 701 n.
piece of one's mind
  reprimand 924 n.
piece rate
  price 809 n.
piece together
  join 45 vb.
  make complete
    54 vb.
  decipher 520 vb.
  repair 656 vb.
piecework
  labour 682 n.
pie chart
  statistics 86 n.
pied-à-terre
  abode 192 n.
pie-eyed
  tipsy 949 adj.
pie in the sky
  fantasy 513 n.
pier
  stable 192 n.
  pillar 218 n.
  stand 218 n.

  support 218 n.
  See **pillar**
  projection 254 n.
  goal 295 n.
  arena 724 n.
pierce
  be sharp 256 vb.
  pierce 263 vb.
  refrigerate 382 vb.
  impress 821 vb.
piercing
  cold 380 adj.
  loud 400 adj.
  strident 407 adj.
pierrot
  entertainer 594 n.
piety
  feeling 818 n.
  piety 979 n.
piffling
  meaningless
    515 adj.
  trivial 639 adj.
pig
  pig 365 n.
  dirty person 649 n.
  cad 938 n.
  sensualist 944 n.
  glutton 947 n.
  police 955 n.
pigeon
  bird 365 n.
  function 622 n.
pigeon-chested
  deformed 246 adj.
pigeon-fancier
  breeder 369 n.
pigeonhole
  class 62 vb.
  sorting 62 n.
  classification 77 n.
  put off 136 vb.
  place 185 n.
  compartment
    194 n.
  receptacle 194 n.
  orifice 263 n.
  be neglectful
    458 vb.
pigeon post
  postal communica-
    tions 531 n.
pigeon-toed
  deformed 246 adj.
pig-farming
  animal husbandry
    369 n.

piggery
  stock farm 369 n.
piggybank
  treasury 799 n.
pig-headed
  obstinate 602 adj.
  wilful 602 adj.
pig in a poke
  uncertainty 474 n.
  gambling 618 n.
piglet
  young creature
    132 n.
  pig 365 n.
pigment
  colour 425 vb.
  pigment 425 n.
pigmentation
  hue 425 n.
  blackness 428 n.
pigmy
  dwarf 196 n.
  dwarfish 196 adj.
  little 196 adj.
pigpen
  stable 192 n.
pig's ear
  bungling 695 n.
pigskin
  skin 226 n.
  bookbinding 589 n.
pigsty
  cattle pen 369 n.
  sink 649 n.
pigswill
  provender 301 n.
pigtail
  hanging object
    217 n.
  crossing 222 n.
  hair 259 n.
  hairdressing 843 n.
pike
  high land 209 n.
  sharp point 256 n.
  fish 365 n.
  spear 723 n.
pikestaff
  high structure
    209 n.
pilaff
  dish 301 n.
pilaster
  pillar 218 n.
pilau
  dish 301 n.

pilchard
fish food 301 n.

pile
fastening 47 n.
accumulation 74 n.
bring together
74 vb.
edifice 164 n.
high structure
209 n.
pillar 218 n.
weaving 222 n.
texture 331 n.
heraldry 547 n.
store 632 vb.
acqulsition 771 n.
funds 797 n.
wealth 800 n.

piledriver
ram 279 n.

pile in
fill 54 vb.
start out 296 vb.
enter 297 vb.

pile it on
exaggerate 546 vb.
superabound
637 vb.

piles
swelling 253 n.
digestive disorders
651 n.

pile up
bring together
74 vb.
exaggerate 546 vb.
store 632 vb.
acquire 771 vb.

pileup
accumulation 74 n.
collision 279 n.

pilfer
steal 788 vb.

pilgrim
traveller 268 n.
pietist 979 n.
worshipper 981 n.

pilgrimage
land travel 267 n.
undertaking 672 n.
piety 979 n.
act of worship
981 n.

pill
contraception
172 n.
sphere 252 n.

874

medicine 658 n.
punishment 963 n.

pillage
plundering 788 n.
rob 788 vb.
booty 790 n.

pillar
fixture 153 n.
high structure
209 n.
pillar 218 n.
monument 548 n.

pillar of society
person of repute
866 n.
good person 937 n.

pillbox
headgear 228 n.
cylinder 252 n.
fort 713 n.

pillion
seat 218 n.

pillory
fetter 747 vb.
lockup 748 n.
satirize 851 vb.
shame 867 vb.
criticize 924 vb.
defame 926 vb.
accuse 928 vb.
punish 963 vb.
pillory 964 n.

pillow
cushion 218 n.
support 218 vb.
softness 327 n.

pilot
precursor 66 n.
driver 268 n.
navigate 269 vb.
navigator 270 n.
aeronaut 271 n.
director 690 n.

pilotage
navigation 269 n.

pilot light
lighter 385 n.

pilot scheme
experiment 461 n.
plan 623 n.
preparation 669 n.

pimp
provide 633 vb.
be impure 951 vb.
bawd 952 n.

pimple
lowness 210 n.

swelling 253 n.
skin disease 651 n.
blemish 845 n.

pimply
convex 253 adj.

PIN
treasury 799 n.

pin
join 45 vb.
fastening 47 n.
sharp point 256 n.
perforator 263 n.
trifle 639 n.
restrain 747 vb.
retain 778 vb.
jewellery 844 n.

pinball
ball game 837 n.

pince-nez
eyeglass 442 n.

pincers
tool 630 n.
pincers 778 n.

pinch
small quantity
33 n.
make smaller
198 vb.
make thin 206 vb.
notch 260 vb.
give pain 377 vb.
pang 377 n.
touch 378 vb.
refrigerate 382 vb.
adversity 731 n.
arrest 747 vb.
steal 788 vb.
poverty 801 n.
economize 814 vb.
be parsimonious
816 vb.

pinched
lean 206 adj.
narrow 206 adj.

pincushion
receptacle 194 n.
porosity 263 n.

pin down
place 187 vb.
compel 740 vb.
retain 778 vb.

pine
tree 366 n.
desire 859 vb.
court 889 vb.

pineapple
fruit and vegetables
301 n.

ping
roll 403 n.
roll 403 vb.
resonance 404 n.
resound 404 vb.

pingpong
ball game 837 n.

pinion
tie 45 vb.
wing 271 n.
fetter 747 vb.
fetter 748 n.
take 786 vb.

pink
moderate 177 adj.
notch 260 vb.
pierce 263 vb.
plant 366 n.
red 431 adj.

pink elephants
alcoholism 949 n.

pink of condition
health 650 n.

pin money
dower 777 n.
money 797 n.
receipt 807 n.

pinnacle
superiority 34 n.
crown 213 vb.
summit 213 n.
perfection 646 n.

pin on
affix 45 vb.
accuse 928 vb.

pin one's hopes on
believe 485 vb.
hope 852 vb.

pinpoint
small thing 33 n.
specify 80 vb.
place 185 n.
place 187 vb.
minuteness 196 n.
orientate 281 vb.

pinprick
small thing 33 n.
shallowness 212 n.
trifle 639 n.
annoyance 827 n.
painfulness 827 n.
enrage 891 vb.
resentment 891 n.

pins-and-needles
pang 377 n.
tingling 378 n.
pin-stripe
pattern 844 n.
pint
metrology 465 n.
pint-size
little 196 adj.
pin-up
picture 553 n.
a beauty 841 n.
pioneer
come before 64 vb.
precursor 66 n.
initiate 68 vb.
settler 191 n.
front 237 n.
traveller 268 n.
preceding 283 n.
prepare 669 vb.
pious
pious 979 adj.
pip
timekeeper 117 n.
flower 366 n.
signal 547 n.
pip at the post
be cunning 698 vb.
pipe
vat 194 n.
cylinder 252 n.
tube 263 n.
conduit 351 n.
blow 352 vb.
air pipe 353 n.
ululate 409 vb.
play music 413 vb.
sing 413 vb.
flute 414 n.
metrology 465 n.
pipe band
orchestra 413 n.
pipe cleaner
tobacco 388 n.
cleaning utensil
648 n.
piped music
music 412 n.
pipe down
cease 145 vb.
be quiescent
266 vb.
be silent 399 vb.
hush 399 int.
be taciturn 582 vb.

pipe dream
insubstantial thing
4 n.
fantasy 513 n.
pleasurableness
826 n.
aspiration 852 n.
pipeline
tube 263 n.
transport 272 n.
conduit 351 n.
store 632 n.
provision 633 n.
pipe of peace
tobacco 388 n.
peace 717 n.
peace offering
719 n.
piper
instrumentalist
413 n.
pipette
vessel 194 n.
tube 263 n.
pipe up
cry 408 vb.
speak 579 vb.
piping
edging 234 n.
hem 234 vb.
tube 263 n.
stridor 407 n.
trimming 844 n.
piping hot
hot 379 adj.
pips
broadcast 531 n.
badge 547 n.
badge of rank
743 n.
pipsqueak
dwarf 196 n.
piquant
pungent 388 adj.
savoury 390 adj.
exciting 821 adj.
witty 839 adj.
impure 951 adj.
pique
excite 821 vb.
hurt 827 vb.
discontent 829 n.
huff 891 vb.
resentment 891 n.
piracy
imitation 20 n.
copy 22 n.

borrowing 785 n.
taking 786 n.
plundering 788 n.
piranha
fish 365 n.
pirate
copy 20 vb.
imitator 20 n.
mariner 270 n.
militarist 722 n.
borrow 785 vb.
appropriate
786 vb.
steal 788 vb.
robber 789 n.
thief 789 n.
bad person 938 n.
pirate radio
broadcasting
531 n.
pirate ship
warship 722 n.
pirouette
rotate 315 vb.
rotation 315 n.
ballet 594 n.
pistil
flower 366 n.
pistol
pistol 723 n.
piston
stopper 264 n.
pit
depth 211 n.
interiority 224 n.
cavity 255 n.
excavation 255 n.
tunnel 263 n.
listener 415 n.
onlookers 441 n.
trap 542 n.
playgoer 594 n.
theatre 594 n.
pitfall 663 n.
workshop 687 n.
stratagem 698 n.
blemish 845 vb.
pit-a-pat
agitation 318 n.
faintness 401 n.
roll 403 n.
pitch
adjust 24 vb.
degree 27 n.
serial place 73 n.
territory 184 n.
place 185 n.

height 209 n.
summit 213 n.
be oblique 220 vb.
obliquity 220 n.
coat 226 vb.
voyage 269 vb.
propel 287 vb.
fluctuation 317 n.
oscillate 317 vb.
be agitated 318 vb.
resin 357 n.
sound 398 n.
harmonize 410 vb.
musical note
410 n.
black thing 428 n.
voice 577 n.
arena 724 n.
sale 793 n.
pitch-dark
dark 418 adj.
pitched
adjusted 24 adj.
pitched battle
fight 716 n.
battle 718 n.
pitcher
vessel 194 n.
pitchfork
propel 287 vb.
farm tool 370 n.
pitch in
aid 703 vb.
cooperate 706 vb.
participate 775 vb.
pitch into
attack 712 vb.
fight 716 vb.
criticize 924 vb.
pitfall
pitfall 663 n.
pith
substance 3 n.
essential part 5 n.
interiority 224 n.
centre 225 n.
pulpiness 356 n.
meaning 514 n.
pithy
substantial 3 adj.
aphoristic 496 adj.
meaningful
514 adj.
concise 569 adj.
witty 839 adj.
pitiable
unhappy 825 adj.

contemptible
    922 adj.
pitiful
    distressing 827 adj.
    lamenting 836 adj.
    disreputable
        867 adj.
    benevolent 897 adj.
pitiless
    pitiless 906 adj.
pits, the
    lowness 210 n.
    misfortune 731 n.
pitta bread
    cereals 301 n.
pittance
    small quantity
        33 n.
    insufficiency 636 n.
    portion 783 n.
pitted
    rough 259 adj.
pitter-patter
    oscillation 317 n.
    faintness 401 n.
pity
    be lenient 736 vb.
    pity 905 n.
    pity 905 vb.
pivot
    pivot 218 n.
pivotal
    crucial 137 adj.
    central 225 adj.
    important 638 adj.
pivot on
    depend 157 vb.
pixel
    image 551 n.
pixie
    elf 970 n.
pixilated
    crazy 503 adj.
    tipsy 949 adj.
pizza
    dish 301 n.
pizzazz
    vigorousness 174 n.
    vigour 571 n.
pizzeria
    café 192 n.
pizzicato
    adagio 412 adv.
placable
    benevolent 897 adj.
placard
    exhibit 522 n.

advertisement
    528 n.
placate
    pacify 719 vb.
place
    state 7 n.
    grade 73 vb.
    serial place 73 n.
    place 185 n.
    place 187 vb.
    house 192 n.
    authority 733 n.
placebo
    medicine 658 n.
place in the sun
    palmy days 730 n.
    desire 859 n.
placement
    location 187 n.
placenta
    sequel 67 n.
    obstetrics 167 n.
place of residence
    locality 187 n.
    abode 192 n.
placid
    inexcitable
        823 adj.
placket
    garment 228 n.
    opening 263 n.
plagiarize
    copy 20 vb.
    repeat 106 vb.
    fake 541 vb.
    borrow 785 vb.
    appropriate
        786 vb.
    steal 788 vb.
plague
    evil 616 n.
    harm 645 vb.
    plague 651 n.
    bane 659 n.
    adversity 731 n.
    oppress 735 vb.
    annoyance 827 n.
    torment 827 vb.
    ruffian 904 n.
plaice
    fish food 301 n.
plaid
    chequer 437 n.
    variegated 437 adj.
plain
    complete 54 adj.
    plain 348 n,

obvious 443 adj.
    manifest 522 adj.
    stylistic 566 adj.
    plain 573 adj.
    ugly 842 adj.
    needlework 844 n.
    temperate 942 adj.
plain as a pikestaff
    obvious 443 adj.
    intelligible 516 adj.
    manifest 522 adj.
plain sailing
    navigation 269 n.
    easy thing 701 n.
plainsong
    vocal music 412 n.
    act of worship
        981 n.
    hymn 981 n.
plaint
    lament 836 n.
    accusation 928 n.
plaintiff
    malcontent 829 n.
    dueness 915 n.
    accuser 928 n.
    litigant 959 n.
plaintive
    lamenting 836 adj.
plait
    tie 45 vb.
    ligature 47 n.
    crossing 222 n.
    weave 222 vb.
    hair 259 n.
    fold 261 n.
plan
    itinerary 267 n.
    structure 331 n.
    guidebook 524 n.
    map 551 n.
    plan 623 n.
    plan 623 vb.
plane
    flat 216 adj.
    flatten 216 vb.
    horizontality
        216 n.
    sharp edge 256 n.
    smooth 258 vb.
    smoother 258 n.
    fly 271 vb.
    aircraft 276 n.
    tree 366 n.
plane sailing
    navigation 269 n.

planet
    rotator 315 n.
    planet 321 n.
planetarium
    astronomy 321 n.
plank
    shelf 218 n.
    conceal 525 vb.
    materials 631 n.
planning
    arrangement 62 n.
    production 164 n.
    plan 623 n.
    preparation 669 n.
plant
    cause 156 vb.
    place 187 vb.
    implant 303 vb.
    plant 366 n.
    vegetate 366 vb.
    cultivate 370 vb.
    trap 542 n.
    equipment 630 n.
    property 777 n.
    false charge 928 n.
plantation
    wood 366 n.
    lands 777 n.
planter
    producer 164 n.
    settler 191 n.
    vessel 194 n.
    farmer 370 n.
    garden 370 n.
plaque
    dirt 649 n.
    honours 866 n.
plasma
    matter 319 n.
    blood 335 n.
    fluid 335 n.
plaster
    adhesive 47 n.
    coat 226 vb.
    covering 226 n.
    facing 226 n.
    doctor 658 vb.
    medicine 658 n.
    See surgical
        dressing
    surgical dressing
        658 n.
plaster cast
    wrapping 226 n.
    sculpture 554 n.

plastered
dead drunk
949 adj.
plasterer
artisan 686 n.
plaster of Paris
surgical dressing
658 n.
plaster saint
paragon 646 n.
plastic
substituted 150 adj.
changeful 152 adj.
flexible 327 adj.
softness 327 n.
spurious 542 adj.
materials 631 n.
borrowing 785 n.
credit 802 n.
impressible
819 adj.
plastic bag
bag 194 n.
carrier 273 n.
Plasticine (tdmk)
softness 327 n.
sculpture 554 n.
plasticity
softness 327 n.
plastic money
borrowing 785 n.
credit 802 n.
plastic surgery
surgery 658 n.
beautification
843 n.
plat du jour
dish 301 n.
plate
plate 194 n.
coat 226 vb.
covering 226 n.
circle 250 n.
tooth 256 n.
photography 551 n.
picture 553 n.
print-type 587 n.
edition 589 n.
plateau
high land 209 n.
vertex 213 n.
horizontality
216 n.
plain 348 n.
plate glass
transparency
422 n.

platelet
blood 335 n.
platform
layer 207 n.
horizontality
216 n.
stand 218 n.
publication 528 n.
publicity 528 n.
policy 623 n.
railway 624 n.
arena 724 n.
platinum
white thing 427 n.
platinum blond(e)
achromatism
426 n.
whitish 427 adj.
yellowness 433 n.
platitude
truth 494 n.
maxim 496 n.
lack of meaning
515 n.
Platonic
pure 950 adj.
Platonic love
love 887 n.
platoon
band 74 n.
formation 722 n.
platter
plate 194 n.
horizontality
216 n.
gramophone 414 n.
plaudits
rejoicing 835 n.
applause 923 n.
plausible
plausible 471 adj.
credible 485 adj.
hypocritical
541 adj.
flattering 925 adj.
play
composition 56 n.
operate 173 vb.
influence 178 n.
range 183 n.
ascend 308 vb.
oscillate 317 vb.
flow 350 VB.
play music 413 vb.
act 594 vb.
stage play 594 n.
action 676 n.

contend 716 vb.
amusement 837 n.
amuse oneself
837 vb.
revel 837 n.
caress 889 vb.
play-acting
duplicity 541 vb.
hypocritical
541 adj.
acting 594 n.
play at
be inattentive
456 vb.
amuse oneself
837 vb.
playback
repetition 106 n.
gramophone 414 n.
play ball
cooperate 706 vb.
playboy, playgirl
beau monde 848 n.
sensualist 944 n.
play down
moderate 177 vb.
underestimate
483 vb.
extenuate 927 vb.
player
musician 413 n.
interpreter 520 n.
actor 594 n.
gambler 618 n.
doer 676 n.
agent 686 n.
player 837 n.
play footsie
caress 889 vb.
play for time
be cunning 698 vb.
be obstructive
702 vb.
playful
merry 833 adj.
witty 839 adj.
innocent 935 adj.
play games
amuse oneself
837 vb.
playground
arena 724 n.
pleasure ground
837 n.
playgroup
school 539 n.

play havoc with
harm 645 vb.
impair 655 vb.
playing
music 412 n.
playing field
arena 724 n.
pleasure ground
837 n.
play into one's hands
blunder 495 vb.
play it by ear
intuit 476 vb.
be cautious 858 vb.
play it by the book
be cautious 858 vb.
play on
use 673 vb.
playmate
colleague 707 n.
chum 880 n.
playroom
chamber 194 n.
play safe
be cautious 858 vb.
play the concertina
play music 413 vb.
play the fool
rampage 61 vb.
be absurd 497 vb.
be foolish 499 vb.
amuse oneself
837 vb.
be ridiculous
849 vb.
be rash 857 vb.
play the game
behave 688 vb.
plaything
plaything 837 n.
plaything of the gods
unlucky person
731 n.
play to the gallery
act 594 vb.
be affected 850 vb.
be ostentatious
875 vb.
play tricks on
fool 542 vb.
play truant
be absent 190 vb.
disappear 446 vb.
run away 620 vb.
relinquish 621 vb.
fail in duty 918 vb.

play up
overestimate
482 vb.
be obstructive
702 vb.
disobey 738 vb.
play upon
motivate 612 vb.
play with fire
be in danger
661 vb.
be rash 857 vb.
playwright
author 589 n.
dramatist 594 n.
plea
testimony 466 n.
argument 475 n.
pretext 614 n.
request 761 n.
vindication 927 n.
litigation 959 n.
plead
testify 466 vb.
argue 475 vb.
plead 614 vb.
do law 958 vb.
plead guilty
assent 488 vb.
confess 526 vb.
accuse 928 vb.
be guilty 936 vb.
stand trial 959 vb.
condemn 961 vb.
pleasant
pleasant 376 adj.
pleasurable
826 adj.
amusing 837 adj.
pleasantry
wit 839 n.
please
please 826 vb.
amuse 837 vb.
pleased
willing 597 adj.
pleased 824 adj.
content 828 adj.
**pleased as a dog with
two tails**
proud 871 adj.
pleased as Punch
pleased 824 adj.
proud 871 adj.
pleasurable
pleasurable
826 adj.

pleasure
pleasure 376 n.
amusement 837 n.
pleat
garment 228 n.
fold 261 n.
plebeian
commoner 869 n.
plebeian 869 adj.
plebiscite
judgment 480 n.
vote 605 n.
decree 737 n.
legislation 953 n.
plectrum
stringed instrument
414 n.
pledge
drink 301 vb.
affirm 532 vb.
oath 532 n.
promise 764 n.
promise 764 vb.
give security
767 vb.
security 767 n.
toast 876 vb.
duty 917 n.
plenary
complete 54 adj.
plenitude
greatness 32 n.
plenitude 54 n.
plenteous
plentiful 635 adj.
liberal 813 adj.
plentiful
great 32 adj.
plentiful 635 adj.
plenty
plenty 635 n.
plethora
redundance 637 n.
satiety 863 n.
pleurisy
respiratory disease
651 n.
pliable
flexible 327 adj.
pliant
conformable
83 adj.
flexible 327 adj.
irresolute 601 adj.
tractable 701 adj.
submitting 721 adj.
servile 879 adj.

pliers
tool 630 n.
pincers 778 n.
plight
state 7 n.
circumstance 8 n.
adversity 731 n.
promise 764 n.
plight one's troth
promise 764 vb.
court 889 vb.
wed 894 vb.
Plimsoll line
limit 236 n.
gauge 465 n.
indicator 547 n.
plimsolls
footwear 228 n.
plinth
base 214 n.
stand 218 n.
plod
walk 267 vb.
move slowly
278 vb.
persevere 600 vb.
work 682 vb.
plonk
wine 301 n.
nonresonance
405 n.
plop
descend 309 vb.
plunge 313 vb.
nonresonance
405 n.
plosive
speech sound
398 n.
plot
piece 53 n.
territory 184 n.
place 185 n.
garden 370 n.
topic 452 n.
represent 551 vb.
narrative 590 n.
dramaturgy 594 n.
plot 623 n.
plot 623 vb.
prepare 669 vb.
lands 777 n.
plot one's course
orientate 281 vb.
plotter
deceiver 545 n.
planner 623 n.

slyboots 698 n.
plough
cut 46 vb.
groove 262 vb.
star 321 n.
cultivate 370 vb.
farm tool 370 n.
disapprove 924 vb.
ploughed
unsuccessful
728 adj.
ploughman
farmer 370 n.
country-dweller
869 n.
ploughman's lunch
meal 301 n.
ploughshare
sharp edge 256 n.
farm tool 370 n.
plough through
travel 267 vb.
ploy
contrivance 623 n.
stratagem 698 n.
pluck
disunite 46 vb.
vitality 162 n.
vigorousness 174 n.
uncover 229 vb.
draw 288 vb.
extract 304 vb.
agitate 318 vb.
cultivate 370 vb.
play music 413 vb.
resolution 599 n.
stamina 600 n.
fleece 786 vb.
take 786 vb.
courage 855 n.
**pluck at one's heart-
strings**
attract 291 vb.
sadden 834 vb.
pluck up courage
take courage
855 vb.
plucky
courageous
855 adj.
plug
covering 226 n.
close 264 vb.
stopper 264 n.
staunch 350 VB.
tobacco 388 n.
advertise 528 vb.

PLU

advertisement
528 n.
emphasize 532 vb.
plug away
persevere 600 vb.
plum
fruit and vegetables
301 n.
purple 436 adj.
purpleness 436 n.
elite 644 n.
trophy 729 n.
taking 786 n.
desired object
859 n.
plumage
plumage 259 n.
plumb
complete 54 adj.
be deep 211 vb.
vertical 215 adj.
measure 465 vb.
plumber
mender 656 n.
artisan 686 n.
plumbing
excretion 302 n.
cleansing 648 n.
plumbline
verticality 215 n.
plumb the depths
be deep 211 vb.
plume
plumage 259 n.
trimming 844 n.
plum in one's mouth
speech defect
580 n.
plummet
verticality 215 n.
be in motion
265 vb.
sailing aid 269 n.
descend 309 vb.
tumble 309 vb.
founder 313 vb.
plunge 313 vb.
plunge 313 vb.
gravity 322 n.
plump
fleshy 195 adj.
plunge 313 vb.
nonresonance
405 n.
plump for
choose 605 vb.

PLY

plump up
enlarge 197 vb.
plunder
acquisition 771 n.
rob 788 vb.
booty 790 n.
plunge
decrease 37 n.
be deep 211 vb.
be in motion
265 vb.
move fast 277 vb.
impel 279 vb.
plunge 313 n.
plunge 313 vb.
be agitated 318 vb.
drench 341 vb.
plunge into
enter 297 vb.
undertake 672 vb.
plunging
deep 211 adj.
aquatics 269 n.
plunging neckline
bareness 229 n.
pluperfect
past time 125 n.
plural
plural 101 adj.
grammatical
564 adj.
pluralism
government 733 n.
plurality
plurality 101 n.
plus
difference 15 n.
in addition 38 adv.
plus fours
trousers 228 n.
plush
softness 327 n.
rich 800 adj.
plushy
ostentatious
875 adj.
plutocrat
rich person 800 n.
plutonium
poison 659 n.
pluvial
humid 341 adj.
ply
layer 207 n.
fold 261 n.
voyage 269 vb.
touch 378 vb.

POC

busy oneself
622 vb.
use 673 vb.
do 676 vb.
ply one's trade
do 676 vb.
plywood
materials 631 n.
pneumatic
soft 327 adj.
gaseous 336 adj.
airy 340 adj.
pneumatic drill
perforator 263 n.
pneumoconiosis
respiratory disease
651 n.
pneumonia
infection 651 n.
respiratory disease
651 n.
poach
cook 301 vb.
encroach 306 vb.
hunt 619 vb.
steal 788 vb.
poacher
hunter 619 n.
thief 789 n.
pocked
mottled 437 adj.
pocket
classification 77 n.
place 185 n.
little 196 adj.
insert 303 vb.
receive 782 vb.
take 786 vb.
steal 788 vb.
be patient 823 vb.
forgive 909 vb.
pocket book
case 194 n.
treasury 799 n.
pocket-handkerchief
little 196 adj.
pocket money
money 797 n.
receipt 807 n.
pocket-size
little 196 adj.
pockmark
cavity 255 n.
make concave
255 vb.
skin disease 651 n.
blemish 845 n.

POI

blemish 845 vb.
pod
receptacle 194 n.
skin 226 n.
uncover 229 vb.
flower 366 n.
podgy
fleshy 195 adj.
soft 327 adj.
podium
stand 218 n.
poem
poem 593 n.
a beauty 841 n.
poet
producer 164 n.
poet 593 n.
poetic
imaginative
513 adj.
poetic 593 adj.
poetic justice
retaliation 714 n.
justice 913 n.
vindication 927 n.
punishment 963 n.
poetic licence
ideality 513 n.
poetry 593 n.
freedom 744 n.
poet laureate
poet 593 n.
poetry
literature 557 n.
poetry 593 n.
po-faced
serious 834 adj.
pogo stick
plaything 837 n.
pogrom
slaughter 362 n.
poignancy
pungency 388 n.
point
juncture 8 n.
degree 27 n.
small thing 33 n.
extremity 69 n.
serial place 73 n.
instant 116 n.
place 185 n.
situation 186 n.
minuteness 196 n.
vertex 213 n.
projection 254 n.
sharpen 256 vb.
sharp point 256 n.

aim 281 vb.
point to 281 vb.
topic 452 n.
reasons 475 n.
gesticulate 547 vb.
indicate 547 vb.
punctuation 547 n.
lettering 586 n.
wit 839 n.
point a finger at
accuse 928 vb.
point at
aim at 617 vb.
not respect 921 vb.
despise 922 vb.
accuse 928 vb.
point blank
towards 281 adv.
point duty
traffic control
305 n.
pointed
keen 174 adj.
sharp 256 adj.
convergent 293 adj.
obvious 443 adj.
rational 475 adj.
meaningful
514 adj.
assertive 532 adj.
witty 839 adj.
pointer
dog 365 n.
indication 547 n.
indicator 547 n.
pointless
prolix 570 adj.
feeble 572 adj.
useless 641 adj.
point of no return
juncture 8 n.
limit 236 n.
goal 295 n.
point of view
view 438 n.
idea 451 n.
bias 481 n.
opinion 485 n.
point out
specify 80 vb.
point to 281 vb.
attract notice
455 vb.
show 522 vb.
inform 524 vb.
indicate 547 vb.

points
advantage 34 n.
divergence 294 n.
railway 624 n.
point the way
come before 64 vb.
indicate 547 vb.
point to
focus 76 vb.
attribute 158 vb.
point to 281 vb.
attract notice
455 vb.
make likely
471 vb.
predict 511 vb.
mean 514 vb.
point-to-point
equitation 267 n.
racing 716 n.
point up
manifest 522 vb.
emphasize 532 vb.
poise
equalize 28 vb.
look 445 n.
conduct 688 vb.
inexcitability
823 n.
poison
destroy 165 vb.
destroyer 168 n.
alcoholic drink
301 n.
murder 362 vb.
be unpalatable
391 vb.
evil 616 n.
badness 645 n.
poison 659 n.
enrage 891 vb.
be malevolent
898 vb.
poisoner
murderer 362 n.
offender 904 n.
poison gas
gas 336 n.
poison 659 n.
weapon 723 n.
poisonous
destructive 165 adj.
deadly 362 adj.
unsavoury 391 adj.
harmful 645 adj.
diseased 651 adj.
toxic 653 adj.

dangerous 661 adj.
paining 827 adj.
poison pen
correspondent
588 n.
detractor 926 n.
poke
bag 194 n.
pierce 263 vb.
touch 378 vb.
gesticulate 547 vb.
poke fun at
be witty 839 vb.
poke one's nose in
interfere 231 vb.
be curious 453 vb.
meddle 678 vb.
poker
furnace 383 n.
card game 837 n.
poker-faced
still 266 adj.
unintelligible
517 adj.
reticent 525 adj.
impassive 820 adj.
inexcitable
823 adj.
serious 834 adj.
poky
little 196 adj.
restraining
747 adj.
polar
ending 69 adj.
topmost 213 adj.
opposite 240 adj.
cold 380 adj.
polar bear
mammal 365 n.
polarity
polarity 14 n.
tendency 179 n.
counteraction
182 n.
contraposition
240 n.
Polaroid (tdmk)
picture 553 n.
**Polaroid (tdmk) cam-
era**
camera 442 n.
polder
land 344 n.
pole
extremity 69 n.

long measure
203 n.
high structure
209 n.
summit 213 n.
verticality 215 n.
pillar 218 n.
pivot 218 n.
centre 225 n.
limit 236 n.
propeller 269 n.
impel 279 vb.
gauge 465 n.
tool 630 n.
poleaxe
kill 362 vb.
slaughter 362 vb.
axe 723 n.
polecat
mammal 365 n.
stench 397 n.
polemics
argument 475 n.
contention 716 n.
pole position
advantage 34 n.
victory 727 n.
poles apart
be contrary 14 vb.
contrariety 14 n.
contrary 14 adj.
different 15 adj.
against 240 adv.
contraposition
240 n.
Pole Star
star 321 n.
pole vault
ascent 308 n.
leap 312 n.
leap 312 vb.
police
order 60 vb.
safeguard 660 vb.
manage 689 vb.
rule 733 vb.
restrain 747 vb.
police 955 n.
police force
police 955 n.
police officer
police 955 n.
police state
despotism 733 n.
police station
lockup 748 n.

policy
policy 623 n.
polio
infection 651 n.
nervous disorders
651 n.
polish
facing 226 n.
smooth 258 vb.
smoother 258 n.
smoothness 258 n.
friction 333 n.
rub 333 vb.
light 417 n.
reflection 417 n.
elegance 575 n.
clean 648 vb.
amendment 654 n.
make better
654 vb.
beauty 841 n.
good taste 846 n.
be ostentatious
875 vb.
ostentation 875 n.
polished
smooth 258 adj.
luminous 417 adj.
undimmed
417 adj.
literary 557 adj.
elegant 575 adj.
clean 648 adj.
polish off
be active 678 vb.
carry through
725 vb.
polite
courteous 884 adj.
respectful 920 adj.
politic
intelligent 498 adj.
wise 498 adj.
advisable 642 adj.
skilful 694 adj.
political
governmental
733 adj.
politician
planner 623 n.
manager 690 n.
expert 696 n.
political party
708 n.
politics
tactics 688 n.
government 733 n.

polka
musical piece
412 n.
dance 837 n.
polka dot
mottle 437 n.
pattern 844 n.
poll
number 86 vb.
numeration 86 n.
statistics 86 n.
head 213 n.
enquiry 459 n.
judgment 480 n.
vote 605 n.
vote 605 vb.
pollard
make smaller
198 vb.
tree 366 n.
pollen
genitalia 167 n.
powder 332 n.
flower 366 n.
pollinate
generate 167 vb.
polling
vote 605 n.
polling booth
electorate 605 n.
polls
vote 605 n.
pollster
enquirer 459 n.
poll tax
tax 809 n.
pollute
harm 645 vb.
make unclean
649 vb.
impair 655 vb.
misuse 675 vb.
pollution
uncleanness 649 n.
infection 651 n.
insalubrity 653 n.
impairment 655 n.
poison 659 n.
misuse 675 n.
slur 867 n.
polo
ball game 837 n.
polo neck
jersey 228 n.
neckline 228 n.
shirt 228 n.

poltergeist
elf 970 n.
ghost 970 n.
spiritualism 984 n.
poltroon
coward 856 n.
poly
academy 539 n.
poly bag
bag 194 n.
carrier 273 n.
polyester
textile 222 n.
polyethylene
materials 631 n.
polygamy
type of marriage
894 n.
polyglot
speaking 579 adj.
polygon
plurality 101 n.
angular figure
247 n.
polymorphous
multiform 82 adj.
polyp
swelling 253 n.
polystyrene
wrapping 226 n.
lining 227 n.
materials 631 n.
polysyllabic
long 203 adj.
diffuse 570 adj.
polytechnic
academy 539 n.
polythene
wrapping 226 n.
materials 631 n.
polythene bag
bag 194 n.
polyunsaturates
food content 301 n.
polyurethane
resin 357 n.
pomade
unguent 357 n.
pomander
scent 396 n.
pomegranate
fruit and vegetables
301 n.
pomelo
fruit and vegetables
301 n.

pommel
handle 218 n.
sphere 252 n.
pomp
pride 871 n.
ostentation 875 n.
**pomp and circum-
stance**
ostentation 875 n.
pompom
trimming 844 n.
pompous
proud 871 adj.
vain 873 adj.
ostentatious
875 adj.
ponce
bawd 952 n.
ponce about
be affected 850 vb.
pond
shallowness 212 n.
lake 346 n.
ponder
meditate 449 vb.
think 449 vb.
estimate 480 vb.
ponderous
weighty 322 adj.
dull 840 adj.
pong
odour 394 n.
smell 394 vb.
stench 397 n.
stink 397 vb.
deteriorate 655 vb.
pontiff
sovereign 741 n.
priest 986 n.
pontificate
dogmatize 473 vb.
affirm 532 vb.
teach 534 vb.
church office 985 n.
pontoon
boat 275 n.
card game 837 n.
pontoon bridge
bridge 624 n.
pony
twenty and over
99 n.
cup 194 n.
pony 273 n.
funds 797 n.
ponytail
hair 259 n.

hairdressing 843 n.
pony-trekking
  sport 837 n.
pooch
  dog 365 n.
poodle
  dog 365 n.
  toady 879 n.
poof
  nonconformist
    84 n.
poofter
  nonconformist
    84 n.
pooh-pooh
  disregard 458 vb.
  underestimate
    483 vb.
  hold cheap 922 vb.
pool
  combine 50 vb.
  lake 346 n.
  store 632 n.
  store 632 vb.
  association 706 n.
  acquisition 771 n.
  joint possession
    775 n.
  ball game 837 n.
pool resources
  cooperate 706 vb.
pools
  gambling 618 n.
pool table
  arena 724 n.
pooped
  fatigued 684 adj.
poor
  incomplete 55 adj.
  weak 163 adj.
  unproductive
    172 adj.
  feeble 572 adj.
  insufficient
    636 adj.
  bad 645 adj.
  unfortunate
    731 adj.
  poor 801 adj.
  unhappy 825 adj.
  disreputable
    867 adj.
poorhouse
  retreat 192 n.
  poverty 801 n.
poor lookout
  adversity 731 n.

hopelessness 853 n.
poorly
  slightly 33 adv.
  weakly 163 adj.
  sick 651 adj.
poor show
  bungling 695 n.
poor turnout
  fewness 105 n.
poor visibility
  dimness 419 n.
  invisibility 444 n.
pop
  paternity 169 n.
  jut 254 vb.
  soft drink 301 n.
  bang 402 n.
  bang 402 vb.
  music 412 n.
  give security
    767 vb.
  borrow 785 vb.
pop art
  art 551 n.
popcorn
  mouthful 301 n.
pope
  sovereign 741 n.
  ecclesiarch 986 n.
pop-eyed
  projecting 254 adj.
pop-fastener
  fastening 47 n.
pop group
  band 74 n.
  orchestra 413 n.
popgun
  plaything 837 n.
pop in
  enter 297 vb.
popinjay
  fop 848 n.
poplar
  tree 366 n.
poplin
  textile 222 n.
pop music
  music 412 n.
  amusement 837 n.
pop off
  die 361 vb.
pop out
  jut 254 vb.
  emerge 298 vb.
popper
  fastening 47 n.

poppet
  darling 890 n.
poppy
  plant 366 n.
  redness 431 n.
poppycock
  empty talk 515 n.
pop singer
  vocalist 413 n.
  entertainer 594 n.
  person of repute
    866 n.
pop the question
  interrogate 459 vb.
  request 761 vb.
  court 889 vb.
populace
  social group 371 n.
  commonalty 869 n.
popular
  general 79 adj.
  native 191 adj.
  governmental
    733 adj.
  reputable 866 adj.
  approved 923 adj.
popularity
  repute 866 n.
  sociability 882 n.
  approbation 923 n.
popular misconception
  error 495 n.
population
  social group 371 n.
populous
  multitudinous
    104 adj.
pop up
  happen 154 vb.
  arrive 295 vb.
  be visible 443 vb.
  appear 445 vb.
porcelain
  brittleness 330 n.
  pottery 381 n.
porch
  entrance 68 n.
  lobby 194 n.
  threshold 234 n.
  doorway 263 n.
  access 624 n.
  church exterior
    990 n.
porcine
  animal 365 adj.

porcupine
  mammal 365 n.
pore
  cavity 255 n.
  orifice 263 n.
  outlet 298 n.
pore over
  scan 438 vb.
  study 536 vb.
pork
  meat 301 n.
porn
  impurity 951 n.
pornographic
  not nice 645 adj.
  erotic 887 adj.
  impure 951 adj.
pornography
  impurity 951 n.
porous
  concave 255 adj.
  porous 263 adj.
porpoise
  mammal 365 n.
porridge
  cereals 301 n.
  pulpiness 356 n.
  detention 747 n.
porringer
  bowl 194 n.
port
  stopping place
    145 n.
  stable 192 n.
  sinistrality 242 n.
  window 263 n.
  wine 301 n.
  redness 431 n.
  shelter 662 n.
portable
  little 196 adj.
  light 323 adj.
  broadcasting
    531 n.
portal
  threshold 234 n.
  doorway 263 n.
portcullis
  barrier 235 n.
  heraldry 547 n.
  obstacle 702 n.
  fort 713 n.
portent
  omen 511 n.
  prodigy 864 n.
portentous
  predicting 511 adj.

frightening
  854 adj.
porter
  doorkeeper 264 n.
  alcoholic drink
    301 n.
  worker 686 n.
  servant 742 n.
portfolio
  bunch 74 n.
  list 87 n.
  case 194 n.
  collection 632 n.
  authority 733 n.
  title deed 767 n.
  estate 777 n.
  jurisdiction 955 n.
porthole
  window 263 n.
portico
  series 71 n.
  lobby 194 n.
portion
  part 53 n.
  piece 53 n.
  fate 596 n.
  provision 633 n.
  portion 783 n.
portion out
  mete out 465 vb.
portly
  fleshy 195 adj.
portmanteau
  box 194 n.
  storage 632 n.
port of call
  stopping place
    145 n.
portrait
  copy 22 n.
  composition 56 n.
  record 548 n.
  picture 553 n.
  description 590 n.
  honours 866 n.
portray
  liken 18 vb.
  imitate 20 vb.
  represent 551 vb.
  paint 553 vb.
portrayal
  assimilation 18 n.
  representation
    551 n.
  description 590 n.

pose
  be an example
    23 vb.
  interrogate 459 vb.
  represent 551 vb.
  behave 688 vb.
  conduct 688 n.
  be difficult 700 vb.
  affectation 850 n.
pose as
  represent 551 vb.
poser
  living model 23 n.
  question 459 n.
  enigma 530 n.
  difficulty 700 n.
poseur
  imitator 20 n.
posh
  fashionable
    848 adj.
  genteel 868 adj.
  ostentatious
    875 adj.
position
  state 7 n.
  order 60 n.
  arrange 62 vb.
  serial place 73 n.
  agency 173 n.
  place 185 n.
  situation 186 n.
  place 187 vb.
  station 187 n.
  opinion 485 n.
  job 622 n.
  prestige 866 n.
positive
  real 1 adj.
  absolute 32 adj.
  numerical 85 adj.
  electricity 160 n.
  positive 473 adj.
  forceful 571 adj.
**positive discrimina-
tion**
  equalization 28 n.
  injustice 914 n.
positive vetting
  protection 660 n.
posse
  band 74 n.
possess
  unite with 45 vb.
  make mad 503 vb.
  possess 773 vb.

appropriate
  786 vb.
possessed
  crazy 503 adj.
  frenzied 503 adj.
  possessed 773 adj.
  excited 821 adj.
  diabolic 969 adj.
possession
  territory 184 n.
  possession 773 n.
  property 777 n.
  spell 983 n.
possessions
  land 344 n.
  property 777 n.
possessive
  avaricious 816 adj.
  loving 887 adj.
  jealous 911 adj.
  selfish 932 adj.
posset
  alcoholic drink
    301 n.
possibility
  possibility 469 n.
possible
  liable 180 adj.
  possible 469 adj.
**POSSLQ (=person
  of opposite sex
  sharing living
  quarters)**
  lover 887 n.
post
  fastening 47 n.
  situation 186 n.
  place 187 vb.
  displace 188 vb.
  pillar 218 n.
  travel 267 vb.
  send 272 vb.
  move fast 277 vb.
  advertise 528 vb.
  *postal communica-
    tions* 531 n.
  correspondence
    588 n.
  employ 622 vb.
  job 622 n.
  commission
    751 vb.
  shame 867 vb.
  impose a duty
    917 vb.
postage
  price 809 n.

postage order
  paper money
    797 n.
postage stamp
  *postal communica-
    tions* 531 n.
postal order
  paper money
    797 n.
postbag
  correspondence
    588 n.
postbox
  *postal communica-
    tions* 531 n.
postcard
  message 529 n.
  correspondence
    588 n.
postcode
  *postal communica-
    tions* 531 n.
  correspondence
    588 n.
post-dated
  anachronistic
    118 adj.
posted, be
  be situated 186 vb.
poster
  advertisement
    528 n.
  picture 553 n.
posterior
  sequential 65 adj.
  subsequent
    120 adj.
  future 124 adj.
  back 238 adj.
  buttocks 238 n.
posterity
  posterity 170 n.
postern
  rear 238 n.
  doorway 263 n.
  fort 713 n.
post-graduate
  student 538 n.
posthaste
  swiftly 277 adv.
posthumous
  subsequent
    120 adj.
  late 136 adj.
postilion
  rider 268 n.
  servant 742 n.

posting
  location 187 n.
  transference 272 n.
  mandate 751 n.
postman's knock
  indoor game 837 n.
post mortem
  death 361 n.
  inquest 364 n.
  enquiry 459 n.
postnatal
  subsequent
    120 adj.
post office
  postal communica-
    tions 531 n.
post on
  send 272 vb.
postpone
  put off 136 vb.
  relinquish 621 vb.
  not complete
    726 vb.
postprandial
  subsequent
    120 adj.
  culinary 301 adj.
postscript
  adjunct 40 n.
  sequel 67 n.
  extremity 69 n.
postulant
  petitioner 763 n.
  nun 986 n.
  lay person 987 n.
postulate
  postulate 475 vb.
  premise 475 n.
  axiom 496 n.
  propound 512 vb.
  suppose 512 vb.
  supposition 512 n.
  request 761 n.
posture
  situation 186 n.
  form 243 n.
  look 445 n.
  behave 688 vb.
  conduct 688 n.
  be affected 850 vb.
postwar
  subsequent
    120 adj.
  peaceful 717 adj.
posy
  bunch 74 n.

ornamentation
    844 n.
  love token 889 n.
pot
  pot 194 n.
  vessel 194 n.
  shorten 204 vb.
  propulsion 287 n.
  shoot 287 vb.
  insert 303 vb.
  pottery 381 n.
  abstract 592 vb.
  drug-taking 949 n.
potash
  fertilizer 171 n.
potato
  opening 263 n.
  fruit and vegetables
    301 n.
pot belly
  stomach 194 n.
  swelling 253 n.
potboiler
  book 589 n.
  novel 590 n.
pot calling the kettle
    black
  equivalent 28 adj.
  See **equivalence**
potency
  power 160 n.
  strength 162 n.
  influence 178 n.
  utility 640 n.
potent
  powerful 160 adj.
  strong 162 adj.
  vigorous 174 adj.
  influential 178 adj.
  heraldry 547 n.
  intoxicating
    949 adj.
potentate
  potentate 741 n.
potential
  quantity 26 n.
  possible 469 adj.
pother
  turmoil 61 n.
  excitable state
    822 n.
pothole
  depth 211 n.
  interiority 224 n.
  cavity 255 n.
  orifice 263 n.
  search 459 n.

  discovery 484 n.
pot-holing
  depth 211 n.
  descent 309 n.
  search 459 n.
  discovery 484 n.
  sport 837 n.
potion
  draught 301 n.
  medicine 658 n.
  magic instrument
    983 n.
potluck
  chance 159 n.
  meal 301 n.
  gambling 618 n.
  nondesign 618 n.
  nonpreparation
    670 n.
  sociability 882 n.
pot or crock of gold
    at the end of the
    rainbow
  objective 617 n.
pot plant
  flower 366 n.
potpourri
  a mixture 43 n.
  medley 43 n.
  scent 396 n.
  musical piece
    412 n.
pots
  great quantity
    32 n.
pot shot
  propulsion 287 n.
potted
  short 204 adj.
potter
  wander 267 vb.
  be inactive 679 vb.
  artisan 686 n.
pottery
  pottery 381 n.
  art 551 n.
potty
  crazy 503 adj.
  latrine 649 n.
pouch
  bag 194 n.
pouffe
  seat 218 n.
poultice
  pulpiness 356 n.
  doctor 658 vb.

surgical dressing
    658 n.
  relieve 831 vb.
poultry
  meat 301 n.
  poultry 365 n.
poultry farming
  animal husbandry
    369 n.
pounce
  move fast 277 vb.
  spurt 277 n.
  descend 309 vb.
  descent 309 n.
  leap 312 vb.
  plunge 313 n.
pounce on
  surprise 508 vb.
  attack 712 vb.
  take 786 vb.
pound
  cut 46 vb.
  rend 46 vb.
  enclosure 235 n.
  strike 279 vb.
  weighing 322 n.
  pulverize 332 vb.
  lockup 748 n.
  coinage 797 n.
pound coin
  coinage 797 n.
pound note
  paper money
    797 n.
pound of fl
  severity 735 n.
  interest 803 n.
  pitilessness 906 n.
pour
  emit 300 vb.
  let fall 311 vb.
  be wet 341 vb.
  flow 350 vb.
  rain 350 vb.
  abound 635 vb.
pouring
  prolific 171 adj.
  flowing 350 adj.
pour oil on troubled
    waters
  assuage 177 vb.
  pacify 719 vb.
pour out
  empty 300 vb.
  let fall 311 vb.
  give 781 vb.

pour scorn on
ridicule 851 vb.
pour with rain
rain 350 vb.
pout
jut 254 vb.
gesticulate 547 vb.
gesture 547 n.
be rude 885 vb.
sullenness 893 n.
poverty
feebleness 572 n.
poverty 801 n.
poverty line
poverty 801 n.
poverty trap
poverty 801 n.
POW
prisoner 750 n.
powder
coat 226 vb.
powder 332 n.
pulverize 332 vb.
medicine 658 n.
beautify 841 vb.
cosmetic 843 n.
primp 843 vb.
powder keg
pitfall 663 n.
arsenal 723 n.
powder puff
cosmetic 843 n.
powder room
latrine 649 n.
powdery
powdery 332 adj.
power
numerical element
85 n.
power 160 n.
strengthen 162 vb.
operate 173 vb.
influence 178 n.
style 566 n.
vigour 571 n.
means 629 n.
authority 733 n.
**power behind the
throne**
cause 156 n.
influence 178 n.
latency 523 n.
authority 733 n.
deputy 755 n.
powerboat
boat 275 n.

power cut
scarcity 636 n.
power-driven
mechanical
630 adj.
powered
dynamic 160 adj.
mechanical
630 adj.
powered gliding
aeronautics 271 n.
powerful
powerful 160 adj.
forceful 571 adj.
notable 638 adj.
authoritative
733 adj.
powerhouse
busy person 678 n.
powerless
impotent 161 adj.
powerless 161 adj.
weak 163 adj.
power station
workshop 687 n.
powers that be
authority 733 n.
officer 741 n.
master 741 n.
powwow
confer 584 vb.
conference 584 n.
advice 691 n.
make terms
766 vb.
pox
venereal disease
651 n.
PR
publicity 528 n.
practicable
possible 469 adj.
useful 640 adj.
practical
possible 469 adj.
useful 640 adj.
advisable 642 adj.
practical criticism
interpretation
520 n.
practicality
use 673 n.
practical joke
foolery 497 n.
trickery 542 n.
witticism 839 n.
ridicule 851 n.

practically
nearly 200 adv.
practice
continuity 71 n.
regularity 81 n.
permanence 144 n.
empiricism 461 n.
practice 610 n.
vocation 622 n.
preparation 669 n.
exercise 682 n.
observance 768 n.
practise
repeat 106 vb.
play music 413 vb.
train 534 vb.
learn 536 vb.
habituate 610 vb.
prepare oneself
669 vb.
use 673 vb.
do 676 vb.
observe 768 vb.
practised
knowing 490 adj.
habituated 610 adj.
usual 610 adj.
prepared 669 adj.
expert 694 adj.
practise medicine
doctor 658 vb.
practise upon
experiment 461 vb.
practising
observant 768 adj.
religious 973 adj.
orthodox 976 adj.
practitioner
doer 676 n.
agent 686 n.
pragmatic
useful 640 adj.
advisable 642 adj.
pragmatism
philosophy 449 n.
good policy 642 n.
prairie
space 183 n.
plain 348 n.
praise
honour 866 vb.
praise 923 n.
praise 923 vb.
praises
thanks 907 n.
praise 923 n.

act of worship
981 n.
praise to the skies
praise 923 vb.
praiseworthy
good 615 adj.
excellent 644 adj.
virtuous 933 adj.
pram
pushcart 274 n.
boat 275 n.
prance
ride 267 vb.
walk 267 vb.
leap 312 n.
leap 312 vb.
be affected 850 vb.
be ostentatious
875 vb.
boast 877 vb.
prang
aeronautics 271 n.
fly 271 vb.
prank
whim 604 n.
revel 837 n.
prating
empty talk 515 n.
prattle
empty talk 515 n.
mean nothing
515 vb.
speak 579 vb.
speech 579 n.
chatter 581 n.
prawn
fish food 301 n.
pray
entreat 761 vb.
deprecate 762 vb.
desire 859 vb.
do penance 941 vb.
be pious 979 vb.
worship 981 vb.
prayer
entreaty 761 n.
request 761 n.
prayers 981 n.
worship 981 n.
prayer book
scripture 975 n.
prayers 981 n.
church utensil
990 n.
prayer meeting
public worship
981 n.

prayers
prayers 981 n.
praying
pious 979 adj.
act of worship
981 n.
praying mantis
insect 365 n.
PR consultant
interpreter 520 n.
preach
teach 534 vb.
orate 579 vb.
preacher
preacher 537 n.
chatterer 581 n.
**preach to the con-
verted**
waste effort
641 adj.
preamble
prelude 66 n.
oration 579 n.
prearrange
do before 119 vb.
predetermine
608 vb.
plan 623 vb.
prepare 669 vb.
prebendary
ecclesiarch 986 n.
precarious
unreliable 474 adj.
unsafe 661 adj.
precaution
protection 660 n.
caution 858 n.
precautions
safeguard 662 n.
preparation 669 n.
precede
precede 283 vb.
precedence
precedence 64 n.
prestige 866 n.
precedent
prototype 23 n.
precedence 64 n.
precursor 66 n.
precursory 66 adj.
rule 81 n.
example 83 n.
prior 119 adj.
priority 119 n.
guide 520 n.
habit 610 n.
legal trial 959 n.

preceding
preceding 64 adj.
preceding 283 n.
precentor
choir 413 n.
church officer
986 n.
precept
precept 693 n.
precinct
place 185 n.
precincts
region 184 n.
surroundings
230 n.
parsonage 986 n.
precious
ornate 574 adj.
valuable 644 adj.
of value 811 adj.
affected 850 adj.
darling 890 n.
precious few
few 105 adj.
precious lamb
darling 890 n.
precious metal
mineral 359 n.
money 797 n.
precious stone
rock 344 n.
gem 844 n.
precipice
high land 209 n.
verticality 215 n.
incline 220 n.
descent 309 n.
pitfall 663 n.
precipitance
rashness 857 n.
precipitate
leavings 41 n.
cause 156 vb.
effect 157 n.
speedy 277 adj.
propel 287 vb.
eject 300 vb.
descend 309 vb.
let fall 311 vb.
be dense 324 vb.
solid body 324 n.
dirt 649 n.
hasty 680 adj.
rash 857 adj.
precipitation
subtraction 39 n.
velocity 277 n.

propulsion 287 n.
ejection 300 n.
lowering 311 n.
condensation
324 n.
rain 350 n.
precipitous
vertical 215 adj.
sloping 220 adj.
précis
shortening 204 n.
translate 520 vb.
translation 520 n.
conciseness 569 n.
compendium
592 n.
precise
arranged 62 adj.
definite 80 adj.
accurate 494 adj.
intelligible 516 adj.
fastidious 862 adj.
formal 875 adj.
pietistic 979 adj.
precisely
truly 494 adv.
precision
touch 378 n.
accuracy 494 n.
intelligibility
516 n.
precision tool
tool 630 n.
preclude
exclude 57 vb.
precocious
early 135 adj.
precocity
anticipation 135 n.
preconceived
biased 481 adj.
preconceived idea
prejudgment 481 n.
preconception
prejudge 481 vb.
prejudgment 481 n.
precooked
ready-made
669 adj.
precursor
precursor 66 n.
predator
killer 362 n.
taker 786 n.
predecease
do before 119 vb.

predecessor
precursor 66 n.
paternity 169 n.
predestination
destiny 155 n.
fate 596 n.
predetermination
608 n.
predestined
impending 155 adj.
fated 596 adj.
predetermined
608 adj.
predetermine
necessitate 596 vb.
predetermine
608 vb.
predicament
predicament 700 n.
predicate
part of speech
564 n.
predict
predict 511 vb.
predictable
unchangeable
153 adj.
prediction
prediction 511 n.
predilection
tendency 179 n.
prejudice 481 n.
choice 605 n.
affections 817 n.
liking 859 n.
love 887 n.
predispose
bias 481 vb.
motivate 612 vb.
predisposition
tendency 179 n.
willingness 597 n.
affections 817 n.
predominant
powerful 160 adj.
influential 178 adj.
authoritative
733 adj.
predominate
predominate 34 vb.
preeminent
supreme 34 adj.
authoritative
733 adj.
noteworthy
866 adj.

preempt
exclude 57 vb.
do before 119 vb.
be early 135 vb.
precede 283 vb.
acquire 771 vb.
preemptive
excluding 57 adj.
preen
primp 843 vb.
decorate 844 vb.
preexistence
existence 1 n.
priority 119 n.
preexisting
prior 119 adj.
prefab
house 192 n.
prefabricated
ready-made
669 adj.
preface
add 38 vb.
come before 64 vb.
put in front 64 vb.
prelude 66 n.
front 237 n.
edition 589 n.
prefatory
preceding 64 adj.
precursory 66 adj.
beginning 68 adj.
prior 119 adj.
prefect
official 690 n.
officer 741 n.
prefer
choose 605 vb.
desire 859 vb.
preferable
excellent 644 adj.
prefer charges
litigate 959 vb.
preference
precedence 64 n.
will 595 n.
choice 605 n.
love 887 n.
**preferential treat-
    ment**
injustice 914 n.
preferment
progression 285 n.
holy orders 985 n.
prefigure
predict 511 vb.
indicate 547 vb.

prefix
add 38 vb.
adjunct 40 n.
affix 45 vb.
put in front 64 vb.
precursor 66 n.
front 237 n.
part of speech
564 n.
pregnancy
fertilized 167 adj.
propagation 167 n.
prolific 171 adj.
meaningful
514 adj.
important 638 adj.
pregnant with
impending 155 adj.
prehensile
tactual 378 adj.
retentive 778 adj.
prehistoric
prior 119 adj.
past 125 adj.
olden 127 adj.
prejudge
do before 119 vb.
prejudge 481 vb.
prejudgment
prejudgment 481 n.
prejudice
influence 178 vb.
tendency 179 n.
bias 481 vb.
prejudice 481 n.
error 495 n.
motivate 612 vb.
affections 817 n.
dislike 861 n.
prejudiced
biased 481 adj.
erroneous 495 adj.
unjust 914 adj.
prejudice the issue
prejudge 481 vb.
prejudicial
evil 616 adj.
harmful 645 adj.
prelate
ecclesiarch 986 n.
preliminaries
beginning 68 n.
preparation 669 n.
preliminary
preceding 64 adj.
precursory 66 adj.
prelude 66 n.

prior 119 adj.
preparatory
669 adj.
prelims
exam 459 n.
edition 589 n.
prelude
prelude 66 n.
preceding 283 n.
musical piece
412 n.
play music 413 vb.
premature
early 135 adj.
ill-timed 138 adj.
immature 670 adj.
prematurely
beforehand
135 adv.
premedication
preparation 669 n.
premeditated
predetermined
608 adj.
premeditated murder
homicide 362 n.
premeditation
foresight 510 n.
predetermination
608 n.
preparation 669 n.
premier
superior 34 n.
director 690 n.
officer 741 n.
premier cru
wine 301 n.
premiere
debut 68 n.
dramaturgy 594 n.
premise
premise 475 n.
premises
place 185 n.
evidence 466 n.
premium
interest 803 n.
receipt 807 n.
price 809 n.
premium bond
equal chance
159 n.
gambling 618 n.
paper money
797 n.
premonition
precursor 66 n.

foresight 510 n.
warning 664 n.
prenatal
prior 119 adj.
preoccupation
attention 455 n.
preoccupied
obsessed 455 adj.
distracted 456 adj.
preordained
fated 596 adj.
predetermined
608 adj.
prep
curriculum 534 n.
study 536 n.
preparation 669 n.
preparation
teaching 534 n.
study 536 n.
medicine 658 n.
preparation 669 n.
Holy Communion
988 n.
preparatory
preceding 64 adj.
preparatory
669 adj.
prepare
prepare 669 vb.
prepared
prepared 669 adj.
prepared, be
foresee 510 vb.
prepare for
prepare 669 vb.
preponderance
inequality 29 n.
preposition
precursor 66 n.
part of speech
564 n.
prepossessing
personable 841 adj.
preposterous
exorbitant 32 adj.
absurd 497 adj.
imaginative
513 adj.
ridiculous 849 adj.
prep school
school 539 n.
prequel
precursor 66 n.
priority 119 n.
front 237 n.
preceding 283 n.

reading matter
589 n.

prerequisite
qualification 468 n.
required 627 adj.
requirement 627 n.

prerogative
authority 733 n.
freedom 744 n.
nobility 868 n.
dueness 915 n.

presage
predict 511 vb.
indicate 547 vb.
threaten 900 vb.

presbyopic
dim-sighted
440 adj.

presbyter
church officer
986 n.
ecclesiarch 986 n.

Presbyterianism
Protestantism
976 n.

presbytery
seniority 131 n.
parish 985 n.
synod 985 n.
the church 985 n.
parsonage 986 n.
church exterior
990 n.

prescribe
doctor 658 vb.
advise 691 vb.
decree 737 vb.

prescript
decree 737 n.

prescription
remedy 658 n.
advice 691 n.
precept 693 n.
dueness 915 n.

prescriptive
due 915 adj.

prescriptive right
dueness 915 n.

preselect
select 605 vb.

presence
presence 189 n.
appearance 445 n.
look 445 n.
conduct 688 n.
ghost 970 n.

present
present 121 adj.
near 200 adj.
show 522 vb.
dramatize 594 vb.
offer 759 n.
offer 759 vb.
gift 781 n.
give 781 vb.
greet 884 vb.

present, the
present time 121 n.

presentable
personable 841 adj.

present arms
greet 884 vb.
show respect
920 vb.

presentation
debut 68 n.
spectacle 445 n.
manifestation
522 n.
report 524 n.
representation
551 n.
offer 759 n.
gift 781 n.
giving 781 n.
celebration 876 n.
reward 962 n.
holy orders 985 n.

present, be
be present 189 vb.

present day
present time 121 n.

present-day
present 121 adj.

presenter
broadcaster 531 n.
speaker 579 n.
giver 781 n.

presentiment
intuition 476 n.
foresight 510 n.
prediction 511 n.

present itself
happen 154 vb.

present oneself
be present 189 vb.

preservation
preservation 666 n.

preservationist
preserver 666 n.

preservative
food content 301 n.
preserver 666 n.

preserve
sweet thing 392 n.
preserve 666 vb.

preserve for posterity
record 548 vb.

preserver
protector 660 n.
preserver 666 n.

preserves
fruit and vegetables
301 n.

preside
direct 689 vb.
be hospitable
882 vb.

presidency
governance 733 n.
*position of author-
ity* 733 n.

president
superior 34 n.
director 690 n.
master 741 n.
officer 741 n.

press
crowd 74 n.
cabinet 194 n.
make smaller
198 vb.
flattener 216 n.
smooth 258 vb.
smoother 258 n.
impel 279 vb.
weigh 322 vb.
press 587 n.
be resolute 599 vb.
compel 740 vb.

press, the
the press 528 n.

press a suit
request 761 vb.

press charges
litigate 959 vb.

press conference
manifestation
522 n.
publication 528 n.

press for time, be
hasten 680 vb.

press forward
progress 285 vb.

pressgang
compel 740 vb.
compulsion 740 n.
take away 786 vb.
taker 786 n.

pressing
weighty 322 adj.
record 548 n.
resolute 599 adj.
compelling
740 adj.

press into service
avail oneself of
673 vb.

press officer
interpreter 520 n.

press on
elapse 111 vb.
progress 285 vb.
lower 311 vb.

press one's suit
be in love 887 vb.
court 889 vb.

press out
extract 304 vb.

press release
report 524 n.
publication 528 n.
news 529 n.

press-stud
fastening 47 n.

**press the panic but-
ton**
fear 854 vb.
frighten 854 vb.
be cowardly
856 vb.

pressure
quantity 26 n.
energy 160 n.
vigorousness 174 n.
influence 178 n.
compression 198 n.
impulse 279 n.
gravity 322 n.
touch 378 n.
resolution 599 n.
inducement 612 n.
instrumentality
628 n.
action 676 n.
exertion 682 n.
adversity 731 n.
restriction 747 n.

pressure-cook
cook 301 vb.

pressure group
influence 178 n.
motivator 612 n.
petitioner 763 n.

pressurize
impel 279 vb.

Prestel (tdmk)
data processing
86 n.
broadcasting
531 n.
prestige
greatness 32 n.
prestige 866 n.
prestigious
reputable 866 adj.
presumably
probably 471 adv.
presume
assume 471 vb.
prejudge 481 vb.
be of the opinion
that 485 vb.
expect 507 vb.
suppose 512 vb.
be insolent 878 vb.
presume on
avail oneself of
673 vb.
be free 744 vb.
presumption
opinion 485 n.
expectation 507 n.
supposition 512 n.
hope 852 n.
rashness 857 n.
insolence 878 n.
arrogation 916 n.
presumptuous
rash 857 adj.
impertinent
878 adj.
insolent 878 adj.
unwarranted
916 adj.
presuppose
put in front 64 vb.
do before 119 vb.
prejudge 481 vb.
suppose 512 vb.
pretence
insubstantial thing
4 n.
foolery 497 n.
supposition 512 n.
duplicity 541 n.
sham 542 n.
pretext 614 n.
ostentation 875 n.
pretend
imitate 20 vb.
imagine 513 vb.
dissemble 541 vb.

be untrue 543 vb.
be affected 850 vb.
pretender
impostor 545 n.
petitioner 763 n.
usurper 916 n.
pretensions
pretension 850 n.
airs 873 n.
ostentation 875 n.
pretentious
absurd 497 adj.
ornate 574 adj.
affected 850 adj.
proud 871 adj.
vain 873 adj.
ostentatious
875 adj.
preternatural
abnormal 84 adj.
See **unusual**
unusual 84 adj.
paranormal 984 n.
pretext
pretext 614 n.
prettiness
beauty 841 n.
pretty
greatly 32 vb.
beautiful 841 adj.
pretty kettle of fish
complexity 61 n.
pretty pass
circumstance 8 n.
predicament 700 n.
pretty penny
dearness 811 n.
pretty speeches
endearment 889 n.
flattery 925 n.
pretty well
greatly 32 vb.
prevail
be 1 vb.
prevail 178 vb.
overmaster 727 vb.
prevailing
powerful 160 adj.
influential 178 adj.
prevailing taste
fashion 848 n.
prevailing winds
wind 352 n.
prevail upon
induce 612 vb.
prevalent
existing 1 adj.

extensive 32 adj.
general 79 adj.
universal 79 adj.
powerful 160 adj.
influential 178 adj.
known 490 adj.
prevaricate
be equivocal
518 vb.
dissemble 541 vb.
be dishonest
930 vb.
prevent
counteract 182 vb.
obstruct 702 vb.
prohibit 757 vb.
preventative
counteraction
182 n.
prevention
counteraction
182 n.
avoidance 620 n.
hindrance 702 n.
restraint 747 n.
preventive
excluding 57 adj.
counteraction
182 n.
prophylactic 658 n.
preventive measure
protection 660 n.
preventive medicine
medical art 658 n.
preservation 666 n.
preview
precursor 66 n.
do before 119 vb.
priority 119 n.
inspection 438 n.
film 445 n.
manifestation
522 n.
dramaturgy 594 n.
previous
preceding 64 adj.
anachronistic
118 adj.
prior 119 adj.
previous engagement
pretext 614 n.
prewar
prior 119 adj.
antiquated 127 adj.
peaceful 717 adj.
prey
animal 365 n.

objective 617 n.
chase 619 n.
sufferer 825 n.
prey on
eat 301 vb.
prey on one's mind
absorb 449 vb.
trouble 827 vb.
frighten 854 vb.
priapism
libido 859 n.
illicit love 951 n.
price
price 809 n.
price 809 vb.
priceless
profitable 640 adj.
valuable 644 adj.
of value 811 adj.
funny 849 adj.
prick
small thing 33 n.
cut 46 vb.
stimulant 174 n.
be sharp 256 vb.
sharp point 256 n.
pierce 263 vb.
give pain 377 vb.
incite 612 vb.
wound 655 n.
wound 655 vb.
excitant 821 n.
prickle
prickle 256 n.
foliage 366 n.
prickly
sharp 256 adj.
irascible 892 adj.
prickly heat
tingling 378 n.
skin disease 651 n.
prick out
implant 303 vb.
cultivate 370 vb.
prick up (one's ears)
elevate 310 vb.
hear 415 vb.
be curious 453 vb.
be attentive 455 vb.
pricy
dear 811 adj.
pride
pride 871 n.
ostentation 875 n.
vice 934 n.
impiety 980 n.

pride (lions)
group 74 n.
pride and joy
favourite 890 n.
pride of place
precedence 64 n.
preceding 283 n.
authority 733 n.
priest
church officer
  986 n.
cleric 986 n.
priest 986 n.
priestess
priest 986 n.
priesthole
retreat 192 n.
hiding-place 527 n.
priesthood
church office 985 n.
ecclesiasticism
  985 n.
clergy 986 n.
prig
prude 950 n.
priggish
affected 850 adj.
prudish 950 adj.
prim
serious 834 adj.
affected 850 adj.
fastidious 862 adj.
prudish 950 adj.
primacy
prestige 866 n.
church office 985 n.
prima donna
superior 34 n.
vocalist 413 n.
actor 594 n.
bigwig 638 n.
proficient person
  696 n.
prima facie evidence
evidence 466 n.
primal
primal 127 adj.
primarily
initially 68 adv.
primary
original 21 adj.
simple 44 adj.
first 68 adj.
fundamental
  156 adj.
educational
  534 adj.

vote 605 n.
important 638 adj.
primary colour
colour 425 n.
primate
superior 34 n.
mammal 365 n.
ecclesiarch 986 n.
prime
numerical 85 adj.
primal 127 adj.
educate 534 vb.
important 638 adj.
elite 644 n.
excellent 644 adj.
make ready
  669 vb.
palmy days 730 n.
church service
  988 n.
primed
informed 524 adj.
prepared 669 adj.
prime minister
superior 34 n.
director 690 n.
officer 741 n.
prime mover
cause 156 n.
producer 164 n.
prime number
number 85 n.
prime of life
salad days 130 n.
middle age 131 n.
adultness 134 n.
primeval
beginning 68 adj.
primal 127 adj.
priming
preparation 669 n.
explosive 723 n.
primitive
past 125 adj.
primal 127 adj.
fundamental
  156 adj.
artist 556 n.
artless 699 adj.
barbaric 869 adj.
primogeniture
priority 119 n.
seniority 131 n.
primordial
original 21 adj.
beginning 68 adj.
primal 127 adj.

fundamental
  156 adj.
primp
primp 843 vb.
primrose
plant 366 n.
yellowness 433 n.
primrose path
way 624 n.
deterioration
  655 n.
wickedness 934 n.
primula
plant 366 n.
primus stove
furnace 383 n.
prince
potentate 741 n.
sovereign 741 n.
aristocrat 868 n.
princely
ruling 733 adj.
liberal 813 adj.
worshipful 866 adj.
noble 868 adj.
Prince of Wales
  check
chequer 437 n.
Prince of Wales's
  feathers
regalia 743 n.
princess
sovereign 741 n.
loved one 887 n.
principal
supreme 34 adj.
first 68 adj.
teacher 537 n.
director 690 n.
master 741 n.
principal boy or girl
acting 594 n.
principality
political organiza-
  tion 733 n.
principally
eminently 34 adv.
principle
essential part 5 n.
rule 81 n.
source 156 n.
element 319 n.
idea 451 n.
premise 475 n.
opinion 485 n.
axiom 496 n.
motive 612 n.

precept 693 n.
probity 929 n.
principles
creed 485 n.
conduct 688 n.
probity 929 n.
virtue 933 n.
prink
dress 228 vb.
beautify 841 vb.
primp 843 vb.
print
copy 22 n.
effect 157 n.
indication 547 n.
photograph 551 vb.
photography 551 n.
picture 553 n.
write 586 vb.
print 587 n.
print 587 vb.
edition 589 n.
pattern 844 n.
printed
printed 587 adj.
printer
publicizer 528 n.
printing
composition 56 n.
reproduction
  166 n.
printing 555 n.
lettering 586 n.
print 587 n.
printing press
publicity 528 n.
press 587 n.
printout
data processing
  86 n.
product 164 n.
print 587 n.
prior
prior 119 adj.
ecclesiarch 986 n.
monk 986 n.
prioress
ecclesiarch 986 n.
nun 986 n.
priori, a
intrinsic 5 adj.
prioritize
order 60 vb.
regularize 62 vb.
priority
priority 119 n.
chief thing 638 n.

importance 638 n.
authority 733 n.

prior to
before 119 adv.

priory
house 192 n.
monastery 986 n.

prism
angular figure 247 n.
colour 425 n.
variegation 437 n.

prismatic
variegated 437 adj.

prison
place 185 n.
prison 748 n.

prisoner
prisoner 750 n.
accused person 928 n.

prisoner of conscience
prisoner 750 n.

prisoner of war
prisoner 750 n.

privacy
invisibility 444 n.
seclusion 883 n.

private
inferior 35 n.
private 80 adj.
special 80 adj.
concealed 525 adj.
soldiery 722 n.
commoner 869 n.
secluded 883 adj.

private detective
detective 459 n.

private enterprise
trade 791 n.

privateer
mariner 270 n.

private eye
detective 459 n.
protector 660 n.

private investigator
detective 459 n.

privately
secretly 525 adv.

private means
independence 744 n.

private parts
genitalia 167 n.

privates
genitalia 167 n.

private school
school 539 n.

privation
loss 772 n.
poverty 801 n.

privatization
transfer 780 n.
trade 791 n.

privatize
assign 780 vb.

privet
tree 366 n.

privet hedge
fence 235 n.

privilege
freedom 744 n.
dueness 915 n.
exempt 919 vb.
nonliability 919 n.

privileged
free 744 adj.
due 915 adj.

privy
latrine 649 n.

Privy Council
council 692 n.

privy purse
receipt 807 n.

privy seal
badge of rule 743 n.

privy to
knowing 490 adj.

prize
benefit 615 n.
objective 617 n.
elite 644 n.
trophy 729 n.
acquisition 771 n.
gift 781 n.
taking 786 n.
booty 790 n.
desired object 859 n.
honour 866 vb.
love 887 vb.
approve 923 vb.
reward 962 n.

prize fighting
pugilism 716 n.

prize-giving
giving 781 n.
reward 962 n.

prize money
reward 962 n.

prize open
force 176 vb.

prizewinner
superior 34 n.
exceller 644 n.
proficient person 696 n.
victor 727 n.
recipient 782 n.

pro
expert 696 n.
prostitute 952 n.

proa
rowing boat 275 n.

probability
probability 471 n.

probable
probable 471 adj.

probably
probably 471 adv.

probation
experiment 461 n.
attempt 671 n.

probationer
beginner 538 n.
offender 904 n.

probation officer
keeper 749·n.

probe
perforator 263 n.
pierce 263 vb.
enquire 459 vb.
enquiry 459 n.
interrogate 459 vb.
search 459 n.
search 459 vb.
be tentative 461 vb.
experiment 461 n.
measure 465 vb.
detector 484 n.

probity
probity 929 n.

problem
topic 452 n.
question 459 n.
enigma 530 n.
difficulty 700 n.
worry 825 n.

problematic
complex 61 adj.
difficult 700 adj.

problematical
uncertain 474 adj.

problematics
topic 452 n.

proboscis
protuberance 254 n.
feeler 378 n.

procedural
ritual 988 adj.

procedure
policy 623 n.
way 624 n.
action 676 n.
conduct 688 n.
ritual 988 n.

proceed
elapse 111 vb.
go on 146 vb.
result 157 vb.
be in motion 265 vb.
travel 267 vb.
progress 285 vb.
do 676 vb.

proceedings
legal process 959 n.

proceeds
earnings 771 n.
receiving 782 n.
receipt 807 n.

process
class 62 vb.
computerize 86 vb.
change 143 n.
modify 143 vb.
convert 147 vb.
produce 164 vb.
production 164 n.
agency 173 n.
photograph 551 vb.
way 624 n.
preserve 666 vb.
conduct 688 vb.
perform ritual 988 vb.

processed
ready-made 669 adj.

processed food
food 301 n.

procession
marching 267 n.
progression 285 n.
pageant 875 n.
ritual act 988 n.

proclaim
manifest 522 vb.
proclaim 528 vb.

proclamation
manifestation 522 n.
publication 528 n.

proclivity
tendency 179 n.

proconsul
governor 741 n.
procrastinate
put off 136 vb.
be neglectful
458 vb.
not act 677 vb.
procrastination
delay 136 n.
negligence 458 n.
unwillingness
598 n.
inactivity 679 n.
procreate
generate 167 vb.
make fruitful
171 vb.
procreation
production 164 n.
reproduction
166 n.
propagation 167 n.
productiveness
171 n.
procreator
propagation 167 n.
paternity 169 n.
proctor
teacher 537 n.
law agent 958 n.
procurator
law agent 958 n.
procurator fiscal
accuser 928 n.
law officer 955 n.
procure
cause 156 vb.
induce 612 vb.
provide 633 vb.
acquire 771 vb.
be impure 951 vb.
procurement
agency 173 n.
acquisition 771 n.
procurer
bawd 952 n.
procuress
bawd 952 n.
prod
stimulant 174 n.
impel 279 vb.
gesticulate 547 vb.
incentive 612 n.
incite 612 vb.
prodigal
prodigal 815 adj.
prodigal 815 n.

prodigal son
prodigal 815 n.
bad person 938 n.
prodigious
prodigious 32 adj.
wonderful 864 adj.
prodigy
intellectual 492 n.
exceller 644 n.
prodigy 864 n.
prodromal
preceding 64 adj.
produce
growth 157 n.
produce 164 vb.
product 164 n.
lengthen 203 vb.
agriculture 370 n.
manifest 522 vb.
dramatize 594 vb.
provision 633 n.
producer
producer 164 n.
stage manager
594 n.
product
numerical result
85 n.
event 154 n.
product 164 n.
production
product 164 n.
production 164 n.
dramaturgy 594 n.
production line
production 164 n.
workshop 687 n.
productive
prolific 171 adj.
productivity
production 164 n.
productiveness
171 n.
diffuseness 570 n.
plenty 635 n.
utility 640 n.
profane
make unclean
649 vb.
impair 655 vb.
shame 867 vb.
cursing 899 adj.
not respect 921 vb.
wicked 934 adj.
irreligious 974 adj.
be impious 980 vb.
profane 980 adj.

profanity
scurrility 899 n.
impiety 980 n.
profess
affirm 532 vb.
plead 614 vb.
profession
assent 488 n.
affirmation 532 n.
pretext 614 n.
vocation 622 n.
promise 764 n.
ostentation 875 n.
duty 917 n.
professional
expert 694 adj.
expert 696 n.
professionalism
skill 694 n.
professor
scholar 492 n.
teacher 537 n.
expert 696 n.
academic title
870 n.
professor emeritus
teacher 537 n.
academic title
870 n.
proffer
offer 759 n.
offer 759 vb.
promise 764 vb.
proficiency
culture 490 n.
skill 694 n.
proficient
knowing 490 adj.
expert 694 adj.
profile
outline 233 n.
outline 233 vb.
laterality 239 n.
form 243 n.
feature 445 n.
estimate 480 n.
picture 553 n.
description 590 n.
profit
growth 157 n.
incentive 612 n.
benefit 615 n.
benefit 615 vb.
utility 640 n.
be expedient
642 vb.
good policy 642 n.

be profitable
771 vb.
gain 771 n.
reward 962 n.
profitable
profitable 640 adj.
beneficial 644 adj.
profit by
profit by 137 vb.
use 673 vb.
profiteer
prosper 730 vb.
prosperous person
730 n.
speculate 791 vb.
overcharge 811 vb.
profligate
prodigal 815 adj.
prodigal 815 n.
vicious 934 adj.
bad person 938 n.
intemperate
943 adj.
sensualist 944 n.
lecherous 951 adj.
profound
great 32 adj.
deep 211 adj.
wise 498 adj.
unclear 568 adj.
profundity
depth 211 n.
thought 449 n.
imperspicuity
568 n.
profuse
many 104 adj.
diffuse 570 adj.
plentiful 635 adj.
liberal 813 adj.
prodigal 815 adj.
profusion
great quantity
32 n.
abundance 171 n.
plenty 635 n.
prodigality 815 n.
progenitor
source 156 n.
paternity 169 n.
progenitrix
maternity 169 n.
progeny
posterity 170 n.
prognosis
foresight 510 n.
prediction 511 n.

medical art 658 n.

prognostication
foresight 510 n.
prediction 511 n.

program
class 62 vb.
computerize 86 vb.
data processing
86 n.

programme
list 87 n.
foresight 510 n.
prediction 511 n.
publication 528 n.
broadcast 531 n.
plan 623 n.
policy 623 n.
undertaking 672 n.
tactics 688 n.

progress
increase 36 n.
continuance 146 n.
motion 265 n.
progress 285 vb.
progression 285 n.
way 624 n.
improvement
654 n.
success 727 n.

progression
order 60 n.
series 71 n.
ratio 85 n.
progression 285 n.

progressive
increasing 36 adj.
continuous 71 adj.
moving 265 adj.
progressive
285 adj.
improving 654 adj.
reformer 654 n.
enterprising
672 adj.

progressiveness
increase 36 n.
continuity 71 n.
progression 285 n.

prohibit
prohibit 757 vb.

prohibition
prohibition 757 n.
temperance 942 n.

prohibitive
excluding 57 adj.
dear 811 adj.

project
make extrinsic
6 vb.
jut 254 vb.
propel 287 vb.
emerge 298 vb.
be visible 443 vb.
curriculum 534 n.
intend 617 vb.
plan 623 n.
plan 623 vb.
undertaking 672 n.

projectile
missile 287 n.
ammunition 723 n.

projecting
projecting 254 adj.

projection
extrinsicality 6 n.
distortion 246 n.
convexity 253 n.
projection 254 n.
propulsion 287 n.
cinema 445 n.
ideality 513 n.
map 551 n.

projector
lamp 420 n.
cinema 445 n.

prolapse
descend 309 vb.

prolepsis
anachronism
118 n.

proletarian
commoner 869 n.
plebeian 869 adj.

proletariat
commonalty 869 n.
lower classes 869 n.

proliferate
grow 36 vb.
be fruitful 171 vb.
abound 635 vb.

prolific
prolific 171 adj.

prolix
prolix 570 adj.

prolixity
diffuseness 570 n.
speech 579 n.
loquacity 581 n.
tedium 838 n.

prologue
prelude 66 n.
oration 579 n.
dramaturgy 594 n.

prolong
augment 36 vb.
continue 71 adj.
sustain 146 vb.
lengthen 203 vb.
preserve 666 vb.

prolongation
sequence 65 n.
protraction 113 n.
continuance 146 n.

prom
music 412 n.

promenade
park 192 n.
land travel 267 n.
See **pedestrian-
ism**

pedestrianism
267 n.
path 624 n.
be ostentatious
875 vb.
pageant 875 n.

promenade concert
music 412 n.

prominence
superiority 34 n.
prominence 254 n.
visibility 443 n.
importance 638 n.
prestige 866 n.

prominent
projecting 254 adj.
obvious 443 adj.
manifest 522 adj.
notable 638 adj.
noteworthy
866 adj.

promiscuity
indiscrimination
464 n.
unchastity 951 n.

promiscuous
indiscriminate
464 adj.
unchaste 951 adj.

promise
be likely 471 vb.
predict 511 vb.
oath 532 n.
promise 764 n.
promise 764 vb.
contract 765 vb.
hope 852 n.

promised
future 124 adj.
expected 507 adj.

affirmative
532 adj.
promised 764 n.

promised land
focus 76 n.
fantasy 513 n.
objective 617 n.
aspiration 852 n.

promises
inducement 612 n.

promise well
progress 285 vb.
be auspicious
730 vb.

promising
probable 471 adj.
predicting 511 adj.
palmy 730 adj.
promising 852 adj.

promontory
projection 254 n.
land 344 n.

promote
concur 181 vb.
promote 285 vb.
make likely
471 vb.
manifest 522 vb.
advertise 528 vb.
be instrumental
628 vb.
be expedient
642 vb.
flatter 925 vb.

promoter
overestimation
482 n.
informant 524 n.
publicizer 528 n.
patron 707 n.
flatterer 925 n.

promotion
progression 285 n.
publicity 528 n.
improvement
654 n.

prompt
early 135 adj.
speedy 277 adj.
remind 505 vb.
reminder 505 n.
hint 524 n.
hint 524 vb.
willing 597 adj.
incite 612 vb.
active 678 adj.
advise 691 vb.

prompter
  reminder 505 n.
  motivator 612 n.
  adviser 691 n.
promptness
  velocity 277 n.
promulgate
  decree 737 vb.
prone
  supine 216 adj.
prong
  bifurcation 92 n.
  sharp point 256 n.
pronoun
  part of speech
  564 n.
pronounce
  judge 480 vb.
  proclaim 528 vb.
  affirm 532 vb.
  voice 577 vb.
  speak 579 vb.
pronounced
  obvious 443 adj.
  manifest 522 adj.
pronounce guilty
  condemn 961 vb.
pronouncement
  judgment 480 n.
  publication 528 n.
pronto
  swiftly 277 adv.
pronunciation
  pronunciation
  577 n.
proof
  hard 326 adj.
  experiment 461 n.
  evidence 466 n.
  certainty 473 n.
  demonstration
  478 n.
  manifestation
  522 n.
  print 587 n.
  reading matter
  589 n.
  necessity 596 n.
  resolute 599 adj.
  amendment 654 n.
  invulnerable
  660 adj.
  legal trial 959 n.
proof against
  impassive 820 adj.
proofreader
  reformer 654 n.

prop
  strengthen 162 vb.
  support 218 vb.
  aircraft 276 n.
  elevate 310 vb.
  rotator 315 n.
propaganda
  argument 475 n.
  publicity 528 n.
  teaching 534 n.
  misteaching 535 n.
  inducement 612 n.
  warfare 718 n.
propagandist
  publicizer 528 n.
  motivator 612 n.
propagate
  augment 36 vb.
  generate 167 vb.
  make fruitful
  171 vb.
  publish 528 vb.
propagator
  propagation 167 n.
  abundance 171 n.
  flower 366 n.
  garden 370 n.
propane
  fuel 385 n.
propel
  propel 287 vb.
propellant
  propellant 287 n.
propeller
  propeller 269 n.
  rotator 315 n.
propensity
  tendency 179 n.
  willingness 597 n.
  liking 859 n.
proper
  relevant 9 adj.
  fit 24 adj.
  component 58 adj.
  advisable 642 adj.
  tasteful 846 adj.
  well-bred 848 adj.
  right 913 adj.
  due 915 adj.
  virtuous 933 adj.
proper fraction
  numerical element
  85 n.
properties
  stage set 594 n.
property
  essential part 5 n.

  ability 160 n.
  lands 777 n.
  property 777 n.
prophecy
  prediction 511 n.
  revelation 975 n.
prophesy
  foresee 510 vb.
  predict 511 vb.
prophet
  sage 500 n.
  oracle 511 n.
  preacher 537 n.
  warner 664 n.
  religious teacher
  973 n.
  worshipper 981 n.
  psychic 984 n.
  priest 986 n.
prophetess
  oracle 511 n.
  priest 986 n.
prophetic
  foreseeing 510 adj.
  predicting 511 adj.
  revelational
  975 adj.
  scriptural 975 adj.
  psychical 984 n.
prophet of doom
  overestimation
  482 n.
prophylactic
  prophylactic 658 n.
  remedial 658 adj.
prophylaxis
  prophylactic 658 n.
  protection 660 n.
  hindrance 702 n.
propinquity
  consanguinity
  11 n.
  nearness 200 n.
propitiate
  pacify 719 vb.
  mediate 720 vb.
  content 828 vb.
  atone 941 vb.
  offer worship
  981 vb.
propitious
  opportune 137 adj.
  beneficial 644 adj.
  palmy 730 adj.
  promising 852 adj.
proportion
  relativeness 9 n.

  correlation 12 n.
  adjust 24 vb.
  fitness 24 n.
  degree 27 n.
  part 53 n.
  ratio 85 n.
  symmetry 245 n.
  elegance 575 n.
  portion 783 n.
proportional
  relative 9 adj.
  correlative 12 adj.
  agreeing 24 adj.
  comparative 27 n.
  numerical 85 adj.
**proportional repre-
  sentation**
  vote 605 n.
  government 733 n.
proportionate
  relative 9 adj.
  correlative 12 adj.
  agreeing 24 adj.
proportioned
  symmetrical
  245 adj.
proportions
  measure 183 n.
  size 195 n.
proposal
  supposition 512 n.
  intention 617 n.
  plan 623 n.
  advice 691 n.
  offer 759 n.
  request 761 n.
  wooing 889 n.
propose
  propound 512 vb.
  select 605 vb.
  intend 617 vb.
  advise 691 vb.
  patronize 703 vb.
  offer 759 vb.
  court 889 vb.
propose marriage
  court 889 vb.
proposition
  topic 452 n.
  supposition 512 n.
  plan 623 n.
  advice 691 n.
  offer 759 n.
  request 761 n.
  debauch 951 vb.
propound
  propound 512 vb.

proprietary
proprietary
777 adj.
proprietary drug
medicine 658 n.
proprieties
etiquette 848 n.
proprietor
owner 776 n.
proprietress
owner 776 n.
proprietrix
owner 776 n.
propriety
relevance 9 n.
fitness 24 n.
elegance 575 n.
good policy 642 n.
good taste 846 n.
etiquette 848 n.
right 913 n.
purity 950 n.
props
stage set 594 n.
propulsion
propulsion 287 n.
prop up
preserve 666 vb.
aid 703 vb.
pro rata
pro rata 783 adv.
prosaic
typical 83 adj.
feeble 572 adj.
plain 573 adj.
prosaic 593 adj.
tedious 838 adj.
dull 840 adj.
pros and cons
reasons 475 n.
proscenium
stage set 594 n.
theatre 594 n.
proscribe
command 737 vb.
prohibit 757 vb.
condemn 961 vb.
proscription
prohibition 757 n.
malediction 899 n.
condemnation
961 n.
penalty 963 n.
prose
prose 593 n.
prosecute
do 676 vb.

indict 928 vb.
litigate 959 vb.
prosecution
accusation 928 n.
legal trial 959 n.
litigation 959 n.
prosecutor
accuser 928 n.
litigant 959 n.
proselyte
learner 538 n.
prosody
prosody 593 n.
prospect
futurity 124 n.
destiny 155 n.
range 183 n.
view 438 n.
search 459 vb.
be tentative 461 vb.
expectation 507 n.
prediction 511 n.
art subject 553 n.
intention 617 n.
prospective
future 124 adj.
expected 507 adj.
foreseeing 510 adj.
prospector
enquirer 459 n.
experimenter
461 n.
detector 484 n.
prospectus
list 87 n.
foresight 510 n.
prediction 511 n.
compendium
592 n.
policy 623 n.
prosper
grow 36 vb.
get better 654 vb.
prosper 730 vb.
prosperity
prosperity 730 n.
prosperous
prosperous 730 adj.
prostate
genitalia 167 n.
prosthesis
precedence 64 n.
substitute 150 n.
leg 267 n.
surgery 658 n.
prostitute
pervert 655 vb.

misuse 675 vb.
debauch 951 vb.
prostitute 952 n.
prostitution
deterioration
655 n.
misuse 675 n.
social evil 951 n.
prostrate
disable 161 vb.
low 210 adj.
flatten 216 vb.
supine 216 adj.
fell 311 vb.
sick 651 adj.
fatigue 684 vb.
fatigued 684 adj.
submitting 721 adj.
suffering 825 adj.
sadden 834 vb.
servile 879 adj.
respectful 920 adj.
prostrated
impotent 161 adj.
prostrate oneself
stoop 311 vb.
greet 884 vb.
show respect
920 vb.
be penitent 939 vb.
worship 981 vb.
perform ritual
988 vb.
prostration
helplessness 161 n.
weakness 163 n.
lowness 210 n.
lowering 311 n.
illness 651 n.
fatigue 684 n.
submission 721 n.
sorrow 825 n.
dejection 834 n.
servility 879 n.
respects 920 n.
piety 979 n.
ritual act 988 n.
prosy
prolix 570 adj.
protagonist
actor 594 n.
protean
multiform 82 adj.
changeful 152 adj.
protect
accompany 89 vb.
screen 421 vb.

safeguard 660 vb.
preserve 666 vb.
defend 713 vb.
befriend 880 vb.
protected
safe 660 adj.
preserved 666 adj.
restrained 747 adj.
protected species
preservation 666 n.
protection
protection 660 n.
safeguard 662 n.
trade 791 n.
protectionism
restriction 747 n.
protection racket
swindling 788 n.
protective clothing
shelter 662 n.
armour 713 n.
protective custody
detention 747 n.
protector
protector 660 n.
master 741 n.
protectorate
territory 184 n.
protection 660 n.
political organiza-
tion 733 n.
protectress
protector 660 n.
protégé(e)
dependant 742 n.
friend 880 n.
protein
food content 301 n.
organism 358 n.
protest
dissent 489 n.
dissent 489 vb.
affirm 532 vb.
negate 533 vb.
negation 533 n.
be unwilling
598 vb.
unwillingness
598 n.
be active 678 vb.
oppose 704 vb.
resist 715 vb.
resistance 715 n.
revolt 738 vb.
refusal 760 n.
refuse 760 vb.
deprecation 762 n.

nonobservance
769 n.
be discontented
829 vb.
disapprobation
924 n.
disapprove 924 vb.
Protestantism
Protestantism
976 n.
protester
dissentient 489 n.
agitator 738 n.
protest march
deprecation 762 n.
prothesis
altar 990 n.
protocol
practice 610 n.
etiquette 848 n.
ostentation 875 n.
proton
minuteness 196 n.
element 319 n.
protoplasm
prototype 23 n.
origin 68 n.
matter 319 n.
organism 358 n.
life 360 n.
prototype
prototype 23 n.
preparation 669 n.
protract
put off 136 vb.
sustain 146 vb.
lengthen 203 vb.
be diffuse 570 vb.
be obstructive
702 vb.
protractor
angular measure
247 n.
gauge 465 n.
protrude
jut 254 vb.
protrusion
convexity 253 n.
protuberance
convexity 253 n.
protuberance
254 n.
protuberant
projecting 254 adj.
proud
proud 871 adj.
vain 873 adj.

proud flesh
swelling 253 n.
prove
happen 154 vb.
expand 197 vb.
demonstrate
478 vb.
be true 494 vb.
vindicate 927 vb.
proven
trustworthy
929 adj.
provenance
origin 68 n.
provender
food 301 n.
provender 301 n.
provisions 301 n.
plant 366 n.
provision 633 n.
prove one's point
demonstrate
478 vb.
proverb
maxim 496 n.
phrase 563 n.
proverbial
known 490 adj.
aphoristic 496 adj.
provide
provide 633 vb.
give 781 vb.
provided
provided 468 adv.
prepared 669 adj.
provided that
thus 8 adv.
provide for
vitalize 360 vb.
providence
foresight 510 n.
divineness 965 n.
provident
foreseeing 510 adj.
providential
opportune 137 adj.
palmy 730 adj.
province
classification 77 n.
district 184 n.
function 622 n.
*political organiza-
tion* 733 n.
parish 985 n.
provinces
district 184 n.

provincial
dweller 191 n.
provincial 192 adj.
narrow-minded
481 adj.
ill-bred 847 adj.
country-dweller
869 n.
plebeian 869 adj.
ecclesiastical
985 adj.
provincialism
narrow mind
481 n.
proving
evidential 466 adj.
proving ground
testing agent
461 n.
provision
foresight 510 n.
provision 633 n.
conditions 766 n.
provisional
inferior 35 adj.
changeable
143 adj.
substituted 150 adj.
experimental
461 adj.
qualifying 468 adj.
provision 633 n.
imperfect 647 adj.
preparatory
669 adj.
conditional
766 adj.
provisionally
provisionally 112
adv.
on terms 766 adv.
provisions
provisions 301 n.
proviso
qualification 468 n.
pretext 614 n.
conditions 766 n.
provisory
conditional
766 adj.
provocation
causation 156 n.
inducement 612 n.
excitation 821 n.
annoyance 827 n.
sauciness 878 n.
resentment 891 n.

provocative
defiant 711 adj.
exciting 821 adj.
impure 951 adj.
provoke
cause 156 vb.
incite 612 vb.
make quarrels
709 vb.
torment 827 vb.
be insolent 878 vb.
provost
master 741 n.
officer 741 n.
law officer 955 n.
prowess
skill 694 n.
prowess 855 n.
prestige 866 n.
prowl
wander 267 vb.
be stealthy 525 vb.
prowler
pedestrian 268 n.
proximate
near 200 adj.
proximity
destiny 155 n.
nearness 200 n.
contiguity 202 n.
proxy
substitute 150 n.
agent 686 n.
commission 751 n.
consignee 754 n.
deputy 755 n.
prude
prude 950 n.
prudence
sagacity 498 n.
foresight 510 n.
economy 814 n.
caution 858 n.
virtues 933 n.
prudent
thoughtful 449 adj.
vigilant 457 adj.
intelligent 498 adj.
wise 498 adj.
foreseeing 510 adj.
advisable 642 adj.
economical
814 adj.
cautious 858 adj.
prudery
pretension 850 n.
purity 950 n.

prudish
  severe 735 adj.
  affected 850 adj.
  modest 874 adj.
  prudish 950 adj.
prune
  subtract 39 vb.
  cut 46 vb.
  make smaller
    198 vb.
  shorten 204 vb.
  fruit and vegetables
    301 n.
  extract 304 vb.
  cultivate 370 vb.
prurient
  inquisitive 453 adj.
  impure 951 adj.
  lecherous 951 adj.
pruritis
  skin disease 651 n.
prussic acid
  poison 659 n.
pry
  scan 438 vb.
  be curious 453 vb.
  enquire 459 vb.
pry into
  search 459 vb.
  meddle 678 vb.
P.S.
  adjunct 40 n.
psalm
  vocal music 412 n.
  hymn 981 n.
psalmody
  vocal music 412 n.
  act of worship
    981 n.
  hymn 981 n.
  public worship
    981 n.
psalter
  vocal music 412 n.
  scripture 975 n.
  hymn 981 n.
  hymnal 988 n.
psaltery
  stringed instrument
    414 n.
psephology
  vote 605 n.
pseud
  impostor 545 n.
pseudo
  simulating 18 adj.
  imitative 20 adj.

  false 541 adj.
pseudonym
  insubstantial thing
    4 n.
  name 561 n.
  misnomer 562 n.
psittacosis
  animal disease
    651 n.
psyche
  self 80 n.
  subjectivity 320 n.
  intellect 447 n.
  spirit 447 n.
  affections 817 n.
psychedelic
  intoxicating
    949 adj.
psychiatry
  psychology 447 n.
  mental disorder
    503 n.
  therapy 658 n.
psychic
  immaterial
    320 adj.
  psychic 984 n.
  psychical 984 n.
psychical
  psychical 984 n.
psychoanalysis
  psychology 447 n.
  therapy 658 n.
psychobabble
  lack of meaning
    515 n.
  unintelligibility
    517 n.
  neology 560 n.
  slang 560 adj.
psychodrama
  psychology 447 n.
  representation
    551 n.
psychography
  spiritualism 984 n.
psychokinesis
  psychics 984 n.
psycholinguistics
  psychology 447 n.
**psychological mo-
  ment**
  crisis 137 n.
**psychological war-
  fare**
  warfare 718 n.

psychology
  psychology 447 n.
  affections 817 n.
psych oneself up
  prepare oneself
    669 vb.
psychopath
  violent creature
    176 n.
  killer 362 n.
  the maladjusted
    504 n.
psychopathology
  psychology 447 n.
  *personality disor-
    der* 503 n.
  medical art 658 n.
psychosis
  psychosis 503 n.
psychosomatic
  diseased 651 adj.
psychotherapy
  psychology 447 n.
  mental disorder
    503 n.
  therapy 658 n.
psychotic
  psychotic 503 adj.
  psychotic 504 n.
psych up
  invigorate 174 vb.
ptarmigan
  table bird 365 n.
pterodactyl
  animal 365 n.
pub
  focus 76 n.
  tavern 192 n.
  social round 882 n.
pub-crawl
  drunkenness 949 n.
puberty
  propagation 167 n.
pubescence
  youth 130 n.
pubic hair
  hair 259 n.
public
  social group 371 n.
  known 490 adj.
  manifest 522 adj.
  shown 522 adj.
  noteworthy
    866 adj.
  formal 875 adj.
  showy 875 adj.

public, the
  commonalty 869 n.
**public address sys-
  tem**
  megaphone 400 n.
  hearing aid 415 n.
  publicity 528 n.
publican
  caterer 633 n.
  receiver 782 n.
publication
  publication 528 n.
  book 589 n.
public baths
  ablutions 648 n.
public convenience
  latrine 649 n.
public domain
  joint possession
    775 n.
public enemy
  enemy 881 n.
  offender 904 n.
public enquiry
  enquiry 459 n.
  adviser 691 n.
public eye
  publicity 528 n.
public figure
  person of repute
    866 n.
public house
  tavern 192 n.
publicist
  exhibitor 522 n.
  publicizer 528 n.
  dissertator 591 n.
publicity
  publicity 528 n.
publicize
  attract notice
    455 vb.
  manifest 522 vb.
  communicate
    524 vb.
  divulge 526 vb.
  advertise 528 vb.
public knowledge
  knowledge 490 n.
public library
  library 589 n.
public life
  vocation 622 n.
**public limited com-
  pany**
  corporation 708 n.

publicly
remarkably 32 vb.
public nuisance
hateful object
888 n.
public opinion
belief 485 n.
consensus 488 n.
tribunal 956 n.
public opinion poll
enquiry 459 n.
public prosecutor
accuser 928 n.
law officer 955 n.
public purse
treasury 799 n.
public relations
publicity 528 n.
public school
school 539 n.
public speaking
oratory 579 n.
public-spirited
patriotic 901 adj.
public transport
vehicle 274 n.
publish
publish 528 vb.
publisher
publicizer 528 n.
bookperson 589 n.
publishing
publication 528 n.
publish the banns
court 889 vb.
marry 894 vb.
puce
brown 430 adj.
purple 436 adj.
Puck
elf 970 n.
fairy 970 n.
puck
missile 287 n.
pucker
become small
198 vb.
fold 261 n.
fold 261 vb.
pudding
sequel 67 n.
dessert 301 n.
dish 301 n.
puddle
shallowness 212 n.
lake 346 n.

pudenda
genitalia 167 n.
pudgy
fleshy 195 adj.
puerile
foolish 499 adj.
trivial 639 adj.
immature 670 adj.
puff
vary 152 vb.
dilation 197 n.
enlarge 197 vb.
emit 300 vb.
pastries and cakes
301 n.
blow 352 vb.
breathe 352 vb.
breeze 352 n.
smoke 388 vb.
overestimate
482 vb.
advertise 528 vb.
advertisement
528 n.
exaggerate 546 vb.
be fatigued 684 vb.
boast 877 vb.
praise 923 n.
praise 923 vb.
flatter 925 vb.
puff adder
reptile 365 n.
puffball
plant 366 n.
puffery
boasting 877 n.
puffin
bird 365 n.
puff out
enlarge 197 vb.
puff up
enlarge 197 vb.
elevate 310 vb.
praise 923 vb.
puffy
fleshy 195 adj.
pug
dog 365 n.
pugilism
pugilism 716 n.
sport 837 n.
pugilistic
warlike 718 adj.
pugnacious
quarrelling
709 adj.
warlike 718 adj.

pugnacity
quarrelsomeness
709 n.
attack 712 n.
bellicosity 718 n.
irascibility 892 n.
pug-nosed
short 204 adj.
puke
voidance 300 n.
vomit 300 vb.
pulchritude
beauty 841 n.
pule
cry 408 vb.
ululate 409 vb.
weep 836 vb.
pull
advantage 34 n.
force 176 vb.
influence 178 n.
move 265 vb.
row 269 vb.
transpose 272 vb.
deflect 282 vb.
propel 287 vb.
propulsion 287 n.
draw 288 vb.
traction 288 n.
attract 291 vb.
attraction 291 n.
extract 304 vb.
extraction 304 n.
smoke 388 vb.
reading matter
589 n.
motivate 612 vb.
doctor 658 vb.
exertion 682 n.
work 682 vb.
pull a fast one
deceive 542 vb.
be cunning 698 vb.
pull a long face
be dejected 834 vb.
pull back
draw 288 vb.
pull down
demolish 165 vb.
pullet
young creature
132 n.
poultry 365 n.
pulley
wheel 250 n.
tool 630 n.

pull in
arrive 295 vb.
pull it off
succeed 727 vb.
pull no punches
be concise 569 vb.
be severe 735 vb.
pull off
print 587 vb.
pull oneself up
lift oneself 310 vb.
pull oneself up by
one's bootstraps
succeed 727 vb.
pull one's leg
fool 542 vb.
be witty 839 vb.
ridicule 851 vb.
pull one's weight
participate 775 vb.
pull out
subtract 39 vb.
displace 188 vb.
enlarge 197 vb.
lengthen 203 vb.
fly 271 vb.
draw 288 vb.
decamp 296 vb.
start out 296 vb.
eject 300 vb.
extract 304 vb.
pull out all the stops
be vigorous 174 vb.
exert oneself
682 vb.
pull out of the hat
surprise 508 vb.
pullover
jersey 228 n.
pull rank
be proud 871 vb.
pull strings
influence 178 vb.
plot 623 vb.
be instrumental
628 vb.
pull the plug on
terminate 69 vb.
pull the rug from
under one's feet
hinder 702 vb.
fire at 712 vb.
pull the wool over
one's eyes
deceive 542 vb.
pull through
be restored 656 vb.

pull tight
  tighten 45 vb.
pull together
  concur 181 vb.
  cooperate 706 vb.
  concord 710 vb.
pull to pieces
  demolish 165 vb.
  argue 475 vb.
  detract 926 vb.
pull towards
  draw 288 vb.
  attract 291 vb.
pull up
  subtract 39 vb.
  cease 145 vb.
  halt 145 vb.
  come to rest
    266 vb.
  arrive 295 vb.
  extract 304 vb.
  elevate 310 vb.
pulmonary embolism
  cardiovascular dis-
    ease 651 n.
pulp
  demolish 165 vb.
  deform 244 vb.
  soften 327 vb.
  thicken 354 vb.
  pulpiness 356 n.
  paper 631 n.
pulpit
  stand 218 n.
  publicity 528 n.
  church interior
    990 n.
  church utensil
    990 n.
pulp literature
  novel 590 n.
pulsar
  star 321 n.
pulsate
  oscillate 317 vb.
  show feeling
    818 vb.
  be excited 821 vb.
pulsation
  periodicity 141 n.
  electricity 160 n.
  impulse 279 n.
  oscillation 317 n.
  feeling 818 n.
pulse
  periodicity 141 n.
  electricity 160 n.

  impulse 279 n.
  oscillate 317 vb.
  oscillation 317 n.
  agitation 318 n.
  be agitated 318 vb.
  spasm 318 n.
pulses
  food 301 n.
  fruit and vegetables
    301 n.
pulverize
  pulverize 332 vb.
puma
  big cat 365 n.
pumice stone
  friction 333 n.
  cleanser 648 n.
pummel
  strike 279 vb.
  fight 716 vb.
pump
  extract 304 vb.
  irrigate 341 vb.
  irrigator 341 n.
  blowing 352 n.
  interrogate 459 vb.
pumpernickel
  cereals 301 n.
pumping
  extraction 304 n.
pump iron
  amuse oneself
    837 vb.
pumpkin
  fruit and vegetables
    301 n.
pump out
  empty 300 vb.
  rarefy 325 vb.
  dry 342 vb.
  blow up 352 vb.
pump rooms
  meeting place
    192 n.
pumps
  footwear 228 n.
pump up
  enlarge 197 vb.
  elevate 310 vb.
  blow up 352 vb.
pun
  assimilation 18 n.
  absurdity 497 n.
  be equivocal
    518 vb.
  equivocalness
    518 n.

  word 559 n.
  be witty 839 vb.
  witticism 839 n.
punch
  mould 23 n.
  a mixture 43 n.
  vigorousness 174 n.
  perforator 263 n.
  pierce 263 vb.
  draught horse
    273 n.
  hammer 279 n.
  knock 279 n.
  strike 279 vb.
  alcoholic drink
    301 n.
  draught 301 n.
  mark 547 vb.
  vigour 571 n.
Punch and Judy
  show
  stage play 594 n.
punch bowl
  bowl 194 n.
puncheon
  pillar 218 n.
punch line
  witticism 839 n.
punchy
  forceful 571 adj.
punctilio
  ostentation 875 n.
  probity 929 n.
punctilious
  attentive 455 adj.
  accurate 494 adj.
  observant 768 adj.
  well-bred 848 adj.
  fastidious 862 adj.
  formal 875 adj.
  obliged 917 adj.
  trustworthy
    929 adj.
punctual
  early 135 adj.
  timely 137 adj.
  periodical 141 adj.
  accurate 494 adj.
punctuality
  punctuality 135 n.
punctuate
  discontinue 72 vb.
  mark 547 vb.
punctuation
  punctuation 547 n.
  grammar 564 n.

punctuation mark
  punctuation 547 n.
puncture
  abate 37 vb.
  make smaller
    198 vb.
  pierce 263 vb.
  abase 311 vb.
  lower 311 vb.
  confute 479 vb.
  wound 655 n.
  wound 655 vb.
  hitch 702 n.
  detract 926 vb.
pundit
  sage 500 n.
  dissertator 591 n.
  expert 696 n.
  jurist 958 n.
pungent
  pungent 388 adj.
  witty 839 adj.
punish
  punish 963 vb.
punishable
  illegal 954 adj.
punishing
  laborious 682 adj.
  paining 827 adj.
punishment
  punishment 963 n.
punishment exercise
  penalty 963 n.
punitive
  severe 735 adj.
  punitive 963 adj.
punk
  nonconformist
    84 n.
  youngster 132 n.
  music 412 n.
  bad 645 adj.
  ruffian 904 n.
punkah
  ventilation 352 n.
punnet
  basket 194 n.
punt
  row 269 vb.
  rowing boat 275 n.
  impel 279 vb.
  propulsion 287 n.
  gamble 618 vb.
punter
  boatman 270 n.
  gambler 618 n.

puny
small 33 adj.
weak 163 adj.
little 196 adj.

pup
young creature
132 n.
reproduce itself
167 vb.
dog 365 n.
insolent person
878 n.

pupa
young creature
132 n.
insect 365 n.

pupil
centre 225 n.
eye 438 n.
learner 538 n.

pupillage
nonage 130 n.
helplessness 161 n.

puppet
dwarf 196 n.
dupe 544 n.
image 551 n.
instrument 628 n.
nonentity 639 n.
auxiliary 707 n.
dependant 742 n.
slave 742 n.
plaything 837 n.
toady 879 n.

puppet-like
obedient 739 adj.
subject 745 adj.

puppetry
drama 594 n.

puppet show
stage play 594 n.
plaything 837 n.

puppy
young creature
132 n.
dog 365 n.
insolent person
878 n.

puppyhood
youth 130 n.

puppy love
love 887 n.

purblind
dim-sighted
440 adj.
misjudging
481 adj.

purchase
influence 178 n.
pivot 218 n.
purchase 792 n.
purchase 792 vb.

purchase tax
tax 809 n.

purdah
womankind 373 n.
concealment 525 n.
seclusion 883 n.

pure
absolute 32 adj.
unmixed 44 adj.
whole 52 adj.
white 427 adj.
genuine 494 adj.
plain 573 adj.
excellent 644 adj.
perfect 646 adj.
salubrious 652 adj.
innocent 935 adj.
pure 950 adj.
pious 979 adj.

purebred
horse 273 n.

puree
hors-d'oeuvres
301 n.
pulpiness 356 n.

purgative
opener 263 n.
purgative 658 n.

purgatory
suffering 825 n.
penance 941 n.
hell 972 n.

purge
slaughter 362 n.
slaughter 362 vb.
purify 648 vb.
purgative 658 n.
capital punishment
963 n.
execute 963 vb.

purification
inodorousness
395 n.
cleansing 648 n.
ritual act 988 n.

purify
purify 648 vb.
perform ritual
988 vb.

purist
people of taste
846 n.

perfectionist 862 n.

Puritan
sectarian 978 adj.
sectarian 978 n.
pietistic 979 adj.
zealot 979 n.

puritanical
severe 735 adj.
fastidious 862 adj.
ascetic 945 adj.

purity
simpleness 44 n.
purity 950 n.

purl
needlework 844 n.

purler
overturning 221 n.
descent 309 n.

purlieus
district 184 n.
locality 187 n.

purloin
defraud 788 vb.
steal 788 vb.

purple
purple 436 adj.
purpleness 436 n.

purple hearts
drug-taking 949 n.

purple prose
imperspicuity
568 n.

purport
mean 514 vb.
meaning 514 n.

purpose
will 595 n.
be resolute 599 vb.
intention 617 n.
aspiration 852 n.

purposeful
resolute 599 adj.

purposeless
useless 641 adj.

purposely
purposely 617 adv.

purpure
heraldic 547 adj.
heraldry 547 n.

purr
faintness 401 n.
sound faint 401 vb.
ululate 409 vb.
sing 413 vb.
rejoice 835 vb.

purse
become small
198 vb.
treasury 799 n.

purse one's lips
gesticulate 547 vb.

purser
consignee 754 n.
treasurer 798 n.

purse strings
finance 797 n.

pursuance
sequence 65 n.
following 284 n.
pursuit 619 n.

pursue
pursue 619 vb.
do 676 vb.

pursuer
hunter 619 n.
dueness 915 n.
accuser 928 n.
litigant 959 n.

pursuit
following 284 n.
pursuit 619 n.
business 622 n.

pursuivant
heraldry 547 n.

purulent
diseased 651 adj.
toxic 653 adj.

purveyor
caterer 633 n.

pus
excrement 302 n.
fluid 335 n.
semiliquidity
354 n.
dirt 649 n.

push
vigorousness 174 n.
move 265 vb.
transpose 272 vb.
impel 279 vb.
impulse 279 n.
propel 287 vb.
propulsion 287 n.
ejection 300 n.
gesture 547 n.
motivate 612 vb.
be active 678 vb.
restlessness 678 n.
haste 680 n.
attack 712 n.
strike at 712 vb.
sell 793 vb.

push around
 impel 279 vb.
push-button
 instrumental
  628 adj.
pushchair
 pushcart 274 n.
pusher
 ram 279 n.
 propellant 287 n.
 busy person 678 n.
 drug-taking 949 n.
push on
 progress 285 vb.
push oneself forward
 be vain 873 vb.
push one's luck
 gamble 618 vb.
 be rash 857 vb.
push out
 eject 300 vb.
pushover
 weakling 163 n.
 dupe 544 n.
 easy thing 701 n.
 victory 727 n.
push too far
 enrage 891 vb.
push up the daisies
 die 361 vb.
pusillanimous
 cowardly 856 adj.
puss
 cat 365 n.
pussy
 cat 365 n.
pussyfoot
 be stealthy 525 vb.
 avoid 620 vb.
 be cautious 858 vb.
pussy willow
 tree 366 n.
pustule
 skin disease 651 n.
put
 firm 45 adj.
 place 187 vb.
put about
 navigate 269 vb.
 circle 314 vb.
 publish 528 vb.
put a brave face on it
 be patient 823 vb.
 take courage
  855 vb.
put across
 convince 485 vb.

put a damper on
 moderate 177 vb.
 depress 834 vb.
**put a false construc-
 tion on**
 be false 541 vb.
put an end to
 terminate 69 vb.
 destroy 165 vb.
 defeat 727 vb.
put aside
 set apart 46 vb.
 exclude 57 vb.
 be neglectful
  458 vb.
 neglected 458 adj.
 store 632 vb.
**put a spoke in one's
 wheel**
 disable 161 vb.
 make useless
  641 adj.
 be obstructive
  702 vb.
put a stop to
 terminate 69 vb.
 halt 145 vb.
 be severe 735 vb.
 restrain 747 vb.
putative
 supposed 512 adj.
put away
 destroy 165 vb.
 *mentally disor-
  dered* 503 adj.
 divorce 896 vb.
put by
 store 632 vb.
put down
 destroy 165 vb.
 suppress 165 vb.
 place 187 vb.
 let fall 311 vb.
 kill 362 vb.
 overmaster 727 vb.
 inglorious 867 adj.
 shame 867 vb.
 humiliate 872 vb.
put-down
 slur 867 n.
put down to
 attribute 158 vb.
put forth
 expand 197 vb.
 propound 512 vb.
put forward
 affirm 532 vb.

 offer 759 vb.
**put in a good word
 for**
 approve 923 vb.
put in an appearance
 be present 189 vb.
put in for
 offer oneself
  759 vb.
 request 761 vb.
put in one's place, be
 be humbled
  872 vb.
put in order
 compose 56 vb.
 arrange 62 vb.
put in perspective
 relate 9 vb.
put in the shade
 abate 37 vb.
 humiliate 872 vb.
put into force
 compel 740 vb.
put into operation
 move 265 vb.
 use 673 vb.
put into practice
 use 673 vb.
 do 676 vb.
 deal with 688 vb.
put in touch
 connect 45 vb.
put in writing
 write 586 vb.
put it another way
 mean 514 vb.
put it bluntly
 affirm 532 vb.
put off
 put off 136 vb.
 influence 178 vb.
 repel 292 vb.
 distracted 456 adj.
 dissuade 613 vb.
 be obstructive
  702 vb.
 cause dislike
  861 vb.
**put off one's stroke,
 be**
 be inattentive
  456 vb.
put off the evil day
 be nervous 854 vb.
put off the scent
 deflect 282 vb.

**put off until to-
 morrow**
 be neglectful
  458 vb.
 be irresolute
  601 vb.
put on
 imitate 20 vb.
 wear 228 vb.
 show 522 vb.
 dissemble 541 vb.
 hypocritical
  541 adj.
 fool 542 vb.
 dramatize 594 vb.
 affected 850 adj.
 be affected 850 vb.
put on a front
 be ostentatious
  875 vb.
put on airs
 be affected 850 vb.
 be vain 873 vb.
 be insolent 878 vb.
put one in mind of
 resemble 18 vb.
 remind 505 vb.
put one in the clear
 justify 927 vb.
put one in the picture
 inform 524 vb.
put one off
 displease 827 vb.
put one off his stroke
 distract 456 vb.
put one on
 be witty 839 vb.
 ridicule 851 vb.
put one on the spot
 be difficult 700 vb.
put one out
 trouble 827 vb.
put one's back into it
 exert oneself
  682 vb.
put one's back up
 cause dislike
  861 vb.
 huff 891 vb.
**put one's best foot
 forward**
 move fast 277 vb.
 undertake 672 vb.
 exert oneself
  682 vb.
**put one's cards on
 the table**

divulge 526 vb.
put one's case
  argue 475 vb.
  affirm 532 vb.
put oneself forward
  be ostentatious
   875 vb.
put oneself out
  exert oneself
   682 vb.
put one's finger on
  place 187 vb.
put one's foot down
  accelerate 277 vb.
  be resolute 599 vb.
  command 737 vb.
  prohibit 757 vb.
put one's foot in it
  blunder 495 vb.
  be clumsy 695 vb.
put one's money on
  expect 507 vb.
put one's nose out of
  joint
  shame 867 vb.
  humiliate 872 vb.
  huff 891 vb.
put one's oar in
  interfere 231 vb.
put one's shoulder to
  the wheel
  begin 68 vb.
  be resolute 599 vb.
  be active 678 vb.
put one's tongue out
  be insolent 878 vb.
put one through it
  torment 827 vb.
put one up
  place 187 vb.
put one wise
  inform 524 vb.
put on ice
  pause 145 vb.
put on one side
  subtract 39 vb.
put on record
  record 548 vb.
put on side
  be affected 850 vb.
  be vain 873 vb.
  be ostentatious
   875 vb.
put on the back-
  burner
  put off 136 vb.
  pause 145 vb.

be neglectful
  458 vb.
disused 674 adj.
stop using 674 vb.
put on the map
  advertise 528 vb.
put on trial
  indict 928 vb.
  litigate 959 vb.
put on view
  show 522 vb.
put on weight
  grow 36 vb.
  expand 197 vb.
put out
  suppress 165 vb.
  eject 300 vb.
  extinguish 382 vb.
  communicate
   524 vb.
  publish 528 vb.
  discontented
   829 adj.
put out of action
  disable 161 vb.
put out of commis-
  sion
  disable 161 vb.
  make useless
   641 vb.
  stop using 674 vb.
  make inactive
   679 vb.
put out the light
  darken 418 vb.
put out to grass
  feed 301 vb.
  stop using 674 vb.
  not retain 779 vb.
put over
  convince 485 vb.
put paid to
  terminate 69 vb.
put pen to paper
  write 586 vb.
put pressure on
  influence 178 vb.
putrefaction
  decay 51 n.
  stench 397 n.
  uncleanness 649 n.
  dilapidation 655 n.
putrefy
  decompose 51 vb.
  deteriorate 655 vb.
putrid
  unsavoury 391 adj.

fetid 397 adj.
not nice 645 adj.
put right
  inform 524 vb.
  rectify 654 vb.
  repair 656 vb.
  remedy 658 vb.
  right 913 adj.
putsch
  revolt 738 n.
putt
  propel 287 vb.
puttees
  legwear 228 n.
put the blame on
  blame 924 vb.
  accuse 928 vb.
put the boot in
  criticize 924 vb.
put the cart before
  the horse
  invert 221 vb.
  act foolishly
   695 vb.
put the cat among
  the pigeons
  make quarrels
   . 709 vb.
put the fear of God
  into
  frighten 854 vb.
put the finishing
  touches to
  crown 213 vb.
put the kibosh on
  destroy 165 vb.
  suppress 165 vb.
put the lid on
  close 264 vb.
  climax 725 vb.
  defeat 727 vb.
put the question
  interrogate 459 vb.
put the screws on
  oppress 735 vb.
  compel 740 vb.
put the skids under
  destroy 165 vb.
put the wind up
  frighten 854 vb.
put through the hoop
  torment 827 vb.
putting
  ball game 837 n.
putting green
  arena 724 n.

put to bed
  place 187 vb.
  print 587 vb.
put to death
  kill 362 vb.
  execute 963 vb.
put to flight
  propel 287 vb.
  defeat 727 vb.
  defeated 728 adj.
put together
  join 45 vb.
  combine 50 vb.
  compose 56 vb.
  bring together
   74 vb.
  produce 164 vb.
put to rights
  regularize 62 vb.
put to sea
  navigate 269 vb.
  voyage 269 vb.
put to shame
  shame 867 vb.
  humiliate 872 vb.
  not respect 921 vb.
  defame 926 vb.
put to sleep
  kill 362 vb.
  render insensible
   375 vb.
  make inactive
   679 vb.
put to the test
  experiment 461 vb.
put to the vote
  vote 605 vb.
put to use
  use 673 vb.
put to work
  initiate 68 vb.
  work 682 vb.
put two and two to-
  gether
  reason 475 vb.
putty
  adhesive 47 n.
  softness 327 n.
  pulpiness 356 n.
putty in one's hands
  willingness 597 n.
  irresolution 601 n.
  persuadability
   612 n.
put under arrest
  arrest 747 vb.

put up
place 187 vb.
place oneself
187 vb.
elevate 310 vb.
select 605 vb.
predetermine
608 vb.
provide 633 vb.
put up a fight
contend 716 vb.
put up for
patronize 703 vb.
put up for sale
offer 759 vb.
sell 793 vb.
put-up job
duplicity 541 n.
predetermination
608 n.
plot 623 n.
false charge 928 n.
put upon
ill-treat 645 vb.
oppress 735 vb.
put up the banns
wed 894 vb.
put up the shutters
terminate 69 vb.
cease 145 vb.
close 264 vb.
screen 421 vb.
put up to
incite 612 vb.
put up with
substitute 150 vb.
acquiesce 488 vb.
knuckle under
721 vb.
be lax 734 vb.
permit 756 vb.
be patient 823 vb.
suffer 825 vb.
forgive 909 vb.
puzzle
complexity 61 n.
puzzle 474 vb.
enigma 530 n.
difficulty 700 n.
worry 825 n.
prodigy 864 n.
puzzling
puzzling 517 adj.
PVC
materials 631 n.
pyelogram
diagnostic 658 n.

pyjamas
nightwear 228 n.
pyknic
thick 205 adj.
pylon
electronics 160 n.
high structure
209 n.
pyramid
series 71 n.
fixture 153 n.
edifice 164 n.
bulk 195 n.
high structure
209 n.
angular figure
247 n.
tomb 364 n.
pyre
interment 364 n.
fire 379 n.
pyrexia
heat 379 n.
illness 651 n.
pyromania
arson 381 n.
pyrotechnics
fire 379 n.
spectacle 445 n.
pageant 875 n.
Pyrrhic victory
victory 727 n.
python
reptile 365 n.

Q

qanat
tunnel 263 n.
irrigator 341 n.
conduit 351 n.
Q.C.
lawyer 958 n.
quack
ululate 409 vb.
ululation 409 n.
dabbler 493 n.
false 541 adj.
impostor 545 n.
doctor 658 n.
unskilled 695 adj.
quad
focus 76 n.
quaternity 96 n.
place 185 n.
meeting place
192 n.

print-type 587 n.
quadrangle
quaternity 96 n.
place 185 n.
meeting place
192 n.
angular figure
247 n.
quadrant
angular measure
247 n.
arc 250 n.
sailing aid 269 n.
gauge 465 n.
measurement
465 n.
quadraphonic sound
sound 398 n.
quadrate
four 96 adj.
quadruple 97 vb.
quadratic
four 96 adj.
quadratic equations
mathematics 86 n.
quadrennial
four 96 adj.
seasonal 141 adj.
quadricentennial
seasonal 141 adj.
quadriga
quaternity 96 n.
carriage 274 n.
quadrilateral
four 96 adj.
quaternity 96 n.
lateral 239 adj.
angular figure
247 n.
quadrille
dance 837 n.
quadrillion
over one hundred
99 n.
quadrisection
quadrisection 98 n.
quadruped
quaternity 96 n.
horse 273 n.
animal 365 n.
quadruple
fourfold 97 adj.
quadruple 97 vb.
quadruplet
quaternity 96 n.
quadruplex
fourfold 97 adj.

quadruplicate
fourfold 97 adj.
quadruple 97 vb.
quaff
drink 301 vb.
get drunk 949 vb.
quagmire
marsh 347 n.
pitfall 663 n.
difficulty 700 n.
quaich
cup 194 n.
quail
recoil 280 vb.
table bird 365 n.
be nervous 854 vb.
quake 854 vb.
be cowardly
856 vb.
quaint
ridiculous 849 adj.
quake
outbreak 176 n.
be cold 380 vb.
show feeling
818 vb.
quake 854 vb.
quake in one's shoes
quake 854 vb.
Quaker
Protestant 976 adj.
Protestant 976 n.
sectarian 978 n.
qualification
fitness 24 n.
ability 160 n.
qualification 468 n.
success 727 n.
dueness 915 n.
qualified
fit 24 adj.
mixed 43 adj.
qualifying 468 adj.
prepared 669 adj.
expert 694 adj.
qualify
modify 143 vb.
moderate 177 vb.
qualify 468 vb.
train 534 vb.
suffice 635 vb.
succeed 727 vb.
qualitative
characteristic
5 adj.
quality
character 5 n.

903

sort 77 n.
tendency 179 n.
excellent 644 adj.
goodness 644 n.
qualms
regret 830 n.
nervousness 854 n.
quandary
circumstance 8 n.
dubiety 474 n.
predicament 700 n.
quango
director 690 n.
council 692 n.
party 708 n.
consignee 754 n.
quantify
specify 80 vb.
measure 465 vb.
quantitative
quantitative 26 adj.
quantities
great quantity
32 n.
quantity
quantity 26 n.
great quantity
32 n.
number 85 n.
quantum
finite quantity
26 n.
element 319 n.
quantum leap
progression 285 n.
success 727 n.
quarantine
disunion 46 n.
set apart 46 vb.
exclude 57 vb.
exclusion 57 n.
prophylactic 658 n.
protection 660 n.
preservation 666 n.
detention 747 n.
imprison 747 vb.
seclude 883 vb.
seclusion 883 n.
quark
minuteness 196 n.
element 319 n.
quarrel
quarrel 709 n.
quarrel 709 vb.
fight 716 vb.
be discontented
829 vb.

quarrelling
dissension 709 n.
quarrelling
709 adj.
quarrelsome
quarrelling
709 adj.
sullen 893 adj.
quarry
source 156 n.
produce 164 vb.
excavation 255 n.
extract 304 vb.
objective 617 n.
chase 619 n.
store 632 n.
workshop 687 n.
quart
quadrisection 98 n.
metrology 465 n.
quarter
cut 46 vb.
sunder 46 vb.
part 53 n.
group 74 n.
quaternity 96 n.
quadrisect 98 vb.
quadrisection 98 n.
period 110 n.
district 184 n.
place 185 n.
place 187 vb.
laterality 239 n.
weighing 322 n.
metrology 465 n.
informant 524 n.
heraldry 547 n.
leniency 736 n.
coinage 797 n.
mercy 905 n.
quarterdeck
layer 207 n.
quarterfinal
contest 716 n.
quartering
quadrisection 98 n.
heraldry 547 n.
quarterly
three 93 adj.
quadrisection 98 n.
journal 528 n.
quartermaster
navigator 270 n.
army officer 741 n.
quarters
locality 187 n.
quarters 192 n.

quartet
quaternity 96 n.
orchestra 413 n.
quarto
quadrisection 98 n.
edition 589 n.
paper 631 n.
quartz
hardness 326 n.
quartz clock
timekeeper 117 n.
quasar
star 321 n.
quash
suppress 165 vb.
abrogate 752 vb.
acquit 960 vb.
quasi
similar 18 adj.
similarly 18 adv.
simulating 18 adj.
imitative 20 adj.
supposed 512 adj.
quaternary
four 96 adj.
quaternion
number 85 n.
quatrain
quaternity 96 n.
verse form 593 n.
quaver
agitation 318 n.
be agitated 318 vb.
roll 403 n.
roll 403 vb.
notation 410 n.
stammer 580 vb.
quake 854 vb.
quay
stable 192 n.
edge 234 n.
shelter 662 n.
queasy
sick 651 adj.
queen
nonconformist
84 n.
pillar 218 n.
sovereign 741 n.
plaything 837 n.
aristocrat 868 n.
queen bee
insect 365 n.
queen it
be proud 871 vb.
be insolent 878 vb.

queenly
ruling 733 adj.
impressive 821 adj.
worshipful 866 adj.
noble 868 adj.
proud 871 adj.
Queen's Bench
lawcourt 956 n.
Queensberry rules
justice 913 n.
Queen's Counsel
lawyer 958 n.
Queen's evidence
disclosure 526 n.
queen size
large 195 adj.
size 195 n.
queer
abnormal 84 adj.
nonconformist
84 n.
unusual 84 adj.
male 372 n.
crazy 503 adj.
sick 651 adj.
ridiculous 849 adj.
wrong 914 adj.
queer one's pitch
harm 645 vb.
Queer Street
poverty 801 n.
quell
suppress 165 vb.
moderate 177 vb.
bring to rest
266 vb.
hinder 702 vb.
overmaster 727 vb.
subjugate 745 vb.
quench
suppress 165 vb.
extinguish 382 vb.
dissuade 613 vb.
sate 863 vb.
quench one's thirst
assuage 177 vb.
quenelles
fish food 301 n.
quernstone
pulverizer 332 n.
querulous
discontented
829 adj.
irascible 892 adj.
query
enquire 459 vb.
question 459 n.

uncertainty 474 n.
punctuation 547 n.
quest
  land travel 267 n.
  search 459 n.
  pursuit 619 n.
  undertaking 672 n.
question
  be curious 453 vb.
  interrogate 459 vb.
  question 459 n.
  doubt 486 vb.
  negate 533 vb.
questionable
  uncertain 474 adj.
  disreputable
   867 adj.
  dishonest 930 adj.
question mark
  question 459 n.
  uncertainty 474 n.
  punctuation 547 n.
question master
  broadcaster 531 n.
questionnaire
  list 87 n.
  question 459 n.
question or quiz
  master
  questioner 459 n.
question paper
  question 459 n.
queue
  retinue 67 n.
  line 203 n.
queue-jumping
  precedence 64 n.
  preceding 283 n.
queue up
  await 507 vb.
quibble
  argue 475 vb.
  sophisticate
   477 vb.
  equivocalness
   518 n.
  pretext 614 n.
quiche
  dish 301 n.
  pastries and cakes
   301 n.
quick
  brief 114 adj.
  speedy 277 adj.
  alive 360 adj.
  intelligent 498 adj.
  willing 597 adj.

active 678 adj.
skilful 694 adj.
witty 839 adj.
irascible 892 adj.
quick-change
  changeful 152 adj.
quicken
  invigorate 174 vb.
  accelerate 277 vb.
  live 360 vb.
  animate 821 vb.
quickie
  draught 301 n.
quick march
  marching 267 n.
  hurry up 680 int.
quickness
  velocity 277 n.
  activity 678 n.
quick on the uptake
  intelligent 498 adj.
quicksand
  marsh 347 n.
quicksilver
  changeable thing
   152 n.
quickstep
  dance 837 n.
  dance 837 vb.
quick-tempered
  irascible 892 adj.
quid
  tobacco 388 n.
  coinage 797 n.
  funds 797 n.
quiddity
  essence 1 n.
  existence 1 n.
  essential part 5 n.
quid pro quo
  interchange 151 n.
  retaliation 714 n.
  witticism 839 n.
  reward 962 n.
quids in
  moneyed 800 adj.
quiescent
  quiescent 266 adj.
quiet
  small 33 adj.
  order 60 n.
  weak 163 adj.
  inert 175 adj.
  assuage 177 vb.
  moderate 177 adj.
  moderation 177 n.

bring to rest
  266 vb.
quiescent 266 adj.
quietude 266 n.
still 266 n.
euphoria 376 n.
hush 399 int.
silence 399 n.
silence 399 vb.
silent 399 adj.
soft-hued 425 adj.
inaction 677 n.
reposeful 683 adj.
peaceful 717 adj.
pleasurable
  826 adj.
modest 874 adj.
secluded 883 adj.
quieten
  bring to rest
   266 vb.
  silence 399 vb.
quiet end
  decease 361 n.
quietness
  quietude 266 n.
  humility 872 n.
quietude
  quietude 266 n.
quietus
  end 69 n.
  death 361 n.
  killing 362 n.
  defeat 728 n.
  acquittal 960 n.
quiff
  hair 259 n.
quill
  prickle 256 n.
  plumage 259 n.
quill-pen
  stationery 586 n.
quilt
  coverlet 226 n.
  variegate 437 vb.
quin
  five 99 n.
quincentennial
  seasonal 141 adj.
quinine
  antidote 658 n.
  prophylactic 658 n.
quinquennial
  periodic 110 adj.
  seasonal 141 adj.
quinquennium
  period 110 n.

quinquereme
  five 99 n.
quintal
  weighing 322 n.
quintessence
  essential part 5 n.
  goodness 644 n.
  perfection 646 n.
quintet
  five 99 n.
  orchestra 413 n.
quintuplet
  five 99 n.
quip
  be witty 839 vb.
  witticism 839 n.
  indignity 921 n.
quire
  paper 631 n.
quirk
  speciality 80 n.
  nonconformity
   84 n.
  eccentricity 503 n.
  whim 604 n.
quisling
  recanter 603 n.
  collaborator 707 n.
  revolter 738 n.
  bad person 938 n.
quit
  separate 46 vb.
  depart 296 vb.
  relinquish 621 vb.
  resign 753 vb.
  fail in duty 918 vb.
quite
  greatly 32 vb.
  slightly 33 adv.
  completely 54 adv.
quite something
  prodigy 864 n.
quite the reverse
  contrariety 14 n.
  inversely 221 adv.
quit one's post
  relinquish 621 vb.
quits
  equal 28 adj.
  equivalence 28 n.
  atonement 941 n.
quiver
  accumulation 74 n.
  case 194 n.
  oscillate 317 vb.
  agitation 318 n.
  be agitated 318 vb.

feel pain 377 vb.
be cold 380 vb.
storage 632 n.
arsenal 723 n.
feeling 818 n.
show feeling
  818 vb.
be excited 821 vb.
quake 854 vb.

quiverful
  contents 193 n.

quixotic
  disinterested
    931 adj.

quiz
  gaze 438 vb.
  watch 441 vb.
  be curious 453 vb.
  interrogate 459 vb.
  interrogation
    459 n.
  broadcast 531 n.
  indoor game 837 n.

quizzical
  enquiring 459 adj.

quod
  prison 748 n.

quoits
  ball game 837 n.

quorum
  finite quantity
    26 n.
  plenitude 54 n.
  electorate 605 n.
  sufficiency 635 n.
  parliament 692 n.

quota
  finite quantity
    26 n.
  part 53 n.
  portion 783 n.

quotable
  relevant 9 adj.

quotation
  referral 9 n.
  part 53 n.
  repetition 106 n.
  evidence 466 n.
  exhibit 522 n.
  price 809 n.

quotation marks
  punctuation 547 n.

quote
  part 53 n.
  exemplify 83 vb.
  repeat 106 vb.
  manifest 522 vb.

quotidian
  seasonal 141 adj.

quotient
  quantity 26 n.
  numerical element
    85 n.

R

rabbet
  join 45 vb.
  furrow 262 n.

rabbi
  theologian 973 n.
  priest 986 n.

rabbit
  mammal 365 n.
  beginner 538 n.
  coward 856 n.

rabbit on
  be diffuse 570 vb.
  be loquacious
    581 vb.

rabbit punch
  knock 279 n.

rabbit warren
  abundance 171 n.

rabble
  rabble 869 n.

rabble-rouser
  motivator 612 n.
  agitator 738 n.
  excitant 821 n.

Rabelaisian
  impure 951 adj.

rabid
  furious 176 adj.
  frenzied 503 adj.
  excitable 822 adj.
  angry 891 adj.

rabies
  animal disease
    651 n.
  infection 651 n. ·

raccoon
  mammal 365 n.

race
  race 11 n.
  travel 267 vb.
  hasten 680 vb.
  conduct 688 n.
  community 708 n.
  contend 716 vb.
  racing 716 n.
  amuse oneself
    837 vb.

race against time
  haste 680 n.

racecourse
  meeting place
    192 n.
  gaming-house
    618 n.
  racing 716 n.
  arena 724 n.

racehorse
  horse 273 n.

racetrack
  path 624 n.
  arena 724 n.

racewalking
  pedestrianism
    267 n.
  racing 716 n.
  sport 837 n.

racial
  ethnic 11 adj.
  parental 169 adj.

racialism
  prejudice 481 n.
  hatred 888 n.

racialist
  biased 481 adj.
  narrow mind
    481 n.
  enemy 881 n.

racing
  speedy 277 adj.
  flowing 350 adj.
  hasty 680 adj.
  racing 716 n.
  sport 837 n.

racism
  prejudice 481 n.
  hatred 888 n.
  injustice 914 n.

racist
  biased 481 adj.
  narrow mind
    481 n.

rack
  compartment
    194 n.
  hanger 217 n.
  shelf 218 n.
  distort 246 vb.
  pain 377 n.
  suffering 825 n.
  torment 827 vb.
  instrument of tor-
    ture 964 n.

rack and ruin
  ruin 165 n.

racket
  turmoil 61 n.
  commotion 318 n.
  loudness 400 n.
  roll 403 n.
  discord 411 n.
  trickery 542 n.
  plot 623 n.
  quarrel 709 n.
  perfidy 930 n.

racketeer
  robber 789 n.
  offender 904 n.
  be dishonest
    930 vb.

rackets
  ball game 837 n.

rack one's brains
  think 449 vb.
  remember 505 vb.

raconteur
  humorist 839 n.

racy
  vigorous 174 adj.
  stylistic 566 adj.
  forceful 571 adj.
  lively 819 adj.
  witty 839 adj.
  impure 951 adj.

radar
  location 187 n.
  sailing aid 269 n.
  detector 484 n.
  telecommunication
    531 n.
  indicator 547 n.

raddle
  redden 431 vb.

radially
  longwise 203 adv.

radian
  angular measure
    247 n.

radiance
  glow 417 n.
  light 417 n.
  beauty 841 n.

radiant
  divergent 294 adj.
  luminous 417 adj.
  happy 824 adj.
  cheerful 833 adj.
  beautiful 841 adj.

radiate
  separate 46 vb.
  be dispersed 75 vb.
  diverge 294 vb.

radiate 417 vb.
radiation
dispersion 75 n.
divergence 294 n.
radiation 417 n.
radiator
heater 383 n.
radical
numerical 85 adj.
revolutionary
149 adj.
revolutionist 149 n.
fundamental
156 adj.
source 156 n.
important 638 adj.
improving 654 adj.
reformer 654 n.
radical mastectomy
surgery 658 n.
Radicals
political party
708 n.
radiesthesia
medical art 658 n.
radio
electronics 160 n.
sound 398 n.
communicate
524 vb.
publicity 528 n.
publish 528 vb.
broadcasting
531 n.
amusement 837 n.
radioactive
insalubrious
653 adj.
dangerous 661 adj.
radioactivity
nucleonics 160 n.
ejection 300 n.
radiation 417 n.
insalubrity 653 n.
poison 659 n.
radioastronomy
astronomy 321 n.
radiogram
gramophone 414 n.
hearing aid 415 n.
radiograph
darkness 418 n.
photography 551 n.
diagnostic 658 n.
radiography
photography 551 n.
medical art 658 n.

radioisotope
radiation 417 n.
radiology
radiation 417 n.
medical art 658 n.
radiopaging
broadcasting
531 n.
radio telescope
astronomy 321 n.
radiotherapy
radiation 417 n.
medical art 658 n.
therapy 658 n.
radio waves
broadcasting
531 n.
radish
fruit and vegetables
301 n.
radius
range 183 n.
line 203 n.
breadth 205 n.
straightness 249 n.
radix
source 156 n.
RAF
air force 722 n.
raffia
ligature 47 n.
fibre 208 n.
raffle
equal chance
159 n.
gamble 618 vb.
gambling 618 n.
gambling game
837 n.
raffle ticket
label 547 n.
raft
carry 273 vb.
rafter
beam 218 n.
materials 631 n.
rag
small thing 33 n.
piece 53 n.
the press 528 n.
trickery 542 n.
book 589 n.
torment 827 vb.
revel 837 n.
ridicule 851 vb.
ragamuffin
slut 61 n.

low fellow 869 n.
ragbag
nonuniformity
17 n.
medley 43 n.
disorder 61 n.
rag day
amusement 837 n.
rag doll
image 551 n.
plaything 837 n.
rage
violence 176 n.
prevail 178 vb.
blow 352 vb.
be active 678 vb.
excitation 821 n.
be excitable
822 vb.
excitable state
822 n.
fashion 848 n.
desire 859 n.
anger 891 n.
be angry 891 vb.
ragged
convoluted 251 adj.
raging
destructive 165 adj.
violent 176 adj.
excited 821 adj.
angry 891 adj.
raglan sleeve
sleeve 228 n.
ragout
a mixture 43 n.
dish 301 n.
rag, tag and bobtail
commonalty 869 n.
ragtime
music 412 n.
ragtime band
orchestra 413 n.
raid
ingress 297 n.
attack 712 n.
attack 712 vb.
warfare 718 n.
taking 786 n.
rob 788 vb.
rail
handle 218 n.
transport 272 n.
orate 579 vb.
curse 899 vb.
criticize 924 vb.
reproach 924 vb.

rail at
cuss 899 vb.
reproach 924 vb.
railcard
cheapness 812 n.
railing
handle 218 n.
fence 235 n.
safeguard 662 n.
raillery
sauciness 878 n.
railroad
carry 273 vb.
impel 279 vb.
railway 624 n.
compel 740 vb.
rails
parallelism 219 n.
fence 235 n.
railway 624 n.
railway
railway 624 n.
railway station
goal 295 n.
raiment
clothing 228 n.
rain
be wet 341 vb.
rain 350 n.
rain 350 vb.
rain blows
strike 279 vb.
rainbow
curve 248 n.
arc 250 n.
camber 253 n.
light 417 n.
colour 425 n.
variegation 437 n.
rain cats and dogs
be wet 341 vb.
rain 350 vb.
raincoat
overcoat 228 n.
raindrop
moisture 341 n.
rainfall
moisture 341 n.
rain 350 n.
rain forest
wood 366 n.
rain or shine
certainly 473 adv.
rainproof
dry 342 adj.
rainy day
adversity 731 n.

907

raise
augment 36 vb.
produce 164 vb.
generate 167 vb.
displace 188 vb.
make higher
  209 vb.
move 265 vb.
impel 279 vb.
progression 285 n.
promote 285 vb.
elevate 310 vb.
lighten 323 vb.
breed stock 369 vb.
incentive 612 n.
acquire 771 vb.
gain 771 n.
levy 786 vb.
relieve 831 vb.
raise a laugh
be witty 839 vb.
be ridiculous
  849 vb.
raise an objection
qualify 468 vb.
raise Cain
be loud 400 vb.
revolt 738 vb.
be angry 891 vb.
raised
projecting 254 adj.
raised voices
quarrel 709 n.
raise expectations
predict 511 vb.
raise objections
dissent 489 vb.
be obstructive
  702 vb.
raise one's eyebrows
gesticulate 547 vb.
deprecate 762 vb.
raise one's glass to
toast 876 vb.
raise one's hand
gesticulate 547 vb.
vote 605 vb.
raise one's hat
greet 884 vb.
raise one's voice
emphasize 532 vb.
speak 579 vb.
raise the alarm
raise the alarm
  665 vb.
frighten 854 vb.

raise the roof
be loud 400 vb.
applaud 923 vb.
raise the wind
acquire 771 vb.
borrow 785 vb.
raise up
elevate 310 vb.
raisin
fruit and vegetables
  301 n.
raison d'être
reason why 156 n.
raita
hors-d'oeuvres
  301 n.
raj
governance 733 n.
rajah
potentate 741 n.
person of rank
  868 n.
rake
displace 188 vb.
thinness 206 n.
smooth 258 vb.
smoother 258 n.
draw 288 vb.
traction 288 n.
pass 305 vb.
cultivate 370 vb.
farm tool 370 n.
male 372 n.
fire at 712 vb.
bad person 938 n.
sensualist 944 n.
libertine 952 n.
rake in
bring together
  74 vb.
rake-off
increment 36 n.
earnings 771 n.
portion 783 n.
receipt 807 n.
price 809 n.
discount 810 n.
reward 962 n.
rake over
search 459 vb.
rake up the past
remember 505 vb.
raki
alcoholic drink
  301 n.
rakish
showy 875 adj.

rakish angle
obliquity 220 n.
rallentando
tempo 410 n.
adagio 412 adv.
rally
cohere 48 vb.
combine 50 vb.
arrange 62 vb.
assemblage 74 n.
bring together
  74 vb.
congregate 74 vb.
continuance 146 n.
propulsion 287 n.
call 547 n.
persevere 600 vb.
incite 612 vb.
get better 654 vb.
be restored 656 vb.
restore 656 vb.
revival 656 n.
aid 703 n.
contest 716 n.
go to war 718 vb.
war measures
  718 n.
command 737 vb.
give courage
  855 vb.
be insolent 878 vb.
rallying
recuperation 656 n.
finance 797 n.
rallying cry
call 547 n.
inducement 612 n.
danger signal
  665 n.
war 718 n.
rallying point
focus 76 n.
rally round
be in order 60 vb.
cooperate 706 vb.
ram
demolish 165 vb.
collide 279 vb.
ram 279 n.
sheep 365 n.
male animal
  372 n.
tool 630 n.
Ramadan
fast 946 n.
holy day 988 n.

ramble
be unrelated 10 vb.
land travel 267 n.
pedestrianism
  267 n.
wander 267 vb.
stray 282 vb.
be insane 503 vb.
be diffuse 570 vb.
amuse oneself
  837 vb.
ramble on
be loquacious
  581 vb.
rambler
traveller 268 n.
wanderer 268 n.
Ramboesque
courageous
  855 adj.
ram down
fill 54 vb.
close 264 vb.
impel 279 vb.
**ram down one's
  throat**
compel 740 vb.
ramekin
bowl 194 n.
ramification
bond 47 n.
branch 53 n.
descendant 170 n.
range 183 n.
filament 208 n.
symmetry 245 n.
divergence 294 n.
ramp
be vertical 215 vb.
incline 220 n.
obliquity 220 n.
ascend 308 vb.
ascent 308 n.
be agitated 318 vb.
trickery 542 n.
be angry 891 vb.
get angry 891 vb.
rampage
rampage 61 vb.
excitable state
  822 n.
anger 891 n.
rampant
furious 176 adj.
violent 176 adj.
vertical 215 adj.
heráldic 547 adj.

rampart
defence 713 n.
fortification 713 n.

ramrod
stopper 264 n.
ram 279 n.
firearm 723 n.

ramshackle
flimsy 163 adj.
dilapidated
655 adj.
unsafe 661 adj.

ranch
stock farm 369 n.
cultivate 370 vb.
farm 370 n.
lands 777 n.

rancid
unsavoury 391 adj.
fetid 397 n.

rancour
enmity 881 n.
hatred 888 n.
resentment 891 n.
malevolence 898 n.

rand
coinage 797 n.

random
nonuniform 17 adj.
mixed 43 adj.
casual 159 adj.
indiscriminate
464 adj.
uncertain 474 adj.

random-access
computerized
86 adj.

random sample
example 83 n.
equal chance
159 n.
empiricism 461 n.

randy
lecherous 951 adj.

range
arrange 62 vb.
series 71 n.
accumulation 74 n.
classification 77 n.
extend 183 vb.
range 183 n.
situation 186 n.
be distant 199 vb.
layer 207 n.
traverse 267 vb.
plain 348 n.
furnace 383 n.

hearing 415 n.
arena 724 n.
be free 744 vb.
merchandise
795 n.

rangefinder
direction 281 n.
telescope 442 n.

range oneself with
join a party
708 vb.

ranger
wanderer 268 n.
keeper 749 n.

rangy
lean 206 adj.
narrow 206 adj.
tall 209 adj.

rani
potentate 741 n.

rank
state 7 n.
relativeness 9 n.
degree 27 n.
graduate 27 vb.
consummate
32 adj.
order 60 n.
arrange 62 vb.
class 62 vb.
grade 73 vb.
serial place 73 n.
classification 77 n.
unsavoury 391 adj.
fetid 397 adj.
estimate 480 vb.
importance 638 n.
bad 645 adj.
have a reputation
866 vb.
prestige 866 n.
nobility 868 n.
heinous 934 adj.

rank and file
soldiery 722 n.
commonalty 869 n.
plebeian 869 adj.

ranking
degree 27 n.
serial place 73 n.
noteworthy
866 adj.
prestige 866 n.

rankle
deteriorate 655 vb.
hurt 827 vb.
huff 891 vb.

be malevolent
898 vb.

ransack
search 459 vb.
take 786 vb.
rob 788 vb.

ransom
restoration 656 n.
deliver 668 vb.
deliverance 668 n.
restitution 787 n.
price 809 n.
tax 809 n.
penalty 963 n.

rant
empty talk 515 n.
mean nothing
515 vb.
be diffuse 570 vb.
grandiloquence
574 n.
orate 579 vb.
oratory 579 n.
be excitable
822 vb.
boast 877 n.
boast 877 vb.
be angry 891 vb.

rant and rave
be diffuse 570 vb.

rap
knock 279 n.
strike 279 vb.
bang 402 n.
crackle 402 vb.
vocal music 412 n.
speak 579 vb.
speech 579 n.
be loquacious
581 vb.
chatter 581 n.
chat 584 n.
converse 584 vb.
interlocution
584 n.

rapacious
avaricious 816 adj.
greedy 859 adj.

rape
unite with 45 vb.
force 176 vb.
district 184 n.
impair 655 vb.
take 786 vb.
taking 786 n.
stealing 788 n.
debauch 951 vb.

rape 951 n.

rapid
speedy 277 adj.

rapidity
velocity 277 n.

rapids
waterfall 350 n.
pitfall 663 n.

rapier
sharp point 256 n.
sidearms 723 n.

rapist
libertine 952 n.

rap over the knuckles
reprimand 924 n.
reprove 924 vb.
corporal punish-
ment 963 n.
spank 963 vb.

rapping
loquacious 581 adj.

rapport
relation 9 n.
agreement 24 n.
concord 710 n.

rapprochement
pacification 719 n.

rapt
attentive 455 adj.
abstracted 456 adj.
impressed 818 adj.

raptorial
thieving 788 adj.

rapture
excitation 821 n.
joy 824 n.
love 887 n.

raptures
rejoicing 835 n.

rapturous
approving 923 adj.

rara avis
rara avis 84 n.

rare
superior 34 adj.
unusual 84 adj.
few 105 adj.
infrequent 140 adj.
culinary 301 adj.
rare 325 adj.
improbable
472 adj.
scarce 636 adj.
excellent 644 adj.
valuable 644 adj.
uncooked 670 adj.
of value 811 adj.

rarefy
make smaller
198 vb.
rarefy 325 vb.

rarely
greatly 32 vb.
here and there
105 adv.
seldom 140 adv.

raring to go
willing 597 adj.
prepared 669 adj.

rarity
nonconformist
84 n.
nonconformity
84 n.
fewness 105 n.
infrequency 140 n.
rarity 325 n.
improbability
472 n.
dearness 811 n.

rascal
low fellow 869 n.
bad person 938 n.

rash
tingling 378 n.
absurd 497 adj.
skin disease 651 n.
rash 857 adj.

rasher
piece 53 n.

rasp
rub 333 vb.
rasp 407 vb.

raspberry
fruit and vegetables
301 n.
gesture 547 n.
reprimand 924 n.

Rastafarian
revolter 738 n.
sectarian 978 adj.

rat
mammal 365 n.
inform 524 vb.
divulge 526 vb.
deceiver 545 n.
apostatize 603 vb.
recanter 603 n.
bad person 938 n.
cad 938 n.

ratatouille
dish 301 n.

ratchet
tooth 256 n.
notch 260 n.

rate
degree 27 n.
graduate 27 vb.
class 62 vb.
grade 73 vb.
velocity 277 n.
estimate 480 vb.
price 809 n.
price 809 vb.
reproach 924 vb.

rateable value
tax 809 n.

rate-capping
restriction 747 n.

ratepayer
resident 191 n.

rates
receipt 807 n.
tax 809 n.

rather
slightly 33 adv.

ratification
certainty 473 n.
assent 488 n.
consent 758 n.
legislation 953 n.

ratify
stabilize 153 vb.
corroborate 466 vb.
make certain
473 vb.
assent 488 vb.
See **endorse**
endorse 488 vb.
permit 756 vb.
consent 758 vb.
contract 765 vb.
approve 923 vb.
make legal 953 vb.

rating
nautical personnel
270 n.
measurement
465 n.
naval man 722 n.
tax 809 n.

ratings
publicity 528 n.

ratio
relativeness 9 n.
degree 27 n.
ratio 85 n.
portion 783 n.

ration
finite quantity
26 n.
degree 27 n.
restrain 747 vb.
apportion 783 vb.
portion 783 n.

rational
numerical 85 adj.
rational 475 adj.
sane 502 adj.

rationale
reason why 156 n.
attribution 158 n.
motive 612 n.
pretext 614 n.

rationalistic
rational 475 adj.
irreligious 974 adj.

rationality
intellect 447 n.
reasoning 475 n.
sanity 502 n.

rationalize
transform 147 vb.
reason 475 vb.
plan 623 vb.
make better
654 vb.
rectify 654 vb.
be irreligious
974 vb.

rationing
restriction 747 n.

rations
provisions 301 n.
provision 633 n.

rat on
accuse 928 vb.

rat race
rotation 315 n.
activity 678 n.
contention 716 n.

rattan
scourge 964 n.

ratting
change of mind
603 n.
chase 619 n.

rattle
come unstuck
49 vb.
derange 63 vb.
impel 279 vb.
oscillate 317 vb.
be loud 400 vb.
loudness 400 n.

crackle 402 vb.
roll 403 n.
roll 403 vb.
gong 414 n.
distract 456 vb.
be loquacious
581 vb.
plaything 837 n.
frighten 854 vb.

rattled
angry 891 adj.

rattle on
speak 579 vb.

rattlesnake
reptile 365 n.

rattletrap
automobile 274 n.
carriage 274 n.

rattling
impulse 279 n.
loud 400 adj.

ratty
angry 891 adj.
irascible 892 adj.

raucous
hoarse 407 adj.
discordant 411 adj.

ravage
impair 655 vb.
attack 712 vb.
go to war 718 vb.
rob 788 vb.

ravaged
unsightly 842 adj.

ravages of time
time 108 n.
dilapidation 655 n.
ugliness 842 n.

rave
overestimate
482 vb.
be absurd 497 vb.
be insane 503 vb.
mean nothing
515 vb.

rave about
advertise 528 vb.
be pleased 824 vb.

ravel
complexity 61 n.
bedevil 63 vb.

raven
eat 301 vb.
bird 365 n.
black thing 428 n.
omen 511 n.

ravening
furious 176 adj.
underfed 636 adj.
ravenous
underfed 636 adj.
hungry 859 adj.
fasting 946 adj.
rave-up
revel 837 n.
ravine
gap 201 n.
narrowness 206 n.
high land 209 n.
valley 255 n.
furrow 262 n.
conduit 351 n.
raving
optimistic 482 adj.
frenzied 503 adj.
frenzy 503 n.
lack of meaning
515 n.
meaningless
515 adj.
impressed 818 adj.
raving mad
mentally disor-
dered 503 adj.
ravioli
dish 301 n.
ravish
unite with 45 vb.
force 176 vb.
delight 826 vb.
debauch 951 vb.
ravishing
pleasurable
826 adj.
raw
incomplete 55 adj.
new 126 adj.
young 130 adj.
uncovered 229 adj.
amorphous
244 adj.
culinary 301 adj.
sentient 374 adj.
painful 377 adj.
cold 380 adj.
florid 425 adj.
ignorant 491 adj.
unhabituated
611 adj.
immature 670 adj.
uncooked 670 adj.
unskilled 695 adj.
sensitive 819 adj.

raw, the
bareness 229 n.
raw-boned
lean 206 adj.
raw deal
misfortune 731 n.
raw material
source 156 n.
amorphism 244 n.
means 629 n.
materials 631 n.
undevelopment
670 n.
ray
small quantity
33 n.
flash 417 n.
ray of hope
hope 852 n.
rayon
fibre 208 n.
textile 222 n.
raze
demolish 165 vb.
obliterate 550 vb.
raze to the ground
demolish 165 vb.
fell 311 vb.
razor
sharp edge 256 n.
cosmetic 843 n.
re
concerning 9 adv.
reach
degree 27 n.
range 183 n.
distance 199 n.
length 203 n.
carry 273 vb.
arrive 295 vb.
pass 305 vb.
hearing 415 n.
acquire 771 vb.
reach new heights
culminate 34 vb.
reach out for
take 786 vb.
reach rock bottom
be deep 211 vb.
react
correlate 12 vb.
counteract 182 vb.
recoil 280 vb.
have feeling
374 vb.
be active 678 vb.
feel 818 vb.

reaction
compensation 31 n.
reversion 148 n.
effect 157 n.
counteraction
182 n.
recoil 280 n.
sense 374 n.
answer 460 n.
retaliation 714 n.
deprecation 762 n.
feeling 818 n.
reactionary
permanent 144 adj.
disobedient
738 adj.
revolter 738 n.
read
gauge 465 vb.
decipher 520 vb.
interpret 520 vb.
study 536 vb.
spell 558 vb.
speak 579 vb.
deal with 688 vb.
readable
intelligible 516 adj.
read between the
lines
decipher 520 vb.
readdress
send 272 vb.
reader
scholar 492 n.
teacher 537 n.
bookperson 589 n.
academic title
870 n.
readership
publicity 528 n.
reading
measurement
465 n.
erudition 490 n.
interpretation
520 n.
lecture 534 n.
study 536 n.
oration 579 n.
read into
misinterpret
521 vb.
readjust
adjust 24 vb.
equalize 28 vb.
read one's hand
divine 511 vb.

read out
teach 534 vb.
speak 579 vb.
read the Riot Act
reprove 924 vb.
read through
scan 438 vb.
ready
early 135 adj.
impending 155 adj.
formed 243 adj.
attentive 455 adj.
vigilant 457 adj.
intelligent 498 adj.
expectant 507 adj.
willing 597 adj.
prepared 669 adj.
ready, the
funds 797 n.
money 797 n.
ready and willing
willing 597 adj.
ready for anything
prepared 669 adj.
courageous
855 adj.
ready-made
formed 243 adj.
ready-made
669 adj.
ready-mixed
ready-made
669 adj.
ready money
funds 797 n.
money 797 n.
payment 804 n.
ready reckoner
counting instru-
ment 86 n.
ready-to-wear
tailored 228 adj.
ready-made
669 adj.
real
real 1 adj.
substantial 3 adj.
material 319 adj.
true 494 adj.
coinage 797 n.
real ale
alcoholic drink
301 n.
real estate
land 344 n.
lands 777 n.

realism
 existence 1 n.
 mimicry 20 n.
 philosophy 449 n.
 accuracy 494 n.
 veracity 540 n.
 representation
  551 n.
 description 590 n.
realistic
 lifelike 18 adj.
 true 494 adj.
 descriptive 590 adj.
reality
 reality 1 n.
realization
 existence 1 n.
 event 154 n.
 materiality 319 n.
 discovery 484 n.
 knowledge 490 n.
 acquisition 771 n.
realize
 make extrinsic
  6 vb.
 specify 80 vb.
 meet with 154 vb.
 materialize 319 vb.
 have feeling
  374 vb.
 perceive 447 vb.
 believe 485 vb.
 know 490 vb.
 understand 516 vb.
 carry out 725 vb.
 acquire 771 vb.
 draw money
  797 vb.
 cost 809 vb.
real-life
 descriptive 590 adj.
real-life story
 biography 590 n.
really
 actually 1 adv.
 substantially 3 adv.
 truly 494 adv.
realm
 territory 184 n.
 nation 371 n.
 function 622 n.
 political organiza-
  tion 733 n.
real McCoy, the
 no imitation 21 n.
real number
 number 85 n.

realpolitik
 cunning 698 n.
real tennis
 ball game 837 n.
real thing
 reality 1 n.
 identity 13 n.
 no imitation 21 n.
 authenticity 494 n.
 love 887 n.
real-time
 computerized
  86 adj.
realty
 lands 777 n.
ream
 enlarge 197 vb.
 paper 631 n.
reap
 cultivate 370 vb.
 store 632 vb.
 acquire 771 vb.
 take 786 vb.
reappear
 reproduce 166 vb.
 be restored 656 vb.
reap the benefit of
 find useful 640 adj.
rear
 be great - large
  32 vb.
 augment 36 vb.
 ending 69 adj.
 produce 164 vb.
 generate 167 vb.
 be high 209 vb.
 be vertical 215 vb.
 back 238 adj.
 buttocks 238 n.
 rear 238 n.
 ascend 308 vb.
 be agitated 318 vb.
 breed stock 369 vb.
 educate 534 vb.
rear-admiral
 naval officer 741 n.
rear end
 buttocks 238 n.
 rear 238 n.
rearguard
 rear 238 n.
 warner 664 n.
 defender 713 n.
 armed force 722 n.
rear its head
 be plain 522 vb.

rearrange
 arrange 62 vb.
 modify 143 vb.
rear up
 ascend 308 vb.
 elevate 310 vb.
 get angry 891 vb.
reason
 reason why 156 n.
 intellect 447 n.
 perceive 447 adj.
 thought 449 n.
 reason 475 vb.
 reasoning 475 n.
 sanity 502 n.
reasonable
 moderate 177 adj.
 possible 469 adj.
 plausible 471 adj.
 rational 475 adj.
 credible 485 adj.
 true 494 adj.
 wise 498 adj.
 sane 502 adj.
 cheap 812 adj.
 just 913 adj.
reasoning
 mental 447 adj.
 rational 475 adj.
 reasoning 475 n.
 wise 498 adj.
reason out
 think 449 vb.
reassemble
 repair 656 vb.
 restore 656 vb.
reassure oneself
 make certain
  473 vb.
reawakening
 revival 656 n.
rebate
 discount 810 n.
rebel
 nonconformist
  84 n.
 dissentient 489 n.
 go to war 718 vb.
 revolt 738 vb.
 revolter 738 n.
 fail in duty 918 vb.
 undutifulness
  918 n.
 schismatic 978 n.
 schismatical
  978 adj.

rebellion
 revolution 149 n.
 revolt 738 n.
 undutifulness
  918 n.
 lawlessness 954 n.
rebellious
 quarrelling
  709 adj.
 defiant 711 adj.
 disobedient
  738 adj.
 insolent 878 adj.
 undutiful 918 adj.
 schismatical
  978 adj.
rebirth
 recurrence 106 n.
 conversion 147 n.
 revival 656 n.
 sanctity 979 n.
reborn
 converted 147 adj.
 sanctified 979 adj.
rebound
 revert 148 vb.
 recoil 280 n.
 recoil 280 vb.
 leap 312 vb.
rebuff
 recoil 280 n.
 repel 292 vb.
 repulsion 292 n.
 reject 607 vb.
 rejection 607 n.
 dissuasion 613 n.
 resist 715 vb.
 resistance 715 n.
 defeat 727 vb.
 defeat 728 n.
 adversity 731 n.
 refusal 760 n.
 refuse 760 vb.
 rudeness 885 n.
 contempt 922 n.
 reprove 924 vb.
rebuild
 reproduce 166 vb.
 restore 656 vb.
rebuke
 humiliation 872 n.
 reprimand 924 n.
 reprove 924 vb.
 punish 963 vb.
rebut
 answer 460 vb.
 tell against 467 vb.

confute 479 vb.
negate 533 vb.

rebuttal
rejoinder 460 n.
counterevidence
467 n.
confutation 479 n.
negation 533 n.
vindication 927 n.
legal trial 959 n.

rebut the charge
justify 927 vb.
accuse 928 vb.

recalcitrant
nonconformist
84 n.
unconformable
84 adj.
unwilling 598 adj.
difficult 700 adj.
opposing 704 adj.
resisting 715 adj.
disobedient
738 adj.

recall
transference 272 n.
remember 505 vb.
remembrance
505 n.
recant 603 vb.
restoration 656 n.
restore 656 vb.
abrogate 752 vb.

recant
dissent 489 vb.
recant 603 vb.
relinquish 621 vb.

recap
compendium
592 n.

recapitulate
repeat 106 vb.
shorten 204 vb.
remind 505 vb.
describe 590 vb.

recapture
remember 505 vb.
imagine 513 vb.
retrieve 656 vb.
acquire 771 vb.

recce
inspection 438 n.
enquiry 459 n.

recede
regress 286 vb.
recede 290 vb.

recede into the distance
regress 286 vb.

receipt
precept 693 n.
title deed 767 n.
payment 804 n.
receipt 807 n.

receive
comprise 78 vb.
meet 295 vb.
admit 299 vb.
receive 782 vb.
be hospitable
882 vb.
greet 884 vb.

receive a standing ovation
act 594 vb.

received
usual 610 adj.

Received Pronunciation
language 557 n.

receiver
hearing aid 415 n.
receiver 782 n.
recipient 782 n.

receiving end
receiving 782 n.

recent
foregoing 125 adj.
new 126 adj.

recent past
past time 125 n.
newness 126 n.

receptacle
receptacle 194 n.
flower 366 n.

reception
arrival 295 n.
reception 299 n.
feasting 301 n.
sound 398 n.
conference 584 n.
celebration 876 n.
social gathering
882 n.
courteous act
884 n.
wedding 894 n.

reception room
chamber 194 n.

receptive
intelligent 498 adj.
studious 536 adj.
willing 597 adj.

recess
compartment
194 n.
angularity 247 n.
hiding-place 527 n.
repose 683 n.
refreshment 685 n.

recesses
interiority 224 n.

recession
decrease 37 n.
contraction 198 n.
recession 290 n.
deterioration
655 n.
inactivity 679 n.
adversity 731 n.
poverty 801 n.

recherché
unusual 84 adj.
excellent 644 adj.

recidivist
offender 904 n.
impious person
980 n.

recipe
cookery 301 n.
contrivance 623 n.
remedy 658 n.
precept 693 n.

recipient
recipient 782 n.

reciprocal
relative 9 adj.
correlative 12 adj.
equivalent 28 adj.
numerical 85 adj.
numerical element
85 n.
periodical 141 adj.

reciprocate
be related 9 vb.
correlate 12 vb.
interchange
151 vb.
fluctuate 317 vb.
cooperate 706 vb.
concord 710 vb.
retaliate 714 vb.

reciprocity
correlation 12 n.
equalization 28 n.
compensation 31 n.
periodicity 141 n.
interchange 151 n.
cooperation 706 n.
concord 710 n.

recital
oration 579 n.
description 590 n.

recitation
oration 579 n.

recite
repeat 106 vb.
speak 579 vb.
describe 590 vb.

reckless
negligent 458 adj.
unwise 499 adj.
defiant 711 adj.
prodigal 815 adj.
rash 857 adj.

reckon
number 86 vb.
measure 465 vb.
be cautious 858 vb.

reckoning
numeration 86 n.
measurement
465 n.
accounts 808 n.
punishment 963 n.

reckon without
misjudge 481 vb.

reclaim
cultivate 370 vb.
restore 656 vb.
retrieve 656 vb.
acquire 771 vb.
appropriate
786 vb.
claim 915 vb.

reclamation
restoration 656 n.
propitiation 941 n.

recline
be horizontal
216 vb.
repose 683 vb.

recluse
solitary 883 n.
ascetic 945 n.
nun 986 n.

recognition
vision 438 n.
knowledge 490 n.
courteous act
884 n.
thanks 907 n.
dueness 915 n.
approbation 923 n.
reward 962 n.

recognizable
visible 443 adj.

intelligible 516 adj.
manifest 522 adj.
recognize
see 438 vb.
notice 455 vb.
discover 484 vb.
know 490 vb.
remember 505 vb.
understand 516 vb.
permit 756 vb.
consent 758 vb.
greet 884 vb.
reward 962 vb.
recoil
recoil 280 n.
recoil 280 vb.
be unwilling
    598 vb.
unwillingness
    598 n.
recollect
remember 505 vb.
recollection
remembrance
    505 n.
imagination 513 n.
recommend
select 605 vb.
advise 691 vb.
patronize 703 vb.
approve 923 vb.
recommendation
credential 466 n.
advice 691 n.
approbation 923 n.
recompense
compensation 31 n.
retaliation 714 n.
reward 962 n.
reward 962 vb.
reconcile
pacify 719 vb.
content 828 vb.
reconciliation
adaptation 24 n.
conformity 83 n.
concord 710 n.
pacification 719 n.
content 828 n.
forgiveness 909 n.
propitiation 941 n.
recondite
puzzling 517 adj.
concealed 525 adj.
recondition
repair 656 vb.

reconnaissance
land travel 267 n.
inspection 438 n.
enquiry 459 n.
reconnaissance party
precursor 66 n.
front 237 n.
armed force 722 n.
reconnoitre
traverse 267 vb.
inspection 438 n.
scan 438 vb.
watch 441 vb.
enquire 459 vb.
enquiry 459 n.
reconsider
meditate 449 vb.
notice 455 vb.
reconstitute
restore 656 vb.
reconstruct
reproduce 166 vb.
restore 656 vb.
record
superior 34 adj.
superiority 34 n.
record 548 n.
record 548 vb.
recording instru-
    ment 549 n.
best 644 adj.
record-breaking
best 644 adj.
wonderful 864 adj.
recorder
flute 414 n.
recorder 549 n.
recording instru-
    ment 549 n.
judge 957 n.
recording
musical piece
    412 n.
gramophone 414 n.
broadcast 531 n.
record 548 n.
record-player
sound 398 n.
gramophone 414 n.
records
record 548 n.
recount
remind 505 vb.
communicate
    524 vb.
describe 590 vb.

recoup
recoup 31 vb.
restitute 787 vb.
recourse
contrivance 623 n.
means 629 n.
recover
recoup 31 vb.
be strong 162 vb.
counteract 182 vb.
get better 654 vb.
be restored 656 vb.
repair 656 vb.
retrieve 656 vb.
deliver 668 vb.
acquire 771 vb.
appropriate
    786 vb.
restitute 787 vb.
recovery
compensation 31 n.
reversion 148 n.
transference 272 n.
improvement
    654 n.
recuperation 656 n.
restoration 656 n.
revival 656 n.
acquisition 771 n.
restitution 787 n.
recreant
bad person 938 n.
recreation
refreshment 685 n.
amusement 837 n.
recreational
amusing 837 adj.
recreation ground
arena 724 n.
pleasure ground
    837 n.
recrimination
retaliation 714 n.
vindication 927 n.
accusation 928 n.
recriminations
reproach 924 n.
recruit
employ 622 vb.
go to war 718 vb.
soldier 722 n.
recruitment
war measures
    718 n.
rectangle
angular figure
    247 n.

rectangular
vertical 215 adj.
rectify
rectify 654 vb.
rectilineal
straight 249 adj.
rectitude
right 913 n.
probity 929 n.
virtue 933 n.
recto
face 237 n.
dextrality 241 n.
edition 589 n.
rector
teacher 537 n.
director 690 n.
church title 986 n.
cleric 986 n.
pastor 986 n.
rectory
parsonage 986 n.
rectum
insides 224 n.
recumbent
low 210 adj.
supine 216 adj.
recuperate
get healthy 650 vb.
be restored 656 vb.
recur
recur 139 vb.
be remembered
    505 vb.
recurrence
continuity 71 n.
recurrence 106 n.
continuance 146 n.
remembrance
    505 n.
relapse 657 n.
recurring
repeated 106 adj.
recurring decimal
numerical element
    85 n.
recurrence 106 n.
noncompletion
    726 n.
recusant
schismatic 978 n.
schismatical
    978 adj.
recycle
repeat 106 vb.
restore 656 vb.
use 673 vb.

RED

acquire 771 vb.
economize 814 vb.
red
revolutionary
149 adj.
culinary 301 adj.
red 431 adj.
revolter 738 n.
red alert
warning 664 n.
danger signal
665 n.
redbrick
educational
534 adj.
redbrick university
academy 539 n.
red cabbage
fruit and vegetables
301 n.
red carpet
floor-cover 226 n.
ostentation 875 n.
respects 920 n.
redcoat
soldier 722 n.
Red Cross
doctor 658 n.
redcurrant
fruit and vegetables
301 n.
redden
redden 431 vb.
get angry 891 vb.
redeem
compensate 31 vb.
restore 656 vb.
deliver 668 vb.
acquire 771 vb.
restitute 787 vb.
purchase 792 vb.
make pious 979 vb.
redeemer
benefactor 903 n.
God the Son 965 n.
redemption
compensation 31 n.
restoration 656 n.
deliverance 668 n.
liberation 746 n.
acquisition 771 n.
propitiation 941 n.
red-eyed
lamenting 836 adj.
angry 891 adj.
red flag
signal 547 n.

RED

danger signal
665 n.
red-handed
murderous 362 adj.
guilty 936 adj.
red herring
irrelevance 10 n.
inattention 456 n.
trickery 542 n.
pretext 614 n.
unimportance
639 n.
stratagem 698 n.
red-hot
violent 176 adj.
hot 379 adj.
red 431 adj.
fervent 818 adj.
Red Indian
redness 431 n.
red-letter day
important matter
638 n.
amusement 837 n.
special day 876 n.
red light
signal light 420 n.
signal 547 n.
dissuasion 613 n.
danger signal
665 n.
prohibition 757 n.
refusal 760 n.
red-light district
brothel 951 n.
redneck
country-dweller
869 n.
redo
restore 656 vb.
redolent
odorous 394 adj.
fragrant 396 adj.
redouble
augment 36 vb.
double 91 vb.
repeat 106 vb.
invigorate 174 vb.
enlarge 197 vb.
redoubtable
frightening
854 adj.
red rag to a bull
dislike 861 n.
resentment 891 n.
redress
compensation 31 n.

RED

restoration 656 n.
remedy 658 n.
justice 913 n.
redress the balance
equalize 28 vb.
red tape
delay 136 n.
habit 610 n.
redundance 637 n.
obstacle 702 n.
governance 733 n.
reduce
abate 37 vb.
decrease 37 vb.
sunder 46 vb.
decompose 51 vb.
render few 105 vb.
convert 147 vb.
weaken 163 vb.
make smaller
198 vb.
shorten 204 vb.
make thin 206 vb.
photograph 551 vb.
abstract 592 vb.
discount 810 vb.
starve 946 vb.
reduced
small 33 adj.
lesser 35 adj.
cheap 812 adj.
reduced visibility
visibility 443 n.
invisibility 444 n.
reduce to
liken 18 vb.
convert 147 vb.
reduce to the ranks
abase 311 vb.
depose 752 vb.
shame 867 vb.
punish 963 vb.
reduction
diminution 37 n.
conversion 147 n.
contraction 198 n.
shortening 204 n.
lowering 311 n.
discount 810 n.
redundancy
identity 13 n.
repetition 106 n.
ejection 300 n.
diffuseness 570 n.
redundance 637 n.
superfluity 637 n.
nonuse 674 n.

REE

leisure 681 n.
deposal 752 n.
redundant
identical 13 adj.
repeated 106 adj.
diffuse 570 adj.
redundant 637 adj.
superfluous
637 adj.
useless 641 adj.
leisurely 681 adj.
reduplicate
double 91 vb.
repeat 106 vb.
redwood
tree 366 n.
reed
grass 366 n.
flute 414 n.
reedy
strident 407 adj.
reef
retard 278 vb.
rock 344 n.
island 349 n.
pitfall 663 n.
reefer
jacket 228 n.
navigator 270 n.
tobacco 388 n.
drug-taking 949 n.
reef knot
ligature 47 n.
reek
gas 336 n.
vaporize 338 vb.
be wet 341 vb.
be hot 379 vb.
odour 394 n.
smell 394 vb.
stench 397 n.
stink 397 vb.
reel
vary 152 vb.
be weak 163 vb.
walk 267 vb.
leap 312 n.
rotate 315 vb.
rotator 315 n.
be agitated 318 vb.
musical piece
412 n.
photography 551 n.
show feeling
818 vb.
dance 837 n.
be drunk 949 vb.

reel in
draw 288 vb.

reel off
specify 80 vb.
exemplify 83 vb.
list 87 vb.
repeat 106 vb.
speak 579 vb.
be loquacious
581 vb.

reentry
space travel 271 n.
return 286 n.
ingress 297 n.

reestablish
restore 656 vb.

refectory
chamber 194 n.

refectory table
stand 218 n.

refer
indicate 547 vb.
consult 691 vb.

referee
witness 466 n.
estimator 480 n.
judge 480 vb.
adviser 691 n.
mediator 720 n.
magistracy 957 n.

reference
referral 9 n.
relation 9 n.
evidence 466 n.
connotation 514 n.
approbation 923 n.

references
credential 466 n.

referendum
judgment 480 n.
vote 605 n.

referral
referral 9 n.

refer to
be related 9 vb.
relate 9 vb.
be included 78 vb.
attribute 158 vb.
inform 524 vb.

refill
store 632 vb.
provision 633 n.
replenish 633 vb.

refine
differentiate 15 vb.
rarefy 325 vb.
purify 648 vb.

make better
654 vb.

refined
soft-hued 425 adj.
personable 841 adj.
tasteful 846 adj.
pure 950 adj.

refinery
workshop 687 n.

refit
restore 656 vb.

reflation
dilation 197 n.
finance 797 n.

reflect
correlate 12 vb.
resemble 18 vb.
imitate 20 vb.
recoil 280 vb.
repel 292 vb.
radiate 417 vb.
meditate 449 vb.
remember 505 vb.
show 522 vb.
represent 551 vb.

reflection
analogue 18 n.
imitation 20 n.
repulsion 292 n.
reflection 417 n.
appearance 445 n.
meditation 449 n.
representation
551 n.
See **image**
slur 867 n.
scurrility 899 n.
reproach 924 n.
detraction 926 n.

reflective
thoughtful 449 adj.

reflector
lamp 420 n.
mirror 442 n.

reflect upon
shame 867 vb.
defame 926 vb.

reflex
copy 22 n.
recoil 280 n.
return 286 n.
sense 374 n.
involuntary
596 adj.
spontaneity 609 n.
habituation 610 n.

reflexive
intrinsic 5 adj.

reflexive verb
part of speech
564 n.

reflexology
medical art 658 n.

reflux
decrease 37 n.
recoil 280 n.
return 286 n.
current 350 n.

reform
modify 143 vb.
transform 147 vb.
change one's mind
603 vb.
amendment 654 n.
get better 654 vb.
make better
654 vb.
rectify 654 vb.
repair 656 vb.
restore 656 vb.
do good 897 adj.
justice 913 n.
be penitent 939 vb.
become pious
979 vb.

reformation
change 143 n.
conversion 147 n.
amendment 654 n.
restoration 656 n.

Reformation, the
Protestantism
976 n.

reformatory
improving 654 adj.
prison 748 n.

refracting telescope
astronomy 321 n.

refraction
deviation 282 n.
reflection 417 n.
visual fallacy
440 n.

refractive
luminous 417 adj.

refractory
wilful 602 adj.
capricious 604 adj.
difficult 700 adj.
opposing 704 adj.
disobedient
738 adj.
sullen 893 adj.

refrain
repetition 106 n.
periodicity 141 n.
cease 145 vb.
tune 412 n.
vocal music 412 n.
verse form 593 n.
avoid 620 vb.
not act 677 vb.
be temperate
942 vb.

refrain from
discontinue 72 vb.

refresh
refresh 685 vb.
delight 826 vb.
relieve 831 vb.

refresher
tonic 658 n.
refreshment 685 n.
price 809 n.
reward 962 n.

refresher course
education 534 n.
study 536 n.

refreshment
meal 301 n.
refreshment 685 n.
enjoyment 824 n.

refreshments
refreshment 685 n.

refresh one's memory
remind 505 vb.

refrigeration
refrigeration 382 n.

refrigerator
refrigerator 384 n.
storage 632 n.

refuel
store 632 vb.
replenish 633 vb.

refuge
retreat 192 n.
reception 299 n.
traffic control
305 n.
refuge 662 n.

refugee
foreigner 59 n.
displacement
188 n.
wanderer 268 n.
escaper 667 n.
outcast 883 n.

refugee camp
abode 192 n.

refulgent
  luminous 417 adj.
refund
  compensation 31 n.
  restitute 787 vb.
  restitution 787 n.
refurbish
  modernize 126 vb.
  make better
    654 vb.
  repair 656 vb.
  restore 656 vb.
refusal
  repulsion 292 n.
  refusal 760 n.
  disapprobation
    924 n.
refuse
  leavings 41 n.
  avoid 620 vb.
  waste 634 n.
  rubbish 641 n.
  dirt 649 n.
  refuse 760 vb.
refute
  confute 479 vb.
  negate 533 vb.
regain
  retrieve 656 vb.
  acquire 771 vb.
regain one's breath
  be refreshed
    685 vb.
regal
  ruling 733 adj.
  impressive 821 adj.
  worshipful 866 adj.
  noble 868 adj.
regale
  delight 826 vb.
regalia
  regalia 743 n.
  ostentation 875 n.
regard
  relation 9 n.
  attention 455 n.
  be mindful 455 vb.
  observe 768 vb.
  honour 866 vb.
  repute 866 n.
  friendliness 880 n.
  love 887 n.
  love 887 vb.
  respect 920 n.
  respect 920 vb.
  approbation 923 n.

regard as
  substitute 150 vb.
  be of the opinion
    that 485 vb.
regarding
  concerning 9 adv.
regardless
  unrelated 10 adj.
  inattentive 456 adj.
  rash 857 adj.
regards
  courteous act
    884 n.
  respects 920 n.
regatta
  racing 716 n.
regency
  authority 733 n.
  governance 733 n.
  government 733 n.
  position of author-
    ity 733 n.
  commission 751 n.
regenerate
  convert 147 vb.
  reproduce 166 vb.
  make better
    654 vb.
  revive 656 vb.
regeneration
  conversion 147 n.
  reproduction
    166 n.
  improvement
    654 n.
  revival 656 n.
  sanctity 979 n.
regent
  potentate 741 n.
reggae
  music 412 n.
regicide
  homicide 362 n.
  revolt 738 n.
régime
  circumstance 8 n.
  dieting 301 n.
  management
    689 n.
  governance 733 n.
regimen
  dieting 301 n.
  therapy 658 n.
  governance 733 n.
regiment
  make uniform
    16 vb.

  band 74 n.
  formation 722 n.
  governance 733 n.
  compel 740 vb.
regimentation
  uniformity 16 n.
  compulsion 740 n.
regina
  sovereign 741 n.
region
  subdivision 53 n.
  region 184 n.
regionalization
  dispersion 75 n.
register
  degree 27 n.
  arrangement 62 n.
  class 62 vb.
  list 87 n.
  musical note
    410 n.
  notice 455 vb.
  understand 516 vb.
  indicate 547 vb.
  record 548 n.
  register 548 vb.
  print 587 vb.
registrar
  recorder 549 n.
  doctor 658 n.
registry
  list 87 n.
  record 548 n.
regress
  reversion 148 n.
  regress 286 vb.
  regression 286 n.
regression
  statistics 86 n.
  regression 286 n.
regret
  regret 830 n.
  regret 830 vb.
regretful
  unwilling 598 adj.
  unhappy 825 adj.
  regretting 830 adj.
  repentant 939 adj.
regrets
  remembrance
    505 n.
  disappointment
    509 n.
  regret 830 n.
regular
  uniform 16 adj.
  equal 28 adj.

  consummate
    32 adj.
  complete 54 adj.
  regular 81 adj.
  frequent 139 adj.
  periodical 141 adj.
  accurate 494 adj.
  habitué 610 n.
  soldier 722 n.
  monk 986 n.
regular army
  army 722 n.
regularity
  uniformity 16 n.
  regularity 81 n.
  periodicity 141 n.
  symmetry 245 n.
  habit 610 n.
regularize
  make uniform
    16 vb.
  regularize 62 vb.
regularly
  often 139 adv.
regulate
  adjust 24 vb.
  order 60 vb.
  regularize 62 vb.
regulation
  rule 81 n.
  management
    689 n.
  precept 693 n.
  legislation 953 n.
regulations
  obstacle 702 n.
  command 737 n.
regurgitate
  regress 286 vb.
  vomit 300 vb.
rehabilitate
  restore 656 vb.
  restitute 787 vb.
  vindicate 927 vb.
rehash
  recurrence 106 n.
  repeat 106 vb.
  repetition 106 n.
rehearsal
  dramaturgy 594 n.
  preparation 669 n.
rehearse
  repeat 106 vb.
  act 594 vb.
  make ready
    669 vb.

prepare oneself
669 vb.
reheat
repeat 106 vb.
reign
date 108 n.
influence 178 n.
governance 733 n.
rule 733 vb.
reimburse
compensate 31 vb.
restitute 787 vb.
pay 804 vb.
rein
moderator 177 n.
fetter 748 n.
reincarnation
recurrence 106 n.
future state 124 n.
transformation
143 n.
reproduction
166 n.
materiality 319 n.
reindeer
mammal 365 n.
reinforce
accrue 38 vb.
strengthen 162 vb.
enlarge 197 vb.
support 218 vb.
replenish 633 vb.
aid 703 vb.
defend 713 vb.
reinforcement
addition 38 n.
adjunct 40 n.
extra 40 n.
expansion 197 n.
repair 656 n.
aid 703 n.
auxiliary 707 n.
reinforcements
aider 703 n.
armed force 722 n.
rein in
retard 278 vb.
restrain 747 vb.
reins
safeguard 662 n.
fetter 748 n.
reinstate
restitute 787 vb.
reissue
duplicate 22 n.
repeat 106 vb.
repetition 106 n.

edition 589 n.
reiterate
repeat 106 vb.
reject
inferior 35 n.
be unwilling
598 vb.
reject 607 vb.
rejection 607 n.
be unsatisfied
636 vb.
rubbish 641 n.
outcast 883 n.
hate 888 vb.
rejection
unwillingness
598 n.
rejection 607 n.
prohibition 757 n.
rejects
leavings 41 n.
cheapness 812 n.
rejoice
delight 826 vb.
please 826 vb.
be content 828 vb.
rejoice 835 vb.
celebrate 876 vb.
rejoice in
be pleased 824 vb.
rejoin
interchange
151 vb.
answer 460 vb.
confute 479 vb.
rejoinder
rejoinder 460 n.
counterevidence
467 n.
confutation 479 n.
rejuvenate
revive 656 vb.
rekindle
revive 656 vb.
relapse
return 286 n.
relapse 657 n.
relapse 657 vb.
be wicked 934 vb.
relate
relate 9 vb.
describe 590 vb.
related
relative 9 adj.
akin 11 adj.
near 200 adj.

relating to
concerning 9 adv.
relation
relation 9 n.
description 590 n.
relations
relation 9 n.
kinsman 11 n.
relationship
relation 9 n.
consanguinity
11 n.
relative
circumstantial
8 adj.
relative 9 adj.
comparative 27 n.
compared 462 adj.
relatively
relatively 9 adv.
slightly 33 adv.
relative to
concerning 9 adv.
relativity
relativeness 9 n.
philosophy 449 n.
relax
disunite 46 vb.
come to rest
266 vb.
decelerate 278 vb.
soften 327 vb.
qualify 468 vb.
not act 677 vb.
repose 683 vb.
be lax 734 vb.
be lenient 736 vb.
liberate 746 vb.
keep calm 823 vb.
relieve 831 vb.
be sociable 882 vb.
relaxation
noncoherence 49 n.
weakness 163 n.
moderation 177 n.
leisure 681 n.
repose 683 n.
laxity 734 n.
liberation 746 n.
amusement 837 n.
relaxed
weak 163 adj.
tranquil 266 adj.
soft 327 adj.
reposeful 683 adj.
lax 734 adj.
free 744 adj.

relay
periodicity 141 n.
publish 528 vb.
broadcast 531 vb.
relay race
cooperation 706 n.
racing 716 n.
release
disunite 46 vb.
transference 272 n.
show 522 vb.
publish 528 vb.
dramatize 594 vb.
deliver 668 vb.
deliverance 668 n.
give scope 744 vb.
liberate 746 vb.
liberation 746 n.
permission 756 n.
permit 756 vb.
nonretention
779 n.
exempt 919 vb.
nonliability 919 n.
release on bail
give bail 767 vb.
relegate
exclude 57 vb.
displace 188 vb.
transpose 272 vb.
relegation
transference 272 n.
ejection 300 n.
relent
show mercy
905 vb.
forgive 909 vb.
relentless
resolute 599 adj.
severe 735 adj.
pitiless 906 adj.
impenitent
940 adj.
relevance
relevance 9 n.
meaning 514 n.
relevant
relevant 9 adj.
reliability
certainty 473 n.
resolution 599 n.
observance 768 n.
probity 929 n.
reliable
unchangeable
153 adj.
evidential 466 adj.

certain 473 adj.
credible 485 adj.
genuine 494 adj.
veracious 540 adj.
resolute 599 adj.
safe 660 adj.
observant 768 adj.
trustworthy
 929 adj.
reliance
 hope 852 n.
relic
 remainder 41 n.
 reminder 505 n.
 trace 548 n.
 talisman 983 n.
relic of the past
 archaism 127 n.
relics
 antiquity 125 n.
 corpse 363 n.
 ritual object 988 n.
relief
 contrariety 14 n.
 substitute 150 n.
 displacement
 188 n.
 outline 233 n.
 form 243 n.
 feature 445 n.
 sculpture 554 n.
 relief 831 n.
relief map
 map 551 n.
relieve
 come after 65 vb.
 relieve 831 vb.
relieve of
 take away 786 vb.
 steal 788 vb.
relieve oneself
 excrete 302 vb.
religion
 religion 973 n.
 piety 979 n.
religious
 observant 768 adj.
 trustworthy
 929 adj.
 divine 965 adj.
 religious 973 adj.
 pietist 979 n.
 pious 979 adj.
 clergy 986 n.
 monk 986 n.
 nun 986 n.

relinquish
 relinquish 621 vb.
 stop using 674 vb.
reliquary
 ritual object 988 n.
relish
 vigorousness 174 n.
 enjoy 376 vb.
 pleasure 376 n.
 taste 386 n.
 condiment 389 n.
 savouriness 390 n.
 be pleased 824 vb.
 enjoyment 824 n.
 pleasurableness
 826 n.
 liking 859 n.
relive the past
 describe 590 vb.
 regret 830 vb.
relocate
 change 143 vb.
 place 187 vb.
 be in motion
 265 vb.
 transpose 272 vb.
relocation
 change 143 n.
 transition 147 n.
 location 187 n.
 transference 272 n.
reluctance
 slowness 278 n.
 dissent 489 n.
 unwillingness
 598 n.
 dislike 861 n.
reluctant
 dissenting 489 adj.
 unwilling 598 adj.
 resisting 715 adj.
rely
 hope 852 vb.
rely on
 be certain 473 vb.
 believe 485 vb.
 take a pledge
 764 vb.
rem
 radiation 417 n.
remain
 be left 41 vb.
 continue 108 vb.
 last 113 vb.
 outlast 113 vb.
 stay 144 vb.
 go on 146 vb.

dwell 192 vb.
be quiescent
 266 vb.
remainder
 remainder 41 n.
 book 589 n.
 sell 793 vb.
remains
 remainder 41 n.
 trace 548 n.
remake
 repeat 106 vb.
 repetition 106 n.
 reproduce 166 vb.
 film 445 n.
 restore 656 vb.
remand
 command 737 vb.
 detention 747 n.
 imprison 747 vb.
remark
 maxim 496 n.
 affirm 532 vb.
 speech 579 n.
remarkable
 remarkable 32 adj.
 unusual 84 adj.
 visible 443 adj.
 wonderful 864 adj.
 noteworthy
 866 adj.
remark on
 notice 455 vb.
remarks
 estimate 480 n.
remarry
 wed 894 vb.
remedial
 improving 654 adj.
 remedial 658 adj.
remedy
 repair 656 vb.
 remedy 658 n.
 remedy 658 vb.
remember
 remember 505 vb.
 give 781 vb.
remembrance
 remembrance
 505 n.
 famousness 866 n.
remembrances
 courteous act
 884 n.
remind
 remind 505 vb.

reminder
 reminder 505 n.
remind oneself
 remember 505 vb.
reminisce
 remember 505 vb.
 describe 590 vb.
reminiscence
 remembrance
 505 n.
 narrative 590 n.
reminiscent
 remembering
 505 adj.
remiss
 negligent 458 adj.
 unwilling 598 adj.
 lax 734 adj.
remission
 fitfulness 142 n.
 lull 145 n.
 moderation 177 n.
 forgiveness 909 n.
remit
 send 272 vb.
 forgive 909 vb.
remittance
 transference 272 n.
 funds 797 n.
 payment 804 n.
remittance man
 recipient 782 n.
remnant
 remainder 41 n.
remnants
 leavings 41 n.
remodel
 transform 147 vb.
 revolutionize
 149 vb.
 rectify 654 vb.
 repair 656 vb.
remonstrance
 dissuasion 613 n.
 deprecation 762 n.
 reprimand 924 n.
remonstrate
 dissuade 613 vb.
 deprecate 762 vb.
 disapprove 924 vb.
 reprove 924 vb.
remorse
 sorrow 825 n.
 regret 830 n.
 pity 905 n.
 guilt 936 n.
 penitence 939 n.

919

remorseful
unhappy 825 adj.
regretting 830 adj.
repentant 939 adj.
remorseless
pitiless 906 adj.
impenitent
940 adj.
remote
irrelevant 10 adj.
inconsiderable
33 adj.
distant 199 adj.
invisible 444 adj.
secluded 883 adj.
remould
modify 143 vb.
reproduce 166 vb.
rectify 654 vb.
removal
subtraction 39 n.
exclusion 57 n.
displacement
188 n.
transference 272 n.
departure 296 n.
extraction 304 n.
deposal 752 n.
taking 786 n.
remove
degree 27 n.
subtract 39 vb.
disunite 46 vb.
exclude 57 vb.
serial place 73 n.
destroy 165 vb.
displace 188 vb.
transpose 272 vb.
depart 296 vb.
extract 304 vb.
class 538 n.
depose 752 vb.
take 786 vb.
take away 786 vb.
remuneration
earnings 771 n.
pay 804 n.
receipt 807 n.
reward 962 n.
remunerative
profitable 640 adj.
gainful 771 adj.
Renaissance
era 110 n.
architectural
192 adj.

renaissance
recurrence 106 n.
life 360 n.
revival 656 n.
rend
rend 46 vb.
demolish 165 vb.
force 176 vb.
hurt 827 vb.
render
convert 147 vb.
transform 147 vb.
coat 226 vb.
liquefy 337 vb.
play music 413 vb.
translate 520 vb.
give 781 vb.
rendering
facing 226 n.
translation 520 n.
building material
631 n.
render null and void
nullify 2 vb.
abrogate 752 vb.
rendezvous
union 45 n.
congregate 74 vb.
focus 76 n.
place 185 n.
goal 295 n.
meet 295 vb.
social round 882 n.
rend the heartstrings
hurt 827 vb.
renegade
recanter 603 n.
bad person 938 n.
renege on
not observe 769 vb.
renew
double 91 vb.
repeat 106 vb.
reproduce 166 vb.
make better
654 vb.
repair 656 vb.
restore 656 vb.
renewal
duplication 91 n.
repetition 106 n.
newness 126 n.
reproduction
166 n.
repair 656 n.
revival 656 n.

renew one's efforts
persevere 600 vb.
renounce
negate 533 vb.
recant 603 vb.
relinquish 621 vb.
resign 753 vb.
not retain 779 vb.
renovate
modernize 126 vb.
reproduce 166 vb.
make better
654 vb.
repair 656 vb.
restore 656 vb.
renovation
newness 126 n.
reproduction
166 n.
amendment 654 n.
repair 656 n.
renown
greatness 32 n.
famousness 866 n.
honour 866 vb.
renowned
renowned 866 adj.
rent
disunion 46 n.
gap 201 n.
assign 780 vb.
purchase 792 vb.
price 809 n.
rental
transfer 780 n.
price 809 n.
rent-boy
libertine 952 n.
prostitute 952 n.
rent out
lease 784 vb.
renunciation
negation 533 n.
recantation 603 n.
relinquishment
621 n.
laxity 734 n.
resignation 753 n.
refusal 760 n.
nonretention
779 n.
seclusion 883 n.
nonliability 919 n.
temperance 942 n.
reorder
modify 143 vb.

reorganization
arrangement 62 n.
revolution 149 n.
amendment 654 n.
restoration 656 n.
reorganize
transform 147 vb.
revolutionize
149 vb.
rectify 654 vb.
restore 656 vb.
rep
textile 222 n.
traveller 268 n.
speaker 579 n.
drama 594 n.
seller 793 n.
repair
adjust 24 vb.
repair 656 n.
repair 656 vb.
relieve 831 vb.
repairer
reformer 654 n.
mender 656 n.
repairs
repair 656 n.
repair to
travel 267 vb.
reparation
compensation 31 n.
repair 656 n.
restoration 656 n.
restitution 787 n.
atonement 941 n.
reward 962 n.
repartee
interchange 151 n.
answer 460 n.
confutation 479 n.
interlocution
584 n.
wit 839 n.
witticism 839 n.
repast
meal 301 n.
repatriate
restitute 787 vb.
repay
compensate 31 vb.
benefit 615 vb.
be profitable
771 vb.
restitute 787 vb.
pay 804 vb.
avenge 910 vb.
reward 962 vb.

repayment
compensation 31 n.
restitution 787 n.
atonement 941 n.
punishment 963 n.

repeal
abrogate 752 vb.
abrogation 752 n.

repeat
duplication 91 n.
repeat 106 vb.
repetition 106 n.
broadcast 531 n.
be diffuse 570 vb.

repeater
timekeeper 117 n.
pistol 723 n.

repel
repel 292 vb.
be unpalatable
  391 vb.
dissuade 613 vb.
resist 715 vb.
displease 827 vb.

repellent
repellent 292 adj.
unpleasant
  827 adj.
ugly 842 adj.
hateful 888 adj.

repent
change one's mind
  603 vb.
be penitent 939 vb.
become pious
  979 vb.

repentance
change of mind
  603 n.
regret 830 n.
penitence 939 n.

repentant
repentant 939 adj.

repercussion
repetition 106 n.
reversion 148 n.
effect 157 n.
counteraction
  182 n.
recoil 280 n.

repertoire
acting 594 n.
collection 632 n.

repertory
drama 594 n.
collection 632 n.

repertory company
actor 594 n.

repetition
repetition 106 n.

repetitious
repeated 106 adj.
diffuse 570 adj.

repetitive
identical 13 adj.
uniform 16 adj.
continuous 71 adj.
repeated 106 adj.
continuing 108 adj.
diffuse 570 adj.
tedious 838 adj.

rephrase
repeat 106 vb.
phrase 563 vb.

replace
substitute 150 vb.
restore 656 vb.
stop using 674 vb.
deputize 755 vb.
not retain 779 vb.

replacement
successor 67 n.
reversion 148 n.
substitute 150 n.
substitution 150 n.
displacement
  188 n.
restoration 656 n.

replace with
substitute 150 vb.

replay
repeat 106 vb.
repetition 106 n.

replenish
fill 54 vb.
replenish 633 vb.

replete
full 54 adj.
filled 635 adj.
redundant 637 adj.
sated 863 adj.

replica
copy 22 n.

reply
reversion 148 n.
answer 460 n.
answer 460 vb.
rejoinder 460 n.
correspond 588 vb.
vindication 927 n.

report
loudness 400 n.
bang 402 n.

communicate
  524 vb.
information 524 n.
report 524 n.
divulge 526 vb.
publicity 528 n.
publish 528 vb.
news 529 n.
correspond 588 vb.
describe 590 vb.
repute 866 n.

reporter
estimator 480 n.
informant 524 n.
publicizer 528 n.
news reporter
  529 n.
chronicler 549 n.

reports
record 548 n.

repose
repose 683 n.
repose 683 vb.

repository
receptacle 194 n.

reprehend
blame 924 vb.
disapprove 924 vb.
reprove 924 vb.

reprehensible
not nice 645 adj.
wrong 914 adj.
blameworthy
  924 adj.
heinous 934 adj.
guilty 936 adj.

represent
represent 551 vb.
deputize 755 vb.

representation
representation
  551 n.
vote 605 n.
commission 751 n.

representative
characteristic
  5 adj.
similar 18 adj.
general 79 adj.
example 83 n.
typical 83 adj.
substitute 150 n.
informant 524 n.
agent 686 n.
councillor 692 n.
mediator 720 n.
consignee 754 n.

delegate 754 n.
envoy 754 n.

**representative gov-
  ernment**
government 733 n.

**representative selec-
  tion**
example 83 n.

repress
suppress 165 vb.
counteract 182 vb.
hinder 702 vb.
subjugate 745 vb.
restrain 747 vb.
prohibit 757 vb.

repression
exclusion 57 n.
counteraction
  182 n.
restraint 747 n.
prohibition 757 n.
moral insensibility
  820 n.

repressive
restraining
  747 adj.

reprieve
delay 136 n.
escape 667 n.
deliverance 668 n.
forgive 909 vb.
forgiveness 909 n.
acquit 960 vb.
acquittal 960 n.

reprimand
reprimand 924 n.
reprove 924 vb.
punish 963 vb.

reprint
copy 20 vb.
duplicate 22 n.
repeat 106 vb.
repetition 106 n.
edition 589 n.

reprisal
retaliation 714 n.
revenge 910 n.
penalty 963 n.
punishment 963 n.

reprisals
revenge 910 n.

reprise
repetition 106 n.
tune 412 n.

reproach
slur 867 n.
reproach 924 n.

reproach 924 vb.
reprove 924 vb.
accuse 928 vb.
reproachful
resentful 891 adj.
disapproving
924 adj.
reproach oneself
regret 830 vb.
be penitent 939 vb.
reprobate
blameworthy
924 adj.
disapprove 924 vb.
wicked 934 adj.
bad person 938 n.
impious 980 adj.
impious person
980 n.
reproduce
reproduce 166 vb.
reproduce itself
reproduce itself
167 vb.
reproduction
reproduction
166 n.
representation
551 n.
picture 553 n.
reprove
reprove 924 vb.
reptile
animal 365 n.
reptile 365 n.
republic
territory 184 n.
nation 371 n.
political organiza-
tion 733 n.
republican
governmental
733 adj.
commoner 869 n.
repudiate
dissent 489 vb.
negate 533 vb.
recant 603 vb.
reject 607 vb.
abrogate 752 vb.
refuse 760 vb.
repudiation
dissent 489 n.
negation 533 n.
rejection 607 n.
abrogation 752 n.

nonobservance
769 n.
nonpayment 805 n.
divorce 896 n.
repugnance
contrariety 14 n.
unwillingness
598 n.
dislike 861 n.
hatred 888 n.
repulse
recoil 280 n.
repel 292 vb.
repulsion 292 n.
reject 607 vb.
defeat 727 vb.
defeat 728 n.
refusal 760 n.
refuse 760 vb.
repulsion
repulsion 292 n.
resistance 715 n.
dislike 861 n.
repulsive
repellent 292 adj.
unclean 649 adj.
ugly 842 adj.
hateful 888 adj.
reputable
reputable 866 adj.
reputation
credit 802 n.
repute 866 n.
pride 871 n.
repute
credit 802 n.
repute 866 n.
request
request 761 n.
request 761 vb.
requiem
obsequies 364 n.
vocal music 412 n.
lament 836 n.
requiem mass
Christian rite
988 n.
require
require 627 vb.
demand 737 vb.
impose a duty
917 vb.
requirement
requirement 627 n.
requisite
necessary 596 adj.
required 627 adj.

requisition
require 627 vb.
requirement 627 n.
dispose of 673 vb.
demand 737 n.
demand 737 vb.
compel 740 vb.
request 761 n.
request 761 vb.
appropriate
786 vb.
taking 786 n.
requite
interchange
151 vb.
reward 962 vb.
rerun
repeat 106 vb.
rescind
recant 603 vb.
abrogate 752 vb.
rescue
restoration 656 n.
restore 656 vb.
safety 660 n.
preserve 666 vb.
escape 667 n.
deliver 668 vb.
deliverance 668 n.
aid 703 n.
defend 713 vb.
liberate 746 vb.
liberation 746 n.
restitution 787 n.
research
be curious 453 vb.
enquire 459 vb.
enquiry 459 n.
experiment 461 vb.
study 536 n.
researcher
enquirer 459 n.
experimenter
461 n.
resection
scission 46 n.
resemblance
similarity 18 n.
resemble
resemble 18 vb.
resent
resent 891 vb.
envy 912 vb.
resentful
resentful 891 adj.
resentment
resentment 891 n.

revengefulness
910 n.
jealousy 911 n.
reservation
qualification 468 n.
doubt 486 n.
dissent 489 n.
conditions 766 n.
seclusion 883 n.
reserve
be early 135 vb.
substitute 150 n.
enclosure 235 n.
doubt 486 n.
concealment 525 n.
keep secret 525 vb.
register 548 vb.
taciturnity 582 n.
select 605 vb.
require 627 vb.
store 632 vb.
not use 674 vb.
restraint 747 n.
lockup 748 n.
acquire 771 vb.
possess 773 vb.
modesty 874 n.
seclusion 883 n.
reserved
reticent 525 adj.
taciturn 582 adj.
restrained 747 adj.
promised 764 adj.
possessed 773 adj.
impassive 820 adj.
inexcitable
823 adj.
modest 874 adj.
unsociable 883 adj.
due 915 adj.
reserves
advantage 34 n.
means 629 n.
store 632 n.
provision 633 n.
armed force 722 n.
funds 797 n.
treasury 799 n.
reservoir
receptacle 194 n.
irrigator 341 n.
lake 346 n.
storage 632 n.
reset
modify 143 vb.
resettlement
location 187 n.

reshape
modify 143 vb.
transform 147 vb.
reside
dwell 192 vb.
reside in
be 1 vb.
residence
presence 189 n.
abode 192 n.
house 192 n.
residency
abode 192 n.
resident
native 191 adj.
resident 191 n.
residual
remaining 41 adj.
numerical result
85 n.
residue
remainder 41 n.
residuum
dirt 649 n.
resign
relinquish 621 vb.
stop using 674 vb.
resign 753 vb.
resignation
recession 290 n.
lack of expectation
508 n.
submission 721 n.
resignation 753 n.
patience 823 n.
hopelessness 853 n.
humility 872 n.
resign oneself
be patient 823 vb.
keep calm 823 vb.
resilient
elastic 328 adj.
resin
grease 357 vb.
resin 357 n.
viol 414 n.
resist
counteract 182 vb.
dissent 489 vb.
be unwilling
598 vb.
resist 715 vb.
restrain 747 vb.
resistance
electricity 160 n.
energy 160 n.
hardness 326 n.

resistance 715 n.
revolter 738 n.
resistant
rigid 326 adj.
dissenting 489 adj.
opposing 704 adj.
resisting 715 adj.
resolute
resolute 599 adj.
resoluteness
resolution 599 n.
courage 855 n.
resolution
separation 46 n.
decomposition
51 n.
topic 452 n.
resolution 599 n.
plan 623 n.
See **policy**
completion 725 n.
resolve
decompose 51 vb.
decipher 520 vb.
be resolute 599 vb.
resolution 599 n.
intend 617 vb.
intention 617 n.
resonant
resonant 404 adj.
resort
convergence 293 n.
contrivance 623 n.
means 629 n.
resort to
congregate 74 vb.
travel 267 vb.
avail oneself of
673 vb.
resounding
sounding 398 adj.
resonant 404 adj.
renowned 866 adj.
resource
contrivance 623 n.
resourceful
progressive
285 adj.
imaginative
513 adj.
skilful 694 adj.
cunning 698 adj.
resources
means 629 n.
materials 631 n.
estate 777 n.
wealth 800 n.

respect
relation 9 n.
observe 768 vb.
respect 920 n.
respect 920 vb.
respectability
repute 866 n.
probity 929 n.
respectable
great 32 adj.
not bad 644 adj.
reputable 866 adj.
honourable
929 adj.
respectful
respectful 920 adj.
respective
relative 9 adj.
respectively
severally 80 adv.
pro rata 783 adv.
respects
courteous act
884 n.
respects 920 n.
respiration
respiration 352 n.
respirator
respiration 352 n.
hospital 658 n.
safeguard 662 n.
preserver 666 n.
respiratory disease
disease 651 n.
respiratory disease
651 n.
respire
breathe 352 vb.
respite
delay 136 n.
lull 145 n.
deliverance 668 n.
repose 683 n.
acquit 960 vb.
resplendent
luminous 417 adj.
splendid 841 adj.
respond
accord 24 vb.
answer 460 vb.
cooperate 706 vb.
concord 710 vb.
feel 818 vb.
respondent
respondent 460 n.
accused person
928 n.

litigant 959 n.
response
effect 157 n.
sense 374 n.
answer 460 n.
feeling 818 n.
friendliness 880 n.
hymn 981 n.
responsible
liable 180 adj.
observant 768 adj.
cautious 858 adj.
obliged 917 adj.
trustworthy
929 adj.
guilty 936 adj.
responsive
sentient 374 adj.
feeling 818 adj.
impressible
819 adj.
rest
be left 41 vb.
remainder 41 n.
be discontinuous
72 vb.
stay 144 vb.
cease 145 vb.
lull 145 n.
pause 145 n.
go on 146 vb.
stability 153 n.
inertness 175 n.
support 218 n.
be quiescent
266 vb.
come to rest
266 vb.
quiescence 266 n.
quietude 266 n.
silence 399 n.
notation 410 n.
inaction 677 n.
be inactive 679 vb.
leisure 681 n.
repose 683 n.
repose 683 vb.
relief 831 n.
rest assured
believe 485 vb.
hope 852 vb.
restate
repeat 106 vb.
restaurant
café 192 n.
cookery 301 n.

restauranteur
caterer 633 n.
restful
tranquil 266 adj.
comfortable
376 adj.
reposeful 683 adj.
restitution
restitution 787 n.
restive
excited 821 adj.
excitable 822 adj.
discontented
829 adj.
restless
transient 114 adj.
fitful 142 adj.
moving 265 adj.
irresolute 601 adj.
active 678 adj.
excited 821 adj.
excitable 822 adj.
restock
replenish 633 vb.
rest on one's laurels
be quiescent
266 vb.
not act 677 vb.
restoration
newness 126 n.
repair 656 n.
restoration 656 n.
dueness 915 n.
vindication 927 n.
penalty 963 n.
restorative
stimulant 174 n.
remedial 658 adj.
tonic 658 n.
restore
compensate 31 vb.
make better
654 vb.
restore 656 vb.
relieve 831 vb.
vindicate 927 vb.
restore one's faith
convince 485 vb.
restrain
restrain 747 vb.
tranquillize
823 vb.
restrained
plain 573 adj.
restrained 747 adj.
restrain oneself
restrain 747 vb.

restraint
moderation 177 n.
restraint 747 n.
restrict
make smaller
198 vb.
limit 236 vb.
qualify 468 vb.
hinder 702 vb.
restrain 747 vb.
prohibit 757 vb.
restricted
small 33 adj.
moderate 177 adj.
concealed 525 adj.
restrained 747 adj.
restricted area
restriction 747 n.
restriction
diminution 37 n.
hindrance 702 n.
restriction 747 n.
prohibition 757 n.
restrictive
excluding 57 adj.
restraining
747 adj.
restrictive practice
restriction 747 n.
restrict oneself
be temperate
942 vb.
rest room
latrine 649 n.
restructuring
arrangement 62 n.
revolution 149 n.
rest with
be one's duty
917 vb.
restyle
hairdressing 843 n.
result
be left 41 vb.
remainder 41 n.
sequel 67 n.
end 69 n.
event 154 n.
effect 157 n.
result 157 vb.
product 164 n.
judgment 480 n.
instrumentality
628 n.
completion 725 n.
resultant
remaining 41 adj.

caused 157 adj.
resultant action
effect 157 n.
result in
result 157 vb.
results
answer 460 n.
resume
repeat 106 vb.
acquire 771 vb.
résumé
abstract 592 vb.
compendium
592 n.
resumption
repetition 106 n.
restoration 656 n.
resurface
repair 656 vb.
resurgence
reproduction
166 n.
revival 656 n.
resurrect
reproduce 166 vb.
revive 656 vb.
resurrection
newness 126 n.
reproduction
166 n.
revival 656 n.
heaven 971 n.
resurrectionist
thief 789 n.
resuscitate
reproduce 166 vb.
revive 656 vb.
animate 821 vb.
retail
communicate
524 vb.
sell 793 vb.
retailer
intermediary
231 n.
seller 793 n.
merchant 794 n.
tradespeople 794 n.
retail price
price 809 n.
retain
stabilize 153 vb.
understand 516 vb.
retain 778 vb.
retainer
inferior 35 n.
retainer 742 n.

reward 962 n.
retake
retrieve 656 vb.
retaliate
retaliate 714 vb.
retaliation
retaliation 714 n.
justice 913 n.
retard
put off 136 vb.
retard 278 vb.
retarded
unintelligent
499 adj.
immature 670 adj.
retch
vomit 300 vb.
retell
repeat 106 vb.
retention
retention 778 n.
retentive
tough 329 adj.
retentive 778 adj.
greedy 859 adj.
reticent
reticent 525 adj.
reticle
network 222 n.
reticulation
network 222 n.
convolution 251 n.
stripe 437 n.
retina
eye 438 n.
retinue
retinue 67 n.
retiral
resignation 753 n.
retire
cease 145 vb.
be quiescent
266 vb.
regress 286 vb.
recede 290 vb.
depart 296 vb.
run away 620 vb.
relinquish 621 vb.
resign 753 vb.
not retain 779 vb.
be modest 874 vb.
retired
prior 119 adj.
former 125 adj.
ageing 131 adj.
disused 674 adj.
leisurely 681 adj.

free 744 adj.
retirement
  disunion 46 n.
  regression 286 n.
  recession 290 n.
  relinquishment
    621 n.
  leisure 681 n.
  resignation 753 n.
  seclusion 883 n.
retiring
  modest 874 adj.
  unsociable 883 adj.
retort
  reversion 148 n.
  interchange 151 n.
  interchange
    151 vb.
  vessel 194 n.
  vaporizer 338 n.
  heater 383 n.
  answer 460 n.
  answer 460 vb.
  testing agent
    461 n.
  confutation 479 n.
  confute 479 vb.
  retaliate 714 vb.
  retaliation 714 n.
  be insolent 878 vb.
retrace
  revert 148 vb.
retrace one's foot-
    steps
  repeat 106 vb.
  turn back 286 vb.
retract
  revert 148 vb.
  draw 288 vb.
  disbelieve 486 vb.
  dissent 489 vb.
  recant 603 vb.
  abrogate 752 vb.
retraction
  reversion 148 n.
  traction 288 n.
  unbelief 486 n.
  dissent 489 n.
  recantation 603 n.
retractor
  traction 288 n.
  unbeliever 486 n.
retreat
  decrease 37 n.
  decrease 37 vb.
  reversion 148 n.
  revert 148 vb.

go away 190 vb.
  retreat 192 n.
  contraction 198 n.
  regress 286 vb.
  regression 286 n.
  recede 290 vb.
  recession 290 n.
  depart 296 vb.
  meditation 449 n.
  run away 620 vb.
  refuge 662 n.
  escape 667 n.
  be defeated 728 vb.
  defeat 728 n.
  seclusion 883 n.
  piety 979 n.
  prayers 981 n.
  worship 981 n.
retrench
  abate 37 vb.
  subtract 39 vb.
  restrain 747 vb.
  economize 814 vb.
retribution
  retaliation 714 n.
  justice 913 n.
  punishment 963 n.
retributive
  punitive 963 adj.
retrieval
  compensation 31 n.
  data processing
    86 n.
  reversion 148 n.
  transference 272 n.
  restoration 656 n.
  deliverance 668 n.
  acquisition 771 n.
retrieve
  retrieve 656 vb.
  deliver 668 vb.
retriever
  dog 365 n.
retroactive
  retrospective
    125 adj.
retrocession
  regression 286 n.
retroflexion
  regression 286 n.
retrogression
  reversion 148 n.
  regression 286 n.
  deterioration
    655 n.
  relapse 657 n.

retrospect
  remembrance
    505 n.
retrospection
  past time 125 n.
  reversion 148 n.
  thought 449 n.
  remembrance
    505 n.
retrospective
  retrospective
    125 adj.
retroussé
  short 204 adj.
  curved 248 adj.
retroversion
  reversion 148 n.
  inversion 221 n.
retrovirus
  infection 651 n.
retsina
  wine 301 n.
return
  recurrence 106 n.
  reversion 148 n.
  revert 148 vb.
  product 164 n.
  inversion 221 n.
  recoil 280 vb.
  turn round 282 vb.
  return 286 n.
  turn back 286 vb.
  propel 287 vb.
  answer 460 n.
  report 524 n.
  vote 605 n.
  vote 605 vb.
  benefit 615 n.
  relapse 657 n.
  relapse 657 vb.
  commission
    751 vb.
  mandate 751 n.
  earnings 771 n.
  restitute 787 vb.
  restitution 787 n.
  receipt 807 n.
  be discontented
    829 vb.
  disapprobation
    924 n.
  disapprove 924 vb.
  reward 962 n.
return a favour
  thank 907 vb.
return a verdict
  judge 480 vb.

return fire
  recoil 280 n.
returns
  answer 460 n.
  record 548 n.
  receipt 807 n.
return the compli-
    ment
  interchange
    151 vb.
  retaliate 714 vb.
reunion
  union 45 n.
  assembly 74 n.
  concord 710 n.
  social gathering
    882 n.
reuse
  use 673 n.
  use 673 vb.
  economize 814 vb.
revamp
  modify 143 vb.
  repair 656 vb.
reveal
  manifest 522 vb.
  inform 524 vb.
  disclose 526 vb.
  publish 528 vb.
  indicate 547 vb.
revealing
  transparent
    422 adj.
  unchaste 951 adj.
reveille
  call 547 n.
revel
  revel 837 n.
  revel 837 vb.
  pageant 875 n.
Revelation
  scripture 975 n.
revelation
  appearance 445 n.
  discovery 484 n.
  lack of expectation
    508 n.
  manifestation
    522 n.
  disclosure 526 n.
  revelation 975 n.
revel in
  enjoy 376 vb.
revels
  festivity 837 n.
revenge
  repetition 106 n.

925

revenge 910 n.
vindicate 927 vb.
revenge oneself
avenge 910 vb.
revenue
means 629 n.
earnings 771 n.
estate 777 n.
receipt 807 n.
reverberate
recoil 280 vb.
roll 403 vb.
resound 404 vb.
revere
honour 866 vb.
love 887 vb.
respect 920 vb.
be pious 979 vb.
worship 981 vb.
reverence
obeisance 311 n.
respect 920 n.
respect 920 vb.
respects 920 n.
piety 979 n.
worship 981 n.
Reverend
title 870 n.
reverend
worshipful 866 adj.
sanctified 979 adj.
cleric 986 n.
reverent
respectful 920 adj.
pious 979 adj.
reverential
respectful 920 adj.
reverie
thought 449 n.
abstractedness
456 n.
fantasy 513 n.
revers
fold 261 n.
reversal
reversion 148 n.
inversion 221 n.
contraposition
240 n.
lack of expectation
508 n.
change of mind
603 n.
reverse
contrariety 14 n.
contrary 14 adj.
modify 143 vb.

revert 148 vb.
be inverted 221 vb.
invert 221 vb.
back 238 adj.
rear 238 n.
contraposition
240 n.
opposite 240 adj.
retard 278 vb.
turn round 282 vb.
regress 286 vb.
defeat 728 n.
adversity 731 n.
abrogate 752 vb.
loss 772 n.
reversion
reversion 148 n.
following 284 n.
restitution 787 n.
revert
revert 148 vb.
deteriorate 655 vb.
revert to
relapse 657 vb.
change hands
780 vb.
review
inspection 438 n.
spectacle 445 n.
attention 455 n.
notice 455 vb.
enquire 459 vb.
enquiry 459 n.
estimate 480 vb.
remember 505 vb.
remembrance
505 n.
interpretation
520 n.
report 524 n.
journal 528 n.
article 591 n.
compendium
592 n.
stage show 594 n.
amendment 654 n.
rectify 654 vb.
pageant 875 n.
reviewer
estimator 480 n.
interpreter 520 n.
bookperson 589 n.
dissertator 591 n.
revile
curse 899 vb.
criticize 924 vb.
reproach 924 vb.

revise
modify 143 vb.
study 536 vb.
print 587 n.
reading matter
589 n.
amendment 654 n.
rectify 654 vb.
revision
inspection 438 n.
study 536 n.
amendment 654 n.
revisit
be present 189 vb.
revitalize
vitalize 360 vb.
revive 656 vb.
revival
repetition 106 n.
dramaturgy 594 n.
improvement
654 n.
revival 656 n.
refreshment 685 n.
revivalism
public worship
981 n.
revive
repeat 106 vb.
revert 148 vb.
be strong 162 vb.
invigorate 174 vb.
live 360 vb.
get better 654 vb.
make better
654 vb.
be restored 656 vb.
revive 656 vb.
be refreshed
685 n.
refresh 685 vb.
animate 821 vb.
revivify
reproduce 166 vb.
revocation
negation 533 n.
recantation 603 n.
abrogation 752 n.
revoke
destroy 165 vb.
suppress 165 vb.
negate 533 vb.
recant 603 vb.
reject 607 vb.
abrogate 752 vb.
prohibit 757 vb.
not retain 779 vb.

revolt
revolt 738 n.
revolt 738 vb.
displease 827 vb.
cause dislike
861 vb.
incur blame
924 vb.
revolt from
hate 888 vb.
revolting
unsavoury 391 adj.
not nice 645 adj.
unpleasant
827 adj.
frightening
854 adj.
hateful 888 adj.
revolution
regular return
141 n.
revolution 149 n.
rotation 315 n.
revolutionary
modern 126 adj.
revolutionary
149 adj.
revolutionist 149 n.
violent creature
176 n.
dissentient 489 n.
reformer 654 n.
disobedient
738 adj.
revolutionist
revolutionist 149 n.
revolutionize
revolutionize
149 vb.
revolve
circle 314 vb.
rotate 315 vb.
revolver
propellant 287 n.
pistol 723 n.
revolving
periodical 141 adj.
rotation 315 n.
revolving doors
doorway 263 n.
revue
spectacle 445 n.
stage show 594 n.
revulsion
reversion 148 n.
recoil 280 n.
recession 290 n.

change of mind
603 n.

rev up
roll 403 vb.
make ready
669 vb.

reward
reward 962 n.
reward 962 vb.

rewind
repeat 106 vb.

reword
repeat 106 vb.
translate 520 vb.
phrase 563 vb.

rewrite
write 586 vb.
rectify 654 vb.

rex
sovereign 741 n.

rhapsodize
imagine 513 vb.

rhapsody
musical piece
412 n.
ideality 513 n.

rhea
bird 365 n.

Rhesus factor
blood 335 n.

rhetoric
vigour 571 n.
grandiloquence
574 n.
ornament 574 n.
oratory 579 n.
ostentation 875 n.

rhetorical
stylistic 566 adj.

rhetorical question
question 459 n.

rheumatic
crippled 163 adj.
diseased 651 adj.

rheumatic fever
rheumatism 651 n.

rheumatics
rheumatism 651 n.

rheumatism
pang 377 n.
rheumatism 651 n.

rheumatoid
diseased 651 adj.

rheumatoid arthritis
pang 377 n.
rheumatism 651 n.

rhinestone
finery 844 n.

rhinitis
respiratory disease
651 n.

rhinoceros
mammal 365 n.

rhinoceros hide
moral insensibility
820 n.

rhinoplasty
surgery 658 n.

rhizome
plant 366 n.

rhododendron
tree 366 n.

rhomboid
obliquity 220 n.

rhubarb
fruit and vegetables
301 n.

rhubarb rhubarb
roll 403 n.
empty talk 515 n.

rhyme
assimilation 18 n.
recurrence 106 n.
poetize 593 vb.
poetry 593 n.
prosody 593 n.

rhyming
repeated 106 adj.
harmonious
410 adj.
poetic 593 adj.

rhyming slang
slang 560 adj.

rhythm
uniformity 16 n.
recurrence 106 n.
periodicity 141 n.
tendency 179 n.
symmetry 245 n.
motion 265 n.
oscillation 317 n.
tempo 410 n.
elegance 575 n.
prosody 593 n.

rhythmic
uniform 16 adj.
continuous 71 adj.
elegant 575 adj.
poetic 593 adj.

ria
gulf 345 n.

rib
ridicule 851 vb.

spouse 894 n.

ribald
vulgar 847 adj.
disreputable
867 adj.
cursing 899 adj.
impure 951 adj.

ribaldry
ridicule 851 n.
scurrility 899 n.
impurity 951 n.

ribband
ligature 47 n.
strip 208 n.

ribbon
ligature 47 n.
strip 208 n.
badge 547 n.
stationery 586 n.
decoration 729 n.
trimming 844 n.
honours 866 n.
love token 889 n.

ribbons
headgear 228 n.
finery 844 n.

ribs
frame 218 n.
laterality 239 n.
meat 301 n.

rib-tickling
witty 839 adj.

rice
cereals 301 n.
food 301 n.
grass 366 n.

rich
prolific 171 adj.
fatty 357 adj.
tasty 386 adj.
florid 425 adj.
diffuse 570 adj.
ornate 574 adj.
plentiful 635 adj.
valuable 644 adj.
rich 800 adj.
splendid 841 adj.
funny 849 adj.

riches
good 615 n.
plenty 635 n.
wealth 800 n.

richness
productiveness
171 n.
diffuseness 570 n.
plenty 635 n.

ornamentation
844 n.

rick
derange 63 vb.
bunch 74 n.
disable 161 vb.

rickets
deformity 246 n.
disease 651 n.

rickety
ageing 131 adj.
flimsy 163 adj.
imperfect 647 adj.
dilapidated
655 adj.
unsafe 661 adj.

rickshaw
cab 274 n.
pushcart 274 n.

ricochet
reversion 148 n.
revert 148 vb.
recoil 280 n.
recoil 280 vb.

ricotta
dairy product
301 n.

rid
eject 300 vb.
deliver 668 vb.

riddance
escape 667 n.
deliverance 668 n.
liberation 746 n.

riddle
pierce 263 vb.
porosity 263 n.
confute 479 vb.
absurdity 497 n.
unintelligibility
517 n.
equivocalness
518 n.
enigma 530 n.
cleaning utensil
648 n.

riddles
indoor game 837 n.

ride
land travel 267 n.
ride 267 vb.
amuse oneself
837 vb.

ride out the storm
navigate 269 vb.

rider
adjunct 40 n.

rider 268 n.
  transport 272 n.
ride roughshod over
  dominate 733 vb.
  oppress 735 vb.
  not observe 769 vb.
  shame 867 vb.
  be insolent 878 vb.
  despise 922 vb.
ridge
  bond 47 n.
  series 71 n.
  narrowness 206 n.
  high land 209 n.
ridicule
  ridicule 851 n.
  ridicule 851 vb.
ridiculous
  ridiculous 849 adj.
riding
  district 184 n.
  motion 265 n.
  equitation 267 n.
  land travel 267 n.
  sport 837 n.
riding habit
  jacket 228 n.
**riding on the crest of
  a wave**
  prosperous 730 adj.
rid oneself
  eject 300 vb.
  escape 667 vb.
  deliver 668 vb.
rife
  existing 1 adj.
  prolific 171 adj.
riffle through
  scan 438 vb.
riffraff
  rabble 869 n.
rifle
  propellant 287 n.
  firearm 723 n.
  rob 788 vb.
  steal 788 vb.
rifle through
  search 459 vb.
rift
  disunion 46 n.
  gap 201 n.
  defect 647 n.
  dissension 709 n.
rig
  dressing 228 n.
  form 243 n.
  carriage 274 n.

  fake 541 vb.
rigging
  support 218 n.
  sail 275 n.
right
  agreeing 24 adj.
  apt 24 adj.
  greatly 32 vb.
  dextrality 241 n.
  straight 249 adj.
  knock 279 n.
  accurate 494 adj.
  true 494 adj.
  truly 494 adv.
  elegant 575 adj.
  repair 656 vb.
  political party
    708 n.
  authority 733 n.
  right 913 adj.
  right 913 n.
right-about turn
  reversion 148 n.
  be inverted 221 vb.
right and proper
  right 913 adj.
right angle
  verticality 215 n.
  angle 247 n.
right as rain
  perfect 646 adj.
right away
  suddenly 135 adv.
righteous
  just 913 adj.
  virtuous 933 adj.
righteousness
  right 913 n.
  virtue 933 n.
rightful
  genuine 494 adj.
  right 913 adj.
  due 915 adj.
right-handed
  handed 378 adj.
**right-hand man, wo-
  man**
  aider 703 n.
  auxiliary 707 n.
  servant 742 n.
  deputy 755 n.
Right Honourable
  title 870 n.
right itself
  cure 656 vb.
right mind
  sanity 502 n.

  orthodox 976 adj.
rightness
  truth 494 n.
  right 913 n.
right now
  at present 121 adv.
right of way
  passage 305 n.
  access 624 n.
  path 624 n.
right royal
  liberal 813 adj.
right time
  juncture 8 n.
  clock time 117 n.
  occasion 137 n.
right wing
  dextrality 241 n.
rightwinger
  dextrality 241 n.
  political party
    708 n.
**right word in the
  right place, the**
  elegance 575 n.
rigid
  rigid 326 adj.
  severe 735 adj.
rigidity
  straightness 249 n.
  quiescence 266 n.
  hardness 326 n.
  severity 735 n.
rigmarole
  lack of meaning
    515 n.
  diffuseness 570 n.
rigor mortis
  decease 361 n.
rigorous
  severe 735 adj.
  fastidious 862 adj.
  pitiless 906 adj.
  ascetic 945 adj.
rigour
  hardness 326 n.
  severity 735 n.
  pitilessness 906 n.
rig-out
  dressing 228 n.
rig the jury
  do wrong 914 adj.
rile
  torment 827 vb.
  enrage 891 vb.
rim
  outline 233 n.

  edge 234 n.
rime
  wintriness 380 n.
rind
  skin 226 n.
rinderpest
  animal disease
    651 n.
ring
  fastening 47 n.
  band 74 n.
  circumscription
    232 n.
  enclose 235 vb.
  enclosure 235 n.
  circle 250 n.
  orifice 263 n.
  be loud 400 vb.
  roll 403 vb.
  resonance 404 n.
  resound 404 vb.
  play music 413 vb.
  communicate
    524 vb.
  message 529 n.
  association 706 n.
  party 708 n.
  arena 724 n.
  badge of rule
    743 n.
  possession 773 n.
  jewellery 844 n.
  love token 889 n.
  wedding 894 n.
ring a bell
  be remembered
    505 vb.
ring-a-ring-o'-roses
  children's games
    837 n.
ring down the curtain
  terminate 69 vb.
  cease 145 vb.
  die 361 vb.
ring for
  desire 859 vb.
ring in
  come before 64 vb.
  initiate 68 vb.
ring off
  terminate 69 vb.
  cease 145 vb.
  be mute 578 vb.
ringer
  substitute 150 n.
ringing
  loud 400 adj.

roll 403 n.
resonance 404 n.
resonant 404 adj.
ringleader
motivator 612 n.
leader 690 n.
agitator 738 n.
ringlet
loop 250 n.
coil 251 n.
hair 259 n.
ringmaster
manager 690 n.
ring road
road 624 n.
circuit 626 n.
ring the changes
repeat 106 vb.
modify 143 vb.
vary 152 vb.
ring true
be true 494 vb.
ring up
communicate
  524 vb.
ringworm
skin disease 651 n.
rink
arena 724 n.
pleasure ground
  837 n.
rinse
drench 341 vb.
clean 648 vb.
hairwash 843 n.
riot
be disordered
  61 vb.
rampage 61 vb.
turmoil 61 n.
abundance 171 n.
violence 176 n.
abound 635 vb.
quarrel 709 n.
fight 716 n.
revolt 738 n.
lawlessness 954 n.
riotous
plentiful 635 adj.
sensual 944 adj.
rip
rend 46 vb.
move fast 277 vb.
wound 655 vb.
libertine 952 n.
ripe
ageing 131 adj.

matured 669 adj.
ripen
impend 155 vb.
get better 654 vb.
mature 669 vb.
carry through
  725 vb.
ripeness
occasion 137 n.
ripe old age
durability 113 n.
old age 131 n.
rip off
deceive 542 vb.
expropriation
  786 n.
fleece 786 vb.
defraud 788 vb.
swindling 788 n.
price 809 n.
dearness 811 n.
overcharge 811 vb.
riposte
recoil 280 n.
answer 460 n.
answer 460 vb.
retaliate 714 vb.
retaliation 714 n.
ripping
super 644 adj.
ripple
convolution 251 n.
crinkle 251 vb.
roughen 259 vb.
roughness 259 n.
furrow 262 n.
agitate 318 vb.
be agitated 318 vb.
wave 350 n.
sound faint 401 vb.
rip-roaring
merry 833 adj.
rise
grow 36 vb.
increase 36 n.
begin 68 vb.
beginning 68 n.
  See **origin**
origin 68 n.
expand 197 vb.
be high 209 vb.
high land 209 n.
be vertical 215 vb.
verticality 215 n.
be oblique 220 vb.
incline 220 n.
fly 271 vb.

progress 285 vb.
progression 285 n.
ascend 308 vb.
ascent 308 n.
lift oneself 310 vb.
make bright
  417 vb.
be duped 544 vb.
incentive 612 n.
flourish 615 vb.
get better 654 vb.
improvement
  654 n.
resist 715 vb.
go to war 718 vb.
succeed 727 vb.
gain 771 n.
show respect
  920 vb.
rise above
be superior 34 vb.
outdo 306 vb.
rise against
withstand 704 vb.
rise to one's feet
be vertical 215 vb.
ascend 308 vb.
show respect
  920 vb.
rise to the bait
be credulous
  487 vb.
rise to the occasion
improvise 609 vb.
suffice 635 vb.
be active 678 vb.
be successful
  727 vb.
succeed 727 vb.
rise up
ascend 308 vb.
revolt 738 vb.
be discontented
  829 vb.
risible
absurd 497 adj.
foolish 499 adj.
laughing 835 adj.
ridiculous 849 adj.
rising
influential 178 adj.
sloping 220 adj.
motion 265 n.
ascent 308 n.
resistance 715 n.
successful 727 adj.
prosperous 730 adj.

revolt 738 n.
respectful 920 adj.
rising damp
moisture 341 n.
rising generation
youth 130 n.
posterity 170 n.
rising ground
high land 209 n.
incline 220 n.
ascent 308 n.
rising star
victor 727 n.
person of repute
  866 n.
risk
gambling 618 n.
danger 661 n.
endanger 661 vb.
speculate 791 vb.
risk-taking
gambling 618 n.
speculative
  618 adj.
rash 857 adj.
risky
uncertain 474 adj.
speculative
  618 adj.
harmful 645 adj.
dangerous 661 adj.
risotto
dish 301 n.
risqué
witty 839 adj.
disreputable
  867 adj.
impure 951 adj.
rissoles
meat 301 n.
rite
order 60 n.
rite 988 n.
rites
act of worship
  981 n.
rite 988 n.
ritual
practice 610 n.
formal 875 adj.
ritual 988 adj.
ritual 988 n.
ritualistic
pietistic 979 adj.
ritualistic 988 adj.
ritual object
ritual object 988 n.

ritzy
  rich 800 adj.
  dear 811 adj.
  fashionable
    848 adj.
  ostentatious
    875 adj.
rival
  opposing 704 adj.
  opponent 705 n.
  contend 716 vb.
  contender 716 n.
  enemy 881 n.
  jealous 911 adj.
  jealousy 911 n.
rivalry
  imitation 20 n.
  opposition 704 n.
  quarrelsomeness
    709 n.
  contention 716 n.
  jealousy 911 n.
  envy 912 n.
rivals
  opposites 704 n.
river
  stream 350 n.
river saga
  narrative 590 n.
rivet
  affix 45 vb.
  fastening 47 n.
Riviera
  pleasure ground
    837 n.
rivulet
  stream 350 n.
roach
  fish 365 n.
  drug-taking 949 n.
road
  transport 272 n.
  direction 281 n.
  gulf 345 n.
  road 624 n.
road block
  closure 264 n.
  obstacle 702 n.
roadhouse
  inn 192 n.
road junction
  crossing 222 n.
road race
  racing 716 n.
road roller
  smoother 258 n.

roadside
  near 200 adj.
  edge 234 n.
  marginal 234 adj.
roadway
  road 624 n.
roam
  wander 267 vb.
  be free 744 vb.
roan
  equine 273 adj.
  horse 273 n.
  brown 430 adj.
  pied 437 adj.
roar
  be agitated 318 vb.
  blow 352 vb.
  be loud 400 vb.
  loudness 400 n.
  roll 403 vb.
  vociferate 408 vb.
  ululate 409 vb.
  emphasize 532 vb.
  voice 577 vb.
  be active 678 vb.
  anger 891 n.
  be angry 891 vb.
  threaten 900 vb.
roaring
  furious 176 adj.
  loudness 400 n.
  excited 821 adj.
  angry 891 adj.
roaring drunk
  drunk 949 adj.
Roaring Forties
  wind 352 n.
roar with laughter
  laugh 835 vb.
roast
  cook 301 vb.
  be hot 379 vb.
  heat 381 vb.
  reprove 924 vb.
roasted
  culinary 301 adj.
  See **cook**
roasting
  burning 381 n.
  reprimand 924 n.
  hot 379 adj.
rob
  weaken 163 vb.
  rob 788 vb.
  steal 788 vb.
  impoverish 801 vb.

robber
  robber 789 n.
  offender 904 n.
robbery
  stealing 788 n.
  loss of right 916 n.
robbery with violence
  stealing 788 n.
robe
  dress 228 vb.
  informal dress
    228 n.
  robe 228 n.
  badge of rule
    743 n.
  canonicals 989 n.
robin
  bird 365 n.
Robin Hood
  robber 789 n.
Robinson Crusoe
  solitary 883 n.
robot
  image 551 n.
  instrument 628 n.
  machine 630 n.
rob Peter to pay Paul
  substitute 150 vb.
robust
  stalwart 162 adj.
  healthy 650 adj.
roc
  rara avis 84 n.
rock
  be unequal 29 vb.
  vary 152 vb.
  fixture 153 n.
  assuage 177 vb.
  bring to rest
    266 vb.
  oscillate 317 vb.
  rock 344 n.
  sweet thing 392 n.
  resolution 599 n.
  pitfall 663 n.
  make inactive
    679 vb.
  aider 703 n.
  gem 844 n.
  pet 889 vb.
  drug-taking 949 n.
rock band or group
  band 74 n.
  orchestra 413 n.
rock bottom
  inferiority 35 n.
  zero 103 n.

base 214 n.
  basis 218 n.
rock-climbing
  ascent 308 n.
  sport 837 n.
rocket
  grow 36 vb.
  rocket 276 n.
  missile 287 n.
  signal light 420 n.
  signal 547 n.
  missile weapon
    723 n.
  reprimand 924 n.
rocketry
  aeronautics 271 n.
  rocket 276 n.
  arms 723 n.
rock garden
  garden 370 n.
rocklike
  permanent 144 adj.
  fixed 153 adj.
  unchangeable
    153 adj.
rock music
  music 412 n.
rock 'n' roll
  agitation 318 n.
  music 412 n.
  dance 837 n.
rock salmon
  fish food 301 n.
rocky
  weakly 163 adj.
  rough 259 adj.
  hard 326 adj.
rococo
  architectural
    192 adj.
  ornamental
    844 adj.
  ornamentation
    844 n.
rod
  long measure
    203 n.
  support 218 n.
  gauge 465 n.
  incentive 612 n.
  pistol 723 n.
  badge of rule
    743 n.
  scourge 964 n.
rodent
  mammal 365 n.

rodeo
contest 716 n.
rod of iron
severity 735 n.
roe
fish food 301 n.
roe deer
mammal 365 n.
roentgen
radiation 417 n.
rogue
trickster 545 n.
ruffian 904 n.
bad person 938 n.
rogue elephant
nonuniformity
17 n.
solitary 883 n.
rogues' gallery
record 548 n.
roguish
merry 833 adj.
witty 839 adj.
roister
revel 837 vb.
role
acting 594 n.
function 622 n.
role-playing
representation
551 n.
conduct 688 n.
roll
piece 53 n.
bunch 74 n.
list 87 n.
elapse 111 vb.
make smaller
198 vb.
textile 222 n.
coil 251 n.
twine 251 vb.
cylinder 252 n.
smooth 258 vb.
hair 259 n.
fold 261 vb.
be in motion
265 vb.
move 265 vb.
voyage 269 vb.
aeronautics 271 n.
fly 271 vb.
propel 287 vb.
cereals 301 n.
rotate 315 vb.
rotation 315 n.
fluctuation 317 n.

oscillate 317 vb.
be agitated 318 vb.
roll 403 n.
roll 403 vb.
record 548 n.
voice 577 vb.
book 589 n.
celebration 876 n.
roll along
travel 267 vb.
rotate 315 vb.
roll back
evolve 316 vb.
roll call
statistics 86 n.
nomenclature
561 n.
roller
flattener 216 n.
wrapping 226 n.
wheel 250 n.
cylinder 252 n.
smoother 258 n.
rotator 315 n.
pulverizer 332 n.
wave 350 n.
rollercoaster
vehicle 274 n.
rollers
hairdressing 843 n.
roller skates
plaything 837 n.
rollicking
merry 833 adj.
roll in
enjoy 376 vb.
superabound
637 vb.
be intemperate
943 vb.
rolling
undulatory
251 adj.
motion 265 n.
rotation 315 n.
fluctuation 317 n.
agitation 318 n.
rolling in it
prosperous 730 adj.
moneyed 800 adj.
rolling in the aisles
laughing 835 adj.
rolling pin
flattener 216 n.
cylinder 252 n.
smoother 258 n.

rolling stone
wanderer 268 n.
rotator 315 n.
rollmops
fish food 301 n.
roll of honour
list 87 n.
honours 866 n.
roll on
continue 108 vb.
go on 146 vb.
be in motion
265 vb.
**roll out the red car-
pet**
celebrate 876 vb.
show respect
920 vb.
roll up
congregate 74 vb.
approach 289 vb.
arrive 295 vb.
rotate 315 vb.
store 632 vb.
roll up one's sleeves
begin 68 vb.
prepare oneself
669 vb.
work 682 vb.
roly-poly
fleshy 195 adj.
dessert 301 n.
Roman
Roman Catholic
976 adj.
roman
written 586 adj.
print-type 587 n.
Roman alphabet
letter 558 n.
Roman Catholicism
Catholicism 976 n.
romance
musical piece
412 n.
fantasy 513 n.
ideality 513 n.
be false 541 vb.
fable 543 n.
narrative 590 n.
novel 590 n.
love affair 887 n.
Romanesque
architectural
192 adj.
ornamental
844 adj.

churchlike 990 adj.
Roman numerals
number 85 n.
romantic
imaginative
513 adj.
visionary 513 n.
literary 557 adj.
feeling 818 adj.
impressible
819 adj.
loving 887 adj.
romanticism
fantasy 513 n.
feeling 818 n.
romanticize
imagine 513 vb.
Romany
wanderer 268 n.
slang 560 adj.
Romeo
lover 887 n.
romp
rampage 61 vb.
leap 312 vb.
be cheerful 833 vb.
amuse oneself
837 vb.
revel 837 n.
caress 889 vb.
rompers
trousers 228 n.
romp home
outstrip 277 vb.
win 727 vb.
rood
cross 222 n.
ritual object 988 n.
church interior
990 n.
roof
home 192 n.
cover 226 vb.
roof 226 n.
shelter 662 n.
rooftop
vertex 213 n.
roof 226 n.
rook
bird 365 n.
deceive 542 vb.
fleece 786 vb.
defraud 788 vb.
rookie
beginner 538 n.
soldier 722 n.

room
room 183 n.
chamber 194 n.
scope 744 n.
rooms
quarters 192 n.
room to swing a cat
room 183 n.
roomy
spacious 183 adj.
roost
dwell 192 vb.
nest 192 n.
repose 683 vb.
rooster
poultry 365 n.
male animal
372 n.
root
numerical element
85 n.
stabilize 153 vb.
source 156 n.
place 187 vb.
base 214 n.
plant 366 n.
word 559 n.
root about
search 459 vb.
root and branch
completely 54 adv.
revolutionary
149 adj.
destructive 165 adj.
rooted
firm 45 adj.
fixed 153 adj.
habitual 610 adj.
rooted to the ground
or spot
fixed 153 adj.
still 266 adj.
root for
incite 612 vb.
patronize 703 vb.
applaud 923 vb.
root out
eject 300 vb.
rootstock
source 156 n.
plant 366 n.
root up
destroy 165 vb.
extract 304 vb.
rope
tie 45 vb.
cable 47 n.

932

fibre 208 n.
tool 630 n.
materials 631 n.
scope 744 n.
fetter 748 n.
jewellery 844 n.
means of execution
964 n.
rope ladder
ascent 308 n.
rope off
circumscribe
232 vb.
enclose 235 vb.
limit 236 vb.
restrain 747 vb.
ropy
thick 205 adj.
bad 645 adj.
Roquefort
dairy product
301 n.
Rorschach or inkblot
test
enquiry 459 n.
rosacea
skin disease 651 n.
blemish 845 n.
rosary
prayers 981 n.
ritual object 988 n.
rose
irrigator 341 n.
plant 366 n.
redness 431 n.
heraldry 547 n.
a beauty 841 n.
roseate
red 431 adj.
rose bowl
bowl 194 n.
rose-coloured
red 431 adj.
cheerful 833 adj.
rose-coloured specta-
cles
misinterpretation
521 n.
hope 852 n.
rosemary
herb 301 n.
roses all the way
palmy days 730 n.
joy 824 n.
rosette
badge 547 n.
decoration 729 n.

trimming 844 n.
rose window
window 263 n.
pattern 844 n.
church interior
990 n.
rosin
friction 333 n.
rub 333 vb.
grease 357 vb.
resin 357 n.
roster
list 87 n.
rostrum
protuberance
254 n.
rosy
red 431 adj.
healthy 650 adj.
palmy 730 adj.
promising 852 adj.
modest 874 adj.
rosy picture
hope 852 n.
rot
decay 51 n.
decompose 51 vb.
absurdity 497 n.
silly talk 515 n.
be unclean 649 vb.
dirt 649 n.
deteriorate 655 vb.
dilapidation 655 n.
impair 655 vb.
blight 659 n.
rota
sequence 65 n.
list 87 n.
regular return
141 n.
rotate
rotate 315 vb.
rotation
rotation 315 n.
rotisserie
café 192 n.
cookery 301 n.
rotor
propeller 269 n.
rotator 315 n.
rotten
unsavoury 391 adj.
not nice 645 adj.
dirty 649 adj.
diseased 651 adj.
dilapidated
655 adj.

vicious 934 adj.
rotten apple
bad person 938 n.
rotten borough
electorate 605 n.
rotter
cad 938 n.
rotund
fleshy 195 adj.
rotund 252 adj.
rotunda
pavilion 192 n.
rouble
coinage 797 n.
roué
bad person 938 n.
libertine 952 n.
rouge
colour 425 vb.
pigment 425 n.
redden 431 vb.
red pigment 431 n.
beautify 841 vb.
cosmetic 843 n.
primp 843 vb.
rouge et noir
gambling 618 n.
gambling game
837 n.
rough
disorderly 61 adj.
violent 176 adj.
violent creature
176 n.
rough 259 adj.
textural 331 adj.
hoarse 407 adj.
harmful 645 adj.
combatant 722 n.
paining 827 adj.
low fellow 869 n.
sullen 893 adj.
cruel 898 adj.
ruffian 904 n.
roughage
food content 301 n.
rough and ready
imperfect 647 adj.
hasty 680 adj.
bungled 695 adj.
rough and tumble
turmoil 61 n.
fight 716 n.
roughcast
coat 226 vb.
facing 226 n.
rough 259 adj.

roughen 259 vb.
rough diamond
  amorphism 244 n.
  undevelopment
   670 n.
roughen
  roughen 259 vb.
rough going
  roughness 259 n.
rough guess
  conjecture 512 n.
roughhewn
  incomplete 55 adj.
  immature 670 adj.
roughhouse
  turmoil 61 n.
  violence 176 n.
  fight 716 n.
roughly
  nearly 200 adv.
roughneck
  low fellow 869 n.
  bad person 938 n.
roughness
  violence 176 n.
  roughness 259 n.
  pungency 388 n.
  stridor 407 n.
  inelegance 576 n.
  painfulness 827 n.
  rudeness 885 n.
rough out
  outline 233 vb.
  represent 551 vb.
rough side of one's
  tongue
  reproach 924 n.
roulette
  gambling 618 n.
  gambling game
   837 n.
roulette wheel
  rotator 315 n.
round
  equal 28 adj.
  part 53 n.
  continuity 71 n.
  serial place 73 n.
  numerical 85 adj.
  recurrence 106 n.
  period 110 n.
  periodicity 141 n.
  fleshy 195 adj.
  be curved 248 vb.
  circle 250 n.
  round 250 adj.
  cylinder 252 n.

land travel 267 n.
  navigate 269 vb.
  circle 314 vb.
  bang 402 n.
  vocal music 412 n.
  circuit 626 n.
  pugilism 716 n.
round about
  around 230 adv.
  round about
   626 adv.
roundabout
  crossing 222 n.
  circle 250 n.
  traffic control
   305 n.
  prolix 570 adj.
  road 624 n.
  roundabout
   626 adj.
roundabout way
  circuition 314 n.
  circuit 626 n.
roundelay
  vocal music 412 n.
rounders
  ball game 837 n.
round number
  number 85 n.
round of applause
  applause 923 n.
round off
  equalize 28 vb.
  make complete
   54 vb.
round on
  attack 712 vb.
  retaliate 714 vb.
  blame 924 vb.
round robin
  continuity 71 n.
  report 524 n.
  correspondence
   588 n.
  request 761 n.
  deprecation 762 n.
roundsman
  traveller 268 n.
  seller 793 n.
round sum
  funds 797 n.
round table
  council 692 n.
round the bend or the
  twist
  crazy 503 adj.

round the clock
  all along 113 adv.
round trip
  reversion 148 n.
  land travel 267 n.
  circuition 314 n.
round up
  bring together
   74 vb.
  break in 369 vb.
roundup
  assemblage 74 n.
round upon
  curse 899 vb.
roup
  sale 793 n.
rouse
  invigorate 174 vb.
  incite 612 vb.
  excite 821 vb.
rouse curiosity
  impress 821 vb.
rousing
  vigorous 174 adj.
  eloquent 579 adj.
  excitation 821 n.
  exciting 821 adj.
rousing cheer
  stimulant 174 n.
  rejoicing 835 n.
rout
  disperse 75 vb.
  confute 479 vb.
  defeat 727 vb.
  defeat 728 n.
  rabble 869 n.
route
  itinerary 267 n.
  passage 305 n.
  route 624 n.
  way 624 n.
route march
  marching 267 n.
routine
  uniformity 16 n.
  order 60 n.
  continuity 71 n.
  regularity 81 n.
  recurrence 106 n.
  regular return
   141 n.
  permanence 144 n.
  habit 610 n.
  habitual 610 adj.
  habituation 610 n.
  practice 610 n.
  way 624 n.

action 676 n.
  conduct 688 n.
  ostentation 875 n.
  ritual 988 n.
roux
  sauce 389 n.
rove
  wander 267 vb.
roving commission
  uncertainty 474 n.
row
  turmoil 61 n.
  series 71 n.
  violence 176 n.
  housing 192 n.
  layer 207 n.
  row 269 vb.
  loudness 400 n.
  discord 411 n.
  quarrel 709 n.
  fight 716 vb.
rowan
  tree 366 n.
rowdy
  violent 176 adj.
  violent creature
   176 n.
  loud 400 adj.
  combatant 722 n.
  rioter 738 n.
  ill-bred 847 adj.
  low fellow 869 n.
  ruffian 904 n.
rowing
  aquatics 269 n.
  water travel 269 n.
    See **aquatics**
  traction 288 n.
  sport 837 n.
rowing boat
  rowing boat 275 n.
rowlock
  pivot 218 n.
royal
  sail 275 n.
  ruling 733 adj.
  liberal 813 adj.
  impressive 821 adj.
  worshipful 866 adj.
  noble 868 adj.
  proud 871 adj.
  ostentatious
   875 adj.
Royal Commission
  council 692 n.
royal jelly
  tonic 658 n.

933

Royal Marines
  naval man 722 n.
Royal Navy
  naval man 722 n.
royalty
  authority 733 n.
  position of author-
    ity 733 n.
  sovereign 741 n.
  receipt 807 n.
  nobility 868 n.
RSVP
  answer 460 vb.
rub
  be contiguous
    202 vb.
  friction 333 n.
  rub 333 vb.
  difficulty 700 n.
rub along with
  be friendly 880 vb.
rub away
  abate 37 vb.
rubber
  elasticity 328 n.
  friction 333 n.
  obliteration 550 n.
  contest 716 n.
rubber band
  elasticity 328 n.
rubbernecking
  inspection 438 n.
  curiosity 453 n.
  desire 859 n.
rubber of bridge
  card game 837 n.
rubber of whist
  card game 837 n.
rubberstamp
  assent 488 vb.
  endorse 488 vb.
rubbery
  elastic 328 adj.
  tough 329 adj.
rubbing
  duplicate 22 n.
rubbish
  absurdity 497 n.
  silly talk 515 n.
  falsehood 541 n.
  rubbish 641 n.
  detract 926 vb.
rubbish bin
  vessel 194 n.
rubble
  piece 53 n.

rub down
  smooth 258 vb.
  rub 333 vb.
  groom 369 vb.
rubella
  infection 651 n.
Rubicon
  limit 236 n.
Rubik's cube (tdmk)
  enigma 530 n.
Rubik's magic
  (tdmk)
  enigma 530 n.
rub in
  rub 333 vb.
  emphasize 532 vb.
rub it in
  aggravate 832 vb.
rub off
  rub 333 vb.
rub one's eyes
  wonder 864 vb.
rub one's hands
  heat 381 vb.
  rejoice 835 vb.
rub one's nose in it
  aggravate 832 vb.
  humiliate 872 vb.
rub out
  destroy 165 vb.
  eject 300 vb.
  rub 333 vb.
  murder 362 vb.
  obliterate 550 vb.
rubric
  redness 431 n.
  creed 485 n.
  label 547 n.
  rite 988 n.
rub salt in the wound
  hurt 827 vb.
  aggravate 832 vb.
rub shoulders with
  be contiguous
    202 vb.
rub up the wrong way
  roughen 259 vb.
  make quarrels
    709 vb.
  hurt 827 vb.
  huff 891 vb.
ruby
  redness 431 n.
  exceller 644 n.
  gem 844 n.
ruby wedding
  anniversary 141 n.

special day 876 n.
ruck
  average 30 n.
  crowd 74 n.
  generality 79 n.
  fold 261 n.
  fold 261 vb.
rucksack
  bag 194 n.
ruction
  turmoil 61 n.
  fight 716 n.
rudder
  sailing aid 269 n.
  aircraft 276 n.
  tool 630 n.
ruddy
  florid 425 adj.
  red 431 adj.
  healthy 650 adj.
rude
  violent 176 adj.
  amorphous
    244 adj.
  ill-bred 847 adj.
  impertinent
    878 adj.
  discourteous
    885 adj.
  disrespectful
    921 adj.
rude health
  health 650 n.
rudeness
  conduct 688 n.
  sauciness 878 n.
  rudeness 885 n.
rudimentary
  beginning 68 adj.
  immature 670 adj.
rudiments
  beginning 68 n.
rue
  unsavouriness
    391 n.
  regret 830 vb.
  be penitent 939 vb.
rueful
  distressing 827 adj.
  regretting 830 adj.
  melancholic
    834 adj.
rue the day
  regret 830 vb.
ruff
  neckwear 228 n.
  plumage 259 n.

ruffian
  low fellow 869 n.
  ruffian 904 n.
ruffle
  derange 63 vb.
  jumble 63 vb.
  edging 234 n.
  roughen 259 vb.
  fold 261 n.
  fold 261 vb.
  agitate 318 vb.
  play music 413 vb.
  torment 827 vb.
  enrage 891 vb.
ruffle one's feathers
  huff 891 vb.
rug
  coverlet 226 n.
  floor-cover 226 n.
rugby
  ball game 837 n.
Rugby football
  ball game 837 n.
rugged
  stalwart 162 adj.
  amorphous
    244 adj.
  difficult 700 adj.
rugger
  ball game 837 n.
ruin
  antiquity 125 n.
  destroy 165 vb.
  ruin 165 n.
  influence 178 n.
  dilapidation 655 n.
  impair 655 vb.
  bane 659 n.
  impoverish 801 vb.
ruination
  ruin 165 n.
  dilapidation 655 n.
  impairment 655 n.
ruined
  nonpaying 805 adj.
  hopeless 853 adj.
ruinous
  destructive 165 adj.
  evil 616 adj.
  harmful 645 adj.
  adverse 731 adj.
ruins
  oldness 127 n.
  ruin 165 n.
rule
  prototype 23 n.
  order 60 n.

rule 81 n.
permanence 144 n.
prevail 178 vb.
line 203 n.
horizontality
    216 n.
judge 480 vb.
creed 485 n.
maxim 496 n.
print-type 587 n.
manage 689 vb.
precept 693 n.
governance 733 n.
rule 733 vb.
command 737 vb.
conditions 766 n.
legislation 953 n.
try a case 959 vb.
rule of thumb
rule 81 n.
empiricism 461 n.
gauge 465 n.
intuition 476 n.
rule out
exclude 57 vb.
make impossible
    470 vb.
exempt 919 vb.
ruler
gauge 465 n.
potentate 741 n.
scourge 964 n.
rules
command 737 n.
right 913 n.
rules and regulations
practice 610 n.
right 913 n.
rules of the game
stratagem 698 n.
rule the roost
dominate 733 vb.
ruling
influential 178 adj.
judgment 480 n.
ruling 733 adj.
legal trial 959 n.
ruling class
master 741 n.
upper class 868 n.
rum
unusual 84 adj.
alcoholic drink
    301 n.
ridiculous 849 adj.
rumba
dance 837 n.

dance 837 vb.
rumble
roll 403 vb.
understand 516 vb.
rumbustious
disorderly 61 adj.
loud 400 adj.
ruminant
animal 365 adj.
animal 365 n.
ruminate
graze 301 vb.
meditate 449 vb.
ruminative
thoughtful 449 adj.
rummage
search 459 vb.
rummy
card game 837 n.
rumour
insubstantial thing
    4 n.
topic 452 n.
rumour 529 n.
rump
remainder 41 n.
buttocks 238 n.
rumple
jumble 63 vb.
roughen 259 vb.
agitate 318 vb.
rumpus
turmoil 61 n.
violence 176 n.
quarrel 709 n.
fight 716 n.
rumpus room
chamber 194 n.
run
come unstuck
    49 vb.
series 71 n.
discontinuity 72 n.
recurrence 106 n.
elapse 111 vb.
continuance 146 n.
operate 173 vb.
be in motion
    265 vb.
gait 265 n.
motion 265 n.
pedestrianism
    267 n.
voyage 269 vb.
water travel 269 n.
move fast 277 vb.
spurt 277 n.

impel 279 vb.
following 284 n.
exude 298 vb.
liquefy 337 vb.
flow 350 VB.
colour 425 vb.
lose colour 426 vb.
edition 589 n.
chase 619 n.
run away 620 vb.
be active 678 vb.
hasten 680 vb.
deal with 688 vb.
manage 689 vb.
amuse oneself
    837 vb.
run across
chance 159 vb.
run after
pursue 619 vb.
desire 859 vb.
court 889 vb.
run aground
fixed 153 adj.
navigate 269 vb.
land 295 vb.
fail 728 vb.
run amok
go mad 503 vb.
strike at 712 vb.
be excitable
    822 vb.
run a risk
gamble 618 vb.
run a temperature
be hot 379 vb.
run away
disappear 446 vb.
run away 620 vb.
wed 894 vb.
runaway
moving 265 adj.
wanderer 268 n.
speedy 277 adj.
recanter 603 n.
avoider 620 n.
escaper 667 n.
runaway victory
victory 727 n.
run away with
take away 786 vb.
run before the wind
navigate 269 vb.
run down
decrease 37 vb.
cease 145 vb.
weakly 163 adj.

collide 279 vb.
underestimate
    483 vb.
sick 651 adj.
dilapidated
    655 adj.
be malevolent
    898 vb.
not respect 921 vb.
criticize 924 vb.
detract 926 vb.
rundown
compendium
    592 n.
rune
indication 547 n.
letter 558 n.
run for
offer oneself
    759 vb.
run for cover
be cowardly
    856 vb.
run for it
run away 620 vb.
rung
degree 27 n.
serial place 73 n.
stand 218 n.
cylinder 252 n.
ascent 308 n.
run in
begin 68 vb.
initiate 68 vb.
enter 297 vb.
arrest 747 vb.
imprison 747 vb.
take 786 vb.
run in one's mind
be remembered
    505 vb.
run in the family
be intrinsic 5 vb.
run into
collide 279 vb.
meet 295 vb.
run its course
elapse 111 vb.
run neck and neck
synchronize
    123 vb.
runner
young plant 132 n.
hanger 217 n.
pedestrian 268 n.
courier 529 n.
contender 716 n.

servant 742 n.

runner beans
  fruit and vegetables
    301 n.
running
  continuous 71 adj.
  continuously
    71 adv.
  motion 265 n.
  speedy 277 adj.
  blood 335 adj.
  flowing 350 adj.
  dramatic 594 adj.
  hasty 680 adj.
  management
    689 n.
  sport 837 n.
running battle
  contention 716 n.
running jump
  leap 312 n.
running repairs
  repair 656 n.
running sore
  outflow 298 n.
  evil 616 n.
  wound 655 n.
  bane 659 n.
  painfulness 827 n.
running track
  path 624 n.
  arena 724 n.
running water
  fluid 335 n.
  water 339 n.
  stream 350 n.
runny
  blood 335 adj.
  flowing 350 adj.
run off
  empty 300 vb.
  flow 350 vb.
  print 587 vb.
run of the mill
  generality 79 n.
run-of-the-mill
  imitative 20 adj.
  ˙*median* 30 adj.
  general 79 adj.
run on
  continue 71 vb.
  go on 146 vb.
  progress 285 vb.
  be loquacious
    581 vb.
  requirement 627 n.

run-on
  continuous 71 adj.
run one's eye over
  scan 438 vb.
run out
  end 69 vb.
  past 125 adj.
  cease 145 vb.
  impel 279 vb.
  dismiss 300 vb.
  not suffice 636 vb.
run out on
  relinquish 621 vb.
run over
  collide 279 vb.
  study 536 vb.
  abstract 592 vb.
run riot
  exaggerate 546 vb.
  superabound
    637 vb.
  be active 678 vb.
  be excitable
    822 vb.
  be intemperate
    943 vb.
  be sensual 944 vb.
run round in circles
  be active 678 vb.
run short
  fall short 307 vb.
runt
  dwarf 196 n.
run the gauntlet
  face danger 661 vb.
  defy 711 vb.
run the risk of
  be liable 180 vb.
  be in danger
    661 vb.
run through
  make uniform
    16 vb.
  pervade 189 vb.
  pierce 263 vb.
  insert 303 vb.
  kill 362 vb.
  strike at 712 vb.
run to
  request 761 vb.
run to seed
  waste 634 vb.
  deteriorate 655 vb.
run up
  produce 164 vb.
  elevate 310 vb.

runway
  air travel 271 n.
  path 624 n.
**run with the hare and
  hunt with the
  hounds**
  be false 541 vb.
  be servile 879 vb.
  be dishonest
    930 vb.
rupee
  coinage 797 n.
rupture
  disagreement 25 n.
  break 46 vb.
  separation 46 n.
  gap 201 n.
  wound 655 n.
  dissension 709 n.
rural
  provincial 192 adj.
ruse
  trickery 542 n.
  stratagem 698 n.
rush
  rampage 61 vb.
  crowd 74 n.
  move fast 277 vb.
  spurt 277 n.
  be agitated 318 vb.
  commotion 318 n.
  flow 350 VB.
  grass 366 n.
  film 445 n.
  be active 678 vb.
  haste 680 n.
  hasten 680 vb.
  hasty 680 adj.
  attack 712 n.
  celebrate 876 vb.
rushed
  hasty 680 adj.
rushed off one's feet
  busy 678 adj.
rush hour
  crowd 74 n.
  period 110 n.
  traffic control
    305 n.
rushing
  excited 821 adj.
**rush in where angels
  fear to tread**
  be rash 857 vb.
rush one's fences
  hasten 680 vb.
  be rash 857 vb.

rusk
  cereals 301 n.
russet
  fruit and vegetables
    301 n.
  brown 430 adj.
  red 431 adj.
Russian roulette
  gambling 618 n.
rust
  abate 37 vb.
  decay 51 n.
  decompose 51 vb.
  oldness 127 n.
  destroyer 168 n.
  blunt 257 vb.
  dim 419 n.
  desuetude 611 n.
  be unclean 649 vb.
  dirt 649 n.
  deteriorate 655 vb.
  dilapidation 655 n.
  impair 655 vb.
  blight 659 n.
  not act 677 vb.
  be inactive 679 vb.
  blemish 845 n.
rustic
  native 191 n.
  provincial 192 adj.
  country-dweller
    869 n.
  plebeian 869 adj.
rustication
  seclusion 883 n.
  penalty 963 n.
rustle
  faintness 401 n.
  sound faint 401 vb.
  hiss 406 vb.
  sibilation 406 n.
  steal 788 vb.
rustler
  thief 789 n.
rusty
  strident 407 adj.
  dim 419 adj.
  red 431 adj.
  unhabituated
    611 adj.
  dilapidated
    655 adj.
  inactive 679 adj.
rut
  continuity 71 n.
  regularity 81 n.
  permanence 144 n.

roughness 259 n.
furrow 262 n.
groove 262 vb.
habit 610 n.
bore 838 n.
desire 859 vb.
libido 859 n.
be impure 951 vb.
ruthless
resolute 599 adj.
cruel 898 adj.
pitiless 906 adj.
rutting
lecherous 951 adj.
rye
alcoholic drink
301 n.
cereals 301 n.
grass 366 n.

S

Sabbath
repose 683 n.
holy day 988 n.
sabbatical
absence 190 n.
leisure 681 n.
repose 683 n.
permit 756 n.
sable
skin 226 n.
black 428 adj.
blackness 428 n.
black thing 428 n.
heraldic 547 adj.
heraldry 547 n.
sabot
footwear 228 n.
sabotage
derange 63 vb.
disable 161 vb.
destroy 165 vb.
destruction 165 n.
waste 634 n.
waste 634 vb.
make useless
641 adj.
impairment 655 n.
be obstructive
702 vb.
hindrance 702 n.
revolt 738 n.
revolt 738 vb.
fail in duty 918 vb.
undutifulness
918 n.

saboteur
destroyer 168 n.
rioter 738 n.
evildoer 904 n.
undutifulness
918 n.
sabre
sidearms 723 n.
sabre-rattling
war 718 n.
frightening
854 adj.
intimidation
854 n.
boasting 877 n.
threat 900 n.
saccharin
sweet thing 392 n.
saccharine
sweet 392 adj.
flattering 925 adj.
sacerdotalism
pietism 979 n.
ecclesiasticism
985 n.
sack
exclude 57 vb.
bag 194 n.
dress 228 n.
transpose 272 vb.
repel 292 vb.
dismiss 300 vb.
ejection 300 n.
wine 301 n.
deposal 752 n.
rob 788 vb.
steal 788 vb.
sackcloth
roughness 259 n.
asceticism 945 n.
sackcloth and ashes
lamentation 836 n.
penitence 939 n.
penance 941 n.
ritual object 988 n.
sacrament
Christian rite
988 n.
rite 988 n.
sacrament, the
the sacrament
988 n.
sacred
worshipful 866 adj.
divine 965 adj.
religious 973 adj.
scriptural 975 adj.

sanctified 979 adj.
sacrifice
substitute 150 n.
kill 362 vb.
killing 362 n.
willingness 597 n.
offer 759 n.
lose 772 vb.
loss 772 n.
give 781 vb.
offering 781 n.
sufferer 825 n.
be disinterested
931 n.
propitiation 941 n.
be pious 979 vb.
act of worship
981 n.
oblation 981 n.
offer worship
981 vb.
idolatry 982 n.
perform ritual
988 vb.
ritual act 988 n.
sacrificial
destructive 165 adj.
disinterested
931 adj.
atoning 941 adj.
sacrilege
impiety 980 n.
sacrilegious
disrespectful
921 adj.
impious 980 adj.
sacristy
church interior
990 n.
sacrosanct
creedal 485 adj.
invulnerable
660 adj.
worshipful 866 adj.
divine 965 adj.
sanctified 979 adj.
sad
funereal 364 adj.
unhappy 825 adj.
distressing 827 adj.
discontented
829 adj.
dejected 834 adj.
melancholic
834 adj.
sadden
sadden 834 vb.

sadder and wiser
regretting 830 adj.
dejected 834 adj.
sad disappointment
disappointment
509 n.
saddle
affix 45 vb.
narrowness 206 n.
high land 209 n.
seat 218 n.
start out 296 vb.
break in 369 vb.
saddlebag
bag 194 n.
saddled
prepared 669 adj.
saddle with
hinder 702 vb.
impose a duty
917 vb.
accuse 928 vb.
sadism
abnormality 84 n.
inhumanity 898 n.
sadist
nonconformist
84 n.
monster 938 n.
sadistic
cruel 898 adj.
pitiless 906 adj.
sadness
sorrow 825 n.
dejection 834 n.
sadomasochism
abnormality 84 n.
safari
land travel 267 n.
safari park
park 192 n.
plain 348 n.
zoo 369 n.
pleasure ground
837 n.
safe
box 194 n.
hiding-place 527 n.
storage 632 n.
safe 660 adj.
treasury 799 n.
safe and sound
undamaged
646 adj.
safe 660 adj.
safe bet
fair chance 159 n.

probability 471 n.
certainty 473 n.
safe-conduct
  protection 660 n.
  preservation 666 n.
  permit 756 n.
safeguard
  protection 660 n.
  safeguard 660 vb.
  safeguard 662 n.
safe house
  hiding-place 527 n.
  refuge 662 n.
safekeeping
  protection 660 n.
  preservation 666 n.
safety
  safety 660 n.
safety belt
  aircraft 276 n.
  safeguard 662 n.
safety catch
  fastening 47 n.
  safeguard 662 n.
safety net
  receptacle 194 n.
  safeguard 662 n.
safety pin
  fastening 47 n.
saffron
  yellowness 433 n.
sag
  be weak 163 vb.
  hang 217 vb.
  be oblique 220 vb.
  be curved 248 vb.
  descend 309 vb.
  be dejected 834 vb.
saga
  broadcast 531 n.
  narrative 590 n.
sagacity
  sagacity 498 n.
sage
  herb 301 n.
  wise 498 adj.
  sage 500 n.
Sahara
  desert 172 n.
sahib
  male 372 n.
  title 870 n.
said
  preceding 64 adj.
  prior 119 adj.
sail
  voyage 269 vb.

water travel 269 n.
sail 275 n.
ship 275 n.
rotator 315 n.
navy 722 n.
amuse oneself
  837 vb.
sail before the mast
  go to sea 269 vb.
sailboard
  sled 274 n.
  amuse oneself
    837 vb.
sailboat
  boat 275 n.
  sailing ship 275 n.
sailing
  aquatics 269 n.
  water travel 269 n.
  sport 837 n.
sailing ship
  water travel 269 n.
  sailing ship 275 n.
sail into
  attack 712 vb.
  fight 716 vb.
sailor
  water travel 269 n.
  mariner 270 n.
  naval man 722 n.
sail too near the wind
  be in danger
    661 vb.
sail under false
  colours
  dissemble 541 vb.
saint
  paragon 646 n.
  benefactor 903 n.
  good person 937 n.
  saint 968 n.
  pietist 979 n.
sainthood
  sanctity 979 n.
saintly
  honourable
    929 adj.
  virtuous 933 adj.
  innocent 935 adj.
  angelic 968 adj.
  pious 979 adj.
Saint's day
  date 108 n.
  anniversary 141 n.
  special day 876 n.
  holy day 988 n.

sake
  alcoholic drink
    301 n.
salaam
  welcome 295 int.
  obeisance 311 n.
  stoop 311 vb.
  courteous act
    884 n.
  greet 884 vb.
  respects 920 n.
salable
  salable 793 adj.
salacious
  impure 951 adj.
salad
  dish 301 n.
  hors-d'oeuvres
    301 n.
salad days
  salad days 130 n.
salamander
  rara avis 84 n.
  amphibian 365 n.
salami
  hors-d'oeuvres
    301 n.
salary
  incentive 612 n.
  earnings 771 n.
  pay 804 n.
  receipt 807 n.
  reward 962 n.
salat
  rite 988 n.
sale
  sale 793 n.
sale of work
  sale 793 n.
sales representative
  seller 793 n.
salesman,-woman
  speaker 579 n.
  seller 793 n.
salesperson
  speaker 579 n.
  servant 742 n.
  seller 793 n.
sales talk
  empty talk 515 n.
  inducement 612 n.
  sale 793 n.
sales tax
  tax 809 n.
salient
  region 184 n.
  projecting 254 adj.

projection 254 n.
saline
  salty 388 adj.
saliva
  excrement 302 n.
  lubricant 334 n.
  fluid 335 n.
  water 339 n.
  moisture 341 n.
salivate
  exude 298 vb.
  excrete 302 vb.
  be wet 341 vb.
  be hungry 859 vb.
sallow
  weakly 163 adj.
  tree 366 n.
  colourless 426 adj.
  whitish 427 adj.
  yellow 433 adj.
  unhealthy 651 adj.
sally
  attack 712 n.
  retaliation 714 n.
  witticism 839 n.
sally forth
  start out 296 vb.
  emerge 298 vb.
salmagundi
  a mixture 43 n.
salmon
  fish food 301 n.
  fish 365 n.
salmonella
  poison 659 n.
salon
  chamber 194 n.
saloon
  tavern 192 n.
  automobile 274 n.
salt
  mariner 270 n.
  pungency 388 n.
  salty 388 adj.
  season 388 vb.
  condiment 389 n.
  white thing 427 n.
  preserve 666 vb.
salt away
  store 632 vb.
saltcellar
  small box 194 n.
  cavity 255 n.
saltire
  cross 222 n.
  heraldry 547 n.

saltlick
provender 301 n.
salt of the earth
elite 644 n.
favourite 890 n.
good person 937 n.
saltpan
marsh 347 n.
saltpetre
explosive 723 n.
salt water
water 339 n.
ocean 343 n.
salty
salty 388 adj.
witty 839 adj.
salubrious
salubrious 652 adj.
salutary
beneficial 644 adj.
salubrious 652 adj.
salutation
allocution 583 n.
courteous act
884 n.
respects 920 n.
salute
obeisance 311 n.
signal 547 vb.
speak to 583 vb.
celebration 876 n.
courteous act
884 n.
greet 884 vb.
congratulation
886 n.
endearment 889 n.
respects 920 n.
show respect
920 vb.
approve 923 vb.
praise 923 vb.
salvage
restoration 656 n.
restore 656 vb.
deliver 668 vb.
deliverance 668 n.
acquire 771 vb.
salvation
restoration 656 n.
preservation 666 n.
deliverance 668 n.
liberation 746 n.
Salvation Army
sect 978 n.
salve
lubricant 334 n.

unguent 357 n.
balm 658 n.
relief 831 n.
salve one's con-
science
justify 927 vb.
atone 941 vb.
do penance 941 vb.
salver
plate 194 n.
ritual object 988 n.
church utensil
990 n.
salvo
bang 402 n.
qualification 468 n.
bombardment
712 n.
celebration 876 n.
sal volatile
pungency 388 n.
tonic 658 n.
samba
dance 837 n.
same
identical 13 adj.
uniform 16 adj.
equal 28 adj.
same here
identically 13 adv.
sameness
identity 13 n.
uniformity 16 n.
equivalence 28 n.
tedium 838 n.
same old story
uniformity 16 n.
same wavelength
consensus 488 n.
friendliness 880 n.
samosa
hors-d'oeuvres
301 n.
samovar
pot 194 n.
sampan
sailing ship 275 n.
samphire
fruit and vegetables
301 n.
sample
prototype 23 n.
example 83 n.
taste 386 vb.
enquire 459 vb.
exhibit 522 n.
diagnostic 658 n.

sampler
enquirer 459 n.
Samson
athlete 162 n.
sanatorium
hospital 658 n.
sanctify
sanctify 979 vb.
sanctimonious
hypocritical
541 adj.
affected 850 adj.
prudish 950 adj.
pietistic 979 adj.
sanctimony
pretension 850 n.
pietism 979 n.
sanction
assent 488 n.
assent 488 vb.
endorse 488 vb.
commission
751 vb.
permission 756 n.
permit 756 vb.
consent 758 n.
consent 758 vb.
approbation 923 n.
approve 923 vb.
sanctions
compulsion 740 n.
sanctity
probity 929 n.
divine attribute
965 n.
sanctity 979 n.
sanctuary
retreat 192 n.
reception 299 n.
protection 660 n.
refuge 662 n.
altar 990 n.
church interior
990 n.
holy place 990 n.
sanctum
retreat 192 n.
chamber 194 n.
refuge 662 n.
seclusion 883 n.
sanctum sanctorum
retreat 192 n.
refuge 662 n.
sand
powder 332 n.
dryer 342 n.
soil 344 n.

sandals
footwear 228 n.
sandalwood
scent 396 n.
sandbag
hammer 279 n.
strike 279 vb.
kill 362 vb.
club 723 n.
scourge 964 n.
sandbank
island 349 n.
sandcastle
weak thing 163 n.
sand-glass
timekeeper 117 n.
sandpaper
smoother 258 n.
roughness 259 n.
pulverizer 332 n.
sands
shore 344 n.
plain 348 n.
sands of time
time 108 n.
sandstone
rock 344 n.
sandstorm
storm 176 n.
powder 332 n.
gale 352 n.
sandwich
meal 301 n.
mouthful 301 n.
sandwich board
advertisement
528 n.
sandy
powdery 332 adj.
dry 342 adj.
red 431 adj.
yellow 433 adj.
sane
sane 502 adj.
sangfroid
moral insensibility
820 n.
inexcitability
823 n.
sanguinary
haematic 335 adj.
murderous 362 adj.
sanguine
red 431 adj.
optimistic 482 adj.
expectant 507 adj.
cheerful 833 adj.

hoping 852 adj.
sanitary
 healthy 650 adj.
 salubrious 652 adj.
sanitation
 cleansing 648 n.
 hygiene 652 n.
sanity
 sanity 502 n.
sanserif
 print-type 587 n.
Sanskrit
 language 557 n.
Santa Claus
 giver 781 n.
 good giver 813 n.
 benefactor 903 n.
sap
 essential part 5 n.
 disable 161 vb.
 weaken 163 vb.
 fluid 335 n.
 moisture 341 n.
 semiliquidity 354 n.
 ninny 501 n.
 dupe 544 n.
 impair 655 vb.
sapient
 wise 498 adj.
sapling
 young plant 132 n.
 tree 366 n.
saponification
 unctuousness 357 n.
sapper
 soldiery 722 n.
sapphire
 blue 435 adj.
 blueness 435 n.
 gem 844 n.
Sapphism
 abnormality 84 n.
sappy
 humid 341 adj.
 foolish 499 adj.
sapwood
 interiority 224 n.
 wood 366 n.
sarcasm
 trope 519 n.
 wit 839 n.
 witticism 839 n.
 ridicule 851 n.
 rudeness 885 n.
 indignity 921 n.

reproach 924 n.
 calumny 926 n.
sarcastic
 keen 174 adj.
 witty 839 adj.
 disrespectful 921 adj.
 disapproving 924 adj.
sarcoma
 swelling 253 n.
 cancer 651 n.
sarcophagus
 box 194 n.
 interment 364 n.
sardine
 fish food 301 n.
sardonic
 disapproving 924 adj.
sari
 robe 228 n.
sarong
 skirt 228 n.
SAS
 brave person 855 n.
sash
 frame 218 n.
 belt 228 n.
 loop 250 n.
 window 263 n.
 badge 547 n.
 decoration 729 n.
 badge of rank 743 n.
sash window
 window 263 n.
Sassenach
 foreigner 59 n.
sassy
 impertinent 878 adj.
 discourteous 885 adj.
Satan
 Satan 969 n.
satanic
 cruel 898 adj.
 wicked 934 adj.
 diabolic 969 adj.
Satanism
 diabolism 969 n.
satchel
 bag 194 n.
satchet
 bag 194 n.

sated, be
 have enough 635 vb.
sateen
 textile 222 n.
satellite
 successor 67 n.
 concomitant 89 n.
 follower 284 n.
 rotator 315 n.
 moon 321 n.
 satellite 321 n.
 dependant 742 n.
 subject 745 adj.
satellite television
 broadcasting 531 n.
satiated
 filled 635 adj.
 bored 838 adj.
 sated 863 adj.
satin
 textile 222 n.
 smoothness 258 n.
satiny
 smooth 258 adj.
 textural 331 adj.
satire
 wit 839 n.
 satire 851 n.
 reproach 924 n.
satirical
 funny 849 adj.
 disrespectful 921 adj.
satirist
 humorist 839 n.
 detractor 926 n.
satirize
 satirize 851 vb.
satisfaction
 payment 804 n.
 enjoyment 824 n.
 content 828 n.
 approbation 923 n.
 atonement 941 n.
 propitiation 941 n.
 reward 962 n.
satisfactory
 sufficient 635 adj.
satisfy
 fill 54 vb.
 demonstrate 478 V.
 convince 485 vb.
 suffice 635 vb.
 pacify 719 vb.

observe 768 vb.
 please 826 vb.
 content 828 vb.
 sate 863 vb.
 reward 962 vb.
satisfying
 pleasant 376 adj.
saturate
 fill 54 vb.
 pervade 189 vb.
 drench 341 vb.
 superabound 637 vb.
 sate 863 vb.
saturated
 full 54 adj.
 sated 863 adj.
saturated fats
 food content 301 n.
saturation
 plenitude 54 n.
 moisture 341 n.
 redundance 637 n.
 satiety 863 n.
saturation point
 plenitude 54 n.
 limit 236 n.
 moisture 341 n.
 redundance 637 n.
 satiety 863 n.
Saturn
 planet 321 n.
 classical deities 967 n.
saturnine
 ugly 842 adj.
 sullen 893 adj.
satyr
 eyesore 842 n.
 libertine 952 n.
 mythical being 970 n.
satyriasis
 personality disorder 503 n.
 libido 859 n.
 illicit love 951 n.
sauce
 cook 301 vb.
 food 301 n.
 sauce 389 n.
 be insolent 878 vb.
 sauciness 878 n.
 rudeness 885 n.
 scurrility 899 n.
saucepan
 pot 194 n.

heater 383 n.
saucer
 plate 194 n.
 circle 250 n.
 cavity 255 n.
saucy
 defiant 711 adj.
 impertinent
  878 adj.
 discourteous
  885 adj.
 disrespectful
  921 adj.
sauna
 chamber 194 n.
 heater 383 n.
 ablutions 648 n.
saunter
 pedestrianism
  267 n.
 wander 267 vb.
 move slowly
  278 vb.
saurian
 animal 365 adj.
sausage
 meat 301 n.
sauté
 cook 301 vb.
Sauternes
 wine 301 n.
savage
 furious 176 adj.
 violent 176 adj.
 violent creature
  176 n.
 ignorant 491 adj.
 ill-treat 645 vb.
 wound 655 vb.
 attack 712 vb.
 severe 735 adj.
 barbaric 869 adj.
 low fellow 869 n.
 discourteous
  885 adj.
 rude person 885 n.
 angry 891 adj.
 cruel 898 adj.
 ruffian 904 n.
 criticize 924 vb.
 monster 938 n.
savagery
 violence 176 n.
 ignorance 491 n.
 inhumanity 898 n.
savages
 humankind 371 n.

savanna
 plain 348 n.
savant(e)
 scholar 492 n.
save
 exclusive of 57 adv.
 store 632 vb.
 preserve 666 vb.
 deliver 668 vb.
 liberate 746 vb.
 acquire 771 vb.
 retain 778 vb.
 economize 814 vb.
 relieve 831 vb.
save by the bell
 deliver 668 vb.
saved
 sanctified 979 adj.
save one's bacon
 be safe 660 vb.
 escape 667 vb.
save one's skin
 deliver 668 vb.
save up
 store 632 vb.
 acquire 771 vb.
saving
 qualifying 468 adj.
 preservation 666 n.
 economical
  814 adj.
 economy 814 n.
saving grace
 virtues 933 n.
savings
 store 632 n.
 gain 771 n.
 economy 814 n.
savings account
 store 632 n.
 funds 797 n.
 accounts 808 n.
Saviour
 God the Son 965 n.
saviour
 preserver 666 n.
 benefactor 903 n.
savoir faire
 knowledge 490 n.
 conduct 688 n.
 skill 694 n.
 etiquette 848 n.
savory
 herb 301 n.
savour
 taste 386 n.
 taste 386 vb.

 be pleased 824 vb.
savour of
 resemble 18 vb.
 taste 386 vb.
 mean 514 vb.
savoury
 dish 301 n.
 mouthful 301 n.
 savouriness 390 n.
 savoury 390 adj.
savoy
 fruit and vegetables
  301 n.
savvy
 know 490 vb.
 knowledge 490 n.
 intelligence 498 n.
 understand 516 vb.
 etiquette 848 n.
saw
 cut 46 vb.
 tooth 256 n.
 notch 260 n.
 rasp 407 vb.
 discord 411 vb.
 play music 413 vb.
 maxim 496 n.
sawdust
 leavings 41 n.
 powder 332 n.
sawmill
 workshop 687 n.
sawn-off
 short 204 adj.
sawn-off shotgun
 firearm 723 n.
sax
 flute 414 n.
saxophone
 flute 414 n.
say
 about 33 adv.
 affirm 532 vb.
 speak 579 vb.
say after
 repeat 106 vb.
say a prayer
 worship 981 vb.
saying
 maxim 496 n.
 affirmation 532 n.
 phrase 563 n.
say in unison
 synchronize
  123 vb.
say of
 attribute 158 vb.

say one is sorry
 be penitent 939 vb.
say so
 decree 737 vb.
say-so
 affirmation 532 n.
 command 737 n.
say what is in one's
 mind
 be artless 699 vb.
scab
 nonconformist
  84 n.
 layer 207 n.
 covering 226 n.
 recanter 603 n.
 wound 655 n.
 revolter 738 n.
 cad 938 n.
scabbard
 case 194 n.
 arsenal 723 n.
scabby
 rough 259 adj.
 unclean 649 adj.
scads
 great quantity
  32 n.
 funds 797 n.
 wealth 800 n.
scaffold
 structure 331 n.
 means of execution
  964 n.
scaffolding
 frame 218 n.
scag
 drug-taking 949 n.
scald
 burn 381 vb.
 ulcer 651 n.
 wound 655 n.
scalding
 hot 379 adj.
 paining 827 adj.
scale
 degree 27 n.
 graduate 27 vb.
 be great - large
  32 vb.
 piece 53 n.
 series 71 n.
 plate 194 n.
 layer 207 n.
 skin 226 n.
 climb 308 vb.
 scales 322 n.

key 410 n.
musical note
410 n.
See key
opacity 423 n.
gauge 465 n.
scale down
abate 37 vb.
render few 105 vb.
scale drawing
plan 623 n.
scalene
unequal 29 adj.
distorted 246 adj.
scalene triangle
angular figure
247 n.
scales
scales 322 n.
scales of justice
justice 913 n.
scallion
fruit and vegetables
301 n.
scallop
edging 234 n.
convolution 251 n.
notch 260 n.
notch 260 vb.
fish food 301 n.
scallywag
bad person 938 n.
scalp
head 213 n.
skin 226 n.
uncover 229 vb.
trophy 729 n.
scalpel
sharp edge 256 n.
scaly
rough 259 adj.
scamp
neglect 458 vb.
not complete
726 vb.
bad person 938 n.
scamped
hasty 680 adj.
uncompleted
726 adj.
scamped work
negligence 458 n.
scamper
move fast 277 vb.
spurt 277 n.
scampi
fish food 301 n.

scan
scan 438 vb.
photograph 551 vb.
photography 551 n.
poetize 593 vb.
scandal
rumour 529 n.
badness 645 n.
slur 867 n.
wrong 914 n.
calumny 926 n.
false charge 928 n.
wickedness 934 n.
scandalize
displease 827 vb.
cause dislike
861 vb.
be wonderful
864 vb.
shame 867 vb.
incur blame
924 vb.
defame 926 vb.
scandal-mongering
detraction 926 n.
scandalous
bad 645 adj.
vulgar 847 adj.
discreditable
867 adj.
wrong 914 adj.
heinous 934 adj.
scanner
enquirer 459 n.
hospital 658 n.
scanning
photography 551 n.
poetic 593 adj.
diagnostic 658 adj.
scansion
prosody 593 n.
scant
small 33 adj.
incomplete 55 adj.
few 105 adj.
insufficient
636 adj.
scant respect
disrespect 921 n.
scanty
small 33 adj.
few 105 adj.
short 204 adj.
insufficient
636 adj.
scapegoat
substitute 150 n.

unlucky person
731 n.
deputy 755 n.
sufferer 825 n.
propitiation 941 n.
oblation 981 n.
scar
high land 209 n.
rock 344 n.
identification
547 n.
indication 547 n.
mark 547 vb.
trace 548 n.
impair 655 vb.
wound 655 n.
blemish 845 n.
blemish 845 vb.
scarce
small 33 adj.
infrequent 140 adj.
unproductive
172 adj.
scarce 636 adj.
of value 811 adj.
scarcely
slightly 33 adv.
seldom 140 adv.
scarcely ever
seldom 140 adv.
scarcity
smallness 33 n.
scarcity 636 n.
scare
false alarm 665 n.
raise the alarm
665 vb.
fear 854 n.
frighten 854 vb.
scarecrow
thinness 206 n.
sham 542 n.
image 551 n.
eyesore 842 n.
intimidation
854 n.
scared
fearing 854 adj.
scared out of one's
wits
fearing 854 adj.
scaremonger
false alarm 665 n.
alarmist 854 n.
coward 856 n.
scarf
wrapping 226 n.

neckwear 228 n.
vestments 989 n.
scarify
notch 260 vb.
wound 655 vb.
scarlet
red 431 adj.
redness 431 n.
unchaste 951 adj.
scarlet fever
infection 651 n.
scarlet woman
loose woman
952 n.
scarp
verticality 215 n.
incline 220 n.
scarper
fail in duty 918 vb.
scatogological
impure 951 adj.
scatter
disunite 46 vb.
separate 46 vb.
be disordered
61 vb.
jumble 63 vb.
be dispersed 75 vb.
disperse 75 vb.
dispersion 75 n.
destroy 165 vb.
displace 188 vb.
move 265 vb.
diverge 294 vb.
let fall 311 vb.
disappear 446 vb.
waste 634 vb.
defeat 727 vb.
scatterbrained
disorderly 61 adj.
light-minded
456 adj.
foolish 499 adj.
crazy 503 adj.
scatter diagram
statistics 86 n.
scattering
separation 46 n.
noncoherence 49 n.
disorder 61 n.
dispersion 75 n.
reflection 417 n.
scatty
light-minded
456 adj.
foolish 499 adj.
crazy 503 adj.

scavenger
  dirty person 649 n.
scenario
  surroundings
    230 n.
  cinema 445 n.
  spectacle 445 n.
  reading matter
    589 n.
  narrative 590 n.
  stage play 594 n.
scene
  situation 186 n.
  surroundings
    230 n.
  view 438 n.
  visibility 443 n.
  spectacle 445 n.
  exhibit 522 n.
  art subject 553 n.
  dramaturgy 594 n.
  stage set 594 n.
  activity 678 n.
  arena 724 n.
  excitable state
    822 n.
  pageant 875 n.
scenery
  spectacle 445 n.
  stage set 594 n.
  beauty 841 n.
scenes
  dissension 709 n.
scenic
  painted 553 adj.
  impressive 821 adj.
  pleasurable
    826 adj.
  beautiful 841 adj.
  ornamental
    844 adj.
  showy 875 adj.
scenic route
  deviation 282 n.
  circuition 314 n.
  circuit 626 n.
scent
  emit 300 vb.
  odour 394 n.
  smell 394 vb.
  scent 396 n.
  knowledge 490 n.
  foresee 510 vb.
  identification
    547 n.
  indication 547 n.
  trace 548 n.

  cosmetic 843 n.
scented
  odorous 394 adj.
  fragrant 396 adj.
scented soap
  scent 396 n.
scent out
  detect 484 vb.
  pursue 619 vb.
sceptic
  unbeliever 486 n.
  impious person
    980 n.
sceptical
  doubting 474 adj.
  dissenting 489 adj.
  irreligious 974 adj.
scepticism
  philosophy 449 n.
  doubt 486 n.
  irreligion 974 n.
sceptre
  badge 547 n.
  regalia 743 n.
schedule
  list 87 n.
  list 87 vb.
  chronology 117 n.
  time 117 vb.
  plan 623 n.
  plan 623 vb.
  policy 623 n.
schematic
  arranged 62 adj.
scheme
  prototype 23 n.
  plan 623 n.
  plot 623 n.
  plot 623 vb.
  be cunning 698 vb.
scheming
  cunning 698 adj.
  dishonest 930 adj.
  perfidious 930 adj.
scherzo
  musical piece
    412 n.
schism
  disunion 46 n.
    See **separation**
  part 53 n.
  dissent 489 n.
  schism 978 n.
schismatic
  dissenting 489 adj.
  quarrelling
    709 adj.

  schismatic 978 n.
  schismatical
    978 adj.
schist
  rock 344 n.
schizoid
  psychotic 503 adj.
  psychotic 504 n.
schizophrenia
  multiformity 82 n.
  psychosis 503 n.
schizophrenic
  multiform 82 adj.
  psychotic 503 adj.
  psychotic 504 n.
schlemiel
  dupe 544 n.
schmaltzy
  feeble 572 adj.
  feeling 818 adj.
  impressible
    819 adj.
  vulgar 847 adj.
schmuck
  dupe 544 n.
schnapps
  alcoholic drink
    301 n.
schnook
  dupe 544 n.
schnozz
  protuberance
    254 n.
schnozzle
  protuberance
    254 n.
scholar
  scholar 492 n.
  learner 538 n.
scholarly
  educational
    534 adj.
  studious 536 adj.
scholarship
  erudition 490 n.
  learning 536 n.
  subvention 703 n.
  receipt 807 n.
  reward 962 n.
scholastic
  intellectual 492 n.
  educational
    534 adj.
  studious 536 adj.
  theologian 973 n.
school
  group 74 n.

  creed 485 n.
  educate 534 vb.
  school 539 n.
schoolboy, -girl
  youngster 132 n.
  learner 538 n.
schooling
  teaching 534 n.
schoolmaster, -mis-
    tress
  master 741 n.
school of thought
  classification 77 n.
schooner
  cup 194 n.
  sailing ship 275 n.
schottische
  dance 837 n.
sciatica
  pang 377 n.
  rheumatism 651 n.
science
  science 490 n.
science fiction
  ideality 513 n.
  novel 590 n.
sci-fi
  novel 590 n.
scimitar
  angularity 247 n.
  curve 248 n.
  sharp edge 256 n.
  sidearms 723 n.
scintillate
  shine 417 vb.
  be witty 839 vb.
scion
  branch 53 n.
  young plant 132 n.
  descendant 170 n.
  tree 366 n.
scission
  scission 46 n.
scissors
  sharp edge 256 n.
sclerosis
  hardness 326 n.
scoff
  food 301 n.
  ridicule 851 n.
  ridicule 851 vb.
  not respect 921 vb.
  despise 922 vb.
  calumny 926 n.
  detract 926 vb.
scoff at
  disbelieve 486 vb.

scold
violent creature
176 n.
cuss 899 vb.
reproach 924 vb.
detractor 926 n.
scolding
irascible 892 adj.
scurrility 899 n.
disapproving
924 adj.
reprimand 924 n.
scolloped
undulatory
251 adj.
sconce
head 213 n.
scone
cereals 301 n.
scoop
ladle 194 n.
information 524 n.
news 529 n.
acquisition 771 n.
scoop out
make concave
255 vb.
scoot
move fast 277 vb.
run away 620 vb.
scooter
conveyance 267 n.
bicycle 274 n.
scope
degree 27 n.
function 622 n.
scope 744 n.
scorch
move fast 277 vb.
dry 342 vb.
be hot 379 vb.
burn 381 vb.
impair 655 vb.
go to war 718 vb.
scorched
dry 342 adj.
hot 379 adj.
scorched earth policy
unproductiveness
172 n.
warfare 718 n.
score
degree 27 n.
cut 46 vb.
compose 56 vb.
composition 56 n.
arrange 62 vb.

arrangement 62 n.
numerical result
85 n.
number 86 vb.
numeration 86 n.
list 87 n.
notch 260 vb.
furrow 262 n.
groove 262 vb.
harmonize 410 vb.
notation 410 n.
music 412 n.
compose music
413 vb.
indication 547 n.
mark 547 vb.
register 548 vb.
wound 655 vb.
triumph 727 vb.
credit 802 n.
accounts 808 n.
score, a
twenty and over
99 n.
score a point
succeed 727 vb.
scoreboard
record 548 n.
score off
confute 479 vb.
triumph 727 vb.
humiliate 872 vb.
scores
multitude 104 n.
scorn
unbelief 486 n.
shame 867 vb.
scurrility 899 n.
disrespect 921 vb.
not respect 921 vb.
contempt 922 n.
despise 922 vb.
detraction 926 n.
impiety 980 n.
scornful
cursing 899 adj.
disrespectful
921 adj.
scorpion
creepy-crawly
365 n.
Scotchtape (tdmk)
adhesive 47 n.
fastening 47 n.
ligature 47 n.

Scotch whisky
alcoholic drink
301 n.
scot-free
free 744 adj.
uncharged 812 adj.
Scotland Yard
police 955 n.
Scottie
dog 365 n.
scoundrel
ruffian 904 n.
bad person 938 n.
cad 938 n.
scour
traverse 267 vb.
pass 305 vb.
rub 333 vb.
search 459 vb.
clean 648 vb.
scourge
evil 616 n.
plague 651 n.
bane 659 n.
adversity 731 n.
oppress 735 vb.
ruffian 904 n.
criticize 924 vb.
flog 963 vb.
scourge 964 n.
scourings
leavings 41 n.
rubbish 641 n.
dirt 649 n.
scout
precursor 66 n.
front 237 n.
traverse 267 vb.
male 372 n.
scan 438 vb.
spectator 441 n.
watch 441 vb.
enquirer 459 n.
warner 664 n.
domestic 742 n.
despise 922 vb.
scout out
watch 441 vb.
scout's honour
veracity 540 n.
scowl
look 438 n.
gesticulate 547 vb.
gesture 547 n.
discontent 829 n.
be rude 885 vb.
rudeness 885 n.

hatred 888 n.
anger 891 n.
be angry 891 vb.
sullenness 893 n.
Scrabble (tdmk)
board game 837 n.
scrabble
search 459 vb.
scraggy
lean 206 adj.
scram
come along
267 int.
decamp 296 vb.
run away 620 vb.
scramble
mix 43 vb.
disorder 61 n.
cook 301 vb.
climb 308 vb.
activity 678 n.
haste 680 n.
fight 716 n.
scrambled eggs
dish 301 n.
scramble for
take 786 vb.
scrap
small quantity
33 n.
piece 53 n.
picture 553 n.
reject 607 vb.
rubbish 641 n.
stop using 674 vb.
fight 716 n.
fight 716 vb.
battle 718 n.
scrapbook
reminder 505 n.
record 548 n.
picture 553 n.
anthology 592 n.
scrape
abate 37 vb.
make smaller
198 vb.
be contiguous
202 vb.
collision 279 n.
stoop 311 vb.
friction 333 n.
rub 333 vb.
touch 378 vb.
rasp 407 vb.
stridor 407 n.
discord 411 vb.

play music 413 vb.
foolery 497 n.
engrave 555 vb.
clean 648 vb.
predicament 700 n.
economize 814 vb.
be parsimonious
    816 vb.
servility 879 n.
respects 920 n.
vice 934 n.
guilty act 936 n.
scrape an acquain-
    tance
befriend 880 vb.
scrape home
win 727 vb.
scraper
sharp edge 256 n.
scrape together
bring together
    74 vb.
acquire 771 vb.
scraping
friction 333 n.
hoarse 407 adj.
discordant 411 adj.
parsimonious
    816 adj.
parsimony 816 n.
servile 879 adj.
respectful 920 adj.
scrappy
fragmentary
    53 adj.
incomplete 55 adj.
scraps
leavings 41 n.
rubbish 641 n.
scratch
cut 46 vb.
rend 46 vb.
shallowness 212 n.
be rough 259 vb.
notch 260 vb.
furrow 262 n.
groove 262 vb.
friction 333 n.
rub 333 vb.
touch 378 vb.
faintness 401 n.
rasp 407 vb.
stridor 407 n.
indication 547 n.
mark 547 vb.
trace 548 n.

change one's mind
    603 vb.
relinquish 621 vb.
trifle 639 n.
ill-treat 645 vb.
wound 655 n.
wound 655 vb.
unprepared
    670 adj.
fight 716 vb.
resign 753 vb.
blemish 845 n.
blemish 845 vb.
scratch a living
be poor 801 vb.
scratch one's back
minister to 703 vb.
flatter 925 vb.
scratch out
eject 300 vb.
obliterate 550 vb.
scratchy
strident 407 adj.
scrawl
lack of meaning
    515 n.
be unintelligible
    517 vb.
unintelligibility
    517 n.
lettering 586 n.
script 586 n.
write 586 vb.
scrawny
lean 206 adj.
scream
blow 352 vb.
be loud 400 vb.
loudness 400 n.
shrill 407 vb.
cry 408 n.
cry 408 vb.
weep 836 vb.
scream, a
funny 849 adj.
scree
piece 53 n.
incline 220 n.
screech
blow 352 vb.
rasp 407 vb.
shrill 407 vb.
stridor 407 n.
cry 408 n.
cry 408 vb.
ululate 409 vb.
ululation 409 n.

screech owl
bird 365 n.
screechy
strident 407 adj.
screed
facing 226 n.
oration 579 n.
script 586 n.
screeds
great quantity
    32 n.
screen
exclusion 57 n.
porosity 263 n.
screen 421 n.
screen 421 vb.
enquire 459 vb.
show 522 vb.
stage set 594 n.
protection 660 n.
defence 713 n.
screening
diagnostic 658 n.
screen off
set apart 46 vb.
exclude 57 vb.
screenplay
cinema 445 n.
reading matter
    589 n.
stage play 594 n.
screw
affix 45 vb.
fastening 47 n.
distort 246 vb.
distortion 246 n.
coil 251 n.
propeller 269 n.
saddle horse 273 n.
propellant 287 n.
rotator 315 n.
tool 630 n.
gaoler 749 n.
earnings 771 n.
rob 788 vb.
debauch 951 vb.
screwdriver
tool 630 n.
screwed up
bungled 695 adj.
screw loose
deficit 55 n.
defect 647 n.
hitch 702 n.
screw loose, a
eccentricity 503 n.

screw on
affix 45 vb.
screw up
tighten 45 vb.
blunder 495 vb.
screw up one's cour-
    age
strengthen 162 vb.
screwy
crazy 503 adj.
scribacious
prolific 171 adj.
diffuse 570 adj.
scribble
lack of meaning
    515 n.
mean nothing
    515 vb.
be unintelligible
    517 vb.
unintelligibility
    517 n.
mark 547 vb.
lettering 586 n.
script 586 n.
write 586 vb.
scribe
mark 547 vb.
recorder 549 n.
instrument 628 n.
theologian 973 n.
zealot 979 n.
scrimmage
quarrel 709 n.
fight 716 n.
fight 716 vb.
scrimp
shorten 204 vb.
be parsimonious
    816 vb.
scrip
title deed 767 n.
paper money
    797 n.
script
cinema 445 n.
lettering 586 n.
script 586 n.
writing 586 n.
book 589 n.
reading matter
    589 n.
stage play 594 n.
scriptural
scriptural 975 adj.
orthodox 976 adj.

secret 530 n.
sea legs
  equilibrium 28 n.
sea level
  lowness 210 n.
  horizontality
    216 n.
sealing wax
  adhesive 47 n.
seal of approval
  repute 866 n.
  approbation 923 n.
seal off
  close 264 vb.
sealskin
  skin 226 n.
seal up
  conceal 525 vb.
  imprison 747 vb.
sealyham
  dog 365 n.
seam
  join 45 vb.
  joint 45 n.
  tie 45 vb.
  dividing line 92 n.
  gap 201 n.
  layer 207 n.
  store 632 n.
seaman
  mariner 270 n.
seamstress
  clothier 228 n.
séance
  manifestation
    522 n.
  council 692 n.
  spiritualism 984 n.
sea of, a
  multitude 104 n.
sea of faces
  crowd 74 n.
  onlookers 441 n.
sea of troubles
  difficulty 700 n.
  adversity 731 n.
sear
  dry 342 vb.
  burn 381 vb.
  heat 381 vb.
search
  search 459 n.
  search 459 vb.
  undertaking 672 n.
search for
  search 459 vb.

searchlight
  flash 417 n.
  lamp 420 n.
search party
  enquirer 459 n.
  search 459 n.
  hunter 619 n.
search warrant
  search 459 n.
  warrant 737 n.
  legal process 959 n.
seared
  dry 342 adj.
seas
  great quantity
    32 n.
sea serpent
  rara avis 84 n.
  reptile 365 n.
seashore
  edge 234 n.
  shore 344 n.
seasick, be
  vomit 300 vb.
seaside
  edge 234 n.
  shore 344 n.
  pleasure ground
    837 n.
season
  mix 43 vb.
  time 108 n.
  period 110 n.
  season 388 vb.
  qualify 468 vb.
  habituate 610 vb.
  mature 669 vb.
  social round 882 n.
seasonal
  seasonal 141 adj.
seasoning
  adjunct 40 n.
  tincture 43 n.
  stimulant 174 n.
  herb 301 n.
  condiment 389 n.
  ripening 669 n.
seasons
  regular return
    141 n.
seat
  equilibrium 28 n.
  situation 186 n.
  locality 187 n.
  place 187 vb.
  station 187 n.
  abode 192 n.

  house 192 n.
  seat 218 n.
  buttocks 238 n.
  apportionment
    783 n.
seat belt
  safeguard 662 n.
  preserver 666 n.
seated, be
  sit down 311 vb.
seating
  room 183 n.
  theatre 594 n.
seaway
  water travel 269 n.
  route 624 n.
seaweed
  plant 366 n.
seaworthy
  marine 275 adj.
  invulnerable
    660 adj.
sebaceous
  fatty 357 adj.
sebaceous cyst
  blemish 845 n.
sebum
  fat 357 n.
secant
  ratio 85 n.
secateurs
  sharp edge 256 n.
  farm tool 370 n.
secco
  art style 553 n.
secede
  dissent 489 vb.
  relinquish 621 vb.
  revolt 738 vb.
  fail in duty 918 vb.
secession
  dissent 489 n.
  change of mind
    603 n.
  relinquishment
    621 n.
  revolt 738 n.
  undutifulness
    918 n.
  schism 978 n.
seclude
  seclude 883 vb.
secluded
  secluded 883 adj.
seclusion
  seclusion 883 n.

second
  small quantity
    33 n.
  inferior 35 adj.
  inferior 35 n.
  sequential 65 adj.
  double 91 vb.
  period 110 n.
  instant 116 n.
  angular measure
    247 n.
  melody 410 n.
  musical note
    410 n.
  measurement
    465 n.
  endorse 488 vb.
  select 605 vb.
  patronize 703 vb.
  deputy 755 n.
  friend 880 n.
secondary
  inferior 35 adj.
  caused 157 adj.
  unimportant
    639 adj.
secondary education
  education 534 n.
secondary growth
  cancer 651 n.
secondary picketing
  hindrance 702 n.
second best
  inferior 35 adj.
  inferior 35 n.
  inferiority 35 n.
  substitute 150 n.
  imperfection 647 n.
  compromise 770 n.
second bite at the cherry
  sequel 67 n.
second chance
  mercy 905 n.
second childhood
  old age 131 n.
  folly 499 n.
second-class
  inferior 35 adj.
second class post
  postal communica-
    tions 531 n.
second cousin
  kinsman 11 n.
seconder
  assenter 488 n.

second fiddle
inferior 35 n.
inferiority 35 n.
nonentity 639 n.
second glance
inspection 438 n.
second-hand
imitative 20 adj.
used 673 adj.
second-hand clothes
clothing 228 n.
second helping
repetition 106 n.
second house
dramaturgy 594 n.
second-in-command
deputy 755 n.
second lieutenant
army officer 741 n.
second nature
habit 610 n.
second place
sequence 65 n.
second-rate
inconsiderable
33 adj.
inferior 35 adj.
trivial 639 adj.
bad 645 adj.
imperfect 647 adj.
seconds
repetition 106 n.
meal 301 n.
cheapness 812 n.
second sight
sense 374 n.
vision 438 n.
intuition 476 n.
foresight 510 n.
occultism 984 n.
psychics 984 n.
seconds out
duel 716 n.
second string
inferior 35 n.
second thoughts
sequel 67 n.
thought 449 n.
doubt 486 n.
change of mind
603 n.
amendment 654 n.
regret 830 n.
nervousness 854 n.
caution 858 n.
second to none
supreme 34 adj.

best 644 adj.
secrecy
secrecy 525 n.
secret
private 80 adj.
dark 418 adj.
occult 523 adj.
concealed 525 adj.
secret 530 n.
cautious 858 adj.
secret agent
secret service
459 n.
secretaire
cabinet 194 n.
secretariat
jurisdiction 955 n.
secretary
recorder 549 n.
stenographer
586 n.
auxiliary 707 n.
deputy 755 n.
secretary of state
official 690 n.
secret ballot
vote 605 n.
secret drawer
hiding-place 527 n.
secrete
emit 300 vb.
excrete 302 vb.
conceal 525 vb.
store 632 vb.
secretion
ejection 300 n.
excretion 302 n.
secretive
reticent 525 adj.
cautious 858 adj.
secretly
secretly 525 adv.
secret police
police enquiry
459 n.
secret service
secret service
459 n.
secret society
latency 523 n.
secrecy 525 n.
society 708 n.
sect
community 708 n.
sect 978 n.
sectarian
sectarian 978 adj.

sectarian 978 n.
section
scission 46 n.
part 53 n.
piece 53 n.
See **part**
subdivision 53 n.
classification 77 n.
region 184 n.
topic 452 n.
edition 589 n.
formation 722 n.
sectional
fragmentary
53 adj.
sector
part 53 n.
subdivision 53 n.
arc 250 n.
secular
lasting 113 adj.
seasonal 141 adj.
irreligious 974 adj.
secure
firm 45 adj.
tied 45 adj.
tighten 45 vb.
be early 135 vb.
fixed 153 adj.
safe 660 adj.
safeguard 660 vb.
give security
767 vb.
acquire 771 vb.
content 828 adj.
securities
estate 777 n.
security
safety 660 n.
security 767 n.
hope 852 n.
dueness 915 n.
legal process 959 n.
security forces
protector 660 n.
security guard
protector 660 n.
security system
protection 660 n.
sedan chair
vehicle 274 n.
sedate
bring to rest
266 vb.
slow 278 adj.
inexcitable
823 adj.

serious 834 adj.
sedative
moderator 177 n.
antidote 658 n.
drug 658 n.
soporific 679 n.
relief 831 n.
sedentary
quiescent 266 adj.
sedge
grass 366 n.
sediment
leavings 41 n.
solid body 324 n.
dirt 649 n.
sedimentary
remaining 41 adj.
indissoluble
324 adj.
sedimentation
subtraction 39 n.
condensation
324 n.
sedition
sedition 738 n.
seditious
revolutionary
149 adj.
disobedient
738 adj.
seduce
attract 291 vb.
bribe 612 vb.
induce 612 vb.
delight 826 vb.
make wicked
934 vb.
debauch 951 vb.
seducer
deceiver 545 n.
motivator 612 n.
lover 887 n.
libertine 952 n.
seduction
attraction 291 n.
inducement 612 n.
liking 859 n.
love affair 887 n.
illicit love 951 n.
unchastity 951 n.
seductive
pleasurable
826 adj.
seductress
motivator 612 n.
a beauty 841 n.

SED

loose woman
952 n.

sedulous
industrious
678 adj.

sedulous ape
imitator 20 n.

see
have feeling
374 vb.
scan 438 vb.
see 438 vb.
church office 985 n.
parish 985 n.

see again
meet 295 vb.

seed
small thing 33 n.
class 62 vb.
origin 68 n.
cause 156 vb.
source 156 n.
product 164 n.
genitalia 167 n.
reproduce itself
167 vb.
posterity 170 n.
fertilizer 171 n.
minuteness 196 n.
powder 332 n.
flower 366 n.

see daylight
detect 484 vb.

seedbed
flower 366 n.
garden 370 n.

seeded
arranged 62 adj.
chosen 605 adj.

seeded player
proficient person
696 n.

seedling
young plant 132 n.

see double
be dim-sighted
440 vb.

seed pearl
gem 844 n.

seed-time
spring 128 n.

seedy
weakly 163 adj.
sick 651 adj.
dilapidated
655 adj.

SEE

see eye to eye
assent 488 vb.
concord 710 vb.

see fit
will 595 vb.

see how the land lies
orientate 281 vb.
be tentative 461 vb.
be cautious 858 vb.

seeing
seeing 438 adj.
vision 438 vb.
visibility 443 n.

seeing you, be
goodbye 296 int.

see it coming
expect 507 vb.
foresee 510 vb.
not wonder 865 vb.

see it through
be resolute 599 vb.
persevere 600 vb.
carry through
725 vb.

seek
enquire 459 vb.
See search
search 459 vb.
pursue 619 vb.
attempt 671 vb.
request 761 vb.

seek advice
consult 691 vb.

seek pastures new
change 143 vb.

seek refuge
seek refuge 662 vb.

seek to
attempt 671 vb.

seem
appear 445 vb.

seeming
similarity 18 n.
simulating 18 adj.
appearance 445 n.
appearing 445 adj.
ostensible 614 adj.
ostentatious
875 adj.

seemingly
probably 471 adv.

seem like
resemble 18 vb.

seemly
circumstantial
8 adj.
fit 24 adj.

SEE

advisable 642 adj.
tasteful 846 adj.

see off
start out 296 vb.
dismiss 300 vb.

see one's way
know 490 vb.

see one through
aid 703 vb.

see out
carry through
725 vb.

seep
infiltrate 297 vb.
be wet 341 vb.

seepage
outflow 298 n.

seep through
exude 298 vb.
pass 305 vb.

seer
sage 500 n.
oracle 511 n.
visionary 513 n.
sorcerer 983 n.
psychic 984 n.

see red
go mad 503 vb.
be excitable
822 vb.
get angry 891 vb.

seersucker
textile 222 n.

seesaw
correlation 12 n.
correlative 12 adj.
fluctuation 317 n.
oscillate 317 vb.
to and fro 317 adv.
be uncertain
474 vb.
dubiety 474 n.
be irresolute
601 vb.

seesaw eating
eating 301 n.

seethe
congregate 74 vb.
effervesce 318 vb.
bubble 355 vb.
be hot 379 vb.
be excited 821 vb.

see the end of
go on 146 vb.
persevere 600 vb.

**see the error of one's
ways**

SEI

be penitent 939 vb.
become pious
979 vb.

see the last of
cease 145 vb.

see the light
discover 484 vb.
know 490 vb.
understand 516 vb.
be penitent 939 vb.
become pious
979 vb.

seething
hot 379 adj.
heating 381 n.
excited 821 adj.
excitable 822 adj.

see things
be insane 503 vb.

seething with
full 54 adj.

see through
know 490 vb.
understand 516 vb.
carry out 725 vb.

see-through
transparent
422 adj.

see to
be mindful 455 vb.
look after 457 vb.
deal with 688 vb.

see you later
goodbye 296 int.

segment
sunder 46 vb.
part 53 n.
part 53 vb.
piece 53 n.
subdivision 53 n.
component 58 n.

segregate
set apart 46 vb.
exclude 57 vb.
seclude 883 vb.

segregation
disunion 46 n.
separation 46 n.
exclusion 57 n.
prejudice 481 n.
seclusion 883 n.

seigneur
master 741 n.
person of rank
868 n.

seine
network 222 n.

seismic
revolutionary
149 adj.
violent 176 adj.
seismograph
oscillation 317 n.
meter 465 n.
seize
halt 145 vb.
arrest 747 vb.
take 786 vb.
seize power
take authority
733 vb.
seize the opportunity
be active 678 vb.
seize up
halt 145 vb.
fail 728 vb.
seizure
spasm 318 n.
illness 651 n.
nervous disorders
651 n.
taking 786 n.
loss of right 916 n.
seldom
seldom 140 adv.
select
abstract 592 vb.
chosen 605 adj.
select 605 vb.
excellent 644 adj.
desire 859 vb.
select committee
director 690 n.
selection
separation 46 n.
accumulation 74 n.
discrimination
463 n.
choice 605 n.
selections
reading matter
589 n.
anthology 592 n.
selective
separate 46 adj.
discriminating
463 adj.
self
identical 13 adj.
self 80 n.
spirit 447 n.
self-assured
positive 473 adj.
assertive 532 adj.

self-centred
vain 873 adj.
selfish 932 adj.
self-complacent
vain 873 adj.
self-confident
positive 473 adj.
resolute 599 adj.
proud 871 adj.
self-conscious
affected 850 adj.
nervous 854 adj.
self-contained
complete 54 adj.
reticent 525 adj.
independent
744 adj.
self-control
moderation 177 n.
will 595 n.
resolution 599 n.
restraint 747 n.
inexcitability
823 n.
temperance 942 n.
self-correcting
compensatory
31 adj.
self-deception
sophistry 477 n.
misjudgment
481 n.
credulity 487 n.
error 495 n.
deception 542 n.
hope 852 n.
self-defence
defence 713 n.
resistance 715 n.
vindication 927 n.
self-delusion
insubstantiality
4 n.
misjudgment
481 n.
credulity 487 n.
self-denying
temperate 942 adj.
self-destruct
destroy 165 vb.
self-determination
will 595 n.
independence
744 n.
self-discipline
temperance 942 n.

act of worship
981 n.
self-effacing
humble 872 adj.
modest 874 adj.
self-employed
independent
744 adj.
self-esteem
pride 871 n.
vanity 873 n.
self-evident
certain 473 adj.
manifest 522 adj.
self-explanatory
intelligible 516 adj.
self-governing
governmental
733 adj.
independent
744 adj.
self-government
government 733 n.
independence
744 n.
self-help
aid 703 n.
self-importance
vanity 873 n.
ostentation 875 n.
self-imposed
voluntary 597 adj.
self-indulgent
selfish 932 adj.
intemperate
943 adj.
self-interest
selfishness 932 n.
selfish
selfish 932 adj.
self-knowledge
knowledge 490 n.
selfless
benevolent 897 adj.
disinterested
931 adj.
self-love
vanity 873 n.
selfishness 932 n.
self-made man
rich person 800 n.
self-opinionated
dogmatist 473 n.
positive 473 adj.
narrow-minded
481 adj.

self-pity
pity 905 n.
selfishness 932 n.
self-possessed
resolute 599 adj.
cautious 858 adj.
self-praise
pride 871 n.
vanity 873 n.
praise 923 n.
selfishness 932 n.
self-preservation
preservation 666 n.
selfishness 932 n.
self-protection
defence 713 n.
self-raising flour
leaven 323 n.
self-reliant
resolute 599 adj.
independent
744 adj.
self-respect
pride 871 n.
self-restraint
resolution 599 n.
restraint 747 n.
temperance 942 n.
self-righteous
affected 850 adj.
pietistic 979 adj.
self-rule
independence
744 n.
self-sacrifice
disinterestedness
931 n.
oblation 981 n.
selfsame
identical 13 adj.
self-satisfied
vain 873 adj.
self-seeking
selfish 932 adj.
selfishness 932 n.
self-service
provision 633 n.
self-service restaurant
café 192 n.
self-styled
named 561 adj.
vain 873 adj.
unwarranted
916 adj.
self-sufficient
complete 54 adj.

sufficient 635 adj.
independent
　744 adj.
self-supporting
independent
　744 adj.
self-taught
studious 536 adj.
unskilled 695 adj.
self-willed
volitional 595 adj.
wilful 602 adj.
disobedient
　738 adj.
sell
advertise 528 vb.
deceive 542 vb.
trickery 542 n.
fable 543 n.
assign 780 vb.
be sold 793 vb.
sell 793 vb.
sell down the river
be dishonest
　930 vb.
seller's market
requirement 627 n.
scarcity 636 n.
prosperity 730 n.
request 761 n.
market 796 n.
selling
sale 793 n.
selling price
price 809 n.
sell like hot cakes
be sold 793 vb.
sell off
not retain 779 vb.
sell 793 vb.
sell oneself
boast 877 vb.
Sellotape (tdmk)
adhesive 47 n.
fastening 47 n.
ligature 47 n.
sell out
sell 793 vb.
be dishonest
　930 vb.
sell-out
dramaturgy 594 n.
playgoer 594 n.
success 727 n.
sale 793 n.
perfidy 930 n.

sell short
detract 926 vb.
sell up
sell 793 vb.
sell well
be published
　528 vb.
be sold 793 vb.
selvedge
weaving 222 n.
edging 234 n.
semantic
semantic 514 adj.
linguistic 557 adj.
semantics
meaning 514 n.
semaphore
communicate
　524 vb.
telecommunication
　531 n.
signal 547 n.
signal 547 vb.
semblance
mimicry 20 n.
copy 22 n.
appearance 445 n.
probability 471 n.
semen
genitalia 167 n.
fertilizer 171 n.
semester
time 108 n.
period 110 n.
semi
house 192 n.
semibreve
notation 410 n.
semicircle
arc 250 n.
semicolon
punctuation 547 n.
semiconductor
electricity 160 n.
semiconscious
insensible 375 adj.
semi-darkness
darkness 418 n.
half-light 419 n.
semidetached house
house 192 n.
semifinal
contest 716 n.
seminar
publicity 528 n.
teaching 534 n.
class 538 n.

conference 584 n.
seminary
monastery 986 n.
semiology
indication 547 n.
semiotics
indication 547 n.
semiprecious stone
rock 344 n.
gem 844 n.
semiquaver
notation 410 n.
semi-skilled
unskilled 695 adj.
semitone
interval 201 n.
musical note
　410 n.
semitransparent
semitransparent
　424 adj.
semolina
dessert 301 n.
senate
seniority 131 n.
parliament 692 n.
senator
councillor 692 n.
master 741 n.
aristocrat 868 n.
senatus
parliament 692 n.
send
send 272 vb.
delight 826 vb.
send a message
communicate
　524 vb.
send an SOS
signal 547 n.
send away
send 272 vb.
eject 300 vb.
**send away with a flea
　in the ear**
repel 292 vb.
dismiss 300 vb.
humiliate 872 vb.
be rude 885 vb.
reprove 924 vb.
send back
reject 607 vb.
send down
eject 300 vb.
send flying
displace 188 vb.
strike 279 vb.

propel 287 vb.
send for
send 272 vb.
command 737 vb.
desire 859 vb.
send home
disperse 75 vb.
send in
admit 299 vb.
send-off
start 68 n.
valediction 296 n.
**send on a wild-goose
　chase**
fool 542 vb.
send one's regards
pay one's respects
　884 vb.
send one to sleep
be tedious 838 vb.
**send out a search
　party**
pursue 619 vb.
send out of the room
punish 963 vb.
send packing
repel 292 vb.
dismiss 300 vb.
**send round the bend
　or the twist**
make mad 503 vb.
send the hat round
aid 703 vb.
send to Coventry
set apart 46 vb.
exclude 57 vb.
disregard 458 vb.
send to prison
imprison 747 vb.
send to sleep
render insensible
　375 vb.
make inactive
　679 vb.
send to the scaffold
kill 362 vb.
execute 963 vb.
send up
augment 36 vb.
elevate 310 vb.
act 594 vb.
satirize 851 vb.
send-up
satire 851 n.
send word
communicate
　524 vb.

senescent
  ageing 131 adj.
senile
  ageing 131 adj.
  impotent 161 adj.
  foolish 499 adj.
senile dementia
  folly 499 n.
  mental disorder
    503 n.
senility
  oldness 127 n.
  old age 131 n.
  helplessness 161 n.
  weakness 163 n.
  folly 499 n.
  dilapidation 655 n.
senior
  superior 34 adj.
  older 131 adj.
  master 741 n.
senior citizen
  old person 133 n.
seniority
  superiority 34 n.
  seniority 131 n.
  authority 733 n.
senior service
  navy 722 n.
senna pods
  purgative 658 n.
señor
  male 372 n.
  title 870 n.
señora
  female 373 n.
  title 870 n.
señorita
  female 373 n.
  title 870 n.
sensation
  sense 374 n.
  news 529 n.
  feeling 818 n.
  prodigy 864 n.
sensational
  dramatic 594 adj.
  excellent 644 adj.
  exciting 821 adj.
  wonderful 864 adj.
  showy 875 adj.
sensationalize
  be ostentatious
    875 vb.
sense
  have feeling
    374 vb.

sense 374 n.
  intellect 447 n.
  perceive 447 adj.
  intuit 476 vb.
  detect 484 vb.
  intelligence 498 n.
  meaning 514 n.
  feel 818 vb.
senseless
  insubstantial 4 adj.
  insensible 375 adj.
  absurd 497 adj.
  foolish 499 adj.
  meaningless
    515 adj.
sense of hearing
  hearing 415 n.
sense of humour
  laughter 835 n.
  wit 839 n.
sense of responsibil-
    ity
  probity 929 n.
sense of smell
  odour 394 n.
sense organ
  sense 374 n.
  instrument 628 n.
senses
  intellect 447 n.
  sanity 502 n.
sensibility
  sensibility 374 n.
  discrimination
    463 n.
sensible
  sentient 374 adj.
  rational 475 adj.
  wise 498 adj.
  useful 640 adj.
  impressible
    819 adj.
sensible of
  knowing 490 adj.
sensitive
  sentient 374 adj.
  discriminating
    463 adj.
  accurate 494 adj.
  feeling 818 adj.
  sensitive 819 adj.
sensitivity
  sensibility 374 n.
  discrimination
    463 n.
  moral sensibility
    819 n.

irascibility 892 n.
sensitized
  sentient 374 adj.
  sensitive 819 adj.
sensorium
  sense 374 n.
sensory
  sentient 374 adj.
  feeling 818 adj.
sensual
  sensual 944 adj.
sensuality
  materiality 319 n.
  pleasure 376 n.
  sensualism 944 n.
sensuous
  sentient 374 adj.
  sensuous 376 adj.
  feeling 818 adj.
sentence
  part 53 n.
  composition 56 n.
  period 110 n.
  judge 480 vb.
  judgment 480 n.
  detention 747 n.
  condemn 961 vb.
  condemnation
    961 n.
  penalty 963 n.
  punish 963 vb.
  punishment 963 n.
sentence to death
  condemn 961 vb.
sententious
  judicial 480 adj.
  forceful 571 adj.
sentient
  sentient 374 adj.
sentiment
  opinion 485 n.
  feeling 818 n.
  excitation 821 n.
  love 887 n.
sentimental
  feeble 572 adj.
  feeling 818 adj.
  impressible
    819 adj.
  loving 887 adj.
sentimental attach-
    ment
  love 887 n.
sentimentality
  feeling 818 n.
  moral sensibility
    819 n.

love 887 n.
sentiments
  moral sensibility
    819 n.
sentinel
  doorkeeper 264 n.
  spectator 441 n.
  surveillance 457 n.
  protector 660 n.
  warner 664 n.
  defender 713 n.
  keeper 749 n.
sentry
  doorkeeper 264 n.
  spectator 441 n.
  surveillance 457 n.
  protector 660 n.
  warner 664 n.
  defender 713 n.
  armed force 722 n.
  keeper 749 n.
sentry box
  compartment
    194 n.
sepal
  flower 366 n.
separate
  unrelated 10 adj.
  subtract 39 vb.
  disunite 46 vb.
  separate 46 adj.
  separate 46 vb.
  decompose 51 vb.
  disperse 75 vb.
  bifurcate 92 vb.
  discriminate
    463 vb.
  select 605 vb.
  divorce 896 vb.
separated
  divergent 294 adj.
  schismatical
    978 adj.
separates
  suit 228 n.
separate the sheep
    from the goats
  discriminate
    463 vb.
separation
  separation 46 n.
  dissension 709 n.
  divorce 896 n.
separatism
  disunion 46 n.
  sectarianism
    978 n.

sepia
  brown pigment
    430 n.

sepia print
  photography 551 n.

sepoy
  soldier 722 n.

sepsis
  infection 651 n.

sept
  race 11 n.
  breed 77 n.

septenary
  over five 99 n.

septennial
  seasonal 141 adj.

septennium
  over five 99 n.

septet
  over five 99 n.

septic
  bad 645 adj.
  unclean 649 adj.
  toxic 653 adj.

septicaemia
  infection 651 n.

septic tank
  stench 397 n.
  sink 649 n.

septuagenarian
  twenty and over
    99 n.

sepulchral
  funereal 364 adj.
  resonant 404 adj.
  hoarse 407 adj.

sepulchre
  tomb 364 n.
  holy place 990 n.

sequel
  sequel 67 n.
  reading matter
    589 n.

sequence
  sequence 65 n.
  poem 593 n.

sequential
  sequential 65 adj.

sequester
  set apart 46 vb.
  exclude 57 vb.
  deprive 786 vb.
  not pay 805 vb.
  seclude 883 vb.

sequestered
  tranquil 266 adj.
  invisible 444 adj.

  latent 523 adj.
  secluded 883 adj.

sequestrate
  levy 786 vb.
  punish 963 vb.

sequin
  circle 250 n.
  finery 844 n.

seraglio
  womankind 373 n.

seraph
  angel 968 n.

seraphic
  virtuous 933 adj.
  angelic 968 adj.
  pietistic 979 adj.

seraphim
  angel 968 n.

sere
  lean 206 adj.
  dry 342 adj.
  dry 342 vb.

serenade
  musical piece
    412 n.
  vocal music 412 n.
  sing 413 vb.
  court 889 vb.
  wooing 889 n.

serendipitous
  casual 159 adj.

serendipity
  chance 159 n.
  discovery 484 n.

serene
  tranquil 266 adj.
  inexcitable
    823 adj.

serenity
  inexcitability
    823 n.
  content 828 n.
  lack of wonder
    865 n.

serf
  farmer 370 n.
  slave 742 n.
  commoner 869 n.

serge
  textile 222 n.

sergeant
  soldiery 722 n.
  army officer 741 n.

sergeant major
  tyrant 735 n.
  army officer 741 n.

serial
  continuous 71 adj.
  recurrence 106 n.
  periodical 141 adj.
  journal 528 n.
  reading matter
    589 n.
  narrative 590 n.

serialize
  continue 71 adj.
  publish 528 vb.

seriate
  continuous 71 adj.

sericulture
  animal husbandry
    369 n.

series
  order 60 n.
  sequence 65 n.
  series 71 n.
  number 85 n.
  recurrence 106 n.
  key 410 n.
  broadcast 531 n.
  edition 589 n.

serif
  print-type 587 n.

serious
  great 32 adj.
  attentive 455 adj.
  resolute 599 adj.
  important 638 adj.
  sick 651 adj.
  dangerous 661 adj.
  serious 834 adj.
  heinous 934 adj.

serjeant-at-law
  lawyer 958 n.

sermon
  lecture 534 n.
  diffuseness 570 n.
  oration 579 n.
  allocution 583 n.
  dissertation 591 n.
  ministration 988 n.

sermonize
  teach 534 vb.
  be pious 979 vb.

serous
  blood 335 adj.
  haematic 335 adj.

serpent
  serpent 251 n.
  reptile 365 n.
  horn 414 n.
  deceiver 545 n.
  bane 659 n.

  slyboots 698 n.
  Satan 969 n.

serpentine
  snaky 251 adj.
  animal 365 adj.

serpigo
  skin disease 651 n.

serrated
  angular 247 adj.
  sharp 256 adj.
  toothed 256 adj.

serried
  cohesive 48 adj.
  dense 324 adj.

serried ranks
  coherence 48 n.

serum
  blood 335 n.
  fluid 335 n.

servant
  servant 742 n.

serve
  unite with 45 vb.
  operate 173 vb.
  concur 181 vb.
  propel 287 vb.
  be instrumental
    628 vb.
  provide 633 vb.
  suffice 635 vb.
  be expedient
    642 vb.
  work 682 vb.
  serve 742 vb.
  be subject 745 vb.
  apportion 783 vb.

serve as
  function 622 vb.

serve notice
  communicate
    524 vb.
  threaten 900 vb.

serve notice on
  litigate 959 vb.

serve up
  provide 633 vb.

serve with a writ
  indict 928 vb.

service
  agency 173 n.
  job 622 n.
  provide 633 vb.
  provision 633 n.
  utility 640 n.
  repair 656 n.
  restore 656 vb.
  preserve 666 vb.

use 673 n.
aid 703 n.
gift 781 n.
public worship
981 n.
church service
988 n.
serviceable
instrumental
628 adj.
useful 640 adj.
service charge
price 809 n.
service flat
flat 192 n.
services
instrumentality
628 n.
services, the
army 722 n.
servile
conformable
83 adj.
plebeian 869 adj.
humble 872 adj.
servile 879 adj.
servility
humility 872 n.
servility 879 n.
serving
serving 742 adj.
servitude
servitude 745 n.
servomechanism
machine 630 n.
servomotor
machine 630 n.
sesquicentenary
special day 876 n.
sesquicentennial
seasonal 141 adj.
sesquipedalian
long 203 adj.
session
council 692 n.
sessions
lawcourt 956 n.
legal trial 959 n.
sestet
verse form 593 n.
set
uniformity 16 n.
affix 45 vb.
firm 45 adj.
join 45 vb.
coherence 48 n.
component 58 n.

arrange 62 vb.
series 71 n.
accumulation 74 n.
band 74 n.
group 74 n.
classification 77 n.
sort 77 n.
inclusion 78 n.
number 85 n.
unit 88 n.
young plant 132 n.
stabilize 153 vb.
tendency 179 n.
place 187 vb.
hang 217 vb.
pendency 217 n.
support 218 vb.
form 243 n.
direction 281 n.
descend 309 vb.
be dense 324 vb.
dense 324 adj.
harden 326 vb.
rigid 326 adj.
cultivate 370 vb.
spectacle 445 n.
be true 494 vb.
educational
534 adj.
class 538 n.
printed 587 adj.
edition 589 n.
stage set 594 n.
usual 610 adj.
collection 632 n.
doctor 658 vb.
make ready
669 vb.
association 706 n.
party 708 n.
contest 716 n.
hairdressing 843 n.
set a course
navigate 269 vb.
set against
set apart 46 vb.
dissuade 613 vb.
make quarrels
709 vb.
cause dislike
861 vb.
set alight
burn 381 vb.
set an example
be an example
23 vb.
motivate 612 vb.

behave 688 vb.
set apart
separate 46 adj.
set apart 46 vb.
exempt 919 vb.
set aside
set apart 46 vb.
displace 188 vb.
reject 607 vb.
store 632 vb.
abrogate 752 vb.
not observe 769 vb.
due 915 adj.
exempt 919 vb.
set at liberty
liberate 746 vb.
exempt 919 vb.
set at naught
defy 711 vb.
set a trap for
ambush 527 vb.
ensnare 542 vb.
set back
put off 136 vb.
setback
descent 309 n.
disappointment
509 n.
dissuasion 613 n.
evil 616 n.
deterioration
655 n.
hitch 702 n.
adversity 731 n.
loss 772 n.
suffering 825 n.
set by the ears
make quarrels
709 vb.
enrage 891 vb.
set down
place 187 vb.
let fall 311 vb.
affirm 532 vb.
set down to
attribute 158 vb.
set fair
warm 379 adj.
be auspicious
730 vb.
palmy 730 adj.
set fire to
burn 381 vb.
kindle 381 vb.
set foot in
enter 297 vb.

set forth
start out 296 vb.
set free
disunite 46 vb.
deliver 668 vb.
disencumber
701 vb.
give scope 744 vb.
liberate 746 vb.
exempt 919 vb.
set in
stay 144 vb.
set in motion
initiate 68 vb.
dispose of 673 vb.
set in one's ways, be
be wont 610 vb.
set in order
compose 56 vb.
make ready
669 vb.
set no store by
underestimate
483 vb.
doubt 486 vb.
hold cheap 922 vb.
set off
correlate 12 vb.
initiate 68 vb.
shoot 287 vb.
show 522 vb.
beautify 841 vb.
decorate 844 vb.
set off on a wild-
goose chase
deflect 282 vb.
set of rules
precept 693 n.
set of teeth
tooth 256 n.
set on
attack 712 vb.
enamoured
887 adj.
set on an even keel
equalize 28 vb.
set one back
hinder 702 vb.
cost 809 vb.
set on edge
roughen 259 vb.
give pain 377 vb.
frighten 854 vb.
set one's cap at
pursue 619 vb.
desire 859 vb.
be in love 887 vb.

court 889 vb.
set one's face against
oppose 704 vb.
refuse 760 vb.
set one's hand to the plough
undertake 672 vb.
set one's heart on
be resolute 599 vb.
desire 859 vb.
be in love 887 vb.
set one's mind at rest
tranquillize 823 vb.
set one's mind on
desire 859 vb.
set one's shoulder to the wheel
undertake 672 vb.
set one's sights
aim 281 vb.
set one's sights on
desire 859 vb.
set one's teeth on edge
be sour 393 vb.
set on fire
burn 381 vb.
excite 821 vb.
set out
arrange 62 vb.
travel 267 vb.
start out 296 vb.
show 522 vb.
dissertate 591 vb.
set piece
pageant 875 n.
set right
disclose 526 vb.
rectify 654 vb.
vindicate 927 vb.
set sail
navigate 269 vb.
start out 296 vb.
set speech
oration 579 n.
set square
angular measure 247 n.
gauge 465 n.
set store by
approve 923 vb.
sett
dwelling 192 n.
paving 226 n.
settee
seat 218 n.

setter
dog 365 n.
set the ball rolling
initiate 68 vb.
set the cat among the pigeons
surprise 508 vb.
set the heather on fire
have a reputation 866 vb.
set theory
mathematics 86 n.
set the pace
motivate 612 vb.
set the seal on
carry through 725 vb.
set the stage
make ready 669 vb.
set the teeth on edge
rasp 407 vb.
displease 827 vb.
set the Thames on fire
attempt the impossible 470 vb.
setting
situation 186 n.
surroundings 230 n.
musical piece 412 n.
view 438 n.
stage set 594 n.
hairdressing 843 n.
ornamental art 844 n.
settle
arrange 62 vb.
terminate 69 vb.
prevail 178 vb.
place oneself 187 vb.
dwell 192 vb.
seat 218 vb.
travel 267 vb.
descend 309 vb.
weigh 322 vb.
murder 362 vb.
answer 460 vb.
make certain 473 vb.
judge 480 vb.
defeat 727 vb.
contract 765 vb.

appropriate 786 vb.
punish 963 vb.
settle an account
pay 804 vb.
set a score
pay 804 vb.
settled
native 191 adj.
quiescent 266 adj.
settled decision
certainty 473 n.
judgment 480 n.
settle down
be quiescent 266 vb.
sleep 679 vb.
settle for
bargain 791 vb.
settle in
enter 297 vb.
settlement
territory 184 n.
location 187 n.
station 187 n.
compact 765 n.
transfer 780 n.
giving 781 n.
payment 804 n.
settle on
choose 605 vb.
settle one's hash
defeat 727 vb.
settler
settler 191 n.
incomer 297 n.
settle upon
possess 773 vb.
settle with
punish 963 vb.
set to
begin 68 vb.
eat 301 vb.
be resolute 599 vb.
undertake 672 vb.
work 682 vb.
fight 716 vb.
set-to
quarrel 709 n.
fight 716 n.
set to music
harmonize 410 vb.
musical 412 adj.
compose music 413 vb.
set to rights
repair 656 vb.

set to work
begin 68 vb.
prepare 669 vb.
set up
compose 56 vb.
arrange 62 vb.
stabilize 153 vb.
cause 156 vb.
strengthen 162 vb.
produce 164 vb.
place 187 vb.
elevate 310 vb.
set-up
circumstance 8 n.
composition 56 n.
structure 331 n.
set upon
resolute 599 adj.
set up shop
undertake 672 vb.
seven
over five 99 n.
seven deadly sins
vice 934 n.
seven-league boots
magic instrument 983 n.
seven lean years
scarcity 636 n.
seven sacraments, the
Christian rite 988 n.
seven seas, the
ocean 343 n.
Seventh-day Adventist
sect 978 n.
seventh heaven
summit 213 n.
happiness 824 n.
heaven 971 n.
seventy
twenty and over 99 n.
seven wonders of the world
prodigy 864 n.
sever
subtract 39 vb.
disunite 46 vb.
several
many 104 adj.
severally
severally 80 adv.
severance
subtraction 39 n.

separation 46 n.
severe
exorbitant 32 adj.
violent 176 adj.
accurate 494 adj.
plain 573 adj.
severe 735 adj.
severity
plainness 573 n.
severity 735 n.
Sèvres china
pottery 381 n.
sew
join 45 vb.
tie 45 vb.
produce 164 vb.
sewage
leavings 41 n.
sewer
tunnel 263 n.
drain 351 n.
stench 397 n.
badness 645 n.
sink 649 n.
insalubrity 653 n.
sewerage
cleansing 648 n.
dirt 649 n.
sewing-bee
assembly 74 n.
sewn
tied 45 adj.
sewn up
completed 725 adj.
sex
coition 45 n.
classification 77 n.
propagation 167 n.
life 360 n.
sexagenarian
twenty and over
99 n.
sexagenary
multifid 100 adj.
sexagesimal
multifid 100 adj.
sex appeal
attraction 291 n.
inducement 612 n.
pleasurableness
826 n.
beauty 841 n.
sex discrimination
prejudice 481 n.
injustice 914 n.
sexism
prejudice 481 n.

pride 871 n.
injustice 914 n.
sexist
biased 481 adj.
narrow mind
481 n.
sexless
impotent 161 adj.
sexology
medical art 658 n.
sext
church service
988 n.
sextant
angular measure
247 n.
arc 250 n.
sailing aid 269 n.
gauge 465 n.
sextennial
seasonal 141 adj.
sextet
over five 99 n.
sexton
interment 364 n.
officer 741 n.
church officer
986 n.
sexual
sensual 944 adj.
impure 951 adj.
sexual abuse
painfulness 827 n.
cruel act 898 n.
rape 951 n.
sexual desire
libido 859 n.
sexual harassment
painfulness 827 n.
cruel act 898 n.
sexual intercourse
coition 45 n.
sexuality
sensualism 944 n.
unchastity 951 n.
**sexually-transmitted
disease**
venereal disease
651 n.
sexy
personable 841 adj.
erotic 887 adj.
impure 951 adj.
sforzando
adagio 412 adv.
sfumato
painted 553 adj.

sh
hush 399 int.
hush 582 int.
shabby
dilapidated
655 adj.
disreputable
867 adj.
dishonest 930 adj.
shack
small house 192 n.
shackle
tie 45 vb.
bond 47 n.
encumbrance
702 n.
hinder 702 vb.
fetter 747 vb.
fetter 748 n.
shade
degree 27 n.
small quantity
33 n.
shade 226 n.
darken 418 vb.
darkness 418 n.
dim 419 vb.
dimness 419 n.
curtain 421 n.
screen 421 vb.
colour 425 vb.
hue 425 n.
qualify 468 vb.
paint 553 vb.
safeguard 660 vb.
ghost 970 n.
shades
shade 226 n.
screen 421 n.
eyeglass 442 n.
ghost 970 n.
shadoof
irrigator 341 n.
shadow
insubstantial thing
4 n.
analogue 18 n.
imitation 20 n.
copy 22 n.
compeer 28 n.
accompany 89 vb.
concomitant 89 n.
thinness 206 n.
be behind 238 vb.
follow 284 vb.
darkness 418 n.
dim 419 vb.

dimness 419 n.
screen 421 vb.
fantasy 513 n.
hunter 619 n.
pursue 619 vb.
auxiliary 707 n.
close friend 880 n.
shadow forth
predict 511 vb.
manifest 522 vb.
shadows
darkness 418 n.
shadowy
immaterial
320 adj.
shadowy 419 adj.
invisible 444 adj.
shady
cold 380 adj.
dark 418 adj.
shadowy 419 adj.
disreputable
867 adj.
dishonest 930 adj.
lawbreaking
954 adj.
shaft
depth 211 n.
handle 218 n.
pillar 218 n.
cavity 255 n.
excavation 255 n.
sharp point 256 n.
tunnel 263 n.
rotator 315 n.
flash 417 n.
tool 630 n.
store 632 n.
missile weapon
723 n.
shag
hair 259 n.
bird 365 n.
tobacco 388 n.
shaggy
hairy 259 adj.
shaggy dog story
fable 543 n.
witticism 839 n.
shagreen
skin 226 n.
Shah
sovereign 741 n.
shake
mix 43 vb.
come unstuck
49 vb.

derange 63 vb.
vary 152 vb.
be weak 163 vb.
force 176 vb.
wriggle 251 vb.
impel 279 vb.
impulse 279 n.
brandish 317 vb.
fluctuation 317 n.
oscillate 317 vb.
agitate 318 vb.
agitation 318 n.
be agitated 318 vb.
blow 352 vb.
be cold 380 vb.
roll 403 vb.
musical note
   410 n.
cause doubt
   486 vb.
show feeling
   818 vb.
impress 821 vb.
frighten 854 vb.
quake 854 vb.
threaten 900 vb.
shake down
   sleep 679 vb.
shakedown
   bed 218 n.
shake hands
   meet 295 vb.
   make peace
     719 vb.
   be friendly 880 vb.
   greet 884 vb.
   forgive 909 vb.
shake off
   outstrip 277 vb.
   eject 300 vb.
   elude 667 vb.
shake oneself free
   achieve liberty
     746 vb.
shake one's faith
   cause doubt
     486 vb.
shake one's fist
   defy 711 vb.
shake one's head
   dissent 489 vb.
   negate 533 vb.
   gesticulate 547 vb.
   refuse 760 vb.
   deprecate 762 vb.
   disapprove 924 vb.

shake on it
   promise 764 vb.
shakes, the
   agitation 318 n.
   illness 651 n.
shake the dust from
   one's feet
   run away 620 vb.
shake up
   agitate 318 vb.
   animate 821 vb.
shake-up
   revolution 149 n.
shaking
   impulse 279 n.
   nervous 854 adj.
   nervousness 854 n.
shaky
   flimsy 163 adj.
   dilapidated
     655 adj.
   unsafe 661 adj.
shale
   brittleness 330 n.
   rock 344 n.
shallots
   fruit and vegetables
     301 n.
shallow
   unproductive
     172 adj.
   shallow 212 adj.
   dabbling 491 adj.
   affected 850 adj.
shallow pretext
   pretext 614 n.
shallows
   shallowness 212 n.
shalom
   welcome 295 int.
sham
   imitate 20 vb.
   imitative 20 adj.
   dissemble 541 vb.
   false 541 adj.
   sham 542 n.
   spurious 542 adj.
   be untrue 543 vb.
   pretension 850 n.
shamble
   walk 267 vb.
shambles
   disorder 61 n.
   turmoil 61 n.
   bungling 695 n.
shame
   evil 616 n.

disrepute 867 n.
   See **slur**
   shame 867 vb.
   slur 867 n.
   humiliation 872 n.
   wrong 914 n.
   improbity 930 n.
   guilt 936 n.
   purity 950 n.
shamefaced
   modest 874 adj.
   guilty 936 adj.
shameful
   evil 616 adj.
   bad 645 adj.
   discreditable
     867 adj.
shame into
   motivate 612 vb.
shameless
   thick-skinned
     820 adj.
   vulgar 847 adj.
   insolent 878 adj.
   dishonest 930 adj.
   unchaste 951 adj.
shamming
   imitative 20 adj.
shammy
   cleaning cloth
     648 n.
shampoo
   rub 333 vb.
   ablutions 648 n.
   clean 648 vb.
   cleanser 648 n.
   hairwash 843 n.
shamrock
   three 93 n.
   plant 366 n.
   heraldry 547 n.
shandy
   alcoholic drink
     301 n.
shanghai
   ensnare 542 vb.
   take away 786 vb.
   steal 788 vb.
Shangri-la
   fantasy 513 n.
shank
   leg 267 n.
   print-type 587 n.
Shanks's pony
   conveyance 267 n.
   pedestrianism
     267 n.

shantung
   textile 222 n.
shanty
   small house 192 n.
   vocal music 412 n.
   poem 593 n.
shanty town
   housing 192 n.
shape
   modality 7 n.
   sort 77 n.
   convert 147 vb.
   produce 164 vb.
   outline 233 n.
   form 243 n.
   form 243 vb.
   appearance 445 n.
   feature 445 n.
   educate 534 vb.
   identification
     547 n.
   represent 551 vb.
   plan 623 vb.
shape a course
   travel 267 vb.
   plan 623 vb.
shapeless
   abnormal 84 adj.
   amorphous
     244 adj.
   unsightly 842 adj.
shapely
   shapely 841 adj.
shape of things to
   come
   prediction 511 n.
shard
   piece 53 n.
share
   part 53 n.
   bisect 92 vb.
   mete out 465 vb.
   title deed 767 n.
   participate 775 vb.
   portion 783 n.
   feel 818 vb.
   be sociable 882 vb.
share and share alike
   participate 775 vb.
shareholder
   participator 775 n.
   owner 776 n.
share in
   participate 775 vb.
share out
   part 53 vb.
   mete out 465 vb.

apportion 783 vb.
share-out
gain 771 n.
participation
775 n.
portion 783 n.
shares
apportionment
783 n.
share shop
stock exchange
618 n.
market 796 n.
sharing
equal 28 adj.
shark
fish 365 n.
trickster 545 n.
taker 786 n.
defrauder 789 n.
sharkskin
textile 222 n.
Sharon fruit
fruit and vegetables
301 n.
sharp
keen 174 adj.
sharp 256 adj.
sentient 374 adj.
sour 393 adj.
musical note
410 n.
discordant 411 adj.
intelligent 498 adj.
descriptive 590 adj.
cunning 698 adj.
paining 827 adj.
unpleasant
827 adj.
witty 839 adj.
hateful 888 adj.
irascible 892 adj.
disapproving
924 adj.
sharp ear
hearing 415 n.
sharpen
sharpen 256 vb.
sharpen the wits
educate 534 vb.
sharper
trickster 545 n.
slyboots 698 n.
defrauder 789 n.
sharp-eyed
seeing 438 adj.
attentive 455 adj.

vigilant 457 adj.
sharply
greatly 32 vb.
sharp note
stridor 407 n.
sharp practice
duplicity 541 n.
trickery 542 n.
cunning 698 n.
perfidy 930 n.
sharp-tempered
irascible 892 adj.
sharp-tongued
irascible 892 adj.
sharp-witted
intelligent 498 adj.
shatter
break 46 vb.
demolish 165 vb.
pulverize 332 vb.
shattering
wonderful 864 adj.
shatterproof
strong 162 adj.
hard 326 adj.
tough 329 adj.
invulnerable
660 adj.
shave
cut 46 vb.
make smaller
198 vb.
shorten 204 vb.
smooth 258 vb.
touch 378 vb.
hairdressing 843 n.
primp 843 vb.
shaver
cosmetic 843 n.
shavings
leavings 41 n.
rubbish 641 n.
she
female 373 adj.
female 373 n.
sheaf
bunch 74 n.
cultivate 370 vb.
shear
subtract 39 vb.
power 160 n.
make smaller
198 vb.
shorten 204 vb.
distortion 246 n.
fleece 786 vb.

shears
sharp edge 256 n.
farm tool 370 n.
sheath
contraception
172 n.
case 194 n.
receptacle 194 n.
covering 226 n.
arsenal 723 n.
sheathe
layer 207 n.
cover 226 vb.
dress 228 vb.
sheath knife
sharp edge 256 n.
shebeen
tavern 192 n.
shed
decrease 37 vb.
small house 192 n.
emit 300 vb.
let fall 311 vb.
disaccustom
611 vb.
relinquish 621 vb.
shed blood
kill 362 vb.
go to war 718 vb.
oppress 735 vb.
shed tears
weep 836 vb.
sheen
light 417 n.
reflection 417 n.
sheep
imitator 20 n.
sheep 365 n.
laity 987 n.
sheepdog
dog 365 n.
sheep farming
animal husbandry
369 n.
sheepfold
stable 192 n.
enclosure 235 n.
cattle pen 369 n.
shelter 662 n.
sheepish
animal 365 adj.
modest 874 adj.
guilty 936 adj.
sheep-like
obedient 739 adj.
sheep's eyes
look 438 n.

desire 859 n.
sheepshank
ligature 47 n.
sheepskin
skin 226 n.
sheer
absolute 32 adj.
simple 44 adj.
vertical 215 adj.
sloping 220 adj.
transparent
422 adj.
sheer off
deviate 282 vb.
recede 290 vb.
sheet
part 53 n.
coverlet 226 n.
dress 228 vb.
edition 589 n.
paper 631 n.
abound 635 vb.
sheet lightning
luminary 420 n.
sheets
great quantity
32 n.
sheikh
potentate 741 n.
person of rank
868 n.
shekel
coinage 797 n.
shekels
shekels 797 n.
shelf
shelf 218 n.
projection 254 n.
storage 632 n.
shelf, the
celibacy 895 n.
shell
remainder 41 n.
emptiness 190 n.
exteriority 223 n.
covering 226 n.
skin 226 n.
uncover 229 vb.
rowing boat 275 n.
missile 287 n.
hardness 326 n.
structure 331 n.
interment 364 n.
horn 414 n.
fire at 712 vb.
ammunition 723 n.
bomb 723 n.

missile weapon
723 n.
seclusion 883 n.
shellac
resin 357 n.
shellback
mariner 270 n.
shellfish
fish food 301 n.
marine life 365 n.
shell out
give 781 vb.
pay 804 vb.
shellshock
neurosis 503 n.
shell-shocked
impotent 161 adj.
shelter
dwell 192 vb.
small house 192 n.
admit 299 vb.
reception 299 n.
screen 421 n.
screen 421 vb.
safeguard 660 vb.
shelter 662 n.
shelter behind
plead 614 vb.
sheltered
safe 660 adj.
sheltered housing
gerontology 131 n.
retreat 192 n.
shelter 662 n.
shelve
put off 136 vb.
pause 145 vb.
be oblique 220 vb.
be neglectful
458 vb.
relinquish 621 vb.
shelving
delay 136 n.
compartment
194 n.
unwillingness
598 n.
shemozzle
turmoil 61 n.
commotion 318 n.
loudness 400 n.
shenanigans
foolery 497 n.
trickery 542 n.
shepherd
bring together
74 vb.

herdsman 369 n.
protector 660 n.
safeguard 660 vb.
leader 690 n.
servant 742 n.
pastor 986 n.
shepherdess
herdsman 369 n.
shepherd's crook
support 218 n.
shepherd's pie
meat 301 n.
sherbet
soft drink 301 n.
sheriff
protector 660 n.
officer 741 n.
law officer 955 n.
judge 957 n.
Sheriff Court
lawcourt 956 n.
Sherlock Holmes
detective 459 n.
sherry
wine 301 n.
Shetland pony
pony 273 n.
Shetland wool
fibre 208 n.
she wolf
violent creature
176 n.
shibboleth
identification
547 n.
instrument 628 n.
shield
covering 226 n.
screen 421 n.
screen 421 vb.
heraldry 547 n.
protection 660 n.
safeguard 660 vb.
shelter 662 n.
armour 713 n.
defend 713 vb.
trophy 729 n.
honours 866 n.
reward 962 n.
shift
subtract 39 vb.
time 108 n.
period 110 n.
periodicity 141 n.
change 143 n.
change 143 vb.
transition 147 n.

displace 188 vb.
displacement
188 n.
dress 228 n.
be in motion
265 vb.
motion 265 n.
move 265 vb.
transference 272 n.
transpose 272 vb.
move fast 277 vb.
deflect 282 vb.
deviation 282 n.
trickery 542 n.
labour 682 n.
change hands
780 vb.
take away 786 vb.
shift for oneself
behave 688 vb.
be free 744 vb.
shifting
changeful 152 adj.
moving 265 adj.
transference 272 n.
shifting sands
changeable thing
152 n.
shift one's ground
change one's mind
603 vb.
shift the blame
be exempt 919 vb.
accuse 928 vb.
shifty
changeful 152 adj.
hypocritical
541 adj.
cunning 698 adj.
disreputable
867 adj.
dishonest 930 adj.
Shi'ites
non-Christian sect
978 n.
shillelagh
club 723 n.
shilling
coinage 797 n.
shilly-shally
vary 152 vb.
be uncertain
474 vb.
be irresolute
601 vb.
shimmer
flash 417 n.

shine 417 vb.
shimmy
wriggle 251 vb.
dance 837 n.
shin
leg 267 n.
meat 301 n.
shindig
turmoil 61 n.
quarrel 709 n.
fight 716 n.
social gathering
882 n.
shine
smooth 258 vb.
smoothness 258 n.
light 417 n.
reflection 417 n.
shine 417 vb.
be skilful 694 vb.
have a reputation
866 vb.
shingle
shorten 204 vb.
coat 226 vb.
roof 226 n.
powder 332 n.
shore 344 n.
hairdressing 843 n.
shingles
skin disease 651 n.
shining
luminous 417 adj.
obvious 443 adj.
clean 648 adj.
shining light
sage 500 n.
good person 937 n.
shin up
climb 308 vb.
shiny
smooth 258 adj.
luminous 417 adj.
ship
load 193 vb.
transfer 272 vb.
carry 273 vb.
ship 275 n.
shipment
contents 193 n.
transport 272 n.
ship of the desert
beast of burden
273 n.
shipping
transport 272 n.
shipping 275 n.

shipping line
shipping 275 n.
shipshape and Bristol fashion
orderly 60 adj.
marine 275 adj.
ship that passes in the night
brief span 114 n.
shipwreck
destroy 165 vb.
ruin 165 n.
shipwright
artisan 686 n.
shipyard
workshop 687 n.
shire
district 184 n.
shire-horse
draught horse 273 n.
shirk
disregard 458 vb.
be unwilling 598 vb.
be irresolute 601 vb.
avoid 620 vb.
be inactive 679 vb.
not observe 769 vb.
fail in duty 918 vb.
shirr
fold 261 vb.
shirt
shirt 228 n.
shirt-tail
extremity 69 n.
shirtwaister
dress 228 n.
shirty
angry 891 adj.
sullen 893 adj.
shiver
small thing 33 n.
break 46 vb.
demolish 165 vb.
strip 208 n.
oscillate 317 vb.
agitation 318 n.
be agitated 318 vb.
feel pain 377 vb.
be cold 380 vb.
quake 854 vb.
shivers
agitation 318 n.
coldness 380 n.
illness 651 n.

nervousness 854 n.
shivery
chilly 380 adj.
shoal
group 74 n.
shoals
shallowness 212 n.
shock
bunch 74 n.
electricity 160 n.
force 176 vb.
violence 176 n.
collision 279 n.
impel 279 vb.
impulse 279 n.
agitation 318 n.
lack of expectation 508 n.
surprise 508 vb.
disappointment 509 n.
illness 651 n.
feeling 818 n.
excitation 821 n.
suffering 825 n.
displease 827 vb.
painfulness 827 n.
fear 854 n.
cause dislike 861 vb.
be wonderful 864 vb.
wonder 864 n.
incur blame 924 vb.
shock absorber
moderator 177 n.
shocked
unexpecting 508 adj.
disapproving 924 adj.
shocked silence
wonder 864 n.
shocking
flagrant 32 adj.
unexpected 508 adj.
not nice 645 adj.
distressing 827 adj.
ugly 842 adj.
frightening 854 adj.
wonderful 864 adj.
discreditable 867 adj.
heinous 934 adj.

shocking-pink
red 431 adj.
shockproof
tough 329 adj.
unfeeling 375 adj.
shock tactics
attack 712 n.
shoddy
inferior 35 adj.
flimsy 163 adj.
spurious 542 adj.
trivial 639 adj.
bad 645 adj.
shoe
footwear 228 n.
shoemaker
clothier 228 n.
shogun
autocrat 741 n.
shoot
branch 53 n.
young plant 132 n.
descendant 170 n.
expand 197 vb.
navigate 269 vb.
move fast 277 vb.
shoot 287 vb.
foliage 366 n.
tree 366 n.
vegetate 366 vb.
give pain 377 vb.
radiate 417 vb.
photograph 551 vb.
be loquacious 581 vb.
amuse oneself 837 vb.
drug oneself 949 vb.
execute 963 vb.
shoot a line
be ostentatious 875 vb.
boast 877 vb.
shoot at
fire at 712 vb.
criticize 924 vb.
shoot down
fell 311 vb.
kill 362 vb.
slaughter 362 vb.
fire at 712 vb.
shoot full of holes
confute 479 vb.
shooting
propulsion 287 n.
killing 362 n.

painful 377 adj.
cinema 445 n.
chase 619 n.
bombardment 712 n.
paining 827 adj.
sport 837 n.
shooting brake
automobile 274 n.
shooting gallery
place of amusement 837 n.
shooting star
brief span 114 n.
meteor 321 n.
luminary 420 n.
omen 511 n.
shooting up
drug-taking 949 n.
shoot one's mouth
boast 877 vb.
shoot-out
fight 716 n.
battle 718 n.
shoot the rapids
navigate 269 vb.
row 269 vb.
pass 305 vb.
shoot up
grow 36 vb.
be high 209 vb.
jut 254 vb.
ascend 308 vb.
elevate 310 vb.
shop
topic 452 n.
inform 524 vb.
workshop 687 n.
purchase 792 vb.
shop 796 n.
shop around
choose 605 vb.
shop assistant
worker 686 n.
servant 742 n.
seller 793 n.
shopfloor
workshop 687 n.
shopkeeper
seller 793 n.
tradespeople 794 n.
shoplifting
stealing 788 n.
shopper
purchaser 792 n.
shopping
purchase 792 n.

shopping basket
purchase 792 n.
shopping centre
meeting place
192 n.
emporium 796 n.
shopping list
requirement 627 n.
purchase 792 n.
shopping mall
meeting place
192 n.
emporium 796 n.
shop-soiled
imperfect 647 adj.
shop steward
official 690 n.
delegate 754 n.
shop window
window 263 n.
exhibit 522 n.
market 796 n.
shore
region 184 n.
support 218 n.
shore 344 n.
shore up
support 218 vb.
preserve 666 vb.
shorn
short 204 adj.
short
incomplete 55 adj.
short 204 adj.
draught 301 n.
deficient 307 adj.
taciturn 582 adj.
irascible 892 adj.
shortage
decrease 37 n.
shortfall 307 n.
requirement 627 n.
scarcity 636 n.
short and sweet
brief 114 adj.
concise 569 adj.
short back and sides
shortness 204 n.
hairdressing 843 n.
shortbread
pastries and cakes
301 n.
shortchange
deceive 542 vb.
overcharge 811 vb.
short-circuit
circuit 626 vb.

shortcoming
shortfall 307 n.
nonobservance
769 n.
vice 934 n.
short commons
insufficiency 636 n.
fasting 946 n.
shortcrust pastry
pastries and cakes
301 n.
short cut
short distance
200 n.
straightness 249 n.
route 624 n.
shorten
shorten 204 vb.
shortfall
deficit 55 n.
shortfall 307 n.
shorthand
writing 586 n.
shorthanded
unprovided
636 adj.
shorthorn
cattle 365 n.
short leet
list 87 n.
choice 605 n.
short list
list 87 n.
choice 605 n.
short-lived
ephemeral 114 adj.
short measure
shortfall 307 n.
short of
less 35 adv.
incomplete 55 adj.
exclusive of 57 adv.
deficient 307 adj.
short run
brief span 114 n.
shorts
shortness 204 n.
trousers 228 n.
underwear 228 n.
short shrift
pitilessness 906 n.
short-sighted
dim-sighted
440 adj.
misjudging
481 adj.

narrow-minded
481 adj.
unwise 499 adj.
short-staffed
deficient 307 adj.
short step
short distance
200 n.
short story
novel 590 n.
short supply
scarcity 636 n.
short-tempered
irascible 892 adj.
short-term
brief 114 adj.
short wave
radiation 417 n.
short with, be
be concise 569 vb.
short work
easy thing 701 n.
shot
mixed 43 adj.
time 108 n.
period 110 n.
stimulant 174 n.
sphere 252 n.
missile 287 n.
propulsion 287 n.
insertion 303 n.
bang 402 n.
conjecture 512 n.
photography 551 n.
gambling 618 n.
hunter 619 n.
medicine 658 n.
ammunition 723 n.
missile weapon
723 n.
drug-taking 949 n.
shot about
periodicity 141 n.
shot across the bows
warning 664 n.
terror tactics 712 n.
shotgun
propellant 287 n.
firearm 723 n.
shotgun wedding
type of marriage
894 n.
shot in one's locker
means 629 n.
shot in the arm
stimulant 174 n.

shot in the dark
empiricism 461 n.
conjecture 512 n.
gambling 618 n.
shot-putter
player 837 n.
shot silk
variegation 437 n.
shoulder
support 218 vb.
carry 273 vb.
impel 279 vb.
propel 287 vb.
meat 301 n.
elevate 310 vb.
print-type 587 n.
undertake 672 vb.
shoulder-length
long 203 adj.
**shoulder one's re-
sponsibility**
incur a duty
917 vb.
shoulder to shoulder
cohesive 48 adj.
shout
be loud 400 vb.
loudness 400 n.
cry 408 n.
vociferate 408 vb.
affirm 532 vb.
emphasize 532 vb.
call 547 n.
voice 577 vb.
defy 711 vb.
rejoice 835 vb.
rejoicing 835 n.
boast 877 vb.
be rude 885 vb.
anger 891 n.
get angry 891 vb.
shout down
vociferate 408 vb.
affirm 532 vb.
make mute 578 vb.
be obstructive
702 vb.
be insolent 878 vb.
criticize 924 vb.
disapprove 924 vb.
shout for
applaud 923 vb.
shouting
loud 400 adj.
loudness 400 n.
cry 408 n.
rudeness 885 n.

shove
  move 265 vb.
  transpose 272 vb.
  impel 279 vb.
  impulse 279 n.
  propel 287 vb.
  gesture 547 n.
  be active 678 vb.
  work 682 vb.
shove ha'penny
  ball game 837 n.
shovel
  ladle 194 n.
  sharp edge 256 n.
  transpose 272 vb.
  conveyor 274 n.
  furnace 383 n.
shove off
  impel 279 vb.
  decamp 296 vb.
shove one's oar in
  meddle 678 vb.
shoving
  hasty 680 adj.
show
  point to 281 vb.
  be visible 443 vb.
  appear 445 vb.
  appearance 445 n.
  spectacle 445 n.
  attract notice
    455 vb.
  evidence 466 vb.
  demonstrate
    478 V.
  exhibit 522 n.
  show 522 vb.
  be disclosed
    526 vb.
  duplicity 541 n.
  stage play 594 n.
  amusement 837 n.
  pride 871 n.
  ostentation 875 n.
  pageant 875 n.
**show a clean pair of
    heels**
  move fast 277 vb.
  run away 620 vb.
show appreciation
  thank 907 vb.
show a profit
  be profitable
    771 vb.
showboat
  ship 275 n.

show business
  drama 594 n.
showcase
  exhibit 522 n.
showdown
  disclosure 526 n.
  fight 716 n.
shower
  crowd 74 n.
  propel 287 vb.
  descend 309 vb.
  descent 309 n.
  let fall 311 vb.
  water 339 n.
  be wet 341 vb.
  drench 341 vb.
  moisten 341 vb.
  rain 350 n.
  rain 350 VB.
  abound 635 vb.
  ablutions 648 n.
  clean 648 vb.
showerproof
  strong 162 adj.
  dry 342 adj.
  invulnerable
    660 adj.
  resisting 715 adj.
shower upon
  give 781 vb.
  be liberal 813 vb.
show fear
  be cowardly
    856 vb.
show girl
  entertainer 594 n.
show in
  admit 299 vb.
showing
  obvious 443 adj.
  visible 443 adj.
  appearing 445 adj.
  manifest 522 adj.
  shown 522 adj.
  dramatic 594 adj.
showing, be
  appear 445 vb.
showing off
  foolery 497 n.
show interest
  be curious 453 vb.
show its face
  be visible 443 vb.
  be plain 522 vb.
  be disclosed
    526 vb.

show its true colours
  be disclosed
    526 vb.
show jumping
  equitation 267 n.
showman
  exhibitor 522 n.
  stage manager
    594 n.
showmanship
  publicity 528 n.
  ostentation 875 n.
show mercy
  show mercy
    905 vb.
shown
  shown 522 adj.
show off
  show 522 vb.
  be affected 850 vb.
  be proud 871 vb.
  be vain 873 vb.
  be ostentatious
    875 vb.
  boast 877 vb.
show-off
  vain person 873 n.
show of force
  brute force 735 n.
show of hands
  vote 605 n.
show one off
  beautify 841 vb.
**show oneself in one's
    true colours**
  be plain 522 vb.
  disclose 526 vb.
show one's face
  be present 189 vb.
  be plain 522 vb.
show one's gratitude
  reward 962 vb.
show one's hand
  divulge 526 vb.
show one's ignorance
  be unskilful
    695 vb.
show one's mettle
  be courageous
    855 vb.
show one's paces
  be vain 873 vb.
  be ostentatious
    875 vb.
show one's respect
  pay one's respects
    884 vb.

show one the ropes
  train 534 vb.
show out
  dismiss 300 vb.
show over
  show 522 vb.
show piece
  exhibit 522 n.
show pity
  pity 905 vb.
showplace
  exhibit 522 n.
show promise
  progress 285 vb.
show respect
  show respect
    920 vb.
showroom
  exhibit 522 n.
show signs of
  evidence 466 vb.
  manifest 522 vb.
  indicate 547 vb.
show the door
  repel 292 vb.
  dismiss 300 vb.
show the flag
  be plain 522 vb.
show the way
  come before 64 vb.
  orientate 281 vb.
  indicate 547 vb.
  prepare 669 vb.
  direct 689 vb.
**show the white
    feather**
  be cowardly
    856 vb.
show the white flag
  submit 721 vb.
show through
  be disclosed
    526 vb.
show up
  be present 189 vb.
  arrive 295 vb.
  be visible 443 vb.
  confute 479 vb.
  be plain 522 vb.
  show 522 vb.
  shame 867 vb.
  accuse 928 vb.
show up well
  be plain 522 vb.
show willing
  be willing 597 vb.
  be active 678 vb.

SHO

cooperate 706 vb.
showy
  florid 425 adj.
  ostentatious
    875 adj.
  showy 875 adj.
shrapnel
  ammunition 723 n.
  missile weapon
    723 n.
shred
  small thing 33 n.
  cut 46 vb.
  piece 53 n.
  fraction 102 n.
  strip 208 n.
  cook 301 vb.
shrew
  mammal 365 n.
  female 373 n.
shrewd
  judicial 480 adj.
  knowing 490 adj.
  intelligent 498 adj.
  skilful 694 adj.
  cunning 698 adj.
shrewd idea
  conjecture 512 n.
shriek
  loudness 400 n.
  stridor 407 n.
  cry 408 n.
  weep 836 vb.
shrieks of laughter
  laughter 835 n.
shrift
  penance 941 n.
  ministration 988 n.
shrike
  bird 365 n.
shrill
  loud 400 adj.
  shrill 407 vb.
  strident 407 adj.
shrimp
  small thing 33 n.
  dwarf 196 n.
  fish food 301 n.
  marine life 365 n.
  hunt 619 vb.
shrine
  tomb 364 n.
  ritual object 988 n.
  temple 990 n.
shrink
  be small 33 vb.
  abate 37 vb.

SHR

decrease 37 vb.
  become small
    198 vb.
  make smaller
    198 vb.
  recoil 280 vb.
  recede 290 vb.
  psychologist 447 n.
  mental disorder
    503 n.
  avoid 620 vb.
  deteriorate 655 vb.
  doctor 658 n.
  be nervous 854 vb.
  quake 854 vb.
  be cowardly
    856 vb.
  be modest 874 vb.
shrinkage
  decrease 37 n.
  contraction 198 n.
  shortness 204 n.
shrink from
  dislike 861 vb.
  hate 888 vb.
shrinking
  decrease 37 n.
  recession 290 n.
  avoidance 620 n.
  nervous 854 adj.
  modest 874 adj.
shrinking violet
  humility 872 n.
  modesty 874 n.
shrinkproof
  unchangeable
    153 adj.
shrink-wrapped
  invulnerable
    660 adj.
shrive
  forgive 909 vb.
  perform ritual
    988 vb.
shrivel
  become small
    198 vb.
  dry 342 vb.
  heat 381 vb.
  deteriorate 655 vb.
shroud
  cover 226 vb.
  wrapping 226 n.
  dress 228 vb.
  grave clothes
    364 n.
  screen 421 vb.

SHU

conceal 525 vb.
Shrove Tuesday
  holy day 988 n.
shrub
  tree 366 n.
shrubbery
  wood 366 n.
  garden 370 n.
shrug
  gesticulate 547 vb.
  gesture 547 n.
shrug off
  underestimate
    483 vb.
  be indifferent
    860 vb.
**shrug one's shoul-
  ders**
  dissent 489 vb.
  not know 491 vb.
  gesticulate 547 vb.
  submit 721 vb.
shrunk
  dwarfish 196 adj.
shudder
  agitation 318 n.
  be agitated 318 vb.
  be cold 380 vb.
  show feeling
    818 vb.
  quake 854 vb.
shudder at
  dislike 861 vb.
shuffle
  mix 43 vb.
  jumble 63 vb.
  substitution 150 n.
  interchange 151 n.
  interchange
    151 vb.
  vary 152 vb.
  be in motion
    265 vb.
  gait 265 n.
  walk 267 vb.
  transpose 272 vb.
  move slowly
    278 vb.
  sophisticate
    477 vb.
  gesticulate 547 vb.
  be excitable
    822 vb.
  dance 837 vb.
  be dishonest
    930 vb.
  perfidy 930 n.

SHU

**shuffle off this mor-
  tal coil**
  die 361 vb.
shuffle the cards
  make ready
    669 vb.
shufti
  inspection 438 n.
shun
  avoid 620 vb.
  dislike 861 vb.
shunt
  transpose 272 vb.
  deflect 282 vb.
shut
  close 264 vb.
shut down
  cease 145 vb.
  close 264 vb.
  lower 311 vb.
shutdown
  stop 145 n.
  inactivity 679 n.
shut-eye
  sleep 679 n.
shut in
  interior 224 adj.
  surround 230 vb.
  close 264 vb.
  imprison 747 vb.
shut one's eyes to
  permit 756 vb.
shut one up
  make mute 578 vb.
shut out
  exclude 57 vb.
shutter
  covering 226 n.
  stopper 264 n.
  darken 418 vb.
  curtain 421 n.
  camera 442 n.
shutters
  shade 226 n.
shut the door on
  exclude 57 vb.
  prohibit 757 vb.
shut the eyes to
  be blind 439 vb.
**shut the stable door
  after the horse
  has bolted**
  lose a chance
    138 vb.
shuttle
  interchange
    151 vb.

vary 152 vb.
weaving 222 n.
travel 267 vb.
fluctuate 317 vb.
fluctuation 317 n.
shuttle diplomacy
periodicity 141 n.
shuttlewise
correlatively
12 adv.
to and fro 317 adv.
shuttling
reversion 148 n.
transference 272 n.
fluctuation 317 n.
shut up
decrease 37 vb.
cease 145 vb.
hush 399 int.
confute 479 vb.
be mute 578 vb.
hush 582 int.
imprison 747 vb.
seclude 883 vb.
shut up shop
terminate 69 vb.
cease 145 vb.
shy
recoil 280 vb.
propel 287 vb.
propulsion 287 n.
reticent 525 adj.
unwilling 598 adj.
be irresolute
601 vb.
avoid 620 vb.
artless 699 adj.
restrained 747 adj.
nervous 854 adj.
quake 854 vb.
cowardly 856 adj.
modest 874 adj.
unsociable 883 adj.
pure 950 adj.
shy from
be cowardly
856 vb.
Shylock
lender 784 n.
shyness
restraint 747 n.
dislike 861 n.
modesty 874 n.
unsociability
883 n.
shy of
incomplete 55 adj.

964

shyster
trickster 545 n.
lawyer 958 n.
Siamese Cat
cat 365 n.
Siamese twins
duality 90 n.
Siberia
coldness 380 n.
sibilant
speech sound
398 n.
sibilation 406 n.
sibling
akin 11 adj.
kinsman 11 n.
Sibyl
oracle 511 n.
sorceress 983 n.
sic
truly 494 adv.
siccative
dryer 342 n.
sick
vomiting 300 n.
sick 651 adj.
vicious 934 adj.
crapulous 949 adj.
sick and tired
bored 838 adj.
sick as a dog
vomiting 300 n.
sick as a parrot
dejected 834 adj.
sicken
be weak 163 vb.
be unpalatable
391 vb.
be ill 651 vb.
deteriorate 655 vb.
displease 827 vb.
cause dislike
861 vb.
sate 863 vb.
sickening
not nice 645 adj.
sick joke
witticism 839 n.
bad taste 847 n.
sickle
angularity 247 n.
curve 248 n.
sharp edge 256 n.
farm tool 370 n.
sick list
list 87 n.

sickly
weakly 163 adj.
colourless 426 adj.
unhealthy 651 adj.
sickness
badness 645 n.
digestive disorders
651 n.
illness 651 n.
sick of
bored 838 adj.
sated 863 adj.
sickroom
hospital 658 n.
sick to one's stomach
vomiting 300 n.
sick with worry
suffering 825 adj.
side
part 53 n.
situation 186 n.
edge 234 n.
flank 239 vb.
lateral 239 adj.
laterality 239 n.
appearance 445 n.
party 708 n.
pride 871 n.
airs 873 n.
vanity 873 n.
ostentation 875 n.
contempt 922 n.
side against
oppose 704 vb.
sidearms
sidearms 723 n.
sideboard
cabinet 194 n.
stand 218 n.
sideburns
hair 259 n.
side by side
cohesive 48 adj.
with 89 adv.
near 200 adv.
sideways 239 adv.
sidecar
bicycle 274 n.
side dish
dish 301 n.
side-effect
effect 157 n.
sidekick
inferior 35 n.
chum 880 n.
sideline
edge 234 n.

laterality 239 n.
sidelong
lateral 239 adj.
sideways 239 adv.
sidereal
celestial 321 adj.
sidereal year
period 110 n.
siderite
meteor 321 n.
side-slip
aeronautics 271 n.
fly 271 vb.
side-splitting
funny 849 adj.
sidestep
be oblique 220 vb.
flank 239 vb.
laterality 239 n.
deviate 282 vb.
deviation 282 n.
avoid 620 vb.
side street
road 624 n.
side to side
to and fro 317 adv.
sidetrack
deflect 282 vb.
sidewalk
paving 226 n.
path 624 n.
road 624 n.
sideways
sideways 239 adv.
directed 281 adj.
sideways look
look 438 n.
side with
assent 488 vb.
join a party
708 vb.
siding
laterality 239 n.
railway 624 n.
sidle
be oblique 220 vb.
flank 239 vb.
deviate 282 vb.
sidle in
enter 297 vb.
siege
circumscription
232 n.
hindrance 702 n.
attack 712 n.
Siegfried Line
defences 713 n.

sierra
  high land 209 n.
  roughness 259 n.
siesta
  sleep 679 n.
sieve
  exclude 57 vb.
  class 62 vb.
  sorting 62 n.
  porosity 263 n.
  discriminate
    463 vb.
  cleaning utensil
    648 n.
  purify 648 vb.
sift
  exclude 57 vb.
  class 62 vb.
  cultivate 370 vb.
  enquire 459 vb.
  discriminate
    463 vb.
  select 605 vb.
  purify 648 vb.
sift through
  search 459 vb.
sigh
  blow 352 vb.
  breathe 352 vb.
  respiration 352 n.
  faintness 401 n.
  sound faint 401 vb.
  cry 408 n.
  cry 408 vb.
  suffer 825 vb.
  be dejected 834 vb.
  melancholy 834 n.
  lament 836 vb.
  lamentation 836 n.
  weep 836 vb.
  be in love 887 vb.
  court 889 vb.
sigh for
  lament 836 vb.
sigh of relief
  relief 831 n.
sight
  sense 374 n.
  see 438 vb.
  vision 438 n.
  telescope 442 n.
  visibility 443 n.
  spectacle 445 n.
  firearm 723 n.
  eyesore 842 n.
  prodigy 864 n.

sight, a
  greatly 32 vb.
sight for sore eyes
  spectacle 445 n.
  pleasurableness
    826 n.
  a beauty 841 n.
sightless
  blind 439 adj.
  invisible 444 adj.
sightly
  personable 841 adj.
sight of, a
  multitude 104 n.
sights
  direction 281 n.
sight-seeing
  inspection 438 n.
  curiosity 453 n.
sigmatism
  speech defect
    580 n.
sign
  number 85 n.
  evidence 466 n.
  testify 466 vb.
  make certain
    473 vb.
  omen 511 n.
  exhibit 522 vb.
  manifestation
    522 n.
  badge 547 n.
  gesticulate 547 vb.
  gesture 547 n.
  indication 547 n.
  label 547 n.
  sign 547 vb.
  signal 547 n.
  letter 558 n.
  warning 664 n.
  command 737 n.
  command 737 vb.
  contract 765 vb.
  give security
    767 vb.
  prodigy 864 n.
signal
  remarkable 32 adj.
  manifest 522 adj.
  hint 524 n.
  gesture 547 n.
  signal 547 n.
  signal 547 vb.
  railway 624 n.
  notable 638 adj.
  command 737 n.

  command 737 vb.
signalize
  dignify 866 vb.
signalling
  telecommunication
    531 n.
signally
  remarkably 32 vb.
signatory
  signatory 765 n.
signature
  key 410 n.
  notation 410 n.
  credential 466 n.
  assent 488 n.
  identification
    547 n.
  label 547 n.
  name 561 n.
  script 586 n.
  edition 589 n.
  compact 765 n.
  title deed 767 n.
signature tune
  tune 412 n.
signet
  label 547 n.
  badge of rule
    743 n.
signet ring
  jewellery 844 n.
significant
  evidential 466 adj.
  meaningful
    514 adj.
  important 638 adj.
signification
  connotation 514 n.
  indication 547 n.
signify
  predict 511 vb.
  mean 514 vb.
  inform 524 vb.
  indicate 547 vb.
sign language
  mimicry 20 n.
  deafness 416 n.
  gesture 547 n.
  language 557 n.
  voicelessness 578 n.
  speech 579 n.
sign off
  resign 753 vb.
sign of the cross
  ritual act 988 n.
sign of the times
  indication 547 n.

sign on
  join a party
    708 vb.
sign one's death warrant
  condemn 961 vb.
sign on the dotted line
  acquiesce 488 vb.
  obey 739 vb.
  promise 764 vb.
  contract 765 vb.
  give security
    767 vb.
  bargain 791 vb.
signor
  male 372 n.
signora
  female 373 n.
  title 870 n.
signore
  title 870 n.
signorina
  female 373 n.
  title 870 n.
signpost
  orientate 281 vb.
  point to 281 vb.
  indicate 547 vb.
  signpost 547 n.
signs of the times
  omen 511 n.
signs of the zodiac
  zodiac 321 n.
sign the pledge
  be sober 948 vb.
sign-writing
  writing 586 n.
Sikh
  religionist 973 n.
silage
  provender 301 n.
silence
  hush 399 int.
  silence 399 n.
  silence 399 vb.
  confute 479 vb.
  defeat 727 vb.
  restrain 747 vb.
  unsociability
    883 n.
silent
  silent 399 adj.
  reticent 525 adj.
  stealthy 525 adj.
  voiceless 578 adj.
  unsociable 883 adj.

disapproving
924 adj.
silent film
film 445 n.
silent majority
commonalty 869 n.
silhouette
outline 233 n.
outline 233 vb.
form 243 n.
form 243 vb.
darken 418 vb.
darkness 418 n.
feature 445 n.
image 551 n.
picture 553 n.
silica
hardness 326 n.
silicosis
respiratory disease
651 n.
silk
fibre 208 n.
textile 222 n.
smoothness 258 n.
lawyer 958 n.
silky
smooth 258 adj.
soft 327 adj.
textural 331 adj.
sill
base 214 n.
shelf 218 n.
threshold 234 n.
projection 254 n.
rock 344 n.
silly
absurd 497 adj.
foolish 499 adj.
fool 501 n.
ridiculous 849 adj.
silly season
absurdity 497 n.
silo
space travel 271 n.
storage 632 n.
gun 723 n.
silt
leavings 41 n.
solid body 324 n.
soil 344 n.
semiliquidity
354 n.
silver
coat 226 vb.
white 427 adj.
whiten 427 vb.

white thing 427 n.
greyness 429 n.
money 797 n.
decorate 844 vb.
ornamentation
844 n.
silver jubilee
anniversary 141 n.
silver lining
relief 831 n.
hope 852 n.
silverplate
coat 226 vb.
silver screen
cinema 445 n.
drama 594 n.
silverside
meat 301 n.
silversmith
artisan 686 n.
silver-tongued
eloquent 579 adj.
silver wedding
anniversary 141 n.
special day 876 n.
wedding 894 n.
silvery
white 427 adj.
grey 429 adj.
simian
animal 365 adj.
similar
similar 18 adj.
similarity
similarity 18 n.
simile
analogue 18 n.
comparison 462 n.
metaphor 519 n.
ornament 574 n.
similitude
similarity 18 n.
comparison 462 n.
simmer
cook 301 vb.
effervesce 318 vb.
bubble 355 vb.
be excited 821 vb.
resent 891 vb.
simony
improbity 930 n.
simoom
gale 352 n.
heat 379 n.
simper
laughter 835 n.

simple
simple 44 adj.
soft-hued 425 adj.
credulous 487 adj.
ignorant 491 adj.
intelligible 516 adj.
plain 573 adj.
tasteful 846 adj.
plebeian 869 adj.
simple interest
gain 771 n.
interest 803 n.
simple-minded
artless 699 adj.
simpleton
ignoramus 493 n.
ninny 501 n.
simplicity
simpleness 44 n.
indiscrimination
464 n.
credulity 487 n.
ignorance 491 n.
intelligibility
516 n.
plainness 573 n.
artlessness 699 n.
facility 701 n.
good taste 846 n.
simplify
simplify 44 vb.
be intelligible
516 vb.
facilitate 701 vb.
simply
singly 88 adv.
simulacrum
sham 542 n.
simulate
imitate 20 vb.
dissemble 541 vb.
simulated
simulating 18 adj.
erroneous 495 adj.
false 541 adj.
hypocritical
541 adj.
spurious 542 adj.
untrue 543 adj.
simultaneous
synchronous
123 adj.
sin
badness 645 n.
disobedience
738 n.
wrong 914 n.

be wicked 934 vb.
vice 934 n.
wickedness 934 n.
be guilty 936 vb.
guilty act 936 n.
be impious 980 vb.
impiety 980 n.
since
subsequently
120 adv.
hence 158 adv.
sincere
simple 44 adj.
veracious 540 adj.
artless 699 adj.
pious 979 adj.
sincerity
no imitation 21 n.
veracity 540 n.
artlessness 699 n.
feeling 818 n.
probity 929 n.
piety 979 n.
sine
ratio 85 n.
sinecure
inaction 677 n.
leisure 681 n.
easy thing 701 n.
sine die
never 109 adv.
sine qua non
essential part 5 n.
speciality 80 n.
concomitant 89 n.
qualification 468 n.
supposition 512 n.
necessity 596 n.
requirement 627 n.
chief thing 638 n.
conditions 766 n.
sinews
vitality 162 n.
sinewy
stalwart 162 adj.
tough 329 adj.
sinful
bad 645 adj.
wrong 914 adj.
heinous 934 adj.
wicked 934 adj.
guilty 936 adj.
impious 980 adj.
sing
roll 403 vb.
resound 404 vb.
ululate 409 vb.

sing 413 vb.
   confess 526 vb.
   be cheerful 833 vb.
   accuse 928 vb.
singe
   burn 381 vb.
   brown 430 vb.
   hairdressing 843 n.
singer
   vocalist 413 n.
singing
   roll 403 n.
   resonance 404 n.
   vocal music 412 n.
   merry 833 adj.
single
   simple 44 adj.
   one 88 adj.
   unit 88 n.
   gramophone 414 n.
   independent
      744 adj.
single file
   line 203 n.
single-handed
   alone 88 adj.
single-minded
   obsessed 455 adj.
   resolute 599 adj.
singleness
   unity 88 n.
   celibacy 895 n.
singleness of purpose
   perseverance 600 n.
single out
   differentiate 15 vb.
   set apart 46 vb.
   select 605 vb.
single parent
   unit 88 n.
   parentage 169 n.
   divorce 896 n.
single state
   celibacy 895 n.
singlet
   underwear 228 n.
single track
   narrow 206 adj.
sing like a canary
   confess 526 vb.
singly
   singly 88 adv.
Sing Sing
   prison 748 n.
sing-song
   uniform 16 adj.
   uniformity 16 n.

singsong
   repeated 106 adj.
   discordant 411 adj.
   music 412 n.
   social gathering
      882 n.
sing the praises
   honour 866 vb.
   praise 923 vb.
singular
   remarkable 32 adj.
   special 80 adj.
   unusual 84 adj.
   one 88 adj.
   grammatical
      564 adj.
singularly
   remarkably 32 vb.
   eminently 34 adv.
sinister
   predicting 511 adj.
   heraldic 547 adj.
   heraldry 547 n.
   evil 616 adj.
   bad 645 adj.
   harmful 645 adj.
   adverse 731 adj.
   frightening
      854 adj.
   dishonest 930 adj.
sinistral
   sinistrality 242 n.
sink
   be inferior 35 vb.
   decrease 37 vb.
   be destroyed
      165 vb.
   destroy 165 vb.
      See **suppress**
   suppress 165 vb.
   be in motion
      265 vb.
   descend 309 vb.
   lower 311 vb.
   sit down 311 vb.
   founder 313 vb.
   plunge 313 vb.
   sink 649 n.
   be ill 651 vb.
   deteriorate 655 vb.
   be fatigued 684 vb.
   defeat 727 vb.
   have trouble
      731 vb.
   lose 772 vb.
   not pay 805 vb.
   be dejected 834 vb.

   lose repute 867 vb.
sinkage
   descent 309 n.
   gravity 322 n.
sink in
   infiltrate 297 vb.
   descend 309 vb.
   cause thought
      449 vb.
   be intelligible
      516 vb.
   impress 821 vb.
sinking
   decrease 37 n.
   decreasing 37 adj.
   ruin 165 n.
   motion 265 n.
   relapse 657 n.
sink into obscurity
   be inferior 35 vb.
sink or swim
   certainly 473 adv.
sunk without trace
   be inferior 35 vb.
   suppress 165 vb.
   descend 309 vb.
   founder 313 vb.
sinner
   evildoer 904 n.
   offender 904 n.
   bad person 938 n.
   devil 969 n.
   impious person
      980 n.
sin of omission
   guilty act 936 n.
sinuous
   convoluted 251 adj.
   snaky 251 adj.
sinus
   cavity 255 n.
sinusitis
   respiratory disease
      651 n.
sip
   small quantity
      33 n.
   draught 301 n.
   drink 301 vb.
   mouthful 301 n.
   taste 386 vb.
siphon
   soft drink 301 n.
   conduit 351 n.
siphon off
   transpose 272 vb.
   empty 300 vb.

sir
   male 372 n.
   name 561 vb.
   speak to 583 vb.
   master 741 n.
   dignify 866 vb.
   title 870 n.
sire
   be akin 11 vb.
   generate 167 vb.
   master 741 n.
   title 870 n.
siren
   rara avis 84 n.
   timekeeper 117 n.
   attraction 291 n.
   sea nymph 343 n.
   loudness 400 n.
   megaphone 400 n.
   signal 547 n.
   motivator 612 n.
   warning 664 n.
   danger signal
      665 n.
   a beauty 841 n.
   nymph 967 n.
sirloin
   meat 301 n.
sirocco
   storm 176 n.
   wind 352 n.
   heat 379 n.
sisal
   fibre 208 n.
sissy
   weakling 163 n.
   male 372 n.
   coward 856 n.
   cowardly 856 adj.
sister
   kinsman 11 n.
   female 373 n.
   nurse 658 n.
   colleague 707 n.
   friend 880 n.
   church title 986 n.
   nun 986 n.
sisterhood
   family 11 n.
   group 74 n.
   community 708 n.
   friendship 880 n.
   sect 978 n.
   nun 986 n.
sisterly
   akin 11 adj.
   friendly 880 adj.

loving 887 adj.
benevolent 897 adj.
Sisyphean labour
hard task 700 n.
noncompletion
726 n.
sit
place oneself
187 vb.
sit down 311 vb.
be inactive 679 vb.
sitar
stringed instrument
414 n.
sit at the feet of
learn 536 vb.
sit back
not act 677 vb.
repose 683 vb.
sitcom
broadcast 531 n.
stage play 594 n.
sit down
be quiescent
266 vb.
sit down 311 vb.
sit-down strike
strike 145 n.
site
place 185 n.
situation 186 n.
locality 187 n.
place 187 vb.
station 187 n.
sit for
be an example
23 vb.
represent 551 vb.
sit in
participate 775 vb.
sit-in
assembly 74 n.
strike 145 n.
presence 189 n.
deprecation 762 n.
malcontent 829 n.
sit in judgment
judge 480 vb.
try a case 959 vb.
sit it out
go on 146 vb.
sit on
predominate 34 vb.
suppress 165 vb.
place oneself
187 vb.
subjugate 745 vb.

restrain 747 vb.
be parsimonious
816 vb.
humiliate 872 vb.
sit on one's tail
come after 65 vb.
follow 284 vb.
approach 289 vb.
obstruct 702 vb.
sit on the fence
be uncertain
474 vb.
be equivocal
518 vb.
be neutral 606 vb.
not act 677 vb.
compromise
770 vb.
be indifferent
860 vb.
sit out
carry through
725 vb.
sitter
living model 23 n.
respondent 460 n.
sit tight
be quiescent
266 vb.
not act 677 vb.
sitting duck
dupe 544 n.
vulnerability 661 n.
easy thing 701 n.
sitting pretty
successful 727 adj.
content 828 n.
sitting tenant
resident 191 n.
situated, be
be situated 186 vb.
situation
circumstance 8 n.
affairs 154 n.
event 154 n.
situation 186 n.
job 622 n.
situation comedy
broadcast 531 n.
stage play 594 n.
sit up
be vertical 215 vb.
sit up and take notice
be attentive 455 vb.
six
over five 99 n.

sixer
over five 99 n.
six feet under
dead 361 adj.
six-footer
tall creature 209 n.
**six of one and half a
dozen of the
other**
equivalence 28 n.
sixpence
coinage 797 n.
six-shooter
pistol 723 n.
sixth
musical note
410 n.
sixth sense
sense 374 n.
intellect 447 n.
intuition 476 n.
occultism 984 n.
sixty
twenty and over
99 n.
**sixty-four- thousand-
dollar question,
the**
question 459 n.
difficulty 700 n.
sizable
great 32 adj.
large 195 adj.
size
make uniform
16 vb.
degree 27 n.
adhesive 47 n.
arrange 62 vb.
size 195 n.
coat 226 vb.
viscidity 354 n.
importance 638 n.
size up
appraise 465 vb.
measure 465 vb.
estimate 480 vb.
sizzle
effervesce 318 vb.
be hot 379 vb.
crackle 402 vb.
hiss 406 vb.
be excited 821 vb.
resent 891 vb.
skate
be in motion
265 vb.

travel 267 vb.
sled 274 n.
fish food 301 n.
amuse oneself
837 vb.
skateboard
sled 274 n.
plaything 837 n.
skate on thin ice
be in danger
661 vb.
skate over
neglect 458 vb.
skating
motion 265 n.
sport 837 n.
skating rink
arena 724 n.
pleasure ground
837 n.
skean-dhu
sidearms 723 n.
skedaddle
come along
267 int.
move fast 277 vb.
decamp 296 vb.
run away 620 vb.
skein
bunch 74 n.
group 74 n.
crossing 222 n.
skeletal
weak 163 adj.
lean 206 adj.
skeleton
remainder 41 n.
chief part 52 n.
incompleteness
55 n.
thinness 206 n.
frame 218 n.
outline 233 n.
structure 331 n.
corpse 363 n.
compendium
592 n.
plan 623 n.
intimidation
854 n.
skeleton at the feast
moper 834 n.
**skeleton in the cup-
board**
secret 530 n.
skeleton key
opener 263 n.

skelter
instrument 628 n.

skelter
move fast 277 vb.

skerry
rock 344 n.
island 349 n.

sketch
copy 22 n.
prototype 23 n.
incompleteness
55 n.
outline 233 n.
outline 233 vb.
form 243 vb.
record 548 n.
represent 551 vb.
representation
551 n.
paint 553 vb.
picture 553 n.
describe 590 vb.
description 590 n.
compendium
592 n.
stage play 594 n.
plan 623 n.
prepare 669 vb.

sketch in the back-
ground
relate 9 vb.

sketch out
outline 233 vb.
represent 551 vb.
abstract 592 vb.
plan 623 vb.

sketchy
incomplete 55 adj.
uncompleted
726 adj.

skew
statistics 86 n.
distort 246 vb.
deflect 282 vb.

skewer
fastening 47 n.
sharp point 256 n.
perforator 263 n.
pierce 263 vb.

ski
be in motion
265 vb.
travel 267 vb.
amuse oneself
837 vb.

skid
gait 265 n.
deviate 282 vb.

skier
pedestrian 268 n.

skiff
boat 275 n.
rowing boat 275 n.

skiffle
music 412 n.

skiing
sport 837 n.

skilful
skilful 694 adj.

skill
skill 694 n.

skillet
pot 194 n.

skim
be contiguous
202 vb.
travel 267 vb.
move fast 277 vb.
purify 648 vb.

skim off
select 605 vb.

skimp
shorten 204 vb.
neglect 458 vb.
be parsimonious
816 vb.

skimpy
small 33 adj.
short 204 adj.
insufficient
636 adj.

skim through
scan 438 vb.

skin
subtract 39 vb.
leavings 41 n.
disunite 46 vb.
skin 226 n.
uncover 229 vb.
rub 333 vb.
fleece 786 vb.
overcharge 811 vb.

skin-and-bone
lean 206 adj.
underfed 636 adj.

skin-deep
shallow 212 adj.
exterior 223 adj.

skin diving
sport 837 n.

skinflick
film 445 n.
impurity 951 n.

skinflint
niggard 816 n.

skinhead
youngster 132 n.
ruffian 904 n.

skinny
weakly 163 adj.
lean 206 adj.
narrow 206 adj.

skin-search
search 459 n.
search 459 vb.

skintight
cohesive 48 adj.

skip
be absent 190 vb.
vessel 194 n.
gait 265 n.
walk 267 vb.
decamp 296 vb.
leap 312 n.
leap 312 vb.
neglect 458 vb.
study 536 vb.
escape 667 vb.
not complete
726 vb.
rejoice 835 vb.

skipper
mariner 270 n.
direct 689 vb.
director 690 n.

skirl
be loud 400 vb.
shrill 407 vb.
stridor 407 n.

skirmish
fight 716 n.
fight 716 vb.
battle 718 n.

skirt
be contiguous
202 vb.
base 214 n.
hanging object
217 n.
skirt 228 n.
edge 234 n.
flank 239 vb.
meat 301 n.
pass 305 vb.
circle 314 vb.
female 373 n.
circuit 626 vb.

skirt round
avoid 620 vb.

skis
sled 274 n.

skit
stage play 594 n.
satire 851 n.
calumny 926 n.

skitter
be in motion
265 vb.

skittish
capricious 604 adj.
excitable 822 adj.

skittle alley
arena 724 n.

skittles
ball game 837 n.

skive
be absent 190 vb.
be inactive 679 vb.
not complete
726 vb.

skivvy
domestic 742 n.
servant 742 n.

skol
bon appétit 301 int.

skua
bird 365 n.

skulduggery
trickery 542 n.
improbity 930 n.

skulk
wander 267 vb.
be stealthy 525 vb.
be cowardly
856 vb.

skull
head 213 n.
dome 253 n.
corpse 363 n.

skull and crossbones
cross 222 n.
flag 547 n.
heraldry 547 n.
intimidation
854 n.

skullcap
headgear 228 n.
canonicals 989 n.

skunk
mammal 365 n.
stench 397 n.
cad 938 n.

sky
space 183 n.
height 209 n.
summit 213 n.
propel 287 vb.
heavens 321 n.

skydiving
  aeronautics 271 n.
sky-high
  enormous 32 adj.
  high 209 adj.
  dear 811 adj.
skyjack
  steal 788 vb.
  stealing 788 n.
skylab
  satellite 321 n.
skylarking
  foolery 497 n.
  revel 837 n.
skylight
  window 263 n.
skyline
  distance 199 n.
  horizontality
    216 n.
  outline 233 n.
  edge 234 n.
  limit 236 n.
  visibility 443 n.
skyscraper
  edifice 164 n.
  high structure
    209 n.
slab
  piece 53 n.
  horizontality
    216 n.
  shelf 218 n.
slabber
  moisture 341 n.
slack
  weak 163 adj.
  inert 175 adj.
  slow 278 adj.
  soft 327 adj.
  coal 385 n.
  negligent 458 adj.
  be inactive 679 vb.
  lazy 679 adj.
  lax 734 adj.
slacken
  decrease 37 vb.
  disunite 46 vb.
  moderate 177 vb.
  decelerate 278 vb.
  be inactive 679 vb.
slacken off
  cease 145 vb.
  decelerate 278 vb.
slacks
  informal dress
    228 n.

  trousers 228 n.
slag
  leavings 41 n.
  slut 61 n.
  rubbish 641 n.
  reproach 924 vb.
slag heap
  rubbish 641 n.
slag off
  cuss 899 vb.
slake
  assuage 177 vb.
  sate 863 vb.
slake one's thirst
  drink 301 vb.
slalom
  racing 716 n.
slam
  close 264 vb.
  impel 279 vb.
  impulse 279 n.
  strike 279 vb.
  propel 287 vb.
  be loud 400 vb.
  loudness 400 n.
  bang 402 n.
  bang 402 vb.
  victory 727 n.
  detract 926 vb.
slammer
  lockup 748 n.
  prison 748 n.
slander
  slur 867 n.
  scurrility 899 n.
  censure 924 n.
  calumny 926 n.
  defame 926 vb.
  false charge 928 n.
slang
  speciality 80 n.
  unintelligibility
    517 n.
  language 557 n.
  slang 560 adj.
  cuss 899 vb.
  criticize 924 vb.
slanging match
  interlocution
    584 n.
  quarrel 709 n.
  scurrility 899 n.
slant
  be oblique 220 vb.
  obliquity 220 n.
  idea 451 n.
  bias 481 n.

slap
  knock 279 n.
  strike 279 vb.
  bang 402 n.
  crackle 402 vb.
  corporal punish-
    ment 963 n.
  spank 963 vb.
slapdash
  negligent 458 adj.
  hasty 680 adj.
  bungled 695 adj.
  clumsy 695 adj.
  rash 857 adj.
slap in the face
  refusal 760 n.
  humiliation 872 n.
  anger 891 n.
  indignity 921 n.
slapstick
  dramatic 594 adj.
  stage play 594 n.
  wit 839 n.
  funny 849 adj.
  ridiculousness
    849 n.
slap-up
  liberal 813 adj.
slash
  cut 46 vb.
  rend 46 vb.
  shorten 204 vb.
  notch 260 vb.
  furrow 262 n.
  wound 655 vb.
  discount 810 vb.
  cheapen 812 vb.
  criticize 924 vb.
slat
  strip 208 n.
slate
  brittleness 330 n.
  greyness 429 n.
  stationery 586 n.
  policy 623 n.
  building material
    631 n.
  criticize 924 vb.
  reproach 924 vb.
  detract 926 vb.
slating
  roof 226 n.
  censure 924 n.
  reprimand 924 n.
slats
  shade 226 n.

slattern
  slut 61 n.
  dirty person 649 n.
  bungler 697 n.
slaughter
  slaughter 362 n.
  slaughter 362 vb.
slave
  instrument 628 n.
  be active 678 vb.
  minister to 703 vb.
  servant 742 n.
  slave 742 n.
  toady 879 n.
slave away
  work 682 vb.
slave-driver
  tyrant 735 n.
slavery
  labour 682 n.
  compulsion 740 n.
  servitude 745 n.
  detention 747 n.
  servility 879 n.
slave to, a
  subject 745 n.
slavish
  imitative 20 adj.
  conformable
    83 adj.
  subjected 745 adj.
  servile 879 adj.
slay
  kill 362 vb.
  amuse 837 vb.
sled
  sled 274 n.
sledge
  be in motion
    265 vb.
  sled 274 n.
sledgehammer
  hammer 279 n.
  pulverizer 332 n.
sleek
  smooth 258 adj.
  personable 841 adj.
sleep
  sleep 679 n.
  sleep 679 vb.
sleep around
  be impure 951 vb.
sleeper
  basis 218 n.
  train 274 n.
  secret service
    459 n.

book 589 n.
sleep in
  fail in duty 918 vb.
sleeping bag
  bag 194 n.
sleeping dog
  latency 523 n.
  pitfall 663 n.
sleeping pill
  moderator 177 n.
  drug 658 n.
  soporific 679 n.
sleepless
  active 678 adj.
sleep on it
  wait 136 vb.
  meditate 449 vb.
sleepwalking
  pedestrianism
    267 n.
  sleep 679 n.
sleep with
  unite with 45 vb.
  debauch 951 vb.
sleepy
  sleepy 679 adj.
sleet
  rain 350 n.
  rain 350 VB.
  wintriness 380 n.
sleeve
  sleeve 228 n.
sleigh
  sled 274 n.
sleight
  sleight 542 n.
sleight of hand
  sleight 542 n.
  skill 694 n.
  cunning 698 n.
slender
  small 33 adj.
  narrow 206 adj.
  insufficient
    636 adj.
  shapely 841 adj.
sleuth
  detective 459 n.
  informer 524 n.
  hunter 619 n.
  pursue 619 vb.
'S' level
  exam 459 n.
slew
  deviate 282 vb.
  deviation 282 n.
  rotate 315 vb.

slice
  cut 46 vb.
  piece 53 n.
  ladle 194 n.
  notch 260 vb.
  deflect 282 vb.
  propel 287 vb.
  be clumsy 695 vb.
  bungling 695 n.
  portion 783 n.
slice (golf)
  propulsion 287 n.
slice of the cake
  portion 783 n.
slick
  smooth 258 adj.
  skilful 694 adj.
  cunning 698 adj.
slick down
  smooth 258 vb.
slide
  fastening 47 n.
  elapse 111 vb.
  obliquity 220 n.
  smoothness 258 n.
  be in motion
    265 vb.
  gait 265 n.
  travel 267 vb.
  descent 309 n.
  photography 551 n.
  deteriorate 655 vb.
  not act 677 vb.
  fail 728 vb.
  hairdressing 843 n.
slide rule
  counting instru-
    ment 86 n.
  gauge 465 n.
sliding
  motion 265 n.
  frail 934 adj.
slight
  inconsiderable
    33 adj.
  small 33 adj.
  weak 163 adj.
  narrow 206 adj.
  shallow 212 adj.
  rare 325 adj.
  disregard 458 vb.
  underestimate
    483 vb.
  trivial 639 adj.
  slur 867 n.
  humiliate 872 vb.
  indignity 921 n.

  not respect 921 vb.
  contempt 922 n.
  hold cheap 922 vb.
  detract 926 vb.
slightly
  slightly 33 adv.
slightly-built
  weak 163 adj.
  narrow 206 adj.
slightness
  weakness 163 n.
slim
  small 33 adj.
  make smaller
    198 vb.
  make thin 206 vb.
  narrow 206 adj.
  shapely 841 adj.
slim down
  render few 105 vb.
slime
  moisture 341 n.
  semiliquidity
    354 n.
  dirt 649 n.
slimming
  dieting 301 n.
slimy
  humid 341 adj.
  viscid 354 adj.
  dirty 649 adj.
  unpleasant
    827 adj.
  servile 879 adj.
  flattering 925 adj.
sling
  bag 194 n.
  propel 287 vb.
  propellant 287 n.
  propulsion 287 n.
  surgical dressing
    658 n.
  missile weapon
    723 n.
sling out
  reject 607 vb.
slings and arrows
  evil 616 n.
slink
  lurk 523 vb.
  be stealthy 525 vb.
slink off
  run away 620 vb.
slinky
  narrow 206 adj.
  shapely 841 adj.

slip
  small thing 33 n.
  come unstuck
    49 vb.
  branch 53 n.
  elapse 111 vb.
  young plant 132 n.
  youngster 132 n.
  dwarf 196 n.
  thinness 206 n.
  underwear 228 n.
  gait 265 n.
  descend 309 vb.
  blunder 495 vb.
  mistake 495 n.
  deteriorate 655 vb.
  failure 728 n.
  be wicked 934 vb.
  guilty act 936 n.
slip away
  go away 190 vb.
  decamp 296 vb.
slip back
  revert 148 vb.
  regress 286 vb.
  fall short 307 vb.
  relapse 657 vb.
slip by
  elapse 111 vb.
slip knot
  ligature 47 n.
slip of the pen
  mistake 495 n.
  solecism 565 n.
slip of the tongue
  mistake 495 n.
  solecism 565 n.
slip one's memory
  be forgotten
    506 vb.
slippage
  deficit 55 n.
  incompleteness
    55 n.
  shortness 204 n.
  shortfall 307 n.
  descent 309 n.
  requirement 627 n.
  insufficiency 636 n.
  scarcity 636 n.
slipper
  footwear 228 n.
slippers
  informal dress
    228 n.
slippery
  smooth 258 adj.

unsafe 661 adj.
cunning 698 adj.
dishonest 930 adj.
slippery slope
  ruin 165 n.
  danger 661 n.
  predicament 700 n.
  wickedness 934 n.
sliproad
  road 624 n.
slips
  workshop 687 n.
slipshod
  negligent 458 adj.
  lax 734 adj.
slip through one's
  fingers
  escape 667 vb.
slip 'twixt the cup
  and the lip
  disappointment
    509 n.
slip up
  blunder 495 vb.
slip–up
  mistake 495 n.
slipway
  smoothness 258 n.
slit
  cut 46 vb.
  disunion 46 n.
  rend 46 vb.
  See **cut**
  sunder 46 vb.
  gap 201 n.
  furrow 262 n.
  wound 655 vb.
slither
  be in motion
    265 vb.
sliver
  small thing 33 n.
  piece 53 n.
slivovitz
  alcoholic drink
    301 n.
Sloane Ranger
  idler 679 n.
  beau monde 848 n.
Sloane Rangers
  elite 644 n.
slob
  bungler 697 n.
  cad 938 n.
slobber
  exude 298 vb.
  emit 300 vb.

excrement 302 n.
excrete 302 vb.
be wet 341 vb.
moisture 341 n.
sloe
  tree 366 n.
  sourness 393 n.
  black thing 428 n.
slog
  strike 279 vb.
  propel 287 vb.
  be active 678 vb.
  work 682 vb.
slogan
  maxim 496 n.
  advertisement
    528 n.
  phrase 563 n.
  instrument 628 n.
slog away
  persevere 600 vb.
sloop
  sailing ship 275 n.
slop
  let fall 311 vb.
  moisten 341 vb.
  semiliquidity
    354 n.
  be clumsy 695 vb.
slope
  high land 209 n.
  be oblique 220 vb.
  obliquity 220 n.
  ascent 308 n.
  descent 309 n.
slope off
  travel 267 vb.
  decamp 296 vb.
  run away 620 vb.
sloping
  sloping 220 adj.
  written 586 adj.
sloppy
  humid 341 adj.
  negligent 458 adj.
  feeble 572 adj.
slosh
  strike 279 vb.
  drench 341 vb.
  flow 350 vb.
sloshed
  dead drunk
    949 adj.
slot
  sorting 62 n.
  serial place 73 n.
  classification 77 n.

place 185 n.
receptacle 194 n.
gap 201 n.
furrow 262 n.
groove 262 vb.
orifice 263 n.
sloth
  inertness 175 n.
  sluggishness 679 n.
  vice 934 n.
slothful
  lazy 679 adj.
slot in
  place 187 vb.
slot machine
  shop 796 n.
  treasury 799 n.
slouch
  move slowly
    278 vb.
  slowcoach 278 n.
  stoop 311 vb.
  be inactive 679 vb.
slough
  leavings 41 n.
  gulf 345 n.
  marsh 347 n.
  relinquish 621 vb.
  dirt 649 n.
  stop using 674 vb.
  difficulty 700 n.
Slough of Despond
  marsh 347 n.
  adversity 731 n.
  dejection 834 n.
slough off
  disaccustom
    611 vb.
slovenly
  negligent 458 adj.
  dirty 649 adj.
  clumsy 695 adj.
slow
  slow 278 adj.
  inexact 495 adj.
  unintelligent
    499 adj.
  impassive 820 adj.
  tedious 838 adj.
  cautious 858 adj.
slowcoach
  slowcoach 278 n.
slow down
  decelerate 278 vb.
  repose 683 vb.
  hinder 702 vb.

slow handclap
  disapprobation
    924 n.
slowly
  slowly 278 adv.
slowly but surely
  by degrees 27 adv.
slow motion
  motion 265 n.
  slowness 278 n.
slow-motion
  slow 278 adj.
slowness
  slowness 278 n.
  unintelligence
    499 n.
  unskilfulness
    695 n.
  moral insensibility
    820 n.
slow on the uptake
  unintelligent
    499 adj.
slow up
  decelerate 278 vb.
slowworm
  reptile 365 n.
slubbed
  rough 259 adj.
sludge
  leavings 41 n.
  semiliquidity
    354 n.
  dirt 649 n.
slug
  knock 279 n.
  strike 279 vb.
  draught 301 n.
  creepy-crawly
    365 n.
  print-type 587 n.
  ammunition 723 n.
sluggard
  slowcoach 278 n.
  idler 679 n.
sluggish
  late 136 adj.
  inert 175 adj.
  slow 278 adj.
  nonactive 677 adj.
  inactive 679 adj.
  lazy 679 adj.
  apathetic 820 adj.
  dejected 834 adj.
  dull 840 adj.
sluice
  outlet 298 n.

drench 341 vb.
irrigator 341 n.
conduit 351 n.
clean 648 vb.
slum
housing 192 n.
sink 649 n.
insalubrity 653 n.
dilapidation 655 n.
poverty 801 n.
slumber
quietude 266 n.
sleep 679 n.
sleep 679 vb.
slump
decrease 37 n.
decrease 37 vb.
unproductiveness
  172 n.
contraction 198 n.
regress 286 vb.
regression 286 n.
fall short 307 vb.
descend 309 vb.
descent 309 n.
tumble 309 vb.
deteriorate 655 vb.
deterioration
  655 n.
be inactive 679 vb.
inactivity 679 n.
adversity 731 n.
poverty 801 n.
cheapness 812 n.
slur
speech defect
  580 n.
stammer 580 vb.
slur 867 n.
censure 924 n.
extenuate 927 vb.
slush
semiliquidity
  354 n.
pulpiness 356 n.
slush fund
incentive 612 n.
gift 781 n.
reward 962 n.
slushy
humid 341 adj.
marshy 347 adj.
slut
slut 61 n.
dirty person 649 n.
loose woman
  952 n.

sly
hypocritical
  541 adj.
cunning 698 adj.
merry 833 adj.
witty 839 adj.
affected 850 adj.
smack
tincture 43 n.
sailing ship 275 n.
knock 279 n.
strike 279 vb.
taste 386 n.
bang 402 n.
crackle 402 vb.
drug-taking 949 n.
corporal punish-
  ment 963 n.
spank 963 vb.
smacker
funds 797 n.
endearment 889 n.
smack of
resemble 18 vb.
taste 386 vb.
indicate 547 vb.
smack one's lips
enjoy 376 vb.
be pleased 824 vb.
rejoice 835 vb.
smack on the wrist
reprimand 924 n.
punish 963 vb.
spank 963 vb.
small
small 33 adj.
lesser 35 adj.
unimportant
  639 adj.
small ad
information 524 n.
advertisement
  528 n.
small arms
firearm 723 n.
small beer
alcoholic drink
  301 n.
nonentity 639 n.
trifle 639 n.
small-beer
lesser 35 adj.
small-built
small 33 adj.
small change
trifle 639 n.
coinage 797 n.

money 797 n.
smaller
small 33 adj.
lesser 35 adj.
smallest room
chamber 194 n.
small fry
inferior 35 n.
child 132 n.
weakling 163 n.
nonentity 639 n.
lower classes 869 n.
smallholding
farm 370 n.
small hours
morning 128 n.
midnight 129 n.
lateness 136 n.
small letter
letter 558 n.
small-mindedness
narrow mind
  481 n.
smallness
smallness 33 n.
invisibility 444 n.
smallpox
infection 651 n.
small print
conditions 766 n.
smalls
underwear 228 n.
small screen
broadcasting
  531 n.
small-sized
small 33 adj.
small talk
chatter 581 n.
chat 584 n.
smarmy
flattering 925 adj.
smart
speedy 277 adj.
feel pain 377 vb.
pang 377 n.
intelligent 498 adj.
active 678 adj.
skilful 694 adj.
cunning 698 adj.
suffer 825 vb.
suffering 825 n.
witty 839 adj.
personable 841 adj.
fashionable
  848 adj.
huff 891 vb.

smart alec
wiseacre 500 n.
vain person 873 n.
smart ass
wiseacre 500 n.
vain person 873 n.
smart-ass
vain 873 adj.
smarten
decorate 844 vb.
smarten up
beautify 841 vb.
smart under
feel 818 vb.
resent 891 vb.
smash
break 46 vb.
demolish 165 vb.
ruin 165 n.
force 176 vb.
collision 279 n.
strike 279 vb.
propel 287 vb.
pulverize 332 vb.
wound 655 vb.
smash (tennis)
propulsion 287 n.
smash and grab raid
stealing 788 n.
smashed
dead drunk
  949 adj.
smash hit
dramaturgy 594 n.
exceller 644 n.
masterpiece 694 n.
success 727 n.
smashing
super 644 adj.
smash up
demolish 165 vb.
smashup
collision 279 n.
smattering
erudition 490 n.
knowledge 490 n.
sciolism 491 n.
smear
coat 226 vb.
dim 419 vb.
make unclean
  649 vb.
blemish 845 n.
blemish 845 vb.
shame 867 vb.
slur 867 n.
calumny 926 n.

973

defame 926 vb.
smear campaign
  discontent 829 n.
  disrepute 867 n.
  detraction 926 n.
smear test
  diagnostic 658 n.
smell
  small quantity
    33 n.
  have feeling
    374 vb.
  sense 374 n.
  odour 394 n.
  smell 394 vb.
  stink 397 vb.
  trace 548 n.
  be unclean 649 vb.
  deteriorate 655 vb.
smell a rat
  detect 484 vb.
  doubt 486 vb.
smelling salts
  pungency 388 n.
  tonic 658 n.
smell of the lamp
  ornament 574 vb.
smell out
  smell 394 vb.
  discover 484 vb.
smelly
  odorous 394 adj.
  fetid 397 adj.
smelt
  liquefy 337 vb.
smelter
  workshop 687 n.
smidgen
  small quantity
    33 n.
  fewness 105 n.
smile
  gesticulate 547 vb.
  gesture 547 n.
  be pleased 824 vb.
  be cheerful 833 vb.
  laughter 835 n.
  smile 835 vb.
  courteous act
    884 n.
  greet 884 vb.
smile on
  be auspicious
    730 vb.
smirch
  defame 926 vb.
  debauch 951 vb.

smirk
  laughter 835 n.
  smile 835 vb.
  flatter 925 vb.
smirk at
  ridicule 851 vb.
smite
  strike 279 vb.
smith
  artisan 686 n.
smithereens
  small thing 33 n.
smitten
  enamoured
    887 adj.
smock
  shirt 228 n.
  fold 261 vb.
smocking
  needlework 844 n.
smog
  powder 332 n.
  cloud 355 n.
  opacity 423 n.
  insalubrity 653 n.
  poison 659 n.
smoke
  emit 300 vb.
  powder 332 n.
  gas 336 n.
  vaporize 338 vb.
  dry 342 vb.
  be hot 379 vb.
  season 388 vb.
  smoke 388 vb.
  tobacco 388 n.
  odour 394 n.
  dirt 649 n.
  make unclean
    649 vb.
  preserve 666 vb.
  mature 669 vb.
  drug oneself
    949 vb.
smokeless
  coal 385 n.
smokeless zone
  air 340 n.
smoke out
  eject 300 vb.
  extract 304 vb.
smoker
  train 274 n.
  tobacco 388 n.
smoke-screen
  screen 421 n.
  opacity 423 n.

  invisibility 444 n.
  concealment 525 n.
  disguise 527 n.
  trickery 542 n.
  pretext 614 n.
  defences 713 n.
smoking
  fiery 379 adj.
  hot 379 adj.
  tobacco 388 n.
  drug-taking 949 n.
smoking jacket
  informal dress
    228 n.
smoky
  dense 324 adj.
  powdery 332 adj.
  vaporific 338 adj.
  heated 381 adj.
  pungent 388 adj.
  fetid 397 adj.
  dim 419 adj.
  opaque 423 adj.
  black 428 adj.
  grey 429 adj.
  dirty 649 adj.
smooch
  caress 889 vb.
smooth
  continuous 71 adj.
  flat 216 adj.
  symmetrical
    245 adj.
  smooth 258 adj.
  smooth 258 vb.
  hypocritical
    541 adj.
  caress 889 vb.
  flatter 925 vb.
  flattering 925 adj.
smooth down
  flatten 216 vb.
smoothen
  smooth 258 vb.
smooth the way
  make possible
    469 vb.
smoothing-iron
  smoother 258 n.
smoothly
  easily 701 adv.
smooth one's ruffled
  feathers
  pacify 719 vb.
smooth over
  assuage 177 vb.
  smooth 258 vb.

smooth sailing
  easy thing 701 n.
smooth-tongued
  hypocritical
    541 adj.
  eloquent 579 adj.
  flattering 925 adj.
smorgasbord
  hors-d'oeuvres
    301 n.
smother
  disable 161 vb.
  suppress 165 vb.
  moderate 177 vb.
  cover 226 vb.
  close 264 vb.
  kill 362 vb.
  murder 362 vb.
  extinguish 382 vb.
  conceal 525 vb.
  pet 889 vb.
smoulder
  be hot 379 vb.
  lurk 523 vb.
  be inactive 679 vb.
  resent 891 vb.
smudge
  blur 440 vb.
  defect 647 n.
  dirt 649 n.
  make unclean
    649 vb.
  blemish 845 n.
  blemish 845 vb.
  slur 867 vb.
smug
  affected 850 adj.
  vain 873 adj.
smuggle
  steal 788 vb.
smuggling
  trade 791 n.
smut
  powder 332 n.
  black thing 428 n.
  dirt 649 n.
  blemish 845 n.
  impurity 951 n.
smutty
  black 428 adj.
  unclean 649 adj.
  impure 951 adj.
snack
  small quantity
    33 n.
  eat 301 vb.
  meal 301 n.

mouthful 301 n.

snaffle
  take 786 vb.
  steal 788 vb.

snag
  defect 647 n.
  danger 661 n.
  pitfall 663 n.
  difficulty 700 n.
  hitch 702 n.
  obstacle 702 n.

snail
  slowcoach 278 n.
  creepy-crawly
    365 n.

snail's pace
  slowness 278 n.

snake
  meander 251 vb.
  serpent 251 n.
  reptile 365 n.
  bane 659 n.
  slyboots 698 n.
  finance 797 n.

snake in the grass
  latency 523 n.
  deceiver 545 n.
  badness 645 n.
  bane 659 n.
  troublemaker
    663 n.
  evildoer 904 n.

snakes and ladders
  board game 837 n.

snaky
  snaky 251 adj.
  animal 365 adj.

snap
  break 46 vb.
  instantaneous
    116 adj.
  vigorousness 174 n.
  bang 402 n.
  crackle 402 vb.
  ululate 409 vb.
  ululation 409 n.
  gesticulate 547 vb.
  photograph 551 vb.
  photography 551 n.
  picture 553 n.
  spontaneous
    609 adj.
  unprepared
    670 adj.
  card game 837 n.
  hatred 888 n.
  anger 891 n.

be angry 891 vb.
sullenness 893 n.

snap decision
  spontaneity 609 n.

snapdragon
  plant 366 n.

snap fastener
  fastening 47 n.

snap one's fingers at
  defy 711 vb.
  not observe 769 vb.
  hold cheap 922 vb.

snap out of it
  be restored 656 vb.
  be cheerful 833 vb.

snappy
  vigorous 174 adj.
  speedy 277 adj.
  aphoristic 496 adj.
  witty 839 adj.
  irascible 892 adj.

snapshot
  photography 551 n.

snap up
  take 786 vb.

snare
  ensnare 542 vb.
  trap 542 n.
  take 786 vb.

Snark
  rara avis 84 n.

snarl
  complexity 61 n.
  distortion 246 n.
  ululate 409 vb.
  ululation 409 n.
  be rude 885 vb.
  hatred 888 n.
  anger 891 n.
  be angry 891 vb.
  sullenness 893 n.
  threat 900 n.
  threaten 900 vb.

snarl-up
  complexity 61 n.

snatch
  small quantity
    33 n.
  arrest 747 vb.
  take 786 vb.

snatch at
  take 786 vb.

snazzy
  fashionable
    848 adj.

sneak
  informer 524 n.

be stealthy 525 vb.
bad person 938 n.

sneakers
  footwear 228 n.

sneak out
  emerge 298 vb.
  escape 667 vb.

sneak thief
  thief 789 n.

sneer
  insolence 878 n.
  contempt 922 n.
  criticize 924 vb.
  reproach 924 n.
  calumny 926 n.

sneer at
  dislike 861 vb.
  be insolent 878 vb.
  detract 926 vb.

sneeze
  breathe 352 vb.

snicker
  laugh 835 vb.
  laughter 835 n.

snide remark
  detraction 926 n.
    See **calumny**

sniff
  absorb 299 vb.
  breathe 352 vb.
  smell 394 vb.
  deprecate 762 vb.
  be insolent 878 vb.
  contempt 922 n.
  disapprove 924 vb.
  calumny 926 n.
  drug oneself
    949 vb.

sniff at
  eat 301 vb.
  reject 607 vb.
  dislike 861 vb.
  despise 922 vb.
  detract 926 vb.

sniffer torch
  testing agent
    461 n.
  detector 484 n.

sniffle
  breathe 352 vb.

sniff out
  discover 484 vb.

snifter
  draught 301 n.

snigger
  cry 408 vb.
  laugh 835 vb.

laughter 835 n.
ridicule 851 n.
ridicule 851 vb.

snip
  small thing 33 n.
  cut 46 vb.
  notch 260 n.
  notch 260 vb.
  cheapness 812 n.

snipe
  shoot 287 vb.
  table bird 365 n.
  fire at 712 vb.

sniper
  attacker 712 n.
  soldier 722 n.
  malcontent 829 n.

snippet
  small thing 33 n.
  piece 53 n.

snitch
  inform 524 vb.
  informer 524 n.
  steal 788 vb.

snivel
  excrete 302 vb.
  weep 836 vb.

snob
  proud person
    871 n.

snobbish
  biased 481 adj.
  proud 871 adj.
  insolent 878 adj.
  disrespectful
    921 adj.

snog
  caress 889 vb.

snood
  headgear 228 n.
  hairdressing 843 n.

snooker
  obstruct 702 vb.
  ball game 837 n.

snoop
  scan 438 vb.
  spectator 441 n.
  be curious 453 vb.
  enquire 459 vb.
  informer 524 n.
  be stealthy 525 vb.

snooper
  detective 459 n.

snooty
  proud 871 adj.
  vain 873 adj.
  insolent 878 adj.

snooze
sleep 679 n.
sleep 679 vb.
snore
rasp 407 vb.
cry 408 vb.
sleep 679 vb.
snort
draught 301 n.
breathe 352 vb.
hiss 406 vb.
rasp 407 vb.
cry 408 vb.
ululate 409 vb.
be insolent 878 vb.
sullenness 893 n.
contempt 922 n.
despise 922 vb.
drug oneself
    949 vb.
snorting
drug-taking 949 n.
snot
excrement 302 n.
dirt 649 n.
snout
protuberance
    254 n.
tobacco 388 n.
snow
softness 327 n.
rain 350 VB.
snow 380 n.
refrigerator 384 n.
white thing 427 n.
abound 635 vb.
drug-taking 949 n.
snowball
grow 36 vb.
increase 36 n.
continuity 71 n.
accumulation 74 n.
expand 197 vb.
missile 287 n.
propel 287 vb.
snow 380 n.
dance 837 n.
snow blindness
snow 380 n.
blindness 439 n.
dim sight 440 n.
snowbound
wintry 129 adj.
snow 380 n.
hindered 702 adj.
restrained 747 adj.

snowdrift
accumulation 74 n.
snow 380 n.
snowdrop
plant 366 n.
snowed-up
hindered 702 adj.
snowfall
snow 380 n.
snowfield
snow 380 n.
snowflake
insubstantial thing
    4 n.
softness 327 n.
powder 332 n.
snow 380 n.
snowman
snow 380 n.
image 551 n.
snowplough
vehicle 274 n.
snow 380 n.
snowstorm
storm 176 n.
snow 380 n.
wintriness 380 n.
snow under
be many 104 vb.
snow-white
white 427 adj.
snowy
cold 380 adj.
white 427 adj.
clean 648 adj.
pure 950 adj.
snub
short 204 adj.
repel 292 vb.
repulsion 292 n.
shame 867 vb.
humiliate 872 vb.
be rude 885 vb.
indignity 921 n.
not respect 921 vb.
contempt 922 n.
despise 922 vb.
reprimand 924 n.
reprove 924 vb.
snub-nosed
short 204 adj.
snuff
tobacco 388 n.
snuff it
die 361 vb.
snuffle
breathe 352 vb.

hiss 406 vb.
snug
retreat 192 n.
tavern 192 n.
chamber 194 n.
little 196 adj.
marine 275 adj.
comfortable
    376 adj.
warm 379 adj.
content 828 adj.
snuggle
caress 889 vb.
so
thus 8 adv.
similarly 18 adv.
greatly 32 vb.
hence 158 adv.
true 494 adj.
soak
pervade 189 vb.
immerse 303 vb.
drench 341 vb.
fleece 786 vb.
overcharge 811 vb.
sate 863 vb.
soak in
descend 309 vb.
soaking wet, be
be wet 341 vb.
soak up
absorb 299 vb.
drink 301 vb.
dry 342 vb.
so and so
person 371 n.
no name 562 n.
soap
softness 327 n.
lubricant 334 n.
lubricate 334 vb.
fat 357 n.
clean 648 vb.
cleanser 648 n.
soapbox
publicity 528 n.
oratory 579 n.
soap opera
broadcast 531 n.
narrative 590 n.
soap powder
cleanser 648 n.
soapsuds
bubble 355 n.
soapy
smooth 258 adj.
bubbly 355 adj.

fatty 357 adj.
white 427 adj.
servile 879 adj.
flattering 925 adj.
soar
be great - large
    32 vb.
be high 209 vb.
fly 271 vb.
ascend 308 vb.
be light 323 vb.
be dear 811 vb.
soar above
outdo 306 vb.
sob
respiration 352 n.
rasp 407 n.
cry 408 n.
cry 408 vb.
voicelessness 578 n.
lamentation 836 n.
weep 836 vb.
sober
moderate 177 vb.
plain 573 adj.
depress 834 vb.
serious 834 adj.
cautious 858 adj.
virtuous 933 adj.
sober 948 adj.
sober as a judge
serious 834 adj.
sober 948 adj.
sobersides
moper 834 n.
sober up
be sober 948 vb.
sobriety
inexcitability
    823 n.
seriousness 834 n.
caution 858 n.
sobriety 948 n.
sobriquet
name 561 n.
sob-stuff
excitation 821 n.
so-called
supposed 512 adj.
spurious 542 adj.
untrue 543 adj.
named 561 adj.
vain 873 adj.
soccer
ball game 837 n.
sociable
sociable 882 adj.

social
national 371 adj.
sociable 882 adj.
social gathering
882 n.
social anthropology
anthropology
371 n.
social butterfly
sociable person
882 n.
social circle
fellowship 882 n.
social class
degree 27 n.
serial place 73 n.
classification 77 n.
community 708 n.
social climber
commoner 869 n.
sociable person
882 n.
social disease
venereal disease
651 n.
social graces
good taste 846 n.
sociability 882 n.
socialism
government 733 n.
joint possession
775 n.
philanthropy
901 n.
Socialists
political party
708 n.
socialite
beau monde 848 n.
sociable person
882 n.
socialize
make better
654 vb.
be sociable 882 vb.
social science
anthropology
371 n.
sociology 901 n.
social security
safety 660 n.
subvention 703 n.
sociology 901 n.
social services
sociology 901 n.
social whirl
festivity 837 n.

social round 882 n.
social work
sociology 901 n.
societal
national 371 adj.
society
accompaniment
89 n.
social group 371 n.
society 708 n.
beau monde 848 n.
fellowship 882 n.
laity 987 n.
sociology
sociology 901 n.
sociopath
the maladjusted
504 n.
sock
strike 279 vb.
drama 594 n.
socket
place 185 n.
receptacle 194 n.
cavity 255 n.
sock it to
strike 279 vb.
socks
legwear 228 n.
sod
piece 53 n.
soil 344 n.
grass 366 n.
soda
soft drink 301 n.
soda water
soft drink 301 n.
water 339 n.
sodomy
illicit love 951 n.
sod's law
rule 81 n.
axiom 496 n.
sofa
seat 218 n.
soft
small 33 adj.
smooth 258 adj.
soft 327 adj.
hush 399 int.
silent 399 adj.
muted 401 adj.
luminous 417 adj.
soft-hued 425 adj.
foolish 499 adj.
lax 734 adj.
lenient 736 adj.

cowardly 856 adj.
pitying 905 adj.
soft drink
soft drink 301 n.
soft drug
drug-taking 949 n.
soften
soften 327 vb.
mute 401 vb.
relieve 831 vb.
extenuate 927 vb.
softening
weakness 163 n.
soft 327 adj.
softening of the brain
mental disorder
503 n.
soften up
weaken 163 vb.
induce 612 vb.
prepare 669 vb.
flatter 925 vb.
soft fruit
fruit and vegetables
301 n.
soft-hearted
impressible
819 adj.
benevolent 897 adj.
pitying 905 adj.
softly
slightly 33 adv.
softly softly
cautiously 858 adv.
soft mark
dupe 544 n.
soft on
enamoured
887 adj.
soft option
easy thing 701 n.
soft-pedal
moderate 177 vb.
move slowly
278 vb.
silence 399 vb.
mute 401 vb.
underestimate
483 vb.
extenuate 927 vb.
soft porn
impurity 951 n.
soft sell
advertisement
528 n.
inducement 612 n.
sale 793 n.

soft-soap
be servile 879 vb.
flatter 925 vb.
soft-spoken
speaking 579 adj.
amiable 884 adj.
soft spot
defect 647 n.
moral sensibility
819 n.
soft touch
dupe 544 n.
easy thing 701 n.
software
data processing
86 n.
soggy
soft 327 adj.
unsavoury 391 adj.
soi-disant
named 561 adj.
vain 873 adj.
soigné(e)
elegant 575 adj.
personable 841 adj.
soil
region 184 n.
soil 344 n.
make unclean
649 vb.
blemish 845 vb.
soirée
evening 129 n.
social gathering
882 n.
sojourn
be present 189 vb.
dwell 192 vb.
visit 882 vb.
solace
relief 831 n.
relieve 831 vb.
amusement 837 n.
solar
celestial 321 adj.
solar heating
heating 381 n.
solarium
arbour 194 n.
heater 383 n.
solar plexus
insides 224 n.
solar system
sun 321 n.
solder
join 45 vb.
adhesive 47 n.

soldier
killer 362 n.
soldier 722 n.
soldier on
stand firm 599 vb.
sold on
enamoured
887 adj.
sold on, be
believe 485 vb.
sole
one 88 adj.
foot 214 n.
fish food 301 n.
solecism
sophism 477 n.
mistake 495 n.
solecism 565 n.
solely
singly 88 adv.
solemn
great 32 adj.
affirmative
532 adj.
serious 834 adj.
formal 875 adj.
sanctified 979 adj.
ritual 988 adj.
solemnity
seriousness 834 n.
prestige 866 n.
ostentation 875 n.
See **formality**
ostentation 875 n.
rite 988 n.
solemnize
celebrate 876 vb.
solfa
vocal music 412 n.
solicit
request 761 vb.
desire 859 vb.
soliciting
request 761 n.
social evil 951 n.
solicitor
petitioner 763 n.
law agent 958 n.
lawyer 958 n.
solicitous
careful 457 adj.
solicitude
attention 455 n.
carefulness 457 n.
worry 825 n.
solid
real 1 adj.

substantial 3 adj.
firm 45 adj.
continuous 71 adj.
strong 162 adj.
formed 243 adj.
material 319 adj.
dense 324 adj.
solid body 324 n.
rigid 326 adj.
certain 473 adj.
genuine 494 adj.
forceful 571 adj.
printed 587 adj.
serious 834 adj.
solidarity
agreement 24 n.
completeness 54 n.
unity 88 n.
association 706 n.
cooperation 706 n.
concord 710 n.
friendship 880 n.
solid-fuel
heating 381 adj.
solid geometry
geometry 465 n.
solidify
cohere 48 vb.
be dense 324 vb.
solidity
substantiality 3 n.
permanence 144 n.
materiality 319 n.
density 324 n.
opacity 423 n.
solidus
coinage 797 n.
soliloquy
soliloquy 585 n.
dramaturgy 594 n.
solitaire
card game 837 n.
gem 844 n.
solitary
unconformable
84 adj.
alone 88 adj.
one 88 adj.
solitary 883 adj.
unsociable 883 adj.
solitary confinement
detention 747 n.
seclusion 883 n.
solitude
unity 88 n.
seclusion 883 n.

solo
unit 88 n.
tune 412 n.
ballet 594 n.
soloist
musician 413 n.
Solomon
sage 500 n.
magistracy 957 n.
so long
goodbye 296 int.
so long as
while 108 adv.
solo whist
card game 837 n.
soluble
mixed 43 adj.
blood 335 adj.
solution
a mixture 43 n.
event 154 n.
solution 337 n.
answer 460 n.
interpretation
520 n.
remedy 658 n.
completion 725 n.
solve
decipher 520 vb.
solvent
liquefaction 337 n.
monetary 797 adj.
moneyed 800 adj.
solvent abuse
drug-taking 949 n.
solvent, be
afford 800 vb.
somatology
anthropology
371 n.
sombre
funereal 364 adj.
dark 418 adj.
dim 419 adj.
black 428 adj.
grey 429 adj.
cheerless 834 adj.
sombrero
headgear 228 n.
some
quantitative 26 adj.
partially 33 adv.
anonymous
562 adj.
no name 562 n.
somebody
substance 3 n.

person 371 n.
bigwig 638 n.
person of repute
866 n.
somebody, be
have a reputation
866 vb.
some hopes
not likely 472 int.
somehow
partially 33 adv.
someone
person 371 n.
someone walking
over one's grave
tingling 378 n.
some other time
different time
122 n.
somersault
overturning 221 n.
something
substance 3 n.
greatly 32 vb.
object 319 n.
something amiss
wrong 914 n.
something between
them
compact 765 n.
love affair 887 n.
something else
variant 15 n.
something else again
variant 15 n.
something in com-
mon
relation 9 n.
something like
similar 18 adj.
something missing
shortfall 307 n.
something on one's
mind
worry 825 n.
something or other
uncertainty 474 n.
something over
superfluity 637 n.
something to be said
for
dueness 915 n.
something to one's
advantage
lack of expectation
508 n.
benefit 615 n.

something to write home about
spectacle 445 n.
something wrong
hitch 702 n.
wrong 914 n.
sometime
prior 119 adj.
former 125 adj.
sometimes
sometimes
139 adv.
somewhat
partially 33 adv.
somewhere
about 33 adv.
somewhere around
nearly 200 adv.
somnambulism
pedestrianism
267 n.
fantasy 513 n.
sleep 679 n.
somnolent
sleepy 679 adj.
son
descendant 170 n.
male 372 n.
son and heir
priority 119 n.
sonar
hearing aid 415 n.
detector 484 n.
sonata
musical piece
412 n.
son et lumière
light 417 n.
lighting 420 n.
spectacle 445 n.
pageant 875 n.
song
cry 408 n.
vocal music 412 n.
poem 593 n.
hymn 981 n.
song and dance
loudness 400 n.
stage show 594 n.
overactivity 678 n.
excitable state
822 n.
sonic
sounding 398 adj.
sonic boom
loudness 400 n.
bang 402 n.

sonnet
verse form 593 n.
wooing 889 n.
sonny
youngster 132 n.
Son of God
God the Son 965 n.
sonority
sound 398 n.
loudness 400 n.
resonance 404 n.
sonorous
sounding 398 adj.
loud 400 adj.
resonant 404 adj.
soon
betimes 135 adv.
soon after
subsequently
120 adv.
soot
powder 332 n.
black thing 428 n.
dirt 649 n.
soothe
assuage 177 vb.
bring to rest
266 vb.
remedy 658 vb.
make inactive
679 vb.
pacify 719 vb.
please 826 vb.
relieve 831 vb.
flatter 925 vb.
soothing
smooth 258 adj.
remedial 658 adj.
relief 831 n.
flattering 925 adj.
soothsayer
oracle 511 n.
sorcerer 983 n.
sooty
powdery 332 adj.
dark 418 adj.
dim 419 adj.
opaque 423 adj.
black 428 adj.
dirty 649 adj.
sop
small quantity
33 n.
mouthful 301 n.
moisture 341 n.
incentive 612 n.

sophisticated
mixed 43 adj.
complex 61 adj.
intelligent 498 adj.
cunning 698 adj.
sophistication
good taste 846 n.
sophistry
sophistry 477 n.
soporific
soporific 679 n.
tedious 838 adj.
sopping, be
be wet 341 vb.
soppy
foolish 499 adj.
feeling 818 adj.
impressible
819 adj.
soprano
stridor 407 n.
vocalist 413 n.
sop to Cerberus
incentive 612 n.
sorbet
dessert 301 n.
sorcery
sorcery 983 n.
sordid
not nice 645 adj.
unclean 649 adj.
vulgar 847 adj.
sore
sentient 374 adj.
painful 377 adj.
evil 616 n.
ulcer 651 n.
wound 655 n.
fatigued 684 adj.
sensitive 819 adj.
painfulness 827 n.
paining 827 adj.
resentful 891 adj.
sore point
moral sensibility
819 n.
painfulness 827 n.
resentment 891 n.
sore pressed
in difficulties
700 adj.
sorghum
cereals 301 n.
grass 366 n.
sorority
family 11 n.
association 706 n.

cooperation 706 n.
community 708 n.
sorrel
horse 273 n.
fruit and vegetables
301 n.
brown 430 adj.
sorrow
sorrow 825 n.
suffer 825 vb.
painfulness 827 n.
lament 836 vb.
pity 905 vb.
sorrowful
unhappy 825 adj.
sorry
unhappy 825 adj.
regretting 830 adj.
melancholic
834 adj.
repentant 939 adj.
sorry, be
regret 830 vb.
sorry sight
painfulness 827 n.
sort
class 62 vb.
sort 77 n.
sortie
outbreak 176 n.
egress 298 n.
attack 712 n.
retaliation 714 n.
sortilege
occultism 984 n.
sorting
sorting 62 n.
sort of
partially 33 adv.
sort out
exclude 57 vb.
render few 105 vb.
discriminate
463 vb.
reject 607 vb.
SOS
signal 547 n.
danger signal
665 n.
so-so
inconsiderable
33 adj.
not bad 644 adj.
middling 732 adj.
sot
drunkard 949 n.

so to speak
  similarly 18 adv.
sotto voce
  muted 401 adj.
sou
  small thing 33 n.
  coinage 797 n.
soufflé
  dessert 301 n.
  dish 301 n.
  bubble 355 n.
sough
  blow 352 vb.
  breeze 352 n.
  faintness 401 n.
  sound faint 401 vb.
sought after
  salable 793 adj.
soul
  essence 1 n.
  insubstantial thing
    4 n.
  essential part 5 n.
  self 80 n.
  interiority 224 n.
  life 360 n.
  person 371 n.
  music 412 n.
  spirit 447 n.
  affections 817 n.
  moral sensibility
    819 n.
soulful
  feeling 818 adj.
soulless
  impassive 820 adj.
  tedious 838 adj.
soul mate
  close friend 880 n.
  loved one 887 n.
  spouse 894 n.
soul music
  music 412 n.
soul-searching
  regret 830 n.
  honourable
    929 adj.
sound
  firm 45 adj.
  whole 52 adj.
  be deep 211 vb.
  gulf 345 n.
  sound 398 n.
  be loud 400 vb.
  play music 413 vb.
  enquire 459 vb.
  be tentative 461 vb.

measure 465 vb.
  genuine 494 adj.
  wise 498 adj.
  access 624 n.
  healthy 650 adj.
  skilful 694 adj.
sound a retreat
  regress 286 vb.
sound as a bell
  strong 162 adj.
  perfect 646 adj.
  healthy 650 adj.
sound asleep
  sleepy 679 adj.
sound a warning
  raise the alarm
    665 vb.
sound barrier
  limit 236 n.
  sound 398 n.
sound board
  gong 414 n.
  musical instrument
    414 n.
  publicity 528 n.
sound effects
  cinema 445 n.
soundless
  still 266 adj.
  silent 399 adj.
soundness
  wisdom 498 n.
  goodness 644 n.
  health 650 n.
  probity 929 n.
soundness of mind
  sanity 502 n.
sound off
  orate 579 vb.
  speak 579 vb.
sound out
  interrogate 459 vb.
soundproof
  silent 399 adj.
sound recording
  listening 415 n.
sound the alarm
  signal 547 vb.
  warn 664 vb.
  raise the alarm
    665 vb.
soundtrack
  sound 398 n.
  cinema 445 n.
sound waves
  sound 398 n.

soup
  a mixture 43 n.
  hors-d'oeuvres
    301 n.
  semiliquidity
    354 n.
  predicament 700 n.
soupçon
  small quantity
    33 n.
  tincture 43 n.
  fewness 105 n.
souped-up
  dynamic 160 adj.
  speedy 277 adj.
sour
  unproductive
    172 adj.
  be sour 393 vb.
  sour 393 adj.
  amiss 616 adv.
  cause discontent
    829 vb.
  melancholic
    834 adj.
source
  source 156 n.
  informant 524 n.
sour grapes
  impossibility
    470 n.
sousaphone
  horn 414 n.
souse
  immerse 303 vb.
  lower 311 vb.
  plunge 313 vb.
  drench 341 vb.
  season 388 vb.
  get drunk 949 vb.
Southern Cross
  star 321 n.
South Pole
  coldness 380 n.
souvenir
  reminder 505 n.
  gift 781 n.
sou'wester
  headgear 228 n.
  gale 352 n.
sovereign
  superior 34 n.
  supreme 34 adj.
  strong 162 adj.
  ruling 733 adj.
  sovereign 741 n.
  coinage 797 n.

godlike 965 adj.
sovereign remedy
  remedy 658 n.
sovereignty
  superiority 34 n.
  governance 733 n.
  divine attribute
    965 n.
sovietism
  government 733 n.
sow
  disperse 75 vb.
  cause 156 vb.
  produce 164 vb.
  let fall 311 vb.
  pig 365 n.
  cultivate 370 vb.
  female animal
    373 n.
sow dissension
  make quarrels
    709 vb.
so what
  Never mind
    860 int.
sow one's wild oats
  revel 837 vb.
  be wicked 934 vb.
  be intemperate
    943 vb.
sow the seeds of
  cause 156 vb.
  educate 534 vb.
**sow the seeds of dis-
    content**
  cause discontent
    829 vb.
soya beans
  fruit and vegetables
    301 n.
soy sauce
  sauce 389 n.
sozzled
  dead drunk
    949 adj.
spa
  hospital 658 n.
space
  disunion 46 n.
  arrange 62 vb.
  time 108 n.
  room 183 n.
  space 183 n.
  interval 201 n.
  space 201 vb.
  opening 263 n.
  world 321 n.

notation 410 n.
print-type 587 n.
storage 632 n.
spacecraft
spaceship 276 n.
space flight
aeronautics 271 n.
space travel 271 n.
space heating
heating 381 n.
space lab
spaceship 276 n.
satellite 321 n.
spaceman, woman
traveller 268 n.
aeronaut 271 n.
space out
grade 73 vb.
space 201 vb.
spaceship
spaceship 276 n.
space station
space travel 271 n.
spaceship 276 n.
follower 284 n.
satellite 321 n.
space travel
space travel 271 n.
spacious
spacious 183 adj.
spade
ladle 194 n.
sharp edge 256 n.
farm tool 370 n.
spadework
source 156 n.
preparation 669 n.
labour 682 n.
spaghetti
dish 301 n.
spaghetti Western
film 445 n.
span
connect 45 vb.
bond 47 n.
group 74 n.
time 108 n.
period 110 n.
extend 183 vb.
range 183 n.
distance 199 n.
length 203 n.
long measure
  203 n.
breadth 205 n.
measure 465 vb.
bridge 624 n.

spangle
flash 417 n.
variegate 437 vb.
finery 844 n.
spaniel
dog 365 n.
toady 879 n.
spank
move fast 277 vb.
strike 279 vb.
spank 963 vb.
spanking
large 195 adj.
knock 279 n.
spanner
tool 630 n.
spanner in the works
hitch 702 n.
spar
hanger 217 n.
support 218 n.
strike 279 vb.
fight 716 vb.
spare
additional 38 adj.
remaining 41 adj.
lean 206 adj.
plain 573 adj.
superfluous
  637 adj.
deliver 668 vb.
be lenient 736 vb.
not retain 779 vb.
give 781 vb.
relieve 831 vb.
show mercy
  905 vb.
exempt 919 vb.
spared, be
live 360 vb.
spare parts
extra 40 n.
safeguard 662 n.
spares
extra 40 n.
spare time
leisure 681 n.
sparing, be
restrain 747 vb.
spark
small quantity
  33 n.
fire 379 n.
flash 417 n.
shine 417 vb.
luminary 420 n.
caress 889 vb.

sparkle
bubble 355 vb.
flash 417 n.
shine 417 vb.
luminary 420 n.
be cheerful 833 vb.
cheerfulness 833 n.
be witty 839 vb.
wit 839 n.
sparkling
light 323 adj.
bubbly 355 adj.
luminous 417 adj.
cheerful 833 adj.
merry 833 adj.
witty 839 adj.
spark off
initiate 68 vb.
cause 156 vb.
sparring partner
pugilist 722 n.
sparrow
bird 365 n.
sparse
few 105 adj.
unproductive
  172 adj.
scarce 636 adj.
sparseness
insubstantiality
  4 n.
smallness 33 n.
fewness 105 n.
Spartan
severe 735 adj.
economical
  814 adj.
abstainer 942 n.
temperate 942 adj.
ascetic 945 adj.
Spartan fare
insufficiency 636 n.
asceticism 945 n.
spasm
brief span 114 n.
spasm 318 n.
illness 651 n.
spasmodic
discontinuous
  72 adj.
periodical 141 adj.
fitful 142 adj.
violent 176 adj.
spastic
diseased 651 adj.
sick person 651 n.

spat
quarrel 709 n.
spate
crowd 74 n.
plenty 635 n.
redundance 637 n.
spats
legwear 228 n.
spatter
disperse 75 vb.
moisten 341 vb.
defame 926 vb.
spatula
ladle 194 n.
spavin
animal disease
  651 n.
spawn
young creature
  132 n.
product 164 n.
generate 167 vb.
reproduce itself
  167 vb.
posterity 170 n.
spay
subtract 39 vb.
unman 161 vb.
speak
communicate
  524 vb.
signal 547 vb.
speak 579 vb.
speakeasy
tavern 192 n.
speaker
megaphone 400 n.
gramophone 414 n.
speaker 579 n.
director 690 n.
master 741 n.
speaker in tongues
zealot 979 n.
speak for
deputize 755 vb.
speak for itself
evidence 466 vb.
be intelligible
  516 vb.
be plain 522 vb.
speaking
speaking 579 adj.
speaking clock
timekeeper 117 n.
speaking in tongues
piety 979 n.

speaking of
concerning 9 adv.
speak of
mean 514 vb.
inform 524 vb.
divulge 526 vb.
publish 528 vb.
speak one's mind
be plain 522 vb.
be truthful 540 vb.
speak 579 vb.
be artless 699 vb.
be courageous
855 vb.
speak out
be plain 522 vb.
affirm 532 vb.
be courageous
855 vb.
speak straight from
the shoulder
speak plainly
573 vb.
speak the truth
be true 494 vb.
confess 526 vb.
speak to
speak to 583 vb.
speak up
affirm 532 vb.
emphasize 532 vb.
speak 579 vb.
be courageous
855 vb.
speak up for
approve 923 vb.
vindicate 927 vb.
speak volumes
evidence 466 vb.
mean 514 vb.
spear
pierce 263 vb.
strike at 712 vb.
spear 723 n.
spearhead
front 237 n.
precede 283 vb.
chief thing 638 n.
leader 690 n.
spearmint
scent 396 n.
special
special 80 adj.
special case
nonuniformity
17 n.
exclusion 57 n.

speciality 80 n.
nonconformity
84 n.
nonliability 919 n.
special effects
cinema 445 n.
specialist
doctor 658 n.
expert 696 n.
speciality
speciality 80 n.
dish 301 n.
specialize
specify 80 vb.
study 536 vb.
specially
greatly 32 vb.
specially 80 adv.
special offer
incentive 612 n.
discount 810 n.
specialty
speciality 80 n.
specie
coinage 797 n.
species
part 53 n.
subdivision 53 n.
group 74 n.
breed 77 n.
sort 77 n.
specific
special 80 adj.
remedy 658 n.
specifically
specially 80 adv.
specification
classification 77 n.
particulars 80 n.
qualification 468 n.
report 524 n.
description 590 n.
specific gravity
gravity 322 n.
density 324 n.
specific heat
heat 379 n.
specify
class 62 vb.
specify 80 vb.
specimen
prototype 23 n.
example 83 n.
exhibit 522 n.
specious
plausible 471 adj.
affected 850 adj.

ostentatious
875 adj.
flattering 925 adj.
specious argument
sophism 477 n.
speck
small thing 33 n.
powder 332 n.
mottle 437 n.
blemish 845 n.
speckled
mottled 437 adj.
specs
eyeglass 442 n.
spectacle
spectacle 445 n.
spectacles
eyeglass 442 n.
spectacular
florid 425 adj.
appearing 445 adj.
showy 875 adj.
spectate
watch 441 vb.
spectator
presence 189 n.
spectator 441 n.
spectral
insubstantial 4 adj.
spooky 970 adj.
spectre
insubstantial thing
4 n.
visual fallacy
440 n.
appearance 445 n.
intimidation
854 n.
ghost 970 n.
spectroscope
astronomy 321 n.
colour 425 n.
spectrum
series 71 n.
light 417 n.
colour 425 n.
variegation 437 n.
speculate
meditate 449 vb.
be tentative 461 vb.
suppose 512 vb.
gamble 618 vb.
attempt 671 vb.
speculate 791 vb.
speculative
thoughtful 449 adj.
uncertain 474 adj.

speculative
618 adj.
speculator
experimenter
461 n.
gambler 618 n.
merchant 794 n.
speculum
mirror 442 n.
speech
language 557 n.
oration 579 n.
speech 579 n.
allocution 583 n.
speeches
diffuseness 570 n.
reading matter
589 n.
speechify
orate 579 vb.
speech impediment
speech defect
580 n.
speechless
silent 399 adj.
voiceless 578 adj.
angry 891 adj.
speech-making
oratory 579 n.
speech therapy
speech defect
580 n.
speed
degree 27 n.
motion 265 n.
move fast 277 vb.
velocity 277 n.
facilitate 701 vb.
drug-taking 949 n.
speed limit
limit 236 n.
restriction 747 n.
speedometer
velocity 277 n.
meter 465 n.
recording instru-
ment 549 n.
speed trap
velocity 277 n.
traffic control
305 n.
detector 484 n.
speed up
augment 36 vb.
accelerate 277 vb.
promote 285 vb.

speedway
racing 716 n.
speedy
speedy 277 adj.
speleology
descent 309 n.
earth sciences 321 n.
mineralogy 359 n.
search 459 n.
discovery 484 n.
sport 837 n.
spell
time 108 n.
period 110 n.
influence 178 n.
predict 511 vb.
mean 514 vb.
imply 523 vb.
indicate 547 vb.
spell 558 vb.
spell 983 n.
spellbinding
eloquent 579 adj.
miracle-working 864 n.
spellbound
still 266 adj.
bewitched 983 adj.
spelling
spelling 558 n.
spell out
specify 80 vb.
decipher 520 vb.
interpret 520 vb.
spell 558 vb.
spend
expend 806 vb.
spendaholic
prodigal 815 n.
spend a penny
excrete 302 vb.
spending spree
expenditure 806 n.
prodigality 815 n.
spendthrift
prodigal 815 adj.
prodigal 815 n.
intemperate 943 adj.
spent
unproductive 172 adj.
feeble 572 adj.
fatigued 684 adj.
lost 772 adj.

sperm
source 156 n.
genitalia 167 n.
fertilizer 171 n.
spermaceti
fat 357 n.
spermatozoa
genitalia 167 n.
sperm bank
storage 632 n.
spermicide
contraception 172 n.
sperm whale
mammal 365 n.
spew
vomit 300 vb.
flow 350 vb.
spew out
eject 300 vb.
sphagnum
plant 366 n.
sphere
degree 27 n.
group 74 n.
classification 77 n.
range 183 n.
region 184 n.
territory 184 n.
sphere 252 n.
world 321 n.
function 622 n.
sphere of influence
influence 178 n.
spherical
round 250 adj.
rotund 252 adj.
sphinx
rara avis 84 n.
secret 530 n.
Sphinx-like
unintelligible 517 adj.
spice
mix 43 vb.
tincture 43 n.
stimulant 174 n.
cook 301 vb.
spice 301 n.
pungency 388 n.
season 388 vb.
spice 389 vb.
make appetizing 390 vb.
pleasurableness 826 n.

spices
interment 364 n.
spick and span
orderly 60 adj.
new 126 adj.
clean 648 adj.
spicy
tasty 386 adj.
savoury 390 adj.
fragrant 396 adj.
exciting 821 adj.
impure 951 adj.
spider
weaving 222 n.
creepy-crawly 365 n.
spider's web
ambush 527 n.
spidery
lean 206 adj.
written 586 adj.
spiel
empty talk 515 n.
speech 579 n.
loquacity 581 n.
inducement 612 n.
sale 793 n.
spiffing
super 644 adj.
spifflicate
destroy 165 vb.
strike 279 vb.
spike
mix 43 vb.
growth 157 n.
vertex 213 n.
sharp point 256 n.
pierce 263 vb.
flower 366 n.
defences 713 n.
hairdressing 843 n.
spike the guns
disable 161 vb.
be obstructive 702 vb.
spiky
sharp 256 adj.
spill
invert 221 vb.
overturning 221 n.
outflow 298 n.
emit 300 vb.
descent 309 n.
let fall 311 vb.
moisten 341 vb.
lighter 385 n.
torch 420 n.

waste 634 vb.
be clumsy 695 vb.
lose 772 vb.
spill the beans
divulge 526 vb.
spillway
conduit 351 n.
spilt milk
loss 772 n.
spin
produce 164 vb.
make thin 206 vb.
weave 222 vb.
land travel 267 n.
aeronautics 271 n.
fly 271 vb.
rotate 315 vb.
rotation 315 n.
fake 541 vb.
spina bifida
nervous disorders 651 n.
spinach
fruit and vegetables 301 n.
spinal
central 225 adj.
back 238 adj.
spin a yarn
be untrue 543 vb.
exaggerate 546 vb.
describe 590 vb.
spindle
pivot 218 n.
rotator 315 n.
tree 366 n.
spindly
lean 206 adj.
spindrift
moisture 341 n.
bubble 355 n.
spin-dry
dry 342 vb.
spine
pillar 218 n.
centre 225 n.
rear 238 n.
prickle 256 n.
hardness 326 n.
bookbinding 589 n.
spine-chilling
exciting 821 adj.
spineless
weak 163 adj.
irresolute 601 adj.
spinet
piano 414 n.

spin fine
make thin 206 vb.
spinnaker
sail 275 n.
spinner
weaving 222 n.
rotator 315 n.
artisan 686 n.
spinney
wood 366 n.
spinning top
cone 252 n.
rotator 315 n.
spinning wheel
weaving 222 n.
rotator 315 n.
spin-off
sequel 67 n.
effect 157 n.
spinose
sharp 256 adj.
spin out
be diffuse 570 vb.
spinster
spinster 895 n.
virgin 950 n.
spiny
sharp 256 adj.
spiral
grow 36 vb.
increase 36 n.
coil 251 n.
coiled 251 adj.
twine 251 vb.
fly 271 vb.
ascend 308 vb.
ascent 308 n.
circle 314 vb.
circuition 314 n.
rotation 315 n.
spiral staircase
ascent 308 n.
spire
high structure
209 n.
vertex 213 n.
sharp point 256 n.
ascend 308 vb.
church exterior
990 n.
spirit
temperament 5 n.
vigorousness 174 n.
life 360 n.
spirit 447 n.
meaning 514 n.
vigour 571 n.

resolution 599 n.
restlessness 678 n.
affections 817 n.
moral sensibility
819 n.
courage 855 n.
ghost 970 n.
spirit away
steal 788 vb.
spirited
forceful 571 adj.
feeling 818 adj.
lively 819 adj.
cheerful 833 adj.
courageous
855 adj.
spirit lamp
lamp 420 n.
spiritless
apathetic 820 adj.
inexcitable
823 adj.
dejected 834 adj.
cowardly 856 adj.
spirit level
horizontality
216 n.
spiritoso
adagio 412 adv.
spirit-raising
sorcery 983 n.
spirit-rapping
psychical 984 n.
spiritualism 984 n.
spirits
state 7 n.
alcoholic drink
301 n.
tonic 658 n.
spiritual
immaterial
320 adj.
vocal music 412 n.
divine 965 adj.
religious 973 adj.
pious 979 adj.
hymn 981 n.
spiritualism
immateriality
320 n.
spirit 447 n.
occultism 984 n.
spiritualism 984 n.
spiritualist
spirit 447 n.
occultist 984 n.

spirituous
intoxicating
949 adj.
spirit writing
spiritualism 984 n.
spirt
ascend 308 vb.
flow 350 vb.
spit
fastening 47 n.
sharp point 256 n.
perforator 263 n.
pierce 263 vb.
emit 300 vb.
eruct 300 vb.
excrement 302 n.
excrete 302 vb.
rotator 315 n.
effervesce 318 vb.
lubricant 334 n.
moisture 341 n.
rain 350 vb.
crackle 402 vb.
hiss 406 vb.
ululate 409 vb.
be angry 891 vb.
threaten 900 vb.
disapprove 924 vb.
spit and polish
cleanness 648 n.
ostentation 875 n.
spite
badness 645 n.
enmity 881 n.
hatred 888 n.
resentment 891 n.
be malevolent
898 vb.
malevolence 898 n.
revengefulness
910 n.
envy 912 n.
detraction 926 n.
spiteful
harmful 645 adj.
hostile 881 adj.
resentful 891 adj.
malevolent
898 adj.
spitfire
violent creature
176 n.
spit on
not respect 921 vb.
spit out
eject 300 vb.

spitting distance
short distance
200 n.
spitting image
identity 13 n.
analogue 18 n.
image 551 n.
representation
551 n.
spittle
excrement 302 n.
lubricant 334 n.
moisture 341 n.
spittoon
sink 649 n.
splash
small quantity
33 n.
disperse 75 vb.
water 339 n.
moisten 341 vb.
flow 350 vb.
hiss 406 vb.
sibilation 406 n.
mottle 437 n.
make unclean
649 vb.
ostentation 875 n.
splashdown
space travel 271 n.
descent 309 n.
splash out
expend 806 vb.
be ostentatious
875 vb.
splatter
moisten 341 vb.
splay
disperse 75 vb.
expand 197 vb.
obliquity 220 n.
diverge 294 vb.
splay-footed
deformed 246 adj.
spleen
insides 224 n.
discontent 829 n.
melancholy 834 n.
resentment 891 n.
sullenness 893 n.
malevolence 898 n.
envy 912 n.
splendid
luminous 417 adj.
excellent 644 adj.
pleasurable
826 adj.

splendid 841 adj.
noteworthy
866 adj.
ostentatious
875 adj.
splendiferous
excellent 644 adj.
ostentatious
875 adj.
splendour
light 417 n.
beauty 841 n.
prestige 866 n.
ostentation 875 n.
splenetic
resentful 891 adj.
irascible 892 adj.
splice
affix 45 vb.
joint 45 n.
tie 45 vb.
cross 222 vb.
introduce 231 vb.
repair 656 vb.
marry 894 vb.
splint
support 218 n.
hardness 326 n.
surgical dressing
658 n.
splinter
small thing 33 n.
break 46 vb.
piece 53 n.
thinness 206 n.
strip 208 n.
splinter group
dissentient 489 n.
party 708 n.
revolter 738 n.
undutifulness
918 n.
schismatic 978 n.
sect 978 n.
split
break 46 vb.
disunion 46 n.
separate 46 vb.
sunder 46 vb.
decompose 51 vb.
discontinuity 72 n.
bisect 92 vb.
bisected 92 adj.
be weak 163 vb.
be destroyed
165 vb.
gap 201 n.

space 201 vb.
furrow 262 n.
open 263 vb.
opening 263 n.
crackle 402 vb.
inform 524 vb.
divulge 526 vb.
dissension 709 n.
quarrel 709 vb.
apportion 783 vb.
portion 783 n.
split hairs
argue 475 vb.
sophisticate
477 vb.
be fastidious
862 vb.
split on
accuse 928 vb.
split one's sides
laugh 835 vb.
split personality
multiformity 82 n.
duality 90 n.
spirit 447 n.
personality disor-
der 503 n.
split second
instant 116 n.
split the difference
average out 30 vb.
compromise
770 vb.
splitting
separation 46 n.
opening 263 n.
brittle 330 adj.
split up
disunite 46 vb.
separate 46 vb.
divorce 896 vb.
splodge
mottle 437 n.
splurge
be prodigal 815 vb.
prodigality 815 n.
be ostentatious
875 vb.
ostentation 875 n.
splutter
emit 300 vb.
hiss 406 vb.
sibilation 406 n.
stammer 580 vb.
Spode china
pottery 381 n.

spoil
derange 63 vb.
modify 143 vb.
tell against 467 vb.
deteriorate 655 vb.
impair 655 vb.
be clumsy 695 vb.
be lax 734 vb.
be lenient 736 vb.
blemish 845 vb.
sate 863 vb.
love 887 vb.
pet 889 vb.
spoilage
impairment 655 n.
spoiled child
satiety 863 n.
favourite 890 n.
spoiler
equilibrium 28 n.
stabilizer 153 n.
spoiling
impairment 655 n.
spoiling for a fight,
be
make quarrels
709 vb.
attack 712 vb.
spoil oneself
be selfish 932 vb.
be sensual 944 vb.
spoils
booty 790 n.
spoils of war
trophy 729 n.
booty 790 n.
spoilsport
dissuasion 613 n.
moper 834 n.
spoilt
inferior 35 adj.
sensual 944 adj.
spoil the ship for a
ha'porth of tar
act foolishly
695 vb.
be parsimonious
816 vb.
spoke
line 203 n.
spoken
informative
524 adj.
linguistic 557 adj.
speaking 579 adj.
spokesman or -wo-
man or -person

interpret 520 vb.
interpreter 520 n.
informant 524 n.
messenger 529 n.
speaker 579 n.
agent 686 n.
deputy 755 n.
sponge
fossil 125 n.
cavity 255 n.
porosity 263 n.
absorb 299 vb.
dry 342 vb.
dryer 342 n.
pulpiness 356 n.
clean 648 vb.
cleaning utensil
648 n.
beg 761 vb.
fleece 786 vb.
be servile 879 vb.
sponge bag
bag 194 n.
sponge on
be servile 879 vb.
sponger
idler 679 n.
beggar 763 n.
toady 879 n.
spongy
concave 255 adj.
porous 263 adj.
rare 325 adj.
soft 327 adj.
marshy 347 adj.
sponsor
witness 466 n.
stage manager
594 n.
aider 703 n.
patronize 703 vb.
patron 707 n.
sponsorship
protection 660 n.
aid 703 n.
security 767 n.
spontaneous
volitional 595 adj.
spontaneous
609 adj.
spontaneousness
will 595 n.
willingness 597 n.
spoof
imitate 20 vb.
mimicry 20 n.
copy 22 n.

deceive 542 vb.
fool 542 vb.
trickery 542 n.
wit 839 n.
witticism 839 n.
satire 851 n.
satirize 851 vb.

spook
spectator 441 n.
secret service
  459 n.
informer 524 n.
intimidation
  854 n.
ghost 970 n.

spooky
spooky 970 adj.

spool
rotate 315 vb.
rotator 315 n.
photography 551 n.

spoon
ladle 194 n.
caress 889 vb.

spoonerism
inversion 221 n.
mistake 495 n.
neology 560 n.
ridiculousness
  849 n.

spoonfeed
aid 703 vb.
be lax 734 vb.
be lenient 736 vb.
pet 889 vb.

spoonful
finite quantity
  26 n.
small quantity
  33 n.

spooning
lovemaking 887 n.
wooing 889 n.

spoor
remainder 41 n.
identification
  547 n.
trace 548 n.

sporadic
nonuniform 17 adj.
infrequent 140 adj.
periodical 141 adj.
uncertain 474 adj.

spore
source 156 n.
powder 332 n.
flower 366 n.

sport
variant 15 n.
nonuniformity
  17 n.
show 522 vb.
trickery 542 n.
be cheerful 833 vb.
amusement 837 n.
sport 837 n.
laughingstock
  851 n.
prodigy 864 n.
be ostentatious
  875 vb.
good person 937 n.

sporting
courageous
  855 adj.
just 913 adj.
honourable
  929 adj.

sporting chance
fair chance 159 n.
probability 471 n.

sportive
merry 833 adj.
witty 839 adj.

sport of kings
racing 716 n.

sports
exercise 682 n.
contention 716 n.
sport 837 n.

sports car
automobile 274 n.

sports centre
meeting place
  192 n.

sports jacket
jacket 228 n.

sportsmanship
sport 837 n.
probity 929 n.

sportswear
clothing 228 n.

sporty
showy 875 adj.

spot
small thing 33 n.
place 185 n.
variegate 437 vb.
see 438 vb.
notice 455 vb.
detect 484 vb.
understand 516 vb.
defect 647 n.

make unclean
  649 vb.
pattern 844 n.
blemish 845 n.
slur 867 n.

spot check
enquiry 459 n.

spotless
perfect 646 adj.
clean 648 adj.
innocent 935 adj.
pure 950 adj.

spotlight
lighting 420 n.
manifest 522 vb.
advertise 528 vb.
publicity 528 n.
publish 528 vb.
theatre 594 n.

spot on
accurate 494 adj.
truly 494 adv.

spots
mottle 437 n.
skin disease 651 n.

spotted
mottled 437 adj.
imperfect 647 adj.

spotty
convex 253 adj.

spouse
spouse 894 n.

spout
projection 254 n.
orifice 263 n.
outlet 298 n.
ascend 308 vb.
flow 350 vb.
stream 350 n.
conduit 351 n.
orate 579 vb.
be loquacious
  581 vb.

sprain
derange 63 vb.
disable 161 vb.
weaken 163 vb.
force 176 vb.
distort 246 vb.
pain 377 n.
impairment 655 n.

sprat
small thing 33 n.

sprats
fish food 301 n.

sprat to catch a
  mackerel

trap 542 n.

sprawl
dispersion 75 n.
expand 197 vb.
lengthen 203 vb.
be horizontal
  216 vb.
repose 683 vb.

sprawling
supine 216 adj.

spray
branch 53 n.
bunch 74 n.
disperse 75 vb.
propellant 287 n.
emit 300 vb.
vaporize 338 vb.
vaporizer 338 n.
irrigator 341 n.
moisten 341 vb.
moisture 341 n.
bubble 355 n.
foliage 366 n.
medicine 658 n.

spread
grow 36 vb.
increase 36 n.
be dispersed 75 vb.
disperse 75 vb.
dispersion 75 n.
generalize 79 vb.
prevail 178 vb.
extend 183 vb.
range 183 n.
pervade 189 vb.
expand 197 vb.
expansion 197 n.
flatten 216 vb.
cover 226 vb.
diverge 294 vb.
divergence 294 n.
feasting 301 n.
meal 301 n.
fat 357 n.
publish 528 vb.

spread abroad
publish 528 vb.

spreadeagled
supine 216 adj.

spread like wildfire
be dispersed 75 vb.
prevail 178 vb.
expand 197 vb.
be published
  528 vb.

spread out
disperse 75 vb.

extend 183 vb.
lengthen 203 vb.
spree
festivity 837 n.
revel 837 n.
drunkenness 949 n.
sprig
branch 53 n.
young plant 132 n.
foliage 366 n.
sprightly
active 678 adj.
cheerful 833 adj.
spring
period 110 n.
spring 128 n.
source 156 n.
coil 251 n.
move fast 277 vb.
spurt 277 n.
recoil 280 n.
outflow 298 n.
ascend 308 vb.
leap 312 n.
leap 312 vb.
elasticity 328 n.
stream 350 n.
machine 630 n.
springboard
recoil 280 n.
springbok
mammal 365 n.
spring-cleaning
cleansing 648 n.
spring from
begin 68 vb.
result 157 vb.
spring onion
fruit and vegetables 301 n.
spring roll
dish 301 n.
spring something on one
surprise 508 vb.
springtime
spring 128 n.
spring to one's feet
lift oneself 310 vb.
spring up
become 1 vb.
grow 36 vb.
begin 68 vb.
happen 154 vb.
expand 197 vb.
lift oneself 310 vb.
leap 312 vb.

be visible 443 vb.
spring upon
surprise 508 vb.
springy
soft 327 adj.
elastic 328 adj.
sprinkle
small quantity 33 n.
mix 43 vb.
disperse 75 vb.
coat 226 vb.
emit 300 vb.
let fall 311 vb.
moisten 341 vb.
rain 350 vb.
sprinkler
irrigator 341 n.
extinguisher 382 n.
sprinkling
small quantity 33 n.
tincture 43 n.
dispersion 75 n.
powderiness 332 n.
ritual act 988 n.
sprint
accelerate 277 vb.
spurt 277 n.
racing 716 n.
sprite
elf 970 n.
spritzer
draught 301 n.
sprocket
tooth 256 n.
notch 260 n.
sprout
grow 36 vb.
begin 68 vb.
young plant 132 n.
result 157 vb.
reproduce itself 167 vb.
descendant 170 n.
expand 197 vb.
vegetate 366 vb.
sprouts
fruit and vegetables 301 n.
spruce
orderly 60 adj.
tree 366 n.
clean 648 adj.
clean 648 vb.
personable 841 adj.

spruce up
make better 654 n.
decorate 844 vb.
sprung
soft 327 adj.
elastic 328 adj.
spry
vigorous 174 adj.
active 678 adj.
cheerful 833 adj.
spumante
wine 301 n.
spume
effervesce 318 vb.
wave 350 n.
bubble 355 n.
bubble 355 vb.
spumy
bubbly 355 adj.
white 427 adj.
spun
narrow 206 adj.
spunk
vitality 162 n.
vigorousness 174 n.
resolution 599 n.
courage 855 n.
spunky
courageous 855 adj.
spur
branch 53 n.
young plant 132 n.
stimulant 174 n.
high land 209 n.
projection 254 n.
sharp point 256 n.
accelerate 277 vb.
impel 279 vb.
break in 369 vb.
incentive 612 n.
incite 612 vb.
hasten 680 vb.
animate 821 vb.
excitant 821 n.
spurious
spurious 542 adj.
bastard 954 adj.
spurn
exclude 57 vb.
reject 607 vb.
refuse 760 vb.
hate 888 vb.
despise 922 vb.
spur of the moment
spontaneity 609 n.

spur on
incite 612 vb.
spurs
decoration 729 n.
badge of rank 743 n.
honours 866 n.
spurt
accelerate 277 vb.
spurt 277 n.
emit 300 vb.
activity 678 n.
hasten 680 vb.
sputnik
spaceship 276 n.
satellite 321 n.
sputter
be agitated 318 vb.
hiss 406 vb.
sibilation 406 n.
sputum
excrement 302 n.
spy
scan 438 vb.
see 438 vb.
spectator 441 n.
watch 441 vb.
be curious 453 vb.
detective 459 n.
enquire 459 vb.
enquirer 459 n.
secret service 459 n.
informer 524 n.
warner 664 n.
revolter 738 n.
spyglass
telescope 442 n.
spying
inspection 438 n.
inquisitive 453 adj.
secret service 459 n.
sedition 738 n.
spy out the land
scan 438 vb.
squabble
quarrel 709 n.
quarrel 709 vb.
squad
band 74 n.
personnel 686 n.
formation 722 n.
squadron
band 74 n.
shipping 275 n.
air force 722 n.

formation 722 n.
navy 722 n.
squadron leader
  air officer 741 n.
squalid
  unclean 649 adj.
  disreputable
    867 adj.
squall
  storm 176 n.
  commotion 318 n.
  gale 352 n.
  cry 408 vb.
  quarrel 709 n.
squalor
  uncleanness 649 n.
  poverty 801 n.
  ugliness 842 n.
squander
  consume 165 vb.
  waste 634 vb.
  misuse 675 vb.
  lose 772 vb.
  be prodigal 815 vb.
square
  equal 28 adj.
  equalize 28 vb.
  compensate 31 vb.
  double 91 vb.
  four 96 adj.
  quaternity 96 n.
  quadruple 97 vb.
  antiquated 127 adj.
  archaism 127 n.
  place 185 n.
  housing 192 n.
  fleshy 195 adj.
  verticality 215 n.
  angular figure
    247 n.
  navigate 269 vb.
  be true 494 vb.
  bribe 612 vb.
  just 913 adj.
  honourable
    929 adj.
square dance
  dance 837 n.
  dancing 837 n.
square deal
  justice 913 n.
square inch
  measure 183 n.
square meal
  meal 301 n.
square metre
  measure 183 n.

square peg in a round
  hole
  unrelatedness 10 n.
  misfit 25 n.
  nonconformist
    84 n.
  displacement
    188 n.
  bungler 697 n.
square root
  numerical element
    85 n.
square the circle
  attempt the impos-
    sible 470 vb.
square up to
  fight 716 vb.
square yard
  measure 183 n.
squash
  crowd 74 n.
  suppress 165 vb.
  make smaller
    198 vb.
  flatten 216 vb.
  fruit and vegetables
    301 n.
  soft drink 301 n.
  abase 311 vb.
  lower 311 vb.
  soften 327 vb.
  pulpiness 356 n.
  confute 479 vb.
  ball game 837 n.
  humiliate 872 vb.
squat
  small 33 adj.
  place oneself
    187 vb.
  dwell 192 vb.
  quarters 192 n.
  fleshy 195 adj.
  dwarfish 196 adj.
  short 204 adj.
  thick 205 adj.
  low 210 adj.
  encroach 306 vb.
  sit down 311 vb.
  possess 773 vb.
  appropriate
    786 vb.
  unsightly 842 adj.
squatter
  intruder 59 n.
  resident 191 n.
  possessor 776 n.
  usurper 916 n.

squaw
  female 373 n.
  spouse 894 n.
squawk
  shrill 407 vb.
  stridor 407 n.
  cry 408 vb.
  ululate 409 vb.
  ululation 409 n.
squeak
  faintness 401 n.
  sound faint 401 vb.
  rasp 407 vb.
  stridor 407 n.
  cry 408 vb.
  ululate 409 vb.
  ululation 409 n.
  deprecate 762 vb.
squeaky
  strident 407 adj.
squeal
  shrill 407 vb.
  cry 408 n.
  ululate 409 vb.
  inform 524 vb.
  divulge 526 vb.
  accuse 928 vb.
squealer
  informer 524 n.
  bad person 938 n.
squeamish
  sick 651 adj.
  fastidious 862 adj.
  prudish 950 adj.
squeeze
  small quantity
    33 n.
  abate 37 vb.
  diminution 37 n.
  crowd 74 n.
  compression 198 n.
  make smaller
    198 vb.
  be dense 324 vb.
  touch 378 n.
  hindrance 702 n.
  obstruct 702 vb.
  oppress 735 vb.
  compel 740 vb.
  restriction 747 n.
  retention 778 n.
  rob 788 vb.
  courteous act
    884 n.
  caress 889 vb.
  endearment 889 n.

squeeze dry
  levy 786 vb.
squeeze in
  fill 54 vb.
  load 193 vb.
  make smaller
    198 vb.
squeeze out
  extract 304 vb.
squelch
  suppress 165 vb.
  be wet 341 vb.
  moisture 341 n.
  hiss 406 vb.
  sibilation 406 n.
squelchy
  soft 327 adj.
  humid 341 adj.
  marshy 347 adj.
squib
  bang 402 n.
squid
  marine life 365 n.
squiffy
  tipsy 949 adj.
squiggle
  coil 251 n.
squinny
  scan 438 vb.
squint
  be oblique 220 vb.
  obliquity 220 n.
  gaze 438 vb.
  look 438 n.
  vision 438 n.
  be blind 439 vb.
  be dim-sighted
    440 vb.
  dim sight 440 n.
  blemish 845 n.
  church interior
    990 n.
squint at
  scan 438 vb.
squint-eyed
  malevolent
    898 adj.
squire
  accompany 89 vb.
  male 372 n.
  minister to 703 vb.
  master 741 n.
  retainer 742 n.
  serve 742 vb.
  owner 776 n.
  aristocrat 868 n.
  be servile 879 vb.

lover 887 n.
court 889 vb.
squirm
wriggle 251 vb.
be agitated 318 vb.
feel pain 377 vb.
be excited 821 vb.
suffer 825 vb.
squirrel
mammal 365 n.
squirt
small quantity
33 n.
dwarf 196 n.
outflow 298 n.
emit 300 vb.
irrigate 341 vb.
irrigator 341 n.
flow 350 vb.
squish
hiss 406 vb.
sibilation 406 n.
S-shaped
snaky 251 adj.
St Bernard
dog 365 n.
dance 837 n.
**St Christopher
medal**
talisman 983 n.
St Valentine's Day
anniversary 141 n.
St Vitus's dance
spasm 318 n.
nervous disorders
651 n.
stab
cut 46 vb.
pierce 263 vb.
kill 362 vb.
give pain 377 vb.
pang 377 n.
ill-treat 645 vb.
wound 655 n.
wound 655 vb.
strike at 712 vb.
suffering 825 n.
stab at
attempt 671 n.
stability
stability 153 n.
stabilize
stabilize 153 vb.
stabilizer
stabilizer 153 n.
stab in the back
attack 712 n.

be dishonest
930 vb.
perfidy 930 n.
stable
equal 28 adj.
group 74 n.
lasting 113 adj.
fixed 153 adj.
strong 162 adj.
dwell 192 vb.
stable 192 n.
horse 273 n.
store 632 vb.
inexcitable
823 adj.
stable companion
concomitant 89 n.
chum 880 n.
staccato
adagio 412 adv.
stack
great quantity
32 n.
bring together
74 vb.
bunch 74 n.
rock 344 n.
store 632 n.
store 632 vb.
acquisition 771 n.
stacks
great quantity
32 n.
funds 797 n.
stack system
gramophone 414 n.
stack the cards
predetermine
608 vb.
stadium
athletics 162 n.
meeting place
192 n.
onlookers 441 n.
theatre 594 n.
racing 716 n.
arena 724 n.
staff
component 58 n.
band 74 n.
support 218 n.
notation 410 n.
employ 622 vb.
personnel 686 n.
director 690 n.
club 723 n.

army officer 741 n.
badge of rule
743 n.
commission
751 vb.
hope 852 n.
vestments 989 n.
staff of life
food 301 n.
life 360 n.
stag
mammal 365 n.
male animal
372 n.
gambler 618 n.
purchaser 792 n.
stage
juncture 8 n.
degree 27 n.
serial place 73 n.
situation 186 n.
layer 207 n.
stand 218 n.
view 438 n.
show 522 vb.
dramatize 594 vb.
stage set 594 n.
theatre 594 n.
arena 724 n.
stage, the
drama 594 n.
**stage a demonstra-
tion**
be ostentatious
875 vb.
stage a strike
halt 145 vb.
stage directions
dramaturgy 594 n.
stage-door Johnny
playgoer 594 n.
stage fright
acting 594 n.
fear 854 n.
stage-manage
cause 156 vb.
lurk 523 vb.
dramatize 594 vb.
be ostentatious
875 vb.
stage manager
stage manager
594 n.
stage name
insubstantial thing
4 n.

misnomer 562 n.
stage set
stage set 594 n.
stage show
stage show 594 n.
stagestruck
dramatic 594 adj.
stage villain
acting 594 n.
stage whisper
voice 577 n.
dramaturgy 594 n.
stage-whisper
voice 577 vb.
stagflation
finance 797 n.
stagger
grade 73 vb.
vary 152 vb.
be weak 163 vb.
obliquity 220 n.
walk 267 vb.
move slowly
278 vb.
oscillate 317 vb.
be agitated 318 vb.
surprise 508 vb.
be fatigued 684 vb.
show feeling
818 vb.
impress 821 vb.
be wonderful
864 vb.
be drunk 949 vb.
staggering
unexpected
508 adj.
drunkenness 949 n.
tipsy 949 adj.
staggers
animal disease
651 n.
staggers, the
inequality 29 n.
stagnant
inert 175 adj.
quiescent 266 adj.
insalubrious
653 adj.
apathetic 820 adj.
stagnate
be quiescent
266 vb.
be inactive 679 vb.
be insensitive
820 vb.

stagnation
  unproductiveness
    172 n.
  inertness 175 n.
  quiescence 266 n.
  nonuse 674 n.
  inaction 677 n.
  inactivity 679 n.
  moral insensibility
    820 n.
stag party
  male 372 n.
  social gathering
    882 n.
staid
  inexcitable
    823 adj.
  serious 834 adj.
stain
  tincture 43 n.
  coat 226 vb.
  facing 226 n.
  colour 425 vb.
  pigment 425 n.
  mark 547 vb.
  trace 548 n.
  defect 647 n.
  dirt 649 n.
  make unclean
    649 vb.
  impair 655 vb.
  blemish 845 n.
  blemish 845 vb.
  shame 867 vb.
  slur 867 n.
stained-glass window
  church interior
    990 n.
stainless
  honourable
    929 adj.
  virtuous 933 adj.
  innocent 935 adj.
stair
  degree 27 n.
  bond 47 n.
  stand 218 n.
  ascent 308 n.
staircase
  series 71 n.
  ascent 308 n.
stairs
  series 71 n.
  ascent 308 n.
  access 624 n.
stairway
  ascent 308 n.

access 624 n.
stake
  fastening 47 n.
  pillar 218 n.
  gamble 618 vb.
  gambling 618 n.
  contend 716 vb.
  promise 764 vb.
  security 767 n.
  estate 777 n.
  property 777 n.
  offering 781 n.
  portion 783 n.
  means of execution
    964 n.
stake, the
  killing 362 n.
  furnace 383 n.
  suffering 825 n.
stake a claim
  claim 915 vb.
stakes
  contest 716 n.
stalactite
  hanging object
    217 n.
stalagmite
  verticality 215 n.
stale
  repeated 106 adj.
  unsavoury 391 adj.
  fetid 397 adj.
  known 490 adj.
  feeble 572 adj.
  insalubrious
    653 adj.
  used 673 adj.
  tedious 838 adj.
  dull 840 adj.
stalemate
  draw 28 n.
  equilibrium 28 n.
  halt 145 vb.
  stop 145 n.
  inaction 677 n.
  obstacle 702 n.
  noncompletion
    726 n.
  defeat 728 n.
stalk
  chief part 52 n.
  filament 208 n.
  support 218 n.
  cylinder 252 n.
  gait 265 n.
  walk 267 vb.
  foliage 366 n.

hunt 619 vb.
  pursue 619 vb.
stall
  put off 136 vb.
  halt 145 vb.
  small house 192 n.
  stable 192 n.
  compartment
    194 n.
  seat 218 n.
  fly 271 vb.
  be equivocal
    518 vb.
  be irresolute
    601 vb.
  be obstructive
    702 vb.
  fail 728 vb.
  shop 796 n.
  church interior
    990 n.
stallion
  horse 273 n.
  male animal
    372 n.
stalls
  listener 415 n.
  onlookers 441 n.
  playgoer 594 n.
  theatre 594 n.
stalwart
  stalwart 162 adj.
  colleague 707 n.
stamen
  flower 366 n.
stamina
  durability 113 n.
  stamina 600 n.
stammer
  pronunciation
    577 n.
  speech defect
    580 n.
  stammer 580 vb.
  guilt 936 n.
stamp
  uniformity 16 n.
  copy 22 n.
  mould 23 n.
  adhesive 47 n.
  sort 77 n.
  form 243 n.
  form 243 vb.
  concavity 255 n.
  make concave
    255 vb.
  walk 267 vb.

knock 279 n.
  leap 312 vb.
  be loud 400 vb.
  assent 488 n.
  gesticulate 547 vb.
  indication 547 n.
  label 547 n.
  mark 547 vb.
  picture 553 n.
  engrave 555 vb.
  print 587 vb.
  correspondence
    588 n.
  deprecate 762 vb.
  give security
    767 vb.
  title deed 767 n.
  mint 797 vb.
  be excitable
    822 vb.
  be angry 891 vb.
  get angry 891 vb.
  applaud 923 vb.
stamp-collector
  collector 492 n.
stamp down
  flatten 216 vb.
stampede
  move fast 277 vb.
  hasten 680 vb.
  defeat 728 n.
  compel 740 vb.
  fear 854 n.
  fear 854 vb.
  frighten 854 vb.
  be cowardly
    856 vb.
stamping
  loudness 400 n.
  applause 923 n.
stamping ground
  focus 76 n.
stamp on
  suppress 165 vb.
  be severe 735 vb.
  oppress 735 vb.
stamp out
  suppress 165 vb.
  extinguish 382 vb.
  subjugate 745 vb.
stance
  form 243 n.
stand
  last 113 vb.
  cease 145 vb.
  be situated 186 vb.
  place 187 vb.

place oneself
187 vb.
be present 189 vb.
meeting place
192 n.
pavilion 192 n.
be vertical 215 vb.
stand 218 n.
support 218 vb.
be quiescent
266 vb.
confute 479 vb.
opinion 485 n.
vote 605 vb.
be inactive 679 vb.
opposition 704 n.
resistance 715 n.
battle 718 n.
arena 724 n.
offer oneself
759 vb.
give 781 vb.
shop 796 n.
expend 806 vb.
be patient 823 vb.
show respect
920 vb.
stand a chance
be possible 469 vb.
be likely 471 vb.
standard
prototype 23 n.
degree 27 n.
median 30 adj.
general 79 adj.
rule 81 n.
typical 83 adj.
high structure
209 n.
testing agent
461 n.
gauge 465 n.
flag 547 n.
linguistic 557 adj.
right 913 adj.
Standard English
language 557 n.
grammar 564 n.
standard error
statistics 86 n.
standardize
make uniform
16 vb.
order 60 vb.
regularize 62 vb.
make conform
83 vb.

gauge 465 vb.
standard lamp
lamp 420 n.
standards
morals 917 n.
stand aside
recede 290 vb.
resign 753 n.
stand by
be present 189 vb.
await 507 vb.
expect 507 vb.
prepare oneself
669 vb.
not act 677 vb.
aid 703 vb.
patronize 703 vb.
defend 713 vb.
keep faith 768 vb.
stand-by
aider 703 n.
stand corrected
incur blame
924 vb.
stand down
cease 145 vb.
relinquish 621 vb.
resign 753 vb.
stand for
indicate 547 vb.
represent 551 vb.
stand in
act 594 vb.
stand-in
substitute 150 n.
deputy 755 n.
stand in for
substitute 150 vb.
function 622 vb.
deputize 755 vb.
standing
state 7 n.
circumstance 8 n.
degree 27 n.
serial place 73 n.
classification 77 n.
permanence 144 n.
permanent 144 adj.
fixed 153 adj.
situation 186 n.
vertical 215 adj.
prestige 866 n.
respectful 920 adj.
standing army
army 722 n.
standing joke
witticism 839 n.

standing order
practice 610 n.
paper money
797 n.
payment 804 n.
standing ovation
victory 727 n.
trophy 729 n.
celebration 876 n.
applause 923 n.
standoffish
proud 871 adj.
unsociable 883 adj.
stand on ceremony
be ostentatious
875 vb.
show respect
920 vb.
stand one's ground
stay 144 vb.
stand firm 599 vb.
oppose 704 vb.
resist 715 vb.
stand on one's own feet
be free 744 vb.
stand on one's own two feet
achieve liberty
746 vb.
stand out
jut 254 vb.
be visible 443 vb.
be plain 522 vb.
be obstinate
602 vb.
not observe 769 vb.
standpipe
water 339 n.
conduit 351 n.
extinguisher 382 n.
standpoint
situation 186 n.
view 438 n.
standstill
lull 145 n.
stop 145 n.
quiescence 266 n.
difficulty 700 n.
stand to reason
be certain 473 vb.
be reasonable
475 vb.
be proved 478 V.
be plain 522 vb.
stand trial
stand trial 959 vb.

stand up
be vertical 215 vb.
ascend 308 vb.
lift oneself 310 vb.
stand up for
patronize 703 vb.
approve 923 vb.
vindicate 927 vb.
stand up to
support 218 vb.
suffice 635 vb.
oppose 704 vb.
withstand 704 vb.
defy 711 vb.
stanza
verse form 593 n.
staple
connect 45 vb.
fastening 47 n.
chief part 52 n.
fibre 208 n.
sharp point 256 n.
texture 331 n.
important 638 adj.
merchandise
795 n.
star
superior 34 n.
star 321 n.
person 371 n.
guide 520 n.
badge 547 n.
act 594 vb.
actor 594 n.
dramatize 594 vb.
bigwig 638 n.
exceller 644 n.
badge of rank
743 n.
trimming 844 n.
desired object
859 n.
have a reputation
866 vb.
honours 866 n.
person of repute
866 n.
favourite 890 n.
starboard
dextrality 241 n.
starch
food content 301 n.
harden 326 vb.
hardness 326 n.
powder 332 n.
thicken 354 vb.
thickening 354 n.

starchy
  rigid 326 adj.
  formal 875 adj.
star-crossed
  unfortunate
    731 adj.
stardom
  famousness 866 n.
stare
  gaze 438 vb.
  look 438 n.
  watch 441 vb.
  not expect 508 vb.
  wonder 864 vb.
  be rude 885 vb.
starfish
  marine life 365 n.
star fruit
  fruit and vegetables
    301 n.
stargazing
  astronomic
    321 adj.
  astronomy 321 n.
  abstracted 456 adj.
  abstractedness
    456 n.
stark
  absolute 32 adj.
  flagrant 32 adj.
  wintry 129 adj.
  uncovered 229 adj.
  florid 425 adj.
  plain 573 adj.
starkers
  bareness 229 n.
  uncovered 229 adj.
stark naked
  uncovered 229 adj.
stark staring mad
  mentally disor-
    dered 503 adj.
starlight
  star 321 n.
  light 417 n.
  luminary 420 n.
starlit
  undimmed
    417 adj.
starry
  celestial 321 adj.
  undimmed
    417 adj.
starry-eyed
  happy 824 adj.
  hoping 852 adj.

stars
  cause 156 n.
  influence 178 n.
  fate 596 n.
Stars and Stripes
  flag 547 n.
start
  begin 68 vb.
  initiate 68 vb.
  start 68 n.
  space 201 vb.
  move fast 277 vb.
  impel 279 vb.
  recoil 280 vb.
  leap 312 vb.
  agitation 318 n.
  be agitated 318 vb.
  not expect 508 vb.
  incite 612 vb.
  be excitable
    822 vb.
  fear 854 vb.
starter
  prelude 66 n.
  beginning 68 n.
  hors-d'oeuvres
    301 n.
starting point
  premise 475 n.
startle
  surprise 508 vb.
  raise the alarm
    665 vb.
  excite 821 vb.
  frighten 854 vb.
  be wonderful
    864 vb.
start up
  initiate 68 vb.
  happen 154 vb.
  ascend 308 vb.
  be visible 443 vb.
  get angry 891 vb.
starvation
  scarcity 636 n.
  hunger 859 n.
  fasting 946 n.
starve
  weaken 163 vb.
  make thin 206 vb.
  be cold 380 vb.
  refrigerate 382 vb.
  be poor 801 vb.
  be hungry 859 vb.
  starve 946 vb.

starving
  necessitous
    627 adj.
  underfed 636 adj.
  hungry 859 adj.
  fasting 946 adj.
Star Wars
  rocket 276 n.
  safeguard 662 n.
  arms 723 n.
  missile weapon
    723 n.
state
  state 7 n.
  district 184 n.
  territory 184 n.
  nation 371 n.
  national 371 adj.
  inform 524 vb.
  affirm 532 vb.
  phrase 563 vb.
  community 708 n.
  political organiza-
    tion 733 n.
  ostentation 875 n.
stately
  elegant 575 adj.
  impressive 821 adj.
  worshipful 866 adj.
  proud 871 adj.
  formal 875 adj.
stately home
  house 192 n.
statement
  list 87 n.
  musical piece
    412 n.
  topic 452 n.
  testimony 466 n.
  report 524 n.
  affirmation 532 n.
  description 590 n.
  pretext 614 n.
  accounts 808 n.
statement of the ob-
    vious
  maxim 496 n.
state of affairs
  circumstance 8 n.
  affairs 154 n.
  event 154 n.
state of health
  state 7 n.
  salubrity 652 n.
state of mind
  state 7 n.
  affections 817 n.

state secret
  secret 530 n.
statesmanship
  sagacity 498 n.
  policy 623 n.
  tactics 688 n.
  management
    689 n.
statesman, -woman
  sage 500 n.
  planner 623 n.
  manager 690 n.
static
  permanent 144 adj.
  quiescent 266 adj.
  radiation 417 n.
static electricity
  electricity 160 n.
station
  degree 27 n.
  serial place 73 n.
  stopping place
    145 n.
  place 185 n.
  situation 186 n.
  place 187 vb.
  station 187 n.
  abode 192 n.
  railway 624 n.
  nobility 868 n.
  duty 917 n.
stationary
  permanent 144 adj.
  quiescent 266 adj.
  nonactive 677 adj.
  inactive 679 adj.
stationed, be
  be situated 186 vb.
stationery
  stationery 586 n.
stations of the cross
  ritual act 988 n.
  ritual object 988 n.
  church interior
    990 n.
station waggon
  automobile 274 n.
statistical
  statistical 86 adj.
statistics
  statistics 86 n.
  accuracy 494 n.
statuary
  sculpture 554 n.
  ornamental art
    844 n.

statue
copy 22 n.
reminder 505 n.
monument 548 n.
image 551 n.
sculpture 554 n.
honours 866 n.

statuesque
beautiful 841 adj.
proud 871 adj.

statuette
image 551 n.
sculpture 554 n.

stature
height 209 n.

status
state 7 n.
circumstance 8 n.
relativeness 9 n.
degree 27 n.
serial place 73 n.
classification 77 n.
prestige 866 n.

status quo
circumstance 8 n.
permanence 144 n.
reversion 148 n.

statute
rule 81 n.
precept 693 n.
legislation 953 n.

statutory
legal 953 adj.

staunch
strong 162 adj.
close 264 vb.
staunch 350 VB.
resolute 599 adj.
friendly 880 adj.
trustworthy
929 adj.

stave
strip 208 n.
notation 410 n.
verse form 593 n.
club 723 n.

stave off
obstruct 702 vb.

stay
bond 47 n.
continue 108 vb.
last 113 vb.
stay 144 vb.
cease 145 vb.
be present 189 vb.
presence 189 n.
dwell 192 vb.

support 218 n.
support 218 vb.
bring to rest
266 vb.
stop 266 int.
social round 882 n.
visit 882 vb.

stay-at-home
solitary 883 n.
unsociable 883 adj.

stay at one's post
do one's duty
917 vb.

staying power
durability 113 n.
power 160 n.
strength 162 n.
stamina 600 n.

stay of execution
delay 136 n.

stay one's hand
cease 145 vb.
pause 145 vb.

stay put
be quiescent
266 vb.
stand firm 599 vb.
be obstinate
602 vb.

stays
underwear 228 n.

stay the course
persevere 600 vb.

steadfast
fixed 153 adj.
resolute 599 adj.
obedient 739 adj.

steading
farm 370 n.

steady
uniform 16 adj.
equal 28 adj.
orderly 60 adj.
regular 81 adj.
frequent 139 adj.
periodical 141 adj.
fixed 153 adj.
unchangeable
153 adj.
support 218 vb.
still 266 adj.
retain 778 vb.
impassive 820 adj.
tranquillize
823 vb.
lover 887 n.

steady state theory
universe 321 n.

steak
piece 53 n.
meat 301 n.

steal
be stealthy 525 vb.
steal 788 vb.
cheapness 812 n.

steal a march on
do before 119 vb.
be early 135 vb.
precede 283 vb.
outdo 306 vb.
deceive 542 vb.
be cunning 698 vb.

steal away
run away 620 vb.
escape 667 vb.

steal one's thunder
abate 37 vb.
precede 283 vb.
outdo 306 vb.

stealth
cunning 698 n.

steal the show
be superior 34 vb.
act 594 vb.
have a reputation
866 vb.

stealthy
muted 401 adj.
stealthy 525 adj.
cautious 858 adj.

steam
energy 160 n.
be in motion
265 vb.
voyage 269 vb.
propellant 287 n.
exude 298 vb.
emit 300 vb.
cook 301 vb.
gas 336 n.
gasify 336 vb.
vaporize 338 vb.
water 339 n.
be wet 341 vb.
bubble 355 vb.
cloud 355 n.
be hot 379 vb.
heat 379 n.
heater 383 n.

steam engine
locomotive 274 n.
machine 630 n.

steamer
pot 194 n.
ship 275 n.

steaming
vaporific 338 adj.
vaporization 338 n.
humid 341 adj.
hot 379 adj.

steamroller
demolish 165 vb.
flattener 216 n.
smoother 258 n.
locomotive 274 n.
compel 740 vb.

steamship
ship 275 n.

steamy
gaseous 336 adj.
vaporific 338 adj.
cloudy 355 adj.
heated 381 adj.

stearin
fat 357 n.

steatopygous
broad 205 adj.

steed
horse 273 n.

steel
a mixture 43 n.
strength 162 n.
strengthen 162 vb.
sharp edge 256 n.
hard 326 adj.
harden 326 vb.
hardness 326 n.
lighter 385 n.
resolution 599 n.

steel band
orchestra 413 n.

steel drum
drum 414 n.

steel oneself
be resolute 599 vb.
be insensitive
820 vb.

steelworks
workshop 687 n.

steely
strong 162 adj.
hard 326 adj.
grey 429 adj.
blue 435 adj.
resolute 599 adj.

steelyard
scales 322 n.
workshop 687 n.

steep
high 209 adj.
high land 209 n.
deep 211 adj.
vertical 215 adj.
verticality 215 n.
sloping 220 adj.
immerse 303 vb.
soften 327 vb.
drench 341 vb.
difficult 700 adj.
dear 811 adj.

steeple
high structure
209 n.
sharp point 256 n.
church exterior
990 n.

steeplechase
leap 312 vb.
chase 619 n.
racing 716 n.

steeplejack
climber 308 n.

steepness
height 209 n.
high land 209 n.
verticality 215 n.
incline 220 n.

steer
navigate 269 vb.
cattle 365 n.
male animal
372 n.
direct 689 vb.

steerage
direction 281 n.

steerage class
lower classes 869 n.

steer a middle course
compromise
770 vb.

steer clear of
deviate 282 vb.

steering
navigation 269 n.
direction 281 n.

steering committee
director 690 n.
consignee 754 n.

stellar
celestial 321 adj.

stem
chief part 52 n.
halt 145 vb.
source 156 n.
genealogy 169 n.

support 218 n.
cylinder 252 n.
staunch 350 VB.
foliage 366 n.
tobacco 388 n.
word 559 n.

stem the tide
withstand 704 vb.
resist 715 vb.
triumph 727 vb.

stench
stench 397 n.

stencil
imitator 20 n.
duplicate 22 n.
mould 23 n.
double 91 vb.
paint 553 n.
script 586 n.
stationery 586 n.

stenography
writing 586 n.

stenosis
compression 198 n.

stentorian
sounding 398 adj.
loud 400 adj.

step
degree 27 n.
serial place 73 n.
short distance
200 n.
long measure
203 n.
stand 218 n.
gait 265 n.
walk 267 vb.
ascent 308 n.
attempt 671 n.
deed 676 n.

step aside
deviate 282 vb.

stepbrother or -sister
kinsman 11 n.

step down
descend 309 vb.

stepfather
paternity 169 n.

step in
interfere 231 vb.
enter 297 vb.
mediate 720 vb.

step ladder
bond 47 n.
ascent 308 n.

stepmother
maternity 169 n.

step on it
accelerate 277 vb.
hurry up 680 int.

steppe
space 183 n.
lowness 210 n.
horizontality
216 n.
land 344 n.
plain 348 n.

stepping-stone
degree 27 n.
bond 47 n.
opportunity 137 n.
passage 305 n.
bridge 624 n.
instrument 628 n.

stepping stones
series 71 n.

stepping up
increase 36 n.
stimulation 174 n.

steps
bond 47 n.
series 71 n.
ascent 308 n.
policy 623 n.
means 629 n.
action 676 n.

step up
augment 36 vb.
invigorate 174 vb.
accelerate 277 vb.

stereo
sound 398 n.
sounding 398 adj.

stereometry
geometry 465 n.

stereophonic
sounding 398 adj.

stereophonic sound
sound 398 n.

stereoscopic
seeing 438 adj.

stereo system
gramophone 414 n.

stereo tower
gramophone 414 n.

stereotype
make uniform
16 vb.
uniformity 16 n.
copy 22 n.
stabilize 153 vb.
printing 555 n.
print 587 n.
print 587 vb.

print-type 587 n.
acting 594 n.

stereotyped
uniform 16 adj.
unchangeable
153 adj.
usual 610 adj.

sterile
impotent 161 adj.
unproductive
172 adj.

sterility
impotence 161 n.
unproductiveness
172 n.

sterilize
purify 648 vb.
make sanitary
652 adj.
doctor 658 vb.

sterling
genuine 494 adj.
valuable 644 adj.
monetary 797 adj.
money 797 n.

stern
buttocks 238 n.
rear 238 n.
resolute 599 adj.
severe 735 adj.
serious 834 adj.
angry 891 adj.
sullen 893 adj.
unkind 898 adj.

sternness
resolution 599 n.
seriousness 834 n.
resentment 891 n.
sullenness 893 n.

steroid
drug 658 n.

stertorous
hoarse 407 adj.

stet
stabilize 153 vb.

stethoscope
hearing aid 415 n.
diagnostic 658 n.

stetson
headgear 228 n.

stevedore
displacement
188 n.
boatman 270 n.
worker 686 n.

stew
a mixture 43 n.

cook 301 vb.
dish 301 n.
lake 346 n.
predicament 700 n.
excitable state
  822 n.
anger 891 n.
steward
aeronaut 271 n.
manager 690 n.
official 690 n.
domestic 742 n.
retainer 742 n.
servant 742 n.
consignee 754 n.
treasurer 798 n.
stewardess
aeronaut 271 n.
servant 742 n.
stewed
tipsy 949 adj.
stick
cohere 48 vb.
halt 145 vb.
go on 146 vb.
be contiguous
  202 vb.
support 218 vb.
pierce 263 vb.
transfer 272 vb.
rub 333 vb.
be wont 610 vb.
club 723 n.
defeat 728 n.
fail 728 vb.
excitant 821 n.
scourge 964 n.
stick at nothing
be resolute 599 vb.
be intemperate
  943 vb.
sticker
adhesive 47 n.
label 547 n.
picture 553 n.
sticking
coherence 48 n.
sticking plaster
adhesive 47 n.
substitute 150 n.
surgical dressing
  658 n.
sticking point
resolution 599 n.
stick insect
insect 365 n.

stick in the mind
be remembered
  505 vb.
stick it out
stand firm 599 vb.
persevere 600 vb.
stickleback
fish 365 n.
stickler
narrow mind
  481 n.
perfectionist 862 n.
stick on
add 38 vb.
affix 45 vb.
accuse 928 vb.
stick one's neck out
face danger 661 vb.
be courageous
  855 vb.
be rash 857 vb.
stick out
jut 254 vb.
emerge 298 vb.
be visible 443 vb.
stick out for
contend 716 vb.
bargain 791 vb.
**stick out like a sore
  thumb**
disagree 25 vb.
jut 254 vb.
attract notice
  455 vb.
sticks
surroundings
  230 n.
racing 716 n.
sticks, the
district 184 n.
stick to
cohere 48 vb.
observe 768 vb.
retain 778 vb.
take 786 vb.
stick together
unite with 45 vb.
concur 181 vb.
stick to one's guns
be certain 473 vb.
argue 475 vb.
affirm 532 vb.
persevere 600 vb.
be obstinate
  602 vb.
stickup
stealing 788 n.

stick up for
patronize 703 vb.
vindicate 927 vb.
stick with it
persevere 600 vb.
sticky
cohesive 48 adj.
tough 329 adj.
viscid 354 adj.
difficult 700 adj.
retentive 778 adj.
sticky-fingered
thieving 788 adj.
sticky tape
adhesive 47 n.
ligature 47 n.
sticky wicket
predicament 700 n.
stiff
impotent 161 adj.
straight 249 adj.
still 266 adj.
rigid 326 adj.
dead 361 adj.
corpse 363 n.
narrow-minded
  481 adj.
ornate 574 adj.
inelegant 576 adj.
fatigued 684 adj.
severe 735 adj.
restraining
  747 adj.
dear 811 adj.
formal 875 adj.
unsociable 883 adj.
stiffen
strengthen 162 vb.
harden 326 vb.
stiffener
support 218 n.
hardness 326 n.
**stiffen one's upper
  lip**
strengthen 162 vb.
stiff-necked
obstinate 602 adj.
defiant 711 adj.
severe 735 adj.
proud 871 adj.
stiff upper lip
resolution 599 n.
feeling 818 n.
moral insensibility
  820 n.
manliness 855 n.

stiff with
full 54 adj.
stifle
disable 161 vb.
suppress 165 vb.
kill 362 vb.
be hot 379 vb.
heat 381 vb.
extinguish 382 vb.
silence 399 vb.
mute 401 vb.
conceal 525 vb.
make mute 578 vb.
hinder 702 vb.
prohibit 757 vb.
stigma
flower 366 n.
indication 547 n.
blemish 845 n.
slur 867 n.
censure 924 n.
detraction 926 n.
false charge 928 n.
stigmata
indication 547 n.
stigmatize
blemish 845 vb.
shame 867 vb.
criticize 924 vb.
defame 926 vb.
accuse 928 vb.
stile
ascent 308 n.
access 624 n.
obstacle 702 n.
stiletto
sharp point 256 n.
perforator 263 n.
sidearms 723 n.
stiletto heels
footwear 228 n.
still
assuage 177 vb.
moderate 177 adj.
quiescent 266 adj.
still 266 adj.
vaporizer 338 n.
heater 383 n.
silence 399 vb.
silent 399 adj.
nevertheless
  468 adv.
photography 551 n.
make mute 578 vb.
inactive 679 adj.
stillborn
dead 361 adj.

unsuccessful
728 adj.
still life
art subject 553 n.
stillroom
chamber 194 n.
storage 632 n.
still water
water 339 n.
stilted
ornate 574 adj.
inelegant 576 adj.
ridiculous 849 adj.
affected 850 adj.
stilts
leg 267 n.
plaything 837 n.
stimulant
stimulant 174 n.
drug 658 n.
refreshment 685 n.
drug-taking 949 n.
intoxicating
949 adj.
stimulate
augment 36 vb.
cause 156 vb.
invigorate 174 vb.
incite 612 vb.
refresh 685 vb.
animate 821 vb.
stimulator
excitant 821 n.
stimulus
cause 156 n.
stimulant 174 n.
incentive 612 n.
sting
be sharp 256 vb.
sharpness 256 n.
sharp point 256 n.
give pain 377 vb.
pang 377 n.
pungency 388 n.
duplicity 541 n.
badness 645 n.
wound 655 vb.
bane 659 n.
fleece 786 vb.
overcharge 811 vb.
excitant 821 n.
excite 821 vb.
suffering 825 n.
torment 827 vb.
enrage 891 vb.
huff 891 vb.

stingray
fish 365 n.
stingy
insufficient
636 adj.
parsimonious
816 adj.
stink
odour 394 n.
stench 397 n.
stink 397 vb.
uncleanness 649 n.
stink bomb
stench 397 n.
stinker
cad 938 n.
stinking
unsavoury 391 adj.
fetid 397 adj.
not nice 645 adj.
unclean 649 adj.
unpleasant
827 adj.
stint
degree 27 n.
time 108 n.
period 110 n.
labour 682 n.
restrain 747 vb.
portion 783 n.
be parsimonious
816 vb.
stipend
subvention 703 n.
reward 962 n.
stipple
variegate 437 vb.
paint 553 vb.
engrave 555 vb.
stipulate
postulate 475 vb.
give terms 766 vb.
stir
mix 43 vb.
stimulation 174 n.
be in motion
265 vb.
motion 265 n.
cook 301 vb.
agitate 318 vb.
be agitated 318 vb.
commotion 318 n.
activity 678 n.
prison 748 n.
excite 821 vb.
stir-fry
cook 301 vb.

dish 301 n.
stir it
make quarrels
709 vb.
stir one's stumps
travel 267 vb.
move fast 277 vb.
be active 678 vb.
stirring
mixture 43 n.
active 678 adj.
busy 678 adj.
exciting 821 adj.
stirrup
support 218 n.
stirrup cup
valediction 296 n.
draught 301 n.
stir up
move 265 vb.
agitate 318 vb.
stir up a hornet's
nest
be in difficulty
700 vb.
stitch
join 45 vb.
tie 45 vb.
fastening 47 n.
component 58 n.
pang 377 n.
needlework 844 n.
stitching
joint 45 n.
bookbinding 589 n.
stitch in time, a
anticipation 135 n.
stoat
mammal 365 n.
stock
race 11 n.
great quantity
32 n.
ligature 47 n.
accumulation 74 n.
source 156 n.
genealogy 169 n.
hors-d'oeuvres
301 n.
animal 365 n.
tree 366 n.
sauce 389 n.
aphoristic 496 adj.
usual 610 adj.
store 632 n.
provide 633 vb.
property 777 n.

merchandise
795 n.
stockade
barrier 235 n.
enclosure 235 n.
protection 660 n.
shelter 662 n.
defences 713 n.
stock and barrel
all 52 n.
stock-breeding
animal husbandry
369 n.
stockbroker
consignee 754 n.
merchant 794 n.
stockbroker belt
district 184 n.
stock car
automobile 274 n.
stock exchange
stock exchange
618 n.
market 796 n.
finance 797 n.
stockholder
participator 775 n.
owner 776 n.
stocking
treasury 799 n.
stockings
legwear 228 n.
stock-in-trade
means 629 n.
equipment 630 n.
store 632 n.
stockpile
store 632 n.
store 632 vb.
stockroom
storage 632 n.
stocks
lockup 748 n.
pillory 964 n.
stocks and shares
means 629 n.
estate 777 n.
stocks and stones
absence of intellect
448 n.
stock-still
still 266 adj.
stock up
store 632 vb.
provide 633 vb.
stocky
stalwart 162 adj.

fleshy 195 adj.
short 204 adj.
stodgy
tedious 838 adj.
dull 840 adj.
stoic
unfeeling person 820 n.
patient 823 adj.
stoical
impassive 820 adj.
patient 823 adj.
Stoicism
philosophy 449 n.
stoicism
feeling 818 n.
moral insensibility 820 n.
inexcitability 823 n.
patience 823 n.
temperance 942 n.
stoke
augment 36 vb.
stoke up
heat 381 vb.
stole
neckwear 228 n.
vestments 989 n.
stolen goods
booty 790 n.
stolid
inactive 679 adj.
impassive 820 adj.
serious 834 adj.
stomach
stomach 194 n.
insides 224 n.
knuckle under 721 vb.
be patient 823 vb.
liking 859 n.
forgive 909 vb.
stomp
dance 837 n.
dance 837 vb.
stone
uncover 229 vb.
strike 279 vb.
missile 287 n.
propel 287 vb.
weighing 322 n.
solid body 324 n.
hardness 326 n.
rock 344 n.
soil 344 n.
sculpture 554 n.

engraving 555 n.
building material 631 n.
ammunition 723 n.
missile weapon 723 n.
unfeeling person 820 n.
gem 844 n.
not respect 921 vb.
Stone Age
era 110 n.
antiquity 125 n.
stoned
insensible 375 adj.
dead drunk 949 adj.
drugged 949 adj.
stone-deaf
deaf 416 adj.
stone's throw
short distance 200 n.
propulsion 287 n.
stone wall
obstacle 702 n.
stonewall
put off 136 vb.
repel 292 vb.
be loquacious 581 vb.
be obstructive 702 vb.
stonework
structure 331 n.
stony
unproductive 172 adj.
rough 259 adj.
hard 326 adj.
unfeeling 375 adj.
impassive 820 adj.
stony broke
poor 801 adj.
stony ground
shallowness 212 n.
stooge
fool 501 n.
dupe 544 n.
instrument 628 n.
nonentity 639 n.
auxiliary 707 n.
dependant 742 n.
humorist 839 n.
laughingstock 851 n.

stooge for
be servile 879 vb.
stool
seat 218 n.
excrement 302 n.
stool of repentance
penitence 939 n.
penance 941 n.
pillory 964 n.
stool pigeon
informer 524 n.
ambush 527 n.
stoop
lobby 194 n.
descend 309 vb.
descent 309 n.
stoop 311 vb.
plunge 313 n.
demean oneself 867 vb.
be humble 872 vb.
stop
end 69 n.
end 69 vb.
terminate 69 vb.
cease 145 vb.
halt 145 vb.
stop 145 n.
stopping place 145 n.
come to rest 266 vb.
stop 266 int.
arrive 295 vb.
goal 295 n.
silence 399 vb.
camera 442 n.
err 495 vb.
punctuation 547 n.
be inactive 679 vb.
obstruct 702 vb.
fail 728 vb.
restrain 747 vb.
prohibit 757 vb.
stop (clock)
be late 136 vb.
stopcock
stopper 264 n.
tool 630 n.
stop dead
halt 145 vb.
stopgap
substitute 150 n.
substituted 150 adj.
preparatory 669 adj.

stop-go
discontinuous 72 adj.
fitful 142 adj.
stop one in the act
hinder 702 vb.
stoppage
stop 145 n.
strike 145 n.
closure 264 n.
quiescence 266 n.
difficulty 700 n.
hitch 702 n.
stopper
close 264 vb.
stopper 264 n.
stopping
contents 193 n.
stopper 264 n.
stopping (dentistry)
lining 227 n.
stopping train
train 274 n.
slowcoach 278 n.
stop short
halt 145 vb.
come to rest 266 vb.
fall short 307 vb.
stop up
obstruct 702 vb.
stopwatch
timekeeper 117 n.
recording instrument 549 n.
storage
accumulation 74 n.
data processing 86 n.
storage 632 n.
store
accumulation 74 n.
store 632 n.
store 632 vb.
shop 796 n.
storehouse
storage 632 n.
storeroom
chamber 194 n.
storage 632 n.
stores
provisions 301 n.
provision 633 n.
storey
series 71 n.
serial place 73 n.

STO

compartment
194 n.
layer 207 n.
stork
obstetrics 167 n.
bird 365 n.
storm
rampage 61 vb.
turmoil 61 n.
crowd 74 n.
storm 176 n.
blow 352 vb.
be loud 400 vb.
take 786 vb.
excitable state
822 n.
anger 891 n.
be angry 891 vb.
storm-bound
windy 352 adj.
storm centre
centre 225 n.
storm cloud
accumulation 74 n.
cloud 355 n.
storm clouds
adversity 731 n.
storm in a teacup
overestimation
482 n.
exaggeration
546 n.
trifle 639 n.
quarrel 709 n.
stormtroops
attacker 712 n.
combatant 722 n.
stormy
violent 176 adj.
windy 352 adj.
excitable 822 adj.
stormy petrel
bird 365 n.
warning 664 n.
story
ideality 513 n.
news 529 n.
fable 543 n.
narrative 590 n.
witticism 839 n.
stoup
cup 194 n.
church utensil
990 n.
stout
stalwart 162 adj.
strong 162 adj.

STR

fleshy 195 adj.
thick 205 adj.
alcoholic drink
301 n.
courageous
855 adj.
stout-hearted
courageous
855 adj.
stoutness
bulk 195 n.
stove
furnace 383 n.
stow
store 632 vb.
stowage
room 183 n.
storage 632 n.
stow away
conceal 525 vb.
store 632 vb.
stowaway
intruder 59 n.
incomer 297 n.
stow it
hush 399 int.
strabismus
dim sight 440 n.
straddle
extend 183 vb.
expand 197 vb.
diverge 294 vb.
pass 305 vb.
strafe
bombardment
712 n.
fire at 712 vb.
reproach 924 vb.
straggle
be dispersed 75 vb.
wander 267 vb.
stray 282 vb.
straggly
hairy 259 adj.
rare 325 adj.
straight
uniform 16 adj.
vertical 215 adj.
straight 249 adj.
towards 281 adv.
accurate 494 adj.
shapely 841 adj.
honourable
929 adj.
**straight and narrow
path**
virtue 933 n.

STR

straighten
straighten 249 vb.
rectify 654 vb.
straighten out
regularize 62 vb.
be horizontal
216 vb.
rectify 654 vb.
straighten up
be vertical 215 vb.
straight-faced
serious 834 adj.
straightforward
directed 281 adj.
intelligible 516 adj.
veracious 540 adj.
plain 573 adj.
artless 699 adj.
trustworthy
929 adj.
straight forwards
towards 281 adv.
**straight from the
shoulder**
genuine 494 adj.
assertive 532 adj.
veracious 540 adj.
straight line
line 203 n.
straightness 249 n.
strain
temperament 5 n.
be unrelated 10 vb.
race 11 n.
quantity 26 n.
small quantity
33 n.
tincture 43 n.
derange 63 vb.
breed 77 n.
power 160 n.
weaken 163 vb.
genealogy 169 n.
agency 173 n.
force 176 vb.
make smaller
198 vb.
distort 246 vb.
distortion 246 n.
exude 298 vb.
overstep 306 vb.
pain 377 n.
sound 398 n.
tune 412 n.
exaggerate 546 vb.
style 566 n.
be resolute 599 vb.

STR

purify 648 vb.
impairment 655 n.
bane 659 n.
attempt 671 vb.
exertion 682 n.
exert oneself
682 vb.
labour 682 n.
fatigue 684 n.
fatigue 684 vb.
affections 817 n.
worry 825 n.
enmity 881 n.
**strain at a gnat and
swallow a camel**
reason badly
477 vb.
act foolishly
695 vb.
strainer
sorting 62 n.
bowl 194 n.
porosity 263 n.
strain every nerve
exert oneself
682 vb.
strain one's eyes
scan 438 vb.
strait
narrow 206 adj.
narrowness 206 n.
gulf 345 n.
access 624 n.
**straitened circum-
stances**
poverty 801 n.
straitjacket
restraint 747 n.
fetter 748 n.
straitlaced
severe 735 adj.
prudish 950 adj.
straits
predicament 700 n.
strand
fibre 208 n.
filament 208 n.
edge 234 n.
hair 259 n.
shore 344 n.
stranded
fixed 153 adj.
hindered 702 adj.
strange
unrelated 10 adj.
extraneous 59 adj.
unusual 84 adj.

unknown 491 adj.
puzzling 517 adj.
ridiculous 849 adj.
wonderful 864 adj.
stranger
foreigner 59 n.
stranger in our midst
intruder 59 n.
stranger to, a
ignorant 491 adj.
strangle
disable 161 vb.
suppress 165 vb.
make smaller
198 vb.
close 264 vb.
kill 362 vb.
murder 362 vb.
retain 778 vb.
execute 963 vb.
stranglehold
retention 778 n.
strangulation
compression 198 n.
closure 264 n.
killing 362 n.
capital punishment
963 n.
strap
tie 45 n.
strip 208 n.
strike 279 vb.
spank 963 vb.
scourge 964 n.
strapping
stalwart 162 adj.
fleshy 195 adj.
support 218 n.
healthy 650 adj.
stratagem
tactics 688 n.
stratagem 698 n.
strategic
planned 623 adj.
Strategic Defence Initiative
rocket 276 n.
arms 723 n.
strategist
motivator 612 n.
planner 623 n.
expert 696 n.
slyboots 698 n.
strategy
sagacity 498 n.
policy 623 n.
tactics 688 n.

warfare 718 n.
strathspey
musical piece
412 n.
dance 837 n.
stratification
covering 226 n.
stratosphere
height 209 n.
atmosphere 340 n.
stratum
layer 207 n.
horizontality
216 n.
stratus
cloud 355 n.
straw
lightness 323 n.
grass 366 n.
flute 414 n.
trifle 639 n.
strawberry
fruit and vegetables
301 n.
strawberry blond(e)
yellowness 433 n.
strawberry mark
identification
547 n.
blemish 845 n.
straw in the wind
indication 547 n.
straw poll
enquiry 459 n.
vote 605 n.
stray
casual 159 adj.
be in motion
265 vb.
wanderer 268 n.
stray 282 vb.
derelict 779 n.
be wicked 934 vb.
streak
small quantity
33 n.
tincture 43 n.
line 203 n.
narrowness 206 n.
strip 208 n.
furrow 262 n.
groove 262 vb.
move fast 277 vb.
flash 417 n.
stripe 437 n.
variegate 437 vb.

make unclean
649 vb.
streaker
stripper 229 n.
streaking
bareness 229 n.
streak of lightning
velocity 277 n.
stream
congregate 74 vb.
crowd 74 n.
group 74 n.
classification 77 n.
tendency 179 n.
be in motion
265 vb.
be wet 341 vb.
flow 350 vb.
rain 350 vb.
stream 350 n.
flash 417 n.
class 538 n.
store 632 n.
abound 635 vb.
streamer
advertisement
528 n.
flag 547 n.
trimming 844 n.
streamers
celebration 876 n.
streamlined
smooth 258 adj.
speedy 277 adj.
stream of consciousness
intellect 447 n.
idea 451 n.
soliloquy 585 n.
narrative 590 n.
streams
great quantity
32 n.
plenty 635 n.
street
locality 187 n.
abode 192 n.
housing 192 n.
road 624 n.
streets ahead
superior 34 adj.
streetwalker
prostitute 952 n.
streetwise
intelligent 498 adj.
strength
greatness 32 n.

strength 162 n.
pungency 388 n.
vigour 571 n.
strengthen
strengthen 162 vb.
strenuous
vigorous 174 adj.
forceful 571 adj.
labouring 682 adj.
stress
quantity 26 n.
power 160 n.
strengthen 162 vb.
distortion 246 n.
pain 377 n.
attract notice
455 vb.
trope 519 n.
affirmation 532 n.
emphasize 532 vb.
vigour 571 n.
pronunciation
577 n.
voice 577 vb.
prosody 593 n.
importance 638 n.
bane 659 n.
exertion 682 n.
fatigue 684 vb.
difficulty 700 n.
worry 825 n.
stretch
be great - large
32 vb.
augment 36 vb.
period 110 n.
range 183 n.
space 183 n.
enlarge 197 vb.
length 203 n.
lengthen 203 vb.
elasticity 328 n.
exaggerate 546 vb.
exertion 682 n.
labour 682 n.
stretchable
flexible 327 adj.
elastic 328 adj.
stretch a point
overstep 306 vb.
be lax 734 vb.
be lenient 736 vb.
not observe 769 vb.
compromise
770 vb.
exempt 919 vb.

999

stretcher
bond 47 n.
bed 218 n.
vehicle 274 n.
hospital 658 n.
stretch one's legs
be refreshed
685 vb.
stretchy
elastic 328 adj.
strew
disperse 75 vb.
striation
furrow 262 n.
stripe 437 n.
stricken
unfortunate
731 adj.
suffering 825 adj.
stricken in years
ageing 131 adj.
strict
orderly 60 adj.
accurate 494 adj.
severe 735 adj.
restraining
747 adj.
obligatory 917 adj.
honourable
929 adj.
orthodox 976 adj.
strictly speaking
truly 494 adv.
stricture
censure 924 n.
reprimand 924 n.
accusation 928 n.
stride
distance 199 n.
gait 265 n.
walk 267 vb.
strident
strident 407 adj.
stridor
stridor 407 n.
stridulation
stridor 407 n.
strife
quarrel 709 n.
contention 716 n.
strike
cease 145 vb.
strike 145 vb.
operate 173 vb.
horizontality
216 n.
strike 279 vb.

lower 311 vb.
be visible 443 vb.
discover 484 vb.
discovery 484 vb.
relinquish 621 vb.
be inactive 679 vb.
be obstructive
702 vb.
revolt 738 n.
revolt 738 vb.
deprecate 762 vb.
acquire 771 vb.
booty 790 n.
strike a bargain
promise 764 vb.
contract 765 vb.
strike a chord
excite 821 vb.
strike dumb
make mute 578 vb.
be wonderful
864 vb.
strike home
be vigorous 174 vb.
strike lucky
have luck 730 vb.
strike off
exclude 57 vb.
eject 300 vb.
depose 752 vb.
strike oil
have luck 730 vb.
strike out
exclude 57 vb.
destroy 165 vb.
swim 269 vb.
start out 296 vb.
striker
revolter 738 n.
player 837 n.
strike up
begin 68 vb.
play music 413 vb.
strike while the iron
is hot
profit by 137 vb.
striking
obvious 443 adj.
expressive 516 adj.
manifest 522 adj.
impressive 821 adj.
wonderful 864 adj.
striking distance
short distance
200 n.
string
adjust 24 vb.

tie 45 vb.
cable 47 n.
ligature 47 n.
continue 71 adj.
series 71 n.
band 74 n.
group 74 n.
fibre 208 n.
pass 305 vb.
harmonize 410 vb.
play music 413 vb.
viol 414 n.
jewellery 844 n.
string along
fool 542 vb.
string band
orchestra 413 n.
stringed instrument
stringed instrument
414 n.
stringent
exorbitant 32 adj.
severe 735 adj.
stringer
news reporter
529 n.
string out
disperse 75 vb.
lengthen 203 vb.
strings
influence 178 n.
orchestra 413 n.
musical instrument
414 n.
latency 523 n.
conditions 766 n.
stringy
tough 329 adj.
strip
abate 37 vb.
subtract 39 vb.
disunite 46 vb.
piece 53 n.
line 203 n.
narrowness 206 n.
strip 208 n.
uncover 229 vb.
deprive 786 vb.
fleece 786 vb.
take 786 vb.
impoverish 801 vb.
shame 867 vb.
stripe
sort 77 n.
line 203 n.
narrowness 206 n.
strip 208 n.

stripe 437 n.
variegate 437 vb.
badge of rank
743 n.
corporal punish-
ment 963 n.
striped
crossed 222 adj.
mottled 437 adj.
stripes
badge 547 n.
strip joint
place of amuse-
ment 837 n.
stripling
youngster 132 n.
male 372 n.
stripper
stripper 229 n.
strip poker
card game 837 n.
strip-search
search 459 n.
search 459 vb.
strip show
stage show 594 n.
striptease
uncovering 229 n.
striptease artist
stripper 229 n.
entertainer 594 n.
strive
attempt 671 vb.
exert oneself
682 vb.
contend 716 vb.
stroboscope
lamp 420 n.
stroke
living model 23 n.
instant 116 n.
helplessness 161 n.
aquatics 269 n.
navigate 269 vb.
row 269 vb.
impulse 279 n.
knock 279 n.
propulsion 287 n.
spasm 318 n.
rub 333 n.
touch 378 n.
touch 378 vb.
gesticulate 547 vb.
indication 547 n.
evil 616 n.
cardiovascular dis-
ease 651 n.

illness 651 n.
nervous disorders
  651 n.
deed 676 n.
please 826 vb.
caress 889 vb.
endearment 889 n.
corporal punish-
  ment 963 n.
stroke of, the
  instant 116 n.
stroke of genius
  deed 676 n.
  masterpiece 694 n.
  success 727 n.
  miracle-working
    864 n.
stroke of luck
  nondesign 618 n.
stroll
  pedestrianism
    267 n.
  wander 267 vb.
  move slowly
    278 vb.
strong
  strong 162 adj.
  influential 178 adj.
  tasty 386 adj.
  pungent 388 adj.
  florid 425 adj.
  healthy 650 adj.
  fervent 818 adj.
  impure 951 adj.
strong-arm tactics
  violence 176 n.
  compulsion 740 n.
strongbox
  treasury 799 n.
stronghold
  refuge 662 n.
  fort 713 n.
strong-minded
  resolute 599 adj.
strong point
  skill 694 n.
strongroom
  storage 632 n.
  treasury 799 n.
strong-willed
  resolute 599 adj.
strontium
  poison 659 n.
strop
  sharpen 256 vb.
strophe
  verse form 593 n.

stroppy
  irascible 892 adj.
  sullen 893 adj.
struck
  impressed 818 adj.
struck all of a heap
  impressed 818 adj.
struck dumb, be
  be mute 578 vb.
  wonder 864 vb.
struck with
  enamoured
    887 adj.
structuralism
  philosophy 449 n.
structure
  edifice 164 n.
  structure 331 n.
struggle
  move slowly
    278 vb.
  attempt 671 vb.
  exertion 682 n.
  exert oneself
    682 vb.
  contend 716 vb.
  contest 716 n.
  fight 716 n.
strum
  play music 413 vb.
strumpet
  prostitute 952 n.
strung
  adjusted 24 adj.
strung up
  excited 821 adj.
strut
  bond 47 n.
  support 218 n.
  gait 265 n.
  walk 267 vb.
  be proud 871 vb.
  be vain 873 vb.
  be ostentatious
    875 vb.
  ostentation 875 n.
  boast 877 vb.
strychnine
  poison 659 n.
stub
  remainder 41 n.
  tobacco 388 n.
  label 547 n.
stubble
  leavings 41 n.
  hair 259 n.
  roughness 259 n.

grass 366 n.
rubbish 641 n.
stubborn
  strong 162 adj.
  rigid 326 adj.
  tough 329 adj.
  obstinate 602 adj.
  difficult 700 adj.
  resisting 715 adj.
  impenitent
    940 adj.
stubby
  short 204 adj.
  thick 205 adj.
stub one's toe
  collide 279 vb.
stub out
  extinguish 382 vb.
stucco
  adhesive 47 n.
  coat 226 vb.
  facing 226 n.
stuck
  firm 45 adj.
  still 266 adj.
  in difficulties
    700 adj.
  hindered 702 adj.
stuck on
  enamoured
    887 adj.
stuck up
  affected 850 adj.
  be proud 871 vb.
  proud 871 adj.
  vain 873 adj.
stuck with
  hindered 702 adj.
stud
  fastening 47 n.
  pillar 218 n.
  roughen 259 vb.
  horse 273 n.
  variegate 437 vb.
  decorate 844 vb.
  jewellery 844 n.
  libertine 952 n.
student
  enquirer 459 n.
  scholar 492 n.
  learner 538 n.
  student 538 n.
studied
  predetermined
    608 adj.
  affected 850 adj.

studies
  study 536 n.
studio
  chamber 194 n.
  workshop 687 n.
studio couch
  seat 218 n.
studious
  studious 536 adj.
  industrious
    678 adj.
study
  retreat 192 n.
  chamber 194 n.
  musical piece
    412 n.
  meditate 449 vb.
  study 536 n.
  study 536 vb.
  picture 553 n.
  dissertation 591 n.
  intend 617 vb.
  prepare oneself
    669 vb.
  workshop 687 n.
  seclusion 883 n.
stuff
  essential part 5 n.
  chief part 52 n.
  fill 54 vb.
  bring together
    74 vb.
  load 193 vb.
  enlarge 197 vb.
  textile 222 n.
  line 227 vb.
  cook 301 vb.
  matter 319 n.
  texture 331 n.
  materials 631 n.
  superabound
    637 vb.
  preserve 666 vb.
  sate 863 vb.
  gluttonize 947 vb.
stuff and nonsense
  absurdity 497 n.
  silly talk 515 n.
stuffed shirt
  insubstantial thing
    4 n.
  vain person 873 n.
stuffing
  increment 36 n.
  adjunct 40 n.
  contents 193 n.
  lining 227 n.

1001

stopper 264 n.
insertion 303 n.
materials 631 n.
satiety 863 n.
gluttonous 947 adj.
stuff oneself
eat 301 vb.
stuffy
warm 379 adj.
fetid 397 adj.
insalubrious
653 adj.
tedious 838 adj.
dull 840 adj.
stuffy (air)
dense 324 adj.
stumble
walk 267 vb.
descent 309 n.
tumble 309 vb.
blunder 495 vb.
be clumsy 695 vb.
be wicked 934 vb.
stumble on, upon
meet with 154 vb.
chance 159 vb.
discover 484 vb.
stumbling block
obstacle 702 n.
restraint 747 n.
stump
remainder 41 n.
piece 53 n.
extremity 69 n.
projection 254 n.
leg 267 n.
walk 267 vb.
puzzle 474 vb.
be difficult 700 vb.
stumped, be
not know 491 vb.
not understand
517 vb.
stumps
leg 267 n.
stump up
pay 804 vb.
stumpy
short 204 adj.
stun
strike 279 vb.
render insensible
375 vb.
be loud 400 vb.
surprise 508 vb.
be wonderful
864 vb.

stung
excited 821 adj.
angry 891 adj.
resentful 891 adj.
stung, be
pay too much
811 vb.
stunned
unexpecting
508 adj.
fearing 854 adj.
stunning
super 644 adj.
stunt
make smaller
198 vb.
shorten 204 vb.
fly 271 vb.
contrivance 623 n.
deed 676 n.
pageant 875 n.
stunted
dwarfish 196 adj.
short 204 adj.
deformed 246 adj.
stunt man or woman
athlete 162 n.
doer 676 n.
brave person 855 n.
stupefaction
wonder 864 n.
stupefy
render insensible
375 vb.
impress 821 vb.
be wonderful
864 vb.
stupendous
prodigious 32 adj.
huge 195 adj.
wonderful 864 adj.
stupid
unintelligent
499 adj.
unskilful 695 adj.
dull 840 adj.
stupidity
unintelligence
499 n.
moral insensibility
820 n.
stupor
insensibility 375 n.
sluggishness 679 n.
moral insensibility
820 n.
wonder 864 n.

sturdy
stalwart 162 adj.
stutter
speech defect
580 n.
stammer 580 vb.
be clumsy 695 vb.
show feeling
818 vb.
quake 854 vb.
sty
stable 192 n.
enclosure 235 n.
stye
swelling 253 n.
style
modality 7 n.
similarity 18 n.
sort 77 n.
chronology 117 n.
form 243 n.
flower 366 n.
engraving 555 n.
name 561 n.
name 561 vb.
style 566 n.
elegance 575 n.
way 624 n.
conduct 688 n.
skill 694 n.
beauty 841 n.
fashion 848 n.
style of address
title 870 n.
styling
hairdressing 843 n.
stylish
elegant 575 adj.
personable 841 adj.
fashionable
848 adj.
stylistic
stylistic 566 adj.
stylite
solitary 883 n.
stylo
stationery 586 n.
stylus
sharp point 256 n.
gramophone 414 n.
stymie
be obstructive
702 vb.
obstruct 702 vb.
Styx
the dead 361 n.
mythic hell 972 n.

suave
smooth 258 adj.
courteous 884 adj.
sub
inferior 35 n.
substitute 150 n.
publish 528 vb.
subaltern
inferior 35 adj.
inferior 35 n.
army officer 741 n.
servant 742 n.
subaqua
sport 837 n.
subconscious
intuition 476 n.
intuitive 476 adj.
latency 523 n.
latent 523 adj.
subconscious, the
spirit 447 n.
subcutaneous
interior 224 adj.
subdivision
scission 46 n.
subdivision 53 n.
subdue
moderate 177 vb.
prevail 178 vb.
overmaster 727 vb.
subjugate 745 vb.
restrain 747 vb.
subedit
publish 528 vb.
rectify 654 vb.
subfusc
formal dress 228 n.
subgroup
subdivision 53 n.
subhuman
animal 365 adj.
cruel 898 adj.
subject
living model 23 n.
inferior 35 adj.
inferior 35 n.
topic 452 n.
part of speech
564 n.
overmaster 727 vb.
subject 742 n.
subject 745 adj.
subject, be
be subject 745 vb.
subjective
intrinsic 5 adj.
intuitive 476 adj.

misjudging
481 adj.
subjectivity
intrinsicality 5 n.
subjectivity 320 n.
subject matter
topic 452 n.
meaning 514 n.
subject to
liable 180 adj.
provided 468 adv.
subject 745 adj.
on terms 766 adv.
subject to terms
conditional
766 adj.
subjoin
insert 303 vb.
sub judice
sub judice 480 adv.
subjugate
prevail 178 vb.
subjugate 745 vb.
sublet
lease 784 vb.
lending 784 n.
sub-lieutenant
nautical personnel
270 n.
naval officer 741 n.
sublimate
vaporize 338 vb.
make better
654 vb.
sublime
high 209 adj.
worshipful 866 adj.
proud 871 adj.
divine 965 adj.
subliminal
latent 523 adj.
involuntary
596 adj.
sublimity
height 209 n.
prestige 866 n.
divine attribute
965 n.
submachine gun
gun 723 n.
submarine
low 210 adj.
deep 211 adj.
depth 211 n.
ship 275 n.
warship 722 n.

submerge
suppress 165 vb.
immerse 303 vb.
descend 309 vb.
plunge 313 vb.
drench 341 vb.
irrigate 341 vb.
be unseen 444 vb.
obliterate 550 vb.
submerse
plunge 313 vb.
submission
argument 475 n.
supposition 512 n.
affirmation 532 n.
submission 721 n.
entreaty 761 n.
submissive
willing 597 adj.
inactive 679 adj.
tractable 701 adj.
peaceful 717 adj.
submitting 721 adj.
obedient 739 adj.
subjected 745 adj.
humble 872 adj.
servile 879 adj.
respectful 920 adj.
submit
propound 512 vb.
affirm 532 vb.
advise 691 vb.
submit 721 vb.
submit a report
communicate
524 vb.
submultiple
numerical element
85 n.
subnormal
inferior 35 adj.
abnormal 84 adj.
unintelligent
499 adj.
*mentally handi-
capped* 503 adj.
subordinate
extrinsic 6 adj.
inferior 35 adj.
inferior 35 n.
servant 742 n.
subject 745 adj.
subordinate clause
subdivision 53 n.
subordination
inferiority 35 n.
order 60 n.

arrangement 62 n.
sequence 65 n.
subjection 745 n.
suborn
bribe 612 vb.
subplot
narrative 590 n.
dramaturgy 594 n.
subpoena
command 737 vb.
warrant 737 n.
legal process 959 n.
subrogation
substitution 150 n.
subscribe
testify 466 vb.
sign 547 vb.
join a party
708 vb.
contract 765 vb.
give security
767 vb.
give 781 vb.
subscriber
assenter 488 n.
signatory 765 n.
giver 781 n.
subscribe to
endorse 488 vb.
patronize 703 vb.
subscription
giving 781 n.
offering 781 n.
pay 804 n.
payment 804 n.
subsection
classification 77 n.
subsequence
posteriority 120 n.
following 284 n.
subsequent
subsequent
120 adj.
subservient
subjected 745 adj.
servile 879 adj.
subset
classification 77 n.
subside
decrease 37 vb.
be quiescent
266 vb.
recede 290 vb.
descend 309 vb.
blow 352 vb.
subsidence
decrease 37 n.

quiescence 266 n.
descent 309 n.
subsidiary
extrinsic 6 adj.
inferior 35 adj.
inferior 35 n.
additional 38 adj.
unimportant
639 adj.
aiding 703 adj.
subsidize
aid 703 vb.
give 781 vb.
subsidy
subvention 703 n.
gift 781 n.
pay 804 n.
subsist
be 1 vb.
pass time 108 vb.
stay 144 vb.
subsistence
existence 1 n.
subsistence level
insufficiency 636 n.
poverty 801 n.
subsoil
base 214 n.
soil 344 n.
subsonic flight
aeronautics 271 n.
subspecies
subdivision 53 n.
breed 77 n.
substance
substance 3 n.
quantity 26 n.
matter 319 n.
structure 331 n.
meaning 514 n.
chief thing 638 n.
importance 638 n.
estate 777 n.
wealth 800 n.
substandard
inferior 35 adj.
abnormal 84 adj.
deficient 307 adj.
cheap 812 adj.
substantial
substantial 3 adj.
great 32 adj.
strong 162 adj.
material 319 adj.
dense 324 adj.
meaningful
514 adj.

substantiate
  specify 80 vb.
  materialize 319 vb.
  corroborate 466 vb.
  demonstrate
    478 V.
  be true 494 vb.
substantive
  part of speech
    564 n.
substitute
  substitute 150 n.
  substitute 150 vb.
  function 622 vb.
  deputy 755 n.
substitution
  substitution 150 n.
subsume
  contain 56 vb.
  class 62 vb.
subtend
  be opposite 240 vb.
subterfuge
  sophistry 477 n.
  concealment 525 n.
  pretext 614 n.
  stratagem 698 n.
subterranean
  low 210 adj.
  deep 211 adj.
  concealed 525 adj.
subtitle
  description 590 n.
subtle
  small 33 adj.
  rare 325 adj.
  cunning 698 adj.
subtle distinction
  differentiation
    15 n.
subtlety
  discrimination
    463 n.
  sophistry 477 n.
  cunning 698 n.
  fastidiousness
    862 n.
subtract
  subtract 39 vb.
suburb
  district 184 n.
  housing 192 n.
suburban
  tedious 838 adj.
  plebeian 869 adj.
suburbia
  dispersion 75 n.

district 184 n.
housing 192 n.
averageness 732 n.
suburbs
  entrance 68 n.
  surroundings
    230 n.
subversion
  disorder 61 n.
  destruction 165 n.
  overturning 221 n.
  lowering 311 n.
  revolt 738 n.
  sedition 738 n.
subversive
  revolutionary
    149 adj.
  destructive 165 adj.
  disobedient
    738 adj.
subvert
  modify 143 vb.
  demolish 165 vb.
  tell against 467 vb.
  impair 655 vb.
subway
  crossing 222 n.
  tunnel 263 n.
  passage 305 n.
  traffic control
    305 n.
  bridge 624 n.
  railway 624 n.
succeed
  come after 65 vb.
  ensue 120 vb.
  substitute 150 vb.
  follow 284 vb.
  succeed 727 vb.
  inherit 771 vb.
  appropriate
    786 vb.
succeeding
  sequential 65 adj.
  subsequent
    120 adj.
succeed to
  inherit 771 vb.
succès de scandale
  disrepute 867 n.
succès fou
  success 727 n.
success
  success 727 n.
success, a
  success 727 n.
  victor 727 n.

successful
  successful 727 adj.
successful, be
  be successful
    727 vb.
  succeed 727 vb.
succession
  sequence 65 n.
  continuity 71 n.
  series 71 n.
  recurrence 106 n.
  posteriority 120 n.
  posterity 170 n.
  following 284 n.
  transfer 780 n.
successive
  sequential 65 adj.
  continuous 71 adj.
  subsequent
    120 adj.
  periodical 141 adj.
successor
  successor 67 n.
  posteriority 120 n.
  beneficiary 776 n.
  recipient 782 n.
success story
  success 727 n.
succinct
  concise 569 adj.
succour
  remedy 658 n.
  aid 703 n.
  aid 703 vb.
succubus
  demon 970 n.
  sorceress 983 n.
succulent
  edible 301 adj.
  plant 366 n.
  savoury 390 adj.
succumb
  be destroyed
    165 vb.
  be fatigued 684 vb.
  knuckle under
    721 vb.
  be dejected 834 vb.
such
  anonymous
    562 adj.
suchlike
  analogue 18 n.
suck
  drink 301 vb.
  extract 304 vb.
  smoke 388 vb.

hiss 406 vb.
oppress 735 vb.
sucker
  branch 53 n.
  young plant 132 n.
  orifice 263 n.
  tree 366 n.
  credulity 487 n.
  ninny 501 n.
  dupe 544 n.
sucking pig
  pig 365 n.
suck up to
  minister to 703 vb.
  be servile 879 vb.
  flatter 925 vb.
sucrose
  food content 301 n.
  sweet thing 392 n.
suction
  energy 160 n.
  attraction 291 n.
  reception 299 n.
  extraction 304 n.
sudden
  brief 114 adj.
  instantaneous
    116 adj.
  unexpected
    508 adj.
  spontaneous
    609 adj.
suddenly
  suddenly 135 adv.
suds
  bubble 355 n.
sue
  demand 737 vb.
  be in love 887 vb.
  court 889 vb.
  claim 915 vb.
  indict 928 vb.
  litigate 959 vb.
suede
  skin 226 n.
suet
  fat 357 n.
suffer
  acquiesce 488 vb.
  be ill 651 vb.
  permit 756 vb.
  be patient 823 vb.
  suffer 825 vb.
sufferance
  permission 756 vb.
suffer a sea change
  differ 15 vb.

be turned to
  147 vb.
suffer defeat
  be defeated 728 vb.
suffice
  suffice 635 vb.
sufficient
  sufficient 635 adj.
suffix
  add 38 vb.
  adjunct 40 n.
  affix 45 vb.
  place after 65 vb.
  sequel 67 n.
  extremity 69 n.
  part of speech
    564 n.
suffocate
  disable 161 vb.
  suppress 165 vb.
  kill 362 vb.
  murder 362 vb.
  be hot 379 vb.
  heat 381 vb.
  extinguish 382 vb.
  superabound
    637 vb.
  hinder 702 vb.
suffrage
  affirmation 532 n.
  vote 605 n.
  prayers 981 n.
suffragette
  female 373 n.
  vote 605 n.
suffusion
  mixture 43 n.
  feeling 818 n.
  humiliation 872 n.
sufi
  pietist 979 n.
  worshipper 981 n.
  monk 986 n.
Sufism
  philosophy 449 n.
  religion 973 n.
sugar
  food content 301 n.
  sweeten 392 vb.
  sweet thing 392 n.
  please 826 vb.
  darling 890 n.
  flatter 925 vb.
sugar cane
  grass 366 n.
sugar daddy
  patron 707 n.

giver 781 n.
  good giver 813 n.
  lover 887 n.
  libertine 952 n.
sugar the pill
  sweeten 392 vb.
  deceive 542 vb.
  flatter 925 vb.
sugary
  sweet 392 adj.
  pleasurable
    826 adj.
  flattering 925 adj.
suggest
  evidence 466 vb.
  remind 505 vb.
  propound 512 vb.
  imply 523 vb.
  hint 524 vb.
  indicate 547 vb.
  represent 551 vb.
  advise 691 vb.
  offer 759 vb.
suggestion
  similarity 18 n.
  small quantity
    33 n.
  knowledge 490 n.
  reminder 505 n.
  latency 523 n.
  hint 524 n.
  plan 623 n.
  advice 691 n.
suggestive
  influential 178 adj.
  meaningful
    514 adj.
  exciting 821 adj.
  impure 951 adj.
suicidal
  destructive 165 adj.
  murderous 362 adj.
  hopeless 853 adj.
  rash 857 adj.
suicide
  kill oneself 362 vb.
  suicide 362 n.
suit
  uniformity 16 n.
  accord 24 vb.
  adjust 24 vb.
  sort 77 n.
  suit 228 n.
  following 284 n.
  beautify 841 vb.
  wooing 889 n.
  accusation 928 n.

litigation 959 n.
suit (of cards)
  series 71 n.
suitable
  circumstantial
    8 adj.
  relevant 9 adj.
  fit 24 adj.
  right 913 adj.
suitcase
  box 194 n.
suite
  series 71 n.
  concomitant 89 n.
  flat 192 n.
  follower 284 n.
  musical piece
    412 n.
suiting
  adaptation 24 n.
  agreeing 24 adj.
  textile 222 n.
suit one down to the
    ground
  accord 24 vb.
  answer 460 vb.
suitor
  concomitant 89 n.
  follower 284 n.
  petitioner 763 n.
  lover 887 n.
  litigant 959 n.
sulk
  be discontented
    829 vb.
  be dejected 834 vb.
  be rude 885 vb.
sulks
  discontent 829 n.
  resentment 891 n.
  sullenness 893 n.
sulky
  carriage 274 n.
  discontented
    829 adj.
  melancholic
    834 adj.
  sullen 893 adj.
sullen
  sullen 893 adj.
sully
  dim 419 vb.
  make unclean
    649 vb.
  make ugly 842 vb.
  blemish 845 vb.
  shame 867 vb.

defame 926 vb.
  be impious 980 vb.
sulphur
  yellowness 433 n.
sulphurous
  fetid 397 adj.
Sultan
  sovereign 741 n.
Sultana
  sovereign 741 n.
sultana
  fruit and vegetables
    301 n.
sultry
  warm 379 adj.
  sullen 893 adj.
sum
  quantity 26 n.
  add 38 vb.
  all 52 n.
  whole 52 n.
  numerical result
    85 n.
  numeration 86 n.
  funds 797 n.
summarize
  shorten 204 vb.
  be concise 569 vb.
  abstract 592 vb.
summary
  brief 114 adj.
  shortening 204 n.
  concise 569 adj.
  description 590 n.
  dissertation 591 n.
  compendium
    592 n.
  lawless 954 adj.
summation
  addition 38 n.
  whole 52 n.
  numeration 86 n.
summer
  pass time 108 vb.
  period 110 n.
  summer 128 n.
  be present 189 vb.
  beam 218 n.
  palmy days 730 n.
summerhouse
  arbour 194 n.
summer solstice
  summer 128 n.
summer time
  clock time 117 n.
summertime
  summer 128 n.

summery
  warm 379 adj.
summing-up
  estimate 480 n.
  judgment 480 n.
  legal trial 959 n.
summit
  summit 213 n.
  conference 584 n.
  council 692 n.
summit conference
  conference 584 n.
summon
  bring together
    74 vb.
  command 737 vb.
  desire 859 vb.
  indict 928 vb.
  litigate 959 vb.
summons
  call 547 n.
  command 737 n.
  warrant 737 n.
  desire 859 n.
  accusation 928 n.
  law 953 n.
  legal process 959 n.
summon up
  excite 821 vb.
sum of money
  funds 797 n.
sump
  receptacle 194 n.
  base 214 n.
  cavity 255 n.
  storage 632 n.
  sink 649 n.
sumptuous
  ostentatious
    875 adj.
sum up
  shorten 204 vb.
  estimate 480 vb.
  judge 480 vb.
  abstract 592 vb.
  try a case 959 vb.
sun
  sun 321 n.
  dry 342 vb.
  dryness 342 n.
  heat 379 n.
  light 417 n.
  luminary 420 n.
sunbathe
  be hot 379 vb.
sunbeam
  light 417 n.

sun bed
  beautification
    843 n.
sunburn
  burning 381 n.
  brown 430 vb.
sundae
  dessert 301 n.
Sunday
  holy day 988 n.
Sunday best
  clothing 228 n.
  finery 844 n.
sunder
  disunite 46 vb.
  sunder 46 vb.
  See **disunite**
sundial
  timekeeper 117 n.
sundown
  evening 129 n.
  darkening 418 n.
sundress
  beachwear 228 n.
  dress 228 n.
sundries
  merchandise
    795 n.
sundry
  multiform 82 adj.
  many 104 adj.
sunflower
  orange 432 n.
sunglasses
  shade 226 n.
  screen 421 n.
  eyeglass 442 n.
  shelter 662 n.
sun hat
  shade 226 n.
  headgear 228 n.
  screen 421 n.
sunk
  concave 255 adj.
  defeated 728 adj.
sunken
  low 210 adj.
  concave 255 adj.
sunken-eyed
  lean 206 adj.
sun lamp
  lamp 420 n.
  beautification
    843 n.
sunlight
  sun 321 n.
  heater 383 n.

  light 417 n.
sunny
  tranquil 266 adj.
  dry 342 adj.
  warm 379 adj.
  undimmed
    417 adj.
  pleasurable
    826 adj.
  cheerful 833 adj.
sunny side
  pleasurableness
    826 n.
sun oneself
  be hot 379 vb.
sunrise
  morning 128 n.
  ascent 308 n.
sunrise industry
  production 164 n.
  business 622 n.
sunscreen
  screen 421 n.
sunset
  evening 129 n.
  descent 309 n.
  glow 417 n.
  darkening 418 n.
  redness 431 n.
sunshade
  shade 226 n.
  screen 421 n.
sunshine
  sun 321 n.
  heat 379 n.
sun spot
  sun 321 n.
sunstroke
  burning 381 n.
sunsuit
  beachwear 228 n.
suntan
  brownness 430 n.
sun-tanning
  beautification
    843 n.
suntan oil
  oil 357 n.
sup
  draught 301 n.
  eat 301 vb.
  taste 386 vb.
super
  supreme 34 adj.
  topmost 213 adj.
  super 644 adj.

superabundant
  great 32 adj.
  many 104 adj.
  diffuse 570 adj.
superannuated
  antiquated 127 adj.
  ageing 131 adj.
  disused 674 adj.
superannuation
  earnings 771 n.
superb
  excellent 644 adj.
  splendid 841 adj.
  ostentatious
    875 adj.
supercharged
  dynamic 160 adj.
supercilious
  proud 871 adj.
  insolent 878 adj.
  disrespectful
    921 adj.
superficial
  insubstantial 4 adj.
  inconsiderable
    33 adj.
  shallow 212 adj.
  exterior 223 adj.
  appearing 445 adj.
  inattentive 456 adj.
  negligent 458 adj.
  dabbling 491 adj.
  irresolute 601 adj.
  trivial 639 adj.
  uncompleted
    726 adj.
superfluity
  greatness 32 n.
  great quantity
    32 n.
  diffuseness 570 n.
  superfluity 637 n.
superfluous
  remaining 41 adj.
  superfluous
    637 adj.
supergiant
  star 321 n.
supergrass
  witness 466 n.
  informer 524 n.
  accuser 928 n.
  bad person 938 n.
superhuman
  divine 965 adj.
  godlike 965 adj.

superimpose
add 38 vb.
modify 143 vb.
cover 226 vb.
superintend
manage 689 vb.
superintendent
manager 690 n.
superior
superior 34 adj.
superior 34 n.
notable 638 adj.
genteel 868 adj.
proud 871 adj.
superiority
superiority 34 n.
contempt 922 n.
superlative
distinctive 15 adj.
supreme 34 adj.
grammatical
  564 adj.
excellent 644 adj.
superman, woman
superior 34 n.
exceller 644 n.
paragon 646 n.
prodigy 864 n.
supermarket
shop 796 n.
supernatural
extraneous 59 adj.
abnormal 84 adj.
unusual 84 adj.
divine 965 adj.
spooky 970 adj.
magical 983 adj.
paranormal 984 n.
supernova
star 321 n.
supernumerary
additional 38 adj.
extra 40 n.
superfluous
  637 adj.
superpower
influence 178 n.
bigwig 638 n.
political organiza-
  tion 733 n.
supersede
substitute 150 vb.
displace 188 vb.
stop using 674 vb.
not retain 779 vb.
supersonic
sounding 398 adj.

supersonic flight
aeronautics 271 n.
velocity 277 n.
superstition
credulity 487 n.
ignorance 491 n.
error 495 n.
heterodoxy 977 n.
idolatry 982 n.
superstitious
misjudging
  481 adj.
erroneous 495 adj.
supertax
tax 809 n.
supervene
accrue 38 vb.
ensue 120 vb.
happen 154 vb.
supervention
addition 38 n.
supervise
manage 689 vb.
supervision
inspection 438 n.
supervisor
manager 690 n.
supine
supine 216 adj.
inactive 679 adj.
submitting 721 adj.
apathetic 820 adj.
indifferent 860 adj.
supper
meal 301 n.
supplant
come after 65 vb.
substitute 150 vb.
supple
flexible 327 adj.
servile 879 adj.
supplement
augment 36 vb.
increment 36 n.
add 38 vb.
addition 38 n.
adjunct 40 n.
make complete
  54 vb.
sequel 67 n.
enlarge 197 vb.
the press 528 n.
edition 589 n.
price 809 n.
supplementary
increasing 36 adj.
additional 38 adj.

supplicant
petitioner 763 n.
worshipper 981 n.
supplicate
entreat 761 vb.
supplies
means 629 n.
provision 633 n.
supply
substitute 150 vb.
store 632 n.
provide 633 vb.
provision 633 n.
support
agency 173 n.
support 218 n.
support 218 vb.
corroborate 466 vb.
assent 488 n.
endorse 488 vb.
act 594 vb.
choose 605 vb.
inducement 612 n.
safeguard 660 vb.
preservation 666 n.
aid 703 n.
aider 703 n.
subvention 703 n.
be patient 823 vb.
approve 923 vb.
vindicate 927 vb.
supporter
follower 284 n.
assenter 488 n.
enthusiast 504 n.
patron 707 n.
benefactor 903 n.
commender 923 n.
supporting
assenting 488 adj.
aiding 703 adj.
approving 923 adj.
supporting role
inferiority 35 n.
supportive
aiding 703 adj.
suppose
suppose 512 vb.
suppose so
suppose 512 vb.
supposing
thus 8 adv.
provided 468 adv.
supposition
supposition 512 n.

suppository
surgical dressing
  658 n.
suppress
suppress 165 vb.
keep secret 525 vb.
overmaster 727 vb.
suppression
exclusion 57 n.
destruction 165 n.
counteraction
  182 n.
lowering 311 n.
concealment 525 n.
restraint 747 n.
abrogation 752 n.
prohibition 757 n.
suppurate
deteriorate 655 vb.
suppuration
excretion 302 n.
infection 651 n.
supra
before 64 adv.
supremacy
superiority 34 n.
importance 638 n.
authority 733 n.
governance 733 n.
divine attribute
  965 n.
supreme
supreme 34 adj.
ending 69 adj.
strong 162 adj.
supremely
greatly 32 vb.
eminently 34 adv.
surcharge
price 809 n.
surd
number 85 n.
numerical 85 adj.
speech sound
  398 n.
voiceless 578 adj.
voicelessness 578 n.
sure
certain 473 adj.
positive 473 adj.
expectant 507 adj.
safe 660 adj.
trustworthy
  929 adj.
surefooted
skilful 694 adj.

sure thing
  fair chance 159 n.
  probability 471 n.
  certainty 473 n.
  necessary 596 adj.
  necessity 596 n.
  easy thing 701 n.
surety
  protection 660 n.
  security 767 n.
  legal process 959 n.
surf
  wave 350 n.
  bubble 355 n.
  amuse oneself
    837 vb.
surface
  space 183 n.
  shallow 212 adj.
  exterior 223 adj.
  exteriority 223 n.
  navigate 269 vb.
  emerge 298 vb.
  ascend 308 vb.
  be light 323 vb.
  texture 331 n.
  be visible 443 vb.
  road 624 n.
surface-to-air missile
  missile weapon
    723 n.
surfboard
  sled 274 n.
  plaything 837 n.
surfeit
  superfluity 637 n.
  sate 863 vb.
  satiety 863 n.
surfing
  aquatics 269 n.
surge
  grow 36 vb.
  increase 36 n.
  congregate 74 vb.
  flow 350 vb.
  be active 678 vb.
surgeon
  doctor 658 n.
surgery
  hospital 658 n.
  surgery 658 n.
surly
  sullen 893 adj.
surmise
  be of the opinion
    that 485 vb.
  opinion 485 n.

  foresee 510 vb.
  conjecture 512 n.
  suppose 512 vb.
surmount
  be superior 34 vb.
  be high 209 vb.
  crown 213 vb.
  climb 308 vb.
surmountable
  possible 469 adj.
surname
  name 561 n.
surpass
  be superior 34 vb.
  outdo 306 vb.
surplice
  vestments 989 n.
surplus
  extra 40 n.
  remainder 41 n.
  remaining 41 adj.
  part 53 n.
  superfluity 637 n.
  superfluous
    637 adj.
surprise
  sequel 67 n.
  lack of expectation
    508 n.
  surprise 508 vb.
  attack 712 n.
  wonder 864 n.
Surrealism
  art 551 n.
  school of painting
    553 n.
  literature 557 n.
surrealistic
  literary 557 adj.
surrender
  relinquish 621 vb.
  nonuse 674 n.
  submission 721 n.
  submit 721 vb.
  resign 753 vb.
  resignation 753 n.
surreptitious
  stealthy 525 adj.
surrogate
  substitute 150 n.
  consignee 754 n.
  deputy 755 n.
surrogate mother
  family 11 n.
  maternity 169 n.
surround
  surround 230 vb.

  outline 233 n.
  enclose 235 vb.
  enclosure 235 n.
  close 264 vb.
  besiege 712 vb.
surroundings
  locality 187 n.
  surroundings
    230 n.
surround-sound sys-
tem
  sound 398 n.
surtax
  tax 809 n.
surveillance
  inspection 438 n.
  surveillance 457 n.
survey
  inspection 438 n.
  scan 438 vb.
  enquire 459 vb.
  enquiry 459 n.
  measure 465 vb.
  estimate 480 vb.
  represent 551 vb.
  dissertate 591 vb.
  dissertation 591 n.
  compendium
    592 n.
surveyor
  enquirer 459 n.
  estimator 480 n.
survivability
  strength 162 n.
  toughness 329 n.
  life 360 n.
  courage 855 n.
survival
  remainder 41 n.
  durability 113 n.
  life 360 n.
survival of the fittest
  biology 358 n.
  contention 716 n.
survive
  be left 41 vb.
  continue 108 vb.
  outlast 113 vb.
  go on 146 vb.
  support 218 vb.
  live 360 vb.
  persevere 600 vb.
  be restored 656 vb.
  escape 667 vb.
survivor
  escaper 667 n.

susceptible
  liable 180 adj.
  sentient 374 adj.
  impressible
    819 adj.
sushi
  fish food 301 n.
sus out
  enquire 459 vb.
suspect
  be uncertain
    474 vb.
  be of the opinion
    that 485 vb.
  doubt 486 vb.
  not know 491 vb.
  offender 904 n.
  wrong 914 adj.
  accused person
    928 n.
suspend
  nullify 2 vb.
  discontinue 72 vb.
  pause 145 vb.
  hang 217 vb.
  stop using 674 vb.
  abrogate 752 vb.
  depose 752 vb.
  prohibit 757 vb.
  make illegal
    954 vb.
  punish 963 vb.
suspended
  powerless 161 adj.
  inert 175 adj.
  hanging 217 adj.
  nonactive 677 adj.
  inactive 679 adj.
  illegal 954 adj.
suspended animation
  insensibility 375 n.
suspender
  fastening 47 n.
  hanger 217 n.
  legwear 228 n.
suspense
  dubiety 474 n.
  expectation 507 n.
suspension
  exclusion 57 n.
  delay 136 n.
  lull 145 n.
  pendency 217 n.
  softness 327 n.
  elasticity 328 n.
  solution 337 n.
  tempo 410 n.

nonuse 674 n.	**swagger**	**swansong**	*oscillate* 317 vb.
inaction 677 n.	*gait* 265 n.	*end* 69 n.	*be agitated* 318 vb.
inactivity 679 n.	*be proud* 871 vb.	*decease* 361 n.	*be uncertain*
abrogation 752 n.	*ostentation* 875 n.	*attempt* 671 n.	474 vb.
prohibition 757 n.	*boast* 877 vb.	*completion* 725 n.	*be irresolute*
penalty 963 n.	*boasting* 877 n.	*lament* 836 n.	601 vb.
suspicion	*be insolent* 878 vb.	**swap**	*motivate* 612 vb.
small quantity	**swain**	*correlate* 12 vb.	*governance* 733 n.
33 n.	*male* 372 n.	*substitute* 150 vb.	**swear**
tincture 43 n.	*country-dweller*	*interchange* 151 n.	*testify* 466 vb.
doubt 486 n.	869 n.	*interchange*	*swear* 532 vb.
knowledge 490 n.	*lover* 887 n.	151 vb.	*take a pledge*
conjecture 512 n.	**swallow**	*barter* 791 n.	764 vb.
hint 524 n.	*absorb* 299 vb.	*trade* 791 vb.	*be rude* 885 vb.
suspicious	*draught* 301 n.	**swarm**	*cuss* 899 vb.
uncertain 474 adj.	*eat* 301 vb.	*grow* 36 vb.	*scurrility* 899 n.
nervous 854 adj.	*mouthful* 301 n.	*congregate* 74 vb.	*be impious* 980 vb.
cautious 858 adj.	*bird* 365 n.	*crowd* 74 n.	**swear by**
jealous 911 adj.	*believe* 485 vb.	*group* 74 n.	*be certain* 473 vb.
dishonest 930 adj.	*be credulous*	*be many* 104 vb.	*believe* 485 vb.
sustain	487 vb.	*be fruitful* 171 vb.	*praise* 923 vb.
continue 108 vb.	*be patient* 823 vb.	*abound* 635 vb.	**swearing**
stay 144 vb.	**swallow one's words**	**swarms**	*oath* 532 n.
sustain 146 vb.	*stammer* 580 vb.	*great quantity*	*discontented*
strengthen 162 vb.	**swamp**	32 n.	829 adj.
support 218 vb.	*fill* 54 vb.	**swarm with**	*cursing* 899 adj.
feed 301 vb.	*be many* 104 vb.	*be many* 104 vb.	*scurrility* 899 n.
corroborate 466 vb.	*destroy* 165 vb.	*superabound*	*impiety* 980 n.
preserve 666 vb.	*drench* 341 vb.	637 vb.	*impious* 980 adj.
aid 703 vb.	*marsh* 347 n.	**swarthy**	**swearword**
sustenance	**swampy**	*dark* 418 adj.	*word* 559 n.
food 301 n.	*marshy* 347 adj.	*blackish* 428 adj.	*scurrility* 899 n.
provisions 301 n.	**swan**	**swashbuckling**	**sweat**
suttee	*bird* 365 n.	*boasting* 877 n.	*exude* 298 vb.
suicide 362 n.	*white thing* 427 n.	**swastika**	*outflow* 298 n.
burning 381 n.	*a beauty* 841 n.	*quaternity* 96 n.	*emit* 300 vb.
oblation 981 n.	**swank**	*cross* 222 n.	*excrement* 302 n.
suture	*be affected* 850 vb.	*heraldry* 547 n.	*excrete* 302 vb.
joint 45 n.	*be proud* 871 vb.	*talisman* 983 n.	*water* 339 n.
tie 45 vb.	*pride* 871 n.	**swat**	*be wet* 341 vb.
svelte	*proud person*	*knock* 279 n.	*be hot* 379 vb.
narrow 206 adj.	871 n.	*strike* 279 vb.	*heat* 379 n.
shapely 841 adj.	*airs* 873 n.	**swatch**	*attempt* 671 vb.
swab	*be vain* 873 vb.	*piece* 53 n.	*do* 676 vb.
dry 342 vb.	*vanity* 873 n.	**swathe**	*labour* 682 n.
dryer 342 n.	*be ostentatious*	*bunch* 74 n.	*work* 682 vb.
clean 648 vb.	875 vb.	*cover* 226 vb.	**sweat blood**
cleaning utensil	*ostentation* 875 n.	*dress* 228 vb.	*exert oneself*
648 n.	*boast* 877 vb.	*fold* 261 vb.	682 vb.
surgical dressing	*boasting* 877 n.	*trace* 548 n.	*work* 682 vb.
658 n.	*be insolent* 878 vb.	**sway**	**sweated labour**
swaddling clothes	**swanky**	*be unequal* 29 vb.	*slave* 742 n.
clothing 228 n.	*fashionable*	*vary* 152 vb.	**sweater**
swag	848 adj.	*power* 160 n.	*jersey* 228 n.
hang 217 vb.	*proud* 871 adj.	*be weak* 163 vb.	**sweatshirt**
descend 309 vb.	*ostentatious*	*influence* 178 n.	*jersey* 228 n.
booty 790 n.	875 adj.	*hang* 217 vb.	*shirt* 228 n.

sweep
range 183 n.
displace 188 vb.
be curved 248 vb.
traverse 267 vb.
propeller 269 n.
propel 287 vb.
propellant 287 n.
scan 438 vb.
clean 648 vb.

sweepstake
equal chance
  159 n.
gambling 618 n.
gambling game
  837 n.

sweep the board
win 727 vb.

sweep under the car-
  pet
conceal 525 vb.

sweet
dessert 301 n.
mouthful 301 n.
sweet 392 adj.
pleasurableness
  826 n.
amiable 884 adj.
benevolent 897 adj.

sweetbreads
meat 301 n.

sweetcorn
fruit and vegetables
  301 n.

sweeten
sweeten 392 vb.

sweetener
gift 781 n.
reward 962 n.

sweetheart
female 373 n.
loved one 887 n.
lover 887 n.
darling 890 n.

sweetmeat
sweets 301 n.

sweetness and light
concord 710 n.

sweet nothings
empty talk 515 n.
endearment 889 n.
flattery 925 n.

sweet on, be
be in love 887 vb.
court 889 vb.

sweets
sweets 301 n.

sweet-talk
be cunning 698 vb.
flattery 925 n.
flatter 925 vb.

sweet-tempered
amiable 884 adj.

sweet tooth
sweetness 392 n.
liking 859 n.

swell
grow 36 vb.
add 38 vb.
expand 197 vb.
swelling 253 n.
elevate 310 vb.
wave 350 n.
super 644 adj.
fop 848 n.
aristocrat 868 n.
be insolent 878 vb.

swelled head
pride 871 n.
proud person
  871 n.
vanity 873 n.

swelling
convex 253 adj.
convexity 253 n.
swelling 253 n.
proud 871 adj.

swell the ranks
accrue 38 vb.
congregate 74 vb.
be included 78 vb.
be many 104 vb.
join a party
  708 vb.

sweltering
hot 379 adj.

swerve
be oblique 220 vb.
obliquity 220 n.
be curved 248 vb.
curvature 248 n.
deviate 282 vb.
deviation 282 n.
change one's mind
  603 vb.

swift
speedy 277 adj.
bird 365 n.

swig
draught 301 n.
drink 301 vb.

swill
drink 301 vb.
get drunk 949 vb.

swim
swim 269 vb.
be light 323 vb.
amuse oneself
  837 vb.

swimming
aquatics 269 n.
sport 837 n.

swimmingly
easily 701 adv.

swimming pool
ablutions 648 n.

swimsuit
beachwear 228 n.
aquatics 269 n.

swindle
deceive 542 vb.
trickery 542 n.
expropriation
  786 n.
fleece 786 vb.
defraud 788 vb.
swindling 788 n.
be dishonest
  930 vb.

swine
pig 365 n.
cad 938 n.
sensualist 944 n.

swing
periodicity 141 n.
reversion 148 n.
vary 152 vb.
agency 173 n.
range 183 n.
hang 217 vb.
hanging object
  217 n.
strike 279 vb.
deviate 282 vb.
deviation 282 n.
fluctuation 317 n.
oscillate 317 vb.
music 412 n.
action 676 n.
scope 744 n.
be punished
  963 vb.

swingeing
exorbitant 32 adj.

swings and round-
  abouts
correlation 12 n.
reversion 148 n.
compromise 770 n.

swing the lead
be false 541 vb.

swipe
knock 279 n.
strike 279 vb.
propulsion 287 n.
strike at 712 vb.
steal 788 vb.

swirl
rotate 315 vb.
vortex 315 n.
eddy 350 n.

swish
faintness 401 n.
sound faint 401 vb.
hiss 406 vb.
sibilation 406 n.
fashionable
  848 adj.

switch
branch 53 n.
substitute 150 vb.
substitution 150 n.
interchange
  151 vb.
hair 259 n.
transpose 272 vb.
deflect 282 vb.
diverge 294 vb.
tool 630 n.
club 723 n.
hairdressing 843 n.
scourge 964 n.

switchback
obliquity 220 n.
meandering 251 n.
undulatory
  251 adj.
vehicle 274 n.

switchboard
focus 76 n.
telecommunication
  531 n.

switch off
terminate 69 vb.
cease 145 vb.

switch on
initiate 68 vb.
operate 173 vb.
move 265 vb.
hear 415 vb.

swivel
pivot 218 n.
rotator 315 n.

swiz
trickery 542 n.
fable 543 n.

swollen
great 32 adj.

convex 253 adj.
diseased 651 adj.
proud 871 adj.
swollen head
pride 871 n.
swoon
helplessness 161 n.
insensibility 375 n.
be fatigued 684 vb.
swoop
move fast 277 vb.
spurt 277 n.
descend 309 vb.
descent 309 n.
plunge 313 n.
swoosh
spurt 277 n.
hiss 406 vb.
sibilation 406 n.
sword
destroyer 168 n.
sharp edge 256 n.
sidearms 723 n.
badge of rank
  743 n.
honours 866 n.
swordfish
fish 365 n.
sword of Damocles
danger 661 n.
intimidation
  854 n.
threat 900 n.
swordstick
sidearms 723 n.
sworn
affirmative
  532 adj.
obedient 739 adj.
contractual
  765 adj.
obliged 917 adj.
sworn enemy
enemy 881 n.
swot
study 536 vb.
learner 538 n.
sycamore
tree 366 n.
sycophant
toady 879 n.
flatterer 925 n.
syllabify
spell 558 vb.
syllable
speech sound
  398 n.

word 559 n.
phrase 563 vb.
voice 577 n.
syllabus
list 87 n.
compendium
  592 n.
syllogize
reason 475 vb.
sylph
fairy 970 n.
sylph-like
narrow 206 adj.
fairylike 970 adj.
symbiosis
union 45 n.
life 360 n.
subjection 745 n.
symbol
insubstantial thing
  4 n.
number 85 n.
substitute 150 n.
metaphor 519 n.
badge 547 n.
indication 547 n.
image 551 n.
letter 558 n.
symbolic
insubstantial 4 adj.
occult 523 adj.
trivial 639 adj.
ritual 988 adj.
symbolism
metaphor 519 n.
latency 523 n.
indication 547 n.
ritual act 988 n.
symbolize
mean 514 vb.
manifest 522 vb.
indicate 547 vb.
represent 551 vb.
symmetry
equality 28 n.
symmetry 245 n.
sympathetic
agreeing 24 adj.
assenting 488 adj.
feeling 818 adj.
friendly 880 adj.
benevolent 897 adj.
pitying 905 adj.
sympathize
imagine 513 vb.
feel 818 vb.
be friendly 880 vb.

pity 905 vb.
sympathize with
love 887 vb.
pity 905 vb.
sympathy
bond 47 n.
attraction 291 n.
imagination 513 n.
cooperation 706 n.
concord 710 n.
participation
  775 n.
feeling 818 n.
liking 859 n.
friendliness 880 n.
love 887 n.
benevolence 897 n.
condolence 905 n.
pity 905 n.
symphonic
harmonious
  410 adj.
musical 412 adj.
symphony
musical piece
  412 n.
symphony orchestra
orchestra 413 n.
symphysis
combination 50 n.
symposium
accumulation 74 n.
assembly 74 n.
argument 475 n.
conference 584 n.
symptom
concomitant 89 n.
visibility 443 n.
evidence 466 n.
omen 511 n.
manifestation
  522 n.
hint 524 n.
indication 547 n.
signal 547 n.
illness 651 n.
diagnostic 658 n.
warning 664 n.
symptomatic
visible 443 adj.
evidential 466 adj.
synagogue
church 990 n.
sync
synchronism 123 n.
synchronize
  123 vb.

synchronism
synchronism 123 n.
synchronize
adjust 24 vb.
combine 50 vb.
synchronize
  123 vb.
syncopated
musical 412 adj.
syncopation
tempo 410 n.
music 412 n.
syncromesh
machine 630 n.
syndicate
publish 528 vb.
association 706 n.
corporation 708 n.
syndrome
concomitant 89 n.
structure 331 n.
evidence 466 n.
omen 511 n.
manifestation
  522 n.
indication 547 n.
signal 547 n.
illness 651 n.
diagnostic 658 n.
synecdoche
trope 519 n.
synergy
concurrence 181 n.
synod
synod 985 n.
synonym
identity 13 n.
equivalence 28 n.
substitute 150 n.
connotation 514 n.
word 559 n.
name 561 n.
synonymous
identical 13 adj.
equivalent 28 adj.
semantic 514 adj.
verbal 559 adj.
synopsis
combination 50 n.
generality 79 n.
list 87 n.
compendium
  592 n.
syntax
composition 56 n.
arrangement 62 n.
grammar 564 n.

synthesis
  union 45 n.
  combination 50 n.
synthesize
  compose 56 vb.
  produce 164 vb.
synthesizer
  musical instrument
  414 n.
synthetic
  simulating 18 adj.
  imitative 20 adj.
  untrue 543 adj.
syphilis
  venereal disease
  651 n.
syphon off
  extract 304 vb.
syringe
  irrigator 341 n.
  moisten 341 vb.
syrup
  soft drink 301 n.
  viscidity 354 n.
  sweet thing 392 n.
system
  whole 52 n.
  order 60 n.
  arrangement 62 n.
  regularity 81 n.
  creed 485 n.
  habit 610 n.
systematic
  orderly 60 adj.
  arranged 62 adj.
  regular 81 adj.
  rational 475 adj.
systems analysis
  mathematics 86 n.
  See **data**
  processing
systems analyst
  planner 623 n.
systole
  contraction 198 n.
syzygy (astronomy)
  contiguity 202 n.

T

ta
  thanks 907 int.
tab
  label 547 n.
  mark 547 vb.
  badge of rank
  743 n.

tabard
  jacket 228 n.
tabby
  cat 365 n.
  mottled 437 adj.
tabernacle
  ritual object 988 n.
  church 990 n.
  temple 990 n.
table
  arrangement 62 n.
  list 87 n.
  put off 136 vb.
  horizontality
  216 n.
  shelf 218 n.
  stand 218 n.
  eating 301 n.
tableau
  spectacle 445 n.
  picture 553 n.
  drama 594 n.
  stage show 594 n.
  pageant 875 n.
tableau vivant
  drama 594 n.
table cloth
  covering 226 n.
table d'hôte
  meal 301 n.
tableland
  high land 209 n.
  vertex 213 n.
  horizontality
  216 n.
  plain 348 n.
tablespoon
  ladle 194 n.
tablet
  horizontality
  216 n.
  monument 548 n.
  medicine 658 n.
table-tapping
  spiritualism 984 n.
table tennis
  ball game 837 n.
table-turning
  spiritualism 984 n.
table water
  soft drink 301 n.
tabloid
  the press 528 n.
taboo
  set apart 46 vb.
  exclude 57 vb.
  exclusion 57 n.

command 737 vb.
  prohibit 757 vb.
  prohibited 757 adj.
  prohibition 757 n.
  bewitch 983 vb.
tabor
  drum 414 n.
tabular
  arranged 62 adj.
tabula rasa
  revolution 149 n.
  emptiness 190 n.
  ignorance 491 n.
tabulate
  class 62 vb.
  list 87 vb.
  register 548 vb.
tachograph
  meter 465 n.
  recording instru-
  ment 549 n.
tachometer
  velocity 277 n.
  meter 465 n.
tachycardia
  cardiovascular dis-
  ease 651 n.
tachymeter
  meter 465 n.
tacit
  tacit 523 adj.
taciturn
  silent 399 adj.
  taciturn 582 adj.
tack
  tie 45 vb.
  fastening 47 n.
  vary 152 vb.
  sharp point 256 n.
  be in motion
  265 vb.
  navigate 269 vb.
  direction 281 n.
  deviate 282 vb.
  deviation 282 n.
  change one's mind
  603 vb.
  route 624 n.
tackle
  begin 68 vb.
  equipment 630 n.
  attempt 671 n.
  attempt 671 vb.
  undertake 672 vb.
  do 676 vb.
tack on
  add 38 vb.

tacky
  cohesive 48 adj.
  viscid 354 adj.
  bad 645 adj.
taco
  cereals 301 n.
  dish 301 n.
tact
  discrimination
  463 n.
  sagacity 498 n.
  management
  689 n.
  good taste 846 n.
tactful
  discriminating
  463 adj.
  wise 498 adj.
  benevolent 897 adj.
tactical
  planned 623 adj.
  cunning 698 adj.
tactics
  tactics 688 n.
tactile
  tactual 378 adj.
tactless
  inattentive 456 adj.
  indiscriminating
  464 adj.
  foolish 499 adj.
  clumsy 695 adj.
  ill-bred 847 adj.
  discourteous
  885 adj.
tadpole
  young creature
  132 n.
  amphibian 365 n.
taekwondo
  wrestling 716 n.
taffeta
  textile 222 n.
tag
  adjunct 40 n.
  ligature 47 n.
  class 62 vb.
  extremity 69 n.
  list 87 n.
  hanging object
  217 n.
  sharp point 256 n.
  maxim 496 n.
  label 547 n.
  mark 547 vb.
  children's games
  837 n.

tagliatelle
  dish 301 n.

tail
  extremity 69 n.
  accompany 89 vb.
  concomitant 89 n.
  hanging object
    217 n.
  be behind 238 vb.
  buttocks 238 n.
  rear 238 n.
  aircraft 276 n.
  follow 284 vb.
  follower 284 n.
  detect 484 vb.
  hunter 619 n.
  pursue 619 vb.

tailback
  retinue 67 n.
  traffic control
    305 n.

tail-end
  back 238 adj.
  rear 238 n.

tail off
  decrease 37 vb.

tailor
  adjust 24 vb.
  clothier 228 n.
  form 243 vb.
  artisan 686 n.

tailor-made
  adjusted 24 adj.
  tailored 228 adj.
  formed 243 adj.

tails
  formal dress 228 n.

tailwind
  wind 352 n.

tainted
  bad 645 adj.
  imperfect 647 adj.
  unclean 649 adj.
  diseased 651 adj.

take
  bring together
    74 vb.
  comprise 78 vb.
  photograph 551 vb.
  subjugate 745 vb.
  arrest 747 vb.
  acquire 771 vb.
  take 786 vb.
  taking 786 n.
  be patient 823 vb.

take aback
  surprise 508 vb.

take a chance
  face danger 661 vb.

take a fancy to
  be pleased 824 vb.
  desire 859 vb.
  be in love 887 vb.

take after
  be intrinsic 5 vb.
  resemble 18 vb.

take a leaf out of an-
  other's book
  do likewise 20 vb.

take amiss
  be discontented
    829 vb.
  resent 891 vb.

take apart
  sunder 46 vb.
  destroy 165 vb.

take a pew
  sit down 311 vb.

take a photo or a pic-
  ture
  photograph 551 vb.

take as
  be of the opinion
    that 485 vb.

take a seat
  sit down 311 vb.

take a shine to
  be in love 887 vb.

take away
  abate 37 vb.
  subtract 39 vb.
  displace 188 vb.
  take away 786 vb.

take-away
  café 192 n.

take away one's good
  name
  shame 867 vb.

take back
  recoup 31 vb.
  recant 603 vb.
  acquire 771 vb.
  take 786 vb.

take by storm
  attack 712 vb.
  take 786 vb.

take care
  be wise 498 vb.

take care of
  be mindful 455 vb.
  look after 457 vb.
  do 676 vb.

take down
  lower 311 vb.

  record 548 vb.
  write 586 vb.
  ridicule 851 vb.

take down a peg
  abase 311 vb.
  depose 752 vb.
  shame 867 vb.
  humiliate 872 vb.

take effect
  operate 173 vb.
  be successful
    727 vb.

take exception to
  deprecate 762 vb.
  resent 891 vb.
  disapprove 924 vb.

take for granted
  assume 471 vb.
  certain 473 adj.
  postulate 475 vb.
  be credulous
    487 vb.
  suppose 512 vb.
  not wonder 865 vb.
  be ungrateful
    908 vb.

take French leave
  be absent 190 vb.
  disappear 446 vb.
  run away 620 vb.
  escape 667 vb.
  disobey 738 vb.
  be free 744 vb.

take hold
  cohere 48 vb.
  prevail 178 vb.
  take 786 vb.

take ill
  be discontented
    829 vb.
  resent 891 vb.

take in
  contain 56 vb.
  comprise 78 vb.
  load 193 vb.
  make smaller
    198 vb.
  absorb 299 vb.
  admit 299 vb.
  scan 438 vb.
  see 438 vb.
  know 490 vb.
  understand 516 vb.
  fool 542 vb.
  store 632 vb.
  safeguard 660 vb.
  receive 782 vb.

  take 786 vb.

take in one's stride
  do easily 701 vb.

take into account
  meditate 449 vb.
  notice 455 vb.
  qualify 468 vb.

take into care
  look after 457 vb.

take into considera-
  tion
  meditate 449 vb.
  notice 455 vb.

take issue with
  go to war 718 vb.

take it
  be of the opinion
    that 485 vb.
  suppose 512 vb.
  knuckle under
    721 vb.

take it easy
  move slowly
    278 vb.
  be neglectful
    458 vb.
  be inactive 679 vb.
  repose 683 vb.

take it on the chin
  suffer 825 vb.

take it or leave it
  have no choice
    606 vb.
  be indifferent
    860 vb.

take it out of
  fatigue 684 vb.

take it upon oneself
  will 595 vb.

taken off guard
  unprepared
    670 adj.

take note
  notice 455 vb.

taken aback, be
  not expect 508 vb.

taken short, be
  excrete 302 vb.

taken to the
  cleaner's, be
  be defeated 728 vb.

taken with, be
  be in love 887 vb.

take off
  imitate 20 vb.
  grow 36 vb.
  subtract 39 vb.

displace 188 vb.
fly 271 vb.
start out 296 vb.
ascend 308 vb.
act 594 vb.
discount 810 vb.
relieve 831 vb.
satirize 851 vb.

takeoff
copy 22 n.
aeronautics 271 n.
air travel 271 n.
departure 296 n.
ascent 308 n.
satire 851 n.

take office
take authority
    733 vb.

take on
admit 299 vb.
train 534 vb.
employ 622 vb.
store 632 vb.
attempt 671 vb.
undertake 672 vb.
do 676 vb.
withstand 704 vb.
contend 716 vb.
fight 716 vb.
be discontented
    829 vb.
lament 836 vb.

take one back
remind 505 vb.

**take one's breath
away**
surprise 508 vb.
make mute 578 vb.
impress 821 vb.
delight 826 vb.
be beautiful
    841 vb.
be wonderful
    864 vb.

take one's ease
repose 683 vb.

take one's hat off to
respect 920 vb.
approve 923 vb.
praise 923 vb.

take one's pick
select 605 vb.

take one's time
wait 136 vb.
move slowly
    278 vb.
be cautious 858 vb.

take one up on
dissent 489 vb.
defy 711 vb.

take on oneself
be resolute 599 vb.
busy oneself
    622 vb.
promise 764 vb.
be insolent 878 vb.
incur a duty
    917 vb.

take on trust
believe 485 vb.
be credulous
    487 vb.

take orders
take orders 986 vb.

take out
subtract 39 vb.
exclude 57 vb.
extract 304 vb.
court 889 vb.

take over
come after 65 vb.
appropriate
    786 vb.
take 786 vb.

takeover
relation 9 n.
transference 272 n.
expropriation
    786 n.
purchase 792 n.

takeover bid
offer 759 n.
purchase 792 n.

take over the reigns
take authority
    733 vb.

take pains
be attentive 455 vb.
be active 678 vb.

take part
be present 189 vb.
cooperate 706 vb.

take pity on
relieve 831 vb.
pity 905 vb.

take pot luck
be sociable 882 vb.

taker
possessor 776 n.
recipient 782 n.
taker 786 n.

take risks
gamble 618 vb.

take root
stay 144 vb.
prevail 178 vb.
place oneself
    187 vb.
be wont 610 vb.

take shape
become 1 vb.

take sides
be biased 481 vb.
choose 605 vb.

take silk
do law 958 vb.

**take something the
wrong way**
be hostile 881 vb.

take steps
prepare 669 vb.
do 676 vb.

take stock of
scan 438 vb.
meditate 449 vb.

take the biscuit
be superior 34 vb.

**take the bit between
one's teeth**
will 595 vb.
be obstinate
    602 vb.
disobey 738 vb.

**take the bull by the
horns**
be resolute 599 vb.
attempt 671 vb.
be active 678 vb.
be courageous
    855 vb.

take the chair
direct 689 vb.

**take the floor or the
stand**
orate 579 vb.

take the helm
direct 689 vb.

take the initiative
initiate 68 vb.

take the lead
come before 64 vb.
initiate 68 vb.
be in front 237 vb.
precede 283 vb.
have a reputation
    866 vb.

take the liberty
permit 756 vb.

**take the line of least
resistance**

do easily 701 vb.
knuckle under
    721 vb.

**take the mickey out
of**
ridicule 851 vb.

take the offensive
attack 712 vb.
go to war 718 vb.

take the opportunity
be early 135 vb.
profit by 137 vb.

take the place of
substitute 150 vb.

take the pledge
be temperate
    942 vb.

take the plunge
initiate 68 vb.
be resolute 599 vb.
be courageous
    855 vb.
wed 894 vb.

take the rap
incur blame
    924 vb.
be punished
    963 vb.

take the veil
become pious
    979 vb.
take orders 986 vb.

**take the wind out of
one's sails**
disable 161 vb.
navigate 269 vb.
abase 311 vb.
be obstructive
    702 vb.
hinder 702 vb.
ridicule 851 vb.

take things easy
keep calm 823 vb.

take time off or out
repose 683 vb.

take to
habituate 610 vb.
desire 859 vb.
befriend 880 vb.
be in love 887 vb.

take to flight
run away 620 vb.
be defeated 728 vb.
fear 854 vb.

take to heart
feel 818 vb.

be discontented
829 vb.
be dejected 834 vb.
resent 891 vb.
take to one's heels
run away 620 vb.
take to pieces
sunder 46 vb.
decompose 51 vb.
make useless
641 adj.
take to task
reprove 924 vb.
take to the cleaners
fleece 786 vb.
take umbrage
be hostile 881 vb.
resent 891 vb.
take up
shorten 204 vb.
elevate 310 vb.
study 536 vb.
be resolute 599 vb.
be wont 610 vb.
busy oneself
622 vb.
undertake 672 vb.
avail oneself of
673 vb.
receive 782 vb.
take 786 vb.
befriend 880 vb.
take up one's cross
suffer 825 vb.
take upon oneself
undertake 672 vb.
take up the challenge
contend 716 vb.
**take up the cudgels
for**
patronize 703 vb.
defend 713 vb.
taking
taking 786 n.
anger 891 n.
takings
earnings 771 n.
receiving 782 n.
taking 786 n.
receipt 807 n.
talc
powder 332 n.
talcum powder
powder 332 n.
cosmetic 843 n.
tale
fable 543 n.

narrative 590 n.
talebearer
informer 524 n.
talent
tendency 179 n.
intelligence 498 n.
aptitude 694 n.
coinage 797 n.
talented
intelligent 498 adj.
gifted 694 adj.
talisman
talisman 983 n.
talk
cry 408 n.
empty talk 515 n.
inform 524 vb.
confess 526 vb.
divulge 526 vb.
rumour 529 n.
broadcast 531 n.
lecture 534 n.
language 557 n.
oration 579 n.
speak 579 vb.
speech 579 n.
be loquacious
581 vb.
allocution 583 n.
chat 584 n.
interlocution
584 n.
talkative
speaking 579 adj.
loquacious 581 adj.
**talk behind one's
back**
defame 926 vb.
talk down
be loquacious
581 vb.
talkdown
aeronautics 271 n.
talkie
film 445 n.
talking head
broadcaster 531 n.
broadcasting
531 n.
talking-to
reprimand 924 n.
talk into
induce 612 vb.
talk it over
confer 584 vb.
talk out of
dissuade 613 vb.

talk round
induce 612 vb.
talks
conference 584 n.
talk shop
be loquacious
581 vb.
**talk through one's
hat**
be absurd 497 vb.
be foolish 499 vb.
talk to oneself
orate 579 vb.
talk turkey
be concise 569 vb.
speak plainly
573 vb.
tall
great 32 adj.
tall 209 adj.
tallboy
cabinet 194 n.
tall order
undertaking 672 n.
hard task 700 n.
tallow
fat 357 n.
tall story
news 529 n.
fable 543 n.
exaggeration
546 n.
tally
accord 24 vb.
numerical result
85 n.
numeration 86 n.
list 87 n.
record 548 n.
credit 802 n.
debt 803 n.
accounts 808 n.
tally-ho
cry 408 n.
chase 619 n.
Talmud
scripture 975 n.
talon
foot 214 n.
sharp point 256 n.
finger 378 n.
pincers 778 n.
tambourine
drum 414 n.
tame
moderate 177 vb.
break in 369 vb.

train 534 vb.
habituate 610 vb.
habituated 610 adj.
oppress 735 vb.
obedient 739 adj.
subjugate 745 vb.
servile 879 adj.
tameness
obedience 739 n.
tammy
headgear 228 n.
tamp
impel 279 vb.
tamp down
close 264 vb.
tamper
derange 63 vb.
ram 279 n.
impair 655 vb.
meddle 678 vb.
tamper with
mix 43 vb.
modify 143 vb.
be false 541 vb.
tampon
stopper 264 n.
surgical dressing
658 n.
tan
be hot 379 vb.
burning 381 n.
colour 425 vb.
brown 430 adj.
brown 430 vb.
spank 963 vb.
tandem
bicycle 274 n.
cooperation 706 n.
tandoori
dish 301 n.
tang
taste 386 n.
pungency 388 n.
odour 394 n.
tangent
ratio 85 n.
contiguity 202 n.
straightness 249 n.
convergence 293 n.
tangential
convergent 293 adj.
tangerine
fruit and vegetables
301 n.
orange 432 n.
tangible
real 1 adj.

substantial 3 adj.
material 319 adj.
tactual 378 adj.
visible 443 adj.
true 494 adj.
tangle
complexity 61 n.
bedevil 63 vb.
roughen 259 vb.
tango
dance 837 n.
dance 837 vb.
tangy
tasty 386 adj.
pungent 388 adj.
tank
vat 194 n.
war chariot 274 n.
storage 632 n.
cavalry 722 n.
tankard
cup 194 n.
tanker
lorry 274 n.
merchant ship
275 n.
tanned
blackish 428 adj.
brown 430 adj.
tanner
coinage 797 n.
tannoy
hearing aid 415 n.
tantalize
tempt 612 vb.
tantamount
equivalent 28 adj.
semantic 514 adj.
tantra
non-Biblical scrip-
ture 975 n.
tantrum
anger 891 n.
tap
stopper 264 n.
impulse 279 n.
knock 279 n.
strike 279 vb.
outlet 298 n.
empty 300 vb.
extract 304 vb.
water 339 n.
conduit 351 n.
touch 378 n.
touch 378 vb.
bang 402 n.
crackle 402 vb.

roll 403 vb.
play music 413 vb.
hear 415 vb.
store 632 n.
acquire 771 vb.
take 786 vb.
tap dancing
dancing 837 n.
tape
cable 47 n.
ligature 47 n.
line 203 n.
strip 208 n.
musical piece
412 n.
gramophone 414 n.
appraise 465 vb.
measure 465 vb.
publish 528 vb.
record 548 n.
record 548 vb.
objective 617 n.
tape measure
counting instru-
ment 86 n.
gauge 465 n.
taper
become small
198 vb.
make smaller
198 vb.
be sharp 256 vb.
converge 293 vb.
convergence 293 n.
lighter 385 n.
torch 420 n.
tape recorder
gramophone 414 n.
recording instru-
ment 549 n.
taper off
decrease 37 vb.
become small
198 vb.
tapestry
hanging object
217 n.
textile 222 n.
art 551 n.
picture 553 n.
tapeworm
creepy-crawly
365 n.
bane 659 n.
tapioca
dessert 301 n.

tar
coat 226 vb.
mariner 270 n.
resin 357 n.
black thing 428 n.
shame 867 vb.
taramasalata
hors-d'oeuvres
301 n.
tar and feather
punish 963 vb.
tarantella
musical piece
412 n.
dance 837 n.
tarantula
creepy-crawly
365 n.
tarboosh
headgear 228 n.
tardy
late 136 adj.
slow 278 adj.
lazy 679 adj.
target
centre 225 n.
limit 236 n.
direction 281 n.
objective 617 n.
tariff
list 87 n.
price 809 n.
tax 809 n.
tarmac
paving 226 n.
smoothness 258 n.
air travel 271 n.
road 624 n.
building material
631 n.
tarn
lake 346 n.
tarnish
make unclean
649 vb.
blemish 845 n.
shame 867 vb.
slur 867 n.
defame 926 vb.
tarot cards
oracle 511 n.
tarpaulin
canopy 226 n.
tarragon
herb 301 n.
tarry
stay 144 vb.

be quiescent
266 vb.
move slowly
278 vb.
tarsus
foot 214 n.
tart
pastries and cakes
301 n.
pungent 388 adj.
sour 393 adj.
irascible 892 adj.
sullen 893 adj.
loose woman
952 n.
tartan
chequer 437 n.
variegated 437 adj.
pattern 844 n.
tartar
sourness 393 n.
dirt 649 n.
tarty
unchaste 951 adj.
**tar with the same
brush**
identify 13 vb.
Tarzan
athlete 162 n.
task
job 622 n.
undertaking 672 n.
deed 676 n.
labour 682 n.
mandate 751 n.
portion 783 n.
duty 917 n.
impose a duty
917 vb.
penalty 963 n.
task force
armed force 722 n.
taskmaster
tyrant 735 n.
TASS
informant 524 n.
tassel
hanging object
217 n.
trimming 844 n.
taste
have feeling
374 vb.
sense 374 n.
taste 386 n.
taste 386 vb.
enquire 459 vb.

tasteful
  elegance 575 n.
  choice 605 n.
  feel 818 vb.
  good taste 846 n.
tasteful
  tasteful 846 adj.
tasteless
  tasteless 387 adj.
  unsavoury 391 adj.
  indiscriminating
    464 adj.
  inelegant 576 adj.
  vulgar 847 adj.
tasty
  tasty 386 adj.
  pleasurable
    826 adj.
ta-ta
  goodbye 296 int.
tatters
  clothing 228 n.
tatting
  network 222 n.
  needlework 844 n.
tattle
  be loquacious
    581 vb.
  chat 584 n.
  converse 584 vb.
tattoo
  periodicity 141 n.
  pierce 263 vb.
  roll 403 n.
  roll 403 vb.
  play music 413 vb.
  colour 425 vb.
  variegate 437 vb.
  call 547 n.
  label 547 n.
  mark 547 vb.
  pageant 875 n.
  celebration 876 n.
  love token 889 n.
tatty
  dilapidated
    655 adj.
taught
  creedal 485 adj.
taunt
  be insolent 878 vb.
  sauciness 878 n.
  enrage 891 vb.
  indignity 921 n.
  not respect 921 vb.
  criticize 924 vb.
  reproach 924 n.
  calumny 926 n.

accusation 928 n.
  accuse 928 vb.
taupe
  greyness 429 n.
taut
  tied 45 adj.
  rigid 326 adj.
tauten
  tighten 45 vb.
  make smaller
    198 vb.
  harden 326 vb.
tautology
  identity 13 n.
  repetition 106 n.
  diffuseness 570 n.
  superfluity 637 n.
tavern
  tavern 192 n.
tawdry
  trivial 639 adj.
  graceless 842 adj.
  vulgar 847 adj.
  showy 875 adj.
tawny
  brown 430 adj.
  yellow 433 adj.
tax
  use 673 vb.
  work 682 vb.
  fatigue 684 vb.
  oppress 735 vb.
  tax 809 n.
  tax 809 vb.
  impose a duty
    917 vb.
taxation
  taking 786 n.
  tax 809 n.
taxes
  earnings 771 n.
  receipt 807 n.
  tax 809 n.
taxi
  be in motion
    265 vb.
  conveyance 267 n.
  fly 271 vb.
  cab 274 n.
taxidermy
  preservation 666 n.
tax one's memory
  remember 505 vb.
taxonomy
  arrangement 62 n.
  classification 77 n.
  botany 368 n.

tax with
  accuse 928 vb.
tea
  meal 301 n.
  soft drink 301 n.
tea-caddy
  small box 194 n.
teach
  educate 534 vb.
  teach 534 vb.
teacher
  teacher 537 n.
tea chest
  box 194 n.
teach-in
  teaching 534 n.
  conference 584 n.
teaching
  teaching 534 n.
teach one a lesson
  retaliate 714 vb.
teach one's grand-
mother to suck
eggs
  be superfluous
    637 vb.
  be insolent 878 vb.
teacup
  cup 194 n.
teak
  hardness 326 n.
  tree 366 n.
teal
  bird 365 n.
tea leaves
  oracle 511 n.
team
  band 74 n.
  group 74 n.
  personnel 686 n.
  party 708 n.
team spirit
  cooperation 706 n.
  concord 710 n.
  fellowship 882 n.
team up
  cooperate 706 vb.
team up with
  combine 50 vb.
  join a party
    708 vb.
tea party
  social gathering
    882 n.
tea planter
  farmer 370 n.

teapot
  pot 194 n.
tear
  disunion 46 n.
  rend 46 vb.
    See **sunder**
  force 176 vb.
  gap 201 n.
  groove 262 vb.
  move fast 277 vb.
  give pain 377 vb.
  ill-treat 645 vb.
  wound 655 vb.
  hurt 827 vb.
  lamentation 836 n.
tear down
  demolish 165 vb.
teardrop
  moisture 341 n.
  lamentation 836 n.
tearful
  unhappy 825 adj.
  melancholic
    834 adj.
  lamenting 836 adj.
tear gas
  poison 659 n.
tearing hurry
  haste 680 n.
tear into
  attack 712 vb.
tear-jerking
  distressing 827 adj.
  lamenting 836 adj.
tear off
  uncover 229 vb.
  move fast 277 vb.
  hasten 680 vb.
tear oneself away
  depart 296 vb.
  be unwilling
    598 vb.
tear one's hair
  gesticulate 547 vb.
  lament 836 vb.
tearoom
  café 192 n.
tear out
  extract 304 vb.
tears
  water 339 n.
  moisture 341 n.
  lamentation 836 n.
tear strips off
  reprove 924 vb.
tear to bits
  demolish 165 vb.

tear up
  demolish 165 vb.
  destroy 165 vb.
  abrogate 752 vb.
tease
  tempt 612 vb.
  excite 821 vb.
  torment 827 vb.
  ridicule 851 vb.
  enrage 891 vb.
  be malevolent
    898 vb.
teaser
  example 83 n.
  priority 119 n.
  advertisement
    528 n.
  difficulty 700 n.
  worry 825 n.
  humorist 839 n.
tea service
  cup 194 n.
tea set
  cup 194 n.
teashop
  café 192 n.
teasing
  exciting 821 adj.
  ridicule 851 n.
teaspoon
  ladle 194 n.
teat
  bosom 253 n.
tea towel
  cleaning cloth
    648 n.
technicality
  means of escape
    667 n.
technician
  machinist 630 n.
  expert 696 n.
Technicolor (tdmk)
  colour 425 n.
  film 445 n.
technique
  painting 553 n.
  way 624 n.
  means 629 n.
  skill 694 n.
technology
  physics 319 n.
  science 490 n.
  business 622 n.
  means 629 n.
technospeak
  neology 560 n.

slang 560 adj.
Ted
  youngster 132 n.
teddy
  underwear 228 n.
teddy bear
  image 551 n.
  plaything 837 n.
tedious
  tedious 838 adj.
  dull 840 adj.
tedium
  tedium 838 n.
tee-hee
  laugh 835 vb.
  laughter 835 n.
teem
  reproduce itself
    167 vb.
  be fruitful 171 vb.
  abound 635 vb.
teem with
  be many 104 vb.
  superabound
    637 vb.
teenage
  young 130 adj.
teenager
  youngster 132 n.
teens
  over five 99 n.
teeny
  small 33 adj.
  dwarf 196 n.
  little 196 adj.
tee shirt
  shirt 228 n.
teeter
  vary 152 vb.
  be weak 163 vb.
  move slowly
    278 vb.
  oscillate 317 vb.
  be agitated 318 vb.
  be uncertain
    474 vb.
  be irresolute
    601 vb.
teeter on the edge
  be in danger
    661 vb.
teeth
  vigorousness 174 n.
  white thing 427 n.
  weapon 723 n.
  pincers 778 n.

teething troubles
  beginning 68 n.
  learning 536 n.
  difficulty 700 n.
  hitch 702 n.
teetotal
  temperate 942 adj.
  sober 948 adj.
tee up
  make ready
    669 vb.
tegument
  skin 226 n.
telecast
  communicate
    524 vb.
  publication 528 n.
  publish 528 vb.
  broadcast 531 n.
telecommunication
  telecommunication
    531 n.
telegram
  information 524 n.
  message 529 n.
  telecommunication
    531 n.
telegraph
  velocity 277 n.
  communicate
    524 vb.
  signal 547 n.
telegraphese
  neology 560 n.
  conciseness 569 n.
telegraphic
  concise 569 adj.
telegraphy
  telecommunication
    531 n.
telekinesis
  spiritualism 984 n.
telemessage
  information 524 n.
  message 529 n.
  telecommunication
    531 n.
tele-ordering
  purchase 792 n.
telepathic
  intuitive 476 adj.
  psychical 984 n.
telepathy
  sense 374 n.
  thought 449 n.
  intuition 476 n.
  psychics 984 n.

telephone
  sound 398 n.
  hearing aid 415 n.
  communicate
    524 vb.
  telecommunication
    531 n.
telephone directory
  directory 87 n.
  guidebook 524 n.
telephonist
  telecommunication
    531 n.
telephony
  telecommunication
    531 n.
telephotography
  photography 551 n.
telephoto lens
  camera 442 n.
teleprinter
  telecommunication
    531 n.
  recording instru-
    ment 549 n.
telescope
  shorten 204 vb.
  astronomy 321 n.
  telescope 442 n.
  be concise 569 vb.
telescopic
  distant 199 adj.
  astronomic
    321 adj.
  visible 443 adj.
teleshopping
  purchase 792 n.
teletext
  data processing
    86 n.
  broadcasting
    531 n.
televise
  show 522 vb.
  communicate
    524 vb.
  publish 528 vb.
television
  electronics 160 n.
  spectacle 445 n.
  publicity 528 n.
  broadcasting
    531 n.
  amusement 837 n.
television channel
  broadcasting
    531 n.

telex
 communicate
  524 vb.
 information 524 n.
 telecommunication
  531 n.
tell
 number 86 vb.
 inform 524 vb.
 divulge 526 vb.
 describe 590 vb.
 command 737 vb.
 accuse 928 vb.
tell against
 tell against 467 vb.
teller
 informant 524 n.
 treasurer 798 n.
tell its own story
 evidence 466 vb.
 be intelligible
  516 vb.
 be plain 522 vb.
tell lies
 be false 541 vb.
 be dishonest
  930 vb.
tell off
 reprove 924 vb.
 punish 963 vb.
tell on
 inform 524 vb.
 divulge 526 vb.
 accuse 928 vb.
telltale
 witness 466 n.
 informer 524 n.
tell tales
 inform 524 vb.
tell-tale sign
 disclosure 526 n.
 indication 547 n.
tell that to the
  marines
 God forbid 489 int.
tell upon
 influence 178 vb.
tellurian
 native 191 adj.
 native 191 n.
telly
 broadcasting
  531 n.
temerity
 rashness 857 n.
temp
 deputy 755 n.

temper
 temperament 5 n.
 state 7 n.
 mix 43 vb.
 strengthen 162 vb.
 moderate 177 vb.
 harden 326 vb.
 qualify 468 vb.
 mature 669 vb.
 affections 817 n.
 excitation 821 n.
 excitable state
  822 n.
 relieve 831 vb.
 anger 891 n.
 be temperate
  942 vb.
tempera
 art style 553 n.
temperament
 temperament 5 n.
 moral sensibility
  819 n.
 irascibility 892 n.
 sullenness 893 n.
temperamental
 nonuniform 17 adj.
 capricious 604 adj.
 excitable 822 adj.
 irascible 892 adj.
 sullen 893 adj.
temperance
 virtue 933 n.
 virtues 933 n.
 temperance 942 n.
temperate
 warm 379 adj.
 temperate 942 adj.
temperature
 illness 651 n.
tempest
 storm 176 n.
 velocity 277 n.
 commotion 318 n.
 excitable state
  822 n.
tempestuous
 disorderly 61 adj.
 violent 176 adj.
 speedy 277 adj.
 windy 352 adj.
 excitable 822 adj.
temple
 head 213 n.
 refuge 662 n.
 honours 866 n.
 church 990 n.

temple 990 n.
tempo
 tendency 179 n.
 motion 265 n.
 velocity 277 n.
 tempo 410 n.
temporal
 continuing 108 adj.
 transient 114 adj.
temporary
 circumstantial
  8 adj.
 inferior 35 adj.
 ephemeral 114 adj.
 substituted 150 adj.
temporary measure
 substitute 150 n.
temporize
 put off 136 vb.
tempt
 cause 156 vb.
 tempt 612 vb.
temptation
 attraction 291 n.
 inducement 612 n.
 difficulty 700 n.
 request 761 n.
 desired object
  859 n.
 liking 859 n.
tempting
 tasty 386 adj.
 savoury 390 adj.
tempting offer
 incentive 612 n.
 reward 962 n.
tempt providence or
  fate
 face danger 661 vb.
 be rash 857 vb.
 be insolent 878 vb.
ten
 over five 99 n.
tenable
 rational 475 adj.
 credible 485 adj.
 invulnerable
  660 adj.
tenacious
 cohesive 48 adj.
 tough 329 adj.
 resolute 599 adj.
 obstinate 602 adj.
 retentive 778 adj.
tenacity
 coherence 48 n.
 toughness 329 n.

 resolution 599 n.
 perseverance 600 n.
 obstinacy 602 n.
 retention 778 n.
 courage 855 n.
tenancy
 time 108 n.
 possession 773 n.
 nonownership
  774 n.
tenant
 resident 191 n.
 dwell 192 vb.
 possessor 776 n.
Ten Commandments
 over five 99 n.
 fixture 153 n.
 precept 693 n.
 code of duty 917 n.
 law 953 n.
 revelation 975 n.
tend
 tend 179 vb.
 look after 457 vb.
 doctor 658 vb.
 serve 742 vb.
tendency
 tendency 179 n.
tender
 locomotive 274 n.
 boat 275 n.
 ship 275 n.
 follower 284 n.
 soft 327 adj.
 sentient 374 adj.
 painful 377 adj.
 soft-hued 425 adj.
 lenient 736 adj.
 offer 759 n.
 offer 759 vb.
 sensitive 819 adj.
 paining 827 adj.
 honour 866 vb.
 loving 887 adj.
 benevolent 897 adj.
 pitying 905 adj.
tender age
 nonage 130 n.
 youth 130 n.
tenderfoot
 intruder 59 n.
 beginner 538 n.
tender-hearted
 feeling 818 adj.
 impressible
  819 adj.
 pitying 905 adj.

tenderize
soften 327 vb.
tender mercies
severity 735 n.
mercy 905 n.
tenderness
weakness 163 n.
softness 327 n.
sensibility 374 n.
pain 377 n.
leniency 736 n.
moral sensibility
819 n.
painfulness 827 n.
love 887 n.
benevolence 897 n.
**tender one's resigna-
tion**
resign 753 vb.
tending
possible 469 adj.
tendon
ligature 47 n.
tendril
ligature 47 n.
branch 53 n.
filament 208 n.
coil 251 n.
foliage 366 n.
pincers 778 n.
tenements
flat 192 n.
housing 192 n.
tenet
precept 693 n.
theology 973 n.
tenets
creed 485 n.
tenner
over five 99 n.
funds 797 n.
tennis
ball game 837 n.
tennis ball
missile 287 n.
tennis court
arena 724 n.
pleasure ground
837 n.
tennis elbow
rheumatism 651 n.
tennis-player
player 837 n.
tenon
projection 254 n.
tenor
degree 27 n.

tendency 179 n.
direction 281 n.
stridor 407 n.
vocalist 413 n.
meaning 514 n.
tenor sax
flute 414 n.
tense
tied 45 adj.
time 108 n.
rigid 326 adj.
grammar 564 n.
feeling 818 n.
fervent 818 adj.
excited 821 adj.
excitable 822 adj.
nervous 854 adj.
tensile
elastic 328 adj.
tension
quantity 26 n.
energy 160 n.
dissension 709 n.
excitation 821 n.
worry 825 n.
enmity 881 n.
tent
dwell 192 vb.
dwelling 192 n.
pavilion 192 n.
small house 192 n.
canopy 226 n.
tentacle
feeler 378 n.
pincers 778 n.
tentative
slow 278 adj.
enquiring 459 adj.
experimental
461 adj.
clumsy 695 adj.
cautious 858 adj.
tenth
multifid 100 adj.
ten to one
probably 471 adv.
tenuous
flimsy 163 adj.
rare 325 adj.
tenure
time 108 n.
possession 773 n.
estate 777 n.
lands 777 n.
benefice 985 n.
church office 985 n.

tepee
dwelling 192 n.
canopy 226 n.
tepid
warm 379 adj.
tequila
alcoholic drink
301 n.
teratogen
poison 659 n.
teratoid
abnormal 84 adj.
unusual 84 adj.
teratology
deformity 246 n.
terce
church service
988 n.
tercentenary
triplication 94 n.
tercentennial
seasonal 141 adj.
tercet
verse form 593 n.
tergiversate
change one's mind
603 vb.
term
end 69 n.
serial place 73 n.
date 108 n.
time 108 n.
period 110 n.
limit 236 n.
word 559 n.
name 561 n.
name 561 vb.
termagant
violent creature
176 n.
terminal
ending 69 adj.
extremity 69 n.
stopping place
145 n.
distant 199 adj.
limit 236 n.
air travel 271 n.
goal 295 n.
deadly 362 adj.
unpromising
853 adj.
**terminal illness or
disease**
decease 361 n.
terminate
terminate 69 vb.

termination
end 69 n.
effect 157 n.
completion 725 n.
**terminological inex-
actitude**
falsehood 541 n.
deception 542 n.
untruth 543 n.
terminology
nomenclature
561 n.
phrase 563 n.
terminus
extremity 69 n.
stopping place
145 n.
limit 236 n.
goal 295 n.
completion 725 n.
termite
insect 365 n.
terms
conditions 766 n.
terms of reference
function 622 n.
mandate 751 n.
conditions 766 n.
tern
bird 365 n.
terotechnology
economy 814 n.
Terpsichorean
dramatic 594 adj.
terrace
housing 192 n.
horizontality
216 n.
terracotta
pottery 381 n.
terra firma
basis 218 n.
land 344 n.
terrain
space 183 n.
region 184 n.
land 344 n.
arena 724 n.
terra incognita
unknown thing
491 n.
secret 530 n.
terrapin
reptile 365 n.
terrarium
zoo 369 n.

terrestrial
native 191 adj.
native 191 n.
terrible
not nice 645 adj.
frightening
854 adj.
terribly
extremely 32 vb.
terrier
dog 365 n.
terrific
prodigious 32 adj.
excellent 644 adj.
terrify
frighten 854 vb.
terrine
bowl 194 n.
hors-d'oeuvres
301 n.
territorial
soldier 722 n.
territorial army
army 722 n.
territorial waters
territory 184 n.
territory
territory 184 n.
land 344 n.
terror
violent creature
176 n.
fear 854 n.
intimidation
854 n.
ruffian 904 n.
respect 920 n.
bad person 938 n.
terrorist
violent creature
176 n.
murderer 362 n.
attacker 712 n.
revolter 738 n.
robber 789 n.
alarmist 854 n.
desperado 857 n.
evildoer 904 n.
bad person 938 n.
terrorize
oppress 735 vb.
frighten 854 vb.
terry towelling
textile 222 n.
terse
short 204 adj.
concise 569 adj.

tertiary
treble 94 adj.
tertiary education
education 534 n.
tessellated
variegated 437 adj.
test
enquire 459 vb.
enquiry 459 n.
exam 459 n.
experiment 461 n.
experiment 461 vb.
diagnostic 658 n.
hard task 700 n.
testament
testimony 466 n.
testator
owner 776 n.
testatrix
owner 776 n.
test case
experiment 461 n.
litigation 959 n.
testicles
genitalia 167 n.
testify
testify 466 vb.
testimonial
credential 466 n.
reminder 505 n.
approbation 923 n.
testimony
testimony 466 n.
test match
contest 716 n.
test tube
vessel 194 n.
testing agent
461 n.
test-tube baby
propagation 167 n.
testy
discontented
829 adj.
irascible 892 adj.
tetanus
spasm 318 n.
infection 651 n.
tetchy
irascible 892 adj.
tête-à-tête
dual 90 adj.
near 200 adv.
chat 584 n.
interlocution
584 n.
advice 691 n.

social gathering
882 n.
tether
affix 45 vb.
tie 45 vb.
place 187 vb.
obstacle 702 n.
fetter 747 vb.
fetter 748 n.
Tethys
ocean 343 n.
classical deities
967 n.
tetrad
quaternity 96 n.
tetragon
quaternity 96 n.
angular figure
247 n.
tetrahedron
quaternity 96 n.
tetrameter
quaternity 96 n.
prosody 593 n.
tetrapod
quaternity 96 n.
tetrarchy
quaternity 96 n.
text
prototype 23 n.
part 53 n.
topic 452 n.
maxim 496 n.
meaning 514 n.
reading matter
589 n.
stage play 594 n.
textile
crossed 222 adj.
textile 222 n.
textural 331 adj.
textual
scriptural 975 adj.
orthodox 976 adj.
texture
weaving 222 n.
texture 331 n.
textured vegetable
protein
meat 301 n.
thank
thank 907 vb.
reward 962 vb.
thank goodness
thanks 907 int.
thank Heaven
thanks 907 int.

thankless
profitless 641 adj.
unpleasant
827 adj.
thankless task
hard task 700 n.
ingratitude 908 n.
thank one's lucky
stars
rejoice 835 vb.
be grateful 907 vb.
thanks
congratulation
886 n.
thanks 907 int.
thanks 907 n.
reward 962 n.
thanksgiving
rejoicing 835 n.
celebration 876 n.
thanks 907 n.
act of worship
981 n.
thanks to
hence 158 adv.
through 628 adv.
thank you
thanks 907 int.
thankyou
thanks 907 n.
thatch
coat 226 vb.
roof 226 n.
hair 259 n.
building material
631 n.
repair 656 vb.
that is
in plain words
520 adv.
that is to say
namely 80 adv.
thaumaturgy
sorcery 983 n.
thaw
come unstuck
49 vb.
soften 327 vb.
liquefaction 337 n.
liquefy 337 vb.
semiliquidity
354 n.
be hot 379 vb.
heat 381 vb.
thaw out
heat 381 vb.

theatre
region 184 n.
meeting place
192 n.
theatre 594 n.
arena 724 n.
place of amusement 837 n.
theatre, the
drama 594 n.
theatregoer
spectator 441 n.
playgoer 594 n.
theatre of war
battle 718 n.
battleground
724 n.
theatrical
dramatic 594 adj.
affected 850 adj.
showy 875 adj.
theft
acquisition 771 n.
stealing 788 n.
theism
deism 973 n.
piety 979 n.
them
master 741 n.
enemy 881 n.
thematic
topical 452 adj.
theme
melody 410 n.
musical piece
412 n.
topic 452 n.
dissertation 591 n.
theme song
tune 412 n.
themselves
self 80 n.
thence
hence 158 adv.
theocracy
government 733 n.
the church 985 n.
theodolite
angular measure
247 n.
gauge 465 n.
theolatry
religion 973 n.
theologian
theologian 973 n.
theology
theology 973 n.

theophany
revelation 975 n.
theorem
topic 452 n.
axiom 496 n.
theoretical
mental 447 adj.
theorize
account for 158 vb.
meditate 449 vb.
suppose 512 vb.
theory
attribution 158 n.
idea 451 n.
opinion 485 n.
supposition 512 n.
theosophy
philosophy 449 n.
religion 973 n.
religious faith
973 n.
occultism 984 n.
therapeutic
remedial 658 adj.
therapeutics
medical art 658 n.
therapy 658 n.
therapy
therapy 658 n.
thereabouts
about 33 adv.
nearly 200 adv.
thereafter
subsequently
120 adv.
therefore
hence 158 adv.
thereupon
subsequently
120 adv.
therm
thermometry
379 n.
thermal
ascent 308 n.
thermal springs
heat 379 n.
thermal underwear
underwear 228 n.
thermodynamics
physics 319 n.
thermometry
379 n.
thermography
thermometry
379 n.

thermoluminescence
glow 417 n.
thermometer
thermometry
379 n.
meter 465 n.
thermonuclear
dynamic 160 adj.
**thermonuclear flask
(tdmk)**
pot 194 n.
preserver 666 n.
thermonuclear reaction
nucleonics 160 n.
thermostat
thermometry
379 n.
thesaurus
word list 87 n.
dictionary 559 n.
reference book
589 n.
collection 632 n.
the sign of, be
indicate 547 vb.
thesis
topic 452 n.
argument 475 n.
supposition 512 n.
affirmation 532 n.
dissertation 591 n.
Thespian
actor 594 n.
dramatic 594 adj.
Thetis
sea nymph 343 n.
nymph 967 n.
they
group 74 n.
authority 733 n.
thick
great 32 adj.
middle 70 n.
multitudinous
104 adj.
thick 205 adj.
dense 324 adj.
dim 419 adj.
opaque 423 adj.
unintelligent
499 adj.
friendly 880 adj.
thick and fast
often 139 adv.
thick as thieves
friendly 880 adj.

**thick as two short
planks**
unintelligent
499 adj.
thicken
augment 36 vb.
grow 36 vb.
enlarge 197 vb.
be dense 324 vb.
thicken 354 vb.
thicket
bunch 74 n.
multitude 104 n.
wood 366 n.
thickness
quantity 26 n.
layer 207 n.
density 324 n.
semiliquidity
354 n.
opacity 423 n.
metrology 465 n.
thick of the action
activity 678 n.
thick of things
middle 70 n.
activity 678 n.
thick on the ground
multitudinous
104 adj.
frequent 139 adj.
thickset
stalwart 162 adj.
short 204 adj.
thick 205 adj.
thick-skinned
thick 205 adj.
unfeeling 375 adj.
thick-skinned
820 adj.
thief
thief 789 n.
bad person 938 n.
thieve
steal 788 vb.
thigh
leg 267 n.
thimbleful
finite quantity
26 n.
small quantity
33 n.
thin
insubstantial 4 adj.
small 33 adj.
incomplete 55 adj.
render few 105 vb.

weak 163 adj.
weaken 163 vb.
make smaller
  198 vb.
lean 206 adj.
narrow 206 adj.
shallow 212 adj.
rare 325 adj.
rarefy 325 vb.
transparent
  422 adj.
feeble 572 adj.
insufficient
  636 adj.
thin air
  insubstantial thing
  4 n.
  air 340 n.
  disappearance
  446 n.
thin end of the wedge
  stratagem 698 n.
thing
  substance 3 n.
  product 164 n.
  object 319 n.
thing, the
  chief thing 638 n.
thingamabob
  no name 562 n.
things
  property 777 n.
thingummy
  no name 562 n.
  tool 630 n.
thin ice
  pitfall 663 n.
think
  think 449 vb.
  be of the opinion
  that 485 vb.
  suppose 512 vb.
think ahead
  plan 623 vb.
think back
  remember 505 vb.
think better of
  meditate 449 vb.
  be penitent 939 vb.
think fit
  will 595 vb.
think highly of
  approve 923 vb.
thinking
  mental 447 adj.
  thought 449 n.
  attentive 455 adj.

opinion 485 n.
wise 498 adj.
desire 859 n.
thinking cap
  thought 449 n.
thinking of, be
  be mindful 455 vb.
think it best to
  choose 605 vb.
think no shame
  demean oneself
  867 vb.
think nothing of
  hold cheap 922 vb.
think of
  be mindful 455 vb.
  remember 505 vb.
  imagine 513 vb.
  intend 617 vb.
think tank
  concurrence 181 n.
  council 692 n.
  consignee 754 n.
think the world of
  love 887 vb.
think through
  think 449 vb.
think twice
  be careful 457 vb.
  be nervous 854 vb.
  be cautious 858 vb.
think up
  produce 164 vb.
  think 449 vb.
  imagine 513 vb.
  plan 623 vb.
thin on the ground
  few 105 adj.
thin on top
  hairless 229 adj.
thin out
  abate 37 vb.
  decrease 37 vb.
  be dispersed 75 vb.
  disperse 75 vb.
  extract 304 vb.
  cultivate 370 vb.
thin red line
  defender 713 n.
  armed force 722 n.
thin-skinned
  sensitive 819 adj.
  irascible 892 adj.
third
  treble 94 adj.
  trisection 95 n.
  interval 201 n.

musical note
  410 n.
third degree
  interrogation
  459 n.
  police enquiry
  459 n.
  corporal punish-
  ment 963 n.
third-rate
  inferior 35 adj.
  trivial 639 adj.
  imperfect 647 adj.
Third World
  three 93 n.
  region 184 n.
  political organiza-
  tion 733 n.
thirst
  dryness 342 n.
  rapacity 786 n.
  be hungry 859 vb.
  desire 859 n.
  hunger 859 n.
thirst for
  desire 859 vb.
thirsty
  dry 342 adj.
  hot 379 adj.
  hungry 859 adj.
thirteen
  over five 99 n.
this moment
  present time 121 n.
this moment in time
  present time 121 n.
this time
  at present 121 adv.
thistle
  prickle 256 n.
  plant 366 n.
  heraldry 547 n.
thistledown
  lightness 323 n.
  softness 327 n.
thither
  towards 281 adv.
thong
  ligature 47 n.
  strip 208 n.
  scourge 964 n.
thorax
  bosom 253 n.
thorn
  prickle 256 n.
  sharp point 256 n.
  foliage 366 n.

suffering 825 n.
thorn in the flesh
  badness 645 n.
  bane 659 n.
  worry 825 n.
  painfulness 827 n.
thorny
  sharp 256 adj.
  difficult 700 adj.
thorough
  consummate
  32 adj.
  complete 54 adj.
  laborious 682 adj.
thoroughbred
  unmixed 44 adj.
  well-bred 848 adj.
  aristocrat 868 n.
  noble 868 adj.
thoroughfare
  road 624 n.
thoroughgoing
  consummate
  32 adj.
  complete 54 adj.
  revolutionary
  149 adj.
thoroughly
  greatly 32 vb.
  completely 54 adv.
thoroughness
  carefulness 457 n.
  completion 725 n.
though
  provided 468 adv.
thought
  small quantity
  33 n.
  thought 449 n.
  opinion 485 n.
thoughtful
  thoughtful 449 adj.
  attentive 455 adj.
  careful 457 adj.
  discriminating
  463 adj.
thoughtless
  inattentive 456 adj.
  negligent 458 adj.
  unwise 499 adj.
  rash 857 adj.
thought-reading
  psychical 984 n.
  psychics 984 n.
thoughts
  thought 449 n.

reading matter
  589 n.
thought-transference
  sense 374 n.
  information 524 n.
  psychics 984 n.
thousand
  over one hundred
  99 n.
thousand and one, a
  many 104 adj.
thrash
  strike 279 vb.
  feasting 301 n.
  meal 301 n.
  pleasure 376 n.
  defeat 727 n.
  enjoyment 824 n.
  amusement 837 n.
  festivity 837 n.
  social gathering
    882 n.
  flog 963 vb.
thrashing
  knock 279 n.
  defeat 728 n.
  corporal punish-
    ment 963 n.
thread
  relevance 9 n.
  small thing 33 n.
  ligature 47 n.
  series 71 n.
  weak thing 163 n.
  thinness 206 n.
  fibre 208 n.
  filament 208 n.
  pass 305 n.
threadbare
  hairless 229 adj.
  used 673 adj.
thread one's way
  travel 267 vb.
thread together
  arrange 62 vb.
threat
  threat 900 n.
threaten
  be to come 124 vb.
  threaten 900 vb.
three
  three 93 adj.
  three 93 n.
three-card trick
  sleight 542 n.
three cheers
  cheers 835 int.

rejoicing 835 n.
  applause 923 n.
  bravo 923 int.
threefold
  treble 94 adj.
three-leaved or leafed
  three 93 adj.
three-line whip
  command 737 n.
Three Musketeers
  close friend 880 n.
threepenny bit
  coinage 797 n.
three-ply
  treble 94 adj.
three R's, the
  curriculum 534 n.
three score
  twenty and over
    99 n.
three score and ten
  twenty and over
    99 n.
three-score years and
  ten
  old age 131 n.
three sheets in the
  wind
  drunk 949 adj.
three-sided
  three 93 adj.
threesome
  three 93 n.
three-star
  fuel 385 n.
threnody
  vocal music 412 n.
thresh
  strike 279 vb.
  cultivate 370 vb.
thresh about
  be agitated 318 vb.
threshold
  entrance 68 n.
  stand 218 n.
  threshold 234 n.
  limit 236 n.
  doorway 263 n.
threshold of pain
  limit 236 n.
  sensibility 374 n.
  pain 377 n.
thrift
  economy 814 n.
thrifty
  economical
    814 adj.

thrill
  agitation 318 n.
  be agitated 318 vb.
  pleasure 376 n.
  feeling 818 n.
  show feeling
    818 vb.
  excitation 821 n.
  excite 821 vb.
  excitable state
    822 n.
  joy 824 n.
  delight 826 vb.
thriller
  film 445 n.
  novel 590 n.
thrill to
  enjoy 376 vb.
  be excited 821 vb.
thrive
  grow 36 vb.
  be vigorous 174 vb.
  flourish 615 vb.
  be healthy 650 vb.
  be active 678 vb.
  prosper 730 vb.
thriving
  vigorous 174 adj.
  prosperity 730 n.
  prosperous 730 adj.
throat
  orifice 263 n.
  air pipe 353 n.
throaty
  hoarse 407 adj.
throb
  periodicity 141 n.
  oscillate 317 vb.
  oscillation 317 n.
  agitation 318 n.
  be agitated 318 vb.
  spasm 318 n.
  give pain 377 vb.
  show feeling
    818 vb.
throes
  violence 176 n.
  pang 377 n.
thrombosis
  condensation
    324 n.
  cardiovascular dis-
    ease 651 n.
throne
  seat 218 n.
  badge 547 n.
  regalia 743 n.

tribunal 956 n.
throng
  congregate 74 vb.
  crowd 74 n.
  be many 104 vb.
  multitude 104 n.
thronged
  multitudinous
    104 adj.
throttle
  disable 161 vb.
  close 264 vb.
  retain 778 vb.
through
  until now 121 adv.
  towards 281 adv.
  through 628 adv.
  by means of
    629 adv.
throughout
  throughout 54 adv.
throughput
  data processing
    86 n.
  transference 272 n.
throughway
  road 624 n.
throw
  move 265 vb.
  impel 279 vb.
  impulse 279 n.
  propel 287 vb.
  propulsion 287 n.
  gambling 618 n.
  exertion 682 n.
throw a fit
  be agitated 318 vb.
throw aside
  reject 607 vb.
throw a spanner in
  the works
  disable 161 vb.
  make useless
    641 vb.
  be obstructive
    702 vb.
throw a tantrum
  be excitable
    822 n.
  get angry 891 vb.
throw away
  eject 300 vb.
  act 594 vb.
  reject 607 vb.
  waste 634 vb.
  stop using 674 vb.
  lose 772 vb.

be prodigal 815 vb.
throwback
　recurrence 106 n.
　reversion 148 n.
　relapse 657 n.
throw cold water on
　moderate 177 vb.
　dissuade 613 vb.
　hinder 702 vb.
throw down
　demolish 165 vb.
　move 265 vb.
　let fall 311 vb.
throw down the gauntlet
　be resolute 599 vb.
　defy 711 vb.
　enrage 891 vb.
throw dust in one's eye
　be unrelated 10 vb.
　deflect 282 vb.
　blind 439 vb.
　deceive 542 vb.
　plead 614 vb.
　avoid 620 vb.
　elude 667 vb.
throw in
　introduce 231 vb.
throw in one's hand
　relinquish 621 vb.
　resign 753 vb.
throw in one's lot with
　choose 605 vb.
throw in one's teeth
　defy 711 vb.
　accuse 928 vb.
throw in the sponge or the towel
　relinquish 621 vb.
　submit 721 vb.
throw into confusion
　bedevil 63 vb.
　derange 63 vb.
throw light on
　make bright 417 vb.
　interpret 520 vb.
　manifest 522 vb.
thrown
　formed 243 adj.
thrown, be
　tumble 309 vb.
thrown-out chest
　ostentation 875 n.

thrown to the lions, be
　endangered 661 adj.
throw off
　disaccustom 611 vb.
throw off one's shackles
　revolt 738 vb.
throw off the scent
　distract 456 vb.
　puzzle 474 vb.
　elude 667 vb.
throw one off the scent
　avoid 620 vb.
throw oneself at
　pursue 619 vb.
throw oneself on another's mercy
　submit 721 vb.
　ask mercy 905 vb.
throw one's hat in the ring
　defy 711 vb.
throw one's weight about
　be vigorous 174 vb.
　be proud 871 vb.
　be insolent 878 vb.
throw open
　open 263 vb.
　admit 299 vb.
　manifest 522 vb.
throw out
　impel 279 vb.
　eject 300 vb.
　reject 607 vb.
throw out the baby with the bath water
　overstep 306 vb.
　waste 634 vb.
　act foolishly 695 vb.
throw over
　fool 542 vb.
　change one's mind 603 vb.
　relinquish 621 vb.
throw the book at
　criticize 924 vb.
　indict 928 vb.
　punish 963 vb.
throw things
　get angry 891 vb.

throw together
　join 45 vb.
throw up
　eject 300 vb.
　vomit 300 vb.
　elevate 310 vb.
　resign 753 vb.
thrum
　roll 403 vb.
　resound 404 vb.
　discord 411 vb.
　play music 413 vb.
thrush
　bird 365 n.
　animal disease 651 n.
　skin disease 651 n.
thrust
　energy 160 n.
　vigorousness 174 n.
　distortion 246 n.
　spurt 277 n.
　impel 279 vb.
　impulse 279 n.
　propellant 287 n.
　be active 678 vb.
　attack 712 n.
　strike at 712 vb.
thrust oneself forward
　be active 678 vb.
thud
　impulse 279 n.
　faintness 401 n.
　sound faint 401 vb.
　nonresonance 405 n.
thug
　violent creature 176 n.
　murderer 362 n.
　robber 789 n.
　ruffian 904 n.
　bad person 938 n.
thumb
　joint 45 n.
　feeler 378 n.
　See **finger**
　finger 378 n.
　touch 378 vb.
　study 536 vb.
　signal 547 vb.
thumb a lift
　ride 267 vb.
　beg 761 vb.
thumb index
　indication 547 n.

edition 589 n.
thumbnail
　small 33 adj.
thumbnail sketch
　miniature 196 n.
　picture 553 n.
　description 590 n.
　compendium 592 n.
thumbscrew
　pain 377 n.
　instrument of torture 964 n.
thumbs down
　prohibition 757 n.
　refusal 760 n.
　condemnation 961 n.
thumbs up
　assent 488 n.
　approbation 923 n.
　acquittal 960 n.
thumb-twiddling
　tedium 838 n.
thump
　knock 279 n.
　strike 279 vb.
　faintness 401 n.
　sound faint 401 vb.
　bang 402 n.
　nonresonance 405 n.
thumping
　large 195 adj.
thunder
　storm 176 n.
　be loud 400 vb.
　loudness 400 n.
　emphasize 532 vb.
　be angry 891 vb.
　malediction 899 n.
　threaten 900 vb.
　criticize 924 vb.
thunder and lightning
　storm 176 n.
thunderbolt
　lack of expectation 508 n.
thunderclap
　loudness 400 n.
　bang 402 n.
　lack of expectation 508 n.
thundering
　large 195 adj.

thunderous
loud 400 adj.
approving 923 adj.
thunderstorm
commotion 318 n.
rain 350 n.
gale 352 n.
thunderstruck
unexpecting
508 adj.
thurible
scent 396 n.
ritual object 988 n.
thus
thus 8 adv.
hence 158 adv.
thwack
knock 279 n.
strike 279 vb.
thwart
halt 145 vb.
disappoint 509 vb.
negate 533 vb.
be obstructive
702 vb.
oppose 704 vb.
trouble 827 vb.
thyme
herb 301 n.
scent 396 n.
tiara
headgear 228 n.
regalia 743 n.
jewellery 844 n.
vestments 989 n.
tibia
leg 267 n.
tic
spasm 318 n.
vision 438 n.
gesture 547 n.
nervous disorders
651 n.
tick
instant 116 n.
periodicity 141 n.
oscillate 317 vb.
insect 365 n.
faintness 401 n.
sound faint 401 vb.
roll 403 vb.
mark 547 vb.
borrowing 785 n.
purchase 792 n.
credit 802 n.
approve 923 vb.

ticket
adjunct 40 n.
list 87 n.
credential 466 n.
label 547 n.
mark 547 vb.
electorate 605 n.
policy 623 n.
precept 693 n.
permit 756 n.
ticket-of-leave man
prisoner 750 n.
offender 904 n.
tickle
touch 378 vb.
incentive 612 n.
delight 826 vb.
amuse 837 vb.
be ridiculous
849 vb.
endearment 889 n.
tickled pink
pleased 824 adj.
merry 833 adj.
tickled to death
pleased 824 adj.
tickle one's fancy
delight 826 vb.
amuse 837 vb.
tickle one's palate
delight 826 vb.
gluttonize 947 vb.
tickle one to death
delight 826 vb.
ticklish
sentient 374 adj.
difficult 700 adj.
tick off
set apart 46 vb.
number 86 vb.
mark 547 vb.
reprove 924 vb.
tick over
move slowly
278 vb.
tidal
changeful 152 adj.
flowing 350 adj.
tidal wave
outbreak 176 n.
oscillation 317 n.
wave 350 n.
pitfall 663 n.
tiddly
tipsy 949 adj.
tiddly-winks
indoor game 837 n.

tide
increase 36 n.
time 108 n.
periodicity 141 n.
progression 285 n.
ocean 343 n.
current 350 n.
tidemark
limit 236 n.
gauge 465 n.
trace 548 n.
tide over
put off 136 vb.
navigate 269 vb.
aid 703 vb.
tidings
news 529 n.
tidy
orderly 60 adj.
arrange 62 vb.
tidy up
arrange 62 vb.
make better
654 vb.
tie
be equal 28 vb.
draw 28 n.
add 38 vb.
tie 45 vb.
bond 47 n.
ligature 47 n.
combine 50 vb.
neckwear 228 n.
obstacle 702 n.
duty 917 n.
tie a knot in one's
handkerchief
remember 505 vb.
tied
equal 28 adj.
tied 45 adj.
restrained 747 adj.
obliged 917 n.
tied house
tavern 192 n.
tie down
compel 740 vb.
tied to one's apron
strings
subject 745 adj.
tie-dyeing
ornamental art
844 n.
tie hand and foot
hinder 702 vb.
restrain 747 vb.

tie in with
be related 9 vb.
tie one's hands
disable 161 vb.
hinder 702 vb.
tiepin
fastening 47 n.
jewellery 844 n.
tier
series 71 n.
classification 77 n.
layer 207 n.
tie the knot
marry 894 vb.
tie-up
relation 9 n.
union 45 n.
association 706 n.
tie up with
relate 9 vb.
connect 45 vb.
tiff
quarrel 709 n.
resentment 891 n.
tig
children's games
837 n.
tiger
violent creature
176 n.
big cat 365 n.
stripe 437 n.
brave person 855 n.
tight
firm 45 adj.
tied 45 adj.
cohesive 48 adj.
narrow 206 adj.
rigid 326 adj.
printed 587 adj.
restraining
747 adj.
retentive 778 adj.
parsimonious
816 adj.
tipsy 949 adj.
tight corner
predicament 700 n.
tighten
tighten 45 vb.
restrain 747 vb.
tighten one's belt
economize 814 vb.
be temperate
942 vb.
starve 946 vb.

tight-fisted
  parsimonious
    816 adj.
tight-fitting
  firm 45 adj.
tight-knit
  concise 569 adj.
tight-lipped
  reticent 525 adj.
  taciturn 582 adj.
tightrope
  narrowness 206 n.
tights
  legwear 228 n.
  trousers 228 n.
tight squeeze
  narrowness 206 n.
tigress
  big cat 365 n.
  female animal
    373 n.
tilde
  punctuation 547 n.
tile
  coat 226 vb.
  headgear 228 n.
  pottery 381 n.
  building material
    631 n.
  plaything 837 n.
till
  counting instrument 86 n.
  while 108 adv.
  box 194 n.
  cultivate 370 vb.
  recording instrument 549 n.
  storage 632 n.
  treasury 799 n.
tillage
  agriculture 370 n.
  ripening 669 n.
till all hours
  late 136 adv.
till blue in the face
  for a long time
    113 adv.
till doomsday
  for ever 115 adv.
tiller
  handle 218 n.
  sailing aid 269 n.
  tool 630 n.
till the cows come home

for a long time
    113 adv.
tilt
  be unequal 29 vb.
  be oblique 220 vb.
  obliquity 220 n.
  canopy 226 n.
  descent 309 n.
tilt at windmills
  waste effort
    641 adj.
tilth
  agriculture 370 n.
timber
  wood 366 n.
  materials 631 n.
timbre
  sound 398 n.
  voice 577 n.
time
  finality 69 n.
  time 108 n.
  era 110 n.
  provisionally 112
    adv.
  time 117 vb.
  destroyer 168 n.
  tempo 410 n.
  detention 747 n.
time after time
  often 139 adv.
time ahead
  futurity 124 n.
time being
  present time 121 n.
time bomb
  timekeeper 117 n.
  pitfall 663 n.
  bomb 723 n.
time-consuming
  wasteful 634 adj.
time-honoured
  habitual 610 adj.
  worshipful 866 adj.
time immemorial
  antiquity 125 n.
**time it or things
    badly**
  mistime 138 vb.
timelag
  interval 201 n.
time-lapse
  slow 278 adj.
timeless
  perpetual 115 adj.
time limit
  limit 236 n.

conditions 766 n.
timely
  early 135 adj.
  timely 137 adj.
time of day
  date 108 n.
  period 110 n.
  clock time 117 n.
time off
  lull 145 n.
  leisure 681 n.
time of life
  date 108 n.
  age 131 n.
time of the month
  untimeliness
    138 n.
  haemorrhage
    302 n.
time of year
  period 110 n.
time on one's hands
  slowness 278 n.
  inaction 677 n.
  leisure 681 n.
time out
  interval 201 n.
timepiece
  timekeeper 117 n.
timer
  timekeeper 117 n.
times, the
  circumstance 8 n.
time-saving
  economical
    814 adj.
  economy 814 n.
timeserver
  recanter 603 n.
time-serving
  servile 879 adj.
  servility 879 n.
timeshare
  abode 192 n.
  amuse oneself
    837 vb.
time-sharing
  data processing
    86 n.
  joint possession
    775 n.
  participation
    775 n.
time signal
  timekeeper 117 n.
  broadcast 531 n.
  signal 547 n.

timetable
  directory 87 n.
  chronology 117 n.
  time 117 vb.
  itinerary 267 n.
  guidebook 524 n.
time to come
  posteriority 120 n.
  futurity 124 n.
time to kill
  leisure 681 n.
  tedium 838 n.
time up
  finality 69 n.
  period 110 n.
  late 136 adj.
time was
  formerly 125 adv.
time without end
  for ever 115 adv.
time-worn
  olden 127 adj.
time zone
  time 108 n.
timid
  nervous 854 adj.
  cowardly 856 adj.
  cautious 858 adj.
  modest 874 adj.
timing
  chronometry
    117 n.
  periodicity 141 n.
  tempo 410 n.
  discrimination
    463 n.
timorous
  nervous 854 adj.
  cowardly 856 adj.
timpani
  drum 414 n.
tin
  small box 194 n.
  cereals 301 n.
  preserve 666 vb.
tincture
  small quantity
    33 n.
  tincture 43 n.
  colour 425 n.
  colour 425 vb.
tinder
  lighter 385 n.
tine
  sharp point 256 n.
ting
  resound 404 vb.

tinge
small quantity
33 n.
mix 43 vb.
tincture 43 n.
colour 425 vb.
hue 425 n.
qualification 468 n.

tingle
have feeling
374 vb.
feel pain 377 vb.
tingling 378 n.
feel 818 vb.
show feeling
818 vb.
be sensitive 819 vb.
be excited 821 vb.

tin god
autocrat 741 n.
insolent person
878 n.

tin hat
headgear 228 n.
armour 713 n.

tinker
impair 655 vb.
meddle 678 vb.
artisan 686 n.
pedlar 794 n.

tinker's cuss
scurrility 899 n.

tinker with
deceive 542 vb.

tinkle
faintness 401 n.
sound faint 401 vb.
resonance 404 n.
resound 404 vb.
message 529 n.

tinkling cymbal
lack of meaning
515 n.

tin Lizzie
automobile 274 n.

tinnitus
resonance 404 n.

tinny
strident 407 adj.

Tin Pan Alley
music 412 n.

tinpot
unimportant
639 adj.

tinsel
flash 417 n.
sham 542 n.

spurious 542 adj.
bauble 639 n.
finery 844 n.
ostentation 875 n.
showy 875 adj.

tin soldier
plaything 837 n.

tint
colour 425 vb.
hue 425 n.
paint 553 vb.
hairwash 843 n.

tintinnabulation
resonance 404 n.
gong 414 n.

tiny
small 33 adj.
little 196 adj.

tip
extra 40 n.
extremity 69 n.
crown 213 vb.
vertex 213 n.
be oblique 220 vb.
obliquity 220 n.
cover 226 vb.
edge 234 n.
lower 311 vb.
touch 378 vb.
hint 524 n.
information 524 n.
message 529 n.
bribe 612 n.
incentive 612 n.
rubbish 641 n.
sink 649 n.
warning 664 n.
advice 691 n.
gift 781 n.
give 781 vb.
pay 804 vb.
thank 907 vb.
thanks 907 n.
reward 962 n.
reward 962 vb.

tip-off
hint 524 n.
information 524 n.
warning 664 n.

tip of the iceberg
ice 380 n.

tippet
hanging object
217 n.
neckwear 228 n.
vestments 989 n.

tipple
alcoholic drink
301 n.
drink 301 vb.
get drunk 949 vb.

tipsy
tipsy 949 adj.

tip the balance
weigh 322 vb.

tip the scales
be unequal 29 vb.
weigh 322 vb.

tip the wink
hint 524 n.
command 737 vb.
permit 756 vb.

tiptoe
walk 267 vb.
be stealthy 525 vb.

tiptop
supreme 34 adj.
topmost 213 adj.
best 644 adj.

tirade
diffuseness 570 n.
oration 579 n.
censure 924 n.

tire
fatigue 684 vb.
trouble 827 vb.

tired
inactive 679 adj.
sleepy 679 adj.
fatigued 684 adj.

tireless
strong 162 adj.
industrious
678 adj.

tire out
fatigue 684 vb.

tiresome
annoying 827 adj.
tedious 838 adj.

tisane
soft drink 301 n.
tonic 658 n.

tissue
chief part 52 n.
thinness 206 n.
textile 222 n.
texture 331 n.
dryer 342 n.
cleaning cloth
648 n.

tissue of lies
untruth 543 n.

tissue paper
weak thing 163 n.
wrapping 226 n.
paper 631 n.

tit
bird 365 n.

titanic
stalwart 162 adj.
huge 195 adj.

titbit
mouthful 301 n.
savouriness 390 n.
news 529 n.
elite 644 n.
pleasurableness
826 n.

titchy
little 196 adj.

tit for tat
correlation 12 n.
equalization 28 n.
interchange 151 n.
retaliation 714 n.
revenge 910 n.

tithe
part 53 n.
multifid 100 adj.
tax 809 n.
benefice 985 n.

titillate
delight 826 vb.
amuse 837 vb.

titivate
make better
654 vb.
beautify 841 vb.
primp 843 vb.
decorate 844 vb.

title
label 547 n.
book 589 n.
edition 589 n.
estate 777 n.
title 870 n.
dueness 915 n.

titled
worshipful 866 adj.
noble 868 adj.

title deed
title deed 767 n.

titles
cinema 445 n.

titter
cry 408 n.
cry 408 vb.
laugh 835 vb.
laughter 835 n.

tittle-tattle
  rumour 529 n.
  chatter 581 n.
  chat 584 n.
tizzy
  excitation 821 n.
  anger 891 n.
T-junction
  road 624 n.
TNT
  explosive 723 n.
toad
  amphibian 365 n.
  eyesore 842 n.
toadstool
  plant 366 n.
toady
  minister to 703 vb.
  knuckle under
    721 vb.
  toady 879 n.
toady to
  be servile 879 vb.
  flatter 925 vb.
to and fro
  to and fro 317 adv.
toast
  cereals 301 n.
  draught 301 n.
  be hot 379 vb.
  brown 430 vb.
  remind 505 vb.
  oration 579 n.
  celebration 876 n.
  toast 876 vb.
  be sociable 882 vb.
  pay one's respects
    884 vb.
  congratulation
    886 n.
toasted
  brown 430 adj.
toaster
  heater 383 n.
**toastmaster or -mis-
    tress**
  speaker 579 n.
toast of the town
  exceller 644 n.
  favourite 890 n.
to a turn
  truly 494 adv.
tobacco
  tobacco 388 n.
tobacconist
  tobacco 388 n.
  tradespeople 794 n.

to be
  subsequent
    120 adj.
  future 124 adj.
to be sure
  certainly 473 adv.
to bits
  apart 46 adv.
toboggan
  be in motion
    265 vb.
  sled 274 n.
  descend 309 vb.
  amuse oneself
    837 vb.
tobogganning
  sport 837 n.
to boot
  in addition 38 adv.
toby
  cup 194 n.
toby jug
  vessel 194 n.
toccata
  musical piece
    412 n.
to come
  subsequent
    120 adj.
  future 124 adj.
  impending 155 adj.
tocsin
  gong 414 n.
to date
  until now 121 adv.
today
  at present 121 adv.
  present time 121 n.
toddle
  be in motion
    265 vb.
  walk 267 vb.
  move slowly
    278 vb.
toddler
  child 132 n.
  pedestrian 268 n.
toddy
  alcoholic drink
    301 n.
to-do
  turmoil 61 n.
  commotion 318 n.
  activity 678 n.
toe
  extremity 69 n.
  base 214 n.

  foot 214 n.
toehold
  retention 778 n.
toe in the water
  empiricism 461 n.
toenail
  foot 214 n.
toe the line
  be uniform 16 vb.
  conform 83 vb.
  acquiesce 488 vb.
  obey 739 vb.
toff
  fop 848 n.
  aristocrat 868 n.
toffee
  mouthful 301 n.
  sweets 301 n.
  brownness 430 n.
toffee-nosed
  proud 871 adj.
tofu
  fruit and vegetables
    301 n.
toga
  robe 228 n.
  badge of rule
    743 n.
together
  continuously
    71 adv.
  together 74 adv.
togetherness
  accompaniment
    89 n.
  friendship 880 n.
  fellowship 882 n.
together with
  in addition 38 adv.
  with 89 adv.
togs
  clothing 228 n.
  finery 844 n.
to hand
  prepared 669 adj.
toil
  move slowly
    278 vb.
  labour 682 n.
  work 682 vb.
toile
  textile 222 n.
toilet
  chamber 194 n.
  dressing 228 n.
  latrine 649 n.

beautification
    843 n.
toilette
  dressing 228 n.
token
  insubstantial 4 adj.
  insubstantial thing
    4 n.
  manifestation
    522 n.
  badge 547 n.
  indication 547 n.
  trivial 639 adj.
  security 767 n.
  gift 781 n.
tokenism
  sham 542 n.
  ostentation 875 n.
tolerable
  inconsiderable
    33 adj.
  not bad 644 adj.
  middling 732 adj.
tolerant
  lax 734 adj.
  lenient 736 adj.
  patient 823 adj.
  benevolent 897 adj.
tolerate
  acquiesce 488 vb.
  assent 488 vb.
    See **acquiesce**
  be lax 734 vb.
  permit 756 vb.
  consent 758 vb.
  be patient 823 vb.
  forgive 909 vb.
toll
  roll 403 vb.
  play music 413 vb.
  raise the alarm
    665 vb.
  receiving 782 n.
  tax 809 n.
tollgate
  access 624 n.
  obstacle 702 n.
tom
  cat 365 n.
  male animal
    372 n.
tomahawk
  axe 723 n.
tomato
  fruit and vegetables
    301 n.
  redness 431 n.

tomb
  tomb 364 n.
tombola
  equal chance
    159 n.
  gambling 618 n.
  gambling game
    837 n.
tomboy
  disorderly 61 adj.
  youngster 132 n.
tombstone
  obsequies 364 n.
Tom, Dick and
    Harry
  commonalty 869 n.
tome
  book 589 n.
tomfoolery
  foolery 497 n.
  folly 499 n.
  wit 839 n.
  ostentation 875 n.
Tommy
  soldier 722 n.
tommy gun
  gun 723 n.
tommyrot
  silly talk 515 n.
tomography
  medical art 658 n.
tomorrow
  futurity 124 n.
Tom Thumb
  dwarf 196 n.
tomtom
  drum 414 n.
ton
  hundred 99 n.
  weighing 322 n.
  funds 797 n.
tone
  tendency 179 n.
  interval 201 n.
  sound 398 n.
  melody 410 n.
  musical note
    410 n.
  hue 425 n.
  painting 553 n.
  style 566 n.
  voice 577 n.
tone-deaf
  deaf 416 adj.
  indiscriminating
    464 adj.

tone down
  moderate 177 vb.
  darken 418 vb.
  misrepresent
    552 vb.
tone in with
  accord 24 vb.
tonga
  cab 274 n.
tongs
  furnace 383 n.
  pincers 778 n.
  hairdressing 843 n.
tongue
  projection 254 n.
  meat 301 n.
  feeler 378 n.
  language 557 n.
  voice 577 n.
  speech 579 n.
tongue-in-cheek
  affected 850 adj.
  flattering 925 adj.
tongue-tied
  voiceless 578 adj.
  taciturn 582 adj.
tonic
  stimulant 174 n.
  vigorous 174 adj.
  musical note
    410 n.
  incentive 612 n.
  remedial 658 adj.
  tonic 658 n.
  excitant 821 n.
tonic solfa
  notation 410 n.
tonnage
  size 195 n.
tonsilitis
  respiratory disease
    651 n.
tonsillectomy
  surgery 658 n.
tonsure
  canonicals 989 n.
too
  in addition 38 adv.
too bad
  evil 616 adj.
  bad 645 adj.
  annoying 827 adj.
  discreditable
    867 adj.
too big for one's
    boots
  vain 873 adj.

too good to be true
  improbable
    472 adj.
  pietistic 979 adj.
tool
  inferior 35 n.
  contrivance 623 n.
  tool 630 n.
  agent 686 n.
  toady 879 n.
tools of the trade
  means 629 n.
  tool 630 n.
too many cooks
  bungling 695 n.
too many irons in the
    fire
  redundance 637 n.
too much
  great quantity
    32 n.
  plenty 635 n.
  redundance 637 n.
  undueness 916 n.
  intemperance
    943 n.
to order
  specially 80 adv.
toot
  loudness 400 n.
  resound 404 vb.
  play music 413 vb.
  raise the alarm
    665 vb.
tooth
  tooth 256 n.
  notch 260 vb.
  liking 859 n.
toothache
  pang 377 n.
tooth for a tooth
  interchange 151 n.
  revenge 910 n.
toothless
  ageing 131 adj.
toothless tiger
  bluntness 257 n.
toothsome
  savoury 390 adj.
tootle
  resound 404 vb.
  play music 413 vb.
too-too
  affected 850 adj.
tootsies
  foot 214 n.

top
  superiority 34 n.
  fill 54 vb.
  put in front 64 vb.
  extremity 69 n.
  crown 213 vb.
  summit 213 n.
  topmost 213 adj.
  vertex 213 n.
  covering 226 n.
  garment 228 n.
  shirt 228 n.
  limit 236 vb.
  cone 252 n.
  stopper 264 n.
  climb 308 vb.
  rotator 315 n.
  completion 725 n.
  plaything 837 n.
topaz
  yellowness 433 n.
  gem 844 n.
top brass
  bigwig 638 n.
  director 690 n.
top drawer
  elite 644 n.
  beau monde 848 n.
  genteel 868 adj.
  upper class 868 n.
top-dressing
  fertilizer 171 n.
  layer 207 n.
  covering 226 n.
tope
  drink 301 vb.
  get drunk 949 vb.
  temple 990 n.
topee
  shade 226 n.
top-heavy
  unequal 29 n.
  weighty 322 adj.
  clumsy 695 adj.
topiarism
  ornamental art
    844 n.
topic
  topic 452 n.
topical
  present 121 adj.
  modern 126 adj.
  topical 452 adj.
topknot
  hair 259 n.
topless
  short 204 adj.

uncovered 229 adj.

top-notch
  supreme 34 adj.
  best 644 adj.
  super 644 adj.
  skilful 694 adj.

topography
  situation 186 n.

topology
  mathematics 86 n.

top out
  crown 213 vb.
  carry through
    725 vb.

topping
  covering 226 n.
  super 644 adj.

topping out
  completion 725 n.

topple
  demolish 165 vb.
  tumble 309 vb.

tops, the
  exceller 644 n.
  favourite 890 n.
  good person 937 n.

top-secret
  occult 523 adj.
  concealed 525 adj.
  secret 530 n.

topsy-turvy
  contrarily 14 adv.
  inversely 221 adv.

top to toe
  longwise 203 adv.

top up
  fill 54 vb.
  store 632 vb.
  replenish 633 vb.

toque
  headgear 228 n.

torch
  lamp 420 n.
  torch 420 n.

toreador
  killer 362 n.
  combatant 722 n.

Tories
  political party
    708 n.

torment
  give pain 377 vb.
  pain 377 n.
  bane 659 n.
  suffering 825 n.
  torment 827 vb.

tornado
  turmoil 61 n.
  storm 176 n.
  vortex 315 n.
  gale 352 n.

torpedo
  suppress 165 vb.
  fire at 712 vb.
  bomb 723 n.

torpid
  inert 175 adj.
  inactive 679 adj.
  inexcitable
    823 adj.

torpor
  inertness 175 n.
  inactivity 679 n.
  sluggishness 679 n.

torque
  quantity 26 n.
  loop 250 n.

torrent
  great quantity
    32 n.
  outbreak 176 n.
  velocity 277 n.
  stream 350 n.

torrential
  violent 176 adj.

torrid
  hot 379 adj.
  warm 379 adj.

torso
  remainder 41 n.
  chief part 52 n.
  piece 53 n.
  incompleteness
    55 n.
  image 551 n.
  sculpture 554 n.

tortilla
  cereals 301 n.
  mouthful 301 n.

tortoise
  slowcoach 278 n.
  animal 365 n.
  reptile 365 n.

tortoiseshell
  covering 226 n.
  variegated 437 adj.
  variegation 437 n.

tortuous
  convoluted 251 adj.
  unclear 568 adj.
  dishonest 930 adj.

torture
  force 176 vb.

violence 176 n.
pain 377 n.
suffering 825 n.
  be malevolent
    898 vb.
  cruel act 898 n.
  corporal punish-
    ment 963 n.
  torture 963 vb.

to scale
  relative 9 adj.
  relatively 9 adv.

tosh
  silly talk 515 n.

toss
  small quantity
    33 n.
  derange 63 vb.
  jumble 63 vb.
  voyage 269 vb.
  propel 287 vb.
  propulsion 287 n.
  oscillate 317 vb.
  agitation 318 n.
  be agitated 318 vb.
  trifle 639 n.

toss and turn
  be excited 821 vb.

toss aside
  not respect 921 vb.

toss one's head
  be proud 871 vb.
  despise 922 vb.

toss up
  elevate 310 vb.
  gamble 618 vb.

toss-up
  equal chance
    159 n.
  uncertainty 474 n.

tot
  dwarf 196 n.
  draught 301 n.

total
  quantity 26 n.
  consummate
    32 adj.
  add 38 vb.
  addition 38 n.
  all 52 n.
  whole 52 adj.
  complete 54 adj.
  inclusive 78 adj.
  numerical result
    85 n.
  number 86 vb.

totalitarianism
  uniformity 16 n.
  despotism 733 n.
  brute force 735 n.

totality
  whole 52 n.
  completeness 54 n.

totalizator
  counting instru-
    ment 86 n.

totally
  completely 54 adv.

tote
  counting instru-
    ment 86 n.
  carry 273 vb.
  gaming-house
    618 n.

totem
  badge 547 n.
    See **indication**
  deity 966 n.
  idol 982 n.

totem pole
  idol 982 n.

to the four winds
  widely 183 adv.

to the letter
  truly 494 adv.

to the point
  relevant 9 adj.
  apt 24 adj.
  brief 114 adj.
  rational 475 adj.
  concise 569 adj.

to the purpose
  apt 24 adj.

to the utmost
  completely 54 adv.

totter
  come unstuck
    49 vb.
  vary 152 vb.
  be weak 163 vb.
  walk 267 vb.
  move slowly
    278 vb.
  oscillate 317 vb.
  be agitated 318 vb.
  deteriorate 655 vb.

tot up to
  number 86 vb.

touch
  be related 9 vb.
  small quantity
    33 n.
  tincture 43 n.

derange 63 vb.
be situated 186 vb.
limit 236 n.
have feeling
  374 vb.
sense 374 n.
touch 378 n.
touch 378 vb.
gesture 547 n.
request 761 vb.
excite 821 vb.
children's games
  837 n.
touch and go
  unreliability 474 n.
  unreliable 474 adj.
  unsafe 661 adj.
touch down
  fly 271 vb.
  land 295 vb.
  descend 309 vb.
touchdown
  aeronautics 271 n.
  air travel 271 n.
  arrival 295 n.
touched
  crazy 503 adj.
  impressed 818 adj.
  impressible
    819 adj.
touch for
  borrow 785 vb.
touching
  concerning 9 adv.
  contiguity 202 n.
  tactual 378 adj.
  borrowing 785 n.
  distressing 827 adj.
touchline
  limit 236 n.
touch off
  cause 156 vb.
  kindle 381 vb.
  excite 821 vb.
touch on
  relate 9 vb.
  notice 455 vb.
  inform 524 vb.
touchpaper
  burning 381 n.
  lighter 385 n.
touchstone
  prototype 23 n.
  testing agent
    461 n.
touch up
  colour 425 vb.

exaggerate 546 vb.
paint 553 vb.
make better
  654 vb.
repair 656 vb.
touchy
  sensitive 819 adj.
  irascible 892 adj.
tough
  violent creature
    176 n.
  tough 329 adj.
  difficult 700 adj.
  resisting 715 adj.
  thick-skinned
    820 adj.
  courageous
    855 adj.
  ruffian 904 n.
toughen
  strengthen 162 vb.
  harden 326 vb.
toupee
  hair 259 n.
  hairdressing 843 n.
tour
  time 108 n.
  period 110 n.
  land travel 267 n.
  travel 267 vb.
  circuition 314 n.
tour de force
  contrivance 623 n.
  deed 676 n.
  masterpiece 694 n.
  success 727 n.
tourism
  land travel 267 n.
tourist
  traveller 268 n.
  bicycle 274 n.
  spectator 441 n.
tournament
  contest 716 n.
  duel 716 n.
  pageant 875 n.
tourniquet
  ligature 47 n.
  stopper 264 n.
  surgical dressing
    658 n.
tousle
  jumble 63 vb.
  roughen 259 vb.
tout
  publicizer 528 n.
  gambler 618 n.

request 761 vb.
petitioner 763 n.
sell 793 vb.
seller 793 n.
commender 923 n.
flatterer 925 n.
tout à fait
  truly 494 adv.
tow
  fibre 208 n.
  navigate 269 vb.
  draw 288 vb.
  traction 288 n.
towards
  towards 281 adv.
towel
  rub 333 vb.
  dryer 342 n.
  cleaning cloth
    648 n.
towelling
  textile 222 n.
  dryer 342 n.
tower
  be great - large
    32 vb.
  fixture 153 n.
  edifice 164 n.
  dwelling 192 n.
  house 192 n.
  be high 209 vb.
  high structure
    209 n.
  ascend 308 vb.
  fort 713 n.
  church exterior
    990 n.
tower block
  flat 192 n.
  high structure
    209 n.
towering
  enormous 32 adj.
  furious 176 adj.
  large 195 adj.
  high 209 adj.
tower over
  be superior 34 vb.
  influence 178 vb.
to wit
  namely 80 adv.
  in plain words
    520 adv.
town
  district 184 n.
  abode 192 n.
  housing 192 n.

town centre
  focus 76 n.
town crier
  megaphone 400 n.
  cry 408 n.
  publicizer 528 n.
  messenger 529 n.
town house
  house 192 n.
towpath
  path 624 n.
towrope
  cable 47 n.
  traction 288 n.
toxaemia
  infection 651 n.
toxic
  toxic 653 adj.
  dangerous 661 adj.
toxin
  poison 659 n.
toxophily
  propulsion 287 n.
toy
  little 196 adj.
  bauble 639 n.
  plaything 837 n.
  caress 889 vb.
toy with
  be inattentive
    456 vb.
toy with one's food
  eat 301 vb.
trace
  copy 20 vb.
  small quantity
    33 n.
  remainder 41 n.
  outline 233 n.
  outline 233 vb.
  detect 484 vb.
  indication 547 n.
  trace 548 n.
tracery
  network 222 n.
  ornamental art
    844 n.
  pattern 844 n.
traces
  fetter 748 n.
trachea
  air pipe 353 n.
tracing
  imitation 20 n.
  copy 22 n.
  outline 233 n.

representation
  551 n.
track
  remainder 41 n.
  continuity 71 n.
  accompany 89 vb.
  water travel 269 n.
  direction 281 n.
  follow 284 vb.
  passage 305 n.
  gramophone 414 n.
  identification
    547 n.
  trace 548 n.
  pursue 619 vb.
  path 624 n.
  railway 624 n.
  route 624 n.
  racing 716 n.
  arena 724 n.
track down
  detect 484 vb.
track record
  conduct 688 n.
tracks
  trace 548 n.
tracksuit
  clothing 228 n.
  suit 228 n.
tract
  region 184 n.
  land 344 n.
  reading matter
    589 n.
  dissertation 591 n.
  lands 777 n.
tractable
  flexible 327 adj.
  tractable 701 adj.
traction
  traction 288 n.
traction engine
  locomotive 274 n.
  traction 288 n.
tractor
  vehicle 274 n.
  traction 288 n.
trad
  music 412 n.
trade
  union 45 n.
  business 622 n.
  vocation 622 n.
  transfer 780 n.
  trade 791 n.
  trade 791 vb.

trade in
  trade 791 vb.
trademark
  speciality 80 n.
  identification
    547 n.
  label 547 n.
trade-off
  correlation 12 n.
  equivalence 28 n.
  interchange 151 n.
  transference 272 n.
  conditions 766 n.
  compromise 770 n.
  transfer 780 n.
  barter 791 n.
  trade 791 n.
trade on
  use 673 vb.
tradesman
  artisan 686 n.
  tradespeople 794 n.
trades union
  society 708 n.
trading
  barter 791 n.
  trade 791 n.
tradition
  tradition 127 n.
  permanence 144 n.
  narrative 590 n.
  habit 610 n.
traditional
  conformable
    83 adj.
  habitual 610 adj.
  usual 610 adj.
  orthodox 976 adj.
traditionalist
  conformist 83 n.
  habitué 610 n.
traduce
  transform 147 vb.
  defame 926 vb.
traffic
  union 45 n.
  motion 265 n.
  conveyance 267 n.
  barter 791 n.
  trade 791 n.
trafficator
  signal light 420 n.
  indicator 547 n.
traffic in
  trade 791 vb.

traffic jam
  traffic control
    305 n.
  obstacle 702 n.
traffic lights
  traffic control
    305 n.
traffic warden
  traffic control
    305 n.
tragedy
  stage play 594 n.
  evil 616 n.
tragic
  dramatic 594 adj.
  evil 616 adj.
  distressing 827 adj.
tragic flaw
  defect 647 n.
  vulnerability 661 n.
tragicomic
  dramatic 594 adj.
trail
  continuity 71 n.
  be dispersed 75 vb.
  hang 217 vb.
  be behind 238 vb.
  be in motion
    265 vb.
  wander 267 vb.
  move slowly
    278 vb.
  follow 284 vb.
  draw 288 vb.
  detect 484 vb.
  identification
    547 n.
  trace 548 n.
  pursue 619 vb.
  path 624 n.
trail-blazer
  precursor 66 n.
trailer
  precursor 66 n.
  retinue 67 n.
  example 83 n.
  priority 119 n.
  small house 192 n.
  cart 274 n.
  follower 284 n.
  traction 288 n.
  film 445 n.
  advertisement
    528 n.
  hunter 619 n.

trail one's coat
  make quarrels
    709 vb.
  enrage 891 vb.
train
  adjunct 40 n.
  retinue 67 n.
  series 71 n.
  make conform
    83 vb.
  hanging object
    217 n.
  garment 228 n.
  rear 238 n.
  conveyance 267 n.
  train 274 n.
  follower 284 n.
  break in 369 vb.
  train 534 vb.
  learn 536 vb.
  habituate 610 vb.
  prepare oneself
    669 vb.
  retainer 742 n.
train-bearer
  retainer 742 n.
  bridal party 894 n.
trained
  habituated 610 adj.
  prepared 669 adj.
  expert 694 adj.
  obedient 739 adj.
trainee
  beginner 538 n.
trainer
  rider 268 n.
  trainer 537 n.
trainers
  footwear 228 n.
training
  teaching 534 n.
  habituation 610 n.
  preparation 669 n.
  exercise 682 n.
training ground
  arena 724 n.
train one's sights on
  aim at 617 vb.
traipse
  wander 267 vb.
trait
  temperament 5 n.
  speciality 80 n.
  nonconformity
    84 n.
  feature 445 n.

identification
547 n.
habit 610 n.
affections 817 n.
traitor
deceiver 545 n.
recanter 603 n.
collaborator 707 n.
revolter 738 n.
enemy 881 n.
evildoer 904 n.
undutifulness
918 n.
bad person 938 n.
traitorous
changeful 152 adj.
disobedient
738 adj.
perfidious 930 adj.
traits
character 5 n.
trajectory
curve 248 n.
route 624 n.
tram
tram 274 n.
tramlines
parallelism 219 n.
habit 610 n.
railway 624 n.
trammel
hinder 702 vb.
fetter 747 vb.
fetter 748 n.
tramp
nonconformist
84 n.
be in motion
265 vb.
pedestrianism
267 n.
walk 267 vb.
wanderer 268 n.
voyage 269 vb.
carrier 273 n.
merchant ship
275 n.
idler 679 n.
beggar 763 n.
poor person 801 n.
low fellow 869 n.
trample
oppress 735 vb.
shame 867 vb.
trample on
ill-treat 645 vb.
subjugate 745 vb.

be insolent 878 vb.
despise 922 vb.
trampoline
recoil 280 n.
trance
quiescence 266 n.
insensibility 375 n.
fantasy 513 n.
sleep 679 n.
tranquil
tranquil 266 adj.
tranquillity
quietude 266 n.
repose 683 n.
inexcitability
823 n.
pleasurableness
826 n.
content 828 n.
lack of wonder
865 n.
tranquillize
assuage 177 vb.
bring to rest
266 vb.
pacify 719 vb.
tranquillize
823 vb.
tranquillizer
moderator 177 n.
quietude 266 n.
drug 658 n.
relief 831 n.
transact
do business 622 vb.
do 676 vb.
deal with 688 vb.
transaction
event 154 n.
action 676 n.
deed 676 n.
trade 791 n.
transcend
be extrinsic 6 vb.
be great - large
32 vb.
be superior 34 vb.
outdo 306 vb.
be good 644 vb.
transcendence
extrinsicality 6 n.
overstepping 306 n.
perfection 646 n.
divine attribute
965 n.
transcendental
supreme 34 adj.

numerical 85 adj.
divine 965 adj.
transcendentalism
philosophy 449 n.
occultism 984 n.
**transcendental medi-
tation**
meditation 449 n.
transcribe
copy 20 vb.
translate 520 vb.
write 586 vb.
transcript
copy 22 n.
script 586 n.
transect
bisect 92 vb.
be oblique 220 vb.
transept
church interior
990 n.
transfer
duplicate 22 n.
transition 147 n.
substitution 150 n.
place 187 vb.
displacement
188 n.
transfer 272 vb.
transference 272 n.
transpose 272 vb.
picture 553 n.
relinquish 621 vb.
mandate 751 n.
not retain 779 vb.
transfer 780 n.
transference
transference 272 n.
metaphor 519 n.
transfigure
modify 143 vb.
transform 147 vb.
make better
654 vb.
beautify 841 vb.
transfixed
fixed 153 adj.
still 266 adj.
transform
modify 143 vb.
transform 147 vb.
transformation
transformation
143 n.
transformer
electronics 160 n.

transfusion
mixture 43 n.
transference 272 n.
surgery 658 n.
transgress
encroach 306 vb.
disobey 738 vb.
not observe 769 vb.
do wrong 914 adj.
be wicked 934 vb.
be guilty 936 vb.
transgression
overstepping 306 n.
wrong 914 n.
vice 934 n.
wickedness 934 n.
guilty act 936 n.
lawbreaking 954 n.
transient
transient 114 adj.
transistor
electronics 160 n.
broadcasting
531 n.
transit
transition 147 n.
motion 265 n.
pass 305 vb.
transition
change 143 n.
transition 147 n.
transference 272 n.
transitional
changeable
143 adj.
converted 147 adj.
moving 265 adj.
transitive verb
part of speech
564 n.
transitory
transient 114 adj.
translate
copy 20 vb.
translate 520 vb.
translation
imitation 20 n.
change 143 n.
transformation
143 n.
transition 147 n.
translation 520 n.
mandate 751 n.
holy orders 985 n.
translator
imitator 20 n.
interpreter 520 n.

transliteration
transference 272 n.
spelling 558 n.

translucent
transparent
422 adj.
semitransparent
424 adj.

transmigration
transference 272 n.

transmission
transference 272 n.
passage 305 n.
sound 398 n.
broadcast 531 n.
transfer 780 n.

transmit
send 272 vb.
transfer 272 vb.
pass 305 vb.
communicate
524 vb.
assign 780 vb.

transmitter
broadcasting
531 n.

transmogrification
transformation
143 n.

transmutation
transformation
143 n.

transom
beam 218 n.
support 218 n.
cross 222 n.
window 263 n.

transparency
transparency
422 n.
photography 551 n.

transparent
transparent
422 adj.
artless 699 adj.
trustworthy
929 adj.

transpire
happen 154 vb.
emerge 298 vb.
vaporize 338 vb.
be plain 522 vb.
be disclosed
526 vb.

transplant
substitute 150 n.
implant 303 vb.

cultivate 370 vb.
surgery 658 n.

transplantation
transference 272 n.

transplant surgery
surgery 658 n.

transport
displace 188 vb.
move 265 vb.
transfer 272 vb.
transport 272 n.
carry 273 vb.
vehicle 274 n.
ship 275 n.
aircraft 276 n.
eject 300 vb.
delight 826 vb.
punish 963 vb.

transportation
motion 265 n.
transport 272 n.
passage 305 n.
penalty 963 n.

transported
pleased 824 adj.

transporter
carrier 273 n.

transpose
displace 188 vb.
invert 221 vb.
move 265 vb.
transpose 272 vb.
harmonize 410 vb.
compose music
413 vb.

transposition
change 143 n.
interchange 151 n.
displacement
188 n.
inversion 221 n.
transference 272 n.
key 410 n.

transubstantiation
transformation
143 n.
the sacrament
988 n.

transverse
crossed 222 adj.

transvestism
abnormality 84 n.

transvestite
nonconformist
84 n.

trap
receptacle 194 n.

orifice 263 n.
close 264 vb.
carriage 274 n.
surprise 508 vb.
ensnare 542 vb.
fool 542 vb.
trap 542 n.
danger 661 n.
imprison 747 vb.
take 786 vb.

trapdoor
covering 226 n.
doorway 263 n.
trap 542 n.

trapeze artist
athlete 162 n.

trapezium
angular figure
247 n.

trapper
killer 362 n.
hunter 619 n.

trappings
adjunct 40 n.
coverlet 226 n.
dressing 228 n.
equipment 630 n.
trimming 844 n.

trash
novel 590 n.
bauble 639 n.
rubbish 641 n.
loose woman
952 n.

trashy
feeble 572 adj.
trivial 639 adj.

trattoria
café 192 n.
inn 192 n.

trauma
disease 651 n.
wound 655 n.
suffering 825 n.

traumatic
distressing 827 adj.

traumatize
wound 655 vb.

travail
adversity 731 n.

travel
be in motion
265 vb.
motion 265 n.
land travel 267 n.
travel 267 vb.

move fast 277 vb.
reading matter
589 n.

travelator
conveyance 267 n.
conveyor 274 n.

traveller
traveller 268 n.
seller 793 n.

traveller's cheque
paper money
797 n.

travelling
land travel 267 n.

**travelling salesman,
woman**
traveller 268 n.
seller 793 n.

travelogue
film 445 n.
guidebook 524 n.
description 590 n.

traverse
counteract 182 vb.
beam 218 n.
traverse 267 vb.
pass 305 vb.
passage 305 n.

travesty
imitate 20 vb.
mimicry 20 n.
copy 22 n.
misinterpretation
521 n.
misrepresentation
552 n.
bungling 695 n.
laughingstock
851 n.
satire 851 n.
satirize 851 vb.
ostentation 875 n.

trawl
network 222 n.
enclosure 235 n.
draw 288 vb.
traction 288 n.
hunt 619 vb.

trawler
mariner 270 n.
fishing boat 275 n.
hunter 619 n.

tray
compartment
194 n.
plate 194 n.

treacherous
uncertain 474 adj.
See **unreliable**
unreliable 474 adj.
false 541 adj.
hypocritical
541 adj.
dangerous 661 adj.
unsafe 661 adj.
malevolent
898 adj.
undutiful 918 adj.
perfidious 930 adj.

treachery
falsehood 541 n.
deception 542 n.
change of mind
603 n.
undutifulness
918 n.
perfidy 930 n.

treacle
viscidity 354 n.
sweet thing 392 n.

treacly
viscid 354 adj.

tread
degree 27 n.
serial place 73 n.
stand 218 n.
be in motion
265 vb.
walk 267 vb.
ascent 308 n.
trace 548 n.

treadmill
uniformity 16 n.
regularity 81 n.
labour 682 n.
bore 838 n.
instrument of tor-
ture 964 n.

tread on eggs
be in difficulty
700 vb.

tread the boards
act 594 vb.

tread water
swim 269 vb.

treason
sedition 738 n.
undutifulness
918 n.
perfidy 930 n.

treasure
store 632 n.
store 632 vb.

exceller 644 n.
funds 797 n.
a beauty 841 n.
honour 866 vb.
love 887 vb.
darling 890 n.
approve 923 vb.

treasure hunt
search 459 n.
racing 716 n.

treasurer
treasurer 798 n.

treasure trove
discovery 484 n.
benefit 615 n.
acquisition 771 n.

treasury
anthology 592 n.
treasury 799 n.

treat
modify 143 vb.
pleasure 376 n.
dissertate 591 vb.
doctor 658 vb.
remedy 658 vb.
behave 688 vb.
contract 765 vb.
give 781 vb.
defray 804 vb.
enjoyment 824 n.
pleasurableness
826 n.
amusement 837 n.

treat as
substitute 150 vb.

treatise
reading matter
589 n.
dissertation 591 vb.

treatment
change 143 n.
painting 553 n.
way 624 n.
use 673 n.
conduct 688 n.

treat with
make terms
766 vb.

treaty
treaty 765 n.

treble
treble 94 adj.
treble 94 vb.
stridor 407 n.
vocalist 413 n.

treble chance
gambling 618 n.

treble figures
hundred 99 n.

trebly
greatly 32 vb.

tree
tree 366 n.

treen
wooden 366 adj.

treetop
vertex 213 n.
foliage 366 n.

trefoil
three 93 n.
heraldry 547 n.
pattern 844 n.

trek
land travel 267 n.
travel 267 vb.
amuse oneself
837 vb.

trellis
frame 218 n.
network 222 n.

trellised
crossed 222 adj.

tremble
vary 152 vb.
be weak 163 vb.
be agitated 318 vb.
be cold 380 vb.
sound faint 401 vb.
roll 403 vb.
show feeling
818 vb.
be excited 821 vb.
quake 854 vb.

tremble in the bal-
ance
be uncertain
474 vb.
be in danger
661 vb.

trembling
agitation 318 n.
See **spasm**
feeling 818 n.
nervous 854 adj.
nervousness 854 n.

tremendous
prodigious 32 adj.

tremolo
roll 403 n.
musical note
410 n.
adagio 412 adv.

tremor
outbreak 176 n.

oscillation 317 n.
agitation 318 n.
feeling 818 n.
nervousness 854 n.

tremulousness
agitation 318 n.

trenail
fastening 47 n.

trench
gap 201 n.
fence 235 n.
excavation 255 n.
furrow 262 n.
conduit 351 n.
cultivate 370 vb.
refuge 662 n.
defences 713 n.

trenchant
keen 174 adj.
assertive 532 adj.
concise 569 adj.
disapproving
924 adj.

trench coat
overcoat 228 n.

trencherman, woman
eater 301 n.
glutton 947 n.

trenches
battleground
724 n.

trend
modality 7 n.
similarity 18 n.
continuity 71 n.
tendency 179 n.
form 243 n.
direction 281 n.
fashion 848 n.
liking 859 n.

trend-setter
living model 23 n.
precursor 66 n.
beau monde 848 n.

trendy
modern 126 adj.
modernist 126 n.
fashionable
848 adj.

trepanning
surgery 658 n.

trepidation
agitation 318 n.
excitable state
822 n.
fear 854 n.
nervousness 854 n.

trespass
  interfere 231 vb.
  ingress 297 n.
  intrude 297 vb.
  encroach 306 vb.
  disobey 738 vb.
  appropriate
    786 vb.
  do wrong 914 adj.
  wrong 914 n.
  arrogation 916 n.
  be wicked 934 vb.
  vice 934 n.
  be guilty 936 vb.
  guilty act 936 n.
  lawbreaking 954 n.
trespasser
  intruder 59 n.
  offender 904 n.
  usurper 916 n.
tresses
  hair 259 n.
trestle
  frame 218 n.
trews
  trousers 228 n.
triad
  three 93 n.
  musical note
    410 n.
trial
  enquiry 459 n.
  empiricism 461 n.
  experiment 461 n.
  experimental
    461 adj.
  bane 659 n.
  preparation 669 n.
  attempt 671 n.
  difficulty 700 n.
  contest 716 n.
  suffering 825 n.
  legal trial 959 n.
  punishment 963 n.
trial and error
  empiricism 461 n.
trial of strength
  hard task 700 n.
  contest 716 n.
trial run
  enquiry 459 n.
  experiment 461 n.
  preparation 669 n.
trials
  experiment 461 n.
  preparation 669 n.
  adversity 731 n.

trials and tribula-
tions
  painfulness 827 n.
triangle
  three 93 n.
  angular figure
    247 n.
  gong 414 n.
triangular
  three 93 adj.
tribal
  ethnic 11 adj.
  national 371 adj.
tribe
  family 11 n.
  race 11 n.
  group 74 n.
  breed 77 n.
  multitude 104 n.
  genealogy 169 n.
  native 191 n.
  community 708 n.
tribesman
  kinsman 11 n.
tribulation
  difficulty 700 n.
  suffering 825 n.
  painfulness 827 n.
tribunal
  tribunal 956 n.
tributary
  inferior 35 adj.
  stream 350 n.
  subject 745 adj.
tribute
  gift 781 n.
  receiving 782 n.
  pay 804 n.
  payment 804 n.
  tax 809 n.
  thanks 907 n.
  dueness 915 n.
  praise 923 n.
  reward 962 n.
trice
  instant 116 n.
trichology
  hairdressing 843 n.
trick
  deceive 542 vb.
  fool 542 vb.
  trickery 542 n.
  habit 610 n.
  contrivance 623 n.
  skill 694 n.
  be cunning 698 vb.
  stratagem 698 n.

  revel 837 n.
  perfidy 930 n.
trick cyclist
  psychologist 447 n.
trickery
  trickery 542 n.
trickle
  small quantity
    33 n.
  fewness 105 n.
  move slowly
    278 vb.
  be wet 341 vb.
  flow 350 vb.
trick out
  primp 843 vb.
  decorate 844 vb.
tricks of the trade
  trickery 542 n.
  stratagem 698 n.
trickster
  trickster 545 n.
tricky
  difficult 700 adj.
tricolour
  three 93 adj.
  flag 547 n.
tricorn
  three 93 adj.
tricycle
  three 93 n.
  bicycle 274 n.
  plaything 837 n.
trident
  three 93 n.
tried
  certain 473 adj.
  matured 669 adj.
  expert 694 adj.
  approved 923 adj.
  trustworthy
    929 adj.
tried and true
  friendly 880 adj.
triennial
  seasonal 141 adj.
triennium
  three 93 n.
trifle
  dessert 301 n.
  be inattentive
    456 vb.
  trifle 639 n.
  be inactive 679 vb.
  caress 889 vb.
trifle with
  not respect 921 vb.

  hold cheap 922 vb.
trifling
  inconsiderable
    33 adj.
  light-minded
    456 adj.
  negligence 458 n.
  trivial 639 adj.
  unimportant
    639 adj.
  contemptible
    922 adj.
trifoliate
  three 93 adj.
triform
  three 93 adj.
trifurcate
  trisect 95 vb.
trigger
  handle 218 n.
  tool 630 n.
  firearm 723 n.
trigger-happy
  murderous 362 adj.
  defiant 711 adj.
  excitable 822 adj.
  rash 857 adj.
  irascible 892 adj.
trigger off
  initiate 68 vb.
  cause 156 vb.
triglyph
  ornamental art
    844 n.
trigonometry
  mathematics 86 n.
  angular measure
    247 n.
  measurement
    465 n.
trihedral
  treble 94 adj.
trike
  bicycle 274 n.
trilateral
  three 93 adj.
  treble 94 adj.
  lateral 239 adj.
trilby
  headgear 228 n.
trill
  flow 350 vb.
  roll 403 n.
  roll 403 vb.
  musical note
    410 n.
  sing 413 vb.

pronunciation
577 n.
voice 577 vb.
trillion
over one hundred
99 n.
trilogy
three 93 n.
stage play 594 n.
trim
adjust 24 vb.
equalize 28 vb.
abate 37 vb.
cut 46 vb.
orderly 60 adj.
arrange 62 vb.
make conform
83 vb.
make smaller
198 vb.
shorten 204 vb.
dressing 228 n.
hem 234 vb.
form 243 n.
be true 494 vb.
beautify 841 vb.
personable 841 adj.
hairdressing 843 n.
decorate 844 vb.
trimester
three 93 n.
period 110 n.
trimming
hairdressing 843 n.
trimming 844 n.
trimmings
adjunct 40 n.
leavings 41 n.
trim the sails
navigate 269 vb.
trinal
treble 94 adj.
trinity
triality 93 n.
trinket
bauble 639 n.
finery 844 n.
trio
three 93 n.
trip
be in motion
265 vb.
land travel 267 n.
walk 267 vb.
descent 309 n.
tumble 309 vb.
blunder 495 vb.

ensnare 542 vb.
be clumsy 695 vb.
excitable state
822 n.
be wicked 934 vb.
tripartite
three 93 adj.
tripe
insides 224 n.
meat 301 n.
silly talk 515 n.
triplane
aircraft 276 n.
triple
treble 94 adj.
treble 94 vb.
triplet
three 93 n.
verse form 593 n.
triple vaccine
prophylactic 658 n.
triplex
treble 94 adj.
triplicate
treble 94 adj.
treble 94 vb.
tripod
three 93 n.
stand 218 n.
tripos
exam 459 n.
trip over
collide 279 vb.
be clumsy 695 vb.
tripper
traveller 268 n.
tripping
melodious 410 adj.
triptych
three 93 n.
picture 553 n.
altar 990 n.
trip up
ensnare 542 vb.
hinder 702 vb.
tripwire
trap 542 n.
obstacle 702 n.
defences 713 n.
trisection
trisection 95 n.
triskaidekaphobia
phobia 854 n.
triste
melancholic
834 adj.

trite
known 490 adj.
aphoristic 496 adj.
meaningless
515 adj.
dull 840 adj.
triteness
lack of meaning
515 n.
triumph
success 727 n.
triumph 727 vb.
victory 727 n.
trophy 729 n.
celebrate 876 vb.
celebration 876 n.
triumphal
successful 727 adj.
triumphant
successful 727 adj.
jubilant 833 adj.
triumph over
humiliate 872 vb.
triumvirate
three 93 n.
government 733 n.
trivet
three 93 n.
stand 218 n.
support 218 n.
furnace 383 n.
trivia
small quantity
33 n.
trifle 639 n.
trivial
irrelevant 10 adj.
inconsiderable
33 adj.
meaningless
515 adj.
trivial 639 adj.
trochee
prosody 593 n.
troglodyte
dweller 191 n.
humankind 371 n.
troika
three 93 n.
carriage 274 n.
Trojan
busy person 678 n.
Trojan horse
ambush 527 n.
trap 542 n.
stratagem 698 n.
enemy 881 n.

perfidy 930 n.
troll
demon 970 n.
elf 970 n.
trolley
stand 218 n.
pushcart 274 n.
train 274 n.
tram 274 n.
trollop
loose woman
952 n.
prostitute 952 n.
trombone
horn 414 n.
trompe l'oeil
art style 553 n.
troop
band 74 n.
congregate 74 vb.
group 74 n.
be many 104 vb.
walk 267 vb.
formation 722 n.
trooper
cavalry 722 n.
troops
armed force 722 n.
soldier 722 n.
See **armed force**
trope
trope 519 n.
trophy
reminder 505 n.
trophy 729 n.
tropical
hot 379 adj.
warm 379 adj.
tropics
heat 379 n.
troposphere
atmosphere 340 n.
trot
gait 265 n.
pedestrianism
267 n.
ride 267 vb.
move fast 277 vb.
troth
promise 764 n.
probity 929 n.
trot out
repeat 106 vb.
manifest 522 vb.
speak 579 vb.
trots, the
defecation 302 n.

digestive disorders
651 n.
Trotskyists
political party
708 n.
trotter
foot 214 n.
horse 273 n.
troubadour
musician 413 n.
vocalist 413 n.
poet 593 n.
entertainer 594 n.
trouble
turmoil 61 n.
derange 63 vb.
attention 455 n.
evil 616 n.
exertion 682 n.
difficulty 700 n.
predicament 700 n.
worry 825 n.
painfulness 827 n.
trouble 827 vb.
dejection 834 n.
troublemaker
troublemaker
663 n.
meddler 678 n.
trouble oneself
exert oneself
682 vb.
troubleshooter
adviser 691 n.
mediator 720 n.
troublesome
annoying 827 adj.
trouble spot
badness 645 n.
bane 659 n.
pitfall 663 n.
trough
inferiority 35 n.
bowl 194 n.
cavity 255 n.
furrow 262 n.
conduit 351 n.
adversity 731 n.
trounce
be superior 34 vb.
destroy 165 vb.
strike 279 vb.
defeat 727 vb.
reprove 924 vb.
spank 963 vb.
trouncing
knock 279 n.

victory 727 n.
defeat 728 n.
reprimand 924 n.
corporal punish-
ment 963 n.
troupe
band 74 n.
actor 594 n.
party 708 n.
trousers
trousers 228 n.
trousseau
clothing 228 n.
store 632 n.
trout
fish food 301 n.
fish 365 n.
trowel
ladle 194 n.
sharp edge 256 n.
conveyor 274 n.
farm tool 370 n.
troy weight
weighing 322 n.
truancy
absence 190 n.
relinquishment
621 n.
escape 667 n.
undutifulness
918 n.
truant
absence 190 n.
absent 190 adj.
avoider 620 n.
escaper 667 n.
undutiful 918 adj.
undutifulness
918 n.
truce
lull 145 n.
interval 201 n.
quiescence 266 n.
deliverance 668 n.
peace 717 n.
pacification 719 n.
truck
carrier 273 n.
carry 273 vb.
lorry 274 n.
pushcart 274 n.
train 274 n.
trudge
walk 267 vb.
move slowly
278 vb.

true
inimitable 21 adj.
straight 249 adj.
accurate 494 adj.
true 494 adj.
artless 699 adj.
patriotic 901 adj.
true blue
conformable
83 adj.
permanent 144 adj.
political party
708 n.
patriotic 901 adj.
trustworthy
929 adj.
true to life
lifelike 18 adj.
true 494 adj.
descriptive 590 adj.
truffle
fruit and vegetables
301 n.
trug
basket 194 n.
truism
truth 494 n.
axiom 496 n.
maxim 496 n.
lack of meaning
515 n.
truly
truly 494 adv.
trump
be superior 34 vb.
masterpiece 694 n.
overmaster 727 vb.
success 727 n.
good person 937 n.
trump card
advantage 34 n.
contrivance 623 n.
chief thing 638 n.
success 727 n.
trumped-up
spurious 542 adj.
untrue 543 adj.
trumpery
bauble 639 n.
trumpet
resound 404 vb.
shrill 407 vb.
ululate 409 vb.
play music 413 vb.
horn 414 n.
proclaim 528 vb.
publicizer 528 n.

call 547 n.
be ostentatious
875 vb.
boast 877 vb.
praise 923 vb.
trump up
fake 541 vb.
truncated
short 204 adj.
concise 569 adj.
truncheon
club 723 n.
badge of rule
743 n.
trundle
move 265 vb.
propel 287 vb.
rotate 315 vb.
trunk
remainder 41 n.
chief part 52 n.
piece 53 n.
incompleteness
55 n.
box 194 n.
support 218 n.
cylinder 252 n.
protuberance
254 n.
tree 366 n.
trunks
beachwear 228 n.
legwear 228 n.
truss
tie 45 vb.
bring together
74 vb.
bunch 74 n.
beam 218 n.
support 218 n.
support 218 vb.
trust
transference 272 n.
transport 272 n.
belief 485 n.
believe 485 vb.
expectation 507 n.
association 706 n.
corporation 708 n.
mandate 751 n.
hope 852 n.
hope 852 vb.
trustee
consignee 754 n.
recipient 782 n.
treasurer 798 n.

trustful
  credulous 487 adj.
trust in
  be certain 473 vb.
trustworthy
  credible 485 adj.
  trustworthy
    929 adj.
trusty
  credible 485 adj.
  trustworthy
    929 adj.
truth
  truth 494 n.
  maxim 496 n.
  veracity 540 n.
  artlessness 699 n.
  divine attribute
    965 n.
truthful
  true 494 adj.
  veracious 540 adj.
  trustworthy
    929 adj.
try
  enquire 459 vb.
  judge 480 vb.
  be willing 597 vb.
  persevere 600 vb.
  attempt 671 n.
  attempt 671 n.
  avail oneself of
    673 vb.
  do 676 vb.
  exert oneself
    682 vb.
  torment 827 vb.
  be tedious 838 vb.
trying
  annoying 827 adj.
try it on
  be tentative 461 vb.
  deceive 542 vb.
  behave 688 vb.
try one's hand at
  attempt 671 vb.
try out
  experiment 461 vb.
trysting
  social round 882 n.
tsarism
  despotism 733 n.
tsetse fly
  insect 365 n.
tub
  vat 194 n.
  vessel 194 n.

1040

bulk 195 n.
  ship 275 n.
  water 339 n.
  ablutions 648 n.
tuba
  horn 414 n.
tubby
  fleshy 195 adj.
  thick 205 adj.
tube
  electronics 160 n.
  excavation 255 n.
  tube 263 n.
  tunnel 263 n.
  railway 624 n.
tuber
  plant 366 n.
tubercular
  diseased 651 adj.
tuberculosis
  infection 651 n.
  respiratory disease
    651 n.
tub-thumping
  eloquent 579 adj.
  oration 579 n.
  oratory 579 n.
tuck
  fold 261 n.
  food 301 n.
tuck in
  place 187 vb.
  load 193 vb.
  eat 301 vb.
tuck into
  insert 303 vb.
tuck up
  place 187 vb.
  shorten 204 vb.
Tudor
  architectural
    192 adj.
tuft
  bunch 74 n.
  fewness 105 n.
  hair 259 n.
tug
  move 265 vb.
  boat 275 n.
  ship 275 n.
  draw 288 vb.
  traction 288 n.
  attract 291 vb.
  attraction 291 n.
  extraction 304 n.
  exertion 682 n.
  work 682 vb.

tugboat
  boat 275 n.
tug of love
  opposition 704 n.
  contest 716 n.
tug of war
  traction 288 n.
  opposition 704 n.
  contest 716 n.
tug one's forelock
  greet 884 vb.
tuition
  teaching 534 n.
tulle
  textile 222 n.
tumble
  unite with 45 vb.
  jumble 63 vb.
  descent 309 n.
  tumble 309 vb.
tumbledown
  flimsy 163 adj.
  dilapidated
    655 adj.
tumble-dry
  dry 342 vb.
tumbler
  athlete 162 n.
  cup 194 n.
tumble to
  discover 484 vb.
  understand 516 vb.
tumbril
  vehicle 274 n.
tumefaction
  dilation 197 n.
tumescence
  dilation 197 n.
  convexity 253 n.
tumid
  convex 253 adj.
tummy
  stomach 194 n.
  insides 224 n.
tumour
  dilation 197 n.
  swelling 253 n.
  cancer 651 n.
tumult
  turmoil 61 n.
  commotion 318 n.
  loudness 400 n.
  discord 411 n.
  activity 678 n.
  revolt 738 n.
tumultuous
  disorderly 61 adj.

violent 176 adj.
tumulus
  earthwork 253 n.
tun
  vat 194 n.
tuna
  fish food 301 n.
tundra
  plain 348 n.
tune
  adjust 24 vb.
  synchronize
    123 vb.
  sound 398 n.
  harmonize 410 vb.
  tune 412 n.
  play music 413 vb.
  make ready
    669 vb.
tuneful
  pleasant 376 adj.
  melodious 410 adj.
tune in
  hear 415 vb.
tuneless
  discordant 411 adj.
tune to
  hear 415 vb.
tune up
  harmonize 410 vb.
tunic
  wrapping 226 n.
  jacket 228 n.
tuning fork
  prototype 23 n.
tunnel
  cavity 255 n.
  make concave
    255 vb.
  pierce 263 vb.
  tunnel 263 n.
  railway 624 n.
tunnel vision
  blindness 439 n.
  dim sight 440 n.
  inattention 456 n.
  narrow mind
    481 n.
  prejudice 481 n.
tunny
  fish food 301 n.
tup
  unite with 45 vb.
  sheep 365 n.
  male animal
    372 n.

tuppence
  trifle 639 n.
turban
  headgear 228 n.
  coil 251 n.
turbid
  opaque 423 adj.
  dirty 649 adj.
turbine
  rotator 315 n.
  machine 630 n.
turbojet
  aircraft 276 n.
turboprop
  aircraft 276 n.
turbot
  fish food 301 n.
  fish 365 n.
turbulence
  turmoil 61 n.
  storm 176 n.
  violence 176 n.
  roughness 259 n.
  commotion 318 n.
  excitability 822 n.
turbulent
  disorderly 61 adj.
  violent 176 adj.
  excitable 822 adj.
tureen
  bowl 194 n.
turf
  piece 53 n.
  soil 344 n.
  grassland 348 n.
  grass 366 n.
  fuel 385 n.
  greenness 434 n.
  gambling 618 n.
  gaming-house
    618 n.
  arena 724 n.
turf accountant
  gambler 618 n.
turf out
  eject 300 vb.
turgid
  convex 253 adj.
  diffuse 570 adj.
  inelegant 576 adj.
  dull 840 adj.
  ostentatious
    875 adj.
turkey
  table bird 365 n.
Turkish bath
  heater 383 n.

  ablutions 648 n.
Turkish delight
  sweets 301 n.
turmeric
  spice 301 n.
turmoil
  turmoil 61 n.
  storm 176 n.
turn
  period 110 n.
  periodicity 141 n.
  change 143 n.
  change 143 vb.
  reversion 148 n.
  revert 148 vb.
  tend 179 vb.
  tendency 179 n.
  form 243 n.
  form 243 vb.
  be curved 248 vb.
  curve 248 n.
  land travel 267 n.
  deviate 282 vb.
  return 286 n.
  circle 314 vb.
  circuition 314 n.
  rotate 315 vb.
  rotation 315 n.
  be agitated 318 vb.
  be sour 393 vb.
  musical note
    410 n.
  stage show 594 n.
  deteriorate 655 vb.
  affections 817 n.
  feeling 818 n.
  dislike 861 n.
turn a blind eye
  be blind 439 vb.
  be inattentive
    456 vb.
  disregard 458 vb.
  avoid 620 vb.
  not act 677 vb.
  permit 756 vb.
  be patient 823 vb.
  forgive 909 vb.
  do wrong 914 adj.
turn about
  revert 148 vb.
  be inverted 221 vb.
  turn round 282 vb.
turn a deaf ear
  be deaf 416 vb.
  disregard 458 vb.
  refuse 760 vb.
  be pitiless 906 vb.

turn against
  change one's mind
    603 vb.
  dissuade 613 vb.
turn and turn about
  correlation 12 n.
  correlatively
    12 adv.
  periodicity 141 n.
turn away
  be curved 248 vb.
  regress 286 vb.
  repel 292 vb.
  dismiss 300 vb.
  disappoint 509 vb.
  refuse 760 vb.
  dislike 861 vb.
turn back
  modify 143 vb.
  revert 148 vb.
  invert 221 vb.
  turn back 286 vb.
turncoat
  recanter 603 n.
turn down
  invert 221 vb.
  refuse 760 vb.
turned
  formed 243 adj.
turned on
  excited 821 adj.
  drugged 949 adj.
  lecherous 951 adj.
turned-up
  curved 248 adj.
turn head over heels
  be inverted 221 vb.
turn in
  be quiescent
    266 vb.
  sleep 679 vb.
turning
  changeableness
    152 n.
  circuition 314 n.
  agitation 318 n.
turning point
  juncture 8 n.
  degree 27 n.
  crisis 137 n.
  reversion 148 n.
  summit 213 n.
  limit 236 n.
  return 286 n.
  important matter
    638 n.

turn inside out
  invert 221 vb.
  search 459 vb.
turn into
  convert 147 vb.
  enter 297 vb.
  translate 520 vb.
turnip
  fruit and vegetables
    301 n.
turnkey
  doorkeeper 264 n.
  gaoler 749 n.
turn of events
  event 154 n.
turn-off
  road 624 n.
turn of phrase
  phrase 563 n.
turn on
  depend 157 vb.
  operate 173 vb.
  excite 821 vb.
    See **animate**
  delight 826 vb.
  drug oneself
    949 vb.
turnon
  motivate 612 vb.
turn one off
  displease 827 vb.
turn one's back on
  disregard 458 vb.
  change one's mind
    603 vb.
  reject 607 vb.
  refuse 760 vb.
  not retain 779 vb.
  be rude 885 vb.
  despise 922 vb.
  disapprove 924 vb.
turn one's coat
  apostatize 603 vb.
turn one's hand to
  busy oneself
    622 vb.
turn one's head
  make mad 503 vb.
  be wonderful
    864 vb.
  flatter 925 vb.
turn one's stomach
  displease 827 vb.
  cause dislike
    861 vb.
turn out
  become 1 vb.

happen 154 vb.
result 157 vb.
produce 164 vb.
displace 188 vb.
eject 300 vb.
search 459 vb.
turnout
production 164 n.
form 243 n.
carriage 274 n.
pageant 875 n.
turn out well
benefit 615 vb.
turn over
be inverted 221 vb.
be curved 248 vb.
fold 261 vb.
transfer 272 vb.
turn over
search 459 vb.
trade 791 vb.
turnover
pastries and cakes
301 n.
earnings 771 n.
receipt 807 n.
reward 962 n.
turn over a new leaf
change 143 vb.
be turned to
147 vb.
change one's mind
603 vb.
get better 654 vb.
be penitent 939 vb.
turn over to
commission
751 vb.
turnpike
road 624 n.
turn Queen's evidence
inform 524 vb.
confess 526 vb.
accuse 928 vb.
turn round
be inverted 221 vb.
turn round 282 vb.
circle 314 vb.
turnstile
barrier 235 n.
recording instrument 549 n.
access 624 n.
obstacle 702 n.
treasury 799 n.

turntable
rotator 315 n.
gramophone 414 n.
turn tail
regress 286 vb.
run away 620 vb.
be cowardly
856 vb.
turn the air blue
cuss 899 vb.
turn the clock back
revert 148 vb.
turn the corner
change 143 vb.
get better 654 vb.
be restored 656 vb.
turn the other cheek
be patient 823 vb.
be humble 872 vb.
forgive 909 vb.
turn the scale
predominate 34 vb.
modify 143 vb.
cause 156 vb.
influence 178 vb.
prevail 178 vb.
dominate 733 vb.
turn the stomach
be unpalatable
391 vb.
turn the tables on
retaliate 714 vb.
accuse 928 vb.
turn to
be turned to
147 vb.
speak to 583 vb.
avail oneself of
673 vb.
turn topsy-turvy
bedevil 63 vb.
be inverted 221 vb.
invert 221 vb.
turn up
happen 154 vb.
chance 159 vb.
be present 189 vb.
shorten 204 vb.
fold 261 vb.
arrive 295 vb.
be visible 443 vb.
turnup
fold 261 n.
turn up one's nose
be unwilling
598 vb.
reject 607 vb.

be fastidious
862 vb.
despise 922 vb.
turn up one's toes
die 361 vb.
turn upside down
bedevil 63 vb.
modify 143 vb.
turn up trumps
be successful
727 vb.
get rich 800 vb.
turpitude
disrepute 867 n.
improbity 930 n.
wickedness 934 n.
turquoise
blue 435 adj.
blueness 435 n.
gem 844 n.
turret
high structure
209 n.
fort 713 n.
turtle
reptile 365 n.
tusk
tooth 256 n.
tussle
contend 716 vb.
contention 716 n.
contest 716 n.
fight 716 n.
tussock
bunch 74 n.
tussore
fibre 208 n.
tutelage
teaching 534 n.
learning 536 n.
protection 660 n.
subjection 745 n.
tutor
educate 534 vb.
teach 534 vb.
teacher 537 n.
domestic 742 n.
keeper 749 n.
tutorial
educational
534 adj.
teaching 534 n.
tutoring
teaching 534 n.
tut-tut
deprecate 762 vb.
deprecation 762 n.

disapprobation
924 n.
disapprove 924 vb.
tutu
skirt 228 n.
tuxedo
formal dress 228 n.
jacket 228 n.
TV
broadcasting
531 n.
twaddle
absurdity 497 n.
silly talk 515 n.
twain
duality 90 n.
twang
sound 398 n.
resound 404 vb.
rasp 407 vb.
stridor 407 n.
play music 413 vb.
pronunciation
577 n.
speech defect
580 n.
tweak
draw 288 vb.
give pain 377 vb.
twee
affected 850 adj.
tweed
textile 222 n.
roughness 259 n.
Tweedledum and Tweedledee
duality 90 n.
tweeds
suit 228 n.
tweet
ululate 409 vb.
tweezers
tool 630 n.
pincers 778 n.
twelfth
multifid 100 adj.
Twelfth Night
holy day 988 n.
twelve
over five 99 n.
twelve noon
noon 128 n.
twelve o'clock
noon 128 n.
twelve tribes
over five 99 n.

twenty
twenty and over
99 n.
twenty-five
twenty and over
99 n.
twenty questions
indoor game 837 n.
twerp
fool 501 n.
twice
double 91 adj.
twice removed
akin 11 adj.
twiddle
rotate 315 vb.
touch 378 vb.
twiddle one's thumbs
not act 677 vb.
be inactive 679 vb.
twig
branch 53 n.
young plant 132 n.
foliage 366 n.
tree 366 n.
know 490 vb.
understand 516 vb.
twilight
evening 129 n.
light 417 n.
darkness 418 n.
dim 419 adj.
half-light 419 n.
deterioration
655 n.
twill
crossed 222 adj.
weave 222 vb.
twin
kinsman 11 n.
identity 13 n.
analogue 18 n.
liken 18 vb.
similar 18 adj.
be equal 28 vb.
compeer 28 n.
concomitant 89 n.
dual 90 adj.
double 91 adj.
double 91 vb.
contemporary
123 n.
synchronous
123 adj.
twine
tie 45 vb.
cable 47 n.

fibre 208 n.
twine 251 vb.
twine round
cohere 48 vb.
twinge
give pain 377 vb.
pang 377 n.
suffering 825 n.
twinkle
instant 116 n.
vary 152 vb.
agitation 318 n.
be agitated 318 vb.
flash 417 n.
shine 417 vb.
gesticulate 547 vb.
gesture 547 n.
laughter 835 n.
smile 835 vb.
twinkling
instant 116 n.
flash 417 n.
twinkling of an eye,
the
instant 116 n.
twins
duality 90 n.
twin set
jersey 228 n.
twirl
coil 251 n.
twine 251 vb.
rotate 315 vb.
rotation 315 n.
twist
tie 45 vb.
complexity 61 n.
derange 63 vb.
make conform
83 vb.
disable 161 vb.
force 176 vb.
bag 194 n.
fibre 208 n.
obliquity 220 n.
deform 244 vb.
distort 246 vb.
distortion 246 n.
coil 251 n.
convolution 251 n.
twine 251 vb.
be in motion
265 vb.
deviate 282 vb.
draw 288 vb.
circle 314 vb.
tobacco 388 n.

bias 481 vb.
eccentricity 503 n.
misinterpret
521 vb.
pervert 655 vb.
dance 837 n.
dance 837 vb.
make ugly 842 vb.
twist and turn
meander 251 vb.
twisted
distorted 246 adj.
convoluted 251 adj.
biased 481 adj.
imperfect 647 adj.
unsightly 842 adj.
twister
gale 352 n.
trickster 545 n.
bad person 938 n.
twist one's arm
induce 612 vb.
compel 740 vb.
twit
fool 501 n.
ridicule 851 vb.
not respect 921 vb.
criticize 924 vb.
accusation 928 n.
twitch
draw 288 vb.
agitate 318 vb.
agitation 318 n.
be agitated 318 vb.
spasm 318 n.
feel pain 377 vb.
gesture 547 n.
twitchiness
agitation 318 n.
twitter
agitation 318 n.
be agitated 318 vb.
ululate 409 vb.
ululation 409 n.
sing 413 vb.
be loquacious
581 vb.
twittering
ululation 409 n.
'twixt
between 231 adv.
two
duality 90 n.
two-a-penny
trivial 639 adj.
cheap 812 adj.

two-edged
double 91 adj.
equivocal 518 adj.
two-edged weapon
inexpedience
643 n.
two-faced
dual 90 adj.
double 91 adj.
hypocritical
541 adj.
dishonest 930 adj.
two-faced person
recanter 603 n.
two-finger gesture
gesture 547 n.
twofold
double 91 adj.
two of a kind
analogue 18 n.
two score
twenty and over
99 n.
two shakes
instant 116 n.
twosome
duality 90 n.
two-time
deceive 542 vb.
two-way
correlative 12 adj.
double 91 adj.
tycoon
bigwig 638 n.
autocrat 741 n.
rich person 800 n.
tyke
dog 365 n.
tympanum
ear 415 n.
church exterior
990 n.
type
character 5 n.
uniformity 16 n.
analogue 18 n.
copy 20 vb.
prototype 23 n.
sort 77 n.
example 83 n.
form 243 n.
person 371 n.
indication 547 n.
image 551 n.
letter 558 n.
write 586 vb.
print-type 587 n.

typeface
print-type 587 n.
typescript
script 586 n.
book 589 n.
typewriter
stationery 586 n.
typhoid
digestive disorders
651 n.
infection 651 n.
typhoon
storm 176 n.
gale 352 n.
typhus
infection 651 n.
typical
characteristic
5 adj.
lifelike 18 adj.
general 79 adj.
typical 83 adj.
typify
be uniform 16 vb.
resemble 18 vb.
predict 511 vb.
manifest 522 vb.
indicate 547 vb.
represent 551 vb.
typist
stenographer
586 n.
typography
composition 56 n.
printing 555 n.
print 587 n.
tyrannical
violent 176 adj.
authoritative
733 adj.
oppressive 735 adj.
insolent 878 adj.
cruel 898 adj.
lawless 954 adj.
tyrannize
ill-treat 645 vb.
meddle 678 vb.
rule 733 vb.
oppress 735 vb.
be malevolent
898 vb.
tyranny
influence 178 n.
despotism 733 n.
brute force 735 n.
insolence 878 n.
arrogation 916 n.

tyrant
tyrant 735 n.
autocrat 741 n.
tyre
wheel 250 n.
tyro
beginner 538 n.

U

U
well-bred 848 adj.
genteel 868 adj.
ubiquitous
ubiquitous 189 adj.
U-boat
ship 275 n.
warship 722 n.
udder
bosom 253 n.
UFO
spaceship 276 n.
unknown thing
491 n.
ugly
deformed 246 adj.
ugly 842 adj.
sullen 893 adj.
ugly customer
troublemaker
663 n.
low fellow 869 n.
ruffian 904 n.
bad person 938 n.
ugly duckling
eyesore 842 n.
ukulele
stringed instrument
414 n.
ulcer
digestive disorders
651 n.
ulcer 651 n.
painfulness 827 n.
ulterior
extraneous 59 adj.
future 124 adj.
distant 199 adj.
ulterior motive
concealment 525 n.
motive 612 n.
ultimate
supreme 34 adj.
ending 69 adj.
fundamental
156 adj.
distant 199 adj.

ultimatum
limit 236 n.
intention 617 n.
requirement 627 n.
warning 664 n.
demand 737 n.
request 761 n.
conditions 766 n.
ultra
extremely 32 vb.
ultrasound
diagnostic 658 n.
ultraviolet radiation
radiation 417 n.
ultra vires
unwarranted
916 adj.
ululation
ululation 409 n.
lamentation 836 n.
umbelliferous
broad 205 adj.
umbilical
central 225 adj.
umbilical cord
bond 47 n.
obstetrics 167 n.
umbrage
foliage 366 n.
resentment 891 n.
umbrella
shade 226 n.
dome 253 n.
protection 660 n.
shelter 662 n.
umlaut
speech sound
398 n.
punctuation 547 n.
umpire
estimator 480 n.
judge 480 vb.
mediate 720 vb.
mediator 720 n.
magistracy 957 n.
umpteen
many 104 adj.
unable
powerless 161 adj.
useless 641 adj.
unskilful 695 adj.
unabridged
intact 52 adj.
unacceptable
unpleasant
827 adj.

unaccompanied
alone 88 adj.
unaccountability
unintelligibility
517 n.
unaccountable
unusual 84 adj.
changeful 152 adj.
unexpected
508 adj.
unintelligible
517 adj.
wonderful 864 adj.
lawless 954 adj.
unaccustomed
unhabituated
611 adj.
unacquainted
ignorant 491 adj.
unadorned
plain 573 adj.
artless 699 adj.
unadulterated
simple 44 adj.
unmixed 44 adj.
genuine 494 adj.
plain 573 adj.
unadventurous
cautious 858 adj.
unaffected
intact 52 adj.
veracious 540 adj.
plain 573 adj.
elegant 575 adj.
artless 699 adj.
impassive 820 adj.
unalienable
intrinsic 5 adj.
unalike
dissimilar 19 adj.
unalterable
unchangeable
153 adj.
unambitious
apathetic 820 adj.
indifferent 860 adj.
inglorious 867 adj.
modest 874 adj.
unanimity
agreement 24 n.
consensus 488 n.
cooperation 706 n.
concord 710 n.
unanimous
agreeing 24 adj.
assenting 488 adj.

unanswerable
lawless 954 adj.
unappetizing
tasteless 387 adj.
unsavoury 391 adj.
unapproachable
infinite 107 adj.
unarguable
undisputed
473 adj.
unarmed
peaceful 717 adj.
unashamed
impenitent
940 adj.
unasked
volitional 595 adj.
voluntary 597 adj.
unwanted 860 adj.
unassailable
fixed 153 adj.
strong 162 adj.
invulnerable
660 adj.
unassuming
plain 573 adj.
artless 699 adj.
humble 872 adj.
modest 874 adj.
unattached
separate 46 adj.
neutral 625 adj.
free 744 adj.
independent
744 adj.
unpossessed
774 adj.
unattainable
impracticable
470 adj.
unattended
neglected 458 adj.
unattractive
unpleasant
827 adj.
graceless 842 adj.
unwanted 860 adj.
unauthorized
powerless 161 adj.
wrong 914 adj.
unwarranted
916 adj.
illegal 954 adj.
unavailable
absent 190 adj.
scarce 636 adj.

unprovided
636 adj.
unavoidable
necessary 596 adj.
compelling
740 adj.
obligatory 917 adj.
unaware
insensible 375 adj.
inattentive 456 adj.
ignorant 491 adj.
unbalanced
unequal 29 adj.
unwise 499 adj.
crazy 503 adj.
*mentally disor-
dered* 503 adj.
excitable 822 adj.
unbaptized
heathenish 974 adj.
unbargained for
unexpected
508 adj.
unbearable
exorbitant 32 adj.
intolerable 827 adj.
unbeatable
strong 162 adj.
best 644 adj.
unbeaten
new 126 adj.
unbecoming
unapt 25 adj.
discreditable
867 adj.
unbeknown
unknown 491 adj.
unbelievable
prodigious 32 adj.
wonderful 864 adj.
unbeliever
unbeliever 486 n.
impious person
980 n.
unbend
repose 683 vb.
be humble 872 vb.
be sociable 882 vb.
forgive 909 vb.
unbiased
judicial 480 adj.
just 913 adj.
unbidden
volitional 595 adj.
voluntary 597 adj.
unbind
disunite 46 vb.

deliver 668 vb.
liberate 746 vb.
not retain 779 vb.
unblemished
unmixed 44 adj.
innocent 935 adj.
unblinking
still 266 adj.
unbolt
open 263 vb.
unborn
unborn 2 adj.
immature 670 adj.
unbowed
vertical 215 adj.
independent
744 adj.
courageous
855 adj.
unbreakable
strong 162 adj.
hard 326 adj.
tough 329 adj.
invulnerable
660 adj.
unbridled
violent 176 adj.
free 744 adj.
unbroken
intact 52 adj.
complete 54 adj.
continuous 71 adj.
unburden
disencumber
701 vb.
unburden oneself
divulge 526 vb.
unbusinesslike
unskilful 695 adj.
unbutton
disunite 46 vb.
uncalled for
voluntary 597 adj.
superfluous
637 adj.
uncanny
spooky 970 adj.
magical 983 adj.
uncap
uncover 229 vb.
open 263 vb.
uncared for
neglected 458 adj.
uncaring
negligent 458 adj.
uncensored
intact 52 adj.

impure 951 adj.
uncensured
approved 923 adj.
unceremonious
discourteous
885 adj.
uncertain
changeful 152 adj.
doubting 474 adj.
uncertain 474 adj.
irresolute 601 adj.
capricious 604 adj.
uncertainty
uncertainty 474 n.
doubt 486 n.
irresolution 601 n.
unchain
disunite 46 vb.
liberate 746 vb.
unchallenged
just 913 adj.
unchanging
characteristic
5 adj.
identical 13 adj.
uniform 16 adj.
perpetual 115 adj.
permanent 144 adj.
unchangeable
153 adj.
trustworthy
929 adj.
unchaperoned
alone 88 adj.
neglected 458 adj.
uncharacteristic
abnormal 84 adj.
uncharitable
parsimonious
816 adj.
unkind 898 adj.
selfish 932 adj.
uncharted
unknown 491 adj.
unchartered
unwarranted
916 adj.
illegal 954 adj.
unchecked
rash 857 adj.
unchivalrous
discourteous
885 adj.
dishonest 930 adj.
unchristian
unkind 898 adj.
heathenish 974 adj.

irreligious 974 adj.
uncial
letter 558 n.
uncivil
impertinent
878 adj.
discourteous
885 adj.
uncivilized
ignorant 491 adj.
ill-bred 847 adj.
barbaric 869 adj.
unclad
uncovered 229 adj.
unclaimed
unpossessed
774 adj.
not retained
779 adj.
unclarified
opaque 423 adj.
unclasp
disunite 46 vb.
unclassified
unrelated 10 adj.
mixed 43 adj.
unknown 491 adj.
uncle
kinsman 11 n.
male 372 n.
lender 784 n.
unclean
unclean 649 adj.
dishonest 930 adj.
impure 951 adj.
unclear
indistinct 444 adj.
unclear 568 adj.
unclench
open 263 vb.
not retain 779 vb.
Uncle Tom Cobbley
and all
everyman 79 n.
unclothe
uncover 229 vb.
unclouded
undimmed
417 adj.
unco
remarkably 32 vb.
unusual 84 adj.
uncoil
lengthen 203 vb.
straighten 249 vb.
recoil 280 vb.
evolve 316 vb.

uncomfortable
suffering 825 adj.
unpleasant
827 adj.
uncommitted
irresolute 601 adj.
neutral 625 adj.
independent
744 adj.
uncommon
remarkable 32 adj.
infrequent 140 adj.
uncommonly
remarkably 32 vb.
uncommunicative
reticent 525 adj.
unsociable 883 adj.
uncompetitive
peaceful 717 adj.
uncomplaining
patient 823 adj.
content 828 adj.
approving 923 adj.
uncompleted
uncompleted
726 adj.
uncomplicated
simple 44 adj.
artless 699 adj.
easy 701 adj.
uncomplimentary
disrespectful
921 adj.
disapproving
924 adj.
uncomprehending
ignorant 491 adj.
uncompromising
resolute 599 adj.
obstinate 602 adj.
severe 735 adj.
unconcealed
manifest 522 adj.
shown 522 adj.
unconcerned
incurious 454 adj.
indifferent 860 adj.
unconditional
obligatory 917 adj.
unconfirmed
weak 163 adj.
heathenish 974 adj.
unconformity
nonconformity
84 n.
uncongenial
cheerless 834 adj.

unsociable 883 adj.
unconnected
unrelated 10 adj.
unconquerable
strong 162 adj.
unconquered
independent
744 adj.
unconscientiousness
improbity 930 n.
unconscionable
exorbitant 32 adj.
lasting 113 adj.
unconscious
impotent 161 adj.
insensible 375 adj.
ignorant 491 adj.
involuntary
596 adj.
inactive 679 adj.
sleepy 679 adj.
impassive 820 adj.
unconsciousness
helplessness 161 n.
insensibility 375 n.
ignorance 491 n.
sleep 679 n.
unconsecrated
heathenish 974 adj.
profane 980 adj.
unconsenting
unwilling 598 adj.
unconstitutional
unwarranted
916 adj.
illegal 954 adj.
uncontaminated
perfect 646 adj.
uncontested
undisputed
473 adj.
uncontrived
artless 699 adj.
uncontrollable
violent 176 adj.
frenzied 503 adj.
wilful 602 adj.
fervent 818 adj.
excited 821 adj.
uncontrolled
independent
744 adj.
intemperate
943 adj.
uncontroversial
undisputed
473 adj.

unconventional
nonuniform 17 adj.
unconformable
84 adj.
unwonted 611 adj.
independent
744 adj.
unconverted
impenitent
940 adj.
heathenish 974 adj.
unconvincing
improbable
472 adj.
feeble 572 adj.
uncooked
uncooked 670 adj.
uncooperative
unwilling 598 adj.
undutiful 918 adj.
uncork
uncover 229 vb.
open 263 vb.
liberate 746 vb.
uncorrected
inexact 495 adj.
uncorroborated
erroneous 495 adj.
uncorrupted
disinterested
931 adj.
innocent 935 adj.
uncounted
many 104 adj.
uncouple
disunite 46 vb.
uncouth
amorphous
244 adj.
clumsy 695 adj.
graceless 842 adj.
ill-bred 847 adj.
plebeian 869 adj.
discourteous
885 adj.
uncover
uncover 229 vb.
open 263 vb.
discover 484 vb.
show respect
920 vb.
uncritical
indiscriminating
464 adj.
approving 923 adj.
uncross (legs)
straighten 249 vb.

unction
lubrication 334 n.
unctuousness
  357 n.
unguent 357 n.
warm feeling
  818 n.
pietism 979 n.
piety 979 n.
unctuous
feeling 818 adj.
servile 879 adj.
flattering 925 adj.
uncultivated
unproductive
  172 adj.
uninstructed
  491 adj.
uncultured
uninstructed
  491 adj.
ill-bred 847 adj.
barbaric 869 adj.
uncurl
straighten 249 vb.
evolve 316 vb.
uncustomary
unusual 84 adj.
uncut
intact 52 adj.
long 203 adj.
immature 670 adj.
uncut gem
gem 844 n.
undamaged
undamaged
  646 adj.
undaughterly
undutiful 918 adj.
undaunted
resolute 599 adj.
undebatable
undisputed
  473 adj.
undeceive
disclose 526 vb.
undecided
doubting 474 adj.
uncertain 474 adj.
irresolute 601 adj.
undecipherable
unintelligible
  517 adj.
undeclared
tacit 523 adj.
undefended
vulnerable 661 adj.

undefiled
unmixed 44 adj.
innocent 935 adj.
pure 950 adj.
undefinable
uncertain 474 adj.
undefined
amorphous
  244 adj.
shadowy 419 adj.
indiscriminate
  464 adj.
uncertain 474 adj.
undemanding
easy 701 adj.
lax 734 adj.
lenient 736 adj.
undemocratic
authoritarian
  735 adj.
insolent 878 adj.
undemonstrative
impassive 820 adj.
undeniable
undisputed
  473 adj.
creedal 485 adj.
undependable
unreliable 474 adj.
dishonest 930 adj.
under
low 210 adj.
under 210 adv.
underachieve
fall short 307 vb.
under-age
young 130 adj.
under arrest
imprisoned
  747 adj.
captive 750 adj.
underbelly
insides 224 n.
undercapitalized
unprovided
  636 adj.
undercarriage
frame 218 n.
support 218 n.
carrier 273 n.
aircraft 276 n.
undercharge
cheapen 812 vb.
underclothes
underwear 228 n.
undercoat
layer 207 n.

pigment 425 n.
under control
obedient 739 adj.
restrained 747 adj.
undercover
latent 523 adj.
concealed 525 adj.
undercover agent
secret service
  459 n.
informer 524 n.
undercurrent
current 350 n.
latency 523 n.
undercurrents
cause 156 n.
undercut
sell 793 vb.
cheapen 812 vb.
underdeveloped
incomplete 55 adj.
immature 670 adj.
underdog
inferior 35 n.
loser 728 n.
unlucky person
  731 n.
underdone
culinary 301 adj.
unsavoury 391 adj.
uncooked 670 adj.
under duress
by force 740 adv.
underemployment
inaction 677 n.
underestimate
underestimate
  483 vb.
underestimation
  483 n.
underexpose
darken 418 vb.
underfed
underfed 636 adj.
underfoot
low 210 adj.
under 210 adv.
underframe
support 218 n.
undergo
meet with 154 vb.
feel 818 vb.
suffer 825 vb.
undergraduate
student 538 n.
underground
low 210 adj.

under 210 adv.
deep 211 adj.
tunnel 263 n.
concealed 525 adj.
hiding-place 527 n.
revolter 738 n.
underground railway
excavation 255 n.
tunnel 263 n.
train 274 n.
railway 624 n.
undergrowth
wood 366 n.
underhand
occult 523 adj.
stealthily 525 adv.
stealthy 525 adj.
dishonest 930 adj.
underinsure
be rash 857 vb.
under investigation
sub judice 480 adv.
underived
original 21 adj.
underlay
layer 207 n.
underlie
cause 156 vb.
lurk 523 vb.
underline
strengthen 162 vb.
attract notice
  455 vb.
emphasize 532 vb.
mark 547 vb.
underling
inferior 35 n.
nonentity 639 n.
servant 742 n.
commoner 869 n.
underlining
vigour 571 n.
underlying
latent 523 adj.
undermanned
deficient 307 adj.
unprovided
  636 adj.
undermine
disable 161 vb.
weaken 163 vb.
make concave
  255 vb.
descend 309 vb.
tell against 467 vb.
plot 623 vb.
impair 655 vb.

be cunning 698 vb.
hinder 702 vb.
revolt 738 vb.
underneath
under 210 adv.
undernourished
underfed 636 adj.
under one's belt
completed 725 adj.
under one's nose
near 200 adv.
obvious 443 adj.
visible 443 adj.
under one's thumb
obedient 739 adj.
subject 745 adj.
underpaid
cheap 812 adj.
unwarranted
   916 adj.
underpants
underwear 228 n.
underpass
crossing 222 n.
tunnel 263 n.
passage 305 n.
bridge 624 n.
underpin
support 218 vb.
underprice
underestimate
   483 vb.
underprivileged
poor 801 adj.
under-privileged, the
lower classes 869 n.
under protest
by force 740 adv.
underrate
underestimate
   483 vb.
not respect 921 vb.
hold cheap 922 vb.
undersea
deep 211 adj.
undershirt
underwear 228 n.
underside
lowness 210 n.
undersign
sign 547 vb.
undersized
small 33 adj.
dwarfish 196 adj.
lean 206 adj.
underskirt
underwear 228 n.

understaffed
unprovided
   636 adj.
understand
perceive 447 adj.
understand 516 vb.
imply 523 vb.
understandable
intelligible 516 adj.
understanding
agreement 24 n.
intellect 447 n.
knowledge 490 n.
intelligence 498 n.
imagination 513 n.
concord 710 n.
pacification 719 n.
compact 765 n.
feeling 818 n.
friendliness 880 n.
friendly 880 adj.
love 887 n.
benevolence 897 n.
pity 905 n.
pitying 905 adj.
understate
underestimate
   483 vb.
under-stated
soft-hued 425 adj.
understood
tacit 523 adj.
usual 610 adj.
understudy
substitute 150 n.
act 594 vb.
actor 594 n.
deputize 755 vb.
deputy 755 n.
undertake
undertake 672 vb.
undertaker
interment 364 n.
doer 676 n.
undertaking
business 622 n.
undertaking 672 n.
promise 764 n.
under-the-counter
stealthily 525 adv.
under the hammer
salable 793 adj.
under the influence
drunk 949 adj.
under the sun
existing 1 adj.
widely 183 adv.

under the weather
weakly 163 adj.
sick 651 adj.
undertone
contrariety 14 n.
faintness 401 n.
musical note
   410 n.
latency 523 n.
voicelessness 578 n.
undervalue
abate 37 vb.
misjudge 481 vb.
underestimate
   483 vb.
not respect 921 vb.
hold cheap 922 vb.
underwater
deep 211 adj.
under way
moving 265 adj.
in preparation
   669 adv.
underwear
underwear 228 n.
underweight
unequal 29 adj.
inferior 35 adj.
weakly 163 adj.
light 323 adj.
underworld
depth 211 n.
lower classes 869 n.
offender 904 n.
wickedness 934 n.
hell 972 n.
underwrite
promise 764 vb.
contract 765 vb.
give security
   767 vb.
undeserved
unwarranted
   916 adj.
undesirability
inexpedience
   643 n.
undesirable
inexpedient
   643 adj.
unpleasant
   827 adj.
unwanted 860 adj.
bad person 938 n.
undetected
latent 523 adj.

undetermined
irresolute 601 adj.
undeveloped
incomplete 55 adj.
latent 523 adj.
imperfect 647 adj.
immature 670 adj.
unskilled 695 adj.
undeviating
uniform 16 adj.
unchangeable
   153 adj.
straight 249 adj.
directed 281 adj.
accurate 494 adj.
orthodox 976 adj.
undies
underwear 228 n.
undifferentiated
uniform 16 adj.
indiscriminate
   464 adj.
undignified
dishonest 930 adj.
undiluted
unmixed 44 adj.
strong 162 adj.
undiminished
intact 52 adj.
undimmed
undimmed
   417 adj.
undiscernible
unintelligible
   517 adj.
undiscerning
blind 439 adj.
inattentive 456 adj.
indiscriminating
   464 adj.
undisciplined
disorderly 61 adj.
disobedient
   738 adj.
intemperate
   943 adj.
undisclosed
concealed 525 adj.
undiscovered
unborn 2 adj.
unknown 491 adj.
latent 523 adj.
occult 523 adj.
undiscriminating
approving 923 adj.
undisguised
obvious 443 adj.

genuine 494 adj.
undisputed
  undisputed
  473 adj.
undissolved
  intact 52 adj.
undistinguished
  indiscriminate
  464 adj.
  middling 732 adj.
undisturbed
  tranquil 266 adj.
undivided
  intact 52 adj.
  complete 54 adj.
  orthodox 976 adj.
undivulged
  tacit 523 adj.
undo
  disunite 46 vb.
  destroy 165 vb.
  counteract 182 vb.
  open 263 vb.
  abrogate 752 vb.
undoing
  separation 46 n.
  destruction 165 n.
  abrogation 752 n.
undomesticated
  unhabituated
  611 adj.
undone
  incomplete 55 adj.
  hopeless 853 adj.
undoubted
  undisputed
  473 adj.
undress
  informal dress
  228 n.
  uniform 228 n.
  uncover 229 vb.
  uncovering 229 n.
undrinkable
  unsavoury 391 adj.
  insalubrious
  653 adj.
undue
  unapt 25 adj.
undulate
  crinkle 251 vb.
  gait 265 n.
  oscillate 317 vb.
undulatory
  undulatory
  251 adj.

unduly
  extremely 32 vb.
undutiful
  undutiful 918 adj.
undying
  existing 1 adj.
  perpetual 115 adj.
  unchangeable
  153 adj.
  remembered
  505 adj.
unearned
  unwarranted
  916 adj.
unearth
  eject 300 vb.
  extract 304 vb.
  exhume 364 vb.
  discover 484 vb.
  manifest 522 vb.
unearthly
  extraneous 59 adj.
  immaterial
  320 adj.
  divine 965 adj.
  spooky 970 adj.
unearthly hour
  earliness 135 n.
unease
  evil 616 n.
uneasy
  clumsy 695 adj.
  nervous 854 adj.
uneatable
  unsavoury 391 adj.
uneconomic
  wasteful 634 adj.
  prodigal 815 adj.
uneconomical
  prodigal 815 adj.
unedited
  intact 52 adj.
uneducated
  uninstructed
  491 adj.
unembellished
  plain 573 adj.
unembroidered
  veracious 540 adj.
unemotional
  impassive 820 adj.
unemployable
  useless 641 adj.
unemployed
  powerless 161 adj.
  quiescent 266 adj.
  nonactive 677 adj.

unending
  perpetual 115 adj.
unenlightened
  ignorant 491 adj.
  unwise 499 adj.
unenterprising
  cautious 858 adj.
unenthusiastic
  unwilling 598 adj.
  apathetic 820 adj.
unequal
  unequal 29 adj.
unequalled
  unequal 29 adj.
  supreme 34 adj.
  best 644 adj.
unequal to
  insufficient
  636 adj.
unequipped
  unequipped
  670 adj.
unequitable
  unequal 29 adj.
unequivocal
  absolute 32 adj.
  certain 473 adj.
  positive 473 adj.
  intelligible 516 adj.
unerring
  certain 473 adj.
  accurate 494 adj.
  innocent 935 adj.
unescorted
  alone 88 adj.
  vulnerable 661 adj.
unethical
  dishonest 930 adj.
uneven
  nonuniform 17 adj.
  unequal 29 adj.
  discontinuous
  72 adj.
  fitful 142 adj.
  rough 259 adj.
  imperfect 647 adj.
  unjust 914 adj.
uneventful
  tranquil 266 adj.
  trivial 639 adj.
unexceptionable
  guiltless 935 adj.
unexceptional
  regular 81 adj.
unexcited
  apathetic 820 adj.

unexciting
  tedious 838 adj.
unexpected
  casual 159 adj.
  unexpected
  508 adj.
unexplained
  uncertain 474 adj.
  unknown 491 adj.
  puzzling 517 adj.
unexplored
  new 126 adj.
  neglected 458 adj.
  unknown 491 adj.
  latent 523 adj.
  secluded 883 adj.
unexposed
  latent 523 adj.
unexpressed
  tacit 523 adj.
unexpurgated
  intact 52 adj.
  impure 951 adj.
unfailing regularity
  uniformity 16 n.
  frequency 139 n.
unfair
  unjust 914 adj.
  dishonest 930 adj.
unfair advantage
  injustice 914 n.
unfaithful
  changeful 152 adj.
  nonobservant
  769 adj.
  hostile 881 adj.
  perfidious 930 adj.
unfaithfulness
  enmity 881 n.
  perfidy 930 n.
  illicit love 951 n.
unfallen
  innocent 935 adj.
  pure 950 adj.
unfallen state
  innocence 935 n.
unfamiliar
  unusual 84 adj.
  unknown 491 adj.
  unhabituated
  611 adj.
  secluded 883 adj.
unfashionable
  unwonted 611 adj.
  plebeian 869 adj.
unfasten
  disunite 46 vb.

unfathomed
deep 211 adj.
unknown 491 adj.
unfavourable
inopportune
138 adj.
opposing 704 adj.
adverse 731 adj.
disapproving
924 adj.
unfeeling
unfeeling 375 adj.
impassive 820 adj.
pitiless 906 adj.
unfeminine
male 372 adj.
unfetter
disunite 46 vb.
disencumber
701 vb.
liberate 746 vb.
unfilial
undutiful 918 adj.
unfilled
unprovided
636 adj.
hungry 859 adj.
unfinished
unfinished 55 adj.
immature 670 adj.
unfit
make useless
641 adj.
useless 641 adj.
inexpedient
643 adj.
imperfect 647 adj.
unskilful 695 adj.
unfit for
unapt 25 adj.
unfitted
unequipped
670 adj.
unfitting
unapt 25 adj.
inexpedient
643 adj.
wrong 914 adj.
undueness 916 n.
unfix
displace 188 vb.
unflagging
strong 162 adj.
unflappable
inexcitable
823 adj.

unflattering
disrespectful
921 adj.
disapproving
924 adj.
unfledged
new 126 adj.
young 130 adj.
immature 670 adj.
unflinching
resolute 599 adj.
courageous
855 adj.
unfold
result 157 vb.
produce 164 vb.
lengthen 203 vb.
straighten 249 vb.
open 263 vb.
extract 304 vb.
evolve 316 vb.
disclose 526 vb.
unforeseeable
uncertain 474 adj.
unreliable 474 adj.
unknown 491 adj.
unforeseen
unexpected
508 adj.
unforgettable
remembered
505 adj.
notable 638 adj.
unforgivable
wrong 914 adj.
heinous 934 adj.
unforgiving
severe 735 adj.
malevolent
898 adj.
unformed
amorphous
244 adj.
immature 670 adj.
unforthcoming
impassive 820 adj.
unsociable 883 adj.
unfortified
unmixed 44 adj.
weak 163 adj.
unfortunate
inopportune
138 adj.
unfortunate
731 adj.
annoying 827 adj.

unfounded
unreal 2 adj.
insubstantial 4 adj.
illogical 477 adj.
erroneous 495 adj.
untrue 543 adj.
unfrequented
secluded 883 adj.
unfriendly
opposing 704 adj.
hostile 881 adj.
unsociable 883 adj.
unkind 898 adj.
unfrock
depose 752 vb.
deprive 786 vb.
disentitle 916 vb.
punish 963 vb.
perform ritual
988 vb.
unfruitful
unproductive
172 adj.
**unfulfilled expecta-
tion**
expectation 507 n.
unfunny
serious 834 adj.
unfurl
lengthen 203 vb.
straighten 249 vb.
evolve 316 vb.
manifest 522 vb.
disclose 526 vb.
unfurnished
unprovided
636 adj.
unequipped
670 adj.
unfussy
plain 573 adj.
ungainly
clumsy 695 adj.
graceless 842 adj.
ungarbled
veracious 540 adj.
ungarnished
uncooked 670 adj.
ungenerous
parsimonious
816 adj.
ungenial
cheerless 834 adj.
ungentlemanly
ill-bred 847 adj.
discourteous
885 adj.

dishonest 930 adj.
ungodly
wicked 934 adj.
irreligious 974 adj.
impious 980 adj.
ungovernable
violent 176 adj.
disobedient
738 adj.
lawless 954 adj.
ungraceful
inelegant 576 adj.
graceless 842 adj.
ungraciousness
conduct 688 n.
rudeness 885 n.
ungrateful
ungrateful 908 adj.
ungrounded
illogical 477 adj.
erroneous 495 adj.
untrue 543 adj.
ungrudging
willing 597 adj.
unguarded
neglected 458 adj.
negligent 458 adj.
vulnerable 661 adj.
unprepared
670 adj.
unguent
unguent 357 n.
ungulate
mammal 365 n.
unhand
not retain 779 vb.
unhappy
inopportune
138 adj.
inexpedient
643 adj.
unfortunate
731 adj.
unhappy 825 adj.
dejected 834 adj.
unharmed
safe 660 adj.
unharness
liberate 746 vb.
unhatched
immature 670 adj.
unhealthy
inexpedient
643 adj.
harmful 645 adj.
unhealthy 651 adj.

insalubrious
   653 adj.
dangerous 661 adj.
unheard
   unknown 491 adj.
   inglorious 867 adj.
   modest 874 adj.
unheated
   cold 380 adj.
unheeded
   neglected 458 adj.
unheeding
   inattentive 456 adj.
unhelpful
   inexpedient
      643 adj.
   unkind 898 adj.
unheralded
   unexpected
      508 adj.
unheroic
   cowardly 856 adj.
   inglorious 867 adj.
unhinge
   derange 63 vb.
   make mad 503 vb.
unhitch
   disunite 46 vb.
unholy
   heathenish 974 adj.
   profane 980 adj.
unhook
   disunite 46 vb.
unhopeful
   dejected 834 adj.
   hopeless 853 adj.
unhouse
   displace 188 vb.
unhurried
   tranquil 266 adj.
   slow 278 adj.
   leisurely 681 adj.
   inexcitable
      823 adj.
unhurt
   undamaged
      646 adj.
unhygienic
   unclean 649 adj.
   insalubrious
      653 adj.
unicameral
   one 88 adj.
unicellular
   one 88 adj.
unicorn
   rara avis 84 n.

animal 365 n.
   heraldry 547 n.
unicycle
   bicycle 274 n.
unidentified
   unrelated 10 adj.
   unknown 491 adj.
unification
   union 45 n.
   combination 50 n.
   unity 88 n.
   association 706 n.
unified
   simple 44 adj.
   combined 50 adj.
uniform
   uniform 16 adj.
   clothing 228 n.
   uniform 228 n.
   badge of rank
      743 n.
uniformity
   uniformity 16 n.
unify
   identify 13 vb.
   join 45 vb.
   combine 50 vb.
unilateral
   unrelated 10 adj.
   one 88 adj.
   lateral 239 adj.
   independent
      744 adj.
unimaginable
   unusual 84 adj.
   impossible 470 adj.
   wonderful 864 adj.
unimaginative
   imitative 20 adj.
   indiscriminating
      464 adj.
   narrow-minded
      481 adj.
   impassive 820 adj.
   thick-skinned
      820 adj.
   dull 840 adj.
unimagined
   unborn 2 adj.
unimpaired
   intact 52 adj.
unimpeachable
   undisputed
      473 adj.
   just 913 adj.
   due 915 adj.
   guiltless 935 adj.

unimportant
   unimportant
      639 adj.
unimposing
   modest 874 adj.
unimpressed
   indifferent 860 adj.
   disapproving
      924 adj.
unimpressive
   modest 874 adj.
uninfluenced
   free 744 adj.
   independent
      744 adj.
uninformative
   reticent 525 adj.
uninformed
   uninstructed
      491 adj.
   unexpecting
      508 adj.
uninhabitable
   empty 190 adj.
uninhabited
   empty 190 adj.
   secluded 883 adj.
uninitiated
   ignorant 491 adj.
   unskilled 695 adj.
uninspired
   feeble 572 adj.
   plain 573 adj.
   prosaic 593 adj.
   apathetic 820 adj.
   impassive 820 adj.
   thick-skinned
      820 adj.
   tedious 838 adj.
uninspiring
   feeble 572 adj.
   dull 840 adj.
unintelligent
   mindless 448 adj.
   unintelligent
      499 adj.
unintelligible
   unintelligible
      517 adj.
unintended
   involuntary
      596 adj.
   unintentional
      618 adj.
unintentional
   unintentional
      618 adj.

uninterested
   incurious 454 adj.
   inattentive 456 adj.
   inactive 679 adj.
   apathetic 820 adj.
   indifferent 860 adj.
uninteresting
   tedious 838 adj.
   dull 840 adj.
uninterrupted
   continuous 71 adj.
   perpetual 115 adj.
uninventive
   dull 840 adj.
uninvestigated
   unknown 491 adj.
uninvited
   unwanted 860 adj.
uninvolved
   unrelated 10 adj.
   incurious 454 adj.
   independent
      744 adj.
   indifferent 860 adj.
union
   agreement 24 n.
   coition 45 n.
   union 45 n.
   coherence 48 n.
   combination 50 n.
   group 74 n.
   unity 88 n.
   business 622 n.
   society 708 n.
   marriage 894 n.
Unionists
   political party
      708 n.
Union Jack
   flag 547 n.
unique
   nonuniform 17 adj.
   dissimilar 19 adj.
   inimitable 21 adj.
   unequal 29 adj.
   special 80 adj.
   unconformable
      84 adj.
   unusual 84 adj.
   one 88 adj.
unisex
   identical 13 adj.
   uniform 16 adj.
   one 88 adj.
unison
   uniformity 16 n.
   agreement 24 n.

melody 410 n.
consensus 488 n.
concord 710 n.
unit
band 74 n.
group 74 n.
unit 88 n.
cabinet 194 n.
person 371 n.
formation 722 n.
unitary
one 88 adj.
unite
simplify 44 vb.
join 45 vb.
combine 50 vb.
bring together
74 vb.
concur 181 vb.
converge 293 vb.
cooperate 706 vb.
united
agreeing 24 adj.
cohesive 48 adj.
combined 50 adj.
united front
coherence 48 n.
association 706 n.
United Reformist
Protestant 976 n.
unity
uniformity 16 n.
agreement 24 n.
unity 88 n.
concord 710 n.
universal
extensive 32 adj.
whole 52 adj.
generality 79 n.
universal 79 adj.
one 88 adj.
cosmic 321 adj.
orthodox 976 adj.
universalism
generality 79 n.
universalize
generalize 79 vb.
universally
greatly 32 vb.
generally 79 adv.
widely 183 adv.
universe
great quantity
32 n.
universe 321 n.
university
academy 539 n.

univocal
one 88 adj.
semantic 514 adj.
unjoined
separate 46 adj.
unjust
bad 645 adj.
unjust 914 adj.
unjustifiable
unjust 914 adj.
wrong 914 adj.
See **unjust**
unwarranted
916 adj.
blameworthy
924 adj.
heinous 934 adj.
unjustified
unwarranted
916 adj.
unkempt
rough 259 adj.
neglected 458 adj.
dirty 649 adj.
unkind
unkind 898 adj.
unkindly
unkind 898 adj.
unkindness
badness 645 n.
inhumanity 898 n.
unknown
number 85 n.
unknown 491 adj.
anonymous
562 adj.
unlace
disunite 46 vb.
unladylike
ill-bred 847 adj.
discourteous
885 adj.
unlatch
disunite 46 vb.
open 263 vb.
unlawful
prohibited 757 adj.
nonobservant
769 adj.
illegal 954 adj.
unleash
disclose 526 vb.
liberate 746 vb.
unless
thus 8 adv.
provided 468 adv.

unlicensed
unwarranted
916 adj.
unlicked cub
undevelopment
670 n.
unlike
different 15 adj.
dissimilar 19 adj.
unlikely
improbable
472 adj.
unlimited
absolute 32 adj.
infinite 107 adj.
intemperate
943 adj.
unlit
unlit 418 adj.
unload
subtract 39 vb.
displace 188 vb.
transpose 272 vb.
empty 300 vb.
extract 304 vb.
disencumber
701 vb.
liberate 746 vb.
take away 786 vb.
unlock
disunite 46 vb.
open 263 vb.
liberate 746 vb.
not retain 779 vb.
unlooked for
unexpected
508 adj.
unloose
disunite 46 vb.
liberate 746 vb.
unloved
hateful 888 adj.
unlucky
inopportune
138 adj.
evil 616 adj.
unfortunate
731 adj.
unhappy 825 adj.
annoying 827 adj.
unmade
unborn 2 adj.
unmalleable
unconformable
84 adj.
rigid 326 adj.

unman
abate 37 vb.
unman 161 vb.
depress 834 vb.
frighten 854 vb.
unmanageable
wilful 602 adj.
difficult 700 adj.
disobedient
738 adj.
unmanifested
latent 523 adj.
unmanly
female 373 adj.
cowardly 856 adj.
unmanned
impotent 161 adj.
fearing 854 adj.
unmannerly
ill-bred 847 adj.
discourteous
885 adj.
unmarked
neglected 458 adj.
undamaged
646 adj.
unmarried
unsociable 883 adj.
unmask
be plain 522 vb.
disclose 526 vb.
unmatched
best 644 adj.
unmeasured
indiscriminate
464 adj.
unmentionable
prohibited 757 adj.
discreditable
867 adj.
impure 951 adj.
unmentionables
underwear 228 n.
unmercenary
disinterested
931 adj.
unmerciful
pitiless 906 adj.
unmerited
unwarranted
916 adj.
unmindful
inattentive 456 adj.
forgetful 506 adj.
unmistakable
visible 443 adj.
certain 473 adj.

intelligible 516 adj.
manifest 522 adj.
unmitigated
consummate
 32 adj.
complete 54 adj.
violent 176 adj.
unmixed
unmixed 44 adj.
unmodified
unmixed 44 adj.
unmoor
separate 46 vb.
navigate 269 vb.
start out 296 vb.
unmotivated
spontaneous
 609 adj.
unmoved
quiescent 266 adj.
apathetic 820 adj.
indifferent 860 adj.
unkind 898 adj.
pitiless 906 adj.
unmoving
still 266 adj.
unmusical
discordant 411 adj.
unnamed
unknown 491 adj.
concealed 525 adj.
anonymous
 562 adj.
unnatural
disagreeing 25 adj.
extraneous 59 adj.
abnormal 84 adj.
unusual 84 adj.
affected 850 adj.
cruel 898 adj.
unnavigable
impracticable
 470 adj.
difficult 700 adj.
unnecessary
superfluous
 637 adj.
unimportant
 639 adj.
unneighbourly
unsociable 883 adj.
unnerve
unman 161 vb.
depress 834 vb.
frighten 854 vb.
unnoticed
invisible 444 adj.

neglected 458 adj.
inglorious 867 adj.
unobjectionable
guiltless 935 adj.
unobservant
inattentive 456 adj.
unobstructed
open 263 adj.
unobtainable
absent 190 adj.
impracticable
 470 adj.
scarce 636 adj.
unobtrusive
modest 874 adj.
unoccupied
empty 190 adj.
nonactive 677 adj.
inactive 679 adj.
leisurely 681 adj.
free 744 adj.
unpossessed
 774 adj.
unofficial
independent
 744 adj.
illegal 954 adj.
lawless 954 adj.
unopened
closed 264 adj.
unorganized
unprepared
 670 adj.
unoriginal
usual 610 adj.
dull 840 adj.
unorthodox
unconformable
 84 adj.
erroneous 495 adj.
unpack
uncover 229 vb.
open 263 vb.
empty 300 vb.
extract 304 vb.
disclose 526 vb.
unpaid
voluntary 597 adj.
unpalatable
unsavoury 391 adj.
unpleasant
 827 adj.
unparalleled
supreme 34 adj.
unusual 84 adj.
best 644 adj.

unpardonable
wrong 914 adj.
heinous 934 adj.
unparliamentary
cursing 899 adj.
unperceived
unknown 491 adj.
unperceiving
blind 439 adj.
unperfumed
odourless 395 adj.
unperson
outcast 883 n.
unpick
disunite 46 vb.
unpleasant
unpleasant
 827 adj.
discourteous
 885 adj.
unplug
disunite 46 vb.
open 263 vb.
liberate 746 vb.
unplumbed
deep 211 adj.
unknown 491 adj.
unpolished
rough 259 adj.
dim 419 adj.
inelegant 576 adj.
immature 670 adj.
plebeian 869 adj.
unpolluted
unmixed 44 adj.
unpopular
unpleasant
 827 adj.
disreputable
 867 adj.
unpossessed
unpossessed
 774 adj.
unpractical
useless 641 adj.
unskilful 695 adj.
unpraiseworthy
blameworthy
 924 adj.
unprecedented
original 21 adj.
first 68 adj.
new 126 adj.
infrequent 140 adj.
unknown 491 adj.
unexpected
 508 adj.

unwonted 611 adj.
wonderful 864 adj.
unpredictable
nonuniform 17 adj.
changeful 152 adj.
uncertain 474 adj.
unreliable 474 adj.
unknown 491 adj.
capricious 604 adj.
unpredicted
unexpected
 508 adj.
unprejudiced
just 913 adj.
unpremeditated
involuntary
 596 adj.
spontaneous
 609 adj.
unintentional
 618 adj.
unprepared
 670 adj.
unprepared
unprepared
 670 adj.
unprepossessing
ugly 842 adj.
unpresentable
ill-bred 847 adj.
unpretentious
veracious 540 adj.
plain 573 adj.
artless 699 adj.
humble 872 adj.
modest 874 adj.
unprincipled
dishonest 930 adj.
wicked 934 adj.
unprintable
prohibited 757 adj.
impure 951 adj.
unprocessed
uncompleted
 726 adj.
unproclaimed
tacit 523 adj.
unproductive
unproductive
 172 adj.
unprofessed
tacit 523 adj.
unprofitable
unproductive
 172 adj.
profitless 641 adj.

inexpedient
643 adj.
unprogressive
nonactive 677 adj.
unpromising
unpromising
853 adj.
unprompted
volitional 595 adj.
voluntary 597 adj.
spontaneous
609 adj.
unpronounceable
inexpressible
517 adj.
unpronounced
tacit 523 adj.
unpropitious
inopportune
138 adj.
opposing 704 adj.
unpromising
853 adj.
unprosperous
unprosperous
731 adj.
unprotected
neglected 458 adj.
vulnerable 661 adj.
unprotesting
humble 872 adj.
unproved
poorly reasoned
477 adj.
unprovided
unprovided
636 adj.
unprovoked
spontaneous
609 adj.
unpublished
tacit 523 adj.
unpunctual
anachronistic
118 adj.
late 136 adj.
ill-timed 138 adj.
unqualified
unmixed 44 adj.
positive 473 adj.
dabbling 491 adj.
unequipped
670 adj.
unskilled 695 adj.
unquestionable
undisputed
473 adj.

true 494 adj.
unquotable
impure 951 adj.
unravel
separate 46 vb.
extract 304 vb.
decipher 520 vb.
unread
neglected 458 adj.
uninstructed
491 adj.
unreal
unreal 2 adj.
imaginary 513 adj.
imaginative
513 adj.
unrealistic
dissimilar 19 adj.
impossible 470 adj.
misjudging
481 adj.
erroneous 495 adj.
unreality
insubstantiality
4 n.
immateriality
320 n.
unreasonable
impossible 470 adj.
illogical 477 adj.
unwise 499 adj.
capricious 604 adj.
wrong 914 adj.
unrecognizable
converted 147 adj.
invisible 444 adj.
unintelligible
517 adj.
disguised 525 adj.
unrecognized
unknown 491 adj.
unreconciled
hostile 881 adj.
impenitent
940 adj.
unredeemed
wicked 934 adj.
unrefined
indiscriminating
464 adj.
inelegant 576 adj.
ill-bred 847 adj.
vulgar 847 adj.
unreformed
impenitent
940 adj.

unrehearsed
spontaneous
609 adj.
unprepared
670 adj.
unrelated
unrelated 10 adj.
unrelenting
obstinate 602 adj.
pitiless 906 adj.
impenitent
940 adj.
unreliable
changeful 152 adj.
weak 163 adj.
unreliable 474 adj.
capricious 604 adj.
undutiful 918 adj.
flattering 925 adj.
dishonest 930 adj.
unrelieved
uniform 16 adj.
unremembered
forgotten 506 adj.
unremitting
continuous 71 adj.
laborious 682 adj.
unrepeated
one 88 adj.
unrepentant
impenitent
940 adj.
unrepresentative
abnormal 84 adj.
unrepresented
absent 190 adj.
unreserved
positive 473 adj.
free 744 adj.
unresisting
inactive 679 adj.
submitting 721 adj.
unresolved
uncertain 474 adj.
irresolute 601 adj.
unresponsive
impassive 820 adj.
indifferent 860 adj.
unrest
motion 265 n.
discontent 829 n.
unrestrained
violent 176 adj.
intemperate
943 adj.
unrestricted
absolute 32 adj.

unrewarding
profitless 641 adj.
unrighteous
wrong 914 adj.
unrightful
unwarranted
916 adj.
unripe
incomplete 55 adj.
young 130 adj.
sour 393 adj.
immature 670 adj.
uncompleted
726 adj.
unrivalled
supreme 34 adj.
unroll
lengthen 203 vb.
straighten 249 vb.
evolve 316 vb.
manifest 522 vb.
disclose 526 vb.
unromantic
true 494 adj.
unruffled
tranquil 266 adj.
impassive 820 adj.
inexcitable
823 adj.
amiable 884 adj.
unruly
disorderly 61 adj.
violent 176 adj.
wilful 602 adj.
disobedient
738 adj.
unsafe
unsafe 661 adj.
unsaid
unknown 491 adj.
tacit 523 adj.
unsalable
profitless 641 adj.
unsanctified
heathenish 974 adj.
profane 980 adj.
unsanctioned
unwarranted
916 adj.
unsated
unprovided
636 adj.
greedy 859 adj.
unsatisfactory
incomplete 55 adj.
disappointing
509 adj.

inexpedient
643 adj.
bad 645 adj.
unpleasant
827 adj.
unsatisfied
greedy 859 adj.
envious 912 adj.
unsavoury
unsavoury 391 adj.
unsay
recant 603 vb.
unscathed
undamaged
646 adj.
unscented
odourless 395 adj.
unscientific
illogical 477 adj.
erroneous 495 adj.
unscramble
simplify 44 vb.
unscrupulous
dishonest 930 adj.
wicked 934 adj.
unseasonable
ill-timed 138 adj.
inexpedient
643 adj.
unseasoned
unmixed 44 adj.
tasteless 387 adj.
immature 670 adj.
unseat
disunite 46 vb.
derange 63 vb.
displace 188 vb.
depose 752 vb.
unseeing
insensible 375 adj.
blind 439 adj.
inattentive 456 adj.
misjudging
481 adj.
impassive 820 adj.
unseemly
unwise 499 adj.
inexpedient
643 adj.
unsightly 842 adj.
wrong 914 adj.
unseen
invisible 444 adj.
unknown 491 adj.
latent 523 adj.
inglorious 867 adj.
modest 874 adj.

secluded 883 adj.
unselective
indiscriminating
464 adj.
unselfconfident
modest 874 adj.
unselfish
benevolent 897 adj.
disinterested
931 adj.
unsentimental
impassive 820 adj.
unsettle
decompose 51 vb.
derange 63 vb.
impress 821 vb.
unsex
unman 161 vb.
unshackle
disencumber
701 vb.
liberate 746 vb.
unshakable
firm 45 adj.
fixed 153 adj.
certain 473 adj.
creedal 485 adj.
resolute 599 adj.
retentive 778 adj.
unshaken
positive 473 adj.
resolute 599 adj.
impassive 820 adj.
unshapely
amorphous
244 adj.
unshaven
hairy 259 adj.
unsheathe
uncover 229 vb.
manifest 522 vb.
unshockable
impassive 820 adj.
unshriven
impenitent
940 adj.
unsightly
unsightly 842 adj.
unsigned
concealed 525 adj.
anonymous
562 adj.
unskilful
unskilful 695 adj.
unskilled
unskilled 695 adj.

unsmiling
serious 834 adj.
sullen 893 adj.
unsociable
unsociable 883 adj.
unsocial
unsociable 883 adj.
unsolicited
voluntary 597 adj.
unsolvable
puzzling 517 adj.
unsophisticated
simple 44 adj.
credulous 487 adj.
artless 699 adj.
ill-bred 847 adj.
unsought
voluntary 597 adj.
unsound
illogical 477 adj.
erroneous 495 adj.
imperfect 647 adj.
unskilled 695 adj.
unsounded
deep 211 adj.
unsound mind
absence of intellect
448 n.
mental disorder
503 n.
unsparing
plentiful 635 adj.
oppressive 735 adj.
severe 735 adj.
liberal 813 adj.
unspeakable
unspeakable
32 adj.
inexpressible
517 adj.
wonderful 864 adj.
unspecified
general 79 adj.
unspiritual
material 319 adj.
sensual 944 adj.
unspoiled
intact 52 adj.
unspoilt
undamaged
646 adj.
unspoken
silent 399 adj.
unknown 491 adj.
tacit 523 adj.
unsporting
dishonest 930 adj.

unsportsmanlike
unjust 914 adj.
dishonest 930 adj.
unstable
fitful 142 adj.
unreliable 474 adj.
foolish 499 adj.
excitable 822 adj.
unstained
honourable
929 adj.
unsteady
fitful 142 adj.
unreliable 474 adj.
irresolute 601 adj.
unsafe 661 adj.
unstick
displace 188 vb.
unstinting
liberal 813 adj.
unstitch
disunite 46 vb.
unstop
open 263 vb.
liberate 746 vb.
unstressed
muted 401 adj.
unstring
disunite 46 vb.
soften 327 vb.
unstructured
amorphous
244 adj.
unstudied
artless 699 adj.
unsubstantial
imaginary 513 adj.
unsubstantiated
erroneous 495 adj.
unsuccessful
unsuccessful
728 adj.
unsuitable
unapt 25 adj.
inexpedient
643 adj.
unsuited
unapt 25 adj.
unsullied
honourable
929 adj.
unsung
tacit 523 adj.
inglorious 867 adj.
unsupported
vulnerable 661 adj.

unsure
  uncertain 474 adj.
unsurpassable
  best 644 adj.
  perfect 646 adj.
unsurpassed
  supreme 34 adj.
unsusceptible
  impassive 820 adj.
unsuspected
  latent 523 adj.
unsuspecting
  credulous 487 adj.
  unexpecting
    508 adj.
unsuspicious
  artless 699 adj.
unsweetened
  sour 393 adj.
unswerving
  straight 249 adj.
  directed 281 adj.
  just 913 adj.
  orthodox 976 adj.
unsymmetrical
  disagreeing 25 adj.
  distorted 246 adj.
unsympathetic
  opposing 704 adj.
  hostile 881 adj.
  unkind 898 adj.
  pitiless 906 adj.
unsystematic
  nonuniform 17 adj.
  fitful 142 adj.
untamed
  disobedient
    738 adj.
  cruel 898 adj.
untarnished
  unmixed 44 adj.
  honourable
    929 adj.
untaught
  uninstructed
    491 adj.
untaxed
  uncharged 812 adj.
unteachable
  unintelligent
    499 adj.
  unwise 499 adj.
untenable
  illogical 477 adj.
untenanted
  empty 190 adj.

unpossessed
    774 adj.
untended
  neglected 458 adj.
untested
  new 126 adj.
  unknown 491 adj.
unthankful
  ungrateful 908 adj.
unthinkable
  impossible 470 adj.
unthinking
  involuntary
    596 adj.
untidy
  nonuniform 17 adj.
  jumble 63 vb.
  agitate 318 vb.
  negligent 458 adj.
  dirty 649 adj.
  make unclean
    649 vb.
untie
  disunite 46 vb.
  deliver 668 vb.
  disencumber
    701 vb.
  liberate 746 vb.
  not retain 779 vb.
until
  while 108 adv.
untilled
  unproductive
    172 adj.
  unprepared
    670 adj.
until now
  before 119 adv.
  until now 121 adv.
untimely
  beforehand
    135 adv.
  ill-timed 138 adj.
  inexpedient
    643 adj.
untitled
  plebeian 869 adj.
untold
  many 104 adj.
  infinite 107 adj.
  unknown 491 adj.
untouchable
  outcast 883 n.
  due 915 adj.
untouched
  intact 52 adj.
  pure 950 adj.

untoward
  ill-timed 138 adj.
  inopportune
    138 adj.
  inexpedient
    643 adj.
  annoying 827 adj.
untraditional
  unwonted 611 adj.
untrained
  uninstructed
    491 adj.
  unhabituated
    611 adj.
  immature 670 adj.
  unprepared
    670 adj.
  unskilled 695 adj.
untranslatable
  inexpressible
    517 adj.
untried
  new 126 adj.
  unknown 491 adj.
untrodden
  new 126 adj.
untroubled
  moderate 177 adj.
  content 828 adj.
untrue
  untrue 543 adj.
  perfidious 930 adj.
untrustworthy
  unreliable 474 adj.
  unsafe 661 adj.
  dishonest 930 adj.
untruth
  error 495 n.
  untruth 543 n.
untruthful
  erroneous 495 adj.
  false 541 adj.
  dishonest 930 adj.
untutored
  uninstructed
    491 adj.
untwist
  evolve 316 vb.
untying
  separation 46 n.
untypical
  dissimilar 19 adj.
  abnormal 84 adj.
unusable
  useless 641 adj.
unused
  remaining 41 adj.

  new 126 adj.
unusual
  nonuniform 17 adj.
  unusual 84 adj.
unutterable
  unspeakable
    32 adj.
  inexpressible
    517 adj.
  wonderful 864 adj.
unvalued
  unwanted 860 adj.
unvarnished
  genuine 494 adj.
  plain 573 adj.
  artless 699 adj.
unvarying
  equal 28 adj.
  unchangeable
    153 adj.
  tedious 838 adj.
unveil
  uncover 229 vb.
  be plain 522 vb.
  disclose 526 vb.
unventilated
  warm 379 adj.
  insalubrious
    653 adj.
unversed
  ignorant 491 adj.
  unskilled 695 adj.
unvoiced
  sounding 398 adj.
  unknown 491 adj.
  tacit 523 adj.
  voiceless 578 adj.
unwanted
  unwanted 860 adj.
unwarrantable
  wrong 914 adj.
  unwarranted
    916 adj.
  illegal 954 adj.
unwarranted
  exorbitant 32 adj.
  illogical 477 adj.
  wrong 914 adj.
  unwarranted
    916 adj.
unwary
  negligent 458 adj.
  rash 857 adj.
unwashed
  dirty 649 adj.

unwavering
unchangeable
153 adj.
resolute 599 adj.
unwelcome
unpleasant
827 adj.
unwanted 860 adj.
hateful 888 adj.
unwell
sick 651 adj.
unwholesome
inexpedient
643 adj.
harmful 645 adj.
insalubrious
653 adj.
impure 951 adj.
unwieldy
unequal 29 adj.
unwieldy 195 adj.
difficult 700 adj.
unwilling
unwilling 598 adj.
unwind
evolve 316 vb.
repose 683 vb.
unwise
unwise 499 adj.
unwish
desire 859 vb.
dislike 861 vb.
unwitting
ignorant 491 adj.
involuntary
596 adj.
unwomanly
male 372 adj.
unwonted
unusual 84 adj.
unwonted 611 adj.
unworkable
powerless 161 adj.
impracticable
470 adj.
useless 641 adj.
unworldly
credulous 487 adj.
ignorant 491 adj.
artless 699 adj.
honourable
929 adj.
innocent 935 adj.
pious 979 adj.
unworthy
inferior 35 adj.

discreditable
867 adj.
dishonest 930 adj.
vicious 934 adj.
wicked 934 adj.
unwrap
uncover 229 vb.
open 263 vb.
extract 304 vb.
disclose 526 vb.
unwritten
tacit 523 adj.
unyielding
strong 162 adj.
resolute 599 adj.
obstinate 602 adj.
difficult 700 adj.
resisting 715 adj.
restraining
747 adj.
unzip
disunite 46 vb.
up
up 308 adv.
up against it
in difficulties
700 adj.
unprosperous
731 adj.
poor 801 adj.
up and about
healthy 650 adj.
up-and-coming
active 678 adj.
prosperous 730 adj.
up and doing
operative 173 adj.
busy 678 adj.
up-and-down
undulatory
251 adj.
upbeat
tempo 410 n.
optimistic 482 adj.
cheerful 833 adj.
upbraid
reproach 924 vb.
up-country
provincial 192 adj.
interiority 224 n.
towards 281 adv.
update
modernize 126 vb.
upend
invert 221 vb.
up for grabs
free 744 adj.

unpossessed
774 adj.
salable 793 adj.
upgrade
promote 285 vb.
make better
654 vb.
repair 656 vb.
dignify 866 vb.
upheaval
disorder 61 n.
revolution 149 n.
elevation 310 n.
uphill
sloping 220 adj.
up 308 adv.
laborious 682 adj.
difficult 700 adj.
with difficulty
700 adv.
uphold
sustain 146 vb.
support 218 vb.
upholstery
lining 227 n.
up in
expert 694 adj.
up in arms
active 678 adj.
opposing 704 adj.
quarrelling
709 adj.
warring 718 adj.
upkeep
subvention 703 n.
upland
space 183 n.
plain 348 n.
uplands
high land 209 n.
uplift
displace 188 vb.
move 265 vb.
elevate 310 vb.
elevation 310 n.
improvement
654 n.
make better
654 vb.
delight 826 vb.
cheer 833 vb.
upmarket
dear 811 adj.
upmost
topmost 213 adj.
upon
meet 295 vb.

up on, be
predominate 34 vb.
be wise 498 vb.
up one's street
fit 24 adj.
upper
superior 34 adj.
excitant 821 n.
upper case
print-type 587 n.
upper-class
genteel 868 adj.
upper class 868 n.
upper classes
upper class 868 n.
upper crust
elite 644 n.
beau monde 848 n.
genteel 868 adj.
upper class 868 n.
uppercut
knock 279 n.
upper hand
advantage 34 n.
influence 178 n.
edge 234 n.
victory 727 n.
Upper House
parliament 692 n.
uppermost
supreme 34 adj.
topmost 213 adj.
uppers
drug-taking 949 n.
uppish
proud 871 adj.
uppity
proud 871 adj.
upright
vertical 215 adj.
verticality 215 n.
written 586 adj.
just 913 adj.
honourable
929 adj.
virtuous 933 adj.
uprising
elevation 310 n.
revolt 738 n.
uproar
turmoil 61 n.
violence 176 n.
loudness 400 n.
fight 716 n.
uproarious
violent 176 adj.
loud 400 adj.

merry 833 adj.

uproot
subtract 39 vb.
exclude 57 vb.
revolutionize
149 vb.
destroy 165 vb.
displace 188 vb.
eject 300 vb.
extract 304 vb.

ups and downs
fluctuation 317 n.

upset
derange 63 vb.
revolution 149 n.
demolish 165 vb.
invert 221 vb.
overturning 221 n.
lowering 311 n.
distract 456 vb.
hinder 702 vb.
impress 821 vb.
trouble 827 vb.
cause discontent
829 vb.
cause dislike
861 vb.
enrage 891 vb.

upshot
event 154 n.
effect 157 n.
judgment 480 n.
completion 725 n.

upside down
contrarily 14 adv.

upsides with
equal 28 adj.

upstage
act 594 vb.
stage set 594 n.
proud 871 adj.
insolent 878 adj.

upstairs
up 308 adv.
intelligence 498 n.

upstanding
vertical 215 adj.

upstart
new 126 adj.
commoner 869 n.
insolent person
878 n.

upsurge
increase 36 n.
ascent 308 n.

upswing
increase 36 n.

elevation 310 n.
improvement
654 n.

up the creek
in difficulties
700 adj.
hindered 702 adj.

up the pole
fertilized 167 adj.
crazy 503 adj.

uptight
excited 821 adj.
nervous 854 adj.
irascible 892 adj.

up to
while 108 adv.
powerful 160 adj.

up-to-date
present 121 adj.
modern 126 adj.

up to one's eyes
busy 678 adj.

up to something
dishonest 930 adj.

up to the mark
sufficient 635 adj.
expert 694 adj.

up-to-the-minute
present 121 adj.
modern 126 adj.
fashionable
848 adj.

upturn
increase 36 n.
invert 221 vb.
ascent 308 n.
improvement
654 n.

upwards
up 308 adv.

upwind
towards 281 adv.

uranium
poison 659 n.

urban blight
housing 192 n.

urbane
cunning 698 adj.
well-bred 848 adj.
sociable 882 adj.
courteous 884 adj.

urbanization
housing 192 n.

urchin
youngster 132 n.

urge
impel 279 vb.

affirm 532 vb.
emphasize 532 vb.
be resolute 599 vb.
incite 612 vb.
hasten 680 vb.
advise 691 vb.
compel 740 vb.
animate 821 vb.
desire 859 n.

urgent
strong 162 adj.
resolute 599 adj.
important 638 adj.
hasty 680 adj.
compelling
740 adj.

urge on
accelerate 277 vb.

Uriah Heep
toady 879 n.

urinal
latrine 649 n.

urinate
excrete 302 vb.

urine
excrement 302 n.

urn
vessel 194 n.
inter 364 vb.
interment 364 n.
pottery 381 n.

urticaria
tingling 378 n.
skin disease 651 n.

us
self 80 n.

usable
useful 640 adj.
used 673 adj.

usage
connotation 514 n.
habit 610 n.
use 673 n.

use
habit 610 n.
instrumentality
628 n.
utility 640 n.
use 673 n.
use 673 vb.

used
used 673 adj.

used to
habituated 610 adj.

useful
useful 640 adj.

useless
useless 641 adj.

user friendly
computerized
86 adj.

use up
disable 161 vb.
dispose of 673 vb.
use 673 vb.
expend 806 vb.

usher
accompany 89 vb.
retainer 742 n.
bridal party 894 n.

usher in
come before 64 vb.
initiate 68 vb.
precede 283 vb.
admit 299 vb.
predict 511 vb.
greet 884 vb.

usual
general 79 adj.
usual 610 adj.

usurer
lender 784 n.

usurp
encroach 306 vb.
take authority
733 vb.
appropriate
786 vb.
deprive 786 vb.

usurper
impostor 545 n.
taker 786 n.
usurper 916 n.

usury
gain 771 n.
lending 784 n.
interest 803 n.

utensil
tool 630 n.

uterus
genitalia 167 n.
insides 224 n.

utilitarian
useful 640 adj.
philanthropic
901 adj.
philanthropist
901 n.
ethical 917 adj.

utility
utility 640 n.

utilize
find useful 640 adj.

use 673 vb.

utmost
limit 236 n.

Utopia
fantasy 513 n.
aspiration 852 n.

utter
consummate
32 adj.
simple 44 adj.
divulge 526 vb.
publish 528 vb.
voice 577 vb.
speak 579 vb.

utterance
voice 577 n.
speech 579 n.

utterly
greatly 32 vb.
completely 54 adv.

uttermost
limit 236 n.

U-turn
change 143 n.
reversion 148 n.
curve 248 n.
return 286 n.
circuition 314 n.
change of mind
603 n.

uxorious
loving 887 adj.

V

vacancy
insubstantiality
4 n.
emptiness 190 n.
job 622 n.
nonownership
774 n.

vacant
insubstantial 4 adj.
empty 190 adj.
unintelligent
499 adj.
free 744 adj.
unpossessed
774 adj.

vacate
go away 190 vb.
relinquish 621 vb.

vacation
absence 190 n.
leisure 681 n.
repose 683 n.

permit 756 n.

vaccinate
implant 303 vb.
doctor 658 vb.
safeguard 660 vb.

vaccine
prophylactic 658 n.

vacillate
change 143 vb.
vary 152 vb.
be uncertain
474 vb.
be irresolute
601 vb.
be capricious
604 vb.

vacuous
insubstantial 4 adj.
empty 190 adj.
mindless 448 adj.

vacuum
nonexistence 2 n.
emptiness 190 n.
rarity 325 n.
clean 648 vb.

vacuum cleaner
cleaning utensil
648 n.

vacuum flask
pot 194 n.

vacuum sealed
invulnerable
660 adj.

vade mecum
guidebook 524 n.

vagabond
wanderer 268 n.
low fellow 869 n.

vagary
foolery 497 n.
ideality 513 n.
whim 604 n.

vagina
genitalia 167 n.
orifice 263 n.

vagrant
changeful 152 adj.
wanderer 268 n.
derelict 779 n.
poor person 801 n.

vague
insubstantial 4 adj.
general 79 adj.
amorphous
244 adj.
shadowy 419 adj.
indistinct 444 adj.

uncertain 474 adj.
reticent 525 adj.
unclear 568 adj.

vain
profitless 641 adj.
useless 641 adj.
unsuccessful
728 adj.
vain 873 adj.

vainglorious
proud 871 adj.
vain 873 adj.

valance
edging 234 n.
trimming 844 n.

vale
valley 255 n.

valediction
valediction 296 n.

valentine
correspondence
588 n.
loved one 887 n.
love token 889 n.
darling 890 n.

valet
clothier 228 n.
clean 648 vb.
minister to 703 vb.
domestic 742 n.
serve 742 vb.

valetudinarian
sick person 651 n.

Valhalla
mythic heaven
971 n.

valiant
courageous
855 adj.

valid
powerful 160 adj.
strong 162 adj.
genuine 494 adj.
useful 640 adj.

validate
stabilize 153 vb.
corroborate 466 vb.
testify 466 vb.
make legal 953 vb.

validity
authenticity 494 n.
legality 953 n.

valise
box 194 n.

Valium (tdmk)
moderator 177 n.
drug 658 n.

valkyrie
soldier 722 n.
mythical being
970 n.

valley
valley 255 n.

valour
courage 855 n.

valuable
valuable 644 adj.

valuables
estate 777 n.

valuation
degree 27 n.
measurement
465 n.
estimate 480 n.

value
degree 27 n.
equivalence 28 n.
appraise 465 vb.
estimate 480 vb.
importance 638 n.
utility 640 n.
goodness 644 n.
account 808 vb.
price 809 n.
price 809 vb.
tax 809 vb.
dearness 811 n.
have taste 846 vb.
honour 866 vb.
love 887 vb.
respect 920 vb.
approve 923 vb.

value-added tax
tax 809 n.

valueless
trivial 639 adj.
profitless 641 adj.

valuer
estimator 480 n.

valve
electronics 160 n.
stopper 264 n.
conduit 351 n.

vamoose
decamp 296 vb.
escape 667 vb.

vamp
play music 413 vb.
improvise 609 vb.
motivator 612 n.
a beauty 841 n.
lover 887 n.
loose woman
952 n.

vampire
taker 786 n.
demon 970 n.

van
beginning 68 n.
lorry 274 n.
preceding 283 n.

vandal
destroyer 168 n.
violent creature
176 n.
troublemaker
663 n.

vandalism
destruction 165 n.
violence 176 n.
waste 634 n.
inhumanity 898 n.

vandalize
waste 634 vb.
impair 655 vb.
make ugly 842 vb.
blemish 845 vb.

vane
weather 340 n.

vanguard
precursor 66 n.
front 237 n.
preceding 283 n.
armed force 722 n.

vanish
pass away 2 vb.
be transient
114 vb.
go away 190 vb.
be unseen 444 vb.
disappear 446 vb.

vanity
insubstantial thing
4 n.
overestimation
482 n.
vanity 873 n.

vanquish
overmaster 727 vb.

vantage
advantage 34 n.

vantage point
view 438 n.

vapid
tasteless 387 adj.
feeble 572 adj.
dull 840 adj.

vaporize
lighten 323 vb.
vaporize 338 vb.

vaporizer
vaporizer 338 n.
air 340 n.

vaporous
gaseous 336 adj.
vaporific 338 adj.
imaginary 513 adj.

vapour
emit 300 vb.
gas 336 n.
cloud 355 n.
fantasy 513 n.
boast 877 vb.

vapours
melancholy 834 n.

variable
circumstantial
8 adj.
nonuniform 17 adj.
unequal 29 adj.
number 85 n.
fitful 142 adj.
changeable
143 adj.
changeful 152 adj.
unreliable 474 adj.
irresolute 601 adj.
capricious 604 adj.

variance
difference 15 n.
disagreement 25 n.
dissension 709 n.

variant
variant 15 n.
changeful 152 adj.

variation
contrariety 14 n.
difference 15 n.
dissimilarity 19 n.
change 143 n.
musical piece
412 n.

varicose veins
cardiovascular dis-
ease 651 n.

variegated
variegated 437 adj.

variety
difference 15 n.
nonuniformity
17 n.
dissimilarity 19 n.
disagreement 25 n.
medley 43 n.
sort 77 n.
multiformity 82 n.

changeableness
152 n.
variegation 437 n.
stage show 594 n.

variform
multiform 82 adj.

variola
infection 651 n.

variorum
commentary 520 n.

various
different 15 adj.
dissimilar 19 adj.
many 104 adj.

varlet
low fellow 869 n.

varnish
coat 226 vb.
facing 226 n.
smooth 258 vb.
smoother 258 n.
smoothness 258 n.
resin 357 n.
sophisticate
477 vb.
untruth 543 n.
exaggerate 546 vb.
plead 614 vb.
cleanser 648 n.
preserve 666 vb.
decorate 844 vb.
ostentation 875 n.
extenuate 927 vb.
justify 927 vb.

vary
differ 15 vb.
be unequal 29 vb.
modify 143 vb.
vary 152 vb.

vascular disease
cardiovascular dis-
ease 651 n.

vase
bowl 194 n.
vessel 194 n.

vasectomy
contraception
172 n.
surgery 658 n.

vassal
dependant 742 n.
subject 742 n.
subject 745 adj.

vast
enormous 32 adj.
spacious 183 adj.
huge 195 adj.

large 195 adj.

VAT
tax 809 n.

vat
vat 194 n.

Vatican
church office 985 n.
the church 985 n.
parsonage 986 n.

vaudeville
stage show 594 n.

vault
cellar 194 n.
depth 211 n.
roof 226 n.
curve 248 n.
dome 253 n.
ascend 308 vb.
ascent 308 n.
leap 312 n.
leap 312 vb.
tomb 364 n.
hiding-place 527 n.
storage 632 n.
church interior
990 n.

vaunt
boast 877 vb.

VCR
broadcasting
531 n.
recording instru-
ment 549 n.

VD
venereal disease
651 n.

VDU
data processing
86 n.

veal
meat 301 n.

vector
number 85 n.
infection 651 n.

veer
change 143 vb.
vary 152 vb.
navigate 269 vb.
deviate 282 vb.
deviation 282 n.
blow 352 vb.

veer round
turn back 286 vb.
change one's mind
603 vb.

vegan
eater 301 n.

feeding 301 adj.
abstainer 942 n.
temperate 942 adj.

vegetable
unfeeling person
820 n.

vegetable-like
impassive 820 adj.
inexcitable
823 adj.

vegetarian
eater 301 n.
feeding 301 adj.
abstainer 942 n.
temperate 942 adj.

vegetate
pass time 108 vb.
be quiescent
266 vb.
vegetate 366 vb.
be inactive 679 vb.
be insensitive
820 vb.

vegetation
inertness 175 n.
vegetable life
366 n.
inaction 677 n.
moral insensibility
820 n.

veggie
eater 301 n.

vehement
vigorous 174 adj.
violent 176 adj.
assertive 532 adj.
forceful 571 adj.
fervent 818 adj.

vehicle
vehicle 274 n.
instrument 628 n.

veil
cover 226 vb.
shade 226 n.
headgear 228 n.
darken 418 vb.
dim 419 vb.
screen 421 n.
screen 421 vb.
be unseen 444 vb.
invisibility 444 n.
conceal 525 vb.
disguise 527 n.
sham 542 n.
vocation 622 n.

veil, the
celibacy 895 n.

veiled
uncertain 474 adj.
unknown 491 adj.
occult 523 adj.
concealed 525 adj.
secluded 883 adj.
monastic 986 adj.

vein
state 7 n.
small quantity
33 n.
tincture 43 n.
tendency 179 n.
narrowness 206 n.
layer 207 n.
filament 208 n.
tube 263 n.
conduit 351 n.
variegate 437 vb.
style 566 n.
diffuseness 570 n.
store 632 n.
affections 817 n.

veld
space 183 n.
plain 348 n.

vellum
stationery 586 n.
bookbinding 589 n.

velocity
velocity 277 n.

velour
textile 222 n.
smoothness 258 n.

velvet
textile 222 n.
smoothness 258 n.
softness 327 n.
palmy days 730 n.

velveteen
textile 222 n.

velvet glove
conduct 688 n.
leniency 736 n.

velvety
smooth 258 adj.
soft 327 adj.

venal
venal 930 adj.

venality
improbity 930 n.

vend
trade 791 vb.
sell 793 vb.

vendetta
quarrel 709 n.
enmity 881 n.

revenge 910 n.

vendor
seller 793 n.

veneer
layer 207 n.
shallowness 212 n.
coat 226 n.
covering 226 n.
facing 226 n.
appearance 445 n.
disguise 527 n.
sham 542 n.
be ostentatious
875 vb.
ostentation 875 n.

venerable
great 32 adj.
olden 127 adj.
ageing 131 adj.

venerate
respect 920 vb.
worship 981 vb.

venereal
conjunctive 45 adj.
diseased 651 adj.
sensual 944 adj.

venereal disease
venereal disease
651 n.

venetian blind
shade 226 n.
curtain 421 n.

vengeance
revenge 910 n.

venial
guiltless 935 adj.

venial sin
vice 934 n.
guilty act 936 n.

venison
meat 301 n.

venogram
diagnostic 658 n.

venom
poison 659 n.
malevolence 898 n.

venomous
toxic 653 adj.
hostile 881 adj.
malevolent
898 adj.
disapproving
924 adj.

vent
orifice 263 n.
outlet 298 n.
air pipe 353 n.

divulge 526 vb.
means of escape
667 n.

ventilate
aerate 340 vb.
blow 352 vb.
divulge 526 vb.
publish 528 vb.
dissertate 591 vb.
purify 648 vb.
make sanitary
652 vb.
refresh 685 vb.

ventilation
ventilation 352 n.
publicity 528 n.
cleansing 648 n.

ventilator
air 340 n.
ventilation 352 n.

vent one's spleen
be angry 891 vb.
resent 891 vb.

ventricle
compartment
194 n.

ventriloquist
imitator 20 n.
entertainer 594 n.

venture
be tentative 461 vb.
gamble 618 vb.
gambling 618 n.
business 622 n.
danger 661 n.
attempt 671 n.
attempt 671 vb.
undertaking 672 n.
speculate 791 vb.
be courageous
855 vb.

venturesome
dangerous 661 adj.
enterprising
672 adj.
courageous
855 adj.
rash 857 adj.

venue
focus 76 n.
locality 187 n.

Venus
planet 321 n.
luminary 420 n.
a beauty 841 n.
mythic deity 966 n.

Olympian deity
967 n.
veracity
veracity 540 n.
verandah
lobby 194 n.
verb
part of speech
564 n.
verbal
testimony 466 n.
semantic 514 adj.
informative
524 adj.
verbal 559 adj.
grammatical
564 adj.
speaking 579 adj.
verbalize
form 243 vb.
phrase 563 vb.
voice 577 vb.
verballed, be
condemn 961 vb.
verbatim
accurate 494 adj.
true 494 adj.
truly 494 adv.
verbally 559 adv.
verbiage
empty talk 515 n.
word 559 n.
imperspicuity
568 n.
diffuseness 570 n.
verbose
verbal 559 adj.
diffuse 570 adj.
loquacious 581 adj.
verboten
prohibited 757 adj.
illegal 954 adj.
verdant
prolific 171 adj.
green 434 adj.
verdict
judgment 480 n.
legal trial 959 n.
verdigris
greenness 434 n.
verdure
foliage 366 n.
grass 366 n.
greenness 434 n.
verge
extremity 69 n.
tend 179 vb.

nearness 200 n.
edge 234 n.
limit 236 n.
road 624 n.
badge of rule
743 n.
verger
officer 741 n.
servant 742 n.
church officer
986 n.
verification
experiment 461 n.
evidence 466 n.
certainty 473 n.
demonstration
478 n.
assent 488 n.
title deed 767 n.
verify
corroborate 466 vb.
make certain
473 vb.
demonstrate
478 V.
give security
767 vb.
verisimilitude
probability 471 n.
accuracy 494 n.
truth 494 n.
veracity 540 n.
verity
truth 494 n.
vermicelli
dish 301 n.
vermicular
animal 365 adj.
vermiform
snaky 251 adj.
vermifuge
antidote 658 n.
vermilion
red 431 adj.
red pigment 431 n.
vermin
insect 365 n.
dirt 649 n.
rabble 869 n.
cad 938 n.
vernacular
native 191 adj.
provincial 192 adj.
language 557 n.
linguistic 557 adj.
dialect 560 adj.
dialectal 560 adj.

plainness 573 n.
vernier
gauge 465 n.
verruca
swelling 253 n.
skin disease 651 n.
versatile
multiform 82 adj.
changeful 152 adj.
useful 640 adj.
skilful 694 adj.
verse
subdivision 53 n.
poetry 593 n.
verse form 593 n.
versed in
knowing 490 adj.
expert 694 adj.
versification
poem 593 n.
poetry 593 n.
See **prosody**
prosody 593 n.
version
sort 77 n.
speciality 80 n.
transformation
143 n.
translation 520 n.
description 590 n.
See **narrative**
verso
rear 238 n.
sinistrality 242 n.
edition 589 n.
versus
towards 281 adv.
in opposition
704 adv.
vertebrae
pillar 218 n.
centre 225 n.
vertebral
central 225 adj.
back 238 adj.
vertebral column
pillar 218 n.
vertebrate
animal 365 adj.
animal 365 n.
vertex
extremity 69 n.
vertex 213 n.
vertical
vertical 215 adj.
vertical takeoff
aeronautics 271 n.

vertigo
weakness 163 n.
illness 651 n.
verve
vigorousness 174 n.
vigour 571 n.
moral sensibility
819 n.
very
greatly 32 vb.
very moment, the
instant 116 n.
very one, the
identity 13 n.
very thing, the
fitness 24 n.
vesicle
sphere 252 n.
swelling 253 n.
vespers
evening 129 n.
church service
988 n.
vessel
vessel 194 n.
ship 275 n.
vest
jacket 228 n.
underwear 228 n.
make legal 953 vb.
vestal
pure 950 adj.
vested
due 915 adj.
vested in, be
belong 773 vb.
vested interest
influence 178 n.
master 741 n.
dueness 915 n.
vestibule
lobby 194 n.
access 624 n.
vestige
small quantity
33 n.
remainder 41 n.
trace 548 n.
vestigial
remaining 41 adj.
vestments
clothing 228 n.
uniform 228 n.
vestments 989 n.
vestry
council 692 n.
synod 985 n.

church interior
990 n.
vet
animal husbandry
369 n.
doctor 658 n.
veteran
olden 127 adj.
old man 133 n.
matured 669 adj.
expert 694 adj.
expert 696 n.
soldier 722 n.
veterinary surgeon
animal husbandry
369 n.
doctor 658 n.
veto
restrain 747 vb.
restraint 747 n.
prohibit 757 vb.
prohibition 757 n.
vetting
protection 660 n.
vex
torment 827 vb.
enrage 891 vb.
vexation
difficulty 700 n.
sorrow 825 n.
annoyance 827 n.
anger 891 n.
vexed
unhappy 825 adj.
discontented
829 adj.
angry 891 adj.
vexed question
question 459 n.
enigma 530 n.
VHF
radiation 417 n.
via
towards 281 adv.
via 624 adv.
viable
alive 360 adj.
possible 469 adj.
viaduct
crossing 222 n.
bridge 624 n.
vial
vessel 194 n.
viands
food 301 n.
vibes
gong 414 n.

feeling 818 n.
vibrant
vigorous 174 adj.
resonant 404 adj.
feeling 818 adj.
vibrate
vary 152 vb.
oscillate 317 vb.
be agitated 318 vb.
roll 403 vb.
resound 404 vb.
show feeling
818 vb.
vibrations
sound 398 n.
feeling 818 n.
vibrato
roll 403 n.
musical note
410 n.
adagio 412 adv.
vibrator
oscillation 317 n.
vicar
deputy 755 n.
church title 986 n.
pastor 986 n.
vicarage
house 192 n.
parsonage 986 n.
vicarious
substituted 150 adj.
vice
badness 645 n.
pincers 778 n.
wrong 914 n.
vice 934 n.
wickedness 934 n.
unchastity 951 n.
vice-captain
deputy 755 n.
vice-like
retentive 778 adj.
vice-president
deputy 755 n.
viceroy
governor 741 n.
deputy 755 n.
vice versa
correlatively
12 adv.
contrarily 14 adv.
inversely 221 adv.
against 240 adv.
vicinity
locality 187 n.
nearness 200 n.

surroundings
230 n.
vicious
furious 176 adj.
bad 645 adj.
malevolent
898 adj.
wrong 914 adj.
vicious 934 adj.
vicious circle
obstacle 702 n.
vicissitude
changeable thing
152 n.
adversity 731 n.
victim
corpse 363 n.
dupe 544 n.
chase 619 n.
unlucky person
731 n.
sufferer 825 n.
laughingstock
851 n.
accused person
928 n.
victimize
fool 542 vb.
ill-treat 645 vb.
oppress 735 vb.
be malevolent
898 vb.
punish 963 vb.
victor
victor 727 n.
Victorian
antiquated 127 adj.
architectural
192 adj.
prude 950 n.
prudish 950 adj.
victorious
superior 34 adj.
strong 162 adj.
successful 727 adj.
victory
victory 727 n.
victuals
food 301 n.
vicuna
fibre 208 n.
textile 222 n.
video
spectacle 445 n.
broadcasting
531 n.
record 548 vb.

amusement 837 n.
videocassette
broadcasting
531 n.
**videocassette re-
corder**
broadcasting
531 n.
*recording instru-
ment* 549 n.
videorecorder
broadcasting
531 n.
videotape
broadcasting
531 n.
record 548 vb.
videotape recorder
*recording instru-
ment* 549 n.
view
inspection 438 n.
scan 438 vb.
see 438 vb.
view 438 n.
watch 441 vb.
appearance 445 n.
estimate 480 n.
opinion 485 n.
intention 617 n.
beauty 841 n.
viewdata
data processing
86 n.
information 524 n.
viewer
spectator 441 n.
broadcasting
531 n.
viewfinder
telescope 442 n.
vie with
oppose 704 vb.
contend 716 vb.
viewpoint
view 438 n.
opinion 485 n.
vigil
precursor 66 n.
surveillance 457 n.
church service
988 n.
vigilance
attention 455 n.
carefulness 457 n.
surveillance 457 n.
sagacity 498 n.

VIG

restlessness 678 n.
vigilant
  seeing 438 adj.
  vigilant 457 adj.
vigilante
  doorkeeper 264 n.
  protector 660 n.
  defender 713 n.
  keeper 749 n.
vigils
  prayers 981 n.
vignette
  picture 553 n.
  description 590 n.
  acting 594 n.
vigorous
  strong 162 adj.
  vigorous 174 adj.
  healthy 650 adj.
vigour
  energy 160 n.
  vitality 162 n.
  vigorousness 174 n.
  vigour 571 n.
  resolution 599 n.
  warm feeling
    818 n.
vile
  bad 645 adj.
  heinous 934 adj.
vilify
  shame 867 vb.
  criticize 924 vb.
  defame 926 vb.
villa
  house 192 n.
village
  district 184 n.
  housing 192 n.
village green
  focus 76 n.
  meeting place
    192 n.
  pleasure ground
    837 n.
village idiot
  country-dweller
    869 n.
villager
  dweller 191 n.
  native 191 n.
villain
  evildoer 904 n.
  offender 904 n.
  bad person 938 n.
villainous
  bad 645 adj.

VIN

vicious 934 adj.
villainy
  improbity 930 n.
  wickedness 934 n.
villein
  farmer 370 n.
  slave 742 n.
  commoner 869 n.
vim
  vitality 162 n.
  vigorousness 174 n.
  vigour 571 n.
vinaigrette
  sauce 389 n.
vinculum
  bond 47 n.
vindicate
  vindicate 927 vb.
vindictive
  resentful 891 adj.
  malevolent
    898 adj.
  punitive 963 adj.
vine
  plant 366 n.
vinegar
  sourness 393 n.
  painfulness 827 n.
  sullenness 893 n.
vinegary
  sour 393 adj.
  irascible 892 adj.
  sullen 893 adj.
vineyard
  farm 370 n.
vingt-et-un
  card game 837 n.
viniculture
  agriculture 370 n.
vino
  wine 301 n.
vinous
  intoxicating
    949 adj.
vintage
  date 108 n.
  olden 127 adj.
  product 164 n.
  agriculture 370 n.
  tasty 386 adj.
  store 632 n.
  excellent 644 adj.
  goodness 644 n.
vintage car
  automobile 274 n.
vinyl
  floor-cover 226 n.

VIR

viol
  viol 414 n.
violate
  unite with 45 vb.
  force 176 vb.
  ill-treat 645 vb.
  misuse 675 vb.
  disobey 738 vb.
  not observe 769 vb.
  debauch 951 vb.
  be impious 980 vb.
violation
  misuse 675 n.
  nonobservance
    769 n.
  undueness 916 n.
  undutifulness
    918 n.
  rape 951 n.
  impiety 980 n.
violent
  great 32 adj.
  violent 176 adj.
  excited 821 adj.
  angry 891 adj.
  lawless 954 adj.
violet
  purple 436 adj.
  purpleness 436 n.
  humility 872 n.
violin
  viol 414 n.
VIP
  person 371 n.
  bigwig 638 n.
  autocrat 741 n.
  person of repute
    866 n.
viper
  reptile 365 n.
  bane 659 n.
virago
  female 373 n.
virgin
  intact 52 adj.
  new 126 adj.
  youngster 132 n.
  female 373 n.
  unknown 491 adj.
  unprepared
    670 adj.
  pure 950 adj.
  virgin 950 n.
virginal
  new 126 adj.
  young 130 adj.
  virtuous 933 adj.

VIS

pure 950 adj.
virginity
  unproductiveness
    172 n.
  celibacy 895 n.
  purity 950 n.
virile
  grown-up 134 adj.
  manly 162 adj.
  vigorous 174 adj.
  male 372 adj.
virility
  adultness 134 n.
  vitality 162 n.
  vigorousness 174 n.
  male 372 n.
virtually
  almost 33 adv.
  on the whole
    52 adv.
virtue
  essential part 5 n.
  ability 160 n.
  utility 640 n.
  goodness 644 n.
  virtue 933 n.
virtuosity
  goodness 644 n.
  skill 694 n.
  good taste 846 n.
virtuoso
  superior 34 n.
  musician 413 n.
  proficient person
    696 n.
virtuous
  virtuous 933 adj.
virulent
  keen 174 adj.
  hostile 881 adj.
  resentful 891 adj.
virus
  disease 651 n.
  illness 651 n.
  infection 651 n.
  poison 659 n.
visa
  credential 466 n.
  assent 488 n.
  permit 756 n.
visage
  face 237 n.
  feature 445 n.
vis-à-vis
  concerning 9 adv.
  against 240 adv.
  opposite 240 adj.

viscera
insides 224 n.
viscid
tough 329 adj.
viscid 354 adj.
viscosity
fluidity 335 n.
viscidity 354 n.
viscount
person of rank
868 n.
viscountess
person of rank
868 n.
viscous
cohesive 48 adj.
blood 335 adj.
viscid 354 adj.
visible
visible 443 adj.
vision
insubstantial thing
4 n.
vision 438 n.
visual fallacy
440 n.
appearance 445 n.
spectacle 445 n.
foresight 510 n.
fantasy 513 n.
manifestation
522 n.
objective 617 n.
a beauty 841 n.
aspiration 852 n.
visionary
unreal 2 adj.
insubstantial 4 adj.
misjudging
481 adj.
imaginary 513 adj.
imaginative
513 adj.
visionary 513 n.
promising 852 adj.
philanthropic
901 adj.
worshipper 981 n.
visit
presence 189 n.
land travel 267 n.
travel 267 vb.
social round 882 n.
visit 882 vb.
do good 897 adj.
haunt 970 vb.

visitation
blight 659 n.
adversity 731 n.
severity 735 n.
suffering 825 n.
punishment 963 n.
visitor
resident 191 n.
traveller 268 n.
arrival 295 n.
incomer 297 n.
sociable person
882 n.
visor
shade 226 n.
screen 421 n.
disguise 527 n.
armour 713 n.
vista
open space 263 n.
view 438 n.
visual
seeing 438 adj.
appearing 445 adj.
visual aid
visibility 443 n.
image 551 n.
visual display unit
data processing
86 n.
visualize
see 438 vb.
imagine 513 vb.
visually challenged
blind 439 adj.
vital
alive 360 adj.
necessary 596 adj.
required 627 adj.
important 638 adj.
lively 819 adj.
cheerful 833 adj.
vitality
vitality 162 n.
life 360 n.
vigour 571 n.
restlessness 678 n.
cheerfulness 833 n.
vitalize
vitalize 360 vb.
vitals
insides 224 n.
vital statistics
statistics 86 n.
beauty 841 n.

vitamins
dieting 301 n.
See **food content**
food content 301 n.
viticulture
agriculture 370 n.
vitreous
hard 326 adj.
vitrify
harden 326 vb.
vitriol
burning 381 n.
poison 659 n.
vitriolic
paining 827 adj.
cursing 899 adj.
vituperate
curse 899 vb.
viva
exam 459 n.
vivacious
forceful 571 adj.
active 678 adj.
feeling 818 adj.
lively 819 adj.
cheerful 833 adj.
vivaciousness
moral sensibility
819 n.
vivacity
vigour 571 n.
restlessness 678 n.
moral sensibility
819 n.
cheerfulness 833 n.
vivarium
zoo 369 n.
viva voce examination
exam 459 n.
vivid
lifelike 18 adj.
vigorous 174 adj.
luminous 417 adj.
florid 425 adj.
obvious 443 adj.
expressive 516 adj.
forceful 571 adj.
descriptive 590 adj.
vivify
vitalize 360 vb.
viviparous animal
mammal 365 n.
vivisection
killing 362 n.
pain 377 n.

vixen
mammal 365 n.
female animal
373 n.
viz.
namely 80 adv.
in plain words
520 adv.
vocabulary
word list 87 n.
dictionary 559 n.
style 566 n.
vocal
musical 412 adj.
speaking 579 adj.
vocalist
vocalist 413 n.
vocation
vocation 622 n.
vociferousness
cry 408 n.
vodka
alcoholic drink
301 n.
vogue
practice 610 n.
fashion 848 n.
repute 866 n.
voguish
fashionable
848 adj.
voice
publish 528 vb.
affirm 532 vb.
affirmation 532 n.
phrase 563 vb.
grammar 564 n.
voice 577 n.
voice 577 vb.
vote 605 n.
voiced
sounding 398 adj.
voiceless
sounding 398 adj.
voiceless 578 adj.
voice-over
sound 398 n.
cinema 445 n.
void
insubstantial 4 adj.
insubstantiality
4 n.
emptiness 190 n.
empty 190 adj.
gap 201 n.
empty 300 vb.
extract 304 vb.

universe 321 n.
rare 325 adj.
abrogate 752 vb.
voidance
voidance 300 n.
voile
textile 222 n.
volatile
transient 114 adj.
changeful 152 adj.
light 323 adj.
gaseous 336 adj.
vaporific 338 adj.
capricious 604 adj.
excitable 822 adj.
vol-au-vent
hors-d'oeuvres
301 n.
volcanic
violent 176 adj.
fiery 379 adj.
excitable 822 adj.
volcano
outbreak 176 n.
fire 379 n.
furnace 383 n.
pitfall 663 n.
vole
mammal 365 n.
volition
will 595 n.
volley
crowd 74 n.
strike 279 vb.
recoil 280 n.
propel 287 vb.
propulsion 287 n.
bang 402 n.
bombardment
712 n.
volleyball
ball game 837 n.
volt
electronics 160 n.
voltage
electronics 160 n.
volte face
reversion 148 n.
return 286 n.
change of mind
603 n.
perfidy 930 n.
voluble
loquacious 581 adj.
volume
quantity 26 n.
greatness 32 n.

subdivision 53 n.
measure 183 n.
space 183 n.
size 195 n.
metrology 465 n.
book 589 n.
voluminous
great 32 adj.
spacious 183 adj.
large 195 adj.
diffuse 570 adj.
voluntarily
willingly 597 adv.
voluntary
musical piece
412 n.
voluntary 597 adj.
voluntary work
voluntary work
597 n.
volunteer
will 595 vb.
be willing 597 vb.
volunteer 597 n.
undertake 672 vb.
soldier 722 n.
offer oneself
759 vb.
voluptuous
sensuous 376 adj.
pleasurable
826 adj.
sensual 944 adj.
vomit
voidance 300 n.
vomit 300 vb.
dislike 861 n.
voodoo
sorcery 983 n.
voracious
greedy 859 adj.
gluttonous 947 adj.
vortex
vortex 315 n.
pitfall 663 n.
votary
lover 887 n.
pietist 979 n.
worshipper 981 n.
vote
vote 605 n.
vote 605 vb.
credit 802 vb.
vote for
endorse 488 vb.
vote of confidence
vote 605 n.

vote of thanks
oration 579 n.
thanks 907 n.
voter
native 191 n.
vote 605 n.
vote with one's feet
cease 145 vb.
vote 605 vb.
legal 953 adj.
voting
list 87 n.
judgment 480 n.
voting paper
electorate 605 n.
voucher
credential 466 n.
record 548 n.
title deed 767 n.
receipt 807 n.
vouch for
promise 764 vb.
give security
767 vb.
vouchsafe
permit 756 vb.
give 781 vb.
vow
affirm 532 vb.
promise 764 n.
promise 764 vb.
offer worship
981 vb.
vowel
speech sound
398 n.
voice 577 n.
vox populi
judgment 480 n.
vote 605 n.
government 733 n.
tribunal 956 n.
voyage
land travel 267 n.
voyage 269 vb.
water travel 269 n.
voyeur
spectator 441 n.
libertine 952 n.
voyeurism
inspection 438 n.
curiosity 453 n.
vroom
move fast 277 vb.
spurt 277 n.
roll 403 vb.

V-sign
gesture 547 n.
sauciness 878 n.
indignity 921 n.
VTR
recording instru-
ment 549 n.
vulcanized
tough 329 adj.
vulgar
general 79 adj.
linguistic 557 adj.
not nice 645 adj.
vulgar 847 adj.
impure 951 adj.
vulgar fraction
numerical element
85 n.
vulgarity
indiscrimination
464 n.
inelegance 576 n.
wit 839 n.
bad taste 847 n.
ill-breeding 847 n.
scurrility 899 n.
vulnerable
weak 163 adj.
vulnerable 661 adj.
vulpine
animal 365 adj.
vulture
eater 301 n.
bird 365 n.
taker 786 n.
glutton 947 n.
vulva
genitalia 167 n.

W

wacky
crazy 503 adj.
wad
piece 53 n.
bunch 74 n.
line 227 vb.
ammunition 723 n.
paper money
797 n.
wadding
contents 193 n.
lining 227 n.
stopper 264 n.
softness 327 n.

waddle
be in motion
265 vb.
gait 265 n.
walk 267 vb.
move slowly
278 vb.
oscillate 317 vb.

wade
walk 267 vb.
swim 269 vb.

waders
footwear 228 n.

wadi
stream 350 n.
conduit 351 n.

wads
great quantity
32 n.
funds 797 n.
wealth 800 n.

wafer
adhesive 47 n.
strip 208 n.
cereals 301 n.

wafer-thin
narrow 206 adj.

waffle
cereals 301 n.
mean nothing
515 vb.
be equivocal
518 vb.
be diffuse 570 vb.
diffuseness 570 n.
be loquacious
581 vb.
chatter 581 n.

waft
carry 273 vb.
be light 323 vb.
blow 352 vb.
breeze 352 n.

wag
brandish 317 vb.
fluctuation 317 n.
oscillate 317 vb.
agitate 318 vb.
be agitated 318 vb.
humorist 839 n.

wage
do 676 vb.
earnings 771 n.
reward 962 n.

wager
uncertainty 474 n.
gamble 618 vb.

gambling 618 n.
contend 716 vb.
contest 716 n.

wages
pay 804 n.
receipt 807 n.
reward 962 n.

waggish
witty 839 adj.

waggle
brandish 317 vb.
oscillate 317 vb.
agitate 318 vb.
be agitated 318 vb.

waggon
cart 274 n.
train 274 n.

wagtail
bird 365 n.

waif
wanderer 268 n.
derelict 779 n.

wail
cry 408 n.
cry 408 vb.
ululate 409 vb.
be discontented
829 vb.
lament 836 vb.
lamentation 836 n.
weep 836 vb.

wain
cart 274 n.

wainscotting
lining 227 n.

waistband
belt 228 n.

waistcoat
jacket 228 n.

waistline
centrality 225 n.
garment 228 n.
See **belt**

wait
continue 108 vb.
wait 136 vb.
go on 146 vb.

wait and see
wait 136 vb.
be tentative 461 vb.
be uncertain
474 vb.
not act 677 vb.

waiter
servant 742 n.

waiting
future 124 adj.

traffic control
305 n.
dubiety 474 n.
expectant 507 adj.
expectation 507 n.

waiting game
caution 858 n.

waiting list
list 87 n.
record 548 n.

waiting room
lobby 194 n.

wait on
result 157 vb.
follow 284 vb.
minister to 703 vb.
court 889 vb.

waitress
servant 742 n.

waits
choir 413 n.

waive
relinquish 621 vb.
not retain 779 vb.

waiver
resignation 753 n.
loss of right 916 n.

wake
adjunct 40 n.
retinue 67 n.
continuity 71 n.
effect 157 n.
rear 238 n.
water travel 269 n.
follower 284 n.
eddy 350 n.
obsequies 364 n.
trace 548 n.
excite 821 vb.
lament 836 n.
condolence 905 n.

wakeful
attentive 455 adj.
active 678 adj.

wake up
have feeling
374 vb.

walk
park 192 n.
gait 265 n.
pedestrianism
267 n.
walk 267 vb.
path 624 n.
conduct 688 n.
haunt 970 vb.

walkabout
pedestrianism
267 n.

walker
pedestrian 268 n.
traveller 268 n.

walkie-talkie
hearing aid 415 n.
telecommunication
531 n.

walking
motion 265 n.
land travel 267 n.
pedestrianism
267 n.

walk it
win 727 vb.

Walkman (tdmk)
gramophone 414 n.

walk off with
win 727 vb.
steal 788 vb.

walk of life
state 7 n.
vocation 622 n.
conduct 688 n.
duty 917 n.

walk out
cease 145 vb.
decamp 296 vb.
relinquish 621 vb.
resist 715 vb.
deprecate 762 vb.
fail in duty 918 vb.

walkout
stop 145 vb.
strike 145 n.
departure 296 n.
egress 298 n.
dissent 489 n.
relinquishment
621 n.

walk out on
change one's mind
603 vb.

walk out with
accompany 89 vb.
court 889 vb.

walkover
easy thing 701 n.
victory 727 n.

wall
exclusion 57 n.
support 218 n.
partition 231 n.
barrier 235 n.
enclose 235 vb.

fence 235 n.
screen 421 n.
obstacle 702 n.
defences 713 n.
fortification 713 n.
wallaby
mammal 365 n.
wallet
case 194 n.
treasury 799 n.
wall-eyed
dim-sighted
440 adj.
wallflower
rejection 607 n.
wall in
cover 226 vb.
wallop
strike 279 vb.
spank 963 vb.
wallow
be agitated 318 vb.
be pleased 824 vb.
be intemperate
943 vb.
wallow in
enjoy 376 vb.
wallpaper
covering 226 n.
line 227 n.
lining 227 n.
wall-to-wall
floor-cover 226 n.
wall up
cover 226 vb.
enclose 235 vb.
kill 362 vb.
obstruct 702 vb.
imprison 747 vb.
wally
fool 501 n.
walnut
fruit and vegetables
301 n.
tree 366 n.
brownness 430 n.
walrus
mammal 365 n.
waltz
rotate 315 vb.
rotation 315 n.
musical piece
412 n.
dance 837 n.
dance 837 vb.
waltz away with
win 727 vb.

waltztime
music 412 n.
wan
weakly 163 adj.
dim 419 adj.
colourless 426 adj.
feeble 572 adj.
wand
badge of rule
743 n.
magic instrument
983 n.
wander
be unrelated 10 vb.
wander 267 vb.
be foolish 499 vb.
be insane 503 vb.
be diffuse 570 vb.
wandering
irrelevant 10 adj.
unrelated 10 adj.
extraneous 59 adj.
unconformable
84 adj.
changeful 152 adj.
mistaken 495 adj.
folly 499 n.
foolish 499 adj.
crazy 503 adj.
frenzied 503 adj.
prolix 570 adj.
wane
decrease 37 n.
decrease 37 vb.
become small
198 vb.
be dim 419 vb.
deteriorate 655 vb.
wangle
fake 541 vb.
deceive 542 vb.
trickery 542 n.
contrivance 623 n.
be cunning 698 vb.
be dishonest
930 vb.
perfidy 930 n.
want
be inferior 35 vb.
deficit 55 n.
fall short 307 vb.
shortfall 307 n.
necessity 596 n.
needfulness 627 n.
require 627 vb.
not suffice 636 vb.
scarcity 636 n.

adversity 731 n.
be poor 801 vb.
poverty 801 n.
desire 859 n.
desire 859 vb.
wanted
absent 190 adj.
desired 859 adj.
wanting
incomplete 55 adj.
absent 190 adj.
deficient 307 adj.
mindless 448 adj.
unintelligent
499 adj.
crazy 503 adj.
insufficient
636 adj.
imperfect 647 adj.
desire 859 n.
wanton
changeful 152 adj.
rash 857 adj.
caress 889 vb.
bad person 938 n.
unchaste 951 adj.
loose woman
952 n.
war
slaughter 362 n.
quarrel 709 n.
contention 716 n.
war 718 n.
warfare 718 n.
warble
ululate 409 vb.
ululation 409 n.
sing 413 vb.
voice 577 vb.
warbler
bird 365 n.
war cry
call 547 n.
danger signal
665 n.
defiance 711 n.
ward
subdivision 53 n.
youth 130 n.
district 184 n.
hospital 658 n.
protection 660 n.
safeguard 660 vb.
dependant 742 n.
detention 747 n.
mandate 751 n.

war dance
defiance 711 n.
dance 837 n.
warden
doorkeeper 264 n.
protector 660 n.
manager 690 n.
defender 713 n.
officer 741 n.
keeper 749 n.
warder
protector 660 n.
defender 713 n.
gaoler 749 n.
ward off
screen 421 vb.
avoid 620 vb.
wardress
gaoler 749 n.
wardrobe
cabinet 194 n.
clothing 228 n.
wardroom
chamber 194 n.
warehouse
storage 632 n.
store 632 vb.
emporium 796 n.
warfare
warfare 718 n.
warhead
rocket 276 n.
explosive 723 n.
warhorse
horse 273 n.
expert 696 n.
warlike
warlike 718 adj.
warlock
sorcerer 983 n.
warm
near 200 adj.
sentient 374 adj.
comfortable
376 adj.
warm 379 adj.
heat 381 vb.
florid 425 adj.
red 431 adj.
fervent 818 adj.
pleasurable
826 adj.
friendly 880 adj.
sociable 882 adj.
angry 891 adj.
resentful 891 adj.
irascible 892 adj.

warm-blooded
fervent 818 adj.
war memorial
obsequies 364 n.
monument 548 n.
trophy 729 n.
warm-hearted
benevolent 897 adj.
warmonger
militarist 722 n.
warmth
heat 379 n.
hue 425 n.
redness 431 n.
vigour 571 n.
desire 859 n.
friendliness 880 n.
anger 891 n.
warmth of heart
benevolence 897 n.
warm to
feel 818 vb.
desire 859 vb.
befriend 880 vb.
be friendly 880 vb.
be in love 887 vb.
warm up
start out 296 vb.
heat 381 vb.
habituate 610 vb.
make ready
  669 vb.
prepare oneself
  669 vb.
warn
attract notice
  455 vb.
warn 664 vb.
warning
prediction 511 n.
information 524 n.
warning 664 n.
danger signal
  665 n.
warning light
signal light 420 n.
signal 547 n.
danger signal
  665 n.
warn off
exclude 57 vb.
prohibit 757 vb.
war of nerves
terror tactics 712 n.
war 718 n.
intimidation
  854 n.

threat 900 n.
warp
break 46 vb.
modify 143 vb.
force 176 vb.
obliquity 220 n.
weaving 222 n.
deform 244 vb.
distort 246 vb.
distortion 246 n.
navigate 269 vb.
deflect 282 vb.
bias 481 n.
bias 481 vb.
impair 655 vb.
pervert 655 vb.
warpaint
pigment 425 n.
cosmetic 843 n.
warpath
warfare 718 n.
warped
distorted 246 adj.
biased 481 adj.
imperfect 647 adj.
warrant
credential 466 n.
make certain
  473 vb.
affirm 532 vb.
affirmation 532 n.
oath 532 n.
safeguard 660 vb.
safety 660 n.
warrant 737 n.
permission 756 n.
permit 756 vb.
promise 764 vb.
give security
  767 vb.
dueness 915 n.
justify 927 vb.
warranted
certain 473 adj.
due 915 adj.
warranty
credential 466 n.
promise 764 n.
security 767 n.
warren
complexity 61 n.
dwelling 192 n.
cavity 255 n.
excavation 255 n.
warrior
combatant 722 n.
soldier 722 n.

brave person 855 n.
war song
defiance 711 n.
wart
swelling 253 n.
hardness 326 n.
skin disease 651 n.
blemish 845 n.
warthog
pig 365 n.
wartime
belligerency 718 n.
warts and all
accuracy 494 n.
true 494 adj.
wary
vigilant 457 adj.
nervous 854 adj.
cautious 858 adj.
wash
facing 226 n.
water travel 269 n.
be wet 341 vb.
drench 341 vb.
moisten 341 vb.
lake 346 n.
flow 350 VB.
wave 350 n.
colour 425 vb.
pigment 425 n.
whiten 427 vb.
be true 494 vb.
trace 548 n.
paint 553 vb.
ablutions 648 n.
clean 648 vb.
balm 658 n.
wash down
drink 301 vb.
clean 648 vb.
washed out
colourless 426 adj.
fatigued 684 adj.
washer
lining 227 n.
circle 250 n.
ablutions 648 n.
washing
painting 553 n.
ablutions 648 n.
cleansing 648 n.
washing machine
ablutions 648 n.
wash one's hands of
avoid 620 vb.
not retain 779 vb.
fail in duty 918 vb.

be exempt 919 vb.
disapprove 924 vb.
washout
failure 728 n.
washroom
chamber 194 n.
ablutions 648 n.
latrine 649 n.
wash up
eject 300 vb.
clean 648 vb.
wasp
insect 365 n.
bane 659 n.
waspish
irascible 892 adj.
wasp-waisted
narrow 206 adj.
wassail
festivity 837 n.
get drunk 949 vb.
wastage
waste 634 n.
rubbish 641 n.
loss 772 n.
waste
decrease 37 vb.
leavings 41 n.
desert 172 n.
unproductive
  172 adj.
space 183 n.
emptiness 190 n.
plain 348 n.
waste 634 n.
waste 634 vb.
rubbish 641 n.
impair 655 vb.
impairment 655 n.
intemperance
  943 n.
waste away
decompose 51 vb.
become small
  198 vb.
wasteful
wasteful 634 adj.
profitless 641 adj.
prodigal 815 adj.
intemperate
  943 adj.
wastelands
desert 172 n.
waste one's time
waste effort
  641 adj.

wastepaper
  rubbish 641 n.
wastepipe
  drain 351 n.
waster
  bad person 938 n.
wastrel
  prodigal 815 n.
  bad person 938 n.
watch
  period 110 n.
  timekeeper 117 n.
  mariner 270 n.
  look 438 n.
  scan 438 vb.
  watch 441 vb.
  attention 455 n.
  be attentive 455 vb.
  invigilate 457 vb.
  surveillance 457 n.
  protection 660 n.
  protector 660 n.
  warner 664 n.
  defend 713 vb.
  defender 713 n.
  keeper 749 n.
  police 955 n.
watchdog
  dog 365 n.
  protector 660 n.
  warner 664 n.
  keeper 749 n.
watchful
  attentive 455 adj.
  vigilant 457 adj.
  intelligent 498 adj.
  active 678 adj.
  observant 768 adj.
  cautious 858 adj.
watchful eye
  surveillance 457 n.
  restlessness 678 n.
watchmaker
  artisan 686 n.
watchman
  spectator 441 n.
  protector 660 n.
  warner 664 n.
  keeper 749 n.
watch one's step
  be careful 457 vb.
  be cautious 858 vb.
watch out for
  scan 438 vb.
  invigilate 457 vb.
  expect 507 vb.

watch over
  safeguard 660 vb.
watchword
  maxim 496 n.
  identification
    547 n.
  instrument 628 n.
water
  cause 156 vb.
  weak thing 163 n.
  soft drink 301 n.
  excrement 302 n.
  element 319 n.
  fluid 335 n.
  water 339 n.
  irrigate 341 vb.
  cultivate 370 vb.
  extinguisher 382 n.
  transparency
    422 n.
  provide 633 vb.
  cleanser 648 n.
water at the mouth
  exude 298 vb.
  eat 301 vb.
  be hungry 859 vb.
  gluttonize 947 vb.
water closet
  cleansing 648 n.
  latrine 649 n.
watercolours
  pigment 425 n.
watercourse
  stream 350 n.
  conduit 351 n.
watercress
  fruit and vegetables
    301 n.
water divining
  discovery 484 n.
water down
  mix 43 vb.
waterfall
  waterfall 350 n.
waterfront
  edge 234 n.
watergate
  conduit 351 n.
waterhole
  lake 346 n.
water lily
  plant 366 n.
waterlogged
  marshy 347 adj.
  hindered 702 adj.
Waterloo
  ruin 165 n.

defeat 728 n.
watermark
  label 547 n.
  pattern 844 n.
waterproof
  strong 162 adj.
  coat 226 vb.
  overcoat 228 n.
  dry 342 adj.
  invulnerable
    660 adj.
  preserve 666 vb.
  resisting 715 adj.
water rat
  mammal 365 n.
watershed
  serial place 73 n.
  reversion 148 n.
  event 154 n.
  summit 213 n.
  partition 231 n.
  limit 236 n.
  divergence 294 n.
water skiing
  aquatics 269 n.
  sport 837 n.
watersports
  aquatics 269 n.
  sport 837 n.
water table
  layer 207 n.
  horizontality
    216 n.
watertight
  dry 342 adj.
waterworks
  excretion 302 n.
  water 339 n.
watery
  weak 163 adj.
  watery 339 adj.
  tasteless 387 adj.
  feeble 572 adj.
  insufficient
    636 adj.
watt
  electronics 160 n.
  metrology 465 n.
wattle
  network 222 n.
wattle and daub
  building material
    631 n.
wave
  vary 152 vb.
  be curved 248 vb.
  crinkle 251 vb.

be in motion
  265 vb.
elevate 310 vb.
brandish 317 vb.
oscillate 317 vb.
agitate 318 vb.
wave 350 n.
blow 352 vb.
gesticulate 547 vb.
gesture 547 n.
hairdressing 843 n.
primp 843 vb.
be ostentatious
  875 vb.
boast 877 vb.
greet 884 vb.
threaten 900 vb.
waveband
  radiation 417 n.
wavelength
  long measure
    203 n.
  oscillation 317 n.
  radiation 417 n.
wave lengths
  broadcasting
    531 n.
wave on
  signal 547 vb.
waver
  vary 152 vb.
  decelerate 278 vb.
  be uncertain
    474 vb.
  doubt 486 vb.
  be irresolute
    601 vb.
wave to
  gesticulate 547 vb.
waving
  gesture 547 n.
  hairdressing 843 n.
wavy
  curved 248 adj.
  undulatory
    251 adj.
wax
  grow 36 vb.
  be turned to
    147 vb.
  changeable thing
    152 n.
  expand 197 vb.
  stripper 229 n.
  smooth 258 vb.
  smoothness 258 n.
  hardness 326 n.

WAX

softness 327 n.
rub 333 vb.
lubricant 334 n.
lubricate 334 vb.
viscidity 354 n.
fat 357 n.
sculpture 554 n.
cleanser 648 n.

wax and wane
change 143 vb.
vary 152 vb.

waxen
fatty 357 adj.
whitish 427 adj.

waxing moon
moon 321 n.

wax lyrical
praise 923 vb.

waxwork
image 551 n.
sculpture 554 n.

waxy
soft 327 adj.
fatty 357 adj.
angry 891 adj.

way
modality 7 n.
degree 27 n.
room 183 n.
water travel 269 n.
direction 281 n.
progression 285 n.
way in 297 n.
habit 610 n.
way 624 n.

wayfarer
traveller 268 n.

way in
approach 289 n.
way in 297 n.

waylay
ambush 527 vb.
ensnare 542 vb.
be cunning 698 vb.

waymark
signpost 547 n.

way out
doorway 263 n.
outlet 298 n.
contrivance 623 n.
means of escape
  667 n.
deliverance 668 n.

way-out
unusual 84 adj.
super 644 adj.

ways
habit 610 n.

ways and means
means 629 n.

wayside
near 200 adj.
edge 234 n.
marginal 234 adj.

wayward
changeful 152 adj.
volitional 595 adj.
wilful 602 adj.
capricious 604 adj.
disobedient
  738 adj.

WC
latrine 649 n.

we
self 80 n.

weak
weak 163 adj.
muted 401 adj.
poorly reasoned
  477 adj.
unintelligent
  499 adj.
feeble 572 adj.
insufficient
  636 adj.
unimportant
  639 adj.
be ill 651 vb.
unwarranted
  916 adj.

weaken
be weak 163 vb.
weaken 163 vb.
tell against 467 vb.

weak-kneed
weak 163 adj.
irresolute 601 adj.

weakling
weakling 163 n.
dwarf 196 n.

weakly
weakly 163 adj.
unhealthy 651 adj.

weakness
weakness 163 n.
tendency 179 n.
liability 180 n.
insufficiency 636 n.
imperfection 647 n.
liking 859 n.

weak-willed
weak 163 adj.
irresolute 601 adj.

weal
swelling 253 n.
trace 548 n.
blemish 845 n.

wealth
abundance 171 n.
money 797 n.
wealth 800 n.

wealthy
rich 800 adj.

wean from
convince 485 vb.
disaccustom
  611 vb.

weapon
contrivance 623 n.
instrument 628 n.
tool 630 n.
weapon 723 n.

wear
decompose 51 vb.
clothing 228 n.
wear 228 vb.
use 673 n.
use 673 vb.
fatigue 684 vb.

wear and tear
decay 51 n.
waste 634 n.
dilapidation 655 n.
use 673 n.
loss 772 n.

wear away
decrease 37 vb.
rub 333 vb.

wear down
induce 612 vb.

wear it
acquiesce 488 vb.

wear on
elapse 111 vb.

wear out
waste 634 vb.
deteriorate 655 vb.
impair 655 vb.
use 673 vb.
fatigue 684 vb.

weary
laborious 682 adj.
fatigue 684 vb.
trouble 827 vb.
discontented
  829 adj.
depress 834 vb.
be tedious 838 vb.
sate 863 vb.

weasel
vehicle 274 n.
mammal 365 n.

weasel word
equivocalness
  518 n.
word 559 n.

weather
storm 176 n.
navigate 269 vb.
weather 340 n.
colour 425 vb.
deteriorate 655 vb.
mature 669 n.

weatherbeaten
tough 329 adj.
dilapidated
  655 adj.

weathered
soft-hued 425 adj.
colourless 426 adj.
matured 669 adj.

weather eye
surveillance 457 n.

weather forecast
weather 340 n.

weathering
achromatism
  426 n.

weatherproof
strong 162 adj.
invulnerable
  660 adj.

weather the storm
navigate 269 vb.
be restored 656 vb.
be safe 660 vb.
escape 667 vb.
triumph 727 vb.

weathervane
changeable thing
  152 n.
weather 340 n.

weave
textile 222 n.
weave 222 vb.
pass 305 vb.
texture 331 n.
fake 541 vb.
pattern 844 n.

weaver
weaving 222 n.
artisan 686 n.

web
complexity 61 n.
filament 208 n.
network 222 n.

textile 222 n.
weaving 222 n.
texture 331 n.
trap 542 n.
webbing
　network 222 n.
web-footed
　deformed 246 adj.
wed
　wed 894 vb.
wedding
　wedding 894 n.
wedding anniversary
　anniversary 141 n.
　special day 876 n.
　wedding 894 n.
wedding day
　wedding 894 n.
wedding march
　musical piece
　　412 n.
wedding ring
　jewellery 844 n.
　love token 889 n.
　wedding 894 n.
　ritual object 988 n.
wedge
　affix 45 vb.
　piece 53 n.
　support 218 n.
　angular figure
　　247 n.
　sharp edge 256 n.
　stopper 264 n.
　tool 630 n.
Wedgwood (tdmk)
　china
　pottery 381 n.
wedlock
　union 45 n.
　marriage 894 n.
wee
　small 33 adj.
　little 196 adj.
weed
　exclude 57 vb.
　render few 105 vb.
　weakling 163 n.
　plant 366 n.
　cultivate 370 vb.
　ninny 501 n.
　disencumber
　　701 vb.
weed-killer
　poison 659 n.
weed out
　abate 37 vb.

eject 300 vb.
extract 304 vb.
weedy
　lean 206 adj.
week
　over five 99 n.
　period 110 n.
weekday
　period 110 n.
weekend
　pass time 108 vb.
　visit 882 vb.
weekly
　periodically
　　141 adv.
　seasonal 141 adj.
　journal 528 n.
weeny
　small 33 adj.
weep
　emit 300 vb.
　excrete 302 vb.
　be wet 341 vb.
　suffer 825 vb.
　be dejected 834 vb.
　weep 836 vb.
weep for
　be sensitive 819 vb.
　pity 905 vb.
weepie
　film 445 n.
weeping
　outflow 298 n.
　water 339 n.
　unhappy 825 adj.
　lamentation 836 n.
　repentant 939 adj.
weeping willow
　tree 366 n.
weevil
　insect 365 n.
weft
　weaving 222 n.
weigh
　elevate 310 vb.
　weigh 322 vb.
　meditate 449 vb.
　notice 455 vb.
　mete out 465 vb.
　estimate 480 vb.
　motivate 612 vb.
weigh against
　tell against 467 vb.
weigh anchor
　navigate 269 vb.
　start out 296 vb.

weighbridge
　scales 322 n.
weigh in
　criticize 924 vb.
weigh on
　lower 311 vb.
　weigh 322 vb.
　oppress 735 vb.
weight
　substantiality 3 n.
　quantity 26 n.
　power 160 n.
　influence 178 n.
　bulk 195 n.
　size 195 n.
　distort 246 vb.
　materiality 319 n.
　gravity 322 n.
　make heavy
　　322 vb.
　scales 322 n.
　vigour 571 n.
　importance 638 n.
　do wrong 914 adj.
weightless
　light 323 adj.
weight-lifting
　exercise 682 n.
　sport 837 n.
weight-training
　sport 837 n.
weight-watching
　dieting 301 n.
weighty
　influential 178 adj.
　material 319 adj.
　weighty 322 adj.
　forceful 571 adj.
　important 638 adj.
weir
　waterfall 350 n.
　conduit 351 n.
　obstacle 702 n.
weird
　unconformable
　　84 adj.
　fate 596 n.
　frightening
　　854 adj.
　wonderful 864 adj.
　spooky 970 adj.
　magical 983 adj.
weirdo
　nonconformist
　　84 n.
welcome
　arrival 295 n.

meet 295 vb.
welcome 295 int.
admit 299 vb.
reception 299 n.
pleasant 376 adj.
assent 488 n.
assent 488 vb.
pleasurable
　826 adj.
desire 859 vb.
desired 859 adj.
celebrate 876 vb.
celebration 876 n.
be friendly 880 vb.
friendliness 880 n.
be hospitable
　882 vb.
sociability 882 n.
courteous act
　884 n.
greet 884 vb.
congratulation
　886 n.
show respect
　920 vb.
applaud 923 vb.
approbation 923 n.
weld
　join 45 vb.
　joint 45 n.
welder
　artisan 686 n.
welfare
　good 615 n.
　prosperity 730 n.
welfare state
　safety 660 n.
　shelter 662 n.
　political organiza-
　　tion 733 n.
　sociology 901 n.
well
　greatly 32 vb.
　receptacle 194 n.
　lowness 210 n.
　depth 211 n.
　excavation 255 n.
　water 339 n.
　lake 346 n.
　flow 350 VB.
　stream 350 n.
　well 615 adv.
　store 632 n.
　healthy 650 adj.
　skilfully 694 adv.
well-adjusted
　adjusted 24 adj.

accurate 494 adj.

well-advised
 wise 498 adj.

well-aimed
 apt 24 adj.
 accurate 494 adj.

well-appointed
 prepared 669 adj.

well-balanced
 symmetrical
  245 adj.

well-behaved
 orderly 60 adj.
 obedient 739 adj.
 amiable 884 adj.

well-being
 euphoria 376 n.
 good 615 n.
 health 650 n.
 salubrity 652 n.
 prosperity 730 n.
 happiness 824 n.

well-born
 worshipful 866 adj.
 noble 868 adj.

well-bred
 well-bred 848 adj.

well-built
 strong 162 adj.
 large 195 adj.
 beautiful 841 adj.

well-chosen
 chosen 605 adj.

well-connected, be
 influence 178 vb.

well-considered
 wise 498 adj.

well-covered
 fleshy 195 adj.

well-cut
 adjusted 24 adj.

well-deserved
 just 913 adj.
 due 915 adj.

well-disposed
 willing 597 adj.

well-documented
 real 1 adj.
 evidential 466 adj.

well done
 bravo 923 int.

well-done
 culinary 301 adj.

well-dressed
 personable 841 adj.
 fashionable
  848 adj.

well-earned
 due 915 adj.

well-endowed
 gifted 694 adj.
 rich 800 adj.
 shapely 841 adj.

well-established
 permanent 144 adj.

well-fed
 fleshy 195 adj.

well-fitting
 adjusted 24 adj.

well-formed
 shapely 841 adj.

well-founded
 fixed 153 adj.
 evidential 466 adj.
 plausible 471 adj.
 certain 473 adj.
 true 494 adj.

well-groomed
 orderly 60 adj.
 clean 648 adj.
 fashionable
  848 adj.

well-grounded
 evidential 466 adj.
 plausible 471 adj.
 certain 473 adj.
 rational 475 adj.
 true 494 adj.

well-heeled
 prosperous 730 adj.
 moneyed 800 adj.
 rich 800 adj.

well-heeled, be
 prosper 730 vb.

well-heeled, the
 rich person 800 n.

wellies
 footwear 228 n.

well-informed
 informed 524 adj.

wellingtons
 footwear 228 n.

well-intentioned
 friendly 880 adj.
 benevolent 897 adj.

well-kept
 orderly 60 adj.

well-known
 usual 610 adj.
 renowned 866 adj.

well-liked
 pleasurable
  826 adj.

well-mannered
 well-bred 848 adj.
 courteous 884 adj.

well-matched
 equal 28 adj.

well-meaning
 friendly 880 adj.

well-meant
 aiding 703 adj.
 benevolent 897 adj.

well-nigh
 nearly 200 adv.

well-off
 prosperous 730 adj.
 rich 800 adj.

well-off, the
 rich person 800 n.

well-paid
 rich 800 adj.

well-placed
 directed 281 adj.

well-preserved
 ageing 131 adj.
 permanent 144 adj.
 preserved 666 adj.

well-proportioned
 symmetrical
  245 adj.
 elegant 575 adj.
 shapely 841 adj.

well-read
 studious 536 adj.

well rid of, be
 escape 667 vb.

well said
 amen 488 int.

well set-up
 stalwart 162 adj.
 prosperous 730 adj.

well-spoken
 speaking 579 adj.
 well-bred 848 adj.
 courteous 884 adj.

wellspring
 source 156 n.

well thought of
 reputable 866 adj.

well-timed
 timely 137 adj.
 advisable 642 adj.

well-to-do
 prosperous 730 adj.
 rich 800 adj.

well-to-do person
 rich person 800 n.

well-turned
 elegant 575 adj.

shapely 841 adj.

well up
 flow 350 vb.

well up in
 expert 694 adj.

well-wisher
 friend 880 n.

well-worn
 dilapidated
  655 adj.
 used 673 adj.

welsh
 run away 620 vb.
 elude 667 vb.
 fleece 786 vb.
 be in debt 803 vb.
 not pay 805 vb.

welsh dresser
 cabinet 194 n.
 stand 218 n.

welsher
 avoider 620 n.
 defrauder 789 n.
 nonpayer 805 n.

**welsh rabbit or rare-
bit**
 dish 301 n.

welt
 edge 234 n.
 swelling 253 n.
 blemish 845 n.

welter
 disorder 61 n.

welterweight
 pugilist 722 n.

weltschmerz
 suffering 825 n.
 discontent 829 n.
 melancholy 834 n.
 tedium 838 n.
 pity 905 n.

wen
 letter 558 n.
 blemish 845 n.

wench
 youngster 132 n.
 female 373 n.
 loose woman
  952 n.

wend
 be in motion
  265 vb.

wend one's way
 travel 267 vb.

werewolf
 demon 970 n.

wersh
weak 163 adj.
tasteless 387 adj.
unsavoury 391 adj.
feeble 572 adj.
insufficient
636 adj.
Western
film 445 n.
novel 590 n.
Westminster
parliament 692 n.
master 741 n.
wet
weakling 163 n.
water 339 n.
watery 339 adj.
humid 341 adj.
moisten 341 vb.
moisture 341 n.
foolish 499 adj.
ninny 501 n.
moderate 625 n.
neutral 625 adj.
political party
708 n.
lax 734 adj.
impressible
819 adj.
wet behind the ears
ignorant 491 adj.
immature 670 adj.
artless 699 adj.
wet blanket
moderator 177 n.
dissuasion 613 n.
moper 834 n.
wether
sheep 365 n.
wet nurse
keeper 749 n.
wet oneself
excrete 302 vb.
wet one's whistle
drink 301 vb.
wetsuit
suit 228 n.
wetted
humid 341 adj.
wet through
drench 341 vb.
whack
finite quantity
26 n.
strike 279 vb.
fatigue 684 vb.
portion 783 n.

spank 963 vb.
whacked
fatigued 684 adj.
whacking
large 195 adj.
whale
giant 195 n.
mammal 365 n.
hunt 619 vb.
whalebone
support 218 n.
hardness 326 n.
whaler
mariner 270 n.
fishing boat 275 n.
hunter 619 n.
wham
strike 279 vb.
propel 287 vb.
bang 402 vb.
wharf
stable 192 n.
edge 234 n.
storage 632 n.
workshop 687 n.
what d'you call it
no name 562 n.
whatnot
cabinet 194 n.
what's his face
no name 562 n.
whatsit
no name 562 n.
tool 630 n.
wheat
cereals 301 n.
food 301 n.
grass 366 n.
wheedle
fool 542 vb.
tempt 612 vb.
request 761 vb.
pet 889 vb.
flatter 925 vb.
wheel
changeable thing
152 n.
wheel 250 n.
move 265 vb.
sailing aid 269 n.
bicycle 274 n.
turn round 282 vb.
propel 287 vb.
circle 314 vb.
rotate 315 vb.
pain 377 n.

instrument of tor-
ture 964 n.
wheel about
turn round 282 vb.
circle 314 vb.
change one's mind
603 vb.
wheel and deal
plot 623 vb.
wheelbarrow
pushcart 274 n.
wheelchair
pushcart 274 n.
wheel clamp
obstacle 702 n.
wheeler-dealing
deception 542 n.
trickery 542 n.
wheeling
circuition 314 n.
rotation 315 n.
wheeling and dealing
cunning 698 n.
wheel of Fortune
changeable thing
152 n.
chance 159 n.
rotator 315 n.
fate 596 n.
nondesign 618 n.
wheel round
be inverted 221 vb.
turn back 286 vb.
wheels within wheels
machine 630 n.
wheelwright
artisan 686 n.
wheeze
breathe 352 vb.
hiss 406 vb.
idea 451 n.
whelk
fish food 301 n.
marine life 365 n.
whelp
young creature
132 n.
reproduce itself
167 vb.
dog 365 n.
when
when 108 adv.
whence
hence 158 adv.
when pigs fly
neverness 109 n.

when the chips are
down
juncture 8 n.
whereabouts
situation 186 n.
presence 189 n.
wherewithal
means 629 n.
funds 797 n.
wherry
sailing ship 275 n.
whet
sharpen 256 vb.
animate 821 vb.
whether
nevertheless
468 adv.
whether or no
nevertheless
468 adv.
whetstone
friction 333 n.
whey
dairy product
301 n.
fluid 335 n.
whey-faced
colourless 426 adj.
whiff
breathe 352 vb.
breeze 352 n.
odour 394 n.
indication 547 n.
Whigs
political party
708 n.
while
time 108 n.
while 108 adv.
while away the time
amuse oneself
837 vb.
whilst
while 108 adv.
whim
ideality 513 n.
whim 604 n.
liking 859 n.
whimper
cry 408 vb.
weep 836 vb.
whimsical
changeful 152 adj.
misjudging
481 adj.
crazy 503 adj.

imaginative
513 adj.
irresolute 601 adj.
capricious 604 adj.
witty 839 adj.
whimsy
nonuniformity
17 n.
foolery 497 n.
ideality 513 n.
whim 604 n.
liking 859 n.
whin
plant 366 n.
whine
shrill 407 vb.
cry 408 n.
cry 408 vb.
ululate 409 vb.
discord 411 vb.
be discontented
829 vb.
weep 836 vb.
whinge
be discontented
829 vb.
weep 836 vb.
whinny
ululate 409 vb.
ululation 409 n.
whip
strike 279 vb.
cook 301 vb.
agitate 318 vb.
break in 369 vb.
give pain 377 vb.
incentive 612 n.
incite 612 vb.
hasten 680 vb.
manager 690 n.
oppress 735 vb.
command 737 n.
officer 741 n.
excitant 821 n.
flog 963 vb.
scourge 964 n.
whipcord
cable 47 n.
whip hand
advantage 34 n.
influence 178 n.
victory 727 n.
governance 733 n.
whippersnapper
youngster 132 n.
insolent person
878 n.

whippet
dog 365 n.
whipping
knock 279 n.
corporal punish-
ment 963 n.
whipping boy
substitute 150 n.
propitiation 941 n.
whip-round
gift 781 n.
payment 804 n.
whip up
thicken 354 vb.
excite 821 vb.
whirl
rotate 315 vb.
rotation 315 n.
vortex 315 n.
be agitated 318 vb.
activity 678 n.
haste 680 n.
excitable state
822 n.
dance 837 vb.
whirligig
changeable thing
152 n.
rotator 315 n.
whirlpool
coil 251 n.
vortex 315 n.
commotion 318 n.
eddy 350 n.
pitfall 663 n.
whirlpool bath
vortex 315 n.
eddy 350 n.
whirlwind
turmoil 61 n.
vortex 315 n.
commotion 318 n.
gale 352 n.
whirlybird
aircraft 276 n.
whirr
be agitated 318 vb.
faintness 401 n.
roll 403 n.
roll 403 vb.
resound 404 vb.
ululate 409 vb.
whisk
move fast 277 vb.
cook 301 vb.
rotate 315 vb.
rotator 315 n.

agitate 318 vb.
whisker
filament 208 n.
feeler 378 n.
whisky
carriage 274 n.
alcoholic drink
301 n.
whisper
small quantity
33 n.
faintness 401 n.
sound faint 401 vb.
imply 523 vb.
hint 524 n.
hint 524 vb.
rumour 529 n.
voice 577 n.
voice 577 vb.
voicelessness 578 n.
speak 579 vb.
detract 926 vb.
detraction 926 n.
whist
hush 399 int.
card game 837 n.
whist drive
amusement 837 n.
whistle
blow 352 vb.
be loud 400 vb.
megaphone 400 n.
hiss 406 vb.
shrill 407 vb.
cry 408 vb.
ululate 409 vb.
play music 413 vb.
sing 413 vb.
flute 414 n.
signal 547 n.
be cheerful 833 vb.
wonder 864 n.
wonder 864 vb.
despise 922 vb.
applaud 923 vb.
disapprobation
924 n.
disapprove 924 vb.
whistle-blowing
warning 664 n.
whistle for
desire 859 vb.
whistle-stop
stopping place
145 n.
whistle-stop tour
vote 605 n.

whit
small quantity
33 n.
trifle 639 n.
white
white 427 adj.
whiten 427 vb.
whiteness 427 n.
eye 438 n.
white-collar worker
worker 686 n.
whited sepulchre
sham 542 n.
deceiver 545 n.
white elephant
bane 659 n.
white feather
cowardice 856 n.
white flag
flag 547 n.
peace offering
719 n.
submission 721 n.
white goods
merchandise
795 n.
white-haired
ageing 131 adj.
white hope
proficient person
696 n.
white horses
wave 350 n.
white-hot
hot 379 adj.
white 427 adj.
fervent 818 adj.
white lie
equivocalness
518 n.
concealment 525 n.
untruth 543 n.
stratagem 698 n.
white lines
traffic control
305 n.
white meat
meat 301 n.
whiten
whiten 427 vb.
whiteness
whiteness 427 n.
cleanness 648 n.
white-out
dimness 419 n.
White Paper
report 524 n.

WHI

record 548 n.
white pepper
  condiment 389 n.
white sauce
  sauce 389 n.
white-skinned
  white 427 adj.
white slave
  prostitute 952 n.
white-tie
  formal 875 adj.
whitewash
  coat 226 vb.
  facing 226 n.
  colour 425 vb.
  pigment 425 n.
  whiten 427 vb.
  sophisticate
    477 vb.
  overestimate
    482 vb.
  mislead 495 vb.
  conceal 525 vb.
  sham 542 n.
  clean 648 vb.
  cleanser 648 n.
  decorate 844 vb.
  extenuate 927 vb.
  justify 927 vb.
  vindication 927 n.
  acquit 960 vb.
whiting
  fish food 301 n.
whitish
  whitish 427 adj.
whittle
  abate 37 vb.
  subtract 39 vb.
  cut 46 vb.
  form 243 vb.
  sculpt 554 vb.
whittle away
  make smaller
    198 vb.
whiz kid
  busy person 678 n.
  victor 727 n.
  prosperous person
    730 n.
  prodigy 864 n.
whizz
  move fast 277 vb.
  spurt 277 n.
  hiss 406 vb.
whoa
  stop 266 int.

WHO

whodunit
  novel 590 n.
whole
  whole 52 adj.
  whole 52 n.
  numerical 85 adj.
  universe 321 n.
whole bang shoot,
  the
  all 52 n.
whole caboodle, the
  all 52 n.
wholefood
  food 301 n.
whole-hearted
  resolute 599 adj.
whole hog
  actively 678 adv.
whole lot
  great quantity
    32 n.
  all 52 n.
wholemeal
  cereals 301 n.
whole number
  whole 52 n.
  number 85 n.
wholesale
  extensive 32 adj.
  greatly 32 vb.
  comprehensive
    52 adj.
  complete 54 adj.
  inclusive 78 adj.
  indiscriminate
    464 adj.
  sell 793 vb.
wholesome
  nourishing 301 adj.
  beneficial 644 adj.
  healthy 650 adj.
  salubrious 652 adj.
  personable 841 adj.
whole truth
  disclosure 526 n.
wholly
  completely 54 adv.
whoop
  loudness 400 n.
  cry 408 n.
  cry 408 vb.
  be cheerful 833 vb.
  rejoice 835 vb.
whoopee
  revel 837 n.
whooping
  loud 400 adj.

WID

whooping-cough
  infection 651 n.
  respiratory disease
    651 n.
whopper
  untruth 543 n.
whore
  be impure 951 vb.
  prostitute 952 n.
whorl
  weaving 222 n.
  coil 251 n.
whosoever
  everyman 79 n.
Who's Who
  directory 87 n.
whydunit
  novel 590 n.
wick
  filament 208 n.
  torch 420 n.
wicked
  evil 616 adj.
  heinous 934 adj.
  wicked 934 adj.
  impure 951 adj.
wickedness
  evil 616 n.
  wickedness 934 n.
wickerwork
  network 222 n.
wicket
  doorway 263 n.
widdershins
  towards 281 adv.
wide
  great 32 adj.
  spacious 183 adj.
  distant 199 adj.
  broad 205 adj.
  mistaken 495 adj.
wide-angle (lens)
  broad 205 adj.
wide-awake
  attentive 455 adj.
  vigilant 457 adj.
wide berth
  avoidance 620 n.
  safety 660 n.
  scope 744 n.
wide-bodied
  broad 205 adj.
wide-eyed
  innocent 935 adj.
widely
  greatly 32 vb.
  widely 183 adv.

WIL

widen
  augment 36 vb.
  generalize 79 vb.
  enlarge 197 vb.
  expand 197 vb.
wide of the mark
  beyond 199 adv.
  distant 199 adj.
  erroneous 495 adj.
  mistaken 495 adj.
wide-open
  open 263 adj.
wide-ranging
  extensive 32 adj.
  spacious 183 adj.
  broad 205 adj.
widespread
  extensive 32 adj.
  comprehensive
    52 adj.
  universal 79 adj.
  spacious 183 adj.
  usual 610 adj.
widow
  female 373 n.
  deprive 786 vb.
widower
  male 372 n.
widow's mite
  small thing 33 n.
  offering 781 n.
widow's peak
  hair 259 n.
width
  quantity 26 n.
  size 195 n.
  breadth 205 n.
wield
  touch 378 vb.
  use 673 vb.
wife
  female 373 n.
  spouse 894 n.
wifely
  loving 887 adj.
wife-swapping
  illicit love 951 n.
wig
  hair 259 n.
wigging
  reprimand 924 n.
wiggle
  oscillate 317 vb.
wigwam
  dwelling 192 n.
wild
  disorderly 61 adj.

desert 172 n.
furious 176 adj.
violent 176 adj.
space 183 n.
erroneous 495 adj.
inexact 495 adj.
absurd 497 adj.
foolish 499 adj.
frenzied 503 adj.
excited 821 adj.
rash 857 adj.
barbaric 869 adj.
unsociable 883 adj.
angry 891 adj.
cruel 898 adj.
unchaste 951 adj.
wild about
enamoured
   887 adj.
wild card
unknown thing
   491 n.
wildcat
big cat 365 n.
independent
   744 adj.
rash 857 adj.
wildcat strike
strike 145 n.
wildebeest
mammal 365 n.
wilderness
desert 172 n.
space 183 n.
emptiness 190 n.
land 344 n.
seclusion 883 n.
wild fire
fire 379 n.
wild chase
inattention 456 n.
folly 499 n.
lost labour 641 n.
bungling 695 n.
failure 728 n.
wild-goose life
animality 365 n.
wildness
folly 499 n.
disobedience
   738 n.
rashness 857 n.
wile
stratagem 698 n.
wiles
trickery 542 n.

wilful
volitional 595 adj.
wilful 602 adj.
will
will 595 n.
will 595 vb.
be resolute 599 vb.
obstinacy 602 n.
title deed 767 n.
bequeath 780 vb.
willies
nervousness 854 n.
willing
volitional 595 adj.
willing 597 adj.
will-o'-the-wisp
glow 417 n.
deception 542 n.
willow
tree 366 n.
willow pattern
pottery 381 n.
willowy
narrow 206 adj.
flexible 327 adj.
shapely 841 adj.
willpower
will 595 n.
resolution 599 n.
willy-nilly
by force 740 adv.
wilt
be weak 163 vb.
deteriorate 655 vb.
be dejected 834 vb.
wily
cunning 698 adj.
wimp
weakling 163 n.
ninny 501 n.
wimple
headgear 228 n.
win
superiority 34 n.
victory 727 n.
win 727 vb.
acquire 771 vb.
gain 771 vb.
appropriate
   786 vb.
wince
recoil 280 vb.
feel pain 377 vb.
show feeling
   818 vb.
suffer 825 vb.
quake 854 vb.

winceyette
textile 222 n.
winch
draw 288 vb.
wind
changeable thing
   152 n.
disable 161 vb.
be curved 248 vb.
voidance 300 n.
circle 314 vb.
rotate 315 vb.
wind 352 n.
play music 413 vb.
musical instrument
   414 n.
empty talk 515 n.
digestive disorders
   651 n.
fatigue 684 vb.
windbag
blowing 352 n.
chatterer 581 n.
windblown
windy 352 adj.
windbreak
wood 366 n.
shelter 662 n.
windcheater
jacket 228 n.
windchill factor
coldness 380 n.
winder
handle 218 n.
rotator 315 n.
windfall
extra 40 n.
lack of expectation
   508 n.
benefit 615 n.
nondesign 618 n.
acquisition 771 n.
gift 781 n.
receiving 782 n.
wind gauge
velocity 277 n.
wind in
draw 288 vb.
winding
complex 61 adj.
convoluted 251 adj.
meandering 251 adj.
dishonest 930 adj.
winding sheet
wrapping 226 n.
grave clothes
   364 n.

windmill
rotator 315 n.
wind one's way
circle 314 vb.
window
window 263 n.
window dressing
publicity 528 n.
duplicity 541 n.
ostentation 875 n.
ostentatious
   875 adj.
window shopping
purchase 792 n.
windowsill
shelf 218 n.
windpipe
respiration 352 n.
air pipe 353 n.
windscreen
window 263 n.
shelter 662 n.
windshield
window 263 n.
wind sock
indicator 547 n.
wind surfing
aquatics 269 n.
sport 837 n.
windswept
windy 352 adj.
wind up
terminate 69 vb.
cease 145 vb.
operate 173 vb.
invigorate 174 vb.
elevate 310 vb.
make ready
   669 vb.
sell 793 vb.
not pay 805 vb.
fear 854 n.
windy
gaseous 336 adj.
windy 352 adj.
diffuse 570 adj.
loquacious 581 adj.
nervous 854 adj.
ostentatious
   875 adj.
wine
wine 301 n.
drunkenness 949 n.
wine and dine
feed 301 vb.
wine cellar
tavern 192 n.

wineglass
cup 194 n.
wine-growing
agriculture 370 n.
winepress
farm tool 370 n.
wineskin
vessel 194 n.
wine-tasting
drinking 301 n.
**wine, women and
  song**
sensualism 944 n.
wing
laterality 239 n.
fly 271 vb.
wing 271 n.
move fast 277 vb.
wound 655 vb.
hinder 702 vb.
air force 722 n.
winge
be discontented
  829 vb.
winger
player 837 n.
wing (of a house)
adjunct 40 n.
wings
stage set 594 n.
theatre 594 n.
win hands down
do easily 701 vb.
win 727 vb.
wink
gaze 438 vb.
look 438 n.
be dim-sighted
  440 vb.
dim sight 440 n.
hint 524 n.
hint 524 vb.
gesticulate 547 vb.
gesture 547 n.
indication 547 n.
warning 664 n.
command 737 vb.
approbation 923 n.
approve 923 vb.
wink at
permit 756 vb.
forgive 909 vb.
do wrong 914 adj.
winkle
fish food 301 n.
marine life 365 n.

winkle out
extract 304 vb.
winner
exceller 644 n.
victor 727 n.
recipient 782 n.
winning
superior 34 adj.
successful 727 adj.
acquiring 771 adj.
acquisition 771 n.
pleasurable
  826 adj.
amiable 884 adj.
winning post
limit 236 n.
objective 617 n.
winnings
gain 771 n.
receiving 782 n.
taking 786 n.
receipt 807 n.
winnow
aerate 340 vb.
cultivate 370 vb.
search 459 vb.
discriminate
  463 vb.
select 605 vb.
win over
convert 147 vb.
convince 485 vb.
induce 612 vb.
pacify 719 vb.
reward 962 vb.
winsome
personable 841 adj.
winter
pass time 108 vb.
period 110 n.
winter 129 n.
wintry 129 adj.
be present 189 vb.
wintriness 380 n.
adversity 731 n.
winterized
heated 381 adj.
winter sports
snow 380 n.
sport 837 n.
win the pools
get rich 800 vb.
win through
triumph 727 vb.
wintry
wintry 129 adj.

wipe
dry 342 vb.
clean 648 vb.
wipe out
nullify 2 vb.
destroy 165 vb.
displace 188 vb.
murder 362 vb.
slaughter 362 vb.
obliterate 550 vb.
defeat 727 vb.
abrogate 752 vb.
wipe up
dry 342 vb.
carry through
  725 vb.
wire
cable 47 n.
narrowness 206 n.
filament 208 n.
communicate
  524 vb.
information 524 n.
message 529 n.
telecommunication
  531 n.
wiredraw
lengthen 203 vb.
make thin 206 vb.
wireless
broadcasting
  531 n.
wire netting
network 222 n.
wire-pulling
influence 178 n.
plot 623 n.
wire service
informant 524 n.
wire-tapping
listening 415 n.
wireworm
creepy-crawly
  365 n.
wiry
stalwart 162 adj.
lean 206 adj.
wisdom
erudition 490 n.
wisdom 498 n.
divine attribute
  965 n.
wisdom tooth
tooth 256 n.
wise
wise 498 adj.

wiseacre
wiseacre 500 n.
wisecrack
be witty 839 vb.
wised-up
informed 524 adj.
wise guy
wiseacre 500 n.
wise man
sage 500 n.
adviser 691 n.
sorcerer 983 n.
wise to
knowing 490 adj.
wise woman
sage 500 n.
sorceress 983 n.
wish
will 595 vb.
desire 859 n.
desire 859 vb.
desired object
  859 n.
wishbone
magic instrument
  983 n.
wishful thinking
misjudgment
  481 n.
credulity 487 n.
error 495 n.
fantasy 513 n.
deception 542 n.
hope 852 n.
wishing well
benevolent 897 adj.
magic instrument
  983 n.
wish on
desire 859 vb.
curse 899 vb.
wishy-washy
weak 163 adj.
tasteless 387 adj.
colourless 426 adj.
feeble 572 adj.
wisp
small thing 33 n.
piece 53 n.
bunch 74 n.
thinness 206 n.
filament 208 n.
hair 259 n.
wispy
flimsy 163 adj.
narrow 206 adj.
hairy 259 adj.

rare 325 adj.
wisteria
tree 366 n.
wit
intelligence 498 n.
humorist 839 n.
wit 839 n.
witch
a beauty 841 n.
eyesore 842 n.
prodigy 864 n.
fairy 970 n.
sorceress 983 n.
witchcraft
power 160 n.
diabolism 969 n.
sorcery 983 n.
witch doctor
sage 500 n.
doctor 658 n.
sorcerer 983 n.
priest 986 n.
witch-hunt
enquiry 459 n.
See **search**
search 459 n.
pursue 619 vb.
pursuit 619 n.
defame 926 vb.
with
in addition 38 adv.
among 43 adv.
with 89 adv.
by means of
629 adv.
with child
fertilized 167 adj.
withdraw
decrease 37 vb.
subtract 39 vb.
cease 145 vb.
revert 148 vb.
go away 190 vb.
regress 286 vb.
recede 290 vb.
depart 296 vb.
extract 304 vb.
dissent 489 vb.
change one's mind
603 vb.
recant 603 vb.
run away 620 vb.
relinquish 621 vb.
stop using 674 vb.
submit 721 vb.
resign 753 vb.
not retain 779 vb.

fail in duty 918 vb.
withdrawal
subtraction 39 n.
disunion 46 n.
separation 46 n.
cessation 145 n.
reversion 148 n.
regression 286 n.
recession 290 n.
extraction 304 n.
dissent 489 n.
recantation 603 n.
relinquishment
621 n.
escape 667 n.
nonuse 674 n.
resignation 753 n.
seclusion 883 n.
schism 978 n.
withdrawal symp-
toms
drug-taking 949 n.
withdrawn
powerless 161 adj.
reticent 525 adj.
taciturn 582 adj.
unsociable 883 adj.
wither
be old 127 vb.
become small
198 vb.
dry 342 vb.
perish 361 vb.
deteriorate 655 vb.
lose repute 867 vb.
wither away
decrease 37 vb.
withering
contraction 198 n.
desiccation 342 n.
disapproving
924 adj.
withers
angularity 247 n.
withhold
keep secret 525 vb.
restrain 747 vb.
refuse 760 vb.
retain 778 vb.
within
inside 224 adv.
within bounds
temperate 942 adj.
within earshot
near 200 adv.
auditory 415 adj.

within one's means
cheap 812 adj.
within reach
near 200 adv.
possibly 469 adv.
easy 701 adj.
within reason
moderate 177 adj.
with it
modern 126 adj.
attentive 455 adj.
intelligent 498 adj.
fashionable
848 adj.
with one, be
understand 516 vb.
without
thus 8 adv.
incomplete 55 adj.
without, be
fall short 307 vb.
without a hitch
easily 701 adv.
without delay
hasty 680 adj.
without doubt
of course 478 adv.
without end
infinite 107 adj.
perpetual 115 adj.
without exception
generally 79 adv.
without fail
certainly 473 adv.
without notice
suddenly 135 adv.
without number
infinite 107 adj.
without rhyme or
reason
absurd 497 adj.
without warning
unexpected
508 adj.
with pleasure
willingly 597 adv.
withstand
counteract 182 vb.
withstand 704 vb.
be hostile 881 vb.
with the crowd
easy 701 adj.
witness
be present 189 vb.
spectator 441 n.
watch 441 vb.
testify 466 vb.

testimony 466 n.
witness 466 n.
wits
intellect 447 n.
intelligence 498 n.
witter
roll 403 n.
witticism
witticism 839 n.
wittingly
purposely 617 adv.
witty
witty 839 adj.
sociable 882 adj.
wizard
sage 500 n.
super 644 adj.
skilful 694 adj.
proficient person
696 n.
prodigy 864 n.
sorcerer 983 n.
wizardry
skill 694 n.
sorcery 983 n.
wizened
ageing 131 adj.
dwarfish 196 adj.
lean 206 adj.
woad
pigment 425 n.
blue pigment
435 n.
wobble
vary 152 vb.
move slowly
278 vb.
oscillate 317 vb.
be agitated 318 vb.
wobbly
flimsy 163 adj.
imperfect 647 adj.
wodge
piece 53 n.
woe
evil 616 n.
bane 659 n.
sorrow 825 n.
woebegone
suffering 825 adj.
unhappy 825 adj.
melancholic
834 adj.
lamenting 836 adj.
woe betide
curse 899 int.

word-perfect
prepared 669 adj.
word-play
equivocalness
518 n.
trope 519 n.
neology 560 n.
wit 839 n.
word processor
data processing
86 n.
word-puzzle
enigma 530 n.
words
phrase 563 n.
quarrel 709 n.
contention 716 n.
anger 891 n.
words, the
reading matter
589 n.
words of one syllable
veracity 540 n.
conciseness 569 n.
word to the wise
hint 524 n.
hush 582 int.
warning 664 n.
advice 691 n.
wordy
prolix 570 adj.
work
energy 160 n.
product 164 n.
agency 173 n.
operate 173 vb.
influence 178 vb.
form 243 vb.
effervesce 318 vb.
bubble 355 vb.
musical piece
412 n.
variegate 437 vb.
stage play 594 n.
business 622 n.
busy oneself
622 vb.
function 622 vb.
job 622 n.
be instrumental
628 vb.
be expedient
642 vb.
use 673 vb.
action 676 n.
deed 676 n.
labour 682 n.

work 682 vb.
be successful
727 vb.
decorate 844 vb.
workable
powerful 160 adj.
possible 469 adj.
workaday
plain 573 adj.
work against
counteract 182 vb.
plot 623 vb.
oppose 704 vb.
workaholic
busy person 678 n.
work at
persevere 600 vb.
busy oneself
622 vb.
deal with 688 vb.
workbox
basket 194 n.
worked up
matured 669 adj.
angry 891 adj.
worker
worker 686 n.
servant 742 n.
worker's cooperative
association 706 n.
workforce
component 58 n.
band 74 n.
means 629 n.
personnel 686 n.
workhouse
retreat 192 n.
poverty 801 n.
work in
introduce 231 vb.
work-in
strike 145 n.
working
instrumental
628 adj.
store 632 n.
action 676 n.
active 678 adj.
labouring 682 adj.
serving 742 adj.
working class
lower classes 869 n.
working day
period 110 n.
job 622 n.
labour 682 n.

working party
enquiry 459 n.
See **enquirer**
consignee 754 n.
workings
structure 331 n.
workmanlike
industrious
678 adj.
work miracles
be successful
727 vb.
be wonderful
864 vb.
work on
influence 178 vb.
work out
happen 154 vb.
result 157 vb.
decipher 520 vb.
mature 669 vb.
deal with 688 vb.
carry through
725 vb.
amuse oneself
837 vb.
work-out
exercise 682 n.
work party
band 74 n.
workroom
chamber 194 n.
workshop 687 n.
works
component 58 n.
structure 331 n.
writing 586 n.
machine 630 n.
workshop 687 n.
works, the
all 52 n.
workshop
teaching 534 n.
class 538 n.
workshop 687 n.
work-shy
lazy 679 adj.
work study
management
689 n.
work to rule
strike 145 n.
work up
excite 821 vb.
work wonders
be active 678 vb.

world
great quantity
32 n.
comprehensive
52 adj.
whole 52 n.
affairs 154 n.
space 183 n.
spacious 183 adj.
universe 321 n.
world 321 n.
world, the
fellowship 882 n.
worldly
material 319 adj.
irreligious 974 adj.
worldly goods
property 777 n.
worldly-wise
intelligent 498 adj.
world of
great quantity
32 n.
world of, a
multitude 104 n.
world-shaking
revolutionary
149 adj.
world-view
generality 79 n.
world war
war 718 n.
world-weary
bored 838 adj.
worldwide
extensive 32 adj.
comprehensive
52 adj.
universal 79 adj.
spacious 183 adj.
worm
coil 251 n.
serpent 251 n.
wriggle 251 vb.
animal 365 n.
creepy-crawly
365 n.
infection 651 n.
cad 938 n.
wormlike
snaky 251 adj.
worm one's way in
infiltrate 297 vb.
worm out
discover 484 vb.

worms
animal disease
651 n.
wormwood
sourness 393 n.
wormy
animal 365 adj.
worn
shown 522 adj.
dilapidated
655 adj.
used 673 adj.
fatigued 684 adj.
worn out
impotent 161 adj.
useless 641 adj.
dilapidated
655 adj.
disused 674 adj.
worried
in difficulties
700 adj.
suffering 825 adj.
dejected 834 adj.
nervous 854 adj.
worries
adversity 731 n.
worry 825 n.
worry
agitate 318 vb.
impress 821 vb.
suffer 825 vb.
worry 825 n.
torment 827 vb.
trouble 827 vb.
worrying
worry 825 n.
annoying 827 adj.
worse for wear, the
weakened 163 adj.
dilapidated
655 adj.
worsen
deteriorate 655 vb.
aggravate 832 vb.
worship
prestige 866 n.
love 887 n.
love 887 vb.
worship 981 n.
worship 981 vb.
worshipper
lover 887 n.
worshipper 981 n.
worst
be superior 34 vb.
defeat 727 vb.

worsted
fibre 208 n.
textile 222 n.
defeated 728 adj.
worst of it, the
defeat 728 n.
wort
plant 366 n.
worth
equivalent 28 adj.
utility 640 n.
goodness 644 n.
price 809 n.
worth, be
cost 809 vb.
worthless
trivial 639 adj.
bad 645 adj.
contemptible
922 adj.
worth one's salt
profitable 640 adj.
worthwhile
good 615 adj.
important 638 adj.
profitable 640 adj.
beneficial 644 adj.
worthwhile, be
be profitable
771 vb.
worthy
excellent 644 adj.
person of repute
866 n.
reputable 866 adj.
virtuous 933 adj.
would-be
hoping 852 adj.
ostentatious
875 adj.
unwarranted
916 adj.
wound
evil 616 n.
wound 655 n.
wound 655 vb.
huff 891 vb.
wounded
suffering 825 adj.
wounds
trophy 729 n.
wound up
excited 821 adj.
woven
correlative 12 adj.
crossed 222 adj.
textural 331 adj.

wow
discord 411 n.
exceller 644 n.
amuse 837 vb.
wrack
ruin 165 n.
plant 366 n.
wraith
ghost 970 n.
wrangle
argue 475 vb.
dissent 489 vb.
quarrel 709 n.
wrap
cover 226 vb.
dress 228 vb.
enclose 235 vb.
fold 261 vb.
wrapped up in
obsessed 455 adj.
wrapped up in one-self
selfish 932 adj.
wrapper
receptacle 194 n.
wrapping 226 n.
informal dress
228 n.
enclosure 235 n.
wrapping
wrapping 226 n.
wrap round
cover 226 vb.
wrapt in thought
thoughtful 449 adj.
wrap up
cover 226 vb.
dress 228 vb.
be hot 379 vb.
wrath
hatred 888 n.
anger 891 n.
wrathful
angry 891 adj.
wreak vengeance
avenge 910 vb.
wreath
crossing 222 n.
loop 250 n.
badge 547 n.
heraldry 547 n.
objective 617 n.
trophy 729 n.
ornamentation
844 n.
honours 866 n.

wreathe
decorate 844 vb.
celebrate 876 vb.
wreck
remainder 41 n.
demolish 165 vb.
destroy 165 vb.
ruin 165 n.
navigate 269 vb.
dilapidation 655 n.
impair 655 vb.
wreckage
remainder 41 n.
ruin 165 n.
wren
bird 365 n.
wrench
disunite 46 vb.
disable 161 vb.
force 176 vb.
impulse 279 n.
draw 288 vb.
extraction 304 n.
tool 630 n.
pincers 778 n.
wrest
distort 246 vb.
wrest from
levy 786 vb.
wrestle
contend 716 vb.
wrestling 716 n.
wrestler
athlete 162 n.
combatant 722 n.
wrestling
wrestling 716 n.
sport 837 n.
wretch
bad person 938 n.
wretched
bad 645 adj.
unfortunate
731 adj.
unhappy 825 adj.
melancholic
834 adj.
wriggle
wriggle 251 vb.
wriggle out of
plead 614 vb.
escape 667 vb.
fail in duty 918 vb.
wring
levy 786 vb.
wringer
smoother 258 n.

dryer 342 n.

wring from
  extract 304 vb.
  compel 740 vb.
wring one's hands
  gesticulate 547 vb.
  regret 830 vb.
  lament 836 vb.
  despair 853 vb.
wring out
  extract 304 vb.
  dry 342 vb.
wrinkle
  jumble 63 vb.
  convolution 251 n.
  crinkle 251 vb.
  roughen 259 vb.
  fold 261 n.
  fold 261 vb.
  furrow 262 n.
  groove 262 vb.
  trickery 542 n.
  indication 547 n.
wrinkled
  ageing 131 adj.
  undulatory
    251 adj.
  rough 259 adj.
  unsightly 842 adj.
wrinkle one's nose
  be fastidious
    862 vb.
  despise 922 vb.
wrinkles
  fold 261 n.
  ugliness 842 n.
wrist
  joint 45 n.
wristwatch
  timekeeper 117 n.
writ
  precept 693 n.
  warrant 737 n.
  mandate 751 n.
  security 767 n.
  law 953 n.
  legal process 959 n.
write
  produce 164 vb.
  communicate
    524 vb.
  write 586 vb.
  describe 590 vb.
write back
  answer 460 vb.
  correspond 588 vb.

write down
  record 548 vb.
  write 586 vb.
  account 808 vb.
write into
  misinterpret
    521 vb.
write off
  relinquish 621 vb.
  stop using 674 vb.
  abrogate 752 vb.
write-off
  nonuse 674 n.
  debt 803 n.
write out
  write 586 vb.
writer
  producer 164 n.
  recorder 549 n.
  author 589 n.
  dissertator 591 n.
write to
  correspond 588 vb.
  be sociable 882 vb.
write up
  advertise 528 vb.
  publish 528 vb.
  account 808 vb.
  praise 923 vb.
write-up
  publicity 528 n.
  article 591 n.
writhe
  vary 152 vb.
  wriggle 251 vb.
  be agitated 318 vb.
  feel pain 377 vb.
  be excited 821 vb.
  suffer 825 vb.
writing
  script 586 n.
  writing 586 n.
writing on the wall
  omen 511 n.
  warning 664 n.
  danger signal
    665 n.
  threat 900 n.
  condemnation
    961 n.
writings
  reading matter
    589 n.
written
  linguistic 557 adj.
  literary 557 adj.
  written 586 adj.

wrong
  unapt 25 adj.
  misjudging
    481 adj.
  erroneous 495 adj.
  amiss 616 adv.
  evil 616 n.
  badly 645 adv.
  ill-treat 645 vb.
  resentment 891 n.
  do wrong 914 adj.
  wrong 914 adj.
  wrong 914 n.
wrong, a
  wrong 914 n.
wrong-doer
  evildoer 904 n.
  offender 904 n.
  wrong 914 n.
wrongdoing
  wickedness 934 n.
  lawbreaking 954 n.
**wrong end of the
  stick**
  misinterpretation
    521 n.
wrongful
  bad 645 adj.
  wrong 914 adj.
  illegal 954 adj.
wrongheaded
  misjudging
    481 adj.
  wrong 914 adj.
wrong moment
  anachronism
    118 n.
wrongness
  error 495 n.
  inexpedience
    643 n.
  wrong 914 n.
wrong side
  contrariety 14 n.
  rear 238 n.
wrong turning
  deviation 282 n.
wroth
  angry 891 adj.
wrought iron
  hardness 326 n.
wrought up
  excited 821 adj.
  angry 891 adj.
wry
  distorted 246 adj.

wynd
  road 624 n.

X

X
  number 85 n.
xanthic
  yellow 433 adj.
xenophobia
  prejudice 481 n.
  phobia 854 n.
  dislike 861 n.
  hatred 888 n.
Xerox (tdmk)
  imitator 20 n.
  copy 22 n.
  duplication 91 n.
  record 548 n.
  recording instru-
    ment 549 n.
  photography 551 n.
  representation
    551 n.
xerox
  copy 20 vb.
  double 91 vb.
X-rated
  grown-up 134 adj.
X-ray
  radiate 417 vb.
  radiation 417 n.
  enquire 459 vb.
  photograph 551 vb.
  photography 551 n.
xylophone
  gong 414 n.

Y

yacht
  go to sea 269 vb.
  boat 275 n.
  sailing ship 275 n.
  amuse oneself
    837 vb.
yachting
  aquatics 269 n.
  water travel 269 n.
  sport 837 n.
**yachtsman or -wo-
  man**
  boatman 270 n.
yackety yack
  empty talk 515 n.
  chatter 581 n.
  loquacity 581 n.

Yahoo
low fellow 869 n.

yak
cattle 365 n.
mean nothing 515 vb.
be loquacious 581 vb.
loquacity 581 n.

yak yak
empty talk 515 n.

yam
fruit and vegetables 301 n.

yammering
empty talk 515 n.

yank
draw 288 vb.

yap
cry 408 vb.
ululate 409 vb.
ululation 409 n.

yard
place 185 n.
long measure 203 n.
support 218 n.
enclosure 235 n.
open space 263 n.
workshop 687 n.

yardstick
prototype 23 n.
counting instrument 86 n.
testing agent 461 n.
gauge 465 n.

yarn
fibre 208 n.
news 529 n.
fable 543 n.
narrative 590 n.
materials 631 n.

yashmak
headgear 228 n.

yaw
vary 152 vb.
navigate 269 vb.
deviate 282 vb.
deviation 282 n.

yawl
sailing ship 275 n.
shrill 407 vb.
cry 408 n.
cry 408 vb.
vociferate 408 vb.
ululate 409 vb.

yawling
ululation 409 n.

yawn
open 263 vb.
opening 263 n.
respiration 352 n.
sleep 679 vb.
be fatigued 684 vb.

yawning
deep 211 adj.
open 263 adj.
opening 263 n.
sleepiness 679 n.
sleepy 679 adj.

yaws
skin disease 651 n.
tropical disease 651 n.

yea
assent 488 n.

year
date 108 n.
period 110 n.
contemporary 123 n.

yearbook
reference book 589 n.

yearling
young creature 132 n.
cattle 365 n.

yearly
periodically 141 adv.
seasonal 141 adj.

yearn
desire 859 vb.

yearning
desire 859 n.
love 887 n.
loving 887 adj.

years
time 108 n.
long duration 113 n.
age 131 n.

yeast
stimulant 174 n.
cereals 301 n.
leaven 323 n.
bubble 355 n.

yell
cry 408 n.
vociferate 408 vb.
weep 836 vb.

yellow
yellow 433 adj.
yellowness 433 n.
cowardly 856 adj.

yellow fever
yellowness 433 n.
tropical disease 651 n.

yellowhammer
bird 365 n.

yellowish
yellow 433 adj.

yellow lines
traffic control 305 n.

yellow-livered
cowardly 856 adj.

Yellow Pages
directory 87 n.
guidebook 524 n.
advertisement 528 n.

yellow press
the press 528 n.
bad taste 847 n.

yellow streak
cowardice 856 n.

yellowy
yellow 433 adj.

yelp
shrill 407 vb.
stridor 407 n.
ululate 409 vb.
ululation 409 n.

yen
coinage 797 n.
desire 859 n.

yeomanry
army 722 n.
cavalry 722 n.
soldier 722 n.

yes
amen 488 int.
assent 488 n.

yes-man
conformist 83 n.
assenter 488 n.
toady 879 n.
flatterer 925 n.

yesterday
priority 119 n.
formerly 125 adv.
past time 125 n.

yet
while 108 adv.
before 119 adv.

nevertheless 468 adv.

Yeti
mythical being 970 n.

yew
tree 366 n.

Y-fronts
underwear 228 n.

yield
be inferior 35 vb.
conform 83 vb.
be weak 163 vb.
product 164 n.
reproduce itself 167 vb.
soften 327 vb.
acquiesce 488 vb.
be irresolute 601 vb.
relinquish 621 vb.
provide 633 vb.
submit 721 vb.
consent 758 vb.
be profitable 771 vb.
not retain 779 vb.
give 781 vb.

yin and yang
polarity 14 n.
duality 90 n.

yob
youngster 132 n.
rude person 885 n.
ruffian 904 n.

yobbo
ruffian 904 n.

yodel
cry 408 n.
sing 413 vb.

yoga
philosophy 449 n.
exercise 682 n.
asceticism 945 n.
religion 973 n.

yoghourt
dairy product 301 n.
dessert 301 n.

yogi
sage 500 n.
ascetic 945 n.
occultist 984 n.

yoke
affix 45 vb.
join 45 vb.
bond 47 n.

YOK

duality 90 n.
pair 90 vb.
support 218 n.
break in 369 vb.
servitude 745 n.
subjection 745 n.
fetter 748 n.

yokel
  native 191 n.
  country-dweller
    869 n.

yon
  distant 199 adj.

yonder
  distant 199 adj.

yoni
  idol 982 n.

yonks
  long duration
    113 n.

young
  young 130 adj.
  product 164 n.
  posterity 170 n.

young creature
  young creature
    132 n.

younger
  inferior 35 n.
  subsequent
    120 adj.
  young 130 adj.

younger generation
  modernist 126 n.
  youth 130 n.

young hopeful
  youngster 132 n.

young person
  youngster 132 n.

youngster
  youngster 132 n.

your honour
  title 870 n.

yourself
  self 80 n.

youth
  youth 130 n.
  youngster 132 n.

youthful
  young 130 adj.
  strong 162 adj.

youth hostel
  inn 192 n.

yowl
  cry 408 vb.
  vociferate 408 vb.
  ululate 409 vb.

ZEB

yoyo
  oscillation 317 n.
  plaything 837 n.

yukky
  unclean 649 adj.

Yule log
  fuel 385 n.

Yuletide
  holy day 988 n.

yummy
  savoury 390 adj.

yuppy
  modernist 126 n.
  beau monde 848 n.

Z

zaitech
  finance 797 n.

zany
  fool 501 n.
  humorist 839 n.
  laughingstock
    851 n.

zap
  move fast 277 vb.
  spurt 277 n.

Z-bend
  obliquity 220 n.
  curve 248 n.

zeal
  curiosity 453 n.
  resolution 599 n.
  warm feeling
    818 n.
  desire 859 n.
  piety 979 n.

zealot
  dogmatist 473 n.
  narrow mind
    481 n.
  enthusiast 504 n.
  zealot 979 n.

zealotry
  opinionatedness
    602 n.

zealous
  active 678 adj.
  fervent 818 adj.

zebra
  mammal 365 n.
  See **cattle**
  stripe 437 n.

zebra crossing
  traffic control
    305 n.
  access 624 n.

ZIG

road 624 n.
refuge 662 n.

Zen
  philosophy 449 n.
  religious faith
    973 n.

zenith
  superiority 34 n.
  completeness 54 n.
  extremity 69 n.
  height 209 n.
  summit 213 n.
  perfection 646 n.
  palmy days 730 n.

zephyr
  breeze 352 n.

zero
  not one 103 adj.
  zero 103 n.

zero-based budgeting
  accounts 808 n.

zero hour
  start 68 n.
  date 108 n.
  departure 296 n.

zero in on
  bring together
    74 vb.
  congregate 74 vb.
  focus 76 vb.
  centralize 225 vb.
  converge 293 vb.
  aim at 617 vb.

zero option
  necessity 596 n.
  choice 605 n.
  no choice 606 n.

zero-rated
  uncharged 812 adj.

zero-rated goods
  tax 809 n.

zest
  vigorousness 174 n.
  pleasure 376 n.
  taste 386 n.
  enjoyment 824 n.
  pleasurableness
    826 n.
  liking 859 n.

zesty
  pungent 388 adj.

zeugma
  ornament 574 n.

ziggurat
  high structure
    209 n.
  temple 990 n.

ZON

zigzag
  be oblique 220 vb.
  obliquity 220 n.
  angular 247 adj.
  angularity 247 n.
  meander 251 vb.
  meandering 251 n.
  deviate 282 vb.
  deviation 282 n.
  to and fro 317 adv.
  pattern 844 n.

zilch
  nonexistence 2 n.
  insubstantiality
    4 n.
  zero 103 n.

zillion
  over one hundred
    99 n.

zing
  vigorousness 174 n.
  move fast 277 vb.
  spurt 277 n.

Zion
  focus 76 n.
  heaven 971 n.
  holy place 990 n.

zip
  fastening 47 n.
  energy 160 n.
  vigorousness 174 n.
  move fast 277 vb.
  spurt 277 n.

zip up
  join 45 vb.
  close 264 vb.

zircon
  gem 844 n.

zit
  blemish 845 n.

zither
  stringed instrument
    414 n.

zloty
  coinage 797 n.

zodiac
  circle 250 n.
  zodiac 321 n.

zombie
  fool 501 n.
  ghost 970 n.

zone
  set apart 46 vb.
  region 184 n.
  territory 184 n.
  layer 207 n.
  land 344 n.

apportion 783 vb.
zonked
　drugged 949 adj.
zoo
　zoo 369 n.
zoological
　biological 358 adj.

animal 365 adj.
zoology
　zoology 367 n.
zoom
　move fast 277 vb.
　spurt 277 n.
　ascend 308 vb.

ascent 308 n.
　photography 551 n.
zoom lens
　camera 442 n.
zoomorphism
　animality 365 n.

idolatry 982 n.
zucchini
　fruit and vegetables
　301 n.
zymotic
　light 323 adj.

FOR THE BEST IN PAPERBACKS, LOOK FOR THE

In every corner of the world, on every subject under the sun, Penguin represents quality and variety – the very best in publishing today.

For complete information about books available from Penguin – including Pelicans, Puffins, Peregrines and Penguin Classics – and how to order them, write to us at the appropriate address below. Please note that for copyright reasons the selection of books varies from country to country.

In the United Kingdom: Please write to *Dept E.P., Penguin Books Ltd, Harmondsworth, Middlesex, UB7 0DA*

If you have any difficulty in obtaining a title, please send your order with the correct money, plus ten per cent for postage and packaging, to *PO Box No 11, West Drayton, Middlesex*

In the United States: Please write to *Dept BA, Penguin, 299 Murray Hill Parkway, East Rutherford, New Jersey 07073*

In Canada: Please write to *Penguin Books Canada Ltd, 2801 John Street, Markham, Ontario L3R 1B4*

In Australia: Please write to the *Marketing Department, Penguin Books Australia Ltd, P.O. Box 257, Ringwood, Victoria 3134*

In New Zealand: Please write to the *Marketing Department, Penguin Books (NZ) Ltd, Private Bag, Takapuna, Auckland 9*

In India: Please write to *Penguin Overseas Ltd, 706 Eros Apartments, 56 Nehru Place, New Delhi, 110019*

In Holland: Please write to *Penguin Books Nederland B.V., Postbus 195, NL–1380AD Weesp, Netherlands*

In Germany: Please write to *Penguin Books Ltd, Friedrichstrasse 10–12, D–6000 Frankfurt Main 1, Federal Republic of Germany*

In Spain: Please write to *Longman Penguin España, Calle San Nicolas 15, E–28013 Madrid, Spain*

In France: Please write to *Penguin Books Ltd, 39 Rue de Montmorency, F-75003, Paris, France*

In Japan: Please write to *Longman Penguin Japan Co Ltd, Yamaguchi Building, 2–12–9 Kanda Jimbocho, Chiyoda-Ku, Tokyo 101, Japan*

FOR THE BEST IN PAPERBACKS, LOOK FOR THE 🐧

PENGUIN REFERENCE BOOKS

The Penguin English Dictionary

Over 1,000 pages long and with over 68,000 definitions, this cheap, compact and totally up-to-date book is ideal for today's needs. It includes many technical and colloquial terms, guides to pronunciation and common abbreviations.

The Penguin Concise Columbia Encyclopedia

The most complete, convenient and authoritative desk encyclopedia for home, school and office. Prepared under the guidance of a distinguished panel of scholars, *The Penguin Concise Columbia Encyclopedia* is a marvel of clarity, convenience and completeness.

The Penguin English Thesaurus   Ed. Betty Kirkpatrick

This new edition of Roget's classic work, now brought up to date for the nineties, will increase anyone's command of the English language. Fully cross-referenced, it includes synonyms of every kind (formal or colloquial, idiomatic and figurative) for almost 900 headings. It is a must for writers and utterly fascinating for any English speaker.

The Penguin Dictionary of Quotations

A treasure-trove of over 12,000 new gems and old favourites, from Aesop and Matthew Arnold to Xenophon and Zola.

The Penguin Wordmaster Dictionary   Manser and Turton

This dictionary puts the pleasure back into word-seeking. Every time you look at a page you get a bonus – a panel telling you everything about a particular word or expression. It is, therefore, a dictionary to be read as well as used for its concise and up-to-date definitions.